THE
OXFORD-DUDEN
PICTORIAL
GERMAN-ENGLISH
DICTIONARY

THE
OXFORD-DUDEN
PICTORIAL
GERMAN-ENGLISH
DICTIONARY

Edited by
the Dudenredaktion and
the German Section of the
Oxford University Press
Dictionary Department

CLARENDON PRESS – OXFORD

Oxford University Press, Walton Street, Oxford OX2 6DP

OXFORD LONDON GLASGOW
NEW YORK TORONTO MELBOURNE AUCKLAND
KUALA LUMPUR SINGAPORE JAKARTA HONG KONG TOKYO
DELHI BOMBAY CALCUTTA MADRAS KARACHI
NAIROBI DAR ES SALAAM CAPE TOWN

Published in the United States by
Oxford University Press, New York

© *Illustrations and German text: Bibliographisches Institut AG, Mannheim 1979*
© *English text: Oxford University Press 1979*
Reprinted 1982

British Library Cataloguing in Publication Data

The Oxford-Duden pictorial German-English dictionary.
1. German language – Dictionaries – English
2. English language – Dictionaries – German
I. Pheby, John II. Dudenredaktion
III. Oxford University Press. Dictionary
Department. German Section IV. Pictorial
German-English dictionary
433'.2'1   PF3640   79-41241
ISBN 0-19-864135-4

The word 'DUDEN' is a registered trademark of the
Bibliographisches Institut for books of any kind

German text edited by Dieter Solf et al., Mannheim
English text edited by John Pheby, Oxford, with the assistance of
Roland Breitsprecher, Michael Clark, Judith Cunningham,
Derek Jordan, and Werner Scholze

Illustrations by Jochen Schmidt, Mannheim

Coordinating editors of the bilingual edition: John Pheby, Oxford, and
Werner Scholze, Mannheim

Typeset by Siemens AG, Munich, Satz AG, Zürich, Bibliographisches Institut AG
Mannheim

Printed in Germany by Klambt-Druck GmbH, Speyer

Foreword

This German-English pictorial dictionary is based on the third, completely revised edition of the German *Bildwörterbuch* published as Volume 3 of the ten-volume *Duden* series of monolingual German dictionaries. The English text represents a direct translation of the German original and follows the original layout and style as closely as possible. It was produced by the German Section of the Oxford University Press Dictionary Department in cooperation with the Dudenredaktion of the Bibliographisches Institut and with the assistance of numerous British companies, institutions, and technical experts.

There are certain kinds of information which can be conveyed more readily and clearly by pictures than by descriptions and explanations, and an illustration will support the simple translation by helping the reader to visualize the object denoted by a given word. This applies both to technical vocabulary sought by the layman and to everyday objects foreign to the general user. In the present dictionary these will be mainly objects from German life which are strange to the English-speaking user – this was dictated by the origin of the text – and the picture will help him to form some impression of the way in which the objects fit into the lives of the German-speaking communities.
Each double page contains a plate illustrating the vocabulary of a whole subject, together with the exact German names and their correct English translations. The arrangement of the text and the presence of alphabetical indexes in German and English allow the dictionary to be used either way: as a German-English or an English-German dictionary. This, together with the wide range of vocabulary, which includes a large proportion of specialized words and technical terms, makes the Oxford-Duden Pictorial Dictionary an indispensable supplement to any German-English or English-German dictionary.

We should like to thank the following individuals and organizations for their help and advice during the preparation of the English text: Mr. N.K. Bowley; British Northrop Ltd.; British Rail, Oxford Region (Area Civil Engineer & Signals Supervisor); The Brush and Compass (Hunts Office Equipment Ltd.); The Careers Information Service of the Army, the Royal Air Force and the Royal Navy; Dr. R. Clark; Mr. G.R. Cunningham; Dentons Cycles Ltd.; Eadie Boyd Ltd.; Mr. P. East; Mr. G. Gilmour, Assistant Librarian, Oxford Polytechnic Library; Greenaway Morris Ltd.; Mr. A.J. Hall, B. Sc., F.R.I.C., F.T.I., F.S.D.C.; George Hattersley & Sons Ltd.; Heel-A-Mat Ltd.; Mr. Simon Howe; Mr. Heinz E. Kiewe, Art Needlework Industries Ltd.; Mather & Platt Ltd.; Melson Wingate Ltd.; Motorworld Garages Ltd.; Mr. W. Napper; Oxfordshire Fire Service (Divisional Headquarters, B Division); Perschke Price Service Organization Ltd.; Rowell & Son; Mr. Robert Sephton, Librarian, Oxford College of Further Education; Mr. W. Slater, Platt, Saco, Lowell Ltd.; Stanton King Organization; Mr. M.J. Trafford; Messrs. R.E. and S.J. Wiblin, Markertow Ltd.

We should also like to extend our thanks to the English staff of the Oxford Dictionaries, in particular Mr. D.J. Edmonds, Dr. D.R. Howlett, Mr. A.M. Hughes, Mr. G. Murray, and Miss S. Raphael.

Oxford, 1980   J. P.

Vorwort

Dieses deutsch-englische Bildwörterbuch entstand auf der Grundlage der 3., vollständig neu bearbeiteten Auflage des deutschen Bildwörterbuches, das als Band 3 der Reihe „Der Duden in 10 Bänden" erschienen ist. Der englische Teil wurde vom German Department des traditionsreichen englischen Verlages Oxford University Press in Zusammenarbeit mit der Dudenredaktion und mit Unterstützung zahlreicher britischer Firmen, Institutionen und Fachwissenschaftler erstellt.

Bilder können bestimmte Informationen schneller und deutlicher vermitteln als Erklärungen und Beschreibungen. Die Abbildung läßt uns häufig sehr viel leichter den Gegenstand erkennen, der mit einem bestimmten Wort bezeichnet wird, als eine noch so treffende Definition des Wortes.

Auch im Umgang mit einer fremden Sprache – ob wir sie nun lernen oder lehren, ob wir sie gut oder weniger gut beherrschen – ist die bildliche Darstellung eine nützliche Hilfe. Die Bildtafeln in diesem Buch zeigen die wichtigsten Dinge aus allen Bereichen des Lebens jeweils in ihrem thematischen Zusammenhang. Auf einer einzig aufgeschlagenen Doppelseite finden wir eine Tafel, die den Wortschatz eines ganzen Gebietes illustriert, dazu die zugehörigen exakten deutschen Bezeichnungen und die korrekten englischen Entsprechungen. Die thematische Gliederung erspart mühsames Nachschlagen der einzelnen Wörter, da man sich über einen ganzen Sachbereich mit einem Blick informieren kann. Außerdem werden alle Wörter noch einmal gesondert in je einem deutschen und einem englischen Register in alphabetischer Reihenfolge verzeichnet.

Diese Konzeption und die Tatsache, daß die Wortauswahl in hohem Maße gerade die speziellen und fachbezogenen Wörter berücksichtigt, machen das Oxford-Duden-Bildwörterbuch zu einer unentbehrlichen Ergänzung jedes deutsch-englischen Wörterbuches.

Wir danken allen Firmen, Institutionen und Fachleuten, die uns bei der Beschaffung und Gestaltung des Bildmaterials unterstützt haben.

Mannheim, 1980
                                  Der Wissenschaftliche Rat
                                        der Dudenredaktion

Abbreviations used in the English text

Am.	*American usage*
c.	*castrated (animal)*
coll.	*colloquial*
f.	*female (animal)*
form.	*formerly*
joc.	*jocular*
m.	*male (animal)*
poet.	*poetic*
sg.	*singular*
sim.	*similar*
y.	*young (animal)*

Abkürzungen im deutschen Text

Im deutschen Text ist bei allen Substantiven das Geschlecht angegeben, soweit es nicht aus der Beugung ersichtlich oder mit dem des unmittelbar vorhergehenden Substantivs identisch ist. Synonyme stehen in Klammern.

ähnl.	ähnlich		*mundartl.*	mundartlich
alem.	alemannisch		*n*	Neutrum
altchristl.	altchristlich		*nd.*	niederdeutsch
automat.	automatisch		*obd.*	oberdeutsch
bayr.	bayrisch		*od.*	oder
bergm.	bergmännisch		*österr.*	österreichisch
Bez.	Bezeichnung		*pl*	Plural
christl.	christlich		*schemat.*	schematisch
darg.	dargestellt		*scherzh.*	scherzhaft
dicht.	dichterisch		*schwäb.*	schwäbisch
dt.	deutsch		*schweiz.*	schweizerisch
elektr.	elektrisch		*seem.*	seemännisch
engl.	englisch		*sg*	Singular
etrusk.	etruskisch		*sog.*	sogenannt
f	Femininum		*südd.*	süddeutsch
fam.	familiär		*südwestd.*	südwestdeutsch
früh.	früher		*stud.*	studentisch
griech.	griechisch		*techn.*	technisch
internat.	international		*ugs.*	umgangssprachlich
landsch.	landschaftlich		*versch.*	verschiedene
m	Maskulinum		*verw.*	verwandt
mitteld.	mitteldeutsch		*z. B.*	zum Beispiel

Inhaltsverzeichnis

Die arabischen Ziffern sind die Nummern der Bildtafeln.

Contents

The arabic numerals are the numbers of the pictures.

Atom, Weltall, Erde
Atom I 1
Atom II 2
Astronomie I 3
Astronomie II 4
Astronomie III 5
Mondlandung 6
Die Atmosphäre 7
Meteorologie I (Wetterkunde) 8
Meteorologie II (Wetterkunde) und Klimakunde 9
Meteorologische Instrumente 10
Allgemeine Geographie I 11
Allgemeine Geographie II 12
Allgemeine Geographie III 13
Landkarte I 14
Landkarte II 15

Mensch und seine Umwelt
Mensch I 16
Mensch II 17
Mensch III 18
Mensch IV 19
Mensch V 20
Erste Hilfe (Unfallhilfe) 21
Arzt I 22
Arzt II 23
Zahnarzt 24
Krankenhaus I 25
Krankenhaus II 26
Krankenhaus III 27
Säuglingspflege und Babyausstattung 28
Kinderkleidung 29
Damenkleidung I (Winterkleidung) 30
Damenkleidung II (Sommerkleidung) 31
Wäsche, Nachtkleidung 32
Herrenkleidung (Männerkleidung) 33
Haar- und Barttrachten 34
Kopfbedeckungen 35
Schmuck 36
Haus und Haustypen 37
Dach und Heizkeller 38
Küche 39
Küchengeräte 40
Diele 41
Wohnzimmer 42
Schlafzimmer 43
Eßzimmer 44
Tafelzubehör 45
Apartment 46
Kinderzimmer 47
Kindergarten (Kindertagesstätte) 48
Bad und Toilette 49
Haushaltsgeräte 50

Natur als Umwelt, Land- und Forstwirtschaft
Ziergarten 51
Nutzgarten 52
Zimmerpflanzen 53
Pflanzenvermehrung 54
Gärtnerei (Gartenbaubetrieb) 55
Gartengeräte 56
Gemüsepflanzen 57
Beeren- und Kernobst 58
Steinobst und Nüsse 59

Atom, Universe, Earth
Atom I 1
Atom II 2
Astronomy I 3
Astronomy II 4
Astronomy III 5
Moon Landing 6
The Atmosphere 7
Meteorology I 8
Meteorology II and Climatology 9
Meteorological Instruments 10
Physical Geography I 11
Physical Geography II 12
Physical Geography III 13
Map I 14
Map II 15

Man and his Social Environment
Man I 16
Man II 17
Man III 18
Man IV 19
Man V 20
First Aid 21
Doctor I 22
Doctor II 23
Dentist 24
Hospital I 25
Hospital II 26
Hospital III 27
Infant Care and Layette 28
Children's Clothes 29
Ladies' Wear I (Winter Wear) 30
Ladies' Wear II (Summer Wear) 31
Underwear, Nightwear 32
Men's Wear 33
Hairstyles and Beards 34
Headgear 35
Jewellery (*Am.* Jewelry) 36
Types of Dwelling 37
Roof and Boiler Room 38
Kitchen 39
Kitchen Utensils and Appliances 40
Hall 41
Living Room (Lounge) 42
Bedroom 43
Dining Room 44
Tableware and Cutlery 45
Flat (Apartment) 46
Children's Room (Nursery) 47
Kindergarten (Day Nursery) 48
Bathroom and Toilet 49
Household Appliances and Utensils 50

Nature as Environment, Agriculture and Forestry
Flower Garden 51
Fruit and Vegetable Garden 52
Indoor Plants (Houseplants) 53
Propagation of Plants 54
Market Garden (*Am.* Truck Garden, Truck Farm) 55
Garden Tools 56
Vegetables (Vegetable Plants) 57
Soft Fruit and Pomes 58
Drupes and Nuts 59

Inhaltsverzeichnis

Contents

Gartenblumen 60
Unkräuter 61
Bauernhof 62
Landwirtschaft 63
Landwirtschaftliche Maschinen I 64
Landwirtschaftliche Maschinen II 65
Landwirtschaftliche Geräte 66
Beregnung 67
Feldfrüchte 68
Futterpflanzen 69
Hunderassen 70
Pferd I 71
Pferd II 72
Haustiere 73
Geflügelhaltung, Eierproduktion 74
Viehhaltung 75
Molkerei 76
Bienen und Bienenzucht 77
Weinbau 78
Weinkeller 79
Garten- und Ackerschädlinge 80
Hausungeziefer, Vorratsschädlinge und
    Schmarotzer 81
Forstschädlinge 82
Schädlingsbekämpfung 83
Forstwirtschaft I 84
Forstwirtschaft II 85
Jagd 86
Jagdwaffen, Jagdgeräte 87
Wild 88
Fischzucht und Angelsport 89

Seefischerei 90

Handwerk und Industrie
Mühlen 91
Mälzerei und Brauerei I 92
Brauerei II 93
Schlachthof 94
Schlachttierteile 95
Fleischerei 96
Bäckerei 97
Lebensmittelgeschäft 98
Supermarkt 99
Schuhmacher 100
Schuhe 101
Handarbeiten 102
Damenschneider 103
Herrenschneider 104
Damenfriseur 105
Herrenfriseur 106
Tabakwaren und Rauchutensilien 107
Gold- und Silberschmied 108
Uhrmacher 109
Uhren 110
Optiker 111
Optische Geräte I 112
Optische Geräte II 113
Fotografie I 114
Fotografie II 115
Fotografie III 116
Schmalfilm 117
Bauplatz I 118
Bauplatz II 119
Zimmerer 120
Dach, Holzverbände 121
Dach und Dachdecker 122
Fußboden, Decke, Treppenbau 123
Glaser 124
Klempner 125
Installateur 126

Garden Flowers 60
Weeds 61
Farm Buildings (*Am.* Farmstead) 62
Agriculture (Farming) 63
Agricultural Machinery I 64
Agricultural Machinery II 65
Agricultural Implements 66
Overhead Irrigation 67
Arable Crops 68
Fodder Plants (Forage Plants) 69
Breeds of Dog 70
Horse I 71
Horse II 72
Domestic Animals 73
Poultry Farming, Egg Production 74
Rearing (*Am.* Raising) of Livestock 75
Dairy 76
Bees and Beekeeping (Apiculture) 77
Wine Growing (Viniculture, Viticulture) 78
Wine Cellar 79
Garden and Field Pests 80
House Insects, Food Pests, and Parasites 81

Forest Pests 82
Pest Control 83
Forestry I 84
Forestry II 85
Hunting 86
Hunting Weapons, Hunting Equipment 87
Game 88
Fish Farming (Fish Culture, Pisciculture) and
    Angling 89
Sea Fishing 90

Trades, Crafts, and Industry
Mills 91
Malting and Brewing I 92
Brewing II 93
Slaughterhouse (Abattoir) 94
Meat Joints 95
Butcher's Shop 96
Bakery 97
Grocer's Shop (*Am.* Grocery Store) 98
Supermarket 99
Shoemaker (Bootmaker) 100
Shoes (Footwear) 101
Needlework 102
Dressmaker 103
Tailor 104
Ladies' Hairdresser 105
Men's Hairdresser (Barber) 106
Tobacco and Smoking Requisites 107
Goldsmith, Silversmith 108
Watchmaker, Clockmaker 109
Clocks and Watches 110
Optician 111
Optical Instruments I 112
Optical Instruments II 113
Photography I 114
Photography II 115
Photography III 116
Cine Film 117
Building Site (Construction Site) I 118
Building Site (Construction Site) II 119
Carpenter 120
Roof, Timber Joints 121
Roof and Roofer 122
Floor, Ceiling, Staircase Construction 123
Glazier 124
Plumber 125
Plumber, Gas Fitter, Heating Engineer 126

Inhaltsverzeichnis

Elektroinstallateur 127
Tapezierer 128
Maler und Lackierer 129
Böttcher und Behälterbauer 130
Kürschner 131
Tischler I 132
Tischler II 133
Heimwerken 134
Drechsler (Elfenbeinschnitzer) 135
Korbmacher (Korbflechter) 136
Schmied I 137
Schmied II (Landfahrzeugtechnik) 138

Freiform- und Gesenkschmiede
  (Warmmassivumformung) 139
Schlosser 140
Autogenschweißer 141
Elektroschweißer 142
Profile, Schrauben und Maschinenteile 143
Steinkohlenbergwerk 144
Erdöl 145
Off-shore-Bohrung 146
Eisenhüttenwerk 147
Eisengießerei und Walzwerk 148
Werkzeugmaschinen I 149
Werkzeugmaschinen II 150
Konstruktionsbüro (Zeichnerbüro) 151
Kraftwerk I 152
Kraftwerk II 153
Kernenergie 154
Neuzeitliche Energiequellen 155
Kokerei 156
Sägewerk 157
Steinbruch 158
Ziegelei (Ziegelwerk) 159
Zementwerk (Zementfabrik) 160
Porzellanherstellung 161
Glasherstellung 162
Baumwollspinnerei I 163
Baumwollspinnerei II 164
Weberei I 165
Weberei II 166
Wirkerei, Strickerei 167
Ausrüstung von Textilien 168
Chemiefasern I 169
Chemiefasern II 170
Textile Bindungen 171
Papierherstellung I 172
Papierherstellung II 173

Graphisches Gewerbe
Setzerei I 174
Setzerei II 175
Setzerei III (Lichtsatz) 176

Fotoreproduktion 177
Galvanoplastik und Klischeeherstellung 178
Offsetkopie 179
Offsetdruck 180
Buchdruck 181
Tiefdruck 182

Buchbinderei I 183
Buchbinderei II 184
Buchbinderei III 185

**Verkehrs- und Nachrichtenwesen,
  Informationstechnik**
Pferdewagen 186

Contents

Electrician 127
Paperhanger 128
Painter 129
Cooper and Tank Construction Engineer 130
Furrier 131
Joiner I 132
Joiner II 133
Do-it-yourself 134
Turner (Ivory Carver) 135
Basket Maker 136
Blacksmith (Smith) I 137
Blacksmith (Smith) II (Farm Vehicle
  Engineering) 138
Hammer Forging (Smith Forging) and
  Drop Forging 139
Metalworker 140
Gas Welder 141
Arc Welder 142
Sections, Bolts, and Machine Parts 143
Coal Mine 144
Mineral Oil (Oil, Petroleum) 145
Offshore Drilling 146
Iron and Steel Works 147
Iron Foundry and Rolling Mill 148
Machine Tools I 149
Machine Tools II 150
Drawing Office 151
Power Plant (Power Station) I 152
Power Plant (Power Station) II 153
Nuclear Energy 154
Modern Sources of Energy 155
Coking Plant 156
Sawmill 157
Quarry 158
Brickworks (Brickyard, Brickfield) 159
Cement Works (Cement Factory) 160
Porcelain and China Manufacture 161
Glass Production 162
Cotton Spinning I 163
Cotton Spinning II 164
Weaving I 165
Weaving II 166
Knitting 167
Finishing of Textile Fabrics 168
Synthetic (Man-made) Fibres (*Am.* Fibers) I 169
Synthetic (Man-made) Fibres (*Am.* Fibers) II 170
Weaves and Knits 171
Papermaking I 172
Papermaking II 173

Printing Industry
Composing Room (Case Room) I 174
Composing Room (Case Room) II 175
Composing Room (Case Room) III
  (Phototypesetting, Photocomposition,
  Photosetting, Filmsetting) 176
Photomechanical Reproduction 177
Electrotyping and Block Making 178
Offset Platemaking 179
Offset Printing 180
Letterpress Printing 181
Photogravure (Gravure Printing, Intaglio
  Printing) 182
Bookbinding I 183
Bookbinding II 184
Bookbinding III 185

**Transport, Communications and Information
  Technology**
Horse-drawn Carriages 186

Inhaltsverzeichnis

Contents

Fahrrad 187
Zweiräder 188
Motorrad (Kraftrad) 189
Verbrennungsmotoren 190
Automobil I 191
Automobil II 192
Automobil III 193
Lastkraftwagen, Omnibusse 194
Kfz-Werkstatt 195
Tankstelle 196
Straßenbahn, elektrische
Überlandbahn 197
Straßenquerschnitt 198
Müllbeseitigung, Straßenreinigung 199

Straßenbau I 200

Straßenbau II 201

Eisenbahnstrecke I 202
Eisenbahnstrecke II (Signalanlagen) 203

Bahnhofshalle 204
Bahnsteig 205
Güterbahnhof 206
Eisenbahnfahrzeuge (Schienenfahrzeuge) I 207
Eisenbahnfahrzeuge (Schienenfahrzeuge) II 208
Eisenbahnfahrzeuge (Schienenfahrzeuge) III 209
Eisenbahnfahrzeuge (Schienenfahrzeuge) IV 210
Eisenbahnfahrzeuge (Schienenfahrzeuge) V 211
Eisenbahnfahrzeuge (Schienenfahrzeuge) VI 212
Eisenbahnfahrzeuge (Schienenfahrzeuge) VII 213
Bergbahnen 214

Brücken 215
Fluß und Flußbau 216
Wasserbau 217
Historische Schiffstypen 218
Segelschiff I 219
Segelschiff II 220
Schiffstypen 221
Schiffbau 222
Motorschiff 223
Navigation 224
Hafen I 225
Hafen II 226
Bergen und Schleppen 227
Rettungswesen 228
Flugzeuge I 229
Flugzeuge II 230
Flugzeuge III 231
Flugzeuge IV 232
Flughafen 233
Raumfahrt I 234
Raumfahrt II 235
Post I 236
Post II (Telefon und Telegrafie) 237
Rundfunk (Hör- und Fernsehfunk) I 238
Rundfunk (Hör- und Fernsehfunk) II 239
Rundfunk III (Fernsehtechnik) 240
Unterhaltungselektronik 241
Unterrichts- und Informationstechnik 242

Audiovision (AV) 243
Rechenzentrum 244

Büro, Bank, Börse
Büro I 245
Büro II 246
Büro III 247
Büro IV 248

Bicycle 187
Motorcycles, Bicycles, Scooters, Mopeds 188
Motorcycle 189
Internal Combustion Engines 190
Motor Car (*Am.* Automobile) I 191
Motor Car (*Am.* Automobile) II 192
Motor Car (*Am.* Automobile) III 193
Lorries (*Am.* Trucks), Vans, Buses 194
Garage (*Am.* Shop) 195
Service Station 196
Tram (*Am.* Streetcar, Trolley), Interurban Electric
Train 197
Cross-section of a Street 198
Refuse Disposal (*Am.* Garbage Disposition), Street
Cleaning 199
Road Construction I (Road Building, Road
Making) 200
Road Construction II (Road Building, Road
Making) 201
Railway Line (*Am.* Railroad Track) I 202
Railway Line (*Am.* Railroad Track) II (Signalling
Equipment) 203
Station Hall 204
Station Platform 205
Goods Station (Freight Depot) 206
Railway Vehicles (Rolling Stock) I 207
Railway Vehicles (Rolling Stock) II 208
Railway Vehicles (Rolling Stock) III 209
Railway Vehicles (Rolling Stock) IV 210
Railway Vehicles (Rolling Stock) V 211
Railway Vehicles (Rolling Stock) VI 212
Railway Vehicles (Rolling Stock) VII 213
Mountain Railways (*Am.* Mountain Railroads) and
Cableways 214
Bridges 215
Rivers and River Engineering 216
Waterway and Hydraulic Engineering 217
Types of Historical Ship 218
Sailing Ship I 219
Sailing Ship II 220
Types of Ship 221
Shipbuilding 222
Motor Ship 223
Navigation 224
Docks, Port, Harbour (*Am.* Harbor) I 225
Docks, Port, Harbour (*Am.* Harbor) II 226
Salvage (Salving) and Towage 227
Life Saving 228
Aircraft I 229
Aircraft II 230
Aircraft III 231
Aircraft IV 232
Airport 233
Space Flight I 234
Space Flight II 235
Post Office I 236
Post Office II (Telephones and Telegraphy) 237
Broadcasting (Radio and Television) I 238
Broadcasting (Radio and Television) II 239
Broadcasting III (Television Engineering) 240
Music Systems (Audio Systems) 241
Teaching Equipment and Information
Technology 242
Audiovision (AV) 243
Computer Centre (*Am.* Center) 244

Office, Bank, Stock Exchange
Office I 245
Office II 246
Office III 247
Office IV 248

Inhaltsverzeichnis

Büro V 249
Bank 250
Börse 251

Öffentlichkeit und Gemeinwesen
Geld (Münzen und Scheine) 252
Fahnen und Flaggen 253
Heraldik, Kronen 254
Streitkräfte I (Heer) 255
Streitkräfte II (Luftwaffe I) 256
Streitkräfte III (Luftwaffe II) 257
Kriegsschiffe I 258
Kriegsschiffe II 259
Schule I (Grund- und Hauptschule) 260
Schule II (Höhere Schule) 261
Universität 262
Wahl 263
Polizei 264
Café 265
Restaurant 266
Hotel 267
Stadt (Innenstadt) 268
Wasserversorgung 269
Feuerwehr 270
Kaufhaus (Warenhaus) 271
Park 272

Freizeit, Spiel, Sport
Kinderspielplatz 273
Kurbad 274
Roulett 275
Brett- und Gesellschaftsspiele 276
Billard 277
Camping 278
Surfing, Tauchen 279
Strandbad 280
Schwimmbad (Freizeitzentrum) 281
Schwimmsport 282
Rudern und Paddeln 283
Segeln I 284
Segeln II 285
Motorboote, Wasserski 286
Segelflug 287
Flugsport 288
Pferdesport 289
Rad- und Motorsport 290
Ballspiele I (Fußball) 291
Ballspiele II 292
Ballspiele III 293
Fechten 294
Freiübungen 295
Geräteturnen I 296
Geräteturnen II (Turnen der Frauen) 297
Leichtathletik 298
Schwerathletik 299
Bergsport 300
Wintersport I (Skisport) 301
Wintersport II 302
Wintersport III 303
Winterlandschaft 304
Verschiedene Sportarten 305

Unterhaltung, Show, Kultur und Kunst
Karneval (Fasching, Fastnacht) 306
Zirkus 307
Rummelplatz 308
Flohmarkt 309

Contents

Office V 249
Bank 250
Stock Exchange 251

Community
Money (Coins and Notes, *Am.* Coins and Bills) 252
Flags 253
Heraldry, Crowns and Coronets 254
Armed Forces I (Army) 255
Armed Forces II (Air Force I) 256
Armed Forces III (Air Force II) 257
Warships I 258
Warships II (Modern Fighting Ships) 259
School I (Primary School) 260
School II (Secondary School, High School) 261
University 262
Election 263
Police 264
Café 265
Restaurant 266
Hotel 267
Town (Town Centre, *Am.* Downtown) 268
Water Supply 269
Fire Service (*Am.* Fire Department) 270
Department Store 271
Park 272

Recreation, Games, Sport
Children's Playground 273
Spa 274
Roulette 275
Board Games and Party Games 276
Billiards 277
Camping and Caravanning (*Am.* Trailering) 278
Surf Riding (Surfing), Skin Diving 279
Bathing Beach 280
Swimming Bath (Leisure Centre, *Am.* Center) 281
Swimming 282
Rowing and Canoeing 283
Sailing (Yachting) I 284
Sailing (Yachting) II 285
Motorboats (Powerboats), Water Skiing 286
Gliding (Soaring) 287
Aerial Sports (Airsports) 288
Horsemanship, Equestrian Sport 289
Cycle Racing and Motorsports 290
Ball Games I (Football, Association Football, Soccer) 291
Ball Games II 292
Ball Games III 293
Fencing 294
Free Exercise 295
Apparatus Gymnastics I 296
Apparatus Gymnastics II (Women's Gymnastics) 297
Athletics (Track and Field Events) 298
Weightlifting and Combat Sports 299
Mountaineering 300
Winter Sports I (Skiing) 301
Winter Sports II 302
Winter Sports III 303
Countryside in Winter 304
Various Sports 305

Entertainment, Culture, and Art
Carnival 306
Circus 307
Fair, Fairground 308
Flea Market 309

Inhaltsverzeichnis   *Contents*

Film I 310
Film II 311
Film III 312
Film IV 313
Ballett 314
Theater I 315
Theater II 316
Diskothek 317
Nachtlokal 318
Stierkampf, Rodeo 319
Musiknotation I 320
Musiknotation II 321
Musikinstrumente I 322
Musikinstrumente II 323
Musikinstrumente III 324
Musikinstrumente IV 325
Musikinstrumente V 326
Fabelwesen 327
Vorgeschichte 328
Ritterwesen (Rittertum) 329
Kirche I 330
Kirche II 331
Kirche III 332
Kunst I 333
Kunst II 334
Kunst III 335
Kunst IV 336
Kunst V 337
Mal- und Zeichenatelier 338
Bildhaueratelier 339
Graphische Kunst 340
Schrift I 341
Schrift II 342
Farbe 343
Mathematik I 344
Mathematik II 345
Mathematik III (Geometrie I) 346
Mathematik IV (Geometrie II) 347
Mathematik V (Mengenlehre) 348
Chemielabor (chemisches Laboratorium) I 349
Chemielabor (chemisches Laboratorium) II 350
Kristalle, Kristallkunde 351
Völkerkunde I 352
Völkerkunde II 353
Völkerkunde III 354
Kostüme, Kleidermoden 355

Tiere und Pflanzen
Zoo (zoologischer Garten) 356
Wirbellose Tiere (Wirbellose) 357
Gliedertiere 358
Vögel I 359
Vögel II (einheimische Vögel) 360
Vögel III (Sperlingsvögel) 361
Vögel IV (Greifvögel) 362
Vögel V (exotische Vögel) 363
Fische, Lurche 364
Schmetterlinge 365
Säugetiere I 366
Säugetiere II 367
Säugetiere III 368
Tiefseefauna 369
Allgemeine Botanik 370
Laubhölzer 371
Nadelhölzer 372
Ziersträucher und Zierbäume I 373
Ziersträucher und Zierbäume II 374
Wiesenblumen und Blumen am Wegrand I 375

Wiesenblumen und Blumen am Wegrand II 376

Films (Motion Pictures) I 310
Films (Motion Pictures) II 311
Films (Motion Pictures) III 312
Films (Motion Pictures) IV 313
Ballet 314
Theatre (*Am.* Theater) I 315
Theatre (*Am.* Theater) II 316
Discotheque 317
Nightclub 318
Bullfighting, Rodeo 319
Musical Notation I 320
Musical Notation II 321
Musical Instruments I 322
Musical Instruments II 323
Musical Instruments III 324
Musical Instruments IV 325
Musical Instruments V 326
Fabulous Creatures (Fabled Beings) 327
Prehistory 328
Chivalry 329
Church I 330
Church II 331
Church III 332
Art I 333
Art II 334
Art III 335
Art IV 336
Art V 337
Artist's Studio 338
Sculptor's Studio 339
Graphic Art 340
Script I 341
Script II 342
Colour (*Am.* Color) 343
Mathematics I 344
Mathematics II 345
Mathematics III (Geometry I) 346
Mathematics IV (Geometry II) 347
Mathematics V (Sets) 348
Chemistry Laboratory I 349
Chemistry Laboratory II 350
Crystals, Crystallography 351
Ethnology I 352
Ethnology II 353
Ethnology III 354
Historical Costumes 355

Animals and Plants
Zoo (Zoological Gardens) 356
Invertebrates 357
Articulates 358
Birds I 359
Birds II (Indigenous Birds, Endemic Birds) 360
Birds III (Passerines) 361
Birds IV (Birds of Prey) 362
Birds V (Exotic Birds) 363
Fish, Amphibia, and Reptiles 364
Lepidoptera (Butterflies and Moths) 365
Mammals I 366
Mammals II 367
Mammals III 368
Deep-sea Fauna 369
General Botany 370
Deciduous Trees 371
Conifers 372
Ornamental Shrubs and Trees I 373
Ornamental Shrubs and Trees II 374
Meadow Flowers and Wayside Flowers (Wild Flowers) I 375
Meadow Flowers and Wayside Flowers (Wild Flowers) II 376

Inhaltsverzeichnis

Wald-, Moor- und Heidepflanzen 377
Alpen-, Wasser- und Sumpfpflanzen 378

Giftpflanzen 379
Heilpflanzen 380
Speisepilze 381
Tropische Genußmittel- und Gewürzpflanzen 382

Industriepflanzen 383
Südfrüchte 384

Contents

Plants of Forest, Marsh and Heathland 377
Alpine Plants, Aquatic Plants (Water Plants),
   and Marsh Plants 378
Poisonous Plants 379
Medicinal Plants 380
Edible Fungi (Esculent Fungi) 381
Tropical Plants used as Stimulants, Spices,
   and Flavourings (*Am.* Flavorings) 382
Plants used in Industry 383
Southern Fruits (Tropical, Subtropical, and
   Mediterranean Fruits) 384

1-8 Atommodelle *n*
- *atom models*
1 das Atommodell des Wasserstoffs *m* (H)
- *model of the hydrogen (H) atom*
2 der Atomkern, ein Proton *n*
- *atomic nucleus, a proton*
3 das Elektron
- *electron*
4 der Elektronenspin
- *electron spin*
5 das Atommodell des Heliums *n* (He)
- *model of the helium (He) atom*
6 die Elektronenschale
- *electron shell*
7 das Pauli-Prinzip
- *Pauli exclusion principle (exclusion principle, Pauli principle)*
8 die abgeschlossene Elektronenschale des Na-Atoms *n* (Natriumatoms)
- *complete electron shell of the Na atom (sodium atom)*
9-14 Molekülstrukturen *f* (Gitterstrukturen)
- *molecular structures (lattice structures)*
9 dér Kochsalzkristall
- *crystal of sodium chloride (of common salt)*
10 das Chlorion
- *chlorine ion*
11 das Natriumion
- *sodium ion*
12 der Cristobalitkristall
- *crystal of cristobalite*
13 das Sauerstoffatom
- *oxygen atom*
14 das Siliciumatom
- *silicon atom*
15 die „Energietreppe" (mögliche Quantensprünge *m*) des Wasserstoffatoms *n*
- *energy levels (possible quantum jumps) of the hydrogen atom*
16 der Atomkern (das Proton)
- *atomic nucleus (proton)*
17 das Elektron
- *electron*
18 das Niveau des Grundzustands *m*
- *ground state level*
19 der angeregte Zustand
- *excited state*
20-25 die Quantensprünge *m*
- *quantum jumps (quantum transitions)*
20 die Lyman-Serie
- *Lyman series*
21 die Balmer-Serie
- *Balmer series*
22 die Paschen-Serie
- *Paschen series*
23 die Bracket-Serie
- *Brackett series*
24 die Pfund-Serie
- *Pfund series*
25 das freie Elektron
- *free electron*
26 das Bohr-Sommerfeldsche Atommodell des H-Atoms *n*
- *Bohr-Sommerfeld model of the H atom*
27 die Energieniveaus *n* des Elektrons *n*
- *energy levels of the electron*

28 der spontane Zerfall eines radioaktiven Materials *n*
- *spontaneous decay of radioactive material*
29 der Atomkern
- *atomic nucleus*
30-31 das Alphateilchen (α, die Alphastrahlung, der Heliumatomkern)
- *alpha particle (α, alpha radiation, helium nucleus)*
30 das Neutron
- *neutron*
31 das Proton
- *proton*
32 das Betateilchen (β, die Betastrahlung, das Elektron)
- *beta particle (β, beta radiation, electron)*
33 die Gammastrahlung (γ, eine harte Röntgenstrahlung)
- *gamma radiation (γ, a hard X-radiation)*
34 die Kernspaltung
- *nuclear fission*
35 der schwere Atomkern
- *heavy atomic nucleus*
36 der Neutronenbeschuß
- *neutron bombardment*
37-38 die Kernbruchstücke *n*
- *fission fragments*
39 das freigesetzte Neutron
- *released neutron*
40 die Gammastrahlung (γ)
- *gamma radiation (γ)*
41 die Kettenreaktion
- *chain reaction*
42 das kernspaltende Neutron
- *incident neutron*
43 der Kern vor der Spaltung
- *nucleus prior to fission*
44 das Kernbruchstück
- *fission fragment*
45 das freigesetzte Neutron
- *released neutron*
46 die wiederholte Kernspaltung
- *repeated fission*
47 das Kernbruchstück
- *fission fragment*
48 die kontrollierte Kettenreaktion in einem Atomreaktor *m*
- *controlled chain reaction in a nuclear reactor*
49 der Atomkern eines spaltbaren Elements *n*
- *atomic nucleus of a fissionable element*
50 der Beschuß durch ein Neutron *n*
- *neutron bombardment*
51 das Kernbruchstück (der neue Atomkern)
- *fission fragment (new atomic nucleus)*
52 das freiwerdende Neutron
- *released neutron*
53 die absorbierten Neutronen *n*
- *absorbed neutrons*
54 der Moderator, eine Bremsschicht aus Graphit *m*
- *moderator, a retarding layer of graphite*
55 die Wärmeableitung (Energiegewinnung)
- *extraction of heat (production of energy)*
56 die Röntgenstrahlung
- *X-radiation*

57 der Beton-Blei-Schutzmantel
- *concrete and lead shield*
58 die Blasenkammer zur Sichtbarmachung der Bahnspuren *f* energiereicher ionisierender Teilchen *n*
- *bubble chamber for showing the tracks of high-energy ionizing particles*
59 die Lichtquelle
- *light source*
60 die Kamera
- *camera*
61 die Expansionsleitung
- *expansion line*
62 der Lichtstrahlengang
- *path of light rays*
63 der Magnet
- *magnet*
64 der Strahlungseintritt
- *beam entry point*
65 der Spiegel
- *reflector*
66 die Kammer
- *chamber*

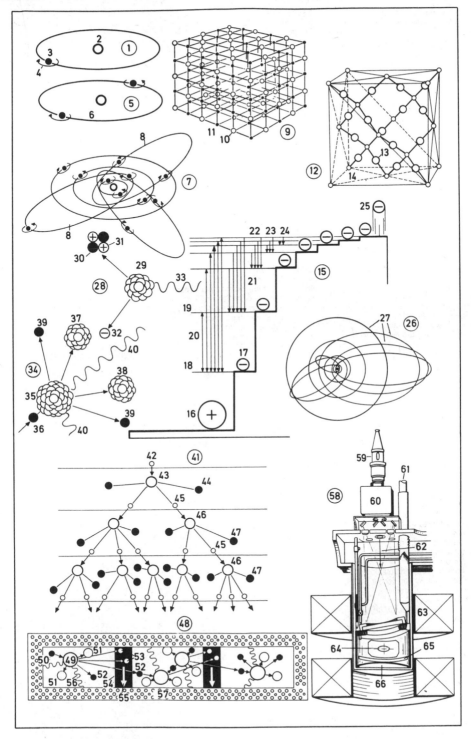

1-23 Strahlungsmeßgeräte *n*
- *radiation detectors (radiation meters)*
1 das Strahlenschutzmeßgerät
- *radiation monitor*
2 die Ionisationskammer
- *ionization chamber (ion chamber)*
3 die Innenelektrode
- *central electrode*
4 der Meßbereichswähler
- *measurement range selector*
5 das Instrumentengehäuse
- *instrument housing*
6 das Ableseinstrument
- *meter*
7 die Nullpunkteinstellung
- *zero adjustment*
8-23 Dosimeter *n*
- *dosimeter (dosemeter)*
8 das Filmdosimeter
- *film dosimeter*
9 der (das) Filter
- *filter*
10 der Film
- *film*
11 das Fingerring-Filmdosimeter
- *film-ring dosimeter*
12 der (das) Filter
- *filter*
13 der Film
- *film*
14 der Deckel mit Filter *m od. n*
- *cover with filter*
15 das Taschendosimeter
- *pocket meter (pen meter, pocket chamber)*
16 die Schauöffnung
- *window*
17 die Ionisationskammer
- *ionization chamber (ion chamber)*
18 die Taschenklemme
- *clip (pen clip)*
19 das Zählrohrgerät (der Geigerzähler)
- *Geiger counter (Geiger-Müller counter)*
20 die Zählrohrfassung
- *counter tube casing*
21 das Zählrohr
- *counter tube*
22 das Instrumentengehäuse
- *instrument housing*
23 der Meßbereichswähler
- *measurement range selector*
24 die Wilsonsche Nebelkammer
- *Wilson cloud chamber (Wilson chamber)*
25 der Kompressionsboden
- *compression plate*
26 die Nebelkammeraufnahme
- *cloud chamber photograph*
27 der Nebelstreifen einer Alphapartikel
- *cloud chamber track of an alpha particle*
28 die Kobaltbestrahlungsapparatur
(*ugs.* Kobaltbombe)
- *telecobalt unit (coll. cobalt bomb)*
29 das Säulenstativ
- *pillar stand*
30 die Halteseile *n*
- *support cables*
31 der Strahlenschutzkopf
- *radiation shield (radiation shielding)*
32 der Abdeckschieber
- *sliding shield*

33 die Lamellenblende
- *bladed diaphragm*
34 das Lichtvisier
- *light-beam positioning device*
35 die Pendelvorrichtung
- *pendulum device (pendulum)*
36 der Bestrahlungstisch
- *irradiation table*
37 die Laufschiene
- *rail (track)*
38 der Kugelmanipulator
(Manipulator)
- *manipulator with sphere unit (manipulator)*
39 der Handgriff
- *handle*
40 der Sicherungsflügel
(Feststellhebel)
- *safety catch (locking lever)*
41 das Handgelenk
- *wrist joint*
42 die Führungsstange
- *master arm*
43 die Klemmvorrichtung
- *clamping device (clamp)*
44 die Greifzange
- *tongs*
45 das Schlitzbrett
- *slotted board*
46 die Bestrahlungsschutzwand, eine Bleisiegelwand [im Schnitt]
- *radiation shield (protective shield, protective shielding), a lead shielding wall [section]*
47 der Greifarm eines Parallelmanipulators *m*
(Master-Slave-Manipulators)
- *grasping arm of a pair of manipulators (of a master/slave manipulator)*
48 der Staubschutz
- *dust shield*
49 das Zyklotron
- *cyclotron*
50 die Gefahrenzone
- *danger zone*
51 der Magnet
- *magnet*
52 die Pumpen *f* zur Entleerung der Vakuumkammer
- *pumps for emptying the vacuum chamber*

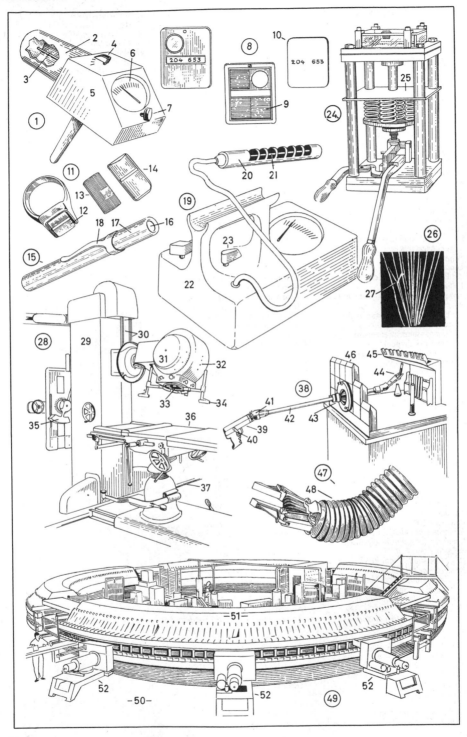

1-35 Sternkarte *f* **des nördlichen Fixsternhimmels** *m* (der nördlichen Hemisphäre), eine Himmelskarte
- *star map of the northern sky (northern hemisphere)*
1-8 Einteilung des Himmelsgewölbes *n*
- *divisions of the sky*
1 der Himmelspol mit dem Polarstern *m* (Nordstern)
- *celestial pole with the Pole Star (Polaris, the North Star)*
2 die Ekliptik (scheinbare Jahresbahn der Sonne)
- *ecliptic (apparent annual path of the sun)*
3 der Himmelsäquator
- *celestial equator (equinoctial line)*
4 der Wendekreis des Krebses *m*
- *tropic of Cancer*
5 der Grenzkreis der Zirkumpolarsterne *m*
- *circle enclosing circumpolar stars*
6-7 die Äquinoktialpunkte *m* (die Tagundnachtgleiche, das Äquinoktium)
- *equinoctial points (equinoxes)*
6 der Frühlingspunkt (Widderpunkt, Frühlingsanfang)
- *vernal equinoctial point (first point of Aries)*
7 der Herbstpunkt (Herbstanfang)
- *autumnal equinoctial point*
8 der Sommersonnenwendepunkt (Sommersolstitialpunkt, das Solstitium, die Sonnenwende)
- *summer solstice (solstice)*
9-48 Sternbilder *n* (*Vereinigung von Fixsternen* m, Gestirnen *n zu Bildern*) **u. Sternnamen** *m*
- *constellations (grouping of fixed stars into figures)* **and names of stars**
9 Adler *m* (Aquila) mit Hauptstern *m* Altair *m* (Atair)
- *Aquila (the Eagle) with Altair the principal star (the brightest star)*
10 Pegasus *m*
- *Pegasus (the Winged Horse)*
11 Walfisch *m* (Cetus) mit Mira *f*, einem veränderlichen Stern *m*
- *Cetus (the Whale) with Mira, a variable star*
12 Fluß *m* Eridanus
- *Eridamus (the Celestial River)*
13 Orion *m* mit Rigel *m*, Beteigeuze u. Bellatrix *f*
- *Orion (the Hunter) with Rigel, Betelgeuse and Bellatrix*
14 der Große Hund (Canis Major) mit
- *Sirius* m, einem Stern 1. Größe
- *Canis Major (the Great Dog, the Greater Dog) with Sirius (the Dog Star), a star of the first magnitude*
15 der Kleine Hund (Canis Minor) mit Prokyon *m*
- *Canis Minor (the Little Dog, the Lesser Dog) with Procyon*
16 Wasserschlange *f* (Hydra)
- *Hydra (the Water Snake, the Sea Serpent)*
17 Löwe *m* (Leo) mit Regulus *m*
- *Leo (the Lion)*
18 Jungfrau *f* (Virgo) mit Spika *f*
- *Virgo (the Virgin) with Spica*

19 Waage *f* (Libra)
- *Libra (the Balance, the Scales)*
20 Schlange *f* (Serpens)
- *Serpens (the Serpent)*
21 Herkules *m* (Hercules)
- *Hercules*
22 Leier *f* (Lyra) mit Wega *f*
- *Lyra (the Lyre) with Vega*
23 Schwan *m* (Cygnus) mit Deneb *m*
- *Cygnus (the Swan, the Northern Cross) with Deneb*
24 Andromeda *f*
- *Andromeda*
25 Stier *m* (Taurus) mit Aldebaran *m*
- *Taurus (the Bull) with Aldebaran*
26 die Plejaden *f* (das Siebengestirn), ein offener Sternhaufen
- *The Pleiades (Pleiads, the Seven Sisters), an open cluster of stars*
27 Fuhrmann *m* (Auriga) mit Kapella *f* (Capella)
- *Auriga (the Wagoner, the Charioteer)*
28 Zwillinge *m* (Gemini) mit Kastor *m* (Castor) u. Pollux *m*
- *Gemini (the Twins) with Castor and Pollux*
29 der Große Wagen (Große Bär, Ursa Major *f*) mit Doppelstern *m* Mizar u. Alkor *m*
- *Ursa Major (the Great Bear, the Greater Bear, the Plough, Charles's Wain, Am. the Big Dipper) with the double star (binary star) Mizar and Alcor*
30 Bootes *m* (Ochsentreiber) mit Arktur *m* (Arcturus)
- *Boötes (the Herdsman)*
31 Nördliche Krone *f* (Corona Borealis)
- *Corona Borealis (the Northern Crown)*
32 Drache *m* (Draco)
- *Draco (the Dragon)*
33 Kassiopeia *f* (Cassiopeia)
- *Cassiopeia*
34 der Kleine Wagen (Kleine Bär, Ursa Minor *f*) mit dem Polarstern *m*
- *Ursa Minor (the Little Bear, Lesser Bear, Am. Little Dipper) with the Pole Star (Polaris, the North Star)*
35 die Milchstraße (Galaxis)
- *the Milky Way (the Galaxy)*
36-48 der südliche Sternhimmel
- *the southern sky*
36 Steinbock *m* (Capricornus)
- *Capricorn (the Goat, the Sea Goat)*
37 Schütze *m* (Sagittarius)
- *Sagittarius (the Archer)*
38 Skorpion *m* (Scorpius)
- *Scorpio (the Scorpion)*
39 Kentaur *m* (Centaurus)
- *Centaurus (the Centaur)*
40 Südliches Dreieck *n* (Triangulum Australe)
- *Triangulum Australe (the Southern Triangle)*
41 Pfau *m* (Pavo)
- *Pavo (the Peacock)*
42 Kranich *m* (Grus)
- *Grus (the Crane)*
43 Oktant *m* (Octans)
- *Octans (the Octant)*
44 Kreuz *n* des Südens, Südliches Kreuz (Crux *f*)
- *Crux (the Southern Cross, the Cross)*

45 Schiff *n* (Argo *f*)
- *Argo (the Celestial Ship)*
46 Kiel *m* des Schiffes *n* (Carina *f*)
- *Carina (the Keel)*
47 Maler *m* (Pictor, Staffelei *f*, Machina Pictoris)
- *Pictor (the Painter)*
48 Netz *n* (Reticulum)
- *Reticulum (the Net)*

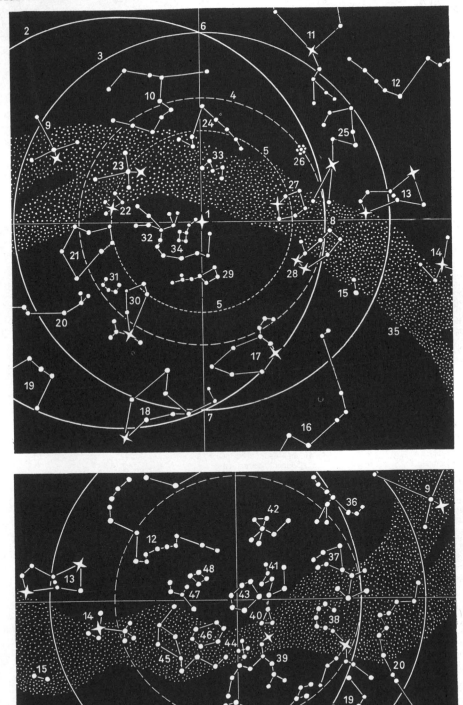

1-9 der Mond
- *the moon*
1 die Mondbahn (der Mondumlauf um die Erde)
- *moon's path (moon's orbit round the earth)*
2-7 die Mondphasen *f* (der Mondwechsel)
- *lunar phases (moon's phases, lunation)*
2 der Neumond
- *new moon*
3 die Mondsichel (der zunehmende Mond)
- *crescent (crescent moon, waxing moon)*
4 der Halbmond (das erste Mondviertel)
- *half-moon (first quarter)*
5 der Vollmond
- *full moon*
6 der Halbmond (das letzte Mondviertel)
- *half-moon (last quarter, third quarter)*
7 die Mondsichel (der abnehmende Mond)
- *crescent (crescent moon, waning moon)*
8 die Erde (Erdkugel)
- *the earth (terrestrial globe)*
9 die Richtung der Sonnenstrahlen *m*
- *direction of the sun's rays*
10-21 die scheinbare Sonnenbahn zu Beginn *m* der Jahreszeiten *f*
- *apparent path of the sun at the beginning of the seasons*
10 die Himmelsachse
- *celestial axis*
11 der Zenit
- *zenith*
12 die Horizontalebene
- *horizontal plane*
13 der Nadir
- *nadir*
14 der Ostpunkt
- *east point*
15 der Westpunkt
- *west point*
16 der Nordpunkt
- *north point*
17 der Südpunkt
- *south point*
18 die scheinbare Sonnenbahn am 21. Dezember *m*
- *apparent path of the sun on 21 December*
19 die scheinbare Sonnenbahn 21. März *m* u. 23. September *m*
- *apparent path of the sun on 21 March and 23 September*
20 die scheinbare Sonnenbahn am 21. Juni *m*
- *apparent path of the sun on 21 June*
21 die Dämmerungsgrenze
- *border of the twilight area*
22-28 die Drehbewegungen *f* der Erdachse
- *rotary motions of the earth's axis*
22 die Achse der Ekliptik
- *axis of the ecliptic*
23 die Himmelssphäre
- *celestial sphere*
24 die Bahn des Himmelspols *m* (Präzession *f* und Nutation *f*)
- *path of the celestial pole (precession and nutation)*

25 die instantane Rotationsachse
- *instantaneous axis of rotation*
26 der Himmelspol
- *celestial pole*
27 die mittlere Rotationsachse
- *mean axis of rotation*
28 die Polhodie
- *polhode*
29-35 Sonnen- und Mondfinsternis [nicht maßstäblich]
- *solar and lunar eclipse [not to scale]*
29 die Sonne
- *the sun*
30 die Erde
- *the earth*
31 der Mond
- *the moon*
32 die Sonnenfinsternis
- *solar eclipse*
33 die Totalitätszone
- *area of the earth in which the eclipse appears total*
34-35 die Mondfinsternis
- *lunar eclipse*
34 der Halbschatten
- *penumbra (partial shadow)*
35 der Kernschatten
- *umbra (total shadow)*
36-41 die Sonne
- *the sun*
36 die Sonnenscheibe
- *solar disc (disk) (solar globe, solar sphere)*
37 Sonnenflecken *m*
- *sunspots*
38 Wirbel *m* in der Umgebung von Sonnenflecken *m*
- *cyclones in the area of sunspots*
39 die Korona (Corona), der bei totaler Sonnenfinsternis oder mit Spezialinstrumenten *n* beobachtbare Sonnenrand
- *corona (solar corona), observable during total solar eclipse or by means of special instruments*
40 Protuberanzen *f*
- *prominences (solar prominences)*
41 der Mondrand bei totaler Sonnenfinsternis
- *moon's limb during a total solar eclipse*
42-52 die Planeten *m* (das Planetensystem, Sonnensystem) [nicht maßstäblich] und die Planetenzeichen *n* (Planetensymbole)
- *planets (planetary system, solar system) [not to scale] and planet symbols*
42 die Sonne
- *the sun*
43 der Merkur
- *Mercury*
44 die Venus
- *Venus*
45 die Erde mit dem Erdmond *m*, ein Satellit *m* (Trabant)
- *Earth, with the moon, a satellite*
46 der Mars mit zwei Monden *m*
- *Mars, with two moons (satellites)*
47 die Planetoiden *m* (Asteroiden)
- *asteroids (minor planets)*
48 der Jupiter mit 14 Monden *m*
- *Jupiter, with 14 moons (satellites)*
49 der Saturn mit 10 Monden *m*
- *Saturn, with 10 moons (satellites)*

50 der Uranus mit fünf Monden *m*
- *Uranus, with five moons (satellites)*
51 der Neptun mit zwei Monden *m*
- *Neptune, with two moons (satellites)*
52 der Pluto
- *Pluto*
53-64 die Tierkreiszeichen *n* (Zodiakussymbole)
- *signs of the zodiac (zodiacal signs)*
53 Widder *m* (Aries)
- *Aries (the Ram)*
54 Stier *m* (Taurus)
- *Taurus (the Bull)*
55 Zwillinge *m* (Gemini)
- *Gemini (the Twins)*
56 Krebs *m* (Cancer)
- *Cancer (the Crab)*
57 Löwe *m* (Leo)
- *Leo (the Lion)*
58 Jungfrau *f* (Virgo)
- *Virgo (the Virgin)*
59 Waage *f* (Libra)
- *Libra (the Balance, the Scales)*
60 Skorpion *m* (Scorpius)
- *Scorpio (the Scorpion)*
61 Schütze *m* (Sagittarius)
- *Sagittarius (the Archer)*
62 Steinbock *m* (Capricornus)
- *Capricorn (the Goat, the Sea Goat)*
63 Wassermann *m* (Aquarius)
- *Aquarius (the Water Carrier, the Water Bearer)*
64 Fische *m* (Pisces)
- *Pisces (the Fish)*

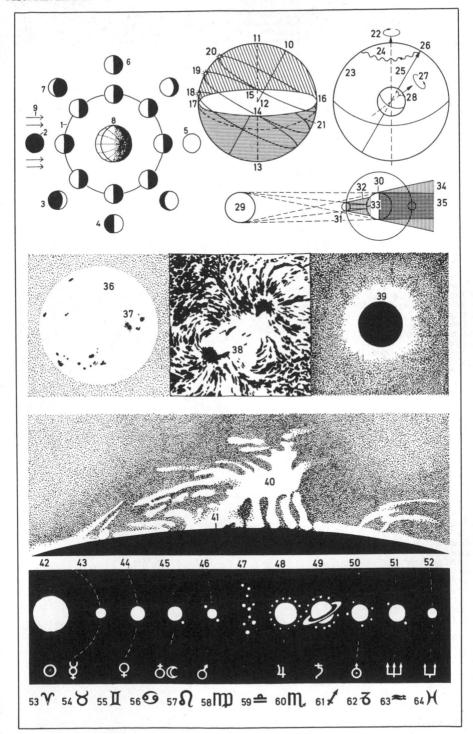

1-16 das Europäische
Südobservatorium (ESO) auf dem
La Silla in *Chile*, eine Sternwarte
(Observatorium *n*) [Schnitt]
- *the European Southern Observatory
(ESO) on* Cerro la Silla, Chile, *an
observatory [section]*
1 der Hauptspiegel von 3,6 m
Durchmesser *m*
- *primary mirror (main mirror) with
a diameter of 3.6 m (144 inches)*
2 die Primärfokuskabine mit der
Halterung für die Sekundärspiegel *m*
- *prime focus cage with mounting for
secondary mirrors*
3 der Planspiegel für den
Coudé-Strahlengang
- *flat mirror for the coudé ray path*
4 die Cassegrain-Kabine
- *Cassegrain cage*
5 der Gitterspektrograph
- *grating spectrograph*
6 die spektrographische Kamera
- *spectrographic camera*
7 der Stundenachsenantrieb
- *hour axis drive*
8 die Stundenachse
- *hour axis*
9 das Hufeisen der Montierung
- *horseshoe mounting*
10 die hydraulische Lagerung
- *hydrostatic bearing*
11 Primär- und
Sekundärfokuseinrichtungen *f*
- *primary and secondary focusing
devices*
12 das Kuppeldach (die Drehkuppel)
- *observatory dome (revolving dome)*
13 der Spalt (Beobachtungsspalt)
- *observation opening*
14 das vertikal bewegliche
Spaltsegment
- *vertically movable dome shutter*
15 der Windschirm
- *wind screen*
16 der Siderostat
- *siderostat*
17-28 das Planetarium *Stuttgart*
[Schnitt]
- *the* Stuttgart *Planetarium [section]*
17 der Verwaltungs-, Werkstatt- und
Magazinbereich
- *administration, workshop, and
store area*
18 die Stahlspinne
- *steel scaffold*
19 die glasvertafelte Pyramide
- *glass pyramid*
20 die drehbare Bogenleiter
- *revolving arched ladder*
21 die Projektionskuppel
- *projection dome*
22 die Lichtblende
- *light stop*
23 der Planetariumsprojektor
- *planetarium projector*
24 der Versenkschacht
- *well*
25 das Foyer
- *foyer*
26 der Filmvorführraum
- *theatre* (Am. *theater*)
27 die Filmvorführkabine
- *projection booth*
28 der Gründungspfahl
- *foundation pile*

29-33 das Sonnenobservatorium *Kitt
Peak* bei *Tucson, Ariz.* [Schnitt]
- *the* Kitt Peak *solar observatory
near* Tucson, Ariz. *[section]*
29 der Sonnenspiegel (Heliostat)
- *heliostat*
30 der teilweise unterirdische
Beobachtungsschacht
- *sunken observation shaft*
31 der wassergekühlte
Windschutzschild
- *water-cooled windshield*
32 der Konkavspiegel
- *concave mirror*
33 der Beobachtungs- und
Spektrographenraum
- *observation room housing the
spectrograph*

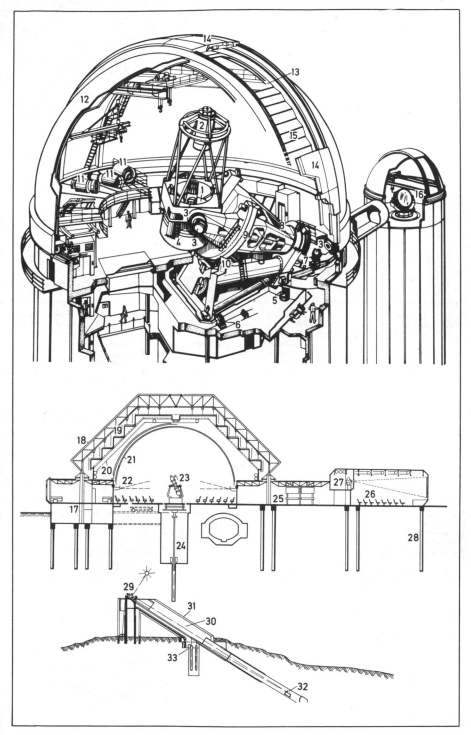

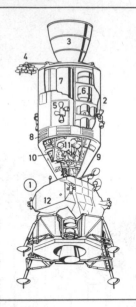
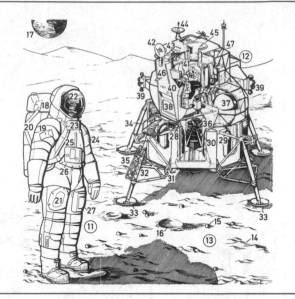

1 die Apollo-Raumeinheit
 - *Apollo spacecraft*
2 die Betriebseinheit (das Service
  module, SM)
 - *service module (SM)*
3 die Düse des
  Hauptraketentriebwerks *n*
 - *nozzle of the main rocket engine*
4 die Richtantenne
 - *directional antenna*
5 der Steuerraketensatz
 - *manoeuvring (Am. maneuvering)*
  rockets
6 die Sauerstoff- und
  Wasserstofftanks *m* für die
  Bordenergieanlage
 - *oxygen and hydrogen tanks for the*
  spacecraft's energy system
7 der Treibstofftank
 - *fuel tank*
8 die Radiatoren *m* der Bordenergieanlage
 - *radiators of the spacecraft's energy*
  system
9 die Kommandoeinheit
  (Apollo-Raumkapsel)
 - *command module (Apollo space*
  capsule)
10 die Einstiegluke der Raumkapsel
 - *entry hatch of the space capsule*
11 der Astronaut
 - *astronaut*
12 die Mondlandeeinheit (das Lunar
  module, LM)
 - *lunar module (LM)*
13 die Mondoberfläche, eine
  Stauboberfläche
 - *moon's surface (lunar surface), a*
  dust-covered surface
14 der Mondstaub
 - *lunar dust*
15 der Gesteinsbrocken
 - *piece of rock*
16 der Meteoritenkrater
 - *meteorite crater*

17 die Erde
 - *the earth*
18-27 der Raumanzug
 - *space suit (extra-vehicular suit)*
18 das Sauerstoffnotgerät
 - *emergency oxygen apparatus*
19 die Sonnenbrillentasche [mit
  Sonnenbrille *f* für den Bordgebrauch]
 - *sunglass pocket [with sunglasses for*
  use on board]
20 das Lebenserhaltungsgerät, ein
  Tornistergerät *n*
 - *life support system (life support*
  pack), a backpack unit
21 die Zugangsklappe
 - *access flap*
22 der Raumanzughelm mit
  Lichtschutzblenden *f*
 - *space suit helmet with sun filters*
23 der Kontrollkasten des
  Tornistergeräts *n*
 - *control box of the life support pack*
24 die Tasche für die Stablampe
 - *penlight pocket*
25 die Zugangsklappe für das
  Spülventil
 - *access flap for the purge valve*
26 Schlauch- und Kabelanschlüsse *m*
  für Radio *n*, Ventilierung *f* und
  Wasserkühlung *f*
 - *tube and cable connections for the*
  radio, ventilation and
  water-cooling systems
27 die Tasche für Schreibutensilien *n*,
  Werkzeug u.ä.
 - *pocket for pens, tools, etc.*
28-36 die Abstiegsstufe
 - *descent stage*
28 der Verbindungsbeschlag
 - *connector*
29 der Treibstofftank
 - *fuel tank*
30 das Triebwerk
 - *engine*

31 die Landegestell-Spreizmechanik
 - *mechanism for unfolding the legs*
32 das Hauptfederbein
 - *main shock absorber*
33 der Landeteller
 - *landing pad*
34 die Ein- und Ausstiegsplattform
 - *ingress/egress platform (hatch*
  platform)
35 die Zugangsleiter
 - *ladder to platform and hatch*
36 das Triebwerkskardan
 - *cardan mount for engine*
37-47 die Aufstiegsstufe
 - *ascent stage*
37 der Treibstofftank
 - *fuel tank*
38 die Ein- und Ausstiegsluke
 - *ingress/egress hatch (entry/exit*
  hatch)
39 die Lageregelungstriebwerke *n*
 - *LM manoeuvring (Am. maneuvering)*
  rockets
40 das Fenster
 - *window*
41 der Besatzungsraum
 - *crew compartment*
42 die Rendezvous-Radarantenne
 - *rendezvous radar antenna*
43 der Trägheitsmeßwertgeber
 - *inertial measurement unit*
44 die Richtantenne für die
  Bodenstelle
 - *directional antenna for ground*
  control
45 die obere Luke
 - *upper hatch (docking hatch)*
46 die Anflugantenne
 - *inflight antenna*
47 der Dockingeinschnitt
 - *docking target recess*

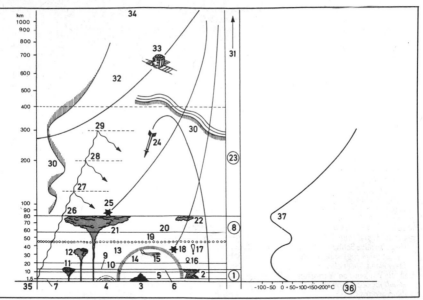

1 die Troposphäre
- *the troposphere*
2 Gewitterwolken *f*
- *thunderclouds*
3 der höchste Berg *Mount Everest* [8 882 m]
- *the highest mountain,*
  Mount Everest [8,882m]
4 der Regenbogen
- *rainbow*
5 die Starkwindschicht
- *jet stream level*
6 die Nullschicht (Umkehr der
  senkrechten Luftbewegungen *f*)
- *zero level (inversion of vertical air*
  movement)
7 die Grundschicht
- *ground layer (surface boundary*
  layer)
8 die Stratosphäre
- *the stratosphere*
9 die Tropopause
- *tropopause*
10 die Trennschicht (Schicht
   schwächerer Luftbewegungen *f*)
- *separating layer (layer of weaker*
  air movement)
11 die Atombombenexplosion
- *atomic explosion*
12 die Wasserstoffbombenexplosion
- *hydrogen bomb explosion*
13 die Ozonschicht
- *ozone layer*
14 die Schallwellenausbreitung
- *range of sound wave propagation*
15 das Stratosphärenflugzeug
- *stratosphere aircraft*
16 der bemannte Ballon
- *manned balloon*
17 der Meßballon
- *sounding balloon*
18 der Meteor
- *meteor*
19 die Obergrenze der Ozonschicht
- *upper limit of ozone layer*

20 die Nullschicht
- *zero level*
21 der Krakatau-Ausbruch
- *eruption of Krakatoa*
22 leuchtende Nachtwolken *f*
- *luminous clouds (noctilucent*
  clouds)
23 die Ionosphäre
- *the ionosphere*
24 der Forschungsraketenbereich
- *range of research rockets*
25 die Sternschnuppe
- *shooting star*
26 die Kurzwelle (Hochfrequenz)
- *short wave (high frequency)*
27 die E-Schicht
- *E-layer (Heaviside-Kennelly*
  Layer)
28 die F₁-Schicht
- *F₁-layer*
29 die F₂-Schicht
- *F₂-layer*
30 das Polarlicht
- *aurora (polar light)*
31 die Exosphäre
- *the exosphere*
32 die Atomschicht
- *atom layer*
33 der Meßsatellitenbereich
- *range of satellite sounding*
34 der Übergang zum Weltraum
- *fringe region*
35 die Höhenskala
- *altitude scale*
36 die Temperaturskala
- *temperature scale (thermometric*
  scale)
37 die Temperaturlinie
- *temperature graph*

1-19 Wolken *f* und Witterung *f*
(Wetter *n*)
- *clouds and weather*
1-4 die Wolken einheitlicher
Luftmassen *f*
- *clouds found in homogeneous air*
  masses
1 der Kumulus (Cumulus, Cumulus
  humilis), eine Quellwolke (flache
  Haufenwolke, Schönwetterwolke)
- *cumulus (woolpack cloud, cumulus*
  humilis, fair-weather cumulus), a
  heap cloud
  (flat-based heap cloud)
2 der Cumulus congestus, eine
  stärker quellende Haufenwolke
- *cumulus congestus, a heap cloud*
  with more marked vertical
  development
3 der Stratokumulus
  (Stratocumulus), eine tiefe,
  gegliederte Schichtwolke
- *stratocumulus, a layer cloud (sheet*
  cloud) arranged in heavy masses
4 der Stratus (Hochnebel), eine tiefe,
  gleichförmige Schichtwolke
- *stratus (high fog), a thick, uniform*
  layer cloud (sheet cloud)
5-12 die Wolken *f* an Warmfronten *f*
- *clouds found at warm fronts*
5 die Warmfront
- *warm front*
6 der Zirrus (Cirrus), eine hohe bis
  sehr hohe Eisnadelwolke, dünn,
  mit sehr mannigfaltigen Formen *f*
- *cirrus, a high to very high*
  ice-crystal cloud, thin and
  assuming a wide variety of forms
7 der Zirrostratus (Cirrostratus), eine
  Eisnadelschleierwolke
- *cirrostratus, an ice-crystal cloud*
  veil
8 der Altostratus, eine mittelhohe
  Schichtwolke
- *altostratus, a layer cloud (sheet*
  cloud) of medium height
9 der Altostratus praecipitans, eine
  Schichtwolke mit Niederschlag *m*
  (Fallstreifen) in der Höhe
- *altostratus praecipitans, a layer*
  cloud (sheet cloud) with
  precipitation in its upper parts
10 der Nimbostratus, eine
  Regenwolke, vertikal sehr
  mächtige Schichtwolke, aus der
  Niederschlag *m* (Regen oder
  Schnee) fällt
- *nimbostratus, a rain cloud, a layer*
  cloud (sheet cloud) of very large
  vertical extent which produces
  precipitation (rain or snow)
11 der Fraktostratus (Fractostratus),
  ein Wolkenfetzen *m* unterhalb des
  Nimbostratus *m*
- *fractostratus, a ragged cloud*
  occurring beneath nimbostratus
12 der Fraktokumulus
  (Fractocumulus), ein
  Wolkenfetzen *m* wie 11, jedoch mit
  quelligen Formen *f*
- *fractocumulus, a ragged cloud like*
  11 but with billowing shapes
13-17 die Wolken *f* an Kaltfronten *f*
- *clouds at cold fronts*
13 die Kaltfront
- *cold front*

14 der Zirrokumulus (Cirrocumulus),
  eine feine Schäfchenwolke
- *cirrocumulus, thin fleecy cloud in*
  the form of globular masses;
  covering the sky: mackerel sky
15 der Altokumulus (Altocumulus),
  eine grobe Schäfchenwolke
- *altocumulus, a cloud in the form of*
  large globular masses
16 der Altocumulus castellanus und
  der Altocumulus floccus,
  Unterformen zu 15
- *altocumulus castellanus and*
  altocumulus floccus, species of 15
17 der Kumulonimbus
  (Cumulonimbus), eine vertikal
  sehr mächtige Quellwolke, bei
  Wärmegewittern *n* unter 1-4
  einzuordnen
- *cumulonimbus, a heap cloud of*
  very large vertical extent, to be
  classified under 1-4 in the case of
  tropical storms
18-19 die Niederschlagsformen *f*
- *types of precipitation*
18 der Landregen oder der verbreitete
  Schneefall, ein gleichförmiger
  Niederschlag *m*
- *steady rain or snow covering a large*
  area, precipitation of uniform
  intensity
19 der Schauerniederschlag (Schauer),
  ein ungleichmäßiger (strichweise
  auftretender) Niederschlag *m*
- *shower, scattered precipitation*

schwarze Pfeile = Kaltluft
black arrow = cold air
weiße Pfeile = Warmluft
white arrow = warm air

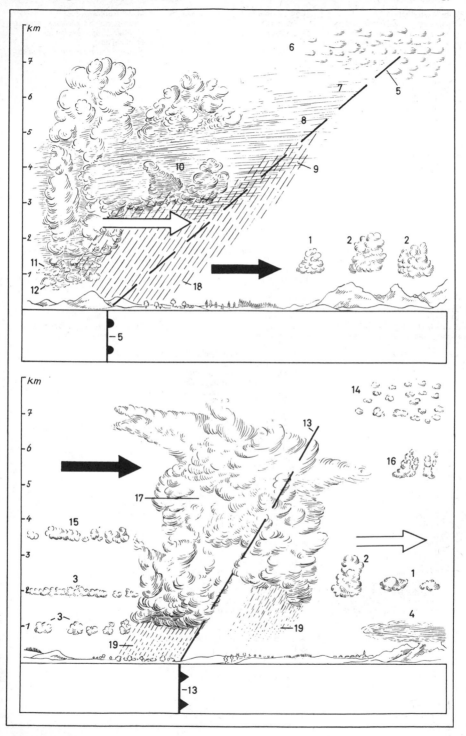

1-39 die Wetterkarte
- *weather chart (weather map, surface chart, surface synoptic chart)*
1 die Isobare (Linie gleichen Luftdrucks *m* im Meeresniveau *n*)
- *isobar (line of equal or constant atmospheric or barometric pressure at sea level)*
2 die Pliobare (Isobare über 1 000 mbar)
- *pleiobar (isobar of over 1,000 mb)*
3 die Miobare (Isobare unter 1 000 mbar)
- *meiobar (isobar of under 1,000 mb)*
4 die Angabe des Luftdrucks *m* in Millibar *n* (mbar)
- *atmospheric (barometric) pressure given in millibars*
5 das Tiefdruckgebiet (Tief, die Zyklone, Depression)
- *low-pressure area (low, cyclone, depression)*
6 das Hochdruckgebiet (Hoch, die Antizyklone)
- *high-pressure area (high, anticyclone)*
7 eine Wetterbeobachtungsstelle (meteorolog. Station, Wetterstation) od. ein Wetterbeobachtungsschiff *n*
- *observatory (meteorological watch office, weather station) or ocean station vessel (weather ship)*
8 die Temperaturangabe
- *temperature*
9-19 die Darstellung des Windes *m*
- *means of representing wind direction (wind-direction symbols)*
9 der Windpfeil zur Bez. der Windrichtung
- *wind-direction shaft (wind arrow)*
10 die Windfahne zur Bez. der Windstärke
- *wind-speed barb (wind-speed feather) indicating wind speed*
11 die Windstille (Kalme)
- *calm*
12 1-2 Knoten *m* (1 Knoten = 1,852 km/h)
- *1-2 knots (1 knot = 1.852 kph)*
13 3-7 Knoten
- *3-7 knots*
14 8-12 Knoten
- *8-12 knots*
15 13-17 Knoten
- *13-17 knots*
16 18-22 Knoten
- *18-22 knots*
17 23-27 Knoten
- *23-27 knots*
18 28-32 Knoten
- *28-32 knots*
19 58-62 Knoten
- *58-62 knots*
20-24 Himmelsbedeckung *f* (Bewölkung)
- *state of the sky (distribution of the cloud cover)*
20 wolkenlos
- *clear (cloudless)*
21 heiter
- *fair*
22 halbbedeckt
- *partly cloudy*
23 wolkig
- *cloudy*
24 bedeckt
- *overcast (sky mostly or completely covered)*

25-29 Fronten *f* u. Luftströmungen *f*
- *fronts and air currents*
25 die Okklusion
- *occlusion (occluded front)*
26 die Warmfront
- *warm front*
27 die Kaltfront
- *cold front*
28 die warme Luftströmung
- *warm airstream (warm current)*
29 die kalte Luftströmung
- *cold airstream (cold current)*
30-39 Wettererscheinungen *f*
- *meteorological phenomena*
30 das Niederschlagsgebiet
- *precipitation area*
31 Nebel *m*
- *fog*
32 Regen *m*
- *rain*
33 Sprühregen *m* (Nieseln *n*)
- *drizzle*
34 Schneefall *m*
- *snow*
35 Graupeln *n*
- *ice pellets (graupel, soft hail)*
36 Hagel *m*
- *hail*
37 Schauer *m*
- *shower*
38 Gewitter *n*
- *thunderstorm*
39 Wetterleuchten *n*
- *lightning*
40-58 die Klimakarte
- *climatic map*
40 die Isotherme (Linie gleicher mittlerer Temperatur)
- *isotherm (line connecting points having equal mean temperature)*
41 die Nullisotherme (Linie durch alle Orte *m* mit 0 °C mittlerer Jahrestemperatur)
- *0 °C (zero) isotherm (line connecting points having a mean annual temperature of 0 °C)*
42 die Isochimene (Linie gleicher mittlerer Wintertemperatur)
- *isocheim (line connecting points having equal mean winter temperature)*
43 die Isothere (Linie gleicher Sommertemperatur)
- *isothere (line connecting points having equal mean summer temperature)*
44 die Isohelie (Linie gleicher Sonnenscheindauer)
- *isohel (line connecting points having equal duration of sunshine)*
45 die Isohyete (Linie gleicher Niederschlagssumme)
- *isohyet (line connecting points having equal amounts of precipitation)*
46-52 die Windsysteme *n*
- *atmospheric circulation (wind systems)*
46-47 die Kalmengürtel *m*
- *calm belts*
46 der äquatoriale Kalmengürtel *m*
- *equatorial trough (equatorial calms, doldrums)*
47 die subtrop. Stillengürtel *m* (Roßbreiten *f*)
- *subtropical high-pressure belts (horse latitudes)*

48 der Nordostpassat
- *north-east trade winds (north-east trades, tropical easterlies)*
49 der Südostpassat
- *south-east trade winds (south-east trades, tropical easterlies)*
50 die Zonen *f* der veränderl. Westwinde *m*
- *zones of the variable westerlies*
51 die Zonen *f* der polaren Winde *m*
- *polar wind zones*
52 der Sommermonsun
- *summer monsoon*
53-58 die Klimate *n* der Erde
- *earth's climates*
53 das äquatoriale Klima: der trop. Regengürtel
- *equatorial climate: tropical zone (tropical rain zone)*
54 die beiden Trockengürtel *m*: die Wüsten- und Steppenzonen *f*
- *the two arid zones (equatorial dry zones): desert and steppe zones*
55 die beiden warm-gemäßigten Regengürtel *m*
- *the two temperate rain zones*
56 das boreale Klima (Schnee-Wald-Klima)
- *boreal climate (snow forest climate)*
57-58 die polaren Klimate *n*
- *polar climates*
57 das Tundrenklima
- *tundra climate*
58 das Klima ewigen Frostes *m*
- *perpetual frost climate*

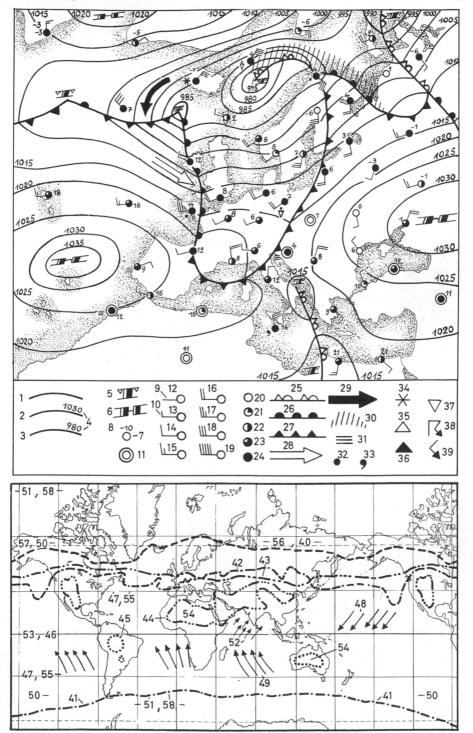

1 das Quecksilberbarometer, ein Heberbarometer *n*, ein Flüssigkeitsbarometer *n*
- *mercury barometer, a siphon barometer, a liquid-column barometer*
2 die Quecksilbersäule
- *mercury column*
3 die Millibarteilung (Millimeterteilung)
- *millibar scale (millimetre, Am. millimeter, scale)*
4 der Barograph, ein selbstschreibendes Aneroidbarometer
- *barograph, a self-registering aneroid barometer*
5 die Trommel
- *drum (recording drum)*
6 der Dosensatz
- *bank of aneroid capsules (aneroid boxes)*
7 der Schreibhebel
- *recording arm*
8 der Hygrograph
- *hygrograph*
9 das Feuchtigkeitsmeßelement (die Haarharfe)
- *hygrometer element (hair element)*
10 die Standkorrektion
- *reading adjustment*
11 die Amplitudeneinstellung
- *amplitude adjustment*
12 der Schreibarm
- *recording arm*
13 die Schreibfeder
- *recording pen*
14 die Wechselräder *n* für das Uhrwerk
- *change gears for the clockwork drive*
15 der Ausschalter für den Schreibarm
- *off switch for the recording arm*
16 die Trommel
- *drum (recording drum)*
17 die Zeitteilung
- *time scale*
18 das Gehäuse
- *case (housing)*
19 der Thermograph
- *thermograph*
20 die Trommel
- *drum (recording drum)*
21 der Schreibhebel
- *recording arm*
22 das Meßelement
- *sensing element*
23 das Silverdisk-Pyrheliometer, ein Instrument *n* zur Messung der Energie der Sonnenstrahlen *m*
- *silver-disc (silver-disk) pyrheliometer, an instrument for measuring the sun's radiant energy*
24 die Silberscheibe
- *silver disc (disk)*
25 das Thermometer
- *thermometer*
26 die isolierende Holzverkleidung
- *wooden insulating casing*
27 der Tubus, mit Diaphragma *n*
- *tube with diaphragm (diaphragmed tube)*
28 das Windmeßgerät (der Windmesser, das Anemometer)
- *wind gauge (Am. gage) (anemometer)*

29 das Gerät zur Anzeige der Windgeschwindigkeit *f*
- *wind-speed indicator (wind-speed meter)*
30 der Schalenstern mit Hohlschalen *f*
- *cross arms with hemispherical cups*
31 das Gerät zur Anzeige der Windrichtung *f*
- *wind-direction indicator*
32 die Windfahne
- *wind vane*
33 das Aspirationspsychrometer
- *aspiration psychrometer*
34 das „trockene" Thermometer
- *dry bulb thermometer*
35 das „feuchte" Thermometer
- *wet bulb thermometer*
36 das Strahlungsschutzrohr
- *solar radiation shielding*
37 das Saugrohr
- *suction tube*
38 der schreibende Regenmesser
- *recording rain gauge (Am. gage)*
39 das Schutzgehäuse
- *protective housing (protective casing)*
40 das Auffanggefäß
- *collecting vessel*
41 das Regendach
- *rain cover*
42 die Registriervorrichtung
- *recording mechanism*
43 das Heberrohr
- *siphon tube*
44 der Niederschlagsmesser (Regenmesser)
- *precipitation gauge (Am. gage) (rain gauge)*
45 das Auffanggefäß
- *collecting vessel*
46 der Sammelbehälter
- *storage vessel*
47 das Meßglas
- *measuring glass*
48 das Schneekreuz
- *insert for measuring snowfall*
49 die Thermometerhütte
- *thermometer screen (thermometer shelter)*
50 der Hygrograph
- *hygrograph*
51 der Thermograph
- *thermograph*
52 das Psychrometer
- *psychrometer (wet and dry bulb thermometer)*
53-54 Extremthermometer *n*
- *thermometers for measuring extremes of temperature*
53 das Maximumthermometer
- *maximum thermometer*
54 das Minimumthermometer
- *minimum thermometer*
55 das Radiosondengespann
- *radiosonde assembly*
56 der Wasserstoffballon
- *hydrogen balloon*
57 der Fallschirm
- *parachute*
58 der Radarreflektor mit Abstandsschnur *f*
- *radar reflector with spacing lines*
59 der Instrumentenkasten mit Radiosonde *f* (ein Kurzwellensender *m*) und Antenne *f*
- *instrument housing with radiosonde (a short-wave transmitter) and antenna*

60 das Transmissometer, ein Sichtweitenmeßgerät *n*
- *transmissometer, an instrument for measuring visibility*
61 das Registriergerät
- *recording instrument (recorder)*
62 der Sender
- *transmitter*
63 der Empfänger
- *receiver*
64 der Wettersatellit (ITOS-Satellit)
- *weather satellite (ITOS satellite)*
65 Wärmeregulierungsklappen *f*
- *temperature regulation flaps*
66 der Solarzellenausleger
- *solar panel*
67 die Fernsehkamera
- *television camera*
68 die Antenne
- *antenna*
69 der Sonnensensor
- *solar sensor (sun sensor)*
70 die Telemetrieantenne
- *telemetry antenna*
71 das Radiometer
- *radiometer*

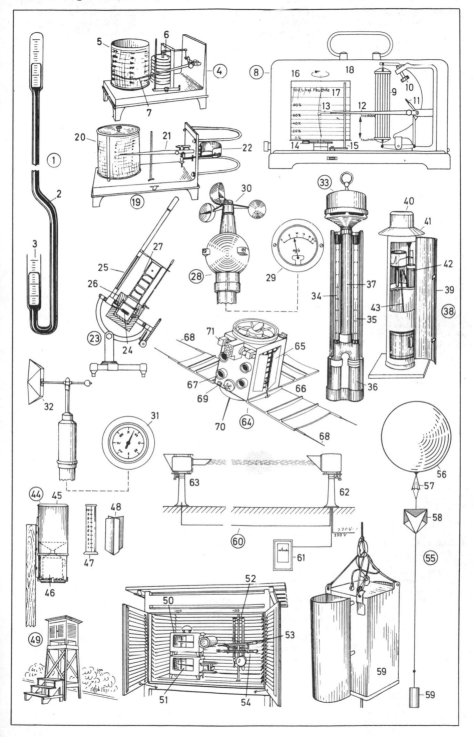

1-5 der Schalenaufbau der Erde
- *layered structure of the earth*
1 die Erdkruste
- *earth's crust (outer crust of the earth, lithosphere, oxysphere)*
2 die Fließzone
- *hydrosphere*
3 der Mantel
- *mantle*
4 die Zwischenschicht
- *sima (intermediate layer)*
5 der Kern (Erdkern)
- *core (earth core, centrosphere, barysphere)*
6-12 die hypsometr. Kurve der Erdoberfläche
- *hypsographic curve of the earth's surface*
6 die Gipfelung
- *peak*
7 die Kontinentaltafel
- *continental mass*
8 der Schelf (Kontinentalsockel)
- *continental shelf (continental platform, shelf)*
9 der Kontinentalabhang
- *continental slope*
10 die Tiefseetafel
- *deep-sea floor (abyssal plane)*
11 der Meeresspiegel
- *sea level*
12 der Tiefseegraben
- *deep-sea trench*
13-28 der Vulkanismus
- *volcanism (vulcanicity)*
13 der Schildvulkan
- *shield volcano*
14 die Lavadecke (der Deckenerguß)
- *lava plateau*
15 der tätige Vulkan, ein Stratovulkan *m* (Schichtvulkan)
- *active volcano, a stratovolcano (composite volcano)*
16 der Vulkankrater (Krater)
- *volcanic crater (crater)*
17 der Schlot (Eruptionskanal)
- *volcanic vent*
18 der Lavastrom
- *lava stream*
19 der Tuff (die vulkan. Lockermassen *f*)
- *tuff (fragmented volcanic material)*
20 der Subvulkan
- *subterranean volcano*
21 der Geysir (Geiser, die Springquelle)
- *geyser*
22 die Wasser-und-Dampf-Fontäne
- *jet of hot water and steam*
23 die Sinterterrassen *f*
- *sinter terraces (siliceous sinter terraces, fiorite terraces, pearl sinter terraces)*
24 der Wallberg
- *cone*
25 das Maar
- *maar (extinct volcano)*
26 der Tuffwall
- *tuff deposit*
27 die Schlotbrekzie
- *breccia*
28 der Schlot des erloschenen Vulkans *m*
- *vent of extinct volcano*
29-31 der Tiefenmagmatismus
- *plutonic magmatism*
29 der Batholit (das Tiefengestein)
- *batholite (massive protrusion)*

30 der Lakkolith, eine Intrusion
- *lacolith, an intrusion*
31 der Lagergang, eine Erzlagerstätte
- *sill, an ore deposit*
32-38 das Erdbeben (*Arten:* das tekton. Beben, vulkan. Beben, Einsturzbeben)
und die Erdbebenkunde (Seismologie)
- *earthquake (kinds: tectonic quake, volcanic quake) and seismology*
32 das Hypozentrum (der Erdbebenherd)
- *earthquake focus (seismic focus, hypocentre, Am. hypocenter)*
33 das Epizentrum (der Oberflächenpunkt senkrecht über dem Hypozentrum *n*)
- *epicentre (Am. epicenter), point on the earth's surface directly above the focus*
34 die Herdtiefe
- *depth of focus*
35 der Stoßstrahl
- *shock wave*
36 die Oberflächenwellen *f* (Erdbebenwellen)
- *surface waves (seismic waves)*
37 die Isoseiste (Verbindungslinie *f* der Orte *m* gleicher Bebenstärke *f*)
- *isoseismal (line connecting points of equal intensity of earthquake shock)*
38 das Epizentralgebiet (makroseism. Schüttergebiet)
- *epicentral area (area of macroseismic vibration)*
39 **der Horizontalseismograph** (Seismometer *n*, Erdbebenmesser *m*)
- *horizontal seismograph (seismometer)*
40 der magnetische Dämpfer
- *electromagnetic damper*
41 der Justierknopf für die Eigenperiode des Pendels *n*
- *adjustment knob for the period of free oscillation of the pendulum*
42 das Federgelenk für die Pendelaufhängung
- *spring attachment for the suspension of the pendulum*
43 die Pendelmasse (stationäre Masse)
- *mass*
44 die Induktionsspulen *f* für den Anzeigestrom des Registriergalvanometers *n*
- *induction coils for recording the voltage of the galvanometer*
45-54 Erdbebenwirkungen *f* (die Makroseismik)
- *effects of earthquakes*
45 der Wasserfall
- *waterfall (cataract, falls)*
46 der Bergrutsch (Erdrutsch, Felssturz)
- *landslide (rockslide, landslip, Am. rock slip)*
47 der Schuttstrom (das Ablagerungsgebiet)
- *talus (rubble, scree)*
48 die Abrißnische
- *scar (scaur, scaw)*
49 der Einsturztrichter
- *sink (sinkhole, swallowhole)*
50 die Geländeverschiebung (der Geländeabbruch)
- *dislocation (displacement)*

51 der Schlammerguß (Schlammkegel)
- *solifluction lobe (solifluction tongue)*
52 die Erdspalte (der Bodenriß)
- *fissure*
53 die Flutwelle, bei Seebeben *n*
- *tsunami (seismic sea wave) produced by seaquake (submarine earthquake)*
54 der gehobene Strand (die Strandterrasse)
- *raised beach*

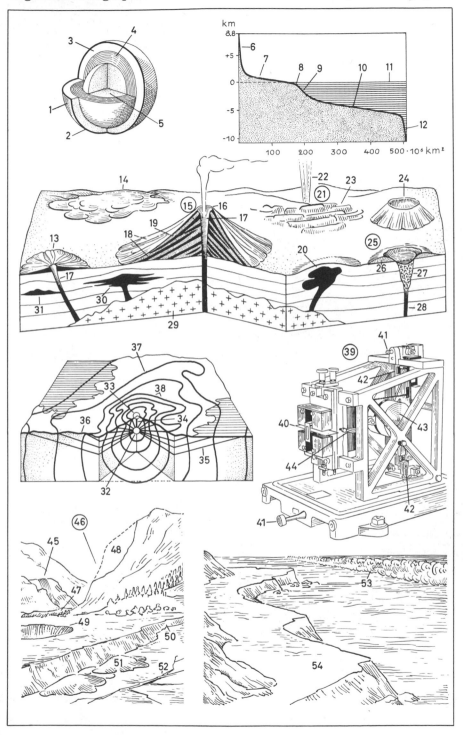

1-33 Geologie
- *geology*
1 die Lagerung der Sedimentgesteine *n*
- *stratification of sedimentary rock*
2 das Streichen
- *strike*
3 das Fallen (die Fallrichtung)
- *dip (angle of dip, true dip)*
4-20 die Gebirgsbewegungen *f*
- **orogeny** *(orogenis, tectogenis,
deformation of rocks by folding
and faulting)*
4-11 das Bruchschollengebirge
- **fault-block mountain** *(block
mountain)*
4 die Verwerfung (der Bruch)
- *fault*
5 die Verwerfungslinie
- *fault line (fault trace)*
6 die Sprunghöhe
- *fault throw*
7 die Überschiebung
- *normal fault (gravity fault, normal
slip fault, slump fault)*
8-11 zusammengesetzte Störungen *f*
- **complex faults**
8 der Staffelbruch
- *step fault (distributive fault,
multiple fault)*
9 die Pultscholle
- *tilt block*
10 der Horst
- *horst*
11 der Grabenbruch
- *graben*
12-20 das Faltengebirge
- **range of fold mountains** *(folded
mountains)*
12 die stehende Falte
- *symmetrical fold (normal fold)*
13 die schiefe Falte
- *asymmetrical fold*
14 die überkippte Falte
- *overfold*
15 die liegende Falte
- *recumbent fold (reclined fold)*
16 der Sattel (die Antiklinale)
- *saddle (anticline)*
17 die Sattelachse
- *anticlinal axis*
18 die Mulde (Synklinale)
- *trough (syncline)*
19 die Muldenachse
- *trough surface (trough plane,
synclinal axis)*
20 das Bruchfaltengebirge
- *anticlinorium*
21 **das gespannte** (artesische)
Grundwasser
- **groundwater under pressure**
(artesian water)
22 die wasserführende Schicht
- *water-bearing stratum (aquifer,
aquafer)*
23 das undurchlässige Gestein
- *impervious rock (impermeable rock)*
24 das Einzugsgebiet
- *drainage basin (catchment area)*
25 die Brunnenröhre
- *artesian well*
26 das emporquellende Wasser, ein
artesischer Brunnen *m*
- *rising water, an artesian spring*
27 **die Erdöllagerstätte** an einer
Antiklinale
- **petroleum reservoir** *in an anticline*

28 die undurchlässige Schicht
- *impervious stratum (impermeable
stratum)*
29 die poröse Schicht als
Speichergestein *n*
- *porous stratum acting as reservoir
rock*
30 das Erdgas, eine Gaskappe
- *natural gas, a gas cap*
31 das Erdöl
- *petroleum (crude oil)*
32 das Wasser (Randwasser)
- *underlying water*
33 der Bohrturm
- *derrick*
34 **das Mittelgebirge**
- **mountainous area**
35 die Bergkuppe
- *rounded mountain top*
36 der Bergrücken (Kamm)
- *mountain ridge (ridge)*
37 der Berghang (Abhang)
- *mountain slope*
38 die Hangquelle
- *hillside spring*
39-47 das Hochgebirge
- **high-mountain region**
39 die Bergkette, ein Bergmassiv *n*
- *mountain range, a massif*
40 der Gipfel (Berggipfel, die
Bergspitze)
- *summit (peak, top of the mountain)*
41 die Felsschulter
- *shoulder*
42 der Bergsattel
- *saddle*
43 die Wand (Steilwand)
- *rock face (steep face)*
44 die Hangrinne
- *gully*
45 die Schutthalde (das Felsgeröll)
- *talus (scree, detritus)*
46 der Saumpfad
- *bridle path*
47 der Paß (Bergpaß)
- *pass (col)*
48-56 das Gletschereis
- **glacial ice**
48 das Firnfeld (Kar)
- *firn field (firn basin, nevé)*
49 der Talgletscher
- *valley glacier*
50 die Gletscherspalte
- *crevasse*
51 das Gletschertor
- *glacier snout*
52 der Gletscherbach
- *subglacial stream*
53 die Seitenmoräne (Wallmoräne)
- *lateral moraine*
54 die Mittelmoräne
- *medial moraine*
55 die Endmoräne
- *end moraine*
56 der Gletschertisch
- *glacier table*

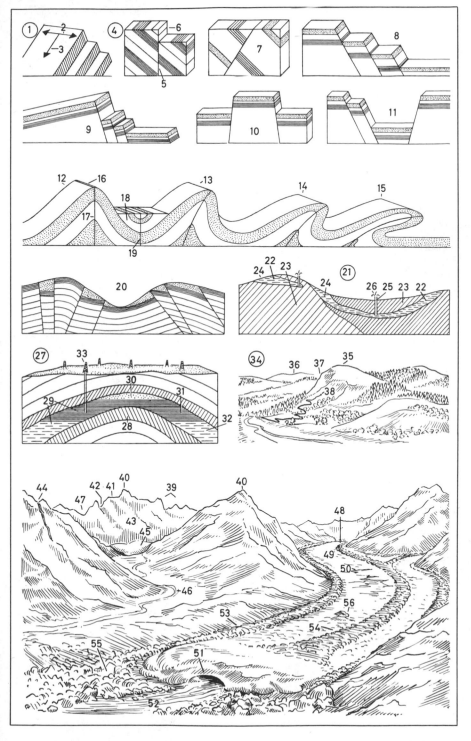

1-13 die Flußlandschaft
- *fluvial topography*
1 die Flußmündung, ein Delta *n*
- *river mouth, a delta*
2 der Mündungsarm, ein Flußarm *m*
- *distributary (distributary channel),*
  a river branch (river arm)
3 der See
- *lake*
4 das Ufer
- *bank*
5 die Halbinsel
- *peninsula (spit)*
6 die Insel
- *island*
7 die Bucht
- *bay (cove)*
8 der Bach
- *stream (brook, rivulet, creek)*
9 der Schwemmkegel
- *levee*
10 die Verlandungszone
- *alluvial plain*
11 der Mäander (die Flußwindung)
- *meander (river bend)*
12 der Umlaufberg
- *meander core (rock island)*
13 die Wiesenaue
- *meadow*
14-24 das Moor
- *bog (marsh)*
14 das Flachmoor
- *low-moor bog*
15 die Muddeschichten *f*
- *layers of decayed vegetable matter*
16 das Wasserkissen
- *entrapped water*
17 der Schilf- und Seggentorf
- *fen peat [consisting of rush and*
  sedge]
18 der Erlenbruchtorf
- *alder-swamp peat*
19 das Hochmoor
- *high-moor bog*
20 die jüngere Moostorfmasse
- *layer of recent sphagnum mosses*
21 der Grenzhorizont
- *boundary between layers (horizons)*
22 die ältere Moostorfmasse
- *layer of older sphagnum mosses*
23 der Moortümpel
- *bog pool*
24 die Verwässerungszone
- *swamp*
25-31 die Steilküste
- *cliffline (cliffs)*
25 die Klippe
- *rock*
26 das Meer (die See)
- *sea (ocean)*
27 die Brandung
- *surf*
28 das Kliff (der Steilhang)
- *cliff (cliff face, steep rock face)*
29 das Brandungsgeröll (Strandgeröll)
- *scree*
30 die Brandungshohlkehle
- *[wave-cut] notch*
31 die Abrasionsplatte
  (Brandungsplatte)
- *abrasion platform (wave-cut*
  platform)
32 das Atoll (das Lagunenriff,
  Kranzriff), ein Korallenriff *n*
- *atoll (ring-shaped coral reef), a*
  coral reef

33 die Lagune
- *lagoon*
34 der Strandkanal
- *breach (hole)*
35-44 die Flachküste (Strandebene,
  der Strand)
- *beach*
35 der Strandwall (die Flutgrenze)
- *high-water line (high-water mark,*
  tidemark)
36 die Uferwellen *f*
- *waves breaking on the shore*
37 die Buhne
- *groyne (Am. groin)*
38 der Buhnenkopf
- *groyne (Am. groin) head*
39 die Wanderdüne, eine Düne
- *wandering dune (migratory dune,*
  travelling, Am. traveling, dune), a
  dune
40 die Sicheldüne
- *barchan (barchane, barkhan,*
  crescentic dune)
41 die Rippelmarken *f*
- *ripple marks*
42 die Kupste
- *hummock*
43 der Windflüchter
- *wind cripple*
44 der Strandsee
- *coastal lake*
45 der Cañon
- *canyon (cañon, coulee)*
46 das Plateau (die Hochfläche)
- *plateau (tableland)*
47 die Felsterrasse
- *rock terrace*
48 das Schichtgestein
- *sedimentary rock (stratified rock)*
49 die Schichtstufe
- *river terrace (bed)*
50 die Kluft
- *joint*
51 der Cañonfluß
- *canyon river*
52-56 Talformen *f [Querschnitt]*
- *types of valley [cross section]*
52 die Klamm
- *gorge (ravine)*
53 das Kerbtal
- *V-shaped valley (V-valley)*
54 das offene Kerbtal
- *widened V-shaped valley*
55 das Sohlental
- *U-shaped valley (U-valley, trough*
  valley)
56 das Muldental
- *synclinal valley*
57-70 die Tallandschaft (das Flußtal)
- *river valley (valleyside)*
57 der Prallhang (Steilhang)
- *scarp (escarpment)*
58 der Gleithang (Flachhang)
- *slip-off slope*
59 der Tafelberg
- *mesa*
60 der Höhenzug
- *ridge*
61 der Fluß
- *river*
62 die Flußaue (Talaue)
- *flood plain*
63 die Felsterrasse
- *river terrace*
64 die Schotterterrasse
- *terracette*

65 die Tallehne
- *pediment*
66 die Anhöhe (der Hügel)
- *hill*
67 die Talsohle (der Talgrund)
- *valley floor (valley bottom)*
68 das Flußbett
- *riverbed*
69 die Ablagerungen *f*
- *sediment*
70 die Felssohle
- *bedrock*
71-83 die Karsterscheinungen *f* im
  Kalkstein *m*
- *karst formation in limestone*
71 die Doline, ein Einsturztrichter *m*
- *dolina, a sink (sinkhole,*
  swallowhole)
72 das Polje
- *polje*
73 die Flußversickerung
- *percolation of a river*
74 die Karstquelle
- *karst spring*
75 das Trockental
- *dry valley*
76 das Höhlensystem
- *system of caverns (system of caves)*
77 der Karstwasserspiegel
- *water level (water table) in a karst*
  formation
78 die undurchlässige Gesteinsschicht
- *impervious rock (impermeable rock)*
79 die Tropfsteinhöhle (Karsthöhle)
- *limestone cave (dripstone cave)*
80-81 Tropfsteine *m*
- *speleothems (cave formations)*
80 der Stalaktit
- *stalactite (dripstone)*
81 der Stalagmit
- *stalagmite*
82 die Sintersäule (Tropfsteinsäule)
- *linked-up stalagmite and stalactite*
83 der Höhlenfluß
- *subterranean river*

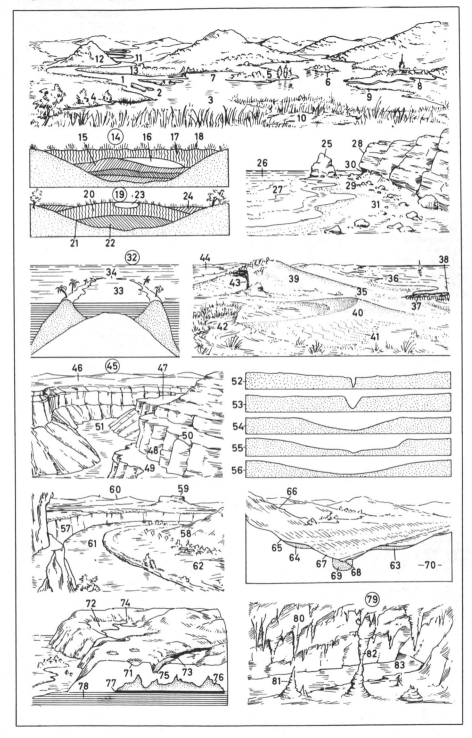

1-7 das Gradnetz der Erde
- *graticule of the earth (network of meridians and parallels on the earth's surface)*
1 der Äquator
- *equator*
2 ein Breitenkreis *m*
- *line of latitude (parallel of latitude, parallel)*
3 der Pol (Nordpol oder Südpol *m*), ein Erdpol *m*
- *pole (North Pole or South Pole), a terrestrial pole (geographical pole)*
4 der Meridian (Längenhalbkreis)
- *line of longitude (meridian of longitude, meridian, terrestrial meridian)*
5 der Nullmeridian
- *Standard meridian (Prime meridian, Greenwich meridian, meridian of Greenwich)*
6 die geographische Breite
- *latitude*
7 die geographische Länge
- *longitude*
8-9 Kartennetzentwürfe *m*
- *map projections*
8 die Kegelprojektion
- *conical (conic) projection*
9 die Zylinderprojektion
- *cylindrical projection (Mercator projection, Mercator's projection)*
10-45 die Erdkarte (Weltkarte)
- *map of the world*
10 die Wendekreise *m*
- *tropics*
11 die Polarkreise *m*
- *polar circles*
12-18 die Erdteile *m* (Kontinente)
- *continents*
12-13 Amerika *n*
- *America*
12 Nordamerika *n*
- *North America*
13 Südamerika *n*
- *South America*
14 Afrika *n*
- *Africa*
15-16 Eurasien *n*
- *Europe and Asia*
15 Europa *n*
- *Europe*
16 Asien *n*
- *Asia*
17 Australien *n*
- *Australia*
18 die Antarktis
- *Antarctica (Antarctic Continent)*
19-26 das Weltmeer
- *ocean (sea)*
19 der Große (Stille, Pazif.) Ozean
- *Pacific Ocean*
20 der Atlantische Ozean
- *Atlantic Ocean*
21 das Nördl. Eismeer
- *Arctic Ocean*
22 das Südl. Eismeer
- *Antarctic Ocean (Southern Ocean)*
23 der Indische Ozean
- *Indian Ocean*
24 die Straße von Gibraltar, eine Meeresstraße
- *Strait of Gibraltar, a sea strait*
25 das Mittelmeer (europäische Mittelmeer)
- *Mediterranean (Mediterranean Sea, European Mediterranean)*

26 die Nordsee, ein Randmeer *n*
- *North Sea, a marginal sea (epeiric sea, epicontinental sea)*
27-29 die Legende (Zeichenerklärung)
- *key (explanation of map symbols)*
27 die kalte Meeresströmung
- *cold ocean current*
28 die warme Meeresströmung
- *warm ocean current*
29 der Maßstab
- *scale*
30-45 die Meeresströmungen *f*
- *ocean (oceanic) currents (ocean drifts)*
30 der Golfstrom
- *Gulf Stream (North Atlantic Drift)*
31 der Kuroschio
- *Kuroshio (Kuro Siwo, Japan Current)*
32 der Nordäquatorialstrom
- *North Equatorial Current*
33 der Äquatoriale Gegenstrom
- *Equatorial Countercurrent*
34 der Südäquatorialstrom
- *South Equatorial Current*
35 der Brasilstrom
- *Brazil Current*
36 der Somalistrom
- *Somali Current*
37 der Agulhasstrom
- *Agulhas Current*
38 der Ostaustralstrom
- *East Australian Current*
39 der Kalifornische Strom
- *California Current*
40 der Labradorstrom
- *Labrador Current*
41 der Kanarienstrom
- *Canary Current*
42 der Humboldtstrom (Perustrom)
- *Peru Current*
43 der Benguellastrom
- *Benguela (Benguella) Current*
44 die Westwinddrift
- *West Wind Drift (Antarctic Circumpolar Drift)*
45 der Westaustralstrom
- *West Australian Current*
46-62 die Vermessung (Landesvermessung, Erdmessung, Geodäsie)
- *surveying (land surveying, geodetic surveying, geodesy)*
46 die Nivellierung (geometrische Höhenmessung)
- *levelling (Am. leveling) (geometrical measurement of height)*
47 die Meßlatte
- *graduated measuring rod (levelling, Am. leveling, staff)*
48 das Nivellierinstrument, ein Zielfernrohr *n*
- *level (surveying level, surveyor's level), a surveyor's telescope*
49 der trigonometrische Punkt
- *triangulation station (triangulation point)*
50 das Standgerüst
- *supporting scaffold*
51 das Signalgerüst
- *signal tower (signal mast)*
52-62 der Theodolit, ein Winkelmeßgerät *n*
- *theodolite, an instrument for measuring angles*

52 der Mikrometerknopf
- *micrometer head*
53 das Mikroskopokular
- *micrometer eyepiece*
54 der Höhenfeintrieb
- *vertical tangent screw*
55 die Höhenklemme
- *vertical clamp*
56 der Seitenfeintrieb
- *tangent screw*
57 die Seitenklemme
- *horizontal clamp*
58 der Einstellknopf für den Beleuchtungsspiegel
- *adjustment for the illuminating mirror*
59 der Beleuchtungsspiegel
- *illuminating mirror*
60 das Fernrohr
- *telescope*
61 die Querlibelle
- *spirit level*
62 die Kreisverstellung
- *circular adjustment*
63-66 die Luftbildmessung (Bildmessung, Fotogrammetrie, Fototopographie)
- *photogrammetry (phototopography)*
63 die Reihenmeßkammer
- *air survey camera for producing overlapping series of pictures*
64 das Stereotop
- *stereoscope*
65 der Storchschnabel (Pantograph)
- *pantograph*
66 der Stereoplanigraph
- *stereoplanigraph*

1-114 die Kartenzeichen einer Karte 1:25 000
- *map signs (map symbols, conventional signs) on a 1:25 000 map*
1 der Nadelwald
- *coniferous wood (coniferous trees)*
2 die Lichtung
- *clearing*
3 das Forstamt
- *forestry office* [no symbol]
4 der Laubwald
- *deciduous wood (non-coniferous trees)*
5 die Heide
- *heath (rough grassland, rough pasture, heath and moor, bracken)*
6 der Sand
- *sand (sand hills)*
7 der Strandhafer
- *beach grass* [no symbol]
8 der Leuchtturm
- *lighthouse*
9 die Wattengrenze
- *mean low water*
10 die Bake
- *beacon*
11 die Tiefenlinien *f* (Isobathen)
- *submarine contours* [no symbol]
12 die Eisenbahnfähre (das Trajekt)
- *train ferry* [no symbol]
13 das Feuerschiff
- *lightship*
14 der Mischwald
- *mixed wood (mixed trees)*
15 das Buschwerk
- *brushwood*
16 die Autobahn mit Auffahrt *f*
- *motorway with slip road (Am. freeway with on-ramp, freeway with acceleration lane)*
17 die Bundesstraße (Fernverkehrsstraße)
- *trunk road*
18 die Wiese
- *grassland* [no symbol]
19 die nasse Wiese
- *marshy grassland* [no symbol]
20 der Bruch (das Moor)
- *marsh*
21 die Hauptstrecke (Hauptlinie, Hauptbahn)
- *main line railway (Am. trunk line)* [no symbol]
22 die Bahnunterführung
- *road over railway*
23 die Nebenbahn
- *branch line* [no symbol]
24 die Blockstelle
- *signal box (Am. switch tower)* [no symbol]
25 die Kleinbahn
- *local line* [no symbol]
26 der Planübergang
- *level crossing*
27 die Haltestelle
- *halt* [no symbol]
28 die Villenkolonie
- *residential area* [no symbol]
29 der Pegel
- *water gauge (Am. gage)* [no symbol]
30 die Straße III. Ordnung
- *good, metalled road*
31 die Windmühle
- *windmill* [labelled: Mill]
32 das Gradierwerk (die Saline)
- *thorn house (graduation house, salina, salt-works* [no symbol]
33 der Funkturm
- *broadcasting station (wireless or television mast)* [no symbol]
34 das Bergwerk
- *mine* [labelled: Mine]
35 das verlassene Bergwerk
- *disused mine* [labelled: Mine (Disused)]
36 die Straße II. Ordnung
- *secondary road (B road)*
37 die Fabrik
- *works* [labelled: Works]

38 der Schornstein
- *chimney*
39 der Drahtzaun
- *wire fence* [no symbol]
40 die Straßenüberfahrt
- *bridge over railway*
41 der Bahnhof
- *railway station (Am. railroad station)*
42 die Bahnüberführung
- *bridge under railway*
43 der Fußweg
- *footpath*
44 der Durchlaß
- *bridge for footpath under railway* [no symbol]
45 der schiffbare Strom
- *navigable river* [no symbol]
46 die Schiffbrücke
- *pontoon bridge* [no symbol]
47 die Wagenfähre
- *vehicle ferry*
48 die Steinmole
- *mole* [no symbol]
49 das Leuchtfeuer
- *beacon*
50 die Steinbrücke
- *stone bridge*
51 die Stadt
- *town (city)*
52 der Marktplatz
- *market place (market square)*
53 die große Kirche mit 2 Türmen *m*
- *large church with two towers* [no symbol]
54 das öffentliche Gebäude
- *public building*
55 die Straßenbrücke
- *road bridge*
56 die eiserne Brücke
- *iron bridge*
57 der Kanal
- *canal*
58 die Kammerschleuse
- *lock*
59 die Landungsbrücke
- *jetty*
60 die Personenfähre
- *foot ferry (foot passenger ferry)*
61 die Kapelle
- *chapel (church) without tower or spire*
62 die Höhenlinien *f* (Isohypsen)
- *contours*
63 das Kloster
- *monastery (convent)* [named]
64 die weit sichtbare Kirche
- *church landmark* [no symbol]
65 der Weinberg
- *vineyard* [no symbol]
66 das Wehr
- *weir*
67 die Seilbahn
- *aerial ropeway*
68 der Aussichtsturm
- *view point* [tower]
69 die Stauschleuse
- *dam*
70 der Tunnel
- *tunnel*
71 der trigonometr. Punkt
- *triangulation station (triangulation point)*
72 die Ruine
- *remains of a building*
73 das Windrad
- *wind pump*
74 die Festung
- *fortress* [castle]
75 das Altwasser
- *ox-bow lake*
76 der Fluß
- *river*
77 die Wassermühle
- *watermill* [labelled: Mill]
78 der Steg
- *footbridge*
79 der Teich
- *pond*
80 der Bach
- *stream (brook, rivulet, creek)*
81 der Wasserturm
- *water tower* [labelled]

82 die Quelle
- *spring*
83 die Straße I. Ordnung
- *main road (A road)*
84 der Hohlweg
- *cutting*
85 die Höhle
- *cave* [labelled: Cave]
86 der Kalkofen
- *lime kiln* [labelled: Lime Works]
87 der Steinbruch
- *quarry*
88 die Tongrube
- *clay pit*
89 die Ziegelei
- *brickworks* [labelled: Brickworks]
90 die Wirtschaftsbahn
- *narrow-gauge (Am. narrow-gage) railway*
91 der Ladeplatz
- *goods depot (freight depot)*
92 das Denkmal
- *monument*
93 das Schlachtfeld
- *site of battle*
94 das Gut, eine Domäne
- *country estate, a demesne*
95 die Mauer
- *wall* [no symbol]
96 das Schloß
- *stately home*
97 der Park
- *park*
98 die Hecke
- *hedge* [no symbol]
99 der unterhaltene Fahrweg
- *poor or unmetalled road*
100 der Ziehbrunnen
- *well*
101 der Einzelhof (Weiler, Einödhof)
- *farm* [named]
102 der Feld- und Waldweg
- *unfenced path (unfenced track)*
103 die Kreisgrenze
- *district boundary*
104 der Damm
- *embankment*
105 das Dorf
- *village*
106 der Friedhof
- *cemetery* [labelled: Cemy]
107 die Dorfkirche
- *church (chapel) with spire*
108 der Obstgarten
- *orchard*
109 der Meilenstein
- *milestone*
110 der Wegweiser
- *guide post*
111 die Baumschule
- *tree nursery* [no symbol]
112 die Schneise
- *ride (aisle, lane, section line)* [no symbol]
113 die Starkstromleitung
- *electricity transmission line*
114 die Hopfenanpflanzung (der Hopfengarten)
- *hop garden* [no symbol]

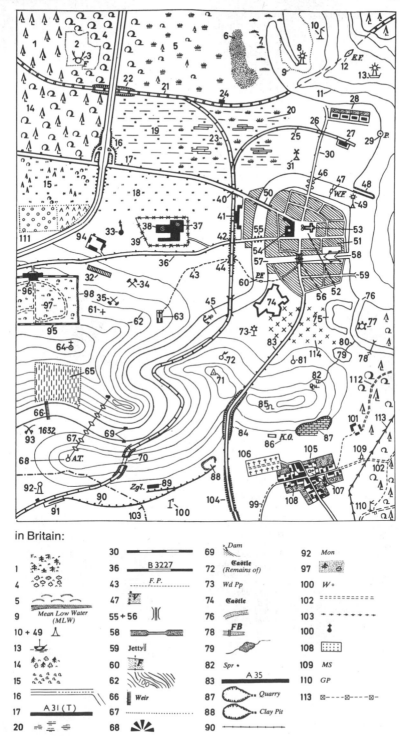

in Britain:

1	30	69 Dam	92 Mon
4	36 B 3227	72 **Castle** (Remains of)	97
5	43 F. P.	73 Wd Pp	100 W ∘
9 Mean Low Water (MLW)	47	74 **Castle**	102
10 + 49	55 + 56)|(	76	103
13	58	78 **FB**	100
14	59 Jetty|	79	108
15	60	82 Spr ∘	109 MS
16	62	83 A 35	110 GP
17 A 31 (T)	66 Weir	87 Quarry	113
20	67	88 Clay Pit	
	68	90	

1-54 der menschliche Körper (Leib)
- *the human body*
1-18 der Kopf (das Haupt)
- *head*
1 der Scheitel (Wirbel)
- *vertex (crown of the head, top of the head)*
2 das Hinterhaupt
- *occiput (back of the head)*
3 das Kopfhaar (Haar)
- *hair*
4-17 das Gesicht (Antlitz)
- *face*
4-5 die Stirn
- *forehead*
4 der Stirnhöcker
- *frontal eminence (frontal protuberance)*
5 der Stirnwulst
- *superciliary arch*
6 die Schläfe
- *temple*
7 das Auge
- *eye*
8 das Jochbein (Wangenbein, der Backenknochen)
- *zygomatic bone (malar bone, jugal bone, cheekbone)*
9 die Wange (Kinnbacke, Backe)
- *cheek*
10 die Nase
- *nose*
11 die Nasen-Lippen-Furche
- *nasolabial fold*
12 das Philtrum (die Oberlippenrinne)
- *philtrum*
13 der Mund
- *mouth*
14 der Mundwinkel
- *angle of the mouth (labial commissure)*
15 das Kinn
- *chin*
16 das Kinngrübchen (Grübchen)
- *dimple (fossette) in the chin*
17 die Kinnlade
- *jaw*
18 das Ohr
- *ear*
19-21 der Hals
- *neck*
19 die Kehle (Gurgel)
- *throat*
20 ugs. die Drosselgrube
- *hollow of the throat*
21 der Nacken (das Genick)
- *nape of the neck*
22-41 der Rumpf
- *trunk*
22-25 der Rücken
- *back*
22 die Schulter
- *shoulder*
23 das Schulterblatt
- *shoulderblade (scapula)*
24 die Lende
- *loins*
25 das Kreuz
- *small of the back*
26 die Achsel (Achselhöhle, Achselgrube)
- *armpit*
27 die Achselhaare *n*
- *armpit hair*
28-30 die Brust (der Brustkorb)
- *thorax (chest)*

28-29 die Brüste (die Brust, Büste)
- *breasts (breast, mamma)*
28 die Brustwarze
- *nipple*
29 der Warzenhof
- *areola*
30 der Busen
- *bosom*
31 die Taille
- *waist*
32 die Flanke (Weiche)
- *flank (side)*
33 die Hüfte
- *hip*
34 der Nabel
- *navel*
35-37 der Bauch (das Abdomen)
- *abdomen (stomach)*
35 der Oberbauch
- *upper abdomen*
36 der Mittelbauch
- *abdomen*
37 der Unterbauch (Unterleib)
- *lower abdomen*
38 die Leistenbeuge (Leiste)
- *groin*
39 die Scham
- *pudenda (vulva)*
40 das Gesäß (die Gesäßbacke, *ugs.* Hinterbacke, das Hinterteil)
- *seat (backside, coll. bottom)*
41 die Afterfurche
- *anal groove (anal cleft)*
42 die Gesäßfalte
- *gluteal fold (gluteal furrow)*
43-54 die Gliedmaßen *f* (Glieder *n*)
- *limbs*
43-48 der Arm
- *arm*
43 der Oberarm
- *upper arm*
44 die Armbeuge
- *crook of the arm*
45 der Ellbogen (Ellenbogen)
- *elbow*
46 der Unterarm
- *forearm*
47 die Hand
- *hand*
48 die Faust
- *fist (clenched fist, clenched hand)*
49-54 das Bein
- *leg*
49 der Oberschenkel
- *thigh*
50 das Knie
- *knee*
51 die Kniekehle (Kniebeuge)
- *popliteal space*
52 der Unterschenkel
- *shank*
53 die Wade
- *calf*
54 der Fuß
- *foot*

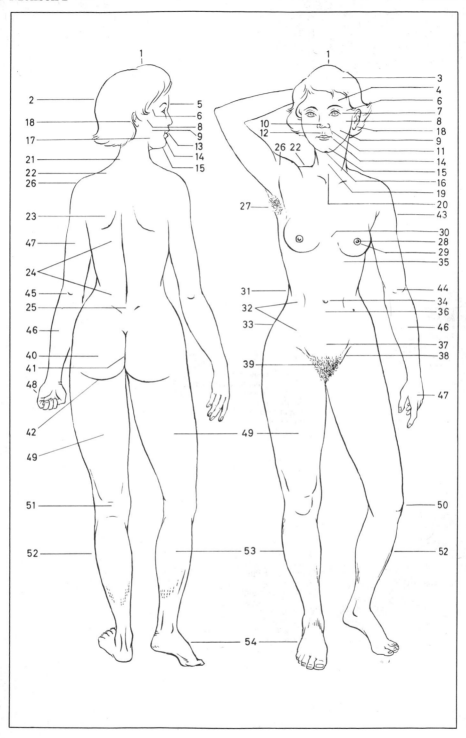

1-29 das Skelett (Knochengerüst,
Gerippe, Gebein, die Knochen *m*)
- *skeleton (bones)*
1 der Schädel
- *skull*
2-5 die Wirbelsäule (das Rückgrat)
- *vertebral column (spinal column,
spine, backbone)*
2 der Halswirbel
- *cervical vertebra*
3 der Brustwirbel
- *dorsal vertebra (thoracic vertebra)*
4 der Lendenwirbel
- *lumbar vertebra*
5 das Steißbein
- *coccyx (coccygeal vertebra)*
6-7 der Schultergürtel
- *shoulder girdle*
6 das Schlüsselbein
- *collarbone (clavicle)*
7 das Schulterblatt
- *shoulderblade (scapula)*
8-11 der Brustkorb
- *thorax (chest)*
8 das Brustbein
- *breastbone (sternum)*
9 die echten Rippen *f* (wahren Rippen)
- *true ribs*
10 die falschen Rippen *f*
- *false ribs*
11 der Rippenknorpel
- *costal cartilage*
12-14 der Arm
- *arm*
12 das Oberarmbein (der
Oberarmknochen)
- *humerus*
13 die Speiche
- *radius*
14 die Elle
- *ulna*
15-17 die Hand
- *hand*
15 der Handwurzelknochen
- *carpus*
16 der Mittelhandknochen
- *metacarpal bone (metacarpal)*
17 der Fingerknochen (das
Fingerglied)
- *phalanx (phalange)*
18-21 das Becken
- *pelvis*
18 das Hüftbein
- *ilium (hip bone)*
19 das Sitzbein
- *ischium*
20 das Schambein
- *pubis*
21 das Kreuzbein
- *sacrum*
22-25 das Bein
- *leg*
22 das Oberschenkelbein
- *femur (thigh bone, thigh)*
23 die Kniescheibe
- *patella (kneecap)*
24 das Wadenbein
- *fibula (splint bone)*
25 das Schienbein
- *tibia (shinbone)*
26-29 der Fuß
- *foot*
26 die Fußwurzelknochen *m*
- *tarsal bones (tarsus)*
27 das Fersenbein
- *calcaneum (heelbone)*

28 die Vorfußknochen *m*
- *metatarsus*
29 die Zehenknochen *m*
- *phalanges*
30-41 der Schädel
- *skull*
30 das Stirnbein
- *frontal bone*
31 das linke Scheitelbein
- *left parietal bone*
32 das Hinterhauptsbein
- *occipital bone*
33 das Schläfenbein
- *temporal bone*
34 der Gehörgang
- *external auditory canal*
35 das Unterkieferbein (der
Unterkiefer)
- *lower jawbone (lower jaw,
mandible)*
36 das Oberkieferbein (der
Oberkiefer)
- *upper jawbone
(upper jaw, maxilla)*
37 das Jochbein
- *zygomatic bone (cheekbone)*
38 das Keilbein
- *sphenoid bone (sphenoid)*
39 das Siebbein
- *ethmoid bone (ethmoid)*
40 das Tränenbein
- *lachrimal (lacrimal) bone*
41 das Nasenbein
- *nasal bone*
42-55 der Kopf [Schnitt]
- *head [section]*
42 das Großhirn
- *cerebrum (great brain)*
43 die Hirnanhangdrüse
- *pituitary gland (pituitary body,
hypophysis cerebri)*
44 der Balken
- *corpus callosum*
45 das Kleinhirn
- *cerebellum (little brain)*
46 die Brücke
- *pons (pons cerebri, pons cerebelli)*
47 das verlängerte Mark
- *medulla oblongata (brain-stem)*
48 das Rückenmark
- *spinal cord*
49 die Speiseröhre
- *oesophagus (esophagus, gullet)*
50 die Luftröhre
- *trachea (windpipe)*
51 der Kehldeckel
- *epiglottis*
52 die Zunge
- *tongue*
53. die Nasenhöhle
- *nasal cavity*
54 die Keilbeinhöhle
- *sphenoidal sinus*
55 die Stirnhöhle
- *frontal sinus*
**56-65 das Gleichgewichts- und
Gehörorgan**
- *organ of equilibrium and hearing*
56-58 das äußere Ohr
- *external ear*
56 die Ohrmuschel
- *auricle*
57 das Ohrläppchen
- *ear lobe*
58 der Gehörgang
- *external auditory canal*

59-61 das Mittelohr
- *middle ear*
59 das Trommelfell
- *tympanic membrane*
60 die Paukenhöhle
- *tympanic cavity*
61 die Gehörknöchelchen *n*: der
Hammer, der Amboß, der
Steigbügel
- *auditory ossicles: hammer, anvil
and stirrup (malleus, incus and
stapes)*
62-64 das innere Ohr
- *inner ear (internal ear)*
62 das Labyrinth
- *labyrinth*
63 die Schnecke
- *cochlea*
64 der Gehörnerv
- *auditory nerve*
65 die Eustachische Röhre
- *eustachian tube*

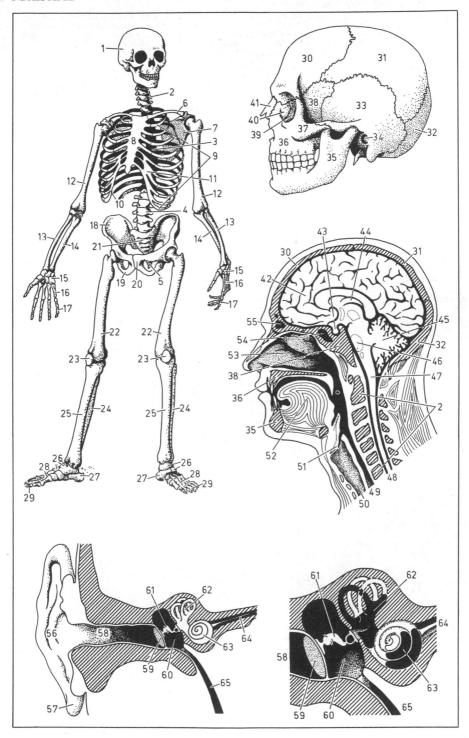

1-21 der Blutkreislauf
- *blood circulation (circulatory system)*
1 die Halsschlagader, eine Arterie
- *common carotid artery, an artery*
2 die Halsblutader, eine Vene
- *jugular vein, a vein*
3 die Schläfenschlagader
- *temporal artery*
4 die Schläfenvene
- *temporal vein*
5 die Stirnschlagader
- *frontal artery*
6 die Stirnvene
- *frontal vein*
7 die Schlüsselbeinschlagader
- *subclavian artery*
8 die Schlüsselbeinvene
- *subclavian vein*
9 die obere Hohlvene
- *superior vena cava*
10 der Aortenbogen (die Aorta)
- *arch of the aorta (aorta)*
11 die Lungenschlagader [mit venösem Blut *n*]
- *pulmonary artery [with venous blood]*
12 die Lungenvene [mit arteriellem Blut *n*]
- *pulmonary vein [with arterial blood]*
13 die Lungen *f*
- *lungs*
14 das Herz
- *heart*
15 die untere Hohlvene
- *inferior vena cava*
16 die Bauchaorta (absteigende Aorta)
- *abdominal aorta (descending portion of the aorta)*
17 die Hüftschlagader
- *iliac artery*
18 die Hüftvene
- *iliac vein*
19 die Schenkelschlagader
- *femoral artery*
20 die Schienbeinschlagader
- *tibial artery*
21 die Pulsschlagader
- *radial artery*

22-33 das Nervensystem
- *nervous system*
22 das Großhirn
- *cerebrum (great brain)*
23 das Zwischenhirn
- *cerebellum (little brain)*
24 das verlängerte Mark
- *medulla oblongata (brain-stem)*
25 das Rückenmark
- *spinal cord*
26 die Brustnerven *m*
- *thoracic nerves*
27 das Armgeflecht
- *brachial plexus*
28 der Speichennerv
- *radial nerve*
29 der Ellennerv
- *ulnar nerve*
30 der Hüftnerv (Beinnerv, Ischiasnerv) [hinten liegend]
- *great sciatic nerve [lying posteriorly]*
31 der Schenkelnerv
- *femoral nerve (anterior crural nerve)*
32 der Schienbeinnerv
- *tibial nerve*

33 der Wadennerv
- *peroneal nerve*
34-64 die Muskulatur
- *musculature (muscular system)*
34 der Kopfhalter (Nicker)
- *sternocleidomastoid muscle (sternomastoid muscle)*
35 der Schultermuskel (Deltamuskel)
- *deltoid muscle*
36 der große Brustmuskel
- *pectoralis major (greater pectoralis muscle, greater pectoralis)*
37 der zweiköpfige Armmuskel (Bizeps)
- *biceps brachii (biceps of the arm)*
38 der dreiköpfige Armmuskel (Trizeps)
- *triceps brachii (triceps of the arm)*
39 der Armspeichenmuskel
- *brachioradialis*
40 der Speichenbeuger
- *flexor carpi radialis (radial flexor of the wrist)*
41 die kurzen Daumenmuskeln *m*
- *thenar muscle*
42 der große Sägemuskel
- *serratus anterior*
43 der schräge Bauchmuskel
- *obliquus externus abdominis (external oblique)*
44 der gerade Bauchmuskel
- *rectus abdominis*
45 der Schneidermuskel
- *sartorius*
46 der Unterschenkelstrecker
- *vastus lateralis and vastus medialis*
47 der Schienbeinmuskel
- *tibialis anterior*
48 die Achillessehne
- *tendo calcaneus (Achilles' tendon)*
49 der Abzieher der großen Zehe, ein Fußmuskel *m*
- *abductor hallucis (abductor of the hallux), a foot muscle*
50 die Hinterhauptmuskeln *m*
- *occipitalis*
51 die Nackenmuskeln *m*
- *splenius of the neck*
52 der Kapuzenmuskel (Kappenmuskel)
- *trapecius*
53 der Untergrätenmuskel
- *infraspinatus*
54 der kleine runde Armmuskel
- *teres minor (lesser teres)*
55 der große runde Armmuskel
- *teres major (greater teres)*
56 der lange Speichenstrecker
- *extensor carpi radialis longus (long radial extensor of the wrist)*
57 der gemeinsame Fingerstrecker
- *extensor communis digitorum (common extensor of the digits)*
58 der Ellenbeuger
- *flexor carpi ulnaris (ulnar flexor of the wrist)*
59 der breite Rückenmuskel
- *latissimus dorsi*
60 der große Gesäßmuskel
- *gluteus maximus*
61 der zweiköpfige Unterschenkelbeuger
- *biceps femoris (biceps of the thigh)*
62 der Zwillingswadenmuskel
- *gastrocnemius, medial and lateral heads*

63 der gemeinsame Zehenstrecker
- *extensor communis digitorum (common extensor of the digits)*
64 der lange Wadenbeinmuskel
- *peroneus longus (long peroneus)*

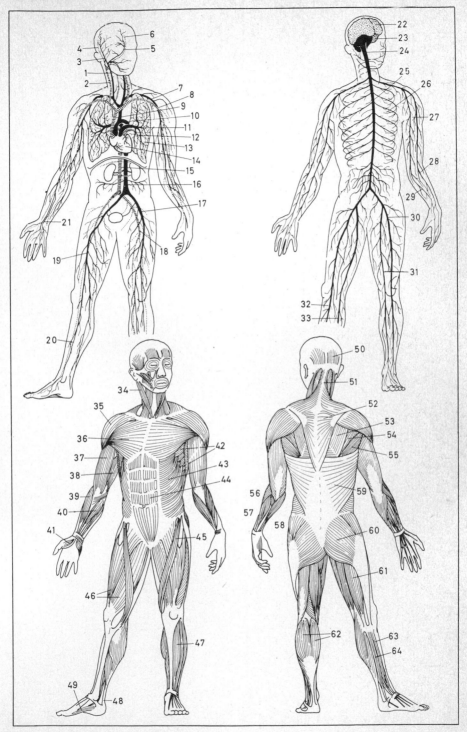

1-13 der Kopf und der Hals
- *head and neck*
1 der Kopfhalter (Kopfnicker, Nicker)
- *sternocleidomastoid muscle (sternomastoid muscle)*
2 der Hinterhauptmuskel
- *occipitalis*
3 der Schläfenmuskel
- *temporalis (temporal, temporal muscle)*
4 der Stirnmuskel
- *occipitofrontalis (frontalis)*
5 der Ringmuskel des Auges *n*
- *orbicularis oculi*
6 mimische Gesichtsmuskeln *m*
- *muscles of facial expression*
7 der große Kaumuskel
- *masseter*
8 der Ringmuskel des Mundes *m*
- *orbicularis oris*
9 die Ohrspeicheldrüse
- *parotid gland*
10 der Lymphknoten; *falsch:* die Lymphdrüse
- *lymph node (submandibular lymph gland)*
11 die Unterkieferdrüse
- *submandibular gland (submaxillary gland)*
12 die Halsmuskeln *m*
- *muscles of the neck*
13 der Adamsapfel [nur beim Mann]
- *Adam's apple (laryngeal prominence) [in men only]*
14-37 der Mund und der Rachen
- *mouth and throat*
14 die Oberlippe
- *upper lip*
15 das Zahnfleisch
- *gum*
16-18 das Gebiß
- *teeth (set of teeth)*
16 die Schneidezähne *m*
- *incisors*
17 der Eckzahn
- *canine tooth (canine)*
18 die Backenzähne *m*
- *premolar (bicuspid) and molar teeth (premolars and molars)*
19 der Mundwinkel
- *angle of the mouth (labial commissure)*
20 der harte Gaumen
- *hard palate*
21 der weiche Gaumen (das Gaumensegel)
- *soft palate (velum palati, velum)*
22 das Zäpfchen
- *uvula*
23 die Gaumenmandel (Mandel)
- *palatine tonsil (tonsil)*
24 die Rachenhöhle (der Rachen)
- *pharyngeal opening (pharynx, throat)*
25 die Zunge
- *tongue*
26 die Unterlippe
- *lower lip*
27 der Oberkiefer
- *upper jaw (maxilla)*
28-37 der Zahn
- *tooth*
28 die Wurzelhaut
- *periodontal membrane (periodontium, pericementum)*

29 der Zement
- *cement (dental cementum, crusta petrosa)*
30 der Zahnschmelz
- *enamel*
31 das Zahnbein
- *dentine (dentin)*
32 das Zahnmark (die Pulpa)
- *dental pulp (tooth pulp, pulp)*
33 die Nerven *m* und Blutgefäße *n*
- *nerves and blood vessels*
34 der Schneidezahn
- *incisor*
35 der Backenzahn
- *molar tooth (molar)*
36 die Wurzel
- *root (fang)*
37 die Krone
- *crown*
38-51 das Auge
- *eye*
38 die Augenbraue
- *eyebrow (supercilium)*
39 das Oberlid
- *upper eyelid (upper palpebra)*
40 das Unterlid
- *lower eyelid (lower palpebra)*
41 die Wimper
- *eyelash (cilium)*
42 die Iris (Regenbogenhaut)
- *iris*
43 die Pupille
- *pupil*
44 die Augenmuskeln *m*
- *eye muscles (ocular muscles)*
45 der Augapfel
- *eyeball*
46 der Glaskörper
- *vitreous body*
47 die Hornhaut
- *cornea*
48 die Linse
- *lens*
49 die Netzhaut
- *retina*
50 der blinde Fleck
- *blind spot*
51 der Sehnerv
- *optic nerve*
52-63 der Fuß
- *foot*
52 die große Zehe (der große Zeh)
- *big toe (great toe, first toe, hallux, digitus I)*
53 die zweite Zehe
- *second toe (digitus II)*
54 die Mittelzehe
- *third toe (digitus III)*
55 die vierte Zehe
- *fourth toe (digitus IV)*
56 die kleine Zehe
- *little toe (digitus minimus, digitus V)*
57 der Zehennagel
- *toenail*
58 der Ballen
- *ball of the foot*
59 der Wadenbeinknöchel (Knöchel)
- *lateral malleolus (external malleolus, outer malleolus, malleolus fibulae)*
60 der Schienbeinknöchel
- *medial malleolus (internal malleolus, inner malleolus, malleolus tibulae, malleolus medialis)*

61 der Fußrücken (Spann, Rist)
- *instep (medial longitudinal arch, dorsum of the foot, dorsum pedis)*
62 die Fußsohle
- *sole of the foot*
63 die Ferse (Hacke, der Hacken)
- *heel*
64-83 die Hand
- *hand*
64 der Daumen
- *thumb (pollex, digitus I)*
65 der Zeigefinger
- *index finger (forefinger, second finger, digitus II)*
66 der Mittelfinger
- *middle finger (third finger, digitus medius, digitus III)*
67 der Ringfinger
- *ring finger (fourth finger, digitus anularis, digitus IV)*
68 der kleine Finger
- *little finger (fifth finger, digitus minimus, digitus V)*
69 der Speichenrand
- *radial side of the hand*
70 der Ellenrand
- *ulnar side of the hand*
71 der Handteller (die Hohlhand)
- *palm of the hand (palma manus)*
72-74 die Handlinien *f*
- *lines of the hand*
72 die Lebenslinie
- *life line (line of life)*
73 die Kopflinie
- *head line (line of the head)*
74 die Herzlinie
- *heart line (line of the heart)*
75 der Daumenballen
- *ball of the thumb (thenar eminence)*
76 das Handgelenk (die Handwurzel)
- *wrist (carpus)*
77 das Fingerglied
- *phalanx (phalange)*
78 die Fingerbeere
- *finger pad*
79 die Fingerspitze
- *fingertip*
80 der Fingernagel (Nagel)
- *fingernail (nail)*
81 das Möndchen
- *lunule (lunula) of the nail*
82 der Knöchel
- *knuckle*
83 der Handrücken
- *back of the hand (dorsum of the hand, dorsum manus)*

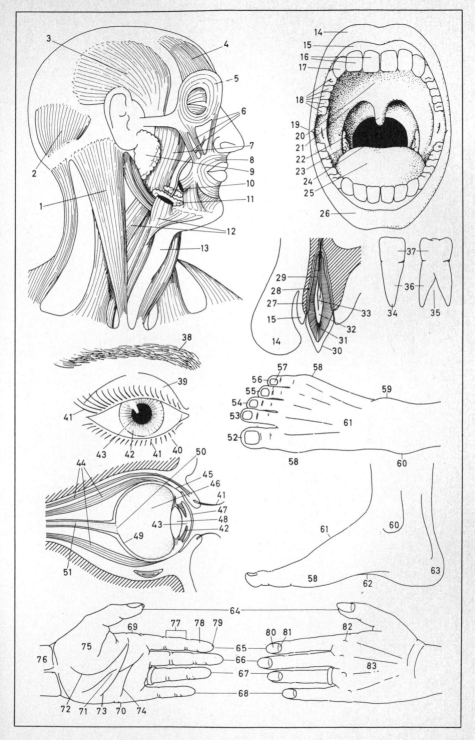

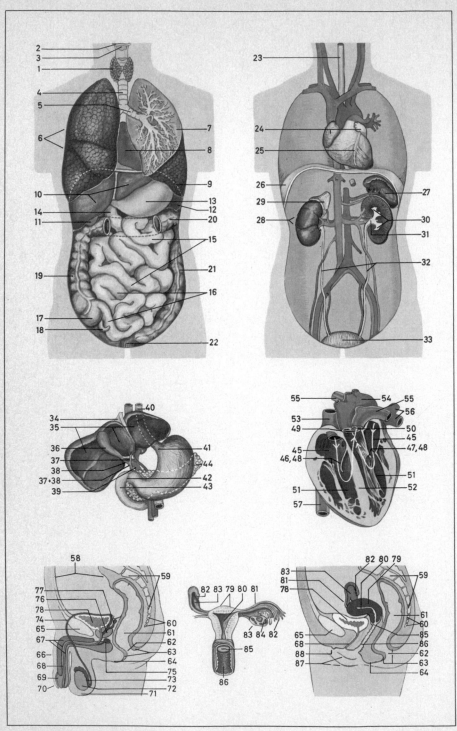

1-57 die inneren Organe n [von vorn]
- *internal organs [front view]*
1 die Schilddrüse
- *thyroid gland*
2-3 der Kehlkopf
- *larynx*
2 das Zungenbein
- *hyoid bone (hyoid)*
3 der Schildknorpel
- *thyroid cartilage*
4 die Luftröhre
- *trachea (windpipe)*
5 der Luftröhrenast
(die Bronchie)
- *bronchus*
6-7 die Lunge
- *lung*
6 der rechte Lungenflügel
- *right lung*
7 der obere Lungenlappen [Schnitt]
- *upper pulmonary lobe (upper lobe
of the lung) [section]*
8 das Herz
- *heart*
9 das Zwerchfell
- *diaphragm*
10 die Leber
- *liver*
11 die Gallenblase
- *gall bladder*
12 die Milz
- *spleen*
13 der Magen
- *stomach*
14-22 der Darm
- *intestines (bowel)*
14-16 der Dünndarm
- *small intestine (intestinum tenue)*
14 der Zwölffingerdarm
- *duodenum*
15 der Leerdarm
- *jejunum*
16 der Krummdarm
- *ileum*
17-22 der Dickdarm
- *large intestine (intestinum crassum)*
17 der Blinddarm
- *caecum (cecum)*
18 der Wurmfortsatz
- *appendix (vermiform appendix)*
19 der aufsteigende Grimmdarm
- *ascending colon*
20 der querliegende Grimmdarm
- *transverse colon*
21 der absteigende Grimmdarm
- *descending colon*
22 der Mastdarm
- *rectum*
23 die Speiseröhre
- *oesophagus (esophagus, gullet)*
24-25 das Herz
- *heart*
24 das Herzohr
- *auricle*
25 die vordere Längsfurche
- *anterior longitudinal cardiac sulcus*
26 das Zwerchfell
- *diaphragm*
27 die Milz
- *spleen*
28 die rechte Niere
- *right kidney*
29 die Nebenniere
- *suprarenal gland*
30-31 die linke Niere [Längsschnitt]
- *left kidney [longitudinal section]*

30 der Nierenkelch
- *calyx (renal calyx)*
31 das Nierenbecken
- *renal pelvis*
32 der Harnleiter
- *ureter*
33 die Harnblase
- *bladder*
34-35 die Leber [hochgeklappt]
- *liver [from behind]*
34 das Leberband
- *falciform ligament of the liver*
35 der Leberlappen
- *lobe of the liver*
36 die Gallenblase
- *gall bladder*
37-38 der gemeinsame Gallengang
- *common bile duct*
37 der Lebergang
- *hepatic duct
(common hepatic duct)*
38 der Gallenblasengang
- *cystic duct*
39 die Pfortader
- *portal vein (hepatic portal vein)*
40 die Speiseröhre
- *oesophagus (esophagus, gullet)*
41-42 der Magen
- *stomach*
41 der Magenmund
- *cardiac orifice*
42 der Pförtner
- *pylorus*
43 der Zwölffingerdarm
- *duodenum*
44 die Bauchspeicheldrüse
- *pancreas*
45-57 das Herz [Längsschnitt]
- *heart [longitudinal section]*
45 der Vorhof
- *atrium*
46-47 die Herzklappen f
- *valves of the heart*
46 die dreizipflige Klappe
- *tricuspid valve (right
atrioventricular valve)*
47 die Mitralklappe
- *bicuspid valve (mitral valve, left
atrioventricular valve)*
48 das Segel
- *cusp*
49 die Aortenklappe
- *aortic valve*
50 die Pulmonalklappe
- *pulmonary valve*
51 die Herzkammer
- *ventricle*
52 die Kammerscheidewand
- *ventricular septum (interventricular
septum)*
53 die obere Hohlvene
- *superior vena cava*
54 die Aorta
- *aorta*
55 die Lungenschlagader
- *pulmonary artery*
56 die Lungenvene
- *pulmonary vein*
57 die untere Hohlvene
- *inferior vena cava*
58 das Bauchfell
- *peritoneum*
59 das Kreuzbein
- *sacrum*
60 das Steißbein
- *coccyx (coccygeal vertebra)*

61 der Mastdarm
- *rectum*
62 der After
- *anus*
63 der Schließmuskel
- *anal sphincter*
64 der Damm
- *perineum*
65 die Schambeinfuge
- *pubic symphisis (symphisis pubis)*
66-77 die männl. Geschlechtsorgane n
[Längsschnitt]
- *male sex organs [longitudinal
section]*
66 das männliche Glied
- *penis*
67 der Schwellkörper
- *corpus cavernosum and spongiosum
of the penis (erectile tissue of the
penis)*
68 die Harnröhre
- *urethra*
69 die Eichel
- *glans penis*
70 die Vorhaut
- *prepuce (foreskin)*
71 der Hodensack
- *scrotum*
72 der rechte Hoden
- *right testicle (testis)*
73 der Nebenhoden
- *epididymis*
74 der Samenleiter
- *spermatic duct (vas deferens)*
75 die Cowper-Drüse
- *Cowper's gland (bulbourethral
gland)*
76 die Vorsteherdrüse
- *prostate (prostate gland)*
77 die Samenblase
- *seminal vesicle*
78 die Harnblase
- *bladder*
79-88 die weibl. Geschlechtsorgane n
[Längsschnitt]
- *female sex organs [longitudinal
section]*
79 die Gebärmutter
- *uterus (matrix, womb)*
80 die Gebärmutterhöhle
- *cavity of the uterus*
81 der Eileiter
- *fallopian tube (uterine tube,
oviduct)*
82 die Fimbrien
- *fimbria (fimbriated extremity)*
83 der Eierstock
- *ovary*
84 das Follikel mit dem Ei n
- *follicle with ovum (egg)*
85 der äußere Muttermund
- *os uteri externum*
86 die Scheide
- *vagina*
87 die Schamlippe
- *lip of the pudendum (lip of the
vulva)*
88 der Kitzler
- *clitoris*

1-13 Notverbände *m*
- *emergency bandages*
1 der Armverband
- *arm bandage*
2 das Dreieckstuch als Armtragetuch *n* (Armschlinge *f*)
- *triangular cloth used as a sling (an arm sling)*
3 der Kopfverband
- *head bandage (capeline)*
4 das Verbandspäckchen
- *first aid kit*
5 der Schnellverband
- *first aid dressing*
6 die keimfreie Mullauflage
- *sterile gauze dressing*
7 das Heftpflaster
- *adhesive plaster (sticking plaster)*
8 die Wunde
- *wound*
9 die Mullbinde
- *bandage*
10 der behelfsmäßige Stützverband eines gebrochenen Gliedes *n*
- *emergency splint for a broken limb (fractured limb)*
11 das gebrochene Bein
- *fractured leg (broken leg)*
12 die Schiene
- *splint*
13 das Kopfpolster
- *headrest*
14-17 Maßnahmen *f* **zur Blutstillung** (die Unterbindung eines Blutgefäßes *n*)
- *measures for stanching the blood flow (tying up of, ligature of, a blood vessel)*
14 die Abdrückstellen *f* der Schlagadern *f*
- *pressure points of the arteries*
15 die Notaderpresse am Oberschenkel *m*
- *emergency tourniquet on the thigh*
16 der Stock als Knebel *m* (Drehgriff)
- *walking stick used as a screw*
17 der Druckverband
- *compression bandage*
18-23 die Bergung und Beförderung eines Verletzten *m* (Verunglückten)
- *rescue and transport of an injured person*
18 der Rautek-Griff (zur Bergung eines Verletzten *m* aus einem Unfallfahrzeug *n*)
- *Rautek grip (for rescue of victim of a car accident)*
19 der Helfer
- *helper*
20 der Verletzte (Verunglückte)
- *injured person (casualty)*
21 der Kreuzgriff
- *chair grip*
22 der Tragegriff
- *carrying grip*
23 die Behelfstrage aus Stöcken *m* und einer Jacke
- *emergency stretcher of sticks and a jacket*
24-27 die Lagerung Bewußtloser *m* **und die künstliche Atmung** (Wiederbelebung)
- *positioning of an unconscious person and artificial respiration (resuscitation)*

24 die stabile Seitenlage (Nato-Lage)
- *coma position*
25 der Bewußtlose
- *unconscious person*
26 die Mund-zu-Mund-Beatmung (*Abart:* Mund-zu-Nase-Beatmung)
- *mouth-to-mouth resuscitation (variation: mouth-to-nose resuscitation)*
27 die Elektrolunge, ein Wiederbelebungsapparat *m*, ein Atemgerät *n*
- *resuscitator (respiratory apparatus, resuscitation apparatus), a respirator (artificial breathing device)*
28-33 die Rettung bei Eisunfällen *m*
- *methods of rescue in ice accidents*
28 der im Eis *n* Eingebrochene
- *person who has fallen through the ice*
29 der Retter
- *rescuer*
30 das Seil
- *rope*
31 der Tisch (o.ä. Hilfsmittel *n*)
- *table (or similar device)*
32 die Leiter
- *ladder*
33 die Selbstrettung
- *self-rescue*
34-38 die Rettung Ertrinkender *m*
- *rescue of a drowning person*
34 der Befreiungsgriff bei Umklammerung *f*
- *method of release (release grip, release) to free rescuer from the clutch of a drowning person*
35 der Ertrinkende
- *drowning person*
36 der Rettungsschwimmer
- *lifesaver*
37 der Achselgriff, ein Transportgriff *m*
- *chest grip, a towing grip*
38 der Hüftgriff
- *tired swimmer grip (hip grip)*

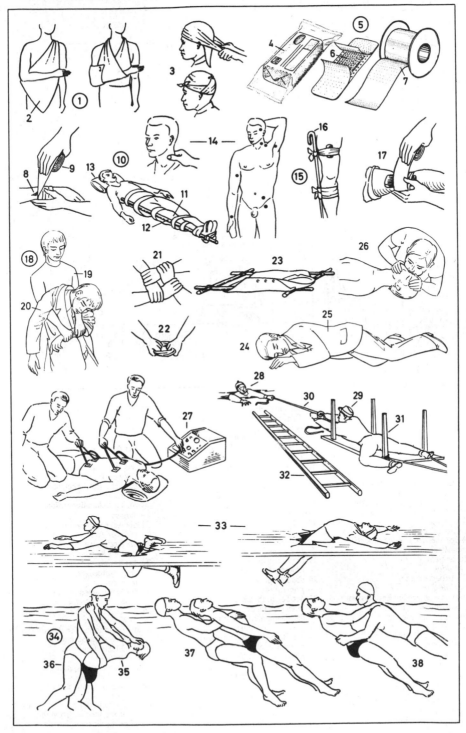

1-74 die Praxis für Allgemeinmedizin f
- *general practice (Am. physician's office)*
1 der Warteraum (das Wartezimmer)
- *waiting room*
2 der Patient
- *patient*
3 die (zur Routineuntersuchung oder Rezepterneuerung) vorbestellten Patienten m
- *patients with appointments (for a routine checkup or renewal of prescription)*
4 die ausgelegten Zeitschriften f
- *magazines [for waiting patients]*
5 die Annahme (Aufnahme, Rezeption)
- *reception*
6 die Patientenkartei
- *patients file*
7 die ausgeschiedenen Karteikarten f
- *eliminated index cards*
8 die Patientenkarte (das Krankenblatt)
- *medical record (medical card)*
9 der Krankenschein
- *health insurance certificate*
10 der Werbekalender
- *advertising calendar (publicity calendar)*
11 das Vorbestellbuch
- *appointments book*
12 der Schriftverkehrsordner
- *correspondence file*

13 der automatische Telefonanrufbeantworter und -aufzeichner
- *automatic telephone answering and recording set (telephone answering device)*
14 das Funksprechgerät
- *radiophone*
15 das Mikrophon
- *microphone*
16 die Schautafel
- *illustrated chart*
17 der Wandkalender
- *wall calendar*
18 das Telefon
- *telephone*
19 die Arzthelferin
- *[doctor's] assistant*
20 das Rezept
- *prescription*
21 der Telefonblock
- *telephone index*
22 das medizinische Wörterbuch
- *medical dictionary*
23 die „Rote Liste" der zugelassenen Arzneimittel n
- *pharmacopoeia (list of registered medicines)*
24 der Postfreistempler
- *franking machine (Am. postage meter)*
25 der Drahthefter
- *stapler*
26 die Diabetikerkartei
- *diabetics file*

27 das Diktiergerät
- *dictating machine*
28 der Locher
- *paper punch*
29 der Arztstempel
- *doctor's stamp*
30 das Stempelkissen
- *ink pad*
31 der Schreibstiftebehälter
- *pencil holder*
32-74 der Behandlungsraum
- *surgery*
32 die Augenhintergrundtafel
- *chart of eyegrounds*
33 die Arzttasche
- *doctor's bag (doctor's case)*
34 das Raumsprechgerät, ein Gegensprechgerät
- *intercom*
35 der Medikamentenschrank
- *medicine cupboard*
36 der Tupferspender
- *swab dispenser*
37 die Luftdusche (der Politzer-Ballon)
- *inflator (Politzer bag)*
38 das Elektrotom
- *electrotome*
39 der Dampfsterilisator
- *steam sterilizer*
40 das Wandschränkchen
- *cabinet*
41 die Ärztemuster n
- *medicine samples (from the pharmaceutical industry)*

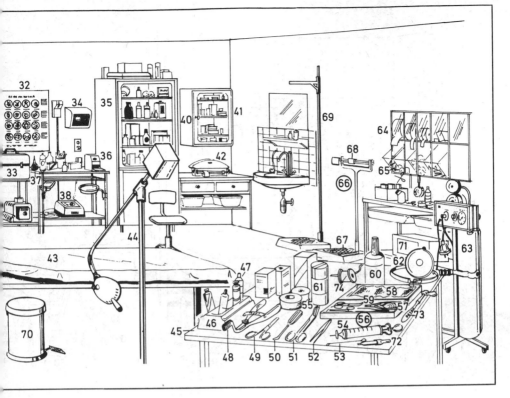

42 die Babywaage
- *baby scales*
43 die Untersuchungsliege
- *examination couch*
44 der Beleuchtungsstrahler
- *directional lamp*
45 der Verbandstisch
- *instrument table*
46 der Tubenständer
- *tube holder*
47 die Salbentube
- *tube of ointment*
48-50 die Behandlungsinstrumente *n*
für die kleine Chirurgie
- *instruments for minor surgery*
48 der Mundsperrer
- *mouth gag*
49 die Kocher-Klemme
- *Kocher's forceps*
50 der scharfe Löffel
- *scoop (curette)*
51 die gekröpfte Schere
- *angled scissors*
52 die Pinzette
- *forceps*
53 die Knopfsonde
- *olive-pointed
(bulb-headed) probe*
54 die Spritze für Spülungen von Ohr
n oder Blase *f*
- *syringe for irrigations of the ear or
bladder*
55 das Heftpflaster
- *adhesive plaster (sticking plaster)*

56 das chirurgische Nahtmaterial
- *surgical suture material*
57 die gebogene chrirurgische Nadel
- *curved surgical needle*
58 die sterile Gaze
- *sterile gauze*
59 der Nadelhalter
- *needle holder*
60 die Sprühdose zur
Hautdesinfektion
- *spray for disinfecting the skin*
61 der Fadenbehälter
- *thread container*
62 der Augenspiegel
- *ophthalmoscope*
63 das Vereisungsgerät für
kryochirurgische Eingriffe *m*
- *freezer for cryosurgery*
64 der Pflaster- und Kleinteilespender
- *dispenser for plasters and small
pieces of equipment*
65 die Einmalinjektionsnadeln *f* und
-spritzen *f*
- *disposable hypodermic needles and
syringes*
66 die Personenwaage, eine
Laufgewichtswaage
- *scales, sliding-weight scales*
67 die Wiegeplattform
- *weighing platform*
68 das Laufgewicht
- *sliding weight (jockey)*
69 der Körpergrößenmesser
- *height gauge (Am. gage)*

70 der Abfalleimer
- *waste bin (Am. trash bin)*
71 der Heißluftsterilisator
- *hot-air sterilizer*
72 die Pipette
- *pipette*
73 der Reflexhammer
- *percussor*
74 der Ohrenspiegel
- *aural speculum (auriscope, aural
syringe)*

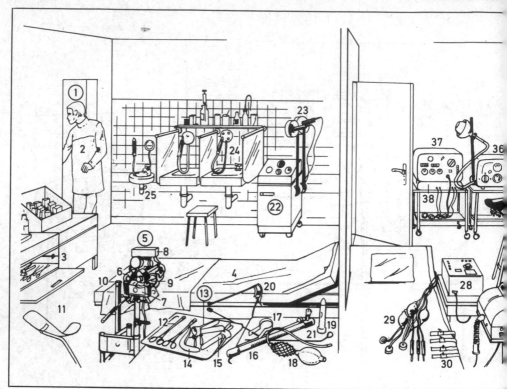

1 das Sprechzimmer
  (Konsultationszimmer)
- *consulting room*
2 der Arzt für Allgemeinmedizin *f*
  (der Allgemeinmediziner; *früh.:*
  der praktische Arzt)
- *general practitioner*
3-21 **gynäkologische und
  proktologische
  Untersuchungsinstrumente** *n*
- *instruments for gynecological and
  proctological examinations*
3 die Vorwärmung der Instrumente *n*
  auf Körpertemperatur *f*
- *warming the instruments up to
  body temperature*
4 die Untersuchungsliege
- *examination couch*
5 das Kolposkop
- *colposcope*
6 der binokulare Einblick
- *binocular eyepiece*
7 die Kleinbildkamera
- *miniature camera*
8 die Kaltlichtbeleuchtung
- *cold light source*
9 der Drahtauslöser
- *cable release*
10 die Öse für den Beinhalter
- *bracket for the leg support*
11 der Beinhalter (Beinkloben)
- *leg support (leg holder)*
12 die Kornzangen *f* (Tupferhalter)
- *holding forceps (sponge holder)*

13 das Scheidenspekulum (der
  Scheidenspiegel)
- *vaginal speculum*
14 das untere Blatt des
  Scheidenspiegels *m*
- *lower blade of the vaginal speculum*
15 die Platinöse (für Abstriche *m*)
- *platinum loop (for smears)*
16 das Rektoskop
- *rectoscope*
17 die Biopsiezange für das Rektoskop
- *biopsy forceps used with the
  rectoscope (proctoscope)*
18 der Luftinsufflator für die
  Rektoskopie
- *insufflator for proctoscopy
  (rectoscopy)*
19 das Proktoskop
- *proctoscope (rectal speculum)*
20 der Harnröhrenkatheter
  (Urethroskop)
- *urethroscope*
21 das Führungsgerät für das
  Proktoskop
- *guide for inserting the proctoscope*
22 das Diathermiegerät
  (Kurzwellengerät,
  Kurzwellenbestrahlungsgerät)
- *diathermy unit (short-wave therapy
  apparatus)*
23 der Radiator
- *radiator*
24 die Inhaliereinrichtung
- *inhaling apparatus (inhalator)*

25 das Spülbecken (für Auswurf *m*)
- *basin (for sputum)*
26-31 **die Ergometrie**
- *ergometry*
26 das Fahrradergometer
- *bicycle ergometer*
27 der Monitor (die
  Leuchtbildanzeige des EKG *n* und
  der Puls- und Atemfrequenz
  während der Belastung)
- *monitor
  (visual display of the ECG
  and of pulse and respiratory rates
  when performing work)*
28 das EKG-Gerät (der
  Elektrokardiograph)
- *ECG (electrocardiograph)*
29 die Saugelektroden *f*
- *suction electrodes*
30 die Anschnallelektroden *f* zur
  Ableitung von den Gliedmaßen *f*
- *strap-on electrodes for the limbs*
31 das Spirometer (zur Messung der
  Atemfunktionen *f*)
- *spirometer (for measuring
  respiratory functions)*
32 die Blutdruckmessung
- *measuring the blood pressure*
33 der Blutdruckmesser
- *sphygmomanometer*
34 die Luftmanschette
- *inflatable cuff*
35 das Stethoskop (Hörrohr)
- *stethoscope*

36 das Mikrowellengerät für
   Bestrahlungen *f*
 - *microwave treatment unit*
37 das Faradisiergerät (Anwendung *f*
   niederfrequenter Ströme *m* mit
   verschiedenen Impulsformen *f*)
 - *faradization unit (application of
   low-frequency currents with
   different pulse shapes)*
38 das automatische Abstimmungsgerät
 - *automatic tuner*
39 das Kurzwellengerät mit Monode *f*
 - *short-wave therapy apparatus*
40 der Kurzzeitmesser
 - *timer*
41-59 **das Labor** (Laboratorium)
 - *laboratory*
41 die medizinisch-technische
   Assistentin (MTA)
 - *medical laboratory technician*
42 der Kapillarständer für die
   Blutsenkung
 - *capillary tube stand for blood
   sedimentation*
43 der Meßzylinder
 - *measuring cylinder*
44 die automatische Pipette
 - *automatic pipette*
45 die Nierenschale
 - *kidney dish*
46 das tragbare EKG-Gerät für den
   Notfalleinsatz
 - *portable ECG machine for
   emergency use*

47 das automatische Pipettiergerät
 - *automatic pipetting device*
48 das thermokonstante Wasserbad
 - *constant temperature water bath*
49 der Wasseranschluß mit
   Wasserstrahlpumpe *f*
 - *tap with water jet pump*
50 die Färbeschale (für die Färbung
   der Blutausstriche *m*, Sedimente *n*
   und Abstriche *m*)
 - *staining dish (for staining blood
   smears, sediments and other smears)*
51 das binokulare Forschungsmikroskop
 - *binocular research microscope*
52 der Pipettenständer für die
   Photometrie
 - *pipette stand for photometry*
53 das Rechen- und Auswertegerät
   für die Photometrie
 - *computer and analyser for
   photometry*
54 das Photometer
 - *photometer*
55 der Kompensationsschreiber
 - *potentiometric recorder*
56 die Transformationsstufe
 - *transforming section*
57 das Laborgerät
 - *laboratory apparatus (laboratory
   equipment)*
58 die Harnsedimentstafel
 - *urine sediment chart*
59 die Zentrifuge
 - *centrifuge*

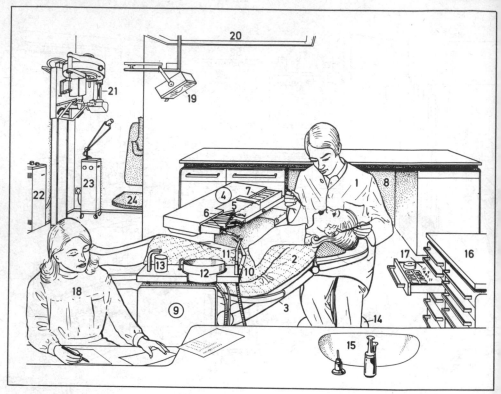

1 der Zahnarzt
- *dentist*
  (dental surgeon)
2 der Patient
- *patient*
3 der Patientenstuhl
  (Behandlungsstuhl)
- *dentist's chair*
4 das Zahnarztgerät
- *dental instruments*
5 der Behandlungstray
- *instrument tray*
6 die Bohrinstrumente *n* mit
  verschiedenen Handstücken *n*
- *drills with different handpieces*
7 die Medikamentenkassette
- *medicine case*
8 die Garage (für das Zahnarztgerät)
- *storage unit (for dental
  instruments)*
9 die Helferineinheit
- *assistant's unit*
10 die Mehrfachfunktionsspritze (für
  kaltes und warmes Wasser, Spray *m*
  oder Luft *f*)
- *multi-purpose syringe (for cold and
  warm water, spray or air)*
11 die Absauganlage
- *suction apparatus*
12 das Speibecken
- *basin*
13 das Wasserglas mit automatischer
  Füllung
- *water glass, filled automatically*

14 der Arbeitssessel
- *stool*
15 das Waschbecken
- *washbasin*
16 der Instrumentenschrank
- *instrument cabinet*
17 das Bohrerfach
- *drawer for drills*
18 die Zahnarzthelferin
- *dentist's assistant*
19 die Behandlungslampe
- *dentist's lamp*
20 die Deckenleuchte
- *ceiling light*
21 das Röntgengerät für
  Panoramaaufnahmen *f*
- *X-ray apparatus for panoramic
  pictures*
22 der Röntgengenerator
- *X-ray generator*
23 das Mikrowellengerät, ein
  Bestrahlungsgerät *n*
- *microwave treatment unit, a
  radiation unit*
24 der Sitzplatz
- *seat*
25 die Zahnprothese (der Zahnersatz,
  das künstliche Gebiß)
- *denture (set of false teeth)*
26 die Brücke (Zahnbrücke)
- *bridge (dental bridge)*
27 der zurechtgeschliffene
  Zahnstumpf
- *prepared stump of the tooth*

28 die Krone (*Arten:* Goldkrone,
  Jacketkrone)
- *crown* (kinds: *gold crown, jacket
  crown)*
29 der Porzellanzahn
- *porcelain tooth (porcelain pontic)*
30 die Füllung (Zahnfüllung, *veralt.:*
  Plombe)
- *filling*
31 der Stiftzahn (Ringstiftzahn)
- *post crown*
32 die Facette
- *facing*
33 der Ring
- *diaphragm*
34 der Stift
- *post*
35 die Carborundscheibe
- *carborundum disc (disk)*
36 die Schmirgelscheibe
- *grinding wheel*
37 Kavitätenbohrer *m*
- *burs*
38 der Finierer (flammenförmige
  Bohrer)
- *flame-shaped finishing bur*
39 Spaltbohrer *m* (Fissurenbohrer)
- *fissure burs*
40 der Diamantschleifer
- *diamond point*
41 der Mundspiegel
- *mouth mirror*
42 die Mundleuchte
- *mouth lamp*

43 der Thermokauter (Kauter)
– *cautery*
44 die Platin-Iridium-Elektrode
– *platinum-iridium electrode*
45 Zahnreinigungsinstrumente *n*
– *tooth scalers*
46 die Sonde
– *probe*
47 die Extraktionszange
– *extraction forceps*
48 der Wurzelheber (Stößel)
– *tooth-root elevator*
49 der Knochenmeißel
– *bone chisel*
50 der Spatel
– *spatula*
51 das Füllungsmischgerät
– *mixer for filling material*
52 die Synchronzeitschaltuhr
– *synchronous timer*
53 die Injektionsspritze zur
Anästhesierung (Nervbetäubung)
– *hypodermic syringe for injection of
local anaesthetic*
54 die Injektionsnadel
– *hypodermic needle*
55 der Matrizenspanner
– *matrix holder*
56 der Abdrucklöffel
– *impression tray*
57 die Spiritusflamme
– *spirit lamp*

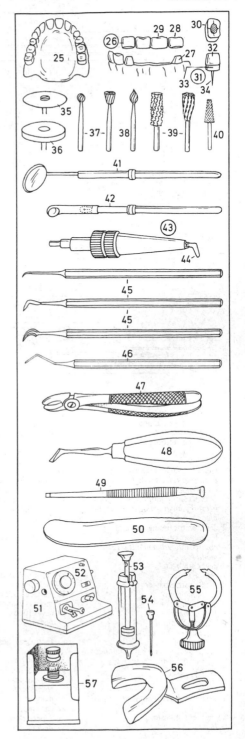

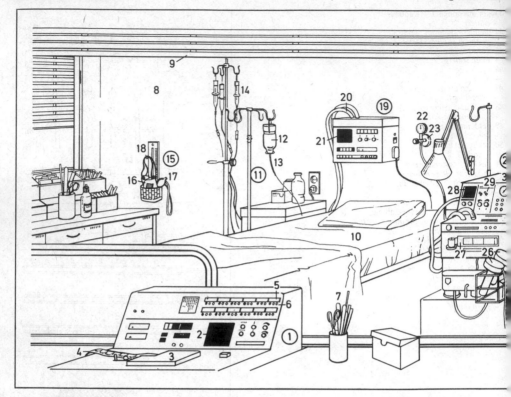

1-30 **die Intensivstation**
(Intensivpflegestation)
- *intensive care unit*
1-9 **der Kontrollraum**
- *control room*
1 die zentrale
Herzüberwachungsanlage zur
Kontrolle von Herzrhythmus *m*
und Blutdruck *m*
- *central control unit for monitoring
heart rhythm (cardiac rhythm) and
blood pressure*
2 der Monitor für die
Herzstromkurve
- *electrocardiogram monitor (ECG
monitor)*
3 das Schreibgerät
- *recorder*
4 das Registrierpapier
- *recording paper*
5 die Patientenkarte
- *patient's card*
6 die Signallampen *f* (mit
Anwahlknöpfen *n* für jeden
Patienten *m*)
- *indicator lights (with call buttons
for each patient)*
7 der Spatel
- *spatula*
8 das Sichtfenster
- *window (observation window, glass
partition)*
9 die Trennjalousie
- *blind*

10 das Patientenbett
- *bed (hospital bed)*
11 der Infusionsgeräteständer
- *stand for infusion apparatus*
12 die Infusionsflasche
- *infusion bottle*
13 der Infusionsschlauch für
Tropfinfusionen *f*
- *tube for intravenous drips*
14 die Infusionseinrichtung für
wasserlösliche Medikamente *n*
- *infusion device for water-soluble
medicaments*
15 der Blutdruckmesser
- *sphygmomanometer*
16 die Manschette
- *cuff*
17 der Aufblasballon
- *inflating bulb*
18 das Quecksilbermanometer
- *mercury manometer*
19 das Bettmonitorgerät
- *bed monitor*
20 das Verbindungskabel zur
zentralen Überwachungsanlage
- *connecting lead to the central
control unit*
21 der Monitor für die
Herzstromkurve
- *electrocardiogram monitor (ECG
monitor)*
22 das Manometer für die
Sauerstoffzufuhr
- *manometer for the oxygen supply*

23 der Wandanschluß für die
Sauerstoffbeatmung
- *wall connection for oxygen
treatment*
24 die fahrbare
Patientenüberwachungseinheit
- *mobile monitoring unit*
25 das Elektrodenkabel zum
passageren Schrittmacher *m*
- *electrode lead to the short-term
pacemaker*
26 die Elektroden *f* zur
Elektroschockbehandlung
- *electrodes for shock treatment*
27 die EKG-Registriereinheit
- *ECG recording unit*
28 der Monitor zur Überwachung der
Herzstromkurve
- *electrocardiogram monitor (ECG
monitor)*
29 die Bedienungsknöpfe *m* für die
Einstellung des Monitors *m*
- *control switches and knobs
(controls) for adjusting the monitor*
30 die Bedienungsknöpfe *m* für die
Schrittmachereinheit
- *control buttons for the pacemaker
unit*

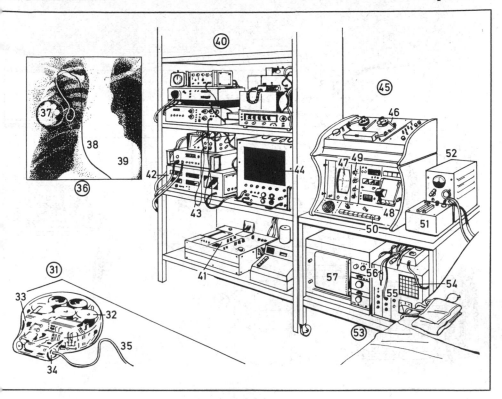

31 **der Herzschrittmacher**
- *pacemaker (cardiac pacemaker)*
32 die Quecksilberbatterie
- *mercury battery*
33 der programmierbare Taktgeber
- *programmed impulse generator*
34 der Elektrodenausgang
- *electrode exit point*
35 die Elektrode
- *electrode*
36 die Herzschrittmacherimplantation
- *implantation of the pacemaker*
37 der intrakorporale
Herzschrittmacher
(Schrittmacher)
- *internal cardiac pacemaker
(internal pacemaker, pacemaker)*
38 die transvenös geführte Elektrode
- *electrode inserted through the vein*
39 die Herzsilhouette im Röntgenbild *n*
- *cardiac silhouette on the X-ray*
40 **die Anlage zur
Schrittmacherkontrolle**
- *pacemaker control unit*
41 der EKG-Schreiber
- *electrocardiograph
(ECG recorder)*
42 der automatische Impulsmesser
- *automatic impulse meter*
43 das Verbindungskabel
(EKG-Kabel) zum Patienten
- *ECG lead to the patient*
44 der Monitor zur optischen
Kontrolle der

Schrittmacherimpulse *m*
- *monitor unit for visual monitoring
of the pacemaker impulses*
45 der EKG-Langzeitanalysator
- *long-term ECG analyser*
46 das Magnetband zur Aufnahme
der EKG-Impulse *m* bei der
Analyse
- *magnetic tape for recording the
ECG impulses during analysis*
47 der Monitor zur EKG-Kontrolle
- *ECG monitor*
48 die automatische
EKG-Rhythmusanalyse auf Papier *n*
- *automatic analysis on paper of the
ECG rhythm*
49 die Einstellung der
EKG-Amplitudenhöhe
- *control knob for the ECG
amplitude*
50 die Programmwahl für die
EKG-Analyse
- *program selector switches for the
ECG analysis*
51 das Ladegerät für die
Antriebsbatterien *f* des
Patientengerätes *n*
- *charger for the pacemaker batteries*
52 das Prüfgerät für die Batterien *f*
- *battery tester*
53 das Druckmeßgerät für den
Rechtsherzkatheter
- *pressure gauge* (Am. *gage*) *for the
right cardiac catheter*

54 der Monitor zur Kurvenkontrolle
- *trace monitor*
55 der Druckanzeiger
- *pressure indicator*
56 das Verbindungskabel zum
Papierschreiber *m*
- *connecting lead to the paper
recorder*
57 der Papierschreiber für die
Druckkurven *f*
- *paper recorder for pressure traces*

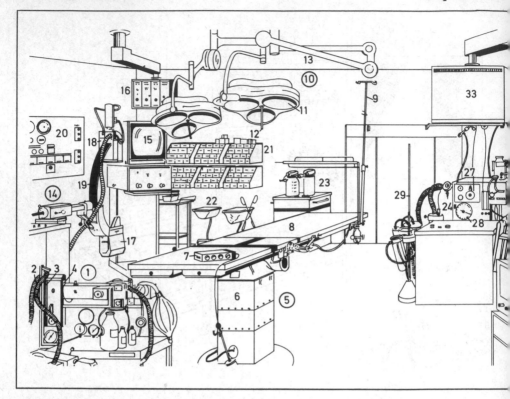

**1-54 die chirurgische Abteilung
(chirurgische Klinik)**
- *surgical unit*
1-33 der Operationssaal (OP-Saal)
- *operating theatre (Am. theater)*
1 der Narkose- und
Dauerbeatmungsapparat
- *anaesthesia and breathing
apparatus (respiratory machine)*
2 die Inhalationsschläuche *m*
- *inhalers (inhaling tubes)*
3 der Durchflußmesser für Lachgas *n*
(Distickstoffoxid, Stickstoffoxydul)
- *flowmeter for nitrous oxide*
4 der Durchflußmesser für
Sauerstoff *m*
- *oxygen flow meter*
5 der aufgeständerte Operationstisch
(OP-Tisch)
- *pedestal operating table*
6 die Tischsäule
- *table pedestal*
7 das Steuergerät
- *control device (control unit)*
8 die verstellbare
Operationstischfläche
- *adjustable top of the operating
table*
9 der Ständer für Tropfinfusionen *f*
- *stand for intravenous drips*
10 die schwenkbare schattenfreie
Operationsleuchte (OP-Lampe)
- *swivel-mounted shadow-free
operating lamp*

11 das Leuchtelement
- *individual lamp*
12 der Handgriff
- *handle*
13 der Schwenkarm
- *swivel arm*
14 der fahrbare
Röntgendurchleuchtungsapparat
- *mobile fluoroscope*
15 der Bildwandlermonitor
- *monitor of the image converter*
16 der Monitor [Rückseite]
- *monitor [back]*
17 die Röhreneinheit
- *tube*
18 die Bildwandlereinheit
- *image converter*
19 der C-Bogen
- *C-shaped frame*
20 die Schalttafel der Klimaanlage
- *control panel for the
air-conditioning*
21 das chirurgische Nahtmaterial
- *surgical suture material*
22 der fahrbare Abfallbehälter
- *mobile waste tray*
23 die Behälter *m* mit unsterilen
Kompressen *f*
- *containers for unsterile
(unsterilized) pads*
24 das Narkose- und
Dauerbeatmungsgerät
- *anaesthesia and respiratory
apparatus*

25 der Respirator
- *respirator*
26 der
Fluothane-(Halothan-)Behälter
- *fluothane container (halothane
container)*
27 die Ventilationseinstellung
- *ventilation control knob*
28 die Registriertafel mit Zeiger *m* für
das Atemvolumen
- *indicator with pointer for
respiratory volume*
29 das Stativ mit
Inhalationsschläuchen *m* und
Druckmessern *m*
- *stand with inhalers (inhaling tubes)
and pressure gauges (Am. gages)*
30 der Katheterbehälter
- *catheter holder*
31 der steril verpackte Katheter
- *catheter in sterile packing*
32 der Pulsschreiber (Sphygmograph)
- *sphygmograph*
33 der Monitor
- *monitor*

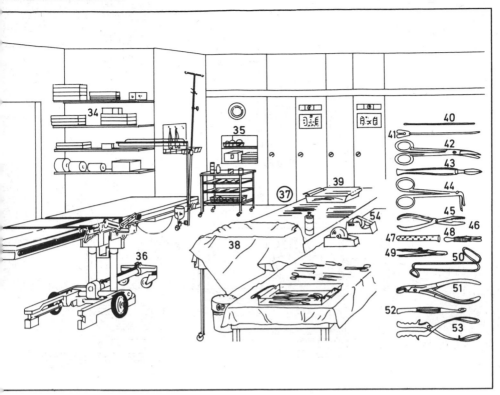

**34-54 der Vorbereitungs- und
Sterilisierraum**
- *preparation and sterilization room*
34 das Verbandsmaterial
- *dressing material*
35 der Kleinsterilisator
- *small sterilizer*
36 das Operationstischfahrgestell
- *carriage of the operating table*
37 der fahrbare Instrumententisch
- *mobile instrument table*
38 das sterile Tuch
- *sterile cloth*
39 der Instrumentenkorb
- *instrument tray*
40-53 die chirurgischen Instrumente *n*
- *surgical instruments*
40 die Knopfsonde
- *olive-pointed
(bulb-headed) probe*
41 die Hohlsonde
- *hollow probe*
42 die gebogene Schere
- *curved scissors*
43 das Skalpell
- *scalpel (surgical knife)*
44 der Ligaturführer
- *ligature-holding forceps*
45 die Sequesterzange
- *sequestrum forceps*
46 die Branche
- *jaw*
47 das Dränrohr (Dränagerohr)
- *drainage tube*

48 die Aderpresse (Aderklemme)
- *surgeon's tourniquet (torcular)*
49 die Arterienpinzette
- *artery forceps*
50 der Wundhaken
- *blunt hook*
51 die Knochenzange
- *bone nippers (bone-cutting forceps)*
52 der scharfe Löffel (die Kürette) für
die Ausschabung (Kürettage)
- *scoop (curette) for erasion
(curettage)*
53 die Geburtszange
- *obstetrical forceps*
54 die Heftpflasterrolle
- *roll of plaster*

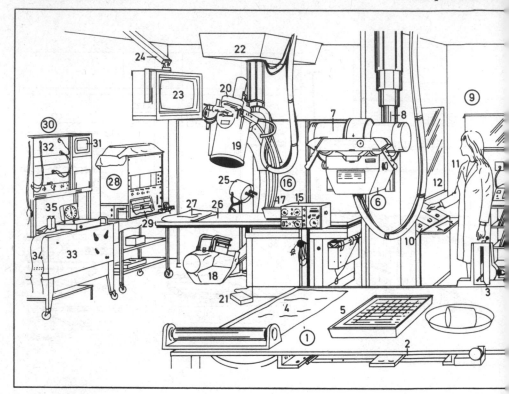

1-35 die Röntgenstation
- *X-ray unit*
1 der Röntgenuntersuchungstisch
- *X-ray examination table*
2 die Röntgenkassettenhalterung
- *support for X-ray cassettes*
3 die Höheneinstellung für den Zentralstrahl bei Seitaufnahmen *f*
- *height adjustment of the central beam for lateral views*
4 die Kompresse bei Nieren- und Gallenaufnahmen *f*
- *compress for pyelography and cholecystography*
5 die Instrumentenschale
- *instrument basin*
6 die Röntgeneinrichtung zur Aufnahme von Nierenkontrastdarstellungen *f*
- *X-ray apparatus for pyelograms*
7 die Röntgenröhre
- *X-ray tube*
8 das ausfahrbare Röntgenstativ
- *telescopic X-ray support*
9 die zentrale Röntgenschaltstelle
- *central X-ray control unit*
10 das Schaltpult
- *control panel (control desk)*
11 die Röntgenassistentin
- *radiographer (X-ray technician)*
12 das Blickfenster zum Angioraum *m* (Angiographieraum)
- *window to the angiography room*

13 das Oxymeter
- *oxymeter*
14 die Kassetten *f* für Nierenaufnahmen *f*
- *pyelogram cassettes*
15 das Druckspritzengerät für Kontrastmittelinjektionen *f*
- *contrast medium injector*
16 das Röntgenbildverstärkergerät
- *X-ray image intensifier*
17 der C-Bogen
- *C-shaped frame*
18 der Röntgenkopf mit der Röntgenröhre
- *X-ray head with X-ray tube*
19 der Bildwandler mit der Bildwandlerröhre
- *image converter with converter tube*
20 die Filmkamera
- *film camera*
21 der Fußschalter
- *foot switch*
22 die fahrbare Halterung
- *mobile mounting*
23 der Monitor
- *monitor*
24 der schwenkbare Monitorarm
- *swivel-mounted monitor support*
25 die Operationslampe (OP-Lampe)
- *operating lamp*
26 der angiographische Untersuchungstisch
- *angiographic examination table*

27 das Kopfkissen
- *pillow*
28 der Acht-Kanal-Schreiber
- *eight-channel recorder*
29 das Registrierpapier
- *recording paper*
30 der Kathetermeßplatz für die Herzkatheterisierung
- *catheter gauge (Am. gage) unit for catheterization of the heart*
31 der Sechs-Kanal-Monitor für Druckkurven *f* und EKG *n*
- *six-channel monitor for pressure graphs and ECG*
32 die Druckwandlereinschübe *m*
- *slide-in units of the pressure transducer*
33 die Papierregistriereinheit mit Entwickler *m* für die Fotoregistrierung
- *paper recorder unit with developer for photographic recording*
34 das Registrierpapier
- *recording paper*
35 der Kurzzeitmesser
- *timer*

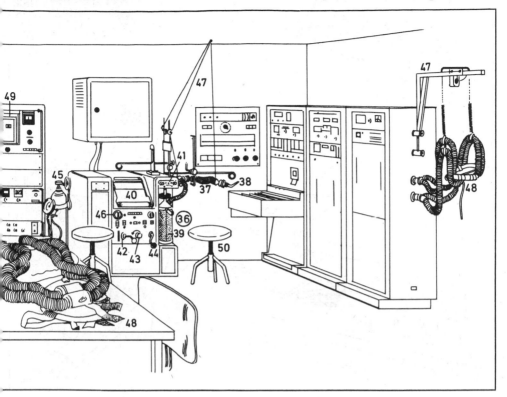

36-50 Spirometrie *f*
- *spirometry*
36 der Spirograph, für die
  Lungenfunktionsprüfung
- *spirograph for pulmonary function
  tests*
37 der Atemschlauch
- *breathing tube*
38 das Mundstück
- *mouthpiece*
39 der Natronkalkabsorber
- *soda-lime absorber*
40 das Registrierpapier
- *recording paper*
41 die Gasversorgungsregulierung
- *control knobs for gas supply*
42 der O_2-Stabilisator
- *O_2-stabilizer*
43 die Drosselklappe
- *throttle valve*
44 die Absorberzuschaltung
- *absorber attachment*
45 die Sauerstoffflasche
- *oxygen cylinder*
46 die Wasserversorgung
- *water supply*
47 die Schlauchhalterung
- *tube support*
48 die Gesichtsmaske
- *mask*
49 der Meßplatz für den CO_2-Verbrauch
- *CO_2 consumption meter*
50 der Patientenhocker
- *stool for the patient*

1 das Kinderreisebett
- *collapsible cot*
2 die Babywippe
- *bouncing cradle*
3 die Säuglingsbadewanne
- *baby bath*
4 der Wickeltischaufsatz
- *changing top*
5 der Säugling (das Baby, Wickelkind)
- *baby (new-born baby)*
6 die Mutter
- *mother*
7 die Haarbürste
- *hairbrush*
8 der Kamm
- *comb*
9 das Handtuch
- *hand towel*
10 die Schwimmente
- *toy duck*
11 die Wickelkommode
- *changing unit*
12 der Beißring
- *teething ring*
13 die Cremedose
- *cream jar*
14 der Puderstreuer
- *box of baby powder*
15 der Lutscher (Schnuller)
- *dummy*
16 der Ball
- *ball*

17 der Babyschlafsack
- *sleeping bag*
18 die Pflegebox (Babybox)
- *layette box*
19 die Milchflasche
- *feeding bottle*
20 der Sauger
- *teat*
21 die Warmhaltebox (Flaschenbox)
- *bottle warmer*
22 die Windelhose für Wegwerfwindeln *f*
- *rubber baby pants for disposable nappies* (Am. *diapers*)
23 das Kinderhemdchen
- *vest*
24 die Strampelhose
- *leggings*
25 das Babyjäckchen
- *baby's jacket*
26 das Häubchen
- *hood*
27 die Kindertasse
- *baby's cup*
28 der Kinderteller, ein Warmhalteteller *m*
- *baby's plate, a stay-warm plate*
29 das Thermometer
- *thermometer*

30 der Stubenwagen, ein Korbwagen *m*
 - *bassinet, a wicker pram*
31 die Stubenwagengarnitur
 - *set of bassinet covers*
32 der Baldachin
 - *canopy*
33 der Kinderstuhl, ein Klappstuhl *m*
 - *baby's high chair, a folding chair*
34 der Sichtfensterkinderwagen
 - *pram (baby-carriage)*
 [with windows]
35 das zurückklappbare Verdeck
 - *folding hood*
36 das Sichtfenster
 - *window*
37 der Sportwagen
 - *pushchair (Am. stroller)*
38 der Fußsack
 - *foot-muff (Am. foot-bag)*
39 der Laufstall (das Laufställchen,
 Ställchen)
 - *play pen*
40 der Laufstallboden
 - *floor of the play pen*
41 die Bauklötze *m*
 - *building blocks*
 (building bricks)
42 das Kleinkind
 - *small child*
43 das Lätzchen
 - *bib*
44 der Rasselring
 - *rattle (baby's rattle)*

45 die Babyschuhe *m*
 - *bootees*
46 der Teddybär
 - *teddy bear*
47 das Töpfchen (der Topf)
 - *potty (baby's pot)*
48 die Babytragetasche
 - *carrycot*
49 das Sichtfenster
 - *window*
50 die Haltegriffe *m*
 - *handles*

1-12 die Babykleidung
- *baby clothes*
1 die Ausfahrgarnitur
- *pram suit*
2 das Mützchen
- *hood*
3 das Ausfahrjäckchen
- *pram jacket (matinée coat)*
4 der Pompon (Bommel)
- *pompon (bobble)*
5 die Babyschuhe *m*
- *bootees*
6 das Achselhemdchen
- *sleeveless vest*
7 das Schlupfhemdchen
- *envelope-neck vest*
8 das Flügelhemdchen
- *wrapover vest*
9 das Babyjäckchen
- *baby's jacket*
10 das Windelhöschen
- *rubber baby pants*
11 das Strampelhöschen (der Babystrampler)
- *playsuit*
12 der zweiteilige Babydress
- *two-piece suit*
13-30 die Kleinkinderkleidung
- *infants' wear*
13 das Sommerkleidchen, ein Trägerkleidchen *n*
- *child's sundress, a pinafore dress*
14 der Flügelärmel
- *frilled shoulder strap*
15 das gesmokte Oberteil
- *shirred top*
16 der Sommerhut (Sonnenhut)
- *sun hat*
17 der einteilige Jerseyanzug
- *one-piece jersey suit*
18 der Vorderreißverschluß
- *front zip*
19 der Overall
- *catsuit (playsuit)*
20 die Applikation
- *motif (appliqué)*
21 das Spielhöschen
- *romper*
22 der Spielanzug
- *playsuit (romper suit)*
23 der Schlaf- und Strampelanzug
- *coverall (sleeper and strampler)*
24 der Bademantel
- *dressing gown (bath robe)*
25 die Kindershorts *pl*
- *children's shorts*
26 die Hosenträger *m*
- *braces (Am. suspenders)*
27 das Kinder-T-Shirt
- *children's T-shirt*
28 das Jerseykleidchen (Strickkleidchen)
- *jersey dress (knitted dress)*
29 die Stickerei
- *embroidery*
30 die Kindersöckchen *n*
- *children's ankle socks*
31-47 die Schulkinderkleidung
- *school children's wear*
31 der Regenmantel (Lodenmantel)
- *raincoat (loden coat)*
32 die Lederhose (Lederhosen *pl*)
- *leather shorts (lederhosen)*
33 der Hirschhornknopf
- *staghorn button*
34 die Lederhosenträger *m*
- *braces (Am. suspenders)*

35 der Hosenlatz
- *flap*
36 das Kinderdirndl
- *girl's dirndl*
37 die Zierkordel (Zierverschnürung)
- *cross lacing*
38 der Schneeanzug (Steppanzug)
- *snow suit (quilted suit)*
39 die Steppnaht
- *quilt stitching (quilting)*
40 die Latzhose
- *dungarees (bib and brace)*
41 der Latzrock
- *bib skirt (bib top pinafore)*
42 die Strumpfhose
- *tights (pantie-hose)*
43 der Nickipulli (Nicki)
- *sweater (jumper)*
44 das Teddyjäckchen
- *pile jacket*
45 die Gamaschenhose
- *leggings*
46 der Mädchenrock
- *girl's skirt*
47 der Kinderpulli
- *child's jumper*
48-68 die Teenagerkleidung
- *teenagers' clothes*
48 die Mädchenüberziehbluse
- *girl's overblouse (overtop)*
49 die Mädchenhose
- *slacks*
50 das Mädchenkostüm
- *girl's skirt suit*
51 die Kostümjacke
- *jacket*
52 der Kostümrock
- *skirt*
53 die Kniestrümpfe *m*
- *knee-length socks*
54 der Mädchenmantel
- *girl's coat*
55 der Mantelgürtel
- *tie belt*
56 die Mädchentasche
- *girl's bag*
57 die Wollmütze
- *woollen (Am. woolen) hat*
58 die Mädchenbluse
- *girl's blouse*
59 der Hosenrock
- *culottes*
60 die Knabenhose
- *boy's trousers*
61 das Knabenhemd
- *boy's shirt*
62 der Anorak
- *anorak*
63 die angeschnittenen Taschen *f*
- *inset pockets*
64 das Kapuzenband
- *hood drawstring (drawstring)*
65 der Strickbund
- *knitted welt*
66 der (die) Wetterparka
- *parka coat (parka)*
67 der Durchziehgürtel
- *drawstring (draw cord)*
68 die aufgesetzten Taschen *f*
- *patch pockets*

1 das Nerzjäckchen
- *mink jacket*
2 der Rollkragenpullover
- *cowl neck jumper*
3 der halsferne Rollkragen
- *cowl collar*
4 der Überziehpullover
- *knitted overtop*
5 der Umschlagkragen
- *turndown collar*
6 der Umschlagärmel
- *turn-up (turnover) sleeve*
7 der Rolli (Unterziehrolli)
- *polo neck jumper*
8 der Kleiderrock
- *pinafore dress*
9 die Reversbluse
- *skirt (with revers collar)*
10 das Hemdblusenkleid, ein
durchgeknöpftes Kleid
- *shirt-waister dress, a
button-through dress*
11 der Kleidergürtel
- *belt*
12 das Winterkleid
- *winter dress*
13 die (der) Paspel
- *piping*
14 die Manschette
- *cuff*
15 der lange Ärmel
- *long sleeve*
16 die Steppweste (wattierte
Steppweste)
- *quilted waistcoat*
17 die Steppnaht
- *quilt stitching (quilting)*
18 der Lederbesatz
- *leather trimming*
19 die lange Winterhose
- *winter slacks*
20 der Ringelpulli
- *striped polo jumper*
21 die Latzhose
- *boiler suit (dungarees, bib and
brace)*
22 die aufgesetzte Tasche
- *patch pocket*
23 die Brusttasche
- *front pocket*
24 der Latz
- *bib*
25 das Wickelkleid
- *wrapover dress (wrap-around dress)*
26 die Polobluse
- *shirt*
27 das Folklorekleid
- *peasant-style dress*
28 die Blümchenborte
- *floral braid*
29 die Tunika (Tunique, das
Tunikakleid)
- *tunic (tunic top, tunic dress)*
30 der Armbund
- *ribbed cuff*
31 das aufgesteppte Muster
- *quilted design*
32 der Plisseerock
- *pleated skirt*
33 das zweiteilige Strickkleid
- *two-piece knitted dress*
34 der Bootsausschnitt, ein
Halsausschnitt *m*
- *boat neck, a neckline*
35 der Ärmelaufschlag
- *turn-up*

36 der angeschnittene Ärmel
- *kimono sleeve*
37 das eingestrickte Muster
- *knitted design*
38 der Lumber
- *lumber-jacket*
39 das Zopfmuster
- *cable pattern*
40 die Hemdbluse (Hemdenbluse,
Bluse)
- *shirt-blouse*
41 der Schlaufenverschluß
- *loop fastening*
42 die Stickerei
- *embroidery*
43 der Stehkragen
- *stand-up collar*
44 die Stiefelhose
- *cossack trousers*
45 das Kasackkleid
- *two-piece combination (shirt top
and long skirt)*
46 die Schleife
- *tie (bow)*
47 die Blende
- *decorative facing*
48 der Ärmelschlitz
- *cuff slit*
49 der Seitenschlitz
- *side slit*
50 das Chasuble
- *tabard*
51 der Seitenschlitzrock
- *inverted pleat skirt*
52 der Untertritt
- *godet*
53 das Abendkleid
- *evening gown*
54 der plissierte Trompetenärmel
- *pleated bell sleeve*
55 die Partybluse
- *party blouse*
56 der Partyrock
- *party skirt*
57 der Hosenanzug
- *trouser suit (slack suit)*
58 die Wildlederjacke
- *suede jacket*
59 der Pelzbesatz
- *fur trimming*
60 der Pelzmantel (*Arten:* Persianer
m, Breitschwanz, Nerz, Zobel)
- *fur coat (kinds: Persian lamb,
broadtail, mink, sable)*
61 der Wintermantel (Tuchmantel)
- *winter coat (cloth coat)*
62 der Ärmelpelzbesatz
- *fur cuff (fur-trimmed cuff)*
63 der Pelzkragen
- *fur collar (fur-trimmed collar)*
64 der Lodenmantel
- *loden coat*
65 die Pelerine
- *cape*
66 die Knebelknöpfe *m*
- *toggle fastenings*
67 der Lodenrock
- *loden skirt*
68 das Ponchocape
- *poncho-style coat*
69 die Kapuze
- *hood*

1 das Kostüm
- *skirt suit*
2 die Kostümjacke
- *jacket*
3 der Kostümrock
- *skirt*
4 die angeschnittene Tasche
- *inset pocket*
5 die Ziernaht
- *decorative stitching*
6 das Jackenkleid
- *dress and jacket combination*
7 die Paspel
- *piping*
8 das Trägerkleid
- *pinafore dress*
9 das Sommerkleid
- *summer dress*
10 der Gürtel (Kleidergürtel)
- *belt*
11 das zweiteilige Kleid
- *two-piece dress*
12 die Gürtelschnalle
- *belt buckle*
13 der Wickelrock
- *wrapover (wrap-around) skirt*
14 die Tubenlinie
- *pencil silhouette*
15 die Schulterknöpfe *m*
- *shoulder buttons*
16 der Fledermausärmel
- *batwing sleeve*
17 das Overdresskleid
- *overdress*
18 die Kimonopasse
- *kimono yoke*
19 der Bindegürtel
- *tie belt*
20 der Sommermantel
- *summer coat*
21 die abknöpfbare Kapuze
- *detachable hood*
22 die Sommerbluse
- *summer blouse*
23 der Revers
- *lapel*
24 der Rock
- *skirt*
25 die Vorderfalte
- *front pleat*
26 das Dirndl (Dirndlkleid)
- *dirndl (dirndl dress)*
27 der Puffärmel
- *puffed sleeve*
28 der Dirndlschmuck
- *dirndl necklace*
29 die Dirndlbluse
- *dirndl blouse*
30 das Mieder
- *bodice*
31 die Dirndlschürze
- *dirndl apron*
32 der Spitzenbesatz (die Spitze), eine Baumwollspitze
- *lace trimming (lace), cotton lace*
33 die Rüschenschürze
- *frilled apron*
34 die Rüsche
- *frill*
35 der Kasack
- *smock overall*
36 das Hauskleid
- *house frock (house dress)*
37 die Popelinejacke
- *poplin jacket*

38 das T-Shirt
- *T-shirt*
39 die Damenshorts *pl*
- *ladies' shorts*
40 der Hosenaufschlag
- *trouser turn-up*
41 der Gürtelbund
- *waistband*
42 der Blouson
- *bomber jacket*
43 der Stretchbund
- *stretch welt*
44 die Bermudas *pl*
- *Bermuda shorts*
45 die Steppnaht
- *saddle stitching*
46 der Rüschenkragen
- *frill collar*
47 der Knoten
- *knot*
48 der Hosenrock
- *culotte*
49 das Twinset
- *twin set*
50 die Strickjacke
- *cardigan*
51 der Pulli
- *sweater*
52 die Sommerhose
- *summer (lightweight) slacks*
53 der Overall
- *jumpsuit*
54 der Ärmelaufschlag
- *turn-up*
55 der Reißverschluß
- *zip*
56 die aufgesetzte Tasche
- *patch pocket*
57 das Nickituch
- *scarf (neckerchief)*
58 der Jeansanzug
- *denim suit*
59 die Jeansweste
- *denim waistcoat*
60 die Jeans *pl* (Blue Jeans)
- *jeans (denims)*
61 die Schlupfbluse
- *overblouse*
62 der Krempelärmel
- *turned-up sleeve*
63 der Stretchgürtel
- *stretch belt*
64 das rückenfreie T-Shirt
- *halter top*
65 der Kasackpullover
- *knitted overtop*
66 der Tunnelgürtel
- *drawstring waist*
67 der Sommerpulli
- *short-sleeved jumper*
68 der V-Ausschnitt
- *V-neck (vee-neck)*
69 der Umlegekragen
- *turndown collar*
70 der Strickbund
- *knitted welt*
71 das Schultertuch (Dreieckstuch)
- *shawl*

1-15 **die Damenunterkleidung**
(Damenunterwäsche,
Damenwäsche, *schweiz.* die
Dessous *n*)
- **ladies' underwear** *(ladies'
underclothes, lingerie)*
1 der Büstenhalter (BH)
- *brassière (bra)*
2 die Miederhose
- *pantie-girdle*
3 das Hosenkorselett
- *pantie-corselette*
4 der Longline-Büstenhalter (lange BH)
- *longline brassière (longline bra)*
5 der Elastikschlüpfer
- *stretch girdle*
6 der Strumpfhalter
- *suspender*
7 das Unterhemd
- *vest*
8 das Hosenhöschen in Slipform *f*
- *pantie briefs*
9 der Damenkniestrumpf
- *ladies' knee-high stocking*
10 der Schlankformschlüpfer
- *long-legged (long leg) panties*
11 die lange Unterhose
- *long pants*
12 die Strumpfhose
- *tights (pantie-hose)*
13 der Unterrock
- *slip*
14 der Halbrock
- *waist slip*
15 der Slip
- *bikini briefs*
16-21 **die Damennachtkleidung**
- **ladies' nightwear**
16 das Nachthemd
- *nightdress (nightgown, nightie)*
17 der zweiteilige Hausanzug
(Schlafanzug)
- *pyjamas* (Am. *pajamas)*
18 das Oberteil
- *pyjama top*
19 die Hose
- *pyjama trousers*
20 der Haus- und Bademantel
- *housecoat*
21 der Schlaf- und Freizeitanzug
- *vest and shorts set [for leisure wear
and as nightwear]*
22-29 **die Herrenunterwäsche**
(Herrenunterkleidung,
Herrenwäsche)
- **men's underwear** *(men's
underclothes)*
22 das Netzhemd (die
Netzunterjacke)
- *string vest*
23 der Netzslip
- *string briefs*
24 der Deckverschluß
- *front panel*
25 die Unterjacke ohne Ärmel *m*
- *sleeveless vest*
26 der Slip
- *briefs*
27 der Schlüpfer
- *trunks*
28 die Unterjacke mit halben Ärmeln *m*
- *short-sleeved vest*
29 die Unterhose mit langen Beinen *n*
- *long johns*
30 der Hosenträger
- *braces* (Am. *suspenders)*

31 der Hosenträgerklipp
- *braces clip*
32-34 **Herrensocken** *f*
- **men's socks**
32 die knielange Socke
- *knee-length sock*
33 der elastische Sockenrand
- *elasticated top*
34 die wadenlange Socke
- *long sock*
35-37 **die Herrennachtkleidung**
- **men's nightwear**
35 der Morgenmantel
- *dressing gown*
36 der Langform-Schlafanzug
- *pyjamas* (Am. *pajamas)*
37 das Schlafhemd
- *nightshirt*
38-47 **Herrenhemden** *n*
- **men's shirts**
38 das Freizeithemd
- *casual shirt*
39 der Gürtel
- *belt*
40 das Halstuch
- *cravat*
41 die Krawatte
- *tie*
42 der Krawattenknoten
- *knot*
43 das Smokinghemd
- *dress shirt*
44 die Rüschen *f* (der Rüschenbesatz)
- *frill (frill front)*
45 die Manschette
- *cuff*
46 der Manschettenknopf
- *cuff link*
47 die Smokingschleife (Fliege)
- *bow-tie*

1-67 die Herrenmode
- *men's fashion*
1 der Einreiher, ein Herrenanzug *m*
- *single-breasted suit, a men's suit*
2 die Jacke (der Rock, das Jackett)
- *jacket (coat)*
3 die Anzughose
- *suit trousers*
4 die Weste
- *waistcoat (vest)*
5 der Aufschlag (Revers)
- *lapel*
6 das Hosenbein mit Bügelfalte
- *trouser leg with crease*
7 der Smoking, ein Abendanzug
- *dinner dress, an evening suit*
8 der Seidenrevers
- *silk lapel*
9 die Brusttasche
- *breast pocket*
10 das Einstecktuch (Ziertaschentuch)
- *dress handkerchief*
11 die Smokingschleife
- *bow-tie*
12 die Seitentasche
- *side pocket*
13 der Frack, ein Gesellschaftsanzug *m*
- *tailcoat (tails), evening dress*
14 der Frackschoß
- *coat-tail*
15 die weiße Frackweste
- *white waistcoat (vest)*
16 die Frackschleife
- *white bow-tie*
17 der Freizeitanzug
- *casual suit*
18 die Taschenklappe (Patte)
- *pocket flap*
19 der Frontsattel
- *front yoke*
20 der Jeansanzug
- *denim suit*
21 die Jeansjacke
- *denim jacket*
22 die Jeans *pl* (Blue Jeans)
- *jeans (denims)*
23 der Hosenbund
- *waistband*
24 der Strandanzug
- *beach suit*
25 die Shorts *pl*
- *shorts*
26 die kurzärmelige Jacke
- *short-sleeved jacket*
27 der Sport-(Trainings-)Anzug
- *tracksuit*
28 die Trainingsjacke mit Reißverschluß *m*
- *tracksuit top with zip*
29 die Trainingshose
- *tracksuit bottoms*
30 die Strickjacke
- *cardigan*
31 der Strickkragen
- *knitted collar*
32 der Herrensommerpulli
- *men's short-sleeved pullover (men's short-sleeved sweater)*
33 das kurzärmelige Hemd
- *short-sleeved shirt*
34 der Hemdenknopf
- *shirt button*
35 der Ärmelaufschlag
- *turn-up*
36 das Strickhemd
- *knitted shirt*

37 das Freizeithemd
- *casual shirt*
38 die aufgesetzte Hemdentasche
- *patch pocket*
39 die Freizeit-(Wander-)Jacke
- *casual jacket*
40 die Kniebundhose
- *knee-breeches*
41 der Kniebund
- *knee strap*
42 der Kniestrumpf
- *knee-length sock*
43 die Lederjacke
- *leather jacket*
44 die Arbeitslatzhose
- *bib and brace overalls*
45 der verstellbare Träger
- *adjustable braces (Am. suspenders)*
46 die Latztasche
- *front pocket*
47 die Hosentasche
- *trouser pocket*
48 der Hosenschlitz
- *fly*
49 die Zollstocktasche
- *rule pocket*
50 das Karohemd
- *check shirt*
51 der Herrenpullover
- *men's pullover*
52 der Skipullover
- *heavy pullover*
53 die Unterziehstrickweste
- *knitted waistcoat (vest)*
54 der Blazer
- *blazer*
55 der Rockknopf
- *jacket button*
56 der Arbeitsmantel (Arbeitskittel, „weiße Kittel")
- *overall*
57 der Regentrenchcoat, ein Trenchcoat *m*
- *trenchcoat*
58 der Mantelkragen
- *coat collar*
59 der Mantelgürtel
- *coat belt*
60 der Popeline-(Übergangs-)Mantel
- *poplin coat*
61 die Manteltasche
- *coat pocket*
62 die verdeckte Knopfleiste
- *fly front*
63 der Tuchcaban
- *car coat*
64 der Mantelknopf
- *coat button*
65 der Schal
- *scarf*
66 der Tuchmantel
- *cloth coat*
67 der Handschuh
- *glove*

1-25 Bart- und Haartrachten *f*
(Frisuren) **des Mannes** *m*
(Männerfrisuren)
- *men's beards and hairstyles*
  (haircuts)
1 das lange, offene Haar
- *long hair worn loose*
2 die Allongeperücke (Staatsperücke,
  Lockenperücke), eine Perücke;
  kürzer und glatter: die
  Stutzperücke (Atzel), die
  Halbperücke (das Toupet)
- *allonge periwig (full-bottomed*
  wig), a wig; shorter and smoother:
  bob wig, toupet
3 die Locken *f*
- *curls*
4 die Haarbeutelperücke (der
  Haarbeutel, Mozartzopf)
- *bag wig (purse wig)*
5 die Zopfperücke
- *pigtail wig*
6 der Zopf
- *queue (pigtail)*
7 die Zopfschleife (das Zopfband)
- *bow (ribbon)*
8 der Schnauzbart (*ugs.* Schnauzer)
- *handlebars (handlebar moustache,*
  Am. *mustache)*
9 der Mittelscheitel
- *centre (Am. center) parting*
10 der Spitzbart, ein Kinnbart *m*
- *goatee (goatee beard), chintuft*
11 der Igelkopf (*ugs.* Stiftenkopf, die
  Bürste)
- *closely-cropped head of hair (crew*
  cut)
12 der Backenbart
- *whiskers*
13 der Henriquatre, ein Spitz- und
  Knebelbart *m*
- *Vandyke beard (stiletto beard,*
  bodkin beard), with waxed
  moustache (Am. mustache)
14 der Seitenscheitel
- *side parting*
15 der Vollbart
- *full beard (circular beard, round*
  beard)
16 der Stutzbart
- *tile beard*
17 die Fliege
- *shadow*
18 der Lockenkopf (Künstlerkopf)
- *head of curly hair*
19 der englische Schnurrbart
- *military moustache (Am. mustache)*
  (English-style moustache)
20 der Glatzkopf
- *partly bald head*
21 die Glatze (*ugs.* Platte)
- *bald patch*
22 der Kahlkopf
- *bald head*
23 der Stoppelbart (die Stoppeln *f*,
  Bartstoppeln)
- *stubble beard (stubble, short beard*
  bristles)
24 die Koteletten *pl; früh.* Favoris
- *side-whiskers (sideboards,*
  sideburns)
25 die glatte Rasur
- *clean shave*
26 der Afro-Look (für Männer u.
  Frauen)
- *Afro look (for men and women)*

27-38 Haartrachten *f* (Frisuren) **der
Frau** (Frauenfrisuren, Damen-
und Mädchenfrisuren)
- *ladies' hairstyles (coiffures,*
  women's and girls' hairstyles)
27 der Pferdeschwanz
- *ponytail*
28 das aufgesteckte Haar
- *swept-back hair (swept-up hair,*
  pinned-up hair)
29 der Haarknoten (Knoten, Chignon,
  ugs. Dutt)
- *bun (chignon)*
30 die Zopffrisur (Hängezöpfe *m*)
- *plaits (bunches)*
31 die Kranzfrisur (Gretchenfrisur)
- *chaplet hairstyle (Gretchen style)*
32 der Haarkranz
- *chaplet (coiled plaits)*
33 das Lockenhaar
- *curled hair*
34 der Bubikopf
- *shingle (shingled hair, bobbed hair)*
35 der Pagenkopf (die Ponyfrisur)
- *pageboy style*
36 die Ponyfransen *f* (*ugs.*
  Simpelfransen)
- *fringe (Am. bangs)*
37 die Schneckenfrisur
- *earphones*
38 die Haarschnecke
- *earphone (coiled plait)*

1-21 Damenhüte *m* **und -mützen** *f*
- *ladies' hats and caps*
1 die Hutmacherin beim Anfertigen
  n eines Hutes *m*
- *milliner making a hat*
2 der Stumpen
- *hood*
3 die Form
- *block*
4 die Putzteile *m od. n*
- *decorative pieces*
5 der Sonnenhut (Sombrero)
- *sombrero*
6 der Mohairhut mit Federputz *m*
- *mohair hat with feathers*
7 der Modellhut mit
  Schmuckgesteck *n*
- *model hat with fancy appliqué*
8 die Leinenmütze
- *linen cap (jockey cap)*
9 die Mütze aus dicker Dochtwolle
- *hat made of thick candlewick yarn*
10 die Strickmütze
- *woollen (Am. woolen) hat (knitted
  hat)*
11 die Mohairstoffkappe
- *mohair hat*
12 der Topfhut mit Steckfedern *f*
- *cloche with feathers*
13 der große Herrenhut aus Sisal *m*
  mit Ripsband *n*
- *large men's hat made of sisal with
  corded ribbon*

14 die Herrenhutform mit
  Schmuckband *n*
- *trilby-style hat with fancy ribbon*
15 der weiche Haarfilzhut
- *soft felt hat*
16 der Japanpanamahut
- *Panama hat with scarf*
17 die Nerzschirmkappe
- *peaked mink cap*
18 der Nerzpelzhut
- *mink hat*
19 die Fuchspelzmütze mit
  Lederkopfteil *m*
- *fox hat with leather top*
20 die Nerzmütze
- *mink cap*
21 der Florentinerhut
- *slouch hat trimmed with flowers*

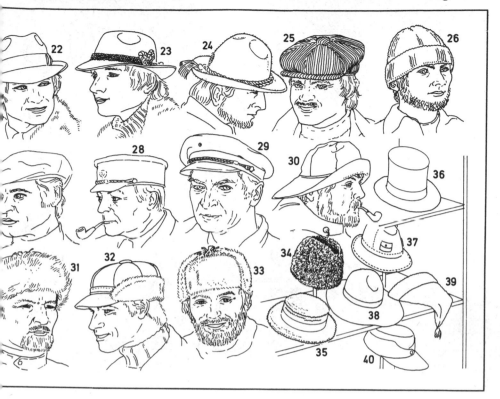

2-40 Herrenhüte *m* **und -mützen** *f*
- *men's hats and caps*
2 der Filzhut im City-Stil *m*
- *trilby hat (trilby)*
3 der Lodenhut
- *loden hat (Alpine hat)*
4 der Rauhhaarfilzhut
mit Quasten *f*
- *felt hat with tassels (Tyrolean hat,
Tyrolese hat)*
5 die Kordmütze
- *corduroy cap*
6 die Wollmütze
- *woollen (Am. woolen) hat*
7 die Baskenmütze
- *beret*
8 die Schiffermütze
(Prinz-Heinrich-Mütze)
- *German sailor's cap ('Prinz
Heinrich' cap)*
9 die Schirmmütze (Seglermütze
- *peaked cap (yachting cap)*
0 der Südwester
- *sou'wester (southwester)*
1 die Fuchsfellmütze mit
Ohrenklappen *f*
- *fox cap with earflaps*
2 die Ledermütze mit
Fellklappen *f*
- *leather cap with fur flaps*
3 die Bisamfellmütze
(Schiwago-Mütze)
- *musquash cap*

34 die Schiffchenmütze, eine Fell-
oder Krimmermütze
- *astrakhan cap, a real or imitation
astrakhan cap*
35 der Strohhut (die Kreissäge)
- *boater*
36 der (graue oder schwarze) Zylinder
(Zylinderhut) aus Seidentaft *m*;
zusammenklappbar: der Klapphut
(Chapeau claque)
- *(grey, Am. gray, or black) top hat
made of silk taffeta; collapsible:
crush hat (opera hat, claque)*
37 der Sommerhut aus Stoff *m* mit
Täschchen *n*
- *sun hat (lightweight hat) made of
cloth with small patch pocket*
38 der breitrandige Hut (Kalabreser,
Zimmermannshut, Künstlerhut)
- *wide-brimmed hat*
39 die Zipfelmütze (Skimütze)
- *toboggan cap (skiing cap, ski cap)*
40 die Arbeitsmütze (für Landwirte
m, Forstbeamte, Handwerker)
- *workman's cap (for farmers,
foresters, craftsmen)*

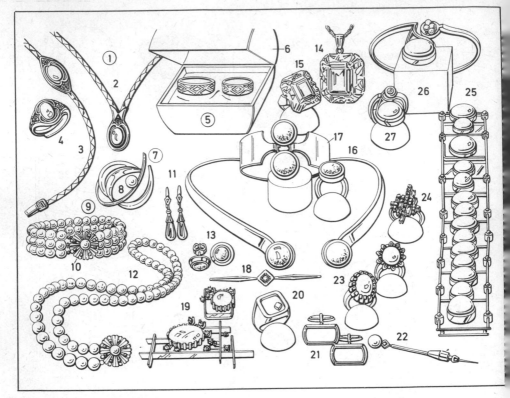

1 die Schmuckgarnitur (das Schmuckset)
- *set of jewellery (Am. jewelry)*
2 das Collier
- *necklace*
3 das Armband
- *bracelet*
4 der Ring
- *ring*
5 die Trauringe *m*
- *wedding rings*
6 das Trauringkästchen
- *wedding ring box*
7 die Brosche, eine Perlenbrosche
- *brooch, a pearl brooch*
8 die Perle
- *pearl*
9 das Zuchtperlenarmband
- *cultured pearl bracelet*
10 die Schließe, eine
   Weißgoldschließe
- *clasp, a white gold clasp*
11 das Ohrgehänge
- *pendant earrings (drop earrings)*
12 das Zuchtperlencollier
- *cultured pearl necklace*
13 die Ohrringe
- *earrings*
14 der Schmucksteinanhänger
   (Edelsteinanhänger)
- *gemstone pendant*
15 der Schmucksteinring (Edelsteinring)
- *gemstone ring*
16 der Halsring
- *choker (collar, neckband)*

17 der Armreif
- *bangle*
18 die Anstecknadel mit Brillant *m*
- *diamond pin*
19 der moderne Ansteckschmuck
- *modern-style brooches*
20 der Herrenring
- *man's ring*
21 die Manschettenknöpfe
- *cuff links*
22 die Krawattennadel
- *tiepin*
23 der Brillantring mit Perle *f*
- *diamond ring with pearl*
24 der moderne Brillantring
- *modern-style diamond ring*
25 das Schmucksteinarmband
   (Edelsteinarmband)
- *gemstone bracelet*
26 der asymmetrische Schmuckreif
- *asymmetrical bangle*
27 der asymmetrische Schmuckring
- *asymmetrical ring*
28 die Elfenbeinkette
- *ivory necklace*
29 die Elfenbeinrose (Erbacher Rose)
- *ivory rose*
30 die Elfenbeinbrosche
- *ivory brooch*
31 die Schmuckkassette
   (Schmuckschatulle, der
   Schmuckkasten, das
   Schmuckkästchen)
- *jewel box (jewel case)*

32 die Perlenkette
- *pearl necklace*
33 die Schmuckuhr
- *bracelet watch*
34 die Echtkorallenkette
- *coral necklace*
35 die Berlocken *f* (das Ziergehänge,
   der Charivari)
- *charms*
36 die Münzenkette
- *coin bracelet*
37 die Goldmünze
- *gold coin*
38 die Münzenfassung
- *coin setting*
39 das Kettenglied
- *link*
40 der Siegelring
- *signet ring*
41 die Gravur
   (das Monogramm)
- *engraving (monogram)*
42-86 die Schleifarten und
   Schliffformen *f*
- *cuts and forms*
42-71 facettierte Steine
- *faceted stones*
42-43 der normal facettierte
   Rundschliff
- *standard round cut*
44 der Brillantschliff
- *brilliant cut*
45 der Rosenschliff
- *rose cut*

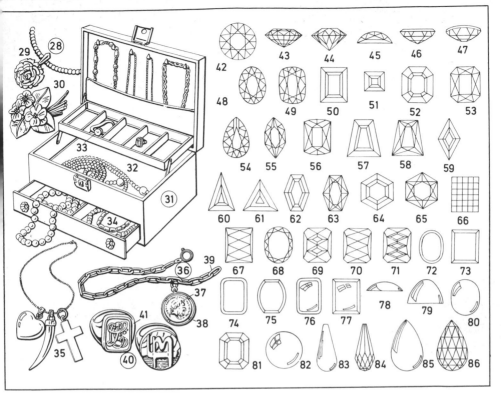

46 die flache Tafel
- *flat table*
47 die gemugelte Tafel
- *table en cabochon*
48 der normal facettierte normale Schliff
- *standard cut*
49 der normal facettierte antike Schliff
- *standard antique cut*
50 der Rechteck-Treppenschliff
- *rectangular step-cut*
51 der Karree-Treppenschliff
- *square step-cut*
52 der Achteck-Treppenschliff
- *octagonal step-cut*
53 der Achteck-Kreuzschliff
- *octagonal cross-cut*
54 die normal facettierte Birnenform
- *standard pear-shape (pendeloque)*
55 die Navette
- *marquise (navette)*
56 die normal facettierte Faßform
- *standard barrel-shape*
57 der Trapez-Treppenschliff
- *trapezium step-cut*
58 der Trapez-Kreuzschliff
- *trapezium cross-cut*
59 das Spießeck (der Rhombus) im Treppenschliff *m*
- *rhombus step-cut*
60-61 das Dreieck *m* (der Triangel) im Treppenschliff
- *triangular step-cut*

62 das Sechseck (Hexagon) im Treppenschliff *m*
- *hexagonal step-cut*
63 das ovale Sechseck (Hexagon) im Kreuzschliff *m*
- *oval hexagonal cross-cut*
64 das runde Sechseck im Treppenschliff *m*
- *round hexagonal step-cut*
65 das runde Sechseck im Kreuzschliff *m*
- *round hexagonal cross-cut*
66 der Schachbrettschliff
- *chequer-board cut*
67 der Triangelschliff
- *triangle cut*
68-71 Phantasieschliffe *m*
- *fancy cuts*
72-77 Ringsteine *m*
- *ring gemstones*
72 die ovale flache Tafel
- *oval flat table*
73 die rechteckige flache Tafel
- *rectangular flat table*
74 die achteckige flache Tafel
- *octagonal flat table*
75 die Faßform
- *barrel-shape*
76 die antike gemugelte Tafel
- *antique table en cabochon*
77 die rechteckige gemugelte Tafel
- *rectangular table en cabochon*
78-81 Cabochons *m*
- *cabochons*

78 der runde Cabochon
- *round cabochon (simple cabochon)*
79 der runde Kegel
- *high dome (high cabochon)*
80 der ovale Cabochon
- *oval cabochon*
81 der achteckige Cabochon
- *octagonal cabochon*
82-86 Kugeln *f* und Pampeln *f*
- *spheres and pear-shapes*
82 die glatte Kugel
- *plain sphere*
83 die glatte Pampel
- *plain pear-shape*
84 die facettierte Pampel
- *faceted pear-shape*
85 der glatte Tropfen
- *plain drop*
86 das facettierte Briolett
- *faceted briolette*

1-53 das freistehende Einfamilienhaus
- *detached house*
1 das Kellergeschoß
- *basement*
2 das Erdgeschoß (Parterre)
- *ground floor (Am. first floor)*
3 das Obergeschoß
- *upper floor (first floor, Am. second floor)*
4 der Dachboden
- *loft*
5 das Dach, ein ungleiches Satteldach *n*
- *roof, a gable roof (saddle roof, saddleback roof)*
6 die Traufe
- *gutter*
7 der First
- *ridge*
8 der Ortgang mit Winddielen *f*
- *verge with bargeboards*
9 der Dachvorsprung (das Dachgesims), ein Sparrengesims *n*
- *eaves, rafter-supported eaves*
10 der Schornstein (Kamin)
- *chimney*
11 der Dachkanal (die Dachrinne)
- *gutter*
12 der Einlaufstutzen
- *swan's neck (swan-neck)*
13 das Regenabfallrohr
- *rainwater pipe (downpipe, Am. downspout, leader)*
14 das Standrohr, ein Gußrohr *n*
- *vertical pipe, a cast-iron pipe*
15 der Giebel (die Giebelseite)
- *gable (gable end)*
16 die Wandscheibe
- *glass wall*
17 der Haussockel
- *base course (plinth)*
18 die Loggia
- *balcony*
19 das Geländer
- *parapet*
20 der Blumenkasten
- *flower box*
21 die zweiflügelige Loggiatür
- *French window (French windows) opening on to the balcony*
22 das zweiflügelige Fenster
- *double casement window*
23 das einflügelige Fenster
- *single casement window*
24 die Fensterbrüstung mit Fensterbank *f*
- *window breast with window sill*
25 der Fenstersturz
- *lintel (window head)*
26 die Fensterleibung
- *reveal*
27 das Kellerfenster
- *cellar window (basement window)*
28 der Rolladen
- *rolling shutter*
29 der Rolladenaussteller
- *rolling shutter frame*
30 der Fensterladen (Klappladen)
- *window shutter (folding shutter)*
31 der Ladenfeststeller
- *shutter catch*
32 die Garage, mit Geräteraum *m*
- *garage with tool shed*
33 das Spalier
- *espalier*
34 die Brettertür
- *batten door (ledged door)*

35 das Oberlicht mit Kreuzsprosse *f*
- *fanlight with mullion and transom*
36 die Terrasse
- *terrace*
37 die Gartenmauer mit Abdeckplatten *f*
- *garden wall with coping stones*
38 die Gartenleuchte
- *garden light*
39 die Gartentreppe
- *steps*
40 der Steingarten
- *rockery (rock garden)*
41 der Schlauchhahn
- *outside tap (Am. faucet) for the hose*
42 der Gartenschlauch
- *garden hose*
43 der Rasensprenger
- *lawn sprinkler*
44 das Planschbecken
- *paddling pool*
45 der Plattenweg
- *stepping stones*
46 die Liegewiese
- *sunbathing area (lawn)*
47 der Liegestuhl
- *deck-chair*
48 der Sonnenschirm (Gartenschirm)
- *sunshade (garden parasol)*
49 der Gartenstuhl
- *garden chair*
50 der Gartentisch
- *garden table*
51 die Teppichstange
- *frame for beating carpets*
52 die Garageneinfahrt
- *garage driveway*
53 die Einfriedung, ein Holzzaun *m*
- *fence, a wooden fence*
54-57 die Siedlung
- *housing estate (housing development)*
54 das Siedlungshaus
- *house on a housing estate (on a housing development)*
55 das Schleppdach
- *pent roof (penthouse roof)*
56 die Schleppgaube (Schleppgaupe)
- *dormer (dormer window)*
57 der Hausgarten
- *garden*
58-63 das Reihenhaus, gestaffelt
- *terraced house [one of a row of terraced houses], stepped*
58 der Vorgarten
- *front garden*
59 der Pflanzenzaun
- *hedge*
60 der Gehweg
- *pavement (Am. sidewalk, walkway)*
61 die Straße
- *street (road)*
62 die Straßenleuchte (Straßenlaterne, Straßenlampe)
- *street lamp (street light)*
63 der Papierkorb
- *litter bin (Am. litter basket)*
64-68 das Zweifamilienhaus
- *house divided into two flats (Am. house divided into two apartments, duplex house)*
64 das Walmdach
- *hip (hipped) roof*
65 die Haustür
- *front door*

66 die Eingangstreppe
- *front steps*
67 das Vordach
- *canopy*
68 das Pflanzen- oder Blumenfenster
- *flower window (window for house plants)*
69-71 das Vier-Familien-Doppelhaus
- *pair of semi-detached houses divided into four flats (Am. apartments)*
69 der Balkon
- *balcony*
70 der Glaserker
- *sun lounge (Am. sun parlor)*
71 die Markise
- *awning (sun blind, sunshade)*
72-76 das Laubenganghaus
- *block of flats (Am. apartment building, apartment house) with access balconies*
72 das Treppenhaus
- *staircase*
73 der Laubengang
- *balcony*
74 die Atelierwohnung
- *studio flat (Am. studio apartment)*
75 die Dachterrasse, eine Liegeterrasse
- *sun roof, a sun terrace*
76 die Grünfläche
- *open space*
77-81 das mehrstöckige Zeilenhaus
- *multi-storey block of flats (Am. multistory apartment building, multistory apartment house)*
77 das Flachdach
- *flat roof*
78 das Pultdach
- *pent roof (shed roof, lean-to roof)*
79 die Garage
- *garage*
80 die Pergola
- *pergola*
81 das Treppenhausfenster
- *staircase window*
82 das Hochhaus
- *high-rise block of flats (Am. high-rise apartment building, high-rise apartment house)*
83 das Penthouse (die Dachterrassenwohnung)
- *penthouse*
84-86 das Wochenendhaus, ein Holzhaus *n*
- *weekend house, a timber house*
84 die waagerechte Bretterschalung
- *horizontal boarding*
85 der Natursteinsockel
- *natural stone base course (natural stone plinth)*
86 das Fensterband
- *strip windows (ribbon windows)*

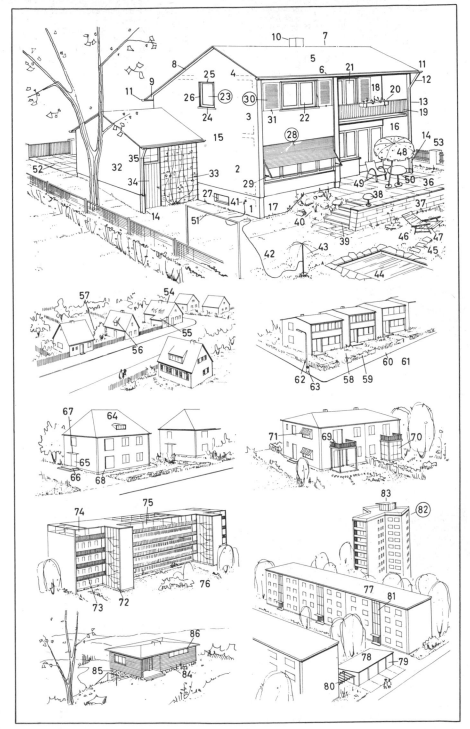

1-29 das Dachgeschoß
- *attic*
1 die Dachhaut
- *roof cladding (roof covering)*
2 das Dachfenster
- *skylight*
3 das Laufbrett
- *gangway*
4 die Steigleiter (Dachleiter)
- *cat ladder (roof ladder)*
5 der Schornstein (Kamin, die Esse)
- *chimney*
6 der Dachhaken
- *roof hook*
7 die Dachgaube (Dachgaupe, Gaube, Gaupe)
- *dormer window (dormer)*
8 das Schneefanggitter
- *snow guard (roof guard)*
9 die Dachrinne
- *gutter*
10 das Fallrohr
- *rainwater pipe (downpipe, Am. downspout, leader)*
11 das Hauptgesims (Dachgesims)
- *eaves*
12 der Spitzboden
- *pitched roof*
13 die Falltür
- *trapdoor*
14 die Bodenluke
- *hatch*
15 die Sprossenleiter
- *ladder*
16 der Holm
- *stile*
17 die Sprosse
- *rung*
18 der Dachboden
- *loft (attic)*
19 der Holzverschlag (Verschlag)
- *wooden partition*
20 die Bodenkammertür
- *lumber room door (boxroom door)*
21 das Vorhängeschloß (Vorlegeschloß)
- *padlock*
22 der Wäschehaken
- *hook [for washing line]*
23 die Wäscheleine
- *clothes line (washing line)*
24 das Ausdehnungsgefäß (Expansionsgefäß) der Heizung
- *expansion tank for boiler*
25 die Holztreppe und das Treppengeländer
- *wooden steps and balustrade*
26 die Wange
- *string (Am. stringer)*
27 die Stufe
- *step*
28 der Handlauf
- *handrail (guard rail)*
29 der Geländerpfosten
- *baluster*
30 der Blitzableiter
- *lightning conductor (lightning rod)*
31 **der Schornsteinfeger** (Kaminkehrer, Essenkehrer)
- ***chimney sweep** (Am. chimney sweeper)*
32 die Sonne mit dem Kugelschlagapparat *m*
- *brush with weight*
33 das Schultereisen
- *shoulder iron*

34 der Rußsack
- *sack for soot*
35 der Stoßbesen
- *flue brush*
36 der Handbesen
- *broom (besom)*
37 der Besenstiel
- *broomstick (broom handle)*
38-81 die Warmwasserheizung, eine Sammelheizung (Zentralheizung)
- *hot-water heating system, full central heating*
38-43 der Heizraum
- *boiler room*
38 die Koksfeuerung
- *coke-fired central heating system*
39 die Aschentür
- *ash box door (Am. cleanout door)*
40 der Fuchs
- *flueblock*
41 das Schüreisen
- *poker*
42 die Ofenkrücke
- *rake*
43 die Kohlenschaufel
- *coal shovel*
44-60 die Ölfeuerung
- *oil-fired central heating system*
44 der Öltank (Ölbehälter)
- *oil tank*
45 der Einsteigschacht
- *manhole*
46 der Schachtdeckel
- *manhole cover*
47 der Einfüllstutzen
- *tank inlet*
48 der Domdeckel
- *dome cover*
49 das Tankbodenventil
- *tank bottom valve*
50 das Heizöl
- *fuel oil (heating oil)*
51 die Entlüftungsleitung
- *air-bleed duct*
52 die Entlüftungskappe
- *air vent cap*
53 die Ölstandsleitung
- *oil level pipe*
54 der Ölstandsanzeiger
- *oil gauge (Am. gage)*
55 die Saugleitung
- *suction pipe*
56 die Rücklaufleitung
- *return pipe*
57 der Zentralheizungskessel (Ölheizungskessel)
- *central heating furnace (oil heating furnace)*
58-60 der Ölbrenner
- *oil burner*
58 das Frischluftgebläse
- *fan*
59 der Elektromotor
- *electric motor*
60 die verkleidete Brenndüse
- *covered pilot light*
61 die Fülltür
- *charging door*
62 das Schauglas (die Kontrollöffnung)
- *inspection window*
63 der Wasserstandsmesser
- *water gauge (Am. gage)*
64 das Kesselthermometer
- *furnace thermometer*

65 der Füll- und Ablaßhahn
- *bleeder*
66 das Kesselfundament
- *furnace bed*
67 die Schalttafel
- *control panel*
68 der Warmwasserboiler (Boiler)
- *hot water tank (boiler)*
69 der Überlauf
- *overflow pipe (overflow)*
70 das Sicherheitsventil
- *safety valve*
71 die Hauptverteilerleitung
- *main distribution pipe*
72 die Isolierung
- *lagging*
73 das Ventil
- *valve*
74 der Vorlauf
- *flow pipe*
75 das Regulierventil
- *regulating valve*
76 der Heizkörper
- *radiator*
77 die Heizkörperrippe (das Element)
- *radiator rib*
78 der Raumthermostat
- *room thermostat*
79 der Rücklauf
- *return pipe (return)*
80 die Rücklaufsammelleitung
- *return pipe [in two-pipe system]*
81 der Rauchabzug
- *smoke outlet (smoke extract)*

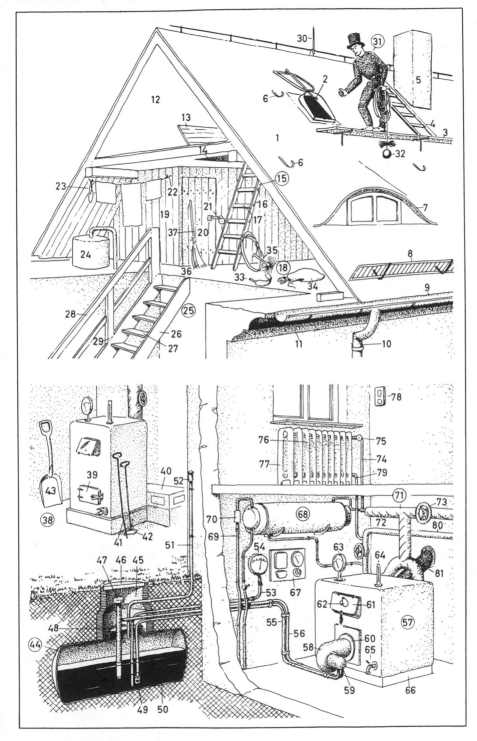

1 die Hausfrau
- *housewife*
2 der Kühlschrank
- *refrigerator (fridge, Am. icebox)*
3 das Kühlfach
- *refrigerator shelf*
4 die Gemüseschale
- *salad drawer*
5 das Kühlaggregat
- *cooling aggregate*
6 das Türfach für Flaschen *f*
- *bottle rack (in storage door)*
7 der Gefrierschrank
(Tiefgefrierschrank)
- *upright freezer*
8 der Oberschrank (Hängeschrank),
ein Geschirrschrank *m*
- *wall cupboard, a kitchen cupboard*
9 der Unterschrank
- *base unit*
10 die Besteckschublade
- *cutlery drawer*
11 der Hauptarbeitsplatz
(Vorbereitungsplatz)
- *working top*
12-17 der Koch- und Backplatz
- *cooker unit*
12 der Elektroherd (*auch:* Gasherd)
- *electric cooker* (also: *gas cooker)*
13 der Backofen
- *oven*
14 das Backofenfenster
- *oven window*
15 die Kochplatte (automatische
Schnellkochplatte)
- *hotplate (automatic high-speed
plate)*

16 der Wasserkessel (Flötenkessel)
- *kettle (whistling kettle)*
17 der Wrasenabzug (Dunstabzug)
- *cooker hood*
18 der Topflappen
- *pot holder*
19 der Topflappenhalter
- *pot holder rack*
20 die Küchenuhr
- *kitchen clock*
21 der Kurzzeitmesser
- *timer*
22 das Handrührgerät (der Handrührer)
- *hand mixer*
23 der Schlagbesen
- *whisk*
24 die elektrische Kaffeemühle, eine
Schlagwerkkaffeemühle
- *electric coffee grinder (with
rotating blades)*
25 die elektrische Zuleitung (das
Leitungskabel)
- *lead*
26 die Wandsteckdose
- *wall socket*
27 der Eckschrank
- *corner unit*
28 das Drehtablett
- *revolving shelf*
29 der Kochtopf
- *pot (cooking pot)*
30 die Kanne
- *jug*
31 das Gewürzregal
- *spice rack*
32 das Gewürzglas
- *spice jar*

33-36 der Spülplatz
- *sink unit*
33 der Abtropfständer
- *dish drainer*
34 der Frühstücksteller
- *tea plate*
35 die Geschirrspüle (Spüle, das
Spülbecken)
- *sink*
36 der Wasserhahn (die
Wassermischbatterie)
- *water tap (Am. faucet) (mixer tap,
Am. mixing faucet)*
37 die Topfpflanze, eine Blattpflanze
- *pot plant, a foliage plant*
38 die Kaffeemaschine (der
Kaffeeautomat)
- *coffee maker*
39 die Küchenlampe
- *kitchen lamp*
40 der Geschirrspülautomat
(Geschirrspüler, die
Geschirrspülmaschine)
- *dishwasher (dishwashing machine)*
41 der Geschirrwagen
- *dish rack*
42 der Eßteller
- *dinner plate*
43 der Küchenstuhl
- *kitchen chair*
44 der Küchentisch
- *kitchen table*

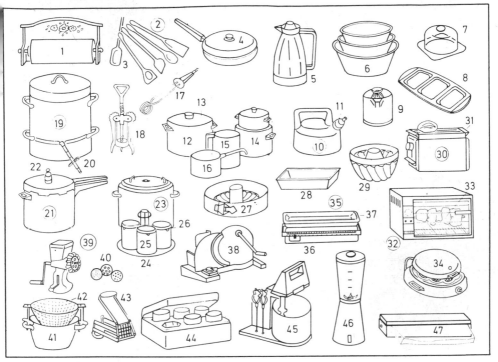

1 der Allzweckabroller mit
  Allzwecktüchern *n*
  (Papiertüchern)
- *general-purpose roll holder with
  kitchen roll (paper towels)*
2 die Kochlöffelgarnitur
- *set of wooden spoons*
3 der Rührlöffel
- *mixing spoon*
4 die Bratpfanne
- *frying pan*
5 die Isolierkanne
- *Thermos jug*
6 Küchenschüsseln *f*
- *set of bowls*
7 die Käseglocke
- *cheese dish with glass cover*
8 das Kabarett
- *three-compartment dish*
9 die Saftpresse für Zitrusfrüchte *f*
- *lemon squeezer*
10 der Flötenkessel
- *whistling kettle*
11 die Flöte
- *whistle*
12-16 die Geschirrserie
- *pan set*
12 der Kochtopf (Fleischtopf)
- *pot (cooking pot)*
13 der Topfdeckel
- *lid*
14 der Bratentopf
- *casserole dish*
15 der Milchtopf
- *milk pot*
16 die Stielkasserolle
- *saucepan*

17 der Tauchsieder
- *immersion heater*
18 der Hebelkorkenzieher
- *corkscrew [with levers]*
19 der Entsafter
- *juice extractor*
20 die Schlauchklemme
- *tube clamp (tube clip)*
21 der Schnellkochtopf
  (Dampfkochtopf)
- *pressure cooker*
22 das Überdruckventil
- *pressure valve*
23 der Einkocher (Einwecker)
- *fruit preserver*
24 der Einweckeinsatz
- *removable rack*
25 das Einweckglas (Weckglas)
- *preserving jar*
26 der Einweckring
- *rubber ring*
27 die Springform
- *spring form*
28 die Kastenkuchenform
- *cake tin*
29 die Napfkuchenform
- *cake tin*
30 der Toaster
- *toaster*
31 der Brötchenröstaufsatz
- *rack for rolls*
32 der Grill
- *rotisserie*
33 der Grillspieß
- *spit*
34 der Waffelautomat
- *electric waffle iron*

35 die Laufgewichtswaage
- *sliding-weight scales*
36 das Laufgewicht
- *sliding weight*
37 die Waagschale
- *scale pan*
38 der Allesschneider
- *food slicer*
39 der Fleischhacker
- *mincer (Am. meat chopper)*
40 die Schneidscheiben *f*
- *blades*
41 der Pommes-frites-Topf
- *chip pan*
42 der Drahteinsatz
- *basket*
43 der Pommes-frites-Schneider
- *potato chipper*
44 der Joghurtbereiter
- *yoghurt maker*
45 die Kleinküchenmaschine
- *mixer*
46 der Mixer
- *blender*
47 das Folienschweißgerät
- *bag sealer*

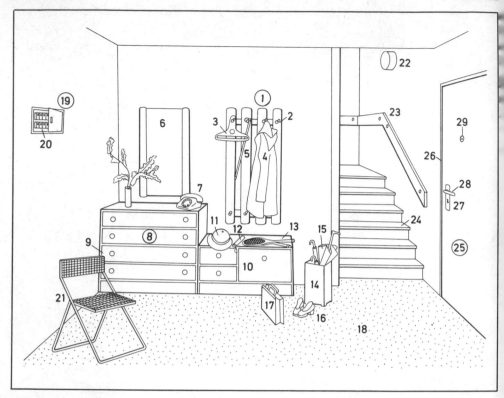

1-29 die Diele (der Flur, Korridor,
   Vorraum, Vorplatz)
- *hall (entrance hall)*
1 die Garderobe (Flurgarderobe,
   Garderobenwand)
- *coat rack*
2 der Kleiderhaken
- *coat hook*
3 der Kleiderbügel
- *coat hanger*
4 das Regencape
- *rain cape*
5 der Spazierstock
- *walking stick*
6 der Garderobenspiegel
- *hall mirror*
7 das Telefon
- *telephone*
8 der Schuh-Mehrzweck-Schrank
- *chest of drawers for shoes, etc.*
9 die Schublade
- *drawer*
10 die Sitzbank
- *seat*
11 der Damenhut
- *ladies' hat*
12 der Taschenschirm
- *telescopic umbrella*
13 die Tennisschläger *m*
- *tennis rackets (tennis racquets)*
14 der Schirmständer
- *umbrella stand*
15 der Regenschirm
- *umbrella*

16 die Schuhe *m*
- *shoes*
17 die Aktentasche
- *briefcase*
18 der Teppichboden
- *fitted carpet*
19 der Sicherungskasten
- *fuse box*
20 der Sicherungsautomat
- *miniature circuit breaker*
21 der Stahlrohrstuhl
- *tubular steel chair*
22 die Treppenleuchte
- *stair light*
23 der Handlauf
- *handrail*
24 die Treppenstufe
- *step*
25 die Abschlußtür (Korridortür)
- *front door*
26 der Türrahmen
- *door frame*
27 das Türschloß
- *door lock*
28 die Türklinke
- *door handle*
29 das Guckloch (der Spion)
- *spyhole*

1 die Stollenanbauwand
  (Schrankwand)
- *wall units*
2 der Stollen
- *side wall*
3 das Bücherregal
- *bookshelf*
4 die Bücherreihe
- *row of books*
5 die Anbauvitrine
- *display cabinet unit*
6 der Unterschrank
- *cupboard base unit*
7 das Schrankelement
- *cupboard unit*
8 der Fernseher
- *television set (TV set)*
9 die Stereoanlage
- *stereo system*
  (stereo equipment)
10 die Lautsprecherbox
- *speaker (loudspeaker)*
11 der Pfeifenständer
- *pipe rack*
12 die Pfeife
- *pipe*
13 der Globus
- *globe*
14 der Messingkessel
- *brass kettle*
15 das Fernrohr
- *telescope*
16 die Aufsatzuhr
- *mantle clock*

17 die Porträtbüste
- *bust*
18 das mehrbändige Lexikon
- *encyclopaedia [in several volumes]*
19 der Raumteiler
- *room divider*
20 der Barschrank (das Barfach)
- *drinks cupboard*
21-26 die Polsterelementgruppe
- *upholstered suite (seating group)*
21 der Polstersessel (Fauteuil)
- *armchair*
22 die Armlehne
- *arm*
23 das Sitzkissen
- *seat cushion (cushion)*
24 das Sofa
- *settee*
25 das Rückenkissen
- *back cushion*
26 die Rundecke
- *[round] corner section*
27 das Sofakissen
- *scatter cushion*
28 der Couchtisch
- *coffee table*
29 der Aschenbecher
- *ashtray*
30 das Tablett
- *tray*
31 die Whiskyflasche
- *whisky (whiskey) bottle*
32 die Sodawasserflasche
- *soda water bottle (soda bottle)*

33-34 die Eßgruppe
- *dining set*
33 der Eßtisch
- *dining table*
34 der Stuhl
- *chair*
35 der Store
- *net curtain*
36 die Zimmerpflanzen *f*
- *indoor plants (houseplants)*

1 der Schlafzimmerschrank, ein
Hochschrank *m*
- *wardrobe (Am. clothes closet)*
2 das Wäschefach
- *linen shelf*
3 der Korbstuhl
- *cane chair*
4-13 das Doppelbett (*ähnl.:* das
französische Bett)
- *double bed (sim.: double divan)*
4-6 das Bettgestell
- *bedstead*
4 das Fußende (der *od.* das Fußteil)
- *foot of the bed*
5 der Bettkasten
- *bed frame*
6 das Kopfende (der *od.* das Kopfteil)
- *headboard*
7 die Tagesdecke
- *bedspread*
8 die Schlafdecke, eine Steppdecke
- *duvet, a quilted duvet*
9 das Bettuch (Bettlaken), ein
Leintuch
- *sheet, a linen sheet*
10 die Matratze, eine
Schaumstoffauflage mit
Drellüberzug *m*
- *mattress, a foam mattress with drill
tick*
11 das Keilkissen
- *[wedge-shaped] bolster*
12-13 das Kopfkissen
- *pillow*

12 der Kopfkissenbezug
- *pillowcase (pillowslip)*
13 das Inlett
- *tick*
14 das Bücherregal
(der Regalaufsatz)
- *bookshelf [attached to the
headboard]*
15 die Leselampe
- *reading lamp*
16 der elektrische Wecker
- *electric alarm clock*
17 die Bettkonsole
- *bedside cabinet*
18 die Schublade
- *drawer*
19 die Schlafzimmerlampe
- *bedroom lamp*
20 das Wandbild
- *picture*
21 der Bilderrahmen
- *picture frame*
22 der Bettvorleger
- *bedside rug*
23 der Teppichboden
- *fitted carpet*
24 der Frisierstuhl
- *dressing stool*
25 die Frisierkommode
- *dressing table*
26 der Parfümzerstäuber
- *perfume spray*
27 das (der) Parfümflakon
- *perfume bottle*

28 die Puderdose
- *powder box*
29 der Frisierspiegel
- *dressing-table mirror (mirror)*

<table>
<tbody>
<tr><td>

1-11 die Eßgruppe
- *dining set*
1 der Eßtisch
- *dining table*
2 das Tischbein
- *table leg*
3 die Tischplatte
- *table top*
4 der (das) Set
- *place mat*
5 das Gedeck
- *place (place setting, cover)*
6 der Suppenteller (tiefe Teller)
- *soup plate (deep plate)*
7 der flache Teller
- *dinner plate*
8 die Suppenterrine
- *soup tureen*
9 das Weinglas
- *wineglass*
10 der Eßzimmerstuhl
- *dining chair*
11 die Sitzfläche
- *seat*
12 die Deckenlampe (Hängelampe)
- *lamp (pendant lamp)*
13 die Übergardinen
- *curtains*
14 die Gardine
- *net curtain*
15 die Gardinenleiste
- *curtain rail*
16 der Bodenteppich
- *carpet*

</td><td>

17 der Hängeschrank
- *wall unit*
18 die Glastür
- *glass door*
19 der Einlegeboden
- *shelf*
20 das Sideboard
- *sideboard*
21 die Besteckschublade
- *cutlery drawer*
22 die Wäscheschublade
- *linen drawer*
23 der Sockel
- *base*
24 das runde Tablett
- *round tray*
25 die Topfpflanze
- *pot plant*
26 der Geschirrschrank (die Vitrine)
- *china cabinet (display cabinet)*
27 das Kaffeegeschirr
- *coffee set (coffee service)*
28 die Kaffeekanne
- *coffee pot*
29 die Kaffeetasse
- *coffee cup*
30 die Untertasse
- *saucer*
31 das Milchkännchen
- *milk jug*
32 die Zuckerdose
- *sugar bowl*
33 das Eßgeschirr
- *dinner set (dinner service)*

</td></tr>
</tbody>
</table>

1 der Eßtisch
- *dining table*
2 das Tafeltuch, ein Damasttuch *n*
- *tablecloth, a damask cloth*
3-12 **das Gedeck**
- *place (place setting, cover)*
3 der Grundteller (Unterteller)
- *bottom plate*
4 der flache Teller (Eßteller)
- *dinner plate*
5 der tiefe Teller (Suppenteller)
- *deep plate (soup plate)*
6 der kleine Teller, für die
  Nachspeise (das Dessert)
- *dessert plate (dessert bowl)*
7 das Eßbesteck
- *knife and fork*
8 das Fischbesteck
- *fish knife and fork*
9 die Serviette (das Mundtuch)
- *serviette (napkin, table napkin)*
10 der Serviettenring
- *serviette ring (napkin ring)*
11 das Messerbänkchen
- *knife rest*
12 die Weingläser *n*
- *wineglasses*
13 die Tischkarte
- *place card*
14 der Suppenschöpflöffel (die
  Suppenkelle)
- *soup ladle*
15 die Suppenschüssel (Terrine)
- *soup tureen (tureen)*

16 der Tafelleuchter (Tischleuchter)
- *candelabra*
17 die Sauciere (Soßenschüssel)
- *sauceboat (gravy boat)*
18 der Soßenlöffel
- *sauce ladle (gravy ladle)*
19 der Tafelschmuck
- *table decoration*
20 der Brotkorb
- *bread basket*
21 das Brötchen
- *roll*
22 die Scheibe Brot *n* (die Brotscheibe)
- *slice of bread*
23 die Salatschüssel
- *salad bowl*
24 das Salatbesteck
- *salad servers*
25 die Gemüseschüssel
- *vegetable dish*
26 die Bratenplatte
- *meat plate (Am. meat platter)*
27 der Braten
- *roast meat (roast)*
28 die Kompottschüssel
- *fruit dish*
29 die Kompottschale
- *fruit bowl*
30 das Kompott
- *fruit (stewed fruit)*
31 die Kartoffelschüssel
- *potato dish*
32 der fahrbare Anrichtetisch
- *serving trolley*

33 die Gemüseplatte
- *vegetable plate (Am. vegetable platter)*
34 der Toast
- *toast*
35 die Käseplatte
- *cheeseboard*
36 die Butterdose
- *butter dish*
37 das belegte Brot
- *open sandwich*
38 der Brotbelag
- *filling*
39 das Sandwich
- *sandwich*
40 die Obstschale
- *fruit bowl*
41 die Knackmandeln *f* (*auch:*
  Kartoffelchips *m*, Erdnüsse *f*)
- *almonds (also: potato crisps,
  peanuts)*
42 die Essig- und Ölflasche
- *oil and vinegar bottle*
43 das Ketchup
- *ketchup (catchup, catsup)*
44 die Anrichte
- *sideboard*
45 die elektrische Warmhalteplatte
- *electric hotplate*
46 der Korkenzieher
- *corkscrew*
47 der Kronenkorköffner, ein
  Flaschenöffner *m*
- *crown cork bottle-opener (crown
  cork opener), a bottle-opener*

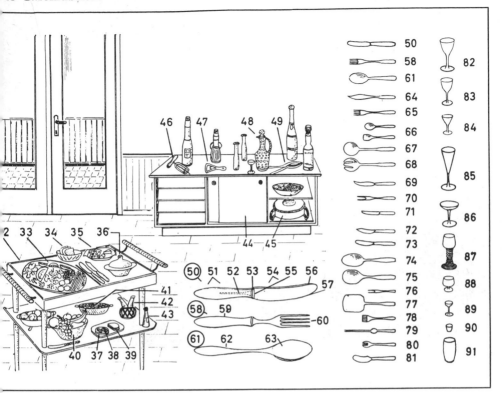

48 die Likörkaraffe
- *liqueur decanter*
49 der Nußknacker
- *nutcrackers (nutcracker)*
50 das Messer
- *knife*
51 das Heft (der Griff)
- *handle*
52 die Angel
- *tang (tongue)*
53 die Zwinge
- *ferrule*
54 die Klinge
- *blade*
55 die Krone
- *bolster*
56 der Rücken
- *back*
57 die Schneide
- *edge (cutting edge)*
58 die Gabel
- *fork*
59 der Stiel
- *handle*
60 die Zinke
- *prong (tang, tine)*
61 der Löffel (Eßlöffel, Suppenlöffel)
- *spoon (dessert spoon, soup spoon)*
62 der Stiel
- *handle*
63 der Schöpfteil
- *bowl*
64 das Fischmesser
- *fish knife*

65 die Fischgabel
- *fish fork*
66 der Dessertlöffel (Kompottlöffel)
- *dessert spoon (fruit spoon)*
67 der Salatlöffel
- *salad spoon*
68 die Salatgabel
- *salad fork*
69-70 das Vorlegebesteck
- *carving set (serving cutlery)*
69 das Vorlegemesser
- *carving knife*
70 die Vorlegegabel
- *serving fork*
71 das Obstmesser
- *fruit knife*
72 das Käsemesser
- *cheese knife*
73 das Buttermesser
- *butter knife*
74 der Gemüselöffel, ein Vorlegelöffel *m*
- *vegetable spoon, a serving spoon*
75 der Kartoffellöffel
- *potato server (serving spoon for
potatoes)*
76 die Sandwichgabel
- *cocktail fork*
77 der Spargelheber
- *asparagus server
(asparagus slice)*
78 der Sardinenheber
- *sardine server*
79 die Hummergabel
- *lobster fork*

80 die Austerngabel
- *oyster fork*
81 das Kaviarmesser
- *caviare knife*
82 das Weißweinglas
- *white wine glass*
83 das Rotweinglas
- *red wine glass*
84 das Südweinglas (Madeiraglas)
- *sherry glass (madeira glass)*
85-86 die Sektgläser
- *champagne glasses*
85 das Spitzglas
- *tapered glass*
86 die Sektschale, ein Kristallglas *n*
- *champagne glass, a crystal glass*
87 der Römer
- *rummer*
88 die Kognakschale
- *brandy glass*
89 die Likörschale
- *liqueur glass*
90 das Schnapsglas
- *spirit glass*
91 das Bierglas
- *beer glass*

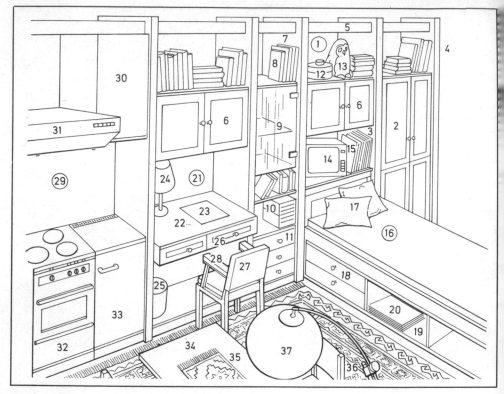

1 die Apartmentwand
(Schrankwand, Regalwand,
Studiowand)
- *wall units (shelf units)*
2 die Schrankfront
- *wardrobe door (Am. clothes closet
door)*
3 der Korpus
- *body*
4 der Stollen
- *side wall*
5 die Blende
- *trim*
6 das zweitürige Schrankelement
- *two-door cupboard unit*
7 das Bücherregal (Vitrinenregal)
- *bookshelf unit (bookcase unit)
[with glass door]*
8 die Bücher *n*
- *books*
9 die Vitrine
- *display cabinet*
10 die Karteikästen *m*
- *card index boxes*
11 die Schublade
- *drawer*
12 die Konfektdose
- *decorative biscuit tin*
13 das Stofftier
- *soft toy animal*
14 der Fernseher
- *television set (TV set)*
15 die Schallplatten *f*
- *records (discs)*

16 die Bettkastenliege
- *bed unit*
17 das Sofakissen
- *scatter cushion*
18 die Bettkastenschublade
- *bed unit drawer*
19 das Bettkastenregal
- *bed unit shelf*
20 die Zeitschriften *f*
- *magazines*
21 der Schreibplatz
- *desk unit (writing unit)*
22 der Schreibtisch
- *desk*
23 die Schreibunterlage
- *desk mat (blotter)*
24 die Tischlampe
- *table lamp*
25 der Papierkorb
- *wastepaper basket*
26 die Schreibtischschublade
- *desk drawer*
27 der Schreibtischsessel
- *desk chair*
28 die Armlehne
- *arm*
29 die Küchenwand (Anbauküche)
- *kitchen unit*
30 der Oberschrank
- *wall cupboard*
31 der Wrasenabzug (die Dunsthaube)
- *cooker hood*
32 der Elektroherd
- *electric cooker*

33 der Kühlschrank
- *refrigerator (fridge, Am. icebox)*
34 der Eßtisch
- *dining table*
35 der Tischläufer
- *table runner*
36 der Orientteppich
- *oriental carpet*
37 die Stehlampe
- *standard lamp*

1 das Kinderbett, ein Doppelbett *n*
   (Etagenbett)
 - *children's bed, a bunk-bed*
2 der Bettkasten
 - *storage box*
3 die Matratze
 - *mattress*
4 das Kopfkissen
 - *pillow*
5 die Leiter
 - *ladder*
6 der Stoffelefant, ein Kuscheltier *n*
   (Schlaftier)
 - *soft toy elephant, a cuddly toy
   animal*
7 der Stoffhund
 - *soft toy dog*
8 das Sitzkissen
 - *cushion*
9 die Ankleidepuppe
 - *fashion doll*
10 der Puppenwagen
 - *doll's pram*
11 die Schlafpuppe
 - *sleeping doll*
12 der Baldachin
 - *canopy*
13 die Schreibtafel
 - *blackboard*
14 die Rechensteine *m*
 - *counting beads*
15 das Plüschpferd zum Schaukeln *n*
   und Ziehen *n*
 - *toy horse for rocking and pulling*

16 die Schaukelkufen *f*
 - *rockers*
17 das Kinderbuch
 - *children's book*
18 das Spielemagazin
 - *compendium of games*
19 das Mensch-ärgere-dich-nicht-Spiel
 - *ludo*
20 das Schachbrett
 - *chessboard*
21 der Kinderzimmerschrank
 - *children's cupboard*
22 die Wäscheschublade
 - *linen drawer*
23 die Schreibplatte
 - *drop-flap writing surface*
24 das Schreibheft
 - *notebook (exercise book)*
25 die Schulbücher *n*
 - *school books*
26 der Bleistift (*auch:* Buntstift *m*,
   Filzstift, Kugelschreiber)
 - *pencil (also: crayon, felt tip pen,
   ballpoint pen)*
27 der Kaufladen (Kaufmannsladen)
 - *toy shop*
28 der Verkaufsstand
 - *counter*
29 der Gewürzständer
 - *spice rack*
30 die Auslage
 - *display*
31 das Bonbonsortiment
 - *assortment of sweets* (Am. *candies*)

32 die Bonbontüte
 - *bag of sweets* (Am. *candies*)
33 die Waage
 - *scales*
34 die Ladenkasse
 - *cash register*
35 das Kindertelefon
 - *toy telephone*
36 das Warenregal
 - *shop shelves (goods shelves)*
37 die Holzeisenbahn
 - *wooden train set*
38 der Muldenkipper, ein
   Spielzeugauto *n*
 - *dump truck, a toy lorry (toy truck)*
39 der Hochbaukran
 - *tower crane*
40 der Betonmischer
 - *concrete mixer*
41 der große Plüschhund
 - *large soft toy dog*
42 der Würfelbecher
 - *dice cup*

1-20 die Vorschulerziehung
- *pre-school education (nursery education)*
1 die Kindergärtnerin
- *nursery teacher*
2 der Vorschüler
- *nursery child*
3 die Bastelarbeit
- *handicraft*
4 der Klebstoff
- *glue*
5 das Aquarellbild
- *watercolour (Am. watercolor) painting*
6 der Aquarellkasten
- *paintbox*
7 der Malpinsel
- *paintbrush*
8 das Wasserglas
- *glass of water*
9 das Puzzle
- *jigsaw puzzle (puzzle)*
10 der Puzzlestein
- *jigsaw puzzle piece*
11 die Buntstifte *m* (Wachsmalstifte)
- *coloured (Am. colored) pencils (wax crayons)*
12 die Knetmasse (Plastilinmasse)
- *modelling (Am. modeling) clay (plasticine)*
13 Knetfiguren *f* (Plastilinfiguren)
- *clay figures (plasticine figures)*
14 das Knetbrett
- *modelling (Am. modeling) board*
15 die Schultafelkreide
- *chalk (blackboard chalk)*
16 die Schreibtafel (Tafel)
- *blackboard*
17 die Rechensteine *m*
- *counting blocks*
18 der Faserschreibstift
- *felt pen (felt tip pen)*
19 das Formlegespiel
- *shapes game*
20 die Spielergruppe
- *group of players*
21-32 das Spielzeug
- *toys*
21 das Kubusspiel
- *building and filling cubes*
22 der mechanische Baukasten
- *construction set*
23 die Kinderbücher *n*
- *children's books*
24 der Puppenwagen, ein Korbwagen
- *doll's pram, a wicker pram*
25 die Babypuppe
- *baby doll*
26 der Baldachin
- *canopy*
27 die Bauklötze *m*
- *building bricks (building blocks)*
28 das hölzerne Bauwerk
- *wooden model building*
29 die Holzeisenbahn
- *wooden train set*
30 der Schaukelteddy
- *rocking teddy bear*
31 der Puppensportwagen
- *doll's pushchair*
32 die Ankleidepuppe
- *fashion doll*
33 das Kind im Kindergartenalter *n*
- *child of nursery school age*
34 die Garderobenablage
- *cloakroom*

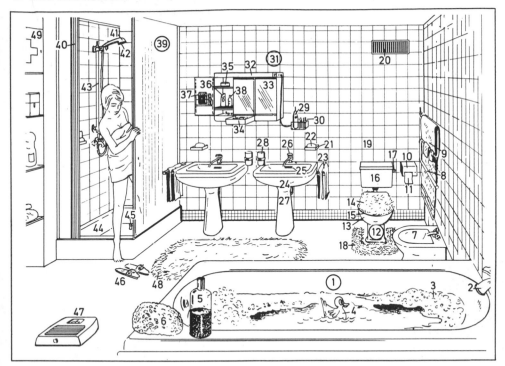

1 die Badewanne
- *bath*
2 die Mischbatterie für kaltes und
  warmes Wasser
- *mixer tap (Am. mixing faucet) for
  hot and cold water*
3 das Schaumbad
- *foam bath (bubble bath)*
4 die Schwimmente
- *toy duck*
5 der Badezusatz
- *bath additive*
6 der Badeschwamm
- *bath sponge (sponge)*
7 das Bidet
- *bidet*
8 der Handtuchhalter
- *towel rail*
9 das Frottierhandtuch
- *terry towel*
10 der Toilettenpapierhalter
- *toilet roll holder (Am. bathroom
  tissue holder)*
11 das Toilettenpapier (Klosettpapier,
   ugs. Klopapier), eine Rolle
   Kreppapier *n*
- *toilet paper (coll. loo paper, Am.
  bathroom tissue), a roll of crepe paper*
12 die Toilette (das Klosett, *ugs.* Klo,
   der Abort, *ugs.* Lokus)
- *toilet (lavatory, W.C., coll. loo)*
13 das Klosettbecken
- *toilet pan (toilet bowl)*
14 der Klosettdeckel mit Frottierüberzug
- *toilet lid with terry cover*
15 die Klosettbrille
- *toilet seat*

16 der Wasserkasten
- *cistern*
17 der Spülhebel
- *flushing lever*
18 die Klosettumrahmung
   (Klosettumrandung)
- *pedestal mat*
19 die Wandkachel
- *tile*
20 die Abluftöffnung
- *ventilator (extraction vent)*
21 die Seifenschale
- *soap dish*
22 die Seife
- *soap*
23 das Handtuch
- *hand towel*
24 das Waschbecken
- *washbasin*
25 der Überlauf
- *overflow*
26 der Kalt- und Warmwasserhahn
- *hot and cold water tap*
27 der Waschbeckenfuß mit dem
   Siphon *m*
- *washbasin pedestal with trap
  (anti-syphon trap)*
28 das Zahnputzglas (der Zahnputzbecher)
- *tooth glass (tooth mug)*
29 die elektrische Zahnbürste
- *electric toothbrush*
30 die Zahnbürsteneinsätze *m*
- *detachable brush heads*
31 der Spiegelschrank
- *mirrored bathroom cabinet*
32 die Leuchtröhre
- *fluorescent lamp*

33 der Spiegel
- *mirror*
34 das Schubfach
- *drawer*
35 die Puderdose
- *powder box*
36 das Mundwasser
- *mouthwash*
37 der elektrische Rasierapparat
- *electric shaver*
38 das Rasierwasser (After-shave, die
   After-shave-Lotion)
- *aftershave lotion*
39 die Duschkabine
- *shower cubicle*
40 der Duschvorhang
- *shower curtain*
41 die verstellbare Handbrause
   (Handdusche)
- *adjustable shower head*
42 der Brausenkopf
- *shower nozzle*
43 die Verstellstange
- *shower adjustment rail*
44 das Fußbecken (die Duschwanne)
- *shower base*
45 der Wannenablauf (das
   Überlaufventil)
- *waste pipe (overflow)*
46 der Badepantoffel
- *bathroom mule*
47 die Personenwaage
- *bathroom scales*
48 der Badevorleger (die Badematte)
- *bath mat*
49 die Hausapotheke
- *medicine cabinet*

1-20 Bügelgeräte *n*
- *irons*
1 der elektrische Bügelautomat
- *electric ironing machine*
2 der elektrische Fußschalter
- *electric foot switch*
3 die Walzenbewicklung
- *roller covering*
4 die Bügelmulde
- *ironing head*
5 das Bettlaken
- *sheet*
6 das elektrische Bügeleisen (der Leichtbügelautomat)
- *electric iron (light-weight iron)*
7 die Bügelsohle
- *sole-plate*
8 der Temperaturwähler
- *temperature selector*
9 der Bügeleisengriff
- *handle (iron handle)*
10 die Anzeigeleuchte
- *pilot light*
11 der Dampf-, Spray- und Trockenbügelautomat
- *steam, spray and dry iron*
12 der Einfüllstutzen
- *filling inlet*
13 die Spraydüse zum Befeuchten *n* der Wäsche
- *spray nozzle for damping the washing*
14 die Dampfaustrittsschlitze
- *steam hole (steam slit)*
15 der Bügeltisch
- *ironing table*
16 das Bügelbrett (die Bügelunterlage)
- *ironing board (ironing surface)*
17 der Bügelbrettbezug
- *ironing-board cover*
18 die Bügeleisenablage
- *iron well*
19 das Aluminiumgestell
- *aluminium* (Am. *aluminum*) *frame*
20 das Ärmelbrett
- *sleeve board*
21 die Wäschetruhe
- *linen bin*
22 die schmutzige Wäsche
- *dirty linen*
23-34 Wasch- und Trockengeräte *n*
- *washing machines and driers*
23 die Waschmaschine (der Waschvollautomat)
- *washing machine (automatic washing machine)*
24 die Waschtrommel
- *washing drum*
25 der Sicherheitstürverschluß
- *safety latch (safety catch)*
26 der Drehwählschalter
- *program selector control*
27 die Mehrkammerfronteinspülung
- *front soap dispenser [with several compartments]*
28 der Trockenautomat, ein Abluftwäschetrockner
- *tumble drier*
29 die Trockentrommel
- *drum*
30 die Fronttür mit den Abluftschlitzen *m*
- *front door with ventilation slits*
31 die Arbeitsplatte
- *work top*

32 der Wäschetrockner (Wäscheständer)
- *airer*
33 die Wäscheleine
- *clothes line (washing line)*
34 der Scherenwäschetrockner
- *extending airer*
35 die Haushaltsleiter, eine Leichtmetalleiter
- *stepladder (steps), an aluminium* (Am. *aluminum*) *ladder*
36 die Wange
- *stile*
37 der Stützschenkel
- *prop*
38 die Stufe (Leiterstufe)
- *tread (rung)*
39-43 Schuhpflegemittel *n*
- *shoe care utensils*
39 die Schuhcremedose
- *tin of shoe polish*
40 der Schuhspray, ein Imprägnierspray *m*
- *shoe spray, an impregnating spray*
41 die Schuhbürste
- *shoe brush*
42 die Auftragebürste für Schuhcreme *f*
- *brush for applying polish*
43 die Schuhcremetube
- *tube of shoe polish*
44 die Kleiderbürste
- *clothes brush*
45 die Teppichbürste
- *carpet brush*
46 der Besen (Kehrbesen)
- *broom*
47 die Besenborsten
- *bristles*
48 der Besenkörper
- *broom head*
49 der Besenstiel
- *broomstick (broom handle)*
50 das Schraubgewinde
- *screw thread*
51 die Spülbürste (Abwaschbürste)
- *washing-up brush*
52 die Kehrschaufel
- *pan (dust pan)*
53-86 die Bodenpflege
- *floor and carpet cleaning*
53 der Handfeger (Handbesen)
- *brush*
54 der Putzeimer (Scheuereimer, Aufwascheimer)
- *bucket (pail)*
55 das Scheuertuch (Putztuch, nd. Feudel)
- *floor cloth (cleaning rag)*
56 die Scheuerbürste
- *scrubbing brush*
57 der Teppichkehrer
- *carpet sweeper*
58 der Handstaubsauger
- *upright vacuum cleaner*
59 die Umschalttaste
- *changeover switch*
60 der Gelenkkopf
- *swivel head*
61 die Staubbeutelfüllanzeige
- *bag-full indicator*
62 die Staubbeutelkassette
- *dust bag container*
63 der Handgriff
- *handle*
64 das Rohr
- *tubular handle*

65 der Kabelhaken
- *flex hook*
66 das aufgewundene Kabel
- *wound-up flex*
67 die Kombidüse
- *all-purpose nozzle*
68 der Bodenstaubsauger
- *cylinder vacuum cleaner*
69 das Drehgelenk
- *swivel coupling*
70 das Ansatzrohr
- *extension tube*
71 die Kehrdüse (*ähnl: Klopfdüse*)
- *floor nozzle (sim.: carpet beater nozzle)*
72 die Saugkraftregulierung
- *suction control*
73 die Staubfüllanzeige
- *bag-full indicator*
74 der Nebenluftschieber zur Luftregulierung
- *sliding fingertip suction control*
75 der Schlauch (Saugschlauch)
- *hose (suction hose)*
76 das Kombinationsteppichpflegegerät
- *combined carpet sweeper and shampooer*
77 die elektrische Zuleitung
- *electric lead (flex)*
78 die Gerätsteckdose
- *plug socket*
79 der Teppichklopfvorsatz (*ähnl.: Teppichschampoiervorsatz, Teppichbürstvorsatz*)
- *carpet beater head (sim.: shampooing head, brush head)*
80 der Allzwecksauger (Trocken- und Naßsauger)
- *all-purpose vacuum cleaner (dry and wet operation)*
81 die Lenkrolle
- *castor*
82 das Motoraggregat
- *motor unit*
83 der Deckelverschluß
- *lid clip*
84 der Grobschmutzschlauch
- *coarse dirt hose*
85 das Spezialzubehör für Grobschmutz *m*
- *special accessory (special attachment) for coarse dirt*
86 der Staubbehälter
- *dust container*
87 der Einkaufswagen
- *shopper (shopping trolley)*

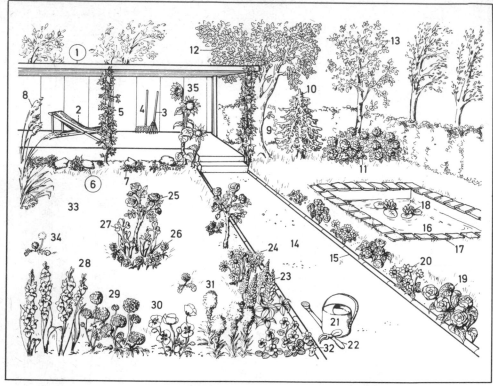

1-35 der Ziergarten (Blumengarten)
- *flower garden*
1 die Pergola
- *pergola*
2 der Liegestuhl (die Gartenliege)
- *deck-chair*
3 der Rasenbesen (Laubbesen, Fächerbesen)
- *lawn rake (wire-tooth rake)*
4 der Rasenrechen
- *garden rake*
5 der Wilde Wein, eine Kletterpflanze
- *Virginia creeper (American ivy, woodbine), a climbing plant (climber, creeper)*
6 der Steingarten
- *rockery (rock garden)*
7 die Steingartenpflanzen f; Arten: Mauerpfeffer m, Hauswurz f, Silberwurz f, Blaukissen n
- *rock plants; varieties: stonecrop (wall pepper), houseleek, dryas, aubretia*
8 das Pampasgras
- *pampas grass*
9 die Gartenhecke
- *garden hedge*
10 die Blaufichte
- *blue spruce*
11 die Hortensien f
- *hydrangeas*
12 die Eiche
- *oak (oak tree)*
13 die Birke
- *birch (birch tree)*

14 der Gartenweg
- *garden path*
15 die Wegeinfassung
- *edging*
16 der Gartenteich
- *garden pond*
17 die Steinplatte
- *flagstone (stone slab)*
18 die Seerose
- *water lily*
19 die Knollenbegonien f
- *tuberous begonias*
20 die Dahlien f
- *dahlias*
21 die Gießkanne
- *watering can (Am. sprinkling can)*
22 der Krehl
- *weeding hoe*
23 die Edellupine
- *lupin*
24 die Margeriten f
- *marguerites (oxeye daisies, white oxeye daisies)*
25 die Hochstammrose
- *standard rose*
26 die Gartengerbera
- *gerbera*
27 die Iris
- *iris*
28 die Gladiolen f
- *gladioli*
29 die Chrysanthemen f
- *chrysanthemums*

30 der Klatschmohn
- *poppy*
31 die Prachtscharte
- *blazing star*
32 das Löwenmäulchen
- *snapdragon (antirrhinum)*
33 der Rasen
- *lawn*
34 der Löwenzahn
- *dandelion*
35 die Sonnenblume
- *sunflower*

1-32 der Kleingarten
(Schrebergarten, Gemüse- und
Obstgarten)
- *allotment (fruit and vegetable
  garden)*
1, 2, 16, 17, 29 Zwergobstbäume *m*
(Spalierobstbäume,
Formobstbäume)
- *dwarf fruit trees (espaliers, espalier
  fruit trees)*
1 die Verrierpalmette, ein
Wandspalierbaum *m*
- *quadruple cordon, a wall espalier*
2 der senkrechte Schnurbaum
(Kordon)
- *vertical cordon*
3 der Geräteschuppen
- *tool shed (garden shed)*
4 die Regentonne
- *water butt (water barrel)*
5 die Schlingpflanze
- *climbing plant (climber, creeper,
  rambler)*
6 der Komposthaufen
- *compost heap*
7 die Sonnenblume
- *sunflower*
8 die Gartenleiter
- *garden ladder (ladder)*
9 die Staude (Blumenstaude)
- *perennial (flowering perennial)*
10 der Gartenzaun (Lattenzaun, das
Staket)
- *garden fence (paling fence, paling)*

11 der Beerenhochstamm
- *standard berry tree*
12 die Kletterrose, am Spalierbogen *m*
- *climbing rose (rambling rose) on
  the trellis arch*
13 die Buschrose (der Rosenstock)
- *bush rose (standard rose tree)*
14 die Sommerlaube (Gartenlaube)
- *summerhouse (garden house)*
15 der Lampion (die Papierlaterne)
- *Chinese lantern (paper lantern)*
16 der Pyramidenbaum, die Pyramide,
ein freistehender Spalierbaum *m*
- *pyramid tree (pyramidal tree,
  pyramid), a free-standing espalier*
17 der zweiarmige, waagerechte
Schnurbaum (Kordon)
- *double horizontal cordon*
18 die Blumenrabatte, ein Randbeet *n*
- *flower bed, a border*
19 der Beerenstrauch
(Stachelbeerstrauch,
Johannisbeerstrauch)
- *berry bush (gooseberry bush,
  currant bush)*
20 die Zementleisteneinfassung
- *concrete edging*
21 der Rosenhochstamm (Rosenstock,
die Hochstammrose)
- *standard rose (standard rose tree)*
22 das Staudenbeet
- *border with perennials*
23 der Gartenweg
- *garden path*

24 der Kleingärtner (Schrebergärtner)
- *allotment holder*
25 das Spargelbeet
- *asparagus patch (asparagus bed)*
26 das Gemüsebeet
- *vegetable patch (vegetable plot)*
27 die Vogelscheuche
- *scarecrow*
28 die Stangenbohne, eine
Bohnenpflanze an Stangen *f*
(Bohnenstangen)
- *runner bean (Am. scarlet runner), a
  bean plant on poles (bean poles)*
29 der einarmige, waagerechte
Schnurbaum (Kordon)
- *horizontal cordon*
30 der Obsthochstamm
(hochstämmige Obstbaum)
- *standard fruit tree*
31 der Baumpfahl
- *tree stake*
32 die Hecke
- *hedge*

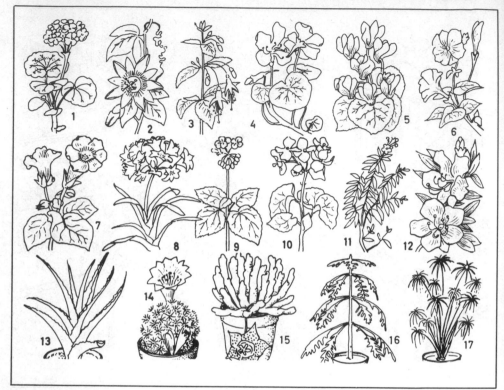

1 die Pelargonie (der Storchschnabel),
ein Geraniengewächs n
- *pelargonium (crane's bill), a
geranium*
2 die Passionsblume (Passiflora),
eine Kletterpflanze f
- *passion flower (Passiflora), a
climbing plant (climber, creeper)*
3 die Fuchsie (Fuchsia), ein
Nachtkerzengewächs n
- *fuchsia, an anagraceous plant*
4 die Kapuzinerkresse
(Blumenkresse, das Tropaeolum)
- *nasturtium (Indian cress,
tropaeolum)*
5 das Alpenveilchen (Cyclamen), ein
Primelgewächs n
- *cyclamen, a primulaceous herb*
6 die Petunie, ein
Nachtschattengewächs n
- *petunia, a solanaceous herb*
7 die Gloxinie (Sinningia), ein
Gesneriengewächs n
- *gloxinia (Sinningia), a
gesneriaceous plant*
8 die Klivie (Clivia), ein
Amaryllisgewächs n
(Narzissengewächs)
- *Clivia minata, an amaryllis
(narcissus)*
9 die Zimmerlinde (Sparmannia),
ein Lindengewächs n
- *African hemp (Sparmannia), a
tiliaceous plant, a linden plant*

10 die Begonie (Begonia, das Schiefblatt) [10]
- *begonia*
11 die Myrte (Brautmyrte, Myrtus)
- *myrtle (common myrtle, Myrtus)*
12 die Azalee (Azalea), ein
Heidekrautgewächs n
- *azalea, an ericaceous plant*
13 die Aloe, ein Liliengewächs n
- *aloe, a liliaceous plant*
14 der Igelkaktus (Kugelkaktus,
Echinopsis, Epsis)
- *globe thistle (Echinops)*
15 der Ordenskaktus (die Stapelia,
eine Aasblume, Aasfliegenblume,
Ekelblume), ein
Seidenpflanzengewächs n
- *stapelia (carrion flower), an
asclepiadaceous plant*
16 die Zimmertanne (Schmucktanne,
eine Araukarie)
- *Norfolk Island pine (an araucaria,
grown as an ornamental)*
17 das Zypergras (der Cyperus
alternifolius), ein Ried- oder
Sauergras n
- *galingale, a cyperacious plant of
the sedge family*

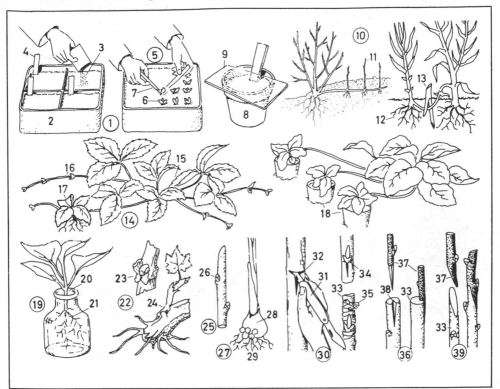

1 die Aussaat
- *seed sowing (sowing)*
2 die Aussaatschale (Saatschale)
- *seed pan*
3 der Samen
- *seed*
4 das Namensschild
- *label*
5 das Verstopfen (Pikieren, Verpflanzen, Umpflanzen, Versetzen, Umsetzen)
- *pricking out (pricking off, transplanting)*
6 der Sämling
- *seedling (seedling plant)*
7 das Pflanzholz
- *dibber (dibble)*
8 der Blumentopf (die Scherbe, *md.* der Blumenasch, *obd.* der Blumenscherben), ein Pflanztopf *m*
- *flower pot (pot)*
9 die Glasscheibe
- *sheet of glass*
10 die Vermehrung durch Ableger *m*
- *propagation by layering*
11 der Ableger
- *layer*
12 der bewurzelte Ableger
- *layer with roots*
13 die Astgabel zur Befestigung
- *forked stick used for fastening*
14 die Vermehrung durch Ausläufer *m*
- *propagation by runners*

15 die Mutterpflanze
- *parent (parent plant)*
16 der Ausläufer (Fechser)
- *runner*
17 der bewurzelte Sproß
- *small rooted leaf cluster*
18 das Absenken in Töpfe *m*
- *setting in pots*
19 der Wassersteckling
- *cutting in water*
20 der Steckling
- *cutting (slip, set)*
21 die Wurzel
- *root*
22 der Augensteckling an der Weinrebe
- *bud cutting on vine tendril*
23 das Edelauge, eine Knospe
- *scion bud, a bud*
24 der ausgetriebene Steckling
- *sprouting (shooting) cutting*
25 der Holzsteckling
- *stem cutting (hardwood cutting)*
26 die Knospe
- *bud*
27 die Vermehrung durch Brutzwiebeln *f*
- *propagation by bulbils (brood bud bulblets)*
28 die alte Zwiebel
- *old bulb*
29 die Brutzwiebel
- *bulbil (brood bud bulblet)*

30-39 die Veredlung
- *grafting (graftage)*
30 die Okulation (das Okulieren)
- *budding (shield budding)*
31 das Okuliermesser
- *budding knife*
32 der T-Schnitt
- *T-cut*
33 die Unterlage
- *support (stock, rootstock)*
34 das eingesetzte Edelauge
- *inserted scion bud*
35 der Bastverband
- *raffia layer (bast layer)*
36 das Pfropfen (Spaltpfropfen)
- *side grafting*
37 das Edelreis (Pfropfreis)
- *scion (shoot)*
38 der Keilschnitt
- *wedge-shaped notch*
39 die Kopulation (das Kopulieren)
- *splice graft (splice grafting)*

1-51 der Gartenbaubetrieb (die
  Gärtnerei, der Erwerbsgartenbau)
- **market garden** (Am. *truck garden,*
  truck farm)
1 der Geräteschuppen
- *tool shed*
2 der Hochbehälter (das
  Wasserreservoir)
- *water tower (water tank)*
3 die Gartenbaumschule, eine
  Baumschule
- *market garden* (Am. *truck garden,*
  truck farm), *a tree nursery*
4 das Treibhaus (Warmhaus,
  Kulturhaus, Kaldarium)
- *hothouse (forcing house, warm*
  house)
5 das Glasdach
- *glass roof*
6 die Rollmatte (Strohmatte,
  Rohrmatte, Schattenmatte)
- *[roll of] matting (straw matting,*
  reed matting, shading)
7 der Heizraum
- *boiler room*
  (boiler house)
8 das Heizrohr (die
  Druckrohrleitung)
- *heating pipe (pressure pipe)*
9 das Deckbrett (der Deckladen, das
  Schattenbrett, Schattierbrett)
- *shading panel (shutter)*
10-11 die Lüftung
- *ventilators (vents)*

10 das Lüftungsfenster (die
  Klapplüftung)
- *ventilation window (window vent,*
  hinged ventilator)
11 die Firstlüftung
- *ridge vent*
12 der Pflanzentisch
- *potting table (potting bench)*
13 der Durchwurf (das Erdsieb,
  Stehsieb, Wurfgitter)
- *riddle (sieve, garden sieve, upright sieve)*
14 die Erdschaufel (Schaufel)
- *garden shovel (shovel)*
15 der Erdhaufen (die kompostierte
  Erde, Komposterde, Gartenerde)
- *heap of earth (composted earth,*
  prepared earth, garden mould, Am.
  mold)
16 das Frühbeet (Mistbeet, Warmbeet,
  Treibbeet, der Mistbeetkasten)
- *hotbed (forcing bed, heated frame)*
17 das Mistbeetfenster (die
  Sonnenfalle)
- *hotbed vent (frame vent)*
18 das Lüftungsholz (Luftholz)
- *vent prop*
19 der Regner (das Beregnungsgerät,
  der Sprenger, Sprinkler)
- *sprinkler (sprinkling device)*
20 der Gärtner (Gartenbauer,
  Gartenbaumeister,
  Handelsgärtner)
- *gardener (nursery gardener, grower,*
  commercial grower)

21 der Handkultivator
- *cultivator (hand cultivator, grubber)*
22 das Laufbrett
- *plank*
23 verstopfte (pikierte) Pflänzchen *n*
- *pricked-out seedlings (pricked-off*
  seedlings)
24 getriebene Blumen *f* [Frühtreiberei]
- *forced flowers [forcing]*
25 Topfpflanzen *f* (eingetopfte,
  vertopfte Pflanzen)
- *potted plants (plants in pots, pot*
  plants)
26 die Bügelgießkanne
- *watering can (Am. sprinkling can)*
27 der Bügel (Schweizerbügel)
- *handle*
28 die Gießkannenbrause
- *rose*
29 das Wasserbassin (der Wasserbehälter)
- *water tank*
30 das Wasserrohr mit Wasser *n*
- *water pipe*

31 der Torfmullballen
- *bale of peat*
32 das Warmhaus
- *warm house (heated greenhouse)*
33 das Kalthaus
- *cold house (unheated greenhouse)*
34 der Windmotor
- *wind generator*
35 das Windrad
- *wind wheel*
36 die Windfahne
- *wind vane*
37 das Staudenbeet, ein Blumenbeet *n*
- *shrub bed, a flower bed*
38 die Ringeinfassung
- *hoop edging*
39 das Gemüsebeet
- *vegetable plot*
40 der Folientunnel (das
   Foliengewächshaus)
- *plastic tunnel (polythene
   greenhouse)*
41 die Lüftungsklappe
- *ventilation flap*
42 der Mittelgang
- *central path*
43 die Gemüseversandsteige
   (Gemüsesteige)
- *vegetable crate*
44 die Stocktomate
   (Tomatenstaude)
- *tomato plant*
45 der Gartenbaugehilfe
- *nursery hand*

46 die Gartenbaugehilfin
- *nursery hand*
47 die Kübelpflanze
- *tub plant*
48 der Kübel
- *tub*
49 das Orangenbäumchen
- *orange tree*
50 der Drahtkorb
- *wire basket*
51 der Setzkasten
- *seedling box*

56 Gartengeräte

Garden Tools 56

1 das Pflanzholz (Setzholz)
- *dibber (dibble)*
2 der Spaten
- *spade*
3 der Gartenbesen
- *lawn rake (wire-tooth rake)*
4 der Rechen (die Harke)
- *rake*
5 die Häufelhacke (der Häufler)
- *ridging hoe*
6 das Erdschäufelchen (die Pflanzkelle)
- *trowel*
7 die Kombihacke
- *combined hoe and fork*
8 die Sichel
- *sickle*
9 das Gartenmesser (die Gartenhippe, Hippe, Asthippe)
- *gardener's knife (pruning knife, billhook)*
10 das Spargelmesser
- *asparagus cutter (asparagus knife)*
11 die Baumschere (Astschere, der Astschneider)
- *tree pruner (long-handled pruner)*
12 der halbautomatische Spaten
- *semi-automatic spade*
13 der Dreizinkgrubber (die Jätekralle)
- *three-pronged cultivator*
14 der Baumkratzer (Rindenkratzer)
- *tree scraper (bark scraper)*
15 der Rasenlüfter
- *lawn aerator (aerator)*
16 die Baumsäge (Astsäge)
- *pruning saw (saw for cutting branches)*
17 die batteriebetriebene Heckenschere
- *battery-operated hedge trimmer*
18 die Motorgartenhacke
- *motor cultivator*
19 die elektrische Handbohrmaschine
- *electric drill*
20 das Getriebe
- *gear*
21 das Anbau-Hackwerkzeug
- *cultivator attachment*
22 der Obstpflücker
- *fruit picker*
23 die Baumbürste (Rindenbürste)
- *tree brush (bark brush)*
24 die Gartenspritze zur Schädlingsbekämpfung
- *sprayer for pest control*
25 das Sprührohr
- *lance*
26 der Schlauchwagen
- *hose reel (reel and carrying cart)*
27 der Gartenschlauch
- *garden hose*
28 der Motorrasenmäher
- *motor lawn mower (motor mower)*
29 der Grasfangkorb
- *grassbox*
30 der Zweitaktmotor
- *two-stroke motor*
31 der elektrische Rasenmäher
- *electric lawn mower (electric mower)*
32 das Stromkabel
- *electric lead (electric cable)*
33 das Messerwerk
- *cutting unit*
34 der Handrasenmäher
- *hand mower*

35 die Messerwalze
- *cutting cylinder*
36 das Messer
- *blade*
37 der Rasentraktor (Aufsitzmäher)
- *riding mower*
38 der Bremsarretierhebel
- *brake lock*
39 der Elektrostarter
- *electric starter*
40 der Fußbremshebel
- *brake pedal*
41 das Schneidwerk
- *cutting unit*
42 der Kippanhänger
- *tip-up trailer*
43 der Kreisregner, ein Rasensprenger *m*
- *revolving sprinkler, a lawn sprinkler*
44 die Drehdüse
- *revolving nozzle*
45 der Schlauchnippel
- *hose connector*
46 der Viereckregner
- *oscillating sprinkler*
47 der Gartenschubkarren
- *wheelbarrow*
48 die Rasenschere
- *grass shears*
49 die Heckenschere
- *hedge shears*
50 die Rosenschere
- *secateurs (pruning shears)*

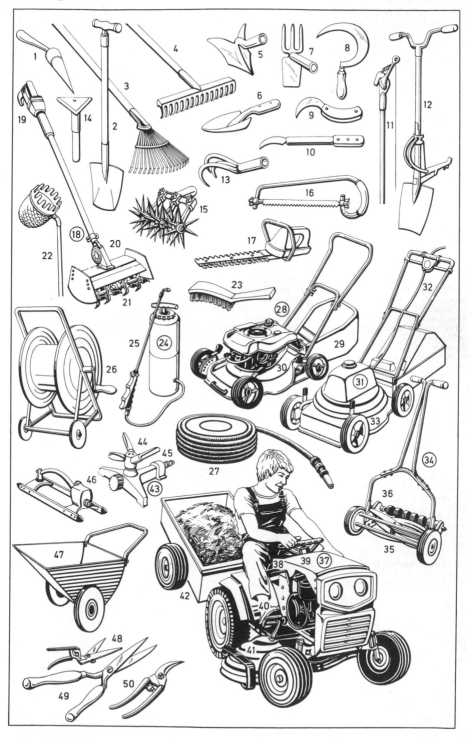

1-11 Hülsenfrüchte *f* **(Leguminosen)**
- *leguminous plants (Leguminosae)*
1 die Erbsenpflanze, ein
  Schmetterlingsblütler *m*
- *pea, a plant with a papilionaceous
  corolla*
2 die Erbsenblüte
- *pea flower*
3 das gefiederte Blatt
- *pinnate leaf*
4 die Erbsenranke, eine Blattranke
- *pea tendril, a leaf tendril*
5 das Nebenblatt
- *stipule*
6 die Hülse, eine Fruchthülle
- *legume (pod), a seed vessel
  (pericarp, legume)*
7 die Erbse [der Samen (Same)]
- *pea [seed]*
8 die Bohnenpflanze, eine
  Kletterpflanze; *Sorten:*
  Gemüsebohne, Kletter- oder
  Stangenbohne, Feuerbohne;
  kleiner: Zwerg- oder Buschbohne
- *bean plant (bean), a climbing plant
  (climber, creeper);* varieties: *broad
  bean (runner bean,* Am. *scarlet
  runner), climbing bean (climber,
  pole bean), scarlet runner bean;
  smaller: dwarf French bean (bush
  bean)*
9 die Bohnenblüte
- *bean flower*
10 der rankende Bohnenstengel
- *twining beanstalk*
11 die Bohne [die Hülse mit den Samen *m*]
- *bean [pod with seeds]*
12 die Tomate (der Liebesapfel,
  Paradiesapfel, *österr.* Paradeis,
  Paradeiser)
- *tomato*
13 die Gurke (*schwäb. Guckummer,
  österr.* der Kümmerling)
- *cucumber*
14 der Spargel
- *asparagus*
15 das Radieschen
- *radish*
16 der Rettich (*bayr.-österr.* Radi)
- *white radish*
17 die Mohrrübe (*obd.* gelbe Rübe,
  md. obd. Möhre, *nd.* Wurzel)
- *carrot*
18 die Karotte
- *stump-rooted carrot*
19 die Petersilie (Federselli, das
  Peterlein)
- *parsley*
20 der Meerrettich (*österr.* Kren)
- *horse-radish*
21 der Porree (Lauch, Breitlauch)
- *leeks*
22 der Schnittlauch
- *chives*
23 der Kürbis; *ähnl.:* die Melone
- *pumpkin (Am. squash);* sim.: *melon*
24 die Zwiebel (Küchenzwiebel,
  Gartenzwiebel)
- *onion*
25 die Zwiebelschale
- *onion skin*
26 der Kohlrabi (Oberkohlrabi)
- *kohlrabi*
27 der (die) Sellerie (Eppich, *österr.*
  Zeller)
- *celeriac*

28-34 Krautpflanzen *f*
- *brassicas (leaf vegetables)*
28 der Mangold
- *chard (Swiss chard, seakale beet)*
29 der Spinat
- *spinach*
30 der Rosenkohl (Brüsseler Kohl)
- *Brussels sprouts (sprouts)*
31 der Blumenkohl (*österr.* Karfiol)
- *cauliflower*
32 der Kohl (Kopfkohl, Kohlkopf),
  ein Kraut *n*; *Zuchtformen:*
  Weißkohl (Weißkraut, *ugs.*
  Kappes), Rotkohl (Rotkraut,
  Blaukraut)
- *cabbage (round cabbage, head of
  cabbage), a brassica;* cultivated
  races (cultivars): *green cabbage,
  red cabbage*
33 der Wirsing (Wirsingkohl,
  Wirsching, das Welschkraut)
- *savoy (savoy cabbage)*
34 der Blätterkohl (Grünkohl,
  Krauskohl, Braunkohl,
  Winterkohl)
- *kale (curly kale, kail), a winter
  green*
35 die Schwarzwurzel
- *scorzonera (black salsify)*
36-40 Salatpflanzen *f*
- *salad plants*
36 der Kopfsalat (Salat, grüner Salat,
  die Salatstaude)
- *lettuce (cabbage lettuce, head of
  lettuce)*
37 das Salatblatt
- *lettuce leaf*
38 der Feldsalat (Ackersalat, die
  Rapunze, Rapunzel, das
  Rapunzlein, Rapünzchen)
- *corn salad (lamb's lettuce)*
39 die Endivie (der Endiviensalat)
- *endive (endive leaves)*
40 die Chicorée (die Zichorie,
  Salatzichorie)
- *chicory (succory, salad chicory)*
41 die Artischocke
- *globe artichoke*
42 der Paprika (spanische Pfeffer)
- *sweet pepper (Spanish paprika)*

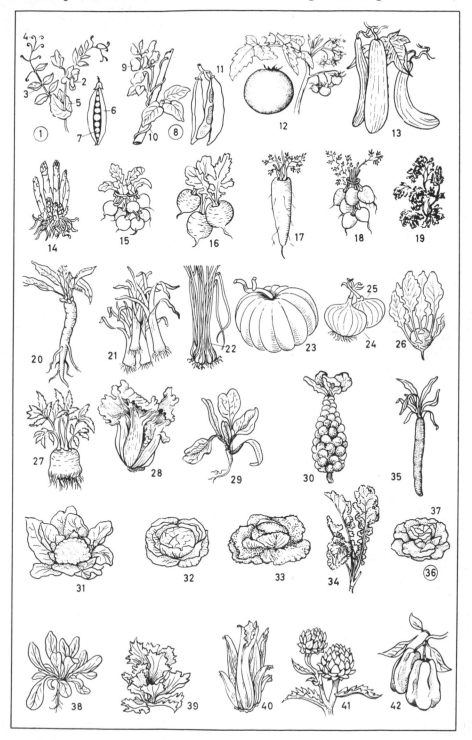

1-30 Beerenobst *n* (Beerensträucher *m*)
– *soft fruit (berry bushes)*
1-15 Steinbrechgewächse *n*
– *Ribes*
1 der Stachelbeerstrauch
– *gooseberry bush*
2 der blühende Stachelbeerzweig
– *flowering gooseberry cane*
3 das Blatt
– *leaf*
4 die Blüte
– *flower*
5 die Stachelbeerspannerraupe
– *magpie moth larva*
6 die Stachelbeerblüte
– *gooseberry flower*
7 der unterständige Fruchtknoten
– *epigynous ovary*
8 der Kelch (die Kelchblätter *n*)
– *calyx (sepals)*
9 die Stachelbeere, eine Beere
– *gooseberry, a berry*
10 der Johannisbeerstrauch
– *currant bush*
11 die Fruchttraube
– *cluster of berries*
12 die Johannisbeere
(*österr.* Ribisel,
schweiz. Trübli *n*)
– *currant*
13 der Fruchtstiel (Traubenstiel)
– *stalk*
14 der blühende Johannisbeerzweig
– *flowering cane of the currant*
15 die Blütentraube
– *raceme*
16 die Erdbeerpflanze; *Arten:* die
Walderdbeere, Gartenerdbeere od.
Ananaserdbeere, Monatserdbeere
– *strawberry plant;* varieties: *wild
strawberry (woodland strawberry),
garden strawberry, alpine
strawberry*
17 die blühende und fruchttragende
Pflanze
– *flowering and fruit-bearing plant*
18 der Wurzelstock
– *rhizome*
19 das dreiteilige Blatt
– *ternate leaf (trifoliate leaf)*
20 der Ausläufer (Seitensproß,
Fechser)
– *runner (prostrate stem)*
21 die Erdbeere, eine Scheinfrucht
– *strawberry, a pseudocarp*
22 der Außenkelch
– *epicalyx*
23 der Samenkern (Samen, Kern)
– *achene (seed)*
24 das Fruchtfleisch
– *flesh (pulp)*
25 der Himbeerstrauch
– *raspberry bush*
26 die Himbeerblüte
– *raspberry flower*
27 die Blütenknospe (Knospe)
– *flower bud (bud)*
28 die Frucht
(Himbeere), eine
Sammelfrucht
– *fruit (raspberry), an aggregate fruit
(compound fruit)*
29 die Brombeere
– *blackberry*
30 die Dornenranke
– *thorny tendril*

31-61 Kernobstgewächse *n*
– *pomiferous plants*
31 der Birnbaum; *wild:* der
Holzbirnbaum
– *pear tree;* wild: *wild pear tree*
32 der blühende Birnbaumzweig
– *flowering branch of the pear tree*
33 die Birne [Längsschnitt]
– *pear [longitudinal section]*
34 der Birnenstiel (Stiel)
– *pear stalk (stalk)*
35 das Fruchtfleisch
– *flesh (pulp)*
36 das Kerngehäuse (Kernhaus)
– *core (carpels)*
37 der Birnenkern (Samen), ein
Obstkern
– *pear pip (seed), a fruit pip*
38 die Birnenblüte
– *pear blossom*
39 die Samenanlage
– *ovules*
40 der Fruchtknoten
– *ovary*
41 die Narbe
– *stigma*
42 der Griffel
– *style*
43 das Blütenblatt (Blumenblatt)
– *petal*
44 das Kelchblatt
– *sepal*
45 das Staubblatt (der Staubbeutel, das
Staubgefäß)
– *stamen (anther)*
46 der Quittenbaum
– *quince tree*
47 das Quittenblatt
– *quince leaf*
48 das Nebenblatt
– *stipule*
49 die Apfelquitte (Quitte) [Längsschnitt]
– *apple-shaped quince [longitudinal
section]*
50 die Birnquitte (Quitte)
[Längsschnitt]
– *pear-shaped quince [longitudinal
section]*
51 der Apfelbaum; *wild:* der
Holzapfelbaum
– *apple tree;* wild: *crab apple tree*
52 der blühende Apfelzweig
– *flowering branch of the apple tree*
53 das Blatt
– *leaf*
54 die Apfelblüte
– *apple blossom*
55 die welke Blüte
– *withered flower*
56 der Apfel [Längsschnitt]
– *apple [longitudinal section]*
57 die Apfelschale
– *apple skin*
58 das Fruchtfleisch
– *flesh (pulp)*
59 das Kerngehäuse (das Kernhaus,
obd. der Apfelbutzen, Butzen, *md.*
Griebs)
– *core (apple core, carpels)*
60 der Apfelkern, ein Obstkern *m*
– *apple pip, a fruit pip*
61 der Apfelstiel (Stiel)
– *apple stalk (stalk)*
62 der Apfelwickler, ein
Kleinschmetterling *m*
– *codling moth (codlin moth)*

63 der Fraßgang
– *burrow (tunnel)*
64 die Larve (Raupe, *ugs.* der Wurm,
die Obstmade) eines
Kleinschmetterlings *m*
– *larva (grub, caterpillar) of a small
moth*
65 das Wurmloch (Bohrloch)
– *wormhole*

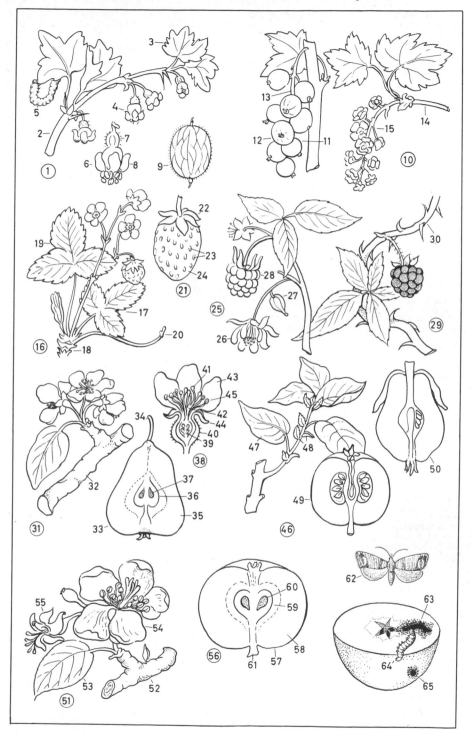

1-36 **Steinobstgewächse** *n*
- *drupes (drupaceous plants)*
1-18 **der Kirschbaum**
- *cherry tree*
1 der blühende Kirschzweig
- *flowering branch of the cherry tree (branch of the cherry tree in blossom)*
2 das Kirschbaumblatt
- *cherry leaf*
3 die Kirschblüte
- *cherry flower (cherry blossom)*
4 der Blütenstengel
- *peduncle (pedicel, flower stalk)*
5 die Kirsche; *Arten:*Süß- oder Herzkirsche, Wild- oder Vogelkirsche, Sauer- oder Weichselkirsche, Schattenmorelle
- *cherry; varieties: sweet cherry (heart cherry), wild cherry (bird cherry), sour cherry, morello cherry (morello)*
6-8 **die Kirsche** (Kirschfrucht) [Querschnitt]
- *cherry (cherry fruit) [cross section]*
6 das Fruchtfleisch
- *flesh (pulp)*
7 der Kirschkern
- *cherry stone*
8 der Samen
- *seed*
9 die Blüte [Querschnitt]
- *flower (blossom) [cross section]*
10 das Staubblatt (der Staubbeutel)
- *stamen (anther)*
11 das Kronblatt (das Blütenblatt)
- *corolla (petal)*
12 das Kelchblatt
- *sepal*
13 das Fruchtblatt (der Stempel)
- *carpel (pistil)*
14 die Samenanlage im mittelständigen Fruchtknoten *m*
- *ovule enclosed in perigynous ovary*
15 der Griffel
- *style*
16 die Narbe
- *stigma*
17 das Blatt
- *leaf*
18 das Blattnektarium (Nektarium, die Honiggrube)
- *nectary (honey gland)*
19-23 **der Zwetschgenbaum**
- *plum tree*
19 der fruchttragende Zweig
- *fruit-bearing branch*
20 die Zwetschge (Zwetsche), eine Pflaume
- *oval, black-skinned plum*
21 das Pflaumenbaumblatt
- *plum leaf*
22 die Knospe
- *bud*
23 der Pflaumenkern (Zwetschgenkern)
- *plum stone*
24 die Reneklode (Reineclaude, Rundpflaume, Ringlotte)
- *greengage*
25 die Mirabelle (Wachspflaume), eine Pflaume
- *mirabelle (transparent gage), a plum*
26-32 **der Pfirsichbaum**
- *peach tree*
26 der Blütenzweig
- *flowering branch (branch in blossom)*

27 die Pfirsichblüte
- *peach flower (peach blossom)*
28 der Blütenansatz
- *flower shoot*
29 das austreibende Blatt
- *young leaf (sprouting leaf)*
30 der Fruchtzweig
- *fruiting branch*
31 der Pfirsich
- *peach*
32 das Pfirsichbaumblatt
- *peach leaf*
33-36 **der Aprikosenbaum** (österr. Marillenbaum)
- *apricot tree*
33 der blühende Aprikosenzweig
- *flowering apricot branch (apricot branch in blossom)*
34 die Aprikosenblüte
- *apricot flower (apricot blossom)*
35 die Aprikose (österr. Marille)
- *apricot*
36 das Aprikosenbaumblatt
- *apricot leaf*
37-51 **Nüsse** *f*
- *nuts*
37-43 **der Walnußbaum** (Nußbaum)
- *walnut tree*
37 der blühende Nußbaumzweig
- *flowering branch of the walnut tree*
38 die Fruchtblüte (weibliche Blüte)
- *female flower*
39 der Staubblütenstand (die männlichen Blüten *f*, das Kätzchen mit den Staubblüten *f*)
- *male inflorescence (male flowers, catkins with stamens)*
40 das unpaarig gefiederte Blatt
- *alternate pinnate leaf*
41 die Walnuß, eine Steinfrucht
- *walnut, a drupe (stone fruit)*
42 die Fruchthülle (Fruchtwand, weiche Außenschale)
- *soft shell (cupule)*
43 die Walnuß (welsche Nuß), eine Steinfrucht
- *walnut, a drupe (stone fruit)*
44-51 **der Haselnußstrauch** (Haselstrauch), ein Windblütler *m*
- *hazel tree (hazel bush), an anemophilous shrub (a wind-pollinating shrub)*
44 der blühende Haselzweig
- *flowering hazel branch*
45 das Staubblütenkätzchen (Kätzchen)
- *male catkin*
46 der Fruchtblütenstand
- *female inflorescence*
47 die Blattknospe
- *leaf bud*
48 der fruchttragende Zweig
- *fruit-bearing branch*
49 die Haselnuß, eine Steinfrucht
- *hazelnut (hazel, cobnut, cob), a drupe (stone fruit)*
50 die Fruchthülle
- *involucre (husk)*
51 das Haselstrauchblatt
- *hazel leaf*

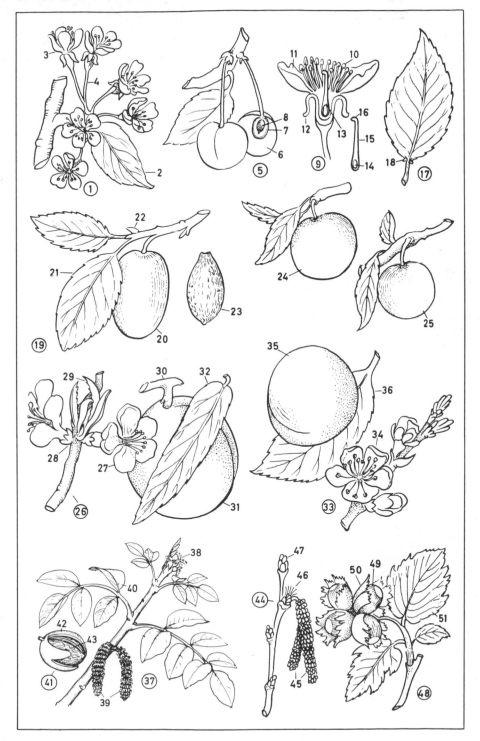

60 Gartenblumen

1 das Schneeglöckchen
(Märzglöckchen, Märzblümchen,
die Märzblume)
- *snowdrop (spring snowflake)*
2 das Gartenstiefmütterchen
(Pensee, Gedenkemein), ein
Stiefmütterchen *n*
- *garden pansy (heartsease pansy), a
pansy*
3 die Trompetennarzisse, eine
Narzisse
- *trumpet narcissus (trumpet
daffodil, Lent lily), a narcissus*
4 die Weiße Narzisse
(Dichternarzisse, Sternblume,
Studentenblume); *ähnl.:* die
Tazette
- *poet's narcissus (pheasant's eye,
poet's daffodil);* sim.: *polyanthus
narcissus*
5 das Tränende Herz (Flammende
Herz, Hängende Herz, Frauenherz,
Jungfernherz, die Herzblume), ein
Erdrauchgewächs *n*
- *bleeding heart (lyre flower), a
fumariaceous flower*
6 die Bartnelke (Büschelnelke,
Fleischnelke, Studentennelke),
eine Nelke (Näglein *n, österr.* Nagerl)
- *sweet william (bunch pink), a
carnation*
7 die Gartennelke
- *gillyflower (gilliflower, clove pink,
clove carnation)*
8 die Wasserschwertlilie (Gelbe
Schwertlilie, Wasserlilie,
Schilflilie, Drachenwurz,
Tropfwurz, Schwertblume, der
Wasserschwertel), eine Schwertlilie
(Iris)
- *yellow flag (yellow water flag,
yellow iris), an iris*
9 die Tuberose (Nachthyazinthe)
- *tuberose*
10 die Gemeine Akelei (Aglei,
Glockenblume, Goldwurz, der
Elfenschuh)
- *columbine (aquilegia)*
11 die Gladiole (Siegwurz, der
Schwertel, *österr.* das Schwertel)
- *gladiolus (sword lily)*
12 die Weiße Lilie, eine Lilie (*obd.*
Gilge, Ilge)
- *Madonna lily (Annunciation lily,
Lent lily), a lily*
13 der Gartenrittersporn, ein
Hahnenfußgewächs *n*
- *larkspur (delphinium), a
ranunculaceous plant*
14 der Staudenphlox, ein Phlox *m*
- *moss pink (moss phlox), a phlox*
15 die Edelrose (Chinesische Rose)
- *garden rose (China rose)*
16 die Rosenknospe, eine Knospe
- *rosebud, a bud*
17 die gefüllte Rose
- *double rose*
18 der Rosendorn, ein Stachel *m*
- *rose thorn, a thorn*
19 die Gaillardie (Kokardenblume)
- *gaillardia*
20 die Tagetes (Samtblume,
Studentenblume, Totenblume,
Tuneserblume, Afrikane)
- *African marigold (tagetes)*

21 der Gartenfuchsschwanz
(Katzenschwanz, das
Tausendschön), ein Amarant *m*
(Fuchsschwanz)
- *love-lies-bleeding, an amaranthine
flower*
22 die Zinnie
- *zinnia*
23 die Pompondahlie, eine Dahlie
(Georgine)
- *pompon dahlia, a dahlia*

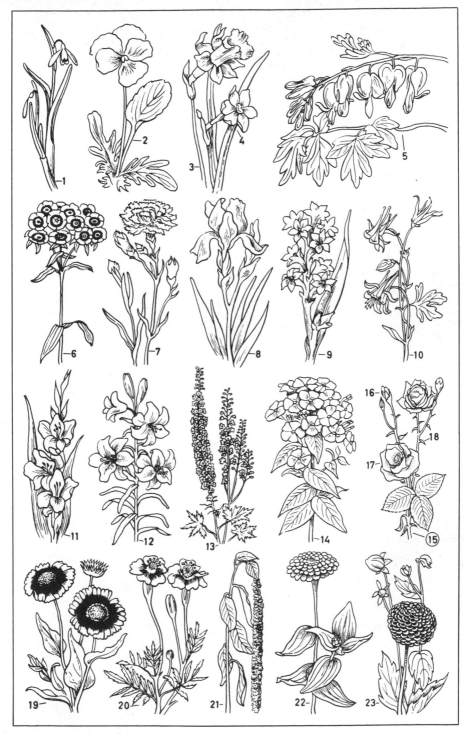

1 die Kornblume (Zyane,
   Kreuzblume, Hungerblume,
   Tremse), eine Flockenblume
 - *corn flower (bluebottle), a centaury*
2 der Klatschmohn (Klappermohn,
   österr. Feldmohn, die Feuerblume,
   schweiz. Kornrose), ein Mohn *m*
 - *corn poppy (field poppy), a poppy*
3 die Knospe
 - *bud*
4 die Mohnblüte
 - *poppy flower*
5 die Samenkapsel (Mohnkapsel) mit
   den Mohnsamen *m*
 - *seed capsule containing
   poppy seeds*
6 die Gemeine Kornrade
   (Kornnelke, Roggenrose)
 - *corn cockle (corn campion,
   crown-of-the-field)*
7 die Saatwucherblume
   (Wucherblume, Goldblume), ein
   Chrysanthemum *n*
 - *corn marigold (field marigold), a
   chrysanthemum*
8 die Ackerkamille (Feldkamille,
   Wilde [Taube] Kamille,
   Hundskamille)
 - *corn camomile (field camomile,
   camomile, chamomile)*
9 das Gemeine Hirtentäschel
   (Täschelkraut, das
   Hirtentäschelkraut, die
   Gänsekresse)
 - *shepherd's purse*
10 die Blüte
 - *flower*
11 die Frucht
   (das Schötchen), in Täschchenform *f*
 - *fruit (pouch-shaped pod)*
12 das Gemeine Kreuzkraut
   (Greiskraut, der Beinbrech)
 - *common groundsel*
13 der Löwenzahn (die Kuhblume,
   Kettenblume, Sonnenblume,
   „Pusteblume", Augenwurz, das
   Milchkraut, der Kuhlattich,
   Hundslattich)
 - *dandelion*
14 das Blütenköpfchen
 - *flower head (capitulum)*
15 der Fruchtstand
 - *infructescence*
16 die Wegrauke, eine Rauke (Ruke,
   Runke)
 - *hedge mustard, a mustard*
17 das Steinkraut (die Steinkresse)
 - *stonecrop*
18 der Ackersenf (Wilde Senf, Falsche
   Hederich)
 - *wild mustard (charlock, runch)*
19 die Blüte
 - *flower*
20 die Frucht, eine Schote
 - *fruit, a siliqua (pod)*
21 der Hederich (Echte Hederich,
   Ackerrettich)
 - *wild radish (jointed charlock)*
22 die Blüte
 - *flower*
23 die Frucht (Schote)
 - *fruit (siliqua, pod)*
24 die Gemeine Melde
 - *common orache (common orach)*
25 der Gänsefuß
 - *goosefoot*

26 die Ackerwinde (Drehwurz), eine
   Winde
 - *field bindweed (wild morning
   glory), a bindweed*
27 der (das) Ackergauchheil (Rote
   Gauchheil, Augentrost, die Rote
   Hühnermyrte, Rote Miere)
 - *scarlet pimpernel (shepherd's
   weatherglass, poor man's
   weatherglass, eye-bright)*
28 die Mäusegerste (Taubgerste,
   Mauergerste)
 - *wild barley (wall barley)*
29 der Flughafer (Windhafer,
   Wildhafer)
 - *wild oat*
30 die Gemeine Quecke (Zwecke, das
   Zweckgras, Spitzgras, der Dort, das
   Pädergras); ähnl.: die
   Hundsquecke, die Binsenquecke
   (der Strandweizen)
 - *common couch grass (couch, quack
   grass, quick grass, quitch grass,
   scutch grass, twitch grass,
   witchgrass); sim.: bearded couch
   grass, sea couch grass*
31 das Kleinblütige Knopfkraut
   (Franzosenkraut, Hexenkraut,
   Goldknöpfchen, die
   Wucherblume)
 - *gallant soldier*
32 die Ackerdistel (Ackerkratzdistel,
   Felddistel, Haferdistel,
   Brachdistel), eine Distel
 - *field eryngo (Watling Street
   thistle), a thistle*
33 die Große Brennessel, eine Nessel
 - *stinging nettle, a nettle*

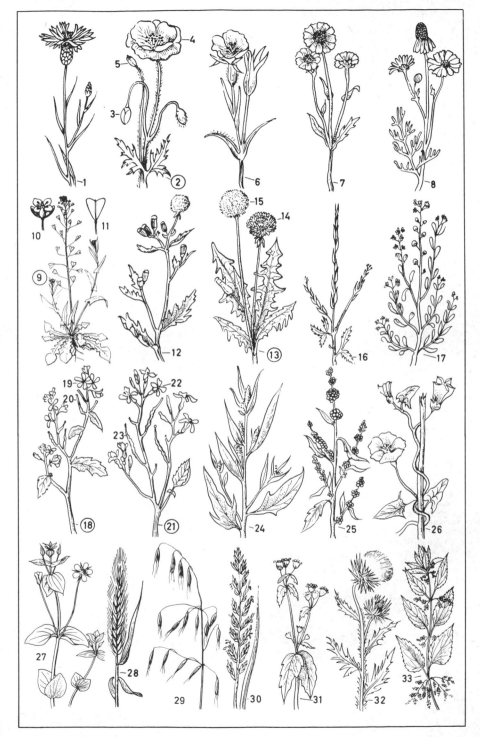

1 das Wohnhaus
- *house*
2 der Reittierstall
- *stable*
3 die Hauskatze
- *house cat (cat)*
4 die Bäuerin
- *farmer's wife*
5 der Besen
- *broom*
6 der Bauer
- *farmer*
7 der Rindviehstall
- *cowshed*
8 der Schweinestall
- *pigsty (sty, Am. pigpen, hogpen)*
9 der Öffenfreßstand
- *outdoor trough*
10 das Schwein
- *pig*
11 der (das) Hochsilo (Futtersilo)
- *above-ground silo (fodder silo)*
12 das Silobeschickungsrohr
- *silo pipe (standpipe for filling the silo)*
13 der (das) Güllesilo
- *liquid manure silo*
14 das Nebengebäude
- *outhouse*
15 der Maschinenschuppen
- *machinery shed*
16 das Schiebetor
- *sliding door*
17 der Zugang zur Werkstatt
- *door to the workshop*
18 der Dreiseitenkipper, ein
  Transportfahrzeug *n*
- *three-way tip-cart, a transport
  vehicle*
19 der Kippzylinder
- *tipping cylinder*
20 die Deichsel
- *shafts*
21 der Stallmiststreuer (Dungstreuer)
- *manure spreader (fertilizer
  spreader, manure distributor)*
22 das Streuaggregat
- *spreader unit (distributor unit)*
23 die Streuwalze
- *spreader cylinder (distributor
  cylinder)*
24 der bewegliche Kratzboden
- *movable scraper floor*
25 die Bordwand
- *side planking (side board)*
26 die Gitterwand
- *wire mesh front*
27 das Beregnungsfahrzeug
- *sprinkler cart*
28 das Regnerstativ
- *sprinkler stand*
29 der Regner (Schwachregner), ein
  Drehstrahlregner
- *sprinkler, a revolving sprinkler*
30 die Regnerschläuche *m* (die
  Schlauchleitung)
- *sprinkler hoses*
31 der Hofraum
- *farmyard*
32 der Hofhund
- *watchdog*
33 das Kalb
- *calf*
34 die Milchkuh
- *dairy cow (milch-cow, milker)*
35 die Hofhecke
- *farmyard hedge*

36 das Huhn (die Henne)
- *chicken (hen)*
37 der Hahn
- *cock (Am. rooster)*
38 der Traktor (Schlepper)
- *tractor*
39 der Schlepperfahrer
- *tractor driver*
40 der Universalladewagen
- *all-purpose trailer*
41 die [hochgeklappe]
  Pick-up-Vorrichtung
- *[folded] pickup attachment*
42 die Entladevorrichtung
- *unloading unit*
43 der (das) Folienschlauchsilo, ein
  Futtersilo *m od. n*
- *polythene silo, a fodder silo*
44 die Viehweide
- *meadow*
45 das Weidevieh
- *grazing cattle*
46 der Elektrozaun (elektrische
  Weidezaun)
- *electrified fence*

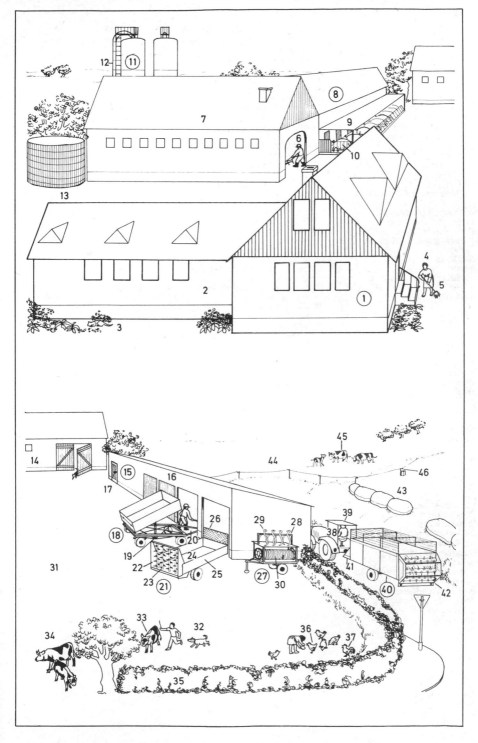

1-41 Feldarbeiten *f*
- *work in the fields*
1 der Brachacker
- *fallow (fallow field, fallow ground)*
2 der Grenzstein
- *boundary stone*
3 der Grenzrain, ein Feldrain *m*
(Rain, Ort)
- *boundary ridge, a balk (baulk)*
4 der Acker (das Feld)
- *field*
5 der Landarbeiter
- *farmworker (agricultural worker, farmhand, farm labourer, Am. laborer)*
6 der Pflug
- *plough (Am. plow)*
7 die Scholle
- *clod*
8 die Ackerfurche (Pflugfurche)
- *furrow*
9 der Lesestein (Feldstein)
- *stone*
10-12 die Aussaat (Bodenbestellung, Bestellung, Feldbestellung, das Säen)
- *sowing*
10 der Sämann
- *sower*
11 das Sätuch
- *seedlip*
12 das Saatkorn (Saatgut)
- *seed corn (seed)*
13 der Flurwächter (Flurhüter, Feldwächter, Feldhüter)
- *field guard*
14 der Kunstdünger (Handelsdünger); *Arten:* Kalidünger, Phosphorsäuredünger, Kalkdünger, Stickstoffdünger
- *chemical fertilizer (artificial fertilizer);* kinds: *potash fertilizer, phosphoric acid fertilizer, lime fertilizer, nitrogen fertilizer*
15 die Fuhre Mist *m* (der Stalldünger, Dung)
- *cartload of manure (farmyard manure, dung)*
16 das Ochsengespann
- *oxteam (team of oxen, Am. span of oxen)*
17 die Flur
- *fields (farmland)*
18 der Feldweg
- *farm track (farm road)*
19-30 die Heuernte
- *hay harvest (haymaking)*
19 der Kreiselmäher mit Schwadablage *f* (der Schwadmäher)
- *rotary mower with swather (swath reaper)*
20 der Verbindungsbalken
- *connecting shaft (connecting rod)*
21 die Zapfwelle
- *power take-off (power take-off shaft)*
22 die Wiese
- *meadow*
23 der Schwad (Schwaden)
- *swath (swathe)*
24 der Kreiselheuer (Kreiselzetter)
- *tedder (rotary tedder)*
25 das gebreitete (gezettete) Heu
- *tedded hay*
26 der Kreiselschwader
- *rotary swather*

27 der Ladewagen mit Pick-up-Vorrichtung
- *trailer with pickup attachment*
28 der Schwedenreuter, ein Heureuter
- *fence rack (rickstand), a drying rack for hay*
29 die Heinze, ein Heureuter
- *rickstand, a drying rack for hay*
30 der Dreibockreuter
- *hay tripod*
31-41 die Getreideernte und Saatbettbereitung *f*
- *grain harvest and seedbed preparation*
31 der Mähdrescher
- *combine harvester*
32 das Getreidefeld
- *cornfield*
33 das Stoppelfeld (der Stoppelacker)
- *stubble field*
34 der Strohballen (Strohpreßballen)
- *bale of straw*
35 die Strohballenpresse, eine Hochdruckpresse
- *straw baler (straw press), a high-pressure baler*
36 der Strohschwad
- *swath (swathe) of straw (windrow of straw)*
37 der hydraulische Ballenlader
- *hydraulic bale loader*
38 der Ladewagen
- *trailer*
39 der Stallmiststreuer
- *manure spreader*
40 der Vierscharbeetpflug
- *four-furrow plough (Am. plow)*
41 die Saatbettkombination
- *combination seed-harrow*

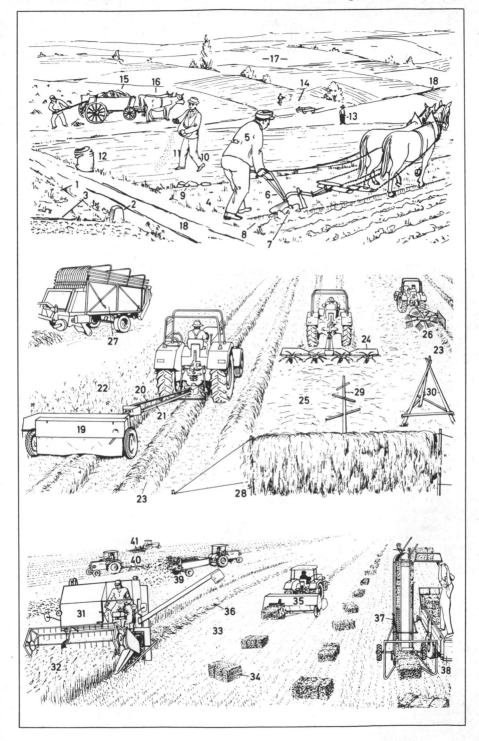

1-33 der **Mähdrescher** (die Kombine)
- *combine harvester (combine)*
1 der Halmteiler
- *divider*
2 die Ährenheber *m*
- *grain lifter*
3 der Messerbalken
- *cutter bar*
4 die Pick-up-Haspel, eine Federzinkenhaspel
- *pickup reel, a spring-tine reel*
5 der Haspelregeltrieb
- *reel gearing*
6 die Einzugswalze
- *auger*
7 der Kettenschrägförderer
- *chain and slat elevator*
8 der Hydraulikzylinder für die Schneidwerkverstellung
- *hydraulic cylinder for adjusting the cutting unit*
9 die Steinfangmulde
- *stone catcher (stone trap)*
10 die Entgrannungseinrichtung
- *awner*
11 der Dreschkorb
- *concave*
12 die Dreschtrommel
- *threshing drum (drum)*
13 die Wendetrommel, zur Strohzuführung
- *revolving beater [for freeing straw from the drum and preparing it for the shakers]*
14 der Hordenschüttler
- *straw shaker (strawwalker)*
15 das Gebläse für die Druckwindreinigung
- *fan for compressed-air winnowing*
16 der Vorbereitungsboden
- *preparation level*
17 das Lamellensieb
- *louvred-type sieve*
18 die Siebverlängerung
- *sieve extension*
19 das Wechselsieb
- *shoe sieve (reciprocating sieve)*
20 die Kornschnecke
- *grain auger*
21 die Überkehrschnecke
- *tailings auger*
22 der Überkehrauslauf
- *tailings outlet*
23 der Korntank
- *grain tank*
24 die Korntankfüllschnecke
- *grain tank auger*
25 die Zubringerschnecken *f* zum Korntankauslauf *m*
- *augers feeding to the grain tank unloader*
26 das Kornauslaufrohr
- *grain unloader spout*
27 die Fenster *n* zur Beobachtung der Tankfüllung
- *observation ports for checking tank contents*
28 der Sechszylinder-Dieselmotor
- *six-cylinder diesel engine*
29 die Hydraulikpumpe mit Ölbehälter *m*
- *hydraulic pump with oil reservoir*
30 das Triebachsvorgelege
- *driving axle gearing*
31 die Triebradbereifung
- *driving wheel tyre (Am. tire)*
32 die Lenkachsbereifung
- *rubber-tyred (Am. rubber-tired) wheel on the steering axle*
33 der Fahrerstand
- *driver's position*

34-39 der **selbstfahrende Feldhäcksler**
- *self-propelled forage harvester (self-propelled field chopper)*
34 die Schneidtrommel (Häckseltrommel)
- *cutting drum (chopper drum)*
35 das Maisgebiß
- *corn head*
36 die Fahrerkabine
- *cab (driver's cab)*
37 der schwenkbare Auswurfturm (Überladeturm)
- *swivel-mounted spout (discharge pipe)*
38 der Auspuff
- *exhaust*
39 die Hinterradlenkung
- *rear-wheel steering system*
40-45 der **Wirbelschwader**
- *rotary swather*
40 die Gelenkwelle
- *cardan shaft*
41 das Laufrad
- *running wheel*
42 der Doppelfederzinken
- *double spring tine*
43 die Handkurbel
- *crank*
44 der Schwadrechen
- *swath rake*
45 der Dreipunktanaubock
- *three-point linkage*
46-58 der **Wirbelwender**
- *rotary tedder*
46 der Ackerschlepper
- *tractor*
47 die Anhängedeichsel
- *draw bar*
48 die Gelenkwelle
- *cardan shaft*
49 die Zapfwelle
- *power take-off (power take-off shaft)*
50 das Getriebe
- *gearing (gears)*
51 das Tragrohr
- *frame bar*
52 der Kreisel
- *rotating head*
53 das Zinkentragrohr
- *tine bar*
54 der Doppelfederzinken
- *double spring tine*
55 der Schutzbügel
- *guard rail*
56 das Laufrad
- *running wheel*
57 die Handkurbel für die Höhenverstellung
- *height adjustment crank*
58 die Laufradverstellung
- *wheel adjustment*
59-84 der **Kartoffelsammelroder** (Kartoffelbunkerroder)
- *potato harvester*
59 die Bedienungsstangen *f* für die Aufzüge *m* des Rodeorgans *n*, des Bunkers *m* und die Deichselverstellung
- *control levers for the lifters of the digger and the hopper and for adjusting the shaft*
60 die höhenverstellbare Zugöse
- *adjustable hitch*
61 die Zugdeichsel
- *drawbar*
62 die Deichselstütze
- *drawbar support*
63 der Gelenkwellenanschluß
- *cardan shaft connection*
64 die Druckwalze
- *press roller*

65 das Getriebe für die Motorhydraulik
- *gearing (gears) for the hydraulic system*
66 das Scheibensech
- *disc (disk) coulter (Am. colter) (rolling coulter)*
67 die Dreiblattschar
- *three-bladed share*
68 der Scheibensechantrieb
- *disc (disk) coulter (Am. colter) drive*
69 das Siebband
- *open-web elevator*
70 die Siebbandklopfeinrichtung
- *agitator*
71 das Mehrstufengetriebe
- *multi-step reduction gearing*
72 die Auflegematte
- *feeder*
73 der Krautabstreifer (die rotierende Flügelwalze)
- *haulm stripper (flail rotor)*
74 das Hubrad
- *rotary elevating drum*
75 die Taumelzellenwalze
- *mechanical tumbling separator*
76 das Krautband mit federnden Abstreifern *m*
- *haulm conveyor with flexible haulm strippers*
77 die Krautbandklopfeinrichtung
- *haulm conveyor agitator*
78 der Krautbandantrieb mit Keilriemen *m*
- *haulm conveyor drive with V-belt*
79 das Gumminoppenband zur Feinkraut-, Erdklumpen- und Steinabsonderung
- *studded rubber belt for sorting vines, clods and stones*
80 das Beimengenband
- *trash conveyor*
81 das Verleseband
- *sorting table*
82 die Gummischeibenwalzen *f* für die Vorsortierung
- *rubber-disc (rubber-disk) rollers for presorting*
83 das Endband
- *discharge conveyor*
84 der Rollbodenbunker
- *endless-floor hopper*
85-96 die **Rübenerntemaschine** (der Bunkerköpfroder)
- *beet harvester*
85 der Köpfer
- *topper*
86 das Tastrad
- *feeler*
87 das Köpfmesser
- *topping knife*
88 das Tasterstützrad mit Tiefenregulierung *f*
- *feeler support wheel with depth adjustment*
89 der Rübenputzer
- *beet cleaner*
90 der Blattelevator
- *haulm elevator*
91 die Hydraulikpumpe
- *hydraulic pump*
92 der Druckluftbehälter
- *compressed-air reservoir*
93 der Ölbehälter
- *oil tank (oil reservoir)*
94 die Spannvorrichtung für den Rübenelevator
- *tensioning device for the beet elevator*
95 das Rübenelevatorband
- *beet elevator belt*
96 der Rübenbunker
- *beet hopper*

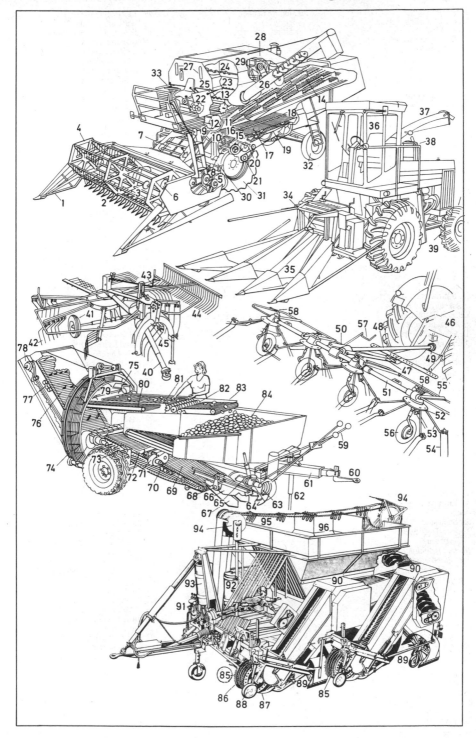

1 **der Karrenpflug,**
ein Einscharpflug *m* [früh.]
- *wheel plough (Am. plow), a*
single-bottom plough [form.]
2 der Handgriff
- *handle*
3 der Pflugsterz (Sterz)
- *plough (Am. plow) stilt (plough*
handle)
4-8 **der Pflugkörper**
- *plough (Am. plow) bottom*
4 das Streichblech (Abstreichblech,
Panzerabstreichblech)
- *mouldboard (Am. moldboard)*
5 das Molterbrett
- *landside*
6 die Pflugsohle (Sohle)
- *sole (slade)*
7 die (das) Pflugschar (Schar)
- *ploughshare (share, Am. plowshare)*
8 die Griessäule
- *frog (frame)*
9 der Grindel (Gründel, Grendel,
Pflugbaum)
- *beam (plough beam, Am. plowbeam)*
10 das Messersech (Pflugmesser, der
od. das Pflugkolter), ein Sech *n*
- *knife coulter (Am. colter), a coulter*
11 der Vorschäler (Vorschneider)
- *skim coulter (Am. colter)*
12 der Führungssteg (Quersteg, das
Querzeug) für die
Kettenselbstführung
- *guide-chain crossbar*
13 die Selbsthaltekette
(Führungskette)
- *guide chain*
14-19 **der Pflugkarren** (Karren, die
Karre)
- *forecarriage*
14 der Stellbügel (Stellbogen, die
Brücke, das Joch)
- *adjustable yoke (yoke)*
15 das Landrad
- *land wheel*
16 das Furchenrad
- *furrow wheel*
17 die Zughakenkette
(Aufhängekette)
- *hake chain*
18 die Zugstange
- *draught beam (drawbar)*
19 der Zughaken
- *hake*
20 **der Schlepper** (Ackerschlepper,
Traktor, Trecker, die
Zugmaschine)
- *tractor (general-purpose tractor)*
21 das Fahrerhausgestänge (der
Überrollbügel)
- *cab frame (roll bar)*
22 der Sattelsitz
- *seat*
23 die Zapfwellenschaltung
- *power take-off gear-change
(gearshift)*
24-29 **die Hubhydraulik** (der Kraftheber)
- *power lift*
24 der Hydraulikkolben
- *ram piston*
25 die Hubstrebenverstellung
- *lifting rod adjustment*
26 der Anschlußrahmen
- *drawbar frame*
27 der obere Lenker
- *top link*

28 der untere Lenker
- *lower link*
29 die Hubstrebe
- *lifting rod*
30 die Anhängekupplung
- *drawbar coupling*
31 die lastschaltbare Motorzapfwelle
(Zapfwelle)
- *live power take-off, live power
take-off shaft*
32 das Ausgleichsgetriebe
- *differential gear (differential)*
33 die Steckachse
- *floating axle*
34 der Wandlerhebel
- *torque converter lever*
35 die Gangschaltung
- *gear-change (gearshift)*
36 das Feinstufengetriebe
- *multi-speed transmission*
37 die hydraulische Kupplung
- *fluid clutch (fluid drive)*
38 das Zapfwellengetriebe
- *power take-off gear*
39 die Fahrkupplung (Kupplung)
- *main clutch*
40 die Zapfwellenschaltung, mit
Zapfwellenkupplung *f*
- *power take-off gear-change
(gearshift) with power take-off clutch*
41 die hydraulische Lenkung mit dem
Wendegetriebe *n*
- *hydraulic power steering and
reversing gears*
42 der Kraftstoffbehälter
- *fuel tank*
43 der Schwimmerhebel
- *float lever*
44 der Vierzylinder-Dieselmotor
- *four-cylinder diesel engine*
45 die Ölwanne mit Pumpe *f* für die
Druckumlaufschmierung
- *oil sump and pump for the
pressure-feed lubrication system*
46 der Frischölbehälter
- *fresh oil tank*
47 die Spurstange
- *track rod (Am. tie rod)*
48 der Vorderachspendelbolzen
- *front axle pivot pin*
49 die Vorderachsfederung
- *front axle suspension*
50 die vordere Anhängevorrichtung
- *front coupling (front hitch)*
51 der Kühler
- *radiator*
52 der Ventilator
- *fan*
53 die Batterie
- *battery*
54 der (das) Ölbadluftfilter
- *oil bath air cleaner (oil bath air
filter)*
55 **der Grubber** (Kultivator)
- *cultivator (grubber)*
56 der Profilrahmen
- *sectional frame*
57 die Federzinke
- *spring tine*
58 die (das) Schar, ein[e]
Doppelherzschar *f u. n* (ähnl.:
Meißelschar)
- *share, a diamond-shaped share
(sim.: chisel-shaped share)*
59 das Stützrad
- *depth wheel*

60 die Tiefeneinstellung
- *depth adjustment*
61 die Anhängevorrichtung
- *coupling (hitch)*
62 **der Volldrehpflug,** ein Anbaupflug *m*
- *reversible plough (Am. plow), a
mounted plough*
63 das Pflugstützrad
- *depth wheel*
64-67 **der Pflugkörper, ein
Universalpflugkörper** *m*
- *plough (Am. plow) bottom, a
general-purpose plough bottom*
64 das Streichblech
- *mouldboard (Am. moldboard)*
65 die (das) Pflugschar (Schar), ein[e]
Spitzschar *f u. n*
- *ploughshare (share, Am.
plowshare), a pointed share*
66 die Pflugsohle
- *sole (slade)*
67 das Molterbrett
- *landside*
68 der Vorschäler
- *skim coulter (Am. colter)*
69 das Scheibensech
- *disc (disk) coulter (Am. colter)
(rolling coulter)*
70 der Pflugrahmen
- *plough (Am. plow) frame*
71 der Grindel
- *beam (plough beam, Am. plowbeam)*
72 die Dreipunktkupplung
- *three-point linkage*
73 die Schwenkvorrichtung (das
Standdrehwerk)
- *swivel mechanism*
74 **die Drillmaschine**
- *drill*
75 der Säkasten
- *seed hopper*
76 das Säschar
- *drill coulter (Am. colter)*
77 das Saatleitungsrohr, ein
Teleskoprohr
- *delivery tube, a telescopic tube*
78 der Saatauslauf
- *feed mechanism*
79 der Getriebekasten
- *gearbox*
80 das Antriebsrad
- *drive wheel*
81 der Spuranzeiger
- *track indicator*
82 **die Scheibenegge,** ein
Aufsattelgerät *n*
- *disc (disk) harrow, a semimounted
implement*
83 die x-förmige Scheibenanordnung
- *discs (disks) in X-configuration*
84 die glatte Scheibe
- *plain disc (disk)*
85 die gezackte Scheibe
- *serrated-edge disc (disk)*
86 die Schnellkupplung
- *quick hitch*
87 **die Saatbettkombination**
- *combination seed-harrow*
88 die dreifeldrige Zinkegge
- *three-section spike-tooth harrow*
89 der dreifeldrige
Zweiwalzenkrümler
- *three-section rotary harrow*
90 der Tragrahmen
- *frame*

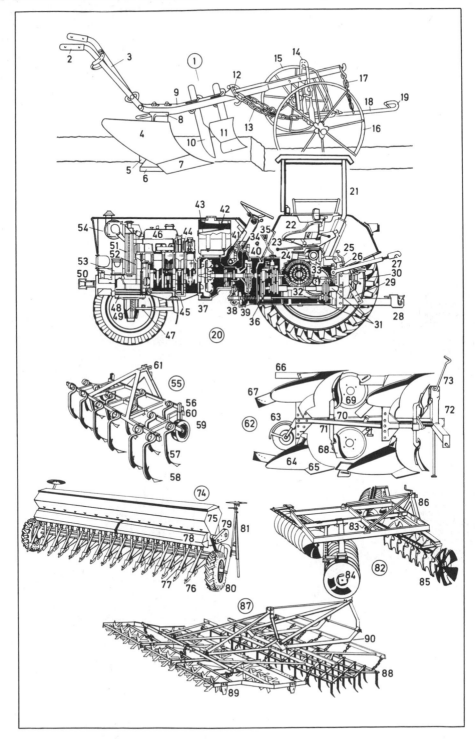

1 die Ziehhacke (Bügelhacke)
- *draw hoe (garden hoe)*
2 der Hackenstiel
- *hoe handle*
3 die dreizinkige Heugabel
  (Heuforke, Forke)
- *three-pronged (three-tined) hay fork (fork)*
4 der Zinken
- *prong (tine)*
5 die Kartoffelgabel (Kartoffelforke, Rübengabel)
- *potato fork*
6 die Kartoffelhacke
- *potato hook*
7 die vierzinkige Mistgabel
  (Mistforke, Forke)
- *four-pronged (four-tined) manure fork (fork)*
8 die Misthacke
- *manure hoe*
9 der Dengelhammer
- *whetting hammer [for scythes]*
10 die Finne
- *peen (pane)*
11 der Dengelamboß
- *whetting anvil [for scythes]*
12 die Sense
- *scythe*
13 das Sensenblatt
- *scythe blade*
14 der Dengel
- *cutting edge*
15 der Sensenbart
- *heel*
16 der Wurf (Sensenstiel)
- *snath (snathe, snead, sneath)*
17 der Sensengriff (Griff)
- *handle*
18 der Sensenschutz (Sensenschuh)
- *scythe sheath*
19 der Wetzstein
- *whetstone (scythestone)*
20 die Kartoffelkralle
- *potato rake*
21 die Kartoffellegewanne
- *potato planter*
22 die Grabgabel
- *digging fork (fork)*
23 der Holzrechen (Rechen, die Heuharke)
- *wooden rake (rake, hayrake)*
24 die Schlaghacke (Kartoffelhacke)
- *hoe (potato hoe)*
25 der Kartoffelkorb, ein Drahtkorb *m*
- *potato basket, a wire basket*
26 die Kleekarre, eine Kleesämaschine
- *clover broadcaster*

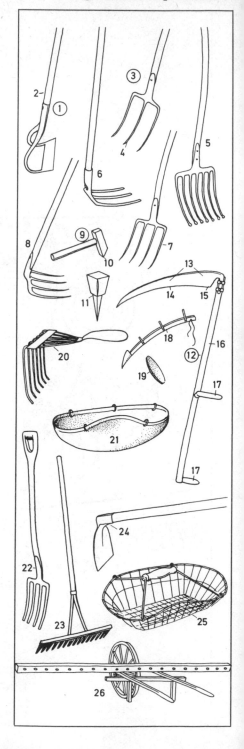

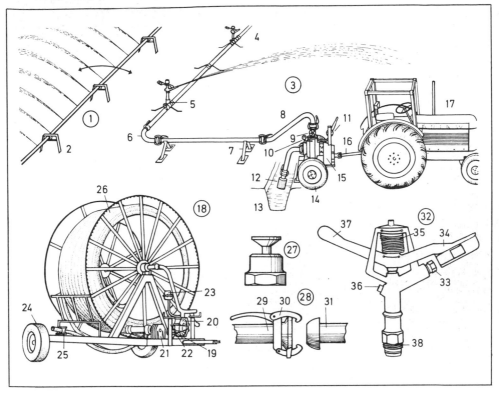

1 das Düsenschwenkrohr
- *oscillating spray line*
2 der Lagerstützbock
- *stand (steel chair)*
3 die vollbewegliche
Beregnungsanlage
- *portable irrigation system*
4 der Kreisregner
- *revolving sprinkler*
5 die Standrohrkupplung
- *standpipe coupler*
6 der Kardanbogen
- *elbow with cardan joint (cardan coupling)*
7 der Stützbock
- *pipe support (trestle)*
8 der Pumpenanschlußbogen
- *pump connection*
9 der Druckanschluß
- *delivery valve*
10 das Manometer
- *pressure gauge (Am. gage) (manometer)*
11 die Evakuierungspumpe
- *centrifugal evacuating pump*
12 der Saugkorb
- *basket strainer*
13 der Graben
- *channel*
14 das Fahrgestell für die
Schlepperpumpe
- *chassis of the p.t.o.-driven pump (power take-off-driven pump)*

15 die Schlepperpumpe
- *p.t.o.-driven (power take-off-driven) pump*
16 die Gelenkwelle
- *cardan shaft*
17 der Schlepper
- *tractor*
18 der Beregnungsautomat für
Großflächen *f*
- *long-range irrigation unit*
19 der Antriebsstutzen
- *drive connection*
20 die Turbine
- *turbine*
21 das Getriebe
- *gearing (gears)*
22 die verstellbare Wagenabstützung
- *adjustable support*
23 die Evakuierungspumpe
- *centrifugal evacuating pump*
24 das Laufrad
- *wheel*
25 die Rohrführung
- *pipe support*
26 das PE-Rohr
(Polyesterrohr)
- *polyester pipe*
27 die Regendüse
- *sprinkler nozzle*
28 das Schnellkupplungsrohr mit
Kardangelenkkupplung *f*
- *quick-fitting pipe connection with cardan joint*

29 der (das) Kardan-M-Teil
- *M-cardan*
30 die Kupplung
- *clamp*
31 das (der) Kardan-V-Teil
- *V-cardan*
32 der Kreisregner, ein Feldregner *m*
- *revolving sprinkler, a field sprinkler*
33 die Düse
- *nozzle*
34 der Schwinghebel
- *breaker*
35 die Schwinghebelfeder
- *breaker spring*
36 der Stopfen
- *stopper*
37 das Gegengewicht
- *counterweight*
38 das Gewinde
- *thread*

1-47 Feldfrüchte *f*
(Ackerbauerzeugnisse *n*,
Landwirtschaftsprodukte)
- **arable crops** *(agricultural produce,*
  farm produce)
1-37 Getreidearten *f* (Getreide *n*,
Körnerfrüchte *f*, Kornfrüchte,
Mehlfrüchte, Brotfrüchte,
Zerealien *pl*)
- **varieties of grain** *(grain, cereals,*
  farinaceous plants, bread-corn)
1 der Roggen (*auch:* das Korn;
„Korn" bedeutet oft
Hauptbrotfrucht *f*, in
Norddeutschland: Roggen *m*, in
Süddeutschland und Italien:
Weizen *m*, in Schweden: Gerste *f*,
in Schottland: Hafer *m*, in
Nordamerika: Mais *m*, in China:
Reis *m*)
- *rye (also: corn, 'corn' often*
  meaning the main cereal of a
  country or region; in Northern
  Germany: rye; in Southern
  Germany and Italy: wheat; in
  Sweden: barley; in Scotland: oats;
  in North America: maize; in
  China: rice)
2 die Roggenähre, eine Ähre
- *ear of rye, a spike (head)*
3 das Ährchen
- *spikelet*
4 das Mutterkorn, ein durch einen
Pilz *m* (Schmarotzer, Parasit)
entartetes Korn *n* (mit
Dauermyzelgeflecht *n*)
- *ergot, a grain deformed by fungus*
  (a parasite) (with mycelium)
5 der bestockte Getreidehalm
- *corn stem after tillering*
6 der Halm
- *culm (stalk)*
7 der Halmknoten
- *node of the culm*
8 das Blatt (Getreideblatt)
- *leaf (grain leaf)*
9 die Blattscheide (Scheide)
- *leaf sheath (sheath)*
10 das Ährchen
- *spikelet*
11 die Spelze
- *glume*
12 die Granne
- *awn (beard, arista)*
13 das Samenkorn (Getreidekorn,
Korn, der Mehlkörper)
- *seed (grain, kernel, farinaceous*
  grain)
14 die Keimpflanze
- *embryo plant*
15 das Samenkorn
- *seed*
16 der Keimling
- *embryo*
17 die Wurzel
- *root*
18 das Wurzelhaar
- *root hair*
19 das Getreideblatt
- *grain leaf*
20 die Blattspreite (Spreite)
- *leaf blade (blade, lamina)*
21 die Blattscheide
- *leaf sheath*
22 das Blatthäutchen
- *ligule (ligula)*

23 der Weizen
- *wheat*
24 der Spelt (Spelz, Dinkel, Blicken,
Fesen, Vesen, das Schwabenkorn)
- *spelt*
25 das Samenkorn; *unreif:* der
Grünkern, eine Suppeneinlage
- *seed; unripe: green spelt, a soup*
  vegetable
26 die Gerste
- *barley*
27 die Haferrispe, eine Rispe
- *oat panicle, a panicle*
28 die Hirse
- *millet*
29 der Reis
- *rice*
30 das Reiskorn
- *rice grain*
31 der Mais (*landsch.* Kukuruz,
türkische Weizen); *Sorten:* Puff-
oder Röstmais, Pferdezahnmais,
Hartmais, Hülsenmais,
Weichmais, Zuckermais
- *maize (Indian corn, Am. corn);*
  varieties: popcorn, dent corn, flint
  corn (flint maize, Am. Yankee
  corn), pod corn (Am. cow corn,
  husk corn), soft corn (Am. flour
  corn, squaw corn), sweet corn
32 der weibliche Blütenstand
- *female inflorescence*
33 die Lieschen *pl*
- *husk (shuck)*
34 der Griffel
- *style*
35 der männliche Blütenstand in
Rispen *f*
- *male inflorescence (tassel)*
36 der Maiskolben
- *maize cob (Am. corn cob)*
37 das Maiskorn
- *maize kernel (grain of maize)*
38-45 Hackfrüchte *f*
- **root crops**
38 die Kartoffel (*österr.* der Erdapfel,
Herdapfel, die Grundbirne,
schweiz. die Erdbirne), eine
Knollenpflanze; *Sorten:* die runde,
rundovale, plattovale, lange
Kartoffel, Nierenkartoffel; nach
Farben: die weiße, gelbe, rote,
blaue Kartoffel
- *potato plant (potato), a tuberous*
  plant; varieties: round, round-oval
  (pear-shaped), flat-oval, long,
  kidney-shaped potato; according
  to colour: white (Am. Irish),
  yellow, red, purple potato
39 die Saatkartoffel (Mutterknolle)
- *seed potato (seed tuber)*
40 die Kartoffelknolle (Kartoffel,
Knolle)
- *potato tuber (potato, tuber)*
41 das Kartoffelkraut
- *potato top (potato haulm)*
42 die Blüte
- *flower*
43 die giftige Beerenfrucht (der
Kartoffelapfel)
- *poisonous potato berry (potato apple)*
44 die Zuckerrübe, eine Runkelrübe
- *sugar beet, a beet*
45 die Wurzel (Rübe, der
Rübenkörper)
- *root (beet)*

46 der Rübenkopf
- *beet top*
47 das Rübenblatt
- *beet leaf*

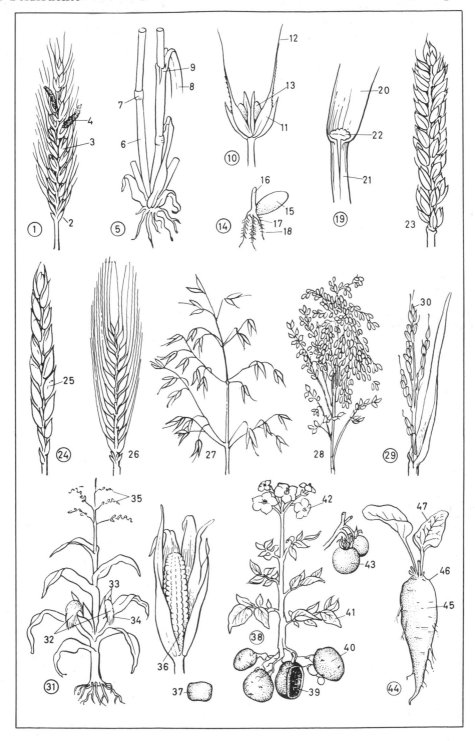

1-28 Futterpflanzen *f* für den Feldfutterbau
- *fodder plants (forage plants) for tillage*
1 der Rotklee (Kopfklee, Rote Wiesenklee, Futterklee, Deutsche Klee, Steyrer Klee)
- *red clover (purple clover)*
2 der Weißklee (Weiße Wiesenklee, Weidenklee, Kriechende Klee)
- *white clover (Dutch clover)*
3 der Bastardklee (Schwedenklee, *nd.* die Alsike)
- *alsike clover (alsike)*
4 der Inkarnatklee (Rosenklee, Blutklee)
- *crimson clover*
5 das vierblättrige Kleeblatt (*volkstüml.:* der Glücksklee)
- *four-leaf (four-leaved) clover*
6 der Wundklee (Wollklee, Tannenklee, Russische Klee, Bärenklee)
- *kidney vetch (lady's finger, lady-finger)*
7 die Kleeblüte
- *flower*
8 die Fruchthülse
- *pod*
9 die Luzerne (der Dauerklee, Welsche Klee, Hohe Klee, Monatsklee)
- *lucerne (lucern, purple medick)*
10 die Esparsette (Esper, der Süßklee, Schweizer Klee)
- *sainfoin (cock's head, cockshead)*
11 die Serradella (Serradelle, der Große Vogelfuß)
- *bird's foot (bird-foot, bird's foot trefoil)*
12 der Ackerspörgel (Feldspörgel, Gemeine Spörgel, Feldspark, Spörgel, Spergel, Spark, Sperk), ein Nelkengewächs *n*
- *corn spurrey (spurrey, spurry), a spurrey (spurry)*
13 der Komfrey (Comfrey), ein Beinwell *m*, Rauhblattgewächs *n*
- *common comfrey, one of the borage family (Boraginaceae)*
14 die Blüte
- *flower (blossom)*
15 die Ackerbohne (Saubohne, Feldbohne, Gemeine Feldbohne, Viehbohne, Pferdebohne, Roßbohne)
- *field bean (broad bean, tick bean, horse bean)*
16 die Fruchthülse
- *pod*
17 die Gelbe Lupine
- *yellow lupin*
18 die Futterwicke (Ackerwicke, Saatwicke, Feldwicke, Gemeine Wicke)
- *common vetch*
19 der Kicherling (die Deutsche Kicher, Saatplatterbse, Weiße Erve)
- *chick-pea*
20 die Sonnenblume
- *sunflower*
21 die Runkelrübe (Futterrübe, Dickrübe, Burgunderrübe, Dickwurz, der Randich)
- *mangold (mangelwurzel, mangoldwurzel, field mangel)*

22 der Hohe Glatthafer (das Französische Raygras, Franzosengras, Roßgras, der Wiesenhafer, Fromental, die Fromändaner Schmale)
- *false oat (oat-grass)*
23 das Ährchen
- *spikelet*
24 der Wiesenschwingel, ein Schwingel *m*
- *meadow fescue grass, a fescue*
25 das Gemeine Knaulgras (Knäuelgras, Knauelgras)
- *cock's foot (cocksfoot)*
26 das Welsche Weidelgras (Italienische Raygras, Italienische Raigras), *ähnl.:* das Deutsche Weidelgras (Englische Raygras, Englische Raigras)
- *Italian ryegrass;* sim.: *perennial ryegrass (English ryegrass)*
27 der Wiesenfuchsschwanz (das Kolbengras), ein Ährenrispengras *n*
- *meadow foxtail, a paniculate grass*
28 der Große Wiesenknopf (Große Pimpernell, Rote Pimpernell, die Bimbernelle, Pimpinelle)
- *greater burnet saxifrage*

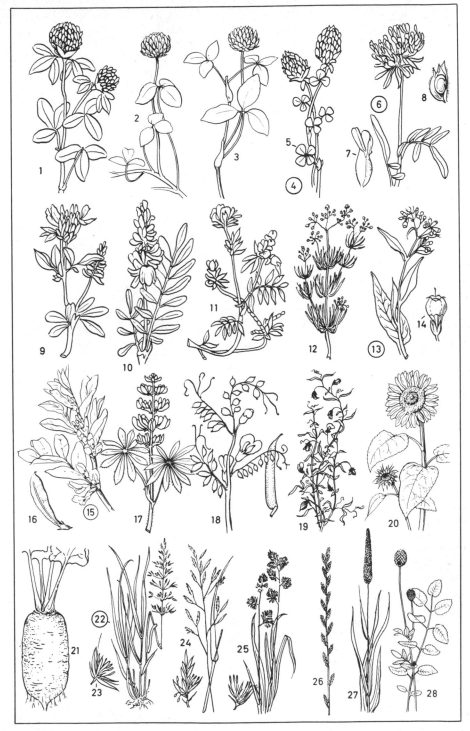

1 die Englische Bulldogge (der
 Bullenbeißer)
– *bulldog*
2 der Behang (das Ohr), ein
 Rosenohr *n*
– *ear, a rose-ear*
3 der Fang (die Schnauze)
– *muzzle*
4 die Nase
– *nose*
5 der Vorderlauf
– *foreleg*
6 die Vorderpfote
– *forepaw*
7 der Hinterlauf
– *hind leg*
8 die Hinterpfote
– *hind paw*
9 der Mops
– *pug (pug dog)*
10 der Boxer
– *boxer*
11 der Widerrist (Schulterblatthöcker)
– *withers*
12 die Rute (der Hundeschwanz), ein
 gestutzter (kupierter) Schwanz *m*
– *tail, a docked tail*
13 die Halsung (das Hundehalsband)
– *collar*
14 die Deutsche Dogge
– *Great Dane*
15 der Foxterrier (Drahthaarfox, Fox)
– *wire-haired fox terrier*

16 der Bullterrier
– *bull terrier*
17 der Scotchterrier (Schottische
 Terrier)
– *Scottish terrier*
18 der Bedlingtonterrier
– *Bedlington terrier*
19 der Pekinese
– *Pekinese (Pekingese, Pekinese dog,*
 Pekingese dog)
20 der Großspitz
– *spitz (Pomeranian)*
21 der Chow-Chow
– *chow (chow-chow)*
22 der Polarhund
– *husky*
23 der Afghane
– *Afghan (Afghan hound)*
24 der Greyhound, ein Hetzhund *m*
– *greyhound (Am. grayhound), a*
 courser
25 der Deutsche Schäferhund
 (Wolfshund), ein Diensthund *m*,
 Wach- und Begleithund
– *Alsatian (German sheepdog, Am.*
 German shepherd), a police dog,
 watch dog, and guide dog
26 die Lefzen *f* (Lippen)
– *flews (chaps)*
27 der Dobermann
– *Dobermann terrier*

28-31 die Hundegarnitur
- *dog's outfit*
28 die Hundebürste
- *dog brush*
29 der Hundekamm
- *dog comb*
30 die Leine (Hundeleine, der
Riemen); *für Jagdzwecke:*
Schweißriemen
- *lead (dog lead, leash); for hunting: leash*
31 der Maulkorb
- *muzzle*
32 der Freßnapf (Futternapf)
- *feeding bowl (dog bowl)*
33 der Knochen
- *bone*
34 der Neufundländer
- *Newfoundland dog*
35 der Schnauzer
- *schnauzer*
36 der Pudel, *ähnl. u. kleiner:* der
Zwergpudel
- *poodle;* sim. and smaller: *pygmy (pigmy) poodle*
37 der Bernhardiner
- *St. Bernard (St. Bernard dog)*
38 der Cockerspaniel
- *cocker spaniel*
39 der Kurzhaardackel
(Dachshund, Teckel),
ein Erdhund *m*
- *dachshund, a terrier*

40 der Deutsche Vorstehhund
- *German pointer*
41 der Setter (Englischer
Vorstehhund)
- *English setter*
42 der Schweißhund (Spürhund)
- *trackhound*
43 der Pointer, ein Spürhund *m*
- *pointer, a trackhound*

1-6 Reitkunst *f* (die Hohe Schule,
    das Schulreiten)
- *equitation (high school riding, haute
    école)*
1 die Piaffe
- *piaffe*
2 der Schulschritt
- *walk*
3 die Passage (der spanische Tritt)
- *passage*
4 die Levade
- *levade (pesade)*
5 die Kapriole
- *capriole*
6 die Kurbette
- *courbette (curvet)*
7-25 das Geschirr
- *harness*
7-13 das Zaumzeug (der Zaum)
- *bridle*
7-11 das Kopfgestell
- *headstall (headpiece, halter)*
7 der Nasenriemen
- *noseband*
8 das Backenstück
- *cheek piece (cheek strap)*
9 der Stirnriemen
- *browband (front band)*
10 das Genickstück
- *crownpiece*
11 der Kehlriemen
- *throatlatch (throatlash)*
12 die Kinnkette (Kandarenkette)
- *curb chain*
13 die Kandare (Schere)
- *curb bit*
14 der Zughaken
- *hasp (hook) of the hame* (Am. *drag
    hook)*
15 das Spitzkumt, ein Kumt *n* (Kummet)
- *pointed collar, a collar*
16 die Schalanken *pl*
- *trappings (side trappings)*
17 der Kammdeckel
- *saddle-pad*
18 der Bauchgurt
- *girth*
19 der Sprenggurt
- *backband*
20 die Aufhaltekette
- *shaft chain (pole chain)*
21 die Deichsel
- *pole*
22 der Strang
- *trace*
23 der Bauchnotgurt
- *second girth (emergency girth)*
24 der Zuggurt
- *trace*
25 die Zügel *m*
- *reins* (Am. *lines)*
26-36 das Sielengeschirr
    (Blattgeschirr)
- *breast harness*
26 die Scheuklappe
- *blinker* (Am. *blinder, winker)*
27 der Aufhaltering
- *breast collar ring*
28 das Brustblatt
- *breast collar (Dutch collar)*
29 die Gabel
- *fork*
30 der Halsriemen
- *neck strap*
31 der Kammdeckel
- *saddle-pad*

32 der Rückenriemen
- *loin strap*
33 der Zügel
- *reins (rein,* Am. *line)*
34 der Schweifriemen
- *crupper (crupper-strap)*
35 der Strang
- *trace*
36 der Bauchgurt
- *girth (belly-band)*
37-49 Reitsättel *m*
- *saddles*
37-44 der Bocksattel
- *stock saddle* (Am. *western saddle)*
37 der Sattelsitz
- *saddle seat*
38 der Vorderzwiesel
- *pommel horn (horn)*
39 der Hinterzwiesel
- *cantle*
40 das Seitenblatt
- *flap* (Am. *fender)*
41 die Trachten *pl*
- *bar*
42 der Bügelriemen
- *stirrup leather*
43 der Steigbügel
- *stirrup (stirrup iron)*
44 der Woilach
- *blanket*
45-49 die Pritsche (der englische
    Sattel)
- *English saddle (cavalry saddle)*
45 der Sitz
- *seat*
46 der Sattelknopf
- *cantle*
47 das Seitenblatt
- *flap*
48 die Pausche
- *roll (knee roll)*
49 das Sattelkissen
- *pad*
50-51 Sporen *pl* [*sg* der Sporn]
- *spurs*
50 der Anschlagsporn
- *box spur (screwed jack spur)*
51 der Anschnallsporn
- *strapped jack spur*
52 das Hohlgebiß
- *curb bit*
53 das Maulgatter
- *gag bit (gag)*
54 der Striegel
- *currycomb*
55 die Kardätsche
- *horse brush (body brush, dandy
    brush)*

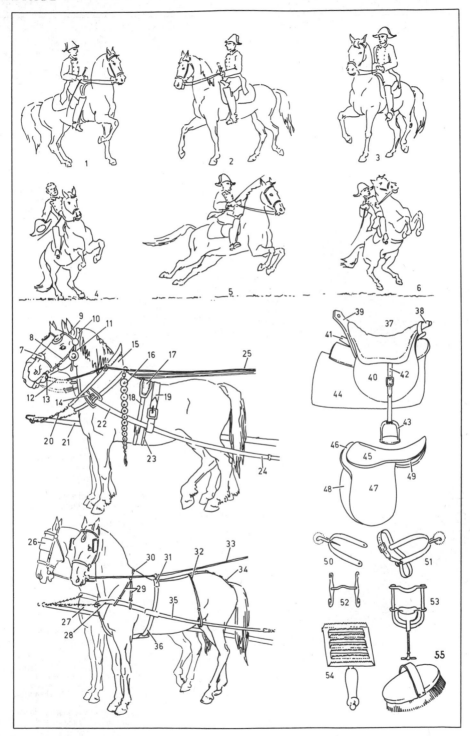

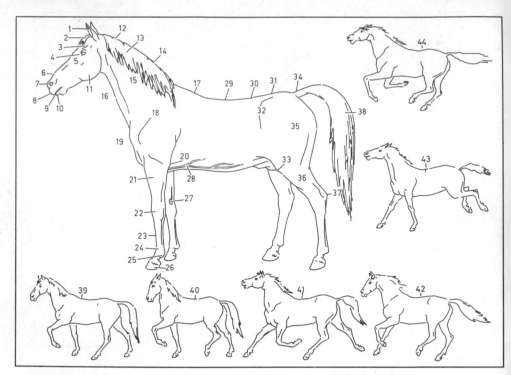

1-38 die äußere Form (das Exterieur) des Pferdes n
- **points of the horse**
1-11 der Kopf (Pferdekopf)
- **head** *(horse's head)*
1 das Ohr
- *ear*
2 der Schopf
- *forelock*
3 die Stirn
- *forehead*
4 das Auge
- *eye*
5 das Gesicht
- *face*
6 die Nase
- *nose*
7 die Nüster
- *nostril*
8 die Oberlippe
- *upper lip*
9 das Maul
- *mouth*
10 die Unterlippe
- *underlip (lower lip)*
11 die Ganasche
- *lower jaw*
12 das Genick
- *crest (neck)*
13 die Mähne (Pferdemähne)
- *mane (horse's mane)*
14 der Kamm (Pferdekamm)
- *crest (horse's crest)*
15 der Hals
- *neck*
16 der Kehlgang (die Kehle)
- *throat (Am. throatlatch, throatlash)*

17 der Widerrist
- *withers*
18-27 die Vorhand
- *forehand*
18 das Schulterblatt
- *shoulder*
19 die Brust
- *breast*
20 der Ellbogen
- *elbow*
21 der Vorarm
- *forearm*
22-26 der Vorderfuß
- *forefoot*
22 das Vorderknie (die Vorderfußwurzel)
- *knee (carpus, wrist)*
23 der Mittelfuß (Röhre)
- *cannon*
24 die Köte (das Kötengelenk)
- *fetlock*
25 die Fessel
- *pastern*
26 der Huf
- *hoof*
27 die Kastanie des Pferdes n, eine Schwiele
- *chestnut (castor), a callosity*
28 die Sporader
- *spur vein*
29 der Rücken (Pferderücken)
- *back*
30 die Lende (Nierengegend)
- *loins (lumbar region)*
31 die Kruppe (Pferdekruppe, das Kreuz)
- *croup (rump, crupper)*
32 die Hüfte
- *hip*

33-37 die Hinterhand
- *hind leg*
33 die Kniescheibe
- *stifle (stifle joint)*
34 die Schweifrübe
- *root (dock) of the tail*
35 die Hinterbacke
- *haunch*
36 die Hose (der Unterschenkel)
- *gaskin*
37 das Sprunggelenk
- *hock*
38 der Schweif (Schwanz, Pferdeschweif, Pferdeschwanz)
- *tail*
39-44 die Gangarten f des Pferdes n
- *gaits of the horse*
39 der Schritt
- *walk*
40 der Paßgang
- *pace*
41 der Trab
- *trot*
42 der Handgalopp (kurze Galopp, Canter)
- *canter (hand gallop)*
43-44 der Vollgalopp (gestreckte Galopp, die Karriere)
- *full gallop*
43 die Karriere beim Auffußen n (Aufsetzen) der beiden Vorderfüße m
- *full gallop at the moment of descent on to the two forefeet*
44 die Karriere beim Schweben n mit allen vier Füßen m
- *full gallop at the moment when all four feet are off the ground*

Abkürzungen:
m. = männlich; *k.* = *kastriert;*
w. = weiblich; *j.* = das Jungtier
Abbreviations:
m. = male; c. = castrated; f. =
female; y. = *young*
1-2 Großvieh *n* (Vieh)
- *cattle*
1 das Rind, ein Horntier *n*, ein
Wiederkäuer *m*; *m.* der Stier (Bulle);
k. der Ochse; *w.* die Kuh; *j.* das Kalb
- *cow, a bovine animal, a horned
animal, a ruminant;* m. *bull;* c. *ox;*
f. *cow;* y. *calf*
2 das Pferd; *m.* der Hengst; *k.* der
Wallach; *w.* die Stute; *j.* das Füllen
(Fohlen)
- *horse;* m. *stallion;* c. *gelding;* f.
mare; y. *foal*
3 der Esel
- *donkey*
4 der Saumsattel (Tragsattel)
- *pack saddle (carrying saddle)*
5 der Saum (die Traglast)
- *pack (load)*
6 der Quastenschwanz
- *tufted tail*
7 die Quaste
- *tuft*
8 das Maultier, ein Bastard *m* von
Eselhengst *m* und Pferdestute *f*
- *mule, a cross between a male
donkey and a mare*
9 das Schwein, ein Paarhufer *m*; *m.*
der Eber; *w.* die Sau; *j.* das Ferkel
- *pig, a cloven-hoofed animal;* m.
boar; f. *sow;* y. *piglet*

10 der Schweinsrüssel (Rüssel)
- *pig's snout (snout)*
11 das Schweinsohr
- *pig's ear*
12 das Ringelschwänzchen
- *curly tail*
13 das Schaf; *m.* der Schafbock (Bock,
Widder); *k.* der Hammel; *j.* das
Lamm
- *sheep;* m. *ram;* c. *wether;* f. *ewe;* y.
lamb
14 die Ziege (Geiß)
- *goat*
15 der Ziegenbart
- *goat's beard*
16 der Hund, ein Leonberger *m*; *m.*
der Rüde; *w.* die Hündin; *j.* der
Welpe
- *dog, a Leonberger;* m. *dog;* f. *bitch;*
y. *pup (puppy, whelp)*
17 die Katze, eine Angorakatze; *m.*
der Kater
- *cat, an Angora cat (Persian cat);* m.
tom (tom cat)
18-36 Kleinvieh *n*
- *small domestic animals*
18 das Kaninchen; *m.* der Rammler
(Bock); *w.* die Häsin
- *rabbit;* m. *buck;* f. *doe*
19-36 Geflügel *n*
- *poultry (domestic fowl)*
19-26 das Huhn
- *chicken*
19 die Henne
- *hen*
20 der Kropf
- *crop (craw)*

21 der Hahn; *k.* der Kapaun
- *cock* (Am. *rooster);* c. *capon*
22 der Hahnenkamm
- *cockscomb (comb, crest)*
23 der Wangenfleck
- *lap*
24 der Kinnlappen
- *wattle (gill, dewlap)*
25 der Sichelschwanz
- *falcate (falcated) tail*
26 der Sporn
- *spur*
27 das Perlhuhn
- *guinea fowl*
28 der Truthahn (Puter); *w.* die
Truthenne (Pute)
- *turkey;* m. *turkey cock (gobbler);* f.
turkey hen
29 das Rad
- *fan tail*
30 der Pfau
- *peacock*
31 die Pfauenfeder
- *peacock's feather*
32 das Pfauenauge
- *eye (ocellus)*
33 die Taube; *m.* der Täuberich
- *pigeon;* m. *cock pigeon*
34 die Gans; *m.* der Gänserich
(Ganser, *nd.* Ganter); *j. nd.* das Gössel
- *goose;* m. *gander;* y. *gosling*
35 die Ente; *m.* der Enterich (Erpel); *j.*
das Entenküken
- *duck;* m. *drake;* y. *duckling*
36 die Schwimmhaut
- *web (palmations) of webbed foot
(palmate foot)*

74 Geflügelhaltung, Eierproduktion

1-27 **die Geflügelhaltung (Intensivhaltung)**
- *poultry farming (intensive poultry management)*
1-17 **die Bodenhaltung**
- *straw yard (strawed yard) system*
1 der Hühneraufzuchtstall (Kükenstall)
- *fold unit for growing stock (chick unit)*
2 das Küken
- *chick*
3 die Schirmglucke
- *brooder (hover)*
4 die verstellbare Futterrinne
- *adjustable feeding trough*
5 der Junghennenstall
- *pullet fold unit*
6 die Tränkrinne
- *drinking trough*
7 der Wasserzulauf
- *water pipe*
8 die Einstreu
- *litter*
9 die Junghenne
- *pullet*
10 die Lüftungsvorrichtung
- *ventilator*
11-17 **die Mastgeflügelzucht**
- *broiler rearing (rearing of broiler chickens)*
11 der Scharraum (Tagesraum)
- *chicken run (Am. fowl run)*
12 das Masthuhn
- *broiler chicken (broiler)*
13 der Futterautomat
- *mechanical feeder (self-feeder, feed dispenser)*
14 die Haltekette
- *chain*
15 das Futterrohr
- *feed supply pipe*
16 die automatische Rundtränke (Selbsttränke)
- *mechanical drinking bowl (mechanical drinker)*
17 die Lüftungsvorrichtung
- *ventilator*
18 die Batteriehaltung (Käfighaltung)
- *battery system (cage system)*
19 die Batterie (Legebatterie)
- *battery (laying battery)*
20 der Etagenkäfig (Stufenkäfig, Batteriekäfig)
- *tiered cage (battery cage, stepped cage)*
21 die Futterrinne
- *feeding trough*
22 die Eierlängssammlung
- *egg collection by conveyor*
23-27 **die automatische Futterzuführung und Entmistung**
- *mechanical feeding and dunging (manure removal, droppings removal)*
23 das Schnellfütterungssystem für die Batteriefütterung (die Futtermaschine)
- *rapid feeding system for battery feeding (mechanical feeder)*
24 der Einfülltrichter
- *feed hopper*
25 das Futtertransportband (die Futtertransportkette, Futterkette)
- *endless-chain feed conveyor (chain feeder)*

26 die Wasserleitung
- *water pipe (liquid feed pipe)*
27 das Kottransportband
- *dunging chain (dunging conveyor)*
28 der Schlupfbrüter
- *[cabinet type] setting and hatching machine*
29 die Vorbruttrommel
- *ventilation drum [for the setting compartment]*
30 der Schlupfteil
- *hatching compartment (hatcher)*
31 der Metallschlupfwagen
- *metal trolley for hatching trays*
32 die Metallschlupfhorde
- *hatching tray*
33 der Vorbruttrommelantrieb
- *ventilation drum motor*
34-53 **die Eierproduktion**
- *egg production*
34 die Eiersammelvorrichtung (Eiersammlung)
- *egg collection system (egg collection)*
35 die Niveauförderung
- *multi-tier transport*
36 die Einquersammlung
- *collection by pivoted fingers*
37 der Antriebsmotor
- *drive motor*
38 die Einsortiermaschine
- *sorting machine*
39 die Rollenzufuhr
- *conveyor trolley*
40 der Durchleuchtungsspiegel
- *fluorescent screen*
41 die Absaugvorrichtung zum Eiertransport m
- *suction apparatus (suction box) for transporting eggs*
42 das Ablagebord für leere und volle Höckereinsätze m
- *shelf for empty and full egg boxes*
43 die Eierwaagen f
- *egg weighers*
44 die Klassensortierung
- *grading*
45 der Höckereinsatz
- *egg box*
46 die vollautomatische Eierverpackungsmaschine
- *fully automatic egg-packing machine*
47 die Durchleuchtungskabine
- *radioscope box*
48 der Durchleuchtungstisch
- *radioscope table*
49-51 **die Auflegevorrichtung**
- *feeder*
49 die Vakuumabsaugvorrichtung
- *suction transporter*
50 der Vakuumschlauch
- *vacuum line*
51 der Anfuhrtisch
- *supply table*
52 die automatische Zählung und Gewichtsklassensortierung f
- *automatic counting and grading*
53 der Verpackungsentstapler
- *packing box dispenser*
54 der Fußring
- *leg ring*
55 die Geflügelmarke
- *wing tally (identification tally)*
56 das Zwerghuhn (Bantamhuhn)
- *bantam*

57 die Legehenne
- *laying hen*
58 das Hühnerei (Ei)
- *hen's egg (egg)*
59 die Kalkschale (Eierschale), eine Eihülle
- *eggshell, an egg integument*
60 die Schalenhaut
- *shell membrane*
61 die Luftkammer
- *air space*
62 das Eiweiß (österr. Eiklar)
- *white [of the egg] (albumen)*
63 die Hagelschnur (Chalaza)
- *chalaza (Am. treadle)*
64 die Dotterhaut
- *vitelline membrane (yolk sac)*
65 die Keimscheibe (der Hahnentritt)
- *blastodisc (germinal disc, cock's tread, cock's treadle)*
66 das Keimbläschen
- *germinal vesicle*
67 der (das) weiße Dotter
- *white*
68 das Eigelb (der od. das gelbe Dotter)
- *yolk*

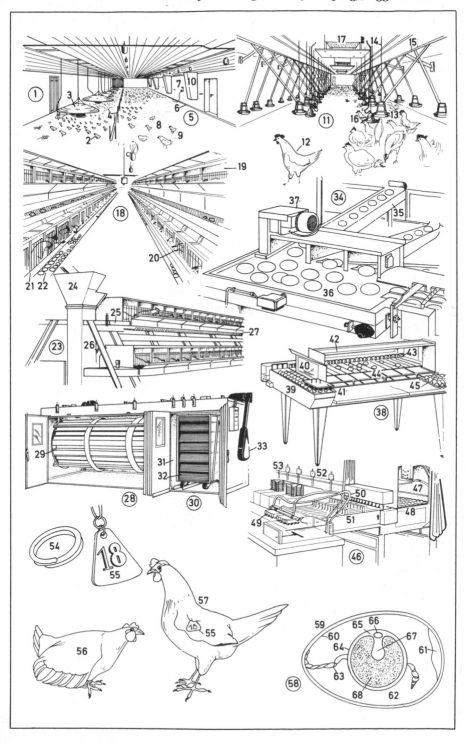

1 **der Pferdestall**
- *stable*
2 der Pferdestand (die Pferdebox, Box)
- *horse stall (stall, horse box, box)*
3 der Futtergang
- *feeding passage*
4 das Reitpony (Pony)
- *pony*
5 die Gitterwand
- *bars*
6 die Einstreu
- *litter*
7 der Strohballen
- *bale of straw*
8 das Oberlicht
- *ceiling light*
9 **der Schafstall**
- *sheep pen*
10 das Mutterschaf
- *mother sheep (ewe)*
11 das Lamm
- *lamb*
12 die Doppelraufe
- *double hay rack*
13 das Heu
- *hay*
14 **der Milchviehstall** (Kuhstall), ein Anbindestall *m*
- *dairy cow shed (cow shed), in which cows require tying*
15-16 die Anbindevorrichtung
- *tether*
15 die Kette
- *chain*
16 der Aufhängeholm
- *rail*
17 die Milchkuh
- *dairy cow (milch-cow, milker)*
18 das Euter
- *udder*
19 die Zitze
- *teat*
20 die Kotrinne
- *manure gutter*
21 die Schubstangenentmistung
- *manure removal by sliding bars*
22 der Kurzstand
- *short standing*
23 **der Melkstand,** ein Fischgrätenmelkstand *m*
- *milking parlour (Am. parlor), a herringbone parlour*
24 die Arbeitsgrube
- *working passage*
25 der Melker
- *milker (Am. milkman)*
26 das Melkgeschirr
- *teat cup cluster*
27 die Milchleitung
- *milk pipe*
28 die Luftleitung
- *air line*
29 die Vakuumleitung
- *vacuum line*
30 der Melkbecher
- *teat cup*
31 das Schauglas
- *window*
32 das Milchsammel- und Luftverteilerstück
- *pulsator*
33 der Entlastungstakt
- *release phase*
34 der Melktakt
- *squeeze phase*

35 **der Schweinestall** (Saustall)
- *pigsty (Am. pigpen, hogpen)*
36 die Läuferbucht (der Läuferkoben, Koben)
- *pen for young pigs*
37 der Futtertrog
- *feeding trough*
38 die Trennwand
- *partition*
39 das Schwein, ein Läufer *m*
- *pig, a young pig*
40 die Abferkel-Aufzucht-Bucht
- *farrowing and store pen*
41 die Muttersau (Sau)
- *sow*
42 die Ferkel *n* (Sauferkel *[bis 8 Wochen]*)
- *piglet (Am. shoat, shote) (sow pig [for first 8 weeks])*
43 das Absperrgitter
- *farrowing rails*
44 die Jaucherinne
- *liquid manure channel*

1-48 **die Molkerei** (der Milchhof)
- *dairy (dairy plant)*
1 **die Milchannahme** (die Abtankhalle)
- *milk reception*
2 der Milchtankwagen
- *milk tanker*
3 die Rohmilchpumpe
- *raw milk pump*
4 der Durchflußmesser (die
   Meßuhr), ein Ovalradzähler *m*
- *flowmeter, an oval (elliptical) gear
   meter*
5 der Rohmilchsilotank
- *raw milk storage tank*
6 der Füllstandmesser
- *gauge (Am. gage)*
7 **die zentrale Schaltwarte**
- *central control room*
8 das Betriebsschaubild
- *chart of the dairy*
9 das Betriebsablaufschema
- *flow chart (flow diagram)*
10 die Füllstandsanzeiger *m* des
   Silotanks
- *storage tank gauges (Am. gages)*
11 das Schaltpult
- *control panel*
12-48 **der Betriebsraum**
- *milk processing area*
12 der Reinigungsseparator (die
   Homogenisiermaschine)
- *sterilizer (homogenizer)*
13 der Milcherhitzer; *ähnl.:* der
   Rahmerhitzer
- *milk heater;* sim.: *cream heater*
14 der Magermilchseparator
- *cream separator*
15 die Trinkmilchtanks
   (Frischmilchtanks)
- *fresh milk tanks*
16 der Tank für die gereinigte Milch
- *tank for sterilized milk*
17 der Magermilchtank
- *skim milk (skimmed milk) tank*
18 der Buttermilchtank
- *buttermilk tank*
19 der Rahmtank
- *cream tank*
20 die Abfüll- und
   Verpackungsanlage für Trinkmilch *f*
- *fresh milk filling and packing plant*
21 die Abfüllmaschine für
   Milchpackungen *f, ähnl.:* der
   Becherfüller
- *filling machine for milk cartons;*
   sim.: *milk tub filler*
22 die Milchpackung (der
   Milchbeutel)
- *milk carton*
23 das Förderband
- *conveyor belt (conveyor)*
24 der Folienschrumpftunnel
- *shrink-sealing machine*
25 die Zwölferpackung in
   Schrumpffolie *f*
- *pack of twelve in shrink foil*
26 die Zehn-Liter-Abfüllanlage
- *ten-litre filling machine*
27 die Folienschweißanlage
- *heat-sealing machine*
28 die Folien *f*
- *plastic sheets*
29 der Schlauchbeutel
- *heat-sealed bag*
30 der Stapelkasten
- *crate*

31 der Rahmreifungstank
- *cream maturing vat*
32 die Butterungs- und Abpackanlage
   (Butterei)
- *butter shaping and packing
   machine*
33 die Butterungsmaschine (der
   Butterfertiger), eine
   Süßrahmbutterungsanlage für
   kontinuierliche Butterung *f*
- *butter churn, a creamery butter
   machine for continuous butter
   making*
34 der Butterstrang
- *butter supply pipe*
35 die Ausformanlage
- *shaping machine*
36 die Verpackungsmaschine
- *packing machine*
37 die Markenbutter in der
   250-g-Packung
- *branded butter in 250 g packets*
38 die Produktionsanlage für
   Frischkäse (die
   Quarkbereitungsanlage)
- *plant for producing curd cheese
   (curd cheese machine)*
39 die Quarkpumpe
- *curd cheese pump*
40 die Rahmdosierpumpe
- *cream supply pump*
41 der Quarkseparator
- *curds separator*
42 der Sauermilchtank
- *sour milk vat*
43 der Rührer
- *stirrer*
44 die Quarkverpackungsmaschine
- *curd cheese packing machine*
45 die Quarkpackung (der Quark,
   Topfen, Weißkäse; *ähnl.:* der
   Schichtkäse)
- *curd cheese packet (curd cheese;*
   sim.: *cottage cheese)*
46 die Deckelsetzstation
- *bottle-capping machine (capper)*
47 der Schnittkäsebetrieb
- *cheese machine*
48 der Labtank
- *rennet vat*

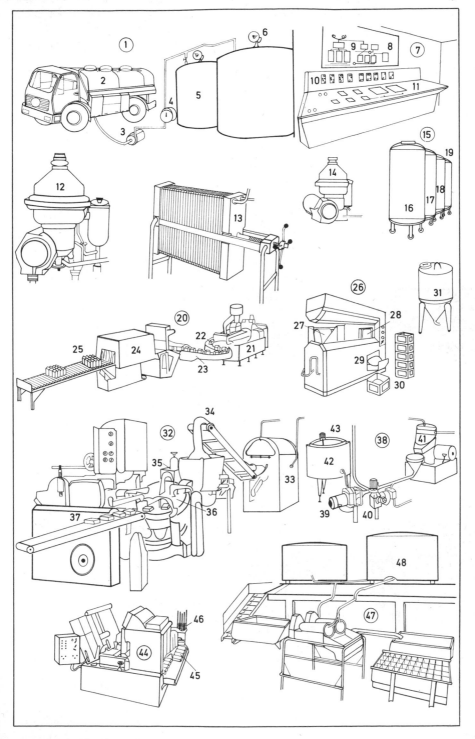

1-25 die Biene (Honigbiene, Imme)
- *bee (honey-bee, hive-bee)*
1, 4, 5 die Kasten *f* (Klassen) der
Biene
- *castes (social classes) of bees*
1 die Arbeiterin (Arbeitsbiene)
- *worker (worker bee)*
2 die drei Nebenaugen *n*
(Stirnaugen)
- *three simple eyes (ocelli)*
3 das Höschen (der gesammelte
Blütenstaub)
- *load of pollen on the hind leg*
4 die Königin (Bienenkönigin, der
Weisel)
- *queen (queen bee)*
5 die Drohne (das Bienenmännchen)
- *drone (male bee)*
**6-9 das linke Hinterbein einer
Arbeiterin**
- *left hind leg of a worker*
6 das Körbchen für den Blütenstaub
- *pollen basket*
7 die Bürste
- *pollen comb (brush)*
8 die Doppelklaue
- *double claw*
9 der Haftballen
- *suctorial pad*
10-19 der Hinterleib der Arbeiterin
- *abdomen of the worker*
10-14 der Stechapparat
- *stinging organs*
10 der Widerhaken
- *barb*
11 der Stachel
- *sting*
12 die Stachelscheide
- *sting sheath*
13 die Giftblase
- *poison sac*
14 die Giftdrüse
- *poison gland*
15-19 der Magen-Darm-Kanal
- *stomachic-intestinal canal*
15 der Darm
- *intestine*
16 der Magen
- *stomach*
17 der Schließmuskel
- *contractile muscle*
18 der Honigmagen
- *honey bag (honey sac)*
19 die Speiseröhre
- *oesophagus (esophagus, gullet)*
20-24 das Facettenauge (Netzauge,
Insektenauge)
- *compound eye*
20 die Facette
- *facet*
21 der Kristallkegel
- *crystal cone*
22 der lichtempfindl. Abschnitt
- *light-sensitive section*
23 die Faser des Sehnervs *m*
- *fibre* (Am. *fiber*) *of the optic nerve*
24 der Sehnerv
- *optic nerve*
25 das Wachsplättchen
- *wax scale*
26-30 die Zelle (Bienenzelle)
- *cell*
26 das Ei
- *egg*
27 die bestiftete Zelle
- *cell with the egg in it*

28 die Made
- *young larva*
29 die Larve
- *larva (grub)*
30 die Puppe
- *chrysalis (pupa)*
31-43 die Wabe (Bienenwabe)
- *honeycomb*
31 die Brutzelle
- *brood cell*
32 die verdeckelte Zelle mit Puppe *f*
(Puppenwiege)
- *sealed (capped) cell with chrysalis
(pupa)*
33 die verdeckelte Zelle mit Honig *m*
(Honigzelle)
- *sealed (capped) cell with honey
(honey cell)*
34 die Arbeiterinnenzellen *f*
- *worker cells*
35 die Vorratszellen *f*, mit Pollen *m*
- *storage cells, with pollen*
36 die Drohnenzellen *f*
- *drone cells*
37 die Königinnenzelle (Weiselwiege)
- *queen cell*
38 die schlüpfende Königin
- *queen emerging [from her cell]*
39 der Deckel
- *cap (capping)*
40 das Rähmchen
- *frame*
41 der Abstandsbügel
- *distance piece*
42 die Wabe
- *[artificial] honeycomb*
43 die Mittelwand (der künstliche
Zellenboden)
- *septum (foundation, comb
foundation)*
44 der Königinnenversandkäfig
- *queen's travelling* (Am. *traveling*) *box*
45-50 der Bienenkasten (die
Ständerbeute, Blätterbeute), ein
Hinterlader *m*, mit Längsbau *m*
(ein Bienenstock *m*, eine Beute)
- *frame hive (movable-frame hive,
movable-comb hive [into which
frames are inserted from the rear],
a beehive (hive))*
45 der Honigraum mit den
Honigwaben *f*
- *super (honey super) with
honeycombs*
46 der Brutraum mit den Brutwaben *f*
- *brood chamber with breeding
combs*
47 das Absperrgitter (der Schied)
- *queen-excluder*
48 das Flugloch
- *entrance*
49 das Flugbrettchen
- *flight board (alighting board)*
50 das Fenster
- *window*
51 veralteter Bienenstand *m*
- *old-fashioned bee shed*
52 der Bienenkorb (Stülpkorb,
Stülper), eine Beute
- *straw hive (skep), a hive*
53 der Bienenschwarm
- *swarm (swarm cluster) of bees*
54 das Schwarmnetz
- *swarming net (bag net)*
55 der Brandhaken
- *hooked pole*

56 das Bienenhaus (Apiarium)
- *apiary (bee house)*
57 der Imker (Bienenzüchter)
- *beekeeper (apiarist,* Am. *beeman)*
58 der Bienenschleier
- *bee veil*
59 die Imkerpfeife
- *bee smoker*
60 die Naturwabe
- *natural honeycomb*
61 die Honigschleuder
- *honey extractor (honey separator)*
62-63 der Schleuderhonig (Honig)
- *strained honey (honey)*
62 der Honigbehälter
- *honey pail*
63 das Honigglas
- *honey jar*
64 der Scheibenhonig
- *honey in the comb*
65 der Wachsstock
- *wax taper*
66 die Wachskerze
- *wax candle*
67 das Bienenwachs
- *beeswax*
68 die Bienengiftsalbe
- *bee sting ointment*

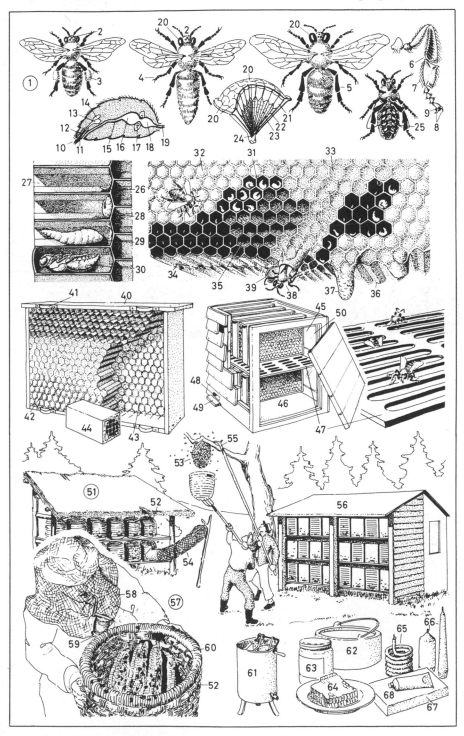

1-21 das Weinbergsgelände
(Weinbaugelände)
- *vineyard area*
1 der Weinberg (Wingert, Weingarten)
in Drahtrahmenspaliererziehung *f*
- *vineyard using wire trellises for
training vines*
2-9 der Rebstock (Weinstock, die
Weinrebe, Rebe)
- *vine (Am. grapevine)*
2 die Weinranke
- *vine shoot*
3 der Langtrieb (Schoß, die Lotte)
- *long shoot*
4 das Weinrebenblatt (Rebenblatt)
- *vine leaf*
5 die Weintraube (Traube) mit den
Weinbeeren *f*
- *bunch of grapes (cluster of grapes)*
6 der Rebenstamm
- *vine stem*
7 der Pfahl (Rebstecken, Stickel,
Weinpfahl)
- *post (stake)*
8 die Drahtrahmenabspannung
- *guy (guy wire)*
9 der Drahtrahmen (das
Drahtrahmengerüst)
- *wire trellis*
10 der Lesebehälter
- *tub for grape gathering*
11 die Weinleserin (Leserin)
- *grape gatherer*

12 die Rebenschere
- *secateurs for pruning vines*
13 der Winzer (Weinbauer)
- *wine grower (viniculturist,
viticulturist)*
14 der Büttenträger
- *dosser carrier*
15 die Bütte (Weinbütte,
Traubenhotte, Tragbütte, die *od.*
das Logel)
- *dosser (pannier)*
16 der Maischetankwagen
- *crushed grape transporter*
17 die Traubenmühle
- *grape crusher*
18 der Trichter
- *hopper*
19 die aufsteckbare Dreiseitenwand
- *three-sided flap extension*
20 das Podest
- *platform*
21 der Weinbergschlepper, ein
Schmalspurschlepper *m*
- *vineyard tractor, a narrow-track
tractor*

1-22 der Weinkeller (Lagerkeller,
Faßkeller, das Faßlager)
- *wine cellar (wine vault)*
1 das Gewölbe
- *vault*
2 das Lagerfaß
- *wine cask*
3 der Weinbehälter, ein
Betonbehälter
- *wine vat, a concrete vat*
4 der Edelstahlbehälter (*auch:*
Kunststofftank)
- *stainless steel vat (also: vat made of
synthetic material)*
5 das Propeller-Schnellrührgerät
- *propeller-type high-speed mixer*
6 der Propellerrührer
- *propeller mixer*
7 die Kreiselpumpe
- *centrifugal pump*
8 der (das) Edelstahl-Schichtfilter
- *stainless steel sediment filter*
9 der halbautomatische Rundfüller
- *semi-automatic circular bottling
machine*
10 die halbautomatische
Naturkorken-Verschließmaschine
- *semi-automatic corking machine*
11 das Flaschenlager
(Flaschengestell)
- *bottle rack*
12 der Kellereigehilfe
- *cellarer's assistant*

13 der Flaschenkorb
- *bottle basket*
14 die Weinflasche
- *wine bottle*
15 die Weinstütze
- *wine jug*
16 die Weinprobe
- *wine tasting*
17 der Weinküfermeister
- *head cellarman*
18 der Weinküfer
- *cellarman*
19 das Weinglas
- *wineglass*
20 das Schnelluntersuchungsgerät
- *inspection apparatus
[for spot-checking samples]*
21 die Horizontaltraubenpresse
- *horizontal wine press*
22 das Sprühgerät
- *humidifier*

1-19 Obstschädlinge *m*
- *fruit pests*
1 der Schwammspinner (Großkopf)
- *gipsy (gypsy) moth*
2 die Eiablage (der Schwamm)
- *batch (cluster) of eggs*
3 die Raupe
- *caterpillar*
4 die Puppe
- *chrysalis (pupa)*
5 die Apfelgespinstmotte, eine Gespinstmotte
- *small ermine moth, an ermine moth*
6 die Larve
- *larva (grub)*
7 das Gespinstnetz (Raupennest)
- *tent*
8 die Raupe beim Skelettierfraß *m*
- *caterpillar skeletonizing a leaf*
9 der Fruchtschalenwickler (Apfelschalenwickler)
- *fruit surface eating tortrix moth (summer fruit tortrix moth)*
10 der Apfelblütenstecher (Apfelstecher, Blütenstecher, Brenner), ein Rüsselkäfer *m*
- *appleblossom weevil, a weevil*
11 die angestochene vertrocknete Blüte
- *punctured, withered flower (blossom)*
12 das Stichloch
- *hole for laying eggs*
13 der Ringelspinner
- *lackey moth*
14 die Raupe
- *caterpillar*
15 die Eier *n*
- *eggs*
16 der Kleine Frostspanner (Frostnachtspanner, Waldfrostspanner, Frostschmetterling), ein Spanner *m*
- *winter moth, a geometrid*
17 die Raupe
- *caterpillar, an inchworm, measuring worm, looper*
18 die Kirschfliege (Kirschfruchtfliege), eine Bohrfliege
- *cherry fruit fly, a borer*
19 die Larve (Made)
- *larva (grub, maggot)*
20-27 Rebenschädlinge *m*
- *vine pests*
20 der Falsche Mehltau, ein Mehltaupilz *m*, eine Blattfallkrankheit
- *downy mildew, a mildew, a disease causing leaf drop*
21 die Lederbeere
- *grape affected with downy mildew*
22 der Traubenwickler
- *grape-berry moth*
23 der Heuwurm, die Raupe der ersten Generation
- *first-generation larva of the grape-berry moth (Am. grape worm)*
24 der Sauerwurm, die Raupe der zweiten Generation
- *second-generation larva of the grape-berry moth (Am. grape worm)*
25 die Puppe
- *chrysalis (pupa)*

26 die Wurzellaus, eine Reblaus
- *root louse, a grape phylloxera*
27 die gallenartige Wurzelanschwellung (Wurzelgalle, Nodosität, Tuberosität)
- *root gall (knotty swelling of the root, nodosity, tuberosity)*
28 der Goldafter
- *brown-tail moth*
29 die Raupe
- *caterpillar*
30 das Gelege
- *batch (cluster) of eggs*
31 das Überwinterungsnest
- *hibernation cocoon*
32 die Blutlaus, eine Blattlaus
- *woolly apple aphid (American blight), an aphid*
33 der Blutlauskrebs, eine Wucherung
- *gall caused by the woolly apple aphid*
34 die Blutlauskolonie
- *woolly apple aphid colony*
35 die San-José-Schildlaus, eine Schildlaus
- *San-José scale, a scale insect (scale louse)*
36 die Larven *f* [männl. länglich, weibl. rund]
- *larvae (grubs)* [male *elongated,* female *round*]
37-55 Ackerschädlinge *m* (Feldschädlinge)
- *field pests*
37 der Saatschnellkäfer, ein Schnellkäfer *m*
- *click beetle, a snapping beetle* (Am. *snapping bug*)
38 der Drahtwurm, die Larve des Saatschnellkäfers *m*
- *wireworm, larva of the click beetle*
39 der Erdfloh
- *flea beetle*
40 die Hessenfliege (Hessenmücke), eine Gallmücke
- *Hessian fly, a gall midge (gall gnat)*
41 die Larve
- *larva (grub)*
42 die Wintersaateule, eine Erdeule
- *turnip moth, an earth moth*
43 die Puppe
- *chrysalis (pupa)*
44 die Erdraupe, eine Raupe
- *cutworm, a caterpillar*
45 der Rübenaaskäfer
- *beet carrion beetle*
46 die Larve
- *larva (grub)*
47 der Große Kohlweißling
- *large cabbage white butterfly*
48 die Raupe des Kleinen Kohlweißlings *m*
- *caterpillar of the small cabbage white butterfly*
49 der Derbrüßler, ein Rüsselkäfer *m*
- *brown leaf-eating weevil, a weevil*
50 die Fraßstelle
- *feeding site*
51 das Rübenälchen, eine Nematode (ein Fadenwurm *m*)
- *sugar beet eelworm, a nematode (a threadworm, hairworm)*
52 der Kartoffelkäfer (Koloradokäfer)
- *Colorado beetle (potato beetle)*
53 die ausgewachsene Larve
- *mature larva (grub)*

54 die Junglarve
- *young larva (grub)*
55 die Eier *n*
- *eggs*

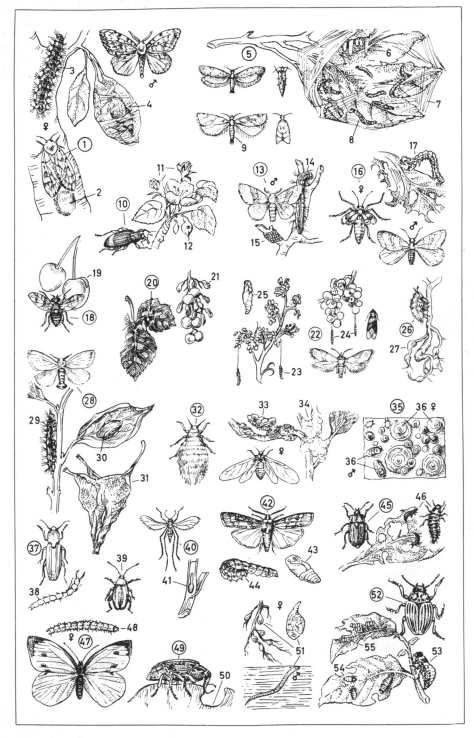

81 Hausungeziefer, Vorratsschädlinge und Schmarotzer

1-14 Hausungeziefer *n*
- *house insects*
1 die Kleine Stubenfliege
- *lesser housefly*
2 die Gemeine Stubenfliege (Große Stubenfliege)
- *common housefly*
3 die Puppe (Tönnchenpuppe)
- *chrysalis (pupa, coarctate pupa)*
4 die Stechfliege (der Wadenstecher)
- *stable fly (biting housefly)*
5 der dreigliedrige Fühler
- *trichotomous antenna*
6 die Kellerassel (Assel), ein Ringelkrebs *m*
- *wood louse (slater, Am. sow bug)*
7 das Heimchen (die Hausgrille), eine Grabheuschrecke
- *house cricket*
8 der Flügel mit Schrillader *f* (Schrillapparat *m*)
- *wing with stridulating apparatus (stridulating mechanism)*
9 die Hausspinne (Winkelspinne)
- *house spider*
10 das Wohnnetz
- *spider's web*
11 der Ohrenkriecher (Ohrenkneifer, Ohrenhöhler, Ohrwurm, Öhrling)
- *earwig*
12 die Hinterleibszange (Raife *pl*, Cerci)
- *caudal pincers*
13 die Kleidermotte, eine Motte
- *clothes moth, a moth*
14 das Silberfischchen (der Zuckergast), ein Borstenschwanz *m*
- *silverfish (Am. slicker), a bristletail*
15-30 Vorratsschädlinge *m*
- *food pests (pests to stores)*
15 die Käsefliege (Fettfliege)
- *cheesefly*
16 der Kornkäfer (Kornkrebs, Kornwurm)
- *grain weevil (granary weevil)*
17 die Hausschabe (Deutsche Schabe, der Schwabe, Franzose, Russe, Kakerlak)
- *cockroach (black beetle)*
18 der Mehlkäfer (Mehlwurm)
- *meal beetle (meal worm beetle, flour beetle)*
19 der Vierfleckige Bohnenkäfer
- *spotted bruchus*
20 die Larve
- *larva (grub)*
21 die Puppe
- *chrysalis (pupa)*
22 der Dornspeckkäfer
- *leather beetle (hide beetle)*
23 der Brotkäfer
- *yellow meal beetle*
24 die Puppe
- *chrysalis (pupa)*
25 der Tabakkäfer
- *cigarette beetle (tobacco beetle)*
26 der Maiskäfer
- *maize billbug (corn weevil)*
27 der Leistenkopfplattkäfer, ein Getreideschädling *m*
- *one of the Cryptolestes, a grain pest*
28 die Dörrobstmotte
- *Indian meal moth*
29 die Getreidemotte
- *Angoumois grain moth (Angoumois moth)*
30 die Getreidemottenraupe im Korn *n*
- *Angoumois grain moth caterpillar inside a grain kernel*
31-42 Schmarotzer *m* des Menschen *m*
- *parasites of man*
31 der Spulwurm
- *round worm (maw worm)*
32 das Weibchen
- *female*
33 der Kopf
- *head*
34 das Männchen
- *male*
35 der Bandwurm, ein Plattwurm *m*
- *tapeworm, a flatworm*
36 der Kopf, ein Haftorgan *n*
- *head, a suctorial organ*
37 der Saugnapf
- *sucker*
38 der Hakenkranz
- *crown of hooks*
39 die Wanze (Bettwanze, Wandlaus)
- *bug (bed bug, Am. chinch)*
40 die Filzlaus (Schamlaus, eine Menschenlaus)
- *crab louse (a human louse)*
41 die Kleiderlaus (eine Menschenlaus)
- *clothes louse (body louse, a human louse)*
42 der Floh (Menschenfloh)
- *flea (human flea, common flea)*
43 die Tsetsefliege
- *tsetse fly*
44 die Malariamücke (Fiebermücke, Gabelmücke)
- *malaria mosquito*

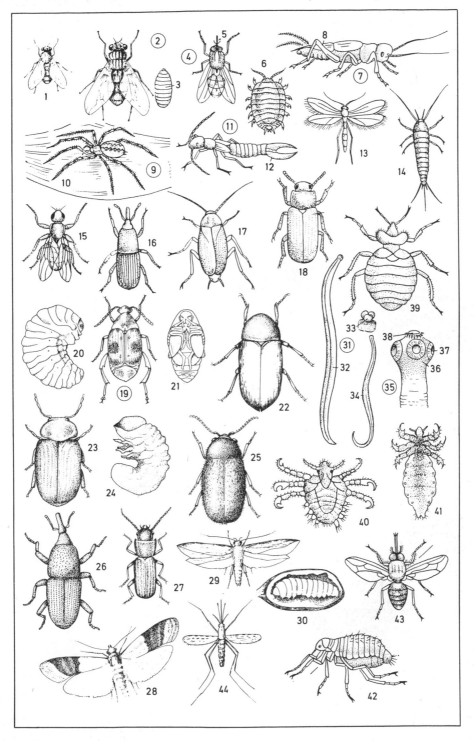

1 der Maikäfer, ein Blatthornkäfer *m*
- *cockchafer (May bug), a lamellicorn*
2 der Kopf
- *head*
3 der Fühler
- *antenna (feeler)*
4 der Halsschild
- *thoracic shield (prothorax)*
5 das Schildchen
- *scutellum*
6-8 die Gliedmaßen *f* (Extremitäten)
- *legs*
6 das Vorderbein
- *front leg*
7 das Mittelbein
- *middle leg*
8 das Hinterbein
- *back leg*
9 der Hinterleib
- *abdomen*
10 die Flügeldecke (der Deckflügel)
- *elytron (wing case)*
11 der Hautflügel (häutige Flügel)
- *membranous wing*
12 der Engerling, eine Larve
- *cockchafer grub, a larva*
13 die Puppe
- *chrysalis (pupa)*
14 der Prozessionsspinner, ein
Nachtschmetterling *m*
- *processionary moth, a nocturnal
moth (night-flying moth)*
15 der Schmetterling
- *moth*
16 die gesellig wandernden Raupen *f*
- *caterpillars in procession*
17 die Nonne (der Fichtenspinner)
- *nun moth (black arches moth)*
18 der Schmetterling
- *moth*
19 die Eier *n*
- *eggs*
20 die Raupe
- *caterpillar*
21 die Puppe
- *chrysalis (pupa) in its cocoon*
22 der Buchdrucker, ein Borkenkäfer *m*
- *typographer beetle, a bark beetle*
23-24 das Fraßbild [Fraßgänge *m*
unter der Rinde]
- *galleries under the bark*
23 der Muttergang
- *egg gallery*
24 der Larvengang
- *gallery made by larva*
25 die Larve
- *larva (grub)*
26 der Käfer
- *beetle*
27 der Kiefernschwärmer
(Fichtenschwärmer, Tannenpfeil),
ein Schwärmer *m*
- *pine hawkmoth, a hawkmoth*
28 der Kiefernspanner, ein Spanner *m*
- *pine moth, a geometrid*
29 der männliche Schmetterling
- *male moth*
30 der weibliche Schmetterling
- *female moth*
31 die Raupe
- *caterpillar*
32 die Puppe
- *chrysalis (pupa)*
33 die Eichengallwespe, eine
Gallwespe
- *oak-gall wasp, a gall wasp*

34 der Gallapfel, eine Galle
- *oak gall (oak apple), a gall*
35 die Wespe
- *wasp*
36 die Larve in der Larvenkammer
- *larva (grub) in its chamber*
37 die Zwiebelgalle an der Buche
- *beech gall*
38 die Fichtengallenlaus
- *spruce-gall aphid*
39 der Wanderer (die Wanderform)
- *winged aphid*
40 die Ananasgalle
- *pineapple gall*
41 der Fichtenrüßler
- *pine weevil*
42 der Käfer
- *beetle (weevil)*
43 der Eichenwickler, ein Wickler *m*
- *green oak roller moth (green oak
tortrix), a leaf roller*
44 die Raupe
- *caterpillar*
45 der Schmetterling
- *moth*
46 die Kieferneule (Forleule)
- *pine beauty*
47 die Raupe
- *caterpillar*
48 der Schmetterling
- *moth*

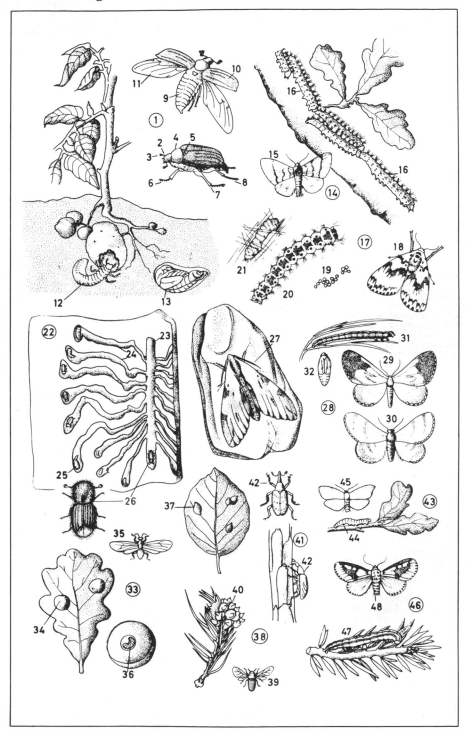

1 die Flächenspritzung
- *area spraying*
2 das Aufbauspritzgerät
- *tractor-mounted sprayer*
3 der Breitspritzrahmen
- *spray boom*
4 die Flachstrahldüse
- *fan nozzle*
5 der Spritzbrühebehälter
- *spray fluid tank*
6 der Schaumstoffbehälter für die Schaummarkierung
- *foam canister for blob marking*
7 die federnde Aufhängung
- *spring suspension*
8 der Sprühnebel
- *spray*
9 der Schaummarkierer
- *blob marker*
10 die Schaumzufuhrleitung
- *foam feed pipe*
11 die Vakuumbegasungsanlage einer Tabakfabrik
- *vacuum fumigator (vacuum fumigation plant) of a tobacco factory*
12 die Vakuumkammer
- *vacuum chamber*
13 die Rohtabakballen *m*
- *bales of raw tobacco*
14 das Gasrohr
- *gas pipe*
15 die fahrbare Begasungskammer zur Blausäurebegasung von Baumschulsetzlingen *m*, Setzreben *f*, Saatgut und leeren Säcken *m*
- *mobile fumigation chamber for fumigating nursery saplings, vine layers, seeds and empty sacks with hydrocyanic (prussic) acid*
16 die Kreislaufanlage
- *gas circulation unit*
17 das Hordenblech
- *tray*
18 die Spritzpistole
- *spray gun*
19 der Drehgriff für die Strahlverstellung
- *twist grip (control grip, handle) for regulating the jet*
20 der Schutzbügel
- *finger guard*
21 der Bedienungshebel
- *control lever (operating lever)*
22 das Strahlrohr
- *spray tube*
23 die Rundstrahldüse
- *cone nozzle*
24 die Handspritze
- *hand spray*
25 der Kunststoffbehälter
- *plastic container*
26 die Handpumpe
- *hand pump*
27 das Pendelspritzgestänge für den Hopfenanbau in Schräglagen *f*
- *pendulum spray for hop growing on slopes*
28 die Pistolenkopfdüse
- *pistol-type nozzle*
29 das Spritzrohr
- *spraying tube*
30 der Schlauchanschluß
- *hose connection*
31 die Giftlegeröhre zum Auslegen *n* von Giftweizen *m*
- *tube for laying poisoned bait*

32 die Fliegenklappe (Fliegenklatsche)
- *fly swat*
33 die Reblauslanze (der Schwefelkohlenstoffinjektor)
- *soil injector (carbon disulphide, Am. carbon disulfide, injector) for killing the vine root louse*
34 der Fußtritt
- *foot lever (foot pedal, foot treadle)*
35 das Gasrohr
- *gas tube*
36 die Mausefalle
- *mousetrap*
37 die Wühlmaus- und Maulwurfsfalle
- *vole and mole trap*
38 die fahrbare Obstbaumspritze, eine Karrenspritze
- *mobile orchard sprayer, a wheelbarrow sprayer (carriage sprayer)*
39 der Spritzmittelbehälter
- *spray tank*
40 der Schraubdeckel
- *screw-on cover*
41 das Pumpenaggregat mit Benzinmotor *m*
- *direct-connected motor-driven pump with petrol motor*
42 das Manometer
- *pressure gauge (Am. gage) (manometer)*
43 die Kolbenrückenspritze
- *plunger-type knapsack sprayer*
44 der Spritzbehälter mit Windkessel *m*
- *spray canister with pressure chamber*
45 der Kolbenpumpenschwengel
- *piston pump lever*
46 das Handspritzrohr mit Düse *f*
- *hand lance with nozzle*
47 das aufgesattelte Sprühgerät
- *semi-mounted sprayer*
48 der Weinbergschlepper
- *vineyard tractor*
49 das Gebläse
- *fan*
50 der Brühebehälter
- *spray fluid tank*
51 die Weinrebenzeile
- *row of vines*
52 der Beizautomat für die Trockenbeizung von Saatgut *n*
- *dressing machine (seed-dressing machine) for dry-seed dressing (seed dusting)*
53 das Entstaubungsgebläse mit Elektromotor *m*
- *dedusting fan (dust removal fan) with electric motor*
54 der (das) Schlauchfilter
- *bag filter*
55 der Absackstutzen
- *bagging nozzle*
56 der Entstaubungsschirm
- *dedusting screen (dust removal screen)*
57 der Sprühwasserbehälter
- *water canister [containing water for spraying]*
58 die Sprüheinrichtung
- *spray unit*
59 das Förderaggregat mit Mischschnecke *f*
- *conveyor unit with mixing screw*

60 der Beizpulverbehälter mit Dosiereinrichtung *f*
- *container for disinfectant powder with dosing mechanism*
61 die Fahrrolle
- *castor*
62 die Mischkammer
- *mixing chamber*

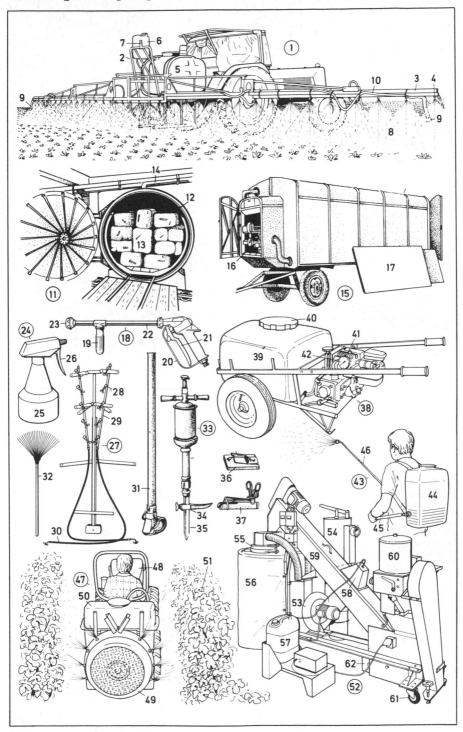

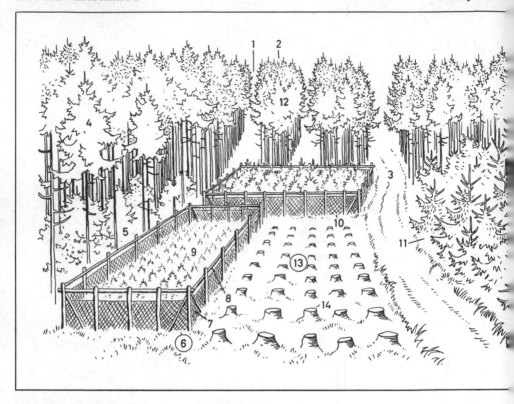

1-34 **der Forst** (das Holz), ein Wald *m*
- *forest, a wood*
1 die Schneise (das Gestell)
- *ride (aisle, lane, section line)*
2 das Jagen (die Abteilung)
- *compartment (section)*
3 der Holzabfuhrweg, ein Waldweg *m*
- *wood haulage way, a forest track*
4-14 **die Kahlschlagwirtschaft**
- *clear-felling system*
4 der Altbestand (das Altholz,
   Baumholz)
- *standing timber*
5 das Unterholz (der Unterstand)
- *underwood (underbrush,
   undergrowth, brushwood,* Am.
   brush)
6 der Saatkamp, ein Kamp *m*
   (Pflanzgarten, Forstgarten,
   Baumschule *f*); *andere Art:* der
   Pflanzkamp
- *seedling nursery, a tree nursery*
7 das Wildgatter (Gatter), ein
   Maschendrahtzaun *m*
   (Kulturzaun)
- *deer fence (fence), a wire netting
   fence (protective fence for
   seedlings);* sim.: *rabbit fence*
8 die Sprunglatte
- *guard rail*
9 die Kultur (Saat)
- *seedlings*
10-11 der Jungbestand
- *young trees*

10 die Schonung (die Kultur nach
   beendeter Nachbesserung *f*,
   Nachpflanzung)
- *tree nursery after transplanting*
11 die Dickung
- *young plantation*
12 das Stangenholz (die Dickung nach
   der Astreinigung)
- *young plantation after brashing*
13 der Kahlschlag (die Schlagfläche,
   Blöße)
- *clearing*
14 der Wurzelstock (Stock, Stubben,
   ugs. Baumstumpf)
- *tree stump (stump, stub)*

15-37 der Holzeinschlag
(Hauungsbetrieb)
- **wood cutting** (timber cutting, tree felling, Am. lumbering)
15 das gerückte (gepolterte) Langholz
- timber skidded to the stack (stacked timber, Am. yarded timber)
16 die Schichtholzbank, ein Raummeter n Holz, der Holzstoß
- stack of logs, one cubic metre (Am. meter) of wood
17 der Pfahl
- post (stake)
18 der Waldarbeiter (Forstwirt) beim Wenden n
- forest labourer (woodsman, Am. logger, lumberer, lumberjack, lumberman, timberjack) turning (Am. canting) timber
19 der Stamm (Baumstamm, das Langholz)
- bole (tree trunk, trunk, stem)
20 der Haumeister beim Numerieren n
- feller numbering the logs
21 die Stahlmeßkluppe
- steel tree calliper (caliper)
22 die Motorsäge (beim Trennen n eines Stammes m)
- power saw (motor saw) cutting a bole
23 der Schutzhelm mit Augenschutz m und Gehörschutzkapseln f
- safety helmet with visor and ear pieces

24 die Jahresringe m
- annual rings
25 der hydraulische Fällheber
- hydraulic felling wedge
26 die Schutzkleidung [orangefarbene Bluse f, grüne Hose f]
- protective clothing [orange top, green trousers]
27 das Fällen mit Motorsäge f
- felling with a power saw (motor saw)
28 die ausgeschnittene Fallkerbe
- undercut (notch, throat, gullet, mouth, sink, kerf, birdsmouth)
29 der Fällschnitt
- back cut
30 die Tasche mit Fällkeil m
- sheath holding felling wedge
31 der Abschnitt
- log
32 das Freischneidegerät zur Beseitigung von Unterholz n und Unkraut n
- free-cutting saw for removing underwood and weeds
33 der Anbausatz mit Kreissäge f (oder Schlagmesser n)
- circular saw (or activated blade) attachment
34 die Motoreinheit
- power unit (motor)
35 das Gebinde mit Sägekettenhaftöl n
- canister of viscous oil for the saw chain

36 der Benzinkanister
- petrol canister (Am. gasoline canister)
37 das Fällen von Schwachholz n (Durchforsten n)
- felling of small timber (of small-sized thinnings) (thinning)

1 die Axt
- *axe (Am. ax)*
2 die Schneide
- *edge (cutting edge)*
3 der Stiel
- *handle (helve)*
4 der Scheitkeil mit Einsatzholz *n* und Ring *m*
- *felling wedge (falling wedge) with wood insert and ring*
5 der Spalthammer
- *riving hammer (cleaving hammer, splitting hammer)*
6 die Sapine (der Sappie, Sappel)
- *lifting hook*
7 der Wendehaken
- *cant hook*
8 das Schäleisen
- *barking iron (bark spud)*
9 der Fällheber mit Wendehaken *m*
- *peavy*
10 der Kluppmeßstock mit Reißer *m*
- *slide calliper (caliper) (calliper square)*
11 die Heppe (das *od.* der Gertel), ein Haumesser *n*
- *billhook, a knife for lopping*
12 der Revolvernumerierschlägel
- *revolving die hammer (marking hammer, marking iron, Am. marker)*
13 die Motorsäge
- *power saw (motor saw)*
14 die Sägekette
- *saw chain*
15 die Sicherheitskettenbremse mit Handschutz *m*
- *safety brake for the saw chain, with finger guard*
16 die Sägeschiene
- *saw guide*
17 die Gashebelsperre
- *accelerator lock*
18 die Entästungsmaschine
- *snedding machine (trimming machine, Am. knotting machine, limbing machine)*
19 die Vorschubwalzen *f*
- *feed rolls*
20 das Gelenkmesser
- *flexible blade*
21 der Hydraulikarm
- *hydraulic arm*
22 der Spitzenabschneider
- *trimming blade*
23 die Stammholzentrindung
- *debarking (barking, bark stripping) of boles*
24 die Vorschubwalze
- *feed roller*
25 der Lochrotor
- *cylinder trimmer*
26 das Rotormesser
- *rotary cutter*
27 der Waldschlepper (zum Transport *m* von Schicht- und Schwachholz *n* innerhalb des Waldes *n*)
- *short-haul skidder*
28 der Ladekran
- *loading crane*
29 der Holzgreifer
- *log grips*
30 die Laderunge
- *post*
31 die Knicklenkung
- *Ackermann steering system*

32 das Rundholzpolter
- *log dump*
33 die Numerierung
- *number (identification number)*
34 der Stammholzschlepper (Skidder)
- *skidder*
35 der Frontschild
- *front blade (front plate)*
36 das überschlagfeste Sicherheitsverdeck
- *crush-proof safety bonnet (Am. safety hood)*
37 die Knicklenkung
- *Ackermann steering system*
38 die Seilwinde
- *cable winch*
39 die Seilführungsrolle
- *cable drum*
40 der Heckschild
- *rear blade (rear plate)*
41 das freihängende Stammholz
- *boles with butt ends held off the ground*
42 der Straßentransport von Langholz *n*
- *haulage of timber by road*
43 der Zugwagen
- *tractor (tractor unit)*
44 der Ladekran
- *loading crane*
45 die hydraulische Ladestütze
- *hydraulic jack*
46 die Seilwinde
- *cable winch*
47 die Runge
- *post*
48 der Drehschemel
- *bolster plate*
49 der Nachläufer
- *rear bed (rear bunk)*

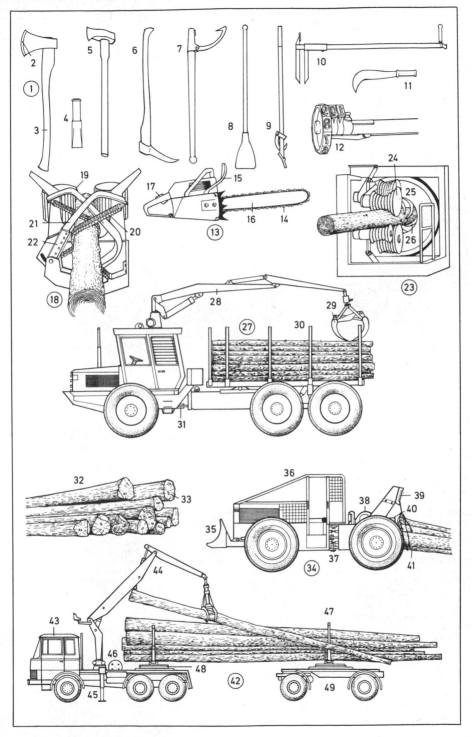

1-52 Jagden *f* (Jagdarten, die Jägerei, das Jagen, Weidwerk*)

1-52 Jagden *f* (Jagdarten, die Jägerei, das Jagen, Weidwerk*)
- *kinds of hunting*
1-8 die Suchjagd (der Pirschgang, das Pirschen im Jagdrevier *n*, Revier)
- *stalking (deer stalking, Am. stillhunting) in the game preserve*
1 der Jäger (Weidmann*, Schütze)
- *huntsman (hunter)*
2 der Jagdanzug
- *hunting clothes*
3 der Rucksack (Weidsack*)
- *knapsack*
4 die Pirschbüchse
- *sporting gun (sporting rifle, hunting rifle)*
5 der Jagdhut (Jägerhut)
- *huntsman's hat*
6 das Jagdglas, ein Fernglas
- *field glasses, binoculars*
7 der Jagdhund
- *gun dog*
8 die Fährte (Spur, das Trittsiegel)
- *track (trail, hoofprints)*
9-12 die Brunftjagd und die Balzjagd
- *hunting in the rutting season and the pairing season*
9 der Jagdschirm (Schirm)
- *hunting screen (screen, Am. blind)*

10 der Jagdstuhl (Ansitzstuhl, Jagdsitz, Jagdstock, Sitzstock)
- *shooting stick (shooting seat, seat stick)*
11 der balzende Birkhahn
- *blackcock, displaying*
12 der Brunfthirsch (brünstige, röhrende Hirsch)
- *rutting stag*
13 das Rottier bei der Äsung
- *hind, grazing*
14-17 der Anstand (Ansitz)
- *hunting from a raised hide (raised stand)*
14 der Hochsitz (Hochstand, die Jagdkanzel, Kanzel, Wildkanzel)
- *raised hide (raised stand, high seat)*
15 das Rudel in Schußweite *f*
- *herd within range*
16 der Wechsel (Wildwechsel)
- *game path (Am. runway)*
17 der Rehbock, durch Blattschuß *m* getroffen und durch Fangschuß *m* getötet
- *roebuck, hit in the shoulder and killed by a finishing shot*
18 der Jagdwagen
- *phaeton*
19-27 Fangjagden *f*
- *types of trapping*
19 der Raubwildfang
- *trapping of small predators*
20 die Kastenfalle (Raubwildfalle)
- *box trap (trap for small predators)*

21 der Köder (Anbiß)
- *bait*
22 der Marder, ein Raubwild *n*
- *marten, a small predator*
23 das Frettieren (die Erdjagd auf Kaninchen *n*)
- *ferreting (hunting rabbits out of their warrens)*
24 das Frettchen (Frett, Kaninchenwiesel)
- *ferret*
25 der Frettchenführer
- *ferreter*
26 der Bau (Kaninchenbau, die Kaninchenhöhle)
- *burrow (rabbit burrow, rabbit hole)*
27 die Haube (Kaninchenhaube, das Netz) über dem Röhrenausgang *m*
- *net (rabbit net) over the burrow opening*

* In der Jägersprache auch Waidwerk, Waidmann, Waidsack

28 die Wildfutterstelle
(Winterfutterstelle)
– *feeding place for game (winter feeding place)*
29 der Wilderer (Raubschütz, Wildfrevler, Jagdfrevler, Wilddieb)
– *poacher*
30 der Stutzen, ein kurzes Gewehr *n*
– *carbine, a short rifle*
31 die Sauhatz (Wildschweinjagd)
– *boar hunt*
32 die Wildsau (Sau, das Wildschwein)
– *wild sow (sow, wild boar)*
33 der Saupacker (Saurüde, Rüde, Hatzrüde, Hetzhund; *mehrere:* die Meute, Hundemeute)
– *boarhound (hound, hunting dog; collectively: pack, pack of hounds)*
34-39 **die Treibjagd** (Kesseljagd, Hasenjagd, das Kesseltreiben)
– **beating** *(driving, hare hunting)*
34 der Anschlag
– *aiming position*
35 der Hase (Krumme, Lampe), ein Haarwild *n*
– *hare, furred game (ground game)*
36 der Apport (das Apportieren)
– *retrieving*
37 der Treiber
– *beater*
38 die Strecke (Jagdbeute)
– *bag (kill)*
39 der Wildwagen
– *cart for carrying game*

40 die Wasserjagd (Entenjagd)
– *waterfowling (wildfowling, duck shooting,* Am. *duck hunting)*
41 der Wildentenzug, das Federwild
– *flight of wild ducks, winged game*
42-46 **die Falkenbeize** (Beizjagd, Beize, Falkenjagd, Falknerei)
– **falconry** *(hawking)*
42 der Falkner (Falkenier, Falkenjäger)
– *falconer*
43 das Zieget, ein Fleischstück *n*
– *reward, a piece of meat*
44 die Falkenhaube (Falkenkappe)
– *falcon's hood*
45 die Fessel
– *jess*
46 der Falke, ein Beizvogel, ein Falkenmännchen *n* (Terzel *m*) beim Schlagen *n* eines Reihers *m*
– *falcon, a hawk, a male hawk (tiercel) swooping (stooping) on a heron*
47-52 **die Hüttenjagd**
– **shooting from a butt**
47 der Einfallbaum
– *tree to which birds are lured*
48 der Uhu (Auf), ein Reizvogel *m* (Lockvogel)
– *eagle owl, a decoy bird (decoy)*
49 die Krücke (Jule)
– *perch*
50 der angelockte Vogel, eine Krähe
– *decoyed bird, a crow*

51 die Krähenhütte (Uhuhütte), eine Hütte (Schießhütte, Ansitzhütte)
– *butt for shooting crows or eagle owls*
52 die Schießluke
– *gun slit*

165

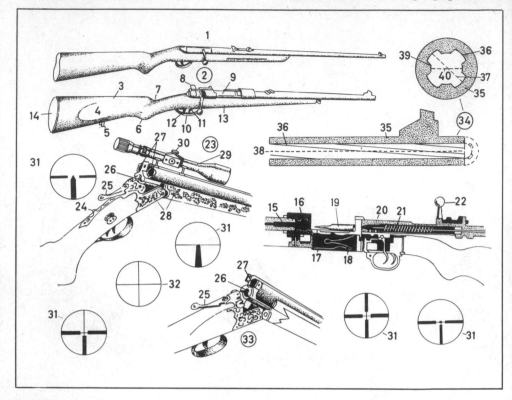

1-40 Sportwaffen *f* (Jagdgewehre *n*)
- *sporting guns* (*sporting rifles, hunting rifles*)

1 der Einzellader
- *single-loader* (*single-loading rifle*)

2 die Repetierbüchse, eine Handfeuerwaffe (Schußwaffe), ein Mehrlader *m* (Magazingewehr *n*)
- *repeating rifle, a small-arm (fire-arm), a repeater* (*magazine rifle, magazine repeater*)

3, 4, 6, 13 die Schäftung
- *stock*

3 der Kolben
- *butt*

4 die Backe [an der linken Seite]
- *cheek* [*on the left side*]

5 der Riemenbügel
- *sling ring*

6 der Pistolengriff
- *pistol grip*

7 der Kolbenhals
- *small of the butt*

8 der Sicherungsflügel
- *safety catch*

9 das Schloß (Gewehrschloß)
- *lock*

10 der Abzugbügel
- *trigger guard*

11 der Druckpunktabzug
- *second set trigger* (*firing trigger*)

12 der Stecher
- *hair trigger* (*set trigger*)

13 der Vorderschaft
- *foregrip*

14 der Rückschlaghinderer (die Gummikolbenkappe)
- *butt plate*

15 das Patronenlager
- *cartridge chamber*

16 der Hülsenkopf
- *receiver*

17 das Patronenmagazin
- *magazine*

18 die Zubringerfeder
- *magazine spring*

19 die Munition
- *ammunition* (*cartridge*)

20 die Kammer
- *chamber*

21 der Schlagbolzen
- *firing pin* (*striker*)

22 der Kammerstengel
- *bolt handle* (*bolt lever*)

23 der Drilling, ein kombiniertes Gewehr *n*, ein Selbstspanner *m*
- *triple-barrelled* (*triple-barreled*) *rifle, a self-cocking gun*

24 der Umschaltschieber (*bei verschiedenen Waffen:* die Sicherung)
- *reversing catch* (*in various guns: safety catch*)

25 der Verschlußhebel
- *sliding safety catch*

26 der Büchsenlauf
- *rifle barrel* (*rifled barrel*)

27 der Schrotlauf
- *smooth-bore barrel*

28 die Jagdgravur
- *chasing*

29 das Zielfernrohr
- *telescopic sight* (*riflescope, telescope sight*)

30 Schrauben *f* für die Absehenverstellung
- *graticule adjuster screws*

31-32 das Absehen (Zielfernrohrabsehen)
- *graticule* (*sight graticule*)

31 versch. Absehensysteme *n*
- *various graticule systems*

32 das Fadenkreuz
- *cross wires* (Am. *cross hairs*)

33 die Bockflinte
- *over-and-under shotgun*

34 der gezogene Gewehrlauf
- *rifled gun barrel*

35 die Laufwandung
- *barrel casing*

36 der Zug
- *rifling*

37 das Zugkaliber
- *rifling calibre* (Am. *caliber*)

38 die Seelenachse
- *bore axis*

39 das Feld
- *land*

40 das Bohrungs- oder Felderkaliber (Kaliber)
- *calibre* (*bore diameter*, Am. *caliber*)

41-48 Jagdgeräte *n*
- *hunting equipment*
41 der Hirschfänger
- *double-edged hunting knife*
42 der Genickfänger (das Weidmesser, Jagdmesser)
- *[single-edged] hunting knife*
43-47 Lockgeräte *n* **zur Lockjagd**
- *calls for luring game (for calling game)*
43 der Fiepblatter (Rehblatter, die Rehfiepe)
- *roe call*
44 die Hasenklage (Hasenquäke)
- *hare call*
45 die Wachtellocke
- *quail call*
46 der Hirschruf
- *stag call*
47 die Rebhuhnlocke
- *partridge call*
48 der Schwanenhals, eine Bügelfalle
- *bow trap (bow gin), a jaw trap*
49 die Schrotpatrone
- *small-shot cartridge*
50 die Papphülse
- *cardboard case*
51 die Schrotladung
- *small-shot charge*
52 der Filzpfropf
- *felt wad*
53 das rauchlose Pulver (*andere Art:* Schwarzpulver)
- *smokeless powder (different kind: black powder)*
54 die Patrone
- *cartridge*
55 das Vollmantelgeschoß
- *full-jacketed cartridge*
56 der Weichbleikern
- *soft-lead core*
57 die Pulverladung
- *powder charge*
58 der Amboß
- *detonator cap*
59 das Zündhütchen
- *percussion cap*
60 das Jagdhorn
- *hunting horn*
61-64 das Waffenreinigungsgerät
- *rifle cleaning kit*
61 der Putzstock
- *cleaning rod*
62 die Laufreinigungsbürste
- *cleaning brush*
63 das Reinigungswerg
- *cleaning tow*
64 die Reinigungsschnur
- *pull-through* (Am. *pull-thru*)
65 die Visiereinrichtung
- *sights*
66 die Kimme
- *notch (sighting notch)*
67 die Visierklappe
- *back sight leaf*
68 die Visiermarke
- *sight scale division*
69 der Visierschieber
- *back sight slide*
70 die Raste
- *notch [to hold the spring]*
71 das Korn
- *front sight (foresight)*
72 die Kornspitze
- *bead*

73 **Ballistik** *f*
- *ballistics*
74 die Mündungswaagerechte
- *azimuth*
75 der Abgangswinkel
- *angle of departure*
76 der Erhöhungswinkel (Elevationswinkel)
- *angle of elevation*
77 die Scheitelhöhe
- *apex (zenith)*
78 der Fallwinkel
- *angle of descent*
79 die ballist. Kurve
- *ballistic curve*

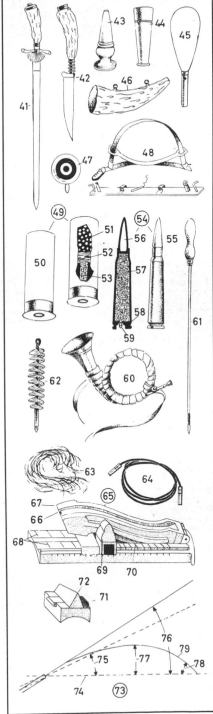

1-27 das Rotwild (Edelwild)
- *red deer*
1 das Tier (Edeltier, Rottier, die Hirschkuh), ein Schmaltier *n* od. ein Geltier *n; mehrere:* Kahlwild *n, das Junge: (weibl.)* Wildkalb *n, (männl.)* Hirschkalb *n*
- *hind (red deer), a young hind or a dam;* collectively: *anterless deer,* (y.): *calf*
2 der Lecker
- *tongue*
3 der Träger (Hals)
- *neck*
4 der Brunfthirsch
- *rutting stag*
5-11 das Geweih
- *antlers*
5 die Rose
- *burr (rose)*
6 die Augensprosse (der Augsproß)
- *brow antler (brow tine, brow point, brow snag)*
7 die Eissprosse (der Eissproß)
- *bez antler (bay antler, bay, bez tine)*
8 die Mittelsprosse (der Mittelsproß)
- *royal antler (royal, tray)*
9 die Krone
- *surroyal antlers (surroyals)*
10 das Ende (die Sprosse)
- *point (tine)*
11 die Stange
- *beam (main trunk)*
12 der Kopf (das Haupt)
- *head*
13 das Geäse (der Äser, das Maul)
- *mouth*
14 die Tränengrube (Tränenhöhle)
- *larmier (tear bag)*
15 das Licht
- *eye*
16 der Lauscher (Loser, Luser)
- *ear*
17 das Blatt
- *shoulder*
18 der Ziemer
- *loin*
19 der Wedel (die Blume)
- *scut (tail)*
20 der Spiegel
- *rump*
21 die Keule
- *leg (haunch)*
22 der Hinterlauf
- *hind leg*
23 das Geäfter (die Afterklaue, Oberklaue, der Heufler, Oberrücken)
- *dew claw*
24 die Schale (Klaue)
- *hoof*
25 der Vorderlauf
- *foreleg*
26 die Flanke
- *flank*
27 der Kragen (Brunftkragen, die Brunftmähne)
- *collar (rutting mane)*
28-39 das Rehwild
- *roe (roe deer)*
28 der Rehbock (Bock)
- *roebuck (buck)*
29-31 das Gehörn (die Krone, bayr.-östr. das Gewichtl)
- *antlers (horns)*

29 die Rose
- *burr (rose)*
30 die Stange mit den Perlen *f*
- *beam with pearls*
31 das Ende
- *point (tine)*
32 der Lauscher
- *ear*
33 das Licht
- *eye*
34 die Ricke (Geiß, Rehgeiß, das Reh), ein Schmalreh *n* (Kitzreh) od. ein Altreh *n* (Geltreh, Altricke *f*, Altgeiß)
- *doe (female roe), a female fawn or a barren doe*
35 der Ziemer (Rehziemer)
- *loin*
36 der Spiegel
- *rump*
37 die Keule
- *leg (haunch)*
38 das Blatt
- *shoulder*
39 das Kitz, *(männl.)* Bockkitz, *(weibl.)* Rehkitz
- *fawn,* (m.) *young buck,* (f.) *young doe*
40-41 das Damwild
- *fallow deer*
40 der Damhirsch (Dambock), ein Schaufler *m, (weibl.)* das Damtier
- *fallow buck, a buck with palmate (palmated) antlers,* (f.) *doe*
41 die Schaufel
- *palm*
42 der Rotfuchs, *(männl.)* Rüde, *(weibl.)* die Fähe (Fähin), *das Junge:* der Welpe
- *red fox,* (m.) *dog,* (f.) *vixen,* (y.) *cub*
43 die Seher *m*
- *eyes*
44 das Gehör
- *ear*
45 der Fang (das Maul)
- *muzzle (mouth)*
46 die Pranten (Branten, Branken)
- *pads (paws)*
47 die Lunte (Standarte, Rute)
- *brush (tail)*
48 der Dachs, *(männl.)* Dachsbär, *(weibl.)* die Dächsin
- *badger,* (f.) *sow*
49 der Pürzel (Bürzel, Schwanz, die Rute)
- *tail*
50 die Prante (Brante, Branke)
- *paws*
51 das Schwarzwild, *(männl.)* der Keiler (das Wildschwein, die Sau) *(weibl.)* die Bache (Sau), *das Junge:* der Frischling
- *wild boar,* (m.) *boar,* (f.) *wild sow (sow),* (y.) *young boar*
52 die Federn *f (der Kamm)*
- *bristles*
53 das Gebrech (Gebräch, der Rüssel)
- *snout*
54 der untere Hauzahn (Hauer), *beide unteren Hauzähne:* das Gewaff, *(bei der Bache)* die Haken, *beide oberen Hauzähne:* die Haderer *f*
- *tusk*
55 das Schild (bes. dicke Haut *f* auf dem Blatt *n*)
- *shield*

56 die Schwarte (Haut)
- *hide*
57 das Geäfter
- *dew claw*
58 der Pürzel (Bürzel, Schmörkel, das Federlein)
- *tail*
59 der Hase (Feldhase), *(männl.)* Rammler, *(weibl.)* Setzhase (die Häsin)
- *hare,* (m.) *buck,* (f.) *doe*
60 der Seher (das Auge)
- *eye*
61 der Löffel
- *ear*
62 die Blume
- *scut (tail)*
63 der Hinterlauf (Sprung)
- *hind leg*
64 der Vorderlauf
- *foreleg*
65 das Kaninchen
- *rabbit*
66 der Birkhahn (Spielhahn, kleine Hahn)
- *blackcock*
67 der Schwanz (das Spiel, der Stoß, die Leier, Schere)
- *tail*
68 die Sichelfedern *f*
- *falcate (falcated) feathers*
69 das Haselhuhn
- *hazel grouse (hazel hen)*
70 das Rebhuhn
- *partridge*
71 das (der) Schild
- *horseshoe (horseshoe marking)*
72 der Auerhahn (Urhahn, große Hahn)
- *wood grouse (capercaillie)*
73 der Federbart (Kehlbart, Bart)
- *beard*
74 der Spiegel
- *axillary marking*
75 der Schwanz (Stoß, Fächer, das Ruder, die Schaufel)
- *tail (fan)*
76 der Fittich (die Schwinge)
- *wing (pinion)*
77 der Edelfasan (Jagdfasan), ein Fasan *m, (männl.)* Fasanenhahn, *(weibl.)* Fasanenhenne
- *common pheasant, a pheasant,* (m.) *cock pheasant (pheasant cock),* (f.) *hen pheasant (pheasant hen)*
78 das Federohr (Horn)
- *plumicorn (feathered ear, ear tuft, ear, horn)*
79 der Fittich (das (der) Schild)
- *wing*
80 der Schwanz (Stoß, das Spiel)
- *tail*
81 das Bein (der Ständer)
- *leg*
82 der Sporn
- *spur*
83 die Schnepfe (Waldschnepfe)
- *snipe*
84 der Stecher (Schnabel)
- *bill (beak)*

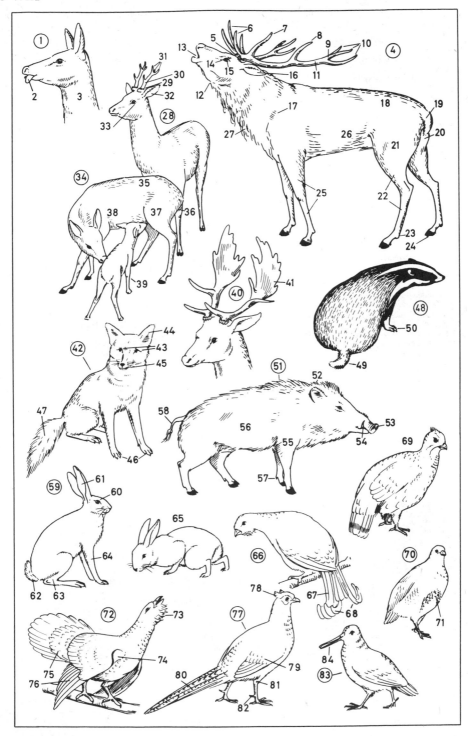

89 Fischzucht und Angelsport

1-19 die Fischzucht
- *fish farming (fish culture, pisciculture)*
1 der Hälter im fließenden Wasser n
- *cage in running water*
2 der Handkescher (Ketscher)
- *hand net (landing net)*
3 das halbovale Fischtransportfaß
- *semi-oval barrel for transporting fish*
4 die Stande
- *vat*
5 der Überlaufrechen
- *trellis in the overflow*
6 der Forellenteich; *ähnl.:* der Karpfenteich, ein Brut-, Vorstreck-, Streck- oder Abwachsteich m
- *trout pond; sim.: carp pond, a fry pond, fattening pond, or cleansing pond*
7 der Wasserzulauf
- *water inlet (water supply pipe)*
8 der Wasserablauf
- *water outlet (outlet pipe)*
9 der Mönch (Teichmönch)
- *monk*
10 das Mönchabsperrgitter
- *screen*
11-19 die Fischbrutanstalt
- *hatchery*
11 das Abstreifen des Laichhechts m
- *stripping the spawning pike (seed pike)*
12 der Fischlaich (Laich, Rogen, die Fischeier n)
- *fish spawn (spawn, roe, fish eggs)*
13 der weibliche Fisch (Rogner)
- *female fish (spawner, seed fish)*
14 die Forellenzucht
- *trout breeding (trout rearing)*
15 der kalifornische Brutapparat
- *Californian incubator*
16 die Forellenbrut
- *trout fry*
17 das Hechtbrutglas
- *hatching jar for pike*
18 der Langstromtrog
- *long incubation tank*
19 die Brandstetterische Eierzählplatte
- *Brandstetter egg-counting board*
20-94 das Sportangeln (die Angelfischerei)
- *angling*
20-31 das Grundangeln
- *bottom fishing (coarse fishing)*
20 der Wurf mit abgezogener Schnur
- *line shooting*
21 die Klänge m
- *coils*
22 das Tuch oder Papier n
- *cloth (rag) or paper*
23 der Rutenhalter
- *rod rest*
24 die Köderdose
- *bait tin*
25 der Fischkorb
- *fish basket (creel)*
26 der Karpfenansitz vom Boot n aus
- *fishing for carp from a boat*
27 das Ruderboot (Fischerboot)
- *rowing boat (fishing boat)*
28 der Setzkescher
- *keep net*
29 die Köderfischsenke
- *drop net*
30 die Stake
- *pole (punt pole, quant pole)*

31 das Wurfnetz
- *casting net*
32 der beidhändige Seitwurf mit Stationärrolle
- *two-handed side cast with fixed-spool reel*
33 die Ausgangsstellung
- *initial position*
34 der Abwurfpunkt
- *point of release*
35 die Bahn der Rutenspitze
- *path of the rod tip*
36 die Flugbahn des Ködergewichts n
- *trajectory of the baited weight*
37-94 Angelgeräte n
- *fishing tackle*
37 die Anglerzange
- *fishing pliers*
38 das Filiermesser
- *filleting knife*
39 das Fischmesser
- *fish knife*
40 der Hakenlöser
- *disgorger (hook disgorger)*
41 die Ködernadel
- *bait needle*
42 der Schonrachenspanner
- *gag*
43-48 Posen f
- *floats*
43 das Korkgleitfloß
- *sliding cork float*
44 die Kunststoffpose
- *plastic float*
45 die Federkielpose
- *quill float*
46 der Schaumstoffschwimmer
- *polystyrene float*
47 die ovale Wasserkugel
- *oval bubble float*
48 die bleibeschwerte Gleitpose
- *lead-weighted sliding float*
49-58 Ruten f
- *rods*
49 die Vollglasrute
- *solid glass rod*
50 der Preßkorkgriff
- *cork handle (cork butt)*
51 der Federstahlring
- *spring-steel ring*
52 der Spitzenring
- *top ring (end ring)*
53 die Teleskoprute
- *telescopic rod*
54 das Rutenteil
- *rod section*
55 das umwickelte Handteil
- *bound handle (bound butt)*
56 der Laufring
- *ring*
57 die Kohlefiberrute, *ähnl.:* die Hohlglasrute
- *carbon-fibre rod; sim.: hollow glass rod*
58 der Weitwurfring, ein Stahlbrückenring
- *all-round ring (butt ring for long cast), a steel bridge ring*
59-64 Rollen f
- *reels*
59 die Multiplikatorrolle (Multirolle)
- *multiplying reel (multiplier reel)*
60 die Schnurführung
- *line guide*
61 die Stationärrolle
- *fixed-spool reel (stationary-drum reel)*

62 der Schnurfangbügel
- *bale arm*
63 die Angelschnur
- *fishing line*
64 die Wurfkontrolle mit dem Zeigefinger m
- *controlling the cast with the index finger*
65-76 Köder m
- *baits*
65 die Fliege
- *fly*
66 der Nymphenköder (die Nymphe)
- *artificial nymph*
67 der Regenwurmköder
- *artificial earthworm*
68 der Heuschreckenköder
- *artificial grasshopper*
69 der einteilige Wobbler
- *single-jointed plug (single-jointed wobbler)*
70 der zweiteilige Langwobbler
- *double-jointed plug (double-jointed wobbler)*
71 der Kugelwobbler
- *round wobbler*
72 der Pilker
- *wiggler*
73 der Blinker (Löffel)
- *spoon bait (spoon)*
74 der Spinner
- *spinner*
75 der Spinner mit verstecktem Haken
- *spinner with concealed hook*
76 der Zocker
- *long spinner*
77 der Wirtel
- *swivel*
78 das Vorfach
- *cast (leader)*
79-87 Haken m
- *hooks*
79 der Angelhaken
- *fish hook*
80 die Hakenspitze mit Widerhaken m
- *point of the hook with barb*
81 der Hakenbogen
- *bend of the hook*
82 das Plättchen (Öhr)
- *spade (eye)*
83 der offene Doppelhaken
- *open double hook*
84 der Limerick
- *limerick*
85 der geschlossene Drilling
- *closed treble hook (triangle)*
86 der Karpfenhaken
- *carp hook*
87 der Aalhaken
- *eel hook*
88-92 Bleigewichte n
- *leads (lead weights)*
88 die Bleiolive
- *oval lead (oval sinker)*
89 die Bleikugeln f
- *lead shot*
90 das Birnenblei
- *pear-shaped lead*
91 das Grundsucherblei
- *plummet*
92 das Seeblei
- *sea lead*
93 der Fischpaß
- *fish ladder (fish pass, fish way)*
94 das Schockernetz
- *stake net*

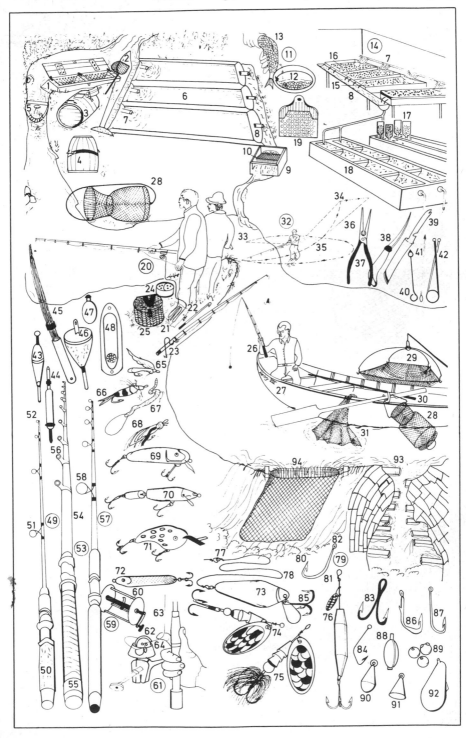

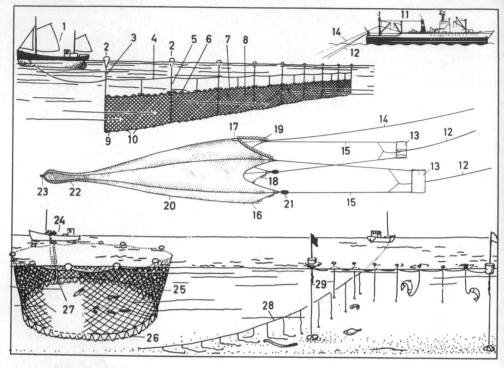

1-23 die Hochseefischerei
- *deep-sea fishing*
1-10 die Treibnetzfischerei
- *drift net fishing*
1 der Heringslogger (Fischlogger, Logger)
- *herring lugger (fishing lugger, lugger)*
2-10 das Heringstreibnetz
- *herring drift net*
2 die Boje (Brail)
- *buoy*
3 das Brailtau
- *buoy rope*
4 das Fleetreep
- *float line*
5 die Zeising
- *seizing*
6 das Flottholz
- *wooden float*
7 das Sperreep
- *headline*
8 das Netz (die Netzwand)
- *net*
9 das Untersimm
- *footrope*
10 die Grundgewichte *n*
- *sinkers (weights)*
11-23 die Schleppnetzfischerei
- *trawl fishing (trawling)*
11 das Fangfabrikschiff, ein Fischtrawler
- *factory ship, a trawler*
12 die Kurrleine
- *warp (trawl warp)*
13 die Scherbretter *n*
- *otter boards*

14 das Netzsondenkabel
- *net sonar cable*
15 der Stander
- *wire warp*
16 der Flügel
- *wing*
17 die Netzsonde
- *net sonar device*
18 das Grundtau
- *footrope*
19 die Kugeln *f*
- *spherical floats*
20 der Bauch (Belly)
- *belly*
21 das 1800-kg-Eisengewicht
- *1,800 kg iron weight*
22 der Stert
- *cod end (cod)*
23 die Codleine zum Schließen *n* des Sterts *m*
- *cod line for closing the cod end*
24-29 die Küstenfischerei
- *inshore fishing*
24 das Fischerboot
- *fishing boat*
25 die Ringwade, ein ringförmig ausgefahrenes Treibnetz *n*
- *ring net cast in a circle*
26 das Drahtseil zum Schließen *n* der Ringwade
- *cable for closing the ring net*
27 die Schließvorrichtung
- *closing gear*
28-29 die Langleinenfischerei
- *long-line fishing (long-lining)*
28 die Langleine
- *long line*

29 die Stellangel
- *suspended fishing tackle*

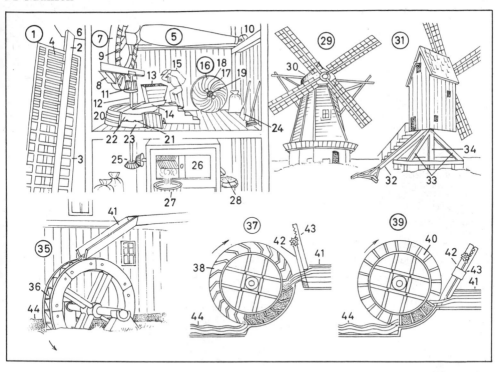

1-34 die Windmühle
- *windmill*
1 der Windmühlenflügel
- *windmill vane (windmill sail, windmill arm)*
2 die Windrute
- *stock (middling, back, radius)*
3 die Saumlatte
- *frame*
4 die Windtür
- *shutter*
5 die Flügelwelle (Radwelle)
- *wind shaft (sail axle)*
6 der Flügelkopf
- *sail top*
7 das Kammrad
- *brake wheel*
8 die Radbremse
- *brake*
9 der Holzzahn
- *wooden cog*
10 das Stützlager
- *pivot bearing (step bearing)*
11 das Windmühlengetriebe (der Trilling)
- *wallower*
12 das Mühleisen
- *mill spindle*
13 die Gosse
- *hopper*
14 der Rüttelschuh
- *shoe (trough, spout)*
15 der Müller
- *miller*
16 der Mühlstein
- *millstone*
17 der Hauschlag (die Luftfurche)
- *furrow (flute)*

18 die Sprengschärfe (Mahlfurche)
- *master furrow*
19 das Mühlsteinauge
- *eye [of the millstone]*
20 die Bütte (das Mahlsteingehäuse)
- *hurst (millstone casing)*
21 der Mahlgang
- *set of stones (millstones)*
22 der Läuferstein (Oberstein)
- *runner (upper millstone)*
23 der Bodenstein
- *bed stone (lower stone, bedder)*
24 die Holzschaufel
- *wooden shovel*
25 der Kegeltrieb (Winkeltrieb)
- *bevel gear (bevel gearing)*
26 der Rundsichter
- *bolter (sifter)*
27 der Holzbottich
- *wooden tub (wooden tun)*
28 das Mehl
- *flour*
29 die holländ. Windmühle
- *smock windmill (Dutch windmill)*
30 die drehbare Windmühlenhaube
- *rotating (revolving) windmill cap*
31 die Bockmühle
- *post windmill (German windmill)*
32 der Stert
- *tailpole (pole)*
33 das Bockgerüst
- *base*
34 der Königsbaum
- *post*
35-44 die Wassermühle
- *watermill*

35 das oberschlächtige Zellenrad, ein Mühlrad *n* (Wasserrad)
- *overshot mill wheel (high-breast mill wheel), a mill wheel (waterwheel)*
36 die Schaufelkammer (Zelle)
- *bucket (cavity)*
37 das mittelschlächtige Mühlrad
- *middleshot mill wheel (breast mill wheel)*
38 die gekrümmte Schaufel
- *curved vane*
39 das unterschlächtige Mühlrad
- *undershot mill wheel*
40 die gerade Schaufel
- *flat vane*
41 das Gerinne
- *headrace (discharge flume)*
42 das Mühlwehr
- *mill weir*
43 der Wasserüberfall
- *overfall (water overfall)*
44 der Mühlbach (Mühlgraben)
- *millstream (millrace, Am. raceway)*

1-41 die Malzbereitung (das Mälzen)
- *preparation of malt (malting)*
1 der Mälzturm (die
  Malzproduktionsanlage)
- *malting tower (maltings)*
2 der Gersteeinlauf
- *barley hopper*
3 die Waschetage mit
  Druckluftwäsche *f*
- *washing floor with compressed-air
  washing unit*
4 der Ablaufkondensator
- *outflow condenser*
5 der Wasserauffangbehälter
- *water-collecting tank*
6 der Weichwasserkondensator
- *condenser for the steep liquor*
7 der Kältemittelsammler
- *coolant-collecting plant*
8 die Weich-Keim-Etage (der
  Feuchtraum, Weichstock, die
  Tenne)
- *steeping floor (steeping tank,
  dressing floor)*
9 der Kaltwasserbehälter
- *cold water tank*
10 der Warmwasserbehälter
- *hot water tank*
11 der Wasserpumpenraum
- *pump room*
12 die Pneumatikanlage
- *pneumatic plant*
13 die Hydraulikanlage
- *hydraulic plant*
14 der Frisch- und Abluftschacht
- *ventilation shaft (air inlet and outlet)*
15 der Exhauster
- *exhaust fan*
16-18 die Darretagen *f*
- ***kilning floors***
16 die Vordarre
- *drying floor*
17 der Brennerventilator
- *burner ventilator*
18 die Nachdarre
- *curing floor*
19 der Darrablaufschacht
- *outlet duct from the kiln*
20 der Fertigmalztrichter
- *finished malt collecting hopper*
21 die Trafostation
- *transformer station*
22 die Kältekompressoren *m*
- *cooling compressors*
23 das Grünmalz (Keimgut)
- *green malt (germinated barley)*
24 die drehbare Horde
- *turner (plough)*
25 die zentrale Schaltwarte mit dem
  Schaltschaubild *n*
- *central control room with flow
  diagram*
26 die Aufgabeschnecke
- *screw conveyor*
27 die Waschetage
- *washing floor*
28 die Weich-Keim-Etage
- *steeping floor*
29 die Vordarre
- *drying kiln*
30 die Nachdarre
- *curing kiln*
31 der Gerstesilo
- *barley silo*
32 die Waage
- *weighing apparatus*

33 der Gersteelevator
- *barley elevator*
34 der Drei-Wege-Kippkasten
- *three-way chute (three-way tippler)*
35 der Malzelevator
- *malt elevator*
36 die Putzmaschine
- *cleaning machine*
37 der Malzsilo
- *malt silo*
38 die Keimabsaugung
- *corn removal by suction*
39 die Absackmaschine
- *sacker*
40 der Staubabscheider
- *dust extractor*
41 die Gersteanlieferung
- *barley reception*
42-53 der Sudprozeß im Sudhaus *n*
- ***mashing process in the mashhouse***
42 der Vormaischer zum Mischen *n*
  von Schrot *n* und Wasser *n*
- *premasher (converter) for mixing
  grist and water*
43 der Maischbottich zum
  Einmaischen *n* des Malzes *n*
- *mash tub (mash tun) for mashing
  the malt*
44 die Maischpfanne (der
  Maischkessel) zum Kochen *n* der
  Maische
- *mash copper (mash tun, Am. mash
  kettle) for boiling the mash*
45 die Pfannenhaube
- *dome of the tun*
46 das Rührwerk
- *propeller (paddle)*
47 die Schiebetür
- *sliding door*
48 die Wasserzuflußleitung
- *water (liquor) supply pipe*
49 der Brauer (Braumeister,
  Biersieder)
- *brewer (master brewer, masher)*
50 der Läuterbottich zum Absetzen *n*
  der Rückstände *m* (Treber) und
  Abfiltrieren *n* der Würze
- *lauter tun for settling the draff
  (grains) and filtering off the wort*
51 die Läuterbatterie zur Prüfung der
  Würze auf Feinheit *f*
- *lauter battery for testing the wort
  for quality*
52 der Hopfenkessel (die
  Würzpfanne) zum Kochen *n* der
  Würze
- *hop boiler (wort boiler) for boiling
  the wort*
53 das Schöpfthermometer
- *ladle-type thermometer (scoop
  thermometer)*

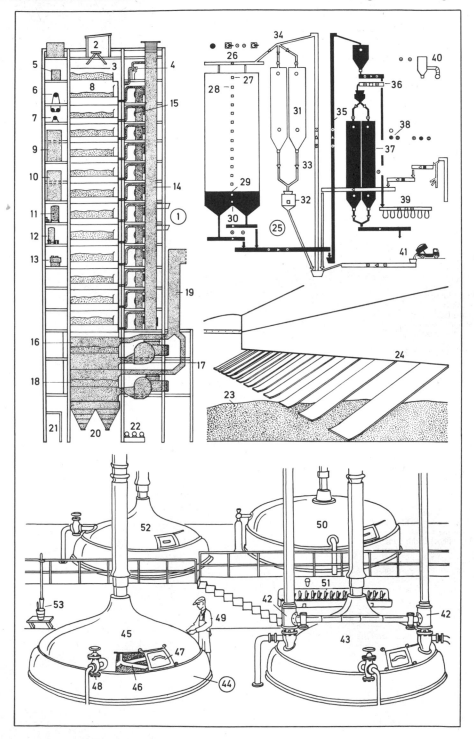

1-31 **die Bierbrauerei** (Brauerei, das
Brauhaus)
- *brewery (brewhouse)*
1-5 **die Würzekühlung und
Trubausscheidung**
- *wort cooling and break removal (trub
removal)*
1 das Steuerpult
- *control desk (control panel)*
2 der Whirlpool zur
Heißtrubausscheidung
- *whirlpool separator for removing
the hot break (hot trub)*
3 das Dosiergefäß für Kieselgur *f*
- *measuring vessel for the kieselguhr*
4 der (das) Kieselgurfilter
- *kieselguhr filter*
5 der Würzekühler
- *wort cooler*
6 der Hefereinzuchtapparat
- *pure culture plant for yeast (yeast
propagation plant)*
7 der Gärkeller
- *fermenting cellar*
8 der Gärbottich
- *fermentation vessel (fermenter)*
9 das Gärthermometer
(Maischethermometer)
- *fermentation thermometer (mash
thermometer)*
10 die Maische
- *mash*
11 das Kühlschlangensystem
- *refrigeration system*
12 der Lagerkeller
- *lager cellar*
13 das Mannloch zum Lagertank *m*
- *manhole to the storage tank*
14 der Anstichhahn
- *broaching tap*
15 der (das) Bierfilter
- *beer filter*
16 das Faßlager
- *barrel store*
17 das Bierfaß, ein Aluminiumfaß *n*
- *beer barrel, an aluminium (*Am.
aluminum*) barrel*
18 die Flaschenreinigungsanlage
- *bottle-washing plant*
19 die Flaschenreinigungsmaschine
- *bottle-washing machine (bottle
washer)*
20 die Schaltanlage
- *control panel*
21 die gereinigten Flaschen *f*
- *cleaned bottles*
22 die Flaschenabfüllung
- *bottling*
23 der Gabelstapler
- *forklift truck (fork truck, forklift)*
24 der Bierkastenstapel
- *stack of beer crates*
25 die Bierdose
- *beer can*
26 die Bierflasche, eine Europaflasche
mit Flaschenbier *n; Biersorten:*
helles Bier, dunkles Bier, Pilsener
Bier, Münchener Bier, Malzbier,
Starkbier (Bockbier, Bock), Porter,
Ale, Stout, Salvator, Gose,
Weißbier (Weizenbier),
Schwachbier (Dünnbier)
- *beer bottle, a Eurobottle with
bottled beer; kinds of beer: light
beer (lager, light ale, pale ale or
bitter), dark beer (brown ale, mild),*

*Pilsener beer, Munich beer, malt
beer, strong beer (bock beer),
porter, ale, stout, Salvator beer,
wheat beer, small beer*
27 der Kronenverschluß
- *crown cork (crown cork closure)*
28 die Einwegpackung
- *disposable pack (carry-home pack)*
29 die Einwegflasche
(Wegwerfflasche)
- *non-returnable bottle (single-trip
bottle)*
30 das Bierglas
- *beer glass*
31 die Schaumkrone
- *head*

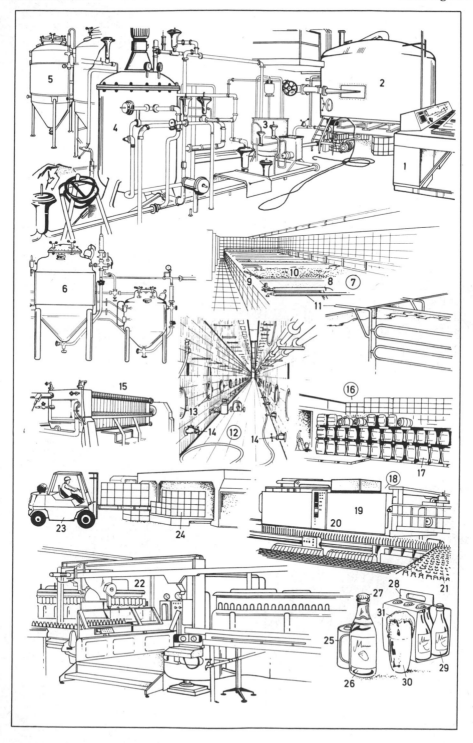

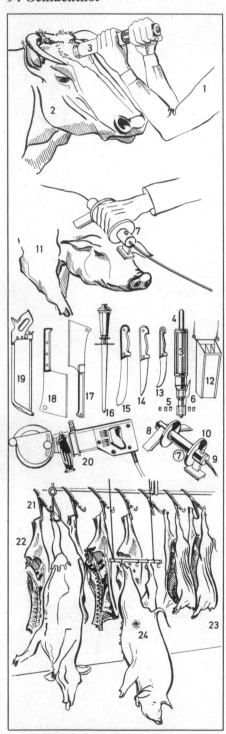

1 der Schlächter (Fleischer, *nordd.* Schlachter, *südd.* Metzger, *österr.* Fleischhauer)
- *slaughterman (Am. slaughterer, killer)*
2 das Schlachtvieh, ein Rind n
- *animal for slaughter, an ox*
3 das Bolzenschußgerät, ein Betäubungsgerät n
- *captive-bolt pistol (pneumatic gun), a stunning device*
4 der Schußbolzen
- *bolt*
5 die Patronen f
- *cartridges*
6 der Auslösebügel
- *release lever (trigger)*
7 das elektrische Betäubungsgerät
- *electric stunner*
8 die Elektrode
- *electrode*
9 die Zuleitung
- *lead*
10 der Handschutz (die Schutzisolierung)
- *hand guard (insulation)*
11 das Schlachtschwein
- *pig (Am. hog) for slaughter*
12 die Messerscheide
- *knife case*
13 das Abhäutemesser
- *flaying knife*
14 das Stechmesser
- *sticking knife (sticker)*
15 das Blockmesser
- *butcher's knife (butcher knife)*
16 der Wetzstahl
- *steel*
17 der Rückenspalter
- *splitter*
18 der Spalter
- *cleaver (butcher's cleaver, meat axe (Am. meat ax))*
19 die Knochensäge
- *bone saw (butcher's saw)*
20 die Fleischzerlegesäge zum Portionieren n von Fleischteilen n
- *meat saw for sawing meat into cuts*
21-24 das Kühlhaus
- ***cold store** (cold room)*
21 der Aufhängebügel
- *gambrel (gambrel stick)*
22 das Rinderviertel
- *quarter of beef*
23 die Schweinehälfte
- *side of pork*
24 der Kontrollstempel des Fleischbeschauers m
- *meat inspector's stamp*

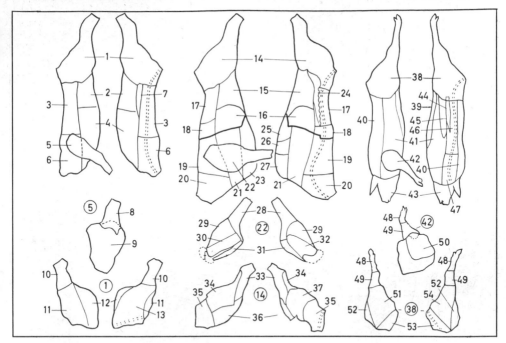

linke Seite: Fleischseite;
rechte Seite: Knochenseite
left: meat side;
right: bone side

1-13 das Kalb
- animal: *calf;* meat: *veal*
1 die Keule mit Hinterhachse *f*
(*südd.* Hinterhaxe *f*)
- *leg with hind knuckle*
2 der Bauch
- *flank*
3 das Kotelett (Kalbskotelett)
- *loin and rib*
4 die Brust (Kalbsbrust)
- *breast (breast of veal)*
5 der Bug mit Vorderhachse *f* (*südd.*
Vorderhaxe *f*)
- *shoulder with fore knuckle*
6 der Hals
- *neck with scrag (scrag end)*
7 das Filet (Kalbsfilet)
- *best end of loin (of loin of veal)*
8 die Vorderhachse
- *fore knuckle*
9 der Bug
- *shoulder*
10 die Hinterhachse (*südd.* Hinterhaxe)
- *hind knuckle*
11 das Nußstück
- *roasting round (oyster round)*
12 das Frikandeau
- *cutlet for frying or braising*
13 die Oberschale
- *undercut (fillet)*
14-37 das Rind
- animal: *ox;* meat: *beef*
14 die Keule mit Hinterhesse *f*
- *round with rump and shank*
15-16 die Lappen *m*
- *flank*
15 die Fleischdünnung
- *thick flank*
16 die Knochendünnung
- *thin flank*
17 das Roastbeef
- *sirloin*
18 die Hochrippe
- *prime rib (fore ribs, prime fore rib)*

19 die Fehlrippe
- *middle rib and chuck*
20 der Kamm
- *neck*
21 die Spannrippe
- *flat rib*
22 der Bug mit Vorderhesse *f*
- *leg of mutton piece (bladebone) with shin*
23 die Brust (Rinderbrust)
- *brisket (brisket of beef)*
24 das Filet (Rinderfilet)
- *fillet (fillet of beef)*
25 die Nachbrust
- *hind brisket*
26 die Mittelbrust
- *middle brisket*
27 das Brustbein
- *breastbone*
28 die Vorderhesse
- *shin*
29 das dicke Bugstück
- *leg of mutton piece*
30 das Schaufelstück
- *part of bladebone*
31 das falsche Filet
- *part of top rib*
32 der Schaufeldeckel
- *part of bladebone*
33 die Hinterhesse
- *shank*
34 das Schwanzstück
- *silverside*
35 die Blume
- *rump*
36 die Kugel
- *thick flank*
37 die Oberschale
- *top side*
38-54 das Schwein
- animal: *pig;* meat: *pork*
38 der Schinken mit dem Eisbein *n*
und dem Spitzbein *n*
- *leg with knuckle and trotter*
39 die Wamme
- *ventral part of the belly*
40 der Rückenspeck
- *back fat*
41 der Bauch
- *belly*

42 der Bug mit Eisbein *n* und
Spitzbein *n*
- *bladebone with knuckle and trotter*
43 der Kopf (Schweinskopf)
- *head (pig's head)*
44 das Filet (Schweinefilet)
- *fillet (fillet of pork)*
45 der Flomen
- *leaf fat (pork flare)*
46 das Kotelett (Schweinekotelett)
- *loin (pork loin)*
47 der Kamm (Schweinekamm)
- *spare rib*
48 das Spitzbein
- *trotter*
49 das Eisbein
- *knuckle*
50 das dicke Stück
- *butt*
51 das Schinkenstück
- *fore end (ham)*
52 die Nuß
- *round end for boiling*
53 der Schinkenspeck
- *fat end*
54 die Oberschale
- *gammon steak*

1-30 **die Fleischerei** (das
Fleischerfachgeschäft, *obd./westd.*
Metzgerei, Schlächterei, *nd.*
Schlachterei)
– *butcher's shop*
1-4 **Fleischwaren** *pl*
– *meat*
1 der Knochenschinken
– *ham on the bone*
2 die Speckseite
– *flitch of bacon*
3 das Dörrfleisch (Rauchfleisch)
– *smoked meat*
4 das Lendenstück
– *piece of loin
(piece of sirloin)*
5 das Schweinefett
(Schweineschmalz)
– *lard*
6-11 **Wurstwaren** *pl*
– *sausages*
6 das Preisschild
– *price label*
7 die Mortadella
– *mortadella*
8 das Brühwürstchen (Würstchen,
Siedewürstchen); *Arten:* „Wiener",
„Frankfurter"
– *scalded sausage;* kinds: *Vienna
sausage (Wiener), Frankfurter
sausage (Frankfurter)*
9 der Preßsack (Preßkopf)
– *collared pork* (Am. *headcheese)*

10 der Fleischwurstring (die „Lyoner")
– *ring of [Lyoner] sausage*
11 die Bratwurst
– *bratwurst (sausage for frying or
grilling)*
12 die Kühltheke
– *cold shelves*
13 der Fleischsalat
– *meat salad (diced meat salad)*
14 die Aufschnittware
– *cold meats* (Am. *cold cuts)*
15 die Fleischpastete
– *pâté*
16 das Hackfleisch (Gehackte,
Schabefleisch, Geschabte, Gewiegte)
– *mince (mincemeat, minced meat)*
17 das Eisbein
– *knuckle of pork*
18 der Sonderangebotskorb
– *basket for special offers*
19 die Sonderpreistafel
– *price list for special offers*
20 das Sonderangebot
– *special offer*
21 die Tiefkühltruhe
– *freezer*
22 das abgepackte Bratenfleisch
– *pre-packed joints*
23 das tiefgefrorene Fertiggericht
– *deep-frozen (deepfreeze)
ready-to-eat meal*
24 das Hähnchen
– *chicken*

25 Konserven *f* (Vollkonserven; *mit
beschränkter Haltbarkeit:*
Präserven *f*)
– *canned food*
26 die Konservendose
– *can*
27 die Gemüsekonserve
– *canned vegetables*
28 die Fischkonserve
– *canned fish*
29 die Remoulade
– *salad cream*
30 die Erfrischungsgetränke *n*
– *soft drinks*

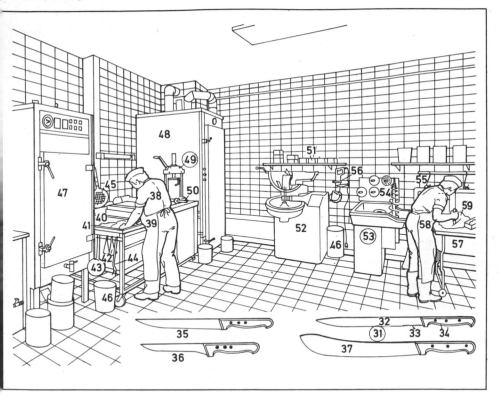

31-59 die Wurstküche (der Zubereitungsraum)
- **kitchen for making sausages**
31-37 Fleischermesser n (Metzgermesser, Schlächtermesser)
- **butcher's knives**
31 das Aufschnittmesser
- slicer
32 die Messerklinge
- knife blade
33 die Sägezahnung
- saw teeth
34 das Messerheft
- knife handle
35 das Fleischmesser
- carver (carving knife)
36 das Ausbeinmesser
- boning knife
37 das Blockmesser
- butcher's knife (butcher knife)
38 der Fleischermeister (Fleischer, obd./westd. Metzger, Schlächter, nd. Schlachter)
- butcher (master butcher)
39 die Fleischerschürze
- butcher's apron
40 die Mengmulde (nd. Schlachtermolle, Molle)
- meat-mixing trough
41 der (das) Bröt (das Bratwurstfüllsel, die Wurstmasse)
- sausage meat

42 die Schabglocke
- scraper
43 der Schaumlöffel
- skimmer
44 die Wurstgabel
- sausage fork
45 das Brühsieb
- scalding colander
46 der Abfalleimer
- waste bin (Am. trash bin)
47 der Kochschrank mit Backeinrichtung f für Dampf m oder Heißluft f
- cooker, for cooking with steam or hot air
48 die Räucherkammer
- smoke house
49 der Handwurstfüller (Tischwurstfüller)
- sausage filler (sausage stuffer)
50 das Füllrohr
- feed pipe (supply pipe)
51 die Gemüsebehälter m
- containers for vegetables
52 der Kutter für die Bräherstellung
- mincing machine for sausage meat
53 der Fleischwolf (die Faschiermaschine)
- mincing machine (meat mincer, mincer, Am. meat grinder)
54 die Passierscheiben f
- plates (steel plates)

55 der Fleischhaken
- meathook (butcher's hook)
56 die Knochensäge
- bone saw
57 die Hackbank
- chopping board
58 der Fleischergeselle beim Zerlegen n
- butcher, cutting meat
59 das Fleischstück
- piece of meat

1-54 der Verkaufsraum der Bäckerei
(Feinbäckerei, Konditorei)
- *baker's shop*
1 die Verkäuferin
- *shop assistant (Am. salesgirl, saleslady)*
2 das Brot (der Brotlaib, Laib)
- *bread (loaf of bread, loaf)*
3 die Krume
- *crumb*
4 die Kruste (Brotrinde)
- *crust (bread crust)*
5 das Endstück (*norddt.* die Kante)
- *crust (Am. heel)*
6-12 Brotsorten *f*
- *kinds of bread (breads)*
6 das Rundbrot (Landbrot, ein
Mischbrot *n*)
- *round loaf, a wheat and rye bread*
7 das kleine Rundbrot
- *small round loaf*
8 das Langbrot, ein Roggenmischbrot *n*
- *long loaf (bloomer), a wheat and
rye bread*
9 das Weißbrot
- *white loaf*
10 das Kastenbrot (*ugs.* Kommißbrot),
ein Vollkornbrot *n*
- *pan loaf, a wholemeal rye bread*
11 der Stollen (Weihnachtsstollen,
Christstollen)
- *yeast bread (Am. stollen)*
12 das französische Weißbrot (die
Baguette)
- *French loaf (baguette, French stick)*

13-16 Brötchen *n (norddt.* **Rundstücke,**
landsch. **Wecke** *m*, **Wecken** *m*, **Semmeln** *f*)
- *rolls*
13 die Semmel (*auch:* der Salzkuchen)
- *roll*
14 das Weizenbrötchen
(Weißbrötchen, *auch:* Salzbrötchen,
Mohnbrötchen, Kümmelbrötchen)
- *[white] roll*
15 das Doppelbrötchen
- *double roll*
16 das Roggenbrötchen
- *rye-bread roll*
17-47 Konditoreiwaren *pl*
- *cakes (confectionery)*
17 die Sahnerolle
- *cream roll*
18 die Pastete, eine Blätterteigpastete
- *vol-au-vent, a puff pastry (Am.
puff paste)*
19 die Biskuitrolle
- *Swiss roll (Am. jelly roll)*
20 das Törtchen
- *tartlet*
21 die Cremeschnitte
- *slice of cream cake*
22-24 Torten *f*
- *flans (Am. pies) and gateaux (torten)*
22 die Obsttorte (*Arten:* Erdbeertorte,
Kirschtorte, Stachelbeertorte;
Pfirsichtorte, Rhabarbertorte)
- *fruit flan (kinds: strawberry flan,
cherry flan, gooseberry flan, peach
flan, rhubarb flan)*

23 die Käsetorte
- *cheesecake*
24 die Cremetorte (*auch:* Sahnetorte,
Arten: Buttercremetorte,
Schwarzwälder Kirschtorte)
- *cream cake (Am. cream pie) (kinds:
butter-cream cake, Black Forest
gateau)*
25 die Tortenplatte
- *cake plate*
26 der Baiser (die Meringe, *schweiz.*
Meringue)
- *meringue*
27 der Windbeutel
- *cream puff*
28 die Schlagsahne (*österr.* das
Schlagobers)
- *whipped cream*
29 der Berliner Pfannkuchen
(Berliner)
- *doughnut (Am. bismarck)*
30 das Schweinsohr
- *Danish pastry*
31 die Salzstange (*auch:* Kümmelstange)
- *saltstick (saltzstange) (also:
caraway roll, caraway stick)*
32 das Hörnchen
- *croissant (crescent roll, Am. crescent)*
33 der Napfkuchen (Topfkuchen,
oberdt. Gugelhupf)
- *ring cake (gugelhupf)*
34 der Kastenkuchen mit
Schokoladenüberzug *m*
- *slab cake with chocolate icing*

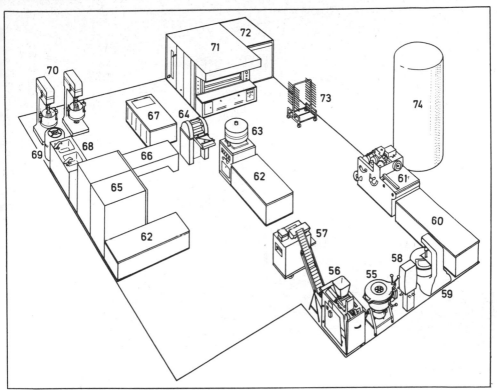

35 das Streuselgebäck
 - *streusel cakes*
36 der Mohrenkopf
 - *marshmallow*
37 die Makrone
 - *coconut macaroon*
38 die Schnecke (*landsch.*
   Schneckennudel)
 - *schnecke*
39 der Amerikaner
 - *[kind of] iced bun*
40 der Einback
 - *sweet bread*
41 der Hefezopf
 - *plaited bun (plait)*
42 der Frankfurter Kranz
 - *Frankfurter garland cake*
43 der Blechkuchen (*Arten:*
   Streuselkuchen,
   Zuckerkuchen,
   Zwetschgenkuchen)
 - *slices* (kinds: *streusel slices,*
   sugared slices,
   plum slices)
44 die Brezel (Laugenbrezel)
 - *pretzel*
45 die Waffel
 - *wafer* (Am. *waffle)*
46 der Baumkuchen
 - *tree cake (baumkuchen)*
47 der Tortenboden
 - *flan case*
48-50 **abgepackte Brotsorten** *f*
 - **wrapped bread**

48 das Vollkornbrot (*auch:*
   Weizenkeimbrot)
 - *wholemeal bread* (also: *wheatgerm*
   bread)
49 der Pumpernickel
 - *pumpernickel (wholemeal rye*
   bread)
50 das Knäckebrot
 - *crispbread*
51 der Lebkuchen
 - *gingerbread* (Am. *lebkuchen)*
52 das Mehl (*Arten:* Weizenmehl,
   Roggenmehl)
 - *flour* (kinds: *wheat flour, rye flour)*
53 die Hefe
 - *yeast (baker's yeast)*
54 der Zwieback (Kinderzwieback)
 - *rusks (French toast)*
55-74 **der Backraum** (die Backstube)
 - **bakery** (*bakehouse)*
55 die Knetmaschine
 - *kneading machine (dough mixer)*
56-57 **die Brotanlage**
 - **bread unit**
56 die Teigteilmaschine
 - *divider*
57 die Wirkanlage
 - *moulder* (Am. *molder)*
58 das Wassermisch- und -meßgerät
 - *premixer*
59 der Mixer
 - *dough mixer*
60 der Arbeitstisch
 - *workbench*

61 die Brötchenanlage
 - *roll unit*
62 der Arbeitstisch
 - *workbench*
63 die Teigteil- und
   Rundwirkmaschine
 - *divider and rounder (rounding*
   machine)
64 die Hörnchenwickelmaschine
 - *crescent-forming machine*
65 Frosteranlagen *f*
 - *freezers*
66 das Fettbackgerät
 - *oven [for baking with fat]*
67-70 **die Konditorei**
 - *confectionery unit*
67 der Kühltisch
 - *cooling table*
68 die Spüle
 - *sink*
69 der Kocher
 - *boiler*
70 die Rühr- und Schlagmaschine
 - *whipping unit [with beater]*
71 der Etagenofen (Backofen)
 - *reel oven (oven)*
72 der Gärraum
 - *fermentation room*
73 der Gärwagen
 - *[fermentation] trolley*
74 die Mehlsiloanlage
 - *flour silo*

1-87 das Lebensmittelgeschäft (die Lebensmittelhandlung, das Feinkostgeschäft, *veraltet:* die Kolonialwarenhandlung), ein Einzelhandelsgeschäft *n*
- *grocer's shop (grocer's, delicatessen shop, Am. grocery store, delicatessen store), a retail shop (Am. retail store)*
1 die Schaufensterauslage
- *window display*
2 das Plakat (Werbeplakat)
- *poster (advertisement)*
3 die Kühlvitrine
- *cold shelves*
4 die Wurstwaren *pl*
- *sausages*
5 der Käse
- *cheese*
6 das Brathähnchen
- *roasting chicken (broiler)*
7 die Poularde, eine gemästete Henne
- *poulard, a fattened hen*
8-11 Backzutaten *f*
- *baking ingredients*
8 die Rosinen *f; ähnl.:* Sultaninen
- *raisins; sim.: sultanas*
9 die Korinthen *f*
- *currants*
10 das Zitronat
- *candied lemon peel*
11 das Orangeat
- *candied orange peel*
12 die Neigungswaage, eine Schnellwaage
- *computing scale, a rapid scale*
13 der Verkäufer
- *shop assistant (Am. salesclerk)*

14 das Warengestell (Warenregal)
- *goods shelves (shelves)*
15-20 Konserven *f*
- *canned food*
15 die Büchsenmilch (Dosenmilch)
- *canned milk*
16 die Obstkonserve
- *canned fruit (cans of fruit)*
17 die Gemüsekonserve
- *canned vegetables*
18 der Fruchtsaft
- *fruit juice*
19 die Ölsardinen *f*, eine Fischkonserve
- *sardines in oil, a can of fish*
20 die Fleischkonserve
- *canned meat (cans of meat)*
21 die Margarine
- *margarine*
22 die Butter
- *butter*
23 das Kokosfett, ein Pflanzenfett *n*
- *coconut oil, a vegetable oil*
24 das Öl; *Arten:* Tafelöl, Salatöl; Olivenöl, Sonnenblumenöl, Weizenkeimöl, Erdnußöl
- *oil; kinds: salad oil, olive oil, sunflower oil, wheatgerm oil, ground-nut oil*
25 der Essig
- *vinegar*
26 der Suppenwürfel
- *stock cube*
27 der Brühwürfel
- *bouillon cube*
28 der Senf
- *mustard*
29 die Essiggurke
- *gherkin (pickled gherkin)*

30 die Suppenwürze
- *soup seasoning*
31 die Verkäuferin
- *shop assistant (Am. salesgirl, saleslady)*
32-34 Teigwaren *pl*
- *pastas*
32 die Spaghetti *pl*
- *spaghetti*
33 die Makkaroni *pl*
- *macaroni*
34 die Nudeln *f*
- *noodles*
35-39 Nährmittel *pl*
- *cereal products*
35 die Graupen *f*
- *pearl barley*
36 der Grieß
- *semolina*
37 die Haferflocken *f*
- *rolled oats (porridge oats, oats)*
38 der Reis
- *rice*
39 der Sago
- *sago*
40 das Salz
- *salt*
41 der Kaufmann (Händler), ein Einzelhändler *m*
- *grocer (Am. groceryman), a shopkeeper, tradesman, retailer (Am. storekeeper)*
42 die Kapern *f*
- *capers*
43 die Kundin
- *customer*
44 der Kassenzettel
- *receipt (sales check)*

45 die Einkaufstasche
- *shopping bag*
46-49 Packmaterial *n*
- *wrapping material*
46 das Einwickelpapier
- *wrapping paper*
47 der Klebestreifen
- *adhesive tape*
48 der Papierbeutel
- *paper bag*
49 die spitze Tüte
- *cone-shaped paper bag*
50 das Puddingpulver
- *blancmange powder*
51 die Konfitüre
- *whole-fruit jam (preserve)*
52 die Marmelade
- *jam*
53-55 Zucker *m*
- *sugar*
53 der Würfelzucker
- *cube sugar*
54 der Puderzucker
- *icing sugar (Am. confectioner's sugar)*
55 der Kristallzucker, eine Raffinade
- *refined sugar in crystals*
56-59 Spirituosen *pl*
- *spirits*
56 der Korn, ein klarer Schnaps *m* (Branntwein)
- *schnapps distilled from grain [usually wheat]*
57 der Rum
- *rum*
58 der Likör
- *liqueur*
59 der Weinbrand (Kognak)
- *brandy (cognac)*

60-64 Wein *m* in Flaschen *f*
- *wine in bottles (bottled wine)*
60 der Weißwein
- *white wine*
61 der Chianti
- *chianti*
62 der Wermut
- *vermouth*
63 der Sekt (Schaumwein)
- *sparkling wine*
64 der Rotwein
- *red wine*
65-68 Genußmittel *n*
- *tea, coffee, etc.*
65 der Kaffee (Bohnenkaffee)
- *coffee (pure coffee)*
66 der Kakao
- *cocoa*
67 die Kaffeesorte
- *coffee*
68 der Teebeutel
- *tea bag*
69 die elektr. Kaffeemühle
- *electric coffee grinder*
70 die Kaffeeröstmaschine
- *coffee roaster*
71 die Rösttrommel
- *roasting drum*
72 die Probierschaufel
- *sample scoop*
73 die Preisliste
- *price list*
74 die Tiefkühltruhe
- *freezer*
75-86 Süßwaren *pl*
- *confectionery* (Am. *candies*)
75 das (der) Bonbon
- *sweet (Am. candy)*

76 die Drops *m*
- *drops*
77 die Karamelle
- *toffees*
78 die Schokoladentafel
- *bar of chocolate*
79 die Bonbonniere
- *chocolate box*
80 die Praline (das Praliné), ein Konfekt *n*
- *chocolate, a sweet*
81 der Nougat (Nugat)
- *nougat*
82 das Marzipan
- *marzipan*
83 die Weinbrandbohne
- *chocolate liqueur*
84 die Katzenzunge
- *cat's tongue*
85 der Krokant
- *croquant*
86 der Schokoladentrüffel
- *truffle*
87 das Tafelwasser (Selterswasser, der Sprudel)
- *soda water*

1-95 der Supermarkt, ein Selbstbedienungsgeschäft *n* für Lebensmittel *n*
- *supermarket, a self-service food store*
1 der Einkaufswagen
- *shopping trolley*
2 der Kunde (Käufer)
- *customer*
3 die Einkaufstasche
- *shopping bag*
4 der Zugang zum Verkaufsraum *m*
- *entrance to the sales area*
5 die Absperrung (Barriere)
- *barrier*
6 das Hundeverbotsschild
- *sign (notice) banning dogs*
7 die angeleinten Hunde *m*
- *dogs tied by their leads*
8 der Verkaufskorb
- *basket*
9 **die Backwarenabteilung** (Brotabteilung, Konditoreiabteilung)
- *bread and cake counter (bread counter, cake counter)*
10 die Backwarenvitrine
- *display counter for bread and cakes*
11 die Brotsorten *f*
- *kinds of bread (breads)*
12 die Brötchen *n*
- *rolls*
13 die Hörnchen *n*
- *croissants (crescent rolls, Am. crescents)*
14 das Landbrot
- *round loaf (strong rye bread)*
15 die Torte
- *gateau*

16 die Jahresbrezel *[südd.]*, eine Hefebrezel
- *pretzel [made with yeast dough]*
17 die Verkäuferin
- *shop assistant (Am. salesgirl, saleslady)*
18 die Kundin (Käuferin)
- *customer*
19 das Angebotsschild
- *sign listing goods*
20 die Obsttorte
- *fruit flan*
21 der Kastenkuchen
- *slab cake*
22 der Napfkuchen
- *ring cake*
23 **die Kosmetikgondel,** eine Gondel (ein Verkaufsregal *n*)
- *cosmetics gondola, a gondola (sales shelves)*
24 der Baldachin
- *canopy*
25 das Strumpffach
- *hosiery shelf*
26 die Strumpfpackung
- *stockings pack (nylons pack)*
27-35 **Körperpflegemittel** (Kosmetika) *n*
- *toiletries (cosmetics)*
27 die Cremedose (Creme; Arten: Feuchtigkeitscreme *f*, Tagescreme *f*, Nachtcreme *f*, Handcreme *f*)
- *cream jar (cream; kinds: moisturising cream, day cream, night-care cream, hand cream)*
28 die Wattepackung
- *cotton wool packet*
29 die Puderdose
- *powder tin*

30 die Packung Wattebäuschchen *n*
- *packet of cotton wool balls*
31 die Zahnpastapackung
- *toothpaste box*
32 der Nagellack
- *nail varnish (nail polish)*
33 die Cremetube
- *cream tube*
34 der Badezusatz
- *bath salts*
35 Hygieneartikel *m*
- *sanitary articles*
36-37 die Tiernahrung
- *pet foods*
36 die Hundevollkost
- *complete dog food*
37 die Packung Hundekuchen *m*
- *packet of dog biscuits*
38 die Packung Katzenstreu *f*
- *bag of cat litter*
39 **die Käseabteilung**
- *cheese counter*
40 der Käselaib
- *whole cheese*
41 der Schweizer Käse (Emmentaler) mit Löchern *n*
- *Swiss cheese (Emmental cheese) with holes*
42 der Edamer (Edamer Käse), ein Rundkäse
- *Edam cheese, a round cheese*
43 die Milchproduktegondel
- *gondola for dairy products*
44 die H-Milch (haltbare, hocherhitzte und homogenisierte Milch)
- *long-life milk (milk with good keeping properties, pasteurized and homogenized milk)*

45 der Milchbeutel	**62 die Back- und Nährmittelgondel**
- plastic milk bag	*- gondola for baking ingredients and*
46 die Sahne	*cereal products*
- cream	**63** das Weizenmehl
47 die Butter	*- wheat flour*
- butter	**64** der Zuckerhut
48 die Margarine	*- sugar loaf*
- margarine	**65** die Packung Suppennudeln *f*
49 die Käseschachtel	*- packet of noodles [for soup]*
- cheese box	**66** das Speiseöl
50 die Eierpackung	*- salad oil*
- egg box	**67** die Gewürzpackung
51 die Frischfleischabteilung	*- spice packet*
(Fleischwarenabteilung)	**68-70 die Genußmittel** *n*
- fresh meat counter (meat counter)	*- tea, coffee, etc.*
52 der Knochenschinken	**68** der Kaffee
- ham on the bone	*- coffee*
53 die Fleischwaren *pl*	**69** die Teeschachtel
- meat (meat products)	*- tea packet*
54 die Wurstwaren *pl*	**70** der lösliche Pulverkaffee
- sausages	(Instantkaffee)
55 der Fleischwurstring	*- instant coffee*
- ring of [pork] sausage	**71 die Getränkegondel**
56 der Rotwurstring	*- drinks gondola*
(die Blutwurst)	**72** der Bierkasten (Kasten Bier *n*)
- ring of blood sausage	*- beer crate (crate of beer)*
57 die Tiefkühlbox	**73** die Bierdose (das Dosenbier)
- freezer	*- beer can (canned beer)*
58-61 das Gefriergut	**74** die Fruchtsaftflasche
- frozen food	*- fruit juice bottle*
58 die Poularde	**75** die Fruchtsaftdose
- poulard	*- fruit juice can*
59 der Putenschlegel	**76** die Weinflasche
- turkey leg (drumstick)	*- bottle of wine*
60 das Suppenhuhn	**77** die Chiantiflasche
- boiling fowl	*- chianti bottle*
61 das Gefriergemüse	**78** die Sektflasche
- frozen vegetables	*- champagne bottle*

79 der Notausgang
- emergency exit
80 die Obst- und Gemüseabteilung
- fruit and vegetable counter
81 der Gemüsekorb
- vegetable basket
82 die Tomaten *f*
- tomatoes
83 die Gurken *f*
- cucumbers
84 der Blumenkohl
- cauliflower
85 die Ananas
- pineapple
86 die Äpfel *m*
- apples
87 die Birnen *f*
- pears
88 die Obstwaage
- scales for weighing fruit
89 die Weintrauben *f*
- grapes (bunches of grapes)
90 die Bananen *f*
- bananas
91 die Konservendose
- can
92 der Kassenstand (die Kasse)
- checkout
93 die Registrierkasse
- cash register
94 die Kassiererin
- cashier
95 die Sperrkette
- chain

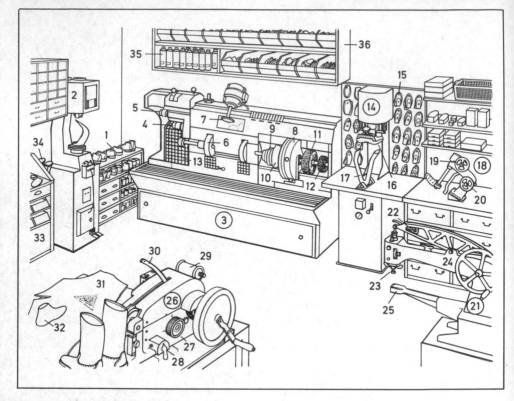

1-68 die Schuhmacherwerkstatt
(*landsch.* Schusterwerkstatt)
- *shoemaker's workshop*
(*bootmaker's workshop*)
1 die fertigen (reparierten) Schuhe *m*
- *finished (repaired) shoes*
2 die Durchnähmaschine
- *auto-soling machine*
3 die Ausputzmaschine
- *finishing machine*
4 der Absatzfräser
- *heel trimmer*
5 die Wechselfräser *m*
- *sole trimmer*
6 die Schleifscheibe
- *scouring wheel*
7 der Bimskreisel
- *naum keag*
8 der Antrieb
- *drive unit*
(*drive wheel*)
9 der Schnittdrücker
- *iron*
10 die Schwabbelscheibe
- *buffing wheel*
11 die Polierbürste
- *polishing brush*
12 die Roßhaarbürste
- *horsehair brush*
13 die Absaugung
- *extractor grid*
14 die automatische Sohlenpresse
- *automatic sole press*

15 die Preßplatte
- *press attachment*
16 das Preßkissen
- *pad*
17 die Andruckbügel *m*
- *press bar*
18 der Ausweitapparat
- *stretching machine*
19 die Verstellvorrichtung für Weite *f*
- *width adjustment*
20 die Verstellvorrichtung für Länge *f*
- *length adjustment*
21 die Nähmaschine
- *stitching machine*
22 die Stärkeverstellung
- *power regulator (power control)*
23 der Fuß
- *foot*
24 das Schwungrad
- *handwheel*
25 der Langarm
- *arm*
26 die Doppelmaschine
- *sole stitcher (sole-stitching machine)*
27 der Fußanheber
- *foot bar lever*
28 die Vorschubeinstellung
- *feed adjustment (feed setting)*
29 die Fadenrolle
- *bobbin (cotton bobbin)*
30 der Fadenführer
- *thread guide (yarn guide)*

31 das Sohlenleder
- *sole leather*
32 der Leisten
- *[wooden] last*
33 der Arbeitstisch
- *workbench*
34 der Eisenleisten
- *last*
35 die Farbsprühdose
- *dye spray*
36 das Materialregal
- *shelves for materials*

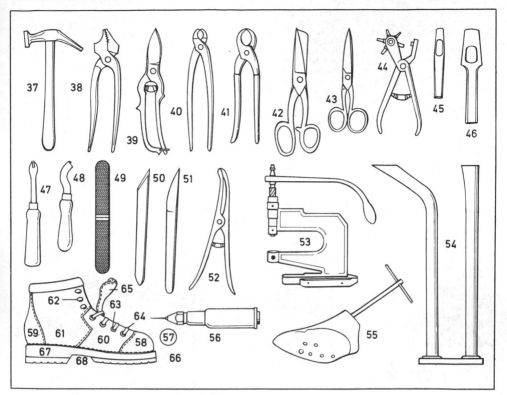

37 der Schusterhammer
- *shoemaker's hammer*
38 die Falzzange
- *shoemaker's pliers (welt pincers)*
39 die Bodenlederschere
- *sole-leather shears*
40 die kleine Beißzange
- *small pincers (nippers)*
41 die große Beißzange (Kneifzange)
- *large pincers (nippers)*
42 die Oberlederschere
- *upper-leather shears*
43 die Fadenschere
- *scissors*
44 die Revolverlochzange
- *revolving punch (rotary punch)*
45 das Locheisen
- *punch*
46 das Henkellocheisen
- *punch [with a handle]*
47 der Stiftenzieher
- *nail puller*
48 das Randmesser
- *welt cutter*
49 die Schuhmacherraspel
- *shoemaker's rasp*
50 das Schustermesser
- *cobbler's knife (shoemaker's knife)*
51 das Schärfmesser
- *skiving knife (skife knife, paring knife)*
52 die Kappenheberzange
- *toecap remover*

53 die Ösen-, Haken- und
   Druckknopfeinsetzmaschine
- *eyelet, hook, and press-stud setter*
54 der Arbeitsständer (Eisenfuß)
- *stand (with iron lasts)*
55 der Weitfixleisten
- *width-setting tree*
56 das Nagelheft
- *nail grip*
57 der Stiefel
- *boot*
58 die Vorderkappe
- *toecap*
59 die Hinterkappe
- *counter*
60 das Vorderblatt
- *vamp*
61 das Seitenteil (das Quartier)
- *quarter*
62 der Haken
- *hook*
63 die Öse
- *eyelet*
64 das Schnürband
- *lace (shoelace, bootlace)*
65 die Zunge
- *tongue*
66 die Sohle
- *sole*
67 der Absatz
- *heel*
68 das Gelenk
- *shank (waist)*

1 der Winterstiefel
- *winter boot*
2 die PVC-Sohle (Kunststoffsohle, Plastiksohle)
- *PVC sole (plastic sole)*
3 das Plüschfutter
- *high-pile lining*
4 das Anoraknylon
- *nylon*
5 der Herrenstiefel
- *men's boot*
6 der Innenreißverschluß
- *inside zip*
7 der Herrenschaftstiefel
- *men's high leg boot*
8 die Plateausohle
- *platform sole (platform)*
9 der Westernstiefel
- *Western boot (cowboy boot)*
10 der Fohlenfellstiefel
- *pony-skin boot*
11 die Schalensohle
- *cemented sole*
12 der Damenstiefel (Damenstraßenstiefel)
- *ladies' boot*
13 der Herrenstraßenstiefel
- *men's high leg boot*
14 der nahtlos gespritzte PVC-Regenstiefel
- *seamless PVC waterproof wellington boot*
15 die Transparentsohle
- *natural-colour (Am. natural-color) sole*
16 die Stiefelkappe
- *toecap*
17 das Trikotfutter
- *tricot lining (knitwear lining)*
18 der Wanderstiefel
- *hiking boot*
19 die Profilsohle
- *grip sole*
20 der gepolsterte Schaftrand
- *padded collar*
21 die Verschnürung
- *tie fastening (lace fastening)*
22 die Badepantolette
- *open-toe mule*
23 das Oberteil aus Frottierstoff
- *terry upper*
24 die Pololaufsohle
- *polo outsole*
25 der Pantoffel
- *mule*
26 das Breitkordoberteil
- *corduroy upper*
27 der Spangenpumps
- *evening sandal (sandal court shoe)*
28 der hohe Absatz (Stöckelabsatz)
- *high heel (stiletto heel)*
29 der Pumps
- *court shoe (Am. pump)*
30 der Mokassin
- *moccasin*
31 der Halbschuh (Schnürschuh)
- *shoe, a tie shoe (laced shoe, Oxford shoe, Am. Oxford)*
32 die Zunge
- *tongue*
33 der Halbschuh mit hohem Absatz
- *high-heeled shoe (shoe with raised heel)*
34 der Slipper
- *casual*
35 der Sportschuh (Turnschuh)
- *trainer (training shoe)*

36 der Tennisschuh
- *tennis shoe*
37 die Kappe
- *counter (stiffening)*
38 die Transparentgummisohle
- *natural-colour (Am. natural-color) rubber sole*
39 der Arbeitsschuh
- *heavy-duty boot (Am. stogy, stogie)*
40 die Schutzkappe
- *toecap*
41 der Hausschuh
- *slipper*
42 der Hüttenschuh aus Wolle
- *woollen (Am. woolen) slip sock*
43 das Strickmuster
- *knit stitch (knit)*
44 der Clog
- *clog*
45 die Holzsohle
- *wooden sole*
46 das Oberteil aus Softrindleder
- *soft-leather upper*
47 der Töffel
- *sabot*
48 die Dianette
- *toe post sandal*
49 die Sandalette
- *ladies' sandal*
50 das orthopädische Fußbett
- *surgical footbed (sock)*
51 die Sandale
- *sandal*
52 die Schuhschnalle
- *shoe buckle (buckle)*
53 der Slingpumps
- *sling-back court shoe (Am. sling pump)*
54 der Stoffpumps
- *fabric court shoe*
55 der Keilabsatz
- *wedge heel*
56 der Lernlaufkinderschuh
- *baby's first walking boot*

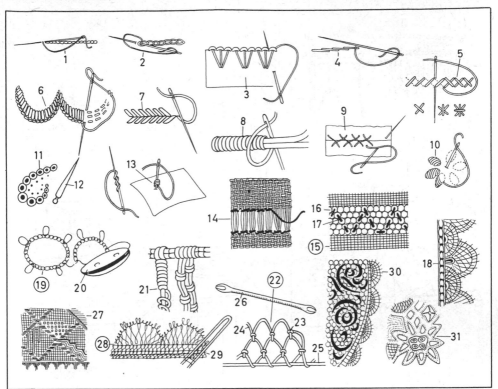

1 die Steppnaht
- *backstitch seam*
2 der Kettenstich
- *chain stitch*
3 der Zierstich
- *ornamental stitch*
4 der Stielstich
- *stem stitch*
5 der Kreuzstich
- *cross stitch*
6 der Langettenstich
- *buttonhole stitch (button stitch)*
7 der Zopfstich
- *fishbone stitch*
8 der Schnurstich
- *overcast stitch*
9 der Hexenstich
- *herringbone stitch (Russian stitch, Russian cross stitch)*
10 die Plattsticharbeit (Flachsticharbeit, Flachstickarbeit)
- *satin stitch (flat stitch)*
11 die Lochstickerei
- *eyelet embroidery (broderie anglaise)*
12 der Lochstecher
- *stiletto*
13 der Knötchenstich (Knotenstich)
- *French knot (French dot, knotted stitch, twisted knot stitch)*
14 die Durchbrucharbeit (der Hohlsaum)
- *hem stitch work*

15 die Tüllarbeit (Tüllspitze)
- *tulle work (tulle lace)*
16 der Tüllgrund (Spitzengrund)
- *tulle background (net background)*
17 der Durchzug
- *darning stitch*
18 die Klöppelspitze; *Arten:* Valenciennesspitzen, Brüsseler Spitzen
- *pillow lace (bobbin lace, bone lace); kinds: Valenciennes, Brussels lace*
19 die Schiffchenarbeit (Frivolitätenarbeit, Okkiarbeit, Occhiarbeit)
- *tatting*
20 das Schiffchen
- *tatting shuttle (shuttle)*
21 die Knüpfarbeit (das Makramee)
- *knotted work (macramé)*
22 die Filetarbeit (Netzarbeit, das Filament)
- *filet (netting)*
23 die Filetschlinge (der Filetknoten)
- *netting loop*
24 der Filetfaden
- *netting thread*
25 der Filetstab
- *mesh pin (mesh gauge)*
26 die Filetnadel (Netznadel, Schütze, Filiernadel)
- *netting needle*
27 die Ajourarbeit (Durchbrucharbeit)
- *open work*

28 die Gabelhäkelei (Gimpenhäkelei)
- *gimping (hairpin work)*
29 die Häkelgabel
- *gimping needle (hairpin)*
30 die Nadelspitzen *f* (Nähspitzen, die Spitzenarbeit); *Arten:* Reticellaspitzen, Venezianerspitzen, Alençonspitzen; *ähnl.* mit Metallfaden *m:* die Filigranarbeit
- *needlepoint lace (point lace, needlepoint); kinds: reticella lace, Venetian lace, Alençon lace; sim. with metal thread: filigree work*
31 die Bändchenstickerei (Bändchenarbeit)
- *braid embroidery (braid work)*

1-27 das Damenschneideratelier
- *dressmaker's workroom*
1 der Damenschneider
- *dressmaker*
2 das Maßband (Bandmaß), ein Metermaß n
- *tape measure (measuring tape), a metre (Am. meter) tape measure*
3 die Zuschneideschere
- *cutting shears*
4 der Zuschneidetisch
- *cutting table*
5 das Modellkleid
- *model dress*
6 die Schneiderpuppe (Schneiderbüste)
- *dressmaker's model (dressmaker's dummy, dress form)*
7 der Modellmantel
- *model coat*
8 die Schneidernähmaschine
- *sewing machine*
9 der Antriebsmotor
- *drive motor*
10 der Treibriemen
- *drive belt*
11 die Fußplatte
- *treadle*
12 das Nähmaschinengarn (die Garnrolle)
- *sewing machine cotton (sewing machine thread) (bobbin)*
13 die Zuschneideschablone
- *cutting template*

14 das Nahtband (Kantenband)
- *seam binding*
15 die Knopfschachtel
- *button box*
16 der Stoffrest
- *remnant*
17 der fahrbare Kleiderständer
- *movable clothes rack*
18 der Flächenbügelplatz
- *hand-iron press*
19 die Büglerin
- *presser (ironer)*
20 das Dampfbügeleisen
- *steam iron*
21 die Wasserzuleitung
- *water feed pipe*
22 der Wasserbehälter
- *water container*
23 die neigbare Bügelfläche
- *adjustable-tilt ironing surface*
24 die Bügeleisenschwebevorrichtung
- *lift device for the iron*
25 die Saugwanne für die Dampfabsaugung
- *steam extractor*
26 die Fußschalttaste für die Absaugung
- *foot switch controlling steam extraction*
27 der aufgebügelte Vliesstoff
- *pressed non-woven woollen (Am. woolen) fabric*

1-32 das Herrenschneideratelier
- *tailor's workroom*
1 der dreiteilige Spiegel
- *triple mirror*
2 die Stoffbahnen *f*
- *lengths of material*
3 der Anzugstoff
- *suiting*
4 das Modejournal
- *fashion journal*
  (fashion magazine)
5 der Aschenbecher
- *ashtray*
6 der Modekatalog
- *fashion catalogue*
7 der Arbeitstisch
- *workbench*
8 das Wandregal
- *wall shelves (wall shelf unit)*
9 die Nähgarnrolle
- *cotton reel*
10 die Nähseidenröllchen *n*
- *small reels of sewing silk*
11 die Handschere
- *hand shears*
12 die kombinierte Elektro- und
   Tretnähmaschine
- *combined electric and treadle*
  sewing machine
13 der Tritt
- *treadle*
14 der Kleiderschutz
- *dress guard*

15 das Schwungrad
- *band wheel*
16 der Unterfadenumspuler
- *bobbin thread*
17 der Nähmaschinentisch
- *sewing machine table*
18 die Nähmaschinenschublade
- *sewing machine drawer*
19 das Kantenband
- *seam binding*
20 das Nadelkissen
- *pincushion*
21 die Anzeichnerei
- *marking out*
22 der Herrenschneider
- *tailor*
23 das Formkissen
- *shaping pad*
24 die Schneiderkreide
- *tailor's chalk (French chalk)*
25 das Werkstück
- *workpiece*
26 der Dampfbügler
- *steam press*
  (steam pressing unit)
27 der Schwenkarm
- *swivel arm*
28 das Bügelformkissen
- *pressing cushion (pressing pad)*
29 das Bügeleisen
- *iron*
30 das Handbügelkissen
- *hand-ironing pad*

31 die Stoffbürste
- *clothes brush*
32 das Bügeltuch
- *pressing cloth*

1-39 der Damenfrisiersalon
  (Damensalon) und Kosmetiksalon
– *ladies' hairdressing salon and beauty*
  salon (Am. *beauty parlor, beauty*
  shop)
1-16 Frisierutensilien *n*
– *hairdresser's tools*
1 die Schale für das Blondiermittel
– *bowl containing bleach*
2 die Strähnenbürste
– *detangling brush*
3 die Blondiermitteltube
– *bleach tube*
4 der Färbelockenwickel
– *curler [used in dyeing]*
5 die Brennschere
– *curling tongs (curling iron)*
6 der Einsteckkamm
– *comb (back comb, side comb)*
7 die Haarschneideschere
– *haircutting scissors*
8 die Effilierschere
– *thinning scissors* (Am. *thinning*
  shears)
9 das Effiliermesser
– *thinning razor*
10 die Haarbürste
– *hairbrush*
11 der Haarclip
– *hair clip*
12 der Lockenwickler (Lockenwickel)
– *roller*
13 die Lockwellbürste
– *curl brush*

14 die Lockenklammer
– *curl clip*
15 der Frisierkamm
– *dressing comb*
16 die Stachelbürste
– *stiff-bristle brush*
17 der verstellbare Frisierstuhl
– *adjustable hairdresser's chair*
18 die Fußstütze
– *footrest*
19 der Frisiertisch
– *dressing table*
20 der Frisierspiegel
– *salon mirror (mirror)*
21 der Haarschneider
– *electric clippers*
22 der Fönkamm
– *warm-air comb*
23 der Handspiegel
– *hand mirror (hand glass)*
24 das Haarspray
  (das Haarfixativ)
– *hair spray (hair-fixing spray)*
25 die Trockenhaube, eine
  Schwenkarmhaube
– *drier, a swivel-mounted drier*
26 der Haubenschwenkarm
– *swivel arm of the drier*
27 der Tellerfuß
– *round base*
28 die Waschanlage
– *shampoo unit*
29 das Haarwaschbecken
– *shampoo basin*

30 die Handbrause
– *hand spray (shampoo spray)*
31 das Serviceplateau
– *service tray*
32 die Shampooflasche
– *shampoo bottle*
33 der Fön
– *hair drier (hand hair drier,*
  hand-held hair drier)
34 der Frisierumhang
– *cape (gown)*
35 die Friseuse
– *hairdresser*
36 die Parfumflasche
– *perfume bottle*
37 die Flasche mit Toilettenwasser *n*
– *bottle of toilet water*
38 die Perücke (Zweitfrisur)
– *wig*
39 der Perückenständer
– *wig block*

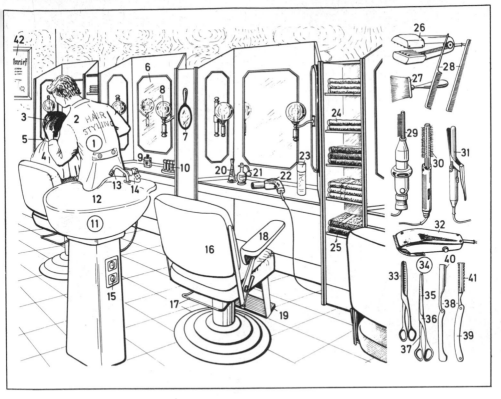

<table>
<tr><td>

15 die Steckdosen *f*, z.B. für den
　　Fönanschluß
- *sockets, e.g. for hair drier*
16 der verstellbare Frisierstuhl
- *adjustable hairdresser's chair*
　(barber's chair)
17 der Verstellbügel
- *height-adjuster bar (height*
　adjuster)
18 die Armlehne
- *armrest*
19 die Fußstütze
- *footrest*
20 das Haarwaschmittel
- *shampoo*
21 der Parfümzerstäuber
- *perfume spray*
22 der Haartrockner (Fön)
- *hair drier (hand hair drier,*
　hand-held hair drier)
23 der Haarfestiger in der Spraydose
- *setting lotion in a spray can*
24 die Handtücher *n*, zur
　　Haartrocknung
- *hand towels for drying hair*
25 die Tücher für
　　Gesichtskompressen *f*
- *towels for face compresses*
26 das Kreppeisen
- *crimping iron*
27 der Nackenpinsel
- *neck brush*
28 der Frisierkamm
- *dressing comb*

</td></tr>
</table>

1-42 der Herrensalon
- *men's salon (men's hairdressing*
　salon, barber's shop, Am. *barbershop)*
1 der Friseur (Friseurmeister,
　schweiz. Coiffeur)
- *hairdresser (barber)*
2 der Arbeitskittel (Friseurkittel)
- *overalls (hairdresser's overalls)*
3 die Frisur (der Haarschnitt)
- *hairstyle (haircut)*
4 der Frisierumhang
　　(Haarschneidemantel)
- *cape (gown)*
5 der Papierkragen
- *paper towel*
6 der Frisierspiegel
- *salon mirror (mirror)*
7 der Handspiegel
- *hand mirror (hand glass)*
8 die Frisierleuchte
- *light*
9 das Toilettenwasser
- *toilet water*
10 das Haarwasser
　　(der Haarwaschzusatz)
- *hair tonic*
11 die Haarwaschanlage
- *shampoo unit*
12 das Waschbecken
- *shampoo basin*
13 die Handdusche (Handbrause)
- *hand spray (shampoo spray)*
14 die Mischbatterie
- *mixer tap (Am. mixing faucet)*

29 der Heißluftkamm
- *warm-air comb*
30 die Thermobürste
- *warm-air brush*
31 der Frisierstab (Lockenformer)
- *curling tongs (hair curler, curling*
　iron)
32 die Haarschneidemaschine
- *electric clippers*
33 die Effilierschere
- *thinning scissors (Am. thinning*
　shears)
34 die Haarschneideschere, *ähnl.:* die
　　Modellierschere
- *haircutting scissors;* sim.: *styling*
　scissors
35 das Scherenblatt
- *scissor-blade*
36 das Schloß
- *pivot*
37 der Schenkel
- *handle*
38 das Rasiermesser
- *open razor (straight razor)*
39 der Messergriff
- *razor handle*
40 die Rasierschneide
- *edge (cutting edge, razor's edge,*
　razor's cutting edge)
41 das Effiliermesser
- *thinning razor*
42 der Meisterbrief
- *diploma*

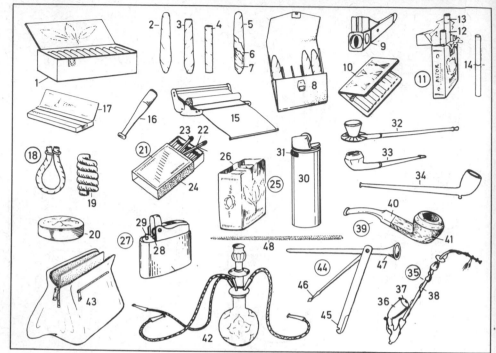

1 die Zigarrenkiste
- *cigar box*
2 die Zigarre; *Arten:* Havanna, Brasil, Sumatra
- *cigar;* kinds: *Havana cigar (Havana), Brazilian cigar, Sumatra cigar*
3 das (der, *ugs.* die) Zigarillo
- *cigarillo*
4 der Stumpen
- *cheroot*
5 das Deckblatt
- *wrapper*
6 das Umblatt
- *binder*
7 die Einlage
- *filler*
8 das Zigarrenetui
- *cigar case*
9 der Zigarrenabschneider
- *cigar cutter*
10 das Zigarettenetui
- *cigarette case*
11 die Zigarettenschachtel
- *cigarette packet* (Am. *pack*)
12 die Zigarette, eine Filterzigarette
- *cigarette, a filter-tipped cigarette*
13 das Mundstück; *Arten:* Korkmundstück, Goldmundstück
- *cigarette tip;* kinds: *cork tip, gold tip*
14 die Papirossa
- *Russian cigarette*
15 die Zigarettenmaschine (der Zigarettenwickler)
- *cigarette roller*
16 die Zigarettenspitze
- *cigarette holder*

17 das Zigarettenpapierheftchen
- *packet of cigarette papers*
18 der Rollentabak
- *pigtail (twist of tobacco)*
19 der Kautabak; *ein Stück:* der Priem
- *chewing tobacco;* a piece: *plug (quid, chew)*
20 die Schnupftabaksdose, mit Schnupftabak *m*
- *snuff box, containing snuff*
21 die Streichholzschachtel (Zündholzschachtel)
- *matchbox*
22 das Streichholz (Zündholz)
- *match*
23 der Schwefelkopf (Zündkopf)
- *head (match head)*
24 die Reibfläche
- *striking surface*
25 das Paket (Päckchen) Tabak *m*; *Arten:* Feinschnitt, Krüllschnitt, Navy Cut
- *packet of tobacco;* kinds: *fine cut, shag, navy plug*
26 die Banderole (Steuerbanderole, Steuermarke)
- *revenue stamp*
27 das Benzinfeuerzeug
- *petrol cigarette lighter (petrol lighter)*
28 der Feuerstein
- *flint*
29 der Docht
- *wick*
30 das Gasfeuerzeug, ein Einwegfeuerzeug (Wegwerffeuerzeug)
- *gas cigarette lighter (gas lighter), a disposable lighter*

31 die Flammenregulierung
- *flame regulator*
32 der Tschibuk
- *chibonk (chibonque)*
33 die kurze Pfeife
- *short pipe*
34 die Tonpfeife
- *clay pipe (Dutch pipe)*
35 die lange Pfeife
- *long pipe*
36 der Pfeifenkopf
- *pipe bowl (bowl)*
37 der Pfeifendeckel
- *bowl lid*
38 das Pfeifenrohr
- *pipe stem (stem)*
39 die Bruyèrepfeife
- *briar pipe*
40 das Pfeifenmundstück
- *mouthpiece*
41 die (sandgestrahlte oder polierte) Bruyèremaserung
- *sand-blast finished or polished briar grain*
42 die (das) Nargileh, eine Wasserpfeife
- *hookah (narghile, narghileh), a water pipe*
43 der Tabaksbeutel
- *tobacco pouch*
44 das Raucherbesteck (Pfeifenbesteck)
- *smoker's companion*
45 der Auskratzer
- *pipe scraper*
46 der Pfeifenreiniger
- *pipe cleaner*
47 der Stopfer
- *tobacco presser*
48 der Pfeifenreinigungsdraht
- *pipe cleaner*

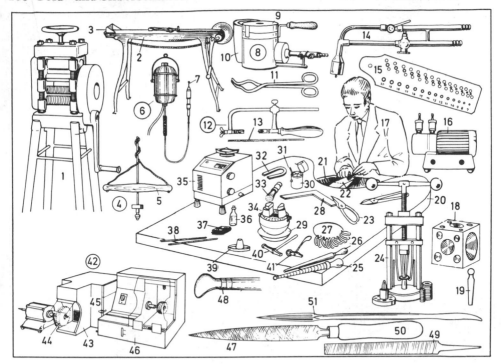

1 die Draht- und Blechwalze
- *wire and sheet roller*
2 die Ziehbank
- *drawbench (drawing bench)*
3 der Draht (Gold- oder Silberdraht)
- *wire (gold or silver wire)*
4 der Dreul (Drillbohrer)
- *archimedes drill (drill)*
5 das Querholz
- *crossbar*
6 die elektrische
Hängebohrmaschine
- *suspended (pendant) electric
drilling machine*
7 der Kugelfräser mit Handstück *n*
- *spherical cutter (cherry)*
8 der Schmelzofen
- *melting pot*
9 der Schamottedeckel
- *fireclay top*
10 der Graphittiegel
- *graphite crucible*
11 die Tiegelzange
- *crucible tongs*
12 die Bogensäge
- *piercing saw (jig saw)*
13 das Laubsägeblatt
- *piercing saw blade*
14 die Lötpistole
- *soldering gun*
15 das Gewindeschneideisen
- *thread tapper*
16 das Zylinderlötgebläse
- *blast burner (blast lamp) for
soldering*
17 der Goldschmied
- *goldsmith*

18 die Würfelanke (Anke, der
Vertiefstempel)
- *swage block*
19 die Punze
- *punch*
20 das Werkbrett
- *workbench (bench)*
21 das Werkbrettfell
- *bench apron*
22 der Feilnagel
- *needle file*
23 die Blechschere
- *metal shears*
24 die Trauringmaschine
(Trauring-Weitenänderungsmaschine)
- *wedding ring sizing machine*
25 der Ringstock
- *ring gauge (Am. gage)*
26 der Ringriegel
- *ring-rounding tool*
27 das Ringmaß
- *ring gauge (Am. gage)*
28 der Stahlwinkel
- *steel set-square*
29 das Linsenkissen,
ein Lederkissen
- *(circular) leather pad*
30 die Punzenbüchse
- *box of punches*
31 die Punze
- *punch*
32 der Magnet
- *magnet*
33 die Brettbürste (der Brettpinsel)
- *bench brush*
34 die Gravierkugel
- *engraving ball (joint vice, clamp)*

35 die Gold- und Silberwaage, eine
Präzisionswaage
- *gold and silver balance (assay
balance), a precision balance*
36 das Lötmittel
- *soldering flux (flux)*
37 die Glühplatte, aus Holzkohle *f*
- *charcoal block*
38 die Lötstange
- *stick of solder*
39 der Lötborax
- *soldering borax*
40 der Fassonhammer
- *shaping hammer*
41 der Ziselierhammer
- *chasing (enchasing) hammer*
42 die Poliermaschine
- *polishing and burnishing machine*
43 der Tischexhaustor
(Tischstaubsauger)
- *dust exhauster (vacuum cleaner)*
44 die Polierbürste
- *polishing wheel*
45 der Staubsammelkasten
- *dust collector (dust catcher)*
46 das Naßbürstgerät
- *buffing machine*
47 die Rundfeile
- *round file*
48 der Blutstein (Roteisenstein)
- *bloodstone (haematite, hematite)*
49 die Flachfeile
- *flat file*
50 das Feilenheft
- *file handle*
51 der Polierstahl
- *polishing iron (burnisher)*

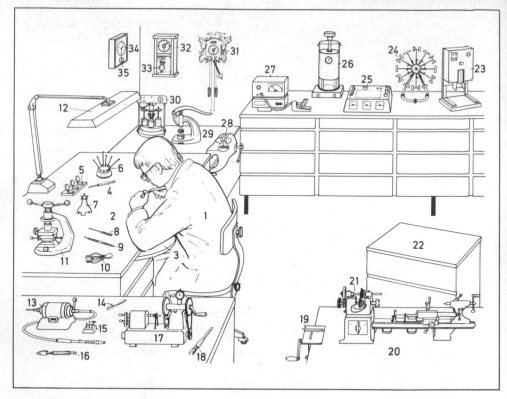

1 der Uhrmacher
- *watchmaker;* also: *clockmaker*
2 der Werktisch
- *workbench*
3 die Armauflage
- *armrest*
4 der Ölgeber
- *oiler*
5 der Ölblock für Kleinuhren *f*
- *oil stand*
6 der Schraubenziehersatz
- *set of screwdrivers*
7 der Zeigeramboß
- *clockmaker's anvil*
8 die Glättahle, eine Reibahle
- *broach, a reamer*
9 das Federstegwerkzeug
- *spring pin tool*
10 der Abheber für
Armbanduhrzeiger *m*
- *hand-removing tool*
11 der Gehäuseschlüssel
- *watchglass-fitting tool [for
armoured, Am. armored, glass]*
12 die Arbeitslampe, eine
Mehrzweckleuchte
- *workbench lamp, a multi-purpose
lamp*
13 der Mehrzweckmotor
- *multi-purpose motor*
14 die Kornzange (Pinzette)
- *tweezers*
15 die Poliermaschinenaufsätze *m*
- *polishing machine attachments*

16 das Stiftenklöbchen
- *pin vice (pin holder)*
17 die Rolliermaschine (der
Rollierstuhl) zum Rollieren *n*,
Polieren *n*, Arrondieren *n* und
Kürzen *n* von Wellen *f*
- *burnisher, for burnishing, polishing
and shortening of spindles*
18 der Staubpinsel
- *dust brush*
19 der Abschneider für
Metallarmbänder *n*
- *cutter for metal watch straps*
20 die Präzisions-Kleindrehmaschine
(Kleindrehbank, der
Uhrmacherdrehstuhl)
- *precision bench lathe
(watchmaker's lathe)*
21 das Keilriemenvorgelege
- *drive-belt gear*
22 der Werkstattmuli für Ersatzteile *n*
- *workshop trolley for spare parts*
23 die Vibrationsreinigungsmaschine
- *ultrasonic cleaner*
24 das Umlaufprüfgerät für
automatische Uhren *f*
- *rotating watch-testing machine for
automatic watches*
25 das Meßpult für die Überprüfung
elektronischer Bauelemente *n*
- *watch-timing machine for
electronic components*
26 das Prüfgerät für wasserdichte Uhren *f*
- *testing device for waterproof watches*

27 die Zeitwaage
- *electronic timing machine*
28 der Schraubstock
- *vice* (Am. *vise*)
29 die Einpreßvorrichtung für
armierte Uhrgläser *n*
- *watchglass-fitting tool for
armoured* (Am. *armored*) *glasses*
30 der Reinigungsautomat für die
konventionelle Reinigung
- *[automatic] cleaning machine for
conventional cleaning*
31 die Kuckucksuhr
(Schwarzwälderuhr)
- *cuckoo clock (Black Forest clock)*
32 die Wanduhr (der Regulator)
- *wall clock (regulator)*
33 das Kompensationspendel
- *compensation pendulum*
34 die Küchenuhr
- *kitchen clock*
35 die Kurzzeituhr (der Kurzzeitwecker)
- *timer*

1 die elektronische Armbanduhr
- *electronic wristwatch*
2 die Digitalanzeige (eine
  Leuchtdiodenanzeige, *auch:*
  Flüssigkristallanzeige)
- *digital readout, a light-emitting
  diode (LED) readout; also: liquid
  crystal readout*
3 der Stunden- und Minutenknopf
- *hour and minute button*
4 der Datums- und Sekundenknopf
- *date and second button*
5 das Armband
- *strap (watch strap)*
6 das Stimmgabelprinzip (Prinzip
  der Stimmgabeluhr *f*)
- *tuning fork principle (principle of
  the tuning fork watch)*
7 die Antriebsquelle (eine
  Knopfzelle)
- *power source (battery cell)*
8 die elektronische Schaltung
- *transformer*
9 das Stimmgabelelement
  (Schwingelement)
- *tuning fork element (oscillating
  element)*
10 das Klinkenrad
- *wheel ratchet*
11 das Räderwerk
- *wheels*
12 der große Zeiger
- *minute hand*
13 der kleine Zeiger
- *hour hand*
14 das Prinzip der elektronischen
  Quarzuhr *f*
- *principle of the electronic quartz
  watch*
15 der Quarz (Schwingquarz)
- *quartz*
16 die Frequenzunterteilung
  (integrierte Schaltungen *f*)
- *integrated circuit*
17 der Schrittschaltmotor
- *oscillation counter*
18 der Decoder
- *decoder*
19 die Terminuhr (der Wecker, die
  Weckuhr)
- *calendar clock (alarm clock)*
20 die Digitalanzeige mit
  Fallblattziffern *f*
- *digital display with flip-over
  numerals*
21 die Sekundenanzeige
- *second indicator*
22 die Abstelltaste
- *stop button*
23 das Stellrad
- *forward and backward wind knob*
24 die Standuhr
- *grandfather clock*
25 das Zifferblatt
- *face*
26 das Uhrgehäuse
- *clock case*
27 das Pendel (das *od.* der
  Perpendikel)
- *pendulum*
28 das Schlaggewicht
- *striking weight*
29 das Ganggewicht
- *time weight*
30 die Sonnenuhr
- *sundial*

31 die Sanduhr (Eieruhr)
- *hourglass (egg timer)*
32-43 **das Springbild der
  automatischen Armbanduhr** *f*
  (Uhr mit automatischem
  Aufzug *m,* Selbstaufzug)
- **components of an
  automatic watch**
  (automatic wristwatch)
32 die Schwingmasse (der Rotor)
- *weight (rotor)*
33 der Stein (Lagerstein), ein
  synthetischer Rubin
- *stone (jewel, jewelled
  bearing), a synthetic ruby*
34 die Spannklinke
- *click*
35 das Spannrad
- *click wheel*
36 das Uhrwerk
- *clockwork
  (clockwork mechanism)*
37 die Werkplatte
- *bottom train plate*
38 das Federhaus
- *spring barrel*
39 die Unruh
- *balance wheel*
40 das Ankerrad
- *escape wheel*
41 das Aufzugsrad
- *crown wheel*
42 die Krone (der Kronenaufzug)
- *winding crown*
43 das Antriebswerk
- *drive mechanism*

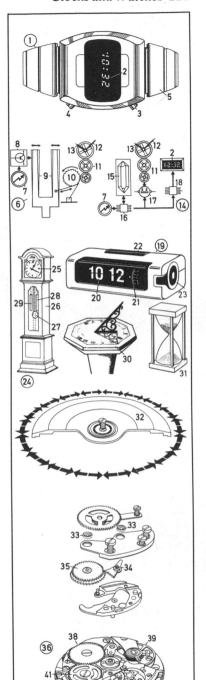

1-19 der Verkaufsraum
- *sales premises*
1-4 die Brillenanprobe
- *spectacle fitting*
1 der Optiker
- *optician*
2 der Kunde
- *customer*
3 das Probegestell
- *trial frame*
4 der Spiegel
- *mirror*
5 der Gestellständer (die
   Gestellauswahl, Brillenauswahl)
- *stand with spectacle frames
   (display of frames, range of
   spectacles)*
6 die Sonnenbrille
- *sunglasses (sun spectacles)*
7 das Metallgestell
- *metal frame*
8 das Horngestell
- *tortoiseshell frame (shell frame)*
9 die Brille
- *spectacles (glasses)*
10-14 das Brillengestell
- *spectacle frame*
10 die Gläserfassung
- *fitting (mount) of the
   frame*
11 der Steg
- *bridge*

12 der Padsteg
- *pad bridge*
13 der Bügel
- *side*
14 das Bügelscharnier
- *side joint*
15 das Brillenglas, ein Bifokalglas *n*
   (Zweistärkenglas)
- *spectacle lens, a bifocal lens*
16 der Handspiegel
- *hand mirror (hand glass)*
17 das Fernglas
- *binoculars*
18 das monokulare Fernrohr (der
   Tubus)
- *monocular telescope (tube)*
19 das Mikroskop
- *microscope*

20-47 die Optikerwerkstatt
- *optician's workshop*
20 der Arbeitstisch
- *workbench*
21 das Universalzentriergerät
- *universal centring (centering) apparatus*
22 die Zentriersaugeraufnahme
- *centring (centering) suction holder*
23 der Zentriersauger
- *sucker*
24 der Brillenglas-Randbearbeitungsautomat
- *edging machine*
25 die Formscheiben *f* für den Randbearbeitungsautomaten *m*
- *formers for the lens edging machine*
26 die eingesetzte Formscheibe
- *inserted former*
27 die mitdrehende Kopierscheibe
- *rotating printer*
28 die Schleifscheibenkombination
- *abrasive wheel combination*
29 das Steuergerät
- *control unit*
30 das Maschinenteil
- *machine part*
31 der Kühlwasseranschluß
- *cooling water pipe*
32 die Reinigungsflüssigkeit
- *cleaning fluid*

33 der Scheitelbrechwertmesser
- *focimeter (vertex refractionometer)*
34 das Zentrier-, Saugerandrück- und Metallaufblockgerät
- *metal-blocking device*
35 Schleifscheibenkombination *f* und Schlifformen *f*
- *abrasive wheel combination and forms of edging*
36 die Vorschleifscheibe
- *roughing wheel for preliminary surfacing*
37 die Feinschleifscheibe für Plus- und Minusfacette *f*
- *fining lap for positive and negative lens surfaces*
38 die Feinschleifscheibe für Spezialfacette *f* und Flachfacette *f*
- *fining lap for special and flat lenses*
39 das Plankonkavglas mit Flachfacette *f*
- *plano-concave lens with a flat surface*
40 das Plankonkavglas mit Spezialfacette *f*
- *plano-concave lens with a special surface*
41 das Konkavkonvexglas mit Spezialfacette *f*
- *concave and convex lens with a special surface*

42 das Konkavkonvexglas mit Minusfacette *f*
- *convex and concave lens with a special surface*
43 der ophthalmologische Prüfplatz
- *ophthalmic test stand*
44 der Phoropter mit Ophthalmometer *n* und Augenrefraktometer *n*
- *phoropter with ophthalmometer and optometer (refractometer)*
45 der Probiergläserkasten
- *trial lens case*
46 der Sehzeichenkollimator
- *collimator*
47 der Sehzeichenprojektor
- *acuity projector*

1 das Laboratoriums- und
Forschungsmikroskop *System
Leitz* [teilweise im Schnitt]
- *laboratory and research
microscope*, Leitz system
2 das Stativ
- *stand*
3 der Stativfuß
- *base*
4 der Grobtrieb
- *coarse adjustment*
5 der Feintrieb
- *fine adjustment*
6 der Beleuchtungsstrahlengang
- *illumination beam path
(illumination path)*
7 die Beleuchtungsoptik
- *illumination optics*
8 die Kondensoreinrichtung
- *condenser*
9 der Mikroskoptisch (Objekttisch)
- *microscope (microscopic, object)
stage*
10 die Kreuztischeinrichtung
- *mechanical stage*
11 der Objektivrevolver
- *objective turret (revolving
nosepiece)*
12 der Binokulartubus
- *binocular head*
13 die Umlenkprismen *n*
- *beam-splitting prisms*
14 das Durchlichtmikroskop mit
Kamera *f* und
Polarisationseinrichtung *f System
Zeiss*
- *transmitted-light microscope with
camera and polarizer*, Zeiss system
15 der Tischsockel
- *stage base*
16 der Aperturblendenschieber
- *aperture-stop slide*
17 der Universaldrehtisch
- *universal stage*
18 die Objektivbrücke
- *lens panel*
19 die Bildweiche
- *polarizing filter*
20 das (der) Kamerateil
- *camera*
21 die Einstellscheibe
- *focusing screen*
22 die Diskussionstubusanordnung
- *discussion tube arrangement*
23 das Großfeld-Metallmikroskop,
ein Auflichtmikroskop *n*
- *wide-field metallurgical
microscope, a reflected-light
microscope (microscope for
reflected light)*
24 die Projektionsmattscheibe
- *matt screen (ground glass screen,
projection screen)*
25 die Großbildkamera
- *large-format camera*
26 die Kleinbildkamera
- *miniature camera*
27 die Bodenplatte
- *base plate*
28 das Lampenhaus
- *lamphouse*
29 der drehbare Kreuztisch
- *mechanical stage*
30 der Objektivrevolver
- *objective turret (revolving
nosepiece)*

31 das Operationsmikroskop
- *surgical microscope*
32 das Säulenstativ
- *pillar stand*
33 die Objektfeldbeleuchtung
- *field illumination*
34 das Fotomikroskop
- *photomicroscope*
35 die Kleinbildkassette
- *miniature film cassette*
36 der zusätzliche Fotoausgang
für Großformat- oder
Fernsehkamera *f*
- *photomicrographic camera
attachment for large-format or
television camera*
37 das Oberflächenprüfgerät
- *surface-finish microscope*
38 der Lichtschnittubus
- *light section tube*
39 der Zahntrieb
- *rack and pinion*
40 das Großfeldstereomikroskop mit
Zoomeinstellung *f*
- *zoom stereomicroscope*
41 das Zoomobjektiv
- *zoom lens*
42 das optische Feinstaubmeßgerät
- *dust counter*
43 die Meßkammer
- *measurement chamber*
44 der Datenausgang
- *data output*
45 der Analogausgang
- *analogue (Am. analog) output*
46 der Meßbereichwähler
- *measurement range selector*
47 die digitale Datenanzeige
- *digital display
(digital readout)*
48 das Eintauchrefraktometer, zur
Nahrungsmitteluntersuchung
- *dipping refractometer for
examining food*
49 das Mikroskopphotometer
- *microscopic photometer*
50 die Photometerlichtquelle
- *photometric light source*
51 die Meßeinrichtung (der
Photovervielfacher)
- *measuring device
(photomultiplier,
multiplier phototube)*
52 die Lichtquelle für die
Übersichtsbeleuchtung
- *light source for survey illumination*
53 der Elektronikschrank
- *remote electronics*
54 das universelle
Großfeldmikroskop
- *universal wide-field microscope*
55 der Fotostutzen, für Kamera *f* oder
Projektionsaufsatz *m*
- *adapter for camera or projector
attachment*
56 der Drehknopf zum Einstellen *n*
des Okularabstandes *m*
- *eyepiece focusing knob*
57 die Filteraufnahme
- *filter pick-up*
58 die Handauflage
- *handrest*
59 das Lampenhaus für die
Auflichtbeleuchtung
- *lamphouse for incident (vertical)
illumination*

60 der Lampenhausanschluß für die
Durchlichtbeleuchtung
- *lamphouse connector for
transillumination*
61 das Großfeldstereomikroskop
- *wide-field stereomicroscope*
62 die Wechselobjektive *n*
- *interchangeable lenses (objectives)*
63 die Auflichtbeleuchtung
- *incident (vertical) illumination
(incident top lighting)*
64 die vollautomatische
Mikroskopkamera, eine
Aufsatzkamera
- *fully automatic microscope camera,
a camera with photomicro mount
adapter*
65 die Filmkassette
- *film cassette*
66 der Universalkondensor zum
Forschungsmikroskop 1 *n*
- *universal condenser for research
microscope 1*
67 die Universalmeßkammer für die
Photogrammetrie (der
Phototheodolit)
- *universal-type measuring machine
for photogrammetry
(phototheodolite)*
68 die Meßbildkamera
- *photogrammetric camera*
69 das Motornivellier, ein
Kompensatornivellier *n*
- *motor-driven level, a compensator
level*
70 das elektro-optische
Streckenmeßgerät
- *electro-optical distance-measuring
instrument*
71 die Stereomeßkammer
- *stereometric camera*
72 die horizontale Basis
- *horizontal base*
73 der Sekundentheodolit
- *one-second theodolite*

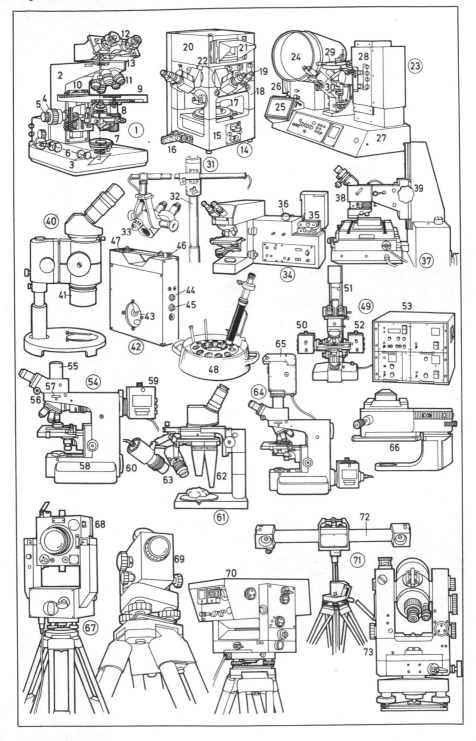

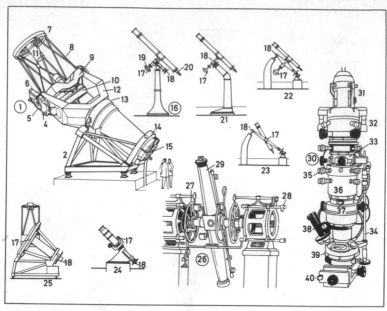

1 **das 2,2-m-Spiegelteleskop**
- *2.2 m reflecting telescope (reflector)*
2 das Untergestell
- *pedestal (base)*
3 die Axial-radial-Lagerung
- *axial-radial bearing*
4 das Deklinationsgetriebe
- *declination gear*
5 die Deklinationsachse
- *declination axis*
6 das Deklinationslager
- *declination bearing*
7 der Frontring
- *front ring*
8 der Tubus
- *tube (body tube)*
9 das Tubusmittelteil
- *tube centre (Am. center) section*
10 der Hauptspiegel
- *primary mirror (main mirror)*
11 der Umlenkspiegel
- *secondary mirror (deviation mirror, corrector plate)*
12 die Gabel
- *fork mounting (fork)*
13 die Abdeckung
- *cover*
14 das Führungslager
- *guide bearing*
15 der Hauptantrieb der Stundenachse
- *main drive unit of the polar axis*
16-25 Fernrohrmontierungen *f*
- *telescope mountings (telescope mounts)*
16 das Linsenfernrohr (der Refraktor) in deutscher Montierung
- *refractor (refracting telescope) on a German-type mounting*
17 die Deklinationsachse
- *declination axis*

18 die Stundenachse
- *polar axis*
19 das Gegengewicht
- *counterweight (counterpoise)*
20 das Okular
- *eyepiece*
21 die Knicksäulenmontierung
- *knee mounting with a bent column*
22 die englische Achsenmontierung
- *English-type axis mounting (axis mount)*
23 die englische Rahmenmontierung
- *English-type yoke mounting (yoke mount)*
24 die Gabelmontierung
- *fork mounting (fork mount)*
25 die Hufeisenmontierung
- *horseshoe mounting (horseshoe mount)*
26 der Meridiankreis
- *meridian circle*
27 der Teilkreis
- *divided circle (graduated circle)*
28 das Ablesemikroskop
- *reading microscope*
29 das Meridianfernrohr
- *meridian telescope*
30 das Elektronenmikroskop
- *electron microscope*
31-39 die Mikroskopröhre
- *microscope tube (microscope body, body tube)*
31 das Strahlenerzeugungssystem (der Strahlkopf)
- *electron gun*
32 die Kondensorlinsen *f*
- *condensers*
33 die Objektschleuse
- *specimen insertion air lock*
34 die Objekttischverstellung (Objektverschiebung)
- *control for the specimen stage adjustment*

35 der Aperturblendentrieb
- *control for the objective apertures*
36 die Objektivlinse
- *objective lens*
37 das Zwischenbildfenster
- *intermediate image screen*
38 die Fernrohrlupe
- *telescope magnifier*
39 das Endbildfenster (der Endbildleuchtschirm)
- *final image tube*
40 die Aufnahmekammer für Film- bzw. Plattenkassetten *f*
- *photographic chamber for film and plate magazines*

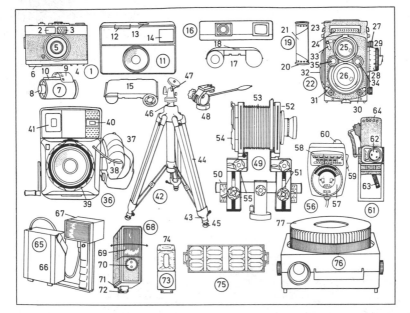

1 die Kleinbild-Kompaktkamera
- *miniature camera (35 mm camera)*
2 der Sucherausblick
- *viewfinder eyepiece*
3 das Belichtungsmesserfenster
- *meter cell*
4 der Zubehörschuh
- *accessory shoe*
5 das versenkbare Objektiv
- *flush lens*
6 die Rückspulkurbel
(Rückwickelkurbel)
- *rewind handle (rewind, rewind crank)*
7 die Kleinbildkassette
(Kleinbildpatrone) 135
- *miniature film cassette (135 film
cassette, 35 mm cassette)*
8 die Filmspule
- *film spool*
9 der Film mit dem
„Einfädelschwanz" m
- *film with leader*
10 das Kassettenmaul
- *cassette slit (cassette exit slot)*
11 die Kassettenkamera
- *cartridge-loading camera*
12 die Auslösetaste
- *shutter release (shutter release
button)*
13 der Blitzwürfelanschluß
- *flash cube contact*
14 der quadratische Sucher
- *rectangular viewfinder*
15 die Filmkassette 126
(Instamatic-Kassette)
- *126 cartridge (instamatic cartridge)*
16 die Pocketkamera
(Kleinstbildkamera)
- *pocket camera (subminiature camera)*
17 die Kleinstbildkassette 110
- *110 cartridge (subminiature
cartridge)*
18 das Bildnummernfenster
- *film window*
19 der Rollfilm 120
- *120 rollfilm*
20 die Rollfilmspule
- *rollfilm spool*
21 das Schutzpapier
- *backing paper*

22 die zweiäugige
Spiegelreflexkamera
- *twin-lens reflex camera*
23 der aufklappbare Sucherschacht
- *folding viewfinder hood (focusing
hood)*
24 das Belichtungsmesserfenster
- *meter cell*
25 das Sucherobjektiv
- *viewing lens*
26 das Aufnahmeobjektiv
- *object lens*
27 der Spulenknopf
- *spool knob*
28 die Entfernungseinstellung
- *distance setting (focus setting)*
29 der Nachführbelichtungsmesser
- *exposure meter using
needle-matching system*
30 der Blitzlichtanschluß
- *flash contact*
31 der Auslöser
- *shutter release*
32 die Filmtransportkurbel
- *film transport (film advance, film
wind)*
33 der Blitzschalter
- *flash switch*
34 das Blendeneinstellrad
- *aperture-setting control*
35 das Zeiteinstellrad
- *shutter speed control*
36 die Großformathandkamera
(Pressekamera)
- *large-format hand camera (press
camera)*
37 der Handgriff
- *grip (handgrip)*
38 der Drahtauslöser
- *cable release*
39 der Rändelring zur
Entfernungseinstellung
- *distance-setting ring (focusing ring)*
40 das Entfernungsmesserfenster
- *rangefinder window*
41 der Mehrformatsucher
- *multiple-frame viewfinder
(universal viewfinder)*
42 das Rohrstativ (Dreibein)
- *tripod*

43 das Stativbein
- *tripod leg*
44 der Rohrschenkel
- *tubular leg*
45 der Gummifuß
- *rubber foot*
46 die Mittelsäule
- *central column*
47 der Kugelgelenkkopf
- *ball and socket head*
48 der Kinonivellierkopf
- *cine camera pan and tilt head*
49 die Großformatbalgenkamera
- *large-format folding camera*
50 die optische Bank
- *optical bench*
51 die Standartenverstellung
- *standard adjustment*
52 die Objektivstandarte
- *lens standard*
53 der Balgen
- *bellows*
54 das Kamerarückteil
- *camera back*
55 die Rückteilverstellung
- *back standard adjustment*
56 der Handbelichtungsmesser
(Belichtungsmesser)
- *hand-held exposure meter
(exposure meter)*
57 die Rechenscheibe
- *calculator dial*
58 die Anzeigeskalen f mit
Anzeigenadel f
- *scales (indicator scales) with
indicator needle
(pointer)*
59 die Meßbereichswippe
- *range switch (high/low range
selector)*
60 die Diffusorkalotte für
Lichtmessungen f
- *diffuser for incident light
measurement*
61 die Belichtungsmeßkassette für
Großbildkameras f
- *probe exposure meter for
large-format cameras*
62 das Meßgerät
- *meter*

63 die Meßsonde
- *probe*
64 der Kassettenschieber
- *dark slide*
65 das zweiteilige
Elektronenblitzgerät
- *battery-portable electronic flash
(battery-portable electronic flash
unit)*
66 das (der) Generatorteil (die
Batterie)
- *powerpack unit (battery)*
67 die Blitzlampe (der Blitzstab)
- *flash head*
68 das einteilige Elektronenblitzgerät
- *single-unit electronic flash
(flashgun)*
69 der schwenkbare Reflektor
- *swivel-mounted reflector*
70 die Photodiode
- *photodiode*
71 der Sucherfuß
- *foot*
72 der Mittenkontakt
- *hot-shoe contact*
73 das Würfelblitzgerät
- *flash cube unit*
74 der Würfelblitz
- *flash cube*
75 die Flashbar (AGFA)
- *flash bar (AGFA)*
76 der Diaprojektor
- *slide projector*
77 das Rundmagazin
- *rotary magazine*

1-105 die Systemkamera
- *system camera*
1 die einäugige
Kleinbild-Spiegelreflexkamera
- *miniature single-lens reflex camera*
2 das Kameragehäuse
- *camera body*
3-8 das Objektiv, ein
Normalobjektiv
- *lens, a normal lens (standard lens)*
3 der Objektivtubus
- *lens barrel*
4 die Entfernungsskala in Metern *m*
und Feet *m*
- *distance scale in metres and feet*
5 der Blendenring
- *aperture ring (aperture-setting ring,
aperture control ring)*
6 die Frontlinsenfassung mit
Filteranschluß *m*
- *front element mount with filter
mount*
7 die Frontlinse
- *front element*
8 der Rändelring zur
Scharfeinstellung
- *focusing ring (distance-setting ring)*
9 die Tragriemenöse
- *ring for the carrying strap*
10 das Batteriefach
- *battery chamber*
11 der Schraubdeckel
- *screw-in cover*
12 die Rückspulkurbel
- *rewind handle (rewind, rewind
crank)*
13 der Batteriehauptschalter
- *battery switch*
14 der Blitzlichtanschluß für F- und
X-Kontakt *m*
- *flash socket for F and X contact*
15 der Spannhebel für den
Selbstauslöser
- *self-time lever (setting lever for the
self-timer, setting lever for the
delayed-action release)*
16 der Schnellschalthebel
- *single-stroke film advance lever*
17 das Bildzählwerk
- *exposure counter (frame counter)*
18 der Auslöseknopf
- *shutter release (shutter release
button)*
19 der Verschlußzeitenknopf
- *shutter speed setting knob (shutter
speed control)*
20 der Zubehörschuh
- *accessory shoe*
21 der Blitzlicht-Mittenkontakt
- *hot-shoe flash contact*
22 der Suchereinblick (das
Sucherokular) mit Korrekturlinse *f*
- *viewfinder eyepiece with correcting
lens*
23 die Kamerarückwand
- *camera back*
24 die Filmandruckplatte
- *pressure plate*
25 der Filmmitnehmer des
Schnelladesystems *n*
- *take-up spool of the rapid-loading
system*
26 die Transportzahntrommel
- *transport sprocket*
27 der Rückspulfreilauf
- *rewind release button (reversing
clutch)*
28 das Filmfenster (Negativfenster,
Bildfenster, die Bildbühne)
- *film window*
29 der Rückspulmitnehmer
- *rewind cam*
30 der Stativgewindeanschluß
- *tripod socket (tripod bush)*
31 das Spiegelreflexsystem
- *reflex system (mirror reflex system)*
32 das Objektiv
- *lens*
33 der Reflexspiegel
- *reflex mirror*
34 das Bildfenster
- *film window*

35 der Bildstrahlengang
- *path of the image beam*
36 der Meßstrahlengang
- *path of the sample beam*
37 die Meßzelle
- *meter cell*
38 der Hilfsspiegel
- *auxiliary mirror*
39 die Einstellscheibe
- *focusing screen*
40 die Bildfeldlinse
- *field lens*
41 das Pentadachkantprisma
- *pentaprism*
42 das Okular
- *eyepiece*
43-105 das Systemzubehör
- *system of accessories*
43 die Wechselobjektive *n*
- *interchangeable lenses*
44 das Fischaugenobjektiv
(Fischauge)
- *fisheye lens (fisheye)*
45 das Weitwinkelobjektiv (die kurze
Brennweite)
- *wide-angle lens (short focal length
lens)*
46 das Normalobjektiv
- *normal lens (standard lens)*
47 die mittlere Brennweite
- *medium focal length lens*
48 das Teleobjektiv (die lange
Brennweite)
- *telephoto lens (long focal length lens)*
49 das Fernobjektiv (die
Fernbildlinse)
- *long-focus lens*
50 das Spiegelobjektiv
- *mirror lens*
51 das Sucherbild
- *viewfinder image*
52 das Signal für die manuelle
Einstellung
- *signal to switch to manual control*
53 der Mattscheibenring
- *matt collar (ground glass collar)*
54 das Mikroprismenraster
(Mikrospaltbildfeld)
- *microprism collar*
55 der Schnittbildindikator (die
Meßkeile *m*)
- *split-image rangefinder (focusing
wedges)*
56 die Blendenskala
- *aperture scale*
57 der Belichtungsmesserzeiger
- *exposure meter needle*
**58-66 auswechselbare
Einstellscheiben *f***
- *interchangeable focusing screens*
58 die Vollmattscheibe mit
Mikroprismenraster
- *all-matt screen (ground glass
screen) with microprism spot*
59 die Vollmattscheibe mit
Prismenraster *n* und
Schnittbildindikator *m*
- *all-matt screen (ground glass
screen) with microprism spot and
split-image rangefinder*
60 die Vollmattscheibe ohne
Einstellhilfsmittel *n*
- *all-matt screen (ground glass
screen) without focusing aids*
61 die Mattscheibe mit Gitterteilung *f*
- *matt screen (ground glass screen)
with reticule*
62 das Prismenraster für Objektive *n*
hoher Öffnung *f*
- *microprism spot for lenses with a
large aperture*
63 das Prismenraster für Objektive ab
Lichtstärke *f* =1:3,5
- *microprism spot for lenses with an
aperture of f = 1 : 3.5 or larger.*
64 die Fresnellinse mit
Mattscheibenring *m* und
Schnittbildindikator *m*
- *Fresnel lens with matt collar
(ground glass collar) and
split-image rangefinder*
65 die Vollmattscheibe mit

feinmattiertem Mittenfleck *m* und
Meßskalen *f*
- *all-matt screen (ground glass
screen) with finely matted central
spot and graduated markings*
66 die Mattscheibe mit Klarglasfleck
m und doppeltem Fadenkreuz *n*
- *matt screen (ground glass screen)
with clear spot and double cross
hairs*
67 die Datenrückwand zum
Einbelichten *n* von
Aufnahmedaten *n*
- *data recording back for exposing
data about shots*
68 der Sucherlichtschacht
- *viewfinder hood (focusing hood)*
69 der auswechselbare Prismensucher
- *interchangeable pentaprism
viewfinder*
70 das Pentadachkantprisma
- *pentaprism*
71 der Winkelsucher
- *right-angle viewfinder*
72 die Korrekturlinse
- *correction lens*
73 die Augenmuschel
(Okularmuschel)
- *eyecup*
74 das Einstellfernrohr
- *focusing telescope*
75 der Batterieanschluß
- *battery unit*
76 der Batteriehandgriff für den
Kameramotor
- *combined battery holder and
control grip for the motor drive*
77 die Schnellschußkamera
- *rapid-sequence camera*
78 der ansetzbare Kameramotor
- *attachable motor drive*
79 die externe Stromversorgung
- *external (outside) power supply*
80 das Zehn-Meter-Filmmagazin
- *ten meter film back (magazine
back)*
81-98 Naheinstell- und Makrogeräte *n*
- *close-up and macro equipment*
81 der Zwischentubus
- *extension tube*
82 der Adapterring
- *adapter ring*
83 der Umkehrring
- *reversing ring*
84 das Objektiv in Retrostellung *f*
- *lens in retrofocus position*
85 das Balgengerät
(Balgennaheinstellgerät)
- *bellows unit (extension bellows,
close-up bellows attachment)*
86 der Einstellschlitten
- *focusing stage*
87 der Diakopiervorsatz
- *slide-copying attachment*
88 der Diakopieradapter
- *slide-copying adapter*
89 der Mikrofotoansatz
- *micro attachment (photomicroscope
adapter)*
90 das Reprostativ
- *copying stand (copy stand,
copypod)*
91 die „Spinnenbeine" *n.*
- *spider legs*
92 das Reproduktionsgestell (der
Reproständer, Kopierständer)
- *copying stand (copy stand)*
93 der Reproarm
- *arm of the copying stand (copy
stand)*
94 das Makrostativ (der
Makroständer)
- *macrophoto stand*
95 die Tischeinsatzplatten *f* für das
Makrostativ
- *stage plates for the macrophoto
stand*
96 die Einlegescheibe
- *insertable disc (disk)*
97 der Lieberkühn-Reflektor
- *Lieberkühn reflector*
98 die Kreuztischeinrichtung

- *mechanical stage*
99 das Tischstativ
- *table tripod (table-top
100 das Schulterstativ
- *rifle grip*
101 der Drahtauslöser
- *cable release*
102 der Doppeldrahtauslös-
- *double cable release*
103 die Kameratasche
(Bereitschaftstasche)
- *camera case (ever-read*
104 der Objektivköcher
- *lens case*
105 der Weichleder-Objekt-
- *soft-leather lens pouch*

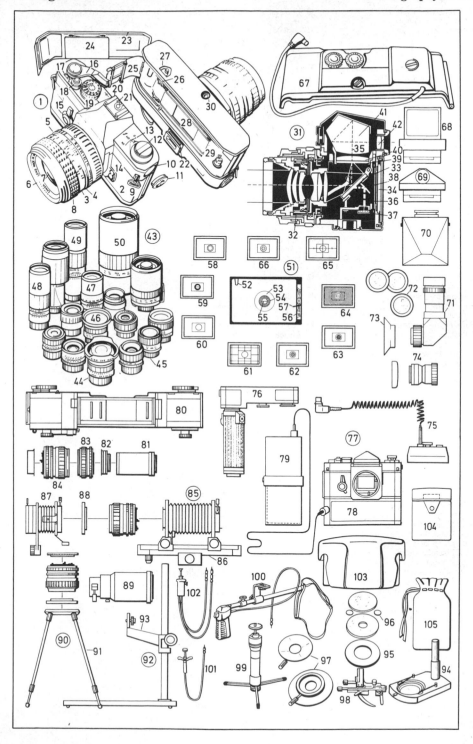

1-60 **Dunkelkammergeräte** *n*
- *darkroom equipment*
1 die Filmentwicklungsdose
- *developing tank*
2 die Einsatzspirale
- *spiral (developing spiral, tank reel)*
3 die Mehretagen-Entwicklungsdose
- *multi-unit developing tank*
4 die Mehretagen-Filmspirale
- *multi-unit tank spiral*
5 die Tageslichteinspuldose
- *daylight-loading tank*
6 das Filmfach
- *loading chamber*
7 der Filmtransportknauf
- *film transport handle*
8 das Entwicklungsthermometer
- *developing tank thermometer*
9 die Faltflasche für
Entwicklerlösung *f*
- *collapsible bottle for developing
solution*
10 die Chemikalienflaschen *f* für
Erstentwickler *m*, Stopphärtebad *n*,
Farbentwickler *m*, Bleichfixierbad *n*,
Stabilisator *m*
- *chemical bottles for first developer,
stop bath, colour developer,
bleach-hardener, stabilizer*
11 die Mensuren *f*
- *measuring cylinders*
12 der Einfülltrichter
- *funnel*
13 das Badthermometer
(Schalenthermometer)
- *tray thermometer (dish
thermometer)*
14 die Filmklammer
- *film clip*
15 die Wässerungswanne (das
Wässerungsgerät, der Bildwascher)
- *wash tank (washer)*
16 der Wasserzulauf
- *water supply pipe*
17 der Wasserablauf
- *water outlet pipe*
18 der Laborwecker
(Kurzzeitwecker)
- *laboratory timer (timer)*
19 der Filmagitator (das
Filmdosenbewegungsgerät)
- *automatic film agitator*
20 die Entwicklungsdose (*auch*: die
Bildtrommel)
- *developing tank*
21 die Dunkelkammerleuchte
- *darkroom lamp (safelight)*
22 die Filterglasscheibe
- *filter screen*
23 der Filmtrockner
- *film drier (drying cabinet)*
24 die Belichtungsschaltuhr
- *exposure timer*
25 die Entwicklungsschale
- *developing dish (developing tray)*
26 der Vergrößerer (das
Vergrößerungsgerät, der
Vergrößerungsapparat)
- *enlarger*
27 das Grundbrett
- *baseboard*
28 die geneigte Tragsäule
- *angled column*
29 der Lampenkopf (das
Lampengehäuse)
- *lamphouse (lamp housing)*

30 die Negativbühne (Filmbühne)
- *negative carrier*
31 der Balgen
- *bellows*
32 das Objektiv
- *lens*
33 der Friktionsfeintrieb
- *friction drive for fine adjustment*
34 die Höhenverstellung
(Maßstabsverstellung)
- *height adjustment (scale
adjustment)*
35 der Vergrößerungsrahmen (die
Vergrößerungskassette)
- *masking frame (easel)*
36 der Coloranalyser (Analyser,
Farbfilterbestimmer)
- *colour (Am. color) analyser*
37 die Farbkontrollampe
- *colour (Am. color) analyser lamp*
38 das Meßkabel
- *probe lead*
39 der Zeitabgleichknopf
- *exposure time balancing knob*
40 der Farbvergrößerer
- *colour (Am. color) enlarger*
41 der Gerätekopf
- *enlarger head*
42 die Profilsäule
- *column*
43-45 der Farbmischkopf
- *colour-mixing (Am. color-mixing)
knob*
43 die Purpurfiltereinstellung
(Magentaeinstellung)
- *magenta filter adjustment (minus
green filter adjustment)*
44 die Gelbfiltereinstellung
- *yellow filter adjustment (minus
blue filter adjustment)*
45 die Blaugrünfiltereinstellung
(Cyaneinstellung)
- *cyan filter adjustment (minus red
filter adjustment)*
46 das (der) Einstellfilter
- *red swing filter*
47 die Entwicklungszange
- *print tongs*
48 die Papierentwicklungstrommel
- *processing drum*
49 der Rollenquetscher
- *squeegee*
50 das Papiersortiment
- *range (assortment) of papers*
51 das Farbvergrößerungspapier, eine
Packung Fotopapier *n*
- *colour (Am. color) printing paper, a
packet of photographic printing
paper*
52 die Farbentwicklungschemikalien *f*
- *colour (Am. color) chemicals
(colour processing chemicals)*
53 der Papierbelichtungsmesser
(Vergrößerungsbelichtungsmesser)
- *enlarging meter (enlarging
photometer)*
54 der Einstellknopf mit Papierindex
m
- *adjusting knob with paper speed
scale*
55 der Meßkopf (die Meßsonde)
- *probe*
56 die halbautomatische
Thermostatentwicklungsschale
- *semi-automatic thermostatically
controlled developing dish*

57 die Schnelltrockenpresse
(Heizpresse)
- *rapid print drier (heated print drier)*
58 die Hochglanzfolie
- *glazing sheet*
59 das Spanntuch
- *pressure cloth*
60 die automatische
Walzenentwicklungsmaschine
- *automatic processor (machine
processor)*

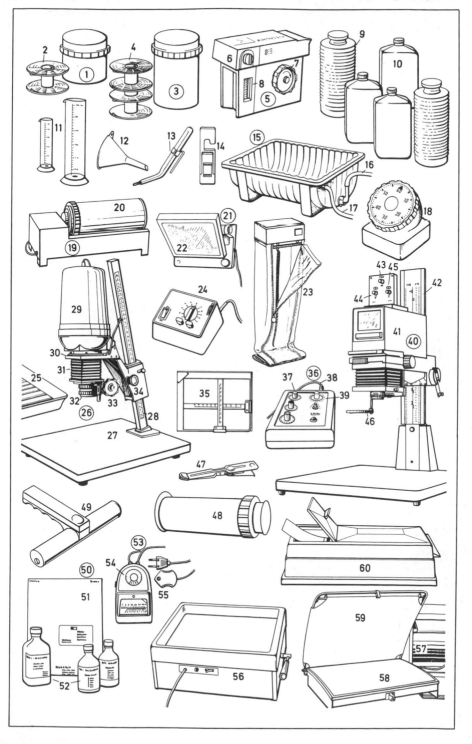

1. **die Schmalfilmkamera**, eine
   Super-8-Tonfilmkamera
 - *cine camera, a Super-8 sound
   camera*
2. das auswechselbare Zoomobjektiv
   (Varioobjektiv)
 - *interchangeable zoom lens (variable
   focus lens, varifocal lens)*
3. die Entfernungseinstellung und die
   manuelle Brennweiteneinstellung
 - *distance setting (focus setting) and
   manual focal length setting*
4. der Blendenring für die manuelle
   Blendeneinstellung
 - *aperture ring (aperture-setting ring,
   aperture control ring) for manual
   aperture setting*
5. der Batteriehandgriff
 - *handgrip with battery chamber*
6. der Auslöser mit
   Drahtauslöseranschluß m
 - *shutter release with cable release socket*
7. der Pilotton- oder
   Impulsgeberanschluß für das
   Tonaufnahmegerät n (beim
   Zweibandverfahren)
 - *pilot tone or pulse generator socket
   for the sound recording equipment
   (with the dual film-tape system)*
8. die Tonanschlußleitung für
   Mikrophon n oder Zuspielgerät n
   (beim Einbandverfahren n)
 - *sound connecting cord for
   microphone or external sound
   source (in single-system recording)*
9. der Fernauslöseranschluß
 - *remote control socket (remote control jack)*
10. der Kopfhöreranschluß
 - *headphone socket (sim.: earphone socket)*
11. der Einstellsystemschalter
 - *autofocus override switch*
12. der Filmgeschwindigkeitsschalter
 - *filming speed selector*
13. der Tonaufnahme-Wahlschalter
    für automatischen oder manuellen Betrieb
 - *sound recording selector switch for
   automatic or manual operation*
14. das Okular mit Augenmuschel f
 - *eyepiece with eyecup*
15. die Dioptrieneinstellung
 - *diopter control ring (dioptric
   adjustment ring)*
16. der Tonaussteuerungsregler
 - *recording level control (audio level
   control, recording sensitivity
   selector)*
17. der Belichtungsmesser-Wahlschalter
 - *manual/automatic exposure
   control switch*
18. die Filmempfindlichkeitseinstellung
 - *film speed setting*
19. die Powerzoomeinrichtung
 - *power zooming arrangement*
20. die Blendenautomatik
 - *automatic aperture control*
21. **das Pistentonsystem**
 - *sound track system*
22. die Tonfilmkamera
 - *sound camera*
23. der ausziehbare
    Mikrophonausleger
 - *telescopic microphone boom*
24. das Mikrophon
 - *microphone*
25. die Mikrophonanschlußleitung
 - *microphone connecting lead
   (microphone connecting cord)*
26. **das Mischpult**
 - *mixing console (mixing desk, mixer)*
27. die Eingänge für verschiedene
    Tonquellen f
 - *inputs from various sound sources*
28. der Kameraausgang
 - *output to camera*
29. **die Super-8-Tonfilmkassette**
 - *Super-8 sound film cartridge*
30. das Kassettenfenster
 - *film gate of the cartridge*
31. die Vorratsspule
 - *feed spool*
32. die Aufwickelspule
 - *take-up spool*

33. der Aufnahmetonkopf
 - *recording head (sound head)*
34. die Transportrolle (der Capstan)
 - *transport roller (capstan)*
35. die Gummiandruckrolle (der
    Gegencapstan)
 - *rubber pinch roller (capstan idler)*
36. die Führungsnut
 - *guide step (guide notch)*
37. die Belichtungssteuernut
 - *exposure meter control step*
38. die Konversionsfiltereingabenut
 - *conversion filter step (colour, Am.
   color, conversion filter step)*
39. **die Single-8-Kassette**
 - *single-8 cassette*
40. die Bildfensteraussparung
 - *film gate opening*
41. der unbelichtete Film
 - *unexposed film*
42. der belichtete Film
 - *exposed film*
43. **die Sechzehn-Millimeter-Kamera**
 - **16 mm camera**
44. der Reflexsucher
 - *reflex finder (through-the-lens
   reflex finder)*
45. das Magazin
 - *magazine*
46-49 **der Objektivkopf**
 - **lens head**
46. der Objektivrevolver
 - *lens turret (turret head)*
47. das Teleobjektiv
 - *telephoto lens*
48. das Weitwinkelobjektiv
 - *wide-angle lens*
49. das Normalobjektiv
 - *normal lens (standard lens)*
50. die Handkurbel
 - *winding handle*
51. **die Super-8-Kompaktkamera**
 - **compact Super-8 camera**
52. die Filmverbrauchsanzeige
 - *footage counter*
53. das Makrozoomobjektiv
 - *macro zoom lens*
54. der Zoomhebel
 - *zooming lever*
55. die Makrovorsatzlinse (Nahlinse)
 - *macro lens attachment (close-up lens)*
56. die Makroschiene (Halterung für
    Kleinvorlagen f)
 - *macro frame (mount for small originals)*
57. **das Unterwassergehäuse**
 - **underwater housing (underwater case)**
58. der Diopter
 - *direct-vision frame finder*
59. der Abstandhalter
 - *measuring rod*
60. die Stabilisationsfläche
 - *stabilizing wing*
61. der Handgriff
 - *grip (handgrip)*
62. der Verschlußriegel
 - *locking bolt*
63. der Bedienungshebel
 - *control lever (operating lever)*
64. das Frontglas
 - *porthole*
65. **der Synchronstart**
 - **synchronization start (sync start)**
66. die Filmberichterkamera
 - *professional press-type camera*
67. der Kameramann
 - *cameraman*
68. der Kameraassistent (Tonassistent)
 - *camera assistant (sound assistant)*
69. der Handschlag zur
    Synchronstartmarkierung
 - *handclap marking sync start*
70. **die Zwei-Band-Film- und Tonaufnahme**
 - **dual film-tape recording using a tape
   recorder**
71. die impulsgebende Kamera
 - *pulse-generating camera*
72. das Impulskabel
 - *pulse cable*
73. der Kassettenrecorder
 - *cassette recorder*
74. das Mikrophon
 - *microphone*

75. **die Zwei-Band-Ton- und
    Filmwiedergabe**
 - **dual film-tape reproduction**
76. die Tonbandkassette
 - *tape cassette*
77. das Synchronsteuergerät
 - *synchronization unit*
78. der Schmalfilmprojektor
 - *cine projector*
79. die Originalfilmspule
 - *film feed spool*
80. die Fangspule, eine Selbstfangspule
 - *take-up reel (take-up spool), an
   automatic take-up reel (take-up spool)*
81. **der Tonfilmprojektor**
 - **sound projector**
82. der Tonfilm (Pistenfilm) mit
    Magnetrandspur f (Tonpiste, Piste)
 - *sound film with magnetic stripe
   (sound track, track)*
83. die Aufnahmetaste
 - *automatic-threading button*
84. die Tricktaste
 - *trick button*
85. der Lautstärkeregler
 - *volume control*
86. die Löschtaste
 - *reset button*
87. der Trickprogrammschalter
 - *fast and slow motion switch*
88. der Betriebsartschalter
 - *forward, reverse, and still projection switch*
89. die Klebepresse für Naßklebungen f
 - *splicer for wet splices*
90. der schwenkbare Filmstreifenhalter
 - *hinged clamping plate*
91. **der Filmbetrachter**
    (Laufbildbetrachter, Editor)
 - **film viewer (animated viewer editor)**
92. der schwenkbare Spulenarm
 - *foldaway reel arm*
93. die Rückwickelkurbel
 - *rewind handle (rewinder)*
94. die Mattscheibe
 - *viewing screen*
95. die Markierungsstanze (Filmstanze)
 - *film perforator (film marker)*
96. **der Sechs-Teller-Film- und
    -Ton-Schneidetisch**
 - **six-turntable film and sound cutting
   table (editing table, cutting bench,
   animated sound editor)**
97. der Monitor
 - *monitor*
98. die Bedienungstasten f (der
    Betätigungsbrunnen)
 - *control buttons (control well)*
99. der Filmteller
 - *film turntable*
100. der erste Tonteller, z.B. für den
     Live-Ton (Originalton)
 - *first sound turntable, e.g. for live sound*
101. der zweite Tonteller, für den
     Zuspielton
 - *second sound turntable for
   post-sync sound*
102. die Bild-Ton-Einheit
 - *film and tape synchronizing head*

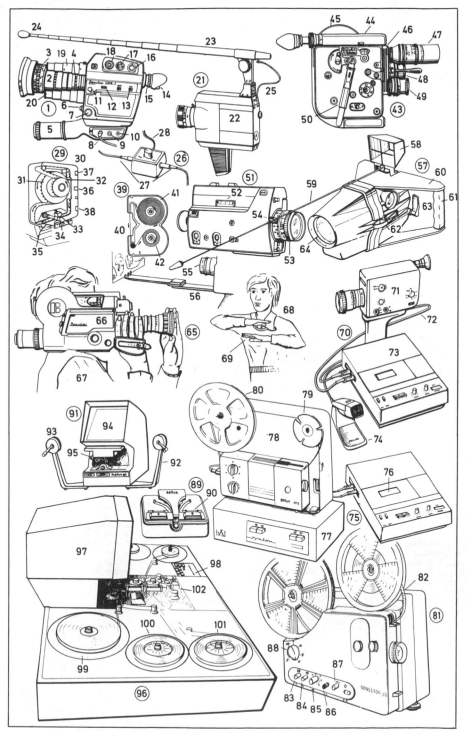

1-49 der Rohbau [Hausbau]
- *carcase (carcass, fabric) [house construction, carcassing]*
1 das Kellergeschoß (Souterrain), aus Stampfbeton *m*
- *basement of tamped (rammed) concrete*
2 der Betonsockel
- *concrete base course*
3 das Kellerfenster
- *cellar window (basement window)*
4 die Kelleraußentreppe
- *outside cellar steps*
5 das Waschküchenfenster
- *utility room window*
6 die Waschküchentür
- *utility room door*
7 das Erdgeschoß
- *ground floor (Am. first floor)*
8 die Backsteinwand (Ziegelsteinwand)
- *brick wall*
9 der Fenstersturz
- *lintel (window head)*
10 die äußere Fensterleibung
- *reveal*
11 die innere Fensterleibung
- *jamb*
12 die Fensterbank (Fenstersohlbank)
- *window ledge (window sill)*
13 der Stahlbetonsturz
- *reinforced concrete lintel*
14 das Obergeschoß
- *upper floor (first floor, Am. second floor)*
15 die Hohlblocksteinwand
- *hollow-block wall*
16 die Massivdecke
- *concrete floor*
17 die Arbeitsbühne
- *work platform (working platform)*
18 der Maurer
- *bricklayer (Am. brickmason)*
19 der Hilfsarbeiter
- *bricklayer's labourer (Am. laborer); also: builder's labourer*
20 der Mörtelkasten
- *mortar trough*
21 der Schornstein
- *chimney*
22 die Treppenhausabdeckung
- *cover (boards) for the staircase*
23 die Gerüststange (der Gerüstständer)
- *scaffold pole (scaffold standard)*
24 die Brüstungsstreiche
- *platform railing*
25 der Gerüstbug
- *angle brace (angle tie) in the scaffold*
26 die Streichstange
- *ledger*
27 der Gerüsthebel
- *putlog (putlock)*
28 der Dielenbelag (Bohlenbelag)
- *plank platform (board platform)*
29 das Sockelschutzbrett
- *guard board*
30 der Gerüstknoten, mit Ketten- od. Seilschließen *f*
- *scaffolding joint with chain or lashing or whip or bond*
31 der Bauaufzug
- *builder's hoist*
32 der Maschinist
- *mixer operator*

33 die Betonmischmaschine, ein Freifallmischer *m*
- *concrete mixer, a gravity mixer*
34 die Mischtrommel
- *mixing drum*
35 der Aufgabekasten
- *feeder skip*
36 die Zuschlagstoffe [Sand *m*, Kies *m*]
- *concrete aggregate [sand and gravel]*
37 die Schiebkarre (Schubkarre, der Schiebkarren, Schubkarren)
- *wheelbarrow*
38 der Wasserschlauch
- *hose (hosepipe)*
39 die Mörtelpfanne (Speispfanne)
- *mortar pan (mortar trough, mortar tub)*
40 der Steinstapel
- *stack of bricks*
41 das gestapelte Schalholz
- *stacked shutter boards (lining boards)*
42 die Leiter
- *ladder*
43 der Sack Zement *m*
- *bag of cement*
44 der Bauzaun, ein Bretterzaun *m*
- *site fence, a timber fence*
45 die Reklamefläche
- *signboard (billboard)*
46 das aushängbare Tor
- *removable gate*
47 die Firmenschilder *n*
- *contractors' name plates*
48 die Baubude (Bauhütte)
- *site hut (site office)*
49 der Baustellenabort
- *building site latrine*
50-57 das Mauerwerkzeug
- *bricklayer's (Am. brickmason's) tools*
50 das Lot (der Senkel)
- *plumb bob (plummet)*
51 der Maurerbleistift
- *thick lead pencil*
52 die Maurerkelle
- *trowel*
53 der Maurerhammer
- *bricklayer's (Am. brickmason's) hammer (brick hammer)*
54 der Schlegel
- *mallet*
55 die Wasserwaage
- *spirit level*
56 die Traufel
- *laying-on trowel*
57 das Reibebrett
- *float*
58-68 Mauerverbände *m*
- *masonry bonds*
58 der NF-Ziegelstein (Normalformat-Ziegelstein)
- *brick (standard brick)*
59 der Läuferverband
- *stretching bond*
60 der Binder- od. Streckerverband
- *heading bond*
61 die Abtreppung
- *racking (raking) back*
62 der Blockverband
- *English bond*
63 die Läuferschicht
- *stretching course*
64 die Binder- od. Streckerschicht
- *heading course*

65 der Kreuzverband
- *English cross bond (Saint Andrew's cross bond)*
66 der Schornsteinverband
- *chimney bond*
67 die erste Schicht
- *first course*
68 die zweite Schicht
- *second course*
69-82 die Baugrube
- *excavation*
69 die Schnurgerüstecke
- *profile (Am. batterboard) [fixed on edge at the corner]*
70 das Schnurkreuz
- *intersection of strings*
71 das Lot
- *plumb bob (plummet)*
72 die Böschung
- *excavation side*
73 die obere Saumdiele
- *upper edge board*
74 die untere Saumdiele
- *lower edge board*
75 der Fundamentgraben
- *foundation trench*
76 der Erdarbeiter
- *navvy (Am. excavator)*
77 das Förderband
- *conveyor belt (conveyor)*
78 der Erdaushub
- *excavated earth*
79 der Bohlenweg
- *plank roadway*
80 der Baumschutz
- *tree guard*
81 der Löffelbagger
- *mechanical shovel (excavator)*
82 der Tieflöffel
- *shovel bucket (bucket)*
83-91 Verputzarbeiten *f*
- *plastering*
83 der Gipser
- *plasterer*
84 der Mörtelkübel
- *mortar trough*
85 das Wurfsieb
- *screen*
86-89 das Leitergerüst
- *ladder scaffold*
86 die Standleiter
- *standard ladder*
87 der Belag
- *boards (planks, platform)*
88 die Kreuzstrebe
- *diagonal strut (diagonal brace)*
89 die Zwischenlatte
- *railing*
90 die Schutzwand
- *guard netting*
91 der Seilrollenaufzug
- *rope-pulley hoist*

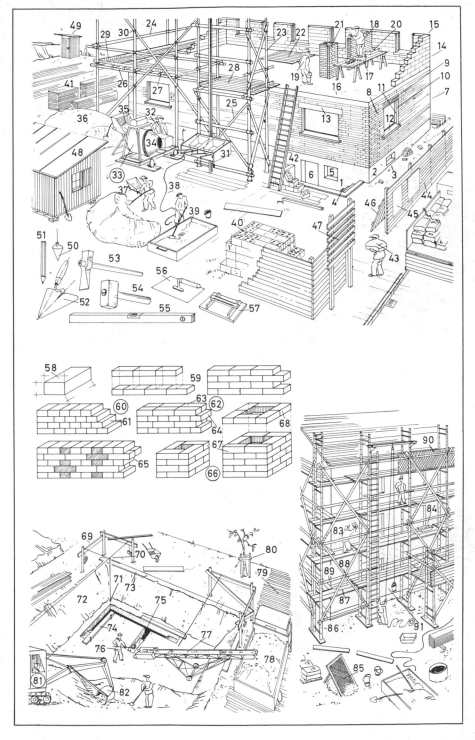

1-89 **der Stahlbetonbau**
- *reinforced concrete (ferroconcrete) construction*
1 das Stahlbetonskelett
- *reinforced concrete (ferroconcrete) skeleton construction*
2 der Stahlbetonrahmen
- *reinforced concrete (ferroconcrete) frame*
3 der Randbalken (Unterzug)
- *inferior purlin*
4 die Betonpfette
- *concrete purlin*
5 der Unterzug
- *ceiling joist*
6 die Voute
- *arch (flank)*
7 die Schüttbetonwand
- *rubble concrete wall*
8 die Stahlbetondecke
- *reinforced concrete (ferroconcrete) floor*
9 der Betonarbeiter, beim Glattstrich *m*
- *concreter (concretor), flattening out*
10 das Anschlußeisen
- *projecting reinforcement (Am. connection rebars)*
11 die Stützenschalung
- *column box*
12 die Unterzugschalung
- *joist shuttering*
13 die Schalungssprieße
- *shuttering strut*
14 die Verschwertung
- *diagonal bracing*
15 der Keil
- *wedge*
16 die Diele
- *board*
17 die Spundwand
- *sheet pile wall (sheet pile, sheet piling)*
18 das Schalholz (die Schalbretter *n*)
- *shutter boards (lining boards)*
19 die Kreissäge
- *circular saw (buzz saw)*
20 der Biegetisch
- *bending table*
21 der Eisenbieger
- *bar bender (steel bender)*
22 die Handeisenschere
- *hand steel shears*
23 das Bewehrungseisen (Armierungseisen)
- *reinforcing steel (reinforcement rods)*
24 der Bimshohlblockstein
- *pumice concrete hollow block*
25 die Trennwand, eine Bretterwand
- *partition wall, a timber wall*
26 die Zuschlagstoffe *m* [Kies *m* und Sand *m* verschiedener Korngröße]
- *concrete aggregate [gravel and sand of various grades]*
27 das Krangleis
- *crane track*
28 die Kipplore
- *tipping wagon (tipping truck)*
29 die Betonmischmaschine
- *concrete mixer*
30 der Zementsilo
- *cement silo*
31 der Turmdrehkran
- *tower crane (tower slewing crane)*
32 das Fahrgestell
- *bogie (Am. truck)*

33 das Gegengewicht (der Ballast)
- *counterweight*
34 der Turm
- *tower*
35 das Kranführerhaus
- *crane driver's cabin (crane driver's cage)*
36 der Ausleger
- *jib (boom)*
37 das Tragseil
- *bearer cable*
38 der Betonkübel
- *concrete bucket*
39 der Schwellenrost
- *sleepers (Am. ties)*
40 der Bremsschuh
- *chock*
41 die Pritsche
- *ramp*
42 die Schubkarre
- *wheelbarrow*
43 das Schutzgeländer
- *safety rail*
44 die Baubude
- *site hut*
45 die Kantine
- *canteen*
46 das Stahlrohrgerüst
- *tubular steel scaffold (scaffolding)*
47 der Ständer
- *standard*
48 der Längsriegel
- *ledger tube*
49 der Querriegel
- *tie tube*
50 die Fußplatte
- *shoe*
51 die Verstrebung
- *diagonal brace*
52 der Belag
- *planking (platform)*
53 die Kupplung
- *coupling (coupler)*
54-76 **Betonschalung** *f* u. Bewehrung *f* (Armierung)
- *formwork (shuttering) and reinforcement*
54 der Schalboden (die Schalung)
- *bottom shuttering (lining)*
55 die Seitenschalung eines Randbalkens *m*
- *side shutter of a purlin*
56 der eingeschnittene Boden
- *cut-in bottom*
57 die Traverse (der Tragbalken)
- *cross beam*
58 die Bauklammer
- *cramp iron (cramp, dog)*
59 der Sprieß, eine Kopfstütze
- *upright member, a standard*
60 die Heftlasche
- *strap*
61 das Schappelholz
- *cross piece*
62 das Drängbrett
- *stop fillet*
63 das Bugbrett
- *strut (brace, angle brace)*
64 das Rahmenholz
- *frame timber (yoke)*
65 die Lasche
- *strap*
66 die Rödelung
- *reinforcement binding*
67 die Stelze (Spange, „Mauerstärke")
- *cross strut (strut)*

68 die Bewehrung (Armierung)
- *reinforcement*
69 der Verteilungsstahl
- *distribution steel*
70 der Bügel
- *stirrup*
71 das Anschlußeisen
- *projecting reinforcement (Am. connection rebars)*
72 der Beton (Schwerbeton)
- *concrete (heavy concrete)*
73 die Stützenschalung
- *column box*
74 das geschraubte Rahmenholz
- *bolted frame timber (bolted yoke)*
75 die Schraube
- *nut (thumb nut)*
76 das Schalbrett
- *shutter board (shuttering board)*
77-89 **Werkzeug** *n*
- *tools*
77 das Biegeeisen
- *bending iron*
78 der verstellbare Schalungsträger
- *adjustable service girder*
79 die Stellschraube
- *adjusting screw*
80 der Rundstahl
- *round bar reinforcement*
81 der Abstandhalter
- *distance piece (separator, spacer)*
82 der Torstahl
- *Torsteel*
83 der Betonstampfer
- *concrete tamper*
84 die Probewürfelform
- *mould (Am. mold) for concrete test cubes*
85 die Monierzange
- *concreter's tongs*
86 die Schalungsstütze
- *sheeting support*
87 die Handschere
- *hand shears*
88 der Betoninnenrüttler
- *immersion vibrator (concrete vibrator)*
89 die Rüttelflasche
- *vibrating cylinder (vibrating head, vibrating poker)*

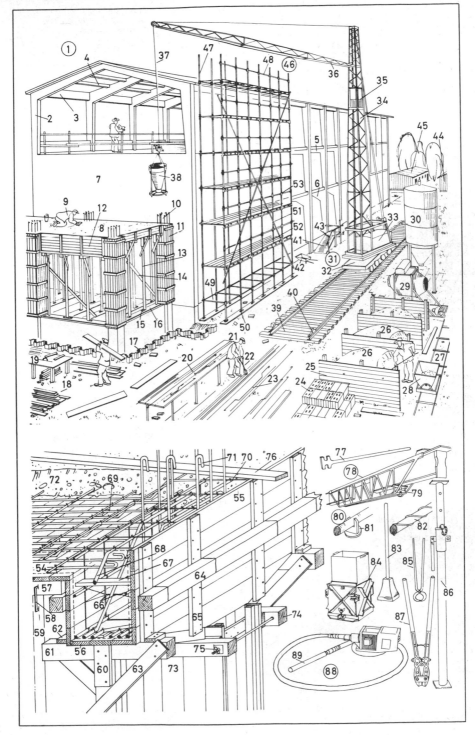

1-59 der Zimmerplatz
(Abbindeplatz)
- *carpenter's yard*
1 der Bretterstapel
- *stack of boards (planks)*
2 das Langholz
- *long timber (Am. lumber)*
3 der Sägeschuppen
- *sawing shed*
4 die Zimmererwerkstatt
- *carpenter's workshop*
5 das Werkstattor
- *workshop door*
6 der Handwagen
- *handcart*
7 der Dachstuhl
- *roof truss*
8 der Richtbaum, mit der Richtkrone
- *tree [used for topping out ceremony], with wreath*
9 die Bretterschalung
- *timber wall*
10 das Kantholz (Bauholz)
- *squared timber (building timber, scantlings)*
11 die Reißbühne (der Reißboden, Schnürboden)
- *drawing floor*
12 der Zimmerer (Zimmermann)
- *carpenter*
13 der Zimmermannshut
- *carpenter's hat*
14 die Ablängsäge, eine Kettensäge
- *cross-cut saw, a chain saw*
15 der Steg
- *chain guide*
16 die Sägekette
- *saw chain*
17 der Stemmapparat (die Kettenfräse)
- *mortiser (chain cutter)*
18 der Auflagerbock
- *trestle (horse)*
19 der aufgebockte Balken
- *beam mounted on a trestle*
20 das Bundgeschirr
- *set of carpenter's tools*
21 die elektrische Bohrmaschine
- *electric drill*
22 das Dübelloch (Dollenloch)
- *dowel hole*
23 das angerissene Dübelloch
- *mark for the dowel hole*
24 der Abbund
- *beams*
25 der Pfosten (Stiel, die Säule)
- *post (stile, stud, quarter)*
26 der Zwischenriegel
- *corner brace*
27 die Strebe
- *brace (strut)*
28 der Haussockel
- *base course (plinth)*
29 die Hauswand
- *house wall (wall)*
30 die Fensteröffnung
- *window opening*
31 die äußere Leibung
- *reveal*
32 die innere Leibung
- *jamb*
33 die Fensterbank (Sohlbank)
- *window ledge (window sill)*
34 der Ringanker
- *cornice*
35 das Rundholz
- *roundwood (round timber)*

36 die Laufdielen *f*
- *floorboards*
37 das Aufzugseil
- *hoisting rope*
38 der Deckenbalken (Hauptbalken)
- *ceiling joist (ceiling beam, main beam)*
39 der Wandbalken
- *wall joist*
40 der Streichbalken
- *wall plate*
41 der Wechsel (Wechselbalken)
- *trimmer (trimmer joist, Am. header, header joist)*
42 der Stichbalken
- *dragon beam (dragon piece)*
43 der Zwischenboden (die Einschubdecke)
- *false floor (inserted floor)*
44 die Deckenfüllung, aus Koksasche *f*, Lehm *m* u.a.
- *floor filling of breeze, loam, etc.*
45 die Traglatte
- *fillet (cleat)*
46 das Treppenloch
- *stair well (well)*
47 der Schornstein
- *chimney*
48 die Fachwerkwand
- *framed partition (framed wall)*
49 die Schwelle
- *wall plate*
50 die Saumschwelle
- *girt*
51 der Fensterstiel, ein Zwischenstiel *m*
- *window jamb, a jamb*
52 der Eckstiel
- *corner stile (corner strut, corner stud)*
53 der Bundstiel
- *principal post*
54 die Strebe, mit Versatz *m*
- *brace (strut) with skew notch*
55 der Zwischenriegel
- *nogging piece*
56 der Brüstungsriegel
- *sill rail*
57 der Fensterriegel (Sturzriegel)
- *window lintel (window head)*
58 das Rähm (Rähmholz)
- *head (head rail)*
59 das ausgemauerte Fach
- *filled-in panel (bay, pan)*
60-82 Handwerkszeug *n* des Zimmerers *m*
- *carpenter's tools*
60 der Fuchsschwanz
- *hand saw*
61 die Handsäge
- *bucksaw*
62 das Sägeblatt
- *saw blade*
63 die Lochsäge
- *compass saw (keyhole saw)*
64 der Hobel
- *plane*
65 der Stangenbohrer
- *auger (gimlet)*
66 die Schraubzwinge
- *screw clamp (cramp, holdfast)*
67 das Klopfholz
- *mallet*
68 die Bundsäge
- *two-handed saw*
69 der Anreißwinkel
- *try square*

70 das Breitbeil
- *broad axe (Am. broadax)*
71 das Stemmeisen
- *chisel*
72 die Bundaxt (Stoßaxt)
- *mortise axe (mortice axe, Am. mortise ax)*
73 die Axt
- *axe (Am. ax)*
74 der Zimmermannshammer
- *carpenter's hammer*
75 die Nagelklaue
- *claw head (nail claw)*
76 der Zollstock
- *folding rule*
77 der Zimmermannsbleistift
- *carpenter's pencil*
78 der Eisenwinkel
- *iron square*
79 das Zugmesser
- *drawknife (drawshave, drawing knife)*
80 der Span
- *shaving*
81 die Gehrungsschmiege (Stellschmiege)
- *bevel*
82 der Gehrungswinkel
- *mitre square (Am. miter square, miter angle)*
83-96 Bauhölzer *n*
- *building timber*
83 der Rundstamm
- *round trunk (undressed timber, Am. rough lumber)*
84 das Kernholz
- *heartwood (duramen)*
85 das Splintholz
- *sapwood (sap, alburnum)*
86 die Rinde
- *bark (rind)*
87 das Ganzholz
- *baulk (balk)*
88 das Halbholz
- *halved timber*
89 die Waldkante (Fehlkante, Baumkante)
- *wane (waney edge)*
90 das Kreuzholz
- *quarter baulk (balk)*
91 das Brett
- *plank (board)*
92 das Hirnholz
- *end-grained timber*
93 das Herzbrett (Kernbrett)
- *heartwood plank (heart plank)*
94 das ungesäumte Brett
- *unsquared (untrimmed) plank (board)*
95 das gesäumte Brett
- *squared (trimmed) board*
96 die Schwarte (der Schwartling)
- *slab (offcut)*

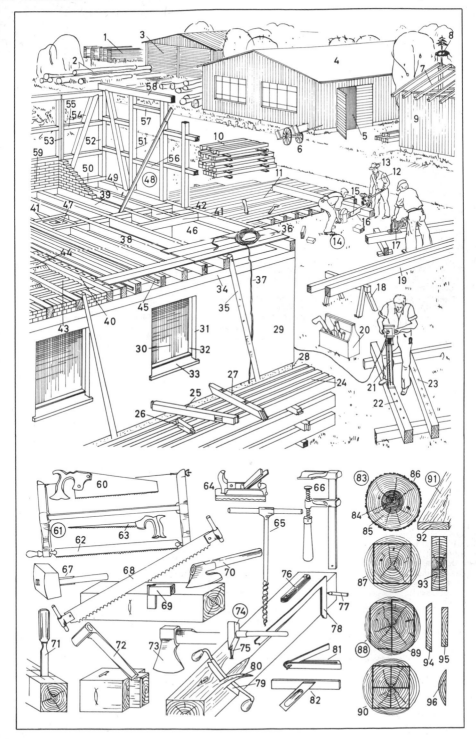

1-26 Dachformen *f* und Dachteile *n*
- *styles and parts of roofs*
1 das Satteldach
- *gable roof (saddle roof, saddleback roof)*
2 der First (Dachfirst)
- *ridge*
3 der Ortgang
- *verge*
4 die Traufe (der Dachfuß)
- *eaves*
5 der Giebel
- *gable*
6 die Dachgaube (Dachgaupe)
- *dormer window (dormer)*
7 das Pultdach
- *pent roof (shed roof, lean-to roof)*
8 das Dachliegefenster
- *skylight*
9 der Brandgiebel
- *fire gable*
10 das Walmdach
- *hip (hipped) roof*
11 die Walmfläche
- *hip end*
12 der Grat (Dachgrat)
- *hip (arris)*
13 die Walmgaube (Walmgaupe)
- *hip (hipped) dormer window*
14 der Dachreiter
- *ridge turret*
15 die Kehle (Dachkehle)
- *valley (roof valley)*
16 das Krüppelwalmdach (der Schopfwalm)
- *hipped-gable roof (jerkin head roof)*
17 der Krüppelwalm
- *partial-hip (partial-hipped) end*
18 das Mansarddach
- *mansard roof (Am. gambrel roof)*
19 das Mansardfenster (Mansardenfenster)
- *mansard dormer window*
20 das Sägedach (Sheddach)
- *sawtooth roof*
21 das Oberlichtband
- *north light*
22 das Zeltdach
- *broach roof*
23 die Fledermausgaube (Fledermausgaupe)
- *eyebrow*
24 das Kegeldach
- *conical broach roof*
25 die Zwiebelkuppel
- *imperial dome (imperial roof)*
26 die Wetterfahne
- *weather vane*
27-83 Dachkonstruktionen *f* aus Holz *n* (Dachverbände *m*)
- *roof structures of timber*
27 das Sparrendach
- *rafter roof*
28 der Sparren
- *rafter*
29 der Dachbalken
- *roof beam*
30 die Windrispe
- *diagonal tie (cross tie, sprocket piece, cocking piece)*
31 der Aufschiebling
- *arris fillet (tilting fillet)*
32 die Außenwand
- *outer wall*
33 der Balkenkopf
- *beam head*

34 das Kehlbalkendach
- *collar beam roof (trussed-rafter roof)*
35 der Kehlbalken
- *collar beam (collar)*
36 der Sparren
- *rafter*
37 zweifachstehender Kehlbalkendachstuhl
- *strutted collar beam roof structure*
38 das Kehlgebälk
- *collar beams*
39 das Rähm (die Seitenpfette)
- *purlin*
40 der Pfosten (Stiel)
- *post (stile, stud)*
41 der Bug
- *brace*
42 einfachstehender Pfettendachstuhl
- *unstrutted (king pin) roof structure*
43 die Firstpfette
- *ridge purlin*
44 die Fußpfette
- *inferior purlin*
45 der Sparrenkopf
- *rafter head (rafter end)*
46 zweifachstehender Pfettendachstuhl, mit Kniestock *m*
- *purlin roof with queen post and pointing sill*
47 der Kniestock (Drempel)
- *pointing sill*
48 die Firstlatte (Firstbohle)
- *ridge beam (ridge board)*
49 die einfache Zange
- *simple tie*
50 die Doppelzange
- *double tie*
51 die Mittelpfette
- *purlin*
52 zweifachliegender Pfettendachstuhl
- *purlin roof structure with queen post*
53 der Binderbalken (Bundbalken)
- *tie beam*
54 der Zwischenbalken (Deckenbalken)
- *joist (ceiling joist)*
55 der Bindersparren (Bundsparren)
- *principal rafter*
56 der Zwischensparren
- *common rafter*
57 der Schwenkbug
- *angle brace (angle tie)*
58 die Strebe
- *brace (strut)*
59 die Zangen *f*
- *ties*
60 Walmdach *n* mit Pfettendachstuhl *m*
- *hip (hipped) roof with purlin roof structure*
61 der Schifter
- *jack rafter*
62 der Gratsparren
- *hip rafter*
63 der Walmschifter
- *jack rafter*
64 der Kehlsparren
- *valley rafter*
65 das doppelte Hängewerk
- *queen truss*
66 der Hängebalken
- *main beam*
67 der Unterzug
- *summer (summer beam)*

68 die Hängesäule
- *queen post (truss post)*
69 die Strebe
- *brace (strut)*
70 der Spannriegel
- *collar beam (collar)*
71 der Wechsel
- *trimmer (Am. header)*
72 der Vollwandträger
- *solid-web girder*
73 der Untergurt
- *lower chord*
74 der Obergurt
- *upper chord*
75 der Brettersteg
- *boarding*
76 die Pfette
- *purlin*
77 die tragende Außenwand
- *supporting outer wall*
78 der Fachwerkbinder
- *roof truss*
79 der Untergurt
- *lower chord*
80 der Obergurt
- *upper chord*
81 der Pfosten
- *post*
82 die Strebe
- *brace (strut)*
83 das Auflager
- *support*
84-98 Holzverbindungen *f*
- *timber joints*
84 die einfache Zapfen
- *mortise (mortice) and tenon joint*
85 der Scherzapfen
- *forked mortise (mortice) and tenon joint*
86 das gerade Blatt
- *halving (halved) joint*
87 das gerade Hakenblatt
- *simple scarf joint*
88 das schräge Hakenblatt
- *oblique scarf joint*
89 die schwalbenschwanzförmige Überblattung
- *dovetail halving*
90 der einfache Versatz
- *single skew notch*
91 der doppelte Versatz
- *double skew notch*
92 der Holznagel
- *wooden nail*
93 der Dollen
- *pin*
94 der Schmiedenagel
- *clout nail (clout)*
95 der Drahtnagel
- *wire nail*
96 die Hartholzkeile *m*
- *hardwood wedges*
97 die Klammer
- *cramp iron (timber dog, dog)*
98 der Schraubenbolzen
- *bolt*

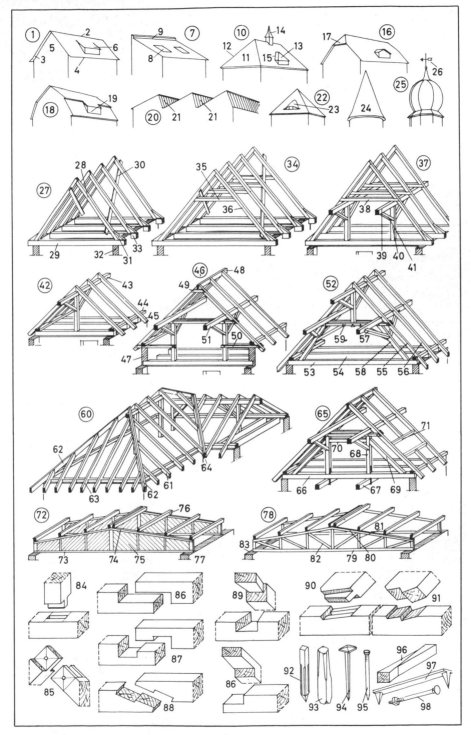

1 das Ziegeldach
- *tiled roof*
2 die Biberschwanz-Doppeldeckung
- *plain-tile double-lap roofing*
3 der Firstziegel
- *ridge tile*
4 der Firstschlußziegel
- *ridge course tile*
5 die Traufplatte
- *under-ridge tile*
6 der Biberschwanz
- *plain (plane) tile*
7 der Lüftungsziegel
- *ventilating tile*
8 der Gratziegel (Walmziegel)
- *ridge tile*
9 die Walmkappe
- *hip tile*
10 die Walmfläche
- *hipped end*
11 die Kehle
- *valley (roof valley)*
12 das Dachliegefenster
- *skylight*
13 der Schornstein
- *chimney*
14 die Schornsteineinfassung, aus Zinkblech n
- *chimney flashing, made of sheet zinc*
15 der Leiterhaken
- *ladder hook*
16 die Schneefangstütze
- *snow guard bracket*
17 die Lattung
- *battens (slating and tiling battens)*
18 die Lattenlehre
- *batten gauge (Am. gage)*
19 der Sparren
- *rafter*
20 der Ziegelhammer
- *tile hammer*
21 das Lattbeil
- *lath axe (Am. ax)*
22 das Deckfaß
- *hod*
23 der Faßhaken
- *hod hook*
24 der Ausstieg
- *opening (hatch)*
25 die Giebelscheibe
- *gable (gable end)*
26 die Zahnleiste
- *toothed lath*
27 das Windbrett
- *soffit*
28 die Dachrinne
- *gutter*
29 das Regenrohr
- *rainwater pipe (downpipe)*
30 der Einlaufstutzen
- *swan's neck (swan-neck)*
31 die Rohrschelle
- *pipe clip*
32 der Rinnenbügel
- *gutter bracket*
33 die Dachziegelschere
- *tile cutter*
34 das Arbeitsgerüst
- *scaffold*
35 die Schutzwand
- *safety wall*
36 das Dachgesims
- *eaves*
37 die Außenwand
- *outer wall*

38 der Außenputz
- *exterior rendering*
39 die Vormauerung
- *frost-resistant brickwork*
40 die Fußpfette
- *inferior purlin*
41 der Sparrenkopf
- *rafter head (rafter end)*
42 die Gesimsschalung
- *eaves fascia*
43 die Doppellatte
- *double lath (tilting lath)*
44 die Dämmplatten f
- *insulating boards*
45-60 **Dachziegel m und Dachziegeldeckungen f**
- *tiles and tile roofings*
45 das Spließdach
- *split-tiled roof*
46 der Biberschwanzziegel
- *plain (plane) tile*
47 die Firstschar
- *ridge course*
48 der Spließ
- *slip*
49 das Traufgebinde
- *eaves course*
50 das Kronendach (Ritterdach)
- *plain-tiled roof*
51 die Nase
- *nib*
52 der Firstziegel
- *ridge tile*
53 das Hohlpfannendach
- *pantiled roof*
54 die Hohlpfanne (S-Pfanne)
- *pantile*
55 der Verstrich
- *pointing*
56 das Mönch-Nonnen-Dach
- *Spanish-tiled roof (Am. mission-tiled roof)*
57 die Nonne
- *under tile*
58 der Mönch
- *over tile*
59 die Falzpfanne
- *interlocking tile*
60 die Flachdachpfanne
- *flat interlocking tile*
61-89 **das Schieferdach**
- *slate roof*
61 die Schalung
- *roof boards (roof boarding, roof sheathing)*
62 die Dachpappe
- *roofing paper (sheathing paper); also: roofing felt (Am. rag felt)*
63 die Dachleiter
- *cat ladder (roof ladder)*
64 der Länghaken
- *coupling hook*
65 der Firsthaken
- *ridge hook*
66 der Dachbock (Dachstuhl)
- *roof trestle*
67 der Bockstrang
- *trestle rope*
68 die Schlinge (der Knoten)
- *knot*
69 der Leiterhaken
- *ladder hook*
70 die Gerüstdiele
- *scaffold board*
71 der Schieferdecker
- *slater*

72 die Nageltasche
- *nail bag*
73 der Schieferhammer
- *slate hammer*
74 der Dachdeckerstift, ein verzinkter Drahtnagel m
- *slate nail, a galvanized wire nail*
75 der Dachschuh, ein Bast- oder Hanfschuh m
- *slater's shoe, a bast or hemp shoe*
76 das Fußgebinde
- *eaves course (eaves joint)*
77 der Eckfußstein
- *corner bottom slate*
78 das Deckgebinde
- *roof course*
79 das Firstgebinde
- *ridge course (ridge joint)*
80 die Ortsteine m
- *gable slate*
81 die Fußlinie
- *tail line*
82 die Kehle
- *valley (roof valley)*
83 die Kastenrinne
- *box gutter (trough gutter, parallel gutter)*
84 die Schieferschere
- *slater's iron*
85 der Schieferstein
- *slate*
86 der Rücken
- *back*
87 der Kopf
- *head*
88 die Brust
- *front edge*
89 das Reiß
- *tail*
90-103 **Pappdeckung f und Wellasbestzementdeckung f**
- *asphalt-impregnated paper roofing and corrugated asbestos cement roofing*
90 das Pappdach
- *asphalt-impregnated paper roof*
91 die Bahn [parallel zur Traufe]
- *width [parallel to the gutter]*
92 die Traufe
- *gutter*
93 der First
- *ridge*
94 der Stoß
- *join*
95 die Bahn [senkrecht zur Traufe]
- *width [at right angles to the gutter]*
96 der Pappnagel
- *felt nail (clout nail)*
97 das Wellasbestzementdach
- *corrugated asbestos cement roof*
98 die Welltafel
- *corrugated sheet*
99 die Firsthaube
- *ridge capping piece*
100 die Überdeckung
- *lap*
101 die Holzschraube
- *wood screw*
102 der Regenzinkhut
- *rust-proof zinc cup*
103 die Bleischeibe
- *lead washer*

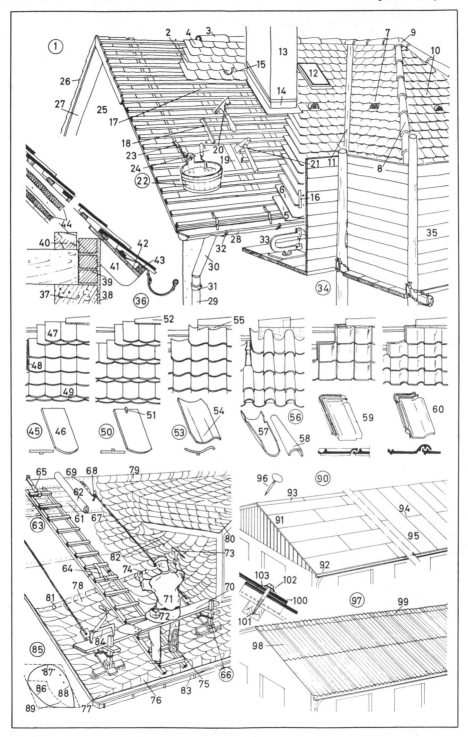

1 die Kellerwand, eine Betonwand
- *basement wall, a concrete wall*
2 das Bankett (der
Fundamentstreifen)
- *footing (foundation)*
3 der Fundamentvorsprung
- *foundation base*
4 die Horizontalisolierung
- *damp course (damp-proof course)*
5 der Schutzanstrich
- *waterproofing*
6 der Bestich (Rapputz, Rauhputz)
- *rendering coat*
7 die Backsteinflachschicht
- *brick paving*
8 das Sandbett
- *sand bed*
9 das Erdreich
- *ground*
10 die Seitendiele
- *shuttering*
11 der Pflock
- *peg*
12 die Packlage (das Gestück)
- *hardcore*
13 der Unterbeton
- *oversite concrete*
14 der Zementglattstrich
(Zementestrich)
- *cement screed*
15 die Untermauerung
- *brickwork base*
16 die Kellertreppe, eine
Massivtreppe
- *basement stairs, solid concrete stairs*
17 die Blockstufe
- *block step*
18 die Antrittsstufe (der Antritt)
- *curtail step (bottom step)*
19 die Austrittsstufe
- *top step*
20 der Kantenschutz
- *nosing*
21 die Sockelplatte
- *skirting (skirting board, Am.
mopboard, washboard, scrub
board, base)*
22 das Treppengeländer, aus
Metallstäben *m*
- *balustrade of metal bars*
23 der Treppenvorplatz
- *ground-floor (Am. first-floor)
landing*
24 die Hauseingangstür
- *front door*
25 der Fußabstreifer
- *foot scraper*
26 der Plattenbelag
- *flagstone paving*
27 das Mörtelbett
- *mortar bed*
28 die Massivdecke, eine
Stahlbetonplatte
- *concrete ceiling, a reinforced
concrete slab*
29 das Erdgeschoßmauerwerk
- *ground-floor (Am. first-floor)
brick wall*
30 die Laufplatte
- *ramp*
31 die Keilstufe
- *wedge-shaped step*
32 die Trittstufe
- *tread*
33 die Setzstufe
- *riser*

34-41 **das Podest** (der Treppenabsatz)
- *landing*
34 der Podestbalken
- *landing beam*
35 die Stahlbetonrippendecke
- *ribbed reinforced concrete floor*
36 die Rippe
- *rib*
37 die Stahlbewehrung
- *steel-bar reinforcement*
38 die Druckplatte
- *subfloor (blind floor)*
39 der Ausgleichestrich
- *level layer*
40 der Feinestrich
- *finishing layer*
41 der Gehbelag
- *top layer (screed)*
42-44 **die Geschoßtreppe, eine
Podesttreppe**
- *dog-legged staircase, a staircase
without a well*
42 die Antrittsstufe
- *curtail step (bottom step)*
43 der Antrittspfosten
- *newel post (newel)*
44 die Freiwange (Lichtwange)
- *outer string (Am. outer stringer)*
45 die Wandwange
- *wall string (Am. wall stringer)*
46 die Treppenschraube
- *staircase bolt*
47 die Trittstufe
- *tread*
48 die Setzstufe
- *riser*
49 das Kropfstück
- *wreath piece (wreathed string)*
50 das Treppengeländer
- *balustrade*
51 der Geländerstab
- *baluster*
52-62 **das Zwischenpodest**
- *intermediate landing*
52 der Krümmling
- *wreath*
53 der Handlauf
- *handrail (guard rail)*
54 der Austrittspfosten
- *head post*
55 der Podestbalken
- *landing beam*
56 das Futterbrett
- *lining board*
57 die Abdeckleiste
- *fillet*
58 die Leichtbauplatte
- *lightweight building board*
59 der Deckenputz
- *ceiling plaster*
60 der Wandputz
- *wall plaster*
61 die Zwischendecke
- *false ceiling*
62 der Riemenboden
- *strip flooring (overlay flooring,
parquet strip)*
63 die Sockelleiste
- *skirting board (Am. mopboard,
washboard, scrub board, base)*
64 der Abdeckstab
- *beading*
65 das Treppenhausfenster
- *staircase window*
66 der Hauptpodestbalken
- *main landing beam*

67 die Traglatte
- *fillet (cleat)*
68-69 die Zwischendecke
- *false ceiling*
68 der Zwischenboden (die
Einschubdecke)
- *false floor (inserted floor)*
69 die Zwischenbodenauffüllung
- *floor filling (plugging, pug)*
70 die Lattung
- *laths*
71 der Putzträger (die Rohrung)
- *lathing*
72 der Deckenputz
- *ceiling plaster*
73 der Blindboden
- *subfloor (blind floor)*
74 der Parkettboden, mit Nut *f* und
Feder *f* (Nut- u. Federriemen *m*)
- *parquet floor with
tongued-and-grooved blocks*
75 die viertelgewendelte Treppe
- *quarter-newelled (Am.
quarter-neweled) staircase*
76 die Wendeltreppe, mit offener
Spindel *f*
- *winding staircase (spiral staircase)
with open newels (open-newel
staircase)*
77 die Wendeltreppe, mit voller
Spindel *f*
- *winding staircase (spiral staircase)
with solid newels (solid-newel
staircase)*
78 die Spindel
- *newel (solid newel)*
79 der Handlauf
- *handrail*

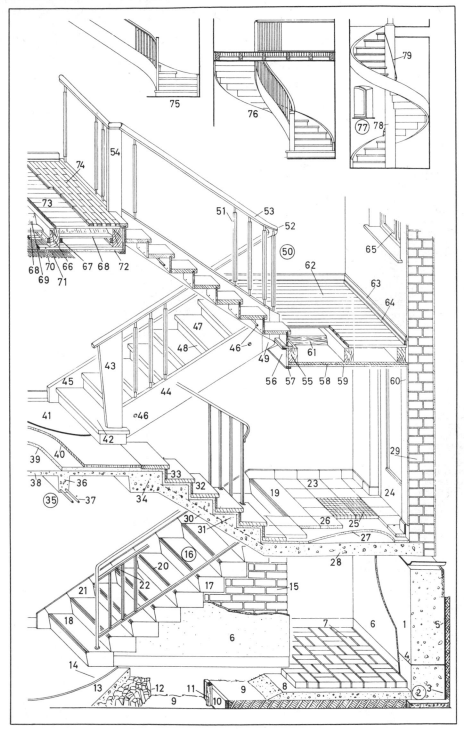

1 die Glaserwerkstatt
- *glazier's workshop*
2 die Leistenproben *f*
(Rahmenproben)
- *frame wood samples (frame samples)*
3 die Leiste
- *frame wood*
4 die Gehrung
- *mitre joint (mitre, Am. miter joint, miter)*
5 das Flachglas; *Arten:* Fensterglas,
Mattglas, Musselinglas,
Kristallspiegelglas, Dickglas,
Milchglas, Verbundglas,
Panzerglas (Sicherheitsglas)
- *sheet glass; kinds: window glass,
frosted glass, patterned glass,
crystal plate glass, thick glass, milk
glass, laminated glass (safety glass,
shatterproof glass)*
6 das Gußglas; *Arten:* Kathedralglas,
Ornamentglas, Rohglas,
Butzenglas, Drahtglas, Linienglas
- *cast glass; kinds: stained glass,
ornamental glass, raw glass,
bull's-eye glass, wired glass, line
glass (lined glass)*
7 die Gehrungssprossenstanze
- *mitring (Am. mitering) machine*
8 der Glaser (z.B. Bauglaser,
Rahmenglaser, Kunstglaser)
- *glassworker (e.g. building glazier,
glazier, decorative glass worker)*

9 die Glastrage (der Glaserkasten)
- *glass holder*
10 die Glasscherbe
- *piece of broken glass*
11 der Bleihammer
- *lead hammer*
12 das Bleimesser
- *lead knife*
13 die Bleirute (Bleisprosse, der Bleisteg)
- *came (lead came)*
14 das Bleiglasfenster
- *leaded light*
15 der Arbeitstisch
- *workbench*
16 die Glasscheibe (Glasplatte)
- *pane of glass*
17 der Glaserkitt (Kitt)
- *putty*
18 der Stifthammer (Glaserhammer)
- *glazier's hammer*
19 die Glaserzange (Glasbrechzange,
Kröselzange)
- *glass pliers*
20 der Schneidewinkel
- *glazier's square*
21 das Schneidelineal (die
Schneideleiste)
- *glazier's rule*
22 der Rundglasschneider
(Zirkelschneider)
- *glazier's beam compass*
23 die Öse
- *eyelet*

24 die Glaserecke
- *glazing sprig*
25-26 Glasschneider *m*
- *glass cutters*
25 der Glaserdiamant (Krösel), ein
Diamantschneider *m*
- *diamond glass cutter*
26 der Stahlrad-Glasschneider
- *steel-wheel (steel) glass cutter*
27 das Kittmesser
- *putty knife*
28 der Stiftdraht
- *pin wire*
29 der Stift
- *panel pin*
30 die Gehrungssäge
- *mitre (Am. miter) block (mitre box)
[with saw]*
31 die Gehrungsstoßlade (Stoßlade)
- *mitre (Am. miter) shoot (mitre board)*

1 die Blechschere
- *metal shears (tinner's snips*, Am.
  tinner's shears)
2 die Winkelschere
- *elbow snips (angle shears)*
3 die Richtplatte
- *gib*
4 die Schlichtplatte
- *lapping plate*
5-7 das Propangaslötgerät
- *propane soldering apparatus*
5 der Propangaslötkolben, ein
  Hammerlötkolben *m*
- *propane soldering iron, a hatchet
  iron*
6 der Lötstein, ein Salmiakstein *m*
- *soldering stone, a sal-ammoniac
  block*
7 das Lötwasser (Flußmittel)
- *soldering fluid (flux)*
8 der Sickenstock, zum Formen *n*
  von Wülsten *m* (Sicken *f*, Sieken,
  Secken)
- *beading iron for forming
  reinforcement beading*
9 die Winkelreibahle,
  eine Reibahle
- *angled reamer*
10 die Werkbank
- *workbench (bench)*
11 der Stangenzirkel
- *beam compass (trammel,* Am. *beam
  trammel)*

12 die elektrische Handschneidkluppe
- *electric hand die*
13 das Locheisen
- *hollow punch*
14 der Sickenhammer
- *chamfering hammer*
15 der Kornhammer
- *beading swage (beading hammer)*
16 die Trennschleifmaschine
- *abrasive-wheel cutting-off
  machine*
17 der Klempner
  (*obd.* Spengler,
  schweiz. Stürzner)
- *plumber*
18 der Holzhammer
- *mallet*
19 das Horn
- *mandrel*
20 die Faust
- *socket (tinner's socket)*
21 der Klotz
- *block*
22 der Amboß
- *anvil*
23 der Tasso
- *stake*
24 die Kreissägemaschine
- *circular saw (buzz saw)*
25 die Sicken-, Bördel- und
  Drahteinlegemaschine
- *flanging, swaging, and wiring
  machine*

26 die Tafelschere (Schlagschere)
- *sheet shears (guillotine)*
27 die Gewindeschneidmaschine
- *screw-cutting machine
  (thread-cutting machine, die
  stocks)*
28 die Rohrbiegemaschine
- *pipe-bending machine (bending
  machine, pipe bender)*
29 der Schweißtransformator
- *welding transformer*
30 die Biegemaschine
  (Rundmaschine) zum Biegen *n* von
  Trichtern *m*
- *bending machine (rounding
  machine) for shaping funnels*

1 der Gas- und Wasserinstallateur
(*ugs.:* Installateur)
- *gas fitter and plumber*
2 die Treppenleiter
- *stepladder*
3 die Sicherheitskette
- *safety chain*
4 das Absperrventil
- *stop valve*
5 die Gasuhr
- *gas meter*
6 die Konsole
- *bracket*
7 die Steigleitung
- *service riser*
8 die Abzweigleitung
- *distributing pipe*
9 die Anschlußleitung
- *supply pipe*
10 die Rohrsägemaschine
- *pipe-cutting machine*
11 der Rohrbock
- *pipe repair stand*
12-25 **Gas- und Wassergeräte** *n*
- **gas and water appliances**
12-13 der Durchlauferhitzer, ein
Heißwasserbereiter
- *geyser, an instantaneous water
heater*
12 der Gasdurchlauferhitzer
- *gas water heater*
13 der Elektrodurchlauferhitzer
- *electric water heater*
14 der Spülkasten der Toilette
- *toilet cistern*
15 der Schwimmer
- *float*
16 das Ablaufventil
- *bell*
17 das Spülrohr
- *flush pipe*
18 der Wasserzufluß
- *water inlet*
19 der Bedienungshebel
- *flushing lever (lever)*
20 der Heizungskörper
(Zentralheizungskörper, Radiator)
- *radiator*
21 die Radiatorrippe
- *radiator rib*
22 das Zweirohrsystem
- *two-pipe system*
23 der Vorlauf
- *flow pipe*
24 der Rücklauf
- *return pipe*
25 der Gasofen
- *gas heater*
26-37 **Armaturen** *f*
- **plumbing fixtures**
26 der Siphon (Geruchsverschluß)
- *trap (anti-syphon trap)*
27 die Einlochmischbatterie für
Waschbecken *n*
- *mixer tap (Am. mixing faucet) for
washbasins*
28 der Warmwassergriff
- *hot tap*
29 der Kaltwassergriff
- *cold tap*
30 die ausziehbare Schlauchbrause
- *extendible shower attachment*
31 der Wasserhahn (das Standventil)
für Waschbecken *n*
- *water tap (pillar tap) for
washbasins*

32 die Spindel
- *spindle top*
33 die Abdeckkappe
- *shield*
34 das Auslaufventil (der
Wasserhahn, Kran, Kranen)
- *draw-off tap* (Am. *faucet*)
35 das Auslaufdoppelventil (der
Flügelhahn)
- *supatap*
36 das Schwenkventil (der
Schwenkhahn)
- *swivel tap*
37 der Druckspüler
- *flushing valve*
38-52 **Fittings** *n*
- *fittings*
38 das Übergangsstück mit
Außengewinde *n*
- *joint with male thread*
39 das Reduzierstück
- *reducing socket
(reducing coupler)*
40 die Winkelverschraubung
- *elbow screw joint (elbow coupling)*
41 das Übergangsreduzierstück mit
Innengewinde *n*
- *reducing socket (reducing coupler)
with female thread*
42 die Verschraubung
- *screw joint*
43 die Muffe
- *coupler (socket)*
44 das T-Stück
- *T-joint (T-junction joint, tee)*
45 die Winkelverschraubung mit
Innengewinde *n*
- *elbow screw joint with female
thread*
46 der Bogen
- *bend*
47 das T-Stück mit
Abgangsinnengewinde *n*
- *T-joint (T-junction joint, tee) with
female taper thread*
48 der Deckenwinkel
- *ceiling joint*
49 der Übergangswinkel
- *reducing elbow*
50 das Kreuzstück
- *cross*
51 der Übergangswinkel mit
Außengewinde *n*
- *elbow joint with male thread*
52 der Winkel
- *elbow joint*
53-57 **Rohrbefestigungen** *f*
- *pipe supports*
53 das Rohrband
- *saddle clip*
54 das Abstandsrohrband
- *spacing bracket*
55 der Dübel
- *plug*
56 einfache Rohrschellen *f*
- *pipe clips*
57 die Abstandsrohrschelle
- *two-piece spacing clip*
58-86 **Installationswerkzeug** *n*
- *plumber's tools, gas fitter's tools*
58 die Brennerzange
- *gas pliers*
59 die Rohrzange
- *footprints*
60 die Kombinationszange
- *combination cutting pliers*

61 die Wasserpumpenzange
- *pipe wrench*
62 die Flachzange
- *flat-nose pliers*
63 der Nippelhalter
- *nipple key*
64 die Standhahnmutternzange
- *round-nose pliers*
65 die Kneifzange
- *pincers*
66 der Rollgabelschlüssel
- *adjustable S-wrench*
67 der Franzose
- *screw wrench*
68 der Engländer
- *shifting spanner*
69 der Schraubendreher
(Schraubenzieher)
- *screwdriver*
70 die Stich- oder Lochsäge
- *compass saw (keyhole saw)*
71 der Metallsägebogen
- *hacksaw frame*
72 der Fuchsschwanz
- *hand saw*
73 der Lötkolben
- *soldering iron*
74 die Lötlampe
- *blowlamp (blowtorch) [for
soldering]*
75 das Dichtband (Gewindeband)
- *sealing tape*
76 das Lötzinn
- *tin-lead solder*
77 der Fäustel
- *club hammer*
78 der Handhammer
- *hammer*
79 die Wasserwaage
- *spirit level*
80 der Schlosserschraubstock
- *steel-leg vice* (Am. *vise*)
81 der Rohrschraubstock
- *pipe vice* (Am. *vise*)
82 der Rohrbieger
- *pipe-bending machine*
83 die Biegeform
- *former (template)*
84 der Rohrabschneider
- *pipe cutter*
85 die Gewindeschneidkluppe
- *hand die*
86 die Gewindeschneidmaschine
- *screw-cutting machine
(thread-cutting machine)*

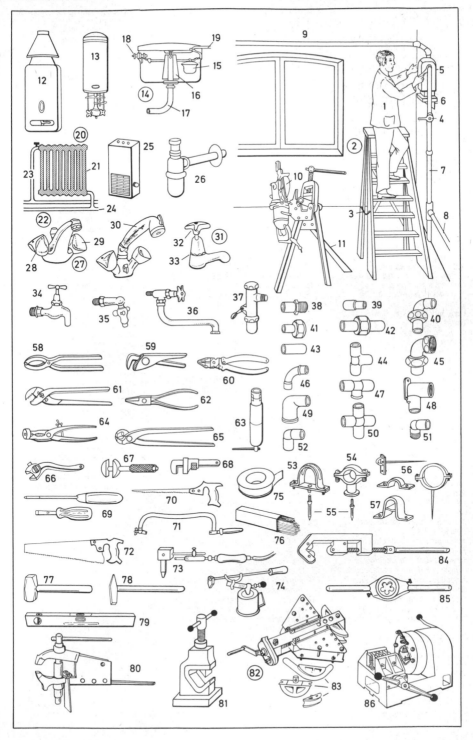

1 der Elektroinstallateur
– *electrician (electrical fitter, wireman)*
2 der Klingeltaster (Türtaster) für Schutzkleinspannung *f* (Schwachstrom *m*)
– *bell push (doorbell) for low-voltage safety current*
3 die Haussprechstelle mit Ruftaste *f*
– *house telephone with call button*
4 der Wippenschalter [für die Unterputzinstallation]
– *[flush-mounted] rocker switch*
5 die Schutzkontaktsteckdose [für die Unterputzinstallation]
– *[flush-mounted] earthed socket (wall socket, plug point, Am. wall outlet, convenience outlet, outlet)*
6 die Schutzkontakt-Doppelsteckdose [für die Aufputzinstallation]
– *[surface-mounted] earthed double socket (double wall socket, double plug point, Am. double wall outlet, double convenience outlet, double outlet)*
7 die Zweifachkombination (Schalter *m* und Schutzkontaktsteckdose *f*)
– *switched socket (switch and socket)*
8 die Vierfachsteckdose
– *four-socket (four-way) adapter (socket)*
9 der Schutzkontaktstecker
– *earthed plug*
10 die Verlängerungsschnur
– *extension lead (Am. extension cord)*
11 der Kupplungsstecker
– *extension plug*
12 die Kupplungsdose
– *extension socket*
13 die dreipolige Steckdose [für Drehstrom *m*] mit Nulleiter *m* und Schutzkontakt *m* für die Aufputzinstallation
– *surface-mounted three-pole earthed socket [for three-phase circuit] with neutral conductor*
14 der Drehstromstecker
– *three-phase plug*
15 das elektrische Läutewerk (der Summer)
– *electric bell (electric buzzer)*
16 der Zugschalter mit Schnur *f*
– *pull-switch (cord-operated wall switch)*
17 der Dimmer [zur stufenlosen Einstellung des Glühlampenlichts *n*]
– *dimmer switch [for smooth adjustment of lamp brightness]*
18 der gußgekapselte Paketschalter
– *drill-cast rotary switch*
19 der Leitungsschutzschalter (Sicherungsschraubautomat)
– *miniature circuit breaker (screw-in circuit breaker, fuse)*
20 der Sicherungsdruckknopf
– *resetting button*
21 die Paßschraube, der Paßeinsatz [für Schmelzsicherungen *f* und Sicherungsschraubautomaten *m*]
– *set screw [for fuses and miniature circuit breakers]*
22 die Unterflurinstallation
– *underfloor mounting (underfloor sockets)*

23 der Kippanschluß für die Starkstrom- und die Fernmeldeleitung
– *hinged floor socket for power lines and communication lines*
24 der Einbauanschluß mit Klappdeckel *m*
– *sunken floor socket with hinged lid (snap lid)*
25 der Anschlußaufsatz
– *surface-mounted socket outlet (plug point) box*
26 die Taschenlampe, eine Stablampe
– *pocket torch, a torch (Am. flashlight)*
27 die Trockenbatterie (Taschenlampenbatterie)
– *dry cell battery*
28 die Kontaktfeder
– *contact spring*
29 die Leuchtenklemme (Buchsenklemme, Lüsterklemme), teilbar, aus thermoplastischem Kunststoff *m*
– *strip of thermoplastic connectors*
30 das Einziehstahlband mit Suchfeder *f* und angenieteter Öse
– *steel draw-in wire (draw wire) with threading key, and ring attached*
31 der Zählerschrank
– *electricity meter cupboard*
32 der Wechselstromzähler
– *electricity meter*
33 die Leitungsschutzschalter *m* (Sicherungsautomaten)
– *miniature circuit breakers (miniature circuit breaker consumer unit)*
34 das Isolierband
– *insulating tape (Am. friction tape)*
35 der Schmelzeinsatzhalter (die Schraubkappe)
– *fuse holder*
36 die Leitungsschutzsicherung (Schmelzsicherung), eine Sicherungspatrone mit Schmelzeinsatz *m*
– *circuit breaker (fuse), a fuse cartridge with fusible element*
37 der Kennmelder [je nach Nennstrom *m* farbig gekennzeichnet]
– *colour (Am. color) indicator [showing current rating]*
38-39 das Kontaktstück
– *contact maker*
40 die Kabelschelle (Plastikschelle)
– *cable clip*
41 das Vielfachmeßgerät (der Spannungs- und Strommesser)
– *universal test meter (multiple meter for measuring current and voltage)*
42 die Feuchtraummantelleitung aus thermoplastischem Kunststoff *m*
– *thermoplastic moisture-proof cable*
43 der Kupferleiter
– *copper conductor*
44 die Stegleitung
– *three-core cable*
45 der elektrische Lötkolben
– *electric soldering iron*
46 der Schraubendreher (Schraubenzieher)
– *screwdriver*
47 die Wasserpumpenzange
– *pipe wrench*

48 der Schutzhelm aus schlagfestem Kunststoff *m*
– *shock-resisting safety helmet*
49 der Werkzeugkoffer
– *tool case*
50 die Rundzange
– *round-nose pliers*
51 der Seitenschneider
– *cutting pliers*
52 die Taschensäge
– *junior hacksaw*
53 die Kombinationszange
– *combination cutting pliers*
54 der Isoliergriff
– *insulated handle*
55 der Spannungssucher (Spannungsprüfer)
– *continuity tester*
56 die elektrische Glühlampe (Allgebrauchslampe, Glühbirne)
– *electric light bulb (general service lamp, filament lamp)*
57 der Glaskolben
– *glass bulb (bulb)*
58 der Doppelwendelleuchtkörper
– *coiled-coil filament*
59 die Schraubfassung (der Lampensockel mit Gewinde *n*)
– *screw base*
60 die Fassung für Glühlampen *f* (Leuchtensockel *m*)
– *lampholder*
61 die Entladungslampe (Leuchtstofflampe)
– *fluorescent tube*
62 die Fassung für Entladungslampen *f*
– *bracket for fluorescent tubes*
63 das Kabelmesser
– *electrician's knife*
64 die Abisolierzange
– *wire strippers*
65 die Bajonettfassung
– *bayonet fitting*
66 die Dreipolsteckdose mit Schalter *m*
– *three-pin socket with switch*
67 der Dreipolstecker
– *three-pin plug*
68 die Sicherung mit Sicherungsdraht *m*
– *fuse carrier with fuse wire*
69 die Glühbirne mit Bajonettfassung *f*
– *light bulb with bayonet fitting*

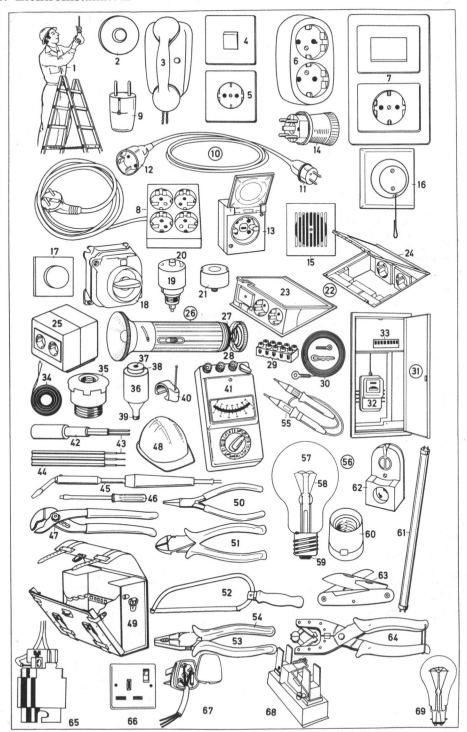

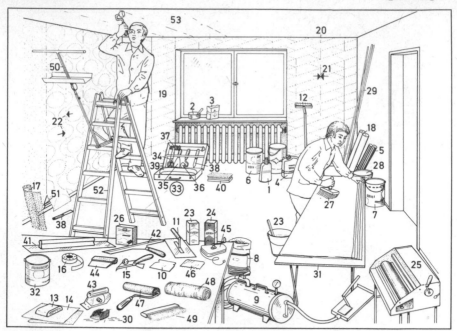

- *preparation of surfaces*
1 der Tapetenablöser
- *wallpaper-stripping liquid (stripper)*
2 der Gips
- *plaster (plaster of Paris)*
3 die Spachtelmasse
- *filler*
4 der Tapetenwechselgrund
- *glue size (size)*
5 die Rollenmakulatur (*ähnl.:*
  Stripmakulatur, Untertapete), ein
  Unterlagsstoff *m*
- *lining paper, a backing paper*
6 das Grundiermittel
- *primer*
7 das Fluatmittel
- *fluate*
8 die Feinmakulatur
- *shredded lining paper*
9 das Tapetenablösegerät
- *wallpaper-stripping machine
  (stripper)*
10 der Japanspachtel
- *scraper*
11 die Glättscheibe
- *smoother*
12 der Tapetenperforator
- *perforator*
13 der Schleifklotz
- *sandpaper block*
14 das Schleifpapier
- *sandpaper*
15 der Tapetenschaber
- *stripping knife*
16 das Indikatorpapier
- *masking tape*
17 die Rißunterlage
- *strip of sheet metal [on which
  wallpaper is laid for cutting]*

18-53 das Tapezieren
- *wallpapering (paper hanging)*
18 die Tapete (*Arten:* Papier-, Rauhfaser-,
  Textil-, Kunststoff-, Metall-,
  Naturwerkstoff-, Wandbildtapete)
- *wallpaper (kinds: wood pulp paper,
  wood chip paper, fabric
  wallhangings, synthetic wallpaper,
  metallic paper, natural (e.g. wood
  or cork) paper, tapestry wallpaper)*
19 die Tapetenbahn
- *length of wallpaper*
20 die Tapetennaht, auf Stoß *m*
- *butted paper edges*
21 der gerade Ansatz (Rapport)
- *matching edge*
22 der versetzte Ansatz
- *non-matching edge*
23 der Tapetenkleister
- *wallpaper paste*
24 der Spezialtapetenkleister
- *heavy-duty paste*
25 das Kleistergerät
- *pasting machine*
26 der Tapeziergerätekleister
- *paste [for the pasting machine]*
27 die Kleisterbürste
- *paste brush*
28 der Dispersionskleber
- *emulsion paste*
29 die Tapetenleiste
- *picture rail*
30 die Leistenstifte
- *beading pins*
31 der Tapeziertisch
- *pasteboard (paperhanger's bench)*
32 der Tapetenschutzlack
- *gloss finish*
33 der Tapezierkasten
- *paperhanging kit*

34 die Tapezierschere
- *shears (bull-nosed scissors)*
35 der Handspachtel
- *filling knife*
36 der Nahtroller
- *seam roller*
37 das Haumesser
- *hacking knife*
38 das Beschneidmesser
- *knife (trimming knife)*
39 die Tapezierschiene
- *straightedge*
40 die Tapezierbürste
- *paperhanging brush*
41 die Wandschneidekelle
- *wallpaper-cutting board*
42 die Abreißschiene
- *cutter*
43 der Nahtschneider
- *trimmer*
44 der Kunststoffspachtel
- *plastic spatula*
45 die Schlagschnur
- *chalked string*
46 der Zahnspachtel
- *spreader*
47 die Tapetenandrückwalze
- *paper roller*
48 das Flanelltuch
- *flannel cloth*
49 der Tapezierwischer
- *dry brush*
50 das Deckentapeziergerät
- *ceiling paperhanger*
51 der Eckenschneidewinkel
- *overlap angle*
52 die Tapeziererleiter
- *paperhanger's trestles*
53 die Deckentapete
- *ceiling paper*

1 das **Maler** (Anstreichen)
- *painting*
2 der Maler (Lackierer)
- *painter*
3 die Streichbürste
- *paintbrush*
4 die Dispersionsfarbe
- *emulsion paint (emulsion)*
5 die Stehleiter (Doppelleiter)
- *stepladder*
6 die Farbendose
- *can (tin) of paint*
7-8 die Farbenkannen *f*
- *cans (tins) of paint*
7 die Kanne mit Handgriff *m*
- *can (tin) with fixed handle*
8 die Kanne mit Traghenkel *m*
- *paint kettle*
9 der Farbenhobbock
- *drum of paint*
10 der Farbeimer
- *paint bucket*
11 der Farbroller (die Farbrolle)
- *paint roller*
12 das Abstreifgitter
- *grill [for removing excess paint from the roller]*
13 die Musterwalze
- *stippling roller*
14 das **Lackieren**
- *varnishing*
15 der Ölsockel
- *oil-painted dado*
16 die Lösungsmittelkanne
- *canister for thinner*
17 der Flächenstreicher
- *flat brush for larger surfaces (flat wall brush)*
18 die Stupfbürste
- *stippler*

19 der Ringpinsel
- *fitch*
20 der Kluppenpinsel
- *cutting-in brush*
21 der Heizkörperpinsel
- *radiator brush (flay brush)*
22 der Malspachtel
- *paint scraper*
23 der Japanspachtel
- *scraper*
24 das Kittmesser
- *putty knife*
25 das Schleifpapier
- *sandpaper*
26 der Schleifklotz
- *sandpaper block*
27 der Fußbodenstreicher
- *floor brush*
28 das **Schleifen und Spritzen** *n*
- *sanding and spraying*
29 die Schleifmaschine
- *grinder*
30 der Rutscher
- *sander*
31 der Spritzkessel
- *pressure pot*
32 die Spritzpistole
- *spray gun*
33 der Kompressor
- *compressor (air compressor)*
34 das Flutgerät zum Fluten *n* von Heizkörpern *m* u.ä.
- *flow coating machine for flow coating radiators, etc.*
35 die Handspritzpistole
- *hand spray*
36 die Anlage für das luftlose Spritzen
- *airless spray unit*
37 die luftlose Spritzpistole
- *airless spray gun*

38 der Auslaufbecher zur Viskositätsmessung
- *efflux viscometer*
39 der Sekundenmesser
- *seconds timer*
40 das **Beschriften und Vergolden** *n*
- *lettering and gilding*
41 der Schriftpinsel
- *lettering brush (signwriting brush, pencil)*
42 das Pausrädchen
- *tracing wheel*
43 das Schablonenmesser
- *stencil knife*
44 das Anlegeöl
- *oil gold size*
45 das Blattgold
- *gold leaf*
46 das Konturieren
- *outline drawing*
47 der Malstock
- *mahlstick*
48 das Aufpausen der Zeichnung
- *pouncing*
49 der Pausebeutel
- *pounce bag*
50 das Vergolderkissen
- *gilder's cushion*
51 das Vergoldermesser
- *gilder's knife*
52 das Anschießen des Blattgoldes *n*
- *sizing gold leaf*
53 das Ausfüllen der Buchstaben *m* mit Stupffarbe *f*
- *filling in the letters with stipple paint*
54 der Stupfpinsel
- *gilder's mop*

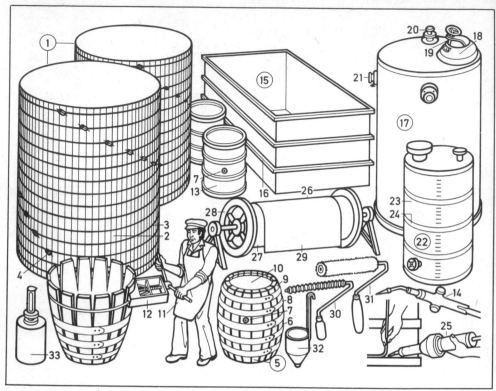

1-33 die Böttcherei und Behälterbauerei
- *cooper's and tank construction engineer's workshops*

1 der Bottich
- *tank*

2 der Mantel aus Umhölzern *n*, Stäben *m*
- *circumference made of staves (staved circumference)*

3 der Rundeisenreifen
- *iron rod*

4 das Spannschloß
- *turnbuckle*

5 das Faß
- *barrel (cask)*

6 der Faßrumpf
- *body of barrel (of cask)*

7 das Spundloch
- *bunghole*

8 der Faßreifen (das Faßband)
- *band (hoop) of barrel*

9 die Faßdaube
- *barrel stave*

10 der Faßboden
- *barrelhead (heading)*

11 der Böttcher
- *cooper*

12 der Faßzieher
- *trusser*

13 das eiserne Rollringfaß
- *drum*

14 der Autogenschweißbrenner
- *gas welding torch*

15 der Beizbottich, aus Thermoplasten *m*
- *staining vat, made of thermoplastics*

16 der Verstärkungsreifen aus Profileisen
- *iron reinforcing band*

17 der Lagerbehälter, aus glasfaserverstärktem Polyesterharz (GFP) *n*
- *storage container, made of glass fibre (Am. glass fiber) reinforced polyester resin*

18 das Mannloch
- *manhole*

19 der Mannlochdeckel, mit Spindel *f*
- *manhole cover with handwheel*

20 der Flanschstutzen
- *flange mount*

21 der Blockflansch
- *flange-type stopcock*

22 der Meßbehälter
- *measuring tank*

23 der Mantel
- *shell (circumference)*

24 der Schrumpfring
- *shrink ring*

25 die Heißluftpistole
- *hot-air gun*

26 das Rohrstück, aus glasfaserverstärktem Kunstharz (GFK) *n*

- *roller made of glass fibre (Am. glass fiber) reinforced synthetic resin*

27 das Rohr
- *cylinder*

28 der Flansch
- *flange*

29 die Glasmatte, das Glasgewebe
- *glass cloth*

30 die Rillenwalze
- *grooved roller*

31 die Lammfellrolle
- *lambskin roller*

32 der Viskosebecher
- *ladle for testing viscosity*

33 das Härterdosiergerät
- *measuring vessel for hardener*

1-25 die Kürschnerwerkstatt
- *furrier's workroom*
1 der Kürschner
- *furrier*
2 die Dampfspritzpistole
- *steam spray gun*
3 das Dampfbügeleisen
- *steam iron*
4 die Klopfmaschine
- *beating machine*
5 die Schneidemaschine zum
  Auslassen *n* der Felle *n*
- *cutting machine for letting out
  furskins*
6 das unzerschnittene Fell
- *uncut furskin*
7 die Auslaßstreifen *m*
- *let-out strips (let-out sections)*
8 die Pelzwerkerin
  (Pelznäherin)
- *fur worker*
9 die Pelznähmaschine
- *fur-sewing machine*
10 das Gebläse für die Auslaßtechnik
- *blower for letting out*
11-21 Felle *n*
- *furskins*
11 das Nerzfell
- *mink skin*
12 die Haarseite
- *fur side*
13 die Lederseite
- *leather side*

14 das geschnittene Fell
- *cut furskin*
15 das Luchsfell vor dem Auslassen *n*
- *lynx skin before letting out*
16 das ausgelassene Luchsfell
- *let-out lynx skin*
17 die Haarseite
- *fur side*
18 die Lederseite
- *leather side*
19 das ausgelassene Nerzfell
- *let-out mink skin*
20 das zusammengesetzte Luchsfell
- *lynx fur, sewn together (sewn)*
21 das Breitschwanzfell
- *broadtail*
22 der Pelzstift
- *fur marker*
23 die Pelzwerkerin (Pelzschneiderin)
- *fur worker*
24 der Nerzmantel
- *mink coat*
25 der Ozelotmantel
- *ocelot coat*

1-73 **die Tischlerwerkstatt**
(Tischlerei; Schreinerei)
- *joiner's workshop*
1-28 **das Tischlerwerkzeug**
- *joiner's tools*
1 die Holzraspel
- *wood rasp*
2 die Holzfeile
- *wood file*
3 die Stichsäge (Lochsäge)
- *compass saw (keyhole saw)*
4 der Fuchsschwanzgriff
- *saw handle*
5 der Vierkantholzhammer (Klüpfel, Klöpfel)
- *[square-headed] mallet*
6 der Tischlerwinkel
- *try square*
7-11 **Beitel** *m*
- *chisels*
7 der Stechbeitel (das Stemmeisen)
- *bevelled-edge chisel (chisel)*
8 der Lochbeitel (das Locheisen)
- *mortise (mortice) chisel*
9 der Hohlbeitel (das Hohleisen)
- *gouge*
10 das Heft
- *handle*
11 der Kantbeitel
- *framing chisel (cant chisel)*
12 der Leimkessel mit Wasserbad *n*
- *glue pot in water bath*
13 der Leimtopf, ein Einsatz *m* für Tischlerleim *m*
- *glue pot (glue well), an insert for joiner's glue*
14 die Schraubzwinge
- *handscrew*
15-28 **Hobel** *m* (Handhobel)
- *planes*
15 der Schlichthobel
- *smoothing plane*
16 der Schrupphobel (Doppelhobel)
- *jack plane*
17 der Zahnhobel
- *toothing plane*
18 die Nase
- *handle (toat)*
19 der Keil
- *wedge*
20 das Hobeleisen (Hobelmesser)
- *plane iron (cutter)*
21 das Keilloch
- *mouth*
22 die Sohle
- *sole*
23 die Wange (Backe)
- *side*
24 der Kasten (Hobelkasten)
- *stock (body)*
25 der Simshobel
- *rebate (rabbet) plane*
26 der Grundhobel
- *router plane (old woman's tooth)*
27 der Schabhobel
- *spokeshave*
28 der Schiffshobel
- *compass plane*
29-37 **die Hobelbank**
- *woodworker's bench*
29 der Fuß
- *foot*
30 die Vorderzange
- *front vice (Am. vise)*
31 der Spannstock
- *vice (Am. vise) handle*

32 die Druckspindel
- *vice (Am. vise) screw*
33 das Zangenbrett
- *jaw*
34 die Bankplatte
- *bench top*
35 die Beilade
- *well*
36 der Bankhaken (das Bankeisen)
- *bench stop (bench holdfast)*
37 die Hinterzange
- *tail vice (Am. vise)*
38 der Tischler (Schreiner)
- *cabinet maker (joiner)*
39 die Rauhbank (der Langhobel)
- *trying plane*
40 die Hobelspäne
- *shavings*
41 die Holzschraube
- *wood screw*
42 das Schränkeisen (der Sägensetzer)
- *saw set*
43 die Gehrungslade
- *mitre (Am. miter) box*
44 der gerade Fuchsschwanz
- *tenon saw*
45 die Dickenhobelmaschine
- *thicknesser (thicknessing machine)*
46 der Dickentisch, mit Tischwalzen *f*
- *thicknessing table with rollers*
47 der Rückschlagschutz
- *kick-back guard*
48 der Späneauswurf
- *chip-extractor opening*
49 die Kettenfräsmaschine
- *chain mortising machine (chain mortiser)*
50 die endlose Fräskette
- *endless mortising chain*
51 die Holzeinspannvorrichtung
- *clamp (work clamp)*
52 die Astlochfräsmaschine
- *knot hole moulding (Am. molding) machine*
53 der Astlochfräser
- *knot hole cutter*
54 das Schnellspannfutter
- *quick-action chuck*
55 der Handhebel
- *hand lever*
56 der Wechselhebel
- *change-gear handle*
57 die Format- und Besäumkreissäge
- *sizing and edging machine*
58 der Hauptschalter
- *main switch*
59 das Kreissägeblatt
- *circular saw (buzz saw) blade*
60 das Handrad zur Höheneinstellung
- *height (rise and fall) adjustment wheel*
61 die Prismaschiene
- *V-way*
62 der Rahmentisch
- *framing table*
63 der Ausleger
- *extension arm (arm)*
64 der Besäumtisch
- *trimming table*
65 der Linealwinkel
- *fence*
66 das Linealhandrädchen
- *fence adjustment handle*
67 der Klemmhebel
- *clamp lever*
68 die Plattenkreissäge
- *board-sawing machine*

69 der Schwenkmotor
- *swivel motor*
70 die Plattenhalterung
- *board support*
71 der Sägeschlitten
- *saw carriage*
72 das Pedal zur Anhebung der Transportrollen *f*
- *pedal for raising the transport rollers*
73 die Tischlerplatte
- *block board*

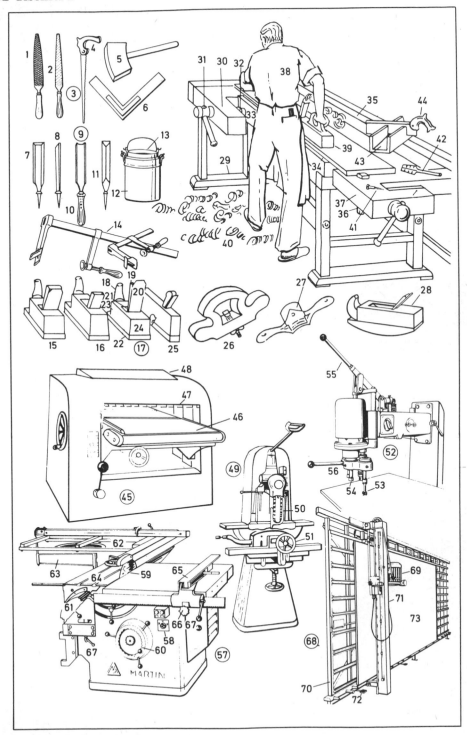

1 die Furnierschälmaschine
- *veneer-peeling machine (peeling machine, peeler)*
2 das Furnier
- *veneer*
3 die Furnierzusammenklebemaschine
- *veneer-splicing machine*
4 der Nylonfadenkops
- *nylon-thread cop*
5 die Nähvorrichtung
- *sewing mechanism*
6 die Dübelbohrmaschine
- *dowel hole boring machine (dowel hole borer)*
7 der Bohrmotor mit Hohlwellenbohrer *m*
- *boring motor with hollow-shaft boring bit*
8 das Handrad für den Spannbügel
- *clamp handle*
9 der Spannbügel
- *clamp*
10 die Spannpratze
- *clamping shoe*
11 die Anschlagschiene
- *stop bar*
12 die Kantenschleifmaschine
- *edge sander (edge-sanding machine)*
13 die Spannrolle mit Ausleger *m*
- *tension roller with extension arm*
14 die Schleifbandregulierschraube
- *sanding belt regulator (regulating handle)*
15 das endlose Schleifband
- *endless sanding belt (sand belt)*
16 der Bandspannhebel
- *belt-tensioning lever*
17 der neigbare Auflagetisch
- *canting table (tilting table)*
18 die Bandwalze
- *belt roller*
19 das Winkellineal für Gehrungen *f*
- *angling fence for mitres (Am. miters)*
20 die aufklappbare Staubhaube
- *opening dust hood*
21 die Tiefenverstellung des Auflagetisches *m*
- *rise adjustment of the table*
22 das Handrad für die Tischhöhenverstellung
- *rise adjustment wheel for the table*
23 die Klemmschraube für die Tischhöhenverstellung
- *clamping screw for the table rise adjustment*
24 die Tischkonsole
- *console*
25 der Maschinenfuß
- *foot of the machine*
26 die Kantenklebemaschine
- *edge-veneering machine*
27 das Schleifrad
- *sanding wheel*
28 die Schleifstaubabsaugung
- *sanding dust extractor*
29 die Klebevorrichtung
- *splicing head*
30 die Einbandschleifmaschine
- *single-belt sanding machine (single-belt sander)*
31 die Bandabdeckung
- *belt guard*
32 die Bandscheibenverkleidung
- *bandwheel cover*

33 der Exhauster
- *extractor fan (exhaust fan)*
34 der Rahmenschleifschuh
- *frame-sanding pad*
35 der Schleiftisch
- *sanding table*
36 die Feineinstellung
- *fine adjustment*
37 die Feinschnitt- und Fügemaschine
- *fine cutter and jointer*
38 der Sägewagen (das Säge- und Hobelaggregat) mit Kettenantrieb *m*
- *saw carriage with chain drive*
39 die nachgeführte Kabelaufhängung
- *trailing cable hanger (trailing cable support)*
40 der Luftabsaugstutzen
- *air extractor pipe*
41 die Transportschiene
- *rail*
42 die Rahmenpresse
- *frame-cramping (frame-clamping) machine*
43 der Rahmenständer
- *frame stand*
44 das Werkstück, ein Fensterrahmen *m*
- *workpiece, a window frame*
45 die Druckluftzuleitung
- *compressed-air line*
46 der Druckzylinder
- *pressure cylinder*
47 der Druckstempel
- *pressure foot*
48 die Rahmeneinspannung
- *frame-mounting device*
49 die Furnierschnellpresse
- *rapid-veneer press*
50 der Preßboden
- *bed*
51 der Preßdeckel
- *press*
52 der Preßstempel
- *pressure piston*

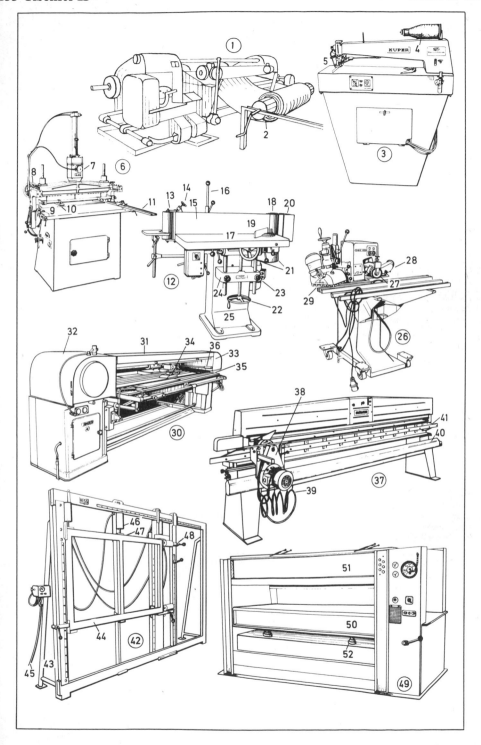

1-34 der Werkzeugschrank für das
Heimwerken (Basteln, Do-it-yourself)
- *tool cupboard (tool cabinet) for
do-it-yourself work*
1 der Schlichthobel
- *smoothing plane*
2 der Gabelschlüsselsatz
- *set of fork spanners (fork wrenches,
open-end wrenches)*
3 die Bügelsäge
- *hacksaw*
4 der Schraubendreher
(Schraubenzieher)
- *screwdriver*
5 der Kreuzschlitzschraubendreher
- *cross-point screwdriver*
6 die Sägeraspel
- *saw rasp*
7 der Hammer
- *hammer*
8 die Holzraspel
- *wood rasp*
9 die Schruppfeile
- *roughing file*
10 der Kleinschraubstock
- *small vice
(Am. vise)*
11 die Wasserpumpenzange
- *pipe wrench*
12 die Eckrohrzange
- *multiple pliers*
13 die Kneifzange
- *pincers*
14 die Kombizange
- *all-purpose wrench*
15 die Entisolierzange
- *wire stripper and cutter*
16 die elektrische Bohrmaschine
- *electric drill*
17 die Stahlsäge
- *hacksaw*
18 der Gipsbecher
- *plaster cup*
19 der Lötkolben
- *soldering iron*
20 der Lötzinndraht
- *tin-lead solder wire*
21 die Lammfellscheibe
(Lammfellpolierhaube)
- *lamb's wool polishing bonnet*
22 der Polierteller (Gummiteller) für
die Bohrmaschine
- *rubber backing disc (disk)*
23 Schleifscheiben *f*
- *grinding wheel*
24 der Drahtbürstenteller
- *wire wheel brush*
25 das Tellerschleifpapier
- *sanding discs (disks)*
26 der Anschlagwinkel
- *try square*
27 der Fuchsschwanz
- *hand saw*
28 der Universalschneider
- *universal cutter*
29 die Wasserwaage
- *spirit level*
30 der Stechbeitel
- *firmer chisel*
31 der Körner
- *centre (Am. center)
punch*
32 der Durchschläger
- *nail punch*
33 der Zollstock (Maßstab)
- *folding rule (rule)*

34 der Kleinteilekasten
- *storage box for small parts*
35 der Werkzeugkasten
(Handwerkskasten)
- *tool box*
36 der Weißleim (Kaltleim)
- *woodworking adhesive*
37 der Malerspachtel
- *stripping knife*
38 das Lassoband (Klebeband)
- *adhesive tape*
39 der Sortimentseinsatz mit Nägeln
m, Schrauben *f* und Dübeln *m*
- *storage box with compartments for
nails, screws and plugs*
40 der Schlosserhammer
- *machinist's hammer*
41 die zusammenlegbare Werkbank
(Heimwerkerbank)
- *collapsible workbench (collapsible
bench)*
42 die Spannvorrichtung
- *jig*
43 die elektrische
Schlagbohrmaschine (der
Elektrobohrer, Schlagbohrer)
- *electric percussion drill (electric
hammer drill)*
44 der Pistolenhandgriff
- *pistol grip*
45 der zusätzliche Handgriff
- *side grip*
46 der Getriebeschalter
- *gearshift switch*
47 der Handgriff mit Abstandshalter *m*
- *handle with depth gauge
(Am. gage)*
48 der Bohrkopf
- *chuck*
49 der Spiralbohrer
- *twist bit (twist drill)*
50-55 Zusatz- und Anbaugeräte zum
Elektrobohrer
- *attachments for an electric drill*
50 die kombinierte Kreis- und
Bandsäge
- *combined circular saw (buzz saw)
and bandsaw*
51 die Drechselbank
- *wood-turning lathe*
52 der Kreissägevorsatz
- *circular saw attachment*
53 der Vibrationsschleifer
- *orbital sanding attachment (orbital
sander)*
54 der Bohrständer
- *drill stand*
55 der Heckenscherenvorsatz
- *hedge-trimming attachment (hedge
trimmer)*
56 die Lötpistole
- *soldering gun*
57 der Lötkolben
- *soldering iron*
58 der Blitzlöter
- *high-speed soldering iron*
59 die Polsterarbeit, das Beziehen
eines Sessels
- *upholstery, upholstering an
armchair*
60 der Bezugsstoff
- *fabric (material) for upholstery*
61 der Heimwerker (Selbstwerker)
- *do-it-yourself enthusiast*

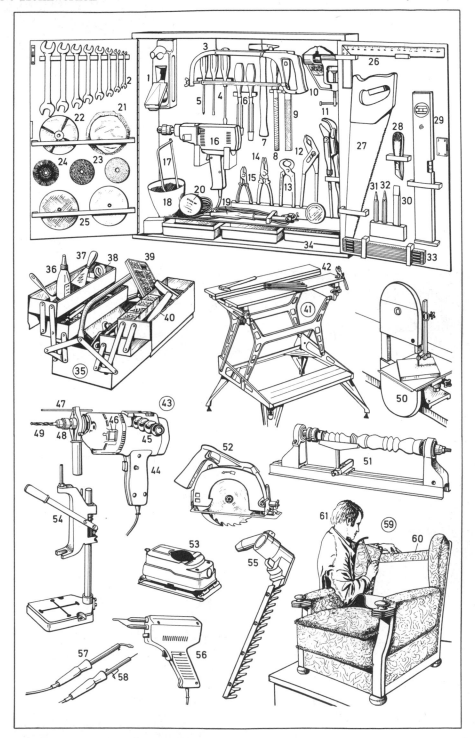

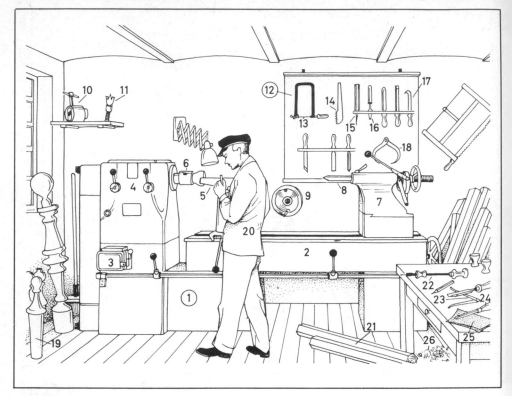

1-26 die Drechslerei
(Drechslerwerkstatt)
- *turnery (turner's workshop)*
1 die Holzdrehbank (Drechselbank)
- *wood-turning lathe (lathe)*
2 die Drechselwange
(Drehbankwange)
- *lathe bed*
3 der Anlaßwiderstand
- *starting resistance (starting resistor)*
4 der Getriebekasten
- *gearbox*
5 die Handvorlage
(Werkzeugauflage)
- *tool rest*
6 das Spundfutter
- *chuck*
7 der Reitstock
- *tailstock*
8 die Spitzdocke
- *centre*
(Am. center)
9 der Wirtel (Quirl), eine Schnurrolle
mit Mitnehmer *m*
- *driving plate with pin*
10 das Zweibackenfutter
- *two-jaw chuck*
11 der Dreizack (Zwirl)
- *live centre (Am. center)*
12 die Laubsäge
- *fretsaw*
13 das Laubsägeblatt
- *fretsaw blade*

14, 15, 24 Drechselwerkzeuge *n*
(Drechslerdrehstähle *m*)
- *turning tools*
14 der Gewindesträhler (Strähler,
Schraubstahl), zum
Holzgewindeschneiden *n*
- *thread chaser, for cutting threads in
wood*
15 die Drehröhre, zum Vordrehen *n*
- *gouge, for rough turning*
16 der Löffelbohrer
(Parallelbohrer)
- *spoon bit (shell bit)*
17 der Ausdrehhaken
- *hollowing tool*
18 der Tastzirkel (Greifzirkel,
Außentaster)
- *outside calliper (caliper)*
19 der gedrechselte Gegenstand
(die gedrechselte Holzware)
- *turned work (turned wood)*
20 der Drechslermeister (Drechsler)
- *master turner (turner)*
21 der Rohling (das unbearbeitete
Holz)
- *[piece of] rough wood*
22 der Drillbohrer
- *drill*
23 der Lochzirkel (Innentaster)
- *inside calliper (caliper)*
24 der Grabstichel (Abstechstahl,
Plattenstahl)
- *parting tool*

25 das Glaspapier (Sandpapier,
Schmirgelpapier)
- *glass paper (sandpaper, emery
paper)*
26 die Drehspäne *m* (Holzspäne)
- *shavings*

1-40 **die Korbmacherei**
(Korbflechterei)
- **basket making** (basketry, basketwork)
1-4 **Flechtarten** f
- **weaves** (strokes)
1 das Drehergeflecht
- randing
2 das Köpergeflecht
- rib randing
3 das Schichtgeflecht
- oblique randing
4 das einfache Geflecht, ein
Flechtwerk n
- randing, a piece of wickerwork
(screen work)
5 der Einschlag
- weaver
6 die Stake
- stake
7 das Werkbrett
- workboard; also: lapboard
8 die Querleiste
- screw block
9 das Einstechloch
- hole for holding the block
10 der Bock
- stand
11 der Spankorb
- chip basket (spale basket)
12 der Span
- chip (spale)
13 der Einweichbottich
- soaking tub

14 die Weidenruten f (Ruten)
- willow stakes (osier stakes)
15 die Weidenstöcke m (Stöcke)
- willow rods (osier rods)
16 der Korb, eine Flechtarbeit
- basket, a piece of wickerwork
(basketwork)
17 der Zuschlag (Abschluß)
- border
18 das Seitengeflecht
- woven side
19 der Bodenstern
- round base
20 das Bodengeflecht
- woven base
21 das Bodenkreuz
- slath
22-24 **die Gestellarbeit**
- **covering a frame**
22 das Gestell
- frame
23 der Splitt
- end
24 die Schiene
- rib
25 das Gerüst
- upsett
26 das Gras; Arten: Espartogras,
Alfagras (Halfagras)
- grass; kinds: esparto grass, alfalfa
grass
27 das Schilf (Rohrkolbenschilf)
- rush (bulrush, reed mace)

28 die Binse (Chinabinsenschnur)
- reed (China reed, string)
29 das Raffiabast (Bast)
- raffia (bast)
30 das Stroh
- straw
31 das Bambusrohr
- bamboo cane
32 das Peddigrohr (span. Rohr, der
Rotang)
- rattan (ratan) chair cane
33 der Korbmacher (Korbflechter)
- basket maker
34 das Biegeeisen
- bending tool
35 der Reißer
- cutting point (bodkin)
36 das Klopfeisen
- rapping iron
37 die Beißzange
- pincers
38 das Putzmesser (der Ausstecher)
- picking knife
39 der Schienenhobel
- shave
40 die Bogensäge
- hacksaw

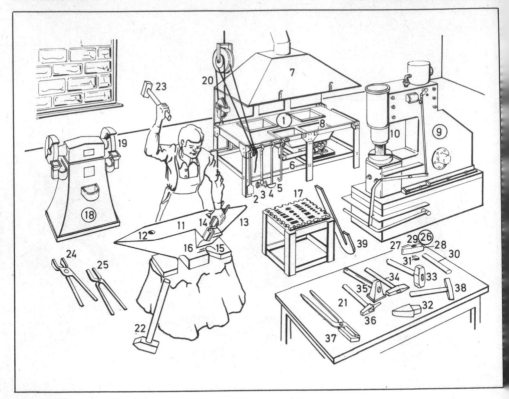

1-8 **die Esse mit dem Schmiedefeuer** *n*
- *hearth (forge) with blacksmith's fire*
1 die Esse
- *hearth (forge)*
2 die Feuerschaufel
- *shovel (slice)*
3 der Löschwedel
- *swab*
4 die Feuerkratze
- *rake*
5 der Schlackenhaken
- *poker*
6 die Luftzuführung
- *blast pipe (tue iron)*
7 der Rauchfang
- *chimney (cowl, hood)*
8 der Löschtrog
- *water trough (quenching trough, bosh)*
9 der Schmiedelufthammer
- *power hammer*
10 der Hammerbär
- *ram (tup)*
11-16 **der Amboß**
- *anvil*
11 der Amboß
- *anvil*
12 das Vierkanthorn
- *flat beak (beck, bick)*
13 das Rundhorn
- *round beak (beck, bick)*
14 der Voramboß
- *auxiliary table*

15 der Backen
- *foot*
16 der Stauchklotz
- *upsetting block*
17 die Lochplatte
- *swage block*
18 der Werkzeugschleifbock
- *tool-grinding machine (tool grinder)*
19 die Schleifscheibe
- *grinding wheel*
20 der Flaschenzug
- *block and tackle*
21 die Werkbank
- *workbench (bench)*
22-39 **Schmiedewerkzeuge** *n*
- *blacksmith's tools*
22 der Vorschlaghammer
- *sledge hammer*
23 der Schmiedehandhammer
- *blacksmith's hand hammer*
24 die Flachzange
- *flat tongs*
25 die Rundzange
- *round tongs*
26 die Teile des Hammers *m*
- *parts of the hammer*
27 die Pinne
- *peen (pane, pein)*
28 die Bahn
- *face*
29 das Auge
- *eye*

30 der Stiel
- *haft*
31 der Keil
- *cotter punch*
32 der Abschroter
- *hardy (hardie)*
33 der Flachhammer
- *set hammer*
34 der Kehlhammer
- *sett (set, sate)*
35 der Schlichthammer
- *flat-face hammer (flatter)*
36 der Rundlochhammer
- *round punch*
37 die Winkelzange
- *angle tongs*
38 der Schrotmeißel
- *blacksmith's chisel (scaling hammer, chipping hammer)*
39 das Dreheisen
- *moving iron (bending iron)*

138 Schmied II (Landfahrzeugtechnik)
Blacksmith (Smith) II (Farm Vehicle Engineering)

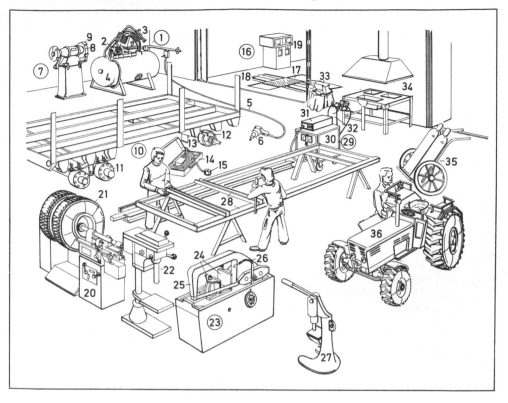

1 die Druckluftanlage
- *compressed-air system*
2 der Elektromotor
- *electric motor*
3 der Kompressor
- *compressor*
4 der Druckluftkessel
- *compressed-air tank*
5 die Druckluftleitung
- *compressed-air line*
6 der Druckluftschlagschrauber
- *percussion screwdriver*
7 das Schleifgerät (die Werkstattschleifmaschine)
- *pedestal grinding machine (floor grinding machine)*
8 die Schleifscheibe
- *grinding wheel*
9 die Schutzhaube
- *guard*
10 der Anhänger
- *trailer*
11 die Bremstrommel
- *brake drum*
12 die Bremsbacke
- *brake shoe*
13 der Bremsbelag
- *brake lining*
14 der Prüfkasten
- *testing kit*

15 das Druckluftmeßgerät
- *pressure gauge* (Am. *gage)*
16 der Bremsprüfstand, ein Rollenbremsprüfstand
- *brake-testing equipment, a rolling road*
17 die Bremsgrube
- *pit*
18 die Bremsrolle
- *braking roller*
19 das Registriergerät
- *meter (recording meter)*
20 die Bremstrommel-Feindrehmaschine
- *precision lathe for brake drums*
21 das Lkw-Rad
- *lorry wheel*
22 das Bohrwerk
- *boring mill*
23 die Schnellsäge, eine Bügelsäge
- *power saw, a hacksaw (power hacksaw)*
24 der Schraubstock
- *vice* (Am. *vise)*
25 der Sägebügel
- *saw frame*
26 die Kühlmittelzuführung
- *coolant supply pipe*
27 die Nietmaschine
- *riveting machine*
28 das Anhängerchassis im Rohbau *m*

- *trailer frame (chassis) under construction*
29 das Schutzgasschweißgerät
- *inert-gas welding equipment*
30 der Gleichrichter
- *rectifier*
31 das Steuergerät
- *control unit*
32 die CO_2-Flasche
- *CO_2 cylinder*
33 der Amboß
- *anvil*
34 die Esse mit dem Schmiedefeuer
- *hearth (forge) with blacksmith's fire*
35 der Autogenschweißwagen
- *trolley for gas cylinders*
36 das Reparaturfahrzeug, ein Traktor *m*
- *vehicle under repair, a tractor*

139 Freiform- und Gesenkschmiede (Warmmassivumformung)

1 der Rillenherd-Durchstoßofen
zum Wärmen *n* von
Rundmaterialien *n*
- *continuous furnace with grid hearth*
  for annealing of round stock
2 die Ausfallöffnung
- *discharge opening (discharge door)*
3 die Gasbrenner *m*
- *gas burners*
4 die Bedienungstür
- *charging door*
5 der Gegenschlaghammer
- *counterblow hammer*
6 der Oberbär
- *upper ram*
7 der Unterbär
- *lower ram*
8 die Bärführung
- *ram guide*
9 der hydraulische Antrieb
- *hydraulic drive*
10 der Ständer
- *column*
11 der Kurzhubgesenkhammer
- *short-stroke drop hammer*
12 der Hammerbär (Bär, Hammer)
- *ram (tup)*
13 der obere Schmiedesattel
(das Obergesenk)
- *upper die block*
14 der untere Schmiedesattel
(das Untergesenk)
- *lower die block*
15 der hydraulische Antrieb
- *hydraulic drive*
16 der Hammerständer
- *frame*
17 die Schabotte (der Amboß)
- *anvil*
18 die Gesenkschmiede- und
Kalibrierpresse
- *forging and sizing press*
19 der Maschinenständer
- *standard*
20 die Tischplatte
- *table*
21 die Lamellenreibungskupplung
- *disc (disk) clutch*
22 die Preßluftzuleitung
- *compressed-air pipe*
23 das Magnetventil
- *solenoid valve*
24 der Lufthammer
- *air-lift gravity hammer (air-lift*
  drop hammer)
25 der Antriebsmotor
- *drive motor*
26 der Schlagbär
- *hammer (tup)*
27 der Fußsteuerhebel
- *foot control (foot pedal)*
28 das freiformgeschmiedete
(vorgeschmiedete) Werkstück
- *preshaped (blocked) workpiece*
29 der Bärführungskopf
- *hammer guide*
30 der Bärzylinder
- *hammer cylinder*
31 die Schabotte
- *anvil*
32 der Schmiedemanipulator
(Manipulator) zum Bewegen *n* des
Werkstücks *n* beim
Freiformschmieden *n*
- *mechanical manipulator to move*
  the workpiece in hammer forging

33 die Zange
- *dogs*
34 das Gegengewicht
- *counterweight*
35 die hydraulische Schmiedepresse
- *hydraulic forging press*
36 der Preßkopf
- *crown*
37 das Querhaupt
- *cross head*
38 der obere Schmiedesattel
- *upper die block*
39 der untere Schmiedesattel
- *lower die block*
40 die Schabotte (der Unteramboß)
- *anvil*
41 der Hydraulikkolben
- *hydraulic piston*
42 die Säulenführung
- *pillar guide*
43 die Wendevorrichtung
- *rollover device*
44 die Krankette
- *burden chain (chain sling)*
45 der Kranhaken
- *crane hook*
46 das Werkstück
- *workpiece*
47 der gasbeheizte Schmiedeofen
- *gas furnace (gas-fired furnace)*
48 der Gasbrenner
- *gas burner*
49 die Arbeitsöffnung
- *charging opening*
50 der Kettenschleier
- *chain curtain*
51 die Aufzugstür
- *vertical-lift door*
52 die Heißluftleitung
- *hot-air duct*
53 der Luftvorwärmer
- *air preheater*
54 die Gaszufuhr
- *gas pipe*
55 die Türaufzugsvorrichtung
- *electric door-lifting mechanism*
56 der Luftschleier
- *air blast*

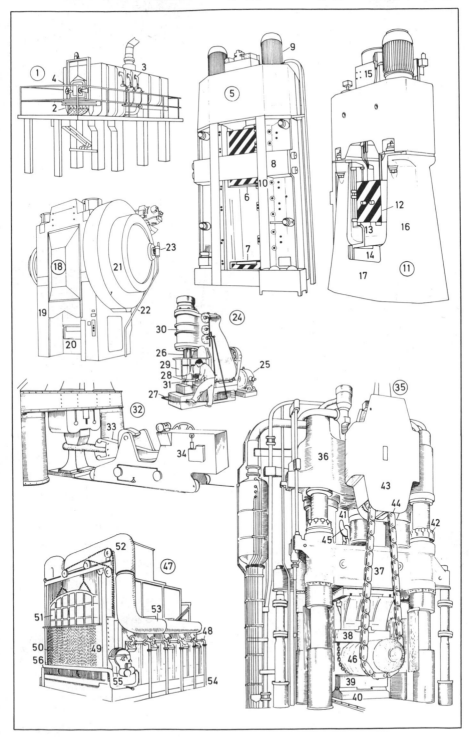

1-22 die Schlosserwerkstatt
- *metalwork shop (mechanic's workshop, fitter's workshop, locksmith's workshop)*
1 der Schlosser (z.B. Maschinenschlosser, Bauschlosser, Stahlbauschlosser, Schloß- und Schlüsselmacher; *früh. auch:* Kunstschlosser), ein Metallbauer *m*
- *metalworker (e.g. mechanic, fitter, locksmith; form. also: wrought-iron craftsman)*
2 der Parallelschraubstock
- *parallel-jaw vice (Am. vise)*
3 die Backe
- *jaw*
4 die Spindel
- *screw*
5 der Knebel
- *handle*
6 das Werkstück
- *workpiece*
7 die Werkbank
- *workbench (bench)*
8 die Feile (*Arten:*Grobfeile, Schlichtfeile, Präzisionsfeile)
- *files (kinds: rough file, smooth file, precision file)*
9 die Bügelsäge
- *hacksaw*
10 der Flachschraubstock, ein Zangenschraubstock *m*
- *leg vice (Am. vise), a spring vice*

11 der Muffelofen (Härteofen), ein Gasschmiedeofen *m*
- *muffle furnace, a gas-fired furnace*
12 die Gaszuführung
- *gas pipe*
13 die Handbohrmaschine
- *hand brace (hand drill)*
14 die Lochplatte (Gesenkplatte)
- *swage block*
15 die Feilmaschine
- *filing machine*
16 die Bandfeile
- *file*
17 das Späneblasrohr
- *compressed-air pipe*
18 die Schleifmaschine
- *grinding machine (grinder)*
19 die Schleifscheibe
- *grinding wheel*
20 die Schutzhaube
- *guard*
21 die Schutzbrille
- *goggles (safety glasses)*
22 der Schutzhelm
- *safety helmet*
23 der Schlosserhammer
- *machinist's hammer*
24 der Feilkloben
- *hand vice* (Am. *vise*)
25 der Kreuzmeißel (Spitzmeißel)
- *cape chisel (cross-cut chisel)*

26 der Flachmeißel
- *flat chisel*
27 die Flachfeile
- *flat file*
28 der Feilenhieb
- *file cut (cut)*
29 die Rundfeile (*auch:* Halbrundfeile)
- *round file (also: half-round file)*
30 das Windeisen
- *tap wrench*
31 die Reibahle
- *reamer*
32 die Schneidkluppe
- *die (die and stock)*
33-35 der Schlüssel
- *key*
33 der Schaft (Halm)
- *stem (shank)*
34 der Griff (die Räute)
- *bow*
35 der Bart
- *bit*
36-43 das Türschloß, ein Einsteckschloß *n*
- *door lock, a mortise (mortice) lock*
36 die Grundplatte (das Schloßblech)
- *back plate*
37 die Falle
- *spring bolt (latch bolt)*
38 die Zuhaltung
- *tumbler*
39 der Riegel
- *bolt*

40 das Schlüsselloch
- *keyhole*
41 der Führungszapfen
- *bolt guide pin*
42 die Zuhaltungsfeder
- *tumbler spring*
43 die Nuß, mit Vierkantloch *n*
- *follower, with square hole*
44 das Zylinderschloß
  (Sicherheitsschloß)
- *cylinder lock (safety lock)*
45 der Zylinder
- *cylinder (plug)*
46 die Feder
- *spring*
47 der Arretierstift
- *pin*
48 der Sicherheitsschlüssel, ein
  Flachschlüssel *m*
- *safety key, a flat key*
49 das Scharnierband
- *lift-off hinge*
50 das Winkelband
- *hook-and-ride band*
51 das Langband
- *strap hinge*
52 der Meßschieber (die Schieblehre)
- *vernier calliper (caliper) gauge*
  (Am. *gage)*
53 die Fünlerlehre
- *feeler gauge (Am. gage)*
54 der Tiefenmeßschieber (die
  Tiefenlehre)
- *vernier depth gauge (Am. gage)*
55 der Nonius
- *vernier*
56 das Haarlineal
- *straightedge*
57 der Meßwinkel
- *square*
58 die Brustleier
- *breast drill*
59 der Spiralbohrer
- *twist bit (twist drill)*
60 der Gewindebohrer (das
  Gewindeeisen)
- *screw tap (tap)*
61 die Gewindebacken *m*
- *halves of a screw die*
62 der Schraubendreher
  (Schraubenzieher)
- *screwdriver*
63 der Schaber
  (*auch:* Dreikantschaber)
- *scraper (also: pointed triangle
  scraper)*
64 der Körner
- *centre (Am. center) punch*
65 der Durchschlag
- *round punch*
66 die Flachzange
- *flat-nose pliers*
67 der Hebelvorschneider
- *detachable-jaw cut nippers*
68 die Rohrzange
- *gas pliers*
69 die Kneifzange
- *pincers*

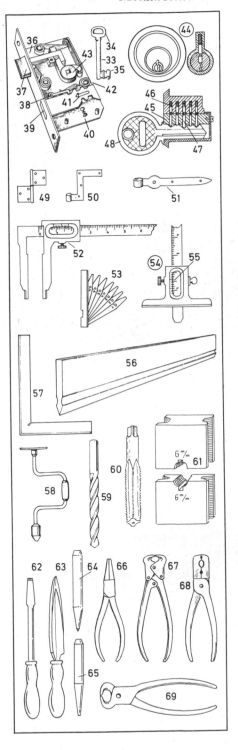

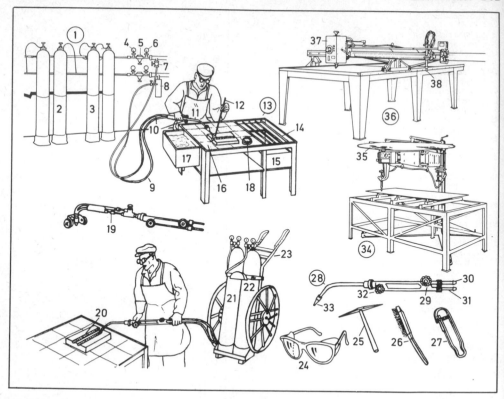

1 die Flaschenbatterie
- *gas cylinder manifold*
2 die Acetylenflasche
- *acetylene cylinder*
3 die Sauerstoffflasche
- *oxygen cylinder*
4 das Hochdruckmanometer
- *high-pressure manometer*
5 das Druckminderventil
- *pressure-reducing valve (reducing valve, pressure regulator)*
6 das Niederdruckmanometer
- *low-pressure manometer*
7 das Absperrventil
- *stop valve*
8 die Niederdruck-Wasservorlage
- *hydraulic back-pressure valve for low-pressure installations*
9 der Gasschlauch
- *gas hose*
10 der Sauerstoffschlauch
- *oxygen hose*
11 der Schweißbrenner
- *welding torch (blowpipe)*
12 der Schweißstab
- *welding rod (filler rod)*
13 der Schweißtisch
- *welding bench*
14 der Schneidrost
- *grating*
15 der Schrottkasten
- *scrap box*

16 der Tischbelag, aus Schamottesteinen m
- *bench covering of chamotte slabs*
17 der Wasserkasten
- *water tank*
18 die Schweißpaste
- *welding paste (flux)*
19 der Schweißbrenner, mit Schneidsatz m und Brennerführungswagen m
- *welding torch (blowpipe) with cutting attachment and guide tractor*
20 das Werkstück
- *workpiece*
21 die Sauerstoffflasche
- *oxygen cylinder*
22 die Acetylenflasche
- *acetylene cylinder*
23 der Flaschenwagen
- *cylinder trolley*
24 die Schweißerbrille
- *welding goggles*
25 der Schlackenhammer
- *chipping hammer*
26 die Drahtbürste
- *wire brush*
27 der Brenneranzünder
- *torch lighter (blowpipe lighter)*
28 der Schweißbrenner
- *welding torch (blowpipe)*
29 das Sauerstoffventil
- *oxygen control*

30 der Sauerstoffanschluß
- *oxygen connection*
31 der Brenngasanschluß
- *gas connection (acetylene connection)*
32 das Brenngasventil
- *gas control (acetylene control)*
33 das Schweißmundstück
- *welding nozzle*
34 die Brennschneidemaschine
- *cutting machine*
35 die Kreisführung
- *circular template*
36 die Universalbrennschneidemaschine
- *universal cutting machine*
37 der Steuerkopf
- *tracing head*
38 die Brennerdüse
- *cutting nozzle*

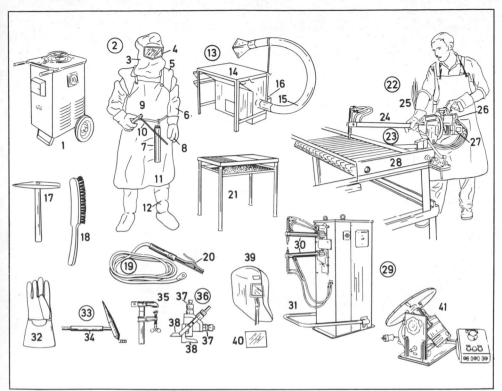

1 der Schweißtransformator
  (Schweißtrafo)
– *welding transformer*
2 der Elektroschweißer
– *arc welder*
3 die Schweißerschutzhaube
– *arc welding helmet*
4 das hochklappbare Schutzglas
– *flip-up window*
5 der Schulterschutz
– *shoulder guard*
6 der Ärmelschutz
– *protective sleeve*
7 der Elektrodenköcher
– *electrode case*
8 der dreifingrige
  Schweißerhandschuh
– *three-fingered welding glove*
9 der Elektrodenhalter
– *electrode holder*
10 die Elektrode
– *electrode*
11 die Lederschürze
– *leather apron*
12 der Schienbeinschutz
– *shin guard*
13 der Absaugeschweißtisch
– *welding table with fume extraction
  equipment*
14 die Absaugetischfläche
– *table top*
15 der Absaugeschwenkrüssel
– *movable extractor duct*

16 der Abluftstutzen
– *extractor support*
17 der Schlackenhammer
– *chipping hammer*
18 die Stahldrahtbürste
– *wire brush*
19 das Schweißkabel
– *welding lead*
20 der Elektrodenhalter
– *electrode holder*
21 der Schweißtisch
– *welding bench*
22 die Punktschweißung
– *spot welding*
23 die Punktschweißzange
– *spot welding electrode holder*
24 der Elektrodenarm
– *electrode arm*
25 die Stromzuführung (das
  Anschlußkabel)
– *power supply
  (lead)*
26 der Elektrodenkraftzylinder
– *electrode-pressure cylinder*
27 der Schweißtransformator
– *welding transformer*
28 das Werkstück
– *workpiece*
29 die fußbetätigte
  Punktschweißmaschine
– *foot-operated spot welder*
30 die Schweißarme *m*
– *welder electrode arms*

31 der Fußbügel für den
  Elektrodenkraftaufbau
– *foot pedal for welding pressure
  adjustment*
32 der fünffingrige
  Schweißerhandschuh
– *five-fingered welding glove*
33 der Schutzgasschweißbrenner für
  die Schutzgasschweißung
  (Inertgasschweißung)
– *inert-gas torch for inert-gas
  welding (gas-shielded arc welding)*
34 die Schutzgaszuführung
– *inert-gas (shielding-gas) supply*
35 die Polzwinge (Werkstückklemme,
  Erdklemme, der Gegenkontakt)
– *work clamp (earthing clamp)*
36 die Kehlnahtmeßlehre
– *fillet gauge (Am. gage) (weld
  gauge) [for measuring throat
  thickness]*
37 die Feinmeßschraube
  (Mikrometerschraube)
– *micrometer*
38 der Meßschenkel
– *measuring arm*
39 das Schutzschild
  (Schweißschutzschild)
– *arc welding helmet*
40 das Schweißhaubenglas
– *filter lens*
41 der Kleindrehtisch
– *small turntable*

[Herstellungsmaterial: Stahl,
Messing, Aluminium, Kunststoff
usw.; als Beispiel wurde im
folgenden Stahl gewählt]
- *[material: steel, brass, aluminium
(Am. aluminum), plastics, etc; in
the following, steel was chosen as
an example]*
1 das Winkeleisen
- *angle iron (angle)*
2 der Schenkel (Flansch)
- *leg (flange)*
3-7 **Eisenträger** (Baustahlträger) *m*
- **steel girders**
3 das T-Eisen
- *T-iron (tee-iron)*
4 der Steg
- *vertical leg*
5 der Flansch
- *flange*
6 das Doppel-T-Eisen
- *H-girder (H-beam)*
7 das U-Eisen
- *E-channel (channel iron)*
8 das Rundeisen
- *round bar*
9 das Vierkanteisen
- *square iron (Am. square stock)*
10 das Flacheisen
- *flat bar*
11 das Bandeisen
- *strip steel*
12 der Eisendraht
- *iron wire*
13-50 **Schrauben** *f*
- **screws and bolts**
13 die Sechskantschraube
- *hexagonal-head bolt*
14 der Kopf
- *head*
15 der Schaft
- *shank*
16 das Gewinde
- *thread*
17 die Unterlegscheibe
- *washer*
18 die Sechskantmutter
- *hexagonal nut*
19 der Splint
- *split pin*
20 die Rundkuppe
- *rounded end*
21 die Schlüsselweite
- *width of head (of flats)*
22 die Stiftschraube
- *stud*
23 die Spitze
- *point (end)*
24 die Kronenmutter
- *castle nut (castellated nut)*
25 das Splintloch
- *hole for the split pin*
26 die Kreuzschlitzschraube, eine
Blechschraube
- *cross-head screw, a sheet-metal
screw (self-tapping screw)*
27 die Innensechskantschraube
- *hexagonal socket head screw*
28 die Senkschraube
- *countersunk-head bolt*
29 die Nase
- *catch*
30 die Gegenmutter (Kontermutter)
- *locknut (locking nut)*
31 der Zapfen
- *bolt (pin)*
32 die Bundschraube
- *collar-head bolt*
33 der Schraubenbund
- *set collar (integral collar)*
34 der Sprengring (Federring)
- *spring washer (washer)*
35 die Lochrundmutter, eine
Stellmutter
- *round nut, an adjusting nut*
36 die Zylinderkopfschraube, eine
Schlitzschraube
- *cheese-head screw, a slotted screw*
37 der Kegelstift
- *tapered pin*
38 der Schraubenschlitz
- *screw slot (screw slit, screw groove)*

39 die Vierkantschraube
- *square-head bolt*
40 der Kerbstift, ein Zylinderstift *m*
- *grooved pin, a cylindrical pin*
41 die Hammerkopfschraube
- *T-head bolt*
42 die Flügelmutter
- *wing nut (fly nut, butterfly nut)*
43 die Steinschraube
- *rag bolt*
44 der Widerhaken
- *barb*
45 die Holzschraube
- *wood screw*
46 der Senkkopf
- *countersunk head*
47 das Holzgewinde
- *wood screw thread*
48 der Gewindestift
- *grub screw*
49 der Stiftschlitz
- *pin slot (pin slit, pin groove)*
50 die Kugelkuppe
- *round end*
51 der Nagel (Drahtstift)
- *nail (wire nail)*
52 der Kopf
- *head*
53 der Schaft
- *shank*
54 die Spitze
- *point*
55 der Dachpappenstift
- *roofing nail*
56 die Nietung (Nietverbindung,
Überlappung)
- *riveting (lap riveting)*
57-60 **die Niete** (der Niet)
- **rivet**
57 der Setzkopf, ein Nietkopf *m*
- *set head (swage head, die head), a
rivet head*
58 der Nietenschaft
- *rivet shank*
59 der Schließkopf
- *closing head*
60 die Nietteilung
- *pitch of rivets*
61 die Welle
- *shaft*
62 die Fase
- *chamfer (bevel)*
63 der Zapfen
- *journal*
64 der Hals
- *neck*
65 der Sitz
- *seat*
66 die Keilnut
- *keyway*
67 der Kegelsitz (Konus)
- *conical seat (cone)*
68 das Gewinde
- *thread*
69 das Kugellager, ein Wälzlager *n*
- *ball bearing, an antifriction bearing*
70 die Stahlkugel
- *steel ball (ball)*
71 der Außenring
- *outer race*
72 der Innenring
- *inner race*
73-74 **die Nutkeile** *m*
- **keys**
73 der Einlegekeil (Federkeil, die Feder)
- *sunk key (feather)*
74 der Nasenkeil
- *gib (gib-headed key)*
75-76 **das Nadellager**
- **needle roller bearing**
75 der Nadelkäfig
- *needle cage*
76 die Nadel
- *needle*
77 die Kronenmutter
- *castle nut (castellated nut)*
78 der Splint
- *split pin*
79 das Gehäuse
- *casing*
80 der Gehäusedeckel
- *casing cover*

81 der Druckschmiernippel
- *grease nipple
(lubricating nipple)*
82-96 **Zahnräder** *n* (Verzahnungen *f*)
- **gear wheels, cog wheels**
82 das Stufenrad
- *stepped gear wheel*
83 der Zahn
- *cog (tooth)*
84 der Zahngrund
- *space between teeth*
85 die Nut (Keilnut)
- *keyway (key seat, key slot)*
86 die Bohrung
- *bore*
87 das Pfeilstirnrad
- *herringbone gear wheel*
88 die Speiche
- *spokes (arms)*
89 die Schrägverzahnung
- *helical gearing (helical spur wheel)*
90 der Zahnkranz
- *sprocket*
91 das Kegelrad
- *bevel gear wheel (bevel wheel)*
92-93 **die Spiralverzahnung**
- **spiral toothing**
92 das Ritzel
- *pinion*
93 das Tellerrad
- *crown wheel*
94 das Planetengetriebe
- *epicyclic gear (planetary gear)*
95 die Innenverzahnung
- *internal toothing*
96 die Außenverzahnung
- *external toothing*
97-107 **Bremsdynamometer** *n*
- **absorption dynamometer**
97 die Backenbremse
- *shoe brake (check brake, block
brake)*
98 die Bremsscheibe
- *brake pulley*
99 die Bremswelle
- *brake shaft (brake axle)*
100 der Bremsklotz (die Bremsbacke)
- *brake block (brake shoe)*
101 die Zugstange
- *pull rod*
102 der Bremslüftmagnet
- *brake magnet*
103 das Bremsgewicht
- *brake weight*
104 die Bandbremse
- *band brake*
105 das Bremsband
- *brake band*
106 der Bremsbelag
- *brake lining*
107 die Stellschraube, zur
gleichmäßigen Lüftung
- *adjusting screw, for even
application of the brake*

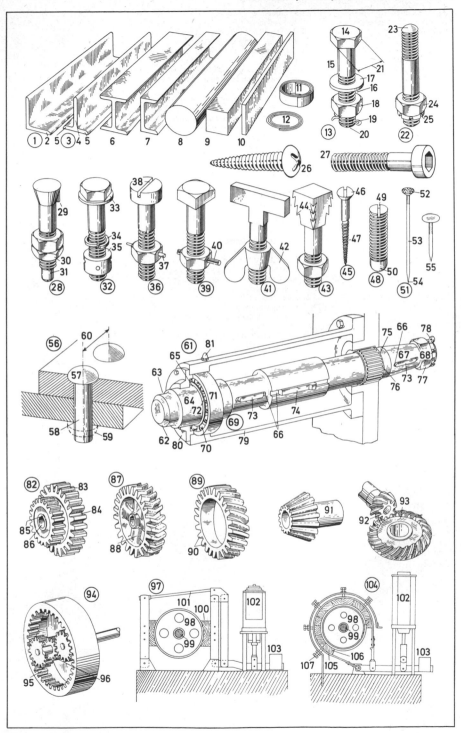

1-51 das Steinkohlenbergwerk (die
Steinkohlengrube, Grube, Zeche)
- *coal mine (colliery, pit)*
1 das Fördergerüst
- *pithead gear (headgear)*
2 das Maschinenhaus
- *winding engine house*
3 der Förderturm
- *pithead frame (head frame)*
4 das Schachtgebäude
- *pithead building*
5 die Aufbereitungsanlage
- *processing plant*
6 die Sägerei
- *sawmill*
7-11 die Kokerei
- *coking plant*
7 die Koksofenbatterie
- *battery of coke ovens*
8 der Füllwagen
- *larry car (larry, charging car)*
9 der Kokskohlenturm
- *coking coal tower*
10 der Kokslöschturm
- *coke-quenching tower*
11 der Kokslöschwagen
- *coke-quenching car*
12 der Gasometer
- *gasometer*
13 das Kraftwerk
- *power plant (power station)*
14 der Wasserturm
- *water tower*
15 der Kühlturm
- *cooling tower*
16 der Grubenlüfter
- *mine fan*
17 der Materiallagerplatz
- *depot*
18 das Verwaltungsgebäude
- *administration building (office
building, offices)*
19 die Bergehalde
- *tip heap (spoil heap)*
20 das Klärwerk (die Kläranlage)
- *cleaning plant*
21-51 die Untertageanlagen *f*
(der Grubenbetrieb)
- *underground workings (underground
mining)*
21 der Wetterschacht
- *ventilation shaft*
22 der Wetterkanal
- *fan drift*
23 die Gestellförderung mit
Förderkörben *m*
- *cage-winding system with cages*
24 der Hauptschacht
- *main shaft*
25 die Gefäßförderanlage
- *skip-winding system*
26 der (*bergm.* das) Füllort
- *winding inset*
27 der Blindschacht
- *staple shaft*
28 die Wendelrutsche
(Wendelrutschenförderung)
- *spiral chute*
29 die Flözstrecke
- *gallery along seam*
30 die Richtstrecke
- *lateral*
31 der Querschlag
- *cross-cut*
32 die Streckenvortriebsmaschine
- *tunnelling (Am. tunneling) machine*

33-37 Strebe *m*
- *longwall faces*
33 der Hobelstreb in flacher Lagerung
- *horizontal ploughed longwall face*
34 der Schrämstreb in flacher.
Lagerung
- *horizontal cut longwall face*
35 der Abbauhammerstreb in steiler
Lagerung
- *vertical pneumatic pick longwall
face*
36 der Rammstreb in steiler Lagerung
- *diagonal ram longwall face*
37 der Alte Mann
- *goaf (gob, waste)*
38 die Wetterschleuse
- *air lock*
39 die Personenfahrung mit
Personenzug *m*
- *transportation of men by cars*
40 die Bandförderung
- *belt conveying*
41 der Rohkohlenbunker
- *raw coal bunker*
42 das Beschickungsband
- *charging conveyor*
43 der Materialtransport mit der
Einschienenhängebahn
- *transportation of supplies by
monorail car*
44 die Personenfahrung mit der
Einschienenhängebahn
- *transportation of men by monorail
car*
45 der Materialtransport mit
Förderwagen *m*
- *transportation of supplies by mine
car*
46 die Wasserhaltung
- *drainage*
47 der Schachtsumpf
- *sump (sink)*
48 das Deckgebirge
- *capping*
49 das Steinkohlengebirge
- *[layer of] coal-bearing rock*
50 das Steinkohlenflöz
- *coal seam*
51 die Verwerfung
- *fault*

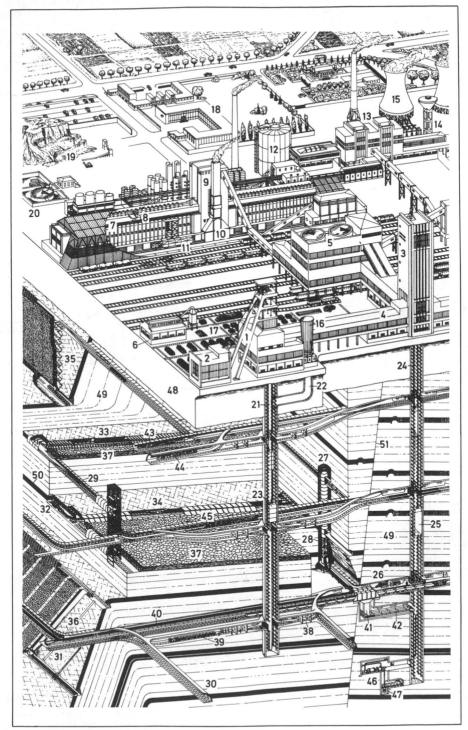

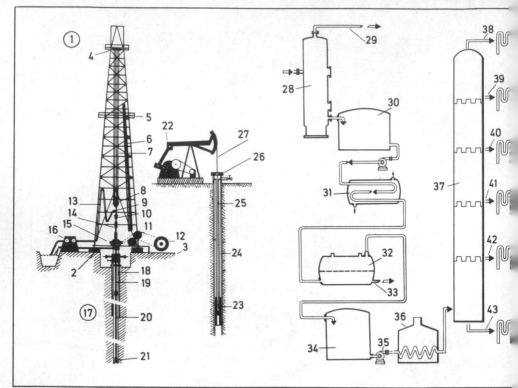

1-21 die Erdölbohrung
- *oil drilling*
1 der Bohrturm
- *drilling rig*
2 der Unterbau
- *substructure*
3 die Arbeitsbühne
- *crown safety platform*
4 die Turmrollen *f*
- *crown blocks*
5 die Gestängebühne, eine Zwischenbühne
- *working platform, an intermediate platform*
6 die Bohrrohre *n*
- *drill pipes*
7 das Bohrseil
- *drilling cable (drilling line)*
8 der Flaschenzug
- *travelling (Am. traveling) block*
9 der Zughaken
- *hook*
10 der Spülkopf
- *[rotary] swivel*
11 das Hebewerk, eine Winde
- *draw works, a hoist*
12 die Antriebsmaschine
- *engine*
13 die Spülleitung
- *standpipe and rotary hose*
14 die Mitnehmerstange
- *kelly*
15 der Drehtisch
- *rotary table*

16 die Spülpumpe
- *slush pump (mud pump)*
17 das Bohrloch
- *well*
18 das Standrohr
- *casing*
19 das Bohrgestänge
- *drilling pipe*
20 die Verrohrung
- *tubing*
21 der Bohrmeißel (Bohrer); Arten: Fischschwanzbohrer *m*, Rollenbohrer, Kernbohrgerät *n*
- *drilling bit; kinds: fishtail (blade) bit, rock (Am. roller) bit, core bit*

22-27 die Erdölgewinnung (Erdölförderung)
- *oil (crude oil) production*
22 der Pumpenantriebsbock
- *pumping unit (pump)*
23 die Tiefpumpe
- *plunger*
24 die Steigrohre *n*
- *tubing*
25 das Pumpgestänge
- *sucker rods (pumping rods)*
26 die Stopfbüchse
- *stuffing box*
27 die Polierstange
- *polish (polished) rod*

28-35 die Rohölaufbereitung [Schema]
- *treatment of crude oil [diagram]*

28 der Gasabscheider
- *gas separator*
29 die Gasleitung
- *gas pipe (gas outlet)*
30 der Naßöltank
- *wet oil tank (wash tank)*
31 der Vorwärmer
- *water heater*
32 die Entwässerungs- und Entsalzungsanlage
- *water and brine separator*
33 die Salzwasserleitung
- *salt water pipe (salt water outlet)*
34 der Reinöltank
- *oil tank*
35 die Transportleitung für Reinöl *n* [zur Raffinerie oder zum Versand *m* mit Kesselwagen *m*, Tankschiff *n*, Pipeline *f*]
- *trunk pipeline for oil [to the refinery or transport by tanker lorry (Am. tank truck), oil tanker, or pipeline]*

36-64 die Rohölverarbeitung (Erdölverarbeitung) [Schema]
- *processing of crude oil [diagram]*
36 der Ölerhitzer (Röhrenofen)
- *oil furnace (pipe still)*
37 die Destillationskolonne (der Fraktionierturm) mit den Kolonnenböden *m*
- *fractionating column (distillation column) with trays*

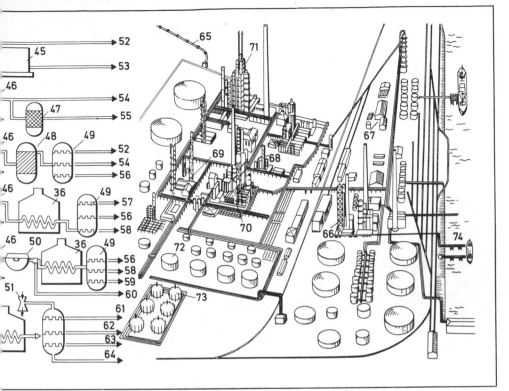

38 die Topgase *n*
- *top gases (tops)*
39 die Leichtbenzinfraktion
- *light distillation products*
40 die Schwerbenzinfraktion
- *heavy distillation products*
41 das Petroleum
- *petroleum*
42 die Gasölfraktion
- *gas oil component*
43 der Rückstand
- *residue*
44 der Kühler
- *condenser (cooler)*
45 der Verdichter (Kompressor)
- *compressor*
46 die Entschwefelungsanlage
- *desulphurizing (desulphurization,*
Am. *desulfurizing, desulfurization)*
plant
47 die Reformieranlage
- *reformer (hydroformer, platformer)*
48 die katalytische Krackanlage
- *catalytic cracker (cat cracker)*
49 die Destillationskolonne
- *distillation column*
50 die Entparaffinierung
- *de-waxing*
(wax separation)
51 der Vakuumanschluß
- *vacuum equipment*
52-64 Erdölerzeugnisse *n*
(Erdölprodukte)
- *oil products*

52 das Heizgas
- *fuel gas*
53 das Flüssiggas
- *liquefied petroleum gas (liquid gas)*
54 das Normalbenzin (Fahrbenzin)
- *regular grade petrol (Am. gasoline)*
55 das Superbenzin
- *super grade petrol (Am. gasoline)*
56 der Dieseltreibstoff
- *diesel oil*
57 das Flugbenzin
- *aviation fuel*
58 das leichte Heizöl
- *light fuel oil*
59 das schwere Heizöl
- *heavy fuel oil*
60 das Paraffin (Tankbodenwachs)
- *paraffin*
(paraffin oil, kerosene)
61 das Spindelöl
- *spindle oil*
62 das Schmieröl
- *lubricating oil*
63 das Zylinderöl
- *cylinder oil*
64 das Bitumen
- *bitumen*
65-74 die Erdölraffinerie
(Ölraffinerie)
- *oil refinery*
65 die Pipeline (Erdölleitung)
- *pipeline (oil pipeline)*
66 die Destillationsanlagen *f*
- *distillation plants*

67 die Schmierölraffinerie
- *lubricating oil refinery*
68 die Entschwefelungsanlage
- *desulphurizing (desulphurization,*
Am. *desulfurizing, desulfurization)*
plant
69 die Gastrennanlage
- *gas-separating plant*
70 die katalytische Krackanlage
- *catalytic cracking plant*
71 die katalytische Reformieranlage
- *catalytic reformer*
72 der Lagertank
- *storage tank*
73 der Kugeltank
- *spherical tank*
74 der Ölhafen
- *tanker terminal*

1-39 die Bohrinsel (Förderinsel)
- *drilling rig (oil rig)*
1-37 die Bohrturmplattform
- *drilling platform*
1 die Energieversorgungsanlage
- *power station*
2 die Abgasschornsteine *m* der
  Generatoranlage
- *generator exhausts*
3 der Drehkran
- *revolving crane (pedestal crane)*
4 das Rohrlager
- *piperack*
5 die Abgasrohre *n* der
  Turbinenanlage
- *turbine exhausts*
6 das Materiallager
- *materials store*
7 das Hubschrauberdeck
- *helicopter deck (heliport deck,
  heliport)*
8 der Fahrstuhl
- *elevator*
9 die Vorrichtung zur Trennung von
  Gas *n* und Öl *n*
- *production oil and gas separator*
10 die Probentrennvorrichtung
- *test oil and gas separators (test
  separators)*
11 die Notfallabfackelanlage
- *emergency flare stack*
12 der Bohrturm
- *derrick*
13 der Dieselkraftstofftank
- *diesel tank*
14 der Bürokomplex
- *office building*
15 die Zementvorrattanks *m*
- *cement storage tanks*
16 der Trinkwassertank
- *drinking water tank*
17 der Vorratstank für Salzwasser *n*
- *salt water tank*
18 die Tanks *m* für
  Hubschrauberkraftstoff *m*
- *jet fuel tanks*
19 die Rettungsboote *n*
- *lifeboats*
20 der Fahrstuhlschacht
- *elevator shaft*
21 der Druckluftbehälter
- *compressed-air reservoir*
22 die Pumpanlage
- *pumping station*
23 der Luftkompressor
- *air compressor*
24 die Klimaanlage
- *air lock*
25 die Meerwasserentsalzungsanlage
- *seawater desalination plant*
26 die Filteranlage für
  Dieselkraftstoff *m*
- *inlet filters for diesel fuel*
27 das Gaskühlaggregat
- *gas cooler*
28 das Steuerpult für die
  Trennvorrichtungen *f*
- *control panel for the separators*
29 die Toiletten *f*
- *toilets (lavatories)*
30 die Werkstatt
- *workshop*
31 die Molchschleuse [der „Molch"
  dient zur Reinigung der Hauptölleitung]
- *pig trap [the 'pig' is used to clean
  the oil pipeline]*

32 der Kontrollraum
- *control room*
33 die Unterkünfte *f*
- *accommodation modules
  (accommodation)*
34 die Hochdruckzementierungspumpen *f*
- *high-pressure cementing pumps*
35 das untere Deck
- *lower deck*
36 das mittlere Deck
- *middle deck*
37 das obere Deck
- *top deck (main deck)*
38 die Stützkonstruktion
- *substructure*
39 der Meeresspiegel
- *mean sea level*

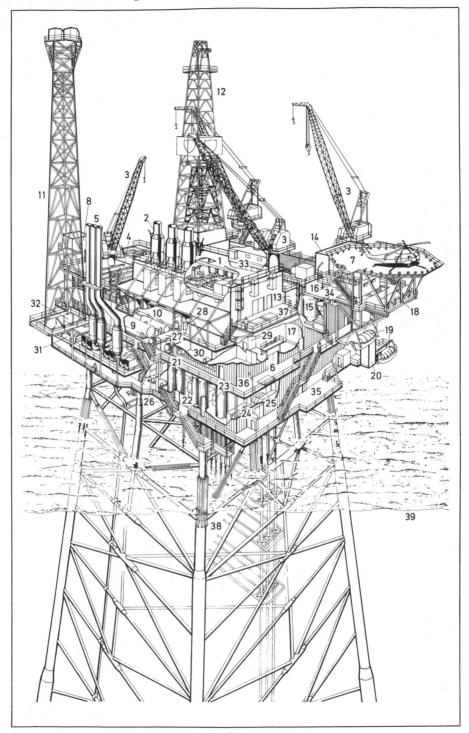

1-20 die Hochofenanlage
- *blast furnace plant*
1 der Hochofen, ein Schachtofen *m*
- *blast furnace, a shaft furnace*
2 der Schrägaufzug für Erz *n* und
  Zuschläge *m* oder Koks *m*
- *furnace incline (lift) for ore and
  flux or coke*
3 die Laufkatze
- *skip hoist*
4 die Gichtbühne
- *charging platform*
5 der Trichterkübel
- *receiving hopper*
6 der Verschlußkegel (die Gichtglocke)
- *bell*
7 der Hochofenschacht
- *blast furnace shaft*
8 die Reduktionszone
- *smelting section*
9 der Schlackenabstich
  (Schlackenabfluß)
- *slag escape*
10 der Schlackenkübel
- *slag ladle*
11 der Roheisenabstich (Roheisenabfluß)
- *pig iron (crude iron, iron) runout*
12 die Roheisenpfanne
- *pig iron (crude iron, iron) ladle*
13 der Gichtgasabzug
- *downtake*
14 der Staubfänger (Staubsack), eine
  Entstaubungsanlage
- *dust catcher, a dust-collecting
  machine*
15 der Winderhitzer
- *hot-blast stove*
16 der außenstehende Brennschacht
- *external combustion chamber*
17 die Luftzuleitung
- *blast main*
18 die Gasleitung
- *gas pipe*
19 die Heizwindleitung
- *hot-blast pipe*
20 die Windform
- *tuyère*
21-69 das Stahlwerk
- *steelworks*
21-30 der Siemens-Martin-Ofen
- *Siemens-Martin open-hearth
  furnace*
21 die Roheisenpfanne
- *pig iron (crude iron, iron) ladle*
22 die Eingußrinne
- *feed runner*
23 der feststehende Ofen
- *stationary furnace*
24 der Ofenraum
- *hearth*
25 die Beschickungsmaschine
- *charging machine*
26 die Schrottmulde
- *scrap iron charging box*
27 die Gasleitung
- *gas pipe*
28 die Gasheizkammer
- *gas regenerator chamber*
29 das Luftzufuhrrohr
- *air feed pipe*
30 die Luftheizkammer
- *air regenerator chamber*
31 die Stahlgießpfanne mit
  Stopfenverschluß *m*
- *[bottom-pouring] steel-casting
  ladle with stopper*

32 die Kokille
- *ingot mould (Am. mold)*
33 der Stahlblock
- *steel ingot*
34-44 die Masselgießmaschine
- *pig-casting machine*
34 das Eingießende
- *pouring end*
35 die Eisenrinne
- *metal runner*
36 das Kokillenband
- *series (strand) of moulds (Am.
  molds)*
37 die Kokille
- *mould (Am. mold)*
38 der Laufsteg
- *catwalk*
39 die Abfallvorrichtung
- *discharging chute*
40 die Massel (das Roheisen)
- *pig*
41 der Laufkran
- *travelling (Am. traveling) crane*
42 die Roheisenpfanne mit
  Obenentleerung *f*
- *top-pouring pig iron (crude iron,
  iron) ladle*
43 der Gießpfannenschnabel
- *pouring ladle lip*
44 die Kippvorrichtung
- *tilting device (tipping device, Am.
  dumping device)*
45-50 der Sauerstoffaufblaskonverter
  (LD-Konverter,
  Linz-Donawitz-Konverter)
- *oxygen-blowing converter (L-D
  converter, Linz-Donawitz converter)*
45 der Konverterhut
- *conical converter top*
46 der Tragring
- *mantle*
47 der Konverterboden
- *solid converter bottom*
48 die feuerfeste Ausmauerung
- *fireproof lining (refractory lining)*
49 die Sauerstofflanze
- *oxygen lance*
50 das Abstichloch
- *tapping hole (tap hole)*
**51-54 der Siemens-Elektro-
  Niederschachtofen**
- *Siemens electric low-shaft furnace*
51 die Begichtung
- *feed*
52 die Elektroden *f* [kreisförmig
  angeordnet]
- *electrodes [arranged in a circle]*
53 die Ringleitung zum Abziehen *n*
  der Ofengase *n*
- *bustle pipe*
54 der Abstich
- *runout*
**55-69 der Thomaskonverter
  (die Thomasbirne)**
- *Thomas converter (basic Bessemer
  converter)*
55 die Füllstellung für flüssiges
  Roheisen *n*
- *charging position for molten pig
  iron*
56 die Füllstellung für Kalk *m*
- *charging position for lime*
57 die Blasstellung
- *blow position*
58 die Ausgußstellung
- *discharging position*

59 die Kippvorrichtung
- *tilting device (tipping device,
  Am. dumping device)*
60 die Kranpfanne
- *crane-operated ladle*
61 der Hilfskranzug
- *auxiliary crane hoist*
62 der Kalkbunker
- *lime bunker*
63 das Fallrohr
- *downpipe*
64 der Muldenwagen
- *tipping car (Am. dump truck)*
65 die Schrottzufuhr
- *scrap iron feed*
66 der Steuerstand
- *control desk*
67 der Konverterkamin
- *converter chimney*
68 das Blasluftzufuhrrohr
- *blast main*
69 der Düsenboden
- *wind box*

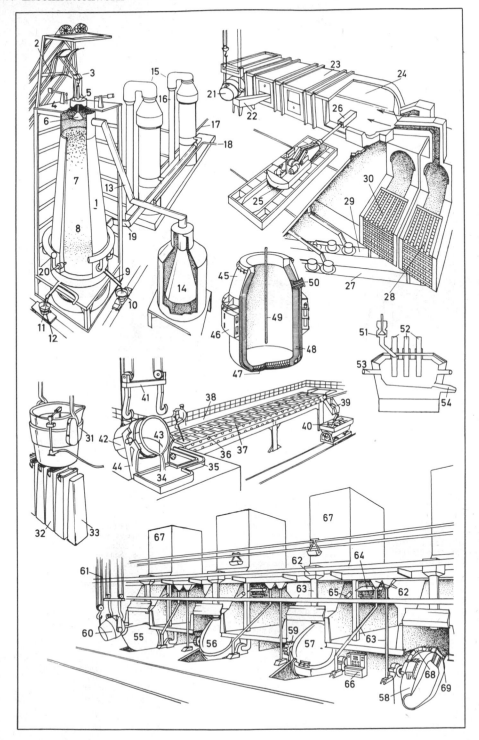

1-45 die Eisengießerei
- *iron foundry*

1-12 der Schmelzbetrieb
- *melting plant*

1 der Kupolofen (Kuppelofen), ein Schmelzofen *m*
- *cupola furnace (cupola), a melting furnace*

2 die Windleitung
- *blast main (blast inlet, blast pipe)*

3 die Abstichrinne
- *tapping spout*

4 das Schauloch
- *spyhole*

5 der kippbare Vorherd
- *tilting-type [hot-metal] receiver*

6 die fahrbare Trommelpfanne
- *mobile drum-type ladle*

7 der Schmelzer
- *melter*

8 der Gießer
- *founder (caster)*

9 die Abstichstange
- *tap bar (tapping bar)*

10 die Stopfenstange
- *bott stick (Am. bot stick)*

11 das flüssige Eisen
- *molten iron*

12 die Schlackenrinne
- *slag spout*

13 die Gießkolonne
- *casting team*

14 die Tragpfanne
- *hand shank*

15 die Traggabel
- *double handle (crutch)*

16 der Tragstiel
- *carrying bar*

17 der Krammstock
- *skimmer rod*

18 der geschlossene Formkasten
- *closed moulding (Am. molding) box*

19 der Oberkasten
- *upper frame (cope)*

20 der Unterkasten
- *lower frame (drag)*

21 der Einguß
- *runner (runner gate, down-gate)*

22 der Steigertrichter
- *riser (riser gate)*

23 die Handpfanne
- *hand ladle*

24-29 der Strangguß
(Senkrechtstrangguß)
- *continuous casting*

24 der absenkbare Gießtisch
- *sinking pouring floor*

25 der erstarrende Metallblock
- *solidifying pig*

26 die feste Phase
- *solid stage*

27 die flüssige Phase
- *liquid stage*

28 die Wasserkühlung
- *water-cooling system*

29 die Kokillenwand
- *mould (Am. mold) wall*

30-37 die Formerei
- *moulding (Am. molding) department (moulding shop)*

30 der Former
- *moulder (Am. molder)*

31 der Preßluftstampfer
- *pneumatic rammer*

32 der Handstampfer
- *hand rammer*

33 der geöffnete Formkasten
- *open moulding (Am. molding) box*

34 die Form (der Modellabdruck)
- *pattern*

35 der Formsand
- *moulding (Am. molding) sand*

36 der Kern
- *core*

37 die Kernmarke
- *core print*

38-45 die Putzerei
- *cleaning shop (fettling shop)*

38 die Zuführung von Stahlkies *m* oder Sand *m*
- *steel grit or sand delivery pipe*

39 das automatische Drehtischgebläse
- *rotary-table shot-blasting machine*

40 der Streuschutz
- *grit guard*

41 der Drehtisch
- *revolving table*

42 das Gußstück
- *casting*

43 der Putzer
- *fettler*

44 die Preßluftschleifmaschine
- *pneumatic grinder*

45 der Preßluftmeißel
- *pneumatic chisel*

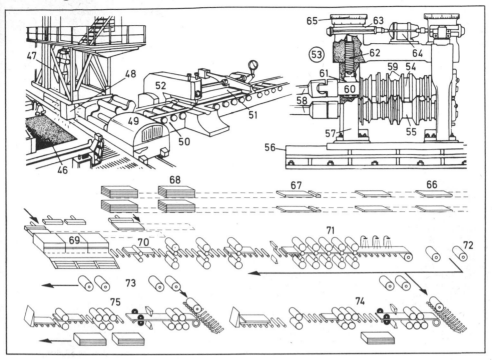

46-75 das Walzwerk
- *rolling mill*
46 der Tiefofen
- *soaking pit*
47 der Tiefofenkran, ein Zangenkran *m* (Stripperkran)
- *soaking pit crane*
48 die Rohbramme (der gegossene Rohstahlblock)
- *ingot*
49 der Blockkippwagen
- *ingot tipper*
50 die Blockstraße (der Rollgang)
- *blooming train (roller path)*
51 das Walzgut (Walzstück)
- *workpiece*
52 die Blockschere
- *bloom shears*
53 das Zweiwalzen-(Duo-)Gerüst
- *two-high mill*
54-55 der Walzensatz
- *set of rolls (set of rollers)*
54 die Oberwalze
- *upper roll (upper roller)*
55 die Unterwalze
- *lower roll (lower roller)*
56-60 das Walzgerüst
- *roll stand*
56 die Grundplatte
- *base plate*
57 der Walzenständer
- *housing (frame)*
58 die Kuppelspindel
- *coupling spindle*
59 das Kaliber
- *groove*

60 das Walzenlager
- *roll bearing*
61-65 die Anstellvorrichtung
- *adjusting equipment*
61 das Einbaustück
- *chock*
62 die Druckschraube
- *main screw*
63 das Getriebe
- *gear*
64 der Motor
- *motor*
65 die Anzeigevorrichtung mit Grob- und Feineinstellung *f*
- *indicator for rough and fine adjustment*
66-75 die Walzenstraße zur Herstellung von Bandstahl *m*
[schematisch]
- *continuous rolling mill train for the manufacture of strip*
[diagram]
66-68 die Halbzeugzurichtung
- *processing of semi-finished product*
66 das Halbzeug
- *semi-finished product*
67 die Autogenschneideanlage
- *gas cutting installation*
68 der Fertigstapel
- *stack of finished steel sheets*
69 die Stoßöfen *m*
- *continuous reheating furnaces*
70 die Vorstraße
- *blooming train*
71 die Fertigstraße
- *finishing train*

72 die Haspel
- *coiler*
73 das Bundlager für den Verkauf
- *collar bearing for marketing*
74 die 5-mm-Scherenstraße
- *5 mm shearing train*
75 die 10-mm-Scherenstraße
- *10 mm shearing train*

1 die Leit- und
  Zugspindeldrehmaschine
  (Drehbank)
- *centre (Am. center) lathe*
2 der Spindelstock mit dem
  Schaltgetriebe
- *headstock with gear control (geared
  headstock)*
3 der Vorlegeschalthebel
- *reduction drive lever*
4 der Hebel für Normal- und Steilgewinde
- *lever for normal and coarse threads*
5 die Drehzahleinstellung
- *speed change lever*
6 der Hebel für das
  Leitspindelwendegetriebe
- *leadscrew reverse-gear lever*
7 der Wechselräderkasten
- *change-gear box*
8 der Vorschubgetriebekasten (das
  Nortongetriebe, der Nortonkasten)
- *feed gearbox (Norton tumbler gear)*
9 die Hebel *m* für die Vorschub- und
  Gewindesteigungen *f*
- *levers for changing the feed and
  thread pitch*
10 der Hebel für das Vorschubgetriebe
- *feed gear lever (tumbler lever)*
11 der Einschalthebel für Rechts-
  oder Linkslauf *m* der Hauptspindel
- *switch lever for right or left hand
  action of main spindle*
12 der Drehmaschinenfuß
- *lathe foot (footpiece)*
13 das Handrad zur
  Längsschlittenbewegung
- *leadscrew handwheel for traversing
  of saddle (longitudinal movement
  of saddle)*
14 der Hebel für das Wendegetriebe
  der Vorschubeinrichtung
- *tumbler reverse lever*
15 die Vorschubspindel
- *feed screw*
16 die Schloßplatte
- *apron (saddle apron, carriage
  apron)*
17 der Längs- und Plangangshebel
- *lever for longitudinal and
  transverse motion*
18 die Fallschnecke zum Einschalten *n*
  der Vorschübe *m*
- *drop (dropping) worm (feed trip,
  feed tripping device) for engaging
  feed mechanisms*
19 der Hebel für das Mutterschloß der
  Leitspindel
- *lever for engaging half nut of
  leadscrew (lever for clasp nut
  engagement)*
20 die Drehspindel (Arbeitsspindel)
- *lathe spindle*
21 der Stahlhalter
- *tool post*
22 der Oberschlitten (Längssupport)
- *top slide (tool slide, tool rest)*
23 der Querschlitten (Quersupport)
- *cross slide*
24 der Bettschlitten (Unterschlitten)
- *bed slide*
25 die Kühlmittelzuführung
- *coolant supply pipe*
26 die Reitstockspitze
- *tailstock centre (Am. center)*
27 die Pinole
- *barrel (tailstock barrel)*

28 der Pinolenfeststellknebel
- *tailstock barrel clamp lever*
29 der Reitstock
- *tailstock*
30 das Pinolenverstellrad
- *tailstock barrel adjusting
  handwheel*
31 das Drehmaschinenbett
- *lathe bed*
32 die Leitspindel
- *leadscrew*
33 die Zugspindel
- *feed shaft*
34 die Umschaltspindel für Rechts-
  und Linkslauf *m* und Ein- und
  Ausschalten *n*
- *reverse shaft for right and left hand
  motion and engaging and
  disengaging*
35 das Vierbackenfutter
- *four-jaw chuck (four-jaw
  independent chuck)*
36 die Spannbacke
- *gripping jaw*
37 das Dreibackenfutter
- *three-jaw chuck (three-jaw
  self-centring, self-centering,
  chuck)*
38 die Revolverdrehmaschine
- *turret lathe*
39 der Querschlitten (Quersupport)
- *cross slide*
40 der Revolverkopf
- *turret*
41 der Mehrfachmeißelhalter
- *combination toolholder (multiple
  turning head)*
42 der Längsschlitten (Längssupport)
- *top slide*
43 das Handkreuz (Drehkreuz)
- *star wheel*
44 die Fangschale für Späne *m* und
  Kühlschmierstoffe *m*
- *coolant tray for collecting coolant
  and swarf*
45-53 Drehmeißel *m* (Drehstähle)
- *lathe tools*
45 der Meißel (Klemmhalter) für
  Wendeschneidplatten *f*
- *tool bit holder (clamp tip tool) for
  adjustable cutting tips*
46 die Wendeschneidplatte
  (Klemmplatte)
  aus Hartmetall *n*
  oder Oxidkeramik *f*
- *adjustable cutting tip (clamp tip) of
  cemented carbide or oxide ceramic*
47 Formen *f* der oxidkeramischen
  Wendeplatten *f*
- *shapes of adjustable oxide ceramic
  tips*
48 der Drehmeißel mit
  Hartmetallschneide *f*
- *lathe tool with cemented carbide
  cutting edge*
49 der Meißelschaft
- *tool shank*
50 die aufgelötete Hartmetallplatte
  (Hartmetallschneide)
- *brazed cemented carbide cutting tip
  (cutting edge)*
51 der Inneneckmeißel
- *internal facing tool (boring tool)
  for corner work*
52 der gebogene Drehmeißel
- *general-purpose lathe tool*

53 der Stechdrehmeißel
  (Abstechdrehmeißel,
  Einstechdrehmeißel)
- *parting (parting-off) tool*
54 das Drehherz
- *lathe carrier*
55 der Mitnehmer
- *driving (driver) plate*
56-72 Meßwerkzeuge *n*
- *measuring instruments*
56 der Grenzlehrdorn (Kaliberdorn)
- *plug gauge (Am. gage)*
57 das Sollmaß
- *'GO' gauging (Am. gaging) member
  (end)*
58 das Ausschußmaß
- *'NOT GO' gauging (Am. gaging)
  member (end)*
59 die Grenzrachenlehre
- *calliper (caliper, snap) gauge
  (Am. gage)*
60 die Gutseite
- *'GO' side*
61 die Ausschußseite
- *'NOT GO' side*
62 die Feinmeßschraube
  (Mikrometerschraube)
- *micrometer*
63 die Meßskala
- *measuring scale*
64 die Meßtrommel
- *graduated thimble*
65 der Meßbügel
- *frame*
66 die Meßspindel
- *spindle (screwed spindle)*
67 der Meßschieber (die Schieblehre)
- *vernier calliper (caliper) gauge
  (Am. gage)*
68 der Tiefenmeßfühler
- *depth gauge (Am. gage) attachment
  rule*
69 die Noniusskala
- *vernier scale*
70 die Außenmeßfühler
- *outside jaws*
71 die Innenmeßfühler
- *inside jaws*
72 der Tiefenmeßschieber
  (die Tiefenlehre)
- *vernier depth gauge (Am. gage)*

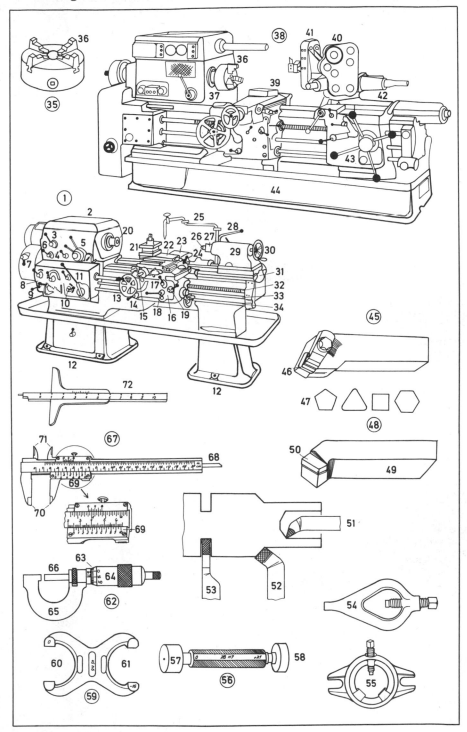

1 die Universalrundschleifmaschine
- *universal grinding machine*
2 der Spindelstock
- *headstock*
3 der Schleifsupport
- *wheelhead slide*
4 die Schleifscheibe
- *grinding wheel*
5 der Reitstock
- *tailstock*
6 das Schleifmaschinenbett
- *grinding machine bed*
7 der Schleifmaschinentisch
- *grinding machine table*
8 die Zweiständer-Langhobelmaschine
- *two-column planing machine*
  (two-column planer)
9 der Antriebsmotor, ein
  Gleichstrom-Regelmotor *m*
- *drive motor,*
  a direct current motor
10 der Ständer
- *column*
11 der Hobeltisch
- *planer table*
12 der Querbalken
- *cross slide (rail)*
13 der Werkzeugsupport
- *tool box*
14 die Bügelsäge
- *hacksaw*
15 die Einspannvorrichtung
- *clamping device*
16 das Sägeblatt
- *saw blade*
17 der Sägebügel
- *saw frame*
18 die Schwenk- oder
  Radialbohrmaschine
- *radial*
  (radial-arm) drilling
  machine
19 die Fußplatte
- *bed (base plate)*
20 der Werkstückaufnahmetisch
- *block for workpiece*
21 der Ständer
- *pillar*
22 der Hubmotor
- *lifting motor*
23 die Bohrspindel
- *drill spindle*
24 der Ausleger
- *arm*
25 das Waagerechtbohr- und -fräswerk
  (Tischbohrwerk)
- *horizontal boring and milling*
  machine
26 der Spindelkasten
- *movable headstock*
27 die Spindel
- *spindle*
28 der Kreuztisch
- *auxiliary table*
29 das Bett
- *bed*
30 der Setzstock
- *fixed steady*
31 der Bohrwerksständer
- *boring mill column*
32 die Universalfräsmaschine
- *universal milling machine*
33 der Frästisch
- *milling machine table*
34 der Tischvorschubantrieb
- *table feed drive*

35 der Hebelschalter für die
  Spindeldrehzahl
- *switch lever for spindle rotation*
  speed
36 der Schaltkasten
- *control box (control unit)*
37 die Senkrechtfrässpindel
- *vertical milling spindle*
38 der Senkrechtantriebskopf
- *vertical drive head*
39 die Waagerechtfrässpindel
- *horizontal milling spindle*
40 das vordere Lager zur
  Stabilisierung der
  Waagerechtspindel
- *end support for steadying*
  horizontal spindle
41 das Bearbeitungszentrum, eine
  Rundtischmaschine
- *machining centre (Am. center), a*
  rotary-table machine
42 der Rundschalttisch
- *rotary (circular) indexing table*
43 der Langlochfräser
- *end mill*
44 der Maschinengewindebohrer
- *machine tap*
45 die Kurzhobelmaschine
- *shaping machine (shaper)*

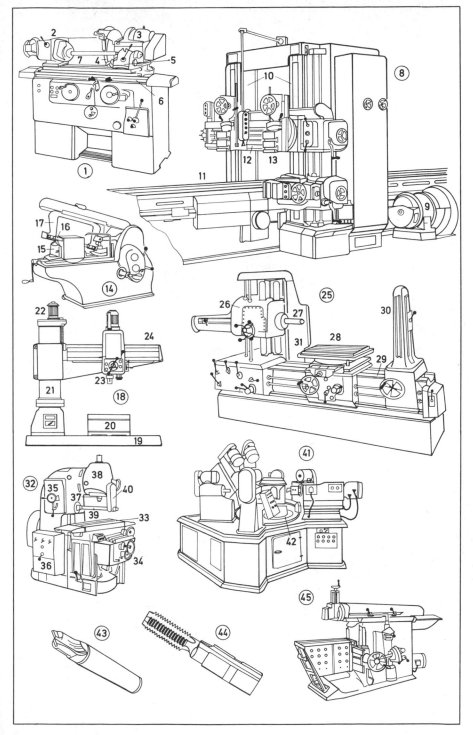

1 das Reißbrett
- *drawing board*
2 die Zeichenmaschine mit
Geradführung *f*
- *drafting machine with parallel motion*
3 der verstellbare Zeichenkopf
- *adjustable knob*
4 das Winkellineal
- *drawing head (adjustable set square)*
5 die Reißbrettverstellung
- *drawing board adjustment*
6 der Zeichentisch
- *drawing table*
7 der Zeichenwinkel (das Dreieck)
- *set square (triangle)*
8 das gleichseitige Dreieck
- *triangle*
9 die Handreißschiene
- *T-square (tee-square)*
10 die Zeichnungsrolle
- *rolled drawing*
11 die graphische Darstellung
(das Diagramm)
- *diagram*
12 die Terminplantafel
- *time schedule*
13 der Papierständer
- *paper stand*
14 die Papierrolle
- *roll of paper*
15 die Abschneidevorrichtung
- *cutter*
16 die technische Zeichnung
- *technical drawing (drawing, design)*
17 die Vorderansicht
- *front view (front elevation)*
18 die Seitenansicht
- *side view (side elevation)*
19 die Draufsicht
- *plan*
20 die unbearbeitete Fläche
- *surface not to be machined*
21 die geschruppte Fläche, eine
bearbeitete Fläche
- *surface to be machined*
22 die feingeschlichtete Fläche
- *surface to be superfinished*
23 die sichtbare Kante
- *visible edge*
24 die unsichtbare Kante
- *hidden edge*
25 die Maßlinie
- *dimension line*
26 der Maßpfeil
- *arrow head*
27 die Schnittverlaufsangabe
- *section line*
28 der Schnitt A-B
- *section A-B*
29 die schraffierte Fläche
- *hatched surface*
30 die Mittellinie
- *centre (Am. center) line*
31 das Schriftfeld
- *title panel (title block)*
32 die Strichliste (die technischen
Daten *pl*)
- *technical data*
33 der Zeichenmaßstab
- *ruler (rule)*
34 der Dreikantmaßstab
- *triangular scale*
35 die Radierschablone
- *erasing shield*

36 die Tuschepatrone
- *drawing ink cartridge*
37 Ständer *m* für Tuschefüller *m*
- *holders for tubular drawing pens*
38 der Arbeitssatz Tuschefüller *m*
- *set of tubular drawing pens*
39 der Feuchtigkeitsmesser
- *hygrometer*
40 die Verschlußkappe mit
Strichstärkenkennzeichnung
- *cap with indication of nib size*
41 der Radierstift
- *pencil-type eraser*
42 der Radiergummi
- *eraser*
43 das Radiermesser
- *erasing knife*
44 die Radierklinge
- *erasing knife blade*
45 der Minenklemmstift
- *clutch-type pencil*
46 die Graphitmine
- *pencil lead
(refill lead, refill, spare lead)*
47 der Radierpinsel
(Glasfaserradierer)
- *glass eraser*
48 die Glasfasern *f*
- *glass fibres (Am. fibers)*
49 die Reißfeder
- *ruling pen*
50 das Kreuzscharnier
- *cross joint*
51 die Teilscheibe
- *index plate*
52 der Einsatzzirkel
- *compass with interchangeable attachments*
53 die Geradführung
- *compass head*
54 der Spitzeneinsatz
(Nadeleinsatz)
- *needle point attachment*
55 der Bleinadeleinsatz
- *pencil point attachment*
56 die Nadel
- *needle*
57 die Verlängerungsstange
- *lengthening arm (extension bar)*
58 der Reißfedereinsatz
- *ruling pen attachment*
59 der Fallnullenzirkel
- *pump compass (drop compass)*
60 die Fallstange
- *piston*
61 der Reißfedereinsatz
- *ruling pen attachment*
62 der Bleieinsatz
- *pencil attachment*
63 der Tuschebehälter
- *drawing ink container*
64 der Schnellverstellzirkel
- *spring bow (rapid adjustment, ratchet-type) compass*
65 das Federringscharnier
- *spring ring hinge*
66 der federgelagerte Bogenfeintrieb
- *spring-loaded fine adjustment for arcs*
67 die gekröpfte Nadel
- *right-angle needle*
68 der Tuschefüllereinsatz
- *tubular ink unit*
69 die Schriftschablone
- *stencil lettering guide (lettering stencil)*

70 die Kreisschablone
- *circle template*
71 die Ellipsenschablone
- *ellipse template*

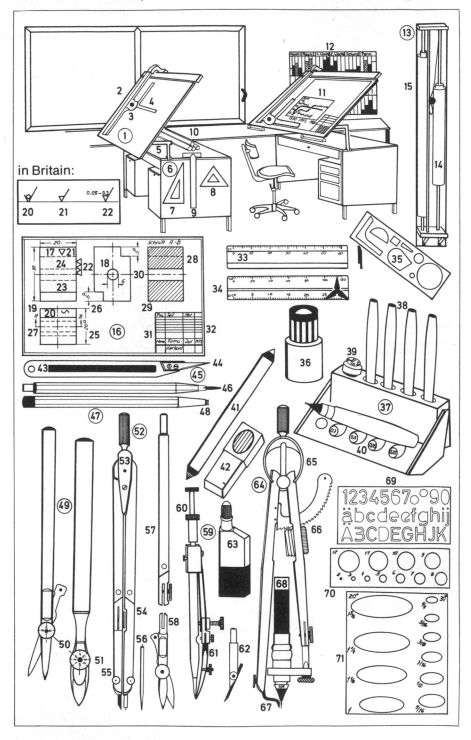

in Britain:

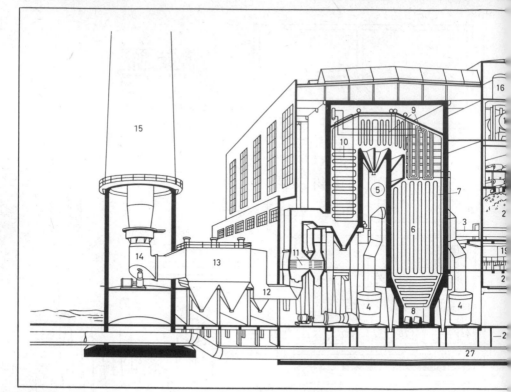

1-28 **das Dampfkraftwerk,** ein
Elektrizitätswerk *n*
– ***steam-generating station,** an electric
power plant*
1-21 **das Kesselhaus**
– ***boiler house***
1 das Kohlenförderband
– *coal conveyor*
2 der Kohlenbunker
– *coal bunker*
3 das Kohlenabzugsband
– *travelling-grate*
　(Am. *traveling-grate) stoker*
4 die Kohlenmühle
– *coal mill*
5 der Dampfkessel, ein Röhrenkessel
　m (Strahlungskessel)
– *steam boiler, a water-tube boiler
　(radiant-type boiler)*
6 die Brennkammer
– *burners*
7 die Wasserrohre *n*
– *water pipes*
8 der Aschenabzug
　(Schlackenabzug)
– *ash pit (clinker pit)*
9 der Überhitzer
– *superheater*
10 der Wasservorwärmer
– *water preheater*
11 der Luftvorwärmer
– *air preheater*
12 der Gaskanal
– *gas flue*

13 der (das) Rauchgasfilter, ein
Elektrofilter *m od. n*
– *electrostatic precipitator*
14 das Saugzuggebläse
– *induced-draught
　(Am. induced-draft) fan*
15 der Schornstein
– *chimney (smokestack)*
16 der Entgaser
– *de-aerator*
17 der Wasserbehälter
– *feedwater tank*
18 die Kesselspeisepumpe
– *boiler feed pump*
19 die Schaltanlage
– *control room*
20 der Kabelboden
– *cable tunnel*
21 der Kabelkeller
– *cable vault*
22 das Maschinenhaus
　(Turbinenhaus)
– *turbine house*
23 die Dampfturbine, mit Generator *m*
– *steam turbine with alternator*
24 der Oberflächenkondensator
– *surface condenser*
25 der Niederdruckvorwärmer
– *low-pressure preheater*
26 der Hochdruckvorwärmer
– *high-pressure preheater
　(economizer)*
27 die Kühlwasserleitung
– *cooling water pipe*

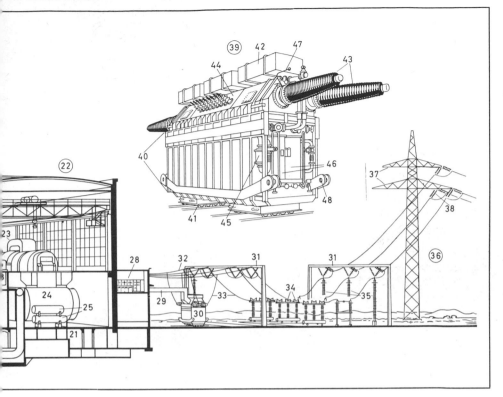

28 die Schaltwarte
- *control room*
29-35 **die Freiluftschaltanlage,** eine
Hochspannungsverteilungsanlage
- *outdoor substation, a substation*
29 die Stromschienen *f*
- *busbars*
30 der Leistungstransformator, ein
Wandertransformator *m*
- *power transformer, a mobile
(transportable) transformer*
31 das Abspannungsgerüst
- *stay poles (guy poles)*
32 das Hochspannungsleitungsseil
- *high-voltage transmission line*
33 das Hochspannungsseil
- *high-voltage conductor*
34 der Druckluftschnellschalter
(Leistungsschalter)
- *air-blast circuit breaker (circuit
breaker)*
35 der Überspannungsableiter
- *surge diverter (Am. lightning
arrester, arrester)*
36 der Freileitungsmast
(Abspannungsmast), ein
Gittermast *m*
- *overhead line support, a lattice steel
tower*
37 der Querträger (die Traverse)
- *cross arm (traverse)*
38 der Abspannisolator (die
Abspannkette)
- *strain insulator*

39 **der Wandertransformator**
(Leistungstransformator,
Transformator, Trafo, Umspanner)
- *mobile (transportable) transformer
(power transformer, transformer)*
40 der Transformator[en]kessel
- *transformer tank*
41 das Fahrgestell
- *bogie (Am. truck)*
42 das Ölausdehnungsgefäß
- *oil conservator*
43 die Oberspannungsdurchführung
- *primary voltage terminal (primary
voltage bushing)*
44 die Unterspannungsdurchführungen *f*
- *low-voltage terminals (low-voltage
bushings)*
45 die Ölumlaufpumpe
- *oil-circulating pump*
46 der Öl-Wasser-Kühler
- *oil cooler*
47 das Funkenhorn
- *arcing horn*
48 die Transportöse
- *transport lug*

1-8 **die Schaltwarte**
- *control room*
1-6 **das Schaltpult**
- *control console (control desk)*
1 der Steuer- und Regelteil, für die
Drehstromgeneratoren *m*
- *control board
(control panel) for
the alternators*
2 der Steuerschalter
- *master switch*
3 der Leuchtmelder
- *signal light*
4 die Anwahlsteuerplatte, zur
Steuerung der
Hochspannungsabzweige *m*
- *feeder panel*
5 die Überwachungsorgane *n*, für die
Steuerung der Schaltgeräte *n*
- *monitoring controls for the
switching systems*
6 die Steuerelemente *n*
- *controls*
7 die Wartentafel, mit den
Meßgeräten *n* der
Rückmeldeanlage
- *revertive signal panel*
8 das Blindschaltbild, zur
Darstellung des Netzzustandes *m*
- *matrix mimic board*
9-18 **der Transformator**
- *transformer*
9 das Ölausdehnungsgefäß
- *oil conservator*
10 die Entlüftung
- *breather*
11 der Ölstandsanzeiger
- *oil gauge (Am. gage)*
12 der Durchführungsisolator
- *feed-through terminal
(feed-through insulator)*
13 der Umschalter, für
Oberspannungsanzapfungen *f*
- *on-load tap changer*
14 das Joch
- *yoke*
15 die Primärwicklung
(Oberspannungswicklung)
- *primary winding (primary)*
16 die Sekundärwicklung
(Unterspannungswicklung)
- *secondary winding (secondary,
low-voltage winding)*
17 der Kern (Schenkel)
- *core*
18 die Anzapfungsverbindung
- *tap (tapping)*
19 **die Transformatorenschaltung**
- *transformer connection*
20 die Sternschaltung
- *star connection (star network,
Y-connection)*
21 die Dreieckschaltung
(Deltaschaltung)
- *delta connection (mesh connection)*
22 der Sternpunkt (Nullpunkt)
- *neutral point*
23-30 **die Dampfturbine,** eine
Dampfturbogruppe
- *steam turbine, a turbogenerator unit*
23 der Hochdruckzylinder
- *high-pressure cylinder*
24 der Mitteldruckzylinder
- *medium-pressure cylinder*
25 der Niederdruckzylinder
- *low-pressure cylinder*

26 der Drehstromgenerator
(Generator)
- *three-phase generator (generator)*
27 der Wasserstoffkühler
- *hydrogen cooler*
28 die Dampfüberströmleitung
- *leakage steam path*
29 das Düsenventil
- *jet nozzle*
30 der Turbinenüberwachungsschrank
mit den Meßinstrumenten *n*
- *turbine monitoring panel with
measuring instruments*
31 der Spannungsregler
- *[automatic] voltage regulator*
32 die Synchronisiereinrichtung
- *synchro*
33 **der Kabelendverschluß**
- *cable box*
34 der Leiter
- *conductor*
35 der Durchführungsisolator
- *feed-through terminal
(feed-through insulator)*
36 die Wickelkeule
- *core*
37 das Gehäuse
- *casing*
38 die Füllmasse
- *filling compound (filler)*
39 der Bleimantel
- *lead sheath*
40 der Einführungsstutzen
- *lead-in tube*
41 das Kabel
- *cable*
42 **das Hochspannungskabel,** für
Dreiphasenstrom *m*
- *high voltage cable, for three-phase
current*
43 der Stromleiter
- *conductor*
44 das Metallpapier
- *metallic paper (metallized paper)*
45 der Beilauf
- *tracer (tracer element)*
46 das Nesselband
- *varnished-cambric tape*
47 der Bleimantel
- *lead sheath*
48 das Asphaltpapier
- *asphalted paper*
49 die Juteumhüllung
- *jute serving*
50 die Stahlband- oder
Stahldrahtarmierung
- *steel tape or steel wire armour
(Am. armor)*
51-62 **der Druckluftschnellschalter,**
ein Leistungsschalter *m*
- *air-blast circuit breaker, a circuit
breaker*
51 der Druckluftbehälter
- *compressed-air tank*
52 das Steuerventil
- *control valve (main operating valve)*
53 der Druckluftanschluß
- *compressed-air inlet*
54 der Hohlstützisolator, ein
Kappenisolator *m*
- *support insulator, a hollow porcelain
supporting insulator*
55 die Schaltkammer (Löschkammer)
- *interrupter*
56 der Widerstand
- *resistor*

57 die Hilfskontakte *m*
- *auxiliary contacts*
58 der Stromwandler
- *current transformer*
59 der Spannungswandler
- *voltage transformer (potential
transformer)*
60 der Klemmenkasten
- *operating mechanism housing*
61 das Funkenhorn
- *arcing horn*
62 die Funkenstrecke
- *spark gap*

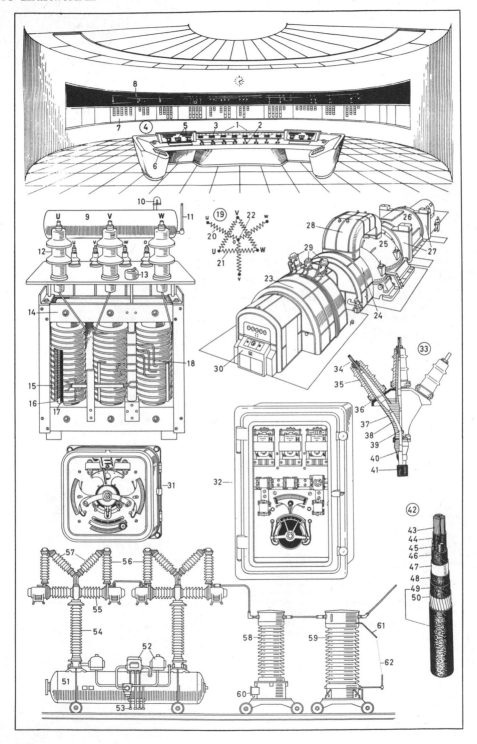

1 **der Brutreaktor** (schnelle Brüter)
[Schema]
- *fast-breeder reactor (fast breeder)
[diagram]*
2 der Primärkreislauf (primäre
Natriumkreislauf)
- *primary circuit (primary loop,
primary sodium system)*
3 der Reaktor
- *reactor*
4 die Brennelementstäbe *m*
(der Kernbrennstoff)
- *fuel rods (fuel pins)*
5 die Primärkreisumwälzpumpe
- *primary sodium pump*
6 der Wärmetauscher
- *heat exchanger*
7 der Sekundärkreislauf (sekundäre
Natriumkreislauf)
- *secondary circuit (secondary loop,
secondary sodium system)*
8 die Sekundärkreisumwälzpumpe
- *secondary sodium pump*
9 der Dampferzeuger
- *steam generator*
10 der Tertiärkreislauf
(Kühlwasserkreislauf)
- *cooling water flow circuit*
11 die Dampfleitung
- *steam line*
12 die Speisewasserleitung
- *feedwater line*
13 die Speisewasserpumpe
- *feed pump*
14 die Dampfturbine
- *steam turbine*
15 der Generator
- *generator*
16 die Netzeinspeisung
- *transmission line*
17 der Kondensator
- *condenser*
18 das Kühlwasser
- *cooling water*
19 **der Kernreaktor,** ein
Druckwasserreaktor *m*
(das Kernkraftwerk, *ugs.*
Atomkraftwerk)
- *nuclear reactor, a pressurized-water
reactor (nuclear power plant,
atomic power plant)*
20 die Betonhülle (das
Reaktorgebäude)
- *concrete shield (reactor building)*
21 der Sicherheitsbehälter aus Stahl *m*
mit Absaugluftspalt *m*
- *steel containment (steel shell) with
air extraction vent*
22 der Reaktordruckbehälter
- *reactor pressure vessel*
23 der Steuerantrieb des Reaktors
- *control rod drive*
24 die Absorberstäbe *m* (Steuerstäbe)
- *control rods*
25 die Hauptkühlmittelpumpe
- *primary coolant pump*
26 der Dampferzeuger
- *steam generator*
27 die Lademaschine für die
Brennelemente *n*
- *fuel-handling hoists*
28 das Lagerbecken für die
Brennelemente *n*
- *fuel storage*
29 die Reaktorkühlmittelleitung
- *coolant flow passage*

30 die Speisewasserleitung
- *feedwater line*
31 die Frischdampfleitung
- *prime steam line*
32 die Personenschleuse
- *manway*
33 der Turbinensatz
- *turbogenerator set*
34 der Drehstromgenerator
- *turbogenerator*
35 der Kondensator
- *condenser*
36 das Nebenanlagengebäude
- *service building*
37 der Abluftkamin
- *exhaust gas stack*
38 der Rundlaufkran
- *polar crane*
39 der Kühlturm, ein
Trockenkühlturm *m*
- *cooling tower, a dry cooling tower*
40 das Druckwasserprinzip [Schema]
- *pressurized-water system*
41 der Reaktor
- *reactor*
42 der Primärkreislauf
- *primary circuit (primary loop)*
43 die Umwälzpumpe
- *circulation pump (recirculation
pump)*
44 der Wärmetauscher
(Dampferzeuger)
- *heat exchanger (steam generator)*
45 der Sekundärkreislauf
(Speisewasser-Dampf-Kreislauf)
- *secondary circuit (secondary loop,
feedwater steam circuit)*
46 die Dampfturbine
- *steam turbine*
47 der Generator
- *generator*
48 das Kühlsystem
- *cooling system*
49 das Siedewasserprinzip [Schema]
- *boiling water system [diagram]*
50 der Reaktor
- *reactor*
51 der Dampf-Kondensat-Kreislauf
- *steam and recirculation water flow
paths*
52 die Dampfturbine
- *steam turbine*
53 der Generator
- *generator*
54 die Umwälzpumpe
- *circulation pump (recirculation
pump)*
55 das Kühlwassersystem (die
Kühlung mit Flußwasser *n*)
- *coolant system (cooling with water
from river)*
56 **die Atommüllagerung** im
Salzbergwerk *n*
- *radioactive waste storage in salt mine*
57-68 die geologischen Verhältnisse *pl*
des als Lagerstätte *f* für radioaktive
Abfälle *m* (Atommüll)
eingerichteten aufgelassenen
Salzbergwerks
- *geological structure of abandoned
salt mine converted for disposal of
radioactive waste (nuclear waste)*
57 der Untere Keuper
- *Lower Keuper*
58 der Obere Muschelkalk
- *Upper Muschelkalk*

59 der Mittlere Muschelkalk
- *Middle Muschelkalk*
60 der Untere Muschelkalk
- *Lower Muschelkalk*
61 die verstürzte
Buntsandsteinscholle
- *Bunter downthrow*
62 die Auslaugungsrückstände *m* des
Zechsteins *m*
- *residue of leached (lixiviated)
Zechstein (Upper Permian)*
63 das Aller-Steinsalz
- *Aller rock salt*
64 das Leine-Steinsalz
- *Leine rock salt*
65 das Staßfurt-Flöz (Kalisalzflöz)
- *Stassfurt seam (potash salt seam,
potash salt bed)*
66 das Staßfurt-Steinsalz
- *Stassfurt salt*
67 der Grenzanhydrit
- *grenzanhydrite*
68 der Zechsteinletten
- *Zechstein shale*
69 der Schacht
- *shaft*
70 die Übertagebauten *m*
- *minehead buildings*
71 die Einlagerungskammer
- *storage chamber*
72 die Einlagerung mittelaktiver
Abfälle *m* im Salzbergwerk *n*
- *storage of medium-active waste in
salt mine*
73 die 511-m-Sohle
- *511 m level*
74 die Strahlenschutzmauer
- *protective screen (anti-radiation
screen)*
75 das Bleiglasfenster
- *lead glass window*
76 die Lagerkammer
- *storage chamber*
77 das Rollreifenfaß mit radioaktivem
Abfall *m*
- *drum containing radioactive waste*
78 die Fernsehkamera
- *television camera*
79 die Beschickungskammer
- *charging chamber*
80 das Steuerpult
- *control desk (control panel)*
81 die Abluftanlage
- *upward ventilator*
82 der Abschirmbehälter
- *shielded container*
83 die 490-m-Sohle
- *490 m level*

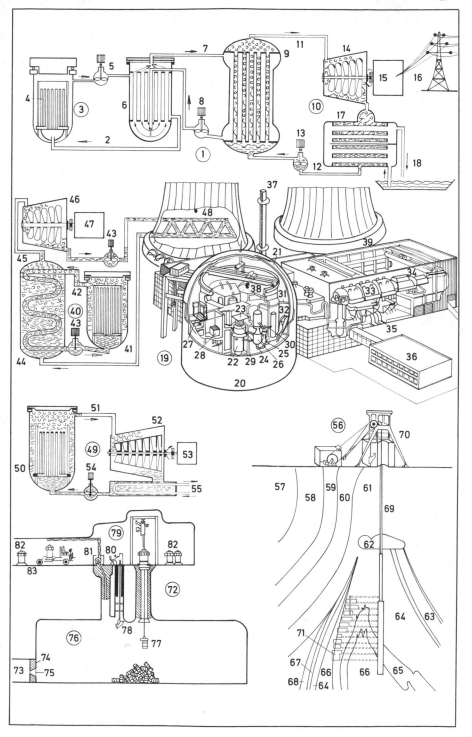

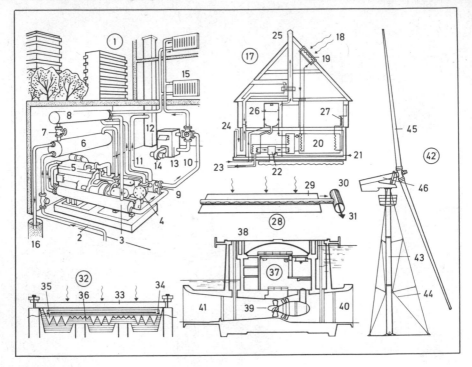

1 das **Wärmepumpensystem**
- *heat pump system*
2 der Grundwasserzufluß
- *source water inlet*
3 der Kühlwasser-Wärmetauscher
- *cooling water heat exchanger*
4 der Kompressor
- *compressor*
5 der Erdgas- oder Dieselmotor
- *natural-gas or diesel engine*
6 der Verdampfer
- *evaporator*
7 das Reduzierventil
- *pressure release valve*
8 der Kondensator
- *condenser*
9 der Abgaswärmetauscher
- *waste-gas heat exchanger*
10 der Vorlauf
- *flow pipe*
11 die Abluftleitung
- *vent pipe*
12 der Kamin
- *chimney*
13 der Heizkessel
- *boiler*
14 das Gebläse
- *fan*
15 der Heizkörper (Radiator)
- *radiator*
16 der Sickerschacht
- *sink*
17-36 die **Sonnenenergienutzung**
- *utilization of solar energy*
17 das mit Sonnenenergie *f* beheizte Haus
- *solar (solar-heated) house*

18 die Sonneneinstrahlung
- *solar radiation (sunlight, insolation)*
19 der Kollektor
- *collector*
20 der Wärmespeicher
- *hot reservoir (heat reservoir)*
21 die Stromzufuhr
- *power supply*
22 die Wärmepumpe
- *heat pump*
23 die Abwasserleitung
- *water outlet*
24 der Luftzutritt
- *air supply*
25 der Abluftkamin
- *flue*
26 die Heißwasserversorgung
- *hot water supply*
27 die Radiatorheizung
- *radiator heating*
28 das Sonnenkraftwerkselement
- *flat plate solar collector*
29 der Schwarzkollektor (mit Asphalt *m* beschichtetes Aluminiumblech)
- *blackened receiver surface with asphalted aluminium (Am. aluminum) foil*
30 das Stahlrohr
- *steel tube*
31 das Wärmetransportmittel
- *heat transfer fluid*
32 der Sonnenziegel
- *flat plate solar collector, containing solar cell*
33 die Glasabdeckung
- *glass cover*

34 die Solarzelle
- *solar cell*
35 die Luftkanäle *m*
- *air ducts*
36 die Isolierung
- *insulation*
37 das **Gezeitenkraftwerk** [Schnitt]
- *tidal power plant [section]*
38 der Staudamm
- *dam*
39 die doppeltwirkende Turbine
- *reversible turbine*
40 der seeseitige Turbineneinlauf
- *turbine inlet for water from the sea*
41 der speicherseitige Turbineneinlauf
- *turbine inlet for water from the basin*
42 das **Windkraftwerk**
- *wind power plant (wind generator, aerogenerator)*
43 der Rohrturm
- *truss tower*
44 die Drahtseilabspannung
- *guy wire*
45 der Rotor
- *rotor blades (propeller)*
46 der Generator und der Richtungsstellmotor
- *generator with variable pitch for power regulation*

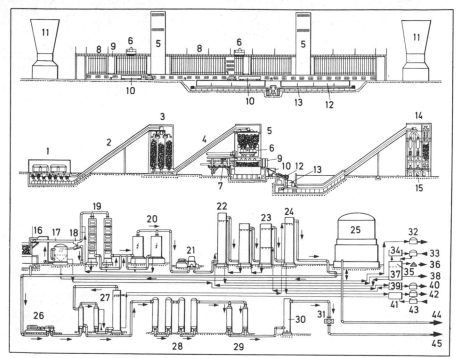

1-15 die Kokerei
- *coking plant*
1 die Kokskohlenentladung
- *dumping of coking coal*
2 der Gurtförderer
- *belt conveyor*
3 der Kokskohlenkomponentenbunker
- *service bunker*
4 der Kohlenturmgurtförderer·
- *coal tower conveyor*
5 der Kohlenturm
- *coal tower*
6 der Füllwagen
- *larry car (larry, charging car)*
7 die Koksausdrückmaschine
- *pusher ram*
8 die Koksofenbatterie
- *battery of coke ovens*
9 der Kokskuchenführungswagen
- *coke guide*
10 der Löschwagen, mit Löschlok *f*
- *quenching car, with engine*
11 der Löschturm
- *quenching tower*
12 die Koksrampe
- *coke loading bay (coke wharf)*
13 das Koksrampenband
- *coke side bench*
14 die Grob- und Feinkokssieberei
- *screening of lump coal and culm*
15 die Koksverladung
- *coke loading*
16-45 die Kokereigasbehandlung
- *coke-oven gas processing*
16 der Gasaustritt aus den Koksöfen *m*
- *discharge (release) of gas from the coke ovens*

17 die Gassammelleitung (Vorlage)
- *gas-collecting main*
18 die Dickteerabscheidung
- *coal tar extraction*
19 der Gaskühler
- *gas cooler*
20 der (das) Elektrofilter
- *electrostatic precipitator*
21 der Gassauger
- *gas extractor*
22 der Schwefelwasserstoffwascher
- *hydrogen sulphide (Am. hydrogen sulfide) scrubber (hydrogen sulphide wet collector)*
23 der Ammoniakwascher
- *ammonia scrubber (ammonia wet collector)*
24 der Benzolwascher
- *benzene (benzol) scrubber*
25 der Gassammelbehälter
- *gas holder*
26 der Gaskompressor
- *gas compressor*
27 die Entbenzolung mit Kühler *m* und Wärmetauscher *m*
- *debenzoling by cooler and heat exchanger*
28 die Druckgasentschwefelung
- *desulphurization (Am. desulfurization) of pressure gas*
29 die Gaskühlung
- *gas cooling*
30 die Gastrocknung
- *gas drying*
31 der Gaszähler
- *gas meter*

32 der Rohteerbehälter
- *crude tar tank*
33 die Schwefelsäurezufuhr
- *sulphuric acid (Am. sulfuric acid) supply*
34 die Schwefelsäureerzeugung
- *production of sulphuric acid (Am. sulfuric acid)*
35 die Ammoniumsulfatherstellung
- *production of ammonium sulphate (Am. ammonium sulfate)*
36 das Ammoniumsulfat
- *ammonium sulphate (Am. ammonium sulfate)*
37 die Regenerieranlage zum Regenerieren *n* der Waschmedien *n*
- *recovery plant for recovering the scrubbing agents*
38 die Abwasserabfuhr
- *waste water discharge*
39 die Entphenolung des Gaswassers *n*
- *phenol extraction from the gas water*
40 der Rohphenolbehälter
- *crude phenol tank*
41 die Rohbenzolerzeugung
- *production of crude benzol (crude benzene)*
42 der Rohbenzoltank
- *crude benzol (crude benzene) tank*
43 der Waschöltank
- *scrubbing oil tank*
44 die Niederdruckgasleitung
- *low-pressure gas main*
45 die Hochdruckgasleitung
- *high-pressure gas main*

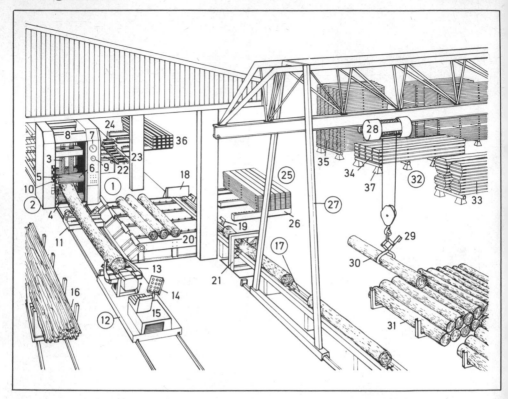

1 das Sägewerk (die Sägehalle)
- *sawmill*
2 das Vollgatter
- *vertical frame saw*
  (Am. *gang mill*)
3 die Sägeblätter *m*
- *saw blades*
4 die Einzugswalze
- *feed roller*
5 die Kletterwalze
- *guide roller*
6 die Riffelung
- *fluting (grooving, grooves)*
7 das Öldruckmanometer
- *oil pressure gauge* (Am. *gage*)
8 der Gatterrahmen
- *saw frame*
9 der Vorschubanzeiger
- *feed indicator*
10 die Skala für die Durchlaßhöhe
- *log capacity scale*
11 der Hilfswagen
- *auxiliary carriage*
12 der Spannwagen
- *carriage*
13 die Spannzange
- *log grips*
14 die Fernbedienung
- *remote control panel*
15 der Antrieb für den Spannwagen
- *carriage motor*
16 der Wagen für die Spreißel *m*
- *truck for splinters (splints)*

17 der Blockzug (Spitzenblockzug)
- *endless log chain*
  (Am. *jack chain*)
18 die Anschlagplatte
- *stop plate*
19 die Blockauswerfer *m*
- *log-kicker arms*
20 der Querförderer
- *cross conveyor*
21 die Waschanlage
- *washer (washing machine)*
22 der Kettenquerförderer für
  Schnittware *f*
- *cross chain conveyor for sawn
  timber*
23 der Rollentisch
- *roller table*
24 die Untertischkappsäge
- *undercut swing saw*
25 die Vorstapelung
- *piling*
26 die Rollenböcke *m*
- *roller trestles*
27 der Portalkran
- *gantry crane*
28 der Kranmotor
- *crane motor*
29 der Schwedengreifer
- *pivoted log grips*
30 das Rundholz
- *roundwood (round timber)*
31 das Rundholzpolter (Sortierpolter)
- *log dump*

32 der Schnittholzplatz
- *squared timber store*
33 die Blockware
- *sawn logs*
34 die Dielen *f*
- *planks*
35 die Bretter *n*
- *boards (planks)*
36 die Kanthölzer *n*
- *squared timber*
37 der Stapelstein
- *stack bearer*

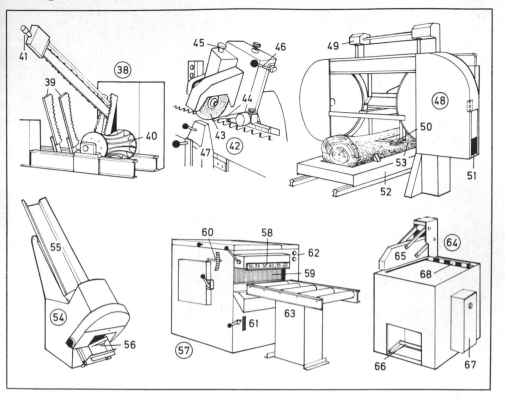

38 die automatische Kettenablängsäge
 - *automatic cross-cut chain saw*
39 die Stammholzhalter *m*
 - *log grips*
40 die Vorschubwalze
 - *feed roller*
41 die Kettenspannvorrichtung
 - *chain-tensioning device*
42 die automatische
 Sägenschärfmaschine
 - *saw-sharpening machine*
43 die Schleifscheibe
 - *grinding wheel (teeth grinder)*
44 die Vorschubklinke
 - *feed pawl*
45 die Tiefeneinstellung für die
 Schärfscheibe
 - *depth adjustment for the teeth
 grinder*
46 der Ausheber für den Schärfkopf
 - *lifter (lever) for the grinder chuck*
47 die Haltevorrichtung für das
 Sägeblatt
 - *holding device for the saw blade*
48 die horizontale Blockbandsäge
 - *horizontal bandsaw for
 sawing logs*
49 die Höheneinstellung
 - *height adjustment*
50 der Spanabstreifer
 - *chip remover*
51 die Späneabsaugung
 - *chip extractor*

52 der Transportschlitten
 - *carriage*
53 das Bandsägeblatt
 - *bandsaw blade*
54 die automatische Brennholzsäge
 - *automatic blocking saw*
55 der Einwurfschacht
 - *feed channel*
56 die Auswurföffnung
 - *discharge opening*
57 die Doppelbesäumsäge
 - *twin edger (double edger)*
58 die Breitenskala
 - *breadth scale (width scale)*
59 die Rückschlagsicherung
 (Lamellen *f*)
 - *kick-back guard (plates)*
60 die Höhenskala
 - *height scale*
61 die Vorschubskala
 - *in-feed scale*
62 die Kontrollampen *f*
 - *indicator lamps*
63 der Aufgabetisch
 - *feed table*
64 die Untertischkappsäge
 - *undercut swing saw*
65 der automatische Niederhalter (mit
 Schutzhaube *f*)
 - *automatic hold-down with
 protective hood*
66 der Fußschalter
 - *foot switch*

67 die Schaltanlage
 - *distribution board (panelboard)*
68 der Längenanschlag
 - *length stop*

1 **der Steinbruch,** ein Tagebau *m*
(Abraumbau)
- *quarry,*
 an open-cast working
2 der Abraum
- *overburden*
3 das anstehende Gestein
- *working face*
4 das Haufwerk (gelöste Gestein)
- *loose rock pile (blasted rock)*
5 der Brecher, ein Steinbrucharbeiter *m*
- *quarryman (quarrier), a quarry*
 worker
6 der Keilhammer
- *sledge hammer*
7 der Keil
- *wedge*
8 der Felsblock
- *block of stone*
9 der Bohrer
- *driller*
10 der Schutzhelm
- *safety helmet*
11 der Bohrhammer (Gesteinsbohrer)
- *hammer drill (hard-rock drill)*
12 das Bohrloch
- *borehole*
13 der Universalbagger
- *universal excavator*
14 die Großraumlore
- *large-capacity truck*
15 die Felswand
- *rock face*

16 der Schrägaufzug
- *inclined hoist*
17 der Vorbrecher
- *primary crusher*
18 das Schotterwerk
- *stone-crushing plant*
19 der Grobkreiselbrecher; *ähnl.:*
 Feinkreiselbrecher
 (Kreiselbrecher)
- *coarse rotary (gyratory) crusher;*
 sim.: *fine rotary (gyratory) crusher*
 (rotary or gyratory crusher)
20 der Backenbrecher
- *hammer crusher (impact crusher)*
21 das Vibrationssieb
- *vibrating screen*
22 das Steinmehl
- *screenings (fine dust)*
23 der Splitt
- *stone chippings*
24 der Schotter
- *crushed stone*
25 der Sprengmeister (Schießmeister)
- *shot firer*
26 der Meßstab
- *measuring rod*
27 die Sprengpatrone
- *blasting cartridge*
28 die Zündschnur
- *fuse (blasting fuse)*
29 der Füllsandeimer
- *plugging sand (stemming sand)*
 bucket

30 der Quaderstein
- *dressed stone*
31 die Spitzhacke
- *pick*
32 die Brechstange
- *crowbar (pinch bar)*
33 die Steingabel
- *fork*
34 der Steinmetz
- *stonemason*
35-38 **Steinmetzwerkzeug** *n*
- *stonemason's tools*
35 der Fäustel
- *stonemason's hammer*
36 der Klöpfel
- *mallet*
37 das Scharriereisen (Breiteisen)
- *drove chisel (drove, boaster, broad*
 chisel)
38 das schwere Flächeneisen
- *dressing axe (Am. ax)*

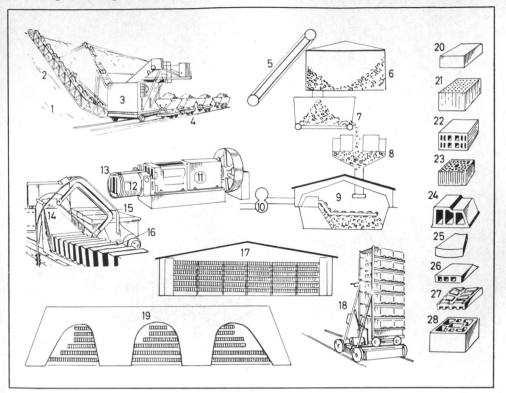

1 die Lehmgrube
- *clay pit*
2 der Lehm, ein unreiner Ton *m*
(Rohton)
- *loam, an impure clay (raw clay)*
3 der Abraumbagger, ein
Großraumbagger *m*
- *overburden excavator, a large-scale
excavator*
4 die Feldbahn, eine
Schmalspurbahn
- *narrow-gauge (Am. narrow-gage)
track system*
5 der Schrägaufzug
- *inclined hoist*
6 das Maukhaus
- *souring chambers*
7 der Kastenbeschicker (Beschicker)
- *box feeder (feeder)*
8 der Kollergang (Mahlgang)
- *edge runner mill (edge mill, pan
grinding mill)*
9 das Walzwerk
- *rolling plant*
10 der Doppelwellenmischer (Mischer)
- *double-shaft trough mixer (mixer)*
11 die Strangpresse (Ziegelpresse)
- *extrusion press (brick-pressing
machine)*
12 die Vakuumkammer
- *vacuum chamber*
13 das Mundstück
- *die*

14 der Tonstrang
- *clay column*
15 der Abschneider (Ziegelschneider)
- *cutter (brick cutter)*
16 der ungebrannte Ziegel (Rohling)
- *unfired brick (green brick)*
17 die Trockenkammer
- *drying shed*
18 der Hubstapler (Absetzwagen)
- *mechanical finger car (stacker
truck)*
19 der Ringofen (Ziegelofen)
- *circular kiln (brick kiln)*
20 der Vollziegel (Ziegelstein,
Backstein, Mauerstein)
- *solid brick (building brick)*
21-22 die Lochziegel *m*
- *perforated bricks and hollow blocks*
21 der Hochlochziegel
- *perforated brick with vertical
perforations*
22 der Langlochziegel
- *hollow clay block with horizontal
perforations*
23 der Gitterziegel
- *hollow clay block with vertical
perforations*
24 der Deckenziegel
- *floor brick*
25 der Schornsteinziegel
(Radialziegel)
- *compass brick (radial brick,
radiating brick)*

26 die Tonhohlplatte (der Hourdi,
Hourdis, Hourdistein)
- *hollow flooring block*
27 die Stallvollplatte
- *paving brick*
28 der Kaminformstein
- *cellular brick [for fireplaces]
(chimney brick)*

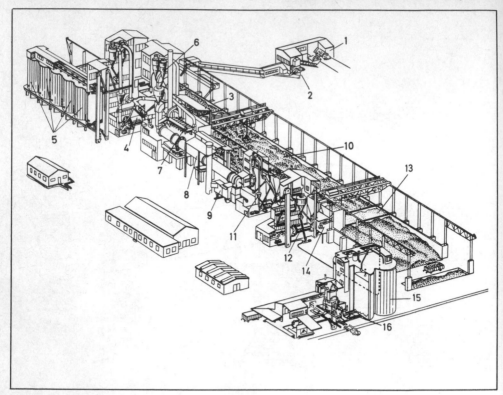

1 die Rohstoffe *m* (Kalkstein *m*, Ton *m* u. Kalksteinmergel *m*)
– *raw materials (limestone, clay and marl)*
2 der Hammerbrecher
– *hammer crusher (hammer mill)*
3 das Rohmateriallager
– *raw material store*
4 die Rohmühle zur Mahlung und gleichzeitigen Trocknung der Rohstoffe *m* unter Verwendung *f* der Wärmetauscherabgase *n*
– *raw mill for simultaneously grinding and drying the raw materials with exhaust gas from the heat exchanger*
5 die Rohmehlsilos *m od. n* (Homogenisiersilos)
– *raw meal silos*
6 die Wärmetauscheranlage (der Zyklonwärmetauscher)
– *heat exchanger (cyclone heat exchanger)*
7 die Entstaubungsanlage (ein Elektrofilter *m od. n*) für die Wärmetauscherabgase *n* aus der Rohmühle
– *dust collector (an electrostatic precipitator) for the heat exchanger exhaust from the raw mill*
8 der Drehrohrofen
– *rotary kiln*
9 der Klinkerkühler
– *clinker cooler*

10 das Klinkerlager
– *clinker store*
11 das Primärluftgebläse
– *primary air blower*
12 die Zementmahlanlage
– *cement-grinding mill*
13 das Gipslager
– *gypsum store*
14 die Gipszerkleinerungsmaschine
– *gypsum crusher*
15 der (das) Zementsilo
– *cement silo*
16 die Zementpackmaschinen *f* für Papierventilsäcke *m*
– *cement-packing plant for paper sacks*

1 die Trommelmühle (Massemühle,
  Kugelmühle), zur
  Naßaufbereitung des
  Rohstoffgemenges *n*
 – *grinding cylinder (ball mill) for the
  preparation of the raw material in
  water*
2 die Probekapsel, mit Öffnung *f* zur
  Beobachtung des Brennvorgangs *m*
 – *sample sagger (saggar, seggar), with
  aperture for observing the firing
  process*
3 der Rundofen [Schema]
 – *bottle kiln (beehive kiln) [diagram]*
4 die Brennform
 – *firing mould (Am. mold)*
5 der Tunnelofen
 – *tunnel kiln*
6 der Segerkegel, zum Messen *n*
  hoher Hitzegrade *m*
 – *Seger cone (pyrometric cone, Am.
  Orton cone) for measuring high
  temperatures*
7 die Vakuumpresse, eine
  Strangpresse
 – *de-airing pug mill (de-airing pug
  press), an extrusion press*
8 der Massestrang
 – *clay column*
9 der Dreher, beim Drehen *n* eines
  Formlings *m*
 – *thrower throwing a ball (bat) of
  clay*

10 der Hubel
 – *slug of clay*
11 die Drehscheibe; *ähnl.:* die
  Töpferscheibe
 – *turntable; sim.: potter's wheel*
12 die Filterpresse
 – *filter press*
13 der Massekuchen
 – *filter cake*
14 das Drehen, mit der
  Drehschablone
 – *jiggering, with a profiling tool;
  sim.: jollying*
15 die Gießform, zum Schlickerguß *m*
 – *plaster mould (Am. mold) for slip
  casting*
16 die Rundtischglasiermaschine
 – *turntable glazing machine*
17 der Porzellanmaler
 – *porcelain painter (china painter)*
18 die handgemalte Vase
 – *hand-painted vase*
19 der Bossierer (Retuscheur)
 – *repairer*
20 das Bossierholz (Modellierholz, der
  Bossiergriffel)
 – *pallet (modelling, Am. modeling,
  tool)*
21 die Porzellanscherben *f* (Scherben)
 – *shards (sherds, potsherds)*

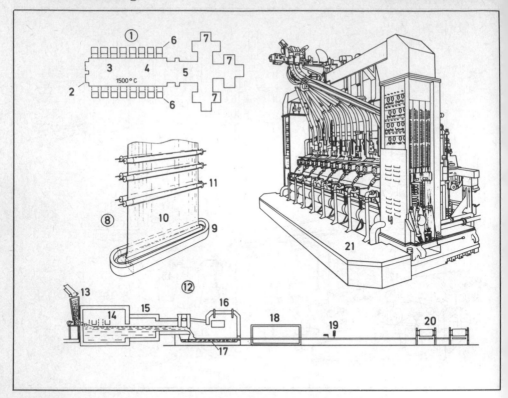

1-20 die Tafelglasherstellung
(Flachglasherstellung)
- *sheet glass production (flat glass production)*
1 die Glasschmelzwanne für das Fourcault-Verfahren [Schema]
- *glass furnace (tank furnace) for the Fourcault process [diagram]*
2 die Einlegevorbauten *m*, für die Gemengeeingabe
- *filling end, for feeding in the batch (frit)*
3 die Schmelzwanne
- *melting bath*
4 die Läuterwanne
- *refining bath (fining bath)*
5 die Arbeitswannen *f*
- *working baths (working area)*
6 die Brenner
- *burners*
7 die Ziehmaschinen *f*
- *drawing machines*
8 die Fourcault-Glasziehmaschine
- *Fourcault glass-drawing machine*
9 die Ziehdüse
- *slot*
10 das aufsteigende Glasband
- *glass ribbon (ribbon of glass, sheet of glass) being drawn upwards*
11 die Transportwalzen *f*
- *rollers (drawing rolls)*
12 der Floatglasprozeß [Schema]
- *float glass process*

13 der Gemengetrichter
- *batch (frit) feeder (funnel)*
14 die Schmelzwanne
- *melting bath*
15 die Abstehwanne
- *cooling tank*
16 das Floatbad unter Schutzgas *n*
- *float bath in a protective inert-gas atmosphere*
17 das geschmolzene Zinn
- *molten tin*
18 der Rollenkühlofen
- *annealing lehr*
19 die Schneidevorrichtung
- *automatic cutter*
20 die Stapler *m*
- *stacking machines*
21 die IS-(Individual-section-)Maschine, eine Flaschenblasmaschine
- *IS (individual-section) machine, a bottle-making machine*

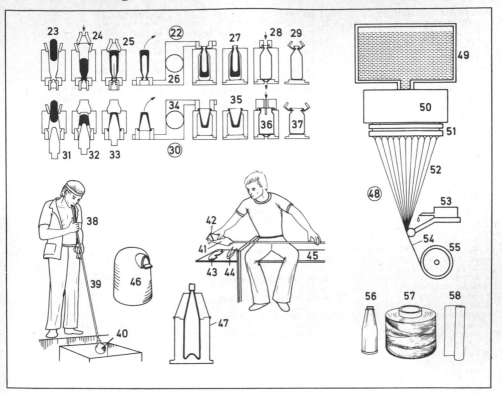

22-37 die Blasschemata *n*
- *blowing processes*
22 der doppelte Blasprozeß
- *blow-and-blow process*
23 die Schmelzgutaufgabe
- *introduction of the gob of molten glass*
24 das Vorblasen
- *first blowing*
25 das Gegenblasen
- *suction*
26 die Überführung von der Preßform in die Blasform
- *transfer from the parison mould (Am. mold) to the blow mould (Am. mold)*
27 die Wiedererhitzung
- *reheating*
28 das Blasen (die Vakuumformung)
- *blowing (suction, final shaping)*
29 der Fertiggutausstoß
- *delivery of the completed vessel*
30 das Preß- und Blasverfahren
- *press-and-blow process*
31 die Schmelzgutaufgabe
- *introduction of the gob of molten glass*
32 der Preßstempel
- *plunger*
33 das Pressen
- *pressing*
34 die Überführung von der Preßform in die Blasform
- *transfer from the press mould (Am. mold) to the blow mould (Am. mold)*

35 das Wiedererhitzen
- *reheating*
36 das Blasen (die Vakuumformung)
- *blowing (suction, final shaping)*
37 der Fertiggutausstoß
- *delivery of the completed vessel*
38-47 das Glasmachen (Mundblasen, die Formarbeit)
- *glassmaking (glassblowing, glassblowing by hand, glass forming)*
38 der Glasmacher (Glasbläser)
- *glassmaker (glassblower)*
39 die Glasmacherpfeife
- *blowing iron*
40 das Kübel (Kölbchen)
- *gob*
41 das mundgeblasene Kelchglas
- *hand-blown goblet*
42 die Pitsche, zum Formen *n* des Kelchglasfußes *m*
- *clappers for shaping the base (foot) of the goblet*
43 die Fassonlehre
- *trimming tool*
44 das Zwackeisen
- *tongs*
45 der Glasmacherstuhl
- *glassmaker's chair (gaffer's chair)*
46 der verdeckte Glashafen
- *covered glasshouse pot*
47 die Form, zum Einblasen *n* des vorgeformten Kübels *n*

- *mould (Am. mold), into which the parison is blown*
48-55 die Herstellung von Textilglas *n*
- *production of glass fibre (Am. glass fiber)*
48 das Düsenziehverfahren
- *continuous filament process*
49 der Glasschmelzofen
- *glass furnace*
50 die Wanne mit Glasschmelze *f*
- *bushing containing molten glass*
51 die Lochnippel *m*
- *bushing tips*
52 die Textilglas-Elementarfäden *m*
- *glass filaments*
53 die Schlichtung
- *sizing*
54 der Spinnfaden
- *strand (thread)*
55 der Spulenkopf
- *spool*
56-58 Textilglasprodukte *n*
- *glass fibre (Am. glass fiber) products*
56 das Textilglasgarn
- *glass yarn (glass thread)*
57 das gefachte Textilglasgarn
- *sleeved glass yarn (glass thread)*
58 die Textilglasmatte
- *glass wool*

1-13 die Baumwollanlieferung
- *supply of cotton*
1 die erntereife Baumwollkapsel
- *ripe cotton boll*
2 der fertige Garnkötzer (Cops, Kops, die Bobine)
- *full cop*
- *(cop wound with weft yarn)*
3 der gepreßte Baumwollballen
- *compressed cotton bale*
4 die Juteumhüllung
- *jute wrapping*
5 der Eisenreifen
- *steel band*
6 die Partienummern *f* des Ballens *m*
- *identification mark of the bale*
7 der Mischballenöffner (Baumwollereiniger)
- *bale opener (bale breaker)*
8 das Zuführlattentuch
- *cotton-feeding brattice*
9 der Füllkasten
- *cotton feed*
10 der Staubsaugtrichter
- *dust extraction fan*
11 die Rohrleitung, zum Staubkeller *m*
- *duct to the dust-collecting chamber*
12 der Antriebsmotor
- *drive motor*
13 das Sammellattentuch
- *conveyor brattice*
14 die Doppelschlagmaschine
- *double scutcher (machine with two scutchers)*
15 die Wickelmulde
- *lap cradle*
16 der Kompressionshaken (Pressionshaken)
- *rack head*
17 der Maschineneinschalthebel
- *starting handle*
18 das Handrad, zum Heben *n* und Senken *n* der Pressionshaken *m*
- *handwheel, for raising and lowering the rack head*
19 das bewegliche Wickelumschlagbrett
- *movable lap-turner*
20 die Preßwalzen *f*
- *calender rollers*
21 die Haube, für das Siebtrommelpaar
- *cover for the perforated cylinders*
22 der Staubkanal
- *dust escape flue (dust discharge flue)*
23 die Antriebsmotoren *m*
- *drive motors (beater drive motors)*
24 die Welle, zum Antrieb *m* der Schlagflügel *m*
- *beater driving shaft*
25 der dreiflüglige Schläger
- *three-blade beater (Kirschner beater)*
26 der Stabrost
- *grid [for impurities to drop]*
27 der Speisezylinder
- *pedal roller (pedal cylinder)*
28 der Mengenregulierhebel, ein Pedalhebel *m*
- *control lever for the pedal roller, a pedal lever*
29 das stufenlose Getriebe
- *variable change-speed gear*
30 der Konuskasten
- *cone drum box*

31 das Hebelsystem, für die Materialregulierung
- *stop and start levers for the hopper*
32 die Holzdruckwalze
- *wooden hopper delivery roller*
33 der Kastenspeiser
- *hopper feeder*
34 die Deckelkrempel (Karde, Kratze)
- *carding machine (card, carding engine)*
35 die Kardenkanne, zur Ablage des Kardenbandes *n*
- *card can (carding can), for receiving the coiled sliver*
36 der Kannenstock
- *can holder*
37 die Kalanderwalzen *f*
- *calender rollers*
38 das Kardenband
- *carded sliver (card sliver)*
39 der Hackerkamm
- *vibrating doffer comb*
40 der Abstellhebel
- *start-stop lever*
41 die Schleiflager *n*
- *grinding-roller bearing*
42 der Abnehmer
- *doffer*
43 die Trommel (der Tambour)
- *cylinder*
44 die Deckelputzvorrichtung
- *flat clearer*
45 die Deckelkette
- *flats*
46 die Spannrollen *f*, für die Deckelkette
- *supporting pulleys for the flats*
47 der Batteurwickel
- *scutcher lap (carded lap)*
48 das Wickelgestell
- *scutcher lap holder*
49 der Antriebsmotor, mit Flachriemen *m*
- *drive motor with flat belt*
50 die Hauptantriebsscheibe
- *main drive pulley (fast-and-loose drive pulley)*
51 das Arbeitsprinzip der Karde
- *principle of the card (of the carding engine)*
52 der Speisezylinder
- *fluted feed roller*
53 der Vorreißer (Briseur)
- *licker-in (taker-in, licker-in roller)*
54 der Vorreißerrost
- *licker-in undercasing*
55 der Tambourrost
- *cylinder undercasing*
56 die Kämmaschine
- *combing machine (comber)*
57 der Getriebekasten
- *drive gearbox (driving gear)*
58 der Kehrstreckenwickel
- *laps ready for combing*
59 die Bandverdichtung
- *calender rollers*
60 das Streckwerk
- *comber draw box*
61 die Zähluhr
- *counter*
62 die Kammzugablage
- *coiler top*
63 das Arbeitsprinzip der Kämmaschine
- *principle of the comber*
64 das Krempelband
- *lap*

65 die Unterzange
- *bottom nipper*
66 die Oberzange
- *top nipper*
67 der Fixkamm
- *top comb*
68 der Kreiskamm
- *combing cylinder*
69 das Ledersegment
- *plain part of the cylinder*
70 das Nadelsegment
- *needled part of the cylinder*
71 die Abreißzylinder *m*
- *detaching rollers*
72 der Kammzug
- *carded and combed sliver*

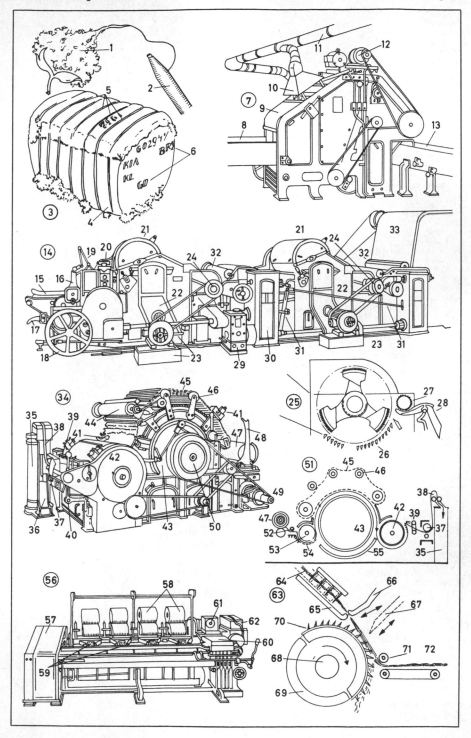

1 **die Strecke**
- *draw frame*
2 der Getriebekasten, mit
eingebautem Motor *m*
- *gearbox with built-in motor*
3 die Kardenkannen *f*
- *sliver cans*
4 die Kontaktwalze, zur Abstellung
der Maschine bei Bandbruch *m*
- *broken thread detector roller*
5 die Doublierung (Doppelung) der
Krempelbänder *n*
- *doubling of the slivers*
6 der Maschinenabstellhebel
- *stopping handle*
7 die Streckwerkabdeckung
- *draw frame cover*
8 die Kontrollampen *f*
- *indicator lamps (signal lights)*
9 das einfache
Vierzylinderstreckwerk [Schema]
- *simple four-roller draw frame
[diagram]*
10 die Unterzylinder *m* (gerillte
Stahlwalzen *f*)
- *bottom rollers (lower rollers), fluted
steel rollers*
11 die mit Kunststoff bezogenen
Oberzylinder *m*
- *top rollers (upper rollers) covered
with synthetic rubber*
12 das grobe Band, vor dem Strecken *n*
- *doubled slivers before drafting*
13 das durch Streckwalzen *f*
verzogene dünne Band
- *thin sliver after drafting*
14 das Hochverzugstreckwerk [Schema]
- *high-draft system (high-draft draw
frame) [diagram]*
15 die Lunteneinführung
(Vorgarneinführung)
- *feeding-in of the sliver*
16 das Laufleder
- *leather apron (composition apron)*
17 die Wendeschiene
- *guide bar*
18 die Durchzugwalze
- *light top roller (guide roller)*
19 der Hochverzugflyer
- *high-draft speed frame (fly frame,
slubbing frame)*
20 die Streckenkannen *f*
- *sliver cans*
21 das Einlaufen der Streckenbänder
n ins Streckwerk *n*
- *feeding of the slivers to the drafting
rollers*
22 das Flyerstreckwerk, mit
Putzdeckel *m*
- *drafting rollers with top clearers*
23 die Flyerspulen *f*
- *roving bobbins*
24 die Flyerin
- *fly frame operator (operative)*
25 der Flyerflügel
- *flyer*
26 das Maschinenendschild
- *frame end plate*
27 der Mittelflyer
- *intermediate yarn-forming frame*
28 das Spulenaufsteckgatter
- *bobbin creel (creel)*
29 die aus dem Streckwerk *n*
austretende Flyerlunte
- *roving emerging from the drafting
rollers*

30 der Spulenantriebswagen
- *lifter rail (separating rail)*
31 der Spindelantrieb
- *spindle drive*
32 der Maschinenabstellhebel
- *stopping handle*
33 der Getriebekasten, mit
aufgesetztem Motor *m*
- *gearbox, with built-on motor*
34 **die Ringspinnmaschine** (Trossel)
- *ring frame (ring spinning frame)*
35 der Kollektordrehstrommotor
- *three-phase motor*
36 die Motorgrundplatte
- *motor base plate (bedplate)*
37 der Transportierring für den Motor
- *lifting bolt [for motor removal]*
38 der Spinnregler
- *control gear for spindle speed*
39 der Getriebekasten
- *gearbox*
40 die Wechselradschere zur
Änderung der
Garnnummerfeinheit
- *change wheels for varying the
spindle speed [to change the yarn
count]*
41 das volle Spulengatter
- *full creel*
42 die Wellen *f* und Stützen *f* für den
Ringbankantrieb
- *shafts and levers for raising and
lowering the ring rail*
43 die Spindeln *f*, mit den
Fadentrennern *m* (Separatoren)
- *spindles with separators*
44 der Sammelkasten der
Fadenabsaugung
- *suction box connected to the front
roller underclearers*
45 **die Standardspindel** der
Ringspinnmaschine
- *standard ring spindle*
46 der Spindelschaft
- *spindle shaft*
47 das Rollenlager
- *roller bearing*
48 der Wirtel
- *wharve (pulley)*
49 der Spindelhaken
- *spindle catch*
50 die Spindelbank
- *spindle rail*
51 die Spinnorgane *n*
- *ring and traveller* (Am. *traveler*)
52 die nackte Spindel
- *top of the ring tube (of the bobbin)*
53 das Garn (der Faden)
- *yarn (thread)*
54 der auf der Ringbank eingelassene
Spinnring
- *ring fitted into the ring rail*
55 der Läufer (Traveller)
- *traveller* (Am. *traveler*)
56 das aufgewundene Garn
- *yarn wound onto the bobbin*
57 **die Zwirnmaschine**
- *doubling frame*
58 das Gatter, mit den aufgesteckten
Fachkreuzspulen *f*
- *creel, with cross-wound cheeses*
59 das Lieferwerk
- *delivery rollers*
60 die Zwirnkopse *m*
- *bobbins of doubled yarn*

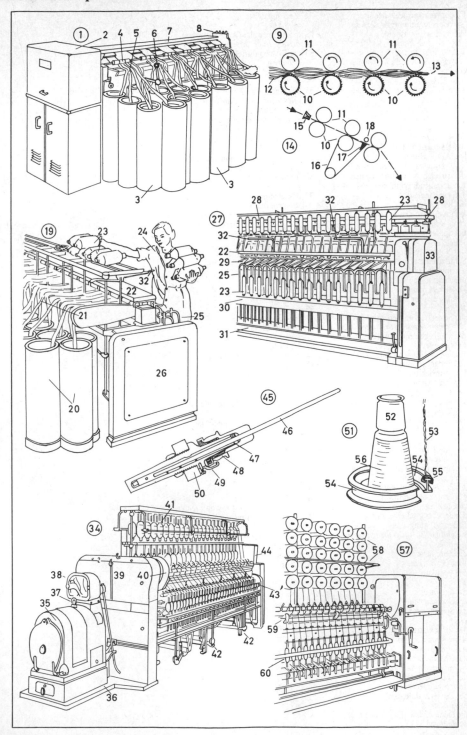

1-57 die Webereivorbereitung
- *processes preparatory to weaving*
1 die Kreuzspulmaschine
- *cone-winding frame*
2 das Wandergebläse
- *travelling (Am. traveling) blower*
3 die Laufschiene, für das
Wandergebläse
- *guide rail, for the travelling (Am.
traveling) blower*
4 das Ventilatorgebläse
- *blowing assembly*
5 die Ausblasöffnung
- *blower aperture*
6 das Haltegestänge, für die
Ventilatorschiene
- *superstructure for the blower rail*
7 die Anzeigevorrichtung, für den
Kreuzspulendurchmesser
- *full-cone indicator*
8 die Kreuzspule, mit
kreuzgeführten Fäden *m*
- *cross-wound cone*
9 der Spulenrahmen
- *cone creel*
10 der Nutenzylinder (die
Schlitztrommel)
- *grooved cylinder*
11 der Zickzackschlitz, zur
Fadenverkreuzung
- *guiding slot for cross-winding the
threads*
12 der Seitentragrahmen, mit Motor *m*
- *side frame, housing the motor*
13 der Stellhebel, zum Abrücken *n* der
Kreuzspule
- *tension and slub-catching device*
14 das Endgestell, mit
Filtereinrichtung *f*
- *off-end framing with filter*
15 der Trosselkops
- *yarn package, a ring tube or mule cop*
16 der Kopsbehälter
- *yarn package container*
17 der Ein- und Ausrücker
- *starting and stopping lever*
18 der Bügel, zur Selbsteinfädlung
- *self-threading guide*
19 die automat. Abstellvorrichtung,
bei Fadenbruch *m*
- *broken thread stop motion*
20 der Schlitzfadenreiniger
- *thread clearer*
21 die Belastungsscheibe, zur
Fadenspannung
- *weighting disc (disk) for tensioning
the thread*
22 die Zettelmaschine
- *warping machine*
23 der Ventilator
- *fan*
24 die Kreuzspule
- *cross-wound cone*
25 das Spulengatter
- *creel*
26 der verstellbare Kamm
(Expansionskamm)
- *adjustable comb*
27 das Zettelmaschinengestell
- *warping machine frame*
28 der Garnmeterzähler
- *yarn length recorder*
29 der Zettel (Zettelbaum)
- *warp beam*
30 die Baumscheibe (Fadenscheibe)
- *beam flange*

31 die Schutzleiste
- *guard rail*
32 die Anlegewalze (Antriebswalze)
- *driving drum (driving cylinder)*
33 der Riemenantrieb
- *belt drive*
34 der Motor
- *motor*
35 das Einschaltfußbrett
- *release for starting the driving drum*
36 die Schraube, zur
Kammbreiteveränderung
- *screw for adjusting the comb setting*
37 die Nadeln *f*, zur Abstellung bei
Fadenbruch *m*
- *drop pins, for stopping the machine
when a thread breaks*
38 die Streifstange
- *guide bar*
39 das Klemmwalzenpaar
- *drop pin rollers*
40 die Indigofärbeschlichtmaschine
- *indigo dying and sizing machine*
41 das Ablaufgestell
- *take-off stand*
42 der Zettelbaum
- *warp beam*
43 die Zettelkette
- *warp*
44 der Netztrog
- *wetting trough*
45 die Tauchwalze
- *immersion roller*
46 die Quetschwalze
- *squeeze roller (mangle)*
47 der Färbetrog
- *dye liquor padding trough*
48 der Luftgang
- *air oxidation passage*
49 der Spültrog
- *washing trough*
50 der Zylindertrockner für die
Vortrocknung
- *drying cylinders for pre-drying*
51 der Speicherkompensator
- *tension compensator (tension
equalizer)*
52 die Schlichtmaschine
- *sizing machine*
53 der Zylindertrockner
- *drying cylinders*
54 das Trockenteilfeld
- *for cotton: stenter; for wool: tenter*
55 die Bäummaschine
- *beaming machine*
56 der geschlichtete Kettbaum
- *sized warp beam*
57 die Preßrollen *f*
- *rollers*

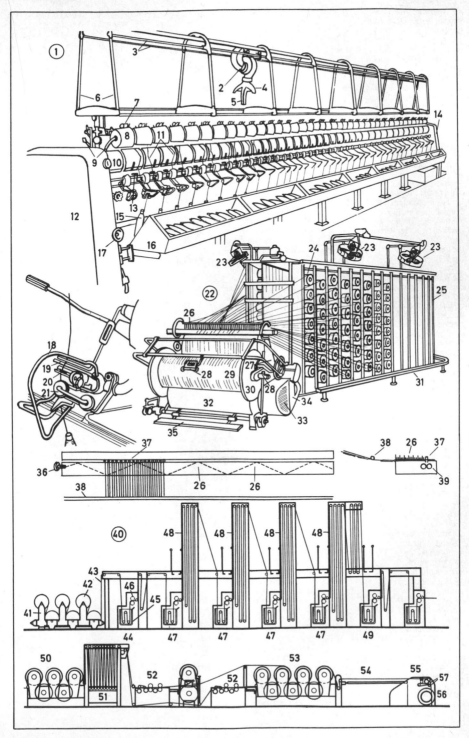

166 Weberei II

Weaving II 166

1 die Webmaschine (der Webstuhl)
- *weaving machine (automatic loom)*
2 der Tourenzähler
- *pick counter (tachometer)*
3 die Führungsschiene der Schäfte *m*
- *shaft (heald shaft, heald frame) guide*
4 die Schäfte *m*
- *shafts (heald shafts, heald frames)*
5 der Schußwechselautomat (Revolverwechsel), zum Kanettenwechsel *m*
- *rotary battery for weft replenishment*
6 der Ladendeckel
- *sley (slay) cap*
7 die Schußspule
- *weft pirn*
8 der Ein- und Ausrückhebel
- *starting and stopping handle*
9 der Schützenkasten, mit Webschützen *m*
- *shuttle box, with shuttles*
10 das Blatt (Riet, der Rietkamm)
- *reed*
11 die Leiste (Warenkante, Webkante, der Webrand, Rand)
- *selvedge (selvage)*
12 die Ware (das fertige Gewebe)
- *cloth (woven fabric)*
13 der Breithalter
- *temple (cloth temple)*
14 der elektr. Fadenfühler
- *electric weft feeler*
15 das Schwungrad
- *flywheel*
16 das Brustbaumbrett
- *breast beam board*
17 der Schlagstock (Schlagarm)
- *picking stick (pick stick)*
18 der Elektromotor
- *electric motor*
19 die Wechselräder *n*
- *cloth take-up motion*
20 der Warenbaum
- *cloth roller (fabric roller)*
21 der Hülsenkasten, für leere Kanetten *f*
- *can for empty pirns*
22 der Schlagriemen, zur Betätigung des Schlagarms *m*
- *lug strap, for moving the picking stick*
23 der Sicherungskasten
- *fuse box*
24 das Webstuhlgestell (der Webstuhlrahmen)
- *loom framing*
25 die Metallspitze
- *metal shuttle tip*
26 der Webschütz
- *shuttle*
27 die Litze (Drahtlitze)
- *heald (heddle, wire heald, wire heddle)*
28 das Fadenauge (Litzenauge)
- *eye (eyelet, heald eyelet, heddle eyelet)*
29 das Fadenauge (Schützenauge)
- *eye (shuttle eye)*
30 die Kanette (Spulenhülse)
- *pirn*
31 die Metallhülse, für Tastfühlerkontakt *m*
- *metal contact sleeve for the weft feeler*

32 die Aussparung, für den Tastfühler
- *slot for the feeler*
33 die Kanettenklemmfeder
- *spring-clip pirn holder*
34 der Kettfadenwächter
- *drop wire*
35 die Webmaschine (der Webstuhl) [schemat. Seitenansicht]
- *weaving machine (automatic loom) [side elevation]*
36 die Schaftrollen *f*
- *heald shaft guiding wheels*
37 der Streichbaum
- *backrest*
38 die Teilschiene
- *lease rods*
39 die Kette (der Kettfaden)
- *warp (warp thread)*
40 das Fach (Webfach)
- *shed*
41 die Weblade
- *sley (slay)*
42 der Ladenklotz
- *race board*
43 der Stecher für die Abstellvorrichtung
- *stop rod blade for the stop motion*
44 der Prellklotz
- *bumper steel*
45 die Pufferabstellstange
- *bumper steel stop rod*
46 der Brustbaum
- *breast beam*
47 die Riffelwalze
- *cloth take-up roller*
48 der Kettbaum
- *warp beam*
49 die Garnscheibe (Baumscheibe)
- *beam flange*
50 die Hauptwelle
- *crankshaft*
51 das Kurbelwellenzahnrad
- *crankshaft wheel*
52 die Ladenschubstange
- *connector*
53 die Ladenstelze
- *sley (slay)*
54 der Spanner (Schaftspanner)
- *lam rods*
55 das Exzenterwellenzahnrad
- *camshaft wheel*
56 die Exzenterwelle
- *camshaft (tappet shaft)*
57 der Exzenter
- *tappet (shedding tappet)*
58 der Exzentertritthebel
- *treadle lever*
59 die Kettbaumbremse
- *let-off motion*
60 die Bremsscheibe
- *beam motion control*
61 das Bremsseil
- *rope of the warp let-off motion*
62 der Bremshebel
- *let-off weight lever*
63 das Bremsgewicht
- *control weight [for the treadle]*
64 der Picker mit Leder- oder Kunstharzpolster *n*
- *picker with leather or bakelite pad*
65 der Schlagarmpuffer
- *picking stick buffer*
66 der Schlagexzenter
- *picking cam*
67 die Exzenterrolle
- *picking bowl*

68 die Schlagstock-Rückholfeder
- *picking stick return spring*

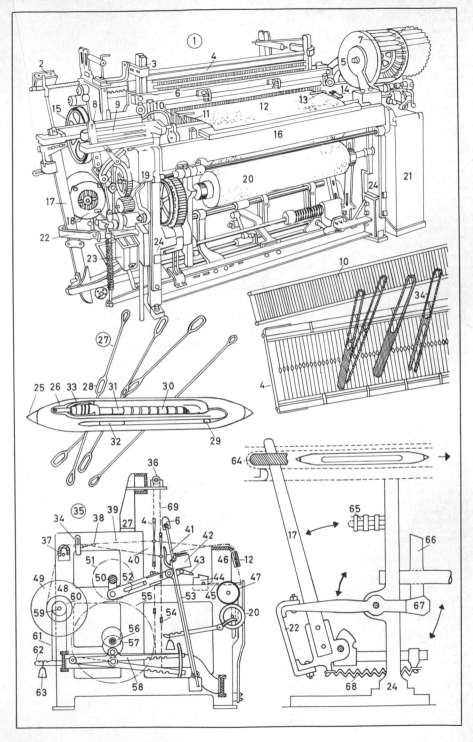

1-66 die Strumpffabrik
- *hosiery mill*
1 der Rundstuhl (die Rundstrickmaschine), zur Herstellung von Schlauchware *f*
- *circular knitting machine for the manufacture of tubular fabric*
2 die Fadenführerhaltestange
- *yarn guide support post (thread guide support post)*
3 der Fadenführer
- *yarn guide (thread guide)*
4 die Flaschenspule
- *bottle bobbin*
5 der Fadenspanner
- *yarn-tensioning device*
6 das Schloß
- *yarn feeder*
7 das Handrad, zur Führung des Fadens *m* hinter die Nadeln *f*
- *handwheel for rotating the machine by hand*
8 der Nadelzylinder
- *needle cylinder (cylindrical needle holder)*
9 der Warenschlauch (die Schlauchware, Maschenware)
- *tubular fabric*
10 der Warenbehälter
- *fabric drum (fabric box, fabric container)*
11 der Nadelzylinder [Schnitt]
- *needle cylinder (cylindrical needle holder) [section]*
12 die radial angeordneten Zungennadeln *f*
- *latch needles arranged in a circle*
13 der Schloßmantel
- *cam housing*
14 die Schloßteile *n* od. *m*
- *needle cams*
15 der Nadelkanal
- *needle trick*
16 der Zylinderdurchmesser; zugleich: Warenschlauchbreite *f*
- *cylinder diameter (also diameter of tubular fabric)*
17 der Faden (das Garn)
- *thread (yarn)*
18 die Cottonmaschine, zur Damenstrumpffabrikation
- *Cotton's patent flat knitting machine for ladies' fully-fashioned hose*
19 die Musterkette
- *pattern control chain*
20 der Seitentragrahmen
- *side frame*
21 die Fontur (der Arbeitsbereich); mehrfonturig: gleichzeitige Herstellung *f* mehrerer Strümpfe *m*
- *knitting head; with several knitting heads: simultaneous production of several stockings*
22 die Griffstange
- *starting rod*
23 die Raschelmaschine (der Fangkettstuhl)
- *Raschel warp-knitting machine*
24 die Kette (der Kettbaum)
- *warp (warp beam)*
25 der Teilbaum
- *yarn-distributing (yarn-dividing) beam*
26 die Teilscheibe
- *beam flange*

27 die Nadelreihe (Zungennadelreihe)
- *row of needles*
28 der Nadelbarren
- *needle bar*
29 die Ware (Raschelware) [Gardinen- und Netzstoffe *m*],, auf dem Warenbaum *m*
- *fabric (Raschel fabric) [curtain lace and net fabrics] on the fabric roll*
30 das Handtriebrad
- *handwheel*
31 die Antriebsräder *n* und der Motor
- *motor drive gear*
32 das Preßgewicht
- *take-down weight*
33 der Rahmen (das Traggestell)
- *frame*
34 die Grundplatte
- *base plate*
35 die Flachstrickmaschine (Handstrickmaschine)
- *hand flat (flat-bed) knitting machine*
36 der Faden (das Garn)
- *thread (yarn)*
37 die Rückholfeder
- *return spring*
38 das Haltegestänge, für die Federn
- *support for springs*
39 der verschiebbare Schlitten
- *carriage*
40 das Schloß
- *feeder-selecting device*
41 die Schiebegriffe *m*
- *carriage handles*
42 die Maschengrößeeinstellskala
- *scale for regulating size of stitches*
43 der Tourenzähler
- *course counter (tachometer)*
44 der Vorsetzhebel
- *machine control lever*
45 die Laufschiene
- *carriage rail*
46 die obere Nadelreihe
- *back row of needles*
47 die untere Nadelreihe
- *front row of needles*
48 der Warenabzug (die Ware)
- *knitted fabric*
49 die Spannleiste (Abzugleiste)
- *tension bar*
50 das Spanngewicht
- *tension weight*
51 das Nadelbett mit Strickvorgang *m*
- *needle bed showing knitting action*
52 die Zähne *m* des Abschlagkamms *m*
- *teeth of knock-over bit*
53 die parallel angeordneten Nadeln *f*
- *needles in parallel rows*
54 der Fadenführer
- *yarn guide (thread guide)*
55 das Nadelbett
- *needle bed*
56 die Abdeckschiene, über den Zungennadeln *f*
- *retaining plate for latch needles*
57 das Nadelschloß
- *guard cam*
58 der Nadelsenker
- *sinker*
59 der Nadelheber
- *needle-raising cam*
60 der Nadelfuß
- *needle butt*
61 die Zungennadel
- *latch needle*

62 die Masche
- *loop*
63 das Durchstoßen der Nadel durch die Masche
- *pushing the needle through the fabric*
64 das Auflegen des Fadens *m* auf die Nadel durch den Fadenführer
- *yarn guide (thread guide) placing yarn in the needle hook*
65 die Maschenbildung
- *loop formation*
66 das Maschenabschlagen
- *casting off of loop*

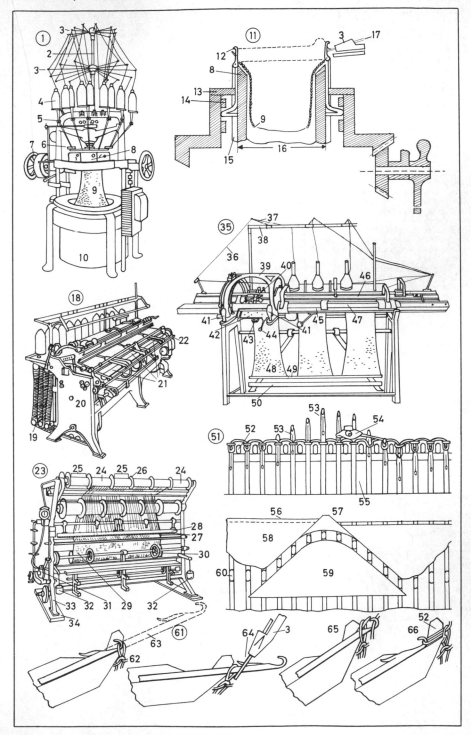

1-65 die Fertigbehandlung von Stoffen *m*
- *finishing*
1 die Zylinderwalke, zur
   Verdichtung der Wollware (des
   Wollgewebes *n*)
- *rotary milling (fulling) machine for
   felting the woollen (Am. woolen)
   fabric*
2 die Gewichtbelastung
- *pressure weights*
3 die obere Zugwalze
- *top milling roller (top fulling roller)*
4 die Antriebsscheibe der unteren
   Zugwalze
- *drive wheel of bottom milling roller
   (bottom fulling roller)*
5 die Warenleitwalze
- *fabric guide roller*
6 die untere Zugwalze
- *bottom milling roller (bottom
   fulling roller)*
7 das Zugbrett (die Brille)
- *draft board*
8 die Breitwaschmaschine, für
   empfindliche Gewebe *n*
- *open-width scouring machine for
   finer fabrics*
9 das Einziehen des Gewebes *n*
- *fabric being drawn off the machine*
10 der Getriebekasten
- *drive gearbox*
11 die Wasserleitung
- *water inlet pipe*
12 die Leitwalze
- *drawing-in roller*
13 der Spannriegel
- *scroll-opening roller*
14 die Pendelzentrifuge, zur
   Gewebeentwässerung
- *pendulum-type hydro-extractor
   (centrifuge), for extracting liquors
   from the fabric*
15 der Grundrahmen
- *machine base*
16 die Säule
- *casing over suspension*
17 das Gehäuse, mit rotierender
   Innentrommel *f*
- *outer casing containing rotating
   cage (rotating basket)*
18 der Zentrifugendeckel
- *hydro-extractor (centrifuge) lid*
19 die Abstellsicherung
- *stop-motion device (stopping
   device)*
20 der Anlauf- und der
   Bremsautomat
- *automatic starting and braking
   device*
21 die Gewebetrockenmaschine
- *for cotton: stenter; for wool: tenter*
22 das feuchte Gewebe
- *air-dry fabric*
23 der Bedienungsstand
- *operator's (operative's) platform*
24 die Gewebebefestigung, durch
   Nadel- oder Kluppenketten *f*
- *feeding of fabric by guides onto
   stenter (tenter) pins or clips*
25 der Elektroschaltkasten
- *electric control panel*
26 der Wareneinlauf in Falten *f*,
   zwecks Eingehens *n* (Schrumpfens,
   Krumpfens) beim Trocknen *n*
- *initial overfeed to produce
   shrink-resistant fabric when dried*

27 das Thermometer
- *thermometer*
28 die Trockenkammer
- *drying section*
29 das Abluftrohr
- *air outlet*
30 der Trocknerauslauf
- *plaiter (fabric-plaiting device)*
31 die Kratzenrauhmaschine, zum
   Aufrauhen *n* der
   Gewebeoberfläche mit Kratzen *f*
   zur Florbildung
- *wire-roller fabric-raising machine
   for producing raised or nap surface*
32 der Antriebskasten
- *drive gearbox*
33 der ungerauhte Stoff
- *unraised cloth*
34 die Rauhwalzen *f*
- *wire-covered rollers*
35 die Gewebeablegevorrichtung (der
   Facher)
- *plaiter (cuttling device)*
36 die gerauhte Ware
- *raised fabric*
37 die Warenbank
- *plaiting-down platform*
38 die Muldenpresse, zum
   Gewebebügeln *n*
- *rotary press (calendering machine),
   for press finishing*
39 das Tuch
- *fabric*
40 die Schaltknöpfe *m* und
   Schalträder *n*
- *control buttons and control wheels*
41 die geheizte Preßwalze
- *heated press bowl*
42 die Gewebeschermaschine
- *rotary cloth-shearing machine*
43 die Scherfasernabsaugung
- *suction slot, for removing loose
   fibres (Am. fibers)*
44 das Schermesser (der
   Scherzylinder)
- *doctor blade (cutting cylinder)*
45 das Schutzgitter
- *protective guard*
46 die rotierende Bürste
- *rotating brush*
47 die Stoffrutsche
- *curved scray entry*
48 das Schalttrittbrett
- *treadle control*
49 die Dekatiermaschine, zur
   Erzielung nichtschrumpfender
   Stoffe *m*
- *[non-shrinking] decatizing
   (decating) fabric-finishing
   machine*
50 die Dekatierwalze
- *perforated decatizing (decating)
   cylinder*
51 das Stück
- *piece of fabric*
52 die Kurbel
- *cranked control handle*
53 die
   Zehnfarben-Walzendruckmaschine
   (Gewebedruckmaschine)
- *ten-colour (Am. color) roller
   printing machine*
54 der Maschinengrundrahmen
- *base of the machine*
55 der Motor
- *drive motor*

56 das Mitläufertuch
- *blanket [of rubber or felt]*
57 die Druckware
- *fabric after printing (printed
   fabric)*
58 die Elektroschaltanlage
- *electric control panel (control unit)*
59 der Gewebefilmdruck
- *screen printing*
60 der fahrbare Schablonenkasten
- *mobile screen frame*
61 der Abstreicher (die Rakel)
- *squeegee*
62 die Druckschablone
- *pattern stencil*
63 der Drucktisch
- *screen table*
64 das aufgeklebte, unbedruckte
   Gewebe
- *fabric gummed down on table
   ready for printing*
65 der Textildrucker
- *screen printing operator (operative)*

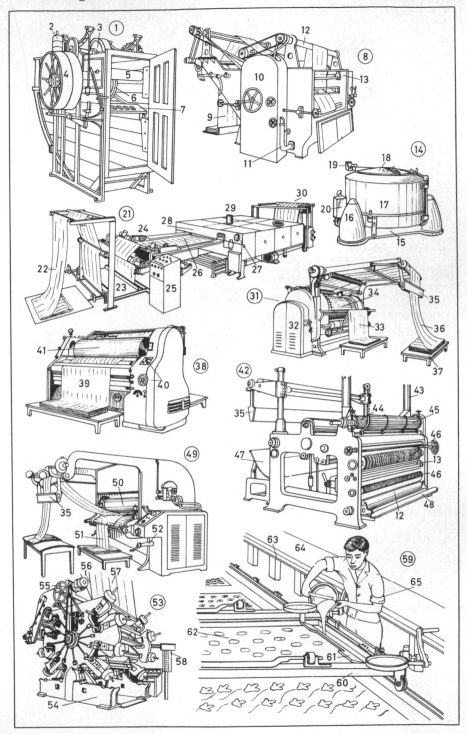

1-34 die Herstellung von
Viskosefasern *f*
(Viskosefilamentgarn *n*) und
Spinnfasern *f* im Viskoseverfahren *n*
- *manufacture of* **continuous filament**
and staple fibre *(Am. fiber) viscose*
rayon yarns by means of the viscose
process
1-12 vom Rohmaterial *n* zur Viskose
- *from raw material to viscose rayon*
1 das Ausgangsmaterial [Buchen-
und Fichtenzellstoff *m* in Blättern
n, Zellstoffplatten *f*]
- *basic material [beech and spruce*
cellulose in form of sheets]
2 die Mischung der Zellstoffblätter *n*
- *mixing cellulose sheets*
3 die Natronlauge
- *caustic soda*
4 das Einlegen der Zellstoffblätter *n*
in Natronlauge *f*
- *steeping cellulose sheets in caustic*
soda
5 das Abpressen der überschüssigen
Natronlauge
- *pressing out excess caustic soda*
6 die Zerfaserung der Zellstoffblätter *n*
- *shredding the cellulose sheets*
7 die Reife der Alkalizellulose
- *maturing (controlled oxidation) of*
the alkali-cellulose crumbs
8 der Schwefelkohlenstoff
- *carbon disulphide (Am. carbon*
disulfide)
9 die Sulfidierung (Umwandlung der
Alkalizellulose in
Zellulosexanthogenat *n*)
- *conversion of alkali-cellulose into*
cellulose xanthate
10 die Auflösung des Xanthogenats *n*
in Natronlauge *f*, zur Erzeugung
der Viskosespinnlösung
- *dissolving the xanthate in caustic*
soda for the preparation of the
viscose spinning solution
11 die Vakuumlagerkessel *m*
- *vacuum ripening tanks*
12 die Filterpressen *f*
- *filter presses*
13-27 von der Viskosespinnmasse
zum Viskosefilamentgarn *n*
- *from viscose to viscose rayon thread*
13 die Spinnpumpe
- *metering pump*
14 die Spinndüse
- *multi-holed spinneret (spinning jet)*
15 das Spinnbad, zur Verwandlung
der zähflüssigen Viskose *f* in
plastische Zellulosefilamente *n*
- *coagulating (spinning) bath for*
converting (coagulating) viscose
(viscous solution) into solid
filaments
16 die Galette, eine Glasrolle
- *Godet wheel, a glass pulley*
17 die Spinnzentrifuge, zur
Vereinigung der Filamente *n*
- *Topham centrifugal pot (box) for*
twisting the filaments into yarn
18 der Spinnkuchen
- *viscose rayon cake*
19-27 die Behandlung des
Spinnkuchens *m*
- *processing of the cake*
19 die Entsäuerung
- *washing*

20 die Entschwefelung
- *desulphurizing (desulphurization,*
Am. *desulfurizing, desulfurization)*
21 das Bleichen
- *bleaching*
22 das Avivieren (Weich- und
Geschmeidigmachen, die
Avivierung)
- *treating of cake to give filaments*
softness and suppleness
23 das Schleudern, zur Entfernung
der überschüssigen Badflüssigkeit
- *hydro-extraction to remove surplus*
moisture
24 das Trocknen, in der
Trockenkammer
- *drying in heated room*
25 das Spulen (die Spulerei)
- *winding yarn from cake into cone*
form
26 die Spulmaschine
- *cone-winding machine*
27 das Viskosefilamentgarn auf
konischer Kreuzspule zur textilen
Weiterverarbeitung
- *viscose rayon yarn on cone ready*
for use
28-34 von der Viskosespinnlösung zur
Spinnfaser
- *from viscose spinning solution to*
viscose rayon staple fibre (Am.
fiber)
28 das Kabel
- *filament tow*
29 die Traufenwascheinrichtung
- *overhead spray washing plant*
30 das Schneidwerk, zum Schneiden *n*
des Kabels *n* auf eine bestimmte
Länge
- *cutting machine for cutting*
filament tow to desired length
31 der Faserbandetagentrockner
- *multiple drying machine for cut-up*
staple fibre (Am. fiber) layer (lap)
32 das Förderband
- *conveyor belt (conveyor)*
33 die Ballenpresse
- *baling press*
34 der versandfertige
Viskosespinnfaserballen
- *bale of viscose rayon ready for*
dispatch (despatch)

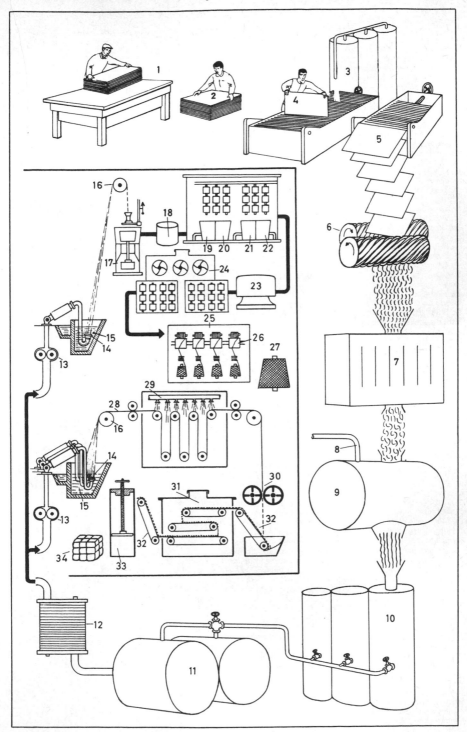

1-62 die Herstellung von
Polyamidfasern
- *manufacture of polyamide (nylon 6,
perlon) fibres* (Am. *fibers*)
1 die Steinkohle [der Rohstoff für die
Polyamidherstellung]
- *coal [raw material for manufacture
of polyamide (nylon 6, perlon)
fibres (Am. fibers)]*
2 die Kokerei, zur
Steinkohletrockendestillation
- *coking plant for dry coal
distillation*
3 die Teer- und Phenolgewinnung
- *extraction of coal tar and phenol*
4 die stufenweise Teerdestillation
- *gradual distillation of tar*
5 der Kühler
- *condenser*
6 die Benzolgewinnung und der
Benzolabtransport
- *benzene extraction and dispatch
(despatch)*
7 das Chlor
- *chlorine*
8 die Benzolchlorierung
- *benzene chlorination*
9 das Chlorbenzol
- *monochlorobenzene
(chlorobenzene)*
10 die Natronlauge
- *caustic soda solution*
11 die Chlorbenzol- und
Natronlaugeverdampfung
- *evaporation of chlorobenzene and
caustic soda*
12 der Reaktionsbehälter (Autoklav)
- *autoclave*
13 das Kochsalz, ein Nebenprodukt *n*
- *sodium chloride (common salt), a
by-product*
14 das Phenol
- *phenol (carbolic acid)*
15 die Wasserstoffzuführung
- *hydrogen inlet*
16 die Phenolhydrierung, zur
Erzeugung von Roh-Cyclohexanol *n*
- *hydrogenation of phenol to produce
raw cyclohexanol*
17 die Destillation
- *distillation*
18 das reine Cyclohexanol
- *pure cyclohexanol*
19 die Dehydrierung
- *oxidation (dehydrogenation)*
20 Bildung *f* von Cyclohexanon *n*
- *formation of cyclohexanone
(pimehinketone)*
21 die Hydroxylaminzuleitung
- *hydroxylamine inlet*
22 Bildung *f* von Cyclohexanonoxim *n*
- *formation of cyclohexanoxime*
23 die Schwefelsäurezusetzung, zur
Molekularumlagerung
- *addition of sulphuric acid* (Am.
*sulfuric acid) to effect molecular
rearrangement*
24 das Ammoniak, zur Aussonderung
der Schwefelsäure
- *ammonia to neutralize sulphuric
acid (Am. sulfuric acid)*
25 Bildung *f* von Laktamöl *n*
- *formation of caprolactam oil*
26 die Ammonsulfatlauge
- *ammonium sulphate (Am.
ammonium sulfate) solution*

27 die Kühlwalze
- *cooling cylinder*
28 das Kaprolaktam
- *caprolactam*
29 die Waage
- *weighing apparatus*
30 der Schmelzkessel
- *melting pot*
31 die Pumpe
- *pump*
32 das (der) Filter
- *filter*
33 die Polymerisation
im Autoklav *m*
(Druckbehälter)
- *polymerization in the autoclave*
34 die Abkühlung des Polyamids *n*
- *cooling of the polyamide*
35 das Schmelzen des Polyamids *n*
- *solidification of the polyamide*
36 der Paternosteraufzug
- *vertical lift* (Am. *elevator)*
37 der Extraktor, zur Trennung des
Polyamids *n* vom restlichen
Laktamöl *n*
- *extractor for separating the
polyamide from the remaining
lactam oil*
38 der Trockner
- *drier*
39 die Polyamidtrockenschnitzel *n*
oder *m*
- *dry polyamide chips*
40 der Schnitzelbehälter
- *chip container*
41 der Schmelzspinnkopf, zum
Schmelzen *n* des Polyamids *n* und
Pressen *n* durch die Spinndüsen *f*
- *top of spinneret for melting the
polyamide and forcing it through
spinneret holes (spinning jets)*
42 die Spinndüsen *f*
- *spinneret holes (spinning jets)*
43 die Erstarrung der
Polyamidfilamente *m*, im
Spinnschacht *m*
- *solidification of polyamide
filaments in the cooling tower*
44 die Garnaufwicklung
- *collection of extruded filaments
into thread form*
45 die Vorzwirnerei
- *preliminary stretching (preliminary
drawing)*
46 die Streckzwirnerei, zur Erzielung
großer Festigkeit *f* und
Dehnbarkeit *f* des
Polyamidfilaments *m*
- *stretching (cold-drawing) of the
polyamide thread to achieve high
tensile strength*
47 die Nachzwirnerei
- *final stretching (final drawing)*
48 die Spulenwäsche
- *washing of yarn packages*
49 der Kammertrockner
- *drying chamber*
50 das Umspulen
- *rewinding*
51 die Kreuzspule
- *polyamide cone*
52 die versandfertige Kreuzspule
- *polyamide cone ready for dispatch
(despatch)*
53 der Mischkessel
- *mixer*

54 die Polymerisation, im
Vakuumkessel *m*
- *polymerization under vacua*
55 das Strecken
- *stretching (drawing)*
56 die Wäscherei
- *washing*
57 die Präparation, zum
Spinnfähigmachen *n*
- *finishing of tow for spinning*
58 die Trocknung des Kabels *n*
- *drying of tow*
59 die Kräuselung des Kabels *n*
- *crimping of tow*
60 das Schneiden des Kabels *n* auf
übliche Faserlänge *f*
- *cutting of tow into normal staple
lengths*
61 die Polyamid-Spinnfaser
- *polyamide staple*
62 der Polyamid-Spinnfaserballen
- *bale of polyamide staple*

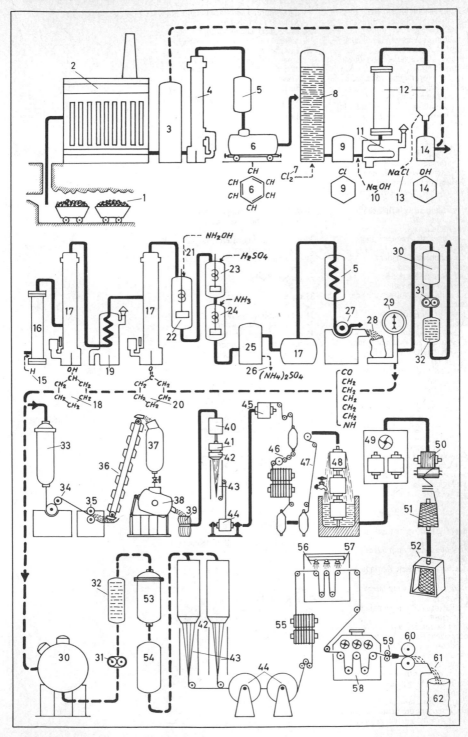

CH
CH⟨6⟩CH
CH　　CH
CH

Cl_2 ⟨7⟩

Cl
⟨9⟩

NaOH
⟨10⟩

NaCl
⟨13⟩

OH
⟨14⟩

NH_2OH

H_2SO_4 ⟨23⟩

NH_3 ⟨24⟩

⟨26⟩ $(NH_4)_2SO_4$

H
OH
⟨15⟩
CH_2 CH_2
CH
CH_2 CH_2
CH_2 CH_2 ⟨18⟩

O
CH_2 CH_2
CH_2 CH_2
CH_2 ⟨20⟩

CO
CH_2
CH_2
CH_2
CH_2
CH_2
NH

1-29 **Gewebebindungen** *f* [schwarze
Quadrate: gehobener Kettfaden,
Schußfaden gesenkt; weiße
Quadrate: gehobener Schußfaden,
Kettfaden gesenkt]
- **weaves** *[black squares: warp thread
raised, weft thread lowered; white
squares: weft thread raised, warp
thread lowered]*
1 die Leinwandbindung
(Tuchbindung) [Gewebedraufsicht]
- *plain weave (tabby weave) [weave
viewed from above]*
2 der Kettfaden
- *warp thread*
3 der Schußfaden
- *weft thread*
4 die Patrone [Vorlage für den
Weber] zur Leinwandbindung
- *draft (point paper design) for plain
weave*
5 der Fadeneinzug in die Schäfte *m*
- *threading draft*
6 der Rieteinzug
- *denting draft (reed-threading
draft)*
7 der gehobene Kettfaden
- *raised warp thread*
8 der gesenkte Kettfaden
- *lowered warp thread*
9 die Schnürung (Aufhängung der
Schäfte *m*)
- *tie-up of shafts in pairs*
10 die Trittfolge
- *treadling diagram*
11 die Patrone zur Panamabindung
(Würfelbindung, englische
Bindung)
- *draft for basket weave (hopsack
weave, matt weave)*
12 der Rapport
(der sich fortlaufend
wiederholende Bindungsteil)
- *pattern repeat*
13 die Patrone für den Schußrips *m*
(Längsrips)
- *draft for warp rib weave*
14 Gewebeschnitt *m* des Schußripses *m*,
ein Kettschnitt *m*
- *section of warp rib fabric, a section
through the warp*
15 der gesenkte Schußfaden
- *lowered weft thread*
16 der gehobene Schußfaden
- *raised weft thread*
17 der erste und zweite Kettfaden
[gehoben]
- *first and second warp threads
[raised]*
18 der dritte und vierte Kettfaden
[gesenkt]
- *third and fourth warp threads
[lowered]*
19 die Patrone für unregelmäßigen
Querrips *m*
- *draft for combined rib weave*
20 der Fadeneinzug in die
Leistenschäfte *m* (Zusatzschäfte
für die Webkante)
- *selvedge (selvage) thread draft
(additional shafts for the selvedge)*
21 der Fadeneinzug in die
Warenschäfte *m*
- *draft for the fabric shafts*
22 die Schnürung der Leistenschäfte *m*
- *tie-up of selvedge (selvage) shafts*

23 die Schnürung der Warenschäfte *m*
- *tie-up of fabric shafts*
24 die Leiste in Tuchbindung *f*
- *selvedge (selvage) in plain weave*
25 Gewebeschnitt *m* des
unregelmäßigen Querripses *m*
- *section through combination rib
weave*
26 die Längstrikotbindung
- *thread interlacing of reversible
warp-faced cord*
27 die Patrone zur
Längstrikotbindung
- *draft (point paper design) for
reversible warp-faced cord*
28 die Gegenbindungsstellen *f*
- *interlacing points*
29 die Waffelbindung für
Waffelmuster *n* in der Ware
- *weaving draft for honeycomb
weave in the fabric*
30-48 **Grundverbindungen** *f* **der
Gewirke** *n* **und Gestricke** *n*
- **basic knits**
30 die Masche, eine offene Masche
- *loop, an open loop*
31 der Kopf
- *head*
32 der Schenkel
- *side*
33 der Fuß
- *neck*
34 die Kopfbindungsstelle
- *head interlocking point*
35 die Fußbindungsstelle
- *neck interlocking point*
36 die geschlossene Masche
- *closed loop*
37 der Henkel
- *mesh [with inlaid yarn]*
38 die schräge Fadenstrecke
- *diagonal floating yarn (diagonal
floating thread)*
39 die Schleife mit Kopfbindung *f*
- *loop interlocking at the head*
40 die Flottung
- *float*
41 die freilaufende Fadenstrecke
- *loose floating yarn (loose floating
thread)*
42 die Maschenreihe
- *course*
43 der Schuß
- *inlaid yarn*
44 der Rechts-links-Fang
- *tuck and miss stitch*
45 der Rechts-links-Perlfang (Köper)
- *pulled-up tuck stitch*
46 der übersetzte
Rechts-links-Perlfang (der
schräge, versetzte Köper)
- *staggered tuck stitch*
47 der Rechts-links-Doppelfang
- *2 x 2 tuck and miss stitch*
48 der Rechts-links-Doppelperlfang
(Doppelköper)
- *double pulled-up tuck stitch*

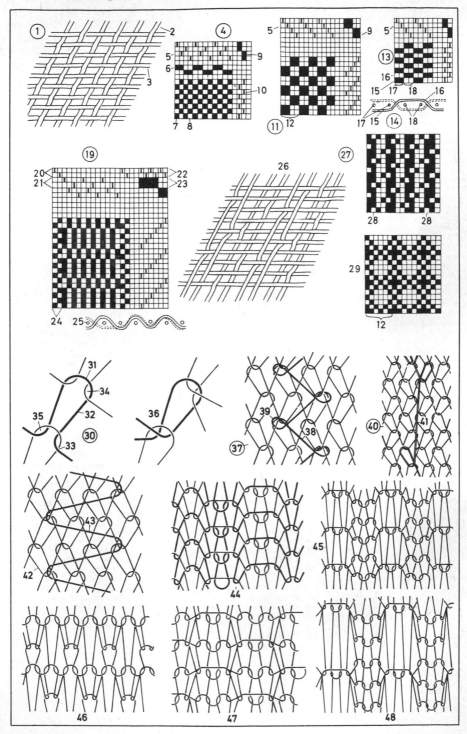

1-52 die Sulfatzellstoffabrik [im Schema]
- *sulphate (Am. sulfate) pulp mill (kraft pulp mill) [in diagram form]*
1 die Hackmaschinen *f* mit Staubabscheider *m*
- *chippers with dust extractor*
2 der Rollsichter
- *rotary screen (riffler)*
3 der Zellenzuteilapparat
- *chip packer (chip distributor)*
4 das Gebläse
- *blower*
5 die Schleudermühle
- *disintegrator (crusher, chip crusher)*
6 die Staubkammer
- *dust-settling chamber*
7 der Zellstoffkocher
- *digester*
8 der Laugenvorwärmer
- *liquor preheater*
9 der Schalthahn
- *control tap*
10 das Schwenkrohr
- *swing pipe*
11 der Diffuseur
- *blow tank (diffuser)*
12 das Spritzventil
- *blow valve*
13 die Diffuseurbütte
- *blow pit (diffuser)*
14 der Terpentinabscheider
- *turpentine separator*
15 der Zentralabscheider
- *centralized separator*
16 der Einspritzkondensator
- *jet condenser (injection condenser)*
17 der Kondensatspeicher
- *storage tank for condensate*
18 der Warmwasserbehälter
- *hot water tank*
19 der Wärmetauscher
- *heat exchanger*
20 der (das) Filter
- *filter*
21 der Vorsortierer
- *presorter*
22 die Sandschleuder
- *centrifugal screen*
23 die umlaufende Sortiermaschine
- *rotary sorter (rotary strainer)*
24 der Entwässerungszylinder
- *concentrator (thickener, decker)*
25 die Bütte
- *vat (chest)*
26 der Sammelbehälter, für Rückwasser *n*
- *collecting tank for backwater (low box)*
27 die Kegelstoffmühle
- *conical refiner (cone refiner, Jordan, Jordan refiner)*
28 der (das) Schwarzlaugenfilter
- *black liquor filter*
29 der Schwarzlaugenbehälter
- *black liquor storage tank*
30 der Kondensator
- *condenser*
31 die Separatoren *m*
- *separators*
32 die Heizkörper *m*
- *heaters (heating elements)*
33 die Laugenpumpe
- *liquor pump*
34 die Dicklaugenpumpe
- *heavy liquor pump*

35 der Mischbehälter
- *mixing tank*
36 der Sulfatbehälter
- *salt cake storage tank (sodium sulphate storage tank)*
37 der Schmelzlöser
- *dissolving tank (dissolver)*
38 der Dampfkessel
- *steam heater*
39 der (das) Elektrofilter
- *electrostatic precipitator*
40 die Luftpumpe
- *air pump*
41 der Behälter für die ungeklärte Grünlauge
- *storage tank for the uncleared green liquor*
42 der Eindicker
- *concentrator (thickener, decker)*
43 der Grünlaugenvorwärmer
- *green liquor preheater*
44 der Wascheindicker
- *concentrator (thickener, decker) for the weak wash liquor (wash water)*
45 der Behälter für die Schwachlauge
- *storage tank for the weak liquor*
46 der Behälter für die Kochlauge
- *storage tank for the cooking liquor*
47 das Rührwerk
- *agitator (stirrer)*
48 der Eindicker
- *concentrator (thickener, decker)*
49 die Kaustifizier-Rührwerke *n*
- *causticizing agitators (causticizing stirrers)*
50 der Klassierer
- *classifier*
51 die Kalklöschtrommel
- *lime slaker*
52 der rückgebrannte Kalk
- *reconverted lime*
53-65 die Holzschleifereianlage [Schema]
- *groundwood mill (mechanical pulp mill) [diagram]*
53 der Stetigschleifer
- *continuous grinder (continuous chain grinder)*
54 der Splitterfänger
- *strainer (knotter)*
55 die Stoffwasserpumpe
- *pulp water pump*
56 die Sandschleuder
- *centrifugal screen*
57 der Sortierer
- *screen (sorter)*
58 der Nachsortierer
- *secondary screen (secondary sorter)*
59 die Grobstoffbütte
- *rejects chest*
60 der Kegelrefiner
- *conical refiner (cone refiner, Jordan, Jordan refiner)*
61 die Entwässerungsmaschine
- *pulp-drying machine (pulp machine)*
62 die Eindickbütte
- *concentrator (thickener, decker)*
63 die Abwasserpumpe
- *waste water pump (white water pump, pulp water pump)*
64 die Dampfschwadenleitung
- *steam pipe*
65 die Wasserleitung
- *water pipe*
66 der Stetigschleifer
- *continuous grinder (continuous chain grinder)*

67 die Vorschubkette
- *feed chain*
68 das Schleifholz
- *groundwood*
69 die Untersetzung für den Vorschubkettenantrieb
- *reduction gear for the feed chain drive*
70 die Steinschärfvorrichtung
- *stone-dressing device*
71 der Schleifstein
- *grinding stone (grindstone, pulpstone)*
72 das Spritzrohr
- *spray pipe*
73 der Steilkegelrefiner (die Kegelmühle)
- *conical refiner (cone refiner, Jordan, Jordan refiner)*
74 das Einstellrad für den Mahlmesserabstand
- *handwheel for adjusting the clearance between the knives (blades)*
75 der rotierende Messerkegel
- *rotating bladed cone (rotating bladed plug)*
76 der stehende Messerkegel
- *stationary bladed shell*
77 der Einlaufanschluß für ungemahlenen Zellstoff *m* bzw. Holzschliff
- *inlet for unrefined cellulose (chemical wood pulp, chemical pulp) or groundwood pulp (mechanical pulp)*
78 der Auslaufanschluß für gemahlenen Zellstoff *m* bzw. Holzschliff
- *outlet for refined cellulose (chemical wood pulp, chemical pulp) or groundwood pulp (mechanical pulp)*
79-86 die Stoffaufbereitungsanlage [Schema]
- *stuff (stock) preparation plant [diagram]*
79 das Förderband zum Aufbringen *n* von Zellstoff *m* bzw. Holzschliff
- *conveyor belt (conveyor) for loading cellulose (chemical wood pulp, chemical pulp) or groundwood pulp (mechanical pulp)*
80 der Zellstoffauflöser
- *pulper*
81 die Ableerbütte
- *dump chest*
82 der Kegelaufschläger
- *cone breaker*
83 die Kegelmühle
- *conical refiner (cone refiner, Jordan, Jordan refiner)*
84 die Reistenmühle
- *refiner*
85 die Fertigbütte
- *stuff chest (stock chest)*
86 die Maschinenbütte
- *machine chest (stuff chest)*

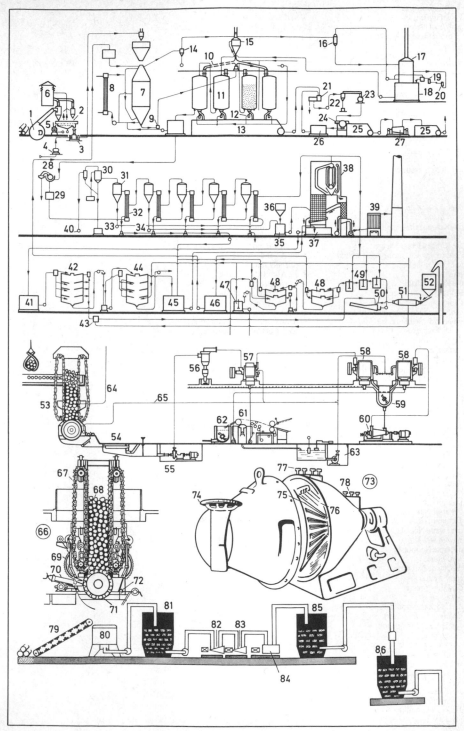

1 die Rührbütte, eine Papierstoffmischbütte
- *stuff chest (stock chest, machine chest), a mixing chest for stuff (stock)*
2-10 Laborgeräte n für die Papierstoff- und die Papieruntersuchung
- *laboratory apparatus (laboratory equipment) for analysing stuff (stock) and paper*
2 der Erlenmeyerkolben
- *Erlenmeyer flask*
3 der Mischzylinder
- *volumetric flask*
4 der Meßzylinder
- *measuring cylinder*
5 der Bunsenbrenner
- *Bunsen burner*
6 der Dreifuß
- *tripod*
7 die Laborschale
- *petri dish*
8 das Reagenzglasgestell
- *test tube rack*
9 die Rohgewichtswaage
- *balance for measuring basis weight*
10 der Dickenmesser
- *micrometer*
11 die Rohrschleudern f vor dem Stoffauflauf m einer Papiermaschine
- *centrifugal cleaners ahead of the breastbox (headbox, stuff box) of a paper machine*
12 das Standrohr
- *standpipe*
13-28 die Papiermaschine (Fertigungsstraße) [Schema]
- *paper machine (production line) [diagram]*
13 die Zuleitung von der Maschinenbütte mit Sand- und Knotenfang m
- *feed-in from the machine chest (stuff chest) with sand table (sand trap, riffler) and knotter*
14 das Sieb
- *wire (machine wire)*
15 der Siebsauger
- *vacuum box (suction box)*
16 die Siebsaugwalze
- *suction roll*
17 der erste Naßfilz
- *first wet felt*
18 der zweite Naßfilz
- *second wet felt*
19 die erste Naßpresse
- *first press*
20 die zweite Naßpresse
- *second press*
21 die Offsetpresse
- *offset press*
22 der Trockenzylinder
- *drying cylinder (drier)*
23 der Trockenfilz (auch: das Trockensieb)
- *dry felt (drier felt)*
24 die Leimpresse
- *size press*
25 der Kühlzylinder
- *cooling roll*
26 die Glättwalzen f
- *calender rolls*
27 die Trockenhaube
- *machine hood*

28 die Aufrollung
- *delivery reel*
29-35 die Rakelstreichmaschine (der Rakelstreicher)
- *blade coating machine (blade coater)*
29 das Rohpapier
- *raw paper (body paper)*
30 die Papierbahn
- *web*
31 die Streichanlage für die Vorderseite
- *coater for the top side*
32 der Infrarottrockenofen
- *infrared drier*
33 die beheizte Trockentrommel
- *heated drying cylinder*
34 die Streichanlage für die Rückseite
- *coater for the underside (wire side)*
35 die fertig gestrichene Papierrolle (der Tambour)
- *reel of coated paper*
36 der Kalander
- *calender (Super-calender)*
37 die Anpreßhydraulik
- *hydraulic system for the press rolls*
38 die Kalanderwalze
- *calender roll*
39 die Abrollvorrichtung
- *unwind station*
40 die Personenhebebühne
- *lift platform*
41 die Aufrollvorrichtung
- *rewind station (rewinder, re-reeler, reeling machine, re-reeling machine)*
42 der Rollenschneider
- *roll cutter*
43 die Schalttafel
- *control panel*
44 der Schneidapparat
- *cutter*
45 die Papierbahn
- *web*
46-51 die Handpapierherstellung
- *papermaking by hand*
46 der Schöpfer (Büttgeselle)
- *vatman*
47 die Bütte (der Trog)
- *vat*
48 die Schöpfform
- *mould (Am. mold)*
49 der Gautscher
- *coucher (couchman)*
50 die Bausch (Pauscht), fertig zum Pressen
- *post ready for pressing*
51 der Filz
- *felt*

1 **die Handsetzerei**
- *hand-setting room*
  (hand-composing room)
2 das Setzregal (Pultregal)
- *composing frame*
3 der Schriftkasten
- *case (typecase)*
4 der Steckschriftkasten
- *case cabinet (case rack)*
5 der Handsetzer (Setzer, Metteur)
- *hand compositor (compositor,*
  typesetter, maker-up)
6 das Manuskript (Typoskript)
- *manuscript (typescript)*
7 die Lettern *f* (Schrift)
- *sorts (types, type characters, characters)*
8 der Kasten, für Stege *m*,
  Füllmaterial *n* (Blindmaterial)
- *rack (case) for furniture (spacing*
  material)
9 das Stehsatzregal
- *standing type rack (standing matter*
  rack)
10 das Abstellbrett (Formbrett)
- *storage shelf (shelf for storing*
  formes, Am. *forms)*
11 der Stehsatz
- *standing type (standing matter)*
12 das Satzschiff
- *galley*
13 der Winkelhaken
- *composing stick (setting stick)*
14 die Setzlinie
- *composing rule (setting rule)*
15 der Satz
- *type (type matter, matter)*
16 die Kolumnenschnur
- *page cord*
17 die Ahle
- *bodkin*
18 die Pinzette
- *tweezers*
19 **die Zeilensetzmaschine „Linotype"** *f*,
  eine Mehrmagazinmaschine
- ***Linotype line-composing**
  (line-casting, slug-composing,
  slug-casting) machine, a
  multi-magazine machine
20 der Ablegemechanismus
- *distributing mechanism (distributor)*
21 die Satzmagazine *n* mit Matrizen *f*
- *type magazines with matrices (matrixes)*
22 der Greifer, zum Ablegen *n* der
  Matrizen *f*
- *elevator carrier for distributing the*
  matrices (matrixes)
23 der Sammler
- *assembler*
24 die Spatienkeile *m*
- *spacebands*
25 das Gießwerk
- *casting mechanism*
26 die Metallzuführung
- *metal feeder*
27 der Maschinensatz (die gegossenen
  Zeilen *f*)
- *machine-set matter (cast lines, slugs)*
28 die Handmatrizen *f*
- *matrices (matrixes) for*
  hand-setting (sorts)
29 die Linotypematrize
- *Linotype matrix*
30 die Zahnung, für den
  Ablegemechanismus *m*
- *teeth for the distributing*
  mechanism (distributor)

31 das Schriftbild (die Matrize)
- *face (type face, matrix)*
32-45 **die Einzelbuchstaben-Setz-
  und -Gießmaschine
  „Monotype"** *f*
- ***monotype single-unit composing**
  (typesetting) **and casting machine**
  (monotype single-unit composition
  caster)
32 die „Monotype"-
  Normalsetzmaschine
  (der Taster)
- *monotype standard composing*
  (typesetting) machine (keyboard)
33 der Papierturm
- *paper tower*
34 der Satzstreifen
- *paper ribbon*
35 die Settrommel
- *justifying scale*
36 der Einheitenzeiger
- *unit indicator*
37 die Tastatur
- *keyboard*
38 der Preßluftschlauch
- *compressed-air hose*
39 die „Monotype"-Gießmaschine
- *monotype casting machine*
  (monotype caster)
40 die automatische Metallzuführung
- *automatic metal feeder*
41 die Pumpendruckfeder
- *pump compression spring (pump*
  pressure spring)
42 der Matrizenrahmen
- *matrix case (die case)*
43 der Papierturm
- *paper tower*
44 das Satzschiff, mit Lettern *f*
  (gegossenen Einzelbuchstaben *m*)
- *galley with types (letters,*
  characters, cast single types, cast
  single letters)
45 die elektrische Heizung
- *electric heater (electric heating unit)*
46 der Matrizenrahmen
- *matrix case (die case)*
47 die Schriftmatrizen *f*
- *type matrices (matrixes) (letter*
  matrices)
48 die Klaue, zum Eingreifen *n* in die
  Kreuzschlittenführung
- *guide block for engaging with the*
  cross-slide guide

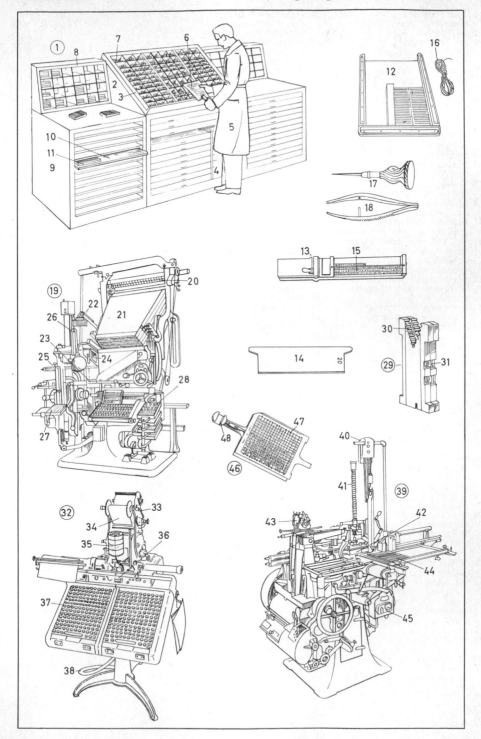

1-17 der Schriftsatz
- *composition (type matter, type)*
1 das Initial (die Initiale)
- *initial (initial letter)*
2 die dreiviertelfette Schrift
  (dreiviertelfett)
- *bold type (bold, boldfaced type,*
  heavy type, boldface)
3 die halbfette Schrift (halbfett)
- *semibold type (semibold)*
4 die Zeile
- *line*
5 der Durchschuß
- *space*
6 die Ligatur
- *ligature (double letter)*
7 die kursive Schrift (kursiv)
- *italic type (italics)*
8 die magere Schrift (mager)
- *light face type (light face)*
9 die fette Schrift (fett)
- *extra bold type (extra bold)*
10 die schmalfette Schrift (schmalfett)
- *bold condensed type (bold condensed)*
11 die Majuskel (der Versalbuchstabe,
   Versal, Großbuchstabe)
- *majuscule (capital letter, capital,*
  upper case letter)
12 die Minuskel (der Kleinbuchstabe)
- *minuscule (small letter, lower case*
  letter)
13 die Sperrung (Spationierung)
- *letter spacing (interspacing)*
14 die Kapitälchen *n*
- *small capitals*
15 der Absatz
- *break*
16 der Einzug
- *indention*
17 der Zwischenraum
- *space*
18 **Schriftgrade** *m* [ein
   typographischer Punkt *m* = 0,376 mm]
- *type sizes [one typographic point =*
  0.376 mm (Didot system), 0.351 mm
  (Pica system). The German
  size-names refer to exact multiples
  of the Didot (Continental) system.
  The English names are now
  obsolete: current English type-sizes
  are exact multiples of the Pica]
19 die Nonplusultra (2 Punkt)
- *six-to-pica (2 points)*
20 die Brillant (3 Punkt)
- *half nonpareil (four-to-pica) (3 points)*
21 die Diamant (4 Punkt)
- *brillant (4 points); sim.: diamond*
  (4½ points)
22 die Perl (5 Punkt)
- *pearl (5 points); sim.: ruby*
  (Am. agate) (5½ points)
23 die Nonpareille (6 Punkt)
- *nonpareil (6 points); sim.:*
  minionette (6½ points)
   die Kolonel (Mignon, 7 Punkt)
- *minion (7 points)*
25 die Petit (8 Punkt)
- *brevier (8 points)*
26 die Borgis (9 Punkt)
- *bourgeois (9 points)*
27 die Korpus (Garmond, 10 Punkt)
- *long primer (10 points)*
28 die Cicero (12 Punkt)
- *pica (12 points)*
29 die Mittel (14 Punkt)
- *English (14 points)*

30 die Tertia (16 Punkt)
- *great primer (two-line brevier,*
  Am. Columbian) (16 points)
31 die Text (20 Punkt)
- *paragon (two-line primer)*
  (20 points)
32-37 die Herstellung von Lettern *f*
- *typefounding (type casting)*
32 der Stempelschneider
- *punch cutter*
33 der Stahlstichel (Stichel)
- *graver (burin, cutter)*
34 die Lupe
- *magnifying glass (magnifier)*
35 der Stempel
- *punch blank (die blank)*
36 der fertige Stahlstempel (die
   Patrize)
- *finished steel punch (finished steel die)*
37 die geprägte Matrize
- *punched matrix (stamped matrix,*
  strike, drive)
38 die Letter
- *type (type character, character)*
39 der Kopf
- *head*
40 das Fleisch
- *shoulder*
41 die Punze
- *counter*
42 das Schriftbild
- *face (type face)*
43 die Schriftlinie
- *type line (bodyline)*
44 die Schrifthöhe
- *height to paper (type height)*
45 die Schulterhöhe
- *height of shank (height of shoulder)*
46 der Kegel
- *body size (type size, point size)*
47 die Signatur
- *nick*
48 die Dickte
- *set (width)*
49 die Matrizenbohrmaschine, eine
   Spezialbohrmaschine
- *matrix-boring machine*
  (matrix-engraving machine), a
  special-purpose boring machine
50 der Ständer
- *stand*
51 der Fräser
- *cutter (cutting head)*
52 der Frästisch
- *cutting table*
53 der Pantographensupport
- *pantograph carriage*
54 die Prismaführung
- *V-way*
55 die Schablone
- *pattern*
56 der Schablonentisch
- *pattern table*
57 der Kopierstift
- *follower*
58 der Pantograph
- *pantograph*
59 die Matrizenspannvorrichtung
- *matrix clamp*
60 die Frässpindel
- *cutter spindle*
61 der Antriebsmotor
- *drive motor*

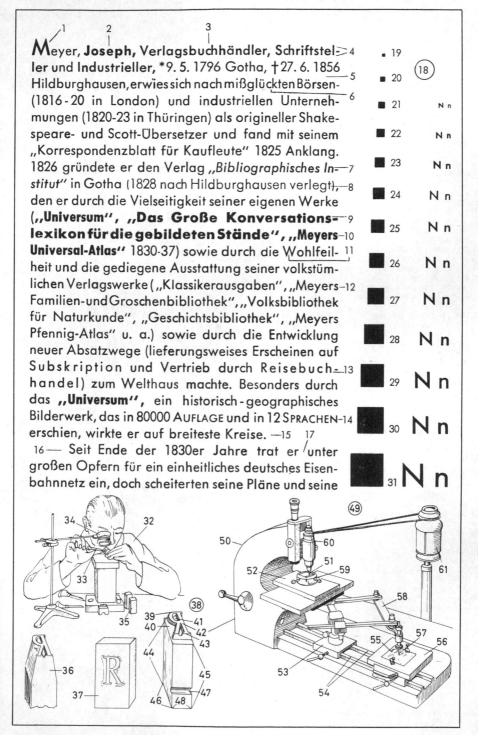

Meyer, **Joseph,** Verlagsbuchhändler, Schriftsteller und Industrieller, *9. 5. 1796 Gotha, †27. 6. 1856 Hildburghausen, erwies sich nach mißglückten Börsen- (1816-20 in London) und industriellen Unternehmungen (1820-23 in Thüringen) als origineller Shakespeare- und Scott-Übersetzer und fand mit seinem „Korrespondenzblatt für Kaufleute" 1825 Anklang. 1826 gründete er den Verlag *„Bibliographisches Institut"* in Gotha (1828 nach Hildburghausen verlegt), den er durch die Vielseitigkeit seiner eigenen Werke (**„Universum", „Das Große Konversationslexikon für die gebildeten Stände", „Meyers Universal-Atlas"** 1830-37) sowie durch die Wohlfeilheit und die gediegene Ausstattung seiner volkstümlichen Verlagswerke („Klassikerausgaben", „Meyers Familien- und Groschenbibliothek", „Volksbibliothek für Naturkunde", „Geschichtsbibliothek", „Meyers Pfennig-Atlas" u. a.) sowie durch die Entwicklung neuer Absatzwege (lieferungsweises Erscheinen auf Subskription und Vertrieb durch Reisebuchhandel) zum Welthaus machte. Besonders durch das **„Universum",** ein historisch-geographisches Bilderwerk, das in 80000 AUFLAGE und in 12 SPRACHEN erschien, wirkte er auf breiteste Kreise. — Seit Ende der 1830er Jahre trat er unter großen Opfern für ein einheitliches deutsches Eisenbahnnetz ein, doch scheiterten seine Pläne und seine

176 Setzerei III (Lichtsatz)

1 das Tastergerät für den Lichtsatz
- *keyboard console (keyboard unit)*
  for phototypesetting
2 die Tastatur
- *keyboard*
3 das Manuskript
- *manuscript (copy)*
4 der Taster
- *keyboard operator*
5 der Lochstreifenlocher
- *tape punch (perforator)*
6 der Lochstreifen
- *punched tape (punch tape)*
7 das Lichtsetzgerät
- *filmsetter*
8 der Lochstreifen
- *punched tape (punch tape)*
9 die Belichtungssteuereinrichtung
- *exposure control device*
10 der Setzcomputer
- *typesetting computer*
11 die Speichereinheit
- *memory unit (storage unit)*
12 der Lochstreifen
- *punched tape (punch tape)*
13 der Lochstreifenabtaster
- *punched tape (punch tape) reader*
14 der Lichtsatzautomat für den
  computergesteuerten Satz
- *photo-unit (photographic unit) for*
  computer-controlled typesetting
  (composition)
15 die Lochstreifenabtastung
- *punched tape (punch tape) reader*
16 die Schriftmatrizen *f*
- *type matrices (matrixes) (letter*
  matrices)
17 der Matrizenrahmen
- *matrix case (film matrix case)*
18 die Führungsklaue
- *guide block*
19 der Synchronmotor
- *synchronous motor*
20 die Schriftscheibe
- *type disc (disk) (matrix disc)*
21 der Spiegelblock
- *mirror assembly*
22 der optische Keil
- *optical wedge*
23 das Objektiv
- *lens*
24 das Spiegelsystem
- *mirror system*
25 der Film
- *film*
26 die Blitzlichtröhren *f*
- *flash tubes*
27 das Diamagazin
- *matrix drum*
28 der Vervielfältigungsautomat für
  Filme *m*
- *automatic film copier*
29 die Lichtsatz-Zentraleinheit für
  den Zeitungssatz
- *central processing unit of a*
  photocomposition system
  (photosetting system) for
  newspaper typesetting
30 das Lochstreifeneingabeelement
- *punched tape (punch tape) input*
  (input unit)
31 der Bedienungsblattschreiber
- *keyboard send-receive teleprinter*
  (Teletype)
32 der Systemresidenz-Plattenspeicher
- *on-line disc (disk) storage unit*
33 der Textplattenspeicher
- *alphanumeric (alphameric) disc*
  (disk) store (alphanumeric disc file)
34 der Plattenstapel
- *disc (disk) stack (disc pack)*

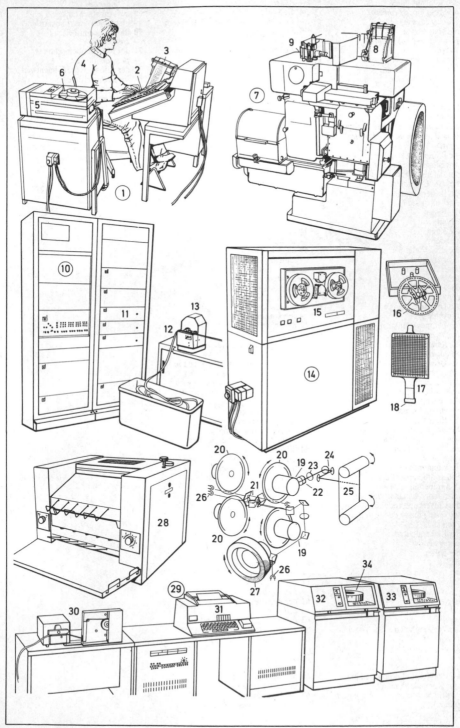

1 die Reproduktionskamera in
  Brückenbauweise *f*
– *overhead process camera (overhead
  copying camera)*
2 die Mattscheibe
– *focusing screen (ground glass
  screen)*
3 der schwenkbare
  Mattscheibenrahmen
– *hinged screen holder*
4 das Achsenkreuz
– *graticule*
5 der Bedienungsstand
– *control console*
6 das schwenkbare Hängeschaltpult
– *hinged bracket-mounted control
  panel*
7 die Prozentskalen *f*
– *percentage focusing charts*
8 der Vakuumfilmhalter
– *vacuum film holder*
9 das Rastermagazin
– *screen magazine*
10 der Balgen
– *bellows*
11 die Standarte
– *standard*
12 die Registriereinrichtung
– *register device*
13 das Brückenstativ
– *overhead gantry*
14 der Originalhalter
– *copyboard*
15 das Originalhaltergestell
– *copyholder*
16 der Lampengelenkarm
– *lamp bracket*
17 die Xenonlampe
– *xenon lamp*
18 das Original
– *copy (original)*
19 der Retuschier- und Montagetisch
– *retouching and stripping desk*
20 die Leuchtfläche
– *illuminated screen*
21 die Höhen- und
  Neigungsverstellung
– *height and angle adjustment*
22 der Vorlagenhalter
– *copyboard*
23 der zusammenlegbare
  Fadenzähler, eine Lupe
  (Vergrößerungsglas *n*)
– *linen tester, a magnifying glass*
24 die Universalreproduktionskamera
– *universal process and reproduction
  camera*
25 der Kamerakasten
– *camera body*
26 der Balgen
– *bellows*
27 der Optikträger
– *lens carrier*
28 die Winkelspiegel *m*
– *angled mirrors*
29 der T-Ständer
– *stand*
30 der Vorlagenhalter
– *copyboard*
31 die Halogenleuchte
– *halogen lamp*
32 die
  Vertikal-Reproduktionskamera,
  eine Kompaktkamera
– *vertical process camera, a compact
  camera*

33 der Kamerakasten
– *camera body*
34 die Mattscheibe
– *focusing screen (ground glass screen)*
35 der Vakuumdeckel
– *vacuum back*
36 die Bedienungstafel
– *control panel*
37 die Vorbelichtungslampe
– *flash lamp*
38 die Spiegeleinrichtung für
  seitenrichtige Aufnahmen *f*
– *mirror for right-reading images*
39 der Scanner (das
  Farbkorrekturgerät)
– *scanner (colour, Am. color,
  correction unit)*
40 das Untergestell
– *base frame*
41 der Lampenraum
– *lamp compartment*
42 das Xenonlampengehäuse
– *xenon lamp housing*
43 die Vorschubmotoren *m*
– *feed motors*
44 der Diaarm
– *transparency arm*
45 die Abtastwalze
– *scanning drum*
46 der Abtastkopf
– *scanning head*
47 der Maskenabtastkopf
– *mask-scanning head*
48 die Maskenwalze
– *mask drum*
49 der Schreibraum
– *recording space*
50 die Tageslichtkassette
– *daylight cassette*
51 der Farbrechner mit Steuersatz *m*
  und selektiver Farbkorrektur *f*
– *colour (Am. color) computer with
  control unit and selective colour
  correction*
52 das Klischiergerät
– *engraving machine*
53 die Nahtausblendung
– *seamless engraving adjustment*
54 die Antriebskupplung
– *drive clutch*
55 der Kupplungsflansch
– *clutch flange*
56 der Antriebsturm
– *drive unit*
57 das Maschinenbett
– *machine bed*
58 der Geräteträger
– *equipment carrier*
59 der Bettschlitten
– *bed slide*
60 das Bedienungsfeld
– *control panel*
61 der Lagerbock
– *bearing block*
62 der Reitstock
– *tailstock*
63 der Abtastkopf
– *scanning head*
64 der Vorlagenzylinder
– *copy cylinder*
65 das Mittellager
– *centre (Am. center) bearing*
66 das Graviersystem
– *engraving system*
67 der Druckzylinder
– *printing cylinder*

68 der Zylinderausleger
– *cylinder arm*
69 der Anbauschrank
– *electronics (electronic) cabinet*
70 die Recheneinheiten *f*
– *computers*
71 der Programmeinschub
– *program input*
72 der automatische Filmentwickler
  für Scannerfilme *m*
– *automatic film processor for
  scanner films*

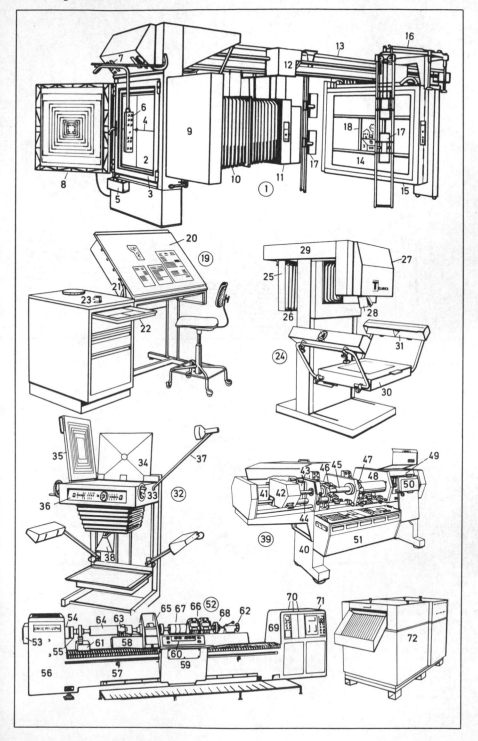

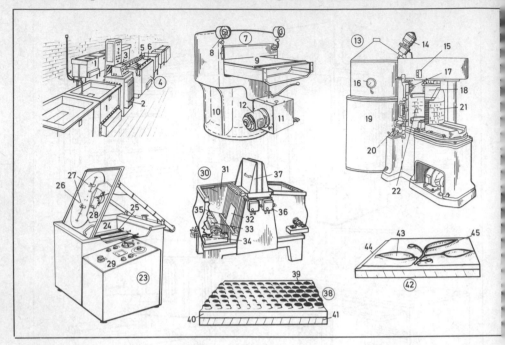

1-6 der galvanische Betrieb
- *electrotyping plant*
1 die Spülwanne
- *cleaning tank*
2 der Gleichrichter
- *rectifier*
3 das Meß- und Regelgerät
- *measuring and control unit*
4 das Galvanisierbecken
- *electroplating tank (electroplating bath, electroplating vat)*
5 die Anodenstange (mit Kupferanoden *f*)
- *anode rod (with copper anodes)*
6 die Warenstange (Kathode)
- *plate rod (cathode)*
7 die hydraulische Matrizenprägepresse
- *hydraulic moulding (Am. molding) press*
8 das Manometer
- *pressure gauge (Am. gage) (manometer)*
9 der Prägetisch
- *apron*
10 der Zylinderfuß
- *round base*
11 die hydraulische Preßpumpe
- *hydraulic pressure pump*
12 der Antriebsmotor
- *drive motor*
13 **das Rundplattengießwerk**
- *curved plate casting machine (curved electrotype casting machine)*
14 der Motor
- *motor*
15 die Antriebsknöpfe
- *control knobs*
16 das Pyrometer
- *pyrometer*

17 der Gießmund
- *mouth piece*
18 der Gießkern
- *core*
19 der Schmelzofen
- *melting furnace*
20 die Einschaltung
- *starting lever*
21 die gegossene Rundplatte für den Rotationsdruck
- *cast curved plate (cast curved electrotype) for rotary printing*
22 die feststehende Gießschale
- *fixed mould (Am. mold)*
23 **die Klischeeätzmaschine**
- *etching machine*
24 der Ätztrog mit der Ätzflüssigkeit und dem Flankenschutzmittel *n*
- *etching tank with etching solution (etchant, mordant) and filming agent (film former)*
25 die Schaufelwalzen *f*
- *paddles*
26 der Rotorteller
- *turntable*
27 die Plattenhalterung
- *plate clamp*
28 der Antriebsmotor
- *drive motor*
29 das Steueraggregat
- *control unit*
30 **die Zwillingsätzmaschine**
- *twin etching machine*
31 der Ätztrog [im Schnitt]
- *etching tank (etching bath) [in section]*
32 die kopierte Zinkplatte
- *photoprinted zinc plate*
33 das Schaufelrad
- *paddle*

34 der Abflußhahn
- *outlet cock (drain cock, Am. faucet)*
35 der Plattenständer
- *plate rack*
36 die Schaltung
- *control switches*
37 der Trogdeckel
- *lid*
38 **die Autotypie,** ein Klischee *n*
- *halftone photoengraving (halftone block, halftone plate), a block (plate, printing plate)*
39 der Rasterpunkt, ein Druckelement
- *dot (halftone dot), a printing element*
40 die geätzte Zinkplatte
- *etched zinc plate*
41 der Klischeefuß (das Klischeeholz)
- *block mount (block mounting, plate mount, plate mounting)*
42 **die Strichätzung**
- *line block (line engraving, line etching, line plate, line cut)*
43 die nichtdruckenden, tiefgeätzten Teile *m* od. *n*
- *non-printing, deep-etched areas*
44 die Klischeefacette
- *flange (bevel edge)*
45 die Ätzflanke (Flanke)
- *sidewall*

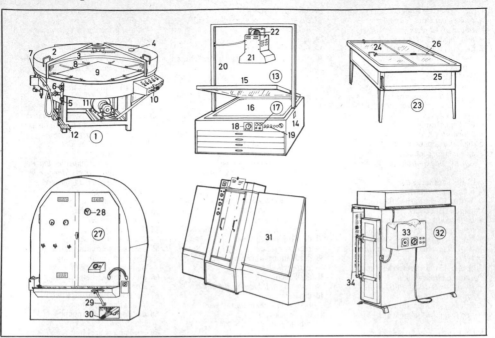

1 die Plattenschleuder
  (Plattenzentrifuge) zum
  Beschichten *n* der Offsetplatten *f*
- *plate whirler (whirler, plate-coating
  machine) for coating offset plates*
2 der Schiebedeckel
- *sliding lid*
3 die Elektroheizung
- *electric heater*
4 das Rundthermometer
- *temperature gauge* (Am. *gage*)
5 der Wasserspülanschluß
- *water connection for the spray unit*
6 die Umlaufspülung
- *spray unit*
7 die Handbrause
- *hand spray*
8 die Plattenhaltestangen *f*
- *plate clamps*
9 die Zinkplatte (*auch:* Magnesium-,
  Kupferplatte)
- *zinc plate (also: magnesium plate,
  copper plate)*
10 das Schaltpult
- *control panel*
11 der Antriebsmotor
- *drive motor*
12 der Bremsfußhebel
- *brake pedal*
13 der pneumatische Kopierrahmen
- *vacuum printing frame (vacuum
  frame, printing-down frame)*
14 das Kopierrahmenuntergestell
- *base of the vacuum printing frame
  (vacuum frame, printing-down
  frame)*
15 das Rahmenoberteil mit der
  Spiegelglasscheibe
- *plate glass frame*

16 die beschichtete Offsetplatte
- *coated offset plate*
17 die Schalttafel
- *control panel*
18 die Belichtungszeiteinstellung
- *exposure timer*
19 die Schalter *m* für die
  Vakuumherstellung
- *vacuum pump switches*
20 das Gestänge
- *support*
21 die Punktlichtkopierlampe, eine
  Metallhalogenlampe
- *point light exposure lamp, a
  quartz-halogen lamp*
22 das Lampengebläse
- *fan blower*
23 der Montagetisch, für die
  Filmmontage
- *stripping table (make-up table) for
  stripping films*
24 die Kristallglasscheibe
- *crystal glass screen*
25 der Beleuchtungskasten
- *light box*
26 die Linealeinrichtung
- *straightedge rules*
27 die Vertikaltrockenschleuder
- *vertical plate-drying cabinet*
28 der Feuchtigkeitsmesser
- *hygrometer*
29 die Geschwindigkeitsregulierung
- *speed control*
30 der Bremsfußhebel
- *brake pedal*
31 die Entwicklungsmaschine für
  vorbeschichtete Platten *f*
- *processing machine for
  presensitized plates*

32 der Brennofen (Einbrennofen) für
  Heißemail- (Diazo-)platten *f*
- *burning-in oven for glue-enamel
  plates (diazo plates)*
33 der Schaltkasten
- *control box (control unit)*
34 die Diazoplatte
- *diazo plate*

1 die Vierfarben-Rollenoffsetmaschine
- *four-colour (Am. four-color) rotary offset press (rotary offset machine, web-offset press)*
2 die unbedruckte Papierrolle
- *roll of unprinted paper (blank paper)*
3 der Rollenstern (Einhängevorrichtung f für die unbedruckte Papierrolle)
- *reel stand (carrier for the roll of unprinted paper)*
4 die Papiertransportwalzen f
- *forwarding rolls*
5 die Bahnkantensteuerung
- *side margin control (margin control, side control, side lay control)*
6-13 die Farbwerke n
- *inking units (inker units)*
6, 8, 10, 12 die Farbwerke n im oberen Druckwerk n
- *inking units (inker units) in the upper printing unit*
6-7 das Gelb-Doppeldruckwerk
- *perfecting unit (double unit) for yellow*
7, 9, 11, 13 die Farbwerke n im unteren Druckwerk n
- *inking units (inker units) in the lower printing unit*
8-9 das Cyan-Doppeldruckwerk
- *perfecting unit (double unit) for cyan*
10-11 das Magenta-Doppeldruckwerk
- *perfecting unit (double unit) for magenta*
12-13 das Schwarz-Doppeldruckwerk
- *perfecting unit (double unit) for black*
14 der Trockenofen
- *drier*
15 der Falzapparat
- *folder (folder unit)*
16 das Schaltpult
- *control desk*
17 der Druckbogen
- *sheet*
18 die Vierfarben-Rollenoffsetmaschine [Schema]
- *four-colour (Am. four-color) rotary offset press (rotary offset machine, web-offset press) [diagram]*
19 der Rollenstern
- *reel stand*
20 die Bahnkantensteuerung
- *side margin control (margin control, side control, side lay control)*
21 die Farbwalzen f
- *inking rollers (ink rollers, inkers)*
22 der Farbkasten
- *ink duct (ink fountain)*
23 die Feuchtwalzen f
- *damping rollers (dampening rollers, dampers, dampeners)*
24 der Gummizylinder
- *blanket cylinder*
25 der Plattenzylinder (Druckträger)
- *plate cylinder*
26 die Papierlaufbahn
- *route of the paper (of the web)*
27 der Trockenofen
- *drier*

28 die Kühlwalzen f
- *chilling rolls (cooling rollers, chill rollers)*
29 der Falzapparat
- *folder (folder unit)*
30 die Vierfarben-Bogenoffsetmaschine [Schema]
- *four-colour (Am. four-color) sheet-fed offset machine (offset press) [diagram]*
31 der Bogenanleger
- *sheet feeder (feeder)*
32 der Anlagetisch
- *feed table (feed board)*
33 der Bogenlauf über Vorgreifer m zur Anlegetrommel
- *route of the sheets through swing-grippers to the feed drum*
34 die Anlegetrommel
- *feed drum*
35 der Druckzylinder
- *impression cylinder*
36 die Übergabetrommeln f
- *transfer drums (transfer cylinders)*
37 der Gummizylinder
- *blanket cylinder*
38 der Plattenzylinder
- *plate cylinder*
39 das Feuchtwerk
- *damping unit (dampening unit)*
40 das Farbwerk
- *inking unit (inker unit)*
41 das Druckwerk
- *printing unit*
42 die Auslegetrommel
- *delivery cylinder*
43 die Kettenauslage
- *chain delivery*
44 die Bogenablage
- *delivery pile*
45 der Bogenausleger
- *delivery unit (delivery mechanism)*
46 die Einfarben-Offsetmaschine (Offsetmaschine)
- *single-colour (Am. single-color) offset press (offset machine)*
47 der Papierstapel (das Druckpapier)
- *pile of paper (sheets, printing paper)*
48 der Bogenanleger, ein automatischer Stapelanleger m
- *sheet feeder (feeder), an automatic pile feeder*
49 der Anlagetisch
- *feed table (feed board)*
50 die Farbwalzen f
- *inking rollers (ink rollers, inkers)*
51 das Farbwerk
- *inking unit (inker unit)*
52 die Feuchtwalzen f
- *damping rollers (dampening rollers, dampers, dampeners)*
53 der Plattenzylinder (Druckträger), eine Zinkplatte
- *plate cylinder, a zinc plate*
54 der Gummizylinder, ein Stahlzylinder m mit Gummidrucktuch n
- *blanket cylinder, a steel cylinder with rubber blanket*
55 der Stapelausleger für die bedruckten Bogen m
- *pile delivery unit for the printed sheets*
56 der Greiferwagen, ein Kettengreifer m
- *gripper bar, a chain gripper*

57 der Papierstapel (mit bedrucktem Papier)
- *pile of printed paper (printed sheets)*
58 das Schutzblech für den Keilriemenantrieb m
- *guard for the V-belt (vee-belt) drive*
59 die Einfarben-Offsetmaschine [Schema]
- *single-colour (Am. single-color) offset press (offset machine) [diagram]*
60 das Farbwerk mit den Farbwalzen f
- *inking unit (inker unit) with inking rollers (ink rollers, inkers)*
61 das Feuchtwerk mit den Feuchtwalzen f
- *damping unit (dampening unit) with damping rollers (dampening rollers, dampers, dampeners)*
62 der Plattenzylinder
- *plate cylinder*
63 der Gummizylinder
- *blanket cylinder*
64 der Druckzylinder
- *impression cylinder*
65 die Auslagetrommel mit dem Greifersystem n
- *delivery cylinder with grippers*
66 die Antriebsscheibe
- *drive wheel*
67 der Bogenzuführungstisch
- *feed table (feed board)*
68 der Bogenanlegeapparat
- *sheet feeder (feeder)*
69 der Papierstapel (mit unbedrucktem Papier)
- *pile of unprinted paper (blank paper, unprinted sheets, blank sheets)*
70 der Kleinoffset-Stapeldrucker
- *small sheet-fed offset press*
71 das Farbwerk
- *inking unit (inker unit)*
72 der Sauganleger
- *suction feeder*
73 die Stapelanlage
- *pile feeder*
74 das Armaturenbrett (Schaltbrett) mit Zähler m, Manometer n, Luftregler m und Schalter m für die Papierzuführung
- *instrument panel (control panel) with counter, pressure gauge (Am. gage), air regulator, and control switch for the sheet feeder (feeder)*
75 die Flachoffsetmaschine (Mailänder Andruckpresse)
- *flat-bed offset press (offset machine) ('Mailänder' proofing press, proof press)*
76 das Farbwerk
- *inking unit (inker unit)*
77 die Farbwalzen f
- *inking rollers (ink rollers, inkers)*
78 das Druckfundament
- *bed (press bed, type bed, forme bed, Am. form bed)*
79 der Zylinder mit Gummidrucktuch;n.
- *cylinder with rubber blanket*
80 der Hebel, für das An- und Abstellen des Druckwerkes n
- *starting and stopping lever for the printing unit*
81 die Druckeinstellung
- *impression-setting wheel (impression-adjusting wheel)*

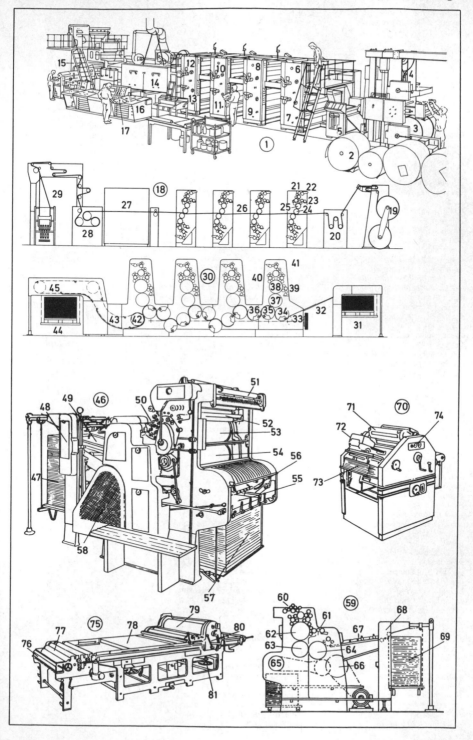

1-65 Maschinen *f* der Buchdruckerei
- *presses (machines) for letterpress printing (letterpress printing machines)*
1 die Zweitouren-Schnellpresse
- *two-revolution flat-bed cylinder press*
2 der Druckzylinder
- *impression cylinder*
3 der Hebel zur Zylinderhebung und -senkung
- *lever for raising or lowering the cylinder*
4 der Anlagetisch
- *feed table (feed board)*
5 der automatische Bogenanleger [mit Saug- und Druckluft *f* betätigt]
- *automatic sheet feeder (feeder) [operated by vacuum and air blasts]*
6 die Luftpumpe, für Bogenan- und -ablage *f*
- *air pump for the feeder and delivery*
7 das Zylinderfarbwerk, mit Verreib- und Auftragwalzen *f*
- *inking unit (inker unit) with distributing rollers (distributor rollers, distributors) and forme rollers (Am. form rollers)*
8 das Tischfarbwerk
- *ink slab (ink plate) inking unit (inker unit)*
9 der Papierablagestapel, für bedrucktes Papier *n*
- *delivery pile for printed paper*
10 der Spritzapparat, zum Bestäuben *n* der Drucke *m*
- *sprayer (anti set-off apparatus, anti set-off spray) for dusting the printed sheets*
11 die Einschießvorrichtung
- *interleaving device*
12 das Pedal, zur Druckan- und -abstellung
- *foot pedal for starting and stopping the press*
13 die Tiegeldruckpresse [Schnitt]
- *platen press (platen machine, platen) [in section]*
14 die Papieran- und -ablage
- *paper feed and delivery (paper feeding and delivery unit)*
15 der Drucktiegel
- *platen*
16 der Kniehebelantrieb
- *toggle action (toggle-joint action)*
17 das Schriftfundament
- *bed (type bed, press bed, forme bed, Am. form bed)*
18 die Farbauftragwalzen *f*
- *forme rollers (Am. form rollers) (forme-inking, Am. form-inking, rollers)*
19 das Farbwerk, zum Verreiben *n* der Druckfarbe
- *inking unit (inker unit) for distributing the ink (printing ink)*
20 die Stoppzylinderpresse (Haltzylinderpresse)
- *stop-cylinder press (stop-cylinder machine)*
21 der Anlagetisch
- *feed table (feed board)*

22 der Anlageapparat
- *feeder mechanism (feeding apparatus, feeder)*
23 der Papierstapel (mit unbedrucktem Papier)
- *pile of unprinted paper (blank paper, unprinted sheets, blank sheets)*
24 das Schutzgitter, für die Papieranlage
- *guard for the sheet feeder (feeder)*
25 der Papierstapel (mit bedrucktem Papier)
- *pile of printed paper (printed sheets)*
26 der Schaltmechanismus
- *control mechanism*
27 die Farbauftragwalzen *f*
- *forme rollers (Am. form rollers) (forme-inking, Am. form-inking, rollers)*
28 das Farbwerk
- *inking unit (inker unit)*
29 die Tiegeldruckpresse [Heidelberger]
- *[Heidelberg] platen press (platen machine, platen)*
30 der Anlagetisch, mit dem unbedruckten Papier *n*
- *feed table (feed board) with pile of unprinted paper (blank paper, unprinted sheets, blank sheets)*
31 der Ablagetisch
- *delivery table*
32 der Druckansteller und Druckabsteller
- *starting and stopping lever*
33 der Ablagebläser
- *delivery blower*
34 die Spritzpistole
- *spray gun (sprayer)*
35 die Luftpumpe, für Saug- und Blasluft *f*
- *air pump for vacuum and air blasts*
36 die geschlossene Form (Satzform)
- *locked-up forme (Am. form)*
37 der Satz
- *type (type matter, matter)*
38 der Schließrahmen
- *chase*
39 das Schließzeug
- *quoin*
40 der Steg
- *length of furniture*
41 die Hochdruck-Rotationsmaschine für Zeitungen *f* bis 16 Seiten *f*
- *rotary letterpress press (rotary letterpress machine, web-fed letterpress machine) for newspapers of up to 16 pages*
42 die Schneidrollen *f*, zum Längsschneiden *n* der Papierbahn
- *slitters for dividing the width of the web*
43 die Papierbahn
- *web*
44 der Druckzylinder
- *impression cylinder*
45 die Pendelwalze
- *jockey roller (compensating roller, compensator, tension roller)*
46 die Papierrolle
- *roll of paper*
47 die automatische Papierrollenbremse
- *automatic brake*

48 das Schöndruckwerk
- *first printing unit*
49 das Widerdruckwerk
- *perfecting unit*
50 das Farbwerk
- *inking unit (inker unit)*
51 der Formzylinder
- *plate cylinder*
52 das Buntdruckwerk
- *second printing unit*
53 der Falztrichter
- *former*
54 das (der) Tachometer, mit Bogenzähler *m*
- *tachometer with sheet counter*
55 der Falzapparat
- *folder (folder unit)*
56 die gefaltete Zeitung
- *folded newspaper*
57 das Farbwerk für die Rotationsmaschine [Schnitt]
- *inking unit (inker unit) for the rotary press (web-fed press) [in section]*
58 die Papierbahn
- *web*
59 der Druckzylinder
- *impression cylinder*
60 der Plattenzylinder
- *plate cylinder*
61 die Farbauftragwalzen *f*
- *forme rollers (Am. form rollers) (forme-inking, Am. form-inking, rollers)*
62 der Farbverreibzylinder
- *distributing rollers (distributor rollers, distributors)*
63 die Farbhebewalze
- *lifter roller (ductor, ductor roller)*
64 die Duktorwalze
- *duct roller (fountain roller, ink fountain roller)*
65 der Farbkasten
- *ink duct (ink fountain)*

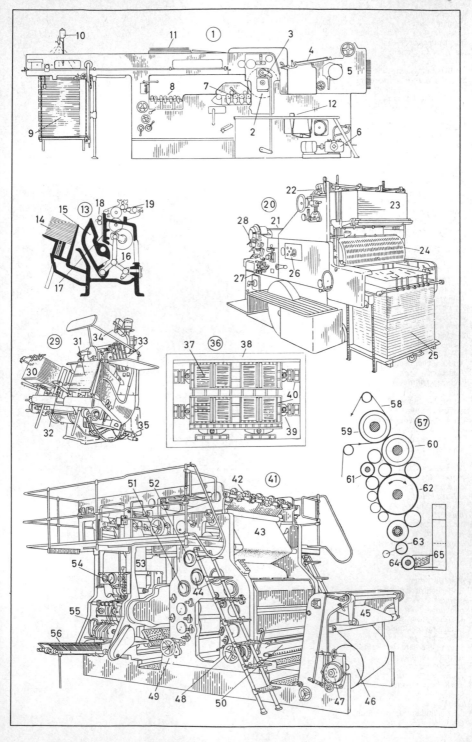

1 die Belichtung des
Pigmentpapiers *n*
- *exposure of the carbon tissue*
(pigment paper)
2 der Vakuumrahmen
- *vacuum frame*
3 die Belichtungslampe, eine
Metallhalogen-Flächenleuchte
- *exposing lamp, a bank of*
quartz-halogen lamps
4 die Punktlichtlampe
- *point source lamp*
5 der Wärmekamin
- *heat extractor*
6 die Pigmentpapierübertragungsmaschine
- *carbon tissue transfer machine*
(laydown machine, laying
machine)
7 der polierte Kupferzylinder
- *polished copper cylinder*
8 die Gummiwalze zum Andrücken
n des kopierten Pigmentpapiers *n*
- *rubber roller for pressing on the*
printed carbon tissue (pigment
paper)
9 die Walzenentwicklungsmaschine
- *cylinder-processing machine*
10 die mit Pigmentpapier *n*
beschichtete Tiefdruckwalze
- *gravure cylinder coated with carbon*
tissue (pigment paper)
11 die Entwicklungswanne
- *developing tank*
12 die Walzenkorrektur
- *staging*
13 die entwickelte Walze
- *developed cylinder*
14 der Retuscheur beim
Abdecken *n*
- *retoucher painting out (stopping*
out)
15 die Ätzmaschine
- *etching machine*
16 der Ätztrog mit der Ätzflüssigkeit
- *etching tank with etching solution*
(etchant, mordant)
17 die kopierte Tiefdruckwalze
- *printed gravure cylinder*
18 der Tiefdruckätzer
- *gravure etcher*
19 die Rechenscheibe
- *calculator dial*
20 die Kontrolluhr
- *timer*
21 die Ätzkorrektur
- *revising (correcting) the cylinder*
22 der geätzte Tiefdruckzylinder
- *etched gravure cylinder*
23 die Korrekturleiste
- *ledge*
24 die Mehrfarben-
Rollentiefdruckmaschine
- *multicolour (Am. multicolor)*
rotogravure press
25 das Abzugsrohr für
Lösungsmitteldämpfe *m*
- *exhaust pipe for solvent fumes*
26 das umsteuerbare Druckwerk
- *reversible printing unit*
27 der Falzapparat
- *folder (folder unit)*
28 das Bedienungs- und
Steuerpult
- *control desk*
29 die Zeitungsaustragvorrichtung
- *newspaper delivery unit*
30 das Förderband
- *conveyor belt (conveyor)*
31 der abgepackte Zeitungsstapel
- *bundled stack of newspapers*

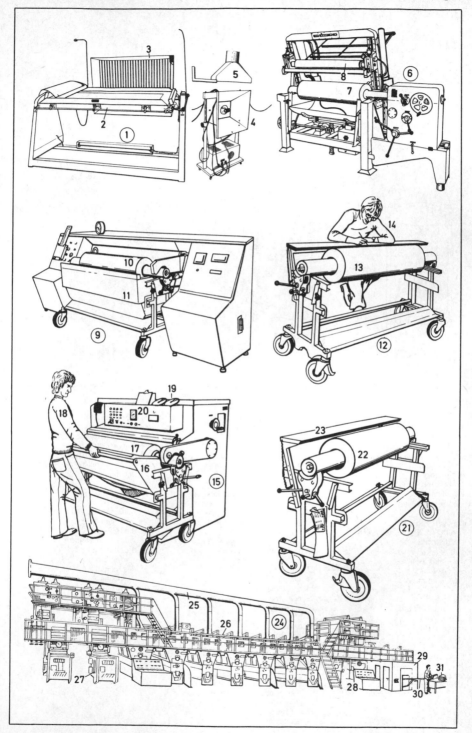

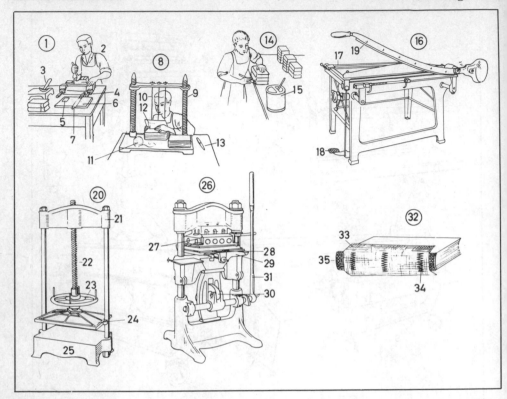

1-35 die Handbuchbinderei
- **hand bookbindery** *(hand bindery)*
1 das Vergolden des Buchrückens *m*
   (die Rückenvergoldung)
- *gilding the spine of the book*
2 der Goldschnittmacher, ein
   Buchbinder *m*
- *gold finisher (gilder),*
   a bookbinder
3 die Filete (Philete)
- *fillet*
4 der Spannrahmen
- *holding press (finishing press)*
5 das Blattgold
- *gold leaf*
6 das Goldkissen
- *gold cushion*
7 das Goldmesser
- *gold knife*
8 das Heften
- *sewing (stitching)*
9 die Heftlade
- *sewing frame*
10 die Heftschnur
- *sewing cord*
11 der (das) Garnknäuel
- *ball of thread (sewing thread)*
12 die Heftlage
- *section (signature)*
13 das Buchbindermesser (der Kneif)
- *bookbinder's knife*
14 die Rückenleimung
- *gluing the spine*

15 der Leimkessel
- *glue pot*
16 die Pappschere
- *board cutter (guillotine)*
17 die Anlegeeinrichtung
- *back gauge (Am. gage)*
18 die Preßeinrichtung, mit
   Fußtritthebel *m*
- *clamp with foot pedal*
19 das Obermesser
- *cutting blade*
20 die Stockpresse, eine Glätt- u.
   Packpresse
- *standing press, a nipping press*
21 das Kopfstück
- *head piece (head beam)*
22 die Spindel
- *spindle*
23 das Schlagrad
- *handwheel*
24 die Preßplatte
- *platen*
25 das Fußstück
- *bed (base)*
26 die Vergolde- und Prägepresse,
   eine Handhebelpresse; *ähnl.:*
   Kniehebelpresse
- *gilding (gold blocking) and*
   embossing press, a hand-lever
   press; sim.: *toggle-joint press*
   (toggle-lever press)
27 der Heizkasten
- *heating box*

28 die ausschiebbare Aushängeplatte
- *sliding plate*
29 der Prägetiegel
- *embossing platen*
30 das Kniehebelsystem
- *toggle action (toggle-joint action)*
31 der Handhebel
- *hand lever*
32 das auf Gaze *f* geheftete Buch (die
   Broschur)
- *book sewn on gauze (mull, scrim)*
   (unbound book)
33 die Heftgaze
- *gauze (mull, scrim)*
34 die Heftung
- *sewing (stitching)*
35 das Kapitalband (Kaptalband)
- *headband*

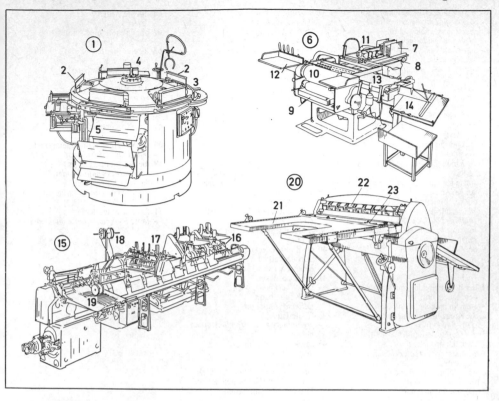

1-23 Buchbindereimaschinen *f*
- *bookbinding machines*
1 der Klebebinder (die
   Klebemaschine) für Kleinauflagen *f*
- *adhesive binder* (perfect binder) *for*
   short runs
2 die Handeinlegestation
- *manual feed station*
3 die Fräs- und Aufrauhstation
- *cutoff knife and roughing station*
4 das Leimwerk
- *gluing mechanism*
5 die Kastenauslage
- *delivery (book delivery)*
6 die Buchdeckenmaschine
- *case maker (case-making machine)*
7 die Magazine *n* für Pappdeckel *m*
- *board feed hopper*
8 die Pappenzieher *m*
- *pickup suckers*
9 der Leimkasten
- *glue tank*
10 der Nutzenzylinder
- *gluing cylinder (glue cylinder, glue*
   roller)
11 der Saugarm
- *picker head*
12 der Stapelplatz für Überzugnutzen
   n [Leinen *n*, Papier *n*, Leder *n*]
- *feed table for covering materials*
   [linen, paper, leather]
13 die Preßeinrichtung
- *pressing mechanism*

14 der Ablegetisch
- *delivery table*
15 der Sammelhefter (die
   Sammeldrahtheftmaschine)
- *gang stitcher (gathering and*
   wire-stitching machine, gatherer
   and wire stitcher)
16 der Bogenanleger
- *sheet feeder (sheet-feeding station)*
17 der Falzanleger
- *folder-feeding station*
18 die Heftdrahtabspulvorrichtung
- *stitching wire feed mechanism*
19 der Auslegetisch
- *delivery table*
20 die Kreispappschere
- *rotary board cutter (rotary*
   board-cutting machine)
21 der Anlegetisch, mit Aussparung *f*
- *feed table with cut-out section*
22 das Kreismesser
- *rotary cutter*
23 das Einführlineal
- *feed guide*

1-35 Buchbindereimaschinen *f*
- *bookbinding machines*
1 der Papierschneideautomat
- *guillotine (guillotine cutter, automatic guillotine cutter)*
2 das Schaltpult
- *control panel*
3 der Preßbalken
- *clamp*
4 der Vorschubsattel
- *back gauge (Am. gage)*
5 die Preßdruckskala
- *calibrated pressure adjustment [to clamp]*
6 die optische Maßanzeige
- *illuminated cutting scale*
7 die Einhandbedienung für den Sattel
- *single-hand control for the back gauge (Am. gage)*
8 die kombinierte Stauch- u. Messerfalzmaschine
- *combined buckle and knife folding machine (combined buckle and knife folder)*
9 der Bogenzuführtisch
- *feed table (feed board)*
10 die Falztaschen *f*
- *fold plates*
11 der Bogenanschlag, zur Bildung der Stauchfalte
- *stop for making the buckle fold*
12 die Kreuzbruchfalzmesser *n*
- *cross fold knives*
13 der Gurtausleger, für Parallelfalzungen *f*
- *belt delivery for parallel-folded signatures*
14 das Dreibruchfalzwerk
- *third cross fold unit*
15 die Dreibruchauslage
- *delivery tray for cross-folded signatures*
16 die Fadenheftmaschine
- *sewing machine (book-sewing machine)*
17 der Spulenhalter
- *spool holder*
18 der Fadenkops (die Fadenspule)
- *thread cop (thread spool)*
19 der Gazerollenhalter
- *gauze roll holder (mull roll holder, scrim roll holder)*
20 die Gaze (Heftgaze)
- *gauze (mull, scrim)*
21 die Körper *m* mit den Heftnadeln *f*
- *needle cylinders with sewing needles*
22 der geheftete Buchblock
- *sewn book*
23 die Auslage
- *delivery*
24 der schwingende Heftsattel
- *reciprocating saddle*
25 der Anleger (Bogenanleger)
- *sheet feeder (feeder)*
26 das Anlegermagazin
- *feed hopper*
27 die Bucheinhängemaschine
- *casing-in machine*
28 der Falzleimapparat
- *joint and side pasting attachment*
29 das Schwert
- *blade*
30 die Vorwärmheizung
- *preheater unit*

31 die Anleimmaschine, für Voll-, Fasson-, Rand- und Streifenbeleimung *f*
- *gluing machine for whole-surface, stencil, edge, and strip gluing*
32 der Leimkessel
- *glue tank*
33 die Leimwalze
- *glue roller*
34 der Einfuhrtisch
- *feed table*
35 die Abtransportvorrichtung
- *delivery*
36 das Buch
- *book*
37 der Schutzumschlag, ein Werbeumschlag *m*
- *dust jacket (dust cover, bookjacket, wrapper), a publisher's wrapper*
38 die Umschlagklappe
- *jacket flap*
39 der Klappentext (Waschzettel)
- *blurb*
40-42 der Bucheinband (Einband)
- *binding*
40 die Einbanddecke (Buchdecke, der Buchdeckel)
- *cover (book cover, case)*
41 der Buchrücken
- *spine (backbone, back)*
42 das Kapitalband
- *tailband (footband)*
43-47 die Titelei
- *preliminary matter (prelims, front matter)*
43 das Schmutztitelblatt
- *half-title*
44 der Schmutztitel (Vortitel)
- *half-title (bastard title, fly title)*
45 das Titelblatt (Haupttitelblatt, die Titelseite, der Innentitel)
- *title page*
46 der Haupttitel
- *full title (main title)*
47 der Untertitel
- *subtitle*
48 das Verlagssignet (Signet, Verlagszeichen, Verlegerzeichen)
- *publisher's imprint (imprint)*
49 das Vorsatzpapier (der od. das Vorsatz)
- *fly leaf (endpaper, endleaf)*
50 die handschriftliche Widmung
- *handwritten dedication*
51 das Exlibris (Bucheignerzeichen)
- *bookplate (ex libris)*
52 das aufgeschlagene Buch
- *open book*
53 die Buchseite (Seite)
- *page*
54 der Falz
- *fold*
55-58 der Papierrand
- *margin*
55 der Bundsteg
- *back margin (inside margin, gutter)*
56 der Kopfsteg
- *head margin (upper margin)*
57 der Außensteg
- *fore edge margin (outside margin, fore edge)*
58 der Fußsteg
- *tail margin (foot margin, tail, foot)*
59 der Satzspiegel
- *type area*
60 die Kapitelüberschrift
- *chapter heading*

61 das Sternchen
- *asterisk*
62 die Fußnote, eine Anmerkung
- *footnote, a note*
63 die Seitenziffer
- *page number*
64 der zweispaltige Satz
- *double-column page*
65 die Spalte (Kolumne)
- *column*
66 der Kolumnentitel
- *running title (running head)*
67 der Zwischentitel
- *caption*
68 die Marginalie (Randbemerkung)
- *marginal note (side note)*
69 die Bogennorm (Norm)
- *signature (signature code)*
70 das feste Lesezeichen
- *attached bookmark (attached bookmarker)*
71 das lose Lesezeichen
- *loose bookmark (loose bookmarker)*

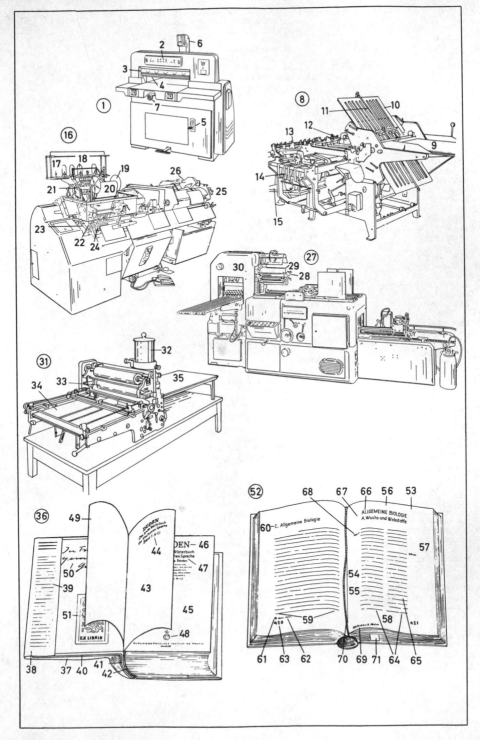

1-54 Wagen *m* (Fahrzeuge *n*,
  Gefährte, Fuhrwerke)
- *carriages (vehicles, conveyances,*
  horse-drawn vehicles)
1-3, 26-39, 45, 51-54 Kutschen *f*
  (Kutschwagen *m*)
- *carriages and coaches (coach wagons)*
1 die Berline
- *berlin*
2 der (das) Break
- *waggonette (larger: brake, break)*
3 das Coupé (Kupee)
- *coupé; sim.: brougham*
4 das Vorderrad
- *front wheel*
5 der Wagenkasten
- *coach body*
6 das Spritzbrett
- *dashboard (splashboard)*
7 die Fußstütze
- *footboard*
8 der Kutschbock (Bock, Bocksitz,
  Kutschersitz)
- *coach box (box, coachman's seat,*
  driver's seat)
9 die Laterne
- *lamp (lantern)*
10 das Fenster
- *window*
11 die Tür (der Wagenschlag,
  Kutschenschlag)
- *door (coach door)*
12 der Türgriff (Griff)
- *door handle (handle)*
13 der Fußtritt (Tritt)
- *footboard (carriage step, coach*
  step, step, footpiece)
14 das feste Verdeck
- *fixed top*
15 die Feder
- *spring*
16 die Bremse (der Bremsklotz)
- *brake (brake block)*
17 das Hinterrad
- *back wheel (rear wheel)*
18 der Dogcart, ein Einspänner *m*
- *dogcart, a one-horse carriage*
19 die Deichsel
- *shafts (thills, poles)*
20 der Lakai (Diener)
- *lackey (lacquey, footman)*
21 der Dieneranzug (die Livree)
- *livery*
22 der Tressenkragen (betreßte Kragen)
- *braided (gallooned) collar*
23 der Tressenrock (betreßte Rock)
- *braided (gallooned) coat*
24 der Tressenärmel (betreßte Ärmel)
- *braided (gallooned) sleeve*
25 der hohe Hut (Zylinderhut)
- *top hat*
26 die Droschke (Pferdedroschke, der
  Fiaker, die Lohnkutsche, der
  Mietwagen)
- *hackney carriage (hackney coach,*
  cab, growler, Am. hack)
27 der Stallknecht (Groom)
- *stableman (groom)*
28 das Kutschpferd (Deichselpferd)
- *coach horse (carriage horse, cab*
  horse, thill horse, thiller)
29 der Hansom (das Hansomcab), ein
  Kabriolett *n*, ein Einspänner *m*
- *hansom cab (hansom), a cabriolet,*
  a one-horse chaise (one-horse
  carriage)

30 die Gabeldeichsel (Deichsel,
  Gabel, Schere)
- *shafts (thills, poles)*
31 der Zügel
- *reins (rein, Am. line)*
32 der Kutscher, mit Havelock *m*
- *coachman (driver) with inverness*
33 der Kremser, ein
  Gesellschaftswagen *m*
- *covered char-a-banc (brake,*
  break), a pleasure vehicle
34 das Cab
- *gig (chaise)*
35 die Kalesche
- *barouche*
36 der Landauer, ein Zweispänner *m*;
  ähnl.: das Landaulett
- *landau, a two-horse carriage; sim.:*
  landaulet, landaulette
37 der Omnibus (Pferdeomnibus,
  Stellwagen)
- *omnibus (horse-drawn omnibus)*
38 der Phaeton (Phaethon)
- *phaeton*
39 die Postkutsche (der Postwagen, die
  Diligence); zugleich: Reisewagen *m*
- *Continental stagecoach (mailcoach,*
  diligence); also: road coach
40 der Postillon (Postillon,
  Postkutscher)
- *mailcoach driver*
41 das Posthorn
- *posthorn*
42 das Schutzdach
- *hood*
43 die Postpferde *n* (Relaispferde)
- *post horses (relay horses, relays)*
44 der Tilbury
- *tilbury*
45 die Troika (das russische
  Dreigespann)
- *troika (Russian three-horse*
  carriage)
46 das Stangenpferd
- *leader*
47 das Seitenpferd
- *wheeler (wheelhorse, pole horse)*
48 der englische Buggy
- *English buggy*
49 der amerikanische Buggy
- *American buggy*
50 das Tandem
- *tandem*
51 der Vis-à-vis-Wagen
- *vis-à-vis*
52 das Klappverdeck
- *collapsible hood (collapsible top)*
53 die Mailcoach (englische
  Postkutsche)
- *mailcoach (English stagecoach)*
54 die Chaise
- *covered (closed) chaise*

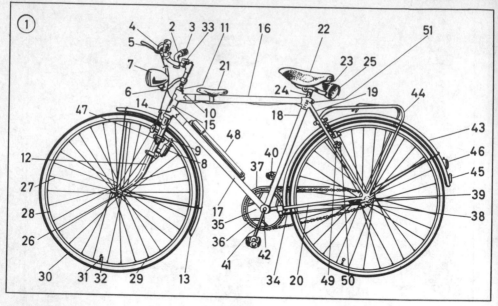

1 das Fahrrad (Rad, Zweirad,
   schweiz. Velo, Veloziped), ein
   Herrenfahrrad *n*, ein Tourenrad *n*
 - *bicycle (cycle,* coll. *bike,* Am.
   *wheel), a gent's bicycle, a touring
   bicycle (touring cycle, roadster)*
2 der Lenker (die Lenkstange), ein
   Tourenlenker *m*
 - *handlebar (handlebars), a touring
   cycle handlebar*
3 der Handgriff (Griff)
 - *handlebar grip (handgrip, grip)*
4 die Fahrradglocke
   (Fahrradklingel)
 - *bicycle bell*
5 die Handbremse
   (Vorderradbremse, eine
   Felgenbremse)
 - *hand brake (front brake), a rim
   brake*
6 der Scheinwerferhalter
 - *lamp bracket*
7 der Scheinwerfer (die
   Fahrradlampe)
 - *headlamp (bicycle lamp)*
8 der Dynamo
   (die Lichtmaschine)
 - *dynamo*
9 das Laufrädchen
 - *pulley*
10-12 die Vorderradgabel
 - *front forks*
10 der Gabelschaft
   (Lenkstangenschaft, das
   Gabelschaftrohr)
 - *handlebar stem*
11 der Gabelkopf
 - *steering head*
12 die Gabelscheiden *f*
 - *fork blades (fork ends)*
13 das vordere Schutzblech
 - *front mudguard (Am. front fender)*

14-20 der Fahrradrahmen (das
   Fahrradgestell)
 - *bicycle frame*
14 das Steuerrohr
   (Steuerkopfrohr)
 - *steering tube (fork column)*
15 das Markenschild
 - *head badge*
16 das obere Rahmenrohr (Oberrohr,
   Scheitelrohr)
 - *crossbar (top tube)*
17 das untere Rahmenrohr
   (Unterrohr)
 - *down tube*
18 das Sattelstützrohr (Sitzrohr)
 - *seat tube*
19 die oberen Hinterradstreben *f*
 - *seat stays*
20 die unteren Hinterradstreben *f*
   (die Hinterradgabel)
 - *chain stays*
21 der Kindersitz
 - *child's seat (child carrier seat)*
22 der Fahrradsattel (Elastiksattel)
 - *bicycle saddle*
23 die Sattelfedern *f*
 - *saddle springs*
24 die Sattelstütze
 - *seat pillar*
25 die Satteltasche (Werkzeugtasche)
 - *saddle bag (tool bag)*
26-32 das Rad (Vorderrad)
 - *wheel (front wheel)*
26 die Nabe
 - *hub*
27 die Speiche
 - *spoke*
28 die Felge
 - *rim (wheel rim)*
29 der Speichennippel
 - *spoke nipple (spoke flange, spoke
   end)*

30 die Bereifung (der Reifen,
   Luftreifen, die Pneumatik, der
   Hochdruckreifen, Preßluftreifen);
   innen: der Schlauch
   (Luftschlauch), *außen:* der Mantel
   (Laufmantel, die Decke)
 - *tyres (Am. tires) (tyre, pneumatic
   tyre, high-pressure tyre);* inside:
   tube (inner tube), outside: *tyre
   (outer case, cover)*
31 das Ventil, ein Schlauchventil *n*,
   mit Ventilschlauch *m* oder ein
   Patentventil *n* mit Kugel *f*
 - *valve, a tube valve with valve tube
   or a patent valve with ball*
32 die Ventilklappe
 - *valve sealing cap*
33 das Fahrradtachometer, mit
   Kilometerzähler *m*
 - *bicycle speedometer with milometer*
34 der Fahrradkippständer
 - *kick stand (prop stand)*
35-42 der Fahrradantrieb
   (Kettenantrieb)
 - *bicycle drive (chain drive)*
35-39 der Kettentrieb
 - *chain transmission*
35 das Kettenrad (das vordere
   Zahnrad)
 - *chain wheel*
36 die Kette, eine Rollenkette
 - *chain, a roller chain*
37 der Kettenschutz (das
   Kettenschutzblech)
 - *chain guard*
38 das hintere Kettenzahnrad (der
   Kettenzahnkranz, Zahnkranz)
 - *sprocket wheel (sprocket)*
39 die Flügelmutter
 - *wing nut (fly nut, butterfly nut)*
40 das Pedal
 - *pedal*

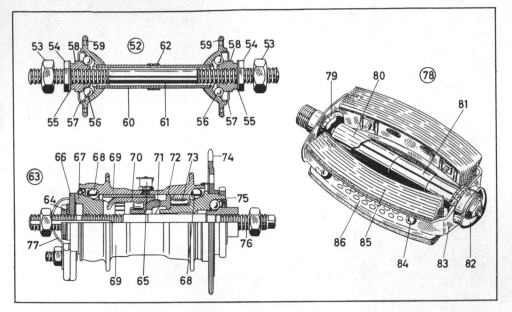

41 die Tretkurbel
- *crank*
42 das Tretkurbellager (Tretlager)
- *bottom bracket bearing*
43 das hintere Schutzblech (der Kotschützer)
- *rear mudguard (Am. rear fender)*
44 der Gepäckträger
- *luggage carrier (carrier)*
45 der Rückstrahler (ugs. das Katzenauge)
- *reflector*
46 das elektr. Rücklicht
- *rear light (rear lamp)*
47 die Fußraste
- *footrest*
48 die Fahrradpumpe (Luftpumpe)
- *bicycle pump*
49 das Fahrradschloß, ein Speichenschloß n
- *bicycle lock, a wheel lock*
50 der Patentschlüssel
- *patent key*
51 die Fahrradnummer (Fabriknummer, Rahmennummer)
- *cycle serial number (factory number, frame number)*
52 die Vorderradnabe
- *front hub (front hub assembly)*
53 die Mutter
- *wheel nut*
54 die Kontermutter, mit Sternprägung f
- *locknut (locking nut)*
55 die Nasenscheibe
- *washer (slotted cone adjusting washer)*
56 die Kugel
- *ball bearing*
57 die Staubkappe
- *dust cap*

58 der Konus
- *cone (adjusting cone)*
59 die Tülle
- *centre (Am. center) hub*
60 das Rohr
- *spindle*
61 die Achse
- *axle*
62 der Ölerklipp
- *clip covering lubrication hole (lubricator)*
63 die Freilaufnabe, mit Rücktrittbremse f
- *free-wheel hub with back-pedal brake (with coaster brake)*
64 die Sicherungsmutter
- *safety nut*
65 der Helmöler (Öler)
- *lubricator*
66 der Bremshebel
- *brake arm*
67 der Hebelkonus
- *brake arm cone*
68 der Kugelring, mit Kugeln f im Kugellager n
- *bearing cup with ball bearings in ball race*
69 die Nabenhülse
- *hub shell (hub body, hub barrel)*
70 der Bremsmantel
- *brake casing*
71 der Bremskonus
- *brake cone*
72 der Walzenführungsring
- *driver*
73 die Antriebswalze
- *driving barrel*
74 der Zahnkranz
- *sprocket*
75 der Gewindekopf
- *thread head*

76 die Achse
- *axle*
77 die Bandage
- *bracket*
78 das Fahrradpedal (Pedal, Rückstrahlpedal, Leuchtpedal, Reflektorpedal)
- *bicycle pedal (pedal, reflector pedal)*
79 die Tülle
- *cup*
80 das Pedalrohr
- *spindle*
81 die Pedalachse
- *axle*
82 die Staubkappe
- *dust cap*
83 der Pedalrahmen
- *pedal frame*
84 der Gummistift
- *rubber stud*
85 der Gummiblock
- *rubber block (rubber tread)*
86 das Rückstrahlglas
- *glass reflector*

1 das Klapprad
- *folding bicycle*
2 das Klappscharnier (*auch:* der Steckverschluß)
- *hinge* (also: *locking lever*)
3 der höhenverstellbare Lenker
- *adjustable handlebar (handlebars)*
4 der höhenverstellbare Sattel
- *adjustable saddle*
5 die Lernstützräder *n*
- *stabilizers*
6 das Mofa
- *motor-assisted bicycle*
7 der Zweitaktmotor mit Fahrtwindkühlung *f*
- *air-cooled two-stroke engine*
8 die Teleskopgabel (Telegabel)
- *telescopic forks*
9 der Rohrrahmen
- *tubular frame*
10 der Treibstofftank
- *fuel tank (petrol tank, Am. gasoline tank)*
11 der hochgezogene Lenker
- *semi-rise handlebars*
12 die Zweigangschaltung
- *two-speed gear-change (gearshift)*
13 der Formsitz
- *high-back polo saddle*
14 die Hinterradschwinge
- *swinging-arm rear fork*
15 der hochgezogene Auspuff
- *upswept exhaust*
16 der Wärmeschutz
- *heat shield*
17 die Antriebskette
- *drive chain*
18 der Sturzbügel
- *crash bar (roll bar)*
19 das (der) Tachometer (der Tacho)
- *speedometer* (coll. *speedo)*
20 das City-Bike (Akku-Bike, ein Elektrofahrzeug *n*)
- *battery-powered moped, an electrically-powered vehicle*
21 der Schwingsattel
- *swivel saddle*
22 der Akkubehälter
- *battery compartment*
23 der Drahtkorb
- *wire basket*
24 das Tourenmoped (Moped)
- *touring moped (moped)*
25 die Tretkurbel (der Tretantrieb, das Startpedal)
- *pedal crank (pedal drive, starter pedal)*
26 der Zweitakt-Einzylindermotor
- *single-cylinder two-stroke engine*
27 der Kerzenstecker
- *spark-plug cap*
28 der Treibstofftank (Gemischtank)
- *fuel tank (petrol tank, Am. gasoline tank)*
29 die Mopedleuchte
- *moped headlamp (front lamp)*
30-35 die Lenkerarmaturen
- *handlebar fittings*
30 der Drehgasgriff (Gasgriff)
- *twist grip throttle control (throttle twist grip)*
31 der Schaltdrehgriff (die Gangschaltung)
- *twist grip (gear-change, gearshift)*
32 der Kupplungshebel
- *clutch lever*

33 der Handbremshebel
- *hand brake lever*
34 das (*ugs.* der) Tachometer (der Tacho)
- *speedometer* (coll. *speedo)*
35 der Rückspiegel
- *rear-view mirror (mirror)*
36 die Vorderrad-Trommelbremse (Trommelbremse)
- *front wheel drum brake (drum brake)*
37 die Bowdenzüge *m*
- *Bowden cables (brake cables)*
38 die Brems- und Rücklichteinheit
- *stop and tail light unit*
39 das Mokick
- *light motorcycle with kickstarter*
40 das Cockpit mit Tachometer *n* und elektronischem Drehzahlmesser *m*
- *housing for instruments with speedometer and electronic rev counter (revolution counter)*
41 die Telegabel mit Faltenbalg *m*
- *telescopic shock absorber*
42 die Doppelsitzbank
- *twin seat*
43 der Kickstarter
- *kickstarter*
44 die Soziusfußraste, eine Fußraste
- *pillion footrest, a footrest*
45 der Sportlenker
- *handlebar (handlebars)*
46 der geschlossene Kettenkasten
- *chain guard*
47 der Motorroller
- *motor scooter (scooter)*
48 die abnehmbare Seitenschale
- *removable side panel*
49 der Rohrrahmen
- *tubular frame*
50 die Blechverkleidung
- *metal fairings*
51 die Raststütze
- *prop stand (stand)*
52 die Fußbremse
- *foot brake*
53 das Signalhorn
- *horn (hooter)*
54 der Haken für Handtasche *f* oder Mappe *f*
- *hook for handbag or briefcase*
55 die Fußschaltung
- *foot gear-change control (foot gearshift control)*
56 der High-riser
- *high-riser;* sim.: *Chopper*
57 der zweigeteilte Lenker
- *high-rise handlebar (handlebars)*
58 die imitierte Motorradgabel
- *imitation motorcycle fork*
59 der Banksattel (Bananensattel)
- *banana saddle*
60 der Chrombügel
- *chrome bracket*

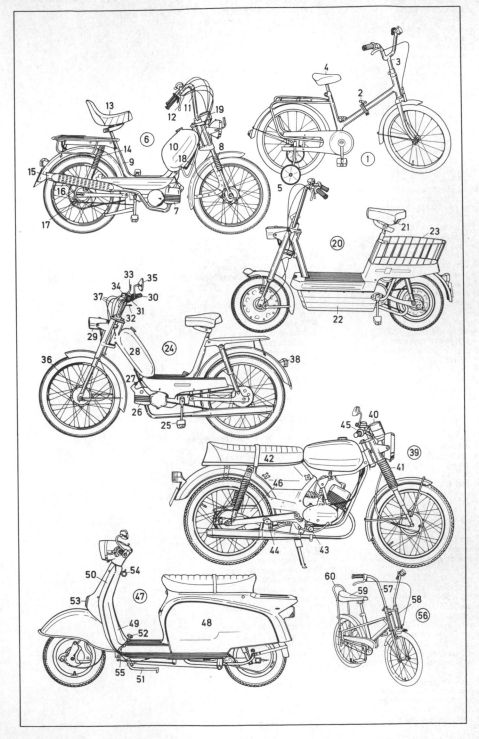

1 das Kleinmotorrad
  (Kleinkraftrad) [50 cm³]
- *lightweight motorcycle (light
  motorcycle) [50 cc]*
2 der Kraftstofftank
- *fuel tank (petrol tank, Am.
  gasoline tank)*
3 der fahrtwindgekühlte
  Einzylinder-Viertaktmotor (mit
  obenliegender Nockenwelle)
- *air-cooled single-cylinder
  four-stroke engine (with overhead
  camshaft)*
4 der Vergaser
- *carburettor (Am. carburetor)*
5 das Ansaugrohr
- *intake pipe*
6 das Fünfganggetriebe
- *five-speed gearbox*
7 die Hinterradschwinge
- *swinging-arm rear fork*
8 das polizeiliche Kennzeichen
- *number plate (Am. license plate)*
9 das Rück- und Bremslicht
- *stop and tail light (rear light)*
10 der Scheinwerfer
- *headlight (headlamp)*
11 die vordere Trommelbremse
- *front drum brake*
12 das Bremsseil, ein Bowdenzug m
- *brake cable (brake line), a Bowden
  cable*
13 die hintere Trommelbremse
- *rear drum brake*
14 die Sportsitzbank
- *racing-style twin seat*
15 der hochgezogene Auspuff
- *upswept exhaust*
16 die Geländemaschine [125 cm³]
  (das Geländesportmotorrad, ein
  leichtes Motorrad)
- *scrambling motorcycle
  (cross-country motorcycle) [125 cc],
  a light motorcycle*
17 der Doppelschleifenrahmen
- *lightweight cradle frame*
18 das Startnummernschild
- *number disc (disk)*
19 die Einmannsitzbank
- *solo seat*
20 die Kühlrippen f
- *cooling ribs*
21 der Motorradständer
- *motorcycle stand*
22 die Motorradkette
- *motorcycle chain*
23 die Teleskopfedergabel
- *telescopic shock absorber*
24 die Speichen f
- *spokes*
25 die Felge
- *rim (wheel rim)*
26 der Motorradreifen
- *motorcycle tyre (Am. tire)*
27 das Reifenprofil
- *tyre (Am. tire) tread*
28 der Gangschaltungshebel
- *gear-change lever (gearshift lever)*
29 der Gasdrehgriff
- *twist grip throttle control (throttle
  twist grip)*
30 der Rückspiegel
- *rear-view mirror (mirror)*
31-58 schwere Motorräder n
- *heavy (heavyweight,
  large-capacity) motorcycles*

31 das Schwerkraftrad mit
  wassergekühltem Motor m
- *heavyweight motorcycle with
  water-cooled engine*
32 die vordere Scheibenbremse
- *front disc (disk) brake*
33 der Scheibenbremssattel
- *disc (disk) brake calliper (caliper)*
34 die Steckachse
- *floating axle*
35 der Wasserkühler
- *water cooler*
36 der Frischöltank
- *oil tank*
37 das Blinklicht (der
  Richtungsanzeiger)
- *indicator (indicator light, turn
  indicator light)*
38 der Kickstarter
- *kickstarter*
39 der wassergekühlte Motor
- *water-cooled engine*
40 der (das) Tachometer
- *speedometer*
41 der Drehzahlmesser
- *rev counter (revolution counter)*
42 das hintere Blinklicht
- *rear indicator (indicator light)*
43 die verkleidete schwere Maschine
  [1000 cm³]
- *heavy (heavyweight,
  high-performance) machine with
  fairing [1000 cc]*
44 das Integral-Cockpit, eine
  integrierte Verkleidung
- *integrated streamlining, an
  integrated fairing*
45 die Blinkleuchte
- *indicator (indicator light, turn
  indicator light)*
46 die Klarsichtscheibe
- *anti-mist windscreen (Am.
  windshield)*
47 der Zweizylinderboxermotor mit
  Kardanantrieb m
- *horizontally-opposed twin engine
  with cardan transmission*
48 das Leichtmetallgußrad
- *light alloy wheel*
49 die Vierzylindermaschine [400 cm³]
- *four-cylinder machine [400 cc]*
50 der fahrtwindgekühlte
  Vierzylinder-Viertaktmotor
- *air-cooled four-cylinder
  four-stroke engine*
51 das Vier-in-einem-Auspuffrohr
- *four-pipe megaphone exhaust pipe*
52 der elektrische Anlasser
- *electric starter button*
53 die Beiwagenmaschine
- *sidecar machine*
54 das Beiwagenschiff
- *sidecar body*
55 die Beiwagenstoßstange
- *sidecar crash bar*
56 die Begrenzungsleuchte
- *sidelight (Am. sidemarker lamp)*
57 das Beiwagenrad
- *sidecar wheel*
58 die Beiwagenwindschutzscheibe
- *sidecar windscreen (Am.
  windshield)*

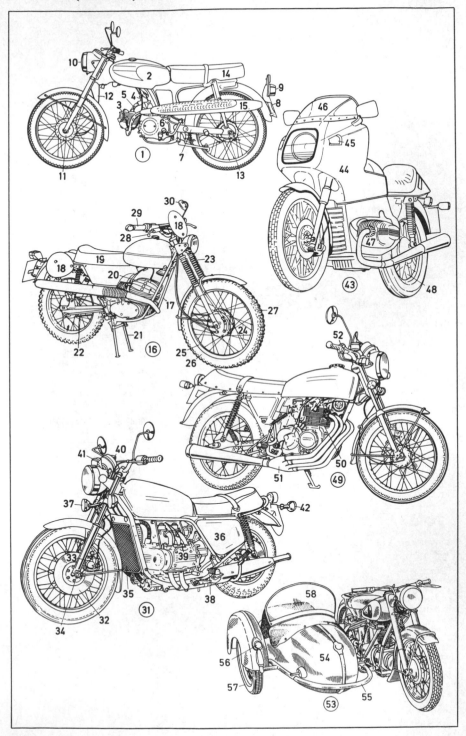

1 der Acht-Zylinder-V-Ottomotor mit Benzineinspritzung *f* im Längsschnitt *m*
- *eight-cylinder V (vee) fuel-injection spark-ignition engine (Otto-cycle engine)*

2 der Ottomotor im Querschnitt *m*
- *cross-section of spark-ignition engine (Otto-cycle internal combustion engine)*

3 der Fünf-Zylinder-Reihen-Dieselmotor im Längsschnitt *m*
- *sectional view of five-cylinder in-line diesel engine*

4 der Dieselmotor im Querschnitt *m*
- *cross-section of diesel engine*

5 der Zwei-Scheiben-Wankelmotor (Rotationskolbenmotor)
- *two-rotor Wankel engine (rotary engine)*

6 der Ein-Zylinder-Zweitakt-Ottomotor
- *single-cylinder two-stroke internal combustion engine*

7 der Lüfter
- *fan*

8 die Viskoselüfterkupplung
- *fan clutch for viscous drive*

9 der Zündverteiler mit Unterdruckdose *f* für die Zündverstellung
- *ignition distributor (distributor) with vacuum timing control*

10 die Zweifach-Rollenkette
- *double roller chain*

11 das Nockenwellenlager
- *camshaft bearing*

12 die Entlüftungsleitung
- *air-bleed duct*

13 das Ölrohr zur Nockenwellenschmierung *f*
- *oil pipe for camshaft lubrication*

14 die Nockenwelle, eine obenliegende Nockenwelle
- *camshaft, an overhead camshaft*

15 der Klappenstutzen
- *venturi throat*

16 der Sauggeräuschdämpfer (Ansauggeräuschdämpfer)
- *intake silencer (absorption silencer, Am. absorption muffler)*

17 der Kraftstoffdruckregler
- *fuel pressure regulator*

18 das Saugrohr (Ansaugrohr)
- *inlet manifold*

19 das Zylinderkurbelgehäuse
- *cylinder crankcase*

20 das Schwungrad
- *flywheel*

21 die Pleuelstange
- *connecting rod (piston rod)*

22 der Kurbelwellenlagerdeckel
- *cover of crankshaft bearing*

23 die Kurbelwelle
- *crankshaft*

24 die Ölablaßschraube
- *oil bleeder screw (oil drain plug)*

25 die Rollenkette des Ölpumpenantriebs *m*
- *roller chain of oil pump drive*

26 der Schwingungsdämpfer
- *vibration damper*

27 die Antriebswelle für den Zündverteiler
- *distributor shaft for the ignition distributor (distributor)*

28 der Öleinfüllstutzen
- *oil filler neck*

29 der Filtereinsatz
- *diaphragm spring*

30 das Reguliergestänge
- *control linkage*

31 die Kraftstoffringleitung
- *fuel supply pipe (Am. fuel line)*

32 das Einspritzventil
- *fuel injector (injection nozzle)*

33 der Schwinghebel
- *rocker arm*

34 die Schwinghebellagerung
- *rocker arm mounting*

35 die Zündkerze mit Entstörstecker *m*
- *spark plug (sparking plug) with suppressor*

36 der Auspuffkrümmer
- *exhaust manifold*

37 der Kolben mit Kolbenringen *m* und Ölabstreifring *m*
- *piston with piston rings and oil scraper ring*

38 der Motorträger
- *engine mounting*

39 der Zwischenflansch
- *dog flange (dog)*

40 das Ölwannenoberteil
- *crankcase*

41 das Ölwannenunterteil
- *oil sump (sump)*

42 die Ölpumpe
- *oil pump*

43 das (der) Ölfilter
- *oil filter*

44 der Anlasser
- *starter motor (starting motor)*

45 der Zylinderkopf
- *cylinder head*

46 das Auslaßventil
- *exhaust valve*

47 der Ölmeßstab (Ölpeilstab)
- *dipstick*

48 die Zylinderkopfhaube
- *cylinder head gasket*

49 die Zweifach-Hülsenkette
- *double bushing chain*

50 der Temperaturgeber
- *warm-up regulator*

51 der Drahtzug der Leerlaufverstellung
- *tapered needle for idling adjustment*

52 die Kraftstoffdruckleitung
- *fuel pressure pipe (fuel pressure line)*

53 die Kraftstoffleckleitung
- *fuel leak line (drip fuel line)*

54 die Einspritzdüse
- *injection nozzle (spray nozzle)*

55 der Heizungsanschluß
- *heater plug*

56 die Auswuchtscheibe
- *thrust washer*

57 die Zwischenradwelle für den Einspritzpumpenantrieb
- *intermediate gear shaft for the injection pump drive*

58 der Spritzversteller (Einspritzversteller)
- *injection timer unit*

59 die Unterdruckpumpe
- *vacuum pump (low-pressure regulator)*

60 die Kurvenscheibe für die Unterdruckpumpe
- *cam for vacuum pump*

61 die Wasserpumpe (Kühlwasserpumpe)
- *water pump (coolant pump)*

62 der Kühlwasserthermostat
- *cooling water thermostat*

63 der Thermoschalter
- *thermo time switch*

64 die Kraftstoff-Handpumpe
- *fuel hand pump*

65 die Einspritzpumpe
- *injection pump*

66 die Glühkerze
- *glow plug*

67 das Ölüberdruckventil
- *oil pressure limiting valve*

68 die Wankelscheibe (der Rotationskolben)
- *rotor*

69 die Dichtleiste
- *seal*

70 der Drehmomentwandler (Föttinger-Wandler)
- *torque converter*

71 die Einscheibenkupplung
- *single-plate clutch*

72 das Mehrganggetriebe (Mehrstufengetriebe)
- *multi-speed gearing (multi-step gearing)*

73 die Portliner *m* im Auspuffkrümmer *m* zur Verbesserung der Abgasentgiftung
- *port liners in the exhaust manifold for emission control*

74 die Scheibenbremse
- *disc (disk) brake*

75 die Achsdifferentialgetriebe
- *differential gear (differential)*

76 die Lichtmaschine
- *generator*

77 die Fußschaltung
- *foot gear-change control (foot gearshift control)*

78 die Mehrscheiben-Trockenkupplung
- *dry multi-plate clutch*

79 der Flachstromvergaser
- *cross-draught (Am. cross-draft) carburettor (Am. carburetor)*

80 die Kühlrippen *f*
- *cooling ribs*

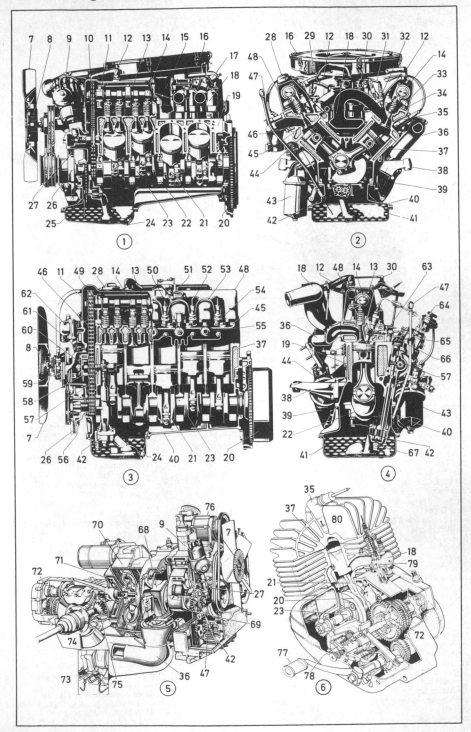

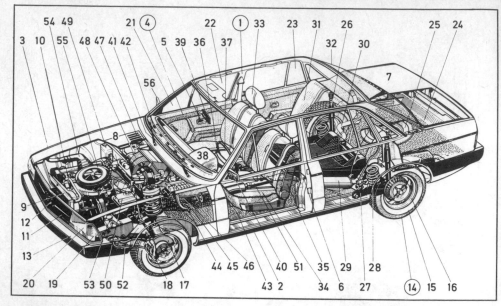

1-56 das Automobil (Auto, Kraftfahrzeug, Kfz, der Kraftwagen, Wagen), ein Personenwagen (Personenfahrzeug *n*)
- *motor car (car, Am. automobile, auto), a passenger vehicle*
1 die selbsttragende Karosserie
- *monocoque body (unitary body)*
2 das Fahrgestell (Chassis), die Bodengruppe der Karosserie
- *chassis, the understructure of the body*
3 der vordere Kotflügel
- *front wing (Am. front fender)*
4 die Autotür (Wagentür)
- *car door*
5 der Türgriff
- *door handle*
6 das Türschloß
- *door lock*
7 der Kofferraumdeckel (die Heckklappe)
- *boot lid (Am. trunk lid)*
8 die Motorhaube
- *bonnet (Am. hood)*
9 der Kühler
- *radiator*
10 die Kühlwasserleitung
- *cooling water pipe*
11 der Kühlergrill
- *radiator grill*
12 das Markenzeichen (die Automarke)
- *badging*
13 die vordere Stoßstange, mit Gummiauflage *f*
- *rubber-covered front bumper (Am. front fender)*
14 das Autorad (Wagenrad), ein Scheibenrad *n*
- *car wheel, a disc (disk) wheel*
15 der Autoreifen
- *car tyre (Am. automobile tire)*
16 die Felge
- *rim (wheel rim)*

17-18 die Scheibenbremse
- *disc (disk) brake*
17 die Bremsscheibe
- *brake disc (disk) (braking disc)*
18 der Bremssattel
- *calliper (caliper)*
19 der vordere Blinker
- *front indicator light (front turn indicator light)*
20 der Scheinwerfer mit Fernlicht *n*, Abblendlicht, Standlicht (Begrenzungsleuchte *f*)
- *headlight (headlamp) with main beam (high beam), dipped beam (low beam), sidelight (side lamp, Am. sidemarker lamp)*
21 die Windschutzscheibe, eine Panoramascheibe
- *windscreen (Am. windshield), a panoramic windscreen*
22 das versenkbare Türfenster
- *crank-operated car window*
23 das ausstellbare Fondfenster
- *quarter light (quarter vent)*
24 der Kofferraum
- *boot (Am. trunk)*
25 das Reserverad
- *spare wheel*
26 der Stoßdämpfer
- *damper (shock absorber)*
27 der Längslenker
- *trailing arm*
28 die Schraubenfeder
- *coil spring*
29 der Auspufftopf
- *silencer (Am. muffler)*
30 die Zwangsentlüftung
- *automatic ventilation system*
31 die Fondsitze *m*
- *rear seats*
32 die Heckscheibe
- *rear window*

33 die verstellbare Kopfstütze
- *adjustable headrest (head restraint)*
34 der Fahrersitz, ein Liegesitz *m*
- *driver's seat, a reclining seat*
35 die umlegbare Rückenlehne
- *reclining backrest*
36 der Beifahrersitz
- *passenger seat*
37 das Lenkrad (Steuerrad, Volant *m* [schweiz. meist *s*])
- *steering wheel*
38 das Cockpit mit Tachometer *n od. m* (Tacho *m*), Drehzahlmesser *m*, Zeituhr *f*, Benzinuhr, Kühlmitteltemperaturanzeige, Öltemperaturanzeige
- *centre (Am. center) console containing speedometer (coll. speedo), revolution counter (rev counter, tachometer), clock, fuel gauge (Am. gage), water temperature gauge, oil temperature gauge*
39 der Innenrückspiegel
- *inside rear-view mirror*
40 der linke Außenspiegel
- *left-hand wing mirror*
41 der Scheibenwischer
- *windscreen wiper (Am. windshield wiper)*
42 die Defrosterdüsen *f*
- *defroster vents*
43 der Bodenteppich
- *carpeting*
44 das Kupplungspedal (*ugs.* die Kupplung)
- *clutch pedal (coll. clutch)*
45 das Bremspedal (*ugs.* die Bremse)
- *brake pedal (coll. brake)*
46 das Gaspedal (*ugs.* das Gas)
- *accelerator pedal (coll. accelerator)*
47 der Lufteinlaßschlitz
- *inlet vent*

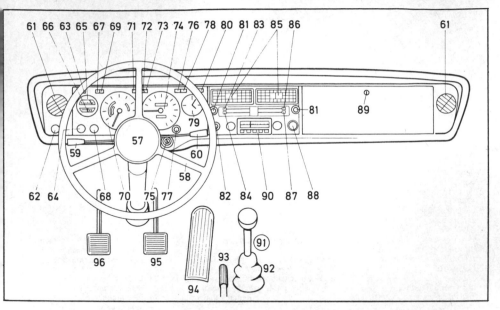

48 das Luftgebläse für die Belüftung
- *blower fan*
49 der Bremsflüssigkeitsbehälter
- *brake fluid reservoir*
50 die Batterie
- *battery*
51 die Auspuffleitung
- *exhaust pipe*
52 das Vorderradfahrwerk, mit
Vorderradantrieb *m*
- *front running gear with front wheel
drive*
53 der Motorträger
- *engine mounting*
54 der Ansauggeräuschdämpfer
- *intake silencer (Am. intake muffler)*
55 der (das) Luftfilter
- *air filter (air cleaner)*
56 der rechte Außenspiegel
- *right-hand wing mirror*
57-90 das Armaturenbrett
- *dashboard (fascia panel)*
57 die Lenkradnabe, als Pralltopf *m*
(Aufprallschutz) ausgebildet
- *controlled-collapse steering column*
58 die Lenkradspeiche
- *steering wheel spoke*
59 der Blink- und Abblendschalter
- *indicator and dimming switch*
60 der Wisch-Wasch- und Hupschalter
- *wiper/washer switch and horn*
61 die Mischdüse für das Seitenfenster
- *side window blower*
62 der Standlicht-, Scheinwerfer- und
Parkleuchtenschalter
- *sidelight, headlight and parking
light switch*
63 die Nebellichtkontrolle
- *fog lamp warning light*
64 der Schalter für die
Nebelscheinwerfer *m* und das
Nebelschlußlicht
- *fog headlamp and rear lamp switch*

65 die Kraftstoffanzeige (Benzinuhr)
- *fuel gauge (Am. gage)*
66 die Kühlmitteltemperaturanzeige
- *water temperature gauge (Am. gage)*
67 die Kontrolle für die
Nebelschlußleuchte
- *warning light for rear fog lamp*
68 der Warnlichtschalter
- *hazard flasher switch*
69 die Fernlichtkontrolle
- *main beam warning light*
70 der elektrische Drehzahlmesser
- *electric rev counter (revolution
counter)*
71 die Kraftstoffkontrollampe
- *fuel warning light*
72 die Kontrolleuchte für die
Handbremse und die
Zweikreisbremsanlage
- *warning light for the hand brake
and dual-circuit brake system*
73 die Öldruckkontrolleuchte
- *oil pressure warning light*
74 das (der) Tachometer mit
Tageskilometerzähler *m*
- *speedometer (coll. speedo) with trip
mileage recorder*
75 das Zünd- und Lenkradschloß
- *starter and steering lock*
76 die Blinker- und Warnlichtkontrolle
- *warning lights for turn indicators
and hazard flashers*
77 der Regler für die
Innenbeleuchtung und Rücksteller
m für den Tageskilometerzähler
- *switch for the courtesy light and reset
button for the trip mileage recorder*
78 die Ladestromkontrolle
- *ammeter*
79 die elektrische Zeituhr
- *electric clock*
80 die Kontrolleuchte für die
Heckscheibenheizung

- *warning light for heated rear
window*
81 der Schalter für die
Fußraumbelüftung
- *switch for the leg space ventilation*
82 der Schalter für die heizbare
Heckscheibe
- *rear window heating switch*
83 der Hebel für die
Gebläseeinstellung
- *ventilation switch*
84 der Hebel für die
Temperaturdosierung
- *temperature regulator*
85 der umstellbare
Frischluftausströmer
- *fresh-air inlet and control*
86 der Hebel für die
Frischluftregulierung
- *fresh-air regulator*
87 der Hebel für die
Warmluftverteilung
- *warm-air regulator*
88 der Zigarrenanzünder
- *cigar lighter*
89 das Handschuhkastenschloß
- *glove compartment (glove box) lock*
90 das Autoradio
- *car radio*
91 der Schalthebel (Schaltknüppel, die
Knüppelschaltung)
- *gear lever (gearshift lever,
floor-type gear-change)*
92 die Ledermanschette
- *leather gaiter*
93 der Handbremshebel
- *hand brake lever*
94 der Gashebel (das Gaspedal)
- *accelerator pedal*
95 das Bremspedal
- *brake pedal*
96 das Kupplungspedal
- *clutch pedal*

1-15 der Vergaser, ein
Fallstromvergaser *m*
- *carburettor* (Am. *carburetor*), a
down-draught (Am. *down-draft*)
carburettor
1 die Leerlaufdüse
- *idling jet (slow-running jet)*
2 die Leerlaufluftdüse
- *idling air jet (idle air bleed)*
3 die Luftkorrekturdüse
- *air correction jet*
4 die Ausgleichsluft
- *compensating airstream*
5 die Hauptluft
- *main airstream*
6 die Starterklappe (Vordrossel)
- *choke flap*
7 der Austrittsarm
- *plunger*
8 der Lufttrichter
- *venturi*
9 die Drosselklappe
- *throttle valve (butterfly valve)*
10 das Mischrohr
- *emulsion tube*
11 die Leerlaufgemischregulierschraube
- *idle mixture adjustment screw*
12 die Hauptdüse
- *main jet*
13 der Kraftstoffzufluß
- *fuel (Am. gasoline inlet) (inlet
manifold)*
14 die Schwimmerkammer
- *float chamber*
15 der Schwimmer
- *float*
16-27 die Druckumlaufschmierung
- *pressure-feed lubricating system*
16 die Ölpumpe
- *oil pump*
17 der Ölvorrat (Ölsumpf)
- *oil sump*
18 das (der) Ölgrobfilter
- *sump filter*
19 der Ölkühler
- *oil cooler*
20 das (der) Feinfilter
- *oil filter*
21 die Hauptölbohrung
- *main oil gallery (drilled gallery)*
22 die Stichleitung
- *crankshaft drilling (crankshaft
tributary, crankshaft bleed)*
23 das Kurbelwellenlager
- *crankshaft bearing (main bearing)*
24 das Nockenwellenlager
- *camshaft bearing*
25 das Pleuellager
- *connecting-rod bearing*
26 die Kurbelzapfenbohrung
- *gudgeon pin (piston pin)*
27 die Nebenleitung
- *bleed*
28-47 das Viergang-Synchrongetriebe
- *four-speed synchromesh gearbox*
28 der Kupplungsfußhebel
- *clutch pedal*
29 die Kurbelwelle
- *crankshaft*
30 die Antriebswelle
- *drive shaft (propeller shaft)*
31 der Anlaßzahnkranz
- *starting gear ring*
32 die Schiebemuffe für den 3. und
4. Gang
- *sliding sleeve for 3rd and 4th gear*

33 der Synchronkegel
(Gleichlaufkegel)
- *synchronizing cone*
34 das Schraubenrad für den 3. Gang
- *helical gear wheel for 3rd gear*
35 die Schiebemuffe für den 1. und
2. Gang
- *sliding sleeve for 1st and 2nd gear*
36 das Schraubenrad für den 1. Gang
- *helical gear wheel for 1st gear*
37 die Vorlegewelle
- *lay shaft*
38 der Tachometerantrieb
- *speedometer drive*
39 das Schraubenrad für den
Tachometerantrieb
- *helical gear wheel for speedometer
drive*
40 die Hauptwelle
- *main shaft*
41 die Schaltstangen *f*
- *gearshift rods*
42 die Schaltgabel für den 1. und
2. Gang
- *selector fork for 1st and
2nd gear*
43 das Schraubenrad für den 2. Gang
- *helical gear wheel for 2nd gear*
44 der Schaltkopf, mit Rückwärtsgang *m*
- *selector head with reverse gear*
45 die Schaltgabel für den 3. und 4.
Gang
- *selector fork for 3rd and 4th gear*
46 der Schalthebel (Schaltknüppel)
- *gear lever (gearshift lever)*
47 das Schaltschema
- *gear-change pattern (gearshift
pattern, shift pattern)*
48-55 die Scheibenbremse
- *disc (disk) brake [assembly]*
48 die Bremsscheibe
- *brake disc (disk) (braking disc)*
49 der Bremssattel, ein Festsattel *m*,
mit den Bremsklötzen *m*
- *calliper (caliper), a fixed calliper
with friction pads*
50 die Servobremstrommel
(Handbremstrommel)
- *servo cylinder (servo unit)*
51 der Bremsbacken
- *brake shoes*
52 der Bremsbelag
- *brake lining*
53 der Bremsleitungsanschluß
- *outlet to brake line*
54 der Radzylinder
- *wheel cylinder*
55 die Rückholfeder
- *return spring*
56-59 das Lenkgetriebe (die
Schneckenlenkung)
- *steering gear (worm-and-nut
steering gear)*
56 die Lenksäule
- *steering column*
57 das Schneckenradsegment
- *worm gear sector*
58 der Lenkstockhebel
- *steering drop arm*
59 das Schneckengewinde
- *worm*
**60-64 die wasserseitig regulierte
Heizanlage** (Wagenheizung)
- *water-controlled heater*
60 der Frischlufteintritt
- *air intake*

61 der Wärmetauscher
- *heat exchanger (heater box)*
62 das Heizgebläse
- *blower fan*
63 die Regulierklappe
- *flap valve*
64 die Defrosterdüse
- *defroster vent*
65-71 die Starrachse
- *live axle (rigid axle)*
65 das Reaktionsrohr
- *propeller shaft*
66 der Längslenker
- *trailing arm*
67 das Gummilager
- *rubber bush*
68 die Schraubenfeder
- *coil spring*
69 der Stoßdämpfer
- *damper (shock absorber)*
70 der Panhardstab
- *Panhard rod*
71 der Stabilisator
- *stabilizer bar*
72-84 das McPherson-Federbein
- *MacPherson strut unit*
72 die Karosserieabstützung
- *body-fixing plate*
73 das Federbeinstützlager
- *upper bearing*
74 die Schraubenfeder
- *suspension spring*
75 die Kolbenstange
- *piston rod*
76 der Federbeinstoßdämpfer
- *suspension damper*
77 die Felge
- *rim (wheel rim)*
78 der Achszapfen
- *stub axle*
79 der Spurstangenhebel
- *steering arm*
80 das Führungsgelenk
- *track-rod ball-joint*
81 die Zugstrebe
- *trailing link arm*
82 das Gummilager
- *bump rubber (rubber bonding)*
83 das Achslager
- *lower bearing*
84 der Vorderachsträger
- *lower suspension arm*

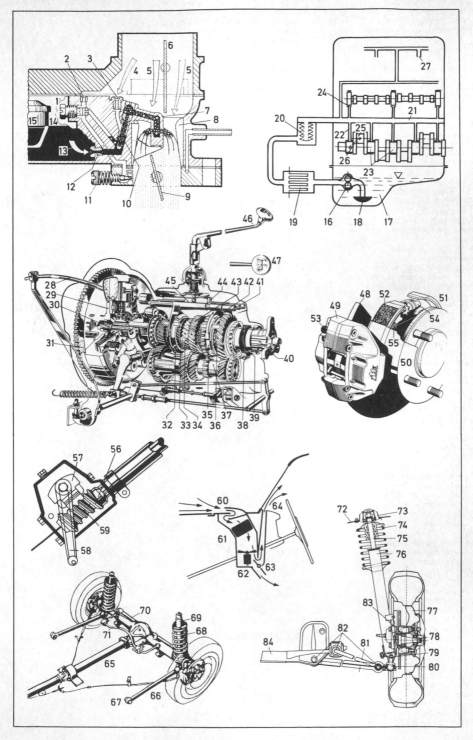

1-36 Autotypen *m*
(Personenwagentypen)
- *car models (Am. automobile models)*

1 die Acht-Zylinder-Pullmannlimousine mit drei Sitzreihen *f*
- *eight-cylinder limousine with three rows of three-abreast seating*

2 die Fahrertür
- *driver's door*

3 die Fondtür
- *rear door*

4 die viertürige Limousine
- *four-door saloon car (Am. four-door sedan)*

5 die Vordertür
- *front door*

6 die Hintertür
- *rear door*

7 die Vordersitzkopfstütze
- *front seat headrest (front seat head restraint)*

8 die Hintersitzkopfstütze
- *rear seat headrest (rear seat head restraint)*

9 die Kabriolimousine
- *convertible*

10 das zurückklappbare Verdeck
- *convertible (collapsible) hood (top)*

11 der Schalensitz (Sportsitz)
- *bucket seat*

12 der Buggy (das Dünenfahrzeug)
- *buggy (dune buggy)*

13 der Überrollbügel
- *roll bar*

14 die Kunststoffkarosserie
- *fibre glass body*

15 der Kombiwagen (das Kombifahrzeug, der Kombinationskraftwagen, Break, Station wagon, *ugs.* Kombi)
- *estate car (shooting brake, estate, . Am. station wagon)*

16 die Heckklappe
- *tailgate*

17 der Laderaum (das Heckabteil)
- *boot space (luggage compartment)*

18 die dreitürige Kombilimousine
- *three-door hatchback*

19 der Kleinwagen (*ugs.* Mini), ein Dreitürer *m*
- *small three-door car (mini)*

20 die Hecktür
- *rear door (tailgate)*

21 die Ladekante
- *sill*

22 die umlegbare Rücksitzbank
- *folding back seat*

23 der Kofferraum
- *boot (luggage compartment, Am. trunk)*

24 das Schiebedach (Stahlschiebedach)
- *sliding roof (sunroof, steel sunroof)*

25 die zweitürige Limousine
- *two-door saloon car (Am. two-door sedan)*

26 der Roadster (das Sportkabrio, Sportkabriolett, Sportcabrio, Sportcabriolet), ein Zweisitzer *m*
- *roadster (hard-top), a two-seater*

27 das Hardtop
- *hard top*

28 das Sportcoupé, ein 2+2-Sitzer *m* (Zweisitzer *m* mit Notsitzen *m*)

- *sporting coupé, a two-plus-two coupé (two-seater with removable back seats)*

29 das Fließheck (der Liftback)
- *fastback (liftback)*

30 die Spoilerkante
- *spoiler rim*

31 die integrierte Kopfstütze
- *integral headrest (integral head restraint)*

32 der Grand-Tourisme-Wagen (GT-Wagen)
- *GT car (gran turismo car)*

33 die integrierte Stoßstange
- *integral bumper (Am. integral fender)*

34 der Heckspoiler
- *rear spoiler*

35 die Heckpartie
- *back*

36 der Frontspoiler
- *front spoiler*

1 der geländegängige Kleinlaster mit
Allradantrieb *m* (Vierradantrieb)
- *light cross-country lorry (light
truck, pickup truck) with all-wheel
drive (four-wheel drive)*
2 das Fahrerhaus
- *cab (driver's cab)*
3 die Ladepritsche
- *loading platform (body)*
4 der Ersatzreifen (Reservereifen),
ein Geländereifen *m*
- *spare tyre (Am. spare tire), a
cross-country tyre*
5 der Kleinlasttransporter
- *light lorry (light truck, pickup
truck)*
6 die Pritschenausführung (der
Pritschenwagen)
- *platform truck*
7 die Kastenausführung (der
Kastenwagen)
- *medium van*
8 die seitliche Schiebetür (Ladetür)
- *sliding side door [for loading and
unloading]*
9 der Kleinbus
- *minibus*
10 das Faltschiebedach
- *folding top (sliding roof)*
11 die Hecktür
- *rear door*
12 die seitliche Klapptür
- *hinged side door*
13 der Gepäckraum
- *luggage compartment*
14 der Fahrgastsitz
- *passenger seat*
15 die Fahrerkabine
- *cab (driver's cab)*
16 der Luftschlitz
- *air inlet*
17 der Reiseomnibus (Autobus, Bus,
schweiz. Autocar)
- *motor coach (coach, bus)*
18 das Gepäckfach
- *luggage locker*
19 das Handgepäck (der Koffer)
- *hand luggage (suitcase, case)*
20 der Schwerlastzug
- *heavy lorry (heavy truck, heavy
motor truck)*
21 das Zugfahrzeug
- *tractive unit (tractor, towing
vehicle)*
22 der Anhänger
- *trailer (drawbar trailer)*
23 die Wechselpritsche
- *swop platform (body)*
24 der Dreiseitenkipper
- *three-way tipper (three-way dump
truck)*
25 die Kipppritsche
- *tipping body (dump body)*
26 der Hydraulikzylinder
- *hydraulic cylinder*
27 die aufgeständerte Containerplatte
- *supported container platform*
28 der Sattelschlepper, ein Tankzug *m*
- *articulated vehicle, a vehicle tanker*
29 die Sattelzugmaschine
- *tractive unit (tractor, towing
vehicle)*
30-33 der Tankauflieger
- *semi-trailer (skeletal)*
30 der Tank
- *tank*

31 das Drehgelenk
- *turntable*
32 das Hilfsfahrwerk
- *undercarriage*
33 das Reserverad
- *spare wheel*
34 der kleine Reise- und Linienbus in
Cityversion *f*
- *midi bus [for short-route town
operations]*
35 die Außenschwingtür
- *outward-opening doors*
36 der Doppeldeckbus
(Doppeldeckomnibus,
Oberdeckomnibus)
- *double-deck bus (double-decker
bus)*
37 das Unterdeck
- *lower deck (lower saloon)*
38 das Oberdeck
- *upper deck (upper saloon)*
39 der Aufstieg
- *boarding platform*
40 der Oberleitungsbus (Trolleybus,
Obus, Oberleitungsomnibus)
- *trolley bus*
41 der Stromabnehmer (Kontaktarm)
- *current collector*
42 die Kontaktrolle (der Trolley)
- *trolley (trolley shoe)*
43 die Zweidrahtoberleitung
(Doppeloberleitung)
- *overhead wires*
44 der Trolleybusanhänger
- *trolley bus trailer*
45 der Gummiwulstübergang
- *pneumatically sprung rubber
connection*

1-55 die Spezialwerkstatt
(Vertragswerkstatt)
- **agent's garage** *(distributor's garage,*
  Am. specialty shop)
1-23 der Diagnosestand
- *diagnostic test bay*
1 das Diagnosegerät
- *computer*
2 der Diagnosestecker
(Zentralstecker)
- *main computer plug*
3 das Diagnosekabel
- *computer harness (computer cable)*
4 der Umschalter für automatischen
oder manuellen Meßbetrieb
- *switch from automatic to manual*
5 der Programmkarteneinschub
- *slot for program cards*
6 der Drucker
- *print-out machine (printer)*
7 das Diagnoseberichtformular
- *condition report (data print-out)*
8 das Handsteuergerät
- *master selector (hand control)*
9 die Bewertungslampen *f* [grün: in
Ordnung; rot: nicht in Ordnung]
- *light readout [green: OK; red: not*
OK]
10 der Aufbewahrungskasten für die
Programmkarten *f*
- *rack for program cards*
11 die Netztaste
- *mains button*

12 die Schnellprogrammtaste
- *switch for fast readout*
13 der Zündwinkeleinschub
- *firing sequence insert*
14 das Ablagefach
- *shelf for used cards*
15 der Kabelgalgen
- *cable boom*
16 das Öltemperaturmeßkabel
- *oil temperature sensor*
17 das Prüfgerät für die Spur- und
Sturzmessung rechts
- *test equipment for wheel and*
steering alignment
18 die Optikplatte rechts
- *right-hand optic plate*
19 die Auslösetransistoren *m*
- *actuating transistors*
20 der Projektorschalter
- *projector switch*
21 die Photoleiste für die
Sturzmessung
- *check light for wheel alignment*
22 die Photoleiste für die
Spurmessung
- *check light for steering alignment*
23 der elektrische Schraubendreher
- *power screwdriver*
24 das Prüfgerät für die
Scheinwerfereinstellung
- *beam setter*
25 die hydraulische Hebebühne
- *hydraulic lift*

26 der verstellbare Hebebühnenarm
- *adjustable arm of hydraulic lift*
27 der Hebebühnenstempel
- *hydraulic lift pad*
28 die Radmulde
- *excavation*
29 der Druckluftmesser
- *pressure gauge (Am. gage)*
30 die Abschmierpresse
- *grease gun*
31 der Kleinteilekasten
- *odds-and-ends box*
32 die Ersatzteilliste
- *wall chart [of spare parts]*

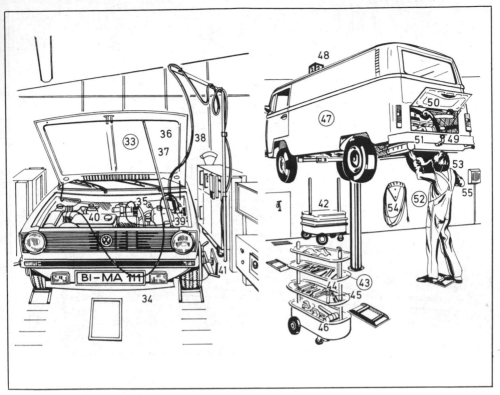

33 die automatische Diagnose
- *automatic computer test*
34 das Kraftfahrzeug (Auto), ein
   Personenwagen *m*
- *motor car (car, Am. automobile,*
   auto), a passenger vehicle
35 der Motorraum
- *engine compartment*
36 die Motorhaube
- *bonnet (Am. hood)*
37 die Motorhaubenstange
- *bonnet support (Am. hood support)*
38 das Diagnosekabel
- *computer harness (computer cable)*
39 die Diagnosesteckbuchse
   (Zentralsteckbuchse)
- *main computer socket*
40 das Öltemperaturfühlerkabel
- *oil temperature sensor*
41 der Radspiegel für die optische
   Spur- und Sturzmessung
- *wheel mirror for visual wheel and*
   steering alignment
42 der Werkzeugwagen
- *tool trolley*
43 das Werkzeug
- *tools*
44 der Schraubenschlüssel
- *impact wrench*
45 der Drehmomentschlüssel
- *torque wrench*
46 der Ausbeulhammer
- *body hammer (roughing-out hammer)*

47 das Reparaturfahrzeug, ein
   Kleinbus *m*
- *vehicle under repair, a minibus*
48 die Reparaturnummer
- *car location number*
49 der Heckmotor
- *rear engine*
50 die Heckmotorklappe
- *tailgate*
51 das Auspuffsystem
- *exhaust system*
52 die Auspuffreparatur
- *exhaust repair*
53 der Kfz-Schlosser
   (Kraftfahrzeugschlosser,
   Kraftfahrzeugmechaniker)
- *motor car mechanic (motor vehicle*
   mechanic, Am. automotive
   mechanic)
54 der Druckluftschlauch
- *air hose*
55 das Durchsagegerät
- *intercom*

1-29 die Tankstelle, eine
Selbstbedienungstankstelle
(Selfservice-Station)
- *service station (petrol station,
filling station, Am. gasoline
station, gas station), a self-service
station*
1 die Zapfsäule
(Tanksäule, *veraltet:*
Benzinpumpe, Rechenkopfsäule)
für Super- und Normalbenzin *n*
(*ähnl.:* für Dieselkraftstoff *m*)
- *petrol (Am. gasoline) pump
(blending pump) for regular and
premium grade petrol
(Am. gasoline) (sim.: for derv)*
2 der Zapfschlauch
- *hose (petrol pump, Am. gasoline
pump, hose)*
3 der Zapfhahn (die Zapfpistole)
- *nozzle*
4 der angezeigte Geldbetrag
- *cash readout*
5 die Füllmengenanzeige
- *volume readout*
6 die Preisangabe
- *price display*
7 das Leuchtzeichen
- *indicator light*
8 der Autofahrer bei der
Selbstbedienung
- *driver using self-service petrol
pump (Am. gasoline pump)*
9 der Feuerlöscher
- *fire extinguisher*
10 der Papiertuchspender
- *paper-towel dispenser*

11 das Papiertuch (Papierhandtuch)
- *paper towel*
12 der Abfallbehälter
- *litter receptacle*
13 der Zweitaktgemischbehälter
- *two-stroke blending pump*
14 das Meßglas
- *meter*
15 das Motoröl
- *engine oil*
16 die Motorölkanne
- *oil can*
17 der Reifendruckprüfer
- *tyre pressure gauge (Am. tire
pressure gage)*
18 die Druckluftleitung
- *air hose*
19 der Luftbehälter
- *static air tank*
20 das Manometer (der
Reifenfüllmesser)
- *pressure gauge (Am. gage)
(manometer)*
21 der Luftfüllstutzen
- *air filler neck*
22 die Autobox
(Reparaturbox)
- *repair bay (repair shop)*
23 der Waschschlauch, ein
Wasserschlauch *m*
- *car-wash hose, a hose (hosepipe)*
24 der Autoshop
- *accessory shop*
25 der Benzinkanister
- *petrol can (Am. gasoline can)*
26 der Regenumhang
- *rain cape*

27 die Autoreifen *m*
- *car tyres (Am. automobile tires)*
28 das Autozubehör
- *car accessories*
29 die Kasse
- *cash desk (console)*

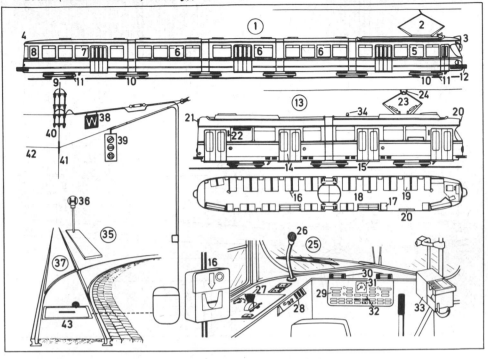

1 der zwölfachsige Gelenktriebwagen
   für den Überlandbetrieb
 - twelve-axle articulated railcar for
   interurban rail service
2 der Stromabnehmer
 - current collector
3 der Wagenbug
 - head of the railcar
4 das Wagenheck
 - rear of the railcar
5 das A-Wagenteil mit Fahrmotor m
 - carriage A containing the motor
6 das B-Wagenteil (auch: C-, D-Wagenteil)
 - carriage B (also: carriages C and D)
7 das E-Wagenteil mit Fahrmotor m
 - carriage E containing the motor
8 der Heckfahrschalter
 - rear controller
9 das Triebdrehgestell
 - bogie
10 das Laufdrehgestell
 - carrying bogie
11 der Radschutz (Bahnräumer)
 - wheel guard
12 die Rammbohle
 - bumper (Am. fender)
13 der sechsachsige Gelenktriebwagen Typ
   „Mannheim" für Straßenbahn-
   und Stadtbahnbetrieb m
 - six-axle articulated railcar
   ('Mannheim' type) for tram (Am.
   streetcar, trolley) and urban rail
   services
14 die Ein- und Ausstiegtür, eine
   Doppelfalttür
 - entrance and exit door, a double
   folding door
15 die Trittstufe
 - step
16 der Fahrscheinentwerter
 - ticket-cancelling machine

17 der Einzelsitzplatz
 - single seat
18 der Stehplatzraum
 - standing room portion
19 der Doppelsitzplatz
 - double seat
20 das Linien- und Zielschild
 - route (number) and destination sign
21 das Linienschild
 - route sign (number sign)
22 der Fahrtrichtungsanzeiger (Blinker)
 - indicator (indicator light)
23 der Scherenstromabnehmer
 - pantograph (current collector)
24 die Schleifstücke, aus Kohle f oder
   Aluminiumlegierung f
 - carbon or aluminium (Am.
   aluminum) alloy trolley shoes
25 der Fahrerstand
 - driver's position
26 das Mikrophon
 - microphone
27 der Sollwertgeber (Fahrschalter)
 - controller
28 das Funkgerät
 - radio equipment (radio
   communication set)
29 die Armaturentafel
 - dashboard
30 die Armaturentafelbeleuchtung
 - dashboard lighting
31 der Geschwindigkeitsanzeiger
 - speedometer
32 die Taster für Türenöffnen n,
   Scheibenwischer m, Innen- und
   Außenbeleuchtung f
 - buttons controlling doors,
   windscreen wipers, internal and
   external lighting
33 der Zahltisch mit Geldwechsler m
 - ticket counter with change machine

34 die Funkantenne
 - radio antenna
35 die Haltestelleninsel
 - tram stop (Am. streetcar stop,
   trolley stop)
36 das Haltestellenschild
 - tram stop sign (Am. streetcar stop
   sign, trolley stop sign)
37 die elektrische Weichenanlage
 - electric change points
38 das Weichenschaltsignal
 - points signal (switch signal)
39 der Weichensignalgeber (die
   Richtungsanzeige)
 - points change indicator
40 der Fahrleitungskontakt
 - trolley wire contact point
41 der Fahrdraht
 - trolley wire (overhead contact wire)
42 die Fahrleitungsquerverspannung
 - overhead cross wire
43 der elektromagnetische (auch:
   elektrohydraulische,
   elektromotorische)
   Weichenantrieb
 - electric (also: electrohydraulic,
   electromechanical) points
   mechanism

1-5 die Fahrbahnschichten *f*
- *road layers*
1 die Frostschutzschicht
- *anti-frost layer*
2 die bituminöse Tragschicht
- *bituminous sub-base course*
3 die untere Binderschicht
- *base course*
4 die obere Binderschicht
- *binder course*
5 die bituminöse Deckschicht
(Fahrbahndecke)
- *bituminous surface*
6 die Bordsteinkante
- *kerb (curb)*
7 der Hochbordstein
- *kerbstone (curbstone)*
8 das Gehwegpflaster
- *paving (pavement)*
9 der Bürgersteig (Gehsteig, Gehweg)
- *pavement* (Am. *sidewalk, walkway*)
10 der Rinnstein
- *gutter*
11 der Fußgängerüberweg
(Zebrastreifen)
- *pedestrian crossing (zebra crossing,* Am. *crosswalk)*
12 die Straßenecke
- *street corner*
13 der Fahrdamm
- *street*
14 die Stromversorgungskabel
- *electricity cables*
15 die Postkabel (Telefonkabel)
- *telephone cables*
16 die Postkabeldurchgangsleitung
- *telephone cable pipeline*

17 der Kabelschacht mit Abdeckung
- *cable manhole with cover (with manhole cover)*
18 der Lichtmast mit der Leuchte
- *lamp post with lamp*
19 das Stromkabel für technische
Anlagen *f*
- *electricity cables for technical installations*
20 die Telefonhausanschlußleitung
- *subscribers'* (Am. *customers') telephone lines*
21 die Gasleitung
- *gas main*
22 die Trinkwasserleitung
- *water main*
23 der Sinkkasten
- *drain*
24 der Ablaufrost
- *drain cover*
25 die Sinkkastenanschlußleitung
- *drain pipe*
26 die
Schmutzwasser-Hausanschlußleitung
- *waste pipe*
27 der Mischwasserkanal
- *combined sewer*
28 die Fernheizleitung
- *district heating main*
29 der U-Bahntunnel
- *underground tunnel*

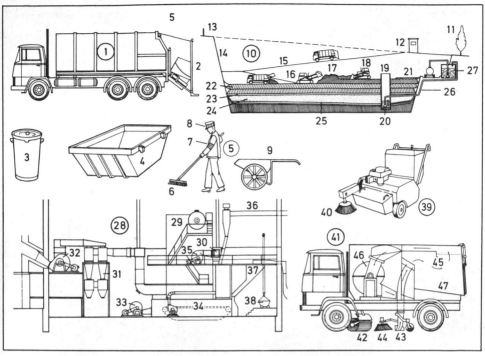

1 der Müllwagen (Müllabfuhrwagen,
das Müllauto, *ugs.* die Müllabfuhr,
schweiz. der Kehrichtabfuhrwagen),
ein Preßmüllfahrzeug *n*
– *refuse collection vehicle* (Am.
garbage truck)
2 die Mülltonnenkippvorrichtung,
ein staubfreies Umleersystem
– *dustbin-tipping device* (Am.
*garbage can dumping device), a
dust-free emptying system*
3 die Mülltonne (Abfalltonne)
– *dustbin* (Am. *garbage can, trash can)*
4 der Müllcontainer
– *refuse container* (Am. *garbage
container)*
5 der Straßenkehrer
– *road sweeper* (Am. *street sweeper)*
6 der Straßenbesen
– *broom*
7 die Verkehrsschutzarmbinde
– *fluorescent armband*
8 die Mütze mit
Verkehrsschutzmarkierung *f*
– *cap with fluorescent band*
9 der Straßenkehrwagen
– *road sweeper's* (Am. *street
sweeper's) barrow*
10 die geordnete Deponie (Mülldeponie)
– *controlled tip* (Am. *sanitary
landfill, sanitary fill)*
11 der Sichtschutz
– *screen*
12 die Eingangskontrolle
– *weigh office*
13 der Wildzaun
– *fence*
14 die Grubenwand
– *embankment*
15 die Zufahrtsrampe
– *access ramp*
16 die Planierraupe
– *bulldozer*
17 der frische Müll (*schweiz.* Kehricht)
– *refuse* (Am. *garbage)*

18 der Deponieverdichter
– *bulldozer for dumping and
compacting*
19 der Pumpenschacht
– *pump shaft*
20 die Abwasserpumpe
– *waste water pump*
21 die poröse Abdeckung
– *porous cover*
22 der verdichtete und verrottete Müll
– *compacted and decomposed refuse*
23 die Kiesfilterschicht
– *gravel filter layer*
24 die Moränenfilterschicht
– *morainic filter layer*
25 die Drainschicht
– *drainage layer*
26 die Abwasserleitung
– *drain pipe*
27 der Abwassersammeltank
– *water tank*
28 die Müllverbrennungsanlage
– *refuse* (Am. *garbage) incineration unit*
29 der Kessel
– *furnace*
30 die Ölfeuerung
– *oil-firing system*
31 der Staubabscheider
– *separation plant*
32 der Saugzugventilator
– *extraction fan*
33 der Unterwindventilator für den Rost
– *low-pressure fan for the grate*
34 der Wanderrost
– *continuous feed grate*
35 das Ölfeuerungsgebläse
– *fan for the oil-firing system*
36 Transporteinrichtung für
Spezialverbrennungsgüter *n*
– *conveyor for separately incinerated
material*
37 die Kohlenbeschickungsanlage
– *coal feed conveyor*
38 der Transportwagen für Bleicherde *f*
– *truck for carrying fuller's earth*

39 die Straßenkehrmaschine
– *mechanical sweeper*
40 die Tellerbürste
– *circular broom*
41 das Kehrfahrzeug
– *road-sweeping lorry
(street-cleaning lorry, street cleaner)*
42 die Kehrwalze
– *cylinder broom*
43 der Saugmund
– *suction port*
44 der Zubringerbesen
– *feeder broom*
45 die Luftführung
– *air flow*
46 der Ventilator
– *fan*
47 der Schmutzbehälter
– *dust collector*

1-54 **Straßenbaumaschinen** *f*
- *road-building machinery*
1 der Hochlöffelbagger
- *shovel (power shovel, excavator)*
2 das Maschinenhaus
- *machine housing*
3 das Raupenfahrwerk
- *caterpillar mounting*
  (Am. *caterpillar tractor*)
4 der Baggerausleger
- *digging bucket arm (dipper stick)*
5 der Baggerlöffel
- *digging bucket (bucket)*
6 die Reißzähne *m* (Grabzähne)
- *digging bucket (bucket) teeth*
7 der Hinterkipper, ein
  Schwerlastwagen *m*
- *tipper (dump truck),*
  a heavy lorry
  (Am. *truck*)
8 die Stahlblechmulde
- *tipping body* (Am. *dump body*)
9 die Verstärkungsrippe
- *reinforcing rib*
10 die verlängerte Stirnwand
- *extended front*
11 das Fahrerhaus
- *cab (driver's cab)*
12 das Schüttgut
- *bulk material*
13 die Schrapperanlage, ein
  Mischgutschrapper *m*
- *concrete scraper, an aggregate*
  scraper
14 der Aufzugkasten
- *skip hoist*
15 der Betonmischer, eine
  Mischanlage
- *mixing drum (mixer drum), a*
  mixing machine
16 die Schürfkübelraupe
- *caterpillar hauling scraper*
17 der Schürfkübel
- *scraper blade*
18 das Planierschild
- *levelling* (Am. *leveling*) *blade*
  (smoothing blade)
19 der Straßenhobel; *auch:* Erdhobel
- *grader (motor grader)*
20 der Straßenaufreißer (Aufreißer)
- *scarifier (ripper, road ripper,*
  rooter)
21 die Hobelschar
- *grader levelling* (Am. *leveling)*
  blade (grader ploughshare, Am.
  plowshare)
22 der Schardrehkranz
- *blade-slewing gear (slew turntable)*
23 die Feldbahn
- *light railway (narrow-gauge,* Am.
  narrow-gage), railway)
24 die Feldbahndiesellokomotive,
  eine Schmalspurlokomotive
- *light railway (narrow-gauge,* Am.
  narrow-gage) diesel locomotive
25 die Anhängerlore (Lore)
- *trailer wagon (wagon truck, skip)*
26 die Explosionsramme, ein
  Bodenstampfer *m*; *schwerer:* der
  Benzinfrosch
  (Explosionsstampfer)
- *tamper (rammer) [with internal*
  combustion engine]; heavier: *frog*
  (frog-type jumping rammer)
27 das Führungsgestänge
- *guide rods*

28 die Planierraupe
- *bulldozer*
29 das Planierschild
- *bulldozer blade*
30 der Schubrahmen
- *pushing frame*
31 der Schotterverteiler
- *road-metal spreading machine*
  (macadam spreader, stone
  spreader)
32 die Schlagbohle
- *tamping beam*
33 die Gleitschuhe *m*
- *sole-plate*
34 das Begrenzungsblech
- *side stop*
35 die Seitenwand des Vorratskübels *m*
- *side of storage bin*
36 die Motordreiradwalze, eine
  Straßenwalze
- *three-wheeled roller, a road roller*
37 die Walze
- *roller*
38 das Allwetterdach
- *all-weather roof*
39 der Dieselkompressorschlepper
- *mobile diesel-powered air*
  compressor
40 die Sauerstoffflasche
- *oxygen cylinder*
41 der selbstfahrende Splittstreuer
- *self-propelled gritter*
42 die Streuklappe
- *spreading flap*
43 der Schwarzdeckenfertiger
- *surface finisher*
44 das Begrenzungsblech
- *side stop*
45 der Materialbehälter
- *bin*
46 die Teerspritzmaschine, mit Teer-
  und Bitumenkocher *m*
- *tar-spraying machine (bituminous*
  distributor) with tar and bitumen
  heater
47 der Teerkessel
- *tar storage tank*
48 die vollautomatische
  Walzasphalt-Trocken-und-Misch-Anlage
- *fully automatic asphalt drying and*
  mixing plant
49 das Aufnahmebecherwerk
- *bucket elevator (elevating conveyor)*
50 die Asphaltmischtrommel
- *asphalt-mixing drum (asphalt*
  mixer drum)
51 der Fülleraufzug
- *filler hoist*
52 die Füllerzugabe
- *filler opening*
53 die Bindemitteleinspritzung
- *binder injector*
54 der Mischasphaltauslauf
- *mixed asphalt outlet*
55 der Regelquerschnitt einer Straße
- *typical cross-section of a*
  bituminous road
56 das Rasenbankett
- *grass verge*
57 die Querneigung
- *crossfall*
58 die Asphaltdecke
- *asphalt surface (bituminous layer,*
  bituminous coating)
59 der Unterbau
- *base (base course)*

60 die Packlage *od.* Kiesbettung, eine
  Frostschutzschicht
- *gravel sub-base course (hardcore*
  sub-base course, Telford base), an
  anti-frost layer
61 die Tiefensickerungsanlage
- *sub-drainage*
62 das gelochte Zementrohr
- *perforated cement pipe*
63 die Entwässerungsrinne
- *drainage ditch*
64 die Humusandeckung
- *soil covering*

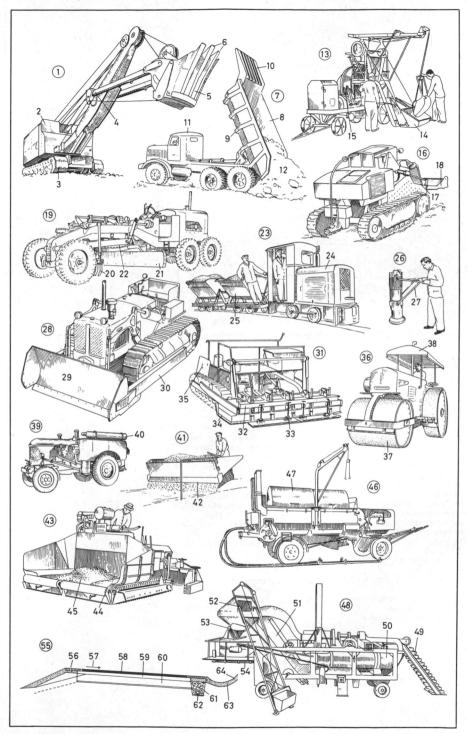

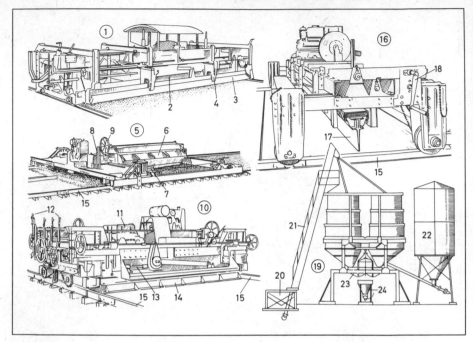

1-24 Betonstraßenbau *m*
(Autobahnbau)
- *concrete road construction (highway construction)*
1 der Planumfertiger, eine Straßenbaumaschine
- *subgrade grader*
2 die Stampfbohle
- *tamping beam (consolidating beam)*
3 die Abgleichbohle (Nivellierbohle)
- *levelling (Am. leveling) beam*
4 die Rollenführung zur Abgleichbohle
- *roller guides for the levelling (Am. leveling) beam*
5 der Betonverteilerwagen
- *concrete spreader*
6 der Betonverteilerkübel
- *concrete spreader box*
7 die Seilführung
- *cable guides*
8 die Steuerhebel *m*
- *control levers*
9 das Handrad zum Entleeren *n* der Kübel *m*
- *handwheel for emptying the boxes*
10 der Vibrationsfertiger
- *concrete-vibrating compactor*
11 das Getriebe
- *gearing (gears)*
12 die Bedienungshebel *m*
- *control levers (operating levers)*
13 die Antriebswelle zu den Vibratoren·*m* des Vibrationsbalkens *m*
- *axle drive shaft to vibrators (tampers) of vibrating beam*
14 der Glättbalken (die Glättbohle)
- *screeding board (screeding beam)*

15 die Laufschienenträger *m*
- *road form*
16 das Fugenschneidgerät (der Fugenschneider)
- *joint cutter*
17 das Fugenschneidmesser (Fugenmesser)
- *joint-cutting blade*
18 die Handkurbel zum Fahrantrieb *m*
- *crank for propelling machine*
19 die Betonmischanlage, eine zentrale Mischstation, eine automatische Verwiege- u. Mischanlage
- *concrete-mixing plant, a stationary central mixing plant, an automatic batching and mixing plant*
20 die Sammelmulde
- *collecting bin*
21 das Aufnahmebecherwerk
- *bucket elevator*
22 der (das) Zementsilo
- *cement store*
23 der Zwangsmischer
- *concrete mixer*
24 der Betonkübel
- *concrete pump hopper*

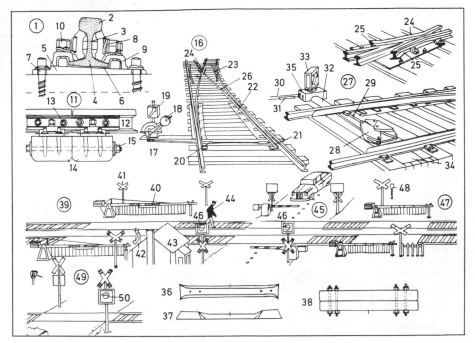

1-38 das Gleis
- *line (track)*
1 die Schiene (Eisenbahnschiene)
- *rail*
2 der Schienenkopf
- *rail head*
3 der Schienensteg
- *web (rail web)*
4 der Schienenfuß
- *rail foot (rail bottom)*
5 die Unterlagsplatte
- *sole-plate (base plate)*
6 die Zwischenlage
- *cushion*
7 die Schwellenschraube
- *coach screw (coach bolt)*
8 die Federringe m
- *lock washers (spring washers)*
9 die Klemmplatte
- *rail clip (clip)*
10 die Hakenschraube
- *T-head bolt*
11 der Schienenstoß
- *rail joint (joint)*
12 die Schienenlasche
- *fishplate*
13 der Laschenbolzen
- *fishbolt*
14 die Kuppelschwelle
- *coupled sleeper (Am. coupled tie, coupled crosstie)*
15 die Kuppelschraube
- *coupling bolt*
16 die Handweiche
- *manually-operated points (switch)*
17 der Handstellbock
- *switch stand*
18 das Stellgewicht
- *weight*

19 das Weichensignal (die Weichenlaterne)
- *points signal (switch signal, points signal lamp, switch signal lamp)*
20 die Stellstange
- *pull rod*
21 die Weichenzunge
- *switch blade (switch tongue)*
22 der Gleitstuhl
- *slide chair*
23 der Radlenker
- *check rail (guard rail)*
24 das Herzstück
- *frog*
25 die Flügelschiene
- *wing rail*
26 die Zwischenschiene
- *closure rail*
27 die fernbediente Weiche
- *remote-controlled points (switch)*
28 der Weichenspitzenverschluß
- *point lock (switch lock)*
29 der Abstützstempel
- *stretcher bar*
30 der Drahtzug
- *point wire*
31 das Spannschloß
- *turnbuckle*
32 der Kanal
- *channel*
33 das elektrisch beleuchtete Weichensignal
- *electrically illuminated points signal (switch signal)*
34 der Weichentrog
- *trough*
35 der Weichenantrieb mit Schutzkasten m
- *points motor with protective casing*
36 die Eisenschwelle
- *steel sleeper (Am. steel tie, steel crosstie)*

37 die Betonschwelle
- *concrete sleeper (Am. concrete tie, concrete crosstie)*
38 die Kuppelschwelle
- *coupled sleeper (Am. coupled tie, coupled crosstie)*
39-50 Bahnübergänge
- *level crossings (Am. grade crossings)*
39 der schienengleiche gesicherte Bahnübergang
- *protected level crossing (Am. protected grade crossing)*
40 die Bahnschranke
- *barrier (gate)*
41 das Warnkreuz (Andreaskreuz)
- *warning cross (Am. crossbuck)*
42 der Schrankenwärter
- *crossing keeper (Am. gateman)*
43 der Schrankenposten
- *crossing keeper's box (Am. gateman's box)*
44 der Streckenwärter
- *linesman (Am. trackwalker)*
45 die Halbschrankenanlage
- *half-barrier crossing*
46 das Blinklicht
- *warning light*
47 die Anrufschranke
- *intercom-controlled crossing; sim.: telephone-controlled crossing*
48 die Wechselsprechanlage
- *intercom system; sim.: telephone*
49 der technisch nicht gesicherte Bahnübergang (unbeschrankte Bahnübergang)
- *unprotected level crossing (Am. unprotected grade crossing)*
50 das Blinklicht
- *warning light*

203 Eisenbahnstrecke II (Signalanlagen)

1-6 Hauptsignale *n*
- *stop signals (main signals)*
1 das Hauptsignal, ein Formsignal *n*
   auf „Zughalt" *m*
- *stop signal (main signal), a*
   semaphore signal in 'stop' position
2 der Signalarm
- *signal arm (semaphore arm)*
3 das elektrische Hauptsignal
   (Lichtsignal) auf „Zughalt" *m*
- *electric stop signal (colour light,*
   Am. color light, signal) at 'stop'
4 die Signalstellung „Langsamfahrt" *f*
- *signal position: 'proceed at low*
   speed'
5 die Signalstellung „Fahrt" *f*
- *signal position: 'proceed'*
6 das Ersatzsignal
- *substitute signal* [German railways
   only]
7-24 Vorsignale *n*
- *distant signals*
7 das Formsignal auf „Zughalt
   erwarten"
- *semaphore signal at 'be prepared to*
   stop at next signal'
8 der Zusatzflügel
- *supplementary semaphore arm*
9 das Lichtvorsignal auf „Zughalt
   erwarten"
- *colour light* (Am. *color light*)
   distant signal at 'be prepared to
   stop at next signal'
10 die Signalstellung „Langsamfahrt
   erwarten"
- *signal position: 'be prepared to*
   proceed at low speed'
11 die Signalstellung „Fahrt erwarten"
- *signal position: 'proceed main*
   signal ahead'
12 das Formvorsignal mit Zusatztafel
   f für Bremswegverkürzung *f* um
   mehr als 5%
- *semaphore signal with indicator*
   plate showing a reduction in
   braking distance of more than 5%
   [German railways only]
13 die Dreiecktafel
- *triangle (triangle sign)* [German
   railways only]
14 das Lichtvorsignal mit Zusatzlicht *n*
   für Bremswegverkürzung *f*
- *colour light* (Am. *color light*)
   distant signal with indicator light
   for showing reduced braking
   distance [German railways only]
15 das weiße Zusatzlicht
- *supplementary white light*
16 die Vorsignalanzeige „Halt
   erwarten" (Notgelb *n*)
- *distant signal indicating 'be*
   prepared to stop at next signal'
   (yellow light)
17 der Vorsignalwiederholer (das
   Vorsignal mit Zusatzlicht *n*, ohne
   Tafel *f*)
- *second distant signal (distant signal*
   with supplementary light, without
   indicator plate)
18 das Vorsignal mit
   Geschwindigkeitsanzeige *f*
- *distant signal with speed indicator*
19 der Geschwindigkeitsvoranzeiger
- *distant speed indicator*
20 das Vorsignal mit
   Richtungsvoranzeige *f*
- *distant signal with route indicator*
21 der Richtungsvoranzeiger
- *route indicator*
22 das Vorsignal ohne Zusatzflügel *m*
   in Stellung *f* „Zughalt erwarten"
- *distant signal without*
   supplementary arm in position: 'be
   prepared to stop at next signal'
23 das Vorsignal ohne Zusatzflügel *m*
   in Stellung *f* „Fahrt erwarten"
- *distant signal without*
   supplementary arm in 'be prepared
   to proceed' position
24 die Vorsignaltafel
- *distant signal identification plate*

25-44 Zusatzsignale *n*
- *supplementary signals*
25 die Trapeztafel zur Kennzeichnung
   des Haltepunkts *m* vor einer
   Betriebsstelle
- *stop board for indicating the*
   stopping point at a control point
   [German railways only]
26-29 die Vorsignalbaken *f*
- *approach signs*
26 die Vorsignalbake in 100 m
   Entfernung *f* vom Vorsignal *n*
- *approach sign 100 m from distant*
   signal
27 die Vorsignalbake in 175 m
   Entfernung *f*
- *approach sign 175 m from distant*
   signal
28 die Vorsignalbake in 250 m
   Entfernung *f*
- *approach sign 250 m from distant*
   signal
29 die Vorsignalbake in einer um 5%
   geringeren Entfernung *f* als der
   Bremsweg der Strecke
- *approach sign at a distance of 5%*
   less than the braking distance on
   the section [German railways only]
30 die Schachbretttafel zur
   Kennzeichnung von
   Hauptsignalen *n*, die nicht
   unmittelbar rechts oder über dem
   Gleis *n* stehen
- *chequered sign indicating stop*
   signals (main signals) not
   positioned immediately to the right
   of or over the line (track) [German
   railways only]
31-32 die Haltetafeln *f* zur
   Kennzeichnung des Halteplatzes *m*
   der Zugspitze
- *stop boards to indicate the stopping*
   point of the front of the train
33 die Haltepunkttafel (ein
   Haltepunkt *m* ist zu erwarten)
- *stop board (be prepared to stop)*
34-35 die Schneepflugtafeln *f*
- *snow plough* (Am. *snowplow*) *signs*
   [German railways only]
34 die Tafel „Pflugschar heben"
- *'raise snow plough* (Am.
   snowplow') *sign* [German railways
   only]
35 die Tafel „Pflugschar senken"
- *'lower snow plough* (Am.
   snowplow') *sign* [German railways only]
36-44 Langsamfahrsignale *n*
- *speed restriction signs*
36-38 die Langsamfahrscheibe
   [Höchstgeschwindigkeit *f*
   3 × 10 = 30 km/h]
- *speed restriction sign [maximum*
   speed 3 × 10 = 30 kph]
36 das Tageszeichen
- *sign for day running*
37 die Geschwindigkeitskennziffer
- *speed code number* [German
   railways only]
38 das Nachtzeichen
- *illuminated sign for night running*
39 der Anfang der vorübergehenden
   Langsamfahrstelle
- *commencement of temporary speed*
   restriction
40 das Ende der vorübergehenden
   Langsamfahrstelle
- *termination of temporary speed*
   restriction
41 die Geschwindigkeit für eine
   ständige Langsamfahrstelle
   [Höchstgeschwindigkeit *f*
   5 × 10 = 50 km/h]
- *speed restriction sign for a section*
   with a permanent speed restriction
   [maximum speed 5 × 10 = 50 kph]
42 der Anfang der ständigen
   Langsamfahrstelle
- *commencement of permanent speed*
   restriction
43 die Geschwindigkeitsankündetafel
   [nur auf Hauptbahnen *f*]

- *speed restriction warning sign [only*
   on main lines] [German railways
   only]
44 das Geschwindigkeitssignal [nur
   auf Hauptbahnen *f*]
- *speed restriction sign [only on main*
   lines] [German railways only]
45-52 Weichensignale *n*
- *points signals (switch signals)*
45-48 einfache Weichen *f*
- *single points (single switches)*
45 der gerade Zweig
- *route straight ahead (main line)*
46 der gebogene Zweig [rechts]
- *[right] branch*
47 der gebogene Zweig [links]
- *[left] branch*
48 der gebogene Zweig [vom
   Herzstück *n* aus gesehen]
- *branch [seen from the frog]*
   [German railways only]
49-52 doppelte Kreuzungsweichen *f*
- *double crossover* [German railways
   only]
49 die Gerade von links nach rechts
- *route straight ahead from left to*
   right [German railways only]
50 die Gerade von rechts nach links
- *route straight ahead from right to*
   left [German railways only]
51 der Bogen von links nach links
- *turnout to the left from the left*
   [German railways only]
52 der Bogen von rechts nach rechts
- *turnout to the right from the right*
   [German railways only]
53 **das mechanische Stellwerk**
- *manually-operated signal box* (Am.
   signal tower, switch tower)
54 das Hebelwerk
- *lever mechanism*
55 der Weichenhebel [blau], ein
   Riegelhebel *m*
- *points lever (switch lever) [blue], a*
   lock lever
56 der Signalhebel [rot]
- *signal lever [red]*
57 die Handfalle
- *catch*
58 der Fahrstraßenhebel
- *route lever*
59 der Streckenblock
- *block instruments*
60 das Blockfeld
- *block section panel*
61 **das elektrische Stellwerk**
- *electrically-operated signal box*
   (Am. *signal tower, switch tower*)
62 die Weichen- und Signalhebel *m*
- *points (switch) and signal knobs*
63 das Verschlußregister
- *lock indicator panel*
64 das Überwachungsfeld
- *track and signal indicator*
65 **das Gleisbildstellwerk**
- *track diagram control layout*
66 der Gleisbildstelltisch
- *track diagram control panel*
   (domino panel)
67 die Drucktasten *f*
- *push buttons*
68 die Fahrstraßen *f*
- *routes*
69 die Wechselsprechanlage
- *intercom system*

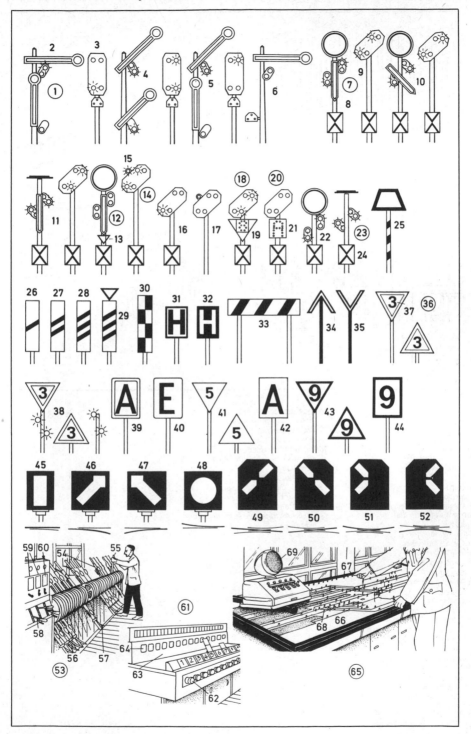

1 die Expreßgutabfertigung
  (Expreßgutannahme und
  -ausgabe)
- *parcels office*
2 das Expreßgut
- *parcels*
3 der Schließkorb
- *basket [with lock]*
4 die Gepäckabfertigung
- *luggage counter*
5 die automatische Zeigerwaage
- *platform scale with dial*
6 der Koffer
- *suitcase (case)*
7 der Gepäckaufkleber
- *luggage sticker*
8 der Gepäckschein
- *luggage receipt*
9 der Abfertigungsbeamte
- *luggage clerk*
10 das Werbeplakat
- *poster (advertisement)*
11 der Bahnhofsbriefkasten
- *station post box (Am. station mailbox)*
12 die Tafel für die Meldung *f*
  verspäteter Züge *m*
- *notice board indicating train delays*
13 das Bahnhofsrestaurant (die
  Bahnhofsgaststätte)
- *station restaurant*
14 der Warteraum (Wartesaal)
- *waiting room*
15 der Stadtplan
- *map of the town (street map)*

16 die Kursbuchtafeln *f*
- *timetable (Am. schedule)*
17 der Hoteldiener
- *hotel porter*
18 der Wandfahrplan
- *arrivals and departures board
  (timetable)*
19 die Ankunftstafel
- *arrival timetable (Am. arrival
  schedule)*
20 die Abfahrtstafel
- *departure timetable (Am. departure
  schedule)*

TO THE TRAINS

TICKETS

CHANGE

21 die Gepäckschließfächer *n*
- *left luggage lockers*
22 der Geldwechselautomat
(Geldwechsler)
- *change machine*
23 der Bahnsteigtunnel
- *tunnel to the platforms*
24 die Reisenden *m u. f*
- *passengers*
25 der Bahnsteigaufgang
- *steps to the platforms*
26 die Bahnhofsbuchhandlung
- *station bookstall (Am. station
bookstand)*
27 die Handgepäckaufbewahrung
- *left luggage office (left luggage)*
28 das Reisebüro; *auch:* der Hotel-
und Zimmernachweis
- *travel centre (Am. center); also:
accommodation bureau*
29 die Auskunft
- *information office (Am.
information bureau)*
30 die Bahnhofsuhr
- *station clock*
31 die Bankfiliale, mit Wechselstelle *f*
- *bank branch with foreign exchange
counter*
32 die Geldkurstabelle
(Währungstabelle)
- *indicator board showing exchange
rates*
33 der Streckennetzplan
- *railway map (Am. railroad map)*

34 die Fahrkartenausgabe
- *ticket office*
35 der Fahrkartenschalter
- *ticket counter*
36 die Fahrkarte
- *ticket (railway ticket, Am. railroad
ticket)*
37 der Drehteller
- *revolving tray*
38 die Sprechmembran
- *grill*
39 der Schalterbeamte
(Fahrkartenverkäufer)
- *ticket clerk (Am. ticket agent)*
40 der Fahrkartendrucker
- *ticket-printing machine
(ticket-stamping machine)*
41 der Handdrucker
- *hand-operated ticket printer*
42 der Taschenfahrplan
- *pocket timetable (Am. pocket train
schedule)*
43 die Gepäckbank
- *luggage rest*
44 die Sanitätswache
- *first aid station*
45 die Bahnhofsmission
- *Travellers' (Am. Travelers') Aid*
46 die öffentliche Fernsprechzelle
(Telefonzelle)
- *telephone box (telephone booth,
telephone kiosk, call box)*
47 der Tabakwarenkiosk
- *cigarettes and tobacco kiosk*

48 der Blumenkiosk
- *flower stand*
49 der Auskunftsbeamte
- *railway information clerk*
50 das amtliche Kursbuch
- *official timetable (official railway
guide, Am. train schedule)*

1 der Bahnsteig	**16** der fahrbare Zeitungsständer	**32** der Gepäckschiebekarren
- *platform*	- *news trolley*	- *barrow*
2 die Bahnsteigtreppe	**17** der Zeitungsverkäufer	**33** der Trinkbrunnen
- *steps to the platform*	- *news vendor* (Am. *news dealer*)	- *drinking fountain*
3 die Bahnsteigüberführung	**18** die Reiselektüre	**34** der elektrische TEE-Zug
- *bridge to the platforms*	- *reading matter for the journey*	(Trans-Europe-Express), *auch*:
4 die Bahnsteignummer	**19** die Bahnsteigkante	IC-Zug (Intercity-Zug)
- *platform number*	- *edge of the platform*	- *electric Trans-Europe Express;*
5 die Bahnsteigüberdachung	**20** der Bahnpolizist	also: *Intercity train*
- *platform roofing*	- *railway policeman* (Am. *railroad*	**35** die E-Lok, eine elektrische
6 die Reisenden *m u. f*	*policeman*)	Schnellzugslokomotive
- *passengers*	**21** der Fahrtrichtungsanzeiger	- *electric locomotive, an express*
7-12 das Reisegepäck	- *destination board*	*locomotive*
- **luggage**	**22** das Feld für den Zielbahnhof	**36** der Stromabnehmerbügel
7 der Handkoffer	- *destination indicator*	- *collector bow (sliding bow)*
- *suitcase (case)*	**23** das Feld für die planmäßige	**37** das Zugsekretariat
8 der Kofferanhänger	Abfahrtszeit	- *secretarial compartment*
- *luggage label*	- *departure time indicator*	**38** das Richtungsschild
9 der Hotelaufkleber *m*	**24** das Feld für die Zugverspätung	- *destination board*
- *hotel sticker*	- *delay indicator*	**39** der Wagenmeister
10 die Reisetasche	**25** der S-Bahnzug, ein Triebwagenzug *m*	- *wheel tapper*
- *travelling* (Am. *traveling*) *bag*	- *suburban train, a railcar*	**40** der Radprüfhammer
11 die Hutschachtel	**26** das Sonderabteil	- *wheel-tapping hammer*
- *hat box*	- *special compartment*	**41** der Aufsichtsbeamte
12 der Schirm (Regenschirm), ein	**27** der Bahnsteiglautsprecher	- *station foreman*
Stockschirm *m*	- *platform loudspeaker*	**42** der Befehlsstab
- *umbrella, a walking-stick umbrella*	**28** das Stationsschild	- *signal*
13 das Empfangsgebäude	- *station sign*	**43** die rote Mütze
(Dienstgebäude)	**29** der Elektrokarren	- *red cap*
- *office*	- *electric trolley (electric truck)*	**44** der Auskunftsbeamte
14 der Hausbahnsteig	**30** der Ladeschaffner	- *inspector*
- *platform*	- *loading foreman*	**45** der Taschenfahrplan
15 der Gleisüberweg	**31** der Gepäckträger	- *pocket timetable*
- *crossing*	- *porter* (Am. *redcap*)	(Am. *pocket train schedule*)

46 die Bahnsteiguhr
- *platform clock*
47 das Abfahrtssignal
- *starting signal*
48 die Bahnsteigbeleuchtung
- *platform lighting*
49 der Bahnsteigkiosk für
   Erfrischungen *f* und
   Reiseverpflegung *f*
- *refreshment kiosk*
50 die Bierflasche
- *beer bottle*
51 die Zeitung
- *newspaper*
52 der Abschiedskuß
- *parting kiss*
53 die Umarmung
- *embrace*
54 die Wartebank
- *platform seat*
55 der Abfallkorb
- *litter bin (Am. litter basket)*
56 der Bahnsteigbriefkasten
- *platform post box (Am. platform
   mailbox)*
57 das Bahnsteigtelefon (der
   Bahnsteigfernsprecher)
- *platform telephone*
58 der Fahrdraht
- *trolley wire (overhead contact wire)*
59-61 das Gleis
- *track*
59 die Schiene
- *rail*

60 die Schwelle
- *sleeper (Am. tie, crosstie)*
61 der Schotter (das Schotterbett)
- *ballast (bed)*

1 die Auffahrtsrampe
(Fahrzeugrampe); *ähnl.:* die
Viehrampe
- *ramp (vehicle ramp);* sim.: *livestock
ramp*
2 der Elektroschlepper
- *electric truck*
3 der Förderwagen
- *trailer*
4 die Stückgüter *n* (Einzelgüter,
Kolli); im Sammelverkehr:
Sammelgut *n* in Sammelladungen *f*
- *part loads (Am. package freight,
less-than-carload freight);* in
general traffic: *general goods in
general consignments (in mixed
consignments)*
5 die Lattenkiste
- *crate*
6 der Stückgutwagen
- *goods van (Am. freight car)*
7 die Güterhalle (der
Güterschuppen)
- *goods shed (Am. freight house)*
8 die Ladestraße
- *loading strip*
9 die Hallenrampe (Laderampe)
- *loading dock*
10 der Torfballen
- *bale of peat*
11 der Leinwandballen
- *bale of linen (of linen cloth)*
12 die Verschnürung
- *fastening (cord)*
13 die Korbflasche
- *wicker bottle (wickered bottle,
demijohn)*
14 der Sack- oder Stechkarren
- *trolley*
15 der Stückgut-Lkw
- *goods lorry (Am. freight truck)*
16 der Gabelstapler
- *forklift truck (fork truck, forklift)*
17 das Ladegleis
- *loading siding*
18 das Sperrgut
- *bulky goods*
19 der bahneigene Kleinbehälter
(Kleincontainer)
- *small railway-owned (Am.
railroad-owned) container*
20 der Schaustellerwagen (*ähnl.:*
Zirkuswagen)
- *showman's caravan (sim.: circus
caravan)*
21 der Flachwagen
- *flat wagon (Am. flat freight car)*
22 das Lademaß
- *loading gauge (Am. gage)*
23 der Strohballen
- *bale of straw*
24 der Rungenwagen
- *flat wagon (Am. flatcar) with side
stakes*
25 der Wagenpark
- *fleet of lorries (Am. trucks)*
26-39 der Güterboden
- ***goods shed***
(*Am. freight house*)
26 die Frachtgutannahme
(Güterabfertigung)
- *goods office (forwarding office,
Am. freight office)*
27 das Stückgut
- *part-load goods (Am. package
freight)*

28 der Stückgutunternehmer
- *forwarding agent (Am. freight
agent, shipper)*
29 der Lademeister
- *loading foreman*
30 der Frachtbrief
- *consignment note (waybill)*
31 die Stückgutwaage
- *weighing machine*
32 die Palette
- *pallet*
33 der Güterbodenarbeiter
- *porter*
34 der Elektrowagen
- *electric cart (electric truck)*
35 der Förderwagen
- *trailer*
36 der Abfertigungsbeamte (die
Ladeaufsicht)
- *loading supervisor*
37 das Hallentor
- *goods shed door (Am. freight house
door)*
38 die Laufschiene
- *rail (slide rail)*
39 die Laufrolle
- *roller*
40 das Wiegehäuschen
- *weighbridge office*
41 die Gleiswaage
- *weighbridge*
42 der Rangierbahnhof
- *marshalling yard (Am.
classification yard, switch yard)*
43 die Rangierlok
- *shunting engine (shunting
locomotive, shunter, Am. switch
engine, switcher)*
44 das Rangierstellwerk
- *marshalling yard signal box (Am.
classification yard switch tower)*
45 der Rangiermeister
- *yardmaster*
46 der Ablaufberg
- *hump*
47 das Rangiergleis
- *sorting siding (classification siding,
classification track)*
48 die Gleisbremse
- *rail brake (retarder)*
49 der Gleishemmschuh
- *slipper brake (slipper)*
50 das Abstellgleis
- *storage siding (siding)*
51 der Prellbock
- *buffer (buffers, Am. bumper)*
52 die Wagenladung
- *wagon load (Am. carload)*
53 das Lagerhaus
- *warehouse*
54 der Containerbahnhof
- *container station*
55 der Portalkran
- *gantry crane*
56 das Hubwerk
- *lifting gear (hoisting gear)*
57 der Container
- *container*
58 der Containertragwagen
- *container wagon (Am. container
car)*
59 der Sattelanhänger
- *semi-trailer*

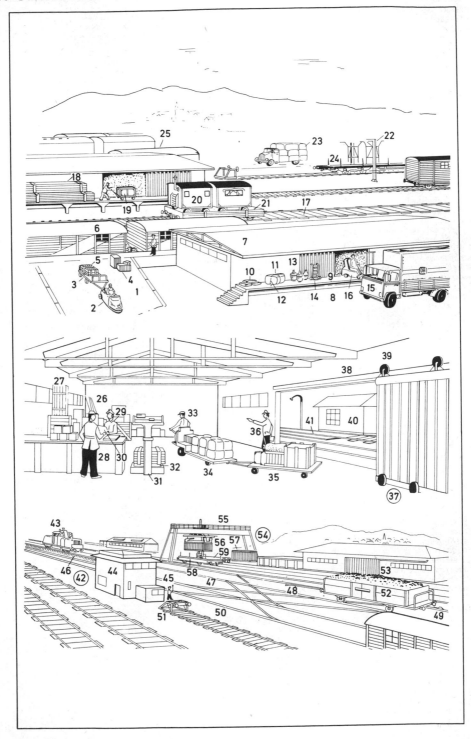

1-21 **der Schnellzugwagen**
(D-Zug-Wagen), ein
Reisezugwagen
- *express train coach (express train carriage, express train car, corridor compartment coach), a passenger coach*
1 die Seitenansicht
- *side elevation (side view)*
2 der Wagenkasten
- *coach body*
3 das Untergestell
- *underframe (frame)*
4 das Drehgestell mit Stahlgummifederung *f* und Stoßdämpfern *m*
- *bogie (truck) with steel and rubber suspension and shock absorbers*
5 die Batteriebehälter *m*
- *battery containers (battery boxes)*
6 der Dampf- und Elektrowärmetauscher für die Heizung
- *steam and electric heat exchanger for the heating system*
7 das Übersetzfenster
- *sliding window*
8 die Gummiwulstdichtung
- *rubber connecting seal*
9 der statische Entlüfter
- *ventilator*
10-21 **der Grundriß**
- *plan*
10 der Zweite-Klasse-Teil
- *second-class section*
11 der Seitengang
- *corridor*
12 der Klappsitz
- *folding seat (tip-up seat)*
13 das Fahrgastabteil (Abteil)
- *passenger compartment (compartment)*
14 die Abteiltür
- *compartment door*
15 der Waschraum
- *washroom*
16 der Abortraum
- *toilet (lavatory, WC)*
17 der Erste-Klasse-Teil
- *first-class section*
18 die Pendeltür
- *swing door*
19 die Stirnwandschiebetür
- *sliding connecting door*
20 die Einstiegstür
- *door*
21 der Vorraum
- *vestibule*
22-32 **der Speisewagen**
- *dining car (restaurant car, diner)*
22-25 **die Seitenansicht**
- *side elevation (side view)*
22 die Einstiegstür
- *door*
23 die Ladetür
- *loading door*
24 der Stromabnehmer für die Energieversorgung bei Stillstand *m*
- *current collector for supplying power during stops*
25 die Batterietröge *m*
- *battery boxes (battery containers)*
26-32 **der Grundriß**
- *plan*
26 der Personalwaschraum
- *staff washroom*

27 der Abstellraum
- *storage cupboard*
28 der Spülraum
- *washing-up area*
29 die Küche
- *kitchen*
30 der Acht-Platten-Elektroherd
- *electric oven with eight hotplates*
31 das Büfett
- *counter*
32 der Speiseraum
- *dining compartment*
33 die Speisewagenküche
- *dining car kitchen*
34 der Küchenmeister (Zugkoch)
- *chef (head cook)*
35 die Anrichte
- *kitchen cabinet*
36 der Schlafwagen
- *sleeping car (sleeper)*
37 die Seitenansicht
- *side elevation (side view)*
38-42 **der Grundriß**
- *plan*
38 das Zwei-Platz-zwei-Bett-Abteil
- *two-seat twin-berth compartment (two-seat two-berth compartment, Am. bedroom)*
39 die Drehfalttür
- *folding doors*
40 der Waschtisch
- *washstand*
41 der Dienstraum
- *office*
42 der Abortraum
- *toilet (lavatory, WC)*
43 das Schnellzugabteil
- *express train compartment*
44 der Ausziehpolstersitz
- *upholstered reclining seat*
45 die Armlehne
- *armrest*
46 der Armlehnenascher
- *ashtray in the armrest*
47 das verstellbare Kopfpolster
- *adjustable headrest*
48 der Leinenbezug
- *antimacassar*
49 der Spiegel
- *mirror*
50 der Kleiderhaken (Mantelhaken)
- *coat hook*
51 die Gepäckablage
- *luggage rack*
52 das Abteilfenster
- *compartment window*
53 das Klapptischchen
- *fold-away table (pull-down table)*
54 die Heizungsregulierung
- *heating regulator*
55 der Abfallbehälter
- *litter receptacle*
56 der Schleudervorhang
- *curtain*
57 die Fußstütze
- *footrest*
58 der Eckplatz
- *corner seat*
59 der Großraumwagen
- *open car*
60 die Seitenansicht
- *side elevation (side view)*
61-72 **der Grundriß**
- *plan*
61 das Großraumabteil
- *open carriage*

62 die Einzelsitzreihe
- *row of single seats*
63 die Doppelsitzreihe
- *row of double seats*
64 der Drehliegesitz
- *reclining seat*
65 das Sitzpolster
- *seat upholstery*
66 die Rückenlehne
- *backrest*
67 der (das) Kopfteil
- *headrest*
68 das Daunenkissen mit Nylonbezug *m*
- *down-filled headrest cushion with nylon cover*
69 die Armlehne, mit Ascher *m*
- *armrest with ashtray*
70 der Garderobenraum
- *cloakroom*
71 der Kofferraum
- *luggage compartment*
72 der WC-Raum
- *toilet (lavatory, WC)*
73 der Quick-Pick-Wagen, ein Selbstbedienungsspeisewagen *m*
- *buffet car (quick-service buffet car), a self-service restaurant car*
74 die Seitenansicht
- *side elevation (side view)*
75 der Stromabnehmer für die Standversorgung
- *current collector for supplying power*
76 der Grundriß
- *plan*
77 der Speiseraum
- *dining compartment*
78-79 **der Angebotsraum**
- *buffet (buffet compartment)*
78 die Gastseite
- *customer area*
79 die Bedienerseite
- *serving area*
80 die Küche
- *kitchen*
81 der Personalraum
- *staff compartment*
82 das Personal-WC
- *staff toilet (staff lavatory, staff WC)*
83 die Speisengefache *n*
- *food compartments*
84 die Teller *m*
- *plates*
85 das Besteck
- *cutlery*
86 die Kasse
- *till (cash register)*

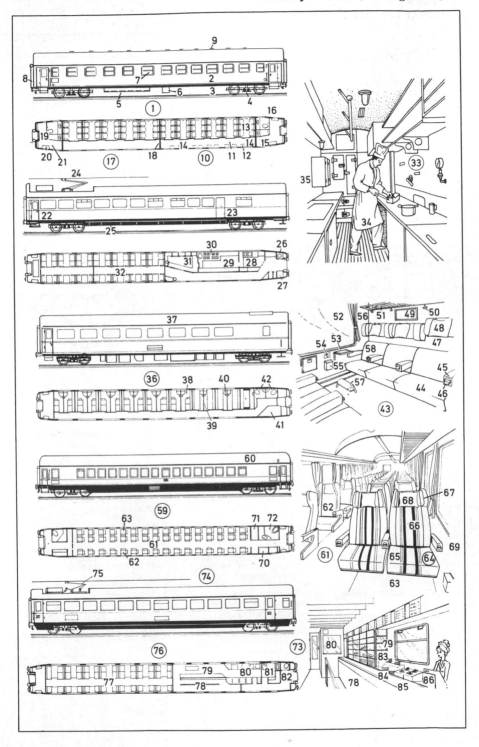

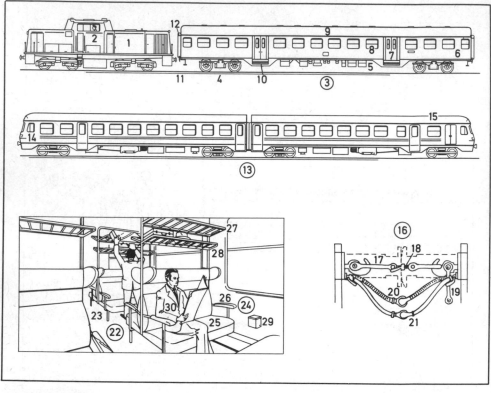

1-30 der Nahverkeh.
- *local train service*

1-12 der Nahverkehrszug
- *local train (short-distance train)*

1 die einmotorige Diesellokomotive (Diesellok)
- *single-engine diesel locomotive*

2 der Lokomotivführer (Lokführer)
- *engine driver (Am. engineer)*

3 der vierachsige Nahverkehrswagen, ein Reisezugwagen *m*
- *four-axled coach (four-axled car) for short-distance routes, a passenger coach (passenger car)*

4 das Drehgestell [mit Scheibenbremsen *f*]
- *bogie (truck) [with disc (disk) brakes]*

5 das Untergestell
- *underframe (frame)*

6 der Wagenkasten mit der Beblechung
- *coach body with metal panelling (Am. paneling)*

7 die Doppeldrehfalttür
- *double folding doors*

8 das Abteilfenster
- *compartment window*

9 der Großraum
- *open carriage*

10 der Einstieg (Einstiegsraum)
- *entrance*

11 der Übergang
- *connecting corridor*

12 die Gummiwulstabdichtung
- *rubber connecting seal*

13 der Leichttriebwagen, ein Nahverkehrstriebwagen *m*, ein Dieseltriebwagen *m*
- *light railcar, a short-distance railcar, a diesel railcar*

14 der Triebwagenführerstand
- *cab (driver's cab, Am. engineer's cab)*

15 der Gepäckraum
- *luggage compartment*

16 die Leitungs- und Wagenkupplung
- *connecting hoses and coupling*

17 der Kupplungsbügel
- *coupling link*

18 die Spannvorrichtung (die Kupplungsspindel mit dem Kupplungsschwengel *m*)
- *tensioning device (coupling screw with tensioning lever)*

19 die nicht eingesenkte Kupplung
- *unlinked coupling*

20 der Heizkupplungsschlauch der Heizleitung
- *heating coupling hose (steam coupling hose)*

21 der Bremskupplungsschlauch der Bremsluftleitung
- *coupling hose (connecting hose) for the compressed-air braking system*

22 der Fahrgastraum 2. Klasse *f*
- *second-class section*

23 der Mittelgang
- *central gangway*

24 das Abteil
- *compartment*

25 die Polsterbank
- *upholstered seat*

26 die Armstütze
- *armrest*

27 die Gepäckablage
- *luggage rack*

28 die Hut- und Kleingepäckablage
- *hat and light luggage rack*

29 der Kippaschenbecher
- *ashtray*

30 der Reisende (Fahrgast)
- *passenger*

209 Eisenbahnfahrzeuge (Schienenfahrzeuge) III
Railway Vehicles (Rolling Stock) III

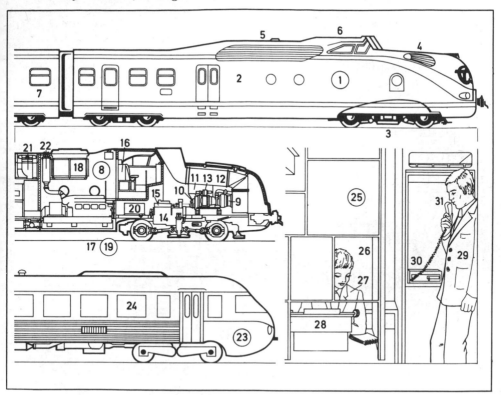

1-22 der TEE-(IC-)Zug
(Trans-Europe-Express-Intercity-Zug)
- *Trans-Europe Express (Intercity train)*
1 der Triebzug (Triebwagenzug) der Deutschen Bundesbahn (DB), ein Dieseltriebzug *m* oder Gasturbinentriebzug *m*
- *German Federal Railway trainset, a diesel trainset or gas turbine trainset*
2 der Triebkopf (Triebwagen)
- *driving unit*
3 der Triebradsatz
- *drive wheel unit*
4 die Vortriebsmaschinenanlage (der Fahrdieselmotor)
- *main engine*
5 die Dieselgeneratoranlage
- *diesel generator unit*
6 der Führerstand
- *cab (driver's cab, Am. engineer's cab)*
7 der Mittelwagen
- *second coach*
8 der Gasturbinentriebkopf [im Schnitt]
- *gas turbine driving unit [diagram]*
9 die Gasturbine
- *gas turbine*
10 das Turbinengetriebe
- *turbine transmission*

11 der Luftansaugkanal
- *air intake*
12 die Abgasleitung mit Schalldämpfer *m*
- *exhaust with silencers (Am. mufflers)*
13 die elektrische Startanlage
- *dynastarter*
14 das Voith-Getriebe
- *Voith transmission*
15 der Wärmetauscher für das Getriebeöl
- *heat exchanger for the transmission oil*
16 der Gasturbinensteuerschrank
- *gas turbine controller*
17 der Kraftstoffbehälter für die Gasturbine
- *gas turbine fuel tank*
18 die Öl-Luft-Kühlanlage für Getriebe *n* und Turbine *f*
- *oil-to-air cooling unit for transmission and turbine*
19 der Hilfsdieselmotor (Hilfsdiesel)
- *auxiliary diesel engine*
20 der Kraftstoffbehälter
- *fuel tank*
21 die Kühlanlage
- *cooling unit*
22 die Auspuffleitung, mit Schalldämpfer *m*
- *exhaust with silencers (Am. mufflers)*

23 der Versuchstriebwagenzug der Société Nationale des Chemin de Fer Français (SNCF), mit Sechszylinder-Unterflurdieselmotor *m* und Zweiwellen-Gasturbine *f*
- *experimental trainset of the Société Nationale des Chemins de Fer Français (SNCF) with six-cylinder underfloor diesel engine and twin-shaft gas turbine*
24 die geräuschgedämpfte Turbinenanlage
- *turbine unit with silencers (Am. mufflers)*
25 das Zugsekretariat
- *secretarial compartment*
26 das Schreibabteil
- *typing compartment*
27 die Zugsekretärin
- *secretary*
28 die Schreibmaschine
- *typewriter*
29 der Geschäftsreisende (reisende Geschäftsmann)
- *travelling (Am. traveling) salesman (businessman on business trip)*
30 das Diktiergerät
- *dictating machine*
31 das Mikrophon
- *microphone*

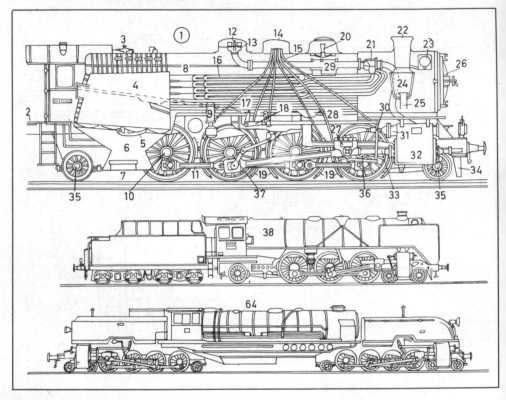

1-69 Dampflokomotiven *f*
(Dampfloks)
- *steam locomotives*

2-37 der Lokomotivkessel und das Loktriebwerk
- *locomotive boiler and driving gear*

2 die Tenderbrücke, mit Kupplung *f*
- *tender platform with coupling*
3 das Sicherheitsventil, für Dampfüberdruck *m*
- *safety valve for excess boiler pressure*
4 die Feuerbüchse
- *firebox*
5 der Kipprost
- *drop grate*
6 der Aschkasten, mit Luftklappen *f*
- *ashpan with damper doors*
7 die Aschkastenbodenklappe
- *bottom door of the ashpan*
8 die Rauchrohre *n*
- *smoke tubes (flue tubes)*
9 die Speisewasserpumpe
- *feed pump*
10 das Achslager
- *axle bearing*
11 die Kuppelstange
- *connecting rod*
12 der Dampfdom
- *steam dome*

13 das Reglerventil
- *regulator valve (regulator main valve)*
14 der Sanddom
- *sand dome*
15 die Sandabfallrohre *n*
- *sand pipes (sand tubes)*
16 der Langkessel
- *boiler (boiler barrel)*
17 die Heiz- oder Siederohre *n*
- *fire tubes or steam tubes*
18 die Steuerung
- *reversing gear (steam reversing gear)*
19 die Sandstreuerrohre *n*
- *sand pipes*
20 das Speiseventil
- *feed valve*
21 der Dampfsammelkasten
- *steam collector*
22 der Schornstein (Rauchaustritt und Abdampfauspuff)
- *chimney (smokestack, smoke outlet and waste steam exhaust)*
23 der Speisewasservorwärmer (Oberflächenvorwärmer)
- *feedwater preheater (feedwater heater, economizer)*
24 der Funkenfänger
- *spark arrester*
25 das Blasrohr
- *blast pipe*

26 die Rauchkammertür
- *smokebox door*
27 der Kreuzkopf
- *cross head*
28 der Schlammsammler
- *mud drum*
29 das Rieselblech
- *top feedwater tray*
30 die Schieberstange
- *combination lever*
31 der Schieberkasten
- *steam chest*
32 der Dampfzylinder
- *cylinder*
33 die Kolbenstange mit Stopfbuchse *f*
- *piston rod with stuffing box (packing box)*
34 der Bahnräumer (Gleisräumer, Schienenräumer)
- *guard iron (rail guard, Am. pilot, cowcatcher)*
35 die Laufachse
- *carrying axle (running axle, dead axle)*
36 die Kuppelachse
- *coupled axle*
37 die Treibachse
- *driving axle*
38 die Schlepptender-Schnellzuglokomotive
- *express locomotive with tender*

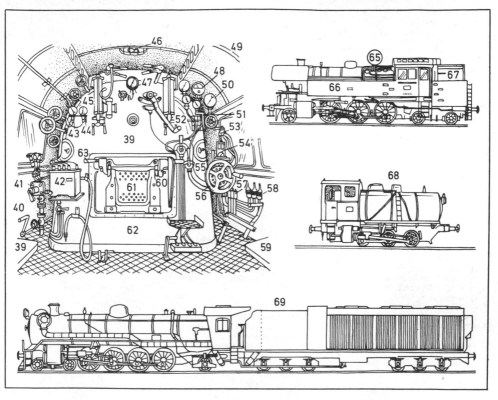

39-63 der Dampflokführerstand
- *cab (driver's cab, Am. engineer's cab)*
39 der Heizersitz
- *fireman's seat*
40 die Kipprostkurbel
- *drop grate lever*
41 die Strahlpumpe
- *line steam injector*
42 die automatische Schmierpumpe
- *automatic lubricant pump (automatic lubricator)*
43 der Vorwärmerdruckmesser
- *preheater pressure gauge (Am. gage)*
44 der Heizdruckmesser
- *carriage heating pressure gauge (Am. gage)*
45 der Wasserstandsanzeiger
- *water gauge (Am. gage)*
46 die Beleuchtung
- *light*
47 der Kesseldruckmesser
- *boiler pressure gauge (Am. gage)*
48 das Fernthermometer
- *distant-reading temperature gauge (Am. gage)*
49 das Lokführerhaus
- *cab (driver's cab, Am. engineer's cab)*
50 der Bremsdruckmesser
- *brake pressure gauge (Am. gage)*

51 der Hebel der Dampfpfeife
- *whistle valve handle*
52 der Buchfahrplan
- *driver's timetable (Am. engineer's schedule)*
53 das Führerbremsventil
- *driver's brake valve (Am. engineer's brake valve)*
54 der Geschwindigkeitsschreiber (Tachograph)
- *speed recorder (tachograph)*
55 der Hahn zum Sandstreuer *m*
- *sanding valve*
56 das Steuerrad
- *reversing wheel*
57 das Notbremsventil
- *emergency brake valve*
58 das Auslöseventil
- *release valve*
59 der Lokführersitz
- *driver's seat (Am. engineer's seat)*
60 der Blendschutz
- *firehole shield*
61 die Feuertür
- *firehole door*
62 der Stehkessel
- *vertical boiler*
63 der Handgriff des Feuertüröffners *m*
- *firedoor handle handgrip*
64 die Gelenklokomotive (Garratlokomotive)

- *articulated locomotive (Garratt locomotive)*
65 die Tenderlok
- *tank locomotive*
66 der Wasserkasten
- *water tank*
67 der Brennstofftender
- *fuel tender*
68 die Dampfspeicherlokomotive (feuerlose Lokomotive)
- *steam storage locomotive (fireless locomotive)*
69 die Kondensationslokomotive
- *condensing locomotive (locomotive with condensing tender)*

211 Eisenbahnfahrzeuge (Schienenfahrzeuge) V

1 die elektrische Lokomotive
   (E-Lok, Ellok)
- *electric locomotive*
2 der Stromabnehmer
- *current collector*
3 der Hauptschalter
- *main switch*
4 der Oberspannungswandler
- *high-tension transformer*
5 die Dachleitung
- *roof cable*
6 der Fahrmotor
- *traction motor*
7 die induktive Zugbeeinflussung
   (Indusi)
- *inductive train control system*
8 die Hauptluftbehälter *m*
- *main air reservoir*
9 das Pfeifsignalinstrument
- *whistle*
10-18 **der Grundriß der Lok**
- *plan of locomotive*
10 der Transformator mit dem
   Schaltwerk *n*
- *transformer with tap changer*
11 der Ölkühler mit dem Lüfter *m*
- *oil cooler with blower*
12 die Ölumlaufpumpe
- *oil-circulating pump*
13 der Schaltwerkantrieb
- *tap changer driving mechanism*
14 der Luftkompressor (Luftpresser)
- *air compressor*
15 der Fahrmotorlüfter
- *traction motor blower*
16 der Klemmenschrank
- *terminal box*
17 Kondensatoren *m* für
   Hilfsmotoren *m*
- *capacitors for auxiliary motors*
18 die Kommutatorklappe
- *commutator cover*
19 der Führerstand (Führerraum)
- *cab (driver's cab, Am. engineer's
   cab)*
20 das Fahrschalterhandrad
- *controller handwheel*
21 der Sicherheitsfahrschalter (Sifa)
- *dead man's handle*
22 das Führerbremsventil
- *driver's brake valve (Am. engineer's
   brake valve)*
23 das Zusatzbremsventil
- *ancillary brake valve (auxiliary
   brake valve)*
24 die Luftdruckanzeige
- *pressure gauge (Am. gage)*
25 der Überbrückungsschalter der
   Sifa
- *bypass switch for the dead man's
   handle*
26 die Zugkraftanzeige
- *tractive effort indicator*
27 die Heizspannungsanzeige
- *train heating voltage indicator*
28 die Fahrdrahtspannungsanzeige
- *contact wire voltage indicator
   (overhead wire voltage indicator)*
29 die Oberstromspannungsanzeige
- *high-tension voltage indicator*
30 der Auf-und-ab-Schalter für den
   Stromabnehmer
- *on/off switch for the current
   collector*
31 der Hauptschalter
- *main switch*

32 der Sandschalter
- *sander switch (sander control)*
33 der Schalter für die
   Schleuderschutzbremse
- *anti-skid brake switch*
34 die optische Anzeige für die
   Hilfsbetriebe *m*
- *visual display for the ancillary
   systems*
35 die Geschwindigkeitsanzeige
- *speedometer*
36 die Fahrstufenanzeige
- *running step indicator*
37 die Zeituhr
- *clock*
38 die Bedienung der Indusi
- *controls for the inductive train
   control system*
39 der Schalter für die
   Führerstandsheizung
- *cab heating switch*
40 der Hebel für das Pfeifsignal
- *whistle lever*
41 **der Fahrleitungsunterhaltungstriebwagen**
   (Regelturmtriebwagen), ein
   Dieseltriebwagen *m*
- *contact wire maintenance vehicle
   (overhead wire maintenance
   vehicle), a diesel railcar*
42 die Arbeitsbühne
- *work platform (working platform)*
43 die Leiter
- *ladder*
44-54 **die Maschinenanlage des
   Fahrleitungsunterhaltungstriebwagens** *m*
- *mechanical equipment of the contact
   wire maintenance vehicle*
44 der Luftkompressor (Luftpresser)
- *air compressor*
45 die Lüfterölpumpe
- *blower oil pump*
46 die Lichtmaschine
- *generator*
47 der Dieselmotor
- *diesel engine*
48 die Einspritzpumpe
- *injection pump*
49 der Schalldämpfer
- *silencer (Am. muffler)*
50 das Schaltgetriebe
- *change-speed gear*
51 die Gelenkwelle
- *cardan shaft*
52 die Spurkranzschmierung
- *wheel flange lubricator*
53 das Achswendegetriebe
- *reversing gear*
54 die Drehmomentenstütze
- *torque converter bearing*
55 **der Akkumulatortriebwagen**
- *accumulator railcar (battery railcar)*
56 der Batterieraum (Batterietrog)
- *battery box (battery container)*
57 der Führerstand
- *cab (driver's cab, Am. engineer's cab)*
58 die Sitzanordnung der zweiten
   Klasse
- *second-class seating arrangement*
59 die Toilette
- *toilet (lavatory, WC)*
60 **der elektrische Schnelltriebzug**
- *fast electric multiple-unit train*
61 der Endtriebwagen
- *front railcar*
62 der Mitteltriebwagen
- *driving trailer car*

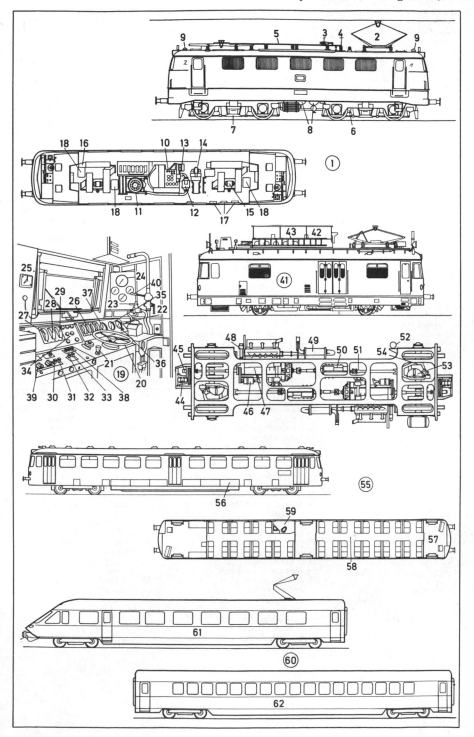

212 Eisenbahnfahrzeuge (Schienenfahrzeuge) VI

1-84 Dieselloks *f*
- *diesel locomotives*

1 die dieselhydraulische Lokomotive,
  eine Streckendiesellokomotive
  (Diesellok) für den mittelschweren
  Reisezug- und Güterzugdienst
- *diesel-hydraulic locomotive, a*
  mainline locomotive (diesel
  locomotive) for medium passenger
  and goods service (freight service)
2 das Drehgestell
- *bogie (truck)*
3 der Radsatz
- *wheel and axle set*
4 der Kraftstoffhauptbehälter
- *main fuel tank*
5 der Führerstand einer Diesellok
- *cab (driver's cab, Am. engineer's*
  cab) of a diesel locomotive
6 das Manometer für die
  Hauptluftleitung
- *main air pressure gauge (Am. gage)*
7 die Bremszylinderdruckanzeige
- *brake cylinder pressure gauge*
  (Am. gage)
8 die Hauptluftbehälter-Druckanzeige
- *main air reservoir pressure gauge*
  (Am. gage)
9 der Geschwindigkeitsmesser
- *speedometer*
10 die Zusatzbremse
- *auxiliary brake*
11 das Führerbremsventil
- *driver's brake valve (Am. engineer's*
  brake valve)
12 das Fahrschalterhandrad
- *controller handwheel*
13 der Sicherheitsfahrschalter (Sifa)
- *dead man's handle*
14 die induktive Zugsicherung
  (Indusi)
- *inductive train control system*
15 die Leuchtmelder *m*
- *signal lights*
16 die Zeituhr
- *clock*
17 der Heizspannungsmesser
- *voltage meter for the train heating*
  system
18 der Heizstrommesser
- *current meter for the train heating*
  system
19 der Motoröltemperaturmesser
- *engine oil temperature gauge*
  (Am. gage)
20 der Getriebeöltemperaturmesser
- *transmission oil temperature gauge*
  (Am. gage)
21 der Kühlwassertemperaturmesser
- *cooling water temperature gauge*
  (Am. gage)
22 der Motordrehzahlmesser
- *revolution counter (rev counter,*
  tachometer)
23 das Zugbahnfunkgerät
- *radio telephone*
24 die dieselhydraulische Lokomotive
  [in Grund- und Aufriß]
- *diesel-hydraulic locomotive [plan*
  and elevation]
25 der Dieselmotor
- *diesel engine*
26 die Kühlanlage
- *cooling unit*
27 das Flüssigkeitsgetriebe
- *fluid transmission*

28 das Radsatzgetriebe
- *wheel and axle drive*
29 die Gelenkwelle
- *cardan shaft*
30 die Lichtanlaßmaschine
- *starter motor*
31 der Gerätetisch
- *instrument panel*
32 das Führerpult
- *driver's control desk*
  (Am. engineer's control desk)
33 die Handbremse
- *hand brake*
34 der Luftpresser mit E-Motor *m*
  (Elektromotor)
- *air compressor with electric motor*
35 der Apparateschrank
- *equipment locker*
36 der Wärmetauscher für das
  Getriebeöl
- *heat exchanger for transmission oil*
37 der Maschinenraumlüfter
- *engine room ventilator*
38 der Indusi-Fahrzeugmagnet
- *magnet for the inductive train*
  control system
39 der Heizgenerator
- *train heating generator*
40 der Heizumrichterschrank
- *casing of the train heating system*
  transformer
41 das Vorwärmgerät
- *preheater*
42 der Abgasschalldämpfer
- *exhaust silencer (Am. exhaust*
  muffler)
43 der Zusatzwärmetauscher für das
  Getriebeöl
- *auxiliary heat exchanger for the*
  transmission oil
44 die hydraulische Bremse
- *hydraulic brake*
45 der Werkzeugkasten
- *tool box*
46 die Anlaßbatterie
- *starter battery*
47 die dieselhydraulische Lokomotive
  für den leichten und mittleren
  Rangierdienst
- *diesel-hydraulic locomotive for light*
  and medium shunting service
48 der Abgasschalldämpfer
- *exhaust silencer (Am. exhaust*
  muffler)
49 das Läutewerk und die Pfeife
- *bell and whistle*
50 das Rangierfunkgerät
- *yard radio*

51-67 der Aufriß der Lok
- *elevation of locomotive*
51 der Dieselmotor mit
  Aufladeturbine *f*
- *diesel engine with supercharged*
  turbine
52 das Flüssigkeitsgetriebe
- *fluid transmission*
53 das Nachschaltgetriebe
- *output gear box*
54 der Kühler
- *radiator*
55 der Wärmetauscher für das
  Motorschmieröl
- *heat exchanger for the engine*
  lubricating oil
56 der Kraftstoffbehälter
- *fuel tank*

57 die Hauptluftbehälter *m*
- *main air reservoir*
58 der Luftpresser
- *air compressor*
59 die Sandkästen *m*
- *sand boxes*
60 der Kraftstoffreservebehälter
- *reserve fuel tank*
61 der Hilfsluftbehälter
- *auxiliary air reservoir*
62 der hydrostatische Lüfterantrieb
- *hydrostatic fan drive*
63 die Sitzbank mit Kleiderkasten *m*
- *seat with clothes compartment*
64 das Handbremsrad
- *hand brake wheel*
65 der Kühlwasserausgleichsbehälter
- *cooling water*
66 der Ausgleichsballast
- *ballast*
67 das Bedienungshandrad für die
  Motor- und Getrieberegulierung
- *engine and transmission control*
  wheel
68 die **Dieselkleinlokomotive** für den
  Rangierdienst
- ***small diesel locomotive** for shunting*
  service
69 der Auspuffendtopf
- *exhaust casing*
70 das Signalhorn (Makrophon)
- *horn*
71 der Hauptluftbehälter
- *main air reservoir*
72 der Luftpresser
- *air compressor*
73 der Acht-Zylinder-Dieselmotor
- *eight-cylinder diesel engine*
74 das Voith-Getriebe mit
  Wendegetriebe *n*
- *Voith transmission with reversing*
  gear
75 der Heizölbehälter
- *heating oil tank (fuel oil tank)*
76 der Sandkasten
- *sand box*
77 die Kühlanlage
- *cooling unit*
78 der Ausgleichsbehälter für das
  Kühlwasser
- *header tank for the cooling water*
79 das Ölbadluftfilter
- *oil bath air cleaner (oil bath air*
  filter)
80 das Handbremsrad
- *hand brake wheel*
81 das Bedienungshandrad
- *control wheel*
82 die Kupplung
- *coupling*
83 die Gelenkwelle
- *cardan shaft*
84 die Klappenjalousie
- *louvred shutter*

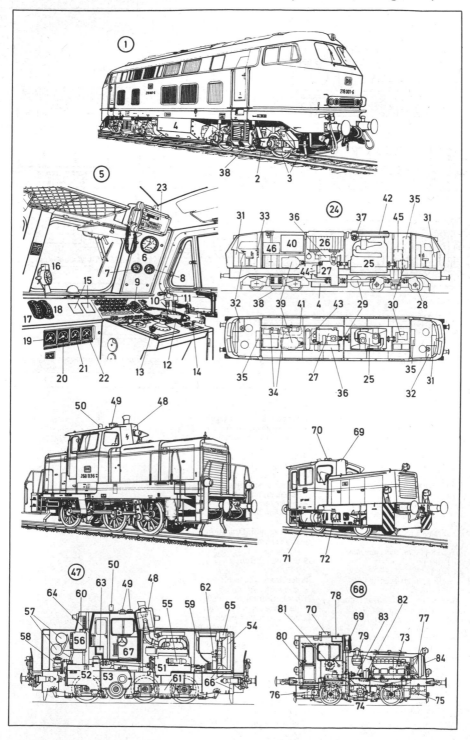

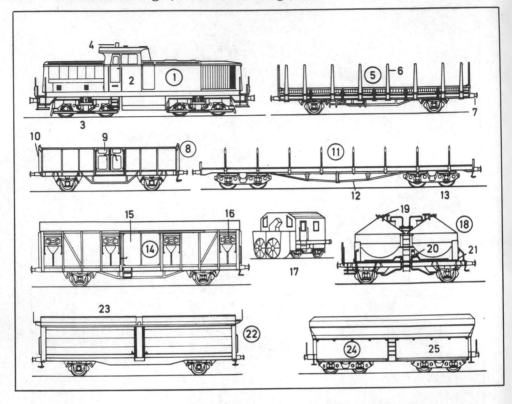

1 die dieselhydraulische Lokomotive
- *diesel-hydraulic locomotive*
2 der Führerstand
- *cab (driver's cab, Am. engineer's cab)*
3 der Radsatz
- *wheel and axle set*
4 die Antenne für die Rangierfunkanlage
- *aerial for the yard radio*
5 der Flachwagen in Regelbauart *f*
- *standard flat wagon (Am. standard flatcar)*
6 die abklappbare Stahlrunge (Runge)
- *hinged steel stanchion (stanchion)*
7 die Puffer *m*
- *buffers*
8 der offene Güterwagen in Regelbauart *f*
- *standard open goods wagon (Am. standard open freight car)*
9 die Seitenwanddrehtüren *f*
- *revolving side doors*
10 die abklappbare Stirnwand
- *hinged front*
11 der Drehgestellflachwagen in Regelbauart *f*
- *standard flat wagon (Am. standard flatcar) with bogies*
12 die Längsträgerverstärkung
- *sole bar reinforcement*
13 das Drehgestell
- *bogie (truck)*

14 der gedeckte Güterwagen
- *covered goods van (covered goods wagon, Am. boxcar)*
15 die Schiebetür
- *sliding door*
16 die Lüftungsklappe
- *ventilation flap*
17 die Schneeschleuder, eine Schienenräummaschine
- *snow blower (rotary snow plough, Am. snowplow), a track-clearing vehicle*
18 der Wagen für Druckluftentladung *f*
- *wagon (Am. car) with pneumatic discharge*
19 die Einfüllöffnung
- *filler hole*
20 der Druckluftanschluß
- *compressed-air supply*
21 der Entleerungsanschluß
- *discharge connection valve*
22 der Schiebedachwagen
- *goods van (Am. boxcar) with sliding roof*
23 die Dachöffnung
- *roof opening*
24 der offene Drehgestell-Selbstentladewagen
- *bogie open self-discharge wagon (Am. bogie open self-discharge freight car)*
25 die Entladeklappe
- *discharge flap (discharge door)*

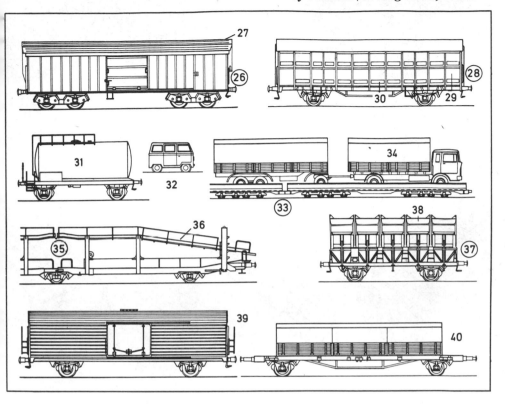

26 der Drehgestell-Schwenkdachwagen
  - *bogie wagon with swivelling
    (Am. swiveling) roof*
27 das Schwenkdach
  - *swivelling (Am. swiveling) roof*
28 der großräumige Verschlagwagen
    für die Beförderung von Kleinvieh *n*
  - *large-capacity wagon
    (Am. large-capacity car) for small
    livestock*
29 die luftdurchlässige Seitenwand
    (Lattenwand)
  - *sidewall with ventilation flaps
    (slatted wall)*
30 die Lüftungsklappe
  - *ventilation flap*
31 der Kesselwagen
  - *tank wagon
    (Am. tank car)*
32 der Gleiskraftwagen
  - *track inspection railcar*
33 die Spezialflachwagen *m*
  - *open special wagons (Am. open
    special freight cars)*
34 der Lastzug
  - *lorry (Am. truck)
    with trailer*
35 der Doppelstockwagen, für den
    Autotransport
  - *two-tier car carrier (double-deck
    car carrier)*
36 die Auffahrmulde
  - *hinged upper deck*

37 der Muldenkippwagen
  - *tipper wagon (Am. dump car) with
    skips*
38 die Kippmulde
  - *skip*
39 der Universalkühlwagen
  - *general-purpose refrigerator wagon
    (refrigerator van, Am. refrigerator
    car)*
40 die Wechselaufbauten *m* für
    Flachwagen *m*
  - *interchangeable bodies for flat
    wagons (Am. flatcars)*

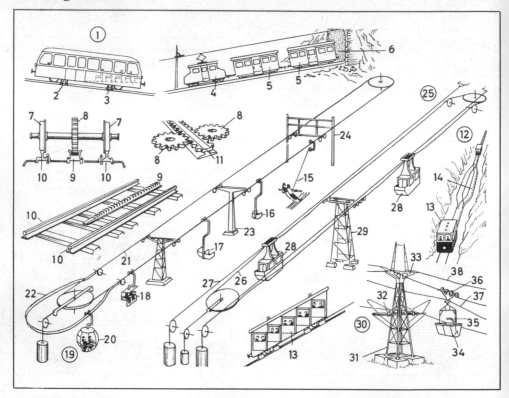

1-14 Schienenbergbahnen *f*
- *mountain railways (Am. mountain railroads)*
1 der Triebwagen, mit forcierter Adhäsion
- *adhesion railcar*
2 der Antrieb
- *drive*
3 die Notbremse
- *emergency brake*
4-5 die Zahnradbergbahn
- *rack mountain railway (rack-and-pinion railway, cog railway, Am. cog railroad, rack railroad)*
4 die elektrische Zahradlokomotive
- *electric rack railway locomotive (Am. electric rack railroad locomotive)*
5 der Zahnradbahnanhänger
- *rack railway coach (rack railway trailer, Am. rack railroad car)*
6 der Tunnel
- *tunnel*
7-11 Zahnstangenbahnen *f* [Systeme]
- *rack railways (rack-and-pinion railways, Am. rack railroads) [systems]*
7 das Laufrad
- *running wheel (carrying wheel)*
8 das Triebzahnrad
- *driving pinion*
9 die Sprossenzahnstange
- *rack [with teeth machined on top edge]*

10 die Schiene
- *rail*
11 die Doppelleiterzahnstange
- *rack [with teeth on both outer edges]*
12 die Standseilbahn
- *funicular railway (funicular, cable railway)*
13 der Standseilbahnwagen
- *funicular railway car*
14 das Zugseil
- *haulage cable*
15-38 Seilschwebebahnen *f* (Schwebebahnen, Drahtseilbahnen, Seilbahnen)
- *cableways (ropeways, cable suspension lines)*
15-24 Einseilbahnen *f*, Umlaufbahn *f*
- *single-cable ropeways (single-cable suspension lines), endless ropeways*
15 der Skischlepplift
- *drag lift*
16-18 der Sessellift
- *chair lift*
16 der Liftsessel, ein Einmannsessel *m*
- *lift chair, a single chair*
17 der Doppelliftsessel, ein Zweimannsessel *m*
- *double lift chair, a two-seater chair*
18 der kuppelbare Doppelsessel
- *double chair (two-seater chair) with coupling*
19 die Kleinkabinenbahn, eine Umlaufbahn
- *gondola cableway, an endless cableway*
20 die Kleinkabine (Umlaufkabine)
- *gondola (cabin)*
21 das Umlaufseil, ein Trag- und Zugseil *n*
- *endless cable, a suspension (supporting) and haulage cable*
22 die Umführungsschiene
- *U-rail*
23 die Einmaststütze
- *single-pylon support*
24 die Torstütze
- *gantry support*
25 die Zweiseilbahn, eine Pendelbahn
- *double-cable ropeway (double-cable suspension line), a suspension line with balancing cabins*
26 das Zugseil
- *haulage cable*
27 das Tragseil
- *suspension cable (supporting cable)*
28 die Fahrgastkabine
- *cabin*
29 die Zwischenstütze
- *intermediate support*
30 die Seilschwebbahn, eine Zweiseilbahn
- *cableway (ropeway, suspension line), a double-cable ropeway (double-cable suspension line)*
31 die Gitterstütze
- *pylon*

32 die Zugseilrolle
- *haulage cable roller*
33 der Seilschuh (das Tragseillauflager)
- *cable guide rail (suspension cable bearing)*
34 der Wagenkasten, ein Kippkasten *m*
- *skip, a tipping bucket (Am. dumping bucket)*
35 der Kippanschlag
- *stop*
36 das Laufwerk
- *pulley cradle*
37 das Zugseil
- *haulage cable*
38 das Tragseil
- *suspension cable (supporting cable)*
39 **die Talstation**
- *valley station (lower station)*
40 der Spanngewichtschacht (Spannschacht)
- *tension weight shaft*
41 das Tragseilspanngewicht
- *tension weight for the suspension cable (supporting cable)*
42 das Zugseilspanngewicht
- *tension weight for the haulage cable*
43 die Spannseilscheibe
- *tension cable pulley*
44 das Tragseil
- *suspension cable (supporting cable)*
45 das Zugseil
- *haulage cable*
46 das Gegenseil (Unterseil)
- *balance cable (lower cable)*
47 das Hilfsseil
- *auxiliary cable (emergency cable)*
48 die Hilfsseilspannvorrichtung
- *auxiliary-cable tensioning mechanism (emergency-cable tensioning mechanism)*
49 die Zugseiltragrollen *f*
- *haulage cable rollers*
50 die Anfahrfederung (der Federpuffer)
- *spring buffer (Am. spring bumper)*
51 der Talstationsbahnsteig
- *valley station platform (lower station platform)*
52 die Fahrgastkabine (Seilbahngondel), eine Großkabine (Großraumkabine)
- *cabin (cableway gondola, ropeway gondola, suspension line gondola), a large-capacity cabin*
53 das Laufwerk
- *pulley cradle*
54 das Gehänge
- *suspension gear*
55 der Schwingungsdämpfer
- *stabilizer*
56 der Abweiser (Abweisbalken)
- *guide rail*
57 **die Bergstation**
- *top station (upper station)*
58 der Tragseilschuh
- *suspension cable guide (supporting cable guide)*
59 der Tragseilverankerungspoller
- *suspension cable anchorage (supporting cable anchorage)*
60 die Zugseilrollenbatterie
- *haulage cable rollers*
61 die Zugseilumlenkscheibe
- *haulage cable guide wheel*

62 die Zugseilantriebsscheibe
- *haulage cable driving pulley*
63 der Hauptantrieb
- *main drive*
64 der Reserveantrieb
- *standby drive*
65 der Führerstand
- *control room*
66 **das Kabinenlaufwerk**
- *cabin pulley cradle*
67 der Laufwerkhauptträger
- *main pulley cradle*
68 die Doppelwiege
- *double cradle*
69 die Zweiradwiege
- *two-wheel cradle*
70 die Laufwerkrollen *f*
- *running wheels*
71 die Tragseilbremse, eine Notbremse bei Zugseilbruch *m*
- *suspension cable brake (supporting cable brake), an emergency brake in case of haulage cable failure*
72 der Gehängebolzen
- *suspension gear bolt*
73 die Zugseilmuffe
- *haulage cable sleeve*
74 die Gegenseilmuffe
- *balance cable sleeve (lower cable sleeve)*
75 der Entgleisungsschutz
- *derailment guard*
76 **Seilbahnstützen** *f* (Zwischenstützen)
- *cable supports (ropeway supports, suspension line supports, intermediate supports)*
77 der Stahlgittermast, eine Fachwerkstütze
- *pylon, a framework support*
78 der Stahlrohrmast, eine Stahlrohrstütze
- *tubular steel pylon, a tubular steel support*
79 der Tragseilschuh (Stützenschuh)
- *suspension cable guide rail (supporting cable guide rail, support guide rail)*
80 der Stützengalgen, ein Montagegerät *n* für Seilarbeiten *f*
- *support truss, a frame for work on the cable*
81 das Stützenfundament
- *base of the support*

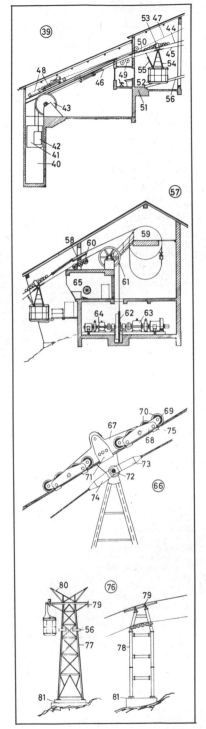

1 der Brückenquerschnitt
- *cross-section of a bridge*
2 die orthogonal anisotrope
(orthotrope) Fahrbahnplatte
- *orthotropic roadway (orthotropic
deck)*
3 das Sprengwerk
- *truss (bracing)*
4 die Verstrebung
- *diagonal brace (diagonal strut)*
5 der Hohlkasten
- *hollow tubular section*
6 das Fahrbahnblech
- *deck slab*
7 die Balkenbrücke
- *solid-web girder bridge (beam
bridge)*
8 die Fahrbahnoberkante
- *road surface*
9 der Obergurt
- *top flange*
10 der Untergurt
- *bottom flange*
11 das feste Lager
- *fixed bearing*
12 das bewegliche Lager
- *movable bearing*
13 die lichte Weite
- *clear span*
14 die Spannweite (Stützweite)
- *span*
15 der Hängesteg (die primitive
Hängebrücke)
- *rope bridge (primitive suspension
bridge)*
16 das Tragseil
- *carrying rope*
17 das Hängeseil
- *suspension rope*
18 der geflochtene Steg
- *woven deck (woven decking)*
19 die steinerne Bogenbrücke
(Steinbrücke),
eine Massivbrücke
- *stone arch bridge, a solid bridge*
20 der Brückenbogen (das
Brückenjoch)
- *arch*
21 der Brückenpfeiler (Strompfeiler)
- *pier*
22 die Brückenfigur
(der Brückenheilige)
- *statue of saint on bridge*
23 die Fachwerkbogenbrücke
- *trussed arch bridge*
24 das Fachwerkelement
- *truss element*
25 der Fachwerkbogen
- *trussed arch*
26 die Bogenspannweite
- *arch span*
27 der Landpfeiler
- *abutment (end pier)*
28 die aufgeständerte Bogenbrücke
- *spandrel-braced arch bridge*
29 der Bogenkämpfer (das
Widerlager)
- *abutment (abutment pier)*
30 der Brückenständer
- *bridge strut*
31 der Bogenscheitel
- *crown*
32 die mittelalterliche Hausbrücke
(der *Ponte Vecchio* in *Florenz*)
- *covered bridge of the Middle Ages
(the* Ponte Vecchio *in* Florence)

33 die Goldschmiedeläden *m*
- *goldsmiths' shops*
34 die Stahlgitterbrücke
- *steel lattice bridge*
35 die Diagonale (Brückenstrebe)
- *counterbrace (crossbrace, diagonal
member)*
36 der Brückenpfosten (die Vertikale)
- *vertical member*
37 der Fachwerkknoten
- *truss joint*
38 das Endportal (Windportal)
- *portal frame*
39 die Hängebrücke
- *suspension bridge*
40 das Tragkabel
- *suspension cable*
41 der Hänger
- *suspender (hanger)*
42 der Pylon (das Brückenportal)
- *tower*
43 die Tragkabelverankerung
- *suspension cable anchorage*
44 das Zugband
[mit der Fahrbahn]
- *tied beam [with roadway]*
45 das Brückenwiderlager
- *abutment*
46 die Schrägseilbrücke
(Zügelgurtbrücke)
- *cable-stayed bridge*
47 das Abspannseil (Schrägseil)
- *inclined tension cable*
48 die Schrägseilverankerung
- *inclined cable anchorage*
49 die Stahlbetonbrücke
- *reinforced concrete bridge*
50 der Stahlbetonbogen
- *reinforced concrete arch*
51 das Schrägseilsystem
(Vielseilsystem)
- *inclined cable system (multiple
cable system)*
52 die Flachbrücke, eine
Vollwandbrücke
- *flat bridge, a plate girder bridge*
53 die Queraussteifung
- *stiffener*
54 der Strompfeiler
- *pier*
55 das Auflager (Brückenlager)
- *bridge bearing*
56 der Eisbrecher
- *cutwater*
57 die Sundbrücke, eine Brücke aus
Fertigbauteilen *m* od. *n*
- *straits bridge, a bridge built of
precast elements*
58 das Fertigbauteil
(Fertigbauelement)
- *precast construction unit*
59 die Hochstraße (aufgeständerte
Straße)
- *viaduct*
60 die Talsohle
- *valley bottom*
61 der Stahlbetonständer
- *reinforced concrete pier*
62 das Vorbaugerüst
- *scaffolding*
63 die Gitterdrehbrücke
- *lattice swing bridge*
64 der Drehkranz
- *turntable*
65 der Drehpfeiler
- *pivot pier*

66 die drehbare Brückenhälfte
(Halbbrücke)
- *pivoting half (pivoting section,
pivoting span, movable half) of
bridge*
67 die Flachdrehbrücke
- *flat swing bridge*
68 das Mittelteil
- *middle section*
69 der Drehzapfen
- *pivot*
70 das Brückengeländer
- *parapet (handrailing)*

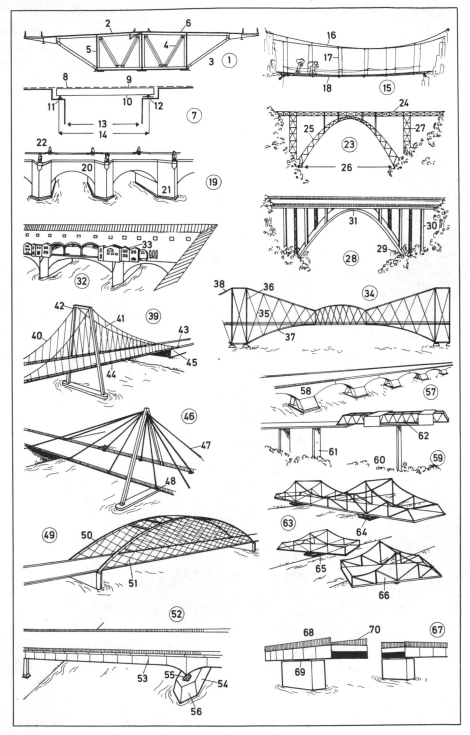

1 die Gierfähre (*mit eigenem Antrieb:*
  Seilfähre; *auch:* Kettenfähre), eine
  Personenfähre
- *cable ferry* (also: *chain ferry*), a
  passenger ferry
2 das Fährseil
- *ferry rope (ferry cable)*
3 der Flußarm
- *river branch (river arm)*
4 die Flußinsel (Strominsel)
- *river island (river islet)*
5 der Uferabbruch am Flußufer *n*,
  ein Hochwasserschaden *m*
- *collapsed section of riverbank,*
  flood damage
6 **die Motorfähre**
- *motor ferry*
7 der Fährsteg (Motorbootsteg)
- *ferry landing stage (motorboat*
  landing stage)
8 die Pfahlgründung
- *pile foundations*
9 die Strömung (der Stromstrich,
  Stromschlauch, Strömungsverlauf)
- *current (flow, course)*
10 **die Pendelfähre** (fliegende Fähre,
   Flußfähre, Stromfähre), eine
   Wagenfähre
- *flying ferry (river ferry), a car ferry*
11 das Fährboot
- *ferry boat*
12 der Schwimmer
- *buoy (float)*
13 die Verankerung
- *anchorage*
14 der Liegehafen (Schutzhafen,
   Winterhafen)
- *harbour* (Am. *harbor*) *for laying up*
   river craft
15 **die Stakfähre,** eine Kahnfähre
- *ferry boat (punt)*
16 die Stake
- *pole (punt pole, quant pole)*
17 der Fährmann
- *ferryman*
18 der Altarm (tote Flußarm)
- *blind river branch (blind river arm)*
19 die Buhne
- *groyne* (Am. *groin*)
20 der Buhnenkopf
- *groyne* (Am. *groin*) *head*
21 die Fahrrinne (Teil *m* des
   Fahrwassers *n*)
- *fairway (navigable part of river)*
22 **der Schleppzug**
- *train of barges*
23 der Flußschleppdampfer (*österr.*
   Remorqueur)
- *river tug*
24 die Schlepptrosse (das Schleppseil)
- *tow rope (tow line, towing hawser)*
25 der Schleppkahn (Frachtkahn,
   Lastkahn, *md.* die Zille)
- *barge (freight barge, cargo barge,*
   lighter)
26 der Schleppschiffer
- *bargeman (bargee, lighterman)*
27 **das Treideln** (der Leinzug)
- *towing (hauling, haulage)*
28 der Treidelmast
- *towing mast*
29 der Treidelmotor
- *towing engine*
30 das Treidelgleis; *früh.* der Leinpfad
- *towing track;* form.: *tow path*
   (towing path)

31 der Fluß, nach der Flußregelung
- *river after river training*
32 **der Hochwasserdeich**
   (Winterdeich)
- *dike (dyke, main dike, flood wall,*
   winter dike)
33 der Entwässerungsgraben
- *drainage ditch*
34 das Deichsiel (die Deichschleuse)
- *dike (dyke) drainage sluice*
35 die Flügelmauer
- *wing wall*
36 der Vorfluter
- *outfall*
37 der Seitengraben (die
   Sickerwasserableitung)
- *drain (infiltration drain)*
38 die Berme (der Deichabsatz)
- *berm (berme)*
39 die Deichkrone
- *top of dike (dyke)*
40 die Deichböschung
- *dike (dyke) batter (dike slope)*
41 das Hochwasserbett
- *flood bed (inundation area)*
42 der Überschwemmungsraum
- *flood containment area*
43 der Strömungsweiser
- *current meter*
44 die Kilometertafel
- *kilometre* (Am. *kilometer*) *sign*
45 das Deichwärterhaus; *auch:*
   Fährhaus
- *dikereeve's (dykereeve's) house*
   (dikereeve's cottage); also:
   ferryman's house (cottage)
46 der Deichwärter
- *dikereeve (dykereeve)*
47 die Deichrampe
- *dike (dyke) ramp*
48 der Sommerdeich
- *summer dike (summer dyke)*
49 der Flußdamm (Uferdamm)
- *levee (embankment)*
50 die Sandsäcke *m*
- *sandbags*
51-55 **die Uferbefestigung**
- *bank protection*
   (bank stabilization,
   revetment)
51 die Steinschüttung
- *riprap*
52 die Anlandung (Sandablagerung)
- *alluvial deposit (sand deposit)*
53 die Faschine (das Zweigebündel)
- *fascine (bundle of wooden sticks)*
54 die Flechtzäune *m*
- *wicker fences*
55 die Steinpackung
- *stone pitching*
56 **der Schwimmbagger,** ein
   Eimerkettenbagger *m*
- *dredger (multi-bucket ladder*
   dredge, floating dredging machine)
57 die Eimerkette
   (das Paternosterwerk)
- *bucket elevator chain*
58 der Fördereimer
- *dredging bucket*
59 **der Saugbagger,** mit Schleppkopf-
   oder Schutensauger *m*
- *suction dredger (hydraulic dredger)*
   with trailing suction pipe or barge
   sucker
60 die Treibwasserpumpe
- *centrifugal pump*

61 der Rückspülschieber
- *back scouring valve*
62 die Saugpumpe, eine Düsenpumpe
   mit Spüldüsen *f*
- *suction pump, a jet pump with*
   scouring nozzles

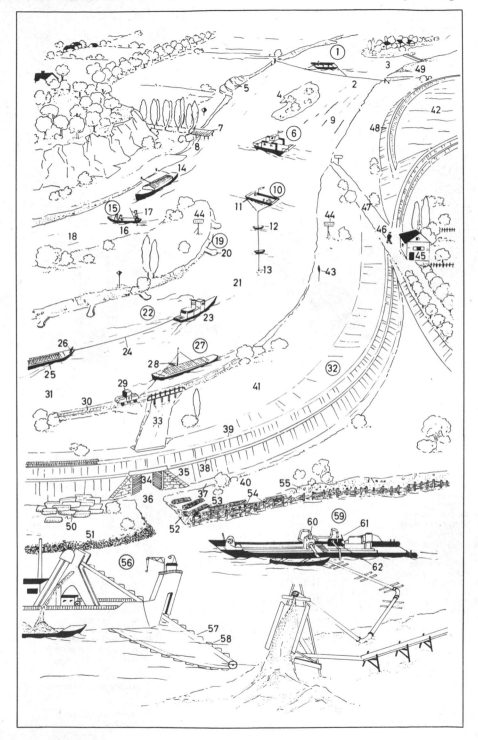

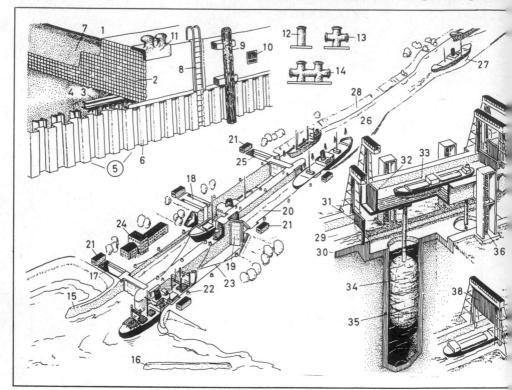

1-14 die Kaimauer
- *quay wall*
1 die Straßendecke
- *road surface*
2 der Mauerkörper
- *body of wall*
3 die Stahlschwelle
- *steel sleeper*
4 der Stahlpfahl
- *steel pile*
5 die Spundwand
- *sheet pile wall (sheet pile bulkhead, sheet piling)*
6 die Spundbohle
- *box pile*
7 die Hinterfüllung
- *backfilling (filling)*
8 die Steigeleiter
- *ladder*
9 der Fender
- *fender (fender pile)*
10 der Nischenpoller
- *recessed bollard*
11 der Doppelpoller
- *double bollard*
12 der Poller
- *bollard*
13 der Kreuzpoller
- *cross-shaped bollard (cross-shaped mooring bitt)*
14 der Doppelkreuzpoller
- *double cross-shaped bollard (double cross-shaped mooring bitt)*

15-28 der Kanal
- *canal*
15-16 die Kanaleinfahrt (Einfahrt)
- *canal entrance*
15 die Mole
- *mole*
16 der Wellenbrecher
- *breakwater*
17-25 die Koppelschleuse
- *staircase of locks*
17 das Unterhaupt
- *lower level*
18 das Schleusentor, ein Schiebetor *n*
- *lock gate, a sliding gate*
19 das Stemmtor
- *mitre (Am. miter) gate*
20 die Schleuse (Schleusenkammer)
- *lock (lock chamber)*
21 das Maschinenhaus
- *power house*
22 das Verholspill, ein Spill *n*
- *warping capstan (hauling capstan), a capstan*
23 die Verholtrosse, eine Trosse
- *warp*
24 die Behörde (z.B. die Kanalverwaltung, die Wasserschutzpolizei, das Zollamt)
- *offices (e.g. canal administration, river police, customs)*
25 das Oberhaupt
- *upper level (head)*
26 der Schleusenvorhafen
- *lock approach*

27 die Kanalweiche (Weiche, Ausweichstelle)
- *lay-by*
28 die Uferböschung
- *bank slope*
29-38 das Schiffshebewerk
- *boat lift (Am. boat elevator)*
29 die untere Kanalhaltung
- *lower pound (lower reach)*
30 die Kanalsohle
- *canal bed*
31 das Haltungstor, ein Hubtor *n*
- *pound lock gate, a vertical gate*
32 das Trogtor
- *lock gate*
33 der Schiffstrog
- *boat tank (caisson)*
34 der Schwimmer, ein Auftriebskörper *m*
- *float*
35 der Schwimmerschacht
- *float shaft*
36 die Hubspindel
- *lifting spindle*
37 die obere Kanalhaltung
- *upper pound (upper reach)*
38 das Hubtor
- *vertical gate*
39-46 das Pumpspeicherwerk
- *pumping plant and reservoir*
39 das Staubecken
- *forebay*
40 das Entnahmebauwerk
- *surge tank*

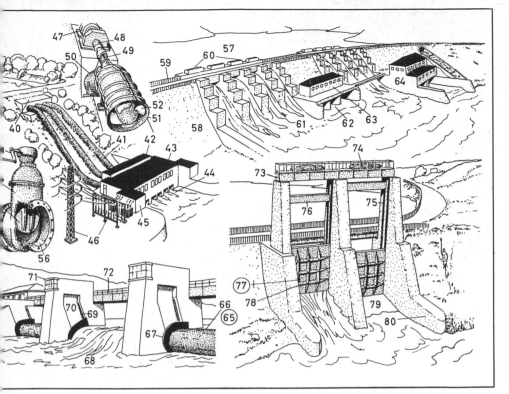

41 die Druckrohrleitung
- *pressure pipeline*
42 das Schieberhaus
- *valve house (valve control house)*
43 das Turbinenhaus (Pumpenhaus)
- *turbine house (pumping station)*
44 das Auslaufbauwerk
- *discharge structure
(outlet structure)*
45 das Schalthaus
- *control station*
46 die Umspannanlage
- *transformer station*
47-52 die Flügelradpumpe
(Propellerpumpe)
- *axial-flow pump (propeller pump)*
47 der Antriebsmotor
- *drive motor*
48 das Getriebe
- *gear*
49 die Antriebswelle
- *drive shaft*
50 das Druckrohr
- *pressure pipe*
51 der Ansaugtrichter
- *suction head*
52 das Flügelrad
- *impeller wheel*
53-56 der Schieber (Absperrschieber)
- *sluice valve (sluice gate)*
53 der Kurbelantrieb
- *crank drive*
54 das Schiebergehäuse
- *valve housing*

55 der Schieber
- *sliding valve (sliding gate)*
56 die Durchflußöffnung
- *discharge opening*
57-64 die Talsperre
- *dam (barrage)*
57 der Stausee
- *reservoir (storage reservoir,
impounding reservoir, impounded
reservoir)*
58 die Staumauer
- *masonry dam*
59 die Mauerkrone
- *crest of dam*
60 der Überfall (die
Hochwasserentlastungsanlage)
- *spillway (overflow spillway)*
61 das Tosbecken
- *stilling basin (stilling box, stilling
pool)*
62 der Grundablaß
- *scouring tunnel (outlet tunnel,
waste water outlet)*
63 das Schieberhaus
- *valve house (valve control house)*
64 das Krafthaus
- *power station*
65-72 das Walzenwehr (Wehr), eine
Staustufe; *anderes System:*
Klappwehr
- *rolling dam (weir), a barrage; other
system: shutter weir*
65 die Walze, ein Staukörper *m*
- *roller, a barrier*

66 die Walzenkrone
- *roller top*
67 der Seitenschild
- *flange*
68 die Versenkwalze
- *submersible roller*
69 die Zahnstange
- *rack track*
70 die Nische
- *recess*
71 das Windwerkshaus
- *hoisting gear cabin*
72 der Bedienungssteg
- *service bridge (walkway)*
73-80 das Schützenwehr
- *sluice dam*
73 die Windwerksbrücke
- *hoisting gear bridge*
74 das Windwerk
- *hoisting gear (winding gear)*
75 die Führungsnut
- *guide groove*
76 das Gegengewicht
- *counterweight (counterpoise)*
77 das Schütz (die Falle)
- *sluice gate (floodgate)*
78 die Verstärkungsrippe
- *reinforcing rib*
79 die Wehrsohle
- *dam sill (weir sill)*
80 die Wangenmauer
- *wing wall*

1-6　**germanisches Ruderschiff**
　[etwa　400 n.Chr.]; das Nydamschiff
- *Germanic rowing boat [ca. AD 400],*
the Nydam boat
1　der Achtersteven
- *stern post*
2　der Steuermann
- *steersman*
3　die Ruderer m
- *oarsman*
4　der Vorsteven
- *stem post (stem)*
5　der Riemen zum Rudern n
- *oar, for rowing*
6　das Ruder, ein Seitenruder n zum
　Steuern n
- *rudder (steering oar), a side rudder,*
for steering
7　**der Einbaum,** ein ausgehöhlter
　Baumstamm m
- *dugout, a hollowed-out tree trunk*
8　das Stechpaddel (die Pagaie)
- *paddle*
9-12　**die Trireme,** ein römisches
　Kriegsschiff n
- *trireme, a Roman warship*
9　der Rammsporn
- *ram*
10　das Kastell
- *forecastle (fo'c'sle)*
11　der Enterbalken, zum Festhalten n
　des Feindschiffs n
- *grapple (grapnel, grappling iron),*
for fastening the enemy ship
alongside
12　die drei Ruderreihen f
- *three banks (tiers) of oars*
13-17　**das Wikingerschiff**
　(der Wikingerdrache,
　das Drachenschiff,
　der Seedrache,
　das Wogenroß) [altnordisch]
- *Viking ship (longship, dragon ship)*
[Norse]
13　der Helm (Helmstock)
- *helm (tiller)*
14　die Zeltschere, mit geschnitzten
　Pferdeköpfen m
- *awning crutch with carved horses'*
heads
15　das Zelt
- *awning*
16　der Drachenkopf
- *dragon figurehead*
17　das Schutzschild (Schild)
- *shield*
18-26　**die Kogge** (Hansekogge)
- *cog (Hansa cog, Hansa ship)*
18　das Ankerkabel (Ankertau)
- *anchor cable (anchor rope, anchor*
hawser)
19　das Vorderkastell
- *forecastle (fo'c'sle)*
20　der Bugspriet
- *bowsprit*
21　das aufgegeite Rahsegel
- *furled (brailed-up) square sail*
22　das Städtebanner
- *town banner (city banner)*
23　das Achterkastell
- *aftercastle (sterncastle)*
24　das Ruder, ein Stevenruder n
- *rudder, a stem rudder*
25　das Rundgattheck
- *rounded prow (rounded bow, bluff*
prow, bluff bow)

26　der Holzfender
- *wooden fender*
27-43　**die Karavelle** [„Santa Maria" 1492]
- *caravel (carvel) ['Santa Maria' 1492]*
27　die Admiralskajüte
- *admiral's cabin*
28　der Besanausleger
- *spanker boom*
29　der Besan, ein Lateinersegel n
- *mizzen (mizen, mutton spanker,*
lateen spanker), a lateen sail
30　die Besanrute
- *lateen yard*
31　der Besanmast
- *mizzen (mizen) mast*
32　die Lasching (Laschung)
- *lashing*
33　das Großsegel, ein Rahsegel n
- *mainsail (main course), a square*
sail
34　das Bonnett, ein abnehmbarer
　Segelstreifen m
- *bonnet, a removable strip of canvas*
35　die Buline (Bulin, Bulien, Buleine)
- *bowline*
36　die Martnets n (Seitengordings f)
- *bunt line (martinet)*
37　die Großrah
- *main yard*
38　das Marssegel
- *main topsail*
39　die Marsrah
- *main topsail yard*
40　der Großmast
- *mainmast*
41　das Focksegel
- *foresail (fore course)*
42　der Fockmast
- *foremast*
43　die Blinde
- *spritsail*
44-50　**die Galeere** [15.-18.Jh.], eine
　Sklavengaleere
- *galley [15th to 18th century], a slave*
galley
44　die Laterne
- *lantern*
45　die Kajüte
- *cabin*
46　der Mittelgang
- *central gangway*
47　der Sklavenaufseher, mit Peitsche f
- *slave driver with whip*
48　die Galeerensklaven m
　(Rudersklaven,
　Galeerensträflinge)
- *galley slaves*
49　die Rambate, eine gedeckte
　Plattform auf dem Vorschiff n
- *covered platform in the forepart of*
the ship
50　das Geschütz
- *gun*
51-60　**das Linienschiff**
　[18./19.Jh.], ein Dreidecker m
- *ship of the line (line-of-battle ship)*
[18th to 19th century], a
three-decker
51　der Klüverbaum
- *jib boom*
52　das Vorbramsegel
- *fore topgallant sail*
53　das Großbramsegel
- *main topgallant sail*
54　das Kreuzbramsegel
- *mizzen (mizen) topgallant sail*

55-57　das Prunkheck
- *gilded stern*
55　der Bovenspiegel
- *upper stern*
56　die Heckgalerie
- *stern gallery*
57　die Tasche, ein Ausbau m mit
　verzierten Seitenfenstern n
- *quarter gallery, a projecting*
balcony with ornamental portholes
58　der Unterspiegel (Spiegel)
- *lower stern*
59　die Geschützpforten f, für
　Breitseitenfeuer n
- *gunports for broadside fire*
60　der Pfortendeckel
- *gunport shutter*

1-72 die Takelung und Besegelung
einer Bark
- *rigging (rig, tackle) and sails of a
bark (barque)*
1-9 die Masten *m*
- *masts*
1 das Bugspriet mit dem
Klüverbaum *m*
- *bowsprit with jib boom*
2-4 der Fockmast
- *foremast*
2 der Fockuntermast
- *lower foremast*
3 die Vorstenge (Vormarsstenge)
- *fore topmast*
4 die Vorbramstenge
- *fore topgallant mast*
5-7 der Großmast
- *mainmast*
5 der Großuntermast
- *lower mainmast*
6 die Großstenge (Großmarsstenge)
- *main topmast*
7 die Großbramstenge
- *main topgallant mast*
8-9 der Besanmast
- *mizzen (mizen) mast*
8 der Besanuntermast
- *lower mizzen (lower mizen)*
9 die Besanstenge
- *mizzen (mizen) topmast*
10-19 das stehende Gut
- *standing rigging*
10 das Stag
- *forestay, mizzen (mizen) stay, mainstay*
11 das Stengestag
- *fore topmast stay, main topmast
stay, mizzen (mizen) topmast stay*
12 das Bramstengestag (Bramstag)
- *fore topgallant stay, mizzen
(mizen) topgallant stay, main
topgallant stay*
13 das Royalstengestag (Royalstag)
- *fore royal stay (main royal stay)*
14 der Klüverleiter
- *jib stay*
15 das Wasserstag
- *bobstay*
16 die Wanten *f*
- *shrouds*
17 die Stengewanten *f*
- *fore topmast rigging (main topmast
rigging, mizzen (mizen) topmast rigging)*
18 die Bramstengewanten *f*
- *fore topgallant rigging (main
topgallant rigging)*
19 die Pardunen *f*
- *backstays*
20-31 die Schratsegel
- *fore-and-aft sails*
20 das Vor-Stengestagsegel
- *fore topmast staysail*
21 der Binnenklüver
- *inner jib*
22 der Klüver
- *outer jib*
23 der Außenklüver
- *flying jib*
24 das Groß-Stengestagsegel
- *main topmast staysail*
25 das Groß-Bramstagsegel
(Bramstengestagsegel)
- *main topgallant staysail*
26 das Groß-Royalstagsegel
(Royalstengestagsegel)
- *main royal staysail*

27 das Besanstagsegel
- *mizzen (mizen) staysail*
28 das Besan-Stengestagsegel
- *mizzen (mizen) topmast staysail*
29 das Besan-Bramstagsegel
(Bramstengestagsegel)
- *mizzen (mizen) topgallant staysail*
30 das Besansegel (der Besan)
- *mizzen (mizen), spanker, driver)*
31 das Gaffeltoppsegel
- *gaff topsail*
32-45 die Rundhölzer *n*
- *spars*
32 die Fockrah
- *foreyard*
33 die Vor-Untermarsrah
- *lower fore topsail yard*
34 die Vor-Obermarsrah
- *upper fore topsail yard*
35 die Vor-Unterbramrah
- *lower fore topgallant yard*
36 die Vor-Oberbramrah
- *upper fore topgallant yard*
37 die Vor-Royalrah
- *fore royal yard*
38 die Großrah
- *main yard*
39 die Groß-Untermarsrah
- *lower main topsail yard*
40 die Groß-Obermarsrah
- *upper main topsail yard*
41 die Groß-Unterbramrah
- *lower main topgallant yard*
42 die Groß-Oberbramrah
- *upper main topgallant yard*
43 die Groß-Royalrah
- *main royal yard*
44 der Besanbaum (Großbaum)
- *spanker boom*
45 die Gaffel
- *spanker gaff*
46 das Fußpferd (Peerd; *pl:* die
Peerden)
- *footrope*
47 die Toppnanten *f*
- *lifts*
48 die Dirk (Besandirk)
- *spanker boom topping lift*
49 der Gaffelstander (Pickstander)
- *spanker peak halyard*
50 die Vor-Marssaling
- *foretop*
51 die Vor-Bramsaling
- *fore topmast crosstrees*
52 die Groß-Marssaling
- *maintop*
53 die Groß-Bramsaling
- *main topmast crosstrees*
54 die Besansaling
- *mizzen (mizen) top*
55-66 die Rahsegel *n*
- *square sails*
55 das Focksegel
- *foresail (fore course)*
56 das Vor-Untermarssegel
- *lower fore topsail*
57 das Vor-Obermarssegel
- *upper fore topsail*
58 das Vor-Unterbramsegel
- *lower fore topgallant sail*
59 das Vor-Oberbramsegel
- *upper fore topgallant sail*
60 das Vor-Royalsegel
- *fore royal*
61 das Großsegel
- *mainsail (main course)*

62 das Groß-Untermarssegel
- *lower main topsail*
63 das Groß-Obermarssegel
- *upper main topsail*
64 das Groß-Unterbramsegel
- *lower main topgallant sail*
65 das Groß-Oberbramsegel
- *upper main topgallant sail*
66 das Groß-Royalsegel
- *main royal sail*
67-71 das laufende Gut
- *running rigging*
67 die Brassen [*sg:* die Braß]
- *braces*
68 die Schoten [*sg:* die Schot]
- *sheets*
69 die Besanschot
- *spanker sheet*
70 die Gaffelgeer [*pl:* die
Gaffelgeerden]
- *spanker vangs*
71 die Gordings *f*
- *bunt line*
72 das Reff
- *reef*

1-5 Segelformen *f*
- *sail shapes*
1 das Gaffelsegel
- *gaffsail*
(small: *trysail, spencer*)
2 das Stagsegel
- *jib*
3 das Lateinersegel
- *lateen sail*
4 das Luggersegel
- *lugsail*
5 das Sprietsegel
- *spritsail*
6-8 Einmaster *m*
- *single-masted sailing boats*
(Am. *sailboats*)
6 die Tjalk
- *tjalk*
7 das Schwert (Seitenschwert)
- *leeboard*
8 der Kutter
- *cutter*
9-10 Eineinhalbmaster *m*
(Anderthalbmaster)
- *mizzen (mizen) masted sailing boats*
(Am. *sailboats*)
9 der Ewer (Ever)
- *ketch-rigged sailing barge*
10 der kurische Reisekahn
- *yawl*
11-17 Zweimaster *m*
- *two-masted sailing boats* (Am.
sailboats)
11-13 der Toppsegelschoner
- *topsail schooner*
11 das Großsegel
- *mainsail*
12 das Schonersegel
- *boom foresail*
13 die Breitfock
- *square foresail*
14 die Schonerbrigg
- *brigantine*
15 der Schonermast mit Schratsegeln *n*
- *half-rigged mast with fore-and-aft
sails*
16 der voll getakelte Mast mit
Rahsegeln *n*
- *full-rigged mast with square sails*
17 die Brigg
- *brig*
18-27 Dreimaster *m*
- *three-masted sailing vessels*
(*three-masters*)
18 der Dreimast-Gaffelschoner
- *three-masted schooner*
19 der Dreimast-Toppsegelschoner
- *three-masted topsail schooner*
20 der Dreimast-Marssegelschoner
- *bark (barque) schooner*
21-23 die Bark [vgl. Takel- und
Segelriß Tafel 219]
- *bark (barque) [cf. illustration of
rigging and sails in plate 219]*
21 der Fockmast
- *foremast*
22 der Großmast
- *mainmast*
23 der Besanmast
- *mizzen (mizen) mast*
24-27 das Vollschiff (Schiff)
- *full-rigged ship*
24 der Kreuzmast
- *mizzen (mizen) mast*
25 die Bagienrah (Begienrah)
- *crossjack yard (crojack yard)*

26 das Bagiensegel (Kreuzsegel)
- *crossjack (crojack)*
27 das Portenband (Pfortenband)
- *ports*
28-31 Viermaster *m*
- *four-masted sailing ships*
(*four-masters*)
28 der Viermast-Gaffelschoner
- *four-masted schooner*
29 die Viermastbark
- *four-masted bark (barque)*
30 der Kreuzmast`
- *mizzen (mizen) mast*
31 das Viermastvollschiff
- *four-masted full-rigged ship*
32-34 die Fünfmastbark
- *five-masted bark (five-masted
barque)*
32 das Skysegel (Skeisel, Skeusel)
- *skysail*
33 der Mittelmast
- *middle mast*
34 der Achtermast
- *mizzen (mizen) mast*
35-37 Entwicklung des Segelschiffes *n*
in 400 Jahren
- *development of sailing ships over
400 years*
35 das Fünfmastvollschiff
„Preußen", 1902-1910
- *five-masted full-rigged ship
'Preussen' 1902-10*
36 der engl. Klipper „Spindrift", 1867
- *English clipper ship 'Spindrift' 1867*
37 die Karavelle „Santa Maria", 1492
- *caravel (carvel) 'Santa Maria' 1492*

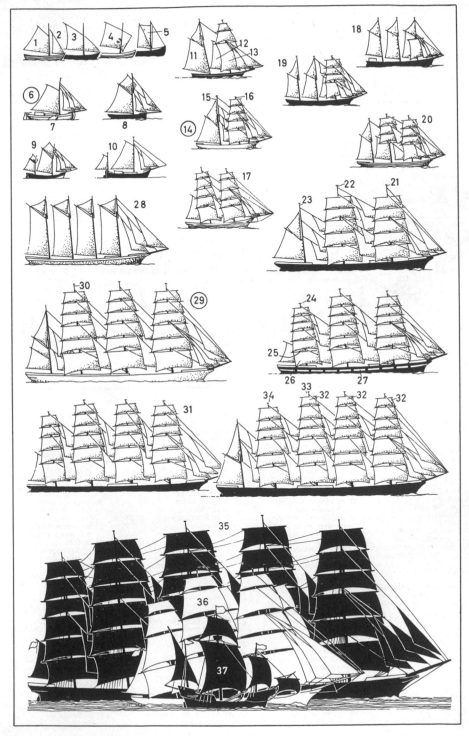

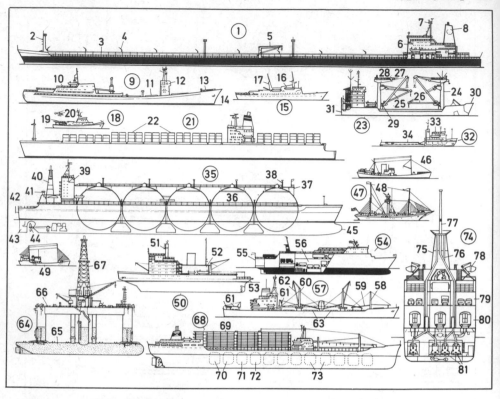

1 **der Mammuttanker** (ULCC, Ultra large crudeoil carrier) vom „All-aft-Typ" *m*
- *ULCC (ultra large crude carrier) of the 'all-aft' type*
2 der vordere Mast
- *foremast*
3 der Laufsteg mit den Rohrleitungen *f*
- *catwalk with the pipes*
4 die Feuerlöschkanone (der Feuerlöschmotor)
- *fire gun (fire nozzle)*
5 der Deckskran
- *deck crane*
6 das Deckshaus mit der Brücke
- *deckhouse with the bridge*
7 der achtere Signal- und Radarmast
- *aft signal (signalling) and radar mast*
8 der Schornstein
- *funnel*
9 **das Kernenergieforschungsschiff** „Otto Hahn", ein Bulkfrachter *m*
- *nuclear research ship 'Otto Hahn', a bulk carrier*
10 der achtere Aufbau (das Maschinenhaus)
- *aft superstructure (engine room)*
11 die Ladeluke für Schüttgut *n*
- *cargo hatchway for bulk goods (bulk cargoes)*
12 die Brücke
- *bridge*
13 die Back
- *forecastle (fo'c'sle)*
14 der Steven
- *stem*
15 **das Seebäderschiff**
- *seaside pleasure boat*

16 der blinde Schornstein
- *dummy funnel*
17 der Abgasmast (Abgaspfosten)
- *exhaust mast*
18 **der Seenotrettungskreuzer**
- *rescue cruiser*
19 die Hubschrauberplattform (das Arbeitsdeck)
- *helicopter platform (working deck)*
20 der Rettungshubschrauber
- *rescue helicopter*
21 **das Vollcontainerschiff**
- *all-container ship*
22 die Containerdecksladung
- *containers stowed on deck*
23 **der Schwerstgutfrachter**
- *cargo ship*
24-29 das Ladegeschirr
- *cargo gear (cargo-handling gear)*
24 der Schwergutpfosten
- *bipod mast*
25 der Schwergutbaum
- *jumbo derrick boom (heavy-lift derrick boom)*
26 der Ladebaum
- *derrick boom (cargo boom)*
27 die Talje (der Flaschenzug)
- *tackle*
28 der Block
- *block*
29 das Widerlager
- *thrust bearing*
30 der Bugtor
- *bow doors*
31 die Heckladeklappe
- *stern loading door*
32 **der Offshore** (Bohrinselversorger)
- *offshore drilling rig supply vessel*
33 der Kompaktaufbau
- *compact superstructure*

34 das Ladedeck (Arbeitsdeck)
- *loading deck (working deck)*
35 **der Flüssiggastanker**
- *liquefied-gas tanker*
36 der Kugeltank
- *spherical tank*
37 der Navigationsfernsehmast
- *navigational television receiver mast*
38 der Abblasemast
- *vent mast*
39 das Deckshaus
- *deckhouse*
40 der Schornstein
- *funnel*
41 der Lüfter
- *ventilator*
42 das Spiegelheck (der Heckspiegel)
- *transom stern (transom)*
43 das Ruderblatt
- *rudder blade (rudder)*
44 die Schiffsschraube
- *ship's propeller (ship's screw)*
45 der Bugwulst (Bulbsteven)
- *bulbous bow*
46 der Fischdampfer (Seitentrawler)
- *steam trawler*
47 **das Feuerschiff**
- *lightship (light vessel)*
48 die Laterne
- *lantern (characteristic light)*
49 der Motorfischkutter
- *smack*
50 **der Eisbrecher**
- *ice breaker*
51 der Turmmast
- *steaming light mast*
52 der Hubschrauberhangar
- *helicopter hangar*

53 die Heckführungsrinne zum Aufnehmen *n* des Bugs *m* geleiteter Schiffe *n*
- *stern towing point, for gripping the bow of ships in tow*
54 **die Ro-ro-Trailerfähre** (der Roll-on-roll-off-Trailer, Roro-Trailer)
- *roll-on roll-off (ro-ro) trailer ferry*
55 die Heckpforte mit Auffahrrampe
- *stern port (stern opening) with ramp*
56 die Lkw-Fahrstühle
- *heavy vehicle lifts (Am. heavy vehicle elevators)*
57 **der Mehrzweckfrachter**
- *multi-purpose freighter*
58 der Lade- und Lüfterpfosten
- *ventilator-type samson (sampson) post (ventilator-type king post)*
59 der Ladebaum (das Ladegeschirr)
- *derrick boom (cargo boom, cargo gear, cargo-handling gear)*
60 der Lademast
- *derrick mast*
61 der Deckskran
- *deck crane*
62 der Schwergutbaum
- *jumbo derrick boom (heavy-lift derrick boom)*
63 die Ladeluke
- *cargo hatchway*
64 **die halbtauchende Bohrinsel**
- *semisubmersible drilling vessel*
65 der Schwimmer mit der Maschinenanlage
- *floating vessel with machinery*
66 die Arbeitsplattform
- *drilling platform*
67 der Bohrturm
- *derrick*

68 der Viehtransporter
(Livestock-Carrier)
- *cattleship (cattle vessel)*
69 der Aufbau für den Tiertransport
- *superstructure for transporting livestock*
70 die Frischwassertanks *m*
- *fresh water tanks*
71 der Treiböltank
- *fuel tank*
72 der Dungtank
- *dung tank*
73 die Futtertanks *m*
- *fodder tanks*
74 die Eisenbahnfähre
(das Trajekt
[im Querschnitt])
- *train ferry [cross section]*
75 der Schornstein
- *funnel*
76 die Rauchzüge *m*
(Abgasleitungen *f*)
- *exhaust pipes*
77 der Mast
- *mast*
78 das Rettungsboot im Patentdavit *m*
- *ship's lifeboat hanging at the davit*
79 das Autodeck
- *car deck*
80 das Eisenbahndeck
(main deck (train deck))
- *main deck (train deck)*
81 die Hauptmotoren *m*
- *main engines*
82 der Passagierdampfer (Liner,
Ocean Liner)
- *passenger liner (liner, ocean liner)*
83 der Atlantiksteven
- *stem*
84 der Gittermantelschornstein
- *funnel with lattice casing*

85 die Flaggengala (der
Flaggenschmuck: über die Toppen
m geflaggt, z.B. auf der
Jungfernfahrt)
- *flag dressing (rainbow dressing,
string of flags extending over
mastheads, e.g., on the maiden
voyage)*
86 der Hecktrawler, ein Fischfang-
und Verarbeitungsschiff *n*
- *trawler, a factory ship*
87 der Heckgalgen
- *gallows*
88 die Heckaufschleppe
- *stern ramp*
89 das Containerschiff
- *container ship*
90 die Verladebrücke
- *loading bridge (loading platform)*
91 das Seefallreep (die Jakobsleiter,
Strickleiter)
- *sea ladder (jacob's ladder, rope
ladder)*
92 der Schubverband, zwei
Binnenwasserfahrzeuge *n*
- *barge and push tug assembly*
93 der Schubschlepper (Schubtrecker)
- *push tug*
94 der Schubleichter
(Schubkahn), ein
Gastankleichter *m*
- *tug-pushed dumb barge
(tug-pushed lighter)*
95 das Lotsenboot
- *pilot boat*
**96 das kombinierte
Fracht-Fahrgast-Schiff**
in Linienfahrt *f*(Kombischiff, der
Linienfrachter)
- *combined cargo and passenger liner*

97 das Ausbooten der Passagiere *m*
- *passengers disembarking by boat*
98 das Fallreep
- *accommodation ladder*
99 das Küstenmotorschiff (Kümo)
- *coaster (coasting vessel)*
100 der Zoll- oder Polizeikreuzer
- *customs or police launch*
101-128 der Ausflugsdampfer (das
Bäderschiff)
- *excursion steamer (pleasure
steamer)*
101-106 die Rettungsbootaufhängung
- *lifeboat launching gear*
101 der Davit
- *davit*
102 der Mittelstander
- *wire rope span*
103 das Manntau
- *lifeline*
104 die Talje
- *tackle*
105 der Block
- *block*
106 der Taljenläufer
- *fall*
107 das Rettungsboot (die Pinasse) mit
der Persenning
- *ship's lifeboat (ship's boat) covered
with tarpaulin*
108 der Steven
- *stem*
109 der Passagier (Fahrgast)
- *passenger*
110 der Stewart
- *steward*
111 der Deckstuhl (Liegestuhl)
- *deck-chair*
112 der Schiffsjunge (*seem.* Moses)
- *deck hand*

113 der Eimer (*seem.* die Pütz)
- *deck bucket*
114 der Bootsmann
- *boatswain (bo's'n, bo'sun, bosun)*
115 die Litewka
- *tunic*
116 das Sonnensegel
- *awning*
117 die Sonnensegelstütze
- *stanchion*
118 die Sonnensegellatte
- *ridge rope (jackstay)*
119 das Bändsel
- *lashing*
120 das Schanzkleid
- *bulwark*
121 die Reling
- *guard rail*
122 der Handläufer
- *handrail (top rail)*
123 der Niedergang
- *companion ladder (companionway)*
124 der Rettungsring (die
Rettungsboje)
- *lifebelt (lifebuoy)*
125 das Nachtrettungslicht
(Wasserlicht)
- *lifebuoy light (lifebelt light, signal
light)*
126 der wachhabende Offizier
(Wachhabende)
- *officer of the watch (watchkeeper)*
127 das Bordjackett
- *reefer (Am. pea jacket)*
128 das Fernglas
- *binoculars*

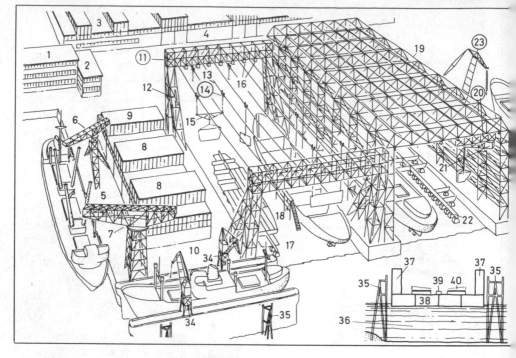

1-43 die Schiffswerft (Werft)
- **shipyard** (shipbuilding yard, dockyard, Am. navy yard)
1 das Verwaltungsgebäude
- administrative offices
2 das Konstruktionsbüro
- ship-drawing office
3-4 die Schiffbauhalle
- shipbuilding sheds
3 der Schnürboden
- mould (Am. mold) loft
4 die Werkhalle
- erection shop
5-9 der Ausrüstungskai
- fitting-out quay
5 der Kai
- quay
6 der Dreibeinkran
- tripod crane
7 der Hammerkran
- hammer-headed crane
8 die Maschinenbauhalle
- engineering workshop
9 die Kesselschmiede
- boiler shop
10 der Reparaturkai
- repair quay
11-26 die Hellinganlagen f (Hellingen f, Helgen m)
- slipways (slips, building berths, building slips, stocks)
11-18 die Kabelkranhelling (Portalhelling), eine Helling (ein Helgen m)
- cable crane berth, a slipway (building berth)
11 das Hellingportal (Portal)
- slipway portal

12 die Portalstütze
- bridge support
13 das Krankabel
- crane cable
14 die Laufkatze
- crab (jenny)
15 die Traverse
- cross piece
16 das Kranführerhaus
- crane driver's cabin (crane driver's cage)
17 die Hellingsohle
- slipway floor
18 die Stelling, ein Baugerüst n
- staging, a scaffold
19-21 die Gerüsthelling
- frame slipway
19 das Hellinggerüst
- slipway frame
20 der Deckenkran
- overhead travelling (Am. traveling) crane (gantry crane)
21 die Drehlaufkatze
- slewing crab
22 der gestreckte Kiel
- keel in position
23 der Drehwippkran, ein Hellingkran m
- luffing jib crane, a slipway crane
24 die Kranbahn
- crane rails (crane track)
25 der Portalkran
- gantry crane
26 die Kranbrücke
- gantry (bridge)
27 der Brückenträger
- trestles (supports)

28 die Laufkatze (der Laufkran)
- crab (jenny)
29 das Schiff in Spanten n
- hull frames in position
30 der Schiffsneubau
- ship under construction
31-33 das Trockendock
- dry dock
31 die Docksohle
- dock floor (dock bottom)
32 das Docktor (der Dockponton, Verschlußponton)
- dock gates (caisson)
33 das Pumpenhaus (Maschinenhaus)
- pumping station (power house)
34-43 das Schwimmdock
- floating dock (pontoon dock)
34 der Dockkran, ein Torkran m
- dock crane (dockside crane), a jib crane
35 die Streichdalben m (Leitdalben)
- fender piling
36-43 der Dockbetrieb
- working of docks
36 die Dockgrube
- dock basin
37-38 der Dockkörper
- dock structure
37 der Seitentank
- side tank (side wall)
38 der Bodentank
- bottom tank (bottom pontoon)
39 der Kielpallen (Kielstapel), ein Dockstapel m
- keel block
40 der Kimmpallen (Kimmstapel)
- bilge block (bilge shore, side support)

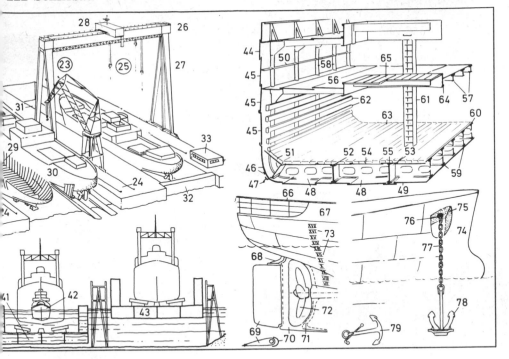

41-43 das Eindocken (Docken) eines
Schiffes n
- docking a ship
41 das geflutete (gefüllte) Schwimmdock
- flooded floating dock
42 der Schlepper beim Bugsieren n
(Schleppen)
- tug towing the ship
43 das gelenzte (leergepumpte) Dock
- emptied (pumped-out) dock
44-61 die Konstruktionselemente n
- structural parts of the ship
44-56 der Längsverband
- longitudinal structure
44-49 die Außenhaut
- shell (shell plating, skin)
44 der Schergang
- sheer strake
45 der Seitengang
- side strake
46 der Kimmgang
- bilge strake
47 der Schlingerkiel (Kimmkiel)
- bilge keel
48 der Bodengang
- bottom plating
49 der Flachkiel
- flat plate keel (keel plate)
50 der Stringer
- stringer (side stringer)
51 die Tankrandplatte (Randplatte)
- tank margin plate
52 der Seitenträger
- longitudinal side girder
53 der Mittelträger
- centre (Am. center) plate girder
(centre girder, kelson, keelson,
vertical keel)

54 die Tankdecke
- tank top plating (tank top, inner
bottom plating)
55 die Mitteldecke
- centre (Am. center) strake
56 die Deckplatte
- deck plating
57 der Deckbalken
- deck beam
58 das Spant
- frame (rib)
59 die Bodenwrange
- floor plate
60 der Doppelboden
- cellular double bottom
61 die Raumstütze
- hold pillar (pillar)
62 u.63 die Garnierung
- dunnage
62 die Seitenwegerung
- side battens (side ceiling, spar
ceiling)
63 die Bodenwegerung
- ceiling (floor ceiling)
64-65 die Luke
- hatchway
64 das Lukensüll
- hatch coaming
65 der Lukendeckel
- hatch cover (hatchboard)
66-72 das Heck
- stern
66 die offene Reling
- guard rail
67 das Schanzkleid
- bulwark
68 der Ruderschaft
- rudder stock

69-70 das Oertz-Ruder
- Oertz rudder
69 das Ruderblatt
- rudder blade (rudder)
70-71 der Achtersteven
(Hintersteven)
- stern frame
70 der Rudersteven (Leitsteven)
- rudder post
71 der Schraubensteven
- propeller post (screw post)
72 die Schiffsschraube
- ship's propeller (ship's screw)
73 die Ahming (Tiefgangsmarke)
- draught (draft) marks
74-79 der Bug
- bow
74 der Vorsteven, ein Wulststeven m
(Wulstbug)
- stem, a bulbous stem (bulbous bow)
75 die Ankertasche (Ankernische)
- hawse
76 die Ankerklüse
- hawse pipe
77 die Ankerkette
- anchor cable (chain cable)
78 der Patentanker
- stockless anchor (patent anchor)
79 der Stockanker
- stocked anchor

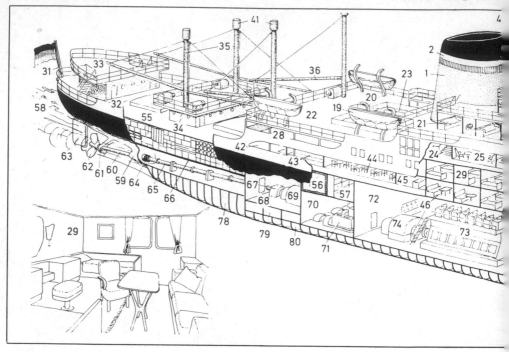

**1–71 das kombinierte
Fracht-Fahrgast-Schiff**
[älteren Typs]
- **combined cargo and passenger ship**
[of the older type]
1 der Schornstein
- *funnel*
2 die Schornsteinmarke
(Schornsteinfarben *pl*)
- *funnel marking*
3 die Sirene (das Typhon)
- *siren (fog horn)*
4–11 das Peildeck
- **compass platform** *(compass bridge,
compass flat, monkey bridge)*
4 die Antennenniederführung
- *antenna lead-in (antenna
down-lead)*
5 die Funkpeilerrahmenantenne
(Peilantenne)
- *radio direction finder (RDF)
antenna (direction finder antenna,
rotatable loop antenna, aural null
loop antenna)*
6 der Magnetkompaß
- *magnetic compass (mariner's
compass)*
7 die Morselampe
- *morse lamp (signalling, Am.
signaling, lamp)*
8 die Radarantenne
- *radar antenna (radar scanner)*
9 das Flaggensignal
- *code flag signal*

10 die Signalleine
- *code flag halyards*
11 das Signalstag
- *triatic stay (signal stay)*
12–18 das Brückendeck (die
Kommandobrücke, Brücke)
- **bridge deck** *(bridge)*
12 der Funkraum
- *radio room*
13 die Kapitänskajüte
- *captain's cabin*
14 der Navigationsraum
- *navigating bridge*
15 die Steuerbord-Seitenlampe [grün;
die Backbord-Seitenlampe rot]
- *starboard sidelight [green; port
sidelight red]*
16 die Brückennock (Nock)
- *wing of bridge*
17 das Schanzkleid (der Windschutz)
- *shelter (weather cloth, dodger)*
18 das Steuerhaus
- *wheelhouse*
19–21 das Bootsdeck
- **boat deck**
19 das Rettungsboot
- *ship's lifeboat*
20 der Davit (Bootskran)
- *davit*
21 die Offizierskajüte
(Offizierskammer)
- *officer's cabin*
22–27 das Promenadendeck
- **promenade deck**

22 das Sonnendeck (Lidodeck)
- *sun deck (lido deck)*
23 das Schwimmbad
- *swimming pool*
24 der Aufgang (Niedergang)
- *companion ladder (companionway)*
25 die Bibliothek
- *library (ship's library)*
26 der Gesellschaftsraum (Salon)
- *lounge*
27 die Promenade
- *promenade*
28–30 das A-Deck
- **A-deck**
28 das halboffene Deck
- *semi-enclosed deck space*
29 die Zweibettkabine, eine Kabine
- *double-berth cabin, a cabin*
30 die Luxuskabine
- *de luxe cabin*
31 der Heckflaggenstock
- *ensign staff*
32–42 das B-Deck (Hauptdeck)
- **B-deck** *(main deck)*
32 das Achterdeck
- *after deck*
33 die Hütte
- *poop*
34 das Deckshaus
- *deckhouse*
35 der Ladepfosten
- *samson (sampson) post (king post)*
36 der Ladebaum
- *derrick boom (cargo boom)*

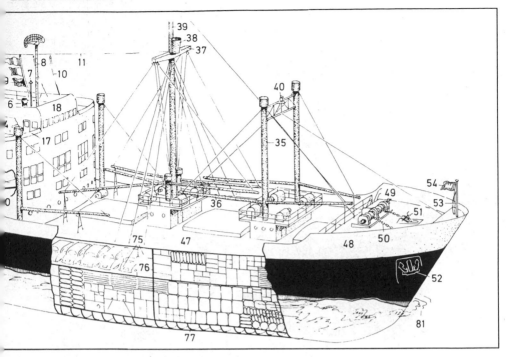

37 die Saling
– *crosstrees (spreader)*
38 der Mastkorb (die Ausgucktonne)
– *crow's nest*
39 die Stenge
– *topmast*
40 das vordere Dampferlicht
– *forward steaming light*
41 der Lüfterkopf
– *ventilator lead*
42 die Kombüse (Schiffsküche)
– *galley (caboose, cookroom, ship's kitchen)*
43 die Pantry (Anrichte)
– *ship's pantry*
44 der Speisesaal
– *dining room*
45 das Zahlmeisterbüro
– *purser's office*
46 die Einbettkabine
– *single-berth cabin*
47 das Vordeck
– *foredeck*
48 die Back
– *forecastle (fo'c'sle)*
49-51 das Ankergeschirr
– *ground tackle*
49 die Ankerwinde
– *windlass*
50 die Ankerkette
– *anchor cable (chain cable)*
51 der Kettenstopper
– *compressor (chain compressor)*
52 der Anker
– *anchor*

53 der Göschstock
– *jackstaff*
54 die Gösch
– *jack*
55 die hinteren (achteren) Laderäume *m*
– *after holds*
56 der Kühlraum
– *cold storage room (insulated hold)*
57 der Proviantraum
– *store room*
58 das Schraubenwasser (Kielwasser)
– *wake*
59 die Wellenhose
– *shell bossing (shaft bossing)*
60 die Schwanzwelle
– *tail shaft (tail end shaft)*
61 der Wellenbock
– *shaft strut (strut, spectacle frame, propeller strut, propeller bracket)*
62 die dreiflügelige Schiffsschraube
– *three-blade ship's propeller (ship's screw)*
63 das Ruderblatt
– *rudder blade (rudder)*
64 die Stopfbüchse
– *stuffing box*
65 die Schraubenwelle
– *propeller shaft*
66 der Wellentunnel
– *shaft alley (shaft tunnel)*
67 das Drucklager
– *thrust block*
68-74 der dieselelektrische Antrieb
– *diesel-electric drive*

68 der E-Maschinenraum
– *electric engine room*
69 der E-Motor
– *electric motor*
70 der Hilfsmaschinenraum
– *auxiliary engine room*
71 die Hilfsmaschinen *f*
– *auxiliary engines*
72 der Hauptmaschinenraum
– *main engine room*
73 die Hauptmaschine, ein Dieselmotor *m*
– *main engine, a diesel engine*
74 der Generator
– *generator*
75 die vorderen Laderäume *m*
– *forward holds*
76 das Zwischendeck
– *tween deck*
77 die Ladung
– *cargo*
78 der Ballasttank, für den Wasserballast
– *ballast tank (deep tank) for water ballast*
79 der Frischwassertank
– *fresh water tank*
80 der Treiböltank
– *fuel tank*
81 die Bugwelle
– *bow wave*

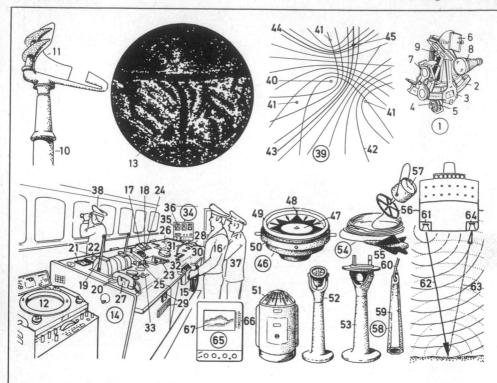

1 **der Sextant**
- *sextant*
2 der Gradbogen
- *graduated arc*
3 die Alhidade
- *index bar (index arm)*
4 die Meßtrommel
- *decimal micrometer*
5 der Nonius
- *vernier*
6 der große Spiegel
- *index mirror*
7 der kleine Spiegel
- *horizon glass (horizon mirror)*
8 das Fernrohr
- *telescope*
9 der Handgriff
- *grip (handgrip)*
10-13 **das Radargerät** (Radar m od. n)
- *radar equipment (radar apparatus)*
10 der Radarmast
- *radar mast*
11 die drehbare Reflektorantenne
- *revolving radar reflector*
12 das Radarsichtgerät
- *radar display unit (radar screen)*
13 das Radarbild
- *radar image (radar picture)*
14-38 **das Steuerhaus** (Ruderhaus)
- *wheelhouse*
14 der Fahr- und Kommandostand
- *steering and control position*
15 das Steuerrad für die Ruderanlage
- *ship's wheel for controlling the rudder mechanism*
16 der Rudergänger
- *helmsman (Am. wheelsman)*
17 der Ruderlagenanzeiger
- *rudder angle indicator*

18 der Sollkurseinsteller
- *automatic pilot (autopilot)*
19 der Betätigungshebel für die Verstellpropeller m
- *control lever for the variable-pitch propeller (reversible propeller, feathering propeller, feathering screw)*
20 das Anzeigegerät für die Propellersteigung
- *propeller pitch indicator*
21 die Umdrehungsanzeige der Hauptmotoren m
- *main engine revolution indicator*
22 die Anzeige der Schiffsgeschwindigkeit
- *ship's speedometer (log)*
23 der Steuerschalter für das Bugstrahlruder
- *control switch for bow thruster (bow-manoeuvring, Am. maneuvering, propeller)*
24 das Echolotanzeigegerät (der Echograph)
- *echo recorder (depth recorder, echograph)*
25 der Doppelmaschinentelegraph
- *engine telegraph (engine order telegraph)*
26 die Steuer- und Kontrollgeräte n für die Schlingerdämpfungsanlage
- *controls for the anti-rolling system (for the stabilizers)*
27 das OB-Telefon (Ortsbatterietelefon)
- *local-battery telephone*
28 das Telefon der Schiffsverkehrs-Fernsprechanlage
- *shipping traffic radio telephone*

29 das Positionslampentableau
- *navigation light indicator panel (running light indicator panel)*
30 die Sprechstelle für die Ruf- und Kommandoanlage
- *microphone for ship's address system*
31 der Kreiselkompaß, ein Tochterkompaß
- *gyro compass (gyroscopic compass), a compass repeater*
32 der Betätigungsknopf für die Schiffssirene
- *control button for the ship's siren (ship's fog horn)*
33 die Überlastkontrolle der Hauptmotoren m
- *main engine overload indicator*
34 das Decca-Gerät zur Positionsbestimmung (der Decca-Navigator)
- *detector indicator unit for fixing the ship's position*
35 die Abstimmgrobanzeige
- *rough focusing indicator*
36 die Abstimmfeinanzeige
- *fine focusing indicator*
37 der Navigationsoffizier
- *navigating officer*
38 der Kapitän
- *captain*
39 **das Decca-Navigator-System**
- *Decca navigation system*
40 die Hauptstation
- *master station*
41 die Nebenstation
- *slave station*
42 die Nullhyperbel
- *null hyperbola*
43 die Hyperbelstandlinie 1
- *hyperbolic position line 1*

44 die Hyperbelstandlinie 2
- *hyperbolic position line 2*
45 der Standort
- *position (fix, ship fix)*
46-53 **Kompasse**
- *compasses*
46 der Fluidkompaß, ein Magnetkompaß
- *liquid compass (fluid compass, spirit compass, wet compass), a magnetic compass*
47 die Kompaßrose
- *compass card*
48 der Steuerstrich
- *lubber's line (lubber's mark, lubber's*
49 der Kompaßkessel
- *compass bowl*
50 die kardanische Aufhängung
- *gimbal ring*
51-53 der Kreiselkompaß (die Kreiselkompaßanlage)
- *gyro compass (gyroscopic compass, gyro compass unit)*
51 der Mutterkompaß
- *master compass (master gyro compass*
52 der Tochterkompaß
- *compass repeater (gyro repeater)*
53 der Tochterkompaß mit Peilaufsatz m
- *compass repeater with pelorus*
54 **das Patentlog**, ein Log n (eine Logge)
- *patent log (screw log, mechanical log, towing log, taffrail log, speedometer), a log*
55 der Logpropeller
- *rotator*
56 der Schwungradregulator
- *governor*
57 das Zählwerk (die Loguhr)
- *log clock*

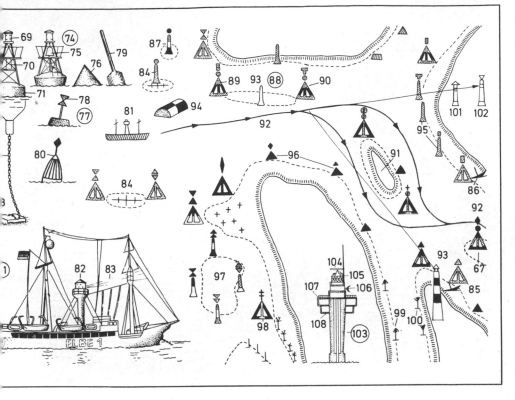

58-67 Lote *n*
- *leads*
58 das Handlot
- *hand lead*
59 der Lotkörper
- *lead (lead sinker)*
60 die Lotleine
- *leadline*
61-67 das Echolot
- *echo sounder (echo sounding machine)*
61 der Schallsender
- *sound transmitter*
62 der Schallwellenimpuls
- *sound wave (sound impulse)*
63 das Echo
- *echo (sound echo, echo signal)*
64 der Echoempfänger
- *echo receiver (hydrophone)*
65 der Echograph (der Echoschreiber)
- *echograph (echo sounding machine recorder)*
66 die Tiefenskala
- *depth scale*
67 das Echobild
- *echogram (depth recording, depth reading)*
68-108 Seezeichen *n*, **zur Betonnung und Befeuerung**
- *sea marks (floating navigational marks) for buoyage and lighting systems*
68-83 Fahrwasserzeichen *n*
- *fairway marks (channel marks)*
68 die Leuchtheultonne
- *light and whistle buoy*
69 die Laterne
- *light (warning light)*
70 der Heulapparat
- *whistle*

71 der Schwimmkörper
- *buoy*
72 die Ankerkette
- *mooring chain*
73 der Tonnenstein (Tonnenanker)
- *sinker (mooring sinker)*
74 die Leuchtglockentonne
- *light and bell buoy*
75 die Glocke
- *bell*
76 die Spitztonne
- *conical buoy*
77 die Stumpftonne
- *can buoy*
78 die Toppzeichen (das Stundenglaszeichen)
- *topmark*
79 die Spierentonne
- *spar buoy*
80 die Bakentonne
- *topmark buoy*
81 das Feuerschiff
- *lightship (light vessel)*
82 der Feuerturm (Laternenträger)
- *lantern mast (lantern tower)*
83 das Leuchtfeuer
- *beam of light*
84-102 die Fahrwasserbezeichnung
- *fairway markings (channel markings) [German type]*
84 Wrack *n* [grüne Betonnung]
- *wreck [green buoys]*
85 Wrack *n* an Steuerbord *n* des Fahrwassers *n*
- *wreck to starboard*
86 Wrack *n* an Backbord *n* des Fahrwassers *n*
- *wreck to port*

87 Untiefe *f*
- *shoals (shallows, shallow water, Am. flats)*
88 Mittelgrund *m* an Backbord *n* des Hauptfahrwassers *n*
- *middle ground to port*
89 Spaltung *f* [der Beginn des Mittelgrundes *m*; Toppzeichen *n*: roter Zylinder *m* über rotem Ball *m*]
- *division (bifurcation) [beginning of the middle ground; topmark: red cylinder above red ball]*
90 Vereinigung *f* [das Ende des Mittelgrundes *m*; Toppzeichen *n*: rotes Antoniuskreuz über rotem Ball *m*]
- *convergence (confluence) [end of the middle ground; topmark: red St. Antony's cross above red ball]*
91 Mittelgrund *m*
- *middle ground*
92 das Hauptfahrwasser
- *main fairway (main navigable channel)*
93 das Nebenfahrwasser
- *secondary fairway (secondary navigable channel)*
94 die Faßtonne
- *can buoy*
95 Backbordtonnen [rot] *f*
- *port hand buoys (port hand marks) [red]*
96 Steuerbordtonnen [schwarz] *f*
- *starboard hand buoys (starboard hand marks) [black]*
97 Untiefe *f* außerhalb des Fahrwassers *n*
- *shoals (shallows, shallow water, Am. flats) outside the fairway*

98 Fahrwassermitte *f* [Toppzeichen *n*: Doppelkreuz]
- *middle of the fairway (mid-channel)*
99 Steuerbordstangen *f* [Besen *m* abwärts]
- *starboard markers [inverted broom]*
100 Backbordstangen *f* [Besen *m* aufwärts]
- *port markers [upward-pointing broom]*
101-102 Richtfeuer *n* (Leitfeuer)
- *range lights (leading lights)*
101 das Unterfeuer
- *lower range light (lower leading light)*
102 das Oberfeuer
- *higher range light (higher leading light)*
103 der Leuchtturm
- *lighthouse*
104 die Radarantenne
- *radar antenna (radar scanner)*
105 die Laterne
- *lantern (characteristic light)*
106 die Richtfunkantenne
- *radio direction finder (RDF) antenna*
107 das Maschinen- und Aufenthaltsdeck
- *machinery and observation platform (machinery and observation deck)*
108 die Wohnräume *m*
- *living quarters*

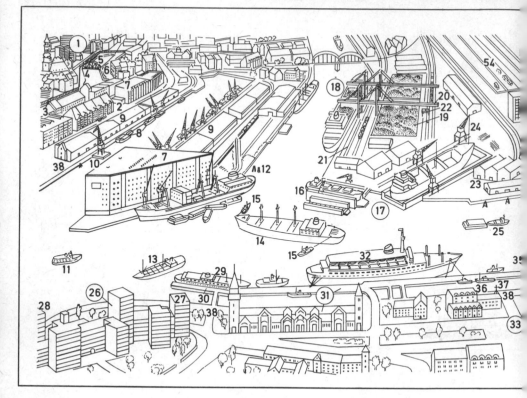

1 das Hafenviertel
- *dock area*
2 der Freihafen
- *free port (foreign trade zone)*
3 die Freihafengrenze (das Zollgitter)
- *free zone frontier (free zone enclosure)*
4 die Zollschranke
- *customs barrier*
5 der Zolldurchlaß
- *customs entrance*
6 das Zollhaus (Hafenzollamt)
- *port custom house*
7 der Speicher
- *entrepôt*
8 die Schute
- *barge (dumb barge, lighter)*
9 der Stückgutschuppen
- *break-bulk cargo transit shed (general cargo transit shed, package cargo transit shed)*
10 der Schwimmkran
- *floating crane*
11 die Hafenfähre (das Fährboot)
- *harbour (Am. harbor) ferry (ferryboat)*
12 die Dalbe (der Dalben, Duckdalben)
- *fender (dolphin)*
13 das Bunkerboot
- *bunkering boat*
14 der Stückgutfrachter
- *break-bulk carrier (general cargo ship)*

15 der Bugsierschlepper
- *tug*
16 das Schwimmdock
- *floating dock (pontoon dock)*
17 das Trockendock
- *dry dock*
18 der Kohlenhafen
- *coal wharf*
19 das Kohlenlager
- *coal bunker*
20 die Verladebrücke
- *transporter loading bridge*
21 die Hafenbahn
- *quayside railway*
22 der Wiegebunker
- *weighing bunker*
23 der Werftschuppen
- *warehouse*
24 der Werftkran
- *quayside crane*
25 die Barkasse mit Leichter *m*
- *launch and lighter*
26 das Hafenkrankenhaus
- *port hospital*
27 die Quarantänestation
- *quarantine wing*
28 das Tropeninstitut (Institut für Tropenmedizin *f*)
- *Institute of Tropical Medicine*
29 der Ausflugsdampfer
- *excursion steamer (pleasure steamer)*
30 die Landungsbrücke
- *jetty*

31 die Fahrgastanlage
- *passenger terminal*
32 das Linienschiff (der Passagierdampfer, Liner, Ocean Liner)
- *liner (passenger liner, ocean liner)*
33 das Meteorologische Amt, eine Wetterwarte
- *meteorological office, a weather station*
34 der Signalmast
- *signal mast (signalling mast)*
35 der Sturmball
- *storm signal*
36 das Hafenamt
- *port administration offices*
37 der Wasserstandsanzeiger
- *tide level indicator*
38 die Kaistraße
- *quayside road (quayside roadway)*
39 der Roll-on-roll-off-Verkehr (Ro-ro-Verkehr, Ro-ro, Roro)
- *roll-on roll-off (ro-ro) system (roll-on roll-off operation)*
40 der Brückenlift
- *gantry*
41 der Truck-to-truck-Verkehr
- *truck-to-truck system (truck-to-truck operation)*
42 die folienverpackten Stapel *m*
- *foil-wrapped unit loads*
43 die Paletten *f*
- *pallets*
44 der Hubstapler
- *forklift truck (fork truck, forklift)*

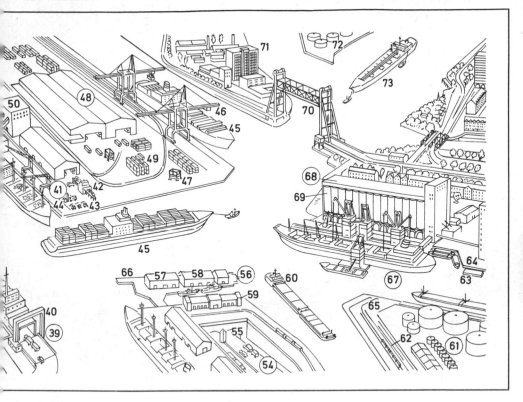

45 das Containerschiff
- *container ship*
46 die Containerbrücke
- *transporter container-loading bridge*
47 der Containerstapler
- *container carrier truck*
48 der (das) Containerterminal
- *container terminal (container berth)*
49 der Containerstapel
- *unit load*
50 das Kühlhaus
- *cold store*
51 das Förderband
- *conveyor belt (conveyor)*
52 der Fruchtschuppen
- *fruit storage shed (fruit warehouse)*
53 das Bürohaus
- *office building*
54 die Stadtautobahn
- *urban motorway (Am. freeway)*
55 die Hafenuntertunnelung
- *harbour (Am. harbor) tunnels*
56 der Fischereihafen
- *fish dock*
57 die Fischhalle
- *fish market*
58 die Versteigerungshalle (Auktionshalle)
- *auction room*
59 die Fischkonservenfabrik
- *fish-canning factory*
60 der Schubschiffverband
- *push tow*

61 das Tanklager
- *tank farm*
62 die Gleisanlage
- *railway siding*
63 der Anlegeponton (Vorleger)
- *landing pontoon (landing stage)*
64 der Kai (die Kaje)
- *quay*
65 das Höft, eine Landspitze
- *breakwater (mole)*
66 die (der) Pier, eine Kaizunge
- *pier (jetty), a quay extension*
67 der Bulkfrachter (Bulkcarrier)
- *bulk carrier*
68 der (das) Silo
- *silo*
69 die Silozelle
- *silo cylinder*
70 die Hubbrücke
- *lift bridge*
71 die Hafenindustrieanlage
- *industrial plant*
72 das Flüssiglager
- *storage tanks*
73 der Tanker
- *tanker*

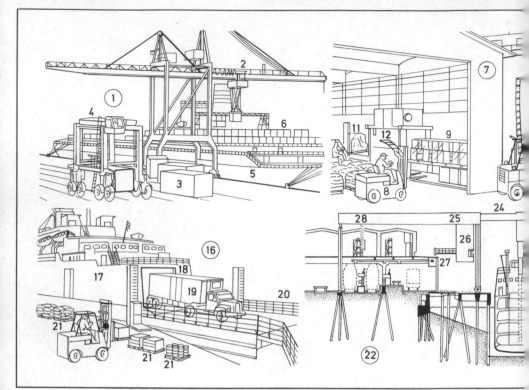

1 das (das) Containerterminal, eine
moderne Güterumschlaganlage
- *container terminal (container
berth), a modern cargo-handling
berth*
2 die Containerbrücke (Ladebrücke),
ähnl.: der Transtainerkran
- *transporter container-loading
bridge (loading bridge); sim.:
transtainer crane (transtainer)*
3 der Container
- *container*
4 der Portalstapler
- *truck (carrier)*
5 das Vollcontainerschiff
- *all-container ship*
6 die Containerdecksladung
- *containers stowed on deck*
7 das Truck-to-truck-handling (der
horizontale rampenlose
Güterumschlag mit Paletten f)
- *truck-to-truck handling (horizontal
cargo handling with pallets)*
8 der Hubstapler (Truck)
- *forklift truck (fork truck, forklift)*
9 die unitisierte folienverpackte
Ladung (das Unitload)
- *unitized foil-wrapped load (unit load)*
10 die Flachpalette, eine Normpalette
- *flat pallet, a standard pallet*
11 das unitisierte Stückgut
- *unitized break-bulk cargo*
12 der Folienschrumpfofen
- *heat sealing machine*

13 der Stückgutfrachter
- *break-bulk carrier (general cargo
ship)*
14 die Ladeluke
- *cargo hatchway*
15 der übernehmende Schiffsstapler
- *receiving truck on board ship*
16 der (das) Allroundterminal
- *multi-purpose terminal*
17 das Roll-on-roll-off-Schiff
(Ro-ro-Schiff, Roro-Schiff)
- *roll-on roll-off ship (ro-ro-ship)*
18 die Heckpforte
- *stern port (stern opening)*
19 die selbstfahrende Ladung, ein
Lastkraftwagen m
- *driven load, a lorry (Am. truck)*
20 die Ro-ro-Abfertigungsanlage
(Ro-ro-Spezialanlage,
Roro-Anlage)
- *ro-ro depot*
21 das unitisierte Packstück
- *unitized load (unitized package)*
22 die Bananenumschlaganlage
[Schnitt]
- *banana-handling terminal [section]*
23 der wasserseitige Turas
- *seaward tumbler*
24 der Ausleger
- *jib*
25 die Elevatorbrücke
- *elevator bridge*
26 das Kettengehänge
- *chain sling*

27 die Leuchtwarte
- *lighting station*
28 der landseitige Turas [für Bahn-
und Lkw-Beladung f]
- *shore-side tumbler for loading
trains and lorries
(Am. trucks)*
29 der Schütt- und Sauggutumschlag
(Massengutumschlag)
- *bulk cargo handling*
30 der Bulkfrachter (Bulkcarrier,
Schüttgutfrachter)
- *bulk carrier*
31 der Schwimmheber
- *floating bulk-cargo elevator*
32 die Saugrohrleitungen f
- *suction pipes*
33 der Rezipient
- *receiver*
34 das Verladerohr
- *delivery pipe*
35 die Massengutschute
- *bulk transporter barge*
36 die Ramme
- *floating pile driver*
37 das Rammgerüst
- *pile driver frame*
38 der Bär (Rammbär, das
Rammgewicht)
- *pile hammer*
39 die Gleitschiene
- *driving guide rail*
40 das Kipplager
- *pile*

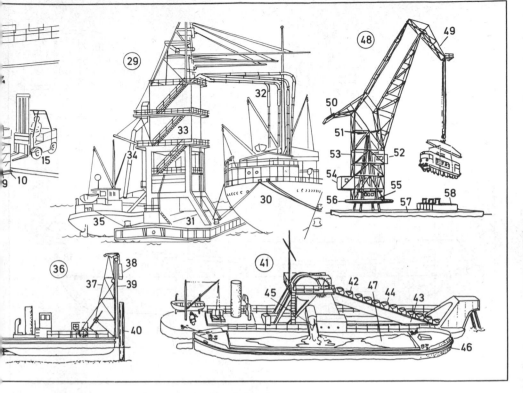

41 der Eimerbagger, ein Bagger *m*
  – *bucket dredger, a dredger*
42 die Eimerkette
  – *bucket chain*
43 die Eimerleiter
  – *bucket ladder*
44 der Baggereimer
  – *dredger bucket*
45 die Schütte (Rutsche)
  – *chute*
46 die Baggerschute
  – *hopper barge*
47 das Baggergut
  – *spoil*
48 der Schwimmkran
  – *floating crane*
49 der Ausleger
  – *jib (boom)*
50 das Gegengewicht
  – *counterweight (counterpoise)*
51 die Verstellspindel
  – *adjusting spindle*
52 der Führerstand (das
    Kranführerhaus)
  – *crane driver's cabin (crane driver's
    cage)*
53 das Krangestell
  – *crane framework*
54 das Windenhaus
  – *winch house*
55 die Kommandobrücke
  – *control platform*
56 die Drehscheibe
  – *turntable*

57 der Ponton, ein Prahm *m*
  – *pontoon, a pram*
58 der Motorenaufbau
  – *engine superstructure (engine
    mounting)*

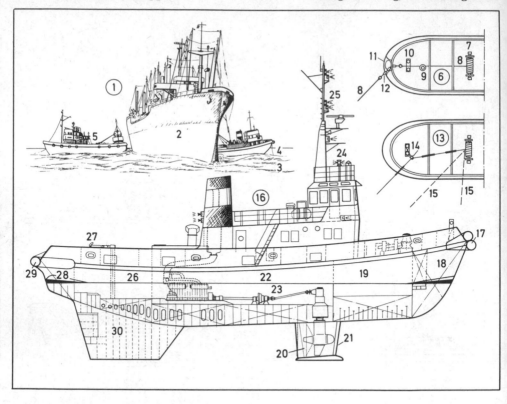

1 die Bergung eines aufgelaufenen
 Schiffes *n*
- salvaging (salving) of a ship run
 aground
2 das aufgelaufene Schiff (der
 Havarist)
- ship run aground (damaged vessel)
3 die Schlickbank; *auch:* der
 Mahlsand
- sandbank; also: quicksand
4 das offene Wasser
- open sea
5 der Schlepper
- tug (salvage tug)
6-15 Schleppgeschirre *n*
- towing gear
6 das Schleppgeschirr für die
 Seeverschleppung
- towing gear for towing at sea
7 die Schleppwinde
- towing winch (towing machine,
 towing engine)
8 die Schlepptrosse (Trosse)
- tow rope
 (tow line, towing hawser)
9 das Schleppkäpsel
- tow rope guide
10 der Kreuzpoller
- cross-shaped bollard
11 die Schleppklüse
- hawse hole
12 die Ankerkette
- anchor cable (chain cable)

13 das Schleppgeschirr für den
 Hafenbetrieb
- towing gear for work in harbours
 (Am. harbors)
14 der Beistopper
- guest rope
15 die Trossenrichtung bei Bruch *m*
 des Beistoppers *m*
- position of the tow rope (tow line,
 towing hawser)
16 der Schlepper (Bugsierschlepper)
 [Aufriß]
- tug (salvage tug) [vertical elevation]
17 der Bugfender
- bow fender (pudding fender)
18 die Vorpiek
- forepeak
19 die Wohnräume *m*
- living quarters
20 der Schottel-Propeller
- Schottel propeller
21 die Kort-Düse
- Kort vent
22 der Maschinen- und
 Propellerraum
- engine and propeller room
23 die Schaltkupplung
- clutch coupling
24 das Peildeck
- compass platform (compass bridge,
 compass flat, monkey bridge)
25 die Feuerlöscheinrichtung
- fire-fighting equipment

26 der Stauraum
- stowage
27 der Schlepphaken
- tow hook
28 die Achterpiek
- afterpeak
29 der Heckfender (die „Maus")
- stern fender
30 der Manövrierkiel
- main manoeuvring (Am.
 maneuvering) keel

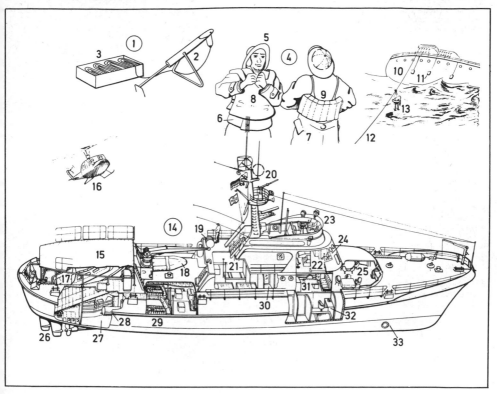

1 der Raketenapparat
- *rocket apparatus (rocket gun, line-throwing gun)*
2 die Rakete
- *life rocket (rocket)*
3 die Rettungsleine (Schießleine)
- *rocket line (whip line)*
4 das Ölzeug
- *oilskins*
5 der Südwester
- *sou'wester (southwester)*
6 die Öljacke
- *oilskin jacket*
7 der Ölmantel
- *oilskin coat*
8 die aufblasbare Schwimmweste
- *inflatable life jacket*
9 die Korkschwimmweste
- *cork life jacket (cork life preserver)*
10 das gestrandete Schiff (der Havarist)
- *stranded ship (damaged vessel)*
11 der Ölbeutel, zum Aufträufeln *n* von Öl *n* auf die Wasseroberfläche
- *oil bag, for trickling oil on the water surface*
12 das Rettungstau
- *lifeline*
13 die Hosenboje
- *breeches buoy*
14 der Seenotkreuzer
- *rescue cruiser*
15 das Hubschrauberarbeitsdeck
- *helicopter landing deck*

16 der Rettungshubschrauber
- *rescue helicopter*
17 das Tochterboot
- *daughter boat*
18 das Schlauchboot
- *inflatable boat (inflatable dinghy)*
19 die Rettungsinsel
- *life raft*
20 die Feuerlöschanlage zur Bekämpfung von Schiffsbränden *m*
- *fire-fighting equipment for fires at sea*
21 das Hospital mit Operationskoje *f* und Unterkühlungsbadewanne *f*
- *hospital unit with operating cabin and exposure bath*
22 der Navigationsraum
- *navigating bridge*
23 der obere Fahrstand
- *upper tier of navigating bridge*
24 der untere Fahrstand
- *lower tier of navigating bridge*
25 die Messe
- *messroom*
26 die Ruder- und Propelleranlage
- *rudders and propeller (screw)*
27 der Stauraum
- *stowage*
28 der Feuerlöschschaumtank
- *foam can*
29 die Seitenmotoren *m*
- *side engines*

30 die Dusche
- *shower*
31 die Vormannkabine
- *coxswain's cabin*
32 die Mannschaftseinzelkabine
- *crew member's single-berth cabin*
33 die Bugschraube
- *bow propeller*

1-14 die Tragflächenanordnung
  (Flügelanordnung)
- *wing configurations*
1 der Hochdecker
- *high-wing monoplane (high-wing plane)*
2 die Spannweite (Flügelspannweite)
- *span (wing span)*
3 der Schulterdecker
- *shoulder-wing monoplane (shoulder-wing plane)*
4 der Mitteldecker
- *midwing monoplane (midwing plane)*
5 der Tiefdecker
- *low-wing monoplane (low-wing plane)*
6 der Dreidecker
- *triplane*
7 der Oberflügel
- *upper wing*
8 der Mittelflügel
- *middle wing (central wing)*
9 der Unterflügel
- *lower wing*
10 der Doppeldecker
- *biplane*
11 der Stiel
- *strut*
12 die Verspannung
- *cross bracing wires*
13 der Anderthalbdecker
- *sesquiplane*
14 der Tiefdecker mit Knickflügeln *m*
- *low-wing monoplane (low-wing plane) with cranked wings (inverted gull wings)*
15-22 Tragflächenformen *f*
  (Flügelformen)
- *wing shapes*
15 der Ellipsenflügel (elliptische Flügel)
- *elliptical wing*
16 der Rechteckflügel
- *rectangular wing*
17 der Trapezflügel
- *tapered wing*
18 der Sichelflügel
- *crescent wing*
19 der Deltaflügel
- *delta wing*
20 der Pfeilflügel mit schwacher positiver Pfeilung
- *swept-back wing with semi-positive sweepback*
21 der Pfeilflügel mit starker positiver Pfeilung
- *swept-back wing with positive sweepback*
22 der Ogivalflügel (Ogeeflügel)
- *ogival wing (ogee wing)*
23-36 die Leitwerksformen *f*
- *tail shapes (tail unit shapes, empennage shapes)*
23 das Normalleitwerk
- *normal tail (normal tail unit)*
24-25 das Seitenleitwerk
- *vertical tail (vertical stabilizer and rudder)*
24 die Seitenflosse
- *vertical stabilizer (vertical fin, tail fin)*
25 das Seitenruder
- *rudder*
26-27 das Höhenleitwerk
- *horizontal tail*

26 die Höhenflosse
- *tailplane (horizontal stabilizer)*
27 das Höhenruder
- *elevator*
28 das Kreuzleitwerk
- *cruciform tail (cruciform tail unit)*
29 das T-Leitwerk
- *T-tail (T-tail unit)*
30 der Verdrängerkörper (die Wirbelkeule)
- *lobe*
31 das V-Leitwerk
- *V-tail (vee-tail, butterfly tail)*
32 das Doppelleitwerk
- *double tail unit (twin tail unit)*
33 die Endscheibe (Seitenscheibe)
- *end plate*
34 das Doppelleitwerk eines Doppelrumpfflugzeugs
- *double tail unit (twin tail unit) of a twin-boom aircraft*
35 das Doppelleitwerk mit hochgestelltem Höhenleitwerk
- *raised horizontal tail with double booms*
36 das Dreifachleitwerk
- *triple tail unit*
37 das Klappensystem
- *system of flaps*
38 der ausfahrbare Vorflügel (Slat)
- *extensible slat*
39 die Störklappe (der Spoiler)
- *spoiler*
40 die Doppelspalt-Fowler-Klappe
- *double-slotted Fowler flap*
41 das äußere Querruder (Langsamflug-Querruder, Low speed aileron)
- *outer aileron (low-speed aileron)*
42 die innere Störklappe *f* (der Landespoiler, Lift dump)
- *inner spoiler (landing flap, lift dump)*
43 das innere Querruder (Allgeschwindigkeits-Querruder, All speed aileron)
- *inner aileron (all-speed aileron)*
44 die Bremsklappe (Luftbremse, Air brakes)
- *brake flap (air brake)*
45 das Grundprofil
- *basic profile*
46-48 die Wölbungsklappen *f*
- *plain flaps (simple flaps)*
46 die Normalklappe
- *normal flap*
47 die Spaltklappe
- *slotted flap*
48 die Doppelspaltklappe
- *double-slotted flap*
49-50 die Spreizklappen
- *split flaps*
49 die einfache Spreizklappe
- *plain split flap (simple split flap)*
50 die Zap-Klappe
- *zap flap*
51 der Doppelflügel
- *extending flap*
52 die Fowler-Klappe
- *Fowler flap*
53 der Vorflügel
- *slat*
54 die profilierte Nasenklappe
- *profiled leading-edge flap (droop flap)*
55 die Krüger-Klappe
- *Krüger flap*

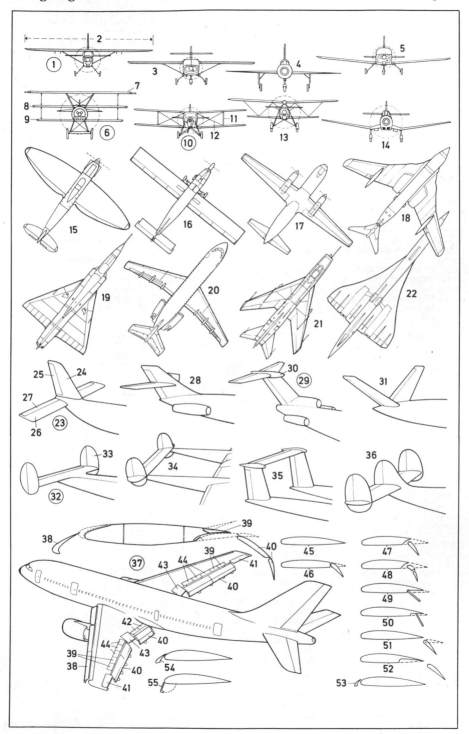

1-31 **das Cockpit** eines einmotorigen
Sport- und Reiseflugzeugs *n*
- *cockpit* of a single-engine
  (single-engined) racing and
  passenger aircraft (racing and
  passenger plane)
1 das Instrumentenbrett (Panel)
- *instrument panel*
2 der Fahrtmesser
  (Geschwindigkeitsmesser)
- *air-speed (Am. airspeed) indicator*
3 der künstliche Horizont
  (Horizontkreisel, Kreiselhorizont)
- *artificial horizon (gyro horizon)*
4 der Höhenmesser
- *altimeter*
5 der Funkkompaß (das
  automatische Peilgerät)
- *radio compass (automatic direction*
  finder)
6 der Magnetkompaß
- *magnetic compass*
7 der Ladedruckmesser
- *boost gauge (Am. gage)*
8 der Drehzahlmesser
- *tachometer (rev counter, revolution*
  counter)
9 die Zylindertemperaturanzeige
- *cylinder temperature gauge*
  (Am. gage)
10 der Beschleunigungsmesser
- *accelerometer*
11 die Borduhr
- *chronometer*
12 der Wendezeiger mit Kugellibelle *f*
- *turn indicator with ball*
13 der Kurskreisel
- *directional gyro*
14 das Variometer
- *vertical speed indicator*
  (rate-of-climb indicator,
  variometer)
15 der VOR-Leitkursanzeiger *[VOR:*
  Very high frequency
  omnidirectional range]
- *VOR radio direction finder [VOR:*
  very high frequency
  omnidirectional range]
16 die Kraftstoffanzeige für den
  linken Tank
- *left tank fuel gauge (Am. gage)*
17 die Kraftstoffanzeige für den
  rechten Tank
- *right tank fuel gauge (Am. gage)*
18 das Amperemeter
- *ammeter*
19 der Kraftstoffdruckmesser
- *fuel pressure gauge (Am. gage)*
20 der Öldruckmesser
- *oil pressure gauge (Am. gage)*
21 die Öltemperaturanzeige
- *oil temperature gauge (Am. gage)*
22 das Sprechfunk- und
  Funknavigationsgerät
- *radio and radio navigation*
  equipment
23 die Kartenbeleuchtung
- *map light*
24 das Handrad (der Steuergriff,
  Steuerknüppel) zur Betätigung der
  Quer- und Höhenruder *n*
- *wheel (control column, control*
  stick) for operating the ailerons
  and elevators
25 das Handrad für den Kopiloten
- *co-pilot's wheel*

26 die Schaltarmaturen *f*
- *switches*
27 die Seitenruderpedale *n*
- *rudder pedals*
28 die Seitenruderpedale *n* für den
  Kopiloten
- *co-pilot's rudder pedals*
29 das Mikrophon für den
  Sprechfunkverkehr
- *microphone for the radio*
30 der Gashebel
- *throttle lever (throttle control)*
31 der Gemischregler (Gemischhebel)
- *mixture control*
32-66 **das einmotorige Sport- und
  Reiseflugzeug**
- *single-engine (single-engined) racing*
  and passenger aircraft (racing and
  passenger plane)
32 der Propeller (die Luftschraube)
- *propeller (airscrew)*
33 die Propellernabenhaube (der
  Spinner)
- *spinner*
34 der Vierzylinder-Boxermotor
- *flat four engine*
35 das Cockpit
- *cockpit*
36 der Pilotensitz
- *pilot's seat*
37 der Kopilotensitz
- *co-pilot's seat*
38 die Passagiersitze *m*
- *passenger seats*
39 die Haube (Kanzelhaube)
- *hood (canopy, cockpit hood,*
  cockpit canopy)
40 das lenkbare Bugrad
- *steerable nose wheel*
41 das Hauptfahrwerk
- *main undercarriage unit (main*
  landing gear unit)
42 die Einstiegstufe
- *step*
43 die Tragfläche (der Flügel)
- *wing*
44 das rechte Positionslicht
- *right navigation light (right position*
  light)
45 der Holm
- *spar*
46 die Rippe
- *rib*
47 der Stringer (die Längsversteifung)
- *stringer*
  (longitudinal reinforcing
  member)
48 der Kraftstofftank
- *fuel tank*
49 der Landescheinwerfer
- *landing light*
50 das linke Positionslicht
- *left navigation light (left position*
  light)
51 der elektrostatische Ableiter
- *electrostatic conductor*
52 das Querruder
- *aileron*
53 die Landeklappe
- *landing flap*
54 der Rumpf
- *fuselage (body)*
55 der Spant
- *frame (former)*
56 der Gurt
- *chord*

57 der Stringer (die Längsversteifung)
- *stringer (longitudinal reinforcing*
  member)
58 das Seitenleitwerk
- *vertical tail (vertical stabilizer and*
  rudder)
59 die Seitenflosse
- *vertical stabilizer (vertical fin, tail*
  fin)
60 das Seitenruder
- *rudder*
61 das Höhenleitwerk
- *horizontal tail*
62 die Höhenflosse
- *tailplane (horizontal stabilizer)*
63 das Höhenruder
- *elevator*
64 das Warnblinklicht
- *warning light (anticollision light)*
65 die Dipolantenne
- *dipole antenna*
66 die Langdrahtantenne
- *long-wire antenna (long-conductor*
  antenna)
67-72 **die Hauptbewegungen** *f* des
  Flugzeugs *n*
- *principal manoeuvres*
  (Am. maneuvers) of the aircraft
  (aeroplane, plane, Am. airplane)
67 das Nicken
- *pitching*
68 die Querachse
- *lateral axis*
69 das Gieren
- *yawing*
70 die Hochachse
- *vertical axis (normal axis)*
71 das Rollen
- *rolling*
72 die Längsachse
- *longitudinal axis*

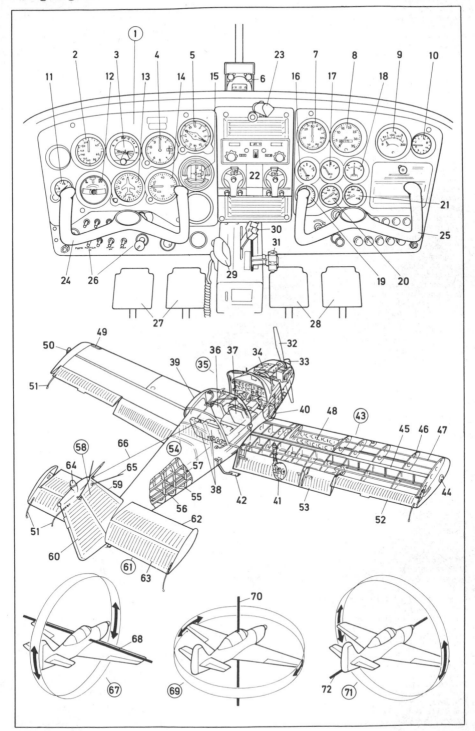

1-33 Flugzeugtypen *m*
- *types of aircraft (aeroplanes, planes,*
  Am. *airplanes)*
1-6 Propellerflugzeuge *n*
- **propeller-driven aircraft**
  (aeroplanes, planes, Am. *airplanes)*
1 das einmotorige Sport- und
  Reiseflugzeug, ein Tiefdecker *m*
- *single-engine (single-engined)*
  racing and passenger aircraft
  (racing and passenger plane), a
  low-wing monoplane (low-wing
  plane)
2 das einmotorige Reiseflugzeug, ein
  Hochdecker *m*
- *single-engine (single-engined)*
  passenger aircraft, a high-wing
  monoplane (high-wing plane)
3 das zweimotorige Geschäfts- und
  Reiseflugzeug
- *twin-engine (twin-engined)*
  business and passenger aircraft
  (business and passenger plane)
4 das Kurz- und
  Mittelstreckenverkehrsflugzeug,
  ein Turbopropflugzeug *n*
  (Turbinen-Propeller-Flugzeug,
  Propeller-Turbinen-Flugzeug)
- *short/medium haul airliner, a*
  turboprop plane (turbopropeller
  plane, propeller-turbine plane)
5 das Turboproptriebwerk
- *turboprop engine (turbopropeller*
  engine)
6 die Kielflosse
- *vertical stabilizer (vertical fin, tail fin)*
7-33 Strahlflugzeuge *n*
  (Düsenflugzeuge, Jets *m*)
- *jet planes (jet aeroplanes, jets,*
  Am. *jet airplanes)*
7 das zweistrahlige Geschäfts- und
  Reiseflugzeug
- *twin-jet business and passenger*
  aircraft (business and passenger
  plane)
8 der Grenzschichtzaun
- *fence*
9 der Flügelspitzentank (Tiptank)
- *wing-tip tank (tip tank)*
10 das Hecktriebwerk
- *rear engine*
11 das zweistrahlige Kurz- und
  Mittelstreckenverkehrsflugzeug
- *twin-jet short/medium haul*
  airliner
12 das dreistrahlige
  Mittelstreckenverkehrsflugzeug
- *tri-jet medium haul airliner*
13 das vierstrahlige
  Langstreckenverkehrsflugzeug
- *four-jet long haul airliner*
14 das
  Großraum-Langstreckenverkehrsflugzeug
  (der Jumbo-Jet)
- *wide-body long haul airliner*
  (jumbo jet)
15 das Überschallverkehrsflugzeug
  [Typ *m Concorde f*]
- *supersonic airliner* [Concorde]
16 die absenkbare Rumpfnase
- *droop nose*
17 **das zweistrahlige**
  Großraumflugzeug für Kurz- und
  Mittelstrecken *f* (der Airbus)
- *twin-jet wide-body airliner for*
  short/medium haul routes (airbus)

18 der Radarbug (die Radarnase, das
   Radom), mit der
   Wetterradarantenne
- *radar nose (radome, radar dome)*
  with weather radar antenna
19 das Cockpit (die Pilotenkanzel)
- *cockpit*
20 die Bordküche
- *galley*
21 der Frachtraum
   (Unterflurstauraum)
- *cargo hold (hold, underfloor hold)*
22 der Passagierraum (Fluggastraum)
   mit Passagiersitzen *m*
- *passenger cabin with passenger*
  seats
23 das einziehbare Bugfahrwerk
- *retractable nose undercarriage unit*
  (retractable nose landing gear unit)
24 die Bugfahrwerksklappe
- *nose undercarriage flap (nose gear*
  flap)
25 die mittlere Passagiertür
- *centre* (Am. *center*) *passenger door*
26 die Triebwerksgondel mit dem
   Triebwerk *n*
   (Turboluftstrahltriebwerk,
   Turbinenluftstrahltriebwerk,
   Düsentriebwerk, die Strahlturbine)
- *engine pod with engine (turbojet*
  engine, jet turbine engine, jet
  engine, jet turbine)
27 die elektrostatischen Ableiter *m*
- *electrostatic conductors*
28 das einziehbare Hauptfahrwerk
- *retractable main undercarriage unit*
  (retractable main landing gear
  unit)
29 das Seitenfenster
- *side window*
30 die hintere Passagiertür
- *rear passenger door*
31 die Toilette
- *toilet (lavatory, WC)*
32 das Druckschott
- *pressure bulkhead*
33 das Hilfstriebwerk (die
   Hilfsgasturbine), für das
   Stromaggregat
- *auxiliary engine (auxiliary gas*
  turbine) for the generator unit

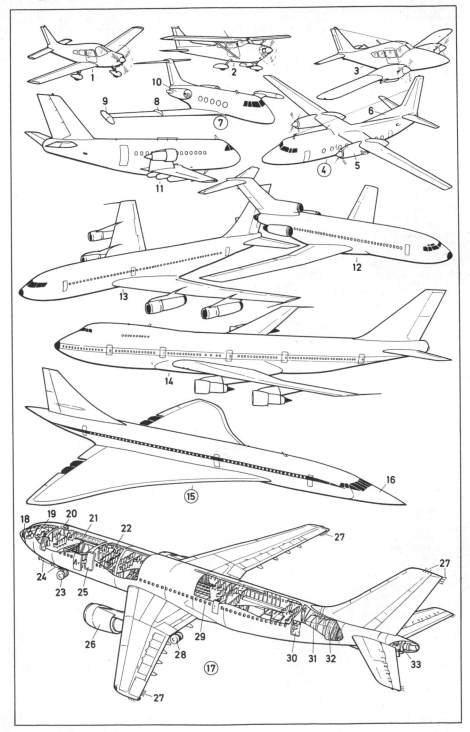

1 das Flugboot, ein Wasserflugzeug *n*
– *flying boat, a seaplane*
2 der Bootsrumpf
– *hull*
3 der Flossenstummel
– *stub wing (sea wing)*
4 die Leitwerkverstrebung
– *tail bracing wires*
5 das Schwimmerflugzeug, ein
Wasserflugzeug *n*
– *floatplane (float seaplane), a
seaplane*
6 der Schwimmer
– *float*
7 die Kielflosse
– *vertical stabilizer (vertical fin, tail
fin)*
8 **das Amphibienflugzeug**
– *amphibian (amphibian flying boat)*
9 der Bootsrumpf
– *hull*
10 das einziehbare Fahrwerk
– *retractable undercarriage
(retractable landing gear)*
11-25 Hubschrauber *m*
– *helicopters*
11 der leichte
Mehrzweckhubschrauber
– *light multirole helicopter*
12-13 der Hauptrotor
– *main rotor*
12 der Drehflügel
– *rotary wing (rotor blade)*
13 der Rotorkopf
– *rotor head*
14 der Heckrotor (Ausgleichsrotor,
die Steuerschraube)
– *tail rotor (anti-torque rotor)*
15 die Landekufen *f*
– *landing skids*
16 der Kranhubschrauber
– *flying crane*
17 die Turbinentriebwerke *n*
– *turbine engines*
18 das Portalfahrwerk
– *lifting undercarriage*
19 die Lastplattform
– *lifting platform*
20 der Zusatztank
– *reserve tank*
21 der Transporthubschrauber
– *transport helicopter*
22 die Rotoren *m* in
Tandemanordnung *f*
– *rotors in tandem*
23 der Rotorträger
– *rotor pylon*
24 das Turbinentriebwerk
– *turbine engine*
25 die Heckladepforte
– *tail loading gate*
26-32 die VSTOL-Flugzeuge *n* (Vertical/
Short-Take-off-and-Landing-Flugzeuge)
– *V/STOL aircraft (vertical/short
take-off and landing aircraft)*
26 das Kippflügelflugzeug, ein
VTOL-Flugzeug *n*
(Vertical-Take-off-and-Landing-Flugzeug,
Senkrechtstarter *m*)
– *tilt-wing aircraft, a VTOL aircraft
(vertical take-off and landing
aircraft)*
27 der Kippflügel in Vertikalstellung *f*
– *tilt wing in vertical position*
28 die gegenläufigen Heckpropeller *m*
– *contrarotating tail propellers*

29 der Kombinationsflugschrauber
– *gyrodyne*
30 das Turboproptriebwerk
– *turboprop engine
(turbopropeller
engine)*
31 das Kipprotorflugzeug
– *convertiplane*
32 der Kipprotor in Vertikalstellung *f*
– *tilting rotor in vertical position*
33-60 Flugzeugtriebwerke *n*
– *aircraft engines (aero engines)*
33-50 Luftstrahltriebwerke *n*
(Düsentriebwerke,
Turboluftstrahltriebwerke,
Turbinenluftstrahltriebwerke,
Strahlturbinen *f*)
– *jet engines (turbojet engines, jet
turbine engines, jet turbines)*
33 das Front-Fan-Triebwerk
(Frontgebläsetriebwerk)
– *front fan-jet*
34 der Fan (das Gebläse, der Bläser)
– *fan*
35 der Niederdruckverdichter
– *low-pressure compressor*
36 der Hochdruckverdichter
– *high-pressure compressor*
37 die Brennkammer
– *combustion chamber*
38 die Fan-Antriebsturbine
– *fan-jet turbine*
39 die Düse (Schubdüse)
– *nozzle (propelling nozzle,
propulsion nozzle)*
40 die Turbinen *f*
– *turbines*
41 der Sekundärstromkanal
– *bypass duct*
42 das Aft-Fan-Triebwerk
(Heckgebläsetriebwerk)
– *aft fan-jet*
43 der Fan
– *fan*
44 der Sekundärstromkanal
– *bypass duct*
45 die Düse (Schubdüse)
– *nozzle (propelling nozzle,
propulsion nozzle)*
46 das Mantelstromtriebwerk
– *bypass engine*
47 die Turbinen *f*
– *turbines*
48 der Mischer
– *mixer*
49 die Düse (Schubdüse)
– *nozzle (propelling nozzle,
propulsion nozzle)*
50 der Sekundärstrom (Mantelstrom,
Nebenstrom)
– *secondary air flow (bypass air flow)*
51 das Turboproptriebwerk, ein
Zweiwellentriebwerk *n*
– *turboprop engine (turbopropeller
engine), a twin-shaft engine*
52 der ringförmige Lufteinlauf
– *annular air intake*
53 die Hochdruckturbine
– *high-pressure turbine*
54 die Niederdruck- und Nutzturbine
– *low-pressure turbine*
55 die Düse (Schubdüse)
– *nozzle (propelling nozzle,
propulsion nozzle)*
56 die Kupplungswelle
– *shaft*

57 die Zwischenwelle
– *intermediate shaft*
58 die Getriebeeingangswelle
– *gear shaft*
59 das Untersetzungsgetriebe
– *reduction gear*
60 die Luftschraubenwelle
– *propeller shaft*

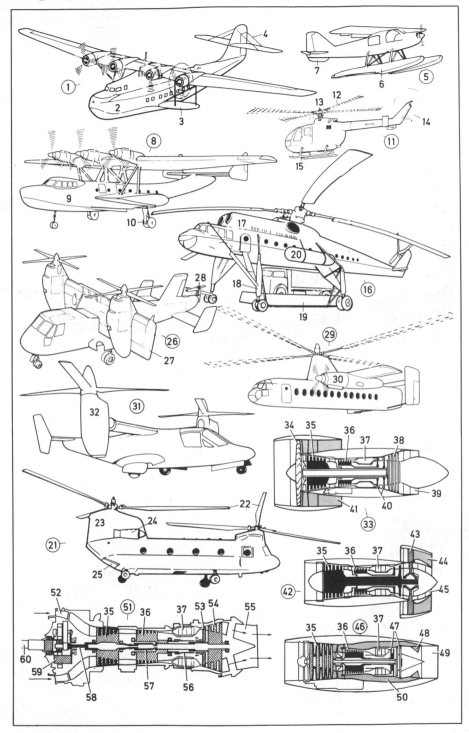

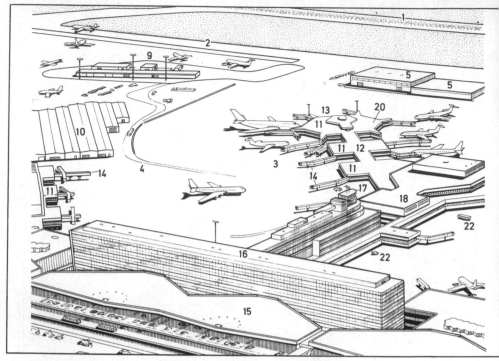

1 die Startbahn (Start- und
 Landebahn, Piste, der Runway)
- *runway*
2 die Rollbahn (der Rollweg,
 Taxiway)
- *taxiway*
3 das Vorfeld (Abfertigungsfeld)
- *apron*
4 die Vorfeldstraße
- *apron taxiway*
5 die Gepäckhalle
- *baggage terminal*
6 die Gepäcktunneleinfahrt
- *tunnel entrance to the baggage
 terminal*
7 die Flughafenfeuerwehr
- *airport fire service*
8 die Gerätehalle
- *fire appliance building*
9 die Fracht- und Posthalle
- *mail and cargo terminal*
10 der Frachthof
- *cargo warehouse*
11 der Flugplatzsammelraum
- *assembly point*
12 der Flugsteig (Fingerflugsteig)
- *pier*
13 der Fingerkopf
- *pierhead*
14 die Fluggastbrücke
- *airbridge*
15 die Abflughalle (das
 Abfertigungsgebäude, der od. das
 Terminal)
- *departure building (terminal)*
16 das Verwaltungsgebäude
- *administration building*
17 der Kontrollturm (Tower)
- *control tower (tower)*
18 die Wartehalle (Lounge)
- *waiting room (lounge)*
19 das Flughafenrestaurant
- *airport restaurant*
20 die Besucherterrasse
- *spectators' terrace*

21 das Flugzeug in
 Abfertigungsposition f, einer
 Nose-in-Position
- *aircraft in loading position (nosed in)*
22 Wartungs- und
 Abfertigungsfahrzeuge n, z.B.
 Gepäckbandwagen m,
 Frischwasserwagen,
 Küchenwagen, Toilettenwagen,
 Bodenstromgerät n,
 Tankwagen m
- *service vehicles, e.g. baggage
 loaders, water tankers, galley
 loaders, toilet-cleaning vehicles,
 ground power units, tankers*
23 der Flugzeugschlepper
- *aircraft tractor (aircraft tug)*
24-53 die Hinweisschilder n
 (Piktogramme) für den
 Flughafenbetrieb
- *airport information symbols
 (pictographs)*
24 „Flughafen" m
- *'airport'*
25 „Abflug" m
- *'departures'*
26 „Ankunft" f
- *'arrivals'*
27 „Umsteiger" m
- *'transit passengers'*
28 „Wartehalle" f
- *'waiting room' ('lounge')*
29 „Treffpunkt" m
- *'assembly point' ('meeting point',
 'rendezvous point')*
30 „Besucherterrasse" f
- *'spectators' terrace'*
31 „Information" f
- *'information'*
32 „Taxi" n
- *'taxis'*
33 „Mietwagen" m
- *'car hire'*
34 „Bahn" f
- *'trains'*

35 „Bus" m
- *'buses'*
36 „Eingang" m
- *'entrance'*
37 „Ausgang" m
- *'exit'*
38 „Gepäckausgabe" f
- *'baggage retrieval'*
39 „Gepäckaufbewahrung" f
- *'luggage lockers'*
40 „Notruf" m
- *'telephone – emergency calls only'*
41 „Fluchtweg" m
- *'emergency exit'*
42 „Paßkontrolle" f
- *'passport check'*
43 „Pressezentrum" n
- *'press facilities'*
44 „Arzt" m
- *'doctor'*
45 „Apotheke" f
- *'chemist' (Am. 'druggist')*
46 „Duschen" f
- *'showers'*
47 „Herrentoilette" f
- *'gentlemen's toilet' ('gentlemen')*
48 „Damentoilette" f
- *'ladies toilet' ('ladies')*
49 „Andachtsraum" m
- *'chapel'*
50 „Restaurant" n
- *'restaurant'*
51 „Geldwechsel" m
- *'change'*
52 „zollfreier Einkauf"
- *'duty free shop'*
53 „Friseur" m
- *'hairdresser'*

411

1 die Saturn-V-Trägerrakete „Apollo" [Gesamtansicht]
- *Saturn V 'Apollo' booster (booster rocket) [overall view]*
2 die Saturn-V-Trägerrakete „Apollo" [Gesamtschnitt]
- *Saturn V 'Apollo' booster (booster rocket) [overall sectional view]*
3 die erste Raketenstufe *S-I C*
- *first rocket stage (S-IC)*
4 F-1-Triebwerke *n*
- *F-1 engines*
5 der Wärmeschutzschild
- *heat shield (thermal protection shield)*
6 die aerodynamische Triebwerksverkleidung
- *aerodynamic engine fairings*
7 aerodynamische Stabilisierungsflossen *f*
- *aerodynamic stabilizing fins*
8 Stufentrenn-Retroraketen *f*, 8 Raketen *f* zu 4 Paaren *n*
- *stage separation retro-rockets, 8 rockets arranged in 4 pairs*
9 der Kerosin-(RP-1-)Tank [811 000 l]
- *kerosene (RP-1) tank [capacity: 811,000 litres]*
10 Flüssigsauerstoff-Förderleitungen *f*, insgesamt 5
- *liquid oxygen (LOX, LO₂) supply lines, total of 5*
11 das Antivortexsystem (Vorrichtung *f* zur Verhinderung einer Wirbelbildung im Treibstoff *m*)
- *anti-vortex system (device for preventing the formation of vortices in the fuel)*
12 der Flüssigsauerstofftank [1 315 000 l]
- *liquid oxygen (LOX, LO₂) tank [capacity: 1,315,000 litres]*
13 die Schwappdämpfung
- *anti-slosh baffles*
14 Druckflaschen für Helium *n*
- *compressed-helium bottles (helium pressure bottles)*
15 der Diffusor für gasförmigen Sauerstoff
- *diffuser for gaseous oxygen*
16 das Tankzwischenstück
- *inter-tank connector (inter-tank section)*
17 Instrumente *n* und Systemüberwachung *f*
- *instruments and system-monitoring devices*
18 die zweite Raketenstufe *S-II*
- *second rocket stage (S-II)*
19 J-2-Triebwerke *n*
- *J-2 engines*
20 der Wärmeschutzschild
- *heat shield (thermal protection shield)*
21 das Triebwerkswiderlager und Schubgerüst
- *engine mounts and thrust structure*
22 Beschleunigungsraketen *f* zum Treibstoffsammeln *n*
- *acceleration rockets for fuel acquisition*
23 die Flüssigwasserstoff-Saugleitung
- *liquid hydrogen (LH₂) suction line*
24 der Flüssigsauerstofftank [1 315 000 l]
- *liquid oxygen (LOX, LO₂) tank [capacity: 1,315,000 litres]*

25 das Standrohr
- *standpipe*
26 der Flüssigwasserstofftank [1 020 000 l]
- *liquid hydrogen (LH₂) tank [capacity; 1,020,000 litres]*
27 der Treibstoffstandsensor
- *fuel level sensor*
28 die Arbeitsbühne
- *work platform (working platform)*
29 der Kabelschacht
- *cable duct*
30 das Mannloch
- *manhole*
31 die S-IC/S-II-Zwischenzelle
- *S-IC/S-II inter-stage connector (inter-stage section)*
32 der Druckgasbehälter
- *compressed-gas container (gas pressure vessel)*
33 die dritte Raketenstufe *S-IV B*
- *third rocket stage (S-IVB)*
34 das J-2-Triebwerk
- *J-2 engine*
35 der Schubkonus
- *nozzle (thrust nozzle)*
36 die S-II/S-IVB-Zwischenzelle
- *S-II/S-IVB inter-stage connector (inter-stage section)*
37 Stufentrenn-Retroraketen *f* für S-II, 4 Raketen *f*
- *four second-stage (S-II) separation retro-rockets*
38 Lageregelungsraketen *f*
- *attitude control rockets*
39 der Flüssigsauerstofftank [77 200 l]
- *liquid oxygen (LOX, LO₂) tank [capacity: 77,200 litres]*
40 der Leitungsschacht
- *fuel line duct*
41 der Flüssigwasserstofftank [253 000 l]
- *liquid hydrogen (LH₂) tank [capacity: 253,000 litres]*
42 Meßsonden *f*
- *measuring probes*
43 Helium-Druckgastanks *m*
- *compressed-helium tanks (helium pressure vessels)*
44 die Tankentlüftung
- *tank vent*
45 der vordere Zellenring
- *forward frame section*
46 die Arbeitsbühne
- *work platform (working platform)*
47 der Kabelschacht
- *cable duct*
48 Beschleunigungsraketen *f* zum Treibstoffsammeln *n*
- *acceleration rockets for fuel acquisition*
49 der hintere Zellenring
- *aft frame section*
50 Helium-Druckgastanks *m*
- *compressed-helium tanks (helium pressure vessels)*
51 die Flüssigwasserstoffleitung
- *liquid hydrogen (LH₂) line*
52 die Flüssigsauerstoffleitung
- *liquid oxygen (LOX, LO₂) line*
53 die Instrumenteneinheit mit 24 Paneelen *n*
- *24-panel instrument unit*
54 der LM-Hangar
- *LM hangar (lunar module hangar)*
55 das LM (Lunar module, die Mondlandeeinheit)
- *LM (lunar module)*

56 das Apollo-SM (Service module), eine Versorgungs- und Geräte-Baugruppe
- *Apollo SM (service module), containing supplies and equipment*
57 das SM-Haupttriebwerk
- *SM (service module) main engine*
58 der Treibstofftank
- *fuel tank*
59 der Stickstofftetroxidtank
- *nitrogen tetroxide tank*
60 das Druckgasfördersystem
- *pressurized gas delivery system*
61 Sauerstofftanks *m*
- *oxygen tanks*
62 Brennstoffzellen *f*
- *fuel cells*
63 Steuerraketengruppen *f*
- *manoeuvring (Am. maneuvering) rocket assembly*
64 die Richtantennengruppe
- *directional antenna assembly*
65 die Raumkapsel (das Kommandoteil)
- *space capsule (command section)*
66 der Rettungsturm für die Startphase
- *launch phase escape tower*

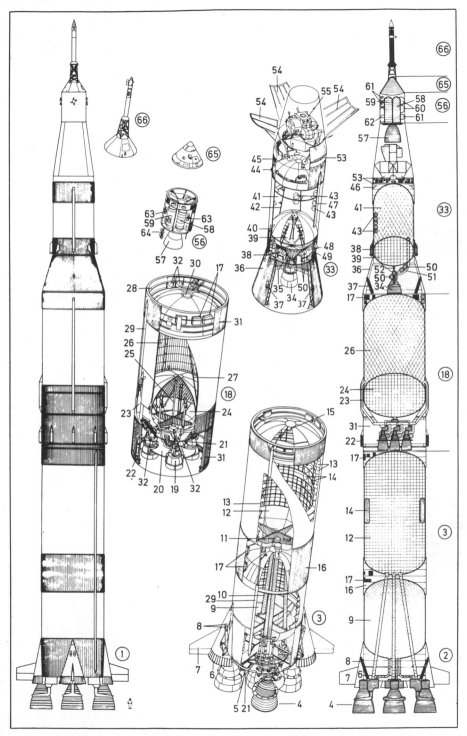

1-45 der Spaceshuttle-Orbiter
(die Weltraumfähre, Raumfähre)
- *Space Shuttle-Orbiter*
1 die zweiholmige Seitenflosse
- *twin-spar (two-spar, double-spar) vertical fin*
2 die Triebwerkraumstruktur
- *engine compartment structure*
3 der Seitenholm
- *fin post*
4 der Rumpfverbindungsbeschlag
- *fuselage attachment [of payload bay doors]*
5 das obere Schubträgergerüst
- *upper thrust mount*
6 das untere Schubträgergerüst
- *lower thrust mount*
7 der Kielträger
- *keel*
8 der Hitzeschild
- *heat shield*
9 der Mittelrumpflängsträger
- *waist longeron*
10 der integral gefräste Hauptspant
- *integrally machined (integrally milled) main rib*
11 die integral versteifte Leichtmetallbeplankung
- *integrally stiffened light alloy skin*
12 die Gitterträger *m*
- *lattice girder*
13 die Isolationsverkleidung des Nutzlastraums *m*
- *payload bay insulation*
14 die Nutzlastraumluke
- *payload bay door*
15 die Kühlschutzverkleidung
- *low-temperature surface insulation*
16 der Besatzungsraum
- *flight deck (crew compartment)*
17 der Sitz des Kommandanten *m*
- *captain's seat (commander's seat)*
18 der Sitz des Piloten *m*
- *pilot's seat (co-pilot's seat)*
19 der vordere Druckspant
- *forward pressure bulkhead*
20 die Rumpfspitze, eine kohlefaserverstärkte Bugklappe
- *nose-section fairings, carbon fibre reinforced nose cone*
21 die vorderen Kraftstofftanks *m*
- *forward fuel tanks*
22 die Avionikkonsolen *f*
- *avionics consoles*
23 das Gerätebrett für die automatische Flugsteuerung
- *automatic flight control panel*
24 die oberen Beobachtungsfenster *n*
- *upward observation windows*
25 die vorderen Beobachtungsfenster *n*
- *forward observation windows*
26 die Einstiegsluke zum Nutzlastraum *m*
- *entry hatch to payload bay*
27 die Luftschleuse
- *air lock*
28 die Leiter zum Unterdeck *n*
- *ladder to lower deck*
29 das Nutzlastbedienungsgerät
- *payload manipulator arm*
30 die hydraulisch steuerbare Bugradeinheit
- *hydraulically steerable nose wheel*
31 das hydraulisch betätigte Hauptfahrwerk
- *hydraulically operated main landing gear*

32 das kohlefaserverstärkte, abnehmbare Flügelnasenteil
- *removable (reusable) carbon fibre reinforced leading edge [of wing]*
33 die beweglichen Elevonteile *n*
- *movable elevon sections*
34 die hitzebeständige Elevonstruktur
- *heat-resistant elevon structure*
35 die Wasserstoffhauptzufuhr
- *main liquid hydrogen (LH₂) supply*
36 der Flüssigkeitsraketen-Hauptmotor
- *main liquid-fuelled rocket engine*
37 die Schubdüse
- *nozzle (thrust nozzle)*
38 die Kühlleitung
- *coolant feed line*
39 das Motorsteuerungsgerät
- *engine control system*
40 der Hitzeschild
- *heat shield*
41 die Hochdruck-Wasserstoffpumpe
- *high-pressure liquid hydrogen (LH₂) pump*
42 die Hochdruck-Sauerstoffpumpe
- *high-pressure liquid oxygen (LOX, LO₂) pump*
43 das Schubsteuerungssystem
- *thrust vector control system*
44 das elektromechanisch steuerbare Raummanöver-Haupttriebwerk
- *electromechanically controlled orbital manoeuvring (Am. maneuvering) main engine*
45 die Schubdüsen-Kraftstofftanks *m*
- *nozzle fuel tanks (thrust nozzle fuel tanks)*
46 der abwerfbare Wasserstoff- und Sauerstoffbehälter
(Treibstoffbehälter)
- *jettisonable liquid hydrogen and liquid oxygen tank (fuel tank)*
47 der integral versteifte Ringspant
- *integrally stiffened annular rib (annular frame)*
48 der Halbkugelendspant
- *hemispherical end rib (end frame)*
49 die hintere Verbindungsbrücke zum Orbiter *m*
- *aft attachment to Orbiter*
50 die Wasserstoffleitung
- *liquid hydrogen (LH₂) line*
51 die Sauerstoffleitung
- *liquid oxygen (LOX, LO₂) line*
52 das Mannloch
- *manhole*
53 das Dämpfungssystem
- *surge baffle system (slosh baffle system)*
54 die Druckleitung zum Wasserstofftank
- *pressure line to liquid hydrogen tank*
55 die Elektriksammelleitung
- *electrical system bus*
56 die Sauerstoffumlaufleitung
- *liquid oxygen (LOX, LO₂) line*
57 die Druckleitung zum Sauerstofftank
- *pressure line to liquid oxygen tank*
58 der wiedergewinnbare Feststoff-Raketenmotor
- *recoverable solid-fuel rocket (solid rocket booster)*
59 der Raum für die Hilfsfallschirme *m*
- *auxiliary parachute bay*

60 der Raum für die Rettungsfallschirme *m* und die vorderen Raketentrennmotoren *m*
- *compartment housing the recovery parachutes and the forward separation rocket motors*
61 der Kabelschacht
- *cable duct*
62 die hinteren Raketentrennmotoren *m*
- *aft separation rocket motors*
63 der hintere Verkleidungskonus
- *aft skirt*
64 die schwenkbare Schubdüse
- *swivel nozzle (swivelling, Am. swiveling, nozzle)*
65 **das Spacelab** (Raumlaboratorium, die Raumstation)
- *Spacelab (space laboratory, space station)*
66 das Allzwecklabor
- *multi-purpose laboratory (orbital workshop)*
67 der Astronaut
- *astronaut*
68 das kardanisch gelagerte Teleskop
- *gimbal-mounted telescope*
69 die Meßgeräteplattform
- *measuring instrument platform*
70 das Raumfahrtmodul
- *spaceflight module*
71 der Schleusentunnel
- *crew entry tunnel*

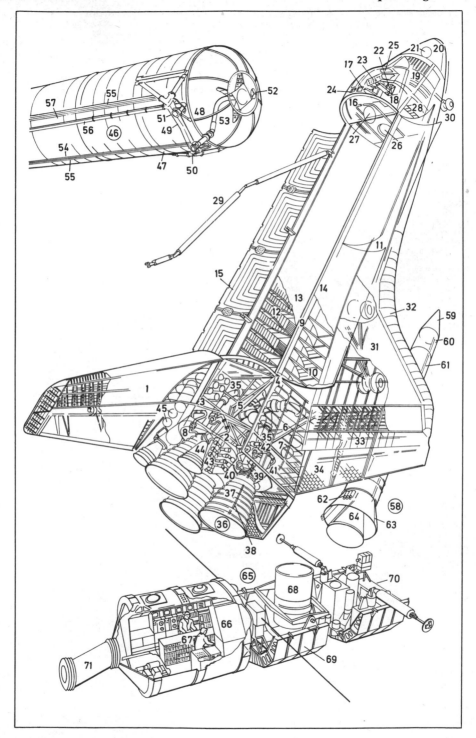

1-30 die Schalterhalle
- *main hall*
1 der Paketschalter (die Paketannahme)
- *parcels counter*
2 die Paketwaage
- *parcels scales*
3 das Paket
- *parcel*
4 die Aufklebeadresse, mit dem Paketnummernzettel *m*
- *stick-on address label with parcel registration slip*
5 der Leimtopf
- *glue pot*
6 das Päckchen
- *small parcel*
7 die Postfreistempelmaschine für Paketkarten *f*
- *franking machine (Am. postage meter) for parcel registration cards*
8 die Telefonzelle (Telefonkabine, Fernsprechkabine)
- *telephone box (telephone booth, telephone kiosk, call box)*
9 der Münzfernsprecher
- *coin-box telephone (pay phone, public telephone)*
10 das Fernsprechbuchgestell
- *telephone directory rack*
11 die Buchschwinge
- *directory holder*
12 das Fernsprechbuch
- *telephone directory (telephone book)*
13 die Postfachanlage
- *post office boxes*
14 das Postfach
- *post office box*
15 der Postwertzeichenschalter (Briefmarkenschalter)
- *stamp counter*
16 der Annahmebeamte
- *counter clerk (counter officer)*
17 der Geschäftsbote
- *company messenger*
18 das Posteinlieferungsbuch
- *record of posting book*
19 der Schalter-Wertzeichengeber
- *counter stamp machine*
20 die Wertzeichenmappe
- *stamp book*
21 der Wertzeichenbogen (Briefmarkenbogen)
- *sheet of stamps*
22 das Wertgelaß
- *security drawer*
23 die Wechselgeldkasse
- *change rack*
24 die Briefwaage
- *letter scales*
25 der Einzahlungs-, Postspar- und Rentenauszahlschalter
- *paying-in (Am. deposit), post office savings, and pensions counter*
26 die Buchungsmaschine
- *accounting machine*
27 die Stempelmaschine für Postanweisungen *f* und Zahlkarten *f*
- *franking machine for money orders and paying-in slips (Am. deposit slips)*
28 der Rückgeldgeber
- *change machine (Am. changemaker)*

29 der Quittungsstempel
- *receipt stamp*
30 die Durchreiche
- *hatch*
31-44 die Briefverteilanlage
- *letter-sorting installation*
31 die Stoffeingabe
- *letter feed*
32 die gestapelten Briefbehälter *m*
- *stacked letter containers*
33 die Stoffzuführungsstrecke
- *feed conveyor*
34 die Aufstellmaschine
- *intermediate stacker*
35 der Codierplatz
- *coding station*
36 die Grobverteilrinne
- *pre-distributor channel*
37 der Prozeßrechner
- *process control computer*
38 die Briefverteilmaschine
- *distributing machine*
39 der Videocodierplatz
- *video coding station*
40 der Bildschirm
- *screen*
41 das Anschriftenbild
- *address display*
42 die Anschrift
- *address*
43 die Postleitzahl
- *post code (postal code, Am. zip code)*
44 die Tastatur
- *keyboard*
45 der Fauststempel
- *handstamp*
46 der Handrollstempel
- *roller stamp*
47 die Stempelmaschine
- *franking machine*
48 die Anlegevorrichtung
- *feed mechanism*
49 die Ablegevorrichtung
- *delivery mechanism*
50-55 die Briefkastenleerung und Postzustellung *f*
- *postal collection and and delivery*
50 der Briefkasten
- *postbox (Am. mailbox)*
51 die Briefsammeltasche
- *collection bag*
52 der Postkraftwagen
- *post office van (mail van)*
53 der Zusteller (Briefträger, Postbote)
- *postman (Am. mail carrier, letter carrier, mailman)*
54 die Zustelltasche
- *delivery pouch (postman's bag, mailbag)*
55 die Briefsendung
- *letter-rate item*
56-60 die Stempelbilder *n*
- *postmarks*
56 der Werbestempelabdruck
- *postmark advertisement*
57 der Tagesstempelabdruck
- *date stamp postmark*
58 der Gebührenstempelabdruck
- *charge postmark*
59 der Sonderstempelabdruck
- *special postmark*
60 der Handrollstempelabdruck
- *roller postmark*

61 die Briefmarke
- *stamp (postage stamp)*
62 die Zähnung
- *perforations*

237 Post II (Telefon und Telegrafie)

1 die Telefonzelle (das Telefonhäuschen, Fernsprechhäuschen), eine öffentliche Sprechstelle
- telephone box (telephone booth, telephone kiosk, call box), a public telephone
2 der Telefonbenutzer (mit eigenem Anschluß: Fernsprechteilnehmer m, Telefonteilnehmer)
- telephone user (with own telephone: telephone subscriber, telephone customer)
3 der Münzfernsprecher für Orts- und Ferngespräche n (Fernwahlmünzfernsprecher m)
- coin-box telephone (pay phone, public telephone) for local and long-distance calls (trunk calls)
4 der Notrufmelder
- emergency telephone
5 das Fernsprechbuch (Telefonbuch)
- telephone directory (telephone book)
6-26 Fernsprecher m (Telefonapparate)
- telephone instruments (telephones)
6 der Fernsprech-Tischapparat in Regelausführung f
- standard table telephone
7 der Telefonhörer (Handapparat)
- telephone receiver (handset)
8 die Hörmuschel
- earpiece
9 die Sprechmuschel
- mouthpiece (microphone)
10 die Wählscheibe (der Nummernschalter)
- dial (push-button keyboard)
11 der Lochkranz (die Fingerlochscheibe)
- finger plate (dial finger plate, dial wind-up plate)
12 der Anschlag
- finger stop (dial finger stop)
13 die Gabel (der Gabelumschalter)
- cradle (handset cradle, cradle switch)
14 die Hörerleitung (Handapparatschnur)
- receiver cord (handset cord)
15 das Telefongehäuse
- telephone casing (telephone cover)
16 der Gebührenanzeiger
- subscriber's (customer's) private meter
17 der Hauptanschlußapparat (die Hauptstelle) für eine Nebenstellen-Reihenanlage
- switchboard (exchange) for a system of extensions
18 die Drucktaste für die Hauptanschlußleitungen f
- push button for connecting main exchange lines
19 die Drucktasten zum Anwählen n der Nebenstellen f
- push buttons for calling extensions
20 das Drucktastentelefon
- push-button telephone
21 die Erdtaste für Nebenstellenanlagen f
- earthing button for the extensions
22-26 die Nebenstellen-Wählanlage
- switchboard with extensions
22 die Hauptstelle
- exchange

23 der Abfrageapparat
- switchboard operator's set
24 der Hauptanschluß
- main exchange line
25 der Schalterschrank (die selbsttätige Vermittlungseinrichtung, Zentrale)
- switching box (automatic switching system, automatic connecting system, switching centre, Am. center)
26 die Nebenstelle
- extension
27-41 das Fernmeldeamt
- telephone exchange
27 der Funkstörungsmeßdienst
- radio interference service
28 der Entstörungstechniker
- interference technician (maintenance technician)
29 der Prüfplatz
- testing board (testing desk)
30 die Telegrafie
- telegraphy
31 der Telegrafenapparat (Telegraf, die Fernschreibmaschine)
- teleprinter (teletypewriter)
32 der Papierstreifen
- paper tape
33 die Fernsprechauskunft
- directory enquiries
34 der Auskunftsplatz
- information position (operator's position)
35 das „Fräulein vom Amt"
- operator
36 das Mikrofilmlesegerät
- microfilm reader
37 die Mikrofilmkartei
- microfilm file
38 die Filmkarte mit den Rufnummern f auf den Projektionsschirm m
- microfilm card with telephone numbers
39 die Datumsanzeige
- date indicator display
40 die Prüf- und Meßstelle
- testing and control station
41 die Vermittlungen f für den Fernsprech-, Fernschreib- und Datendienst
- switching centre (Am. center) for telephone, telex and data transmission services
42 der Wähler (Edelmetall-Motor-Drehwähler, EMD-Wähler, zukünftig: die elektronische Wähleinrichtung)
- selector (motor uniselector made of noble metals; in the future: electronic selector)
43 der Kontaktring
- contact arc (bank)
44 der Kontaktarm
- contact arm (wiper)
45 das Kontaktfeld
- contact field
46 das Kontaktglied
- contact arm tag
47 der Elektromagnet
- electromagnet
48 der Wählermotor
- selector motor
49 das Einstellglied
- restoring spring (resetting spring)

50 Nachrichtenverbindungen f
- communication links
51-52 der Satellitenfunk
- satellite radio link
51 die Erdfunkstelle mit Richtfunkantenne f
- earth station with directional antenna
52 der Fernmeldesatellit mit Richtfunkantenne f
- communications satellite with directional antenna
53 die Küstenfunkstelle
- coastal station
54-55 der Überseefunk
- intercontinental radio link
54 die Kurzwellenstation
- short-wave station
55 die Ionosphäre
- ionosphere
56 das Tiefseekabel
- submarine cable (deep-sea cable)
57 der Unterwasserverstärker
- underwater amplifier
58 die Datenfernverarbeitung (die Datendienste)
- data transmission (data services)
59 das Ein-/Ausgabegerät für Datenträger m
- input/output device for data carriers
60 die Datenverarbeitungsanlage
- data processor
61 der Datendrucker
- teleprinter
62-64 Datenträger m
- data carriers
62 der Lochstreifen
- punched tape (punch tape)
63 das Magnetband
- magnetic tape
64 die Lochkarte
- punched card (punch card)
65 der Telexanschluß
- telex link
66 die Fernschreibmaschine (der Blattschreiber)
- teleprinter (page printer)
67 das Fernschaltgerät
- dialling (Am. dialing) unit
68 der Fernschreiblochstreifen zur Übermittlung des Textes m mit Höchstgeschwindigkeit f
- telex tape (punched tape, punch tape) for transmitting the text at maximum speed
69 das Fernschreiben
- telex message
70 das Tastenfeld
- keyboard

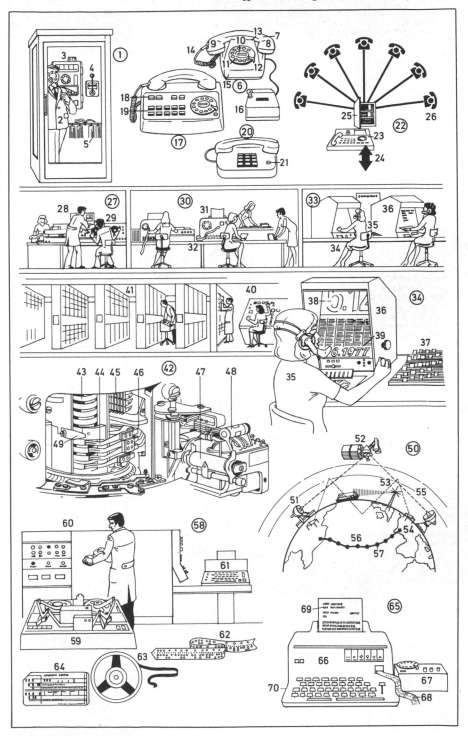

1-6 der zentrale Tonträgerraum beim Hörfunk m
- *central recording channel of a radio station*
1 das Kontroll- und Monitorfeld
- *monitoring and control panel*
2 das Datensichtgerät (der Videomonitor) zur optischen Anzeige f des rechnergesteuerten Programms n
- *data display terminal (video data terminal, video monitor) for visual display of computer-controlled programmes (Am. programs)*
3 der Verstärker- und Netzgeräteträger
- *amplifier and mains power unit*
4 das Magnetton-Aufnahme- und -Wiedergabelaufwerk für Viertelzollmagnetband n
- *magnetic sound recording and playback deck for ¼" magnetic tape*
5 das Magnetband, ein Viertelzollband n
- *magnetic tape, a ¼" tape*
6 der Filmspulenhalter
- *film spool holder*
7-15 der Betriebsraum des Hörfunksternpunkts m
- *radio switching centre (Am. center) control room*
7 das Kontroll- und Monitorfeld
- *monitoring and control panel*
8 der Kommandolautsprecher
- *talkback speaker*
9 das Ortsbatterietelefon (OB-Telefon)
- *local-battery telephone*
10 das Kommandomikrophon
- *talkback microphone*
11 das Datensichtgerät
- *data display terminal (video data terminal)*
12 der Fernschreiber
- *teleprinter*
13 die Eingabetastatur für Rechnerdaten pl
- *input keyboard for computer data*
14 die Tastatur für die Betriebsfernsprechanlage
- *telephone switchboard panel*
15 die Abhörlautsprecher m
- *monitoring speaker (control speaker)*
16-26 der Rundfunksendekomplex
- *broadcasting centre (Am. center)*
16 der Tonträgerraum
- *recording room*
17 der Regieraum
- *production control room (control room)*
18 der Sprecherraum
- *studio*
19 der Toningenieur
- *sound engineer (sound control engineer)*
20 das Tonregiepult
- *sound control desk (sound control console)*
21 der Nachrichtensprecher
- *newsreader (newscaster)*
22 der Sendeleiter
- *duty presentation officer*
23 das Reportagetelefon
- *telephone for phoned reports*

24 die Schallplatten-Abspielapparatur
- *record turntable*
25 das Mischpult des Tonträgerraumes m
- *recording room mixing console (mixing desk, mixer)*
26 die Tontechnikerin
- *sound technician (sound mixer, sound recordist)*
27-53 das Nachsynchronisierstudio beim Fernsehen n
- *television post-sync studio*
27 der Tonregieraum
- *sound production control room (sound control room)*
28 das Synchronstudio
- *dubbing studio (dubbing theatre, Am. theater)*
29 der Sprechertisch
- *studio table*
30 die optische Signalanzeige
- *visual signal*
31 die elektronische Stoppuhr
- *electronic stopclock*
32 die Projektionsleinwand
- *projection screen*
33 der Bildmonitor
- *monitor*
34 das Sprechermikrophon
- *studio microphone*
35 die Geräuschorgel
- *sound effects box*
36 die Mikrophonanschlußtafel
- *microphone socket panel*
37 der Einspiellautsprecher
- *recording speaker (recording loudspeaker)*
38 das Regiefenster
- *control room window (studio window)*
39 das Kommandomikrophon für den Produzenten
- *producer's talkback microphone*
40 das Ortsbatterietelefon (OB-Telefon)
- *local-battery telephone*
41 das Tonregiepult
- *sound control desk (sound control console)*
42 die Gruppenschalter m
- *group selector switch*
43 das Lichtzeigerinstrument
- *visual display*
44 das Begrenzerinstrument
- *limiter display (clipper display)*
45 die Schalt- und Regelkassetten f
- *control modules*
46 die Vorhörtasten f
- *pre-listening buttons*
47 der Flachbahnregler
- *slide control*
48 die Universalentzerrer m
- *universal equalizer (universal corrector)*
49 die Eingangswahlschalter m
- *input selector switch*
50 der Vorhörlautsprecher
- *pre-listening speaker*
51 der Pegeltongenerator
- *tone generator*
52 der Kommandolautsprecher
- *talkback speaker*
53 das Kommandomikrophon
- *talkback microphone*

54-59 der Vormischraum für Überspielungen f und Mischungen f von perforierten Magnetfilmen m 16 mm, 17,5 mm, 35 mm
- *pre-mixing room for transferring and mixing 16 mm, 17.5 mm, 35 mm perforated magnetic film*
54 das Tonregiepult
- *sound control desk (sound control console)*
55 die Magnetton-Aufnahme- und -Wiedergabe-Kompaktanlage
- *compact magnetic tape recording and playback equipment*
56 das Einzellaufwerk für die Wiedergabe
- *single playback deck*
57 das zentrale Antriebsgerät
- *central drive unit*
58 das Einzellaufwerk für Aufnahme f und Wiedergabe f
- *single recording and playback deck*
59 der Umrolltisch
- *rewind bench*
60-65 der Bildendkontrollraum
- *final picture quality checking room*
60 der Vorschaumonitor
- *preview monitor*
61 der Programmonitor
- *programme (Am. program) monitor*
62 die Stoppuhr
- *stopclock*
63 das Bildmischpult
- *vision mixer (vision-mixing console, vision-mixing desk)*
64 die Kommandoanlage
- *talkback system (talkback equipment)*
65 der Kameramonitor
- *camera monitor (picture monitor)*

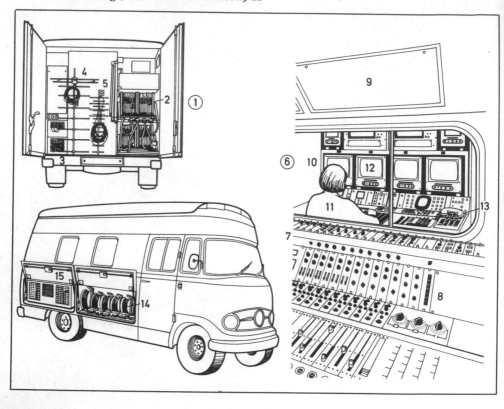

1-15 der Ü-Wagen
(Fernsehübertragungswagen;
auch: Tonreportagewagen *m*)
- *outside broadcast (OB) vehicle*
(television OB van; also: sound OB
van, radio OB van)
1 die Heckeinrichtung des
Ü-Wagens *m*
- *rear equipment section of the OB*
vehicle
2 die Kamerakabel *n*
- *camera cable*
3 die Kabelanschlußtafel
- *cable connection panel*
4 die Fernsehempfangsantenne für
das erste Programm
- *television (TV) reception aerial*
(receiving aerial) for Channel I
5 die Fernsehantenne für das zweite
Programm
- *television (TV) reception aerial*
(receiving aerial) for Channel II
6 die Inneneinrichtung des
Ü-Wagens *m*
- *interior equipment (on-board*
equipment) of the OB vehicle
7 der Tonregieraum
- *sound production control room*
(sound control room)
8 das Tonregiepult
- *sound control desk*

(sound control
console)
9 der Kontrollautsprecher
- *monitoring loudspeaker*
10 der Bildregieraum
- *vision control room (video control*
room)
11 die Videotechnikerin
- *video controller (vision controller)*
12 der Kameramonitor
- *camera monitor (picture monitor)*
13 das Bordtelefon
- *on-board telephone*
(intercommunication telephone)
14 die Mikrophonkabel *n*
- *microphone cable*
15 die Klimaanlage
- *air-conditioning equipment*

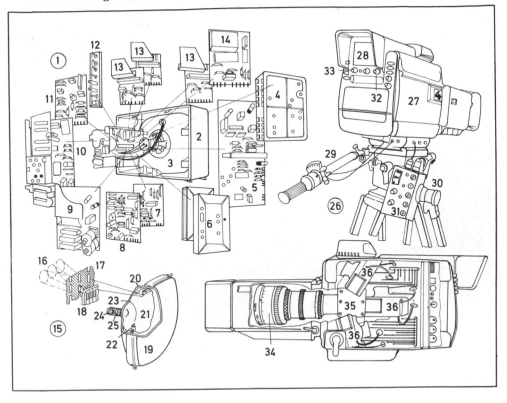

1 der **Farbfernsehempfänger**
(Farbfernseher, das
Farbfernsehgerät) in
Modulbauweise *f*
- *colour (Am. color) television (TV)*
  receiver (colour television set) of
  modular design
2 das Fernsehergehäuse
- *television cabinet*
3 die Fernsehröhre
- *television tube (picture tube)*
4 der ZF-Verstärkermodul
- *IF (intermediate frequency)*
  amplifier module
5 der Farbdecodermodul
- *colour (Am. color)*
  decoder module
6 die VHF- und UHF-Tuner *m*
- *VHF and UHF tuner*
7 der Horizontalsynchronmodul
- *horizontal synchronizing module*
8 der Vertikalablenkmodul
- *vertical deflection module*
9 der Ost-West-Modul
- *horizontal linearity control module*
10 der Horizontalablenkmodul
- *horizontal deflection module*
11 der Regelmodul
- *control module*
12 der Konvergenzmodul
- *convergence module*

13 der Farbendstufenmodul
- *colour (Am. color) output stage module*
14 der Tonmodul
- *sound module*
15 der Farbbildschirm
- *colour (Am. color) picture tube*
16 die Elektronenstrahlen *m*
- *electron beams*
17 die Maske mit Langlöchern *n*
- *shadow mask with elongated holes*
18 die Leuchtstoffstreifen *m*
- *strip of fluorescent (luminescent,*
  phosphorescent) material
19 die Leuchtstoffschicht
- *coating (film) of fluorescent*
  material
20 die innere magnetische
Abschirmung
- *inner magnetic screen (screening)*
21 das Vakuum
- *vacuum*
22 die temperaturkompensierte
Maskenaufhängung
- *temperature-compensated shadow*
  mask mount
23 der Zentrierring für die
Ablenkeinheit
- *centring (centering) ring for the*
  deflection system
24 die Elektronenstrahlsysteme *n*
- *electron gun assembly*

25 die Schnellheizkathode
- *rapid heat-up cathode*
26 die **Fernsehkamera**
- *television (TV) camera*
27 der Kamerakopf
- *camera head*
28 der Kameramonitor
- *camera monitor*
29 der Führungshebel
- *control arm (control lever)*
30 die Scharfeinstellung
- *focusing adjustment*
31 die Bedienungstafel
- *control panel*
32 die Kontrastregelung
- *contrast control*
33 die Helligkeitsregelung
- *brightness control*
34 das Zoomobjektiv
- *zoom lens*
35 das Strahlenteilungsprisma (der
Strahlenteiler)
- *beam-splitting prism (beam*
  splitter)
36 die Aufnahmeeinheit (Farbröhre)
- *pickup unit (colour, Am. color,*
  pickup tube)

1 **der Radiorecorder**
- *radio cassette recorder*
2 der Tragbügel
- *carrying handle*
3 die Drucktasten *f* für das (den)
Kassettenteil
- *push buttons for the cassette
recorder unit*
4 die Stationstasten *f*
- *station selector buttons (station
preset buttons)*
5 das eingebaute Mikrophon
- *built-in microphone*
6 das Kassettenfach
- *cassette compartment*
7 die Frequenzskala
- *tuning dial*
8 der Flachbahnregler
- *slide control
[for volume or tone]*
9 der Frequenzwähler
- *tuning knob (tuning control, tuner)*
10 **die Kompaktkassette**
(Compact-Cassette)
- *compact cassette*
11 der Kassettenbehälter (die
Kassettenbox)
- *cassette box (cassette holder,
cassette cabinet)*
12 das Kassettenband
- *cassette tape*
13-48 **die Stereoanlage** (*auch:*
Quadroanlage *f*) aus
HiFi-Komponenten *f*
(HiFi-Bausteinen *m*)
- *stereo system (also: quadraphonic
system) made up of Hi-Fi
components*
13-14 **die Stereoboxen** *f*
- *stereo speakers*
14 die Lautsprecherbox, eine
Dreiwegebox mit
Frequenzweichen *f*
- *speaker (loudspeaker), a three-way
speaker with crossover (crossover
network)*
15 der Hochtonlautsprecher
(Hochtöner, ein
Kalottenhochtöner *m*)
- *tweeter*
16 der Mitteltonlautsprecher
- *mid-range speaker*
17 der Baßlautsprecher (Baß,
Tieftöner)
- *woofer*
18 **der Plattenspieler** (die
Phonokomponente, der
Phonobaustein)
- *record player (automatic record
changer, auto changer)*
19 das Plattenspielerchassis
- *record player housing (record player
base)*
20 der Plattenteller
- *turntable*
21 der Tonarm
- *tone arm*
22 das Balancegewicht
- *counterbalance (counterweight)*
23 die kardanische Aufhängung
- *gimbal suspension*
24 die Auflagekraftverstellung
- *stylus pressure control (stylus force
control)*
25 die Antiskatingeinstellung
- *anti-skate control*

26 das magnetische Tonabnehmersystem
mit der (konischen oder biradialen)
Abtastnadel, einem Diamanten *m*
- *magnetic cartridge with (conical or
elliptical) stylus, a diamond*
27 die Tonarmarretierung
- *tone arm lock*
28 der Tonarmlift
- *tone arm lift*
29 der Umdrehungszahlwähler
- *speed selector (speed changer)*
30 der Starter
- *starter switch*
31 der Tonhöhenabstimmer
- *treble control*
32 die Abdeckhaube
- *dust cover*
33 **das Stereokassettendeck**
- *stereo cassette deck*
34 das Kassettenfach
- *cassette compartment*
35-36 die Aussteuerungsanzeigen *f*
- *recording level meters (volume unit
meters, VU meters)*
35 das Aussteuerungsinstrument für
den linken Kanal
- *left-channel recording level meter*
36 das Aussteuerungsinstrument für
den rechten Kanal
- *right-channel recording level meter*
37 **der Tuner**
- *tuner*
38 die UKW-Stationstasten *f*
- *VHF (FM) station selector buttons*
39 das Leuchtinstrument für die
Senderabstimmung
- *tuning meter*
40 **der Verstärker; Tuner u. Verstärker
kombiniert:** der Receiver (das
Steuergerät)
- *amplifier; tuner and amplifier
together: receiver (control unit)*
41 der Lautstärkeregler
- *volume control*
42 der Vierkanal-Balanceregler *m*
(Pegelregler *m*)
- *four-channel balance control (level
control)*
43 die Höhen- und
Tiefenabstimmung
- *treble and bass tuning*
44 der Eingangswähler
- *input selector*
45 **der Vierkanaldemodulator** für
CD4-Schallplatten *f*
- *four-channel demodulator for CD4
records*
46 der Quadro-/Stereo-Umschalter
- *quadra/stereo converter*
47 die Kassettenbox
- *cassette box (cassette holder,
cassette cabinet)*
48 die Schallplattenfächer *n*
- *record storage slots (record storage
compartments)*
49 **das Mikrophon**
- *microphone*
50 die Einsprechöffnungen *f*
- *microphone screen*
51 der Mikrophonfuß
- *microphone base (microphone stand)*
52 **die Dreifach-Kompaktanlage** (das
Phono-Kassetten-Steuergerät)
- *three-in-one stereo component
system (automatic record changer,
cassette deck, and stereo receiver)*

53 die Tonarmwaage
- *tone arm balance*
54 die Abstimmungsregler *m*
- *tuning meters*
55 die Leuchtanzeige für die
automatische Eisenoxid-/
Chromdioxid-Umschaltung
- *indicator light for automatic FeO/
CrO₂ tape switch-over*
56 **das Spulentonbandgerät,** ein Zwei-
oder Vierspurgerät *n*
- *open-reel-type recorder, a two or
four-track unit*
57 die Bandspule
- *tape reel (open tape reel)*
58 das Spulentonband (Tonband, ein
Viertelzollband *n*)
- *open-reel tape (recording tape, ¼"
tape)*
59 das Tonkopfgehäuse mit
Löschkopf *m*, Sprechkopf *m* und
Hörkopf *m* (*oder:* Kombikopf *m*)
- *sound head housing with erasing
head (erase head), recording head,
and reproducing head (or:
combined head)*
60 der Bandumlenker und
Endabschalter
- *tape deflector roller and end switch
(limit switch)*
61 die Aussteuerungskontrolle
- *recording level meter (VU meter)*
62 der Bandgeschwindigkeitsschalter
- *tape speed selector*
63 der Ein-/Ausschalter
- *on/off switch*
64 das Bandzählwerk
- *tape counter*
65 die Stereomikrophoneingänge *m*
- *stereo microphone sockets (stereo
microphone jacks)*
66 **der Kopfhörer**
- *headphones (headset)*
67 der gepolsterte Kopfhörerbügel
- *padded headband (padded
headpiece)*
68 die Membran
- *membrane*
69 die Ohrmuschel
- *earcups (earphones)*
70 der Kopfhörerstecker, ein
Normstecker *m* (*anders:* der
Klinkenstecker)
- *headphone cable plug, a standard
multi-pin plug (not the same as a
phono plug)*
71 die Anschlußleitung
- *headphone cable (headphone cord)*

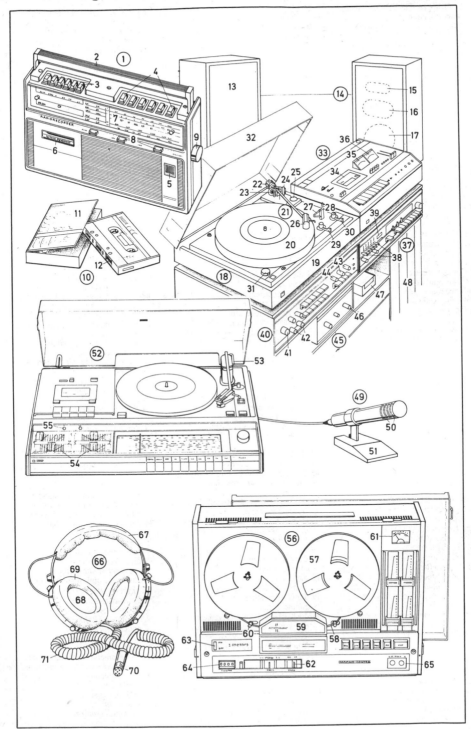

1 der Gruppenunterricht mit einem
 Lehrautomaten *m*
- *group instruction using a **teaching
 machine***
2 der Lehrertisch mit der zentralen
 Steuereinheit
- *instructor's desk with central
 control unit*
3 der Klassenspiegel mit
 Individualanzeigen *f* und
 Quersummenzähler *m*
- *master control panel with
 individual diplays and cross total
 counters*
4 das Schülereingabegerät in der
 Hand des Schülers *m* (Adressaten)
- *student input device (student
 response device) in the hand of a
 student*
5 der Lehrschrittzähler
- *study step counter (progress counter)*
6 der Arbeitsprojektor
 (Overheadprojektor)
- *overhead projector*
7 die Einrichtung für die audiovisuelle
 Lernprogrammherstellung
- *apparatus for producing
 audio-visual learning programmes
 (Am. programs)*
8-10 die Bildkodiereinrichtung
- *frame coding device*
8 der Filmbetrachter
- *film viewer*
9 die Speichereinheit
- *memory unit (storage unit)*
10 die Filmperforationseinrichtung
- *film perforator*
11-14 die Tonkodiereinrichtung
- *audio coding equipment (sound
 coding equipment)*
11 das Tastenfeld für die Kodierung
- *coding keyboard*
12 das Zweispur-Tonbandgerät
- *two-track tape recorder*
13 das Vierspur-Tonbandgerät
- *four-track tape recorder*
14 die Pegelaussteuerung
- *recording level meter*
15 das P.I.P.-System *[P.I.P.:
 Programmed Individual Presentation f]*
- *PIP (programmed individual
 presentation) system*
16 der AV-Projektor für die
 programmierte Unterweisung
- *AV (audio-visual) projector for
 programmed instruction*
17 die Tonkassette
- *audio cassette*
18 die Bildkassette
- *video cassette*
19 die Datenstation
- *data terminal*
20 die Fernsprechverbindung zur
 zentralen Datenerfassung
- *telephone connection with the
 central data collection station*
21 **das Bildtelefon** (der Bildfernsprecher)
- *video telephone*
22 die Konferenzschaltung
- *conference circuit (conference
 hook-up, conference connection)*
23 die Eigenbildtaste
- *camera tube switch (switch for
 transmitting speaker's picture)*
24 die Sprechtaste
- *talk button (talk key, speaking key)*

25 die Wähltastatur
- *touch-tone buttons (touch-tone pad)*
26 der Telefonbildschirm
- *video telephone screen*
27 die Infrarotübertragung von
 Fernsehton *m*
- *infrared transmission of television sound*
28 das Fernsehgerät
- *television receiver (television set, TV set)*
29 der Infrarottonsender
- *infrared sound transmitter*
30 der drahtlose Infrarottonkopfhörer
 mit Akkuspeisung *f*
- *cordless battery-powered infrared
 sound headphones (headset)*
31 **die Mikrofilmaufzeichnungsanlage**
 [im Schema]
- *microfilming system [diagram]*
32 die Magnetbandstation
 (Datenspeicheranlage)
- *magnetic tape station (data storage unit)*
33 der Pufferspeicher
- *buffer storage*
34 die Anpassungseinheit
- *adapter unit*
35 die digitale Steuerung
 (Digitalsteuerung)
- *digital control*
36 die Kamerasteuerung
- *camera control*
37 der Schriftspeicher
- *character storage*
38 die Analogsteuerung
- *analogue (Am. analog) control*
39 die Bildröhrengeometrie-Korrektur
- *correction (adjustment) of picture
 tube geometry*
40 die Kathodenstrahlröhre
- *cathode ray tube (CRT)*
41 die Optik
- *optical system*
42 das Formulardia zur Einblendung
 von Formularen
- *slide (transparency) of a form for
 mixing-in images of forms*
43 die Blitzlampe
- *flash lamp*
44 die Universalfilmkassetten *f*
- *universal film cassettes*
45-84 **Demonstrations- und Lehrgeräte** *n*
- *demonstration and teaching
 equipment*
45 das Demonstrationsmodell eines
 Viertaktmotors *m*
- *demonstration model of a
 four-stroke engine*
46 der Kolben
- *piston*
47 der Zylinderkopf
- *cylinder head*
48 die Zündkerze
- *spark plug (sparking plug)*
49 der Unterbrecher
- *contact breaker*
50 die Kurbelwelle mit Gegengewicht *n*
- *crankshaft with balance weights
 (counterbalance weights)
 (counterbalanced crankshaft)*
51 der Kurbelkasten
- *crankcase*
52 das Einlaßventil
- *inlet valve*
53 das Auslaßventil
- *exhaust valve*
54 die Kühlwasserbohrungen *f*
- *coolant bores (cooling water bores)*

55 das Demonstrationsmodell eines
 Zweitaktmotors *m*
- *demonstration model of a
 two-stroke engine*
56 der Nasenkolben
- *deflector piston*
57 der Überströmschlitz
- *transfer port*
58 der Auslaßschlitz
- *exhaust port*
59 die Kurbelkastenspülung
- *crankcase scavenging*
60 die Kühlrippen *f*
- *cooling ribs*
61-67 Molekülmodelle *n*
- *models of molecules*
61 das Äthylenmolekül
- *ethylene molecule*
62 das Wasserstoffatom
- *hydrogen atom*
63 das Kohlenstoffatom
- *carbon atom*
64 das Formaldehydmolekül
- *formaldehyde atom*
65 das Sauerstoffmolekül
- *oxygen molecule*
66 der Benzolring
- *benzene ring*
67 das Wassermolekül
- *water molecule*
68-72 Schaltungen *f* aus Bauelementen *n*
- *electronic circuits made up of
 modular elements*
68 der Logikbaustein, ein integrierter
 Schaltkreis
- *logic element (logic module), an
 integrated circuit*
69 die Stecktafel für elektronische
 Bausteine *m*
- *plugboard for electronic elements
 (electronic modules)*
70 die Bausteinverbindung
- *linking (link-up, joining,
 connection) of modules*
71 der Magnetkontakt
- *magnetic contact*
72 der Schaltungsaufbau mit
 Magnethaftsteinen *m*
- *assembly (construction) of a circuit,
 using magnetic modules*
73 das Vielfachmeßgerät für Strom *m*,
 Spannung *f* und Widerstand *m*
- *multiple meter for measuring
 current, voltage and resistance*
74 der Meßbereichwählschalter
- *measurement range selector*
75 die Meßskala
- *measurement scale (measurement dial)*
76 die Anzeigenadel
- *indicator needle (pointer)*
77 das Strom- und Spannungsmeßgerät
- *current/voltage meter*
78 die Justierschraube
- *adjusting screw*
79 die optische Bank
- *optical bench*
80 die Dreikantschiene
- *triangular rail*
81 das Lasergerät (der Schul-Laser)
- *laser (teaching laser, instruction laser)*
82 die Lochblende
- *diaphragm*
83 das Linsensystem
- *lens system*
84 der Auffangschirm
- *target (screen)*

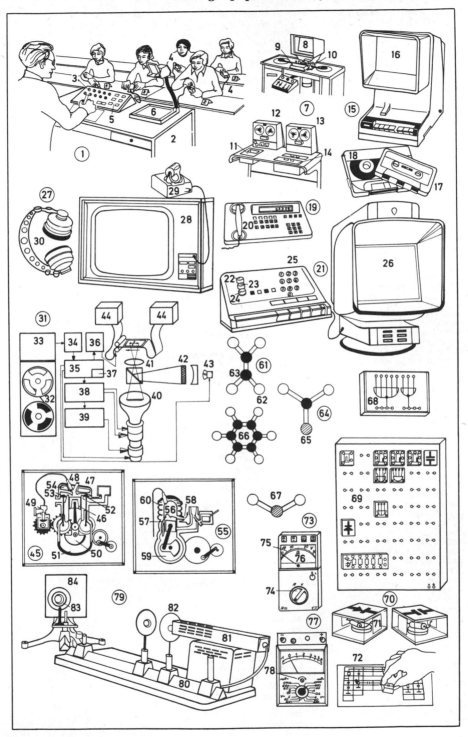

1-4 die AV-Kamera mit Recorder *m*
- *AV (audio-visual) camera with recorder*
1 die Kamera
- *camera*
2 das Objektiv
- *lens*
3 das eingebaute Mikrophon
- *built-in microphone*
4 der tragbare Videorecorder (für Viertelzoll-Spulenmagnetband *n*)
- *portable video (videotape) recorder for ¼" open-reel magnetic tape*
5-36 das VCR-/Video-Cassette-Recorder-)System
- *VCR (video cassette recorder) system*
5 die VCR-Kassette (für Halbzoll-Magnetband)
- *VCR cassette (for ½" magnetic tape)*
6 der Heimfernseher (*auch:* der Monitor)
- *domestic television receiver (also: monitor)*
7 der Videokassettenrecorder
- *video cassette recorder*
8 der Kassettenlift
- *cassette compartment*
9 das Bandzählwerk
- *tape counter*
10 der Bildstandsregler
- *centring (centering) control*
11 die Tonaussteuerung
- *sound (audio) recording level control*
12 die Aussteuerungsanzeige
- *recording level indicator*
13 die Bedienungstasten *f*
- *control buttons (operating keys)*
14 die Anzeigelampe der Bandeinfädelung
- *tape threading indicator light*
15 die Umschalter *m* für die Audio-/Videoaussteuerungsanzeige
- *changeover switch for selecting audio or video recording level display*
16 die Ein-/Ausschalter *m*
- *on/off switch*
17 die Stationstasten *f*
- *station selector buttons (station preset buttons)*
18 die eingebaute Schaltuhr
- *built-in timer switch*
19 die VCR-Kopftrommel
- *VCR (video cassette recorder) head drum*
20 der Löschkopf
- *erasing head (erase head)*
21 der Führungsstift
- *stationary guide (guide pin)*
22 das Bandlineal
- *tape guide*
23 die Tonwelle
- *capstan*
24 der Audiosynchronkopf
- *audio sync head*
25 die Andruckrolle
- *pinch roller*
26 der Videokopf
- *video head*
27 die Riefen *f* in der Kopftrommelwand für die Luftpolsterbildung
- *grooves in the wall of the head drum to promote air cushion formation*

28 das VCR-Spurschema
- *VCR (video cassette recorder) track format*
29 die Bandvorschubsrichtung
- *tape feed*
30 die Videokopf-Bewegungsrichtung
- *direction of video head movement*
31 die Videospur, eine Schrägspur
- *video track, a slant track*
32 die Tonspur
- *sound track (audio track)*
33 die Synchronspur
- *sync track*
34 der Synchronkopf
- *sync head*
35 der Tonkopf
- *sound head (audio head)*
36 der Videokopf
- *video head*
37-45 das TED-(Television-Disc-)Bildplattensystem
- *TED (television disc) system*
37 der Bildplattenspieler (das Bildplattenabspielgerät)
- *video disc player*
38 der Plattenschlitz mit der eingeschobenen Bildplatte
- *disc slot with inserted video disc*
39 der Programmwähler
- *programme (Am. program) selector*
40 die Programmskala
- *programme (Am. program) scale (programme dial)*
41 die Betriebstaste (,,*Play*")
- *operating key ('play')*
42 die Taste für Szenenwiederholung *f* (,,*Select*")
- *key for repeating a scene (scene-repeat key, 'select')*
43 die Stoptaste
- *stop key*
44 die Bildplatte
- *video disc*
45 die Bildplattenhülle
- *video disc jacket*
46-60 das VLP-(Video-Long-Play-)Bildplattensystem
- *VLP (video long play) video disc system*
46 der Bildplattenspieler
- *video disc player*
47 die Deckelzunge (*darunter:* der Abtastbereich)
- *cover projection (below it: scanning zone)*
48 die Betriebstasten *f*
- *operating keys*
49 der Zeitlupenregler
- *slow motion control*
50 das optische System [im Schema]
- *optical system [diagram]*
51 die VLP-Bildplatte
- *VLP video disc*
52 das Objektiv
- *lens*
53 der Laserstrahl
- *laser beam*
54 der Drehspiegel
- *rotating mirror*
55 der teildurchlässige Spiegel
- *semi-reflecting mirror*
56 die Photodiode
- *photodiode*
57 der Helium-Neon-Laser
- *helium-neon laser*

58 die Videosignale *n* der Plattenoberfläche
- *video signals on the surface of the video disc*
59 die Signalspur
- *signal track*
60 das einzelne Signalelement (,,Pit")
- *individual signal element ('pit')*

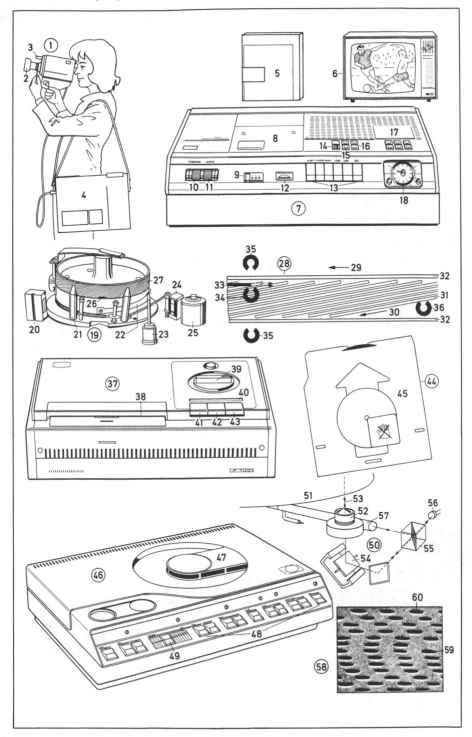

1 der Magnetplattenspeicher
- *disc (disk) store (magnetic disc
  store)*
2 das Magnetband
- *magnetic tape*
3 der Konsoloperator (Chefoperator)
- *console operator (chief operator)*
4 die Konsolschreibmaschine
- *console typewriter*
5 die Gegensprechanlage
- *intercom
  (intercom system)*
6 die Zentraleinheit mit
  Hauptspeicher *m* und Rechenwerk *n*
- *central processor with main
  memory and arithmetic unit*
7 die Operations- und
  Fehleranzeigen *f*
- *operation and error indicators*
8 die Leseeinheit für Disketten *f*
- *floppy disc (disk) reader*
9 die Magnetbandeinheit
- *magnetic tape unit*
10 die Magnetbandspule
- *magnetic tape reel*
11 die Betriebsanzeigen *f*
- *operating indicators*
12 der Lochkartenleser und -stanzer
- *punched card (punch card) reader
  and punch*
13 das Ablagefach für verarbeitete
   Lochkarten *f*
- *card stacker*

14 der Operator
- *operator*
15 die Bedienungsanleitungen *f*
- *operating instructions*

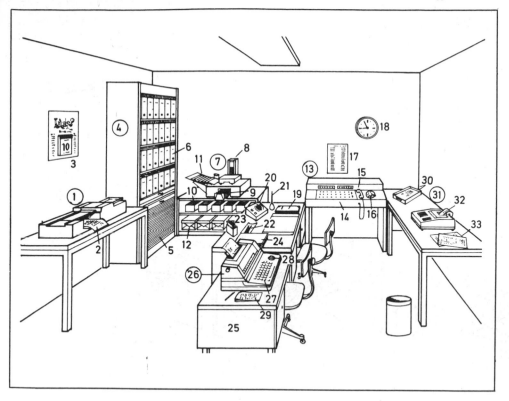

1-33 das Vorzimmer
(Sekretärinnenzimmer)
- *receptionist's office (secretary's office)*
1 das Telekopiersystem (der Faksimiletransceiver)
- *facsimile telegraph*
2 die Telekopie (Empfangskopie)
- *transmitted copy (received copy)*
3 der Wandkalender
- *wall calendar*
4 der Aktenschrank
- *filing cabinet*
5 die Rolltür
- *tambour door (roll-up door)*
6 der Aktenordner
- *file (document file)*
7 die Umdruck-Adressiermaschine
- *transfer-type addressing machine*
8 der Schablonenaufnahmeschacht
- *vertical stencil magazine*
9 die Schablonenablage
- *stencil ejection*
10 die Schablonenaufbewahrungslade
- *stencil storage drawer*
11 die Papierzuführung
- *paper feed*
12 der Briefpapiervorrat
- *stock of notepaper*
13 die Hauszentrale (Telefonzentrale)
- *switchboard (internal telephone exchange)*

14 das Drucktastenfeld für die Hausanschlüsse *m*
- *push-button keyboard for internal connections*
15 der Hörer
- *handset*
16 die Wählscheibe
- *dial*
17 das Hausanschlußverzeichnis
- *internal telephone list*
18 die Normaluhr
- *master clock (main clock)*
19 die Unterschriftenmappe
- *folder containing documents, correspondence, etc. for signing (to be signed)*
20 die Sprechanlage
- *intercom (office intercom)*
21 der Schreibstift
- *pen*
22 die Schreibschale
- *pen and pencil tray*
23 der Zettelkasten
- *card index*
24 der Formularstoß
- *stack (set) of forms*
25 der Schreibmaschinentisch
- *typing desk*
26 die Speicherschreibmaschine
- *memory typewriter*
27 das Schreibtastenfeld (Typenfeld)
- *keyboard*

28 der Drehschalter für den Arbeitsspeicher und die Magnetbandschleife
- *rotary switch for the main memory and the magnetic tape loop*
29 der Stenoblock (Stenogrammblock)
- *shorthand pad (Am. steno pad)*
30 das Ablagekörbchen
- *letter tray*
31 der Bürorechner
- *office calculator*
32 das Druckwerk
- *printer*
33 der Geschäftsbrief
- *business letter*

1-36 das Chefzimmer
- *executive's office*
1 der Schreibtischsessel
- *swivel chair*
2 der Schreibtisch
- *desk*
3 die Schreibplatte
- *writing surface (desk top)*
4 die Schreibtischschublade
- *desk drawer*
5 das Klappengefach
- *cupboard (storage area) with door*
6 die Schreibunterlage
- *desk mat (blotter)*
7 der Geschäftsbrief
- *business letter*
8 der Terminkalender
- *appointments diary*
9 die Schreibschale
- *desk set*
10 das Wechselsprechgerät
- *intercom (office intercom)*
11 die Schreibtischlampe
- *desk lamp*
12 der Taschenrechner
(Elektronikrechner)
- *pocket calculator (electronic calculator)*
13 das Telefon, eine
Chef-Sekretär-Anlage
- *telephone, an executive-secretary
system*
14 die Wählscheibe, *auch:* das
Drucktastenfeld
- *dial; ..also: push-button keyboard*

15 die Schnellruftasten *f*
- *call buttons*
16 der Hörer (Telefonhörer)
- *receiver (telephone receiver)*
17 das Diktiergerät
- *dictating machine*
18 die Diktatlängenanzeige
- *position indicator*
19 die Bedienungstasten *f*
- *control buttons (operating keys)*
20 der Truhenschrank
- *cabinet*
21 der Besuchersessel
- *visitor's chair*
22 der Geldschrank (Panzerschrank,
Tresor)
- *safe*
23 die Zuhaltung
- *bolts
(locking mechanism)*
24 die Panzerung (Panzerwand)
- *armour (Am. armor) plating*
25 die vertraulichen Unterlagen *f*
- *confidential documents*
26 die Patentschrift
- *patent*
27 das Bargeld
- *petty cash*
28 das Wandbild
- *picture*
29 der Barschrank
- *bar (drinks cabinet)*
30 das (der) Barset
- *bar set*

31-36 die Besprechungsgruppe
(Konferenzgruppe)
- *conference grouping*
31 der Konferenztisch
(Besprechungstisch)
- *conference table*
32 das Taschendiktiergerät
(Kleindiktiergerät)
- *pocket-sized dictating machine
(micro cassette recorder)*
33 der Aschenbecher
- *ashtray*
34 der Ecktisch
- *corner table*
35 die Tischleuchte (Tischlampe)
- *table lamp*
36 der Konferenzsessel
- *two-seater sofa [part of the
conference grouping]*

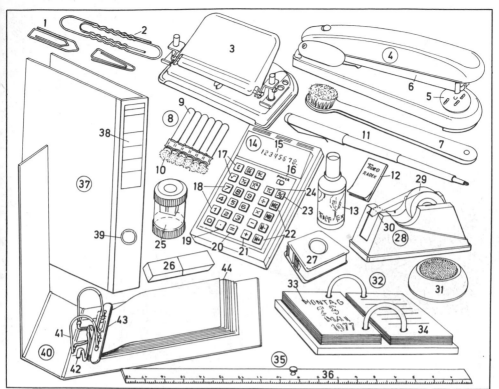

1-44 Büromaterial *n*
- **office equipment** *(office supplies, office materials)*
1 die Büroklammer (Briefklammer)
- *[small] paper clip*
2 die Aktenklammer
- *[large] paper clip*
3 der Locher
- *punch*
4 der Hefter (die Büroheftmaschine)
- *stapler (stapling machine)*
5 die Matrize
- *anvil*
6 der Ladeschieber
- *spring-loaded magazine*
7 die Reinigungsbürste für Schreibmaschinentypen *f*
- *type-cleaning brush for typewriters*
8 der Typenreiniger *m*
- *type cleaner (type-cleaning kit)*
9 der Flüssigkeitsbehälter
- *fluid container (fluid reservoir)*
10 die Reinigungsbürste
- *cleaning brush*
11 der Filzschreiber (Filzstift)
- *felt tip pen*
12 das Tippfehlerkorrekturblatt
- *correcting paper [for typing errors]*
13 die Tippfehlerkorrekturflüssigkeit
- *correcting fluid [for typing errors]*
14 der elektronische Taschenrechner
- *electronic pocket calculator*
15 die achtstellige Leuchtanzeige
- *eight-digit fluorescent display*

16 der Ein-/Ausschalter
- *on/off switch*
17 die Funktionstasten *f*
- *function keys*
18 die Zifferntasten
- *number keys*
19 die Kommataste
- *decimal key*
20 die Ist-gleich-Taste
- *'equals' key*
21 die Vorschriftstasten *f* (Rechenbefehlstasten)
- *instruction keys (command keys)*
22 die Speichertasten *f*
- *memory keys*
23 die Prozentrechnungstaste
- *percent key (percentage key)*
24 die π-Taste für Kreisberechnungen *f*
- *π-key (pi-key) for mensuration of circles*
25 der Bleistiftspitzer
- *pencil sharpener*
26 das Schreibmaschinenradiergummi (Maschinengummi)
- *typewriter rubber*
27 der Klebestreifenspender
- *adhesive tape dispenser*
28 der Klebestreifenhalter
- *adhesive tape holder (roller-type adhesive tape dispenser)*
29 die Klebestreifenrolle
- *roll of adhesive tape*
30 die Abreißkante
- *tear-off edge*

31 der Anfeuchter
- *moistener*
32 der Tischkalender
- *desk diary*
33 das Datumsblatt (Kalenderblatt)
- *date sheet (calendar sheet)*
34 das Notizblatt (Vormerkblatt)
- *memo sheet*
35 das Lineal
- *ruler*
36 die Zentimeter- und Millimeterteilung
- *centimetre and millimetre (Am. centimeter and millimeter) graduations*
37 der Aktenordner
- *file (document file)*
38 das Rückenschild
- *spine label (spine tag)*
39 das Griffloch
- *finger hole*
40 der Belegordner
- *arch board file*
41 die Ordnermechanik
- *arch unit*
42 der Griffhebel
- *release lever (locking lever, release/lock lever)*
43 der Klemmbügel
- *compressor*
44 der Kontoauszug
- *bank statement (statement of account)*

1-48 das Großraumbüro
- *open plan office*
1 die Trennwand
- *partition wall (partition screen)*
2 die Registraturtheke mit der Hängetrogregistratur
- *filing drawer with suspension file system*
3 die Behältertasche (der Hängeordner)
- *suspension file*
4 der Kartenreiter
- *file tab*
5 der Aktenordner
- *file (document file)*
6 die Archivkraft
- *filing clerk*
7 die Sachbearbeiterin
- *clerical assistant*
8 die Aktennotiz
- *note for the files*
9 das Telefon
- *telephone*
10 das Aktenregal
- *filing shelves*
11 der Sachbearbeitertisch
- *clerical assistant's desk*
12 der Büroschrank
- *office cupboard*
13 die Pflanzengondel
- *plant stand (planter)*
14 die Zimmerpflanzen *f*
- *indoor plants (houseplants)*

15 die Programmiererin
- *programmer*
16 das Datensichtgerät
- *data display terminal (visual display unit)*
17 der Kundendienstsachbearbeiter
- *customer service representative*
18 der Kunde
- *customer*
19 die Computergraphik
- *computer-generated design (computer-generated art)*
20 die Schallschlucktrennwand
- *sound-absorbing partition*
21 die Schreibkraft
- *typist*
22 die Schreibmaschine
- *typewriter*
23 die Karteiwanne
- *filing drawer*
24 die Kundenkartei
- *customer card index*
25 der Bürostuhl, ein Drehstuhl *m*
- *office chair, a swivel chair*
26 der Maschinentisch
- *typing desk*

27 der Karteikasten
– *card index box*
28 das Vielzweckregal
– *multi-purpose shelving*
29 der Chef
– *proprietor*
30 der Geschäftsbrief
– *business letter*
31 die Chefsekretärin
– *proprietor's secretary*
32 der Stenogrammblock
– *shorthand pad (Am. steno pad)*
33 die Phonotypistin
– *audio typist*
34 das Diktiergerät
– *dictating machine*
35 der Ohrhörer
[in der Ohrmuschel]
– *earphone [worn in ear]*
36 das statistische Schaubild (die
Statistik)
– *statistics chart*
37 der Schreibtischunterschrank
– *pedestal containing a cupboard or
drawers*
38 der Schiebetürenschrank
– *sliding-door cupboard*
39 die Büroelemente *n* in
Winkelbauweise *f*
– *office furniture arranged in an
angular configuration*
40 das Hängeregal
– *wall-mounted shelf*

41 der Ablagekorb
– *letter tray*
42 der Wandkalender
– *wall calendar*
43 die Datenzentrale
– *data centre (Am. center)*
44 der Informationsabruf vom
Datensichtgerät *n*
– *calling up information on the data
display terminal (visual display
unit)*
45 der Papierkorb
– *waste paper basket*
46 die Umsatzstatistik
– *sales statistics*
47 das EDV-Blatt (die ausgedruckten
Daten *pl*), ein Leporello *m*
– *EDP print-out, a continuous
fan-fold sheet*
48 das Verbindungselement
– *connecting element*

1 die elektrische Schreibmaschine,
eine Kugelkopfschreibmaschine
- *electric typewriter*, a golf ball
typewriter
2-6 das Blocktastenfeld (die
Tastatur)
- *keyboard*
2 die Leertaste
- *space bar*
3 die Umschalttaste für die
Großbuchstaben *m*
- *shift key*
4 der Zeilenschalter
- *line space and carrier return key*
5 der Umschaltfeststeller
- *shift lock*
6 die Randlösetaste
- *margin release key*
7 die Tabulatortaste
- *tabulator key*
8 die Tabulatorlöschtaste
- *tabulator clear key*
9 der Ein-/Ausschalter
- *on/off switch*
10 der Anschlagstärkeeinsteller
- *striking force control (impression
control)*
11 der Farbbandwähler
- *ribbon selector*
12 die Randeinstellung
- *margin scale*
13 der vordere (linke) Randsteller
- *left margin stop*
14 der hintere (rechte) Randsteller
- *right margin stop*
15 der Kugelkopf (Schreibkopf) mit
den Typen *f*
- *golf ball (spherical typing element)
bearing the types*
16 die Farbbandkassette
- *ribbon cassette*
17 der Papierhalter mit den
Führungsrollen *f*
- *paper bail with rollers*
18 die Schreibwalze
- *platen*
19 das Schreibfenster
- *typing opening (typing window)*
20 der Papiereinwerfer
- *paper release lever*
21 die Schreibwerkrückführung
(Schlittenrückführung)
- *carrier return lever*
22 der Walzendrehknopf
- *platen knob*
23 der Zeileneinsteller
- *line space adjuster*
24 der Walzenlöser
- *variable platen action lever*
25 der Walzenstechknopf
- *push-in platen variable*
26 die Radierauflage
- *erasing table*
27 die transparente
Gehäuseabdeckung
- *transparent cover*
28 der Austauschkugelkopf
- *exchange golf ball (exchange typing
element)*
29 die Type
- *type*
30 der Schreibkopfdeckel
- *golf ball cap (cap of typing
element)*
31 die Zahnsegmente *n*
- *teeth*

32 **der Rollenkopierautomat**
- ***web-fed automatic copier***
33 das Rollenmagazin
- *magazine for paper roll*
34 die Formateinstellung
- *paper size selection (format
selection)*
35 die Kopienvorwahl
- *print quantity selection*
36 der Kontrastregler
- *contrast control*
37 der Hauptschalter
- *main switch (on/off switch)*
38 der Bedienungsschalter
- *start print button*
39 das Vorlagenfenster
- *document glass*
40 das Übertragungstuch
- *transfer blanket*
41 die Tonerwalze
- *toner roll*
42 das Belichtungssystem
- *exposure system*
43 der Kopienausstoß
- *print delivery (copy delivery)*
44 **die Brieffaltmaschine**
- ***letter-folding machine***
45 die Papiereingabe
- *paper feed*
46 die Falteinrichtung
- *folding mechanism*
47 der Auffangtisch
- *receiving tray*
48 **der Kleinoffsetdrucker**
- ***small offset press***
49 die Papieranlage
- *paper feed*
50 der Hebel für die
Druckplatteneinfärbung
- *lever for inking the plate cylinder*
51-52 das Farbwerk
- *inking unit (inker unit)*
51 der Verreiber
- *distributing roller (distributor)*
52 die Auftragswalze
- *ink roller (inking roller, fountain
roller)*
53 die Druckhöhenverstellung
- *pressure adjustment*
54 die Papierablage
- *sheet delivery (receiving table)*
55 die Druckgeschwindigkeitseinstellung
- *printing speed adjustment*
56 der Rüttler zum Glattstoßen *n* der
Papierstapel *m*
- *jogger for aligning the piles of sheets*
57 der Papierstapel
- *pile of paper (pile of sheets)*
58 die Falzmaschine
- *folding machine*
59 die Bogenzusammentragemaschine
für Kleinauflagen *f*
- *gathering machine (collating
machine, assembling machine) for
short runs*
60 die Zusammentragestation
- *gathering station (collating station,
assembling station)*
61 der Klebebinder für die
Thermobindung
- *adhesive binder (perfect binder) for
hot adhesives*
62 **das Magnetband-Diktiergerät**
- ***magnetic tape dictating machine***
63 der Kopfhörer (Ohrhörer)
- *headphones (headset, earphones)*

64 der Ein-/Ausschalter
- *on/off switch*
65 der Mikrophonbügel
- *microphone cradle*
66 die Fußschalterbuchse
- *foot control socket*
67 die Telefonbuchse
- *telephone adapter socket*
68 die Kopfhörerbuchse
- *headphone socket (earphone socket,
headset socket)*
69 die Mikrophonbuchse
- *microphone socket*
70 der eingebaute Lautsprecher
- *built-in loudspeaker*
71 die Kontrollampe
- *indicator lamp (indicator light)*
72 das Kassettenfach
- *cassette compartment*
73 die Vorlauf-, Rücklauf- und
Stopptasten *f*
- *forward wind, rewind and stop
buttons*
74 die Zeitskala mit Indexstreifen *m*
- *time scale with indexing marks*
75 der Zeitskalastopp
- *time scale stop*

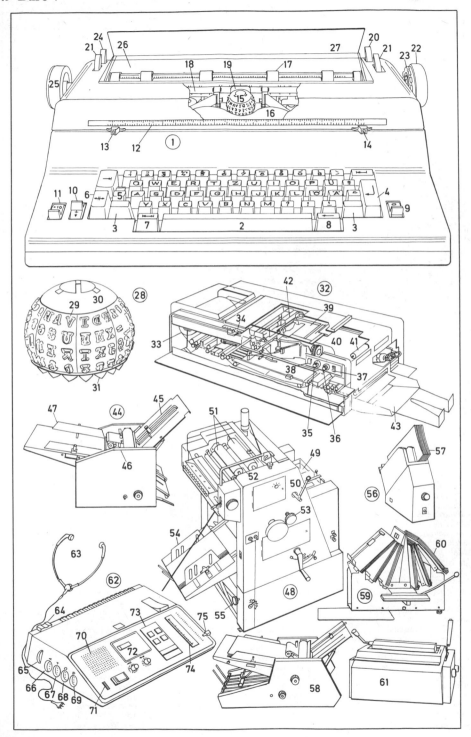

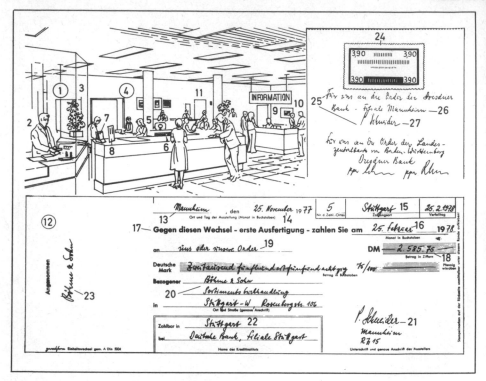

1-11 die Kundenhalle
- *main hall*
1 die Kasse
- *cashier's desk (cashier's counter)*
2 der Kassierer
- *teller (cashier)*
3 das schußsichere Panzerglas
- *bullet-proof glass*
4 die Servicegruppe (Bedienung *f* und Beratung *f* für Sparkonten *n*, Privat- und Firmenkonten *n*, persönliche Kredite *m*)
- *service counters (service and advice for savings accounts, private and company accounts, personal loans)*
5 die Bankangestellte
- *bank clerk*
6 die Bankkundin
- *customer*
7 die Prospektfaltblätter *m*
- *brochures*
8 der Kurszettel
- *stock list (price list, list of quotations)*
9 der Informationsstand
- *information counter*
10 der Geldwechselschalter
- *foreign exchange counter*
11 der Durchgang zum Tresorraum *m*
- *entrance to strong room*
12 **der Wechsel;** *hier:* ein gezogener Wechsel *m* (Tratte *f*), ein angenommener Wechsel *m* (das Akzept)
- *bill of exchange (bill); here: a draft, an acceptance (a bank acceptance)*

13 der Ausstellungsort
- *place of issue*
14 der Ausstellungstag
- *date of issue*
15 der Zahlungsort
- *place of payment*
16 der Verfalltag
- *date of maturity (due date)*
17 die Wechselklausel (Bezeichnung der Urkunde als Wechsel *m*)
- *bill clause (draft clause)*
18 die Wechselsumme (der Wechselbetrag)
- *value*
19 die Order (der Wechselnehmer, Remittent)
- *order (payee, remitter)*

20 der Bezogene (Adressat, Trassat)
- *drawee (payer)*
21 der Aussteller (Trassant)
- *drawer*
22 der Domizilvermerk (die Zahlstelle)
- *domicilation (paying agent)*
23 der Annahmevermerk (das Akzept)
- *acceptance*
24 die Wechselstempelmarke
- *stamp*
25 das Indossament (der Übertragungsvermerk)
- *endorsement (indorsement, transfer entry)*
26 der Indossatar (Indossat, Girat)
- *endorsee (indorsee)*
27 der Indossant (Girant)
- *endorser (indorser)*

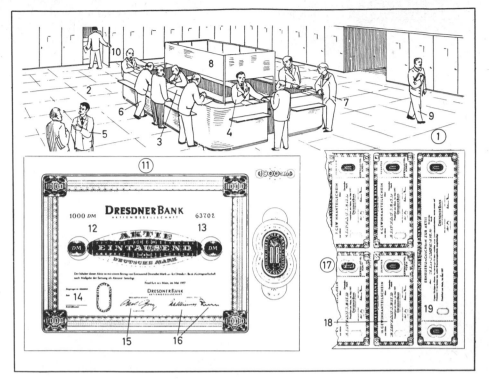

1-10 die Börse (Effekten-, Wertpapier- oder Fondsbörse)
- *stock exchange (exchange for the sale of securities, stocks, and bonds)*
1 der Börsensaal
- *exchange hall (exchange floor)*
2 der Markt für Wertpapiere *n*
- *market for securities*
3 die Maklerschranke (der Ring)
- *broker's post*
4 der vereidigte Kursmakler (Börsenmakler, Effektenmakler, Sensal), ein Handelsmakler *m*
- *sworn stockbroker (exchange broker, stockbroker, Am. specialist), an inside broker*
5 der freie Kursmakler (Agent), für Freiverkehr *m*
- *kerbstone broker (kerbstoner, curbstone broker, curbstoner, outside broker), a commercial broker dealing in unlisted securities*
6 das Börsenmitglied, ein zum Börsenhandel *m* zugelassener Privater *m*
- *member of the stock exchange (stockjobber, Am. floor trader, room trader)*
7 der Börsenvertreter (Effektenhändler), ein Bankangestellter *m*
- *stock exchange agent (boardman), a bank employee*

8 die Kursmaklertafel (Kurstafel, Maklertafel, der Kursanzeiger)
- *quotation board*
9 der Börsendiener
- *stock exchange attendant (waiter)*
10 die Telefonzelle (Fernsprechkabine)
- *telephone box (telephone booth, telephone kiosk, call box)*
11-19 Wertpapiere *n* (Effekten *pl*): Arten: Aktie *f*, festverzinsliches Wertpapier, Rente *f*, Anleihe *f*, Pfandbrief *m*, Kommunalobligation *f*, Industrieobligation *f*, Wandelschuldverschreibung *f*
- *securities; kinds: share (Am. stock), fixed-income security, annuity, bond, debenture bond, municipal bond (corporation stock), industrial bond, convertible bond*
11 die Aktienurkunde (der Mantel); *hier:* die Inhaberaktie
- *share certificate (Am. stock certificate); here: bearer share (share warrant)*
12 der Nennwert der Aktie
- *par (par value, nominal par, face par) of the share*
13 die laufende Nummer
- *serial number*
14 die Seitennummer der Eintragung im Aktienbuch *n* der Bank
- *page number of entry in bank's share register (bank's stock ledger)*

15 die Unterschrift des Aufsichtsratsvorsitzers *m*
- *signature of the chairman of the board of governors*
16 die Unterschrift des Vorstandsvorsitzers *m*
- *signature of the chairman of the board of directors*
17 der Bogen (Kuponbogen)
- *sheet of coupons (coupon sheet, dividend coupon sheet)*
18 der Dividendenschein (Gewinnanteilschein)
- *dividend warrant (dividend coupon)*
19 der Erneuerungsschein (Talon)
- *talon*

252 Geld (Münzen und Scheine)

1-28 Münzen *f* (Geldstücke *n*,
Hartgeld; *Arten:* Gold-, Silber-,
Nickel-, Kupfer- od.
Aluminiummünzen *f*)
- **coins** *(coin, coinage, metal money,
specie, Am. hard money;* kinds:
*gold, silver, nickel, copper, or
aluminium, Am. aluminum, coins)*
1 Athen: Tetradrachme *f* in
Nuggetform *f*
- *Athens: nugget-shaped tetradrachm
(tetradrachmon, tetradrachma)*
2 die Eule (der Stadtvogel von
Athen)
- *the owl (emblem of the city of
Athens)*
3 Aureus *m* Konstantins des Großen
- *aureus of Constantine the Great*
4 Brakteat *m* Kaiser Friedrichs I.
Barbarossa
- *bracteate of Emperor Frederick I
Barbarossa*
5 Frankreich: Louisdor *m*
Ludwigs XIV.
- *Louis XIV louis-d'or*
6 Preußen: 1 Reichstaler *m*
Friedrichs des Großen
- *Prussia: 1 reichstaler (speciestaler)
of Frederick the Great*
7 Bundesrepublik Deutschland:
5 Deutsche Mark *f* (DM);
1 DM *f* = 100 Pfennige *m*
- *Federal Republic of Germany:
5 Deutschmarks (DM);
1 DM = 100 pfennigs*
8 die Vorderseite (der Avers)
- *obverse*
9 die Rückseite (der Revers)
- *reverse (subordinate side)*
10 das Münzzeichen (der
Münzbuchstabe)
- *mint mark (mintage, exergue)*
11 die Randinschrift
- *legend (inscription on the edge of a
coin)*
12 das Münzbild, ein Landeswappen *n*
- *device (type), a provincial coat of
arms*
13 Österreich: 25 Schilling *m*;
1 Sch. *m* = 100 Groschen *m*
- *Austria: 25 schillings;
1 sch = 100 groschen*
14 die Länderwappen *n*
- *provincial coats of arms*
15 Schweiz: 5 Franken *m*; 1 Franken *m*
(franc, franco) = 100 Rappen *m*
(Centimes, centimes)
- *Switzerland: 5 francs; 1 franc =
100 centimes*
16 Frankreich: 1 Franc *m* (franc) =
100 Centimes *m* (centimes)
- *France: 1 franc = 100 centimes*
17 Belgien: 100 Francs *m* (francs)
- *Belgium: 100 francs*
18 Luxemburg: 1 Franc *m* (franc)
- *Luxembourg (Luxemburg): 1 franc*
19 Niederlande: 2½ Gulden *m*;
1 Gulden *m* (florin) = 100 Cents *m*
(cents)
- *Netherlands: 2½ guilders;
1 guilder (florin, gulden) = 100 cents*
20 Italien 10 Lire *f* (lire, *sg.* Lira)
- *Italy: 10 lire (sg. lira)*
21 Vatikanstaat: 10 Lire *f*
(lire, *sg* Lira)
- *Vatican City: 10 lire (sg. lira)*

22 Spanien: 1 Peseta *f* (peseta) =
100 Céntimos *m* (céntimos)
- *Spain: 1 peseta = 100 céntimos*
23 Portugal: 1 Escudo *m* (escudo) =
100 Centavos *m* (centavos)
- *Portugal: 1 escudo =
100 centavos*
24 Dänemark: 1 Krone *f* (krone) =
100 Öre *n* (øre)
- *Denmark: 1 krone = 100 öre*
25 Schweden: 1 Krone *f* (krona) =
100 Öre *n* (öre)
- *Sweden: 1 krona = 100 öre*
26 Norwegen: 1 Krone *f* (krone) =
100 Öre *n* (øre)
- *Norway: 1 krone = 100 öre*
27 Tschechoslowakei: 1 Krone *f*
(koruna) = 100 Halèr *m* (halèřu)
- *Czechoslovakia: 1 koruna =
100 heller*
28 Jugoslawien: 1 Dinar *m* (dinar) =
100 Para *m* (para)
- *Yugoslavia: 1·dinar = 100 paras*
29-39 Banknoten *f* (Papiergeld *n*,
Noten *f*, Geldscheine *m*, Scheine)
- **banknotes** *(Am. bills) (paper
money, notes, treasury notes)*
29 Bundesrepublik Deutschland: 20 DM *f*
- *Federal Republic of Germany: 20 DM*
30 die Notenbank
- *bank of issue (bank of circulation)*
31 das Porträtwasserzeichen
- *watermark [a portrait]*
32 die Wertbezeichnung
- *denomination*
33 USA: 1 Dollar *m* (dollar. $) = *100
Cents m (cents)*
- *USA: 1 dollar ($ 1) = 100 cents*
34 die Faksimileunterschriften *f*
- *facsimile signatures*
35 der Kontrollstempel
- *impressed stamp*
36 die Reihenbezeichnung
- *serial number*
37 Vereinigtes Königreich
Großbritannien und Nordirland:
1 Pfund Sterling *m* (£)=100 New
Pence *m* (new pence, p; *sg* New
Penny)
- *United Kingdom of Great Britain
and Northern Ireland: 1 pound
sterling (£ 1) = 100 new pence (100p.)
(sg. new penny, new p)*
38 das Guillochenwerk
- *guilloched pattern*
39 Griechenland: 1 000 Drachmen *f*
(drachmai); 1 Drachme *f* =
100 Lepta *n* (lepta; *sg* Lepton)
- *Greece: 1,000 drachmas
(drachmae); 1 drachma = 100 lepta
(sg. lepton)*
40-44 die Münzprägung
- *striking of coins (coinage, mintage)*
40-41 die Prägestempel *m*
- *coining dies (minting dies)*
40 der Oberstempel
- *upper die*
41 der Unterstempel
- *lower die*
42 der Prägering
- *collar*
43 das Münzplättchen (Blankett,
Rondell)
- *coin disc (disk) (flan, planchet, blank)*
44 der Prägetisch
- *coining press (minting press)*

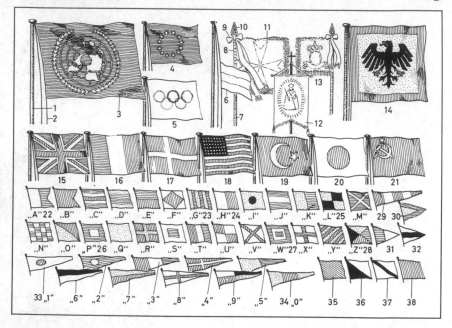

1-3 die Flagge der Vereinten Nationen *f*
- *flag of the United Nations*
1 der Flaggenstock (Flaggenmast) mit dem Flaggenknopf *m*
- *flagpole (flagstaff) with truck*
2 die Flaggenleine (Flaggleine)
- *halyard (halliard, haulyard)*
3 das Flaggentuch
- *bunting*
4 die Flagge des Europarates *m* (Europaflagge)
- *flag of the Council of Europe*
5 die Olympiaflagge
- *Olympic flag*
6 die Flagge halbstock[s] (halbmast) [zur Trauer]
- *flag at half-mast (Am. at half-staff) [as a token of mourning]*
7-11 die Fahne
- *flag*
7 der Fahnenschaft
- *flagpole (flagstaff)*
8 der Fahnennagel
- *ornamental stud*
9 das Fahnenband
- *streamer*
10 die Fahnenspitze
- *pointed tip of the flagpole*
11 das Fahnentuch
- *bunting*
12 das Banner
- *banner (gonfalon)*
13 die Reiterstandarte (das Feldzeichen der Kavallerie)
- *cavalry standard (flag of the cavalry)*
14 die Standarte des dt. Bundespräsidenten [das Abzeichen eines Staatsoberhaupts *n*]
- *standard of the German Federal President [ensign of head of state]*

15-21 Nationalflaggen *f*
- *national flags*
15 der Union Jack (Großbritannien)
- *the Union Jack (Great Britain)*
16 die Trikolore (Frankreich)
- *the Tricolour (Am. Tricolor) (France)*
17 der Danebrog (Dänemark)
- *the Danebrog (Dannebrog) (Denmark)*
18 das Sternenbanner (USA)
- *the Stars and Stripes (Star-Spangled Banner) (USA)*
19 der Halbmond (Türkei)
- *the Crescent (Turkey)*
20 das Sonnenbanner (Japan)
- *the Rising Sun (Japan)*
21 Hammer und Sichel (UdSSR)
- *the Hammer and Sickle (USSR)*
22-34 Signalflaggen *f*, ein Stell *n* Flaggen *f*
- *signal flags, a hoist*
22-28 Buchstabenflaggen *f*
- *letter flags*
22 Buchstabe A, ein gezackter Stander
- *letter A, a burgee (swallow-tailed flag)*
23 G, das Lotsenrufsignal
- *G, pilot flag*
24 H („Lotse ist an Bord")
- *H ('pilot on board')*
25 L („Stop, wichtige Mitteilung")
- *L ('you should stop, I have something important to communicate')*
26 P, der Blaue Peter, ein Abfahrtssignal *n*
- *P, the Blue Peter ('about to set sail')*
27 W („benötige ärztliche Hilfe")
- *W ('I require medical assistance')*
28 Z, ein rechteckiger Stander
- *Z, an oblong pennant (oblong pendant)*

29 der Signalbuchwimpel, ein Wimpel *m* des internat. Signalbuchs *n*
- *code pennant (code pendant), used in the International Signals Code*
30-32 Hilfsstander *m*, dreieckige Stander
- *substitute flags (repeaters), triangular flags (pennants, pendants)*
33-34 Zahlenwimpel *m*
- *numeral pennants (numeral pendants)*
33 die Zahl 1
- *number 1*
34 die Zahl 0
- *number 0*
35-38 Zollflaggen *f*
- *customs flags*
35 der Zollstander von Zollbooten *n*
- *customs boat pennant (customs boat pendant)*
36 „Schiff zollamtlich abgefertigt"
- *'ship cleared through customs'*
37 das Zollrufsignal
- *customs signal flag*
38 die Pulverflagge [„feuergefährliche Ladung"]
- *powder flag ['inflammable (flammable) cargo']*

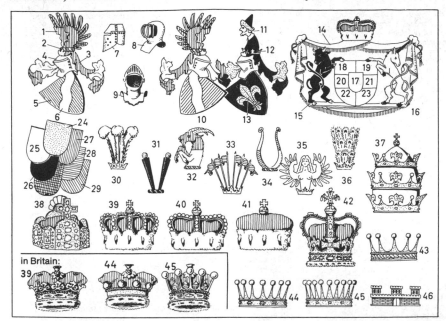

1-36 Heraldik *f* (Wappenkunde)
- *heraldry (blazonry)*
1, 11, 30-36 Helmzier *f*
(Helmzeichen *n*, Helmkleinod, Zimier)
- *crests*
1-6 das Wappen
- *coat-of-arms (achievement of arms, hatchment, achievement)*
1 die Helmzier
- *crest*
2 der Wulst
- *wreath of the colours* (Am. *colors*)
3 die Decke (Helmdecke)
- *mantle (mantling)*
4, 7-9 Helme *m*
- *helmets (helms)*
4 der Stechhelm
- *tilting helmet (jousting helmet)*
5 der Wappenschild
- *shield*
6 der schräglinke Wellenbalken
- *bend sinister wavy*
7 der Kübelhelm
- *pot-helmet (pot-helm, heaume)*
8 der Spangenhelm
- *barred helmet (grilled helmet)*
9 der offene Helm
- *helmet affronty with visor open*
10-13 das Ehewappen
(Allianzwappen, Doppelwappen)
- *marital achievement (marshalled, Am. marshaled, coat-of-arms)*
10 das Wappen des Mannes *m*
- *arms of the baron (of the husband)*
11-13 das Wappen der Frau
- *arms of the family of the femme (of the wife)*
11 der Menschenrumpf
- *demi-man;* also: *demi-woman*
12 die Laubkrone (Helmkrone)
- *crest coronet*

13 die Lilie
- *fleur-de-lis*
14 das Wappenzelt
(der Wappenmantel)
- *heraldic tent (mantling)*
15-16 Schildhalter *m*, Wappentiere *n*
- *supporters (heraldic beasts)*
15 der Stier
- *bull*
16 das Einhorn
- *unicorn*
17-23 die Wappenbeschreibung
(Blasonierung, Wappenfeldordnung)
- *blazon*
17 das Herzschild
- *inescutcheon (heart-shield)*
18-23 erstes bis sechstes Feld
(Wappenfeld)
- *quarterings one to six*
18, 20, 22 vorn, rechts
- *dexter, right*
18-19 oben
- *chief*
19, 21, 23 hinten, links
- *sinister, left*
22-23 unten
- *base*
24-29 die Tinkturen *f*
- *tinctures*
24-25 Metalle *n*
- *metals*
24 Gold *n* [gelb]
- *or (gold) [yellow]*
25 Silber *n* [weiß]
- *argent (silver) [white]*
26 schwarz
- *sable*
27 rot
- *gules*
28 blau
- *azure*

29 grün
- *vert*
30 die Straußenfedern *f*
- *ostrich feathers (treble plume)*
31 der Kürißprügel
- *truncheon*
32 der wachsende Bock
- *demi-goat*
33 die Turnierfähnchen *n*
- *tournament pennons*
34 die Büffelhörner *pl*
- *buffalo horns*
35 die Harpyie
- *harpy*
36 der Pfauenbusch
- *plume of peacock's feathers*
37, 38, 42-46 Kronen *f*
- *crowns and coronets [continental type]*
37 die Tiara
- *tiara (papal tiara)*
38 die Kaiserkrone [dt. bis 1806]
- *Imperial Crown [German, until 1806]*
39 der Herzogshut
- *ducal coronet (duke's coronet)*
40 der Fürstenhut
- *prince's coronet*
41 der Kurfürstenhut (Kurhut)
- *elector's coronet*
42 die engl. Königskrone
- *English Royal Crown*
43-45 Rangkronen *f*
- *coronets of rank*
43 die Adelskrone
- *baronet's coronet*
44 die Freiherrnkrone
- *baron's coronet (baronial coronet)*
45 die Grafenkrone
- *count's coronet*
46 die Mauerkrone eines Stadtwappens *n*
- *mauerkrone (mural crown) of a city crest*

1-98 die Bewaffnung des Heeres *n*
- *army armament (army weaponry)*
1-39 Handwaffen *f*
- *hand weapons*
1 die Pistole P1
- *P1 pistol*
2 das Rohr (der Lauf)
- *barrel*
3 das Korn
- *front sight (foresight)*
4 der Schlaghebel
- *hammer*
5 der Abzug
- *trigger*
6 das Griffstück
- *pistol grip*
7 der Magazinhalter
- *magazine holder*
8 die Maschinenpistole MP2
- *MP 2 machine gun*
9 die Schulterstütze
- *shoulder rest (butt)*
10 das Gehäuse
- *casing (mechanism casing)*
11 die Rohrhaltemutter
- *barrel clamp (barrel-clamping nut)*
12 der Spannschieber
- *cocking lever (cocking handle)*
13 der Handschutz
- *palm rest*
14 die Handballensicherung
- *safety catch*
15 das Magazin
- *magazine*
16 das Gewehr G3-A3
- *G3-A3 self-loading rifle*
17 das Rohr (der Lauf)
- *barrel*
18 der Mündungsfeuerdämpfer
- *flash hider (flash eliminator)*
19 der Handschutz
- *palm rest*
20 die Abzugsvorrichtung
- *trigger mechanism*
21 das Magazin
- *magazine*
22 die Kimme (das Visier)
- *notch (sighting notch, rearsight)*
23 der Kornhalter mit Korn *n*
- *front sight block (foresight block)
  with front sight (foresight)*
24 der Gewehrkolben (Kolben)
- *rifle butt (butt)*
25 die Panzerfaust 44
- *44 mm anti-tank rocket launcher*
26 die Granate
- *rocket (projectile)*
27 das Rückstoßrohr
- *buffer*
28 das Zielfernrohr
- *telescopic sight
  (telescope sight)*
29 die Abfeuerungseinrichtung
- *firing mechanism*
30 der Wangenschutz
- *cheek rest*
31 die Schulterstütze
- *shoulder rest (butt)*
32 das Maschinengewehr MG3
- *MG3 machine gun (Spandau)*
33 das Gehäuse
- *barrel casing*
34 der Rückstoßverstärker
- *gas regulator*
35 die Rohrwechselklappe
- *belt-changing flap*

36 das Visier
- *rearsight*
37 der Kornhalter mit Korn *n*
- *front sight block (foresight block)
  with front sight (foresight)*
38 das Griffstück
- *pistol grip*
39 die Schulterstütze
- *shoulder rest (butt)*
40-95 Schwere Waffen *f*
- *heavy weapons*
40 der Mörser 120 mm AM 50
- *120 mm AM 50 mortar*
41 das Rohr
- *barrel*
42 das Zweibein
- *bipod*
43 das Fahrgestell
- *gun carriage*
44 der Rückstoßdämpfer
- *buffer (buffer ring)*
45 der Richtaufsatz
- *sight (sighting mechanism)*
46 die Grundplatte
- *base plate*
47 die Kugelpfanne
- *striker pad*
48 die Richtkurbel
- *traversing handle*
49-74 Artilleriewaffen *f* auf
  Selbstfahrlafetten *f*
- *artillery weapons mounted on
  self-propelled gun carriages*
49 die Kanone 175 mm SF M 107
- *175 mm SFM 107 cannon*
50 das Antriebsrad
- *drive wheel*
51 der Hubzylinder
- *elevating piston*
52 die Rohrbremse
- *buffer (buffer recuperator)*
53 die Hydraulikanlage
- *hydraulic system*
54 das Bodenstück
- *breech ring*
55 der Schaufelsporn
- *spade*
56 der Schaufelzylinder
- *spade piston*
57 die Panzerhaubitze 155 mm M 109 G
- *155 mm M 109 G self-propelled gun*
58 die Mündungsbremse
- *muzzle*
59 der Rauchabsauger
- *fume extractor*
60 die Rohrwiege
- *barrel cradle*
61 der Rohrvorholer
- *barrel recuperator*
62 die Rohrstütze
- *barrel clamp*
63 das Fla-Maschinengewehr
- *light anti-aircraft (AA) machine
  gun*
64 der Raketenwerfer *Honest John* M 386
- *Honest John M 386 rocket launcher*
65 die Rakete, mit Sprengkopf *m*
- *rocket with warhead*
66 die Startrampe
- *launching ramp*
67 die Höhenrichteinrichtung
- *elevating gear*
68 die Fahrzeugstütze
- *jack*
69 die Seilwinde
- *cable winch*

70 der Raketenwerfer 110 SF
- *110 SF rocket launcher*
71 das Rohrpaket
- *disposable rocket tubes*
72 die Rohrpanzerung
- *tube bins*
73 die Drehringlafette
- *turntable*
74 die Zielzeigereinrichtung
- *fire control system*
75 das Feldarbeitsgerät 2,5 t
- *2.5 tonne construction vehicle*
76 die Hubeinrichtung
- *lifting arms (lifting device)*
77 die Räumschaufel
- *shovel*
78 das Gegengewicht
- *counterweight (counterpoise)*
79-95 Panzer
- *armoured* (Am. *armored*) *vehicles*
79 der Sanitätspanzer M 113
- *M113 armoured (Am. armored)
  ambulance*
80 der Kampfpanzer *Leopard* 1 A 3
- *Leopard 1 A 3 tank*
81 die Walzenblende
- *protection device*
82 der
  Infrarot-Weißlicht-Zielscheinwerfer
- *infrared laser rangefinder*
83 die Nebelwurfbecher *m*
- *smoke canisters (smoke dispensers)*
84 der Panzerturm
- *armoured* (Am. *armored*) *turret*
85 die Kettenblende
- *skirt*
86 die Laufrolle
- *road wheel*
87 die Kette
- *track*
88 der Kanonenjagdpanzer
- *anti-tank tank*
89 der Rauchabsauger
- *fume extractor*
90 die Rohrblende
- *protection device*
91 der Schützenpanzer *Marder*
- *Marder armoured (Am. armored)
  personnel carrier*
92 die Maschinenkanone
- *cannon*
93 der Bergepanzer *Standard*
- *Standard armoured (Am. armored)
  recovery vehicle*
94 die Räum- und Stützschaufel
- *levelling (Am. leveling) and support
  shovel*
95 der Kranausleger
- *jib*
96 der Mehrzweck-Lkw 0,25 t
- *.25 tonne all-purpose vehicle*
97 die abklappbare
  Windschutzscheibe
- *drop windscreen (Am. drop
  windshield)*
98 das Planenverdeck
- *canvas cover*

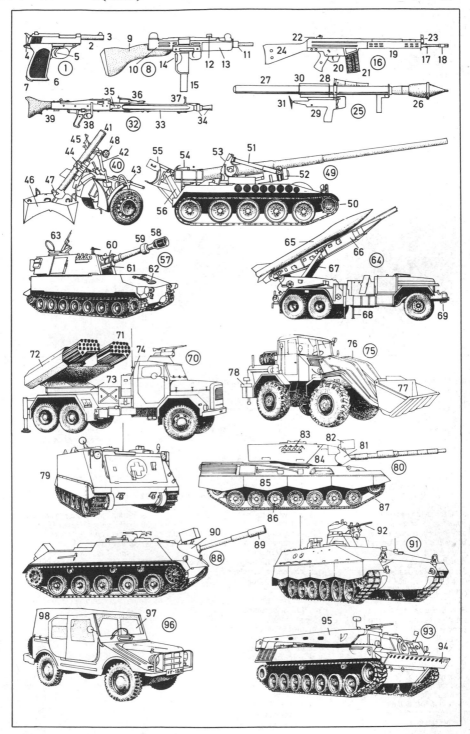

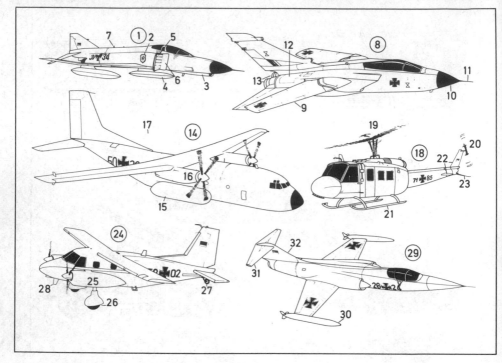

1 **der Abfangjäger und Jagdbomber**
McDonnell-Douglas F-4F
Phantom II
– McDonnell-Douglas F-4F
Phantom II *interceptor and*
fighter-bomber
2 **das Geschwaderabzeichen**
– *squadron marking*
3 die Bordkanone
– *aircraft cannon*
4 der Flügeltank (Unterflügeltank)
– *wing tank (underwing tank)*
5 der Lufteinlaß
– *air intake*
6 die Grenzschichtschneide
– *boundary layer control flap*
7 der Flugbetankungsstutzen
– *in-flight refuelling (Am. refueling)*
probe (flight refuelling probe, air
refuelling probe)
8 **das Mehrzweckkampfflugzeug**
(MRCA, Multirole Combat
Aircraft) *Panavia 200 Tornado*
– Panavia 2000 Tornado *multirole*
combat aircraft (MRCA)
9 die schwenkbare Tragfläche (der
Schwenkflügel)
– *swing wing*
10 die Radarnase (der Radarbug, das
Radom)
– *radar nose (radome, radar dome)*
11 das Staurohr
– *pitot-static tube (pitot tube)*
12 die Bremsklappe (Luftbremse)
– *brake flap (air brake)*
13 die Nachbrennerdüsen *f* der
Triebwerke *n*

– *afterburner exhaust nozzles of the*
engines
14 **das**
Mittelstreckentransportflugzeug *C*
160 Transall
– C160 Transall *medium-range*
transport aircraft
15 die Fahrwerkgondel
– *undercarriage housing (landing*
gear housing)
16 das Propeller-Turbinen-Triebwerk
(Turboproptriebwerk)
– *propeller-turbine engine (turboprop*
engine)
17 die Antenne
– *antenna*
18 **der leichte Transport- und**
Rettungshubschrauber *Bell*
UH-1D Iroquois
– Bell UH-ID Iroquois *light transport*
and rescue helicopter
19 der Hauptrotor
– *main rotor*
20 der Heckrotor
(die Steuerschraube)
– *tail rotor*
21 die Landekufen
– *landing skids*
22 die Stabilisierungsflossen *f*
– *stabilizing fins*
(stabilizing
surfaces, stabilizers)
23 der Sporn
– *tail skid*
24 **das STOL-Transport- und**
Verbindungsflugzeug *Dornier DO*
28 D-2 Skyservant

– Dornier DO 28 D-2 Skyservant
transport and communications
aircraft
25 die Triebwerksgondel
– *engine pod*
26 das Hauptfahrwerk
– *main undercarriage unit (main*
landing gear unit)
27 das Spornrad
– *tail wheel*
28 die Schwertantenne
– *sword antenna*
29 **der Jagdbomber** *F-104 G*
Starfighter
– F-104 G Starfighter *fighter-bomber*
30 der Flügelspitzentank (Tiptank)
– *wing-tip tank (tip tank)*
31-32 das T-Leitwerk
– *T-tail (T-tail unit)*
31 die Höhenflosse (der Stabilisator)
– *tailplane (horizontal stabilizer,*
stabilizer)
32 die Seitenflosse
– *vertical stabilizer (vertical fin, tail*
fin)

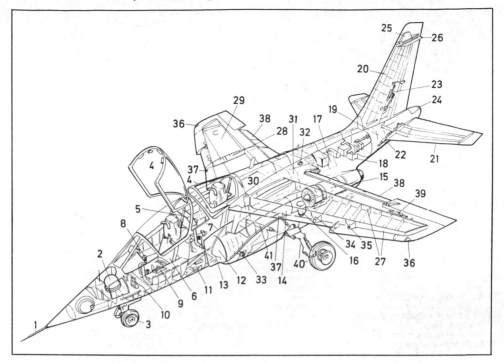

1-41 der deutsch-französische
  Strahltrainer
  Dornier-Dassault-Breguet Alpha Jet
- Dornier-Dassault-Breguet Alpha
  Jet *Franco-German jet trainer*
1 das Staurohr
- *pitot-static tube (pitot tube)*
2 der Sauerstoffbehälter
- *oxygen tank*
3 das vorwärts einfahrende Bugrad
- *forward-retracting nose wheel*
4 die Kabinenhaube
- *cockpit canopy (cockpit hood)*
5 der Haubenzylinder
- *canopy jack*
6 der Flugzeugführersitz
  (Schülersitz), ein Schleudersitz *m*
- *pilot's seat (student pilot's seat), an
  ejector seat (ejection seat)*
7 der Kampfbeobachtersitz
  (Lehrersitz), ein Schleudersitz *m*
- *observer's seat (instructor's seat),
  an ejector seat (ejection seat)*
8 der Steuerknüppel
- *control column (control stick)*
9 die Leistungshebel *m*
- *thrust lever*
10 die Seitenruderpedale *n* mit Bremsen *f*
- *rudder pedals with brakes*
11 der Frontavionikraum
- *front avionics bay*
12 der Triebwerkslufteinlauf
- *air intake to the engine*
13 die Grenzschicht-Trennzunge
- *boundary layer control flap*
14 der Lufteinlaufkanal
- *air intake duct*

15 das Turbinentriebwerk
- *turbine engine*
16 der Hydraulikspeicher
- *reservoir for the hydraulic system*
17 der Batterieraum
- *battery housing*
18 der Heckavionikraum
- *rear avionics bay*
19 der Gepäckraum
- *baggage compartment*
20 der dreiholmige Leitwerkaufbau
- *triple-spar tail construction*
21 das Höhenleitwerk
- *horizontal tail*
22 die Höhenleitwerk-Rudermaschine
- *servo-actuating mechanism for the
  elevator*
23 die Seitenrudermaschine
- *servo-actuating mechanism for the
  rudder*
24 der Bremsschirmkasten
- *brake chute housing (drag chute
  housing)*
25 die VHF-Antenne
  (UKW-Antenne) *[VHF: Very high
  frequency]*
- *VHF (very high frequency) antenna
  (UHF antenna)*
26 die VOR-Antenne *[VOR: Very
  high frequency omnidirectional range]*
- *VOR (very high frequency
  omnidirectional range) antenna*
27 der zweiholmige
  Tragflächenaufbau
- *twin-spar wing construction*
28 die holmintegrierte Beplankung
- *former with integral spars*

29 die Integralflächentanks *m*
- *integral wing tanks*
30 der Rumpfzentraltank
- *centre-section* (Am. *center-section)
  fuel tank*
31 die Rumpftanks *m*
- *fuselage tanks*
32 der Schwerkraftfüllstutzen
- *gravity fuelling* (Am. *fueling) point*
33 der Druckbetankungsanschluß
- *pressure fuelling* (Am. *fueling)
  point*
34 die innere Flügelaufhängung
- *inner wing suspension*
35 die äußere Flügelaufhängung
- *outer wing suspension*
36 die Positionsleuchten *f*
- *navigation lights (position lights)*
37 die Landescheinwerfer *m*
- *landing lights*
38 die Landeklappe
- *landing flap*
39 die Querruderbetätigung
- *aileron actuator*
40 das vorwärts einfahrende
  Hauptfahrwerk
- *forward-retracting main
  undercarriage unit (main landing
  gear unit)*
41 der Fahrwerk-Ausfahrzylinder
- *undercarriage hydraulic cylinder
  (landing gear hydraulic cylinder)*

1-63 leichte Kampfschiffe *n*
- *light battleships*
1 der Raketenzerstörer
- *destroyer*
2 der Glattdecksrumpf
(Flushdecksrumpf)
- *hull of flush-deck vessel*
3 der Bug (Steven)
- *bow (stem)*
4 der Flaggenstock (Göschstock)
- *flagstaff (jackstaff)*
5 der Anker, ein Patentanker *m*
- *anchor, a stockless anchor (patent anchor)*
6 das Ankerspill
- *anchor capstan (windlass)*
7 der Wellenbrecher
- *breakwater (Am. manger board)*
8 das (*auch:* der) Knickspant
- *chine strake*
9 das Hauptdeck
- *main deck*
10-28 die Aufbauten *pl*
- *superstructures*
10 das Aufbaudeck
- *superstructure deck*
11 die Rettungsinseln *f*
- *life rafts*
12 der Kutter (das Beiboot)
- *cutter (ship's boat)*
13 der Davit (Bootsaussetzkran)
- *davit (boat-launching crane)*
14 die Brücke (Kommandobrücke, der Brückenaufbau)
- *bridge (bridge superstructure)*
15 die Positionsseitenlampe
- *side navigation light (side running light)*
16 die Antenne
- *antenna*
17 der Funkpeilrahmen
- *radio direction finder (RDF) frame*
18 der Gittermast
- *lattice mast*
19 der vordere Schornstein
- *forward funnel*
20 der achtere (hintere) Schornstein
- *aft funnel*
21 die Schornsteinkappe
- *cowl*
22 der achtere (hintere) Aufbau (die Hütte)
- *aft superstructure (poop)*
23 das Spill
- *capstan*
24 der Niedergang (das Luk)
- *companion ladder (companionway, companion hatch)*
25 der Heckflaggenstock
- *ensign staff*
26 das Heck, ein Spiegelheck *n*
- *stern, a transom stern*
27 die Wasserlinie
- *waterline*
28 der Scheinwerfer
- *searchlight*
29-37 die Bewaffnung
- *armament*
29 der Geschützturm (Turm) 100 mm
- *100 mm gun turret*
30 der U-Boot-Abwehr-Raketenwerfer, ein Vierling *m*
- *four-barrel anti-submarine rocket launcher (missile launcher)*
31 die Zwillingsflak 40 mm
- *40 mm twin anti-aircraft (AA) gun*

32 der Flugabwehrraketenstarter MM 38, im Abschußcontainer *m*
- *MM 38 anti-aircraft (AA) rocket launcher (missile launcher) in launching container*
33 das U-Boot-Jagd-Torpedorohr
- *anti-submarine torpedo tube*
34 die Wasserbombenablaufbühne
- *depth-charge thrower*
35 der Waffenleitradar
- *weapon system radar*
36 die Radarantenne
- *radar antenna (radar scanner)*
37 der optische Entfernungsmesser
- *optical rangefinder*
38 der Raketenzerstörer
- *destroyer*
39 der Buganker
- *bower anchor*
40 der Schraubenschutz
- *propeller guard*
41 der Dreibeingittermast
- *tripod lattice mast*
42 der Pfahlmast
- *pole mast*
43 die Lüfteröffnungen *f*
- *ventilator openings (ventilator grill)*
44 das Rauchabzugsrohr
- *exhaust pipe*
45 die Pinaß
- *ship's boat*
46 die Antenne
- *antenna*
47 die radargesteuerte Allzielkanone 127 mm im Geschützturm *m*
- *radar-controlled 127 mm all-purpose gun in turret*
48 das Allzielgeschütz 127 mm
- *127 mm all-purpose gun*
49 der Raketenstarter für Tartar-Flugkörper *m*
- *launcher for Tartar missiles*
50 der Asroc-Starter (U-Boot-Abwehr-Raketenwerfer)
- *anti-submarine rocket (ASROC) launcher (missile launcher)*
51 die Feuerleitradar-Antennen *f*
- *fire control radar antennas*
52 das Radom (der Radardom)
- *radome (radar dome)*
53 die Fregatte
- *frigate*
54 die Ankerklüse
- *hawse pipe*
55 die Dampferlaterne (das Dampferlicht)
- *steaming light*
56 die Positionslampe (das Positionslicht)
- *navigation light (running light)*
57 der Luftansaugschacht
- *air extractor duct*
58 der Schornstein
- *funnel*
59 der Rauchabweiser (die Schornsteinkappe)
- *cowl*
60 die Peitschenantenne
- *whip antenna (fishpole antenna)*
61 der Kutter
- *cutter*
62 die Hecklaterne
- *stern light*
63 der Schraubenschutzwulst
- *propeller guard boss*

64-91 Kampfboote *n*
- *fighting ships*
64 das Unterseeboot (U-Boot)
- *submarine*
65 die durchflutete Back
- *flooded foredeck*
66 der Druckkörper
- *pressure hull*
67 der Turm
- *turret*
68 die Ausfahrgeräte *n*
- *retractable instruments*
69 das Flugkörperschnellboot
- *E-boat (torpedo boat)*
70 das Allzielgeschütz 76 mm mit Turm *m*
- *76 mm all-purpose gun with turret*
71 der Flugkörperstartcontainer
- *missile-launching housing*
72 das Deckshaus
- *deckhouse*
73 die Fla-Kanone 40 mm
- *40 mm anti-aircraft (AA) gun*
74 die Schraubenschutzleiste
- *propeller guard moulding (Am. molding)*
75 das Flugkörperschnellboot E-boat (torpedo boat)
76 der Wellenbrecher
- *breakwater (Am. manger board)*
77 das Radom (der Radardom)
- *radome (radar dome)*
78 das Torpedorohr
- *torpedo tube*
79 die Abgasöffnung
- *exhaust escape flue*
80 das Minenjagdboot
- *mine hunter*
81 die Scheuerleiste, mit Verstärkungen *f*
- *reinforced rubbing strake*
82 das Schlauchboot
- *inflatable boat (inflatable dinghy)*
83 der Bootsdavit
- *davit*
84 das Schnelle Minensuchboot
- *minesweeper*
85 die Kabeltrommelwinde
- *cable winch*
86 die Schleppwinde (Winsch)
- *towing winch (towing machine, towing engine)*
87 das Minenräumgerät (die Ottern *m*, Schwimmer)
- *mine-sweeping gear (paravanes)*
88 der Kran
- *crane (davit)*
89 das Landungsboot
- *landing craft*
90 die Bugrampe
- *bow ramp*
91 die Heckrampe
- *stern ramp*
92-97 Hilfsschiffe *n*
- *auxiliaries*
92 der Tender
- *tender*
93 der Versorger
- *servicing craft*
94 der Minentransporter
- *minelayer*
95 das Schulschiff
- *training ship*
96 der Hochseebergungsschlepper
- *deep-sea salvage tug*
97 der Betriebsstofftanker
- *fuel tanker (replenishing ship)*

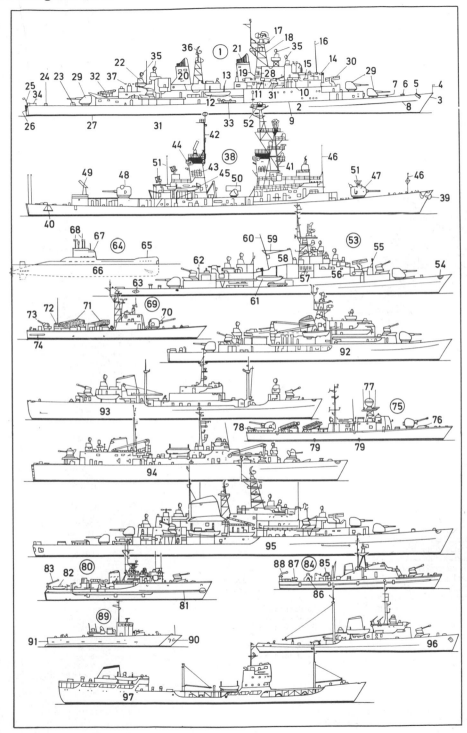

259 Kriegsschiffe II (moderne Kampfschiffe)

1 der atomgetriebene Flugzeugträger
„Nimitz ICVN 68" (USA)
- **nuclear-powered aircraft carrier**
'Nimitz ICVN68' *(USA)*
2-11 der Seitenriß
- *body plan*
2 das Flugdeck
- *flight deck*
3 die Insel (Kommandobrücke)
- *island (bridge)*
4 der Flugzeugaufzug
- *aircraft lift (Am. aircraft elevator)*
5 der Achtfach-Flarak-Starter
- *eight-barrel anti-aircraft (AA)
rocket launcher (missile launcher)*
6 der Pfahlmast (Antennenträger)
- *pole mast (antenna mast)*
7 die Antenne
- *antenna*
8 die Radarantenne
- *radar antenna (radar scanner)*
9 der vollgeschlossene Orkanbug
- *fully enclosed bow*
10 der Bordkran
- *deck crane*
11 das Spiegelheck
- *transom stern*
12-20 der Decksplan
- *deck plan*
12 das Winkeldeck (Flugdeck)
- *angle deck (flight deck)*
13 der Flugzeugaufzug
- *aircraft lift (Am. aircraft elevator)*
14 das Doppelstartkatapult
- *twin launching catapult*
15 die versenkbare Flammenschutzwand
- *hinged (movable) baffle board*
16 das Landefangseil (Bremsseil)
- *arrester wire*
17 die Barriere (das Notauffangnetz)
- *emergency crash barrier*
18 der Catgang
- *safety net*
19 das Schwalbennest
- *caisson (cofferdam)*
20 der Achtfach-Flarak-Starter
- *eight-barrel anti-aircraft (AA)
rocket launcher (missile launcher)*
21 der Raketenkreuzer der
„Kara"-Klasse (UdSSR)
- 'Kara' class **rocket cruiser** *(missile
cruiser) (USSR)*
22 der Glattdecksrumpf
- *hull of flush-deck vessel*
23 der Deckssprung
- *sheer*
24 der U-Jagdraketensalvenwerfer,
ein Zwölfling *m*
- *twelve-barrel underwater salvo
rocket launcher (missile launcher)*
25 der Flugabwehrraketenstarter, ein
Zwilling *m*
- *twin anti-aircraft (AA) rocket
launcher (missile launcher)*
26 der Startbehälter für 4
Kurzstreckenraketen *f*
- *launching housing for 4
short-range rockets (missiles)*
27 die Flammenschutzwand
- *baffle board*
28 die Brücke
- *bridge*
29 die Radarantenne
- *radar antenna (radar scanner)*
30 der Fla-Zwillingsturm 76 mm
- *twin 76 mm anti-aircraft (AA) gun turret*
31 der Gefechtsturm
- *turret*

32 der Schornstein
- *funnel*
33 der Fla-Raketenstarterzwilling
- *twin anti-aircraft (AA) rocket
launcher (missile launcher)*
34 die Fla-Maschinenkanone
- *automatic anti-aircraft (AA) gun*
35 das Beiboot
- *ship's boat*
36 der U-Jagdtorpedofünflingssatz
- *underwater 5-torpedo housing*
37 der U-Jagdraketensalvenwerfer,
ein Sechsling *m*
- *underwater 6-salvo rocket launcher
(missile launcher)*
38 der Hubschrauberhangar
- *helicopter hangar*
39 die Hubschrauberlandeplattform
- *helicopter landing platform*
40 das tiefenveränderbare Sonargerät (VDS)
- *variable depth sonar (VDS)*
41 der atomgetriebene
Raketenkreuzer der
„California"-Klasse (USA)
- 'California' class **rocket cruiser**
(missile cruiser) (USA)
42 der Rumpf
- *hull*
43 der vordere Gefechtsturm
- *forward turret*
44 der achtere (hintere) Gefechtsturm
- *aft turret*
45 der Backsaufbau
- *forward superstructure*
46 die Landungsboote
- *landing craft*
47 die Antenne
- *antenna*
48 die Radarantenne
- *radar antenna (radar scanner)*
49 das Radom (der Radardom)
- *radome (radar dome)*
50 der Luftzielraketenstarter
- *surface-to-air rocket launcher
(missile launcher)*
51 der U-Jagdraketentorpedostarter
- *underwater rocket launcher (missile
launcher)*
52 das Geschütz 127 mm mit Geschützturm *m*
- *127 mm gun with turret*
53 die Hubschrauberlandeplattform
- *helicopter landing platform*
54 das U-Jagd-Atom-U-Boot (der
Subsubkiller)
- **nuclear-powered fleet submarine**
55-74 die Mittelschiffsektion [schematisch]
- *middle section [diagram]*
55 der Druckkörper
- *pressure hull*
56 der Hilfsmaschinenraum
- *auxiliary engine room*
57 die Kreiselturbopumpe
- *rotary turbine pump*
58 der Dampfturbinengenerator
- *steam turbine generator*
59 die Schraubenwelle
- *propeller shaft*
60 das Drucklager
- *thrust block*
61 das Untersetzungsgetriebe
- *reduction gear*
62 die Hoch- und Niederdruckturbine
- *high and low pressure turbine*
63 das Hochdruckdampfrohr des
Sekundärkreislaufs *m*
- *high-pressure steam pipe for the
secondary water circuit (auxiliary
water circuit)*

64 der Kondensator
- *condenser*
65 der Primärkreislauf
- *primary water circuit*
66 der Wärmetauscher
- *heat exchanger*
67 der Atomreaktormantel
- *nuclear reactor casing (atomic pile
casing)*
68 der Reaktorkern
- *reactor core*
69 die Steuerelemente *n*
- *control rods*
70 die Bleiabschirmung
- *lead screen*
71 der Turm
- *turret*
72 der Schnorchel
- *snorkel (schnorkel)*
73 die Lufteintrittsöffnung
- *air inlet*
74 die Ausfahrgeräte *n*
- *retractable instruments*
75 das Einhüllen-Küsten-U-Boot mit
konventionellem
(dieselelektrischem) Antrieb *m*
- **patrol submarine** *with conventional
(diesel-electric) drive*
76 der Druckkörper
- *pressure hull*
77 die durchflutete Back
- *flooded foredeck*
78 die Mündungsklappe
- *outer flap (outer doors) [for
torpedoes]*
79 das Torpedorohr
- *torpedo tube*
80 die Bugraumbilge
- *bow bilge*
81 der Anker
- *anchor*
82 die Ankerwinsch
- *anchor winch*
83 die Batterie
- *battery*
84 Wohnräume *m* mit Klappkojen *f*
- *living quarters with folding bunks*
85 der Kommandantenraum (das
Kommandantenschapp)
- *commanding officer's cabin*
86 das Zentralluk
- *main hatchway*
87 der Flaggenstock
- *flagstaff*
88-91 die Ausfahrgeräte *n*
- *retractable instruments*
88 das A-Sehrohr (Angriffssehrohr)
- *attack periscope*
89 die Antenne
- *antenna*
90 der Schnorchel
- *snorkel (schnorkel)*
91 die Radarantenne
- *radar antenna (radar scanner)*
92 die Abgaslippen *f*
- *exhaust outlet*
93 der Wintergarten
- *heat space (hot-pipe space)*
94 das Dieselaggregat
- *diesel generators*
95 das hintere Tiefen- und
Seitenruder
- *aft diving plane and vertical rudder*
96 das vordere Tiefenruder
- *forward vertical rudder*

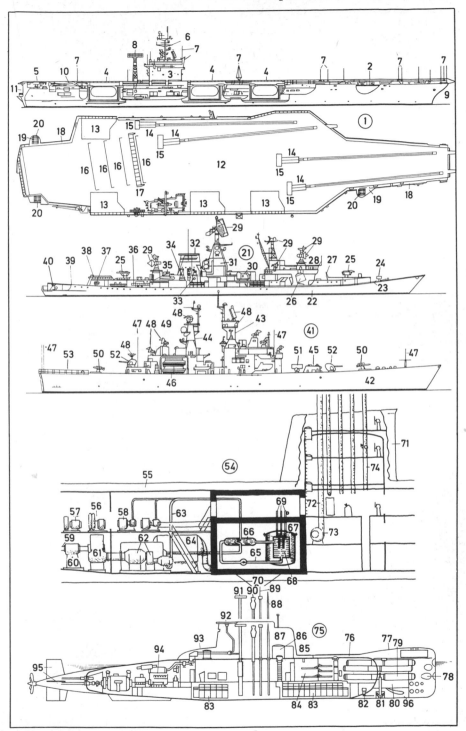

1-85 die Grund- und Hauptschule
(ugs. Volksschule)
- *primary school*
1-45 das Klassenzimmer (der
Klassenraum)
- *classroom*
1 die Tischaufstellung in
Hufeisenform *f*
- *arrangement of desks in a
horseshoe*
2 der Doppeltisch
- *double desk*
3 die Schüler *m* in
Gruppenanordnung *f*
- *pupils (children) in a group (sitting
in a group)*
4 das Übungsheft
- *exercise book*
5 der Bleistift (Zeichenstift)
- *pencil*
6 der Wachsmalstift
- *wax crayon*
7 die Schultasche (Schulmappe)
- *school bag*
8 der Traggriff (Griff, Henkel)
- *handle*
9 der Schulranzen (Ranzen)
- *school satchel (satchel)*
10 das Vorfach
- *front pocket*
11 der Tragriemen (Schulterriemen)
- *strap (shoulder strap)*
12 das Federmäppchen (die
Federmappe)
- *pen and pencil case*
13 der Reißverschluß
- *zip*
14 der Füllfederhalter (Füllhalter,
Füller)
- *fountain pen (pen)*
15 das Ringbuch (der Ringhefter)
- *loose-leaf file (ring file)*
16 das Lesebuch
- *reader*
17 das Rechtschreibungsbuch
- *spelling book*
18 das Schreibheft
- *notebook (exercise book)*
19 der Filzstift
- *felt tip pen*
20 das Melden (Handheben)
- *raising the hand*
21 der Lehrer
- *teacher*
22 der Lehrertisch
- *teacher's desk*
23 das Klassenbuch
- *register*
24 die Schreibschale
- *pen and pencil tray*
25 die Schreibunterlage
- *desk mat (blotter)*
26 die Fenstermalerei in Fingerfarben
f (die Fingermalerei *f*)
- *window painting with finger paints
(finger painting)*
27 die Schüleraquarelle *n*
- *pupils' (children's) paintings
(watercolours)*
28 das Kreuz
- *cross*
29 die dreiflügelige Tafel (Schultafel,
Wandtafel)
- *three-part blackboard*
30 der Kartenhalter
- *bracket for holding charts*

31 die Kreideablage
- *chalk ledge*
32 die (weiße) Kreide
- *(white) chalk*
33 die Tafelzeichnung
- *blackboard drawing*
34 die Schemazeichnung
- *diagram*
35 die umklappbare Seitentafel
- *reversible side blackboard*
36 die Projektionsfläche
(Projektionswand)
- *projection screen*
37 das Winkellineal
- *triangle*
38 der Winkelmesser
- *protractor*
39 die Gradeinteilung
- *divisions*
40 der Tafelzirkel (Kreidezirkel)
- *blackboard compass*
41 die Schwammschale
- *sponge tray*
42 der Tafelschwamm (Schwamm)
- *blackboard sponge (sponge)*
43 der Klassenschrank
- *classroom cupboard*
44 die Landkarte (Wandkarte)
- *map (wall map)*
45 die Backsteinwand
- *brick wall*
46-85 der Werkraum
- *craft room*
46 der Werktisch
- *workbench*
47 die Schraubzwinge
- *vice* (Am. *vise*)
48 der Zwingenknebel
- *vice* (Am. *vise*) *bar*
49 die Schere
- *scissors*
50-52 die Klebearbeit
- *working with glue (sticking paper,
cardboard, etc.)*
50 die Klebefläche
- *surface to be glued*
51 die Klebstofftube
(ugs. der Alleskleber)
- *tube of glue*
52 der Tubenverschluß
- *tube cap*
53 die Laubsäge
- *fretsaw*
54 das Laubsägeblatt (Sägeblatt)
- *fretsaw blade (saw blade)*
55 die Holzraspel (Raspel)
- *wood rasp (rasp)*
56 das eingespannte Holzstück
- *piece of wood held in the vice*
(Am. *vise*)
57 der Leimtopf
- *glue pot*
58 der Hocker
- *stool*
59 der Kehrbesen
- *brush*
60 die Kehrschaufel
- *pan (dust pan)*
61 die Scherben *f*
- *broken china*
62 die Emailarbeit (Emaillearbeit)
- *enamelling*
(Am. *enameling*)
63 der elektrische Emaillierofen
- *electric enamelling*
(Am. *enameling*) *stove*

64 der Kupferrohling
- *unworked copper*
65 das Emailpulver
- *enamel powder*
66 das Haarsieb
- *hair sieve*
67-80 die Schülerarbeiten *f*
- *pupils' (childrens) work*
67 die Tonplastiken *f* (Formarbeiten)
- *clay models (models)*
68 der Fensterschmuck aus farbigem
Glas *n*
- *window decoration of coloured
(Am. colored) glass*
69 das Glasmosaikbild
- *glass mosaic picture (glass mosaic)*
70 das Mobile
- *mobile*
71 der Papierdrachen (Drachen,
Flugdrachen)
- *paper kite (kite)*
72 die Holzkonstruktion
- *wooden construction*
73 der Polyeder
- *polyhedron*
74 die Kasperlefiguren *f*
- *hand puppets*
75 die Tonmasken *f*
- *clay masks*
76 die gegossenen Kerzen *f*
(Wachskerzen)
- *cast candles (wax candles)*
77 die Holzschnitzerei
- *wood carving*
78 der Tonkrug
- *clay jug*
79 die geometrischen Formen *f* aus
Ton *m*
- *geometrical shapes made of clay*
80 das Holzspielzeug
- *wooden toys*
81 das Arbeitsmaterial
- *materials*
82 der Holzvorrat
- *stock of wood*
83 die Druckfarben *f*, für
Holzschnitte *m*
- *inks for wood cuts*
84 die Malpinsel *m*
- *paintbrushes*
85 der Gipssack
- *bag of plaster of Paris*

1-45 das Gymnasium, *auch:* der Gymnasialzweig einer Gesamtschule
- *grammar school; also: upper band of a comprehensive school (Am. alternative school)*

1-13 der Chemieunterricht
- *chemistry*

1 der Chemiesaal mit ansteigenden Sitzreihen *f*
- *chemistry lab (chemistry laboratory) with tiered rows of seats*

2 der Chemielehrer
- *chemistry teacher*

3 der Experimentiertisch
- *demonstration bench (teacher's bench)*

4 der Wasseranschluß
- *water pipe*

5 die gekachelte Arbeitsfläche
- *tiled working surface*

6 das Ausgußbecken
- *sink*

7 der Videomonitor, ein Bildschirm *m* für Lehrprogramme *n*
- *television monitor, a screen for educational programmes (Am. programs)*

8 der Overheadprojektor (Arbeitsprojektor)
- *overhead projector*

9 die Auflagefläche für die Transparente *n*
- *projector top for skins*

10 die Projektionsoptik, mit Winkelspiegel *m*
- *projection lens with right-angle mirror*

11 der Schülertisch mit Experimentiereinrichtung *f*
- *pupils' (Am. students') bench with experimental apparatus*

12 der Stromanschluß (die Steckdose)
- *electrical point (socket)*

13 der Projektionstisch
- *projection table*

14-34 der Vorbereitungsraum für den Biologieunterricht
- *biology preparation room (biology prep room)*

14 das Skelett (Gerippe)
- *skeleton*

15 die Schädelsammlung, Nachbildungen *f* (Abgüsse *m*) von Schädeln *m*
- *collection of skulls, models (casts) of skulls*

16 die Kalotte (das Schädeldach) des Pithecanthropus erectus *m*
- *calvarium of Pithecanthropus erectus*

17 der Schädel des Homo steinheimensis *m*
- *skull of Steinheim man*

18 die Kalotte (das Schädeldach) des Sinanthropus *m*
- *calvarium of Peking man (of Sinanthropus)*

19 der Neanderthalerschädel, ein Altmenschenschädel *m*
- *skull of Neanderthal man, a skull of primitive man*

20 der Australopithecusschädel
- *australopithecine skull (skull of Australopithecus)*

21 der Schädel des Jetztmenschen *m*
- *skull of present-day man*

22 der Präpariertisch
- *dissecting bench*

23 die Chemikalienflaschen *f*
- *chemical bottles*

24 der Gasanschluß
- *gas tap*

25 die Petrischale
- *petri dish*

26 der Meßzylinder
- *measuring cylinder*

27 die Arbeitsbogen *m* (das Lehrmaterial)
- *work folder (teaching material)*

28 das Lehrbuch
- *textbook*

29 die bakteriologischen Kulturen
- *bacteriological cultures*

30 der Brutschrank
- *incubator*

31 der Probierglastrockner
- *test tube rack*

32 die Gaswaschflasche
- *washing bottle*

33 die Wasserschale
- *water tank*

34 der Ausguß
- *sink*

35 das Sprachlabor
- *language laboratory*

36 die Wandtafel
- *blackboard*

37 die Lehrereinheit (das zentrale Schaltpult)
- *console*

38 der Kopfhörer
- *headphones (headset)*

39 das Mikrophon
- *microphone*

40 die Ohrmuschel
- *earcups*

41 der gepolsterte Kopfhörerbügel
- *padded headband (padded headpiece)*

42 der Programmrecorder, ein Kassettenrecorder *m*
- *programme (Am. program) recorder, a cassette recorder*

43 der Lautstärkeregler für die Schülerstimme
- *pupil's (Am. student's) volume control*

44 der Programmlautstärkeregler
- *master volume control*

45 die Bedienungstasten *f*
- *control buttons (operating keys)*

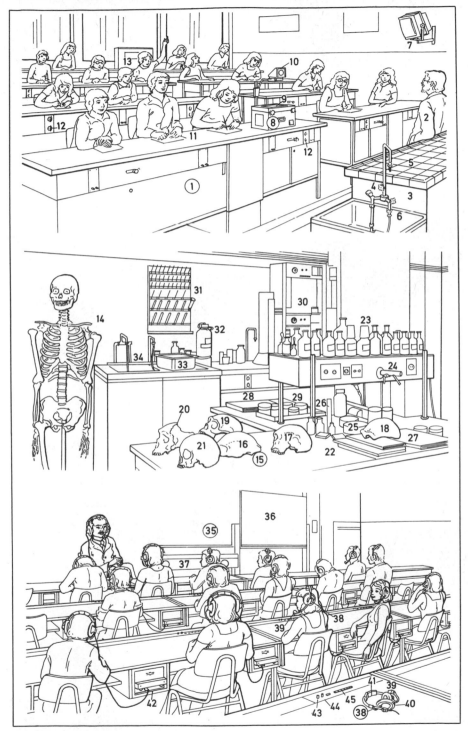

1-25 die Universität
(Hochschule; *stud.* Uni)
- *university (college)*
1 die Vorlesung (das Kolleg)
- *lecture*
2 der Hörsaal (das Auditorium)
- *lecture room (lecture theatre,*
Am. *theater)*
3 der Dozent (Hochschullehrer), ein
Universitätsprofessor *m* oder Lektor
- *lecturer (university lecturer, college*
lecturer, Am. *assistant professor),*
a university professor or assistant
lecturer
4 das (der) Katheder (das Vortragspult)
- *lectern*
5 das Manuskript
- *lecture notes*
6 der Assistent
- *demonstrator*
7 der hilfswissenschaftliche Assistent
(Famulus)
- *assistant*
8 das Lehrbild
- *diagram*
9 der Student
- *student*
10 die Studentin
- *student*
11-25 die Universitätsbibliothek;
ähnl.: Staatsbibliothek,
wissenschaftliche Landes- oder
Stadtbibliothek

- *university library;* sim.: *national*
library, regional or municipal
scientific library
11 das Büchermagazin, mit den
Bücherbeständen *pl*
- *stack (book stack) with the stock of*
books
12 das Bücherregal, ein Stahlregal *n*
- *bookshelf, a steel shelf*
13 der Lesesaal
- *reading room*
14 die Aufsicht, eine Bibliothekarin
- *member of the reading room staff,*
a librarian
15 das Zeitschriftenregal, mit
Zeitschriften *f*
- *periodicals rack with periodicals*
16 das Zeitungsregal
- *newspaper shelf*
17 die Präsenzbibliothek
(Handbibliothek), mit
Nachschlagewerken *n*
(Handbüchern, Lexika,
Enzyklopädien *f,* Wörterbüchern *n*)
- *reference library with reference*
books (handbooks, encyclopedias,
dictionaries)
18 die Bücherausleihe (der
Ausleihsaal) und der Katalograum
- *lending library and catalogue*
(Am. *catalog) room*
19 der Bibliothekar
- *librarian*

20 das Ausleihpult
- *issue desk*
21 der Hauptkatalog
- *main catalogue (*Am. *catalog)*
22 der Karteischrank
- *card catalogue (*Am. *catalog)*
23 der Karteikasten
- *card catalogue (*Am. *catalog)*
drawer
24 der Bibliotheksbenutzer
- *library user*
25 der Leihschein
- *borrower's ticket (library ticket)*

1-15 die Wahlversammlung
  (Wählerversammlung), eine
  Massenversammlung
- *election meeting, a public meeting*
1-2 der Vorstand
- *committee*
1 der Versammlungsleiter
- *chairman*
2 der Beisitzer
- *committee member*
3 der Vorstandstisch
- *committee table*
4 die Glocke
- *bell*
5 der Wahlredner
- *election speaker (speaker)*
6 das Rednerpult
- *rostrum*
7 das Mikrophon
- *microphone*
8 die Versammlung (Volksmenge)
- *meeting (audience)*
9 der Flugblattverteiler
- *man distributing leaflets*
10 der Saalschutz
  (ein Ordner *m*)
- *stewards*
11 die Armbinde
- *armband (armlet)*
12 das Spruchband
- *banner*
13 das Wahlschild
- *placard*

14 der Aufruf
- *proclamation*
15 der Zwischenrufer
- *heckler*
16-30 die Wahl
- *election*
16 das Wahllokal (der Wahlraum)
- *polling station (polling place)*
17 der Wahlhelfer
- *election officer*
18 die Wählerkartei (Wahlkartei)
- *electoral register*
19 die Wählerkarte, mit der
  Wahlnummer
- *polling card with registration
  number (polling number)*
20 der Stimmzettel, mit den Namen *m*
  der Parteien *f* und
  Parteikandidaten *m*
- *ballot paper with the names of the
  parties and candidates*
21 der Abstimmungsumschlag
- *ballot envelope*
22 die Wählerin
- *voter*
23 die Wahlzelle (Wahlkabine)
- *polling booth*
24 der Wähler mit Stimmrecht *n*
  (Wahlberechtigte *m*,
  Stimmberechtigte *m*)
- *elector (qualified voter)*
25 die Wahlordnung
- *election regulations*

26 der Schriftführer
- *clerk*
27 der Führer der Gegenliste
- *clerk with the duplicate list*
28 der Wahlvorsteher
  (Abstimmungsleiter)
- *election supervisor*
29 die Wahlurne
- *ballot box*
30 der Urnenschlitz
- *slot*

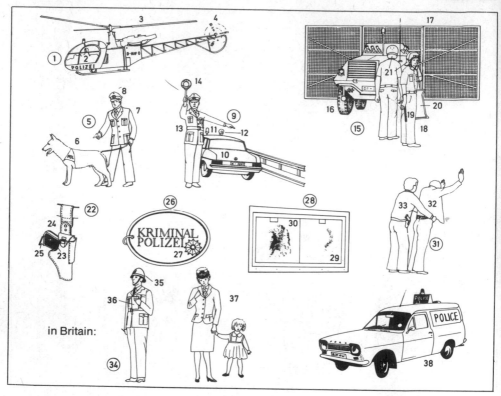

in Britain:

1-33 der Polizeivollzugsdienst
- *police duties*
1 der Polizeihubschrauber
  (Verkehrshubschrauber), zur
  Verkehrsüberwachung aus der
  Luft
- *police helicopter (traffic helicopter)
  for controlling (Am. controling)
  traffic from the air*
2 die Pilotenkanzel
- *cockpit*
3 der Rotor (Hauptrotor)
- *rotor (main rotor)*
4 der Heckrotor
- *tail rotor*
5 der Polizeihundeeinsatz
- *use of police dogs*
6 der Polizeihund
- *police dog*
7 die Uniform (Dienstkleidung)
- *uniform*
8 die Dienstmütze, eine
  Schirmmütze mit Kokarde *f*
- *uniform cap, a peaked cap with
  cockade*
9 die Verkehrskontrolle einer
  motorisierten Verkehrsstreife
- *traffic control by a mobile traffic
  patrol*
10 der Streifenwagen
- *patrol car*
11 das Blaulicht
- *blue light*

12 der Lautsprecher
- *loud hailer (loudspeaker)*
13 der Streifenbeamte
- *patrolman (police patrolman)*
14 die Polizeikelle
- *police signalling (Am. signaling)
  disc (disk)*
15 der Demonstrationseinsatz
- *riot duty*
16 der Sonderwagen
- *special armoured
  (Am. armored)
  car*
17 das Räumgitter
- *barricade*
18 der Polizeibeamte in
  Schutzkleidung *f*
- *policeman (police officer) in riot
  gear*
19 die Hiebwaffe (ugs.
  der Gummiknüppel)
- *truncheon (baton)*
20 der Schutzschild
- *riot shield*
21 der Schutzhelm
- *protective helmet (helmet)*
22 die Dienstpistole
- *service pistol*
23 der Pistolengriff
- *pistol grip*
24 das Schnellziehholster
  (die Pistolentasche)
- *quick-draw holster*

25 das Pistolenmagazin
- *magazine*
26 die Dienstmarke der
  Kriminalpolizei *f*
- *police identification disc (disk)*
27 der Polizeistern
- *police badge*
28 der Fingerabdruckvergleich
  (die Daktyloskopie)
- *fingerprint identification
  (dactyloscopy)*
29 der Fingerabdruck
- *fingerprint*
30 die Leuchttafel
- *illuminated screen*
31 die körperliche Durchsuchung
  (Leibesvisitation)
- *search*
32 der Verdächtige
- *suspect*
33 der Kriminalbeamte in
  Zivilkleidung *f*
- *detective (plainclothes policeman)*
34 der englische Bobby
- *English policeman*
35 der Helm
- *helmet*
36 das Notizbuch
- *pocket book*
37 die Polizistin
- *policewoman*
38 der Polizeiwagen
- *police van*

1-26 das Café (Kaffee, Kaffeehaus) mit Konditorei *f*; *ähnl.*: das Espresso, die Teestube
- *café, serving cakes and pastries;* sim.: *espresso bar, tea room*
1 das Büfett (Kuchenbüfett, Konditoreibüfett, *österr.* Büffet)
- *counter (cake counter)*
2 die Großkaffeemaschine
- *coffee urn*
3 der Zahlteller
- *tray for the money*
4 die Torte
- *gateau*
5 das Baiser (*obd.* und *österr.* die Meringe, *schweiz.* Meringue), ein Zuckerschaumgebäck *n* mit Schlagsahne *f* (Schlagrahm *m*, *bayr.-österr.* Schlagobers *n*, Obers)
- *meringue with whipped cream*
6 der Auszubildende (Azubi); *früh.*: Konditoreilehrling
- *trainee pastry cook*
7 das Büfettfräulein (die Büfettdame, *österr.* Büffetdame)
- *girl (lady) at the counter*
8 der Zeitungsschrank (das Zeitungsregal)
- *newspaper shelves (newspaper rack)*
9 die Wandleuchte
- *wall lamp*
10 die Eckbank, eine Polsterbank
- *corner seat, an upholstered seat*

11 der Kaffeehaustisch
- *café table*
12 die Marmorplatte
- *marble top*
13 die Serviererin
- *waitress*
14 das Tablett (Auftragetablett, Serviertablett, Servierbrett)
- *tray*
15 die Limonadenflasche
- *bottle of lemonade*
16 das Limonadenglas
- *lemonade glass*
17 die Schachspieler *m* bei der Schachpartie (Partie Schach *n*)
- *chess players playing a game of chess*
18 das Kaffeegedeck
- *coffee set*
19 die Tasse Kaffee *m*
- *cup of coffee*
20 das Zuckerschälchen
- *small sugar bowl*
21 das Sahnekännchen (der Sahnegießer)
- *cream jug* (Am. *creamer*)
22-24 Cafégäste *m* (Kaffeehausgäste, Kaffeehausbesucher)
- *café customers*
22 der Herr
- *gentleman*
23 die Dame
- *lady*

24 der Zeitungsleser
- *man reading a newspaper*
25 die Zeitung
- *newspaper*
26 der Zeitungshalter
- *newspaper holder*

1-29 das Restaurant (*veraltet:* die
Restauration; *weniger
anspruchsvoll:* die Wirtschaft,
Trinkstube)
- *restaurant*
1-11 der Ausschank (die Theke, das
Büfett, *österr.* Büffet)
- *bar (counter)*
1 der Bierdruckapparat
(Selbstschenker)
- *beer pump (beerpull)*
2 die Tropfplatte
- *drip tray*
3 der Bierbecher, ein Becherglas *n*
- *beer glass, a tumbler*
4 der Bierschaum (die Blume)
- *froth (head)*
5 die Aschenkugel für Tabakasche *f*
- *spherical ashtray for cigarette and
cigar ash*
6 das Bierglas
- *beer glass (beer mug)*
7 der Bierwärmer
- *beer warmer*
8 der Büfettier (*österr.* Büffetier)
- *bartender (barman, Am. barkeeper,
barkeep)*
9 das Gläserregal
- *shelf for glasses*
10 das Flaschenregal
- *shelf for bottles*
11 der Tellerstapel (Geschirrstapel)
- *stack of plates*

12 der Kleiderständer
(Garderobenständer)
- *coat stand*
13 der Huthaken
- *hat peg*
14 der Kleiderhaken
- *coat hook*
15 der Wandventilator
(Wandlüfter)
- *wall ventilator*
16 die Flasche
- *bottle*
17 das Tellergericht
- *complete meal*
18 die Bedienung (Kellnerin,
Serviererin, *schweiz.* Saaltochter)
- *waitress*
19 das Tablett
- *tray*
20 der Losverkäufer
- *lottery ticket seller*
21 die Speisekarte (Tageskarte,
Menükarte, *schweiz.* Menukarte)
- *menu (menu card)*
22 die Menage
- *cruet stand*
23 der Zahnstocherbehälter
- *toothpick holder*
24 der Streichholzständer
(Zündholzständer)
- *matchbox holder*
25 der Gast
- *customer*

26 der Bieruntersetzer (Bierdeckel)
- *beer mat*
27 das Gedeck
- *meal of the day*
28 die Blumenverkäuferin (das
Blumenmädchen)
- *flower seller (flower girl)*
29 der Blumenkorb
- *flower basket*
30-44 die Weinstube (das Weinlokal,
Weinrestaurant)
- *wine restaurant (wine bar)*
30 der Weinkellner, ein Oberkellner *m*
(*ugs.* Ober)
- *wine waiter, a head waiter*
31 die Weinkarte
- *wine list*
32 die Weinkaraffe
- *wine carafe*
33 das Weinglas
- *wineglass*
34 der Kachelofen
- *tiled stove*
35 die Ofenkachel
- *stove tile*
36 die Ofenbank
- *stove bench*
37 das Holzpaneel (Paneel)
- *wooden panelling (Am. paneling)*
38 die Eckbank
- *corner seat*
39 der Stammtisch
- *table reserved for regular customers*

40 der Stammgast
- *regular customer*
41 die Besteckkommode (Kommode)
- *cutlery chest*
42 der Weinkühler
- *wine cooler*
43 die Weinflasche
- *bottle of wine*
44 die Eisstückchen *n*
- *ice cubes (ice, lumps of ice)*
45-78 das Selbstbedienungsrestaurant
(SB-Restaurant, die
Selbstbedienungsgaststätte,
SB-Gaststätte)
- *self-service restaurant*
45 der Tablettstapel
- *stack of trays*
46 die Trinkhalme *m*
- *drinking straws (straws)*
47 die Servietten *f*
- *serviettes (napkins)*
48 die Besteckentnahmefächer *n*
- *cutlery holders*
49 der Kühltresen für kalte Gerichte *n*
- *cool shelf*
50 das Honigmelonenstück
- *slice of honeydew melon*
51 der Salatteller
- *plate of salad*
52 der Käseteller
- *plate of cheeses*
53 das Fischgericht
- *fish dish*

54 das belegte Brötchen
- *roll [with topping]*
55 das Fleischgericht mit Beilagen *f*
- *meat dish with trimmings*
56 das halbe Hähnchen
- *half chicken*
57 der Früchtekorb
- *basket of fruit*
58 der Fruchtsaft
- *fruit juice*
59 das Getränkefach
- *drinks shelf*
60 die Milchflasche
- *bottle of milk*
61 die Mineralwasserflasche
- *bottle of mineral water*
62 das Rohkostmenü
(Diätmenü)
- *vegetarian meal (diet meal)*
63 das Tablett
- *tray*
64 die Tablettablage
- *tray counter*
65 die Speiseübersicht
- *food price list*
66 die Küchendurchreiche
- *serving hatch*
67 das warme Gericht
- *hot meal*
68 der Bierzapfapparat
- *beer pump (beerpull)*
69 die Kasse
- *cash desk*

70 die Kassiererin
- *cashier*
71 der Besitzer (Chef)
- *proprietor*
72 die Barriere
- *rail*
73 der Speiseraum
- *dining area*
74 der Eßtisch
- *table*
75 das Käsebrot
- *bread and cheese*
76 der Eisbecher
- *ice-cream sundae*
77 die Salz- und Pfefferstreuer *m*
- *salt cellar and pepper pot*
78 der Tischschmuck
(Blumenschmuck)
- *table decoration (flower
arrangement)*

1-26 das Vestibül
(der Empfangsraum, Anmelderaum)
- *vestibule*
  (foyer, reception hall)
1 der Portier
- *doorman (commissionaire)*
2 die Postablage, mit den
  Postfächern *n*
- *letter rack with pigeon holes*
3 das Schlüsselbrett
- *key rack*
4 die Kugelleuchte, eine
  Mattglaskugel
- *globe lamp, a frosted glass globe*
5 der Nummernkasten
  (Klappenkasten)
- *indicator board (drop board)*
6 das Lichtrufsignal
- *indicator light*
7 der Empfangschef
  (Geschäftsführer)
- *chief receptionist*
8 das Fremdenbuch
- *register (hotel register)*
9 der Zimmerschlüssel
- *room key*
10 das Nummernschild, mit der
  Zimmernummer
- *number tag*
  (number tab) showing
  room number
11 die Hotelrechnung
- *hotel bill*

12 der Anmeldeblock, mit
  Meldezetteln *m*
  (Anmeldeformularen *n*)
- *block of registration forms*
13 der Reisepaß
- *passport*
14 der Hotelgast
- *hotel guest*
15 der Luftkoffer, ein Leichtkoffer *m*
  für Flugreisen *f*
- *lightweight suitcase, a light suitcase*
  for air travel
16 das Wandschreibpult (Wandpult)
- *wall desk*
17 der Hausdiener (Hausknecht)
- *porter* (Am. *baggage man*)
18-26 die Halle (Hotelhalle)
- *lobby (hotel lobby)*
18 der Hotelboy (Hotelpage, Boy,
  Page)
- *page (pageboy,* Am. *bell boy)*
19 der Hoteldirektor
- *hotel manager*
20 der Speisesaal (das
  Hotelrestaurant)
- *dining room (hotel restaurant)*
21 der Kronleuchter, eine
  mehrflammige Leuchte
- *chandelier*
22 die Kaminecke
- *fireside*
23 der Kamin
- *fireplace*

24 der (das) Kaminsims
- *mantelpiece (mantelshelf)*
25 das offene Feuer
- *fire (open fire)*
26 der Klubsessel
- *armchair*
27-38 das Hotelzimmer, ein
  Doppelzimmer *n* mit Bad *n*
- *hotel room, a double room with bath*
27 die Doppeltür
- *double door*
28 die Klingeltafel
- *service bell panel*
29 der Schrankkoffer
- *wardrobe trunk*
30 das Kleiderabteil
- *clothes compartment*
31 das Wäscheabteil
- *linen compartment*
32 das Doppelwaschbecken
- *double washbasin*
33 der Zimmerkellner
- *room waiter*
34 das Zimmertelefon
- *room telephone*
35 der Veloursteppich
- *velour (velours) carpet*
36 der Blumenschemel
- *flower stand*
37 das Blumenarrangement
- *flower arrangement*
38 das Doppelbett
- *double bed*

39 der Gesellschaftssaal (Festsaal)
- *banquet room*
40-43 die Tischgesellschaft
  (geschlossene Gesellschaft) beim
  Festessen *n* (Mahl, Bankett)
- *party (private party) at table (at a*
  banquet)
40 der Festredner, beim Trinkspruch
  m (Toast)
- *speaker proposing a toast*
41 der Tischnachbar von 42
- *42's neighbour (Am. neighbor)*
42 der Tischherr von 43
- *43's partner*
43 die Tischdame von 42
- *42's partner*
44-46 der Fünfuhrtee (Five o'clock
  tea), im Hotelfoyer *n*
- *thé dansant (tea dance) in the foyer*
44 das Bartrio (die Barband)
- *bar trio*
45 der Stehgeiger
- *violinist*
46 das Paar beim Tanzen *n* (Tanzpaar)
- *couple dancing (dancing couple)*
47 der Ober (Kellner)
- *waiter*
48 das Serviertuch
- *napkin*
49 der Zigarren-und-Zigaretten-Boy
- *cigar and cigarette boy*
50 der Tragladen (Bauchladen)
- *cigarette tray*

51 die Hotelbar
- *hotel bar*
52 die Fußleiste
- *foot rail*
53 der Barhocker
- *bar stool*
54 die Bartheke (Theke)
- *bar*
55 der Bargast
- *bar customer*
56 das Cocktailglas
- *cocktail glass*
  (Am. highball glass)
57 das Whiskyglas
- *whisky (whiskey) glass*
58 der Sektkork
- *champagne cork*
59 der Sektkübel (Sektkühler)
- *champagne bucket (champagne*
  cooler)
60 das Meßglas
- *measuring beaker (measure)*
61 der Cocktailshaker (Mixbecher)
- *cocktail shaker*
62 der Mixer (Barmixer)
- *bartender (barman, Am. barkeeper,*
  barkeep)
63 die Bardame
- *barmaid*
64 das Flaschenbord
- *shelf for bottles*
65 das Gläserregal
- *shelf for glasses*

66 die Spiegelverkleidung
- *mirrored panel*
67 der Eisbehälter
- *ice bucket*

1 die Parkuhr (das Parkometer)
- *parking meter*
2 der Stadtplan
- *map of the town (street map)*
3 die beleuchtete Schautafel
- *illuminated board*
4 die Legende
- *key*
5 der Abfallkorb (Abfallbehälter, Papierkorb)
- *litter bin (Am. litter basket)*
6 die Straßenlaterne (Straßenleuchte, Straßenlampe)
- *street lamp (street light)*
7 das Straßenschild mit dem Straßennamen *m*
- *street sign showing the name of the street*
8 der Gully
- *drain*
9 das Textilgeschäft (der Modesalon)
- *clothes shop (fashion house)*
10 das Schaufenster
- *shop window*
11 die Schaufensterauslage
- *window display (shop window display)*
12 die Schaufensterdekoration
- *window decoration (shop window decoration)*
13 der Eingang
- *entrance*

14 das Fenster
- *window*
15 der Blumenkasten
- *window box*
16 die Leuchtreklame
- *neon sign*
17 die Schneiderwerkstatt
- *tailor's workroom*
18 der Passant
- *pedestrian*
19 die Einkaufstasche
- *shopping bag*
20 der Straßenkehrer
- *road sweeper (Am. street sweeper)*
21 der Straßenbesen (Kehrbesen)
- *broom*
22 der Abfall (Straßenschmutz, Kehricht)
- *rubbish (litter)*
23 die Straßenbahnschienen
- *tramlines (Am. streetcar tracks)*
24 der Fußgängerüberweg (*ugs.* der Zebrastreifen)
- *pedestrian crossing (zebra crossing, Am. crosswalk)*
25 die Straßenbahnhaltestelle
- *tram stop (Am. streetcar stop, trolley stop)*
26 das Haltestellenschild
- *tram stop sign (Am. streetcar stop sign, trolley stop sign)*
27 der Straßenbahnfahrplan
- *tram timetable (Am. streetcar schedule)*

28 der Fahrscheinautomat
- *ticket machine*
29 das Hinweiszeichen „Fußgängerüberweg" *m*
- *'pedestrian crossing' sign*
30 der Verkehrspolizist bei der Verkehrsregelung
- *traffic policeman on traffic duty (point duty)*
31 der weiße Ärmel
- *traffic control cuff*
32 die weiße Mütze
- *white cap*
33 das Handzeichen
- *hand signal*
34 der Motorradfahrer
- *motorcyclist*
35 das Motorrad
- *motorcycle*
36 die Beifahrerin (Sozia)
- *pillion passenger (pillion rider)*
37 die Buchhandlung
- *bookshop*
38 das Hutgeschäft
- *hat shop (hatter's shop); for ladies' hats: milliner's shop*
39 das Ladenschild
- *shop sign*
40 das Versicherungsbüro
- *insurance company office*
41 das Kaufhaus (Warenhaus, Magazin)
- *department store*

42 die Schaufensterfront
- *shop front*
43 die Reklametafel
- *advertisement*
44 die Beflaggung
- *flags*
45 die Dachreklame aus
 Leuchtbuchstaben *m*
- *illuminated letters*
46 der Straßenbahnzug
- *tram (Am. streetcar, trolley)*
47 der Möbelwagen
- *furniture lorry (Am. furniture truck)*
48 die Straßenüberführung
- *flyover*
49 die Straßenbeleuchtung, eine
 Mittenleuchte
- *suspended street lamp*
50 die Haltlinie
- *stop line*
51 die Fußgängerwegmarkierung
- *pedestrian crossing (Am. crosswalk)*
52 die Verkehrsampel
- *traffic lights*
53 der Ampelmast
- *traffic light post*
54 die Lichtzeichenanlage
- *set of lights*
55 die Fußgängerlichtzeichen *n*
- *pedestrian lights*
56 die Telefonzelle
- *telephone box (telephone booth, telephone kiosk, call box)*

57 das Kinoplakat
- *cinema advertisement (film poster)*
58 die Fußgängerzone
- *pedestrian precinct (paved zone)*
59 das Straßencafé
- *street café*
60 die Sitzgruppe
- *group seated (sitting) at a table*
61 der Sonnenschirm
- *sunshade*
62 der Niedergang zu den Toiletten *f*
- *steps to the public lavatories (public conveniences)*
63 der Taxistand (Taxenstand)
- *taxi rank (taxi stand)*
64 das Taxi (die Taxe, *schweiz.* der Taxi)
- *taxi (taxicab, cab)*
65 das Taxischild
- *taxi sign*
66 das Verkehrszeichen „Taxenstand" *m*
- *traffic sign showing 'taxi rank' ('taxi stand')*
67 das Taxentelefon
- *taxi telephone*
68 das Postamt
- *post office*
69 der Zigarettenautomat
- *cigarette machine*
70 die Litfaßsäule
- *advertising pillar*
71 das Werbeplakat
- *poster (advertisement)*

72 die Fahrbahnbegrenzung
- *white line*
73 der Einordnungspfeil „links abbiegen"
- *lane arrow for turning left*
74 der Einordnungspfeil „geradeaus"
- *lane arrow for going straight ahead*
75 der Zeitungsverkäufer
- *news vendor (Am. news dealer)*

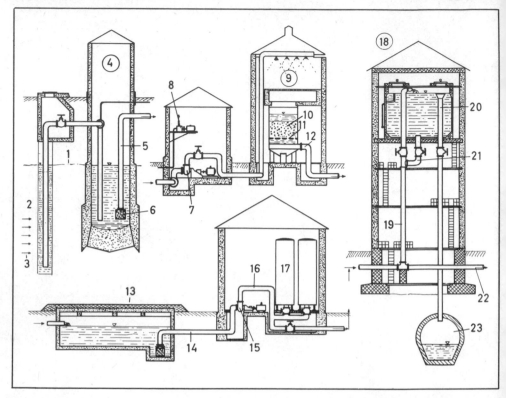

1-66 die Trinkwasserversorgung
- *drinking water supply*
1 der Grundwasserspiegel
- *water table (groundwater level)*
2 die wasserführende Schicht
- *water-bearing stratum (aquifer, aquafer)*
3 der Grundwasserstrom
- *groundwater stream (underground stream)*
4 der Sammelbrunnen für das Rohwasser
- *collector well for raw water*
5 die Saugleitung
- *suction pipe*
6 der Saugkorb mit Fußventil *n*
- *pump strainer with foot valve*
7 die Schöpfpumpe mit Motor *m*
- *bucket pump with motor*
8 die Vakuumpumpe mit Motor *m*
- *vacuum pump with motor*
9 die Schnellfilteranlage
- *rapid-filter plant*
10 der Filterkies
- *filter gravel (filter bed)*
11 der Filterboden, ein Rost *m*
- *filter bottom, a grid*
12 die Ablaufleitung für filtriertes Wasser *n*
- *filtered water outlet*
13 der Reinwasserbehälter
- *purified water tank*

14 die Saugleitung mit Saugkorb *m* und Fußventil *n*
- *suction pipe with pump strainer and foot valve*
15 die Hauptpumpe mit Motor *m*
- *main pump with motor*
16 die Druckleitung
- *delivery pipe*
17 der Windkessel
- *compressed-air vessel (air vessel, air receiver)*
18 der Wasserturm (Wasserhochbehälter, das Wasserhochreservoir)
- *water tower*
19 die Steigleitung
- *riser pipe (riser)*
20 die Überlaufleitung
- *overflow pipe*
21 die Falleitung
- *outlet*
22 die Leitung in das Verteilungsnetz
- *distribution main*
23 der Abwasserkanal
- *excess water conduit*
24-39 die Fassung einer Quelle
- *tapping a spring*
24 die Quellstube
- *chamber*
25 der Sandfang
- *chamber wall*
26 der Einsteigschacht
- *manhole*

27 der Entlüfter
- *ventilator*
28 die Steigeisen *n*
- *step irons*
29 die Ausschüttung
- *filling (backing)*
30 das Absperrventil
- *outlet control valve*
31 der Entleerungsschieber
- *outlet valve*
32 der Seiher
- *strainer*
33 der Überlauf
- *overflow pipe (overflow)*
34 der Grundablaß
- *bottom outlet*
35 die Tonrohre *n*
- *earthenware pipes*
36 die wasserundurchlässige Schicht
- *impervious stratum (impermeable stratum)*
37 vorgelagerte Feldsteine *m*
- *rough rubble*
38 die wasserführende Schicht
- *water-bearing stratum (aquifer, aquafer)*
39 die Stampflehmpackung
- *loam seal (clay seal)*
40-52 die Einzelwasserversorgung
- *individual water supply*
40 der Brunnen
- *well*

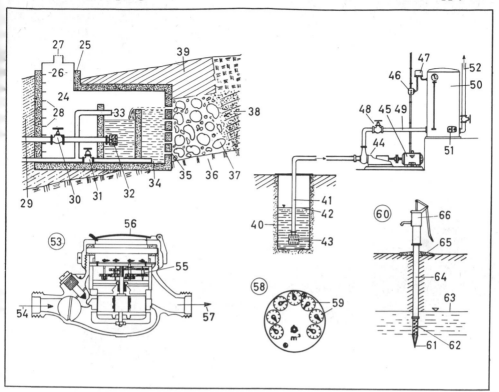

41 die Saugleitung
 – *suction pipe*
42 der Grundwasserspiegel
 – *water table (groundwater level)*
43 der Saugkorb mit Fußventil *n*
 – *pump strainer with foot valve*
44 die Kreiselpumpe
 – *centrifugal pump*
45 der Motor
 – *motor*
46 der Motorschaltschutz
 – *motor safety switch*
47 der Druckwächter, ein Schaltgerät *n*
 – *manostat, a switching device*
48 der Absperrschieber
 – *stop valve*
49 die Druckleitung
 – *delivery pipe*
50 der Windkessel
 – *compressed-air vessel (air vessel, air receiver)*
51 das Mannloch
 – *manhole*
52 die Leitung zum Verbraucher *m*
 – *delivery pipe*
53 die Wasseruhr (der Wasserzähler, Wassermesser), ein Flügelradwasserzähler *m*
 – *water meter, a rotary meter*
54 der Wasserzufluß
 – *water inlet*
55 das Zählwerk
 – *counter gear assembly*

56 die Haube mit Glasdeckel *m*
 – *cover with glass lid*
57 der Wasserabfluß
 – *water outlet*
58 das Zifferblatt des Wasserzählers *m*
 – *water-meter dial*
59 das Zählwerk
 – *counters*
60 der Rammbrunnen
 – *driven well (tube well, drive well)*
61 die Rammspitze
 – *pile shoe*
62 das (der) Filter
 – *filter*
63 der Grundwasserspiegel
 – *water table (groundwater level)*
64 das Brunnenrohr (Mantelrohr)
 – *well casing*
65 die Brunnenumrandung
 – *well head*
66 die Handpumpe
 – *hand pump*

1-46 **die Feuerwehrübung** (Lösch-,
Steig-, Leiter-, Rettungsübung)
- *fire service drill (extinguishing,
climbing, ladder, and rescue work)*
1-3 die Feuerwache
- *fire station*
1 die Fahrzeughalle und das
Gerätehaus
- *engine and appliance room*
2 die Mannschaftsunterkunft
(Unterkunft)
- *firemen's quarters*
3 der Übungsturm
- *drill tower*
4 die Feuersirene (Alarmsirene)
- *fire alarm (fire alarm siren, fire
siren)*
5 das Löschfahrzeug (die
Kraftspritze, Motorspritze)
- *fire engine*
6 das Blaulicht (Warnlicht), ein
Blinklicht *n*
- *blue light (warning light), a
flashing light
(Am. flashlight)*
7 das Signalhorn
- *horn (hooter)*
8 die Motorpumpe, eine
Kreiselpumpe
- *motor pump, a centrifugal pump*
9 die Kraftfahrdrehleiter
- *motor turntable ladder (Am. aerial
ladder)*

10 der Leiterpark, eine Stahlleiter
(mechanische Leiter)
- *ladder, a steel ladder (automatic
extending ladder)*
11 das Leitergetriebe
- *ladder mechanism*
12 die Abstützspindel
- *jack*
13 der Maschinist
- *ladder operator*
14 die Schiebeleiter
- *extension ladder*
15 der Einreißhaken
- *ceiling hook (Am. preventer)*
16 die Hakenleiter
- *hook ladder (Am. pompier ladder)*
17 die Haltemannschaft
- *holding squad*
18 das Sprungtuch
- *jumping sheet (sheet)*
19 der Rettungswagen (Unfallwagen),
ein Krankenkraftwagen *m*
(*ugs.* das Sanitätsauto, Krankenauto,
die Ambulanz)
- *ambulance car (ambulance)*
20 das Wiederbelebungsgerät, ein
Sauerstoffgerät
- *resuscitator (resuscitation
equipment), oxygen apparatus*
21 der Sanitäter
- *ambulance attendant (ambulance man)*
22 die Armbinde
- *armband (armlet, brassard)*

23 die Tragbahre (Krankenbahre)
- *stretcher*
24 der Bewußtlose
- *unconscious man*
25 der Unterflurhydrant
- *pit hydrant*
26 das Standrohr
- *standpipe (riser, vertical pipe)*
27 der Hydrantenschlüssel
- *hydrant key*
28 die fahrbare Schlauchhaspel
- *hose reel
(Am. hose cart, hose
wagon, hose truck, hose carriage)*
29 die Schlauchkupplung
- *hose coupling*
30 die Saugleitung, eine
Schlauchleitung
- *soft suction hose*
31 die Druckleitung
- *delivery hose*
32 das Verteilungsstück
- *dividing breeching*
33 das Strahlrohr
- *branch*
34 der Löschtrupp
- *branchmen*
35 der Überflurhydrant
- *surface hydrant (fire plug)*
36 der Brandmeister
- *officer in charge*
37 der Feuerwehrmann
- *fireman (Am. firefighter)*

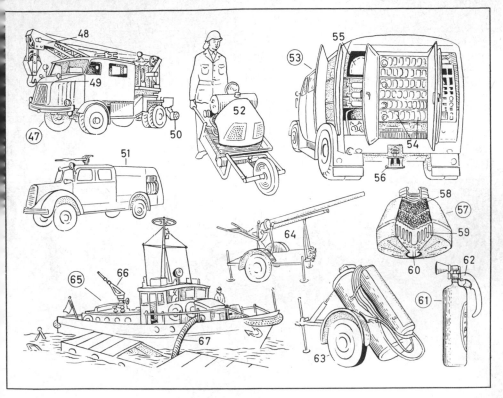

38 der Feuerschutzhelm, mit dem
Nackenschutz *m*
- *helmet (fireman's helmet, Am. fire
hat) with neck guard (neck flap)*
39 das Atemschutzgerät
- *breathing apparatus*
40 die Gasmaske
- *face mask*
41 das tragbare Funksprechgerät
- *walkie-talkie set*
42 der Handscheinwerfer
- *hand lamp*
43 das Feuerwehrbeil
- *small axe (Am. ax, pompier
hatchet)*
44 der Hakengurt
- *hook belt*
45 die Fangleine (Rettungsleine)
- *beltline*
46 die Schutzkleidung
(Wärmeschutzkleidung) aus
Asbest *m* (Asbestanzug) oder
Metallstoff *m*
- *protective clothing of asbestos
(asbestos suit) or of metallic fabric*
47 der Kranwagen
- *breakdown lorry (Am. crane truck,
wrecking crane)*
48 der Bergungskran
- *lifting crane*
49 der Zughaken
- *load hook (draw hook, Am. drag
hook)*

50 die Stützrolle
- *support roll*
51 das Tanklöschfahrzeug
(der Tanklöschwagen)
- *water tender*
52 die Tragkraftspritze
- *portable pump*
53 der Schlauch- und Gerätewagen
- *hose layer*
54 die Rollschläuche *m*
- *flaked lengths of hose*
55 die Kabeltrommel
- *cable drum*
56 das Spill
- *winch*
57 der (das) Gasmaskenfilter
- *face mask filter*
58 die Aktivkohle
- *active carbon (activated carbon,
activated charcoal)*
59 der (das) Staubfilter
- *dust filter*
60 die Lufteintrittsöffnung
- *air inlet*
61 der Handfeuerlöscher
- *portable fire extinguisher*
62 das Pistolenventil
- *trigger valve*
63 das fahrbare Löschgerät
- *large mobile extinguisher (wheeled
fire extinguisher)*
64 der Luftschaum- und Wasserwerfer
- *foam-making branch (Am. foam gun)*

65 das Feuerlöschboot
- *fireboat*
66 die Wasserkanone
- *monitor (water cannon)*
67 der Saugschlauch
- *suction hose*

1 die Kassiererin
- *cashier*
2 die elektrische Registrierkasse (Ladenkasse, Tageskasse)
- *electric cash register (till)*
3 die Zifferntasten *f*
- *number keys*
4 der Auslöschknopf
- *cancellation button*
5 der Geldschub (Geldkasten)
- *cash drawer (till)*
6 die Geldfächer *n*, für Hartgeld *n* und Banknoten *f*
- *compartments (money compartments) for coins and notes (Am. bills)*
7 der quittierte Kassenzettel (Kassenbon, Bon)
- *receipt (sales check)*
8 die Zahlung (registrierte Summe)
- *amount [to be paid]*
9 das Zählwerk
- *adding mechanism*
10 die Ware
- *goods*
11 der Lichthof
- *glass-roofed well*
12 die Herrenartikelabteilung
- *men's wear department*
13 die Schauvitrine (Innenauslage)
- *showcase (display case, indoor display window)*
14 die Warenausgabe
- *wrapping counter*

15 das Warenkörbchen
- *tray for purchases*
16 die Kundin (Käuferin)
- *customer*
17 die Strumpfwarenabteilung
- *hosiery department*
18 die Verkäuferin
- *shop assistant (Am. salesgirl, saleslady)*
19 das Preisschild
- *price card*
20 der Handschuhständer
- *glove stand*
21 der Dufflecoat, ein dreiviertellanger Mantel
- *duffle coat, a three-quarter length coat*
22 die Rolltreppe
- *escalator*
23 die Leuchtstoffröhre (Leuchtstofflampe)
- *fluorescent light (fluorescent lamp)*
24 das Büro (z.B. Kreditbüro, Reisebüro, Direktionsbüro)
- *office (e.g. customer accounts office, travel agency, manager's office)*
25 das Werbeplakat
- *poster (advertisement)*
26 die Theater- und Konzertkartenverkaufsstelle (Kartenvorverkaufsstelle)
- *theatre (Am. theater) and concert booking office (advance booking office)*

27 das Regal
- *[set of] shelves*
28 die Damenkonfektionsabteilung (Abteilung für Damenkleidung)
- *ladies' wear department*
29 das Konfektionskleid (*ugs.* Kleid von der Stange)
- *ready-made dress (ready-to-wear dress, coll. off-the-peg dress)*
30 der Staubschutz
- *dust cover*
31 die Kleiderstange
- *clothes rack*
32 die Ankleidekabine (Ankleidezelle, der Anproberaum)
- *changing booth (fitting booth)*
33 der Empfangschef
- *shop walker (Am. floorwalker, floor manager)*
34 die Modepuppe
- *dummy*
35 der Sessel
- *seat (chair)*
36 das Modejournal (die Modezeitschrift)
- *fashion journal (fashion magazine)*
37 der Schneider, beim Abstecken *n*
- *tailor marking a hemline*
38 das Metermaß (Bandmaß)
- *measuring tape (tape measure)*
39 die Schneiderkreide
- *tailor's chalk (French chalk)*

40 der Rocklängenmesser
   (Rockrunder)
 - hemline marker
41 der lose Mantel
 - loose-fitting coat
42 das Verkaufskarree
 - sales counter
43 der Warmluftvorhang
 - warm-air curtain
44 der Portier (Pförtner)
 - doorman (commissionaire)
45 der Personenaufzug (Lift)
 - lift (Am. elevator)
46 der Fahrstuhl (die Fahrkabine)
 - lift cage (lift car, Am. elevator car)
47 der Fahrstuhlführer
   (Aufzugführer, Liftboy)
 - lift operator (Am. elevator operator)
48 die Steuerung
 - controls (lift controls, Am. elevator
   controls)
49 der Stockwerkanzeiger
 - floor indicator
50 die Schiebetür
 - sliding door
51 der Aufzugschacht
 - lift shaft (Am. elevator shaft)
52 das Tragseil
 - bearer cable
53 das Steuerseil
 - control cable
54 die Führungsschiene
 - guide rail

55 der Kunde (Käufer)
 - customer
56 die Wirkwaren pl
 - hosiery
57 die Weißwaren pl (Tischwäsche f
   und Bettwäsche f)
 - linen goods (table linen and bed
   linen)
58 das Stofflager (die Stoffabteilung)
 - fabric department
59 der Stoffballen (Tuchballen)
 - roll of fabric (roll of material, roll
   of cloth)
60 der Abteilungsleiter (Rayonchef)
 - head of department (department
   manager)
61 die Verkaufstheke
 - sales counter
62 die Bijouteriewarenabteilung
   (Galanteriewarenabteilung)
 - jewellery (Am. jewelry) department
63 die Neuheitenverkäuferin
 - assistant (Am. salesgirl, saleslady),
   selling new lines (new products)
64 der Sondertisch
 - special counter (extra counter)
65 das Plakat mit dem Sonderangebot n
 - placard advertising special offers
66 die Gardinenabteilung
 - curtain department
67 die Rampendekoration
 - display on top of the shelves

1-40 der französische Park
(Barockpark), ein Schloßpark *m*
- *formal garden (French Baroque
  garden), palace gardens*
1 die Grotte
- *grotto (cavern)*
2 die Steinfigur, eine Quellnymphe
- *stone statue, a river nymph*
3 die Orangerie
- *orangery (orangerie)*
4 das Boskett
- *boscage (boskage)*
5 der Irrgarten (das Labyrinth aus
  Heckengängen *m*)
- *maze (labyrinth of paths and
  hedges)*
6 das Naturtheater
- *open-air theatre (Am. theater)*
7 das Barockschloß
- *Baroque palace*
8 die Wasserspiele *n* (Wasserkünste *f*)
- *fountains*
9 die Kaskade (der stufenförmige
  künstliche Wasserfall)
- *cascade (broken artificial waterfall,
  artificial falls)*
10 das Standbild (die Statue), ein
  Denkmal *n*
- *statue, a monument*
11 der Denkmalsockel
- *pedestal (base of statue)*
12 der Kugelbaum
- *globe-shaped tree*

13 der Kegelbaum
- *conical tree*
14 der Zierstrauch
- *ornamental shrub*
15 der Wandbrunnen
- *wall fountain*
16 die Parkbank
- *park bench*
17 die Pergola (der Laubengang)
- *pergola (bower, arbour, Am. arbor)*
18 der Kiesweg
- *gravel path (gravel walk)*
19 der Pyramidenbaum
- *pyramid tree (pyramidal tree)*
20 die Amorette
- *cupid (cherub, amoretto, amorino)*
21 der Springbrunnen
- *fountain*
22 die Fontäne (der Wasserstrahl)
- *fountain (jet of water)*
23 das Überlaufbecken
- *overflow basin*
24 das Bassin
- *basin*
25 der Brunnenrand
  (die Ummauerung)
- *kerb (curb)*
26 der Spaziergänger
- *man out for a walk*
27 die Fremdenführerin (Hostess)
- *tourist guide*
28 die Touristengruppe
- *group of tourists*

29 die Parkordnung
- *park by-laws (bye-laws)*
30 der Parkwächter
- *park keeper*
31 das Parktor (Gittertor), ein
  schmiedeeisernes Tor *n*
- *garden gates, wrought iron gates*
32 der Parkeingang
- *park entrance*
33 das Parkgitter
- *park railings*
34 der Gitterstab
- *railing (bar)*
35 die Steinvase
- *stone vase*
36 die Rasenfläche (Grünfläche, der
  Rasen)
- *lawn*
37 die Wegeinfassung, eine
  beschnittene Hecke
- *border, a trimmed (clipped) hedge*
38 der Parkweg
- *park path*
39 die Parterreanlage
- *parterre*
40 die Birke
- *birch (birch tree)*

41-72 der englische Park (englische
Garten, Landschaftspark)
- *landscaped park (jardin anglais)*
41 die Blumenrabatte
- *flower bed*
42 die Gartenbank
- *park bench (garden seat)*
43 der Abfallkorb
- *litter bin (Am. litter basket)*
44 die Spielwiese
- *play area*
45 der Wasserlauf
- *stream*
46 der Steg
- *jetty*
47 die Brücke
- *bridge*
48 der bewegliche Parkstuhl
- *park chair*
49 das Wildgehege (Tiergehege)
- *animal enclosure*
50 der Teich
- *pond*
51-54 das Wassergeflügel
- *waterfowl*
51 die Wildente mit Jungen *n*
- *wild duck with young*
52 die Gans
- *goose*
53 der Flamingo
- *flamingo*
54 der Schwan
- *swan*

55 die Insel
- *island*
56 die Seerose
- *water lily*
57 das Terrassencafé
- *open-air café*
58 der Sonnenschirm
- *sunshade*
59 der Parkbaum
- *park tree (tree)*
60 die Baumkrone
- *treetop (crown)*
61 die Baumgruppe
- *group of trees*
62 die Wasserfontäne
- *fountain*
63 die Trauerweide
- *weeping willow*
64 die moderne Plastik
- *modern sculpture*
65 das Tropengewächshaus
(Pflanzenschauhaus)
- *hothouse*
66 der Parkgärtner
- *park gardener*
67 der Laubbesen
- *broom*
68 die Minigolfanlage
- *minigolf course*
69 der Minigolfspieler
- *minigolf player*
70 die Minigolfbahn
- *minigolf hole*

71 die Mutter mit Kinderwagen *m*
- *mother with pram (baby carriage)*
72 das Liebespaar (Pärchen)
- *courting couple (young couple)*

1 das Tischtennisspiel
- *table tennis game*
2 der Tisch
- *table*
3 das Tischtennisnetz
- *table tennis net*
4 der Tischtennisschläger
- *table tennis racket (raquet) (table tennis bat)*
5 der Tischtennisball
- *table tennis ball*
6 das Federballspiel
- *badminton game (shuttlecock game)*
7 der Federball
- *shuttlecock*
8 der Rundlaufpilz
- *maypole swing*
9 das Kinderfahrrad
- *child's bicycle*
10 das Fußballspiel
- *football game (soccer game)*
11 das Fußballtor
- *goal (goalposts)*
12 der Fußball
- *football*
13 der Torschütze
- *goal scorer*
14 der Torwart
- *goalkeeper*
15 das Seilhüpfen (Seilspringen)
- *skipping*
  (Am. jumping rope)

16 das Hüpfseil (Springseil)
- *skipping rope (Am. skip rope, jump rope, jumping rope)*
17 der Kletterturm
- *climbing tower*
18 die Reifenschaukel
- *rubber tyre (Am. tire) swing*
19 der Lkw-Reifen
- *lorry tyre (Am. truck tire)*
20 der Hüpfball
- *bouncing ball*
21 der Abenteuerspielplatz
- *adventure playground*
22 die Rundholzleiter
- *log ladder*
23 der Ausguck
- *lookout platform*
24 die Rutschbahn
- *slide*
25 der Abfallkorb
- *litter bin (Am. litter basket)*
26 der Teddybär
- *teddy bear*
27 die Holzeisenbahn
- *wooden train set*
28 das Planschbecken
- *paddling pool*
29 das Segelboot
- *sailing boat (yacht, Am. sailboat)*
30 die Spielzeugente
- *toy duck*
31 der Kinderwagen
- *pram (baby carriage)*

32 das Reck
- *high bar (bar)*
33 das Go-Kart (die Seifenkiste)
- *go-cart (soap box)*
34 die Starterflagge
- *starter's flag*
35 die Wippe
- *seesaw*
36 der Roboter
- *robot*

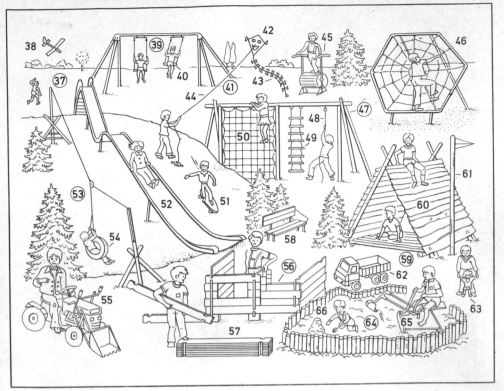

37 der Modellflug
- *flying model aeroplanes*
  (Am. *airplanes*)
38 das Modellflugzeug
- *model aeroplane*
  (Am. *airplane*)
39 die Doppelschaukel
- *double swing*
40 der Schaukelsitz
  (das Schaukelbrett)
- *swing seat*
41 das Drachensteigenlassen
- *flying kites*
42 der Drachen
- *kite*
43 der Drachenschwanz
- *tail of the kite*
44 die Drachenschnur
- *kite string*
45 die Lauftrommel
- *revolving drum*
46 das Spinnennetz
- *spider's web*
47 das Klettergerüst
- *climbing frame*
48 das Kletterseil
- *climbing rope*
49 die Strickleiter
- *rope ladder*
50 das Kletternetz
- *climbing net*
51 das Rollbrett (Skateboard)
- *skateboard*

52 die Berg-und-Tal-Rutschbahn
- *up-and-down slide*
53 die Reifendrahtseilbahn
- *rubber tyre (Am. tire) cable car*
54 der Sitzreifen
- *rubber tyre (Am. tire)*
55 der Traktor, ein Tretauto *n*
- *tractor, a pedal car*
56 das Aufbauhäuschen
- *den*
57 die Steckbretter *n*
- *presawn boards*
58 die Bank
- *seat (bench)*
59 die Winnetouhütte
- *Indian hut*
60 das Kletterdach
- *climbing roof*
61 die Fahnenstange
- *flagpole (flagstaff)*
62 das Spielzeugauto
- *toy lorry (Am. toy truck)*
63 die Laufpuppe
- *walking doll*
64 der Sandkasten
- *sandpit (Am. sandbox)*
65 der Spielzeugbagger
- *toy excavator (toy digger)*
66 der Sandberg
- *sandhill*

1-21 der Kurpark
- *spa gardens*
1-7 die Saline
- *salina (salt works)*
1 das Gradierwerk
(Rieselwerk)
- *thorn house (graduation house)*
2 das Dornreisig
- *thorns (brushwood)*
3 die Verteilungsrinne für die Sole
- *brine channels*
4 die Solezuleitung vom Pumpwerk
- *brine pipe from the pumping station*
5 der Gradierwärter
- *salt works attendant*
6-7 die Inhalationskur
- *inhalational therapy*
6 das Freiinhalatorium
- *open-air inhalatorium (outdoor
inhalatorium)*
7 der Kranke, beim Inhalieren *n*
(bei der Inhalation)
- *patient inhaling (taking an
inhalation)*
8 das Kurhaus, mit dem Kursaal *m*
(Kasino *n*)
- *hydropathic (pump room) with
kursaal (casino)*
9 die Wandelhalle (der Säulengang,
die Kolonnade)
- *colonnade*
10 die Kurpromenade
- *spa promenade*

11 die Brunnenallee
- *avenue leading to the mineral
spring*
12-14 die Liegekur
- *rest cure*
12 die Liegewiese
- *sunbathing area (lawn)*
13 der Liegestuhl
- *deck-chair*
14 das Sonnendach
- *sun canopy*
15 der Brunnenpavillon (das
Brunnenhaus, der Quellpavillon)
- *pump room*
16 der Gläserstand
- *rack for glasses*
17 die Zapfstelle
- *tap*
18 der Kurgast (Badegast), bei der
Trinkkur
- *patient taking the waters*
19 der Konzertpavillon
- *bandstand*
20 die Kurkapelle, beim Kurkonzert *n*
- *spa orchestra giving a concert*
21 der Kapellmeister (Dirigent)
- *conductor*

1-33 das Roulett
(Roulette), ein
Glücksspiel *n* (Hasardspiel)
- *roulette, a game of chance
(gambling game)*
1 der Roulettspielsaal (Spielsaal), in
der Spielbank (im Spielkasino *n*)
- *gaming room in the casino (in the
gambling casino)*
2 die Kasse
- *cash desk*
3 der Spielleiter (Chef de partie)
- *tourneur (dealer)*
4 der Handcroupier (Croupier)
- *croupier*
5 das Rateau (die Geldharke)
- *rake*
6 der Kopfcroupier
- *head croupier*
7 der Saalchef
- *hall manager*
8 der Roulettspieltisch
- *roulette table (gaming table,
gambling table)*
9 das Tableau (der Spielplan)
- *roulette layout*
10 die Roulettmaschine
- *roulette wheel*
11 die Tischkasse (Bank)
- *bank*
12 der Jeton (die Plaque, Spielmarke,
das Stück)
- *chip (check, plaque)*

13 der Einsatz
- *stake*
14 der Kasinoausweis
- *membership card*
15 der Roulettspieler
- *roulette player*
16 der Privatdetektiv (Hausdetektiv)
- *private detective (house detective)*
17 der Roulettspielplan
- *roulette layout*
18 die (das) Zero (Null *f*, 0)
- *zero (nought, O)*
19 das Passe (Groß) [Zahlen von 19-36]
- *passe (high) [numbers 19 to 36]*
20 das Pair [gerade Zahlen]
- *pair (even numbers)*
21 das Noir (Schwarz)
- *noir (black)*
22 das Manque (Klein)
[Zahlen von 1-18]
- *manque (low) [numbers 1 to 18]*
23 das Impair [ungerade Zahlen]
- *impair [odd numbers]*
24 das Rouge (Rot)
- *rouge (red)*
25 das Douze premier (erstes
Dutzend) [Zahlen von 1 bis 12]
- *douze premier (first dozen)
[numbers 1 to 12]*
26 das Douze milieu (mittleres
Dutzend) [Zahlen von 13 bis 24]
- *douze milieu (second dozen)
[numbers 13 to 24]*

27 das Douze dernier (letztes
Dutzend) [Zahlen von 25 bis 36]
- *douze dernier (third dozen)
[numbers 25 to 36]*
28 die Roulettmaschine (das Roulett)
- *roulette wheel (roulette)*
29 der Roulettkessel
- *roulette bowl*
30 das Hindernis
- *fret (separator)*
31 die Drehscheibe, mit den
Nummern *f* 0 bis 36
- *revolving disc (disk) showing
numbers 0 to 36*
32 das Drehkreuz
- *spin*
33 die Roulettkugel
- *roulette ball*

1-16 **das Schachspiel** (Schach,
königliche Spiel), ein
Kombinationsspiel *n* oder
Positionsspiel *n*
- **chess,** *a game involving
combinations of moves, a
positional game*
1 das Schachbrett (Spielbrett), mit
den Figuren *f* in der
Ausgangsstellung
- *chessboard (board) with the men
(chessmen) in position*
2 das weiße Feld (Schachbrettfeld,
Schachfeld)
- *white square (chessboard square)*
3 das schwarze Feld
- *black square*
4 die weißen Schachfiguren *f*
(Figuren, die Weißen) als
Schachfigurensymbole *n* [weiß = W]
- *white chessmen (white pieces)
[white = W]*
5 die schwarzen Schachfiguren *f*
(die Schwarzen) als
Schachfigurensymbole *n* [schwarz = S]
- *black chessmen (black pieces)
[black = B]*
6 die Buchstaben *m* und Zahlen *f* zur
Schachfelderbezeichnung, zur
Niederschrift (Notation) von
Schachpartien *f* (Zügen *m*) und
Schachproblemen *n*
- *letters and numbers for designating
chess squares for the notation of
chess moves and chess problems*
7 die einzelnen Schachfiguren *f*
(Steine *m*)
- *individual chessmen (individual
pieces)*
8 der König
- *king*
9 die Dame (Königin)
- *queen*
10 der Läufer
- *bishop*
11 der Springer
- *knight*
12 der Turm
- *rook (castle)*
13 der Bauer
- *pawn*
14 die Gangarten *f* (Züge) der
einzelnen Figuren *f*
- *moves of the individual pieces*
15 das Matt (Schachmatt), ein
Springermatt *n* [S f 3 ≠]
- *mate (checkmate), a mate by knight
[kt f 3 ≠]*
16 die Schachuhr, eine Doppeluhr für
Schachturniere *n*
(Schachmeisterschaften *f*)
- *chess clock, a double clock for
chess matches (chess
championships)*
17-19 **das Damespiel** (Damspiel)
- **draughts** *(Am. checkers)*
17 das Damebrett
- *draughtboard
(Am. checkerboard)*
18 der weiße Damestein; *auch:*
Spielstein *m* für Puff- und
Mühlespiel *n*
- *white draughtsman (Am. checker,
checkerman); also: piece for
backgammon and nine men's
morris*

19 der schwarze Damestein
- *black draughtsman (Am. checker,
checkerman)*
20 **das Saltaspiel** (Salta)
- *salta*
21 der Saltastein
- *salta piece*
22 das Spielbrett, für das **Puffspiel**
(Puff, Tricktrack)
- *backgammon board*
23-25 **das Mühlespiel**
- **nine men's morris**
23 das Mühlebrett
- *nine men's morris board*
24 die Mühle
- *mill*
25 die Zwickmühle (Doppelmühle)
- *double mill*
26-28 **das Halmaspiel**
- **halma**
26 das Halmabrett
- *halma board*
27 der Hof
- *yard (camp, corner)*
28 die verschiedenfarbigen
Halmafiguren *f* (Halmasteine *m*)
- *halma pieces (halma men) of
various colours (Am. colors)*
29 **das Würfelspiel** (Würfeln,
Knobeln)
- *dice (dicing)*
30 der Würfelbecher (Knobelbecher)
- *dice cup*
31 die Würfel *m* (*landsch.* Knobel)
- *dice*
32 die Augen *n*
- *spots (pips)*
33 **das Dominospiel** (Domino)
- **dominoes**
34 der Dominostein
- *domino (tile)*
35 der Pasch
- *double*
36 **Spielkarten** *f*
- **playing cards**
37 die französische Spielkarte (das
Kartenblatt)
- *French playing card (card)*
38-45 die Farben *f* (Serienzeichen *n*)
- *suits*
38 Kreuz *n* (Treff)
- *clubs*
39 Pik *n* (Pique, Schippen)
- *spades*
40 Herz *n* (Cœur)
- *hearts*
41 Karo *n* (Eckstein *m*)
- *diamonds*
42-45 die deutschen Farben *f*
- *German suits*
42 Eichel *f* (Ecker)
- *acorns*
43 Grün *n* (Blatt, Gras, Grasen)
- *leaves*
44 Rot *n* (Herz)
- *hearts*
45 Schellen *n*
- *bells (hawkbells)*

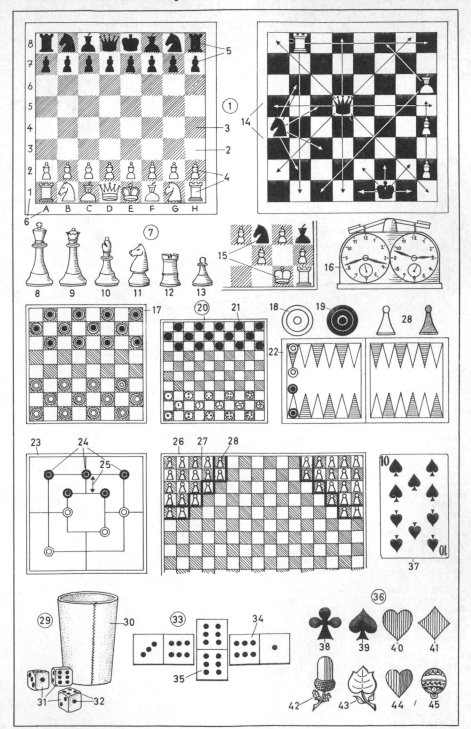

1-19 das Billard (Billardspiel)
- *game of billiards (billiards)*
1 die Billardkugel (der Billardball), eine Elfenbein- oder Kunststoffkugel
- *billiard ball, an ivory or plastic ball*
2-6 Billardstöße *m*
- *billiard strokes (forms of striking)*
2 der Mittelstoß (Horizontalstoß)
- *plain stroke (hitting the cue ball dead centre, Am. center)*
3 der Hochstoß [ergibt Nachläufer *m*]
- *top stroke [promotes extra forward rotation]*
4 der Tiefstoß [ergibt Rückzieher *m*]
- *screw-back [imparts a direct recoil or backward motion]*
5 der Effetstoß
- *side (running side, Am. English)*
6 der Kontereffetstoß
- *check side*
7-19 das Billardzimmer
- *billiard room (Am. billiard parlor, billiard saloon, poolroom)*
7 das französische Billard (Karambolagebillard); *ähnl.:* das deutsche oder englische Billard (Lochbillard)
- *French billiards (carom billiards, carrom billiards);* sim.: *German or English billiards (pocket billiards, Am. poolbilliards)*
8 der Billardspieler
- *billiard player*
9 das Queue (der Billardstock)
- *cue (billiard cue, billiard stick)*

10 die Queuekuppe, eine Lederkuppe
- *leather cue tip*
11 der weiße Spielball
- *white cue ball*
12 der rote Stoßball
- *red object ball*
13 der weiße Punktball
- *white spot ball (white dot ball)*
14 der Billardtisch (das Brett)
- *billiard table*
15 die Spielfläche mit grüner Tuchbespannung *f*
- *table bed with green cloth (billiard cloth, green baize covering)*
16 die Bande (Gummibande)
- *cushions (rubber cushions, cushioned ledge)*
17 das Billardtaxi, eine Kontrolluhr
- *billiard clock, a timer*
18 die Anschreibetafel
- *billiard marker*
19 der Queueständer
- *cue rack*

1-59 der Campingplatz
- *camp site (camping site, Am. campground)*
1 die Rezeption (Anmeldung, das Büro)
- *reception (office)*
2 der Campingplatzwart
- *.camp site attendant*
3 der Klappwohnwagen (Klappanhänger, Klappcaravan, Faltwohnwagen, Faltcaravan)
- *folding caravan (collapsible caravan, collapsible trailer)*
4 die Hängematte
- *hammock*
5-6 der Sanitärtrakt (die Sanitäranlagen *pl*)
- *washing and toilet facilities*
5 die Toiletten *f* und Waschräume *m*
- *toilets and washrooms (Am. lavatories)*
6 die Wasch- und Spülbecken *n*
- *washbasins and sinks*
7 der Bungalow (*schweiz.* das Chalet)
- *bungalow (chalet)*
8-11 das Pfadfinderlager (Pfadfindertreffen, Jamboree)
- *scout camp*
8 das Rundzelt
- *bell tent*
9 der Fahrtenwimpel
- *pennon*
10 das Lagerfeuer
- *camp fire*
11 der Pfadfinder (Boy-Scout)
- *boy scout (scout)*
12 das Segelboot (die Segeljolle, Jolle)
- *sailing boat (yacht, Am. sailboat)*
13 der Landungssteg (Landesteg)
- *landing stage (jetty)*
14 das Sportschlauchboot, ein Schlauchboot *n*
- *inflatable boat (inflatable dinghy)*

15 der Außenbordmotor (Außenborder)
- *outboard motor (outboard)*
16 der Trimaran (das Dreirumpfboot)
- *trimaran*
17 die Ducht (das Sitzbrett)
- *thwart (oarsman's bench)*
18 die Dolle
- *rowlock (oarlock)*
19 der Riemen (das Ruder)
- *oar*
20 der Bootsanhänger (Bootswagen, Boottransporter, Trailer)
- *boat trailer (boat carriage)*
21 **das Hauszelt**
- *ridge tent*
22 das Überdach
- *flysheet*
23 die Zeltspannleine (Zeltleine)
- *guy line (guy)*
24 der Zeltpflock (Hering, Zelthering)
- *tent peg (peg)*
25 der Zeltpflockhammer (Heringshammer)
- *mallet*
26 der Zeltspannring
- *groundsheet ring*
27 die Apsis (Zeltapsis, Gepäckapsis)
- *bell end*
28 das ausgestellte Vordach
- *erected awning*
29 die Zeltlampe, eine Petroleumlampe
- *storm lantern, a paraffin lamp*
30 der Schlafsack
- *sleeping bag*
31 die Luftmatratze (aufblasbare Liegematratze)
- *air mattress (inflatable air-bed)*
32 der Wassersack (Trinkwassersack)
- *water carrier (drinking water carrier)*

33 der zweiflammige Gaskocher für Propangas *n* oder Butangas *n*
- *double-burner gas cooker for propane gas or butane gas*
34 die Propan-(Butan-)gasflasche
- *propane or butane gas bottle*
35 der Dampfkochtopf
- *pressure cooker*
36 **das Bungalowzelt** (Steilwandzelt)
- *frame tent*
37 das Vordach
- *awning*
38 die Zeltstange
- *tent pole*
39 der Rundbogeneingang
- *wheelarch doorway*
40 die Lüftungsfenster
- *mesh ventilator*
41 das Klarsichtfenster
- *transparent window*
42 die Platznummer
- *pitch number*
43 der Campingstuhl, ein Klappstuhl *m*
- *folding camp chair*
44 der Campingtisch, ein Klapptisch *m*
- *folding camp table*
45 das Campinggeschirr
- *camping eating utensils*
46 der Camper
- *camper*
47 der Holzkohlengrill
- *charcoal grill (barbecue)*
48 die Holzkohle
- *charcoal*
49 der Blasebalg
- *bellows*
50 der Dachgepäckträger
- *roof rack*
51 die Gepäckspinne
- *roof lashing*

52 **der Wohnwagen** (Wohnhänger, Caravan)
- *caravan (Am. trailer)*
53 der Gasflaschenkasten (Deichselkasten)
- *box for gas bottle*
54 das Buglaufrad
- *jockey wheel*
55 die Anhängekupplung
- *drawbar coupling*
56 der Dachlüfter
- *roof ventilator*
57 das Wohnwagenvorzelt
- *caravan awning*
58 das aufblasbare Igluzelt
- *inflatable igloo tent*
59 die Campingliege
- *camp bed (Am. camp cot)*

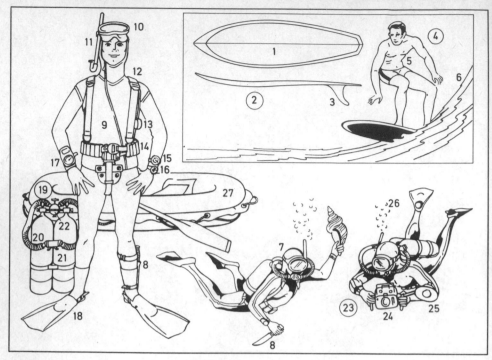

1-6 das Surfing (Wellenreiten,
Brandungsreiten)
- *surf riding (surfing)*
1 das Surfbrett (Surfboard) in der
Draufsicht
- *plan view of surfboard*
2 das Surfbrett (Surfboard) im
Schnitt *m*
- *section of surfboard*
3 das Schwert
- *skeg (stabilizing fin)*
4 das Big-wave-riding (Reiten in der
Superbrandung)
- *big wave riding*
5 der Surfer
- *surfboarder (surfer)*
6 die Brandungswelle
- *breaker*
7-27 das Tauchen
- *skin diving (underwater swimming)*
7 der Taucher
- *skin diver (underwater swimmer)*
8-22 die Taucherausrüstung
- *underwater swimming set*
8 das Tauchermesser
- *knife*
9 der Neopren-Tauchanzug, ein
Kälteschutzanzug *m*
- *neoprene wetsuit*
10 die Tauchmaske (Tauchermaske,
Maske), eine
Druckausgleichsmaske
- *diving mask (face mask, mask), a
pressure-equalizing mask*
11 der Schnorchel
- *snorkel (schnorkel)*

12 die Bebänderung des
Preßlufttauchgeräts *n*
- *harness of diving apparatus*
13 der Druckmesser für den
Flascheninhalt
- *compressed-air pressure gauge
(Am. gage)*
14 der Bleigürtel
- *weight belt*
15 der Tiefenmesser
- *depth gauge
(Am. gage)*
16 die Taucheruhr zur
Tauchzeitüberwachung
- *waterproof watch for checking
duration of dive*
17 das Dekometer zur Anzeige der
Auftauchstufen *f*
(Dekompressionsstufen)
- *decometer for measuring stages of
ascent*
18 die Schwimmflosse
- *fin (flipper)*
19 das Tauchgerät (*auch:* die
Aqualunge), ein Zweiflaschengerät
- *diving apparatus (also: aqualung,
scuba), with two cylinders (bottles)*
20 der Zweischlauch-Lungenautomat
- *two-tube demand regulator*
21 die Preßluftflasche
- *compressed-air cylinder
(compressed-air bottle)*
22 das Flaschenventil
- *on/off valve*
23 die Unterwasserfotografie
- *underwater photography*

24 das Unterwassergehäuse für die
Kamera
(*ähnl.:* die Unterwasserkamera)
- *underwater camera housing
(underwater camera case);*
sim.: *underwater camera*
25 das Unterwasserblitzgerät
- *underwater flashlight*
26 die Ausatmungsluft
- *exhaust bubbles*
27 das Schlauchboot
- *inflatable boat (inflatable dinghy)*

1 der Badewärter
- *lifesaver (lifeguard)*
2 das Rettungsseil
- *lifeline*
3 der Rettungsring
- *lifebelt (lifebuoy)*
4 der Sturmball
- *storm signal*
5 der Zeitball
- *time ball*
6 die Warnungstafel
- *warning sign*
7 die Gezeitentafel, eine
Anzeigetafel für Ebbe *f* und Flut *f*
- *tide table, a notice board showing
times of low tide and high tide*
8 die Tafel, mit Wasser- und
Lufttemperaturangabe *f*
- *board showing water and air
temperature*
9 der Badesteg
- *bathing platform*
10 der Wimpelmast
- *pennon staff*
11 der Wimpel
- *pennon*
12 das Wasservelo (Wassertretrad,
Wasserfahrrad, Pedalo)
- *paddle boat (peddle boat)*
13 das Surfbrettfahren, hinter dem
Motorboot *n*
- *surf riding (surfing) behind motorboat*
14 der Surfer
- *surfboarder (surfer)*
15 das Surfbrett
- *surfboard*

16 der Wasserski
- *water ski*
17 die Schwimmatratze
- *inflatable beach mattress*
18 der Wasserball
- *beach ball*
19-23 Strandkleidung *f*
- *beachwear*
19 der Strandanzug
- *beach suit*
20 der Strandhut
- *beach hat*
21 die Strandjacke
- *beach jacket*
22 die Strandhose
- *beach trousers*
23 der Strandschuh (Badeschuh)
- *beach shoe (bathing shoe)*
24 die Strandtasche (Badetasche)
- *beach bag*
25 der Bademantel
- *bathing gown (bathing wrap)*
26 der Bikini (zweiteilige
Damenbadeanzug)
- *bikini (ladies' two-piece bathing suit)*
27 das Badehöschen
- *bikini bottom*
28 der Büstenhalter
- *bikini top*
29 die Badehaube (Bademütze,
Schwimmkappe)
- *bathing cap (swimming cap)*
30 der Badegast
- *bather*
31 das Ringtennis
- *deck tennis (quoits)*

32 der Gummiring
- *rubber ring (quoit)*
33 das Schwimmtier, ein
Aufblasartikel *m*
- *rubber animal, an inflatable
animal*
34 der Strandwärter
- *beach attendant*
35 die Sandburg (Strandburg)
- *sand den [built as a wind-break]*
36 der Strandkorb
- *roofed wicker beach chair*
37 der Unterwasserjäger
- *underwater swimmer*
38 die Tauchbrille
- *diving goggles*
39 der Schnorchel
- *snorkel (schnorkel)*
40 die Handharpune (der Fischspeer)
- *hand harpoon (fish spear, fish
lance)*
41 die Tauchflosse (Schwimmflosse,
zum Sporttauchen *n*
- *fin (flipper) for diving (for
underwater swimming)*
42 der Badeanzug (Schwimmanzug)
- *bathing suit (swimsuit)*
43 die Badehose (Schwimmhose)
- *bathing trunks (swimming trunks)*
44 die Badekappe (Schwimmkappe)
- *bathing cap (swimming cap)*
45 das Strandzelt, ein Hauszelt *n*
- *beach tent, a ridge tent*
46 die Rettungsstation
- *lifeguard station*

281 Schwimmbad (Freizeitzentrum)

1-9 das Brandungsbad (Wellenbad),
ein Hallenbad n
- swimming pool with artificial
waves, an indoor pool
1 die künstliche Brandung
- artificial waves
2 die Strandzone
- beach area
3 der Beckenrand
- edge of the pool
4 der Bademeister
- swimming pool attendant (pool
attendant, swimming bath
attendant)
5 der Liegesessel
- sun bed
6 der Schwimmring
- lifebelt
7 die Schwimmanschetten f
- water wings
8 die Badehaube
- bathing cap
9 die Schleuse zum Sprudelbad n im
Freien n
- channel to outdoor mineral bath
10 das Solarium (künstliche
Sonnenbad)
- solarium
11 die Liegefläche
- sunbathing area
12 die Sonnenbadende
- sun bather
13 die künstliche Sonne
- sun ray lamp
14 das Badetuch
- bathing towel
15 das Freikörperkulturgelände
(FKK-Gelände, Nudistengelände,
ugs. „Abessinien")
- nudist sunbathing area
16 der Nudist (Freund textilfreier
Lebensart)
- nudist (naturist)
17 der Sichtschutzraum
- screen (fence)
18 die Sauna (finnische Sauna, das
finnische Heißluftbad), eine
Gemeinschaftssauna
- sauna (mixed sauna)
19 die Holzauskleidung
- wood panelling (Am. paneling)
20 die Sitz- und Liegestufen f
- tiered benches
21 der Saunaofen
- sauna stove
22 die Feldsteine m
- stones
23 das Hygrometer
(der Feuchtigkeitsmesser)
- hygrometer
24 das Thermometer
- thermometer
25 das Sitztuch
- towel
26 der Bottich für die Befeuchtung der
Ofensteine m
- water tub for moistening the stones
in the stove
27 die Birkenruten f zum Schlagen n
der Haut
- birch rods (birches) for beating the
skin
28 der Abkühlungsraum, zur
Abkühlung nach der Sauna
- cooling room for cooling off
(cooling down) after the sauna

29 die temperierte Dusche
- lukewarm shower
30 das Kaltwasserbecken
- cold bath
31 der Hot-Whirl-Pool (das
Unterwassermassagebad)
- hot whirlpool (underwater massage
bath)
32 die Einstiegstufe
- step into the bath
33 das Massagebad
- massage bath
34 das Jetgebläse
- jet blower
35 der Hot-Whirl-Pool [Schema]
- hot whirlpool [diagram]
36 der Beckenquerschnitt
- section of the bath
37 der Einstieg
- step
38 die umlaufende Sitzbank
- circular seat
39 die Wasserabsaugung
- water extractor
40 der Wasserdüsenkanal
- water jet pipe
41 der Luftdüsenkanal
- air jet pipe

1-32 **die Badeanstalt**
(Schwimmanstalt, das
Schwimmbad, die
Schwimmanlage), ein Freibad *n*
- *swimming pool*, *an open-air
swimming pool*
1 die Badezelle (Zelle, Badekabine,
Kabine)
- *changing cubicle*
2 die Dusche (Brause)
- *shower (shower bath)*
3 der Umkleideraum
- *changing room*
4 das Sonnenbad *od.* Luftbad
- *sunbathing area*
5-10 **die Sprunganlage**
- *diving boards (diving apparatus)*
5 der Turmspringer
- *diver (highboard diver)*
6 der Sprungturm
- *diving platform*
7 die Zehnmeterplattform
- *ten-metre (Am. ten-meter)
platform*
8 die Fünfmeterplattform
- *five-metre (Am. five-meter)
platform*
9 das Dreimeterbrett (Sprungbrett)
- *three-metre (Am. three-meter)
springboard (diving board)*
10 das Einmeterbrett, ein Trampolin *n*
- *one-metre (Am. one-meter)
springboard, a trampoline*
11 das Sprungbecken
- *diving pool*
12 der gestreckte Kopfsprung
- *straight header*
13 der Fußsprung
- *feet-first jump*
14 der Paketsprung
- *tuck jump (haunch jump)*
15 der Bademeister
- *swimming pool attendant (pool
attendant, swimming bath
attendant)*
16-20 **der Schwimmunterricht**
- *swimming instruction*
16 der Schwimmlehrer
(Schwimmeister)
- *swimming instructor (swimming
teacher)*
17 der Schwimmschüler, beim
Schwimmen *n*
- *learner-swimmer*
18 das Schwimmkissen
- *float;* sim.: *water wings*
19 der Schwimmgürtel (Korkgürtel,
Tragegürtel, die Korkweste)
- *swimming belt (cork jacket)*
20 das Trockenschwimmen
- *land drill*
21 das Nichtschwimmerbecken
- *non-swimmers' pool*
22 die Laufrinne
- *footbath*
23 das Schwimmerbecken
- *swimmers' pool*
24-32 **das Freistilwettschwimmen**
einer Schwimmstaffel
- *freestyle relay race*
24 der Zeitnehmer
- *timekeeper (lane timekeeper)*
25 der Zielrichter
- *placing judge*
26 der Wenderichter
- *turning judge*

27 der Startblock (Startsockel)
- *starting block (starting place)*
28 der Anschlag eines
Wettschwimmers *m*
- *competitor touching the finishing
line*
29 der Startsprung
- *starting dive (racing dive)*
30 der Starter
- *starter*
31 die Schwimmbahn
- *swimming lane*
32 die Korkleine
- *rope with cork floats*
33-39 **die Schwimmarten** *f*
(Schwimmstile *m*, Schwimmlagen *f*,
Stilarten *f*)
- *swimming strokes*
33 das Brustschwimmen
- *breaststroke*
34 das Schmetterlingsschwimmen
(Butterfly)
- *butterfly stroke*
35 das Delphinschwimmen
- *dolphin butterfly stroke*
36 das Seitenschwimmen
- *side stroke*
37 das Kraulschwimmen (Crawlen,
Kraulen, Kriechstoßschwimmen);
ähnl.: das
Handüberhandschwimmen
- *crawl stroke (crawl);* sim.: *trudgen
stroke (trudgen, double overarm
stroke)*
38 das Tauchen
(Unterwasserschwimmen)
- *diving (underwater swimming)*
39 das Wassertreten
- *treading water*
40-45 **das Wasserspringen**
(Wasserkunstspringen,
Turmspringen, Kunstspringen, die
Wassersprünge *m*)
- *diving (acrobatic diving, fancy
diving, competitive diving,
highboard diving)*
40 der Hechtsprung aus dem Stand *m*
- *standing take-off pike dive*
41 der Auerbachsprung vorwärts
- *one-half twist isander (reverse dive)*
42 der Salto (Doppelsalto) rückwärts
- *backward somersault (double
backward somersault)*
43 die Schraube mit Anlauf *m*
- *running take-off twist dive*
44 der Bohrer
- *screw dive*
45 der Handstandsprung
- *armstand dive (handstand dive)*
46-50 **das Wasserballspiel**
- *water polo*
46 das Wasserballtor
- *goal*
47 der Tormann
- *goalkeeper*
48 der Wasserball
- *water polo ball*
49 der Verteidiger
- *back*
50 der Stürmer
- *forward*

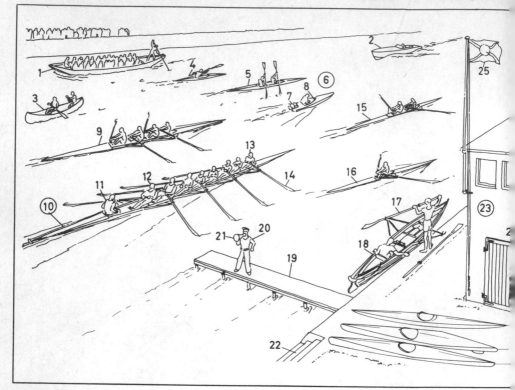

1-18 die Auffahrt zur Regatta
  (Ruderregatta, zum Wettrudern *n*)
– *taking up positions for the regatta*
1 der Stechkahn, ein
  Vergnügungsboot *n*
– *punt, a pleasure boat*
2 das Motorboot
– *motorboat*
3 der Kanadier, ein Kanu *n*
– *Canadian canoe*
4 der (das) Kajak (der Grönländer),
  ein Paddelboot *n*
– *kayak (Alaskan canoe, slalom
  canoe), a canoe*
5 der (das) Doppelkajak
– *tandem kayak*
6 das Außenbordmotorboot
– *outboard motorboat (outboard
  speedboat, outboard)*
7 der Außenbordmotor
– *outboard motor (outboard)*
8 die Plicht (das Kockpit, Cockpit,
  der Sitzraum)
– *cockpit*
9-16 Rennboote *n* (Sportboote,
  Auslegerboote)
– *racing boats (sportsboats,
  outriggers)*
9-15 Riemenboote *n*
– *shells (rowing boats, Am. rowboats)*
9 der Vierer ohne Steuermann *m*
  (Vierer ohne), ein Kraweelboot *n*
– *coxless four, a carvel-built boat*

10 der Achter (Rennachter)
– *eight (eight-oared racing shell)*
11 der Steuermann
– *cox*
12 der Schlagmann, ein Ruderer *m*
– *stroke, an oarsman*
13 der Bugmann (die „Nummer Eins")
– *bow ('number one')*
14 der Riemen
– *oar*
15 der Zweier (Riemenzweier)
– *coxless pair*
16 der Einer (Renneiner *das Skiff*)
– *single sculler
  (single skuller, racing
  sculler, racing skuller, skiff)*
17 das Skull
– *scull (skull)*
18 der Einer mit Steuermann *m*, ein
  Klinkereiner *m*
– *coxed single, a clinker-built single*
19 der Steg (Bootssteg, Landungssteg,
  Anlegesteg)
– *jetty (landing stage, mooring)*
20 der Rudertrainer
– *rowing coach*
21 das Megaphon (Sprachrohr,
  scherzh.: die Flüstertüte)
– *megaphone*
22 die Bootstreppe
– *quayside steps*
23 das Bootshaus (Klubhaus)
– *clubhouse (club)*

24 der Bootsschuppen
– *boathouse*
25 die Klubflagge (der Klubstander)
– *club's flag*
26-33 der Gigvierer, ein Gigboot *n*
  (Dollenboot, Tourenboot)
– *four-oared gig, a touring boat*
26 das Ruder
– *oar*
27 der Steuersitz
– *cox's seat*
28 die Ducht (Ruderbank)
– *thwart (seat)*
29 die Dolle (Riemenauflage)
– *rowlock (oarlock)*
30 der Dollbord
– *gunwale (gunnel)*
31 der Duchtweger
– *rising*
32 der Kiel (Außenkiel)
– *keel*
33 die Außenhaut [geklinkert]
– *skin (shell, outer skin)
  [clinker-built]*
34 das einfache Paddel (Stechpaddel,
  die Pagaie)
– *single-bladed paddle (paddle)*
35-38 der Riemen (das Skull)
– *oar (scull, skull)*
35 der Holm (Riemenholm)
– *grip*
36 die Belederung
– *leather sheath*

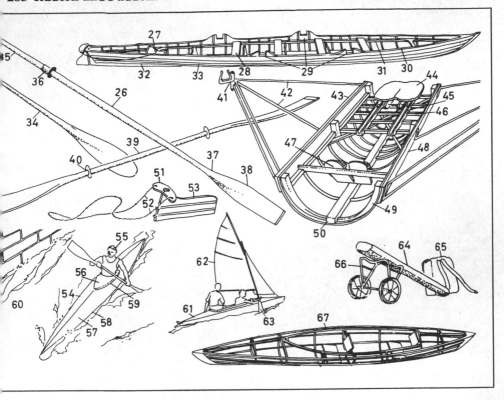

37 der Riemenhals
- *shaft (neck)*
38 das Blatt (Riemenblatt)
- *blade*
39 das Doppelpaddel
- *double-bladed paddle (double-ended paddle)*
40 der Tropfring
- *drip ring*
41-50 der Rollsitz (Rudersitz)
- *sliding seat*
41 die Dolle (Drehdolle)
- *rowlock (oarlock)*
42 der Ausleger
- *outrigger*
43 das Spülbord
- *saxboard*
44 der Rollsitz
- *sliding seat*
45 die Rollschiene (Rollbahn)
- *runner*
46 die Versteifung
- *strut*
47 das Stemmbrett
- *stretcher*
48 die Außenhaut
- *skin (shell, outer skin)*
49 der (das) Spant
- *frame (rib)*
50 der Kiel (Innenkiel)
- *kelson (keelson)*
51-53 das Ruder (Steuer)
- *rudder (steering rudder)*

51 das Ruderjoch (Steuerjoch)
- *yoke*
52 die Steuerleine
- *lines (steering lines)*
53 das Blatt (Ruderblatt, Steuerblatt)
- *blade (rudder blade, rudder)*
54-66 Faltboote n
- *folding boats (foldboats, canoes)*
54 der Faltbooteiner, ein Sporteiner m
- *one-man kayak*
55 der Faltbootfahrer
- *canoeist*
56 die Spritzdecke
- *spraydeck*
57 das Verdeck
- *deck*
58 die Gummihaut (Außenhaut, Bootshaut)
- *rubber-covered canvas hull*
59 der Süllrand
- *cockpit coaming (coaming)*
60 die Floßgasse am Wehr n
- *channel for rafts alongside weir*
61 der Faltbootzweier, ein Tourenzweier m (Wanderzweier)
- *two-seater folding kayak, a touring kayak*
62 das Faltbootsegel
- *sail of folding kayak*
63 das Seitenschwert
- *leeboard*
64 die Stabtasche
- *bag for the rods*

65 der Bootsrucksack
- *rucksack*
66 der Bootswagen
- *boat trailer (boat carriage)*
67 das Faltbootgerüst
- *frame of folding kayak*
68-70 Kajaks m od. n
- *kayaks*
68 der (das) Eskimokajak
- *Eskimo kayak*
69 der (das) Wildwasserrennkajak
- *wild-water racing kayak*
70 der (das) Wanderkajak
- *touring kayak*

1-9 **das Windsurfing**
- *windsurfing*
1 der Windsurfer
- *windsurfer*
2 das Segel
- *sail*
3 das Klarsichtfenster
- *transparent window (window)*
4 der Mast
- *mast*
5 das Surfbrett
- *surfboard*
6 das bewegliche Lager für die
  Mastneigung und die Steuerung
- *universal joint (movable bearing)*
  for adjusting the angle of the mast
  and for steering
7 der Gabelbaum
- *boom*
8 das (einholbare) Hauptschwert
- *retractable centreboard*
  (Am. centerboard)
9 das Hilfsschwert
- *rudder*
10-48 **das Segelboot**
- *yacht (sailing boat, Am. sailboat)*
10 das Vordeck
- *foredeck*
11 der Mast
- *mast*
12 der Trapezdraht
- *trapeze*
13 die Saling
- *crosstrees (spreader)*
14 der Wanthänger
- *hound*
15 das Vorstag
- *forestay*
16 die Fock (Genua)
- *jib (Genoa jib)*
17 der Fockniederholer
- *jib downhaul*
18 die Want
- *side stay (shroud)*
19 der Wantenspanner
- *lanyard (bottlescrew)*
20 der Mastfuß
- *foot of the mast*
21 der Baumniederholer
- *kicking strap (vang)*
22 die Fockschotklemme
- *jam cleat*
23 die Fockschot
- *foresheet (jib sheet)*
24 der Schwertkasten
- *centreboard (Am. centerboard) case*
25 der Knarrpoller
- *bitt*
26 das Schwert
- *centreboard (Am. centerboard)*
27 der Traveller
- *traveller (Am. traveler)*
28 die Großschot
- *mainsheet*
29 die Fockschotleitschiene
- *fairlead*
30 die Ausreitgurte *m*
- *toestraps (hiking straps)*
31 der Pinnenausleger
- *tiller extension (hiking stick)*
32 die Pinne
- *tiller*
33 der Ruderkopf
- *rudderhead (rudder stock)*
34 das Ruderblatt
- *rudder blade (rudder)*

35 der Spiegel (das Spiegelheck)
- *transom*
36 das Lenzloch
- *drain plug*
37 der Großsegelhals
- *gooseneck*
38 das Segelfenster
- *window*
39 der Baum
- *boom*
40 das Unterliek
- *foot*
41 das Schothorn
- *clew*
42 das Vorliek
- *luff (leading edge)*
43 die Lattentasche
- *leech pocket (batten cleat, batten*
  pocket)
44 die Latte
- *batten*
45 das Achterliek
- *leech (trailing edge)*
46 das Großsegel
- *mainsail*
47 der Großsegelkopf
- *headboard*
48 der Verklicker
- *racing flag (burgee)*
49-65 **die Bootsklassen** *f*
- *yacht classes*
49 der Flying Dutchman
- *Flying Dutchman*
50 die Olympiajolle
- *O-Joller*
51 das Finndingi
- *Finn dinghy (Finn)*
52 der Pirat
- *pirate*
53 das 12-m²-Sharpie
- *12.00 m² sharpie*
54 das Tempest
- *tempest*
55 der Star
- *star*
56 das (der) Soling
- *soling*
57 der Drachen
- *dragon*
58 die 5,5-m-Klasse
- *5.5-metre (Am. 5.5-meter) class*
59 die 6-m-R-Klasse
- *6-metre (Am. 6-meter) R-class*
60 der 30-m²-Schärenkreuzer
- *30.00 m² cruising yacht (coastal*
  cruiser)
61 der 30-m²-Jollenkreuzer
- *30.00 m² dinghy cruiser*
62 die 25-m²-Einheitskieljacht
- *25.00 m² one-design keelboat*
63 die KR-Klasse
- *KR-class*
64 der Katamaran
- *catamaran*
65 der Doppelrumpf
- *twin hull*

1-13 Segelstellungen *f* und Windrichtungen *f*
- *points of sailing and wind directions*
1 das Segeln vor dem Wind *m*
- *sailing downwind*
2 das Großsegel
- *mainsail*
3 die Fock
- *jib*
4 die Schmetterlingsstellung der Segel *n*
- *ballooning sails*
5 die Mittschiffslinie
- *centre (Am. center) line*
6 die Windrichtung
- *wind direction*
7 das Boot ohne Fahrt *f*
- *yacht tacking*
8 das killende Segel
- *sail, shivering*
9 das Segeln am Wind *m* (das Anluven)
- *luffing*
10 das Segeln hart (hoch) am Wind *m*
- *sailing close-hauled*
11 das Segeln mit halbem Wind *m*
- *sailing with wind abeam*
12 das Segeln mit raumem Wind *m*
- *sailing with free wind*
13 die Backstagsbrise
- *quartering wind (quarter wind)*
14-24 der Regattakurs
- *regatta course*
14 die Start- und Zieltonne (Start- und Zielboje)
- *starting and finishing buoy*
15 das Startschiff
- *committee boat*
16 der Dreieckskurs (die Regattastrecke)
- *triangular course (regatta course)*
17 die Wendeboje (Wendemarke)
- *buoy (mark) to be rounded*
18 die Kursboje
- *buoy to be passed*
19 der erste Umlauf
- *first leg*
20 der zweite Umlauf
- *second leg*
21 der dritte Umlauf
- *third leg*
22 die Kreuzstrecke
- *windward leg*
23 die Vormwindstrecke
- *downwind leg*
24 die Umwindstrecke
- *reaching leg*
25-28 das Kreuzen
- *tacking*
25 die Kreuzstrecke
- *tack*
26 das Halsen
- *gybing (jibing)*
27 das Wenden
- *going about*
28 der Verlust an Höhe *f* beim Halsen *n*
- *loss of distance during the gybe (jibe)*
29-41 Rumpfformen *f* von Segelbooten *n*
- *types of yacht hull*
29-34 die Fahrtenkieljacht
- *cruiser keelboat*
29 das Heck
- *stern*
30 der Löffelbug
- *spoon bow*
31 die Wasserlinie
- *waterline*
32 der Kiel (Ballastkiel)
- *keel (ballast keel)*
33 der Ballast
- *ballast*
34 das Ruder
- *rudder*
35 die Rennkieljacht
- *racing keelboat*
36 der Bleikiel
- *lead keel*
37-41 die Jolle, eine Schwertjacht
- *keel-centreboard (Am. centerboard) yawl*
37 das aufholbare Ruder
- *retractable rudder*
38 die Plicht (das Cockpit)
- *cockpit*
39 der Kajütenaufbau (die Kajüte)
- *cabin superstructure (cabin)*
40 der gerade Steven (Auf-und-nieder-Steven)
- *straight stem*
41 das aufholbare Schwert
- *retractable centreboard (Am. centerboard)*
42-49 Heckformen *f* von Segelbooten *n*
- *types of yacht stern*
42 das Jachtheck
- *yacht stern*
43 der Jachtspiegel
- *square stern*
44 das Kanuheck
- *canoe stern*
45 das Spitzgatheck
- *cruiser stern*
46 das Namensschild
- *name plate*
47 das Totholz
- *deadwood*
48 das Spiegelheck
- *transom stern*
49 der Spiegel
- *transom*
50-57 die Beplankung von Holzbooten *n*
- *timber planking*
50-52 die Klinkerbeplankung
- *clinker planking (clench planking)*
50 die Außenhautplanke
- *outside strake*
51 das Spant, ein Querspant *n*
- *frame (rib)*
52 der Klinknagel
- *clenched nail (riveted nail)*
53 die Kraweelbeplankung
- *carvel planking*
54 der Nahtspantenbau
- *close-seamed construction*
55 der Nahtspant, ein Längsspant *n*
- *stringer*
56 die Diagonalkraweelbeplankung
- *diagonal carvel planking*
57 die innere Beplankung
- *inner planking*

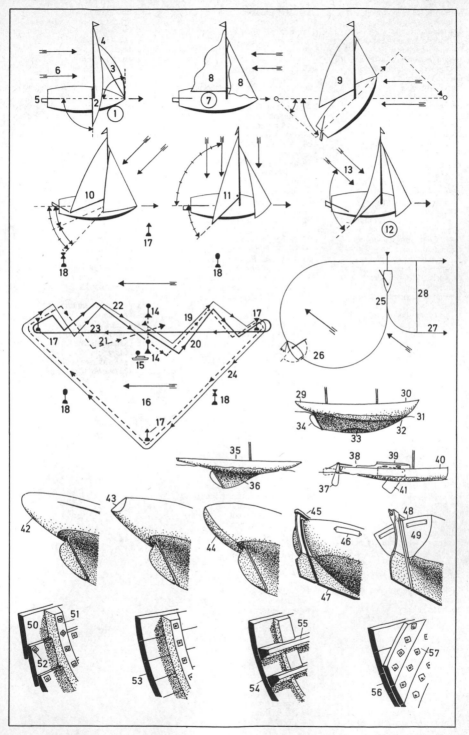

1-5 Motorboote *n* (Sportboote)
- *motorboats (powerboats, sportsboats)*
1 das Sportschlauchboot mit Außenbordmotor *m*
- *inflatable sportsboat with outboard motor (outboard inflatable)*
2 das Inbord-Sportboot [mit Z-Antrieb *m*]
- *Z-drive motorboat (outdrive motorboat)*
3 das Kajütboot
- *cabin cruiser*
4 der Motorkreuzer
- *motor cruiser*
5 die 30-m-Hochseejacht
- *30-metre (Am. 30-meter) ocean-going cruiser*
6 die Verbandsflagge
- *association flag*
7 der Bootsname (*oder:* die Zertifikatsnummer)
- *name of craft* (or: *registration number*)
8 die Clubzugehörigkeit und der Heimathafen
- *club membership and port of registry* (Am. *home port*)
9 die Verbandsflagge an der Steuerbordsaling
- *association flag on the starboard crosstrees*
10-14 die Lichterführung auf Sportbooten *n* für Küsten- und Seegewässer *n* (die Positionslaternen *f*)
- *navigation lights of sportsboats in coastal and inshore waters*
10 das weiße Topplicht
- *white top light*
11 das grüne Steuerbordlicht (die Steuerbordlaterne)
- *green starboard sidelight*
12 das rote Backbordlicht (die Backbordlaterne)
- *red port sidelight*
13 das grünrote Buglicht
- *green and red bow light (combined lantern)*
14 das weiße Hecklicht
- *white stern light*
15-18 Anker *m*
- *anchors*
15 der Stockanker (Admiralitätsanker), ein Schwergewichtsanker *m*
- *stocked anchor (Admiralty anchor), a bower anchor*
16-18 Leichtgewichtsanker *m*
- *lightweight anchor*
16 der Pflugscharanker
- *CQR anchor (plough,* Am. *plow, anchor)*
17 der Patentanker
- *stockless anchor (patent anchor)*
18 der Danforth-Anker
- *Danforth anchor*
19 die Rettungsinsel (das Rettungsfloß)
- *life raft*
20 die Schwimmweste
- *life jacket*
21-44 Motorbootrennen *n*
- *powerboat racing*
21 der Außenbordkatamaran
- *catamaran with outboard motor*

22 das Hydroplane-Rennboot
- *hydroplane*
23 der Rennaußenbordmotor
- *racing outboard motor*
24 die Ruderpinne
- *tiller*
25 die Benzinleitung
- *fuel pipe*
26 der Heckspiegel (das Heckbrett)
- *transom*
27 der Tragschlauch
- *buoyancy tube*
28 Start *m* und Ziel *n*
- *start and finish*
29 die Startzone
- *start*
30 die Start- und Ziellinie
- *starting and finishing line*
31 die Wendeboje
- *buoy to be rounded*
32-37 Verdrängungsboote *n*
- *displacement boats*
32-34 das Rundspantboot
- *round-bilge boat*
32 die Bodenansicht
- *view of hull bottom*
33 der Vorschiffquerschnitt
- *section of fore ship*
34 der Achterschiffquerschnitt
- *section of aft ship*
35-37 das V-Boden-Boot
- *V-bottom boat (vee-bottom boat)*
35 die Bodenansicht
- *view of hull bottom*
36 der Vorschiffquerschnitt
- *section of fore ship*
37 der Achterschiffquerschnitt
- *section of aft ship*
38-44 Gleitboote *n*
- *planing boats (surface skimmers, skimmers)*
38-41 das Stufenboot
- *stepped hydroplane (stepped skimmer)*
38 die Seitenansicht
- *side view*
39 die Bodenansicht
- *view of hull bottom*
40 der Vorschiffquerschnitt
- *section of fore ship*
41 der Achterschiffquerschnitt
- *section of aft ship*
42 das Dreipunktboot
- *three-point hydroplane*
43 die Flosse
- *fin*
44 die Tatze
- *float*
45-62 Wasserski *m*
- *water skiing*
45 die Wasserskiläuferin
- *water skier*
46 der Tiefwasserstart
- *deep-water start*
47 das Seil (Schleppseil)
- *tow line (towing line)*
48 die Hantel
- *handle*
49-55 die Wasserskisprache (die Handzeichen *n* des Wasserskiläufers *m*)
- *water-ski signalling (code of hand signals from skier to boat driver)*
49 das Zeichen „Schneller"
- *signal for 'faster'*

50 das Zeichen „Langsamer"
- *signal for 'slower' ('slow down')*
51 das Zeichen „Tempo in Ordnung"
- *signal for 'speed OK'*
52 das Zeichen „Wenden"
- *signal for 'turn'*
53 das Zeichen „Halt"
- *signal for 'stop'*
54 das Zeichen „Motor abstellen"
- *signal for 'cut motor'*
55 der Wink „Zurück zum Liegeplatz"
- *signal for 'return to jetty' ('back to dock')*
56-62 Wasserski *m*
- *types of water ski*
56 der Figurenski, ein Monoski
- *trick ski (figure ski), a monoski*
57-58 die Gummibindung
- *rubber binding*
57 der Vorfußgummi
- *front foot binding*
58 der Fersengummi
- *heel flap*
59 die Stegschlaufe für den zweiten Fuß
- *strap support for second foot*
60 der Slalomski
- *slalom ski*
61 der Kiel (die Flosse)
- *skeg (fixed fin, fin)*
62 der Sprungski
- *jump ski*
63 das Luftkissenfahrzeug
- *hovercraft (air-cushion vehicle)*
64 die Luftschraube
- *propeller*
65 das angeblasene Ruder
- *rudder*
66 das Luftkissen (Luftpolster)
- *skirt enclosing air cushion*

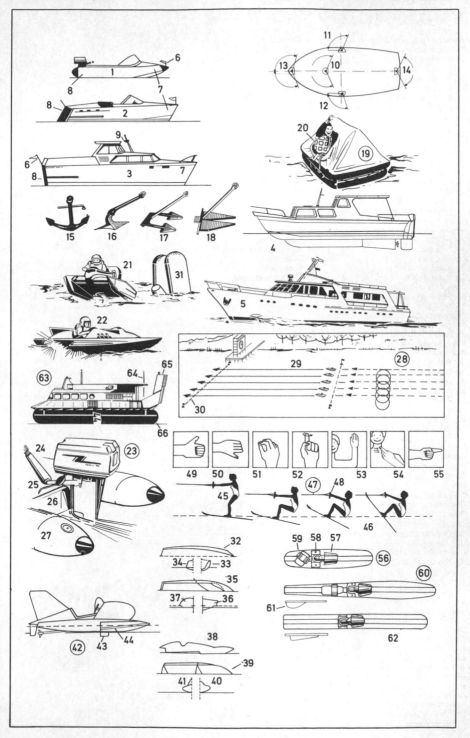

1 der Flugzeugschleppstart
(Flugzeugschlepp, Schleppflug,
Schleppstart)
- *aeroplane (Am. airplane) tow
launch (aerotowing)*
2 das Schleppflugzeug, ein
Motorflugzeug *n*
- *tug (towing plane)*
3 das geschleppte Segelflugzeug
(Segelflugzeug im Schlepp *m*)
- *towed glider (towed sailplane)*
4 das Schleppseil
- *tow rope*
5 der Windenstart
- *winched launch*
6 die Motorwinde
- *motor winch*
7 der Seilfallschirm
- *cable parachute*
8 der Motorsegler
- *motorized glider (powered glider)*
9 das Hochleistungssegelflugzeug
- *high-performance glider
(high-performance sailplane)*
10 das T-Leitwerk
- *T-tail (T-tail unit)*
11 der Windsack
- *wind sock (wind cone)*
12 der Kontrollturm
- *control tower (tower)*
13 das Segelfluggelände
- *glider field*
14 die Flugzeughalle (der Hangar)
- *hangar*
15 die Start- und Landebahn für
Motorflugzeuge *n*
- *runway for aeroplanes (Am. airplanes)*
16 das Wellensegeln
- *wave soaring*
17 die Leewellen *f* (Föhnwellen)
- *lee waves (waves, wave system)*
18 der Rotor
- *rotor*
19 die Lentikulariswolken *f*
- *lenticular clouds (lenticulars)*
20 das Thermiksegeln
- *thermal soaring*
21 der Aufwindschlauch
(Thermikschlauch, thermische
Aufwind, „Bart")
- *thermal*
22 die Kumuluswolke (Haufenwolke,
Quellwolke, der Kumulus)
- *cumulus cloud (heap cloud,
cumulus, woolpack cloud)*
23 das Frontsegeln (Frontensegeln,
Gewittersegeln)
- *storm-front soaring*
24 die Gewitterfront
- *storm front*
25 der Frontaufwind
- *frontal upcurrent*
26 die Kumulonimbuswolke
(der Kumulonimbus)
- *cumulonimbus cloud
(cumulonimbus)*
27 das Hangsegeln
- *slope soaring*
28 der Hangaufwind
- *hill upcurrent (orographic lift)*
29 der Holmflügel, eine Tragfläche
- *multispar wing, a wing*
30 der Hauptholm, ein Kastenholm
- *main spar, a box spar*
31 der Anschlußbeschlag
- *connector fitting*

32 die Wurzelrippe
- *anchor rib*
33 der Schrägholm
- *diagonal spar*
34 die Nasenleiste
- *leading edge*
35 die Hauptrippe
- *main rib*
36 die Hilfsrippe
- *nose rib (false rib)*
37 die Endleiste
- *trailing edge*
38 die Bremsklappe (Störklappe,
Sturzflugbremse)
- *brake flap (spoiler)*
39 die Torsionsnase
- *torsional clamp*
40 die Bespannung
- *covering (skin)*
41 das Querruder
- *aileron*
42 der Randbogen
- *wing tip*
43 das Drachenfliegen
- *hang gliding*
44 der Drachen (Hanggleiter,
Deltagleiter)
- *hang glider*
45 der Drachenflieger
- *hang glider pilot*
46 die Haltestange
- *control frame*

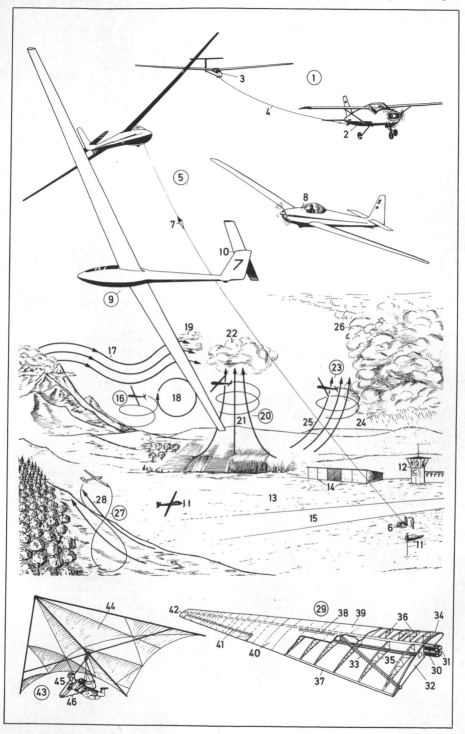

1-9 **der Kunstflug** (die
　　Kunstflugfiguren *f*)
- **aerobatics** *(aerobatic manoeuvres,*
　Am. *maneuvers)*
1 der Looping
- *loop*
2 die liegende Loopingacht
- *horizontal eight*
3 der Rollenkreis
- *rolling circle*
4 der Turn
- *stall turn (hammer head)*
5 das Männchen
- *tail slide (whip stall)*
6 die Schraube
- *vertical flick spin*
7 das Trudeln
- *spin*
8 die Rolle
- *horizontal slow roll*
9 der Rückenflug
- *inverted flight (negative flight)*
10 **das Cockpit**
- *cockpit*
11 das Instrumentenbrett
- *instrument panel*
12 der Kompaß
- *compass*
13 die Funk- und
　　Navigationseinrichtung
- *radio and navigation equipment*
14 der Steuerknüppel
- *control column (control stick)*
15 der Gashebel
- *throttle lever (throttle control)*
16 der Gemischregulierhebel
- *mixture control*
17 das Funksprechgerät
- *radio equipment*
18 **der Sport- und Kunstflugzweisitzer**
- **two-seater plane for racing and**
　aerobatics
19 die Kabine
- *cabin*
20 die Antenne
- *antenna*
21 die Seitenflosse
- *vertical stabilizer (vertical fin, tail fin)*
22 das Seitenruder
- *rudder*
23 die Höhenflosse
- *tailplane (horizontal stabilizer)*
24 das Höhenruder
- *elevator*
25 die Trimmklappe
- *trim tab (trimming tab)*
26 der Rumpf
- *fuselage (body)*
27 der Tragflügel (die Tragfläche)
- *wing*
28 das Querruder
- *aileron*
29 die Landeklappe
- *landing flap*
30 die Trimmklappe
- *trim tab (trimming tab)*
31 die Positionslampe [rot]
- *navigation light (position light)*
　[red]
32 der Landescheinwerfer
- *landing light*
33 das Hauptfahrwerk
- *main undercarriage unit (main*
　landing gear unit)
34 das Bugrad
- *nose wheel*

35 das Triebwerk
- *engine*
36 der Propeller (die Luftschraube)
- *propeller (airscrew)*
37-62 **das Fallschirmspringen** (der
　　Fallschirmsport, das
　　Fallschirmsportspringen)
- **skydiving** *(parachuting, sport*
　parachuting)
37 der Fallschirm (Sprungfallschirm)
- *parachute*
38 die Schirmkappe
- *canopy*
39 der Hilfsschirm
- *pilot chute*
40 die Fangleinen *f*
- *suspension lines*
41 die Steuerleine
- *steering line*
42 der Haupttragegurt
- *riser*
43 das Gurtzeug
- *harness*
44 der Verpackungssack
- *pack*
45 das Schlitzsystem des
　　Sportfallschirms *m*
- *system of slots of the sports*
　parachute
46 die Steuerschlitze *m*
- *turn slots*
47 der Scheitel
- *apex*
48 die Basis
- *skirt*
49 das Stabilisierungspaneel
- *stabilizing panel*
50-51 das Stilspringen
- *style jump*
50 das Rückwärtssalto
- *back loop*
51 die Spirale (Drehung)
- *spiral*
52-54 die ausgelegten Sichtsignale *n*
- *ground signals*
52 das Zeichen „Sprungerlaubnis" *f*
　　(das Zielkreuz)
- *signal for 'permission to jump'*
　('conditions are safe') (target cross)
53 das Zeichen „Sprungverbot *n* –
　　neuer Anflug" *m*
- *signal for 'parachuting suspended –*
　repeat flight'
54 das Zeichen „Sprungverbot *n* –
　　sofort landen"
- *signal for 'parachuting suspended –*
　aircraft must land'
55 der Zielsprung
- *accuracy jump*
56 das Zielkreuz
- *target cross*
57 der innere Zielkreis
　　[Radius *m* 25 m]
- *inner circle [radius 25 m]*
58 der mittlere Zielkreis
　　[Radius *m* 50 m]
- *middle circle [radius 50 m]*
59 der äußere Zielkreis
　　[Radius *m* 100 m]
- *outer circle [radius 100 m]*
60-62 Freifallhaltungen *f*
- *free-fall positions*
60 die X-Lage
- *full spread position*
61 die Froschlage
- *frog position*

62 die T-Lage
- *T position*
63-84 **das Ballonfahren**
　　(Freiballonfahren)
- **ballooning**
63 der Gasballon
- *gas balloon*
64 die Gondel (der Ballonkorb)
- *gondola (balloon basket)*
65 der Ballast (die Sandsäcke)
- *ballast (sandbags)*
66 die Halteleine (das Halteseil)
- *mooring line*
67 der Korbring
- *hoop*
68 die Bordinstrumente *n*
- *flight instruments (instruments)*
69 das Schlepptau
- *trail rope*
70 der Füllansatz
- *mouth (neck)*
71 die Füllansatzleinen *f*
- *neck line*
72 die Notreißbahn
- *emergency rip panel*
73 die Notreißleine
- *emergency ripping line*
74 die Gänsefüße *m*
- *network (net)*
75 die Reißbahn
- *rip panel*
76 die Reißleine (Reißbahnleine)
- *ripping line*
77 das Ventil
- *valve*
78 die Ventilleine
- *valve line*
79 der Heißluftballon
- *hot-air balloon*
80 die Brennerplattform
- *burner platform*
81 die Füllöffnung
- *mouth*
82 das Ventil
- *vent*
83 die Reißbahn
- *rip panel*
84 der Ballonaufstieg (Ballonstart)
- *balloon take-off*
85-91 **der Modellflugsport**
- **flying model aeroplanes**
　(Am. airplanes)
85 der funkferngesteuerte Modellflug
- *radio-controlled model flight*
86 das ferngesteuerte Freiflugmodell
- *remote-controlled free flight model*
87 die Funkfernsteuerung (das
　　Fernsteuerfunkgerät)
- *remote control radio*
88 die Antenne (Sendeantenne)
- *antenna (transmitting antenna)*
89 das Fesselflugmodell
- *control line model*
90 die Eindrahtfesselflugsteuerung
- *mono-line control system*
91 die fliegende Hundehütte, ein
　　Groteskflugmodell *n*
- *flying kennel, a K9-class model*

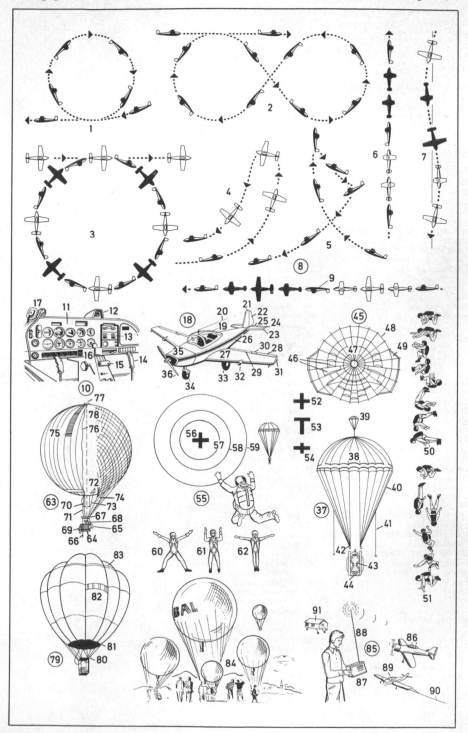

1-7 **das Dressurreiten**
- *dressage*
1 das Dressurviereck
- *arena (dressage arena)*
2 die Bande
- *rail*
3 das Dressurpferd
- *school horse*
4 der dunkle Reitfrack (*od.* schwarze Rock)
- *dark coat (black coat)*
5 die weiße Stiefelhose
- *white breeches*
6 der Zylinder (*od.* runde Hut)
- *top hat*
7 die Gangart (*auch:* die Hufschlagfigur)
- *gait (also: school figure)*
8-14 **das Springreiten** (Jagdspringen)
- *show jumping*
8 das Hindernis (Gatter), ein halbfestes Hindernis; *ähnl.:* das Rick, das Koppelrick, die Palisade, der Oxer, die Hürde, der Wall, die Mauer
- *obstacle (fence), an almost-fixed obstacle; sim.: gate, gate and rails, palisade, oxer, mound, wall*
9 das Springpferd
- *jumper*
10 der Springsattel
- *jumping saddle*
11 der Sattelgurt
- *girth*
12 die Trense
- *snaffle*
13 der rote (*auch:* schwarze) Rock
- *red coat (hunting pink, pink; also: dark coat)*
14 die Jagdkappe
- *hunting cap (riding cap)*
15 die Bandage
- *bandage*
16-19 **die Military**
- *three-day event*
16 der Geländeritt
- *endurance competition*
17 die Querfeldeinstrecke
- *cross-country*
18 der Sturzhelm (*auch:* die verstärkte Reitkappe)
- *helmet (also: hard hat, hard hunting cap)*
19 die Streckenmarkierung
- *course markings*
20-22 **das Hindernisrennen** (Jagdrennen)
- *steeplechase*
20 die Hecke (mit Wassergraben *m*), ein festes Hindernis
- *water jump, a fixed obstacle*
21 der Sprung
- *jump*
22 die Reitgerte
- *riding switch*
23-40 **das Trabrennen**
- *harness racing (harness horse racing)*
23 die Trabrennbahn (Traberbahn, der Track, das Geläuf)
- *harness racing track (track)*
24 der Sulky
- *sulky*
25 das Speichenrad mit Plastikscheibenschutz *m*
- *spoke wheel (spoked wheel) with plastic wheel disc (disk)*

26 der Fahrer, im Trabdreß *m*
- *driver in trotting silks*
27 die Fahrleine
- *rein*
28 das Traberpferd (der Traber)
- *trotter*
29 der Scheck
- *piebald horse*
30 der Bodenblender
- *shadow roll*
31 die Kniegamasche
- *elbow boot*
32 der Gummischutz
- *rubber boot*
33 die Startnummer
- *number*
34 die verglaste Tribüne mit den Totalisatorschaltern *m* (Totokassen *f*)
- *glass-covered grandstand with totalizator windows (tote windows) inside*
35 die Totalisatoranzeigetafel (Totoanzeigetafel)
- *totalizator (tote)*
36 die Starternummer
- *number [of each runner]*
37 die Eventualquote
- *odds (price, starting price, price offered)*
38 die Siegeranzeige
- *winners' table*
39 die Siegquote
- *winner's price*
40 die Zeitanzeige
- *time indicator*
41-49 **das Jagdreiten, eine Schleppjagd;** *ähnl.:* Fuchsjagd *f*, Schnitzeljagd
- **hunt, a drag hunt;** *sim.: fox hunt, paper chase (paper hunt, hare-and-hounds)*
41 das Feld (die Gruppe)
- *field*
42 der rote Jagdrock
- *hunting pink*
43 der Piqueur
- *whipper-in (whip)*
44 das Jagdhorn (Hifthorn)
- *hunting horn*
45 der Master
- *Master (Master of foxhounds, MFH)*
46 die Hundemeute (Meute, Koppel)
- *pack of hounds (pack)*
47 der Hirschhund
- *staghound*
48 der „Fuchs"
- *drag*
49 die Schleppe (künstliche Fährte)
- *scented trail (artificial scent)*
50 **das Galopprennen**
- **horse racing (racing)**
51 das Feld (die Rennpferde *n*)
- *field (racehorses)*
52 der Favorit
- *favourite (Am. favorite)*
53 der Outsider (Außenseiter)
- *outsider*

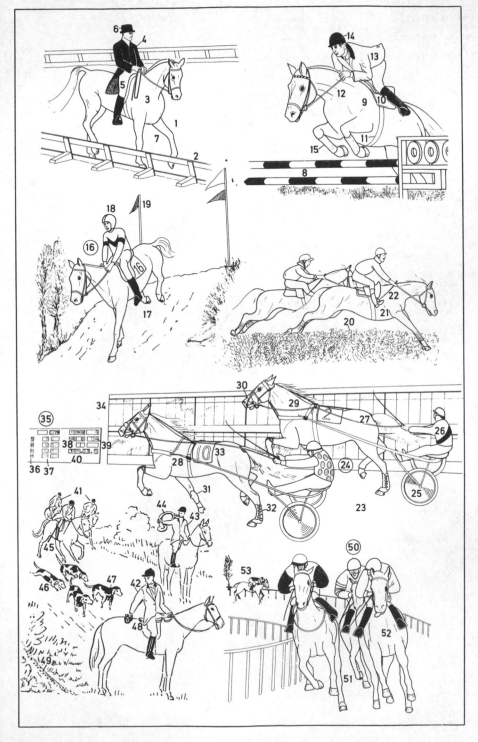

1-23 **Radsport** *m*
- *cycle racing*
1 die Radrennbahn; *hier:* Hallenbahn *f*
- *cycling track (cycle track); here:*
  indoor track
2-7 das Sechstagerennen
- *six-day race*
2 der Sechstagefahrer, ein
  Bahnrennfahrer *m* im Feld *n*
- *six-day racer, a track racer (track*
  rider) on the track
3 der Sturzhelm
- *crash hat*
4 die Rennleitung
- *stewards*
5 der Zielrichter
- *judge*
6 der Rundenzähler
- *lap scorer*
7 die Rennfahrerkabine
- *rider's box (racer's box)*
8-10 das Straßenrennen
- *road race*
8 der Straßenfahrer, ein
  Radrennfahrer *m*
- *road racer, a racing cyclist*
9 das Rennfahrertrikot
- *racing jersey*
10 die Trinkflasche
- *water bottle*
11-15 das Steherrennen
  (Dauerrennen)
- *motor-paced racing (long-distance*
  racing)
11 der Schrittmacher, ein
  Motorradfahrer *m*
- *pacer, a motorcyclist*
12 die Schrittmachermaschine (das
  Schrittmachermotorrad)
- *pacer's motorcycle*
13 die Rolle, eine Schutzvorrichtung
- *roller, a safety device*
14 der Steher (Dauerfahrer)
- *stayer (motor-paced track rider)*
15 die Stehermaschine, ein Rennrad *n*
- *motor-paced cycle, a racing cycle*
16 das Rennrad (die Rennmaschine)
  für Straßenrennen *n*
- *racing cycle (racing bicycle) for*
  road racing (road race bicycle)
17 der Rennsattel, ein ungefederter
  Sattel
- *racing saddle, an unsprung saddle*
18 der Rennlenker
- *racing handlebars (racing*
  handlebar)
19 der Schlauchreifen (Rennreifen)
- *tubular tyre (Am. tire) (racing tyre)*
20 die Schaltungskette
- *chain*
21 der Rennhaken
- *toe clip (racing toe clip)*
22 der Riemen
- *strap*
23 der Ersatzschlauchreifen
- *spare tubular tyre (Am. tire)*
24-38 **Motorsport** *m*
- *motorsports*
24-28 das Motorradrennen;
  Disziplinen: Grasbahnrennen *n*,
  Straßenrennen, Sandbahnrennen,
  Zementbahnrennen,
  Aschenbahnrennen, Bergrennen,
  Eisrennen (ein Speedway *n*),
  Geländesport *m*, Trial *n*,
  Moto-Cross

- *motorcycle racing; disciplines:*
  grasstrack racing, road racing,
  sand track racing, cement track
  racing, speedway [on ash or shale
  tracks], mountain racing, ice racing
  (ice speedway), scramble racing,
  trial, moto cross
24 die Sandbahn
- *sand track*
25 der Motorradrennfahrer
- *racing motorcyclist (rider)*
26 die Lederschutzkleidung
- *leather overalls (leathers)*
27 die Rennmaschine, eine
  Solomaschine
- *racing motorcycle, a solo machine*
28 die Startnummer
- *number (number plate)*
29 das Seitenwagengespann, in der
  Kurve
- *sidecar combination on the bend*
30 der Seitenwagen
- *sidecar*
31 die verkleidete Rennmaschine [500 cm³]
- *streamlined racing motorcycle [500 cc.]*
32 das Gymkhana, ein
  Geschicklichkeitswettbewerb *m*;
  hier: der Motorradfahrer beim
  Sprung *m*
- *gymkhana, a competition of skill;*
  here: motorcyclist performing a
  jump
33 die Geländefahrt, eine
  Leistungsprüfung
- *cross-country race, a test in*
  performance
34-38 Rennwagen *m*
- *racing cars*
34 der Formel-I-Rennwagen
  (ein Monoposto *m*)
- *Formula One racing car (a mono*
  posto)
35 der Heckspoiler
- *rear spoiler (aerofoil, Am. airfoil)*
36 der Formel-II-Rennwagen (ein
  Rennsportwagen *m*)
- *Formula Two racing car (a racing car)*
37 der Super-V-Rennsportwagen
- *Super-Vee racing car*
38 der Prototyp, ein Sportwagen *m*
- *prototype, a racing car*

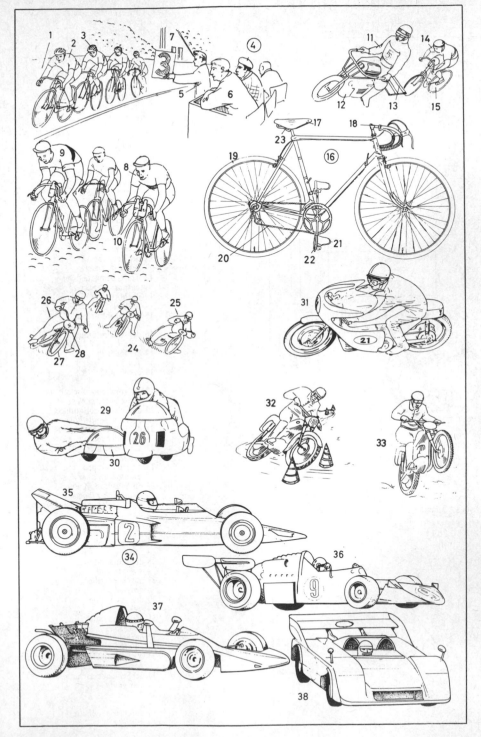

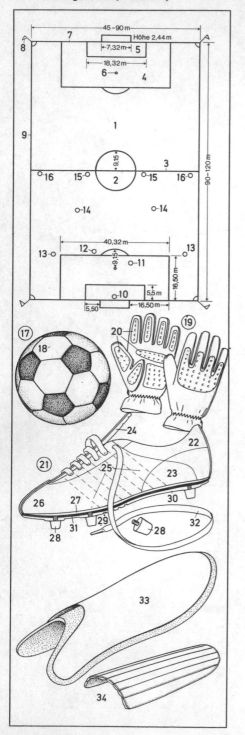

1-16 der Fußballplatz
- *football pitch*
1 das Spielfeld
- *field (park)*
2 der Mittelkreis
- *centre (Am. center) circle*
3 die Mittellinie
- *half-way line*
4 der Strafraum (Sechzehnmeterraum)
- *penalty area*
5 der Torraum
- *goal area*
6 der Elfmeterpunkt (die Strafstoßmarke)
- *penalty spot*
7 die Torlinie
- *goal line (by-line)*
8 die Eckfahne
- *corner flag*
9 die Seitenlinie
- *touch line*
10 der Tormann (Torwart)
- *goalkeeper*
11 der Libero
- *spare man*
12 der Vorstopper
- *inside defender*
13 der Außenverteidiger
- *outside defender*
14 die Mittelfeldspieler *m*
- *midfield players*
15 der Innenstürmer
- *inside forward (striker)*
16 der Außenstürmer
- *outside forward (winger)*
17 der Fußball
- *football*
18 das Ventil
- *valve*
19 die Torwarthandschuhe *m*
- *goalkeeper's gloves*
20 die Schaumstoffauflage
- *foam rubber padding*
21 der Fußballschuh
- *football boot*
22 das Lederfutter
- *leather lining*
23 die Hinterkappe
- *counter*
24 die Schaumstoffzunge
- *foam rubber tongue*
25 die Gelenkzugriemen *m*
- *bands*
26 der Oberlederschaft
- *shaft*
27 die Einlegesohle
- *insole*
28 der Schraubstollen
- *screw-in stud*
29 die Gelenkrille
- *groove*
30 die Nylonsohle
- *nylon sole*
31 die Brandsohle
- *inner sole*
32 der Schnürsenkel
- *lace (bootlace)*
33 die Beinschiene mit Knöchelschutz *m*
- *football pad with ankle guard*
34 der Schienbeinschutz
- *shin guard*
35 das Tor
- *goal*
36 die Querlatte (Latte)
- *crossbar*

37 der Pfosten (Torpfosten)
- *post (goalpost)*
38 der Abstoß
- *goal kick*
39 die Faustabwehr
- *save with the fists*
40 der Strafstoß (ugs. Elfmeter)
- *penalty (penalty kick)*
41 der Eckstoß (Eckball)
- *corner (corner kick)*
42 das Abseits
- *offside*
43 der Freistoß
- *free kick*
44 die Mauer
- *wall*
45 der Fallrückzieher
- *bicycle kick
(overhead bicycle kick)*
46 der Kopfball (Kopfstoß)
- *header*
47 die Ballabgabe
- *pass (passing the ball)*
48 die Ballannahme
- *receiving the ball (taking a pass)*
49 der Kurzpaß (Doppelpaß)
- *short pass (one-two)*
50 das Foul (die Regelwidrigkeit)
- *foul (infringement)*
51 das Sperren
- *obstruction*
52 das Dribbling (der Durchbruch)
- *dribble*

53 der Einwurf
- *throw-in*
54 der Ersatzspieler
- *substitute*
55 der Trainer
- *coach*
56 das Trikot
- *shirt (jersey)*
57 die Sporthose
- *shorts*
58 der Sportstrumpf
- *sock (football sock)*
59 der Linienrichter
- *linesman*
60 die Handflagge
- *linesman's flag*
61 der Platzverweis
- *sending-off*
62 der Schiedsrichter (Unparteiische)
- *referee*
63 die Verweiskarte (rote Karte; zur
Verwarnung *auch*: die gelbe Karte)
- *red card; as a caution also: yellow
card*
64 die Mittelfahne
- *centre (Am. center) flag*

1 **der Handball** (Hallenhandball, das
   Handballspiel, Hallenhandballspiel)
- *handball (indoor handball)*
2 der Handballspieler, ein
   Feldspieler *m*
- *handball player, a field player*
3 der Kreisspieler, beim Sprungwurf *m*
- *attacker, making a jump throw*
4 der Abwehrspieler
- *defender*
5 die Freiwurflinie
- *penalty line*
6 **das Hockey** (Hockeyspiel)
- *hockey*
7 das Hockeytor
- *goal*
8 der Tormann
- *goalkeeper*
9 der Beinschutz (Schienbein-,
   Knieschutz)
- *pad (shin pad, knee pad)*
10 der Kickschuh
- *kicker*
11 die Gesichtsmaske
- *face guard*
12 der Handschuh
- *glove*
13 der Hockeyschläger (Hockeystock)
- *hockey stick*
14 der Hockeyball
- *hockey ball*
15 der Hockeyspieler
- *hockey player*
16 der Schußkreis
- *striking circle*
17 die Seitenlinie
- *sideline*
18 die Ecke
- *corner*
19 **das Rugby** (Rugbyspiel)
- *rugby (rugby football)*
20 das Gedränge
- *scrum (scrummage)*
21 der Rugbyball
- *rugby ball*
22 **der Football** (das Footballspiel)
- *American football (Am. football)*
23 der Ballträger, ein Footballspieler *m*
- *player carrying the ball, a football
   player*
24 der Helm
- *helmet*
25 der Gesichtsschutz
- *face guard*
26 die gepolsterte Jacke
- *padded jersey*
27 der Ball
- *ball (pigskin)*
28 **der Basketball** (Korbball, das
   Basketballspiel, Korbballspiel)
- *basketball*
29 der Basketball
- *basketball*
30 das Korbbrett (Spielbrett)
- *backboard*
31 der Korbständer
- *basket posts*
32 der Korb
- *basket*
33 der Korbring
- *basket ring*
34 die Zielmarkierung
- *target rectangle*
35 der Korbleger, ein
   Basketballspieler *m*
- *basketball player shooting*

36 die Endlinie
- *end line*
37 der Freiwurfraum
- *restricted area*
38 die Freiwurflinie
- *free-throw line*
39 die Auswechselspieler *m*
- *substitute*
40-69 **der Baseball** (das Baseballspiel)
- *baseball*
40-58 das Spielfeld
- *field (park)*
40 die Zuschauergrenze
- *spectator barrier*
41 der Außenfeldspieler
- *outfielder*
42 der Halbspieler
- *short stop*
43 das zweite Mal
- *second base*
44 der Malspieler
- *baseman*
45 der Läufer
- *runner*
46 das erste Mal
- *first base*
47 das dritte Mal
- *third base*
48 die Foullinie (Fehllinie)
- *foul line (base line)*
49 das Wurfmal
- *pitcher's mound*
50 der Werfer (Pitcher)
- *pitcher*
51 das Schlägerfeld (die Home base)
- *batter's position*
52 der Schlagmann (Batter)
- *batter*
53 das Schlagmal
- *home base (home plate)*
54 der Fänger (Catcher)
- *catcher*
55 der Chefschiedsrichter
- *umpire*
56 die Coach-box
- *coach's box*
57 der Coach (Mannschaftsbetreuer,
   Trainer)
- *coach*
58 die nachfolgenden Schlagmänner
- *batting order*
59-60 Baseballhandschuhe *m*
- *baseball gloves (baseball mitts)*
59 der Handschuh des Feldspielers *m*
- *fielder's glove (fielder's mitt)*
60 der Handschuh des Fängers *m*
- *catcher's glove (catcher's mitt)*
61 der Baseball
- *baseball*
62 die Schlagkeule
- *bat*
63 der Schlagmann beim
   Schlagversuch *m*
- *batter at bat*
64 der Fänger
- *catcher*
65 der Schiedsrichter
- *umpire*
66 der Läufer
- *runner*
67 das Malkissen
- *base plate*
68 der Werfer
- *pitcher*
69 die Werferplatte
- *pitcher's mound*

70-76 **das Kricket** (Kricketspiel,
   Cricket)
- *cricket*
70 das Krickettor (Mal) mit dem
   Querstab *m*
- *wicket with bails*
71 die Wurflinie
- *back crease (bowling crease)*
72 die Schlaglinie
- *crease (batting crease)*
73 der Torwächter der Fangpartei
- *wicket keeper of the fielding side*
74 der Schlagmann
- *batsman*
75 das Schlagholz
- *bat (cricket bat)*
76 der Außenspieler (Werfer)
- *fielder (bowler)*
77-82 **das Krocket** (Krocketspiel,
   Croquet)
- *croquet*
77 der Zielpfahl
- *winning peg*
78 das Krockettor
- *hoop*
79 der Wendepfahl
- *corner peg*
80 der Krocketspieler
- *croquet player*
81 der Krockethammer
- *croquet mallet*
82 die Krocketkugel
- *croquet ball*

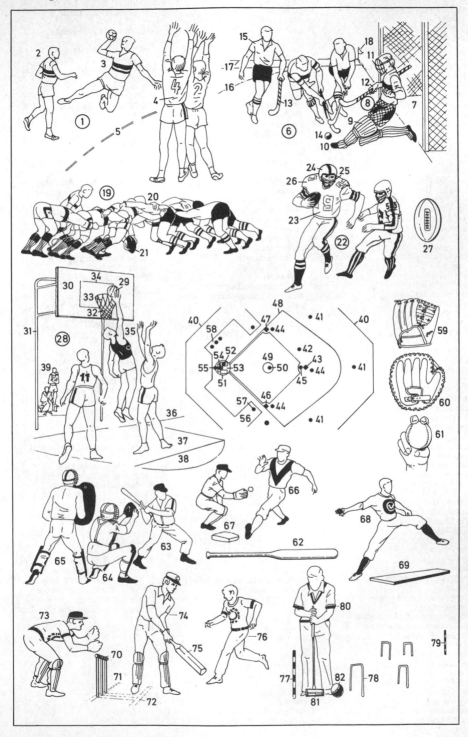

1-42 das Tennis (Tennisspiel)
- *tennis*
1 der Tennisplatz
- *tennis court*
2 *bis* 3 die Seitenlinie für das Doppelspiel (Doppel; Herrendoppel, Damendoppel, gemischte Doppel)
- *sideline for doubles match (doubles; men's doubles, women's doubles, mixed doubles) (doubles sideline)*
3 *bis* 10 die Grundlinie
- *base line*
4 *bis* 5 die Seitenlinie für das Einzelspiel (Einzel; Herreneinzel, Dameneinzel)
- *sideline for singles match (singles; men's singles, women's singles) (singles sideline)*
6 *bis* 7 die Aufschlaglinie
- *service line*
8 *bis* 9 die Mittellinie
- *centre (Am. center) line*
11 das Mittelzeichen
- *centre (Am. center) mark*
12 das Aufschlagfeld
- *service court*
13 das Netz (Tennisnetz)
- *net (tennis net)*
14 der Netzhalter
- *net strap*
15 der Netzpfosten
- *net post*
16 der Tennisspieler
- *tennis player*
17 der Schmetterball
- *smash*
18 der Partner
- *opponent*
19 der Schiedsrichter
- *umpire*
20 der Schiedsrichterstuhl
- *umpire's chair*
21 das Schiedsrichtermikrophon
- *umpire's microphone*
22 der Balljunge
- *ball boy*
23 der Netzrichter
- *net-cord judge*
24 der Seitenlinienrichter
- *foot-fault judge*
25 der Mittellinienrichter
- *centre (Am. center) line judge*
26 der Grundlinienrichter
- *base line judge*
27 der Aufschlaglinienrichter
- *service line judge*
28 der Tennisball
- *tennis ball*
29 der Tennisschläger (Schläger, das Racket)
- *tennis racket (tennis racquet, racket, racquet)*
30 der Schlägerschaft (Racketschaft)
- *racket handle (racquet handle)*
31 die Saitenbespannung (Schlagfläche)
- *strings (striking surface)*
32 der Spanner
- *press (racket press, racquet press)*
33 die Spannschraube
- *tightening screw*
34 die Anzeigetafel
- *scoreboard*
35 die Spielerergebnisse *n*
- *results of sets*
36 der Spielername
- *player's name*
37 die Zahl der Sätze *m*
- *number of sets*
38 der Spielstand
- *state of play*
39 der Rückhandschlag
- *backhand stroke*
40 der Vorhandschlag
- *forehand stroke*
41 der Flugball (normalhohe Vorhandflugball)
- *volley (forehand volley at normal height)*
42 der Aufschlag
- *service*
43-44 das Federballspiel (Badminton)
- *badminton*
43 der Federballschläger (Badmintonschläger)
- *badminton racket (badminton racquet)*
44 der Federball
- *shuttle (shuttlecock)*
45-55 das Tischtennis (Tischtennisspiel)
- *table tennis*
45 der Tischtennisschläger
- *table tennis racket (racquet) (table tennis bat)*
46 der Schlägergriff
- *racket (racquet) handle (bat handle)*
47 die Auflage der Schlagfläche
- *blade covering*
48 der Tischtennisball
- *table tennis ball*
49 die Tischtennisspieler *m*; hier: das gemischte Doppel (Mixed)
- *table tennis players; here: mixed doubles*
50 der Rückschläger
- *receiver*
51 der Aufschläger
- *server*
52 der Tischtennistisch
- *table tennis table*
53 das Tischtennisnetz
- *table tennis net*
54 die Mittellinie
- *centre (Am. center) line*
55 die Seitenlinie
- *sideline*
56-71 das Volleyballspiel
- *volleyball*
56-57 die richtige Haltung der Hände *f*
- *correct placing of the hands*
58 der Volleyball
- *volleyball*
59 das Servieren des Volleyballs *m*
- *serving the volleyball*
60 der Grundspieler (Abwehrspieler)
- *blocker*
61 der Aufgaberaum
- *service area*
62 der Aufgeber
- *server*
63 der Netzspieler (Angriffsspieler)
- *front-line player*
64 die Angriffszone
- *attack area*
65 die Angriffslinie
- *attack line*
66 die Verteidigungszone
- *defence (Am. defense) area*
67 der erste Schiedsrichter
- *referee*
68 der zweite Schiedsrichter
- *umpire*
69 der Linienrichter
- *linesman*
70 die Anzeigetafel
- *scoreboard*
71 der Anschreiber
- *scorer*
72-78 das Faustballspiel
- *faustball*
72 die Angabelinie
- *base line*
73 die Leine
- *tape*
74 der Faustball
- *faustball*
75 der Schlagmann (Angriffsspieler, Vorderspieler, Überschläger)
- *forward*
76 der Mittelspieler (Mittelmann)
- *centre (Am. center)*
77 der Hintermann (Abwehrspieler, Hinterspieler)
- *back*
78 der Hammerschlag
- *hammer blow*
79-93 das Golfspiel (Golf)
- *golf*
79-82 die Spielbahn (die Löcher *n*)
- *course (golf course, holes)*
79 der Abschlag (Abschlagplatz)
- *teeing ground*
80 das Rough
- *rough*
81 der Bunker (die Sandgrube)
- *bunker (Am. sand trap)*
82 das Grün (Green, Golfgrün, Puttergrün)
- *green (putting green)*
83 der Golfspieler, beim Treibschlag *m* (Weitschlag)
- *golfer, driving*
84 der Durchschwung
- *follow-through*
85 der Golfwagen (Caddywagen)
- *golf trolley*
86 das Einlochen (Putten)
- *putting (holing out)*
87 das Loch (Hole)
- *hole*
88 die Flagge
- *flagstick*
89 der Golfball
- *golf ball*
90 der Aufsatz
- *tee*
91 der (bleigefüllte) Holzschläger (das Holz, Wood), ein Treiber *m* (Driver); *ähnl.:* der Brassie
- *wood, a driver; sim.: brassie (brassy, brassey)*
92 der Eisenschläger (das Eisen, Iron)
- *iron*
93 der Putter
- *putter*

1-33 das Sportfechten
- *fencing (modern fencing)*
1-18 das Florettfechten
- *foil*
1 der Fechtmeister
- *fencing master (fencing instructor)*
2 die Fechtbahn (Kampfbahn, Piste, Planche)
- *piste*
3 die Startlinie
- *on guard line*
4 die Mittellinie
- *centre (Am. center) line*
5-6 die Fechter *m* (Florettfechter) beim Freigefecht *n* (Assaut *m* od. *n*)
- *fencers (foil fencers, foilsmen, foilists) in a bout*
5 der Angreifer in der Ausfallstellung (im Ausfall *m*)
- *attacker (attacking fencer) in lunging position (lunging)*
6 der Angegriffene in der Parade (Abwehr, Deckung)
- *defender (defending fencer), parrying*
7 der gerade Stoß (Coup droit, die Botta dritta), eine Fechtaktion
- *straight thrust, a fencing movement*
8 die Terz- bzw. Sixtdeckung (Terz-, Sixtparade)
- *parry of the tierce*
9 die Gefechtslinie
- *line of fencing*
10 die drei Fechtabstände *m* zum Gegner *m* (weiter, mittlerer, naher Abstand)
- *three fencing measures (short, medium and long measure)*
11 das Florett, eine Stoßwaffe
- *foil, a thrust weapon*
12 der Fechthandschuh
- *fencing glove*
13 die Fechtmaske
- *fencing mask (foil mask)*
14 der Halsschutz an der Fechtmaske
- *neck flap (neck guard) on the fencing mask*
15 die Metallweste
- *metallic jacket*
16 die Fechtjacke
- *fencing jacket*
17 die absatzlosen Fechtschuhe *m*
- *heelless fencing shoes*
18 die Grundstellung zum Fechtergruß *m* und zur Fechtstellung
- *first position for fencer's salute (initial position, on guard position)*
19-24 das Säbelfechten
- *sabre (Am. saber) fencing*
19 der Säbelfechter
- *sabreurs (sabre fencers, Am. saber fencers)*
20 der (leichte) Säbel
- *(light) sabre (Am. saber)*
21 der Säbelhandschuh
- *sabre (Am. saber) glove (sabre gauntlet)*
22 die Säbelmaske
- *sabre (Am. saber) mask*
23 der Kopfhieb
- *cut at head*
24 die Quintparade
- *parry of the fifth (quinte)*

25-33 das Degenfechten mit elektrischer Trefferanzeige
- *épée, with electrical scoring equipment*
25 der Degenfechter
- *épéeist*
26 der Elektrodegen; *auch:* das Elektroflorett
- *electric épée; also: electric foil*
27 die Degenspitze
- *épée point*
28 die optische Trefferanzeige
- *scoring lights*
29 die Laufrolle (Kabelrolle)
- *spring-loaded wire spool*
30 die Anzeigelampe
- *indicator light*
31 das Rollenkabel
- *wire*
32 das Anzeigegerät (der Meldeapparat)
- *electronic scoring equipment*
33 die Auslage
- *on guard position*
34-45 die Fechtwaffen *f*
- *fencing weapons*
34 der leichte Säbel (Sportsäbel), eine Hieb- und Stoßwaffe
- *light sabre (Am. saber), a cut and thrust weapon*
35 die Glocke
- *guard*
36 der Degen, eine Stoßwaffe
- *épée, a thrust weapon*
37 das französische Florett, eine Stoßwaffe
- *French foil, a thrust weapon*
38 die Glocke
- *guard (coquille)*
39 das italienische Florett
- *Italian foil*
40 der Florettknauf
- *foil pommel*
41 der Griff
- *handle*
42 die Parierstange
- *cross piece (quillons)*
43 die Glocke
- *guard (coquille)*
44 die Klinge
- *blade*
45 die Spitze
- *button*
46 die Klingenbindungen *f*
- *engagements*
47 die Quartbindung
- *quarte (carte) engagement*
48 die Terzbindung (*auch:* Sixtbindung)
- *tierce engagement (also: sixte engagement)*
49 die Cerclebindung
- *circling engagement*
50 die Sekondbindung (*auch:* Oktavbindung)
- *seconde engagement (also: octave engagement)*
51-53 die gültigen Treffflächen *f*
- *target areas*
51 der gesamte Körper beim Degenfechten *n* (Herren *m*)
- *the whole body in épée fencing (men)*
52 Kopf *m* und Oberkörper *m* bis zu den Leistenfurchen *f* beim Säbelfechten *n* (Herren *m*)

- *head and upper body down to the groin in sabre (Am. saber) fencing (men)*
53 der Rumpf vom Hals *m* bis zu den Leistenfurchen *f* beim Florettfechten *n* (Damen *f* u. Herren *m*)
- *trunk from the neck to the groin in foil fencing (ladies and men)*

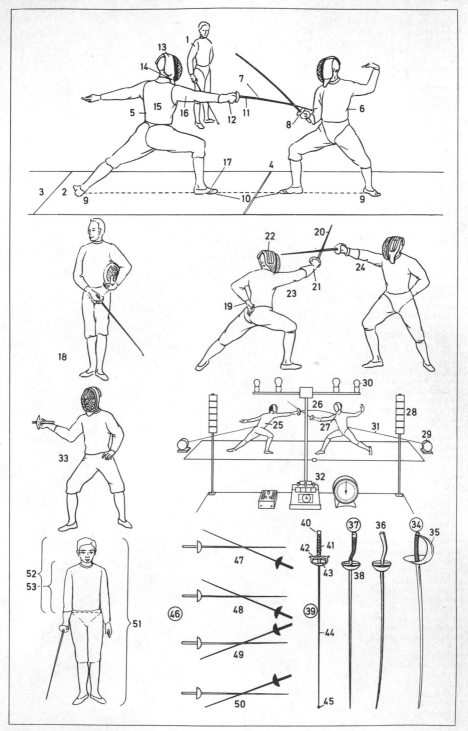

1 die Grundstellung
- *basic position (starting position)*
2 die Laufstellung
- *running posture*
3 die Seitgrätschstellung
- *side straddle*
4 die Quergrätschstellung
- *straddle (forward straddle)*
5 der Ballenstand
- *toe stand*
6 der Hockstand
- *crouch*
7 der Kniestand
- *upright kneeling position*
8 der Fersensitz
- *kneeling position, seat on heels*
9 der Hocksitz
- *squat*
10 der Strecksitz
- *L-seat (long sitting)*
11 der Schneidersitz
- *tailor seat (sitting tailor-style)*
12 der Hürdensitz
- *hurdle (hurdle position)*
13 der Spitzwinkelsitz
- *V-seat*
14 der Seitspagat
- *side split*
15 der Querspagat
- *forward split*
16 der Winkelstütz
- *L-support*
17 der Spitzwinkelstütz
- *V-support*
18 der Grätschwinkelstütz
- *straddle seat*
19 die Brücke
- *bridge*
20 die Bank (der Knieliegestütz)
- *kneeling front support*
21 der Liegestütz vorlings
- *front support*
22 der Liegestütz rücklings
- *back support*
23 der Hockliegestütz
- *crouch with front support*
24 der Winkelliegestütz
- *arched front support*
25 der Liegestütz seitlings
- *side support*
26 der Unterarmstand
- *forearm stand (forearm balance)*
27 der Handstand
- *handstand*
28 der Kopfstand
- *headstand*
29 der Nackenstand (die Kerze)
- *shoulder stand (shoulder balance)*
30 die Waage vorlings
- *forward horizontal stand (arabesque)*
31 die Waage rücklings
- *rearward horizontal stand*
32 die Rumpfbeuge seitwärts
- *trunk-bending sideways*
33 die Rumpfbeuge vorwärts
- *trunk-bending forwards*
34 die Rumpfbeuge rückwärts
- *arch*
35 der Strecksprung
- *astride jump (butterfly)*
36 der Hocksprung
- *tuck jump*
37 der Grätschsprung
- *astride jump*
38 der Winkelsprung
- *pike*

39 der Schersprung
- *scissor jump*
40 der Rehsprung
- *stag jump (stag leap)*
41 der Laufschritt
- *running step*
42 der Ausfallschritt
- *lunge*
43 der Nachstellschritt
- *forward pace*
44 die Rückenlage
- *lying on back*
45 die Bauchlage
- *prone position*
46 die Seitlage (Flankenlage)
- *lying on side*
47 die Tiefhalte der Arme *m*
- *holding arms downwards*
48 die Seithalte der Arme *m*
- *holding (extending) arms sideways*
49 die Hochhalte der Arme *m*
- *holding arms raised upward*
50 die Vorhalte der Arme *m*
- *holding (extending) arms forward*
51 die Rückhalte der Arme *m*
- *arms held (extended) backward*
52 die Nackenhalte der Arme *m*
- *hands clasped behind the head*

1-11 **die Turngeräte** *n* **im olympischen Turnen** *n* **der Männer** *m*
- *gymnastics apparatus in men's Olympic gymnastics*
1 das Langpferd ohne Pauschen *f* (das Sprungpferd)
- *long horse (horse, vaulting horse)*
2 der Barren
- *parallel bars*
3 der Barrenholm
- *bar*
4 die Ringe
- *rings (stationary rings)*
5 das Seitpferd mit Pauschen *f* (das Pauschenpferd)
- *pommel horse (side horse)*
6 die Pausche
- *pommel*
7 das Reck (Spannreck)
- *horizontal bar (high bar)*
8 die Reckstange
- *bar*
9 die Recksäule
- *upright*
10 die Verspannung
- *stay wires*
11 der Boden (die 12x12-m-Bodenfläche)
- *floor (12 m x 12 m floor area)*
12-21 **Hilfsgeräte** *n* **und Geräte** *n* **des Schul- und Vereinsturnens** *n*
- *auxiliary apparatus and apparatus for school and club gymnastics*
12 das Sprungbrett (Reutherbrett)
- *springboard (Reuther board)*
13 die Niedersprungmatte
- *landing mat*
14 die Bank
- *bench*
15 der Sprungkasten
- *box*
16 der kleine Sprungkasten
- *small box*
17 der Bock
- *buck*
18 die Weichbodenmatte
- *mattress*
19 das Klettertau
- *climbing rope (rope)*
20 die Sprossenwand
- *wall bars*
21 die Gitterleiter
- *window ladder*
22-39 **das Verhalten zum Gerät** *n* (die Haltungen *f*, Positionen)
- *positions in relation to the apparatus*
22 der Seitstand vorlings
- *side, facing*
23 der Seitstand rücklings
- *side, facing away*
24 der Querstand vorlings
- *end, facing*
25 der Querstand rücklings
- *end, facing away*
26 der Außenseitstand vorlings
- *outside, facing*
27 der Innenquerstand
- *inside, facing*
28 der Stütz vorlings
- *front support*
29 der Stütz rücklings
- *back support*
30 der Grätschsitz
- *straddle position*
31 der Außenseitsitz
- *seated position outside*

32 der Außenquersitz
- *riding seat outside*
33 der Streckhang vorlings
- *hang*
34 der Streckhang rücklings
- *reverse hang*
35 der Beugehang
- *hang with elbows bent*
36 der Sturzhang
- *piked reverse hang*
37 der Sturzhang gestreckt
- *straight inverted hang*
38 der Streckstütz
- *straight hang*
39 der Beugestütz
- *bent hang*
40-46 **die Griffarten** *f*
- *grasps (kinds of grasp)*
40 der Ristgriff am Reck *n*
- *overgrasp on the horizontal bar*
41 der Kammgriff am Reck *n*
- *undergrasp on the horizontal bar*
42 der Zwiegriff am Reck *n*
- *combined grasp on the horizontal bar*
43 der Kreuzgriff am Reck *n*
- *cross grasp on the horizontal bar*
44 der Ellgriff am Reck *n*
- *rotated grasp on the horizontal bar*
45 der Speichgriff am Barren *m*
- *outside grip on the parallel bars*
46 der Ellgriff am Barren *m*
- *rotated grasp on the parallel bars*
47 der lederne Reckriemen
- *leather handstrap*
48-60 **Übungen** *f* **an den Geräten** *n*
- *exercises*
48 der Hechtsprung am Sprungpferd *n*
- *long-fly on the horse*
49 das Übergrätschen am Barren *m*
- *rise to straddle on the parallel bars*
50 der Seitspannhang (Kreuzhang) an den Ringen *m*
- *crucifix on the rings*
51 die Schere am Pauschenpferd *n*
- *scissors (scissors movement) on the pommel horse*
52 das Heben in den Handstand am Boden *m*
- *legs raising into a handstand on the floor*
53 die Hocke am Sprungpferd *n*
- *squat vault on the horse*
54 die Kreisflanke am Pauschenpferd *n*
- *double leg circle on the pommel horse*
55 das Schleudern (der Überschlag rückwärts) an den Ringen *m*
- *hip circle backwards on the rings*
56 die Hangwaage vorlings an den Ringen *m*
- *lever hang on the rings*
57 die Schwungstemme rückwärts am Barren *m*
- *rearward swing on the parallel bars*
58 die Oberarmkippe am Barren *m*
- *forward kip into upper arm hang on the parallel bars*
59 der Unterschwung vorlings rückwärts am Reck *n*
- *backward underswing on the horizontal bar*
60 die Riesenfelge vorlings rückwärts am Reck *n*
- *backward grand circle on the horizontal bar*

61-63 **die Turnkleidung**
- *gymnastics kit*
61 das Turnhemd
- *singlet (vest, Am. undershirt)*
62 die Turnhose
- *gym trousers*
63 die Turnschuhe *m* (Gymnastikschuhe)
- *gym shoes*
64 die Bandage
- *wristband*

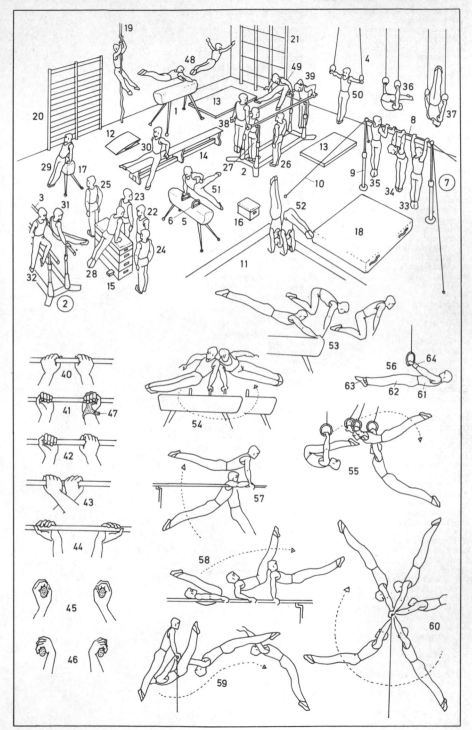

297 Geräteturnen II (Turnen der Frauen)

1-6 die Turngeräte *n* im olympischen Turnen *n* der Frauen *f*
- *gymnastics apparatus in women's Olympic gymnastics*
1 das Seitpferd ohne Pauschen *f* (das Sprungpferd)
- *horse (vaulting horse)*
2 der Schwebebalken
- *beam*
3 der Stufenbarren (das Doppelreck, der Spannbarren)
- *asymmetric bars (uneven bars)*
4 der Barrenholm
- *bar*
5 die Verspannung
- *stay wires*
6 der Boden (die 12×12-m-Bodenfläche)
- *floor (12 m × 12 m floor area)*
7-14 **Hilfsgeräte** *n* und Geräte *n* des Schul- und Vereinsturnens
- **auxiliary apparatus** *and apparatus for school and club gymnasties*
7 die Niedersprungmatte
- *landing mat*
8 das Sprungbrett (Reutherbrett)
- *springboard (Reuther board)*
9 der kleine Sprungkasten
- *small box*
10 das Trampolin
- *trampoline*
11 das Sprungtuch
- *sheet (web)*
12 der Rahmen
- *frame*
13 die Gummizüge
- *rubber springs*
14 das Absprungtrampolin
- *springboard trampoline*
15-32 **Übungen** *f* an den Geräten *n*
- **apparatus exercises**
15 der Salto rückwärts gehockt
- *backward somersault*
16 die Hilfestellung
- *spotting position (standing-in position)*
17 der Salto rückwärts gestreckt am Trampolin *n*
- *vertical backward somersault on the trampoline*
18 der Salto vorwärts gehockt am Absprungtrampolin *n*
- *forward somersault on the springboard trampoline*
19 die Rolle vorwärts am Boden *m*
- *forward roll on the floor*
20 die Hechtrolle am Boden *m*
- *long-fly to forward roll on the floor*
21 das Rad (der Überschlag seitwärts) am Schwebebalken *m*
- *cartwheel on the beam*
22 der Handstandüberschlag vorwärts am Sprungpferd *n*
- *handspring on the horse*
23 der Bogengang rückwärts am Boden *m*
- *backward walkover*
24 der Flickflack (Handstandüberschlag rückwärts) am Boden *m*
- *back flip (flik-flak) on the floor*
25 der Schmetterling (freie Überschlag vorwärts) am Boden *m*
- *free walkover forward on the floor*
26 der Schrittüberschlag vorwärts am Boden *m*
- *forward walkover on the floor*
27 die Kopfkippe (der Kopfüberschlag) am Boden *m*
- *headspring on the floor*
28 die Schwebekippe am Stufenbarren *m*
- *upstart on the asymmetric bars*
29 die freie Felge am Stufenbarren *m*
- *free backward circle on the asymmetric bars*
30 die Wende am Sprungpferd *n*
- *face vault over the horse*
31 die Flanke am Sprungpferd *n*
- *flank vault over the horse*
32 die Kehre am Sprungpferd *n*
- *back vault (rear vault) over the horse*
33-50 **Gymnastik** *f* mit Handgerät *n*
- **gymnastics with hand apparatus**
33 der Bogenwurf
- *hand-to-hand throw*
34 der Gymnastikball
- *gymnastic ball*
35 der Hochwurf
- *high toss*
36 das Prellen
- *bounce*
37 das Handkreisen mit zwei Keulen *f*
- *hand circling with two clubs*
38 die Gymnastikkeule
- *gymnastic club*
39 das Schwingen
- *swing*
40 der Schlußhocksprung
- *tuck jump*
41 der Gymnastikstab
- *bar*
42 der Durchschlag
- *skip*
43 das Sprungseil
- *rope (skipping rope)*
44 der Kreuzdurchschlag
- *criss-cross skip*
45 das Springen mit Durchschlag
- *skip through the hoop*
46 der Gymnastikreifen
- *gymnastic hoop*
47 das Handumkreisen
- *hand circle*
48 die Schlange
- *serpent*
49 das Gymnastikband
- *gymnastic ribbon*
50 die Spirale
- *spiral*
51-52 die Turnkleidung (Gymnastikkleidung)
- *gymnastics kit*
51 der Turnanzug (Gymnastikanzug)
- *leotard*
52 die Turnschuhe *m* (Gymnastikschuhe)
- *gym shoes*

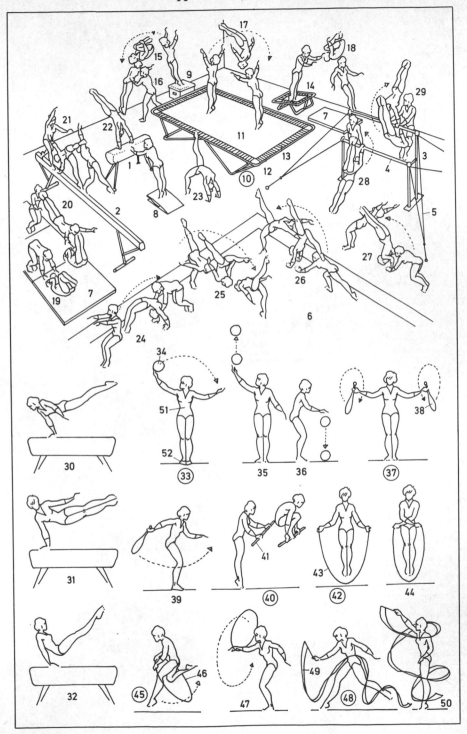

1-8 das Laufen
- *running*
1-6 der Start
- *start*
1 der Startblock
- *starting block*
2 die (verstellbare) Fußstütze
- *(adjustable) block (pedal)*
3 der Startplatz
- *start*
4 der Tiefstart
- *crouch start*
5 der Läufer, ein Sprinter *m*
 (Kurzstreckenläufer); *auch:*
 Mittelstreckenläufer *m*
 (Mittelstreckler),
 Langstreckenläufer
 (Langstreckler)
- *runner, a sprinter;* also:
 *middle-distance runner,
 long-distance runner*
6 die Laufbahn, eine Aschenbahn *f*
 od. Kunststoffbahn *f*
- *running track (track), a cinder track
 or synthetic track*
7-8 das Hürdenlaufen (der
 Hürdenlauf); *ähnl.:* das
 Hindernislaufen (der
 Hindernislauf)
- *hurdles (hurdle racing);* sim.:
 steeplechase
7 das Überlaufen
- *clearing the hurdle*
8 die Hürde
- *hurdle*
9-41 das Springen
- *jumping and vaulting*
9-27 der Hochsprung
- *high jump*
9 der Fosbury-Flop
- *Fosbury flop (Fosbury, flop)*
10 der Hochspringer
- *high jumper*
11 die Drehung um die Körperlängs-
 und -querachse
- *body rotation (rotation on the
 body's longitudinal and latitudinal
 axes)*
12 die Schulterlandung
- *shoulder landing*
13 der Sprungständer
- *upright*
14 die Sprunglatte (Latte)
- *bar (crossbar)*
15 der Parallelrückenrollsprung
- *Eastern roll*
16 der Rückenrollsprung
- *Western roll*
17 der Rollsprung
- *roll*
18 die Rolltechnik
- *rotation*
19 die Landung
- *landing*
20 die Höhenmarkierung
- *height scale*
21 die Scher-Kehr-Technik
- *Eastern cut-off*
22 der Schersprung
- *scissors (scissor jump)*
23 der Wälzsprung
- *straddle (straddle jump)*
24 die Wälztechnik
- *turn*
25 die Sechsuhrstellung
- *vertical free leg*
26 der Absprung
- *take-off*
27 das Schwungbein
- *free leg*
28-36 der Stabhochsprung
- *pole vault*
28 der Sprungstab
 (Stabhochsprungstab)
- *pole (vaulting pole)*
29 der Stabhochspringer in der
 Aufschwungphase
- *pole vaulter (vaulter) in the pull-up
 phase*
30 die Schwungtechnik (das Flyaway)
- *swing*
31 das Überqueren der Latte
- *crossing the bar*
32 die Hochsprunganlage
- *high jump apparatus (high jump
 equipment)*
33 der Sprungständer
- *upright*
34 die Sprunglatte
- *bar (crossbar)*
35 der Einstichkasten
- *box*
36 der Sprunghügel (das
 Sprungkissen)
- *landing area (landing pad)*
37-41 der Weitsprung
- *long jump*
37 der Absprung
- *take-off*
38 der Absprungbalken
- *take-off board*
39 die Sprunggrube
- *landing area*
40 die Laufsprungtechnik
- *hitch-kick*
41 die Hangtechnik
- *hang*
42-47 der Hammerwurf
- *hammer throw*
42 der Hammer
- *hammer*
43 der Hammerkopf
- *hammer head*
44 der Verbindungsdraht
- *handle*
45 der Hammergriff
- *grip*
46 die Hammergriffhaltung
- *holding the grip*
47 der Handschuh
- *glove*
48 das Kugelstoßen
- *shot put*
49 die Kugel
- *shot (weight)*
50 die O'Brien-Technik
- *O'Brien technique*
51-53 der Speerwurf
- *javelin throw*
51 der Daumenzeigefingergriff
- *grip with thumb and index finger*
52 der Daumenmittelfingergriff
- *grip with thumb and middle finger*
53 der Zangengriff
- *horseshoe grip*
54 die Wicklung
- *binding*

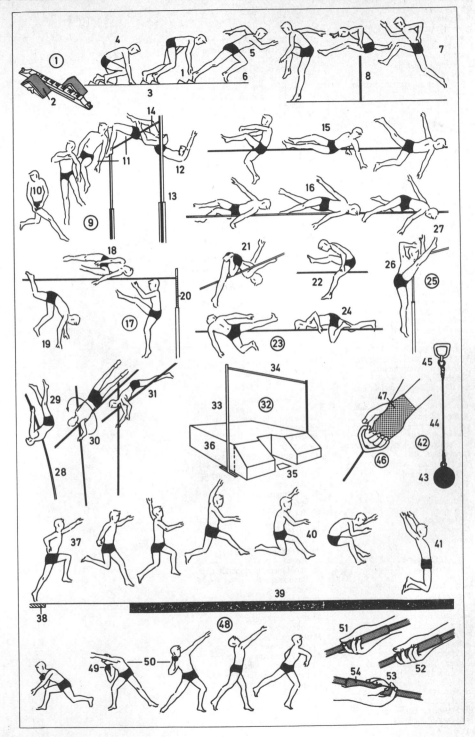

1-5 **das Gewichtheben**
- *weightlifting*
1 das Hockereißen
- *squat-style snatch*
2 der Gewichtheber
- *weightlifter*
3 die Scheibenhantel
- *disc (disk) barbell*
4 das Stoßen mit Ausfallschritt *m*
- *jerk with split*
5 die fixierte Last
- *maintained lift*
6-12 **das Ringen** (der Ringkampf)
- *wrestling*
6-9 der griechisch-römische Ringkampf
- *Greco-Roman wrestling*
6 der Standkampf
- *standing wrestling (wrestling in standing position)*
7 der Ringer (Ringkämpfer)
- *wrestler*
8 der Bodenkampf (*hier:* der Ansatz zum Aufreißen *n*)
- *on-the-ground wrestling (*here: the referee's position)*
9 die Brücke
- *bridge*
10-12 das Freistilringen
- *freestyle wrestling*
10 der seitliche Armhebel mit Einsteigen *n*
- *bar arm (arm bar) with grapevine*
11 der Beinsteller
- *double leg lock*
12 die Ringmatte (Matte)
- *wrestling mat (mat)*
13-17 **das Judo** (*ähnl.:* das Jiu-Jitsu)
- *judo (*sim.: *ju-jitsu, jiu jitsu, ju-jutsu)*
13 das Gleichgewichtsbrechen nach rechts vorn
- *drawing the opponent off balance to the right and forward*
14 der Judoka
- *judoka (judoist)*
15 der farbige Gürtel, als Abzeichen *n* für den Dan-Grad
- *coloured (Am.* colored*) belt, as a symbol of Dan grade*
16 der Unparteiische
- *referee*
17 der Judowurf
- *judo throw*
18-19 **das Karate**
- *karate*
18 der Karateka
- *karateka*
19 der Seitfußstoß, eine Fußtechnik
- *side thrust kick, a kicking technique*
20-50 **das Boxen** (der Boxkampf, Faustkampf, das *od.* der Boxmatch)
- *boxing (boxing match)*
20-24 die Trainingsgeräte *n*
- *training apparatus (training equipment)*
20 der Doppelendball
- *[spring-supported] punch ball*
21 der Sandsack
- *punch bag (Am.* punching bag*)*
22 der Punktball
- *speed ball*
23 die Maisbirne (Boxbirne)
- *[suspended] punch ball*

24 der Plattformball (Birnball, Punchingball)
- *punch ball*
25 der Boxer, ein Amateurboxer *m* (kämpft mit Trikot *n*), od. ein Berufsboxer *m* (Professional; kämpft ohne Trikot *n*)
- *boxer, an amateur boxer (boxes in a singlet, vest, Am.* undershirt*) or a professional boxer (boxes without singlet)*
26 der Boxhandschuh
- *boxing glove*
27 der Sparringspartner (Trainingspartner)
- *sparring partner*
28 der gerade Stoß (die Gerade)
- *straight punch (straight blow)*
29 das Abducken und Seitneigen *n*
- *ducking and sidestepping*
30 der Kopfschutz
- *headguard*
31 der Nahkampf; *hier:* der Clinch
- *infighting;* here: *clinch*
32 der Haken (Aufwärtshaken)
- *uppercut*
33 der Kopfhaken (Seitwärtshaken)
- *hook to the head (hook, left hook or right hook)*
34 der Tiefschlag, ein verbotener Schlag *m*
- *punch below the belt, a foul punch (illegal punch, foul)*
35-50 die Boxveranstaltung, ein Titelkampf *m*
- *boxing match (boxing contest), a title fight (title bout)*
35 der Boxring (Ring, Kampfring)
- *boxing ring (ring)*
36 die Seile *n*
- *ropes*
37 die Seilverspannung
- *stay wire (stay rope)*
38 die neutrale Ecke
- *neutral corner*
39 der Sieger
- *winner*
40 der durch Niederschlag *m* (Knockout, k.o.) Besiegte (k.o.-geschlagene Gegner)
- *loser by a knockout*
41 der Ringrichter
- *referee*
42 das Auszählen
- *counting out*
43 der Punktrichter
- *judge*
44 der Sekundant (Helfer)
- *second*
45 der Manager (Veranstalter, Boxmanager)
- *manager*
46 der Gong
- *gong*
47 der Zeitnehmer
- *timekeeper*
48 der Protokollführer
- *record keeper*
49 der Pressefotograf
- *press photographer*
50 der Sportreporter (Reporter)
- *sports reporter (reporter)*

1-57 **das Bergsteigen** (Bergwandern,
  der Hochtourismus)
- *mountaineering (mountain
  climbing, Alpinism)*
1 das Unterkunftshaus (die
  Alpenvereinshütte, Schutzhütte,
  Berghütte, der Stützpunkt)
- *hut (Alpine Club hut, mountain
  hut, base)*
2-13 **das Klettern** (Felsgehen,
  Klettern im Fels *m*) [Felstechnik *f*,
  Klettertechnik]
- *climbing (rock climbing) [rock
  climbing technique]*
2 die Wand (Felswand, Steilstufe)
- *rock face (rock wall)*
3 der Riß (Längs-, Quer- od.
  Diagonalriß)
- *fissure (vertical, horizontal or
  diagonal fissure)*
4 das Band (Fels-, Gras-, Geröll-,
  Schnee- od. Eisband)
- *ledge (rock ledge, grass ledge, scree
  ledge, snow ledge, ice ledge)*
5 der Bergsteiger (Kletterer,
  Felsgeher, Alpinist, Hochtourist)
- *mountaineer (climber, mountain
  climber, Alpinist)*
6 der Anorak (Hochtourenanorak,
  das Schneehemd, die Daunenjacke)
- *anorak (high-altitude anorak,
  snowshirt, padded jacket)*
7 die Bundhose (Kletterhose)
- *breeches (climbing breeches)*
8 der Kamin
- *chimney*
9 der Felskopf
- *belay (spike, rock spike)*
10 die Selbstsicherung
- *belay*
11 die Seilschlinge (Schlinge)
- *rope sling (sling)*
12 das Bergseil (Seil)
- *rope*
13 die Leiste
- *spur*
14-21 **das Eisgehen** (Klettern im Eis *n*)
  [Eistechnik *f*]
- *snow and ice climbing [snow and ice
  climbing technique]*
14 die Eiswand (der Firnhang)
- *ice slope (firn slope)*
15 der Eisgeher
- *snow and ice climber*
16 der Pickel
- *ice axe (Am. ax)*
17 die Stufe (der Tritt im Eis *n*)
- *step (ice step)*
18 die Gletscherbrille (Schneebrille)
- *snow goggles*
19 die Kapuze (Anorakkapuze)
- *hood (anorak hood)*
20 die Wächte (Schneewächte,
  Firnwächte)
- *cornice (snow cornice)*
21 der Grat (Eisgrat, Firngrat)
- *ridge (ice ridge)*
22-27 **die Seilschaft** [das Gehen am
  Seil *n*]
- *rope (roped party) [roped trek]*
22 der Gletscher
- *glacier*
23 die Gletscherspalte
- *crevasse*
24 die Schneebrücke (Firnbrücke)
- *snow bridge*

25 der Seilerste
- *leader*
26 der Seilzweite
- *second man (belayer)*
27 der Seildritte (Schlußmann)
- *third man (non-belayer)*
28-30 **das Abseilen**
- *roping down (abseiling, rapelling)*
28 die Abseilschlinge
- *abseil sling*
29 der Karabinersitz
- *sling seat*
30 der Dülfersitz
- *Dülfer seat*
31-57 **die Bergsteigerausrüstung**
  (alpine Ausrüstung, hochalpine
  Ausrüstung, Kletterausrüstung,
  Eistourenausrüstung)
- *mountaineering equipment (climbing
  equipment, snow and ice climbing
  equipment)*
31 der Pickel
- *ice axe (Am. ax)*
32 der Handriemen
- *wrist sling*
33 die Haue
- *pick*
34 die Schaufel
- *adze (Am. adz)*
35 das Karabinerloch
- *karabiner hole*
36 das Eisbeil
- *short-shafted ice axe (Am. ax)*
37 der Eishammer (der
  Kombihammer für Eis *n* und Fels
  m, Hammer)
- *hammer axe (Am. ax)*
38 der Universalkletterhaken
- *general-purpose piton*
39 der Abseilhaken (Ringhaken)
- *abseil piton (ringed piton)*
40 die Eisschraube
  (Halbrohreissschraube)
- *ice piton (semi-tubular screw ice
  piton, corkscrew piton)*
41 die Eisspirale
- *drive-in ice piton*
42 der Bergschuh
- *mountaineering boot*
43 die Profilsohle
- *corrugated sole*
44 der Kletterschuh
- *climbing boot*
45 die aufgerauhte Hartgummikante
- *roughened stiff rubber upper*
46 der Karabiner
- *karabiner*
47 die Schraubsicherung
- *screwgate*
48 die Steigeisen *n* (Leichtsteigeisen,
  Zwölfzacker, Zehnzacker)
- *crampons (lightweight crampons,
  twelve-point crampons, ten-point
  crampons)*
49 die Frontalzacken
- *front points*
50 der Zackenschutz
- *point guards*
51 die Steigeisenriemen
- *crampon strap*
52 die Steigeisenkabelbindung
- *crampon cable fastener*
53 der Steinschlaghelm
- *safety helmet (protective helmet)*
54 die Stirnlampe
- *helmet lamp*

55 die Schneegamaschen *f*
- *snow gaiters*
56 der Klettergürtel
- *climbing harness*
57 der Sitzgurt
- *sit harness*

1-72 der Skisport (Skilauf, das
  Skilaufen, Skifahren)
- *skiing*
1 der Kompaktski
- *compact ski*
2 die Sicherheitsskibindung
- *safety binding (release binding)*
3 der Fangriemen
- *strap*
4 die Stahlkante
- *steel edge*
5 der Skistock
- *ski stick (ski pole)*
6 der Stockgriff
- *grip*
7 die Handschlaufe
- *loop*
8 der Stockteller
- *basket*
9 der einteilige Damenskianzug
- *ladies' one-piece ski suit*
10 die Skimütze
- *skiing cap (ski cap)*
11 die Skibrille
- *skiing goggles*
12 der Schalenskistiefel
- *cemented sole skiing boot*
13 der Skihelm
- *crash helmet*
14-20 die Langlaufausrüstung
- *cross-country equipment*
14 der Langlaufski
- *cross-country ski*
15 die Langlauf-Rattenfallbindung
- *cross-country rat trap binding*
16 der Langlaufschuh
- *cross-country boot*
17 der Langlaufanzug
- *cross-country gear*
18 die Schirmmütze
- *peaked cap*
19 die Sonnenbrille
- *sunglasses*
20 die Langlaufstöcke *m*, aus
  Tonkinrohr *n*
- *cross-country poles made of
  bamboo*
21-24 Skiwachsutensilien *pl*
- *ski-waxing equipment*
21 das Skiwachs
- *ski wax*
22 der Wachsbügler (die Lötlampe)
- *waxing iron
  (blowlamp, blowtorch)*
23 der Wachskorken
- *waxing cork*
24 das Wachskratzeisen
- *wax scraper*
25 der Rennstock
- *downhill racing pole*
26 der Grätenschritt, zur Ersteigung
  eines Hanges *m*
- *herringbone, for climbing a slope*
27 der Treppenschritt, zur Ersteigung
  eines Hanges *m*
- *sidestep, for climbing a slope*
28 die Hüfttasche
- *ski bag*
29 der Torlauf
- *slalom*
30 die Torstange
- *gate pole*
31 der Rennanzug
- *racing suit*
32 der Abfahrtslauf
- *downhill racing*

33 das „Ei", die Idealabfahrtshaltung
- *'egg' position, the ideal downhill
  racing position*
34 der Abfahrtsski
- *downhill ski*
35 der Sprunglauf
- *ski jumping*
36 der „Fisch", die Flughaltung
- *lean forward*
37 die Startnummer
- *number*
38 der Sprungski
- *ski jumping ski*
39 die Führungsrillen *f* (3 bis 5 Rillen *f*)
- *grooves (3 to 5 grooves)*
40 die Kabelbindung
- *cable binding*
41 der Sprungstiefel
- *ski jumping boots*
42 der Langlauf
- *cross-country*
43 der Rennoverall
- *cross-country stretch-suit*
44 die Loipe
- *course*
45 das Markierungsfähnchen (die
  Loipenmarkierung)
- *course-marking flag*
46 die Schichten *f* (Lamellen) eines
  modernen Skis *m*
- *layers of a modern ski*
47 der Spezialkern
- *special core*
48 die Laminate *n*
- *laminates*
49 die Dämpfungsschicht
- *stabilizing layer (stabilizer)*
50 die Stahlkante
- *steel edge*
51 die Aluoberkante
  (Aluminiumoberkante)
- *aluminium (Am. aluminum) upper
  edge*
52 die Kunststofflauffläche
- *synthetic bottom (artificial bottom)*
53 der Sicherheitsbügel
- *safety jet*
54-56 die Bindungselemente *n*
- *parts of the binding*
54 die Fersenautomatik
- *automatic heel unit*
55 der Backen
- *toe unit*
56 der Skistopper
- *ski stop*
57-63 der Skilift
- *ski lift*
57 der Doppelsessellift
- *double chair lift*
58 der Sicherheitsbügel,
  mit Fußstütze *f*
- *safety bar with footrest*
59 der Schlepplift
- *ski lift*
60 die Schleppspur
- *track*
61 der Schleppbügel
- *hook*
62 der Seilrollautomat
- *automatic cable pulley*
63 das Schleppseil
- *haulage cable*
64 der Slalomlauf
- *slalom*
65 das offene Tor
- *open gate*

66 das blinde vertikale Tor
- *closed vertical gate*
67 das offene vertikale Tor
- *open vertical gate*
68 das schräge Doppeltor
- *transversal chicane*
69 die Haarnadel
- *hairpin*
70 das versetzte vertikale Doppeltor
- *elbow*
71 der Korridor
- *corridor*
72 die Allais-Schikane (Chicane
  Allais)
- *Allais chicane*

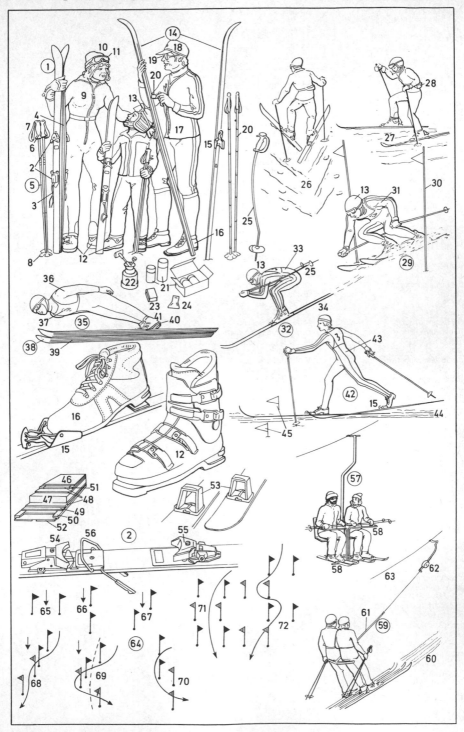

1-26 das Eislaufen
(Schlittschuhlaufen, der Eislauf)
- *ice skating*
1 die Eisläuferin (der Eisläufer,
Schlittschuhläufer, ein
Einzelläufer *m*)
- *ice skater, a solo skater*
2 das Standbein
- *tracing leg*
3 das Spielbein
- *free leg*
4 die Paarläufer *m*
- *pair skaters*
5 die Todesspirale
- *death spiral*
6 der Bogen
- *pivot*
7 der Rehsprung
- *stag jump (stag leap)*
8 die eingesprungene Sitzpirouette
- *jump-sit-spin*
9 die Waagepirouette
- *upright spin*
10 das Fußanfassen
- *holding the foot*
11-19 die Pflichtfiguren *f*
- *compulsory figures*
11 der Bogenachter
- *curve eight*
12 der Schlangenbogen
- *change*
13 der Dreier
- *three*
14 der Doppeldreier
- *double-three*
15 die Schlinge
- *loop*
16 die Schlangenbogenschlinge
- *change-loop*
17 der Gegendreier
- *bracket*
18 die Gegenwende
- *counter*
19 die Wende
- *rocker*
20-25 Schlittschuhe *m*
- *ice skates*
20 das Eisschnellaufcomplet
(der Schnellaufschlittschuh)
- *speed skating set (speed skate)*
21 die Kante
- *edge*
22 der Hohlschliff
- *hollow grinding (hollow ridge,
concave ridge)*
23 das Eishockeycomplet
- *ice hockey set (ice hockey skate)*
24 der Eislaufstiefel
- *ice skating boot*
25 der Schoner
- *skate guard*
26 der Eisschnelläufer
- *speed skater*
27-28 das Schlittschuhsegeln
- *skate sailing*
27 der Schlittschuhsegler
- *skate sailor*
28 das Handsegel
- *hand sail*
29-37 das Eishockey
- *ice hockey*
29 der Eishockeyspieler
- *ice hockey player*
30 der Eishockeyschläger
(Eishockeystock)
- *ice hockey stick*

31 der Schlägerschaft
- *stick handle*
32 das Schlägerblatt
- *stick blade*
33 der Schienbeinschutz
- *shin pad*
34 der Kopfschutz
- *headgear (protective helmet)*
35 die Eishockeyscheibe (der Puck,
eine Hartgummischeibe)
- *puck, a vulcanized rubber disc
(disk)*
36 der Torwart (der Tormann)
- *goalkeeper*
37 das Tor
- *goal*
38-40 das Eisstockschießen
- *ice-stick shooting (Bavarian curling)*
38 der Eisstockschütze
- *ice-stick shooter (Bavarian curler)*
39 der Eisstock
- *ice stick*
40 die Daube
- *block*
41-43 das Curling
- *curling*
41 der Curlingspieler
- *curler*
42 der Curlingstein
- *curling stone (granite)*
43 der Curlingbesen
- *curling brush (curling broom,
besom)*
44-46 das Eissegeln
- *ice yachting (iceboating, ice sailing)*
44 die Eisjacht (das Eissegelboot)
- *ice yacht (iceboat)*
45 die Eiskufe
- *steering runner*
46 der Ausleger
- *outrigged runner*

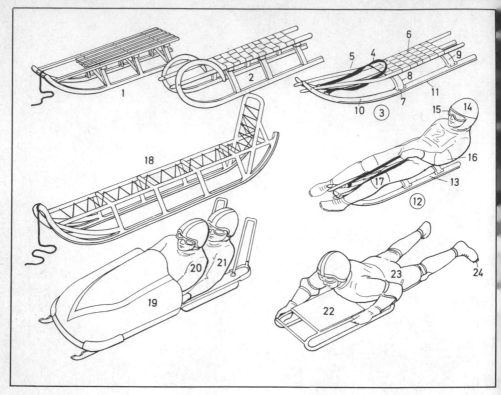

1　der starre Schlitten (Volksrodel)
- *toboggan*
　(sledge, Am. sled)
2　der Volksrodel mit Gurtsitz *m*
- *toboggan (sledge, Am. sled) with*
　seat of plaid straps
3　der Jugendrodel
- *junior luge toboggan (junior luge,*
　junior toboggan)
4　der Lenkgurt
- *rein*
5　der Holm (die Spange)
- *bar (strut)*
6　der Sitz
- *seat*
7　das Kappenblech
- *bracket*
8　der Vorderfuß
- *front prop*
9　der Hinterfuß
- *rear prop*
10　die bewegliche Kufe
- *movable runner*
11　die Schiene
- *metal face*
12　der Rennrodler
- *luge tobogganer*
13　der Rennrodel
- *luge toboggan (luge, toboggan)*
14　der Sturzhelm
- *crash helmet*
15　die Rennbrille
- *goggles*

16　der Ellbogenschützer
- *elbow pad*
17　der Knieschützer
- *knee pad*
18　der Nansenschlitten, ein
　Polarschlitten *m*
- *Nansen sledge, a polar sledge*
19-21　Bobsport *m*
- *bobsleigh (bobsledding)*
19　der Bobschlitten, ein Zweierbob *m*
- *bobsleigh (bobsled), a two-man*
　bobsleigh (a boblet)
20　der Steuermann (Bobführer)
- *steersman*
21　der Bremser
- *brakeman*
22-24　das Skeletonfahren
- *skeleton tobogganing (Cresta*
　tobogganing)
22　der Skeleton (Skeletonschlitten)
- *skeleton (skeleton toboggan)*
23　der Skeletonfahrer
- *skeleton rider*
24　das Kratzeisen, zum Lenken *n* und
　Bremsen *n*
- *rake, for braking and steering*

1 die Schneelawine (Lawine); *Arten:*
   Staublawine *f*, Grundlawine
 - *avalanche (snow avalanche, Am.*
   snowslide); kinds: wind avalanche,
   ground avalanche
2 der Lawinenbrecher, eine
   Ablenkmauer; *ähnl.:* der
   Lawinenkeil
 - *avalanche wall, a deflecting wall*
   (diverting wall); sim.: avalanche
   wedge
3 die Lawinengalerie
 - *avalanche gallery*
4 das Schneetreiben
 - *snowfall*
5 die Schneeverwehung
   (Schneewehe)
 - *snowdrift*
6 der Schneezaun
 - *snow fence*
7 der Bannwald
 - *avalanche forest [planted as*
   protection against avalanches]
8 der Straßenreinigungswagen
 - *street-cleaning lorry (street cleaner)*
9 der Vorbauschneepflug
   (Schneepflug)
 - *snow plough*
   (Am. snowplow)
   attachment
10 die Schneekette (Gleitschutzkette)
 - *snow chain (skid chain, tyre chain,*
   Am. tire chain)

11 die Kühlerhaube
 - *radiator bonnet (Am. radiator*
   hood)
12 das Kühlerhaubenfenster und die
   Fensterklappe (Jalousie)
 - *radiator shutter and shutter*
   opening (louvre shutter)
13 der Schneemann
 - *snowman*
14 die Schneeballschlacht
 - *snowball fight*
15 der Schneeball
 - *snowball*
16 der Skibob
 - *ski bob*
17 die Schlitterbahn (Schleife, *bayr.*
   Ranschel)
 - *slide*
18 der Junge, beim Schlittern *n*
   (Schleifen, *bayr.* Ranscheln)
 - *boy, sliding*
19 das Glatteis
 - *icy surface*
   (icy ground)
20 die Schneedecke, auf dem Dach *n*
 - *covering of snow, on the roof*
21 der Eiszapfen
 - *icicle*
22 der Schneeschipper
   (Schneeschaufler), beim Schippen *n*
   (Schneeschippen,
   Schneeschaufeln)
 - *man clearing snow*

23 die Schneeschippe
   (Schneeschaufel)
 - *snow push (snow shovel)*
24 der Schneehaufen
 - *heap of snow*
25 der Pferdeschlitten
 - *horse-drawn sleigh (horse sleigh)*
26 die Schlittenschellen *f* (Schellen,
   das Schellengeläut)
 - *sleigh bells (bells, set of bells)*
27 der Fußsack
 - *foot muff (Am. foot bag)*
28 die Ohrenklappe (der
   Ohrenschützer)
 - *earmuff*
29 der Stuhlschlitten (Stehschlitten,
   Tretschlitten); *ähnl.:* der
   Stoßschlitten (Schubschlitten)
 - *handsledge (tread sledge); sim.:*
   push sledge
30 der Schneematsch (geschmolzene
   Schnee, Matschschnee)
 - *slush*

1-13 das **Sportkegeln**
- *skittles*
1-11 die Kegelaufstellung (der Kegelstand)
- *skittle frame*
1 der Vordereckkegel (Erste)
- *front pin (front)*
2 der linke Vordergassenkegel, eine Dame
- *left front second pin (left front second)*
3 die linke Vordergasse
- *running three [left]*
4 der rechte Vordergassenkegel, eine Dame
- *right front second pin (right front second)*
5 die rechte Vordergasse
- *running three [right]*
6 der linke Eckkegel, ein Bauer *m*
- *left corner pin (left corner), a corner (copper)*
7 der König
- *landlord*
8 der rechte Eckkegel, ein Bauer *m*
- *right corner pin (right corner), a corner (copper)*
9 der linke Hintergassenkegel, eine Dame
- *back left second pin (back left second)*
10 der rechte Hintergassenkegel, eine Dame
- *back right second pin (back right second)*
11 der Hintereckkegel (Letzte)
- *back pin (back)*
12 der Kegel
- *pin*
13 der Kegelkönig (König)
- *landlord*
14-20 das **Bowling**
- *tenpin bowling*
14 die Bowlingaufstellung (der Bowlingstand)
- *frame*
15 die Bowlingkugel (Lochkugel)
- *bowling ball (ball with finger holes)*
16 das Griffloch
- *finger hole*
17-20 die Wurfarten *f*
- *deliveries*
17 der Straight-Ball (Straight)
- *straight ball*
18 der Hook-Ball (Hook, Hakenwurf)
- *hook ball (hook)*
19 der Curve-Ball (Bogenwurf)
- *curve*
20 der Back-up-Ball (Rückhandbogenwurf)
- *back-up ball (back-up)*
21 das **Boulespiel** (Cochonnet); *ähnl.*: das ital. Bocciaspiel (das *od.* die Boccia), das engl. Bowlspiel
- ***boules;*** *sim.: Italian game of boccie, green bowls (bowls)*
22 der Boulespieler
- *boules player*
23 die Malkugel (Zielkugel, der Pallino, Lecco)
- *jack (target jack)*
24 die gerillte Wurfkugel
- *grooved boule*
25 die Spielergruppe
- *group of players*
26 das **Gewehrschießen**
- *rifle shooting*
27-29 Anschlagsarten *f*
- *shooting positions*
27 der stehende Anschlag
- *standing position*
28 der kniende Anschlag
- *kneeling position*
29 der liegende Anschlag
- *prone position*

30-33 Schießscheiben *f* (Zielscheiben, Ringscheiben)
- *targets*
30 die Gewehrscheibe für 50m Schußweite *f*
- *target for 50 m events (50 m target)*
31 der Ring
- *circle*
32 die Gewehrscheibe für 100m Schußweite *f*
- *target for 100 m events (100 m target)*
33 die laufende Scheibe (der Keiler)
- *bobbing target (turning target, running-boar target)*
34-39 die Sportmunition
- *ammunition*
34 das Diabologeschoß für Luftgewehr *n*
- *air rifle cartridge*
35 die Randzünderpatrone für Zimmerstutzen *m*
- *rimfire cartridge for zimmerstutzen (indoor target rifle), a smallbore German single-shot rifle*
36 die Patronenhülse
- *case head*
37 die Randkugel
- *caseless round*
38 die Patrone Kaliber *n* 22 *long rifle*
- *22 long rifle cartridge*
39 die Patrone Kaliber *n* 222 *Remington*
- *.222 Remington cartridge*
40-49 Sportgewehre *n*
- *sporting rifles*
40 das Luftgewehr
- *air rifle*
41 der Diopter
- *optical sight*
42 das Korn
- *front sight (foresight)*
43 das Kleinkaliberstandardgewehr
- *smallbore standard rifle*
44 die internationale freie Kleinkaliberwaffe
- *international smallbore free rifle*
45 die Handstütze für den stehenden Anschlag
- *palm rest for standing position*
46 die Kolbenkappe mit Haken *m*
- *butt plate with hook*
47 der Lochschaft
- *butt with thumb hole*
48 das Kleinkalibergewehr für die laufende Scheibe
- *smallbore rifle for bobbing target (turning target)*
49 das Zielfernrohr
- *telescopic sight (riflescope, telescope sight)*
50 die Dioptervisierung mit Ringkorn *n*
- *optical ring sight*
51 die Dioptervisierung mit Balkenkorn *n*
- *optical ring and bead sight*
52-66 das **Bogenschießen**
- ***archery*** *(target archery)*
52 der Abschuß
- *shot*
53 der Bogenschütze
- *archer*
54 der Turnierbogen
- *competition bow*
55 der Wurfarm
- *riser*
56 das Visier
- *point-of-aim mark*
57 der Handgriff
- *grip (handle)*
58 der Stabilisator
- *stabilizer*

59 die Bogensehne (Sehne)
- *bow string (string)*
60 der Pfeil
- *arrow*
61 die Pfeilspitze
- *pile (point) of the arrow*
62 die Steuerfedern *f* (Truthahnfedern, die Befiederung)
- *fletching*
63 die Nocke
- *nock*
64 der Schaft
- *shaft*
65 das Schützenzeichen
- *cresting*
66 die Scheibe
- *target*
67 das bask. **Pelotaspiel** (die Jai alai)
- *Basque game of pelota (jai alai)*
68 der Pelotaspieler
- *pelota player*
69 der Schläger (die Cesta)
- *wicker basket (cesta)*
70-78 das **Skeet** (Skeetschießen), ein Wurftaubenschießen *n* (Tontaubenschie
- ***skeet*** *(skeet shooting), a kind of clay pigeon shooting*
70 die Skeet-Bockdoppelflinte
- *skeet over-and-under shotgun*
71 die Laufmündung mit Skeetbohrung *f*
- *muzzle with skeet choke*
72 der Gewehranschlag bei Abruf *m* (die Jagdstellung)
- *ready position on call*
73 der fertige Anschlag
- *firing position*
74 die Skeetanlage (Taubenwurfanlage)
- *shooting range*
75 das Hochhaus
- *high house*
76 das Niederhaus
- *low house*
77 die Wurfrichtung
- *target's path*
78 der Schützenstand
- *shooting station (shooting box)*
79 das **Rhönrad**
- ***aero wheel***
80 der Griff
- *handle*
81 das Fußbrett
- *footrest*
82 das **Go-Karting**
- ***go-karting*** *(karting)*
83 das Go-Kart
- *go-kart (kart)*
84 die Startnummer
- *number plate (number)*
85 die Pedale *n*
- *pedals*
86 der profillose Reifen (Slick)
- *pneumatic tyre (Am. tire)*
87 der Benzintank
- *petrol tank (Am. gasoline tank)*
88 der Rahmen
- *frame*
89 das Lenkrad
- *steering wheel*
90 der Schalensitz
- *bucket seat*
91 die Feuerschutzwand
- *protective bulkhead*
92 der Zweitaktmotor
- *two-stroke engine*
93 der Schalldämpfer
- *silencer (Am. muffler)*

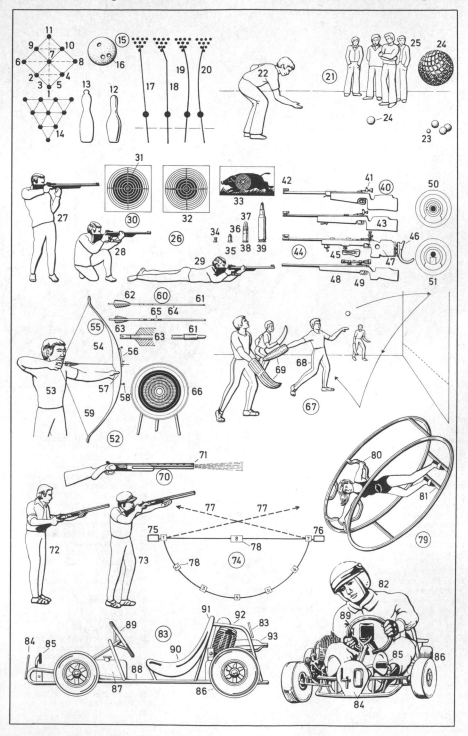

1-48 der Maskenball (das Maskenfest, Narrenfest, Kostümfest)
- *masked ball (masquerade, fancy-dress ball)*
1 der Ballsaal (Festsaal, Saal)
- *ballroom*
2 das Poporchester (die Popband), ein Tanzorchester *n*
- *pop group, a dance band*
3 der Popmusiker
- *pop musician*
4 der (das) Lampion (die Papierlaterne)
- *paper lantern*
5 die Girlande
- *festoon (string of decorations)*
6-48 die Maskierung (Verkleidung) bei der Maskerade
- *disguise (fancy dress) at the masquerade*
6 die Hexe
- *witch*
7 die Gesichtsmaske (Maske)
- *mask*
8 der Trapper (Pelzjäger)
- *fur trapper (trapper)*
9 das Apachenmädchen
- *Apache girl*
10 der Netzstrumpf
- *net stocking*
11 der Hauptgewinn der Tombola (Verlosung), ein Präsentkorb *m*

- *first prize in the tombola (raffle), a hamper*
12 die Pierrette
- *pierette*
13 die Larve
- *half mask (domino)*
14 der Teufel
- *devil*
15 der Domino
- *domino*
16 das Hawaiimädchen
- *hula-hula girl (Hawaii girl)*
17 die Blumenkette
- *garland*
18 der Bastrock
- *grass skirt (hula skirt)*
19 der Pierrot
- *pierrot*
20 die Halskrause
- *ruff*
21 die Midinette
- *midinette*
22 das Biedermeierkleid
- *Biedermeier dress*
23 der Schutenhut
- *poke bonnet*
24 das Dekolleté mit Schönheitspflästerchen *n* (Musche *f*, Mouche)
- *décolletage with beauty spot*
25 die Bajadere (indische Tänzerin)
- *bayadère (Hindu dancing girl)*

26 der Grande
- *grandee*
27 die Kolombine (Kolumbine)
- *Columbine*
28 der Maharadscha
- *maharaja (maharajah)*
29 der Mandarin, ein chines. Würdenträger
- *mandarin, a Chinese dignitary*
30 die Exotin
- *exotic girl (exotic)*
31 der Cowboy; *ähnl.:* Gaucho
- *cowboy; sim.: gaucho (vaquero)*
32 der Vamp, im Phantasiekostüm *n*
- *vamp, in fancy dress*
33 der Stutzer (Dandy, Geck, *österr.* das Gigerl), eine Charaktermaske
- *dandy (fop, beau), a disguise*
34 die Ballrosette (das Ballabzeichen)
- *rosette*
35 der Harlekin
- *harlequin*
36 die Zigeunerin
- *gipsy (gypsy) girl*
37 die Kokotte (Halbweltdame)
- *cocotte (demi-monde, demi-mondaine, demi-rep)*
38 der Eulenspiegel, ein Narr *m* (Schelm, Schalk, Possenreißer)
- *owl-glass, a fool (jester, buffoon)*
39 die Narrenkappe (Schellenkappe)
- *foolscap (jester's cap and bells)*
40 die Rassel (Klapper)
- *rattle*

41 die Odaliske (Orientalin), eine
   orientalische Haremssklavin
  - *odalisque, Eastern female slave in*
   Sultan's seraglio
42 die Pluderhose
  - *chalwar (pantaloons)*
43 der Seeräuber (Pirat)
  - *pirate (buccaneer)*
44 die Tätowierung
  - *tattoo*
45 die Papiermütze
  - *paper hat*
46 die Pappnase
  - *false nose*
47 die Knarre (Ratsche, Rätsche)
  - *clapper (rattle)*
48 die Pritsche (Narrenpritsche)
  - *slapstick*
49-54 Feuerwerkskörper *m*
  - *fireworks*
49 das Zündblättchen
   (Knallblättchen)
  - *percussion cap*
50 das (der) Knallbonbon
  - *cracker*
51 die Knallerbse
  - *banger*
52 der Knallfrosch
  - *jumping jack*
53 der Kanonenschlag
  - *cannon cracker (maroon, marroon)*
54 die Rakete
  - *rocket*

55 die Papierkugel
  - *paper ball*
56 der Schachterlteufel
   (Jack-in-the-box, ein
   Scherzartikel *m*)
  - *jack-in-the-box, a joke*
57-70 der Karnevalszug
   (Faschingszug)
  - *carnival procession*
57 der Karnevalswagen
   (Faschingswagen)
  - *carnival float (carnival truck)*
58 der Karnevalsprinz (Prinz
   Karneval, Faschingsprinz)
  - *King Carnival*
59 das Narrenzepter
  - *bauble (fool's sceptre,* Am. *scepter)*
60 der Narrenorden
   (Karnevalsorden)
  - *fool's badge*
61 die Karnevalsprinzessin
   (Faschingsprinzessin)
  - *Queen Carnival*
62 das Konfetti
  - *confetti*
63 die Riesenfigur, eine Spottgestalt
  - *giant figure, a satirical figure*
64 die Schönheitskönigin
  - *beauty queen*
65 die Märchenfigur
  - *fairy-tale figure*
66 die Papierschlange
  - *paper streamer*

67 das Funkenmariechen
  - *majorette*
68 die Prinzengarde
  - *king's guard*
69 der Hanswurst, ein Spaßmacher *m*
  - *buffoon, a clown*
70 die Landsknechttrommel
  - *lansquenet's drum*

1-63 der Wanderzirkus
- *travelling (Am. traveling) circus*
1 das Zirkuszelt (Spielzelt, Chapiteau), ein Viermastzelt *n*
- *circus tent (big top), a four-pole tent*
2 der Zeltmast
- *tent pole*
3 der Scheinwerfer
- *spotlight*
4 der Beleuchter
- *lighting technician*
5 der Artistenstand
- *platform [for the trapeze artists]*
6 das Trapez (Schaukelreck)
- *trapeze*
7 der Luftakrobat (Trapezkünstler, „fliegende Mensch")
- *trapeze artist*
8 die Strickleiter
- *rope ladder*
9 die Musikertribüne (Orchestertribüne)
- *bandstand*
10 die Zirkuskapelle
- *circus band*
11 der Manegeneingang
- *ring entrance (arena entrance)*
12 der Sattelplatz (Aufsitzplatz)
- *wings*
13 die Stützstange (Zeltstütze)
- *tent prop (prop)*
14 das Sprungnetz, ein Sicherheitsnetz *n*
- *safety net*

15 der Zuschauerraum
- *seats for the spectators*
16 die Zirkusloge
- *circus box*
17 der Zirkusdirektor
- *circus manager*
18 der Artistenvermittler (Agent)
- *artiste agent (agent)*
19 der Eingang und Ausgang
- *entrance and exit*
20 der Aufgang
- *steps*
21 die Manege (Reitbahn)
- *ring (arena)*
22 die Bande (Piste)
- *ring fence*
23 der Musikclown
- *musical clown (clown)*
24 der Clown (Spaßmacher)
- *clown*
25 die „komische Nummer", eine Zirkusnummer
- *comic turn (clown act), a circus act*
26 die Kunstreiter *m*
- *circus riders (bareback riders)*
27 der Manegendiener, ein Zirkusdiener *m*
- *ring attendant, a circus attendant*
28 die Pyramide
- *pyramid*
29 der Untermann
- *support*

30-31 die Freiheitsdressur
- *performance by liberty horses*
30 das Zirkuspferd in Levade *f*
- *circus horse, performing the levade (pesade)*
31 der Dresseur, ein Stallmeister *m*
- *ringmaster, a trainer*
32 der Voltigereiter (Voltigeur)
- *vaulter*
33 der Notausgang
- *emergency exit*
34 der Wohnwagen (Zirkuswagen)
- *caravan (circus caravan, Am. trailer)*
35 der Schleuderakrobat
- *springboard acrobat (springboard artist)*
36 das Schleuderbrett
- *springboard*
37 der Messerwerfer
- *knife thrower*
38 der Kunstschütze
- *circus marksman*
39 die Assistentin
- *assistant*
40 die Seiltänzerin
- *tightrope dancer*
41 das Drahtseil
- *tightrope*
42 die Balancierstange (Gleichgewichtsstange)
- *balancing pole*
43 die Wurfnummer (Schleudernummer)
- *throwing act*

44 der Balanceakt
- *balancing act*
45 der Untermann
- *support*
46 die Perche (Bambusstange)
- *pole (bamboo pole)*
47 der Akrobat
- *acrobat*
48 der Äquilibrist
- *equilibrist (balancer)*
49 der Raubtierkäfig, ein Rundkäfig *m*
- *wild animal cage, a round cage*
50 das Raubtiergitter
- *bars of the cage*
51 der Laufgang (Gittergang,
Raubtiergang)
- *passage (barred passage, passage
for the wild animals)*
52 der Dompteur (Tierbändiger,
Tierlehrer)
- *tamer (wild animal tamer)*
53 die Bogenpeitsche (Peitsche)
- *whip*
54 die Schutzgabel
- *fork (protective fork)*
55 das Piedestal
- *pedestal*
56 das Raubtier (der Tiger, der Löwe)
- *wild animal (tiger, lion)*
57 das Setzstück
- *stand*
58 der Springreifen
- *hoop (jumping hoop)*

59 die Wippe
- *seesaw*
60 die Laufkugel
- *ball*
61 die Zeltstadt
- *camp*
62 der Käfigwagen
- *cage caravan*
63 die Tierschau
- *menagerie*

1-69 der Jahrmarkt (die Kirchweih,
  nd. Kirmes, *südwestdt.* die Messe,
  Kerwe, *bayr.* die Dult)
- *fair (annual fair)*
1 der Festplatz (die Festwiese, Wiese)
- *fairground*
2 das Kinderkarussell, ein Karussell
  n (*österr.* ein Ringelspiel *n, md./*
  schweiz. eine Reitschule)
- *children's merry-go-round,*
  (whirligig), a roundabout (Am.
  carousel)
3 die Erfrischungsbude (Getränkebude,
  der Getränkeausschank)
- *refreshment stall (drinks stall)*
4 das Kettenkarussell (der Kettenflieger)
- *chairoplane*
5 die Berg-und-Tal-Bahn, eine
  Geisterbahn
- *up-and-down roundabout, a ghost train*
6 die Schaubude
- *show booth (booth)*
7 die Kasse
- *box (box office)*
8 der Ausrufer (Ausschreier)
- *barker*
9 das Medium
- *medium*
10 der Schausteller
- *showman*
11 der Stärkemesser (Kraftmesser,
  „Lukas")
- *try-your-strength machine*

12 der ambulante Händler
- *hawker*
13 der Luftballon
- *balloon*
14 die Luftschlange
- *paper serpent*
15 die Federmühle, ein Windrad *n*
- *windmill*
16 der Taschendieb (Dieb)
- *pickpocket (thief)*
17 der Verkäufer
- *vendor*
18 der türkische Honig
- *Turkish delight*
19 das Abnormitätenkabinett
- *freak show*
20 der Riese
- *giant*
21 die Riesendame
- *fat lady*
22 die Liliputaner *m* (Zwerge)
- *dwarfs (midgets)*
23 das Bierzelt
- *beer marquee*
24 die Schaustellerbude (das
  Schaustellerzelt)
- *sideshow*
25-28 Artisten *m* (fahrende Leute *pl*,
  Fahrende *m*)
- *travelling* (Am. *traveling*) *artistes*
  (travelling show people)
25 der Feuerschlucker
- *fire eater*

26 der Schwertschlucker
- *sword swallower*
27 der Kraftmensch
- *strong man*
28 der Entfesselungskünstler
- *escapologist*
29 die Zuschauer *m*
- *spectators*
30 der Eisverkäufer (*ugs.* Eismann)
- *ice-cream vendor (ice-cream man)*
31 die Eiswaffel (Eistüte), mit Eis *n*
  (Speiseeis)
- *ice-cream cornet, with ice cream*
32 der Bratwurststand (die
  Würstchenbude)
- *sausage stand*
33 der Bratrost (Rost)
- *grill* (Am. *broiler)*
34 die Rostbratwurst (Bratwurst)
- *bratwurst (grilled sausage,* Am.
  broiled sausage)
35 die Wurstzange
- *sausage tongs*
36 die Kartenlegerin, eine
  Wahrsagerin
- *fortune teller*
37 das Riesenrad
- *big wheel (Ferris wheel)*
38 die Kirmesorgel (automatische
  Orgel), ein Musikwerk *n*
  (Musikautomat *m*)
- *orchestrion (automatic organ), an*
  automatic musical instrument

39 die Achterbahn (Gebirgsbahn)
- *scenic railway (switchback)*
40 die Turmrutschbahn (Rutschbahn)
- *toboggan slide (chute)*
41 die Schiffsschaukel (Luftschaukel)
- *swing boats*
42 die Überschlagschaukel
- *swing boat, turning full circle*
43 der Überschlag
- *full circle*
44 die Spielbude
- *lottery booth (tombola booth)*
45 das Glücksrad
- *wheel of fortune*
46 die Teufelsscheibe (das Taifunrad)
- *devil's wheel (typhoon wheel)*
47 der Wurfring
- *throwing ring (quoit)*
48 die Gewinne *m*
- *prizes*
49 der Stelzenläufer
- *sandwich man on stilts*
50 das Reklameplakat
- *sandwich board*
  (placard)
51 der Zigarettenverkäufer, ein
  fliegender Händler
- *cigarette seller, an itinerant trader*
  (a hawker)
52 der Bauchladen
- *tray*
53 der Obststand
- *fruit stall*

54 der Todesfahrer (Steilwandfahrer)
- *wall-of-death rider*
55 das Lachkabinett (Spiegelkabinett)
- *hall of mirrors*
56 der Konkavspiegel
- *concave mirror*
57 der Konvexspiegel
- *convex mirror*
58 die Schießbude
- *shooting gallery*
59 der (das) Hippodrom
- *hippodrome*
60 der Trödelmarkt (Altwarenmarkt)
- *junk stalls (second-hand stalls)*
61 das Sanitätszelt (die Sanitätswache)
- *first aid tent (first aid post)*
62 die Skooterbahn (das Autodrom)
- *dodgems (bumper cars)*
63 der Skooter (Autoskooter)
- *dodgem car (bumper car)*
64-66 der Topfmarkt
- *pottery stand*
64 der Marktschreier
- *barker*
65 die Marktfrau
- *market woman*
66 die Töpferwaren *f*
- *pottery*
67 die Jahrmarktbummler *m*
- *visitors to the fair*
68 das Wachsfigurenkabinett
  (Panoptikum)
- *waxworks*

69 die Wachsfigur (Wachspuppe)
- *wax figure*

1 die Tretnähmaschine
- *treadle sewing machine*
2 die Blumenvase
- *flower vase*
3 der Wandspiegel
- *wall mirror*
4 der Kanonenofen
- *cylindrical stove*
5 das Ofenrohr
- *stovepipe*
6 der Ofenrohrkrümmer
- *stovepipe elbow*
7 die Ofentür
- *stove door*
8 der Ofenschirm
- *stove screen*
9 der Kohlenfüller
- *coal scuttle*
10 der Holzkorb
- *firewood basket*
11 die Puppe
- *doll*
12 der Teddybär
- *teddy bear*
13 die Drehorgel
- *barrel organ*
14 das Orchestrion (der Musikautomat)
- *orchestrion*
15 die Metallscheibe (das Notenblatt)
- *metal disc (disk)*
16 der Rundfunkempfänger (das
Radio, Radiogerät,
Rundfunkgerät, der Radioapparat,
scherzh.: „Dampfradio"), ein

Superheterodynempfänger *m*
(Superhet)
- *radio (radio set,* joc.: *'steam
radio'), a superheterodyne
(superhet)*
17 die Schallwand
- *baffle board*
18 das „magische Auge", eine
Abstimmanzeigeröhre
- *'magic eye', a tuning indicator valve*
19 die Schallöffnung
- *loudspeaker aperture*
20 die Stationstasten *f*
- *station selector buttons (station
preset buttons)*
21 der Abstimmungsknopf
- *tuning knob*
22 die Frequenzeinstellskalen *f*
- *frequency bands*
23 die Detektoranlage (der
Detektorempfänger)
- *crystal detector (crystal set)*
24 der Kopfhörer
- *headphones (headset)*
25 die Balgenkamera (Klappkamera)
- *folding camera*
26 der Balgen
- *bellows*
27 der Klappdeckel
- *hinged cover*
28 die Springspreizen *f*
- *spring extension*
29 der Verkäufer
- *salesman*

30 die Boxkamera (Box)
- *box camera*
31 das Grammophon (der
Grammophonapparat)
- *gramophone*
32 die Schallplatte
(Grammophonplatte)
- *record (gramophone record)*
33 die Schalldose mit der
Grammophonnadel
- *needle head with gramophone
needle*
34 der Schalltrichter
- *horn*
35 das Grammophongehäuse
- *gramophone box*
36 der Schallplattenständer
- *record rack*
37 das Tonbandgerät, ein
Tonbandkoffer *m*
- *tape recorder, a portable tape
recorder*
38 das Blitzlichtgerät (Blitzgerät)
- *flashgun*
39 das Blitzbirnchen (die Blitzbirne)
- *flash bulb*
40–41 das Elektronenblitzgerät
(Röhrenblitzgerät)
- *electronic flash (electronic
flashgun)*
40 der Lampenstab
- *flash head*
41 der (das) Akkuteil
- *accumulator*

42 der Diaprojektor
   (Diapositivprojektor)
 - *slide projector*
43 der Diaschieber
 - *slide holder*
44 das Lampengehäuse
 - *lamphouse*
45 der Leuchter
 - *candlestick*
46 die Jakobsmuschel (Pilgermuschel)
 - *scallop shell*
47 das Besteck
 - *cutlery*
48 der Souvenirteller
 - *souvenir plate*
49 der Trockenständer für Fotoplatten *f*
 - *drying rack for photographic plates*
50 die Fotoplatte
 - *photographic plate*
51 der Selbstauslöser
 - *delayed-action release*
52 die Zinnsoldaten *m* (*ähnl.*:
   Bleisoldaten *m*)
 - *tin soldiers* (sim.: *lead soldiers*)
53 der Bierseidel
 - *beer mug (stein)*
54 die Trompete
 - *bugle*
55 die antiquarischen Bücher *n*
 - *second-hand books*
56 die Standuhr
 - *grandfather clock*
57 das Uhrengehäuse
 - *clock case*

58 das Uhrenpendel (der *od.* das
   Perpendikel)
 - *pendulum*
59 das Ganggewicht
 - *time weight*
60 das Schlaggewicht
 - *striking weight*
61 der Schaukelstuhl
 - *rocking chair*
62 der Matrosenanzug
 - *sailor suit*
63 die Matrosenmütze
 - *sailor's hat*
64 das Waschservice
 - *washing set*
65 die Waschschüssel
 - *washing basin*
66 die Wasserkanne
 - *water jug*
67 der Waschständer
 - *washstand*
68 der Wäschestampfer
 - *dolly*
69 die Waschwanne
   (Waschbütte)
 - *washtub*
70 das Waschbrett
 - *washboard*
71 der Brummkreisel
 - *humming top*
72 die Schiefertafel
 - *slate*
73 der Griffelkasten
 - *pencil box*

74 die Addier- und Saldiermaschine
 - *adding and subtracting machine*
75 die Papierrolle
 - *paper roll*
76 die Zahlentasten *f*
 - *number keys*
77 die Rechenmaschine
 - *abacus*
78 das Tintenfaß, ein Klapptintenfaß *n*
 - *inkwell, with lid*
79 die Schreibmaschine
 - *typewriter*
80 die mechanische Rechenmaschine
 - *[hand-operated] calculating
   machine (calculator)*
81 die Antriebskurbel
 - *operating handle*
82 das Resultatwerk
 - *result register (product register)*
83 das Umdrehungszählwerk
 - *rotary counting mechanism (rotary
   counter)*
84 die Küchenwaage
 - *kitchen scales*
85 der Pettycoat
 - *waist slip (underskirt)*
86 der Leiterwagen
 - *wooden handcart*
87 die Wanduhr
 - *wall clock*
88 die Wärmflasche
 - *bed warmer*
89 die Milchkanne
 - *milk churn*

1-13 die Filmstadt
- *film studios (studio complex, Am. movie studios)*
1 das Freigelände (Außenbaugelände)
- *lot (studio lot)*
2 die Kopierwerke *n*
- *processing laboratories (film laboratories, motion picture laboratories)*
3 die Schneidehäuser *n*
- *cutting rooms*
4 das Verwaltungsgebäude
- *administration building (office building, offices)*
5 der Filmlagerbunker (das Filmarchiv)
- *film (motion picture) storage vault (film library, motion picture library)*
6 die Werkstätten *f*
- *workshop*
7 die Filmbauten *m*
- *film set (Am. movie set)*
8 die Kraftstation
- *power house*
9 die technischen und Forschungslaboratorien *n*
- *technical and research laboratories*
10 die Filmateliergruppen *f*
- *groups of stages*
11 das Betonbassin für Wasseraufnahmen *f*
- *concrete tank for marine sequences*

12 der Rundhorizont
- *cyclorama*
13 der Horizonthügel
- *hill*
14-60 Filmaufnahmen *f*
- *shooting (filming)*
14 das Musikatelier
- *music recording studio (music recording theatre, Am. theater)*
15 die „akustische" Wandbekleidung
- *'acoustic' wall lining*
16 die Bildwand
- *screen (projection screen)*
17 das Filmorchester
- *film orchestra*
18 die Außenaufnahme (Freilichtaufnahme)
- *exterior shooting (outdoor shooting, exterior filming, outdoor filming)*
19 die quarzgesteuerte Synchronkamera
- *camera with crystal-controlled drive*
20 der Kameramann
- *cameraman*
21 die Regieassistentin
- *assistant director*
22 der Mikrophonassistent (Mikromann)
- *boom operator (boom swinger)*
23 der Tonmeister
- *recording engineer (sound recordist)*
24 das tragbare quarzgesteuerte Tonaufnahmegerät

- *portable sound recorder with crystal-controlled drive*
25 der Mikrophongalgen
- *microphone boom*
26-60 die Atelieraufnahme im Tonfilmatelier *n* (Spielfilmatelier *n*, in der Aufnahmehalle)
- *shooting (filming) in the studio (on the sound stage, on the stage, in the filming hall)*
26 der Produktionsleiter
- *production manager*
27 die Hauptdarstellerin (Filmschauspielerin, der Filmstar, Filmstern, Star);
früh.: die Diva (Filmdiva)
- *leading lady (film actress, film star, star)*
28 der Hauptdarsteller (Filmschauspieler, Filmheld, Held)
- *leading man (film actor, film star, star)*
29 der Filmkomparse (Filmstatist, Komparse, Statist)
- *film extra (extra)*
30 die Mikrophonanordnung für Stereo- und Effektaufnahme *f*
- *arrangement of microphones for stereo and sound effects*
31 das Ateliermikrophon
- *studio microphone*
32 das Mikrophonkabel
- *microphone cable*

33 die Filmkulisse und der Prospekt
  (die Hintergrundkulisse)
 - *side flats and background*
34 der Klappenmann
 - *clapper boy*
35 die Synchronklappe, mit Tafel *f* für
  Filmtitel *m*, Einstellungsnummer *f*
  und Nummer *f* der Wiederholung
 - *clapper board (clapper) with slates
   (boards) for the film title, shot
   number (scene number) and take
   number*
36 der Maskenbildner (Filmfriseur)
 - *make-up artist (hairstylist)*
37 der Beleuchter
 - *lighting electrician (studio
   electrician, lighting man, Am. gaffer)*
38 die Streuscheibe
 - *diffusing screen*
39 das Skriptgirl (Scriptgirl, die
  Ateliersekretärin)
 - *continuity girl (script girl)*
40 der Filmregisseur (Regisseur)
 - *film director (director)*
41 der Kameramann
 - *cameraman (first cameraman)*
42 der Schwenker
  (Kameraschwenker,
  Kameraführer), ein
  Kameraassistent *m*
 - *camera operator, an assistant
   cameraman (camera assistant)*
43 der Filmarchitekt
 - *set designer (art director)*

44 der Aufnahmeleiter
 - *director of photography*
45 das Filmdrehbuch (Drehbuch,
  Filmmanuskript, Manuskript,
  Skript, Script)
 - *filmscript (script, shooting script,
   Am. movie script)*
46 der Regieassistent
 - *assistant director*
47 die schalldichte Filmkamera
  (Bildaufnahmekamera), eine
  Breitbildkamera
  (Cinemascope-Kamera)
 - *soundproof film camera
   (soundproof motion picture
   camera), a wide screen camera
   (cinemascope camera)*
48 der Schallschutzkasten (Blimp)
 - *soundproof housing (soundproof
   cover, blimp)*
49 der Kamerakran (Dolly)
 - *camera crane (dolly)*
50 das Pumpstativ
 - *hydraulic stand*
51 die Abdeckblende, zum Abdecken
  n von Fehllicht *n* (der Neger)
 - *mask (screen) for protection from
   spill light (gobo, nigger)*
52 der Stativscheinwerfer
  (Aufheller)
 - *tripod spotlight (fill-in light, filler
   light, fill light, filler)*
53 die Scheinwerferbrücke
 - *spotlight catwalk*

54 der Tonmeisterraum
 - *recording room*
55 der Tonmeister
 - *recording engineer (sound recordist)*
56 das Mischpult
 - *mixing console (mixing desk)*
57 der Tonassistent
 - *sound assistant (assistant sound
   engineer)*
58 das Magnettonaufzeichnungsgerät
 - *magnetic sound recording
   equipment (magnetic sound
   recorder)*
59 die Verstärker- und
  Trickeinrichtung, z.B. für Nachhall
  m und Effektton *m*
 - *amplifier and special effects
   equipment, e.g. for echo and sound
   effects*
60 die Tonkamera (Lichttonkamera)
 - *sound recording camera (optical
   sound recorder)*

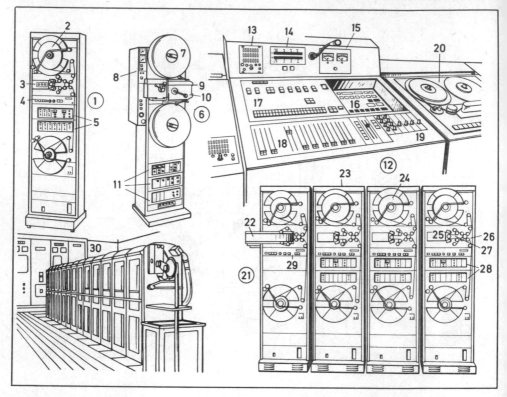

1-46 Tonaufzeichnung *f* und Kopie *f*
- *sound recording and re-recording (dubbing)*
1 das Magnettonaufzeichnungsgerät
- *magnetic sound recording equipment (magnetic sound recorder)*
2 die Magnetfilmspule
- *magnetic film spool*
3 der Magnetkopfträger
- *magnetic head support assembly*
4 das Schaltfeld
- *control panel*
5 der Magnetton-Aufnahme- und -Wiedergabeverstärker
- *magnetic sound recording and playback amplifier*
6 die Lichttonkamera (Tonkamera, das Lichttonaufnahmegerät)
- *optical sound recorder (sound recording camera, optical sound recording equipment)*
7 die Tageslichtfilmkassette
- *daylight film magazine*
8 das Steuer- und Kontrollfeld
- *control and monitoring panel*
9 das Okular zur optischen Kontrolle der Lichttonaufzeichnung
- *eyepiece for visual control of optical sound recording*
10 das Laufwerk
- *deck*

11 die Aufnahmeverstärker *m* und das (der) Netzteil
- *recording amplifier and mains power unit*
12 das Schalt- und Regelpult
- *control desk (control console)*
13 der Abhörlautsprecher
- *monitoring loudspeaker (control loudspeaker)*
14 die Aussteuerinstrumente *n*
- *recording level indicators*
15 die Kontrollinstrumente *n*
- *monitoring instruments*
16 das Klinkenfeld
- *jack panel*
17 das Schaltfeld
- *control panel*
18 die Flachbahnregler *m*
- *sliding control*
19 die Entzerrer *m*
- *equalizer*
20 das Magnettonlaufwerk
- *magnetic sound deck*
21 die Mischanlage für Magnetfilm *m*
- *mixer for magnetic film*
22 der Filmprojektor
- *film projector*
23 das Aufnahme- und Wiedergabegerät
- *recording and playback equipment*
24 die Filmspule
- *film reel (film spool)*

25 der Kopfträger für den Aufnahme-, den Wiedergabe- und den Löschkopf
- *head support assembly for the recording head, playback head, and erasing head (erase head)*
26 der Filmantrieb
- *film transport mechanism*
27 der (das) Gleichlauffilter
- *synchronizing filter*
28 die Magnettonverstärker *m*
- *magnetic sound amplifier*
29 das Steuerfeld
- *control panel*
30 die Filmentwicklungsmaschinen *f* im Kopierwerk *n*
- *film-processing machines (film-developing machines) in the processing laboratory (film laboratory, motion picture laboratory)*

31 der Hallraum
- *echo chamber*
32 der Hallraumlautsprecher
- *echo chamber loudspeaker*
33 das Hallraummikrophon
- *echo chamber microphone*
34-36 die Tonmischung (Mischung
   mehrerer Tonstreifen *m*)
- *sound mixing (sound dubbing,*
   mixing of several sound tracks)
34 das Mischatelier
- *mixing room (dubbing room)*
35 das Mischpult, für Einkanalton *m*
   oder Stereoton *m*
- *mixing console (mixing desk) for*
   mono or stereo sound
36 die Mischtonmeister *m*
   (Tonmeister), bei der Mischarbeit
- *dubbing mixers (recording*
   engineers, sound recordists)
   dubbing (mixing)
37-41 die Synchronisation
   (Nachsynchronisierung)
- *synchronization (syncing, dubbing,*
   post-synchronization,
   post-syncing)
37 das Synchronisierungsatelier
- *dubbing studio (dubbing theatre,*
   Am. *theater)*
38 der Synchronregisseur
- *dubbing director*
39 die Synchronsprecherin
- *dubbing speaker (dubbing actress)*

40 das Galgenmikrophon
- *boom microphone*
41 das Tonkabel
- *microphone cable*
42-46 der Schnitt
- *cutting (editing)*
42 der Schneidetisch
- *cutting table (editing table, cutting*
   bench)
43 der Schnittmeister (Cutter)
- *film editor (cutter)*
44 die Filmteller *m* für die Bild- und
   Tonstreifen *m*
   film turnables, for picture and
   sound tracks
45 die Bildprojektion
- *projection of the picture*
46 der Lautsprecher
- *loudspeaker*

1-23 die Filmwiedergabe
- *film projection (motion picture projection)*
1 das Lichtspielhaus (Lichtspieltheater, Filmtheater, Kino)
- *cinema (picture house, Am. movie theater, movie house)*
2 die Kinokasse
- *cinema box office (Am. movie theater box office)*
3 die Kinokarte
- *cinema ticket (Am. movie theater ticket)*
4 die Platzanweiserin
- *usherette*
5 die Kinobesucher *m* (das Filmpublikum)
- *cinemagoers (filmgoers, cinema audience, Am. moviegoers, movie audience)*
6 die Sicherheitsbeleuchtung (Notbeleuchtung)
- *safety lighting (emergency lighting)*
7 der Notausgang
- *emergency exit*
8 die Rampe (Bühne)
- *stage*
9 die Sitzreihen *f*
- *rows of seats (rows)*
10 der Bühnenvorhang (Bildwandvorhang)
- *stage curtain (screen curtain)*

11 die Bildwand (Projektionswand, „Leinwand")
- *screen (projection screen)*
12 der Bildwerferraum (Filmvorführraum, die Vorführkabine)
- *projection room (projection booth)*
13 die Linksmaschine
- *lefthand projector*
14 die Rechtsmaschine
- *righthand projector*
15 das Kabinenfenster, mit Projektions- und Schauöffnung *f*
- *projection room window with projection window and observation port*
16 die Filmtrommel
- *reel drum (spool box)*
17 der Saalverdunkler (Saalbeleuchtungsregler)
- *house light dimmers (auditorium lighting control)*
18 der Gleichrichter, ein Selen- oder Quecksilberdampfgleichrichter *m* für die Projektionslampen *f*
- *rectifier, a selenium or mercury vapour rectifier for the projection lamps*
19 der Verstärker
- *amplifier*
20 der Filmvorführer
- *projectionist*
21 der Umrolltisch, zur Filmumspulung

- *rewind bench for rewinding the film*
22 der Filmkitt
- *film cement (splicing cement)*
23 der Diaprojektor, für Werbediapositive *n*
- *slide projector for advertisements*

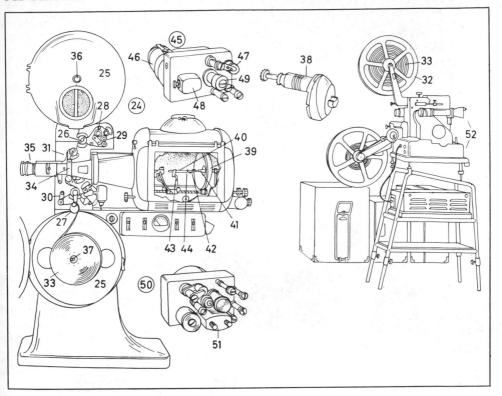

24-52 Filmprojektoren *m*
- *film projectors*
24 der Tonfilmprojektor
   (Filmbildwerfer, Kinoprojektor,
   Filmvorführungsapparat, die
   Theatermaschine, Kinomaschine)
- *sound projector (film projector,*
  cinema projector, theatre projector,
  Am. movie projector)
25-38 das Filmlaufwerk
- *projector mechanism*
25 die Feuerschutztrommeln *f*
   (Filmtrommeln), mit
   Umlaufölkühlung *f*
- *fireproof reel drums (spool boxes)*
  with circulating oil cooling system
26 die Vorwickel-Filmzahntrommel
- *feed sprocket (supply sprocket)*
27 die Nachwickel-Filmzahntrommel
- *take-up sprocket*
28 das Magnetonabnehmersystem
- *magnetic head cluster*
29 die Umlenkrolle, mit
   Bildstrichverstellung *f*
- *guide roller (guiding roller) with*
  framing control
30 der Schleifenbildner, zur
   Filmvorberuhigung; *auch:*
   Filmrißkontakt *m*
- *loop former for smoothing out the*
  intermittent movement; also: film
  break detector
31 die Filmgleitbahn
- *film path*

32 die Filmspule
- *film reel (film spool)*
33 die Filmrolle
- *reel of film*
34 das Bildfenster (Filmfenster), mit
   Filmkühlgebläse *n*
- *film gate (picture gate, projector*
  gate) with cooling fan
35 das Projektionsobjektiv
- *projection lens (projector lens)*
36 die Abwickelachse
- *feed spindle*
37 die Aufwickelfriktionsachse
- *take-up spindle with friction drive*
38 das Malteserkreuzgetriebe
- *maltese cross mechanism (maltese*
  cross movement, Geneva
  movement)
39-44 das Lampenhaus
- *lamphouse*
39 die Spiegelbogenlampe, mit
   asphärischem Hohlspiegel *m* und
   Blasmagnet *m* zur
   Lichtbogenstabilisierung (*auch:*
   die Xenon-Höchstdrucklampe)
- *mirror arc lamp, with aspherical*
  (non-spherical) concave mirror and
  blowout magnet for stabilizing the
  arc (also: high-pressure xenon arc
  lamp)
40 die Positivkohle
- *positive carbon (positive carbon rod)*
41 die Negativkohle
- *negative carbon (negative carbon rod)*

42 der Lichtbogen
- *arc*
43 der Kohlenhalter
- *carbon rod holder*
44 der Krater (Kohlenkrater)
- *crater (carbon crater)*
45 das Lichttongerät [auch für
   Mehrkanal-Lichtton-Stereophonie
   f und für Gegentaktspur *f*
   vorgesehen]
- *optical sound unit [also designed*
  for multi-channel optical
  stereophonic sound and for
  push-pull sound tracks]
46 die Lichttonoptik
- *sound optics*
47 der Tonkopf
- *sound head*
48 die Tonlampe, im Gehäuse *n*
- *exciter lamp in housing*
49 die Photozelle (in der Hohlachse)
- *photocell in hollow drum*
50 das Vierkanal-Magnettonzusatzgerät
   (der Magnettonabtaster)
- *attachable four-track magnetic*
  sound unit (penthouse head,
  magnetic sound head)
51 der Vierfachmagnetkopf
- *four-track magnetic head*
52 die Schmalfilmtheatermaschine,
   für Wanderkino *n*
- *narrow-gauge (Am. narrow-gage)*
  cinema projector for mobile
  cinema

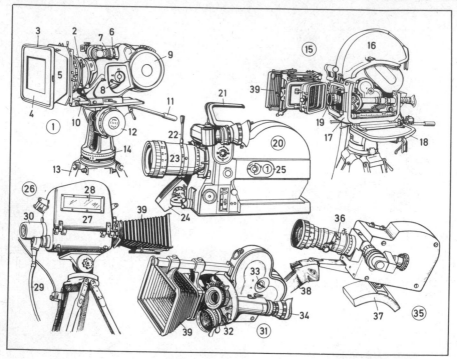

1-39 Filmkameras *f*
- *motion picture cameras (film cameras)*
1 die Normalfilmkamera
  (35-mm-Filmkamera)
- *standard-gauge (Am.*
  standard-gage) motion picture
  camera (standard-gauge, Am.
  standard-gage, 35 mm camera)
2 das Objektiv (die Aufnahmeoptik)
- *lens (object lens, taking lens)*
3 das Kompendium (die
  Sonnenblende), mit Filter- und
  Kaschbühne *f*
- *lens hood (sunshade) with matte box*
4 der Kasch
- *matte (mask)*
5 der Gegenlichttubus
- *lens hood barrel*
6 das Sucherokular
- *viewfinder eyepiece*
7 die Okulareinstellung
- *eyepiece control ring*
8 der Schließer für die Sektorenblende
- *opening control for the segment*
  disc (disk) shutter
9 das Filmkassettengehäuse
- *magazine housing*
10 die Kompendiumschiene
- *slide bar for the lens hood*
11 der Führungshebel
- *control arm (control lever)*
12 der Kinoneiger
- *pan and tilt head*
13 das Holzstativ
- *wooden tripod*
14 die Gradeinteilung
- *degree scale*

15 die schalldichte (geblimpte)
  Filmkamera
- *soundproof (blimped) motion*
  picture camera (film camera)
16-18 das Schallschutzgehäuse (der Blimp)
- *soundproof housing (blimp)*
16 das Schallschutzoberteil
- *upper section of the soundproof*
  housing
17 das Schallschutzunterteil
- *lower section of the soundproof*
  housing
18 die abgeklappte Schallschutzseitenwand
- *open sidewall of the soundproof*
  housing
19 das Kameraobjektiv
- *camera lens*
20 die leichte Bildkamera
- *lightweight professional motion*
  picture camera
21 der Handgriff
- *grip (handgrip)*
22 der Zoomverstellhebel
- *zooming lever*
23 das Zoomobjektiv (Varioobjektiv)
  mit stufenlos veränderlicher
  Brennweite
- *zoom lens (variable focus lens,*
  varifocal lens) with infinitely
  variable focus
24 der Auslösehandgriff
- *handgrip with shutter release*
25 die Kameratür
- *camera door*
26 die Bild-Ton-Kamera
  (Reportagekamera) für Bild- und
  Tonaufnahme *f*

- *sound camera (newsreel camera) for*
  recording sound and picture
27 das Schallschutzgehäuse (der Blimp)
- *soundproof housing (blimp)*
28 das Beobachtungsfenster für die
  Bildzähler *m* und Betriebsskalen *f*
- *window for the frame counters and*
  indicator scales
29 das Synchronkabel (Pilottonkabel)
- *pilot tone cable (sync pulse cable)*
30 der Pilottongeber
- *pilot tone generator (signal*
  generator, pulse generator)
31 die Schmalfilmkamera, eine
  16-mm-Kamera
- *professional narrow-gauge (Am.*
  narrow-gage) motion picture
  camera, a 16 mm camera
32 der Objektivrevolver
- *lens turret (turret head)*
33 die Gehäuseverriegelung
- *housing lock*
34 die Okularmuschel
- *eyecup*
35 die Hochgeschwindigkeitskamera,
  eine Schmalfilmspezialkamera
- *high-speed camera, a special*
  narrow-gauge (Am. narrow-gage)
  camera
36 der Zoomhebel
- *zooming lever*
37 die Schulterstütze
- *rifle grip*
38 der Auslösehandgriff
- *handgrip with shutter release*
39 der Faltenbalg des Kompendiums *n*
- *lens hood bellows*

1-6 die fünf Positionen *f*
- *the five positions (ballet positions)*
1 die erste Position
- *first position*
2 die zweite Position
- *second position*
3 die dritte Position
- *third position*
4 die vierte Position [offen]
- *fourth position [open]*
5 die vierte Position [gekreuzt; weite fünfte Position]
- *fourth position [crossed; extended fifth position]*
6 die fünfte Position
- *fifth position*
7-10 die Ports de bras *n* (Armhaltungen *f*)
- *ports de bras (arm positions)*
7 das Port de bras à coté
- *port de bras à coté*
8 das Port de bras en bas
- *port de bras en bas*
9 das Port de bras en avant
- *port de bras en avant*
10 das Port de bras en haut
- *port de bras en haut*
11 das Degagé à la quatrième devant
- *dégagé à la quatrième devant*
12 das Degagé à la quatrième derrière
- *dégagé à la quatrième derrière*
13 das Effacé
- *effacé*
14 das Sur le cou-de-pied
- *sur le cou-de-pied*
15 das Ecarté
- *écarté*

16 das Croisé
- *croisé*
17 die Attitude
- *attitude*
18 die Arabeske
- *arabesque*
19 die ganze Spitze
- *à pointe (on full point)*
20 das (der) Spagat
- *splits*
21 die Kapriole
- *cabriole (capriole)*
22 das Entrechat (Entrechat quatre)
- *entrechat (entrechat quatre)*
23 die Préparation [z.B. zur Pirouette]
- *préparation [e.g. for a pirouette]*
24 die Pirouette
- *pirouette*
25 das Corps de ballet (die Balletttruppe)
- *corps de ballet*
26 die Ballettänzerin (Balletteuse)
- *ballet dancer (ballerina)*
27-28 der Pas de trois
- *pas de trois*
27 die Primaballerina
- *prima ballerina*
28 der erste Solotänzer (erste Solist)
- *principal male dancer (leading soloist)*
29 das Tutu
- *tutu*
30 der Spitzenschuh, ein Ballettschuh *m*
- *point shoe, a ballet shoe (ballet slipper)*
31 der Ballerinenrock
- *ballet skirt*

1-4 **die Vorhangzüge** *m*
- *types of curtain operation*
1 der griechische Zug
- *draw curtain (side parting)*
2 der italienische Zug
- *tableau curtain (bunching up sideways)*
3 der deutsche Zug
- *fly curtain (vertical ascent)*
4 der kombinierte (griechisch-deutsche) Zug
- *combined fly and draw curtain*
5-11 **die Garderobenhalle**
- *cloakroom hall (Am. checkroom hall)*
5 die Garderobe (Kleiderablage)
- *cloakroom (Am. checkroom)*
6 die Garderobenfrau (Garderobiere)
- *cloakroom attendant (Am. checkroom attendant)*
7 die Garderobenmarke (Garderobennummer)
- *cloakroom ticket (Am. check)*
8 der Theaterbesucher
- *playgoer (theatregoer, Am. theatergoer)*
9 das Opernglas
- *opera glass (opera glasses)*
10 der Kontrolleur
- *commissionaire*
11 die Theaterkarte (das Theaterbillett), eine Einlaßkarte
- *theatre (Am. theater) ticket, an admission ticket*
12-13 **das Foyer** (die Wandelhalle, der Wandelgang)
- *foyer (lobby, crush room)*
12 der Platzanweiser; *früh.:* Logenschließer *m*
- *usher; form.: box attendant*
13 das Programmheft (Programm)
- *programme (Am. program)*
14-27 **der Theaterraum**
- *auditorium and stage*
14 die Bühne
- *stage*
15 das Proszenium
- *proscenium*
16-20 **der Zuschauerraum**
- *auditorium*
16 der dritte Rang (die Galerie)
- *gallery (balcony)*
17 der zweite Rang
- *upper circle*
18 der erste Rang
- *dress circle (Am. balcony, mezzanine)*
19 das Parkett
- *front stalls*
20 der Sitzplatz (Zuschauerplatz, Theaterplatz)
- *seat (theatre seat, Am. theater seat)*
21-27 **die Probe** (Theaterprobe)
- *rehearsal (stage rehearsal)*
21 der Theaterchor (Chor)
- *chorus*
22 der Sänger
- *singer*
23 die Sängerin
- *singer*
24 der Orchesterraum (die Orchesterversenkung)
- *orchestra pit*
25 das Orchester
- *orchestra*

26 der Dirigent
- *conductor*
27 der Taktstock (Dirigentenstab)
- *baton (conductor's baton)*
28-42 **der Malersaal**, eine Theaterwerkstatt
- *paint room, a workshop*
28 der Bühnenarbeiter
- *stagehand (scene shifter)*
29 die Arbeitsbrücke
- *catwalk (bridge)*
30 das Setzstück (Versatzstück)
- *set piece*
31 die Versteifung
- *reinforcing struts*
32 die Kaschierung
- *built piece (built unit)*
33 der Prospekt
- *backcloth (backdrop)*
34 der tragbare Malerkasten (die Handpalette)
- *portable box for paint containers*
35 der Bühnenmaler, ein Dekorationsmaler *m*
- *scene painter, a scenic artist*
36 die fahrbare Palette
- *paint trolley*
37 der Bühnenbildner
- *stage designer (set designer)*
38 der Kostümbildner
- *costume designer*
39 der Kostümentwurf
- *design for a costume*
40 die Figurine
- *sketch for a costume*
41 die Modellbühne
- *model stage*
42 das Bühnenbildmodell
- *model of the set*
43-52 **die Schauspielergarderobe**
- *dressing room*
43 der Schminkspiegel
- *dressing room mirror*
44 das Schminktuch
- *make-up gown*
45 der Schminktisch
- *make-up table*
46 der Schminkstift
- *greasepaint stick*
47 der Chefmaskenbildner
- *chief make-up artist (chief make-up man)*
48 der Maskenbildner (Theaterfriseur)
- *make-up artist (hairstylist)*
49 die Perücke
- *wig*
50 die Requisiten *n*
- *props (properties)*
51 das Theaterkostüm
- *theatrical costume*
52 die Signallampe (der Inspizientenruf)
- *call light*

1-60 das Bühnenhaus mit der Maschinerie (Ober- und Untermaschinerie)
- *stagehouse with machinery (machinery in the flies and below stage)*
1 die Stellwarte
- *control room*
2 das Steuerpult (die Lichtstellanlage) mit Speichereinrichtung *f* zur Speicherung der Lichtstimmung
- *control console (lighting console, lighting control console) with preset control for presetting lighting effects*
3 der Stellwartenzettel (die Kontente)
- *lighting plot (light plot)*
4 der Schnürboden (Rollenboden)
- *grid (gridiron)*
5 die Arbeitsgalerie (der Arbeitssteg)
- *fly floor (fly gallery)*
6 die Berieselungsanlage, zum Feuerschutz *m*
- *sprinkler system for fire prevention (for fire protection)*
7 der Schnürbodenmeister
- *fly man*
8 die Züge *m* (Prospektzüge)
- *fly lines (lines)*
9 der Rundhorizont (Bühnenhimmel)
- *cyclorama*
10 der Prospekt (Bühnenhintergrund, das Hinterhängestück)
- *backcloth (backdrop, background)*
11 der Bogen, ein Zwischenhängestück *n*
- *arch, a drop cloth*
12 die Soffitte (das Deckendekorationsstück)
- *border*
13 das Kastenoberlicht
- *compartment (compartment-type, compartmentalized) batten (Am. border light)*
14 die szenischen Beleuchtungskörper *m*
- *stage lighting units (stage lights)*
15 die Horizontbeleuchtung (Prospektbeleuchtung)
- *horizon lights (backdrop lights)*
16 die schwenkbaren Spielflächenscheinwerfer *m*
- *adjustable acting area lights (acting area spotlights)*
17 die Bühnenbildprojektionsapparate *m*
- *scenery projectors (projectors)*
18 die Wasserkanone (eine Sicherheitseinrichtung)
- *monitor (water cannon) (a piece of safety equipment)*
19 die fahrbare Beleuchtungsbrücke
- *travelling (Am. traveling) lighting bridge (travelling lighting gallery)*
20 der Beleuchter
- *lighting operator (lighting man)*
21 der Portal-(Turm-)Scheinwerfer
- *portal spotlight (tower spotlight)*
22 der verstellbare Bühnenrahmen (das Portal, der Mantel)
- *adjustable proscenium*
23 der Vorhang (Theatervorhang)
- *curtain (theatrical curtain)*
24 der eiserne Vorhang
- *iron curtain (safety curtain, fire curtain)*

25 die Vorbühne (*ugs.* Rampe)
- *forestage (apron)*
26 das Rampenlicht (die Fußrampenleuchten *f*)
- *footlight (footlights, floats)*
27 der Souffleurkasten
- *prompt box*
28 die Souffleuse (*männl.:* der Souffleur, Vorsager)
- *prompter*
29 der Inspizientenstand
- *stage manager's desk*
30 der Spielwart (Inspizient)
- *stage director (stage manager)*
31 die Drehbühne
- *revolving stage*
32 die Versenköffnung
- *trap opening*
33 der Versenktisch
- *lift (Am. elevator)*
34 das Versenkpodium, ein Stockwerkpodium *n*
- *bridge (Am. elevator), a rostrum*
35 die Dekorationsstücke *n*
- *pieces of scenery*
36 die Szene (der Auftritt)
- *scene*
37 der Schauspieler (Darsteller)
- *actor*
38 die Schauspielerin (Darstellerin)
- *actress*
39 die Statisten *m*
- *extras (supers, supernumeraries)*
40 der Regisseur (Spielleiter)
- *director (producer)*
41 das Rollenheft
- *prompt book (prompt script)*
42 der Regietisch
- *director's table (producer's table)*
43 der Regieassistent
- *assistant director (assistant producer)*
44 das Regiebuch
- *director's script (producer's script)*
45 der Bühnenmeister
- *stage carpenter*
46 der Bühnenarbeiter
- *stagehand (scene shifter)*
47 das Setzstück (Versatzstück)
- *set piece*
48 der Spiegellinsenscheinwerfer
- *mirror spot (mirror spotlight)*
49 der Farbscheibenwechsler (mit Farbscheibe *f*)
- *automatic filter change (with colour filters, colour mediums, gelatines)*
50 die hydraulische Druckstation
- *hydraulic plant room*
51 der Wasserbehälter
- *water tank*
52 die Saugleitung
- *suction pipe*
53 die hydraulische Druckpumpe
- *hydraulic pump*
54 die Druckleitung
- *pressure pipe*
55 der Druckkessel (Akkumulator)
- *pressure tank (accumulator)*
56 das Kontaktmanometer
- *pressure gauge (Am. gage)*
57 der Flüssigkeitsstandanzeiger
- *level indicator (liquid level indicator)*
58 der Steuerhebel
- *control lever*

59 der Maschinenmeister
- *operator*
60 die Drucksäulen *f* (Plunger *m*)
- *rams*

1 die Bar
- *bar*
2 die Bardame
- *barmaid*
3 der Barhocker
- *bar stool*
4 das Flaschenregal
- *shelf for bottles*
5 das Gläserregal
- *shelf for glasses*
6 das Bierglas
- *beer glass*
7 Wein- und Likörgläser *n*
- *wine and liqueur glasses*
8 der Bierzapfhahn (Zapfhahn)
- *beer tap (tap)*
9 die Bartheke (Theke)
- *bar*
10 der Kühlschrank
- *refrigerator
(fridge, Am. icebox)*
11 die Barlampen *f*
- *bar lamps*
12 die indirekte Beleuchtung
- *indirect lighting*
13 die Lichtorgel
- *colour (Am. color) organ (clavilux)*
14 die Tanzflächenbeleuchtung
- *dance floor lighting*
15 die Lautsprecherbox
- *speaker (loudspeaker)*
16 die Tanzfläche
- *dance floor*

17-18 das Tanzpaar
- *dancing couple*
17 die Tänzerin
- *dancer*
18 der Tänzer
- *dancer*
19 der Plattenspieler
- *record player*
20 das Mikrophon
- *microphone*
21 das Tonbandgerät
- *tape recorder*
22-23 die Stereoanlage
- *stereo system (stereo equipment)*
22 der Tuner
- *tuner*
23 der Verstärker
- *amplifier*
24 die Schallplatten
- *records (discs)*
25 der Diskjockey
- *disc jockey*
26 das Mischpult
- *mixing console (mixing desk, mixer)*
27 das Tamburin
- *tambourine*
28 die Spiegelwand
- *mirrored wall*
29 die Deckenverkleidung
- *ceiling tiles*
30 die Belüftungsanlagen
- *ventilators*

31 die Toiletten *f*
- *toilets (lavatories, WC)*
32 der Longdrink
- *long drink*
33 der Cocktail
- *cocktail (Am. highball)*

1-33 **das Nachtlokal** (der Nightclub, Nachtklub)
- *nightclub (night spot)*
1 die Garderobe
- *cloakroom (Am. checkroom)*
2 die Garderobenfrau
- *cloakroom attendant (Am. checkroom attendant)*
3 die Band (Combo)
- *band*
4 die Klarinette
- *clarinet*
5 der Klarinettist
- *clarinettist (Am. clarinetist)*
6 die Trompete
- *trumpet*
7 der Trompeter
- *trumpeter*
8 die Gitarre
- *guitar*
9 der Gitarrist (Gitarrenspieler)
- *guitarist (guitar player)*
10 das Schlagzeug
- *drums*
11 der Schlagzeuger
- *drummer*
12 die Lautsprecherbox (der Lautsprecher)
- *speaker (loudspeaker)*
13 die Bar
- *bar*
14 die Bardame (Bedienung)
- *barmaid*

15 die Bartheke
- *bar*
16 der Barhocker
- *bar stool*
17 das Tonbandgerät
- *tape recorder*
18 der Receiver
- *receiver*
19 die Spirituosen *pl*
- *spirits*
20 der Schmalfilmprojektor für Pornofilme *m* (Sexfilme)
- *cine projector for porno films (sex films, blue movies)*
21 .der Leinwandkasten mit der Leinwand
- *box containing screen*
22 die Bühne
- *stage*
23 die Bühnenbeleuchtung
- *stage lighting*
24 der Bühnenscheinwerfer
- *spotlight*
25 die Sofittenbeleuchtung
- *festoon lighting*
26 die Sofittenlampe
- *festoon lamp (lamp, light bulb)*
27-32 der Striptease (die Entkleidungsnummer)
- *striptease act (striptease number)*
27 die Stripteasetänzerin (Stripperin, Stripteuse)
- *striptease artist (stripper)*

28 der Straps
- *suspender (Am. garter)*
29 der Büstenhalter
- *brassière (bra)*
30 die Pelzstola
- *fur stole*
31 die Handschuhe *m*
- *gloves*
32 der Strumpf
- *stocking*
33 die Animierdame
- *hostess*

1-33 **der Stierkampf** (die Corrida)
- *bullfight (corrida, corrida de toros)*
1 die Spielszene
- *mock bullfight*
2 der Nachwuchstorero (Novillero)
- *novice (aspirant matador, novillero)*
3 die Stierattrappe
- *mock bull (dummy bull)*
4 der Nachwuchsbanderillero
- *novice banderillero (apprentice banderillero)*
5 die Stierkampfarena
 (Plaza de toros) [Schema]
- *bullring (plaza de toros) [diagram]*
6 der Haupteingang
- *main entrance*
7 die Logen *f*
- *boxes*
8 die Sitzplätze *m*
- *stands*
9 die Arena (der Ruedo)
- *arena (ring)*
10 der Eingang der Stierkämpfer *m*
- *bullfighters' entrance*
11 der Einlaß der Stiere *m*
- *torril door*
12 die Abgangspforte für die getöteten
 Stiere *m*
- *exit gate for killed bulls*
13 die Schlachterei
- *slaughterhouse*
14 die Stierställe *m*
- *bull pens (corrals)*
15 der Pferdehof
- *paddock*
16 der Lanzenreiter (Picador)
- *lancer on horseback (picador)*
17 die Lanze
- *lance (pike pole, javelin)*
18 das gepanzerte Pferd
- *armoured (Am. armored) horse*
19 der stählerne Beinpanzer
- *leg armour
 (Am. armor)*
20 der runde Picadorhut
- *picador's round hat*
21 der Banderillero, ein Torero *m*
- *banderillero, a torero*
22 die Banderillas *f*
 (die Wurfpfeile *m*)
- *banderillas (barbed darts)*
23 die Leibbinde
- *shirtwaist*
24 der Stierkampf
- *bullfight*
25 der Matador, ein Torero *m*
- *matador (swordsman), a torero*
26 das Zöpfchen, ein
 Standesabzeichen *n* des Matadors *m*
- *queue, a distinguishing mark of the
 matador*
27 das rote Tuch (die Capa)
- *red cloak (capa)*
28 der Kampfstier („el toro")
- *fighting bull*
29 der Stierkämpferhut
- *montera [hat made of tiny black
 silk chenille balls]*
30 das Töten des Stiers *m*
 (die Estocada)
- *killing the bull (kill)*
31 der Matador bei
 Wohltätigkeitsveranstaltungen *f*
 [ohne Tracht *f*]
- *matador in charity performances
 [without professional uniform]*

32 der Degen (die Espada, Estoque)
- *estoque (sword)*
33 die Muleta
- *muleta*
34 **das Rodeo**
- *rodeo*
35 der Jungstier
- *young bull*
36 der Cowboy
- *cowboy*
37 der Stetson (Stetsonhut)
- *stetson (stetson hat)*
38 das Halstuch
- *scarf (necktie)*
39 der Rodeoreiter
- *rodeo rider*
40 das Lasso
- *lasso*

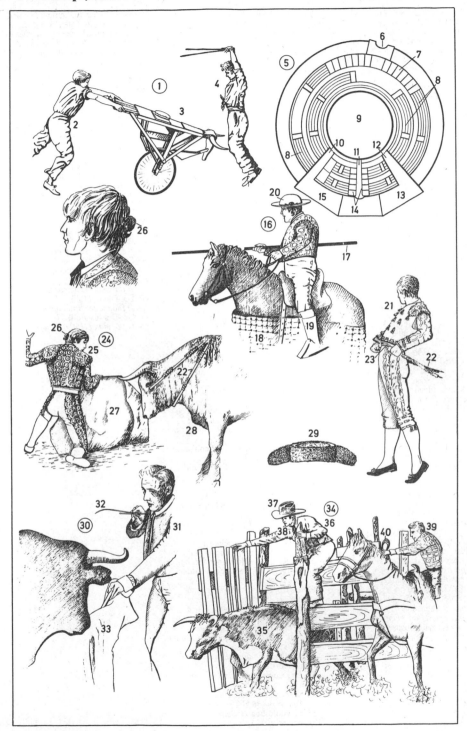

1-2 mittelalterliche Noten *f*
- *medieval (mediaeval) notes*
1 die Choralnotation
   (die Quadratnotation)
- *plainsong notation (neumes,*
   neums, pneumes, square notation)
2 die Mensuralnotation
- *mensural notation*
3-7 die Musiknote (Note)
- *musical note (note)*
3 der Notenkopf
- *note head*
4 der Notenhals
- *note stem (note tail)*
5 das Notenfähnchen
- *hook*
6 der Notenbalken
- *stroke*
7 der Verlängerungspunkt
- *dot indicating augmentation of*
   note's value
8-11 die Notenschlüssel *m*
- *clefs*
8 der Violinschlüssel (G-Schlüssel)
- *treble clef (G-clef, violin clef)*
9 der Baßschlüssel (F-Schlüssel)
- *bass clef (F-clef)*
10 der Altschlüssel (C-Schlüssel)
- *alto clef (C-clef)*
11 der Tenorschlüssel (C-Schlüssel)
- *tenor clef*
12-19 die Notenwerte *m*
- *note values*
12 die Doppelganze (*früh.*: Brevis)
- *breve (brevis, Am. double-whole note)*
13 die ganze Note (*früh.*: Semibrevis)
- *semibreve (Am. whole note)*
14 die halbe Note (*früh.*: Minima)
- *minim (Am. half note)*
15 die Viertelnote (*früh.*:
   Semiminima)
- *crotchet (Am. quarter note)*
16 die Achtelnote (*früh.*: Fusa)
- *quaver (Am. eighth note)*
17 die Sechzehntelnote (*früh.*:
   Semifusa)
- *semiquaver (Am. sixteenth note)*
18 die Zweiunddreißigstelnote
- *demisemiquaver (Am. thirty-second*
   note)
19 die Vierundsechzigstelnote
- *hemidemisemiquaver (Am.*
   sixty-fourth note)
20-27 die Pausenzeichen *n* (Pausen *f*)
- *rests*
20 die Pause für die Doppelganze
- *breve rest*
21 die ganze Pause
- *semibreve rest (Am. whole rest)*
22 die halbe Pause
- *minim rest (Am. half rest)*
23 die Viertelpause
- *crotchet rest (Am. quarter rest)*
24 die Achtelpause
- *quaver rest (Am. eighth rest)*
25 die Sechzehntelpause
- *semiquaver rest (Am. sixteenth rest)*
26 die Zweiunddreißigstelpause
- *demisemiquaver rest*
   (Am. thirty-second rest)
27 die Vierundsechzigstelpause
- *hemidemisemiquaver rest*
   (Am. sixty-fourth rest)
28-42 der Takt (die Taktart)
- *time (time signatures, measure,*
   Am. *meter)*

28 der Zweiachteltakt
- *two-eight time*
29 der Zweivierteltakt
- *two-four time*
30 der Zweihalbetakt
- *two-two time*
31 der Vierachteltakt
- *four-eight time*
32 der Viervierteltakt
- *four-four time (common time)*
33 der Vierhalbetakt
- *four-two time*
34 der Sechsachteltakt
- *six-eight time*
35 der Sechsvierteltakt
- *six-four time*
36 der Dreiachteltakt
- *three-eight time*
37 der Dreivierteltakt
- *three-four time*
38 der Dreihalbetakt
- *three-two time*
39 der Neunachteltakt
- *nine-eight time*
40 der Neunvierteltakt
- *nine-four time*
41 der Fünfvierteltakt
- *five-four time*
42 der Taktstrich
- *bar (bar line, measure line)*
43-44 das Liniensystem
- *staff (stave)*
43 die Notenlinie
- *line of the staff*
44 der Zwischenraum
- *space*
45-49 die Tonleitern *f*
- *scales*
45 die C-Dur-Tonleiter Stammtöne:
   c, d, e, f, g, a, h, c
- *C major scale naturals: c, d, e, f, g,*
   a, b, c
46 die a-Moll-Tonleiter [natürlich]
   Stammtöne: a, h, c, d, e, f, g, a
- *A minor scale [natural] naturals: a,*
   b, c, d, e, f, g, a
47 die a-Moll-Tonleiter [harmonisch]
- *A minor scale [harmonic]*
48 die a-Moll-Tonleiter [melodisch]
- *A minor scale [melodic]*
49 die chromatische Tonleiter
- *chromatic scale*
50-54 die Versetzungszeichen *n*
   (die Vorzeichen)
- *accidentals (inflections, key*
   signatures)
50-51 die Erhöhungszeichen *n*
- *signs indicating the raising of a note*
50 das Kreuz (die Halbtonerhöhung)
- *sharp (raising the note a semitone*
   or half-step)
51 das Doppelkreuz (die Erhöhung
   um 2 Halbtöne *m*)
- *double sharp (raising the note a*
   tone or full-step)
52-53 die Erniedrigungszeichen
- *signs indicating the lowering of a note*
52 das B (die Halbtonerniedrigung)
- *flat (lowering the note a semitone*
   or half-step)
53 das Doppel-B (die Erniedrigung
   um 2 Halbtöne *m*)
- *double flat (lowering the note a*
   tone or full-step)
54 das Auflösungszeichen
- *natural*

55-68 die Tonarten (Durtonarten und
   die ihnen parallelen Molltonarten,
   jeweils mit gleichem Vorzeichen *n*)
- *keys (major keys and the related*
   minor keys having the same
   signature)
55 C-Dur (a-Moll)
- *C major (A minor)*
56 G-Dur (e-Moll)
- *G major (E minor)*
57 D-Dur (h-Moll)
- *D major (B minor)*
58 A-Dur (fis-Moll)
- *A major (F sharp minor)*
59 E-Dur (cis-Moll)
- *E major (C sharp minor)*
60 H-Dur (gis-Moll)
- *B major (G sharp minor)*
61 Fis-Dur (dis-Moll)
- *F sharp major (D sharp minor)*
62 C-Dur (a-Moll)
- *C major (A minor)*
63 F-Dur (d-Moll)
- *F major (D minor)*
64 B-Dur (g-Moll)
- *B flat major (G minor)*
65 Es-Dur (c-Moll)
- *E flat major (C minor)*
66 As-Dur (f-Moll)
- *A flat major (F minor)*
67 Des-Dur (b-Moll)
- *D flat major (B flat minor)*
68 Ges-Dur (es-Moll)
- *G flat major (E flat minor)*

1-5 der Akkord
- *chord*
1-4 Dreiklänge *m*
- *triad*
1 der Durdreiklang
- *major triad*
2 der Molldreiklang
- *minor triad*
3 der verminderte Dreiklang
- *diminished triad*
4 der übermäßige Dreiklang
- *augmented triad*
5 der Vierklang,
ein Septimenakkord *m*
- *chord of four notes, a chord of the
seventh (seventh chord, dominant
seventh chord)*
6-13 die Intervalle *n*
- *intervals*
6 die Prime (der Einklang)
- *unison (unison interval)*
7 die große Sekunde
- *major second*
8 die große Terz
- *major third*
9 die Quarte
- *perfect fourth*
10 die Quinte
- *perfect fifth*
11 die große Sexte
- *major sixth*
12 die große Septime
- *major seventh*
13 die Oktave
- *perfect octave*
14-22 die Verzierungen *f*
- *ornaments (graces, grace notes)*
14 der lange Vorschlag
- *long appoggiatura*
15 der kurze Vorschlag
- *acciaccatura
(short appoggiatura)*
16 der Schleifer
- *slide*
17 der Triller ohne Nachschlag *m*
- *trill (shake) without turn*
18 der Triller mit Nachschlag *m*
- *trill (shake) with turn*
19 der Pralltriller
- *upper mordent (inverted mordent,
pralltriller)*
20 der Mordent
- *lower mordent (mordent)*
21 der Doppelschlag
- *turn*
22 das Arpeggio
- *arpeggio*
23-26 andere Notationszeichen *n*
- *other signs in musical notation*
23 die Triole; entspr.: Duole,
Quartole, Quintole, Sextole,
Septole (Septimole)
- *triplet; corresponding groupings:
duplet (couplet), quadruplet,
quintuplet, sextolet (sextuplet),
septolet (septuplet, septimole)*
24 der Bindebogen
- *tie (bind)*
25 die Fermate, ein Halte- und
Ruhezeichen *n*
- *pause (pause sign)*
26 das Wiederholungszeichen
- *repeat mark*
27-41 Vortragsbezeichnungen *f*
- *expression marks (signs of relative
intensity)*

27 marcato (markiert, betont)
- *marcato (marcando, markiert,
attack, strong accent)*
28 presto (schnell)
- *presto (quick, fast)*
29 portato (getragen)
- *portato (lourer, mezzo staccato,
carried)*
30 tenuto (gehalten)
- *tenuto (held)*
31 crescendo (anschwellend)
- *crescendo (increasing gradually in
power)*
32 decrescendo (abschwellend)
- *decrescendo (diminuendo,
decreasing or diminishing
gradually in power)*
33 legato (gebunden)
- *legato (bound)*
34 staccato (abgestoßen)
- *staccato (detached)*
35 piano (leise)
- *piano (soft)*
36 pianissimo (sehr leise)
- *pianissimo (very soft)*
37 pianissimo piano (so leise wie
möglich)
- *pianissimo piano (as soft as
possible)*
38 forte (stark)
- *forte (loud)*
39 fortissimo (sehr stark)
- *fortissimo (very loud)*
40 forte fortissimo (so stark wie
möglich)
- *forte fortissimo (double fortissimo,
as loud as possible)*
41 fortepiano (stark ansetzend, leise
weiterklingend)
- *forte piano (loud and immediately
soft again)*
42-50 die Einteilung des Tonraums *m*
- *divisions of the compass*
42 die Subkontraoktave
- *subcontra octave (double contra
octave)*
43 die Kontraoktave
- *contra octave*
44 die große Oktave
- *great octave*
45 die kleine Oktave
- *small octave*
46 die 1gestrichene Oktave
- *one-line octave*
47 die 2gestrichene Oktave
- *two-line octave*
48 die 3gestrichene Oktave
- *three-line octave*
49 die 4gestrichene Oktave
- *four-line octave*
50 die 5gestrichene Oktave
- *five-line octave*

1 die Lure, ein Bronzehorn *n*
- *lur, a bronze trumpet*
2 die Panflöte (Panpfeife, Syrinx)
- *panpipes (Pandean pipes, syrinx)*
3 der Diaulos, eine doppelte Schalmei
- *aulos, a double shawm*
4 der Aulos
- *aulos pipe*
5 die Phorbeia (Mundbinde)
- *phorbeia (peristomion, capistrum, mouth band)*
6 das Krummhorn
- *crumhorn (crummhorn, cromorne, krumbhorn, krummhorn)*
7 die Blockflöte
- *recorder (fipple flute)*
8 die Sackpfeife (der Dudelsack); ähnl.: die Musette
- *bagpipe;* sim.: *musette*
9 der Windsack
- *bag*
10 die Melodiepfeife
- *chanter (melody pipe)*
11 der Stimmer (Brummer, Bordun)
- *drone (drone pipe)*
12 der krumme Zink
- *curved cornett (zink)*
13 der Serpent
- *serpent*
14 die Schalmei; *größer:* der Bomhart (Pommer, die Bombarde)
- *shawm (schalmeyes);* larger: *bombard (bombarde, pommer)*
15 die Kithara; *ähnl. u. kleiner:* die Lyra (Leier)
- *cythara (cithara);* sim. and smaller: *lyre*
16 der Jocharm
- *arm*
17 der Steg
- *bridge*
18 der Schallkasten
- *sound box (resonating chamber, resonator)*
19 das Plektron (Plektrum), ein Schlagstäbchen *n*
- *plectrum, a plucking device*
20 die Pochette (Taschengeige, Sackgeige, Stockgeige)
- *kit (pochette), a miniature violin*
21 die Sister (Cister), ein Zupfinstrument *n*; *ähnl.:* die Pandora
- *cittern (cithern, cither, cister, citole), a plucked instrument;* sim.: *pandora (bandora, bandore)*
22 das Schalloch
- *sound hole*
23 die Viola, eine Gambe; *größer:* die Viola da Gamba, der (die) Violone
- *viol (descant viol, treble viol), a viola da gamba;* larger: *tenor viol, bass viol (viola da gamba, gamba), violone (double bass viol)*
24 der Violenbogen
- *viol bow*
25 die Drehleier (Radleier, Bauernleier, Bettlerleier, Vielle, das Organistrum)
- *hurdy-gurdy (vielle à roue, symphonia, armonie, organistrum)*
26 das Streichrad
- *friction wheel*
27 der Schutzdeckel
- *wheel cover (wheel guard)*

28 die Klaviatur
- *keyboard (keys)*
29 der Resonanzkörper
- *resonating body (resonator, sound box)*
30 die Melodiesaiten *f*
- *melody strings*
31 die Bordunsaiten *f*
- *drone strings (drones, bourdons)*
32 das Hackbrett (Cimbalom, die Zimbal, Cimbal, Cymbal, Zymbal, Zimbel)
- *dulcimer*
33 die Zarge
- *rib (resonator wall)*
34 der Schlegel zum Walliser Hackbrett *n*
- *beater for the Valasian dulcimer*
35 die Rute zum Appenzeller Hackbrett *n*
- *hammer (stick) for the Appenzell dulcimer*
36 das Klavichord (Clavichord); *Arten:* das gebundene oder das bundfreie Klavichord
- *clavichord; kinds: fretted or unfretted clavichord*
37 die Klavichordmechanik
- *clavichord mechanism*
38 der Tastenhebel
- *key (key lever)*
39 der Waagebalken
- *balance rail*
40 das Führungsplättchen
- *guiding blade*
41 der Führungsschlitz
- *guiding slot*
42 das Auflager
- *resting rail*
43 die Tangente
- *tangent*
44 die Saite
- *string*
45 das Clavicembalo (Cembalo, Klavizimbel), ein Kielflügel *m*; *ähnl.:* das Spinett (Virginal)
- *harpsichord (clavicembalo, cembalo), a wing-shaped stringed keyboard instrument;* sim.: *spinet (virginal)*
46 das obere Manual
- *upper keyboard (upper manual)*
47 das untere Manual
- *lower keyboard (lower manual)*
48 die Cembalomechanik
- *harpsichord mechanism*
49 der Tastenhebel
- *key (key lever)*
50 die Docke (der Springer)
- *jack*
51 der Springerrechen (Rechen)
- *slide (register)*
52 die Zunge
- *tongue*
53 der Federkiel (Kiel)
- *quill plectrum*
54 der Dämpfer
- *damper*
55 die Saite
- *string*
56 das Portativ, eine tragbare Orgel; *größer:* das Positiv
- *portative organ, a portable organ;* larger: *positive organ (positive)*
57 die Pfeife
- *pipe (flue pipe)*

58 der Balg
- *bellows*

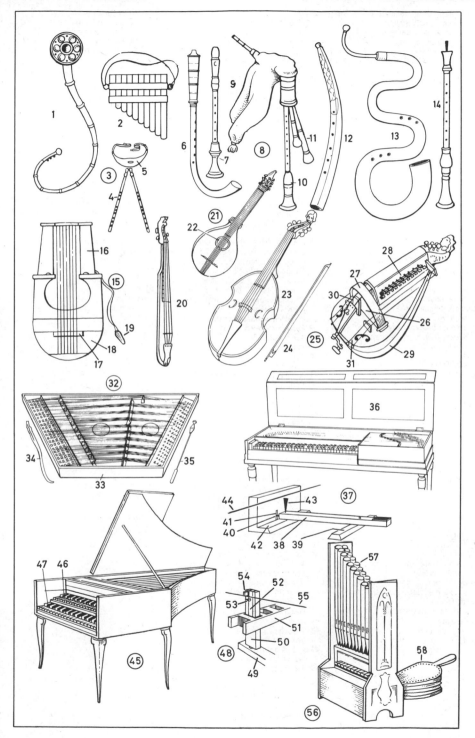

1-62 Orchesterinstrumente *n*
- *orchestral instruments*
1-27 Saiteninstrumente *n*,
Streichinstrumente
- *stringed instruments, bowed instruments*
1 die Violine (Geige, *früh.*: Fiedel *f*)
- *violin*
2 der Geigenhals (Hals)
- *neck of the violin*
3 der Resonanzkörper
(Geigenkörper, Geigenkorpus)
- *resonating body (violin body, sound box of the violin)*
4 die Zarge
- *rib (side wall)*
5 der Geigensteg (Steg)
- *violin bridge*
6 das F-Loch, ein Schalloch *n*
- *F-hole, a sound hole*
7 der Saitenhalter
- *tailpiece*
8 die Kinnstütze
- *chin rest*
9 die Saiten *f* (Violinsaiten, der
Bezug): die G-Saite, D-Saite,
A-Saite, E-Saite
- *strings (violin strings, fiddle strings): G-string, D-string, A-string, E-string*
10 der Dämpfer (die Sordine)
- *mute (sordino)*
11 das Kolophonium
- *resin (rosin, colophony)*
12 der Violinbogen (Geigenbogen,
Bogen, *früh.*: Fiedelbogen)
- *violin bow (bow)*
13 der Frosch
- *nut (frog)*
14 die Stange
- *stick (bow stick)*
15 der Geigenbogenbezug, ein
Roßhaarbezug *m*
- *hair of the violin bow (horsehair)*
16 das Violincello (Cello), eine Kniegeige
- *violoncello (cello), a member of the da gamba violin family*
17 die Schnecke
- *scroll*
18 der Wirbel
- *tuning peg (peg)*
19 der Wirbelkasten
- *pegbox*
20 der Sattel
- *nut*
21 das Griffbrett
- *fingerboard*
22 der Stachel
- *spike (tailpin)*
23 der Kontrabaß (die Baßgeige,
Violone *m od. f*)
- *double bass (contrabass, violone, double bass viol, Am. bass)*
24 die Decke
- *belly (top, soundboard)*
25 die Zarge
- *rib (side wall)*
26 der Flödel (die Einlage)
- *purfling (inlay)*
27 die Bratsche
- *viola*
28-38 Holzblasinstrumente *n*
- *woodwind instruments (woodwinds)*
28 das Fagott; *größer*: das
Kontrafagott
- *bassoon; larger: double bassoon (contrabassoon)*

29 das S-Rohr, mit dem
Doppelrohrblatt *n*
- *tube with double reed*
30 die Pikkoloflöte (Piccoloflöte,
kleine Flöte)
- *piccolo (small flute, piccolo flute, flauto piccolo)*
31 die große Flöte, eine Querflöte
- *flute (German flute), a cross flute (transverse flute, side-blown flute)*
32 die Klappe
- *key*
33 das Tonloch (Griffloch)
- *fingerhole*
34 die Klarinette; *größer*: die
Baßklarinette
- *clarinet; larger: bass clarinet*
35 die Brille (Klappe)
- *key (brille)*
36 das Mundstück
- *mouthpiece*
37 das Schallstück (die Stürze)
- *bell*
38 die Oboe (Hoboe); *Arten*: Oboe
d'amore; die Tenoroboen: Oboe da
caccia, das Englischhorn; das
Heckelphon (die Baritonoboe)
- *oboe (hautboy); kinds: oboe d'amore; tenor oboes: oboe da caccia, cor anglais; heckelphone (baritone oboe)*
39-48 Blechblasinstrumente *n*
- *brass instruments (brass)*
39 das Tenorhorn
- *tenor horn*
40 das Ventil
- *valve*
41 das Waldhorn (Horn), ein
Ventilhorn *n*
- *French horn (horn, waldhorn), a valve horn*
42 der Schalltrichter (Schallbecher)
- *bell*
43 die Trompete; *größer*: die
Baßtrompete; *kleiner*: das Kornett
(Piston)
- *trumpet; larger: B♭ cornet; smaller: cornet*
44 die Baßtuba (Tuba, das
Bombardon); *ähnl.*: das Helikon
(Pelitton), die Kontrabaßtuba
- *bass tuba (tuba, bombardon); sim.: helicon (pellitone), contrabass tuba*
45 der Daumenring
- *thumb hold*
46 die Zugposaune (Posaune,
Trombone); *Arten*: Altposaune *f*,
Tenorposaune, Baßposaune
- *trombone; kinds: alto trombone, tenor trombone, bass trombone*
47 der Posaunenzug (Zug, die
Posaunenstangen *f*)
- *trombone slide (slide)*
48 das Schallstück
- *bell*
49-59 Schlaginstrumente *n*
- *percussion instruments*
49 der Triangel
- *triangle*
50 das Becken (die Tschinellen *f*,
türkischen Teller *m*)
- *cymbals*
51-59 Membraphone *n*
- *membranophones*

51 die kleine Trommel
(Wirbeltrommel)
- *side drum (snare drum)*
52 das Fell (Trommelfell, Schlagfell)
- *drum head (head, upper head, batter head, vellum)*
53 die Stellschraube (Spannschraube)
- *tensioning screw*
54 der Trommelschlegel
(Trommelstock)
- *drumstick*
55 die große Trommel (türkische
Trommel)
- *bass drum (Turkish drum)*
56 der Schlegel
- *stick (padded stick)*
57 die Pauke (Kesselpauke), eine
Schraubenpauke; *ähnl.*:
Maschinenpauke *f*
- *kettledrum (timpano), a screw-tensioned drum; sim.: machine drum (mechanically tuned drum)*
58 das Paukenfell
- *kettledrum skin (kettledrum vellum)*
59 die Stimmschraube
- *tuning screw*
60 die Harfe, eine Pedalharfe
- *harp, a pedal harp*
61 die Saiten *f*
- *strings*
62 das Pedal (Harfenpedal)
- *pedal*

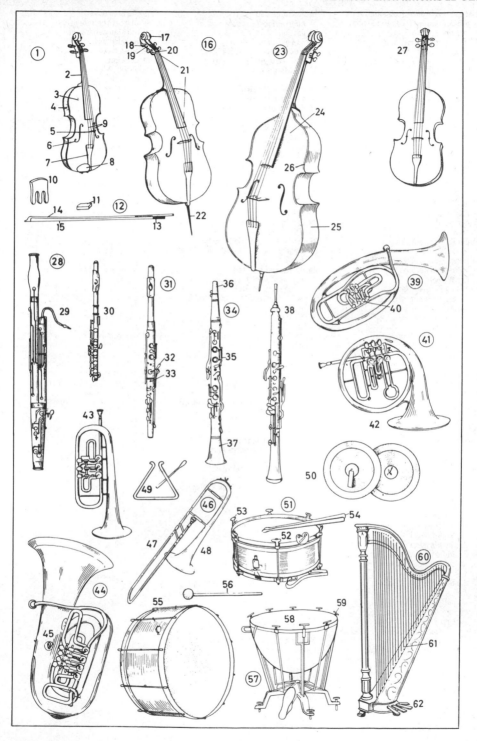

1-46 Volksmusikinstrumente *n*
- *popular musical instruments (folk instruments)*
1-31 Saiteninstrumente *n*
- *stringed instruments*
1 die Laute; *größer:* die Theorbe, Chitarrone
- *lute; larger: theorbo, chitarrone*
2 der Schallkörper
- *resonating body (resonator)*
3 das Dach
- *soundboard (belly, table)*
4 der Querriegel (Saitenhalter)
- *string fastener (string holder)*
5 das Schalloch (die Schallrose)
- *sound hole (rose)*
6 die Saite, eine Darmsaite
- *string, a gut (catgut) string*
7 der Hals
- *neck*
8 das Griffbrett
- *fingerboard*
9 der Bund
- *fret*
10 der Kragen (Knickkragen, Wirbelkasten)
- *head (bent-back pegbox, swan-head pegbox, pegbox)*
11 der Wirbel
- *tuning peg (peg, lute pin)*
12 die Gitarre (Zupfgeige, Klampfe)
- *guitar*
13 der Saitenhalter
- *string holder*
14 die Saite, eine Darm- oder Perlonsaite
- *string, a gut (catgut) or nylon string*
15 der Schallkörper (Schallkasten)
- *resonating body (resonating chamber, resonator, sound box)*
16 die Mandoline
- *mandolin (mandoline)*
17 der Ärmelschoner
- *sleeve protector (cuff protector)*
18 der Hals
- *neck*
19 das Wirbelbrett
- *pegdisc*
20 das Spielplättchen (Plektron, die Penna)
- *plectrum*
21 die Zither (Schlagzither)
- *zither (plucked zither)*
22 der Stimmstock
- *pin block (wrest pin block, wrest plank)*
23 der Stimmnagel
- *tuning pin (wrest pin)*
24 die Melodiesaiten *f* (Griffsaiten)
- *melody strings (fretted strings, stopped strings)*
25 die Begleitsaiten *f* (Baßsaiten, Freisaiten)
- *accompaniment strings (bass strings, unfretted strings, open strings)*
26 die Ausbuchtung des Resonanzkastens *m*
- *semicircular projection of the resonating sound box (resonating body)*
27 der Schlagring
- *ring plectrum*
28 die Balalaika
- *balalaika*
29 das Banjo
- *banjo*

30 das Tamburin
- *tambourine-like body*
31 das Fell
- *parchment membrane*
32 die Okarina, eine Gefäßflöte
- *ocarina, a globular flute*
33 das Mundstück
- *mouthpiece*
34 das Tonloch (Griffloch)
- *fingerhole*
35 die Mundharmonika
- *mouth organ (harmonica)*
36 das Akkordeon (die Handharmonika, das Schifferklavier, Matrosenklavier); *ähnl.:* die Ziehharmonika, Konzertina, das Bandoneon, die Bandonika
- *accordion; sim.: piano accordion, concertina, bandoneon*
37 der Balg
- *bellows*
38 der Balgverschluß
- *bellows strap*
39 der Diskantteil (die Melodieseite)
- *melody side (keyboard side, melody keys)*
40 die Klaviatur
- *keyboard (keys)*
41 das Diskantregister
- *treble stop (treble coupler, treble register)*
42 die Registertaste
- *stop lever*
43 der Baßteil (die Begleitseite)
- *bass side (accompaniment side, bass studs, bass press-studs, bass buttons)*
44 das Baßregister
- *bass stop (bass coupler, bass register)*
45 das Schellentamburin (Tamburin)
- *tambourine*
46 die Kastagnetten *f*
- *castanets*
47-78 Jazzinstrumente *n*
- *jazz band instruments (dance band instruments)*
47-58 Schlaginstrumente *n*
- *percussion instruments*
47-54 die Jazzbatterie (das Schlagzeug)
- *drum kit (drum set, drums)*
47 die große Trommel
- *bass drum*
48 die kleine Trommel
- *small tom-tom*
49 das Tomtom
- *large tom-tom*
50 das Hi-Hat (High-Hat, Charleston), ein Becken *n*
- *high-hat cymbals (choke cymbals, Charleston cymbals, cup cymbals)*
51 das Becken (Cymbel)
- *cymbal*
52 der Beckenhalter
- *cymbal stand (cymbal holder)*
53 der Jazzbesen, ein Stahlbesen *m*
- *wire brush*
54 die Fußmaschine
- *pedal mechanism*
55 die Conga (Tumba)
- *conga drum (conga)*
56 der Spannreifen
- *tension hoop*
57 die Timbales *m*
- *timbales*

58 die Bongos *m*
- *bongo drums (bongos)*
59 die Maracas *f; ähnl.:* Rumbakugeln *f*
- *maracas; sim.: shakers*
60 der Guiro
- *guiro*
61 das Xylophon (die Holzharmonika); *früh.:* die Strohfiedel; *ähnl.:* das Marimbaphon, Tubaphon
- *xylophone; form.: straw fiddle; sim.: marimbaphone (steel marimba), tubaphone*
62 der Holzstab
- *wooden slab*
63 der Resonanzkasten
- *resonating chamber (sound box)*
64 der Klöppel
- *beater*
65 die Jazztrompete
- *jazz trumpet*
66 das Ventil
- *valve*
67 der Haltehaken
- *finger hook*
68 der Dämpfer
- *mute (sordino)*
69 das Saxophon
- *saxophone*
70 der Trichter
- *bell*
71 das Ansatzrohr
- *crook*
72 das Mundstück
- *mouthpiece*
73 die Schlaggitarre (Jazzgitarre)
- *struck guitar (jazz guitar)*
74 die Aufsazseite
- *hollow to facilitate fingering*
75 das Vibraphon
- *vibraphone (Am. vibraharp)*
76 der Metallrahmen
- *metal frame*
77 die Metallplatte
- *metal bar*
78 die Metallröhre
- *tubular metal resonator*

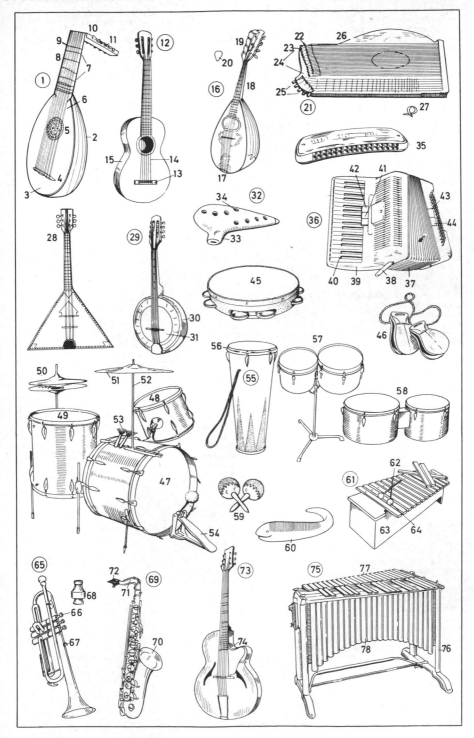

1 **das Klavier** (Piano, Pianino, Pianoforte, Fortepiano), ein Tasteninstrument *n; niedere Form:* das Kleinklavier; *Vorformen:* das Pantaleon, das Hammerklavier; die Celesta, mit Stahlplättchen *n* an Stelle der Saiten *f*
- **piano** *(pianoforte, upright piano, upright, vertical piano, spinet piano, console piano), a keyboard instrument (keyed instrument); smaller form: cottage piano (pianino); earlier forms: pantaleon; celesta, with steel bars instead of strings*
2-18 die Pianomechanik (Klaviermechanik)
- *piano action (piano mechanism)*
2 der Eisenrahmen
- *iron frame*
3 der Hammer (Klavierhammer, Saitenhammer, Filzhammer); *alle:* das Hammerwerk
- *hammer;* collectively: *striking mechanism*
4-5 die Klaviatur (die Klaviertasten *f*, Tasten, die Tastatur)
- *keyboard (piano keys)*
4 die weiße Taste (Elfenbeintaste)
- *white key (ivory key)*
5 die schwarze Taste (Ebenholztaste)
- *black key (ebony key)*
6 das Klaviergehäuse
- *piano case*
7 der Saitenbezug (die Klaviersaiten *f*)
- *strings (piano strings)*
8-9 die Klavierpedale *n*
- *piano pedals*
8 das rechte Pedal (*ungenau:* Fortepedal), zur Aufhebung der Dämpfung
- *right pedal (sustaining pedal, damper pedal;* loosely: *forte pedal, loud pedal) for raising the dampers*
9 das linke Pedal (*ungenau:* Pianopedal), zur Verkürzung des Anschlagweges *m* der Hämmer *m*
- *left pedal (soft pedal;* loosely: *piano pedal) for reducing the striking distance of the hammers on the strings*
10 die Diskantsaiten *f*
- *treble strings*
11 der Diskantsteg
- *treble bridge (treble belly bridge)*
12 die Baßsaiten *f*
- *bass strings*
13 der Baßsteg
- *bass bridge (bass belly bridge)*
14 der Plattenstift
- *hitch pin*
15 die Hammerleiste
- *hammer rail*
16 die Mechanikbacke
- *brace*
17 der Stimmnagel (Stimmwirbel, Spannwirbel)
- *tuning pin (wrest pin, tuning peg)*
18 der Stimmstock
- *pin block (wrest pin block, wrest plank)*
19 das Metronom (der Taktmesser)
- *metronome*
20 der Stimmschlüssel (Stimmhammer)
- *tuning hammer (tuning key, wrest)*

21 der Stimmkeil
- *tuning wedge*
22-39 die Tastenmechanik
- *key action (key mechanism)*
22 der Mechanikbalken
- *beam*
23 die Abhebestange
- *damper-lifting lever*
24 der Hammerkopf (Hammerfilz)
- *felt-covered hammer head*
25 der Hammerstiel
- *hammer shank*
26 die Hammerleiste
- *hammer rail*
27 der Fanger
- *check (back check)*
28 der Fangerfilz
- *check felt (back check felt)*
29 der Fangerdraht
- *wire stem of the check (wire stem of the back check)*
30 die Stoßzunge (der Stößer)
- *sticker (hopper, hammer jack, hammer lever)*
31 der Gegenfanger
- *button*
32 das Hebeglied (die Wippe)
- *action lever*
33 die Pilote
- *pilot*
34 der Pilotendraht
- *pilot wire*
35 der Bändchendraht
- *tape wire*
36 das Bändchen (Litzenband)
- *tape*
37 die Dämpferpuppe (das Filzdöckchen, der Dämpfer, die Dämpfung)
- *damper (damper block)*
38 der Dämpferarm
- *damper lifter*
39 die Dämpferpralleiste
- *damper rest rail*
40 **der Flügel** (Konzertflügel für den Konzertsaal; *kleiner:* der Stutzflügel, Zimmerflügel; *Nebenform:* das Tafelklavier)
- **grand piano** *(horizontal piano, grand, concert grand, for the concert hall;* smaller: *baby grand piano, boudoir piano;* other form: *square piano, table piano)*
41 die Flügelpedale *n;* das rechte Pedal zur Aufhebung der Dämpfung; das linke Pedal zur Tondämpfung (Verschiebung der Klaviatur; nur eine Saite wird angeschlagen „una corda")
- *grand piano pedals; right pedal for raising the dampers; left pedal for softening the tone (shifting the keyboard so that only one string is struck 'una corda')*
42 der Pedalstock (die Lyrastütze, Lyra)
- *pedal bracket*
43 **das Harmonium**
- **harmonium** *(reed organ, melodium)*
44 der Registerzug
- *draw stop (stop, stop knob)*
45 der Kniehebel (Schweller)
- *knee lever (knee swell, swell)*
46 das Tretwerk (der Tretschemel, Bedienungstritt des Blasebalgs *m*)
- *pedal (bellows pedal)*

47 das Harmoniumgehäuse
- *harmonium case*
48 das Manual
- *harmonium keyboard (manual)*

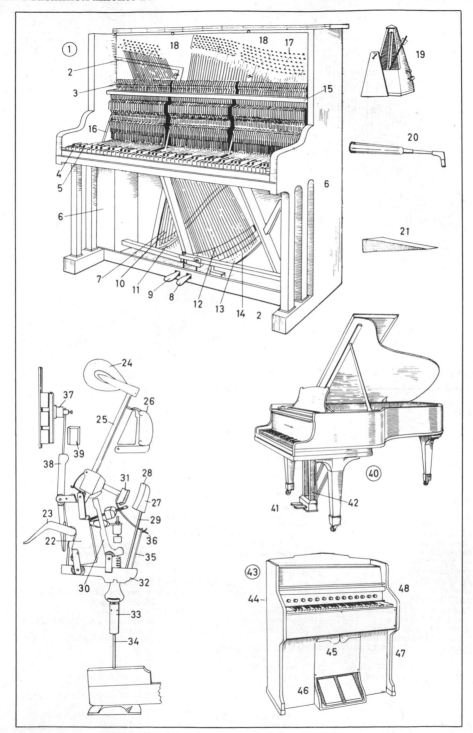

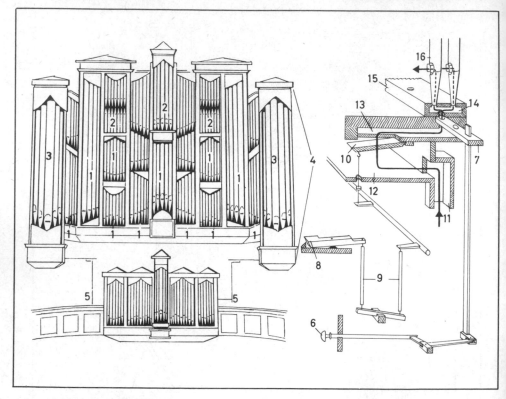

1-52 die Orgel (Kirchenorgel)
- **organ** *(church organ)*
1-5 der Prospekt (Orgelprospekt, das Orgelgehäuse)
- *front view of organ (organ case) [built according to classical principles]*
1-3 die Prospektpfeifen *f*
- *display pipes (face pipes)*
1 das Hauptwerk
- *Hauptwerk (*approx. English equivalent: *great organ)*
2 das Oberwerk
- *Oberwerk (*approx. English equivalent: *swell organ)*
3 die Pedalpfeifen *f*
- *pedal pipes*
4 der Pedalturm
- *pedal tower*
5 das Rückpositiv
- *Rückpositiv (*approx. English equivalent: *choir organ)*
6-16 die mechanische Traktur (Spielmechanik); *andere Arten:* die pneumatische Traktur, elektr. Traktur)
- *tracker action (mechanical action);* other systems: *pneumatic action, electric action*
6 der Registerzug
- *draw stop (stop, stop knob)*
7 die Registerschleife
- *slider (slide)*

8 die Taste
- *key (key lever)*
9 die Abstrakte
- *sticker*
10 das Ventil (Spielventil)
- *pallet*
11 der Windkanal
- *wind trunk*
12-14 die Windlade, eine Schleiflade; *andere Arten:* Kastenlade *f*, Springlade, Kegellade, Membranenlade
- *wind chest, a slider wind chest;* other types: *sliderless wind chest (unit wind chest), spring chest, kegellade chest (cone chest), diaphragm chest*
12 die Windkammer
- *wind chest (wind chest box)*
13 die Kanzelle (Tonkanzelle)
- *groove*
14 die Windverführung
- *upper board groove*
15 der Pfeifenstock
- *upper board*
16 die Pfeife eines Registers *n*
- *pipe of a particular stop*
17-35 die Orgelpfeifen *f* (Pfeifen)
- *organ pipes (pipes)*
17-22 die Zungenpfeife (Zungenstimme) aus Metall *n*, eine Posaune
- *metal reed pipe (set of pipes: reed stop), a posaune stop*

17 der Stiefel
- *boot*
18 die Kehle
- *shallot*
19 die Zunge
- *tongue*
20 der Bleikopf
- *block*
21 die Stimmkrücke (Krücke)
- *tuning wire (tuning crook)*
22 der Schallbecher
- *tube*
23-30 die offene Lippenpfeife aus Metall *n*, ein Salicional *n*
- *open metal flue pipe, a salicional*
23 der Fuß
- *foot*
24 der Kernspalt
- *flue pipe windway (flue pipe duct)*
25 der Aufschnitt
- *mouth (cutup)*
26 die Unterlippe (das Unterlabium)
- *lower lip*
27 die Oberlippe (das Oberlabium)
- *upper lip*
28 der Kern
- *languid*
29 der Pfeifenkörper (Körper)
- *body of the pipe (pipe)*
30 die Stimmrolle (der Stimmlappen), eine Stimmvorrichtung
- *tuning flap (tuning tongue), a tuning device*

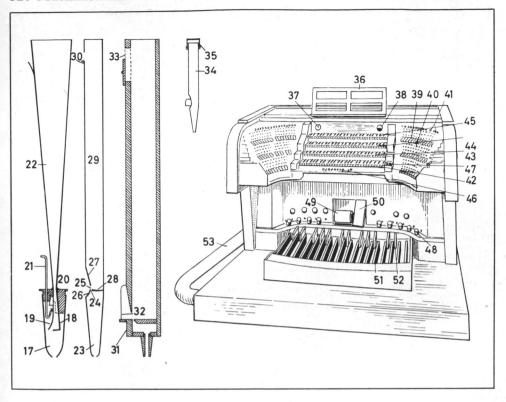

31-33 die offene Lippenpfeife aus
    Holz *n*, ein Prinzipal *n*
– *open wooden flue pipe (open
    wood), principal (diapason)*
31 der Vorschlag
– *cap*
32 der Bart
– *ear*
33 der Stimmschlitz, mit Schieber *m*
– *tuning hole (tuning slot), with slide*
34 die gedackte (gedeckte)
    Lippenpfeife
– *stopped flue pipe*
35 der Metallhut
– *stopper*
36-52 der Orgelspieltisch (Spieltisch)
    einer elektrisch gesteuerten Orgel
– *organ console (console) of an
    electric action organ*
36 das Notenpult
– *music rest
    (music stand)*
37 die Kontrolluhr für die
    Walzenstellung
– *crescendo roller indicator*
38 die Kontrolluhr für die
    Stromspannung
– *voltmeter*
39 die Registertaste
– *stop tab (rocker)*
40 die Taste für freie Kombination *f*
– *free combination stud (free
    combination knob)*

41 die Absteller *m* für Zunge *f*,
    Koppel *f* usw.
– *cancel buttons for reeds, couplers
    etc.*
42 das I. Manual, für das Rückpositiv
– *manual I, for the Rückpositiv
    (choir organ)*
43 das II. Manual, für das Hauptwerk
– *manual II, for the Hauptwerk
    (great organ)*
44 das III. Manual, für das Oberwerk
– *manual III, for the Oberwerk
    (swell organ)*
45 das IV. Manual, für das
    Schwellwerk
– *manual IV,
    for the Schwellwerk
    (solo organ)*
46 die Druckknöpfe *m* und
    Kombinationsknöpfe *m*, für die
    Handregistratur, freie, feste
    Kombinationen *f* und
    Setzerkombinationen *f*
– *thumb pistons controlling the
    manual stops (free or fixed
    combinations) and buttons for
    setting the combinations*
47 die Schalter *m*, für Wind *m* und
    Strom *m*
– *switches for current to blower and
    action*
48 der Fußtritt, für die Koppel
– *toe piston, for the coupler*

49 der Rollschweller
    (Registerschweller)
– *crescendo roller (general crescendo
    roller)*
50 der Jalousieschweller
– *balanced swell pedal*
51 die Pedaluntertaste (Pedaltaste)
– *pedal key [natural]*
52 die Pedalobertaste
– *pedal key [sharp or flat]*
53 das Kabel
– *cable (transmission cable)*

1-61 Fabelwesen n (Fabeltiere),
  mytholog. Tiere n und Figuren f
- *fabulous creatures (fabulous*
  animals), mythical creatures
1 der Drache (Drachen, Wurm,
  Lindwurm, Lintwurm, *bayr./*
  österr. Tatzelwurm)
- *dragon*
2 der Schlangenleib
- *serpent's body*
3 die Klaue
- *claws (claw)*
4 der Fledermausflügel
- *bat's wing*
5 das doppelzüngige Maul
- *fork-tongued mouth*
6 die gespaltene Zunge
- *forked tongue*
7 das Einhorn [Symbol n der
  Jungfräulichkeit]
- *unicorn [symbol of virginity]*
8 das gedrehte Horn
- *spirally twisted horn*
9 der Vogel Phönix (Phönix)
- *Phoenix*
10 die Flamme oder Asche der
  Wiedergeburt
- *flames or ashes of resurrection*
11 der Greif
- *griffin (griffon, gryphon)*
12 der Adlerkopf
- *eagle's head*
13 die Greifenklaue
- *griffin's claws*
14 der Löwenleib
- *lion's body*
15 die Schwinge
- *wing*
16 die Chimära (Schimäre), ein
  Ungeheuer n
- *chimera (chimaera), a monster*
17 der Löwenkopf
- *lion's head*
18 der Ziegenkopf
- *goat's head*
19 der Drachenleib
- *dragon's body*
20 die Sphinx, eine symbol. Gestalt
- *sphinx, a symbolic figure*
21 das Menschenhaupt
- *human head*
22 der Löwenrumpf
- *lion's body*
23 die Nixe (Wassernixe, das
  Meerweib, die Meerfrau,
  Meerjungfrau, Meerjungfer,
  Meerfee, Seejungfer, das
  Wasserweib, die Wasserfrau,
  Wasserjungfer, Wasserfee, Najade,
  Quellnymphe, Wassernymphe,
  Flußnixe); *ähnl.:* Nereide f,
  Ozeanide (Meergottheiten,
  Meergöttinnen); *männl.* der Nix
  (Nickel, Nickelmann,
  Wassermann)
- *mermaid (nix, nixie, water nixie,*
  sea maid, sea maiden, naiad, water
  nymph, water elf, ocean nymph,
  sea nymph, river nymph); sim.:
  Nereids, Oceanids (sea divinities,
  sea deities, sea goddesses); male:
  nix (merman, seaman)
24 der Mädchenleib
- *woman's trunk*
25 der Fischschwanz (Delphinschwanz)
- *fish's tail (dolphin's tail)*

26 der Pegasus (das Dichterroß,
  Musenroß, Flügelroß); *ähnl.:* der
  Hippogryph
- *Pegasus (favourite,* Am. *favorite,*
  steed of the Muses, winged horse);
  sim.: *hippogryph*
27 der Pferdeleib
- *horse's body*
28 die Flügel m
- *wings*
29 der Zerberus (Kerberos,
  Höllenhund)
- *Cerberus (hellhound)*
30 der dreiköpfige Hundeleib
- *three-headed dog's body*
31 der Schlangenschweif
- *serpent's tail*
32 die Hydra von Lerna (Lernäische
  Schlange)
- *Lernaean (Lernean) Hydra*
33 der neunköpfige Schlangenleib
- *nine-headed serpent's body*
34 der Basilisk
- *basilisk (cockatrice) [in English*
  legend usually with two legs]
35 der Hahnenkopf
- *cock's head*
36 der Drachenleib
- *dragon's body*
37 der Gigant (Titan), ein Riese m
- *giant (titan)*
38 der Felsbrocken
- *rock*
39 der Schlangenfuß
- *serpent's foot*
40 der Triton, ein Meerwesen n
- *triton, a merman (demigod of the*
  sea)
41 das Muschelhorn
- *conch shell trumpet*
42 der Pferdefuß
- *horse's hoof*
43 der Fischschwanz
- *fish's tail*
44 der Hippokamp (das Seepferd)
- *hippocampus*
45 der Pferderumpf
- *horse's trunk*
46 der Fischschwanz
- *fish's tail*
47 der Seestier, ein Seeungeheuer n
- *sea ox, a sea monster*
48 der Stierleib
- *monster's body*
49 der Fischschwanz
- *fish's tail*
50 der siebenköpfige Drache der
  Offenbarung (Apokalypse)
- *seven-headed dragon of St. John's*
  Revelation (Revelations,
  Apocalypse)
51 der Flügel
- *wing*
52 der Zentaur (Kentaur), ein
  Mischwesen n
- *centaur (hippocentaur), half man*
  and half beast
53 der Menschenleib mit Pfeil m und
  Bogen m
- *man's body with bow and arrow*
54 der Pferdekörper
- *horse's body*
55 die Harpyie, ein Windgeist m
- *harpy, a winged monster*
56 der Frauenkopf
- *woman's head*

57 der Vogelleib
- *bird's body*
58 die Sirene, ein Dämon m
- *siren, a daemon*
59 der Mädchenleib
- *woman's body*
60 der Flügel
- *wing*
61 die Vogelklaue
- *bird's claw*

1-40 vorgeschichtliche
(prähistorische) Fundgegenstände
m (Funde *m*)
- *prehistoric finds*
1-9 die Altsteinzeit (das Paläolithikum)
und **die Mittelsteinzeit**
(das Mesolithikum)
- *Old Stone Age (Palaeolithic,
Paleolithic, period)
and Mesolithic period*
1 der Faustkeil, aus Stein *m*
- *hand axe (Am. ax) (fist hatchet), a
stone tool*
2 die Geschoßspitze, aus Knochen *m*
- *head of throwing spear, made of
bone*
3 die Harpune, aus Knochen *m*
- *bone harpoon*
4 die Spitze
- *head*
5 die Speerschleuder, aus der
Geweihstange des Rentiers *n*
- *harpoon thrower, made of reindeer
antler*
6 der bemalte Kieselstein
- *painted pebble*
7 der Kopf des Wildpferdes, eine
Schnitzerei
- *head of a wild horse, a carving*
8 das Steinzeitidol, eine
Elfenbeinstatuette
- *Stone Age idol (Venus), an ivory
statuette*
9 der Wisent, ein Felsbild *n*
(Höhlenbild) [Höhlenmalerei *f*]
- *bison, a cave painting (rock
painting) [cave art, cave painting]*
10-20 die Jungsteinzeit
(das Neolithikum)
- *New Stone Age
(Neolithic period)*
10 die Amphore [Schnurkeramik *f*]
- *amphora [corded ware]*
11 der Kumpf [Hinkelsteingruppe *f*]
- *bowl [menhir group]*
12 die Kragenflasche
[Trichterbecherkultur *f*]
- *collared flask [Funnel-Beaker
culture]*
13 das spiralverzierte Gefäß
[Bandkeramik *f*]
- *vessel with spiral pattern [spiral
design pottery]*
14 der Glockenbecher
[Glockenbecherkultur *f*]
- *bell beaker [beaker pottery]*
15 das Pfahlhaus, ein Pfahlbau *m*
- *pile dwelling (lake dwelling,
lacustrine dwelling)*
16 der Dolmen, ein Megalithgrab *n*
(ugs. Hünengrab); *andere Arten:*
das Ganggrab, Galeriegrab; *mit*
Erde, Kies, Steinen überdeckt: der
Tumulus (das Hügelgrab)
- *dolmen (cromlech), a megalithic
tomb (coll.: giant's tomb); other
kinds: passage grave, gallery grave
(long cist); when covered with
earth: tumulus (barrow, mound)*
17 das Steinkistengrab mit
Hockerbestattung *f*
(ein Hockergrab *n*)
- *stone cist, a contracted burial*
18 der Menhir (*landsch.* Hinkelstein
m, ein Monolith *m*)
- *menhir (standing stone), a monolith*

19 die Bootaxt, eine Streitaxt aus Stein *m*
- *boat axe (Am. ax), a stone battle axe*
20 die menschl. Figur aus gebranntem
Ton *m* (ein Idol *n*)
- *clay figurine (an idol)*
21-40 die Bronzezeit und **die Eisenzeit**;
Epochen: die Hallstattzeit,
La-Tène-Zeit
- *Bronze Age and Iron Age; epochs:
Hallstatt period, La Tène period*
21 die bronzene Lanzenspitze
- *bronze spear head*
22 der Bronzedolch mit Vollgriff *m*
- *hafted bronze dagger*
23 das Tüllenbeil, eine Bronzeaxt mit
Ösenschäftung *f*
- *socketed axe (Am. ax), a bronze axe
with haft fastened to rings*
24 die Gürtelscheibe
- *girdle clasp*
25 der Halskragen
- *necklace (lunula)*
26 der goldene Halsring
- *gold neck ring*
27 die Violinbogenfibel, eine Fibel
(Bügelnadel)
- *violin-bow fibula (safety pin)*
28 die Schlangenfibel; *andere Arten:*
die Kahnfibel, die Armbrustfibel
- *serpentine fibula; other kinds: boat
fibula, arc fibula*
29 die Kugelkopfnadel, eine
Bronzenadel
- *bulb-head pin, a bronze pin*
30 die zweiteilige Doppelspiralfibel;
ähnl.: die Plattenfibel
- *two-piece spiral fibula; sim.: disc
(disk) fibula*
31 das Bronzemesser mit Vollgriff *m*
- *hafted bronze knife*
32 der eiserne Schlüssel
- *iron key*
33 die Pflugschar
- *ploughshare (Am. plowshare)*
34 die Situla aus Bronzeblech *n*, eine
Grabbeigabe *f*
- *sheet-bronze situla, a funerary
vessel*
35 die Henkelkanne
[Kerbschnittkeramik *f*]
- *pitcher [chip-carved pottery]*
36 der Miniaturkultwagen
(Kultwagen)
- *miniature ritual cart (miniature
ritual chariot)*
37 die keltische Silbermünze
- *Celtic silver coin*
38 die Gesichtsurne, eine
Aschenurne; *andere Arten:* die
Hausurne, die Buckelurne
- *face urn, a cinerary urn; other
kinds: domestic urn, embossed urn*
39 das Urnengrab in Steinpackung *f*
- *urn grave in stone chamber*
40 die Zylinderhalsurne
- *urn with cylindrical neck*

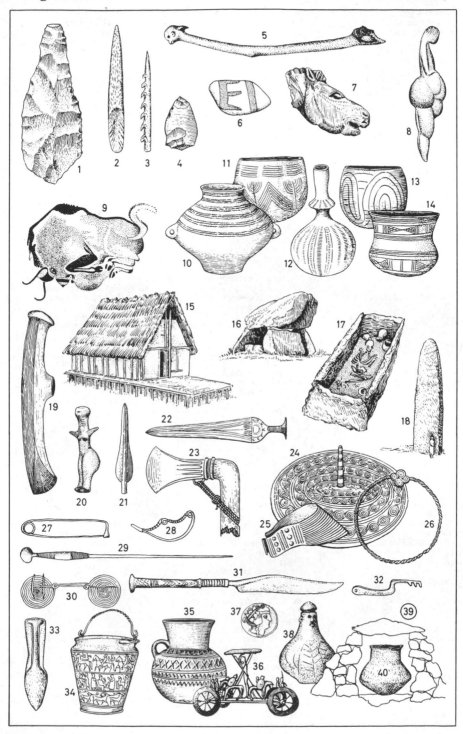

1 die Ritterburg (Burg, Feste, *früh.*:
 Veste, das Ritterschloß)
 - *knight's castle (castle)*
2 der Burghof
 - *inner ward (inner bailey)*
3 der Ziehbrunnen
 - *draw well*
4 der Bergfried (Hauptturm,
 Wachtturm, Wartturm)
 - *keep (donjon)*
5 das Verlies
 - *dungeon*
6 der Zinnenkranz
 - *battlements (crenellation)*
7 die Zinne
 - *merlon*
8 die Wehrplatte
 - *tower platform*
9 der Türmer
 - *watchman*
10 die Kemenate (das Frauenhaus)
 - *ladies' apartments (bowers)*
11 das Zwerchhaus
 - *dormer window (dormer)*
12 der Söller
 - *balcony*
13 das Vorratshaus (Mushaus)
 - *storehouse (magazine)*
14 der Eckturm (Mauerturm)
 - *angle tower*
15 die Ringmauer (Mantelmauer, der
 Zingel)
 - *curtain wall (curtains, enclosure
 wall)*
16 die Bastion
 - *bastion*
17 der Scharwachturm
 - *angle tower*
18 die Schießscharte
 - *crenel (embrasure)*
19 die Schildmauer
 - *inner wall*
20 der Wehrgang
 - *battlemented parapet*
21 die Brustwehr
 - *parapet (breastwork)*
22 das Torhaus
 - *gatehouse*
23 die Pechnase (der Gußerker)
 - *machicolation (machicoulis)*
24 das Fallgatter
 - *portcullis*
25 die Zugbrücke (Fallbrücke)
 - *drawbridge*
26 die Mauerstrebe (Mauerstütze)
 - *buttress*
27 das Wirtschaftsgebäude
 - *offices and service rooms*
28 das Mauertürmchen
 - *turret*
29 die Burgkapelle
 - *chapel*
30 der Palas (die Dürnitz)
 - *great hall*
31 der Zwinger
 - *outer ward (outer bailey)*
32 das Burgtor
 - *castle gate*
33 der Torgraben
 - *moat (ditch)*
34 die Zugangsstraße
 - *approach*
35 der Wartturm
 - *watchtower (turret)*
36 der Pfahlzaun (die Palisade)
 - *palisade (pallisade, palisading)*

37 der Ringgraben (Burggraben,
 Wallgraben)
 - *moat (ditch, fosse)*
38-65 die Ritterrüstung
 - *knight's armour (Am. armor)*
38 der Harnisch, ein Panzer *m*
 - *suit of armour (Am. armor)*
39-42 der Helm
 - *helmet*
39 die Helmglocke
 - *skull*
40 das Visier
 - *visor (vizor)*
41 das Kinnreff
 - *beaver*
42 das Kehlstück
 - *throat piece*
43 die Halsberge
 - *gorget*
44 der Brechrand (Stoßkragen)
 - *epaulière*
45 der Vorderflug
 - *pallette (pauldron, besageur)*
46 das Bruststück (der Brustharnisch)
 - *breastplate (cuirass)*
47 die Armberge (Ober- und
 Unterarmschiene)
 - *brassard*
 (rear brace and vambrace)
48 die Armkachel
 - *cubitière (coudière, couter)*
49 der Bauchreifen
 - *tasse (tasset)*
50 der Panzerhandschuh (Gantelet)
 - *gauntlet*
51 der Panzerschurz
 - *habergeon (haubergeon)*
52 der Diechling
 - *cuisse (cuish, cuissard, cuissart)*
53 der Kniebuckel
 - *knee cap (knee piece, genouillère,
 poleyn)*
54 die Beinröhre
 - *jambeau (greave)*
55 der Bärlatsch
 - *solleret (sabaton, sabbaton)*
56 der Langschild
 - *pavis (pavise, pavais)*
57 der Rundschild
 - *buckler (round shield)*
58 der Schildbuckel (Schildstachel)
 - *boss (umbo)*
59 der Eisenhut
 - *iron hat*
60 die Sturmhaube
 - *morion*
61 die Kesselhaube (Hirnkappe)
 - *light casque*
62 Panzer *m*
 - *types of mail and armour
 (Am. armor)*
63 der Kettenpanzer (die Brünne)
 - *mail (chain mail, chain armour,
 Am. armor)*
64 der Schuppenpanzer
 - *scale armour (Am. armor)*
65 der Schildpanzer
 - *plate armour (Am. armor)*
66 der Ritterschlag (die Schwertleite)
 - *accolade (dubbing, knighting)*
67 der Burgherr, ein Ritter *m*
 - *liege lord, a knight*
68 der Knappe
 - *esquire*
69 der Mundschenk
 - *cup bearer*

70 der Minnesänger
 - *minstrel (minnesinger, troubadour)*
71 das Turnier
 - *tournament (tourney, joust, just,
 tilt)*
72 der Kreuzritter
 - *crusader*
73 der Tempelritter
 - *Knight Templar*
74 die Schabracke
 - *caparison (trappings)*
75 der Grießwärtel
 - *herald (marshal at tournament)*
76 das Stechzeug
 - *tilting armour (Am. armor)*
77 der Stechhelm
 - *tilting helmet (jousting helmet)*
78 der Federbusch
 - *panache (plume of feathers)*
79 die Stechtartsche
 - *tilting target (tilting shield)*
80 der Rüsthaken
 - *lance rest*
81 die Stechlanze (Lanze)
 - *tilting lance (lance)*
82 die Brechscheibe
 - *vamplate*
83-88 der Roßharnisch
 - *horse armour (Am. armor)*
83 das Halsstück (der Kanz)
 - *neck guard (neck piece)*
84 der Roßkopf
 - *chamfron (chaffron, chafron,
 chamfrain, chanfron)*
85 der Fürbug
 - *poitrel*
86 das Flankenblech
 - *flanchard (flancard)*
87 der Kürißsattel
 - *tournament saddle*
88 das Gelieger
 - *rump piece (quarter piece)*

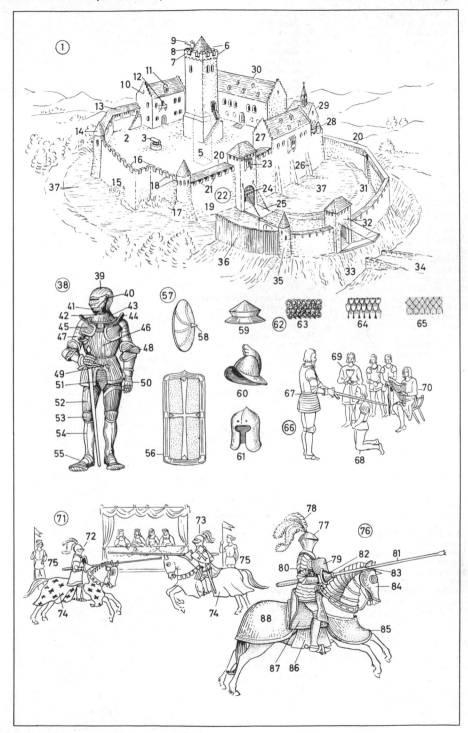

1-30 **die protestantische
(evangelische) Kirche**
- *Protestant church*
1 der Altarplatz
- *chancel*
2 das Lesepult
- *lectern*
3 der Altarteppich
- *altar carpet*
4 der Altar (Abendmahlstisch)
- *altar (communion table, Lord's
table, holy table)*
5 die Altarstufen *f*
- *altar steps*
6 die Altardecke (Altarbekleidung)
- *altar cloth*
7 die Altarkerze
- *altar candle*
8 die Hostiendose (Pyxis)
- *pyx (pix)*
9 der Hostienteller (die Patene)
- *paten (patin, patine)*
10 der Kelch
- *chalice (communion cup)*
11 die Bibel (Heilige Schrift)
- *Bible (Holy Bible, Scriptures, Holy
Scripture)*
12 das Altarkreuz
- *altar crucifix*
13 das Altarbild
- *altarpiece*
14 das Kirchenfenster
- *church window*
15 die Glasmalerei
- *stained glass*
16 der Wandleuchter
- *wall candelabrum*
17 die Sakristeitür
- *vestry door (sacristy door)*
18 die Kanzeltreppe
- *pulpit steps*
19 die Kanzel
- *pulpit*
20 das Antependium
- *antependium*
21 der Kanzeldeckel (Schalldeckel)
- *canopy (soundboard, sounding
board)*
22 der Prediger (Pastor, Pfarrer,
Geistliche, Seelsorger) im Ornat *m*
- *preacher (pastor, vicar, clergyman,
rector) in his robes (vestments,
canonicals)*
23 die Kanzelbrüstung
- *pulpit balustrade*
24 die Nummerntafel mit den
Liedernummern *f*
- *hymn board showing hymn
numbers*
25 die Empore
- *gallery*
26 der Küster (Kirchendiener)
- *verger (sexton, sacristan)*
27 der Mittelgang
- *aisle*
28 die Kirchenbank (Bank);
insgesamt: das Kirchengestühl
(Gestühl)
- *pew;* collectively: *pews (seating)*
29 der Kirchenbesucher
(Kirchgänger, Andächtige);
insgesamt: die Gemeinde
- *churchgoer (worshipper);*
collectively: *congregation*
30 das Gesangbuch
- *hymn book*

31-62 **die katholische Kirche**
- *Roman Catholic church*
31 die Altarstufen *f*
- *altar steps*
32 das Presbyterium (der Chor)
- *presbytery (choir, chancel,
sacrarium, sanctuary)*
33 der Altar
- *altar*
34 die Altarkerzen *f*
- *altar candles*
35 das Altarkreuz
- *altar cross*
36 das Altartuch
- *altar cloth*
37 der Ambo (das Predigtpult)
- *lectern*
38 das Missale (Meßbuch)
- *missal (mass book)*
39 der Priester
- *priest*
40 der Ministrant (Meßdiener)
- *server*
41 die Sedilien *f* (Priestersitze *m*)
- *sedilia*
42 der Tabernakel
- *tabernacle*
43 die Stele
- *stele (stela)*
44 die Osterkerze
- *paschal candle (Easter candle)*
45 der Osterkerzenständer
- *paschal candlestick (Easter
candlestick)*
46 die Sakristeiglocke
- *sanctus bell*
47 das Vortragkreuz
- *processional cross*
48 der Altarschmuck (Grünschmuck,
Blumenschmuck)
- *altar decoration (foliage, flower
arrangement)*
49 das Ewige Licht (die Ewige Lampe)
- *sanctuary lamp*
50 das Altarbild, ein Christusbild *n*
- *altarpiece, a picture of Christ*
51 die Madonnenstatue
- *Madonna, statue of the Virgin
Mary*
52 der Opferkerzentisch
- *pricket*
53 die Opferkerzen *f*
- *votive candles*
54 die Kreuzwegstation (Station des
Kreuzwegs *m*)
- *station of the Cross*
55 der Opferstock
- *offertory box*
56 der Schriftenstand
- *literature stand*
57 die Schriften *f* (Traktate *n*)
- *literature (pamphlets, tracts)*
58 der Mesner (Sakristan)
- *verger (sexton, sacristan)*
59 der Klingelbeutel
- *offertory bag*
60 das Almosen (die Opfergabe)
- *offering*
61 der Gläubige (Betende)
- *Christian (man praying)*
62 das Gebetbuch
- *prayer book*

1 die Kirche
- *church*
2 der Kirchturm
- *steeple*
3 der Kirchturmhahn
- *weathercock*
4 die Wetterfahne (Windfahne)
- *weather vane (wind vane)*
5 der Turmknauf
- *spire ball*
6 die Kirchturmspitze
- *church spire (spire)*
7 die Kirchturmuhr
- *church clock (tower clock)*
8 das Schalloch
- *belfry window*
9 die elektrisch betriebene Glocke
- *electrically operated bell*
10 das Firstkreuz
- *ridge cross*
11 das Kirchendach
- *church roof*
12 die Gedenkkapelle
(Gnadenkapelle)
- *memorial chapel*
13 die Sakristei, ein Anbau *m*
- *vestry (sacristy), an annexe (annex)*
14 die Gedenktafel (Gedenkplatte,
der Gedenkstein, das Epitaph)
- *memorial tablet (memorial plate,
wall memorial, wall stone)*
15 der Seiteneingang
- *side entrance*
16 das Kirchenportal (die Kirchentür)
- *church door (main door, portal)*
17 der Kirchgänger
- *churchgoer*
18 die Friedhofsmauer
(Kirchhofmauer)
- *graveyard wall (churchyard wall)*
19 das Friedhofstor (Kirchhoftor)
- *graveyard gate (churchyard gate,
lichgate, lychgate)*
20 das Pfarrhaus
- *vicarage (parsonage, rectory)*
21-41 der Friedhof (Kirchhof,
Gottesacker)
- *graveyard (churchyard, God's acre,
Am. burying ground)*
21 das Leichenhaus (die Leichenhalle,
Totenhalle, Leichenkapelle,
Parentationshalle)
- *mortuary*
22 der Totengräber
- *grave digger*
23 das Grab (die Grabstelle,
Grabstätte, Begräbnisstätte)
- *grave (tomb)*
24 der Grabhügel
- *grave mound*
25 das Grabkreuz
- *cross*
26 der Grabstein (Gedenkstein,
Leichenstein, das Grabmal)
- *gravestone (headstone, tombstone)*
27 das Familiengrab
(Familienbegräbnis)
- *family grave (family tomb)*
28 die Friedhofskapelle
- *graveyard chapel*
29 das Kindergrab
- *child's grave*
30 das Urnengrab
- *urn grave*
31 die Urne
- *urn*

32 das Soldatengrab
- *soldier's grave*
33-41 die Beerdigung (Beisetzung, das
Begräbnis, Leichenbegängnis)
- *funeral (burial)*
33 die Trauernden *m u. f* (Trauergäste *m*)
- *mourners*
34 die Grube
- *grave*
35 der Sarg
- *coffin* (Am. *casket*)
36 die Sandschaufel
- *spade*
37 der Geistliche
- *clergyman*
38 die Hinterbliebenen *m u. f*
- *the bereaved*
39 der Witwenschleier, ein
Trauerschleier *m*
- *widow's veil, a mourning veil*
40 die Sargträger *m*
- *pallbearers*
41 die Totenbahre
- *bier*
42-50 die Prozession
- *procession (religious procession)*
42 das Prozessionskreuz, ein
Tragkreuz *n*
- *processional crucifix*
43 der Kreuzträger
- *cross bearer (crucifer)*
44 die Prozessionsfahne, eine
Kirchenfahne
- *processional banner, a church
banner*
45 der Ministrant
- *acolyte*
46 der Baldachinträger
- *canopy bearer*
47 der Priester
- *priest*
48 die Monstranz, mit dem
Allerheiligsten *n* (Sanktissimum)
- *monstrance with the Blessed
Sacrament (consecrated Host)*
49 der Traghimmel (Baldachin)
- *canopy (baldachin, baldaquin)*
50 die Nonnen *f*
- *nuns*
51 die Prozessionsteilnehmer *m*
- *participants in the procession*
52-58 das Kloster
- *monastery*
52 der Kreuzgang
- *cloister*
53 der Klosterhof (Klostergarten)
- *monastery garden*
54 der Mönch, ein Benediktiner *m*
- *monk, a Benedictine monk*
55 die Kutte
- *habit (monk's habit)*
56 die Kapuze
- *cowl (hood)*
57 die Tonsur
- *tonsure*
58 das Brevier
- *breviary*
59 die Katakombe (das Zömeterium),
eine unterirdische, altchristliche
Begräbnisstätte
- *catacomb, an early Christian
underground burial place*
60 die Grabnische (das Arkosolium)
- *niche (tomb recess, arcosolium)*
61 die Steinplatte
- *stone slab*

1 die christliche Taufe
- *Christian baptism (christening)*
2 die Taufkapelle (das Baptisterium)
- *baptistery (baptistry)*
3 der protestantische (evangelische)
  Geistliche
- *Protestant clergyman*
4 der Talar (Ornat)
- *robes (vestments, canonicals)*
5 das Beffchen
- *bands*
6 der Halskragen
- *collar*
7 der Täufling
- *child to be baptized
  (christened)*
8 das Taufkleid
- *christening robe (christening dress)*
9 der Taufschleier
- *christening shawl*
10 der Taufstein
- *font*
11 das Taufbecken
- *font basin*
12 das Taufwasser
- *baptismal water*
13 die Paten *m*
- *godparents*
14 die kirchliche Trauung
- *church wedding (wedding
  ceremony, marriage ceremony)*
15-16 das Brautpaar
- *bridal couple*
15 die Braut
- *bride*
16 der Bräutigam
- *bridegroom (groom)*
17 der Ring (Trauring, Ehering)
- *ring (wedding ring)*
18 der Brautstrauß (das Brautbukett)
- *bride's bouquet (bridal bouquet)*
19 der Brautkranz
- *bridal wreath*
20 der Schleier (Brautschleier)
- *veil (bridal veil)*
21 das Myrtensträußchen
- *[myrtle] buttonhole*
22 der Geistliche
- *clergyman*
23 die Trauzeugen *m*
- *witnesses [to the marriage]*
24 die Brautjungfer
- *bridesmaid*
25 die Kniebank
- *kneeler*
26 das Abendmahl
- *Holy Communion*
27 die Kommunizierenden *m u. f*
- *communicants*
28 die Hostie (Oblate)
- *Host (wafer)*
29 der Abendmahlskelch
- *communion cup*
30 der Rosenkranz
- *rosary*
31 die Vater-unser-Perle
- *paternoster*
32 die Ave-Maria-Perle; *je 10:* ein
  Gesätz *n*
- *Ave Maria; set of 10: decade*
33 das Kruzifix
- *crucifix*
34-54 liturgische Geräte *n* (kirchliche
  Geräte)
- *liturgical vessels (ecclesiastical
  vessels)*

34 die Monstranz
- *monstrance*
35 die Hostie (große Hostie, das
  heilige Sakrament, Allerheiligste,
  Sanktissimum)
- *Host (consecrated Host, Blessed
  Sacrament)*
36 die Lunula
- *lunula (lunule)*
37 der Strahlenkranz
- *rays*
38 die Rauchfaßgarnitur (das
  Weihrauchfaß, Räucherfaß,
  Rauchfaß) für liturgische
  Räucherungen *f* (Inzensationen)
- *censer (thurible), for offering
  incense (for incensing)*
39 die Rauchfaßkette
- *thurible chain*
40 der Rauchfaßdeckel
- *thurible cover*
41 die Rauchfaßschale, ein
  Feuerbecken *n*
- *thurible bowl*
42 das Weihrauchschiffchen
- *incense boat*
43 der Weihrauchlöffel
- *incense spoon*
44 die Meßgarnitur
- *cruet set*
45 das Meßkännchen für Wasser *n*
- *water cruet*
46 das Meßkännchen für Wein *m*
- *wine cruet*
47 der Weihwasserkessel
- *holy water basin*
48 das Ciborium (der Speisekelch) mit
  den kleinen Hostien *f*
- *ciborium containing the sacred
  wafers*
49 der Kelch
- *chalice*
50 die Hostienschale
- *dish for communion wafers*
51 die Patene
- *paten (patin, patine)*
52 die Altarschelle (die Glocken *f*)
- *altar bells*
53 die Hostiendose (Pyxis)
- *pyx (pix)*
54 das Aspergill (der Weihwedel)
- *aspergillum*
55-72 christl. Kreuzformen *f*
- *forms of Christian crosses*
55 das lateinische Kreuz (Passionskreuz)
- *Latin cross (cross of the Passion)*
56 das griechische Kreuz
- *Greek cross*
57 das russische Kreuz
- *Russian cross*
58 das Petruskreuz
- *St. Peter's cross*
59 das Antoniuskreuz (Taukreuz,
  ägyptisches Kreuz)
- *St. Anthony's cross (tau cross)*
60 das Andreaskreuz (Schrägkreuz,
  der Schragen, das burgundische
  Kreuz)
- *St. Andrew's cross (saltire cross)*
61 das Schächerkreuz (Gabelkreuz,
  Deichselkreuz)
- *Y-cross*
62 das Lothringer Kreuz
- *cross of Lorraine*
63 das Henkelkreuz
- *ansate cross*

64 das Doppelkreuz (erzbischöfliches
  Kreuz)
- *patriarchal cross*
65 das Kardinalkreuz
  (Patriarchenkreuz)
- *cardinal's cross*
66 das päpstliche Kreuz (Papstkreuz)
- *Papal cross*
67 das konstantinische Kreuz, ein
  Christusmonogramm *n* (CHR)
- *Constantinian cross, a monogram of
  Christ (CHR)*
68 das Wiederkreuz
- *crosslet*
69 das Ankerkreuz
- *cross moline*
70 das Krückenkreuz
- *cross of Jerusalem*
71 das Kleeblattkreuz (Lazaruskreuz,
  Brabanter Kreuz)
- *cross botonnée (cross treflée)*
72 das Jerusalemer Kreuz
- *fivefold cross (quintuple cross)*

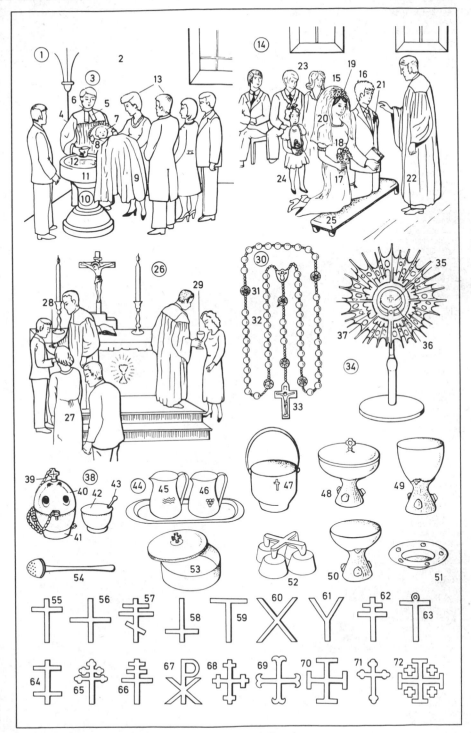

1-18 ägyptische Kunst *f*
- *Egyptian art*
1 die Pyramide, eine Spitzpyramide, ein Königsgrab *n*
- *pyramid, a royal tomb*
2 die Königskammer
- *king's chamber*
3 die Königinnenkammer
- *queen's chamber*
4 der Luftkanal
- *air passage*
5 die Sargkammer
- *coffin chamber*
6 die Pyramidenanlage
- *pyramid site*
7 der Totentempel
- *funerary temple*
8 der Taltempel
- *valley temple*
9 der Pylon (Torbau)
- *pylon, a monumental gateway*
10 die Obelisken *m*
- *obelisks*
11 der ägyptische Sphinx
- *Egyptian sphinx*
12 die geflügelte Sonnenscheibe
- *winged sun disc (sun disk)*
13 die Lotossäule
- *lotus column*
14 das Knospenkapitell
- *knob-leaf capital (bud-shaped capital)*
15 die Papyrussäule
- *papyrus column*
16 das Kelchkapitell
- *bell-shaped capital*
17 die Palmensäule
- *palm column*
18 die Bildsäule
- *ornamented column*
19-20 babylonische Kunst *f*
- *Babylonian art*
19 der babylonische Fries
- *Babylonian frieze*
20 der glasierte Reliefziegel
- *glazed relief tile*
21-28 Kunst *f* **der Perser** *m*
- *art of the Persians*
21 das Turmgrab
- *tower tomb*
22 die Stufenpyramide
- *stepped pyramid*
23 die Stiersäule
- *double bull column*
24 der Blattüberfall
- *projecting leaves*
25 das Palmettenkapitell
- *palm capital*
26 die Volute
- *volute (scroll)*
27 der Schaft
- *shaft*
28 das Stierkapitell
- *double bull capital*
29-36 Kunst *f* **der Assyrer** *m*
- *art of the Assyrians*
29 die Sargonsburg, eine Palastanlage
- *Sargon's Palace, palace buildings*
30 die Stadtmauer
- *city wall*
31 die Burgmauer
- *castle wall*
32 der Tempelturm (Zikkurat), ein Stufenturm *m*
- *temple tower (ziggurat), a stepped (terraced) tower*

33 die Freitreppe
- *outside staircase*
34 das Hauptportal
- *main portal*
35 die Portalbekleidung
- *portal relief*
36 die Portalfigur
- *portal figure*
37 kleinasiatische Kunst *f*
- *art of Asia Minor*
38 das Felsgrab
- *rock tomb*

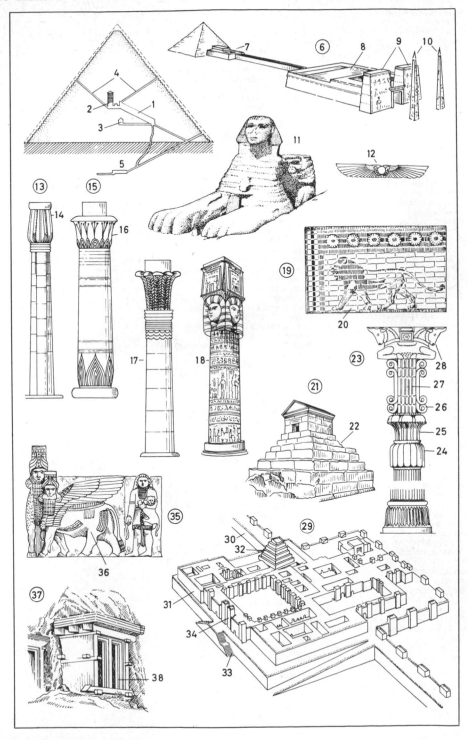

1-48 griechische Kunst *f*
- *Greek art*
1-7 die Akropolis
- *the Acropolis*
1 der Parthenon, ein dorischer Tempel
- *the Parthenon, a Doric temple*
2 das Peristyl (der Säulenumgang)
- *peristyle*
3 der Aetos (das Giebeldreieck)
- *pediment*
4 das Krepidoma (der Unterbau)
- *crepidoma (stereobate)*
5 das Standbild
- *statue*
6 die Tempelmauer
- *temple wall*
7 die Propyläen *pl* (Torbauten *m*)
- *propylaea (propylaeum, propylon)*
8 die dorische Säule
- *Doric column*
9 die ionische Säule
- *Ionic column*
10 die korinthische Säule
- *Corinthian column*
11-14 das Kranzgesims
- *cornice*
11 die Sima (Traufleiste)
- *cyma*
12 das Geison
- *corona*
13 der Mutulus (Dielenkopf)
- *mutule*
14 der Geisipodes (Zahnschnitt)
- *dentils*
15 die Triglyphe (der Dreischlitz)
- *triglyph*
16 die Metope, eine Friesverzierung
- *metope, a frieze decoration*
17 die Regula (Tropfenplatte)
- *regula*
18 das Epistyl (der Architrav)
- *epistyle (architrave)*
19 das Kyma (Kymation)
- *cyma (cymatium, kymation)*
20-25 das Kapitell (Kapitäl)
- *capital*
20 der Abakus
- *abacus*
21 der Echinus (Igelwulst)
- *echinus*
22 das Hypotrachelion (der Säulenhals)
- *hypotrachelium (gorgerin)*
23 die Volute
- *volute (scroll)*
24 das Volutenpolster
- *volute cushion*
25 der Blattkranz
- *acanthus*
26 der Säulenschaft
- *column shaft*
27 die Kannelierung
- *flutes (grooves, channels)*
28-31 die Basis (der Säulenfuß)
- *base*
28 der Toros (Torus, Wulst)
- *[upper] torus*
29 der Trochilus (die Hohlkehle)
- *trochilus (concave moulding, Am. molding)*
30 die Rundplatte
- *[lower] torus*
31 die Plinthe (der Säulensockel)
- *plinth*

32 der Stylobat
- *stylobate*
33 die Stele
- *stele (stela)*
34 das Akroterion; *am Giebel:* die Giebelverzierung
- *acroterion (acroterium, acroter)*
35 die Herme (der Büstenpfeiler)
- *herm (herma, hermes)*
36 die Karyatide; *männl.:* der Atlant
- *caryatid; male: Atlas*
37 die griech. Vase
- *Greek vase*
38-43 griech. Ornamente *n*
- *Greek ornamentation (Greek decoration, Greek decorative designs)*
38 die Perlschnur, ein Zierband *n*
- *bead-and-dart moulding (Am. molding), an ornamental band*
39 das Wellenband
- *running dog (Vitruvian scroll)*
40 das Blattornament
- *leaf ornament*
41 die Palmette
- *palmette*
42 das Eierstabkyma
- *egg and dart (egg and tongue, egg and anchor) cyma*
43 der Mäander
- *meander*
44 das griech. Theater (Theatron)
- *Greek theatre (Am. theater)*
45 die Skene (das Bühnengebäude)
- *scene*
46 das Proskenium (der Bühnenplan)
- *proscenium*
47 die Orchestra (der Tanzplatz)
- *orchestra*
48 die Thymele (der Opferstein)
- *thymele (altar)*
49-52 etruskische Kunst *f*
- *Etruscan art*
49 der etrusk. Tempel
- *Etruscan temple*
50 die Vorhalle
- *portico*
51 die Zella (der Hauptraum)
- *cella*
52 das Gebälk
- *entablature*
53-60 römische Kunst *f*
- *Roman art*
53 der Aquädukt
- *aqueduct*
54 der Wasserkanal
- *conduit (water channel)*
55 der Zentralbau
- *centrally-planned building (centralized building)*
56 der Portikus
- *portico*
57 das Gesimsband
- *reglet*
58 die Kuppel
- *cupola*
59 der Triumphbogen
- *triumphal arch*
60 die Attika
- *attic*
61-71 altchristl. Kunst *f*
- *Early Christian art*
61 die Basilika
- *basilica*
62 das Mittelschiff
- *nave*

63 das Seitenschiff
- *aisle*
64 die Apsis (Altarnische)
- *apse*
65 der Kampanile
- *campanile*
66 das Atrium
- *atrium*
67 der Säulengang
- *colonnade*
68 der Reinigungsbrunnen
- *fountain*
69 der Altar
- *altar*
70 der Lichtgaden
- *clerestory (clearstory)*
71 der Triumphbogen
- *triumphal arch*
72-75 byzantinische Kunst *f*
- *Byzantine art*
72-73 das Kuppelsystem
- *dome system*
72 die Hauptkuppel
- *main dome*
73 die Halbkuppel
- *semidome*
74 der Hängezwickel (Pendentif)
- *pendentive*
75 das Auge, eine Lichtöffnung
- *eye, a lighting aperture*

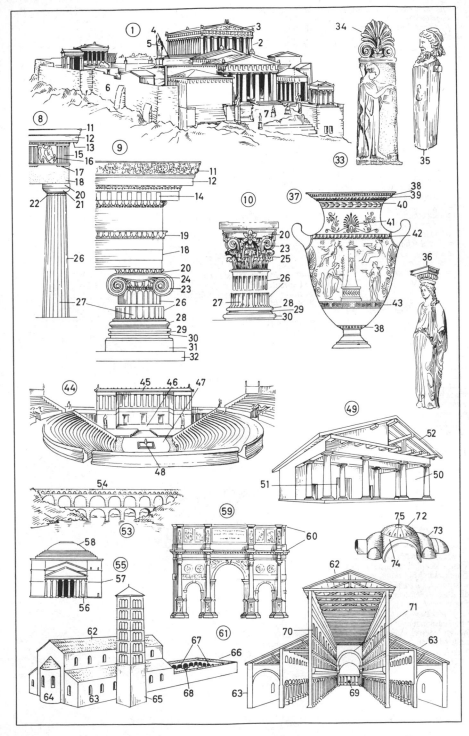

1-21 romanische Kunst *f* (Romanik)
- *Romanesque art*
1-13 die romanische Kirche, ein
Dom *m*
- *Romanesque church, a cathedral*
1 das Mittelschiff
- *nave*
2 das Seitenschiff
- *aisle*
3 das Querschiff (Querhaus)
- *transept*
4 der Chor
- *choir (chancel)*
5 die Apsis (Chornische)
- *apse*
6 der Vierungsturm
- *central tower*
(Am. *center tower)*
7 der Turmhelm
- *pyramidal tower roof*
8 die Zwergarkaden *f*
- *arcading*
9 der Rundbogenfries
- *frieze of round arcading*
10 die Blendarkade
- *blind arcade (blind arcading)*
11 die Lisene, ein senkrechter
Wandstreifen *m*
- *lesene, a pilaster strip*
12 das Rundfenster
- *circular window*
13 das Nebenportal (Seitenportal, die
Nebenpforte, Seitenpforte)
- *side entrance*
14-16 roman. Ornamente *n*
- *Romanesque ornamentation
(Romanesque decoration,
Romanesque decorative designs)*
14 das Schachbrettornament
- *chequered* (Am. *checkered) pattern
(chequered design)*
15 das Schuppenornament
- *imbrication (imbricated design)*
16 das Zackenornament
(Zickzackornament)
- *chevron design*
17 das roman. Wölbungssystem
- *Romanesque system of vaulting*
18 der Gurtbogen
- *transverse arch*
19 der Schildbogen
- *barrel vault (tunnel vault)*
20 der Pfeiler
- *pillar*
21 das Würfelkapitell
- *cushion capital*
22-41 gotische Kunst *f* (Gotik)
- *Gothic art*
22 die gotische Kirche [Westwerk *n*,
Westfassade *f*], ein Münster *n*
- *Gothic church [westwork, west end,
west façade], a cathedral*
23 die Rosette (Fensterrose)
- *rose window*
24 das Kirchenportal, ein
Gewändeportal *n*
- *church door (main door, portal), a
recessed portal*
25 die Archivolte
- *archivolt*
26 das Bogenfeld (Tympanon)
- *tympanum*
27-35 das got. Bausystem
- *Gothic structural system*
27-28 das Strebewerk
- *buttresses*

27 der Strebepfeiler
- *buttress*
28 der Strebebogen (Schwibbogen)
- *flying buttress*
29 die Fiale (das Pinakel), ein
Pfeileraufsatz *m*
- *pinnacle*
30 der Wasserspeier
- *gargoyle*
31-32 das Kreuzgewölbe
- *cross vault (groin vault)*
31 die Gewölberippen *f*
(Kreuzrippen)
- *ribs (cross ribs)*
32 der Schlußstein (Abhängling)
- *boss (pendant)*
33 das Triforium (der Laufgang)
- *triforium*
34 der Bündelpfeiler
- *clustered pier (compound pier)*
35 der Dienst
- *respond (engaged pillar)*
36 der Wimperg (Ziergiebel)
- *pediment*
37 die Kreuzblume
- *finial*
38 die Kriechblume (Krabbe)
- *crocket*
39-41 das Maßwerkfenster, ein
Lanzettfenster *n*
- *tracery window, a lancet window*
39-40 das Maßwerk
- *tracery*
39 der Vierpaß
- *quatrefoil*
40 der Fünfpaß
- *cinquefoil*
41 das Stabwerk
- *mullions*
42-54 Kunst *f* **der Renaissance**
- *Renaissance art*
42 die Renaissancekirche
- *Renaissance church*
43 der Risalit, ein vorspringender
Gebäudeteil *m* od. *n*
- *projection, a projecting part of the
building*
44 die Trommel (der Tambour)
- *drum*
45 die Laterne
- *lantern*
46 der Pilaster (Halbpfeiler)
- *pilaster (engaged pillar)*
47 der Renaissancepalast
- *Renaissance palace*
48 das Kranzgesims
- *cornice*
49 das Giebelfenster
- *pedimental window*
50 das Segmentfenster
- *pedimental window [with round
gable]*
51 das Bossenwerk (die Rustika)
- *rustication (rustic work)*
52 das Gurtgesims
- *string course*
53 der Sarkophag (die Tumba)
- *sarcophagus*
54 das Feston (die Girlande)
- *festoon (garland)*

1-8 Kunst ƒ **des Barocks** *m od. n*
- *Baroque art*
1 die Barockkirche
- *Baroque church*
2 das Ochsenauge
- *bull's eye*
3 die welsche Haube
- *bulbous cupola*
4 die Dachgaube
- *dormer window (dormer)*
5 der Volutengiebel
- *curved gable*
6 die gekuppelte Säule
- *twin columns*
7 die Kartusche
- *cartouche*
8 das Rollwerk
- *scrollwork*
9-13 die Kunst ƒ **des Rokokos** *n*
- *Rococo art*
9 die Rokokowand
- *Rococo wall*
10 die Volute, eine Hohlkehle
- *coving, a hollow moulding (Am. molding)*
11 das Rahmenwerk
- *framing*
12 die Sopraporte (Supraporte)
- *ornamental moulding (Am. molding)*
13 die Rocaille, ein Rokokoornament *n*
- *rocaille, a Rococo ornament*
14 der Tisch im Louis-seize-Stil *m*
- *table in Louis Seize style (Louis Seize table)*
15 das Bauwerk des Klassizismus *m* (im klassizistischen Stil *m*), ein Torbau *m*
- *neoclassical building (building in neoclassical style), a gateway*
16 der Empiretisch (Tisch im Empirestil *m*)
- *Empire table (table in the Empire style)*
17 das Biedermeiersofa (Sofa im Biedermeierstil *m*)
- *Biedermeier sofa (sofa in the Biedermeier style)*
18 der Lehnstuhl im Jugendstil *m*
- *Art Nouveau easy chair (easy chair in the Art Nouveau style)*
19-37 Bogenformen ƒ
- *types of arch*
19 der Bogen (Mauerbogen)
- *arch*
20 das Widerlager
- *abutment*
21 der Kämpfer (Kämpferstein)
- *impost*
22 der Anfänger, ein Keilstein *m*
- *springer, a voussoir (wedge stone)*
23 der Schlußstein
- *keystone*
24 das Haupt (die Stirn)
- *face*
25 die Leibung
- *pier*
26 der Rücken
- *extrados*
27 der Rundbogen
- *round arch*
28 der Flachbogen
- *segmental arch (basket handle)*
29 der Parabelbogen
- *parabolic arch*

30 der Hufeisenbogen
- *horseshoe arch*
31 der Spitzbogen
- *lancet arch*
32 der Dreipaßbogen (Kleeblattbogen)
- *trefoil arch*
33 der Schulterbogen
- *shouldered arch*
34 der Konvexbogen
- *convex arch*
35 der Vorhangbogen
- *tented arch*
36 der Kielbogen (Karniesbogen); ähnl.: Eselsrücken *m*
- *ogee arch (keel arch)*
37 der Tudorbogen
- *Tudor arch*
38-50 Gewölbeformen ƒ
- *types of vault*
38 das Tonnengewölbe
- *barrel vault (tunnel vault)*
39 die Kappe
- *crown*
40 die Wange
- *side*
41 das Klostergewölbe
- *cloister vault (cloistered vault)*
42 das Kreuzgratgewölbe
- *groin vault (groined vault)*
43 das Kreuzrippengewölbe
- *rib vault (ribbed vault)*
44 das Sterngewölbe
- *stellar vault*
45 das Netzgewölbe
- *net vault*
46 das Fächergewölbe
- *fan vault*
47 das Muldengewölbe
- *trough vault*
48 die Mulde
- *trough*
49 das Spiegelgewölbe
- *cavetto vault*
50 der Spiegel
- *cavetto*

1-6 chinesische Kunst *f*
- *Chinese art*
1 die Pagode (Stockwerkpagode), ein
  Tempelturm *m*
- *pagoda (multi-storey, multistory,*
  pagoda), a temple tower
2 das Stufendach
- *storey (story) roof*
  (roof of storey)
3 der Pailou, ein Ehrentor *n*
- *pailou (pailoo), a memorial*
  archway
4 der Durchgang
- *archway*
5 die Porzellanvase
- *porcelain vase*
6 die geschnittene Lackarbeit
- *incised lacquered work*
7-11 japanische Kunst *f*
- *Japanese art*
7 der Tempel
- *temple*
8 der Glockenturm
- *bell tower*
9 das Traggebälk
- *supporting structure*
10 der Bodhisattwa, ein
  buddhistischer Heiliger
- *bodhisattva (boddhisattva), a*
  Buddhist saint
11 das Torii, ein Tor *n*
- *torii, a gateway*
12-18 islamische Kunst *f*
- *Islamic art*
12 die Moschee
- *mosque*
13 das Minarett, ein Gebetsturm *m*
- *minaret, a prayer tower*
14 der Mikrab (die Betnische)
- *mihrab*
15 der Mimbar (Predigtstuhl)
- *minbar (mimbar, pulpit)*
16 das Mausoleum, eine Grabstätte
- *mausoleum, a tomb*
17 das Stalaktitengewölbe
- *stalactite vault (stalactitic vault)*
18 das arabische Kapitell
- *Arabian capital*
19-28 indische Kunst *f*
- *Indian art*
19 der tanzende Schiwa, ein indischer
  Gott
- *dancing Siva (Shiva), an Indian*
  god
20 die Buddhastatue
- *statue of Buddha*
21 der Stupa (die indische Pagode), ein
  Kuppelbau *m*, ein buddhistischer
  Sakralbau
- *stupa (Indian pagoda), a mound*
  (dome), a Buddhist shrine
22 der Schirm
- *umbrella*
23 der Steinzaun
- *stone wall (Am. stone fence)*
24 das Eingangstor
- *gate*
25 die Tempelanlage
- *temple buildings*
26 der Schikhara (Tempelturm)
- *shikara (sikar, sikhara, temple*
  tower)
27 die Tschaitjahalle
- *chaitya hall*
28 die Tschaitja, ein kleiner Stupa
- *chaitya, a small stupa*

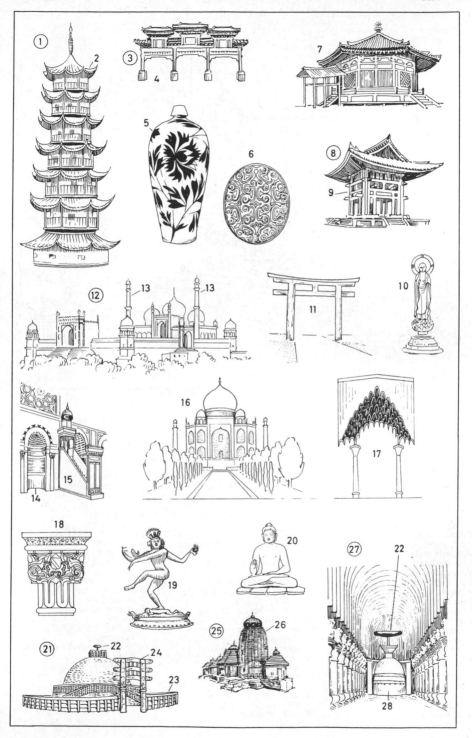

1-43 das Atelier (Studio)
- *studio*
1 das Atelierfenster
- *studio skylight*
2 der Kunstmaler, ein Künstler *m*
- *painter, an artist*
3 die Atelierstaffelei
- *studio easel*
4 die Kreideskizze, mit dem
Bildaufbau *m*
- *chalk sketch, with the composition
(rough draft)*
5 der Kreidestift
- *crayon (piece of chalk)*
6-19 Malutensilien *n; meist pl*
(Malgeräte *n*)
- *painting materials*
6 der Flachpinsel
- *flat brush*
7 der Haarpinsel
- *camel hair brush*
8 der Rundpinsel
- *round brush*
9 der Grundierpinsel
- *priming brush*
10 der Malkasten
- *box of paints (paintbox)*
11 die Farbtube mit Ölfarbe *f*
- *tube of oil paint*
12 der Firnis
- *varnish*
13 das Malmittel
- *thinner*

14 das Palettenmesser
- *palette knife*
15 der (die) Malspachtel
- *spatula*
16 der Kohlestift
- *charcoal pencil (charcoal, piece of
charcoal)*
17 die Temperafarbe (Gouachefarbe)
- *tempera (gouache)*
18 die Aquarellfarbe (Wasserfarbe)
- *watercolour (Am. watercolor)*
19 der Pastellstift
- *pastel crayon*
20 der Keilrahmen (Blendrahmen)
- *wedged stretcher (canvas stretcher)*
21 die Leinwand (das Malleinen)
- *canvas*
22 die Malpappe, mit dem Malgrund *m*
- *piece of hardboard, with painting
surface*
23 die Holzplatte
- *wooden board*
24 die Holzfaserplatte
(Preßholzplatte)
- *fibreboard (Am. fiberboard)*
25 der Maltisch
- *painting table*
26 die Feldstaffelei
- *folding easel*
27 das Stilleben, ein Motiv *n*
- *still life group, a motif*
28 die Handpalette
- *palette*

29 der Palettenstecker
- *palette dipper*
30 das (der) Podest
- *platform*
31 die Gliederpuppe
- *lay figure (mannequin, manikin)*
32 das Aktmodell (Modell, der Akt)
- *nude model (model, nude)*
33 der Faltenwurf
- *drapery*
34 der Zeichenbock
- *drawing easel*
35 der Zeichenblock (Skizzenblock)
- *sketch pad*
36 die Ölstudie
- *study in oils*
37 das Mosaik
- *mosaic (tessellation)*
38 die Mosaikfigur
- *mosaic figure*
39 die Mosaiksteine *m*
- *tesserae*
40 das Fresko (Wandbild)
- *fresco (mural)*
41 das Sgraffito (die Kratzmalerei, der
Kratzputz)
- *sgraffito*
42 der Putz
- *plaster*
43 der Entwurf
- *cartoon*

1-38 das Atelier
1 der Bildhauer
- *sculptor*
2 der Proportionszirkel
- *proportional dividers*
3 der Tastzirkel
- *calliper (caliper)*
4 das Gipsmodell, ein Gipsguß *m*
- *plaster model, a plaster cast*
5 der Steinblock (Rohstein)
- *block of stone (stone block)*
6 der Modelleur (Tonbildner)
- *modeller (Am. modeler)*
7 die Tonfigur, ein Torso *m*
- *clay figure, a torso*
8 die Tonrolle, eine Modelliermasse
- *roll of clay, a modelling (Am.
  modeling) substance*
9 der Modellierbock
- *modelling (Am. modeling) stand*
10 das Modellierholz
- *wooden modelling (Am. modeling)
  tool*
11 die Modellierschlinge
- *wire modelling (Am. modeling) tool*
12 das Schlagholz
- *beating wood*
13 das Zahneisen
- *claw chisel (toothed chisel, tooth
  chisel)*
14 das Schlageisen (der
   Kantenmeißel)
- *flat chisel*

15 das Punktiereisen
- *point (punch)*
16 der Eisenhammer
   (Handfäustel)
- *iron-headed hammer*
17 der Hohlbeitel
- *gouge (hollow chisel)*
18 das gekröpfte Eisen
- *spoon chisel*
19 der Kantbeitel, ein Stechbeitel *m*
- *wood chisel, a bevelled-edge chisel*
20 der Geißfuß
- *V-shaped gouge*
21 der Holzhammer (Schlegel)
- *mallet*
22 das Gerüst
- *framework*
23 die Fußplatte
- *baseboard*
24 das Gerüsteisen
- *armature support (metal rod)*
25 der Knebel (Reiter)
- *armature*
26 die Wachsplastik
- *wax model*
27 der Holzblock
- *block of wood*
28 der Holzbildhauer (Bildschnitzer)
- *wood carver (wood sculptor)*
29 der Sack mit Gipspulver *n* (Gips *m*)
- *sack of gypsum powder (gypsum)*
30 die Tonkiste
- *clay box*

31 der Modellierton (Ton)
- *modelling (Am. modeling) clay
  (clay)*
32 die Statue, eine Skulptur (Plastik)
- *statue, a sculpture*
33 das Flachrelief (Basrelief, Relief)
- *low relief (bas-relief)*
34 das Modellierbrett
- *modelling (Am. modeling) board*
35 das Drahtgerüst, ein Drahtgeflecht *n*
- *wire frame, wire netting*
36 das Rundmedaillon (Medaillon)
- *circular medallion (tondo)*
37 die Maske
- *mask*
38 die Plakette
- *plaque*

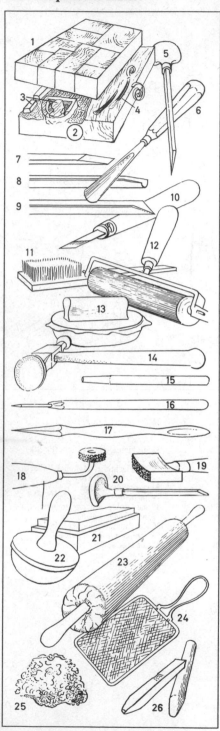

1-13 die Holzschneidekunst
(Xylographie, der Holzschnitt), ein
Hochdruckverfahren *n*
- *wood engraving (xylography), a
relief printing method (a letterpress
printing method)*
1 die Hirnholzplatte für Holzstich *m*,
ein Holzstock *m*
- *end-grain block for wood
engravings, a wooden block*
2 die Langholzplatte für Holzschnitt *m*,
eine Holzmodel
- *wooden plank for woodcutting, a
relief image carrier*
3 der Positivschnitt
- *positive cut*
4 der Langholzschnitt
- *plank cut*
5 der Konturenstichel (Linienstichel,
Spitzstichel)
- *burin (graver)*
6 das Rundeisen
- *U-shaped gouge*
7 das Flacheisen
- *scorper (scauper, scalper)*
8 das Hohleisen
- *scoop*
9 der Geißfuß
- *V-shaped gouge*
10 das Konturenmesser
- *contour knife*
11 die Handbürste
- *brush*
12 die Gelatinewalze
- *roller (brayer)*
13 der Reiber
- *pad (wiper)*
14-24 der Kupferstich
(die Chalkographie), ein
Tiefdruckverfahren *n*; *Arten:* die
Radierung, die Schabkunst (das
Mezzotinto), die Aquatinta, die
Kreidemanier (Krayonmanier)
- *copperplate engraving
(chalcography), an intaglio
process;* kinds: *etching, mezzotint,
aquatint, crayon engraving*
14 der Punzenhammer
- *hammer*
15 die Punze
- *burin*
16 die Radiernadel (Graviernadel)
- *etching needle (engraver)*
17 der Polierstahl, mit dem Schaber *m*
- *scraper and burnisher*
18 das Kornroulett (Punktroulett, der
Punktroller)
- *roulette*
19 das Wiegemesser (Wiegeeisen, die
Wiege, der Granierstahl)
- *rocking tool (rocker)*
20 der Rundstichel (Boll-,
Bolzstichel), ein Grabstichel *m*
- *round-headed graver, a graver (burin)*
21 der Ölstein
- *oilstone*
22 der Tampon (Einschwärzballen)
- *dabber (inking ball, ink ball)*
23 die Lederwalze
- *leather roller*
24 das Spritzsieb
- *sieve*
25-26 die Lithographie (der Steindruck),
ein Flachdruckverfahren *n*
- *lithography (stone lithography), a
planographic printing method*

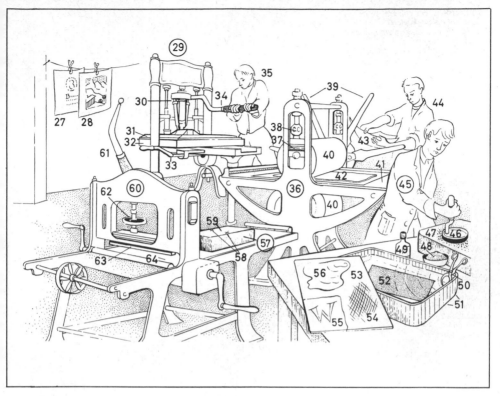

25 der Wasserschwamm (Schwamm),
    zum Anfeuchten *n* des
    Lithosteines *m*
  – *sponge for moistening the*
    lithographic stone
26 die Lithokreide (Fettkreide), eine
    Kreide
  – *lithographic crayons (greasy chalk)*
27-64 **die graphische Werkstatt**, eine
    Druckerei
  – ***graphic art studio,*** *a printing*
    office (Am. *printery*)
27 der Einblattdruck
  – *broadside (broadsheet, single sheet)*
28 der Mehrfarbendruck (Farbdruck,
    die Chromolithographie)
  – *full-colour* (Am. *full-color) print*
    (colour print, chromolithograph)
29 die Tiegeldruckpresse, eine
    Handpresse
  – *platen press, a hand press*
30 das Kniegelenk
  – *toggle*
31 der Tiegel, eine Preßplatte
  – *platen*
32 die Druckform
  – *type forme* (Am. *form)*
33 die Durchziehkurbel
  – *feed mechanism*
34 der Bengel
  – *bar (devil's tail)*
35 der Drucker
  – *pressman*

36 die Kupferdruckpresse
  – *copperplate press*
37 die Pappzwischenlage
  – *tympan*
38 der Druckregler
  – *pressure regulator*
39 das Sternrad
  – *star wheel*
40 die Walze
  – *cylinder*
41 der Drucktisch
  – *bed*
42 das Filztuch
  – *felt cloth*
43 der Probeabzug (Probedruck,
    Andruck)
  – *proof (pull)*
44 der Kupferstecher
  – *copperplate engraver*
45 der Lithograph,
    beim Steinschliff *m*
  – *lithographer (litho artist), grinding*
    the stone
46 die Schleifscheibe
  – *grinding disc (disk)*
47 die Körnung
  – *grain (granular texture)*
48 der Glassand
  – *pulverized glass*
49 die Gummilösung
  – *rubber solution*
50 die Greifzange
  – *tongs*

51 das Ätzbad, zum Ätzen *n* der
    Radierung
  – *etching bath for etching*
52 die Zinkplatte
  – *zinc plate*
53 die polierte Kupferplatte
  – *polished copperplate*
54 die Kreuzlage
  – *cross hatch*
55 der Ätzgrund
  – *etching ground*
56 der Deckgrund
  – *non-printing area*
57 der Lithostein
  – *lithographic stone*
58 die Paßzeichen *n* (Nadelzeichen)
  – *register marks*
59 die Bildplatte
  – *printing surface (printing image*
    carrier)
60 die Steindruckpresse
  – *lithographic press*
61 der Druckhebel
  – *lever*
62 die Reiberstellung
  – *scraper adjustment*
63 der Reiber
  – *scraper*
64 das Steinbett
  – *bed*

1-20 Schriften *f* der Völker *n*
- *scripts of various peoples*
1 altägyptische Hieroglyphen *f*, eine Bilderschrift
- *ancient Egyptian hieroglyphics, a pictorial system of writing*
2 arabisch
- *Arabic*
3 armenisch
- *Armenian*
4 georgisch
- *Georgian*
5 chinesisch
- *Chinese*
6 japanisch
- *Japanese*
7 hebräisch
- *Hebrew (Hebraic)*
8 Keilschrift *f*
- *cuneiform script*
9 Devanagari *n* (die Schrift des Sanskrit *n*)
- *Devanagari, script employed in Sanskrit*
10 siamesisch
- *Siamese*
11 tamulisch (Tamul *n*)
- *Tamil*
12 tibetisch
- *Tibetan*
13 Sinaischrift *f*
- *Sinaitic script*
14 phönizisch
- *Phoenician*
15 griechisch
- *Greek*
16 lateinische (romanische) Kapitalis *f* (Kapitalschrift)
- *Roman capitals*
17 Unzialis *f* (Unziale, Unzialschrift)
- *uncial (uncials, uncial script)*
18 karolingische Minuskel *f*
- *Carolingian (Carlovingian, Caroline) minuscule*
19 Runen *f*
- *runes*
20 russisch
- *Russian*
21-26 alte **Schreibgeräte** *n*
- *ancient writing implements*
21 indischer Stahlgriffel *m*, ein Ritzer *m* für Palmblattschrift *f*
- *Indian steel stylus for writing on palm leaves*
22 altägyptischer Schreibstempel *m*, eine Binsenrispe
- *ancient Egyptian reed pen*
23 Rohrfeder *f*
- *writing cane*
24 Schreibpinsel *m*
- *brush*
25 römische Metallfeder *f* (Stilus *m*)
- *Roman metal pen (stylus)*
26 Gänsefeder *f*
- *quill (quill pen)*

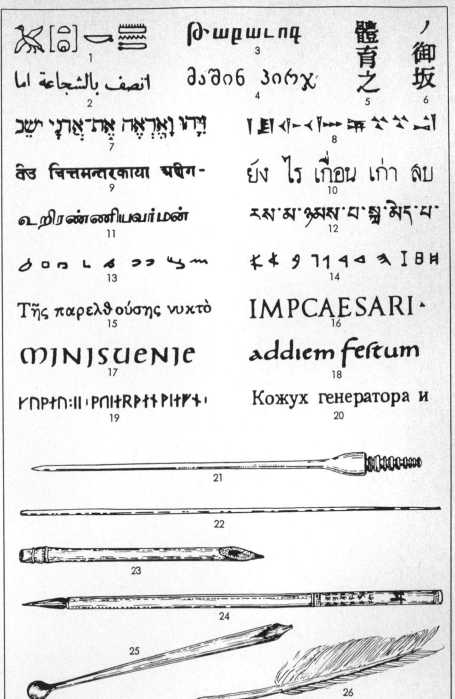

1-20: scripts
21-26: writing implements

1-15 Schriften *f*
- *types (type faces)*
1 die gotische Schrift
- *Gothic type (German black-letter type)*
2 die Schwabacher Schrift (Schwabacher)
- *Schwabacher type (German black-letter type)*
3 die Fraktur
- *Fraktur (German black-letter type)*
4 die Renaissanceantiqua (Mediaeval)
- *Humanist (Mediaeval)*
5 die vorklassizistische Antiqua (Barockantiqua)
- *Transitional*
6 die klassizistische Antiqua
- *Didone*
7 die Grotesk (Groteskschrift)
- *Sanserif (Sanserif type, Grotesque)*
8 die Egyptienne
- *Egyptian*
9 die Schreibmaschinenschrift
- *typescript (typewriting)*
10 die englische Schreibschrift
- *English hand (English handwriting, English writing)*
11 die deutsche Schreibschrift
- *German hand (German handwriting, German writing)*
12 die lateinische Schreibschrift
- *Latin script*
13 die Kurzschrift (Stenographie)
- *shorthand (shorthand writing, stenography)*
14 die Lautschrift (phonetische Umschrift)
- *phonetics (phonetic transcription)*
15 die Blindenschrift
- *Braille*
16-29 Satzzeichen *n*
- *punctuation marks (stops)*
16 der Punkt
- *full stop (period, full point)*
17 der Doppelpunkt (das Kolon)
- *colon*
18 das Komma
- *comma*
19 der Strichpunkt (das Semikolon)
- *semicolon*
20 das Fragezeichen
- *question mark (interrogation point, interrogation mark)*
21 das Ausrufezeichen
- *exclamation mark (Am. exclamation point)*
22 der Apostroph
- *apostrophe*
23 der Gedankenstrich
- *dash (em rule)*
24 die runden Klammern *f*
- *parentheses (round brackets)*
25 die eckigen Klammern *f*
- *square brackets*
26 das Anführungszeichen (die Anführungsstriche *m*, ugs. die Gänsefüßchen *n*)
- *quotation mark (double quotation marks, paired quotation marks, inverted commas)*
27 das französische Anführungszeichen
- *guillemet (French quotation mark)*
28 der Bindestrich
- *hyphen*

29 die Fortführungspunkte *m*
- *marks of omission (ellipsis)*
30-35 Akzente *m* **und Aussprachezeichen** *n*
- *accents and diacritical marks (diacritics)*
30 der Accent aigu (der Akut)
- *acute accent (acute)*
31 der Accent grave (der Gravis)
- *grave accent (grave)*
32 der Accent circonflexe (der Zirkumflex)
- *circumflex accent (circumflex)*
33 die Cedille [unter c]
- *cedilla [under c]*
34 das Trema [über e]
- *diaeresis (Am. dieresis) [over e]*
35 die Tilde [über n]
- *tilde [over n]*
36 das Paragraphenzeichen
- *section mark*
37-70 die Zeitung, eine überregionale Tageszeitung
- *newspaper, a national daily newspaper*
37 die Zeitungsseite
- *newspaper page*
38 die Frontseite
- *front page*
39 der Zeitungskopf
- *newspaper heading*
40 die Kopfleiste mit dem Impressum *n*
- *head rules and imprint*
41 der Untertitel
- *subheading*
42 das Ausgabedatum
- *date of publication*
43 die Postzeitungsnummer
- *Post Office registration number*
44 die Schlagzeile (Artikelüberschrift)
- *headline*
45 die Spalte
- *column*
46 die Spaltenüberschrift
- *column heading*
47 die Spaltenlinie
- *column rule*
48 der Leitartikel
- *leading article (leader, editorial)*
49 der Artikelhinweis
- *reference to related article*
50 die Kurznachricht
- *brief news item*
51 der politische Teil
- *political section*
52 die Seitenüberschrift
- *page heading*
53 die Karikatur
- *cartoon*
54 der Korrespondentenbericht
- *report by newspaper's own correspondent*
55 das Agentursignum
- *news agency's sign*
56 die Werbeanzeige (ugs. Reklame *f*)
- *advertisement (coll. ad)*
57 der Sportteil
- *sports section*
58 das Pressefoto
- *press photo*
59 die Bildunterschrift
- *caption*
60 der Sportbericht
- *sports report*
61 die Sportnachricht
- *sports news item*

62 der überregionale Teil
- *home and overseas news section*
63 die vermischten Nachrichten *f*
- *news in brief (miscellaneous news)*
64 das Fernsehprogramm (die Programmvorschau)
- *television programmes (Am. programs)*
65 der Wetterbericht
- *weather report*
66 die Wetterkarte
- *weather chart (weather map)*
67 der Feuilletonteil (das Feuilleton)
- *arts section (feuilleton)*
68 die Todesanzeige
- *death notice*
69 der Anzeigenteil (Annoncenteil)
- *advertisements (classified advertising)*
70 die Stellenanzeige, ein Stellenangebot *n*
- *job advertisement, a vacancy (a situation offered)*

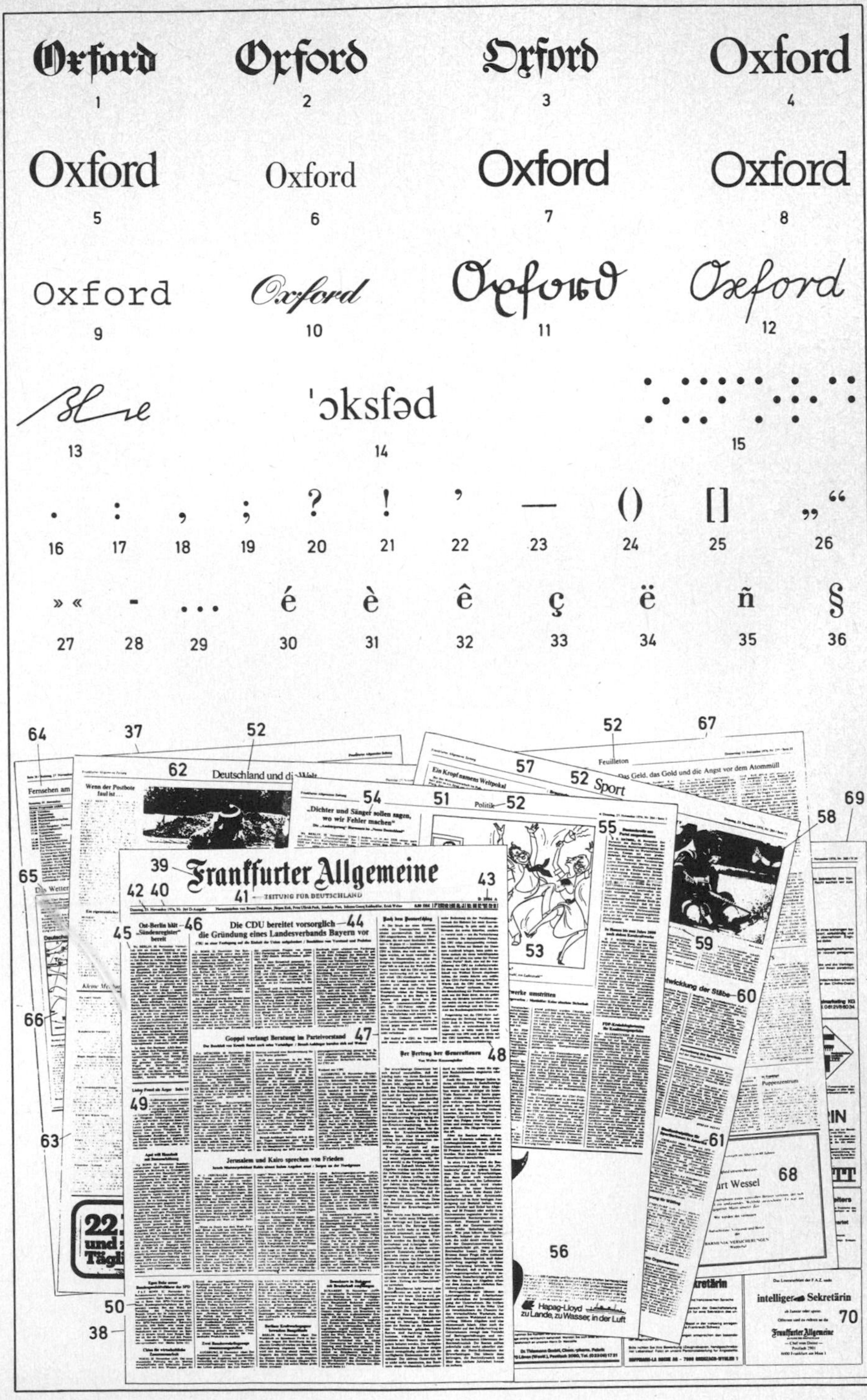
Oxford 1
Oxford 2
Oxford 3
Oxford 4
Oxford 5
Oxford 6
Oxford 7
Oxford 8
Oxford 9
Oxford 10
Oxford 11
Oxford 12
13
ˈɔksfəd 14
15
. 16
: 17
, 18
; 19
? 20
! 21
’ 22
— 23
() 24
[] 25
„“ 26
»« 27
- 28
... 29
é 30
è 31
ê 32
ç 33
ë 34
ñ 35
§ 36
Frankfurter Allgemeine
ZEITUNG FÜR DEUTSCHLAND
Die CDU bereitet vorsorglich die Gründung eines Landesverbands Bayern vor
Ost-Berlin hält „Sündenregister“ bereit
Goppel verlangt Beratung im Parteivorstand
Jerusalem und Kairo sprechen von Frieden
Der Vertrag der Generationen
Deutschland und die Welt
Wenn der Postbote faul ist ...
„Dichter und Sänger sollen sagen, wo wir Fehler machen“
Politik
Ein Kropf namens Weltpokal
Sport
Feuilleton
Das Geld, das Gold und die Angst vor dem Atommüll
Fernsehen am
Das Wetter
Puppenzentrum
Hapag-Lloyd
zu Lande, zu Wasser, in der Luft
Sekretärin
intelligente Sekretärin
Frankfurter Allgemeine
37 38 39 40 41 42 43 44 45 46 47 48 49 50 51 52 53 54 55 56 57 58 59 60 61 62 63 64 65 66 67 68 69 70

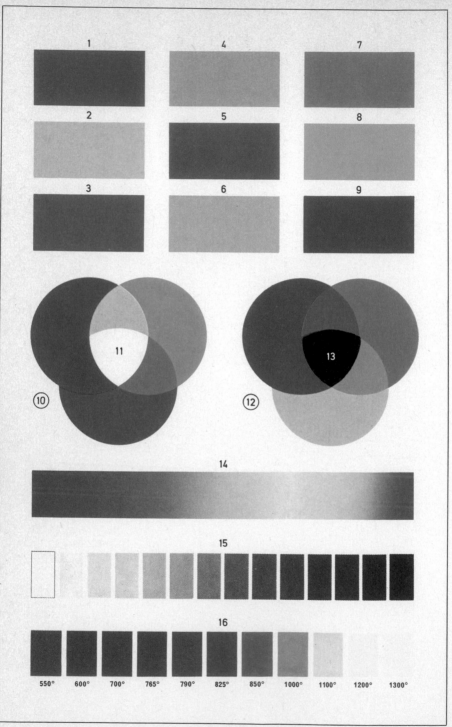

1 rot
- *red*
2 gelb
- *yellow*
3 blau
- *blue*
4 rosa
- *pink*
5 braun
- *brown*
6 himmelblau
- *azure (sky blue)*
7 orange
- *orange*
8 grün
- *green*
9 violett
- *violet*
10 die additive Farbmischung
- *additive mixture of colours*
  (Am. *colors)*
11 weiß
- *white*
12 die subtraktive Farbmischung
- *subtractive mixture of colours*
  (Am. *colors)*
13 schwarz
- *black*
14 das Sonnenspektrum
  (die Regenbogenfarben *f)*
- *solar spectrum (colours,* Am. *colors,*
  of the rainbow)
15 die Grauleiter (der Stufengraukeil)
- *grey (Am. gray) scale*
16 die Glühfarben *f*
- *heat colours (Am. colors)*

① I II III IV V VI VII VIII IX X
② 1 2 3 4 5 6 7 8 9 10

① XX XXX XL XLIX IL L LX LXX LXXX XC
② 20 30 40 49 50 60 70 80 90

① XCIX IC C CC CCC CD D DC DCC DCCC
② 99 100 200 300 400 500 600 700 800

① CM CMXC M
② 900 990 1000

③ 9658 ④ 5 kg. ⑤ 2 ⑥ 2. ⑦ +5 ⑧ −5

1-26 Arithmetik *f*
- *arithmetic*
1-22 die Zahl
- *numbers*
1 die römischen Ziffern *f* (Zahlzeichen *n*)
- *Roman numerals*
2 die arabischen Ziffern *f*
- *Arabic numerals*
3 die reine (unbenannte) Zahl, eine vierstellige Zahl [8: die Einerstelle, 5: die Zehnerstelle, 6: die Hunderterstelle, 9: die Tausenderstelle]
- *abstract number, a four-figure number [8: units; 5: tens; 6: hundreds; 9: thousands]*
4 die benannte Zahl
- *concrete number*
5 die Grundzahl (Kardinalzahl)
- *cardinal number (cardinal)*
6 die Ordnungszahl (Ordinalzahl)
- *ordinal number (ordinal)*
7 die positive Zahl [mit dem positiven Vorzeichen *n*]
- *positive number [with plus sign n]*
8 die negative Zahl [mit dem negativen Vorzeichen *n*]
- *negative number [with minus sign]*
9 allgemeine Zahlen *f*
- *algebraic symbols*

10 die gemischte Zahl [3: die ganze Zahl, ⅓ der Bruch (die Bruchzahl, gebrochene Zahl, ein Zahlenbruch *m*)]
- *mixed number [3: whole number (integer); ⅓: fraction]*
11 gerade Zahlen *f*
- *even numbers*
12 ungerade Zahlen *f*
- *odd numbers*
13 Primzahlen *f*
- *prime numbers*
14 die komplexe Zahl [3: die reelle Zahl, 2 √−1̄ : die imaginäre Zahl]
- *complex number [3: real part; 2√−1̄ : imaginary part)*
15-16 gemeine Brüche *m*
- *vulgar fractions*
15 der echte Bruch [2: der Zähler, der Bruchstrich, 3: der Nenner]
- *proper fraction [2: numerator, horizontal line; 3: denominator]*
16 der unechte Bruch, zugleich der Kehrwert (reziproke Wert) von 15
- *improper fraction, also the reciprocal of item 15*
17 der Doppelbruch
- *compound fraction (complex fraction)*
18 der uneigentliche Bruch [ergibt beim „Kürzen" *n* eine ganze Zahl]
- *improper fraction [when cancelled down produces a whole number]*

19 ungleichnamige Brüche *m* [35: der Hauptnenner (gemeinsame Nenner)]
- *fractions of different denominations [35: common denominator*
20 der endliche Dezimalbruch (Zehnerbruch) mit Komma *n* und Dezimalstellen *f* [3: die Zehntel *n*, 5: die Hundertstel, 7: die Tausendstel]
- *proper decimal fraction with decimal point [in German: comma] and decimal places [3: tenths; 5: hundredths; 7: thousandths]*
21 der unendliche periodische Dezimalbruch
- *recurring decimal*
22 die Periode
- *recurring decimal*
23-26 das Rechnen (die Grundrechnungsarten *f*)
- *fundamental arithmetical operations*
23 das Zusammenzählen (Addieren, die Addition); [3 u. 2: die Summanden *m*, +: das Pluszeichen, =: das Gleichheitszeichen, 5: die Summe (das Ergebnis, Resultat)]
- *addition (adding) [3 and 2: the terms of the sum; +: plus sign; =: equals sign, : 5: the sum]*

⑨ a,b,c... ⑩ $3\frac{1}{3}$ ⑪ 2,4,6,8 ⑫ 1,3,5,7

⑬ 3,5,7,11 ⑭ $3+2\sqrt{-1}$ ⑮ $\frac{2}{3}$ ⑯ $\frac{3}{2}$

⑰ $\dfrac{\frac{5}{6}}{\frac{3}{4}}$ ⑱ $\frac{12}{4}$ ⑲ $\frac{4}{5}+\frac{2}{7}=\frac{38}{35}$ ⑳ 0,357

㉑ $0,6666....=0,\overline{6}$ ㉒ ㉓ $3+2=5$

㉔ $3-2=1$ ㉕ $3\cdot2=6$ ㉖ $6:2=3$

$3\times2=6$

in Britain:

⑥ 2nd ⑳ 0·357 ㉑ $0·6666...=0·\overline{6}$ ㉒

㉖ $6\div2=3$

---

24 das Abziehen (Subtrahieren, die
Subtraktion); [3: der Minuend, −:
das Minuszeichen,
2: der Subtrahend, 1: der Rest
(die Differenz)]
- *subtraction (subtracting); [3: the*
minuend; − : minus sign; 2: the
subtrahend; 1: the remainder
(difference)]

25 das Vervielfachen (Malnehmen,
Multiplizieren, die
Multiplikation); [3: der
Multiplikand, · od. ×: das
Malzeichen, 2: der Multiplikator, 2
u. 3: Faktoren *m*, 6: das Produkt]
- *multiplication (multiplying); [3: the*
multiplicand; × (in German ·):
multiplication sign; 2: the
multiplier; 2 and 3: factors; 6: the
product]

26 das Teilen (Dividieren, die
Division); [6: der Dividend (die
Teilungszahl), : = das
Divisionszeichen, 2: der Teiler
(Divisor), 3: der Quotient
(Teilwert)]
- *division (dividing); [6: the dividend:*
÷ (in German :): division sign; 2: the
divisor; 3: the quotient

① $3^2 = 9$ ② $\sqrt[3]{8} = 2$ ③ $\sqrt{4} = 2$

④ $3x + 2 = 12$

⑤ $4a + 6ab - 2ac = 2a\,(2 + 3b - c)$ ⑥ $\log_{10} 3 = 0{,}4771$

oder $\lg 3 = 0{,}4771$

⑦ $\dfrac{k\,[1000\,\text{DM}]\cdot\ p\,[5\,\%]\cdot\ t\,[2\,\text{Jahre}]}{100} = z\,[100\,\text{DM}]$

in Britain:

⑥ $\log_{10} 3 = 0\cdot 4771$

1-24 Arithmetik *f*
– *arithmetic*
1-10 höhere Rechnungsarten *f*
– **advanced arithmetical operations**
1 die Potenzrechnung
  (das Potenzieren); [3 hoch 2: die Potenz,
  3: die Basis, 2: der Exponent (die
  Hochzahl), 9: der Potenzwert]
– *raising to a power [three squared
  (3^2): the power; 3: the base; 2: the
  exponent (index); 9: value of the
  power]*
2 die Wurzelrechnung
  (das Radizieren, das Wurzelziehen);
  [3.Wurzel *f* aus 8: die Kubikwurzel,
  8: der Radikand (die Grundzahl),
  3: der Wurzelexponent
  (Wurzelgrad), √ : das Wurzelzeichen,
  2: der Wurzelwert]
– *evolution (extracting a root);
  [cube root of 8: cube root; 8: the
  radical; 3: the index (degree) of the
  root; √ : radical sign; 2: value of
  the root]*
3 die Quadratwurzel (Wurzel)
– *square root*
4-5 die Buchstabenrechnung (Algebra)
– *algebra*
4 die Bestimmungsgleichung [3, 2:
  die Koeffizienten *m*, x: die Unbekannte]
– *simple equation [3, 2: the
  coefficients; x: the unknown
  quantity]*

5 die identische Gleichung
  (Identität, Formel); [a, b, c: die
  allgemeinen Zahlen *f*]
– *identical equation; [a, b, c:
  algebraic symbols]*
6 die Logarithmenrechnung (das
  Logarithmieren); [log: das Zeichen
  für den Logarithmus, lg: das Zeichen
  für den Zehnerlogarithmus, 3: der
  Numerus, 10: die Grundzahl
  (Basis), 0: die Kennziffer, 4771: die
  Mantisse, 0,4771: der Logarithmus]
– *logarithmic calculation (taking the
  logarithm, log); [log: logarithm
  sign; 3: number whose logarithm is
  required; 10: the base; 0: the
  characteristic; 4771: the mantissa;
  0.4771: the logarithm]*
7 die Zinsrechnung; [k: das Kapital
  (der Grundwert), p: der Zinsfuß
  (Prozentsatz, Hundertsatz), t: die
  Zeit, z: die Zinsen *pl* (Prozente *n*,
  der Zins, Gewinn), %: das
  Prozentzeichen]
– *simple interest formula; [P: the
  principal; R: rate of interest; T:
  time; I: interest (profit); % :
  percentage sign]*
8-10 die Schlußrechnung
  (Dreisatzrechnung, Regeldetri);
  [≙: entspricht]
– *rule of three (rule-of-three sum,
  simple proportion)*

8 der Ansatz mit der Unbekannten x
– *statement with the unknown
  quantity x*
9 die Gleichung
  (Bestimmungsgleichung)
– *equation (conditional equation) .*
10 die Lösung
– *solution*
11-14 höhere Mathematik
– **higher mathematics**
11 die arithmetische Reihe mit den
  Gliedern *n* 2, 4, 6, 8
– *arithmetical series with the
  elements 2, 4, 6, 8*
12 die geometrische Reihe
– *geometrical series*
13-14 die Infinitesimalrechnung
– *infinitesimal calculus*
13 der Differentialquotient (die
  Ableitung); [dx, dy: die
  Differentiale *n*, d: das
  Differentialzeichen]
– *derivative [dx, dy: the differentials;
  d: differential sign]*
14 das Integral (die Integration); [x:
  die Veränderliche (der Integrand),
  C: die Integrationskonstante, *∫* das
  Integralzeichen, dx: das
  Differential]
– *integral (integration); [x: the
  variable; C: constant of
  integration; ∫: the integral sign;
  dx: the differential]*

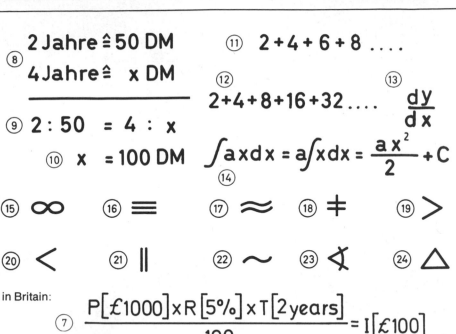

⑧ 2 Jahre ≙ 50 DM
  4 Jahre ≙ x DM

⑨ 2 : 50 = 4 : x

⑩ x = 100 DM

⑪ 2 + 4 + 6 + 8 . . . .

⑫ 2 + 4 + 8 + 16 + 32 . . . .

⑬ $\dfrac{dy}{dx}$

⑭ $\displaystyle\int a\,x\,dx = a\!\int x\,dx = \dfrac{a\,x^{2}}{2} + C$

⑮ ∞   ⑯ ≡   ⑰ ≈   ⑱ ≠   ⑲ >

⑳ <   ㉑ ∥   ㉒ ∼   ㉓ ∢   ㉔ △

in Britain:

⑦ $\dfrac{P\,[£1000] \times R\,[5\%] \times T\,[2\,years]}{100} = I\,[£100]$

㉓ ∢

15-24 mathematische Zeichen *n*
- *mathematical symbols*
15 unendlich
- *infinity*
16 identisch (das Identitätszeichen)
- *identically equal to (the sign of identity)*
17 annähernd gleich
- *approximately equal to*
18 ungleich (das Ungleichheitszeichen)
- *unequal to*
19 größer als
- *greater than*
20 kleiner als
- *less than*
21-24 geometrische Zeichen *n*
- *geometrical symbols*
21 parallel (das Parallelitätszeichen)
- *parallel (sign of parallelism)*
22 ähnlich (das Ähnlichkeitszeichen)
- *similar to (sign of similarity)*
23 das Winkelzeichen
- *angle symbol*
24 das Dreieckszeichen
- *triangle symbol*

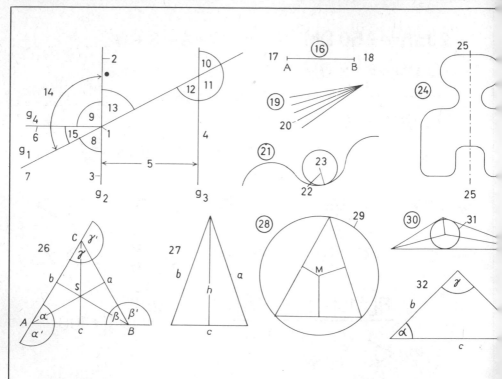

1-58 die Planimetrie (elementare, euklidische Geometrie)
- *plane geometry (elementary geometry, Euclidian geometry)*

1-23 Punkt *m*, **Linie** *f*, **Winkel** *m*
- *point, line, angle*

1 der Punkt [Schnittpunkt von g_1 und g_2], der Scheitelpunkt von 8
- *point [point of intersection of g_1 and g_2], the angular point of 8*

2, 3 die Gerade g_2
- *straight line g_2*

4 die Parallele zu g_2
- *the parallel to g_2*

5 der Abstand der Geraden *f* g_2 und g_3
- *distance between the straight lines g_2 and g_3*

6 die Senkrechte (g_4) auf g_2
- *perpendicular (g_4) on g_2*

7, 3 die Schenkel *m* von 8
- *the arms of 8*

8, 13 Scheitelwinkel *m*
- *vertically opposite angles*

8 der Winkel
- *angle*

9 der rechte Winkel [90]
- *right angle [90°]*

10, 11, 12 der überstumpfe Winkel
- *reflex angle*

10 der spitze Winkel, zugl. Wechselwinkel zu 8
- *acute angle, also the alternate angle to 8*

11 der stumpfe Winkel
- *obtuse angle*

12 der Gegenwinkel zu 8
- *corresponding angle to 8*

13, 9, 15 der gestreckte Winkel [180°]
- *straight angle [180°]*

14 der Nebenwinkel; *hier:* Supplementwinkel *m* zu 13
- *adjacent angle; here: supplementary angle to 13*

15 der Komplementwinkel zu 8
- *complementary angle to 8*

16 die Strecke AB
- *straight line AB*

17 der Endpunkt A
- *end A*

18 der Endpunkt B
- *end B*

19 das Strahlenbündel
- *pencil of rays*

20 der Strahl
- *ray*

21 die krumme (gekrümmte) Linie
- *curved line*

22 ein Krümmungshalbmesser *m*
- *radius of curvature*

23 ein Krümmungsmittelpunkt *m*
- *centre* (Am. *center*) *of curvature*

24-58 die ebenen Flächen *f*
- *plane surfaces*

24 die symmetrische Figur
- *symmetrical figure*

25 die Symmetrieachse
- *axis of symmetry*

26-32 Dreiecke *n*
- *plane triangles*

26 das gleichseitige Dreieck; [A, B, C die Eckpunkte *m*; a, b, c die Seiten *f*; α (Alpha), β (Beta), γ (Gamma) die Innenwinkel *m*; α', β', γ' die Außenwinkel *m*; S der Schwerpunkt]
- *equilateral triangle; [A, B, C: the vertices; a, b, c: the sides; α (alpha), β (beta), γ (gamma): the interior angles; α', β', γ': the exterior angles; S: the centre (Am. center)]*

27 das gleichschenklige Dreieck: [a, b die Schenkel *m*; c die Basis (Grundlinie), h die Achse, eine Höhe]
- *isosceles triangle [a, b: the sides (legs); c: the base; h: the perpendicular, an altitude]*

28 das spitzwinklige Dreieck mit den Mittelsenkrechten *f*
- *acute-angled triangle with perpendicular bisectors of the sides*

29 der Umkreis
- *circumcircle (circumscribed circle)*

30 das stumpfwinklige Dreieck mit den Winkelhalbierenden *f*
- *obtuse-angled triangle with bisectors of the angles*

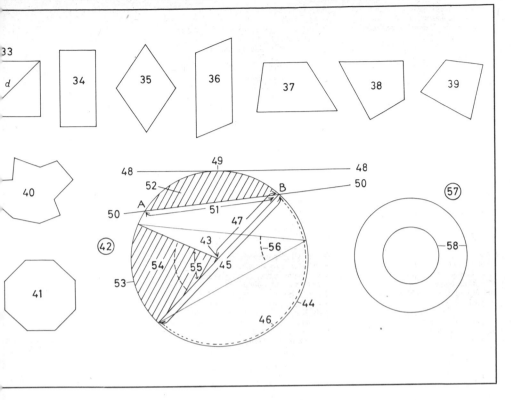

31 der Inkreis
- *inscribed circle*
32 das rechtwinklige Dreieck und die trigonometrischen Winkelfunktionen f; [a, b die Katheten f; c die Hypotenuse; γ der rechte Winkel; $a{:}c = \sin\alpha$ (Sinus); $b{:}c = \cos\alpha$ (Kosinus); $a{:}b = \operatorname{tg}\alpha$ (Tangens); $b{:}a = \operatorname{ctg}\alpha$ (Kotangens)]
- *right-angled triangle and the trigonometrical functions of angles; [a, b: the catheti; c: the hypotenuse; γ; the right angle; $\frac{a}{c} = \sin\alpha$ (sine); $\frac{b}{c} = \cos\alpha$ (cosine); $\frac{a}{b} = \tan\alpha$ (tangent); $\frac{b}{a} = \cot\alpha$ (cotangent)]*
33-39 **Vierecke** *n*
- *quadrilaterals*
33-36 **Parallelogramme** *n*
- *parallelograms*
33 das Quadrat [d eine Diagonale]
- *square [d: a diagonal]*
34 das Rechteck
- *rectangle*
35 der Rhombus (die Raute)
- *rhombus (rhomb, lozenge)*
36 das Rhomboid
- *rhomboid*
37 das Trapez
- *trapezium*
38 das Deltoid (der Drachen)
- *deltoid (kite)*
39 das unregelmäßige Viereck
- *irregular quadrilateral*
40 das Vieleck
- *polygon*
41 das regelmäßige Vieleck
- *regular polygon*
42 **der Kreis**
- *circle*
43 der Mittelpunkt (das Zentrum)
- *centre (Am. center)*
44 der Umfang (die Peripherie, Kreislinie)
- *circumference (periphery)*
45 der Durchmesser
- *diameter*
46 der Halbkreis
- *semicircle*
47 der Halbmesser (Radius, r)
- *radius (r)*
48 die Tangente
- *tangent*
49 der Berührungspunkt (P)
- *point of contact (P)*
50 die Sekante
- *secant*
51 die Sehne AB
- *the chord AB*
52 das Segment (der Kreisabschnitt)
- *segment*
53 der Kreisbogen
- *arc*
54 der Sektor (Kreisausschnitt)
- *sector*
55 der Mittelpunktswinkel (Zentriwinkel)
- *angle subtended by the arc at the centre (Am. center) (centre, Am. center, angle)*
56 der Umfangswinkel (Peripheriewinkel)
- *circumferential angle*
57 der Kreisring
- *ring (annulus)*
58 konzentrische Kreise *m*
- *concentric circles*

1 das rechtwinklige
   Koordinatensystem
- *system of right-angled coordinates*
2-3 das Achsenkreuz
- *axes of coordinates (coordinate
   axes)*
2 die Abszissenachse (x-Achse)
- *axis of abscissae (x-axis)*
3 die Ordinatenachse (y-Achse)
- *axis of ordinates (y-axis)*
4 der Koordinatennullpunkt
- *origin of ordinates*
5 der Quadrant [I-IV der 1. bis
   4.Quadrant]
- *quadrant [I - IV: 1st to 4th
   quadrant]*
6 die positive Richtung
- *positive direction*
7 die negative Richtung
- *negative direction*
8 die Punkte m[P_1 und P_2 im
   Koordinatensystem n; x_1 und y_1
   [bzw. x_2 und y_2 ihre Koordinaten f
- *points [P_1 and P_2] in the system of
   coordinates; x_1 and y_1 [and x_2 and
   y_2 respectively] their coordinates*
9 der Abszissenwert [x_1 bzw. x_2 (die
   Abszissen f)
- *values of the abscissae [x_1 and x_2]
   (the abscissae)*
10 der Ordinatenwert [y_1 bzw. y_2] (die
   Ordinaten f)
- *values of the ordinates [y_1 and y_2]
   (the ordinates)*
11-29 **die Kegelschnitte** m
- *conic sections*
11 **die Kurven** f im
   Koordinatensystem n
- *curves in the system of coordinates*
12 lineare Kurven f[a die Steigung der
   Kurve, b der Ordinatendurchgang
   der Kurve, c die Wurzel der Kurve]
- *plane curves [a: the gradient (slope)
   of the curve; b: the ordinates'
   intersection of the curve; c: the root
   of the curve]*
13 gekrümmte Kurven f
- *inflected curves*
14 **die Parabel,** eine Kurve zweiten
   Grades m
- *parabola, a curve of the second
   degree*
15 die Äste m der Parabel
- *branches of the parabola*
16 der Scheitelpunkt (Scheitel) der
   Parabel
- *vertex of the parabola*
17 die Achse der Parabel
- *axis of the parabola*
18 **eine Kurve dritten Grades** m
- *a curve of the third degree*
19 das Kurvenmaximum
- *maximum of the curve*
20 das Kurvenminimum
- *minimum of the curve*
21 der Wendepunkt
- *point of inflexion (of inflection)*
22 **die Ellipse**
- *ellipse*
23 die große Achse
- *transverse axis (major axis)*
24 die kleine Achse
- *conjugate axis (minor axis)*
25 Die Brennpunkte m der Ellipse
   [F_1 und F_2]
- *foci of the ellipse [F_1 and F_2],*

26 **die Hyperbel**
- *hyperbola*
27 die Brennpunkte m [F_1 u. F_2]
- *foci [F_1 and F_2]*
28 die Scheitelpunkte m [S_1 u. S_2]
- *vertices [S_1 and S_2]*
29 die Asymptoten f [a und b]
- *asymptotes [a and b]*
30-46 **geometrische Körper** m
- *solids*
30 der Würfel
- *cube*
31 das Quadrat, eine Fläche
- *square, a plane (plane surface)*
32 die Kante
- *edge*
33 die Ecke
- *corner*
34 die Säule (das quadratische Prisma)
- *quadratic prism*
35 die Grundfläche
- *base*
36 der Quader
- *parallelepiped*
37 das Dreikantprisma
- *triangular prism*
38 der Zylinder, ein gerader Zylinder
- *cylinder, a right cylinder*
39 die Grundfläche, eine Kreisfläche
- *base, a circular plane*
40 der Mantel
- *curved surface*
41 die Kugel
- *sphere*
42 das Rotationsellipsoid
- *ellipsoid of revolution*
43 der Kegel
- *cone*
44 die Kegelhöhe (Höhe des Kegels m)
- *height of the cone (cone height)*
45 der Kegelstumpf
- *truncated cone (frustum of a cone)*
46 die vierseitige Pyramide
- *quadrilateral pyramid*

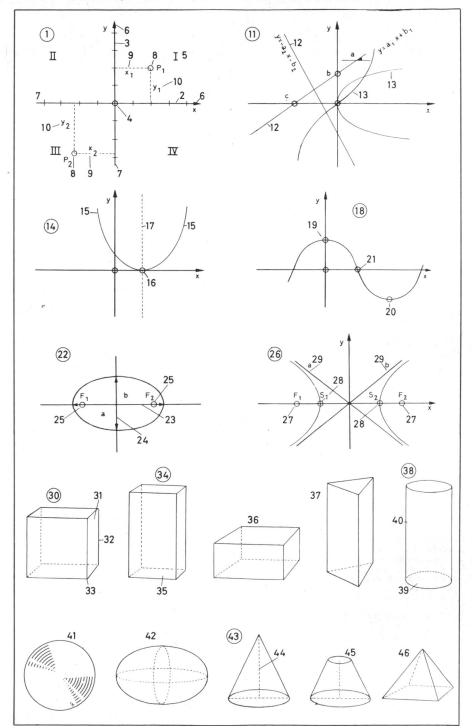

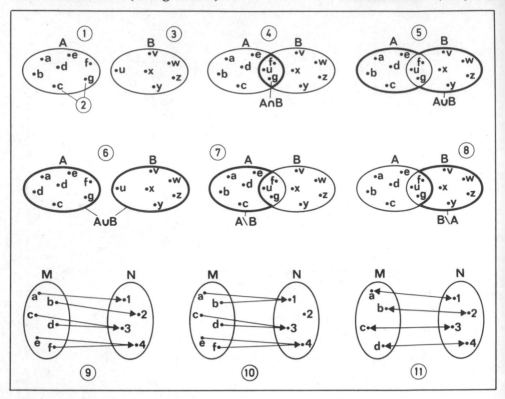

1 die Menge A, die Menge
  |a,b,c,d,e,f,g|
 - *the set A, the set |a, b, c, d, e, f, g|*
2 die Elemente *n* der Menge A
 - *elements (members) of the set A*
3 die Menge B, die Menge
  |u, v, w, x, y, z|
 - *the set B, the set |u, v, w, x, y, z|*
4 die Schnittmenge (der
  Durchschnitt, die
  Durchschnittsmenge) A∩B=|f, g, u|
 - *intersection of the sets A and B,*
  $A \cap B = |f, g, u|$
5-6 die Vereinigungsmenge A∪B =
  |a, b, c, d, e, f, g, u, v, w, x, y, z|
 - *union of the sets A and B, A∪B =*
  |a, b, c, d, e, f, g, u, v, w, x, y, z|
7 die Differenzmenge (Restmenge)
  A∖B = |a, b, c, d|
 - *complement of the set B, B' = |a, b,*
  c, d, e|
8 die Differenzmenge B∖A =
  |v, w, x, y, z|
 - *complement of the set A, A' =*
  |v, w, x, y, z|
9-11 Abbildungen *f*
 - *mappings*
9 die Abbildung der Menge M *auf*
  die Menge N
 - *mapping of the set M* onto *the set N*
10 die Abbildung der Menge M *in* die
  Menge N
 - *mapping of the set M* into *the set N*

11 die eineindeutige (umkehrbar
   eindeutige) Abbildung der Menge
   M auf die Menge N
 - *one-to-one mapping of the set M*
   onto the set N

610

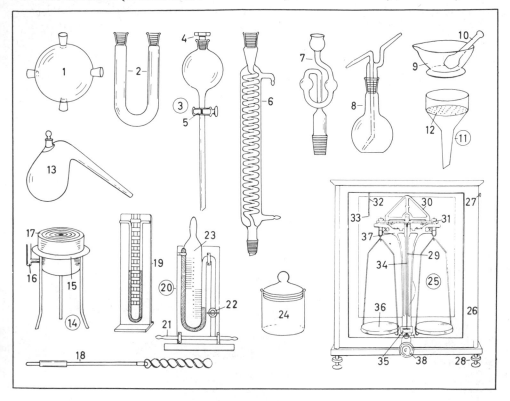

1-38 die Laborgeräte *n*
- **laboratory apparatus** *(laboratory equipment)*
1 die Scheidtsche Kugel
- *Scheidt globe*
2 das U-Rohr
- *U-tube*
3 der Scheidetrichter (Tropftrichter)
- *separating funnel*
4 der Achtkantschliffstöpsel
- *octagonal ground-glass stopper*
5 der Hahn
- *tap* (Am. *faucet*)
6 der Schlangenkühler
- *coiled condenser*
7 das Sicherheitsrohr (der Gäraufsatz)
- *air lock*
8 die Spritzflasche
- *wash-bottle*
9 der Mörser
- *mortar*
10 das Pistill (der Stampfer, die Keule)
- *pestle*
11 die Nutsche (der Büchner-Trichter)
- *filter funnel (Büchner funnel)*
12 das Filtersieb
- *filter (filter plate)*
13 die Retorte
- *retort*
14 das Wasserbad
- *water bath*

15 der Dreifuß
- *tripod*
16 der Wasserstandszeiger
- *water gauge* (Am. *gage*)
17 die Einlegeringe *m*
- *insertion rings*
18 der Rührer
- *stirrer*
19 das Über- und Unterdruckmanometer (Manometer)
- *manometer for measuring positive and negative pressures*
20 das Spiegelglasmanometer, für kleine Drücke *m*
- *mirror manometer for measuring small pressures*
21 die Ansaugleitung
- *inlet*
22 der Hahn
- *tap* (Am. *faucet*)
23 die verschiebbare Skala
- *sliding scale*
24 das Wägeglas
- *weighing bottle*
25 die Analysenwaage
- *analytical balance*
26 das Gehäuse
- *case*
27 die Vorderwand, zum Hochschieben *n*
- *sliding front panel*
28 die Dreipunktauflage
- *three-point support*

29 der Ständer
- *column (balance column)*
30 der Waagebalken
- *balance beam (beam)*
31 die Reiterschiene
- *rider bar*
32 die Reiterauflage
- *rider holder*
33 der Reiter
- *rider*
34 der Zeiger
- *pointer*
35 die Skala
- *scale*
36 die Wägeschale
- *scale pan*
37 die Arretierung
- *stop*
38 der Arretierungsknopf
- *stop knob*

1-63 **die Laborgeräte** n
- *laboratory apparatus (laboratory equipment)*
1 der Bunsenbrenner
- *Bunsen burner*
2 das Gaszuführungsrohr
- *gas inlet (gas inlet pipe)*
3 die Luftregulierung
- *air regulator*
4 der Teclu-Brenner
- *Teclu burner*
5 der Anschlußstutzen
- *pipe union*
6 die Gasregulierung
- *gas regulator*
7 der Kamin
- *stem*
8 die Luftregulierung
- *air regulator*
9 der Gebläsebrenner
- *bench torch*
10 der Mantel
- *casing*
11 die Sauerstoffzufuhr
- *oxygen inlet*
12 die Wasserstoffzufuhr
- *hydrogen inlet*
13 die Sauerstoffdüse
- *oxygen jet*
14 der Dreifuß
- *tripod*
15 der Ring
- *ring (retort ring)*
16 der Trichter
- *funnel*
17 das Tondreieck
- *pipe clay triangle*
18 das Drahtnetz
- *wire gauze*
19 das Asbestdrahtnetz
- *wire gauze with asbestos centre (Am. center)*
20 das Becherglas (der Kochbecher)
- *beaker*
21 die Bürette, zum Abmessen n von Flüssigkeit f
- *burette (for measuring the volume of liquids)*
22 das Bürettenstativ
- *burette stand*
23 die Bürettenklemme
- *burette clamp*
24 die Meßpipette
- *graduated pipette*
25 die Vollpipette (Pipette)
- *pipette*
26 der Meßzylinder (das Meßglas)
- *measuring cylinder (measuring glass)*
27 der Meßkolben
- *measuring flask*
28 der Mischzylinder
- *volumetric flask*
29 die Abdampfschale, aus Porzellan n
- *evaporating dish (evaporating basin), made of porcelain*
30 die Schlauchklemme (der Quetschhahn)
- *tube clamp (tube clip, pinchcock)*
31 der Tontiegel, mit Deckel m
- *clay crucible with lid*
32 die Tiegelzange
- *crucible tongs*
33 die Klemme (Klammer)
- *clamp*

34 das Reagenzglas (Probierglas)
- *test tube*
35 das Reagenzglasgestell (der Reagenzglashalter)
- *test tube rack*
36 der Stehkolben
- *flat-bottomed flask*
37 der Schliffansatz
- *ground glass neck*
38 der Rundkolben, mit langem Hals m
- *long-necked round-bottomed flask*
39 der Erlenmeyerkolben
- *Erlenmeyer flask (conical flask)*
40 die Filtrierflasche
- *filter flask*
41 der (das) Faltenfilter
- *fluted filter*
42 der Einweghahn
- *one-way tap*
43 die Chlorkalziumröhre
- *calcium chloride tube*
44 der Hahnstopfen
- *stopper with tap*
45 der Zylinder
- *cylinder*
46 der Destillierapparat
- *distillation apparatus (distilling apparatus)*
47 der Destillierkolben
- *distillation flask (distilling flask)*
48 der Kühler
- *condenser*
49 der Rücklaufhahn, ein Zweiwegehahn m
- *return tap, a two-way tap*
50 der Destillierkolben
- *distillation flask (distilling flask, Claisen flask)*
51 der Exsikkator
- *desiccator*
52 der Tubusdeckel
- *lid with fitted tube*
53 der Schlußhahn
- *tap*
54 der Exsikkatoreneinsatz, aus Porzellan n
- *desiccator insert made of porcelain*
55 der Dreihalskolben
- *three-necked flask*
56 das Verbindungsstück
- *connecting piece (Y-tube)*
57 die Dreihalsflasche
- *three-necked bottle*
58 die Gaswaschflasche
- *gas-washing bottle*
59 der Gasentwicklungsapparat (Kippsche Apparat)
- *gas generator (Kipp's apparatus, Am. Kipp generator)*
60 der Überlaufbehälter
- *overflow container*
61 der Substanzbehälter
- *container for the solid*
62 der Säurebehälter
- *acid container*
63 die Gasentnahme
- *gas outlet*

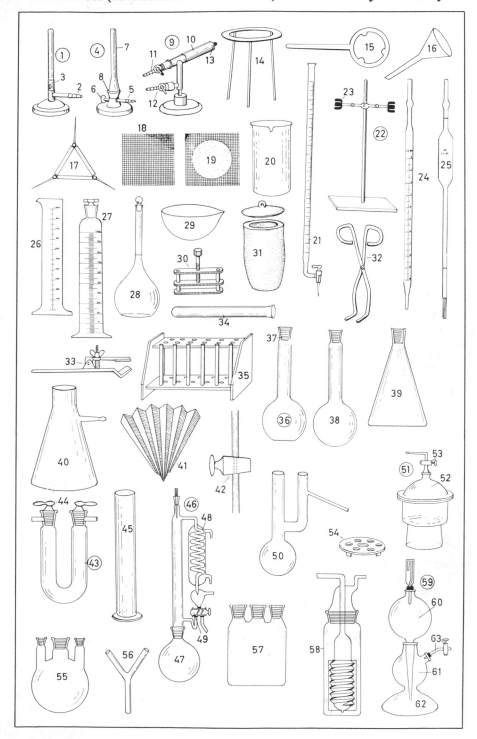

1-26 **Kristallgrundformen** *f* **und**
Kristallkombinationen *f*
(Kristallstruktur *f*, Kristallbau *m*)
- *basic crystal forms and crystal*
combinations (structure of crystals)
1-17 **das reguläre** (kubische,
tesserale, isometrische)
Kristallsystem
- *regular (cubic, tesseral, isometric)*
crystal system
1 das Tetraeder (der Vierflächner)
[Fahlerz *n*]
- *tetrahedron (four-faced*
polyhedron) [tetrahedrite, fahlerz,
fahl ore]
2 das Hexaeder (der Würfel,
Sechsflächner), ein Vollflächner *m*
(Holoeder) [Steinsalz *n*]
- *hexahedron (cube, six-faced*
polyhedron), a holohedron [rock
salt]
3 das Symmetriezentrum (der
Kristallmittelpunkt)
- *centre (Am. center) of symmetry*
(crystal centre)
4 eine Symmetrieachse (Gyre)
- *axis of symmetry (rotation axis)*
5 eine Symmetrieebene
- *plane of symmetry*
6 das Oktaeder (der Achtflächner)
[Gold *n*]
- *octahedron (eight-faced*
polyhedron) [gold]
7 das Rhombendodekaeder
(Granatoeder) [Granat *m*]
- *rhombic dodecahedron [garnet]*
8 das Pentagondodekaeder [Pyrit *m*]
- *pentagonal dodecahedron [pyrite,*
iron pyrites]
9 ein Fünfeck *n* (Pentagon)
- *pentagon (five-sided polygon)*
10 das Pyramidenoktaeder
[Diamant *m*]
- *triakis-octahedron [diamond]*
11 das Ikosaeder (der
Zwanzigflächner), ein
regelmäßiger Vielflächner
- *icosahedron (twenty-faced*
polyhedron), a regular polyhedron
12 das Ikositetraeder (der
Vierundzwanzigflächner) [Leuzit *m*]
- *icositetrahedron*
(twenty-four-faced polyhedron)
[leucite]
13 das Hexakisoktaeder (der
Achtundvierzigflächner)
[Diamant *m*]
- *hexakis-octahedron*
(hexoctahedron, forty-eight-faced
polyhedron) [diamond]
14 das Oktaeder mit Würfel *m*
[Bleiglanz *m*]
- *octahedron with cube [galena]*
15 ein Hexagon *n* (Sechseck)
- *hexagon (six-sided polygon)*
16 der Würfel mit Oktaeder *n*
[Flußspat *m*]
- *cube with octahedron [fluorite,*
fluorspar]
17 ein Oktogon *n* (Achteck)
- *octagon (eight-sided polygon)*
18-19 **das tetragonale Kristallsystem**
- *tetragonal crystal system*
18 die tetragonale Pyramide
- *tetragonal dipyramid (tetragonal*
bipyramid)

19 das Protoprisma mit
Protopyramide *f* [Zirkon *m*]
- *protoprism with protopyramid*
[zircon]
20-22 **das hexagonale Kristallsystem**
- *hexagonal crystal system*
20 das Protoprisma mit Proto- und
Deuteropyramide *f* und Basis *f*
[Apatit *m*]
- *protoprism with protopyramid,*
deutero-pyramid and basal
pinacoid [apatite]
21 das hexagonale Prisma
- *hexagonal prism*
22 das hexagonale (ditrigonale)
Prisma, mit Rhomboeder *n*
[Kalkspat *m*]
- *hexagonal (ditrigonal) biprism with*
rhombohedron [calcite]
23 die rhombische Pyramide (das
rhombische Kristallsystem)
[Schwefel *m*]
- *orthorhombic pyramid (rhombic*
crystal system) [sulphur,
Am. *sulfur]*
24-25 **das monkline Kristallsystem**
- *monoclinic crystal system*
24 das monkline Prisma mit
Klinopinakoid *n* und
Hemipyramide *f* (Teilflach *n*,
Hemieder *n*) [Gips *m*]
- *monoclinic prism with*
clinoprinacoid and hemipyramid
(hemihedron) [gypsum]
25 das Orthopinakoid
(Schwalbenschwanz-Zwillingskristall
m) [Gips *m*]
- *orthopinacoid (swallow-tail twin*
crystal) [gypsum]
26 trikline Pinakoiden (das trikline
Kristallsystem) [Kupfersulfat *n*]
- *triclinic pinacoids (triclinic crystal*
system) [copper sulphate,
Am. *copper sulfate]*
27-33 **Apparate** *m* **zur**
Kristallmessung
(zur Kristallometrie)
- *apparatus for measuring crystals (for*
crystallometry)
27 das Anlegegoniometer
(Kontaktgoniometer)
- *contact goniometer*
28 das Reflexionsgoniometer
- *reflecting goniometer*
29 der Kristall
- *crystal*
30 der Kollimator
- *collimator*
31 das Beobachtungsfernrohr
- *observation telescope*
32 der Teilkreis
- *divided circle (graduated circle)*
33 die Lupe, zum Ablesen *n* des
Drehungswinkels *m*
- *lens for reading the angle of*
rotation

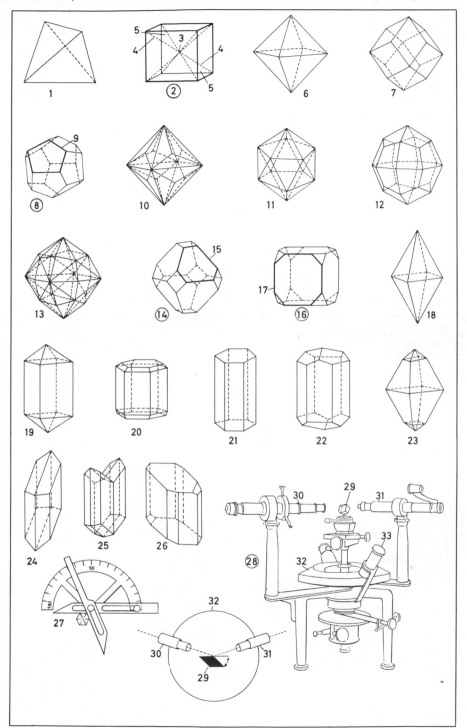

1 der Totempfahl (Wappenpfahl)
- *totem pole*
2 das Totem, eine geschnitzte u.
bemalte bildliche od. symbolische
Darstellung
- *totem, a carved and painted
pictorial or symbolic representation*
3 der Prärieindianer
- *plains Indian*
4 der Mustang, ein Steppenpferd n
- *mustang, a prairie horse*
5 der (das) Lasso, ein langer
Wurfriemen m mit leicht
zusammenziehbarer Schlinge
- *lasso, a long throwing-rope with
running noose*
6 die Friedenspfeife
- *pipe of peace*
7 das Tipi
- *wigwam (tepee, teepee)*
8 die Zeltstange
- *tent pole*
9 die Rauchklappe
- *smoke flap*
10 die Squaw, eine Indianerfrau
- *squaw, an Indian woman*
11 der Indianerhäuptling
- *Indian chief*
12 der Kopfschmuck, ein
Federschmuck m
- *headdress, an ornamental feather
headdress*
13 die Kriegsbemalung
- *war paint*
14 die Halskette, aus Bärenkrallen f
- *necklace of bear claws*
15 der Skalp (die abgezogene
Kopfhaut des Gegners m), ein
Siegeszeichen n
- *scalp (cut from enemy's head), a
trophy*
16 der Tomahawk, eine Streitaxt
- *tomahawk, a battle axe (Am. ax)*
17 die Leggins pl (Leggings,
Wildledergamaschen f)
- *leggings*
18 der Mokassin, ein Halbschuh m
(aus Leder n und Bast m)
- *moccasin, a shoe of leather and bast*
19 das Kanu der Waldlandindianer m
- *canoe of the forest Indians*
20 der Mayatempel, eine
Stufenpyramide
- *Maya temple, a stepped pyramid*
21 die Mumie
- *mummy*
22 das Quipu (die Knotenschnur,
Knotenschrift der Inka m)
- *quipa (knotted threads, knotted
code of the Incas)*
23 der Indio (Indianer Mittel- u.
Südamerikas); *hier:*
Hochlandindianer m
- *Indio (Indian of Central and South
America);* here: *highland Indian*
24 der Poncho, eine Decke mit
Halsschlitz m als ärmelloser,
mantelartiger Überwurf
- *poncho, a blanket with a head
opening used as an armless
cloak-like wrap*
25 der Indianer der tropischen
Waldgebiete n
- *Indian of the tropical forest*
26 das Blasrohr
- *blowpipe*

27 der Köcher
- *quiver*
28 der Pfeil
- *dart*
29 die Pfeilspitze
- *dart point*
30 der Schrumpfkopf, eine
Siegestrophäe
- *shrunken head, a trophy*
31 die Bola, ein Wurf- und Fanggerät n
- *bola (bolas), a throwing and
entangling device*
32 die in Leder gehüllte Stein- od.
Metallkugel
- *leather-covered stone or metal ball*
33 die Pfahlbauhütte
- *pile dwelling*
34 der Dukduk-Tänzer, ein Mitglied
m eines Männergeheimbundes m
- *duk-duk dancer, a member of a
duk-duk (men's secret society)*
35 das Auslegerboot
- *outrigger canoe (canoe with
outrigger)*
36 der Schwimmbalken
- *outrigger*
37 der eingeborene Australier
- *Australian aborigine*
38 der Gürtel aus Menschenhaar n
- *loincloth of human hair*
39 der Bumerang, ein Wurfholz n
- *boomerang, a wooden missile*
40 die Speerschleuder mit Speeren m
- *throwing stick (spear thrower) with
spears*

1 der Eskimo
- *Eskimo*
2 der Schlittenhund,
ein Polarhund *m*
- *sledge dog (sled dog), a husky*
3 der Hundeschlitten
- *dog sledge (dog sled)*
4 der (das) Iglu, eine kuppelförmige
Schneehütte
- *igloo, a dome-shaped snow hut*
5 der Schneeblock
- *block of snow*
6 der Eingangstunnel
- *entrance tunnel*
7 die Tranlampe
- *blubber-oil lamp*
8 das Wurfbrett
- *wooden missile*
9 die Stoßharpune
- *lance*
10 die einspitzige Harpune
- *harpoon*
11 der Luftsack
- *skin float*
12 der (das) Kajak, ein leichtes
Einmannboot *n*
- *kayak, a light one-man canoe*
13 das fellbespannte Holz- oder
Knochengerüst
- *skin-covered wooden or bone frame*
14 das Paddel
- *paddle*
15 das Rengespann
- *reindeer harness*
16 das Rentier
- *reindeer*
17 der Ostjake
- *Ostyak (Ostiak)*
18 der Ständerschlitten
- *passenger sledge*
19 die Jurte, ein Wohnzelt *n* der west-
und zentralasiatischen Nomaden *m*
- *yurt (yurta), a dwelling tent of the
western and central Asiatic nomads*
20 die Filzbedeckung
- *felt covering*
21 der Rauchabzug
- *smoke outlet*
22 der Kirgise
- *Kirghiz*
23 die Schaffellmütze
- *sheepskin cap*
24 der Schamane
- *shaman*
25 der Fransenschmuck
- *decorative fringe*
26 die Rahmentrommel
- *frame drum*
27 der Tibeter
- *Tibetan*
28 die Gabelflinte
- *flintlock with bayonets*
29 die Gebetsmühle
- *prayer wheel*
30 der Filzstiefel
- *felt boot*
31 das Hausboot (der Sampan)
- *houseboat (sampan)*
32 die Dschunke
- *junk*
33 das Mattensegel
- *mat sail*
34 die Rikscha
- *rickshaw (ricksha)*
35 der Rikschakuli
- *rickshaw coolie (cooly)*

36 der (das) Lampion
- *Chinese lantern*
37 der Samurai
- *samurai*
38 die wattierte Rüstung
- *padded armour* (Am. *armor)*
39 die Geisha
- *geisha*
40 der Kimono
- *kimono*
41 der Obi
- *obi*
42 der Fächer
- *fan*
43 der Kuli
- *coolie (cooly)*
44 der Kris, ein malaiischer Dolch
- *kris (creese, crease), a Malayan
dagger*
45 der Schlangenbeschwörer
- *snake charmer*
46 der Turban
- *turban*
47 die Flöte
- *flute*
48 die tanzende Schlange
- *dancing snake*

1 die Kamelkarawane
- *camel caravan*
2 das Reittier
- *riding animal*
3 das Lasttier (Tragtier)
- *pack animal*
4 die Oase
- *oasis*
5 der Palmenhain
- *grove of palm trees*
6 der Beduine
- *bedouin (beduin)*
7 der Burnus
- *burnous*
8 der Massaikrieger
- *Masai warrior*
9 die Haartracht
- *headdress (hairdress)*
10 der Schild
- *shield*
11 die bemalte Rindshaut
- *painted ox hide*
12 die Lanze mit langer Klinge
- *long-bladed spear*
13 der Neger
- *negro*
14 die Tanztrommel
- *dance drum*
15 das Wurfmesser
- *throwing knife*
16 die Holzmaske
- *wooden mask*
17 die Ahnenfigur
- *figure of an ancestor*
18 die Signaltrommel
- *slit gong*
19 der Trommelstab
- *drumstick*
20 der Einbaum, ein aus einem
   Baumstamm *m* ausgehöhltes Boot
- *dugout, a boat hollowed out of a*
   tree trunk
21 die Negerhütte
- *negro hut*
22 die Negerin
- *negress*
23 die Lippenscheibe
- *lip plug (labret)*
24 der Mahlstein
- *grinding stone*
25 die Hererofrau
- *Herero woman*
26 die Lederhaube
- *leather cap*
27 die Kalebasse
- *calabash (gourd)*
28 die Bienenkorbhütte
- *beehive-shaped hut*
29 der Buschmann
- *bushman*
30 der Ohrpflock
- *earplug*
31 der Lendenschurz
- *loincloth*
32 der Bogen
- *bow*
33 der Kirri, eine Keule mit rundem,
   verdicktem Kopf *m*
- *knobkerry (knobkerrie), a club with*
   round, knobbed end
34 die Buschmannfrau beim
   Feuerbohren *n*
- *bushman woman making a fire by*
   twirling a stick
35 der Windschirm
- *windbreak*

36 der Zulu im Tanzschmuck *m*
- *Zulu in dance costume*
37 der Tanzstock
- *dancing stick*
38 der Beinring
- *bangle*
39 das Kriegshorn aus Elfenbein *n*
- *ivory war horn*
40 die Amulett-und-Würfel-Kette
- *string of amulets and bones*
41 der Pygmäe
- *pigmy*
42 die Zauberpfeife zur
   Geisterbeschwörung
- *magic pipe for exorcising evil spirits*
43 der Fetisch
- *fetish*

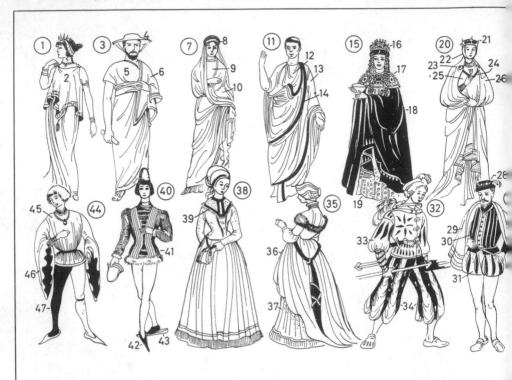

1 Griechin f
- Greek woman
2 der Peplos
- peplos
3 Grieche m
- Greek
4 der Petasos (thessalische Hut)
- petasus (Thessalonian hat)
5 der Chiton, ein Leinenrock m als
Untergewand n
- chiton, a linen gown worn as a
basic garment
6 das Himation, ein wollener
Überwurfmantel
- himation, woollen (Am. woolen) cloak
7 Römerin f
- Roman woman
8 das Stirntoupet
- toupee wig (partial wig)
9 die Stola
- stola
10 die Palla, ein farbiger Umwurf
- palla, a coloured (Am. colored)
wrap
11 Römer m
- Roman
12 die Tunika
- tunica (tunic)
13 die Toga
- toga
14 der Purpursaum
- purple border (purple band)
15 byzantinische Kaiserin f
- Byzantine empress

16 das Perlendiadem
- pearl diadem
17 das Schmuckgehänge
- jewels
18 der Purpurmantel
- purple cloak
19 das Gewand
- long tunic
20 deutsche Fürstin f [13.Jh.]
- German princess [13th cent.]
21 das Diadem (der Schapel)
- crown (diadem)
22 das Kinnband (Gebände, Gebende)
- chinband
23 die Tassel
- tassel
24 die Mantelschnur
- cloak cord
25 das gegürtete Kleid
- girt-up gown (girt-up surcoat,
girt-up tunic)
26 der Mantel
- cloak
27 Deutscher in spanischer Tracht f
[um 1575]
- German dressed in the Spanish
style [ca. 1575]
28 das Barett
- wide-brimmed cap
29 der kurze Mantel (die Kappe)
- short cloak (Spanish cloak, short cape)
30 das ausgestopfte Wams
- padded doublet (stuffed doublet,
peascod)

31 die gepolsterte Oberschenkelhose
- stuffed trunk-hose
32 Landsknecht m [um 1530]
- lansquenet (German mercenary
soldier) [ca. 1530]
33 das Schlitzwams
- slashed doublet (paned doublet)
34 die Pluderhose
- Pluderhose (loose breeches, paned
trunk-hose, slops)
35 Baslerin f [um 1525]
- woman of Basle [ca. 1525]
36 das Überkleid
- overgown (gown)
37 das Untergewand
- undergown (petticoat)
38 Nürnbergerin f [um 1500]
- woman of Nuremberg [ca. 1500]
39 der Schulterkragen (Goller, Koller)
- shoulder cape
40 Burgunder m [15.Jh.]
- Burgundian [15th cent.]
41 das kurze Wams
- short doublet
42 die Schnabelschuhe m
- piked shoes (peaked shoes, copped
shoes, crackowes, poulaines)
43 die Holzunterschuhe m (Trippen f)
- pattens (clogs)
44 junger Edelmann [um 1400]
- young nobleman [ca. 1400]
45 die kurze Schecke
- short, padded doublet (short,
quilted doublet, jerkin)

46 die Zaddelärmel *m*
- *dagged sleeves (petal-scalloped
  sleeves)*
47 die Strumpfhose
- *hose*
48 Augsburger Patrizierin *f* [um 1575]
- *Augsburg patrician lady [ca. 1575]*
49 die Ärmelpuffe
- *puffed sleeve*
50 das Überkleid (die Marlotte)
- *overgown (gown, open gown,
  sleeveless gown)*
51 franz. Dame *f* [um 1600]
- *French lady [ca. 1600]*
52 der Mühlsteinkragen
- *millstone ruff (cartwheel ruff, ruff)*
53 die geschnürte Taille
  (Wespentaille)
- *corseted waist (wasp waist)*
54 Herr *m* (um 1650)
- *gentleman [ca. 1650]*
55 der schwed. Schlapphut
- *wide-brimmed felt hat (cavalier hat)*
56 der Leinenkragen
- *falling collar (wide-falling collar)
  of linen*
57 das Weißzeugfutter
- *white lining*
58 die Stulpenstiefel *m*
- *jack boots (bucket-top boots)*
59 Dame *f* [um 1650]
- *lady [ca. 1650]*
60 die gepufften Ärmel *m* (Puffärmel)
- *full puffed sleeves (puffed sleeves)*

61 Herr *m* [um 1700]
- *gentleman [ca. 1700]*
62 der Dreispitz (Dreieckhut,
  Dreimaster)
- *three-cornered hat*
63 der Galanteriedegen
- *dress sword*
64 Dame *f* [um 1700]
- *lady [ca. 1700]*
65 die Spitzenhaube
- *lace fontange (high headdress of lace)*
66 der Spitzenumhang
- *lace-trimmed loose-hanging gown
  (loose-fitting housecoat, robe de
  chambre, negligée, contouche)*
67 der Stickereisaum
- *band of embroidery*
68 Dame *f* [um 1880]
- *lady [ca. 1880]*
69 die Turnüre (der Cul de Paris)
- *bustle*
70 Dame *f* [um 1858]
- *lady [ca. 1858]*
71 die Schute (der Schutenhut)
- *poke bonnet*
72 der runde Reifrock (die Krinoline)
- *crinoline*
73 Herr *m* der Biedermeierzeit
- *gentleman of the Biedermeier
  period*
74 der hohe Kragen (Vatermörder)
- *high collar (choker collar)*
75 die geblümte Weste
- *embroidered waistcoat (vest)*

76 der Schoßrock
- *frock coat*
77 die Zopfperücke
- *pigtail wig*
78 das Zopfband (die Zopfschleife)
- *ribbon (bow)*
79 Damen *f* im Hofkleid *n* [um 1780]
- *ladies in court dress [ca. 1780]*
80 die Schleppe
- *train*
81 die Rokokofrisur
- *upswept Rococo coiffure*
82 der Haarschmuck
- *hair decoration*
83 der flache Reifrock
- *panniered overskirt*

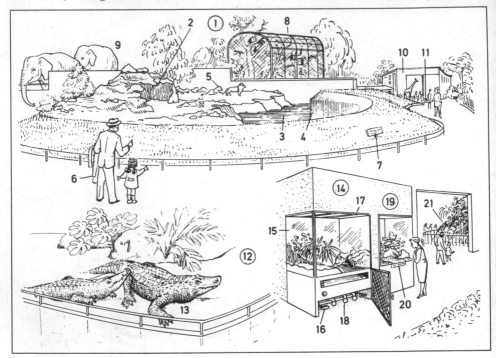

1 das Freigehege (die Freianlage)
– *outdoor enclosure (enclosure)*
2 der Naturfelsen
– *rocks*
3 der Absperrgraben, ein
Wassergraben *m*
– *moat*
4 die Schutzmauer
– *enclosing wall*
5 die gezeigten Tiere *n; hier:* ein
Löwenrudel *n*
– *animals on show;* here: *a pride of
lions*
6 der Zoobesucher
– *visitor to the zoo*
7 die Hinweistafel
– *notice*
8 die Voliere (das Vogelgehege)
– *aviary*
9 das Elefantengehege
– *elephant enclosure*
10 das Tierhaus (z.B. Raubtierhaus,
Giraffenhaus, Elefantenhaus,
Affenhaus)
– *animal house (e.g. carnivore house,
giraffe house, elephant house,
monkey house)*
11 der Außenkäfig (Sommerkäfig)
– *outside cage (summer quarters)*
12 das Reptiliengehege
– *reptile enclosure*
13 das Nilkrokodil
– *Nile crocodile*
14 das Terra-Aquarium
– *terrarium and aquarium*
15 der Glasschaukasten
– *glass case*

16 die Frischluftzuführung
– *fresh-air inlet*
17 der Luftabzug (die Entlüftung)
– *ventilator*
18 die Bodenheizung
– *underfloor heating*
19 das Aquarium
– *aquarium*
20 die Erläuterungstafel
– *information plate*
21 die Klimalandschaft
– *flora in artificially maintained
climate*

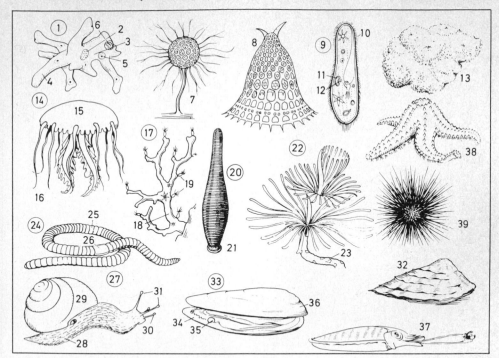

1-12 Einzeller *m* (Einzellige *pl*, Protozoen *n*, Urtierchen)
- **unicellular (one-celled, single-celled) animals** *(protozoans)*
1 die Amöbe (das Wechseltierchen), ein Wurzelfüßler *m*
- *amoeba, a rhizopod*
2 der Zellkern
- *cell nucleus*
3 das Protoplasma
- *protoplasm*
4 das Scheinfüßchen
- *pseudopod*
5 das Absonderungsbläschen (die pulsierende Vakuole, eine Organelle)
- *excretory vacuole (contractile vacuole, an organelle)*
6 das Nahrungsbläschen (die Nahrungsvakuole)
- *food vacuole*
7 das Gittertierchen, ein Sonnentierchen *n*
- *Actinophrys, a heliozoan*
8 das Strahlentierchen (die Radiolarie); *darg.:* das Kieselsäureskelett
- *radiolarian; here: siliceous skeleton*
9 das Pantoffeltierchen, ein Wimperinfusorium *n* (Wimpertierchen)
- *slipper animalcule, a Paramecium (ciliate infusorian)*
10 die Wimper
- *cilium*
11 der Hauptkern (Großkern)
- *macronucleus (meganucleus)*
12 der Nebenkern (Kleinkern)
- *micronucleus*
13-39 Vielzeller *m* (Gewebetiere *n*, Metazoen)
- **multicellular animals** *(metazoans)*

13 der Badeschwamm, ein Schwammtier *n* (Schwamm *m*)
- *bath sponge, a porifer (sponge)*
14 die Meduse, eine Scheibenqualle (Schirmqualle, Qualle), ein Hohltier *n*
- *medusa, a discomedusa (jellyfish), a coelenterate*
15 der Schirm
- *umbrella*
16 der Fangarm (der *od.* das Tentakel)
- *tentacle*
17 die Edelkoralle, ein Korallentier *n* (Blumentier, Riffbildner *m*)
- *red coral (precious coral), a coral animal (anthozoan, reef-building animal)*
18 der Korallenstock
- *coral colony*
19 der Korallenpolyp
- *coral polyp*
20-26 Würmer *m*
- **worms** *(Vermes)*
20 der Blutegel, ein Ringelwurm *m* (Gliederwurm)
- *leech, an annelid*
21 die Saugscheibe
- *sucker*
22 der Spirographis, ein Borstenwurm *m*
- *Spirographis, a bristle worm*
23 die Röhre
- *tube*
24 der große Regenwurm (Tauwurm, Pier)
- *earthworm*
25 das Körperglied (Segment)
- *segment*
26 das Clitellum [der Begattung dienende Region]

- *clitellum [accessory reproductive organ]*
27-36 Weichtiere *n* (Mollusken *f*)
- *molluscs* (Am. *mollusks*)
27 die Weinbergschnecke, eine Schnecke
- *edible snail, a snail*
28 der Kriechfuß
- *creeping foot*
29 die Schale (das Gehäuse, Schneckenhaus)
- *shell (snail shell)*
30 die Stielauge
- *stalked eye*
31 die Fühler *m*
- *tentacle (horn, feeler)*
32 die Auster
- *oyster*
33 die Flußperlmuschel
- *freshwater pearl mussel*
34 die Perlmutter (das Perlmutt)
- *mother-of-pearl (nacre)*
35 die Perle
- *pearl*
36 die Muschelschale
- *mussel shell*
37 der gemeine Tintenfisch, ein Kopffüßer *m*
- *cuttlefish, a cephalopod*
38-39 Stachelhäuter *m* (Echinodermen)
- *echinoderms*
38 der Seestern
- *starfish (sea star)*
39 der Seeigel
- *sea urchin (sea hedgehog)*

1-23 **Gliederfüßer** *m*
- *arthropods*
1-2 **Krebstiere** *n* (Krebse *m*,
  Krustentiere *n*)
- *crustaceans*
1 die Wollhandkrabbe, eine Krabbe
- *mitten crab, a crab*
2 die Wasserassel
- *water slater*
3-23 **Insekten** *n* (Kerbtiere, Kerfe *m*)
- *insects*
3 die Seejungfer, ein Gleichflügler
  m, eine Libelle (Wasserjungfer)
- *water nymph (dragonfly), a
  homopteran (homopterous insect),
  a dragonfly*
4 der Wasserskorpion, eine
  Wasserwanze, ein Schnabelkerf *m*
- *water scorpion (water bug), a
  rhynchophore*
5 das Raubbein
- *raptorial leg*
6 die Eintagsfliege
- *mayfly (dayfly, ephemerid)*
7 das Facettenauge
- *compound eye*
8 das Grüne Heupferd (die
  Heuschrecke, der Heuspringer,
  Heuhüpfer, Grashüpfer), eine
  Springheuschrecke, ein
  Geradflügler *m*
- *green grasshopper (green locust,
  meadow grasshopper), an
  orthopteron (orthopterous insect)*
9 die Larve
- *larva (grub)*
10 das geschlechtsreife Insekt, eine
  Imago, ein Vollkerf *m*
- *adult insect, an imago*
11 das Springbein
- *leaping hind leg*
12 die Große Köcherfliege (eine
  Köcherfliege, Wassermotte,
  Frühlingsfliege, ein Haarflügler),
  ein Netzflügler *m*
- *caddis fly (spring fly, water moth),
  a neuropteran*
13 die Blattlaus (Röhrenlaus), eine
  Pflanzenlaus
- *aphid (greenfly), a plant louse*
14 die ungeflügelte Blattlaus
- *wingless aphid*
15 die geflügelte Blattlaus
- *winged aphid*
16-20 **Zweiflügler** *m*
- *dipterous insects (dipterans)*
16 die Stechmücke (*obd.* Schnake,
  österr. Gelse, der Moskito), eine Mücke
- *gnat (mosquito, midge), a culicid*
17 der Stechrüssel
- *proboscis (sucking organ)*
18 die Schmeißfliege (der Brummer),
  eine Fliege
- *bluebottle (blowfly), a fly*
19 die Made
- *maggot (larva)*
20 die Puppe
- *chrysalis (pupa)*
21-23 **Hautflügler** *m*
- *Hymenoptera*
21-22 die Ameise
- *ant*
21 das geflügelte Weibchen
- *winged female*
22 der Arbeiter
- *worker*

23 die Hummel
- *bumblebee (humblebee)*
24-39 **Käfer** *m* (Deckflügler)
- *beetles (Coleoptera)*
24 der Hirschkäfer (*obd.* Schröter,
  Feuerschröter, Hornschröter, *md.*
  Hausbrenner, *schweiz.*
  Donnerkäfer, *österr.* Schmidkäfer),
  ein Blatthornkäfer *m*
- *stag beetle, a lamellicorn beetle*
25 die Kiefer *m* (Zangen *f*)
- *mandibles*
26 die Freßwerkzeuge *n*
- *trophi*
27 der Fühler
- *antenna (feeler)*
28 der Kopf
- *head*
29-30 die Brust (der Thorax)
- *thorax*
29 der Halsschild
- *thoracic shield (prothorax)*
30 das Schildchen
- *scutellum*
31 der Hinterleibsrücken
- *tergites*
32 die Atemöffnung
- *stigma*
33 der Flügel (Hinterflügel)
- *wing (hind wing)*
34 die Flügelader
- *nervure*
35 die Knickstelle
- *point at which the wing folds*
36 der Deckflügel (Vorderflügel)
- *elytron (forewing)*
37 der Siebenpunkt, ein Marienkäfer
  m (Herrgottskäfer, Glückskäfer,
  Sonnenkälbchen *n*, *md.*
  Gottesgiebchen, *schweiz.*
  Frauenkäfer *m*)
- *ladybird (ladybug), a coccinellid*
38 der Zimmermannsbock
  (Zimmerbock), ein Bockkäfer *m*
  (Bock)
- *Ergates faber, a longicorn beetle
  (longicorn)*
39 der Mistkäfer, ein
  Blatthornkäfer *m*
- *dung beetle, a lamellicorn beetle*
40-47 **Spinnentiere** *n*
- *arachnids*
40 der Hausskorpion (Italienischer
  Skorpion), ein Skorpion *m*
- *Euscorpius flavicandus, a scorpion*
41 das Greifbein mit Schere
- *cheliped with chelicer*
42 der Kieferfühler
- *maxillary antenna (maxillary
  feeler)*
43 der Schwanzstachel
- *tail sting*
44-46 **Spinnen** (*md.* Kanker *m*)
- *spiders*
44 der Holzbock (die Waldzecke,
  Hundezecke), eine Milbe, Zecke
- *wood tick (dog tick), a tick*
45 die Kreuzspinne (Gartenspinne),
  eine Radnetzspinne
- *cross spider (garden spider), an orb
  spinner*
46 die Spinndrüsenregion
- *spinneret*
47 das Spinnengewebe (das
  Spinnennetz, *österr.* das Spinnweb)
- *spider's web (web)*

48-56 **Schmetterlinge** *m* (Falter)
- *Lepidoptera (butterflies and moths)*
48 der Maulbeerseidenspinner, ein
  Seidenspinner *m*
- *mulberry-feeding moth (silk moth),
  a bombycid moth*
49 die Eier *n*
- *eggs*
50 die Seidenraupe
- *silkworm*
51 der Kokon
- *cocoon*
52 der Schwalbenschwanz, ein
  Edelfalter *m* (Ritter)
- *swallowtail, a butterfly*
53 der Fühler
- *antenna (feeler)*
54 der Augenfleck
- *eyespot*
55 der Ligusterschwärmer, ein
  Schwärmer *m*
- *privet hawkmoth, a hawkmoth
  (sphinx)*
56 der Rüssel
- *proboscis*

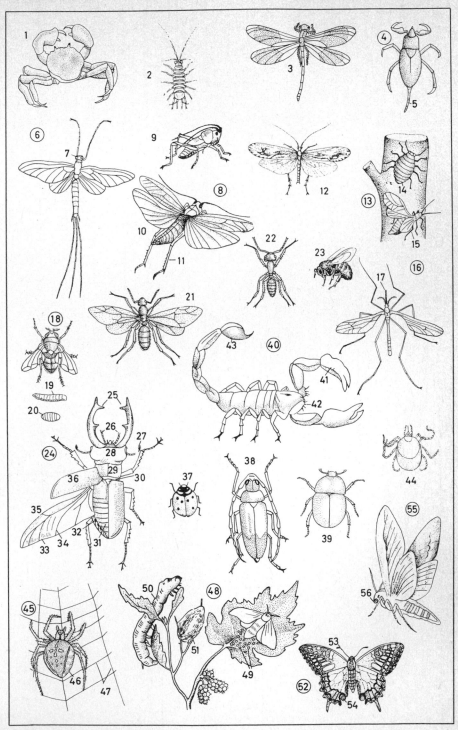

1-3 **Straußvögel** *m* (flugunfähige
  Vögel *m*)
- *flightless birds*
1 der Helmkasuar, ein Kasuar *m*;
  ähnl.: der Emu
- *cassowary;* sim.: *emu*
2 der Strauß
- *ostrich*
3 das Straußengelege [12-14 Eier *n*]
- *clutch of ostrich eggs [12 - 14 eggs]*
4 der Kaiserpinguin
  (Riesenpinguin), ein Pinguin *m*
  (Flossentaucher, Fettaucher; ein
  flugunfähiger Vogel)
- *king penguin, a penguin, a*
  flightless bird
5-10 **Ruderfüßer** *m*
- *web-footed birds*
5 der Rosapelikan (Gemeine
  Pelikan, Nimmersatt, die
  Kropfgans, Löffelgans, Meergans,
  Beutelgans), ein Pelikan *m*
- *white pelican (wood stork, ibis,*
  wood ibis, spoonbill, brent-goose,
  Am. *brant-goose, brant), a pelican*
6 der Ruderfuß (Schwimmfuß)
- *webfoot (webbed foot)*
7 die Schwimmhaut
- *web (palmations) of webbed foot*
  (palmate foot)
8 der Unterschnabel, mit dem
  Kehlsack *m* (Hautsack)
- *lower mandible with gular pouch*
9 der Baßtölpel (Weiße Seerabe, die
  Bassangans), ein Tölpel *m*
- *northern gannet (gannet, solan*
  goose), a gannet
10 die Krähenscharbe, ein Kormoran
  m (eine Scharbe), mit gespreizten
  Flügeln *m* „posierend"
- *green cormorant (shag), a*
  cormorant displaying with spread
  wings
11-14 **Langflügler** *m* (Seeflieger,
  Meeresvögel)
- *long-winged birds (seabirds)*
11 die Zwergschwalbe (Kleine
  Schwalbenmöwe), eine
  Seeschwalbe, beim Tauchen *n* nach
  Nahrung *f*
- *common sea swallow, a sea swallow*
  (tern), diving for food
12 der Eissturmvogel
- *fulmar*
13 die Trottellumme (Dumme
  Lumme, das Dumme Tauchhuhn),
  eine Lumme, ein Alk *m*
- *guillemot, an auk*
14 die Lachmöwe (Haffmöwe,
  Kirrmöwe, Fischmöwe,
  Speckmöwe, Seekrähe, der
  Mohrenkopf), eine Möwe
- *black-headed gull (mire crow), a gull*
15-17 **Gänsevögel** *m*
- *Anseres*
15 der Gänsesäger (Ganner, die
  Sägegans, Sägeente, Schnarrgans),
  ein Säger *m*
- *goosander (common merganser), a*
  sawbill
16 der Höckerschwan (Wildschwan,
  Stumme Schwan, alem. Elbs, Ölb),
  ein Schwan *m*
- *mute swan, a swan*
17 der Schnabelhöcker
- *knob on the bill*

18 der Fischreiher (Graureiher,
  Kammreiher), ein Reiher *m*, ein
  Storchvogel *m*
- *common heron, a heron*
19-21 **Regenpfeiferartige** *pl*
- *plovers*
19 der Stelzenläufer (Strandreiter, die
  Storchschnepfe)
- *stilt (stilt bird, stilt plover)*
20 das Bleßhuhn (Wasserhuhn,
  Moorhuhn, die Weißblässe,
  Bläßente), eine Ralle
- *coot, a rail*
21 der Kiebitz (*nd.* Kiewitt)
- *lapwing (green plover, peewit,*
  pewit)
22 die Wachtel, ein Hühnervogel *m*
- *quail, a gallinaceous bird*
23 die Turteltaube, eine Taube
- *turtle dove, a pigeon*
24 der Mauersegler (Mauerhäkler, die
  Mauerschwalbe, Kirchenschwalbe,
  Turmschwalbe, Kreuzschwalbe),
  ein Segler *m*
- *swift*
25 der Wiedehopf (Kuckucksküster,
  Kuckucksknecht, Heervogel,
  Wehrhahn, Dreckvogel, Kotvogel,
  Stinkvogel), ein Ra[c]kenvogel
- *hoopoe, a roller*
26 der aufrichtbare Federschopf
- *erectile crest*
27 der Buntspecht (Rotspecht,
  Großspecht, Fleckspecht), ein
  Specht *m* (Holzhacker); *verw.:* der
  Wendehals (Drehhals, Drehvogel,
  Regenvogel)
- *spotted woodpecker, a woodpecker;*
  related: *wryneck*
28 das Nestloch
- *entrance to the nest*
29 die Bruthöhle
- *nesting cavity*
30 der Kuckuck (Gauch, Gutzgauch)
- *cuckoo*

1, 3, 4, 5, 7, 9, 10 Singvögel *m*
- *songbirds*
1 der Stieglitz (Distelfink), ein
Finkenvogel *m*
- *goldfinch, a finch*
2 der Bienenfresser
- *bee eater*
3 das Gartenrotschwänzchen
(Rotschwänzchen), ein
Drosselvogel *m*
- *redstart (star finch), a thrush*
4 die Blaumeise, eine Meise, ein
Standvogel *m*
- *bluetit, a tit (titmouse), a resident
bird (non-migratory bird)*
5 der Gimpel (Dompfaff)
- *bullfinch*
6 die Blauracke (Mandelkrähe)
- *common roller (roller)*
7 der Pirol, ein Zugvogel *m*
- *golden oriole, a migratory bird*
8 der Eisvogel
- *kingfisher*
9 die Weiße Bachstelze, eine Stelze
- *white wagtail, a wagtail*
10 der Buchfink (Edelfink)
- *chaffinch*

1-20 Singvögel *m*
- *songbirds*
1-3 Rabenvögel *m* (Raben)
- *Corvidae (corvine birds, crows)*
1　der Eichelhäher (Eichelhabicht, Nuß-, Spiegelhäher, Holzschreier), ein Häher *m*
- *jay (nutcracker)*
2　die Saatkrähe (Feld-, Haferkrähe), eine Krähe
- *rook, a crow*
3　die Elster (Alster, Gartenkrähe, schweiz. Atzel)
- *magpie*
4　der Star (Rinderstar, Starmatz)
- *starling (pastor, shepherd bird)*
5　der Haussperling (Dach-, Kornsperling, Spatz)
- *house sparrow*
6-8 Finkenvögel *m*
- *finches*
6-7 Ammern *f*
- *buntings*
6　die Goldammer (Gelbammer, der Kornvogel, Grünschling)
- *yellowhammer (yellow bunting)*
7　der Ortolan (Gärtner, die Garten-, Sommerammer)
- *ortolan (ortolan bunting)*
8　der Erlenzeisig (Erdfink, Strumpfwirker, Leineweber), ein Zeisig *m*
- *siskin (aberdevine)*

9　die Kohlmeise (Spiegel-, Rollmeise, der Schlosserhahn), eine Meise
- *great titmouse (great tit, ox eye), a titmouse (tit)*
10　das Wintergoldhähnchen (Safranköpfchen); *ähnl.:* das Sommergoldhähnchen (Goldköpfchen), ein Goldhähnchen *n* (Goldhämmerchen, Sommerkönig *m*)
- *golden-crested wren (goldcrest); sim.: firecrest, one of the Regulidae*
11　der Kleiber (Blauspecht, Baumrutscher)
- *nuthatch*
12　der Zaunkönig (Zaunschlüpfer, Dorn-, Vogel-, Winterkönig)
- *wren*
13-17 Drosselvögel *m* (Drosseln *f*, Erdsänger *m*)
- *thrushes*
13　die Amsel (Schwarz-, Dreckamsel, Graudrossel, schweiz. Amstel)
- *blackbird*
14　die Nachtigall (Wassernachtigall, der Rotvogel, *dicht.* Philomele *f*)
- *nightingale (poet.: philomel, philomela)*
15　das Rotkehlchen (Rötel)
- *robin (redbreast, robin redbreast)*

16　die Singdrossel (Wald-, Weißdrossel, Zippe)
- *song thrush (throstle, mavis)*
17　der Sprosser (Sproßvogel)
- *thrush nightingale*
18-19 Lerchen *f*
- *larks*
18　die Heidelerche (Baum-, Steinlerche)
- *woodlark*
19　die Haubenlerche (Kamm-, Dreck-, Hauslerche)
- *crested lark (tufted lark)*
20　die Rauchschwalbe (Dorf-, Lehmschwalbe) (eine Schwalbe)
- *common swallow (barn swallow, chimney swallow), a swallow*

1-13 Greifvögel *m (früh.:* Tagraubvögel *m)*
- *diurnal birds of prey*
1-4 Falken *m*
- *falcons*
1 der Merlin (Zwergfalke)
- *merlin*
2 der Wanderfalke
- *peregrine falcon*
3 die „Hose" (Unterdeckfedern *f*, das Schenkelgefieder)
- *leg feathers*
4 der Lauf
- *tarsus*
5-9 Adler *m*
- *eagles*
5 der Seeadler (Meeradler)
- *white-tailed sea eagle (white-tailed eagle, grey sea eagle, erne)*
6 der Hakenschnabel
- *hooked beak*
7 der Fang
- *claw (talon)*
8 der Stoß (Schwanz)
- *tail*
9 der Mäusebussard (Mauser)
- *common buzzard*
10-13 Habichtartige *pl*
- *accipiters*
10 der Habicht (Hühnerhabicht)
- *goshawk*
11 der Rote Milan (die Gabel-, Königsweihe)
- *common European kite (glede, kite)*

12 der Sperber (Sperlingstößer)
- *sparrow hawk (spar-hawk)*
13 die Rohrweihe (Sumpf-, Rostweihe)
- *marsh harrier (moor buzzard, moor harrier, moor hawk)*
14-19 Eulen *f*
- *owls (nocturnal birds of prey)*
14 die Waldohreule (Goldeule, der Kleine Uhu)
- *long-eared owl (horned owl)*
15 der Uhu
- *eagle-owl (great horned owl)*
16 das Federohr
- *plumicorn (feathered ear, ear tuft, ear, horn)*
17 die Schleiereule
- *barn owl (white owl, silver owl, yellow owl, church owl, screech owl)*
18 der „Schleier" (Federkranz)
- *facial disc (disk)*
19 der Steinkauz (das Käuzchen, der Totenvogel)
- *little owl (sparrow owl)*

1　der Gelbhaubenkakadu, ein
　Papageienvogel *m*
–　*sulphur-crested cockatoo, a parrot*
2　der Ararauna
–　*blue-and-yellow macaw*
3　der blaue Paradiesvogel
–　*blue bird of paradise*
4　der Sappho-Kolibri
–　*sappho*
5　der Kardinal
–　*cardinal (cardinal bird)*
6　der Tukan (Rotschnabeltukan,
　Pfefferfresser), ein Spechtvogel *m*
–　*toucan (red-billed toucan), one of
　the Piciformes*

1-18 Fische *m*
- *fishes*
1 der Menschenhai (Blauhai), ein Haifisch *m* (Hai)
- *man-eater (blue shark, requin), a shark*
2 die Nase
- *nose (snout)*
3 die Kiemenspalte
- *gill slit (gill cleft)*
4 der Teichkarpfen (Flußkarpfen), ein Spiegelkarpfen *m* (Karpfen)
- *carp, a mirror carp (carp)*
5 der Kiemendeckel
- *gill cover (operculum)*
6 die Rückenflosse
- *dorsal fin*
7 die Brustflosse
- *pectoral fin*
8 die Bauchflosse
- *pelvic fin (abdominal fin, ventral fin)*
9 die Afterflosse
- *anal fin*
10 die Schwanzflosse
- *caudal fin (tail fin)*
11 die Schuppe
- *scale*
12 der Wels (Flußwels, Wallerfisch, Waller, Weller)
- *catfish (sheatfish, sheathfish, wels)*
13 der Bartfaden
- *barbel*
14 der Hering
- *herring*
15 die Bachforelle (Steinforelle, Bergforelle), eine Forelle
- *brown trout (German brown trout), a trout*
16 der Gemeine Hecht (Schnock, Wasserwolf)
- *pike (northern pike)*
17 der Flußaal (Aalfisch, Aal)
- *freshwater eel (eel)*
18 das Seepferdchen (der Hippokamp, Algenfisch)
- *sea horse (Hippocampus, horsefish)*
19 die Büschelkiemen *f*
- *tufted gills*
20-26 Lurche *m* (Amphibien *f*)
- *Amphibia (amphibians)*
20-22 Schwanzlurche *m*
- *salamanders*
20 der Kammolch, ein Wassermolch *m*
- *greater water newt (crested newt), a water newt*
21 der Rückenkamm
- *dorsal crest*
22 der Feuersalamander, ein Salamander *m*
- *fire salamander, a salamander*
23-26 Froschlurche *m*
- *salientians (anurans, batrachians)*
23 die Erdkröte, eine Kröte (*nd.* Padde, *obd.* ein Protz *m*)
- *European toad, a toad*
24 der Laubfrosch
- *tree frog (tree toad)*
25 die Schallblase
- *vocal sac (vocal pouch, croaking sac)*
26 die Haftscheibe
- *adhesive disc (disk)*
27-41 Kriechtiere *n* (Reptilien)
- *reptiles*

27, 30-37 Echsen *f*
- *lizards*
27 die Zauneidechse
- *sand lizard*
28 die Karettschildkröte
- *hawksbill turtle (hawksbill)*
29 der Rückenschild
- *carapace (shell)*
30 der Basilisk
- *basilisk*
31 der Wüstenwaran, ein Waran *m*
- *desert monitor, a monitor lizard (monitor)*
32 der Grüne Leguan, ein Leguan *m*
- *common iguana, an iguana*
33 das Chamäleon, ein Wurmzüngler *m*
- *chameleon, one of the Chamaeleontidae (Rhiptoglossa)*
34 der Klammerfuß
- *prehensile foot*
35 der Rollschwanz
- *prehensile tail*
36 der Mauergecko, ein Gecko *m* (Haftzeher)
- *wall gecko, a gecko*
37 die Blindschleiche, eine Schleiche
- *slowworm (blindworm), one of the Anguidae*
38-41 Schlangen *f*
- *snakes*
38 die Ringelnatter, eine Natter (eine Schwimmnatter; Wassernatter; Wasserschlange)
- *ringed snake (ring snake, water snake, grass snake), a colubrid*
39 die Mondflecken *m*
- *collar*
40-41 Vipern *f* (Ottern)
- *vipers (adders)*
40 die Kreuzotter (Otter, Höllennatter), eine Giftschlange
- *common viper, a poisonous (venomous) snake*
41 die Aspisviper
- *asp (asp viper)*

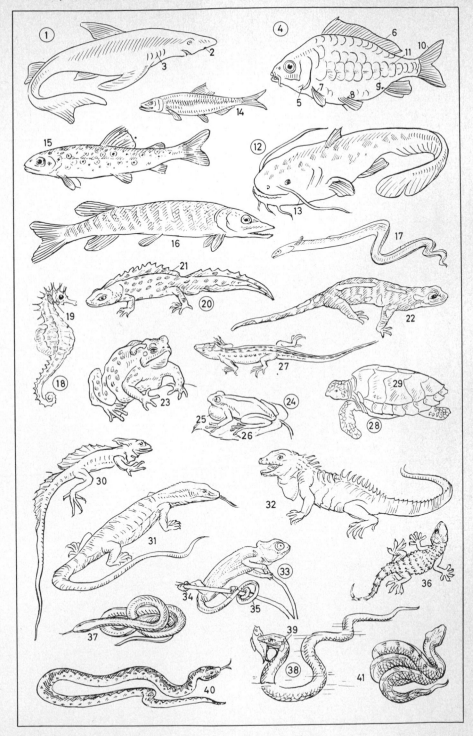

1-6 Tagfalter *m*
- *butterflies*
1 der Admiral
- *red admiral*
2 das Tagpfauenauge
- *peacock butterfly*
3 der Aurorafalter
- *orange tip (orange tip butterfly)*
4 der Zitronenfalter
- *brimstone (brimstone butterfly)*
5 der Trauermantel
- *Camberwell beauty (mourning cloak, mourning cloak butterfly)*
6 der Bläuling
- *blue (lycaenid butterfly, lycaenid)*
7-11 Nachtfalter *m*
  (Nachtschmetterlinge)
- *moths (Heterocera)*
7 der Braune Bär
- *garden tiger*
8 das Rote Ordensband
- *red underwing*
9 der Totenkopf
  (Totenkopfschwärmer), ein
  Schwärmer *m*
- *death's-head moth (death's-head hawkmoth), a hawkmoth (sphinx)*
10 die Raupe
- *caterpillar*
11 die Puppe
- *chrysalis (pupa)*

1 das Schnabeltier, ein Kloakentier *n*
   (Eileger *m*)
- *platypus (duck-bill, duck-mole), a
   monotreme (oviparous mammal)*
2-3 **Beuteltiere** *n*
- *marsupial mammals
   (marsupials)*
2 das Nordamerikanische Opossum,
   eine Beutelratte
- *New World opossum, a didelphid*
3 das Rote Riesenkänguruh, ein
   Känguruh *n*
- *red kangaroo (red flyer), a
   kangaroo*
4-7 **Insektenfresser** *m*
   (Kerbtierfresser)
- *insectivores (insect-eating
   mammals)*
4 der Maulwurf
- *mole*
5 der Igel
- *hedgehog*
6 der Stachel
- *spine*
7 die Hausspitzmaus, eine Spitzmaus
- *shrew (shrew mouse), one of the
   Soricidae*
8 das Neunbindengürteltier
- *nine-banded armadillo (peba)*
9 die Ohrenfledermaus, eine
   Glattnase, ein Flattertier *n* (eine
   Fledermaus)
- *long-eared bat (flitter-mouse), a
   flying mammal (chiropter,
   chiropteran)*
10 das Steppenschuppentier, ein
   Schuppentier *n*
- *pangolin (scaly ant-eater), a scaly
   mammal*
11 das Zweizehenfaultier
- *two-toed sloth (unau)*
12-19 **Nagetiere** *n*
- *rodents*
12 das Meerschweinchen
- *guinea pig (cavy)*
13 das Stachelschwein
- *porcupine*
14 die Biberratte
- *beaver*
15 die Wüstenspringmaus
- *jerboa*
16 der Hamster
- *hamster*
17 die Wühlmaus
- *water vole*
18 das Murmeltier
- *marmot*
19 das Eichhörnchen
- *squirrel*
20 der Afrikanische Elefant, ein
   Rüsseltier *n*
- *African elephant, a proboscidean
   (proboscidian)*
21 der Rüssel
- *trunk (proboscis)*
22 der Stoßzahn
- *tusk*
23 der Lamantin, eine Sirene
- *manatee (manati, lamantin), a
   sirenian*
24 der südafrikanische Klippschliefer,
   ein Schliefer *m* (Klippdachs)
- *South African dassie (das, coney,
   hyrax), a procaviid*
25-31 **Huftiere** *n*
- *ungulates*

25-27 **Unpaarhufer** *m*
- *odd-toed ungulates*
25 das Spitzmaulnashorn, ein
   Nashorn *n*
- *African black rhino, a rhinoceros
   (nasicorn)*
26 der Flachlandtapir, ein Tapir *m*
- *Brazilian tapir, a tapir*
27 das Zebra
- *zebra*
28-31 **Paarhufer** *m*
- *even-toed ungulates*
28-30 **Wiederkäuer** *m*
- *ruminants*
28 das Lama
- *llama*
29 das Trampeltier (zweihöckrige
   Kamel)
- *Bactrian camel (two-humped
   camel)*
30 der Guanako
- *guanaco*
31 das Nilpferd
- *hippopotamus*

1-10 Huftiere *n*, **Wiederkäuer** *m*
- *ungulates, ruminants*
1 der Elch
- *elk (moose)*
2 der Wapiti
- *wapiti (Am. elk)*
3 die Gemse (Gams)
- *chamois*
4 die Giraffe
- *giraffe*
5 die Hirschziegenantilope, eine Antilope
- *black buck, an antelope*
6 das Mufflon
- *mouflon (moufflon)*
7 der Steinbock
- *ibex (rock goat, bouquetin, steinbock)*
8 der Hausbüffel
- *water buffalo (Indian buffalo, water ox)*
9 der Bison
- *bison*
10 der Moschusochse
- *musk ox*
11-22 Raubtiere *n*
- *carnivores (beasts of prey)*
11-13 Hundeartige *pl*
- *Canidae*
11 der Schabrackenschakal (Schakal)
- *black-backed jackal (jackal)*
12 der Rotfuchs
- *red fox*
13 der Wolf
- *wolf*
14-17 Marder *m*
- *martens*
14 der Steinmarder
- *stone marten (beach marten)*
15 der Zobel
- *sable*
16 das Wiesel
- *weasel*
17 der Seeotter, ein Otter *m*
- *sea otter, an otter*
18-22 Robben *f* (Flossenfüßler *m*)
- *seals (pinnipeds)*
18 der Seebär (die Bärenrobbe)
- *fur seal (sea bear, ursine seal)*
19 der Seehund
- *common seal (sea calf, sea dog)*
20 das Polarmeerwalroß
- *walrus (morse)*
21 das Barthaar
- *whiskers*
22 der Hauer
- *tusk*
23-29 Wale *m*
- *whales*
23 der Tümmler
- *bottle-nosed dolphin (bottle-nose dolphin)*
24 der Gemeine Delphin
- *common dolphin*
25 der Pottwal
- *sperm whale (cachalot)*
26 das Atemloch
- *blowhole (spout hole)*
27 die Fettflosse
- *dorsal fin*
28 die Brustflosse
- *flipper*
29 die Schwanzflosse
- *tail flukes (tail)*

1-11 Raubtiere *n*
- *carnivores (beasts of prey)*
1 die Streifenhyäne, eine Hyäne
- *striped hyena, a hyena*
2-8 Katzen *f*
- *felines (cats)*
2 der Löwe
- *lion*
3 die Mähne (Löwenmähne)
- *mane (lion's mane)*
4 die Tatze
- *paw*
5 der Tiger
- *tiger*
6 der Leopard
- *leopard*
7 der Gepard
- *cheetah (hunting leopard)*
8 der Luchs
- *lynx*
9-11 Bären *m*
- *bears*
9 der Waschbär
- *raccoon (racoon, Am. coon)*
10 der Braunbär
- *brown bear*
11 der Eisbär
- *polar bear (white bear)*
12-16 Herrentiere *n*
- *primates*
12-13 Affen *m*
- *monkeys*
12 der Rhesusaffe
- *rhesus monkey (rhesus, rhesus macaque)*
13 der Pavian
- *baboon*
14-16 Menschenaffen *m*
- *anthropoids (anthropoid apes, great apes)*
14 der Schimpanse
- *chimpanzee*
15 der Orang-Utan
- *orang-utan (orang-outan)*
16 der Gorilla
- *gorilla*

1 Gigantocypris agassizi (der
Riesenmuschelkrebs)
- *Gigantocypris agassizi*
2 Macropharynx longicaudatus (der
Pelikanaal)
- *Macropharynx longicaudatus
(pelican eel)*
3 Pentacrinus [der Haarstern], eine
Seelilie, ein Stachelhäuter
- *Pentacrinus (feather star), a sea
lily, an echinoderm*
4 Thaumatolampas diadema (die
Wunderlampe), ein Tintenfisch *m*
[leuchtend]
- *Thaumatolampas diadema, a
cuttlefish [luminescent]*
5 Atolla, eine Tiefseemeduse, ein
Hohltier *n*
- *Atolla, a deep-sea medusa, a
coelenterate*
6 Melanocetes, ein Armflossler *m*
[leuchtend]
- *Melanocetes, a pediculate
[luminescent]*
7 Lophocalyx philippensis, ein
Glasschwamm *m*
- *Lophocalyx philippensis, a glass
sponge*
8 Mopsea, eine Hornkoralle
[Kolonie *f*]
- *Mopsea, a sea fan [colony]*
9 Hydrallmania, ein Hydroidpolyp
m, ein Polyp *m*, ein Hohltier *n*
[Kolonie *f*]
- *Hydrallmania, a hydroid polyp, a
coelenterate [colony]*
10 Malacosteus indicus, ein
Großmaul *n* [leuchtend]
- *Malacosteus indicus, a stomiatid
[luminescent]*
11 Brisinga endecacnemos, ein
Schlangenstern *m*, ein
Stachelhäuter *m* [nur gereizt
leuchtend]
- *Brisinga endecacnemos, a sand star
(brittle star), an echinoderm
[luminescent only when stimulated]*
12 Pasiphaea, eine Garnele, ein Krebs *m*
- *Pasiphaea, a shrimp, a crustacean*
13 Echiostoma, ein Großmaul *n*, ein
Fisch *m* [leuchtend]
- *Echiostoma, a stomiatid, a fish
[luminescent]*
14 Umbellula encrinus, eine Seefeder,
ein Hohltier *n* [Kolonie *f*
leuchtend]
- *Umbellula encrinus, a sea pen (sea
feather), a coelenterate [colony,
luminescent]*
15 Polycheles, ein Krebs *m*
- *Polycheles, a crustacean*
16 Lithodes, ein Krebs *m*, eine Krabbe
- *Lithodes, a crustacean, a crab*
17 Archaster, ein Seestern *m*, ein
Stachelhäuter *m*
- *Archaster, a starfish (sea star), an
echinoderm*
18 Oneirophanta, eine Seegurke, ein
Stachelhäuter *m*
- *Oneirophanta, a sea cucumber, an
echinoderm*
19 Palaeopneustes niasicus, ein
Seeigel *m*, ein Stachelhäuter *m*
- *Palaeopneustes niasicus, a sea
urchin (sea hedgehog), an
echinoderm*

20 Chitonactis, eine Seeanamone, ein
Hohltier *n*
- *Chitonactis, a sea anemone
(actinia), a coelenterate*

1 der Baum
- *tree*
2 der Baumstamm (Stamm)
- *bole (tree trunk, trunk, stem)*
3 die Baumkrone
- *crown of tree (crown)*
4 der Wipfel
- *top of tree (treetop)*
5 der Ast
- *bough (limb, branch)*
6 der Zweig
- *twig (branch)*
7 der Baumstamm [Querschnitt]
- *bole (tree trunk) [cross section]*
8 die Rinde (Borke)
- *bark (rind)*
9 der Bast
- *phloem (bast sieve tissue, inner fibrous bark)*
10 das Kambium (der Kambiumring)
- *cambium (cambium ring)*
11 die Markstrahlen m
- *medullary rays (vascular rays, pith rays)*
12 das Splintholz
- *sapwood (sap, alburnum)*
13 das Kernholz
- *heartwood (duramen)*
14 das Mark
- *pith*
15 **die Pflanze**
- *plant*
16-18 die Wurzel
- *root*
16 die Hauptwurzel
- *primary root*
17 die Nebenwurzel (Seitenwurzel)
- *secondary root*
18 das Wurzelhaar
- *root hair*
19-25 der Sproß
- *shoot (sprout)*
19 das Blatt
- *leaf*
20 der Stengel
- *stalk*
21 der Seitensproß
- *side shoot (offshoot)*
22 die Endknospe
- *terminal bud*
23 die Blüte
- *flower*
24 die Blütenknospe
- *flower bud*
25 die Blattachsel, mit der Achselknospe
- *leaf axil with axillary bud*
26 **das Blatt**
- *leaf*
27 der Blattstiel (Stiel)
- *leaf stalk (petiole)*
28 die Blattspreite (Spreite)
- *leaf blade (blade, lamina)*
29 die Blattaderung
- *venation (veins, nervures, ribs)*
30 die Blattrippe
- *midrib (nerve)*
31-38 Blattformen f
- *leaf shapes*
31 linealisch
- *linear*
32 lanzettlich
- *lanceolate*
33 rund
- *orbicular (orbiculate)*
34 nadelförmig
- *acerose (acerous, acerate, acicular, needle-shaped)*
35 herzförmig
- *cordate*

36 eiförmig
- *ovate*
37 pfeilförmig
- *sagittate*
38 nierenförmig
- *reniform*
39-42 geteilte Blätter n
- *compound leaves*
39 gefingert
- *digitate (digitated, palmate, quinquefoliolate)*
40 fiederteilig
- *pinnatifid*
41 paarig gefiedert
- *abruptly pinnate*
42 unpaarig gefiedert
- *odd-pinnate*
43-50 Blattrandformen f
- *leaf margin shapes*
43 ganzrandig
- *entire*
44 gesägt
- *serrate (serrulate, saw-toothed)*
45 doppelt gesägt
- *doubly toothed*
46 gekerbt
- *crenate*
47 gezähnt
- *dentate*
48 ausgebuchtet
- *sinuate*
49 gewimpert
- *ciliate (ciliated)*
50 die Wimper
- *cilium*
51 **die Blüte**
- ***flower***
52 der Blütenstiel
- *flower stalk (flower stem, scape)*
53 der Blütenboden
- *receptacle (floral axis, thalamus, torus)*
54 der Fruchtknoten
- *ovary*
55 der Griffel
- *style*
56 die Narbe
- *stigma*
57 das Staubblatt
- *stamen*
58 das Kelchblatt
- *sepal*
59 das Kronblatt
- *petal*
60 Fruchtknoten m und Staubblatt n [Schnitt]
- *ovary and stamen [section]*
61 die Fruchtknotenwand
- *ovary wall*
62 die Fruchtknotenhöhle
- *ovary cavity*
63 die Samenanlage
- *ovule*
64 der Embryosack
- *embryo sac*
65 der Pollen (Blütenstaub)
- *pollen*
66 der Blütenschlauch
- *pollen tube*
67-77 Blütenstände m
- *inflorescences*
67 die Ähre
- *spike (racemose spike)*
68 die geschlossene Traube
- *raceme (simple raceme)*
69 die Rispe
- *panicle*
70 die Trugdolde
- *cyme*

71 der Kolben
- *spadix (fleshy spike)*
72 die Dolde
- *umbel (simple umbel)*
73 das Köpfchen
- *capitulum*
74 das Körbchen
- *composite head (discoid flower head)*
75 der Blütenkrug
- *hollow flower head*
76 die Schraubel
- *bostryx (helicoid cyme)*
77 der Wickel
- *cincinnus (scorpioid cyme, curled cyme)*
78-82 Wurzeln f
- *roots*
78 die Adventivwurzeln f
- *adventitious roots*
79 die Speicherwurzel
- *tuber (tuberous root, swollen taproot)*
80 die Kletterwurzeln f
- *adventitious roots (aerial roots)*
81 die Wurzeldornen m
- *root thorns*
82 die Atemwurzeln f
- *pneumatophores*
83-85 der Grashalm
- *blade of grass*
83 die Blattscheide
- *leaf sheath*
84 das Blatthäutchen
- *ligule (ligula)*
85 die Blattspreite
- *leaf blade (lamina)*
86 der Keimling
- *embryo (seed, germ)*
87 das Keimblatt
- *cotyledon (seed leaf, seed lobe)*
88 die Keimwurzel
- *radicle*
89 die Keimsproßachse
- *hypocotyl*
90 die Blattknospe
- *plumule (leaf bud)*
91-102 Früchte f
- *fruits*
91-96 Öffnungsfrüchte f
- *dehiscent fruits*
91 die Balgfrucht
- *follicle*
92 die Hülse
- *legume (pod)*
93 die Schote
- *siliqua (pod)*
94 die Spaltkapsel
- *schizocarp*
95 die Deckelkapsel
- *pyxidium (circumscissile seed vessel)*
96 die Porenkapsel
- *poricidal capsule (porose capsule)*
97-102 Schließfrüchte f
- *indehiscent fruits*
97 die Beere
- *berry*
98 die Nuß
- *nut*
99 die Steinfrucht (Kirsche)
- *drupe (stone fruit) (cherry)*
100 die Sammelnußfrucht (Hagebutte)
- *aggregate fruit (compound fruit) (rose hip)*
101 die Sammelsteinfrucht (Himbeere)
- *aggregate fruit (compound fruit) (raspberry)*
102 die Sammelbalgfrucht (Apfel m)
- *pome (apple)*

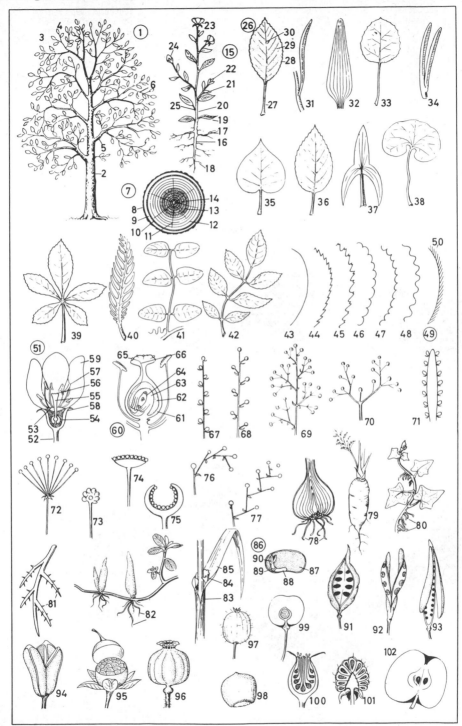

1-73 Laubbäume *m*
- *deciduous trees*
1 die Eiche
- *oak (oak tree)*
2 der Blütenzweig
- *flowering branch*
3 der Fruchtzweig
- *fruiting branch*
4 die Frucht (Eichel)
- *fruit (acorn)*
5 der Becher (die Cupula)
- *cupule (cup)*
6 die weibliche Blüte
- *female flower*
7. die Braktee
- *bract*
8 der männliche Blütenstand
- *male inflorescence*
9 die Birke
- *birch (birch tree)*
10 der Zweig mit Kätzchen *n*, ein
　Blütenzweig *m*
- *branch with catkins, a flowering*
　branch
11 der Fruchtzweig
- *fruiting branch*
12 die Fruchtschuppe
- *scale (catkin scale)*
13 die weibliche Blüte
- *female flower*
14 die männliche Blüte
- *male flower*
15 die Pappel
- *poplar*
16 der Blütenzweig
- *flowering branch*
17 die Blüte
- *flower*
18 der Fruchtzweig
- *fruiting branch*
19 die Frucht
- *fruit*
20 der Samen
- *seed*
21 das Blatt der Zitterpappel (Espe)
- *leaf of the aspen (trembling poplar)*
22 der Fruchtstand
- *infructescence*
23 das Blatt der Silberpappel
- *leaf of the white poplar (silver*
　poplar, silverleaf)
24 die Salweide
- *sallow*
　(goat willow)
25 der Zweig mit den Blütenknospen *f*
- *branch with flower buds*
26 das Blütenkätzchen mit
　Einzelblüte *f*
- *catkin with single flower*
27 der Blattzweig
- *branch with leaves*
28 die Frucht
- *fruit*
29 der Blattzweig der Korbweide
- *osier branch with leaves*
30 die Erle
- *alder*
31 der Fruchtzweig
- *fruiting branch*
32 der Blütenzweig mit vorjährigem
　Zapfen *m*
- *branch with previous year's cone*
33 die Buche
- *beech (beech tree)*
34 der Blütenzweig
- *flowering branch*

35 die Blüte
- *flower*
36 der Fruchtzweig
- *fruiting branch*
37 die Ecker (Buchenfrucht)
- *beech nut*
38 die Esche
- *ash (ash tree)*
39 der Blütenzweig
- *flowering branch*
40 die Blüte
- *flower*
41 der Fruchtzweig
- *fruiting branch*
42 die Eberesche
- *mountain ash (rowan, quickbeam)*
43 der Blütenstand
- *inflorescence*
44 der Fruchtstand
- *infructescence*
45 die Frucht [Längsschnitt]
- *fruit [longitudinal section]*
46 die Linde
- *lime (lime tree, linden, linden tree)*
47 der Fruchtzweig
- *fruiting branch*
48 der Blütenstand
- *inflorescence*
49 die Ulme (Rüster)
- *elm (elm tree)*
50 der Fruchtzweig
- *fruiting branch*
51 der Blütenzweig
- *flowering branch*
52 die Blüte
- *flower*
53 der Ahorn
- *maple (maple tree)*
54 der Blütenzweig
- *flowering branch*
55 die Blüte
- *flower*
56 der Fruchtzweig
- *fruiting branch*
57 der Ahornsamen mit Flügel *m*
- *maple seed with wings (winged*
　maple seed)
58 die Roßkastanie
- *horse chestnut (horse chestnut tree,*
　chestnut, chestnut tree, buckeye)
59 der Zweig mit jungen Früchten *f*
- *branch with young fruits*
60 die Kastanie (der Kastaniensamen)
- *chestnut (horse chestnut)*
61 die reife Frucht
- *mature (ripe) fruit*
62 die Blüte [Längsschnitt]
- *flower [longitudinal section]*
63 die Hainbuche (Weißbuche)
- *hornbeam (yoke elm)*
64 der Fruchtzweig
- *fruiting branch*
65 der Samen
- *seed*
66 der Blütenzweig
- *flowering branch*
67 die Platane
- *plane (plane tree)*
68 das Blatt
- *leaf*
69 der Fruchtstand und die Frucht
- *infructescence and fruit*
70 die Robinie
- *false acacia (locust tree)*
71 der Blütenzweig
- *flowering branch*

72 Teil *m* des Fruchtstandes *m*
- *part of the infructescence*
73 der Blattansatz mit Nebenblättern *n*
- *base of the leaf stalk with stipules*

1-71 Nadelbäume *m* (Koniferen *f*)
- *coniferous trees (conifers)*
1 die Edeltanne (Weißtanne)
- *silver fir (European silver fir, common silver fir)*
2 der Tannenzapfen, ein Fruchtzapfen *m*
- *fir cone, a fruit cone*
3 die Zapfenachse
- *cone axis*
4 der weibliche Blütenzapfen
- *female flower cone*
5 die Deckschuppe
- *bract scale (bract)*
6 der männliche Blütensproß
- *male flower shoot*
7 das Staubblatt
- *stamen*
8 die Zapfenschuppe
- *cone scale*
9 der Samen mit Flügel *m*
- *seed with wing (winged seed)*
10 der Samen [Längsschnitt]
- *seed [longitudinal section]*
11 die Tannennadel (Nadel)
- *fir needle (needle)*
12 die Fichte
- *spruce (spruce fir)*
13 der Fichtenzapfen
- *spruce cone*
14 die Zapfenschuppe
- *cone scale*
15 der Samen
- *seed*
16 der weibliche Blütenzapfen
- *female flower cone*
17 der männliche Blütenstand
- *male inflorescence*
18 das Staubblatt
- *stamen*
19 die Fichtennadel
- *spruce needle*
20 die Kiefer (Gemeine Kiefer, Föhre)
- *pine (Scots pine)*
21 die Zwergkiefer
- *dwarf pine*
22 der weibliche Blütenzapfen
- *female flower cone*
23 der zweinadlige Kurztrieb
- *short shoot with bundle of two leaves*
24 die männlichen Blütenstände *m*
- *male inflorescences*
25 der Jahrestrieb
- *annual growth*
26 der Kiefernzapfen
- *pine cone*
27 die Zapfenschuppe
- *cone scale*
28 der Samen
- *seed*
29 der Fruchtzapfen der Zirbelkiefer
- *fruit cone of the arolla pine (Swiss stone pine)*
30 der Fruchtzapfen der Weymouthskiefer (Weimutskiefer)
- *fruit cone of the Weymouth pine (white pine)*
31 der Kurztrieb [Querschnitt]
- *short shoot [cross section]*
32 die Lärche
- *larch*
33 der Blütenzweig
- *flowering branch*

34 die Schuppe des weiblichen Blütenzapfens *m*
- *scale of the female flower cone*
35 der Staubbeutel
- *anther*
36 der Zweig mit Lärchenzapfen *m* (Fruchtzapfen)
- *branch with larch cones (fruit cones)*
37 der Samen
- *seed*
38 die Zapfenschuppe
- *cone scale*
39 der Lebensbaum
- *arbor vitae (tree of life, thuja)*
40 der Fruchtzweig
- *fruiting branch*
41 der Fruchtzapfen
- *fruit cone*
42 die Schuppe
- *scale*
43 der Zweig mit männlichen und weiblichen Blüten *f*
- *branch with male and female flowers*
44 der männliche Sproß
- *male shoot*
45 die Schuppe, mit Pollensäcken *m*
- *scale with pollen sacs*
46 der weibliche Sproß
- *female shoot*
47 der Wacholder
- *juniper (juniper tree)*
48 der weibliche Sproß [Längsschnitt]
- *female shoot [longitudinal section]*
49 der männliche Sproß
- *male shoot*
50 die Schuppe, mit Pollensäcken *m*
- *scale with pollen sacs*
51 der Fruchtzweig
- *fruiting branch*
52 die Wacholderbeere (Krammetsbeere)
- *juniper berry*
53 die Frucht [Querschnitt]
- *fruit [cross section]*
54 der Samen
- *seed*
55 die Pinie
- *stone pine*
56 der männliche Sproß
- *male shoot*
57 der Fruchtzapfen mit Samen [Längsschnitt]
- *fruit cone with seeds [longitudinal section]*
58 die Zypresse
- *cypress*
59 der Fruchtzweig
- *fruiting branch*
60 der Samen
- *seed*
61 die Eibe
- *yew (yew tree)*
62 männlicher Blütensproß und weiblicher Blütenzapfen
- *male flower shoot and female flower cone*
63 der Fruchtzweig
- *fruiting branch*
64 die Frucht
- *fruit*
65 die Zeder
- *cedar (cedar tree)*
66 der Fruchtzweig
- *fruiting branch*

67 die Fruchtschuppe
- *fruit scale*
68 männlicher Blütensproß und weiblicher Blütenzapfen
- *male flower shoot and female flower cone*
69 der Mammutbaum
- *mammoth tree (Wellingtonia, sequoia)*
70 der Fruchtzweig
- *fruiting branch*
71 der Samen
- *seed*

1 die Forsythie
- *forsythia*
2 der Fruchtknoten und das
  Staubblatt
- *ovary and stamen*
3 das Blatt
- *leaf*
4 der Gelbblühende Jasmin
- *yellow-flowered jasmine (jasmin,*
  jessamine)
5 die Blüte [Längsschnitt] mit Griffel
  m, Fruchtknoten *m* und
  Staubblättern *n*
- *flower [longitudinal section] with*
  styles, ovaries and stamens
6 der Gemeine Liguster
- *privet (common privet)*
7 die Blüte
- *flower*
8 der Fruchtstand
- *infructescence*
9 der Wohlriechende Pfeifenstrauch
- *mock orange (sweet syringa)*
10 der Gemeine Schneeball
- *snowball (snowball bush, guelder*
  rose)
11 die Blüte
- *flower*
12 die Früchte *f*
- *fruits*
13 der Oleander
- *oleander (rosebay, rose laurel)*
14 die Blüte [Längsschnitt]
- *flower [longitudinal section]*
15 die Rote Magnolie
- *red magnolia*
16 das Blatt
- *leaf*
17 die Japanische Quitte
- *japonica (Japanese quince)*
18 die Frucht
- *fruit*
19 der Gemeine Buchsbaum
- *common box (box, box tree)*
20 die weibliche Blüte
- *female flower*
21 die männliche Blüte
- *male flower*
22 die Frucht [Längsschnitt]
- *fruit [longitudinal section]*
23 die Weigelie
- *weigela (weigelia)*
24 die Palmlilie [Teil *m* des
  Blütenstands *m*]
- *yucca [part of the inflorescence]*
25 das Blatt
- *leaf*
26 die Hundsrose
- *dog rose (briar rose, wild briar)*
27 die Frucht
- *fruit*
28 die Kerrie
- *kerria*
29 die Frucht
- *fruit*
30 die Rötästige Kornelkirsche
- *cornelian cherry*
31 die Blüte
- *flower*
32 die Frucht (Kornelkirsche,
  Kornelle)
- *fruit (cornelian cherry)*
33 der Echte Gagel
- *sweet gale (gale)*

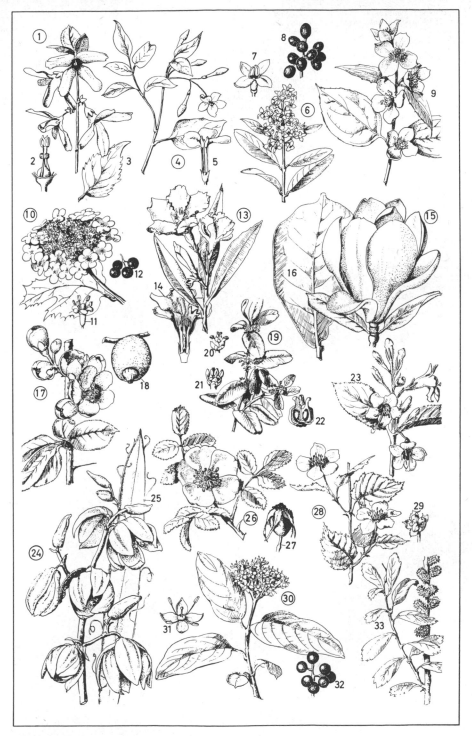

1 der Gemeine Tulpenbaum
- *tulip tree (tulip poplar, saddle tree, whitewood)*
2 die Fruchtblätter *n*
- *carpels*
3 das Staubblatt
- *stamen*
4 die Frucht
- *fruit*
5 der Ysop
- *hyssop*
6 die Blüte [von vorn]
- *flower [front view]*
7 die Blüte
- *flower*
8 der Kelch mit Frucht *f*
- *calyx with fruit*
9 der Gemeine Hülsstrauch (die Stechpalme)
- *holly*
10 die Zwitterblüte
- *androgynous (hermaphroditic, hermaphrodite) flower*
11 die männliche Blüte
- *male flower*
12 die Frucht mit bloßgelegten Steinen *m*
- *fruit with stones exposed*
13 das Echte Geißblatt (Jelängerjelieber *m* od. *n*)
- *honeysuckle (woodbine, woodbind)*
14 die Blütenknospen *f*
- *flower buds*
15 die Blüte [aufgeschnitten]
- *flower [cut open]*
16 die Gemeine Jungfernrebe (der Wilde Wein)
- *Virginia creeper (American ivy, woodbine)*
17 die geöffnete Blüte
- *open flower*
18 der Fruchtstand
- *infructescence*
19 die Frucht [Längsschnitt]
- *fruit [longitudinal section]*
20 der Echte Besenginster
- *broom*
21 die Blüte nach Entfernung *f* der Blumenblätter *n*
- *flower with the petals removed*
22 die unreife Hülse
- *immature (unripe) legume (pod)*
23 der Spierstrauch (die Spiräe)
- *spiraea*
24 die Blüte [Längsschnitt]
- *flower [longitudinal section]*
25 die Frucht
- *fruit*
26 das Fruchtblatt
- *carpel*
27 die Schlehe (der Schwarzdorn, Schlehdorn)
- *blackthorn (sloe)*
28 die Blätter *n*
- *leaves*
29 die Früchte *f*
- *fruits*
30 der Eingriffelige Weißdorn
- *single-pistilled hawthorn (thorn, may)*
31 die Frucht
- *fruit*
32 der Goldregen
- *laburnum (golden chain, golden rain)*
33 die Blütentraube
- *raceme*
34 die Früchte *f*
- *fruits*
35 der Schwarze Holunder (Holunderbusch, Holderbusch, Holder, Holler)
- *black elder (elder)*
36 die Holunderblüten *f* (Holderblüten, Hollerblüten), Blütentrugdolden *f*
- *elder flowers (cymes)*
37 die Holunderbeeren *f* (Holderbeeren, Hollerbeeren)
- *elderberries*

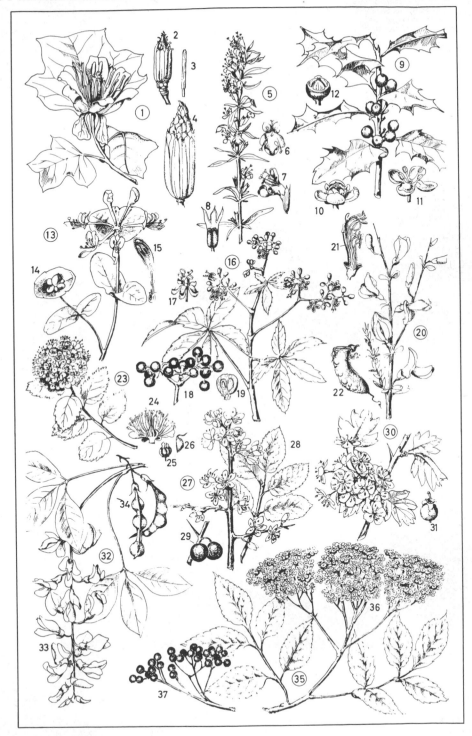

1 der Rundblätterige Steinbrech
- *rotundifoliate (rotundifolious)*
  saxifrage (rotundifoliate
  breakstone)
2 das Blatt
- *leaf*
3 die Blüte
- *flower*
4 die Frucht
- *fruit*
5 die Gemeine Kuhschelle
- *anemone (windflower)*
6 die Blüte [Längsschnitt]
- *flower [longitudinal section]*
7 die Frucht
- *fruit*
8 der Scharfe Hahnenfuß
- *buttercup (meadow buttercup,*
  butterflower, goldcup, king cup,
  crowfoot)
9 das Grundblatt
- *basal leaf*
10 die Frucht
- *fruit*
11 das Wiesenschaumkraut
- *lady's smock (ladysmock, cuckoo*
  flower)
12 das grundständige Blatt
- *basal leaf*
13 die Frucht
- *fruit*
14 die Glockenblume
- *harebell (hairbell, bluebell)*
15 das Grundblatt
- *basal leaf*
16 die Blüte [Längsschnitt]
- *flower [longitudinal section]*
17 die Frucht
- *fruit*
18 die Efeublätterige Gundelrebe (der
  Gundermann)
- *ground ivy (ale hoof)*
19 die Blüte [Längsschnitt]
- *flower [longitudinal section]*
20 die Blüte [von vorn]
- *flower [front view]*
21 der Scharfe Mauerpfeffer
- *stonecrop*
22 das (der) Ehrenpreis
- *speedwell*
23 die Blüte
- *flower*
24 die Frucht
- *fruit*
25 der Samen
- *seed*
26 das Pfennigkraut
- *moneywort*
27 die aufgesprungene Fruchtkapsel
- *dehisced fruit*
28 der Samen
- *seed*
29 die Taubenskabiose
- *small scabious*
30 das Grundblatt
- *basal leaf*
31 die Strahlblüte
- *ray floret (flower of outer series)*
32 die Scheibenblüte
- *disc (disk) floret (flower of inner*
  series)
33 der Hüllkelch mit Kelchborsten *f*
- *involucral calyx with pappus*
  bristles
34 der Fruchtknoten mit Kelch *m*
- *ovary with pappus*

35 die Frucht
- *fruit*
36 das Scharbockskraut
- *lesser celandine*
37 die Frucht
- *fruit*
38 die Blattachsel mit Brutknollen *n*
- *leaf axil with bulbil*
39 das Einjährige Rispengras
- *annual meadow grass*
40 die Blüte
- *flower*
41 das Ährchen [von der Seite]
- *spikelet [side view]*
42 das Ährchen [von vorn]
- *spikelet [front view]*
43 die Karyopse (Nußfrucht)
- *caryopsis (indehiscent fruit)*
44 der Grasbüschel
- *tuft of grass (clump of grass)*
45 der Gemeine Beinwell (die
  Schwarzwurz)
- *comfrey*
46 die Blüte [Längsschnitt]
- *flower [longitudinal section]*
47 die Frucht
- *fruit*

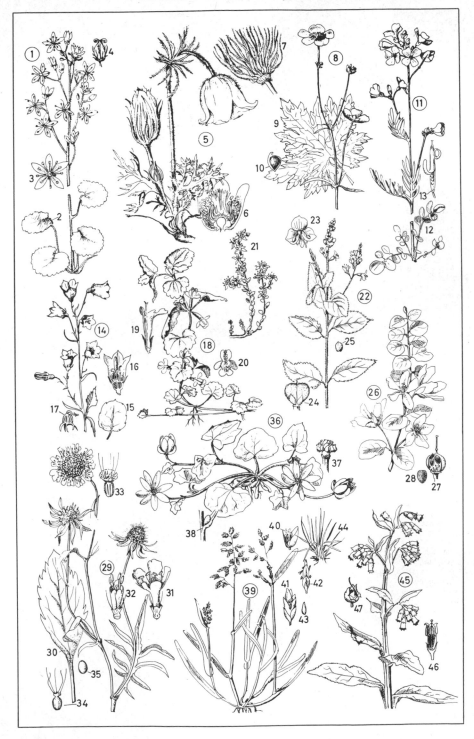

1 das Gänseblümchen
(Maßliebchen)
- *daisy (Am. English daisy)*
2 die Blüte
- *flower*
3 die Frucht
- *fruit*
4 die Wucherblume (Margerite)
- *oxeye daisy (white oxeye daisy,*
marguerite)
5 die Blüte
- *flower*
6 die Frucht
- *fruit*
7 die Sterndolde
- *masterwort*
8 die Schlüsselblume (Primel, das
Himmelsschlüsselchen)
- *cowslip*
9 die Königskerze (Wollblume, das
Wollkraut)
- *great mullein (Aaron's rod,*
shepherd's club)
10 der Wiesenknöterich (Knöterich)
- *bistort (snakeweed)*
11 die Blüte
- *flower*
12 die Wiesenflockenblume
- *knapweed*
13 die Wegmalve (Malve)
- *common mallow*
14 die Frucht
- *fruit*
15 die Schafgarbe
- *yarrow*
16 die Braunelle
- *self-heal*
17 der Hornklee
- *bird's foot trefoil (bird's foot*
clover)
18 der Ackerschachtelhalm [ein Sproß *m*]
- *horsetail (equisetum) [a shoot]*
19 die Blüte
- *flower (strobile)*
20 die Pechnelke
- *campion (catchfly)*
21 die Kuckuckslichtnelke
- *ragged robin (cuckoo flower)*
22 die Osterluzei
- *birth-wort*
23 die Blüte
- *flower*
24 der Storchschnabel
- *crane's bill*
25 die Wegwarte (Zichorie)
- *wild chicory (witloof, succory, wild*
endive)
26 das Nickende Leinkraut
- *common toadflax*
(butter-and-eggs)
27 der Frauenschuh
- *lady's slipper (Venus's slipper,*
Am. *moccasin flower)*
28 das Knabenkraut, eine Orchidee
- *orchis (wild orchid), an orchid*

1 das Buschwindröschen (die
  Anemone, *schweiz.* das Schneeglöggli)
- *wood anemone (anemone,*
  windflower)
2 das Maiglöckchen (die Maiblume,
  schweiz. das Maierisli, Knopfgras,
  Krallegras)
- *lily of the valley*
3 das Katzenpfötchen
  (Himmelfahrtsblümchen); *ähnl.:*
  die Sandstrohblume
- *cat's foot (milkwort);* sim.:
  sandflower (everlasting)
4 der Türkenbund
- *turk's cap (turk's cap lily)*
5 der Waldgeißbart
- *goatsbeard (goat's beard)*
6 der Bärenlauch (*österr.* Faltigron,
  Faltrian, Feltrian)
- *ramson*
7 das Lungenkraut
- *lungwort*
8 der Lerchensporn
- *corydalis*
9 die Große Fetthenne (der
  Schmerwurz, Donnerbart, *schweiz.*
  Schuhputzer)
- *orpine (livelong)*
10 der Seidelbast
- *daphne*
11 das Große Springkraut
  (Rührmichnichtan)
- *touch-me-not*
12 der Keulige Bärlapp
- *staghorn (stag horn moss, stag's*
  horn, stag's horn moss, coral
  evergreen)
13 das Fettkraut, eine
  insektenfressende Pflanze
- *butterwort, an insectivorous plant*
14 der Sonnentau; *ähnl.:* die
  Venusfliegenfalle
- *sundew;* sim.: *Venus's flytrap*
15 die Bärentraube
- *bearberry*
16 der Tüpfelfarn, ein Farnkraut *n*
  (Farn *m*); *ähnl.:* der Wurmfarn,
  Adlerfarn, Königsfarn
- *polypody (polypod), a fern;* sim.:
  male fern, brake (bracken, eagle
  fern), royal fern (royal osmund,
  king's fern, ditch fern)
17 das Goldene Frauenhaar, ein Moos *n*
- *haircap moss (hair moss, golden*
  maidenhair), a moss
18 das Wollgras
- *cotton grass (cotton rush)*
19 das Heidekraut (die Erika); *ähnl.:*
  die Glockenheide (Sumpfheide,
  Moorheide)
- *heather (heath, ling);* sim.: *bell*
  heather (cross-leaved heather)
20 das Heideröschen (Sonnenröschen)
- *rock rose (sun rose)*
21 der Sumpfporst
- *marsh tea*
22 der Kalmus
- *sweet flag (sweet calamus, sweet sedge)*
23 die Heidelbeere (Schwarzbeere,
  Blaubeere); *ähnl.:* die Preiselbeere,
  Moorbeere, Krähenbeere
  (Rauschbeere)
- *bilberry (whortleberry, huckleberry,*
  blueberry); sim.: cowberry (red
  whortleberry), bog bilberry (bog
  whortleberry), crowberry (crakeberry)

1-13 Alpenpflanzen *f*
- *alpine plants*
1 die Alpenrose
- *alpine rose (alpine rhododendron)*
2 der Blütenzweig
- *flowering shoot*
3 das Alpenglöckchen
- *alpine soldanella (soldanella)*
4 die ausgebreitete Blütenkrone
- *corolla opened out*
5 die Samenkapsel mit dem Griffel *m*
- *seed vessel with the style*
6 die Edelraute
- *alpine wormwood*
7 der Blütenstand
- *inflorescence*
8 die Aurikel
- *auricula*
9 das Edelweiß
- *edelweiss*
10 die Blütenformen *f*
- *flower shapes*
11 die Frucht mit dem Haarkelch *m*
- *fruit with pappus tuft*
12 der Teilblütenkorb
- *part of flower head (of capitulum)*
13 der Stengellose Enzian
- *stemless alpine gentian*
14-57 Wasser- u. Sumpfpflanzen *f*
- *aquatic plants* (water plants) and
  marsh plants
14 die Seerose
- *white water lily*
15 das Blatt
- *leaf*
16 die Blüte
- *flower*
17 die Victoria regia
- *Queen Victoria water lily (Victoria
  regia water lily, royal water lily,
  Amazon water lily)*
18 das Blatt
- *leaf*
19 die Blattunterseite
- *underside of the leaf*
20 die Blüte
- *flower*
21 das Schilfrohr (der Rohrkolben)
- *reed mace bulrush (cattail, cat's
  tail, cattail flag, club rush)*
22 der männliche Teil des Kolbens *m*
- *male part of the spadix*
23 die männliche Blüte
- *male flower*
24 der weibliche Teil
- *female part*
25 die weibliche Blüte
- *female flower*
26 das Vergißmeinnicht
- *forget-me-not*
27 der blühende Zweig
- *flowering shoot*
28 die Blüte [Schnitt]
- *flower [section]*
29 der Froschbiß
- *frog's bit*
30 die Brunnenkresse
- *watercress*
31 der Stengel mit Blüten *f* und
  jungen Früchten *f*
- *stalk with flowers and immature
  (unripe) fruits*
32 die Blüte
- *flower*
33 die Schote mit Samen *m*
- *siliqua (pod) with seeds*

34 zwei Samen *m*
- *two seeds*
35 die Wasserlinse
- *duckweed (duck's meat)*
36 die blühende Pflanze
- *plant in flower*
37 die Blüte
- *flower*
38 die Frucht
- *fruit*
39 die Schwanenblume
- *flowering rush*
40 die Blütendolde
- *flower umbel*
41 die Blätter *n*
- *leaves*
42 die Frucht
- *fruit*
43 die Grünalge
- *green alga*
44 der Froschlöffel
- *water plantain*
45 das Blatt
- *leaf*
46 die Blütenrispe
- *panicle*
47 die Blüte
- *flower*
48 der Zuckertang, eine Braunalge
- *honey wrack, a brown alga*
49 der Laubkörper (Thallus, das
  Thallom)
- *thallus (plant body, frond)*
50 das Haftorgan
- *holdfast*
51 das Pfeilkraut
- *arrow head*
52 die Blattformen *f*
- *leaf shapes*
53 der Blütenstand mit männlichen
  Blüten *f* [oben] und weiblichen
  Blüten *f* [unten]
- *inflorescence with male flowers
  [above] and female flowers [below]*
54 das Seegras
- *sea grass*
55 der Blütenstand
- *inflorescence*
56 die Wasserpest
- *Canadian waterweed (Canadian
  pondweed)*
57 die Blüte
- *flower*

1 der Eisenhut (Sturmhut)
- *aconite (monkshood, wolfsbane, helmet flower)*
2 der Fingerhut (die Digitalis)
- *foxglove (Digitalis)*
3 die Herbstzeitlose (*österr.* Lausblume, das Lauskraut, *schweiz.* die Herbstblume, Winterblume)
- *meadow saffron (naked lady, naked boys)*
4 der Schierling
- *hemlock (Conium)*
5 der Schwarze Nachtschatten (*österr.* Mondscheinkraut, Saukraut)
- *black nightshade (common nightshade, petty morel)*
6 das Bilsenkraut
- *henbane*
7 die Tollkirsche (Teufelskirsche, *schweiz.* Wolfsbeere, Wolfskirsche, Krottenblume, Krottenbeere, *österr.* Tintenbeere, Schwarzbeere), ein Nachtschattengewächs *n*
- *deadly nightshade (belladonna, banewort, dwale), a solanaceous herb*
8 der Stechapfel (Dornapfel, die Stachelnuß)
- *thorn apple (stramonium, stramony, Am. jimson weed, jimpson weed, Jamestown weed, stinkweed)*
9 der Aronsstab
- *cuckoo pint (lords-and-ladies, wild arum, wake-robin)*
10-13 Giftpilze *m*
- *poisonous fungi (poisonous mushrooms, toadstools)*
10 der Fliegenpilz, ein Blätterpilz *m*
- *fly agaric (fly amanita, fly fungus), an agaric*
11 der Knollenblätterpilz
- *amanita*
12 der Satanspilz
- *Satan's mushroom*
13 der Giftreizker
- *woolly milk cap*

1 die Kamille (Deutsche Kamille,
   Echte Kamille)
 - *camomile (chamomile, wild
   camomile)*
2 die Arnika
 - *arnica*
3 die Pfefferminze
 - *peppermint*
4 der Wermut
 - *wormwood (absinth)*
5 der Baldrian
 - *valerian (allheal)*
6 der Fenchel
 - *fennel*
7 der Lavendel (*schweiz.* Valander *m*,
   die Balsamblume)
 - *lavender*
8 der Huflattich (Pferdefuß,
   Brustlattich)
 - *coltsfoot*
9 der Rainfarn
 - *tansy*
10 das Tausendgüldenkraut
 - *centaury*
11 der Spitzwegerich
 - *ribwort (ribwort plantain, ribgrass)*
12 der Eibisch
 - *marshmallow*
13 der Faulbaum
 - *alder buckthorn (alder dogwood)*
14 der Rizinus
 - *castor-oil plant (Palma Christi)*
15 der Schlafmohn
 - *opium poppy*
16 der Sennesblätterstrauch (die
   Kassie); *die getrockneten Blätter:*
   Sennesblätter *n*
 - *senna (cassia);* the dried leaflets:
   senna leaves
17 der Chinarindenbaum
 - *cinchona (chinchona)*
18 der Kampferbaum
 - *camphor tree (camphor laurel)*
19 der Betelnußbaum
 - *betel palm (areca, areca palm)*
20 die Betelnuß
 - *betel nut (areca nut)*

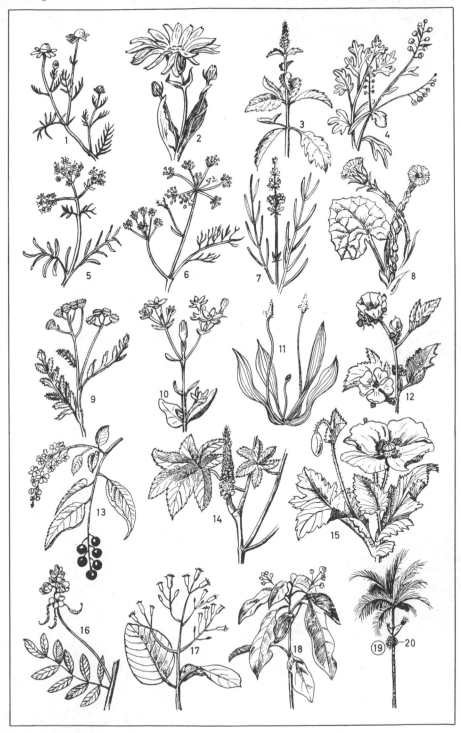

1 der Feldchampignon
- *meadow mushroom (field mushroom)*
2 das Fadengeflecht (Pilzgeflecht, Myzelium, Myzel) mit Fruchtkörpern *m* (Pilzen)
- *mycelial threads (hyphae, mycelium) with fruiting bodies (mushrooms)*
3 Pilz *m* [Längsschnitt]
- *mushroom [longitudinal section]*
4 der Hut mit Lamellen *f*
- *cap (pileus) with gills*
5 der Schleier (das Velum)
- *veil (velum)*
6 die Lamelle [Schnitt]
- *gill [section]*
7 die Sporenständer *m* (Basidien *f*) [vom Lamellenrand *m* mit Sporen *f*]
- *basidia [on the gill with basidiospores]*
8 die keimenden Sporen *f*
- *germinating basidiospores (spores)*
9 die Trüffel
- *truffle*
10 der Pilz [von außen]
- *truffle [external view]*
11 der Pilz [Schnitt]
- *truffle [section]*
12 Inneres *n* mit den Sporenschläuchen *m* [Schnitt]
- *interior showing asci [section]*
13 zwei Sporenschläuche *m* mit den Sporen *f*
- *two asci with the ascospores (spores)*
14 der Pfifferling
- *chanterelle (chantarelle)*
15 der Maronenpilz
- *Chestnut Boletus*
16 der Steinpilz
- *cep (cepe, squirrel's bread, Boletus edulis)*
17 die Röhrenschicht
- *layer of tubes (hymenium)*
18 der Stiel
- *stem (stipe)*
19 der Eierbovist
- *puffball (Bovista nigrescens)*
20 der Flaschenbovist
- *devil's tobacco pouch (common puffball)*
21 der Butterpilz
- *Brown Ring Boletus (Boletus luteus)*
22 der Birkenpilz
- *Birch Boletus (Boletus scaber)*
23 der Speisetäubling
- *Russula vesca*
24 der Habichtschwamm
- *scaled prickle fungus*
25 der Mönchskopf
- *slender funnel fungus*
26 der Speisemorchel
- *morel (Morchella esculenta)*
27 der Spitzmorchel
- *morel (Morchella conica)*
28 der Hallimasch
- *honey fungus*
29 der Grünreizker
- *saffron milk cap*
30 der Parasolpilz
- *parasol mushroom*
31 der Semmelpilz
- *hedgehog fungus (yellow prickle fungus)*

32 der Gelbe Ziegenbart
- *yellow coral fungus (goatsbeard, goat's beard, coral Clavaria)*
33 das Stockschwämmchen
- *little cluster fungus*

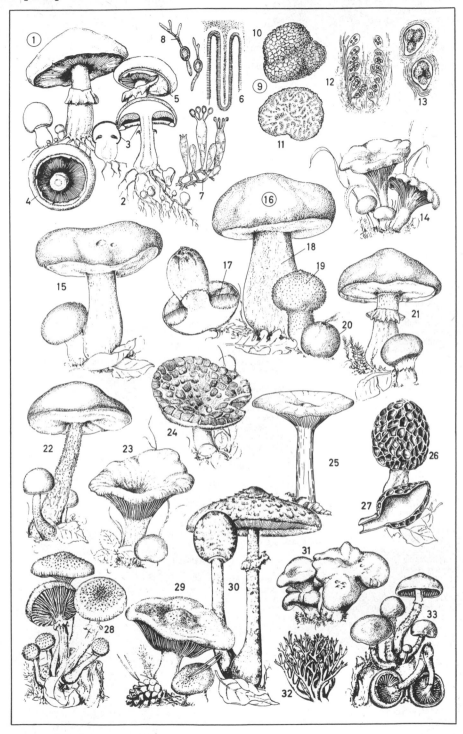

1 der Kaffeestrauch
- *coffee tree (coffee plant)*
2 der Fruchtzweig
- *fruiting branch*
3 der Blütenzweig
- *flowering branch*
4 die Blüte
- *flower*
5 die Frucht mit den beiden Bohnen
  f[Längsschnitt]
- *fruit with two beans [longitudinal
  section]*
6 die Kaffeebohne; *nach
  Verarbeitung:* der Kaffee
- *coffee bean; when processed:
  coffee*
7 der Teestrauch
- *tea plant (tea tree)*
8 der Blütenzweig
- *flowering branch*
9 das Teeblatt; *nach Verarbeitung:*
  der Tee
- *tea leaf; when processed: tea*
10 die Frucht
- *fruit*
11 der Matestrauch
- *maté shrub (maté, yerba maté,
  Paraguay tea)*
12 der Blütenzweig mit den
  Zwitterblüten *f*
- *flowering branch with androgynous
  (hermaphroditic, hermaphrodite)
  flowers*
13 die männl. Blüte
- *male flower*
14 die Zwitterblüte
- *androgynous (hermaphroditic,
  hermaphrodite) flower*
15 die Frucht
- *fruit*
16 der Kakaobaum
- *cacao tree (cacao)*
17 der Zweig mit Blüten *f* und
  Früchten *f*
- *branch with flowers and fruits*
18 die Blüte [Längsschnitt]
- *flower [longitudinal section]*
19 die Kakaobohnen *f; nach
  Verarbeitung:* der Kakao, das
  Kakaopulver
- *cacao beans (cocoa beans); when
  processed: cocoa, cocoa powder*
20 der Samen [Längsschnitt]
- *seed [longitudinal section]*
21 der Embryo
- *embryo*
22 der Zimtbaum
- *cinnamon tree (cinnamon)*
23 der Blütenzweig
- *flowering branch*
24 die Frucht
- *fruit*
25 die Zimtrinde; *zerstoßen:* der Zimt
- *cinnamon bark; when crushed:
  cinnamon*
26 der Gewürznelkenbaum
- *clove tree*
27 der Blütenzweig
- *flowering branch*
28 die Knospe; *getrocknet:* die
  Gewürznelke, „Nelke"
- *flower bud; when dried: clove*
29 die Blüte
- *flower*
30 der Muskatnußbaum
- *nutmeg tree*

31 der Blütenzweig
- *flowering branch*
32 die weibl. Blüte [Längsschnitt]
- *female flower [longitudinal section]*
33 die reife Frucht
- *mature (ripe) fruit*
34 die Muskatblüte, ein Samen *m* mit
  geschlitztem Samenmantel *m*
  (Macis)
- *nutmeg with mace, a seed with
  laciniate aril*
35 der Samen [Querschnitt];
  getrocknet: die Muskatnuß
- *seed [cross section]; when dried:
  nutmeg*
36 der Pfefferstrauch
- *pepper plant*
37 der Fruchtzweig
- *fruiting branch*
38 der Blütenstand
- *inflorescence*
39 die Frucht [Längsschnitt] mit
  Samen *m* (Pfefferkorn); *gemahlen:*
  der Pfeffer
- *fruit [longitudinal section] with
  seed (peppercorn); when ground:
  pepper*
40 die Virginische Tabakpflanze
- *Virginia tobacco plant*
41 der Blütenzweig
- *flowering shoot*
42 die Blüte
- *flower*
43 das Tabakblatt; *verarbeitet:* der
  Tabak
- *tobacco leaf; when cured: tobacco*
44 die reife Fruchtkapsel
- *mature (ripe) fruit capsule*
45 der Samen
- *seed*
46 die Vanillepflanze
- *vanilla plant*
47 der Blütenzweig
- *flowering shoot*
48 die Vanilleschote; *nach
  Verarbeitung:* die Vanillestange
- *vanilla pod; when cured: stick of
  vanilla*
49 der Pistazienbaum
- *pistachio tree*
50 der Blütenzweig mit den weibl.
  Blüten *f*
- *flowering branch with female
  flowers*
51 die Steinfrucht (Pistazie)
- *drupe (pistachio, pistachio nut)*
52 das Zuckerrohr
- *sugar cane*
53 die Pflanze (der Habitus) während
  der Blüte
- *plant (habit) in bloom*
54 die Blütenrispe
- *panicle*
55 die Blüte
- *flower*

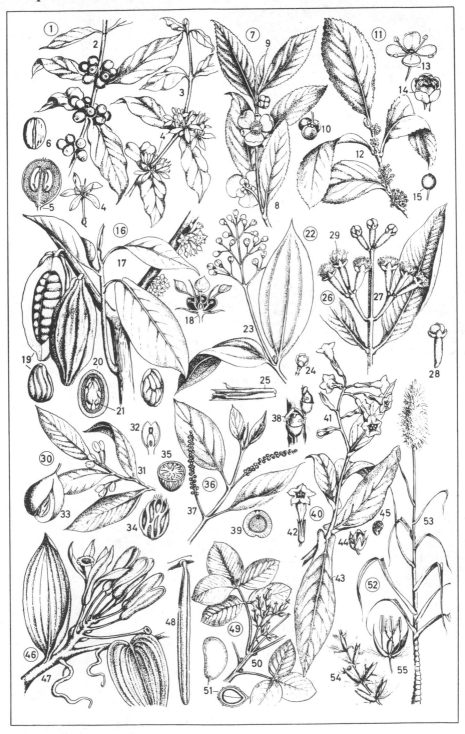

1 der Raps
- *rape (cole, coleseed)*
2 das Grundblatt
- *basal leaf*
3 die Blüte [Längsschnitt]
- *flower [longitudinal section]*
4 die reife Fruchtschote
- *mature (ripe) siliqua (pod)*
5 der ölhaltige Samen
- *oleiferous seed*
6 der Flachs (Lein)
- *flax*
7 der Blütenstengel
- *peduncle (pedicel, flower stalk)*
8 die Fruchtkapsel
- *seed vessel (boll)*
9 der Hanf
- *hemp*
10 die fruchtende weibliche Pflanze
- *fruiting female (pistillate) plant*
11 der weibliche Blütenstand
- *female inflorescence*
12 die Blüte
- *flower*
13 der männliche Blütenstand
- *male inflorescence*
14 die Frucht
- *fruit*
15 der Samen
- *seed*
16 die Baumwolle
- *cotton*
17 die Blüte
- *flower*
18 die Frucht
- *fruit*
19 das Samenhaar [die Wolle]
- *lint [cotton wool]*
20 der Kapokbaum
- *silk-cotton tree (kapok tree, capoc tree, ceiba tree)*
21 die Frucht
- *fruit*
22 der Blütenzweig
- *flowering branch*
23 der Samen
- *seed*
24 der Samen [Längsschnitt]
- *seed [longitudinal section]*
25 die Jute
- *jute*
26 der Blütenzweig
- *flowering branch*
27 die Blüte
- *flower*
28 die Frucht
- *fruit*
29 der Olivenbaum (Ölbaum)
- *olive tree (olive)*
30 der Blütenzweig
- *flowering branch*
31 die Blüte
- *flower*
32 die Frucht
- *fruit*
33 der Gummibaum
- *rubber tree (rubber plant)*
34 der Zweig mit Früchten *f*
- *fruiting branch*
35 die Feige
- *fig*
36 die Blüte
- *flower*
37 der Guttaperchabaum
- *gutta-percha tree*

38 der Blütenzweig
- *flowering branch*
39 die Blüte
- *flower*
40 die Frucht
- *fruit*
41 die Erdnuß
- *peanut (ground nut, monkey nut)*
42 der Blütenzweig
- *flowering shoot*
43 die Wurzel mit Früchten *f*
- *root with fruits*
44 die Frucht [Längsschnitt]
- *nut (kernel) [longitudinal section]*
45 die Sesampflanze
- *sesame plant (simsim, benniseed)*
46 der Zweig mit Blüten *f* und Früchten *f*
- *flowers and fruiting branch*
47 die Blüte [Längsschnitt]
- *flower [longitudinal section]*
48 die Kokospalme
- *coconut palm (coconut tree, coco palm, cocoa palm)*
49 der Blütenstand
- *inflorescence*
50 die weibliche Blüte
- *female flower*
51 die männliche Blüte [Längsschnitt]
- *male flower [longitudinal section]*
52 die Frucht [Längsschnitt]
- *fruit [longitudinal section]*
53 die Kokosnuß
- *coconut (cokernut)*
54 die Ölpalme
- *oil palm*
55 der männliche Blütenkolben mit der Blüte
- *male spadix*
56 der Fruchtstand mit der Frucht
- *infructescence with fruit*
57 der Samen mit den Keimlöchern *n*
- *seed with micropyles (foramina) (foraminate seeds)*
58 die Sagopalme
- *sago palm*
59 die Frucht
- *fruit*
60 das Bambusrohr
- *bamboo stem (bamboo culm)*
61 der Blattzweig
- *branch with leaves*
62 die Blütenähre
- *spike*
63 das Halmstück mit Knoten *m*
- *part of bamboo stem with joints*
64 die Papyrusstaude
- *papyrus plant (paper reed, paper rush)*
65 der Blütenschopf
- *umbel*
66 die Blütenähre
- *spike*

384 Südfrüchte

1 die Dattelpalme
- *date palm (date)*
2 die fruchttragende Palme
- *fruiting palm*
3 der Palmwedel
- *palm frond*
4 der männliche Blütenkolben
- *male spadix*
5 die männliche Blüte
- *male flower*
6 der weibliche Blütenkolben
- *female spadix*
7 die weibliche Blüte
- *female flower*
8 ein Zweig *m* des Fruchtstandes *m*
- *stand of fruit*
9 die Dattel
- *date*
10 der Dattelkern (Samen)
- *date kernel (seed)*
11 die Feige
- *fig*
12 der Zweig mit Scheinfrüchten *f*
- *branch with pseudocarps*
13 die Feige mit Blüten *f*
[Längsschnitt]
- *fig with flowers [longitudinal
section]*
14 die weibliche Blüte
- *female flower*
15 die männliche Blüte
- *male flower*
16 der Granatapfel
- *pomegranate*
17 der Blütenzweig
- *flowering branch*
18 die Blüte [Längsschnitt,
Blütenkrone entfernt]
- *flower [longitudinal section, corolla
removed]*
19 die Frucht
- *fruit*
20 der Samen (Kern) [Längsschnitt]
- *seed [longitudinal section]*
21 der Samen [Querschnitt]
- *seed [cross section]*
22 der Embryo
- *embryo*
23 die Zitrone (Limone); *ähnl.:*
Mandarine *f*, Apfelsine *f*,
Pampelmuse *f* (Grapefruit *f*)
- *lemon; sim.: tangerine (mandarin),
orange, grapefruit*
24 der Blütenzweig
- *flowering branch*
25 die Apfelsinenblüte
(Orangenblüte) [Längsschnitt]
- *orange flower [longitudinal section]*
26 die Frucht
- *fruit*
27 die Apfelsine (Orange)
[Querschnitt]
- *orange [cross section]*
28 die Bananenstaude
- *banana plant (banana tree)*
29 die Blätterkrone
- *crown*
30 der Scheinstamm mit den
Blattscheiden *f*
- *herbaceous stalk with overlapping
leaf sheaths*
31 der Blütenstand mit jungen
Früchten *f*
- *inflorescence with young fruits*
32 der Fruchtstand
- *infructescence (bunch of fruit)*

33 die Banane
- *banana*
34 die Bananenblüte
- *banana flower*
35 das Bananenblatt [Schema]
- *banana leaf [diagram]*
36 die Mandel
- *almond*
37 der Blütenzweig
- *flowering branch*
38 der Fruchtzweig
- *fruiting branch*
39 die Frucht
- *fruit*
40 die Steinfrucht mit dem Samen *m*
[der Mandel]
- *drupe containing seed [almond]*
41 das Johannisbrot
- *carob*
42 der Zweig mit weibl. Blüten *f*
- *branch with female flowers*
43 die weibliche Blüte
- *female flower*
44 die männliche Blüte
- *male flower*
45 die Frucht
- *fruit*
46 die Fruchtschote [Querschnitt]
- *siliqua (pod) [cross section]*
47 der Samen
- *seed*
48 die Edelkastanie
- *sweet chestnut (Spanish chestnut)*
49 der Blütenzweig
- *flowering branch*
50 der weibliche Blütenstand
- *female inflorescence*
51 die männliche Blüte
- *male flower*
52 der Fruchtbecher (die Cupula) mit
den Samen *m* [den Kastanien *f*,
Maronen *f*]
- *cupule containing seeds (nuts,
chestnuts)*
53 die Paranuß
- *Brazil nut*
54 der Blütenzweig
- *flowering branch*
55 das Blatt
- *leaf*
56 die Blüte [Aufsicht]
- *flower [from above]*
57 die Blüte [Längsschnitt]
- *flower [longitudinal section]*
58 der geöffnete Fruchttopf mit
einliegenden Samen *m*
- *opened capsule, containing seeds
(nuts)*
59 die Paranuß [Querschnitt]
- *Brazil nut [cross section]*
60 die Nuß [Längsschnitt]
- *nut [longitudinal section]*
61 die Ananaspflanze (Ananas)
- *pineapple plant (pineapple)*
62 die Scheinfrucht mit der
Blattrosette
- *pseudocarp with crown of leaves*
63 die Blütenähre
- *syncarp*
64 die Ananasblüte
- *pineapple flower*
65 die Blüte [Längsschnitt]
- *flower [longitudinal section]*

Für freundliche Unterstützung und Mitarbeit haben wir zu danken:

ADB GmbH, Bestwig; AEG-Telefunken, Abteilung Werbung, Wolfenbüttel; Agfa-Gevaert AG, Presse-Abteilung, Leverkusen; Eduard Ahlborn GmbH, Hildesheim; AID, Land- und Hauswirtschaftlicher Auswertungs- und Informationsdienst e. V., Bonn-Bad Godesberg; Arbeitsausschuß der Waldarbeitsschulen beim Kuratorium für Waldarbeit und Forsttechnik, Bad Segeberg; Arnold & Richter KG, München; Atema AB, Härnösand (Schweden); Audi NSU Auto-Union AG, Presseabteilung, Ingolstadt; Bêché & Grohs GmbH, Hückeswagen/Rhld.; Big Dutchman (Deutschland) GmbH, Bad Mergentheim und Calveslage über Vechta; Biologische Bundesanstalt für Land- und Forstwirtschaft, Braunschweig; Black & Decker, Idstein/Ts.; Braun AG, Frankfurt am Main; Bolex GmbH, Ismaning; Maschinenfabrik zum Bruderhaus GmbH, Reutlingen; Bund Deutscher Radfahrer e. V., Gießen; Bundesanstalt für Arbeit, Nürnberg; Bundesanstalt für Wasserbau, Karlsruhe; Bundesbahndirektion Karlsruhe, Presse- u. Informationsdienst, Karlsruhe; Bundesinnungsverband des Deutschen Schuhmacher-Handwerks, Düsseldorf; Bundeslotsenkammer, Hamburg; Bundesverband Bekleidungsindustrie e. V., Köln; Bundesverband der Deutschen Gas- und Wasserwirtschaft e. V., Frankfurt am Main; Bundesverband der Deutschen Zementindustrie e. V., Köln; Bundesverband Glasindustrie e. V., Düsseldorf; Bundesverband Metall, Essen-Kray und Berlin; Burkhardt + Weber KG, Reutlingen; Busatis-Werke KG, Remscheid; Claas GmbH, Harsewinkel; Copygraph GmbH, Hannover; Dr. Irmgard Correll, Mannheim; Daimler-Benz AG, Presse-Abteilung, Stuttgart; Dalex-Werke Niepenberg & Co. GmbH, Wissen; Elisabeth Daub, Mannheim; John Deere Vertrieb Deutschland, Mannheim; Deutsche Bank AG, Filiale Mannheim, Mannheim; Deutsche Gesellschaft für das Badewesen e. V., Essen; Deutsche Gesellschaft für Schädlingsbekämpfung mbH, Frankfurt am Main; Deutsche Gesellschaft zur Rettung Schiffbrüchiger, Bremen; Deutsche Milchwirtschaft, Molkerei- und Käserei-Zeitung (Verlag Th. Mann), Gelsenkirchen-Buer; Deutsche Eislauf-Union e. V., München; Deutscher Amateur-Box-Verband e. V., Essen; Deutscher Bob- und Schlittensportverband e. V., Berchtesgaden; Deutscher Eissport-Verband e. V., München; Deutsche Reiterliche Vereinigung e. V., Abteilung Sport, Warendorf; Deutscher Fechter-Bund e. V., Bonn; Deutscher Fußball-Bund, Frankfurt am Main; Deutscher Handball-Bund, Dortmund; Deutscher Hockey-Bund e. V., Köln; Deutscher Leichtathletik Verband, Darmstadt; Deutscher Motorsport Verband e. V., Frankfurt am Main; Deutscher Schwimm-Verband e. V., München; Deutscher Turner-Bund, Würzburg; Deutscher Verein von Gas- und Wasserfachmännern e. V., Eschborn; Deutscher Wetterdienst, Zentralamt, Offenbach; DIN Deutsches Institut für Normung e. V., Köln; Deutsches Institut für Normung e. V., Fachnormenausschuß Theatertechnik, Frankfurt am Main; Deutsche Versuchs- und Prüf-Anstalt für Jagd- und Sportwaffen e. V., Altenbeken-Buke; Friedrich Dick GmbH, Esslingen; Dr. Maria Dose, Mannheim; Dual Gebrüder Steidinger, St. Georgen/Schwarzwald; Durst AG, Bozen (Italien); Gebrüder Eberhard, Pflug- und Landmaschinenfabrik, Ulm; Gabriele Echtermann, Hemsbach; Dipl.-Ing. W. Ehret GmbH, Emmendingen-Kollmarsreute; Eichbaum-Brauereien AG, Worms/Mannheim; ER-WE-PA, Maschinenfabrik und Eisengießerei GmbH, Erkrath bei Düsseldorf; Escher Wyss GmbH, Ravensburg; Eumuco Aktiengesellschaft für Maschinenbau, Leverkusen; Euro-Photo GmbH, Willich; European Honda Motor Trading GmbH, Offenbach; Fachgemeinschaft Feuerwehrfahrzeuge und -geräte, Verein Deutscher Maschinenbau-Anstalten e. V., Frankfurt am Main; Fachnormenausschuß Maschinenbau im Deutschen Normenausschuß DNA, Frankfurt am Main; Fachnormenausschuß Schmiedetechnik in DIN Deutsches Institut für Normung e. V., Hagen; Fachverband des Deutschen Tapetenhandels e. V., Köln; Fachverband der Polstermöbelindustrie e. V., Herford; Fachverband Rundfunk und Fernsehen im Zentralverband der Elektrotechnischen Industrie e. V., Frankfurt am Main; Fahr AG Maschinenfabrik, Gottmadingen; Fendt & Co., Agrartechnik, Marktoberndorf; Fichtel & Sachs AG, Schweinfurt; Karl Fischer, Pforzheim; Heinrich Gerd Fladt, Ludwigshafen am Rhein; Forschungsanstalt für Weinbau, Gartenbau, Getränketechnologie und Landespflege, Geisenheim am Rhein; Förderungsgemeinschaft des Deutschen Bäckerhandwerks e. V., Bad Honnef; Forschungsinstitut der Zementindustrie, Düsseldorf; Johanna Förster, Mannheim; Stadtverwaltung Frankfurt am Main, Straßen- und Brückenbauamt, Frankfurt am Main; Freier Verband Deutscher Zahnärzte e. V., Bonn-Bad Godesberg; Fuji Photo Film (Europa) GmbH, Düsseldorf; Gesamtverband der Deutschen Maschen-Industrie e. V., Gesamtmasche, Stuttgart; Gesamtverband des Deutschen Steinkohlenbergbaus, Essen; Gesamtverband der Textilindustrie in der BRD, Gesamttextil, e. V., Frankfurt am Main; Geschwister-Scholl-Gesamtschule, Mannheim-Vogelstang; Eduardo Gomez, Mannheim; Gossen GmbH, Erlangen; Rainer Götz, Hemsbach; Grapha GmbH, Ostfildern; Ines Groh, Mannheim; Heinrich Groos, Geflügelzuchtbedarf, Bad Mergentheim; A. Gruse, Fabrik für Landmaschinen, Großberkel; Hafen Hamburg, Informationsbüro, Hamburg; Hagedorn Landmaschinen GmbH, Warendorf/Westf.; kino-hähnel GmbH, Erftstadt Liblar; Dr. Adolf Hanle, Mannheim; Hauptverband Deutscher Filmtheater e. V., Hamburg; Dr.-Ing. Rudolf Hell GmbH, Kiel; W. Helwig Söhne KG, Ziegenhain; Geflügelfarm Hipp, Mannheim; Gebrüder Holder, Maschinenfabrik, Metzingen; Horten Aktiengesellschaft, Düsseldorf; IBM Deutschland GmbH, Zentrale Bildstelle, Stuttgart; Innenministerium Baden-Württemberg, Pressestelle, Stuttgart; Industrieverband Gewebe, Frankfurt am Main; Industrievereinigung Chemiefaser e. V., Frankfurt am Main; Instrumentation Marketing Corporation, Burbank (Calif.); ITT Schaub-Lorenz Vertriebsgesellschaft mbH, Pforzheim; M. Jakoby KG, Maschinenfabrik, Hetzerath/Mosel; Jenoptik Jena GmbH, Jena (DDR); Brigitte Karnath, Wiesbaden; Wilhelm Kaßbaum, Hockenheim; Van Katwijk's Industrieën N. V., Staalkat Div., Aalten (Holland); Kernforschungszentrum Karlsruhe; Leo Keskari, Offenbach; Dr. Rolf Kiesewetter, Mannheim; Ev. Kindergarten, Hohensachsen; Klambt-Druck GmbH, Offset-Abteilung, Speyer; Maschinenfabrik Franz Klein, Salzkotten; Dr. Klaus-Friedrich Klein, Mannheim; Klimsch + Co., Frankfurt am Main; Kodak AG, Stuttgart; Alfons Kordecki, Eckernförde; Heinrich Kordecki, Mannheim; Krefelder Milchhof GmbH, Krefeld; Dr. Dieter Krickeberg, Musikinstrumenten-Museum, Berlin; Bernard Krone GmbH, Spelle; Pelz-Kunze, Mannheim; Kuratorium für Technik und Bauwesen in der Landwirtschaft, Darmstein-Kranichstein; Landesanstalt für Pflanzenschutz, Stuttgart; Landesinnungsverband des Schuhmacherhandwerks Baden-Württemberg, Stuttgart; Landespolizeidirektion Karlsruhe, Karlsruhe; Landwirtschaftskammer, Hannover; Metzgerei Lebold, Mannheim; Ernst Leitz Wetzlar GmbH, Wetzlar; Louis Leitz, Stuttgart; Christa Leverkinck, Mannheim; Franziska Liebisch, Mannheim; Linhof GmbH, München; Franz-Karl Frhr. von Linden, Mannheim; Loewe Opta GmbH, Kronach; Beate Lüdicke, Mannheim; MAN AG, Werk Augsburg, Augsburg; Mannheimer Verkehrs-Aktiengesellschaft (MVG), Mannheim; Milchzentrale Mannheim-Heidelberg AG, Mannheim; Ing. W. Möhlenkamp, Melle; Adolf Mohr Maschinenfabrik, Hofheim; Mörtl Schleppergerätebau AG, Gemünden/Main; Hans-Heinrich Müller, Mannheim; Müller Martini AG, Zofingen; Gebr. Nubert KG, Spezialeinrichtungen, Schwäbisch Gmünd; Nürnberger Hercules-Werke GmbH, Nürnberg; Olympia Werke AG, Wilhelmshaven; Ludwig Pani Lichttechnik und Projektion, Wien (Österreich); Ulrich Papin, Mannheim; Pfalzmilch Nord GmbH, Ludwigshafen/Albisheim; Adolf Pfeiffer GmbH, Ludwigshafen am Rhein; Philips Pressestelle, Hamburg; Carl Platz GmbH Maschinenfabrik, Frankenthal/Pfalz; Posttechnisches Zentralamt, Darmstadt; Rabe-Werk Heinrich Clausing, Bad Essen; Rahdener Maschinenfabrik August Kolbus, Rahden; Rank Strand Electric, Wolfenbüttel; Stephan Reinhardt, Worms; Nic. Reisinger, Graphische Maschinen, Frankfurt-Rödelheim; Rena Büromaschinenfabrik GmbH & Co., Deisenhofen bei München; Werner Ring, Speyer; Ritter Filmgeräte GmbH, Mannheim; Röber Saatreiniger KG, Minden; Rollei Werke, Braunschweig; Margarete Rossner, Mannheim; Roto-Werke GmbH, Königslutter; Ruhrkohle Aktiengesellschaft, Essen; Papierfabrik Salach GmbH, Salach/Württ.; Dr. Karl Schaifers, Heidelberg; Oberarzt Dr. med. Hans-Jost Schaumann, Städt. Krankenanstalten, Mannheim; Schlachthof, Mannheim; Dr. Schmitz + Apelt, Industrieofenbau GmbH, Wuppertal; Maschinenfabrik Schmotzer GmbH, Bad Windsheim; Mälzerei Schragmalz, Berghausen b. Speyer; Schutzgemeinschaft Deutscher Wald, Bonn; Siemens AG, Bereich Meß- und Prozeßtechnik, Bildund Tontechnik, Karlsruhe; Siemens AG, Dental-Depot, Mannheim; Siemens-Reiniger-Werke, Erlangen; Sinar AG Schaffhausen, Feuerthalen (Schweiz); Spitzenorganisation der Filmwirtschaft e. V., Wiesbaden; Stadtwerke – Verkehrsbetriebe, Mannheim; W. Steenbeck & Co., Hamburg; Streitkräfteamt, Dezernat Werbemittel, Bonn-Duisdorf; Bau- und Möbelschreinerei Fritz Ströbel, Mannheim; Gebrüder Sucker GmbH & Co. KG, Mönchengladbach; Gebrüder Sulzer AG, Winterthur (Schweiz); Dr. med. Alexander Tafel, Weinheim; Klaus Thome, Mannheim; Prof. Dr. med. Michael Trede, Städt. Krankenanstalten, Mannheim; Trepel AG, Wiesbaden; Verband der Deutschen Hochseefischereien e. V., Bremerhaven; Verband der Deutschen Schiffbauindustrie e. V., Hamburg; Verband der Korbwaren-, Korbmöbel- und Kinderwagenindustrie e. V., Coburg; Verband des Deutschen Drechslerhandwerks e. V., Nürnberg; Verband des Deutschen Faß- und Weinküfer-Handwerks, München; Verband Deutscher Papierfabriken e. V., Bonn; Verband Kommunaler Städtereinigungsbetriebe, Köln-Marienburg; Verband technischer Betriebe für Film und Fernsehen e. V., Berlin; Verein Deutscher Eisenhüttenleute, Düsseldorf; Verein Deutscher Zementwerke, Düsseldorf; Vereinigung Deutscher Elektrizitätswerke, VDEW, e. V., Frankfurt am Main; Verkehrsverein, Weinheim/Bergstr.; J. M. Voith GmbH, Heidenheim; Helmut Volland, Erlangen; Dr. med. Dieter Walter, Weinheim; W. E. G. Wirtschaftsverband Erdöl- und Erdgasgewinnung e. V., Hannover; Einrichtungshaus für die Gastronomie Jürgen Weiss & Co., Düsseldorf; Wella Aktiengesellschaft, Darmstadt; Optik-Welzer, Mannheim; Werbe & Graphik Team, Schriesheim; Wiegand Karlsruhe GmbH, Ettlingen; Dr. Klaus Wiemann, Gevelsburg; Wirtschaftsvereinigung Bergbau, Bonn; Wirtschaftsvereinigung Eisen- und Stahlindustrie, Düsseldorf; Wolf-Dietrich Wyrwas, Mannheim; Yashica Europe GmbH, Hamburg; Zechnersche Buchdruckerei, Speyer; Carl Zeiss, Oberkochen; Zentralverband der Deutschen Elektrohandwerke, ZVEH, Frankfurt am Main; Zentralverband der deutschen Seehafenbetriebe e. V., Hamburg; Zentralverband der elektrotechnischen Industrie e. V., Fachverband Phonotechnik, Hamburg; Zentralverband des Deutschen Bäckerhandwerks e. V., Bad Honnef; Zentralverband des Deutschen Friseurhandwerks, Köln; Zentralverband des Deutschen Handwerks ZDH, Pressestelle, Bonn; Zentralverband des Kürschnerhandwerks, Bad Homburg; Zentralverband für das Juwelier-, Gold- und Silberschmiedehandwerk der BRD, Ahlen; Zentralverband für Uhren, Schmuck und Zeitmeßtechnik, Bundesinnungsverband des Uhrmacherhandwerks, Königstein; Zentralverband Sanitär-, Heizungs- und Klimatechnik, Bonn; Erika Zöller, Edingen; Zündapp-Werke GmbH, München.

Register

Die halbfetten Zahlen hinter den Stichwörtern sind die Nummern der Bildtafeln, die mageren die auf diesen Tafeln erscheinenden Bildnummern. Gleichlautende Wörter mit verschiedenen Bedeutungen werden durch kursiv gesetzte Bereichsangaben oder Bedeutungshinweise unterschieden.

Folgende Abkürzungen und Kurzformen wurden für die Bereichsangaben verwendet:

Anat.:	Anatomie	*Med.:*	Medizin
Astr.:	Astronomie	*Mil.:*	Militärwesen
AV:	Audiovision	*Müllbes.:*	Müllbeseitigung
Bau:	Bauwesen	*Mus.:*	Musik
Bot.:	Botanik	*Papier:*	Papierherstellung
Buchb.:	Buchbinderei	*Porzellan:*	Porzellanherstellung
Chem.:	Chemie	*Repro:*	Fotoreproduktion
Druck:	Druckerei	*Schädlingsbek.:*	Schädlingsbekämpfung
Eisenb.:	Eisenbahnwesen	*Tech.:*	Technik
Elektr.:	Elektroinstallateur	*Textilw.:*	Textilwesen
Fotogr.:	Fotografie	*U-Elektronik:*	Unterhaltungselektronik
Geld:	Geldwesen	*Walz.:*	Walztechnik
Glas:	Glasherstellung	*Wasservers.:*	Trinkwasserversorgung
Infotechnik:	Informationstechnik	*Web.:*	Weberei
Hütt.:	Hüttenwerk	*Werkzeugmasch.:*	Werkzeugmaschinen
Landw.:	Landwirtschaft	*Winter:*	Winterlandschaft
Masch.:	Maschinenteile	*Zeichn.:*	Zeichnerbüro
Math.:	Mathematik	*Zool.:*	Zoologie

A

Aal 364 17
~fisch 364 17
~haken 89 87
Aas-blume 53 15
~fliegenblume 53 15
Abakus 334 20
Abbauhammerstreb 144 35
Abbildung 348 9-11, 9, 10, 11
Abbindeplatz 120 1-59
Abblasemast 221 38
Abblend-licht 191 20
~schalter 191 59
Abbund 120 24
Abdampf-auspuff 210 22
~schale 350 29
Abdeckblende 310 51
Abdecken *Druck* 182 14
~ *Film* 310 51
Abdeck-haube 241 32
~kappe 126 33
~leiste 123 57
~platte 37 37
~schieber 2 32
~schiene 167 56
~stab 123 64
Abdeckung *Optik* 113 13
~ *Straße* 198 17
~ *Müllbes.* 199 21
Abdomen 16 35-37
Abdrucklöffel 24 56
Abdrückstelle 21 14
Abducken 299 29
Abend-anzug 33 7
~kleid 30 53
Abendmahl 332 26
Abendmahls-kelch 332 29
~tisch 330 4
Abenteuerspielplatz 273 21
Abfahrts-lauf 301 32

~signal *Eisenb.* 205 47
~signal *Flaggen* 253 26
~ski 301 34
~tafel 204 20
~zeit 205 23
Abfall 268 22
~, mittelaktiver 154 72
~, radioaktiver 154 77
~behälter 26 22; 196 12; 207 55; 268 5
Abfälle, radioaktive 154 57-68
Abfall-eimer 22 70; 96 46
~korb 205 55; 268 5; 272 43; 273 25
~tonne 199 3
~vorrichtung 147 39
Abfangjäger 256 1
Abferkel-Aufzucht-Bucht 75 40
Abfertigungs-beamter 204 9; 206 36
~fahrzeug 233 22
~feld 233 3
~gebäude 233 15
~position 233 21
Abfeuerungseinrichtung 255 29
Abfiltrieren 92 50
Abflug 233 25
~halle 233 15
Abflußhahn 178 34
Abfrageapparat 237 23
Abfüll-anlage 76 20
~maschine 76 21
~ und Verpackungsanlage 76 20
Abgangs-innengewinde 126 47
~pforte 319 12
~winkel 87 75
Abgas-entgiftung 190 73

~leitung *Eisenb.* 209 12
~leitung *Schiff* 221 76
~lippe 259 92
~mast 221 17
~öffnung 258 79
~pfosten 221 17
~rohr 146 5
~schalldämpfer 212 42, 48
~schornstein 146 2
~wärmetauscher 155 9
abgestoßen 321 34
Abgleichbohle 201 3, 4
Abguß 261 15
Abhang 12 37
Abhängling 335 32
Abhäutemesser 94 13
Abheber 109 10
Abhebestange 325 23
Abhörlautsprecher *Radio* 238 15
Abisolierzange 127 64
Abkühlung *Textil* 170 34
~ *Schwimmbad* 281 28
Abkühlungsraum 281 28
Ablage-bläser 181 33
~bord 74 42
~fach *Auto* 195 14
~fach *Rechenzentrum* 244 13
~korb 248 41
~körbchen 245 30
Ablagerung 13 69
Ablagerungsgebiet 11 47
Ablagetisch 181 31
Ablängsäge 120 14
Ablaßhahn 38 65
Ablauf-berg 206 46
~gestell 116 47
~kondensator 92 4
~leitung 269 12
~rost 198 24
~ventil 126 16

Ableerbütte 172 81
Ablegemechanismus 174 20, 30
Ableger 54 10, 11, 12
Ablegetisch 184 14
~vorrichtung 236 49
Ableiter, elektrostatischer 230 51; 231 27
Ableitung 345 13
Ablenk-einheit 240 23
~mauer 304 2
Ablese-instrument 2 6
~mikroskop 113 28
Abluft-anlage 154 81
~kamin 154 37; 155 25
~leitung 155 11
~öffnung 49 20
~rohr 168 29
~schacht 92 14
~schlitz 50 30
~stutzen 142 16
~wäschetrockner 50 28
Abmessen 350 21
abnehmender Mond 4 7
Abnehmer 163 42
Abnormitätenkabinett 308 19
Abort 49 12
~raum 207 16, 42
Abpackanlage 76 32
Abrasionsplatte 13 31
Abraum 158 2
~bagger 159 3
~bau 158 1
Abreiß-kante 247 30
~schiene 128 42
~zylinder 163 71
Abrißnische 11 48
Abrollvorrichtung 173 39
Abrücken (der Kreuzspule) 165 13
Abruf 305 72
Absack-maschine 92 39

~stutzen 83 55
Absatz *Schuhmacher* 100 67
~ *Setzerei* 175 15
~, hoher 101 28, 33
~fräser 100 4
Absauganlage 24 11
Absauge-schweißtisch 142 13
~schwenkrüssel 142 15
~tischfläche 142 14
Absaugluftspalt 154 21
Absaugung *Schuhmacher* 100
13
~ *Schneiderei* 103 26
Absaugvorrichtung 74 41
Abschiedskuß 205 52
Abschirmbehälter 154 82
Abschirmung, magnetische
240 27
Abschlag 293 79
~kamm 167 52
~platz 293 79
Abschluß 136 17
~tür 41 25
Abschmierpresse 195 30
Abschneider *Uhrmacher* 109
19
~ *Ziegelei* 159 15
Abschneidevorrichtung 151
15
Abschnitt 84 31
~, lichtempfindlicher 77 22
Abschroter 137 32
Abschuß 305 52
~container 258 32
abschwellend 321 32
Absehen 87 31-32
~system 87 31
~verstellung 87 30
Abseilen 300 28-30
Abseil-haken 300 39
~schlinge 300 28
Abseits 291 42
Absenken 54 18
Absetzen 92 50
Absetzwagen 159 18
Absonderungsbläschen 357 5
Absorber-stab 154 24
~zuschaltung 27 44
absorbiertes Neutron 1 53
Abspann-isolator 152 38
~kette 152 38
~seil 215 47
Abspannungs-gerüst 152 31
~mast 152 36
Absperr-gitter *Landw.* 75 43
~gitter *Imker* 77 47
~graben 356 3
~schieber *Wasserbau* 217
53-56
~schieber *Wasservers.* 269 48
Absperrung 99 5
Absperrventil *Installateur*
126 4
~ *Schweiß.* 141 7
~ *Wasservers.* 269 30
Absprung 298 26, 37
~balken 298 38
~trampolin 297 14, 18
Abstand 346 5
~halter *Film* 117 59
~halter *Bau* 119 81
Abstands-bügel 77 41
~halter 134 47
~rohrband 126 54
~rohrschelle 126 57
~schnur 10 58
Abstech-drehmeißel 149 53
~stahl 135 24
Abstecken 271 37
Abstehwanne 162 15
Abstellbrett 174 10
Absteller 326 41
Abstell-gleis 206 50

~hebel 163 40
~raum 207 27
~sicherung 168 19
~taste 110 22
~vorrichtung 165 19; 166 43
Abstich 147 54
~loch 147 50
~rinne 148 3
~stange 148 9
Abstiegsstufe 6 28-36
Abstimm-anzeigeröhre 309 18
~feinanzeige 224 36
~grobanzeige 224 35
Abstimmungsgerät 23 38
~knopf 309 21
~leiter 263 28
~regler 241 54
~umschlag 263 21
Abstoß 291 38
Abstrakte 326 9
Abstreichblech 65 4
Abstreicher 168 61
Abstreifen (des Laichhechts)
89 11
Abstreifer 64 76
Abstreifgitter 129 12
Abstrich 23 15, 50
Abstütz-spindel 270 12
~stempel 202 29
Abszisse 347 9
Abszissen-achse 347 2
~wert 347 9
Abtankhalle 76 1
Abtast-bereich 243 47
~kopf 177 46, 63
~nadel, konische 241 26
~walze 177 45
Abteil 207 13; 208 24
~fenster 207 52; 208 8
~tür 207 14
Abteilung 84 2
~, chirurgische 26 1-54
~ für Damenkleidung 271 28
Abteilungsleiter 271 60
Abtransportvorrichtung 185
35
Abtreppung 118 61
Abtropfständer 39 33
Abwachsteich 89 6
Abwaschbürste 50 51
Abwasser-abfuhr 156 38
~kanal 269 23
~leitung *Energieversorgung*
155 23
~leitung *Müllbes.* 199 26
~pumpe *Papier* 172 63
~pumpe *Müllbes.* 199 20
~sammeltank 199 27
Abwehr 294 6
~spieler 292 4; 293 60, 77
Abweisbalken 214 56
Abweiser 214 56
Abwickelachse 312 36
Abwurfpunkt 89 34
Abzeichen 299 15
Abziehen *Hütt.* 147 53
~ *Math.* 344 24
Abzieher der großen Zehe 18
49
Abzug 255 5
~bügel 87 10
~leiste 167 49
Abzugs-rohr 182 25
~vorrichtung 255 20
Abzweigleitung 126 8
Accent aigu 342 30
~ circonflexe 342 32
~ grave 342 31
Acetylenflasche 141 2, 22
Achillessehne 18 48
Achsdifferentialgetriebe 190
75
Achse *Astr.* 4 22

~ *Fahrrad* 187 61, 76
~ *Math.* 346 27; 347 17, 23, 24
Achsel 16 26
~griff 21 37
~grube 16 26
~haare 16 27
~hemdchen 29 6
~höhle 16 26
~knospe 370 25
Achsen-kreuz *Repro* 177 4
~kreuz *Math.* 347 2-3
~montierung 113 22
Achs-lager *Auto* 192 83
~lager *Eisenb.* 210 10
~wendegetriebe 211 53
~zapfen 192 78
Achteck 351 17
~-Kreuzschliff 36 53
~-Treppenschliff 36 52
Achtel-note 320 16
~pause 320 24
Achter 283 10
~bahn 308 39
~deck 223 32
~kastell 218 23
~liek 284 45
~mast 220 34
~piek 227 28
~schiffquerschnitt 286 34, 37,
41
~steven 218 1; 222 70-71
Achtfach-Flarak-Starter 259
5, 20
Acht-flächner 351 6
~-Kanal-Schreiber 27 28
~kantschliffstöpsel 349 4
~-Platten-Elektroherd 207 30
Achtundvierzigflächner 351
13
Acht-Zylinder~Dieselmotor
212 73
~-Pullmannlimousine 193 1
~-V-Ottomotor 190 1
Acker 63 4
~bauerzeugnis 68 1-47
~bohne 69 15
~distel 61 32
~furche 63 8
~gauchheil 61 27
~kamille 61 8
~kratzdistel 61 32
~rettich 61 21
~salat 57 38
~schachtelhalm 376 18
~schädling 80 37-55
~schlepper 64 46; 65 20
~senf 61 18
~spörgel 69 12
~wicke 69 18
~winde 61 26
Adamsapfel 19 13
Adapterring 115 82
Addieren 344 23
Addier- und Saldiermaschine
309 74
Addition 344 23
additive Farbmischung 343 10
A-Deck 223 28-30
Adelskrone 254 43
Ader-klemme 26 48
~presse 26 48
Adhäsion 214 1
Adler *Astr.* 3 9
~ *Vögel* 362 5-9
~farn 377 16
~kopf 327 12
Admiral 365 1
Admiralitätsanker 286 15
Admiralskajüte 218 27
Adressat *Infotechnik* 242 4
~ *Bank* 250 19
A-Dur 320 58
Adventivwurzel 370 78

Aetos 334 3
Affe 368 12-13
Affenhaus 356 10
Afghane 70 23
Afrika 14 14
Afrikane 60 20
Afrikanischer Elefant 366 20
Afro-Look 34 26
After 20 62
~flosse 364 9
~furche 16 41
~klaue 88 23
After-shave 49 38
~-Lotion 49 38
Aft-Fan-Triebwerk 232 42
Agent *Börse* 251 5
~ *Zirkus* 307 18
Agentursignum 342 55
Aglei 60 10
Agulhasstrom 14 37
Ahle 174 17
Ahming 222 73
Ahnenfigur 354 17
ähnlich 345 22
Ähnlichkeitszeichen 345 22
Ahorn 371 53
~samen 371 57
Ährchen *Landw.* 68 3, 10
~ *Bot.* 69 23; 375 41, 42
Ähre *Landw.* 68 2
~ *Bot.* 370 67
Ähren-heber 64 2
~rispengras 69 27
Air brakes 229 44
Airbus 231 17
Ajourarbeit 102 27
Akelei, Gemeine 60 10
Akkord 321 1-5
Akkordeon 324 36
Akku-behälter 188 22
~-Bike 188 20
Akkumulator 316 55
~triebwagen 211 55
Akku-speisung 242 30
~teil 309 41
Akrobat 307 47
Akropolis 334 1-7
Akroterion 334 34
Akt 338 32
Akten-klammer 247 2
~notiz 248 8
~ordner 245 6; 247 37; 248 5
~regal 248 10
~schrank 245 4
~tasche 41 17
Aktie 251 11-19
Aktien-buch 251 14
~urkunde 251 11
Aktivkohle 270 58
Aktmodell 338 32
Akut 342 30
Akzent 342 30-35
Akzept 250 12, 23
Alarmsirene 270 4
Aldebaran 3 25
Ale 93 26
Alençonspitze 102 30
Alfagras 136 26
Algebra 345 4-5
Algenfisch 364 10
Alhidade 224 3
Alk 359 13
Alkalizellulose 169 7, 9
Alkor 3 29
All-aft-Typ 221 1
Allais-Schikane 301 72
Allerheiligstes 331 48; 332 35
Aller-Steinsalz 154 63
Alles-kleber 260 51
~schneider 40 38
Allgebrauchslampe 127 56
Allgemein-medizin 22 1-74;
23 2

~mediziner 23 2
Allgeschwindigkeits-
  Querruder 229 43
Allianzwappen 254 10-13
Allongeperücke 34 2
Allradantrieb 194 1
Allroundterminal 226 16
All speed aileron 229 43
Allwetterdach 200 38
Allziel-geschütz 258 48, 70
~kanone 258 47
Allzweck-abroller 40 1
~labor 235 66
~sauger 50 80
~tuch 40 1
Almosen 330 60
Aloe 53 13
Alpen-glöckchen 378 3
~pflanze 378 1-13
~rose 378 1
~veilchen 53 5
Alpenvereinshütte 300 1
Alpha-partikel 2 27
~strahlung 1 30-31
~teilchen 1 30-31
alpine Ausrüstung 300
  31-57
Alpinist 300 5
Alsike 69 3
Alster 361 3
Altair 3 9
Altar Kirche 330 4, 33
~ Kunst 334 69
~bekleidung 330 6
~bild 330 13, 50
~decke 330 6
~kerze 330 7, 34
~kreuz 330 12, 35
Altarm 216 18
Altar-nische 334 64
~platz 330 1
~schelle 332 52
~schmuck 330 48
~stufe 330 5, 31
~teppich 330 3
~tuch 330 36
Altbestand 84 4
Alter Mann 144 37
Alt-geiß 88 34
~holz 84 4
~menschenschädel 261 19
Altocumulus 8 15
~ castellanus 8 16
~ floccus 8 16
Altokumulus 8 15
Altostratus 8 8
~ praecipitans 8 9
Alt-posaune 323 46
~reh 88 34
~ricke 88 34
~schlüssel 320 10
~steinzeit 328 1-9
~warenmarkt 308 60
~wasser 15 75
Aluminium-blech 155 29
~faß 93 17
~gestell 50 19
~legierung 197 24
~münze 252 1-28
~oberkante 301 51
Aluoberkante 301 51
Amarant 60 21
Amaryllisgewächs 53 8
Amateurboxer 299 25
Ambo 330 37
Amboß Anat. 17 61
~ Jagd 87 58
~ Klempner 125 22
~ Schmied 137 11-16; 138 33
~ Tech. 139 17
ambulanter Händler 308 12
Ambulanz 270 19
Ameise 358 21-22

Amerika 14 12-13
Amerikaner 97 39
Ammer 361 6-7
Ammoniak 170 24
~wascher 156 23
Ammoniumsulfat 156 36
~herstellung 156 35
Ammonsulfatlauge 170 26
Amöbe 357 1
a-Moll 320 55, 62
~-Tonleiter 320 46, 47, 48
Amorette 272 20
Ampelmast 268 53
Amperemeter 230 18
Amphibie 364 20-26
Amphibienflugzeug 232 8
Amphore 328 10
Amplitudeneinstellung 10 11
Amsel 361 13
Amstel 361 13
Amt, Meteorologisches 225
  33
Amulett-und-Würfel-Kette
  354 40
Analog-ausgang 112 45
~steuerung 242 38
Analyse 25 46
Analysenwaage 349 25
Analyser 116 36
Ananas 99 85; 384 61
~blüte 384 64
~erdbeere 58 16
~galle 82 40
~pflanze 384 61
Anästhesierung 24 53
Anbau 331 13
~gerät 134 50-55
~-Hackwerkzeug 56 21
~küche 46 29
~pflug 65 62
~satz 84 33
~schrank 177 69
~vitrine 42 5
Anbinde-stall 75 14
~vorrichtung 75 15-16
Anbiß 86 21
Andächtiger 330 29
Andachtsraum 233 49
Anderthalb-decker 229 13
~master 220 9-10
Andreaskreuz Eisenb. 202 41
~ Kirche 332 60
Andromeda 3 24
Andruck 340 43
~bügel 100 17
Andrücken 182 8
Andruck-presse, Mailänder
  180 75
~rolle 243 25
Anemometer 10 28
Anemone 377 1
Aneroidbarometer 10 4
Anfahrfederung 214 50
Anfänger 336 22
Anfeuchter 247 31
Anflugantenne 6 46
Anfuhrtisch 74 51
Anführungs-strich 342 26
~zeichen 342 26, 27
Angabelinie 293 72
Angebots-raum 207 78-79
~schild 99 19
Angegriffener 294 6
Angel 45 52
~fischerei 89 20-94
~gerät 89 37-94
~haken 89 79
~schnur 89 63
~sport 89
angeregter Zustand 1 19
Angiographieraum 27 12
Angioraum 27 12
Anglerzange 89 37

Angorakatze 73 17
Angreifer 294 5
Angriffs-linie 293 65
~sehrohr 259 88
~spieler 293 63, 75
~zone 293 64
Anhänge-deichsel 64 47
~kupplung Landmaschinen
  65 30
~kupplung Camping 278 55
Anhänger 138 10; 194 22
~chassis 138 28
~lore 200 25
Anhängevorrichtung 65 50,
  61
Anhöhe 13 66
Animierdame 318 33
anisotrop 215 2
Anke 108 18
Anker 223 52; 258 5; 259 81;
  286 15-18
~geschirr 223 49-51
~kabel 218 18
~kette 222 77; 223 50; 224 72;
  227 12
~klüse 222 76; 258 54
~kreuz 332 69
~nische 222 75
~rad 110 40
~spill 258 6
~tasche 222 75
~tau 218 18
~winde 223 49
~winsch 259 82
Ankleide-kabine 271 32
~puppe 47 9; 48 32
~zelle 271 32
Ankunft 233 26
Ankunftstafel 204 19
Anlage-apparat 181 22
~tisch 180 32, 49; 181 4, 21, 30
Anlandung 216 52
Anlaßbatterie 212 46
Anlasser 190 44
~, elektrischer 189 52
Anlaß-widerstand 135 3
~zahnkranz 192 31
Anlauf 282 43
~automat 168 20
Anlege-einrichtung 183 17
~goniometer 351 27
~ponton 225 63
Anleger 185 25
~magazin 185 26
~steg 283 19
~tisch 184 21
~trommel 180 33, 34
~vorrichtung 236 48
~walze 165 32
Anleihe 251 11-19
Anlehnmaschine 185 31
Anleimmaschine 185 31
Anluven 285 9
Anmelde-block 267 12
~formular 267 12
~raum 267 1-26
Anmeldung 278 1
Anmerkung 185 62
annähernd gleich 345 17
Annahme 67 2
~beamter 236 16
~vermerk 250 23
Annoncenteil 342 69
Anodenstange 178 5
Anorak Kleidung 29 62
~ Sport 300 6
~kapuze 300 19
~nylon 101 4
Anpassungseinheit 242 34
Anpreßhydraulik 173 37
Anproberaum 271 32
Anreißwinkel 120 69
Anrichte Haushalt 45 44

~ Eisenb. 207 35
~ Schiff 223 43
~tisch 45 32
Anrufschranke 202 47
Ansatz Tapezierer 128 21, 22
~ Sport 299 8
~ Math. 345 8
~rohr Haushalt 50 70
~rohr Mus. 324 71
Ansaug-geräuschdämpfer
  190 16; 191 54
~leitung 349 21
~rohr 189 5; 190 18
~trichter 217 51
Anschießen 129 52
Anschlag Jagd 86 34
~ Post 237 12
~ Sport 282 28; 305 27, 28, 29,
  45, 73
~platte 157 18
Anschlagsart 305 27-29
Anschlag-schiene 133 11
~sporn 71 50
~stärkeeinsteller 249 10
~weg 325 9
~winkel 134 26
Anschluß 237 2
~aufsatz 127 25
~beschlag 287 31
~eisen 119 10, 71
~kabel 142 25
~leitung Installateur 126 9
~leitung U-Elektronik 241 71
~rahmen 65 26
~stutzen 350 5
Anschnall-elektrode 23 30
~sporn 71 51
Anschreiber 293 71
Anschreibetafel 277 18
Anschrift 236 42
Anschriftenbild 236 41
anschwellend 321 31
Ansitz 86 14-17
~hütte 86 51
~stuhl 86 10
Anstand 86 14-17
Ansteck-nadel 36 18
~schmuck 36 19
Anstellvorrichtung 148 61-65
Anstichhahn 93 14
Anstreichen 129 1
Antarktis 14 18
Antenne Meteorol. 10 59, 68
~ Eisenb. 213 4
~ Mil. 256 17; 258 16, 46; 259
  7, 47, 89
~ Sport 288 20, 88
Antennen-niederführung 223
  4
~träger 259 6
Antependium 330 20
Antiklinale 12 16, 27
Antilope 367 5
Antiqua 342 5, 6
antiquarisches Buch 309 55
Anti-skatingeinstellung 241
  25
~vortexsystem 234 11
~zyklone 9 6
Antlitz 16 4-17
Antoniuskreuz Schiff 224 90
~ Kirche 332 59
Antrieb Schuhmacher 100 8
~ Sägewerk 157 15
~ Spinnerei 163 24
~ Bergbahnen 214 2
~, dieselelektrischer 223
  68-74; 259 75
~, hydraulischer 139 9, 15
~, konventioneller 259 75
Antriebs-batterie 25 51
~gerät 238 57
~kasten 168 32

~kette 188 17
~knopf 178 15
~kupplung 177 54
~kurbel 309 81
~maschine 145 12
Antriebsmotor *Landw.* 74 37
~ *Schneiderei* 103 9
~ *Tech.* 139 25
~ *Werkzeugmasch.* 150 9
~ *Spinnerei* 163 12, 23, 49
~ *Setzerei* 175 61
~ *Druck* 178 12, 28; 179 11
~ *Wasserbau* 217 47
Antriebsquelle 110 7
~rad *Landmaschinen* 65 80
~rad *Textil* 167 31
~rad *Mil.* 255 50
~scheibe *Textil* 168 4
~scheibe *Druck* 180 66
~stutzen 67 19
~turbine 232 38
~turm 177 56
~walze *Web.* 165 32
~walze *Fahrrad* 187 73
~welle *Motor* 190 27
~welle *Auto* 192 30
~welle *Straßenbau* 201 13
~welle *Wasserbau* 217 49
~werk 110 43
Antritt 123 18
Antrittspfosten 123 43
~stufe 123 18, 42
Anwählen 237 19
Anwahl-knopf 25 6
~steuerplatte 153 4
Anzapfungsverbindung 153 18
Anzeichnerei 104 21
Anzeige 224 22
~, optische 238 2
~gerät *Schiff* 224 20
~gerät *Sport* 294 32
~lampe *AV* 243 14
~lampe *Sport* 294 30
~leuchte 50 10
~nadel *Fotogr.* 114 58
~nadel *Infotechnik* 242 76
Anzeigenteil 342 69
Anzeige-skala 114 58
~strom 11 44
~tafel *Strandbad* 280 7
~tafel *Sport* 293 34, 70
~vorrichtung *Walz.* 148 65
~vorrichtung *Web.* 165 7
Anzug-hose 33 3
~stoff 104 3
Aorta 18 10, 16; 20 54
Aorten-bogen 18 10
~klappe 20 49
Apachenmädchen 306 9
Apartment 46
~wand 46 1
Apatit 351 20
Aperturblenden-schieber 112 16
~trieb 113 35
Apfel 58 56; 99 86; 370 102
~baum 58 51
~blüte 58 54
~blütenstecher 80 10
~butzen 58 59
~gespinstmotte 80 5
~kern 58 60
~quitte 58 49
~schale 58 57
~schalenwickler 80 9
Apfelsine 384 23, 27
Apfelsinenblüte 384 25
Apfel-stecher 80 10
~stiel 58 61
~wickler 58 62
~zweig 58 52
Apiarium 77 56

Apokalypse 327 50
Apollo-Raumeinheit 6 1
~-Raumkapsel 6 9
~-SM 234 56
Apostroph 342 22
Apotheke 233 45
Apparateschrank 212 35
Appenzeller Hackbrett 322 35
Applikation 29 20
Apport 86 36
Apportieren 86 36
Aprikose 59 35
Aprikosen-baum 59 33-36
~baumblatt 59 36
~blüte 59 34
~zweig 59 33
Apsis *Camping* 278 27
~ *Kunst* 334 64; 335 5
Aquädukt 334 53
Aqualunge 279 19
Aquarell-bild 48 5
~farbe 338 18
~kasten 48 6
Aquarium 356 19
Aquarius 4 63
Aquatinta 340 14-24
Äquator 14 1
Äquatorialer Gegenstrom 14 33
äquatorialer Kalmengürtel 9 46
äquatoriales Klima 9 53
Aquila 3 9
Äquilibrist 307 48
Äquinoktialpunkt 3 6-7
Äquinoktium 3 6-7
Arabeske 314 18
arabisch 341 2
arabische Ziffer 344 2
Ararauna 363 2
Araukarie 53 16
Arbeiter 358 22
Arbeiterin 77 1
Arbeiterinnenzelle 77 34
Arbeits-bereich 167 21
~biene 77 1
~bogen 261 27
~brücke 315 29
~bühne *Bau* 118 17
~bühne *Erdöl* 145 3
~bühne *Eisenb.* 211 42
~bühne *Raumfahrt* 234 28, 46
~deck 221 19, 34
~fläche 261 5
~galerie 316 5
~gerüst 122 34
~grube 75 24
~kittel *Kleidung* 33 56
~kittel *Friseur* 106 2
~lampe 109 12
~latzhose 33 44
~mantel 33 56
~material 260 81
~mütze 35 40
~öffnung 139 49
Arbeitspindel 149 20
Arbeits-platte 50 31
~plattform 221 66
~prinzip (der Karde) 163 51
~prinzip (der Kämmaschine) 163 63
~projektor *Infotechnik* 242 6
~projektor *Schule* 261 8
~satz 151 38
~schuh 101 39
~sessel 24 14
~speicher 245 28
~ständer 100 54
~steg 316 5
~tisch *Bäckerei* 97 60, 62
~tisch *Schuhmacher* 100 33
~tisch *Schneiderei* 104 7

~tisch *Optiker* 111 20
~tisch *Glaser* 124 15
~wanne 162 5
Archaster 369 17
Architrav 334 18
Archivkraft 248 6
Archivolte 335 25
Arcturus 3 30
Arena 319 9
Argo 3 45
Aries 4 53
Arithmetik 344 1-26; 345 1-24
Arkosolium 331 60
Arktur 3 30
Arm 16 43-48; 17 12-14
Armatur 126 26-37
Armaturen-brett *Druck* 180 74
~brett *Auto* 191 57-90
~tafel 197 29
~tafelbeleuchtung 197 30
Armauflage 109 3
Armband *Schmuck* 36 3
~ *Uhr* 110 5
Armbanduhr, automatische 110 32-43
~, elektronische 110 1
Armbanduhrzeiger 109 10
Arm-berge 329 47
~beuge 16 44
~binde *Wahl* 263 11
~binde *Feuerwehr* 270 22
Armbrustfibel 328 28
Armbund 30 30
Ärmel 32 25; 268 31
~, angeschnittener 30 36
~, betreßter 186 24
~, gepuffter 355 60
~, halber 32 28
~, langer 30 15
~aufschlag 30 35; 31 54; 33 35
~brett 50 20
~pelzbesatz 30 62
~puffe 355 49
~schlitz 30 48
~schoner 324 17
~schutz 142 6
armenisch 341 3
Arm-flossler 369 6
~geflecht 18 27
~haltung 314 7-10
~hebel 299 10
Armierung 119 54-76, 68
Armierungseisen 119 23
Arm-kachel 329 48
~lehne 42 22; 46 28; 106 18; 207 45, 69
~lehnenascher 207 46
~muskel 18 54, 55
~muskel, dreiköpfiger 18 38
~muskel, zweiköpfiger 18 37
~reif 36 17
~schlinge 21 2
~speichenmuskel 18 39
~stütze 208 26
~tragetuch 21 2
~verband 21 1
Arnika 380 2
Aronsstab 379 9
Arpeggio 321 22
Arretierstift 140 47
Arretierung 349 37
Arretierungsknopf 349 38
Arrondieren 109 17
Arterie 18 1
arterielles Blut 18 12
Arterienpinzette 26 49
artesischer Brunnen 12 26
artesisches Grundwasser 12 21
Artikel-hinweis 342 49
~überschrift 342 44

Artilleriewaffe 255 49-74
Artischocke 57 41
Artist 308 25-28
Artisten-stand 307 5
~vermittler 307 18
Arzneimittel 22 23
Arzt 22; 23; 233 44
~, praktischer 23 2
Ärztemuster 22 41
Ärztehelferin 22 19
ärztliche Hilfe 253 27
Arzt-stempel 22 29
~tasche 22 33
A-Saite 323 9
Asbest 270 46
~anzug 270 46
~drahtnetz 350 19
Asche 327 10
Aschen-abzug 152 8
~bahn 298 6
~bahnrennen 290 24-28
~becher 42 29; 104 5; 246 33
~kugel 266 5
~tür 38 39
~urne 328 38
Ascher 207 69
Aschkasten 210 6
~bodenklappe 210 7
As-Dur 320 66
A-Sehrohr 259 88
Äser 88 13
Asien 14 16
Aspergill 332 54
Asphalt 155 29
~decke 200 58
~mischtrommel 200 50
~papier 153 48
asphärischer Hohlspiegel 312 39
Aspirationspsychrometer 10 33
Aspisviper 364 41
Asroc-Starter 258 50
Assaut 294 5-6
Assel 81 6
Assistent 262 6, 7
Assistentin 307 39
Assyrer 333 29-36
Ast *Math.* 347 15
~ *Bot.* 370 5
Asteroid 4 47
Ast-gabel 54 13
~hippe 56 9
~lochfräser 132 53
~lochfräsmaschine 132 52
~reinigung 84 12
Astronaut 6 11; 235 67
Astronomie 3; 4; 5
Ast-säge 56 16
~schere 56 11
~schneider 56 11
Äsung 86 13
Asymptote 347 29
Atair 3 9
Atelier 338 1-43; 339 1-38
~aufnahme 310 26-60
~fenster 338 1
~mikrophon 310 31
~sekretärin 310 39
~staffelei 338 3
~wohnung 37 74
Atem-frequenz 23 27
~funktion, Messung der 23 31
~gerät 21 27
~loch 367 26
~öffnung 358 32
~schlauch 27 37
~schutzgerät 270 39
~volumen 26 28
~wurzel 370 82
Äthylenmolekül 242 61
Atlant 334 36

Atlantiksteven **221** 83
Atlantischer Ozean **14** 20
Atmosphäre **7**
Atmung, künstliche **21** 24-27
Atoll **13** 32
Atolla **369** 5
Atom **1 ; 2**
~bombenexplosion **7** 11
~kern **1** 2, 16, 29, 49, 51
~kern, schwerer **1** 35
~kraftwerk **154** 19
~modell **1** 1, 1-8, 5, 26
~müll **154** 57-68
~müllagerung **154** 56
~reaktor **1** 48
~reaktormantel **259** 67
~schicht **7** 32
Atrium **334** 66
Attika **334** 60
Attitude **314** 17
Ätzbad **340** 51
Atzel Perücke **34** 2
~ Vögel **361** 3
Ätzen **340** 51
Ätz-flanke **178** 45
~flüssigkeit **178** 24 ; **182** 16
~grund **340** 55
~korrektur **182** 21
~maschine **182** 15
~trog **178** 24, 31 ; **182** 16
Audio-synchronkopf **243** 24
~-/Videoaussteuerungsan-
  zeige **243** 15
~vision **243**
audiovisuelle Lernprogramm-
  herstellung **242** 7
Auditorium **262** 2
Auerbachsprung **282** 41
Auerhahn **88** 72
Auf **86** 48
Aufbau **221** 10, 69 ; **258** 22
~deck **258** 10
~häuschen **273** 56
~spritzgerät **83** 2
Aufbauten **258** 10-28
Aufbereitungsanlage **144** 5
Aufbewahrungskasten **195** 10
Aufblas-artikel **280** 33
~ballon **25** 17
Aufenthaltsdeck **224** 107
Auffahr-mulde **213** 36
~rampe **221** 55
Auffahrt **15** 16
Auffahrtsrampe **206** 1
Auffang-gefäß **10** 40, 45
~schirm **242** 84
Auffüßen **72** 43
Aufgabe-kasten **118** 35
~raum **293** 61
~schnecke **92** 26
~tisch **157** 63
Aufgang Schiff **223** 24
~ Zirkus **307** 20
Aufgeber **293** 62
Aufhalte-kette **71** 20
~ring **71** 27
Aufhänge-bügel **94** 21
~holm **75** 16
~kette **65** 17
Aufhängung Schädlingsbek.
  83 7
~ Textilw. **171** 9
~, kardanische Schiff **224** 50
~, kardanische U-Elektronik
  241 23
Aufheller **310** 52
Aufklebeadresse **236** 4
Aufladeturbine **212** 51
Auflage **293** 47
~fläche **261** 9

Auflagekraftverstellung **241** 24
Auflager Bau **121** 83
~ Brücken **215** 55
~ Mus. **322** 42
~bock **120** 18
Auflagetisch **133** 17, 21
Auflege-matte **64** 72
~vorrichtung **74** 49-51
Auflicht-beleuchtung **112** 59, 63
~mikroskop **112** 23
Auflösung **169** 10
Auflösungszeichen **320** 54
Aufnahme Med. **22** 5
~ Repro **177** 38
~ TV **238** 58
~becherwerk **200** 49 ; **201** 21
~daten **115** 67
~einheit **240** 36
~gerät **311** 23
~halle **310** 26-60
~kammer **113** 40
~kopf **311** 25
~leiter **310** 44
~objektiv **114** 26
~optik **313** 2
~taste **117** 83
~tonkopf **117** 33
~- und Wiedergabegerät **311** 23
~verstärker **311** 11
Aufpausen **129** 48
Aufprallschutz **191** 57
Aufputzinstallation **127** 6, 13
Aufrauhen **168** 31
Aufrauhstation **184** 3
Aufreißen **299** 8
Aufreißbar **200** 20
Aufrollung **173** 28
Aufruf **263** 14
Aufsattelgerät **65** 82
Aufsatz **293** 90
~kamera **112** 64
~seite **324** 74
~uhr **42** 16
Aufschiebling **121** 31
Aufschlag Kleidung **33** 5
~ Sport **293** 42
Aufschläger **293** 51
Aufschlag-feld **293** 12
~linie **293** 6 bis 7
~linienrichter **293** 27
Aufschnitt **326** 25
~messer **96** 31
~ware **96** 14
Aufschwungphase **298** 29
Aufsetzen **72** 43
Aufsicht **262** 14
Aufsichtsbeamter **205** 41
Aufsichtsratsvorsitzer **251** 15
Aufsitz-mäher **56** 37
~platz **307** 12
Aufstellmaschine **236** 34
Aufstieg **194** 39
Aufstiegsstufe **6** 37-47
Auftauchstufe **279** 17
Auftrage-bürste **50** 42
~tablett **50** 34
Auftragswalze **249** 52
Auftragwalze **181** 7
Aufträufeln **228** 11
Auftriebskörper **217** 34
Auftritt **316** 36
Auf-und-ab-Schalter **211** 30
Auf-und-nieder-Steven **285** 40
Aufwärtshaken **299** 32
Aufwascheimer **50** 54
Aufwickel-friktionsachse **312** 37
~spule **117** 32

Aufwind, thermischer **287** 21
~schlauch **287** 21
Aufzug **64** 59
~, automatischer **110** 32-43
~führer **271** 47
~kasten **200** 14
~schacht **271** 51
~seil **120** 37
Aufzugs-rad **110** 41
~tür **139** 51
Augapfel **19** 45
Auge Anat. **16** 7 ; **19** 5, 38-51
~ Pferd **72** 4
~ Jagd **88** 60
~ Schmied **137** 29
~ Spiele **276** 32
~ Kunst **334** 75
Augen-braue **19** 38
~fleck **358** 54
~hintergrundstafel **22** 32
~muschel **115** 73 ; **117** 14
~muskel **19** 44
~refraktometer **111** 44
~schutz **84** 23
~spiegel **22** 62
~sprosse **88** 6
~steckling **54** 22
~trost **61** 27
~wurz **61** 13
Augsburger Patrizierin **355** 48
Augsproß **88** 6
Auktionshalle **225** 58
Aulos **322** 4
Aureus **252** 3
Auriga **3** 27
Aurikel **378** 8
Aurorafalter **365** 3
Ausatmungsluft **279** 26
Ausbau **218** 57
Ausbeinmesser **96** 36
Ausbeulhammer **195** 46
Ausblasöffnung **165** 5
Ausbooten **221** 97
Ausbuchtung **324** 26
Ausdehnungsgefäß **38** 24
Ausdrehhaken **135** 17
Ausfahr-garnitur **29** 1
~gerät **258** 68 ; **259** 74, 88-91
~jäckchen **29** 3
Ausfall **294** 5
~öffnung **139** 2
~schritt **295** 42 ; **299** 4
~stellung **294** 5
Ausflugsdampfer **221** 101-128 ; **225** 29
Ausformanlage **76** 35
Ausfüllen **129** 53
~gerät **237** 59
Ausgabe-datum **342** 42
~gerät **237** 59
Ausgang Piktogramm **233** 37
~ Zirkus **307** 19
Ausgangs-material **169** 1
~stellung Angelsport **89** 33
~stellung Spiele **276** 1
ausgebuchtet **370** 48
Ausgleichestrich **123** 39
Ausgleichs-ballast **212** 66
~behälter **212** 78
~getriebe **65** 32
~luft **192** 4
~rotor **232** 14
Ausguck **273** 23
~tonne **223** 38
Ausguß **261** 34
~becken **261** 6
~stellung **147** 58
Aushängeplatte **183** 28
Ausheber **157** 46
Auskratzer **107** 45
Auskunft **204** 29
Auskunfts-beamter **204** 49 ; **205** 44

~platz **237** 34
Auslage Kaufmannsladen **47** 30
~ Buchb. **185** 23
~ Sport **294** 33
~trommel **180** 65
Auslassen **131** 5, 15
Auslaß-schlitz **242** 58
~streifen **131** 7
~technik **131** 10
~ventil Motor **190** 46
~ventil Infotechnik **242** 53
Auslauf-anschluß **172** 78
~bauwerk **217** 44
~becher **129** 38
~doppelventil **126** 35
Ausläufer **54** 14, 16 ; **58** 20
Auslaufventil **126** 34
Auslaugungsrückstand **154** 62
Ausleger Bau **119** 36
~ Tischler **132** 63 ; **133** 13
~ Werkzeugmasch. **150** 24
~ Hafen **226** 24, 49
~ Sport **283** 42 ; **302** 46
~boot Sportboote **283** 9-16
~boot Völkerkunde **352** 35
Auslege-tisch **184** 19
~trommel **180** 42
Ausleih-pult **262** 20
~saal **262** 18
Auslöschknopf **271** 4
Auslöse-bügel **94** 6
~handgriff **313** 24, 38
~knopf **115** 18
Auslöser **114** 31 ; **117** 6
Auslöse-taste **114** 12
~transistor **195** 19
~ventil **210** 58
Ausmauerung **147** 48
Auspuff **64** 38 ; **188** 15 ; **189** 15
~endtopf **212** 69
~krümmer **190** 36, 73
~leitung Auto **191** 51
~leitung Eisenb. **209** 22
~reparatur **195** 52.
~rohr **189** 51
~system **195** 51
~topf **191** 29
Ausputzmaschine **100** 3
Ausreitgurte **284** 30
Ausrücker **165** 17
Ausrückhebel **166** 8
Ausrufer **308** 8
Ausrufezeichen **342** 21
Ausrüstung **300** 31-57
~ (von Textilien) **168**
Ausrüstungskai **222** 5-9
Aussaat **54** 1 ; **63** 10-12
~schale **54** 2
Ausschabung **26** 52
Ausschalter **10** 15
Ausschank **266** 1-11
Ausschreier **308** 8
Ausschuß-maß **149** 58
~seite **149** 61
Ausschüttung **269** 29
Außen-aufnahme **310** 18
~baugelände **310** 1
~beleuchtung **197** 32
~border **278** 15
~bordkatamaran **286** 21
~bordmotor **278** 15 ; **283** 7 ; **286** 1
~bordmotorboot **283** 6
~feldspieler **292** 41
~gewinde **126** 38, 51
~haut **222** 44-49 ; **283** 33, 48, 58
~hautplanke **285** 50
~käfig **356** 11
~kelch **58** 22
~kiel **283** 32

~klüver 219 23
~meßfühler 149 70
~putz 122 38
~quersitz 296 32
~ring 143 71
~schale 59 42
~schwingtür 194 35
~seiter 289 53
~seitsitz 296 31
~seitstand 296 26
~spiegel 191 40, 56
~spieler 292 76
~steg 185 57
~stürmer 291 16
~taster 135 18
~verteidiger 291 13
~verzahnung 143 96
~wand 121 32; 122 37
~wand, tragende 121 77
~winkel 346 26
äußere Form (des Pferdes) 72
1-38
Aussichtsturm 15 68
Aussonderung 170 24
Aussparung Web. 166 32
~ Buchb. 184 21
Aussprachezeichen 342 30-35
Ausstecher 136 38
Aussteller 250 21
Ausstellungsort 250 13
~tag 250 14
Aussteuerinstrument 311 14
Aussteuerungsanzeige 241
35-36; 243 12
~instrument 241 35, 36
~kontrolle 241 61
Ausstieg 122 24
Ausstiegsluke 6 38
~plattform 6 34
Ausstiegtür 197 14
Austauschkugelkopf 249 28
Auster 357 32
Austerngabel 45 80
Australien 14 17
Australier 352 37
Australopithecusschädel 261
20
Austrittsarm 192 7
~pfosten 123 54
~stufe 123 19
Auswechselspieler 292 39
Ausweichstelle 217 27
Ausweitapparat 100 18
Auswertegerät 23 53
Auswuchtscheibe 190 56
Auswurf 23 25
~öffnung 157 56
~turm 64 37
Auszählen 299 42
Ausziehpolstersitz 207 44
Auszubildender 265 6
Auto 191 1-56; 195 34
~bahn 15 16
~bahnbau 201 1-24
~box 196 22
~bus 194 17
~car 194 17
~deck 221 79
Autodrom 308 62
Autofahrer 196 8
Autogen-schneideanlage 148
67
~schweißbrenner 130 14
~schweißer 141
~schweißwagen 138 35
Autoklav 170 12, 33
Automarke 191 12
automatische Orgel 308 38
automatischer
Telefonanrufaufzeichner
22 13
~ Telefonanrufbeantworter
22 13

automatische
Schnellkochplatte 39 15
Automobil 191 1-56; 192; 193
Auto-rad 191 14
~radio 191 90
~reifen 191 15; 196 27
~shop 196 24
~skooter 308 63
~transport 213 35
~tür 191 4
~typ 193 1-36
Autotypie 178 38
Autozubehör 196 28
AV 243
Ave-Maria-Perle 332 32
Avers 252 8
Avionikkonsole 235 22
Avivieren 169 22
Avivierung 169 22
AV-Kamera 243 1-4
AV-Projektor 242 16
Axial-radial-Lagerung 113 3
Axt Forstw. 85 1
~ Bau 120 73
Azalea 53 12
Azalee 53 12
Azubi 265 6

B

B 320 52
Baby 28 5
~ausstattung 28
~box 28 18
~dress, zweiteiliger 29 12
~jäckchen 28 25; 29 9
~kleidung 29 1-12
~puppe 48 25
~schlafsack 28 17
~schuh 28 45; 29 5
~strampler 29 11
~tragetasche 28 48
~waage 22 42
~wippe 28 2
Bach 13 8; 15 80
Bache 88 51
Bachforelle 364 15
Bachstelze, Weiße 360 9
Back 221 13; 223 48; 258 65;
259 77
Backbord 224 88
~laterne 286 12
~licht 286 12
~-Seitenlampe 223 15
~stange 224 100
~tonne 224 95
Backe Anat. 16 9
~ Jagd 87 4
~ Tischler 132 23
~ Schlosser 140 3
Backeinrichtung 96 47
Backen Schmied 137 15
~ Sport 301 55
~bart 34 12
~brecher 158 20
~bremse 143 97
~knochen 16 8
~stück 71 8
~zahn 19 18, 35
Bäckerei 97
Back-mittelgondel 99 62
~ofen 39 13; 97 71
~ofenfenster 39 14
~platz 39 12-17
~raum 97 55-74
Backsaufbau 259 45
Backstagsbrise 285 13
Backstein 159 20
~flachschicht 123 7
~wand 118 8; 260 45
Back-stube 97 55-74
~- und Nährmittelgondel 99
62

Back-up-Ball 305 20
Back-warenabteilung 99 9
~warenvitrine 99 10
~zutat 98 8-11
Bad 49; 267 27-38
Bade-anstalt 282 1-32
~anzug 280 42
~gast 274 18; 280 30
~haube 280 29; 281 8
~höschen 280 27
~hose 280 43
~kabine 282 1
~kappe 280 44
~mantel 29 24; 32 20;
280 25
~matte 49 48
~meister 281 4; 282 15
~mütze 280 29
~pantoffel 49 46
~pantolette 101 22
Bäderschiff 221 101-128
Bade-schuh 280 23
~schwamm Haushalt 49 6
~schwamm Zool. 357 13
~steg 280 9
~tasche 280 24
~tuch 281 14
~vorleger 49 48
~wanne 49 1
~wärter 280 1
~zelle 282 1
~zusatz 49 5; 99 34
Badflüssigkeit 169 23
Badminton 293 43-44
~schläger 293 43
Badthermometer 116 13
Bagger 226 41
~ausleger 200 4
~eimer 226 44
~gut 226 47
~löffel 200 5
~schute 226 46
Bagien-rah 220 25
~segel 220 4
Baguette 97 12
Bahn 122 91, 95
~ Schmied 137 28
~ Flughafen 233 34
~beladung 226 28
Bahnhof 15 41
Bahnhofs-briefkasten 204 11
~buchhandlung 204 26
~gaststätte 204 13
~halle 204
~mission 204 45
~restaurant 204 13
~uhr 204 30
Bahn-kantensteuerung 180 5,
20
~polizist 205 20
~räumer 197 11; 210 34
~rennfahrer 290 2
~schranke 202 40
~spur 1 58
Bahnsteig 205
~aufgang 204 25
~beleuchtung 205 48
~briefkasten 205 56
~fernsprecher 205 57
~kante 205 19
~kiosk 205 49
~lautsprecher 205 27
~nummer 205 4
~telefon 205 57
~treppe 205 2
~tunnel 204 23
~überdachung 205 5
~überführung 205 3
~uhr 205 46
Bahn-überführung 15 42
~übergang 202 39-50
~übergang, schienengleicher
202 39

~übergang, unbeschrankter
202 49
~unterführung 15 22
Baiser 97 26; 265 5
Bajadere 306 25
Bajonettfassung 127 65, 69
Bake 15 10
Bakentonne 224 80
bakteriologische Kulturen
261 29
Balalaika 324 28
Balance-akt 307 44
~gewicht 241 22
Balancierstange 307 42
Baldachin Babyausstattung
28 32; 47 12; 48 26
~ Supermarkt 99 24
~ Kirche 331 49
~träger 331 46
Baldrian 380 5
Balg 322 58; 324 37
Balgen 114 53; 116 31; 177
10, 26; 309 26
~gerät 115 85
~kamera 309 25
~naheinstellgerät 115 85
Balgfrucht 370 91
~verschluß 324 38
Balken Anat. 17 44
~ Bau 120 19
~brücke 215 7
~kopf 121 33
~korn 305 51
Balkon 37 69
Ball 28 16; 292 27
~abgabe 291 47
~abzeichen 306 34
~annahme 291 48
~ Sport 285 33; 288 65
~kiel 285 32
~tank 223 78
Ballen Anat. 19 58
~ Spinnerei 163 6
~lader 63 37
~presse 169 33
~stand 295 5
Ballerinenrock 314 31
Ballett 314
Balletttänzerin 314 26
Balletteuse 314 26
Ballett-schuh 314 30
~truppe 314 25
Ballistik 87 73
ballistische Kurve 87 79
Balljunge 293 22
Ballon, bemannter 7 16
~aufstieg 288 84
~fahren 288 63-84
~korb 288 64
~start 288 84
Ball-rosette 306 34
~saal 306 1
~spiel 291; 292; 293
~träger 292 23
Balmer-Serie 1 21
Balsamblume 380 7
Balzjagd 86 9-12
Bambus-rohr Korbmacher 136
31
~rohr Bot. 383 60
~stange 307 46
Banane 99 90; 384 33
Bananen-blatt 384 35
~blüte 384 34
~sattel 188 59
~staude 384 28
~umschlaganlage 226 22
Band Sport 300 4
~ Nachtlokal 318 3
~, dünnes 146 13
~, grobes 164 12
~abdeckung 133 31

Bandage *Fahrrad* 187 77
~ *Sport* 289 15; 296 64
Band-bremse 143 104
~bruch 164 4
Bändchen 325 36
~arbeit 102 31
~draht 325 35
~stickerei 102 31
Bande *Billard* 277 16
~ *Sport* 289 2
~ *Zirkus* 307 22
Band-einfädelung 243 14
~eisen 143 11
Banderilla 319 22
Banderillero 319 21
Banderole 107 26
Band-feile 140 16
~förderung 144 40
~geschwindigkeitsschalter 241 62
~keramik 328 13
~lineal 243 22
~maß *Schneiderei* 103 2
~maß *Warenhaus* 271 38
Bandoneon 324 36
Bandonika 324 36
Band-säge 134 50
~sägeblatt 157 53
~scheibenverkleidung 133 32
Bändsel 221 119
Band-spannhebel 133 16
~spule 241 57
~stahl 148 66-75
~umlenker 241 60
~verdichtung 163 59
~vorschubsrichtung 243 29
~walze 133 18
Bandwurm 81 35
Bandzählwerk 241 64; 243 9
Banjo 324 29
Bank *Geldinstitut* 250; 251 14
~ *Spielplatz* 273 58
~ *Roulett* 275 11
~ *Sport* 295 20; 296 14
~ *Kirche* 330 28
~, optische *Fotogr.* 114 50
~, optische *Infotechnik* 242 79
~angestellte 250 5
~angestellter 251 7
~eisen 132 36
Bankett *Bau* 123 2
~ *Festessen* 267 40-43
Bank-filiale 204 31
~haken 132 36
~kundin 250 6
~note 252 29-39; 271 6
~platte 132 34
~sattel 188 59
Banner 253 12
Bannwald 304 7
Bantamhuhn 74 56
Baptisterium 332 2
Bar 317 1; 318 13
Bär *Tech.* 139 12
~ *Hafen* 226 38
~ *Zool.* 368 9-11
~, Brauner 365 7
~, Großer 3 29
~, Kleiner 3 34
Bar-band 267 44
~dame 267 63; 317 2; 318 14
Bären-klee 69 6
~kralle 352 14
~lauch 377 6
~robbe 367 18
~traube 377 15
Barett 355 28
Barfach 42 20
Bärführung 139 8
Bärführungskopf 139 29
Bargast 267 55
Bargeld 246 27

Barhocker 267 53; 317 3; 318 16
Baritonoboe 323 38
Bark 220 21-23
~, Takelung und Besegelung einer 219 1-72
Barkasse 225 25
Barlampe 317 11
Bärlapp, Keuliger 377 12
Bärlatsch 329 55
Barmixer 267 62
Barock, Kunst des ~s 336 1-8
~antiqua 342 5
~kirche 336 1
~park 272 1-40
~schloß 272 7
Barograph 10 4
Barren 296 2, 45, 46, 49, 57, 58
~holm 296 3; 297 4
Barriere *Supermarkt* 99 5
~ *Mil.* 259 17
~ *Restaurant* 266 72
Bar-schrank 42 20; 246 29
~set 246 30
Bart *Jagd* 88 73
~ *Schlosser* 140 35
~ *Sport* 287 21
~ *Mus.* 326 32
~faden 364 13
~haar 367 21
Bartheke 267 54; 317 9; 318 15
Bartnelke 60 6
Bartrio 267 44
Bart-stoppel 34 23
~tracht 34 1-25
Bärzylinder 139 30
Baseball 292 40-69, 61
~handschuh 292 59-60
~spiel 292 40-69
Basidie 381 7
Basilika 334 61
Basilisk *Fabelwesen* 327 34
~ *Zool.* 364 30
Basis *Sport* 288 48
~ *Architektur* 334 28-31
~ *Math.* 345 1, 6; 346 27
~ *Kristallkunde* 351 20
~, horizontale 112 72
Baskenmütze 35 27
Basketball 292 28, 29
~spiel 292 28
~spieler 292 35
Baslerin 355 35
Basrelief 339 33
Baß 241 17
Bassangans 359 9
Baßgeige 323 23
Bassin 272 24
Baß-klarinette 323 34
~lautsprecher 241 17
~posaune 323 46
~register 324 44
~saite 324 25; 325 12
~schlüssel 320 9
~steg 325 13
~teil 324 43
Baßtölpel 359 9
Baß-trompete 323 43
~tuba 323 44
Bast *Korbmacher* 136 29
~ *Völkerkunde* 352 18
~ *Bot.* 370 9
Bastard 73 8
~klee 69 3
Bastelarbeit 48 3
Basteln 134 1-34
Bastion 329 16
Bast-rock 306 18
~schuh 122 75
~verband 54 35
Batholit 11 29
Batter 292 52

Batterie *Med.* 25 52
~ *Landmaschinen* 65 53
~ *Landw.* 74 19
~ *Fotogr.* 114 66
~ *Auto* 191 50
~ *Mil.* 259 83
~anschluß 115 75
~behälter 207 5
~fach 115 10
~fütterung 74 23
~haltung 74 18
~handgriff 115 76; 117 5
~hauptschalter 115 13
~käfig 74 20
~raum *Eisenb.* 211 56
~raum *Mil.* 257 17
~trog 207 25; 211 56
Batteurwickel 163 47
Bau 86 26
~aufzug 118 31
~bude 118 48; 119 44
Bauch *Anat.* 16 35-37
~ *Fischerei* 90 20
~ *Fleischerei* 95 2, 41
~aorta 18 16
~fell 20 58
~flosse 364 8
~gurt 71 18, 36
~laden 267 50; 308 52
~lage 295 45
~muskel 18 43, 44
~notgurt 71 23
~reifen 329 49
~speicheldrüse 20 44
Bauelement, elektronisches 109 25
Bauer *Landw.* 62 6
~ *Spiele* 276 13
~ *Kegeln* 305 6, 8
Bäuerin 62 4
Bauern-hof 62
~leier 322 25
Bau-gerüst 222 18
~glaser 124 8
~grube 118 69-82
~holz 120 10, 83-96
~hütte 118 48
~kasten 48 22
~klammer 119 58
~klotz 28 41; 48 27
Baum *Segeln* 284 39
~ *Bot.* 370 1
~bürste 56 23
~gruppe 272 61
~holz 84 4
~kante 120 89
~kratzer 56 14
~krone 272 60; 370 3
~kuchen 97 46
~lerche 361 18
Bäummaschine 165 55
Baum-niederholer 284 21
~pfahl 52 31
~rutscher 361 11
~säge 56 16
~scheibe 165 30; 166 49
~schere 56 11
~schule *Landkarte* 15 111
~schule *Gärtner* 55 3
~schule *Forstw.* 84 6
~schulsetzling 83 15
~schutz 118 80
~stamm *Forstw.* 84 19
~stamm *Schiff* 218 7
~stamm *Völkerkunde* 354 20
~stamm *Bot.* 370 2, 7
~stumpf 84 14
Baumwoll-anlieferung 163 1-13
~ballen 163 3
Baumwolle 383 16
~reiniger 163 7
Baumwoll-kapsel 163 1

~spinnerei 163; 164
~spitze 31 32
Bau-platz 118; 119
~schlosser 140 1
Bauscht 173 50
Baustahlträger 143 3-7
Baustein, elektronischer 242 69
~verbindung 242 70
Baustellenabort 118 49
Bausystem, gotisches 335 27-35
Bauwerk 48 28; 336 15
Bauzaun 118 44
B-Deck 223 32-42
B-Dur 320 64
Bearbeitungszentrum 150 41
Bebänderung 279 12
Bebenstärke 11 37
Beblechung 208 6
Becher 371 5
~füller 76 21
~glas *Restaurant* 266 3
~glas *Chem.* 350 20
Becken *Anat.* 17 18-21
~ *Mus.* 323 50; 324 50, 51
~halter 324 52
~querschnitt 281 36
~rand 281 3
bedeckt 9 24
Bedienerseite 207 79
Bedienung 211 38; 266 18; 318 14
Bedienungs-anleitung 244 15
~blattschreiber 176 31
~feld 177 60
~handrad 212 67, 81
~hebel *Schädlingsbek.* 83 21
~hebel *Film* 117 63
~hebel *Installateur* 126 19
~hebel *Straßenbau* 201 12
~knopf 25 29, 30
~pult 182 28
~schalter 249 38
~stand *Textil* 168 23
~stand *Repro* 177 5
~stange 217 72
~tafel *Repro* 177 36
~tafel *Fernsehtechnik* 240 31
~taste *Film* 117 98
~taste *A V* 243 13
~taste *Büro* 246 19
~taste *Sprachlabor* 261 45
~tritt 325 46
~tür 139 4
~- und Steuerpult 182 28
Bedlingtonterrier 70 18
Beduine 354 6
Beerdigung 331 33-41
Beere 58 9; 370 97
Beeren-frucht 68 43
~hochstamm 52 11
~obst 58 1-30
~strauch 52 19; 58 1-30
Befehlsstab 205 42
Befeuchten 50 13
Befeuchtung 281 26
Befeuerung 224 68-108
Beffchen 332 5
Befiederung 305 62
Beflaggung 268 44
Befreiungsgriff 21 34
Begasungskammer 83 15
Begattung 357 26
Begichtung 147 51
Beginrah 220 25
Begleit-hund 70 25
~saite 324 25
~seite 324 43
Begonia 53 10
Begonie 53 10
Begräbnis 331 33-41

~stätte 331 23, 59
Begrenzerinstrument 238 44
Begrenzungs-blech 200 34, 44
~leuchte *Motorrad* 189 56
~leuchte *Auto* 191 20
Behälter 172 41, 45, 46
~bauer 130
~bauerei 130 1-33
~tasche 248 3
Behandlungs-instrument 22 48-50
~lampe 24 19
~raum 22 32-74
~stuhl 24 3
~tray 24 5
Behang 70 2
Behelfstrage 21 23
Behörde 217 24
Beiboot 258 12; 259 35
Beifahrerin 268 36
Beifahrersitz 191 36
Beilade 132 35
Beilage 266 55
Beilauf 153 45
Beimengenband 64 80
Bein *Anat.* 16 49-54; 17 22-25
~ *Med.* 21 11
~ *Jagd* 88 81
~, langes 32 29
Beinbrech 61 12
Bein-halter 23 10, 11
~kloben 23 11
~nerv 18 30
~panzer 319 19
~ring 354 38
~röhre 329 54
~schiene 291 33
~schutz 292 9
~steller 299 11
Beinwell 69 13
~, Gemeiner 375 45
Beisetzung 331 33-41
Beisitzer 263 2
Beiß-ring 28 12
~zange 100 40, 41; 136 37
Beistopper 227 14, 15
Beitel 132 7-11
Beiwagen-maschine 189 53
~rad 189 57
~schiff 189 54
~stoßstange 189 55
~windschutzscheibe 189 58
Beiz-automat 83 52
~bottich 130 15
Beize 86 42-46
Beiz-jagd 86 42-46
~pulverbehälter 83 60
~vogel 86 46
Belag 118 87; 119 52
Belastung 23 27
Belastungsscheibe 165 21
Belederung 283 36
Belegordner 247 40
belegtes Brot 45 37
~ Brötchen 266 54
Beleuchter 307 4; 310 37; 316 20
Beleuchtung 210 46; 317 12
Beleuchtungs-brücke 316 19
~kasten 179 25
~körper 316 14
~optik 112 7
~spiegel 14 58, 59
~strahlengang 112 6
~strahler 22 44
belichteter Film 117 42
Belichtung 182 1
Belichtungs-lampe 182 3
~messer 114 56
~messerfenster 114 3, 24
~messer-Wahlschalter 117 17
~messerzeiger 115 57
~meßkassette 114 61

~schaltuhr 116 24
~steuereinrichtung 176 9
~steuernut 117 37
~system 249 42
~zeiteinstellung 179 18
Bellatrix 3 13
Belly 90 20
Belüftung 191 48
Belüftungsanlage 317 30
Benediktiner 331 54
Bengel 340 34
Benguellastrom 14 43
Benzin-einspritzung 190 1
~feuerzeug 107 27
~frosch 200 26
~kanister 84 36; 196 25
~leitung 286 25
~motor 83 41
~pumpe 196 1
~tank 345 87
~uhr 191 38, 65
Benzol-abtransport 170 6
~chlorierung 170 8
~gewinnung 170 6
~ring 242 66
~wascher 156 24
Beobachtungs-fenster *Raumfahrt* 235 24, 25
~fenster *Film* 313 28
~fernrohr 351 31
~raum 5 33
~schacht 5 30
~spalt 5 13
Beplankung 257 28; 285 50-57, 57
Beregnung 67
Beregnungs-anlage 67 3
~automat 67 18
~fahrzeug 62 27
~gerät 55 19
Bereifung 187 30
Bereitschaftstasche 115 103
Bergbahn 214
Bergehalde 144 19
Bergen 227
Bergepanzer 255 93
Berg-forelle 364 15
~fried 329 4
~gipfel 12 40
~hang 12 37
~hütte 300 1
~kette 12 39
~kuppe 12 35
~massiv 12 39
~paß 12 47
~rennen 290 24-28
~rücken 12 36
~rutsch 11 46
~sattel 12 42
~schuh 300 42
~seil 300 12
~spitze 12 40
~sport 300
~station 214 57
~steigen 300 1-57
Bergsteiger 300 5
~ausrüstung 300 31-57
Berg-und-Tal-Bahn 308 5
~-Rutschbahn 273 52
Bergung *Erste Hilfe* 21 18
~ *Schiff* 227 1
~ eines Verletzten 21 18-23
Bergungskran 270 48
Bergwandern 300 1-57
Bergwerk 15 34
~, verlassenes 15 35
Berieselungsanlage 316 6
Berline 186 1
Berliner 97 29
~ Pfannkuchen 97 29
Berlocke 36 35
Berme 216 38
Bermudas 31 44

Bernhardiner 70 37
Berufsboxer 299 25
Berührungspunkt 346 49
Besan 218 29; 219 30
~ausleger 218 28
~baum 219 44
~-Bramstagsegel 219 29
~dirk 219 48
~mast 218 31; 219 8-9; 220 23
~rute 218 30
~saling 219 54
~schot 219 69
~segel 219 30
~stagsegel 219 27
~stenge 219 9
~-Stengestagsegel 219 28
~untermast 219 8
Besatzungsraum 6 41; 235 16
Besäumtisch 132 64
Beschichten 179 1
Beschicker 159 7
Beschickungs-band 144 42
~kammer 154 79
~maschine 147 25
Beschleunigungs-messer 230 10
~rakete 234 22, 48
Beschneidemesser 128 38
Beschriften 129 40
Beschuß 1 50
Besegelung einer Bark 219 1-72
Besen *Haushalt* 50 46
~ *Landw.* 62 5
~ *Navigation* 224 99, 100
~borste 50 47
Besenginster, Echter 374 20
Besen-körper 50 48
~stiel 38 37; 50 49
Besiegter 299 40
Besitzer 266 71
Bespannung 287 40
Besprechungs-gruppe 246 31-36
~tisch 246 31
Bestäuben 181 10
Besteck 207 85; 309 47
~entnahmefach 266 48
~kommode 266 41
~schublade 39 10; 44 21
Bestellung 63 10-12
Bestich 123 6
Bestimmungsgleichung 345 4, 9
Bestrahlung 23 36
Bestrahlungs-gerät 24 23
~schutzwand 2 46
~tisch 2 36
Besucher-sessel 246 21
~terrasse 233 20, 30
Beta-strahlung 1 32
~teilchen 1 32
Betätigungs-brunnen 117 98
~hebel 224 19
~knopf 224 32
Betäubungsgerät 94 3
~, elektrisches 94 7
Beteigeuze 3 13
Betelnuß 380 20
~baum 380 19
Betender 330 61
Betnische 337 14
Beton 119 72
~arbeiter 119 9
~bassin 310 11
~behälter 79 3
~-Blei-Schutzmantel 1 57
~hülle 154 20
~innenrüttler 119 88
~kübel 119 38; 201 24
~mischanlage 201 19
~mischer 47 40; 200 15

~mischmaschine 118 33; 119 29
Betonnung 224 68-108, 84
Beton-pfette 119 4
~schalung 119 54-76
~schutzmantel 1 57
~schwelle 202 37
~sockel 118 2
~stampfer 119 83
~straßenbau 201 1-24
betont 321 27
Beton-verteilerkübel 201 6
~verteilerwagen 201 5
~wand 123 1
Betrieb, automatischer 117 13
~, manueller 117 13
Betriebs-ablaufschema 76 9
~anzeige 244 11
Betriebsartschalter 117 88
Betriebs-einheit 6 2
~fernsprechanlage 238 14
~raum *Molkerei* 76 12-48
~raum *Rundfunk* 238 7-15
~schaubild 76 8
~skala 313 28
~stelle 203 25
Betriebsstofftanker 258 97
Betriebstaste 243 41, 48
Bett 150 29
~, französisches 43 4-13
~gestell 43 4-6
~kasten 43 5; 47 2
~kastenliege 46 16
~kastenregal 46 19
~kastenschublade 46 18
~konsole 43 17
~laken 43 9; 50 5
Bettlerleier 322 25
Bett-monitorgerät 25 19
~schlitten *Werkzeugmasch.* 149 24
~schlitten *Repro* 177 59
Bettuch 43 9
Bett-vorleger 43 22
~wanze 81 39
~wäsche 271 57
Beuge-hang 296 35
~eine 296 39
~stütz 296 39
Beute 77 45-50, 52
Beutel-gans 359 5
~ratte 366 2
~tier 366 2-3
Bewaffnung 258 29-37
~ des Heeres 255 1-98
Bewehrung 119 54-76, 68
Bewehrungseisen 119 23
Bewertungslampe 195 9
Bewölkung 9 20-24
Bewußtloser 21 24-27, 25; 270 24
Beziehen 134 59
Bezogener 250 20
Bezug 323 9
Bezugsstoff 134 60
BH 32 1
~, langer 32 4
Bibel 330 11
Biberratte 366 14
Biberschwanz 122 46
~-Doppeldeckung 122 2
~ziegel 122 46
Bibliothek 223 25
Bibliothekar 262 19
Bibliothekarin 262 14
Bibliotheksbenutzer 262 24
Bidet 49 7
Biedermeier-kleid 306 22
~sofa 336 17
~stil 336 17
~zeit 355 73
Biege-eisen *Bau* 119 77
~eisen *Korbmacher* 136 34

~form 126 83
~maschine 125 30
Biegen 125 30
Biegetisch 119 20
Biene 77 1-25
Bienen 77
~fresser 360 2
~giftsalbe 77 68
~haus 77 56
~kasten 77 45-50
~königin 77 4
~korb 77 52
~korbhütte 354 28
~männchen 77 5
~schleier 77 58
~schwarm 77 53
~stand, veralteter 77 51
~stock 77 45-50
~wabe 77 31-43
~wachs 77 67
~zelle 77 26-30
~zucht 77
~züchter 77 57
Bier 99 72
~, dunkles 93 26
~, helles 93 26
~, Münchener 93 26
~, Pilsener 93 26
~becher 266 3
~brauerei 93 1-31
~deckel 266 26
~dose 93 25; 99 73
~druckapparat 266 1
~faß 93 17
~filter 93 15
~flasche 93 26; 205 50
~glas 45 91; 93 30; 266 6; 317 6
~kasten 99 72
~kastenstapel 93 24
~schaum 266 4
~seidel 309 53
~sieder 92 49
~untersetzer 266 26
~wärmer 266 7
~zapfapparat 266 68
~zapfhahn 317 8
~zelt 308 23
Bifokalglas 111 15
Big-wave-riding 279 4
Bijouteriewarenabteilung 271 62
Bikini 280 26
Bild-aufbau 338 4
~aufnahme 313 26
~aufnahmekamera 310 47
~bühne 115 28
~endkontrollraum 238 60-65
Bilder-rahmen 43 21
~schrift 341 1
Bild-feldlinse 115 40
~fenster 115 34; 312 34
~fensteraussparung 117 40
~fernsprecher 242 21
Bildhauer 339 1
~atelier 339
Bild-kamera 313 20
~kassette 242 18
~kodiereinrichtung 242 8-10
~messung 14 63-66
~mischpult 238 63
~monitor 238 33
~nummernfenster 114 18
~platte A V 243 38, 44
~platte Graphik 340 59
~plattenabspielgerät 243 37
~plattenhülle 243 45
~plattenspieler 243 37, 46
~projektion 311 45
~regieraum 239 10
~röhrengeometrie-
   Korrektur 242 39
~säule 333 18

~schirm 236 40; 261 7
~schnitzer 339 28
~standsregler 243 10
~strahlengang 115 35
~streifen 311 44
~strichverstellung 312 29
~telefon 242 21
~-Ton-Einheit 117 102
~-Ton-Kamera 313 26
~trommel 116 20
~- und Tonstreifen 311 44
~unterschrift 342 59
~wand 310 16; 312 11
Bildwandler 27 19
~einheit 26 18
~monitor 26 15
~röhre 27 19
Bild-wandvorhang 312 10
~wascher 116 15
~weiche 112 19
~werferraum 312 12
~zähler 313 28
~zählwerk 115 17
Billard 277 1-19, 7
~ball 277 1
~kugel 277 1
~spiel 277 1-19
~spieler 277 8
~stock 277 9
~stoß 277 2-6
~taxi 277 17
~tisch 277 14
~zimmer 277 7-19
Bilsenkraut 379 6
Bimbernelle 69 28
Bims-hohlblockstein 119 24
~kreisel 100 7
Binde-bogen 321 24
~gürtel 31 19
~mitteleinspritzung 200 53
Binder-balken 121 53
~schicht Bau 118 64
~schicht Straße 198 3, 4
~sparren 121 55
~verband 118 60
Bindestrich 342 28
Bindung, englische 171 11
~, textile 171
Bindungs-element 301 54-56
~teil 171 12
Binnen-klüver 219 21
~wasserfahrzeug 221 92
binokularer Einblick 23 6
Binokulartubus 112 12
Binse 136 28
Binsen-quecke 61 30
~rispe 341 22
Biologieunterricht 261 14-34
Biopsiezange 23 17
Birke 51 13; 272 40; 371 9
~rute 281 27
Birkahn 86 11; 88 66
Birn-ball 299 24
~baum 58 31
~baumzweig 58 32
Birne 58 33; 99 87
Birnen-blei 89 90
~blüte 58 38
~form, normal facettierte 36 54
~kern 58 37
~stiel 58 34
Birnquitte 58 50
Bisamflitmütze 35 33
Biskuitrolle 97 19
Bison 367 9
Bitumen 145 64
~kocher 200 46
Bizeps 18 37
Blankett 252 43
Blase 22 54
Blasebalg Camping 278 49

~ Mus. 325 46
Blasen 162 28, 36
~kammer 1 58
Bläser 232 34
Blas-form 162 26, 34
~luft 181 35
~luftzufuhrrohr 147 68
~magnet 312 39
Blasonierung 254 17-23
Blas-prozeß, doppelter 162 22
~rohr Eisenb. 210 25
~rohr Völkerkunde 352 26
~schema 162 22-37
Bläßente 359 20
Blas-stellung 147 57
~verfahren 162 30
Blatt Landw. 57 3; 68 8
~ Bot. 58 3, 19, 53; 59 17, 40;
   370 19, 26; 371 21, 23, 68;
   373 3, 16, 25; 374 28; 375 2,
   12; 378 15, 18, 41, 45; 384 55
~ Jagd 88 17, 38, 55
~ Bau 121 86
~ Web. 166 10
~ Textilw. 169 1
~ Spiele 276 43
~ Sport 283 38, 53
~, austreibendes 59 29
~achsel 370 25; 375 38
~aderung 370 29
~ansatz 371 73
~elevator 64 90
Blätter-beute 77 45-50
~kohl 57 34
~krone 384 29
~pilz 379 10
Blätterteigpastete 97 18
Blatt-fallkrankheit 80 20
~form 370 31-38; 378 52
~geschirr 71 26-36
~gold 129 45, 52; 183 5
~häutchen 68 22; 370 84
~hornkäfer 82 1; 358 24, 39
~knospe 59 47; 370 90
~kranz 334 25
~laus 80 32; 358 13, 14, 15
~nektarium 59 18
~ornament 334 40
~pflanze 39 37
~randform 370 43-50
~ranke 57 4
~rippe 370 30
~rosette 384 62
~scheide 68 9, 21; 370 83; 384 30
~schreiber 237 66
~schuß 86 17
~spreite 68 20; 370 28, 85
~stiel 370 27
~überfall 333 24
~unterseite 378 19
~zweig 371 27, 29; 383 61
blau Heraldik 254 28
~ Farbe 343 3
Blaubeere 377 23
Blauer Peter 253 26
Blau-fichte 51 10
~grünfiltereinstellung 116 45
~hai 364 1
~kissen 51 7
~kraut 57 32
~licht Polizei 264 11
~licht Feuerwehr 270 6
Bläuling 365 6
Blau-meise 360 4
~racke 360 6
~säurebegasung 83 15
~specht 361 11
Blazer 33 54
Blech-blasinstrument 323 39-48
~kuchen 97 43

~schere 108 23; 125 1
~schraube 143 26
~verkleidung 188 50
~walze 108 1
Bleiabschirmung 259 70
Bleichen 169 21
Bleich-erde 199 38
~fixierbad 116 10
Blei-einsatz 151 62
~gewicht 89 88-92
~glanz 351 14
~glasfenster 124 14; 154 75
~gürtel 279 14
~hammer 124 11
~kiel 285 36
~kopf 326 20
~kugel 89 89
~mantel 153 39, 47
~messer 124 12
~nadeleinsatz 151 55
~olive 89 88
~rute 124 13
~scheibe 122 103
~schutzmantel 1 57
~siegelwand 2 46
~soldat 309 52
~sprosse 124 13
~steg 124 13
~stift 47 26; 260 5
~stiftspitzer 247 25
Blendarkade 335 10
Blende Kleidung 30 47
~ Möbel 46 5
Blenden-automatik 117 20
~einstellrad 114 34
~einstellung 117 4
~ring 115 5; 117 4
~skala 115 56
Blend-rahmen 338 20
~schutz 210 60
Bleßhuhn 359 20
Blicken 68 24
Blickfenster 27 12
Blimp 310 48; 313 16-18, 27
Blindboden 123 73
Blinddarm 20 17
Blinde 218 43
Blindenschrift 342 15
blinder Fleck 19 50
~ Schornstein 221 16
Blind-material 174 8
~schacht 144 27
~schaltbild 153 8
Blindschleiche 364 37
Blinker Angelsport 89 73
~ Auto 191 19
~ Straßenbahn 197 22
~kontrolle 191 76
~- und Warnlichtkontrolle 191 76
Blink-leuchte 189 45
~licht Motorrad 189 37, 42
~licht Eisenb. 202 46, 50
~licht Feuerwehr 270 6
~schalter 191 59
~- und Abblendschalter 191 59
Blitz-ableiter 38 30
~birnchen 309 39
~birne 309 39
~gerät 309 38
~lampe Fotogr. 114 67
~lampe Infotechnik 242 43
Blitzlicht-anschluß 114 30; 115 14
~gerät 309 38
~-Mittenkontakt 115 21
~röhre 176 26
Blitz-löter 134 58
~schalter 114 33
~stab 114 67
~würfelanschluß 114 13
Block 221 28, 105

~auswerfer 157 19
~bandsäge 157 48
~feld 203 60
~flansch 130 21
~flöte 322 7
~kippwagen 148 49
~messer 94 15; 96 37
~schere 148 52
~stelle 15 24
~straße 148 50
~stufe 123 17
~tastenfeld 249 2-6
~verband 118 62
~ware 157 33
~zug 157 17
Blondiermittel 105 1
~tube 105 3
Blöße 84 13
Blouson 31 42
Blue Jeans 31 60; 33 22
Blümchenborte 30 28
Blume *Pflanze* 55 24; 375; 376
~ *Jagd* 88 19, 62
~ *Fleischerei* 95 35
~ *Restaurant* 266 4
Blumen-arrangement 267 37
~asch 54 8
~beet 55 37
~blatt 58 43; 374 21
~fenster 37 68
~garten 51 1-35
~kasten 37 20; 268 15
~kette 306 17
~kiosk 204 48
~kohl 57 31; 99 84
~korb 266 29
~kresse 53 4
~mädchen 266 28
~rabatte 52 18; 272 41
~schemel 267 36
~scherben 54 8
~schmuck 266 78; 330 48
~staude 52 9
~tier 357 17
~topf 54 8
~vase 309 2
~verkäuferin 266 28
Bluse 30 40; 84 26
Blut, arterielles 18 12
~, venöses 18 11
~ausstrich 23 50
~druck 25 1
~druckmesser 23 33; 25 15
~druckmessung 23 32
Blüte *Teil der Pflanze* 58 4; 59 9; 61 10, 19, 22; 68 42; 69 14; 80 11; 370 23, 51; 371 6, 13, 14, 17, 35, 40, 52, 55, 62; 372 43; 373 5, 7, 11, 14, 20, 21, 31; 374 6, 7, 11, 15, 17, 21, 24; 375 3, 6, 16, 19, 20, 23, 40, 46; 376 2, 5, 11, 19, 23; 378 16, 20, 23, 25, 28, 31, 32, 37, 47, 53, 57; 382 4, 13, 17, 18, 29, 32, 42, 50, 55; 383 3, 12, 17, 27, 31, 36, 39, 46, 47, 50, 51, 55; 384 5, 7, 13, 14, 15, 18, 42, 43, 44, 51, 56, 57, 65
~ *Blütezeit* 382 53
~, männliche 59 39
~, weibliche 59 38
~, welke 58 55
Blutegel 357 20
Blütenähre 383 62, 66; 384 63
~ansatz 59 28
~blatt 58 43; 59 11
~boden 370 53
~dolde 378 40
~form 378 10
~kätzchen 371 26
~knospe 58 27; 370 24; 371

25; 374 14
~kolben 383 55; 384 4, 6
~köpfchen 61 14
~krone 378 4; 384 18
~krug 370 75
~rispe 378 46; 382 54
~schlauch 370 66
~schopf 383 65
~sproß 372 6, 62, 68
~stand 370 67-77; 371 8, 43, 48; 372 17, 24; 373 24; 378 7, 53, 55; 382 38; 383 11, 13, 49; 384 31, 50
~stand, männlicher 68 35
~stand, weiblicher 68 32
~staub *Bienenzucht* 77 3, 6
~staub *Bot.* 370 65
~stecher 80 10
~stengel 59 4; 383 7
~stiel 370 52
~traube 58 15; 374 33
~trugdolde 374 36
~zapfen 372 4, 16, 22, 34, 62, 68
~zweig 59 26; 371 2, 10, 16, 32, 34, 39, 51, 54, 66, 71; 372 33; 378 2; 382 3, 8, 12, 23, 27, 31, 41, 47, 50; 383 22, 26, 30, 38, 42; 384 17, 24, 37, 49, 54
Blut-gefäß 19 33
~klee 69 4
~kreislauf 18 1-21
Blutlaus 80 32
~kolonie 80 34
~krebs 80 33
Blut-senkung 23 42
~stein 108 48
~stillung 21 14-17
~wurst 99 56
b-Moll 320 67
Bobby 264 34
Bobführer 303 20
Bobine 163 2
Bob-schlitten 303 19
~sport 303 19-21
Boccia 305 21
~spiel 305 21
Bock *Zool.* 73 13, 18; 358 38
~ *Jagd* 88 28
~ *Brauerei* 93 26
~ *Korbmacher* 136 10
~ *Wagen* 186 8
~ *Sport* 296 17
~, wachsander 254 32
~bier 93 26
~flinte 87 33
~gerüst 91 33
~käfer 358 38
~kitz 88 39
~mühle 91 31
~sattel 71 37-44
~sitz 186 8
~strang 122 67
Boden 296 11, 52; 297 6, 19, 20, 23, 24, 25, 26, 27
~, eingeschnittener 119 56
~ansicht 286 32, 35, 39
~bestellung 63 10-12
~blender 289 30
~fläche 296 11; 297 6
~gang 222 48
~geflecht 136 20
~gruppe der Karosserie 191 2
~haltung 74 1-17
~heizung 356 18
~kammertür 38 20
~kampf 299 8
~kreuz 136 21
~lederschere 100 39
~luke 38 14
~pflege 50 53-86
~platte 112 27

~riß 11 52
~stampfer 200 26
~staubsauger 50 68
~stein 91 23
~stelle 6 44
~stern 136 19
~stromgerät 233 22
~stück 255 54
~tank 222 38
~teppich *Wohnung* 44 16
~teppich *Auto* 191 43
~wegerung 222 63
~wrange 222 59
Bodhisattwa 337 10
Bogen *Installateur* 126 46
~ *Druck* 180 55
~ *Eisenb.* 203 51, 52
~ *Börse* 251 17
~ *Sport* 302 6
~ *Theater* 316 11
~ *Mus.* 323 12
~ *Fabelwesen* 327 53
~ *Kunst* 336 19
~ *Völkerkunde* 354 32
~ablage 180 44; 181 6
~achter 302 11
~anlage 181 6
~anlegeapparat 180 68
~anleger *Druck* 180 31, 48; 181 5
~anleger *Buchb.* 184 16; 185 25
~anschlag 185 11
~ausleger 180 45
~brücke 215 19, 28
~feintrieb 151 66
~feld 335 26
~form 336 19-37
~gang 297 23
~kämpfer 215 29
~lauf 180 33
~leiter 5 20
~norm 185 69
~offsetmaschine 180 30
~peitsche 307 53
~säge 108 12; 136 40
~scheitel 215 31
~schießen 305 52-66
~schütze 305 53
~sehne 305 59
~spannweite 215 26
~wurf 297 33; 305 19
~zähler 181 54
~zuführtisch 185 9
~zuführungstisch 180 67
~zusammentragemaschine 249 59
Bohlen-belag 118 28
~weg 118 79
Bohne *Landw.* 57 11
~ *Bot.* 382 5
Bohnen-blüte 57 9
~käfer, Vierfleckiger 81 19
~kaffee 98 65
~pflanze 52 28; 57 8
~stange 52 28
~stengel 57 10
Bohrer *Med.* 24 38
~ *Erdöl* 145 21
~ *Steinbruch* 158 9
~ *Sport* 282 44
~fach 24 17
Bohr-fliege 80 18
~gestänge 145 19
~hammer 158 11
~insel 146 1-39; 221 64
~inselversorger 221 32
~instrument 24 6
~kopf 134 48
Bohrloch *Bot.* 58 65
~ *Erdöl* 145 17
~ *Steinbruch* 158 12
Bohr-maschine 120 21; 134

16, 22
~meißel 145 21
~motor 133 7
~rohr 145 6
~seil 145 7
Bohr-Sommerfeldsches Atommodell 1 26
Bohr-spindel 150 23
~ständer 134 54
~turm *Landkarte* 12 33
~turm *Erdöl* 145 1; 146 12; 221 67
~turmplattform 146 1-37
Bohrung 143 86
Bohrungskaliber 87 40
Bohr-werk 138 22
~werksständer 150 31
Boiler 38 68
Boje 90 2
Bola 352 31
Bollstichel 340 20
Bolzenschußgerät 94 3
Bolzstichel 340 20
Bombarde 322 14
Bombardon 323 44
Bomhart 322 14
Bommel 29 4
Bon 271 7
Bonbon 98 75
Bonbonniere 98 79
Bonbon-sortiment 47 31
~tüte 47 32
Bongo 324 58
Bonnett 218 34
Boot 89 26; 285 7; 354 20
~axt 328 19
Bootes 3 30
Boots-anhänger 278 20
~ausschnitt 30 34
~aussetzkran 258 13
~davit 258 83
~deck 223 19-21
~haus 283 23
~haut 283 58
~klasse 284 49-65
~kran 223 20
~mann 221 114
~name 286 7
~rucksack 283 65
~rumpf 232 2, 9
~schuppen 283 24
~steg 283 19
~treppe 283 22
~wagen 278 20; 283 66
Boottransporter 278 20
Bord-energieanlage 6 6, 8
~gebrauch 6 19
~instrument 288 68
~jackett 221 127
~kanone 256 3
~kran 259 10
~küche 231 20
Bordsteinkante 198 6
Bord-telefon 239 13
~uhr 230 11
Bordun 322 11
~saite 322 31
Bordwand 62 25
boreales Klima 9 56
Borgis 175 26
Borke 370 8
Borkenkäfer 82 22
Börse 251 1-10
Börsen-diener 251 9
~handel 251 6
~makler 251 4
~mitglied 251 6
~saal 251 1
~vertreter 251 7
Borsten-schwanz 81 14
~wurm 357 22
Böschung 118 72
Boskett 272 4

Bossenwerk 335 51
Bossierer 161 19
Bossier-griffel 161 20
~holz 161 20
Botanik, allgemeine 370
Botta dritta 294 7
Böttcher 130 11
Böttcherei 130 1-33
Bottich *Böttcher* 130 1
~ *Schwimmbad* 281 26
Boule-spiel 305 21
~spieler 305 22
Bovenspiegel 218 55
Bowdenzug 188 37; 189 12
Bowling 305 14-20
~aufstellung 305 14
~kugel 305 15
~stand 305 14
Bowlspiel 305 21
Box *Landw.* 75 2
~ *Flohmarkt* 309 30
~birne 299 23
Boxen 299 20-50
Boxer *Zool.* 70 10
~ *Sport* 299 25
~motor 230 34
Box-handschuh 299 26
~kamera 309 30
~kampf 299 20-50
~manager 299 45
~match 299 20-50
~ring 299 35
~veranstaltung 299 35-50
Boy 267 18
Boy-Scout 278 11
Brach-acker 63 1
~distel 61 32
Bracket-Serie 1 23
Brail 90 2
~tau 90 3
Brakteat 252 4
Braktee 371 7
Bram-stag 219 12
~stengestag 219 12
~stengstagsegel 219 25, 29
~stengewant 219 18
Branche 26 46
Brand-giebel 121 9
~haken 77 55
~meister 270 36
~sohle 291 31
Brandstettersche
. Eierzählplatte 89 19
Brandung 13 27
~, künstliche 281 1
Brandungs-bad 281 1-9
~geröll 13 29
~hohlkehle 13 30
~platte 13 31
~reiten 279 1-6
~welle 279 6
Branke 88 46, 50
Branntwein 98 56
Brante 88 46, 50
Brasil 107 2
Brasilstrom 14 35
Braß 219 67
Brassie 293 91
Brät 96 41
Braten 45 27
~fleisch 96 22
~platte 45 26
~topf 40 14
Brathähnchen 98 6
Brätherstellung 96 52
Brat-pfanne 40 4
~rost 308 33
Bratsche 323 27
Bratwurst 96 11; 308 34
~füllsel 96 41
~stand 308 32
Brauer 92 49
Brauerei 92; 93 1-31

Brau-haus 93 1-31
~meister 92 49
braun 343 5
Braun-alge 378 48
~bär 368 10
Braunelle 376 16
Brauner Bär 365 7
Braunkohl 57 34
Brause 282 2
Brausenkopf 49 42
Braut 332 15
~bukett 332 18
Bräutigam 332 16
Braut-jungfer 332 24
~kranz 332 19
~myrte 53 11
~paar 332 15-16
~schleier 332 20
~strauß 332 18
Break *Wagen* 186 2
~ *Auto* 193 15
Brecher 158 5
Brech-rand 329 44
~scheibe 329 82
~stange 158 32
Breit-beil 120 70
~bildkamera 310 47
Breite, geographische 14 6
Breiteisen 158 37
Breiten-kreis 14 2
~skala 157 58
Breit-fock 220 13
~halter 166 13
~kordoberteil 101 26
~lauch 57 21
~schwanz 30 60
~schwanzfell 131 21
~seitenfeuer 218 59
~spritzrahmen 83 3
~waschmaschine 168 8
Brems-arretierhebel 56 38
~automat 168 20
~backe *Schmied* 138 12
~backe *Masch.* 143 100
~backen 192 51
~band 143 105
~belag *Schmied* 138 13
~belag *Masch.* 143 106
~belag *Auto* 192 52
~druckmesser 210 50
~dynamometer 143 97-107
Bremse *Wagen* 186 16
~ *Auto* 191 45
~ *Eisenb.* 212 44
~ *Mil.* 257 10
Bremsen 303 24
Bremser 303 21
Brems-flüssigkeitsbehälter
    191 49
~fußhebel 179 12, 30
~gewicht *Masch.* 143 103
~gewicht *Web.* 166 63
~grube 138 17
~hebel *Web.* 166 62
~hebel *Fahrrad* 187 66
~klappe *Flugzeug* 229 44
~klappe *Mil.* 256 12
~klappe *Sport* 287 38
~klotz *Masch.* 143 100
~klotz *Wagen* 186 16
~klotz *Auto* 192 49
~konus 187 71
~kupplungsschlauch 208 21
~leitungsanschluß 192 53
~licht 189 9
~luftleitung 208 21
~luftmagnet 143 102
~mantel 187 70
~pedal 191 45, 95
~prüfstand 138 16
~rolle 138 18
~sattel 191 18; 192 49
~scheibe *Masch.* 143 98

~scheibe *Web.* 166 60
~scheibe *Auto* 191 17; 192 48
~schicht 1 54
~schirmkasten 257 24
~schuh 119 40
~seil *Web.* 166 61
~seil *Motorrad* 189 12
~seil *Mil.* 259 16
~trommel 138 11
~trommel-
    Feindrehmaschine 138 20
~- und Rücklichteinheit 188
    38
~weg 203 29
~wegverkürzung 203 12, 14
~welle 143 99
~zylinderdruckanzeige 212 7
Brenn-düse 38 60
~element 154 27, 28
~elementstab 154 4
Brenner *Landw.* 80 10
~ *Glas* 162 6
~anzünder 141 27
~düse 141 38
~führungswagen 141 19
~plattform 288 80
~ventilator 92 17
~zange 126 58
Brennessel, Große 61 33
Brenn-form 161 4
~gasanschluß 141 31
~gasventil 141 32
~holzsäge 157 54
~kammer *Kraftwerk* 152 6
~kammer *Flugzeug* 232 37
~ofen 179 32
~punkt 347 25, 27
~schacht 147 16
~schere 105 5
~schneidemaschine 141 34
Brennstoff-tender 210 67
~zelle 234 62
Brenn-vorgang 161 2
~weite 115 45, 47, 48; 313 23
~weiteneinstellung 117 3
Brett *Bau* 120 91
~ *Sägewerk* 157 35
~ *Billard* 277 14
~, gesäumtes 120 95
~, ungesäumtes 120 94
~bürste 108 33
Bretter-schalung *Haus* 37 84
~schalung *Bau* 120 9
~stapel 121 1
~steg 121 75
~tür 37 34
~wand 119 25
~zaun 118 44
Brett-pinsel 108 33
~spiel 276
Brevier 331 58
Brevis 320 12
Brezel 97 44
Brief-behälter 236 32
~faltmaschine 249 44
~kasten 236 50
~kastenleerung 236 50-55
~klammer 247 1
~marke 236 61
~markenbogen 236 21
~markenschalter 236 15
~papiervorrat 245 12
~sammeltaste 236 51
~sendung 236 55
~träger 236 53
~verteilanlage 236 31-44
~verteilmaschine 236 38
~waage 236 24
Brigg 220 17
Brillant-behälter *Schmuck* 36 18
~ *Setzerei* 175 20
~ring 36 23, 24
~schliff 36 44

Brille *Optiker* 111 9
~ *Textilw.* 168 7
~ *Mus.* 323 35
Brillen-anprobe 111 1-4
~auswahl 111 5
~gestell 111 10-14
Brillenglas 111 15
~-Randbearbeitungsautomat
    111 24
Briolett, facettiertes 36 86
Briseur 163 53
Brisinga endecacnemos 369
    11
Brombeere 58 29
Bronchie 20 5
Bronze-axt 328 23
~blech 328 34
~dolch 328 22
~horn 322 1
~messer 328 31
~nadel 328 29
~zeit 328 21-40
Brosche 36 7
Broschur 183 32
Brot 43 22; 97 2
~, belegtes 45 37
~abteilung 99 9
~anlage 97 56-57
~belag 45 38
Brötchen 45 21; 97 13-16; 99
    12
~, belegtes 266 54
~anlage 97 61
~röstaufsatz 40 31
Brot-frucht 68 1-37
~käfer 81 23
~korb 45 20
~laib 97 2
~rinde 97 4
~scheibe 45 22
~sorte 97 6-12, 48-50; 99 11
Bruch *Geogr.* 12 4; 15 20
~ *Schiff* 227 15
~ *Math.* 344 10
~, echter 344 15
~, gemeiner 344 15-16
~, unechter 344 16
~, uneigentlicher 344 18
~, ungleichnamiger 344 19
~faltengebirge 12 20
~schollengebirge 12 4-11
~strich 344 15
~zahl 344 10
Brücke *Geogr.* 15 56
~ *Anat.* 17 46
~ *Med.* 24 26
~ *Landmaschinen* 65 14
~ *Brücken* 215 57
~ *Schiff* 221 6, 12; 223 12-18
~ *Mil.* 258 14; 259 28
~ *Park* 272 47
~ *Sport* 295 19; 299 9
Brücken-aufbau 258 14
~bauweise 177 1
~bogen 215 20
~deck 223 12-18
~figur 215 22
~geländer 215 70
~hälfte 215 66
~heilige 215 22
~joch 215 20
~lager 215 55
~lift 225 40
~nock 223 16
~pfeiler 215 21
~pfosten 215 36
~portal 215 42
~querschnitt 215 1
~ständer 215 30
~stativ 177 13
~strebe 215 35
~träger 222 27
~widerlager 215 45

Brühebehälter 83 50
Brüh·sieb 96 45
~würfel 98 27
~würstchen 96 8
Brummer *Mus.* 322 11
~ *Zool.* 358 18
Brunft·hirsch 86 12; 88 4
~jagd 86 9-12
~kragen 88 27
~mähne 88 27
Brünne 329 63
Brunnen 269 40
~, artesischer 12 26
~allee 274 11
~haus 274 15
~kresse 378 30
~pavillon 274 15
~rand 272 25
~rohr 269 64
~röhre 12 25
~umrandung 269 65
Brüsseler Kohl 57 30
~ Spitze 102 18
Brust *Anat.* 16 28-29, 28-30
~ *Pferd* 72 19
~ *Fleischerei* 95 4, 23
~ *Bau* 122 88
~ *Zool.* 358 29-30
~baum 166 46
~baumbrett 166 16
~bein *Anat.* 17 8
~bein *Fleischerei* 95 27
~blatt 71 28
Brüste 16 28-29
Brust·flosse 364 7; 367 28
~harnisch 329 46
~korb 16 28-30; 17 8-11
~lattich 380 8
~leier 140 58
~muskel 18 36
~nerv 18 26
~schwimmen 282 33
~stück 329 46
~tasche 30 23; 33 9
Brüstungs·riegel 120 56
~streiche 118 24
Brust·warze 16 28
~wehr 329 21
~wirbel 17 3
Brutapparat 89 15
Brüter, schneller 154 1
Brut·höhle 359 29
~knollen 375 38
~raum 77 46
~reaktor 154 1
~schrank 261 30
~teich 89 6
~wabe 77 46
~zelle 77 31
~zwiebel 54 27, 29
Bruyère·maserung 107 41
~pfeife 107 39
Bubikopf 34 34
Buch 46 8; 183 32; 185 36, 52
~, antiquarisches 309 55
Buchbinder 183 2
Buchbinderei 183; 184; 185
~maschine 184 1-23; 185
1-35
Buchbindermesser 183 13
Buch·block 185 22
~decke 185 40
~deckel 185 40
~deckenmaschine 184 6
~druck 181
~drucker 82 22
~druckerei, Maschinen der
181 1-65
Buche 82 37; 371 33
Buch·eignerzeichen 185 51
~einband 185 40-42
~einhängemaschine 185 27
Buchen·frucht 371 37

~zellstoff 169 1
Bücher·ausleihe 262 18
~bestände 262 11
~magazin 262 11
~regal 42 3; 43 14; 46 7; 262
12
~reihe 42 4
Buchfahrplan 210 52
Buchfink 360 10
Buchhandlung 268 37
Büchner·Trichter 349 11
Buchrücken 183 1; 185 41
Buchsbaum, Gemeiner 373
19
Buch·schwinge 236 11
~seite 185 53
Buchsenklemme 127 29
Büchsen·lauf 87 26
~milch 98 15
Buchstabe 129 53
Buchstaben·flagge 253 22-28
~rechnung 345 4-5
Bucht 13 7
Buchungsmaschine 236 26
Buckelurne 328 38
Buddhastatue 337 20
Büfett 207 31; 265 1; 266
1-11
~dame 265 7
~fräulein 265 7
Büfettier 266 8
Büffelhörner 254 34
Büffet 265 1; 266 1-11
~dame 265 7
Büffetier 266 8
Bug *Fleischerei* 95 5, 9, 22, 42
~ *Bau* 121 41
~ *Schiff* 222 74-79; 258 3
~anker 258 39
~brett 119 63
Bügel *Gärtner* 55 27
~ *Optiker* 111 13
~ *Bau* 119 70
~ *Web.* 165 18
~automat 50 1
~brett 50 16
~brettbezug 50 17
Bügeleisen 50 6; 104 29
~ablage 50 18
~griff 50 9
~schwebevorrichtung 103 24
Bügel·falle 87 48
~falte 33 6
~fläche 103 23
~formkissen 104 28
~gerät 50 1-20
~gießkanne 55 26
~hacke 66 1
~mulde 50 4
~nadel 328 27
~riemen 71 42
~säge *Heimwerker* 134 3
~säge *Schmied* 138 23
~säge *Schlosser* 140 9
~säge *Werkzeugmasch.* 150 14
~scharnier 111 14
~sohle 50 7
~tisch 50 15
~tuch 104 32
~unterlage 50 16
Bug·fahrwerk 231 23
~fahrwerksklappe 231 24
~fender 227 17
Buggy 193 12
~, amerikanischer 186 49
~, englischer 186 48
Bug·klappe 235 20
~laufrad 278 54
Büglerin 103 19
Bug·licht 286 13
~mann 283 13
~rad 230 40; 257 3; 288 34
~radeinheit 235 30

~rampe 258 90
~raumbilge 259 80
~schraube 228 33
Bugsieren 222 42
Bugsierschlepper 225 15; 227
16
Bug·spriet 218 20; 219 1
~strahlruder 224 23
~stück, dickes 95 29
~tor 221 30
~welle 223 81
~wulst 221 45
Buhne *Geogr.* 13 37
~ *Fluß* 216 19
Bühne 312 8; 315 14; 318 22
Bühnen·arbeiter 315 28; 316
46
~beleuchtung 318 23
~bildmodell 315 42
~bildner 315 37
~bildprojektionsapparat 316
17
~gebäude 334 45
~haus 316 1-60
~himmel 316 9
~hintergrund 316 10
~kopf *Geogr.* 13 38
~ *Fluß* 216 20
Bühnen·maler 315 35
~meister 316 45
~plan 334 46
~rahmen 316 22
~scheinwerfer 318 24
~vorhang 312 10
Bulbsteven 221 45
Buleine 218 35
Bulien 218 35
Bulin 218 35
Buline 218 35
Bulk·carrier 225 67; 226 30
~frachter 221 9; 225 67; 226
30
Bulldogge, Englische 70 1
Bulle 73 1
Bullenbeißer 70 1
Bullterrier 70 16
Bumerang 352 39
Bund 324 9
~axt 120 72
~balken 121 53
Bündelpfeiler 335 34
Bundes·präsident 253 14
~straße 15 17
Bund·geschirr 120 20
~hose 300 7
~lager 148 73
~säge 120 68
~schraube 143 32
~sparren 121 55
~steg 185 55
~stiel 120 53
Bungalow 278 7
~zelt 278 36
Bunker *Landmaschinen* 64 59
~ *Sport* 293 81
~boot 225 13
~köpfroder 64 85-96
Bunsenbrenner 173 5; 350 1
Bunt·druckwerk 181 52
~sandsteinscholle 154 61
~specht 359 27
~stift 47 26; 48 11
Bürette 350 21
Büretten·klemme 350 23
~stativ 350 22
Burg 329 1
Bürgersteig 198 9
Burg·graben 329 37
~herr 329 67
~hof 329 2
~kapelle 329 29
~mauer 333 31
~tor 329 32

Burgunder 355 40
~rübe 69 21
Burnus 354 7
Büro 245; 246; 247; 248;
249; 271 24; 278 1
~element 248 39
~haus 225 53
~heftmaschine 247 4
~klammer 247 1
~komplex 146 14
~material 247 1-44
~rechner 245 31
~schrank 248 12
~stuhl 248 25
Bürste *Haarschnitt* 34 11
~ *Zool.* 77 7
~, rotierende 168 46
Bürzel 88 49, 58
Bus *Auto* 194 17
~ *Piktogramm* 233 35
Buschbohne 57 8
Büschel·kieme 364 19
~nelke 60 6
Buschmann 354 29
~frau 354 34
Busch·rose 52 13
~werk 15 15
~windröschen 377 1
Busen 16 30
Büste 16 28-29
Büstenhalter 32 1, 4; 280 28;
318 29
Büstenpfeiler 334 35
Butangas 278 33
~flasche 278 34
Bütte *Weinbau* 78 15
~ *Mühle* 91 20
~ *Papier* 172 25; 173 47
Büttenträger 78 14
Butter 98 22; 99 47
~cremetorte 97 24
~dose 45 36
Butterei 76 32
Butterfertiger 76 33
Butterfly 282 34
Butter·messer 45 73
~milchtank 76 18
~pilz 381 21
~strang 76 34
Butterung 76 33
Butterungs·anlage 76 32
~maschine 76 33
~ und Abpackanlage 76 32
Büttgeselle 173 46
Butzen 58 59
Butzenglas 124 6

C

Cab 186 34
Cabochon 36 78-81
~, achteckiger 36 81
~, ovaler 36 80
~, runder 36 78
Caddywagen 293 85
Café 265 1-26
~gast 265 22-24
Camper 278 46
Camping 278
~geschirr 278 45
~liege 278 59
~platz 278 1-59
~platzwart 278 2
~stuhl 278 43
~tisch 278 44
Cancer 4 56
Canis Major 3 14
~ Minor 3 15
Cañon 13 45
~fluß 13 51
Canter 72 42
Capa 319 27

Capella 3 27
Capricornus 3 36; 4 62
Capstan 117 34
Caravan 278 52
Carborundscheibe 24 35
Carina 3 46
Cassegrain-Kabine 5 4
Cassiopeia 3 33
Castor 3 28
Catcher 292 54
Catgang 259 18
C-Bogen 26 19; 27 17
CD4-Schallplatte 241 45
C-Dur 320 55, 62
~-Tonleiter 320 45
Cedille 342 33
Celesta 325 1
Cello 323 16
Cembalo 322 45
~mechanik 322 48
cent 252 19, 33
Cent 252 19, 33
Centaurus 3 39
centavo 252 23
Centavo 252 23
centime 252 15, 16
Centime 252 15, 16
céntimo 252 22
Céntimo 252 22
Cerci 81 12
Cerclebindung 294 49
Cesta 305 69
Chaise 186 54
Chalaza 74 63
Chalet 278 7
Chalkographie 340 14-24
Chamäleon 364 33
Chapeau claque 35 36
Chapiteau 307 1
Charaktermaske 306 33
Charivari 36 35
Charleston 324 50
Chassis 191 2
Chasuble 30 50
Chef Büro 248 29
~ Restaurant 266 71
~ de partie 275 3
~maskenbildner 315 47
~operator 244 3
~schiedsrichter 292 55
~-Sekretär-Anlage 246 13
~sekretärin 248 31
~zimmer 246 1-36
Chemiefaser 169; 170
~labor 349; 350
~lehrer 261 2
~saal 261 1
~unterricht 261 1-13
Chemikalienflasche 116 10;
  261 23
Chianti 98 61
~flasche 99 77
Chicane Allais 301 72
Chicorée 57 40
Chignon 34 29
Chimära 327 16
China-binsenschnur 136 28
~rindenbaum 380 17
chinesisch 341 5
Chinesische Rose 60 15
Chirurgie, kleine 22 48-50
chirurgische Abteilung 26
  1-54
~ Klinik 26 1-54
chirurgisches Instrument 26
  40-53
~ Nahtmaterial 22 56; 26 21
Chitarrone 324 1
Chiton 355 5
Chitonactis 369 20
Chlor 170 7
~benzol 170 9
~benzol- und

Natronlaugeverdampfung
  170 11
~benzolverdampfung 170 11
~ion 1 10
~kalziumröhre 350 43
Chor Theat. 315 21
~ Kirche 330 32
~ Kunst 335 4
Choralnotation 320 1
Chornische 335 5
Chow-Chow 70 21
Christstollen 97 11
Christus-bild 330 50
~monogramm 332 67
chromatische Tonleiter 320
  49
Chrombügel 188 60
Chromolithographie 340 28
Chrysantheme 51 29
Chrysanthemum 61 7
Ciborium 332 48
Cicero 175 28
Cimbal 322 32
Cimbalom 322 32
Cinemascope-Kamera 310 47
Cirrocumulus 8 14
Cirrostratus 8 7
Cirrus 8 6
cis-Moll 320 59
Cister 322 21
City-Bike 188 20
~-Stil 35 22
~version 194 34
Clavicembalo 322 45
Clavichord 322 36
Clinch 299 31
Clitellum 357 26
Clivia 53 8
Clog 101 44
Clown 307 24
Clubzugehörigkeit 286 8
c-Moll 320 65
Coach 292 57
~-box 292 56
Cochonnet 305 21
Cockerspaniel 70 38
Cockpit Motorrad 188 40; 189
  44
~ Auto 191 38
~ Flugzeug 230 1-31, 35; 231
  19
~ Sport 283 8; 285 38; 288 10
Cocktail 317 33
~glas 267 56
~shaker 267 61
Codierplatz 236 35
Codleine 90 23
Cœur 276 40
CO2-Flasche 138 32
Coiffeur 106 1
Collier 36 2
Coloranalyser 116 36
Combo 318 3
Comfrey 69 13
Compact-Cassette 241 10
computergesteuerter Satz 176
  14
Computergraphik 248 19
Conga 324 55
Container 206 57; 226 3
~bahnhof 206 54
~brücke 225 46; 226 2
~decksladung 221 22; 226 6
~platte 194 27
~schiff 221 89; 225 45
~stapel 225 49
~stapler 225 47
~terminal 225 48; 226 1
~tragwagen 206 58
Cops 163 2
Corona 4 39
~ Borealis 3 31
Corps de ballet 314 25

Corrida 319 1-33
Cottonmaschine 167 18
Couchtisch 42 28
Coudé-Strahlengang 5 3
Coup droit 294 7
Coupé 186 3
CO2-Verbrauch 27 49
Cowboy Karneval 306 31
~ Rodeo 319 36
Cowper-Drüse 20 75
Crawlen 282 37
Creme 99 27
~dose 28 13; 99 27
~schnitte 97 21
~torte 97 24
~tube 99 33
crescendo 321 31
Cricket 292 70-76
Cristobalitkristall 1 12
Croisé 314 16
Croquet 292 77-82
Croupier 275 4
Crux 3 44
C-Schlüssel 320 10, 11
Cul de Paris 355 69
Cumulonimbus 8 17
Cumulus 8 1
~ congestus 8 2
~ humilis 8 1
Cupula 371 5; 384 52
Curling 302 41-43
~besen 302 43
~spieler 302 41
~stein 302 42
Curve-Ball 305 19
Cutter 311 43
Cyan-Doppeldruckwerk 180
  8-9
~einstellung 116 45
Cyclamen 53 5
Cyclo-hexanol 170 18
~hexanon 170 20
~hexanonoxim 170 22
Cygnus 3 23
Cymbal 322 32
Cymbel 324 51
Cyperus alternifolius 53 17

D

Dach Haus 37 5; 38; 121; 122
~ Mus. 324 3
~balken 121 29
~bock 122 66
~boden 37 4; 38 18
~decker 122
~deckerstift 122 74
~fenster 38 2
~first 121 2
~formen 121 1-26
~fuß 121 4
~gaube 38 7; 121 6; 336 4
~gaupe 38 7; 121 6
~gepäckträger 278 50
~geschoß 38 1-29
~gesims 37 9; 38 11; 122 36
~grat 121 12
~haken 38 6
~haut 38 1
~kanal 37 11
~kehle 121 15
~konstruktion 121 27-83
~leiter 38 4; 122 63
~leitung 121 5
~liegefenster 121 8; 122 12
~lüfter 278 56
~öffnung 213 23
~pappe 122 62
~pappenstift 143 55
~reiter 121 14
~reklame 268 45
~rinne 37 11; 38 9; 122 28

Dachs 88 48
~bär 88 48
Dachschuh 122 75
Dachshund 70 39
Dächsin 88 48
Dach-sperling 361 5
~stuhl 120 7; 122 66
~teile 121 1-26
~terrasse 37 75
~terrassenwohnung 37 83
~verband 121 27-83
~vorsprung 37 9
~ziegel 122 45-60
~ziegeldeckung 122 45-60
~ziegelschere 122 33
Dahlie 51 20; 60 23
Daktyloskopie 264 28
Dalbe 225 12
Dalben 225 12
Damasttuch 45 2
Dambock 88 40
Dame Spiele 265 23; 276 9
~ Sport 305 2, 4, 9, 10
~ Kostüme 355 59, 64, 68, 70,
  79
~, franz. 355 51
~brett 276 17
Damen-badeanzug 280 26
~doppel 293 2 bis 3
~einzel 293 4 bis 5
~friseur 105
~frisiersalon 105 1-39
~frisur 34 27-38
~hut 35 1-21; 41 11
~kleidung 30; 31; 271 28
~kniestrumpf 32 9
~konfektionsabteilung 271 28
~mütze 35 1-21
~nachtkleidung 32 16-21
~salon 105 1-39
~schneider 103 1
~schneideratelier 103 1-27
~shorts 31 39
~skianzug 301 9
~stiefel 101 12
~straßenstiefel 101 12
~strumpffabrikation 167 18
~toilette 233 48
~unterkleidung 32 1-15
~unterwäsche 32 1-15
~wäsche 32 1-15
Damespiel 276 17-19
~stein 276 18, 19
Damhirsch 88 40
Damm Landkarte 15 104
~ Anat. 20 64
Dämmerungsgrenze 4 21
Dämmplatte 122 44
Dämon 327 58
Dampf 96 47
~absaugung 103 25
~austrittsschlitz 50 14
~bügeleisen 103 20; 131 3
~bügler 104 26
~dom 210 12
Dämpfer 322 54; 323 10; 324
  68; 325 37
~, magnetischer 11 40
~arm 325 38
Dampfer-laterne 258 55
~licht 223 40; 258 55
Dämpfer-pralleiste 325 39
~puppe 325 37
Dampf-erzeuger 154 9, 26, 44
~kessel Kraftwerk 152 5
~kessel Papier 172 38
~kochtopf 40 21; 278 35
~-Kondensat-Kreislauf 154
  51
~kraftwerk 152 1-28
~leitung 154 11
~lok 210 1-69
~lokführerstand 210 39-63

~lokomotive 210 1-69
~pfeife 210 51
~radio 309 16
~sammelkasten 210 21
~schwadenleitung 172 64
~speicherlokomotive 210 68
~~, Spray- und
Trockenbügelautomat 50
11
~spritzpistole 131 2
~sterilisator 22 39
~turbine 152 23; 154 14, 46,
52
~turbinengenerator 259 58
~turbogruppe 153 23-30
~überdruck 210 3
~überströmleitung 153 28
~- und
Elektrowärmetauscher 207
6
Dämpfung 325 8, 37, 41
Dämpfungsschicht 301 49
~system 235 53
Dampfzylinder 210 32
Damspiel 276 17-19
Dam·tier 88 40
~wild 88 40-41
Dandy 306 33
Danebrog 253 17
Danforth-Anker 286 18
Dan-Grad 299 15
Darm Anat. 20 14-22
~ Zool. 77 15
~saite 324 6, 14
Darrablaufschacht 92 19
Darretage 92 16-18
Darsteller 316 37
Darstellerin 316 38
Daten 248 47
~, technische 151 32
~anzeige 112 47
~ausgang 112 44
~dienst 237 41, 58
~drucker 237 61
~erfassung, zentrale 242 20
~fernverarbeitung 237 58
~rückwand 115 67
~sichtgerät Rundfunk 238 2,
11
~sichtgerät Büro 248 16, 44
~speicheranlage 242 32
~station 242 19
~träger 237 59, 62-64
~verarbeitungsanlage 237 60
~zentrale 248 43
Dattel 384 9
~kern 384 10
~palme 384 1
Datumsanzeige 237 39
~blatt 247 33
~knopf 110 4
~- und Sekundenknopf 110 4
Daube 302 40
Dauer·beatmungsapparat 26 1
~beatmungsgerät 26 24
~fahrer 290 14
~klee 69 9
~myzelgeflecht 68 4
~rennen 290 11-15
Daumen 19 64
~ballen 19 75
~mittelfingergriff 298 52
~muskel 18 41
~ring 323 45
~zeigefingergriff 298 51
Daunen·jacke 300 6
~kissen 207 68
Davit 221 101; 223 20; 258 13
D-Dur 320 57
Decca-Gerät 224 34
~-Navigator 224 34
~-Navigator-System 224 39
Deck 146 35, 36, 37

~, halboffenes 223 28
~balken 222 57
~blatt 107 5
~brett 55 9
Decke Bau 123
~ Fahrrad 187 30
~ Heraldik 254 3
~ Mus. 323 24
Deckel Atom 2 14
~ Zool. 77 39
~ Chem. 350 31
~kapsel 370 95
~kette 163 45, 46
~krempel 163 34
~putzvorrichtung 163 44
~setzstation 76 46
~verschluß 50 83
~zunge 243 47
Decke mit Halsschlitz 352 24
Decken·balken 120 38; 121 54
~dekorationsstück 316 12
~erguß 11 14
~füllung 120 44
~kran 222 20
~lampe 44 12
~leuchte 24 20
~putz 123 59, 72
~tapete 128 53
~tapeziergerät 128 50
~verkleidung 317 29
~winkel 126 48
~ziegel 159 24
Deck·faß 122 22
~flügel 82 10; 358 36
~flügler 358 24-39
~gebinde 122 78
~gebirge 144 48
~grund 340 56
~laden 55 9
~platte 222 56
~schicht 198 5
~schuppe 372 5
Decks·haus 221 6, 39; 223 34;
258 72
~kran 221 5, 61
~plan 259 12-20
~sprung 259 23
Deckstuhl 221 111
Deckung 294 6
Deckverschluß 32 24
Decoder 110 18
decrescendo 321 32
Defrosterdüse 191 42; 192 64
Degagé à la quatrième
derrière 314 12
~ à la quatrième devant 314
11
Degen Sport 294 36
~ Stierkampf 319 32
~fechten 294 25-33, 51
~fechter 294 25
~spitze 294 27
Dehnbarkeit 170 46
Dehydrierung 170 19
Deich·absatz 216 38
~böschung 216 40
~krone 216 39
~rampe 216 47
~schleuse 216 34
Deichsel 62 20; 71 21; 186 19,
30
~kasten 278 53
~kreuz 332 61
~pferd 186 28
~stütze 64 62
~verstellung 64 59
Deich·siel 216 34
~wärter 216 46
~wärterhaus 216 45
Dekatier·maschine 168 49
~walze 168 50
Deklinationsachse 113 5, 17
~getriebe 113 4

~lager 113 6
Dekolleté 306 24
Dekometer 279 17
Dekompressionsstufe 279 17
Dekorationsstück 316 35
Delphin, Gemeiner 367 24
~schwanz 327 25
~schwimmen 282 35
Delta 13 1
~flügel 229 19
~gleiter 287 44
~muskel 18 35
~schaltung 153 21
Deltoid 346 38
Demonstrations·einsatz 264
15
~gerät 242 45-84
~modell 242 45, 55
Deneb 3 23
Dengel 66 14
~amboß 66 11
~hammer 66 9
Denkmal Landkarte 15 92
~ Park 272 10
~sockel 272 11
Deponie 199 10
~verdichter 199 18
Depression 9 5
Derbrüßler 80 49
Des-Dur 320 67
Dessert 45 6
~löffel 45 66
Dessous 32 1-15
Destillation 170 17
Destillations·anlage 145 66
~kolonne 145 37, 49
Destillier·apparat 350 46
~kolben 350 47, 50
Detektor·anlage 309 23
~empfänger 309 23
Deuteropyramide 351 20
Deutsche Dogge 70 14
deutsche Farben 276 42-45
Deutsche Kamille 380 1
~ Kicher 69 19
~ Mark 252 7
deutsche Montierung 113 16
Deutscher 355 27
~ Klee 69 1
~ Schäferhund 70 25
~ Vorstehhund 70 40
deutscher Zug 315 3
Deutsche Schabe 81 17
Deutsches Weidelgras 69 26
Devanagari 341 9
Dezimal·bruch 344 20
~bruch, unendlicher
periodischer 344 21
~stelle 344 20
Diaarm 177 44
Diabetikerkartei 22 26
Diabologeschoß 305 34
Diadem 355 21
Diagnose 195 33
~berichtformular 195 7
~gerät 195 1
~kabel 195 3, 38
~stand 195 1-23
~steckbuchse 195 39
~stecker 195 2
Diagonale Brücken 215 35
~ Math. 346 33
Diagonal·kraweelbeplankung
285 56
~riß 300 3
Diagramm 151 11
Diakopier·adapter 115 88
~vorsatz 115 87
Diamagazin 176 27
Diamant Setzerei 175 21
~ U-Elektronik 241 26
~ Kristallkunde 351 10, 13
~schleifer 24 40

~schneider 124 25
Dianette 101 48
Diaphragma 10 27
Diapositivprojektor 309 42
Diaprojektor 114 76; 309 42;
312 23
Diaschieber 309 43
Diathermiegerät 23 22
Diätmenü 266 62
Diaulos 322 3
Diazoplatte 179 32, 34
Dichtband 126 75
Dichter·narzisse 60 4
~roß 327 26
Dichtleiste 190 69
Dickdarm 20 17-22
Dicken·hobelmaschine 132 45
~messer 173 10
~tisch 132 46
dickes Bugstück 95 29
~ Stück 95 50
Dick·glas 124 5
~laugenpumpe 172 34
~rübe 69 21
Dickte 175 48
Dickteerabscheidung 156 18
Dickung 84 11, 12
Dickwurz 69 21
Dieb 308 16
Diechling 329 52
Diele Wohnung 41 1-29
~ Bau 119 16
~ Sägewerk 157 34
Dielen·belag 118 28
~kopf 334 13
Diener 186 20
~anzug 186 21
Dienst 335 35
~gebäude 205 13
~hund 70 25
~kleidung 264 7
~marke 264 26
~mütze 264 8
~pistole 264 22
~raum 207 41
Dieselaggregat 259 94
dieselelektrischer Antrieb
223 68-74
Diesel·generatoranlage 209 5
~kleinlokomotive 212 68
~kompressorschlepper 200 39
~kraftstoff 146 26; 196 1
~kraftstofftank 146 13
~lok 208 1; 212 1-84, 1, 5
~lokomotive 208 1
~motor 155 5; 190 3, 4; 211
47; 212 25, 51; 223 73
~treibstoff 145 56
~triebwagen 208 13; 211 41
~triebzug 209 1
Differential 345 13, 14
~quotient 345 13
~zeichen 345 13
Differenz 344 24
~menge 348 7, 8
Diffuseur 172 11
~bütte 172 13
Diffusor 234 15
~kalotte 114 60
Digitalanzeige 110 2, 20
digitale Datenanzeige 112 47
~ Steuerung 242 35
Digitalis 379 2
Digitalsteuerung 242 35
Diktatlangenanzeige 246 18
Diktiergerät 22 27; 209 30;
246 17; 248 34
Diligence 186 39
Dimmer 127 17
dinar 252 28
Dinar 252 28
Dinkel 68 24
Diopter Film 117 58

~ *Sport* 305 41
~visierung 305 50, 51
Dioptrieneinstellung 117 15
Dipolantenne 230 65
Direktionsbüro 271 24
Dirigent 274 21; 315 26
Dirigentenstab 315 27
Dirk 219 48
Dirndl 31 26
~bluse 31 29
~kleid 31 26
~schmuck 31 28
~schürze 31 31
Diskant-register 324 41
~saite 325 10
~steg 325 11
~teil 324 39
Diskette 244 8
Diskjockey 317 25
Diskothek 317
Diskussionstubusanordnung
  112 22
dis-Moll 320 61
Dispersions-farbe 129 4
~kleber 128 28
Distel 61 32
~fink 360 1
Distickstoffoxid 26 3
Diva 310 27
Dividend 344 26
Dividendenschein 251 18
Dividieren 344 26
Division 344 26
Divisionszeichen 344 26
Divisor 344 26
DM 252 7, 29
d-Moll 320 63
Dobermann 70 27
Docht 107 29
~wolle 35 9
Dock 222 43
~betrieb 222 36-43
Docke 322 50
Docken 222 41-43
Dockgrube 222 36
Dockingeinschnitt 6 47
Dock-körper 222 37-38
~kran 222 34
~ponton 222 32
~sohle 222 31
~stapel 222 39
~tor 222 32
Dogcart 186 18
Dogge, Deutsche 70 14
Do-it-yourself 134 1-34
Dolch 353 44
Dolde 370 72
Doline 13 71
dollar 252 33
Dollar 252 33
Dollbord 283 30
Dolle 278 18; 283 29, 41
Dollen 121 93
~boot 283 26-33
~loch 120 22
Dolly 310 49
Dolmen 328 16
Dom 335 1-13
Domäne 15 94
Domdeckel 38 48
Domino *Spiele* 276 33
~ *Karneval* 306 15
~spiel 276 33
~stein 276 34
Domizilvermerk 250 22
Dompfaff 360 5
Dompteur 307 52
Donnerbart 377 9
Donnerkäfer 358 24
Doppel *Sport* 293 2 *bis* 3, 49
~, gemischtes 293 2 *bis* 3
~-B 320 53
~besäumsäge 157 57

~bett 43 4-13; 47 1; 267 38
~boden 222 60
~brötchen 97 15
~bruch 344 17
~deckbus 194 36
~decker 229 10
~deckomnibus 194 36
~deckung 122 2
~drahtauslöser 115 102
~drehfalttür 208 7
~dreier 302 14
~druckwerk 180 6-7, 8-9,
  10-11, 12-13
~endball 299 20
~falttür 197 14
~fang 171 47
~federzinken 64 42, 54
~flügel 229 51
~ganze 320 12, 20
~haken, offener 89 83
~haus 37 56-71
~herzschar 65 58
~hobel 132 16
~kajak 283 5
~klaue 77 8
~köper 171 48
~kreuz *Schiff* 224 98
~kreuz *Mus.* 320 51
~kreuz *Kirche* 332 64
~kreuzpoller 217 14
~latte 122 43
~leiter 129 5
~leiterzahnstange 214 11
~leitwerk 229 32, 34, 35
~liftsessel 214 17
~maschine 100 26
~maschinentelegraph 224 25
~mühle 276 25
~oberleitung 194 43
~paddel 283 39
~paß 291 49
~perlfang 171 48
~poller 217 11
~punkt 342 17
~raufe 75 12
~reck 297 3
~rohrblatt 323 29
~rumpf 284 65
~rumpfflugzeug 229 34
~salto 282 42
~schaukel 273 39
~schlag 321 21
~schlagmaschine 163 14
~schleifenrahmen 189 17
~sessel 214 18
~sessellift 301 57
~sitzbank 188 42
~sitzplatz 197 19
~sitzreihe 207 63
~spalt-Fowler-Klappe 229 40
~spaltklappe 229 48
~spiel 293 2 *bis* 3
~spiralfibel 328 30
~startkatapult 259 14
~steckdose 127 6
~stern 3 29
~stockwagen 213 35
doppelt gesägt 370 45
Doppel-tisch 260 2
~tor 301 68, 70
~tür 227 27
~uhr 276 16
Doppelung 164 5
Doppel-wappen 254 10-13
~waschbecken 267 32
~wellenmischer 159 10
~wendelleuchtkörper 127 58
~wiege 214 68
~zange 121 50
~zimmer 267 27-38
Dorf 15 105
~kirche 15 107

~schwalbe 361 20
dorischer Tempel 334 1
dorische Säule 334 8
Dornapfel 379 8
Dornenranke 58 30
Dorn-könig 361 12
~reisig 274 2
~speckkäfer 81 22
Dörr-fleisch 96 3
~obstmotte 81 28
Dort 61 30
Dosen-bier 99 73
~milch 98 15
~satz 10 6
Dosiereinrichtung 83 60
~gefäß 93 3
Dosimeter 2 8-23
Dotter, gelber 74 68
~, weißer 74 67
~haut 74 64
Doublierung 164 5
Douze dernier 275 27
~ milieu 275 26
~ premier 275 25
Dozent 262 3
Drache *Astr.* 3 32
~ *Fabelwesen* 327 1, 50
Drachen *Schule* 260 71
~ *Spielplatz* 273 42
~ *Sport* 284 57; 287 44
~ *Fabelwesen* 327 1
~ *Math.* 346 38
~fliegen 287 43
~flieger 287 45
~kopf 218 16
~leib 327 19, 36
~schiff 218 13-17
~schnur 273 44
~schwanz 273 43
~steigenlassen 273 41
~wurz 60 8
Drachme 252 39
Drachmen 252 39
Draco 3 32
Draht 108 3
~auslöser 23 9; 114 38; 115
  101
~auslöseranschluß 117 6
~bürste 141 26
~bürstenteller 134 24
~einsatz 40 42
~geflecht 339 35
~gerüst 339 35
~glas 124 6
~haarfox 70 15
~hefter 22 25
~korb *Gärtner* 55 50
~korb *Landw.* 66 25
~korb *Zweirad* 188 23
~litze 166 27
~nagel 121 95; 122 74
~netz 350 18
~rahmen 78 9
~rahmenabspannung 78 8
~rahmengerüst 78 9
~rahmenspaliererziehung 78
  1
~seil *Fischerei* 90 26
~seil *Zirkus* 307 41
~seilabspannung 155 44
~seilbahn 214 15-38
~stift 143 51
~- und Blechwalze 108 1
~walze 108 1
~wurm 80 38
~zaun 15 39
~zug *Motor* 190 51
~zug *Eisenb.* 202 30
Drainschicht 199 25
Dränagerohr 26 47
Drängbrett 119 62
Dränrohr 26 47
Draufsicht 151 19

Drechsel-bank 134 51; 135 1
~wange 135 2
~werkzeuge 135 14,15,24
Drechsler 135 20
~drehstähle 135 14,15,24
Drechslerei 135 1-26
Drechsler-meister 135 20
~werkstatt 135 1-26
Dreck-amsel 361 13
~lerche 361 19
~vogel 359 25
Drehbank 149 1
~wange 135 2
Dreh-bewegung 4 22-28
~buch 310 45
~bühne 316 31
~dolle 283 41
~düse 56 44
~eisen 137 39
Drehen 161 9, 14
Dreher 161 9
~geflecht 136 1
Dreh-falttür 207 39
~flügel 232 12
~gasgriff 188 30
~gelenk *Staubsauger* 50 69
~gelenk *Auto* 194 31
Drehgestell 207 4; 208 4; 212
  2; 213 13
~flachwagen 213 11
~-Schwenkdachwagen 213 26
~-Selbstentladewagen 213 24
Dreh-griff 21 16
~griff *Schädlingsbek.* 83 19
~hals 359 27
~herz 149 54
~knopf 112 56
~kran 146 3
~kranz 215 64
~kreuz *Werkzeugmasch.* 149
  43
~kreuz *Roulett* 275 32
~kuppel 5 12
~laufkatze 222 21
~leier 322 25
~liegesitz 207 64
Drehmaschinen-bett 149 31
~fuß 149 12
Drehmeißel 149 45-53, 48, 52
Drehmomentstütze 211 54
Drehmoment-schlüssel 195 45
~wandler 190 70
Dreh-orgel 309 13
~pfeiler 215 65
~ringlafette 255 73
~röhre 135 15
~rohrofen 160 8
~schablone 161 14
~schalter 245 28
~scheibe *Porzellan* 161 11
~scheibe *Hafen* 226 56
~scheibe *Roulett* 275 31
~schemel 85 48
~span 135 26
~spiegel 243 54
~spindel 149 20
~stahl 149 45-53
~strahlregner 62 29
Drehstrom 127 13
~generator 153 1, 26; 154 34
~stecker 127 14
Dreh-stuhl 248 25
~tablett 39 28
~teller 204 37
~tisch *Erdöl* 145 15
~tisch *Eisengießerei* 148 41
~tischgebläse 148 39
Drehung 288 51; 298 11
Drehungswinkel 351 33
Dreh-vogel 359 27
~wählschalter 50 26
~wippkran 222 23
~wurz 61 26

Drehzahl-einstellung 149 5
~messer 188 40; 189 41; 191
38, 70; 230 8
Drehzapfen 215 69
Drei-achteltakt 320 36
~backenfutter 149 37
~bein 114 42
~beingittermast 258 41
~beinkran 222 6
~blattschar 64 67
~bockreuter 63 30
~bruchauslage 185 15
~bruchfalzwerk 185 14
~decker *Schiff* 218 51-60
~decker *Flugzeug* 229 6
Dreieck 36 60-61; 151 7, 8;
346 26-32
~, gleichschenkliges 346 27
~, gleichseitiges 346 26
~, rechtwinkliges 346 32
~, spitzwinkliges 346 28
~, stumpfwinkliges 346 30
~hut 355 62
~schaltung 153 21
Dreiecks-kurs 285 16
~tuch *Med.* 21 2
~tuch *Kleidung* 31 71
~zeichen 345 24
Dreieckstafel 203 13
Dreier 302 13
Dreifach~Kompaktanlage
241 52
~leitwerk 229 36
Drei-fuß *Papier* 173 6
~fuß *Chem.* 349 15; 350 14
~gespann, russisches 186 45
~halbetakt 320 38
~halsflasche 350 57
~halskolben 350 55
Dreikant-maßstab 151 34
~prisma 347 37
~schaber 140 63
~schiene 242 80
Dreiklang 321 1-4
Dreimaster *Schiff* 220 18-27
~ *Kostüme* 355 62
Dreimast~Gaffelschoner 220
18
~-Marssegelschoner 220 20
~-Toppsegelschoner 220 19
Drei-meterbrett 282 9
~paßbogen 336 32
Dreiphasenstrom 153 42
dreipolige Steckdose 127 13
Drei-polsteckdose 127 66
~polstecker 127 67
~punktanbaubock 64 45
~punktauflage 349 28
~punktboot 286 42
~punktkupplung 65 72
~rumpfboot 278 16
~satzrechnung 345 8-10
~schlitz 334 15
~seitenkipper *Landw.* 62 18
~seitenkipper *Auto* 194 24
~seitenwand 78 19
~spitz 355 62
dreiteiliger Spiegel 104 1
Dreitürer 193 19
dreiviertelfett 175 2
Dreivierteltakt 320 37
Drei-wegebox 241 14
~-Wege-Kippkasten 92 34
~zack 135 11
~zinkgrubber 56 13
Drellüberzug 43 10
Drempel 121 47
Dresch-korb 64 11
~trommel 64 12
Dresseur 307 31
Dressur-pferd 289 3
~reiten 289 1-7
~viereck 289 1

Dreul 108 4
Dribbling 291 52
Drillbohrer 108 4; 135 22
Drilling 87 23
~, geschlossener 89 85
Drillmaschine 65 74
Driver 293 91
Drohne 77 5
Drohnenzelle 77 36
Drops 98 76
Droschke 186 26
Drossel 361 13-17
~grube 16 20
~klappe *Med.* 27 43
~klappe *Auto* 192 9
~vogel 360 3; 361 13-17
Druck *Druck* 181 10
~ *Chem.* 349 20
~absteller 181 32
~abstellung 181 12
~anschluß 67 9
~ansteller 181 32
~anstellung 181 12
~anzeiger 25 55
~ausgleichsmaske 279 10
~behälter 170 33
~betankungsanschluß 257 33
~bogen 180 17
~einstellung 180 81
~element 178 39
Drucker *Auto* 195 6
~ *Graphik* 340 35
Druckerei 340 27-64
Druck-farbe *Druck* 181 19
~farbe *Schule* 260 83
~flasche 234 14
~form 340 32
~fundament 180 78
~gasbehälter 234 32
~gasentschwefelung 156 28
~gasfördersystem 234 60
~geschwindigkeitseinstellung
249 55
~hebel 340 61
~höhenverstellung 249 53
~kessel 316 55
~knopf 326 46
~knopfeinsetzmaschine 100
53
~körper 258 66; 259 55, 76
~kurve 25 57; 27 31
~lager *Schiff* 223 67; 259 60
~leitung *Raumfahrt* 235 54,
57
~leitung *Wasservers.* 269 16,
49
~leitung *Feuerwehr* 270 31
~leitung *Theater* 316 54
Druckluft 181 5
~anlage 138 1
~anschluß *Kraftwerk* 153 53
~anschluß *Eisenb.* 213 20
~behälter *Landmaschinen* 64
92
~behälter *Erdöl* 146 21
~behälter-*Kraftwerk* 153 51
~entladung 213 18
~kessel 138 4
~leitung *Schmied* 138 5
~leitung *Auto* 196 18
~messer 195 29
~meßgerät 138 5
~schlagschrauber 138 6
~schlauch 195 54
~schnellschalter 152 34; 153
51-62
~wäsche 92 3
~zuleitung 133 45
Druck-messer *Med.* 26 29
~messer *Sporttauchen* 279 13
~meßgerät 25 53
~minderventil 141 5
~papier 180 47

~platte 123 38
~platteneinfärbung 249 50
~pumpe 316 53
~punktabzug 87 11
~regler 340 38
~rohr 217 50
~rohrleitung *Gärtner* 55 8
~rohrleitung *Wasserbau* 217
41
~säule 316 60
~schablone 168 62
~schmiernippel 143 81
~schott 231 32
~schraube 148 62
~spant 235 19
~spindel 132 32
~spritzengerät 27 15
~spüler 126 37
~station 316 50
~stempel 133 47
~taste *Eisenb.* 203 67
~taste *Post* 237 18, 19
~taste *U-Elektronik* 241 3
~tastenfeld 245 14; 246 14
~tastentelefon 237 20
~tiegel 181 15
~tisch *Textil* 168 63
~tisch *Graphik* 340 41
~träger 180 25, 53
~umlaufschmierung 65 45;
192 16-27
~verband 21 17
~wächter 269 47
~walze 64 64
~wandlereinschub 27 32
~ware 168 57
~wasserprinzip 154 40
~wasserreaktor 154 19
Druckwerk *Druck* 180 41, 80;
182 26
~ *Büro* 245 32
~, oberes 180 6,8,10,12
~, unteres 180 7,9,11,13
Druck-windreinigung 64 15
~zylinder *Tischler* 133 46
~zylinder *Repro* 177 67
~zylinder *Druck* 180 35, 64;
181 2, 44, 59
D-Saite 323 9
Dschunke 353 32
Dübel 126 55; 134 39
~bohrmaschine 133 6
~loch 120 22, 23
Ducht 278 17; 283 28
~weger 283 31
Duckdalben 225 12
Dudelsack 322 8
Dufflecoat 271 21
Dukduk-Tänzer 352 34
Duktorwalze 181 64
Dülfersitz 300 30
Dult 308 1-69
Dumme Lumme 359 13
Dummes Tauchhuhn 359 13
Düne 13 39
Dünenfahrzeug 193 12
Dung 63 15
~streuer 62 21
~tank 221 72
Dunkelkammer-gerät 116
1-60
~leuchte 116 21
dunkles Bier 93 26
Dünn-bier 93 26
~darm 20 14-16
Dunst-abzug 39 17
~haube 46 31
Duole 321 23
Durchbruch 291 52
~arbeit 102 14, 27
Durchfluß-messer *Med.* 26 3,
4
~messer *Molkerei* 76 4

~öffnung 217 56
Durchforsten 84 37
Durchführungsisolator 153
12, 35
Durchgang *Bank* 250 11
~ *Kunst* 337 4
Durchlaß 15 44
~höhe 157 10
Durchlauferhitzer 126 12-13
Durchleuchtungs-kabine 74
47
~spiegel 74 40
~tisch 74 48
Durchlicht-beleuchtung 112
60
~mikroskop 112 14
Durchmesser 346 45
Durchnähmaschine 100 2
Durchreiche 236 30
Durchsagegerät 195 55
Durchschlag *Schlosser* 140 65
~ *Sport* 297 42, 45
Durchschläger 134 32
Durchschnitt 348 4
Durchschnittsmenge 348 4
Durchschuß 175 5
Durchschwung 293 84
Durchsuchung 264 31
Durchwurf 55 13
Durchzieh-gürtel 29 67
~kurbel 340 33
Durchzug 102 17
~walze 164 18
Durdreiklang 321 1
Dürnitz 329 30
Durtonart 320 55-68
Dusche 228 30; 233 46; 281
29; 282 2
Dusch-kabine 49 39
~vorhang 49 40
~wanne 49 44
Düse *Raumfahrt* 6 3
~ *Landw.* 67 33
~ *Schädlingsbek.* 83 46
~ *Flugzeug* 232 39, 45, 49, 55
Düsen-boden 147 69
~flugzeug 231 7-33
~pumpe 216 62
~schwenkrohr 67 1
~triebwerk 231 26; 232 33-50
~ventil 153 29
~ziehverfahren 162 48
Dutt 34 29
Dynamo 187 8
D-Zug-Wagen 207 1-21

E

Ebbe 280 7
Ebenholztaste 325 5
Eber 73 9
Eberesche 371 42
Ecarté 314 15
Echinoderme 357 38-39
Echinopsis 53 14
Echinus 334 21
Echiostoma 369 13
Echo 224 63
~bild 224 67
~empfänger 224 64
~graph 224, 65
~lot 224 61-67
~lotanzeigegerät 224 24
~schreiber 224 65
Echse 364 27,30-37
Echte Kamille 380 1
Echter Besenginster 374 20
~ Gagel 373 33
~ Hederich 61 21
echte Rippe 17 9
Echtes Geißblatt 374 13
Echtkorallenkette 36 34

Eck-ball 291 41
~bank 265 10; 266 38
Ecke Sport 292 18; 299 38
~ Math. 347 33
Eckenschneidewinkel 128 51
Ecker Spiele 276 42
~ Bot. 371 37
Eck-fahne 291 8
~fußstein 122 77
~kegel 305 6, 8
~platz 207 58
~punkt 346 26
~rohrzange 134 12
~schrank 39 27
~stein 276 41
~stiel 120 52
~stoß 291 41
~tisch 246 34
~turm 329 14
~zahn 19 17
Edamer 99 42
~ Käse 99 42
Edel-auge 54 23, 34
~falter 358 52
~fasan 88 77
~fink 360 10
~kastanie 384 48
~koralle 357 17
~lupine 51 23
~mann 355 44
~metall-Motor-Drehwähler
   237 42
~raute 378 6
~reis 54 37
~rose 60 15
~stahlbehälter 79 4
~stahl-Schichtfilter 79 8
~steinanhänger 36 14
~steinarmband 36 25
~steinring 36 15
~tanne 372 1
~tier 88 1
~weiß 378 9
~wild 88 1-27
Editor 117 91
E-Dur 320 59
EDV-Blatt 248 47
Efeublätterige Gundelrebe
   375 18
Effacé 314 13
Effektaufnahme 310 30
Effekten 251 11-19
~börse 251 1-10
~händler 251 7
~makler 251 4
Effektton 310 59
Effetstoß 277 5
Effilier-messer 105 9; 106 41
~schere 105 8; 106 33
Egyptienne 342 8
Ehe-ring 332 17
~wappen 254 10-13
Ehrenpreis 375 22
Ehrentor 337 3
Ei Anat. 20 84
~ Landw. 74 58; 77 26; 80 15,
   55; 82 19; 358 49; 359 3
~ Sport 301 33
~ablage 80 2
Eibe 372 61
Eibisch 380 12
Eiche 51 12; 371 1
Eichel Anat. 20 69
~ Spiele 276 42
~ Bot. 371 4
~habicht 361 1
~häher 361 1
Eichen-gallwespe 82 33
~wickler 82 43
Eichhörnchen 366 19
Eier-bovist 381 19
~längssammlung 74 22
~packung 99 50

~produktion 74 34-53
~sammelvorrichtung 74 34
~sammlung 74 34
~schale 74 59
~stabkyma 334 42
~stock 20 83
~transport 74 41
~uhr 110 31
~verpackungsmaschine 74 46
~waage 74 43
~zählplatte 89 19
eiförmig 370 36
Eigelb 74 68
Eigen-bildtaste 242 23
~periode 11 41
Eihülle 74 59
Eiklar 74 62
Eileger 366 1
Eileiter 20 81
Eimer 221 113
~bagger 226 41
~kette 216 57; 226 42
~kettenbagger 216 56
~leiter 226 43
einäugige
   Spiegelreflexkamera 115 1
Ein-/Ausgabegerät 237 59
Ein-/Ausschalter 241 63;
   243 16; 247 16; 249 9, 64
Einback 97 40
Einband 185 40-42
~decke 185 40
~schleifmaschine 133 30
~verfahren 117 8
Einbauanschluß 127 24
Einbaum 218 7; 354 20
Einbaustück 148 61
Einbelichten 115 67
Einbettkabine 223 46
Einblasen 162 47
Einblattdruck 340 27
Einblendung (von
   Formularen) 242 42
Einblick, binokularer 23 6
Einbrennofen 179 32
Eindickbütte 172 62
Eindicker 172 42, 48
Eindocken 222 41-43
Eindrahtfesselflugsteuerung
   288 90
Eineinhalbmaster 220 9-10
Einer 283 16
~ mit Steuermann 283 18
Einerstelle 344 3
Einfädelschwanz 114 9
Einfahrt 217 15-16
Einfallbaum 86 47
Einfamilienhaus 37 1-53
Einfarben-Offsetmaschine
   180 46, 59
Einfriedung 37 53
Einführlineal 184 23
Einfuhrtisch 185 34
Einführungsstutzen 153 40
~stutzen Öltank 38 47
~stutzen Haushalt 50 12
~trichter Landw. 74 24
~trichter Fotogr. 116 12
Eingabe-gerät 237 59
~tastatur 238 13
Eingang Film 117 27
~ Piktogramm 233 36
~ Stadt 268 13
~ Zirkus 307 19
Eingangs-kontrolle 199 12
~tor 337 24
~treppe 37 66
~tunnel 353 6
~wähler 241 44
~wahlschalter 238 49
Eingebrochener 21 28
Eingehen 168 26

Eingießende 147 34
Eingreifen 174 48
Eingriffeliger Weißdorn 374
   30
Einguß 148 21
~rinne 147 22
Einhandbedienung 185 7
Einhängevorrichtung 180 3
Einheitenzeiger 174 36
Einheitskieljacht, 25-m²-
   284 62
Einhorn Heraldik 254 16
~ Fabelwesen 327 7
Einhüllen-Küsten-U-Boot
   259 75
Einjähriges Rispengras 375
   39
Einkanalton 311 35
Einkauf, zollfreier 233 52
Einkaufstasche 98 45; 99 3;
   268 19
~wagen Haushalt 50 87
~wagen Supermarkt 99 1
Einklang 321 6
Einkocher 40 23
Einlage Zigarre 107 7
~ Mus. 323 26
Einlagerung 154 72
Einlagerungskammer 154 71
Einlaß-karte 315 11
~ventil 242 52
Einlaufanschluß 172 77
Einlaufen (der
   Streckenbänder) 164 21
Einlaufstutzen 37 12; 122 30
Einlege-boden 44 19
~keil 143 73
~ring 349 17
~scheibe 115 96
~sohle 291 27
~vorbau 162 2
Einlochen 293 86
Einlochmischbatterie 126 27
Einmaischen 92 43
Einmal-injektionsnadel 22 65
~injektionsspritze 22 65
Einmann-boot 353 12
~sessel 214 16
~sitzbank 189 19
Einmaster 220 6-8
Einmaststütze 214 23
Einmeterbrett 282 10
Einödhof 15 101
Einordnungspfeil 268 73, 74
Einpreßvorrichtung 109 29
Einquersammlung 74 36
Einreiher 33 1
Einreißhaken 270 15
Einrücker 165 17
Einrückhebel 166 8
Einsatz 275 13
~holz 85 4
~spirale 116 2
~zirkel 151 52
Einschalt-Fußbrett 165 35
~hebel 149 11
Einschaltung 178 20
Einscharpflug 65 1
Einscheibenkupplung 190 71
Einschienenhängebahn 144
   43, 44
Einschießvorrichtung 181 11
Einschlag 136 5
Einschubdecke 120 43; 123 68
Einschwärzballen 340 22
Einseilbahn 214 15-24
Einsortiermaschine 74 38
Einspänner 186 18, 29
Einspannvorrichtung 150 15
Einspaltlautsprecher 238 37
Einsprechöffnung 241 50
Einspritz-düse 190 54
~kondensator 172 16

~pumpe Motor 190 65
~pumpe Eisenb. 211 48
~pumpenantrieb 190 57
~ventil 190 32
~versteller 190 58
Einstechdrehmeißel 149 53
Einsteck-kamm 105 6
~loch 136 9
~schloß 140 36-43
~tuch 33 10
Einsteigen 299 10
Einsteigschacht Öltank 38 45
~ Wasservers. 269 26
Einstell-fernrohr 115 74
~filter 116 46
~glied 237 49
~hilfsmittel 115 60
~knopf 14 58; 116 54
~rad 172 74
~scheibe 112 21; 115 39,
   58-66
~schlitten 115 86
~systemschalter 117 11
Einstellung, manuelle 115 52
~, stufenlose 127 17
Einstellungsnummer 310 35
Einstichkasten 298 35
Einstieg Eisenb. 208 10
~ Schwimmbad 281 37
~luke 6 10
Einstiegs-luke 6 38; 235 26
~plattform 6 34
~raum 208 10
Einstiegstufe Flugzeug 230 42
~ Schwimmbad 281 32
Einstiegstür 207 20, 22
Einstieg 197 14
Einstreu 74 8; 75 6
Einsturz-beben 11 32-38
~trichter 11 49; 13 71
Eintagsfliege 358 6
Eintauchrefraktometer 112
   48
Eintragung 251 14
Ein- und Ausrücker 165 17
Ein- und Ausrückhebel 166 8
Ein- und Ausschalten 149 34
Ein- und Ausstiegsluke 6 38
Ein- und Ausstiegsplattform
   6 34
Ein- und Ausstiegstür 197 14
Einweckeinsatz 40 24
Einwecker 40 23
Einweck-glas 40 25
~ring 40 26
Einweg-feuerzeug 107 30
~flasche 93 29
~hahn 350 42
~packung 93 28
Einweichbottich 136 13
Einwickelpapier 98 46
Einwurf 291 53
~schacht 157 55
Einzahlungsschalter 236 25
Einzel 293 4 bis 5
~blüte 371 26
~buchstabe, gegossener 174
   44
~buchstaben-Setz-und-
   Gießmaschine 174 32-45
~gut 206 4
~handelsgeschäft 98 1-87
~händler 98 41
~hof 15 101
~lader 87 1
~läufer 302 1
~laufwerk 238 56, 58
~zeller 357 1-12
Einzellige 357 1-12
Einzel-sitzplatz 197 17
~sitzreihe 207 62
~spiel 293 4 bis 5
~wasserversorgung 269 40-52

Einziehstahlband 127 30
Einzug 175 16
Einzugsgebiet 12 24
~walze Landmaschinen 64 6
~walze Sägewerk 157 4
Einzylindermotor 188 26
Einzylinder-Viertaktmotor 189 3
Ein-Zylinder-Zweitakt-Ottomotor 190 6
Eis Erste Hilfe 21 28
~ Sport 300 17, 37
~ Rummelplatz 308 31
~, Klettern im 300 14-21
~band Straßenbau 200 4
~band Sport 300 4
~bär 368 11
~becher 266 76
~behälter 267 67
~beil 300 36
~bein 95 38, 42, 49; 96 17
~brecher Brücken 215 56
~brecher Schiff 221 50
Eisen Eisengießerei 148 11
~ Sport 293 92
~, gekröpftes 339 18
Eisenbahn-deck 221 80
~fähre Landkarte 15 12
~fähre Schiff 221 74
~fahrzeug 207; 208; 209; 210; 211; 212; 213
~schiene 202 1
~strecke 202; 203
Eisen-bieger 119 21
~draht 143 12
~fuß 100 54
~gewicht 90 21
~gießerei 148 1-45
~hammer 339 16
~hut Ritterwesen 329 59
~hut Bot. 379 1
~hüttenwerk 147
~leisten 100 34
~oxid-/Chromdioxid-Umschaltung 241 55
~rahmen 325 2
~reifen 163 5
~rinne 147 35
~schläger 293 92
~schwelle 202 36
~träger 143 3-7
~winkel 120 78
~zeit 328 21-40
eiserner Vorgang 316 24
Eisgehen 300 14-21
~geher 300 15
~grat 300 21
~hammer 300 37
Eishockey 302 29-37
~complet 302 23
~scheibe 302 35
~schläger 302 30
~spieler 302 29
~stock 302 30
Eis-jacht 302 44
~kufe 302 45
~lauf 302 1-26
~laufen 302 1-26
~läufer 302 1
~läuferin 302 1
~laufstiefel 302 24
~mann 308 30
Eismeer, Nördliches 14 21
~, Südliches 14 22
Eis-nadelschleierwolke 8 7
~nadelwolke 8 6
~rennen 290 24-28
~schnellaufcomplet 302 20
~schnelläufer 302 26
~schraube 300 40
~segelboot 302 44
~segeln 302 44-46
~spirale 300 41

~sproß 88 7
~sprosse 88 7
~stock 302 39
~stockschießen 302 38-40
~stockschütze 302 38
~stückchen 266 44
~sturmvogel 359 12
~technik 300 14-21
~tourenausrüstung 300 31-57
~tüte 308 31
~unfall 21 28-33
~verkäufer 308 30
~vogel 360 8
~waffel 308 31
~wand 300 14
~zapfen 304 21
Eiweiß 74 62
Ekelblume 53 15
EKG 23 27; 27 31
~-Amplitudenhöhe 25 49
~-Analyse 25 50
~-Gerät 23 28, 46
~-Impuls 25 46
~-Kabel 25 43
~-Kontrolle 25 47
~-Langzeitanalysator 25 45
~-Registriereinheit 25 27
~-Rhythmusanalyse 25 48
~-Schreiber 25 41
Ekliptik 3 2; 4 22
Elastik-sattel 187 22
~schlüpfer 32 5
Elbs 359 16
Elch 367 1
Elefant, Afrikanischer 366 20
Elefanten-gehege 356 9
~haus 356 10
Elektriksammelleitung 235 55
elektrischer Rasierapparat 49 37
~ Weidezaun 62 46
elektrisches Läutewerk 127 15
elektrische Zahnbürste 49 29
~ Zuleitung 39 25; 50 77
Elektrizitätswerk 152 1-28
Elektrobohrer 134 43
Elektrode 25 26, 35, 38; 94 8; 142 10; 147 52
Elektrodegen 294 26
Elektroden-arm 142 24
~ausgang 25 34
~halter 142 9, 20
~kabel 25 25
~köcher 142 7
~kraftaufbau 142 31
~kraftzylinder 142 26
Elektro-durchlauferhitzer 126 13
~fahrzeug 188 20
~filter Kraftwerk 152 13
~filter Kokerei 156 20
~filter Zement 160 7
~filter Papier 172 39
~florett 294 26
~heizung 179 3
~herd 39 12; 46 32
~installateur 127
~kardiograph 23 28
~karren 205 29
~lunge 21 27
~magnet 237 47
~motor 38 59; 83 53; 138 2; 166 18; 212 34
Elektron 3, 17, 27, 32
~, freies 1 25
Elektronähmaschine 104 12
Elektronen-blitzgerät 114 65, 68; 309 40-41
~mikroskop 113 30
~schale 1 6, 8

~spin 1 4
~strahl 240 16
~strahlsystem 240 24
Elektronik-rechner 246 12
~schrank 112 53
elektronischer Baustein 242 69
elektro-optisches Streckenmeßgerät 112 70
Elektro-schaltanlage 168 58
~schaltkasten 168 25
~schlepper 206 2
~schockbehandlung 25 26
~schweißer 142
~starter 56 39
Elektrotom 22 38
Elektro- und Tretnähmaschine 104 12
~wagen 206 34
~zaun 62 46
Element Heizung 38 77
~ Math. 348 2
~, spaltbares 1 49
Elementarfaden 162 52
Elevationswinkel 87 76
Elevatorbrücke 226 25
Elevon-struktur 235 34
~teil 235 33
Elfenbein 354 39
~brosche 36 30
~kette 36 28
~kugel 277 1
~rose 36 29
~schnitzer 135
~statuette 328 8
~taste 325 4
Elfenschuh 60 10
Elfmeter 291 40
~punkt 291 6
Ellbogen Anat. 16 45
~ Pferd 72 20
~schützer 303 16
Elle 17 14
Ellen-beuger 18 58
~bogen 16 45
~nerv 18 29
~rand 19 70
Ellgriff 296 44, 46
Ellipse 347 22, 25
Ellipsen-flügel 229 15
~schablone 151 71
elliptische Flügel 229 15
Ellok 211 1
E-Lok 205 35; 211 1
Elster 361 3
Emailarbeit 260 62
Emaillearbeit 260 62
Emaillierofen 260 63
Emailpulver 260 65
E-Maschinenraum 223 68
Embryo 382 21; 384 22
~sack 370 64
EMD-Wähler 237 42
Emmentaler 99 41
e-Moll 320 56
E-Motor 212 34; 223 69
Empfänger 10 63
Empfangs-chef Hotel 267 7
~chef Warenhaus 271 33
~gebäude 205 13
~kopie 245 2
~raum 267 1-26
Empire-stil 336 16
~tisch 336 16
Empore 330 25
Emu 359 1
End-abschalter 241 60
~band 64 83
~bildfenster 113 39
~bildschirm 113 39
Ende 88 10, 31
Endgestell 165 14
Endivie 57 39

Endiviensalat 57 39
End-knospe 370 22
~leiste 287 37
~linie 292 36
~moräne 12 55
~portal 215 38
~punkt 346 17, 18
~scheibe 229 33
~stück 97 5
~triebwagen 211 61
Energie-gewinnung 1 55
~niveau 1 27
~quelle, neuzeitliche 155
~treppe 1 15
~versorgung 207 24
~versorgungsanlage 146 1
Engerling 82 12
Engländer 126 68
englische Achsenmontierung 113 22
~ Bindung 171 11
Englische Bulldogge 70 1
englische Rahmenmontierung 113 23
englischer Garten 272 41-72
~ Park 272 41-72
Englischer Vorstehhund 70 41
Englisches Raigras 69 26
~ Raygras 69 26
Englischhorn 323 38
Entästungsmaschine 85 18
Entbenzolung 156 27
Ente 73 35
Enten-jagd 86 40
~küken 73 35
Enterbalken 218 11
Enterich 73 35
Entfernung 169 23
Entfernungs-einstellung 114 28, 39; 117 3
~messer 258 37
~messerfenster 114 40
~skala 115 4
Entfesselungskünstler 308 28
Entgaser 152 16
Entgleisungsschutz 214 75
Entgrannungseinrichtung 64 10
Entisolierzange 134 15
Entkleidungsnummer 318 27-32
Entlade-klappe 213 25
~vorrichtung 62 42
Entladungslampe 127 61
Entlastungstakt 75 33
Entleerungs-anschluß 213 21
~schieber 269 31
Entlüfter Eisenb. 207 9
~ Wasservers. 269 27
Entlüftung 153 10; 356 17
Entlüftungs-kappe 38 52
~leitung Heizung 38 51
~leitung Motor 190 12
Entmistung 74 23-27
Entnahmebauwerk 217 40
Entparaffinierung 145 50
Entphenolung 156 39
Entrechat 314 22
~ quatre 314 22
Entsafter 40 19
Entsalzungsanlage 145 32
Entsäuerung 169 19
Entschweflung 169 20
Entschwefelungsanlage 145 46, 68
Entstaubungs-anlage Hütt. 147 14
~anlage Zementwerk 160 7
~gebläse 83 53
~schirm 83 56
Entstörstecker 190 35

Entstörungstechniker 237 28
Entwässerungsanlage 145 32
~graben 216 33
~maschine 172 61
~rinne 200 63
~ und Entsalzungsanlage
  145 32
~zylinder 172 24
Entwickler 27 33
~lösung 116 9
Entwicklungsdose 116 20
~maschine 179 31
~schale 116 25
~thermometer 116 8
~wanne 182 11
~zange 116 47
Entwurf 338 43
Entzerrer 311 19
Enzian, Stengelloser 378 13
Enzyklopädie 262 17
Epistyl 334 18
Epitaph 331 14
Epizentralgebiet 11 38
Epizentrum 11 33
Eppich 57 27
Epsis 53 14
Erbacher Rose 36 29
Erbse 57 7
Erbsen-blüte 57 2
~pflanze 57 1
~ranke 57 4
Erd-achse 4 22-28
~apfel 68 38
~arbeiter 118 76
~aushub 118 78
Erdbeben 11 32-38
~herd 11 32
~kunde 11 32-38
~messer 11 39
~welle 11 36
~wirkungen 11 45-54
Erdbeere 58 21
Erdbeer-pflanze 58 16
~torte 97 22
Erdbirne 68 38
Erde 4 8, 30, 45 ; 6 17
~, kompostierte 55 15
Erd-eule 80 42
~fink 361 8
~floh 80 39
~funkstelle 237 51
~gas 12 30
~gasmotor 155 5
~geschoß 37 2 ; 118 7
~geschoßmauerwerk 123 29
~haufen 55 15
~hobel 200 19
~hund 70 39
~jagd 86 23
~karte 14 10-45
~kern 11 5
~klemme 142 35
~klumpenabsonderung 64 79
~kröte 364 23
~kruste 11 1
~kugel 4 8
~messung 14 46-62
~mond 4 45
Erdnuß 45 41 ; 383 41
~öl 98 24
Erdoberfläche 11 6-12
Erdöl 12 31 ; 145
~bohrung 145 1-21
~erzeugnis 145 52-64
~förderung 145 22-27
~gewinnung 145 22-27
~lagerstätte 12 27
~leitung 145 65
~produkt 145 52-64
~raffinerie 145 65-74
~verarbeitung 145 36-64
Erd-pol 14 3
~rauchgewächs 60 5

~raupe 80 44
~reich 123 9
~rutsch 11 46
~sänger 361 13-17
~schaufel 55 14
~schäufelchen 56 6
~sieb 55 13
~spalte 11 52
~taste 237 21
~teil 14 12-18
Erfrischung 205 49
Erfrischungs-bude 308 3
~getränk 96 30
Ergebnis 344 23
Ergometrie 23 26-31
Erhöhung 320 51
Erhöhungs-winkel 87 76
~zeichen 320 50-51
Eridanus 3 12
Erika 377 19
Erläuterungstafel 356 20
Erle 371 30
Erlenbruchtorf 13 18
Erlenmeyerkolben 173 2 ; 350
  39
Erlenzeisig 361 8
erloschener Vulkan 11 28
Erneuerungsschein 251 19
Erniedrigung 320 53
Erniedrigungszeichen 320
  52-53
Erpel 73 35
Ersatz-reifen 194 4
~schlauchreifen 290 23
~signal 203 6
~spieler 291 54
~teil 109 22
~teilliste 195 32
Erstarrung 170 43
Erste Hilfe 21
Erste-Klasse-Teil 207 17
Erstentwickler 116 10
Erster 305 1
Ertrinkender 21 35
Eruptionskanal 11 17
Erve, Weiße 69 19
Erwerbsgartenbau 55 1-51
Erz 147 2
~lagerstätte 11 31
E-Saite 323 9
Esche 371 38
E-Schicht 7 27
escudo 252 23
Escudo 252 23
Es-Dur 320 65
Esel 73 3
~hengst 73 8
Eselsrücken 336 36
Eskimo 353 1
~kajak 283 68
es-Moll 320 68
Espada 319 32
Esparsette 69 10
Espartogras 136 26
Espe 371 21
Esper 69 10
Espresso 265 1-26
Eßbesteck 45 7
Esse 38 5 ; 137 1-8, 1 ; 138 34
Essenkehrer 38 31
Eß-geschirr 44 33
~gruppe 42 33-34 ; 44 1-11
Essig 98 25
~flasche 45 42
~gurke 98 29
Eß-löffel 45 61
~teller 39 7 ; 45 4
~tisch 42 33 ; 44 1 ; 45 1 ; 46
  34 ; 266 74
~zimmer 44
~zimmerstuhl 44 10
Estocada 319 30
Estoque 319 32

Etagen-bett 47 1
~käfig 74 20
~ofen 97 71
Eule 252 2 ; 362 14-19
Eulenspiegel 306 38
Eurasien 14 15-16
Europa 14 15
~flagge 253 4
~flasche 93 26
~rat 253 4
Eustachische Röhre 17 65
Euter 75 18
Evakuierungspumpe 67 11,
  23
evangelische Kirche 330 1-30
Eventualquote 289 37
Ever 220 9
Ewer 220 9
Ewige Lampe 330 49
ewiger Frost 9 58
Ewiges Licht 330 49
Exhauster Mälzerei 92 15
~ Tischler 133 33
Exlibris 185 51
Exosphäre 7 31
Exotin 306 30
Expansions-gefäß 38 24
~kamm 165 26
~leitung 1 61
Experimentier-einrichtung
  261 11
~tisch 261 3
Explosions-ramme 200 26
~stampfer 200 26
Exponent 345 1
Expreßgut 204 2
~abfertigung 204 1
~annahme 204 1
~ausgabe 204 1
Exsikkator 350 51
Exsikkatoreneinsatz 350 54
Exterieur (des Pferdes) 72
  1-38
Extraktionszange 24 47
Extraktor 170 37
Extremität 82 6-8
Extremthermometer 10
  53-54
Exzenter 166 57
~rolle 166 67
~tritthebel 166 58
~welle 166 56
~wellenzahnrad 166 55

F

Fabel-tier 327 1-61
~wesen 327 1-61
Fabrik 15 37
~nummer 187 51
Facette Med. 24 32
~ Zool. 77 20
Facettenauge 77 20-24 ; 358 7
facettierter Stein 36 42-71
Fach 166 40
~, ausgemauertes 120 59
Facher 168 35
Fächer Jagd 88 75
~ Völkerkunde 353 42
~besen 51 3
~gewölbe 336 46
Fachkreuzspule 164 58
Fachwerk-binder 121 78
~bogen 215 25
~bogenbrücke 215 23
~element 215 24
~knoten 215 37
~stütze 214 77
~wand 120 48
Faden 164 53 ; 165 8 ; 167 7,
  17, 36, 64
~absaugung 164 44
~auge 166 28, 29

~behälter 22 61
~bruch 165 19, 37
~einzug 171 5, 20, 21
~fühler 166 14
Fadenführer Schuhmacher
  100 30
~ Textil 167 3, 54, 64
~haltestange 167 2
Faden-geflecht 381 2
~heftmaschine 185 16
~kops 185 18
~kreuz Jagd 87 32
~kreuz Fotogr. 115 66
~rolle 100 29
~scheibe 165 30
~schere 100 43
~spanner 167 5
~spannung 165 21
~spule 185 18
~strecke 171 38, 41
~trenner 164 43
~verkreuzung 165 11
~wurm 80 51
~zähler 177 23
Fagott 323 28
Fähe 88 42
Fähin 88 42
Fahlerz 351 1
Fahne 253 7-11
Fahnen-band 253 9
~nagel 253 8
~schaft 253 7
~spitze 253 10
~stange 273 61
~tuch 253 11
Fahrantrieb 201 18
Fahrbahn-begrenzung 268 72
~blech 215 6
~decke 198 5
~oberkante 215 8
~platte 215 2
~schicht 198 1-5
Fahrbenzin 145 54
Fährboot 216 11 ; 225 11
Fahrdamm 198 13
~dieselmotor 209 4
Fahrdraht 197 41 ; 205 58
~spannungsanzeige 211 28
Fähre 216 10
fahrende Leute 308 25-28
Fahrender 308 25-28
Fahrer 289 26
~haus 194 2 ; 200 11
~hausgestänge 65 21
~kabine 64 36 ; 194 15
~sitz 191 34
~stand 64 33 ; 197 25
~tür 193 2
Fahrgast Eisenb. 208 30
~ Schiff 221 109
~abteil 207 13
~anlage 225 31
~kabine 214 28, 52
~raum 208 22
~sitz 194 14
Fahrgestell Landw. 67 14
~ Bau 119 32
~ Kraftwerk 152 41
~ Auto 191 2
~ Geschütz 255 43
Fährhaus 216 45
Fahr-kabine 271 46
~karte 204 36
~kartenausgabe 204 34
~kartendrucker 204 40
~kartenschalter 204 35
~kartenverkäufer 204 39
~kupplung 65 39
~leine 289 27
Fahrleitungs-kontakt 197 40
~querverspannung 197 42
~unterhaltungstriebwagen
  211 41, 44-54

Fährmann 216 17
Fahrmotor 197 5, 7; 211 6
~lüfter 211 15
Fahrrad 187 1
~antrieb 187 35-42
~ergometer 23 26
~gestell 187 14-20
~glocke 187 4
~kippständer 187 34
~klingel 187 4
~lampe 187 7
~nummer 187 51
~pedal 187 78
~pumpe 187 48
~rahmen 187 14-20
~sattel 187 22
~schloß 187 49
~tachometer 187 33
Fahr·rinne 216 21
~rolle 83 61
Fahrschalter 197 27
~handrad 211 20; 212 12
Fahrscheinautomat 268 28
~entwerter 197 16
Fährseil 216 2
Fahrstand 228 23, 24
Fährsteg 216 7
Fahrstraße 203 68
Fahrstraßenhebel 203 58
Fahrstufenanzeige 211 36
Fahrstuhl 146 8; 271 46
~, LKW- 221 56
~führer 271 47
~schacht 146 20
Fahrt Eisenb. 203 5
~ Sport 285 7
Fährte Jagd 86 8
~ Sport 289 49
Fahrten·kieljacht 285 29-34
~wimpel 278 9
Fahrt·messer 230 2
~richtungsanzeiger 197 22;
   205 21
~windkühlung 188 7
Fahr- und Kommandostand
   224 14
Fahrwasser 216 21; 224 85, 97
~bezeichnung 224 84-102
~mitte 224 98
~zeichen 224 68-83
Fahrweg 15 99
Fahrwerk 232 10
~-Ausfahrzylinder 257 41
~gondel 256 15
Fahrzeug 186 1-54
~halle 270 1
~rampe 206 1
~stütze 255 68
Faksimiletransceiver 245 1
~unterschrift 252 34
Faktor 344 25
Falke 86 46; 362 1-4
Falkenbeize 86 42-46
~haube 86 44
Falkenier 86 42
Falken·jagd 86 42-46
~jäger 86 42
~kappe 86 44
~männchen 86 46
Falkner 86 42
Falknerei 86 42-46
Fall·blattziffer 110 20
~brücke 329 25
Falle Schlosser 140 37
~ Wasserbau 217 77
Falleitung 269 21
Fallen 12 3
Fällen 84 27, 37
Fallgatter 329 24
Fäll·heber 85 9
~heber, hydraulischer 84 25
~keil 84 30
Fall·kerbe 84 28

~nullenzirkel 151 59
~reep 221 98
~richtung 12 3
~rohr Haus 38 10
~rohr Hütt. 147 63
~rückzieher 291 45
Fallschirm 10 57; 288 37
~sport 288 37-62
~sportspringen 288 37-62
~springen 288 37-62
Fallschnecke 149 18
Fällschnitt 84 29
Fall·stange 151 60
~streifen 8 9
~stromvergaser 192 1-15
~tür 38 13
~winkel 87 78
Falscher Hederich 61 18
falsche Rippe 17 10
Falscher Mehltau 80 20
falsches Filet 95 31
Faltboot 283 54-66
~einer 283 54
~fahrer 283 55
~gerüst 283 67
~segel 283 62
~zweier 283 61
Faltcaravan 278 3
Falte 168 22
~, liegende 12 15
~, schiefe 12 13
~, stehende 12 12
~, überkippte 12 14
Falteinrichtung 249 46
Falten·balg Motorrad 188 41
~balg Film 313 39
~filter 350 41
~gebirge 12 12-20
~wurf 338 33
Falter 358 48-56
Faltflasche 116 9
Faltigron 377 6
Faltrian 377 6
Falt·schiebedach 194 10
~wohnwagen 278 3
Falz 185 54
~anleger 184 17
~apparat 180 15, 29; 181 55;
   182 27
~leimapparat 185 28
~maschine 249 58
~pfanne 122 59
~tasche 185 10
~trichter 181 53
~zange 100 38
Familien·begräbnis 331 27
~grab 331 27
Famulus 262 7
Fan 232 34, 43
~-Antriebsturbine 232 38
Fang Zool. 70 3
~ Jagd 88 45
~ Textil 171 44
~ Vögel 362 7
~arm 357 16
Fanger 325 27
Fänger 292 54, 60, 64
Fanger·draht 325 29
~filz 325 28
Fang·fabrikschiff 90 11
~gerät 352 31
~jagd 86 19-27
~kettstuhl 167 23
~leine Feuerwehr 270 45
~leine Sport 288 40
~partei 292 73
~riemen 301 3
~schale 149 44
~schuß 86 17
~spule 117 80
Faradisiergerät 23 37
Farbauftragwalze 181 18, 27,
   61

Farbband·kassette 249 16
~wähler 249 11
Farb·bildschirm 240 15
~decodermodul 240 5
~druck 340 28
Farbe 276 38-45; 343
Farbeimer 129 10
Färbelockenwickel 105 4
Farben, deutsche 276 42-45
~dose 129 6
Farbendstufenmodul 240 13
Farben·hobbock 129 9
~kanne 129 7-8
Farb·entwickler 116 10
~entwicklungschemikalien
   116 52
Färbe·schale 23 50
~trog 165 47
Farb·fernsehempfänger 240 1
~fernseher 240 1
~fernsehgerät 240 1
~filterbestimmer 116 36
~hebewalze 181 63
~kasten 180 22; 181 65
~kontrollampe 116 37
~korrektur, selektive 177 51
~korrekturgerät 177 39
~mischkopf 116 43-45
~mischung, additive 343 10
~mischung, subtraktive 343
   12
~rechner 177 51
~röhre 240 36
~rolle 129 11
~roller 129 11
~scheibe 316 49
~scheibenwechsler 316 49
~sprühdose 100 35
~tube 181 8
~vergrößerer 116 40
~vergrößerungspapier 116
   51
~verreibzylinder 181 62
~walze 181 21, 50, 60, 77
~werk 180 6-13, 40, 51, 60,
   71, 76; 181 19, 28, 50, 57;
   249 51-52
Farn 377 16
~kraut 377 16
Fasan 88 77
Fasanen·hahn 88 77
~henne 88 77
Faschiermaschine 96 53
Faschine 216 53
Fasching 306
Faschings·prinz 306 58
~prinzessin 306 61
~wagen 306 57
~zug 306 57-70
Fase 143 62
Faser 77 23
~bandegentrockner 169 31
~länge 170 60
~schreibstift 48 18
Faß 130 5
~band 130 8
~boden 130 10
~daube 130 9
Faßform 36 75
~, normal facettierte 36 56
Faß·haken 122 23
~keller 79 1-22
~lager Weinkeller 79 1-22
~lager Brauerei 93 16
Fasson·beleimung 185 31
~hammer 108 40
~lehre 162 43
Faß·reifen 130 8
~rumpf 130 6
~tonne 224 94
Fassung 127 60, 62
~ einer Quelle 269 24-39
Faßzieher 130 12

Fastnacht 306
Faulbaum 380 13
Faust Anat. 16 48
~ Klempner 125 20
~abwehr 291 39
~ball 293 74
~ballspiel 293 72-78
Fäustel 126 77; 158 35
Faust·kampf 299 20-50
~keil 328 1
~stempel 236 45
Fauteuil 42 21
Favoris 34 24
Favorit 289 52
F-Dur 320 63
Fechser 54 16; 58 20
Fecht·abstand 294 10
~aktion 294 7
~bahn 294 2
Fechten 294
Fechter 294 5-6
~gruß 294 18
Fecht·handschuh 294 12
~jacke 294 16
~maske 294 13, 14
~meister 294 1
~schuh 294 17
~stellung 294 18
~waffe 294 34-45
Feder Jagd 88 52
~ Bau 123 74
~ Schlosser 140 46
~ Masch. 143 73
~ Textil 167 38
~ Wagen 186 15
~ball 273 7; 293 44
~ballschläger 293 43
~ballspiel 273 6; 293 43-44
~bart 88 73
~bein 192 72-84
~beinstoßdämpfer 192 76
~beinstützlager 192 73
~busch 329 78
~gelenk 11 42
~haus 110 38
~keil 143 73
~kiel 322 53
~kielpose 89 45
~kranz 362 18
~leine Feuerwehr 270 45
~leine Sport 288 40
~mäppchen 260 12
~mappe 260 12
~mühle 308 15
~ohr 88 78; 362 16
~puffer 214 50
~putz 35 6
~ring Masch. 143 34
~ring Eisenb. 202 8
~ringscharnier 151 65
~schmuck 352 12
~schopf 359 26
~selli 57 19
~stahlring 89 51
~stegwerkzeug 109 9
~wild 86 41
~zinke 65 57
~zinkenhaspel 64 4
Fehleranzeige 244 7
Fehl·kante 120 89
~licht 310 51
~linie 292 48
~rippe 95 19
Feige 383 35; 384 11, 13
Feile 140 8
Feilen·heft 108 50
~hieb 140 28
Feil·kloben 140 24
~maschine 140 15
~nagel 108 22
Feinbäckerei 97 1-54
Feindschiff 218 11
Fein·einstellung Tischler 133
   36

~einstellung *Walz.* 148 65
~estrich 123 40
~filter 192 20
Feinheit 92 51
Feinkokssieberei 156 14
Feinkostgeschäft 98 1-87
Fein-krautabsonderung 64 79
~kreiselbrecher 158 19
~makulatur 128 8
~meßschraube *Schweiß.* 142 37
~meßschraube *Meßwerkzeug* 149 62
~schleifscheibe 111 37, 38
~schnitt 107 25
~schnitt- und Fügemaschine 133 37
~staubmeßgerät 112 42
~stufengetriebe 65 36
~trieb 112 5
Feld *Landw.* 63 4
~ *Jagd* 87 39
~ *Heraldik* 254 18-23
~ *Sport* 289 41, 51; 290 2
~, schwarzes 276 3
~, weißes 276 2
~arbeit 63 1-41
~arbeitsgerät 255 75
Feldbahn *Ziegelei* 159 4
~ *Straßenbau* 200 23
~diesellokomotive 200 24
Feld-bestellung 63 10-12
~bohne 69 15
~bohne, Gemeine 69 15
~champignon 381 1
~distel 61 32
Felderkaliber 87 40
Feld-frucht 68 1-47
~futterbau 69 1-28
~häcksler 64 34-39
~hase 88 59
~hüter 63 13
~kamille 61 8
~krähe 361 2
~mohn 61 2
~rain 63 3
~regner 67 32
~salat 57 38
~schädling 80 37-55
~spark 69 12
~spieler 292 2, 59
~spörgel 69 12
~staffelei 338 26
~stein *Landw.* 63 9
~stein *Wasservers.* 269 37
~stein *Schwimmbad* 281 22
~wächter 63 13
~weg *Landkarte* 15 102
~weg *Landw.* 63 18
~wicke 69 18
~zeichen 253 13
Felge *Fahrrad* 187 28; 189 25; 191 16; 192 77
~ *Sport* 297 29
Felgenbremse 187 5
Fell *Kürschner* 131 5, 6, 11-21, 14
~ *Mus.* 323 52; 324 31
~klappe 35 32
~mütze 35 34
Fels 300 37
~, Klettern im 300 2-13
~band *Straßenbau* 200 4
~band *Bergsteigen* 300 4
~bild 328 9
~block 158 8
~brocken 327 38
~gehen 300 2-13
~geher 300 5
~geröll 12 45
~grab 333 38
~kopf 300 9
~schulter 12 41

~sohle 13 70
~sturz 11 46
~technik 300 2-13
~terrasse 13 47, 63
~wand 158 15; 300 2
Feltrian 377 6
Fenchel 380 6
Fender 217 9
Fenster *Raumfahrt* 6 40
~ *Haus* 37 22, 23; 268 14
~ *Landmaschinen* 64 27
~ *Imker* 77 50
~ *Wagen* 186 10
~band 37 86
~bank 37 24; 118 12; 120 33
~brüstung 37 24
~glas 124 5
~klappe 304 12
~laden 37 30
~leibung 37 26; 118 10, 11
~malerei 260 26
~öffnung 120 30
~rahmen 133 44
~riegel 120 57
~rose 335 23
~schmuck 260 68
~sohlbank 118 12
~stiel 120 51
~sturz 37 25; 118 9
Ferkel 73 9; 75 42
Fermate 321 25
Fern-auslöseranschluß 117 9
~bedienung 157 14
~bildlinse 115 49
~gespräch 237 3
~glas 86 6; 111 17; 221 128
~heizleitung 198 28
~licht 191 20
~lichtkontrolle 191 69
Fernmelde-amt 237 27-41
~leitung 127 23
~satellit 237 52
Fernobjektiv 115 49
Fernrohr 14 60; 42 15; 111 18; 224 8
~lupe 113 38
~montierung 113 16-25
Fernschaltgerät 237 67
Fernschreibdienst 237 41
Fernschreiben 237 69
Fernschreiber 238 12
Fernschreib-lochstreifen 237 68
~maschine 237 31, 66
Fernseh-antenne 239 5
~empfangsantenne 239 4
Fernsehen 238 27-53
Fernseher 42 8; 46 14
~gehäuse 240 2
Fernseh-funk 238; 239
~gerät 242 28
~kamera 10 67; 112 36; 154 78; 240 26
~programm 342 64
~röhre 240 3
~technik 240
~ton 242 27
~übertragungswagen 239 1-15
Fernsprech-auskunft 237 33
~buch 236 12; 237 5
~buchgestell 236 10
~dienst 237 41
Fernsprecher 237 6-26
Fernsprech-häuschen 237 1
~kabine 236 8; 251 10
~teilnehmer 237 2
~Tischapparat 237 6
~verbindung 242 20
~zelle, öffentliche 204 46
Fern-steuerfunkgerät 288 87
~thermometer 210 48
~verkehrsstraße 15 17

~wahlmünzfernsprecher 237 3
Ferse 19 63
Fersen-automatik 301 54
~bein 17 27
~gummi 286 58
~sitz 295 8
~bauelement 215 58
~bauteil 215 57, 58
~behandlung 168 1-65
~bütte 172 85
~gericht, tiefgefrorenes 96 23
~gutausstoß 162 29, 37
~malztrichter 92 20
~stapel 148 68
~straße 148 71
Fertigungsstraße 173 13-28
Fesen 68 24
Fessel *Pferd* 72 25
~ *Jagd* 86 45
~flugmodell 288 89
Feste 329 1
feste Phase 148 26
Festessen 267 40-43
Festigkeit 170 46
Feston 335 54
Fest-platz 308 1
~redner 267 40
~saal 267 39; 306 1
~sattel 192 49
Feststellhebel 2 40
Feststoff-Raketenmotor 235 58
Festung 15 74
festverzinsliches Wertpapier 251 11-19
Festwiese 308 1
Fetisch 354 43
fett 175 9
Fettaucher 359 4
Fett-backgerät 97 66
~fliege 81 15
~flosse 367 27
~henne, Große 377 9
~kraut 377 13
~kreide 340 26
Feuchtigkeits-creme 99 27
~meßelement 10 9
~messer *Zeichn.* 151 39
~messer *Druck* 179 28
~messer *Schwimmbad* 281 23
Feucht-raum 92 8
~raummantelleitung 127 42
~walze 180 23, 52, 61
~werk 180 39, 61
Feudel 50 55
Feuer, offenes 267 25
~becken 332 41
~blume 61 2
~bohne 57 8
~bohren 354 34
~büchse 210 4
feuergefährliche Ladung 253 38
Feuer-kratze 137 4
~leitradar-Antenne 258 51
Feuerlösch-anlage 228 20
~boot 270 65
~einrichtung 227 25
Feuerlöscher 79 9
Feuerlösch-kanone 221 4
~motor 221 4
~schaumtank 228 28
feuerlose Lokomotive 210 68
Feuersalamander 364 22
Feuer-schaufel 137 2
~schiff *Landkarte* 15 13
~schiff *Schiff* 221 47; 224 81
~schlucker 308 25
~schröter 358 24
~schutz 316 6
~schutzhelm 270 38
~schutztrommel 312 25

~schutzwand 305 91
~sirene 270 4
~stein 107 28
~tür 210 61
~turm 224 82
~türöffner 210 63
~wache 270 1-3
Feuerwehr 270
~beil 270 43
~mann 270 37
~übung 270 1-46
Feuerwerkskörper 306 49-54
Feuilleton 342 67
~teil 342 67
Fiaker 186 26
Fiale 335 29
Fibel 328 27
Fichte 372 12
Fichten-gallenlaus 82 38
~nadel 372 19
~rüßler 82 41
~schwärmer 82 27
~spinner 82 17
~zapfen 372 13
~zellstoff 169 1
Fiebermücke 81 44
Fiedel 323 1
~bogen 323 12
fiederteilig 370 40
Fiepblatter 87 43
Figur 276 1, 4, 14
~, menschliche 328 20
~, mythologische 327 1-61
~, symmetrische 346 24
Figurenski 286 56
Figurine 315 40
Filament 102 22; 169 17
Filet 95 7, 24, 44
~, falsches 95 31
~arbeit 102 22
Filete 183 3
Filet-faden 102 24
~knoten 102 23
~nadel 102 26
~schlinge 102 23
~stab 102 25
Filier-messer 89 38
~nadel 102 26
Filigranarbeit 102 30
Film 2 10, 13; 114 9; 176 25, 28; 310; 311; 312; 313
~, belichteter 117 42
~, unbelichteter 117 41
~agitator 116 19
~andruckplatte 115 24
~antrieb 311 26
~architekt 310 43
~archiv 310 5
~ateliergruppe 310 10
~aufnahme 310 14-60
~bauten 310 7
~berichterkamera 117 66
~betrachter 117 91; 242 8
~bildwerfer 312 24
~bühne 116 30
~diva 310 27
~dosenbewegungsgerät 116 19
~dosimeter 2 8, 11
~drehbuch 310 45
~empfindlichkeitseinstellung 117 18
Filmentwickler 177 72
Filmentwicklungs-dose 116 1
~maschine 311 30
Film-fach 116 4
~fenster 115 28; 312 34
~friseur 310 36
~geschwindigkeitsschalter 117 12
~gleitbahn 312 31
~held 310 28
~kamera 27 20; 310 47; 313 1-39, 15

~kamera, 35-mm- 313 1
~karte 237 38
~kassette 112 65; 113 40; 114
  15
~kassettengehäuse 313 9
~kitt 312 22
~klammer 116 14
~komparse 310 29
~kühlgebläse 312 34
~kulisse 310 33
~lagerbunker 310 5
~laufwerk 312 25-38
~magazin 115 80
~manuskript 310 45
~mitnehmer 115 25
~montage 179 23
~orchester 310 17
~perforationseinrichtung
  242 10
~projektor 311 22;
  312 24-52
~publikum 312 5
~regisseur 310 40
~rißkontakt 312 30
~rolle 312 33
~schauspieler 310 28
~schauspielerin 310 27
~spule 114 8; 311 24; 312 32
~spulenhalter 238 6
~stadt 310 1-13
~stanze 117 95
~star 310 27
~statist 310 29
~stern 310 27
~streifenhalter 117 90
~teller 117 99; 311 44
~theater 312 1
~titel 310 35
~transportknauf 116 7
~transportkurbel 114 32
~trockner 116 23
~trommel 312 16, 25
~umspulung 312 21
~verbrauchsanzeige 117 52
~voberuhigung 312 30
~vorführer 312 20
~vorführkabine 5 27
~vorführraum 5 26; 312 12
~vorführungsapparat 312 24
~wiedergabe 312 1-23
Filter Atom 2 9, 12, 14
~ Textil 170 32
~ Papier 172 20
~ Wasservers. 269 62
~anlage 146 26
~anschluß 115 6
~aufnahme 112 57
~boden 269 11
~bühne 313 3
~einrichtung 165 14
~einsatz 190 29
~glasscheibe 116 22
~kies 269 10
~presse Porzellan 161 12
~presse Textil 169 12
~sieb 349 12
~zigarette 107 12
Filtrierflasche 350 40
filtriertes Wasser 269 12
Filz 173 51
~bedeckung 353 20
~döckchen 325 37
~hammer 325 3
~hut 35 22
~laus 81 40
~pfropf 87 52
~schreiber 247 11
~stiefel 353 30
~stift 47 26; 247 11; 260 19
Filztuch 340 42
Fimbrien 20 82
Finger, kleiner 19 68
~abdrucke 264 29

~abdruckvergleich 264 28
~beere 19 78
~farbe 260 26
~flugsteig 233 12
~glied 17 17; 19 77
~hut 379 2
~knochen 17 17
~kopf 233 13
~lochscheibe 237 11
~malerei 260 26
~nagel 19 80
~ring-Filmdosimeter 2 11
~spitze 19 79
~strecker 18 57
Finierer 24 38
Finkenvogel 360 1; 361 6-8
Finndingi 284 51
Finne 66 10
finnische Sauna 281 18
Firmen-konto 250 4
~schild 118 47
Firn-brücke 300 24
~feld 12 48
~grat 300 21
~hang 300 14
Firnis 338 12
Firnwächte 300 20
First 37 7; 121 2; 122 93
~bohle 121 48
~gebinde 122 79
~haken 122 65
~haube 122 99
~kreuz 331 10
~latte 121 48
~lüftung 55 11
~pfette 121 43
~schar 122 47
~schlußziegel 122 4
~ziegel 122 3, 52
Fisch 89 13; 301 36; 364 1-18;
  369 13
~auge 115 44
~augenobjektiv 115 44
~besteck 45 8
~brutanstalt 89 11-19
~dampfer 221 46
Fische 4 64
Fischei 89 12
Fischerboot 89 27; 90 24
Fischereihafen 225 56
Fisch-fang- und
  Verarbeitungsschiff 221 86
~gabel 45 65
~gericht 266 53
~grätenmelkstand 75 23
~halle 225 57
~konserve 96 28; 98 19
~konservenfabrik 225 59
~korb 89 25
~laich 89 12
~logger 90 1
~messer 45 64; 89 39
~möwe 359 14
~paß 89 93
~reiher 359 18
~schwanz 327 25, 43, 46, 49
~schwanzbohrer 145 21
~speer 280 40
~transportfaß 89 3
~trawler 90 11
~zucht 89 1-19
Fis-Dur 320 61
fis-Moll 320 58
Fissurenbohrer 24 39
Fittich 88 76, 79
Fitting 126 38-52
Five o'clock tea 267 44-46
Fix-kamm 163 67
~stern 3 9-48
~sternhimmel, nördlicher 3
  1-35
FKK-Gelände 281 15
F-Kontakt 115 14

Flach-bahnregler 238 47; 241
  8; 311 18
~bogen 336 28
~brücke 215 52
~dach 37 73
~dachpfanne 122 60
~drehbrücke 215 67
~druckverfahren 340 25-26
Fläche 347 31
~, bearbeitete 151 21
~, ebene 346 24-58
~, feingeschlichtete 151 22
~, geschruppte 151 21
~, schraffierte 151 29
~, unbearbeitete 151 20
Flacheisen Masch. 143 10
~ Graphik 340 7
Flächen-bügelplatz 103 18
~eisen 158 38
~leuchte 182 3
~spritzung 83 1
~streicher 129 17
flacher Teller 44 7; 45 4
Flach-facette 111 38, 39
~feile 108 49; 140 27
~glas 124 5
~glasherstellung 162 1-20
~hammer 137 33
~hang 13 58
~kiel 222 49
~küste 13 35-44
~landtapir 366 26
~meißel 140 26
~moor 13 14
~offsetmaschine 180 75
~palette 226 10
~pinsel 338 6
~relief 339 33
~riemen 163 49
Flachs 383 6
Flach-schlüssel 140 48
~schraubstock 140 10
~sticharbeit 102 10
~stickarbeit 102 10
~strahldüse 83 4
~strickmaschine 167 35
~stromvergaser 190 79
~wagen 206 21; 213 5, 40
~zange 126 62; 137 24; 140 66
Flagge 253 1-3, 4, 6; 293 88
Flaggen-gala 221 85
~knopf 253 1
~leine 253 2
~mast 253 1
~schmuck 221 85
~signal 223 9
~stock 253 1; 258 4; 259 87
~tuch 253 3
Flaggleine 253 2
Fla--Kanone 258 73
~Maschinengewehr 255 63
~Maschinenkanone 259 34
Flamingo 272 53
Flamme 327 10
Flammendes Herz 60 5
Flammen-regulierung 107 31
~schutzwand 259 15, 27
Flanelltuch 128 48
Flanke Anat. 16 32
~schutzmittel 178 24
Flansch Böttcher 130 28
~ Masch. 143 2, 5
~stutzen 130 20
Fla-Raketenstarterzwilling
  259 33
Flasche 93 21; 98 60-64; 105
  37; 266 16
Flaschen-abfüllung 93 22

~batterie 141 1
~bier 93 26
~blasmaschine 162 21
~bord 267 64
~bovist 381 20
~box 28 21
~gestell 79 11
~inhalt 279 13
~korb 79 13
~lager 79 11
~öffner 45 47
~regal 266 10; 317 4
~reinigungsanlage 93 18
~reinigungsmaschine 93 19
~spule 167 4
~ventil 279 22
~wagen 141 23
~zug 137 20; 145 8; 221 27
Flashbar 114 75
Flattertier 366 9
Fla-Zwillingsturm 259 30
Flecht-arbeit 136 16
~art 136 1-4
~werk 136 4
~zaun 216 54
Fleck, blinder 19 50
~specht 359 27
Fledermaus 366 9
~ärmel 31 16
~flügel 327 4
~gaube 121 23
~gaupe 121 23
Fleetreep 90 4
Fleisch 175 40
~beschauer 94 24
~dünnung 95 15
Fleischer 94 1; 96 38
Fleischerei 96 1-30
Fleischer-fachgeschäft 96
  1-30
~geselle 96 58
~meister 96 38
~messer 96 31-37
~schürze 96 39
Fleisch-gericht 266 55
~hacker 40 39
~haken 96 55
~hauer 94 1
~konserve 98 20
~messer 96 35
~nelke 60 6
~pastete 96 15
~salat 96 13
~stück 86 43; 96 59
~teile 94 20
~topf 40 12
~waren 96 1-4; 99 53
~warenabteilung 99 51
~wolf 96 53
~wurstring 96 10; 99 55
~zerlegesäge 94 20
Flickfilz 297 24
Fliege Kleidung 32 47
~ Bart 34 1
~ Angelsport 89 65
~ Zool. 358 18
fliegende Fähre 216 10
~ Hundehütte 288 91
fliegender Händler 308 51
~ Mensch 307 7
Fliegen-klappe 83 32
~klatsche 83 32
~pilz 379 10
fließendes Wasser 89 1
~zone 11 2
Float-bad 162 16
~glasprozeß 162 12
F-Loch 323 6
Flockenblume 61 1
Flödel 323 26
Floh 81 42
~markt 309

Flomen 95 45
Florbildung 168 31
Florentinerhut 35 21
Florett 294 11, 37, 39
~fechten 294 1-18, 53
~fechter 294 5-6
~knauf 294 40
florin 252 19
Flosse 286 43, 61
Flossen-füßler 367 18-22
~stummel 232 3
~taucher 359 4
Floßgasse 283 60
Flöte Küchengeräte 40 11
~ Mus. 323 30, 31
~ Völkerkunde 353 47
Flötenkessel 39 16; 40 10
Flottholz 90 6
Flottung 171 40
Flöz 154 65
~strecke 144 29
Fluatmittel 128 7
Fluchtweg 233 41
Flug-abwehrraketenstarter
    258 32; 259 25
~bahn 89 36
~ball 293 41
~benzin 145 57
~betankungsstutzen 256 7
~blattverteiler 263 9
~boot 232 1
~brettchen 77 49
~deck 259 2, 12
~drachen 260 71
Flügel Zool. 81 8; 82 11; 327
    28, 51, 60; 358 33; 359 10
~ Fischerei 90 16
~ Flugzeug 230 43
~ Mus. 325 40
~ Bot. 371 57; 372 9
~, elliptischer 229 15
~ader 358 34
~anordnung 229 1-14
~ärmel 29 14
~aufhängung 257 34, 35
~decke 82 10
~form 229 15-22
~hahn 126 35
~hemdchen 29 8
~kopf 91 6
~mauer 216 35
~mutter 143 42; 187 39
~nasenteil 235 32
~pedal 325 41
~rad 217 52
~radpumpe 217 47-52
~radwasserzähler 269 53
~roß 327 26
~schiene 202 25
~spannweite 229 2
~spitzentank 231 9; 256 30
~tank 256 4
~walze 64 73
~welle 91 5
Fluggast-brücke 233 14
~raum 231 22
Flughafen 233
~betrieb, Hinweisschilder für
    den 233 24-53
~feuerwehr 233 7
~restaurant 233 19
Flug-hafer 61 29
~haltung 301 36
~körperschnellboot 258 69,
    75
~körperstartcontainer 258 71
~loch 77 48
~platzsammelraum 233 11
~reise 267 15
~sport 288
~steig 233 12
~steuerung, automatische
    235 23

Flugzeug 229; 230 67-72;
    231; 232; 233 21
~aufzug 259 4, 13
~führersitz 257 6
~halle 287 14
~schlepp 287 1
~schlepper 233 23
~schleppstart 287 1
~träger, atomgetriebener 259
    1
~triebwerk 232 33-60
~typ 231 1-33
Fluidkompaß 224 46
Fluothane-~-(Halothan-)
    Behälter 26 26
~-Behälter 26 26
Flur Haus 41 1-29
~ Landw. 63 17
~garderobe 41 1
~hüter 63 13
~wächter 63 13
Flushdecksrumpf 258 2
Fluß Astr. 3 12
~ Geogr. 13 61; 15 76; 216 31
~aal 364 17
~arm 13 2; 216 3, 18
~aue 13 62
~bau 216
~bett 13 68
~damm 216 49
~fähre 216 10
flüssige Phase 148 27
flüssiges Eisen 148 11
~ Roheisen 147 55
Flüssiggas 145 53
~tanker 221 35
Flüssigkeit 350 21
Flüssigkeits-barometer 10 1
~behälter 247 9
~getriebe 212 27, 52
~raketen-Hauptmotor 235 36
~standanzeiger 316 57
Flüssig-kristallanzeige 110 2
~lager 225 72
~sauerstoff-Förderleitung
    234 10
~sauerstoffleitung 234 52
~sauerstofftank 234 12, 24, 39
~wasserstoffleitung 234 51
~wasserstoff-Saugleitung 234
    23
~wasserstofftank 234 26, 41
Fluß-insel 216 4
~karpfen 364 4
~landschaft 13 1-13
~mittel 125 7
~mündung 13 1
~nixe 327 23
~perlmuschel 357 33
~regelung 216 31
~schleppdampfer 216 23
~spat 351 16
~tal 13 57-70
~ufer 216 5
~versickerung 13 73
~wasser 154 55
~wels 364 12
~windung 13 11
Flüstertüte 283 21
Flut 280 7
Fluten 129 34
Flut-gerät 129 34
~grenze 13 35
~welle 11 53
Flyaway 298 30
Flyerflügel 164 25
Flyerin 164 24
Flyer-lunte 164 29
~spule 164 23
~streckwerk 164 22
Flying Dutchman 284 49
f-Moll 320 66
Fock 284 16; 285 3

~mast 218 42; 219 2-4; 220 21
~niederholer 284 17
~rah 219 32
~schot 284 23
~schotklemme 284 22
~schotleitschiene 284 29
~segel 218 41; 219 55
~untermast 219 2
Fohlen 73 2
~fellstiefel 101 10
Föhnwelle 287 17
Föhre 372 20
Folie 76 28
Folien-gewächshaus 55 40
~schlauchsilo 62 43
~schrumpfofen 226 12
~schrumpftunnel 76 24
~schweißanlage 76 27
~schweißgerät 40 47
~tunnel 55 40
Folklorekleid 30 27
Follikel 20 84
Fön 105 33; 106 22
~anschluß 106 15
Fond-fenster 191 23
~sitz 191 31
~tür 193 3
Fönkamm 105 22
Fontäne 272 22
Fontur 167 21
Football 292 22
~spiel 292 22
~spieler 292 23
Förder-aggregat 83 59
~band Molkerei 76 23
~band Bau 118 77
~band Textil 169 32
~band Papier 172 79
~band Druck 182 30
~band Hafen 225 51
~eimer 216 58
~gerüst 144 1
~insel 146 1-39
~korb 144 23
~turm 144 3
~wagen Bergbau 144 45
~wagen Eisenb. 206 3, 35
Forelle 364 15
Forellen-brut 89 16
~teich 89 6
~zucht 89 14
Forke 66 3, 7
Forleule 82 46
Form Hutmacher 35 3
~ Eisengießerei 148 34
~ Glas 162 47
~ Druck 181 36
~, äußere (des Pferdes) 72
    1-38
~, geometrische 260 79
Formaldehydmolekül 242 64
Form-arbeit Glas 162 38-47
~arbeit Schule 260 67
~arbeiten 260 67
Format-einstellung 249 34
~- und Besäumkreissäge 132
    57
Formbrett 174 10
Formel 345 5
~-I-Rennwagen 290 34
~-II-Rennwagen 290 36
Formen 162 42
Former 148 30
Formerei 148 30-37
Form-kasten 148 18, 33
~kissen 104 23
~legespiel 48 19
Formling 161 9
Form-obstbaum 52
    1, 2, 16, 17, 29
~sand 148 35
~scheibe 111 25, 26
~signal 203 1, 7

~sitz 188 13
Formular 242 42
~dia 242 42
~stoß 245 24
Form-vorsignal 203 12
~zylinder 181 51
Forschungs-laboratorium 310
    9
~mikroskop 23 51; 112 1, 66
~raketenbereich 7 24
Forst 84 1-34
~amt 15 3
~beamter 35 40
~garten 84 6
~schädling 82
~wirt 84 18
~wirtschaft 84; 85
Forsythie 373 1
forte 321 38
~ fortissimo 321 40
Fortepedal 325 8
fortepiano 321 41
Fortepiano 325 1
Fortführungspunkt 342 29
fortissimo 321 39
Fosbury-Flop 298 9
Fotoausgang 112 36
Fotografie 114; 115; 116
Foto-grammetrie 14 63-66
~mikroskop 112 34
~papier 116 51
~platte 309 49, 50
~registrierung 27 33
~reproduktion 177
~stutzen 112 55
~topographie 14 63-66
Föttinger-Wandler 190 70
Foul 291 50
~linie 292 48
Fourcault-
    Glasziehmaschine 162 8
~-Verfahren 162 1
Fowler-Klappe 229 52
Fox 70 15
~terrier 70 15
Foyer Astr. 5 25
~ Theater 315 12-13
Fracht-brief 206 30
~-Fahrgast-Schiff 221 96;
    223 1-71
~gutannahme 206 26
~halle 233 9
~hof 233 10
~kahn 216 25
~raum 231 21
~- und Posthalle 233 9
Frack 33 13
~schleife 33 16
~schoß 33 14
~weste 33 15
Fractocumulus 8 12
Fractostratus 8 11
Fragezeichen 342 20
Fraktionierturm 145 37
Fraktokumulus 8 12
Fraktostratus 8 11
Fraktur 342 3
franc 252 15, 16, 17, 18
Franc 252 16, 17, 18
franco 252 15
Franken 252 15
Frankfurter 96 8
~ Kranz 97 42
Fransenschmuck 353 25
Franzose Zool. 81 17
~ Installateur 126 67
Franzosen-gras 69 22
~kraut 61 31
französischer Park 272 1-40
französisches Bett 43 4-13
Französisches Raygras 69 22
französisches Weißbrot 97 12
Fräser 175 51

Fräskette 132 50
Fraß-bild 82 23-24
~gang *Bot.* 58 63
~gang *Zool.* 82 23-24
Frässpindel 175 60
Fraßstelle 80 50
Fräs-station 184 3
~tisch *Werkzeugmasch.* 150 33
~tisch *Setzerei* 175 52
~- und Aufrauhstation 184 3
Frauen-frisur 34 27-38
~haar, Goldenes 377 17
~haus 329 10
~herz 60 5
~käfer 358 37
~kopf 327 56
~schuh 376 27
Fräulein vom Amt 237 35
Fregatte 258 53
Frei-anlage 356 1
~bad 282 1-32
~ballonfahren 288 63-84
freie Kleinkaliberwaffe 305 44
freier Überschlag 297 25
freies Elektron 1 25
Freifall-haltung 288 60-62
~mischer 118 33
Freiflugmodell 288 86
freiformgeschmiedetes Werkstück 139 28
Freiform-schmiede 139
~schmieden 139 32
Frei-gefecht 294 5-6
~gehege 356 1
~gelände 310 1
freigesetztes Neutron 1 39, 45
Frei-hafen 225 2
~hafengrenze 225 3
Freiheitsdressur 307 30-31
Freiherrnkrone 254 44
Frei-inhalatorium 274 6
~körperkulturgelände 281 15
Freilaufnabe 187 63
Freileitungsmast 152 36
Freilichtaufnahme 310 18
Freiluftschaltanlage 152 29-35
Frei-saite 324 25
~schneidegerät 84 32
Freistil-ringen 299 10-12
~wettschwimmen 282 24-32
Frei-stoß 291 43
~treppe 333 33
~übungen 295
~verkehr 251 5
~wange 123 44
freiwerdendes Neutron 1 52
Freiwurf-linie 292 5, 38
~raum 292 37
Freizeit-~(Wander-)Jacke 33 39
~anzug 32 21; 33 17
~hemd 32 38; 33 37
~jacke 33 39
~zentrum 281
Fremden-buch 267 8
~führerin 272 27
Frequenz-einstellskala 309 22
~skala 241 7
~unterteilung 110 16
~wähler 241 9
~weiche 241 14
Fresko 338 40
Fresnellinse 115 64
Freß-napf 70 32
~werkzeug 358 26
Frett 86 24
Frettchen 86 24
~führer 86 25
Frettieren 86 23
Friedenspfeife 352 6

Friedhof 15 106; 331 21-41
Friedhofs-kapelle 331 28
~mauer 331 18
~tor 331 19
Fries, babylonischer 333 19
~verzierung 334 16
Frikandeau 95 12
Friktionsfeintrieb 116 33
Frisch-dampfleitung 154 31
~fleischabteilung 99 51
~käse 76 38
Frischling 88 51
Frischluft-ausströmer 191 85
~eintritt 192 60
~gebläse 38 58
~regulierung 191 86
~schacht 92 14
~zuführung 356 16
Frisch-milchtank 76 15
~ölbehälter 65 46
~öltank 189 36
~- und Abluftschacht 92 14
~wassertank 221 70; 223 79
~wasserwagen 233 22
Friseur *Friseur* 106 1
~ *Piktogramm* 233 53
~kittel 106 2
~meister 106 1
Friseuse 105 35
Frisier-kamm 105 15; 106 28
~kommode 43 25
~leuchte 106 8
~spiegel *Wohnung* 43 29
~spiegel *Friseur* 105 20; 106 6
~stab 106 31
~stuhl *Wohnung* 43 24
~stuhl *Friseur* 105 17; 106 16
~tisch 105 19
~umhang 105 34; 106 4
~utensil 105 1-16
Frisur 34 1-25, 27-38; 106 3
Frivolitätenarbeit 102 19
Fromändaner Schmale 69 22
Fromental 69 22
Frontalzacken 300 49
Front-aufwind 287 25
~avionikraum 257 11
Fronten 9 25-29
~segeln 287 23
Front-Fan-Triebwerk 232 33
~gebläsetriebwerk 232 33
~glas 117 64
~linse 115 7
~linsenfassung 115 6
~ring 113 7
~sattel 33 19
~schild 85 35
~segeln 287 23
~seite 342 38
~spoiler 193 36
~tür 50 30
Frosch 323 13
~biß 378 29
~lage 288 61
~löffel 378 44
~lurch 364 23-26
Frost, ewiger 9 58
Frosteranlage 97 65
~nachtspanner 80 16
~schmetterling 80 16
~schutzschicht 198 1; 200 60
~spanner, Kleiner 80 16
Frottier-handtuch 49 9
~stoff 101 23
~überzug 49 14
Frucht 58 28; 61 11, 20, 23;
    370 91-102; 371 4, 19, 28,
    45, 59, 61, 69; 372 53, 64;
    373 12, 18, 22, 27, 29, 32;
    374 4, 8, 12, 19, 25, 29, 31,
    34; 375 4, 7, 10, 13, 17, 24,
    35, 37, 47; 376 3, 6, 14; 378
    11, 31, 38, 42; 382 5, 10, 15,

17, 24, 33, 39; 383 14, 18,
21, 28, 32, 34, 40, 43, 44, 46,
52, 56, 59; 384 19, 26, 31,
39, 45
~becher 384 52
~blatt 59 13; 374 2, 26
~blüte 59 38
~blütenstand 59 46
Früchtekorb 266 57
Frucht-fleisch 58 24, 35, 58; 59 6
~hülle 57 6; 59 42, 50
~hülse 69 8, 16
~kapsel 375 27; 382 44; 383 8
Fruchtknoten 58 40; 370 54,
    60; 373 2, 5; 375 34
~, mittelständiger 59 14
~, unterständiger 58 7
~höhle 370 62
~wand 370 61
Frucht-körper 381 2
~saft 98 18; 266 58
~saftdose 99 75
~saftflasche 99 74
~schalenwickler 80 9
~schote 383 4; 384 46
~schuppe 371 12; 372 67
~schuppen 225 52
~stand 61 15; 371 22, 44, 69,
    72; 373 8; 374 18; 383 56;
    384 8, 32
~stiel 58 13
~topf 384 58
~traube 58 11
~wand 59 42
~zapfen 372 2, 29, 30, 36, 41,
    57
~zweig 59 30; 371 3, 11, 18,
    31, 36, 41, 47, 50, 56, 64;
    372 40, 51, 59, 63, 66, 70;
    382 2, 37; 384 38
Frühbeet 55 16
Frühlings-anfang 3 6
~fliege 358 12
~punkt 3 6
Frühstückskeller 39 34
Frühtreiberei 55 24
F₁-Schicht 7 28
F₂-Schicht 7 29
F-Schlüssel 320 9
Fuchs *Heizung* 38 40
~ *Sport* 289 48
~fellmütze 35 31
Fuchsia 53 3
Fuchsie 53 3
Fuchs-jagd 289 41-49
~pelzmütze 35 19
~schwanz *Bot.* 60 21
~schwanz *Werkzeug* 120 60;
    126 72; 132 44; 134 27
~schwanzgriff 132 4
Fugen-messer 201 17
~schneider 201 16
~schneidgerät 201 16
~schneidmesser 201 17
Fühler 81 5; 82 3; 357 31; 358
    27, 53
~lehre 140 53
Fuhre Mist 63 15
Führer-bremsventil 210 53;
    211 22; 212 11
~ der Gegenliste 263 27
~pult 212 32
~raum 211 19
~stand *Eisenb.* 209 6; 211 19,
    57; 212 5; 213 2
~stand *Bergbahnen* 214 65
~stand *Hafen* 226 52
~standsheizung 211 39
Fuhrmann 3 27
Führungs-gelenk 192 80
~gerät 23 21
~gestänge 200 27

~hebel 240 29; 313 11
~kette 65 13
~klaue 176 18
~lager 113 14
~nut *Film* 117 36
~nut *Wasserbau* 217 75
~plättchen 322 40
~rille 301 39
~rolle 249 17
~schiene *Web.* 166 3
~schiene *Aufzug* 271 54
~schlitz 322 41
~stange 2 42
~steg 65 12
~stift 243 21
~zapfen 140 41
Fuhrwerk 186 1-54
Füll-ansatz 288 70
~ansatzleine 288 71
Füllen 73 2
Füller 260 14
~aufzug 200 51
~zugabe 200 52
Füll-federhalter 260 14
~hahn 38 65
~halter 260 14
~kasten 163 9
~masse 153 38
~material 174 8
~mengenanzeige 196 5
~öffnung 288 81
~ort 144 26
~rohr 96 50
~sandeimer 158 29
~standmesser 76 6
~standsanzeige 76 10
~stellung 147 55, 56
~tür 38 61
~- und Ablaßhahn 38 65
Füllung 24 30
Füllungsmischgerät 24 51
Füllwagen 144 8; 156 6
Fund 328 1-40
Fundament-graben 118 75
~streifen 123 2
~vorsprung 123 3
Fundgegenstand,
    prähistorischer 328
    1-40
F- und X-Kontakt 115 14
Fünf-eck 351 9
~ganggetriebe 189 6
~mastbark 220 32-34
~mastvollschiff 220 35
~meterplattform 282 8
~paß 335 40
~uhrtee 267 44-46
~vierteltakt 320 41
~-Zylinder-Reihen-
    Dieselmotor 190 3
Funk-antenne 197 34
~einrichtung 288 13
Funken-fänger 210 24
~horn 152 47; 153 61
~mariechen 306 67
~strecke 153 62
Funk-fernsteuerung 288 87
~gerät 197 28
~kompaß 230 5
~navigationsgerät 230 22
~peilerrahmenantenne 223 5
~peilrahmen 258 17
~raum 223 12
~sprechgerät 22 14; 270 41;
    288 17
~störungsmeßdienst 237 27
Funktionstaste 247 17
Funk-turm 15 33
~- und Navigationsein-
    richtung 288 13
Fürbug 329 85
Furchenrad 65 16
Furnier 133 2

~schälmaschine 133 1
~schnellpresse 133 49
~zusammenklebemaschine 133 3
Fürstenhut 254 40
Fürstin 355 20
Fusa 320 16
Fuß *Anat.* 16 54; 17 26-29; 19 52-63
~ *Schuhmacher* 100 23
~ *Tischler* 132 29
~ *Textil* 171 33
~ *Mus.* 326 23
~abstreifer 123 25
~anfassen 302 10
~anheber 100 27
Fußball 273 12; 291
~platz 291 1-16
~schuh 291 21
~spiel 273 10
~tor 273 11
Fuß-becken 49 44
~bett 101 50
~bindungsstelle 171 35
Fußboden 123
~streicher 129 27
Fuß-bremse 188 52
~bremshebel 56 40
~brett 305 81
~bügel 142 31
~ende 43 4
Fußgänger-lichtzeichen 268 55
~überweg 198 11; 268 24, 29
~wegmarkierung 268 51
~zone 268 58
Fuß-gebinde 122 76
~leiste 267 52
~linie 122 81
~maschine 324 54
~muskel 18 49
~note 185 62
~pferd 219 46
~pfette 121 44; 122 40
~platte *Schneiderei* 103 11
~platte *Bau* 119 50
~platte *Werkzeugmasch.* 150 19
~platte *Bildhauerei* 339 23
~rampenleuchte 316 26
~raste 187 47; 188 44
~raumbelüftung 191 81
~ring 74 54
~rücken 19 61
~sack 28 38; 304 27
~schalter 27 21; 50 2; 157 66
~schalterbuchse 249 66
~schalttaste 103 26
~schaltung 188 55; 190 77
~sohle 19 62
~sprung 282 13
~steg 185 58
~steuerhebel 139 27
~stück 183 25
~stütze *Friseur* 105 18; 106 19
~stütze *Wagen* 186 7
~stütze *Eisenb.* 207 57
~stütze *Sport* 298 2; 301 58
~technik 299 19
~teil 43 4
~tritt *Schädlingsbek.* 83 34
~tritt *Wagen* 186 13
~tritt *Mus.* 326 48
~tritthebel 183 18
~ventil 269 6, 14, 43
~weg 15 43
~wurzelknochen 17 26
Futterautomat 74 13
~brett 123 56
~gang 75 3
~kette 74 25
~klee 69 1
~maschine 74 23

~napf 70 32
~pflanze 69 1-28
~rinne 74 4, 21
~rohr 74 15
~rübe 69 21
~silo 62 11, 43
~tank 221 73
~transportband 74 25
~transportkette 74 25
~trog 75 37
~wicke 69 18
~zuführung 74 23-27

G

Gabel *Haushalt* 45 58; 71 29
~ *Optik* 113 12
~ *Wagen* 186 30
~ *Post* 237 13
~baum 284 7
~deichsel 186 30
~flinte 353 28
~häkelei 102 28
~kopf 187 11
~kreuz 332 61
~montierung 113 24
~mücke 81 44
~schaft 187 10
~schaftrohr 187 10
~scheide 187 12
~schlüsselsatz 134 2
~stapler 93 23; 206 16
~umschalter 237 13
~weihe 362 11
Gaffel 219 45
~geer 219 70
~segel 220 1
~stander 219 49
~toppsegel 219 31
Gagel, Echter 373 33
Gaillardie 60 19
Galanterie-degen 355 63
~warenabteilung 271 62
Galaxis 3 35
Galeere 218 44-50
Galeerensklave 218 48
~sträfling 218 48
Galerie 315 16
~grab 328 16
Galette 169 16
Galgenmikrophon 311 40
Gallapfel 82 34
Galle 82 34
Gallen-aufnahme 27 4
~blase 20 11, 36
~blasengang 20 38
~gang 20 37-38
Gall-mücke 80 40
~wespe 82 33
Galopp, gestreckter 72 43-44
~, kurzer 72 42
~rennen 289 50
galvanischer Betrieb 178 1-6
Galvanisierbecken 178 4
Galvanoplastik 178
Gamaschenhose 29 45
Gambe 322 23
Gammastrahlung 1 33, 40
Gams 367 3
Ganasche 72 11
Gang 192 32, 34, 35, 36, 42, 43, 45
~art 289 7
~arten 72 39-44
~gewicht 110 29; 309 59
~grab 328 16
~schaltung 65 35; 188 31
~schaltungshebel 189 28
Ganner 359 15
Gans 73 34; 272 52
Gänse-blümchen 376 1
~feder 341 26

~fuß *Bot.* 61 25
~fuß *Sport* 288 74
~füßchen 342 26
~kresse 61 9
Ganser 73 34
Gänserich 73 34
Gänse-säger 359 15
~vogel 359 15-17
Gantelet 329 50
Ganter 73 34
ganze Note 320 13
~ Pause 320 21
Ganzholz 120 87
ganzrandig 370 43
Garage *Med.* 24 8
~ *Haus* 37 32, 79
Garageneinfahrt 37 52
Gär-aufsatz 349 7
~bottich 93 8
Garderobe *Wohnung* 41 1
~ *Theater* 315 5
~ *Nachtlokal* 318 1
Garderoben-ablage 48 34
~frau *Theater* 315 6
~frau *Nachtlokal* 318 2
~halle 315 5-11
~marke 315 7
~nummer 315 7
~raum 207 70
~spiegel 41 6
~ständer 266 12
~wand 41 1
Garderobiere 315 6
Gardine 44 14
Gardinen-abteilung 271 66
~leiste 44 15
~stoff 167 29
Gärkeller 93 7
Garmond 175 27
Garn 164 53, 56; 167 17, 36
~aufwicklung 170 44
Garnele 369 12
Garnierung 222 62u.63
Garn-knäuel 183 11
~kötzer 163 2
~meterzähler 165 28
~nummernfeinheit 164 40
~rolle 103 12
~scheibe 166 49
Garratlokomotive 210 64
Gärraum 97 72
Garten, englischer 272 41-72
~ammer 361 7
~bank 272 42
~baubetrieb 55 1-51
~bauer 55 20
~baugehilfe 55 45
~baugehilfin 55 46
~baumeister 55 20
~baumschule 55 3
~besen 56 3
~blume 60 19
~erdbeere 58 16
~erde 55 15
~fuchsschwanz 60 21
~gerät 56
~gerbera 51 26
~hecke 51 9
~hippe 56 9
~krähe 361 3
~laube 52 14
~leiter 52 8
~leuchte 37 38
~liege 51 2
~mauer 37 37
~messer 56 9
~nelke 60 7
~rittersporn 60 13
~rotschwänzchen 360 3
~schädling 80
~schirm 37 48
~schlauch 37 42; 56 27
~schubkarren 56 47

~spinne 358 45
~spritze 56 24
~stiefmütterchen 60 2
~stuhl 37 49
~teich 51 16
~tisch 37 50
~treppe 37 39
~weg 51 14; 52 23
~zaun 52 10
~zwiebel 57 24
Gärthermometer 93 9
Gärtner *Beruf* 55 20
~ *Vögel* 361 7
Gärtnerei 55 1-51
Gärwagen 97 73
Gas *Erdöl* 146 9
~ *Auto* 191 46
~abscheider 145 28
~anschluß 261 24
~austritt 156 16
~ballon 288 63
~brenner 139 3, 48
~drehgriff 189 29
~durchlauferhitzer 126 12
~entnahme 350 63
~entwicklungsapparat 350 59
~feuerzeug 107 30
~flaschenkasten 278 53
~gerät 126 12-25
~griff 188 30
Gashebel *Auto* 191 94
~ *Flugzeug* 230 30; 288 15
~sperre 85 17
Gas-heizkammer 147 28
~herd 39 12
~kanal 152 12
~kappe 12 30
~kocher 278 33
~kompressor 156 26
~kühlaggregat 146 27
~kühler 156 19
~kühlung 156 29
~leitung *Erdöl* 145 29
~leitung *Hütt.* 147 18, 27
~leitung *Straße* 198 21
~maske 270 40
~maskenfilter 270 57
~ofen 126 25
~ölfraktion 145 42
Gasometer 144 12
Gas-pedal 191 46, 94
~regulierung 350 6
~rohr 83 14, 35
~sammelbehälter 156 25
~sammelleitung 156 17
~sauger 156 21
~schlauch 141 9
~schmiedeofen 140 11
Gast 266 25
Gas-tankleichter 221 94
~trennanlage 145 69
~trocknung 156 30
Gastseite 207 78
Gas-turbine 209 9, 17
~turbinensteuerschrank 209 16
~turbinentriebkopf 209 8
~turbinentriebzug 209 1
~uhr 126 5
~ und Wasserinstallateur 126 1
~versorgungsregulierung 27 41
~waschflasche 261 32; 350 58
~wasser 156 39
~zähler 156 31
~zufuhr 139 54
~zuführung 140 12
~zuführungsrohr 350 2
Gatter *Forstw.* 84 7
~ *Spinnerei* 164 53
~ *Sport* 289 8
~rahmen 157 8

Gaube 38 7
Gauch 359 30
Gauchheil, Roter 61 27
~, Rotes 61 27
Gaucho 306 31
Gaumen, harter 19 20
~, weicher 19 21
~mandel 19 23
~segel 19 21
Gaupe 38 7
Gautscher 173 49
Gaze Med. 22 58
~ Buchb. 183 32; 185 20
~rollenhalter 185 19
G-Dur 320 56
Geäfter 88 23, 57
Geäse 88 13
Gebälk 334 52
Gebände 355 22
Gebärmutter 20 79
~höhle 20 80
Gebäudeteil 335 43
Gebein 17 1-29
Gebende 355 22
Gebetbuch 330 62
Gebets·mühle 353 29
~turm 337 13
Gebinde 84 35
Gebirgs·bahn 308 39
~bewegungen 12 4-20
Gebiß 19 16-18
~, künstliches 24 25
Gebläse Landmaschinen 64
  15
~ Schädlingsbek. 83 49
~ Kürschner 131 10
~ Wärmepumpe 155 14
~ Papier 172 4
~ Flugzeug 232 34
~brenner 350 9
~einstellung 191 83
geblimpte Filmkamera 313
  15
Gebräch 88 53
Gebrech 88 53
Gebühren·anzeiger 237 16
~stempelabdruck 236 58
gebunden 321 33
Geburtszange 26 53
Geck 306 33
Gecko 364 36
gedackte Lippenpfeife 326 34
Gedankenstrich 342 23
Gedeck 44 5; 45 3-12; 266 27
gedeckter Güterwagen 213 14
Gedenkemein 60 2
Gedenk·kapelle 331 12
~platte 331 14
~stein 331 14, 26
~tafel 331 14
Gedränge 292 20
gedrechselte Holzware 135 19
Gefahrenzone 2 50
Gefährt 186 1-54
Gefäß 328 13
~flöte 324 32
~förderanlage 144 25
Gefechts·linie 294 9
~turm 259 31, 43, 44
gefiedert, paarig 370 41
~, unpaarig 370 42
gefingert 370 39
Geflecht 136 4
Geflügel 73 19-36
~haltung 74
~marke 74 55
Gefrier·gemüse 99 61
~gut 99 58-61
~schrank 39 7
Gegen·bindungsstelle 171 28
~blasen 162 25
~capstan 117 35
~dreier 302 17

~fanger 325 31
Gegengewicht Landw. 67 37
~ Optik 113 19
~ Bau 119 33
~ Tech. 139 34
~ Wasserbau 217 76
~ Hafen 226 50
~ Infotechnik 242 50
~ Mil. 255 78
Gegenkontakt 142 35
Gegenlichttubus 313 5
Gegen·liste 263 27
~mutter 143 30
~schlaghammer 139 5
~seil 214 46
~seilmuffe 214 74
~sprechanlage 244 5
~sprechgerät 22 34
Gegentaktspur 312 45
Gegen·wende 302 18
~winkel 346 12
Gegner 294 10; 299 40
Gehacktes 96 16
gehalten 321 30
Gehänge 214 54
~bolzen 214 72
Gehäuse Meteorol. 10 18
~ Masch. 143 79
~ Kraftwerk 153 37
~ Textil 168 17
~ Mil. 255 10, 33
~ Film 312 48
~ Chem. 349 26
~ Zool. 357 29
~abdeckung 249 27
~deckel 143 80
~schlüssel 109 11
~verriegelung 313 33
Gehbelag 123 41
Gehen am Seil 300 22-27
Gehör 88 44
~gang 17 34, 58
~knöchelchen 17 61
Gehörn 88 29-31
Gehör·nerv 17 64
~organ 17 56-65
~schutzkapsel 84 23
Gehrung 124 4; 133 19
Gehrungs·lade 132 43
~säge 124 30
~schmiege 120 81
~sprossenstanze 124 7
~stoßlade 124 31
~winkel 120 82
Geh·steig 198 9
~weg 37 60; 198 9
~wegpflaster 198 5
Geige 323 1
Geigen·bogen 323 12
~bogenbezug 323 15
~hals 323 2
~körper 323 3
~korpus 323 3
~steg 323 5
Geigerzähler 2 19
Geiser 11 21
Geisha 353 39
Geisipodes 334 14
Geison 334 12
Geiß Zool. 73 14
~ Jagd 88 34
Geißblatt, Echtes 374 13
Geißfuß 339 20; 340 9
Geister·bahn 308 5
~beschwörung 354 42
Geistlicher 330 22; 331 37;
  332 3, 22
gekerbt 370 46
Gelände·abbruch 11 50
~fahrt 290 33
~maschine 189 16
Geländer 37 19
Gelände·reifen 194 4

~ritt 289 16
Geländer·pfosten 38 29
~stab 123 51
Gelände·sport 290 24-28
~sportmotorrad 189 16
~verschiebung 11 50
Gelatinewalze 340 12
Geläuf 289 23
gelb 343 2
Gelb·ammer 361 6
~blühender Jasmin 373 4
~-Doppeldruckwerk 180 6-7
gelbe Karte 291 63
Gelbe Lupine 69 17
gelber Dotter 74 68
gelbe Rübe 57 17
Gelber Ziegenbart 381 32
Gelbe Schwertlilie 60 8
Gelb·filtereinstellung 116 44
~haubenkakadu 363 1
Geld 252
~betrag 196 4
~fach 271 6
~harke 275 5
~kasten 271 5
~kurstabelle 204 32
~schein 252 29-39
~schrank 246 22
~schub 271 5
~stück 252 1-28
~wechsel 233 51
~wechselautomat 204 22
~wechselschalter 250 10
~wechsler 197 33; 204 22
Gelege 80 30
Gelenk 100 68
~kopf 50 60
~lokomotive 210 64
~messer 85 20
~rille 291 29
~triebwagen 197 1, 13
~welle 64 40, 48; 67 16; 211
  51; 212 29, 83
~wellenanschluß 64 63
~zugriemen 291 25
Gelieger 329 88
Gelse 358 16
Gelt·reh 88 34
~tier 88 1
Gemeinde 330 29
Gemeine Akelei 60 10
~ Feldbohne 69 15
~ Jungfernrebe 374 16
~ Kornrade 61 6
~ Kuhschelle 375 5
~ Melde 61 24
~ Quecke 61 30
Gemeiner Beinwell 375 45
~ Buchsbaum 373 19
~ Delphin 367 24
~ Hecht 364 16
~ Hülsstrauch 374 9
~ Liguster 373 6
~ Pelikan 359 5
~ Schneeball 373 10
~ Spörgel 69 12
~ Tulpenbaum 374 1
Gemeines Hirtentäschel 61 9
~ Knaulgras 69 25
~ Kreuzkraut 61 12
Gemeine Stubenfliege 81 2
~ Wicke 69 18
Gemeinschaftssauna 281 18
Gemenge·eingabe 162 2
~trichter 162 13
Gemini 3 28; 4 55
Gemisch·hebel 230 31
~regler 230 31
~regulierhebel 288 16
~tank 188 28
Gemse 367 3
Gemüse·abteilung 99 80
~beet 52 26; 55 39

~behälter 96 51
~bohne 57 8
~garten 52 1-32
~konserve 96 27; 98 17
~korb 99 81
~löffel 45 74
~pflanze 57
~platte 45 33
~schale 39 4
~schüssel 45 25
~steige 55 43
~- und Obstgarten 52 1-32
~versandsteige 55 43
Generator 152 23; 153 26;
  154 15, 47, 53; 155 46; 223
  74
~anlage 146 2
~teil 114 66
Genick Anat. 16 21
~ Pferd 72 12
~fänger 87 42
~stück 71 10
Genua 284 16
Genußmittel 98 65-68; 99
  68-70
~pflanze, tropische 382
Geodäsie 14 46-62
Geographie 11; 12; 13
geographische Breite 14 6
~ Länge 14 7
Geologie 12 1-33
Geometrie 346; 347
~, elementare 346 1-58
~, euklidische 346 1-58
geometrische Form 260 79
geometrischer Körper 347
  30-46
geometrisches Zeichen 345
  21-24
Georgine 60 23
georgisch 341 4
Gepäck·abfertigung 204 4
~ablage 207 51; 208 27
~apsis 278 27
~aufbewahrung 233 39
~aufkleber 204 7
~ausgabe 233 38
~bandwagen 233 22
~bank 204 43
~fach 194 18
~halle 233 5
~raum Auto 194 13
~raum Eisenb. 208 15
~raum Flugzeug 257 19
~schein 204 8
~schiebekarren 205 32
~schließfach 204 21
~spinne 278 51
~träger Fahrrad 187 44
~träger Eisenb. 205 34
~tunneleinfahrt 233 6
Gepard 368 7
Gerade Eisenb. 203 49, 50
~ Sport 299 28
~ Math. 346 2-3, 5
Gerad·flügler 358 8
~führung 151 2, 53
Gerät 296 48-60; 297 15-32
~, landwirtschaftliches 66
Geräte, kirchliche 332 34-54
~, liturgische 332 34-54
~, optische 112; 113
~-Baugruppe 234 56
~brett 235 3
~halle 233 8
~haus 270 1
~kopf 116 41
~raum 37 32
~schuppen 52 3; 55 1
~tisch 212 31
~träger 177 58
~turnen 296; 297

~wagen 270 53
Gerätsteckdose 50 78
Geräuschorgel 238 35
Gericht 266 49, 67
Gerinne 91 41
Gerippe 17 1-29; 261 14
germanisches Ruderschiff
  218 1-6
Geröllband 300 4
Gerste 68 1, 26
~anlieferung 92 41
~einlauf 92 2
~elevator 92 33
~silo 92 31
Gertel 85 11
Geruchsverschluß 126 26
Gerüst Korbmacher 136 25
~ Bildhauerei 339 22
~bug 118 25
~diele 122 70
~eisen 339 24
~hebel 118 27
~helling 222 19-21
~knoten 118 30
~ständer 118 23
~stange 118 23
gesägt 370 44
~, doppelt 370 45
Gesamtschule 261 1-45
Gesangbuch 330 30
Gesäß 16 40
~backe 16 40
~falte 16 42
~muskel 18 60
Gesätz 332 32
Geschabtes 96 16
Geschäfts-bote 236 17
~brief 245 33; 246 7; 248 30
~flugzeug 231 3, 7
~führer 267 7
~reisender 209
~- und Reiseflugzeug 231 3, 7
Geschicklichkeitswettbewerb
  290 32
Geschirr 71 7-25
~schrank 39 8; 44 26
~serie 40 12-16
~spülautomat 39 40
~spüle 39 35
~spüler 39 40
~spülmaschine 39 40
~stapel 266 11
~wagen 39 41
Geschlechtsorgan, männl. 20
  66-77
~, weibl. 20 79-88
geschlossene Gesellschaft 267
  40-43
Geschmeidigmachen 169 22
geschmolzener Schnee 304
  30
Geschoß-spitze 328 2
~treppe 123 42-44
Geschütz 218 50; 259 52
~pforte 218 59
~turm 258 29, 47; 259 52
Geschwaderabzeichen 256 2
Geschwindigkeit 203 41
Geschwindigkeits · ankünde-
  tafel 203 43
~anzeige 203 18; 211 35
~anzeiger 197 31
~kennziffer 203 37
~messer Eisenb. 212 9
~messer Flugzeug 230 2
~regulierung 179 29
~schreiber 210 54
~signal 203 44
~voranzeiger 203 19
Ges-Dur 320 68
Gesellschaft, geschlossene
  267 40-43
Gesellschafts-anzug 33 13

~raum 223 26
~saal 267 39
~spiel 276
~wagen 186 33
Gesenk-platte 140 14
~schmiede 139
~schmiedepresse 139 18
~schmiede- und
  Kalibrierpresse 139 18
Gesicht Anat. 16 4-17
~ Pferd 72 5
Gesichts-kompresse 106 25
~maske Med. 27 48
~maske Sport 292 11
~maske Karneval 306 7
~muskel, mimischer 19 6
~schutz 292 25
~urne 328 38
Gesims-band 334 57
~schalung 122 42
Gesneriengewächs 53 7
gespanntes Grundwasser 12
  21
Gespinst-motte 80 5
~netz 80 7
Gestalt, symbolische 327 20
Gestänge 179 20
~bühne 145 5
Gestein, anstehendes 158 3
~, gelöstes 158 4
~, undurchlässiges 12 23
Gesteins-bohrer 158 11
~brocken 6 15
~schicht, undurchlässige 13
  78
Gestell Forstw. 84 1
~ Korbmacher 136 22
~arbeit 136 22-24
~auswahl 111 5
~förderung 144 23
~ständer 111 5
Gestirn 3 9-48
Gestricke 171 30-48
Gestück 123 12
Gestühl 330 28
geteilte Blätter 370 39-42
getragen 321 29
Getränke-ausschank 308 3
~bude 308 3
~fach 266 59
~gondel 99 71
Getreide 68 1-37
~art 68 1-37
~blatt 68 8, 19
~ernte 63 31-41
~feld 63 32
~halm 68 5
~korn 68 13
~motte 81 29
~mottenraupe 81 30
~schädling 81 27
Getriebe Gartengeräte 56 20
~ Landw. 64 50, 65; 67 21
~ Walz. 148 63
~ Spinnerei 163 29
~ Straßenbau 201 11
~ Eisenb. 209 18
~ Wasserbau 217 48
~eingangswelle 232 58
~kasten Landw. 65 79
~kasten Drechsler 135 4
~kasten Spinnerei 163 57; 164
  2, 33, 39
~kasten Textil 168 10
~öl 209 15; 212 36, 43
~öltemperaturmesser 212 20
~regulierung 212 67
~schalter 134 46
Gewaff 88 54
Gewand 355 19
Gewändeportal 335 24
Gewebe 166 12; 168 8, 9, 22,
  64

~ablegevorrichtung 168 35
~befestigung 168 24
~bindung 171 1-29
~bügeln 168 38
~druckmaschine 168 53
~entwässerung 168 14
~filmdruck 168 59
~oberfläche 168 31
~schermaschine 168 42
~schnitt 171 14, 25
~tier 357 13-39
~trockenmaschine 168 21
Gewehr 86 30; 255 16
~, kombiniertes 87 23
~anschlag 305 72
~kolben 255 24
~lauf, gezogener 87 34
~scheibe 305 30, 32
~schießen 305 26
~schloß 87 9
Geweih 88 5-11
~stange 328 5
Gewicht-belastung 168 2
~heben 299 1-5
~heber 299 2
Gewichtl 88 29-31
Gewichtsklassensortierung
  74 52
Gewiegtes 96 16
gewimpert 370 49
Gewinde Landw. 67 38
~ Masch. 143 16, 68
~backen 140 61
~band 126 75
~bohrer 140 60
~eisen 140 60
~kopf 187 75
~schneideisen 108 15
~schneidkluppe 126 85
~schneidmaschine 125 27;
  126 86
~steigung 149 9
~stift 143 48
~strähler 135 14
Gewinn Rummelplatz 308 48
~ Math. 345 7
~anteilschein 251 18
Gewirke 171 30-48
Gewitter 9 38
~front 287 24
~segeln 287 23
~wolke 7 2
Gewölbe 79 1
~form 336 38-50
~rippe 335 31
Gewürzglas 39 32
~nelke 382 28
~nelkenbaum 382 26
~packung 99 67
~pflanze, tropische 382
~regal 39 31
~ständer 47 29
Geysir 11 21
gezähnt 370 47
Gezeiten-kraftwerk 155 37
~tafel 280 7
GFK 130 26
GFP 130 17
Gicht-bühne 147 4
~gasabzug 147 13
~glocke 147 6
Giebel 37 15; 121 5
~dreieck 334 3
~fenster 335 49
~scheibe 122 25
~seite 37 15
~verzierung 334 34
Gieren 230 69
Gierfähre 216 1
Gießer 148 8
Gieß-form 161 15
~kanne 51 21
~kannenbrause 55 28

~kern 178 18
~kolonne 148 13
~maschine 174 39
~mund 178 17
~pfannenschnabel 147 43
~schale 178 22
~tisch 148 24
~werk 174 25
Gift-blase 77 13
~drüse 77 14
~leger öhre 83 31
~pflanze 379
~pilz 379 10-13
~reizker 379 13
~schlange 364 40
~weizen 83 13
Gigant 327 37
Gigantocypris agassizi 369 1
Gigboot 283 26-33
Gigerl 306 33
Gigvierer 283 26-33
Gilge 60 12
Gimpel 360 5
Gimpenhäkelei 102 28
Gipfel 12 40
Gipfelung 11 6
Gips Tapezierer 128 2
~ Bildhauerei 339 29
~ Kristallkunde 351 24, 25
~becher 134 18
Gipser 118 83
Gips-guß 339 4
~lager 160 13
~modell 339 4
~pulver 339 29
~sack 260 85
~zerkleinerungsmaschine
  160 14
Giraffe 367 4
Giraffenhaus 356 10
Girant 250 27
Girat 250 26
Girlande Karneval 306 5
~ Kunst 335 54
gis-Moll 320 60
Gitarre 318 8; 324 12
Gitarrenspieler 318 9
Gitarrist 318 9
Gitter-drehbrücke 215 63
~gang 307 51
~leiter 296 21
~mantelschornstein 221 84
~mast Kraftwerk 152 36
~mast Mil. 258 18
~spektrograph 5 5
~stab 272 34
~struktur 1 9-14
~stütze 214 31
~teilung 115 61
~tierchen 357 7
~tor 272 31
~träger 235 12
~wand 62 26; 75 5
~ziegel 159 23
Gladiole 51 28; 60 11
Glas, farbiges 260 68
~abdeckung 155 33
~band 162 10
~bläser 162 38
~brechzange 124 19
~dach 55 5
~deckel 269 56
Glaser 124 8
~diamant 124 25
~ecke 124 24
Gläserfassung 111 10
Glaser-hammer 124 18
~kasten 124 9
Glaserker 37 70
Glaserkitt 124 17
Gläser-regal 266 9; 267 65;
  317 5
~stand 274 16

Glaser-werkstatt 124 1
~zange 124 19
Glasfaser 151 48
~radierer 151 47
glasfaserverstärktes
    Kunstharz 130 26
~ Polyesterharz 130 17
Glasgewebe 130 29
~hafen 162 46
~herstellung 162
~kolben 127 57
~körper 19 46
~machen 162 38-47
~macher 162 38
~macherpfeife 162 39
~macherstuhl 162 45
~malerei 330 15
~matte 130 29
~mosaikbild 260 69
~papier 135 25
~platte 124 16
~rolle 169 16
~sand 340 48
~schaukasten 356 15
~scheibe 54 9; 124 16
~scherbe 124 10
~schmelze 162 16
~schmelzofen 162 49
~schmelzwanne 162 1
~schneider 124 25-26
~schwamm 369 7
~trage 124 9
~tür 44 18
glasvertafelt 5 19
Glätt·ahle 109 8
~balken 201 14
~bohle 201 14
Glatt·decksrumpf 258 2; 259
    22
~eis 304 19
~hafer, Hoher 69 22
~nase 366 9
Glätt·presse 183 20
~scheibe 128 11
Glatt·stoßen 249 56
~strich 119 9
Glättwalze 173 26
Glatze 34 21
Glatzkopf 34 20
Gläubiger 330 61
gleich, annähernd 345 17
Gleichflügler 358 3
Gleichgewichts·brechen 299
    13
~organ 17 56-65
~stange 307 42
Gleichheitszeichen 344 23
Gleichlauf·filter 311 27
~kegel 192 33
Gleichrichter Schmied 138 30
~ Druck 178 2
~ Film 312 18
Gleichstrom-Regelmotor 150
    9
Gleichung 345 9
~, identische 345 5
Gleis 202 1-38; 205 59-61
~anlage 225 62
~bildstelltisch 203 66
~bildstellwerk 203 65
~bremse 206 48
~hemmschuh 206 49
~kraftwagen 213 32
~räumer 210 34
~überweg 205 15
~waage 206 41
Gleit·boot 286 38-41, 38-44
~hang 13 58
~pose 89 48
~schiene 226 39
~schuh 200 33
~schutzkette 304 10
~stuhl 202 22

Gletscher 300 22
~bach 12 52
~brille 300 18
~eis 12 48-56
~spalte 12 50; 300 23
~tisch 12 56
~tor 12 51
Glied Med. 21 10
~ Math. 345 11
~, männliches 20 66
Glieder 16 43-54
~füßer 358 1-23
~puppe 338 31
~tier 358
~wurm 357 20
Gliedmaße 82 6-8
Gliedmaßen 16 43-54
Globus 42 13
Glocke 224 75; 263 4; 294 35,
    38, 43; 331 9; 332 52
Glocken·becher 328 14
~becherkultur 328 14
~blume 60 10; 375 14
~heide 377 19
~turm 337 8
Gloxinie 53 7
Glücks·käfer 358 37
~klee 69 5
~rad 308 45
~spiel 275 1-33
Glüh·birne 127 56, 69
~farbe 343 16
~kerze 190 66
~lampe 127 56
~lampenlicht 127 17
~platte 108 37
g-Moll 320 64
Gnadenkapelle 331 12
Go-Kart Spielplatz 273 33
~ Sport 305 83
Go-Karting 305 82
Gold Heraldik 254 24
~ Kristallkunde 351 6
~after 80 28
~ammer 361 6
~blume 61 7
~draht 108 3
Goldenes Frauenhaar 377 17
Gold·eule 362 14
~hähnchen 361 10
~hämmerchen 361 10
~kissen 183 6
~knöpfchen 61 31
~köpfchen 361 10
~krone 24 28
~messer 183 7
~mundstück 107 13
~münze 36 37; 252 1-28
~regen 374 32
~schmied 108 17
~schmiedeladen 215 33
~schnittmacher 183 2
~- und Silberschmied 108
~- und Silberwaage 108 35
~waage 108 35
~wurz 60 10
Golf 293 79-93
~ball 293 89
~grün 293 82
~spiel 293 79-93
~spieler 293 83
~strom 14 30
~wagen 293 85
Goller 355 39
Gondel Supermarkt 99 23
~ Sport 288 64
Gong 299 46
Gording 219 71
Gorilla 368 16
Gösch 223 54
~stock 223 53; 258 4
Gose 93 26
Gosse 91 13

Gössel 73 34
Gotik 335 22-41
gotische Schrift 342 1
Gott, indischer 337 19
Gottesacker 331 21-41
Gottesgiebchen 358 37
Gouachefarbe 338 17
Grab 331 23
~beigabe 328 34
Graben 67 13
~bruch 12 11
Grab·gabel 66 22
~heuschrecke 81 7
~hügel 331 24
~kreuz 331 25
~mal 331 26
~nische 331 60
~stätte Kirche 331 23
~stätte Kunst 337 16
~stein 331 26
~stelle 331 23
~stichel Drechsler 135 24
~stichel Graphik 340 20
~zahn 200 6
Gradbogen 224 2
Gradeinteilung Schule 260 39
~ Film 313 14
Gradier·wärter 274 5
~werk Landkarte 15 32
~werk Kurbad 274 1
Gradnetz 14 1-7
Grafenkrone 254 45
Grammophon 309 31
~apparat 309 31
~gehäuse 309 35
~nadel 309 33
~platte 309 32
Granat 351 7
~apfel 384 16
Granate 255 26
Granatoeder 351 7
Grande 306 26
Grand-Tourisme-Wagen 193
    32
Granierstahl 340 19
Granne 68 12
Grapefruit 384 23
graphische Darstellung 151
    11
~ Kunst 340
~ Werkstatt 340 27-64
Graphit 1 54
~mine 151 46
~tiegel 108 10
Gras Korbmacher 136 26
~ Spiele 276 43
~bahnrennen 290 24-28
~band 200 4; 300 4
~büschel 375 44
Grasen 276 43
Gras·fangkorb 56 29
~halm 370 83-85
~hüpfer 358 8
Grat Bau 121 12
~ Bergsport 300 21
Grätenschritt 301 26
Grätsch·sitz 296 30
~sprung 295 37
~winkelstütz 295 18
Grat·sparren 121 62
~ziegel 122 2
Grau·drossel 361 13
~leiter 343 15
Graupe 98 35
Graupeln 9 35
Graureiher 359 18
Gravier-kugel 108 34
~nadel 340 16
~system 177 66
Gravis 342 31
Gravur 36 41
Green 293 82
Greif 327 11

~arm 2 47
~bein 358 41
Greifenklaue 327 13
Greifer 174 22
~system 180 65
~wagen 180 56
Greif·vogel 362 1-13
~zange Atom 2 44
~zange Graphik 340 50
~zirkel 135 18
Greiskraut 61 12
Grendel 65 9
Grenz·anhydrit 154 67
~horizont 13 21
~kreis 3 5
~lehrdorn 149 56
~rachenlehre 149 59
~rain 63 3
Grenzschicht·schneide 256 6
~-Trennzunge 257 13
~zaun 231 8
Grenzstein 63 2
Gretchenfrisur 34 31
Greyhound 70 24
Griebs 58 59
Grieche 355 3
Griechin 355 1
griechisch 341 15
griechischer Zug 315 1
griechisch-römischer
    Ringkampf 299 6-9
Grieß 98 36
Griessäule 65 8
Grießwärtel 329 75
Griff Messergriff 45 51
~ Landw. 66 17
~ Schlosser 140 34
~ Wagen 186 12
~ Fahrrad 187 3
~ Schule 260 9
~ Sport 294 41; 305 80
~art 296 40-46
~brett 323 21; 324 8
Griffel 58 42; 59 15; 68 34;
    370 55; 373 5; 378 5
~kasten 309 73
Griff·hebel 247 42
~loch Büro 247 39
~loch Sport 305 16
~loch Mus. 323 33; 324 34
~saite 324 24
~stange 167 22
~stück 255 6, 38
Grill 40 32
~spieß 40 33
Grimmdarm 20 19, 20, 21
Grindel 65 9, 71
Grob·einstellung 148 65
~feile 140 8
~kokssieberei 156 14
~kreiselbrecher 158 19
~schmutz 50 18
~schmutzschlauch 50 84
~stoffbütte 172 59
~trieb 112 4
~- und Feinkokssieberei 156
    14
~verteilrinne 236 36
Grönländer 283 4
Groom 186 27
Groschen 252 13
Groß 275 19
~baum 219 44
~bildkamera 112 25; 114 61
~Bramsaling 219 53
~bramsegel 219 25
~Bramstagsegel 219 25
~bramstenge 219 7
~buchstabe 175 11; 249 3
Große Fetthenne 377 9
große Hostie 332 35
Große Köcherfliege 358 12
große Oktave 321 44

größer als 345 19
Großer Bär 3 29
großer Hahn 88 72
Großer Hund 3 14
~ Kohlweißling 80 47
~ Ozean 14 19
~ Pimpernell 69 28
~ Vogelfuß 69 11
~ Wagen 3 29
~ Wiesenknopf 69 28
große Sekunde 321 7
~ Septime 321 12
~ Sexte 321 11
Großes Springkraut 377 11
Große Stubenfliege 81 2
große Terz 321 8
Großfeld-Metallmikroskop 112 23
~mikroskop 112 54
~stereomikroskop 112 40, 61
Großfläche 67 18
Großformat-balgenkamera 114 49
~handkamera 114 36
~kamera 112 36
Groß-hirn 17 42; 18 22
~kabine 214 52
~kaffeemaschine 265 2
~kern 357 11
~kopf 80 1
~-Marssaling 219 52
~marsstenge 219 6
~mast 218 40; 219 5-7; 220 22
~maul 369 10, 13
~-Oberbramrah 219 42
~-Oberbramsegel 219 65
~-Obermarsrah 219 40
~-Obermarssegel 219 63
~rah 218 37; 219 38
Großraum 208 9
~abteil 207 61
~bagger 159 3
~büro 248 1-48
~flugzeug 231 17
~kabine 214 52
~-Langstrecken-
verkehrsflugzeug 231 14
~lore 158 14
~wagen 207 59
Groß-Royalrah 219 43
~-Royalsegel 219 66
~-Royalstagsegel 219 26
~schot 284 28
~segel 218 33; 219 61; 220 11; 284 46; 285 2
~segelhals 284 37
~segelkopf 284 47
~specht 359 27
~spitz 70 20
~stenge 219 4
~-Stengestagsegel 219 24
~-Unterbramrah 219 41
~-Unterbramsegel 219 64
~-Untermarsrah 219 39
~-Untermarssegel 219 62
~untermast 219 5
~vieh 73 1-2
Grotesk 342 7
~flugmodell 288 91
~schrift 342 7
Grotte 272 1
Grubber 65 55
Grübchen 16 16
Grube Bergb. 144 1-51
~ Kirche 331 34
Gruben-betrieb 144 21-51
~lüfter 144 16
~wand 199 14
grün Heraldik 254 29
~ Farbe 343 8
Grün Spiele 276 43
~ Sport 293 82

~alge 378 43
Grund-ablaß Wasserbau 217 62
~ablaß Wasservers. 269 34
~angeln 89 20-31
~birne 68 38
~blatt 375 9, 15, 30; 383 2
~brett 116 27
Gründel 65 9
Grund-fläche 347 35, 39
~gewicht 90 10
~hobel 132 26
Grundier-mittel 128 6
~pinsel 338 9
Grund-lawine 304 1
~linie Sport 293 3 bis 10
~linie Math. 346 27
~linienrichter 293 26
~platte Schlösser 140 36
~platte Walz. 148 56
~platte Textil 167 34
~platte Mil. 255 46
~profil 229 45
~rahmen 168 15
~rechnungsart 344 23-26
~riß 207 76
~schicht 7 7
~schule 260 1-85
~spieler 293 60
~stellung 294 18; 295 1
~sucherblei 89 91
~tau 90 18
~teller 45 3
~- und Hauptschule 260 1-85
Gründungspfahl 5 28
Grundverbindung 171 30-48
Grundwasser, artesisches 12 21
~, gespanntes 12 21
~spiegel 269 1, 42, 63
~strom 269 3
~zufluß 155 2
Grund-wert 345 7
~zahl 344 5; 345 2, 6
~zustand 1 18
Grüner Leguan 364 32
grüner Salat
Grünes Heupferd 358 8
Grün-fläche 37 76; 272 36
~kern 68 25
~kohl 57 34
~lauge 172 41
~laugenvorwärmer 172 43
~malz 92 23
~reizker 381 29
~schling 361 6
~schmuck 330 48
Gruppe 289 41
Gruppen-anordnung 260 3
~schalter 238 42
~unterricht 242 1
Grus 3 42
G-Saite 323 9
G-Schlüssel 320 8
GT-Wagen 193 32
Guanako 366 30
Guckloch 41 29
Guckummer 57 13
Gugelhupf 97 33
Guillochenwerk 252 38
Guiro 324 60
Gulden 252 19
Güllesilo 62 13
Gully 268 8
Gummi-andruckrolle 117 35
~auflage 191 13
~bande 277 16
~baum 383 33
~bindung 286 57-58
~block 177 6
~drucktuch 180 54, 79
~fuß 114 45
~haut 283 58

~knüppel 264 19
~kolbenkappe 87 14
~lager 192 67, 82
~lösung 340 49
~noppenband 64 79
~ring 280 32
~scheibenwalze 64 82
~schutz 289 32
~stift 187 84
~teller 134 22
~walze 182 8
~wulstabdichtung 208 12
~wulstdichtung 207 8
~wulstübergang 194 45
~zug 297 13
~zylinder 180 24, 37, 54, 63
Gundelrebe, Efeublätterige 375 18
Gundermann 375 18
Gurgel 16 19
Gurke 57 13; 99 83
Gurt 230 56
~ausleger 185 13
~bogen 335 18
Gürtel 31 10; 32 39; 299 15; 352 38
~bund 31 41
~scheibe 328 24
~schnalle 31 12
Gurt-förderer 156 2
~gesims 335 52
~sitz 303 2
~zeug 288 33
Gußerker 329 23
gußgekapselter Paketschalter 127 18
Guß-glas 124 6
~rohr 37 14
~stück 148 42
Gut 15 94
~, laufendes 219 67-71
~, stehendes 219 10-19
Güter-abfertigung 206 26
~bahnhof 206
~boden 206 26-39
~bodenarbeiter 206 33
~halle 206 7
~schuppen 206 7
~umschlag 226 7
~umschlaganlage 226 1
~wagen 213 8, 14
~zugdienst 212 1
Gutseite 149 60
Guttaperchabaum 383 37
Gutzgauch 359 30
Gymkhana 290 32
Gymnasialzweig 261 1-45
Gymnasium 261 1-45
Gymnastik 297 33-50
~anzug 297 51
~ball 297 34
~band 297 49
~keule 297 38
~kleidung 297 51-52
~reifen 297 46
~schuh 296 63; 297 52
~stab 297 41
gynäkologisches Untersuchungsinstrument 23 3-21
Gyre 351 4

H

Haar 16 3
~, aufgestecktes 34 28
~, offenes 34 1
~beutel 34 4
~beutelperücke 34 4
~bürste 28 7; 105 10
~clip 105 11
~festiger 106 23

~filzhut 35 15
~fixativ 105 24
~flügler 358 12
~harfe 10 9
~kelch 378 11
~knoten 34 29
~kranz 34 32
~lineal 140 56
~nadel 301 69
~pinsel 338 7
~schmuck 355 82
~schnecke 34 38
~schneidemantel 106 4
~schneidemaschine 106 32
~schneider 105 21
~schneideschere 105 7; 106 34
~schnitt 106 3
~seite 131 12, 17
~sieb 260 66
~spray 105 24
~stern 369 3
~tracht 34 1-25, 27-38; 354 9
~trockner 106 22
~trocknung 106 24
~waschanlage 106 11
~waschbecken 105 29
~waschmittel 106 20
~waschzusatz 106 10
~wasser 106 10
~wild 86 35
Habicht 362 10
~artige 362 10-13
~schwamm 381 24
Habitus 382 53
Hack-bank 96 57
~brett 322 32, 34, 35
Hacke 19 63
Hacken 19 63
~stiel 66 2
Hackerkamm 163 39
Hack-fleisch 96 16
~frucht 68 38-45
~maschine 172 1
Häckseltrommel 64 34
Haderer 88 54
Hafen 225; 226
~amt 225 36
~bahn 225 21
~betrieb 227 13
~fähre 225 11
~industrieanlage 225 71
~krankenhaus 225 26
~untertunnelung 225 55
~viertel 225 1
~zollamt 225 6
Hafer 68 1
~distel 61 32
~flocke 98 37
~krähe 361 2
~rispe 68 27
Haffmöwe 359 14
Haft-ballen 77 9
~organ Zool. 81 36
~organ Bot. 378 50
~scheibe 364 26
~zeher 364 36
Hagebutte 370 100
Hagel 9 36
~schnur 74 63
Häher 361 1
Hahn Landw. 62 37
~ Zool. 73 21
~ Eisenb. 210 55
~ Chem. 349 5, 22
~, großer 88 72
~, kleiner 88 66
Hähnchen 96 24; 266 56
Hahnenfuß, Scharfer 375 8
~gewächs 60 13
Hahnen-kamm 73 22
~kopf 327 35
~tritt 74 65
Hahnstopfen 350 44

Hai 364 1
~fisch 364 1
Hainbuche 371 63
Häkelgabel 102 29
Haken *Jagd* 88 54; 89 79-87
~ *Schuhmacher* 100 62
~ *Motorroller* 188 54
~ *Sport* 299 32; 305 46
~, versteckter 89 75
~blatt 121 87, 88
~bogen 89 81
~einsetzmaschine 100 53
~gurt 270 44
~kranz 81 38
~leiter 270 16
~löser 89 40
~schnabel 362 6
~schraube 202 10
~spitze 89 80
~wurf 305 18
halbbedeckt 9 22
Halbbrücke 215 66
halbe Note 320 14
~ Pause 320 22
halber Wind 285 11
halbfett 175 3
Halb-holz 120 88
~insel 13 5
~kreis 346 46
~kugelendspant 235 48
~kuppel 334 73
halbmast 253 6
Halb-messer 346 47
~mond 4 4, 6; 253 19
~perücke 34 2
~pfeiler 335 46
~rock 32 14
~rohreissschraube 300 40
~rundfeile 140 29
~schatten 4 34
~schrankenanlage 202 45
~schuh 101 31, 33; 352 18
~spieler 292 42
halbstock[s] 253 6
Halbton 320 51, 53
~erhöhung 320 50
~erniedrigung 320 52
Halb-weltdame 306 37
~zeug 148 66
~zeugzurichtung 148 66-68
~zoll-Magnetband 243 5
Halèr 252 27
Halfagras 136 26
Halle 267 18-26
Hallen-bad 281 1-9
~bahn 290 1
~handball 292 1
~handballspiel 292 1
~rampe 206 9
~tor 206 37
Hallimasch 381 28
Hallraum 311 31
~lautsprecher 311 32
~mikrophon 311 33
Hallstattzeit 328 21-40
Halm *Landw.* 68 6
~ *Schlosser* 140 33
Halma-brett 276 24
~figur 276 28
~spiel 276 26-28
~stein 276 28
Halm-knoten 68 7
~stück 383 63
~teiler 64 1
Halogenleuchte 177 31
Halothanbehälter 26 26
Hals *Anat.* 16 19-21; 19 1-13
~ *Pferd* 72 15
~ *Jagd* 88 3
~ *Fleischerei* 95 6
~ *Masch.* 143 64
~ *Sport* 294 53
~ *Mus.* 323 2; 324 7, 18

~ *Chem.* 350 38
~ausschnitt 30 34
~berge 329 43
~blutader 18 2
Halsen 285 26, 28
Hals-kette 352 14
~kragen *Vorgeschichte* 328 25
~kragen *Kirche* 332 6
~krause 306 20
~muskel 19 12
~riemen 71 30
~ring 36 16; 328 26
~schild 82 4; 358 29
~schlagader 18 1
~schutz 294 14
~tuch 32 40; 319 38
Halsung 70 13
Halswirbel 17 2
Halte-gestänge 165 6; 167 38
~griff 28 50
~haken 324 67
~kette 74 14
~leine 288 66
~mannschaft 270 17
~platz 203 31-32
~punkt 203 25, 33
~punkttafel 203 33
Hälter 89 1
Halterung *Astr.* 5 2
~ *Med.* 27 22
Halte-seil *Bestrahlungsgerät* 2
   30
~seil *Sport* 288 66
~stange 287 46
Haltestelle 15 27
Haltestellen-insel 197 35
~schild 197 36; 268 26
Halte-tafel 203 31-32
~ *und* Ruhezeichen 321 25
~vorrichtung 157 47
~zeichen 321 25
Haltlinie 268 50
Haltung 296 22-39
Haltungsstör 217 31
Haltzylinderpresse 181 20
Hammel 73 13
Hammer *Anat.* 17 61
~ *Heimwerken* 134 7
~ *Schmied* 137 26
~ *Tech.* 139 12
~ *Sport* 298 42; 300 37
~ *Mus.* 325 3, 9
~bär 137 10; 139 12
~brecher 160 2
~filz 325 24
~griff 298 45
~griffhaltung 298 46
~klavier 325 1
~kopf *Sport* 298 43
~kopf *Mus.* 325 24
~kopfschraube 143 41
~kran 222 7
~leiste 325 15, 26
~lötkolben 125 5
~schlag 293 78
~ständer 139 16
~stiel 325 25
Hammer und Sichel 253 21
Hammer-werk 325 3
~wurf 298 42-47
Hamster 366 16
Hand 16 47; 17 15-17; 19
   64-83
~apparat 237 7
~apparatschnur 237 14
Handarbeit 102
Hand-auflage 112 58
~ball 292 1
~ballensicherung 255 14
~ballspiel 292 1
~ballspieler 292 2
~belichtungsmesser 114 56
~besen 38 36; 50 53

~bibliothek 262 17
~bohrmaschine 140 13
~bohrmaschine, elektrische
   56 19
~brause 49 41; 105 30; 106
   13; 179 7
~bremse *Fahrrad* 187 5
~bremse *Auto* 191 72
~bremse *Eisenb.* 212 33
~bremshebel *Moped* 188 33
~bremshebel *Auto* 191 93
~bremsrad 212 64, 80
~bremstrommel 192 50
~buch 262 17
~buchbinderei 183 1-35
~bügelkissen 104 30
~bürste 340 11
~creme 99 27
~croupier 275 4
~drucker 204 41
~dusche 49 41; 106 13
~einlegestation 184 2
~eisenschere 119 22
Handels-dünger 63 14
~gärtner 55 20
~makler 251 4
Hand-falle 203 57
~fäustel 339 16
~feger 50 53
~feuerlöscher 270 61
~feuerwaffe 87 2
~flagge 291 60
~galopp 72 42
~gelenk 2 41; 19 76
~gepäck 194 19
~gepäckaufbewahrung 204 27
~gerät 297 33-50
~griff 2 39; 26 12; 50 63; 65 2;
   114 37; 117 61; 129 7; 134
   45; 187 3; 210 63; 224 9;
   305 57; 313 21
~hammer 126 78
~harmonika 324 36
~harpune 280 40
~hebel *Tischler* 132 55
~hebel *Buchb.* 183 31
~hebelpresse 183 26
~heben 260 20
~hobel 132 15-28
~kescher 89 2
~koffer 205 7
~kreisen 297 37
~kreuz 149 43
~kultivator 55 21
~kurbel 64 43, 57; 117 50;
   201 18
~lauf 38 28; 41 23; 123 53, 79
~läufer 221 122
Händler 98 41; 308 12, 51
Hand-linie 19 72-74
~lot 224 58
~matrize 174 28
~palette 315 34; 338 28
~papierherstellung 173 46-51
~pfanne 148 23
~presse 340 29
~pumpe *Schädlingsbek.* 83 26
~pumpe *Motor* 190 64
~pumpe *Wasservers.* 269 66
~rad *Tischler* 132 60; 133 8, 22
~rad *Werkzeugmasch.* 149 13
~rad *Spinnerei* 163 18
~rad *Textil* 167 57
~rad *Straßenbau* 201 9
~rad *Flugzeug* 230 24, 25
~rasenmäher 56 34
~registratur 236 46
~reißschiene 151 9
~riemen 300 32
~rollstempel 236 46
~rollstempelabdruck 236 60
~rücken 19 83
~rührer 39 22

~rührgerät 39 22
~säge 120 61
~scheinwerfer 270 42
~schere *Schneiderei* 104 11
~schere *Bau* 119 87
~schlag 117 69
~schlaufe 301 7
~schneidkluppe 125 12
Handschuh *Kleidung* 33 67;
   318 31
~ *Sport* 292 12, 59, 60; 298 47
~kastenschloß 191 89
~ständer 271 20
Hand-schutz *Forstw.* 85 15
~schutz *Schlachthof* 94 10
~schutz *Mil.* 255 13, 19
~segel 302 28
~setzer 174 5
~setzerei 174 1
~spachtel 128 35
~spiegel 105 23; 106 7; 111 16
~spritze 83 24
~spritzpistole 129 35
~spritzrohr 83 46
~stampfer 148 32
Handstand 295 27; 296 52
~sprung 282 45
~überschlag 297 22, 24
Hand-staubsauger 50 58
~stellbock 202 17
~steuergerät 195 8
~strickmaschine 167 35
~stück *Med.* 24 6
~stück *Goldschmied* 108 7
~stütze 305 45
~tasche 188 54
~teil 89 55
~teller 19 71
~triebrad 167 30
Handtuch 28 9; 49 23; 106 24
~halter 49 8
Hand-überhandschwimmen
   282 37
~umkreisen 297 47
~vorlage 135 5
~waffe 255 1-39
~wagen 120 6
~weiche 202 16
~werker 35 40
Handwerks-kasten 134 35
~zeug 120 60-82
Hand-wurstfüller 96 49
~wurzel 19 76
~wurzelknochen 17 15
~zeichen 268 33; 286 49-55
Hanf 383 9
~schuh 122 75
Hang 301 26, 27
Hangar 287 14
Hangaufwind 287 28
Hänge-balken 121 66
~bohrmaschine, elektrische
   108 6
~brücke 215 15, 39
~lampe 44 12
~matte 278 4
Hängendes Herz 60 5
Hängeordner 248 3
Hänger 215 41
Hänge-regal 248 40
~säule 121 68
~schaltpult 177 6
~schrank 39 8; 44 17
~seil 215 17
~steg 215 15
~trogregistratur 248 2
~werk 121 65
~zopf 34 30
~zwickel 334 74
Hang-gleiter 287 44
~quelle 12 38
~rinne 12 44
~segeln 287 27

~technik 298 41
~waage 296 56
Hansekogge 218 18-26
Hansom 186 29
~cab 186 29
Hanswurst 306 69
Hantel 286 48
Hardtop 193 27
Haremssklavin 306 41
Harfe 323 60
Harfenpedal 323 62
Harke 56 4
Harlekin 306 35
Harmonium 325 43
~gehäuse 325 47
Harnblase 20 33, 78
Harnisch 329 38
Harn-leiter 20 32
~röhre 20 68
~röhrenkatheter 23 20
~sedimentstafel 23 58
Harpune 328 3; 353 10
Harpyie 254 35; 327 55
Härteofen 140 11
Härterdosiergerät 130 33
harte Röntgenstrahlung 1 33
Hart-geld 252 1-28; 271 6
~gummikante 300 45
~gummischeibe 302 35
~holzkeil 121 96
~mais 68 31
Hartmetall 149 46
~platte 149 50
~schneide 149 48, 50
Hasardspiel 275 1-33
Hase 86 35; 88 59
Hasel-huhn 88 69
~nuß 59 49
~nußstrauch 59 44-51
~strauch 59 44-51
~strauchblatt 59 51
~zweig 59 44
Hasen-jagd 86 34-39
~klage 87 44
~quäke 87 44
Häsin 73 18; 88 59
Haspel 148 72
~regeltrieb 64 5
Hatzrüde 86 33
Häubchen 28 26
Haube Jagd 86 27
~ Spinnerei 163 21
~ Flugzeug 230 39
~ Wasservers. 269 56
Hauben-lerche 361 19
~schwenkarm 105 26
~zylinder 257 5
Haue 300 33
Hauer 88 54; 367 22
Häufelhacke 56 5
Haufenwolke 8 1, 2; 287 22
Häufler 56 5
Haufwerk 158 4
Haumeister 84 20
Haumesser Forstw. 85 11
~ Tapezierer 128 37
Haupt Anat. 16 1-18
~ Jagd 88 12
~ Kunst 336 24
Hauptanschluß 237 24
~apparat 237 17
~leitung 237 18
Hauptantrieb Optik 113 15
~ Bergbahnen 214 63
Hauptantriebsscheibe 163 50
Haupt-arbeitsplatz 39 11
~bahn Landkarte 15 21
~bahn Eisenb. 203 43, 44
~balken 120 38
~bewegung 230 67-72
~brotfrucht 68 1
~darsteller 310 28
~darstellerin 310 27

~deck 223 32-42; 258 9
~düse 192 12
~eingang 319 6
~fahrwasser 224 88, 92
~fahrwerk 230 41; 231 28;
    235 31; 256 26; 257 40; 288
    33
~federbein 6 32
~gesims 38 11
~gewinn 306 11
~holm 287 30
~katalog 262 21
~kern 357 11
~kühlmittelpumpe 154 25
~kuppel 334 72
~linie 15 21
Hauptluft 192 5
~behälter 211 8; 212 57, 71
~behälter-Druckanzeige 212
    8
~leitung 212 6
Haupt-maschine 223 73
~maschinenraum 223 72
~motor 221 81; 224 21, 33
~nenner 344 19
~ölbohrung 192 21
~ölleitung 146 31
~podestbalken 123 66
~portal 333 34
~pumpe 269 15
~raketentriebwerk 6 3
~raum 334 51
~rippe 287 35
~rotor 232 12-13; 256 19; 264
    3
~schacht 144 24
~schalter Tischler 132 58
~schalter Eisenb. 211 3, 31
~schalter Büro 249 37
~schule 260 1-85
~schwert 284 8
~signal 203 1-6, 3, 30
~spant 235 10
~speicher 244 6
~spiegel 5 1; 113 10
~spindel 149 11
~station 224 40
~stelle 237 17, 22
~stern 3 9
~strecke 15 21
~titel 185 46
~titelblatt 185 45
~tragegurt 288 42
~triebwerk 234 57; 235 44
~turm 329 4
~verteilerleitung 38 71
~welle Web. 166 50
~welle Auto 192 40
~werk 326 1, 43
~wurzel 370 16
Haus 37; 155 17
Hausanschluß 245 14
~verzeichnis 245 17
Hausanzug, zweiteiliger 32
    17
~apotheke 49 49
~bahnsteig 205 14
~bau 118 1-49
~boot 353 31
~brenner 358 24
~brücke 215 32
~büffel 367 8
Hauschlag 91 17
Hausdetektiv 275 16
~diener 267 17
~eingangstür 123 24
~frau 39 1
~garten 37 57
~grille 81 17
Haushalts-gerät 50
~leiter 50 35
Haus-katze 62 3
~kleid 31 36

~knecht 267 17
~lerche 361 19
~mantel 32 20
~schabe 81 17
~schuh 101 41
~skorpion 358 40
~sockel 37 17; 120 28
~sperling 361 5
~spinne 81 9
~spitzmaus 366 7
~sprechstelle 127 3
~tier 73
~tür 37 65
~typ 37
~- und Bademantel 32 20
~ungeziefer 81 1-14
~urne 328 38
~wand 120 29
~wurz 51 7
~zelt 278 21; 280 45
~zentrale 245 13
Haut 88 56
~desinfektion 22 60
~flügel 82 11
~flügler 358 21-23
~sack 359 8
Hauungsbetrieb 84 15-37
Hauzahn 88 54
Havanna 107 2
Havarist 227 2; 228 10
Havelock 186 32
Hawaiimädchen 306 16
Hebe-bühne 195 25
~bühnenarm 195 26
~bühnenstempel 195 27
~glied 325 32
Hebel Druck 180 80; 181 3
~ Auto 191 83, 84, 86, 87
~konus 187 67
~korkenzieher 40 18
~schalter 150 35
~system 163 31
~vorschneider 140 67
~werk 203 54
Heben 296 52
Heber-barometer 10 1
~rohr 10 43
Hebewerk 145 11
hebräisch 341 7
Hecht, Gemeiner 364 16
~brutglas 89 17
~rolle 297 20
~sprung 282 40; 296 48
Heck 222 66-72; 258 26; 285
    29
~abteil 193 17
~aufschleppe 221 88
~avionikraum 257 18
~brett 286 26
Hecke Landkarte 15 98
~ Garten 52 32; 272 37
~ Reitsport 289 20
Heckeinrichtung 239 1
Heckelphon 323 38
Hecken-gang 272 5
~schere 56 49
~schere, batteriebetriebene
    56 17
~scherenvorsatz 134 55
Heck-fahrschalter 197 8
~fender 227 29
~flaggenstock 223 31; 258 25
~form 285 42-49
~führungsrinne 221 53
~galerie 218 56
~galgen 221 87
~gebläsetriebwerk 232 42
~klappe 191 7; 193 16
~ladeklappe 221 31
~ladepforte 232 25
~laterne 258 62
~licht 286 10

~motor 195 49
~motorklappe 195 50
~partie 193 35
~pforte 221 55; 226 18
~propeller 232 28
~rampe 258 91
~rotor 232 14; 256 20; 264 4
~scheibe 191 32, 82
~scheibenheizung 191 80
~schild 85 40
~spiegel 221 42; 286 26
~spoiler 193 34; 290 35
~trawler 221 86
~triebwerk 231 10
~tür 193 20; 194 11
Hederich, Echter 61 21
~, Falscher 61 18
Heer 255 1-98
~vogel 359 25
Hefe 97 53
~brezel 99 16
~reinzuchtapparat 93 6
~zopf 97 41
Heft 45 51; 132 10
~drahtabspulvorrichtung 184
    18
Heften 183 8
Hefter 247 4
Heft-gaze 183 33; 185 20
~lade 183 9
~lage 183 12
~lasche 119 60
~nadel 185 21
~pflaster 21 7; 22 55
~pflasterrolle 26 54
~sattel 185 24
~schnur 183 10
Heftung 183 34
Heide 15 5
~kraut 377 19
~krautgewächs 53 12
Heidelbeere 377 23
Heide-lerche 361 18
~pflanze 377
~röschen 377 20
Heiliger, buddhistischer 337
    10
Heilige Schrift 330 11
heiliges Sakrament 332 35
Heilpflanze 380
Heimathafen 286 8
Heimchen 81 7
Heim-fernseher 243 6
~werken 134 1-34
~werker 134 61
~werkerbank 134 41
Heinze 63 29
Heiß-email-(Diazo-)platte
    179 32
~emailplatte 179 32
Heißluft 96 47
~bad 281 18
~ballon 288 79
~kamm 106 29
~leitung 139 52
~pistole 130 25
~sterilisator 22 71
Heißtrubausscheidung 93 2
Heißwasser-bereiter 126
    12-13
~versorgung 155 26
heiter 9 21
Heiz-anlage 192 60-64
~druckmesser 210 44
Heizersitz 210 39
Heiz-gas 145 52
~gebläse 192 62
~generator 212 39
~kasten 183 27
~keller 38
~kessel 155 13
Heizkörper 38 76; 129 34;
    155 15; 172 32

~pinsel 129 21
~rippe 38 77
Heiz-kupplungsschlauch 208 20
~leitung 208 20
~öl 38 50
~öl, leichtes 145 58
~öl, schweres 145 59
~ölbehälter 212 75
~presse 116 57
~raum 38 38-43; 55 7
~rohr Gärtner 55 8
~rohr Eisenb. 210 17
~spannungsanzeige 211 27
~spannungsmesser 212 17
~strommesser 212 18
~umrichterschrank 212 40
Heizung Haus 38 24
~ Setzerei 174 45
~ Eisenb. 207 6
Heizungs-anschluß 190 55
~körper 126 20
~regulierung 207 54
Heizwindleitung 147 19
Held 310 28
Helfer Erste Hilfe 21 19
~ Sport 299 44
Helferineinheit 24 9
Helgen 222 11-26, 11-18
Helikon 323 44
Heliostat 5 29
Helium 1 5; 234 14
~atomkern 1 30-31
~-Druckgastank 234 43, 50
~-Neon-Laser 243 57
helles Bier 93 26
Helligkeitsregelung 240 33
Helling 222 11-26, 11-18
~anlage 222 11-26
~gerüst 222 19
~kran 222 23
~portal 222 11
~sohle 222 17
Helm Schiff 218 13
~ Heraldik 254 4, 7-9, 9
~ Polizei 264 35
~ Sport 292 24
~ Ritterwesen 329 39-42
~decke 254 3
~glocke 329 39
~kasuar 359 1
~kleinod 254 1,11,30-36
~krone 254 12
~öler 187 65
~stock 218 13
~zeichen 254 1,11,30-36
~zier 254 1,11,30-36
Hemd, kurzärmeliges 33 33
~bluse 30 40
~blusenkleid 30 10
Hemden-bluse 30 40
~knopf 33 34
~tasche, aufgesetzte 33 38
Hemieder 351 24
Hemipyramide 351 24
Hemisphäre, nördliche 3 1-35
Hengst 73 2
Henkel Textil 171 37
~ Schule 260 8
~kanne 328 35
~kreuz 332 63
~locheisen 100 46
Henne 62 36; 73 19; 98 7
Henriquatre 34 13
Heppe 85 11
Heraldik 254 1-36
Herbst-anfang 3 7
~blume 379 3
~punkt 3 7
~zeitlose 379 3
Hercules 3 21
Herd-apfel 68 38

~tiefe 11 34
Hererofrau 354 25
Hering Camping 278 24
~ Zool. 364 14
Herings-hammer 278 25
~logger 90 1
~treibnetz 90 2-10
Herkules 3 21
Herme 334 35
Herr 265 22; 355 54, 61, 73
Herren-anzug 33 1
~artikelabteilung 271 12
~doppel 293 2 bis 3
~einzel 293 4 bis 5
~fahrrad 187 1
~friseur 106
~hemd 32 38-47
~hut 35 13, 22-40
~hutform 35 14
~kleidung 33
~mode 33 1-67
~mütze 35 22-40
~nachtkleidung 32 35-37
~pullover 33 51
~ring 36 20
~salon 106 1-42
~schaftstiefel 101 7
~schneider 104 22
~schneideratelier 104 1-32
~socke 32 32-34
~sommerpulli 33 32
~stiefel 101 5
~straßenstiefel 101 13
~tier 368 12-16
~toilette 233 47
~unterkleidung 32 22-29
~unterwäsche 32 22-29
~wäsche 32 22-29
Herrgottskäfer 358 37
Herz Anat. 18 14; 20 8, 24-25, 45-57
~ Spiele 276 40, 44
~blume 60 5
~brett 120 93
herzförmig 370 35
Herz-kammer 20 51
~katheterisierung 27 30
~kirsche 59 5
~klappen 20 46-47
~linie 19 74
Herzogshut 254 39
Herz-ohr 20 24
~rhythmus 25 1
~schild 254 17
Herzschrittmacher 25 31
~, intrakorporaler 25 37
~implantation 25 36
Herz-silhouette 25 39
~stromkurve 25 2, 21, 28
~stück 202 24; 203 48
~überwachungsanlage 25 1
Hessen-fliege 80 40
~mücke 80 40
Hetzhund 70 24; 86 33
Heu 63 25; 75 13
~ernte 63 19-30
Heufler 88 23
Heu-forke 66 3
~gabel 66 3
~harke 66 23
~hüpfer 358 8
Heulapparat 224 70
Heu-pferd, Grünes 358 8
~reuter 63 28, 29
~schrecke 358 8
~schreckenköder 89 68
~springer 358 8
~wurm 80 23
Hexaeder 351 2
Hexagon Schmuck 36 62, 63
~ Kristallkunde 351 15
~, ovales 36 63
Hexakisoktaeder 351 13

Hexe 306 6
Hexen-kraut 61 31
~stich 102 9
Hieb- und Stoßwaffe 294 34
Hiebwaffe Polizei 264 19
~ Sport 294 34
Hieroglyphe 341 1
HiFi-Baustein 241 13-48
~-Komponente 241 13-48
Hifthorn 289 44
High-Hat 324 50
~riser 188 56
Hi-Hat 324 50
Hilfe, ärztliche 253 27
~, Erste 21
~stellung 297 16
Hilfs-arbeiter 118 19
~betrieb 211 34
~diesel 209 19
~dieselmotor 209 19
~fahrwerk 194 32
~fallschirm 235 59
~gasturbine 231 33
~gerät 296 12-21; 297 7-14
~kontakt 153 57
~kranzug 147 61
~luftbehälter 212 61
~maschine 223 71
~maschinenraum 223 70; 259 56
~mittel 21 31
~motor 211 17
~rippe 287 36
~schiff 258 92-97
~schirm 288 39
~schwert 284 9
~seil 214 47
~seilspannvorrichtung 214 48
~spiegel 115 38
~stander 253 30-32
~triebwerk 231 33
~wagen 157 11
hilfswissenschaftlicher Assistent 262 7
Himation 355 6
Himbeerblüte 58 26
Himbeere 58 28; 370 101
Himbeerstrauch 58 25
himmelblau 343 6
Himmelfahrtsblümchen 377 3
Himmels-achse 4 10
~äquator 3 3
~bedeckung 9 20-24
~gewölbe 3 1-8
~karte 3 1-35
~pol 3 1; 4 24, 26
~schlüsselchen 376 8
~sphäre 4 23
Hindernis Roulette 275 30
~ Sport 289 8, 20
~lauf 298 7-8
~laufen 298 7-8
~rennen 289 20-22
Hinkelstein 328 18
~gruppe 328 11
Hinter-backe Anat. 16 40
~backe Pferd 72 35
~bein 77 6-9; 82 8
Hinterbliebene 331 38
Hinterbliebener 331 38
Hintereckegel 305 11
~flügel 358 33
~füllung 217 7
~fuß 303 9
~gassenkegel 305 9, 10
~grundkulisse 310 33
~hachse 95 1, 10
~hand 72 33-37
~hängestück 316 10
~haupt 16 2
~hauptmuskel 18 50; 19 2
~hauptsbein 17 32

~haxe 95 1, 10
~hesse 95 14, 33
~kappe 100 59; 291 23
~kipper 200 7
~lader 77 45-50
~lauf 70 7; 88 22, 63
~leib 82 9
~leib (der Arbeiterin) 77 10-19
~leibsrücken 358 31
~leibszange 81 12
~mann 293 77
~pfote 70 8
Hinterrad 186 17
~gabel 187 20
~lenkung 64 39
~schwinge 188 14; 189 7
~strebe 187 19, 20
Hinter-sitzkopfstütze 193 8
~spieler 293 77
~steven 222 70-71
~teil 16 40
~tür 193 6
~zange 132 37
~zwiesel 71 39
Hinweis-schild 233 24-53
~tafel 356 7
~zeichen 268 29
Hippe 56 9
Hippodrom 308 59
Hippogryph 327 26
Hippokamp Fabelwesen 327 44
~ Zool. 364 18
Hirn-anhangdrüse 17 43
~holz 120 92
~holzplatte 340 1
~kappe 329 61
Hirsch 86 12
~fänger 87 41
~hornknopf 29 33
~hund 289 47
~käfer 358 24
~kalb 88 1
~kuh 88 1
~ruf 87 46
~ziegenantilope 367 5
Hirse 68 28
Hirtentäschel, Gemeines 61 9
~kraut 61 9
Hitze-grad 161 6
~schild 235 8, 40
H-Milch 99 44
h-Moll 320 57
Hobel 120 64; 132 15-28
~aggregat 133 38
~bank 132 29-37
~eisen 132 20
~kasten 132 24
~messer 132 20
~schar 200 21
~span 132 40
~streb 144 33
~tisch 150 11
Hoboe 323 38
Hoch 9 6
~achse 230 70
hochalpine Ausrüstung 300 31-57
Hoch-baukran 47 39
~behälter 55 2
~bordstein 198 7
~decker 229 1; 231 2
Hochdruck-dampfrohr 259 63
~gasleitung 156 45
~gebiet 9 6
~manometer 141 4
~presse 63 35
~reifen 187 30
~-Rotationsmaschine 181 41
~-Sauerstoffpumpe 235 42
~turbine 232 53; 259 62

~verdichter 232 36
~verfahren 340 1-13
~vorwärmer 152 26
~-Wasserstoffpumpe 235 41
~zementierungspumpe 146 34
~zylinder 153 23
Hoch-fläche 13 46
~frequenz 7 26
~gebirge 12 39-47
~geschwindigkeitskamera 313 35
~glanzfolie 116 58
~halte 295 49
~haus 37 82; 305 75
~landindianer 352 23
~leistungssegelflugzeug 287 9
~lochziegel 159 21
~löffelbagger 200 1
~moor 13 19
~nebel 8 4
Hochofen 147 1
~anlage 147 1-20
~schacht 147 7
Hoch-rippe 95 18
~schrank 43 1
~schule 262 1-25
~schullehrer 262 3
Hochsee-bergungsschlepper 258 96
~fischerei 90 1-23
~jacht, 30-m- 286 5
Hoch-silo 62 11
~sitz 86 14
Hochspannungs-abzweig 153 4
~kabel 153 42
~leitungsseil 152 32
~seil 152 33
~verteilungsanlage 152 29-35
Hoch-springer 298 10
~sprung 298 9-27
~sprunganlage 298 32
~stammrose 51 25; 52 21
~stand 86 14
Höchstgeschwindigkeit 203 36-38, 41; 237 68
Hoch-stoß 277 3
~straße 215 59
~töner 241 15
~tonlautsprecher 241 15
~tourenanorak 300 6
~tourismus 300 1-57
~tourist 300 5
~- und Niederdruckturbine 259 62
~verzugflyer 164 19
~verzugstreckwerk 164 14
Hochwasser-bett 216 41
~deich 216 32
~entlastungsanlage 217 60
~schaden 216 5
Hoch-wurf 297 35
~zahl 345 1
Hocke 296 53
Hocker 260 58
~bestattung 328 17
Höckereinsatz 74 42, 45
Hockereißen 299 1
Hockergrab 328 17
Höckerschwan 359 16
Hockey 292 6
~ball 292 14
~schläger 292 13
~spiel 292 6
~spieler 292 15
~stock 292 13
~tor 292 7
Hock-liegestütz 295 23
~sitz 295 9
~sprung 295 36
~stand 295 6
Hoden 20 72

~sack 20 71
Hof 276 27
~hecke 62 35
~hund 62 32
~kleid 355 79
~raum 62 31
Höft 225 65
Höhe Sport 285 28
~ Math. 346 27
~ des Kegels 347 44
Höhen-abstimmung 241 43
~einstellung Med. 27 3
~einstellung Tischler 132 60
~einstellung Sägewerk 157 49
~feintrieb 14 54
~flosse Flugzeug 229 26; 230 62
~flosse Mil. 256 31
~flosse Sport 288 23
~klemme 14 55
Höhenleitwerk 229 26-27, 35; 230 61; 257 21
~-Rudermaschine 257 22
Höhen-linie 15 62
~markierung 298 20
~messer 230 4
~messung 14 46
~richteinrichtung 255 67
~ruder Flugzeug 229 27; 230 24, 63
~ruder Sport 288 24
~skala Atmosphäre 7 35
~skala Sägewerk 157 60
~- und Neigungsverstellung 177 21
~- und Tiefenabstimmung 241 43
~verstellung Landmaschinen 64 57
~verstellung Fotogr. 116 34
~verstellung Repro 177 21
~zug 13 60
Höhere Schule 261
Hoher Glatthafer 69 22
~ Klee 69 9
Hohe Schule 71 1-6
Hohl-achse 312 49
~beitel Tischler 132 9
~beitel Bildhauerei 339 17
~blocksteinwand 118 15
Höhle 15 85
Hohl-eisen Tischler 132 9
~eisen Graphik 340 8
Höhlen-bild 328 9
~fluß 13 83
~malerei 328 9
~system 13 76
Hohl-gebiß 71 52
~glasrute 89 57
~hand 19 71
~kasten 215 5
~kehle 334 29; 336 10
~pfanne 122 54
~pfannendach 122 53
~saum 102 14
~schale 10 30
~schliff 302 22
~sonde 26 41
~spiegel 312 39
~stützisolator 153 54
~tier 357 14; 369 5, 9, 14, 20
~vene 18 9, 15; 20 53, 57
~weg 15 84
~wellenbohrer 133 7
Holder 374 35
~beere 374 37
~blüte 374 36
~busch 374 35
Hole 293 87
Höllen-hund 327 29
~natter 364 40
Holler 374 35
~beere 374 37

~blüte 374 36
Holm Leiter 38 16
~ Flugzeug 230 45
~ Sport 283 35; 303 5
~flügel 287 29
Holoeder 351 2
Holunder, Schwarzer 374 35
~beere 374 37
~blüte 374 36
~busch 374 35
Holz Forstw. 84 1-34, 16
~ Golf 293 91
~, unbearbeitetes 135 21
~abfuhrweg 84 3
~apfelbaum 58 51
~auskleidung 281 19
~bildhauer 339 28
~birnbaum 58 31
~blasinstrument 323 28-38
~block 339 27
~bock 358 44
~boot 285 50-57
~bottich 91 27
~drehbank 135 1
~druckwalze 163 32
~einschlag 84 15-37
~einspannvorrichtung 132 51
~eisenbahn 47 37; 48 29; 273 27
~faserplatte 338 24
~feile 132 2
~fender 218 26
~gerüst 353 13
~gewinde 143 47
~gewindeschneiden 135 14
~greifer 85 29
~hacker 359 27
~hammer 125 18; 339 21
~harmonika 324 61
~haus 37 84-86
~kohle 108 37; 278 48
~kohlengrill 278 47
~konstruktion 260 72
~korb 309 10
~maske 354 16
~model 340 2
~nagel 121 92
~paneel 266 37
~platte 338 23
~raspel 132 1; 134 8; 260 55
~rechen 66 23
~schaufel 91 24
~schläger 293 91
~schleifereianlage 172 53-65
~schliff 172 77, 78, 79
~schneidekunst 340 1-13
~schnitt 260 83; 340 1-13, 2
~schnitzerei 260 77
~schraube 122 101; 132 41; 143 45
~schreier 361 1
~sohle 101 45
~span 135 26
~spielzeug 260 80
~stab 324 62
~stativ 313 13
~steckling 54 25
~stich 340 1
~stock 340 1
~stoß 84 16
~stück 260 56
~treppe 38 25
~unterschuh 355 43
~verbände 121
~verbindung 121 84-98
~verkleidung 10 26
~verschlag 38 19
~vorrat 260 82
~ware 135 19
~zahn 91 9
~zaun 37 53
Home base 292 51
Homogenisier-maschine 76

12
~silo 160 5
Homo steinheimensis 261 17
Honig 77 33, 62-63
~behälter 77 62
~biene 77 1-25
~glas 77 63
~grube 59 18
~magen 77 18
~melonenstück 266 50
~raum 77 45
~schleuder 77 61
~wabe 77 45
~zelle 77 33
Hook 305 18
~-Ball 305 18
Hopfen-anbau 83 27
~anpflanzung 15 114
~garten 15 114
~kessel 92 52
Horde 92 24
Horden-blech 83 17
~schüttler 64 14
Hörer 245 15; 246 16
~leitung 237 14
Hörfunk 238 1-6; 239
~sternpunkt 238 7-15
Horizont, künstlicher 230 3
Horizontal-ablenkmodul 240 10
~ebene 4 12
~isolierung 123 4
~seismograph 11 39
~stoß 277 2
~synchronmodul 240 7
~traubenpresse 79 21
Horizont-beleuchtung 316 15
~hügel 310 13
~kreisel 230 3
Hör-kopf 241 59
~muschel 237 8
Horn Jagd 88 78
~ Klempner 125 19
~ Mus. 323 41
~, gedrehtes 327 8
Hörnchen 97 32; 99 13
~wickelmaschine 97 64
Horn-gestell 111 8
~haut 19 47
~klee 376 17
~koralle 369 8
~schröter 358 24
~tier 73 1
Hör-rohr 23 35
~saal 262 2
Horst 12 10
Hortensie 51 11
Höschen 77 3
Hose Kleidung 32 19
~ Pferd 72 36
~ Vögel 362 3
Hosen-anzug 30 57
~aufschlag 31 40
~bein 33 6
~boje 228 13
~bund 33 23
~höschen 32 8
~korselett 32 3
~latz 29 35
~rock 29 59; 31 48
~schlitz 33 48
~tasche 33 47
~träger 29 26; 32 30
~trägerklipp 32 31
Hospital 228 21
Hostess 272 27
Hostie 332 28, 35
~, große 332 35
~, kleine 332 48
Hostien-dose 330 8; 332 53
~schale 332 50
~teller 330 9
Hotel 267

~aufkleber 205 9
~bar 267 51
~boy 267 18
~diener 204 17
~direktor 267 19
~foyer 267 44-46
~gast 267 14
~halle 267 18-26
~nachweis 204 28
~page 267 18
~rechnung 267 11
~restaurant 267 20
~zimmer 267 27-38
Hot-Whirl-Pool 281 31, 35
Hourdi 159 26
Hourdis 159 26
Hourdistein 159 26
Hub-brücke 225 70
~einrichtung 255 76
Hubel 161 10
Hub-hydraulik 65 24-29
~motor 150 22
~rad 64 74
Hubschrauber 232 11-25
~arbeitsdeck 228 15
~deck 146 7
~hangar 221 52; 259 38
~kraftstoff 146 18
~landeplattform 259 39, 53
~plattform 221 19
Hub-spindel 217 36
~stapler 159 18; 225 44; 226 8
~strebe 65 29
~strebenverstellung 65 25
~tor 217 31, 38
~werk 206 56
~zylinder 255 51
Huf 72 26
Hufeisen 5 9
~bogen 336 30
~form 260 1
~montierung 113 25
Huflattich 380 8
Hufschlagfigur 289 7
Hüftbein 17 18
Hüfte *Anat.* 16 33
~ *Pferd* 72 32
Hüftgriff 21 38
Huftier 366 25-31; 367 1-10
Hüft-nerv 18 30
~schlagader 18 17
~tasche 301 28
~vene 18 18
Hügel 13 66
~grab 328 16
Huhn 62 36; 73 19-26
Hühner-aufzuchtstall 74 1
~ei 74 58
~habicht 362 10
~myrte, Rote 61 27
~vogel 359 22
Hüllkelch 375 33
Hülse 57 6, 11; 370 92; 374 22
Hülsen-frucht 57 1-11
~kasten 166 21
~kette 190 49
~kopf 87 16
~mais 68 31
Hülsstrauch, Gemeiner 374 9
Humboldtstrom 14 42
Hummel 358 23
Hummergabel 45 79
Humusandeckung 200 64
Hund 73 16; 99 7
~, Großer 3 14
~, Kleiner 3 15
Hundeartige 367 11-13
~bürste 70 18
~garnitur 70 28-31
~halsband 70 13
~kamm 70 29
~kuchen 99 37
~leib 327 30

~leine 70 30
~meute 86 33; 289 46
~rasse 70
Hunderterstelle 344 3
Hundertsatz 345 7
Hundertstel 344 20
Hunde-schlitten 353 3
~schwanz 70 12
~verbotsschild 99 6
~vollkost 99 36
~zecke 358 44
Hündin 73 16
Hunds-kamille 61 8
~lattich 61 13
~quecke 61 30
~rose 373 26
Hünengrab 328 16
Hungerblume 61 1
Hüpf-ball 273 20
~seil 273 16
Hupschalter 191 60
Hürde 289 8; 298 8
Hürden-lauf 298 7-8
~laufen 298 7-8
~sitz 295 12
Hut *Kopfbedeckung* 35 1
~ *Sport* 289 6
~ *Bot.* 381 4
~, breitrandiger 35 38
~, hoher 186 25
~, thessalischer 355 4
~ablage 208 28
~geschäft 268 38
~haken 266 13
~macherin 35 1
~schachtel 205 11
Hütte *Jagd* 86 51
~ *Schiff* 223 33; 258 22
Hütten-jagd 86 47-52
~schuh 101 42
Hyäne 368 1
Hydra *Astr.* 3 16
~ *Fabelwesen* 327 32
Hydrallmania 369 9
Hydrantenschlüssel 270 27
Hydraulik-anlage *Mälzerei* 92
  13
~anlage *Mil.* 255 53
~arm 85 21
~kolben 65 24; 139 41
~pumpe 64 29, 91
~speicher 257 16
~zylinder 64 8; 194 26
hydraulische Bremse 212 44
~ Lagerung 5 10
hydraulischer Antrieb 139 9,
  15
hydraulische Schmiedepresse
  139 35
Hydroidpolyp 369 9
Hydroplane-Rennboot 286
  22
hydrostatischer Lüfterantrieb
  212 62
Hydroxylaminzuleitung 170
  21
Hygieneartikel 99 35
Hygrograph 10 8, 50
Hygrometer 281 23
Hyperbel 347 26
~standlinie 224 43, 44
Hypotenuse 346 32
Hypotrachelion 334 22
Hypozentrum 11 32, 33
hypsometrische Kurve 11
  6-12

I

IC-Zug 205 34
Idealabfahrtshaltung 301 33
identisch 345 16

Identität 345 5
Identitätszeichen 345 16
Idol 328 20
Igel 366 5
~kaktus 53 14
~kopf 34 11
~wulst 334 21
Iglu 353 4
~zelt 278 58
Ikosaeder 351 11
Ikositetraeder 351 12
Ilge 60 12
Imago 358 10
Imker 77 57
~pfeife 77 59
Imme 77 1-25
Impair 275 23
Imprägnierspray 50 40
Impressum 342 40
Impulsform 23 37
impulsgebende Kamera 117
  71
Impuls-geberanschluß 117 7
~kabel 117 72
~messer 25 42
Inbord-Sportboot 286 2
Indexstreifen 249 74
Indianer 352 23, 25
~frau 352 10
~häuptling 352 11
Indigofärbeschlichtmaschine
  165 40
Indikatorpapier 128 16
Indio 352 23
indirekte Beleuchtung 317 12
Indischer Ozean 14 23
indische Tänzerin 306 25
Individual-section-
  Maschine 162 21
Indossament 250 25
Indossant 250 27
Indossat 250 26
Indossator 250 26
Induktionsspule 11 44
induktive Zugbeeinflussung
  211 7
Indusi 211 7, 38; 212 14
~-Fahrzeugmagnet 212 38
Industrie-obligation 251
  11-19
~pflanze 383
Inertgasschweißung 142 33
Infinitesimalrechnung 345
  13-14
Information 233 31
Informations-abruf 248 44
~stand 250 9
~technik 242
Infrarot-tonkopfhörer 242 30
~tonsender 242 29
~trockenofen 173 32
~übertragung 242 27
~-Weißlicht-
  Zielscheinwerfer 255 82
Infusions-einrichtung 25 14
~flasche 25 12
~geräteständer 25 11
~schlauch 25 13
Inhaberaktie 251 11
Inhalation 274 7
Inhalations-kur 274 6-7
~schlauch 26 2, 29
Inhalier-einrichtung 23 24
Inhalieren 274 7
Initial 175 1
Initiale 175 1
Injektions-nadel 24 54
~spritze 24 53
Inka 352 22
Inkarnatklee 69 4
Inkreis 346 31
Inlett 43 13

Innen-auslage 271 13
~beleuchtung 191 77; 197 32
~eckmeißel 149 51
~einrichtung 239 6
~elektrode 2 3
~gewinde 126 41, 45
~kiel 283 50
~meßfühler 149 71
~querstand 296 27
~reißverschluß 101 6
~ring 143 72
~rückspiegel 191 39
~sechskantschraube 143 27
~stadt 268
~stürmer 291 15
~taster 135 23
~titel 185 45
~trommel 168 17
~- und Außenbeleuchtung
  197 32
~verzahnung 143 95
~winkel 346 26
innere Organe 20 1-57
Insekt 358 3-23, 10
Insektenauge 77 20-24
insektenfressende Pflanze
  377 13
Insektenfresser 366 4-7
Insel 13 6; 259 3; 272 55
Inspizient 316 30
Inspizienten-ruf 315 52
~stand 316 29
Installateur 126 1
Installationswerkzeug 126
  58-86
Instamatic-Kassette 114 15
instantane Rotationsachse 4
  25
Instantkaffee 99 70
Institut für Tropenmedizin
  225 28
Instrument *Med.* 23 3
~ *Raumfahrt* 234 17
~, chirurgisches 26 40-53
Instrumenten-brett 230 1; 288
  11
~einheit 234 53
~gehäuse 2 5, 22
~kasten 10 59
~korb 26 39
~schale 27 5
~schrank 24 16
~tisch 26 37
Integral 345 14
~-Cockpit 189 44
~flächentank 257 29
~zeichen 345 14
Integrand 345 14
Integration 345 14
Integrationskonstante 345 14
integrierter Schaltkreis 242
  68
integrierte Schaltung 110 16
Intensiv-haltung 74 1-27
~pflegestation 25 1-30
~station 25 1-30
Intercity-Zug 205 34
Intervall 321 6-13
Intrusion 11 30
Inzensation 332 38
Ionisationskammer 2 2, 17
ionische Säule 334 9
ionisierende Teilchen 1 58
Ionosphäre 7 23; 237 55
Iris *Anat.* 19 42
~ *Bot.* 51 27; 60 8
Iron 293 92
Irrgarten 272 5
Ischiasnerv 18 30
IS-Maschine 162 21
Isobare 9 1
Isobathe 15 11
Isochimene 9 42

Isohelie 9 44
Isohyete 9 45
Isohypse 15 62
Isolationsverkleidung 235 13
Isolier-band 127 34
~griff 127 54
~kanne 40 5
Isolierung 38 72; 155 36
isometrisches Kristallsystem
351 1-17
Isoseiste 11 37
Isothere 9 43
Isotherme 9 40
Ist-gleich-Taste 247 20
Italienischer Skorpion 358 40
italienischer Zug 315 2
Italienisches Raigras 69 26
~ Raygras 69 26
ITOS-Satellit 10 64

J

Jacht-heck 285 42
~spiegel 285 43
Jacke 21 23; 33 2
~, gepolsterte 292 26
~, kurzärmelige 33 26
Jackenkleid 31 6
Jacketkrone 24 28
Jackett 33 2
Jack-in-the-box 306 56
Jagd 86 1-52
~anzug 86 2
~art 86 1-52
~beute 86 38
~bomber 256 1, 29
~fasan 88 77
~frevler 86 29
~gerät 87
~geräte 87 41-48
~gewehr 87 1-40
~glas 86 6
~gravur 87 28
~horn 87 60; 289 44
~hund 86 7
~hut 86 5
~kanzel 86 14
~kappe 289 14
~messer 87 42
~reiten 289 41-49
~rennen 289 20-22
~revier 86 1-8
~rock 289 42
~schirm 86 9
~sitz 86 10
~springen 289 8-14
~stellung 305 72
~stock 86 10
~stuhl 86 10
~waffe 87
~wagen 86 18
Jagen 84 2; 86 1-52
Jäger 86 1
Jägerei 86 1-52
Jägerhut 86 5
Jahres-bahn 3 2
~brezel 99 16
~ring 84 24
~temperatur 9 41
~trieb 372 25
~zeit 4 10-21
Jahrmarkt 308 1-69
~bummler 308 67
Jai alai 305 67
Jakobs-leiter 221 91
~muschel 309 46
Jalousie 304 12
~schweller 326 50
Jamboree 278 8-11
japanisch 341 6
Japanische Quitte 373 17
Japan-panamahut 35 16

~spachtel 128 10; 129 23
Jasmin, Gelbblühender 373 4
Jätekralle 56 13
Jaucherinne 75 44
Jazz-batterie 324 47-54
~besen 324 53
~gitarre 324 73
~instrument 324 47-78
~trompete 324 65
Jeans 31 60; 33 22
~anzug 31 58; 33 20
~jacke 33 21
~weste 31 59
Jelängerjelieber 374 13
Jersey-anzug, einteiliger 29 17
~kleidchen 29 28
Jet 231 7-33
~gebläse 281 34
Jeton 275 12
Jetztmensch 261 21
Jiu-Jitsu 299 13-17
Joch Landmaschinen 65 14
~ Kraftwerk 153 14
~arm 322 16
~bein 16 8; 17 37
Joghurtbereiter 40 44
Johannisbeere 58 12
Johannisbeer-strauch 52 19;
58 10
~zweig 58 14
Johannisbrot 384 41
Jolle 278 12; 285 37-41
Jollenkreuzer, 30-m²- 284 61
J-2-Triebwerk 234 34
Judo 299 13-17
Judoka 299 14
Judowurf 299 17
Jugend-rodel 303 3
~stil 336 18
Jule 86 49
Jumbo-Jet 231 14
Jungbestand 84 10-11
Junges 272 51
Jungfern-fahrt 221 85
~herz 60 5
~rebe, Gemeine 374 16
Jungfrau 3 18; 4 58
Jungfräulichkeit 327 7
Jung-henne 74 9
~hennenstall 74 5
~larve 80 54
~steinzeit 328 10-20
~stier 319 35
Jupiter 4 48
Jurte 353 19
Justier-knopf 11 41
~schraube 242 78
Jute 383 25
~umhüllung 153 49; 163 4

K

Kabarett 40 8
Kabel 50 66; 153 41; 169 28,
30; 170 58, 59, 60; 326 53
~anschluß 6 26
~anschlußtafel 239 3
~aufhängung 133 39
~bindung 301 40
~boden 152 20
~endverschluß 153 33
~galgen 195 15
~haken 50 65
~keller 152 21
~kranhelling 222 11-18
~messer 127 63
~rolle 294 29
~schacht Straßenbau 198 17
~schacht Raumfahrt 234 29,
47; 235 61
~schelle 127 40
~trommel 270 55

~trommelwinde 258 85
Kabine 223 29; 282 1; 288 19
Kabinen-fenster 312 15
~haube 257 4
~laufwerk 214 66
Kabriolett 186 29
Kabriolimousine 193 9
Kachelofen 266 34
Käfer 82 26, 42; 358 24-39
Kaffee Getränk 98 65; 99 68;
265 1-26, 19
~ Bot. 382 6
~automat 39 38
~bohne 382 6
~gedeck 265 18
~geschirr 44 27
Kaffeehaus 265 1-26
~besucher 265 22-24
~gast 265 22-24
~tisch 265 11
Kaffee-kanne 44 28
~maschine 39 38
~mühle, elektrische 39 24; 98
69
~röstmaschine 98 70
~sorte 98 67
~strauch 382 1
~tasse 44 29
Käfig-haltung 74 18
~wagen 307 62
Kahl-kopf 34 22
~schlag 84 13
~schlagwirtschaft 84 4-14
~wild 88 1
Kahn-fähre 216 15
~fibel 328 28
Kai 222 5; 225 64
~mauer 217 1-14
Kaiserin 355 15
Kaiser-krone 254 38
~pinguin 359 4
Kai-straße 225 38
~zunge 225 66
Kajak 283 4, 68-70; 353 12
Kaje 225 64
Kajütboot 286 3
Kajüte 218 45; 285 39
Kajütenaufbau 285 39
Kakao Getränk 98 66
~ Bot. 382 19
~baum 382 16
~bohne 382 19
~pulver 382 19
Kakerlak 81 17
Kalabreser 35 38
Kalander 173 36
~walze Spinnerei 163 37
~walze Papier 173 38
Kalb Zool. 62 33; 73 1
~ Fleischerei 95 1-13
Kalbs-brust 95 4
~filet 95 7
~kotelett 95 3
Kaldarium 55 4
Kalebasse 354 27
Kalenderblatt 247 33
Kalesche 186 35
Kaliber Jagd 87 40
~ Walz. 148 59
~ Sport 305 38, 39
~dorn 149 56
Kalibrierpresse 139 18
Kalidünger 63 14
Kalifornischer Strom 14 39
Kalisalzflöz 154 65
Kalk 147 56
~, rückgebrannter 172 52
~bunker 147 62
~dünger 63 14
~löschtrommel 172 51
~ofen 15 86
~schale 74 59
~spat 351 22

~stein 13 71-83; 160 1
~steinmergel 160 1
Kalme 9 11
Kalmengürtel 9 46-47
~, äquatorialer 9 46
Kalmus 377 22
Kalotte 261 16, 18
Kalottenhochtöner 241 15
Kälte-kompressor 92 22
~mittelsammler 92 7
~schutzanzug 279 9
Kalt-front 8 13-17, 13; 9 27
~haus 55 33
~leim 134 36
~lichtbeleuchtung 23 8
Kalt- und Warmwasserhahn
49 26
Kaltwasser-becken 281 30
~behälter 92 9
~griff 126 29
~hahn 49 26
Kambium 370 10
~ring 370 10
Kamel, zweihöckriges 366 29
~karawane 354 1
Kamera 1 60; 112 55; 243 1;
279 24; 313 31
~, impulsgebende 117 71
~assistent 117 68; 310 42
~ausgang 117 28
~führer 310 42
~gehäuse 115 2
~kabel 239 2
~kasten 177 25, 33
~kopf 240 27
~kran 310 49
~mann 117 67; 310 20, 41
~monitor 238 65; 239 12; 240
28
~motor 115 76, 78
~objektiv 313 19
~rückteil 114 54
~rückwand 115 23
~schwenker 310 42
~steuerung 242 36
~tasche 115 103
~teil 112 20
~tür 313 25
Kamille 380 1
~, Taube 61 8
~, Wilde 61 8
Kamin Haus 37 10; 38 5; 155
12; 267 23
~ Bergsport 300 8
~ Chem. 350 7
~ecke 267 22
~formstein 159 28
~kehrer 38 31
~sims 267 24
Kamm Geogr. 12 36
~ Hausrat 28 8
~ Pferd 72 14
~ Jagd 88 52
~ Fleischerei 95 20, 47
~, verstellbarer 165 26
Kämmaschine 163 56, 63
Kamm-breiteveränderung
165 36
~deckel 71 17, 31
Kammer Atom 1 66
~ Gewehr 87 20
~scheidewand 20 52
~schleuse 15 58
~stengel 87 22
~trockner 170 49
Kamm-griff 296 41
~lerche 361 19
Kammolch 364 20
Kamm-rad 91 7
~reiher 359 18
Kammzug 163 72
~ablage 163 62
Kamp 84 6

Kampanile 334 65
Kampf-bahn 294 2
~beobachtersitz 257 7
~boot 258 64-91
Kämpfer 336 21
Kampferbaum 380 18
Kämpferstein 336 21
Kampf-panzer 255 80
~ring 299 35
~schiff 259
~stier 319 28
Kanadier 283 3
Kanal Landkarte 15 57
~ Eisenb. 202 32
~ Wasserbau 217 15-28
~ U-Elektronik 241 35, 36
~einfahrt 217 15-16
~haltung 217 29, 37
~sohle 217 30
~verwaltung 217 24
~weiche 217 27
Kanarienstrom 14 41
Kandare 71 13
Kandarenkette 71 12
Kanette 166 21, 30
Kanetten-klemmfeder 166 33
~wechsel 166 5
Känguruh 366 3
Kaninchen 73 18; 86 23; 88 65
~bau 86 26
~haube 86 27
~höhle 86 26
~wiesel 86 24
Kanker 358 44-46
Kanne 39 30; 129 7, 8
Kannelierung 334 27
Kannenstock 163 36
Kanone 255 49
Kanonen-jagdpanzer 255 88
~ofen 309 4
~schlag 306 53
Kantbeitel Tischler 132 11
~ Bildhauerei 339 19
Kante Brotstück 97 5
~ Zeichn. 151 23, 24
~ Sport 302 21
~ Math. 347 32
Kanten-band 103 14; 104 19
~klebemaschine 133 26
~meißel 339 14
~schleifmaschine 133 12
~schutz 123 20
Kantholz 120 10; 157 36
Kantine 119 45
Kanu Sport 283 3
~ Völkerkunde 352 19
~heck 285 44
Kanz 329 83
Kanzel Jagd 86 14
~ Kirche 330 19
~brüstung 330 23
~deckel 330 21
~haube 230 39
Kanzelle 326 13
Kanzeltreppe 330 18
Kapaun 73 21
Kapella 3 27
Kapelle 15 61
Kapellmeister 274 21
Kapern 98 42
Kapillarständer 23 42
Kapital 345 7
Kapitäl 334 20-25
Kapitalband 183 35; 185 43
Kapitälchen 175 14
Kapitalis 341 16
Kapitalschrift 341 16
Kapitän 224 38
Kapitänskajüte 223 13
Kapitell 334 20-25
~, arabisches 337 18
Kapitelüberschrift 185 60

Kapokbaum 383 20
Kappe Schuh 101 37
~ Kunst 336 39
~ Kostüme 355 29
Kappen-blech 303 7
~heberzange 100 52
~isolator 153 54
~muskel 18 52
Kappes 57 32
Kapriole Reitkunst 71 5
~ Ballett 314 21
Kaprolaktam 170 28
Kaptalband 183 35
Kapuze 30 69; 300 19; 331 56
~, abknöpfbare 31 21
Kapuzen-band 29 64
~muskel 18 52
Kapuzinerkresse 53 4
Kar 12 48
Karabiner 300 46
~loch 300 35
~sitz 300 29
Karambolagebillard 277 7
Karamelle 98 77
Karate 299 18-19
Karateka 299 18
Karavelle 218 27-43; 220 37
Kardan-antrieb 189 47
~bogen 67 6
~gelenkkupplung 67 28
kardanische Aufhängung Schiff 224 50
~ Aufhängung U-Elektronik 241 23
Kardan~M-Teil 67 29
~-V-Teil 67 31
Kardätsche 71 55
Karde 163 34, 51
Karden-band 163 35, 38
~kanne 163 35; 164 3
Kardinal 363 5
~kreuz 332 65
~zahl 344 5
Karettschildkröte 364 28
Karfiol 57 31
Karikatur 342 53
Karneval 306
Karnevals-orden 306 60
~prinz 306 58
~prinzessin 306 61
~wagen 306 57
~zug 306 57-70
Karniesbogen 336 36
Karo 276 41
~hemd 33 50
karolingische Minuskel 341 18
Karosserie 191 2
~, selbsttragende 191 1
~abstützung 192 72
Karotte 57 18
Karpfen 364 4
~ansitz 89 26
~haken 89 86
~teich 89 6
Karre 65 14-19
Karree-Treppenschliff 36 51
Karren 65 14-19
~pflug 65 1
~spritze 83 38
Karriere 72 43-44
Karst-erscheinungen 13 71-83
~höhle 13 79
~quelle 13 74
~wasserspiegel 13 77
Karte, gelbe 291 63
~, rote 291 63
Kartei-karte 22 7
~kasten 46 10; 248 27; 262 23
~schrank 262 22
~wanne 248 23
Karten-beleuchtung 230 23
~blatt 276 37

~halter 260 30
~legerin 308 36
~netzentwurf 14 8-9
~reiter 248 4
~vorverkaufsstelle 271 26
~zeichen 15 1-114
Kartoffel 68 38, 40
~apfel 68 43
~bunkerroder 64 59-84
~chip 45 41
~forke 66 5
~gabel 66 5
~hacke 66 6, 24
~käfer 80 52
~knolle 68 40
~korb 66 25
~kralle 66 5
~kraut 68 41
~legewanne 66 21
~löffel 45 75
~sammelroder 64 59-84
~schüssel 45 31
Kartusche 336 7
Karussell 308 2
Karyatide 334 36
Karyopse 375 43
Kasack 31 35
~kleid 30 45
~pullover 31 65
Kasch 33 4
~bühne 313 3
Kaschierung 315 32
Käse 98 5
~abteilung 99 39
~brot 266 75
~fliege 81 15
~glocke 40 7
~laib 99 40
~messer 45 72
~platte 45 35
~schachtel 99 49
~teller 266 52
~torte 97 23
Kasino 274 8
~ausweis 275 14
Kaskade 272 9
Kasperlefigur 260 74
Kasse 99 92; 196 29; 207 86; 250 1; 266 69; 275 2; 308 7
~stand 99 92
~zettel 98 44; 271 7
Kassette 27 14; 117 39
Kassetten-band 241 12
~behälter 241 11
~box 241 11, 47
~fach 241 6, 34; 249 72
~fenster 117 30
~lift 243 8
~maul 114 10
~recorder 117 73; 261 42
~schieber 114 64
~teil 241 3
Kassie 380 16
Kassierer 250 2
Kassiererin 99 94; 266 70; 271 1
Kassiopeia 3 33
Kastagnette 324 46
Kastanie Bot. 371 60; 384 52
~ Pferd 72 27
Kastaniensamen 371 60
Kaste 77 1,4,5
Kastell 218 10
Kasten Tischler 132 24
~ Setzerei 174 8
~ausführung 194 7
~auslage 184 5
~beschicker 159 7
~ Bier 99 72
~brot 97 10
~falle 86 20

~holm 287 30
~kuchen 97 34; 99 21
~kuchenform 40 28
~lade 326 12-14
~oberlicht 316 13
~rinne 122 83
~speiser 163 33
~wagen 194 7
Kastor 3 28
Kasuar 359 1
Katakombe 331 59
Katalograum 262 18
katalytische Krackanlage 145 48, 70
~ Reformieranlage 145 71
Katamaran 284 64
Kater 73 17
Katheder 262 4
Kathedralglas 124 6
Kathete 346 32
Katheter 26 31
~behälter 26 30
~meßplatz 27 30
Kathode 178 6
Kathodenstrahlröhre 242 40
katholische Kirche 330 31-62
Kätzchen 59 39, 45; 371 10
Katze 73 17; 368 2-8
Katzen-auge 187 45
~pfötchen 377 3
~schwanz 60 21
~streu 99 38
~zunge 98 84
Käufer 99 2; 271 55
Käuferin 99 18; 271 16
Kauf-haus 268 41; 271
~laden 47 27
~mann 98 41
~mannsladen 47 27
Kaumuskel 19 7
Kaustifizier-Rührwerk 172 49
Kautabak 107 19
Kauter 24 43
Käuzchen 362 19
Kavallerie 253 13
Kaviarmesser 45 81
Kavitätenbohrer 24 37
Kegel Setzerei 175 46
~ Sport 305 12
~ Math. 347 43
~, runder 36 79
~aufschläger 172 82
~aufstellung 305 1-11
~baum 272 13
~dach 121 24
~höhe 347 44
~könig 305 13
~lade 326 12-14
~mühle 172 73, 83
~projektion 14 8
~rad 143 91
~refiner 172 60
~schnitte 347 11-29
~sitz 143 67
~stand 305 1-11
~stift 143 37
~stoffmühle 172 27
~stumpf 347 45
~trieb 91 25
Kehlbalken 121 35
~dach 121 34
~dachstuhl 121 37
Kehl-bart 88 73
~deckel 17 51
Kehle Anat. 16 19
~ Pferd 72 16
~ Bau 121 15; 122 11, 82
~ Mus. 326 18
Kehl-gang 72 16
~gebälk 121 38
~hammer 137 34
~kopf 20 2-3

~nahtmeßlehre 142 36
~riemen 71 11
~sack 359 8
~sparren 121 64
~stück 329 42
Kehr-besen 50 46; 260 59; 268 21
~düse 50 71
Kehre 297 32
Kehrfahrzeug 199 41
Kehricht 199 17; 268 22
~abfuhrwagen 199 1
Kehr-schaufel 50 52; 260 60
~streckenwickel 163 58
~walze 199 42
~wert 344 16
Keil Bau 119 15
~ Tischler 132 19
~ Schmied 137 31
~ Steinbruch 158 7
~, optischer 176 22
~absatz 101 55
~bein 17 38
~beinhöhle 17 54
Keiler 88 51; 305 33
Keil-hammer 158 6
~kissen 43 11
~loch 132 21
~nut 143 66, 85
~rahmen 338 20
Keilriemen 64 78
~antrieb 180 58
~vorgelege 109 21
Keil-schnitt 54 38
~schrift 341 8
~stein 336 22
~stufe 123 31
Keim-absaugung 92 38
~bläschen 74 66
~blatt 370 87
~gut 92 23
Keimling 68 16; 370 86
Keim-loch 383 57
~pflanze 68 14
~scheibe 74 65
~sproßachse 370 89
~wurzel 370 88
Kelch Bot. 58 8; 374 8; 375 34
~ Kirche 330 10; 332 49
~blatt 58 8, 44; 59 12; 370 58
~borste 375 33
~glas 162 41
~glasfuß 162 42
~kapitell 333 16
Keller-assel 81 6
~außentreppe 118 4
Kellereigehilfe 79 12
Keller-fenster 37 27; 118 3
~geschoß 37 1; 118 1
~treppe 123 16
~wand 123 1
Kellner 267 47
Kellnerin 266 18
Kemenate 329 10
Kennmelder 127 37
Kennzeichen, polizeiliches 189 8
Kennziffer 345 6
Kentaur Astr. 3 39
~ Fabelwesen 327 52
Kerberos 327 29
Kerb-schnittkeramik 328 35
~stift 143 40
~tal 13 53, 54
~tier 358 3-23
~tierfresser 366 4-7
Kerf 358 3-23
Kern Atom 1 43
~ Geogr. 11 5
~ Bot. 58 23; 384 20
~ Gieß. 148 36
~ Kraftwerk 153 17
~ Mus. 326 28

~bohrgerät 145 21
~brennstoff 154 4
~brett 120 93
~bruchstück 1 37-38, 44, 47, 51
~energie 154
~energieforschungsschiff 221 9
~gehäuse 58 36, 59
~haus 58 36, 59
~holz Bau 120 84
~holz Bot. 370 13
~kraftwerk 154 19
~marke 148 37
~obst 58
~obstgewächs 58 31-61
~reaktor 154 19
~schatten 4 35
~spalt 326 24
kernspaltendes Neutron 1 42
Kernspaltung 1 34, 46
Kerosin-(RP-1-)Tank 234 9
Kerrie 373 28
Kerwe 308 1-69
Kerze Wachskerze 260 76
~ Sport 295 29
Kerzenstecker 188 27
Kessel 199 29
~druckmesser 210 47
~fundament 38 66
~haube 329 61
~haus 152 1-21
~jagd 86 34-39
~pauke 323 57
~schmiede 222 9
~speisepumpe 152 18
~thermometer 38 64
~treiben 86 34-39
~wagen 145 35; 213 31
Ketchup 45 43
Ketscher 89 2
Kettbaum 165 56; 166 48; 167 24
~bremse 166 59
Kette Landw. 75 15
~ Web. 166 39; 167 24
~ Fahrrad 187 36
~ Mil. 255 87
Ketten-ablängsäge 157 38
~antrieb Tischler 133 38
~antrieb Fahrrad 187 35-42
~auslage 180 43
~blende 255 85
~blume 61 13
~fähre 216 1
~flieger 308 4
~fräse 120 17
~fräsmaschine 132 49
~gehänge 226 26
~glied 36 39
~greifer 180 56
~karussell 308 4
~kasten 188 46
~panzer 329 63
~querförderer 157 22
~rad 187 35
~säge 120 14
~schleier 139 50
~schließe 118 30
~schrägförderer 64 7
~schutz 187 37
~schutzblech 187 37
~selbstführung 65 12
~spannvorrichtung 157 41
~stich 102 2
~stopper 223 51
~trieb 187 35-39
~zahnkranz 187 38
~zahnrad 187 38
Kettfaden 166 39; 171 1-29, 2, 17, 18
~, gehobener 171 7

~, gesenkter 171 8
~wächter 166 34
Kettschnitt 171 14
Keule Jagd 88 21, 37
~ Fleischerei 95 1, 14
~ Sport 297 37
~ Chem. 349 10
~ Völkerkunde 354 33
Keuliger Bärlapp 377 12
Keuper, Unterer 154 57
Kfz 191 1-56
~-Schlosser 195 53
~-Werkstatt 195
Kicherling 69 19
Kick-schuh 292 10
~starter 188 43; 189 38
Kiebitz 359 21
Kiefer Zool. 358 25
~ Bot. 372 20
~fühler 358 42
Kiefern-eule 82 46
~schwärmer 82 27
~spanner 82 28
~zapfen 372 26
Kiel Sport 283 32, 50; 285 32; 286 61
~ Mus. 322 53
~, gestreckter 222 22
~bogen 336 36
~ des Schiffes 3 46
~flosse 231 6; 232 7
~flügel 322 45
~pallen 222 39
~stapel 222 39
~träger 235 7
~wasser 223 58
Kiemen-deckel 364 5
~spalte 364 3
Kies 118 36; 119 26
~bettung 200 60
Kieselgur 93 3
~filter 93 4
Kieselsäureskelett 357 8
Kieselstein 328 6
Kies-filterschicht 199 23
~weg 272 18
Kiewitt 359 21
killendes Segel 285 8
Kilometer-tafel 216 44
~zähler 187 33
Kimme 87 66; 255 22
Kimm-gang 222 46
~kiel 222 47
~pallen 222 40
~stapel 222 40
Kimono 353 40
~passe 31 18
Kind 48 33
Kinder-bett 47 1
~buch 47 17; 48 23
~dirndl 29 36
~fahrrad 273 9
~garten 48
~gartenleiter 48 33
~gärtnerin 48 1
~grab 331 29
~hemdchen 28 23
~karussell 308 2
~kleidung 29
~pulli 29 47
~reisebett 28 1
~shorts 29 25
~sitz 187 21
~söckchen 29 30
~spielplatz 273
~stuhl 28 33
~tagesstätte 48
~tasse 28 27
~telefon 47 35
~teller 28 28
~-T-Shirt 29 27
~wagen 272 71; 273 31
~zimmer 47

~zimmerschrank 47 21
~zwieback 97 54
Kinn 16 15
~backe 16 9
~band 355 22
~bart 34 10
~grübchen 16 16
~kette 71 12
~lade 16 17
~lappen 73 24
~reff 329 41
~stütze 323 8
Kino 312 1
~besucher 312 5
~karte 312 3
~kasse 312 2
~maschine 312 24
~neiger 313 12
~nivellierkopf 114 48
~plakat 268 57
~projektor 312 24
Kipp-anhänger 56 42
~anschlag 214 35
~anschluß 127 23
~aschenbecher 208 29
~flügel 232 27
~flügelflugzeug 232 26
~kasten 214 34
~lager 226 40
~lore 119 28
~mulde 213 38
~pritsche 194 25
~rost 210 5
~rostkurbel 210 40
~rotor 232 32
~rotorflugzeug 232 31
Kippscher Apparat 350 59
Kipp-vorrichtung 147 44, 59
~zylinder 62 19
Kirche 15 53, 64; 330; 331; 332; 335 1-13
~, evangelische 330 1-30
~, gotische 335 22
~, katholische 330 31-62
~, protestantische 330 1-30
~, romanische 335 1-13
Kirchen-bank 330 28
~besucher 330 29
~dach 331 11
~diener 330 26
~fahne 331 44
~fenster 330 14
~gestühl 330 28
~orgel 326 1-52
~portal 331 16; 335 24
~schwalbe 359 24
~tür 331 16
Kirchgänger 330 29; 331 17
Kirchhof 331 21-41
~mauer 331 18
~tor 331 19
kirchliche Geräte 332 34-54
Kirchturm 331 2
~hahn 331 3
~spitze 331 6
~uhr 331 7
Kirchweih 308 1-69
Kirgise 353 22
Kirmes 308 1-69
~orgel 308 24
Kirri 354 33
Kirrmöwe 359 14
Kirsch-baum 59 1-18
~baumblatt 59 2
~blüte 59 3
Kirsche 59 5, 6-8; 370 99
Kirsch-fliege 80 18
~frucht 59 6-8
~fruchtfliege 80 18
~kern 59 7
~torte 97 22
~torte, Schwarzwälder 97 24
~zweig 59 1

Kithara 322 15
Kitt 124 17
Kittel, weißer 33 56
Kittmesser 124 27; 129 24
Kitz 88 39
Kitzler 20 88
Kitzreh 88 34
Klamm 13 52
Klammer *Bau* 121 97
~ *Chem.* 350 33
~, eckige 342 25
~, runde 342 24
~fuß 364 34
Klampfe 324 12
Klang 89 21
Klappanhänger 278 3
~caravan 278 3
~deckel *Elektr.* 127 24
~deckel *Kamera* 309 27
Klappe *Anat.* 20 46
~ *Mus.* 323 32, 35
Klappen-gefach 246 5
~jalousie 212 84
~kasten 267 5
~mann 310 34
~stutzen 190 15
~system 229 37
~text 185 39
Klapper 306 40
~mohn 61 2
Klapp-hut 35 36
~kamera 309 25
~koje 259 84
~laden 37 30
~lüftung 55 10
~rad 188 1
~scharnier 188 2
~sitz 207 12
~stuhl *Babyausstattung* 28 33
~stuhl *Camping* 278 43
~tintenfaß 309 78
~tisch 278 44
~tischchen 207 53
~tür 194 12
~verdeck 186 52
~wehr 217 65-72
~wohnwagen 278 3
Kläranlage 144 20
klarer Schnaps 98 56
Klarglasfleck 115 66
Klarinette 318 4; 323 34
Klarinettist 318 5
Klarsicht-fenster 278 41; 284 3
~scheibe 189 46
Klärwerk 144 20
Klasse 77 1,4,5
~, 5,5-m- 284 58
Klassen-buch 260 23
~raum 260 1-45
~schrank 260 43
~sortierung 74 44
~spiegel 242 3
~zimmer 260 1-45
Klassierer 172 50
Klassizismus 336 15
klassizistischer Stil 336 15
Klatschmohn 51 30; 61 2
Klaue *Jagd* 88 24
~ *Setzerei* 174 48
~ *Fabelwesen* 327 3
Klaviatur 322 28; 324 40; 325 4-5, 41
Klavichord 322 36
~mechanik 322 37
Klavier 325 1
~gehäuse 325 6
~hammer 325 3
~mechanik 325 2-18
~pedal 325 8-9
~saite 325 7
~taste 325 4-5
Klavizimbel 322 45

Klebe-arbeit 260 50-52
~band 134 38
~binder 184 1; 249 61
~fläche 260 50
~maschine 184 1
~presse 117 89
~streifen 98 47
~streifenhalter 247 28
~streifenrolle 247 29
~streifenspender 247 27
~vorrichtung 133 29
Klebstoff 48 4
~tube 260 51
Klee, Deutscher 69 1
~, Hoher 69 9
~, Kriechender 69 2
~, Russischer 69 6
~, Schweizer 69 10
~, Steyrer 69 1
~, Welscher 69 9
Kleeblatt, vierblättriges 69 5
~bogen 336 32
~kreuz 332 71
Klee-blüte 69 7
~karre 66 26
~sämaschine 66 26
Kleiber 361 11
Kleid 30 10; 271 29
~, gegürtetes 355 25
~, zweiteiliges 31 11
Kleider-ablage 315 5
~abteil 267 30
~bügel 41 3
~bürste 50 44
~gürtel 30 11; 31 10
~haken 41 2; 207 50; 266 14
~kasten 212 63
~laus 81 41
~mode 355
~motte 81 13
~rock 30 8
~schutz 104 14
~ständer *Schneiderei* 103 17
~ständer *Restaurant* 266 12
~stange 271 31
Klein 275 22
~auflage 184 1; 249 59
~bahn 15 25
~behälter 206 19
Kleinbild-kamera 23 7; 112 26
~kassette 112 35; 114 7
~-Kompaktkamera 114 1
~patrone 114 7
~-Spiegelreflexkamera 115 1
Kleinblütiges Knopfkraut 61 31
Klein-buchstabe 175 12
~bus 194 9; 195 47
~container 206 19
~diktiergerät 246 32
~drehbank 109 20
~drehtisch 142 41
kleine Hostie 332 48
~ Oktave 321 45
kleiner als 345 20
Kleiner Bär 3 34
kleiner Finger 19 68
Kleiner Frostspanner 80 16
kleiner Hahn 88 66
Kleiner Hund 3 15
~ Kohlweißling 80 48
~ Uhu 362 14
~ Wagen 3 34
Kleine Schwalbenmöwe 359 11
~ Stubenfliege 81 1
Klein-garten 52 1-32
~gärtner 52 24
~gepäckablage 208 28
~hirn 17 45
~kabine 214 20
~kabinenbahn 214 19

Kleinkaliber-gewehr 305 48
~standardgewehr 305 43
~waffe 305 44
Klein-kern 357 12
~kind 28 42
~kinderkleidung 29 13-30
~klavier 325 1
~kraftrad 189 1
~küchenmaschine 40 45
~laster 194 1
~lasttransporter 194 5
~motorrad 189 1
~offsetdrucker 249 48
~offset-Stapeldrucker 180 70
~schmetterling 58 62, 64
~schraubstock 134 10
Kleinst-bildkamera 114 16
~bildkassette 114 17
Kleinsterilisator 26 35
Kleinteile-kasten 134 34; 195 31
~spender 22 64
Klein-uhr 109 5
~vieh 73 18-36; 213 28
~vorlage 117 56
~wagen 193 19
Kleister-bürste 128 27
~gerät 128 25
Klemmbügel 247 43
Klemme 350 33
Klemmen-kasten 153 60
~schrank 211 16
Klemm-halter 149 45
~hebel 132 67
~platte *Werkzeugmasch.* 149 46
~platte *Eisenb.* 202 9
~schraube 133 23
~vorrichtung 2 43
~walzenpaar 165 39
Klempner 125 17
Kletterausrüstung 300 31-57
~bohne 57 8
~dach 273 60
Kletterer 300 5
Klettergerüst 273 47
~gürtel 300 56
~hose 300 7
Klettern 300 2-13
Kletternetz 273 50
Klettern im Eis 300 14-21
~ im Fels 300 2-13
Kletterpflanze 51 5; 53 2; 57 8
~rose 52 12
~schuh 300 44
~seil 273 48
~tau 296 19
~technik 300 2-13
~turm 273 17
~walze 157 5
~wurzel 370 80
Kliff 13 53
Klima 9 53-58
~, äquatoriales 9 53
~, boreales 9 56
~, polares 9 57-58
~anlage 26 20; 146 24; 239 15
~karte 9 40-58
~kunde 9
~landschaft 356 21
Klinge *Messerklinge* 45 54
~ *Sport* 294 44
~ *Völkerkunde* 354 12
Klingel-beutel 330 59
~tafel 267 28
~taster 127 2
Klingenbindung 294 46
Klinik, chirurgische 26 1-54
Klinken-feld 311 16
~rad 110 10
~stecker 241 70
Klinker-beplankung 285 50-52

~einer 283 18
~kühler 160 9
~lager 160 10
Klinknagel 285 52
Klinopinakoid 351 24
Klippdachs 366 24
Klippe 13 25
Klipper 220 36
Klippschliefer 366 24
Klischee 178 38
~ätzmaschine 178 23
~facette 178 44
~fuß 178 41
~herstellung 178
~holz 178 41
Klischiergerät 177 52
Klivie 53 8
Klo 49 12
Kloakentier 366 1
Klopapier 49 11
Klopf-düse 50 71
~eisen 136 36
Klöpfel *Tischler* 132 5
~ *Steinbruch* 158 36
Klopf-holz 120 67
~maschine 131 4
Klöppel 324 64
~spitze 102 18
Klosett 49 12
~becken 49 13
~brille 49 15
~deckel 49 14
~papier 49 11
~umrahmung 49 18
~umrandung 49 18
Kloster 15 63; 331 52-58
~garten 331 53
~gewölbe 336 41
~hof 331 53
Klotz 125 21
Klub-flagge 283 25
~haus 283 23
~sessel 267 26
~stander 283 25
Kluft 13 50
Klüpfel 132 5
Kluppen-kette 168 24
~pinsel 129 20
Kluppmeßstock 85 10
Klüver 219 22
~baum 218 51; 219 1
~leiter 219 14
Knaben-hemd 29 61
~hose 29 60
~kraut 376 28
Knäckebrot 97 50
Knackmandel 45 41
Knall-blättchen 306 49
~bonbon 306 50
~erbse 306 51
~frosch 306 52
Knappe 329 68
Knarre 306 47
Knarrpoller 284 25
Knäuelgras 69 25
Knäuelgras 69 25
Knaulgras, Gemeines 69 25
Knebel *Med.* 21 16
~ *Schlosser* 140 5
~ *Bildhauerei* 339 25
~bart 34 13
~knopf 30 66
Kneif 183 13
~zange 100 41; 126 65; 134 13; 140 69
Knet-brett 48 14
~figur 48 13
~maschine 97 55
~masse 48 12
Knick-flügel 229 14
~kragen 324 10
~lenkung 85 31, 37

~säulenmontierung 113 21
~spant 258 8
~stelle 358 35
Knie 16 50
~bank 332 25
~beuge 16 51
~buckel 329 53
~bund 33 41
~bundhose 33 40
~gamasche 289 31
~geige 323 16
~gelenk 340 30
Kniehebel 325 45
~antrieb 181 16
~presse 183 26
~system 183 30
Knie-kehle 16 51
~liegestütz 295 20
~scheibe *Anat.* 17 23
~scheibe *Pferd* 72 33
~schutz 292 9
~schützer 303 17
~stand 295 7
~stock 121 46, 47
~strumpf 29 53; 33 42
Knobel 276 31
~becher 276 30
Knobeln 276 29
Knöchel 19 59, 82
~schutz 291 33
Knochen 17 1-29; 70 33; 328 2, 3
~dünnung 95 16
~gerüst 17 1-29; 353 13
~meißel 24 49
~säge 94 19; 96 56
~schinken 96 1; 99 52
~zange 26 51
Knockout 299 40
Knolle 68 40
Knollen-begonie 51 19
~blätterpilz 379 11
~pflanze 68 38
Knopf-gras 377 2
~kraut, Kleinblütiges 61 31
~leiste, verdeckte 33 62
~schachtel 103 15
~sonde 22 53; 26 40
~zelle 110 7
Knospe 54 23, 26; 58 27; 59 22; 60 16; 61 3; 382 28
Knospenkapitell 333 14
Knötchenstich 102 13
Knoten *Meteorol.* 9 12
~ *Kleidung* 31 47
~ *Haartracht* 34 29
~ *Bau* 122 68
~ *Bot.* 383 63
~fang 173 13
~schnur 352 22
~schrift 352 22
~stich 102 13
Knöterich 376 10
Knüpfarbeit 102 21
Knüppelschaltung 191 91
Kobalt-bestrahlungsapparat 2 28
~bombe 2 28
Koben 75 36
Kochbecher 350 20
Kocher 97 69
Köcher 352 27
~fliege, Große 358 12
Kocher-Klemme 22 49
Koch-lauge 172 46
~löffelgarnitur 40 2
~platte 39 15
~platz 39 12-17
~salz 170 13
~salzkristall 1 9
~schrank 96 47
~topf 39 29; 40 12
~ und Backplatz 39 12-17

Kockpit 283 8
Köder 86 21; 89 65-76
~dose 89 24
~fischsenke 89 29
~gewicht 89 36
~nadel 89 41
Kodierung 242 11
Koeffizient 345 4
Koffer 194 19; 204 6
~anhänger 205 8
~raum *Auto* 191 24; 193 23
~raum *Eisenb.* 207 71
~raumdeckel 191 7
Kogge 218 18-26
Kognak 98 59
~schale 45 88
Kohl 57 32
~, Brüsseler 57 30
Kohle 197 24
~fiberrute 89 57
Kohlen-abzugsband 152 3
~beschickungsanlage 199 37
~bunker 152 2
~förderband 152 1
~füller 309 9
~hafen 225 18
~halter 312 43
~krater 312 44
~lager 225 19
~mühle 152 4
~schaufel 38 43
Kohlenstoffatom 242 63
Kohlenturm 156 5
~gurtförderer 156 4
Kohlestift 338 16
Kohl-kopf 57 32
~meise 361 9
~rabi 57 26
~weißling, Großer 80 47
~weißling, Kleiner 80 48
Kokarde 264 8
Kokardenblume 60 19
Kokerei 144 7-11; 156 1-15; 170 2
~gasbehandlung 156 16-45
Kokille 147 32, 37
Kokillen-band 147 36
~wand 148 29
Kokon 358 51
Kokos-fett 98 23
~nuß 383 53
~palme 383 48
Kokotte 306 37
Koks 147 2
~asche 120 44
~ausdrückmaschine 156 7
~feuerung 38 38
Kokskohlen-entladung 156 1
~komponentenbunker 156 3
~turm 144 9
Koks-kuchenführungswagen 156 9
~löschturm 144 10
~löschwagen 144 11
~ofen 156 16
~ofenbatterie 144 7; 156 8
~rampe 156 12
~rampenband 156 13
~verladung 156 15
Kölbchen 162 40
Kolben *Gewehr* 87 3
~ *Motor* 190 37
~ *Infotechnik* 242 46
~ *Mil.* 255 24
~ *Bot.* 370 71; 378 22
~gras 69 27
~hals 87 7
~kappe 305 46
~pumpenschwengel 83 45
~ring 190 37
~rückenspritze 83 43
~stange *Auto* 192 75
~stange *Eisenb.* 210 33

Kolleg 262 1
Kollektor 155 19
~drehstrommotor 164 35
Koller 355 39
~gang 159 8
Kollimator 351 30
Kollo 206 4
Kolombine 306 27
Kolon 342 17
Kolonel 175 24
Kolonialwarenhandlung 98 1-87
Kolonie 369 8, 9, 14
Kolonnade 274 9
Kolonnenboden 145 37
Kolophonium 323 11
Koloradokäfer 80 52
Kolposkop 23 5
Kolumbine 306 27
Kolumne 185 65
Kolumnen-schnur 174 16
~titel 185 66
Kombi 193 15
~düse 50 67
~fahrzeug 193 15
~hacke 56 7
~hammer 300 37
~kopf 241 59
~limousine, dreitürige 193 18
Kombination 326 40, 46
Kombinations-flugschrauber 232 29
~knopf 326 46
~kraftwagen 193 15
~spiel 276 1-16
~teppichpflegegerät 50 76
~zange 126 60; 127 53
Kombine 64 1-33
kombinierter Zug 315 4
Kombi-schiff 221 96
~wagen 193 15
~zange 134 14
Kombüse 223 42
Komfrey 69 13
komische Nummer 307 25
Komma *Schrift* 342 18
~ *Math.* 344 20
Kommandant 235 17
Kommandanten-raum 259 85
~schapp 259 85
Kommando-anlage 238 64
~brücke 223 12-18; 226 55; 258 14; 259 3
~einheit 6 9
~lautsprecher 238 8, 52
~mikrophon 238 10, 39, 53
~stand 224 14
~teil 234 65
Kommataste 247 19
Kommißbrot 97 10
Kommode 266 41
Kommunalobligation 251 11-19
Kommunizierender 332 27
Kommutatorklappe 211 18
Kompakt-aufbau 221 33
~kamera 117 51; 177 32
~kassette 241 10
~ski 301 1
Komparase 310 29
Kompaß 224 46-53; 288 12
~kessel 224 49
~rose 224 47
Kompendium 313 3, 39
~schiene 313 10
Kompensations-pendel 109 33
~schreiber 23 55
Kompensatornivellier 112 69
Komplementwinkel 346 15
Kompost-erde 55 15
~haufen 52 6
Kompott 45 30
~löffel 45 66

~schale 45 29
~schüssel 45 28
Kompresse 26 23; 27 4
Kompressions-boden 2 25
~haken 163 16
Kompressor 129 33; 138 3; 145 45; 155 4
Kondensationslokomotive 210 69
Kondensator *Kernenergie* 154 17, 35
~ *Wärmepumpe* 155 8
~ *Papier* 172 30
~ *Eisenb.* 211 17
~ *Mil.* 259 64
Kondensatspeicher 172 17
Kondensor-einrichtung 112 8
~linse 113 32
Konditorei 97 1-54, 67-70; 265 1-26
~abteilung 99 9
~büfett 265 1
~lehrling 265 6
~waren 97 17-47
Konfekt 98 80
~dose 46 12
Konfektionskleid 271 29
Konferenz-gruppe 246 31-36
~schaltung 242 22
~sessel 246 36
~tisch 246 31
Konfetti 306 62
Konfitüre 98 51
Konifere 372 1-71
König *Spiele* 276 8
~ *Kegelsport* 305 7, 13
Königin *Zool.* 77 4, 38
~ *Spiele* 276 9
Königinnen-kammer 333 3
~versandkäfig 77 44
~zelle 77 37
Königs-baum 91 34
~farn 377 16
~grab 333 1
~kammer 333 2
~kerze 376 9
~krone 254 42
~weihe 362 11
Konkav-konvexglas 111 41, 42
~spiegel *Astr.* 5 32
~spiegel *Rummelplatz* 308 56
Konserve 96 25; 98 15-20
Konservendose 96 26; 99 91
Konsole 126 6
Konsol-operator 244 3
~schreibmaschine 244 4
Konstruktions-büro 151; 222 2
~element 222 44-61
Konsultationszimmer 23 1
Kontakt-arm *Auto* 194 41
~arm *Telefon* 237 44
~feder 127 28
~feld 237 45
~glied 237 46
~goniometer 351 27
~manometer 316 56
~ring 237 43
~rolle 194 42
~stück 127 38-39
~walze 164 4
Kontente 316 3
Konter-effetstoß 277 6
~mutter 143 30; 187 54
Kontinental-abhang 11 9
~sockel 11 8
~tafel 11 7
Kontinente 14 12-18
Kontoauszug 247 44
Kontra-baß 323 23
~baßtuba 323 44
~fagott 323 28

~oktave 321 43
Kontrast-mittelinjektion 27 15
~regelung 240 32
~regler 249 36
Kontrollampe 157 62; 164 8; 249 71
Kontrollautsprecher 239 9
Kontrolle 191 67
~, optische 25 44
Kontrolleuchte 191 72, 80
Kontrolleur 315 10
Kontroll-feld Radio 238 1, 7
~feld Film 311 8
~gerät 224 26
~instrument 311 15
~kasten 6 23
~öffnung 38 62
~raum 25 1-9; 146 32
~stempel 94 24; 252 35
~turm 233 17; 287 12
~uhr Druck 182 20
~uhr Billard 277 17
~uhr Mus. 326 37, 38
~ und Monitorfeld 238 1, 7
Konturen-messer 340 10
~stichel 340 5
Konturieren 129 46
Konus 143 67; 187 58
~kasten 163 30
Konvergenzmodul 240 12
Konversionsfiltereingabenut 117 38
Konverter-boden 147 47
~hut 147 45
~kamin 147 67
Konvex-bogen 336 34
~spiegel 308 57
Konzertflügel 325 40
Konzertina 324 36
Konzert-kartenverkaufsstelle 271 26
~pavillon 274 19
~saal 325 40
Koordinate 347 8
Koordinaten-nullpunkt 347 4
~system 347 8, 11
~system, rechtwinkliges 347 1
Köper 171 45
~, schräger 171 46
~, versetzter 171 46
~geflecht 136 2
Kopf Anat. 16 1-18; 17 42-55; 19 1-13
~ Pferd 72 1-11
~ Zool. 81 33, 36; 82 2; 358 28
~ Jagd 88 12
~ Fleischerei 95 43
~ Bau 122 87
~ Masch. 143 14, 52
~ Textil 171 31
~ Setzerei 175 39
~ Sport 294 52
~ball 291 46
~bedeckung 35
~bindung 171 39
~bindungsstelle 171 34
Köpfchen 370 73
Kopf-croupier 275 6
~ende 43 6
Köpfer 64 85
Kopf-füßer 357 37
~gestell 71 7-11
~haar 16 3
~haken 299 33
~halter 18 34; 19 1
~haut, abgezogene 352 15
~hieb 294 23
Kopfhörer 241 66; 249 63; 261 38; 309 24
~anschluß 117 10
~buchse 249 68
~bügel 241 67; 261 41

~stecker 241 70
Kopf-kippe 297 27
~kissen 27 27; 43 12-13; 47 4
~kissenbezug 43 12
~klee 69 1
~kohl 57 32
~leiste 342 40
~linie 19 73
Köpfmesser 64 87
Kopf-nicker 19 1
~polster Med. 21 13
~polster Eisenb. 207 47
~salat 57 36
~schmuck 352 12
~schutz 299 30; 302 34
~sprung 282 12
~stand 295 28
~steg 185 56
~stoß 291 46
~stück 183 21
~stütze Bau 119 59
~stütze Auto 191 33; 193 7, 8
~stütze, integrierte 193 31
~teil Bett 43 6
~teil Eisenb. 207 67
~träger 311 25
~trommelwand 243 27
~überschlag 297 27
~verband 21 3
Kopie 111 1-46
Kopien-ausstoß 249 43
~vorwahl 249 35
Kopier-rahmen 179 13
~rahmenuntergestell 179 14
~scheibe 111 27
~ständer 115 92
~stift 175 57
~werk 310 2; 311 30
Kopilot 230 25, 28
Kopilotensitz 230 37
Koppel Pferdesport 289 46
~ Mus. 326 41, 48
~rick 289 8
~schleuse 217 17-25
Kops 163 2
~behälter 165 16
Kopulation 54 39
Kopulieren 54 39
Korallen-polyp 357 19
~riff 13 32
~stock 357 18
~tier 357 17
Korb Korbmacher 136 16
~ Sport 292 32
Korbball 292 28
~spiel 292 28
Korbbrett 292 30
Körbchen Zool. 77 6
~ Bot. 370 74
Korb-flasche 206 13
~flechter 136 33
~flechterei 136 1-40
~leger 292 35
~macher 136 33
~macherei 136 1-40
~ring 288 67; 292 33
~ständer 292 31
~stuhl 43 3
~wagen 28 30; 48 24
~weide 371 29
Kordmütze 35 25
Kordon 52 2, 17, 29
korinthische Säule 334 10
Korkenzieher 45 46
Kork-gleitfloß 89 43
~gürtel 282 19
~leine 282 32
~mundstück 107 13
~schwimmweste 228 9
~weste 282 19
Kormoran 359 10
Korn Landw. 68 1, 13
~ Zool. 81 30

~ Jagd 87 71
~ Branntwein 98 56
~ Mil. 255 3, 23, 37
~ Sport 305 42
~, entartetes 68 4
Kornblume 61 1
Kornelkirsche 373 32
~, Rotästige 373 30
Kornelle 373 32
Körner 134 31; 140 64
~frucht 68 1-37
Kornett 323 43
Korn-frucht 68 1-37
~größe 119 26
~halter 255 23, 37
~hammer 125 15
~käfer 81 16
~krebs 81 16
~nelke 61 6
~rade, Gemeine 61 6
~rose 61 2
~roulett 340 18
~schnecke 64 20
~sperling 361 5
~spitze 87 72
Korntank 64 23
~auslauf 64 25
~auslaufrohr 64 26
~füllschnecke 64 24
Körnung 340 47
Korn-vogel 361 6
~wurm 81 16
~zange Med. 23 12
~zange Uhrmacher 109 14
Korona 4 39
Körper Buchb. 185 21
~ Mus. 326 29
~, geometrischer 347 30-46
~, menschlicher 16 1-54
~glied 357 25
~größenmesser 22 69
~längsachse 298 11
~pflegemittel 99 27-35
~querachse 298 11
~temperatur 23 3
Korpus Möbel 46 3
~ Setzerei 175 27
Korrekturleiste 182 23
~linse 115 22, 72
Korrespondentenbericht 342 54
Korridor Haus 41 1-29
~ Sport 301 71
~tür 41 25
Kort-Düse 227 21
koruna 252 27
Kosinus 346 32
Kosmetik-gondel 99 23
~salon 105 1-39
Kosmetikum 99 27-35
Kostüm Kleidung 31 1
~ Kleidermoden 355
~bildner 315 38
~entwurf 315 39
~fest 306 1-48
~jacke 29 51; 31 2
~rock 29 52; 31 3
Kotangens 346 32
Köte 72 24
Kotelett 95 3, 46
Koteletten 34 24
Kötengelenk 72 24
Kot-flügel 191 3
~rinne 75 20
~schützer 187 43
~transportband 74 27
~vogel 359 25
Krabbe Kunst 335 38
~ Zool. 358 1; 369 16
Krackanlage 145 48, 70
Kraftfahrdrehleiter 270 9
Kraftfahrzeug 191 1-56; 195 34

~mechaniker 195 53
~schlosser 195 53
Kraft-haus 217 64
~heber 65 24-29
~mensch 308 27
~messer 308 11
~rad 189
~spritze 270 5
~station 310 8
Kraftstoff-anzeige 191 65; 230 16, 17
~behälter 65 42; 209 17, 20; 212 56
~druckleitung 190 52
~druckmesser 230 19
~druckregler 190 17
~-Handpumpe 190 64
~hauptbehälter 212 4
~kontrollampe 191 71
~leckleitung 190 53
~reservebehälter 212 60
~ringleitung 190 31
~tank 189 2; 230 48; 235 21
~zufluß 192 13
Kraft-wagen 191 1-56
~werk 144 13; 152; 153
Kragen Jagd 88 27
~ Mus. 324 10
~ Kostüme 355 74
~, betreßter 186 22
~flasche 328 12
Krähe 86 50; 361 2
Krähen-beere 377 23
~hütte 86 51
~scharbe 359 10
Krakatau-Ausbruch 7 21
Krallegras 377 2
Krammetsbeere 372 52
Krammstock 148 17
Kran Installateur 126 34
~ Mil. 258 88
~ausleger 255 95
~bahn 222 24
~brücke 222 26
Kranen 126 34
Kran-führerhaus 119 35; 222 16; 226 52
~gestell 226 53
~gleis 119 27
~haken 139 45
~hubschrauber 232 16
Kranich 3 42
Krankabel 222 13
Kranken-auto 270 19
~bahre 270 23
~blatt 22 8
~haus 25; 26; 27
~kraftwagen 270 19
~schein 22 9
Kranker 274 7
Kran-kette 139 44
~motor 157 28
~pfanne 147 60
~wagen 270 67
Kranz, Frankfurter 97 42
~frisur 34 31
~gesims 334 11-14; 335 48
~riff 13 32
Krater Geogr. 11 16
~ Film 312 44
Kratzboden 62 24
Kratze 163 34; 168 31
Kratzeisen 303 24
Kratzenrauhmaschine 168 31
Kratz-malerei 338 41
~putz 338 41
Kraulen 282 37
Kraulschwimmen 282 37
Kräuselung 170 59
Krauskohl 57 34
Kraut 57 32
~abstreifer 64 73

~band 64 76
~bandantrieb 64 78
~bandklopfeinrichtung 64 77
~pflanze 57 28-34
Krawatte 32 41
Krawatten-knoten 32 42
~nadel 36 22
Kraweel-beplankung 285 53
~boot 283 9
Krayonmanier 340 14-24
Krebs *Astr.* 3 4; 4 56
~ *Zool.* 358 1-2; 369 12, 15, 16
~tier 358 1-2
Kredit 250 4
~büro 271 24
Krehl 51 22
Kreide *Schule* 260 32
~ *Graphik* 340 26
~ablage 260 31
~manier 340 14-24
~skizze 338 4
~stift 338 5
~zirkel 260 40
Kreis 346 42
~, konzentrischer 346 58
~abschnitt 346 52
~ausschnitt 346 54
~berechnung 247 24
~bogen 346 53
Kreisel 64 52
~brecher 158 19
~heuer 63 24
~horizont 230 3
~kompaß 224 31, 51-53
~kompaßanlage 224 51-53
~mäher 63 19
~pumpe 79 7; 269 44; 270 8
~schwader 63 26
~turbopumpe 259 57
~zetter 63 24
Kreis-fläche 347 39
~flanke 296 54
~führung 141 35
~grenze 15 103
~kamm 163 68
~laufanlage 83 16
~linie 346 44
~messer 184 22
~pappschere 184 20
~regner 56 43; 67 4, 32
~ring 346 57
Kreissäge *Hut* 35 35
~ *Forstw.* 84 33
~ *Bau* 119 19
~ *Heimwerken* 134 50
~blatt 132 59
~maschine 125 24
~vorsatz 134 52
Kreis-schablone 151 70
~spieler 292 3
~verstellung 14 62
Krempelärmel 31 62
~band 163 64; 164 5
Kremser 186 33
Kren 57 20
Krepidoma 334 4
Kreppapier 49 11
Kreppeisen 106 26
Kreuz *Anat.* 16 25
~ *Pferd* 72 31
~ *Schule* 260 28
~ *Spiele* 276 38
~ *Mus.* 320 50
~, ägyptisches 332 59
~, Brabanter 332 71
~, burgundisches 332 60
~, erzbischöfliches 332 64
~, griechisches 332 56
~, Jerusalemer 332 72
~, konstantinisches 332 67
~, lateinisches 332 55
~, Lothringer 332 62
~, päpstliches 332 66

~, russisches 332 57
~bein 17 21; 20 59
~blume *Bot.* 61 1
~blume *Kunst* 335 37
~bramsegel 218 54
~bruchfalzmesser 185 12
~ des Südens 3 44
~durchschlag 297 44
Kreuzen 285 25-28
Kreuz-form, christl. 332
55-72
~gang 331 52
~gewölbe 335 31-32
~gratgewölbe 336 42
~griff *Med.* 21 21
~griff *Sport* 296 43
~hang 296 50
~holz 120 90
~kopf 210 27
~kraut, Gemeines 61 12
~lage 340 54
~leitwerk 229 28
~mast 220 24, 30
~meißel 140 25
~otter 364 40
~poller 217 13; 227 10
~rippe 335 31
~rippengewölbe 336 43
~ritter 329 72
~scharnier 151 50
~schliff 36 63, 65
~schlittenführung 174 48
~schlitzschraube 143 26
~schlitzschraubendreher
134 5
~schwalbe 359 24
~segel 220 26
~spinne 358 45
~sprosse 37 35
~spule 165 8, 13, 24; 169 27;
170 51, 52
~spulendurchmesser 165 7
~spulmaschine 165 1
~stich 102 5
~strebe 118 88
~strecke 285 22, 25
~stück 126 50
Kreuztisch *Optik* 112 29
~ *Werkzeugmasch.* 150 28
~einrichtung 112 10; 115 98
Kreuzträger 331 43
Kreuzungsweichen 203 49-52
Kreuz-verband 118 65
~weg 330 54
~wegstation 330 54
Kricket 292 70-76
~spiel 292 70-76
~tor 292 70
Kriechblume 335 38
Kriechender Klee 69 2
Kriech-fuß 357 28
~stoßschwimmen 282 37
~tier 364 27-41
Kriegs-bemalung 352 13
~horn 354 39
~schiff 258; 259
~schiff, römisches 218 9-12
Kriminal-beamter 264 33
~polizei 264 26
Krimmermütze 35 34
Krinoline 355 72
Kris 353 44
Kristall 351 29
~bau 351 1-26
~glas 45 86
~glasscheibe 179 24
~grundform 351 1-26
~kegel 77 21
~kombination 351 1-26
~kunde 351
~messung 351 27-33
~mittelpunkt 351 3
Kristallometrie 351 27-33

Kristall-spiegelglas 124 5
~struktur 351 1-26
Kristallsystem, hexagonales
351 20-22
~, isometrisches 351 1-17
~, kubisches 351 1-17
~, monklines 351 24-25
~, reguläres 351 1-17
~, rhombisches 351 23
~, tesserales 351 1-17
~, tetragonales 351 18-19
~, triklines 351 26
Kristallzucker 98 55
KR-Klasse 284 63
Krocket 292 77-82
~hammer 292 81
~kugel 292 82
~spiel 292 77-82
~spieler 292 80
~tor 292 78
Krokant 98 85
krona 252 25
Kronblatt 59 11; 370 59
krone 252 24, 26
Krone *Anat.* 19 37
~ *Zahnarzt* 24 28
~ *Messerkrone* 45 55
~ *Jagd* 88 9, 29-31
~ *Uhr* 110 42
~ *Geld* 252 24, 25, 26, 27
~ *Herrscherkrone* 254
37,38,42-46
Kronen-aufzug 110 42
~dach 122 50
~korköffner 45 47
~mutter 143 24, 77
~verschluß 93 27
Kronleuchter 267 21
Kropf 73 20
~gans 359 5
~stück 123 49
Krösel 124 25
~zange 124 19
Kröte 364 23
Krotten-beere 379 7
~blume 379 7
Krücke *Jagd* 86 49
~ *Mus.* 326 21
Krückenkreuz 332 70
Krüger-Klappe 229 55
Krüllschnitt 107 25
Krume 97 3
Krummdarm 20 16
Krumme 86 35
Krummhorn 322 6
Krümmling 123 52
Krümmungs-halbmesser 346
22
~mittelpunkt 346 23
Krumpfen 168 26
Kruppe 72 31
Krüppelwalm 121 17
~dach 121 16
Kruste 97 4
Krustentier 358 1-2
Kruzifix 332 33
kryochirurgischer Eingriff 22
63
Kübel *Gärtner* 55 48
~ *Straßenbau* 201 9
~helm 254 7
~pflanze 55 47
Kubikwurzel 345 2
Kubusspiel 48 21
Küche 39; 207 29, 80
Kuchenbüfett 265 1
Küchen-durchreiche 266 66
~gerät 40
~lampe 39 39
~meister 207 34
~schüssel 40 6
~stuhl 39 43
~tisch 39 44

Kristall-spiegelglas 124 5
~uhr 39 20; 109 34
~waage 309 84
~wagen 233 22
~wand 46 29
~zwiebel 57 24
Kuckuck 359 30
Kuckucks-knecht 359 25
~küster 359 25
~lichtnelke 376 21
~uhr 109 31
Kufe 303 10
Kugel *Schmuck* 36 82-86
~ *Fischerei* 90 19
~ *Fleischerei* 95 36
~ *Fahrrad* 187 31, 56, 68
~ *Sport* 298 49
~ *Math.* 347 41
~, glatte 36 82
~baum 272 12
~fräser 108 7
~gelenkkopf 114 47
~kaktus 53 14
~kopf 249 15
~kopfnadel 328 29
~kopfschreibmaschine 249 1
~kuppe 143 50
~lager 143 69; 187 68
~leuchte 267 4
~libelle 230 12
~manipulator 2 38
~mühle 161 1
~pfanne 255 47
~ring 187 68
~schlagapparat 38 32
~schreiber 47 26
~stoßen 298 48
~tank 145 73; 221 36
~wobbler 89 71
Kuh 73 1
~blume 61 13
Kühl-aggregat 39 5
~anlage 209 21; 212 26, 77
Kuhlattich 61 13
Kühler *Landmaschinen* 65 51
~ *Erdöl* 145 44
~ *Kokerei* 156 27
~ *Textil* 170 5
~ *Auto* 191 9
~ *Eisenb.* 212 54
~ *Chem.* 350 48
~grill 191 11
~haube 304 11
~haubenfenster 304 12
Kühl-fach 39 3
~haus *Fleischerei* 94 21-24
~haus *Hafen* 225 50
~leitung 235 38
~mitteltemperaturanzeige
191 38, 66
~mittelzuführung *Schmied*
138 26
~mittelzuführung
Werkzeugmasch. 149 25
~raum 223 56
~rippe 189 20; 190 80; 242 60
~schlangensystem 93 11
~schmierstoff 149 44
~schrank 39 2; 46 33; 317 10
~schutzverkleidung 235 15
~system 154 48
~theke 96 12
~tisch 97 67
~tresen 266 49
~turm 144 15; 154 39
Kühlung 154 55
Kühl-vitrine 98 3
~walze *Textil* 170 27
~walze *Druck* 180 28
Kühlwasser *Kernenergie* 154
18
~ *Eisenb.* 212 78
~anschluß 111 31
~ausgleichsbehälter 212 65

~bohrung 242 54
~kreislauf 154 10
~leitung *Kraftwerk* 152 27
~leitung *Auto* 191 10
~pumpe 190 61
~system 154 55
~temperaturmesser 212 21
~thermostat 190 62
~-Wärmetauscher 155 3
Kühlzylinder 173 25
Kuh-schelle, Gemeine 375 5
~stall 75 14
Küken 74 2
~stall 74 1
Kukuruz 68 31
Külbel 162 40, 47
Kuli 353 43
Kultivator 65 55
Kultur 84 9, 10
Kulturen, bakteriologische 261 29
Kultur-haus 55 4
~zaun 84 7
Kultwagen 328 36
Kümmel-brötchen 97 14
~stange 97 31
Kümmerling 57 13
Kummet 71 15
Kümo 221 99
Kumpf 328 11
Kumt 71 15
Kumulonimbus 8 17; 287 26
~wolke 287 26
Kumulus 8 1; 287 22
~wolke 287 22
Kunde 99 2; 111 2; 248 18; 271 55
Kundendienstsachbearbeiter 248 17
Kunden-halle 250 1-11
~kartei 248 24
Kundin 98 43; 99 18; 271 16
Kunst 333; 334; 335; 336; 337
~, ägyptische 333 1-18
~, altchristliche 334 61-71
~, babylonische 333 19-20
~, byzantinische 334 72-75
~, chinesische 337 1-6
~, etruskische 334 49-52
~, gotische 335 22-41
~, graphische 340
~, griechische 334 1-48
~, indische 337 19-28
~, islamische 337 12-18
~, japanische 337 7-11
~, kleinasiatische 333 37
~, romanische 335 1-21
~, römische 334 53-60
~ der Perser 333 21-28
~ der Renaissance 335 42-54
~ des Barocks 336 1-8
~ des Rokokos 336 9-13
~dünger 63 14
~flug 288 1-9
~flugzeug 288 1-9
~flugweisitzer 288 18
~glaser 124 8
Kunstharz, glasfaserverstärktes 130 26
~polster 166 64
Künstler 338 2
~hut 35 38
~kopf 34 18
künstliche Atmung 21 24-27
künstlicher Horizont 230 3
künstliches Gebiß 24 25
künstliche Sonne 281 13
Kunst-maler 338 2
~reiter 307 26
~schlosser 140 1
~schütze 307 38
~springen 282 40-45

Kunststoff 164 11
~, schlagfester 127 48
~, thermoplastischer 127 29
~bahn 298 6
~behälter 83 25
~karosserie 193 14
~kugel 277 1
~lauffläche 301 52
~pose 89 44
~sohle 101 2
~spachtel 128 44
~tank 79 4
~tapete 128 18
Kupee 186 3
Kupfer-anode 178 5
~druckpresse 340 36
~leiter 127 43
~münze 252 1-28
~platte 179 9; 340 53
~rohling 260 64
~stecher 340 44
~stich 340 14-24
~sulfat 351 26
~zylinder 182 7
Kupolofen 148 1
Kuponbogen 251 17
Kuppel 334 58
~achse 210 36
~bau 337 21
~dach 5 12
~ofen 148 1
~schraube 202 15
~schwelle 202 14, 38
~spindel 148 58
~stange 210 11
~system 334 72-73
Kupplung *Landmaschinen* 65 39; 67 30
~ *Bau* 119 53
~ *Auto* 191 44
~ *Eisenb.* 208 19; 210 2; 212 82
~, hydraulische 65 37
Kupplungsbügel 208 17
~dose 127 12
~flansch 177 55
~fußhebel 192 28
~hebel 188 32
~pedal 191 44, 96
~schwengel 208 18
~spindel 208 18
~stecker 127 11
~welle 232 56
Kupste 13 42
Kurbad 274
Kurbel 168 52
~antrieb 217 53
~kasten 242 51
~kastenspülung 242 59
~welle 190 23; 192 29; 242 50
~wellenlager 192 23
~wellenlagerdeckel 190 22
~wellenzahnrad 166 51
~zapfenbohrung 192 26
Kurbette 71 6
Kürbis 57 23
Kürettage 26 52
Kürette 26 52
Kurfürstenhut 254 41
Kurgast 274 18
~haus 274 8
Kurhut 254 41
kurischer Reisekahn 220 10
Kürißprügel 254 31
Kürißsattel 329 87
Kur-kapelle 274 20
~konzert 274 20
Kuroschio 14 31
Kur-park 274 1-21
~promenade 274 10
Kurrleine 90 12
Kursaal 274 8
Kurs-anzeiger 251 8

~boje 285 18
~buch 204 50
~buchtafel 204 16
Kürschner 131 1
~werkstatt 131 1-25
kursiv 175 7
Kurs-kreisel 230 13
~makler 251 4, 5
~maklertafel 251 8
~tafel 251 8
~zettel 250 8
Kurve 347 11, 12, 13, 14, 18
~, ballistische 87 79
Kurven-kontrolle 25 54
~maximum 347 19
~minimum 347 20
~scheibe 190 60
Kürzen *Uhrmacher* 109 17
~ *Math.* 344 18
Kurzhaardackel 70 39
Kurz-hobelmaschine 150 45
~hubgesenkhammer 139 11
~nachricht 342 50
~paß 291 49
~schrift 342 13
~stand 75 22
~strecke 231 17
~streckenläufer 298 5
~streckenrakete 259 26
~streckenverkehrsflugzeug 231 4, 11
~trieb 372 23, 31
Kurz- und Mittelstrecken-verkehrsflugzeug 231 4, 11
Kurzwelle 7 26
Kurzwellen-bestrahlungsgerät 23 22
~gerät 23 22, 39
~sender 10 59
~station 237 54
Kurzzeit-messer 23 40; 27 35; 39 21
~uhr 109 35
~wecker 109 35; 116 18
Kuscheltier 47 6
Küsten-fischerei 90 24-29
~funkstelle 237 53
~gewässer 286 10-14
~motorschiff 221 99
Küster 330 26
Kutschbock 186 8
Kutsche 186 1-3,26-39,45,51-54
Kutschenschlag 186 11
Kutscher 186 32
~sitz 186 8
Kutsch-pferd 186 28
~wagen 186 1-3,26-39,45,51-54
Kutte 331 55
Kutter *Fleischerei* 96 52
~ *Schiff* 220 8; 258 12, 61
Kyma 334 19
Kymation 334 19

L

Labor 23 41-59
Laboratorium 23 41-59; 349; 350
~, technisches 310 9
Laboratoriums-mikroskop 112 1
~- und Forschungsmikroskop 112 1
Labor-gerät 23 57; 173 2-10; 349 1-38; 350 1-63
~schale 173 7
~wecker 116 18
Labradorstrom 14 40

Labtank 76 48
Labyrinth *Anat.* 17 62
~ *Park* 272 5
Lach-gas 26 3
~kabinett 308 55
~möwe 359 14
Lackarbeit 337 6
Lackieren 129 14
Lackierer 129 2
Lade-aufsicht 206 36
~baum 221 26, 59; 223 36
~brücke 226 2
~deck 221 34
~druckmesser 230 7
~gerät 25 51
~geschirr 221 24-29, 59
~gleis 206 17
~kante 193 21
~kran 85 28, 44
~luke 221 11, 63; 226 14
~maschine 154 27
~maß 206 22
~mast 221 60
~meister 206 29
Laden-deckel 166 6
~feststeller 37 31
~kasse 47 34; 271 2
~klotz 166 42
~schild 268 39
~schubstange 166 52
~stelze 166 53
Lade-pfosten 221 58; 223 35
~platz 15 91
~pritsche 194 3
~ rampe 206 9
~raum *Auto* 193 17
~raum *Schiff* 223 55, 75
~runge 85 30
~schaffner 205 30
~schieber 247 6
~straße 206 8
~stromkontrolle 191 78
~stütze 85 45
~tür *Auto* 194 8
~tür *Eisenb.* 207 23
~ und Lüfterpfosten 221 58
~wagen 63 27, 38
Ladung 223 77; 226 9, 19
~, feuergefährliche 253 38
Lager *Werkzeugmasch.* 150 40
~ *Brücken* 215 11, 12
~ *Sport* 284 6
~, bewegliches 215 12
~, festes 215 11
~becken 154 28
~behälter 130 17
~bock 177 61
Lageregelungs-rakete 234 38
~triebwerk 6 39
Lager-faß 79 2
~feuer 278 10
~gang 11 31
~haus 206 53
~kammer 154 76
~keller 79 1-22; 93 12
~stätte 154 57-68
~stein 110 33
~stützbock 67 2
~tank 93 13; 145 72
Lagerung 144 33, 34, 35, 36
~ Bewußtloser 21 24-27
Lagune 13 33
Laguneriff 13 32
Laib 97 2
Laich 89 12
~hecht 89 11
Lakai 186 20
Lakkolith 11 30
Laktamöl 170 25, 37
Lama 366 28
Lamantin 366 23
Lamelle *Sägewerk* 157 59
~ *Sport* 301 46

~ *Bot.* 381 4, 6
Lamellen-blende 2 33
~rand 381 7
~reibungskupplung 139 21
~sieb 64 17
Laminat 301 48
Lamm 73 13; 75 11
Lammfell-polierhaube 134 21
~rolle 130 31
~scheibe 134 21
Lampe 86 35
Lampen-gebläse 179 22
~gehäuse 116 29; 309 44
~gelenkarm 177 16
~haus 112 28, 59; 312 39-44
~hausanschluß 112 60
~kopf 116 29
~raum 177 41
~sockel 127 59
~stab 309 40
Lampion 52 15; 306 4; 353 36
Landarbeiter 63 5
Landauer 186 36
Landaulett 186 36
Landbrot 97 6; 99 14
Lande-bahn 233 1; 287 15
~fangseil 259 16
~gestell-Spreizmechanik 6 31
~klappe 230 53; 257 38; 288
  29
~kufe 232 15; 256 21
Länderwappen 252 14
Landesbibliothek,
  wissenschaftliche 262
  11-25
Landes-scheinwerfer 230 49;
  257 37; 288 32
~spoiler 229 42
~steg 278 13
Landes-vermessung 14
  46-62
~wappen 252 12
Landeteller 6 33
Land-fahrzeugtechnik 138
~karte 14; 15; 260 44
~pfeiler 215 27
~rad 65 15
~regen 8 18
Landschaftspark 272 41-72
Landsknecht 355 32
~trommel 306 70
Landspitze 225 65
Landung 298 19
Landungs-boot 258 89; 259
  46
~brücke *Landkarte* 15 59
~brücke *Hafen* 225 30
~steg 278 13; 283 19
Landwirt 35 40
Landwirtschaft 63
landwirtschaftliche Maschine
  64; 65
landwirtschaftliches Gerät 66
Landwirtschaftsprodukt 68
  1-47
Lang-arm 100 25
~band 140 51
~brot 97 8
~drahtantenne 230 66
Länge 100 20
~, geographische 14 7
Längen-anschlag 157 68
~halbkreis 14 4
langer Ärmel 30 15
Langettenstich 102 6
lange Unterhose 32 11
Lang-flügler 359 11-14
~form-Schlafanzug 32 36
Länghaken 122 64
Langhobel 132 39
Langholz *Forstw.* 84 15, 19;
  85 42
~ *Bau* 120 2

~platte 340 2
~schnitt 340 4
Langkessel 210 16
Langlauf 301 42
~anzug 301 17
~ausrüstung 301 14-20
~-Rattenfallbindung 301 15
~schuh 301 16
~ski 301 14
~stock 301 20
Lang-leine 90 28
~leinenfischerei 90 28-29
Langloch 240 17
~fräser 150 43
~ziegel 159 22
Langpferd 296 1
Längsachse 230 72
Langsam-fahrscheibe 203
  36-38
~fahrsignal 203 36-44
~fahrstelle 203 39, 40, 41, 42
~fahrt 203 4
~flug-Querruder 229 41
Längsbau 77 45-50
Langschild 329 56
Längs-furche 20 25
~lenker 191 27; 192 66
~riegel 119 48
~rips 171 13
~riß 300 3
~schlitten 149 42
~schlittenbewegung 149 13
~schneiden 181 42
~schnitt 190 1, 3
~spant 285 55
~support 149 22, 42
~trägerverstärkung 213 12
Lang-streckenläufer 298 5
~streckenverkehrsflugzeug
  231 13
~streckler 298 5
Längstrikotbindung 171 26,
  27
Langstromtrog 89 18
Längs- und Plangangshebel
  149 17
Langwand 222 44-56
~versteifung 230 47, 57
Langtrieb 78 3
~wobbler, zweiteiliger 89 70
Lanze *Stierkampf* 319 17
~ *Ritterwesen* 329 81
~ *Völkerkunde* 354 12
Lanzen-reiter 319 16
~spitze 328 21
Lanzettfenster 335 39-41
lanzettlich 370 32
Lappen 95 15-16
Lärche 372 32
Lärchenzapfen 372 36
Larve *Zool.* 58 64; 77 29; 80 6,
  19, 36, 38, 41, 46, 53; 81 20;
  82 12, 25, 36; 358 9
~ *Karneval* 306 13
Larven-gang 82 24
~kammer 82 36
Lasche 119 65
Laschenbolzen 202 13
Lasching 218 32
Laschung 218 32
Laser-gerät 242 81
~strahl 243 53
Lasso 319 40; 352 5
~band 134 38
Last 299 5
~kahn 216 25
~kraftwagen 194; 226 19
~plattform 232 19
~tier 354 3
~zug 213 34
Lateinersegel 218 29; 220 3
La-Tène-Zeit 328 21-40
Laterne *Wagen* 186 9

~ *Schiff* 218 44; 221 48; 224
  69, 105
~ *Kunst* 335 45
Laternenträger 224 82
Lattbeil 122 21
Latte 284 44; 291 36; 298 14,
  31
Latten-kiste 206 5
~lehre 122 18
~tasche 284 43
~wand 213 29
~zaun 52 10
Lattung 122 17; 123 70
Latz 30 24
Lätzchen 28 43
Latz-hose 29 40; 30 21
~rock 29 41
~tasche 33 46
Laub-baum 371 1-73
~besen 51 3; 272 67
Laubengang 37 73; 272 17
~haus 37 72-76
Laub-frosch 364 24
~hölzer 371
~körper 378 49
~krone 254 12
~säge 135 12; 260 53
~sägeblatt 108 13; 135 13;
  260 54
~wald 15 4
Lauch 57 21
Lauf *Mil.* 255 2, 17
~ *Vögel* 362 4
~achse 210 35
~bahn 298 6
~bildbetrachter 117 91
~brett *Dach* 38 3
~brett *Gärtner* 55 22
~diele 120 36
~drehgestell 197 10
Laufen 298 1-8
laufende Nummer 251 13
~ Scheibe 305 33, 48
laufendes Gut 219 67-71
Läufer *Landw.* 75 39
~ *Spinnerei* 164 55
~ *Spiele* 276 10
~ *Sport* 292 45, 66; 298 5
~bucht 75 36
~koben 75 36
~schicht 118 63
~stein 91 22
~verband 118 59
Lauf-gang *Zirkus* 307 51
~gang *Kunst* 335 33
~gewicht 22 68; 40 36
~gewichtswaage 22 66; 40 35
~katze 147 3; 222 14, 28
~kran 147 41; 222 28
~kugel 307 60
~leder 164 16
~mantel 187 30
~mündung 305 71
~platte 123 30
~puppe 273 63
~rad *Landw.* 64 41, 56; 67 24
~rad *Bergbahnen* 214 7
~rädchen 187 9
~radverstellung 64 58
~reinigungsbürste 87 62
~ring 89 56
~rinne 282 22
~rolle *Eisenb.* 206 39
~rolle *Mil.* 255 86
~rolle *Sport* 294 29
~schiene *Atom* 2 37
~schiene *Web.* 165 3
~schiene *Textil* 167 45
~schiene *Eisenb.* 206 38
~schienenträger 201 15
~schritt 295 41
~sprungtechnik 298 40
~stall 28 39

~stallboden 28 40
~ställchen 28 39
~steg *Hütt.* 147 38
~steg *Schiff* 221 3
~stellung 295 2
~trommel 273 45
~wandung 87 35
Laufwerk *Bergbahnen* 214 36,
  53
~ *Film* 311 10
~hauptträger 214 67
~rolle 214 70
Laugen-brezel 97 44
~pumpe 172 33
~vorwärmer 172 8
Lausblume 379 3
Lauscher 88 16, 32
Lauskraut 379 3
Laute 324 1
Läuter-batterie 92 51
~bottich 92 50
~wanne 162 4
Läutewerk 127 15
Lautschrift 342 14
Lautsprecher 249 70; 264 12;
  311 46; 318 12
~box 42 10; 241 14; 317 15;
  318 12
Lautstärkeregler 117 85; 241
  41; 261 43
Läutwerk 212 49
Lava-decke 11 14
~strom 11 18
Lavendel 380 7
Lawine 304 1
Lawinen-brecher 304 2
~galerie 304 3
~keil 304 2
Lazaruskreuz 332 71
LD-Konverter 147 45-50
Lebens-art, textilfreie 281 16
~baum 372 39
~erhaltungsgerät 6 20
~linie 19 72
Lebensmittel 99 1-96
~geschäft 98 1-87
~handlung 98 1-87
Leber 20 10, 34-35
~band 20 34
~gang 20 37
~lappen 20 35
Lebkuchen 97 51
Lecco 305 23
Lecker 88 2
Leder *Buchb.* 184 12
~ *Völkerkunde* 352 18
~beere 80 21
~besatz 30 18
~futter 291 22
~haube 354 26
~hose 29 32
~hosen 29 32
~hosenträger 29 34
~jacke 33 43
~kissen 108 29
~kopfteil 35 19
~kuppe 277 10
~manschette 191 92
~mütze 35 32
~polster 166 64
~schürze 142 11
~schutzkleidung 290 26
~segment 163 69
~seite 131 13, 18
~walze 340 23
Leerdarm 20 15
Leerlauf-düse 192 1
~gemischregulierschraube
  192 11
~luftdüse 192 2
~verstellung 190 51
Leertaste 249 2
Leewelle 287 17

Lefze 70 26
legato 321 33
Lege-batterie 74 19
~henne 74 57
Legende 14 27-29; 268 4
Leggings 352 17
Leggins 352 17
Leguan 364 32
~, Grüner 364 32
Leguminose 57 1-11
Lehm 120 44; 159 2
~grube 159 1
~schwalbe 361 20
Lehnstuhl 336 18
Lehr-automat 242 1
~bild 262 8
~buch 261 28
Lehrer 260 21
~einheit 261 37
~sitz 257 7
~tisch 242 2; 260 22
Lehr-gerät 242 45-84
~material 261 27
~programm 261 7
~schrittzähler 242 5
Leib 16 1-54
~binde 319 23
Leibesvisitation 264 31
Leibung 120 31, 32; 336 25
Leichen-begängnis 331 33-41
~halle 331 21
~haus 331 21
~kapelle 331 21
~stein 331 26
Leicht-athletik 298
~bauplatte 123 58
~benzinfraktion 145 39
~bügelautomat 50 6
Leichter 225 25
Leicht-gewichtsanker 286
16-18
~koffer 267 15
~metallbeplankung 235 11
~metalleiter 50 35
~metallgußrand 189 48
~steigeisen 300 48
~triebwagen 208 13
Leier Astr. 3 22
~ Jagd 88 67
~ Mus. 322 15
Leihschein 262 25
Leim-kasten 184 9
~kessel 132 12; 183 15; 185 32
~presse 173 24
~topf 132 13; 236 5; 260 57
~walze 185 33
~werk 184 4
Lein 383 6
Leine Hundeleine 70 30
~ Sport 293 73
Leinen 184 12
~bezug 207 48
~kragen 355 56
~mütze 35 8
~rock 355 5
Leine-Steinsalz 154 64
Leineweber 361 8
Lein-kraut, Nickendes 376 26
~pfad 216 30
~tuch 43 9
Leinwand Film 312 11
~ Nachtlokal 318 21
~ Malerei 338 21
~ballen 206 11
~bindung 171 1, 4
~kasten 318 21
Leinzug 216 27
leise 321 35
Leiste Anat. 16 38
~ Glaser 124 3
~ Web. 166 11
~ Textil 171 24
~ Bergsport 300 13

Leisten 100 32
~beuge 16 38
~furche 294 52, 53
~kopfplattkäfer 81 27
~probe 124 2
~schaft 171 20, 22
~stift 128 30
Leistungs-hebel 257 9
~prüfung 290 33
~schalter 152 34; 153 51-62
~transformator 152 30, 39
Leit-artikel 342 48
~dalbe 222 35
Leiter 21 32; 47 5; 118 42; 211
43; 235 28; 270 10
~ Kraftwerk 153 34
~gerüst 118 86-89
~getriebe 270 11
~haken 122 15, 69
~park 270 10
~stufe 50 38
~übung 270 1-46
~wagen 309 86
Leit-feuer 224 101-102
~spindel 149 19, 32
~spindelwendegetriebe 149 6
~steven 222 70
Leit- und
Zugspindeldrehmaschine
149 1
Leitung 269 22, 52
Leitungs-kabel 39 25
~kupplung 208 16
~schacht 234 40
~schutzschalter 127 19, 33
~schutzsicherung 127 36
Leit-walze 168 12
~werkaufbau 257 20
~werksform 229 23-36
~werkverstrebung 232 4
Lektor 262 3
Lende Anat. 16 24
~ Pferd 72 30
Lenden-schurz 354 31
~stück 96 4
~wirbel 17 4
Lenkachsbereifung 64 32
Lenken 303 24
Lenker 65 27, 28; 187 2; 188
3, 11, 57
~armaturen 188 30-35
Lenk-getriebe 192 56-59
~gurt 303 4
Lenkrad 191 37; 305 89
~nabe 191 57
~schloß 191 75
~speiche 191 58
Lenk-rolle 50 81
~säule 192 56
~stange 187 2
~stangenschaft 187 10
~stockhebel 192 58
Lenkung, hydraulische 65 41
Lentikulariswolke 287 19
Lenzloch 284 36
Leo 3 17; 4 57
Leonberger 73 16
Leopard 368 6
Leporello 248 47
Lepton 252 39
Lerche 361 18-19
Lerchensporn 377 8
Lernäische Schlange 327 32
Lern-laufkinderschuh 101 56
~programmherstellung,
audiovisuelle 242 7
~stützgerät 188 5
Lese-behälter 78 10
~buch 260 16
~einheit 244 8
~lampe 43 15
~pult 330 2
Leserin 78 11

Lese-saal 262 13
~stein 63 9
~zeichen, festes 185 70
~zeichen, loses 185 71
Letter 174 7, 44; 175 32-37,
38
Letzter 305 11
Leucht-anzeige 241 55; 247 15
~bildanzeige 23 27
~buchstabe 268 45
~diodenanzeige 110 2
Leuchte 198 18; 267 21
Leuchtelement 26 11
leuchtende Nachtwolken 7 22
Leuchten-klemme 127 29
~sockel 127 60
Leuchter 309 45
—Leucht-feuer Landkarte 15 49
~feuer Schiff 224 83
~fläche 177 20
~glockentonne 224 74
~heultonne 224 68
~instrument 241 39
~melder Kraftwerk 153 2
~melder Eisenb. 212 15
~pedal 187 78
~reklame 268 16
~röhre 49 32
Leuchtstoff-lampe 127 61;
271 23
~röhre 271 23
~schicht 240 19
~streifen 240 18
Leucht-tafel 264 30
~turm Landkarte 15 8
~turm Schiff 224 103
~warte 226 27
~zeichen 196 7
Leuzit 351 12
Levade 71 4; 307 30
Lexika 262 17
Lexikon 42 18; 262 17
Libelle 358 3
Libero 291 11
Libra 3 19; 4 59
Licht 88 15, 33
~anlaßmaschine 212 30
~blende 5 22
Lichtbogen 312 42
~stabilisierung 312 39
lichtempfindlicher Abschnitt
77 22
Lichterführung 286 10-14
lichte Weite 215 13
Licht-gaden 334 70
~hof 271 11
~maschine 187 8; 190 76; 211
46
~mast 198 18
~messung 114 60
~öffnung 334 75
~orgel 317 11
~quelle 1 59; 112 52
~rufsignal 267 6
Lichtsatz 176 1
~automat 176 14
~-Zentraleinheit 176 29
Licht-schnittubus 112 38
~schutzblende 6 22
~setzgerät 176 7
~signal 203 3
~spielhaus 312 1
~spieltheater 312 1
~stärke 115 63
~stellanlage 316 2
~stimmung 316 2
~strahlengang 1 62
Lichtton-aufnahmegerät 311
6
~aufzeichnung 311 9
~gerät 312 45
~kamera 310 60; 311 6
~optik 312 46

Lichtung 15 2
Licht-visier 2 34
~vorsignal 203 9, 14
~wange 123 44
~zeichenanlage 268 54
~zeigerinstrument 238 43
Lidodeck 223 22
Lieberkühn-Reflektor 115 97
Liebes-apfel 57 12
~paar 272 72
Liedernummer 330 24
Lieferwerk 164 59
Liege-fläche 281 11
~hafen 216 14
~kur 274 12-14
~matratze 278 31
~sessel 281 5
~sitz 191 34
~stufe 281 20
~stuhl 37 47; 51 2; 221 111;
274 13
~stütz 295 21, 22, 25
~terrasse 37 75
~wiese 37 46; 274 12
Lieschen 68 33
Lift 271 45
~back 193 29
~boy 271 47
~ dump 229 42
~sessel 214 16
Ligatur 175 6
~führer 26 44
Liguster, Gemeiner 373 6
~schwärmer 358 55
Likör 98 58
~glas 317 7
~karaffe 45 48
~schale 45 89
Lilie Bot. 60 12
~ Heraldik 254 13
Liliengewächs 53 13
Liliputaner 308 22
Limerick 89 84
Limonaden-flasche 265 15
~glas 265 16
Limone 384 23
Limousine, viertürige 193 4
~, zweitürige 193 25
Linde 371 46
Lindengewächs 53 9
Lindwurm 327 1
Lineal 247 35
~einrichtung 179 26
~handrädchen 132 66
linealisch 370 31
Linealwinkel 132 65
Liner 221 82; 225 32
Linie 346 1-23
~, gekrümmte 346 21
~, krumme 346 21
Linien-bus 194 34
~fahrt 221 96
~frachter 221 96
~glas 124 6
~richter 291 59; 293 69
~schiff 218 51-60; 225 32
~schild 197 20, 21
~stichel 340 5
~system 320 43-44
Links-lauf 149 11
~maschine 312 13
Linotype 174 19
~matrize 174 29
Linse 19 48
Linsen-fernrohr 113 16
~kissen 108 29
~system 242 83
Lintwurm 327 1
Linz-Donawitz-Konverter
147 45-50
Lippe 70 26
Lippen-pfeife 326 23-30,
31-33, 34

~scheibe 354 23
Lira 252 20, 21
Lisene 335 11
Litewka 221 115
Litfaßsäule 268 70
Lithodes 369 16
Lithograph 340 45
Lithographie 340 25-26
Lithokreide 340 26
Lithostein 340 25, 57
liturgische Geräte 332 34-54
~ Räucherung 332 38
Litze 166 27
Litzen-auge 166 28
~band 325 36
Livestock-Carrier 221 68
Live-Ton 117 100
Livree 186 21
Lkw--Beladung 226 28
~Fahrstuhl 221 56
~Rad 138 21
~Reifen 273 19
LM 6 12; 234 55
LM-Hangar 234 54
Loch Käse 99 41
~ Golf 293 79-82, 87
~beitel 132 8
~billard 277 7
~blende 242 82
~eisen 100 45; 125 13; 132 8
Locher 22 28; 247 3
Lochkarte 237 64; 244 13
Lochkarten-leser 244 12
~leser und -stanzer 244 12
~stanzer 244 12
Loch-kranz 237 11
~kugel 305 15
~nippel 162 51
~platte 137 17; 140 14
~rotor 85 25
~rundmutter 143 35
~säge 120 63; 126 70; 132 3
~schaft 305 47
~stecher 102 12
~stickerei 102 11
Lochstreifen 176 6, 8, 12; 237 62
~abtaster 176 13
~abtastung 176 15
~eingabeelement 176 30
~locher 176 5
Loch-ziegel 159 21-22
~zirkel 135 23
Locke 34 3
Locken-former 106 31
~haar 34 33
~klammer 105 14
~kopf 34 18
~perücke 34 2
~wickel 105 12
~wickler 105 12
Lockermasse, vulkanische 11 19
Lock-geräte 87 43-47
~jagd 87 43-47
~vogel 86 48
~wellbürste 105 13
Loden-hut 35 23
~mantel 29 31; 30 64
~rock 30 67
Löffel Med. 22 50
~ Hausrat 45 61
~ Jagd 88 61
~ Angelsport 89 73
~, scharfer 22 50; 26 52
~bagger 118 81
~bohrer 135 16
~bug 285 30
~gans 359 5
Log 224 54
Logarithmenrechnung 345 6
Logarithmieren 345 6
Logarithmus 345 6

Loge 319 7
Logel 78 15
Logenschließer 315 12
Logge 224 54
Logger 90 1
Loggia 37 18
~tür 37 21
Logikbaustein 242 68
Log-propeller 224 55
~uhr 224 57
Lohnkutsche 186 26
Loipe 301 44
Loipenmarkierung 301 45
Lok 211 10-18; 212 51-67
~führer 208 2
~führerhaus 210 49
~führersitz 210 59
Lokomotive 211 1; 212 1, 24, 47; 213 1
Lokomotiv-führer 208 2
~kessel 210 2-37
Loktriebwerk 210 2-37
Lokus 49 12
Longdrink 317 32
Longline-Büstenhalter 32 4
Looping 288 1
~acht 288 2
Lophocalyx philippensis 369 7
Lore 200 25
Lösch-fahrzeug 270 5
~gerät 270 63
~kammer 153 55
~kopf 241 59; 243 20; 311 25
~lok 156 10
~taste 117 86
~trog 137 8
~trupp 270 34
~turm 156 11
~übung 270 1-46
~wagen 156 10
~wedel 137 3
Loser 88 16
Lösung 345 10
Lösungsmittel-dampf 182 25
~kanne 129 16
Losverkäufer 266 20
Lot Bau 118 50, 71
~ Schiff 224 58-67
Löt-borax 108 39
~kolben 126 73; 127 45; 134 19, 57
Lotkörper 224 59
Lötlampe 126 74; 301 22
Lotleine 224 60
Lötmittel 108 36
Lotossäule 333 13
Lötpistole 108 14; 134 56
Lotse ist an Bord 253 24
Lotsen-boot 221 95
~rufsignal 253 23
Lötstange 108 38
~stein 125 6
Lotte 78 3
Löt-wasser 125 7
~zinn 126 76
~zinndraht 134 20
Louisdor 252 5
Louis-seize-Stil 336 14
Lounge 233 18
Löwe Astr. 3 17; 4 57
~ Zool. 307 56; 368 2
Löwen-kopf 327 17
~leib 327 14
~mähne 368 3
~mäulchen 51 32
~rudel 356 5
~rumpf 327 22
~zahn 51 34; 61 13
Low speed aileron 229 41
Luchs 368 8
~fell 131 15, 16, 20
Luft-absaugstutzen 133 40

~abzug 356 17
~akrobat 307 7
~ansaugkanal 209 11
~ansaugschacht 258 57
~bad 282 4
~ballon 308 13
~behälter 196 19
~bewegung 7 6, 10
~bildmessung 14 63-66
~bremse 229 44; 256 12
~druck 9 1, 4
~druckanzeige 211 24
~dusche 22 37
~düsenkanal 281 41
~einlaß 256 5
~einlaßschlitz 191 47
~einlauf 232 52
~einlaufkanal 257 14
~eintrittsöffnung 259 73; 270 60
Lüfter Motor 190 7
~ Eisenb. 211 11
~ Schiff 221 41
~antrieb 212 62
~kopf 223 41
~kupplung 190 8
~öffnung 258 43
~ölpumpe 211 45
~pfosten 221 58
Luft-filter 191 55
~führung 199 45
~füllstutzen 196 21
~furche 91 17
~gang 165 48
~gebläse 191 48
~gewehr 305 34, 40
~hammer 139 24
~heizkammer 147 30
~holz 55 18
~insufflator 23 18
~kammer 74 61
~kanal Sonnenziegel 155 35
~kanal Kunst 333 4
~kissen 286 60
~kissenfahrzeug 286 63
~klappe 210 6
~koffer 267 15
~kompressor 146 23; 211 14, 44
~korrekturdüse 192 3
~leitung 75 28
~loses Spritzen 129 36
Luft-manschette 23 34
~massen 8 1-4
~matratze 278 31
~polster 286 66
~polsterbildung 243 27
~presser 211 14, 44; 212 34, 58, 72
~pumpe Papier 172 40
~pumpe Druck 181 6, 35
~pumpe Fahrrad 187 48
~regler 180 74
~regulierung Staubsauger 50 74
~regulierung Chem. 350 3, 8
~reifen 187 30
~röhre 17 50; 20 4
~röhrenast 20 5
~sack 353 10
~schaukel 308 41
~schaum- und Wasserwerfer 270 64
~schaumwerfer 270 64
~schlange 308 14
~schlauch 187 30
~schleier 139 56
~schleuse 235 27
~schlitz 194 16
~schraube 330 32; 286 64; 288 36
~schraubenwelle 232 60
~strahltriebwerk 232 33-50

~strömung 9 28, 29
~strömungen 9 25-29
~temperaturangabe 280 8
~trichter 192 8
Lüftung Gewächshaus 55 10-11
~ Masch. 143 107
Lüftungs-fenster 55 10; 278 40
~holz 55 18
~klappe Gärtner 55 41
~klappe Eisenb. 213 16, 30
~vorrichtung 74 10, 17
~ziegel 122 7
Luft-verteilerstück 75 32
~vorwärmer 139 53; 152 11
~waffe 256; 257
~zielraketenstarter 259 50
~zufuhrrohr 147 29
~zuführung 137 6
~zuleitung 147 17
~zutritt 155 24
Luggersegel 220 4
Luk 258 24
Lukas 308 11
Luke 6 45; 222 64-65
Luken-deckel 222 65
~süll 222 64
Lumber 30 38
Lumme 359 13
Lunar module 6 12; 234 55
Lunge 18 13; 20 6-7
Lungen-flügel 20 6
~funktionsprüfung 27 36
~kraut 377 7
~lappen 20 7
~schlagader 18 11; 20 55
~vene 18 12; 20 56
Lunte 88 47
Lunteneinführung 164 15
Lunula 332 36
Lupe 175 34; 177 23; 351 33
Lupine, Gelbe 69 17
Lurch 364 20-26
Lure 322 1
Luser 88 16
Lüsterklemme 127 29
Lutscher 28 15
Luxuskabine 223 30
Luzerne 69 9
Lyman-Serie 1 20
Lymph-drüse 19 10
~knoten 19 10
Lyoner 96 10
Lyra Astr. 3 22
~ Mus. 322 15; 325 42

M

Mäander Geogr. 13 11
~ Kunst 334 43
Maar 11 25
Machina Pictoris 3 47
Macis 382 34
Macropharynx longicaudatus 369 2
Mädchen-bluse 29 58
~frisur 34 27-38
~hose 29 49
~kostüm 29 50
~leib 327 24, 59
~mantel 29 54
~rock 29 46
~tasche 29 56
~überziehbluse 29 48
Made 77 28; 80 19; 358 19
Madeiraglas 45 84
Madonnenstatue 330 51
Magazin Film 117 45
~ Buchb. 184 7
~ Mil. 255 15, 21
~ Kaufhaus 268 41

~bereich 5 17
~gewehr 87 2
~halter 255 7
Magen *Anat.* 20 13, 41-42
~ *Zool.* 77 16
~-Darm-Kanal 77 15-19
~mund 20 41
Magenta-Doppeldruckwerk 180 10-11
~einstellung 116 43
mager 175 8
Magermilch-separator 76 14
~tank 76 17
magisches Auge 309 18
Magnesiumplatte 179 9
Magnet 1 63; 2 51; 108 32
Magnetband 25 46; 237 63; 238 5; 244 2
~-Diktiergerät 249 62
~einheit 244 9
~schleife 245 28
~spule 244 10
~station 242 32
Magnet-film 238 54-59; 311 21
~filmspule 311 2
~haftstein 242 72
magnetischer Dämpfer 11 40
Magnet-kompaß 223 6; 224 46; 230 6
~kontakt 242 71
~kopfträger 311 3
~plattenspeicher 244 1
~randspur 117 82
Magnetton-abnehmersystem 312 28
~abtaster 312 50
~-Aufnahme-
Kompaktanlage 238 55
~-Aufnahmelaufwerk 238 4
~-Aufnahme- und -
Wiedergabelaufwerk 238 4
~-Aufnahme- und -
Wiedergabe-
Kompaktanlage 238 55
~-Aufnahme- und -
Wiedergabeverstärker 311 5
~-Aufnahmeverstärker 311 5
~aufzeichnungsgerät 310 58; 311 1
~laufwerk 311 20
~verstärker 311 28
~-Wiedergabe-
Kompaktanlage 238 55
~-Wiedergabelaufwerk 238 4
~-Wiedergabeverstärker 311 5
Magnetventil 139 23
Magnolie, Rote 373 15
Maharadscha 306 28
Mähdrescher 63 31; 64 1-33
Mahl 267 40-43
~furche 91 18
~gang *Mühle* 91 21
~gang *Ziegelei* 159 8
~messerabstand 172 74
~sand 227 3
~stein 354 24
~steingehäuse 91 20
Mahlung 160 4
Mähne *Pferd* 72 13
~ *Löwe* 368 3
Maiblume 377 2
Maierisli 377 2
Maiglöckchen 377 2
Maikäfer 82 1
Mailänder Andruckpresse 180 75
Mailcoach 186 53
Mais 68 1, 31
~birne 299 23
Maischbottich 92 43

Maische 92 44; 93 10
~tankwagen 87 16
~thermometer 93 9
Maisch-kessel 92 44
~pfanne 92 44
Mais-gebiß 64 35
~käfer 81 26
~kolben 68 36
~korn 68 37
Majuskel 175 11
Makkaroni 98 33
Makler-schranke 251 3
~tafel 251 8
Makramee 102 21
Makrogerät 115 81-98
Makrone 97 37
Makro-phon 212 70
~schiene 117 56
~seismik 11 45-54
makroseismisches
Schüttergebiet 11 38
Makro-ständer 115 94
~stativ 115 94
~vorsatzlinse 117 55
~zoomobjektiv 117 53
Mal 292 43, 46, 47, 70
Malacosteus indicus 369 10
Malariamücke 81 44
Malatelier 338
Malen 129 1
Maler *Astr.* 3 47
~ *Beruf* 129 2
~kasten 315 34
~saal 315 28-42
~spachtel 134 37
Mal-gerät 338 1-28
~grund 338 22
~kasten 338 10
~kissen 292 67
~kugel 305 23
~leinen 338 21
~mittel 338 13
Malnehmen 344 25
Mal-pappe 338 22
~pinsel 48 7; 260 84
~spachtel 129 22; 338 15
Malspieler 292 44
Malstock 129 47
Malteserkreuzgetriebe 312 38
Mal-tisch 338 25
~utensil 338 6-19
Malve 376 13
Malz 92 43
~bereitung 92 1-41
~bier 93 26
Malzeichen 344 25
Malzelevator 92 35
Mälzen 92 1-41
Mälzerei 92
Malz-produktionsanlage 92 1
~silo 92 37
Mälzturm 92 1
Mammut-baum 372 69
~tanker 221 1
Manager 299 45
Mandarin 306 29
Mandarine 384 23
Mandel *Anat.* 19 23
~ *Bot.* 384 36, 40
~krähe 360 6
Mandoline 324 16
Manege 307 21
Manegen-diener 307 27
~eingang 307 11
Mangold 57 28
Manipulator *Atom* 2 38
~ *Tech.* 139 32
Männchen *Zool.* 81 34
~ *Flugsport* 288 5
Männer-frisur 34 1-25
~geheimbund 352 34
~kleidung 33
männliche Blüte 59 39

männlicher Blütenstand 68 35
männliches Glied 20 66
Mannloch *Brauerei* 93 13
~ *Böttcher* 130 18
~ *Raumfahrt* 234 30; 235 52
~ *Wasservers.* 269 51
~deckel 130 19
Mannschafts-betreuer 292 57
~einzelkabine 228 32
~unterkunft 270 2
Manntau 221 103
Manometer 25 22; 67 10; 83 42; 178 8; 180 74; 196 20; 212 6; 349 19
Manövrierkiel 227 30
Manque 275 22
Mansarddach 121 18
Mansardenfenster 121 19
Mansardfenster 121 19
Manschette *Med.* 25 16
~ *Kleidung* 30 14; 32 45
Manschettenknopf 32 46; 36 21
Mantel *Geogr.* 11 3
~ *Böttcher* 130 2, 23
~ *Fahrrad* 187 30
~ *Börse* 251 11
~ *Warenhaus* 271 41
~ *Theater* 316 22
~ *Math.* 347 40
~ *Chem.* 350 10
~ *Kostüme* 355 26, 29
~, dreiviertellanger 271 21
~gürtel 29 55; 33 59
~haken 207 50
~knopf 33 64
~kragen 33 58
~mauer 329 15
~rohr 269 64
~schnur 355 24
~strom 232 50
~stromtriebwerk 232 46
~tasche 33 61
Mantisse 345 6
Manual 322 46, 47; 325 48; 326 42, 43, 44, 45
Manuskript 174 6; 176 3; 262 5; 310 45
Mappe 188 54
Maraca 324 59
marcato 321 27
Märchenfigur 306 65
Marder 86 22; 367 14-17
Margarine 98 21; 99 48
Margerite 51 24; 376 4
Marginalie 185 68
Marienkäfer 358 37
Marille 59 35
Marillenbaum 59 33-36
Marimbaphon 324 61
Mark *Geld* 252 7
~ *Bot.* 370 14
~, verlängertes 17 47; 18 24
Marken-butter 76 37
~schild 187 15
~zeichen 191 12
markiert 321 27
Markierungs-fähnchen 301 45
~stanze 117 95
Markise 37 71
Markstrahl 370 11
Markt 251 2
~frau 308 65
~platz 15 52
~schreier 308 64
Marlotte 355 50
Marmelade 98 52
Marmorplatte 265 12
Marone 384 52
Maronenpilz 381 15
Mars 4 46
~rah 218 39

~segel 218 38
Martnet 218 36
März-blümchen 60 1
~blume 60 1
~glöckchen 60 1
Marzipan 98 82
Masche 167 62, 63
~, geschlossene 171 36
~, offene 171 30
Maschen-abschlagen 167 66
~bildung 167 65
~drahtzaun 84 7
~größeneinstellskala 167 42
~reihe 171 42
~ware 167 9
Maschine 181 1-65
~, landwirtschaftliche 64; 65
~, schwere 189 43
Maschinen-abstellhebel 164 6, 32
~anlage *Eisenb.* 211 44-54
~anlage *Schiff* 221 65
~bauhalle 222 8
~bett 177 57
~bütte 172 86; 173 13
~deck 224 107
~einschalthebel 163 17
~endschild 164 26
~fuß 133 25
~gewehr 255 32
~gewindebohrer 150 44
~grundrahmen 168 54
~gummi 247 26
~haus *Bergb.* 144 2
~haus *Kraftwerk* 152 22
~haus *Straßenbau* 200 2
~haus *Wasserbau* 217 21
~haus *Schiff* 221 10; 222 33
~kanone 255 92
~meister 316 59
~pauke 323 57
~pistole 255 8
~raum 227 22
~raumlüfter 212 37
~satz 174 27
~schlosser 140 1
~schuppen 62 15
~ständer 139 19
~teil 111 30; 143
~tisch 248 26
~- und Propellerraum 227 22
Maschinerie 316 1-60
Maschinist *Bau* 118 32
~ *Feuerwehr* 270 13
Maske *Fernsehtechnik* 240 17
~ *Sport* 279 10
~ *Karneval* 306 7
~ *Bildhauerei* 339 37
Masken-abtastkopf 177 47
~aufhängung 240 22
~ball 306 1-48
~bildner 310 36; 315 48
~fest 306 1-48
~walze 177 48
Maskerade 306 6-48
Maskierung 306 6-48
Massagebad 281 33
Massaikrieger 354 8
Maß-anzeige 185 6
~band 103 2
Massekuchen 161 13
Massel 147 40
~gießmaschine 147 34-44
Massemühle 161 1
Massengut-schute 226 35
~umschlag 226 29
Massenversammlung 263 1-15
Massestrang 161 8
Massiv-brücke 215 19
~decke 118 16; 123 28
~treppe 123 16
Maßliebchen 376 1

Maß-linie 151 25
~pfeil 151 26
Maßstab Geogr. 14 29
~ Zollstock 134 33
Maßstabsverstellung 116 34
Maßwerk 335 39-40
~fenster 335 39-41
Mast 219 1-9; 220 16; 221 2, 77; 284 4, 11
~darm 20 22, 61
Master 289 45
Master-Slave-Manipulator 2 47
Mast-fuß 284 20
~geflügelzucht 74 11-17
~huhn 74 12
~korb 223 38
~neigung 284 6
Matador 319 25, 26, 31
Material-behälter 200 45
~lager 146 6
~lagerplatz 144 17
~regal 100 36
~regulierung 163 31
~transport 144 43, 45
Matestrauch 382 11
Mathematik 344; 345; 346; 347; 348
~, höhere 345 11-14
mathematisches Zeichen 345 15-24
Matratze 43 10; 47 3
Matrize Setzerei 174 21, 22, 31; 175 37
~ Heftmaschine 247 5
Matrizen-bohrmaschine 175 49
~prägepresse 178 7
~rahmen 174 42, 46; 176 17
~spanner 24 55
~spannvorrichtung 175 59
Matrosen-anzug 309 62
~klavier 324 36
~mütze 309 63
Matschschnee 304 30
Matt 276 15
Matte 299 12
Mattensegel 353 33
Matt-glas 124 5
~glaskugel 267 4
~scheibe 115 61, 66; 117 94; 177 2, 34
~scheibenrahmen 177 3
~scheibenring 115 53, 64
Mauer Landkarte 15 95
~ Pferdesport 289 8; 291 44
~bogen 336 19
~gecko 364 36
~gerste 61 28
~häkler 359 24
~körper 217 2
~krone Wasserbau 217 59
~krone Kronen 254 46
~pfeffer 51 7
~pfeffer, Scharfer 375 21
~schwalbe 359 24
~segler 359 24
~stärke 119 67
~stein 159 20
~strebe 329 26
~stütze 329 26
~turm 329 14
~türmchen 329 28
~verbände 118 58-68
~werkzeug 118 50-57
Maukhaus 159 6
Maul Pferd 72 9
~ Jagd 88 13, 45
~, doppelzüngiges 327 5
Maulbeerseidenspinner 358 48
Maul-gatter 71 53
~korb 70 31

~tier 73 8
~wurf 366 4
~wurfsfalle 83 37
Maurer 118 18
~bleistift 118 51
~hammer 118 53
~kelle 118 52
Maus 227 29
Mäusebussard 362 9
Mausefalle 83 36
Mäusegerste 61 28
Mauser 362 9
Mausoleum 337 16
Maximumthermometer 10 53
Mayatempel 352 20
McPherson-Federbein 192 72-84
Mechanik-backe 325 16
~balken 325 22
Medaillon 339 36
Mediaeval 342 4
Medikament, wasserlösliches 25 14
Medikamenten-kassette 24 7
~schrank 22 35
Medium 308 9
medizinisches Wörterbuch 22 22
medizinisch-technische Assistentin 23 41
Meduse 357 14
Meer 13 26
~adler 362 5
Meeres-niveau 9 1
~spiegel Geogr. 11 11
~spiegel Erdöl 146 39
~straße 14 24
~strömung 14 27, 28, 30-45
~vogel 359 11-14
Meer-fee 327 23
~frau 327 23
~gans 359 5
~gottheit 327 23
~göttin 327 23
~jungfer 327 23
~jungfrau 327 23
Meerrettich 57 20
Meerschweinchen 366 12
Meer-wasserentsalzungsanlage 146 25
~weib 327 23
~wesen 327 40
Megalithgrab 328 16
Megaphon 283 21
Mehl 91 28; 97 52
~frucht 68 1-37
~käfer 81 18
~körper 68 13
~siloanlage 97 74
Mehltau, Falscher 80 20
~pilz 80 20
Mehlwurm 81 18
Mehretagen-Entwicklungsdose 116 3
~-Filmspirale 116 4
Mehrfach-funktionsspritze 24 10
~meißelhalter 149 41
Mehrfarben-druck 340 28
~-Rollentiefdruckmaschine 182 24
Mehrformatsucher 114 41
~ganggetriebe 190 72
~kammerfronteinspülung 50 27
Mehrkanal-Lichtton-Stereophonie 312 45
Mehr-lader 87 2
~magazinmaschine 174 19
Mehrscheiben-Trockenkupplung 190 78
Mehrstufengetriebe 64 71; 190 72

Mehrzweck-frachter 221 57
~hubschrauber 232 11
~kampfflugzeug 256 8
~leuchte 109 12
~-Lkw 255 96
~motor 109 13
Meilenstein 15 109
Meise 360 4; 361 9
Meißel 149 45
~schaft 149 49
~schar 65 58
Meisterbrief 106 42
Melanocetes 369 6
Melde, Gemeine 61 24
Meldeapparat 294 32
Melden 260 20
Meldezettel 267 12
Melkbecher 75 30
Melker 75 25
Melk-geschirr 75 26
~stand 75 23
~takt 75 34
Melodie-pfeife 322 10
~saite 322 30; 324 24
~seite 324 39
Melone 57 23
Membran 241 68
Membranenlade 326 12-14
Membraphon 323 51-59
Menage 266 22
Menge 348 1, 2, 3, 9, 10, 11
Mengen-lehre 348
~regulierhebel 163 28
Mengmulde 96 40
Menhir 328 18
Mensch 16; 17; 18; 19; 20
Mensch-ärgere-dich-nicht-Spiel 47 19
Menschen-affe 368 14-16
~floh 81 42
~haar 352 38
~hai 364 1
~haupt 327 21
~laus 81 40, 41
~leib 327 53
~rumpf 254 11
menschliche Figur 328 20
menschlicher Körper 16 1-54
Mensur 116 11
Mensuralnotation 320 2
Menukarte 266 21
Menükarte 266 21
Meridian 14 4
~fernrohr 113 29
~kreis 113 26
Meringe 97 26; 265 5
Meringue 97 26; 265 5
Merkur 4 43
Merlin 362 1
Mesner 330 58
Mesolithikum 328 1-9
Meß-ballon 7 17
~behälter 130 22
~bereichswähler 2 4, 23
~bereichswippe 114 59
~bereichwähler 112 46
~bereichwählschalter 242 74
~betrieb, automatischer 195 4
~betrieb, manueller 195 4
~bildkamera 112 68
~buch 330 38
~bügel 149 65
~diener 330 40
Messe Schiff 228 25
~ Jahrmarkt 308 1-69
Meß-einrichtung 112 51
~element 10 22
Messen 161 6
Messer 45 50; 56 36
~balken 64 3
~bänkchen 45 11
~falzmaschine 185 8

~griff 106 39
~heft 96 34
~kegel, rotierender 172 75
~kegel, stehender 172 76
~klinge 96 32
~scheide 94 12
~sech 65 10
~walze 56 35
~werfer 307 37
~werk 56 33
Meß-garnitur 332 44
~gerät Fotogr. 114 62
~gerät Kraftwerk 153 7
~gerät Druck 178 3
~geräteplattform 235 69
~glas 10 47; 196 14; 267 60; 350 26
Messingkessel 42 14
Meß-instrument 153 30
~kabel 116 38
~kammer 112 43
~kännchen 332 45, 46
~keile 115 55
~kolben 350 27
~kopf 116 55
~latte 14 47
~pipette 350 24
~platz 27 49
~pult 109 25
~satellitenbereich 7 33
~schenkel 142 38
~schieber 140 52; 149 67
~skala 115 65; 149 63; 242 75
~sonde Fotogr. 114 63; 116 55
~sonde Raumfahrt 234 42
~spindel 149 66
~stab 158 26
~stelle 237 40
~strahlengang 115 36
~trommel Meßwerkzeug 149 64
~trommel Sextant 224 4
~uhr 76 4
~- und Regelgerät 178 3
Messung der Atemfunktion 23 31
Meß-werkzeug 149 56-72
~winkel 140 57
~zelle 115 37
~zylinder 23 43; 173 4; 261 26; 350 26
Metall 254 24-25
~armband 109 19
~bauer 140 1
~block 148 25
~faden 102 30
~feder 341 25
~gestell 111 7
~halogen-Flächenleuchte 182 3
~halogenlampe 179 21
~hülse 166 31
~hut 326 35
~kugel 352 32
~papier 153 44
~platte 324 77
~rahmen 324 76
~röhre 324 78
~sägebogen 126 71
~scheibe 309 15
~schlupfhorde 74 32
~schlupfwagen 74 31
~spitze 166 25
~stab 123 22
~stoff 270 46
~tapete 128 18
~weste 294 15
~zuführung 174 26, 40
Metazoen 357 13-39
Metazoon 357 13-39
Meteor 7 18
Meteoritenkrater 6 16
Meteorologie 8; 9

meteorologische Instrumente 10
Meteorologisches Amt 225 33
meteorologische Station 9 7
Metermaß 103 2; 271 38
Metope 334 16
Metronom 325 19
Metteur 174 5
Metzger 94 1; 96 38
Metzgerei 96 1-30
Metzgermesser 96 31-37
Meute 86 33; 289 46
Mezzotinto 340 14-24
Midinette 306 21
Mieder 31 30
~hose 32 2
Miere, Rote 61 27
Mietwagen 186 26; 233 33
Mignon 175 24
Mikrab 337 14
Mikrofilm·aufzeichnungsan-
  lage 242 31
~kartei 237 37
~lesegerät 237 36
Mikro·fotoansatz 115 89
~mann 310 22
Mikrometer·knopf 14 52
~schraube 142 37; 149 62
Mikrophon 22 15; 117 8, 24,
  74; 197 26; 209 31; 230 29;
  241 49; 243 3; 261 39; 263
  7; 317 20
~, eingebautes 241 5
~anordnung 310 30
~anschlußleitung 117 25
~anschlußtafel 238 36
~assistent 310 22
~ausleger 117 23
~buchse 249 69
~bügel 249 65
~fuß 241 51
~galgen 310 25
~kabel 239 14; 310 32
Mikroprismenraster 115 54,
  58
Mikroskop 111 19
~kamera 112 64
~okular 14 53
~photometer 112 49
~röhre 113 31-39
~tisch 112 9
Mikrospaltbildfeld 115 54
Mikrowellengerät 23 36; 24
  23
Milan, Roter 362 11
Milbe 358 44
Milch 76 16; 99 44
~annahme 76 1
~beutel 76 22; 99 45
~erhitzer 76 13
~flasche 28 19; 266 60
~glas 124 5
~hof 76 1-48
~kännchen 44 31
~kanne 309 89
~kraut 61 13
~kuh 62 34; 75 17
~leitung 75 27
~packung 76 21, 22
~produktgondel 99 43
~sammelstück 75 32
~sammel- und
  Luftverteilerstück 75 32
~straße 3 35
~tankwagen 76 2
~topf 40 15
~viehstall 75 14
Military 289 16-19
Millibar 9 4
~teilung 10 3
Millimeterteilung 10 3; 247
  36
Milz 20 12, 27

Mimbar 337 15
Minarett 337 13
Minen·jagdboot 258 80
~klemmstift 151 45
~räumgerät 258 87
~suchboot, Schnelles 258 84
~transporter 258 94
Mineralwasserflasche 266 61
Mini 193 19
Miniaturkultwagen 328 36
Minigolf·anlage 272 68
~bahn 272 70
~spieler 272 69
Minima 320 14
Minimumthermometer 10 54
Ministrant 330 40; 331 45
Minnesänger 329 70
Minuend 344 24
Minusfacette 111 37, 42
Minuskel 175 12
~, karolingische 341 18
Minuszeichen 344 24
Minutenknopf 110 3
Miobare 9 3
Mira 3 11
Mirabelle 59 25
Misch·anlage Straßenbau 200
  15; 201 19
~anlage Film 311 21
~arbeit 311 36
~asphaltauslauf 200 54
~atelier 311 34
~ballenöffner 163 7
~batterie 49 2; 106 14
~behälter 172 35
~brot 97 6
~düse 191 61
Mischen 92 42
Mischer Ziegelei 159 10
~ Flugzeug 232 48
Misch·gutschrapper 200 13
~kammer 83 62
~kessel 170 53
~pult 117 26; 238 25; 310 56;
  311 35; 317 26
~rohr 192 10
~schnecke 83 59
~station 201 19
~tonmeister 311 36
~trommel 118 34
Mischung 238 54-59
Misch·wald 15 14
~wasserkanal 198 27
~wesen 327 52
~zylinder 173 3; 350 28
Missale 330 38
Mist·beet 55 16
~beetfenster 55 17
~beetkasten 55 16
~forke 66 7
~gabel 66 7
~hacke 66 8
~käfer 358 39
Mitlauftuch 168 56
Mitnehmer 135 9; 149 55
~stange 145 14
Mitralklappe 20 47
Mittel 175 29
mittelaktiver Abfall 154 72
mittelalterliche Noten 320
  1-2
Mittel·bauch 16 36
~bein 82 7
~brust 95 26
~decke 222 55
~decker 229 4
~druckzylinder 153 24
~fahne 291 64
~feldspieler 291 14
~finger 19 66
~flügel 229 8
~flyer 164 27
~fuß 72 23

~gang Gärtner 55 42
~gang Eisenb. 208 23
~gang Schiff 218 46
~gang Kirche 330 27
~gebirge 12 34
~handknochen 17 16
~kreis 291 2
~lager 177 65
~linie Zeichn. 151 30
~linie Sport 291 3; 293 8 bis
  9, 54; 294 4
~linienrichter 293 25
~mann 293 76
~mast 220 33
~meer 14 25
~moräne 12 54
~ohr 17 59-61
~pfette 121 51
~punkt 346 43
~punktswinkel 346 55
~rumpflängsträger 235 9
~säule 14 46
~scheitel 34 9
~schiff 334 62; 335 1
~schiffsektion 259 55-74
mittelschlächtiges Mühlrad
  91 37
Mittel·senkrechte 346 28
~spieler 293 76
~sproß 88 8
~sprosse 88 8
~stander 221 102
mittelständiger Fruchtknoten
  59 14
Mittel·steinzeit 328 1-9
~stoß 277 2
~strecke 231 17
~streckenläufer 298 5
~streckentransportflugzeug
  256 14
~streckenverkehrsflugzeug
  231 4, 11, 12
~streckler 298 5
~teil 215 68
~tonlautsprecher 241 16
~träger 222 53
~triebwagen 211 62
~wagen 209 7
~wand 77 43
~zehe 19 54
~zeichen 293 11
Mitten·fleck 115 65
~kontakt 114 72; 115 21
~leuchte 268 49
Mittlerer Muschelkalk 154 59
Mittschiffslinie 285 5
Mixbecher 267 61
Mixed 293 49
Mixer Küchengerät 40 46
~ Bäckerei 97 59
~ Barmixer 267 62
Mizar 3 29
Möbelwagen 268 47
Mobile 260 70
Mode·journal 104 4; 271 36
~katalog 104 6
Modell 338 32
~abdruck 148 34
~bühne 315 41
Modelleur 339 6
Modell·flug 273 37; 288 85
~flugsport 288 85-91
~flugzeug 273 38
~hut 35 7
Modellier·bock 339 9
~brett 339 34
~holz Porzellan 161 20
~holz Bildhauerei 339 10
~masse 339 8
~schere 106 34
~schlinge 339 11
~ton 339 31

Modell·kleid 103 5
~mantel 103 7
Modepuppe 271 34
Moderator 1 54
Mode·salon 268 9
~zeitschrift 271 36
Modulbauweise 240 1
Mofa 188 6
Mohair·hut 35 6
~stoffkappe 35 11
Mohn 61 2
~blüte 61 4
~brötchen 97 14
~kapsel 61 5
~samen 61 5
Möhre 57 17
Mohrenkopf Gebäck 97 36
~ Vögel 359 14
Mohrrübe 57 17
Mokassin 101 30; 352 18
Mokick 188 39
Molch 146 31
~schleuse 146 31
Mole 217 15
Molekularumlagerung 170 23
Molekül·modell 242 61-67
~struktur 1 9-14
Molkerei 76 1-48
Molldreiklang 321 2
Molle 96 40
Molltonart 320 55-68
Molluske 357 27-37
Molterbrett 65 5, 67
Monatserdbeere 58 16
~klee 69 9
Mönch Fischzucht 89 9
~ Bau 122 58
~ Kirche 331 54
~absperrgitter 89 10
~Nonnen-Dach 122 56
Mönchskopf 381 25
Mond 4 1-9, 31
~, abnehmender 4 7
~, zunehmender 4 3
~bahn 4 1
Möndchen 19 81
Mond·finsternis 4 29-35,
  34-35
~fleck 364 39
~landeeinheit 6 12; 234 55
~landung 6
~oberfläche 6 13
~phasen 4 2-7
~rand 4 41
~scheinkraut 379 5
~sichel 4 3, 7
~staub 6 14
~umlauf 4 1
~viertel 4 4, 6
~wechsel 4 2-7
Monierzange 119 85
Monitor 23 27; 25 2, 21, 28,
  29, 44, 47, 54; 26 16, 33; 27
  23; 243 6
~arm 27 24
~feld 238 1, 7
Monode 23 39
Monogramm 36 41
Monolith 328 18
Monoposto 290 34
Monoski 286 56
Monotype 174 32-45, 32, 39
„Monotype"-
  Normalsetzmaschine 174
  32
Monstranz 331 48; 332 34
Montage·gerät 214 80
~tisch 177 19; 179 23
Moor 14 24; 15 20
~beere 377 23
~heide 377 19
~huhn 359 20
~pflanze 377

~tümpel 13 23
Moos 377 17
~torfmasse 13 20, 22
Moped 188 24
~leuchte 188 29
Mops 70 9
Mopsea 369 8
Moränenfilterschicht 199 24
Mordent 321 20
Morgenmantel 32 35
Morselampe 223 7
Mörser *Mil.* 255 40
~ *Chem.* 349 9
Mortadella 96 7
Mörtel-bett 123 27
~kasten 118 20
~kübel 118 84
~pfanne 118 39
Mosaik 338 37
~figur 338 38
~stein 338 39
Moschee 337 12
Moschusochse 367 10
Moses 221 112
Moskito 358 16
Motiv 338 27
Moto-Cross 290 24-28
Motor 148 64; 164 2, 33, 37;
  165 12, 34; 167 31; 168 55;
  178 14; 189 31, 39; 269 7, 8,
  15, 45
~aggregat 50 82
~boot 280 13; 283 2; 286 1-5
~bootrennen 286 21-44
~bootsteg 216 7
~drehzahlmesser 212 22
~dreiradwalze 200 36
~einheit 84 34
Motorenaufbau 226 58
Motor-fähre 216 6
~fischkutter 221 49
~flugzeug 287 2, 15
~gartenhacke 56 18
~grundplatte 164 36
~haube 191 8; 195 36
~haubenstange 195 37
~hydraulik 64 65
motorisierte Verkehrsstreife
  264 9
Motor-kreuzer 286 4
~nivellier 112 69
~öl 196 15
~ölkanne 196 16
~öltemperaturmesser 212 19
~pumpe 270 8
Motorrad 189; 268 35
~, leichtes 189 16
~, schweres 189 31-58
~fahrer 268 34; 290 11, 32
~gabel, imitierte 188 58
~kette 189 22
~reifen 189 26
~rennen 290 24-28
~rennfahrer 290 25
~ständer 189 21
Motor-rasenmäher 56 28
~raum 195 35
~regulierung 212 67
~roller 188 47
~säge 84 22, 27; 85 13
~schaltschutz 269 46
~schiff 223
~schmieröl 212 55
~segler 287 8
~sport 290 24-38
~spritze 270 5
~steuerungsgerät 235 39
~träger 190 38; 191 53
~winde 287 6
~zapfwelle 65 31
Motte 81 13
Mouche 306 24
Möwe 359 14

Mozartzopf 34 4
MRCA 256 8
MTA 23 41
Mücke 358 16
Muddeschicht 13 15
Muffe 126 43
Muffelofen 140 11
Mufflon 367 6
Mühlbach 91 44
Mühle *Bauwerk* 91
~ *Spiele* 276 24
~brett 276 23
Mühleisen 91 12
Mühlespiel 276 18, 23-25
Mühl-graben 91 44
~rad 91 35
~rad, mittelschlächtiges 91
  37
~rad, unterschlächtiges 91 39
~stein 91 16
~steinauge 91 19
~steinkragen 355 52
~wehr 91 42
Mulde *Geogr.* 12 18
~ *Kunst* 336 48
Mulden-achse 12 19
~gewölbe 336 47
~kipper 47 38
~kippwagen 213 37
~presse 168 38
~tal 13 56
~wagen 147 64
Muleta 319 33
Müll 199 17, 22
~abfuhr 199 1
~abfuhrwagen 199 1
Mullauflage 21 6
Müll-auto 199 1
~beseitigung 199
Mullbinde 21 9
Müll-container 199 4
~deponie 199 10
Müller 91 15
Müll-tonne 199 3
~tonnenkippvorrichtung 199
  2
~verbrennungsanlage 199 28
~wagen 199 1
Multiplikand 344 25
Multiplikation 344 25
Multiplikator 344 25
~rolle 89 59
Multiplizieren 344 25
Multirole Combat Aircraft
  256 8
Multirolle 89 59
Mumie 352 21
Münchener Bier 93 26
Mund 16 13; 19 8, 14-37
~binde 322 5
~blasen 162 38-47
~harmonika 324 35
~leuchte 24 42
~schenk 329 69
~sperrer 22 48
~spiegel 24 41
Mundstück *Med.* 27 38
~ *Zigarette* 107 13
~ *Ziegelei* 159 13
~ *Mus.* 323 36; 324 33, 72
Mundtuch 45 9
Mündungs-arm 13 2
~bremse 255 58
~feuerdämpfer 255 18
~klappe 259 78
~waagerechte 87 74
Mund-wasser 49 36
~winkel 16 14; 19 19
~zu-Mund-Beatmung 21 26
~zu-Nase-Beatmung 21 26
Munition 87 19
Münster 335 22
Münz-bild 252 12

~buchstabe 252 10
Münze 252 1-28
Münzen-fassung 36 38
~kette 36 36
Münz-fernsprecher 236 9; 237
  3
~plättchen 252 43
~prägung 252 40-44
~zeichen 252 10
Murmeltier 366 18
Musche 306 24
Muschel-horn 327 41
~kalk, Mittlerer 154 59
~kalk, Oberer 154 58
~kalk, Unterer 154 60
~schale 357 36
Musenroß 327 26
Musette 322 8
Mushaus 329 13
Musik-atelier 310 14
~automat 308 38; 309 14
~clown 307 23
Musikertribüne 307 9
Musik-instrument 322; 323;
  324; 325; 326
~notation 320; 321
~note 320 3-7
~werk 308 38
Muskat-blüte 382 34
~nuß 382 35
~nußbaum 382 30
Muskulatur 18 34-64
Musselinglas 124 5
Mustang 352 4
Muster, aufgestepptes 30 31
~, eingestricktes 30 37
~kette 167 19
~walze 129 13
Mutter *Frau* 28 6; 272 71
~ *Fahrrad* 187 53
~gang 82 23
~knolle 68 39
~kompaß 224 51
~korn 68 4
~mund 20 85
~pflanze 54 15
~sau 75 41
~schaf 75 10
~schloß 149 19
Mutulus 334 13
Mützchen 29 2
Mütze 35 9; 268 32
Myrte 53 11
Myrtensträußchen 332 21
Myrtus 53 11
mythologische Figur 327 1-61
mythologische Tier 327 1-61
Myzel 381 2
Myzelium 381 2

N

Nabe 187 26
Nabel 16 34
Nabenhülse 187 69
Nach-besserung 84 10
~bildung 261 15
~brennerdüse 256 13
~brust 95 25
~darre 92 18, 30
~führbelichtungsmesser 114
  29
~hall 310 59
~läufer *Forstw.* 85 49
~läufer *Billard* 277 3
~pflanzung 84 10
Nachricht, vermischte 342 63
Nachrichten-sprecher 238 21
~verbindung 237 50
Nach-schaltgetriebe 212 53
~schlag 321 17, 18
~schlagewerk 262 17

~sortierer 172 58
~speise 45 6
~stellschritt 295 43
~synchronisierstudio 238
~synchronisierung 311 37-41
Nacht-creme 99 27
~falter 365 7-11
~hemd 32 16
~hyazinthe 60 9
Nachtigall 361 14
Nacht-kerzengewächs 53 3
~kleidung 32
~klub 318 1-33
~lokal 318 1-33
~rettungslicht 221 125
Nachtschatten, Schwarzer
  379 5
~gewächs 53 6; 379 7
Nacht-schmetterling 82 14;
  365 7-11
~wolken, leuchtende 7 22
~zeichen 203 38
Nachwickel-
  Filmzahntrommel 312 27
Nachwuchs-banderillero 319
  4
~torero 319 2
Nachzwirnerei 170 47
Nacken 16 21
~halte 295 52
~muskel 18 51
~pinsel 106 27
~schutz 270 38
~stand 295 29
Nadel *Masch.* 143 76
~ *Zeichn.* 151 56
~ *Textilw.* 165 37; 167 7, 53,
  63, 64
~ *Bot.* 372 11
~, chirurgische 22 57
~, gekröpfte 151 67
~barren 167 28
~baum 372 1-71
~bett 167 51, 55
~einsatz 151 54
nadelförmig 370 34
Nadel-fuß 167 60
~halter 22 59
~heber 167 59
~hölzer 372
~käfig 143 75
~kanal 167 15
~kette 168 24
~kissen 104 20
~lager 143 75-76
~reihe 167 27, 46, 47
~schloß 167 57
~segment 163 70
~senker 167 58
~spitze 102 30
~wald 15 1
~zeichen 340 58
~zylinder 167 8, 11
Nadir 4 13
Nagel *Anat.* 19 80
~ *Masch.* 134 39; 143 51
~heft 100 56
~klaue 120 75
~lack 99 32
~tasche 122 72
Nagel 60 6
Nagetier 366 12-19
Näglein 60 6
Naheinstellgerät 115 81-98
Nähgarnrolle 104 9
Näh-kampf 299 31
~linse 117 55
Nähmaschine 100 21
Nähmaschinen-garn 103 12
~schublade 104 18
~tisch 104 17
Nährmittel 98 35-39

~gondel 99 62
Nahrungs-bläschen 357 6
~mitteluntersuchung 112 48
~vakuole 357 6
Näh-seidenröllchen 104 10
~spitze 102 30
Naht-ausblendung 177 53
~band 103 14
~material, chirurgisches 22
56; 26 21
~roller 128 36
~schneider 128 43
~spant 285 55
~spantenbau 285 54
Nahverkehr 208 1-30
Nahverkehrs-triebwagen 208
13
~wagen 208 3
~zug 208 1-12
Nähvorrichtung 133 5
Najade 327 23
Namensschild *Pflanzen* 54 4
~ *Segeln* 285 46
Nansenschlitten 303 18
Napfkuchen 97 33; 99 22
~form 40 29
Narbe 58 41; 59 16; 370 56
Nargileh 107 42
Narkose-apparat 26 1
~gerät 26 24
~- und
Dauerbeatmungsapparat
26 1, 24
Narr 306 38
Narren-fest 306 1-48
~kappe 306 39
~orden 306 60
~pritsche 306 48
~zepter 306 59
Narzisse 60 3
~, Weiße 60 4
Narzissengewächs 53 8
Nase *Anat.* 16 10
~ *Zool.* 70 4; 364 2
~ *Pferd* 72 6
~ *Bau* 122 51
~ *Tischler* 132 18
~ *Masch.* 143 29
Nasen-bein 17 41
~höhle 17 53
~keil 143 74
~klappe 229 54
~kolben 242 56
~leiste 287 34
~-Lippen-Furche 16 11
~riemen 71 7
~scheibe 187 55
Nashorn 366 25
Naß-aufbereitung 161 1
~bürstgerät 108 46
nasse Wiese 15 19
Naß-filz 173 17, 18
~klebung 117 89
~öltank 145 30
~presse 173 19, 20
Nationalflagge 253 15-21
Nato-Lage 21 24
Natrium-atom 1 8
~ion 1 11
~kreislauf, primärer 154 2
~kreislauf, sekundärer 154 7
Natron-kalkabsorber 27 39
~lauge 169 3, 4, 5, 10; 170 10
~laugeverdampfung 170 11
Natter 364 38
Natur-felsen 356 2
~korken-
Verschließmaschine,
halbautomatische 79 10
~steinsockel 37 85
~theater 272 6
~wabe 77 60
~werkstofftapete 128 18

Navette 36 55
Navigation 224
Navigations-einrichtung 288
13
~fernsehmast 221 37
~offizier 224 37
~raum 223 14; 228 22
Navy Cut 107 25
Neanderthalerschädel 261 19
Nebel 9 31
~kammer, Wilsonsche 2 24
~kammeraufnahme 2 26
~lichtkontrolle 191 63
~scheinwerfer 191 64
~schlußleuchte 191 67
~schlußlicht 191 64
~streifen 2 27
~wurfbecher 255 83
Neben-anlagengebäude 154
36
~auge 77 2
~bahn 15 23
~blatt 57 5; 58 48; 371 73
~fahrwasser 224 93
~gebäude 62 14
~hoden 20 73
~kern 357 12
~leitung 192 27
~luftschieber 50 74
~niere 20 29
~pforte 335 13
~portal 335 13
~produkt 170 13
~station 224 41
~stelle 237 19, 26
~stellenanlage 237 21
~stellen-Reihenanlage 237
17
~stellen-Wählanlage 237
22-26
~strom 232 50
~winkel 346 14
~wurzel 370 17
Negativ-bühne 116 30
~fenster 115 28
~kohle 312 21
Neger *Film* 310 51
~ *Völkerkunde* 354 13
~hütte 354 21
Negerin 354 22
Neigungs-verstellung 177 21
~waage 98 12
Nektarium 59 18
Nelke 60 6; 382 28
Nelkengewächs 69 12
Nematode 80 51
Nenner 344 15
~, gemeinsamer 344 19
Nenn-strom 127 37
~wert 251 12
Neolithikum 328 10-20
Neopren-Tauchanzug 279 9
Neptun 4 51
Nereide 327 23
Nerv 19 33
~betäubung 24 53
Nervensystem 18 22-33
Nerz 30 60
~fell 131 11, 19
~jäckchen 30 1
~mantel 131 24
~mütze 35 2
~pelzhut 35 18
~schirmkappe 35 17
Nessel 61 33
~band 153 46
Nestloch 359 28
Netz *Astr.* 3 48
~ *Jagd* 86 27
~ *Fischerei* 90 8
~ *Sport* 293 13
~arbeit 102 22
~auge 77 20-24

~einspeisung 154 16
~flügler 358 12
~geräteträger 238 3
~gewölbe 336 45
~halter 293 14
~haut 19 49
~hemd 32 22
~nadel 102 26
~pfosten 293 15
~richter 293 23
~slip 32 23
~sonde 90 17
~sondenkabel 90 14
~spieler 293 63
~stoff 167 29
~strumpf 306 10
~taste 195 11
~teil 311 11
~trog 165 44
~unterjacke 32 22
~wand 90 42
~zustand 153 8
Neufundländer 70 34
Neumond 4 2
Neunachteltakt 320 39
Neunbindengürteltier 366 8
Neunvierteltakt 320 40
Neutron 1 30, 50
~, absorbiertes 1 53
~, freigesetztes 1 39, 45
~, freiwerdendes 1 52
~, kernspaltendes 1 42
Neutronenbeschuß 1 36
New Penny 252 37
NF-Ziegelstein 118 58
nichtdruckender Teil 178 43
Nichtschwimmerbecken 282
21
Nickel 327 23
~mann 327 23
~münze 252 1-28
Nicken 230 67
Nickendes Leinkraut 376 26
Nicker 18 34; 19 1
Nicki 29 43
~pulli 29 43
~tuch 31 57
Niederdruck-gasleitung 156
44
~manometer 141 6
~turbine 232 54; 259 62
~- und Nutzturbine 232 54
~verdichter 232 35
~vorwärmer 152 25
~-Wasservorlage 141 8
~zylinder 153 25
niederfrequenter Strom 23 37
Nieder-gang *Schiff* 221 123;
223 24; 258 24
~gang *Stadt* 268 62
~halter 157 65
~haus 305 76
~schachtofen 147 51-54
Niederschlag *Meteorol.* 8 9,
10, 18, 19
~ *Sport* 299 40
Niederschlags-formen 8 18-19
~gebiet 9 30
~messer 10 44
~summe 9 45
Niederschrift 276 6
Niedersprungmatte 296 13;
297 7
Niere 20 28, 30-31
Nieren-aufnahme 27 4, 14
~becken 20 31
nierenförmig 370 38
Nieren-gegend 72 30
~kartoffel 68 38
~kelch 20 30
~kontrastdarstellung 27 6
~schale 23 45

Nieseln 9 33
Niet 143 57-60
Niete 143 57-60
Nietenschaft 143 58
Niet-kopf 143 57
~maschine 138 27
~teilung 143 60
Nietung 143 56
Nietverbindung 143 56
Nightclub 318 1-33
Nil-krokodil 356 13
~pferd 366 31
Nimbostratus 8 10, 11
Nimmersatt 359 5
Nippelhalter 126 63
Nische 217 70
Nischenpoller 217 10
Niveau 1 18
~förderung 74 35
Nivellier-bohle 201 3
~instrument 14 48
Nivellierung 14 46
Nix 327 23
Nixe 327 23
Nock 223 16
Nocke 305 63
Nockenwelle 189 3; 190 14
~, obenliegende 190 14
Nockenwellen-lager 190 11;
192 24
~schmierung 190 13
Nodosität 80 27
Noir 275 21
Nomade 353 19
Nonius *Schlosser* 140 55
~ *Schiff* 224 5
~skala 149 69
Nonne *Zool.* 82 17
~ *Bau* 122 57
~ *Kirche* 331 50
Non-pareille 175 23
~plusultra 175 19
Nordamerika 14 12
Nordamerikanisches
Opossum 366 2
Nordäquatorialstrom 14 32
nördliche Hemisphäre 3 1-35
Nördliche Krone 3 31
nördlicher Fixsternhimmel 3
1-35
Nördliches Eismeer 14 21
Nord-ostpassat 9 48
~pol 14 3
~punkt 4 16
~see 14 26
~stern 3 1
Norm 185 69
Normal-benzin 145 54; 196 1
~filmkamera 313 1
~format-Ziegelstein 118 58
~gewinde 149 4
~klappe 229 46
~leitwerk 229 23
~objektiv 115 3-8, 46; 117 49
~setzmaschine 174 32
~uhr 245 18
Norm-palette 226 10
~stecker 241 70
Norton-getriebe 149 8
~kasten 149 8
Nose-in-Position 233 21
Notaderpresse 21 15
Notation 276 6
Notationszeichen 321 23-26
Not-auffangnetz 259 17
~ausgang 99 79; 307 33; 312 7
~beleuchtung 312 6
~bremse 214 3, 71
~bremsventil 210 57
Note 252 29-39; 320 3-7
Noten, mittelalterliche 320
1-2
~balken 320 6

~bank 252 30
~blatt 309 15
~fähnchen 320 5
~hals 320 4
~kopf 320 3
~linie 320 43
~pult 326 36
~schlüssel 320 8-11
~wert 320 12-19
Notfall-abfackelanlage 146 11
~einsatz 23 46
Notgelb 203 16
Notiz-blatt 247 34
~buch 264 36
Not-reißbahn 288 72
~reißleine 288 73
~ruf 233 40
~rufmelder 237 4
~sitz 193 28
~verband 21 1-13
Nougat 98 81
Novillero 319 2
Nudel 98 34
Nudist 281 16
Nudistengelände 281 15
Nugat 98 81
Nuggetform 252 1
Null 275 18
Nulleiter 127 13
Null-hyperbel 224 42
~isotherme 9 41
~meridian 14 5
~punkt 153 22
~punkteinstellung 2 7
~schicht 7 6, 20
Numerieren 84 20
Numerierung 85 33
Numerus 345 6
Nummer, komische 307 25
~, laufende 251 13
Nummern-kasten 267 5
~schalter 237 10
~schild 267 10
~tafel 330 24
Nürnbergerin 355 38
Nuß Bot. 59 37-51; 370 98;
    384 60
~ Fleischerei 95 52
~ Schlosser 140 43
~, welsche 59 43
~baum 59 37-43
~baumzweig 59 37
~frucht 375 43
~häher 361 1
~knacker 45 49
~stück 95 11
Nüster 72 7
Nut Bau 123 74
~ Masch. 143 85
Nutation 4 24
Nutenzylinder 165 10
Nutkeil 143 73-74
Nutsche 349 11
Nut- u. Federriemen 123 74
Nutzenzylinder 184 10
Nutz-garten 52
~lastbedienungsgerät 235 29
~lastraum 235 13, 26
~lastraumluke 235 14
~turbine 232 54
Nydamschiff 218 1-6
Nylon-bezug 207 68
~fadenkops 133 4
~sohle 291 30
Nymphe 89 66
Nymphenköder 89 66

O

Oase 354 4
Obelisk 333 10
Obenentleerung 147 42
Ober 266 30; 267 47

Oberarm 16 43
~bein 17 12
~kippe 296 58
~knochen 17 12
~schiene 329 47
Oberbär 139 6
Oberbauch 16 35
Oberdeck 194 38
~omnibus 194 36
Oberer Muschelkalk 154 58
Oberfeuer 224 102
Oberflächen-kondensator 152
    24
~prüfgerät 112 37
~punkt 11 33
~vorwärmer 210 23
~welle 11 36
Ober-flügel 229 7
~geschoß 37 3; 118 14
~gesenk 139 13
~gurt Bau 121 74, 80
~gurt Brücken 215 9
~haupt 217 25
~kasten 148 19
~kellner 266 30
~kiefer 17 36; 19 27
~kieferbein 17 36
~klaue 88 23
~kohlrabi 57 26
~körper 294 52
~labium 326 27
~lederschaft 291 26
~lederschere 100 42
Oberleitungs-bus 194 40
~omnibus 194 40
Oberlicht 37 35; 75 8
~band 121 21
Ober-lid 19 39
~lippe Anat. 19 14
~lippe Pferd 72 8
~lippe Mus. 326 27
~lippenrinne 16 12
~maschinerie 316 1-60
~messer 183 19
~rohr 187 16
~rücken 88 23
Obers 265 5
Oberschale 95 13, 37, 54
Oberschenkel 16 49; 21 15
~bein 17 22
~hose 355 31
oberschlächtiges Zellenrad 91
    35
Ober-schlitten 149 22
~schrank 39 8; 46 30
Oberspannungs-anzapfung
    153 13
~durchführung 152 43
~wandler 211 4
~wicklung 153 15
Ober-stein 91 22
~stempel 252 40
~stromspannungsanzeige 211
    29
Oberteil Kleidung 32 18
~ Schuh 101 23, 46
~, gesmoktes 29 15
Ober-walze 148 54
~werk 326 2, 44
~zange 163 66
~zylinder 164 11
Obi 353 41
Objektfeldbeleuchtung 112
    33
Objektiv 114 5; 115 3-8, 32,
    84; 116 32; 176 23; 243 2,
    52; 313 2
~brücke 112 18
~köcher 115 104
~kopf 117 46-49
~linse 113 36
~revolver 112 11, 30; 117 46;
    313 32

~standarte 114 52
~tubus 115 3
Objekt-schleuse 113 33
~tisch 112 9
~tischverstellung 113 34
~verschiebung 113 34
Oblate 332 28
Oboe 323 38
~ da caccia 323 38
~ d'amore 323 38
O'Brien-Technik 298 50
Observatorium 5 1-16
Obst-abteilung 99 80
~baum 52 30
~baumspritze, fahrbare
    83 38
~garten 15 108; 52 1-32
~hochstamm 52 30
~kern 58 37, 60
~konserve 98 16
~made 58 64
~messer 45 71
~pflücker 56 22
~schädling 80 1-19
~schale 45 40
~stand 308 53
~torte 97 22; 99 20
~ und Gemüseabteilung 99
    80
~waage 99 88
OB-Telefon 224 27; 238 9, 40
Obus 194 40
Occhiarbeit 102 19
Ocean Liner 221 82; 225 32
Ochse 73 1
Ochsen-auge 336 2
~gespann 63 16
~treiber 3 30
Octans 3 43
Odalisque 306 41
Oertz-Ruder 222 69-70
Ofen 147 23
~bank 266 36
~gas 147 53
~kachel 266 35
~krücke 38 42
~raum 147 24
~rohr 309 5
~rohrkrümmer 309 6
~schirm 309 8
~stein 281 26
~tür 309 7
Offenbarung 327 50
offenes Feuer 267 25
~ Wasser 227 4
Offenfreßstand 62 9
öffentliche Fernsprechzelle
    204 46
öffentliches Gebäude 15 54
öffentliche Sprechstelle 237 1
Offizier, wachhabender 221
    126
Offiziers-kajüte 223 21
~kammer 223 21
Öffnung Fotogr. 115 62
~ Porzellan 161 2
Öffnungsfrucht 370 91-96
Offset-druck 180
~kopie 179
~maschine 180 1, 18, 30, 46,
    59
~platte 179 1, 16
~presse 173 21
Offshore 221 32
Off-shore-Bohrung 146
Ogeeflügel 229 22
Ogivalflügel 229 22
Ohr 16 18; 22 54; 70 2; 72 1
Ohr, äußeres 17 56-58
~, inneres 17 62-64
Öhr 89 82
Ohren-fledermaus 366 9
~höhler 81 11

~klappe 35 31; 304 28
~kneifer 81 11
~kriecher 81 11
~schützer 304 28
~spiegel 22 74
Ohr-gehänge 36 11
~hörer 248 35; 249 63
~läppchen 17 57
Öhrling 81 11
Ohr-muschel Anat. 17 56
~muschel Kopfhörer 241 69;
    248 35; 261 40
~pflock 354 30
~ring 36 13
~speicheldrüse 19 9
~wurm 81 11
Okarina 324 32
Okkiarbeit 102 19
Okklusion 9 25
Oktaeder 351 6, 14, 16
Oktant 3 43
Oktave 321 13, 46, 47, 48, 49,
    50
~, große 321 44
~, kleine 321 45
Oktogon 351 17
Okular 113 20; 115 42; 117
    14; 311 9
~abstand 112 56
~einstellung 313 7
~muschel 115 73; 313 34
Okulation 54 30
Okulieren 54 30
Okuliermesser 54 31
Öl Speiseöl 98 24
~ Erdöl 146 9
~ Schiff 228 11
~ablaßschraube 190 24
~abstreifring 190 37
~ausdehnungsgefäß 152 42;
    153 9
Ölb 359 16
Öl-badluftfilter 65 54; 212 79
~baum 383 29
~behälter 38 44; 64 29, 93
~beutel 228 11
~block 109 5
~brenner 38 58-60
Öldruck-kontrolleuchte 191
    73
~manometer 157 7
~messer 230 20
Oleander 373 13
Öleinfüllstutzen 190 28
Öler 187 65
Ölerhitzer 145 36
Ölerklipp 187 62
Öl-farbe 338 11
~feuerung 38 44-60; 199 30
~feuerungsgebläse 199 35
~filter 190 43
~flasche 45 42
~geber 109 4
~grobfilter 192 18
~hafen 145 74
~heizungskessel 38 57
Oliven-baum 383 29
~öl 98 24
Öl-jacke 228 6
~kühler 192 19; 211 11
~-Luft-Kühlanlage 209 18
~mantel 228 7
~meßstab 190 47
~palme 383 54
~peilstab 190 47
~pumpe 190 42; 192 16
~pumpenantrieb 190 25
~raffinerie 145 65-74
~rohr 190 13
~sardine 98 19
~sockel 129 15
~standsanzeiger 38 54; 153
    11

~standsleitung 38 53
~stein 340 21
~studie 338 36
~sumpf 192 17
~tank 38 44
Öltemperatur-anzeige 191 38; 230 21
~fühlerkabel 195 40
~meßkabel 195 16
Öl-überdruckventil 190 67
~umlaufpumpe 152 45; 211 12
~vorrat 192 17
~wanne 65 45
~wannenoberteil 190 40
~wannenunterteil 190 41
~-Wasser-Kühler 152 46
Olympia-flagge 253 5
~jolle 284 50
olympisches Turnen 296 1-11; 297 1-6
Ölzeug 228 4
Omnibus 186 37; 194
Oneirophanta 369 18
Operations-anzeige 244 7
~koje 228 21
~lampe 27 25
~leuchte 26 10
~mikroskop 112 31
~saal 26 1-33
~tisch 26 5
~tischfahrgestell 26 36
~tischfläche 26 8
~ und Fehleranzeige 244 7
Operator 244 14
Opernglas 315 9
Opfer-gabe 330 60
~kerze 330 53
~kerzentisch 330 52
~stein 334 48
~stock 330 55
ophthalmologischer Prüfplatz 111 43
Ophthalmometer 111 44
OP-Lampe 26 10; 27 25
Opossum, Nordamerikanisches 366 2
OP-Saal 26 1-33
Optik 242 41
Optiker 111 1
~werkstatt 111 20-47
Optik-platte 195 18
~träger 177 27
OP-Tisch 26 5
optische Anzeige 238 2
~ Bank 242 79
~ Geräte 112; 113
~ Kontrolle 25 44
optisches System 243 50
orange 343 7
Orange 384 27
Orangeat 98 11
Orangen-bäumchen 55 49
~blüte 384 25
Orangerie 272 3
Orang-Utan 368 15
Orbiter 235 49
Orchester 315 25
~instrument 323 1-62
~raum 315 24
~tribüne 307 9
~versenkung 315 24
Orchestra 334 47
Orchestrion 309 14
Orchidee 376 28
Ordens-band, Rotes 365 8
~kaktus 53 15
Order 250 19
Ordinalzahl 344 6
Ordinate 347 10
Ordinaten-achse 347 3
~durchgang 347 12

~wert 347 10
Ordner 263 10
~mechanik 247 41
Ordnungszahl 344 6
öre 252 25
Öre 252 24, 25, 26
Organe, innere 20 1-57
Organelle 357 5
Organistrum 322 25
Orgel 308 38; 322 56; 326 1-52, 36-52
~gehäuse 326 1-5
~pfeife 326 17-35
~prospekt 326 1-5
~spieltisch 326 36-52
Orientalin 306 41
Orientteppich 46 36
Original 177 18
~filmspule 117 79
~halter 177 14
~haltergestell 177 15
~ton 117 100
Orion 3 13
Orkanbug 259 9
Ornament, griechisches 334 38-43
~, romanisches 335 14-16
~glas 124 6
Ornat 330 22; 332 4
Ort 63 3
~gang 37 8; 121 3
orthogonal 215 2
Orthopinakoid 351 25
orthotrop 215 2
Ortolan 361 7
Orts-batterietelefon 224 27; 238 9, 40
~gespräch 237 3
Ortstein 122 80
Öse Med. 23 10
~ Schuhmacher 100 63
~ Glaser 124 23
~ Elektr. 127 30
Ösen-einsetzmaschine 100 53
~schäftung 328 23
O₂-Stabilisator 27 42
Ostaustralstrom 14 38
Oster-kerze 330 44
~kerzenständer 330 45
~luzei 376 22
Ost-jake 353 17
~punkt 4 14
~-West-Modul 240 9
Otter Mil. 258 87
~ Zool. 364 40-41, 40; 367 17
Ottomotor 190 1, 2, 6
Outsider 289 53
ovales Hexagon 36 63
Ovalradzähler 76 4
Overall 29 19; 31 53
Overdresskleid 31 17
Overheadprojektor Infotechnik 242 6
~ Schule 261 8
Oxer 289 8
Oxidkeramik 149 46
oxidkeramische Wendeplatte 149 47
Oxymeter 27 13
Ozean 14 19, 20, 23
Ozeanide 327 23
Ozelotmantel 131 25
Ozonschicht 7 13, 19

P

p 252 37
Paar 267 46
~hufer 73 9; 366 28-31
paarig gefiedert 370 41
Paarläufer 302 4
Päckchen 236 6
Pack-lage 123 12; 200 60

~material 98 46-49
~presse 183 20
~stück, unitisiertes 226 21
Packung 99 30, 37, 38, 65
Padde 364 23
Paddel 283 34; 353 14
~boot 283 4
Paddeln 283
Pädergras 61 30
Padsteg 111 12
Pagaie 218 8; 283 34
Page 267 18
Pagenkopf 34 35
Pagode 337 1, 21
Pailou 337 3
Pair 275 20
Paket 107 25; 236 3
~annahme 236 1
~karte 236 7
~nummernzettel 236 4
~schalter Elektr. 127 18
~schalter Post 236 1
~sprung 282 14
~waage 236 2
Palaeopneustes niasicus 369 19
Paläolithikum 328 1-9
Palas 329 30
Palastanlage 333 29
Palette Eisenb. 206 32
~ Hafen 225 43; 226 7
~ Theater 315 36
Paletten-messer 338 14
~stecker 338 29
Palisade Sport 289 8
~ Ritterwesen 329 36
Palla 355 10
Pallino 305 23
Palmblattschrift 341 21
Palme 384 2
Palmen-hain 354 5
~säule 333 17
Palmette 334 41
Palmettenkapitell 333 25
Palm-lilie 373 24
~wedel 384 3
Pampasgras 51 8
Pampel 36 82-86
~, facettierte 36 84
~, glatte 36 83
Pampelmuse 384 23
Panamabindung 171 11
Pandora 322 21
Paneel Raumfahrt 234 53
~ Restaurant 266 37
Panel 230 1
Panflöte 322 2
Panhardstab 192 70
Panoptikum 308 68
Panorama-aufnahme 24 21
~scheibe 191 21
Panpfeife 322 2
Pantaleon 325 1
Pantoffel 101 25
~tierchen 357 9
Pantograph 14 65; 175 58
~graphensupport 175 53
Pantry 223 43
Panzer Mil. 255 79-95
~ Ritterwesen 329 38, 62
~abstreichblech 65 4
~faust 255 25
~glas 124 5; 250 3
~handschuh 329 50
~haubitze 255 57
~schrank 246 22
~schurz 329 51
~turm 255 84
Panzerung 246 24
Panzerwand 246 24
Papageienvogel 363 1
Papier 89 22; 180 57, 69; 181 9, 23, 25, 30; 184 12

~ablage 181 14; 249 54
~ablagestapel 181 9
~anlage 181 14, 24; 249 49
~bahn 173 30, 45; 181 42, 43, 58
~belichtungsmesser 116 53
~beutel 98 48
~drachen 260 71
~eingabe 249 45
~einwerfer 249 20
~entwicklungstrommel 116 48
~geld 252 29-39
~halter 249 17
~handtuch 196 11
~herstellung 172; 173
~index 116 54
~korb 37 63; 46 25; 248 45; 268 5
~kragen 106 5
~kugel 306 55
~laterne 52 15; 306 4
~laufbahn 180 26
~maschine 173 11, 13-28
~mütze 306 45
~rand 185 55-58
~registriereinheit 27 33
~rolle 151 14; 173 35; 180 2, 3; 181 46; 309 75
~rollenbremse 181 47
~schlange 306 66
~schneideautomat 185 1
~schreiber 25 56, 57
~sortiment 116 50
~ständer 151 13
~stapel 180 47, 57, 69; 181 23, 25; 249 56, 57
~stoffmischbütte 173 1
~stoffuntersuchung 173 2-10
~streifen 237 32
~tapete 128 18
~transportwalze 180 4
~tuch 40 1; 196 11
~tuchspender 196 10
~turm 174 33, 43
~untersuchung 173 2-10
~ventilsack 160 16
~zuführung 180 74; 245 11
Papirossa 107 14
Papp-dach 122 90
~deckel 184 7
~deckung 122 90-103
Pappel 371 15
Pappenzieher 184 8
Papp-hülse 87 50
~nagel 122 96
~nase 306 46
~schere 183 16
~zwischenlage 340 37
Paprika 57 42
Papstkreuz 332 66
Papyrus-säule 333 15
~staude 383 64
para 252 28
Para 252 28
Parabel 347 14, 15, 16, 17
~bogen 336 29
Parade 294 6
Paradeis 57 12
Paradeiser 57 12
Paradiesapfel 57 12
~vogel 363 3
Paraffin 145 60
Paragraphenzeichen 342 36
parallel 345 21
Parallelbohrer 135 16
Parallele 346 4
Parallelfalzung 185 13
Parallelitätszeichen 345 21
Parallelmanipulator 2 47
Parallelogramm 346 33-36
Parallel-rückenrollsprung 298 15

~schraubstock **140** 2
Paranuß **384** 53, 59
Parasit **68** 4
Parasolpilz **381** 30
Pärchen **272** 72
Pardune **219** 19
Parentationshalle **331** 21
Parfümflakon **43** 27
Parfumflasche **105** 36
Parfümzerstäuber **43** 26;
　　106 21
Parierstange **294** 42
Park **15** 97; **272**
~, englischer **272** 41-72
~, französischer **272** 1-40
~bank **272** 16
~baum **272** 59
~eingang **272** 32
Parkett **315** 19
~boden **123** 74
Park-gärtner **272** 66
~gitter **272** 33
Parkleuchtenschalter **191**
　　62
Parkometer **268** 1
Park-ordnung **272** 29
~stuhl **272** 48
~tor **272** 31
Parkuhr **268** 1
Park-wächter **272** 30
~weg **272** 38
Partei **263** 20
~kandidat **263** 20
Parterre **37** 2
~anlage **272** 39
Parthenon **334** 1
Partienummer **163** 6
Partner **293** 18
Party-bluse **30** 55
~rock **30** 56
Pasch **276** 35
Paschen-Serie **1** 22
Pas de trois **314** 27-28
Pasiphaea **369** 12
Paspel **30** 13; **31** 7
Paß **12** 47
Passage **71** 3
passagerer Schrittmacher
　　25 25
Passagier **221** 97, 109
~dampfer **221** 82; **225** 32
~raum **231** 22
~sitz **230** 38; **231** 22
~tür **231** 25, 30
Passant **268** 18
Passe **275** 19
Paß-einsatz **127** 21
~gang **72** 40
Passierscheibe **96** 54
Passiflora **53** 2
Passions-blume **53** 2
~kreuz **332** 55
Paßkontrolle **233** 42
~schraube **127** 21
~zeichen **340** 58
Pastellstift **338** 19
Pastete **97** 18
Pastor **330** 22
Pate **332** 13
Patene **330** 9; **332** 51
Patent-anker **222** 78; **258** 5;
　　286 17
~davit **221** 78
~log **224** 54
~schlüssel **187** 50
~schrift **246** 26
~ventil **187** 31
Paternosteraufzug **170** 36
~werk **216** 57
Patient **22** 2, 3; **24** 2; **25** 43
Patienten-bett **25** 10
~gerät **25** 51
~hocker **27** 50

~karte **22** 8; **25** 5
~kartei **22** 6
~stuhl **24** 3
~überwachungseinheit **25** 24
Patriarchenkreuz **332** 65
Patrize **175** 36
Patrizierin, Augsburger **355**
　　48
Patrone *Munition* **87** 54; **94** 5;
　　305 38, 39
~ *Textilw.* **171** 4, 11, 13, 19, 27
Patronen-hülse **305** 36
~lager **187** 15
~magazin **87** 17
Patte **33** 18
Pauke **323** 57
Paukenfell **323** 58
Paukenhöhle **17** 60
Pauli-Prinzip **1** 7
Pausche *Pferd* **71** 48
~ *Sport* **296** 1, 5, 6; **297** 1
Pauschenpferd **296** 5, 51, 54
Pauscht **173** 50
Pause **320** 20-27, 20
~beutel **129** 49
Pausenzeichen **320** 20-27
Pausrädchen **129** 42
Pavian **368** 13
Pavo **3** 41
Pazifischer Ozean **14** 19
Pech-nase **329** 23
~nelke **376** 20
Pedal *Tischler* **132** 72
~ *Druck* **181** 12
~ *Fahrrad* **187** 40, 78
~ *Sport* **305** 85
~ *Mus.* **323** 62; **325** 8, 9, 41
~achse **187** 81
~harfe **323** 60
~hebel **163** 28
Pedalo **280** 12
Pedal-obertaste **326** 52
~pfeife **326** 3
~rahmen **187** 83
~rohr **187** 80
~stock **325** 42
~taste **326** 51
~turm **326** 4
~untertaste **326** 51
Peddigrohr **136** 32
Peerd **219** 46
Pegasus *Astr.* **3** 10
Pegel **15** 29
~aussteuerung **242** 14
~regler **241** 42
~tongenerator **238** 51
Peil-antenne **223** 5
~aufsatz **224** 53
~deck **223** 4-11; **227** 24
~gerät **230** 5
Peitsche **218** 47; **307** 53
Peitschenantenne **258** 60
Pekinese **70** 19
Pelargonie **53** 1
Pelerine **30** 65
Pelikan **359** 5
~, Gemeiner **359** 5
~aal **369** 2
Pelitton **323** 44
Pelota-spiel **305** 67
~spieler **305** 68
Pelz-besatz **30** 59
~jäger **306** 8
~kragen **30** 63
~mantel **30** 60
~näherin **131** 8
~nähmaschine **131** 9
~schneiderin **131** 23
~stift **131** 22
~stola **318** 30
~werkerin **131** 8, 23
Pendel *Geogr.* **11** 41

~ *Uhr* **110** 27
~aufhängung **11** 42
~bahn **214** 25
~fähre **216** 10
~masse **11** 43
~spritzgestänge **83** 27
~tür **207** 18
~vorrichtung **2** 35
~walze **181** 45
~zentrifuge **168** 14
Pendentif **334** 74
Penna **324** 20
Penny **252** 37
Pensee **60** 2
Pentacrinus **369** 3
Pentadachkantprisma **115** 41,
　　70
Pentagon **351** 9
~dodekaeder **351** 8
Penthouse **37** 83
Peplos **355** 2
Perche **307** 46
Pergola **37** 80; **51** 1; **272** 17
Periode **344** 22
Peripherie **346** 44
~winkel **346** 56
Peristyl **334** 2
Perl **175** 22
Perle *Schmuck* **36** 8, 23
~ *Jagd* **88** 30
~ *Zool.* **357** 35
Perlen-brosche **36** 7
~diadem **355** 16
~kette **36** 32
Perlfang **171** 45, 46
Perlhuhn **73** 27
Perlmutt **357** 34
Perlmutter **357** 34
Perlonsaite **324** 14
Perlschnur **334** 38
PE-Rohr **67** 26
Perpendikel **110** 27; **309** 58
Persenning **221** 107
Perser, Kunst der **333** 21-28
Persianer **30** 60
Personal-raum **207** 81
~waschraum **207** 26
~WC **207** 82
Personen-aufzug **271** 45
~fähre *Landkarte* **15** 60
~fähre *Fluß* **216** 1
~fahrung **14** 39, 44
~fahrzeug **191** 1-56
~hebebühne **173** 40
~schleuse **154** 32
~waage **22** 66; **49** 47
~wagen **191** 1-56; **195** 34
~wagentyp **193** 1-36
~zug **144** 39
Perücke **34** 2; **105** 38; **315** 49
Perückenständer **105** 39
Perustrom **14** 42
peseta **252** 22
Peseta **252** 22
Petasos **355** 4
Peter, Blauer **253** 26
Peterlein **57** 19
Petersilie **57** 19
Petit **175** 25
Petrischale **261** 25
Petroleum **145** 41
~lampe **278** 29
Petruskreuz **332** 58
Pettycoat **309** 85
Petunie **53** 6
Pfadfinder **278** 11
~lager **278** 8-11
~treffen **278** 8-11
Pfahl **78** 7; **84** 17
~bau **328** 15
~bauhütte **352** 33
~gründung **216** 8
~haus **328** 15

~mast **258** 42; **259** 6
~zaun **329** 36
Pfandbrief **251** 11-19
Pfannenhaube **92** 45
Pfannkuchen, Berliner **97** 29
Pfarrer **330** 22
Pfarrhaus **331** 20
Pfau *Astr.* **3** 41
~ *Zool.* **73** 30
Pfauen-auge **73** 32
~busch **254** 36
~feder **73** 31
Pfeffer **382** 39
~, spanischer **57** 42
~fresser **363** 6
~korn **382** 39
Pfefferminze **380** 3
Pfeffer-strauch **382** 36
~streuer **266** 77
Pfeife *Tabakspfeife* **42** 12
~ *Eisenb.* **212** 49
~ *Mus.* **322** 57; **326** 16, 17-35
~, kurze **107** 33
~, lange **107** 35
Pfeifen-besteck **107** 44
~deckel **107** 37
~kopf **107** 36
~körper **326** 29
~mundstück **107** 40
~reiniger **107** 46
~reinigungsdraht **107** 48
~rohr **107** 38
~ständer **42** 11
~stock **326** 15
~strauch, Wohlriechender
　　373 9
Pfeifsignal **211** 40
~instrument **211** 9
Pfeil **305** 60; **327** 53; **352** 28
Pfeiler **335** 20
~aufsatz **335** 29
Pfeilflügel **229** 20, 21
pfeilförmig **370** 37
Pfeil-kraut **378** 15
~spitze **305** 61; **352** 29
~stirnrad **143** 87
Pfeilung, positive **229** 20, 21
Pfennig **252** 7
Pfennigkraut **375** 26
Pferd **71**; **72**; **73** 2; **319** 18
~, Fabelwesen **327** 26
~box **75** 2
~droschke **186** 26
~fuß *Fabelwesen* **327** 42
~fuß *Bot.* **380** 8
~hof **319** 15
~kamm **72** 14
~kopf **72** 1-11
~kopf, geschnitzter **218** 14
~körper **327** 54
~kruppe **72** 31
~leib **327** 27
~mähne **72** 13
~omnibus **186** 37
~rücken **72** 29
~rumpf **327** 45
~schlitten **304** 25
~schwanz *Frisur* **34** 27
~schwanz *Pferd* **72** 38
~schweif **72** 38
~sport **289**
~stall **75** 1
~stand **75** 2
~stute **73** 8
~wagen **186**
~zahnmais **68** 31
Pfette **121** 76
Pfettendachstuhl **121** 60
~, einfachstehender **121** 42
~, zweifachliegender **121** 52
~, zweifachstehender **121** 46
Pfifferling **381** 14
Pfirsich **59** 31

~baum 59 26-32
~baumblatt 59 32
~blüte 59 27
~torte 97 22
Pflänzchen 55 23
Pflanze 370 15; 378 36; 382 53; 383 10
~, blühende 58 17
~, eingetopfte 55 25
~, fruchttragende 58 17
~, insektenfressende 377 13
~, vertopfte 55 25
Pflanzen-fenster 37 68
~fett 98 23
~gondel 248 13
~laus 358 13
~schauhaus 272 65
~tisch 55 12
~vermehrung 54
~zaun 37 59
Pflanz-garten 84 6
~holz 54 7; 56 1
~kamp 84 6
~kelle 56 6
~topf 54 8
Pflaster-spender 22 64
~- und Kleinteilespender 22 64
Pflaume 59 20, 25
Pflaumen-baumblatt 59 21
~kern 59 23
Pflegebox 28 18
Pflichtfigur 302 11-19
Pflock 123 11
Pflug 63 6
~baum 65 9
~furche 63 8
~karren 65 14-19
~kolter 65 10
~körper 65 4-8, 64-67
~messer 65 10
~rahmen 65 70
~schar Landmaschinen 65 7, 65
~schar Eisenb. 203 34, 35
~schar Vorgeschichte 328 33
~scharanker 286 16
~sohle 65 6, 66
~sterz 65 3
~stützrad 65 63
Pfortader 20 39
Pforten-band 220 27
~deckel 218 60
Pförtner Anat. 20 42
~ Warenhaus 271 44
Pfosten Bau 120 25; 121 40, 81
~ Sport 291 37
Pfropfen, das 54 36
Pfropfreis 54 37
Pfund 252 37
Pfund-Serie 1 24
Pfund Sterling 252 37
Phaethon 186 38
Phaeton 186 38
Phantasie-kostüm 306 32
~schliff 36 68-71
Phase, feste 148 26
~, flüssige 148 27
Phenol 170 14
~gewinnung 170 3
~hydrierung 170 16
Philete 183 3
Philomele 361 14
Philtrum 16 12
Phlox 60 14
phonetische Umschrift 342 14
Phönix 327 9
phönizisch 341 14
Phono-baustein 241 18
~-Kassetten-Steuergerät 241 52

~komponente 241 18
~typistin 248 33
Phorbeia 322 5
Phoropter 111 44
Phosphorsäuredünger 63 14
Photo-diode 114 70; 243 56
~grammetrie 112 67
~leiste 195 21, 22
~meter 23 54
~meterlichtquelle 112 50
~metrie 23 52, 53
~theodolit 112 67
~vervielfacher 112 51
~zelle 312 49
Piaffe 71 1
Pianino 325 1
pianissimo 321 36
~ piano 321 37
piano 321 35
Piano 325 1
~forte 325 1
~mechanik 325 2-18
~pedal 325 9
Picador 319 16
~hut 319 20
Piccoloflöte 323 30
Pickel 300 16, 31
Picker 166 64
Pickstander 219 49
Pick-up~Haspel 64 4
~-Vorrichtung 62 41; 63 27
Pictor 3 47
Piedestal 307 55
Pier Hafen 225 66
~ Zool. 357 24
Pierrette 306 12
Pierrot 306 19
Pigment-papier 182 1, 8, 10
~papierübertragungsmaschine 182 6
Pik 276 39
Pikieren 54 5
Pikkoloflöte 323 30
Piktogramm 233 24-53
Pilaster 335 46
Pilgermuschel 309 46
Pilker 89 72
Pilot 235 18
Pilote 335 33
Piloten-draht 325 34
~kanzel 231 19; 264 2
~sitz 230 36
Pilotton-anschluß-117 7
~geber 313 30
~kabel 313 29
Pilsener Bier 93 26
Pilz 68 4; 381 2, 3, 10, 11
~geflecht 381 2
Pimpernell, Großer 69 28
~, Roter 69 28
Pimpinelle 69 28
Pinakel 335 29
Pinakoid, triklines 351 26
Pinaß 258 45
Pinasse 221 107
Pinguin 359 4
Pinie 372 55
Pinne Schmied 137 27
~ Sport 284 32
Pinnenausleger 284 31
Pinole 149 27
Pinolen-feststellknebel 149 28
~verstellrad 149 30
Pinzette 22 52; 109 14; 174 18
Pipeline 145 35, 65
Pipette 22 72; 23 44; 350 25
Pipettenständer 23 52
Pipettiergerät 23 47
P.I.P.-System 242 15
Pique 276 39
Piqueur 289 43
Pirat Segelsport 284 52
~ Karneval 306 43

Pirol 360 7
Pirouette 314 23, 24
Pirschbüchse 86 4
Pirschen 86 1-8
Pirschgang 86 1-8
Pisces 4 64
Pistazie 382 51
Pistazienbaum 382 49
Piste Film 117 82
~ Flughafen 233 1
~ Sport 294 2
~ Zirkus 307 22
Pisten-film 117 82
~tonsystem 117 21
Pistill 349 10
Pistole 255 1
Pistolen-griff 87 6; 264 23
~handgriff 134 44
~kopfdüse 83 28
~magazin 264 25
~tasche 264 24
~ventil 270 62
Piston 323 43
Pit 243 60
Pitcher 292 50
Pithecanthropus erectus 261 16
Pitsche 162 42
Plakat 98 2; 271 65
Plakette 339 38
Planche 294 2
Planenverdeck 255 98
Planet 4 42-52
Planetarium 5 17-28
Planetariumsprojektor 5 23
Planeten-getriebe 143 94
~symbole 4 42-52
~system 4 42-52
~zeichen 4 42-52
Planetoid 4 47
Planier-raupe 199 16; 200 28
~schild 200 18, 29
Planimetrie 346 1-58
Plankonkavglas 111 39, 40
planmäßige Abfahrtszeit 205 23
Planschbecken 37 44; 273 28
Plan-spiegel 5 3
~übergang 15 26
Planumfertiger 201 1
Plaque 275 12
Plastik 272 64; 339 32
~scheibenschutz 289 25
~schelle 127 40
~sohle 101 8
Plastilin-figur 48 13
~masse 48 12
Platane 371 67
Plateau 13 46
~sohle 101 8
Platin~Iridium-Elektrode 24 44
~öse 23 15
Plättchen 89 82
Platte 179 31
Platten-belag 123 26
~fibel 328 30
~halterung 132 70; 178 27
~haltestange 179 8
~kassette 113 40
~kreissäge 132 68
~oberfläche 243 58
~schleuder 179 1
~schlitz 243 38
~speicher 176 32
~spieler 241 18; 317 19
~spielerchassis 241 19
~stahl 135 24
~ständer 178 35
~stapel 176 34
~stift 325 14
~teller 241 20
~weg 37 45

~zentrifuge 179 1
~zylinder 180 25, 38, 53, 62; 181 60
Plattform 218 49
~ball 299 24
Platt-sticharbeit 102 10
~wurm 81 35
Platz-anweiser 315 12
~anweiserin 312 4
~nummer 278 42
~verweis 291 61
Play 243 41
Plaza de toros 319 5
Plejade 3 26
Plektron 322 19; 324 20
Plektrum 322 19
Pleuel-lager 192 25
~stange 190 21
Plicht 283 8; 285 38
Plinthe 334 31
Pliobare 9 2
Plisseerock 30 32
Plombe 24 30
Pluderhose 306 42; 355 34
Plunger 316 60
Plüsch-futter 101 3
~hund 47 41
~pferd 47 15
Plus-facette 111 37
~zeichen 344 23
Pluto 4 52
Pneumatik 187 30
~anlage 92 12
Pochette 322 20
Pocketkamera 114 16
Podest 78 20; 123 34-41; 338 30
~balken 123 34, 55
~treppe 123 42-44
Pointer 70 43
Pol 14 3
polare Winde 9 51
Polarhund 70 22; 353 2
Polarisationseinrichtung 112 14
Polar-kreis 14 11
~licht 7 30
~meerwalroß 367 20
~schlitten 303 18
~stern 3 1, 34
Polhodie 4 28
Polierbürste 100 11; 108 44
Polieren 109 17
Polier-maschine 108 42
~maschinenaufsatz 109 15
~stahl 108 51; 340 17
~stange 145 27
~teller 134 22
Politzer-Ballon 22 37
Polizei 264
~beamter 264 18
~hubschrauber 264 1
~hund 264 6
~hundeeinsatz 264 5
~kelle 264 14
~kreuzer 221 100
~stern 264 27
~vollzugsdienst 264 1-33
Polizeiwagen 264 38
Polizistin 264 37
Polje 13 72
Pollen 77 35; 370 65
~sack 372 45, 50
Poller 217 12
Pollux 3 28
Polo-bluse 30 26
~laufsohle 101 24
Polster-arbeit 134 59
~bank 208 25; 265 10
~elementgruppe 42 21-26
~sessel 42 21
Polyamid 170 34, 35, 37, 41
~faser 170 1-62

~filament 170 43, 46
~herstellung 170 1
~Spinnfaser 170 61
~Spinnfaserballen 170 62
~trockenschnitzel 170 39
Polycheles 369 15
Polyeder 260 73
Polyester-harz,
　glasfaserverstärktes 130
　17
~rohr 67 26
Polymerisation 170 33, 54
Polyp 369 9
Polzwinge 142 35
Pommer 322 14
Pommes-frites-Schneider 40
　43
~-Topf 40 41
Pompon 29 4
~dahlie 60 23
Poncho 352 24
~cape 30 68
Ponton 226 57
Pony 75 4
~franse 34 36
~frisur 34 35
Popband 306 2
Popeline-jacke 31 37
~mantel 33 60
Pop-musiker 306 3
~orchester 306 2
Porenkapsel 370 96
Pornofilm 318 20
poröse Schicht 12 29
Porree 57 21
Portal Schiffbau 222 11
~ Theater 316 22
~bekleidung 333 35
~fahrwerk 232 18
~figur 333 36
~helling 222 11-18
~kran 157 27; 206 55; 222 25
~scheinwerfer 316 21
~stapler 226 4
~stütze 222 12
Portativ 322 56
portato 321 29
Port de bras 314 7-10
~ de bras à coté 314 7
~ de bras en avant 314 9
~ de bras en bas 314 8
~ de bras en haut 314 10
Portenband 220 27
Porter 93 26
Portier 267 1; 271 44
Portikus 334 56
Portliner 190 73
Porträt-büste 42 17
~wasserzeichen 252 31
Porzellan 350 29, 54
~herstellung 161
~maler 161 17
~scherbe 161 21
~vase 337 5
~zahn 24 29
Posaune 323 46; 326 17-22
Posaunen-stange 323 47
~zug 323 47
Pose 89 43-48
Position Turnen 296 22-39
~ Ballett 314 1-6, 1, 2, 3, 4, 5, 6
Positions-bestimmung 224 34
~lampe 258 56; 288 31
~lampentableau 224 29
~laternen 286 10-14
~leuchte 257 36
~licht 230 44, 50; 258 56
~seitenlampe 258 15
~spiel 276 1-16
Positiv 322 56
~kohle 312 40
~schnitt 340 3
Possenreißer 306 38

Post 236; 237
~ablage 267 2
~amt 268 68
~anweisung 236 27
~bote 236 53
~einlieferungsbuch 236 18
~fach Post 236 14
~fach Hotel 267 2
~fachanlage 236 13
~freistempelmaschine 236 7
~freistempler 22 24
~halle 233 9
~horn 186 41
Postillion 186 40
Postillon 186 40
Post-kabel 198 15
~kabeldurchgangsleitung 198
　16
~kraftwagen 236 52
~kutsche 186 39
~kutsche, englische 186 53
~kutscher 186 40
~leitzahl 236 43
~pferd 186 43
~sparschalter 236 25
~wagen 186 39
~wertzeichenschalter 236 15
~zeitungsnummer 342 43
~zustellung 236 50-55
Potenz 345 1
Potenzieren 345 1
Potenz-rechnung 345 1
~wert 345 1
Pottwal 367 25
Poularde 98 7; 99 58
Powerzoomeinrichtung 117 19
Prachtscharte 51 31
Präge-presse 183 26
~ring 252 42
~stempel 252 40-41
~tiegel 183 29
~tisch 178 9; 252 44
prähistorischer
　Fundgegenstand 328 1-40
Prahm 226 57
praktischer Arzt 23 2
Praline 98 80
Praliné 98 80
Prall-hang 13 57
~topf 191 57
~triller 321 19
Prante 88 46, 50
Präparation 170 57
Präpariertisch 261 22
Prärieindianer 352 3
Präsentkorb 306 11
Präsenzbibliothek 262 17
Präserve 96 25
Praxis 22 1-74
Präzession 4 24
Präzisions-feile 140 8
~-Kleindrehmaschine 109 20
~waage 108 35
Prediger 330 22
Predigt-pult 330 37
~stuhl 337 15
Preisangabe 196 6
Preiselbeere 377 23
Preis-liste 98 73
~schild 96 6; 271 19
Prellbock 206 51
Prellen 297 36
Prellklotz 166 44
Préparation 314 23
Presbyterium 330 32
Preß-balken 185 3
~boden 133 50
~deckel 133 51
~druckskala 185 5
Presse-foto 342 58
~fotograf 299 49
Preßeinrichtung 183 18;
　184 13

Pressekamera 114 36
Pressen Glas 162 33
~ Textil 170 41
~ Papier 173 50
Pressezentrum 233 43
Preß-form 162 26, 34
~gewicht 167 32
~holzplatte 338 24
Pressionshaken 163 16, 18
Preß-kissen 100 16
~kopf Fleischerei 96 9
~kopf Tech. 139 36
~korkgriff 89 50
Preßluft-flasche 279 21
~meißel 148 45
~reifen 187 30
~schlauch 174 38
~schleifmaschine 148 44
~stampfer 148 31
~tauchgerät 279 12
~zuleitung 139 22
Preß-müllfahrzeug 199 1
~platte Schuhmacher 100 15
~platte Buchb. 183 24
~platte Graphik 340 31
~pumpe 178 11
~rolle 165 57
~sack 96 9
~stempel Tischler 133 52
~stempel Glas 162 32
~- und Blasverfahren 162
　30
~verfahren 162 30
~walze 163 20; 168 41
presto 321 28
Priem 107 19
Priester 331 47
~sitz 330 41
Primaballerina 314 27
Primär-fokuseinrichtung 5 11
~fokuskabine 5 2
~kreislauf 154 2, 42; 259 65
~kreisumwälzpumpe 154 5
~luftgebläse 160 11
~wicklung 153 15
Prime 321 6
Primel 376 8
~gewächs 53 5
Primzahl 344 13
Prinzengarde 306 68
Prinz-Heinrich-Mütze 35 28
Prinzipal 326 31-33
Prinz Karneval 306 58
Prisma, ditrigonales 351 22
~, hexagonales 351 21, 22
~, monklines 351 24
~, quadratisches 347 34
~führung 175 54
~schiene 132 61
Prismen-raster 115 59, 62, 63
~sucher 115 69
Pritsche Pferd 71 45-49
~ Bau 119 41
~ Karneval 306 48
Pritschen-ausführung 194 6
~wagen 194 6
Privatdetektiv 275 16
Privater 251 6
Privatkonto 250 4
Probe 315 21-27
~abzug 340 43
~druck 340 43
~gestell 111 3
~kapsel 161 2
Probentrennvorrichtung 146
　10
Probewürfelform 119 84
Probier-glas 350 34
~gläserkasten 111 45
~glastrockner 261 31
~schaufel 98 72
Produkt 344 25
Produktions-anlage 76 38

~leiter 310 26
Produzent 238 39
Professional 299 25
Profil 143
~eisen 130 16
~rahmen 65 56
~säule 116 42
~sohle 101 19; 300 43
Programm 315 13
~, rechnergesteuertes 238 2
~einschub 177 71
~heft 315 13
Programmiererin 248 15
programmierte
　Unterweisung 242 16
Programm-karte 195 10
~karteneinschub 195 5
~lautstärkeregler 261 44
Programmonitor 238 61
Programm-recorder 261 42
~skala 243 40
~vorschau 342 64
~wahl 25 50
~wähler 243 39
Projektions-aufsatz 112 55
~fläche 260 36
~kuppel 5 21
~lampe 312 18
~leinwand 238 32
~mattscheibe 112 24
~objektiv 312 35
~öffnung 312 15
~optik 261 10
~schirm 237 38
~tisch 261 13
~wand 260 36; 312 11
Projektorschalter 195 20
proktologisches
　Untersuchungsinstrument
　23 3-21
Proktoskop 23 19, 21
Prokyon 3 15
Promenade 223 27
Promenadendeck 223 22-27
Propangas 278 33
~flasche 278 34
~lötgerät 125 5-7
~lötkolben 125 5
Propeller 230 32; 288 36
~anlage 228 26
~flugzeug 231 1-6
~nabenhaube 230 33
~pumpe 217 47-52
~raum 227 22
~rührer 79 6
~-Schnellrührgerät 79 5
~steigung 224 20
~-Turbinen-Flugzeug 231 4
~-Turbinen-Triebwerk 256
　16
Proportionszirkel 339 2
Propyläen 334 7
Proskenium 334 46
Prospekt Film 310 33
~ Theater 315 33; 316 10
~ Mus. 326 1-5
~beleuchtung 316 15
~faltblätter 250 7
~pfeife 326 1-3
~zug 316 8
Proszenium 315 15
protestantische Kirche 330
　1-30
Protokollführer 299 48
Proton 1 2, 16, 31
Proto-plasma 357 3
~prisma 351 19, 20
~pyramide 351 19, 20
~typ 290 38
~- und Deuteropyramide 351
　20
~zoen 357 1-12
~zoon 357 1-12

Protuberanz 4 40
Protz 364 23
Proviantraum 223 57
Prozent 345 7
~rechnungstaste 247 23
~satz 345 7
~skala 177 7
~zeichen 345 7
Prozession 331 42-50
Prozessions-fahne 331 44
~kreuz 331 42
~spinner 82 14
~teilnehmer 331 51
Prozeßrechner 236 37
Prüf-art 25 52; 109 26; 195 17, 24
~kasten 138 14
~platz 237 29
~platz, ophthalmologischer 111 43
~stelle 237 40
~- und Meßstelle 237 40
Prüfung 92 51
Prunkheck 218 55-57
Psychrometer 10 52
Puck 302 35
Puddingpulver 98 50
Pudel 70 36
Puder-dose 43 28; 49 35; 99 29
~streuer 28 14
~zucker 98 54
Puff 276 22
Puffärmel 31 27; 355 60
Puffer 213 7
~abstellstange 166 45
~speicher 242 33
Puffmais 68 31
Puffspiel 276 18, 22
Pulli 31 51
Pullmannlimousine 193 1
Pulmonalklappe 20 50
Pulpa 19 32
Puls-frequenz 23 27
~schlagader 18 21
~schreiber 26 32
~- und Atemfrequenz 23 27
Pult-dach 37 78; 121 7
~regal 174 2
~scholle 12 9
Pulver 87 53
~flagge 253 38
~kaffee 99 70
~ladung 87 57
Pumpanlage 146 22
Pumpe 2 52; 65 45; 170 31
Pumpen-aggregat 83 41
~anschlußbogen 67 8
~antriebsbock 145 22
~druckfeder 174 41
~haus Wasserbau 217 43
~haus Schiff 222 33
~schacht 199 19
Pumpernickel 97 49
Pumpgestänge 145 25
Pumps 101 29
Pump-speicherwerk 217 39-46
~stativ 310 50
~werk 274 4
Punchingball 299 24
Punkt Setzerei 175 19, 20, 21, 22, 23, 24, 25, 26, 27, 28, 29, 30, 31
~ Schrift 342 16
~ Math. 346 1-23, 1; 347 8
~, trigonometrischer 14 49; 15 71
~, typographischer 175 18
~ball Billard 277 13
~ball Sport 299 22
Punktiereisen 339 15
Punkt-lichtkopierlampe 179 21

~lichtlampe 182 4
~richter 299 43
~roller 340 18
~roulette 340 18
~schweißmaschine 142 29
~schweißung 142 22
~schweißzange 142 23
Punze Goldschmied 108 19, 31
~ Setzerei 175 41
~ Graphik 340 15
Punzen-büchse 108 30
~hammer 340 14
Pupille 19 43
Puppe Zool. 77 30, 32; 80 4, 25, 43; 81 3, 21, 24; 82 13, 21, 32; 358 20; 365 11
~ Flohmarkt 309 11
Puppen-sportwagen 48 31
~wagen 47 10; 48 24
~wiege 77 32
Purpur-filtereinstellung 116 43
~mantel 355 18
~saum 355 14
Pürzel 88 49, 58
Pusteblume 61 13
Pute 73 28
Putenschlegel 99 59
Puter 73 28
Putten 293 86
Putter 293 93
~grün 293 82
Putz 338 42
Pütz 221 113
Putz-deckel 164 22
~eimer 50 54
Putzer 148 43
Putzerei 148 38-45
~maschine 92 36
~messer 136 38
~stock 87 61
~teil 35 4
~träger 123 71
~tuch 50 55
Puzzle 48 9
~stein 48 10
PVC-Regenstiefel 101 14
~Sohle 101 2
Pygmäe 354 41
Pylon Brücken 215 42
~ Kunst 333 9
Pyramide Astr. 5 19
~ Garten 52 16
~ Zirkus 307 28
~ Kunst 333 1
~ Math. 347 46
~, rhombische 351 23
~, tetragonale 351 18
Pyramiden-anlage 333 6
~baum 52 16; 272 19
~oktaeder 351 10
Pyrit 351 7
Pyrometer 178 16
Pyxis 330 8; 332 53

Q

Quader 347 36
~stein 158 30
Quadrant 347 5
Quadrat 346 33; 347 31
~notation 320 1
~wurzel 345 3
Quadroanlage 241 13-48
Quadro-/Stereo-Umschalter 241 46
Qualle 357 14
Quantensprung 1 15, 20-25
Quarantänestation 225 27
Quark 76 45
~bereitungsanlage 76 38

~packung 76 45
~pumpe 76 39
~separator 76 41
~verpackungsmaschine 76 44
Quartbindung 294 47
Quarte 321 9
Quartier 100 61
Quartole 321 23
Quarz 110 15
~uhr, elektronische 110 14
~batterie 25 32
~dampfgleichrichter 312 18
~manometer 25 18
~säule 10 2
Quelle 15 82; 269 24-39
Quell-nymphe 272 2; 327 23
~pavillon 274 15
~stube 269 24
~wolke 8 1, 17; 287 22
Querachse 230 68
~aussteifung 215 53
~balken 150 12
~feldeinstrecke 289 17
~flöte 323 31
~förderer 157 20
~grätschstellung 295 4
~haupt 139 37
~haus 335 3
~holz 108 5
~latte 291 36
~leiste 136 8
~libelle 14 61
~neigung 200 57
~riegel Bau 119 49
~riegel Mus. 324 4
~rips 171 19, 25
~riß 300 3
Querruder 229 41, 43; 230 24, 52; 287 41; 288 28
~betätigung 257 39
Querschiff 335 3
~schlag 144 31
~schlitten 149 23, 39
~schnitt 190 2, 4
~spagat 295 15
~spant 285 51
~stab 292 70
~stand 296 24, 25
~steg 65 12
~summenzähler 242 3
~support 149 23, 39
~träger 152 37
~- und Höhenruder 230 24
~zeug 65 12
Quetsch-hahn 350 30
~walze 165 46
Queue 277 9
~kuppe 277 10
~ständer 277 19
Quick-Pick-Wagen 207 73
Quinte 321 10
Quintole 321 23
Quintparade 294 24
Quipu 352 22
Quirl 135 9
Quitte 58 49, 50
~, Japanische 373 17
Quitten-baum 58 46
~blatt 58 47
Quittungsstempel 236 29
Quotient 344 26

R

Rabe 361 1-3
Rabenvogel 361 1-3
Rachen 19 14-37, 24

~höhle 19 24
Rackenvogel 359 25
Racket 293 29
~schaft 293 30
Rad Zool. 73 29
~ Fahrrad 187 1, 26-32
~ Sport 297 21
Radar 224 10-13
~antenne 223 8; 224 104; 258 36; 259 8, 29, 48, 91
~bild 224 13
~bug 231 18; 256 10
~dom 258 52, 77; 259 49
~gerät 224 10-13
~mast 221 7; 224 10
~nase 231 18; 256 10
~reflektor 10 58
~sichtgerät 224 12
Radbremse 91 8
Räderwerk 110 11
Radi 57 16
Radial-bohrmaschine 150 18
~ziegel 159 25
Radiator Mondlandung 6 8
~ Med. 23 23
~ Installateur 126 20; 155 15
~heizung 155 27
~rippe 126 21
Radier-auflage 249 26
~gummi 151 42
~klinge 151 44
~messer 151 43
~nadel 340 16
~pinsel 151 47
~schablone 151 35
~stift 151 41
Radierung 340 14-24, 51
Radieschen 57 15
Radikand 345 2
Radio 6 26; 309 16
radioaktive Abfälle 154 57-68
radioaktiver Abfall 154 77
radioaktives Material 1 28
Radio-apparat 309 16
~gerät 309 16
Radiolarie 357 8
Radio-meter 10 71
~recorder 241 1
~sonde 10 59
~sondengespann 10 55
Radius 346 47
Radizieren 345 2
Rad-leier 322 25
~lenker 202 23
~mulde 195 28
Radnetzspinne 358 45
Radom 231 18; 256 10; 258 52, 77; 259 49
Rad-prüfhammer 205 40
~rennbahn 290 1
~rennfahrer 290 8
~satz 212 3; 213 3
~satzgetriebe 212 28
~schutz 197 11
~spiegel 195 41
~sport 290 1-23
~welle 91 5
~zylinder 192 54
Raffiabast 136 29
Raffinade 98 55
Raffinerie 145 35
Rähm 120 58; 121 39
Rähmchen 77 40
Rahmdosierpumpe 76 40
Rahmen Textilw. 167 33
~ Sport 297 12; 305 88
~einspannung 133 48
~glaser 124 8
~holz 119 64, 74
~montierung 113 23
~nummer 187 51
~oberteil 179 15
~presse 133 42

~probe 124 2
~rohr 187 16, 17
~schleifschuh 133 34
~ständer 133 43
~tisch 132 62
~trommel 353 26
~werk 336 11
Rahmerhitzer 76 13
Rähmholz 120 58
Rahm-reifungstank 76 31
~tank 76 19
Rahsegel 218 21, 33; 219
　55-66; 220 16
Raife 81 12
Raigras, Englisches 69 26
~, Italienisches 69 26
Rain 63 3
~farn 380 9
Rakel 168 61
~streicher 173 29-35
~streichmaschine 173 29-35
Rakenvogel 359 25
Rakete Schiff 228 2
~ Raumfahrt 234 8, 37
~ Mil. 255 65
~ Karneval 306 54
Raketen-apparat 228 1
~kreuzer 259 21
~kreuzer, atomgetriebener
　259 41
~starter 258 49
~stufe 234 3, 18, 33
~trennmotor 235 60, 62
~werfer 255 64, 70
~zerstörer 258 1, 38
Ralle 359 20
Rambate 218 49
Ramm-bär 226 38
~bohle 197 12
~brunnen 269 60
Ramme 226 36
Ramm-gerüst 226 37
~gewicht 226 38
Rammler 73 18; 88 59
Ramm-spitze 269 61
~sporn 218 9
~streb 144 36
Rampe 312 8; 316 25
Rampen-dekoration 271 67
~licht 316 26
Rand 166 11
~balken 119 3, 55
~bearbeitungsautomat 111 25
~beet 52 18
~beleimung 185 31
~bemerkung 185 68
~bogen 287 42
~einstellung 249 12
Rändelring 114 39; 115 8
Randich 69 21
Rand-inschrift 252 11
~kugel 305 37
~lösetaste 249 6
~meer 14 26
~messer 100 48
~platte 222 51
~steller 249 13, 14
~wasser 12 32
~zünderpatrone 305 35
Rang 315 16, 17, 18
Rangier-bahnhof 206 42
~dienst 212 47, 68
~funkanlage 213 4
~funkgerät 212 50
~gleis 206 47
~lok 206 43
~meister 206 45
~stellwerk 206 44
Rangkrone 254 43-45
Ranschel 304 17
Ranscheln 304 18
Ranzen 260 9
Rappen 252 15

Rapport Tapezierer 128 21
~ Textilw. 171 12
Rapputz 123 6
Raps 383 1
Rapünzchen 57 38
Rapunze 57 38
Rapunzel 57 38
Rapunzlein 57 38
Raschel-maschine 167 23
~ware 167 29
Rasen 51 33; 272 36
~bankett 200 56
~besen 51 3
~fläche 272 36
~lüfter 56 15
~mäher 56 31
~rechen 51 4
~schere 56 48
~sprenger 37 43; 56 43
~traktor 56 37
Rasier-apparat, elektrischer
　49 37
~messer 106 38
~schneide 106 40
~wasser 49 38
Raspel 260 55
Rassel 306 40
~ring 28 44
Raste 87 70
Raster-magazin 177 9
~punkt 178 39
Raststütze 188 51
Rasur 34 25
Rateau 275 5
Ratsche 306 47
Rätsche 306 47
Raub-bein 358 5
~schütz 86 29
Raubtier 307 56; 367 11-22;
　368 1-11
~gang 307 51
~gitter 307 50
~haus 356 10
~käfig 307 49
Raubvogel 362 1-13
Raubwild 86 22
~falle 86 20
~fang 86 19
Rauch-absauger 255 59, 89
~abweiser 258 59
~abzug 38 81; 353 21
~abzugsrohr 258 44
~austritt 210 22
Raucherbesteck 107 44
Räucher-faß 332 38
~kammer 96 48
Räucherung, liturgische 332
　38
Rauchfang 137 7
Rauchfaß 332 38
~deckel 332 40
~garnitur 332 38
~kette 332 39
~schale 332 41
Rauch-fleisch 96 3
~gasfilter 152 13
~kammertür 210 26
~klappe 352 9
~rohr 210 8
~schwalbe 361 20
~utensil 107
~zug 221 76
Rauh-bank 132 39
~blattgewächs 69 13
~fasertapete 128 18
~haarfilzhut 35 24
~putz 123 6
~walze 168 34
Rauke 61 16
Raumanzug 6 18-27
~helm 6 22
raumer Wind 285 12
Raumfähre 235 1-45

Raumfahrt 234; 235
~modul 235 70
Räumgitter 264 17
Raum-kapsel 6 10; 234 65
~laboratorium 235 65
~manöver-Hauptriebwerk
　235 44
~meter 84 16
Räumschaufel 255 77, 94
Raum-sprechgerät 22 34
~station 235 65
~stütze 222 61
~teiler 42 19
~thermostat 38 78
Räum- und Stützschaufel 255
　94
Raupe 58 64; 80 3, 8, 14, 17,
　29, 44, 48; 82 16, 20, 31, 44,
　47; 365 10
~ der ersten Generation 80
　23
~ der zweiten Generation 80
　24
Raupen-fahrwerk 200 3
~nest 80 7
Rauschbeere 377 23
Raute 346 35
Räute 140 34
Rautek-Griff 21 18
Raygras, Englisches 69 26
~, Französisches 69 22
~, Italienisches 69 26
Rayonchef 271 60
Reagenzglas 350 34
~gestell 173 8; 350 35
~halter 350 35
Reaktions-behälter 170 12
~rohr 192 65
Reaktor 154 3, 23, 41, 50
~druckbehälter 154 22
~gebäude 154 20
~kern 259 68
~kühlmittelleitung 154 29
Rebe 78 2-9
Reben-blatt 78 4
~schädling 80 20-27
~schere 78 12
~stamm 78 6
Rebhuhn 88 70
~locke 87 47
Reblaus 80 26
~lanze 83 33
Reb-stecken 78 7
~stock 78 2-9
Receiver 241 40; 318 18
Rechen Gartengerät 56 4; 66
　23
~ Mus. 322 51
~befehlstaste 247 21
~einheit 177 70
~gerät 23 53
~kopfsäule 196 1
~maschine 309 77, 80
~scheibe Fotogr. 114 57
~scheibe Druck 182 19
~stein 47 14; 48 17
~- und Auswertegerät 23 53
~werk 244 6
~zentrum 244
Rechnen 344 23-26
Rechnerdaten 238 13
Rechnungsart, höhere 345
　1-10
Rechteck 346 34
~flügel 229 16
~-Treppenschliff 36 50
Rechtschreibungsbuch 260 17
Rechts-herzkatheter 25 53
~lauf 149 11
Rechts-links-Doppelfang
　171 47
~-Doppelperlfang 171 48
~-Fang 171 44

~-Perlfang 171 45
~-Perlfang, übersetzter 171
　46
Rechts-maschine 312 14
~- und Linkslauf 149 34
Reck 273 32; 296 7, 40, 41, 42,
　43, 44, 59, 60
~riemen 296 47
~säule 296 9
~stange 296 8
Recorder 243 1-4
Rednerpult 263 6
Reduktionszone 147 8
Reduzier-stück 126 39
~ventil 155 7
Reff 219 72
Reflektor 114 69; 115 97
~antenne 224 11
~pedal 187 78
Reflexhammer 22 73
Reflexionsgoniometer 351 28
Reflex-spiegel 115 33
~sucher 117 44
Reformieranlage 145 47, 71
Refraktor 113 16
Regal 271 27
~aufsatz 43 14
~wand 46 1
Regatta 283 1-18
~, Auffahrt zur 283 1-18
~kurs 285 14-24
~strecke 285 16
Regel-ausführung 237 6
~bauart 213 5, 8, 11
~detri 345 8-10
~gerät 178 3
~kassette 238 45
~modul 240 11
~pult 311 12
~querschnitt 200 55
~teil 153 1
~turmtriebwagen 211 41
~widrigkeit 291 50
Regen 8 10; 9 32
~abfallrohr 37 13
Regenbogen 7 4
~farbe 343 14
~haut 19 42
Regen-cape 41 4
~dach 10 41
~düse 67 27
Regenerieranlage 156 37
Regenerieren 156 37
Regen-gürtel, tropischer 9 53
~gürtel, warm-gemäßigter 9
　55
~mantel 29 31
~messer 10 38, 44
~pfeiferartige 359 19-21
~rohr 122 29
~schirm 41 15; 205 12
~stiefel 101 14
~tonne 52 4
~trenchcoat 33 57
~umhang 196 26
~vogel 359 27
~wolke 8 10
~wurm 357 24
~wurmköder 89 67
~zinkhut 122 102
Regie-assistent 310 46; 316 43
~assistentin 310 21
~buch 316 46
~fenster 238 38
~raum 238 17
~tisch 316 42
Regisseur 310 40; 316 40
Register 326 16
~schleife 326 7
~schweller 326 49
~taste 324 42; 326 39
~zug 325 44; 326 6
Registraturtheke 248 2

Registrier-einrichtung 177 12
~galvanometer 11 44
~gerät Meteorol. 10 61
~gerät Schmied 138 19
~kasse 99 93; 271 2
~papier 25 4; 27 29, 34, 40
~tafel 26 28
~vorrichtung 10 42
Reglerventil 210 13
Regner 55 19; 62 29
~schlauch 62 30
~stativ 62 28
Regula 334 17
Regulator 109 32
Regulier-gestänge 190 30
~klappe 192 63
~ventil 38 75
Regulus 3 17
Reh 88 34
~blatter 87 43
~bock 86 17; 88 28
~fiepe 87 43
~geiß 88 34
~kitz 88 39
~sprung 295 40; 302 7
~wild 88 28-39
~ziemer 88 35
Reibahle 109 8; 125 9; 140 31
Reibebrett 118 57
Reiber 340 13, 63
~stellung 340 62
Reibfläche 107 24
Reichstaler 252 6
Reife 169 7
Reifen Fahrrad 187 30
~ Sport 305 86
~drahtseilbahn 273 53
~druckprüfer 196 17
~füllmesser 196 20
~profil 189 27
~schaukel 273 18
Reifrock 355 72, 83
Reihe, arithmetische 345 11
~, geometrische 345 12
Reihen-bezeichnung 252 36
~-Dieselmotor 190 3
~haus, gestaffeltes 37 58-63
~meßkammer 14 63
Reiher 86 46; 359 18
Reineclaude 59 24
Reinigung 109 30
Reinigungsautomat 109 30
~brunnen 334 68
~bürste 247 7, 10
~flüssigkeit 111 32
~schnur 87 64
~separator 76 12
~werg 87 63
Rein-öl 145 35
~öltank 145 34
~wasserbehälter 269 13
Reis 68 1, 29; 98 38
Reise-büro 204 28; 271 24
~bus 194 34
~flugzeug 230 1-31, 32-66;
231 1, 2, 3, 7
~gepäck 205 7-12
~kahn, kurischer 220 10
~lektüre 205 18
Reisende 204 24; 205 6
Reisender 208 30
reisender Geschäftsmann 209
29
Reise-omnibus 194 17
~paß 267 13
~tasche 205 10
~- und Linienbus 194 34
~verpflegung 205 49
~wagen 186 39
~zugdienst 212 1
~zugwagen 207 1-21; 208 3
Reiskorn 68 30
Reiß 122 89

~bahn 288 75, 83
~bahnleine 288 76
~boden 120 11
~brett 151 1
~brettverstellung 151 5
~bühne 120 11
Reißer Forstw. 85 10
~ Korbmacher 136 35
Reiß-feder 151 49
~federeinsatz 151 58, 61
~leine 288 76
~verschluß 31 55; 33 28; 260
13
~zahn 200 6
Reistenmühle 172 84
Reitbahn 307 21
Reiten in der Superbrandung
279 4
Reiter Bildhauerei 339 25
~ Chem. 349 33
~auflage 349 32
~schiene 349 31
~standarte 253 13
Reit-frack 289 4
~gerte 289 22
~kappe 289 18
~kunst 71 1-6
~pony 75 4
~sattel 71 37-49
~schule 308 2
~stock 135 7; 149 29; 150 5;
177 62
~stockspitze 149 26
~tier 354 2
~tierstall 62 2
Reizvogel 86 48
Reklame 342 56
~fläche 118 45
~plakat 308 50
~tafel 268 43
Rektoskop 23 16, 17
Rektoskopie 23 18
Relaispferd 186 43
Relief 339 33
~ziegel 333 20
Reling 221 121
~, offene 222 66
Remittent 250 19
Remorqueur 216 23
Remoulade 96 29
Renaissance, Kunst der 335
42-54
~antiqua 342 4
~kirche 335 42
~palast 335 47
Rendezvous-Radarantenne 6
42
Reneklode 59 24
Rengespann 353 15
Renn-achter 283 10
~anzug 301 31
~außenbordmotor 286 23
~boot 283 9-16
~brille 303 15
~einer 283 16
~fahrerkabine 290 7
~fahrertrikot 290 9
~haken 290 21
~kieljacht 285 35
~leitung 290 4
~lenker 290 18
~maschine 290 16, 27, 31
~overall 301 43
~pferd 289 51
~rad 290 15, 16
~reifen 290 19
~rodel 303 13
~rodler 303 12
~sattel 290 17
~sportwagen 290 36
~stock 301 25
~wagen 290 34-38
Rente 251 11-19

Rentenauszahlschalter 236 25
Rentier 328 5; 353 16
Reparatur-box 196 22
~fahrzeug 138 36; 195 47
~kai 222 10
~nummer 195 48
Repetierbüchse 87 2
Reportage-kamera 313 26
~telefon 238 23
Reporter 299 50
Reproarm 115 93
Reproduktions-gestell 115 92
~kamera 177 1, 24, 32
Repro-ständer 115 92
~stativ 115 90
Reptilie 364 27-41
Reptiliengehege 356 12
Requisit 315 50
Reserve-antrieb 214 64
~rad 191 25; 194 33
~reifen 194 4
Resonanz-kasten 324 26, 63
~körper 322 29; 323 3
Respirator 26 25
Rest 344 24
Restaurant Piktogramm 233
50
~ Gaststätte 266 1-29
Restauration 266 1-29
Restmenge 348 7
Resultat 344 23
~werk 309 82
Reticellaspitze 102 30
Reticulum 3 48
Retorte 349 13
Retrostellung 115 84
Retter 21 29
Rettich 57 16
Rettung bei Eisunfällen 21
28-33
~ Ertrinkender 21 34-38
Rettungs-boje 221 124
~boot 146 19; 221 78, 107;
223 19
~bootaufhängung 221
101-106
~fallschirm 235 60
~floß 286 19
~hubschrauber 221 20; 228
16; 256 18
~insel 228 19; 258 11; 286 19
~leine 228 3; 270 45
~ring 221 124; 280 3
~schwimmer 21 36
~seil 280 2
~station 280 46
~tau 228 12
~turm 234 66
~übung 270 1-46
~wagen 270 19
~wesen 228
Retuscher Porzellan 161 19
~ Druck 182 14
Retuschier-tisch 177 19
~- und Montagetisch 177 19
Reuherbrett 296 12; 297 8
Revers Kleidung 31 23; 33 5
~ Geld 252 9
~bluse 30 9
Revier 86 1-8
Revolver-drehmaschine 149
38
~kopf 149 40
~lochzange 100 44
~numerierschlägel 85 12
~wechsel 166 5
Rezept 22 20
~erneuerung 22 3
Rezeption Med. 22 5
~ Camping 278 1
Rezipient 226 33
reziproker Wert 344 16
Rhabarbertorte 97 22

Rhesusaffe 368 12
Rhombendodekaeder 351 7
Rhomboeder 351 22
Rhomboid 346 36
Rhombus Schmuck 36 59
~ Math. 346 35
Rhönrad 305 79
Ribisel 58 12
Richt-antenne 6 4, 44
~antennengruppe 234 64
~aufsatz 255 45
~baum 120 8
~feuer 224 101-102
~funkantenne 224 106; 237
51, 52
~krone 120 8
~kurbel 255 48
~platte 125 3
~strecke 144 30
Richtung 347 6, 7
Richtungs-anzeige 197 39
~anzeiger 189 37
~schild 205 38
~stellmotor 155 46
~voranzeige 203 20
~voranzeiger 203 21
Rick 289 8
Ricke 88 34
Riedgras 53 17
Riefe 243 27
Riegel 140 39
~hebel 203 55
Riemen Hundeleine 70 30
~ Schiff 218 5; 278 19; 283 14,
35-38
~ Sport 290 22
~antrieb 165 33
~auflage 283 29
~blatt 283 38
~boden 123 62
~boot 283 9-15
~bügel 87 5
~hals 283 37
~holm 283 35
~zweier 283 15
Riese 308 20; 327 37
Riesel-blech 210 29
~werk 274 1
Riesen-dame 308 21
~felge 296 60
~figur 306 63
~känguruh, Rotes 366 3
~muschelkrebs 369 1
~pinguin 359 4
~rad 308 37
Riet 166 10
~einzug 171 6
~kamm 166 10
Riffbildner 357 17
Riffelung 157 6
Riffelwalze 166 47
Rigel 3 13
Rikscha 353 34
~kuli 353 35
Rillen-herd-Durchstoßofen
139 1
~walze 130 30
Rind 73 1; 94 2; 95 14-37
Rinde 120 86; 370 8
Rinden-bürste 56 23
~kratzer 56 14
Rinder-brust 95 23
~filet 95 24
~star 361 4
~viertel 94 22
Rindshaut 354 11
Rindviehstall 62 7
Ring Med. 24 33
~ Schmuck 36 4
~ Forstw. 85 4
~ Börse 251 3
~ Sport 299 35; 305 31
~ Kirche 332 17

~ *Chem.* 350 15
~anker 120 34
Ringbank 164 54
~antrieb 164 42
Ringbuch 260 15
Ringe 296 4, 50, 55, 56
Ringeinfassung 55 38
Ringel-krebs 81 6
~natter 364 38
~pulli 30 20
~schwänzchen 73 12
~spiel 308 2
~spinner 80 13
~wurm 357 20
Ringen 299 6-12
Ringer 299 7
Ring-finger 19 67
~graben 329 37
~haken 300 39
~hefter 260 15
~kampf, griechisch-
  römischer 299 6-9
~kämpfer 299 7
~korn 305 50
~leitung 147 53
Ringlotte 59 24
Ring-maß 108 27
~matte 299 12
~mauer 329 15
~muskel 19 5, 8
~ofen 159 19
~pinsel 129 19
~richter 299 41
~riegel 108 26
~scheibe 305 30-33
~spant 235 47
~spinnmaschine 164 34, 45
~stein 36 72-77
~stiftzahn 24 31
~stock 108 25
~tennis 280 31
~wade 90 25, 26
Rinnenbügel 122 32
Rinnstein 198 10
Rippe *Bau* 123 36
~ *Flugzeug* 230 46
~, echte 17 9
~, falsche 17 10
~, wahre 17 9
Rippelmarke 13 41
Rippenknorpel 17 11
Ripsband 35 13
Risalit 335 43
Rispe 68 27, 35; 370 69
Rispengras, Einjähriges 375
  39
Riß 300 3
~unterlage 128 17
Rist 19 61
~griff 296 40
Ritter *Ritterwesen* 329 67
~ *Zool.* 358 52
~burg 329 1
~dach 122 50
~rüstung 329 38-65
~schlag 329 66
~schloß 329 1
Rittertum 329
Ritterwesen 329
Ritzel 143 92
Ritzer 341 21
Rizinus 380 14
R-Klasse, 6-m- 284 59
Roadster 193 26
Roastbeef 95 17
Robbe 367 18-22
Robinie 371 70
Roboter 273 36
Rocaille 336 13
Rock 31 24; 33 2; 289 4, 13
~, betreßter 186 23
~knopf 33 55
~längenmesser 271 40

~runder 271 40
Rödelung 119 66
Rodeo 319 34
~reiter 319 39
Rodeorgan 64 59
Rogen 89 12
~ähre 68 2
~brötchen 97 16
~mehl 97 52
~mischbrot 97 8
~rose 61 6
Rogner 89 13
Roh-bau *Bau* 118 1-49
~bau *Schmied* 138 28
~benzolerzeugung 156 41
~benzoltank 156 42
~bramme 148 48
~-Cyclohexanol 170 16
Roheisen 147 40, 55
~abfluß 147 11
~abstich 147 11
~pfanne 147 12, 21, 42
Roh-gewichtswaage 173 3
~glas 124 6
~kohlenbunker 144 41
~kostmenü 266 62
Rohling *Drechsler* 135 21
~ *Ziegelei* 159 16
Roh-material 169 1-12
~materiallager 160 3
~mehlsilo 160 5
~milchpumpe 76 3
~milchsilotank 76 5
~mühle 160 4, 7
~ölaufbereitung 145 28-35
~ölverarbeitung 145 36-64
~papier 173 29
~phenolbehälter 156 40
Rohr *Haushalt* 50 64
~ *Böttcher* 130 27
~ *Fahrrad* 187 60
~ *Mil.* 255 2, 17, 41
~, spanisches 136 32
~abschneider 126 84
~band 126 53
~befestigung 126 53-57
~biegemaschine 125 28
~bieger 126 82
~blende 255 90
~bock 126 11
~bremse 255 52
Röhre *Pferd* 72 23
~ *Zool.* 357 23
Röhren-ausgang 86 27
~blitzgerät 309 40-41
~einheit 26 17
~kessel 152 5
~laus 358 13
~ofen 145 36
~schicht 381 17
Rohr-feder 341 23
~führung 67 25
~haltemutter 255 11
~kolben 378 21
~kolbenschilf 136 27
~lager 146 4
~leitung 163 11; 221 3
~matte 55 6
~paket 255 71
~panzerung 255 72
~rahmen 188 9, 49
~sägemaschine 126 10
~schelle 122 31; 126 56
~schenkel 114 44
~schleuder 173 11
~schraubstock 126 81
~stativ 114 42
~stück 130 26
~stütze 255 62
~turm 155 43
Rohrung 123 71
Rohr-vorholer 255 61

~wechselklappe 255 35
~weihe 362 13
~wiege 255 60
~zange 126 59; 140 68
Roh-stahlblock 148 48
~stein 339 5
Rohstoff 160 1, 4; 170 1
~gemenge 161 1
Roh-tabakballen 83 13
~teerbehälter 156 32
~ton 159 2
~wasser 269 4
Rokoko, Kunst des ~s 336
  9-13
~frisur 355 81
~ornament 336 13
~wand 336 9
Rolladen 37 28
~aussteller 37 29
Roll-bahn *Flughafen* 233 2
~bahn *Sport* 283 45
~bodenbunker 64 84
~brett 273 51
Rolle *Angelsport* 89 59-64
~ *Sport* 288 8; 290 13; 297 19
Rollen 230 71
~bock 157 26
~boden 316 4
~bohrer 145 21
~bremsprüfstand 138 16
~führung 201 4
~heft 316 41
~kabel 294 31
~kette 187 36; 190 10, 25
~kopierautomat 249 32
~kreis 288 3
~kühlofen 162 18
~lager 164 47
~magazin 249 33
~makulatur 128 5
~offsetmaschine 180 1, 18
~quetscher 116 49
~schneider 173 42
~stern 180 3, 19
~tabak 107 18
~tiefdruckmaschine 182 24
~tisch 157 23
~zufuhr 74 39
Rollfilm 114 19
~spule 114 20
Roll-gabelschlüssel 126 66
~gang 148 50
Rolli 30 7
Rollieren 109 17
Rollier-maschine 109 17
~stuhl 109 17
Rollkragen, halsferner 30 3
~pullover 30 2
Roll-matte 55 6
~meise 361 9
Roll-on-roll-off-Schiff 226
  17
~-Trailer 221 54
~Verkehr 225 39
Roll-reifenfaß 154 77
~ringfaß 130 13
~schiene 283 45
~schlauch 270 54
~schwanz 364 35
~schweller 326 49
~sichter 172 2
~sitz 283 41-50, 44
~sprung 298 1
~technik 298 18
~treppe 271 22
~tür 245 5
~weg 233 2
~werk 336 8
Romanik 335 1-21
Römer *Trinkglas* 45 87
~ *Kostüme* 355 11
Römerin 355 7
römisches Kriegsschiff 218

9-12
römische Ziffer 344 1
Rondell 252 43
Röntgen-assistentin 27 11
~bild 25 39
~bildverstärkergerät 27 16
~durchleuchtungsapparat 26
  14
~einrichtung 27 6
~generator 24 22
~gerät 24 21
~kassettenhalterung 27 2
~kopf 27 18
~röhre 27 7, 18
~schaltstelle 27 9
~station 27 1-35
~stativ 27 8
~strahlung 1 56
~strahlung, harte 1 33
~untersuchungstisch 27 1
Ro-ro 225 39
Roro 225 39
Ro-ro-Abfertigungsanlage
  226 20
Roro-Anlage 226 20
Ro-ro-Schiff 226 17
Roro-Schiff 226 17
Ro-ro-Spezialanlage 226 20
Ro-ro-Trailer 221 54
Ro-ro-Trailerfähre 221 54
~Verkehr 225 39
rosa 343 4
Rosapelikan 359 5
Rose 88 5, 29
~, Chinesische 60 15
~, gefüllte 60 17
Rosen-dorn 60 18
~hochstamm 52 21
~klee 69 4
~knospe 60 16
~kohl 57 30
~kranz 332 30
~ohr 70 2
~schere 56 50
~schliff 36 45
~stock 52 13, 21
Rosette 335 23
Rosine 98 8
Roßbohne 69 15
Roßbreiten 9 47
Roßgras 69 22
Roßhaar-bezug 323 15
~bürste 100 12
Roßharnisch 329 83-88
Roßkastanie 371 58
Roßkopf 329 84
Rost *Straßenreinigung* 199 33
~ *Wasservers.* 269 11
~ *Rummelplatz* 308 33
~bratwurst 308 34
Röst-mais 68 31
~trommel 98 71
Rostweihe 362 13
rot *Heraldik* 254 27
~ *Farbe* 343 1
Rot *Roulett* 275 24
~ *Spiele* 276 44
Rotang 136 32
Rotästige Kornelkirsche 373
  30
Rotations-achse 4 25, 27
~druck 178 21
~ellipsoid 347 42
~kolben 190 68
~kolbenmotor 190 5
~maschine 181 41, 57
Rote Hühnermyrte 61 27
Roteisenstein 108 48
rote Karte 291 63
Rötel 361 15
Rote Liste 22 23
~ Magnolie 373 15
~ Miere 61 27

rote Mütze 205 43
Roter Gauchheil 61 27
~ Milan 362 11
~ Pimpernell 69 28
~ Wiesenklee 69 1
Rotes Gauchheil 61 27
~ Ordensband 365 8
~ Riesenkänguruh 366 3
rotes Tuch 319 27
Rot-fuchs 88 42; 367 12
~kehlchen 361 15
~klee 69 1
~kohl 57 32
~kraut 57 32
Rotor *Uhr* 110 32
~ *Windkraftwerk* 155 45
~ *Hubschrauber* 232 22; 264 3
~ *Flugsport* 287 18
~kopf 232 13
~messer 85 26
~teller 178 26
~träger 232 23
Rot-schnabeltukan 363 6
~schwänzchen 360 3
~specht 359 27
~tier 86 13; 88 1
~vogel 361 14
~wein 98 64
~weinglas 45 83
~wild 88 1-27
~wurstring 99 56
Rouge 275 24
Rough 293 80
Roulett 275 1-33, 28
Roulette 275 1-33
Roulett-kessel 275 29
~kugel 275 33
~maschine 275 10, 28
~spieler 275 15
~spielplan 275 17
~spielsaal 275 1
~spieltisch 275 8
Routineuntersuchung 22 3
Royal-stag 219 13
~stengestag 219 13
~stengestagsegel 219 26
Rübe 68 45
~, gelbe 57 17
Rüben-aaskäfer 80 45
~älchen 80 51
~blatt 68 47
~bunker 64 96
~elevator 64 94
~elevatorband 64 95
~erntemaschine 64 85-96
~gabel 66 5
~kopf 68 46
~körper 68 45
~putzer 64 89
Rubin 110 33
Rücken *Anat.* 16 22-25
~ *Messerrücken* 45 56
~ *Pferd* 72 29
~ *Bau* 122 86
~ *Kunst* 336 26
~flosse 364 6
~flug 288 9
~kamm 364 21
~kissen 42 25
~lage 295 44
~lehne 191 35; 207 66
~leimung 183 14
~mark 17 48; 18 25
~muskel 18 59
~riemen 71 32
~rollsprung 298 16
~schild *Büro* 247 38
~schild *Zool.* 364 29
~spalter 94 17
~speck 95 40
~vergoldung 183 1
Rückgeldgeber 236 28
Rückgrat 17 2-5

Rückhalte 295 51
Rück-handbogenwurf 305 20
~handschlag 293 39
~holfeder 166 68; 167 37; 192
55
Rücklauf 38 79; 126 24
~hahn 350 49
~leitung 38 56
~sammelleitung 38 80
~taste 249 73
Rück-licht 187 46; 189 9
~meldeanlage 153 7
~positiv 326 5, 42
Rucksack 86 3
Rückschläger 293 50
Rückschlag-hinderer 87 14
~schutz 132 47
~sicherung 157 59
Rück-seite 252 9
~sitzbank 193 22
~spiegel 188 35; 189 30
~spulfreilauf 115 27
~spulkurbel 114 6; 115 12
~spulmitnehmer 115 29
~spülschieber 216 61
~stand *Brauerei* 92 50
~stand *Erdöl* 145 43
~steller 191 77
~stoßdämpfer 255 44
~stoßrohr 255 27
~stoßverstärker 255 34
~strahler 187 45
~strahlglas 187 2
~strahlpedal 187 78
~teilverstellung 114 55
~trittbremse 187 63
Rückwärts-gang 192 44
~salto 288 50
Rück-wasser 172 26
~wickelkurbel 114 6; 117 93
~zieher 277 4
Rüde 73 16; 86 33; 88 42
Rudel 86 15
Ruder *Jagd* 88 75
~ *Schiff* 218 6, 24; 278 19; 283
26, 51-53; 285 34, 37; 286
65
~anlage 224 15; 228 26
~bank 283 28
~blatt 221 43; 222 69; 223 63;
283 53; 284 34
~boot 89 27
Ruderer 218 3; 283 12
Ruder-fuß 359 6
~füßer 359 5-10
~gänger 224 16
~haus 224 14-38
~joch 283 51
~kopf 284 3
~lagenanzeiger 224 17
Rudern 218 5; 283
Ruder-pinne 286 24
~regatta 283 1-18
~reihe 218 12
~schaft 222 68
~schiff, germanisches 218
1-6
~sitz 283 41-50
~sklave 218 48
~steven 222 70
~trainer 283 20
~ und Propelleranlage 228
26
Ruedo 319 9
Ruf-nummer 237 38
~taste 127 3
~ und Kommandoanlage
224 30
Rugby 292 19
~ball 292 21
~spiel 292 19
Ruhezeichen 321 25
Rührbütte 173 1

Rührer *Molkerei* 76 43
~ *Chem.* 349 18
Rühr-löffel 40 3
~maschine 97 70
~michnichtan 377 11
~ und Schlagmaschine 97 70
~werk *Brauerei* 92 46
~werk *Papier* 172 47, 49
Ruine 15 72
Ruke 61 16
Rum 98 57
Rumbakugel 324 59
Rummelplatz 308
Rumpf *Anat.* 16 22-41
~ *Flugzeug* 230 54
~ *Schiff* 259 42
~ *Sport* 288 26; 294 53
~beuge 295 32, 33, 34
~form 285 29-41
~nase 231 16
~spitze 235 20
~tank 257 31
~verbindungsbeschlag 235 4
~zentraltank 257 30
rund 370 33
Rundblätteriger Steinbrech
375 1
Rundbogen 336 27
~eingang 278 39
~fries 335 9
Rund-brot 97 6, 7
~ecke 42 26
~eisen 143 8; 340 6
~eisenreifen 130 3
Rundenzähler 290 6
Rund-feile 108 47; 140 29
~fenster 335 12
~füller, halbautomatischer
79 9
Rundfunk 238; 239; 240
~empfänger 309 16
~gerät 309 16
~sendekomplex 238 16-26
Rund-gattheck 218 25
~glasschneider 124 22
~holz *Bau* 120 35
~holz *Sägewerk* 157 30
~holz *Schiff* 219 32-45
~holzleiter 273 22
~holzpolter 85 32; 157 31
~horizont 310 12; 316 9
~horn 137 13
~käfig 307 49
~käse 99 42
~kolben 350 34
~kuppe 143 20
~laufkran 154 38
~laufpilz 273 8
~lochhammer 137 36
~magazin 114 77
~maschine 125 30
~materialien 139 1
~medaillon 339 36
~ofen 161 3
~pflaume 59 24
~pinsel 338 8
~platte *Druck* 178 21
~platte *Kunst* 334 30
~plattengießwerk 178 13
~schalttisch 150 42
~schild 329 57
~schliff, normal facettierter
36 42-43
~sichter 91 26
~spantboot 286 32-34
~stahl 119 80
~stamm 120 83
~stichel 340 20
~strahldüse 83 23
~strickmaschine 167 1
~stück 97 13-16
~stuhl 167 1
~thermometer 179 4

~tischglasiermaschine 161 16
~tischmaschine 150 41
~tränke 74 16
~wirkmaschine 97 63
~zange *Elektr.* 127 50
~zange *Schmied* 137 25
~zelt 278 8
Rune 341 19
Runge 85 47; 213 6
Rungenwagen 206 24
Runke 61 16
Runkelrübe 68 44; 69 21
Runway 233 1
Rüsche 31 34; 32 44
Rüschen-besatz 32 44
~kragen 31 46
~schürze 31 33
Russe 81 17
Rüssel 73 10; 88 53; 358 56;
366 21
~käfer 80 10, 49
~tier 366 20
russisch 341 20
Russischer Klee 69 6
Rußsack 38 34
Rüster 371 49
Rüsthaken 329 80
Rustika 335 51
Rüstung 353 38
Rute *Zool.* 70 12; 88 47, 49
~ *Angelsport* 89 49-58
~ *Korbmacher* 136 14
~ *Mus.* 322 35
Ruten-halter 89 23
~spitze 89 35
~teil 89 54
Rutschbahn 273 24; 308 40
Rutsche 226 45
Rutscher 129 30
Rüttel-flasche 119 89
~schuh 91 14
Rüttler 249 56

S

Saal 306 1
~beleuchtungsregler 312 17
~chef 275 7
~schutz 263 10
~tochter 266 18
~verdunkler 312 17
Saat 84 9
~auslauf 65 78
Saatbett-bereitung 63 31-41
~kombination 63 41; 65 87
Saat-gut 63 12; 83 15, 52
~kamp 84 6
~kartoffel 68 39
~korn 63 12
~krähe 361 2
~leitungsrohr 65 77
~platterbse 69 19
~schale 54 2
~schnellkäfer 80 37, 38
~wicke 69 18
~wucherblume 61 7
Säbel 294 20, 34
~fechten 294 19-24, 52
~fechter 294 19
~handschuh 294 21
~maske 294 22
Sachbearbeiterin 248 7
Sachbearbeitertisch 248 11
Sack 339 29
~geige 322 20
~karren 206 14
~pfeife 322 8
Säen 63 10-12
Safranköpfchen 361 10
Saftpresse 40 9
Säge-aggregat 133 38
~blatt 120 62; 150 16; 157 3,

47; 260 54
~bügel 138 25; 150 17
~dach 121 20
~ente 359 15
~gans 359 15
~halle 157 1
~kette 85 14; 120 16
~kettenhaftöl 84 35
~muskel 18 42
Sägen-schärfmaschine 157 42
~setzer 132 42
Säger 359 15
Sägeraspel 134 6
Sägerei 144 6
Säge-schiene 85 16
~schlitten 132 71
~schuppen 120 3
~wagen 133 38
~werk 157 1
~zahnung 96 33
Sagittarius 3 37; 4 61
Sago 98 39
~palme 383 58
Sahne 99 46
~gießer 265 21
~kännchen 265 21
~rolle 97 17
~torte 97 24
Saite 322 44, 55; 323 9, 61; 324
  6, 14
Saiten-bespannung 293 31
~bezug 325 7
~halter 323 7; 324 4, 13
~hammer 325 3
~instrument 323 1-27; 324
  1-31
Säkasten 65 75
Sakralbau 337 21
Sakrament, heiliges 332 35
Sakristan 330 58
Sakristei 331 13
~glocke 330 46
~tür 330 17
Salamander 364 22
Salat, grüner 57 36
~besteck 45 24
~blatt 57 37
~gabel 45 68
~löffel 45 67
~öl 98 24
~pflanze 57 36-40
~schüssel 45 23
~staude 57 36
~teller 266 51
~zichorie 57 40
Salbentube 22 47
Salicional 326 23-30
Saline 15 32; 274 1-7
Saling 223 37; 284 13
Salmiakstein 125 6
Salon 223 26
Salta 276 20
~spiel 276 20
~stein 276 21
Salto 282 42; 297 15, 17, 18
Salvator 93 26
Salweide 371 24
Salz 98 40
~bergwerk 154 56, 72
~bergwerk, aufgelassenes
  154 57-68
~brötchen 97 14
~kuchen 97 13
~stange 97 31
~streuer 266 77
~wasser 146 17
~wasserleitung 145 33
Sämann 63 10
Samen 54 3; 58 23, 37; 59 8;
  371 20, 65; 372 9, 10, 15, 28,
  37, 54, 57, 60, 71; 375 25,
  28; 378 33, 34; 382 20, 34,
  35, 39, 45; 383 5, 15, 23, 24,

57; 384 10, 20, 21, 40, 47,
  52, 58
~anlage 58 39; 59 14; 370 63
~blase 20 77
~haar 383 19
~kapsel 61 5; 378 5
~kern 58 23
~korn 68 13, 15, 25
~leiter 20 74
~mantel 382 34
Sämling 54 6
Sammel-balgfrucht 370 102
~behälter Meteorol. 10 46
~behälter Papier 172 26
~brunnen 269 4
~drahtheftmaschine 184 15
~frucht 58 28
~gut 206 4
~hefter 184 15
~heizung 38 38-81
~kasten 164 44
~ladung 206 4
~lattentuch 163 13
~mulde 201 20
~nußfrucht 370 100
~steinfrucht 370 101
~verkehr 206 4
Sammler 174 23
Sampan 353 31
Samtblume 60 20
Samurai 353 37
Sand 15 6; 118 36; 119 26;
  148 38
~abfallrohr 210 15
~ablagerung 216 52
Sandale 101 51
Sandalette 101 49
Sand-bahn 290 24
~bahnrennen 290 24-28
~berg 273 66
~bett 123 8
~burg 280 35
~dom 210 14
~fang 173 13; 269 25
~grube 293 81
~kasten Eisenb. 212 59, 76
~kasten Spielplatz 273 64
~papier 135 25
~sack 216 50; 288 65; 299 21
~schalter 211 32
~schaufel 331 36
~schleuder 172 22, 56
~streuer 210 55
~streuerrohr 210 19
~strohblume 377 3
~uhr 110 31
~- und Knotenfang 173 13
Sandwich 45 39
~gabel 45 76
Sänger 315 22
Sängerin 315 23
Sanitär-anlagen 278 5-6
~trakt 278 5-6
Sanitäter 270 21
Sanitäts-auto 270 19
~panzer 255 79
~wache 204 44; 308 61
~zelt 308 61
San-José-Schildlaus 80 35
Sanktissimum 331 48; 332 35
Sanskrit 341 9
Sapine 85 6
Sappel 85 6
Sappho-Kolibri 363 4
Sardinenheber 45 78
Sarg 331 35
~kammer 333 5
Sargonsburg 333 29
Sargträger 331 40
Sarkophag 335 53
Säschar 65 76
Satanspilz 379 12
Satellit 4 45

Satellitenfunk 237 51-52
Sattel Geogr. 12 16
~ Buchb. 185 7
~ Fahrrad 187 22; 188 4; 290
  17
~ Mus. 323 20
~, englischer 71 45-49
~achse 12 17
~anhänger 206 59
~dach 37 5; 121 1
~feder 187 23
~gurt 289 11
~kissen 71 49
~knopf 71 46
~platz 307 12
~schlepper 194 28
~sitz Landmaschinen 65 22
~sitz Pferd 71 37
~stütze 187 24
~stützrohr 187 18
~tasche 187 25
~zugmaschine 194 29
Sätuch 63 11
Saturn 4 49
Saturn-V-Trägerrakete 234
  1, 2
Satz Setzerei 174 15; 181 37
~ Sport 293 37
~, computergesteuerter 176
  14
~, zweispaltiger 185 64
~form 181 36
~magazin 174 21
~schiff 174 12, 44
~spiegel 185 59
~streifen 174 34
~zeichen 342 16-29
Sau 73 9; 75 41; 86 32; 88 51
~bohne 69 15
Sauciere 45 17
Sauer-gras 53 17
~kirsche 59 5
~milchtank 76 42
Sauerstoff 26 4; 234 15
~anschluß 141 30
~atom 1 13
~aufblaskonverter 147 45-50
~beatmung 25 23
~behälter 235 46; 257 2
~düse 350 13
~flasche 27 45; 141 3, 21; 200
  40
~gerät 270 20
~lanze 147 49
~leitung 235 51
~molekül 242 65
~notgerät 6 18
~pumpe 235 42
~schlauch 141 10
~tank 6 6; 234 61; 235 57
~umlaufleitung 235 56
~ventil 141 29
~zufuhr 25 22; 350 11
Sauerwurm 80 24
Sauferkel 75 42
Saug-anleger 180 72
~arm 184 11
~bagger 216 59
~elektrode 23 29
Sauger 28 20
Säugetier 366; 367; 368
Saug-geräuschdämpfer 190 16
~gutumschlag 226 29
~korb 67 12; 269 6, 14, 43
~kraftregulierung 50 72
~leitung 38 55; 269 5, 14, 41;
  270 30; 316 52
Säugling 28 37
Säuglings-badewanne 28 3
~pflege 28 28
Saug-luft 181 5, 35
~mund 199 43
~napf 81 37

~pumpe 216 62
~rohr Meteorol. 10 37
~rohr Motor 190 18
~rohrleitung 226 32
~scheibe 357 21
~schlauch Haushalt 50 75
~schlauch Feuerwehr 270 67
~wanne 103 25
~zuggebläse 152 14
~zugventilator 199 32
Sau-hatz 86 31
~kraut 379 5
Säule Bau 120 25
~ Textil 168 16
~ Math. 347 34
~, dorische 334 8
~, gekuppelte 336 6
~, ionische 334 9
~, korinthische 334 10
Säulen-führung 139 42
~fuß 334 28-31
~gang 274 9; 334 67
~hals 334 22
~schaft 334 26
~sockel 334 31
~stativ 2 29; 112 32
~umgang 334 2
Saum 73 5
~diele 118 73, 74
~latte 91 3
~pfad 12 46
~sattel 73 4
~schwelle 120 50
Sauna 281 18, 28
~, finnische 281 18
~ofen 281 21
Saupacker 86 33
Säurebehälter 350 62
Sau-rüde 86 33
~stall 75 35
Saxophon 324 69
S-Bahnzug 205 25
SB-Gaststätte 266 45-78
SB-Restaurant 266 45-78
Scanner 177 39
~film 177 72
Schabe, Deutsche 81 17
Schabefleisch 96 16
Schaber 140 63; 340 17
Schab-glocke 96 42
~hobel 132 27
~kunst 340 14-24
Schablone 175 55
Schablonen-ablage 245 9
~aufbewahrungslade 245 10
~aufnahmeschacht 245 8
~kasten 168 60
~messer 129 43
~tisch 175 56
Schabotte 139 17, 31, 40
Schabracke 329 74
Schabrackenschakal 367 11
Schach 265 17; 276 1-16
Schachbrett 47 20; 276 1
Schachbrettafel 203 30
Schachbrett-feld 276 2
~ornament 335 14
Schächerkreuz 332 61
Schach-feld 276 2
~felderbezeichnung 276 6
~figur 276 4, 5, 7
~figurensymbol 276 4, 5
~matt 276 15
~meisterschaft 276 16
~partie 265 17; 276 6
~problem 276 6
~spiel 276 1-16
~spieler 265 17
Schacht 154 69
~deckel 38 46
Schachtelteufel 306 56
Schacht-gebäude 144 4

~ofen 147 1
~sumpf 144 47
Schach-turnier 276 16
~uhr 276 16
Schädel 17 1, 30-41; 261 15, 17, 21
~dach 261 16, 18
~sammlung 261 15
Schädlingsbekämpfung 56 24; 83
Schaf 73 13
~bock 73 13
Schäfchenwolke 8 14, 15
Schäferhund, Deutscher 70 25
Schaf-fellmütze 353 23
~garbe 376 15
~stall 75 9
Schaft *Schlosser* 140 33
~ *Masch.* 143 15, 53
~ *Textil* 166 3, 4; 171 5, 9
~ *Sport* 305 64
~ *Kunst* 333 27
~rand 101 20
~rolle 166 36
~spanner 166 54
Schäftung 87 3,4,6,13
Schakal 367 11
Schal 33 65
Schalanken 71 16
Schal-boden 119 54
~brett 119 18, 76
Schale *Jagd* 88 24
~ *Friseur* 105 1
~ *Zool.* 357 29
Schäleisen 85 8
Schalen-aufbau 11 1-5
~haut 74 60
~sitz 193 11; 305 90
~skistiefel 301 12
~sohle 101 11
~stern 10 30
~thermometer 116 13
Schalholz 118 41; 119 18
Schalk 306 38
Schall-becher 323 42; 326 22
~blase 364 25
~dämpfer *Eisenb.* 209 12, 22; 211 49
~dämpfer *Sport* 305 93
~deckel 330 21
~dose 309 33
~kasten 322 18; 324 15
~körper 324 2, 15
Schalloch *Mus.* 322 22; 323 6; 324 5
~ *Kirche* 331 8
Schall-öffnung 309 19
~platte 46 15; 309 32; 317 24
Schallplatten-
    Abspielapparatur 238 24
~fach 241 48
~ständer 309 36
Schall-rose 324 5
~schlucktrennwand 248 20
Schallschutz-gehäuse 313 16-18, 27
~kasten 310 48
~oberteil 313 16
~seitenwand 313 18
~unterteil 313 17
Schall-sender 224 61
~stück 323 37, 48
~trichter 309 34; 323 42
~wand 309 17
~wellenausbreitung 7 14
~wellenimpuls 224 62
Schalmei 322 3, 14
Schalt-anlage 93 20; 152 19; 157 67
~armatur 230 26
~brett 180 74
~drehgriff 188 31

Schalter 127 7, 66; 179 19; 180 74; 191 64, 81, 82; 326 47
~beamter 204 39
~halle 236 1-30
~schrank 237 25
~-Wertzeichengeber 236 19
Schalt-feld 311 4, 17
~gabel 192 42, 45
~gerät 153 5; 269 47
~getriebe 149 2; 211 50
~hahn 172 9
~haus 217 45
~hebel 191 91; 192 46
~kammer 153 55
~kassette 238 45
~kasten 150 36; 179 33
~knopf 168 40
~knüppel 191 91; 192 46
~kopf 192 44
~kreis, integrierter 242 68
~kupplung 227 23
~mechanismus 181 26
~pult 27 10; 76 11; 153 1-6; 179 10; 180 16; 185 2; 261 37; 311 12
~rad 168 40
~schaubild 92 25
~schema 192 47
~stange 192 41
~tafel 26 20; 38 67; 173 43; 179 17
~trittbrett 168 48
~uhr 243 18
~- und Regelkassette 238 45
~- und Regelpult 311 12
Schaltung 178 36; 242 68-72
~, elektronische 110 8
~, integrierte 110 16
Schaltungs-aufbau 242 72
~kette 290 20
Schalt-warte 76 7; 92 25; 152 28; 153 1-8
~werk 211 10
~werkantrieb 211 13
Schalung 119 54; 122 61
Schalungs-sprieße 119 13
~stütze 119 86
~träger 119 78
Scham 16 39
Schamane 353 24
Scham-bein 17 20
~beinfuge 20 65
~laus 81 40
~lippe 20 87
Schamotte-deckel 108 9
~stein 141 16
Schanzkleid 221 120; 222 67; 223 17
Schapel 355 21
Schappelholz 119 61
Schar 65 7, 58, 65
Scharbe 359 10
Scharbockskraut 375 36
Schardrehkranz 200 22
Schärenkreuzer, 30-m²- 284 60
Scharfeinstellung 115 8; 240 30
Scharfer Hahnenfuß 375 8
scharfer Löffel 22 50; 26 52
Scharfer Mauerpfeffer 375 21
Schärf-kopf 157 46
~messer 100 51
~scheibe 157 45
Scharnierband 140 49
Scharraum 74 11
Scharriereisen 158 37
Scharwachturm 329 17
Schatten-brett 55 9
~matte 55 6
~morelle 59 5
Schattierbrett 55 9

Schau-bild 248 36
~bude 308 6
Schauer 8 19; 9 37
~niederschlag 8 19
Schaufel *Gärtner* 55 14
~ *Jagd* 88 41, 75
~ *Mühlrad* 91 38, 40
~ *Bergsport* 300 34
~deckel 95 32
~kammer 91 36
~rad 178 33
~sporn 255 55
~stück 95 30
~walze 178 25
~zylinder 255 56
Schaufenster 268 10
~auslage 98 1; 268 11
~dekoration 268 12
~front 268 42
Schaufler 88 40
Schauglas *Heizung* 38 62
~ *Landw.* 75 31
Schaukel-brett 273 40
~kufe 47 16
~reck 307 6
~sitz 273 40
~stuhl 309 61
~teddy 48 30
Schauloch 148 4
Schaum-bad 49 3
~krone 93 31
~löffel 96 43
~markierer 83 9
~markierung 83 6
Schaumstoff-auflage
    Schlafzimmer 43 10
~auflage *Sport* 291 20
~behälter 83 6
~schwimmer 89 46
~zunge 291 24
Schaum-wein 98 63
~zuführleitung 83 10
Schauöffnung 2 16; 312 15
Schauspieler 316 37
~garderobe 315 43-52
Schauspielerin 316 38
Schausteller 308 10
~bude 308 24
~wagen 206 20
~zelt 308 24
Schau-tafel *Med.* 22 16
~tafel *Stadt* 268 3
~vitrine 271 13
Scheck 289 29
Schecke 355 45
Scheibe *Landmaschinen* 65 84, 85
~ *Sport* 305 66
~, laufende 305 33, 48
~ *Brot* 45 22
Scheiben-anordnung 65 83
~blüte 375 32
~bremse 189 32; 190 74; 191 17-18; 192 48-55
~bremsen 208 4
~bremssattel 189 33
~egge 65 82
~hantel 299 3
~honig 77 64
~qualle 357 14
~rad 191 14
~sech 64 66; 65 69
~sechantrieb 64 68
~wischer 191 41; 197 32
Scheide *Anat.* 20 86
~ *Landw.* 68 9
Scheiden-spekulum 23 13
~spiegel 23 13, 14
Scheidetrichter 349 3
Scheidsche Kugel 349 1
Schein 252 29-39
~frucht 58 21; 384 12, 62
~füßchen 357 4

~stamm 384 30
Scheinwerfer *Fahrzeug* 187 7; 189 10; 191 20; 258 28
~ *Zirkus* 307 3
~brücke 310 53
~einstellung 195 24
~halter 187 6
~schalter 191 62
Scheitel *Anat.* 16 1
~ *Flugsport* 288 47
~ *Math.* 347 16
~bein 17 31
~brechwertmesser 111 33
~höhe 87 77
~punkt 346 1; 347 16, 28
~rohr 187 16
~winkel 346 8-13
Scheitkeil 85 4
Schelf 11 8
Schelle 304 26
Schellen 276 45
~geläut 304 26
~kappe 306 39
~tamburin 324 45
Schelm 306 38
Schemazeichnung 260 34
Schenkel *Friseur* 106 37
~ *Masch.* 143 2
~ *Kraftwerk* 153 17
~ *Textil* 171 32
~ *Math.* 346 7 u. 3, 27
~gefieder 362 3
~nerv 18 31
~schlagader 18 19
Scherbe 54 8; 161 21; 260 61
Scherbrett 90 13
Schere *Med.* 22 51
~ *Pferd* 71 13
~ *Jagd* 88 67
~ *Wagen* 186 30
~ *Schule* 260 49
~ *Sport* 296 51
~ *Zool.* 358 41
~, gebogene 26 42
~, gekröpfte 22 51
Scheren-blatt 106 35
~straße 148 74, 75
~stromabnehmer 197 23
~wäschetrockner 50 34
Scher-fasernabsaugung 168 43
~gang 222 44
~messer 168 44
~sprung 295 39; 298 22
~zapfen 121 85
Scherzartikel 306 56
Scherzylinder 168 44
Scheuer-bürste 50 56
~eimer 50 54
~leiste 258 81
~tuch 50 55
Scheuklappe 71 26
Schicht *Bau* 118 67, 68
~ *Sport* 301 46
~, poröse 12 29
~, undurchlässige 12 28
~, wasserführende 12 22; 269 2, 38
~, wasserundurchlässige 269 36
~filter 79 8
~geflecht 136 3
~gestein 13 48
~holz 85 27
~holzbank 84 16
~käse 76 45
~stufe 13 49
~vulkan 11 15
~wolke 8 3, 4, 8, 9, 10
Schiebe-dach 193 24
~dachwagen 213 22
~deckel 179 2
~griff 167 41
~leiter 270 14

~muffe 192 32, 35
Schieber *Wasserbau* 217
   53-56, 55
~ *Mus.* 326 33
~gehäuse 217 54
~haus 217 42, 63
~kasten 210 31
~stange 210 30
Schiebe-tor 62 16; 217 18
~tür 92 47; 194 8; 213 15; 271
   50
~türenschrank 248 38
Schieb-karre 118 37
~karren 118 37
~lehre 140 52; 149 67
Schied 77 47
Schiedsrichter 291 62; 292 65;
   293 19, 67, 68
~mikrophon 293 21
~stuhl 293 20
Schiefblatt 53 10
Schiefer-dach 122 61-89
~decker 122 71
~hammer 122 73
~schere 122 84
~stein 122 85
~tafel 309 72
Schienbein 17 25
~knöchel 19 60
~muskel 18 47
~nerv 18 32
~schlagader 18 20
~schutz 142 12; 291 34; 292
   9; 302 33
Schiene *Med.* 21 12
~ *Korbmacher* 136 24
~ *Eisenb.* 202 1; 205 59; 214
   10
~ *Sport* 303 11
Schienen-bergbahn 214 1-14
~fahrzeug 207; 208; 209;
   210; 211; 212; 213
~fuß 202 4
schienengleicher
   Bahnübergang 202 39
Schienen-hobel 136 39
~kopf 202 2
~lasche 202 12
~räumer 210 34
~räummaschine 213 17
~steg 202 3
~stoß 202 11
Schierling 379 4
Schieß-bude 308 58
~hütte 86 51
~leine 228 3
~luke 86 52
~meister 158 25
~scharte 329 18
~scheibe 305 30-33
Schiff *Astr.* 3 45, 46
~ *Fahrzeug* 220 24-27; 222 29
~, aufgelaufenes 227 1, 2
~, geleitetes 221 53
~, gestrandetes 228 10
schiffbarer Strom 15 45
Schiff-bau 222
~bauhalle 222 3-4
~brücke 15 46
Schiffchen 102 20
~arbeit 102 19
~mütze 35 34
Schiffer-klavier 324 36
~mütze 35 28
Schiffs-brand 228 20
~geschwindigkeit 224 22
~hebewerk 217 29-38
~hobel 132 28
~junge 221 112
~küche 223 42
~neubau 222 30
~schaukel 308 41
~schraube 221 44; 222 72; 223

   62
~sirene 224 32
~stapler 226 15
~trog 217 33
~typ 221
~typen, historische 218
~verkehrs-Fernsprechanlage
   224 28
~werft 222 1-43
Schifter 121 61
Schikhara 337 26
Schild *Jagd* 88 55, 71, 79
~ *Schiff* 218 17
~ *Völkerkunde* 354 10
~bogen 335 19
~buckel 329 58
Schildchen 82 5; 358 30
Schild-drüse 20 1
~halter 254 15-16
~knorpel 20 3
~laus 80 35
~mauer 329 19
~panzer 329 65
~stachel 329 58
~vulkan 11 13
Schilf 136 27
~lilie 60 8
~rohr 378 21
~- und Seggentorf 13 17
Schilling 252 13
Schimäre 327 16
Schimpanse 368 14
Schinken 95 38
~speck 95 53
~stück 95 51
Schippen *Spiele* 276 39
~ *Winter* 304 22
Schirm *Jagd* 86 9
~ *Eisenb.* 205 12
~ *Kunst* 337 22
~ *Zool.* 357 15
~glucke 74 3
~kappe 288 38
~mütze 35 29; 264 8; 301 18
~quaile 357 14
~ständer 41 14
Schiwa 337 19
Schiwago-Mütze 35 33
Schlachter 94 1; 96 38
Schlächter 94 1; 96 38
Schlachterei 96 1-30; 319 13
Schlächterei 96 1-30
Schlächtermesser 96 31-37
Schlachtermolle 96 40
Schlacht-feld 15 93
~hof 94
~schwein 94 11
~tierteil 95
~vieh 94 2
Schlacken-abfluß 147 9
~abstich 147 9
~abzug 152 8
~haken 137 5
~hammer 141 25; 142 17
~kübel 147 10
~rinne 148 12
Schlaf-anzug 29 23; 32 17, 21,
   36
~decke 43 8
Schläfe 16 6
Schläfen-bein 17 33
~muskel 19 3
~schlagader 18 3
~vene 18 4
Schlaf-hemd 32 37
~mohn 380 15
~puppe 47 11
~sack 278 30
~tier 47 6
~- und Freizeitanzug 32 21
~- und Strampelanzug 29 23
~wagen 207 36
Schlafzimmer 43

~lampe 43 19
~schrank 43 1
Schlag 299 34
~ader 21 14
~arm 166 17, 22
~armpuffer 166 65
~bär 139 26
~besen 39 23
~bohle 200 32
~bohrer 134 43
~bohrmaschine 134 43
~bolzen 87 21
~eisen 339 14
Schlagen 86 46
Schläger *Spinnerei* 163 25
~ *Sport* 293 29; 305 69
~blatt 302 32
~feld 292 51
~griff 293 46
~schaft 293 30; 302 31
Schlag-exzenter 166 66
~fell 323 52
schlagfester Kunststoff 127
   48
Schlag-fläche *Forstw.* 84 13
~fläche *Sport* 293 31, 47
~flügel 163 24
~gewicht 110 28; 309 60
~gitarre 324 73
~hacke 66 24
~hebel 255 4
~holz *Sport* 292 75
~holz *Bildhauerei* 339 12
~instrument 323 49-59; 324
   47-58
~keule 292 62
~linie 292 72
~mal 292 53
~mann 283 12; 292 52, 58, 63,
   74; 293 75
~maschine 97 70
~messer 84 33
~obers 97 28; 265 5
~rad 183 23
~rahm 265 5
~riemen 166 22
~ring 324 27
~sahne 97 28; 265 5
~schere 125 26
~schnur 128 45
~stäbchen 322 19
~stock 166 17
~stock-Rückholfeder 166 68
~versuch 292 63
~werkkaffeemühle 39 24
~zeile 342 44
~zeug 318 10; 324 47-54
~zeuger 318 11
~zither 324 21
Schlamm-erguß 11 51
~kegel 11 51
~sammler 210 28
Schlange *Astr.* 3 20
~ *Sport* 297 48
~ *Zool.* 364 38-41
~, tanzende 353 48
Schlangen-beschwörer 353 45
~bogen 302 12
~bogenschlinge 302 16
~fibel 328 28
~fuß 327 39
~kühler 349 6
~leib 327 2, 33
~schweif 327 31
~stern 369 11
Schlankformschlüpfer 32 10
Schlapphut 355 55
Schlauch *Haushalt* 50 75
~ *Fahrrad* 187 30
~anschluß 6 26; 83 30
~beutel 76 29
~boot 228 18; 258 82; 278 14;
   279 27

~brause 126 30
~filter 83 54
~hahn 37 41
~halterung 27 47
~haspel 270 28
~klemme 40 20; 350 30
~kupplung 270 29
~leitung *Landw.* 62 30
~leitung *Feuerwehr* 270 30
~nippel 56 45
~reifen 290 19
~- und Gerätewagen 270 53
~ventil 187 31
~wagen *Gartengerät* 56 26
~wagen *Feuerwehr* 270 53
~ware 167 1, 9
Schlaufenverschluß 30 41
Schlegel *Bau* 118 54
~ *Mus.* 322 34; 323 56
~ *Bildhauerei* 339 21
Schlehdorn 374 27
Schlehe 374 27
Schleiche 364 37
Schleier *Kirche* 332 20
~ *Vögel* 362 18
~ *Bot.* 381 5
~eule 362 17
Schleif-arten 36 42-86
~band 133 15
~bandregulierschraube 133
   14
Schleife *Kleidung* 30 46
~ *Textil* 171 39
~ *Winter* 304 17
Schleifen *Lackierer* 129 28
~ *Winter* 304 18
~bildner 312 30
Schleifer 321 16
Schleif-gerät 138 7
~holz 172 68
~klotz 128 13; 129 26
~lade 326 12-14
~lager 163 41
~maschine 129 29; 140 18
~maschinenbett 150 6
~maschinentisch 150 7
~papier 128 14; 129 25
~rad 133 27
~scheibe 100 6; 134 23; 137
   19; 138 8; 140 19; 150 4;
   157 43; 340 46
~scheibenkombination 111
   28, 35
~staubabsaugung 133 28
~stein 172 71
~stück 197 24
~support 150 3
~tisch 133 35
Schlepp 273 3
~bügel 301 61
~dach 37 55
Schleppe *Sport* 289 49
~ *Kostüme* 355 80
Schleppen 222 42; 227
Schlepper *Landmaschinen* 62
   38; 65 20; 67 17
~ *Schiff* 222 42; 227 5, 16
~fahrer 62 39
~pumpe 67 14, 15
Schlepp-flug 287 1
~flugzeug 287 2
~gaube 37 56
~gaupe 37 56
~geschirr 227 6-15, 6, 13
~haken 227 27
~jagd 289 41-49
~kahn 216 25
~käpsel 227 9
~klüse 227 11
~kopfsauger 216 59
~lift 301 59
~netzfischerei 90 11-23
~schiffer 216 26

~seil 216 24; 286 47; 287 4; 301 63
~spur 301 60
~start 287 1
~tau 288 69
~tender-Schnellzuglokomotive 210 38
~trosse 216 24; 227 8
~winde 227 7; 258 86
~zug 216 22
Schleuderakrobat 307 35
~brett 307 36
~honig 77 62-63
~mühle 172 5
Schleudern Textil 169 23
~ Sport 296 55
Schleuder-nummer 307 43
~schutzbremse 211 33
~sitz 257 6, 7
~vorhang 207 56
Schleuse Wasserbau 217 20
~ Schwimmbad 281 9
Schleusen-kammer 217 20
~tor 217 18
~tunnel 235 71
~vorhafen 217 26
Schlicht-feile 140 8
~hammer 137 35
~hobel 132 15; 134 1
~maschine 165 52
~platte 125 4
Schlichtung 162 53
Schlickbank 227 3
Schlickerguß 161 15
Schliefer 366 24
Schließe 36 10
Schließbart 313 8
Schließ-frucht 370 97-102
~kopf 143 59
~korb 204 3
~muskel Anat. 20 63
~muskel Zool. 77 17
~rahmen 181 38
~vorrichtung 90 27
~zeug 181 39
Schliff, facettierter antiker 36 49
~, facettierter normaler 36 48
~ansatz 350 37
Schlifform 111 35
Schliffformen 36 42-86
Schlinge Bau 122 68
~ Sport 300 11; 302 15
~ Völkerkunde 352 5
Schlinger-dämpfungsanlage 224 26
~kiel 222 47
Schlingpflanze 52 5
Schlitten Textil 167 39
~ Sport 303 1
~hund 353 2
~rückführung 249 21
~schelle 304 26
Schlitterbahn 304 17
Schlittern 304 18
Schlittschuh 302 20-25
~laufen 302 1-26
~läufer 302 1
~segeln 302 27-28
~segler 302 27
Schlitz-brett 2 45
~fadenreiniger 165 20
~schraube 143 36
~system 288 45
~trommel 165 10
~wams 355 33
Schloß Landkarte 15 96
~ Jagd 87 9
~ Friseur 106 36
~ Textil 167 6, 40
~blech 140 36
Schlosser 140 1

~hahn 361 9
~hammer 134 40; 140 23
~schraubstock 126 80
~werkstatt 140 1-22
Schloß-macher 140 1
~mantel 167 13
~park 272 1-40
~platte 149 16
~teil 167 14
~ und Schlüsselmacher 140 1
Schlot 11 17, 28
~brekzie 11 27
Schlupf-bluse 31 61
~brüter 74 28
Schlüpfer 32 27
Schlupf-hemdchen 29 7
~teil 74 30
Schlüssel 140 33-35; 328 32
Schlüsselbein 17 6
~schlagader 18 7
~vene 18 8
Schlüssel-blume 376 8
~brett 267 3
~loch 140 40
~macher 140 1
~weite 143 21
Schluß-hahn 350 53
~hocksprung 297 40
~mann 300 27
~rechnung 345 8-10
~stein 335 32; 336 23
Schmale, Fromändaner 69 22
schmalfett 175 10
Schmalfilm 117
~kamera 117 1; 313 31
~projektor 117 78; 318 20
~spezialkamera 313 35
~theatermaschine 312 52
Schmalreh 88 34
Schmalspur-bahn 159 4
~lokomotive 200 24
~schlepper 78 21
Schmaltier 88 1
Schmarotzer 68 4; 81 31-42
Schmeißfliege 358 18
Schmelz-betrieb 148 1-12
~einsatz 127 36
~einsatzhalter 127 35
Schmelzen 170 35, 41
Schmelzer 148 7
Schmelz-gutaufgabe 162 23, 31
~kessel 170 30
~löser 172 37
~ofen 108 8; 148 1; 178 19
~sicherung 127 21, 36
~spinnkopf 170 41
~wanne 162 3, 14
Schmerwurz 377 9
Schmetterling 293 17
Schmetterling Zool. 82 15, 18, 45, 48; 358 48-56; 365
~ Sport 297 25
~, männlicher 82 29
~, weiblicher 82 30
Schmetterlings-blütler 57 1
~schwimmen 282 34
~stellung 285 4
Schmidkäfer 358 24
Schmied 137; 138
Schmiede-feuer 137 1-8; 138 34
~handhammer 137 23
~lufthammer 137 9
~manipulator 139 32
~nagel 121 94
~ofen 139 47
~presse 139 35
~sattel 139 13, 14, 38, 39
~werkzeug 137 22-39
Schmieröl 145 62
~ölraffinerie 145 67

~pumpe 210 42
Schmink-spiegel 315 43
~stift 315 46
~tisch 315 45
~tuch 315 44
Schmirgel-papier 135 25
~scheibe 24 36
Schmörkel 88 58
Schmuck 36
~band 35 14
~garnitur 36 1
~gehänge 355 17
~gesteck 35 7
~kassette 36 31
~kästchen 36 31
~kasten 36 31
~reif 36 26
~ring 36 27
~schatulle 36 31
~set 36 1
~steinanhänger 36 14
~steinarmband 36 25
~steinring 36 15
~tanne 53 16
~uhr 36 33
Schmutz-behälter 199 47
~titel 185 44
~titelblatt 185 43
~wasser-Hausanschlußleitung 198 26
Schnabel 88 84
~höcker 359 17
~kerf 358 4
~schuh 355 42
~tier 366 1
Schnake 358 16
Schnaps, klarer 98 56
~glas 45 90
Schnarrgans 359 15
Schnauzbart 34 8
Schnauze 70 3
Schnauzer Schnurrbart 34 8
~ Zool. 70 35
Schnecke Anat. 17 63
~ Bäckerei 97 38
~ Mus. 323 17
~ Zool. 357 27
Schnecken-frisur 34 37
~gewinde 192 59
~haus 357 29
~lenkung 192 56-59
~nudel 97 38
~radsegment 192 57
Schnee 8 10
~, geschmolzener 304 30
~anzug 29 38
~ball 304 15
~ball, Gemeiner 373 10
~ballschlacht 304 14
~band 200 4; 300 4
~block 353 5
~brille 300 18
~brücke 300 24
~decke 304 20
~fall 8 18; 9 34
~fanggitter 38 8
~fangstütze 122 16
~gamasche 300 55
~glöckchen 60 1
~glöggli 377 1
~haufen 304 24
~hemd 300 6
~hütte 353 4
~kette 304 10
~kreuz 10 48
~lawine 304 1
~mann 304 13
~matsch 304 30
~pflug 304 9
~pflugtafel 203 34-35
~schaufel 304 23
~schaufeln 304 22

~schaufler 304 22
~schippe 304 23
~schippen 304 22
~schipper 304 22
~schleuder 213 17
~treiben 304 4
~verwehung 304 5
~wächte 300 20
~-Wald-Klima 9 56
~wehe 304 5
~zaun 304 6
Schneidapparat 173 44
Schneide 45 57; 85 2
~haus 310 3
~leiste 124 21
~lineal 124 21
~maschine 131 5
Schneiden 170 60
~ (des Kabels) 169 30
Schneider 271 37
~büste 103 6
~kreide 104 24; 271 39
~muskel 18 45
~nähmaschine 103 8
~puppe 103 6
~sitz 295 11
~werkstatt 268 17
Schneide-tisch 117 96; 311 42
~vorrichtung 162 19
~winkel 124 20
~zahn 19 16, 34
Schneid-kluppe 140 32
~rolle 181 42
~rost 141 14
~satz 141 19
~scheibe 40 40
~trommel 64 34
~werk Gartengerät 56 41
~werk Textil 169 30
~werkverstellung 64 8
Schneise Landkarte 15 112
~ Forstw. 84 1
schnell 321 28
Schnelladesystem 115 25
Schnellaufschlittschuh 302 20
schneller Brüter 154 1
Schnell-filteranlage 269 9
~fütterungssystem 74 23
~heizkathode 240 25
~käfer 80 37
~kochplatte 39 15
~kochtopf 40 21
~kupplung 65 86
~kupplungsrohr 67 28
~presse 181 1
~programmtaste 195 12
~ruftaste 246 15
~säge 138 23
~schalthebel 115 16
~schußkamera 115 77
~spannfutter 132 54
~triebzug 211 60
~trockenpresse 116 57
~untersuchungsgerät 79 20
~verband 21 5
~verstellzirkel 151 64
~waage 98 12
~ziehholster 264 24
~zugabteil 207 43
~zuglokomotive 205 35
~zugwagen 207 1-21
Schnepfe 88 83
Schnitt Zeichn. 151 28
~ Druck 178 31
~ Film 311 42-46
~bildindikator 115 55, 59, 64
~drücker 100 9
~holzplatz 157 32
~käsebetrieb 76 47
~lauch 57 22
~meister 311 43
~menge 348 4
~punkt 346 1

~verlaufsangabe 151 27
~ware 157 22
Schnitzel-behälter 170 40
~jagd 289 41-49
Schnitzerei 328 7
Schnock 364 16
Schnorchel *Mil.* 259 72, 90
~ *Sport* 279 11; 280 39
Schnuller 28 15
Schnupftabak 107 20
Schnupftabaksdose 107 20
Schnur *Angelsport* 89 20
~ *Elektr.* 127 16
Schnürband 100 64
Schnurbaum 52 2, 17, 29
Schnürboden *Bau* 120 11
~ *Schiff* 222 3
~ *Theater* 316 4
~meister 316 7
Schnur-fangbügel 89 62
~führung 89 60
~gerüstecke 118 69
~keramik 328 10
~kreuz 118 70
Schnurrbart 34 19
Schnurrolle 135 9
Schnür-schuh 101 31
~senkel 291 32
Schnurstich 102 8
Schnürung 171 9, 22, 23
Schockernetz 89 94
Schokoladen-tafel 98 78
~trüffel 98 86
~überzug 97 34
Scholle 63 7
Schöndruckwerk 181 48
Schoner 302 25
~brigg 220 14
~mast 220 15
~segel 220 12
Schönheits-königin 306 64
~pflästerchen 306 24
Schonrachenspanner 89 42
Schonung 84 10
Schönwetterwolke 8 1
Schopf 72 2
Schöpfer 173 46
Schöpf-form 173 48
~pumpe 269 7
~teil 45 63
~thermometer 92 53
Schopfwalm 121 16
Schornstein *Gebäude* 15 38; 37 10; 38 5; 118 21; 120 47; 122 13; 152 15
~ *Fahrzeug* 210 22; 221 8, 40, 75; 223 1; 258 19, 20, 58; 259 32
~, blinder 221 16
~einfassung 122 14
~farben 223 2
~feger 38 31
~kappe 258 21, 59
~marke 223 2
~verband 118 66
~ziegel 159 25
Schoß 78 3
~rock 355 76
Schot 219 68
Schötchen 61 11
Schote 61 20, 23; 370 93; 378 33
Schothorn 284 41
Schottel-Propeller 227 20
Schotter 158 24; 205 61
~bett 205 61
~terrasse 13 64
~verteiler 200 31
~werk 158 18
Schottischer Terrier 70 17
Schrägaufzug 147 2; 158 16; 159 5
Schragen 332 60

Schräg-holm 287 33
~kreuz 332 60
~lage 83 27
Schrägseil 215 47
~brücke 215 46
~system 215 51
~verankerung 215 48
Schräg-spur 243 31
~verzahnung 143 89
Schrämstreb 144 34
Schränkeisen 132 42
Schrankelement 42 7; 46 6
Schranken-posten 202 43
~wärter 202 42
Schrank-front 46 2
~koffer 267 29
~wand 42 1; 46 1
Schrapperanlage 200 13
Schratsegel 219 20-31; 220 15
Schraubdeckel 83 40; 115 11
Schraube *Jagd* 87 30
~ *Bau* 119 75
~ *Heimwerker* 134 39; 143
~ *Textilw.* 165 36
~ *Sport* 282 43; 288 6
Schraubel 370 76
Schrauben 143 13-50
~bolzen 121 98
~bund 143 33
~dreher 126 69; 127 46; 134 4; 140 62
~dreher, elektrischer 195 23
~feder 191 28; 192 68, 74
~pauke 323 57
~rad 192 34, 36, 39, 43
~schlitz 143 38
~schlüssel 195 44
~schutz 258 40
~schutzleiste 258 74
~schutzwulst 258 63
~steven 222 71
~wasser 223 58
~welle 223 65; 259 59
~zieher 126 69; 127 46; 134 4; 140 62
~ziehersatz 109 6
Schraub-fassung 127 59
~gewinde 50 50
~kappe 127 35
~sicherung 300 47
~stahl 135 14
~stock 109 28; 138 24
~stollen 291 28
~zwinge 120 66; 132 14; 260 47
Schreber-garten 52 1-32
~gärtner 52 24
Schreib-abteil 209 26
~arm 10 12, 15
~feder 10 13
~fenster 249 19
~gerät 249 3; 341 21-26
~hebel 10 7, 21
~heft 47 24; 260 18
~kopf 249 15
~kopfdeckel 249 30
~kraft 248 21
Schreibmaschine 209 28; 248 22; 309 79
~, elektrische 249 1
Schreibmaschinen-radiergummi 247 26
~schrift 342 9
~tisch 245 25
~type 247 7
Schreib-pinsel 341 24
~platte 47 23; 246 3
~platz 46 21
~raum 177 49
~schale 245 22; 246 9; 260 24
~schrift, deutsche 342 11
~schrift, englische 342 10
~schrift, lateinische 342 12

~stempel 341 22
~stift 245 21
~stiftebehälter 22 31
~tafel 47 13; 48 16
~tastenfeld 245 27
Schreibtisch 46 22; 246 2
~lampe 246 11
~schublade 46 26; 246 4
~sessel 46 27; 246 1
~unterschrank 248 37
Schreib-unterlage 46 23; 246 6; 260 25
~utensilien 6 27
~walze 249 18
~werkrückführung 249 21
Schreiner 132 38
Schreinerei 132 1-73
Schrift *Setzerei* 174 7; 175 2, 3, 7, 8, 9, 10
~ *Kirche* 330 57
~ *Schriftzeichen* 341; 342 1-15
~bild 174 31; 175 42
Schriftenstand 330 56
Schrift-feld 151 31
~führer 263 26
~fundament 181 17
~grad 175 18
~höhe 175 44
~kasten 174 3
~linie 175 43
~matrize 174 47; 176 16
~pinsel 129 41
~satz 175 1-17
~schablone 151 69
~scheibe 176 20
~speicher 242 37
~verkehrsordner 22 12
Schrillader 81 8
Schrillapparat 81 8
Schritt 72 39
Schrittmacher *Med.* 25 37
~ *Sport* 290 11
~, passagerer 25 25
~einheit 25 30
~impuls 25 44
~kontrolle 25 40
~maschine 290 12
~motorrad 290 12
Schritt-schaltmotor 110 17
~überschlag 297 26
Schrot 92 42
Schröter 358 24
Schrot-ladung 87 51
~lauf 87 27
~meißel 137 38
~patrone 87 49
Schrott-kasten 141 15
~mulde 147 26
~zufuhr 147 65
Schrumpfen 168 26
Schrumpf-folie 76 25
~kopf 352 30
~ring 130 24
Schrupp-feile 134 9
~hobel 132 16
Schub-düse 232 39, 45, 49, 55; 235 37, 64
~düsen-Kraftstofftank 235 45
~fach 49 34
~gerüst 234 21
~kahn 221 94
~karre 118 37; 119 42
~karren 118 37
~konus 234 35
~lade 41 9; 43 18; 46 11
~leichter 221 94
~rahmen 200 30
~schiffverband 225 60
~schlepper 221 93
~schlitten 304 29
~stangenentmistung 75 21

~steuerungssystem 235 43
~trägergerüst 235 5, 6
~trecker 221 93
~verband 221 92
Schuh 41 16; 100 1; 101
~bürste 50 41
Schuhcreme 50 42
~dose 50 39
~tube 50 43
Schuhmacher 100
~werkstatt 100 1-68
Schuh-Mehrzweck-Schrank 41 8
~pflegemittel 50 39-43
~putzer 377 9
~schnalle 101 52
~spray 50 40
Schulbuch 47 25
Schule 260; 261
~, Höhere 261
Schüler 242 4; 260 3
~aquarell 260 27
~arbeit 260 67-80
~eingabegerät 242 4
~sitz 257 6
~stimme 261 43
~tisch 261 11
Schul-kinderkleidung 29 31-47
~Laser 242 81
~mappe 260 7
~ranzen 260 9
~reiten 71 1-6
~schiff 258 95
~schritt 71 2
~tafel 260 29
~tafelkreide 48 15
~tasche 260 7
Schulter 16 22
~blatt *Anat.* 16 23; 17 7
~blatt *Pferd* 72 18
~blatthöcker 70 11
~bogen 336 33
~decker 229 3
~eisen 38 33
~gürtel 17 6-7
~höhe 175 45
~knopf 31 15
~kragen 355 39
~landung 298 12
~muskel 18 35
~riemen 260 11
~schutz 142 5
~stativ 115 100
~stütze *Mil.* 255 9, 31, 39
~stütze *Film* 313 37
~tuch 31 71
Schulturnen 296 12-21; 297 7-14
Schuppe *Zool.* 364 11
~ *Bot.* 372 34, 42, 45, 50
Schuppen-ornament 335 15
~panzer 329 64
~tier 366 10
Schüreisen 38 41
Schürfkübel 200 17
~raupe 200 16
Schuß 171 43
~bolzen 94 4
Schußfaden 171 1-29, 3
~, gehobener 171 16
~, gesenkter 171 15
Schuß-kreis 292 16
~rips 171 13, 14
~spule 166 7
~waffe 87 2
~wechselautomat 166 5
~weite 86 15; 305 30, 32
Schuster-hammer 100 37
~messer 100 50
~werkstatt 100 1-68
Schute *Hafen* 225 8

~ *Kostüme* 355 71
Schuten-hut 306 23; 355 71
~sauger 216 59
Schüttbetonwand 119 7
Schütte 226 45
Schüttergebiet,
　makroseismisches 11 38
Schüttgut 200 12; 221 11
~frachter 226 30
~umschlag 226 29
Schutt-halde 12 45
~strom 11 47
Schütt- und
　Sauggutumschlag 226 29
Schütz 217 77
Schutz-anstrich 123 5
~blech *Druck* 180 58
~blech *Fahrrad* 187 13, 43
~brille 140 21
~bügel 64 55; 83 20
~dach 186 42
~deckel 322 27
Schütze *Astr.* 3 37; 4 61
~ *Jagd* 86 1
~ *Handarbeit* 102 26
Schützen-auge 166 29
~kasten 166 9
~panzer 255 91
~stand 305 78
~wehr 217 73-80
~zeichen 305 65
Schutzgabel 307 54
Schutzgas 162 16
~schweißbrenner 142 33
~schweißgerät 138 29
~schweißung 142 33
~zuführung 142 34
Schutz-gehäuse 10 39
~geländer 119 43
~gitter 168 45; 181 24
~glas 142 4
~hafen 216 14
~haube 138 9; 140 20; 157 65
~helm 84 23; 127 48; 140 22;
　158 10; 264 21
~hütte 300 1
~isolierung 94 10
~kappe 101 40
~kasten 202 35
~kleidung 84 26; 264 18; 270
　46
~kleinspannung 127 2
~kontakt 127 13
~kontakt-Doppelsteckdose
　127 6
~kontaktsteckdose 127 5, 7
~kontaktstecker 127 9
~leiste 165 31
~mauer 356 4
~papier 114 21
~schild *Schweißtechnik* 142
　39
~schild *Schiff* 218 17
~schild *Polizei* 264 20
~umschlag 185 37
~wand 118 90; 122 35
Schwabacher Schrift 342 2
Schwabbelscheibe 100 10
Schwabe 81 17
Schwabenkorn 68 24
Schwach-bier 93 26
~holz 84 37; 85 27
~lauge 172 45
~regner 62 29
~strom 127 2
Schwad 63 23
~ablage 63 19
Schwaden 63 23
Schwad-mäher 63 19
~rechen 64 44
Schwalbe 361 20
Schwalbenmöwe, Kleine 359
　11

Schwalbennest 259 19
Schwalbenschwanz 358 52
~-Zwillingskristall 351 25
Schwamm *Landw.* 80 2
~ *Schule* 260 42
~ *Graphik* 340 25
~ *Zool.* 357 13
~schale 260 41
~spinner 80 1
~tier 357 13
Schwan *Astr.* 3 23
~ *Vögel* 272 54; 359 16
~, Stummer 359 16
Schwanen-blume 378 39
~hals 87 48
Schwanz 70 12; 72 38; 88 49,
　67, 75, 80; 362 8
~flosse 364 10; 367 29
~lurch 364 20-22
~stachel 358 43
~stück 95 34
~welle 223 60
Schwappdämpfung 234 13
Schwärmer 82 27; 358 55; 365
　9
Schwarmnetz 77 54
Schwarte *Jagd* 88 56
~ *Bau* 120 96
Schwartling 120 96
schwarz *Heraldik* 254 26
~ *Farbe* 343 13
Schwarz 275 21
~amsel 361 13
~beere 377 23; 379 7
~deckenfertiger 200 43
~-Doppeldruckwerk 180
　12-13
~dorn 374 27
Schwarzer Holunder 374 35
~ Nachtschatten 379 5
schwarzes Feld 276 3
Schwarz-kollektor 155 29
~laugenbehälter 172 29
~laugenfilter 172 28
~pulver 87 53
Schwarzwälder Kirschtorte
　97 24
~uhr 109 31
Schwarz-wild 88 51
~wurz 375 45
~wurzel 57 35
Schwebe-bahn 214 15-38
~balken 297 2, 21
~kippe 297 28
Schweben 72 44
Schweden-greifer 157 29
~klee 69 3
~reuter 63 28
Schwefel 351 23
~kohlenstoff 169 8
~kohlenstoffinjektor 83 33
~kopf 107 23
Schwefelsäure 170 24
~erzeugung 156 34
~zufuhr 156 33
~zusetzung 170 23
Schwefelwasserstoffwascher
　156 22
Schweif 72 38
~riemen 71 34
~rübe 72 34
Schwein 62 10; 73 9; 75 39; 95
　38-54
Schweine-fett 96 5
~filet 95 44
~hälfte 94 23
~kamm 95 42
~kotelett 95 46
~schmalz 96 5
~stall 62 8; 75 35
Schweinskopf 95 43
~ohr *Zool.* 73 11
~ohr *Bäckerei* 97 30

~rüssel 73 10
Schweiß-arm 142 30
~brenner 141 11, 19, 28
Schweißer-brille 141 24
~handschuh 142 8, 32
~schutzhaube 142 3
Schweiß-haubenglas 142 40
~hund 70 42
~kabel 142 19
~mundstück 141 33
~paste 141 18
~riemen 70 30
~schutzschild 142 39
~stab 141 12
~tisch 141 13; 142 21
~trafo 142 1
~transformator 125 29; 142 1,
　27
Schweizerbügel 55 27
Schweizer Käse 99 41
~ Klee 69 10
Schwelle *Bau* 120 49
~ *Eisenb.* 205 60
Schwellen-rost 119 39
~schraube 202 7
Schweller 325 45
Schwell-körper 20 67
~werk 326 45
Schwemmkegel 13 9
Schwenk-arm 26 13; 104 27
~armhaube 105 25
~bohrmaschine 150 18
~bug 121 57
~dach 213 27
Schwenker 310 42
Schwenk-flügel 256 9
~hahn 126 36
~motor 132 69
~rohr 172 10
~ventil 126 36
~vorrichtung 65 73
Schwer-athletik 299
~benzinfraktion 145 40
~beton 119 72
schwerer Atomkern 1 35
Schwere Waffe 255 40-95
Schwer-gewichtsanker 286 15
~gutbaum 221 25, 62
~gutposten 221 24
~kraftfüllstutzen 257 32
~kraftrad 189 31
~lastwagen 200 7
~lastzug 194 20
~punkt 346 26
Schwerstgutfrachter 221 23
Schwert *Buchb.* 185 29
~ *Schiff* 220 7; 279 3; 284 26;
　285 41
~antenne 256 28
~blume 60 8
Schwertel 60 11
Schwert-jacht 285 37-41
~kasten 284 24
~leite 329 66
~lilie 60 8
~lilie, Gelbe 60 8
~schlucker 308 26
Schwibbogen 335 28
Schwiele 72 27
Schwimmanlage 282 1-32
Schwimmanschette 281 7
Schwimm-anstalt 282 1-32
~anzug 280 42
~art 282 33-39
Schwimmatratze 280 17
Schwimm-bad 223 23; 281;
　282 1-32
~bagger 216 56
~bahn 282 31
~balken 352 36
~dock 222 34-43, 41; 225 16
Schwimmeister 282 16
Schwimmen 282 17

Schwimmente 28 10; 49 4
Schwimmer *Installateur* 126
　15
~ *Auto* 192 15
~ *Fluß* 216 12
~ *Wasserbau* 217 34
~ *Schiff* 221 65
~ *Flugzeug* 232 6
~ *Mil.* 258 87
~becken 282 23
~flugzeug 232 5
~hebel 65 43
~kammer 192 14
~schacht 217 35
Schwimm-flosse 279 18; 280
　41
~fuß 359 6
~gürtel 282 19
~haut 73 36; 359 7
~heber 226 31
~hose 280 43
~kappe 280 29, 44
~kissen 282 18
~körper 224 71
~kran 225 10; 226 48
~lage 282 33-39
~lehrer 282 16
~natter 364 38
~ring 281 6
~schüler 282 17
~sport 282
~staffel 282 24-32
~stil 282 33-39
~tier 280 33
~unterricht 282 16-20
~weste 286 20
~weste, aufblasbare 228 8
Schwinge 88 76; 327 15
Schwingel 69 24
Schwingelement 110 9
Schwingen 297 39
Schwinghebel 67 34; 190 33
~feder 67 35
~lagerung 190 34
Schwing-masse 110 32
~quarz 110 15
~sattel 188 21
Schwingungsdämpfer 190
　26; 214 55
Schwungbein 298 27
Schwungrad 100 24; 104 15;
　166 15; 190 20
~regulator 224 56
Schwung-stemme 296 57
~technik 298 30
Scorpius 3 38; 4 60
Scotchterrier 70 17
Script 310 45
~girl 310 39
Sech 65 10
sechsachsiger
　Gelenktriebwagen 197 13
Sechsachteltakt 320 34
Sechseck 36 62; 351 15
~, ovales 36 63
~, rundes 36 64, 65
Sechsflächner 351 2
~-Kanal-Monitor 27 31
Sechskant-mutter 143 18
~schraube 143 13
Sechsling 259 37
Sechstage-fahrer 290 2
~rennen 290 2-7
Sechs-~Teller-Film- und -
　Ton-Schneidetisch 117 96
~uhrstellung 298 25
~vierteltakt 320 35
Sechszylinder-~Dieselmotor
　64 28
~-Unterflurdieselmotor 209
　23
Sechzehn-meterraum 291 4
~-Millimeter-Kamera 117 43

Sechzehntel-note 320 17
~pause 320 25
Secke 125 8
Sedilie 330 41
Sediment 23 50
~gestein 12 1
See 13 3, 26
~adler 362 5
~anamone 369 20
~bäderschiff 221 15
~bär 367 18
~beben 11 53
~blei 89 92
~drache 218 13-17
~fallreep 221 91
~feder 369 14
~fischerei 90
~flieger 359 11-14
~gewässer 286 10-14
~gras 378 54
~gurke 369 18
~hund 367 19
~igel 357 39; 369 19
~jungfer Fabelwesen 327 23
~jungfer Zool. 358 3
~krähe 359 14
Seelenachse 87 38
Seelilie 369 3
Seelsorger 330 22
See-notkreuzer 228 14
~notrettungskreuzer 221 18
~otter 367 17
~pferd 327 44
~pferdchen 364 18
~rabe, Weißer 359 9
~räuber 306 43
~rose 51 18; 272 56; 378 14
~schwalbe 359 11
~stern 357 38; 369 17
~stier 327 47
~ungeheuer 327 47
~verschleppung 227 6
~zeichen 224 68-108
Segel Anat. 20 48
~ Sport 284 2; 285 4, 8
~boot 273 29; 278 12; 284
    10-48; 285 29-41, 42-49
~fenster 284 38
~flug 287
~fluggelände 287 13
~flugzeug 287 3
~form 220 1-5
~jolle 278 12
Segeln 284; 285 1, 9, 10, 11,
    12
Segel-schiff 219; 220 35-37
~stellung 285 1-13
~streifen 218 34
Segerkegel 161 6
Segler 359 24
~mütze 35 29
Segment Math. 346 52
~ Zool. 357 25
~fenster 335 50
Seher 88 43, 60
Sehne Sport 305 59
~ Math. 346 51
Sehnerv Anat. 19 51
~ Zool. 77 23, 24
Sehzeichen-kollimator 111 46
~projektor 111 47
Seidelbast 377 10
Seiden-pflanzengewächs 53 15
~raupe 358 50
~revers 33 6
~spinner 358 48
~taft 35 36
Seife 49 22
Seifen-kiste 273 33
~schale 49 21
Seiher 269 32
Seil 21 30; 286 47; 299 36;
    300 12

~, Gehen am 300 22-27
~arbeiten 214 80
Seilbahn 15 67;
    214 15-38
~gondel 214 52
~stütze 214 76
Seil-dritter 300 27
~erster 300 25
~fähre 216 1
~fallschirm 287 7
~führung 201 7
~führungsrolle 85 39
~hüpfen 273 15
~rollautomat 301 62
~rollenaufzug 118 91
~schaft 300 22-27
~schließe 118 30
~schlinge 300 11
~schuh 214 33
~schwebbahn 214 30
~schwebebahn 214 15-38
~springen 273 15
~tänzerin 307 40
~verspannung 299 37
~winde 85 38, 46; 255 69
~zweiter 300 26
Seismologie 11 32-38
Seismometer 11 39
Seitaufnahme 27 3
Seite Buch 185 53
~ Math. 346 26
Seiten-ansicht 151 18; 166 35;
    207 1, 37, 60, 74; 286 38
~blatt 71 40, 47
~diele 123 10
~eingang 331 15
~feintrieb 14 56
~fenster Auto 191 61
~fenster Schiff 218 57
~fenster Flugzeug 231 29
~flosse 229 24; 230 59; 235 1;
    256 32; 288 21
~gang 207 11; 222 45
~geflecht 136 18
~gording 218 36
~graben 216 37
~holm 235 3
~klemme 14 57
~lage, stabile 21 24
~leitwerk 229 24-25; 230 58
~linie 291 9; 292 17; 293 2
    bis 3, 4 bis 5, 55
~linienrichter 293 24
~moräne 12 53
~motor 228 29
~nummer 251 14
~pferd 186 47
~pfette 121 39
~pforte 335 13
~portal 335 13
~riß 259 2-11
Seitenruder 218 6; 229 25;
    230 60; 259 95; 288 22
~maschine 257 23
~pedal 230 27, 28; 257 10
Seiten-schale 188 48
~schalung 119 55
~scheibe 229 33
~scheitel 34 14
~schiff 334 63; 335 2
~schild 217 67
~schlitz 30 49
~schlitzrock 30 51
~schneider 127 51
~schwert 220 7; 283 63
~schwimmen 282 36
~sproß 58 20; 370 21
~tafel 260 35
~tank 222 37
~tasche 33 12
~teil 100 61
~träger 222 52
~tragrahmen 165 12; 167 20

~trawler 221 46
~überschrift 342 52
~wagen 290 30
~wagengespann 290 29
~wand 213 29
~wanddrehtür 213 9
~wegerung 222 62
~wurzel 370 17
~ziffer 185 63
Seit-fußstoß 299 19
~grätschstellung 295 3
~halte 295 48
~lage 295 46
~neigen 299 29
~pferd 296 5; 297 1
~spagat 295 14
~spannung 296 50
~stand 296 22, 23
Seitwärtshaken 299 33
Seitwurf 89 32
Sekante 346 50
Sekondbindung 294 50
Sekretärinnenzimmer 245
    1-33
Sekt 98 63
~flasche 99 78
~glas 45 85-86
~kork 267 58
~kübel 267 59
~kühler 267 59
Sektor 346 54
Sektorenblende 313 8
Sektschale 45 86
Sekundant 299 44
Sekundär-fokuseinrichtung 5
    11
~kreislauf 154 7, 45; 259 63
~kreisumwälzpumpe 154 8
~spiegel 5 2
~strom 232 50
~stromkanal 232 41, 44
~wicklung 153 16
Sekunde, große 321 7
Sekunden-anzeige 110 21
~knopf 110 4
~messer 129 39
~theodolit 112 73
Selbst-aufzug 110 32-43
~auslöser 115 15; 309 51
~bedienung 196 8
Selbstbedienungs-gaststätte
    266 45-78
~geschäft 99 1-96
~restaurant 266 45-78
~speisewagen 207 73
~tankstelle 196 1-29
Selbst-einfädelung 165 18
~fahrlafette 255 49-74
~fangspule 117 80
~haltekette 65 13
~rettung 21 33
~schenker 266 1
~sicherung 300 10
~spanner 87 23
~tränke 74 16
~werker 134 61
Select 243 42
Selengleichrichter 312 18
Selfservice-Station 196 1-29
Sellerie 57 27
Selterswasser 98 87
Semibrevis 320 13
Semifloa 320 30
Semifusa 320 17
Semikolon 342 19
Semiminima 320 15
Semmel 97 13, 13-16
~pilz 381 31
Sende-antenne 288 88
~leiter 238 22
Sender 10 62
~abstimmung 241 39
Senf 98 28
~, Wilder 61 18

Senkel 118 50
Senkkopf 143 46
Senkrechtantriebskopf 150 38
Senkrechte 346 6
Senkrecht-frässpindel 150 37
~starter 232 26
~strangguß 148 24-29
Senkschraube 143 28
Sennes-blatt 380 16
~blätterstrauch 380 16
Sensal 251 4
Sense 66 12
Sensen-bart 66 15
~blatt 66 13
~griff 66 17
~schuh 66 18
~schutz 66 18
~stiel 66 16
Separator Spinnerei 164 43
~ Papier 172 31
Septime, große 321 12
Septimenakkord 321 5
Septimole 321 23
Septole 321 23
Sequesterzange 26 45
Serienzeichen 276 38-45
Serpens 3 20
Serpent 322 13
Serradella 69 11
Serradelle 69 11
Servicegruppe 250 4
Service module 6 2; 234 56
Serviceplateau 105 31
Servierbrett 265 14
Servieren 293 59
Serviererin 266 13; 266 18
Servier-tablett 265 14
~tuch 267 48
Serviette 45 9; 266 47
Serviettenring 45 10
Servobremstrommel 192 50
Sesampflanze 383 45
Sessel 134 59; 271 35
~lift 214 16-18
Set 44 4
Setter 70 41
Settrommel 174 35
Setzer 174 5
Setzerei 174 5; 175; 176
Setzerkombination 326 46
Setz-hase 88 59
~holz 56 1
~kasten 55 51
~kescher 89 28
~kopf 143 57
~linie 174 14
~maschine 174 32-45
~rebe 83 15
~regal 174 2
~stock 150 30
~stück Zirkus 307 57
~stück Theat. 315 30; 316 47
~stufe 123 33, 48
~-und Gießmaschine 174
    32-45
Sexfilm 318 20
Sextant 224 1
Sexte, große 321 11
Sextole 321 23
Sgraffito 338 41
Shampooflasche 105 32
Sharpie, 12-m²- 284 53
Sheddach 121 20
Shorts 33 25
siamesisch 341 10
Sichel 56 8
~düne 13 40
~feder 88 68
~flügel 229 18
~schwanz 73 25
Sicherheits-behälter 154 21
~beleuchtung 312 6

~bügel 301 53, 58
~einrichtung 316 18
~fahrschalter 211 21; 212 13
~glas 124 5
~kette 126 3
~kettenbremse 85 15
~netz 307 14
~rohr 349 7
~schloß 140 44
~schlüssel 140 48
~skibindung 301 2
~türverschluß 50 25
~ventil 38 70; 210 3
~verdeck 85 36
Sicherung *Jagd* 87 24
~ *Elektr.* 127 68
Sicherungs-automat 41 20;
127 33
~draht 127 68
~druckknopf 127 20
~flügel 2 40; 87 8
~kasten 41 19; 166 23
~mutter 187 64
~patrone 127 36
~schraubautomat 127 19, 21
Sicht-fenster 25 8; 28 36, 49
~fensterkinderwagen 28 34
~schutz 199 11
~schutzraum 281 17
~signale 288 52-54
~weitenmeßgerät 10 60
Sicke 125 8
Sicken-~, Bördel- und
Drahteinlegemaschine 125
25
~hammer 125 14
~stock 125 8
Sicker-schacht 155 16
~wasserableitung 216 37
Sideboard 44 20
Siderostat 5 16
Sieb 173 14
~band 64 69
~bandklopfeinrichtung 64 70
~bein 17 39
Sieben-gestirn 3 26
~punkt 358 37
Sieb-sauger 173 15
~saugwalze 173 16
~trommelpaar 163 21
~verlängerung 64 18
Siede-rohr 210 17
~wasserprinzip 154 49
~würstchen 96 8
Siedlung 37 54-57
Siedlungshaus 37 54
Siegelring 36 40
Sieger 299 39
~anzeige 289 38
Sieges-trophäe 352 30
~zeichen 352 15
Siegquote 289 39
~wurz 60 11
Sieke 125 8
Sielengeschirr 71 26-36
Siemens-Elektro-
Niederschachtofen 147
51-54
~-Martin-Ofen 147 21-30
Sifa 211 21, 25; 212 13
Signal 115 52
~anlage 203
~anzeige, optische 238 30
~arm 203 2
~buch 253 29
~buchwimpel 253 29
~element 243 60
~flagge 253 22-34
~gerüst 14 51
~hebel 203 56, 62
~horn 188 53; 212 70; 270 7
~lampe 25 6; 315 52
~leine 223 10

~mast 221 7; 225 34
~spur 243 59
~stag 223 11
~stellung 203 4, 5, 10, 11
~trommel 354 18
Signatur 175 47
Signet 185 48
Silber 254 25
~draht 108 3
~fischchen 81 14
~münze 252 1-28; 328 37
~pappel 371 23
~scheibe 10 24
~schmied 108
~waage 108 35
~wurz 51 7
Siliciumatom 1 14
Silo 225 68
~beschickungsrohr 62 12
~tank 76 10
~zelle 225 69
Silverdisk-Pyrheliometer 10
23
Sima 334 11
Simpelfranse 34 36
Simshobel 132 25
Sinaischrift 341 13
Sinanthropus 261 18
Singdrossel 361 16
Single-8-Kassette 117 39
Singvogel 360 1,3,4,5,7,9,10;
361 1-20
Sinkkasten 198 23
~anschlußleitung 198 25
Sinningia 53 7
Sinter-säule 13 82
~terrasse 11 23
Sinus 346 32
Siphon 49 27; 126 26
Sirene *Schiff* 223 3
~ *Fabelwesen* 327 58
~ *Zool.* 366 23
Sirius 3 14
Sisal 35 13
Sister 322 21
Situla 328 34
Sitz *Pferd* 71 45
~ *Masch.* 143 65
~ *Fahrzeug* 235 17, 18; 303 6
~anordnung 211 58
~bank 41 10; 212 63; 281 38
~bein 17 19
~brett 278 17
~fläche 44 11
~gruppe 268 60
~gurt 300 57
~kissen 42 23; 47 8
~pirouette 302 8
~platz 24 24; 315 20; 319 8
~polster 207 65
~raum 283 8
~reifen 273 54
~reihe 193 1; 261 1; 312 9
~rohr 187 18
~stock 86 10
~stufe 281 20
~tuch 281 25
~- und Liegestufe 281 20
Sixt-bindung 294 48
~deckung 294 8
~parade 294 8
Skala 110; 349 23, 35
Skalp 352 15
Skalpell 26 43
Skateboard 273 51
Skeet 305 70-78
~anlage 305 74
~-Bockdoppelflinte 305 70
~bohrung 305 71
~schießen 305 70-78
Skeisel 220 32
Skeleton 303 22
~fahren 303 22-24

~fahrer 303 23
~schlitten 303 22
Skelett 17 1-29; 261 14
Skelettierfraß 80 8
Skene 334 45
Skeusel 220 32
Ski 301 46
~bob 304 16
~brille 301 11
Skidder 85 34
Ski-fahren 301 1-72
~helm 301 13
~lauf 301 1-72
~laufen 301 1-72
~lift 301 57-63
~mütze 35 39; 301 10
~pullover 33 52
~schlepplift 214 15
~sport 301 1-72
~stock 301 5
~stopper 301 56
~wachs 301 21
~wachsutensilien 301 21-24
Skizzenblock 338 35
Sklaven-aufseher 218 47
~galeere 218 44-50
Skooter 308 63
~bahn 308 62
Skorpion 3 38; 4 60
~, Italienischer 358 40
Skript 310 45
~girl 310 39
Skull 283 17, 35-38
Skulptur 339 32
Skysegel 220 32
Slalom-lauf 301 64
~ski 286 60
Slat 229 38
Slick 305 86
Slingpumps 101 53
Slip 32 15, 26
~form 32 8
Slipper 101 34
SM 6 2
SM-Hauptriebwerk 234 57
Smoking 33 7
~hemd 32 43
~schleife 32 47; 33 11
Socke, knielange 32 32
~, wadenlange 32 34
Sockel 44 23
~leiste 123 63
~platte 123 21
~schutzbrett 118 29
Sockenrand 32 33
Sodawasserflasche 42 32
Sofa 42 24; 336 17
~kissen 42 27; 46 17
Soffitte 316 12
Sofitten-beleuchtung 318 25
~lampe 318 26
Softrindleder 101 46
Sohlbank 120 33
Sohle *Landmaschinen* 65 6
~ *Schuhmacher* 100 66
~ *Tischler* 132 22
~ *Atommüllagerung* 154 73,
83
Sohlen-leder 100 31
~presse 100 14
~tal 13 55
Solarium 281 11
Solar-zelle 155 34
~zellenausleger 10 66
Soldatengrab 331 32
Sole 274 3
~zuleitung 274 4
Soling 284 56
Solist 314 28
Söller 329 12
Soll-kurseinsteller 224 18
~maß 149 57
~wertgeber 197 27

Solo-maschine 290 27
~tänzer 314 28
Solstitium 3 8
Somalistrom 14 36
Sombrero 35 5
Sommer-ammer 361 7
~bluse 31 22
~deich 216 48
~goldhähnchen 361 10
~hose 31 52
~hut 29 16; 35 37
~käfig 356 11
~kleid 31 9
~kleidchen 29 13
~kleidung 31
~könig 361 10
~laube 52 14
~mantel 31 20
~monsun 9 52
~pulli 31 67
~solstitialpunkt 3 8
~sonnenwendepunkt 3 8
~temperatur 9 43
Sonargerät 259 40
Sonde 24 46
Sonder-abteil 205 26
~angebot 96 20; 271 65
~angebotskorb 96 18
~preistafel 96 19
~stempelabdruck 236 59
~tisch 271 64
~wagen 264 16
Sonne 3 2; 4 29, 36-41, 42; 38
32
~, künstliche 281 13
Sonnen-bad 282 4
~bad, künstliches 281 10
~badende 281 12
~bahn 4 18, 19, 20
~bahn, scheinbare 4 10-21
~banner 253 20
~blende 313 3
~blume 51 35; 52 7; 61 13; 69
20
~blumenöl 98 24
~brille 6 19; 111 6; 301 19
~brillentasche 6 19
~dach 274 14
~deck 223 22
~einstrahlung 155 18
~energie 155 17
~energienutzung 155 17-36
~falle 55 17
~finsternis 4 29-35, 32, 39, 41
~fleck 4 37, 38
~hut 29 16; 35 5
~kälbchen 358 37
~kraftwerkselement 155 28
~observatorium 5 29-33
~rand 4 39
~röschen 377 20
~scheibe 4 36
~scheibe, geflügelte 333 12
~scheindauer 9 44
~schirm 37 48; 268 61; 272 58
Sonnensegel 221 116
~latte 221 118
~stütze 221 117
Sonnen-sensor 10 69
~spektrum 343 14
~spiegel 5 29
~strahl 4 9
~system 4 42-52
~tau 377 14
~tierchen 357 7
~uhr 110 30
~wende 3 8
~ziegel 155 32
Sopraporte 336 12
Sordine 323 10
Sortierer 172 57
Sortier-maschine 172 23
~polter 157 31

Sortimentseinsatz 134 39
Soßen-löffel 45 18
~schüssel 45 17
Souffleur 316 28
~kasten 316 27
Souffleuse 316 28
Souterrain 118 1
Souvenirteller 309 48
Sozia 268 36
Soziusfußraste 188 44
Spacelab 235 65
Spaceshuttle-Orbiter 235
  1-45
Spachtelmasse 128 3
Spagat 314 20
Spaghetti 98 32
Spalier 37 33
~baum 52 16
~bogen 52 12
~obstbaum 52 1,2,16,17,29
Spalt 5 13
spaltbares Element 1 49
Spaltbohrer 24 39
Spalte 185 65; 342 45
Spalten-linie 342 47
~überschrift 342 46
Spalter 94 18
~kapsel 370 94
~klappe 229 47
~pfropfen 54 36
~segment 5 14
Spaltung Atom 1 43
~ Schiff 224 89
Span 120 80; 136 12; 149 44
~abstreifer 157 50
Späne-absaugung 157 51
~auswurf 132 48
~blasrohr 140 17
Spange Bau 119 67
~ Sport 303 5
Spangen-helm 254 8
~pumps 101 27
spanischer Pfeffer 57 42
~ Tritt 71 3
spanisches Rohr 136 32
Spankorb 136 11
Spann 19 61
~backe 149 36
~barren 297 3
~bügel 133 8, 9
Spanner Zool. 80 16; 82 28
~ Web. 166 54
~ Sport 293 32
Spann-gewicht 167 50
~gewichtschacht 214 40
~hebel 115 15
~klinke 110 34
~leiste 167 49
~pratze 133 10
~rad 110 35
~rahmen 183 4
~reck 296 7
~reifen 324 56
~riegel Bau 121 70
~riegel Textil 168 13
~rippe 95 21
~rolle Tischler 133 13
~rolle Spinnerei 163 46
~schacht 214 40
~schieber 255 12
~schloß Böttcher 130 4
~schloß Eisenb. 202 31
~schraube Sport 293 33
~schraube Mus. 323 53
~seilscheibe 214 43
~stock 132 31
~tuch 116 59
Spannung 242 73
Spannungs-messer 127 41
~meßgerät 242 77
~prüfer 127 55
~regler 153 31

~sucher 127 55
~wandler 153 59
Spann-vorrichtung
  Landmaschinen 64 94
~vorrichtung Heimwerker
  134 42
~vorrichtung Eisenb. 208 18
~wagen 157 12, 15
~weite Brücken 215 14
~weite Flugzeug 229 2
~wirbel 325 17
~zange 157 13
Spant 222 29, 58; 230 55; 283
  49; 285 51
Spargel 57 14
~beet 52 25
~heber 45 77
~messer 56 10
Spark 69 12
Sparkonto 250 4
Sparmannia 53 9
Sparren 121 28, 36; 122 19
~dach 121 27
~gesims 37 9
~kopf 121 45; 122 41
Sparringspartner 299 27
Spaßmacher 306 69; 307 24
Spatel 24 50; 25 7
Spaten 56 2
~, halbautomatischer 56 12
Spatienkeil 174 24
Spationierung 175 13
Spatz 361 5
Spazier-gänger 272 26
~stock 41 5
Specht 359 27
~vogel 363 6
Speck-möwe 359 14
~seite 96 2
Speedway 290 24-28
Speer 352 40
~schleuder 328 5; 352 40
~wurf 298 51-53
Speibecken 24 12
Speiche Anat. 17 13
~ Masch. 143 88
~ Fahrrad 187 27
~ Motorrad 189 24
Speichen-beuger 18 40
~nerv 18 28
~nippel 187 29
~rad 289 25
~rand 19 69
~schloß 187 49
~strecker 18 56
Speicher 225 7
~einheit 176 11; 242 9
~einrichtung 316 2
~gestein 12 29
~kompensator 165 51
~schreibmaschine 245 26
~taste 247 22
Speicherung 316 2
Speicherwurzel 370 79
Speichgriff 296 45
Speise-eis 308 31
~karte 266 21
~kelch 332 48
~morchel 381 26
Speisen-gefach 207 83
~übersicht 266 65
Speise-öl 99 66
~pilz 381
~raum 207 32, 77; 266 73
~röhre 17 49; 20 23, 40
~röhre Zool. 77 19
~saal 223 44; 267 20
~täubling 381 23
~ventil 210 20
Speisewagen 207 22-32
~küche 207 33
Speisewasser-Dampf-
  Kreislauf 154 45

~leitung 154 12, 30
~pumpe 154 13; 210 9
~vorwärmer 210 23
Speisezylinder 163 27, 52
Speispfanne 118 39
Spektrographenraum 5 33
spektrographische Kamera 5
  6
Spelt 68 24
Spelz 68 24
Spelze 68 11
Spengler 125 17
Sperber 362 12
Spergel 69 12
Sperk 69 12
Sperlingstößer 362 12
Sperlingsvogel 361
Sperreep 90 7
Sperren 291 51
Sperr-gut 206 18
~kette 99 95
Sperrung 175 13
Spezial-bohrmaschine 175 49
~facette 111 38, 40, 41
~flachwagen 213 33
~kern 301 47
~tapetenkleister 128 24
~verbrennungsgüter 199 36
~werkstatt 195 1-55
~zubehör 50 85
S-Pfanne 122 54
Sphinx 327 20
~, ägyptische 333 11
Sphygmograph 26 32
Spiegel Optik 1 65; 49 33; 111
  4; 207 49; 224 6, 7; 243 55
~ Jagd 88 20, 36, 74
~ Schiff 218 58; 284 35; 285
  49
~ Kunst 336 50
~, dreiteiliger 104 1
~block 176 21
~bogenlampe 312 39
~einrichtung 177 38
~gewölbe 336 49
~glasmanometer 349 20
~glasscheibe 179 15
~häher 361 1
~heck 221 42; 258 26; 259 11;
  284 35; 285 48
~kabinett 308 55
~karpfen 364 4
~linsenscheinwerfer 316 48
~meise 361 9
~objektiv 115 50
Spiegelreflex-kamera 114 22;
  115 1
~system 115 31
Spiegel-schrank 49 31
~system 176 24
~teleskop 113 1
~verkleidung 267 66
~wand 317 28
Spiel 88 67, 80
~anzug 29 22
~bahn 293 79-82
~ball 277 11
~bank 275 1
~bein 302 3
~brett Spiele 276 1, 22
~brett Sport 292 30
~bude 308 44
Spielemagazin 47 18
Spielerergebnis 293 35
~gruppe 48 20; 305 25
~name 293 36
Spiel-feld 291 1; 292 40-58
~filmatelier 310 26-60
~fläche 277 15
~flächenscheinwerfer 316 16
~hahn 88 66
~höschen 29 21
~karte 276 36, 37

~kasino 275 1
~leiter Roulett 275 3
~leiter Theater 316 40
~marke 275 12
~mechanik 326 6-16
~plan 275 9
~plättchen 324 20
~saal 275 1
~stand 293 38
~stein 276 18
~szene 319 1
~tisch 326 36-52
~ventil 326 10
~wart 316 30
~wiese 272 44
~zelt 307 1
Spielzeug 48 21-32
~auto 47 38; 273 62
~bagger 273 65
~ente 273 30
Spierentonne 224 79
Spierstrauch 374 23
Spießbeck 36 59
Spika 3 18
Spill Schiff 217 22; 258 23
~ Feuerwehr 270 56
Spinat 57 29
Spindel Bau 123 76, 77, 78
~ Installateur 126 32
~ Böttcher 130 19
~ Schlosser 140 4
~ Werkzeugmasch. 150 27
~ Buchb. 183 22
~antrieb 164 31
~bank 164 50
~drehzahl 150 35
~haken 164 49
~kasten 150 26
~öl 145 61
~schaft 164 46
~stock 149 2; 150 2
Spinett 322 45
Spinn-bad 169 15
~drüsenregion 358 46
~düse 169 14; 170 41, 42
Spinne 358 44-46
Spinnen-bein 115 91
~gewebe 358 47
~netz Spielplatz 273 46
~netz Zool. 358 47
~tier 358 40-47
Spinner Angelsport 89 74, 75
~ Flugzeug 230 33
Spinn-faden 162 54
~fähigmachen 170 57
~faser 169 1-34, 28-34; 170
  61
~faserballen 170 62
~kuchen 169 18, 19-27
~organ 164 51
~pumpe 169 13
~regler 164 38
~ring 164 54
~schacht 170 43
~web 358 47
~zentrifuge 169 17
Spion 41 29
Spiräe 374 23
Spiralbohrer 134 49; 140 59
Spirale 288 51; 297 50
Spiralverzahnung 143 92-93
Spirituosen 98 56-59; 318 19
Spiritusflamme 24 57
Spirograph 27 36
Spirographis 357 22
Spirometer 23 31
Spirometrie 27 36-50
Spitz-bart 34 10, 13
~bein 95 38, 42, 48
~boden 38 12
~bogen 336 31
~docke 135 8

Spitze *Kleidung* 31 32; 102 18
~ *Masch.* 143 23, 54
~ *Sport* 294 45
~ *Ballett* 314 19
~ *Vorgeschichte* 328 4
Spitzen-abschneider 85 22
~arbeit 102 30
~besatz 31 32
~blockzug 157 17
~einsatz 151 54
~grund 102 16
~haube 355 65
~ring 89 52
~schuh 314 30
~umhang 355 66
Spitz-gattheck 285 45
~glas 45 85
~gras 61 30
~hacke 158 31
~kumt 71 15
~maulnashorn 366 25
~maus 366 7
~meißel 140 25
~morchel 381 27
~pyramide 333 1
~schar 65 65
~stichel 340 5
~tonne 224 76
~- und Knebelbart 34 13
~wegerich 380 11
~winkelsitz 295 13
~winkelstütz 295 17
Spließ 122 48
~dach 122 45
Splint 143 19, 78
~holz 120 85; 370 12
~loch 143 25
Splitt *Korbmacher* 136 23
~ *Steinbruch* 158 23
Splitterfänger 172 54
Splittstreuer 200 41
Spoiler 193 34, 36; 229 39, 42
~kante 193 30
spontaner Zerfall 1 28
Sporader 72 28
Spore 381 7, 8, 13
Sporen 71 50-51
~schlauch 381 12, 13
~ständer 381 7
Spörgel 69 12
~, Gemeiner 69 12
Sporn *Pferd* 71 50-51
~ *Zool.* 73 26; 88 82
~ *Mil.* 256 23
~rad 256 27
Sport-angeln 89 20-94
~anzug 33 27
~art 305
~bericht 342 60
~boot 283 9-16; 286 1-5,
    10-14
~cabrio 193 26
~cabriolet 193 26
~coupé 193 28
~einer 283 54
~fallschirm 288 45
~fechten 294 1-33
~flugzeug 230 1-31, 32-66;
    231 1
~flugzweisitzer 288 18
~gewehr 305 40-49
~hose 291 57
~kabrio 193 26
~kabriolett 193 26
~kegeln 305 1-13
~lenker 188 45
~munition 305 34-39
~nachricht 342 61
~reporter 299 50
~säbel 294 34
~schlauchboot 278 14; 286 1
~schuh 101 35
~sitz 193 11

~sitzbank 189 14
~strumpf 291 58
~tauchen 280 41
~teil 342 57
~- und Reiseflugzeug 230
    1-31, 32-66; 231 1
~waffe 87 1-40
~wagen *Kinderwagen* 28 37
~wagen *Sport* 290 38
Spottgestalt 306 63
Sprach-labor 261 35
~rohr 283 21
Spray 24 10
~dose 106 23
~düse 50 13
Sprechanlage 245 20
Sprecher-mikrophon 238 34
~raum 238 18
~tisch 238 29
Sprechfunk-gerät 230 22
~- und Funknavigationsgerät
    230 22
~verkehr 230 29
Sprech-kopf 241 59
~membran 204 38
~muschel 237 9
~stelle 224 30
~stelle, öffentliche 237 1
~taste 242 24
~zimmer 23 1
Spreißel 157 16
Spreite 68 20; 370 28
Spreizklappe 229 49, 50
Sprenger 55 19
Spreng-gurt 71 19
~kopf 255 65
~meister 158 25
~patrone 158 27
~ring 143 34
~schärfe 91 18
~werk 215 3
Sprieß 119 59
Sprietsegel 220 5
Spring-bein 358 11
~bild 110 32-43
~brunnen 272 21
Springen 297 45; 298 9-41
Springer *Spiele* 276 11
~ *Mus.* 322 50
~matt 276 15
~rechen 322 51
Spring-form 40 27
~heuschrecke 358 8
~kraut, Großes 377 11
~lade 326 12-14
~pferd 289 9
~quelle 11 21
~reifen 307 58
~reiten 289 8-14
~sattel 289 10
~seil 273 16
~spreize 309 28
Sprinkler 55 19
Sprinter 298 5
Spritz-apparat 181 10
~behälter 83 44
~brett 186 6
~brühebehälter 83 5
~decke 283 56
Spritze 22 54
Spritzen 129 28
~, luftloses 129 36
Spritz-flasche 349 8
~kessel 129 31
~mittelbehälter 83 39
~pistole 83 18; 129 32, 37;
    181 34
~rohr *Schädlingsbek.* 83 29
~rohr *Papier* 172 72
~sieb 340 24
~ventil 172 12
~versteller 190 58
Sproß 54 17; 370 19-25; 372

    44, 46, 48, 49, 56; 376 18
Sprosse *Leiter* 38 17
~ *Jagd* 88 10
Sprossen-leiter 38 15
~wand 296 20
~zahnstange 214 9
Sprosser 361 17
Sproßvogel 361 17
Spruchband 263 12
Sprudel 98 87
~bad 281 9
Sprüh-dose 22 60
~einrichtung 83 58
~gerät 79 22
~gerät, aufgesatteltes 83 47
~nebel 83 8
~regen 9 33
~rohr 56 25
~wasserbehälter 83 57
Sprung *Jagd* 88 63
~ *Sport* 289 21; 290 32
~anlage 282 5-10
~becken 282 11
~brett 282 9; 296 12; 297 8
~erlaubnis 288 52
~fallschirm 288 37
~gelenk 72 37
~grube 298 39
~höhe 12 6
~hügel 298 36
~kasten 296 15, 16; 297 9
~kissen 298 36
~latte *Forstw.* 84 8
~latte *Sport* 298 14, 34
~lauf 301 35
~netz 307 14
~pferd 296 1, 48, 53; 297 1, 22,
    30, 31, 32
~seil 297 43
~ski 286 62; 301 38
~stab 298 28
~ständer 298 13, 33
~stiefel 301 41
~tuch *Feuerwehr* 270 18
~tuch *Sport* 297 11
~turm 282 6
~verbot 288 53, 54
~wurf 292 3
Spül-becken 23 25; 39 35; 278
    6
~bord 283 43
~bürste 50 51
~düse 216 62
Spüle 39 35; 97 68
Spulen 169 25
~antriebswagen 164 30
~arm 117 92
~aufsteckgatter 164 28
~gatter 164 41; 165 25
~halter 185 17
~hülse 166 30
~knopf 114 27
~kopf 162 55
~rahmen 165 9
~tonband 241 58
~tonbandgerät 241 56
~wäsche 170 48
Spulerei 169 25
Spül-hebel 49 17
~kasten 126 14
~kopf 145 10
~leitung 145 13
Spulmaschine 169 26
Spül-platz 39 33-36
~pumpe 145 16
~raum 207 28
~rohr 126 17
~trog 165 49
Spülung 22 54
Spül-ventil 6 25
~wanne 178 1
Spulwurm 81 31
Spund-bohle 217 6

~futter 135 6
~loch 130 7
~wand 119 17; 217 5
Spur 86 8
~anzeiger 65 81
Spürhund 70 42, 43
Spur-kranzschmierung 211 52
~messung 195 17, 22, 41
~stange 65 47
~stangenhebel 192 79
~- und Sturzmessung 195 17
Squaw 352 10
S-Rohr 323 29
Staats-bibliothek 262 11-25
~oberhaupt 253 14
~perücke 34 2
Stab 130 2
~hochspringer 298 29
~hochsprung 298 28-36
~hochsprungstab 298 28
stabile Seitenlage 21 24
Stabilisationsfläche 117 60
Stabilisator *Fotogr.* 116 10
~ *Auto* 192 71
~ *Mil.* 256 31
~ *Sport* 305 58
Stabilisierung 150 40
Stabilisierungs-flosse 234 7;
    256 22
~paneel 288 49
Stab-lampe 6 24; 127 26
~rost 163 26
~tasche 283 64
~werk 335 41
staccato 321 34
Stachel *Bot.* 60 18
~ *Zool.* 77 11; 366 6
~ *Mus.* 323 22
Stachelbeerblüte 58 6
Stachelbeere 58 9
Stachelbeer-spannerraupe 58
    5
~strauch 52 19; 58 1
~torte 97 22
~zweig 58 2
Stachel-bürste 105 16
~häuter 357 38-39; 369 3, 11,
    17, 18, 19
~nuß 379 8
~scheide 77 12
~schwein 366 13
Stadt 15 51; 268
~autobahn 225 54
~bahnbetrieb 197 13
~bibliothek,
    wissenschaftliche 262
    11-25
Städtebanner 218 22
Stadt-mauer 333 30
~plan 204 15; 268 2
~wappen 254 46
Staffelbruch 12 8
Staffelei 3 47
Stag 219 10
~segel 220 2
Stahl 154 21
~bandarmierung 153 50
~bauschlosser 140 1
~besen 324 53
Stahlbeton-bau 119 1-89
~bogen 215 50
~brücke 215 49
~decke 119 8
~platte 123 28
~rahmen 119 2
~rippendecke 123 35
~skelett 119 1
~ständer 215 61
~sturz 118 13
Stahl-bewehrung 123 37
~blechmulde 200 8
~block 147 33
~brückenring 89 58

Stahldraht-armierung 153 50
~bürste 142 18
Stahlgießpfanne 147 31
Stahlgitter-brücke 215 34
~mast 214 77
Stahl-griffel 341 21
~gummifederung 207 4
~halter 149 21
~kante 301 4, 50
~kies 148 38
~kugel 143 70
~leiter 270 10
~meßkluppe 84 21
~pfahl 217 4
~plättchen 325 1
~rad-Glasschneider 124 26
~regal 262 12
Stahlrohr 155 30
~gerüst 119 46
~mast 214 77
~stuhl 41 21
~stütze 214 78
Stahl-runge 213 6
~säge 134 17
~schiebedach 193 24
~schwelle 217 3
~spinne 5 18
~stempel 175 36
~stichel 175 33
~walze 164 10
~werk 147 21-69
~winkel 108 28
~zylinder 180 54
Stake Boot 89 30; 216 16
~ Korbmacher 136 6
Staket 52 10
Stakfähre 216 15
Stalagmit 13 81
Stalaktit 13 80
Stalaktitengewölbe 337 17
Ställchen 28 39
Stall-dünger 63 15
~knecht 186 27
~meister 307 31
~miststreuer 62 21; 63 39
~vollplatte 159 27
Stamm 84 19, 22; 370 2
~gast 266 40
Stammholz 85 41
~entrindung 85 23
~halter 157 39
~schlepper 85 34
Stammtisch 266 39
Stampf-beton 118 1
~bohle 201 2
Stampfer 349 10
Stampflehmpackung 269 39
Stand 282 40
Standardspindel 164 45
Standarte Jagd 88 47
~ Repro 177 11
~ des dt. Bundespräsidenten 253 14
Standartenverstellung 114 51
Stand-bein 302 2
~bild 272 10; 334 5
~drehwerk 65 73
Stande 89 4
Stander 90 15
Stander, dreieckiger 253 30-32
~, gezackter 253 22
~, rechteckiger 253 28
Ständer Med. 26 9
~ Jagd 88 81
~ Bau 119 47
~ Tech. 139 10; 150 10, 21; 175 50; 349 29
~ Zeichn. 151 37
~beute 77 45-50
~schlitten 353 18
Standesabzeichen 319 26
Stand-gerüst 14 50

~hahnmutternzange 126 64
~kampf 299 6
~korrektion 10 10
~leiter 118 86
Standlicht 191 20
~schalter 191 62
Standort 224 45
Standrohr Haus 37 14
~ Erdöl 145 18
~ Papier 173 12
~ Raumfahrt 234 25
~ Feuerwehr 270 26
~kupplung 67 5
Stand-seilbahn 214 12
~seilbahnwagen 214 13
~uhr 110 24; 309 56
~ventil 126 31
~versorgung 207 75
~vogel 360 4
Stange Garten 52 28
~ Jagd 88 11, 30
~ Mus. 323 14
Stangen-bohne 52 28; 57 8
~bohrer 120 65
~holz 84 12
~pferd 186 46
~zirkel 125 11
Stapel 225 42
~anlage 180 73
~anleger 180 48
~ausleger 180 55
~drucker 180 70
Stapelia 53 15
Stapel-kasten 76 30
~platz 184 12
~stein 157 37
Stapler Glas 162 20
~ Hafen 226 15
Star Segelsport 284 55
~ Film 310 27
~ Vögel 361 4
stark 321 38
Starkbier 93 26
Stärke-messer 308 11
~verstellung 100 22
Starkstromleitung Landkarte 15 113
~ Elektr. 127 23
Starkwindschicht 7 5
Starmatz 361 4
Starrachse 192 65-71
Start 286 28; 298 1-6
~anlage 209 13
~bahn 233 1; 287 15
~behälter 259 26
~block 282 27; 298 1
~boje 285 14
Starter U-Elektronik 241 30
~ Sport 282 30
~flagge 273 34
~klappe 192 6
~nummer 289 36
Start-linie 286 30; 294 3
~nummer 289 33; 290 28; 301 37; 305 84
~nummernschild 189 18
~pedal 188 25
~phase 234 66
~platz 298 3
~rampe 255 66
~schiff 285 15
~sockel 282 27
~sprung 282 29
~tonne 285 14
~- und Landebahn 233 1
~- und Zielboje 285 14
~- und Ziellinie 286 30
~- und Zieltonne 285 14
~zone 286 29
Staßfurt-Flöz 154 65
~-Steinsalz 154 66
stationäre Masse 11 43
Stationärrolle 89 32, 61

Station des Kreuzwegs 330 54
Stations-schild 205 28
~taste 241 4; 243 17; 309 20
Station wagon 193 15
Statist 310 29; 316 39
Statistik 248 36
Stativ 26 29; 112 2
~bein 114 43
~fuß 112 3
~gewindeanschluß 115 30
~scheinwerfer 310 52
Statue 272 10; 339 32
Staub-abscheider Mälzerei 92 40
~abscheider Papier 172 1
~abscheider Müllbes. 199 31
~behälter 50 86
~beutel 58 45; 59 10; 372 35
~beutelfüllanzeige 50 61
~beutelkassette 50 62
~blatt 58 45; 59 10; 370 57, 60; 372 7, 18; 373 2, 5; 374 3
~blüte 59 39
~blütenkätzchen 59 45
~blütenstand 59 39
~ecken 217 39
~fänger 147 14
~filter 270 59
~füllanzeige 50 73
~gefäß 58 45
~haube 133 20
~kammer 172 6
~kanal 163 22
~kappe 187 57, 82
~keller 163 11
~lawine 304 1
~oberfläche 6 13
~pinsel 109 18
~sack 147 14
~sammelkasten 108 45
~saugtrichter 163 10
~schutz Atom 2 48
~schutz Warenhaus 271 30
Stauch-falte 185 11
~falzmaschine 185 8
~klotz 137 16
~- u. Messerfalzmaschine 185 8
Staudamm 155 38
Staude 52 9
Stauden-beet 52 22; 55 37
~phlox 60 14
Stau-körper 217 65
~mauer 217 58
~raum 227 26; 228 27
~rohr 256 11; 257 1
~schleuse 15 69
~see 217 57
~stufe 217 65-72
Stech-apfel 379 8
~apparat 77 10-14
~beitel 132 7; 134 30; 339 19
~drehmeißel 149 53
Stecher Jagd 87 12; 88 84
~ Web. 166 43
Stech-fliege 81 4
~helm 254 4; 329 77
~kahn 283 1
~karren 206 14
~lanze 329 81
~messer 94 14
~mücke 358 16
~paddel 218 8; 283 34
~palme 374 9
~rüssel 358 17
~tartsche 329 79
~zeug 329 76
Steck-achse 65 33; 189 34
~brett 273 57
~dose 106 15; 127 13; 261 12
~feder 35 12
Steckling 54 20, 24
Steck-schriftkasten 174 4

~tafel 242 69
~verschluß 188 2
Steg Landkarte 15 78
~ Optiker 111 11
~ Bau 120 15
~ Masch. 143 4
~ Setzerei 174 8
~ Druck 181 40
~ Brücken 215 18; 272 46
~ Mus. 322 17; 323 5
~leitung 127 44
~schlaufe 286 59
stehendes Gut 219 10-19
Steher 290 14
~maschine 290 15
~rennen 290 11-15
Steh-geiger 267 45
~kessel 210 62
~kolben 350 36
~kragen 30 43
~lampe 46 37
~leiter 129 5
~platzraum 197 18
~satz 174 11
~satzregal 174 9
~schlitten 304 29
~sieb 55 13
Steig-bügel Anat. 17 61
~bügel Pferd 71 43
Steigeisen Wasservers. 269 28
~ Bergsport 300 48
~kabelbindung 300 52
~riemen 300 51
Steigeleiter 217 8
Steigertrichter 148 22
Steig-leiter 38 4
~leitung 126 7; 269 19
~rohr 145 24
~übung 270 1-46
Steigung 347 12
Steil-gewinde 149 4
~hang 13 28, 57
~kegelrefiner 172 73
~küste 13 25-31
~stufe 300 2
~wand 12 43
~wandfahrer 308 54
~wandzelt 278 36
Stein Uhr 110 33
~ Spiele 276 7
~ Vorgeschichte 328 1, 19
~ Bot. 374 12
~, facettierter 36 42-71
~absonderung 64 79
~bett 340 64
~block 339 5
~bock Astr. 3 36; 4 62
~bock Zool. 367 7
~brech, Rundblätteriger 375 1
~brechgewächs 58 1-15
~bruch 15 87; 158 1
~brucharbeiter 158 5
~brücke 15 50; 215 19
~druck 340 25-26
~druckpresse 340 60
~fangmulde 64 9
~figur 272 2
~forelle 364 15
~frucht 59 41, 43, 49; 370 99; 382 51; 384 40
~gabel 158 33
~garten 37 40; 51 6
~gartenpflanze 51 7
~kauz 362 19
~kistengrab 328 17
Steinkohle 170 1
Steinkohlen-bergwerk 144 1-51
~flöz 144 50
~gebirge 144 49
~grube 144 1-51

Steinkohletrockendestillation 170 2
Stein·kraut 61 17
~kresse 61 17
~kugel 352 32
~lerche 361 18
~marder 367 14
~mehl 158 22
Steinmetz 158 34
~werkzeug 158 35-38
Stein·mole 15 48
~obst 59 59
~obstgewächs 59 1-36
~packung Fluß 216 55
~packung Vorgeschichte 328 39
~pilz 381 16
~platte 51 17; 331 61
~salz 154 63, 64, 66; 351 2
~schärfvorrichtung 172 70
~schlaghelm 300 53
~schliff 340 45
~schraube 143 43
~schüttung 216 51
~stapel 118 40
~vase 272 35
~zaun 337 23
Steinzeitidol 328 8
Steißbein 17 5; 20 60
Stele 330 43; 334 33
Stell 253 22-34
~angel 90 29
~bogen 65 14
~bügel 65 14
Stellen·angebot 342 70
~anzeige 342 70
Stell·gewicht 202 18
~hebel 165 13
Stelling 222 18
Stell·mutter 143 35
~rad 110 23
~schmiege 120 81
~schraube 119 79; 143 107; 323 53
~stange 202 20
~wagen 186 37
~warte 316 1
~wartenzettel 316 3
Stellwerk 203 53, 61
Stelze Bau 119 67
~ Vögel 360 9
Stelzenläufer Rummelplatz 308 49
~ Vögel 359 19
Stemm·apparat 120 17
~brett 283 47
~eisen 120 71; 132 7
~tor 217 19
Stempel Bot. 59 13
~ Setzerei 175 35
~bild 236 56-60
~kissen 22 30
~maschine 236 27, 47
~schneider 175 32
Stenge 223 18
Stengel 370 20; 378 31
Stengelloser Enzian 378 13
Stenge·stag 219 11
~want 219 17
Steno·block 245 29
~grammblock 245 29; 248 32
~graphie 342 13
Steppanzug 29 38
~decke 43 8
Steppen·pferd 352 4
~schuppentier 366 10
~zone 9 54
Stepp·naht 29 39; 30 17; 31 45; 102 1
~weste 30 16
Stereo·anlage 42 9; 241 13-48; 317 22-23
~aufnahme 310 30

~box 241 13-14
~kassettendeck 241 33
~meßkammer 112 71
~mikrophoneingang 241 65
~planigraph 14 66
~ton 311 35
Stereotop 14 64
steriles Tuch 26 38
Sterilisierraum 26 34-54
Sterling 252 37
Stern, veränderlicher 3 11
~bild 3 9-48
~blume 60 4
Sternchen 185 61
Sterndolde 376 7
Sternenbanner 253 18
Stern·gewölbe 336 44
~haufen 3 26
~himmel, südlicher 3 36-48
~karte 3 1-35
~namen 3 9-48
~prägung 187 54
~punkt 153 22
~rad 340 39
~schaltung 153 20
~schnuppe 7 25
~warte 5 1-16
Stert Fischerei 90 22, 23
~ Mühle 91 32
Sterz 65 3
Stethoskop 23 35
Stetigschleifer 172 53, 66
Stetson 319 37
~hut 319 37
Steuer 283 51-53
~aggregat 178 29
~antrieb 154 23
~banderole 107 26
~blatt 283 53
Steuerbord 224 85
~laterne 286 11
~licht 286 11
~saling 286 9
~-Seitenlampe 223 15
~stange 224 99
~tonne 224 96
Steuereinheit 242 2
~element 153 6; 259 69
~feder 305 62
~feld 311 8, 29
Steuergerät Med. 26 7
~ Optiker 111 29
~ Schmied 138 31
~ Schiff 224 26
Steuer·griff 230 24
~haus 223 18; 224 14-38
~hebel 201 8; 316 58
~joch 283 51
~knüppel 230 24; 257 8; 288 14
~kopf 141 37
~kopfrohr 187 14
~leine 283 52; 288 41
~mann 218 2; 283 11; 303 20
~marke 107 26
Steuern 218 6
Steuer·pult 93 1; 146 28; 154 80; 182 28; 316 2
~rad Auto 191 37
~rad Eisenb. 210 56
~rad Schiff 224 15
~raketengruppe 234 63
~raketensatz 6 5
~rohr 187 14
~satz 177 51
~schalter Kraftwerk 153 2
~schalter Schiff 224 23
~schlitz 288 46
~schraube 232 14; 256 20
~seil 271 53
~sitz 283 27
~stab 154 24

~stand 147 66
~strich 224 48
~teil 153 1
~- und Kontrollfeld 311 8
~- und Kontrollgeräte 224 26
~- und Regelteil 153 1
Steuerung Kraftwerk 153 4, 5
~ Eisenb. 210 18
~ Fahrstuhl 271 48
~ Segelsport 284 6
~, digitale 242 35
Steuerventil 153 52
Steven 221 14, 108; 258 3; 285 40
~ruder 218 24
Stewart 221 110
Steyrer Klee 69 1
Stichbalken 120 42
Stichel 175 33
Stich·leitung 192 22
~loch 80 12
~säge 126 70; 132 3
Stickel 78 7
Stickerei 29 29; 30 42
~saum 355 67
Stickstoff·dünger 63 14
~oxydul 26 3
~tetroxidtank 234 59
Stiefel Schuhmacher 100 57
~ Mus. 326 17
~hose 30 44; 289 5
~kappe 101 16
Stiefmütterchen 60 2
Stieglitz 360 1
Stiel Besteck 45 59, 62
~ Bot. 58 34, 61; 370 27; 381 18
~ Forstw. 85 3
~ Bau 120 25; 121 40
~ Schmied 137 30
~ Flugzeug 229 11
~auge 357 30
~kasserolle 40 16
~stich 102 4
Stier Astr. 3 25; 4 54
~ Zool. 73 1
~ Heraldik 254 15
~ Stierkampf 319 11, 12
~attrappe 319 3
~kampf 319 1-33, 24
~kamparena 319 5
~kämpfer 319 10
~kämpferhut 319 29
~kapitell 333 28
~leib 327 48
~säule 333 23
~stall 319 14
Stift Med. 24 34
~ Glaser 124 29
~draht 124 28
Stiften·klöbchen 109 16
~kopf 34 11
~zieher 100 47
Stift·hammer 124 18
~schlitz 143 49
~schraube 143 22
~zahn 24 31
Stilart 282 33-39
Stilleben 182 1
Stillengürtel 9 47
Stiller Ozean 14 19
Stillstand 207 24
Stilspringen 288 50-51
Stilus 341 25
Stimm·berechtigte 263 24
~berechtigter 263 24
Stimmer 322 11
Stimmgabel·element 110 9
~prinzip 110 6
~uhr 110 6
Stimm·hammer 325 20
~keil 325 21
~krücke 326 21

~lappen 326 30
~nagel 324 23; 325 17
~recht 263 24
s-rolle 326 30
~schlitz 326 33
~schlüssel 325 20
~schraube 323 59
~stock 324 22; 325 18
~vorrichtung 326 30
~wirbel 325 17
~zettel 263 20
Stinkvogel 359 25
Stirn Anat. 16 4-5
~ Pferd 72 3
~ Kunst 336 24
~auge 77 2
~bein 17 30
~höcker 16 4
~höhle 17 55
~lampe 300 54
~muskel 19 4
~riemen 71 9
~schlagader 18 5
~toupet 355 8
~vene 18 6
~wand Straßenbau 200 10
~wand Eisenb. 213 10
~wandschiebetür 207 19
~wulst 16 5
Stock Med. 21 23
~ Forstw. 84 14
~ Korbmacher 136 15
~anker 222 79; 286 15
Stöckelabsatz 101 28
Stock·geige 322 20
~griff 301 6
~presse 183 20
~schirm 205 12
~schwämmchen 381 33
~teller 301 8
~tomate 55 44
Stockwerk·anzeiger 271 49
~pagode 337 1
~podium 316 34
Stoff 168 33
~, nichtschrumpfender 168 49
~abteilung 271 58
~aufbereitungsanlage 172 79-86
~auflauf 173 11
~bahn 104 2
~ballen 271 59
~bürste 104 31
~eingabe 236 31
~elefant 47 6
~hund 47 7
~lager 271 58
~pumps 101 54
~rest 103 16
~rutsche 168 47
~tier 46 13
~wasserpumpe 172 55
~zuführungsstrecke 236 33
Stola 355 9
Stollen 42 2; 46 4; 97 11
~anbauwand 42 1
STOL-Transportflugzeug 256 24
STOL-Verbindungsflugzeug 256 24
Stop, wichtige Mitteilung 253 25
Stopfbuchse 210 33
Stopfbüchse Erdöl 145 26
~ Schiff 223 64
Stopfen 67 36
~stange 148 10
~verschluß 147 31
Stopfer 107 47
Stoppel 34 23
~acker 63 33
~bart 34 23

~feld 63 33
Stopp-härtebad 116 10
~taste 249 73
~uhr 238 62
~uhr, elektronische 238 31
~zylinderpresse 181 20
Stoptaste 243 43
Storch-schnabel *Geogr.* 14 65
~schnabel *Bot.* 53 1; 376 24
~schnepfe 359 19
~vogel 359 18
Store 42 35
Störklappe 229 39, 42; 287 38
Störung, zusammengesetzte 12 8-11
Stoß *Vögel* 88 67, 75, 80; 362 8
~ *Bau* 122 94
~ *Tapezierer* 128 20
~ *Sport* 294 7; 299 28
~axt 120 72
~ball 277 12
~besen 38 35
~dämpfer 191 26; 192 69, 76; 207 4
Stößel 24 48
Stoßen 299 4
Stößer 325 30
Stoß-harpune 353 9
~kragen 329 44
~lade 124 31
~ofen 148 69
~schlitten 304 29
~stange 191 13
~stange, integrierte 193 33
~strahl 11 35
~waffe 294 11, 34, 36, 37
~zahn 366 22
~zunge 325 30
Stout 93 26
Straf-raum 291 4
~stoß 291 4
~stoßmarke 291 6
Strahl 346 20
~blüte 375 31
Strahlen-bündel 346 19
~erzeugungssystem 113 31
~flugzeug 231 7-33
~gang 5 3
~kranz 332 37
Strahlenschutz-kopf 2 31
~mauer 154 74
~meßgerät 2 1
Strahlen-teiler 240 35
~teilungsprisma 240 35
~tierchen 357 8
Strähler 135 14
Strahl-kopf 113 31
~pumpe 210 41
~rohr *Schädlingsbek.* 83 22
~rohr *Feuerwehr* 270 33
~trainer 257 1-41
~turbine 231 26; 232 33-50
Strahlungs-eintritt 1 64
~kessel 152 5
~meßgerät 2 1-23
~schutzrohr 10 36
Strahlverstellung 83 19
Strähnenbürste 105 2
Straight 305 17
~-Ball 305 17
Strampel-anzug 29 23
~höschen 29 11
~hose 28 24
Strand 11 54; 13 35-44
~anzug 33 24; 280 19
~bad 280
~burg 280 35
~ebene 13 35-44
~geröll 13 29
~hafer 15 7
~hose 280 22
~hut 280 20
~jacke 280 21

~kanal 13 34
~kleidung 280 19-23
~korb 280 36
~reiter 359 19
~schuh 280 23
~see 13 44
~tasche 280 24
~terrasse 11 54
~wall 13 35
~wärter 280 34
~weizen 61 30
~zelt 280 45
~zone 281 2
Strang 71 22, 35
~guß 148 24-29
~presse 159 11; 161 7
Straps 318 28
Straße 37 61; 200 55; 215 59
Straßenaufreißer 200 20
Straßenbahn 197
~betrieb 197 13
~fahrplan 268 27
~haltestelle 268 25
~schienen 268 23
~zug 268 46
Straßen-bau 200; 201
~baumaschine 200 1-54; 201 1
~beleuchtung 268 49
~besen 199 6; 268 21
~brücke 15 55
~café 268 59
~decke 217 1
~ecke 198 12
~fahrer 290 8
~hobel 200 19
~kehrer 199 5; 268 20
~kehrmaschine 199 39
~kehrwagen 199 9
~lampe 37 62; 268 6
~laterne 37 62; 268 6
~leuchte 37 62; 268 6
~name 268 7
~querschnitt 198
~reinigung 199
~reinigungswagen 304 8
~rennen 290 8-10, 16, 24-28
~schild 268 7
~schmutz 268 22
~transport 85 42
~überfahrt 15 40
~überführung 268 48
~walze 200 36
Straße I. Ordnung 15 83
~ II. Ordnung 15 36
~ III. Ordnung 15 30
~ von Gibraltar 14 24
Strato-cumulus 8 3
~kumulus 8 3
~sphäre 7 8
~sphärenflugzeug 7 15
~vulkan 11 15
Stratus 8 4
Strauß 359 2
Straußen-feder 254 30
~gelege 359 3
Straußvogel 359 1-3
Streb 144 33-37
Strebe 120 27, 54; 121 58, 69, 82
~bogen 335 28
~pfeiler 335 27
~werk 335 27-28
Strecke *Jagd* 86 38
~ *Spinnerei* 164 1
~ *Math.* 346 16
Strecken 164 12; 170 55
~band 164 21
~block 203 59
~diesellokomotive 212 1
~kanne 164 20
~markierung 289 19
~meßgerät 112 70

~netzplan 204 33
~vortriebsmaschine 144 32
~wärter 202 44
Strecker-schicht 118 64
~verband 118 60
Streck-hang 296 33, 34
~sitz 295 10
~sprung 295 35
~stütz 296 38
~teich 89 6
~walze 164 13
~werk 163 60; 164 21, 29
~werkabdeckung 164 7
~zwirnerei 170 46
Streich-anlage 173 31, 34
~balken 120 40
~baum 166 37
~blech 65 4, 64
~bürste 129 3
~dalbe 222 35
Streichen 12 2
Streichholz 107 22
~schachtel 107 21
~ständer 266 24
Streich-instrument 323 1-27
~rad 322 26
~stange 118 26
Streifen-beamter 264 13
~beleimung 185 31
~hyäne 368 1
~wagen 264 10
Streifstange 165 38
Streit-axt 328 19; 352 16
~kräfte 255; 256; 257
Stretch-bund 31 43
~gürtel 31 63
Streu-aggregat 62 22
~klappe 200 42
~scheibe 310 38
~schutz 148 40
Streusel-gebäck 97 35
~kuchen 97 43
Streuwalze 62 23
Strich-ätzung 178 42
~liste 151 32
~punkt 342 19
~stärkenkennzeichnung 151 40
Strickbund 29 65; 31 70
Strickerei 167
Strick-hemd 33 36
~jacke 31 50; 33 30
~kleid 30 33
~kleidchen 29 28
~kragen 33 31
~leiter 221 91; 273 49; 307 8
~muster 101 43
~mütze 35 10
~vorgang 167 51
Striegel 71 54
Stringer *Schiff* 222 50
~ *Flugzeug* 230 47, 57
Stripmakulatur 128 5
Stripperin 318 27
Stripperkran 148 47
Striptease 318 27-32
~tänzerin 318 27
Stripteuse 318 27
Stroh 136 30
~ballen 63 34; 75 7; 206 23
~ballenpresse 63 35
~fiedel 324 61
~hut 35 35
~matte 55 6
~preßballen 63 34
~schwad 63 36
~zuführung 64 13
Strom 242 73; 326 47
~, niederfrequenter 23 37
~, schiffbarer 15 45
Stromabnehmer *Auto* 194 41
~ *Straßenbahn* 197 2
~ *Eisenb.* 207 24, 75; 211 2, 30

~bügel 205 36
Strom-aggregat 231 33
~anschluß 261 12
~fähre 216 10
~insel 216 4
~kabel 56 32; 198 19
~leiter 153 43
~messer 127 41
~meßgerät 242 77
~pfeiler 215 21, 54
~schiene 152 29
~schlauch 216 9
~spannung 326 38
~strich 216 9
~- und Spannungsmeßgerät 242 77
Strömung 216 9
Strömungs-verlauf 216 9
~weiser 216 43
Strom-versorgung 115 79
~versorgungskabel 198 14
~wandler 153 58
~zufuhr 155 21
~zuführung 142 25
Strumpf 167 21; 318 32
~fabrik 167 1-66
~fach 99 25
~halter 32 6
~hose 29 42; 32 12; 355 47
~packung 99 26
~warenabteilung 271 17
~wirker 361 8
Stubben 84 14
Stubenfliege, Gemeine 81 2
~, Große 81 2
~, Kleine 81 1
Stubenwagen 28 30
~garnitur 28 31
Stück *Textilw.* 168 51
~ *Roulett* 275 12
~, dickes 95 50
Stückgut 206 4, 27; 226 11
~frachter 225 14; 226 13
~-Lkw 206 15
~schuppen 225 9
~unternehmer 206 28
~waage 206 31
~wagen 206 6
Student 262 9
Studenten-blume 60 4, 20
~nelke 60 6
Studentin 262 10
Studio 338 1-43
~wand 46 1
Stufe *Haus* 38 27
~ *Haushalt* 50 38
~ *Bergsport* 300 17
Stufen-barren 297 3, 28, 29
~boot 286 38-41
~dach 337 2
~graukeil 343 15
~käfig 74 20
stufenlose Einstellung 127 17
Stufen-pyramide 333 22; 352 20
~rad 143 82
~trenn-Retrorakete 234 8, 37
~turm 333 32
Stuhl 42 34
~schlitten 304 29
Stulpenstiefel 355 58
Stülper 77 52
Stülpkorb 77 52
Stummer Schwan 359 16
Stumpen 35 2; 107 4
Stumpftonne 224 77
Stunden-achse 5 8; 113 15, 18
~achsenantrieb 5 7
~glaszeichen 224 78
~knopf 110 3
~- und Minutenknopf 110 3
Stupa 337 21, 28
Stupf-bürste 129 18

~farbe 129 53
~pinsel 129 54
Sturmball 225 35; 280 4
Stürmer 282 50
Sturm-haube 329 60
~hut 379 1
Sturzbügel 188 18
Stürze 323 37
Sturz-flugbremse 287 38
~hang 296 36, 37
~helm 289 18; 290 3; 303 14
~messung 195 17, 21, 41
Stürzner 125 17
Sturzriegel 120 57
Stute 73 2
Stütz 296 28, 29
Stutzbart 34 16
Stützbock 67 7
Stütze 164 42
Stutzen 86 30
Stützen-fundament 214 81
~galgen 214 80
~schalung 119 11, 73
~schuh 214 79
Stutzer 306 33
Stutzflügel 325 40
Stütz-konstruktion 146 38
~lager 91 10
Stutzperücke 34 2
Stütz-punkt 300 1
~rad 65 59
~rolle 270 50
~schaufel 255 94
~schenkel 50 37
~stange 307 13
~verband 21 10
~weite 215 14
Stylobat 334 32
Subkontraoktave 321 42
Substanzbehälter 350 61
Subsubkiller 259 54
Subtrahend 344 24
Subtrahieren 344 24
Subtraktion 344 24
subtraktive Farbmischung 343 12
subtropischer Stillengürtel 9 47
Subvulkan 11 20
Sucher 114 14
~ausblick 114 2
~bild 115 51
~einblick 115 22
~fuß 114 71
~lichtschacht 115 68
~objektiv 114 25
~okular 115 22; 313 6
~schacht 114 23
Such-feder 127 30
~jagd 86 1-8
Süd-amerika 14 13
~äquatorialstrom 14 34
~früchte 384
Sudhaus 92 42-53
südlicher Sternhimmel 3 36-48
Südliches Dreieck 3 40
~ Eismeer 14 22
~ Kreuz 3 44
Süd-ostpassat 9 49
~pol 14 3
Sudprozeß 92 42-53
Süd-punkt 4 17
~weinglas 45 84
~wester 35 30; 228 5
Sulfat-behälter 172 36
~zellstoffabrik 172 1-52
Sulfidierung 169 9
Sulky 289 24
Süllrand 283 59
Sultanine 98 8
Sumatra 107 2
Summand 344 23

Summe 271 8; 344 23
Summer 127 15
Sumpf-heide 377 19
~pflanze 378 14-57
~porst 377 21
~weihe 362 13
Sundbrücke 215 57
Super-benzin 145 55; 196 1
~brandung 279 4
~het 309 16
~heterodynempfänger 309 16
~-8-Kompaktkamera 117 51
~markt 99 1-96
~-8-Tonfilmkamera 117 1
~-8-Tonfilmkassette 117 29
~-V-Rennsportwagen 290 37
Suppen-einlage 68 25
~huhn 99 60
~kelle 45 14
~löffel 45 61
~nudeln 99 65
~schöpflöffel 45 14
~schüssel 45 15
~teller 44 6; 45 5
~terrine 44 8
~würfel 98 26
~würze 98 30
Supplementwinkel 346 14
Supraporte 336 12
Surf-board 279 1, 2
~brett 279 1, 2; 280 15; 284 5
~brettfahren 280 13
Surfer 279 5; 280 14
Surfing 279 1-6
Sur le cou-de-pied 314 14
Süß-kirsche 59 5
~klee 69 10
~rahmbutterungsanlage 76 33
~waren 98 75-86
symbolische Gestalt 327 20
Symmetrie-achse 346 25; 351 4
~ebene 351 5
~zentrum 351 3
Synchrongetriebe 192 28-47
Synchronisation 311 37-41
Synchronisiereinrichtung 153 32
Synchronisierungsatelier 311 37
Synchron-kabel 313 29
~kamera 310 19
~kegel 192 33
~klappe 310 35
~kopf 243 34
~motor 176 19
~regisseur 311 38
~sprecherin 311 39
~spur 243 33
~start 117 65
~startmarkierung 117 69
~steuergerät 117 77
~studio 238 28
~zeitschaltuhr 24 52
Synklinale 12 18
synthetischer Rubin 110 33
Syrinx 322 2
System, optisches 243 50
~kamera 115 1-105
~residenz-Plattenspeicher 176 32
~überwachung 234 17
~zubehör 115 43-105
Szene 316 36
Szenenwiederholung 243 42

T

Tabak 107 25; 382 43
~asche 266 5
~blatt 382 43

~fabrik 83 11
~käfer 81 25
~pflanze 382 40
Tabaksbeutel 107 43
Tabakwaren 107
~kiosk 204 47
Tabernakel 330 42
Tableau 275 9
Tablett 42 30; 44 24; 265 14; 266 19, 63
~ablage 266 64
~stapel 266 45
Tabulator-löschtaste 249 8
~taste 249 7
Tacho 188 19, 34; 191 38
~graph 210 54
Tachometer 181 54; 188 19, 34, 40; 189 40; 191 38, 74
~antrieb 192 38, 39
Tafel 48 16; 260 29; 280 8; 310 35
~, achteckige flache 36 74
~, antike gemugelte 36 76
~, flache 36 46
~, gemugelte 36 47
~, ovale flache 36 72
~, rechteckige flache 36 73
~, rechteckige gemugelte 36 77
~berg 13 59
~glasherstellung 162 1-20
~klavier 325 40
~leuchter 45 16
~öl 98 24
~schere 125 26
~schmuck 45 19
~schwamm 260 42
~tuch 45 2
~wasser 98 87
~zeichnung 260 33
~zirkel 260 40
~zubehör 45
Tagebau 158 1
Tages-creme 99 27
~decke 43 7
~karte 266 21
~kasse 271 2
~kilometerzähler 191 74, 77
Tageslicht-einspuldose 116 5
~filmkassette 311 7
~kassette 117 50
Tages-raum 74 11
~stempelabdruck 236 57
~zeichen 203 36
~zeitung 342 37-70
Tagetes 60 20
Tag-falter 365 1-6
~pfauenauge 365 2
~raubvogel 362 1-13
~undnachtgleiche 3 6-7
Taifunrad 308 46
Taille 16 31
~, geschnürte 355 53
Takelung 219 1-72
Takt 320 28-42
~art 320 28-42
~geber 25 33
~messer 325 19
~stock 315 27
~strich 320 42
Talar 332 4
Tal-aue 13 60
~formen 13 52-56
~gletscher 12 49
~grund 13 67
Talje 221 27, 104
Taljenläufer 221 106
Tal-landschaft 13 57-70
~lehne 13 65
Talon 251 19
Tal-sohle 13 67; 215 60
~sperre 217 57-64
~station 214 39

~stationsbahnsteig 214 51
~tempel 333 8
Tambour Spinnerei 163 43
~ Papier 173 35
~ Kunst 335 44
~rost 163 55
Tamburin 317 27; 324 30, 45
Tampon 340 22
Tamul 341 11
tamulisch 341 11
Tandem 186 50
~anordnung 232 22
Tangente Mus. 322 43
~ Math. 346 48
Tank 76 16; 146 18; 194 30; 230 16, 17
~auflieger 194 30-33
~bodenventil 38 49
~bodenwachs 145 60
~decke 222 54
~entlüftung 234 44
Tanker 225 73
Tank-füllung 64 27
~lager 225 61
~löschfahrzeug 270 51
~löschwagen 270 51
~randplatte 222 51
~säule 196 1
~schiff 145 35
~stelle 196 1-29
~wagen 233 22
~zug 194 28
~zwischenstück 234 16
Tannen-klee 69 6
~nadel 372 11
~pfeil 82 27
~zapfen 372 2
Tanzen 267 46
Tänzer 317 18
Tänzerin 317 17
~, indische 306 25
Tanz-fläche 317 16
~flächenbeleuchtung 317 14
~orchester 306 2
~paar 267 46; 317 17-18
~platz 334 47
~schmuck 354 36
~stock 354 37
~trommel 354 14
Tapete 128 18
Tapeten-ablösegerät 128 9
~ablöser 128 1
~andrückwalze 128 47
~bahn 128 19
~kleister 128 23
~leiste 128 29
~naht 128 20
~perforator 128 12
~schaber 128 15
~schutzlack 128 32
~wechselgrund 128 4
Tapezierbürste 128 40
Tapezieren 128 18-53
Tapezierer 128
~leiter 128 52
Tapezier-geräteleister 128 26
~kasten 128 33
~schere 128 34
~schiene 128 39
~tisch 128 31
~wischer 128 49
Tapir 366 26
Tartar-Flugkörper 258 49
Täschchenform 61 11
Tasche 218 57
~, angeschnittene 29 63; 31 4
~, aufgesetzte 29 68; 30 22; 31 56
Täschelkraut 61 9
Taschen-dieb 308 16
~diktiergerät 246 32
~dosimeter 2 15
~fahrplan 204 42; 205 45

~geige 322 20
~klappe 33 18
~klemme 2 18
~lampe 127 26
~lampenbatterie 127 27
~rechner 246 12; 247 14
~säge 127 52
~schirm 41 12
Tassel 355 23
Tasso 125 23
Tastatur 174 37; 176 2; 236
44; 238 14; 249 2-6; 325
4-5
Taste *A V* 243 42
~ *Mus.* 325 4, 5; 326 8, 40
Tasten-feld 237 70; 242 11
~hebel 322 38, 49
~instrument 325 1
~mechanik 325 22-39
Taster *Setzerei* 174 32; 176 4
~ *Straßenbahn* 197 32
~gerät 176 1
~stützrad 64 88
Tast-fühler 166 32
~fühlerkontakt 166 31
~rad 64 86
~zirkel 135 18; 339 3
tätiger Vulkan 11 15
Tätowierung 306 44
Tatze *Motorboot* 286 44
~ *Zool.* 368 4
Tatzelwurm 327 1
Taube 73 33; 359 23
Taube Kamille 61 8
Tauben-skabiose 375 29
~wurfanlage 305 74
Täuberich 73 33
Taubgerste 61 28
Tauchbrille 280 38
Tauchen 279 7-27; 282 38;
359 11
Taucher 279 7
~ausrüstung 279 8-22
~maske 279 10
~messer 279 8
~uhr 279 16
Tauch-flosse 280 41
~gerät 279 19
~huhn, Dummes 359 13
~maske 279 10
~sieder 40 17
~walze 165 45
~zeitüberwachung 279 16
Taufbecken 332 11
Taufe 332 1
Tauf-kapelle 332 2
~kleid 332 8
Täufling 332 7
Tauf-schleier 332 9
~stein 332 10
~wasser 332 12
Taukreuz 332 59
Taumelzellenwalze 64 75
Taurus 3 25; 4 54
Tausenderstelle 344 3
Tausend-güldenkraut 380 10
~schön 60 21
Tausendstel 344 20
Tauwurm 357 24
Taxe 268 64
Taxen-stand 268 63, 66
~telefon 268 67
Taxi 233 32; 268 64
~schild 268 65
~stand 268 63
~way 233 2
Tazette 60 4
technische Daten 151 32
technisches Laboratorium
310 9
technische Zeichnung 151 16
Teckel 70 39
Teclu-Brenner 350 4

TED-Bildplattensystem 243
37-45
Teddy-bär 28 46; 273 26; 309
12
~jäckchen 29 44
Tee 382 9
~beutel 98 68
~blatt 382 9
Teenagerkleidung 29 48-68
Teer-destillation 170 4
~gewinnung 170 3
~kessel 200 47
~kocher 200 46
~spritzmaschine 200 46
~- und Bitumenkocher 200
46
~- und Phenolgewinnung 170
3
Tee-schachtel 99 69
~strauch 382 7
~stube 265 1-26
TEE-Zug 205 34; 209 1-22
Teich *Landkarte* 15 79
~ *Park* 272 50
~karpfen 364 4
~mönch 89 9
Teig-teilmaschine 97 56, 63
~teil- und
Rundwirkmaschine 97 63
~waren 98 32-34
Teil, nichtdruckender 178 43
~, politischer 342 51
~, tiefgeätzter 178 43
~, überregionaler 342 62
~baum 167 25
~blütenkorb 378 12
Teilchen, ionisierende 1 58
Teilen 344 26
Teiler 344 26
Teil-flach 351 24
~kreis 113 27; 351 32
~scheibe *Zeichn.* 151 51
~scheibe *Textilw.* 167 26
~schiene 166 38
Teilungszahl 344 26
Teilwert 344 26
T-Eisen 143 3
tektonisches Beben 11 32-38
Telefon 22 18; 41 7; 224 28;
237; 246 13; 248 9
~anrufaufzeichner,
automatischer 22 13
~anrufbeantworter,
automatischer 22 13
~anrufbeantworter und -
aufzeichner 22 13
~apparat 237 6-26
~benutzer 237 2
~bildschirm 242 26
~block 22 21
~buch 237 5
~buchse 249 67
~gehäuse 237 15
~hausanschlußleitung 198 20
~maschinen 237 1
~hörer 237 7; 246 16
~kabel 198 15
~kabine 236 8
~teilnehmer 237 2
~zelle 204 46; 236 8; 237 1;
251 10; 268 56
~zentrale 245 13
Tele-gabel 188 8, 41
~graf 237 31
~grafenapparat 237 31
~grafie 237 30
~kopie 245 2
~kopiersystem 245 1
~metreantenne 10 70
~objektiv 115 48; 117 47
Teleskop 235 68
~federgabel 189 23
~gabel 188 8

~rohr 65 77
~rute 89 53
Television-Disc-
Bildplattensystem 243
37-45
Telexanschluß 237 65
Teller *Haushalt* 45 6
~ *Eisenb.* 207 84
~, flacher 44 7; 45 4
~, tiefer 44 6; 45 5
~bürste 199 40
~fuß 105 27
~gericht 266 17
~rad 143 93
~schleifpapier 134 25
~stapel 266 11
Tempel 337 7
~, dorischer 334 1
~, etruskischer 334 49
~anlage 337 25
~mauer 334 6
~ritter 329 73
~turm 333 32; 337 1, 26
Temperafarbe 338 17
Temperatur 9 40
~angabe 9 8
~dosierung 191 84
~geber 190 50
~linie 7 37
~skala 7 36
~wähler 50 8
Tempest 284 54
Tender 258 92
~brücke 210 2
~lok 210 65
Tenne 92 8
Tennis 293 1-42
~ball 293 28
~netz 293 13
~platz 293 1
~schläger 41 13; 293 29
~schuh 101 36
~spiel 293 1-42
~spieler 293 16
Tenor-horn 323 39
~oboe 323 38
~posaune 323 46
~schlüssel 320 11
Tentakel 357 16
tenuto 321 30
Teppich-boden 41 18; 43 23
~bürste 50 45
~kehrer 50 57
~klopfvorsatz 50 79
~schamponiervorsatz 50 79
~stange 37 51
Terminal 233 15
Termin-kalender 246 8
~plantafel 151 12
~uhr 110 19
Terpentinabscheider 172 14
Terra-Aquarium 356 14
Terrasse 37 36
Terrassencafé 272 57
Terrier, Schottischer 70 17
Terrine 45 15
Tertia 175 30
Tertiärkreislauf 154 10
Terz, große 321 8
~bindung 294 48
~deckung 294 8
Terzel 86 46
Terzparade 294 8
Tetradrachme 252 1
Tetraeder 351 1
Teufel 306 14
Teufels-kirsche 379 7
~scheibe 308 46
Text 175 31
Textildrucker 168 65
textile Bindung 171
textilfreie Lebensart 281 16

Textilgeschäft 268 9
Textilglas 162 48-55
~-Elementarfaden 162 52
~garn 162 56
~garn, gefachtes 162 57
~matte 162 58
~produkt 162 56-58
Textilien 168
Textiltapete 128 18
Textplattenspeicher 176 33
Thallom 378 49
Thallus 378 49
Thaumatolampas diadema
369 4
Theater 315; 316; 334 44
~, griechisches 334 44
~besucher 315 8
~billett 315 11
~chor 315 21
~friseur 315 48
~karte 315 11
~kartenverkaufsstelle 271 26
~kostüm 315 51
~maschine 312 24
~platz 315 20
~probe 315 21-27
~raum 315 14-27
~- und
Konzertkartenverkaufsstelle
271 26
~vorhang 316 23
~werkstatt 315 28-42
Theatron 334 44
Theke 266 1-11; 267 54; 317
9
Theodolit 14 52-62
Theorbe 324 1
Thermik-schlauch 287 21
~segeln 287 20
thermischer Aufwind 287 21
Thermo-bindung 249 61
~bürste 106 30
~graph 10 19, 51
~kauter 24 43
thermokonstantes Wasserbad
23 48
Thermometer 10 25, 34, 35;
28 29; 168 27; 281 24
~hütte 10 49
Thermoplast 130 15
thermoplastischer Kunststoff
127 29
Thermoschalter 190 63
Thermostatentwicklungsschale
116 56
Thomas-birne 147 55-69
~konverter 147 55-69
Thorax 358 29-30
Thymele 334 48
Tiara 254 37
Tibeter 353 27
tibetisch 341 12
Tief 9 5
~decker 229 5, 14; 231 1
Tiefdruck 182
~ätzer 182 18
~gebiet 9 5
~verfahren 340 14-24
~walze 182 10, 17
~zylinder 182 22
Tiefen-abstimmung 241 43
~einstellung 65 60; 157 45
~gestein 11 29
~lehre 140 54; 149 72
~linie 15 11
~magnetismus 11 29-31
~messer 279 15
~meßfühler 149 68
~meßschieber 140 54; 149 72
~ruder 259 95, 96
~sickerungsanlage 200 61
~skala 224 66
~- und Seitenruder 259 95

~verstellung 133 21
tiefer Teller 44 6; 45 5
Tiefgangsmarke 222 73
tiefgeätzter Teil 178 43
Tiefgefrierschrank 39 7
tiefgefrorenes Fertiggericht
   96 23
Tiefhalte 295 47
Tiefkühl-box 99 57
~truhe 96 21; 98 74
Tieflöffel 118 82
Tiefofen 148 46
~kran 148 47
Tief-pumpe 145 23
~schlag 299 34
Tiefsee-fauna 369
~graben 11 12
~kabel 237 56
~meduse 369 5
~tafel 11 10
Tief-start 298 4
~stoß 277 4
~töner 241 17
~wasserstart 286 46
Tiegel 340 31
~druckpresse 181 13, 29; 340
   29
~zange 108 11; 350 32
Tier 88 1; 356 5
~, mythologisches 327 1-61
~, wirbelloses 357
~bändiger 307 52
~gehege 272 49
~haus 356 10
~kreiszeichen 4 53-64
~lehrer 307 52
~nahrung 99 36-37
~schau 307 63
~transport 221 69
Tiger 307 56; 368 5
Tilbury 186 44
Tilde 342 35
Timbale 324 57
Tinktur 25 24-29
Tinten-beere 379 7
~faß 309 78
~fisch 357 37; 369 4
Tipi 352 7
Tippfehlerkorrektur-blatt 247
   12
~flüssigkeit 247 13
Tiptank 231 9; 256 30
Tisch 21 31; 273 2; 336 14, 16
~aufstellung 260 1
~bein 44 2
~belag 141 16
~bohrwerk 150 25
~dame 267 43
~einsatzplatten 115 95
~exhauster 108 43
~farbwerk 181 8
~gesellschaft 267 40-43
~herr 267 42
~höhenverstellung 133 22, 23
~kalender 247 32
~karte 45 13
~kasse 275 11
~konsole 133 24
~lampe 46 24; 246 35
~läufer 46 35
Tischler 132 38; 133
Tischlerei 132 1-73
Tischler-leim 132 13
~platte 132 73
~werkstatt 132 1-73
~werkzeug 132 1-28
~winkel 132 6
Tisch-leuchte 246 35
~leuchter 45 16
~nachbar 267 41
~platte 44 3; 139 20
~säule 26 6
~schmuck 266 78

~sockel 112 15
~stativ 115 99
~staubsauger 108 43
Tischtennis 293 45-55
~ball 273 5; 293 48
~netz 273 3; 293 53
~schläger 273 4; 293 45
~spiel 273 1; 293 45-55
~spieler 293 49
~tisch 293 52
Tisch-vorschubantrieb 150 34
~walze 132 46
~wäsche 271 57
~wurstfüller 96 49
Titan 327 37
Titelblatt 185 45
Titelei 185 43-47
Titel-kampf 299 35-50
~seite 185 45
Tjalk 220 6
T-Lage 288 62
T-Leitwerk 229 29; 256
   31-32; 287 10
Toast Brot 45 34
~ Trinkspruch 267 40
Toaster 40 30
Tochter-boot 228 17
~kompaß 224 31, 52
Todes-anzeige 342 68
~fahrer 308 54
~spirale 302 5
Töffel 101 47
Toga 355 13
Toilette 49 12; 126 14; 146 29;
   211 59; 231 31; 268 62; 278
   5; 317 31
Toiletten-papier 49 11
~papierhalter 49 10
~wagen 233 22
~wasser 105 37; 106 9
Tollkirsche 379 7
Tölpel 359 9
Tomahawk 352 16
Tomate 57 12; 99 82
Tomatenstaude 55 44
Tombola 306 11
Tomtom 324 49
Ton 159 2; 160 1; 260 79; 328
   20; 339 31
~, gebrannter 328 20
Tonabnehmersystem,
   magnetisches 241 26
Tonanschlußleitung 117 8
Tonarm 241 21
~arretierung 241 27
~lift 241 28
~waage 241 53
Ton-art 320 55-68
~assistent 117 68; 310 57
Tonaufnahme 313 26
~gerät 117 7; 310 24
~-Wahlschalter 117 13
Ton-aufzeichnung 311 1-46
~aussteuerung 243 11
~aussteuerungsregler 117 16
Tonband 241 58
~gerät 309 37; 317 21; 318 17
~kassette 117 76
~koffer 309 37
Ton-bildner 339 6
~dämpfung 325 41
~dreieck 350 17
Tonerwalze 249 41
Tonfigur 339 7
Tonfilm 117 82
~atelier 310 26-60
~kamera 117 1, 22
~kassette 117 29
~projektor 117 81; 312 24
Ton-grube 15 88
~höhenabstimmer 241 31
~hohlplatte 159 26
~ingenieur 238 19

~kabel 311 41
~kamera 310 60; 311 6
~kanzelle 326 13
~kassette 242 17
Tonkinrohr 301 20
Ton-kiste 339 30
~kodiereinrichtung 242
   11-14
~kopf 243 35; 312 47
~kopfgehäuse 241 59
~krug 260 78
~lampe 312 48
~leiter 320 45-49
~loch 323 33; 324 34
~maske 260 75
~meister 310 23, 55; 311 36
~meisterraum 310 54
~mischung 311 34-36
~modul 240 14
Tönnchenpuppe 81 3
Tonnen-anker 224 73
~gewölbe 336 38
~stein 224 73
Ton-pfeife 107 34
~piste 117 82
~plastik 260 67
~quelle 117 27
~raum 321 42-50
~regiepult 238 20, 41, 54; 239
   8
~regieraum 238 27; 239 7
~reportagewagen 239 1-15
~rohr 269 35
~rolle 339 8
~spur 243 32
~strang 159 14
~streifen 311 34-36, 44
Tonsur 331 57
Ton-taubenschießen 305
   70-78
~technikerin 238 26
~teller 117 100, 101
~tiegel 350 31
~trägerraum 238 1-6, 16, 25
~welle 243 23
Topf Babyausstattung 28 47
~ Pflanzen 54 18
Töpfchen 28 47
Topfdeckel 40 13
Topfen 76 45
Töpfer-scheibe 161 11
~ware 308 66
Topf-hut 35 12
~kuchen 97 33
~lappen 39 18
~lappenhalter 39 19
~markt 308 64-66
~pflanze 39 37; 44 25; 55 25
Topgas 145 38
Topp 221 85
~licht 286 10
~nante 219 47
~segelschoner 220 11-13
~zeichen 224 78, 89, 90, 98
Tor Park 272 31
~ Sport 291 35; 301 65, 66, 67;
   302 37
~ Kunst 337 11
~, aushängbares 118 46
~bau 333 9; 336 15
~bauten 334 7
Torero 319 21, 25
Torf-ballen 206 10
~mullballen 55 31
Tor-graben 329 33
~haus 329 22
Torii 337 11
Tor-kran 222 34
~lauf 301 29
~linie 291 7
~mann 282 47; 291 10; 292 8;
   302 36
Tornistergerät 6 20, 23

Toros 334 28
Torpedorohr 258 78; 259 79
Tor-pfosten 291 37
~raum 291 5
~schütze 273 13
Torsionsnase 287 39
Torso 339 7
Tor-stahl 119 82
~stange 301 30
~stütze 214 24
Törtchen 97 20
Torte 97 22-24; 99 15; 265 4
Torten-boden 97 47
~platte 97 25
Torus 334 28
Tor-wächter 292 73
~wart 273 14; 291 10; 302 36
~warthandschuh 291 19
Tosbecken 217 61
totale Sonnenfinsternis 4 39
Totalisator-anzeigetafel 289
   35
~schalter 289 34
Totalitätszone 4 33
Totem 352 2
~pfahl 352 1
Toten-bahre 331 41
~blume 60 20
~gräber 331 22
~halle 331 21
~kopf 365 9
~kopfschwärmer 365 9
~tempel 333 7
~vogel 362 19
toter Flußarm 216 18
Totholz 285 47
Toto-anzeigetafel 289 35
~kasse 289 34
Toupet 34 2
Touren-boot 283 26-33
~lenker 187 2
~moped 188 24
~rad 187 1
~zähler 166 2; 167 43
~zweier 283 61
Touristengruppe 272 28
Tower 233 17
Trab 72 41
Trabant 4 45
Trabdreß 289 26
Traber 289 28
~bahn 289 23
~pferd 289 28
Trab-rennbahn 289 23
~rennen 289 23-40
Tracht 319 31; 355 27
~, spanische 355 27
Trachten 71 41
Track 289 23
Trafo 152 39
~station 92 21
Trag-bahre 270 23
~balken 119 57
~bügel 241 2
~bütte 78 15
Trage-griff 21 22
~gürtel 28 29
Träger Kleidung 33 45
~ Jagd 88 3
~kleid 31 8
~kleidchen 29 13
~rakete 234 1, 2
Tragfläche 230 43; 256 9; 287
   29; 288 27
Tragflächen-anordnung 229
   1-14
~aufbau 257 27
~form 229 15-22
Tragflügel 288 27
~gabel 148 15
~gebälk 337 9
~gestell 167 33
~griff 260 8

Trägheitsmeßwertgeber 6 43
Trag-henkel 129 8
~himmel 331 49
~kabel 215 40
~kabelverankerung 215 43
~kraftspritze 270 52
~kreuz 331 42
~laden 267 50
~last 73 5
~latte 120 45; 123 67
~pfanne 148 14
~rahmen 65 90
~riemen 260 11
~riemenöse 115 9
~ring 147 46
~rohr 64 51
~sattel 73 4
~säule 116 28
~schicht 198 2
~schlauch 286 27
Tragseil Bau 119 37
~ Bergbahnen 214 21, 27, 38, 44
~ Brücken 215 16
~ Fahrstuhl 271 52
~bremse 214 71
~lauflager 214 33
~schuh 214 58, 79
~spanngewicht 214 41
~verankerungspoller 214 59
Trag-stiel 148 16
~tier 354 3
Trailer 278 20
Trainer 291 55; 292 57
Trainings-anzug 33 27
~gerät 299 20-24
~hose 33 29
~jacke 33 28
~partner 299 27
Trajekt Landkarte 15 12
~ Schiff 221 74
Traktat 330 57
Traktor 62 38; 65 20; 138 36; 273 55
Traktur 326 6-16
Trampeltier 366 29
Trampolin 282 10; 297 10, 17
Tränenbein 17 40
Tränendes Herz 60 5
Tränen-grube 88 14
~höhle 88 14
Tränkrinne 74 6
Tranlampe 353 7
Trans-Europe-Express 205 34
~-Express-Intercity-Zug 209 1-22
Transformationsstufe 23 56
Transformator 152 39; 153 9-18; 211 10
Transformator[en]kessel 152 40
Transformatorenschaltung 153 19
Transmissometer 10 60
Transparent 261 9
~gummisohle 101 38
~sohle 101 15
Transport-einrichtung 199 36
~fahrzeug 62 18
~griff 21 37
~hubschrauber 232 21; 256 18
Transportierring 164 37
Transport-leitung 145 35
~öse 152 48
~rolle Film 117 34
~rolle Tischler 132 72
~schiene 133 41
~schlitten 157 52
~- und Rettungshubschrauber 256 18

~wagen 199 38
~walze 162 11
~zahntrommel 115 26
Transtainerkran 226 2
Trapez Zirkus 307 6
~ Math. 346 37
~draht 284 12
~flügel 229 17
~-Kreuzschliff 36 58
~künstler 307 7
~tafel 203 25
~-Treppenschliff 36 57
Trapper 306 8
Trassant 250 21
Trassat 250 20
Tratte 250 12
Traube 78 5; 370 68
Trauben-hotte 78 15
~mühle 78 17
~stiel 58 13
~wickler 80 22
Trauer-gast 331 33
~mantel 365 5
Trauernder 331 33
Trauer-schleier 331 39
~weide 272 63
Traufe 37 6; 121 4; 122 92
Traufel 118 56
Traufenwascheinrichtung 169 23
Trauf-gebinde 122 49
~leiste 334 11
~platte 122 5
Trauring 36 5; 332 17
~kästchen 36 6
~maschine 108 24
~- Weiteränderungs- maschine 108 24
Trauung, kirchliche 332 14
Trauzeuge 332 23
Traveller Spinnerei 164 55
~ Segelsport 284 27
Traverse Bau 119 57
~ Kraftwerk 152 37
~ Schiff 222 15
Treber 92 50
Trecker 65 20
Treff 276 38
Trefferanzeige 294 25-33, 28
Treff-fläche 294 51-53
~punkt 223 29
Treib-achse 210 37
~beet 55 16
Treiber Jagd 86 37
~ Sport 293 91
Treib-haus 55 4
~jagd 86 34-39
~netz 90 25
~netzfischerei 90 1-10
~öltank 221 71; 223 80
~riemen 103 10
~schlag 293 83
Treibstoff-behälter 235 46
~sammeln 234 22, 48
~standsensor 234 27
~tank 6 7, 29, 37; 188 10, 28; 234 58
Treibwasserpumpe 216 60
Treidel-gleis 216 30
~mast 216 28
~motor 216 29
Treideln 216 27
Trema 342 34
Tremse 61 1
Trenn-jalousie 25 9
~schicht 7 10
~schleifmaschine 125 16
Trennung 170 37
Trenn-vorrichtung 146 28
~wand 75 38; 119 25; 248 1
Trense 289 12
Treppe 123 75

Treppen-absatz 123 34-41
~bau 123
~geländer 38 25; 123 22, 50
Treppenhaus 37 72
~abdeckung 118 22
~fenster 37 81; 123 65
Treppen-leiter 126 2
~leuchte 41 22
~loch 120 46
~schliff 36 59, 60-61, 62, 64
~schraube 123 46
~schritt 301 27
~stufe 41 24
~vorplatz 123 23
Tresor 246 22
~raum 250 11
Tressen-ärmel 186 24
~kragen 186 22
~rock 186 23
Tret-antrieb 188 25
~auto 273 55
~kurbel 187 41; 188 25
~kurbellager 187 42
~lager 187 42
~nähmaschine 104 12; 309 1
~schemel 325 46
~schlitten 304 29
~werk 325 46
Trial 290 24-28
Triangel Schmuck 36 60-61
~ Mus. 323 49
~schliff 36 67
Triangulum Australe 3 40
Tribüne 289 34
Trichter 78 18; 125 30; 324 70; 350 16
~becherkultur 328 12
~kübel 147 5
Trick-einrichtung 310 59
~programmschalter 117 87
~taste 117 84
~track 276 22
Triebachsvorgelege 64 30
~drehgestell 197 9
~kopf 209 2
Triebrad-bereifung 64 31
~satz 209 3
Triebwagen 209 2; 214 1
~führerstand 208 14
~zug 205 25; 209 1
Triebwerk 6 30; 231 26; 234 4, 19, 34; 256 13; 288 35
~raumstruktur 235 2
Triebwerks-gondel 231 26; 256 25
~kardan 6 36
~lufteinlauf 257 12
~verkleidung 234 6
~widerlager 234 21
Triebzahnrad 214 8
~zug 209 1
Triforium 335 33
Triglyphe 334 15
trigonometrischer Punkt 14 49; 15 71
Trikolore 253 16
Trikot 291 56; 299 25
~futter 101 17
Triller 321 17, 18
Trilling 91 11
Trimaran 278 16
Trimmklappe 288 25, 30
Trink-brunnen 205 33
~flasche 290 10
~halm 266 46
~kur 274 18
~milch 76 20
~milchtank 76 15
~spruch 267 40
~stube 266 1-29
Trinkwasser-leitung 198 22
~sack 278 32
~tank 146 16

~versorgung 269 1-66
Triole 321 23
Trippe 355 43
Trireme 218 9-12
Triton 327 40
Tritt Schneiderei 104 13
~ Wagen 186 13
~ Bergsport 300 17
~, spanischer 71 3
~folge 171 10
~siegel 86 8
~stufe 123 32, 47; 197 15
Triumphbogen 334 59, 71
Trizeps 18 38
Trochilus 334 29
Trocken-automat 50 28
~batterie 127 27
~beizung 83 52
~dock 222 31-33; 225 17
~filz 173 23
~gerät 50 23-34
~gürtel 9 54
~haube Friseur 105 25
~haube Papier 173 27
~kammer Ziegelei 159 17
~kammer Textilw. 168 28; 169 24
~kühlturm 154 39
~kupplung 190 78
~ofen 180 14, 27
~schwimmen 282 20
~sieb 173 23
~ständer 309 49
~tal 13 75
~teilfeld 165 54
~trommel Haushalt 50 29
~trommel Papier 173 33
~- und Naßsauger 50 80
~zylinder 173 22
Trocknen 168 26; 169 24
Trockner 170 38
~auslauf 168 30
Trocknung 160 4; 170 58
Trödelmarkt 308 60
Trog 173 47
~deckel 178 37
~tor 217 32
Troika 186 45
Trolley 194 42
~bus 194 40
~busanhänger 194 44
Trombone 323 46
Trommel Meteorol. 10 5, 16, 20
~ Spinnerei 163 43
~ Mus. 323 51, 55; 324 47, 48
~ Kunst 335 44
~bremse 188 36; 189 11, 13
~fell Anat. 17 59
~fell Mus. 323 52
~mühle 161 1
~pfanne 148 6
~schlegel 323 54
~stab 354 19
~stock 323 54
Trompete 309 54; 318 6; 323 43
Trompeten-ärmel, plissierter 30 54
~narzisse 60 3
Trompeter 318 7
Tropaeolum 53 4
Tropen-gewächshaus 272 65
~institut 225 28
~medizin 225 28
Tropfen, glatter 36 85
~platte 334 17
Tropf-infusion 25 13; 26 9
~platte 266 2
~ring 283 40
Tropfstein 13 80-81
~höhle 13 79

~säule 13 82
Tropf-trichter 349 3
~wurz 60 8
tropische
  Genußmittelpflanze 382
~ Gewürzpflanze 382
tropischer Regengürtel 9 53
Tropo-pause 7 9
~sphäre 7 1
Trosse 217 23; 227 8
Trossel 164 34
~kops 165 15
Trossenrichtung 227 15
Trottellumme 359 13
Trubausscheidung 93 1-5
Trübli 58 12
Truck 226 8
~-to-truck-handling 226 7
~-to-truck-Verkehr 225 41
Trudeln 288 7
Trüffel 381 9
Trugdolde 370 70
Truhenschrank 246 20
Truthahn 73 28
~feder 305 62
Truthenne 73 28
Tschaitja 337 28
~halle 337 27
Tschibuk 107 32
Tschinelle 323 50
T-Schnitt 54 32
Tsetsefliege 81 43
T-Shirt 31 38
~, rückenfreies 31 64
T-Ständer 177 29
T-Stück 126 44, 47
Tuba 323 44
Tubaphon 324 61
Tuben-linie 31 14
~ständer 22 46
~verschluß 260 52
Tuberose 60 9
Tuberosität 80 27
Tubus 10 27; 111 18; 113 8
~deckel 350 52
~mittelteil 113 9
Tuch 89 22; 106 25; 168 39
~, steriles 26 38
~ballen 271 59
~bespannung 277 15
~bindung 171 1, 24
~caban 33 63
~mantel 30 61; 33 66
Tudorbogen 336 37
Tuff 11 19
~wall 11 26
Tukan 363 6
Tüllarbeit 102 15
Tülle 187 59, 79
Tüllenbeil 328 23
Tüll-grund 102 16
~spitze 102 15
Tulpenbaum, Gemeiner 374 1
Tumba Mus. 324 55
~ Kunst 335 53
Tümmler 367 23
Tumulus 328 16
Tundrenklima 9 57
Tuner 241 37, 40; 317 22
Tuneserblume 60 20
Tunika 30 29; 355 12
~kleid 30 29
Tunique 30 29
Tunnel 15 70; 214 6
~gürtel 31 66
~ofen 161 5
Tüpfelfarn 377 16
Tupfer-halter 23 12
~spender 22 36
Tür 186 11
Turas 226 23, 28
Türaufzugsvorrichtung 139
  55

Turban 353 46
Turbine 67 20; 155 39; 209
  18; 232 40, 47
Turbinen-anlage 146 5; 209
  24
~einlauf 155 40, 41
~getriebe 209 10
~haus 152 22; 217 43
~luftstrahltriebwerk 231 26;
  232 33-50
~-Propeller-Flugzeug 231 4
~satz 154 33
~triebwerk 232 17, 24; 257 15
~überwachungsschrank 153·
  30
Turbo-luftstrahltriebwerk
  231 26; 232 33-50
~propflugzeug 231 4
~proptriebwerk 231 5; 232
  30, 51; 256 16
Tür-fach 39 6
~fenster 191 22
~griff 186 12; 191 5
Türkenbund 377 4
türkischer Honig 308 18
~ Teller 323 50
~ Weizen 68 31
türkische Trommel 323 55
Türklinke 41 28
Turm Landkarte 15 53
~ Bau 119 34
~ Mil. 258 29, 67, 70; 259 71
~ Spiele 276 12
~drehkran 119 31
Türmer 329 9
Turm-grab 333 21
~helm 335 7
~knauf 331 5
~mast 221 51
~rolle 145 4
~rutschbahn 308 40
~scheinwerfer 316 21
~schwalbe 359 24
~springen 282 40-45
~springer 282 5
Turn 288 4
Turnanzug 297 51
Turnen 297
~, olympisches 296 1-11; 297
  1-6
Turn-gerät 296 1-11; 297 1-6
~hemd 296 61
~hose 296 62
Turnier 329 71
~bogen 305 54
~fähnchen 254 33
Turn-kleidung 296 61-63; 297
  51-52
~schuh 101 35; 296 63; 297 52
Turnüre 355 69
Tür-rahmen 41 26
~schloß 41 27; 140 36-43;
  191 6
~taster 127 2
Turteltaube 359 23
Tusche-behälter 151 63
~füller 151 37, 38
~füllereinsatz 151 68
~patrone 151 36
Tüte 314 29
Tutu 314 29
Twinset 31 49
Tympanon 335 26
Type 249 15, 29
Typen-feld 245 27
~reiniger 247 8
Typhon 223 3
typographischer Punkt 175 18
Typoskript 174 6

U

U-Bahntunnel 198 29
Überblattung 121 89
Überbrückungsschalter 211
  25
Überdach 278 22
Überdeckung 122 100
Überdruck-manometer 349 19
~ventil 40 22
Überfall 217 60
Überflurhydrant 270 35
Überführung 162 26, 34
Übergabetrommel 180 36
Übergang 208 11
Übergangs-mantel 33 60
~reduzierstück 126 41
~stück 126 38
~winkel 126 49, 51
Übergardine 44 13
Übergrätschen 296 49
Überhitzer 152 9
Überkehrauslauf 64 22
Überkehrschnecke 64 21
Überkleid 355 36, 50
Überladeturm 64 37
Überland-bahn, elektrische
  197
~betrieb 197 1
Überlappung 143 56
Überlastkontrolle 224 33
Überlauf 38 69; 49 25; 269 33
~becken 272 23
~behälter 350 60
Überlaufen 298 7
Überlauf-leitung 269 20
~rechen 89 5
~ventil 49 45
übermäßiger Dreiklang 321 4
Übermittlung 237 68
Überqueren 298 31
Überrollbügel 65 21; 193 13
Überschallverkehrsflugzeug
  231 15
Überschiebung 12 7
Überschlag 296 55; 297 21;
  308 43
~, freier 297 25
Überschläger 293 75
Überschlagschaukel 308 42
Überschwemmungsraum 216
  42
Überseefunk 237 54-55
Übersetzfenster 207 7
Übersichtsbeleuchtung 112
  52
Überspannungsableiter 152
  35
Überspielung 238 54-59
Überströmschlitz 242 57
Übertagebau 154 70
Übertragungs-tuch 249 40
~vermerk 250 25
Über- und
  Unterdruckmanometer
  349 19
Überwachungs-anlage 25 20
~feld 203 64
~organ 153 5
Überwinterungsnest 80 31
Überwurf 352 24
~mantel 33 60
Überziehpullover 30 4
Überzugnutzen 184 12
U-Boot 258 64
~-Abwehr-Raketenwerfer
  258 30, 50
~-Jagd-Torpedorohr 258 33
Übungs-heft 260 4
~turm 270 3
U-Eisen 143 7
Ufer 13 4
~abbruch 216 5

~befestigung 216 51-55
~böschung 217 28
~damm 216 49
~welle 13 36
UHF-Tuner 240 6
Uhr 110
~, automatische 109 24
~, wasserdichte 109 26
Uhren-gehäuse 309 57
~pendel 309 58
Uhr-gehäuse 110 26
~glas 109 29
~macher 109 1
~macherdrehstuhl 109 20
~werk 10 14; 110 36
Uhu 86 48; 362 15
~, Kleiner 362 14
~hütte 86 51
U-Jagd-~Atom-U-Boot 259
  54
~raketensalvenwerfer 259 24,
  37
~raketentorpedostarter 259
  51
~torpedofünflingssatz 259 36
UKW-Antenne 257 25
~-Stationstaste 241 38
ULCC 221 1
Ulme 371 49
Ultra large crudeoil carrier
  221 1
Umarmung 205 53
Umbellula encrinus 369 14
Umblatt 107 6
Umdrehungs-anzeige 224 21
~zahlwähler 241 29
~zähler 309 83
Umdruck-
  Adressiermaschine 245 7
Umfang 346 44
Umfangswinkel 346 56
Umführungsschiene 214 22
Umholz 130 2
Umkehrring 115 83
Umklammerung 21 34
Umkleideraum 282 3
Umkreis 346 29
Umlauf 285 19, 20, 21
~bahn 314 15-24, 19
~berg 13 12
~kabine 214 20
~ölkühlung 312 25
~prüfgerät 109 24
~seil 214 21
~spülung 179 6
Umleersystem 199 2
Umlegekragen 31 69
Umlenk-prisma 112 13
~rolle 312 29
~spiegel 113 11
Ummauerung 272 25
Umpflanzen 54 5
Umrolltisch 238 59; 312 21
Umsatzstatistik 248 46
Umschalter Kraftwerk 153 13
~ Auto 195 4
~ AV 243 15
Umschalt-feststeller 249 5
~schieber 87 24
~spindel 149 34
~taste 50 59; 249 3
Umschlagärmel 30 6
~klappe 185 38
~kragen 30 5
Umschrift 342 14
Umsetzen 54 5
Umspannanlage 217 46
Umspanner 152 39
Umspulen 170 50
Umsteiger 233 27
Umwälzpumpe 154 43, 54
Umwandlung 169 9
Umwindstrecke 285 24

Umwurf 355 10
Unbekannte 345 4, 8
unbelichteter Film 117 41
unbeschrankter
　Bahnübergang 202 49
undurchlässige
　Gesteinsschicht 13 78
~ Schicht 12 28
undurchlässiges Gestein 12 23
unendlich 345 15
Unfall-fahrzeug 21 18
~hilfe 21
~wagen 270 19
Ungeheuer 327 16
ungleich 345 18
Ungleichheitszeichen 345 18
Uni 262 1-25
Uniform 264 7
Union Jack 253 15
Unitload 226 9
Universal-bagger 158 13
~brennschneidemaschine 141
　36
~drehtisch 112 17
~entzerrer 238 48
~filmkassette 242 44
~fräsmaschine 150 32
~kletterhaken 300 38
~kondensor 112 66
~kühlwagen 213 39
~ladewagen 62 40
~meßkammer 112 67
~pflugkörper 65 64-67
~reproduktionskamera 177
　24
~rundschleifmaschine 150 1
~schneider 134 28
~zentriergerät 111 21
Universität 262 1-25
Universitäts-bibliothek 262
　11-25
~professor 262 3
Unkraut 61; 84 32
Unpaarhufer 366 25-27
unpaarig gefiedert 370 42
Unparteiischer 291 62; 299 16
Unruh 110 39
Unter-amboß 139 40
~arm 16 46
~armschiene 329 47
~armstand 295 26
~bär 139 7
~bau Erdöl 145 2
~bau Straßenbau 200 59
~bau Kunst 334 4
~bauch 16 37
~beton 123 13
Unterbindung eines
　Blutgefäßes 21 14-17
Unterbrecher 242 49
Unterdeck Auto 194 37
~ Raumfahrt 235 28
~feder 362 3
Unterdruck-dose 190 9
~manometer 349 19
~pumpe 190 59, 60
Unterer Keuper 154 57
~ Muschelkalk 154 60
Unterfadenumspuler 104 16
Unterfeuer 224 101
Unterflügel 229 9
~tank 256 4
Unterflur-hydrant 270 25
~installation 127 22
~stauraum 231 21
Unter-gesenk 139 14
~gestell Optik 113 2
~gestell Repro 177 40
~gestell Eisenb. 207 3; 208 5
~gewand 355 5, 37
~grätenmuskel 18 53
~grundvorbehandlung 128
　1-17

~gurt 121 73, 79; 215 10
Unterhaltungselektronik
　241
Unter-haupt 217 17
~hemd 32 7
~holz 84 5, 32
~hose 32 29
~hose, lange 32 11
~jacke 32 25, 28
~kasten 148 20
Unterkiefer 17 35
~bein 17 35
~drüse 19 11
Unter-kühlungsbadewanne
　228 21
~kunft 146 33; 270 2
~kunftshaus 300 1
~labium 326 26
~lage 54 33
~lage, vertrauliche 246 25
Unterlags-platte 202 5
Unter-legscheibe 143 17
~leib 16 37
~lid 19 40
~liek 284 40
~lippe Anat. 19 26
~lippe Pferd 72 10
~lippe Mus. 326 26
~mann 307 29, 45
~maschinerie 316 1-60
~mauerung 123 15
~putzinstallation 127 4, 5
Unterrichtstechnik 242
Unter-rock 32 13
~rohr 187 17
Unterschenkel Anat. 16 52
~ Pferd 72 36
~beuger 18 61
~strecker 18 46
unterschlächtiges Mühlrad
　91 39
Unter-schlitten 149 24
~schnabel 359 8
~schrank 39 9; 42 6
~schrift 251 15, 16
~schriftenmappe 245 19
~schwung 296 59
~seeboot 258 64
~seil 214 46
~setzung 172 69
~setzungsgetriebe 232 59;
　259 61
~simm 90 9
Unterspannungs-durchführung
　152 44
~wicklung 153 16
Unter-spiegel 218 58
~stand 84 5
unterständiger Fruchtknoten
　58 7
Unterstempel 252 41
Untersuchungs-instrument 23
　3-21
~liege 22 43; 23 4
~tisch, angiographischer 27
　26
Unter-tageanlage 144 21-51
~tapete 128 5
~tasse 44 30
~teller 45 3
~tischkappsäge 157 24, 64
~titel 185 47; 342 41
~tritt 30 52
~walze 148 55
Unterwasser-blitzgerät 279 25
~fotografie 279 23
~gehäuse 117 57; 279 24
~jäger 280 37
~kamera 279 24
~massagebad 281 31
~schwimmen 282 38
~verstärker 237 57

Unterweisung,
　programmierte 242 16
Unter-windventilator 199 33
~zange 163 65
Unterzieh-rolli 30 7
~strickweste 33 53
Unterzug 119 3, 5; 121 67
~schalung 119 12
Unterzylinder 164 10
Untiefe 224 87, 97
Unziale 341 17
Unzialis 341 17
Unzialschrift 341 17
Uranus 4 50
Urethroskop 23 20
Urhahn 88 72
Urkunde 250 17
Urne 331 31
Urnen-grab 328 39; 331 30
~schlitz 263 30
U-Rohr 349 2
Ursa Major 3 29
~ Minor 3 34
Urtierchen 357 1-12
Ü-Wagen 239 1-15, 1, 6

V

Vakuole 357 5
Vakuum 240 21
~absaugvorrichtung 74 49
~anschluß 145 51
~begasungsanlage 83 11
~deckel 177 35
~filmhalter 177 8
~formung 162 28, 36
~herstellung 179 19
~kammer 2 52; 83 12; 159 12
~kessel 170 54
~lagerkessel 169 11
~leitung 75 29
~presse 161 7
~pumpe 269 8
~rahmen 182 2
~schlauch 74 50
Valander 380 7
Valenciennesspitze 102 18
Vamp 306 32
Vanille-pflanze 382 46
~schote 382 48
~stange 382 48
Variometer 230 14
Varioobjektiv 117 2; 313 23
Vase 161 18
~, griechische 334 37
Vatermörder 355 74
Vater-unser-Perle 332 31
V-Ausschnitt 31 68
VCR–Kassette 243 5
~Kopftrommel 243 19
~Spurschema 243 28
~System 243 5-36
VDS 259 40
Velo 187 1
Velourteppich 267 35
Veloziped 187 1
Velum 381 5
Vene 18 2
Venezianerspitze 102 30
venöses Blut 18 11
Ventil Heizung 38 73
~ Fahrrad 187 31
~ Sport 298 77, 82; 291 18
~ Mus. 323 40; 324 66; 326 10
Ventilationseinstellung 26 27
Ventilator 65 52; 165 23; 199
　46
~gebläse 165 4
~schiene 165 6
Ventilhorn 323 41
Ventilierung 6 26

Ventil-klappe 187 32
~leine 288 78
~schlauch 187 31
Venus 4 44
Venusfliegenfalle 377 14
Veränderliche 345 14
veränderlicher Stern 3 11
Verankerung 216 13
Veranstalter 299 45
Verarbeitungsschiff 221 86
Verbands-flagge 286 6, 9
~material 26 34
~päckchen 21 4
~tisch 22 45
Verbindungs-balken 63 20
~beschlag 6 28
~brücke 235 49
~draht 298 44
~element 248 48
~kabel 25 20, 43, 56
~stück 350 56
Verbraucher 269 52
Verbrennungsmotor 190
Verbundglas 124 5
Verdächtiger 264 32
Verdampfer 155 6
Verdeck Kinderwagen 28 35
~ Wagen 186 14
~ Sport 283 57
~, zurückklappbares 193 10
Verdichter 145 45
verdichteter Müll 199 22
Verdichtung 168 1
Verdrängerkörper 229 30
Verdrängungsboot 286 32-37
Veredlung 54 30-39
Vereinigung 224 90
Vereinigungsmenge 348 5-6
Vereinsturnen 296 12-21; 297
　7-14
Vereinte Nationen 253 1-3
Vereisungsgerät 22 63
Verfalltag 250 16
Vergaser 189 4; 192 1-15
Vergißmeinnicht 378 26
Vergnügungsboot 283 1
Vergolden Maler 129 40
~ Buchb. 183 1
Vergoldepresse 183 26
Vergolder-kissen 129 50
~messer 129 51
Vergolde- und Prägepresse
　183 26
Vergrößerer 116 26
Vergrößerungs-apparat 116 26
~belichtungsmesser 116 53
~gerät 116 26
~glas 177 23
~kassette 116 35
~rahmen 116 35
Verhalten zum Gerät 296
　22-39
Verhol-spill 217 22
~trosse 217 23
Verkauf 148 73
Verkäufer 98 13; 308 17; 309
　29
Verkäuferin 97 1; 98 31; 99
　17; 271 18
Verkaufs-karree 271 42
~korb 99 8
~raum 97 1-54; 99 4; 111
　1-19
~regal 99 23
~stand 47 28
~theke 271 61
Verkehrs-ampel 268 52
~hubschrauber 264 1
~kontrolle 264 9
~polizist 268 30
~regelung 268 30
~schutzarmbinde 199 7
~schutzmarkierung 199 8

~streife 264 9
~überwachung 264 1
~zeichen 268 66
Verkleidung *Motorrad* 189 44
~ *Karneval* 306 6-48
Verkleidungskonus 235 63
Verklicker 284 48
Verlade·brücke 221 90; 225 20
~rohr 226 34
Verlags·signet 185 48
~zeichen 185 48
Verlandungszone 13 10
Verlängerungs·punkt 320 7
~schnur 127 10
~stange 151 57
verlassenes Bergwerk 15 35
Verlegerzeichen 185 48
Verleseband 64 81
Verletzter 21 18-23, 18, 20
Verlies 329 5
Verlosung 306 11
Verlust 285 28
Vermehrung 54 10, 14, 27
Vermessung 14 46-62
verminderter Dreiklang 321 3
Vermittlung 237 41
Vermittlungseinrichtung 237 25
Verpackungs·anlage 76 20
~entstapler 74 53
~maschine 76 36
~sack 288 44
Verpflanzen 54 5
Verputzarbeiten 118 83-91
Verreiber 249 51
Verreibwalze 181 7
Verrierpalmette 52 1
Verrohrung 145 20
verrotteter Müll 199 22
Versal 175 11
~buchstabe 175 11
Versammlung 263 8
Versammlungsleiter 263 1
Versand 145 35
Versatz 120 54; 121 90, 91
~stück 315 30; 316 47
Verschlag 38 19
~wagen 213 28
Verschluß·hebel 87 25
~kappe 151 40
~kegel 147 6
~ponton 222 32
~register 203 63
~riegel 117 62
~zeitenknopf 115 19
Verschnürung *Schuh* 101 21
~ *Eisenb.* 206 12
Verschraubung 126 42
Verschwertung 119 14
versenkbares Objektiv 114 5
Versenk·öffnung 316 32
~podium 316 34
~schacht 5 24
~tisch 316 33
~walze 217 68
Versetzen 54 5
Versetzungszeichen 320 50-54
Versicherungsbüro 268 40
Versorger 258 93
Versorgungs·Baugruppe 234 56
~- und Geräte-Baugruppe 234 56
Verspannung *Flugzeug* 229 12
~ *Sport* 296 10; 297 5
Verstärker 241 40; 312 19; 317 23
~einrichtung 310 59
~träger 238 3
~- und Netzgeräteträger 238 3

Verstärkung 258 81
Verstärkungs·reifen 130 16
~rippe 200 9; 217 78
Versteifung *Sport* 283 46
~ *Theater* 315 31
Versteigerungshalle 225 58
Verstell·bügel 106 17
~propeller 224 19
~spindel 226 51
~stange 49 43
~vorrichtung 100 19, 20
Verstopfen 54 5
Verstrebung *Bau* 119 51
~ *Brücken* 215 4
Verstrich 122 55
Versuchstriebwagenzug 209 23
Verteidiger 282 49
Verteidigungszone 293 66
Verteilungs·netz 269 22
~rinne 274 3
~stahl 119 69
~stück 270 32
Vertical·/Short-Take-off-and-Landing-Flugzeug 232 26-32
~-Take-off-and-Landing-Flugzeug 232 26
Vertiefstempel 108 18
Vertikalablenkmodul 240 8
Vertikale 215 36
Vertikal·Reproduktionskamera 177 32
~stellung 232 27, 32
~trockenschleuder 179 27
Vertragswerkstatt 195 1-55
vertrauliche Unterlage 246 25
Verunglückter 21 18-23, 20
Vervielfachen 344 25
Vervielfältigungsautomat 176 28
Verwaltungs·bereich 5 17
~gebäude 144 18; 222 1; 233 16; 310 4
Verwarnung 291 63
Verwässerungszone 13 24
Verweiskarte 291 63
Verwerfung 12 4; 144 51
Verwerfungslinie 12 5
Verwiegeanlage 201 19
Verzahnung 143 82-96
Verzierung 321 14-22
Vesen 68 24
Veste 329 1
Vestibül 267 1-26
VHF·Antenne 257 25
~-Tuner 240 6
Vibraphon 324 75
Vibrations·balken 201 13
~fertiger 201 10
~reinigungsmaschine 109 23
~schleifer 134 53
~sieb 158 21
Vibrator 201 13
Victoria regia 378 17
Video·Cassette-Recorder-System 243 5-36
~codierplatz 236 39
~kassettenrecorder 243 7
~kopf 243 26, 36
~kopf-Bewegungsrichtung 243 30
~-Long-Play-Bildplattensystem 243 46-60
~monitor 238 2; 261 7
~recorder 243 4
~signal 243 58
~spur 243 3
~technikerin 239 11
Vieh 73 1-2
~bohne 69 15

~haltung 75
~rampe 206 1
~transporter 221 68
~weide 62 44
Vieleck 346 40
~, regelmäßiges 346 41
Vielfachmeßgerät 127 41; 242 73
Vielflächner 351 11
Vielle 322 25
Viel·seilsystem 215 51
~zeller 357 13-39
Vielzweckregal 248 28
Vier·achteltakt 320 31
~backenfutter 149 35
vierblättriges Kleeblatt 69 5
Viereck 346 33-39
~, unregelmäßiges 346 39
~regner 56 46
Vierer ohne Steuermann 283 9
Vierfach·magnetkopf 312 51
~steckdose 127 8
Vier-Familien-Doppelhaus 37 69-71
Vierfarben-Bogenoffsetmaschine 180 30
~-Rollenoffsetmaschine 180 1, 18
Vierflächner 351 1
Vierfleckiger Bohnenkäfer 81 19
Vier·gang-Synchrongetriebe 192 28-47
~halbetakt 320 33
~-in-einem-Auspuffrohr 189 51
Vierkanal·Balanceregler 241 42
~demodulator 241 45
~-Magnetonzusatzgerät 312 50
Vierkant·eisen 143 9
~holzhammer 132 5
~horn 137 22
~loch 140 43
~schraube 143 39
Vierklang 321 5
Vierling 258 30
Vier·mastbark 220 29
~master 220 28-31
~mast-Gaffelschoner 220 28
~mastvollschiff 220 31
~mastzelt 307 1
~paß 335 39
~radantrieb 194 1
~scharbeetpflug 63 40
~spurgerät 241 56
~spur-Tonbandgerät 242 13
~taktmotor 189 3, 50; 242 45
viertelgewendelte Treppe 123 75
Viertel·note 320 15
~pause 320 23
Viertelzoll·band 238 5; 241 58
~magnetband 238 4
~-Spulenmagnetband 243 4
Vierundsechzigstel·note 320 19
~pause 320 27
Vierundzwanzigflächner 351 12
Vierungsturm 335 6
Viervierteltakt 320 32
Vierzylinder·Boxermotor 230 34
~-Dieselmotor 65 44
~maschine 189 49
~streckwerk 164 9
~-Viertaktmotor 189 50
Villenkolonie 15 28
Viola 322 23

~ da Gamba 322 23
Violenbogen 322 24
violett 343 9
Violin·bogen 323 12
~bogenfibel 328 27
~cello 323 16
Violine 323 1
Violin·saite 323 9
~schlüssel 320 8
Violone 322 23; 323 23
Viper 364 40-41
Virginal 322 45
Virginische Tabakpflanze 382 40
Virgo 3 18; 4 58
Vis-à-vis-Wagen 186 51
Visier *Mil.* 255 22, 36
~ *Sport* 305 56
~ *Ritterwesen* 329 40
~einrichtung 87 65
~klappe 87 67
~marke 87 68
~schieber 87 69
Viskose 169 1-12, 15
~becher 130 32
~faser 169 1-34
Viskosefilamentgarn 169 1-34, 13-27, 17
Viskose·lüfterkupplung 190 ß
~spinnfaserballen 169 34
~spinnlösung 169 10, 28-34
~spinnmasse 169 13-27
~verfahren 169 1-34
Viskositätsmessung 129 38
Vitrine 44 26; 46 9
Vitrinenregal 46 7
V-Leitwerk 229 31
Vliesstoff 103 27
VLP-Bildplatte 243 51
VLP-Bildplattensystem 243 46-60
Vogel 359; 360; 361; 362; 363
~, angelockter 86 50
~, einheimischer 360
~, exotischer 363
~, flugunfähiger 359 1-3, 4
Vogelfuß, Großer 69 11
Vogel·gehege 356 8
~kirsche 59 5
~klaue 327 61
~könig 361 12
~leib 327 57
~ Phönix 327 9
~scheuche 52 27
Voith-Getriebe 209 14; 212 74
Volant 191 37
Voliere 356 8
Völkerkunde 352; 353; 354
Volks·menge 263 8
~musikinstrument 324 1-46
~rodel 303 1, 2
~schule 260 1-85
Voll·bart 34 15
~beleimung 185 31
~containerschiff 221 21; 226 5
~drehpflug 65 62
Volleyball 293 58, 59
~spiel 293 56-71
Voll·flächner 351 2
~galopp 72 43-44
~gatter 157 2
~glasrute 89 49
~griff 328 22, 31
~kerf 358 10
~konserve 96 25
~kornbrot 97 10, 48
~mantelgeschoß 87 55
~mattscheibe 115 58, 59, 60, 65
~mond 4 5
~pipette 350 25

~schiff 220 24-27
~wandbrücke 215 52
~wandträger 121 72
~ziegel 159 20
Voltigereiter 307 32
Voltigeur 307 32
Volute 333 26; 334 23; 336 10
Voluten-giebel 336 5
~polster 334 24
Voramboß 137 14
VOR-Antenne 257 26
Vorarm 72 21
Vorbau-gerüst 215 62
~schneepflug 304 9
Vorbelichtungslampe 177 37
Vorbereitungs-boden 64 16
~platz 39 11
~raum *Med.* 26 34-54
~raum *Schule* 261 14-34
Vorbestellbuch 22 11
Vorblasen 162 24
Vor-Bramsaling 219 51
Vorbram-segel 218 52
~stenge 219 4
Vorbrecher 158 17
Vorbrut-trommel 74 29
~trommelantrieb 74 33
Vorbühne 316 25
Vordach 37 67; 278 28, 37
Vordarre 92 16, 29
Vordeck 223 47; 284 10
Vorder-achsfederung 65 49
~achspendelbolzen 65 48
~achsträger 192 84
~ansicht 151 17
~bein 82 6
~blatt 100 60
~eckkegel 305 1
~falte 31 25
~flug 329 45
~flügel 358 36
~fuß 72 22-26, 43; 303 8
~fußwurzel 72 22
~gasse 303 5, 6
~gassenkegel 305 2, 4
~hachse 95 5, 8
~haxe 95 5
~hesse 95 22, 28
~kappe 100 58
~kastell 218 19
~knie 72 22
~lauf 70 5; 88 25, 64
~pfote 70 6
Vorderrad 186 4; 187 26-32
~antrieb 191 52
~bremse 187 5
~fahrwerk 191 52
~gabel 187 10-12
~nabe 187 52
~-Trommelbremse 188 36
Vorder-reißverschluß 29 18
~schaft 87 13
~seite 252 8
~sitzkopfstütze 193 7
~spieler 293 75
~tür 193 5
~wand 349 27
~zange 132 30
~zwiesel 71 38
Vordrehen 135 15
Vordrossel 192 6
Vorfach *Angelsport* 89 78
~ *Schule* 260 10
Vorfeld 233 3
~straße 233 4
Vorflügel 229 38, 53
Vorfluter 216 36
Vorführkabine 312 12
Vorfuß-gummi 286 57
~knochen 17 24
Vorgarneinführung 164 15
Vorgarten 37 58

Vorgeschichte 328
vorgeschmiedetes Werkstück 139 28
Vorgreifer 180 33
Vorhalle 334 50
Vorhalte 295 50
Vorhand 72 18-27
~flugball 293 41
~schlag 293 40
Vorhang 316 23, 24
~bogen 336 35
Vorhängeschloß 38 21
Vorhangzug 315 1-4
Vorhaut 20 70
Vorherd 148 5
Vorhof 20 45
Vorhör-lautsprecher 238 50
~taste 238 46
Vorlage 156 17
Vorlagen-fenster 249 39
~halter 177 22, 30
~zylinder 177 64
Vorlauf 38 74; 126 23; 155 10
~taste 249 73
Vorlege-besteck 45 69-70
~gabel 45 70
~löffel 45 74
~messer 45 69
Vorleger 225 63
Vorlegeschalthebel 149 3
~schloß 38 21
~welle 192 37
VOR-Leitkursanzeiger 230 15
Vorlesung 262 1
Vorliek 284 42
Vormaischer 92 42
Vormannkabine 228 31
Vor-Marssaling 219 50
Vormarsstenge 219 3
Vormauerung 122 39
Vormerkblatt 247 34
Vormischraum 238 54-59
Vormwindstrecke 285 23
Vor-Oberbramrah 219 36
Vor-Oberbramsegel 219 59
Vor-Obermarsrah 219 34
Vor-Obermarssegel 219 57
Vorpiek 227 18
Vorplatz 41 1-29
Vorrats-haus 329 13
~kübel 200 35
~schädling 81 15-30
~spule 117 31
~tank 146 17
~zelle 77 35
Vorraum *Haus* 41 1-29
~ *Eisenb.* 207 21
Vorreißer 163 53
~rost 163 54
Vor-Royalrah 219 37
Vor-Royalsegel 219 60
Vorsager 316 28
Vorsatz 185 49
~papier 185 49
Vorschäler 65 11, 68
Vorschaumonitor 238 60
Vorschiff 218 49
~querschnitt 286 33, 36, 40
Vorschlag 321 14, 15; 326 31
~hammer 137 22
Vorschleifscheibe 111 36
Vorschneider 65 11
Vorschub 149 18
~anzeiger 157 9
~einrichtung 149 14
~einstellung 100 28
~getriebe 149 10
~getriebekasten 149 8
~kette 172 67
~kettenantrieb 172 69
~klinke 157 44

~motor 177 43
~sattel 185 4
~skala 157 61
~spindel 149 15
~steigung 149 9
~walze 85 19, 24; 157 40
Vorschüler 48 2
Vorschulerziehung 48 1-20
Vorsetzhebel 167 44
Vorsignal 203 7-24, 17, 18, 20, 22, 23
~anzeige 203 16
~bake 203 26, 27, 28, 29
~tafel 203 24
~wiederholer 203 17
Vorsortierer 172 21
Vorstag 284 15
Vorstand 263 1-2
Vorstands-tisch 263 3
~vorsitzer 251 16
Vorstapelung 157 25
Vorsteherdrüse 20 76
Vorstehhund, Deutscher 70 40
~, Englischer 70 41
Vorstenge 219 3
Vor-Stengestagsegel 219 20
Vorsteven 218 4; 222 74
Vorstopper 291 12
Vorstraße 148 70
Vorstreckteich 89 6
Vortitel 185 44
Vortragkreuz 330 47
Vortrags-bezeichnung 321 27-41
~pult 262 4
Vortriebsmaschinenanlage 209 4
Vortrocknung 165 50
Vor-Unterbramrah 219 35
Vor-Unterbramsegel 219 58
Vor-Untermarsrah 219 33
Vor-Untermarssegel 219 56
Vorwärmer 145 31
~druckmesser 210 43
Vorwärm-gerät 212 41
~heizung 185 30
Vorwärmung 23 3
Vorwickel-Filmzahntrommel 312 26
Vorzeichen *Mus.* 320 50-54, 55-68
~ *Math.* 344 7, 8
Vorzimmer 245 1-33
Vorzwirnerei 170 45
Voute 119 6
VSTOL-Flugzeug 232 26-32
VTOL-Flugzeug 232 26
Vulkan, erloschener 11 28
~, tätiger 11 15
vulkanische Lockermasse 11 19
vulkanisches Beben 11 32-38
Vulkanismus 11 13-28
Vulkankrater 11 16

W

Waage *Astr.* 3 19; 4 59
~ *Gerät* 47 33; 92 32; 170 29
~ *Sport* 295 30, 31
~balken *Mus.* 322 39
~balken *Chem.* 349 30
~pirouette 302 9
Waagerecht-bohr- und -fräswerk 150 25
~frässpindel 150 39
~spindel 150 40
Waagschale 40 37
Wabe 77 31-43, 42
Wach-habende 221 126
~habender 221 126

~hund 70 25
Wacholder 372 47
~beere 372 52
Wachsbügler 301 22
wachsender Bock 254 32
Wachs-figur 308 69
~figurenkabinett 308 68
~kerze 77 66; 260 76
~korken 301 23
~kratzeisen 301 24
~malstift 48 11; 260 6
~pflaume 59 25
~plastik 339 26
~plättchen 77 25
~puppe 308 69
~stock 77 65
Wächte 300 20
Wachtel 359 22
~locke 87 45
Wachtturm 329 4
Wach- und Begleithund 70 25
Wade 16 53
Wadenbein 17 24
~knöchel 19 59
~muskel 18 64
Waden-nerv 18 33
~stecher 81 4
Waffe, Schwere 255 40-95
Waffel 97 45
~automat 40 34
~bindung 171 29
~muster 171 29
Waffen-leitradar 258 35
~reinigungsgerät 87 61-64
Wägeglas 349 24
Wagen *Sägewerk* 157 16
~ *Pferdewagen* 186 1-54; 191 1-56
~ *Eisenb.* 213 18
~, Großer 3 29
~, Kleiner 3 34
~abstützung 67 22
~bug 197 3
~fähre 15 47; 216 10
~heck 197 4
~heizung 192 60-64
~kasten *Wagen* 186 5
~kasten *Eisenb.* 207 2; 208 6
~kasten *Bergbahnen* 214 34
~kupplung 208 16
~ladung 206 52
~meister 205 39
~park 206 25
~rad 191 14
~schlag 186 11
~teil 197 5
~tür 191 4
Wägeschale 349 36
Wahl 263 16-30
~berechtigte 263 24
~berechtigter 263 24
Wahleinrichtung, elektronische 237 42
Wähler 257 37 42
~ *Wahl* 263 24
Wählerin 263 22
Wähler-karte 263 19
~kartei 263 18
~motor 237 48
~versammlung 263 1-15
Wahl-helfer 263 17
~kabine 263 23
~kartei 263 18
~lokal 263 16
~nummer 263 19
~ordnung 263 25
~raum 263 16
~redner 263 5
~schalter 117 13
Wählscheibe 237 10; 245 16; 246 14
Wahlschild 263 13
Wähltastatur 242 25

Wahl·urne 263 29
~versammlung 263 1-15
~vorsteher 263 28
~zelle 263 23
wahre Rippe 17 9
Wahrsagerin 308 36
Währungstabelle 204 32
Wal 367 23-29
Wald 84 1-34
~arbeiter 84 18
~drossel 361 16
~erdbeere 58 16
~frostspanner 80 16
~geißbart 377 5
~horn 323 41
~kante 120 89
~landindianer 352 19
~ohreule 362 14
~pflanze 377
~schlepper 85 27
~schnepfe 88 83
~weg Landkarte 15 102
~weg Forstw. 84 3
~zecke 358 44
Walfisch 3 11
Wall 289 8
Wallach 73 2
Wallberg 11 24
Waller 364 12
~fisch 364 12
Wallgraben 329 37
Walliser Hackbrett 322 34
Wallmoräne 12 53
Walm·dach 37 64; 121 10, 60
~fläche 121 11; 122 10
~gaube 121 13
~gaupe 121 13
~kappe 122 9
~schifter 121 63
~ziegel 122 8
Walnuß 59 41, 43
~baum 59 37-43
Walzasphalt-Trocken-und-
    Misch-Anlage 200 48
Walze Druck 182 13
~ Straßenbau 200 37
~ Wasserbau 217 65
~ Graphik 340 40
Walzen·bewicklung 50 3
~blende 255 81
~drehknopf 249 22
~druckmaschine 168 53
~entwicklungsmaschine
    Fotogr. 116 60
~entwicklungsmaschine
    Druck 182 9
~führungsring 187 72
~korrektur 182 12
~krone 217 66
~lager 148 60
~löser 249 24
~satz 148 54-55
~ständer 148 57
~stechknopf 249 25
~stellung 326 37
~straße 148 66-75
~wehr 217 65-72
Walz·gerüst 148 56-60
~gut 148 51
Wälz·lager 143 69
~sprung 298 23
Walzstück 148 51
Wälztechnik 298 24
Walzwerk Eisenverarbeitung
    148 46-75
~ Ziegelei 159 9
Wamme 95 39
Wams 355 30, 41
Wand Geogr. 12 43
~ Bergsport 300 2
~anschluß 25 23
~balken 120 39
~bekleidung 310 15

~bild 43 20; 246 28; 338 40
~bildtapete 128 18
~brunnen 272 15
Wandel·gang 315 12-13
~halle 274 9; 315 12-13
~schuldverschreibung 251
    11-19
Wanderdüne 13 39
Wanderer 82 39
Wander·falke 362 2
~form 82 39
~gebläse 165 2, 3
~jacke 33 39
~kajak 283 70
~kino 312 52
~rost 199 34
~stiefel 101 18
~transformator 152 30, 39
~zirkus 307 1-63
~zweier 283 61
Wand·fahrplan 204 18
~kachel 49 19
~kalender 22 17; 245 3; 248
    42
~karte 260 44
~laus 81 39
Wandlerhebel 65 34
Wand·leuchte 265 9
~leuchter 330 16
~lüfter 266 15
~pult 267 16
~putz 123 60
~regal 104 8
~scheibe 37 16
~schneidekelle 128 41
~schränkchen 22 40
~schreibpult 267 16
~spalierbaum 52 1
~spiegel 309 3
~steckdose 39 26
~streifen 335 11
~tafel 260 29; 261 36
~uhr 109 32; 309 87
~ventilator 266 15
~wange 123 45
Wange Anat. 16 9
~ Leiter 38 26; 50 36
~ Tischler 132 23
~ Kunst 336 40
Wangen·bein 16 8
~fleck 73 23
~mauer 217 80
~schutz 255 30
Wankel·motor 190 5
~scheibe 190 68
Wanne 162 50
Wannenablauf 49 45
Want 284 18
Wante 219 16
Wantenspanner 284 19
Wanthänger 284 14
Wanze 81 39
Wapiti 367 2
Wappen 254 1-6
~beschreibung 254 17-23
~feld 254 18-23
~feldordnung 254 17-23
~kunde 254 1-36
~mantel 254 14
~pfahl 352 1
~schild 254 5
~tier 254 15-16
~zelt 254 14
Waran 364 31
Ware Textilw. 166 12; 167 29,
    48; 171 29
~ Warenhaus 271 10
~, geraubte 168 36
Waren·abzug 167 48
~ausgabe 271 14
~bank 168 37
~baum 166 20; 167 29
~behälter 167 10

~einlauf 168 26
~gestell 98 14
~haus 268 41; 271
~kante 166 11
~körbchen 271 15
~leitwalze 168 5
~regal 47 36; 98 14
~schaft 171 21, 23
~schlauch 167 9
~schlauchbreite 167 16
~stange 178 6
Warmbeet 55 16
Wärme·ableitung 1 55
~gewitter 8 17
~kamin 182 5
Wärmen 139 1
Wärme·pumpe 155 22
~pumpensystem 155 1
~regulierungsklappe 10 65
Wärmeschutz 188 16
~kleidung 270 46
~schild 234 5, 20
Wärmespeicher 155 20
Wärmetauscher
    Energieversorgung 154 6,
    44; 155 3
~ Kokerei 156 27
~ Papier 172 19
~ Auto 192 61
~ Eisenb. 209 15; 212 36, 55
~ Mil. 259 66
~abgas 160 4, 7
~anlage 160 6
Wärmetransportmittel 155 31
Wärmflasche 309 88
Warmfront 8 5-12, 5; 9 26
warm·gemäßigter
    Regengürtel 9 55
Warm·haltebox 28 21
~halteplatte 45 45
~halteteller 28 28
~haus 55 4, 32
Warmluft·verteilung 191 87
~vorhang 271 43
Warmmassivumformung 139
Warmwasser·behälter 92 10;
    172 18
~boiler 38 68
~griff 126 28
~hahn 49 26
~heizung 38 38-81
Warn·blinklicht 230 64
~kreuz 202 41
Warnlicht 270 6
~kontrolle 191 76
~schalter 191 68
Warnungstafel 280 6
Warte·bank 205 54
~halle 233 18, 28
Wartentafel 153 7
Warte·raum Med. 22 1
~raum Eisenb. 204 14
~saal 204 14
~zimmer 22 1
Wartturm 329 4, 35
Wartungs·fahrzeug 233 22
~- und Abfertigungs-
    fahrzeuge 233 22
Warzenhof 16 29
Wasch·anlage Friseur 105 28
~anlage Sägewerk 157 21
~bär 368 9
~becken 24 15; 49 24; 106 12;
    126 27, 31; 278 6
~beckenfuß 49 27
~brett 309 70
~bütte 309 69
Wäsche Kleidung 32
~ Haushalt 50 13
~, schmutzige 50 22
~abteil 267 31
~fach 43 2
~haken 38 22

Wascheindicker 172 44
Wäscheleine 38 23;
    50 33
Wäscherei 170 56
Wäsche-schublade 44 22; 47
    22
~stampfer 309 68
~ständer 50 32
Waschetage 92 3, 27
Wäsche·trockner 50 32
~truhe 50 21
Wasch·gerät 50 23-34
~küchenfenster 118 5
~küchentür 118 6
~maschine 50 23
~medien 156 37
~öltank 156 43
~raum 207 15; 278 5
~schalter 191 60
~schlauch 196 23
~schüssel 309 65
~service 309 64
~ständer 309 67
~tisch 207 40
~trommel 50 24
~- und Spülbecken 278 6
~vollautomat 50 23
~wanne 309 69
~zettel 185 39
Wasser 12 32; 49 2; 55 30; 92
    42; 332 45
~, emporquellendes 12 26
~, filtriertes 269 12
~, fließendes 89 1
~, offenes 227 4
~abfluß 269 57
~ablauf Fischzucht 89 8
~ablauf Fotogr. 116 17
~absaugung 281 39
~anschluß 23 49; 261 4
~assel 358 2
~auffangbehälter 92 5
~aufnahme 310 11
~bad 132 12; 349 14
~bad, thermokonstantes 23
    48
Wasserball Strandbad 280 18
~ Sport 282 48
Wasserballast 223 78
Wasserball·spiel 282 46-50
~tor 282 46
Wasser-bassin 55 29
~behälter 55 29; 103 22; 152
    17; 316 51
~bombenablaufbühne 258 34
~düsenkanal 281 40
~fahrrad 280 12
~fall 11 45
~fall, künstlicher 272 9
~farbe 338 18
~fee 327 23
~flugzeug 232 1, 5
~fontäne 272 62
~frau 327 23
wasserführende Schicht 12
    22; 269 2, 38
Wasser·geflügel 272 51-54
~gerät 126 12-25
~glas 24 13; 48 8
~graben 289 20; 356 3
~hahn 39 36; 126 31, 34
~haltung 144 46
~hochbehälter 269 18
~hochreservoir 269 18
~huhn 359 20
~jagd 86 40
~jungfer Fabelwesen 327 23
~jungfer Zool. 358 3
~kanal 334 54
~kanne 309 66
~kanone 270 66; 316 18
~kasten Toilette 49 16

~kasten Schweiß. 141 17
~kasten Eisenb. 210 66
~kessel 39 16
~kissen 13 16
~kugel 89 47
~kühler 189 35
~kühlung Mondlandung 6 26
~kühlung Eisengießerei 148 28
~künste 272 8
~kunstspringen 282 40-45
~lauf 272 45
~leitung 74 26; 168 11; 172 65
~licht 221 125
~lilie 60 8
~linie 258 27; 285 31
~linse 378 35
wasserlösliches Medikament 25 14
Wassermann Astr. 4 63
~ Fabelwesen 327 23
Wasser-messer 269 53
~meßgerät 97 58
~mischbatterie 39 36
~mischgerät 97 58
~misch- und -meßgerät 97 58
~molch 364 20
~molekül 242 67
~motte 358 12
~mühle 15 77; 91 35-44
~nachtigall 361 14
~natter 364 38
~nixe 327 23
~nymphe 327 23
~oberfläche 228 11
~pest 378 56
~pfeife 107 42
~pflanze 378 14-57
~pumpe 190 61
~pumpenraum 92 11
~pumpenzange 126 61; 127 47; 134 11
~rad 91 35
~reservoir 55 2
~rohr 55 30; 152 7
~sack 278 32
~schale 261 33
~schlange Astr. 3 16
~schlange Zool. 364 38
~schlauch 118 38; 196 23
~schutzpolizei 217 24
~schwamm 340 25
~schwertel 60 8
~schwertlilie 60 8
Wasserski 280 16; 286 45-62, 56-62
~läufer 286 49-55
~läuferin 286 45
~sprache 286 49-55
Wasser-skorpion 358 4
~speier 335 30
~spiele 272 8
~springen 282 40-45
~sprung 282 40-45
~spülanschluß 179 5
~stag 219 15
Wasserstands-anzeiger Eisenb. 210 45
~anzeiger Hafen 225 37
~messer 38 63
~zeiger 349 16
Wassersteckling 54 19
Wasserstoff 1 1
~atom 1 15; 242 62
~ballon 10 56
~behälter 235 46
~bombenexplosion 7 12
~hauptzufuhr 235 35
~kühler 153 27
~leitung 235 50
~pumpe 235 41
~tank 6 6; 235 54
~- und Sauerstoffbehälter

235 46
~zufuhr 350 12
~zuführung 170 15
Wasser-strahl 272 22
~strahlpumpe 23 49
~temperaturangabe 280 8
~treten 282 39
~tretrad 280 12
~turm 15 81; 144 14; 269 18
~überfall 91 43
~uhr 269 53
~-und-Dampf-Fontäne 11 22
~- und Lufttemperatur-angabe 280 8
wasserundurchlässige Schicht 269 36
Wässerungs-gerät 116 15
~wanne 116 15
Wasser-velo 280 12
~versorgung 27 46; 269
~vorwärmer 152 10
~waage 118 55; 126 79; 134 29
~wanze 358 4
~weib 327 23
~werfer 270 64
~wolf 364 16
~zähler 269 53, 58
~zufluß 126 18; 269 54
~zuflußleitung 92 48
~zulauf 74 7; 89 7; 116 16
~zuleitung 103 21
Wattebäuschchen 99 30
Wattengrenze 15 9
Wattepackung 99 28
wattierte Steppweste 30 16
WC-Raum 207 72
Weber 171 4
Weberei 165; 166
~vorbereitung 165 1-57
Web-fach 166 40
~kante 166 11; 171 20
~lade 166 41
~maschine 166 1, 35
~rand 166 11
~schütz 166 9, 26
Webstuhl 166 1, 35
~gestell 166 24
~rahmen 166 24
Wechsel Jagd 86 16
~ Bau 120 41; 121 71
~ Bank 250 17
~, angenommener 250 12
~, gezogener 250 12
~aufbau 213 40
~balken 120 41
~betrag 250 18
~fräser 100 5
~geldkasse 236 23
~hebel 132 56
~klausel 250 17
~nehmer 250 19
~objektiv 112 62; 115 43
~pritsche 194 23
~rad 10 14; 166 19
~räderkasten 149 7
~radschere 164 40
~sieb 64 19
~sprechanlage 202 48; 203 69
~sprechgerät 246 10
~stelle 204 31
~stempelmarke 250 24
~stromzähler 127 32
~summe 250 18
~tierchen 357 1
~winkel 346 10
Weck 97 13-16
Wecken 97 13-16
Wecker 43 16; 110 19
Weck-glas 40 25
~uhr 110 19

Wedel 88 19
Wega 3 22
Weg-einfassung 51 15; 272 37
~malve 376 13
~rauke 61 16
~warte 376 25
~weiser 15 110
Wegwerf-feuerzeug 107 30
~flasche 93 29
~windel 28 22
Wehr 15 66; 217 65-72; 283 60
~gang 329 20
~hahn 359 25
~platte 329 8
~sohle 217 79
Weibchen 81 32; 358 21
weibliche Blüte 59 38
weiblicher Blütenstand 68 32
Weich-bleikern 87 56
~bodenmatte 296 18
Weiche Anat. 16 32
~ Eisenb. 202 27; 203 45-48
~ Wasserbau 217 27
Weichen-anlage 197 37
~antrieb 197 43; 202 35
~hebel 203 55, 62
~laterne 202 19
~schaltsignal 197 38
~signal 202 19, 33; 203 45-48
~signalgeber 197 39
~spitzenverschluß 202 28
~trog 202 34
~- und Signalhebel 203 62
~zunge 202 21
Weich-Keim-Etage 92 8, 28
~leder-Objektivköcher 115 105
~machen 169 22
~mais 68 31
Weichselkirche 59 5
Weich-stock 92 8
~tier 357 27-37
~- und Geschmeidigmachen 169 22
~wasserkondensator 92 6
Weidelgras, Deutsches 69 26
~, Welsches 69 26
Weiden-klee 69 2
~rute 136 14
~stock 136 15
Weide-vieh 62 45
~zaun, elektrischer 62 46
Weid-mann 86 1
~messer 87 42
~sack 86 3
~werk 86 1-52
Weigelie 373 23
Weihnachtsstollen 97 11
Weihrauch-faß 332 38
~löffel 332 43
~schiffchen 332 42
Weihwasserkessel 332 47
Weihwedel 332 54
Weiler 15 101
Weimutskiefer 372 30
Wein 98 60-64; 332 46
~, Wilder 51 5; 374 16
~bau 78
~bauer 78 13
~baugelände 78 1-21
~beere 78 5
~behälter 79 3
Weinberg 15 65; 78 1
~schlepper 78 21; 83 48
~schnecke 357 27
Weinbergsgelände 78 1-21
Wein-brand 98 59
~brandbohne 98 83
~bütte 78 15
~flasche 79 14; 99 76; 266 43
~garten 78 1
~glas 44 9; 45 12; 79 19; 266

33; 317 7
~karaffe 266 32
~karte 266 31
~keller 79 1-22
~kellner 266 30
~küfer 79 18
~küfermeister 79 17
~kühler 266 42
~leserin 78 11
~lokal 266 30-44
~pfahl 78 7
~probe 79 16
~ranke 78 2
~rebe 54 22; 78 2-9
~rebenblatt 78 4
~rebenzeile 83 51
~restaurant 266 30-44
~stock 78 2-9
~stube 266 30-44
~stütze 79 15
~traube 78 5; 99 89
Weisel 77 4
~wiege 77 37
weiß 343 11
Weiß-bier 93 26
~blässe 359 20
~brot 97 9
~brot, französisches 97 12
~brötchen 97 14
~buche 371 63
~dorn, Eingriffeliger 374 30
~drossel 361 16
Weiße Bachstelze 360 9
~ Erve 69 19
~ Lilie 60 12
~ Narzisse 60 4
weißer Dotter 74 67
~ Kittel 33 56
Weißer Seerabe 359 9
~ Wiesenklee 69 2
weißes Feld 276 2
Weiß-goldschließe 36 10
~käse 76 45
~klee 69 2
~kohl 57 32
~kraut 57 32
~leim 134 36
~tanne 372 1
~waren 271 57
~wein 98 60
~weinglas 45 82
~zeugfutter 355 57
Weite 100 19
Weiterverarbeitung, textile 169 27
Weit-fixleisten 100 55
~schlag 293 83
~sprung 298 37-41
~winkelobjektiv 115 45; 117 48
~wurfring 89 58
Weizen 68 1, 23
~, türkischer 68 31
~bier 93 26
~brötchen 97 14
~keimbrot 97 48
~keimöl 98 24
~mehl 97 52; 99 63
Wellasbest-zementdach 122 97
~zementdeckung 122 90-103
Welle 109 17; 143 61; 163 24; 164 42
Wellen-bad 281 1-9
~balken 254 6
~band 334 39
~bock 223 61
~brecher 217 16; 258 7, 76
~hose 223 59
~reiten 279 1-6
~segeln 278 10
~tunnel 223 66
Weller 364 12

Welltafel 122 98
Welpe 73 16; 88 42
Wels 364 12
welsche Haube 336 3
~ Nuß 59 43
Welscher Klee 69 9
Welsches Weidelgras 69 26
Welschkraut 57 33
Welt-karte 14 10-45
~meer 14 19-26
Weltraum 7 34
~fähre 235 1-45
Wende 297 30; 302 19
~boje 285 17; 286 31
~getriebe 65 41; 149 14; 212 74
~haken 85 7, 9
~hals 359 27
~kreis 3 4; 14 10
Wendel-rutsche 144 28
~rutschenförderung 144 28
~treppe 123 76, 77
Wendemarke 285 17
Wenden Forstw. 84 18
~ Segelsport 285 27
Wende-pflahl 292 79
~platte 149 47
~punkt 347 21
~richter 282 26
~schiene 164 17
~schneidplatte 149 45, 46
~trommel 64 13
~vorrichtung 139 43
~zeiger 230 12
Werbe-anzeige 342 56
~diapositiv 312 23
~kalender 22 10
~plakat 98 2; 204 10; 268 71; 271 25
~stempelabdruck 236 56
~umschlag 185 37
Werfer 292 50, 68, 76
~platte 292 69
Werft 222 1-43
~kran 225 24
~schuppen 225 23
Werk-bank 125 10; 134 41; 137 21; 140 7
~brett 108 20; 136 7
~brettfell 108 21
~halle 222 4
~platte 110 37
~raum 260 46-85
Werkstatt 62 17; 146 30; 195; 310 6
~, graphische 340 27-64
~bereich 5 17
~muli 109 22
Werkstattor 120 5
Werkstattschleifmaschine 138 7
Werkstück 104 25; 133 44; 139 28, 32, 46; 140 6; 141 20; 142 28
~aufnahmetisch 150 20
~klemme 142 35
Werktisch 109 2; 260 46
Werkzeug 6 27; 119 77-89; 195 43
~auflage 135 5
~kasten 134 35; 212 45
~koffer 127 49
~maschine 149; 150
~schleifbock 137 18
~schrank 134 1-34
~support 150 13
~tasche 187 25
~wagen 195 42
Wermut Getränk 98 62
~ Bot. 380 4
Wert, reziproker 344 16
~bezeichnung 252 32
~gelaß 236 22

Wertpapier 251 2, 11-19
~, festverzinsliches 251 11-19
~börse 251 1-10
Wertzeichen-bogen 236 21
~mappe 236 20
Wespe 82 35
Wespentaille 355 53
Westaustralstrom 14 45
Weste 33 4; 355 75
West-fassade 335 22
~punkt 4 15
~werk 335 22
~wind 9 50
~winddrift 14 44
Wetter 8 1-19
~beobachtungsschiff 9 7
~beobachtungsstelle 9 7
~bericht 342 65
~erscheinungen 9 30-39
~fahne 121 26; 331 4
~kanal 144 22
~karte 9 1-39; 342 66
~kunde 8; 9
~leuchten 9 39
~parka 29 66
~radarantenne 231 18
~satellit 10 64
~schacht 144 21
~schleuse 144 38
~station 9 7
~warte 225 33
Wett-rudern 283 1-18
~schwimmer 282 28
Wetz-stahl 94 16
~stein 66 19
Weymouthskiefer 372 30
Whirlpool 93 2
Whisky-flasche 42 31
~glas 267 57
Wicke, Gemeine 69 18
Wickel 370 77
~gestell 163 48
~keule 153 36
~kind 28 5
~kleid 30 25
~kommode 28 11
~mulde 163 15
~rock 31 13
~tischaufsatz 28 4
~umschlagbrett 163 19
Wickler 82 43
Wicklung 298 54
Widder Astr. 4 53
~punkt 3 6
Widerdruckwerk 181 49
Widerhaken Zool. 77 10
~ Angelsport 89 80
~ Masch. 143 44
Widerlager Brücken 215 29
~ Schiff 221 29
~ Kunst 336 20
Widerrist 70 11; 72 17
Widerstand 153 56; 242 73
Widmung 185 50
Wiedehopf 359 25
Wieder-belebung 21 24-27
~belebungsapparat 21 27
~belebungsgerät 270 20
~erhitzen 162 19
~erhitzung 162 27
Wiedergabe 238 56, 58
~gerät 311 23
~kopf 311 25
Wiedergeburt 327 10
Wiederholung 310 35
Wiederholungszeichen 321 26
Wieder-käuer 73 1; 366 28-30; 367 1-10
~kreuz 332 68
Wiege 340 19

~bunker 225 22
~eisen 340 19
~häuschen 206 40
~messer 340 19
~plattform 22 67
Wiener 96 8
Wiese Landkarte 15 18
~ Landw. 63 22
~ Rummelplatz 308 1
~, nasse 15 19
Wiesel 367 16
Wiesen-aue 13 13
~blume 375; 376
~flockenblume 376 12
~fuchsschwanz 69 27
~klee, Roter 69 1
~klee, Weißer 69 2
~knopf, Großer 69 28
~knöterich 376 10
~schaumkraut 375 11
~schwingel 69 24
Wikinger-drache 218 13-17
~schiff 218 13-17
Wild 88
~dieb 86 29
Wilde Kamille 61 8
Wild-ente 272 51
~entenzug 86 41
Wilderer 86 29
Wilder Senf 61 18
~ Wein 51 5; 374 16
Wild-frevler 86 29
~futterstelle 86 28
~gatter 84 7
~gehege 272 49
~hafer 61 29
~kalb 88 1
~kanzel 86 14
~kirsche 59 5
Wildleder-gamasche 352 17
~jacke 30 58
Wild-pferd 328 7
~sau 86 32
~schwan 359 16
~schwein 86 32; 88 51
~schweinjagd 86 31
~wagen 86 39
~wasserrennkajak 283 69
~wechsel 86 16
~zaun 199 13
Wilsonsche Nebelkammer 2 24
Wimpel 253 29; 280 11
~mast 280 10
Wimper Anat. 19 41
~ Zool. 357 10
~ Bot. 370 50
Wimperg 335 36
Wimper-infusorium 357 9
~tierchen 357 9
Wind 9 9-19; 285 1, 9; 326 47
~, halber 285 11
~, raumer 285 12
~beutel 97 27
~blütler 59 44-51
~brett 122 27
~diele 37 8
Winde Bot. 61 26
~ Erdöl 145 11
~, polare 9 51
Windeisen 140 30
Windel-höschen 29 10
~hose 28 22
Winden-haus 226 54
~start 287 5
Wind-erhitzer 147 15
~fahne 9 10; 10 32; 55 36; 331 4
~flüchter 13 43
~form 147 20
~geist 327 55
~geschwindigkeit 10 29

~hafer 61 29
~kammer 326 12
~kanal 326 11
~kessel 83 44; 269 17, 50
~kraftwerk 155 42
~lade 326 12-14
~leitung 148 2
~messer 10 28
~meßgerät 10 28
~motor 55 34
Windmühle 15 31; 91 1-34
~, holländische 91 29
Windmühlen-flügel 91 1
~getriebe 91 11
~haube 91 30
Wind-pfeil 9 9
~portal 215 38
~rad 15 73; 55 35; 308 15
~richtung 9 9; 10 31; 285 1-13, 6
~rispe 121 30
~rute 91 2
~sack Segelflug 287 11
~sack Mus. 322 9
~schirm Astr. 5 15
~schirm Völkerkunde 354 35
Windschutz 223 17
~scheibe 191 21; 255 97
~schild 5 31
Wind-stärke 9 10
~stille 9 11
~surfer 284 1
~surfing 284 1-9
~systeme 9 46-52
~tür 91 4
~verführung 326 14
~werk 217 74
~werksbrücke 217 73
~werkshaus 217 71
Wingert 78 1
Winkel Installateur 126 52
~ Math. 346 1-23, 8
~, gestreckter 346 13,9-15
~, rechter 346 9, 32
~, spitzer 346 10
~, stumpfer 346 11
~, überstumpfer 346 10,11-12
~band 140 50
~bauweise 248 39
~deck 259 12
~eisen 143 1
~funktion 346 32
~haken 174 13
~halbierende 346 30
~liegestütz 295 24
~lineal 133 19; 151 4; 260 37
~messer 260 38
~meßgerät 14 52-62
~reibahle 125 9
~schere 125 2
~spiegel 177 28; 261 10
~spinne 81 9
~sprung 295 38
~stütz 295 16
~sucher 115 71
~trieb 91 25
~verschraubung 126 40, 45
~zange 137 37
~zeichen 345 23
Winnetouhütte 273 59
Winsch 258 86
Winter-blume 379 3
~deich 216 32
~futterstelle 86 28
~garten 259 93
~goldhähnchen 361 10
~hafen 216 14
~hose 30 19
~kleid 30 12
~kleidung 30
~kohl 57 34
~könig 361 12

~landschaft 304
~mantel 30 61
~saateule 80 42
~sport 301; 302; 303
~stiefel 101 1
~temperatur 9 42
Winzer 78 13
Wipfel 370 4
Wippe Spielplatz 273 35
~ Zirkus 307 59
~ Mus. 325 32
Wippenschalter 127 4
Wirbel Astr. 4 38
~ Anat. 16 1
~ Mus. 323 18; 324 11
~bildung 234 11
~brett 324 19
~kasten 323 19; 324 10
~keule 229 30
Wirbellose 357
wirbelloses Tier 357
Wirbelsäule 17 2-5
~schwader 64 40-45
~trommel 323 51
~wender 64 46-58
Wirkanlage 97 57
Wirkerei 167
Wirkwaren 271 56
Wirsching 57 33
Wirsing 57 33
~kohl 57 33
Wirtel Angelsport 89 77
~ Drechsler 135 9
~ Spinnerei 164 48
Wirtschaft 266 1-29
Wirtschafts-bahn 15 90
~gebäude 329 27
Wisch-Waschschalter 191 60
~-Wasch- und Hupschalter
   191 60
Wisent 328 9
Witterung 8 1-19
Witwenschleier 331 39
Wobbler, einteiliger 89 69
Wochenendhaus 37 84-86
Wogenroß 218 13-17
Wohlriechender
   Pfeifenstrauch 373 9
Wohltätigkeitsveranstaltung
   319 31
Wohn-anhänger 278 52
~haus 62 1
~netz 81 10
~raum 224 108; 227 19; 259
   84
~wagen Camping 278 52
~wagen Zirkus 307 34
~wagenvorzelt 278 57
~zelt 353 19
~zimmer 42
Woilach 71 44
Wölbungs-klappe 229 46-48
~system, roman. 335 17
Wolf 367 13
Wolfs-beere 379 7
~hund 70 25
~kirsche 379 7
Wolken 8 1-19
~fetzen 8 11, 12
wolkenlos 9 20
wolkig 9 23
Wollblume 376 9
Wolle Schuh 101 42
~ Bot. 383 19
Woll-gewebe 168 1
~gras 377 18
~handkrabbe 358 1
~klee 69 6
~kraut 376 9
~mütze 29 57; 35 26
~ware 168 1
Wood 293 91
Wörterbuch 262 17

~, medizinisches 22 22
Wrack 224 84, 85, 86
Wrasenabzug 39 17; 46 31
Wucherblume 61 7, 31; 376 4
Wucherung 80 33
Wühlmaus 366 17
~falle 83 37
~- und Maulwurfsfalle 83 37
Wulst Klempner 125 8
~ Heraldik 254 2
~ Kunst 334 28
~bug 222 74
~steven 222 74
Wunde 21 8
Wunderlampe 369 4
Wund-haken 26 50
~klee 69 6
Würdenträger 306 29
Wurf Landw. 66 16
~ Angelsport 89 20
~arm 305 52
~art 305 17-20
~brett 353 8
Würfel Spiele 276 31
~ Math. 347 30
~ Kristallkunde 351 2, 14, 16
~anke 108 18
~becher 47 42; 276 30
~bindung 171 11
~blitz 114 74
~blitzgerät 114 73
~kapitell 335 21
Würfeln 276 29
Würfel-spiel 276 29
~zucker 98 53
Wurf-gerät 352 31
~gitter 55 13
~holz 352 39
~kontrolle 89 64
~kugel 305 24
~linie 292 71
~mal 292 49
~messer 354 15
~netz 89 31
~nummer 307 43
~pfeil 319 22
~richtung 305 77
~riemen 352 5
~ring 308 47
~sieb 118 85
~taubenschießen 305 70-78
~- und Fanggerät 352 31
Wurm Zool. 58 64; 357 20-26
~ Fabelwesen 327 1
~farn 377 16
~fortsatz 20 18
~loch 58 65
~züngler 364 33
Würstchen 96 8
~bude 308 32
Wurst-gabel 96 44
~küche 96 31-59
~masse 96 41
~waren 96 6-11; 98 4; 99 54
~zange 308 35
Würze 92 50, 51, 52
~kühler 93 5
~kühlung 93 1-5
Wurzel Anat. 19 36
~ Bot. 54 21; 57 17; 68 17, 45;
   370 16-18, 78-82; 383 43
~ Math. 345 2, 3; 347 12
~anschwellung 80 27
~dorn 370 81
~exponent 345 2
~füßler 357 1
~galle 80 27
~grad 345 2
~haar 68 18; 370 18
~haut 19 28
~heber 24 48
~laus 80 26
~rechnung 345 2

~rippe 287 32
~stock 58 18; 84 14
~wert 345 2
~zeichen 345 2
~ziehen 345 2
Würzpfanne 92 52
Wüsten-springmaus 366 15
~waran 364 31
~zone 9 54

X

x-Achse 347 2
Xanthogenat 169 10
Xenon-Höchstdrucklampe
   312 39
~lampe 177 17
~lampengehäuse 177 42
X-Kontakt 115 14
X-Lage 288 60
Xylographie 340 1-13
Xylophon 324 61

Y

y-Achse 347 3
Ysop 374 5

Z

Zacken-ornament 335 16
~schutz 300 50
Zaddelärmel 355 46
Zahl 344 1-22, 3
~, allgemeine 344 9; 345 5
~, benannte 344 4
~, ganze 344 10, 18
~, gebrochene 344 10
~, gemischte 344 10
~, gerade 344 11
~, imaginäre 344 14
~, komplexe 344 14
~, negative 344 8
~, positive 344 7
~, reelle 344 14
~, ungerade 344 12
Zahlen-bruch 344 10
~taste 309 76
~wimpel 253 33-34
Zähler Druck 180 74
~ Math. 344 15
~schrank 127 31
Zahl-karte 236 27
~meisterbüro 223 45
Zählrohr 2 21
~fassung 2 20
~gerät 2 19
Zahl-stelle 250 22
~teller 265 3
~tisch 197 33
Zähluhr 163 61
Zahlung 271 8
Zählung, automatische 74 52
Zahlungsort 250 15
Zählwerk 224 57; 269 55, 59;
   271 9
Zahlzeichen 344 1
Zahn Anat. 19 28-37
~ Masch. 143 83
~ Textilw. 167 52
Zahnarzt 24 1
~gerät 24 4, 8
~helferin 24 18
Zahn-bein 19 31
~brücke 24 26
~bürste, elektrische 49 29
~bürsteneinsatz 49 30
~eisen 339 13
~ersatz 24 25
~fleisch 19 15

~füllung 24 30
~grund 143 84
~hobel 132 17
~kranz 143 90; 187 38, 74
~leiste 122 26
~mark 19 32
~pastapackung 99 31
~prothese 24 25
~putzbecher 49 28
~putzglas 49 28
Zahnrad 143 82-96; 187 35
~bahnanhänger 214 5
~bergbahn 214 4-5
Zahn-reinigungsinstrument
   24 45
~schmelz 19 30
~schnitt 334 14
~segment 249 31
~spachtel 128 46
~stange 217 69
~stangenbahn 214 7-11
~stocherbehälter 266 23
~stumpf 24 27
~trieb 112 39
Zahnung 174 30
Zähnung 236 62
Zahnradlokomotive 214 4
Zange Bau 121 49, 59
~ Tech. 139 33
~ Zool. 358 25
Zangen-brett 132 33
~griff 298 53
~kran 148 47
~schraubstock 140 10
Z-Antrieb 286 2
Zäpfchen 19 22
Zapfen Bau 121 84
~ Masch. 143 31, 63
~ Bot. 371 32
~achse 372 3
~schuppe 372 8, 14, 27, 38
Zapf-hahn Tankstelle 196 3
~hahn Diskothek 317 8
~pistole 196 3
~säule 196 1
~schlauch 196 2
~stelle 274 17
Zapfwelle 63 21; 64 49;
   65 31
Zapfwellen-getriebe 65 38
~kupplung 65 40
~schaltung 65 23, 40
Zap-Klappe 229 50
Zarge 322 33; 323 4, 25
Zauberpfeife 354 42
Zaum 71 7-13
~zeug 71 7-13
Zaun-eidechse 364 27
~könig 361 12
~schlüpfer 361 12
Zebra 366 27
~streifen 198 11; 268 24
Zeche 144 1-51
Zechstein 154 62
~letten 154 68
Zecke 358 44
Zeder 372 65
Zeh 19 52
Zehe 19 52, 53, 55, 56
Zehen-knochen 17 29
~nagel 19 57
~strecker 18 63
Zehner-bruch 344 20
~logarithmus 345 6
~stelle 344 3
Zehnfarben-Walzendruck-
   maschine 168 53
Zehn-Liter-Abfüllanlage 76
   26
~-Meter-Filmmagazin 115
   80
~meterplattform 282 7
Zehntel 344 20

Zehnzacker 300 48
Zeichen, geometrisches 345 21-24
~, mathematisches 345 15-24
~atelier 338
~block 338 35
~bock 338 34
~erklärung 14 27-29
~kopf 151 3
~maschine 151 2
~maßstab 151 33
~stift 260 5
~tisch 151 6
~winkel 151 7
Zeichnerbüro 151
Zeichnung 129 48
~, technische 151 16
Zeichnungsrolle 151 10
Zeigefinger 19 65
Zeiger 26 28; 349 34
~, großer 110 12
~, kleiner 110 13
~amboß 109 7
~waage 204 5
Zeile 175 4
~, gegossene 174 27
Zeilen-einsteller 249 23
~haus 37 77-81
~schalter 249 4
~setzmaschine 174 19
Zeisig 361 8
Zeising 90 5
Zeit 345 7
~abgleichknopf 116 39
~anzeige 289 40
~ball 280 5
~einstellrad 114 35
~lupenregler 243 49
~nehmer 282 24; 299 47
~schrift 22 4; 46 20; 262 15
~schriftenregal 262 15
~skala 249 74
~skalastopp 249 75
~teilung 10 17
~uhr 191 38; 211 37; 212 16
~uhr, elektrische 191 79
Zeitung 181 41, 56; 205 51; 265 25; 342 37-70
Zeitungs-austragvorrichtung 182 29
~halter 265 26
~kopf 342 39
~leser 265 24
~regal 262 16; 265 8
~satz 176 29
~schrank 265 8
~seite 342 37
~ständer 205 16
~stapel 182 31
~verkäufer 205 17; 268 75
Zeitwaage 109 27
Zella 334 51
Zelle Zool. 77 26-30, 27, 32, 33
~ Mühlen 91 36
~ Schwimmbad 282 1
Zellenboden, künstlicher 77 43
Zellenrad, oberschlächtiges 91 35
Zellen-ring 234 45, 49
~zuteilapparat 172 3
Zeller 57 27
Zellkern 357 2
Zellstoff 172 77, 78, 79
~auflöser 172 80
~blatt 169 2, 4, 6
~kocher 172 7
~platte 169 1
Zellulosefilament 169 15
Zellulosexanthogenat 169 9
Zelt 218 15
~apsis 278 27

~dach 121 22
~hering 278 24
~lampe 278 29
~leine 278 23
~mast 307 2
~pflock 278 24
~pflockhammer 278 25
~schere 218 14
~spannleine 278 23
~spannring 278 26
~stadt 307 61
~stange 278 38; 352 8
~stütze 307 13
Zement Anat. 19 29
~ Bau 118 43
~bahnrennen 290 24-28
~estrich 123 14
~fabrik 160
~glattstrich 123 14
~leisteneinfassung 52 20
~mahlanlage 160 12
~packmaschine 160 16
~rohr 200 62
~silo 119 30; 160 15; 201 22
~vorrattank 146 15
~werk 160
Zenit 4 11
Zentaur 327 52
Zentimeter-teilung 247 36
~- und Millimeterteilung 247 36/
Zentral-abscheider 172 15
~bau 334 55
Zentrale 237 25
Zentraleinheit 176 29; 244 6
zentrale Steuereinheit 242 2
Zentral-heizung 38 38-81
~heizungskessel 38 57
~heizungskörper 126 20
~luk 259 86
~steckbuchse 195 39
~stecker 195 2
~strahl 27 3
Zentrier-~, Saugerandrück- und Metallaufblockgerät 111 34
~ring 240 23
~sauger 111 23
~saugeraufnahme 111 22
Zentrifuge 23 59
Zentrifugendeckel 168 18
Zentriwinkel 346 55
Zentrum 346 43
Zerberus 327 29
Zerealien 68 1-37
Zerfall, spontaner 1 28
Zerfaserung 169 6
Zerlegen 96 58
Zero 275 18
Zertifikatsnummer 286 7
Zettel 165 29
~baum 165 29, 42
~kasten 245 23
~kette 165 43
~maschine 165 22
~maschinengestell 165 27
ZF-Verstärkermodul 240 4
Zichorie 57 40; 376 25
Zickzack-ornament 335 16
~schlitz 155 11
Ziege 73 14
Ziegel, ungebrannter 159 16
~dach 122 1
Ziegelei 15 89; 159
Ziegel-hammer 122 20
~ofen 159 19
~presse 159 11
~schneider 159 15
~stein 159 20
~steinwand 118 8
~werk 159
Ziegenbart 73 15
~, Gelber 381 32

Ziegenkopf 327 18
Zieget 86 43
Zieh-bank 108 2
~brunnen 15 100; 329 3
~düse 162 9
~hacke 66 1
~harmonika 324 36
~maschine 162 7
Ziel 286 28
~bahnhof 205 22
~boje 285 14
Zielfernrohr 14 48; 87 29; 255 28; 305 49
~absehen 87 31-32
Ziel-kreis 288 57, 58, 59
~kreuz 288 56
~kugel 305 23
~linie 286 30
~markierung 292 34
~pfahl 292 77
~richter 282 25; 290 5
~scheibe 305 30-33
~schild 197 20
~sprung 288 55
~tonne 285 14
~zeigereinrichtung 255 74
Ziemer 88 18, 35
Zier-band 334 38
~baum 373; 374
~garten 51 1-35
~gehänge 36 35
~giebel 335 36
~kordel 29 37
~naht 31 5
~stich 102 3
~strauch 272 14; 373; 374
~taschentuch 33 10
~verschnürung 29 3
Ziffer, arabische 344 2
~, römische 344 1
~blatt 110 25; 269 58
Zifferntaste 247 18; 271 3
Zigarette 107 12
Zigaretten-automat 268 69
~etui 107 10
~maschine 107 15
~papierheftchen 107 17
~schachtel 107 11
~spitze 107 16
~verkäufer 308 51
~wickler 107 15
Zigarillo 107 3
Zigarre 107 2
Zigarren-abschneider 107 9
~anzünder 191 88
~etui 107 8
~kiste 107 1
~-und-Zigaretten-Boy 267 49
Zigeunerin 306 36
Zikkurat 333 32
Zille 216 25
Zimbal 322 32
Zimbel 322 32
Zimier 254 1,11,30-36
Zimmerbock 358 38
Zimmerer 120 12
~werkstatt 120 4
Zimmer-kellner 267 33
~klavier 325 40
~linde 53 9
~mann 120 12
Zimmermanns-bleistift 120 77
~bock 358 38
~hammer 120 74
~hut 35 38; 120 13
Zimmer-nachweis 204 28
~nummer 267 10
~pflanze 42 36; 53; 248 14
~platz 120 1-59
~schlüssel 267 9
~stutzen 305 35

~tanne 53 16
~telefon 267 34
Zimt 382 25
~baum 382 22
~rinde 382 25
Zingel 329 15
Zink 322 12
~blech 122 14
Zinke 45 60
Zinkegge 65 88
Zinken 66 4
~tragrohr 64 53
Zinkplatte 178 32, 40; 179 9; 180 53; 340 52
Zinn, geschmolzenes 162 17
Zinne 329 7
Zinnenkranz 329 6
Zinnie 60 22
Zinnsoldat 309 52
Zins 345 7
Zinsen 345 7
Zins-fuß 345 7
~rechnung 345 7
Zipfelmütze 35 39
Zippe 361 16
Zirbelkiefer 372 29
Zirkelschneider 124 22
Zirkon 351 19
Zirkumflex 342 32
Zirkumpolarstern 3 5
Zirkus 307
~diener 307 27
~direktor 307 17
~kapelle 307 10
~loge 307 16
~nummer 307 25
~pferd 307 30
~wagen 206 20; 307 34
~zelt 307 1
Zirrokumulus 8 14
Zirrostratus 8 7
Zirrus 8 6
Ziselierhammer 108 41
Zither 324 21
Zitronat 98 10
Zitrone 384 23
Zitronenfalter 365 4
Zitrusfrucht 40 9
Zitterpappel 371 21
Zitze 75 19
Zivilkleidung 264 33
Zobel 30 60; 367 15
Zocker 89 76
Zodiakussymbole 4 53-64
Zoll-amt 217 24
~boot 253 35
~durchlaß 225 5
~flagge 253 35-38
zollfreier Einkauf 233 52
Zoll-gitter 225 3
~haus 225 6
~kreuzer 221 100
~rufsignal 253 37
~schranke 225 4
~stander 253 35
~stock 120 76; 134 33
~stocktasche 33 49
Zömeterium 331 59
Zoo 356
~besucher 356 6
zoologischer Garten 356
Zoom-einstellung 112 40
~hebel 117 54; 313 36
~objektiv 112 41; 117 2; 240 34; 313 23
~verstellhebel 313 22
Zopf 34 6
~band 34 7; 355 78
Zöpfchen 319 26
Zopf-frisur 34 30
~muster 30 39
~perücke 34 5; 355 77
~schleife 34 7; 355 78

~stich 102 7
Zubehörschuh 114 4; 115 20
Zubereitungsraum 96 31-59
Zubringer-besen 199 44
~feder 87 18
~schnecke 64 25
Zuchtperlen-armband 36 9
~collier 36 12
Zucker 98 53-55
~dose 44 32
~gast 81 14
~hut 99 64
~kuchen 97 43
~mais 68 31
~rohr 382 52
~rübe 68 44
~schälchen 265 20
~schaumgebäck 265 5
~tang 378 48
Zufahrtsrampe 199 15
Zuführlattentuch 163 8
Zuführung 148 38
Zug Jagd 87 36
~ Eisenb. 204 12
~ Spiele 276 6, 14
~ Theater 316 8
~ Mus. 323 47
Zugang 62 17; 99 4
Zugangs-klappe 6 21, 25
~leiter 6 35
~straße 329 34
Zug-bahnfunkgerät 212 23
~band 215 44
~beeinflussung, induktive
  211 7
~brett 168 7
~brücke 329 25
~deichsel 64 61
Zügel 71 25, 33; 186 31
~gurtbrücke 215 46
Zug-fahrzeug 194 21
~gurt 71 24
~haken Landmaschinen 65 19
~haken Pferd 71 14
~haken Erdöl 145 9
~haken Feuerwehr 270 49
~hakenkette 65 17
~halt 203 1, 3
~kaliber 87 37
~koch 207 34
Zugkraftanzeige 211 26
Zug-maschine 65 20
~messer 120 79
~öse 64 60
~posaune 323 46
~schalter 127 16
Zugseil 214 14, 21, 26, 37, 45
~antriebsscheibe 214 62
~bruch 214 71
~muffe 214 73
~rolle 214 32
~rollenbatterie 214 60
~spanngewicht 214 42
~tragrolle 214 49
~umlenkscheibe 214 61
Zug-sekretariat 205 37; 209 25
~sekretärin 209 27
~sicherung 212 14
~spindel 149 33
~spitze 203 31-32
~stange 65 18; 143 101
~strebe 192 81
~verspätung 205 24
~vogel 360 7
~wagen 85 43
~walze 168 3, 4, 6
Zuhaltung Schlosser 140 38
~ Büro 246 23
Zuhaltungsfeder 140 42
Zuleitung Schlachthof 94 9
~ Papier 173 13
~, elektrische 39 25; 50 77
Zulu 354 36

Zündblättchen 306 49
Zündholz 107 22
~schachtel 107 21
~ständer 266 24
Zünd-hütchen 87 59
~kerze 190 35; 242 48
~kopf 107 23
~schloß 191 75
~schnur 158 28
~- und Lenkradschloß 191 75
~verstellung 190 9
~verteiler 190 9, 27
~winkeleinschub 195 13
zunehmender Mond 4 3
Zunge Anat. 17 52; 19 25
~ Schuh 100 65; 101 32
~ Mus. 322 52; 326 19, 41
~, gespaltene 327 6
Zungenbein 20 2
Zungennadel 167 12, 56, 61
~reihe 167 27
Zungen-pfeife 326 17-22
~stimme 326 17-22
Zupf-geige 324 12
~instrument 322 21
Zusammentragestation 249
  60
Zusammenzählen 344 23
Zusatz-bremse 212 10
~bremsventil 211 23
~flügel 203 8, 22, 23
~gerät 134 50-55
~licht 203 14, 15, 17
~schaft 171 20
~signal 203 25-44
~tafel 203 12
~tank 232 20
~wärmetauscher 212 43
Zuschauer 308 29
~grenze 292 40
~platz 315 20
~raum 307 15; 315 16-20
Zuschlag Korbmacher 136 17
~ Hütt. 147 2
Zuschlagstoff 118 36; 119 26
Zuschneide-schablone 103 13
~schere 103 3
~tisch 103 4
Zuspiel-gerät 117 8
~ton 117 101
Zustand, angeregter 1 19
Zusteller 236 53
Zustelltasche 236 54
Zwackeisen 162 44
Zwangs-entlüftung 191 30
~mischer 201 23
Zwanzigflächner 351 11
Zwecke 61 30
Zweckgras 61 30
Zweiachteltakt 320 28
zweiäugige
  Spiegelreflexkamera 114
  22
Zweibackenfutter 135 10
Zwei-Band-Film- und -
  Tonaufnahme 117 70
~-Ton- und -
  Filmwiedergabe 117 75
Zwei-bandverfahren 117 7
~bein 255 42
~bettkabine 223 29
~drahtoberleitung 194 43
Zweier 283 15
~bob 303 19
Zweifach~-Hülsenkette 190
  49
~kombination 127 7
~-Rollenkette 190 10
Zwei-familienhaus 37 64-68
~flaschengerät 279 19
~flügler 358 16-20
Zweig 59 19, 48; 370 6; 371 10,
  25, 59; 372 36, 43; 378 27;

  382 17; 383 34, 46; 384 8,
  12, 42
Zweig, gebogener 203 46, 47
Zweig, gerader 203 45
Zweigangschaltung 188 12
Zweigebündel 216 53
Zwei-halbetakt 320 30
~kreisbremsanlage 191 72
~mannsessel 214 17
~master 220 11-17
~-Platz-zwei-Bett-Abteil
  207 38
~rad 187 1; 188
~radwiege 214 69
~rohrsystem 126 22
~-Scheiben-Wankelmotor
  190 5
~schlauch-Lungenautomat
  279 20
~seilbahn 214 25, 30
~sitzer 193 26, 28
~spänner 186 36
~spurgerät 241 56
~spur-Tonbandgerät 242 12
~ständer-
  Langhobelmaschine 150 8
~stärkenglas 111 15
Zweitakt-Einzylindermotor
  188 26
~gemischbehälter 196 13
~motor 56 30; 188 7; 242 55;
  305 92
~-Ottomotor 190 6
Zweite-Klasse-Teil 207 10
Zweitfrisur 105 38
Zweitouren-Schnellpresse
  181 1
Zweiunddreißigstel-note 320
  18
~pause 320 26
Zweivierteltakt 320 29
Zweiwalzen~-(Duo-)Gerüst
  148 53
~krümler 65 89
Zwei-wegehahn 350 49
~wellen-Gasturbine 209 23
~wellentriebwerk 232 51
~zehenfaultier 366 11
Zweizylinderboxermotor 189
  47
Zwerchfell 20 9, 26
Zwerchhaus 329 11
Zwerg 308 22
~arkade 335 8
~bohne 57 8
~falke 362 1
~huhn 74 56
~kiefer 372 21
~obstbaum 52 1,2,16,17,29
~- oder Buschbohne 57 8
~pudel 70 36
~schwalbe 359 11
Zwetsche 59 20
Zwetschge 59 20
Zwetschgen-baum 59 19-23
~kern 59 23
~kuchen 97 43
Zwickmühle 276 25
Zwieback 97 54
Zwiebel 54 28; 57 24
~galle 82 37
~kuppel 121 25
~schale 57 25
Zwiegriff 296 42
Zwilling 259 25
Zwillinge 3 28; 4 55
Zwillingsätzmaschine 178 30
~flak 258 31
~wadenmuskel 18 62
Zwinge 45 53
Zwingenknebel 260 48
Zwinger 329 31
Zwirl 135 11

Zwirn-kops 164 60
~maschine 164 57
Zwischen-balken 121 54
~bildfenster 113 37
~boden 120 43; 123 68
~bodenauffüllung 123 69
~bühne 145 5
~deck 223 76
~decke 123 61, 68-69
~flansch 190 39
~hängestück 316 11
~hirn 18 23
~lage 202 6
~latte 118 89
~podest 123 52-62
~radwelle 190 57
~raum Setzerei 175 17
~raum Mus. 320 44
~riegel 120 26, 55
~rufer 263 15
~schicht 11 4
~schiene 202 26
~sparren 121 56
~stiel 120 51
~stütze 214 29, 76
~titel 185 67
~tubus 115 81
~welle 232 57
~zelle 234 31, 36
Zwitterblüte 374 10; 382 12,
  14
zwölfachsiger
  Gelenktriebwagen 197 1
Zwölferpackung 76 25
Zwölffingerdarm 20 14, 43
Zwölfling 259 24
Zwölfzacker 300 48
Zyane 61 1
Zyklone 9 5
Zyklonwärmetauscher 160 6
Zyklotron 2 49
Zylinder Kopfbedeckung 35
  36; 289 6
~ Schlosser 140 45
~ Druck 180 79
~ Math. 347 38
~ Chem. 350 45
~ausleger 177 68
~durchmesser 167 16
~farbwerk 181 7
~fuß 178 10
~halsurne 328 40
~hebung 181 3
~hut 35 36; 186 25
Zylinderkopf 190 45; 242 47
~haube 190 48
~schraube 143 36
Zylinder-kurbelgehäuse 190
  19
~lötgebläse 108 16
~öl 145 63
~projektion 14 9
~schloß 140 44
~senkung 181 3
~stift 143 40
~temperaturanzeige 230 9
~trockner 165 50, 53
~walke 168 1
Zymbal 322 32
Zypergras 53 17
Zypresse 372 58

Index

Ordering

In this index the entries are ordered as follows:
1. Entries consisting of single words, e.g.: 'hair'.
2. Entries consisting of noun + adjective. Within this category the adjectives are entered alphabetically, e.g. 'hair, bobbed' is followed by 'hair, closely-cropped'.
   Where adjective and noun are regarded as elements of a single lexical item, they are not inverted, e.g.: 'blue spruce', not 'spruce, blue'.
3. Entries consisting of other phrases, e.g. 'hair curler', 'ham on the bone', are alphabetized as headwords.

Where a whole phrase makes the meaning or use of a headword highly specific, the whole phrase is entered alphabetically. For example 'ham on the bone' follows 'hammock'.

References

The numbers in bold type refer to the sections in which the word may be found, and those in normal type refer to the items named in the pictures. Homonyms, and in some cases uses of the same word in different fields, are distinguished by section headings (in italics), some of which are abbreviated, to help to identify at a glance the field required. In most cases the full form referred to by the abbreviations will be obvious. Those which are not are explained in the following list:

Agr.	Agriculture/Agricultural	*Hydr. Eng.*	Hydraulic Engineering
Alp. Plants	Alpine Plants	*Impl.*	Implements
Art. Studio	Artist's Studio	*Inf. Tech.*	Information Technology
Bldg.	Building	*Intern. Combust. Eng.*	Internal Combustion Engine
Carp.	Carpenter	*Moon L.*	Moon Landing
Cement Wks.	Cement Works	*Music Not.*	Musical Notation
Cost.	Costumes	*Overh. Irrign.*	Overhead Irrigation
Cyc.	Cycle	*Platem.*	Platemaking
Decid.	Deciduous	*Plant Propagn.*	Propagation of Plants
D.I.Y.	Do-it-yourself	*Rm.*	Room
Dom. Anim.	Domestic Animals	*Sp.*	Sports
Equest.	Equestrian Sport	*Text.*	Textile[s]
Gdn.	Garden	*Veg.*	Vegetable[s]

A

Aaron's rod 376 9
abacus 309
abacus *Art* 334 20
abattoir 94
abdomen *Man* 16 35-37, 36
abdomen *Bees* 77 10-19
abdomen *Forest Pests* 82 9
abdomen, lower ~ 16 37
abdomen, upper ~ 16 35
abductor hallucis 18 49
abductor of the hallux 18 49
aberdevine 361 8
aborigine, Australian ~ 352 37
abrasion platform 13 31
abrasive wheel combination 111 28, 35
abscissa 347 9
abseiling 300 28-30
abseil piton 300 39
abseil sling 300 28
absinth 380 4
absorber attachment 27 44
absorption dynamometer 143 97-107
absorption muffler 190 16
absorption silencer 190 16
abutment *Bridges* 215 27, 29, 45
abutment *Art* 336 20
abutment pier 215 29
acanthus 334 25
acceleration lane 15 16
acceleration rocket 234 22, 48
accelerator 191 46
accelerator lock 85 17
accelerator pedal 191 46, 94
accelerometer 230 10
accent, acute ~ 342 30

accent, circumflex ~ 342 32
accent, grave ~ 342 31
accent, strong ~ 321 27
accents 342 30-35
acceptance 250 12, 23
access balcony 37 72-76
access flap 6 21, 25
accessories 115 43-105
accessory shoe 114 4; 115 20
accessory shop 196 24
access ramp 199 15
acciaccatura 321 15
accipiters 362 10-13
accolade 329 66
accommodation 146 33
accommodation bureau 204 28
accommodation ladder 221 98
accomodation module 146 33
accompaniment side 324 43
accompaniment string 324 25
accordion 324 36
account, private ~ 250 4
accounting machine 236 26
accumulator 309 41
accumulator *Theatre* 316 55
accumulator railcar 211 55
accuracy jump 288 55
acerate 370 34
acerose 370 34
acerous 370 34
acetylene connection 141 31
acetylene control 141 32
acetylene cylinder 141 2, 22
achene 58 23
achievement 254 1-6
achievement, marital ~ 254 10-13
achievement of arms 254 1-6
Achilles' tendon 18 48
acicular 370 34

acid container 350 62
Ackermann steering system 85 31, 37
acolyte 331 45
aconite 379 1
acorn 371 4
acorns 276 42
acrobat 307 47
Acropolis 334 1-7
acroter 334 34
acroterion 334 34
acroterium 334 34
acting area light 316 16
acting area spotlight 316 16
actinia 369 20
Actinophrys 357 7
action 326 6-16
action lever 325 32
activated blade attachment 84 33
actor 316 37
actress 316 38
actuating transistor 195 19
acuity projector 111 47
acute 342 30
ad 342 56
Adam's apple 19 13
adapter 112 55
adapter, four-socket ~ 127 8
adapter, four-way ~ 127 8
adapter ring 115 82
adapter unit 242 34
adders 364 40-41
adding 344 23
adding and subtracting machine 309 74
adding mechanism 271 9
addition 344 23
address 236 42
address display 236 41
addressing machine, transfer-type ~ 245 7

address label 236 4
address system, ship's ~ 224 30
A-deck 223 28-30
adhesion railcar 214 1
adhesive, hot ~ 249 61
adhesive binder *Bookbind.* 184 1
adhesive binder *Office* 249 61
adhesive tape dispenser 247 27
adhesive tape dispenser, roller-type ~ 247 28
adhesive tape holder 247 28
adjusting cone 187 58
adjusting equipment 148 61-65
adjusting knob 116 54
adjusting nut 143 35
adjusting screw *Bldg. Site* 119 79
adjusting screw *Mach. Parts etc.* 143 107
adjusting screw *Inf. Tech.* 242 78
adjusting spindle 226 51
adjusting washer 187 55
adjustment, circular ~ 14 62
adjustment, coarse ~ 112 4
adjustment, fine ~ *Optic. Instr.* 112 5
adjustment, fine ~ *Photog.* 116 33
adjustment, fine ~ *Joiner* 133 36
adjustment, fine ~ *Drawing Off.* 151 66
adjustment knob 11 41
administration area 5 17
administration building *Coal* 144 18
administration building

Airport **233** 16
administration building
    Films **310** 4
Admiralty anchor **286** 15
admission ticket **315** 11
adult insect **358** 10
advance booking office **271**
    26
adventure playground **273** 21
advertisement **98** 2; **204** 10;
    268 43, 71; **271** 25; **312** 23;
    342 56, 69
advertising, classified ~ **342**
    69
advertising calendar **22** 10
advertising pillar **268** 70
adze **300** 34
aerator **56** 15
aerial **213** 4
aerial ladder **270** 9
aerial sports **288**
aerobatic manoeuvres **288** 1-9
aerobatics **288** 1-9
aero engines **232** 33-60
aerofoil, rear ~ **290** 35
aerogenerator **155** 42
aeroplane **230** 67-72
aeroplane, propeller-driven ~
    231 1-6
aeroplane, types of ~ **231** 1-33
aeroplane tow launch **287** 1
aerotowing **287** 1
aero wheel **305** 79
Afghan **70** 23
Afghan hound **70** 23
A flat major **320** 66
Africa **14** 14
African hemp **53** 9
African marigold **60** 20
Afro look **34** 26
afterburner exhaust nozzle
    256 13
aftercastle **218** 23
after deck **223** 32
afterpeak **227** 28
aftershave lotion **49** 38
aft fan-jet **232** 42
aft ship **286** 34, 37, 41
agaric **379** 10
agate **175** 22
agent **307** 18
aggregate scraper **200** 13
agitator *Agr. Mach.* **64** 70
agitator *Paperm.* **172** 47
agricultural implements **66**
agricultural machinery **64**; **65**
agricultural worker **63** 5
agriculture **63**
Agulhas Current **14** 37
aileron **230** 52; **287** 41; **288** 28
aileron, inner ~ **229** 43
aileron, outer ~ **229** 41
aileron actuator **257** 39
aiming position **86** 34
air-bed, inflatable ~ **278** 31
air blast **139** 56
air-blast circuit breaker **152**
    34; **153** 51-62
air-bleed duct *Roof &*
    Boilerr. **38** 51
air-bleed duct *Intern.*
    Combust. Eng. **190** 12
air blower, primary ~ **160** 11
air brake **229** 44; **256** 12
airbridge **233** 14
airbus **231** 17
air cleaner **191** 55
air compressor *Painter* **129** 33
air compressor *Offshore*
    Drill. **146** 23
air compressor *Railw.* **211** 14,
    44; **212** 34, 58, 72
air compressor, diesel-

powered ~ **200** 39
air compressor, mobile ~ **200**
    39
air-conditioning **26** 20
air-conditioning equipment
    239 15
air correction jet **192** 3
aircraft **229**; **230**; **231**; **232**
aircraft, propeller-driven ~
    231 1-6
aircraft, single-engine ~ **230**
    1-31, 32-66; **231** 1, 2
aircraft, tilt-wing ~ **232** 26
aircraft, twin-boom ~ **229** 34
aircraft, twin-engine ~ **231** 3
aircraft, twin-jet ~ **231** 7
aircraft, types of ~ **231** 1-33
aircraft cannon **256** 3
aircraft carrier, nuclear-
    powered ~ **259** 1
aircraft elevator **259** 4, 13
aircraft engines **232** 33-60
aircraft lift **259** 4, 13
aircraft tractor **233** 23
aircraft tug **233** 23
air currents **9** 25-29
air cushion **286** 66
air-cushion vehicle **286** 63
air duct **155** 35
airer **50** 32
airer, extending ~ **50** 34
air extraction vent **154** 21
air extractor duct **258** 57
air extractor pipe **133** 40
air feed pipe **147** 29
air filler neck **196** 21
air filter **191** 55
air flow **199** 45
air flow, secondary ~ **232** 50
air force **256**; **257**
air hose *Garage* **195** 54
air hose *Serv. Stat.* **196** 18
air inlet *Lorries etc.* **194** 16
air inlet *Warships* **259** 73
air inlet *Fire Brig.* **270** 60
air inlet and outlet **92** 14
air intake *Car* **192** 60
air intake *Railw.* **209** 11
air intake *Air Force* **256** 5; **257**
    12
air intake, annular ~ **232** 52
air intake duct **257** 14
air jet pipe **281** 41
air line **75** 28
airliner, four-jet ~ **231** 13
airliner, supersonic ~ **231** 15
airliner, tri-jet ~ **231** 12
airliner, twin-jet ~ **231** 11, 17
airliner, wide-body ~ **231** 14,
    17
air lock *Coal* **144** 38
air lock *Offshore Drill.* **146** 24
air lock *Space* **235** 27
air lock *Chem.* **349** 7
air masses, homogeneous ~ **8**
    1-4
air mattress **278** 31
air outlet **168** 29
air oxidation passage **165** 48
air passage **333** 4
airplane *see* aeroplane
airport **233**
'airport' **233** 24
airport fire service **233** 7
airport information symbols
    233 24-53
airport restaurant **233** 19
air preheater *Forging* **139** 53
air preheater *Power Plant* **152**
    11
air pump *Paperm.* **172** 40
air pump *Letterpress* **181** 6, 35
air receiver **269** 17, 50

air refuelling probe **256** 7
air regenerator chamber **147**
    30
air regulator *Offset Print.* **180**
    74
air regulator *Chem.* **350** 3, 8
air reservoir, auxiliary ~ **212**
    61
air reservoir, main ~ **211** 8;
    212 57, 71
air rifle **305** 40
air rifle cartridge **305** 34
airscrew **230** 32; **288** 36
air space **74** 61
air-speed indicator **230** 2
airsports **288**
airstream, cold ~ **9** 29
airstream, main ~ **192** 5
airstream, warm ~ **9** 28
air supply **155** 24
air survey camera **14** 63
air temperature **280** 8
air vent cap **38** 52
air vessel **269** 17, 50
aisle *Map* **15** 112
aisle *Forestry* **84** 1
aisle *Church* **330** 27
aisle *Art* **334** 63; **335** 2
alarm clock **110** 19
alarm clock, electric ~ **43** 16
albumen **74** 62
alburnum *Carp.* **120** 85
alburnum *Bot.* **370** 12
Alcor **3** 29
Aldebaran **3** 25
alder **371** 30
alder buckthorn **380** 13
alder dogwood **380** 13
alder-swamp peat **13** 18
ale **93** 26
ale hoof **375** 18
Alençon lace **102** 30
alfalfa grass **136** 26
alga, brown ~ **378** 48
alga, green ~ **378** 43
algebra **345** 4-5
alighting board **77** 49
alkali-cellulose **169** 9
alkali-cellulose crumbs **169** 7
Allais chicane **301** 72
all-container ship **221** 21;
    226 5
Aller rock salt **154** 63
allheal **380** 5
allonge periwig **34** 2
allotment **52** 1-32
allotment holder **52** 24
all-purpose gun **258** 70
all-purpose gun, radar-
    controlled ~ **258** 47, 48
all-purpose trailer **62** 40
all-purpose vehicle **255** 96
all-speed aileron **229** 43
alluvial deposit **216** 52
all-weather roof **200** 38
all-wheel drive **194** 1
almond *Tablew. etc.* **45** 41
almond *South. Fruits* **384** 36
aloe **53** 13
alphanumeric disc store **176**
    33
alpha particle **1** -31; **227**
alpha radiation **1** 30-31
Alpine Club hut **300** 1
alpine rhododendron **378** 1
alpine rose **378** 1
alpine soldanella **378** 3
alpine strawberry **58** 16
alpine wormwood **378** 6
Alpinism **300** 1-57
Alpinist **300** 5
Alsatian **70** 25
alsike **69** 3

alsike clover **69** 3
Altair **3** 9
altar **330** 4, 33; **334** 48, 69
altar bell **332** 52
altar candle **330** 7, 34
altar carpet **330** 3
altar cloth **330** 6, 36
altar cross **330** 35
altar crucifix **330** 12
altar decoration **330** 48
altarpiece **330** 13, 50
altar steps **330** 5, 31
alternative school **261** 1-45
alternator **152** 23; **153** 1
altimeter **230** 4
altitude **346** 27
altitude scale **7** 35
alto clef **320** 10
altocumulus **8** 15
altocumulus castellanus **8** 16
altocumulus floccus **8** 16
altostratus **8** 8
altostratus praecipitans **8** 9
alto trombone **323** 46
aluminium foil, asphalted ~
    155 29
aluminum *see* aluminium
A major **320** 58
amanita **379** 11
amaryllis **53** 8
Amazon water lily **378** 17
ambulance **270** 19
ambulance, armoured ~ **255**
    79
ambulance attendant **270** 21
ambulance car **270** 19
ambulance man **270** 21
America **14** 12-13
American blight **80** 32
American football **292** 22
American ivy **51** 5; **374** 16
A minor **320** 55, 62
A minor scale **320** 46, 47, 48
ammeter *Car* **191** 78
ammeter *Aircraft* **230** 18
ammonia **170** 24
ammonia scrubber **156** 23
ammonia wet collector **156** 23
ammonium sulphate **156** 36
ammonium sulphate,
    production of ~ **156** 35
ammonium sulphate solution
    170 26
ammunition **87** 19; **305** 34-49
amoeba **357** 1
amoretto **272** 20
amorino **272** 20
amount **271** 8
Amphibia **364**; **364** 20-26
amphibian **232** 8
amphibians **364** 20-26
amplifier **241** 40; **312** 19; **317**
    23
amplifier, underwater ~ **237** 57
amplifier and mains power
    unit **238** 3
amplifier equipment **310** 59
amplitude adjustment **10** 11
amulet **354** 40
anaesthesia and breathing
    apparatus **26** 1
anaesthesia and respiratory
    apparatus **26** 24
anaesthetic, local ~ **24** 53
analog *see* analogue
analogue control **242** 38
analogue output **112** 45
analyser **23** 53
analysis, automatic ~ **25** 48
analytical balance **349** 25
anchor **223** 52; **259** 81
anchor, lightweight ~ **286**
    16-18

anchor, stocked ~ **222** 79; **286** 15
anchor, stockless ~ **222** 78; **258** 5; **286** 17
anchorage **216** 13
anchor cable **218** 18; **222** 77; **223** 50; **227** 12
anchor capstan **258** 6
anchor hawser **218** 18
anchor rib **287** 32
anchor rope **218** 18
anchors **286** 15-18
anchor winch **259** 82
ancillary brake valve **211** 23
Andromeda **3** 24
anemometer **10** 28
anemone **375** 5; **377** 1
aneroid barometer **10** 4
aneroid box **10** 6
aneroid capsule **10** 6
angiographic examination table **27** 26
angiography room **27** 12
angle *Mach. Parts etc.* **143** 1
angle *Maths.* **346** 1-23; **346** 8-13, 8, 55
angle, acute ~ **346** 10
angle, adjacent ~ **346** 14
angle, alternate ~ **346** 10
angle, circumferential ~ **346** 56
angle, exterior ~ **346** 26
angle, interior ~ **346** 26
angle, obtuse ~ **346** 11
angle, straight ~ **346** 13,9-15
angle brace **118** 25; **119** 63; **121** 57
angle deck **259** 12
angle iron **143** 1
angle of departure **87** 75
angle of descent **87** 78
angle of dip **12** 3
angle of elevation **87** 76
angle of rotation **351** 33
angle of the mouth **16** 14; **19** 19
angle shears **125** 2
angle symbol **345** 23
angle tie **118** 25; **121** 57
angle tongs **137** 37
angle tower **329** 14, 17
angling **89** 20-94
angling fence **133** 19
Angora cat **73** 17
Angoumois grain moth **81** 29
Angoumois grain moth caterpillar **81** 30
Angoumois moth **81** 29
Anguidae **364** 37
animal, bovine ~ **73** 1
animal, cloven-hoofed ~ **73** 9
animal, horned ~ **73** 1
animal, inflatable ~ **280** 33
animal, rubber ~ **280** 33
animal, toy ~ **46** 13; **47** 6
animal, wild ~ **307** 56
animal enclosure **272** 49
animal house **356** 10
animals, domestic ~ **73** 18-36
animals, fabulous ~ **327** 1-61
animals, multicellular ~ **357** 13-39
animals, one-celled ~ **357** 1-12
animals, single-celled ~ **357** 1-12
animals, unicellular ~ **357** 1-12
ankle guard **291** 33
ankle sock, children's ~ **29** 30
annealing lehr **162** 18
annelid **357** 20

annexe **331** 13
annuity **251** 11-19
annulus **346** 57
Annunciation lily **60** 12
anode, copper ~ **178** 5
anode rod **178** 5
anorak *Child. Clothes* **29** 62
anorak *Mountain.* **300** 6
anorak hood **300** 19
Anseres **359** 15-17
ant **358** 21-22
Antarctica **14** 18
Antarctic Circumpolar Drift **14** 44
Antarctic Continent **14** 18
Antarctic Ocean **14** 22
antelope **367** 5
antenna *Meteorol. Instr.* **10** 59, 68
antenna *Forest Pests* **82** 3
antenna *Air Force* **256** 17
antenna *Warships* **258** 16, 46; **259** 7, 47, 89
antenna *Airsports* **288** 20, 88
antenna *Articulates* **358** 27, 53
antenna, maxillary ~ **358** 42
antenna, trichotomous ~ **81** 5
antenna down-lead **223** 4
antenna lead-in **223** 4
antenna mast **259** 6
antependium **330** 20
anthozoan **357** 17
anther *Soft Fruit* **58** 45
anther *Drupes & Nuts* **59** 10
anther *Conifers* **372** 35
anthropoid apes **368** 14-16
anthropoids **368** 14-16
anti-aircraft gun **258** 73
anti-aircraft gun, automatic ~ **259** 34
anti-aircraft machine gun **255** 63
anti-aircraft missile launcher **258** 32; **259** 5, 20
anti-aircraft rocket launcher **258** 32; **259** 5, 20
anticline **12** 16, 27
anticlinorium **12** 20
anticollision light **230** 64
anticyclone **9** 6
antifriction bearing **143** 69
anti-frost layer **198** 1; **200** 60
antimacassar **207** 48
anti-mist windscreen **189** 46
anti-mist windshield **189** 46
anti-radiation screen **154** 74
anti-rolling system **224** 26
antirrhinum **51** 32
anti set-off apparatus **181** 10
anti set-off spray **181** 10
anti-skate control **241** 25
anti-skid brake switch **211** 33
anti-slosh baffle **234** 13
anti-submarine missile launcher **258** 30, 50
anti-submarine rocket launcher **258** 30, 50
anti-submarine torpedo tube **258** 33
anti-syphon trap *Bathrm. etc.* **49** 27
anti-syphon trap *Plumb. etc.* **126** 26
anti-tank rocket launcher **255** 25
anti-tank tank **255** 88
anti-torque rotor **232** 14
anti-vortex system **234** 11
antler, palmate ~ **88** 40
antler, royal ~ **88** 8
antler, surroyal ~ **88** 9
antlers **88** 5-11, 29-31
anurans **364** 23-26

anus **20** 62
anvil *Plumb.* **125** 22
anvil *Blacksm.* **137** 11, 11-16; **138** 33
anvil *Forging* **139** 17, 31, 40
anvil *Office* **247** 5
anvil, clockmaker's ~ **109** 7
aorta **18** 10; **20** 54
aorta, abdominal ~ **18** 16
Apache girl **306** 9
apartment **37** 64-68, 69-71; **46**
apartment, ladies' ~ **329** 10
apartment building **37** 72-76
apartment building, high-rise ~ **37** 82
apartment building, multistory ~ **37** 77-81
apartment house **37** 72-76
apartment house, high-rise ~ **37** 82
apartment house, multistory ~ **37** 77-81
apatite **351** 20
aperture **115** 62, 63
aperture control, automatic ~ **117** 20
aperture control ring **115** 5; **117** 4
aperture ring **115** 5; **117** 4
aperture scale **115** 56
aperture setting **117** 4
aperture-setting control **114** 34
aperture-setting ring **115** 5; **117** 4
aperture-stop slide **112** 16
apex *Hunt.* **87** 77
apex *Airsports* **288** 47
aphid **80** 32; **358** 13
aphid, winged ~ **82** 39; **358** 15
aphid, wingless ~ **358** 14
apiarist **77** 57
apiary **77** 56
apiculture **77**
à pointe **314** 19
Apollo booster **234** 1, 2
Apollo service module **234** 56
Apollo space capsule **6** 9
Apollo spacecraft **6** 1
apostrophe **342** 22
apparatus, auxiliary ~ **296** 12-21; **297** 7-14
apparatus exercises **297** 15-32
apparatus gymnastics **296**; **297**
appendix **20** 18
appendix, vermiform ~ **20** 18
Appenzell dulcimer **322** 35
apple **58** 56; **99** 86; **370** 102
apple blossom **58** 54
appleblossom weevil **80** 10
apple core **58** 59
apple pip **58** 60
apple skin **58** 57
apple stalk **58** 61
apple tree **58** 51, 52
appliance room **270** 1
appliqué **29** 20
appoggiatura **321** 14, 15
appointments book **22** 11
appointments diary **246** 8
approach **329** 3
approach sign **203** 26, 27, 28, 29
approach signs **203** 26-29
apricot **59** 35
apricot blossom **59** 34
apricot branch, flowering ~ **59** 33
apricot flower **59** 34
apricot leaf **59** 36
apricot tree **59** 33-36

apron *Mach. Tools* **149** 16
apron *Electrotyp. etc.* **178** 9
apron *Airport* **233** 3
apron *Theatre* **316** 25
apron, butcher's ~ **96** 39
apron, composition ~ **164** 16
apron, frilled ~ **31** 33
apron, leather ~ *Arc Weld.* **142** 11
apron, leather ~ *Cotton Spin.* **164** 16
apron taxiway **233** 4
apse **334** 64; **335** 5
aquafer **12** 22; **269** 2, 38
aqualung **279** 19
aquarium **356** 14, 19
Aquarius **4** 63
aquatint **340** 14-24
aqueduct **334** 53
aquifer **12** 22; **269** 2, 38
Aquila **3** 9
aquilegia **60** 10
arabesque *Free Exerc.* **295** 30
arabesque *Ballet* **314** 18
arachnids **358** 40-47
araucaria **53** 16
arbor **272** 17
arbor vitae **372** 39
arbour **272** 17
arc *Films* **312** 42
arc *Maths.* **346** 53, 55
arc, graduated ~ **224** 2
arcade, blind ~ **335** 10
arcading **335** 8
arcading, blind ~ **335** 10
arcading, round ~ **335** 9
arc fibula **328** 24
arch *Bldg. Site* **119** 6
arch *Bridges* **215** 20
arch *Free Exerc.* **295** 34
arch *Theatre* **316** 11
arch *Art* **336** 19
arch, convex ~ **336** 34
arch, longitudinal ~ **19** 61
arch, parabolic ~ **336** 29
arch, reinforced concrete ~ **215** 50
arch, round ~ **336** 27
arch, segmental ~ **336** 28
arch, shouldered ~ **336** 33
arch, superciliary ~ **16** 5
arch, tented ~ **336** 35
arch, transverse ~ **335** 18
arch, trellis ~ **52** 12
arch, triumphal ~ **334** 59, 71
arch, trussed ~ **215** 25
arch, Tudor ~ **336** 37
arch, types of ~ **336** 19-37
Archaster **369** 17
arch board file **247** 40
arch bridge, spandrel-braced ~ **215** 28
arch bridge, stone ~ **215** 19
arched front support **295** 24
Archer *Astron.* **3** 37; **4** 61
archer *Sports* **305** 53
archery **305** 52-66
archimedes drill **108** 4
architrave **334** 18
archivolt **335** 25
arch span **215** 26
arch unit **247** 41
archway **337** 4
archway, memorial ~ **337** 3
arcing horn **152** 47; **153** 61
arcosolium **331** 60
Arctic Ocean **14** 21
arc welder **142** 2
arc welding, gas-shielded ~ **142** 33
arc welding helmet **142** 3, 39
area, epicentral ~ **11** 38
area spraying **83** 1

areca 380 19
areca nut 380 20
areca palm 380 19
arena *Equest.* 289 1
arena *Circus* 307 21
arena *Bullfight. etc.* 319 9
arena entrance 307 11
areola 16 29
argent 254 25
Argo 3 45
Aries 4 53
aril, laciniate ~ 382 34
arista 68 12
arithmetic 344 1-26; 345 1-24
arithmetic unit 244 6
arm *Man* 16 43-48; 17 12-14
arm *Living Rm.* 42 22
arm *Flat* 46 28
arm *Shoem.* 100 25
arm *Photog.* 115 93
arm *Joiner* 132 63
arm *Mach. Parts etc.* 143 88
arm *Mach. Tools* 150 24
arm *Music. Instr.* 322 16
arm *Maths.* 346 7-3
arm, adjustable ~ 195 26
arm, hydraulic ~ 85 21
arm, supplementary ~ 203 22, 23
arm, upper ~ 16 43
armadillo 366 8
armament 258 29-37
armature 339 25
armature support 339 24
armband 311; 270 22
armband, fluorescent ~ 199 7
arm bandage 21 1
arm bar 299 10
armchair 42 21; 267 26
armed forces 255; 256; 257
armlet 263 11; 270 22
armonie 322 25
armor *see* armour
armour 329 38, 62
armour, knight's ~ 329 38-65
armour, padded ~ 353 38
armour, steel tape ~ 153 50
armour, steel wire ~ 153 50
armoured car 264 16
armoured vehicles 255 79-95
armour plating 246 24
armpit 16 26
armpit hair 16 27
arm positions 314 7-10
armrest 106 18; 109 3; 207 45, 69; 208 26
arm sling 21 2
arms of the baron 254 10
arms of the family of the femme 254 11-13
arms of the family of the wife 254 11-13
arms of the husband 254 10
armstand dive 282 45
army 255
army armament 255 1-98
army weaponry 255 1-98
arnica 380 2
A road 15 83
arolla pine 372 29
arpeggio 321 22
arrangement of desks 260 1
arrester 152 35
arrester wire 259 16
arris 121 12
arris fillet 121 31
'arrivals' 233 26
arrivals and departures board 204 18
arrival schedule 204 19
arrival timetable 204 19
arrow 305 60

arrow head *Drawing Off.* 151 26
arrow head *Alp. Plants etc.* 378 51
art 333; 334; 335; 336; 337
art, Babylonian ~ 333 19-20
art, Baroque ~ 336 1-8
art, Byzantine ~ 334 72-75
art, Chinese ~ 337 1-6
art, computer-generated ~ 248 19
art, Early Christian ~ 334 61-71
art, Egyptian ~ 333 1-18
art, Etruscan ~ 334 49-52
art, Gothic ~ 335 22-41
art, Greek ~ 334 1-48
art, Indian ~ 337 19-28
art, Islamic ~ 337 12-18
art, Japanese ~ 337 7-11
art, Renaissance ~ 335 42-54
art, Rococo ~ 336 9-13
art, Roman ~ 334 53-60
art, Romanesque ~ 335 1-21
art director 310 43
artery, carotid ~ 18 1
artery, femoral ~ 18 19
artery, frontal ~ 18 5
artery, iliac ~ 18 17
artery, pulmonary ~ 18 11; 20 55
artery, radial ~ 18 21
artery, subclavian ~ 18 7
artery, temporal ~ 18 3
artery, tibial ~ 18 20
artery forceps 26 49
arthropods 358 1-23
articulates 358
artillery weapons 255 49-74
artist 338 2
artiste agent 307 18
artistes, travelling ~ 308 25-28
Art Nouveau easy chair 336 18
art of Asia Minor 333 37
art of the Assyrians 333 29-36
art of the Persians 333 21-28
arts section 342 67
ascent, vertical ~ 315 3
ascent stage 6 37-47
ascospore 381 13
ascus 381 12, 13
ash box door 38 39
ashpan 210 6, 7
ash pit 152 8
ashtray 42 29; 104 5; 207 46, 69; 208 29; 246 33
ashtray, spherical ~ 266 5
ash tree 371 38
Asia 14 16
asp 364 41
asparagus 57 14
asparagus bed 52 25
asparagus cutter 56 10
asparagus knife 56 10
asparagus patch 52 25
asparagus server 45 77
asparagus slice 45 77
aspen 371 21
aspergillum 332 54
asphalt drying and mixing plant 200 48
asphalt mixer drum 200 50
asphalt-mixing drum 200 50
aspiration psychrometer 10 33
asp viper 364 41
assay balance 108 35
assembler 174 23
assembling machine 249 59
assembling station 249 60
assembly of a circuit 242 72
assembly point 233 11, 29

assistant *Univ.* 262 7
assistant *Store* 271 63
assistant *Circus* 307 39
assistant, cellarer's ~ 79 12
assistant, dentist's ~ 24 18
assistant, doctor's ~ 22 19
assistant cameraman 310 42
assistant director *Films* 310 21, 46
assistant director *Theatre* 316 43
assistant lecturer 262 3
assistant producer 316 43
assistant professor 262 3
assistant sound engineer 310 57
association flag 286 6, 9
association football 291
asterisk 185 61
asteroids 4 47
astride jump 295 35, 37
astronaut 6 11; 235 67
astronomy 3; 4; 5
asymmetric bars 297 3
asymptote 347 29
athletics 298
Atlantic Ocean 14 20
Atlas 334 36
atmosphere 7
atoll 13 32
Atolla 369 5
atom 1; 2
atomic pile casing 259 67
atomic power plant 154 19
atom layer 7 32
atom models 1 1-8
atrium *Man* 20 45
atrium *Art* 334 66
attachment to Orbiter 235 49
attack 321 27
attack area 293 64
attacker *Ball Games* 292 3
attacker *Fencing* 294 5
attacking fencer 294 5
attack line 293 65
attack periscope 259 88
attic 38 1-29, 18; 334 60
attitude 314 17
attitude control rocket 234 38
aubretia 51 7
auction room 225 58
audience 263 8
audio cassette 242 17
audio coding equipment 242 11-14
audio head 243 35
audio level control 117 16
audio recording level control 243 11
audio sync head 243 24
audio systems 241
audio track 243 32
audio typist 248 33
audiovision 243
audio-visual camera 243 1-4
audio-visual projector 242 16
auditorium 315 14-27, 16-20
auditorium lighting control 312 17
auger *Agr. Mach.* 64 6, 25
auger *Carp.* 120 65
augmented triad 321 4
auk 359 13
aulos 322 3
aulos pipe 322 4
aural syringe 22 74
aureus 252 3
auricle 17 56; 20 24
auricula 378 8
Auriga 3 27
auriscope 22 74
aurora 7 30
Australia 14 17

Australopithecus 261 20
auto 191 1-56; 195 34
auto changer 241 18
autoclave 170 12, 33
autofocus override switch 117 11
automatic flight control panel 235 23
automatic-threading button 117 83
automobile 191 1-56; 192; 193; 195 34
automobile models 193 1-36
automobile tire 191 15; 196 27
automotive mechanic 195 53
autopilot 224 18
auto-soling machine 100 2
auxiliaries 258 92-97
auxiliary brake valve 211 23
auxiliary-cable tensioning mechanism 214 48
auxiliary engine room 223 70; 259 56
auxiliary parachute bay 235 59
AV 243
avalanche 304 1
avalanche forest 304 7
avalanche gallery 304 3
avalanche wall 304 2
avalanche wedge 304 2
Ave Maria 332 32
avenue 274 11
aviary 356 8
aviation fuel 145 57
avionics bay, front ~ 257 11
avionics bay, rear ~ 257 18
avionics console 235 22
awn 68 12
awner 64 10
awning *Dwellings* 37 71
awning *Ship* 218 15; 221 116
awning *Camping* 278 28, 37
awning crutch 218 14
ax *see* axe
axe 85 1; 120 73; 270 43
axe, bronze ~ 328 23
axe, socketed ~ 328 23
axial-flow pump 217 47-52
axis *Astron.* 4 22
axis *Maths.* 347 17
axis, anticlinal ~ 12 17
axis, celestial ~ 4 10
axis, conjugate ~ 347 24
axis, coordinate ~ 347 2-3
axis, earth's ~ 4 22-28
axis, floral ~ 370 53
axis, lateral ~ 230 68
axis, longitudinal ~ 230 72
axis, major ~ 347 23
axis, minor ~ 347 24
axis, normal ~ 230 70
axis, polar ~ 113 15, 18
axis, synclinal ~ 12 19
axis, transverse ~ 347 23
axis, vertical ~ 230 70
axis mount, English-type ~ 113 22
axis mounting, English-type ~ 113 22
axis of abscissae 347 2
axis of ordinates 347 3
axis of rotation, instantaneous ~ 4 25
axis of rotation, mean ~ 4 27
axis of symmetry *Maths.* 346 25
axis of symmetry *Crystals* 351 4
axle 187 61, 76, 81
axle, coupled ~ 210 36
axle, floating ~ *Agr. Mach.* 65 33

axle, floating ~ *Motorcycle* 189 34
axle, live ~ 192 65-71
axle, rigid ~ 192 65-71
axle bearing 210 10
axle drive shaft 201 13
azalea 53 12
azimuth 87 74
azure *Heraldry* 254 28
azure *Colour* 343 6

B

baboon 368 13
baby 28 5
baby bath 28 3
baby carriage 28 34; 272 71; 273 31
baby clothes 29 1-12
baby doll 48 25
baby grand piano 325 40
baby pants 28 22
baby pants, rubber ~ 29 10
baby powder 28 14
baby scales 22 42
back *Man* 16 22-25
back *Tablew. etc.* 45 56
back *Horse* 72 29
back *Mills* 91 2
back *Roof* 122 86
back *Bookbind.* 185 41
back *Car* 193 35
back *Swim.* 282 49
back *Ball Games* 293 77
back *Sports* 305 11
backband 71 19
backboard 292 30
backbone *Man* 17 2-5
backbone *Bookbind.* 185 41
back check 325 27
back check felt 325 28
backcloth 315 33; 316 10
back comb 105 6
back crease 292 71
back cushion 42 25
back cut 84 29
backdrop 315 33; 316 10
backdrop light 316 15
back fat 95 40
backfilling 217 7
back flip 297 24
backgammon 276 18
backgammon board 276 22
back gauge 183 17; 185 4, 7
background *Films* 310 33
background *Theatre* 316 10
backhand stroke 293 39
backing 269 29
backing disc, rubber ~ 134 22
backing paper *Photog.* 114 21
backing paper *Paperhanger* 128 5
back left second pin 305 9
back loop 288 50
back of the hand 19 83
backpack unit 6 20
back-pedal brake 187 63
back pin 305 11
back plate 140 36
back-pressure valve, hydraulic ~ 141 8
backrest *Weaving* 166 37
backrest *Railw.* 207 66
backrest, reclining ~ 191 35
back right second pin 305 10
back scouring valve 216 61
backside 16 40
back sight leaf 87 67
back sight slide 87 69
back standard adjustment 114 55

backstay 219 19
backstitch seam 102 1
back support 295 22; 296 29
back-up ball 305 20
back vault 297 32
backward grand circle 296 60
backward somersault *Swim.* 282 42
backward somersault *Gymn.* 297 15
backward underswing 296 59
backward walkover 297 23
backwater 172 26
bacon 96 2
Bactrian camel 366 29
badge, fool's ~ 306 60
badger 88 48
badging 191 12
badminton 293 43-44
badminton game 273 6
badminton racket 293 43
badminton racquet 293 43
baffle board *Warships* 259 27
baffle board 309 17
baffle board, hinged ~ 259 15
baffle board, movable ~ 259 15
bag *Doc.* 22 33
bag *Hunt.* 86 38
bag *Music. Instr.* 322 9
bag, girl's ~ 29 56
bag, heat-sealed ~ 76 29
bag, paper ~ 98 48
bag, postman's ~ 236 54
bag filter 83 54
bag-full indicator 50 61, 73
baggage compartment 257 19
baggage loader 233 22
baggage man 267 17
'baggage retrieval' 233 38
baggage terminal 233 5, 16
bagging nozzle 83 55
bag net 77 54
bagpipe 322 8
bag sealer 40 47
baguette 97 12
bag wig 34 4
bail 292 70
bailey, inner ~ 329 2
bailey, outer ~ 329 31
bait 86 21
bait, poisoned ~ 83 31
bait, weighted ~ 89 36
bait needle 89 41
baits 89 65-76
bait tin 89 24
bakehouse 97 55-74
baker's shop 97 1-54
bakery 97 55-74
baking ingredient 99 62
baking ingredients 98 8-11
balalaika 324 28
Balance *Astron.* 3 19; 4 59
balance *Paperm.* 173 9
balance beam 349 30
balance cable 214 46
balance cable sleeve 214 74
balance column 349 29
balancer 307 48
balance rail 322 39
balance weight 242 50
balance wheel 110 39
balancing act 307 44
balancing cabins 214 25
balancing knob 116 39
balancing pole 307 42
balcony *Dwellings* 37 18, 69, 73
balcony *Theatre* 315 16; 315 18
balcony *Chivalry* 329 12
balcony, projecting ~ 218 57
baldachin 331 49

baldaquin 331 49
bald patch 34 21
bale 55 31; 63 34; 75 7; 83 13; 169 34; 170 62; 206 10, 11, 23
bale arm 89 62
bale breaker 163 7
bale loader, hydraulic ~ 63 37
bale opener 163 7
baler, high-pressure ~ 63 35
baling press 169 33
balk 63 3
ball *Infant Care etc.* 28 16
ball *Bicycle* 187 31
ball *Aircraft* 230 12
ball *Ball Games* 292 27
ball *Circus* 307 60
ball, ivory ~ 277 1
ball, metal ~ 352 32
ball, paper ~ 306 55
ball, plastic ~ 277 1
ball, steel ~ 143 70
ball, stone ~ 352 32
ball and socket head 114 47
ballast *Station* 205 61
ballast *Railw.* 212 66
ballast *Sailing* 285 33
ballast *Airsports* 288 65
ballast keel 285 32
ballast tank 223 78
ball bearing 143 69; 187 56, 68
ball boy 293 22
ballerina 314 26
ballet 314
ballet dancer 314 26
ballet positions 314 1-6
ballet shoe 314 30
ballet skirt 314 31
ballet slipper 314 30
ball games 291; 292; 293
ballistics 87 73
ball mill 161 1
ball of clay 161 9
ball of the foot 19 58
ball of the thumb 19 75
balloon 308 13
balloon, gas ~ 288 63
balloon, hot-air ~ 288 79
balloon, manned ~ 7 16
balloon basket 288 64
ballooning 288 63-84
ballot box 263 29
ballot envelope 263 21
ballot paper 263 20
ball race 167 68
ballroom 306 1
Balmer series 1 21
baluster 38 29; 123 51
balustrade 38 25; 123 22, 50
bamboo cane 136 31
bamboo culm 383 60
bamboo stem 383 60, 63
banana 99 90; 384 33
banana flower 384 34
banana-handling terminal 226 22
banana leaf 384 35
banana plant 384 28
banana saddle 188 59
banana tree 384 28
band *Ball Games* 291 25
band *Nightclub* 318 3
band *Church* 332 5
band, fluorescent ~ 199 8
band, iron ~ 130 16
band, ornamental ~ 334 38
band, steel ~ 163 5
bandage *First Aid* 21 9
bandage *Equest.* 289 15
bandages, emergency ~ 21 1-13
band brake 143 104

banderilla 319 22
banderillero 319 4, 21
band of barrel 130 8
bandoneon 324 36
bandora 322 21
bandsaw 134 50; 157 48
bandsaw, horizontal ~ 157 48
bandsaw blade 157 53
bandstand 274 19; 307 9
band wheel 104 15
bandwheel cover 133 32
banewort 379 7
banger 306 51
bangle *Jewell.* 36 17
bangle *Ethnol.* 354 38
bangle, asymmetrical ~ 36 26
bangs 34 36
banjo 324 29
bank *Phys. Geog.* 13 4
bank *Post* 237 43
bank *Bank* 250
bank *Roulette* 275 11
bank acceptance 250 12
bank branch 204 31
bank clerk 250 5
bank employee 251 7
banknotes 252 29-39
bank of circulation 252 30
bank of issue 252 30
bank of oars 218 12
bank protection 216 51-55
bank slope 217 28
bank stabilization 216 51-55
bank statement 247 44
banner *Flags* 253 12
banner *Election* 263 12
banner, processional ~ 331 44
banquet room 267 39
bantam 74 56
baptism, Christian ~ 332 1
baptistery 332 2
bar *Horse* 71 41
bar *Office* 246 29
bar *Restaurant* 266 1-11
bar *Hotel* 267 54
bar *Park* 272 34
bar *Playground* 273 32
bar *Gymn.* 296 3, 8; 297 4, 41
bar *Athletics* 298 14, 34
bar *Winter Sp.* 303 5
bar *Circus* 307 50
bar *Disco* 317 1, 9
bar *Nightclub* 318 13, 15
bar *Music. Not.* 320 42
bar *Graphic Art* 340 34
bar, flat ~ 143 10
bar, metal ~ 324 77
bar, round ~ 143 8
bar, sliding ~ 75 21
bar arm 299 10
barb *Bees* 77 10
barb *Fish Farm.* 89 80
barb *Mach. Parts etc.* 143 44
barbecue 278 47
barbel 364 13
bar bender 119 21
barber 106 1
barber's shop 106 1-42
barchan 13 40
barchane 13 40
bar customer 267 55
bareback rider 307 26
barge 216 22, 25; 225 8
barge and push tug assembly 221 92
bargeboard 37 8
bargee 216 26
bargeman 216 26
barge sucker 216 59
bark *Carp.* 120 86
bark *Ship* 219 1-72; 220 21-23
bark *Bot.* 370 8

bark, five-masted ~ 220 32-34
bark, four-masted ~ 220 29
bark beetle 82 22
bark brush 56 23
barkeep 266 8; 267 62
barkeeper 266 8; 267 62
barker 308 8, 64
barkhan 13 40
barking 85 23
barking iron 85 8
bark schooner 220 20
bark scraper 56 14
bark spud 85 8
bark stripping 85 23
bar lamp 317 11
barley 68 1, 26
barley, germinated ~ 92 23
barley elevator 92 33
barley hopper 92 2
barley reception 92 41
barley silo 92 31
bar line 320 42
barmaid 267 63; 317 2; 318 14
barman 266 8; 267 62
barn owl 362 17
barn swallow 361 20
barograph 10 4
barouche 186 35
barque 219 1-72; 220 21-23
barque, five-masted ~ 220 32-34
barque, four-masted ~ 220 29
barque schooner 220 20
barrage 217 57-64, 65-72
barrel Cooper 130 5
barrel Mach. Tools 149 27
barrel Army 255 2, 17, 41
barrel, aluminium ~ 93 17
barrel, rifled ~ 87 26
barrel, semi-oval ~ 89 3
barrel, smooth-bore ~ 87 27
barrel casing 87 35; 255 33
barrel clamp 255 11, 62
barrel-clamping nut 255 11
barrel cradle 255 60
barrelhead 130 10
barrel organ 309 13
barrel recuperator 255 61
barrel-shape 36 75
barrel-shape, standard ~ 36 56
barrel stave 130 9
barrel store 93 16
barrel vault 335 19; 336 38
barricade 264 17
barrier Supermkt. 99 5
barrier Railw. 202 40
barrier Hydr. Eng. 217 65
barrow Station 205 32
barrow Prehist. 328 16
barrow, road sweeper's ~ 199 9
barrow, street sweeper's ~ 199 9
bars 75 5
bar set 246 30
bar stool 267 53; 317 3; 318 16
bartender 266 8; 267 62
bar trio 267 44
barysphere 11 5
basal pinacoid 351 20
base Dining Rm. 44 23
base Mills 91 33
base Optic. Instr. 112 3; 113 2
base Floor etc. Constr. 123 21, 63
base Bookbind. 183 25
base Road Constr. 200 59
base Heraldry 254 22-23
base Mountain. 300 1
base Art 334 28-31

base Maths. 345 1, 6; 346 27; 347 35, 39
base, horizontal ~ 112 72
base, round ~ Hairdresser 105 27
base, round ~ Basketm. 136 19
base, round ~ Electrotyp. etc. 178 10
base, woven ~ 136 20
baseball 292 40-69, 61
baseball glove 292 59-60
baseball mitt 292 59-60
baseboard Photog. 116 27
baseboard Sculpt. Studio 339 23
base course Dwellings 37 17
base course Carp. 120 28
base course Street Sect. 198 3
base course Road Constr. 200 59
base course, concrete ~ 118 2
base course, natural stone ~ 37 85
base frame 177 40
base line 292 48; 293 3 - 10, 72
base line judge 293 26
baseman 292 44
basement 37 1; 118 1
basement stairs 123 16
basement wall 123 1
basement window 37 27; 118 3
base of goblet 162 42
base of machine 168 54
base of statue 272 11
base of support 214 81
base plate Optic. Instr. 112 27
base plate Iron Foundry etc. 148 56
base plate Mach. Tools 150 19
base plate Knitting 167 34
base plate Railw. 202 5
base plate Army 255 46
base plate Ball Games 292 67
base unit 39 9
basic knits 171 30-48
basic position 295 1
basidia 381 7
basidiospore 381 8
basilica 334 61
basilisk Fabul. Creat. 327 34
basilisk Fish etc. 364 30
basin Doc. 23 25
basin Dent. 24 12
basin Park 272 24
basis weight 173 9
basket Kitch. Utensils 40 42
basket Butch. 96 18
basket Supermkt. 99 8
basket Basketm. 136 16
basket Station 204 3
basket Ball Games 292 32
basket Winter Sp. 301 8
basket, rotating ~ 168 17
basket, wicker ~ 305 69
basket, wire ~ 55 50; 66 25; 188 23
basketball 292 28, 29
basketball player 292 35
basket handle 336 28
basket maker 136 33
basket making 136 1-40
basket post 292 31
basket ring 292 33
basketry 136 1-40
basket weave 171 11
basketwork 136 1-40, 16
bas-relief 339 33
bass 323 23
bass belly bridge 325 13
bass bridge 325 13
bass button 324 43

bass clarinet 323 34
bass clef 320 9
bass coupler 324 44
bass drum 323 55; 324 47
bassinet 28 30
bassinet covers 28 31
bassoon 323 28
bass press-stud 324 43
bass register 324 44
bass side 324 43
bass stop 324 44
bass string 324 25; 325 12
bass stud 324 43
bass trombone 323 46
bass tuba 323 44
bass tuning 241 43
bass viol 322 23
bast 136 29
bastard title 185 44
bastion 329 16
bat 292 62, 75
batch 162 2
batch feeder 162 13
batch funnel 162 13
batching and mixing plant, automatic ~ 201 19
batch of eggs 80 2, 30
bath Bathrm. etc. 49 1
bath Hotel 267 27-38
bath Swim. 281 36
bath, cold ~ 281 30
bath handle 293 46
bather 280 30
bathing beach 280
bathing cap 280 29, 44; 281 8
bathing gown 280 25
bathing platform 280 9
bathing shoe 280 23
bathing suit 280 42
bathing suit, two-piece ~ 280 26
bathing towel 281 14
bathing trunks 280 43
bathing wrap 280 25
bath mat 49 48
batholite 11 29
bath robe 29 24
bathroom 49
bathroom cabinet, mirrored ~ 49 31
bathroom mule 49 46
bathroom scales 49 47
bathroom tissue 49 11
bathroom tissue holder 49 10
bath salts 99 34
bath sponge Bathrm. etc. 49 6
bath sponge Invertebr. 357 13
bat of clay 161 9
baton 264 19
baton, conductor's ~ 315 27
batrachians 364 23-26
batsman 292 74
batten Roof 122 17
batten Sailing 284 44
batten, compartmentalized ~ 316 13
batten, compartment-type ~ 316 13
batten cleat 284 43
batten door 37 34
batten gauge 122 18
batten pocket 284 43
batter 292 52, 63
batterboard 118 69
batter's position 292 51
battery Agr. Mach. 65 53
battery Poultry Farm 74 19
battery Photog. 114 66
battery Car 191 50
battery Warships 259 83
battery, rotary ~ 166 5
battery box 207 5, 25; 211 56

bass clarinet 323 34
battery cage 74 20
battery cell 110 7
battery chamber Photog. 115 10
battery chamber Cine Film 117 5
battery compartment 188 22
battery container 207 5, 25; 211 56
battery feeding 74 23
battery holder 115 76
battery housing 257 17
battery railcar 211 55
battery switch 115 13
battery system 74 18
battery tester 25 52
battery unit 115 75
batting crease 292 72
batting order 292 58
battle axe 352 16
battle axe, stone ~ 328 19
battlement 329 6
battleships, light ~ 258 1-63
bauble 306 59
baulk Agr. 63 3
baulk Carp. 120 87
baumkuchen 97 46
Bavarian curler 302 38
Bavarian curling 302 38-40
bay Phys. Geog. 13 7
bay Game 88 7
bay Carp. 120 59
bayadère 306 25
bay antler 88 7
bayonet 353 28
bayonet fitting 127 65, 69
B-deck 223 32-42
beach 13 35-44
beach, raised ~ 11 54
beach area 281 2
beach attendant 280 34
beach bag 280 24
beach ball 280 18
beach chair, roofed ~ 280 36
beach chair, wicker ~ 280 36
beach grass 15 7
beach hat 280 20
beach jacket 280 21
beach marten 367 14
beach mattress, inflatable ~ 280 17
beach shoe 280 23
beach suit 33 24; 280 19
beach tent 280 45
beach trousers 280 22
beachwear 280 19-23
beacon 15 10, 49
bead 87 72
bead-and-dart moulding 334 38
beading 123 64
beading hammer 125 15
beading iron 125 8
beading pin 128 30
beading swage 125 15
beak 88 84
beak, flat ~ 137 12
beak, hooked ~ 362 6
beak, round ~ 137 13
beaker 350 20
beaker pottery 328 14
beam Agr. Mach. 65 9, 71
beam Game 88 11, 30
beam Carp. 120 19, 24
beam Gymn. 297 2
beam Music. Instr. 325 22
beam Chem. 349 30
beam, central ~ 27 3
beam, dipped ~ 191 20
beam, high ~ 191 20
beam, low ~ 191 20
beam, main ~ Carp. 120 38
beam, main ~ Roof 121 66

beam, main ~ *Car* 191 20
beam, tied ~ 215 44
beam bridge 215 7
beam compass 125 11
beam compass, glaziers ~ 124 22
beam entry point 1 64
beam flange 165 30; 166 49; 167 26
beam head 121 33
beaming machine 165 55
beam motion control 166 60
beam of light 224 83
beam setter 195 24
beam splitter 240 35
beam-splitting prism *Optic. Instr.* 112 13
beam-splitting prism *Broadcast.* 240 35
beam trammel 125 11
bean 57 8, 11
bean, bush ~ 57 8
bean, climbing ~ 57 8
bean flower 57 9
bean plant 52 28; 57 8
bean pole 52 28
beanstalk 57 10
bearberry 377 15
beard *Arable Crops* 68 12
beard *Dom. Anim.* 73 15
beard *Game* 88 73
beard, circular ~ 34 15
beard, full ~ 34 15
beard, round ~ 34 15
bearded couch grass 61 30
beards 34 1-25
bearer cable 119 37; 271 52
bearer share 251 11
bearing, axial-radial ~ 113 3
bearing, centre ~ 177 65
bearing, fixed ~ 215 11
bearing, hydrostatic ~ 5 10
bearing, jewelled ~ 110 33
bearing, lower ~ 192 83
bearing, main ~ 192 23
bearing, movable ~ *Bridges* 215 12
bearing, movable ~ *Sailing* 284 6
bearing, upper ~ 192 73
bearing block 177 61
bearing cup 187 68
bears 368 9-11
beasts of prey 367 11-22; 368 1-11
beater *Hunt.* 86 37
beater *Bakery* 97 70
beater *Music. Instr.* 322 34; 324 64
beater, revolving ~ 64 13
beater, three-blade ~ 163 25
beater drive motor 163 23
beater driving shaft 163 24
beating 86 34-39
beating machine 131 4
beating wood 339 12
beau 306 33
beauty parlor 105 1-39
beauty queen 306 64
beauty salon 105 1-39
beauty shop 105 1-39
beauty spot 306 24
beaver *Chivalry* 329 41
beaver *Mammals* 366 14
beck, flat ~ 137 12
beck, round ~ 137 13
bed *Phys. Geog.* 13 49
bed *Hosp.* 25 10
bed *Joiner* 133 50
bed *Mach. Tools* 150 19, 29
bed *Offset Print.* 180 78
bed *Letterpress* 181 17
bed *Bookbind.* 183 25

bed *Station* 205 61
bed *Graphic Art* 340 41, 64
bed, children's ~ 47 1
bed, double ~ 43 4-13; 267 38
bed, rear ~ 85 49
bed bug 81 39
bedder 91 23
bed frame 43 5
bed linen 271 57
Bedlington terrier 70 18
bed monitor 25 19
bedouin 354 6
bedrock 13 70
bedroom 43
bedroom, twin-berth 207 38
bedroom, two-berth ~ 207 38
bedroom, two-seat ~ 207 38
bedroom lamp 43 19
bedside cabinet 43 17
bedside rug 43 22
bed slide 149 24
bedspread 43 7
bedstead 43 4-6
bed stone 91 23
beduin 354 6
bed unit 46 16
bed unit drawer 46 18
bed unit shelf 46 19
bed warmer 309 88
bee 77 1-25
bee, male ~ 77 5
beech cellulose 169 1
beech gall 82 37
beech nut 371 37
beech tree 371 33
bee eater 360 2
beef 95 14-37
beehive 77 45-50
beehive kiln 161 3
bee house 77 56
beekeeper 77 57
beekeeping 77
beeman 77 57
beer 99 72
beer, bottled ~ 93 26
beer, canned ~ 99 73
beer barrel 93 17
beer bottle 93 26; 205 50
beer can 93 25; 99 73
beer crate 93 24; 99 72
beer filter 93 15
beer glass 45 91; 93 30; 266 3, 6; 317 6
beer marquee 308 23
beer mat 266 26
beer mug 266 6; 309 53
beerpull 266 1, 68
beer pump 266 1, 68
beer tap 317 8
beer warmer 266 7
bees 77
bee shed 77 51
bee smoker 77 59
bee sting ointment 77 68
beeswax 77 67
beet 68 44, 45
beet carrion beetle 80 45
beet cleaner 64 89
beet elevator 64 94
beet elevator belt 64 95
beet harvester 64 85-96
beet hopper 64 96
beetle 82 26, 42
beet leaf 68 47
beetles 358 24-39
beet top 68 46
bee veil 77 58
begonia 53 10
begonia, tuberous ~ 51 19
belay 300 9, 10
belayer 300 26
belfry window 331 8
bell *Plumb. etc.* 126 16

bell *Iron & Steel* 147 6
bell *Railw.* 212 49
bell *Navig.* 224 75
bell *Election* 263 4
bell *Winter Countr.* 304 26
bell *Music. Instr.* 323 37, 42, 48; 324 70
bell, electric ~ 127 15
bell, electrically operated ~ 331 9
belladonna 379 7
Bellatrix 3 13
bell beaker 328 14
bell boy 267 18
bell end 278 27
bellows *Photog.* 114 53; 116 31
bellows *Photomech. Reprod.* 177 10, 26
bellows *Camping* 278 49
bellows *Flea Market* 309 26
bellows *Music. Instr.* 322 58; 324 37
bellows pedal 325 46
bellows strap 324 38
bellows unit 115 85
bell push 127 2
bells 276 45
bell sleeve, pleated ~ 30 54
bell tent 278 8
bell tower 337 8
belly *Sea Fish.* 90 20
belly *Meat* 95 39, 41
belly *Music. Instr.* 323 24; 324 3
belly-band 71 36
belt 30 11; 31 10; 32 39
belt, coloured ~ 299 15
belt, flat ~ 163 49
belt, stretch ~ 31 63
belt buckle 31 12
belt-changing flap 255 35
belt conveying 144 40
belt conveyor 156 2
belt delivery 185 13
belt drive 165 33
belt guard 133 31
beltline 270 45
belt roller 133 18
belt-tensioning lever 133 16
bench *Goldsm. etc.* 108 20
bench *Plumb.* 125 10
bench *Blacksm.* 137 21
bench *Metalwkr.* 140 7
bench *Playground* 273 58
bench *Gymn.* 296 14
bench, collapsible ~ 134 41
bench, oarsman's ~ 278 17
bench, paperhanger's ~ 128 31
bench, pupil's ~ 261 11
bench, student's ~ 261 11
bench, teacher's ~ 261 3
bench, tiered ~ 281 20
bench, woodworker's ~ 132 29-37
bench apron 108 21
bench brush 108 33
bench covering 141 16
bench holdfast 132 36
bench stop 132 36
bench top 132 34
bench torch 350 9
bend 126 46
bending iron *Bldg. Site* 119 77
bending iron *Blacksm.* 137 39
bending machine 125 28, 30
bending table 119 20
bending tool 136 34
bend of hook 89 81
bend sinister wavy 254 6
Benguela Current 14 43
benniseed 383 45

bent hang 296 39
benzene chlorination 170 8
benzene extraction 170 6
benzene ring 242 66
benzene scrubber 156 24
benzol scrubber 156 24
beret 35 27
berlin 186 1
berm 216 38
Bermuda shorts 31 44
berry 58 9, 11; 370 97
berry bush 52 19
berry bushes 58 1-30
berry tree, standard ~ 52 11
besageur 329 45
besom *Roof & Boiler.* 38 36
besom *Winter Sp.* 302 43
Bessemer converter 147 55-69
best end of loin 95 7
beta particle 1 32
beta radiation 1 32
Betelgeuse 3 13
betel nut 380 20
betel palm 380 19
bevel *Carp.* 120 81
bevel *Mach. Parts etc.* 143 62
bevel edge 178 44
bevel gear 91 25
bevel gearing 91 25
bevel gear wheel 143 91
bevel wheel 143 91
bez antler 88 7
bez tine 88 7
B flat major 320 64
B flat minor 320 67
bib *Infant Care etc.* 28 43
bib *Ladies' Wear* 30 24
bib and brace *Child. Clothes* 29 40
bib and brace *Ladies' Wear* 30 21
bib and brace overalls 33 44
Bible 330 11
bib skirt 29 41
biceps brachii 18 37
biceps femoris 18 61
bick, flat ~ 137 12
bick, round ~ 137 13
bicycle 187
bicycle, child's ~ 273 9
bicycle, folding ~ 188 1
bicycle, gent's ~ 187 1
bicycle, motor-assisted ~ 188 6
bicycle bell 187 4
bicycle drive 187 35-42
bicycle frame 187 14-20
bicycle kick 291 45
bicycle lamp 187 7
bicycle lock 187 49
bicycle pedal 187 78
bicycle pump 187 48
bicycles 188
bicycle saddle 187 22
bicycle speedometer 187 33
bidet 49 7
Biedermeier dress 306 22
Biedermeier sofa 336 17
bier 331 41
bifurcation 224 89
Big Dipper 3 29
big top 307 1
big wave riding 279 4
big wheel 308 37
bike 187 1
bikini 280 26
bikini bottom 280 27
bikini briefs 32 15
bikini top 280 28
bilberry 377 23
bile duct, common ~ 20 37-38
bilge block 222 40

bilge keel **222** 47
bilge shore **222** 40
bilge strake **222** 46
bill *Game* **88** 84
bill *Bank* **250** 12
bill *Birds* **359** 17
billboard **118** 45
bill clause **250** 17
billhook **56** 9; **85** 11
billiard ball **277** 1
billiard clock **277** 17
billiard cloth **277** 15
billiard cue **277** 9
billiard marker **277** 18
billiard parlor **277** 7-19
billiard player **277** 8
billiard room **277** 7-19
billiards **277** 1-19
billiards, English ~ **277** 7
billiards, French ~ **277** 7
billiards, German ~ **277** 7
billiard saloon **277** 7-19
billiard stick **277** 9
billiard strokes **277** 2-6
billiard table **277** 14
bill of exchange **250** 12
bills **252** 29-39
bin **200** 45
bind **321** 24
binder **107** 6
binder course **198** 4
binder injector **200** 53
binding *Bookbind.* **185** 40-42
binding *Athletics* **298** 54
binding, parts of ~ **301** 54-56
binding, rubber ~ **286** 57-58
bindweed **61** 26
binoculars **86** 6; **111** 17; **221** 128
biology preparation room **261** 14-34
biopsy forceps **23** 17
biplane **229** 10
bipod **255** 42
bipod mast **221** 24
biprism **351** 22
biprism, hexagonal ~ **351** 22
bipyramid, tetragonal ~ **351** 18
birch **51** 13; **272** 40; **281** 27
Birch Boletus **381** 22
birch rod **281** 27
birch tree **51** 13; **272** 40; **371** 9
bird **86** 50
bird, flightless ~ **359** 4
bird, gallinaceous ~ **359** 22
bird, migratory ~ **360** 7
bird, non-migratory ~ **360** 4
bird, resident ~ **360** 4
bird cherry **59** 5
bird-foot **69** 11
birds **359**; **361**; **362**; **363**
birds, corvine ~ **361** 1-3
birds, endemic ~ **360**
birds, exotic ~ **363**
birds, flightless ~ **359** 1-3
birds, indigenous ~ **360**
birds, long-winged ~ **359** 11-14
birds, web-footed ~ **359** 5-10
bird's foot **69** 11
bird's foot clover **376** 17
bird's foot trefoil **69** 11; **376** 17
birdsmouth **84** 28
birds of prey **362**
birds of prey, diurnal ~ **362** 1-13
birds of prey, nocturnal ~ **362** 14-19
birth-wort **376** 22
biscuit tin, decorative ~ **46** 12
bisector **346** 28, 30

bishop **276** 10
bismarck **97** 29
bison **328** 9; **367** 9
bistort **376** 10
bit **140** 35
bitch **73** 16
biting housefly **81** 4
bitt **284** 25
bitter **93** 26
bitumen **145** 64
bituminous distributor **200** 46
black **343** 13
black arches moth **82** 17
black-backed jackal **367** 11
black beetle **81** 17
blackberry **58** 29
blackbird **361** 13
blackboard **47** 13; **48** 16; **261** 36
blackboard, three-part ~ **260** 29
blackboard chalk **48** 15
blackboard compass **260** 40
blackboard drawing **260** 33
blackboard sponge **260** 42
black buck **367** 5
blackcock **86** 11; **88** 66
black elder **374** 35
Black Forest clock **109** 31
Black Forest gateau **97** 24
black-headed gull **359** 14
black liquor filter **172** 28
black liquor storage tank **172** 29
black nightshade **379** 5
black rhino **366** 25
black salsify **57** 35
blacksmith **137**; **138**
blacksmith's tools **137** 22-39
blackthorn **374** 27
bladder **20** 33, 78
blade *Kitch. Utensils* **40** 40
blade *Tablew. etc.* **45** 54
blade *Gdn. Tools* **56** 36
blade *Arable Crops* **68** 20
blade *Paperm.* **172** 74
blade *Bookbind.* **185** 29
blade *Rowing* **283** 38, 53
blade *Fencing* **294** 44
blade *Bot.* **370** 28
blade, flexible ~ **85** 20
blade, front ~ **85** 35
blade, lower ~ **23** 14
blade, rear ~ **85** 40
blade, rotating ~ **39** 24
blade bit **145** 21
bladebone **95** 22, 30, 32, 42
blade coater **173** 29-35
blade coating machine **173** 29-35
blade covering **293** 47
bladed cone, rotating ~ **172** 75
bladed plug, rotating ~ **172** 75
bladed shell, stationary ~ **172** 76
blade of grass **370** 83-85
blade-slewing gear **200** 22
blancmange powder **98** 50
blank **252** 43
blanket **71** 44; **168** 56
blanket, rubber ~ **180** 54, 79
blanket cylinder **180** 24, 37, 54, 63
blast burner **108** 16
blast furnace **147** 1
blast furnace plant **147** 1-20
blast furnace shaft **147** 7
blasting cartridge **158** 27
blasting fuse **158** 28
blast inlet **148** 2
blast lamp **108** 16
blast main **147** 17, 68; **148** 2
blastodisc **74** 65

blast pipe *Blacksm.* **137** 6
blast pipe *Iron Foundry etc.* **148** 2
blast pipe *Railw.* **210** 25
blazer **33** 54
blazing star **51** 31
blazon **254** 17-23
blazonry **254** 1-36
bleach **105** 1
bleach-hardener **116** 10
bleaching **169** 21
bleach tube **105** 3
bleed **192** 27
bleeder **38** 65
bleeding heart **60** 5
blender **40** 46
blending pump **196** 1
Blessed Sacrament **331** 48; **332** 35
blimp **310** 48; **313** 16-18, 27
blind *Hosp.* **25** 9
blind *Hunt.* **86** 9
blinder **71** 26
blind spot **19** 50
blindworm **364** 37
blinker **71** 26
blob marker **83** 9
blob marking **83** 6
block *Headgear* **35** 3
block *Plumb.* **125** 21
block *Mach. Tools* **150** 20
block *Ship* **221** 28, 105
block *Winter Sp.* **302** 40
block *Music. Instr.* **326** 20
block, adjustable ~ **298** 2
block, charcoal ~ **108** 37
block, clay ~ **159** 22, 23
block, hollow ~ **119** 24; **159** 21-22, 22, 23
block, pumice concrete ~ **119** 24
block, rubber ~ **187** 85
block, tongued and grooved ~ **123** 74
block, travelling ~ **145** 8
block, wooden ~ **340** 1
block and tackle **137** 20
block board **132** 73
block brake **143** 97
blocker **293** 60
blocking saw **157** 54
block instruments **203** 59
block making **178**
block mount **178** 41
block mountain **12** 4-11
block mounting **178** 41
block of flats **37** 72-76
block of flats, high-rise ~ **37** 82
block of flats, multi-storey ~ **37** 77-81
block section panel **203** 60
block step **123** 17
blood, arterial ~ **18** 12
blood, venous ~ **18** 11
blood circulation **18** 1-21
blood pressure **23** 32; **25** 1
blood sausage **99** 56
blood sedimentation **23** 42
blood smear **23** 50
bloodstone **108** 48
blood vessel **19** 33
bloomer **97** 8
blooming train **148** 50, 70
bloom shears **148** 52
blossom **59** 9; **69** 14; **80** 11
blotter **46** 23; **246** 6; **260** 25
blouse, girl's ~ **29** 58
blow, straight ~ **299** 28
blow-and-blow process **162** 22
blower *Furrier* **131** 10

blower *Paperm.* **172** 4
blower *Railw.* **211** 11
blower, travelling ~ **165** 2, 3
blower aperture **165** 5
blower fan **191** 48; **192** 62
blower oil pump **211** 45
blower rail **165** 6
blowfly **358** 18
blowhole **367** 26
blowing **162** 28, 36
blowing, first ~ **162** 24
blowing assembly **165** 4
blowing iron **162** 39
blowing processes **162** 22-37
blowlamp **126** 74; **301** 22
blow mould **162** 26, 34
blowout magnet **312** 39
blowpipe *Gas Weld.* **141** 11, 19; **141** 28
blowpipe *Ethnol.* **352** 26
blowpipe lighter **141** 27
blow pit **172** 13
blow position **147** 57
blow tank **172** 11
blowtorch **126** 74; **301** 22
blow valve **172** 12
blubber-oil lamp **353** 7
blue *Colour* **343** 3
blue *Lepidopt.* **365** 6
blue-and-yellow macaw **363** 2
bluebell **375** 14
blueberry **377** 23
blue bird of paradise **363** 3
bluebottle **61** 1; **358** 18
blue light **264** 11; **270** 6
Blue Peter **253** 26
blue shark **364** 1
blue spruce **51** 10
bluetit **360** 4
bluff bow **218** 25
bluff prow **218** 25
blurb **185** 39
B minor **320** 57, 60
boar *Dom. Anim.* **73** 9
boar *Game* **88** 51
boar, young ~ **88** 51
board *Bldg. Site* **118** 22, 87; **119** 16
board *Carp.* **120** 1, 91
board *Sawmill* **157** 35
board *Games* **276** 1
board, illuminated ~ **268** 3
board, presawn ~ **273** 57
board, squared ~ **120** 95
board, unsquared ~ **120** 94
board, wooden ~ **338** 23
board cutter **183** 16
board cutter, rotary ~ **184** 20
board-cutting machine, rotary ~ **184** 20
board feed hopper **184** 7
board games **276**
boarding **121** 75
boarding, horizontal ~ **37** 84
boarding platform **194** 39
boardman **251** 7
board platform **118** 28
board-sawing machine **132** 68
board support **132** 70
boarhound **86** 33
boar hunt **86** 31
boaster **158** 37
boat, carvel-built ~ **283** 9
boat, inflatable ~ **228** 18; **258** 82; **278** 14; **279** 27
boat, ship's ~ **221** 107; **258** 12, 45; **259** 35
boat, V-bottom ~ **286** 35-37
boat, vee-bottom ~ **286** 35-37
boat axe **328** 19
boat carriage **278** 20; **283** 66

boat deck 223 19-21
boat elevator 217 29-38
boater 35 35
boat fibula 328 28
boathouse 283 24
boat-launching crane 258 13
boat lift 217 29-38
boat neck 30 34
boats, folding ~ 283 54-66
boatswain 221 114
boat tank 217 33
boat trailer 278 20; 283 66
bobbin *Shoem.* 100 29
bobbin *Dressm.* 103 12
bobbin *Cotton Spin.* 164 52,
  56, 60
bobbin creel 164 28
bobbin lace 102 18
bobbin thread 104 16
bobble 29 4
boblet 303 19
bobsled 303 19
bobsledding 303 19-21
bobsleigh 303 19-21
bobsleigh, two-man ~ 303 19
bobstay 219 15
bob wig 34 2
boccie 305 21
bock beer 93 26
bodhisattva 337 10
bodice 31 30
bodkin *Basketm.* 136 35
bodkin *Composing Rm.* 174
  17
bodkin beard 34 13
body *Flat* 46 3
body *Joiner* 132 24
body *Lorries etc.* 194 3, 23
body *Aircraft* 230 54
body *Airsports* 288 26
body, bird's ~ 327 57
body, dog's ~ 327 30
body, dragon's ~ 327 19, 36
body, fibre glass ~ 193 14
body, horse's ~ 327 27, 54
body, human ~ 16 1-54
body, interchangeable ~ 213
  40
body, lion's ~ 327 14, 22
body, man's ~ 327 53
body, monocoque ~ 191 1
body, monster's ~ 327 48
body, pituitary ~ 17 43
body, serpent's ~ 327 2, 33
body, tambourine-like ~ 324
  30
body, unitary ~ 191 1
body, woman's ~ 327 59
body brush 71 55
body-fixing plate 192 72
body hammer 195 46
bodyline 175 43
body louse 81 41
body of barrel 130 6
body of wall 217 2
body paper 173 29
body plan 259 2-11
body rotation 298 11
body size 175 46
body temperature 23 3
body tube 113 8, 31-39
bog 13 14-24
bog bilberry 377 23
bogie *Bldg. Site* 119 32
bogie *Power Plant* 152 41
bogie *Tram* 197 9
bogie *Railw.* 207 4; 208 4; 212
  2; 213 11, 13
bogie open freight car 213 24
bogie open wagon 213 24
bogie wagon 213 26
bog pool 13 23
bog whortleberry 377 23

Bohr-Sommerfeld model 1
  26
boiler *Roof & Boilerr.* 38 24,
  68
boiler *Bakery* 97 69
boiler *Energy Sources* 155 13
boiler *Railw.* 210 16
boiler, radiant-type ~ 152 5
boiler, vertical ~ 210 62
boiler barrel 210 16
boiler feed pump 152 18
boiler house *Market Gdn.* 55
  7
boiler house *Power Plant* 152
  1-21
boiler pressure 210 3
boiler pressure gauge 210 47
boiler room *Roof & Boilerr.*
  38 38-43
boiler room *Market Gdn.* 55 7
boiler shop 222 9
boiler suit 30 21
boiling fowl 99 60
boiling water system 154 49
bola 352 31
bolas 352 31
bold 175 2
bold condensed 175 10
boldface 175 2
bole 84 19, 22; 85 23, 41; 370
  2, 7
Boletus edulis 381 16
Boletus luteus 381 21
Boletus scaber 381 22
boll 383 8
bollard 217 12
bollard, cross-shaped ~ 217
  13, 14; 227 10
bollard, double ~ 217 11, 14
bollard, recessed ~ 217 10
bolster *Bedrm.* 43 11
bolster *Tablew. etc.* 45 55
bolster plate 85 48
bolt *Slaughterho.* 94 4
bolt *Roof* 121 98
bolt *Metalwkr.* 140 39
bolt *Mach. Parts etc.* 143 31
bolt *Office* 246 23
bolt, collar-head ~ 143 32
bolt, countersunk-head ~ 143
  28
bolt, hexagonal-head ~ 143
  13
bolt, square-head ~ 143 39
bolt, T-head ~ 143 41
bolter 91 26
bolt guide pin 140 41
bolt handle 87 22
bolt lever 87 22
bolts 143 13-50
bombard 322 14
bombardon 323 44
bomber jacket 31 42
bombycid moth 358 48
bond *Bldg. Site* 118 30
bond *Stock Exch.* 251 1-10,
  11-19
bond, convertible ~ 251 11-19
bond, English ~ 118 62
bond, industrial ~ 251 11-19
bond, municipal ~ 251 11-19
bonding, rubber ~ 192 82
bone 70 33; 354 40
bone, ethmoid ~ 17 39
bone, frontal ~ 17 30
bone, hyoid ~ 20 2
bone, jugal ~ 16 8
bone, lachrimal ~ 17 40
bone, malar ~ 16 8
bone, metacarpal ~ 17 16
bone, nasal ~ 17 41
bone, occipital ~ 17 32
bone, parietal ~ 17 31

bone, sphenoid ~ 17 38
bone, tarsal ~ 17 26
bone, temporal ~ 17 33
bone, zygomatic ~ 16 8; 17 37
bone chisel 24 49
bone-cutting forceps 26 51
bone lace 102 18
bone nippers 26 51
bones 17 1-29
bone saw *Slaughterho.* 94 19
bone saw *Butch.* 96 56
bongo drum 324 58
boning knife 96 36
bonnet *Car* 191 8
bonnet *Garage* 195 36
bonnet *Ship* 218 34
bonnet support 195 37
book 42 4; 46 8; 185 36
book, children's ~ 47 17; 48
  23
book, open ~ 185 52
book, second-hand ~ 309 55
book, sewn ~ 185 22
book, unbound ~ 183 32
bookbinder 183 2
bookbinding 183; 184; 185
bookbinding machines 184
  1-23; 185 1-35
bookcase unit 46 7
book cover 185 40
book delivery 184 5
bookjacket 185 37
bookmark, attached ~ 185 70
bookmark, loose ~ 185 71
bookmarker, attached ~ 185
  70
bookmarker, loose ~ 185 71
bookplate 185 51
book-sewing machine 185 16
bookshelf 42 3; 43 14; 262 12
bookshelf unit 46 7
bookshop 268 37
book stack 262 11
boom *Bldg. Site* 119 36
boom *Docks* 226 49
boom *Sailing* 284 7, 39
boom, double ~ 229 35
boom foresail 220 12
boom microphone 311 40
boom operator 310 22
boom swinger 310 22
booster rocket 234 1, 2
boost gauge 230 7
boot *Car* 191 24; 193 23
boot *Music. Instr.* 326 17
boot, baby's ~ 101 56
boot, felt ~ 353 30
boot, ladies' ~ 101 12
boot, men's ~ 101 5
boot, pony-skin ~ 101 10
boot, rubber ~ 289 32
boot, Western ~ 101 9
bootee 28 45; 29 5
booth 308 6
bootlace 100 64; 291 32
boot lid 191 7
bootmaker 100
boot space 193 17
borage family 69 13
Boraginaceae 69 13
border *Fruit & Veg. Gdn.* 52
  18, 22
border *Basketm.* 136 17
border *Park* 272 37
border *Theatre* 316 12
border light 316 13
bore 143 86
bore axis 87 38
bore diameter 87 40
borehole 158 12

borer 80 18
boring machine 175 49
boring mill 138 22
boring mill column 150 31
boring motor 133 7
boring tool 149 51
borrower's ticket 262 25
boscage 272 4
bosh 137 8
bo's'n 221 114
bosom 16 30
boss *Chivalry* 329 58
boss *Art* 335 32
bostryx 370 76
bo'sun 221 114
botany 370
bottle *Brew.* 93 21
bottle *Restaurant* 266 16
bottle *Swim.* 279 19
bottle, collapsible ~ 116 9
bottle, non-returnable ~ 93
  29
bottle, three-necked ~ 350 57
bottle, wicker ~ 206 13
bottle, wickered ~ 206 13
bottle basket 79 13
bottle bobbin 167 4
bottle-capping machine 76 46
bottle kiln 161 3
bottle-making machine 162
  21
bottle-nosed dolphin 367 23
bottle-opener 45 47
bottle rack *Kitch.* 39 6
bottle rack *Wine Cell.* 79 11
bottlescrew 284 19
bottle warmer 28 21
bottle washer 93 19
bottle-washing machine 93
  19
bottle-washing plant 93 18
bottling 93 22
bottling machine, circular ~
  79 9
bottling machine, semi-
  automatic ~ 79 9
bottom 16 40
bottom, artificial ~ 301 52
bottom, cellular ~ 222 60
bottom, cut-in ~ 119 56
bottom, double ~ 222 60
bottom, synthetic ~ 301 52
bottom bracket bearing 187
  42
bottom fishing 89 20-31
bottom outlet 269 34
bottom plating 222 48
bottom plating, inner ~ 222
  54
bott stick 148 10
boudoir piano 325 40
bough 370 5
bouillon cube 98 27
boule, grooved ~ 305 24
boules 305 21
boules player 305 22
bounce 297 36
bouncing ball 273 20
boundary layer control flap
  256 6; 257 13
boundary ridge 63 3
boundary stone 63 2
bouquet, bridal ~ 332 18
bouquetin 367 7
bourgeois 175 26
bout 294 5-6
Bovista nigrescens 381 19
bow *Ladies' Wear* 30 46
bow *Hairst. etc.* 34 7
bow *Metalwkr.* 140 34
bow *Shipbuild.* 222 74-79
bow *Warships* 258 3
bow *Rowing* 283 13

bow *Music. Instr.* **323** 12
bow *Ethnol.* **354** 32
bow *Hist. Cost.* **355** 78
bow, bulbous ~ **221** 45; **222** 74
bow, fully enclosed ~ **259** 9
bow, rounded ~ **218** 25
bow, sliding ~ **205** 36
bow and arrow **327** 53
bow bilge **259** 80
Bowden cable **188** 37; **189** 12
bow door **221** 30
bowed instruments **323** 1-27
bowel **20** 14-22
bower **272** 17
bower, ladies' ~ **329** 10
bower anchor **258** 39; **286** 15
bow fender **227** 17
bow gin **87** 48
bowl **40** 6; **45** 63; **105** 1; **107** 36
bowler **292** 76
bow light, green and red ~ **286** 13
bowline **218** 35
bowling ball **305** 15
bowling crease **292** 71
bowl lid **107** 37
bowls **305** 21
bow-manoeuvring propeller **224** 23
bow propeller **228** 33
bow ramp **258** 90
bowsprit **218** 20; **219** 1
bow stick **323** 14
bow string **305** 59
bow thruster **224** 23
bow-tie **32** 47; **33** 11, 16
bow trap **87** 48
bow wave **223** 81
box *Livestock* **75** 2
box *Carriages* **186** 8
box *Gymn.* **296** 15
box *Athletics* **298** 35
box *Fair* **308** 7
box *Bullfight. etc.* **319** 7
box, centrifugal ~ **169** 17
box, coach's ~ **292** 56
box, crossing keeper's ~ **202** 43
box, gateman's ~ **202** 43
box, racer's ~ **290** 7
box, rider's ~ **290** 7
box, small ~ **296** 16; **297** 9
box attendant **315** 12
box camera **309** 30
boxcar **213** 14, 22
boxer *Dog* **70** 10
boxer *Sports* **299** 25
box feeder **159** 7
box gutter **122** 83
boxing **299** 20-50
boxing contest **299** 35-50
boxing glove **299** 26
boxing match **299** 20-50, 35-50
boxing ring **299** 35
box office **308** 7
box pile **217** 6
boxroom door **38** 20
box spar **287** 30
box spur **71** 50
box trap **86** 20
box tree **373** 29
boy scout **278** 11
bra **32** 1; **318** 29
bra, longline ~ **32** 4
brace *Bldg. Site* **119** 63
brace *Carp.* **120** 27, 54
brace *Roof* **121** 41, 58, 69, 82
brace *Ship* **219** 67
brace *Music. Instr.* **325** 16
brace, diagonal ~ *Bldg. Site* **118** 88; **119** 51

brace, diagonal ~ *Bridges* **215** 4
bracelet **36** 3
bracelet, cultured pearl ~ **36** 9
bracelet, gemstone ~ **36** 25
bracelet watch **36** 33
braces **29** 26, 34; **32** 30
braces, adjustable ~ **33** 45
braces clip **32** 31
brachioradialis **18** 39
bracing **215** 3
bracing, diagonal ~ **119** 14
bracken **15** 5; **377** 16
bracket *Doc.* **23** 10
bracket *Plumb. etc.* **126** 6
bracket *Bicycle* **187** 77
bracket *School* **260** 30
bracket *Winter Sp.* **302** 17; **303** 7
bracket, chrome ~ **188** 60
bracket, round ~ **342** 24
bracket, square ~ **342** 25
Brackett series **1** 23
bract **371** 7; **372** 5
bracteate **252** 4
bract scale **372** 5
braid, floral ~ **30** 28
braid embroidery **102** 31
braid work **102** 31
Braille **342** 15
brain-stem **17** 47; **18** 24
brake *Mills* **91** 8
brake *Carriages* **186** 2, 16
brake *Car* **191** 45
brake *Air Force* **257** 10
brake *Forest Plants etc.* **377** 16
brake, automatic ~ **181** 47
brake, auxiliary ~ **212** 10
brake, covered ~ **186** 33
brake, front ~ **187** 5
brake, hydraulic ~ **212** 44
brake arm **187** 66
brake arm cone **187** 67
brake axle **143** 99
brake band **143** 105
brake block *Mach. Parts etc.* **143** 100
brake block *Carriages* **186** 16
brake cable **188** 37; **189** 12
brake casing **187** 70
brake chute housing **257** 24
brake cone **187** 71
brake cylinder pressure gauge **212** 7
brake disc **191** 17; **192** 48
brake drum **138** 11, 20
brake flap *Aircraft* **229** 44
brake flap *Air Force* **256** 12
brake flap *Gliding* **287** 38
brake fluid reservoir **191** 49
brake line *Motorcycle* **189** 12
brake line *Car* **192** 53
brake lining *Blacksm.* **138** 13
brake lining *Mach. Parts etc.* **143** 106
brake lining *Car* **192** 52
brake lock **56** 38
brake magnet **143** 102
brakeman **303** 21
brake pedal *Gdn. Tools* **56** 40
brake pedal *Offset Platem.* **179** 12, 30
brake pedal *Car* **191** 45, 95
brake pressure gauge **210** 50
brake pulley **143** 98
brake shaft **143** 99
brake shoe *Blacksm.* **138** 12
brake shoe *Mach. Parts etc.* **143** 100
brake shoe *Car* **192** 51
brake system, dual-circuit ~ **191** 72

brake-testing equipment **138** 16
brake weight **143** 103
brake wheel **91** 7
braking disc **191** 17; **192** 48
braking distance **203** 29
braking roller **138** 18
branch *Railw.* **203** 48
branch *Fire Brig.* **270** 33
branch *Maths.* **347** 15
branch *Bot.* **370** 5, 6
branch *Decid. Trees* **371** 10, 25, 27, 32, 59
branch *Conifers* **372** 36, 43
branch *Trop. Plants* **382** 17
branch *Industr. Plants* **383** 61
branch *South. Fruits* **384** 12, 42
branch, flowering ~ **58** 32, 52; **59** 1, 26, 37
branch, fruit-bearing ~ **59** 19, 48
branch, fruiting ~ **59** 30
branch, left ~ **203** 47
branch, right ~ **203** 46
branch line **15** 23
branchman **270** 34
brandy **98** 59
brandy glass **45** 88
brant **359** 5
brant-goose **359** 5
brashing **84** 12
brass **323** 39-48
brassard *Fire Brig.* **270** 22
brassard *Chivalry* **329** 47
brassica **57** 32
brassicas **57** 28-34
brassie **293** 91
brassière **32** 1; **318** 29
brassière, longline ~ **32** 4
brass instruments **323** 39-48
bratwurst **96** 11; **308** 34
brayer **340** 12
Brazil Current **14** 35
Brazil nut **384** 53, 59
breach **13** 34
bread **45** 22; **97** 2
bread, kinds of ~ **97** 6-12; **99** 11
bread, wrapped ~ **97** 48-50
bread and cheese **266** 75
bread basket **45** 20
bread-corn **68** 1-37
bread counter **99** 9
bread crust **97** 4
breadth scale **157** 58
bread unit **97** 56-57
break *Brew.* **93** 2
break *Composing Rm.* **175** 15
break *Carriages* **186** 2
break, covered ~ **186** 33
break-bulk cargo, unitized ~ **226** 11
break-bulk cargo elevator, floating ~ **226** 31
break-bulk cargo transit shed **225** 9
break-bulk carrier **225** 14; **226** 13
breakdown lorry **270** 47
breaker *Overh. Irrign.* **67** 34
breaker *Swim.* **279** 6
breaker spring **67** 35
break removal **93** 1-5
breakstone, rotundifoliate ~ **375** 1
breakwater *Hydr. Eng.* **217** 16
breakwater *Docks* **225** 65
breakwater *Warships* **258** 7, 76
breast *Man* **16** 28-29
breast *Horse* **72** 19
breast beam **166** 46

breast beam board **166** 16
breastbone *Man* **17** 8
breastbone *Meat* **95** 27
breastbox **173** 11
breast collar **71** 28
breast collar ring **71** 27
breast drill **140** 58
breast harness **71** 26-36
breast of veal **95** 4
breastplate **329** 46
breast pocket **33** 9
breasts **16** 28-29
breaststroke **282** 33
breastwork **329** 21
breather **153** 10
breathing apparatus **26** 1; **270** 39
breathing tube **27** 37
breccia **11** 27
breeches **300** 7
breeches, loose ~ **355** 34
breeches, white ~ **289** 5
breeches buoy **228** 13
breech ring **255** 54
breeding comb **77** 46
breeds **70**
breeze **120** 44
brent-goose **359** 5
breve **320** 12
breve rest **320** 20
breviary **331** 58
brevier **175** 25
brevis **320** 12
brewer **92** 49
brewery **93** 1-31
brewhouse **93** 1-31
brewing **92**; **93**
briar grain **107** 41
briar rose **373** 26
brick **118** 40
brick, cellular ~ **159** 28
brick, green ~ **159** 16
brick, perforated ~ **159** 21-22, 21
brick, radial ~ **159** 25
brick, radiating ~ **159** 25
brick, solid ~ **159** 20
brick, standard ~ **118** 58
brick, unfired ~ **159** 16
brick cutter **159** 15
brickfield **159**
brick hammer **118** 53
brick kiln **159** 19
bricklayer **118** 18
bricklayer's tools **118** 50-57
brickmason **118** 18
brickmason's tools **118** 50-57
brick-pressing machine **159** 11
brickwork, frost-resistant ~ **122** 39
brickwork base **123** 15
brickworks *Map* **15** 89
brickworks **159**
brickyard **159**
bride **332** 15
bridegroom **332** 16
bridesmaid **332** 24
bridge *Map* **15** 44
bridge *Optician* **111** 11
bridge *Station* **205** 3
bridge *Ship* **221** 6, 12; **223** 12-18
bridge *Shipbuild.* **222** 26
bridge *Warships* **258** 14; **259** 3, 28
bridge *Park* **272** 47
bridge *Free Exerc.* **295** 19
bridge *Sports* **299** 9
bridge *Theatre* **315** 29; **316** 34
bridge *Music. Instr.* **322** 17
bridge, cable-stayed ~ **215** 46

bridge, covered ~ **215** 32
bridge, cross-section of ~ **215** 1
bridge, dental ~ **24** 26
bridge, flat ~ **215** 52
bridge, iron ~ **15** 56
bridge, reinforced concrete ~ **215** 49
bridge, rope ~ **215** 15
bridge, solid ~ **215** 19
bridge, stone ~ **15** 50
bridge bearing **215** 55
bridge deck **223** 12-18
bridge over railway **15** 40
bridge ring **89** 58
bridges **215**
bridge strut **215** 30
bridge superstructure **258** 14
bridge support **222** 12
bridge under railway **15** 42
bridle **71** 7-13
bridle path **12** 46
briefcase **41** 17
briefs **32** 26
brig **220** 17
brigantine **220** 14
brightness control **240** 33
brille **323** 35
brilliant **175** 21
brilliant cut **36** 44
brimstone butterfly **365** 4
brine channel **274** 3
brine pipe **274** 4
briolette, faceted ~ **36** 86
Brisinga endecacnemos **369** 11
brisket, hind ~ **95** 25
brisket, middle ~ **95** 26
brisket of beef **95** 23
bristle **88** 52
bristles *Hairst. etc.* **34** 23
bristles *Household* **50** 47
bristletail **81** 14
bristle worm **357** 22
broach **109** 8
broaching tap **93** 14
broach roof **121** 22
broach roof, conical ~ **121** 24
B road **15** 36
broad axe **120** 70
broad bean *Veg.* **57** 8
broad bean *Fodder Plants* **69** 15
broadcasting **238**; **239**; **240**
broadcasting centre **238** 16-26
broadcasting station **15** 33
broadsheet **340** 27
broadside **340** 27
broadside fire **218** 59
broadtail *Ladies' Wear* **30** 60
broadtail *Furrier* **131** 21
brochure **250** 7
broderie anglaise **102** 11
broiler **98** 6; **308** 33
broiler chicken **74** 12
broiler rearing **74** 11-17
broken thread detector roller **164** 4
broken thread stop motion **165** 19
broker, commercial ~ **251** 5
broker, inside ~ **251** 4
broker, outside ~ **251** 5
bronchus **20** 5
Bronze Age **328** 21-40
brooch, ivory ~ **36** 30
brooch, modern-style ~ **36** 19
brooch, pearl ~ **36** 7
brood bud bulblet **54** 27, 29
brood cell **77** 31
brood chamber **77** 46
brooder **74** 3

brook **13** 8; **15** 80
broom **38** 36; **50** 46; **62** 5; **199** 6; **268** 21; **272** 67
broom *Shrubs etc.* **374** 20
broom, circular ~ **199** 40
broom, cylinder ~ **199** 42
broom, inverted ~ **224** 99
broom, upward-pointing ~ **224** 100
broom handle **38** 37; **50** 49
broom head **50** 48
broomstick **38** 37; **50** 49
brougham **186** 3
brow antler **88** 6
browband **71** 9
brown **343** 5
brown ale **93** 26
brown bear **368** 10
brown leaf-eating weevil **80** 49
Brown Ring Boletus **381** 21
brown-tail moth **80** 28
brown trout **364** 15
brow point **88** 6
brow snag **88** 6
brow tine **88** 6
brush *Roof & Boilerr.* **38** 32
brush *Household* **50** 42, 53
brush *Bees* **77** 7
brush *Forestry* **84** 5
brush *Game* **88** 47
brush *School* **260** 59
brush *Graphic Art* **340** 11
brush *Script* **341** 24
brush, camel hair ~ **338** 7
brush, dry ~ **128** 49
brush, flat ~ *Painter* **129** 17
brush, flat ~ *Art. Studio* **338** 6
brush, rotating ~ **168** 46
brush, round ~ **338** 8
brush, stiff-bristle ~ **105** 16
brush, wire ~ *Gas Weld.* **141** 26
brush, wire ~ *Arc Weld.* **142** 18
brush, wire ~ *Music. Instr.* **324** 53
brush head **50** 79
brush head, detachable ~ **49** 30
brushwood *Map* **15** 15
brushwood *Forestry* **84** 5
brushwood *Spa* **274** 2
Brussels lace **102** 18
Brussels sprout **57** 30
bubble bath **49** 3
bubble chamber **1** 58
bubble float, oval ~ **89** 47
buccaneer **306** 43
Büchner funnel **349** 11
buck *Dom. Anim.* **73** 18
buck *Game* **88** 28, 40, 59
buck *Gymn.* **296** 17
buck, young ~ **88** 39
bucket *Household* **50** 54
bucket *Mills* **91** 36
bucket *Bldg. Site* **118** 82
bucket *Road Constr.* **200** 5
bucket chain **226** 42
bucket dredger **226** 41
bucket elevator **200** 49; **201** 21
bucket elevator chain **216** 57
bucket ladder **226** 43
bucket pump **269** 7
bucket seat *Car* **193** 11
bucket seat *Sports* **305** 90
bucket teeth **200** 6
bucket-top boot **355** 58
buckeye **371** 58
buckle **101** 52
buckle and knife folder **185** 8
buckle and knife folding machine **185** 8

buckle fold **185** 11
buckler **329** 57
bucksaw **120** 61
bud **54** 23, 26; **58** 27; **59** 22; **60** 16; **61** 3
bud, axillary ~ **370** 25
bud, terminal ~ **370** 22
bud cutting **54** 22
Buddha **337** 20
budding **54** 30
budding knife **54** 31
buffalo **367** 8
buffalo horn **254** 34
buffer *Station* **206** 51
buffer *Railw.* **213** 7
buffer *Army* **255** 27, 44, 52
buffer recuperator **255** 52
buffer ring **255** 44
buffer storage **242** 33
buffet **207** 78-79
buffet car, quick-service ~ **207** 73
buffet compartment **207** 78-79
buffing machine **108** 46
buffing wheel **100** 10
buffoon **306** 38, 69
bug **81** 39
buggy **193** 12
buggy, American ~ **186** 49
buggy, English ~ **186** 48
bugle **309** 54
building, centralized ~ **334** 55
building, centrally-planned ~ **334** 55
building, model ~ **48** 28
building, neoclassical ~ **336** 15
building, public ~ **15** 54
building berth **222** 11-18
building berths **222** 11-26
building block **28** 41; **48** 27
building board, lightweight ~ **123** 58
building brick *Infant Care etc.* **28** 41
building brick *Kindergart.* **48** 27
building brick *Brickwks.* **159** 20
building glazier **124** 8
building site **118**; **119**
building slips **222** 11-26
building timber **120** 10, 83-96
built piece **315** 32
built unit **315** 32
bulb, glass ~ **127** 57
bulb, old ~ **54** 28
bulb-head pin **328** 29
bulbil **54** 27, 29; **375** 38
bulk cargo **221** 11
bulk cargo handling **226** 29
bulk carrier *Ship* **221** 9
bulk carrier *Docks* **225** 67; **226** 30
bulk goods **221** 11
bulkhead, protective ~ **305** 91
bulk material **200** 12
bulk transporter barge **226** 35
Bull *Astron.* **3** 25; **4** 54
bull *Dom. Anim.* **73** 1
bull *Heraldry* **254** 15
bull, mock ~ **319** 3
bull, young ~ **319** 35
bulldog **70** 1
bulldozer **199** 16; **200** 28
bulldozer blade **200** 29
bulldozer for dumping and compacting **199** 18
bullfight **319** 1-33, 24
bullfight, mock ~ **319** 1
bullfighting **319**
bullfinch **360** 5

bull pen **319** 14
bullring **319** 5
bull's eye **336** 2
bull's-eye glass **124** 6
bull terrier **70** 16
bulrush **136** 27
bulwark **221** 120; **222** 67
bumblebee **358** 23
bumper *Tram* **197** 12
bumper *Station* **206** 51
bumper, front ~ **191** 13
bumper, integral ~ **193** 33
bumper car **308** 62, 63
bumper steel **166** 44
bumper steel stop rod **166** 45
bump rubber **192** 82
bun **34** 29
bun, plaited ~ **97** 41
bunches **34** 30
bunch of fruit **384** 32
bunch of grapes **78** 5; **99** 89
bunch pink **60** 6
bungalow **278** 7
bunghole **130** 7
bunk, folding ~ **259** 84
bunk, rear ~ **85** 49
bunk-bed **47** 1
bunker **293** 81
bunkering boat **225** 13
Bunsen burner **173** 5; **350** 1
Bunter downthrow **154** 61
bunting **253** 3, 11
buntings **361** 6-7
bunt line **218** 36; **219** 71
buoy **90** 2; **216** 12; **224** 71; **285** 17, 18; **286** 31
buoy, conical ~ **224** 76
buoy, green ~ **224** 84
buoy, port hand ~ **224** 95
buoy, starboard hand ~ **224** 96
buoyancy tube **286** 27
buoy rope **90** 3
bur **24** 37
burden chain **139** 44
burette **350** 21
burette clamp **350** 23
burette stand **350** 22
burgee **253** 22; **284** 48
Burgundian **355** 40
burial **331** 33-41
burial place, underground ~ **331** 59
burin **175** 33; **340** 5, 15, 20
burner *Power Plant* **152** 6
burner *Glass Prod.* **162** 6
burner, gas ~ **139** 3, 48
burner platform **288** 80
burner ventilator **92** 17
burning-in oven **179** 32
burnisher *Goldsm. etc.* **108** 51
burnisher *Watchm.* **109** 17
burnishing **109** 17
burnous **354** 7
burr **88** 5, 29
burrow *Soft Fruit* **58** 63
burrow *Hunt.* **86** 26
burying ground **331** 21-41
bus **194** 17
bus, double-deck ~ **194** 36
bus, double-decker ~ **194** 36
bus, electrical system ~ **235** 55
busbar **152** 29
buses *Lorries etc.* **194**
'buses' *Airport* **233** 35
bush, rubber ~ **192** 67
bushing **162** 50
bushing chain, double ~ **190** 49
bushing tip **162** 51
bushman **354** 29
bushman woman **354** 34
business and passenger aircraft **231** 3, 7

business letter 245 33; 246 7; 248 30
business trip 209 29
bust 42 17
bustle 355 69
bustle pipe 147 53
butane gas 278 33
butane gas bottle 278 34
butcher 96 38, 58
butcher knife 94 15; 96 37
butcher's shop 96 1-30
butt *Hunt.* 86 47-52, 51; 87 3, 7
butt *Meat* 95 50
butt *Army* 255 9, 24, 31, 39
butt *Sports* 305 47
butt, bound ~ 89 55
butt, cork ~ 89 50
butt end 85 41
butter 98 22; 99 47
butter, branded ~ 76 37
butter-and-eggs 376 26
butter churn 76 33
butter-cream cake 97 24
buttercup 375 8
butter dish 45 36
butterflies 358 48-56; 365 1-6
butterflower 375 8
butterfly *Free Exerc.* 295 35
butterfly *Articulates* 358 52
butterfly nut 143 42; 187 39
butterfly stroke 282 34
butterfly tail 229 31
butterfly valve 192 9
butter knife 45 73
butter-making, continuous ~ 76 33
buttermilk tank 76 18
butter shaping and packing machine 76 32
butter supply pipe 76 34
butterwort 377 13
button *Tram* 197 32
button *Fencing* 294 45
button *Music. Instr.* 325 31
button, staghorn ~ 29 33
button box 103 15
buttonhole 332 21
buttonhole stitch 102 6
button stitch 102 6
butt plate *Hunt.* 87 14
butt plate *Sports* 305 46
buttress *Chivalry* 329 26
buttress *Art* 335 27
buttresses 335 27-28
butt ring 89 58
buzzer, electric ~ 127 15
buzz saw 119 19; 125 24; 134 50
buzz saw blade 132 59
by-line 291 7
bypass air flow 232 50
bypass duct 232 41, 44
bypass engine 232 46
bypass switch 211 25

C

cab *Carriages* 186 26, 28
cab *Lorries etc.* 194 2
cab *Town* 268 64
cab, driver's ~ 64 36; 194 2, 15; 200 11; 208 14; 209 6; 210 39-63, 49; 211 19, 57; 212 5; 213 2
cab, engineer's ~ 208 14; 209 6; 210 39-63, 49; 211 19, 57; 212 5; 213 2
cabbage, green ~ 57 32
cabbage, red ~ 57 32
cabbage, round ~ 57 32

cabbage lettuce 57 36
cabbage white butterfly 80 47, 48
cab frame 65 21
cab heating switch 211 39
cab horse 186 28
cabin *Railw.* 214 20, 28
cabin *Ship* 218 45
cabin *Sailing* 285 39
cabin *Airsports* 288 19
cabin, admiral's ~ 218 27
cabin, captain's ~ 223 13
cabin, commanding officer's ~ 259 85
cabin, coxswain's ~ 228 31
cabin, crane driver's ~ 119 35; 222 16; 226 52
cabin, de luxe ~ 223 30
cabin, double-berth ~ 223 29
cabin, large-capacity ~ 214 52
cabin, officer's ~ 223 21
cabin, single-berth ~ 223 46; 228 32
cabin cruiser 286 3
cabinet 22 40; 246 20
cabinet maker 132 38
cabin pulley cradle 214 66
cabin superstructure 285 39
cable *Sea Fish.* 90 26
cable *Power Plant* 153 41
cable *Music. Instr.* 326 53
cable, auxiliary ~ 214 47
cable, electric ~ 56 32
cable, endless ~ 214 21
cable, high-voltage ~ 153 42
cable, lower ~ 214 46
cable, moisture-proof ~ 127 42
cable, submarine ~ 237 56
cable, thermoplastic ~ 127 42
cable, three-core ~ 127 44
cable binding 301 40
cable boom 195 15
cable box 153 33
cable clip 127 40
cable connection 6 26
cable connection panel 239 3
cable crane berth 222 11-18
cable drum 85 39; 270 55
cable duct 234 29, 47; 235 61
cable ferry 216 1
cable guide 201 7
cable guide rail 214 33
cable manhole 198 17
cable parachute 287 7
cable pattern 30 39
cable pulley, automatic ~ 301 62
cable railway 214 12
cable release 23 9; 114 38; 115 101
cable release, double ~ 115 102
cable release socket 117 6
cable support 214 76
cable suspension lines 214 15-38
cable tunnel 152 20
cable vault 152 21
cableway 214 30
cableway, endless ~ 214 19
cableway gondola 214 52
cableways 214 15-38
cable winch 85 38, 46; 255 69; 258 85
cabochon, high ~ 36 79
cabochon, octagonal ~ 36 81
cabochon, oval ~ 36 80
cabochon, round ~ 36 78
cabochon, simple ~ 36 78
cabochons 36 78-81
caboose 223 42
cabriole 314 21

cabriolet 186 29
cacao bean 382 19
cacao tree 382 16
cachalot 367 25
caddis fly 358 12
caecum 20 17
café 265 1-26
café, open-air ~ 272 57
café customers 265 22-24
café table 265 11
cage *Fish Farm.* 89 1
cage *Coal* 144 23
cage *Circus* 307 50
cage, crane driver's ~ 119 35; 222 16; 226 52
cage, outside ~ 356 11
cage, rotating ~ 168 17
cage, round ~ 307 49
cage, stepped ~ 74 20
cage, tiered ~ 74 20
cage caravan 307 62
cage system 74 18
cage-winding system 144 23
caisson 217 33; 222 32; 259 19
cake 169 19-27, 22
cake counter 99 9; 265 1
cake plate 97 25
cakes 97 17-47
cake tin 40 28, 29
calabash 354 27
calcaneum 17 27
calcite 351 22
calcium chloride tube 350 43
calculating machine 309 80
calculation, logarithmic ~ 345 6
calculator 309 80
calculator, electronic ~ 246 12
calculator dial *Photog.* 114 57
calculator dial *Photograv.* 182 19
calculus, infinitesimal ~ 345 13-14
calendar 22 10
calendar clock 110 19
calendar sheet 247 33
calender 173 36
calendering machine 168 38
calender roll 173 26, 38
calender roller 163 20, 37, 59
calf *Man* 16 53
calf *Farm Bldgs.* 62 33
calf *Dom. Anim.* 73 1
calf *Game* 88 1
calf *Meat* 95 1-13
caliber 87 40
calibre 87 40
California Current 14 39
caliper *see* calliper
call, local ~ 237 3
call, long-distance ~ 237 3
call box 204 46; 236 8; 237 1; 251 10; 268 56
call button 25 6; 127 3; 246 15
calliper *Car* 191 18
calliper *Sculpt. Studio* 339 3
calliper, fixed ~ 192 49
calliper, inside ~ 135 23
calliper, outside ~ 135 18
calliper gauge 149 59
calliper square 85 10
call light 315 52
callosity 72 27
calls for luring game 87 43-47
calm 9 11
calm belts 9 46-47
calms, equatorial ~ 9 46
calvarium 261 16, 18
calyx 58 8; 374 8
calyx, involucral ~ 375 33
calyx, renal ~ 20 30
cam 190 60

Camberwell beauty 365 5
cambium ring 370 10
came 124 13
camel 366 29
camel caravan 354 1
camera *Atom* 1 60
camera *Optic. Instr.* 112 14, 20
camera *Cine Film* 117 28
camera *Audiovis.* 243 1
camera *Films* 310 19
camera, cartridge-loading ~ 114 11
camera, compact ~ *Cine Film* 117 51
camera, compact ~ *Photomech. Reprod.* 177 32
camera, folding ~ 114 49; 309 25
camera, high-speed ~ 313 35
camera, large-format ~ *Optic. Instr.* 112 25, 36
camera, large-format ~ *Photog.* 114 49, 61
camera, miniature ~ *Doc.* 23 7
camera, miniature ~ *Optic. Instr.* 112 26
camera, miniature ~ *Photog.* 114 1; 115 1
camera, 35 mm ~ *Photog.* 114 1
camera, 16 mm ~ *Cine Film* 117 43
camera, 35 mm ~ *Films* 313 1
camera, 16 mm ~ *Films* 313 31
camera, narrow-gauge ~ 313 35
camera, photogrammetric ~ 112 68
camera, professional press-type ~ 117 66
camera, rapid-sequence ~ 115 77
camera, single-lens reflex ~ 115 1
camera, spectrographic ~ 5 6
camera, stereometric ~ 112 71
camera, subminiature ~ 114 16
camera, Super-8 ~ 117 51
camera, underwater ~ 279 24
camera assistant 117 68; 310 42
camera back 114 54; 115 23
camera body *Photog.* 115 2
camera body *Photomech. Reprod.* 177 25, 33
camera cable 239 2
camera case 115 103
camera case, underwater ~ 279 24
camera control 242 36
camera crane 310 49
camera door 313 25
camera head 240 27
camera housing, underwater ~ 279 24
camera lens 313 19
cameraman 117 67; 310 20
cameraman, first ~ 310 41
camera monitor 238 65; 239 12; 240 28
camera operator 310 42
camera tube switch 242 23
cam housing 167 13
camomile *Weeds* 61 8
camomile *Med. Plants* 380 1
camp *Games* 276 27
camp *Circus* 307 61
campanile 334 65
camp bed 278 59

camp chair, folding ~ 278 vp
camp cot 278 59
camper 278 46
camp fire 278 10
campground 278 1-59
camphor laurel 380 18
camphor tree 380 18
camping 278
camping eating utensils 278 45
camping site 278 1-59
campion 376 20
camp site 278 1-59
camp site attendant 278 2
camp table, folding ~ 278 44
camshaft 166 56; 190 11, 14
camshaft bearing 192 24
camshaft lubrication 190 13
camshaft wheel 166 55
can Butch. 96 26
can Supermkt. 99 91
can Painter 129 7
can Weaving 166 21
Canadian pondweed 378 56
Canadian waterweed 378 56
canal Map 15 57
canal Hydr. Eng. 217 15-28
canal, auditory ~ 17 34, 58
canal, stomachic-intestinal ~ 77 15-19
canal administration 217 24
canal bed 217 30
canal entrance 217 15-16
Canary Current 14 41
can buoy 224 77, 94
cancel button 326 41
cancellation button 271 4
Cancer 4 56
candelabra 45 16
candidate 263 20
candies 47 31, 32
candies Grocer 98 75-86
candle, cast ~ 260 76
candle, paschal ~ 330 44
candle, wax ~ 77 66; 260 76
candlestick 309 45
candlestick, paschal ~ 330 45
candlewick yarn 35 9
candy 98 75
cane, flowering ~ 58 14
can holder 163 36
Canidae 367 11-13
Canina 3 46
canine 19 17
Canis Major 3 14
Canis Minor 3 15
canister 84 35; 129 16
canned vegetables 98 17
cannon Horse 72 23
cannon Army 255 49, 92
cannon cracker 306 53
canoe 352 19
canoe, Alaskan ~ 283 4
canoe, Canadian ~ 283 3
canoeing 283
canoeist 283 55
canoes 283 54-66
canoe stern 285 44
canoe with outrigger 352 35
cañon 13 45
canonicals Church 330 22; 332 4
canopy Infant Care etc. 28 32
canopy Dwellings 37 67
canopy Child. Rm. 47 12
canopy Supermkt. 99 24
canopy Aircraft 230 39
canopy Airsports 288 38
canopy Church 330 21; 331 49
canopy bearer 331 46
canopy jack 257 5
cant chisel 132 11

canteen 119 45
canter 72 42
cant hook 85 7
canting table 133 17
cantle 71 39, 46
canvas 338 21
canvas hull, rubber-covered ~ 283 58
canvas stretcher 338 20
canyon 13 45
canyon river 13 51
cap Bees 77 39
cap Drawing Off. 151 40
cap Refuse Coll. 199 8
cap Music. Instr. 326 31
cap Edib. Fungi 381 4
cap, astrakhan ~ 35 34
cap, corduroy ~ 35 25
cap, fox ~ 35 31
cap, leather ~ 35 32; 354 26
cap, linen ~ 35 8
cap, mink ~ 35 17, 20
cap, musquash ~ 35 33
cap, peaked ~ 35 17, 29; 264 8; 301 18
cap, sailor's ~ 35 28
cap, sheepskin ~ 353 23
cap, white ~ 268 32
cap, wide-brimmed ~ 355 28
capa 319 27
capacitor 211 17
cap and bells 306 39
caparison 329 74
cape 30 65; 105 34; 106 4
cape, short ~ 355 29
cape chisel 140 25
capeline 21 3
caper 98 42
capercaillie 88 72
capillary tube stand 23 42
capistrum 322 5
capital Composing Rm. 175 11
capital Art 334 20-25
capital, Arabian ~ 337 18
capital, bell-shaped ~ 333 16
capital, bud-shaped ~ 333 14
capital, Roman ~ 341 16
capital, small ~ 175 14
capitulum 61 14; 370 73; 378 12
capoc tree 383 20
cap of typing element 249 30
capon 73 21
capper 76 46
capping Bees 77 39
capping Coal 144 48
Capricorn 3 36; 4 62
capriole 71 5
caprolactam 170 28
caprolactam oil 170 25
caps, ladies' ~ 35 1-21
caps, men's ~ 35 22-40
capstan Cine Film 117 34
capstan Hydr. Eng. 217 22
capstan Audiovis. 243 23
capstan Warships 258 23
capstan idler 117 35
capsule 384 58
capsule, poricidal ~ 370 96
capsule, porose ~ 370 96
captain 224 38
caption 185 67; 342 59
car Car 191 1-56
car Garage 195 34
car Railw. 213 18
car, four-axled ~ 208 3
car, large-capacity ~ 213 28
car, open ~ 207 59
car accessory 196 28
carapace 364 29
caravan 278 52; 307 34
caravan, collapsible ~ 278 3

caravan, showman's ~ 206 20
caravan awning 278 57
caravanning 278
caravel 218 27-43; 220 37
caraway roll 97 31
caraway stick 97 31
carbide, cemented ~ 149 46
carbine 86 30
carbolic acid 170 14
carbon, active ~ 270 58
carbon, negative ~ 312 41
carbon, positive ~ 312 40
carbon atom 242 63
carbon crater 312 44
carbon disulfide 169 8
carbon disulphide 169 8
carbon disulphide injector 83 33
carbon rod, negative ~ 312 41
carbon rod, positive ~ 312 40
carbon rod holder 312 43
carbon tissue 182 1, 10
carbon tissue, printed ~ 182 8
carbon tissue transfer machine 182 6
carburetor see carburettor
carburettor 189 4; 192 1-15
carburettor, cross-draught ~ 190 79
car carrier, double-deck ~ 213 35
car carrier, two-tier ~ 213 35
carcase 118 1-49
carcass 118 1-49
carcassing 118 1-49
car coat 33 63
card Cotton Spin. 163 34, 51
card Games 276 37
card, patient's ~ 25 5
card, used ~ 195 14
cardan coupling 67 6
cardan joint 67 6, 28
cardan mount 6 36
cardan shaft 64 40, 48; 67 16; 211 51; 212 29, 83
cardan shaft connection 64 63
cardan transmission 189 47
cardboard 260 50-52
card can 163 35
card catalogue 262 22
card catalogue drawer 262 23
car deck 221 79
cardiac rhythm 25 1
cardiac sulcus, longitudinal ~ 20 25
cardigan 31 50; 33 30
cardinal Maths. 344 5
cardinal Birds 363 5
cardinal bird 363 5
card index 245 23
card index box 46 10; 248 27
carding can 163 35
carding engine 163 34, 51
carding machine 163 34
car door 191 4
card sliver 163 38
card stacker 244 13
car ferry 216 10
cargo 223 77
cargo and passenger liner 221 96
cargo and passenger ship 223 1-71
cargo barge 216 25
cargo boom 221 26, 59; 223 36
cargo gear 221 24-29, 59
cargo handling, horizontal ~ 226 7
cargo-handling berth 226 1
cargo-handling gear 221 24-29, 59
cargo hatchway 221 11, 63; 226 14

cargo hold 231 21
cargo ship 221 23
cargo warehouse 233 10
'car hire' 233 33
carload 206 52
car location number 195 48
car models 193 1-36
carnation 60 6
carnival 306
carnival float 306 57
carnival procession 306 57-70
carnival truck 306 57
carnivore house 356 10
carnivores 367 11-22; 368 1-11
carob 384 41
carom billiards 277 7
carousel 308 2
carp 89 26; 364 4
carpel 58 36, 59; 59 13; 374 2, 26
carpenter 120 12
carpenter's tools 120 60-82
carpenter's yard 120 1-59
carpet 44 16
carpet, fitted ~ 41 18; 43 23
carpet, oriental ~ 46 36
carpet, velour ~ 267 35
carpet beater head 50 79
carpet beater nozzle 50 71
carpet brush 50 45
carpet cleaning 50 53-86
carpeting 191 43
carpet sweeper 50 57
carpet sweeper and shampooer, combined ~ 50 76
carp hook 89 86
carp pond 89 6
carpus Man 17 15; 19 76
carpus Horse 72 22
car radio 191 90
carriage Hosp. 26 36
carriage Sawmill 157 12, 52
carriage Knitting 167 39
carriage Tram 197 5, 6, 7
carriage, auxiliary ~ 157 11
carriage, one-horse ~ 186 18, 29
carriage, open ~ 207 61; 208 9
carriage, three-horse ~ 186 45
carriage, two-horse ~ 186 36
carriage apron 149 16
carriage handle 167 41
carriage heating pressure gauge 210 44
carriage horse 186 28
carriage motor 157 15
carriage rail 167 45
carriages 186 1-54,
1-3,26-39,45,51-54
carriages, horse-drawn ~ 186
carriage sprayer 83 38
carriage step 186 13
carrier Bicycle 187 44
carrier Docks 226 4
carrier return lever 249 21
carrion flower 53 15
carrot 57 17
carrot, stump-rooted ~ 57 18
carrycot 28 48
carry-home pack 93 28
carrying axle 210 35
carrying bogie 197 10
carrying cart 56 26
carrying grip 21 22
carrying handle 241 2
carrying rope 215 16
carrying saddle 73 4
carrying strap 115 9
carrying wheel 214 7
cart 86 39

cart, electric ~ **206** 34
carte engagement **294** 47
cartilage, costal ~ **17** 11
cartilage, thyroid ~ **20** 3
cartoon *Art. Studio* **338** 43
cartoon *Script* **342** 53
cartouche **336** 7
cartridge *Hunt.* **87** 19, 54
cartridge *Slaughterho.* **94** 5
cartridge *Cine Film* **117** 30
cartridge, full-jacketed ~ **87** 55
cartridge, instamatic ~ **114** 15
cartridge, magnetic ~ **241** 26
cartridge, subminiature ~ **114** 17
cartridge chamber **87** 15
cartwheel **297** 21
cartwheel ruff **355** 52
car tyre **191** 15; **196** 27
carvel **218** 27-43; **220** 37
carvel planking **285** 53
carvel planking, diagonal ~ **285** 56
carver **96** 35
carving knife **45** 69; **96** 35
carving set **45** 69-70
car-wash hose **196** 23
car wheel **191** 14
car window, crank-operated ~ **191** 22
caryatid **334** 36
caryopsis **375** 43
cascade **272** 9
case *Meteorol. Instr.* **10** 18
case *Doc.* **22** 33
case *Composing Rm.* **174** 3, 8
case *Bookbind.* **185** 40
case *Lorries etc.* **194** 19
case *Station* **204** 6; **205** 7
case *Chem.* **349** 26
case, cardboard ~ **87** 50
case cabinet **174** 4
case head **305** 36
case maker **184** 6
case-making machine **184** 6
case rack **174** 4
case room **174**; **175**; **176**
cash desk **196** 29; **266** 69; **275** 2
cash drawer **271** 5
cashier **99** 94; **250** 2; **266** 70; **271** 1
cash readout **196** 4
cash register **47** 34; **99** 93; **207** 86
cash register, electric ~ **271** 2
casing *Mach. Parts etc.* **143** 79
casing *Oil, Petr.* **145** 18
casing *Power Plant* **153** 37
casing *Text. Finish.* **168** 16
casing *Army* **255** 10
casing *Chem.* **350** 10
casing, outer ~ **168** 17
casing, protective ~ *Meteorol. Instr.* **10** 39
casing, protective ~ *Railw.* **202** 35
casing cover **143** 80
casing-in machine **185** 27
casino **274** 8; **275** 1
cask **130** 5
casket **331** 35
casque, light ~ **329** 61
Cassegrain cage **5** 4
casserole dish **40** 14
cassette, compact ~ **241** 50
cassette, daylight ~ **177** 50
cassette, 35 mm ~ **114** 7
cassette, single-8 ~ **117** 39
cassette box **241** 11, 47
cassette cabinet **241** 11, 47
cassette compartment **241** 6, 34; **243** 8; **249** 72

cassette deck **241** 52
cassette exit slot **114** 10
cassette holder **241** 11, 47
cassette recorder **117** 73; **261** 42
cassette recorder unit **241** 3
cassette slit **114** 10
cassette tape **241** 12
cassia **380** 16
Cassiopeia **3** 33
cassowary **359** 1
cast **89** 64, 78
cast, long ~ **89** 58
castanets **324** 46
caster **148** 8
castes of bees **77** 1,4,5
cast glass **124** 6
casting **148** 42
casting, continuous ~ **148** 24-29
casting mechanism **174** 25
casting net **89** 31
casting off **167** 66
casting team **148** 13
castle *Map* **15** 74
castle *Games* **276** 12
castle, knight's ~ **329** 1
castle gate **329** 32
castle nut **143** 77
castle wall **333** 31
cast line **174** 27
cast of skull **261** 15
castor *Household* **50** 81
castor *Horse* **72** 27
castor *Pest Contr.* **83** 61
Castor and Pollux **3** 28
castor-oil plant **380** 14
casual **101** 34
casualty **21** 20
cat **62** 3; **73** 17
catacomb **331** 59
catalogue, main ~ **262** 21
catalogue room **262** 18
catalytic cracking plant **145** 70
catamaran **284** 64; **286** 21
cataract **11** 45
catch *Mach. Parts etc.* **143** 29
catch *Railw.* **203** 57
catcher **292** 54, 64
catchfly **376** 20
catchment area **12** 24
catchup **45** 43
cat cracker **145** 48
caterpillar **58** 64; **82** 16, 20, 31, 44, 47; **365** 10; **80** 3, 8, 14, 17, 29, 44, 48
caterpillar hauling scraper **200** 16
caterpillar mounting **200** 3
caterpillar tractor **200** 3
catfish **364** 12
cathedral **335** 1-13, 22
catheter **26** 31
catheter, cardiac ~ **25** 53
catheter gauge unit **27** 30
catheter holder **26** 30
catheterization **27** 30
cathetus **346** 32
cathode **178** 6
cathode ray tube **242** 40
catkin **59** 39; **371** 10, 26
catkin, male ~ **59** 45
catkin scale **371** 12
cat ladder **38** 4; **122** 63
cat litter **99** 38
cats **368** 2-8
cat's foot **377** 3
cat's tail **378** 21
cat's tongue **98** 84
catsuit **29** 19
catsup **45** 43
cattail **378** 21

cattail flag **378** 21
cattle **62** 45; **73** 1-2
cattleship **221** 68
cattle vessel **221** 68
catwalk *Iron & Steel* **147** 38
catwalk *Ship* **221** 3
catwalk *Theatre* **315** 29
cauliflower **57** 31; **99** 84
causticizing agitator **172** 49
causticizing stirrer **172** 49
caustic soda **169** 3, 4, 5, 10; **170** 11
caustic soda solution **170** 10
cautery **24** 43
cavalier hat **355** 55
cavalry saddle **71** 45-49
cavalry standard **253** 13
cave *Phys. Geog.* **13** 76
cave *Map* **15** 85
cave, dripstone ~ **13** 79
cave, limestone ~ **13** 79
cave art **328** 9
cave formations **13** 80-81
cave painting **328** 9
cavern *Phys. Geog.* **13** 76
cavern *Park* **272** 1
cavetto **336** 50
cavetto vault **336** 49
caviare knife **45** 81
cavity **91** 36
cavity, nasal ~ **17** 53
cavity, tympanic ~ **17** 60
cavity of the uterus **20** 80
cavy **366** 12
C-clef **320** 10
cecum **20** 17
cedar tree **372** 65
cedilla **342** 33
ceiba tree **383** 20
ceiling **222** 63
ceiling, concrete ~ **123** 28
ceiling, false ~ **123** 61, 68-69
ceiling beam **120** 38
ceiling construction **123**
ceiling hook **270** 15
ceiling joint **126** 48
ceiling joist **119** 5; **120** 38; **121** 54
ceiling light **24** 20; **75** 8
ceiling paper **128** 53
ceiling paperhanger **128** 50
ceiling plaster **123** 59, 72
ceiling tile **317** 29
celeriac **57** 27
celesta **325** 1
Celestial River **3** 12
Celestial Ship **3** 45
cell **77** 26-30, 27
cell, sealed ~ **77** 32, 33
cella **334** 51
cellarman **79** 18
cellar steps, outside ~ **118** 4
cellar window **37** 27; **118** 3
cell nucleus **357** 2
cello **323** 16
cellulose, refined ~ **172** 78
cellulose, unrefined ~ **172** 77
cellulose sheet **169** 2, 4, 6
cellulose xanthate **169** 9
cembalo **322** 45
cement *Man* **19** 29
cement *Bldg. Site* **118** 43
cement factory **160**
cement-grinding mill **160** 12
cementing pump, high-pressure ~ **146** 34
cement-packing plant **160** 16
cement screed **123** 14
cement silo **119** 30; **160** 15
cement storage tank **146** 15
cement store **201** 22
cement track racing **290** 24-28

cementum, dental ~ **19** 29
cement works **160**
cemetery **15** 106
censer **332** 38
cent **252** 19, 33
Centaur *Astron.* **3** 39
centaur *Fabul. Creat.* **327** 52
Centaurus **3** 39
centaury **61** 1; **380** 10
centavo **252** 23
center *see* centre
centerboard *see* centreboard
centering *see* centring
centime **252** 15, 16
centimeter *see* centimetre
centimetre graduation **247** 36
céntimo **252** 22
central heating, full ~ **38** 38-81
central heating furnace **38** 57
central heating system, coke-fired ~ **38** 38
central heating system, oil-fired ~ **38** 44-60
centre *Turner* **135** 8
centre *Ball Games* **293** 76
centre *Maths.* **346** 26, 43, 55
centre, asbestos ~ **350** 19
centre, live ~ **135** 11
centre angle **346** 55
centreboard **284** 26
centreboard, retractable ~ **284** 8; **285** 41
centreboard case **284** 24
centre circle **291** 2
centre console **191** 38
centre flag **291** 64
centre girder **222** 53
centre lathe **149** 1
centre line *Drawing Off.* **151** 30
centre line *Sailing* **285** 5
centre line *Ball Games* **293** 8 - 9, 54
centre line *Fencing* **294** 4
centre line judge **293** 25
centre mark **293** 11
centre of curvature **346** 23
centre of symmetry **351** 3
centre plate girder **222** 53
centre punch **134** 31; **140** 64
centre-section fuel tank **257** 30
centre strake **222** 55
centrifuge **23** 59
centrifuge, pendulum-type ~ **168** 14
centrifuge lid **168** 18
centring apparatus, universal ~ **111** 21
centring control **243** 10
centring ring **240** 23
centring suction holder **111** 22
centrosphere **11** 5
cep **381** 16
cepe **381** 16
cephalopod **357** 37
Cerberus **327** 29
cereal **68** 1
cereal product **99** 62
cereal products **98** 35-39
cereals **68** 1-37
cerebellum **17** 45; **18** 23
cerebrum **17** 42; **18** 22
cesta **305** 69
Cetus **3** 11
chaffinch **360** 10
chaffron **329** 84
chafron **329** 84
chain **74** 14; **75** 15; **99** 95; **118** 30

chain *Bicycle* 187 36
chain *Cyc. Racing* 290 20
chain armour 329 63
chain cable 222 77; 223 50;
  227 12
chain compressor 223 51
chain curtain 139 50
chain cutter 120 17
chain delivery 180 43
chain drive 187 35-42
chain feeder 74 25
chain ferry 216 1
chain grinder, continuous ~
  172 53, 66
chain gripper 180 56
chain guard 187 37; 188 46
chain guide 120 15
chain mail 329 63
chain mortiser 132 49
chain mortising machine 132
  49
chain reaction 1 41, 48
chain saw 120 14
chain sling *Forging* 139 44
chain sling *Docks* 226 26
chain stay 187 20
chain stitch 102 2
chain-tensioning device 157
  41
chain transmission 187 35-39
chain wheel 187 35
chair 42 34; 271 35
chair, adjustable ~ 105 17;
  106 16
chair, barber's ~ 106 16
chair, cane ~ 43 3
chair, dentist's ~ 24 3
chair, double ~ 214 18
chair, folding ~ 28 33
chair, gaffer's ~ 162 45
chair, glassmaker's ~ 162 45
chair, hairdresser's ~ 105 17;
  106 16
chair, single ~ 214 16
chair, steel ~ 67 2
chair, tubular steel ~ 41 21
chair, two-seater ~ 214 17, 18
chair, umpire's ~ 293 20
chair, visitor's ~ 246 21
chair grip 21 21
chair lift 214 16-18
chair lift, double ~ 301 57
chairman 263 1
chairman of board of
  directors 251 16
chairman of board of
  governors 251 15
chairoplane 308 4
chaise 186 34
chaise, closed ~ 186 54
chaise, covered ~ 186 54
chaise, one-horse ~ 186 29
chaitya 337 28
chaitya hall 337 27
chalaza 74 63
chalcography 340 14-24
chalet 278 7
chalice 330 10; 332 49
chalk 48 15; 260 32; 338 5
chalk, French ~ 104 24
chalk, tailor's ~ 104 24
chalk ledge 260 31
chalk sketch 338 4
chalwar 306 42
Chamaeleontidae 364 33
chamber *Atom* 1 66
chamber *Forest Pests* 82 36
chamber *Hunt.* 87 20
chamber *Water* 269 24
chamber, king's ~ 333 2
chamber, photographic ~ 113
  40
chamber, queen's ~ 333 3

chamber, stone ~ 328 39
chamber wall 269 25
chameleon 364 33
chamfer 143 62
chamfering hammer 125 14
chamfrain 329 84
chamfron 329 84
chamois 367 3
chamomile 61 8; 380 1
chamotte slab 141 16
champagne bottle 99 78
champagne bucket 267 59
champagne cooler 267 59
champagne cork 267 58
champagne glass 45 86
champagne glasses 45 85-86
chancel 330 1, 32; 335 4
chandelier 267 21
chanfron 329 84
'change' *Airport* 233 51
change *Winter Sp.* 302 12
change-gear box 149 7
change-gear handle 132 56
change gears 10 14
change-loop 302 16
change machine 197 33; 204
  22; 236 28
changemaker 236 28
changeover switch 50 59; 243
  15
change points, electric ~ 197
  37
change rack 236 23
change-speed gear 163 29;
  211 50
change wheel 164 40
changing booth 271 32
changing cubicle 282 1
changing room 282 3
changing top 28 4
changing unit 28 11
channel *Overh. Irrign.* 67 13
channel *Railw.* 202 32
channel *Swim.* 281 9
channel *Rowing* 283 60
channel *Art* 334 27
channel, distributary ~ 13 2
channel, navigable ~ 224 92,
  93
channel iron 143 7
channel markings 224 84-102
channel marks 224 68-83
chantarelle 381 14
chanter 322 10
chanterelle 381 14
chapel *Map* 15 61, 107
'chapel' *Airport* 233 49
chapel *Chivalry* 329 29
chaplet 34 32
chaplet hairstyle 34 31
chaps 70 26
chapter heading 185 60
char-a-banc, covered ~ 186
  33
character 174 7, 44; 175 38
characteristic 345 6
characteristic light 221 48;
  224 105
character storage 242 37
charcoal 278 48
charcoal, activated ~ 270 58
charcoal grill 278 47
charcoal pencil 338 16
chard 57 28
charge bottom feeder 236 58
charger 25 51
charging car 144 8; 156 6
charging chamber 154 79
charging conveyor 144 42
charging door 38 61; 139 4
charging machine 147 25
charging opening 139 49
charging platform 147 4

charging position 147 55, 56
Charioteer 3 27
charity performance 319 31
Charles's Wain 3 29
Charleston cymbals 324 50
charlock 61 18
charm 36 35
chart 22 32; 76 8; 260 30
chart, illustrated ~ 22 16
chase 181 38
chasing 87 28
chasing hammer 108 41
chassis *Overh. Irrign.* 67 14
chassis *Blacksm.* 138 28
chassis *Car* 191 2
check *Roulette* 275 12
check *Theatre* 315 7
check *Music. Instr.* 325 27
check brake 143 97
checker 276 18, 19
checkerboard 276 17
checkerman 276 18, 19
checkers 276 17-19
check felt 325 28
check light 195 21, 22
checkmate 276 15
checkout 99 92
check rail 202 23
checkroom 315 5; 318 1
checkroom attendant 315 6;
  318 2
checkroom hall 315 5-11
check side 277 6
cheek *Man* 16 9
cheek *Hunt.* 87 4
cheekbone 16 8; 17 37
cheek piece 71 8
cheek rest 255 30
cheek strap 71 8
cheese 98 5; 266 52
cheese, cross-wound ~ 164 58
cheese, round ~ 99 42
cheese, whole ~ 99 40
cheeseboard 45 35
cheese box 99 49
cheesecake 97 23
cheese counter 99 39
cheese dish 40 7
cheesefly 81 15
cheese knife 45 72
cheese machine 76 47
cheetah 368 7
chef 207 34
chelicer 358 41
cheliped 358 41
chemical bottle 116 10; 261
  23
'chemist' 233 45
chemistry 261 1-13
chemistry laboratory 261 1;
  349; 350
chemistry teacher 261 2
chequer-board cut 36 66
cheroot 107 4
cherry *Drupes & Nuts* 59 5,
  6-8
cherry *Goldsm. etc.* 108 7
cherry *Bot.* 370 99
cherry blossom 59 3
cherry flan 97 22
cherry flower 59 3
cherry fruit 59 6-8
cherry fruit fly 80 18
cherry leaf 59 2
cherry stone 59 7
cherry tree 59 1, 11-18
cherub 272 20
chess 265 17; 276 1-16
chessboard 47 20; 276 1
chessboard square 276 2
chess championship 276 16
chess clock 276 16
chessman 276 1, 4, 5, 7

chess match 276 16
chess move 276 6
chess player 265 17
chess problem 276 6
chess square 276 6
chest *Man* 16 28-30; 17 8-11
chest *Paperm.* 172 25
chest grip 21 37
chestnut *Horse* 72 27
chestnut *Decid. Trees* 371 60
chestnut *South. Fruits* 384 52
Chestnut Boletus 381 15
chestnut tree 371 58
chest of drawers 41 8
chevron design 335 16
chew 107 19
chewing tobacco 107 19
chianti 98 61
chianti bottle 99 77
chibonk 107 32
chibonque 107 32
chick 74 2
chicken 62 36; 73 19-26; 96
  24
chicken run 74 11
chick-pea 69 19
chick unit 74 1
chicory 57 40
chief 254 18-19
chignon 34 29
child 260 3
child, small ~ 28 42
child carrier seat 187 21
children's room 47
chilling roll 180 28
chill roller 180 28
chimera 327 16
chimney *Map* 15 38
chimney *Dwellings* 37 10
chimney *Roof & Boilerr.* 38 5
chimney *Bldg. Site* 118 21
chimney *Carp.* 120 47
chimney *Roof* 122 13
chimney *Blacksm.* 137 7
chimney *Power Plant* 152 15
chimney *Energy Sources* 155
  12
chimney *Railw.* 210 22
chimney *Mountain.* 300 8
chimney bond 118 66
chimney brick 159 28
chimney flashing 122 14
chimney swallow 361 20
chimney sweep 38 31
chimney sweeper 38 31
chimpanzee 368 14
chin 16 15
china, broken ~ 260 61
china cabinet 44 26
china manufacture 161
china painter 161 17
China reed 136 28
China rose 60 15
chinaband 355 22
chinch 81 39
chinchona 380 17
Chinese lantern 52 15
chine strake 258 8
chin rest 323 8
chintuft 34 10
chip *Basketm.* 136 12
chip *Roulette* 275 12
chip basket 136 11
chip container 170 40
chip crusher 172 5
chip distributor 172 3
chip extractor 157 51
chip-extractor opening 132 48
chip packer 172 3
chip pan 40 41
chipper 172 1
chipping hammer *Blacksm.*
  137 38

chipping hammer *Gas Weld.* 141 25
chipping hammer *Arc Weld.* 142 17
chip remover 157 50
chiropter 366 9
chiropteran 366 9
chisel 120 71
chisel, bevelled-edge ~ 132 7; 339 19
chisel, blacksmith's ~ 137 38
chisel, broad ~ 158 37
chisel, flat ~ 140 26; 339 14
chisel, hollow ~ 339 17
chisel, pneumatic ~ 148 45
chisel, toothed ~ 339 13
chisels 132 7-11
chitarrone 324 1
chiton 355 5
Chitonactis 369 20
chivalry 329
chive 57 22
chlorine 170 7
chlorine ion 1 10
chlorobenzene 170 9, 11
chock *Bldg. Site* 119 40
chock *Iron Foundry etc.* 148 61
chocolate 98 80
chocolate, bar of ~ 98 78
chocolate box 98 79
chocolate liqueur 98 83
choir 330 32; 335 4
choir organ 326 5, 42
choke cymbals 324 50
choke flap 192 6
choker 36 16
choker collar 355 74
cholecystography 27 4
Chopper 188 56
chopper drum 64 34
chopping board 96 57
chord *Aircraft* 230 56
chord *Music. Not.* 321 1-5, 5
chord *Maths.* 346 51
chord, lower ~ 121 73, 79
chord, upper ~ 121 74, 80
chorus 315 21
chow 70 21
christening 332 1
christening dress 332 8
christening robe 332 8
christening shawl 332 9
Christian 330 61
chromatic scale 320 49
chromolithograph 340 28
chronometer 230 11
chrysalis 77 30, 32; 80 4, 25, 43; 81 3, 21, 24; 82 13, 21, 32; 358 20; 365 11
chrysanthemum 51 29; 61 7
chuck *Meat* 95 19
chuck *D.I.Y.* 134 48
chuck *Turner* 135 6
chuck, four-jaw ~ 149 35
chuck, independent ~ 149 35
chuck, quick-action ~ 132 54
chuck, self-centring ~ 149 37
chuck, three-jaw ~ 149 37
chuck, two-jaw ~ 135 10
church 15 53, 61, 107; 330; 331 1; 332
church, Baroque ~ 336 1
church, Gothic ~ 335 22
church, Protestant ~ 330 1-30
church, Renaissance ~ 335 42
church, Roman Catholic ~ 330 31-62
church, Romanesque ~ 335 1-13
church banner 331 44
church clock 331 7
church door *Church* 331 16

church door *Art* 335 24
churchgoer 330 29; 331 17
church landmark 15 64
church organ 326 1-52
church owl 362 17
church roof 331 11
church spire 331 6
church wedding 332 14
church window 330 14
churchyard 331 21-41
churchyard gate 331 19
churchyard wall 331 18
chute *Docks* 226 45
chute *Fair* 308 40
chute, spiral ~ 144 28
chute, three-way ~ 92 34
ciborium 332 48
cigar, Brazilian ~ 107 2
cigar and cigarette boy 267 49
cigar box 107 1
cigar case 107 8
cigar cutter 107 9
cigarette, filter-tipped ~ 107 12
cigarette, Russian ~ 107 14
cigarette beetle 81 25
cigarette case 107 10
cigarette holder 107 16
cigarette lighter 107 27, 30
cigarette machine 268 69
cigarette packet 107 11
cigarette paper 107 17
cigarette roller 107 15
cigarettes and tobacco kiosk 204 47
cigarette seller 308 51
cigarette tip 107 13
cigarette tray 267 50
cigarillo 107 3
cigar lighter 191 88
ciliate 370 49
ciliate infusorian 357 9
cilium *Man* 19 41
cilium *Invertebr.* 357 10
cilium *Bot.* 370 50
cinchona 380 17
cincinnus 370 77
cine camera 117 1
cine film 117
cinema 312 1
cinema, mobile ~ 312 52
cinema advertisement 268 57
cinema audience 312 5
cinema box office 312 2
cinemagoer 312 5
cinema projector 312 24
cinema projector, narrow-gauge ~ 312 52
cinemascope camera 310 47
cinema ticket 312 3
cine projector 117 78; 318 20
cinnamon 382 25
cinnamon bark 382 25
cinnamon tree 382 22
cinquefoil 335 40
circle *Sports* 305 31
circle *Maths.* 346 42
circle, circumscribed ~ 346 29
circle, divided ~ *Optic. Instr.* 113 27
circle, divided ~ *Crystals* 351 32
circle, graduated ~ *Optic. Instr.* 113 27
circle, graduated ~ *Crystals* 351 32
circle, inner ~ 288 57
circle, inscribed ~ 346 31
circle, middle ~ 288 58
circle, outer ~ 288 59
circle, upper ~ 315 17
circles, concentric ~ 346 58
circles, polar ~ 14 11

circle template 151 70
circling engagement 294 49
circuit, integrated ~ *Clocks* 110 16
circuit, integrated ~ *Inf. Tech.* 242 68
circuit, primary ~ 154 2, 42
circuit, secondary ~ 154 7, 45
circuit breaker 127 19, 33, 36; 152 34; 153 51-62
circuit breaker, miniature ~ 41 20
circuit breaker consumer unit 127 33
circular broom 199 40
circular saw attachment 84 33; 134 52
circular saw blade 132 59
circulation, atmospheric ~ 9 46-52
circulation pump 154 43, 54
circulatory system 18 1-21
circumcircle 346 29
circumference *Cooper* 130 23
circumference *Maths.* 346 44
circumference, staved ~ 130 2
circumflex 342 32
circus 307
circus, travelling ~ 307 1-63
circus act 307 25
circus attendant 307 27
circus band 307 10
circus box 307 16
circus caravan 206 20; 307 34
circus horse 307 30
circus manager 307 17
circus marksman 307 38
circus rider 307 26
circus tent 307 1
circus trailer 307 34
cirrocumulus 8 14
cirrostratus 8 7
cirrus 8 6
cist, long ~ 328 16
cist, stone ~ 328 17
cistern 49 16
cithara 322 15
cittern 322 21
city 15 51
city banner 218 22
city wall 333 30
Claisen flask 350 50
clamp *Atom* 2 43
clamp *Overh. Irrign.* 67 30
clamp *Goldsm. etc.* 108 34
clamp *Joiner* 132 51; 133 9
clamp *Bookbind.* 183 18; 185 3
clamp *Chem.* 350 33
clamp, horizontal ~ 14 57
clamp, vertical ~ 14 55
clamp handle 133 8
clamping device *Atom* 2 43
clamping device *Mach. Tools* 150 15
clamping plate, hinged ~ 117 90
clamping screw 133 23
clamping shoe 133 10
clamp lever 132 67
clamp tip 149 46
clamp tip tool 149 45
clapper *Carnival* 306 47
clapper *Films* 310 35
clapper board 310 35
clapper boy 310 34
clappers 162 42
clarinet 318 4; 323 34
clarinettist 318 5
clasp, white gold ~ 36 10
clasp nut 149 19
classes, social ~of bees 77 1,4,5

classification siding 206 47
classification track 206 47
classification yard 206 42
classification yard switch tower 206 44
classifier 172 50
classroom 260 1-45
classroom cupboard 260 43
clavicembalo 322 45
clavichord 322 36
clavichord mechanism 322 37
clavicle 17 6
clavilux 317 13
claw 327 3; 362 7
claw, bird's ~ 327 61
claw, double ~ 77 8
claw chisel 339 13
claw head 120 75
claws, griffin's ~ 327 13
clay 160 1; 260 79; 339 8, 31
clay, impure ~ 159 2
clay, raw ~ 159 2
clay box 339 30
clay column *Brickwks.* 159 14
clay column *Porcelain Manuf.* 161 8
clay pigeon shooting 305 70-78
clay pit *Map* 15 88
clay pit *Brickwks.* 159 1
cleaner, centrifugal ~ 173 11
cleaner, ultrasonic ~ 109 23
cleaning brush *Hunt.* 87 62
cleaning brush *Office* 247 10
cleaning fluid 111 32
cleaning machine *Brew.* 92 36
cleaning machine *Watchm.* 109 30
cleaning plant 144 20
cleaning rag 50 55
cleaning rod 87 61
cleaning shop 148 38-45
cleaning tank 178 1
cleaning tow 87 63
cleanout door 38 39
cleansing pond 89 6
clear-felling system 84 4-14
clearing *Map* 15 2
clearing *Forestry* 84 13
clearstory 334 70
cleat *Carp.* 120 45
cleat *Floor etc. Constr.* 123 67
cleaver, butcher's ~ 94 18
cleaving hammer 85 5
clefs 320 8-11
cleft, anal ~ 16 41
clench planking 285 50-52
clerestory 334 70
clergyman 330 22; 331 37; 332 22
clergyman, Protestant ~ 332 3
clerical assistant 248 7
clerk 263 26, 27
clew 284 41
click 110 34
click beetle 80 37, 38
click wheel 110 35
cliff 13 28
cliff face 13 28
cliffline 13 25-31
cliffs 13 25-31
climate, artificially maintained ~ 356 21
climate, boreal ~ 9 56
climate, equatorial ~ 9 53
climates 9 53-58
climates, polar ~ 9 57-58
climatic map 9 40-58
climatology 9
climber *Flower Gdn.* 51 5
climber *Fruit & Veg. Gdn.* 52 5

climber *Indoor Plants* 53 2
climber *Veg.* 57 8
climber *Mountain.* 300 5
climbing 300 2-13
climbing boot 300 44
climbing breeches 300 7
climbing equipment 300 31-57
climbing frame 273 47
climbing harness 300 56
climbing net 273 50
climbing plant 53 2
climbing roof 273 60
climbing rope 273 48; 296 19
climbing tower 273 17
clinch 299 31
clinker cooler 160 9
clinker pit 152 8
clinker planking 285 50-52
clinker store 160 10
clinoprinacoid 351 24
clip *Atom* 2 18
clip *Bicycle* 187 62
clip *Railw.* 202 9
clipper display 238 44
clippers, electric ~ 105 21; 106 32
clipper ship, English ~ 220 36
clitellum 357 26
clitoris 20 88
Clivia minata 53 8
cloak 355 18, 26
cloak, red ~ 319 27
cloak, short ~ 355 29
cloak, Spanish ~ 355 29
cloak, woollen ~ 355 6
cloak cord 355 24
cloakroom 48 34; 207 70; 315 5; 318 1
cloakroom attendant 315 6; 318 2
cloakroom hall 315 5-11
cloakroom ticket 315 7
cloche 35 12
clock 191 38; 211 37; 212 16
clock, double ~ 276 16
clock, electric ~ 191 79
clock, main ~ 245 18
clock case 110 26; 309 57
clockmaker 109 1
clocks 110
clockwork 110 36
clockwork drive 10 14
clockwork mechanism 110 36
clod 63 7
clog 101 44; 355 43
cloister 331 52
cloister vault 336 41
closed vertical gate 301 66
close-up bellows attachment 115 85
close-up equipment 115 81-98
close-up lens 117 55
closing gear 90 27
closing head 143 59
closure rail 202 26
cloth 166 12; 271 59
cloth, damask ~ 45 2
cloth, felt ~ 340 42
cloth, flannel ~ 128 48
cloth, linen ~ 206 11
cloth, sterile ~ 26 38
cloth, unraised ~ 168 33
clothes, children's ~ 29
clothes, teenagers' ~ 29 48-68
clothes brush 50 44; 104 31
clothes closet 43 1
clothes closet door 46 2
clothes compartment 212 63; 267 30
clothes line 38 23; 50 33
clothes louse 81 41

clothes moth 81 13
clothes rack 271 31
clothes rack, movable ~ 103 17
clothes shop 268 9
clothing, protective ~ 84 26; 270 46
cloth roller 166 20
cloth-shearing machine, rotary ~ 168 42
cloth take-up motion 166 19
cloth take-up roller 166 47
cloth temple 166 13
cloud, lenticular ~ 287 19
cloud chamber photograph 2 26
cloud chamber track 2 27
cloud cover 9 20-24
clouds 8 1-19, 1-4, 5-12, 13-17
clouds, luminous ~ 7 22
clouds, noctilucent ~ 7 22
clout 121 94
clout nail 121 94; 122 96
clove 382 28
clove carnation 60 7
clove pink 60 7
clover, four-leaf ~ 69 5
clover broadcaster 66 26
clove tree 382 26
clown 306 69; 307 24
clown, musical ~ 307 23
clown act 307 25
club 283 23
club hammer 126 77
clubhouse 283 23
club membership 286 8
club rush 378 21
clubs 276 38
clump of grass 375 44
cluster of eggs 80 2, 30
cluster of grapes 78 5
cluster of stars 3 26
clutch 191 44
clutch, dry ~ 190 78
clutch, fluid ~ 65 37
clutch, main ~ 65 39
clutch, multi-plate ~ 190 78
clutch, single-plate ~ 190 71
clutch coupling 227 23
clutch flange 177 55
clutch lever 188 32
clutch pedal 191 44, 96; 192 28
C major 320 55, 62
C major scale 320 45
C minor 320 65
coach *Lorries etc.* 194 17
coach *Ball Games* 291 55; 292 57
coach, four-axled ~ 208 3
coach, second ~ 209 7
coach body 186 5; 207 2; 208 6
coach bolt 202 7
coach box 186 8
coach door 186 11
coaches 186 1-3,26-39,45,51-54
coach horse 186 28
coachman 186 32
coach screw 202 7
coach step 186 13
coach wagons 186 1-3,26-39,45,51-54
coagulating bath 169 15
coal 170 1
coal bunker 152 2; 225 19
coal conveyor 152 1
coal distillation, dry ~ 170 2
coal feed conveyor 199 37
coal mill 152 4
coal mine 144 1-51

coal scuttle 309 9
coal seam 144 50
coal shovel 38 43
coal tar 170 3
coal tar extraction 156 18
coal tower 156 5
coal tower conveyor 156 4
coal wharf 225 18
coaming 283 59
coarse dirt hose 50 84
coarse fishing 89 20-31
coastal cruiser 284 60
coastal lake 13 44
coaster 221 99
coaster brake 187 63
coasting vessel 221 99
coat 29 54; 30 60; 33 2
coat, black ~ 289 4
coat, braided ~ 186 23
coat, cloth ~ 30 61; 33 66
coat, dark ~ 289 4, 13
coat, fur ~ 30 60
coat, gallooned ~ 186 23
coat, loden ~ 29 31; 30 64
coat, loose-fitting ~ 271 41
coat, mink ~ 131 24
coat, ocelot ~ 131 25
coat, oilskin ~ 228 7
coat, poncho-style ~ 30 68
coat, poplin ~ 33 60
coat, red ~ 289 13
coat, three-quarter length ~ 271 21
coat belt 33 59
coat button 33 64
coat collar 33 58
coater 173 31, 34
coat hanger 41 3
coat hook 41 2; 207 50; 266 14
coating, bituminous ~ 200 58
coating of fluorescent material 240 19
coat-of-arms 254 1-6
coat-of-arms, marshalled ~ 254 10-13
coat-of-arms, provincial ~ 252 12, 14
coat pocket 33 61
coat rack 41 1
coat stand 266 12
coat-tail 33 14
cob 59 49
cobalt bomb 2 28
cobnut 59 49
coccinellid 358 37
coccyx 17 5; 20 60
cochlea 17 63
cock *Farm Bldgs.* 62 37
cock *Dom. Anim.* 73 21
cockade 264 8
cockatrice 327 34
cockchafer 82 1
cockchafer grub 82 12
cocker spaniel 70 38
cocking handle 255 12
cocking lever 255 12
cocking piece 121 30
cock pheasant 88 77
cock pigeon 73 33
cockpit *Aircraft* 230 1-31, 35; 231 19
cockpit *Police* 264 2
cockpit *Rowing* 283 8
cockpit *Sailing* 285 38
cockpit *Airsports* 288 10
cockpit canopy 230 39; 257 4
cockpit coaming 283 59
cockpit hood 230 39; 257 4
cockroach 81 17
cockscomb 73 22
cock's foot 69 25
cock's head 69 10

cock's tread 74 65
cocktail 317 33
cocktail fork 45 76
cocktail glass 267 56
cocktail shaker 267 61
cocoa *Grocer* 98 66
cocoa *Trop. Plants* 382 19
cocoa bean 382 19
cocoa palm 383 48
cocoa powder 382 19
coconut 383 53
coconut oil 98 23
coconut palm 383 48
coconut tree 383 48
cocoon *Forest Pests* 82 21
cocoon *Articulates* 358 51
coco palm 383 48
cocotte 306 37
cod 90 22
code flag halyard 223 10
code flag signal 223 9
cod end 90 22
code pendant 253 29
code pennant 253 29
coding keyboard 242 11
coding station 236 35
cod line 90 23
codling moth 58 62
codlin moth 58 62
coefficient 345 4
coelenterate 357 14; 369 5, 9, 14, 20
coffee 98 65-68, 67; 99 68-70, 68; 265 19
coffee *Trop. Plants* 382 6
coffee, instant ~ 99 70
coffee, pure ~ 98 65
coffee bean 382 6
coffee cup 44 29
coffee grinder, electric ~ 39 24; 98 69
coffee maker 39 38
coffee plant 382 1
coffee pot 44 28
coffee roaster 98 70
coffee service 44 27
coffee set 44 27; 265 18
coffee table 42 28
coffee tree 382 1
coffee urn 265 2
cofferdam 259 19
coffin 331 35
coffin chamber 333 5
cog *Mach. Parts etc.* 143 83
cog *Ship* 218 18-26
cog, wooden ~ 91 9
cog railroad 214 4-5
cog railway 214 4-5
cog wheels 143 82-96
coiffure, upswept ~ 355 81
coiffures 34 27-38
coil 89 21
coiled-coil filament 127 58
coiler 148 72
coiler top 163 62
coil spring 191 28; 192 68
coin 252 1-28
coin, Celtic ~ 328 37
coin, gold ~ 36 37
coin, silver ~ 328 37
coinage 252 1-28, 40-44
coin-box telephone 236 9; 237 3
coin bracelet 36 36
coin disc 252 43
coining dies 252 40-41
coining press 252 44
coins 252 1-28
coins, aluminium ~ 252 1-28
coins, copper ~ 252 1-28
coins, gold ~ 252 1-28
coins, nickel ~ 252 1-28

coins, silver ~ **252** 1-28
coin setting **36** 38
coke **147** 2
coke guide **156** 9
coke loading **156** 15
coke loading bay **156** 12
coke oven **144** 7; **156** 8, 16
coke-oven gas processing **156** 16-45
coke-quenching car **144** 11
coke-quenching tower **144** 10
cokernut **383** 53
coke side bench **156** 13
coke wharf **156** 12
coking coal **156** 1
coking coal tower **144** 9
coking plant *Coal* **144** 7-11
coking plant *Coking* **156** 1-15
coking plant *Synth. Fibres* **170** 2
col **12** 47
cold-drawing **170** 46
cold house **55** 33
cold light source **23** 8
cold room **94** 21-24
cold shelf **96** 12; **98** 3
cold storage room **223** 56
cold store **94** 21-24; **225** 50
cold tap **126** 29
cold water tank **92** 9
cole **383** 1
Coleoptera **358** 24-39
coleseed **383** 1
collar *Jewell.* **36** 16
collar *Dog* **70** 13
collar *Game* **88** 27
collar *Roof* **121** 35, 70
collar *Money* **252** 42
collar *Church* **332** 6
collar *Fish etc.* **364** 39
collar, braided ~ **186** 22
collar, cowl ~ **30** 3
collar, Dutch ~ **71** 28
collar, fur ~ **30** 63
collar, fur-trimmed ~ **30** 63
collar, galloaned ~ **186** 22
collar, ground glass ~ **115** 53, 64
collar, high ~ **355** 74
collar, integral ~ **143** 33
collar, knitted ~ **33** 31
collar, matt ~ **115** 53, 64
collar, padded ~ **101** 20
collar, pointed ~ **71** 15
collar, stand-up ~ **30** 43
collar, turndown ~ **30** 5; **31** 69
collar, wide-falling ~ **355** 56
collar beam **121** 35, 38, 70
collar beam roof **121** 34
collar beam roof structure **121** 37
collar bearing **148** 73
collarbone **17** 6
collating machine **249** 59
collating station **249** 60
collecting bin **201** 20
collecting hopper **92** 20
collecting tank **172** 26
collecting vessel **10** 40, 45
collection **74** 36
collection bag **236** 51
collector **155** 19
collector bow **205** 36
collector well **269** 4
college **262** 1-25
college lecturer **262** 3
colliery **144** 1-51
collimator **111** 46; **351** 30
colon **342** 17
colon, ascending ~ **20** 19
colon, descending ~ **20** 21
colon, transverse ~ **20** 20
colonnade **274** 9; **334** 67

colophony **323** 11
color *see* colour
Colorado beetle **80** 52
colour **343**
colour analyser **116** 36
colour analyser lamp **116** 37
colour chemicals **116** 52
colour computer **177** 51
colour conversion filter step **117** 38
colour correction, selective ~ **177** 51
colour correction unit **177** 39
colour decoder module **240** 5
colour developer **116** 10
colour enlarger **116** 40
colour filter **316** 49
colour indicator **127** 37
colour light distant signal **203** 9, 14
colour light signal **203** 3
colour medium **316** 49
colour-mixing knob **116** 43-45
colour organ **317** 13
colour output stage module **240** 13
colour pickup tube **240** 36
colour picture tube **240** 15
colour print **340** 28
colour printing paper **116** 51
colour processing chemicals **116** 52
colours of the rainbow **343** 14
colour television receiver **240** 1
colour television set **240** 1
colposcope **23** 5
coltsfoot **380** 8
colubrid **364** 38
Columbian **175** 30
columbine *Gdn. Flowers* **60** 10
Columbine *Carnival* **306** 27
column *Photog.* **116** 42
column *Forging* **139** 10
column *Mach. Tools* **150** 10
column *Bookbind.* **185** 65
column *Script* **342** 45
column *Chem.* **349** 29
column, angled ~ **116** 28
column, bent ~ **113** 21
column, central ~ **114** 46
column, Corinthian ~ **334** 10
column, Doric ~ **334** 8
column, Ionic ~ **334** 9
column, ornamented ~ **333** 18
column, spinal ~ **17** 2-5
column, vertebral ~ **17** 2-5
column box **119** 11, 73
column heading **342** 46
column rule **342** 47
column shaft **334** 26
coma position **21** 24
comb *Infant Care etc.* **28** 8
comb *Dom. Anim.* **73** 22
comb *Hairdresser* **105** 6
comb, adjustable ~ **165** 26
comb, top ~ **163** 67
combat sports **299**
comber **163** 56, 63
comber draw box **163** 60
comb foundation **77** 43
combination, two-piece ~ **30** 45
combination cutting pliers **126** 60; **127** 53
combination lever **210** 30
combination rib weave **171** 25
combination toolholder **149** 41
combine **64** 1-33
combined grasp **296** 42

combine harvester **63** 31; **64** 1-33
combing cylinder **163** 68
combing machine **163** 56
comb setting **165** 36
combustion chamber **232** 37
combustion chamber, external ~ **147** 16
comfrey **375** 45
comic turn **307** 25
comma **342** 18
command key **247** 21
command module **6** 9
command section **234** 65
commencement of speed restriction **203** 39, 42
commissionaire **267** 1; **271** 44; **315** 10
commissure, labial ~ **16** 14; **19** 19
committee **263** 1-2
committee boat **285** 15
committee member **263** 2
committee table **263** 3
common box **373** 19
common buzzard **362** 9
common comfrey **69** 13
common denominator **344** 19
common dolphin **367** 24
common European kite **362** 11
common flea **81** 42
common groundsel **61** 12
common heron **359** 18
common housefly **81** 2
common iguana **364** 32
common mallow **376** 13
common merganser **359** 15
common myrtle **53** 11
common nightshade **379** 5
common orache **61** 24
common pheasant **88** 77
common privet **373** 6
common puffball **381** 20
common roller **360** 6
common salt **170** 13
common sea-swallow **359** 11
common silver fir **372** 1
common swallow **361** 20
common time **320** 32
common toadflax **376** 26
common vetch **69** 18
common viper **364** 40
communicant **332** 27
communication line **127** 23
communication link **237** 50
communications satellite **237** 52
communion cup **330** 10; **332** 29
communion table **330** 4
communion wafer **332** 50
commutator cover **211** 18
companion hatch **258** 24
companion ladder **221** 123; **223** 24; **258** 24
companionway **221** 123; **222** 23; **223** 24; **258** 24
company account **250** 4
company messenger **236** 17
compartment *Forestry* **84** 2
compartment *Railw.* **207** 13; **208** 24
compartment *Store* **271** 6
compartment, secretarial ~ **205** 37; **209** 25
compartment, special ~ **205** 26
compartment, twin-berth ~ **207** 38
compartment, two-berth ~ **207** 38

compartment, two-seat ~ **207** 38
compartment batten **316** 13
compartment door **207** 14
compartment window **207** 52; **208** 8
compass *Drawing Off.* **151** 52
compass *Airsports* **288** 12
compass, divisions of ~ **321** 42-50
compass, fluid ~ **224** 46
compass, gyroscopic ~ **224** 31, 51-53
compass, liquid ~ **224** 46
compass, magnetic ~ **223** 6; **224** 46; **230** 6
compass, mariner's ~ **223** 6
compass, ratchet-type ~ **151** 64
compass, spirit ~ **224** 46
compass, wet ~ **224** 46
compass bowl **224** 49
compass brick **159** 25
compass bridge **223** 4-11; **227** 24
compass card **224** 47
compasses **224** 46-53
compass flat **223** 4-11; **227** 24
compass head **151** 53
compass plane **132** 28
compass platform **223** 4-11; **227** 24
compass repeater **224** 31, 52, 53
compass saw **120** 63; **126** 70; **132** 3
compendium of games **47** 18
compensating airstream **192** 4
compensating roller **181** 45
compensation pendulum **109** 33
compensator **181** 45
compensator level **112** 69
competition bow **305** 54
competitor **282** 28
complementary angle **346** 15
complement of set **348** 7, 8
composing frame **174** 2
composing room **174**; **175**; **176**
composing rule **174** 14
composing stick **174** 13
composition *Composing Rm.* **175** 1-17
composition *Art. Studio* **338** 4
composition, computer-controlled ~ **176** 14
compositor **174** 5
compost heap **52** 6
comprehensive school **261** 1-45
compress **27** 4
compressed-air bottle **279** 21
compressed-air braking system **208** 21
compressed-air cylinder **279** 21
compressed-air hose **174** 38
compressed-air inlet **153** 53
compressed-air line *Joiner* **133** 45
compressed-air line *Blacksm.* **138** 5
compressed-air pipe *Forging* **139** 22
compressed-air pipe *Metalwkr.* **140** 17
compressed-air pressure gauge **279** 13
compressed-air reservoir *Agr. Mach.* **64** 92
compressed-air reservoir *Offshore Drill.* **146** 21

compressed-air supply 213 20
compressed-air system 138 1
compressed-air tank
Blacksm. 138 4
compressed-air tank Power
Plant 153 51
compressed-air vessel 269 17,
50
compressed-gas container
234 32
compressed-helium bottle
234 14
compressed-helium tank 234
43, 50
compression bandage 21 17
compression plate 2 25
compressor Painter 129 33
compressor Blacksm. 138 3
compressor Oil, Petr. 145 45
compressor Energy Sources
155 4
compressor Ship 223 51
compressor Office 247 43
compressor, high-pressure ~
232 36
compressor, low-pressure ~
232 35
computer 23 53 ; 177 70 ; 195 1
computer cable 195 3, 38
computer centre 244
computer data 238 13
computer harness 195 3, 38
computer socket, main ~
195 2, 39
computer test, automatic ~
195 33
computing scale 98 12
concave 64 11
concave ridge 302 22
concentrator 172 24, 42, 44,
48, 62
concert grand 325 40
concertina 324 36
conch shell trumpet 327 41
concrete, heavy ~ 119 72
concrete, rammed ~ 118 1
concrete, tamped ~ 118 1
concrete aggregate 118 36;
119 26
concrete bucket 119 38
concrete mixer 47 40; 118 33;
119 29; 201 23
concrete-mixing plant 201 19
concrete pump hopper 201 24
concreter 119 9
concrete road construction
201 1-24
concrete scraper 200 13
concrete spreader 201 5
concrete spreader box 201 6
concrete tamper 119 83
concrete test cube 119 84
concrete-vibrating
compactor 201 10
concrete vibrator 119 88
condensate 172 17
condenser Brew. 92 6
condenser Optic. Instr. 112 8;
113 32
condenser Oil, Petr. 145 44
condenser Nucl. Energy 154
17, 35
condenser Energy Sources
155 8
condenser Synth. Fibres 170 5
condenser Paperm. 172 30
condenser Warships 259 64
condenser Chem. 350 48
condenser, coiled ~ 349 6
condenser, universal ~ 112 66
condensing locomotive 210
69
condensing tender 210 69

condition report 195 7
conductor Power Plant 153 34,
43
conductor Spa 274 21
conductor Theatre 315 26
conductor, copper ~ 127 43
conductor, electrostatic ~ 230
51 ; 231 27
conductor, high-voltage ~
152 33
conduit 334 54
cone Phys. Geog. 11 24
cone Mach. Parts etc. 143 67
cone Synth. Fibres 169 27
cone Bicycle 187 58
cone Maths. 347 43
cone Decid. Trees 371 32
cone, cross-wound ~ 165 8, 24
cone, pyrometric ~ 161 6
cone, truncated ~ 347 45
cone axis 372 3
cone breaker 172 82
cone chest 326 12-14
cone creel 165 9
cone drum box 163 30
cone height 347 44
cone nozzle 83 23
cone refiner 172 27, 60, 73, 83
cone scale 372 8, 14, 27, 38
cone-winding frame 165 1
cone-winding machine 169
26
coney 366 24
confectionery 97 17-47; 98
75-86
confectionery unit 97 67-70
conference circuit 242 22
conference connection 242 22
conference grouping 246
31-36
conference hook-up 242 22
conference table 246 31
confetti 306 62
configuration, angular ~ 248
39
confluence 224 90
conga drum 324 55
congregation 330 29
conifers 372 1-71
Conium 379 4
connecting corridor 208 11
connecting door, sliding ~
207 19
connecting element 248 48
connecting hose 208 16, 21
connecting lead 25 20, 56
connecting piece 350 56
connecting rod Agr. 63 20
connecting rod Intern.
Combust. Eng. 190 21
connecting rod Railw. 210 11
connecting-rod bearing 192
25
connecting seal, rubber ~ 207
8; 208 12
connecting shaft 63 20
connecting system, automatic
~ 237 25
connection, internal ~ 245 14
connection, pneumatically
sprung ~ 194 45
connection, rubber ~ 194 45
connection of modules 242 70
connection rebar 119 10, 71
connector Moon L. 6 28
connector Weaving 166 52
connector, thermoplastic ~
127 29
connector fitting 287 31
consignment, general ~ 206 4
consignment, mixed ~ 206 4
consignment note 206 30
console Joiner 133 24

console Serv. Stat. 196 29
console School 261 37
console Music. Instr. 326
36-52
console operator 244 3
console piano 325 1
console typewriter 244 4
consolidating beam 201 2
constant of integration 345 14
constellations 3 9-48
construction, close-seamed ~
285 54
construction, wooden ~ 260
72
construction of circuit 242 72
construction set 48 22
construction site 118; 119
construction unit, precast ~
215 58
construction vehicle 255 75
consulting room 23 1
contact, auxiliary ~ 153 57
contact, magnetic ~ 242 71
contact arc 237 43
contact arm 237 44
contact arm tag 237 46
contact breaker 242 49
contact field 237 45
contact goniometer 351 27
contact maker 127 38-39
contact sleeve, metal ~ 166 31
contact spring 127 28
contact wire maintenance
vehicle 211 41, 44-54
contact wire voltage indicator
211 28
container 206 57 ; 221 22 ; 226
3, 6
container Chem. 350 61
container, plastic ~ 83 25
container, railroad-owned ~
206 19
container, railway-owned ~
206 19
container, shielded ~ 154 82
container berth 225 48; 226 1
container car 206 58
container carrier truck 225 47
container for vegetables 96 51
container platform 194 27
container ship 221 89; 225 45
container station 206 54
container terminal 225 48;
226 1
container wagon 206 58
containment, steel ~ 154 21
continents 14 12-18
continuity girl 310 39
continuity tester 127 55
continuous feed grate 199 34
continuous filament process
162 48
continuous reheating furnace
148 69
continuous rolling mill train
148 66-75
contouche 355 66
contour 15 62
contour, submarine ~ 15 11
contour knife 340 10
contrabass 323 23
contrabassoon 323 28
contrabass tuba 323 44
contracted burial 328 17
contractile vacuole 357 5
contra octave 321 43
contrast control 240 32 ; 249
36
contrast medium injector 27
15
control, digital ~ 242 35
control, manual ~ 115 52
control, sliding ~ 311 18

control and monitoring panel
311 8
control arm 240 29 ; 313 11
control board 153 1
control box Moon L. 6 23
control box Mach. Tools 150
36
control box Offset Platem.
179 33
control button Hosp. 25 30
control button Cine Film 117
98
control button Text. Finish.
168 40
control button Navig. 224 32
control button Audiovis. 243
13
control button Office 246 19
control button School 261 45
control cable 271 53
control column 230 24 ; 257
8; 288 14
control console Power Plant
153 1-6
control console Photomech.
Reprod. 177 5
control console Films 311 12
control console Theatre 316 2
control desk Hosp. 27 10
control desk Brew. 93 1
control desk Iron & Steel 147
66
control desk Power Plant 153
1-6
control desk Nucl. Energy 154
80
control desk Offset Print. 180
16
control desk Photograv. 182
28
control desk Films 311 12
control desk, driver's ~ 212 32
control desk, engineer's ~ 212
32
control device 26 7
control frame 287 46
control gear 164 38
control grip Pest Contr. 83 19
control grip Photog. 115 76
control handle, cranked ~ 168
52
control knob Hosp. 25 49 ; 27
41
control knob Electrotyp. etc.
178 15
controller 197 27
controller, rear ~ 197 8
controller handwheel 211 20;
212 12
control lever Agr. Mach. 64
59
control lever Pest Contr. 83 21
control lever Cine Film 117 63
control lever Cotton Spin. 163
28
control lever Road Constr.
201 8, 12
control lever Navig. 224 19
control lever Broadcast. 240
29
control lever Films 313 11
control lever Theatre 316 58
control line model 288 89
control linkage 190 30
control loudspeaker 311 13
control mechanism 181 26
control module 238 45 ; 240 11
control panel Hosp. 26 20 ; 27
10
control panel Roof & Boilerr.
38 67
control panel Dairy. 76 11
control panel Brew. 93 1, 20

control panel *Offshore Drill.* 146 28
control panel *Power Plant* 153 1
control panel *Nucl. Energy* 154 80
control panel *Paperm.* 173 43
control panel *Photomech. Reprod.* 177 36, 60
control panel *Offset Platem.* 179 10, 17
control panel *Offset Print.* 180 74
control panel *Bookbind.* 185 2
control panel *Broadcast.* 240 31
control panel *Films* 311 4, 17, 29
control panel, bracket-mounted ~ 177 6
control panel, electric ~ 168 25, 58
control panel, hinged ~ 177 6
control platform 226 55
control point 203 25
control rod *Nucl. Energy* 154 24
control rod *Warships* 259 69
control rod drive 154 23
control room *Hosp.* 25 1-9
control room *Offshore Drill.* 146 32
control room *Power Plant* 152 19, 28; 153 1-8
control room *Railw.* 214 65
control room *Broadcast.* 238 17
control room *Theatre* 316 1
control room, central ~ *Dairy.* 76 7
control room, central ~ *Brew.* 92 25
control room window 238 38
controls 25 29; 153 6; 271 48
control speaker 238 15
control station 217 45
control stick 230 24; 257 8; 288 14
control switch *Hosp.* 25 29
control switch *Offset Print.* 180 74
control switch *Navig.* 224 23
control tap 172 9
control tower 233 17; 287 12
control unit *Hosp.* 26 7
control unit *Opticn.* 111 29
control unit *Blacksm.* 138 31
control unit *Mach. Tools* 150 36
control unit *Photomech. Reprod.* 177 51
control unit *Electrotyp. etc.* 178 29
control unit *Offset Platem.* 179 33
control unit *Audio* 241 40
control unit, central ~ *Hosp.* 25 1, 20
control unit, central ~ *Inf. Tech.* 242 2
control unit, electric ~ 168 58
control valve 153 52
control weight 166 63
control well 117 98
control wheel *Text. Finish.* 168 40
control wheel *Railw.* 212 81
convenience outlet 127 5
convenience outlet, double ~ 127 6
convent 15 63
convergence 224 90
convergence module 240 12

conversion filter step 117 38
converter 92 42
converter bottom, solid ~ 147 47
converter chimney 147 67
converter top, conical ~ 147 45
converter tube 27 19
convertible 193 9
convertiplane 232 31
conveyances 186 1-54
conveyor *Poultry Farm* 74 22
conveyor *Dairy.* 76 23
conveyor *Bldg. Site* 118 77
conveyor *Synth. Fibres* 169 32
conveyor *Paperm.* 172 79
conveyor *Photograv.* 182 30
conveyor *Refuse Coll.* 199 36
conveyor *Docks* 225 51
conveyor belt *Dairy.* 76 23
conveyor belt *Bldg. Site* 118 77
conveyor belt *Synth. Fibres* 169 32
conveyor belt *Paperm.* 172 79
conveyor belt *Photograv.* 182 30
conveyor belt *Docks* 225 51
conveyor brattice 163 13
conveyor trolley 74 39
conveyor unit 83 59
cook, head ~ 207 34
cooker 96 47
cooker, calor gas ~ 278 33
cooker, double-burner ~ 278 33
cooker, electric ~ 39 12; 46 32
cooker, gas ~ 39 12; 278 33
cooker hood 39 17; 46 31
cooker unit 39 12-17
cooking liquor 172 46
cooking pot 39 29; 40 12
cookroom 223 42
coolant 149 44
coolant bore 242 54
coolant-collecting plant 92 7
coolant feed line 235 38
coolant flow passage 154 29
coolant pump 190 61
coolant pump, primary ~ 154 25
coolant supply pipe 138 26; 149 25
coolant system 154 55
coolant tray 149 44
cooler *Oil, Petr.* 145 44
cooler *Coking* 156 27
coolie 353 43
cooling 170 34
cooling aggregate 39 5
cooling compressor 92 22
cooling cylinder 170 27
cooling fan 312 34
cooling rib 189 20; 190 80; 242 60
cooling roll 173 25
cooling roller 180 28
cooling room 281 28
cooling system 154 48
cooling table 97 67
cooling tank 162 15
cooling tower *Coal* 144 15
cooling tower *Nucl. Energy* 154 39
cooling tower *Synth. Fibres* 170 43
cooling unit 209 21; 212 26, 77
cooling water *Nucl. Energy* 154 18
cooling water *Railw.* 212 65, 78
cooling water bore 242 54
cooling water flow circuit 154 10

cooling water heat exchanger 155 3
cooling water pipe *Opticn.* 111 31
cooling water pipe *Power Plant* 152 27
cooling water pipe *Car* 191 10
cooling water temperature gauge 212 21
cooling water thermostat 190 62
cool shelf 266 49
coon 368 9
cooper 130 11
coordinate 347 2-3, 8
coordinate, right-angled ~ 347 1
coot 359 20
cop, full ~ 163 2
cope 148 19
copier, automatic ~ 249 32
copier, web-fed ~ 249 32
coping stone 37 37
copper 305 6, 18
copper, unworked ~ 260 64
copper cylinder, polished ~ 182 7
copper plate 179 9
copperplate, polished ~ 340 53
copperplate engraver 340 44
copperplate engraving 340 14-24
copperplate press 340 36
copper sulphate 351 26
copy 176 3; 177 18
copy, received ~ 245 2
copy, transmitted ~ 245 2
copyboard 177 14, 22, 30
copy cylinder 177 64
copy delivery 249 43
copyholder 177 15
copying camera, overhead ~ 177 1
copying stand 115 90, 92, 93
copypod 115 90
copy stand 115 90, 92, 93
coquille 294 38, 43
coral, precious ~ 357 17
coral, red ~ 357 17
coral animal 357 17
coral Clavaria 381 32
coral colony 357 18
coral evergreen 377 12
coral polyp 357 19
coral reef 13 32
cor anglais 323 38
cord 206 12
cord, warp-faced ~ 171 26, 27
cordate 370 35
corded ware 328 10
cordon, horizontal ~ 52 17, 29
cordon, quadruple ~ 52 1
cordon, vertical ~ 52 2
core *Phys. Geog.* 11 5
core *Soft Fruit* 58 36, 59
core *Iron Foundry etc.* 148 36
core *Power Plant* 153 17, 36
core *Electrotyp. etc.* 178 18
core, soft-lead ~ 87 56
core, special ~ 301 47
core bit 145 21
core print 148 37
corking machine, semi-automatic ~ 79 10
corkscrew 40 18; 45 46
corkscrew piton 300 40
cormorant 359 10
corn 68 1, 31
corn camomile 61 8
corn campion 61 6
corn cob 68 36

corn cockle 61 6
cornea 19 47
cornelian cherry 373 30, 32
corner *Games* 276 27
corner *Ball Games* 291 41; 292 18
corner *Sports* 305 6; 305 8
corner *Maths.* 347 33
corner bottom slate 122 77
corner brace 120 26
corner flag 291 8
corner kick 291 41
corner peg 292 79
corner seat 207 58; 265 10; 266 38
corner section 42 26
corner stile 120 52
corner strut 120 52
corner stud 120 52
corner table 246 34
corner unit 39 27
corner work 149 51
cornet 323 43
cornett, curved ~ 322 12
cornfield 63 32
corn flower 61 1
corn head 64 35
cornice *Carp.* 120 34
cornice *Mountain.* 300 20
cornice *Art* 334 11-14; 335 48
corn marigold 61 7
corn poppy 61 2
corn removal 92 38
corn salad 57 38
corn spurrey 69 12
corn stem 68 5
corn weevil 81 26
corolla 59 11; 378 4
corolla, papilionaceous ~ 57 1
corona 334 12
corona, solar ~ 4 39
Corona Borealis 3 31
coronet, baronet's ~ 254 43
coronet, baronial ~ 254 44
coronet, count's ~ 254 45
coronet, ducal ~ 254 39
coronet, elector's ~ 254 41
coronet, prince's ~ 254 40
coronets 254; 254 37,38,42-46
coronets of rank 254 43-45
corporation stock 251 11-19
corps de ballet 314 25
corpus callosum 17 44
corpus cavernosum and spongiosum 20 67
corral 319 14
correcting fluid 247 13
correcting lens 115 22
correcting paper 247 12
correction lens 115 72
corrector, universal ~ 238 48
corrector plate 113 11
correspondence 245 19
correspondence file 22 12
correspondent 342 54
corresponding angle 346 12
corrida 319 1-33
corridor *Railw.* 207 11
corridor *Winter Sp.* 301 71
corridor compartment coach 207 1-21
Corvidae 361 1-3
corydalis 377 8
cosine 346 32
cosmetics 99 27-35
cosmetics gondola 99 23
cossack trousers 30 44
costume, theatrical ~ 315 51
costume designer 315 38
costumes, historical ~ 355
cot, collapsible ~ 28 1
cotangent 346 32

cottage, dikereeve's ~ **216** 45
cottage, ferryman's ~ **216** 45
cottage cheese **76** 45
cottage piano **325** 1
cotter punch **137** 31
cotton *Cotton Spin.* **163** 1-13
cotton *Industr. Plants* **383** 16
cotton bale, compressed ~ **163** 3
cotton bobbin **100** 29
cotton boll, ripe ~ **163** 1
cotton feed **163** 9
cotton-feeding brattice **163** 8
cotton grass **377** 18
cotton reel **104** 9
cotton rush **377** 18
cotton spinning **163**; **164**
cotton wool ball **99** 30
cotton wool packet **99** 28
cotyledon **370** 87
couch *Doc.* **22** 43
couch *Weeds* **61** 30
coucher **173** 49
couch grass **61** 30
couchman **173** 49
coudé ray path **5** 3
coudière **329** 48
coulee **13** 45
coulter **65** 10
coulter, disc ~ **64** 66; **65** 69
coulter, drill ~ **65** 76
coulter, rolling ~ **64** 66; **65** 69
coulter, skim ~ **65** 68
counter *Child. Rm.* **47** 28
counter *Shoem.* **100** 59
counter *Shoes* **101** 37
counter *Cotton Spin.* **163** 61
counter *Composing Rm.* **175** 41
counter *Offset Print.* **180** 74
counter *Railw.* **207** 31
counter *Café* **265** 1
counter *Restaurant* **266** 1-11
counter *Water* **269** 59
counter *Ball Games* **291** 23
counter *Winter Sp.* **302** 18
counter *Flea Market* **309** 83
counter, cashier's ~ **250** 1
counter, extra ~ **271** 64
counter, special ~ **271** 64
counterbalance **241** 22
counterbalance weight **242** 50
counterblow hammer **139** 5
counterbrace **215** 35
counter clerk **236** 16
counter gear assembly **269** 55
counter officer **236** 16
counterpoise *Optic. Instr.* **113** 19
counterpoise *Hydr. Eng.* **217** 76
counterpoise *Docks* **226** 50
counterpoise *Army* **255** 78
counter stamp machine **236** 19
counter tube **2** 21
counter tube casing **2** 20
counterweight *Overh. Irrign.* **67** 37
counterweight *Optic. Instr.* **113** 19
counterweight *Bldg. Site* **119** 33
counterweight *Forging* **139** 34
counterweight *Hydr. Eng.* **217** 76
counterweight *Docks* **226** 50
counterweight *Audio* **241** 22
counterweight *Army* **255** 78
counting, automatic ~ **74** 52
counting beads **47** 14
counting blocks **48** 17
counting mechanism **309** 83

counting out **299** 42
country estate **15** 94
countryside in winter **304**
coupé *Carriages* **186** 3
coupé *Car* **193** 28
couple **267** 46; **272** 72; **317** 17-18
couple, bridal ~ **332** 15-16
coupler *Bldg. Site* **119** 53
coupler *Plumb. etc.* **126** 43
coupler *Music. Instr.* **326** 41
couplet **321** 23
coupling *Agr. Mach.* **65** 61
coupling *Bldg. Site* **119** 53
coupling *Railw.* **208** 16; **210** 2; **212** 82; **214** 18
coupling, front ~ **65** 50
coupling, unlinked ~ **208** 19
coupling bolt **202** 15
coupling hook **122** 64
coupling hose **208** 21
coupling link **208** 17
coupling screw **208** 18
coupling spindle **148** 58
coupon **251** 17
coupon sheet **251** 17
courbette **71** 6
course *Weaves* **171** 42
course *Rivers* **216** 9
course *Ball Games* **293** 79-82
course *Winter Sp.* **301** 44
course, damp-proof ~ **123** 4
course, first ~ **118** 67
course, second ~ **118** 68
course, triangular ~ **285** 16
course counter **167** 43
course-marking flag **301** 45
course markings **289** 19
courser **70** 24
court dress **355** 79
courtesy light **191** 77
court shoe **101** 29
court shoe, fabric ~ **101** 54
court shoe, sling-back ~ **101** 53
couter **329** 48
cove **13** 7
cover *Dining Rm.* **44** 5
cover *Tablew. etc.* **45** 3-12
cover *Optic. Instr.* **113** 13
cover *Photog.* **115** 11
cover *Bldg. Site* **118** 22
cover *Bookbind.* **185** 40
cover *Bicycle* **187** 30
cover *Water* **269** 56
cover, canvas ~ **255** 98
cover, glass ~ *Kitch. Utensils* **40** 7
cover, glass ~ *Energy Sources* **155** 33
cover, hinged ~ **309** 27
cover, nylon ~ **207** 68
cover, porous ~ **199** 21
cover, screw-in ~ **115** 11
cover, screw-on ~ **83** 40
cover, soundproof ~ **310** 48
cover, terry ~ **49** 14
cover, transparent ~ **249** 27
coverall **29** 23
covering **287** 40
covering, felt ~ **353** 20
covering, green baize ~ **277** 15
covering material **184** 12
cover projection **243** 47
cover with filter **2** 14
coving **336** 10
cow **73** 1
cowberry **377** 23
cowboy **306** 31; **319** 36
cowboy boot **101** 9
cowcatcher **210** 34
cow corn **68** 31
cowl *Blacksm.* **137** 7

cowl *Warships* **258** 21, 59
cowl *Church* **331** 56
cowl collar **30** 3
cowl neck jumper **30** 2
Cowper's gland **20** 75
cowshed *Farm Bldgs.* **62** 7
cowshed *Livestock* **75** 14
cowslip **376** 8
cox **283** 11
coxed single **283** 18
coxless four **283** 9
coxless pair **283** 15
CQR anchor **286** 16
Crab *Astron.* **4** 56
crab *Shipbuild.* **222** 14, 28
crab *Articulates* **358** 1
crab *Deep Sea Fauna* **369** 16
crab apple tree **58** 51
crab louse **81** 40
cracker **306** 50
cracker, catalytic ~ **145** 48
crackowe **355** 42
cradle **237** 13
cradle, bouncing ~ **28** 2
cradle, double ~ **214** 68
cradle, two-wheel ~ **214** 69
cradle frame, lightweight ~ **189** 17
cradle switch **237** 13
craft room **260** 46-85
crakeberry **377** 23
cramp **119** 58; **120** 66
cramp iron **119** 58; **121** 97
crampon **300** 48
crampon cable fastener **300** 52
crampon strap **300** 51
Crane *Astron.* **3** 42
crane *Warships* **258** 88
crane, floating ~ **225** 10; **226** 48
crane, flying ~ **232** 16
crane, hammer-headed ~ **222** 7
crane, overhead ~ **222** 20
crane, polar ~ **154** 38
crane, revolving ~ **146** 3
crane, travelling ~ **147** 41; **222** 20
crane cable **222** 13
crane framework **226** 53
crane hoist, auxiliary ~ **147** 61
crane hook **139** 45
crane motor **157** 28
crane's bill **53** 1; **376** 24
crane track **119** 27
crane truck **270** 47
crank *Agr. Mach.* **64** 43
crank *Bicycle* **187** 41
crank *Road Constr.* **201** 18
crankcase **190** 40; **242** 51
crankcase scavenging **242** 59
crank drive **217** 53
crankshaft **166** 50; **190** 23; **192** 29
crankshaft, counterbalanced ~ **242** 50
crankshaft bearing **190** 22; **192** 23
crankshaft bleed **192** 22
crankshaft drilling **192** 22
crankshaft tributary **192** 22
crankshaft wheel **166** 51
crash bar **188** 18
crash barrier **259** 17
crash hat **290** 3
crash helmet **301** 13; **303** 14
crate **76** 30; **206** 5
crater **312** 44
crater, volcanic ~ **11** 16
cravat **32** 40
craw **73** 20
crawl **282** 37

crawl stroke **282** 37
crayon **47** 26; **338** 5
crayon, wax ~ **48** 11; **260** 6
crayon engraving **340** 14-24
cream **99** 27, 46
cream, whipped ~ **97** 28; **265** 5
cream cake **97** 21, 24
creamer **265** 21
creamery butter machine **76** 33
cream heater **76** 13
cream jar **28** 13; **99** 27
cream jug **265** 21
cream maturing vat **76** 31
cream pie **97** 24
cream puff **97** 27
cream roll **97** 17
cream separator **76** 14
cream supply pump **76** 40
cream tank **76** 19
cream tube **99** 33
crease *Men's Wear* **33** 6
crease *Ball Games* **292** 72
crease *Ethnol.* **353** 44
creatures, fabulous ~ **327** 1-61
creatures, mythical ~ **327** 1-61
creek *Phys. Geog.* **13** 8
creek *Map* **15** 80
creel *Fish Farm.* **89** 25
creel *Cotton Spin.* **164** 28, 58
creel *Weaving* **165** 25
creel, full ~ **164** 41
creeper **51** 5; **52** 5; **53** 2; **57** 8
creeping foot **357** 28
creese **353** 44
crenate **370** 46
crenel **329** 18
crenellation **329** 6
crepe paper **49** 11
crepidoma **334** 4
crescendo **321** 31
crescendo roller **326** 49
crescendo roller indicator **326** 37
crescent *Astron.* **4** 3, 7
crescent *Bakery* **97** 32
crescent *Supermkt.* **99** 13
Crescent *Flags* **253** 19
crescent-forming machine **97** 64
crescent moon **4** 3, 7
crescent roll **97** 32; **99** 13
crescent wing **229** 18
crest *Horse* **72** 12, 14
crest *Dom. Anim.* **73** 22
crest *Heraldry* **254** 1
crest, dorsal ~ **364** 21
crest, erectile ~ **359** 26
Cresta tobogganing **303** 22-24
crest coronet **254** 12
crested lark **361** 19
crested newt **364** 20
cresting **305** 65
crest of dam **217** 59
crests **254** 1,11,30-36
crevasse **12** 50; **300** 23
crew compartment **6** 41; **235** 16
crew cut **34** 11
crew entry tunnel **235** 71
cricket **292** 70-76
cricket bat **292** 75
crimping **170** 59
crimping iron **106** 26
crimson clover **69** 4
crinoline **355** 72
crispbread **97** 50
criss-cross skip **297** 44
cristobalite **1** 12
croaking sac **364** 25

crocket 335 38
croisé 314 16
croissant 97 32; 99 13
crojack 220 26
crojack yard 220 25
cromlech 328 16
crook 324 71
crook of the arm 16 44
crop 73 20
crops, arable ~ 68
croquant 98 85
croquet 292 77-82
croquet ball 292 82
croquet mallet 292 81
croquet player 292 80
Cross Astron. 3 44
cross Plumb. etc. 126 50
cross School 260 28
cross Church 331 25
cross, ansate ~ 332 63
cross, cardinal's ~ 332 65
cross, Constantinian ~ 332 67
cross, fivefold ~ 332 72
cross, Greek ~ 332 56
cross, Latin ~ 332 55
cross, Papal ~ 332 66
cross, patriarchal ~ 332 64
cross, processional ~ 330 47
cross, quintuple ~ 332 72
cross, Russian ~ 332 57
cross, saltire ~ 332 60
cross, St. Andrew's ~ 332 60
cross, St. Anthony's ~ 332 59
cross, St. Peter's ~ 332 58
cross arm 152 37
cross arms 10 30
crossbar Goldsm. etc. 108 5
crossbar Bicycle 187 16
crossbar Ball Games 291 36
crossbar Athletics 298 14, 34
cross beam 119 57
cross bearer 331 43
cross bond, English ~ 118 65
cross botonnée 332 71
crossbrace 215 35
cross bracing wire 229 12
crossbuck 202 41
cross chain conveyor 157 22
cross conveyor 157 20
cross-country Equest. 289 17
cross-country Winter Sp. 301 42
cross-country binding 301 15
cross-country boot 301 16
cross-country equipment 301 14-20
cross-country gear 301 17
cross-country lorry 194 1
cross-country motorcycle 189 16
cross-country pole 301 20
cross-country race 290 33
cross-country ski 301 14
cross-country stretch-suit 301 43
cross-country tyre 194 4
cross-cut 144 31
cross-cut, octagonal ~ 36 53
cross-cut, oval hexagonal ~ 36 63
cross-cut, round hexagonal ~ 36 65
cross-cut, trapezium ~ 36 58
cross-cut chain saw 157 38
cross-cut chisel 140 25
cross-cut saw 120 14
crosses, Christian ~ 332 55-72
crossfall 200 57
cross fold knife 185 12
cross fold unit, third ~ 185 14
cross grasp 296 43
cross hairs 87 32
cross hairs, double ~ 115 66

cross hatch 340 54
cross head Forging 139 37
cross head Railw. 210 27
crossing 205 15
crossing, intercom-controlled ~ 202 47
crossing, telephone-controlled ~ 202 47
crossing keeper 202 42
crossing the bar 298 31
crossjack 220 26
crossjack yard 220 25
cross joint 151 50
cross lacing 29 37
crosslet 332 68
cross moline 332 69
cross of Jerusalem 332 70
cross of Lorraine 332 62
cross of the Passion 332 55
crossover 241 14
crossover, double ~ 203 49-52
crossover network 241 14
cross piece Bldg. Site 119 61
cross piece Shipbuild. 222 15
cross piece Fencing 294 42
cross rib 335 31
cross slide 149 23, 39; 150 12
cross-slide guide 174 48
cross spider 358 45
cross stitch 102 5
cross stitch, Russian ~ 102 9
cross strut 119 67
cross tie Roof 121 30
crosstie Station 205 60
crosstie, concrete ~ 202 37
crosstie, coupled ~ 202 14, 38
crosstie, steel ~ 202 36
cross total counter 242 3
crosstrees 223 37; 284 13
crosstrees, starboard ~ 286 9
cross treflée 332 71
cross vault 335 31-32
crosswalk 198 11; 268 24, 51
cross-winding the threads 165 11
cross wire, overhead ~ 197 42
cross wires 87 32
crotchet 320 15
crotchet rest 320 23
crouch 295 6, 23
crouch start 298 4
croup 72 31
croupier 275 4
croupier, head ~ 275 6
crowbar 158 32
crowberry 377 23
crowfoot 375 8
crown Man 16 1; 19 37
crown Dent. 24 28
crown Forging 139 36
crown Bridges 215 31
crown Park 272 60
crown Art 336 39
crown Hist. Cost. 355 21
crown South. Fruits 384 29
crown, gold ~ 24 28
crown, mural ~ 254 46
crown block 145 4
crown cork 93 27
crown cork bottle-opener 45 47
crown cork closure 93 27
crown cork opener 45 47
crown of hooks 81 38
crown-of-the-field 61 6
crown of tree 370 3
crownpiece 71 10
crowns 254 37,38,42-46
crown safety platform 145 3
crown wheel Clocks 110 41
crown wheel Mach. Parts etc. 143 93

crows 361 1-3
crow's nest 223 38
crucible, clay ~ 350 31
crucible, graphite ~ 108 10
crucible tongs 108 11; 350 32
crucifer 331 43
crucifix Gymn. 296 50
crucifix Church 332 33
crucifix, processional ~ 331 42
crude benzene, production of ~ 156 41
crude benzene tank 156 42
crude benzol, production of ~ 156 41
crude benzol tank 156 42
crude oil production 145 22-27
crude phenol tank 156 40
crude tar tank 156 32
cruet set 332 44
cruet stand 266 22
cruiser 286 5
cruiser keelboat 285 29-34
cruiser stern 285 45
cruising yacht 284 60
crumb 97 3
crumhorn 322 6
crupper 71 34; 72 31
crupper-strap 71 34
crusader 329 72
crushed grape transporter 78 16
crusher 172 5
crusher, coarse ~ 158 19
crusher, fine ~ 158 19
crusher, gyratory ~ 158 19
crusher, primary ~ 158 17
crusher, rotary ~ 158 19
crush hat 35 36
crush room 315 12-13
crust 97 4, 5
crust, earth's ~ 11 1
crust, outer ~ 11 1
crustacean 369 12, 15, 16
crustaceans 358 1-2
crusta petrosa 19 29
crutch 148 15
Crux 3 44
cryosurgery 22 63
Cryptolestes 81 27
crystal 351 29
crystal centre 351 3
crystal combinations 351 1-26
crystal cone 77 21
crystal detector 309 23
crystal forms 351 1-26
crystallography 351
crystallometry 351 27-33
crystal plate glass 124 5
crystals 351 1-26
crystal set 309 23
crystal system 351 1-17
cub 88 42
cube Kindergart. 48 21
cube Maths. 347 30
cube Crystals 351 2, 14, 16
cube root 345 2
cube sugar 98 53
cubic crystal system 351 1-17
cubitière 329 48
cuckoo 359 30
cuckoo clock 109 31
cuckoo flower 375 11; 376 21
cuckoo pint 379 9
cucumber 57 13; 99 83
cue 277 9
cue ball, white ~ 277 11
cue rack 277 19
cue tip, leather ~ 277 10

cuff 25 16; 30 14; 32 45
cuff, fur ~ 30 62
cuff, fur-trimmed ~ 30 62
cuff, inflatable ~ 23 34
cuff, ribbed ~ 30 30
cuff link 32 46; 36 21
cuff protector 324 17
cuff slit 30 48
cuirass 329 46
cuish 329 52
cuissard 329 52
cuisse 329 52
culicid 358 16
culm Arable Crops 68 6
culm Coking 156 14
culotte 31 48; 29 59
cultivator Market Gdn. 55 21
cultivator Agr. Mach. 65 55
cultivator, three-pronged ~ 56 13
cultivator attachment 56 21
culture, bacteriological ~ 261 29
cumulonimbus 8 17; 287 26
cumulonimbus cloud 287 26
cumulus 8 1; 287 22
cumulus cloud 287 22
cumulus congestus 8 2
cumulus humilis 8 1
cup Bicycle 187 79
cup Decid. Trees 371 5
cup, baby's ~ 28 27
cup, hemispherical ~ 10 30
cup, rust-proof ~ 122 102
cup, zinc ~ 122 102
cup bearer 329 69
cupboard 246 5
cupboard, children's ~ 47 21
cupboard, sliding-door ~ 248 38
cupboard base unit 42 6
cupboard unit 42 7
cupboard unit, two-door ~ 46 6
cup cymbals 324 50
cupid 272 20
cupola Iron Foundry etc. 148 1
cupola Art 334 58
cupola, bulbous ~ 336 3
cupola furnace 148 1
cupule 59 42; 371 5; 384 52
curb 198 6; 272 25
curb bit 71 13, 52
curb chain 71 12
curbstone 198 7
curbstone broker 251 5
curbstoner 251 5
curd cheese 76 38, 45
curd cheese machine 76 38
curd cheese packet 76 45
curd cheese packing machine 76 44
curd cheese pump 76 39
curds separator 76 41
curettage 26 52
curette 22 50; 26 52
curing floor 92 18
curing kiln 92 30
curl 34 3
curl brush 105 13
curl clip 105 14
curler Hairdresser 105 4
curler Winter Sp. 302 41
curling 302 41-43
curling broom 302 43
curling brush 302 43
curling iron 105 5; 106 31
curling stone 302 42
curling tongs 105 5; 106 31
curly kale 57 34
currant 58 12, 14; 98 9
currant bush 52 19; 58 10

current 216 9
current, cold ~ 9 29
current, three-phase ~ 153 42
current, warm ~ 9 28
current collector Lorries etc.
194 41
current collector Tram 197 2,
23
current collector Railw. 207
24, 75; 211 2, 30
current meter Railw. 212 18
current meter Rivers 216 43
current rating 127 37
currents, oceanic ~ 14 30-45
current transformer 153 58
current/voltage meter 242
77
currycomb 71 54
curtail step 123 18, 42
curtain Dining Rm. 44 13
curtain Railw. 207 56
curtain Chivalry 329 15
curtain, iron ~ 316 24
curtain, theatrical 316 23
curtain department 271 66
curtain lace 167 29
curtain operation, types of ~
315 1-4
curtain rail 44 15
curtain wall 329 15
curvature 346 22
curve Sports 305 19
curve Maths. 347 11, 18
curve, ballistic ~ 87 79
curve, hypsographic ~ 11
6-12
curve, inflected ~ 347 13
curve, plane ~ 347 12
curved electrotype casting
machine 178 13
curved plate casting machine
178 13
curve eight 302 11
curvet 71 6
cushion 42 23; 47 8; 202 6
cushion, gilder's ~ 129 50
cushion, rubber ~ 277 16
cushion capital 335 21
cusp 20 48
customer 98 43; 99 2, 18; 111
2; 248 18; 250 6; 266 25;
271 16, 55
customer accounts office 271
24
customer area 207 78
customer card index 248 24
customer service
representative 248 17
customs 217 24
customs barrier 225 4
customs boat pendant 253 35
customs boat pennant 253 35
customs entrance 225 5
customs flags 253 35-38
customs launch 221 100
customs signal flag 253 37
cut Metalwkr. 140 28
cut Fencing 294 23
cut, antique ~ 36 49
cut, cold ~ 96 14
cut, positive ~ 340 3
cut, round ~ 36 42-43
cut, standard ~ 36 48
cut and thrust weapon 294 34
cutlery 45; 309 47
cutlery chest 266 41
cutlery drawer 39 10; 44 21
cutlery holder 266 48
cutlet 95 12
cut nippers, detachable-jaw ~
140 67
cutoff knife and roughing
station 184 3

cuts 36 42-86
cuts, fancy ~ 36 68-71
cutter Paperhanger 128 42
cutter Joiner 132 20
cutter Drawing Off. 151 15
cutter Brickwks. 159 15
cutter Paperm. 173 44
cutter Composing Rm. 175 33,
51
cutter Ship 220 8
cutter Warships 258 12, 61
cutter Films 311 43
cutter, automatic ~ 162 19
cutter, fine ~ 133 37
cutter, rotary ~ Forestry 85 26
cutter, rotary ~ Bookbind. 184
22
cutter, spherical ~ 108 7
cutter, universal ~ 134 28
cutter bar 64 3
cutter for metal watch straps
109 19
cutter spindle 175 60
cutting Map 15 84
cutting Plant Propagn. 54 19,
20
cutting Synth. Fibres 170 60
cutting Films 311 42-46
cutting, shooting ~ 54 24
cutting, sprouting ~ 54 24
cutting attachment 141 19
cutting bench 117 96; 311 42
cutting blade 183 19
cutting cylinder Gdn. Tools
56 35
cutting cylinder Text. Finish.
168 44
cutting drum 64 34
cutting edge 45 57; 66 14; 85
2
cutting edge, cemented
carbide ~ 149 48, 50
cutting edge, razor's ~ 106 40
cutting head 175 51
cutting-in brush 129 20
cutting machine Furrier 131 5
cutting machine Gas Weld.
141 34
cutting machine Synth. Fibres
169 30
cutting machine, universal ~
141 36
cutting nozzle 141 38
cutting-off machine 125 16
cutting pliers 127 51
cutting point 136 35
cutting room 310 3
cutting scale, illuminated ~
185 6
cutting shears 103 3
cutting table Dressm. 103 4
cutting table Cine Film 117 96
cutting table Composing Rm.
175 52
cutting table Films 311 42
cutting template 103 13
cutting tip, adjustable ~ 149
45, 46
cutting tip, cemented carbide
~ 149 50
cutting unit Gdn. Tools 56 33,
41
cutting unit Agr. Mach. 64 8
cuttlefish 357 37; 369 4
cuttling device 168 35
cutup 326 25
cutwater 215 56
cutworm 80 44
cyan filter adjustment 116 45
cyclamen 53 5
cycle 187 1
cycle, motor-paced ~ 290 15
cycle racing 290 1-23

cycle serial number 187 51
cycle track 290 1
cycling track 290 1
cyclohexanol, pure ~ 170 18
cyclohexanol, raw ~ 170 16
cyclohexanone 170 20
cyclohexanoxime 170 22
cyclone 4 38; 9 5
cyclone heat exchanger 160 6
cyclorama 310 12; 316 9
cyclotron 2 49
Cygnus 3 23
cylinder Cooper 130 27
cylinder Metalwkr. 140 45
cylinder Cotton Spin. 163 43
cylinder Offset Print. 180 79
cylinder Railw. 210 32
cylinder Swim. 279 19
cylinder Graphic Art 340 40
cylinder Chem. 350 45
cylinder, developed ~ 182 13
cylinder, grooved ~ 165 10
cylinder, high-pressure ~ 153
23
cylinder, hydraulic ~ 64 8;
194 26
cylinder, low-pressure ~ 153
25
cylinder, medium-pressure ~
153 24
cylinder, perforated ~ 163 21
cylinder, right ~ 347 38
cylinder, steel ~ 180 54
cylinder arm 177 68
cylinder crankcase 190 19
cylinder diameter 167 16
cylinder head 190 45; 242 47
cylinder head gasket 190 48
cylinder lock 140 44
cylinder oil 145 63
cylinder-processing machine
182 9
cylinder temperature gauge
230 9
cylinder trimmer 85 25
cylinder trolley 141 23
cylinder undercasing 163 55
cyma 334 11, 19
cymatium 334 19
cymbal 324 51
cymbal holder 324 52
cymbals 323 50
cymbal stand 324 52
cyme 370 70; 374 36
cyme, curled ~ 370 77
cyme, helicoid ~ 370 76
cyme, scorpioid ~ 370 77
cypress 372 58
cythara 322 15

D

dabber 340 22
dachshund 70 39
dactyloscopy 264 28
dado, oil-painted ~ 129 15
daemon 327 58
da gamba violin 323 16
dagger, bronze ~ 328 22
dagger, hafted ~ 328 22
dagger, Malayan ~ 353 44
dahlia 51 20; 60 23
dairy 76 1-48
dairy cow 62 34; 75 17
dairy cow shed 75 14
dairy plant 76 1-48
dairy product 99 43
daisy 376 1
dam Map 15 69
dam Game 88 1
dam Energy Sources 155 38
dam Hydr. Eng. 217 57-64

damp course 123 4
dampener 180 23, 52, 61
dampening roller 180 23, 52,
61
dampening unit 180 39, 61
damper Offset Print. 180 23,
52, 61
damper Car 191 26; 192 69
damper Music. Instr. 322 54;
325 37
damper, electromagnetic ~ 11
40
damper block 325 37
damper door 210 6
damper lifter 325 38
damper-lifting lever 325 23
damper pedal 325 8
damper rest rail 325 39
damping roller 180 23, 52, 61
damping unit 180 39, 61
dam sill 217 79
dance band 306 2
dance band instruments 324
47-78
dance costume 354 36
dance drum 354 14
dance floor 317 16
dance floor lighting 317 14
dancer 317 17, 18
dancer, principal ~ 314 28
dancing girl, Hindu ~ 306 25
dancing snake 353 48
dancing stick 354 37
dandelion 51 34; 61 13
dandy 306 33
dandy brush 71 55
Danebrog 253 17
Danforth anchor 286 18
danger zone 2 50
Dan grade 299 15
Danish pastry 97 30
Dannebrog 253 17
daphne 377 10
dark beer 93 26
darkroom equipment 116
1-60
darkroom lamp 116 21
dark slide 114 64
darning stitch 102 17
dart 352 28
dart, barbed ~ 319 22
dart point 352 29
das 366 24
dash 342 23
dashboard Carriages 186 6
dashboard Car 191 57-90
dashboard Tram 197 29
dashboard lighting 197 30
dassie 366 24
data, technical ~ 151 32
data carrier 237 59, 62-64
data centre 248 43
data collection station,
central ~ 242 20
data display terminal 238 2,
11; 248 16, 44
data output 112 44
data print-out 195 7
data processor 237 60
data recording back 115 67
data service 237 58
data storage unit 242 32
data terminal 242 19
data transmission 237 58
data transmission service 237
41
date 384 9
date and second button 110 4
date indicator display 237 39
date kernel 384 10
date of issue 250 14
date of maturity 250 16
date of publication 342 42

date palm **384** 1
date sheet **247** 33
date stamp postmark **236** 57
daughter boat **228** 17
davit **221** 78, 101; **223** 20; **258** 13, 83, 88
day cream **99** 27
dayfly **358** 6
daylight film magazine **311** 7
daylight-loading tank **116** 5
day nursery **48**
dead axle **210** 35
deadly nightshade **379** 7
dead man's handle **211** 21; **212** 13
deadwood **285** 47
de-aerator **152** 16
de-airing pug mill **161** 7
de-airing pug press **161** 7
dealer **275** 3
death notice **342** 68
death's-head hawkmoth **365** 9
death's-head moth **365** 9
death spiral **302** 5
debarking **85** 23
debenture bond **251** 11-19
debenzoling **156** 27
decade **332** 32
decatizing cylinder, perforated ~ **168** 50
decay, spontaneous ~ **1** 28
Decca navigation system **224** 39
decimal, recurring ~ **344** 21, 22
decimal fraction, proper ~ **344** 20
decimal key **247** 19
decimal place **344** 20
decimal point **344** 20
deck *Rowing* **283** 57
deck *Films* **311** 10
deck, lower ~ *Offshore Drill.* **146** 35
deck, lower ~ *Lorries etc.* **194** 37
deck, lower ~ *Space* **235** 28
deck, main ~ *Offshore Drill.* **146** 37
deck, main ~ *Ship* **221** 80; **223** 32-42
deck, main ~ *Warships* **258** 9
deck, middle ~ **146** 36
deck, orthotropic ~ **215** 2
deck, top ~ **146** 37
deck, upper ~ *Lorries etc.* **194** 38
deck, upper ~ *Railw.* **213** 36
deck, woven ~ **155** 18
deck beam **222** 57
deck bucket **221** 113
deck-chair **37** 47; **51** 2; **221** 111; **274** 13
deck crane **221** 5, 61
deck crane *Warships* **259** 10
decker **172** 24, 42, 44, 48, 62
deck hand **221** 112
deckhouse **221** 6, 39; **223** 34; **258** 72
decking, woven ~ **215** 18
deck plan **259** 12-20
deck plating **222** 56
deck slab **215** 6
deck space **223** 28
deck tennis **280** 31
declination axis **113** 5, 17
declination bearing **113** 6
declination gear **113** 4
decoder **110** 18
décolletage **306** 24
decometer **279** 17
decoration, Greek ~ **334** 38-43

decoration, Romanesque ~ **335** 14-16
decorative glass worker **124** 8
decorative pieces **35** 4
decoy bird **86** 48
decrescendo **321** 32
dedication, handwritten ~ **185** 50
dedusting fan **83** 53
dedusting screen **83** 56
deep-sea cable **237** 56
deep-sea fauna **369**
deep-sea fishing **90** 1-23
deep-sea floor **11** 10
deep-sea medusa **369** 5
deep-sea salvage tug **258** 96
deep-sea trench **11** 12
deep tank **223** 78
deep-water start **286** 46
deer, antlerless ~ **88** 1
deer fence **84** 7
deer stalking **86** 1-8
defence area **293** 66
defender *Ball Games* **292** 4
defender *Fencing* **294** 6
defending fencer **294** 6
deflection system **240** 23
deflector piston **242** 56
defroster vent **191** 42; **192** 64
dégagé **314** 11, 12
degree **345** 2
degree scale **313** 14
dehydrogenation **170** 19
delayed-action release **115** 15
delay indicator **205** 24
delicatessen shop **98** 1-87
deliveries **305** 17-20
delivery **184** 5; **185** 23, 35
delivery blower **181** 33
delivery cylinder **180** 42, 65
delivery hose **270** 31
delivery mechanism *Offset Print.* **180** 45
delivery mechanism *Post* **236** 49
delivery pile **180** 44; **181** 9
delivery pipe *Docks* **226** 34
delivery pipe *Water* **269** 16, 49, 52
delivery pouch **236** 54
delivery reel **173** 28
delivery roller **164** 59
delivery table **181** 31; **184** 14, 19
delivery tray **185** 15
delivery tube **65** 77
delivery unit **180** 45
delivery valve **67** 9
delphinium **60** 13
delta **13** 1
delta connection **153** 21
delta wing **229** 19
deltoid **346** 38
demand regulator, two-tube ~ **279** 20
demesne **15** 94
demi-goat **254** 32
demigod **327** 40
demijohn **206** 13
demi-man **254** 11
demi-mondaine **306** 37
demi-monde **306** 37
demi-rep **306** 37
demisemiquaver **320** 18
demisemiquaver rest **320** 26
demi-woman **254** 11
demonstration bench **261** 3
demonstration equipment **242** 45-84
demonstration model **242** 45, 55

demonstrator **262** 6
den **273** 56
Deneb **3** 23
denims **31** 60; **33** 22
denomination *Money* **252** 32
denomination *Maths.* **344** 19
denominator **344** 15
dental surgeon **24** 1
dentate **370** 47
dent corn **68** 31
dentil **334** 14
dentine **19** 31
denting draft **171** 6
dentist **24** 1
denture **24** 25
department manager **271** 60
department store **268** 41; **271**
departure building **233** 15
'departures' **233** 25
departure schedule **204** 20
departure time indicator **205** 23
departure timetable **204** 20
deposit counter **236** 25
deposit slip **236** 27
depot **144** 17
depression **9** 5
depth adjustment **64** 88; **65** 60; **157** 45
depth-charge thrower **258** 34
depth gauge *D.I.Y.* **134** 47
depth gauge *Swim.* **279** 15
depth gauge attachment rule **149** 68
depth of focus **11** 34
depth reading **224** 67
depth recorder **224** 24
depth recording **224** 67
depth scale **224** 66
depth wheel **65** 59, 63
derailment guard **214** 75
derivative **345** 13
derrick *Phys. Geog.* **12** 33
derrick *Offshore Drill.* **146** 12
derrick *Ship* **221** 67
derrick boom **221** 26, 59; **223** 36
derrick boom, heavy-lift ~ **221** 25, 62
derrick mast **221** 60
descant viol **322** 23
descent stage **6** 28-36
desert monitor **364** 31
desert zone **9** 54
desiccator **350** 51
desiccator insert **350** 54
design **151** 16
design, chequered ~ **335** 14
design, computer-generated ~ **248** 19
design, imbricated ~ **335** 15
design, knitted ~ **30** 37
design, modular ~ **240** 1
design, quilted ~ **30** 31
design for costume **315** 39
designs, decorative ~ **334** 38-43; **335** 14-16
desk **46** 22; **246** 2
desk, cashier's ~ **250** 1
desk, clerical assistant's ~ **248** 11
desk, double ~ **260** 2
desk, instructor's ~ **242** 2
desk, stage manager's ~ **316** 29
desk, teacher's ~ **260** 22
desk chair **46** 27
desk diary **247** 32
desk drawer **46** 26; **246** 4
desk lamp **246** 11
desk mat **46** 23; **246** 6; **260** 25
desk set **246** 9

desk top **246** 3
desk unit **46** 21
dessert bowl **45** 6
dessert plate **45** 6
dessert spoon **45** 61, 66
destination board **205** 21, 38
destination indicator **205** 22
destination sign **197** 20
destroyer **258** 1, 38
desulfurization see desulphurization
desulfurizing see desulphurizing
desulphurization **156** 28
desulphurizing **169** 20
desulphurizing plant **145** 46, 68
detaching roller **163** 71
detangling brush **105** 2
detective **264** 33
detector indicator unit **224** 34
detonator cap **87** 58
detritus **12** 45
deutero-pyramid **351** 20
Deutschmark **252** 7
Devanagari **341** 9
developer **27** 33
developer, first ~ **116** 10
developing dish **116** 25
developing dish, semi-automatic ~ **116** 56
developing dish, thermostatically controlled ~ **116** 56
developing solution **116** 9
developing spiral **116** 2
developing tank *Photog.* **116** 1, 20
developing tank *Photograv.* **182** 11
developing tank, multi-unit ~ **116** 3
developing tank thermometer **116** 8
developing tray **116** 25
deviation mirror **113** 11
device **252** 12
devil **306** 14
devil's tail **340** 34
devil's tobacco pouch **381** 20
devil's wheel **308** 46
de-waxing **145** 50
dew claw **88** 23, 57
dewlap **73** 24
dexter **254** 18, 20, 22
D flat major **320** 67
diabetics file **22** 26
diacritics **342** 30-35
diadem **355** 21
diadem, pearl ~ **355** 16
diaeresis **342** 34
diagnostic test bay **195** 1-23
diagonal **346** 33
diagram *Drawing Off.* **151** 11
diagram *School* **260** 34
diagram *Univ.* **262** 8
dial **204** 5; **237** 10; **245** 16
dial finger plate **237** 11
dial finger stop **237** 12
dialling unit **237** 67
dial wind-up plate **237** 11
diameter **346** 45
diamond *Composing Rm.* **175** 21
diamond *Audio* **241** 26
diamond *Crystals* **351** 10, 13
diamonds **276** 41
diaper, disposable ~ **28** 22
diaphragm *Meteorol. Instr.* **10** 27
diaphragm *Man* **20** 9, 26
diaphragm *Dent.* **24** 33
diaphragm *Inf. Tech.* **242** 82

diaphragm, bladed ~ 2 33
diaphragm chest 326 12-14
diaphragm spring 190 29
diathermy unit 23 22
diazo plate 179 32, 34
dibber 54 7; 56 1
dibble 54 7; 56 1
dice 276 29, 31
dice cup 47 42; 276 30
dicing 276 29
dictating machine 22 27; 209
  30; 246 17; 248 34
dictating machine, pocket-
  sized ~ 246 32
dictionary 262 17
dictionary, medical ~ 22 22
didelphid 366 2
Didone 342 6
die Metalwkr. 140 32
die Brickwks. 159 13
die, lower ~ 252 41
die, steel ~ 175 36
die, upper ~ 252 40
die and stock 140 32
die blank 175 35
die block, lower ~ 139 14, 39
die block, upper ~ 139 13, 38
die case 174 42, 46
die head 143 57
diesel-electric drive 223
  68-74; 259 75
diesel engine Energy Sources
  155 5
diesel engine Intern.
  Combust. Eng. 190 4
diesel engine Railw. 211 47;
  212 25, 51
diesel engine Ship 223 73
diesel engine, auxiliary ~ 209
  19
diesel engine, eight-cylinder
  ~ 212 73
diesel engine, five-cylinder
  in-line ~ 190 3
diesel engine, four-cylinder ~
  65 44
diesel engine, six-cylinder ~
  Agr. Mach. 64 28
diesel engine, six-cylinder ~
  Railw. 209 23
diesel engine, underfloor ~
  209 23
diesel fuel 146 26
diesel generator 259 94
diesel generator unit 209 5
diesel-hydraulic locomotive
  212 1, 24, 47; 213 1
diesel locomotive 212 1, 68
diesel locomotive, single-
  engine ~ 208 1
diesel locomotives 212 1-84
diesel oil 145 56
diesel railcar 208 13; 211 41
diesel tank 146 13
diesel trainset 209 1
die stock 125 27
diet meal 266 62
difference 344 24
differential Agr. Mach. 65 32
differential Intern. Combust.
  Eng. 190 75
differential Maths. 345 13, 14
differential gear 65 32; 190
  75
differential sign 345 13
diffuser Photog. 114 60
diffuser Paperm. 172 11, 13
diffuser Space 234 15
diffusing screen 310 38
digester 172 7
digger 64 59
digger, toy ~ 273 65
digging bucket 200 5

digging bucket arm 200 4
digging bucket teeth 200 6
digging fork 66 22
Digitalis 379 2
digital readout Clocks 110 2
digital readout Optic. Instr.
  112 47
digitate 370 39
digitated 370 39
digitus I 19 52, 64
digitus II 19 53, 65
digitus III 19 54, 66
digitus IV 19 55, 67
digitus V 19 56, 68
digitus anularis 19 67
digitus medius 19 66
digitus minimus 19 56, 68
dike 216 34, 39
dike, main ~ 216 32
dike batter 216 40
dike ramp 216 47
dikereeve 216 46
dike slope 216 40
diligence 186 39
dimension line 151 25
diminished triad 321 3
diminuendo 321 32
dimmer switch 127 17
dimple 16 16
dinar 252 28
diner 207 22-32
dinghy, inflatable ~ 228 18;
  258 82; 278 14; 279 27
dinghy cruiser 284 61
dining area 266 73
dining car 207 22-32
dining car kitchen 207 33
dining chair 44 10
dining compartment 207 32,
  77
dining room 44; 223 44; 267
  20
dining set 42 33-34; 44 1-11
dining table 42 33; 44 1; 45 1;
  46 34
dinner dress 33 7
dinner plate 39 42; 44 7; 45 4
dinner service 44 33
dinner set 44 33
diopter control ring 117 15
dioptric adjustment ring 117
  15
dip, true ~ 12 3
diploma 106 42
dipole antenna 230 65
dipper stick 200 4
dipstick 190 47
dipterans 358 16-20
dipyramid, tetragonal ~ 351 18
direct current motor 150 9
direction, negative ~ 347 7
direction, positive ~ 347 6
directional antenna Moon L.
  6 4, 44
directional antenna Post 237
  51, 52
directional antenna assembly
  234 64
directional gyro 230 13
direction finder, automatic ~
  230 5
direction finder antenna 223
  5
director 310 40; 316 40
director of photography 310
  44
directory enquiries 237 33
directory holder 236 11
direct-vision frame finder
  117 58
dirndl 31 26
dirndl, girl's ~ 29 36
dirndl apron 31 31

dirndl blouse 31 29
dirndl dress 31 26
dirndl necklace 31 28
disc Flat 46 15
disc Agr. Mach. 65 83
disc Disco 317 24
disc, adhesive ~ 364 26
disc, carborundum ~ 24 35
disc, facial ~ 362 18
disc, germinal ~ 74 65
disc, insertable ~ 115 96
disc, metal ~ 309 15
disc, plain ~ 65 84
disc, revolving ~ 275 31
disc, serrated-edge ~ 65 85
disc, silver ~ 10 24
disc, solar ~ 4 36
disc barbell 299 3
disc brake Intern. Combust.
  Eng. 190 74
disc brake Car 191 17-18; 192
  48-55
disc brake Railw. 208 4
disc brake, front ~ 189 32
disc brake calliper 189 33
disc clutch 139 21
disc coulter drive 64 68
disc fibula 328 30
disc floret 375 32
discharge, pneumatic ~ 213
  18
discharge connection valve
  213 21
discharge conveyor 64 83
discharge door 139 2; 213 25
discharge flap 213 25
discharge flume 91 41
discharge opening Forging
  139 2
discharge opening Sawmill
  157 56
discharge opening Hydr. Eng.
  217 56
discharge pipe 64 37
discharge structure 217 44
discharging chute 147 39
discharging position 147 58
disc jockey 317 25
discomedusa 357 14
discotheque 317
disc pack 176 34
disc slot 243 38
disc stack 176 34
disc store 244 1
discussion tube arrangement
  112 22
disc wheel 191 14
disgorger 89 40
disguise 306 6-48, 33
dish 332 50
dish, three-compartment ~
  40 8
dish drainer 39 33
dish rack 39 41
dish thermometer 116 13
dishwasher 39 40
dishwashing machine 39 40
disinfectant powder 83 60
disintegrator 172 5
disk see disc
dislocation 11 50
dispenser 22 64
displacement 11 50
displacement boats 286 32-37
display 47 30; 271 67
display, digital ~ Clocks 110
  20
display, digital ~ Optic. Instr.
  112 47
display, individual ~ 242 3
display, visual ~ Railw. 211 34
display, visual ~ Broadcast.
  238 2, 43

display cabinet 44 26; 46 9
display cabinet unit 42 5
display case 271 13
display counter 99 10
display pipes 326 1-3
display window, indoor ~ 271
  13
dissecting bench 261 22
dissolver 172 37
dissolving tank 172 37
distance 346 5
distance-measuring
  instrument 112 70
distance piece Bees 77 41
distance piece Bldg. Site 119
  81
distance scale 115 4
distance setting 114 28;
  117 3
distance-setting ring 114 39;
  115 8
distant signal identification
  plate 203 24
distillation 170 17
distillation, gradual ~ 170 4
distillation apparatus 350 46
distillation column 145 37, 49
distillation flask 350 47, 50
distillation plant 145 66
distillation product, heavy ~
  145 40
distillation product, light ~
  145 39
distilling apparatus 350 46
distilling flask 350 47, 50
distributary 13 2
distributing machine 236 38
distributing mechanism 174
  20
distributing pipe 126 8
distributing roller 181 7, 62;
  249 51
distribution board 157 67
distribution main 269 22
distribution pipe, main ~ 38
  71
distribution steel 119 69
distributor Composing Rm.
  174 20
distributor Letterpress 181 7,
  62
distributor Intern. Combust.
  Eng. 190 9, 27
distributor Office 249 51
distributor cylinder 62 23
distributor roller 181 7, 62
distributor shaft 190 27
distributor unit 62 22
district boundary 15 103
district heating main 198 28
ditch 329 33, 37
ditch fern 377 16
divan, double ~ 43 4-13
diver 282 5
dividend 344 26
dividend coupon 251 18
dividend coupon sheet 251 17
dividend warrant 251 18
divider Agr. Mach. 64 1
divider Bakery 97 56
divider and rounder 97 63
dividing 344 26
dividing breeching 270 32
diving 282 38
diving, acrobatic ~ 282 40-45
diving, competitive ~ 282
  40-45
diving, fancy ~ 282 40-45
diving apparatus 279 12, 19;
  282 5-10
diving board 282 9
diving boards 282 5-10
diving goggles 280 38

diving mask **279** 10
diving plane, aft ~ **259** 95
diving platform **282** 6
diving pool **282** 11
division *Navig.* **224** 89
division *School* **260** 39
division *Maths.* **344** 26
division sign **344** 26
divisor **344** 26
D major **320** 57
D minor **320** 63
Dobermann terrier **70** 27
dock *Horse* **72** 34
dock *Shipbuild.* **222** 36-43
dock, emptied (pumped-out) ~ **222** 43
dock, floating ~ *Shipbuild.* **222** 34-43, 41
dock, floating ~ *Docks* **225** 16
dock area **225** 1
dock basin **222** 36
dock bottom **222** 31
dock crane **222** 34
dock floor **222** 31
dock gate **222** 32
docking a ship **222** 41-43
docking hatch **6** 45
docking target recess **6** 47
docks **225**; **226**
dockside crane **222** 34
dock structure **222** 37-38
dockyard **222** 1-43
doctor **22**; **23**
'doctor' **233** 44
doctor blade **168** 44
document **245** 19
document, confidential ~ **246** 25
document file **245** 6; **247** 37; **248** 5
document glass **249** 39
dodecahedron, pentagonal ~ **351** 8
dodecahedron, rhombic ~ **351** 7
dodgem **308** 62
dodgem car **308** 63
dodger **223** 17
doe *Dom. Anim.* **73** 18
doe *Game* **88** 40, 59
doe, barren ~ **88** 34
doe, young ~ **88** 39
doffer **163** 42
doffer comb, vibrating ~ **163** 39
dog *Dom. Anim.* **73** 16
dog *Game* **88** 42
dog *Bldg. Site* **119** 58
dog *Roof* **121** 97
dog *Intern. Combust. Eng.* **190** 39
dog, three-headed ~ **327** 30
dog, toy ~ **47** 7, 41
dog biscuit **99** 37
dog bowl **70** 32
dog brush **70** 28
dogcart **186** 18
dog comb **70** 29
dog flange **190** 39
dog food **99** 36
dog lead **70** 30
dog rose **373** 26
dogs *Dog* **70**
dogs *Forging* **139** 33
dog sled **353** 3
dog sledge **353** 3
dog's outfit **70** 28-31
Dog Star **3** 14
dog tick **358** 44
do-it-yourself **134**
do-it-yourself enthusiast **134** 61
do-it-yourself work **134** 1-34

doldrums **9** 46
dolina **13** 71
doll **309** 11
doll, sleeping ~ **47** 11
doll, walking ~ **273** 63
dollar **252** 33
doll's pram **47** 10; **48** 24
dolly *Flea Market* **309** 68
dolly *Films* **310** 49
dolmen **328** 16
dolphin **225** 12
dolphin butterfly stroke **282** 35
dome *Brew.* **92** 45
dome *Art* **337** 21
dome, high ~ **36** 79
dome, imperial ~ **121** 25
dome, main ~ **334** 72
dome, revolving ~ **5** 12
dome cover **38** 48
dome shutter **5** 14
dome system **334** 72-73
domicilation **22**
dominant seventh chord **321** 5
domino *Games* **276** 34
domino *Carnival* **306** 13, 15
dominoes **276** 33
domino panel **203** 66
donjon **329** 4
donkey **73** 3
door *Farm Bldgs.* **62** 17
door *Carriages* **186** 11
door *Tram* **197** 32
door *Railw.* **207** 20, 22
door, bottom ~ **210** 7
door, double ~ *Tram* **197** 14
door, double ~ *Railw.* **208** 7
door, double ~ *Hotel* **267** 27
door, driver's ~ **193** 2
door, folding ~ *Tram* **197** 14
door, folding ~ *Railw.* **207** 39; **208** 7
door, front ~ *Dwellings* **37** 65
door, front ~ *Hall* **41** 25
door, front ~ *Household* **50** 30
door, front ~ *Floor etc. Constr.* **123** 24
door, front ~ *Car* **193** 5
door, glass ~ **44** 18
door, hinged ~ **194** 12
door, ledged ~ **37** 34
door, main ~ *Church* **331** 16
door, main ~ *Art* **335** 24
door, outer ~ **259** 78
door, outward-opening ~ **194** 35
door, rear ~ *Car* **193** 3, 6, 20
door, rear ~ *Lorries etc.* **194** 11
door, revolving ~ **213** 9
door, side ~ *Lorries etc.* **194** 8, 12
door, side ~ *Railw.* **213** 9
door, sliding ~ *Farm Bldgs.* **62** 16
door, sliding ~ *Brew.* **92** 47
door, sliding ~ *Lorries etc.* **194** 8
door, sliding ~ *Railw.* **213** 15
door, vertical-lift ~ **139** 51
doorbell **127** 2
door frame **41** 26
door handle *Hall* **41** 28
door handle *Carriages* **186** 12
door handle *Car* **191** 5
door-lifting mechanism **139** 55
door lock *Hall* **41** 27
door lock *Metalwkr.* **140** 36-43
door lock *Car* **191** 6
doorman **267** 1; **271** 44

dormer **37** 56; **38** 7; **121** 6; **329** 11; **336** 4
dormer window **37** 56; **38** 7; **121** 6; **329** 11; **336** 4
dormer window, hipped ~ **121** 13
dorsum manus **19** 83
dorsum of the foot **19** 61
dorsum of the hand **19** 83
dorsum pedis **19** 61
dosimeter **2** 8-23
dosing mechanism **83** 60
dosser **78** 15
dosser carrier **78** 14
dot **178** 39
dot, French ~ **102** 13
dot ball, white ~ **277** 13
double **276** 35
double backward somersault **282** 42
double bass **323** 23
double bassoon **323** 28
double bass viol **322** 23; **323** 23
double bull capital **333** 28
double bull column **333** 23
double edger **157** 57
double flat **320** 53
double-lap roofing **122** 2
double leg circle **296** 54
double leg lock **299** 11
double mill **276** 25
double overarm stroke **282** 37
doubles **293** 2-3
doubles, mixed ~ **293** 49
double sharp **320** 51
doubles match **293** 2-3
doubles sideline **293** 2-3
doublet, padded ~ **355** 30, 45
doublet, paned ~ **355** 33
doublet, quilted ~ **355** 45
doublet, short ~ **355** 41, 45
doublet, slashed ~ **355** 33
doublet, stuffed ~ **355** 30
double-three **302** 14
double unit for black **180** 12-13
double unit for cyan **180** 8-9
double unit for magenta **180** 10-11
double unit for yellow **180** 6-7
double-whole note **320** 12
doubling frame **164** 57
doubling of slivers **164** 5
dough mixer **97** 55, 59
doughnut **97** 29
douze dernier **275** 27
douze milieu **275** 26
douze premier **275** 25
dovetail halving **121** 89
dowel hole **120** 22, 23
dowel hole borer **133** 6
dowel hole boring machine **133** 6
down-draught carburettor **192** 1-15
down-gate **148** 21
downhill racing **301** 32
downhill racing pole **301** 25
downhill racing position **301** 33
downhill ski **301** 34
downpipe **37** 13; **38** 10; **122** 29; **147** 63
downspout **37** 13; **38** 10
downtake **147** 13
down-town **268**
down tube **187** 17
downy mildew **80** 20, 21
drachma **252** 39
Draco **3** 32
draff **92** 50

draft *Weaves* **171** 4, 11, 13, 19, 21, 27
draft *Bank* **250** 12
draft *see* draught
draft, rough ~ **338** 4
draft board **168** 7
draft clause **250** 17
drafting **164** 12, 13
drafting machine **151** 2
drafting roller **164** 21, 22, 29
draft mark **222** 73
drag *Iron Foundry etc.* **148** 20
drag *Equest.* **289** 48
drag chute housing **257** 24
drag hook *Horse* **71** 14
drag hook *Fire Brig.* **270** 49
drag hunt **289** 41-49
drag lift **214** 15
Dragon *Astron.* **3** 32
dragon *Sailing* **284** 57
dragon *Fabul. Creat.* **327** 1, 50
dragon, seven-headed ~ **327** 50
dragon beam **120** 42
dragon figurehead **218** 16
dragonfly **358** 3
dragon piece **120** 42
dragon ship **218** 13-17
drain *Street Sect.* **198** 23
drain *Rivers* **216** 37
drain *Town* **268** 8
drainage **144** 46
drainage basin **12** 24
drainage ditch *Rivers* **216** 33
drainage ditch *Road Constr.* **200** 63
drainage layer **199** 25
drainage sluice **216** 34
drainage tube **26** 47
drain cock **178** 34
drain cover **198** 24
drain pipe **198** 25; **199** 26
drain plug **284** 36
drake **73** 35
drapery **338** 33
draught beam **65** 18
draughtboard **276** 17
draught mark **222** 73
draughts **276** 17-19
draughtsman **276** 18, 19
drawbar **64** 47, 61; **65** 18
drawbar coupling *Agr. Mach.* **65** 30
drawbar coupling *Camping* **278** 55
drawbar frame **65** 26
drawbar support **64** 62
drawbar trailer **194** 22
drawbench **108** 2
drawbridge **329** 25
draw cord **29** 67
draw curtain **315** 1
drawee **250** 20
drawer *Dent.* **24** 17
drawer *Hall* **41** 9
drawer *Bedrm.* **43** 18
drawer *Flat* **46** 11
drawer *Bathrm. etc.* **49** 34
drawer *Bank* **250** 21
draw frame **164** 1
draw frame, four-roller ~ **164** 9
draw frame, simple ~ **164** 9
draw frame cover **164** 7
draw hoe **66** 1
draw hook **270** 49
drawing *Drawing Off.* **151** 16
drawing *Synth. Fibres* **170** 55
drawing, final ~ **170** 47
drawing, preliminary ~ **170** 45
drawing, rolled ~ **151** 10
drawing bench **108** 2

drawing board 151 1
drawing board adjustment 151 5
drawing easel 338 34
drawing floor 120 11
drawing head 151 4
drawing ink cartridge 151 36
drawing ink container 151 63
drawing-in roller 168 12
drawing knife 120 79
drawing machine 162 7
drawing office 151
drawing pen, tubular ~ 151 37, 38
drawing roll 162 11
drawing table 151 6
draw-in wire 127 30
drawknife 120 79
draw-off tap 126 34
drawshave 120 79
draw stop 325 44; 326 6
drawstring 29 64, 67
drawstring waist 31 66
draw well 329 3
draw wire 127 30
draw works 145 11
dredger 216 56; 226 41
dredger, hydraulic ~ 216 59
dredger bucket 226 44
dredging bucket 216 58
dredging machine, floating 216 56
dress 31 9
dress, button-through ~ 30 10
dress, jersey ~ 29 28
dress, knitted ~ 29 28; 30 33
dress, off-the-peg ~ 271 29
dress, peasant-style ~ 30 27
dress, ready-made ~ 271 29
dress, ready-to-wear ~ 271 29
dress, shirt-waister ~ 30 10
dress, two-piece ~ 30 33; 31 11
dress, wrap-around ~ 30 25
dress, wrapover ~ 30 25
dressage 289 1-7
dressage arena 289 1
dress and jacket combination 31 6
dress circle 315 18
dress form 103 6
dress guard 104 14
dressing, sterile gauze ~ 21 6
dressing axe 158 38
dressing comb 105 15; 106 28
dressing floor 92 8
dressing gown 29 24; 32 35
dressing machine 83 52
dressing material 26 34
dressing room 315 43-52
dressing room mirror 315 43
dressing stool 43 24
dressing table 43 25; 105 19
dressing-table mirror 43 29
dressmaker 103 1
dress shirt 32 43
dress sword 355 63
dribble 291 52
drier Synth. Fibres 170 38
drier Paperm. 173 22
drier Offset Print. 180 14, 27
drier, swivel-mounted ~ 105 25
drier felt 173 23
driers 50 23-34
drift net fishing 90 1-10
drill Dent. 24 6, 17
drill Agr. Mach. 65 74
drill Goldsm. etc. 108 4
drill Turner 135 20
drill, electric ~ 56 19; 120 21; 134 16, 50-55
driller 158 9

drilling bit 145 21
drilling cable 145 7
drilling line 145 7
drilling machine, electric ~ 108 6
drilling machine, radial-arm ~ 150 18
drilling machine, suspended ~ 108 6
drilling pipe 145 19
drilling platform 146 1-37; 221 66
drilling rig 145 1; 146 1-39
drilling vessel, semisubmersible ~ 221 64
drill pipe 145 6
drill spindle 150 23
drill stand 134 54
drill tower 270 3
drink, soft ~ 96 30
drinker, mechanical ~ 74 16
drinking bowl, mechanical ~ 74 16
drinking fountain 205 33
drinking straw 266 46
drinking trough 74 6
drinking water carrier 278 32
drinking water supply 269 1-66
drinking water tank 146 16
drinks cabinet 246 29
drinks cupboard 42 20
drinks gondola 99 71
drinks shelf 266 59
drinks stall 308 3
drip, intravenous ~ 25 13; 26 9
drip fuel line 190 53
drip ring 283 40
dripstone 13 80
drip tray 266 2
drive Composing Rm. 175 37
drive Railw. 214 2
drive, clockwork ~ 10 14
drive, conventional ~ 259 75
drive, crystal-controlled ~ 310 19, 24
drive, fluid ~ 65 37
drive, hydraulic ~ 139 9, 15
drive, main ~ 214 63
drive belt 103 10
drive-belt gear 109 21
drive chain 188 17
drive clutch 177 54
drive connection 67 19
drive gearbox 163 57; 168 10, 32
drive mechanism 110 43
drive motor Poultry Farm 74 37
drive motor Dressm. 103 9
drive motor Forging 139 25
drive motor Mach. Tools 150 9
drive motor Cotton Spin. 163 12, 23, 49
drive motor Text. Finish. 168 55
drive motor Composing Rm. 175 61
drive motor Electrotyp. etc. 178 12, 28
drive motor Offset Platem. 179 11
drive motor Hydr. Eng. 217 47
drive pulley, fast-and-loose ~ 163 50
drive pulley, main ~ 163 50
driver Carriages 186 32
driver Bicycle 187 72
driver Serv. Stat. 196 8
driver Ship 219 30

driver Equest. 289 26
driver Ball Games 293 91
driver plate 149 55
driver's brake valve 210 53; 211 22; 212 11
driver's position Agr. Mach. 64 33
driver's position Tram 197 25
drive shaft Car 192 30
drive shaft Hydr. Eng. 217 49
drive unit Shoem. 100 8
drive unit Photomech. Reprod. 177 56
drive unit, central ~ 238 57
drive well 269 60
drive wheel Agr. Mach. 65 80
drive wheel Shoem. 100 8
drive wheel Text. Finish. 168 4
drive wheel Offset Print. 180 66
drive wheel Army 255 50
drive wheel unit 209 3
driving 86 34-39
driving axle 210 37
driving axle gearing 64 30
driving barrel 187 73
driving cylinder 165 32
driving drum 165 32, 35
driving gear Cotton Spin. 163 57
driving gear Railw. 210 2-37
driving guide rail 226 39
driving pinion 214 8
driving plate Turner 135 9
driving plate Mach. Tools 149 55
driving shaft 163 24
driving trailer car 211 62
driving unit 209 2
driving wheel tyre 64 31
drizzle 9 33
drone Bees 77 5
drone Music. Instr. 322 11
drone cell 77 36
drone pipe 322 11
drone string 322 31
droop flap 229 54
droop nose 231 16
drop 98 76
drop, plain ~ 36 85
drop board 267 5
drop cloth 316 11
drop compass 151 59
drop forging 139
drop grate 210 5
drop grate lever 210 40
drop hammer, air-lift ~ 139 24
drop hammer, short-stroke ~ 139 11
drop net 89 29
drop pin 165 37
droppings removal 74 23-27
dropping worm 149 18
drop pin roller 165 39
drop windscreen 255 97
drop windshield 255 97
drop wire 166 34
drop worm 149 18
drove 158 37
drove chisel 158 37
'druggist' 233 45
drum Meteorol. Instr. 10 5, 16, 20
drum Household 50 29
drum Agr. Mach. 64 12
drum Painter 129 9
drum Cooper 130 13
drum Nucl. Energy 154 77
drum Nightclub 318 10
drum Music. Instr. 323 57
drum Art 335 44

drum, hollow ~ 312 49
drum, lansquenet's ~ 306 70
drum, revolving ~ 273 45
drum brake 188 36
drum brake, front ~ 189 11
drum brake, rear ~ 189 13
drum head 323 52
drum kit 324 47-54
drummer 318 11
drum of paint 129 9
drums 324 47-54
drum set 324 47-54
drumstick Supermkt. 99 59
drumstick Music. Instr. 323 54
drumstick Ethnol. 354 19
drupe 59 41, 43, 49; 370 99; 382 51; 384 40
drupes 59 59, 1-36
dryas 51 7
dry bulb thermometer 10 34
dry cell battery 127 27
dry cooling tower 154 39
dry dock 222 31-33; 225 17
drying 169 24; 170 58
drying cabinet 116 23
drying chamber 170 49
drying cylinder 165 50, 53; 173 22
drying cylinder, heated ~ 173 33
drying floor 92 16
drying kiln 92 16
drying machine 169 31
drying rack Agr. 63 28, 29
drying rack Flea Market 309 49
drying section 168 28
drying shed 159 17
dry-seed dressing 83 52
dry zone, equatorial ~ 9 54
D sharp minor 320 61
dual film-tape recording 117 70
dual film-tape reproduction 117 75
dual film-tape system 117 7
dubbing Films 311 1-46, 37-41
dubbing Chivalry 329 66
dubbing actress 311 39
dubbing director 311 38
dubbing mixer 311 36
dubbing room 311 34
dubbing speaker 311 39
dubbing studio Broadcast. 238 28
dubbing studio Films 311 37
dubbing theatre Broadcast. 238 28
dubbing theatre Films 311 37
duck 73 35
duck, toy ~ 49 4; 273 30
duck, wild ~ 86 41; 272 51
duck-bill 366 1
duck hunting 86 40
ducking 299 29
duckling 73 35
duck-mole 366 1
duck shooting 86 40
duck's meat 378 35
duckweed 378 35
duct 163 11
duct, cystic ~ 20 38
duct, hepatic ~ 20 37
duct, spermatic ~ 20 74
ductor 181 63
ductor roller 181 63
duct roller 181 64
due date 250 16
duffle coat 271 21
dugout 218 7; 354 20
duk-duk dancer 352 34

dulcimer 322 32
Dülfer seat 300 30
dumb barge 225 8
dumb barge, tug-pushed ~ 221 94
dummy *Infant Care etc.* 28 15
dummy *Store* 271 34
dummy, dressmaker's ~ 103 6
dummy bull 319 3
dummy funnel 221 16
dump body 194 25; 200 8
dump car 213 37
dump chest 172 81
dumping bucket 214 34
dumping device 147 44, 59
dump truck 47 38; 147 64; 200 7
dump truck, three-way ~ 194 24
dune, crescentic ~ 13 40
dune, migratory ~ 13 39
dune, travelling ~ 13 39
dune, wandering ~ 13 39
dune buggy 193 12
dung 63 15
dungarees 29 40; 30 21
dung beetle 358 39
dungeon 329 5
dunging, mechanical ~ 74 23-27
dunging chain 74 27
dunging conveyor 74 27
dung tank 221 72
dunnage 222 62u.63
duodenum 20 14, 43
duplet 321 23
duplicate list 263 27
duramen 120 84; 370 13
dust, fine ~ 158 22
dust, lunar ~ 6 14
dust bag container 50 62
dustbin 199 3
dustbin-tipping device 199 2
dust brush 109 18
dust cap 187 57, 82
dust catcher *Goldsm. etc.* 108 45
dust catcher *Iron & Steel* 147 14
dust-collecting chamber 163 11
dust-collecting machine 147 14
dust collector *Goldsm. etc.* 108 45
dust collector *Cement Wks.* 160 7
dust collector *Refuse Coll.* 199 47
dust container 50 86
dust counter 112 42
dust cover *Bookbind.* 185 37
dust cover *Audio* 241 32
dust cover *Store* 271 30
dust discharge flue 163 22
dust escape flue 163 22
dust exhauster 163 10
dust extraction fan 163 10
dust extractor 92 40; 172 1
dust filter 270 59
dust hood 133 20
dust jacket 185 37
dust pan 50 52; 260 60
dust removal fan 83 53
dust removal screen 83 56
dust-settling chamber 172 6
dust shield 2 48
Dutch clover 69 2
'duty free shop' 233 52
duty presentation officer 238 22
duvet, quilted ~ 43 8
dwale 379 7

dwarf 308 22
dwarf French bean 57 8
dwarf pine 372 21
dwelling 37
dwelling, lacustrine ~ 328 15
dye liquor padding trough 165 47
dye spray 100 35
dyke *see* dike
dynamo 187 8
dynastarter 209,13

E

Eagle 3 9
eagle fern 377 16
eagle owl *Hunt.* 86 48, 51
eagle owl *Birds* 362 15
eagles 362 5-9
ear *Man* 16 18
ear *Arable Crops* 68 2
ear *Dog* 70 2
ear *Horse* 72 1
ear *Dom. Anim.* 73 11
ear *Game* 88 16, 32, 44, 61
ear *Music. Instr.* 326 32
ear *Birds* 362 16
ear, external ~ 17 56-58
ear, feathered ~ *Game* 88 78
ear, feathered ~ *Birds* 362 16
ear, internal ~ 17 62-64
ear, middle ~ 17 59-61
earcup 241 69; 261 40
earflap 35 31
ear lobe 17 57
earmuff 304 28
earphone *Hairst. etc.* 34 38
earphone *Audio* 241 69
earphone *Office* 248 35; 249 63
earphones 34 37
earphone socket *Cine Film* 117 10
earphone socket *Office* 249 68
ear piece *Forestry* 84 23
earpiece *Post* 237 8
earplug 354 30
earrings 36 13
earrings, drop ~ 36 11
earrings, pendant ~ 36 11
earth 4 8, 30
Earth 4 45
earth 6 17
earth, composted ~ 55 15
earth, excavated ~ 118 78
earth, prepared ~ 55 15
earth core 11 5
earthing button 237 21
earthing clamp 142 35
earth moth 80 42
earthquake 11 32-38
earthquake, submarine ~ 11 53
earthquake focus 11 32
earth station 237 51
earthworm 357 24
earthworm, artificial ~ 89 67
ear tuft 362 16
earwig 81 11
easel 116 35
easel, folding ~ 338 26
East Australian Current 14 38
Easter candle 330 44
Easter candlestick 330 45
easterlies 9 48, 49
Eastern cut-off 298 21
Eastern roll 298 15
east point 4 14
easy chair 336 18
eaves 38 11; 121 4; 122 36
eaves, rafter-supported ~ 37 9

eaves course 122 49, 76
eaves fascia 122 42
eaves joint 122 76
E-boat 258 69, 75
écarté 314 15
ECG 23 28
ECG amplitude 25 49
ECG analyser 25 45
ECG analysis 25 50
ECG impulse 25 46
ECG lead 25 43
ECG machine, portable ~ 23 46
ECG monitor 25 2, 21, 28, 47
ECG recorder 25 41
ECG recording unit 25 27
ECG rhythm 25 48
E-channel 143 7
echinoderm 369 3, 11, 17, 18, 19
echinoderms 357 38-39
Echinops 53 14
echinus 334 21
Echiostoma 369 13
echo 224 63
echo chamber 311 31
echo chamber loudspeaker 311 32
echo chamber microphone 311 33
echogram 224 67
echograph 224 24, 65
echo receiver 224 64
echo recorder 224 24
echo signal 224 63
echo sounder 224 61-67
echo sounding machine 224 61-67
echo sounding machine recorder 224 65
eclipse 4 33
eclipse, lunar ~ 4 29-35, 34-35
eclipse, solar ~ 4 29-35, 32, 39, 41
ecliptic 3 2; 4 22
economizer *Power Plant* 152 26
economizer *Railw.* 210 23
Edam cheese 99 42
edelweiss 378 9
edge *Tablew. etc.* 45 57
edge *Forestry* 85 2
edge *Winter Sp.* 302 21
edge *Maths.* 347 32
edge, aluminium ~ 301 51
edge, front ~ 122 88
edge, hidden ~ 151 24
edge, matching ~ 128 21
edge, non-matching ~ 128 22
edge, razor's ~ 106 40
edge, steel ~ 301 4, 50
edge, upper ~ 301 51
edge, visible ~ 151 23
edge board, lower ~ 118 74
edge board, upper ~ 118 73
edge mill 159 8
edge of platform 205 19
edge of pool 281 3
edge runner mill 159 8
edge sander 133 12
edge-sanding machine 133 12
edge-veneering machine 133 26
edging *Flower Gdn.* 51 15
edging *Optician* 111 35
edging, concrete ~ 52 20
edging, hoop ~ 55 38
edging machine 111 24
editing 311 42-46
editing table 117 96; 311 42
editorial 342 48
EDP print-out 248 47

education, nursery ~ 48 1-20
education, pre-school ~ 48 1-20
eel 364 17
eel hook 89 87
effacé 314 13
efflux viscometer 129 38
E flat major 320 65
E flat minor 320 68
egg *Man* 20 84
egg *Poultry Farm* 74 58
egg *Bees* 77 26, 27
egg *Gdn. Pests* 80 15, 55
egg *Forest Pests* 82 19
egg *Articulates* 358 49
egg and anchor cyma 334 42
egg and dart cyma 334 42
egg and tongue cyma 334 42
egg box 74 42, 45; 99 50
egg collection 74 22, 34
egg collection system 74 34
egg-counting board 89 19
egg gallery 82 23
egg integument 74 59
egg-packing machine, fully automatic ~ 74 46
egg position 301 33
egg production 74 34-53
eggshell 74 59
egg timer 110 31
egg weigher 74 43
Egyptian 342 8
eight 283 10
eighth note 320 16
eighth rest 320 24
ejection seat 257 6, 7
ejector seat 257 6, 7
E-layer 7 27
elbow *Man* 16 45
elbow *Overh. Irrign.* 67 6
elbow *Horse* 72 20
elbow *Winter Sp.* 301 70
elbow boot 289 31
elbow coupling 126 40
elbow joint 126 51, 52
elbow pad 303 16
elbow screw joint 126 40, 45
elbow snips 125 2
elder 374 35
elderberry 374 37
elder flower 374 36
election 263 16-30
election meeting 263 1-15
election officer 263 17
election regulations 263 25
election speaker 263 5
election supervisor 263 28
elector 263 24
electoral register 263 18
electric action organ 326 36-52
electrical fitter 127 1
electrical point 261 12
electrical socket 261 12
electrical system bus 235 55
electric engine room 223 68
electrician 127 1
electricity cable 198 14, 19
electricity meter 127 32
electricity meter cupboard 127 31
electricity transmission line 15 113
electric light bulb 127 56
electric power plant 152 1-28
electrocardiogram monitor 25 2, 21, 28
electrocardiograph 23 28; 25 41
electrode *Hosp.* 25 26, 35, 38
electrode *Slaughterho.* 94 8
electrode *Arc Weld.* 142 10
electrode *Iron & Steel* 147 52

electrode, central ~ 2 3
electrode, platinum-iridium
~ 24 44
electrode, strap-on ~ 23 30
electrode arm 142 24
electrode case 142 7
electrode exit point 25 34
electrode holder 142 9, 20
electrode lead 25 25
electromagnet 237 47
electron 1 3, 17, 27, 32
electron, free ~ 1 25
electron beam 240 16
electron gun 113 31
electron gun assembly 240 24
electronic circuits 242 68-72
electronics, remote ~ 112 53
electronics cabinet 177 69
electron microscope 113 30
electron shell 1 6, 8
electron spin 1 4
electroplating bath 178 4
electroplating tank 178 4
electroplating vat 178 4
electrotome 22 38
electrotype, curved ~ 178 21
electrotyping 178
electrotyping plant 178 1-6
element, electronic ~ 242 69
element, fissionable ~ 1 49
element, front ~ 115 7
element, fusible ~ 127 36
element, oscillating ~ 110 9
element of set 348 2
elephant 366 20
elephant, toy ~ 47 6
elephant enclosure 356 9
elephant house 356 10
elevating conveyor 200 49
elevating drum, rotary ~ 64
74
elevating gear 255 67
elevating piston 255 51
elevation, front ~ 151 17
elevation, side ~ 151 18
elevator Offshore Drill. 146 8
elevator Synth. Fibres 170 36
elevator Aircraft 229 27; 230
63
elevator Air Force 257 22
elevator Store 271 45
elevator Airsports 288 24
elevator Theatre 316 33, 34
elevator, chain and slat ~ 64
7
elevator, open-web ~ 64 69
elevator bridge 226 25
elevator car 271 46
elevator carrier 174 22
elevator controls 271 48
elevator operator 271 47
elevator shaft Offshore Drill.
146 20
elevator shaft Store 271 51
elevon section, movable ~ 235
33
elevon structure, heat-
resistant ~ 235 34
elk 367 1, 2
ellipse 347 22
ellipse template 151 71
ellipsis 342 29
ellipsoid of revolution 347 42
elm tree 371 49
elytron 82 10; 358 36
E major 320 59
embankment Map 15 104
embankment Refuse Coll.
199 14
embankment Rivers 216 49
embossing platen 183 29
embrace 205 53
embrasure 329 18

embroidery 29 29; 30 42; 355
67
embryo Arable Crops 68 16
embryo Bot. 370 86
embryo Trop. Plants 382 21
embryo South. Fruits 384 22
embryo plant 68 14
embryo sac 370 64
emergency brake 214 3, 71
emergency brake valve 210 57
emergency cable 214 47
emergency-cable tensioning
mechanism 214 48
emergency crash barrier 259 17
'emergency exit' 233 41
emergency exit 307 33; 312 7
emergency flare stack 146 11
emergency lighting 312 6
emergency telephone 237 4
emery paper 135 25
eminence, frontal ~ 16 4
eminence, thenar ~ 19 75
E minor 320 56
emission control 190 73
Emmental cheese 99 41
empennage shapes 229 23-36
Empire table 336 16
empress, Byzantine ~ 355 15
emptying system, dust-free ~
199 2
em rule 342 23
emu 359 1
emulsion 129 4
emulsion paint 129 4
emulsion paste 128 28
emulsion tube 192 10
enamel 19 30
enamelling 260 62
enamelling stove, electric ~
260 63
enamel powder 260 65
enchasing hammer 108 41
enclosing wall 356 4
enclosure, outdoor ~ 356 1
enclosure wall 329 15
encyclopaedia 42 18; 262 17
end Basketm. 136 23
end, hipped ~ 122 10
end, partial-hipped ~ 121 17
end, round ~ 143 50
end, rounded ~ 143 50
end, west ~ 335 22
end frame, hemispherical ~
235 48
end-grain block 340 1
endive 57 39
endive leaf 57 39
endleaf 185 49
end line 292 36
end moraine 12 55
endorsee 250 26
endorsement 250 25
endorser 250 27
endpaper 185 49
end pier 215 27
end plate 229 33
end rib, hemispherical ~ 235
48
end ring 89 52
end support 150 40
end switch 241 60
endurance competition 289
16
energy 1 55
energy, solar ~ 155 17-36
energy level 1 15, 27
energy system 6 6, 8
engagement 294 46
engine Moon L. 6 30
engine Oil, Petr. 145 12
engine Aircraft 231 26

engine Airsports 288 35
engine, air-cooled ~ 188 7;
189 3, 50
engine, auxiliary ~ Ship 223
71
engine, auxiliary ~ Aircraft
231 33
engine, eight-cylinder ~ 190 1
engine, four-cylinder ~ 189
50
engine, four-stroke ~ 189 3,
50
engine, main ~ Railw. 209 4
engine, main ~ Ship 221 81;
223 73
engine, rear ~ Garage 195 49
engine, rear ~ Aircraft 231 10
engine, side ~ 228 29
engine, single-cylinder ~ 188
26; 189 3
engine, twin-shaft ~ 232 51
engine, two-stroke ~ 188 7,
26; 242 55; 305 92
engine, water-cooled ~ 189
31, 39
engine and propeller room
227 22
engine and transmission
control wheel 212 67
engine compartment 195 35
engine compartment
structure 235 2
engine control system 235 39
engine driver 208 2
engineer 208 2
engineering workshop 222 8
engineer's brake valve 210 53;
211 22; 212 11
engine fairing, aerodynamic
~ 234 6
engine mount 234 21
engine mounting 190 38; 191
53; 226 58
engine oil 196 15
engine oil temperature gauge
212 19
engine order telegraph 224 25
engine pod 231 26; 256 25
engine room Ship 221 10
engine room Fire Brig. 270 1
engine room ventilator 212 37
engine superstructure 226 58
engine telegraph 224 25
English Composing Rm. 175
29
English Billiards 277 5
English daisy 376 1
English hand 342 10
English ryegrass 69 26
English setter 70 41
engraver 340 16
engraving 36 41
engraving ball 108 34
engraving machine 177 52
engraving system 177 66
enlarger 116 26
enlarger head 116 41
enlarging meter 116 53
enlarging photometer 116 53
ensign of head of state 253 14
ensign staff 223 31; 258 25
entablature 334 52
entire 370 43
entrance 77 48; 99 4; 208 10
'entrance' 233 36
entrance 307 19
entrance, bullfighters' ~ 319
10
entrance, main ~ 319 6
entrance, side ~ 331 15; 335
13
entrance and exit door 197 14
entrance hall 41 1-29

entrance tunnel 353 6
entrechat 314 22
entrepôt 225 7
entry/exit hatch 6 38
entry hatch 6 10; 235 26
epaulière 329 44
épée 294 25-33, 36
épée, electric ~ 294 26
épéeist 294 25
épée point 294 27
ephemerid 358 6
epicalyx 58 22
epicenter 11 33
epicentre 11 33
epididymis 20 73
epiglottis 17 51
epistyle 334 18
equalizer 311 19
equalizer, universal ~ 238 48
'equals' key 247 20
equals sign 344 23
equation, conditional ~ 345 9
equation, identical ~ 345 5
equation, simple ~ 345 4
equator 14 1
equator, celestial ~ 3 3
Equatorial Countercurrent 14
33
equestrian sport 289
equilibrist 307 48
equinoxes 3 6-7
equipment carrier 177 58
equipment locker 212 35
equipment section 239 1
equisetum 376 18
equitation 71 1-6
erase head 241 59; 243 20;
311 25
eraser 151 42
eraser, glass ~ 151 47
eraser, pencil-type ~ 151 41
erasing head 241 59; 243 20;
311 25
erasing knife 151 43
erasing knife blade 151 44
erasing shield 151 35
erasing table 249 26
erasion 26 52
erection shop 222 4
Ergates faber 358 38
ergometer, bicycle ~ 23 26
ergometry 23 26-31
ergot 68 4
Eridamus 3 12
Erlenmeyer flask 173 2; 350
39
ermine moth 80 5
erne 362 5
error indicator 244 7
eruption 7 21
escalator 271 22
escape wheel 110 40
escapologist 308 28
escarpment 13 57
escudo 252 23
Eskimo 353 1
Eskimo kayak 283 68
esophagus 17 49
espalier 37 33; 52 1,2,16,17,29
espalier, free-standing ~ 52
16
espalier fruit tree 52
1,2,16,17,29
esparto grass 136 26
espresso bar 265 1-26
esquire 329 68
estate 193 15
estate car 193 15
estoque 319 32
etchant 178 24; 182 16
etching 340 14-24
etching bath 178 31; 340 51
etching ground 340 55

etching machine *Electrotyp. etc.* 178 23
etching machine *Photograv.* 182 15
etching needle 340 16
etching solution 178 24; 182 16
etching tank 178 24, 31; 182 16
ethmoid 17 39
ethnology 352; 353; 354
ethylene molecule 242 61
Eurobottle 93 26
Europe 14 15
European silver fir 372 1
European Southern Observatory 5 1-16
European toad 364 23
Euscorpius flavicandus 358 40
evacuating pump, centrifugal ~ 67 11, 23
evaporating basin 350 29
evaporating dish 350 29
evaporator 155 6
evening dress 33 13
evening gown 30 53
evening sandal 101 27
evening suit 33 7
everlasting 377 3
ever-ready case 115 103
evolution 345 2
ewe 73 13; 75 10
examination couch 22 43; 23 4
examination table 27 1, 26
excavation *Bldg. Site* 118 69-82
excavation side 118 72
excavator 118 76, 81; 200 1
excavator, large-scale ~ 159 3
excavator, toy ~ 273 65
excavator, universal ~ 158 13
excess water conduit 269 23
exchange *Post* 237 17, 22
exchange *Stock Exch.* 251 1-10
exchange broker 251 4
exchange floor 251 1
exchange golf ball 249 28
exchange hall 251 1
exchange rate 204 32
exchange typing element 249 28
excited state 1 19
exciter lamp 312 48
exclamation mark 342 21
exclamation point 342 21
exclusion principle 1 7
excretory vacuole 357 5
excursion steamer 221 101-128; 225 29
executive-secretary system 246 13
exercise book 47 24; 260 4, 18
exercises 296 48-60
exergue 252 10
exhaust *Agr. Mach.* 64 38
exhaust *Railw.* 209 12, 22
exhaust, upswept ~ 188 15; 189 15
exhaust bubbles 279 26
exhaust casing 212 69
exhaust escape flue 258 79
exhaust fan *Brew.* 92 15
exhaust fan *Joiner* 133 33
exhaust gas 160 4
exhaust gas stack 154 37
exhaust manifold 190 36, 73
exhaust mast 221 17
exhaust muffler 212 42, 48
exhaust outlet 259 92

exhaust pipe *Photograv.* 182 25
exhaust pipe *Car* 191 51
exhaust pipe *Ship* 221 76
exhaust pipe *Warships* 258 44
exhaust pipe, four-pipe ~ 189 51
exhaust port 242 58
exhaust repair 195 52
exhaust silencer 212 42, 48
exhaust system 195 51
exhaust valve 190 46; 242 53
'exit' 233 37
exit 307 19
exit, emergency ~ 99 79
exit gate 319 12
ex libris 185 51
exosphere 7 31
exotic 306 30
expansion line 1 61
expansion tank 38 24
experimental apparatus 261 11
explosion, atomic ~ 7 11
exponent 345 1
exposing lamp 182 3
exposure bath 228 21
exposure control device 176 9
exposure control switch 117 17
exposure counter 115 17
exposure meter 114 29
exposure meter, hand-held ~ 114 56
exposure meter control step 117 37
exposure meter needle 115 57
exposure system 249 42
exposure time balancing knob 116 39
exposure timer 116 24; 179 18
expression marks 321 27-41
express locomotive 205 35
express train car 207 1-21
express train carriage 207 1-21
express train coach 207 1-21
express train compartment 207 43
extension *Joiner* 133 13
extension *Post* 237 17, 19, 21, 22-26, 26
extension arm 132 63
extension bar 151 57
extension bellows 115 85
extension cord 127 10
extension ladder 270 14
extension lead 127 10
extension plug 127 11
extension socket 127 12
extension tube *Household* 50 70
extension tube *Photog.* 115 81
extensor, common ~ 18 57, 63
extensor, radial ~ 18 56
extensor carpi radialis longus 18 56
extensor communis digitorum 18 57, 63
extinguisher, mobile ~ 270 63
extra 310 29; 316 39
extra bold 175 9
extracting a root 345 2
extraction fan 199 32
extraction forceps 24 47
extraction of phenol 170 3
extraction vent 49 20
extractor 170 37
extractor duct, movable ~ 142 15
extractor fan 133 33
extractor grid 100 13

extractor support 142 16
extrados 336 26
extremity, fimbriated ~ 20 82
extrusion press 159 11; 161 7
eye *Man* 16 7; 19 38-51
eye *Horse* 72 4
eye *Dom. Anim.* 73 32
eye *Game* 88 15, 33, 43, 60
eye *Fish Farm.* 89 82
eye *Mills* 91 19
eye *Blacksm.* 137 29
eye *Weaving* 166 28, 29
eye *Art* 334 75
eye, compound ~ *Bees* 77 20-24
eye, compound ~ *Articulates* 358 7
eye, simple ~ 77 2
eye, stalked ~ 357 30
eyeball 19 45
eye-bright 61 27
eyebrow *Man* 19 38
eyebrow *Roof* 121 23
eyecup 115 73; 117 14; 313 34
eyeground 22 32
eyelash 19 41
eyelet *Shoem.* 100 63
eyelet *Glaz.* 124 23
eyelet *Weaving* 166 28
eyelet, hook, and press-stud setter 100 53
eyelet embroidery 102 11
eyelid, lower ~ 19 40
eyelid, upper ~ 19 39
eye muscles 19 44
eyepiece 113 20; 115 42; 117 14; 311 9
eyepiece, binocular ~ 23 6
eyepiece control ring 313 7
eyepiece focusing knob 112 56
eyespot 358 54

F

fabled beings 327
fabric *Bldg. Site* 118 1-49
fabric *Knitting* 167 29, 48
fabric *Text. Finish.* 168 39, 51, 64
fabric *Weaves* 171 29
fabric *Store* 271 59
fabric, air-dry ~ 168 22
fabric, metallic ~ 270 46
fabric, non-woven ~ 103 27
fabric, printed ~ 168 57
fabric, raised ~ 168 36
fabric, shrink-resistant ~ 168 26
fabric, tubular ~ 167 1, 9
fabric, woollen ~ *Dressm.* 103 27
fabric, woollen ~ *Text. Finish.* 168 1
fabric, woven ~ 166 12
fabric box 167 10
fabric container 167 10
fabric department 271 58
fabric drum 167 10
fabric-finishing machine, decatizing ~ 168 49
fabric for upholstery 134 60
fabric guide roller 168 5
fabric-plaiting device 168 30
fabric-raising machine 168 31
fabric roll 167 29
fabric roller 166 20
fabric shaft 171 21, 23
fabric wallhanging 128 18
fabulous creatures 327
façade, west ~ 335 22

face *Man* 16 4-17
face *Horse* 72 5
face *Clocks* 110 25
face *Blacksm.* 137 28
face *Composing Rm.* 174 31; 175 42
face *Art* 336 24
face, metal ~ 303 11
face compress 106 25
face guard 292 11, 25
face mask *Fire Brig.* 270 40
face mask *Swim.* 279 10
face mask filter 270 57
face par 251 12
face pipes 326 1-3
facet 77 20
face urn 328 38
face vault 297 30
facing 24 32
facing, decorative ~ 30 47
facsimile signature 252 34
facsimile telegraph 245 1
factor 344 25
factory number 187 51
factory ship *Sea Fish.* 90 11
factory ship *Ship* 221 86
fahlerz 351 1
fahl ore 351 1
fair 308
fair, annual ~ 308 1-69
fairground 308 1
fairing 189 43
fairing, integrated ~ 189 44
fairing, metal ~ 188 50
fairlead 284 29
fairway 216 21
fairway, main ~ 224 92
fairway, secondary ~ 224 93
fairway markings 224 84-102
fairway marks 224 68-83
fair-weather cumulus 8 1
fairy-tale figure 306 65
falcon 86 46
falconer 86 42
falconry 86 42-46
falcons 362 1-4
fall 221 106
falling wedge 85 4
fallow 63 1
fallow buck 88 40
fallow deer 88 40-41
falls 11 45
falls, artificial ~ 272 9
false acacia 371 70
false oat 69 22
family grave 331 27
family tomb 331 27
fan *Roof & Boiler.* 38 58
fan *Agr. Mach.* 64 15; 65 52
fan *Pest Contr.* 83 49
fan *Game* 88 75
fan *Energy Sources* 155 14
fan *Weaving* 165 23
fan *Intern. Combust. Eng.* 190 7
fan *Refuse Coll.* 199 35, 46
fan *Aircraft* 232 34, 43
fan *Ethnol.* 353 42
fan, low-pressure ~ 199 33
fan blower 179 22
fan clutch 190 8
fancy appliqué 35 7
fancy dress 306 6-48, 32
fancy-dress ball 306 1-48
fan drift 144 22
fan drive, hydrostatic ~ 212 62
fan fold sheet, continuous ~ 248 47
fang 19 36
fan-jet turbine 232 38
fanlight 37 35
fan nozzle 83 4

fan tail **73** 29
fan vault **336** 46
faradization unit **23** 37
farm **15** 101
farm buildings **62**
farmer **62** 6
farmhand **63** 5
farming **63**
farm labourer **63** 5
farmland **63** 17
farm produce **68** 1-47
farm road **63** 18
farmstead **62**
farm track **63** 18
farm vehicle engineering **138**
farmworker **63** 5
farmyard **62** 31
farmyard hedge **62** 35
farmyard manure **63** 15
farrowing and store pen **75** 40
farrowing rails **75** 43
fascia panel **191** 57-90
fascine **216** 53
fashion catalogue **104** 6
fashion doll **47** 9; **48** 32
fashion house **268** 9
fashion journal **104** 4; **271** 36
fashion magazine **104** 4; **271** 36
fast and slow motion switch **117** 87
fastback **193** 29
fast breeder **154** 1
fast-breeder reactor **154** 1
fastening *Plant Propagn.* **54** 13
fastening *Station* **206** 12
fat end **95** 53
fat lady **308** 21
fattening pond **89** 6
faucet *Kitch.* **39** 36
faucet *Plumb. etc.* **126** 34
faucet *Electrotyp. etc.* **178** 34
faucet *Chem.* **349** 5, 22
faucet, outside ~ **37** 41
fault *Phys. Geog.* **12** 4
fault *Coal* **144** 51
fault, distributive ~ **12** 8
fault, multiple ~ **12** 8
fault, normal ~ **12** 7
fault-block mountain **12** 4-11
faulting **12** 4-20
fault line **12** 5
faults, complex ~ **12** 8-11
fault throw **12** 6
fault trace **12** 5
faustball **293** 72-78, 74
favorite **289** 52
favourite **289** 52
fawn **88** 39
fawn, female ~ **88** 34
F-clef **320** 9
F-contact **115** 14
feather *Headgear* **35** 6, 12
feather *Dom. Anim.* **73** 31
feather *Mach. Parts etc.* **143** 73
feather *Chivalry* **329** 78
feather, falcate ~ **88** 68
feather, peacock's ~ **254** 36
feather star **369** 3
feed *Iron & Steel* **147** 51
feed *Mach. Tools* **149** 9
feed adjustment **100** 28
feed board **180** 32, 49, 67; **181** 4, 21, 30; **185** 9
feed chain **180** 72
feed chain drive **172** 69
feed channel **157** 55
feed conveyor **236** 33
feed conveyor, endless-chain ~ **74** 25
feed dispenser **74** 13

feed drum **180** 33, 34
feeder *Agr. Mach.* **64** 72
feeder *Poultry Farm* **74** 49-51
feeder *Brickwks.* **159** 7
feeder *Offset Print.* **180** 31, 48, 68, 74
feeder *Letterpress* **181** 22, 24
feeder *Bookbind.* **185** 25
feeder, automatic ~ **181** 5
feeder, mechanical ~ **74** 13, 23
feeder broom **199** 44
feeder mechanism **181** 22
feeder panel **153** 4
feeder-selecting device **167** 40
feeder skip **118** 35
feed gearbox **149** 8
feed gear lever **149** 10
feed guide **184** 23
feed hopper *Poultry Farm* **74** 24
feed hopper *Bookbind.* **185** 26
feed-in **173** 13
feed indicator **157** 9
feeding, mechanical ~ **74** 23-27
feeding apparatus **181** 22
feeding bottle **28** 19
feeding bowl **70** 32
feeding-in **164** 15
feeding passage **75** 3
feeding place **86** 28
feeding site **80** 50
feeding trough *Poultry Farm* **74** 21
feeding trough *Livestock* **75** 37
feeding trough, adjustable ~ **74** 4
feed mechanism *Agr. Mach.* **65** 78
feed mechanism *Mach. Tools* **149** 18
feed mechanism *Post* **236** 48
feed mechanism *Graphic Art* **340** 33
feed motor **177** 43
feed pawl **157** 44
feed pipe **96** 50
feed pump *Nucl. Energy* **154** 13
feed pump *Railw.* **210** 9
feed roll **85** 19
feed roller **85** 24; **157** 4, 40
feed roller, fluted ~ **163** 52
feed runner **147** 22
feed screw **149** 15
feed setting **100** 28
feed shaft **149** 33
feed spindle **312** 36
feed spool **117** 31
feed sprocket **312** 26
feed supply pipe **74** 15
feed table *Sawmill* **157** 63
feed table *Offset Print.* **180** 32, 49, 67
feed table *Letterpress* **181** 4, 21, 30
feed table *Bookbind.* **184** 12, 21; **185** 9, 34
feed-through insulator **153** 12, 35
feed-through terminal **153** 12, 35
feed trip **149** 18
feed tripping device **149** 18
feed valve **210** 20
feedwater heater **210** 23
feedwater line **154** 12, 30
feedwater preheater **210** 23
feedwater steam circuit **154** 45
feedwater tank **152** 17

feedwater tray, top ~ **210** 29
feeler *Agr. Mach.* **64** 86
feeler *Forest Pests* **82** 3
feeler *Weaving* **166** 32
feeler *Invertebr.* **357** 31
feeler *Articulates* **358** 27, 53
feeler, maxillary ~ **358** 42
feeler gauge **140** 53
feeler support wheel **64** 88
feet-first jump **282** 13
felines **368** 2-8
feller **84** 20
felling **84** 27
felling wedge **84** 4, 30
felling wedge, hydraulic ~ **84** 25
felt **173** 51
felt, dry ~ **173** 23
felt nail **122** 96
felt pen **48** 18
felt tip pen **247** 11; **260** 19
female, winged ~ **358** 21
femur **17** 22
fence *Joiner* **132** 65
fence *Refuse Coll.* **199** 13
fence *Aircraft* **231** 8
fence *Swim.* **281** 17
fence *Equest.* **289** 8
fence, electrified ~ **62** 46
fence, paling ~ **52** 10
fence, protective ~ **84** 7
fence, stone ~ **337** 23
fence, timber ~ **118** 44
fence, wicker ~ **216** 54
fence, wire ~ **15** 39
fence, wire netting ~ **84** 7
fence, wooden ~ **37** 53
fence adjustment handle **132** 66
fence rack **63** 28
fencers **294** 5-6
fencer's salute **294** 18
fencing **294**
fencing, modern ~ **294** 1-33
fencing glove **294** 12
fencing instructor **294** 1
fencing jacket **294** 16
fencing mask **294** 13, 14
fencing master **294** 1
fencing measure **294** 10
fencing movement **294** 7
fencing shoe, heelless ~ **294** 17
fencing weapons **294** 34-45
fender *Horse* **71** 40
fender *Tram* **197** 12
fender *Hydr. Eng.* **217** 9
fender *Docks* **225** 12
fender, front ~ *Bicycle* **187** 13
fender, front ~ *Car* **191** 3; **191** 3, 13
fender, integral ~ **193** 33
fender, wooden ~ **218** 26
fender pile *Hydr. Eng.* **217** 9
fender pile *Shipbuild.* **222** 35
F-1 engine **234** 4
fennel **380** 6
fen peat **13** 17
fermentation room **97** 72
fermentation thermometer **93** 9
fermentation trolley **97** 73
fermentation vessel **93** 8
fermenter **93** 8
fermenting cellar **93** 7
fern **377** 16
ferret **86** 24
ferreter **86** 25
ferreting **86** 23
ferries **221**
Ferris wheel **308** 37
ferroconcrete construction **119** 1-89

ferrule **45** 53
ferry, flying ~ **216** 10
ferryboat **216** 11, 15; **225** 11
ferry cable **216** 2
ferry landing stage **216** 7
ferryman **216** 17
ferry rope **216** 2
fertilizer, artificial ~ **63** 14
fertilizer, chemical ~ **63** 14
fertilizer, lime ~ **63** 14
fertilizer, nitrogen ~ **63** 14
fertilizer, phosphoric acid ~ **63** 14
fertilizer, potash ~ **63** 14
fertilizer spreader **62** 21
fescue **69** 24
festoon *Carnival* **306** 5
festoon *Art* **335** 54
festoon lamp **318** 26
festoon lighting **318** 25
fetish **354** 43
fetlock **72** 24
fettler **148** 43
fettling shop **148** 38-45
feuilleton **342** 67
F-hole **323** 6
fiber *see* fibre
fibre **77** 23
fibre, glass ~ **151** 48
fibre, loose ~ **168** 43
fibreboard **338** 24
fibula **17** 24
fibula, serpentine ~ **328** 28
fibula, spiral ~ **328** 30
fibula, two-piece ~ **328** 30
fiddle string **323** 9
field *Agr.* **63** 4, 17
field *Equest.* **289** 41, 51
field *Ball Games* **291** 1; **292** 40-58
field, fallow ~ **63** 1
field bean **69** 15
field bindweed **61** 26
field camomile **61** 8
field chopper, self-propelled ~ **64** 34-39
fielder **292** 76
field eryngo **61** 32
field glasses **86** 6
field guard **63** 13
field illumination **112** 33
fielding side **292** 73
field lens **115** 40
field mangel **69** 21
field marigold **61** 7
field mushroom **381** 1
field pests **80** 37-55
field player **292** 2
field poppy **61** 2
field sprinkler **67** 32
fig **383** 35; **384** 11, 13
fighter-bomber **256** 1, 29
fighting bull **319** 28
fighting ships **258** 64-91
fighting ships, modern ~ **259**
figure, clay ~ **48** 13; **339** 7
figure, plasticine ~ **48** 13
figure, satirical ~ **306** 63
figure, symbolic ~ **327** 20
figure, symmetrical ~ **346** 24
figure, wax ~ **308** 69
figurehead **218** 16
figures, compulsory ~ **302** 11-19
figure ski **286** 56
figurine, clay ~ **328** 20
filament **169** 17, 22; **170** 44
filament, continuous ~ **169** 1-34
filament, solid ~ **169** 15
filament lamp **127** 56
filament tow **169** 28, 30
file *Doc.* **22** 12, 26

file *Metalwkr.* **140** 16
file *Office* **245** 6; **247** 37; **248** 5
file, flat ~ **108** 49; **140** 27
file, half-round ~ **140** 29
file, rough ~ **140** 8
file, round ~ **108** 47; **140** 29
file, smooth ~ **140** 8
file handle **108** 50
filet **102** 22
file tab **248** 4
filigree work **102** 30
filing cabinet **245** 4
filing clerk **248** 6
filing drawer **248** 2, 23
filing machine **140** 15
filing shelf **248** 10
fill, sanitary ~ **199** 10
filler *Tobacc. etc.* **107** 7
filler *Paperhanger* **128** 3
filler *Power Plant* **153** 38
filler *Films* **310** 52
filler hoist **200** 51
filler hole **213** 19
filler light **310** 52
filler opening **200** 52
filler rod **141** 12
fillet *Meat* **95** 13
fillet *Carp.* **120** 45
fillet *Floor etc. Constr.* **123** 57, 67
fillet *Bookbind.* **183** 3
fillet, tilting ~ **121** 31
fillet gauge **142** 36
filleting knife **89** 38
fillet of beef **95** 24
fillet of pork **95** 44
filling *Dent.* **24** 30
filling *Tablew. etc.* **45** 38
filling *Hydr. Eng.* **217** 7
filling *Water* **269** 29
filling compound **153** 38
filling end **162** 2
filling inlet **50** 12
filling knife **128** 35
filling machine **76** 21, 26
filling material **24** 51
filling station **196** 1-29
fill-in light **310** 52
fill light **310** 52
film *Atom* **2** 10, 13
film *Photog.* **114** 9
film *Composing Rm.* **176** 25
film, cine ~ **117** 26
film, exposed ~ **117** 42
film, unexposed ~ **117** 41
film actor **310** 28
film actress **310** 27
film advance **114** 32
film advance lever, single-stroke ~ **115** 16
film agitator, automatic ~ **116** 19
film and sound cutting table **117** 96
film and tape synchronizing head **117** 102
film back **115** 80
film break detector **312** 30
film camera **27** 20
film camera, soundproof ~ **310** 47; **313** 15
film cameras **313** 1-39
film cassette **112** 65
film cassette, miniature ~ **114** 7
film cassette, universal ~ **242** 44
film cement **312** 22
film clip **116** 14
film copier, automatic ~ **176** 28
film-developing machine **311** 30

film director **310** 40
film dosimeter **2** 8
film drier **116** 23
film editor **311** 43
film extra **310** 29
film feed spool **117** 79
film former **178** 24
film gate **117** 30; **312** 34
film gate opening **117** 40
filmgoer **312** 5
filming **310** 14-60, 26-60
filming, exterior ~ **310** 18
filming, outdoor ~ **310** 18
filming agent **178** 24
filming speed selector **117** 12
film laboratory **310** 2, 30
film library **310** 5
film magazine **113** 40
film marker **117** 95
film matrix case **176** 17
film of fluorescent material **240** 19
film orchestra **310** 17
film path **312** 31
film perforator **117** 95; **242** 10
film poster **268** 57
film-processing machine **311** 30
film processor, automatic ~ **177** 72
film projection **312** 1-23
film projector **311** 22; **312** 24
film projectors **312** 24-52
film reel **311** 24; **312** 32
film-ring dosimeter **2** 11
films **310**; **311**; **312**; **313**
filmscript **310** 45
filmsetter **176** 1
filmsetting **176**
film speed setting **117** 18
film spool **114** 8; **311** 24; **312** 32
film spool holder **238** 6
film star **310** 27, 28
film storage vault **310** 5
film studios **310** 1-13
film title **310** 35
film transport **114** 32
film transport handle **116** 7
film transport mechanism **311** 26
film turntable **117** 99; **311** 44
film viewer **117** 91; **242** 8
film wind **114** 32
film window **114** 18; **115** 28, 34
filter *Atom* **2** 9, 12, 14
filter *Weaving* **165** 14
filter *Synth. Fibres* **170** 32
filter *Paperm.* **172** 20
filter *Water* **269** 62
filter *Chem.* **349** 12
filter, fluted ~ **350** 41
filter adjustment **116** 43, 44, 45
filter bed **269** 10
filter bottom **269** 11
filter cake **161** 13
filter change, automatic ~ **316** 49
filtered water outlet **269** 12
filter flask **350** 40
filter funnel **349** 11
filter gravel **269** 10
filter lens **142** 40
filter mount **115** 6
filter pick-up **112** 57
filter plate **349** 12
filter press *Porcelain Manuf.* **161** 12

filter press *Synth. Fibres* **169** 12
filter screen **116** 22
fimbria **20** 82
fin *Swim.* **279** 18
fin *Bathing* **280** 41
fin *Motorboats etc.* **286** 43
fin, abdominal ~ **364** 8
fin, anal ~ **364** 9
fin, caudal ~ **364** 10
fin, dorsal ~ *Fish etc.* **364** 6
fin, dorsal ~ *Mammals* **367** 27
fin, fixed ~ **286** 61
fin, pectoral ~ **364** 7
fin, pelvic ~ **364** 8
fin, ventral ~ **364** 8
fin, vertical ~ *Aircraft* **229** 24; **230** 59; **231** 6; **232** 7
fin, vertical ~ *Space* **235** 1
fin, vertical ~ *Air Force* **256** 32
fin, vertical ~ *Airsports* **288** 21
final image tube **113** 39
final picture quality checking room **238** 60-65
finch **360** 1
finches **361** 6-8
finds, prehistoric ~ **328** 1-40
fine cut **107** 25
fine focusing indicator **224** 36
finger, fifth ~ **19** 68
finger, fourth ~ **19** 67
finger, little ~ **19** 68
finger, middle ~ **19** 66
finger, pivoted ~ **74** 36
finger, second ~ **19** 65
finger, third ~ **19** 66
fingerboard **323** 21; **324** 8
finger guard **83** 20; **85** 15
finger hole *Office* **247** 39
finger hole *Sports* **305** 16
fingerhole *Music. Instr.* **323** 33; **324** 34
finger hook **324** 67
fingernail **19** 80
finger pad **19** 78
finger paint **260** 26
finger painting **260** 26
finger plate **237** 11
fingerprint **264** 29
fingerprint identification **264** 28
finger stop **237** 12
fingertip **19** 79
finial **335** 37
fining bath **162** 4
fining lap **111** 37, 38
finish **286** 28
finish, gloss ~ **128** 32
finished malt collecting hopper **92** 20
finishing **168** 1-65; **170** 57
finishing bur **24** 38
finishing layer **123** 40
finishing line **282** 28; **286** 30
finishing machine **100** 3
finishing of textile fabrics **168**
finishing press **183** 4
finishing train **148** 71
Finn **284** 51
Finn dinghy **284** 51
fin post **235** 3
fipple flute **322** 7
fir cone **372** 2
fire, blacksmith's ~ **137** 1-8; **138** 34
fire, open ~ **267** 25
fire alarm **270** 4
fire alarm siren **270** 4
fire appliance building **233** 8
fire-arm **87** 2
fireboat **270** 65
firebox **210** 4
fire control radar antenna **258** 51

fire control system **255** 74
fire crest **361** 10
fire curtain **316** 24
fire department **270**
firedoor handle handgrip **210** 63
fire eater **308** 25
fire engine **270** 5
fire extinguisher **196** 9
fire extinguisher, portable ~ **270** 61
fire extinguisher, wheeled ~ **270** 63
firefighter **270** 37
fire-fighting equipment **227** 25; **228** 20
fire gable **121** 9
fire gun **221** 4
fire hat **270** 38
firehole door **210** 61
firehole shield **210** 60
fireman **270** 37
fire nozzle **221** 4
fireplace **267** 23
fire plug **270** 35
fire prevention **316** 6
fire protection **316** 6
fire salamander **364** 22
fire service **270**
fire service drill **270** 1-46
fireside **267** 22
fire siren **270** 4
fire station **270** 1-3
fire tube **210** 17
firewood basket **309** 10
fireworks **306** 49-54
firing mechanism **255** 29
firing mould **161** 4
firing pin **87** 21
firing position **305** 73
firing process **161** 2
firing sequence insert **195** 13
firing trigger **87** 11
firmer chisel **134** 30
firn basin **12** 48
fir needle **372** 11
firn field **12** 48
firn slope **300** 14
first aid **21**
first aid dressing **21** 5
first aid kit **21** 4
first aid post **308** 61
first aid station **204** 44
first aid tent **308** 61
first base **292** 46
first-class section **207** 17
first floor **37** 2; **118** 7
first-floor landing **123** 23
first position **294** 18
Fish *Astron.* **4** 64
fish *Grocer* **98** 19
fish *Fish etc.* **364**
fish, canned ~ **96** 28
fish, female ~ **89** 13
fish basket **89** 25
fishbolt **202** 13
fishbone stitch **102** 7
fish-canning factory **225** 59
fish culture **89** 1-19
fish dish **266** 53
fish dock **225** 56
fish egg **89** 12
fishes **364** 1-18
fisheye **115** 44
fish farming **89** 1-19
fish fork **45** 8, 65
fish hook **89** 79
fishing **89** 26
fishing boat **89** 27; **90** 24
fishing line **89** 63
fishing lugger **90** 1
fishing pliers **89** 37

fishing tackle 89 37-94
fishing tackle, suspended ~ 90 29
fish knife *Tablew. etc.* 45 8, 64
fish knife *Fish Farm.* 89 39
fish ladder 89 93
fish lance 280 40
fish market 225 57
fish pass 89 93
fishplate 202 12
fishpole antenna 258 60
fish spawn 89 12
fish spear 280 40
fishtail bit 145 21
fish way 89 93
fission 1 43, 46
fission, nuclear ~ 1 34
fission fragment 1 44, 47, 51
fission fragments 1 37-38
fissure 11 52
fissure, diagonal ~ 300 3
fissure, horizontal ~ 300 3
fissure, vertical ~ 300 3
fissure bur 24 39
fist 16 48
fist hatchet 328 1
fitch 129 19
fitter 140 1
fitting booth 271 32
fitting of the frame 111 10
fitting-out quay 222 5-9
fittings 126 38-52
five-four time 320 41
fix 224 45
flag *Flags* 253 7-11
flag *Town* 268 44
flag, club's ~ 283 25
flag, linesman's ~ 291 60
flag, Olympic ~ 253 5
flag, swallow-tailed ~ 253 22
flag at half-mast 253 6
flag at half-staff 253 6
flag dressing 221 85
flag of the Council of Europe 253 4
flag of the United Nations 253 1-3
flagpole 253 1, 7; 273 61
flags 253
flags, national ~ 253 15-21
flags, triangular ~ 253 30-32
flagstaff 253 1, 7; 258 4; 259 87; 273 61
flagstick 293 88
flagstone 51 17
flail rotor 64 73
flame regulator 107 31
flamingo 272 53
flan 252 43
flancard 329 86
flan case 97 47
flanchard 329 86
flange *Cooper* 130 28
flange *Mach. Parts etc.* 143 2, 5
flange *Electrotyp. etc.* 178 44
flange *Hydr. Eng.* 217 67
flange, bottom ~ 215 10
flange, top ~ 215 9
flange mount 130 20
flanging, swaging, and wiring machine 125 25
flank *Man* 16 32
flank *Game* 88 26
flank *Meat* 95 2, 15-16
flank *Bldg. Site* 119 6
flank, thick ~ 95 15, 36
flank, thin ~ 95 16
flank vault 297 31
flans 97 22-24
flap *Child. Clothes* 29 35
flap *Horse* 71 40, 47
flap *Aircraft* 229 37

flap, double-slotted ~ 229 48
flap, extending ~ 229 51
flap, fur ~ 35 32
flap, normal ~ 229 46
flap, outer ~ 259 78
flap, slotted ~ 229 47
flap, split ~ 229 49
flap extension 78 19
flaps, plain ~ 229 46-48
flaps, simple ~ 229 46-48
flaps, split ~ 229 49-50
flap valve 192 63
flare, pork ~ 95 45
flash, battery-portable ~ 114 65
flash, electronic ~ 114 65, 68; 309 40-41
flash, single-unit ~ 114 68
flash bar 114 75
flash bulb 309 39
flash contact 114 30
flash cube 114 74
flash cube contact 114 13
flash cube unit 114 73
flash eliminator 255 18
flashgun 114 68; 309 38
flashgun, electronic ~ 309 40-41
flash head 114 67; 309 40
flash hider 255 18
flash lamp *Photomech. Reprod.* 177 37
flash lamp *Inf. Tech.* 242 43
flashlight *Electr.* 127 26
flashlight *Fire Brig.* 270 6
flashlight, underwater ~ 279 25
flash socket 115 14
flash switch 114 33
flash tube 176 26
flask, collared ~ 328 12
flask, conical ~ 350 39
flask, flat-bottomed ~ 350 36
flask, long-necked ~ 350 38
flask, round-bottomed ~ 350 38
flask, three-necked ~ 350 55
flask, volumetric ~ 173 3
flat *Dwellings* 37 64-68, 69-71
flat *Flat* 46
flat *Music. Not.* 320 52
flat-bed cylinder press, two-revolution ~ 181 1
flat-bed knitting machine 167 35
flat-bed offset machine 180 75
flat-bed offset press 180 75
flatcar 206 24; 213 5, 11, 40
flat clearer 163 44
flat four engine 230 34
flat glass production 162 1-20
flat plate keel 222 49
flats *Cotton Spin.* 163 45, 46
flats *Navig.* 224 87, 97
flatter 137 35
flatworm 81 35
flauto piccolo 323 30
flavourings 382
flax 383 6
flay brush 129 21
flaying knife 94 13
flea 81 42
flea beetle 80 39
flea market 309
fleet of lorries 206 25
fleet submarine, nuclear-powered ~ 259 54
flesh *Soft Fruit* 58 24, 35, 58
flesh *Drupes & Nuts* 59 6
fletching 305 62
fleur-de-lis 254 13
flews 70 26

flex 50 66, 77
flex hook 50 65
flexor, radial ~ 18 40
flexor, ulnar ~ 18 58
flexor carpi radialis 18 40
flexor carpi ulnaris 18 58
flies 316 1-60
flight, negative ~ 288 9
flight board 77 49
flight deck *Space* 235 16
flight deck *Warships* 259 2, 12
flight instrument 288 68
flight of wild ducks 86 41
flight refuelling probe 256 7
flik-flak 297 24
flint 107 28
flint corn 68 31
flintlock 353 28
flint maize 68 31
flip-over numeral 110 20
flipper *Swim.* 279 18
flipper *Bathing* 280 41
flipper *Mammals* 367 28
flip-up window 142 4
flitch of bacon 96 2
flitter-mouse 366 9
float *Bldg. Site* 118 57
float *Plumb. etc.* 126 15
float *Weaves* 171 40
float *Car* 192 15
float *Rivers* 216 12
float *Hydr. Eng.* 217 34
float *Aircraft* 232 6
float *Swim.* 282 18
float *Motorboats etc.* 286 44
float *Theatre* 316 26
float, cork ~ *Fish Farm.* 89 43
float, cork ~ *Swim.* 282 32
float, lead-weighted ~ 89 48
float, plastic ~ 89 44
float, polystyrene ~ 89 46
float, quill ~ 89 45
float, skin ~ 353 11
float, sliding ~ 89 43, 48
float, spherical ~ 90 19
float, wooden ~ 90 6
float bath 162 16
float chamber 192 14
float glass process 162 12
floating thread, diagonal ~ 171 38
floating thread, loose ~ 171 41
floating vessel 221 65
floating yarn, diagonal ~ 171 38
floating yarn, loose ~ 171 41
float lever 65 43
float line 90 4
floatplane 232 5
floats 89 43-48
float seaplane 232 5
float shaft 217 35
flood bed 216 41
flood containment area 216 42
flood damage 216 5
floodgate 217 77
flood plain 13 62
flood wall 216 32
floor 296 11; 297 6
floor, blind ~ 123 38, 73
floor, concrete ~ 118 16
floor, false ~ 120 43; 123 68
floor, ferroconcrete ~ 119 8
floor, first ~ 37 2, 3; 118 7, 14
floor, inserted ~ 120 43; 123 68
floor, reinforced concrete ~ 119 8; 123 35
floor, ribbed ~ 123 35
floor, second ~ 37 3; 118 14
floor, upper ~ 37 3; 118 14
floor and carpet cleaning 50 53-86

floorboard 120 36
floor brick 159 24
floor brush 129 27
floor ceiling 222 63
floor cleaning 50 53-86
floor cloth 50 55
floor construction 123
floor filling 120 44; 123 69
floor grinding machine 138 7
floor indicator 271 49
flooring block, hollow ~ 159 26
floor manager 271 33
floor nozzle 50 71
floor plate 222 59
floor socket 127 23
floor socket, sunken ~ 127 24
floor trader 251 6
floorwalker 271 33
flop 298 9
floppy disc reader 244 8
flora 356 21
florin 252 19
flour 91 28; 97 52
flour beetle 81 18
flour corn 68 31
flour silo 97 74
flow 216 9
flow chart 76 9
flow coating machine 129 34
flow diagram 76 9; 92 25
flower *Soft Fruit* 58 4
flower *Drupes & Nuts* 59 9
flower *Weeds* 61 10, 19, 22
flower *Arable Crops* 68 42
flower *Fodder Plants* 69 7, 14
flower *Gdn. Pests* 80 11
flower *Bot.* 370 23, 51
flower *Decid. Trees* 371 17, 26, 35, 40, 52, 55, 62
flower *Shrubs etc.* 373 5, 7, 11, 14, 31; 374 6, 7, 15, 21, 24
flower *Flowers etc.* 375 3, 6, 16, 19, 20, 23, 40, 46; 376 2, 5, 11, 19, 23
flower *Alp. Plants etc.* 378 16, 20, 28, 31, 32, 37, 47, 57
flower *Trop. Plants* 382 4, 17, 18, 29, 42, 55
flower *Industr. Plants* 383 12, 17, 27, 31, 36, 39, 46, 47
flower *South. Fruits* 384 13, 18, 56, 57, 65
flower, amaranthine ~ 60 21
flower, androgynous ~ *Shrubs etc.* 374 10
flower, androgynous ~ *Trop. Plants* 382 12, 14
flower, female ~ *Drupes & Nuts* 59 38
flower, female ~ *Decid. Trees* 371 6, 13
flower, female ~ *Conifers* 372 43
flower, female ~ *Shrubs etc.* 373 20
flower, female ~ *Alp. Plants etc.* 378 25; 378 53
flower, female ~ *Trop. Plants* 382 32, 50
flower, female ~ *Industr. Plants* 383 50
flower, female ~ *South. Fruits* 384 7, 14, 42, 43
flower, forced ~ 55 24
flower, fumariaceous ~ 60 5
flower, hermaphroditic ~ *Shrubs etc.* 374 10
flower, hermaphroditic ~ *Trop. Plants* 382 12, 14
flower, male ~ *Drupes & Nuts* 59 39

flower, male ~ *Decid. Trees* 371 14
flower, male ~ *Conifers* 372 43
flower, male ~ *Shrubs etc.* 373 21; 374 11
flower, male ~ *Alp. Plants etc.* 378 23, 53
flower, male ~ *Trop. Plants* 382 13
flower, male ~ *Industr. Plants* 383 51
flower, male ~ *South. Fruits* 384 5, 15, 44, 51
flower, open ~ 374 17
flower, withered ~ 58 55
flower arrangement 266 78; 267 37; 330 48
flower basket 266 29
flower bed *Fruit & Veg. Gdn.* 52 18
flower bed *Market Gdn.* 55 37
flower bed *Park* 272 41
flower box 37 20
flower bud *Soft Fruit* 58 27
flower bud *Bot.* 370 24
flower bud *Decid. Trees* 371 25
flower bud *Shrubs etc.* 374 14
flower bud *Trop. Plants* 382 28
flower cone, female ~ 372 4, 16, 22, 34, 62, 68
flower garden 51 1-35
flower girl 266 28
flower head *Weeds* 61 14
flower head *Alp. Plants etc.* 378 14
flower head, discoid ~ 370 74
flower head, hollow ~ 370 75
flowering branch *Decid. Trees* 371 2, 10, 16, 34, 39, 51, 54, 66, 71
flowering branch *Conifers* 372 33
flowering branch *Trop. Plants* 382 8, 12, 23, 27, 31, 50
flowering branch *Industr. Plants* 383 22, 26, 30, 38
flowering branch *South. Fruits* 384 17, 24, 37, 49, 54
flowering rush 378 39
flowering shoot *Alp. Plants etc.* 378 2, 27
flowering shoot *Trop. Plants* 382 41, 47
flowering shoot *Industr. Plants* 383 42
flower pot 54 8
flowers, wild ~ 375; 376
flower seller 266 28
flower shoot 59 28
flower shoot, male ~ 372 6, 62, 68
flower stalk *Drupes & Nuts* 59 4
flower stalk *Bot.* 370 52
flower stalk *Industr. Plants* 383 7
flower stand 204 48; 267 36
flower stem 370 52
flower umbel 378 40
flower vase 309 2
flower window 37 68
flowmeter *Hosp.* 26 3
flowmeter *Dairy.* 76 4
flow path 154 51
flow pipe *Roof & Boiler.* 38 74
flow pipe *Plumb. etc.* 126 23
flow pipe *Energy Sources* 155 10
fluate 128 7

flue 155 25
flueblock 38 40
flue brush 38 35
flue pipe 322 57
flue pipe, metal ~ 326 23-30
flue pipe, open ~ 326 23-30, 31-33
flue pipe, stopped ~ 326 34
flue pipe, wooden ~ 326 31-33
flue pipe duct 326 24
flue pipe windway 326 24
flue tube 210 8
fluid container 247 9
fluid reservoir 247 9
fluid transmission 212 27, 52
fluorescent display, eight-digit ~ 247 15
fluorescent material 240 18
fluorescent tube 127 61, 62
fluorite 351 16
fluoroscope, mobile ~ 26 14
fluorspar 351 16
fluothane container 26 26
flush-deck vessel 258 2; 259 22
flushing lever *Bathrm. etc.* 49 17
flushing lever *Plumb. etc.* 126 19
flushing valve 126 37
flush pipe 126 17
flute *Mills* 91 17
flute *Music. Instr.* 323 31
flute *Art* 334 27
flute *Ethnol.* 353 47
flute, globular ~ 324 32
flute, small ~ 323 30
fluting 157 6
flux *Goldsm. etc.* 108 36
flux *Plumb.* 125 7
flux *Gas Weld.* 141 18
flux *Iron & Steel* 147 2
fly *Men's Wear* 33 48
fly *Fish Farm.* 89 65
fly *Articulates* 358 18
fly gallery 316 5
fly amanita 379 10
fly and draw curtain 315 4
fly curtain 315 3
flyer 164 25
fly floor 316 5
fly frame 164 19
fly frame operative 164 24
fly frame operator 164 24
fly front 33 62
fly fungus 379 10
fly gallery 316 5
flying boat 232 1
flying boat, amphibian ~ 232 8
flying buttress 335 28
Flying Dutchman 284 49
fly leaf 185 49
fly line 316 8
fly man 316 7
fly nut *Mach. Parts etc.* 143 42
fly nut *Bicycle* 187 39
flyover 268 48
flysheet 278 22
fly swat 83 32
fly title 185 44
flywheel *Weaving* 166 15
flywheel *Intern. Combust. Eng.* 190 20
F major 320 63
F minor 320 66
foal 73 2
foam bath 49 3
foam can 228 28
foam canister 83 6
foam feed pipe 83 10
foam gun 270 64
foam-making branch 270 64
focal length setting 117 3

focimeter 111 33
fo'c'sle 218 10, 19; 221 13; 223 48
focus 347 25, 27
focus, seismic ~ 11 32
focusing adjustment 240 30
focusing aid 115 60
focusing device 5 11
focusing hood 114 23; 115 68
focusing ring 114 39; 115 8
focusing screen *Optic. Instr.* 112 21
focusing screen *Photog.* 115 39
focusing screen *Photomech. Reprod.* 177 2, 34
focusing screens, interchangeable ~ 115 58-66
focusing stage 115 86
focusing telescope 115 74
focusing wedge 115 55
focus setting 114 28; 117 3
fodder plants 69 1-28
fodder silo 62 11, 43
fodder tank 221 73
fog 9 31
fog, high ~ 8 4
fog headlamp and rear lamp switch 191 64
fog horn 223 3
fog horn, ship's ~ 224 32
fog lamp, rear ~ 191 67
fog lamp warning light 191 63
foil 294 1-18, 11
foil, electric ~ 294 26
foil, French ~ 294 37
foil, Italian ~ 294 39
foil fencers 294 5-6
foilists 294 5-6
foil mask 294 13
foil pommel 294 40
foilsmen 294 5-6
fold 185 54
fold, asymmetrical ~ 12 13
fold, gluteal ~ 16 42
fold, nasolabial ~ 16 11
fold, normal ~ 12 12
fold, reclined ~ 12 15
fold, recumbent ~ 12 15
fold, symmetrical ~ 12 12
fold-away table 207 53
foldboats 283 54-66
folder *Offset Print.* 180 15, 29
folder *Letterpress* 181 55
folder *Photograv.* 182 27
folder *Office* 245 19
folder-feeding station 184 17
folder unit *Offset Print.* 180 15, 29
folder unit *Letterpress* 181 55
folder unit *Photograv.* 182 27
folding 12 4-20
folding machine 249 58
folding mechanism 249 46
fold mountains 12 12-20
fold plate 185 10
fold unit 74 1
foliage 330 48
foliage plant 39 37
folk instruments 324 1-46
follicle *Man* 20 84
follicle *Bot.* 370 91
follower *Metalwkr.* 140 43
follower *Composing Rm.* 175 57
follow-through 293 84
font 332 10
fontange, lace ~ 355 65
font basin 332 11
food, canned ~ 96 25; 98 15-20
food, frozen ~ 99 58-61

food compartment 207 83
food pests 81 15-30
food price list 266 65
food slicer 40 38
food store, self-service ~ 99 1-96
food vacuole 357 6
fool 306 38
foolscap 306 39
foot *Man* 16 54; 17 26-29; 19 52-63
foot *Shoem.* 100 23
foot *Photog.* 114 71
foot *Joiner* 132 29
foot *Blacksm.* 137 15
foot *Bookbind.* 185 58
foot *Sailing* 284 40
foot *Music. Instr.* 326 23
foot, palmate ~ 73 36; 359 7
foot, prehensile ~ 364 34
foot, rubber ~ 114 45
foot, second ~ 286 59
foot, serpent's ~ 327 39
foot, webbed ~ 73 36; 359 6, 7
footage counter 117 52
foot bag *Infant Care etc.* 28 34
foot bag *Winter Countr.* 304 27
football 273 12; 291 17; 292 22
football boot 291 21
football game 273 10
football pad 291 33
football pitch 291 1-16
football player 292 23
football sock 291 58
footband 185 42
foot bar lever 100 27
footbath 282 22
footbed, surgical ~ 101 50
foot binding, front ~ 286 57
footboard 186 7, 13
foot brake 188 52
footbridge 15 78
foot control 139 27
foot control socket 249 66
foot-fault judge 293 24
foot ferry 15 60
foot gear-change control 188 55; 190 77
foot gearshift control 188 55; 190 77
footing 123 2
foot lever 83 34
footlight 316 26
footman 186 20
foot margin 185 58
foot muff *Infant Care etc.* 28 38
foot muff *Winter Countr.* 304 27
foot muscle 18 49
footnote 185 62
foot of bed 43 4
foot of goblet 162 42
foot of machine 133 25
foot of mast 284 20
foot passenger ferry 15 60
footpath 15 43
footpath under railway 15 44
foot pedal *Pest Contr.* 83 34
foot pedal *Forging* 139 27
foot pedal *Arc Weld.* 142 31
foot pedal *Letterpress* 181 12
foot pedal *Bookbind.* 183 18
footpiece *Mach. Tools* 149 12
footpiece *Carriages* 186 13
footprints 126 59
foot rail 267 52
footrest *Hairdresser* 105 18; 106 19
footrest *Bicycle* 187 47
footrest *Motorcycles etc.* 188 44

footrest *Railw.* 207 57
footrest *Winter Sp.* 301 58
footrest *Sports* 305 81
footrope *Sea Fish.* 90 9, 18
footrope *Ship* 219 46
foot scraper 123 25
foot switch *Hosp.* 27 21
foot switch *Dressm.* 103 26
foot switch *Sawmill* 157 66
foot switch, electric ~ 50 2
foot treadle 83 34
foot valve 269 6, 14, 43
footwear 101
fop 306 33
forage harvester, self-
  propelled ~ 64 34-39
forage plants 69 1-28
foramen 383 57
forceps 22 52
forceps, obstetrical ~ 26 53
forcing 55 24
forcing bed 55 16
forcing house 55 4
forearm *Man* 16 46
forearm *Horse* 72 21
forearm balance 295 26
forearm stand 295 26
forebay 217 39
forecarriage 65 14-19
forecastle 218 10, 19; 221 13;
  223 48
fore course 218 41; 219 55
foredeck 223 47; 284 10
foredeck, flooded ~ 258 65;
  259 77
fore edge 185 57
fore edge margin 185 57
fore end 95 51
forefinger 19 65
forefoot 72 22-26
foregrip 87 13
forehand 72 18-27
forehand stroke 293 40
forehand volley 293 41
forehead *Man* 16 4-5
forehead *Horse* 72 3
foreign counter 204 31
foreign exchange counter
  204 31; 250 10
foreign trade zone 225 2
foreleg 70 5; 88 25, 64
forelock 72 2
foremast 218 42; 219 2-4; 220
  21; 221 2
foremast, lower ~ 219 2
forepart 218 49
forepaw 70 6
forepeak 227 18
fore royal 219 60
fore royal stay 219 13
fore royal yard 219 37
foresail 218 41; 219 55
foresail, square ~ 220 13
foresheet 284 23
fore ship 286 33, 36, 40
foresight 255 3, 23, 37; 305 42
foresight block 255 23, 37
foreskin 20 70
forest 84 1-34
forestage 316 25
forestay 219 10; 284 15
forest Indian 352 19
forest labourer 84 18
forest pests 82
forestry 84; 85
forestry office 15 3
forest track 84 3
foretop 219 50
fore topgallant mast 219 4
fore topgallant rigging 219 18
fore topgallant sail 218 52
fore topgallant stay 219 12
fore topmast 219 3

fore topmast crosstrees 219 51
fore topmast rigging 219 17
fore topmast stay 219 11
fore topmast staysail 219 20
forewing 358 36
foreyard 219 32
forge 137 1-8, 1, 34
forget-me-not 378 26
forging and sizing press 139
  18
forging press, hydraulic ~ 139
  35
fork *Tablew. etc.* 45 7, 58
fork *Agr. Impl.* 66 3, 7, 22
fork *Horse* 71 29
fork *Optic. Instr.* 113 12
fork *Quarry* 158 33
fork, protective ~ 307 54
fork, rear ~ 188 14; 189 7
fork, swinging-arm ~ 188 14;
  189 7
fork blade 187 12
fork column 187 14
fork end 187 12
forklift 93 23; 206 16; 225 44;
  226 8
forklift truck 93 23; 206 16;
  225 44; 226 8
fork mount 113 24
fork mounting 113 12, 24
forks, front ~ 187 10-12
forks, telescopic ~ 188 8
fork spanner 134 2
fork truck 93 23; 206 16; 225
  44; 226 8
fork wrench 134 2
form *Office* 245 24
form *see* forme
formaldehyde atom 242 64
format selection 249 34
forme 174 10
forme, locked up ~ 181 36
forme bed 180 78; 181 17
forme-inking roller 181 18,
  27, 61
former *Optic.* 111 25, 26
former *Plumb. etc.* 126 83
former *Letterpress* 181 53
former *Aircraft* 230 55
former *Air Force* 257 28
forme roller 181 7, 18, 27
forms 36 42-86
Formula One racing car 290
  34
Formula Two racing car 290
  36
formwork 119 54-76
forsythia 373 1
forte 321 38
forte fortissimo 321 40
forte pedal 325 8
forte piano 321 41
fortissimo 321 39
fortress 15 74
fortune teller 308 36
forward *Swim.* 282 50
forward *Ball Games* 293 75
forward, reverse and still
  projection switch 117 88
forward horizontal stand 295
  30
forwarding agent 206 28
forwarding office 206 26
forwarding roll 180 4
forward kip 296 58
forward pace 295 43
forward roll 297 19, 20
forward somersault 297 18
forward split 295 15
forward straddle 295 4
forward walkover 297 26
forward wind button 249 73
Fosbury flop 298 9

fosse 329 37
fossette 16 16
foul 291 50; 299 34
foul line 292 48
foundation *Bees* 77 43
foundation *Floor etc. Constr.*
  123 2
foundation base 123 3
foundation pile 5 28
foundation trench 118 75
founder 148 8
fountain 272 8, 21, 22, 62; 334
  68
fountain pen 260 14
fountain roller 181 64; 249 52
Fourcault glass-drawing
  machine 162 8
Fourcault process 162 1
four-channel balance control
  241 42
four-channel demodulator
  241 45
four-channel level control
  241 42
four-eight time 320 31
four-four time 320 32
four-masters 220 28-31
four-to-pica 175 20
four-two time 320 33
four-wheel drive 194 1
fowl, domestic ~ 73 19-36
fowl run 74 11
Fowler flap 229 52
Fowler flap, double-slotted ~
  229 40
fowl run 74 11
foxglove 379 2
fox hunt 289 41-49
fox terrier, wire-haired ~ 70
  15
foyer 5 25; 267 1-26, 44-46;
  315 12-13
fraction 344 10, 19
fraction, complex ~ 344 17
fraction, compound ~ 344 17
fraction, improper ~ 344 16,
  18
fraction, proper ~ 344 15
fractionating column 145 37
fractions, vulgar 344 15-16
fractocumulus 8 12
fractostratus 8 11
Fraktur 342 3
frame *Agr. Mach.* 65 8, 90
frame *Bees* 77 40
frame *Mills* 91 3
frame *Optic.* 111 5
frame *Basketm.* 136 22
frame *Forging* 139 7
frame *Iron Foundry etc.* 148
  57
frame *Mach. Tools* 149 65
frame *Knitting* 167 33
frame *Railw.* 207 3; 208 5
frame *Shipbuild.* 222 58
frame *Aircraft* 230 55
frame *Rowing* 283 49, 67
frame *Sailing* 285 51
frame *Gymn.* 297 12
frame *Sports* 305 14, 88
frame, aluminium ~ 50 19
frame, annular ~ 235 47
frame, bone ~ 353 13
frame, C-shaped ~ 26 19; 27 17
frame, ferroconcrete ~ 119 2
frame, heated ~ 55 16
frame, iron ~ 325 2
frame, lower ~ 148 20
frame, metal ~ *Opticn.* 111 7
frame, metal ~ *Music. Instr.*
  324 76
frame, plate glass ~ 179 15
frame, reinforced concrete ~
  119 2

frame, sectional ~ 65 56
frame, shell ~ 111 8
frame, tortoiseshell ~ 111 8
frame, tubular ~ 188 9, 49
frame, upper ~ 148 19
frame, wire ~ 339 35
frame, wooden ~ 353 13
frame bar 64 51
frame-clamping machine 133
  42
frame-coding device 242
  8-10
frame counter 115 17; 313 28
frame-cramping machine
  133 42
frame drum 353 26
frame end plate 164 26
frame hive 77 45-50
frame-mounting device 133
  48
frame number 187 51
frame sample 124 2
frame-sanding pad 133 34
frame saw, vertical ~ 157 2
frame section, aft ~ 234 49
frame section, forward ~ 234
  45
frame slipway 222 19-21
frame stand 133 43
frame tent 278 36
frame timber 119 64
frame timber, bolted ~ 119
  74
frame vent 55 17
frame wood 124 3
frame wood sample 124 2
framework 339 22
framework support 214 77
framing 336 11
framing chisel 132 11
framing control 312 29
framing table 132 62
franc 252 15, 16, 17, 18
Frankfurter 96 8
Frankfurter garland cake 97
  42
Frankfurter sausage 96 8
franking machine 22 24; 236
  7, 27, 47
freak show 308 19
free backward circle 297 29
free combination knob 326 40
free combination stud 326 40
free exercise 295
free-fall positions 288 60-62
free flight model, remote-
  controlled ~ 288 86
free kick 291 43
free leg *Athletics* 298 27
free leg *Winter Sp.* 302 3
free leg, vertical ~ 298 25
free port 225 2
freestyle relay race 282 24-32
freestyle wrestling 299 10-12
free-throw line 292 38
free walkover forward 297 25
freeway *Map* 15 16
freeway *Docks* 225 54
free-wheel hub 187 63
freezer 22 63; 96 21; 97 65; 98
  74; 99 53
freezer, upright ~ 39 7
free zone enclosure 225 3
free zone frontier 225 3
freight agent 206 28
freight barge 216 25
freight car 206 6
freight car, flat ~ 206 21
freight car, open ~ 213 8, 33
freight car, special ~ 213 33
freight depot *Map* 15 91
freight depot *Station* 206
freighter 221 57

freight house **206** 7, 26-39
freight house door **206** 37
freight office **206** 26
freight truck **206** 15
French chalk **271** 39
French horn **323** 41
French lady **355** 51
French toast **97** 54
French window **37** 21
frequency band **309** 22
fresco **338** 40
fresh-air inlet **356** 16
fresh-air inlet and control **191** 85
fresh-air regulator **191** 86
fresh meat counter **99** 51
fresh milk filling and packing plant **76** 20
fresh milk tank **76** 15
fresh oil tank **65** 46
freshwater eel **364** 17
freshwater pearl mussel **357** 33
fresh water tank **221** 70; **223** 79
Fresnel lens **115** 64
fret *Roulette* **275** 30
fret *Music. Instr.* **324** 9
fretsaw **135** 12; **260** 53
fretsaw blade **135** 13; **260** 54
friction drive **116** 33; **312** 37
friction pad **192** 49
friction tape **127** 34
friction wheel **322** 26
fridge *Kitch.* **39** 2
fridge *Flat* **46** 33
fridge *Disco* **317** 10
frieze **335** 9
frieze, Babylonian ~ **333** 19
frieze decoration **334** 16
frigate **258** 53
frill **31** 34; **32** 44
frill collar **31** 46
frill front **32** 44
fringe **34** 36
fringe, decorative ~ **353** 25
fringe region **7** 34
frit **162** 2
frit feeder **162** 13
frit funnel **162** 13
frock coat **355** 76
frog *Agr. Mach.* **65** 8
frog *Road Constr.* **200** 26
frog *Railw.* **202** 24
frog *Music. Instr.* **323** 13
frog position **288** 61
frog's bit **378** 29
frond **378** 49
front **305** 1
front, cold ~ **8** 13; **9** 27
front, extended ~ **200** 10
front, hinged ~ **213** 10
front, occluded ~ **9** 25
front, warm ~ **8** 5; **9** 26
frontalis **19** 4
front axle pivot pin **65** 48
front axle suspension **65** 49
front band **71** 9
front element mount **115** 6
front fan-jet **232** 33
front-line player **293** 63
front panel, sliding ~ **349** 27
front roller undercleaner **164** 44
fronts **9** 25-29
fronts, cold ~ **8** 13-17
fronts, warm ~ **8** 5-12
front seat headrest **193** 7
front seat head restraint **193** 7
front sight block **255** 23, 37
front support *Free Exerc.* **295** 21, 23
front support *Gymn.* **296** 28

front wheel drive **191** 52
front wheel drum brake **188** 36
froth **266** 4
fruit *Weeds* **61** 11, 20, 23
fruit *Restaurant* **266** 57
fruit *Decid. Trees* **371** 4, 19, 28, 45, 69
fruit *Conifers* **372** 53, 64
fruit *Shrubs etc.* **373** 12, 18, 22, 27, 29, 32; **374** 4, 8, 12, 19, 25, 29, 31, 34
fruit *Flowers etc.* **375** 4, 7, 10, 13, 17, 24, 35, 37, 47; **376** 3, 6, 14
fruit *Alp. Plants etc.* **378** 11, 38, 42
fruit *Trop. Plants* **382** 3, 5, 10, 15, 17, 24, 39
fruit *Industr. Plants* **383** 14, 18, 21, 28, 32, 40, 43, 52, 56, 59
fruit *South. Fruits* **384** 19, 26, 39, 45
fruit, aggregate ~ *Soft Fruit* **58** 28
fruit, aggregate ~ *Bot.* **370** 100, 101
fruit, canned ~ **98** 16
fruit, compound ~ *Soft Fruit* **58** 28
fruit, compound ~ *Bot.* **370** 100, 101
fruit, dehisced ~ **375** 27
fruit, immature ~ **378** 31
fruit, indehiscent ~ **375** 43
fruit, mature ~ *Decid. Trees* **371** 61
fruit, mature ~ *Trop. Plants* **382** 33
fruit, ripe ~ *Decid. Trees* **371** 61
fruit, ripe ~ *Trop. Plants* **382** 33
fruit, soft ~ **58** 1-30
fruit, stewed ~ **45** 30
fruit, unripe ~ **378** 31
fruit, young ~ *Decid. Trees* **371** 59
fruit, young ~ *South. Fruits* **384** 31
fruit and vegetable counter **99** 80
fruit and vegetable garden **52** 1-32
fruit bowl **45** 29, 40
fruit capsule, mature ~ **382** 44
fruit capsule, ripe ~ **382** 44
fruit cone **372** 2, 29, 30, 36, 41, 57
fruit dish **45** 28
fruit flan **97** 22; **99** 20
fruit garden **52**
fruiting body **381** 2
fruiting branch *Decid. Trees* **371** 3, 11, 18, 31, 36, 41, 47, 50, 56, 64
fruiting branch *Conifers* **372** 40, 51, 59, 63, 66, 70
fruiting branch *Trop. Plants* **382** 2, 37
fruiting branch *Industr. Plants* **383** 34, 46
fruiting branch *South. Fruits* **384** 38
fruiting palm **384** 2
fruit juice **98** 18; **266** 58
fruit juice bottle **99** 74
fruit juice can **99** 75
fruit knife **45** 71
fruit pests **80** 1-19
fruit picker **56** 22
fruit pip **58** 37, 60

fruit preserver **40** 23
fruits **370** 91-102
fruits, dehiscent ~ **370** 91-96
fruits, indehiscent ~ **370** 97-102
fruits, Mediterranean ~ **384**
fruits, southern ~ **384**
fruits, subtropical ~ **384**
fruits, tropical ~ **384**
fruit scale **372** 67
fruit spoon **45** 66
fruit stall **308** 53
fruit storage shed **225** 52
fruit tree, standard ~ **52** 30
fruit trees, dwarf ~ **52** 1,2,16,17,29
fruit warehouse **225** 52
frustum of a cone **347** 45
frying pan **40** 4
fry pond **89** 6
F sharp major **320** 61
F sharp minor **320** 58
fuchsia **53** 3
fuel cell **234** 62
fuel gas **145** 52
fuel gauge **191** 38, 65
fuel-handling hoist **154** 27
fuel hand pump **190** 64
fuel-injection engine **190** 1
fuel injector **190** 32
fuel inlet **192** 13
fuel leak line **190** 53
fuel level sensor **234** 27
fuel line **190** 31
fuel line duct **234** 40
fuel oil **38** 50
fuel oil, heavy ~ **145** 59
fuel oil, light ~ **145** 58
fuel oil tank **212** 75
fuel pin **154** 4
fuel pipe **286** 25
fuel pressure gauge **230** 19
fuel pressure line **190** 52
fuel pressure pipe **190** 52
fuel pressure regulator **190** 17
fuel rod **154** 4
fuel storage **154** 28
fuel supply pipe **190** 31
fuel tank *Moon L.* **6** 7, 29, 37
fuel tank *Agr. Mach.* **65** 42
fuel tank *Motorcycles etc.* **188** 10, 28
fuel tank *Motorcycle* **189** 2
fuel tank *Railw.* **209** 20; **212** 56
fuel tank *Ship* **221** 71; **223** 80
fuel tank *Aircraft* **230** 48
fuel tank *Space* **234** 58
fuel tank, forward ~ **235** 21
fuel tank, jettisonable ~ **235** 46
fuel tank, main ~ **212** 4
fuel tanker **258** 97
fuel tender **210** 67
fuel warning light **191** 71
full circle **308** 43
full-colour print **340** 28
full-cone indicator **165** 7
fuller's earth **199** 38
fulling machine, rotary ~ **168** 1
fulling roller, bottom ~ **168** 6
fulling roller, top ~ **168** 3
full point **342** 16
full spread position **288** 60
full-step **320** 51, 53
full stop **342** 16
full title **185** 46
fulmar **359** 12
fume extraction equipment **142** 13
fume extractor **255** 59, 89
fumigation chamber, mobile ~ **83** 15

fumigation plant, vacuum ~ **83** 11
fumigator, vacuum ~ **83** 11
function, trigonometrical ~ **346** 32
function key **247** 17
funeral **331** 33-41
fungi, edible ~ **381**
fungi, esculent ~ **381**
fungi, poisonous ~ **379** 10-13
funicular **214** 12
funicular railway car **214** 13
funnel *Photog.* **116** 12
funnel *Ship* **221** 8, 40, 75, 84; **223** 1
funnel *Warships* **258** 58; **259** 32
funnel *Chem.* **350** 16
funnel, aft ~ **258** 20
funnel, forward ~ **258** 19
Funnel-Beaker culture **328** 12
funnel marking **223** 2
fur marker **131** 22
furnace **199** 29
furnace, continuous ~ **139** 1
furnace, electric ~ **147** 51-54
furnace, gas ~ **139** 47
furnace, gas-fired ~ **139** 47; **140** 11
furnace, low-shaft ~ **147** 51-54
furnace, stationary ~ **147** 23
furnace bed **38** 66
furnace incline **147** 2
furnace lift **147** 2
furnace thermometer **38** 64
furniture **174** 8; **181** 40
furniture lorry **268** 47
furniture truck **268** 47
furrier **131** 1
furrow *Agr.* **63** 8
furrow *Mills* **91** 17
furrow, gluteal ~ **16** 42
furrow wheel **65** 16
fur seal **367** 18
fur-sewing machine **131** 9
fur side **131** 12, 17
furskin **131** 5
furskin, cut ~ **131** 14
furskin, uncut ~ **131** 6
furskins **131** 11-21
fur trapper **306** 8
fur worker **131** 8, 23
fuse *Electr.* **127** 19, 36
fuse *Quarry* **158** 28
fuse box *Hall* **41** 19
fuse box *Weaving* **166** 23
fuse carrier **127** 68
fuse cartridge **127** 36
fuse holder **127** 35
fuselage **230** 54; **288** 26
fuselage attachment **235** 4
fuselage tank **257** 31
fuse wire **127** 68

G

gable **37** 15; **121** 5; **122** 25
gable, curved ~ **336** 5
gable, round ~ **335** 50
gable end **37** 15; **122** 25
gable roof **37** 5; **121** 1
gable slate **122** 80
gaffer **310** 37
gaffsail **220** 1
gaff topsail **219** 31
gag *Horse* **71** 53
gag *Fish Farm.* **89** 42
gag bit **71** 53
gage *see* gauge

gaillardia **60** 19
gait **289** 7
gaiter, leather ~ **191** 92
gaits of the horse **72** 39-44
Galaxy **3** 35
gale **373** 33
galena **351** 14
galingale **53** 17
gall *Gdn. Pests* **80** 33
gall *Forest Pests* **82** 34
gallant soldier **61** 31
gall bladder **20** 11, 36
galleries under bark **82** 23-24
gallery *Forest Pests* **82** 24
gallery *Coal* **144** 29
gallery *Theatre* **315** 16
gallery *Church* **330** 25
gallery, drilled ~ **192** 21
gallery grave **328** 16
galley *Composing Rm.* **174** 12, 44
galley *Ship* **218** 44-50; **223** 42
galley *Aircraft* **231** 20
galley loader **233** 22
galley slave **218** 48
gall gnat **80** 40
gall midge **80** 40
gallop, full ~ **72** 43-44, 43, 44
gallows **221** 87
gall wasp **82** 33
galvanometer **11** 44
gamba **322** 23
gambling casino **275** 1
gambling game **275** 1-33
gambling table **275** 8
gambrel **94** 21
gambrel roof **121** 18
gambrel stick **94** 21
game **86** 28; **88**
game, furred ~ **86** 35
game, positional ~ **276** 1-16
game, winged ~ **86** 41
game of chance **275** 1-33
game path **86** 16
game preserve **86** 1-8
gaming room **275** 1
gaming table **275** 8
gamma radiation **1** 33, 40
gammon steak **95** 54
gander **73** 34
gang mill **157** 2
gang stitcher **184** 15
gangway **38** 3
gangway, central ~ *Railw.* **208** 23
gangway, central ~ *Ship* **218** 46
gannet **359** 9
gantry *Photomech. Reprod.* **177** 13
gantry *Shipbuild.* **222** 26
gantry *Docks* **225** 40
gantry crane **157** 27; **206** 55; **222** 20, 25
gantry support **214** 24
garage *Dwellings* **37** 32, 79
garage *Garage* **195**
garage, agent's ~ **195** 1-55
garage, distributor's ~ **195** 1-55
garage driveway **37** 52
garbage **199** 17
garbage can **199** 3
garbage can dumping device **199** 2
garbage container **199** 4
garbage disposition **199**
garbage incineration unit **199** 28
garbage truck **199** 1
garden **37** 57
garden, Baroque ~ **272** 1-40
garden, formal ~ **272** 1-40

garden, front ~ **37** 58
garden chair **37** 49
gardener **55** 20
garden fence **52** 10
garden flowers **60**
garden gate **272** 31
garden hedge **51** 9
garden hoe **66** 1
garden hose **37** 42; **56** 27
garden house **52** 14
garden ladder **52** 8
garden light **37** 38
garden mould **55** 15
garden pansy **60** 2
garden parasol **37** 48
garden path **51** 14; **52** 23
garden pests **80**
garden pond **51** 16
garden rake **51** 4
garden rose **60** 15
garden seat **272** 42
garden shed **52** 3
garden shovel **55** 14
garden sieve **55** 13
garden spider **358** 45
garden strawberry **58** 16
garden table **37** 50
garden tiger **365** 7
garden tools **56**
garden wall **37** 37
gargoyle **335** 30
garland **306** 17; **335** 54
garnet **351** 7
Garratt locomotive **210** 64
garter **318** 28
gas, liquid ~ **145** 53
gas, natural ~ **12** 30
gas appliances **126** 12-25
gas bottle **278** 53
gas cap **12** 30
gas circulation unit **83** 16
gas-collecting main **156** 17
gas compressor **156** 26
gas connection **141** 31
gas control **141** 32
gas cooler *Offshore Drill.* **146** 27
gas cooler *Coking* **156** 19
gas cooling **156** 29
gas cutting installation **148** 67
gas cylinder **138** 35
gas cylinder manifold **141** 1
gas drying **156** 30
gas extractor **156** 21
gas fitter **126** 1
gas fitter's tools **126** 58-86
gas flue **152** 12
gas generator **350** 59
gas hose **141** 9
gas inlet **350** 2
gas inlet pipe **350** 2
gaskin **72** 36
gas lighter **107** 30
gas main **198** 21
gas main, high-pressure ~ **156** 45
gas main, low-pressure ~ **156** 44
gas meter *Plumb. etc.* **126** 5
gas meter *Coking* **156** 31
gas oil component **145** 42
gasoline can **196** 25
gasoline canister **84** 36
gasoline inlet **192** 13
gasoline pump **196** 1
gasoline pump, self-service ~ **196** 8
gasoline pump hose **196** 2
gasoline station **196** 1-29
gasoline tank **188** 10, 28; **189** 2; **305** 87
gasometer **144** 12

gas outlet *Oil, Petr.* **145** 29
gas outlet *Chem.* **350** 63
gas pipe *Pest Contr.* **83** 14
gas pipe *Forging* **139** 54
gas pipe *Metalwkr.* **140** 12
gas pipe *Oil, Petr.* **145** 29
gas pipe *Iron & Steel* **147** 18, 27
gas pliers *Plumb. etc.* **126** 58
gas pliers *Metalwkr.* **140** 68
gas pressure vessel **234** 32
gas regenerator chamber **147** 28
gas regulator **255** 34; **350** 6
gas-separating plant **145** 69
gas separator **145** 28
gas station **196** 1-29
gas supply **27** 41
gas tap **261** 24
gastrocnemius **18** 62
gas tube **83** 35
gas turbine **209** 9
gas turbine, auxiliary ~ **231** 33
gas turbine, twin-shaft ~ **209** 23
gas turbine controller **209** 16
gas turbine driving unit **209** 8
gas turbine fuel tank **209** 17
gas turbine trainset **209** 1
gas-washing bottle **350** 58
gas water **156** 39
gas welder **141**
gas welding torch **130** 14
gate **202** 40; **289** 8; **337** 24
gate, removable ~ **118** 46
gate, sliding ~ **217** 18, 55
gate, vertical ~ **217** 31, 38
gate, wrought iron ~ **272** 31
gate and rails **289** 8
gateau **99** 15; **265** 4
gateaux **97** 22-24
gatehouse **329** 22
gateman **202** 42
gate pole **301** 30
gateway **336** 15; **337** 11
gateway, monumental ~ **333** 9
gatherer and wire stitcher **184** 15
gathering and wire-stitching machine **184** 15
gathering machine **249** 59
gathering station **249** 60
gaucho **306** 31
gauge **76** 6
gauntlet **329** 50
gauze **183** 33; **185** 20
gauze, sterile ~ **22** 58
gauze, wire ~ **350** 18, 19
gauze roll holder **185** 19
G-clef **320** 8
gear *Gdn. Tools* **56** 20
gear *Iron Foundry etc.* **148** 63
gear *Road Constr.* **201** 11
gear *Hydr. Eng.* **217** 48
gear, epicyclic ~ **143** 94
gear, planetary ~ **143** 94
gearbox *Agr. Mach.* **65** 79
gearbox *Turner* **135** 4
gearbox *Cotton Spin.* **164** 2, 33, 39
gearbox, five-speed ~ **189** 6
gear-change *Agr. Mach.* **65** 35
gear-change *Motorcycles etc.* **188** 31
gear-change, floor-type ~ **191** 91
gear-change, two-speed ~ **188** 12
gear-change lever **189** 28
gear-change pattern **192** 47
gear control **149** 2
gearing *Agr. Mach.* **64** 50, 65

gearing *Overh. Irrign.* **67** 21
gearing *Road Constr.* **201** 11
gearing, helical ~ **143** 89
gearing, multi-speed ~ **190** 72
gearing, multi-step ~ **190** 72
gear lever **191** 91; **192** 46
gear meter **76** 4
gears *Agr. Mach.* **64** 50, 65
gears *Overh. Irrign.* **67** 21
gear shaft **232** 58
gear shaft, intermediate ~ **190** 57
gearshift **65** 23, 35; **188** 31
gearshift, two-speed ~ **188** 12
gearshift lever *Motorcycle* **189** 28
gearshift lever *Car* **191** 91; **192** 46
gearshift pattern **192** 47
gearshift rod **192** 41
gearshift switch **134** 46
gear wheel, helical ~ **192** 34, 36, 39, 43
gear wheel, herringbone ~ **143** 87
gear wheel, stepped ~ **143** 82
gear wheels **143** 82-96
gecko **364** 36
Geiger counter **2** 19
Geiger-Müller counter **2** 19
geisha **353** 39
gelatine **316** 49
gelding **73** 2
Gemini **3** 28; **4** 55
general cargo ship **225** 14; **226** 13
general cargo transit shed **225** 9
general practice **22** 1-74
general practitioner **23** 2
general service lamp **127** 56
generator *Nucl. Energy* **154** 15, 47, 53
generator *Energy Sources* **155** 46
generator *Intern. Combust. Eng.* **190** 76
generator *Railw.* **211** 46
generator *Ship* **223** 74
generator exhaust **146** 2
generator unit **231** 33
Geneva movement **312** 38
Genoa jib **284** 16
genouillère **329** 53
gentleman *Café* **265** 22
gentleman *Hist. Cost.* **355** 54, 61, 73
'gentlemen' **233** 47
'gentlemen's toilet' **233** 47
geodesy **14** 46-62
geography, physical ~ **11**; **12**; **13**
geology **12** 1-33
geometrical shape **260** 79
geometrid **80** 16; **82** 28
geometry **346**; **347**
geometry, elementary ~ **346** 1-58
geometry, Euclidian ~ **346** 1-58
geranium **53** 1
gerbera **51** 26
germ **370** 86
German brown trout **364** 15
German hand **342** 11
German pointer **70** 40
German sheepdog **70** 25
German shepherd **70** 25
geyser *Phys. Geog.* **11** 21
geyser *Plumb. etc.* **126** 12-13
G flat major **320** 68
gherkin, pickled ~ **98** 29
ghost train **308** 5

giant **308** 20; **327** 37
giant figure **306** 63
gib *Plumb.* **125** 3
gib *Mach. Parts etc.* **143** 74
gig **186** 34
gig, four-oared ~ **283** 26-33
Gigantocypris agassizi **369** 1
gilder **183** 2
gilding *Painter* **129** 40
gilding *Bookbind.* **183** 1
gilding and embossing press **183** 26
gill *Dom. Anim.* **73** 24
gill *Edib. Fungi* **381** 4, 6
gill, tufted ~ **364** 19
gill cleft **364** 3
gill cover **364** 5
gill slit **364** 3
gillyflower **60** 7
gimbal ring **224** 50
gimbal suspension **241** 23
gimlet **120** 65
gimping **102** 28
gimping needle **102** 29
gingerbread **97** 51
gipsy girl **306** 36
gipsy moth **80** 1
giraffe **367** 4
giraffe house **356** 10
girder, steel ~ **143** 3-7
girdle **32** 5
girdle clasp **328** 24
girl, exotic ~ **306** 30
girt **120** 50
girth **71** 18, 36; **289** 11
girth, emergency ~ **71** 23
girth, second ~ **71** 23
glacier *Phys. Geog.* **12** 49
glacier *Mountain.* **300** 22
glacier snout **12** 51
glacier table **12** 56
gladiolus **51** 28; **60** 11
gland, bulbourethral ~ **20** 75
gland, parotid ~ **19** 9
gland, pituitary ~ **17** 43
gland, prostate ~ **20** 76
gland, submandibular ~ **19** 11
gland, submaxillary ~ **19** 11
gland, suprarenal ~ **20** 29
gland, thyroid ~ **20** 1
glans penis **20** 69
glass **54** 9
glass, armoured ~ **109** 29
glass, bullet-proof ~ **250** 3
glass, coloured ~ **260** 68
glass, crystal ~ **45** 86
glass, frosted ~ **124** 5
glass, laminated ~ **124** 5
glass, lined ~ **124** 6
glass, molten ~ **162** 23, 31, 50
glass, ornamental ~ **124** 6
glass, patterned ~ **124** 5
glass, pulverized ~ **340** 48
glass, raw ~ **206** 6
glass, shatterproof ~ **124** 5
glass, stained ~ **124** 6; **330** 15
glass, tapered ~ **45** 85
glass, thick ~ **124** 5
glass, wired ~ **124** 6
glassblower **162** 38
glassblowing **162** 38-47
glass case **356** 15
glass cloth **130** 29
glass cutter, diamond ~ **124** 25
glass cutter, steel ~ **124** 26
glass cutters **124** 25-26
glass-drawing machine **162** 8
glasses **111** 9
glass fibre, production of ~ **162** 48-55
glass fibre products **162** 56-58
glass filament **162** 52
glass forming **162** 38-47

glass furnace **162** 1, 49
glass holder **124** 9
glasshouse pot, covered ~ **162** 46
glassmaker **162** 38
glassmaking **162** 38-47
glass mosaic picture **260** 69
glass paper **135** 25
glass pliers **124** 19
glass ribbon **162** 10
glass sponge **369** 7
glass wool **162** 58
glassworker **124** 8
glazier **124**; **124** 8
glazing sheet **116** 58
glazing sprig **124** 24
glede **362** 11
glider **287** 3
glider, high-performance ~ **287** 9
glider, motorized ~ **287** 8
glider, powered ~ **287** 8
glider field **287** 13
gliding **287**
globe **42** 13
globe, frosted glass ~ **267** 4
globe, solar ~ **4** 36
globe, terrestrial ~ **4** 8
globe artichoke **57** 41
globe lamp **267** 4
globe thistle **53** 14
glove **33** 67; **292** 12; **298** 47; **318** 31
glove, catcher's ~ **292** 60
glove, fielder's ~ **292** 59
glove, goalkeeper's ~ **291** 19
glove box lock **191** 89
glove compartment lock **191** 89
glove stand **271** 20
glow plug **190** 66
gloxinia **53** 7
glue **48** 4; **260** 50-52, 51
glue, joiner's ~ **132** 13
glue cylinder **184** 10
glue-enamel plate **179** 32
glue pot **132** 12, 13; **183** 15; **236** 5; **260** 57
glue roller **184** 10; **185** 33
glue size **128** 4
glue tank **184** 9; **185** 32
glue well **132** 13
gluing **183** 14
gluing cylinder **184** 10
gluing machine **185** 31
gluing mechanism **184** 4
glume **68** 11
gluteus maximus **18** 60
G major **320** 56
G minor **320** 64
gnat **358** 16
goaf **144** 37
goal *Playground* **273** 11
goal *Ball Games* **282** 46
goal *Ball Games* **291** 35; **292** 7
goal *Winter Sp.* **302** 37
goal area **291** 5
goalkeeper *Playground* **273** 14
goalkeeper *Swim.* **282** 47
goalkeeper *Ball Games* **291** 10; **292** 8
goalkeeper *Winter Sp.* **302** 36
goal kick **291** 38
goal line **291** 7
goalpost **273** 11; **291** 37
goal scorer **273** 13
Goat *Astron.* **3** 36; **4** 62
goatee beard **34** 10
goat's beard *Forest Plants etc.* **377** 5
goatsbeard *Forest Plants etc.* **377** 5

goat's beard *Edib. Fungi* **381** 32
goatsbeard *Edib. Fungi* **381** 32
goat willow **371** 24
gob *Coal* **144** 37
gob *Glass Prod.* **162** 40
gobbler **73** 28
goblet, hand-blown ~ **162** 41
gobo **310** 51
gob of molten glass **162** 23, 31
go-cart **273** 33
god, Indian ~ **337** 19
godet **30** 52
Godet wheel **169** 16
godparent **332** 13
God's acre **331** 21-41
'GO' gauging member **149** 57
goggles **140** 21; **303** 15
going about **285** 27
go-kart **305** 83
go-karting **305** 82
gold *Heraldry* **254** 24
gold *Crystals* **351** 6
gold and silver balance **108** 35
goldcrest **361** 10
goldcup **375** 8
gold cushion **183** 6
golden chain **374** 32
golden crested wren **361** 10
golden maidenhair **377** 17
golden oriole **360** 7
golden rain **374** 32
goldfinch **360** 1
gold finisher **183** 2
gold knife **183** 7
gold leaf **129** 45, 52; **183** 5
gold size **129** 44
goldsmith **108** 17
golf **293** 79-93
golf ball *Office* **249** 15
golf ball *Ball Games* **293** 89
golf ball cap **249** 30
golf ball typewriter **249** 1
golf course **293** 79-82
golfer **293** 83
golf trolley **293** 85
gondola *Supermkt.* **99** 23, 43, 62
gondola *Railw.* **214** 20
gondola *Airsports* **288** 64
gondola cableway **214** 19
gonfalon **253** 12
gong **299** 46
goods **271** 10
goods, bulky ~ **206** 18
goods, general ~ **206** 4
goods depot **15** 91
goods lorry **206** 15
goods office **206** 26
goods shed **206** 7, 26-39
goods shed door **206** 37
goods shelf **47** 36; **98** 14
goods station **206**
goods van **206** 6; **213** 22
goods van, covered ~ **213** 14
goods wagon, covered ~ **213** 14
goods wagon, open ~ **213** 8
goosander **359** 15
goose **73** 34; **272** 52
gooseberry **58** 9
gooseberry bush **52** 19; **58** 1
gooseberry cane, flowering ~ **58** 2
gooseberry flan **97** 22
gooseberry flower **58** 6
goosefoot **61** 25
gooseneck **284** 37
gorge **13** 52
gorgerin **334** 22
gorget **329** 43
gorilla **368** 16
goshawk **362** 10

'GO' side **149** 60
gosling **73** 34
gouache **338** 17
gouge **132** 9; **135** 15; **339** 17
gouge, U-shaped ~ **340** 6
gouge, V-shaped ~ **339** 20; **340** 9
gourd **354** 27
governor **224** 56
gown **105** 34; **106** 4; **355** 25, 36, 66
gown, linen ~ **355** 5
gown, open ~ **355** 50
gown, sleeveless ~ **355** 50
graben **12** 11
grace notes **321** 14-22
graces **321** 14-22
grade crossing, protected ~ **202** 39
grade crossing, unprotected ~ **202** 49
grade crossings **202** 39-50
grader **200** 19
grader levelling blade **200** 21
grader ploughshare **200** 21
gradient **347** 12
grading **74** 44
grading, automatic ~ **74** 52
graduated measuring rod **14** 47
graduation house *Map* **15** 32
graduation house *Spa* **274** 1
graftage **54** 30-39
grafting **54** 30-39
grain *Arable Crops* **68** 1-37, 4, 37
grain *Brew.* **92** 50
grain *Graphic Art* **340** 47
grain, farinaceous ~ **68** 13
grain auger **64** 20
grain harvest **63** 31-41
grain leaf **68** 8, 19
grain lifter **64** 2
grain pest **81** 27
grain tank **64** 23
grain tank auger **64** 24
grain tank unloader **64** 25
grain unloader spout **64** 26
grain weevil **81** 16
grammar school **261** 1-45
gramophone **309** 31
gramophone box **309** 35
gramophone needle **309** 33
gramophone record **309** 32
granary weevil **81** 16
grand **325** 40
grandee **306** 26
grandfather clock **110** 24; **309** 56
grand piano **325** 40
grand piano pedal **325** 41
grandstand, glass-covered ~ **289** 34
granite **302** 42
gran turismo car **193** 32
granular texture **340** 47
grape **80** 21; **99** 89
grape-berry moth **80** 22, 23, 24
grape crusher **78** 17
grapefruit **384** 23
grape gatherer **78** 11
grape phylloxera **80** 26
grapevine *Wine Grow.* **78** 2-9
grapevine *Sports* **299** 10
grape worm **80** 23, 24
graphic art **340**
graphic art studio **340** 27-64
graphite **1** 54
grapnel **218** 11
grapple **218** 11
grappling iron **218** 11
grasp, kinds of ~ **296** 40-46

grasping arm 2 47
grass 136 26
grass, paniculate ~ 69 27
grassbox 56 29
grasshopper, artificial ~ 89 68
grassland 15 18
grassland, marshy ~ 15 19
grassland, rough ~ 15 5
grass ledge 300 4
grass shears 56 48
grass snake 364 38
grasstrack racing 290 24-28
grass verge 200 56
grate 199 33
graticule Map 14 1-7
graticule Hunt. 87 31-32
graticule Photomech. Reprod. 177 4
graticule adjuster screw 87 30
graticule system 87 31
grating 141 14
grating spectrograph 5 5
graupel 9 35
grave Church 331 23, 34
grave Script 342 31
grave, child's ~ 331 29
grave, soldier's ~ 331 32
grave digger 331 22
gravel 118 36; 119 26
gravel filter layer 199 23
grave mound 331 24
graver 175 33; 340 5
graver, round-headed ~ 340 20
gravestone 331 26
graveyard 331 21-41
graveyard chapel 331 28
graveyard gate 331 19
graveyard wall 331 18
gravity fault 12 7
gravity fuelling point 257 32
gravity hammer, air-lift ~ 139 24
gravity mixer 118 33
gravure cylinder 182 10
gravure cylinder, etched ~ 182 22
gravure cylinder, printed ~ 182 17
gravure etcher 182 18
gravure printing 182
gravy boat 45 17
gravy ladle 45 18
gray see grey
grayhound 70 24
grease gun 195 30
grease nipple 143 81
greasepaint stick 315 46
greasy chalk 340 26
great apes 368 14-16
Great Bear 3 29
great brain 17 42; 18 22
Great Dane 70 14
Great Dog 3 14
Greater Bear 3 29
greater burnet saxifrage 69 28
Greater Dog 3 14
greater water newt 364 20
great hall 329 30
great horned owl 362 15
great mullein 376 9
great organ 326 1, 43
great primer 175 30
great tit 361 9
great titmouse 361 9
greave 329 54
Greek 355 3
Greek woman 355 1
green Ball Games 293 82
green Colour 343 8
green bowls 305 21
green cloth 277 15
green cormorant 359 10

greenfly 358 13
greengage 59 24
green grasshopper 358 8
greenhouse, heated ~ 55 32
greenhouse, polythene ~ 55 40
greenhouse, unheated ~ 55 33
green liquor, uncleared ~ 172 41
green liquor preheater 172 43
green locust 358 8
green oak roller moth 82 43
green oak tortrix 82 43
green plover 359 21
Greenwich meridian 14 5
grenzanhydrite 154 67
Gretchen style 34 31
greyhound 70 24
grey scale 343 15
grey sea eagle 362 5
grid Cotton Spin. 163 26
grid Water 269 11
grid Theatre 316 4
grid hearth 139 1
gridiron 316 4
griffin 327 11
grill Painter 129 12
grill Station 204 38
grill Fair 308 33
grinder Painter 129 29
grinder Metalwkr. 140 18
grinder, continuous ~ 172 53, 66
grinder, pneumatic ~ 148 44
grinder chuck 157 46
grinding, hollow ~ 302 22
grinding cylinder 161 1
grinding disc 340 46
grinding machine 140 18
grinding machine, universal ~ 150 1
grinding machine bed 150 6
grinding machine table 150 7
grinding-roller bearing 163 41
grinding stone Paperm. 172 71
grinding stone Ethnol. 354 24
grinding wheel Dent. 24 36
grinding wheel D.I.Y. 134 23
grinding wheel Blacksm. 137 19; 138 8
grinding wheel Metalwkr. 140 19
grinding wheel Mach. Tools 150 4
grinding wheel Sawmill 157 43
grindstone 172 71
grip Photog. 114 37
grip Cine Film 117 61
grip Bicycle 187 3
grip Navig. 224 9
grip Rowing 283 35
grip Athletics 298 45
grip Winter Sp. 301 6
grip Sports 305 57
grip Films 313 21
gripper 180 65
gripper bar 180 56
gripping jaw 149 36
grip sole 101 19
grist 92 42
grit guard 148 40
gritter, self-propelled ~ 200 41
grocer 98 41
grocer's shop 98 1-87
groceryman 98 41
grocery store 98 1-87
groin 16 38
groin see groyne
groin vault 335 31-32; 336 42

groom Carriages 186 27
groom Church 332 16
groove Iron Foundry etc. 148 59
groove Sawmill 157 6
groove Ball Games 291 29
groove Winter Sp. 301 39
groove Music. Instr. 326 13
groove Art 334 27
groove, anal ~ 16 41
grooving 157 6
groschen 252 13
Grotesque 342 7
grotto 272 1
ground 123 9
ground, fallow ~ 63 1
ground, icy ~ 304 19
ground avalanche 304 1
ground control 6 44
ground floor 37 2; 118 7
ground-floor landing 123 23
ground game 86 35
ground ivy 375 18
ground layer 7 7
ground nut 383 41
ground-nut oil 98 24
ground power unit 233 22
groundsheet ring 278 26
ground signals 288 52-54
ground state level 1 18
ground tackle 223 49-51
groundwater 12 21
groundwater level 269 1, 42, 63
groundwater stream 269 3
groundwood 172 68
groundwood mill 172 53-65
groundwood pulp 172 77, 78
group 260 3; 268 60
group instruction 242 1
group selector switch 238 42
grove 354 5
grower 55 20
grower, commercial ~ 55 20
growing stock 74 1
growler 186 26
growth, annual ~ 372 25
groyne Phys. Geog. 13 37
groyne Rivers 216 19
groyne head Phys. Geog. 13 38
groyne head Rivers 216 20
grub 58 64; 77 29; 81 20; 358 9; 80 6, 19, 36, 41, 46, 53, 54; 82 25, 36
grubber 55 21; 65 55
grub screw 143 48
Grus 3 42
G sharp minor 320 60
GT car 193 32
guanaco 366 30
guard Metalwkr. 140 20
guard Fencing 294 35, 38, 43
guard, king's ~ 306 68
guard, protective ~ 168 45
guard board 118 29
guard cam 167 57
guard for V-belt 180 58
guard iron 210 34
guard netting 118 90
guard rail Roof & Boilerr. 38 28
guard rail Agr. Mach. 64 55
guard rail Forestry 84 8
guard rail Floor etc. Constr. 123 53
guard rail Weaving 165 31
guard rail Railw. 202 23
guard rail Ship 221 121
guard rail Shipbuild. 222 66
gudgeon pin 192 26
guelder rose 373 10

guest rope 227 14
gugelhupf 97 33
guide 23 21
guide, stationary ~ 243 21
guide bar Cotton Spin. 164 17
guide bar Weaving 165 38
guide bearing 113 14
guide block 174 48; 176 18
guide chain 65 13
guide-chain crossbar 65 12
guide dog 70 25
guide groove 217 75
guide notch 117 36
guide pin 243 21
guide post 15 110
guide rail Weaving 165 3
guide rail Railw. 214 56
guide rail Store 271 54
guide roller Cotton Spin. 157 5
guide roller Cotton Spin. 164 18
guide roller Films 312 29
guide step 117 36
guide tractor 141 19
guiding blade 322 40
guiding roller 312 29
guiding slot Weaving 165 11
guiding slot Music. Instr. 322 41
guilder 252 19
guillemet 342 27
guillemot 359 13
guillotine Plumb. 125 26
guillotine Bookbind. 183 16; 185 1
guillotine cutter, automatic ~ 185 1
guinea fowl 73 27
guinea pig 366 12
guiro 324 60
guitar 318 8; 324 12, 73
guitarist 318 9
guitar player 318 9
gulden 252 19
gules 254 27
Gulf Stream 14 30
gull 359 14
gullet Man 17 49; 20 23, 40
gullet Bees 77 19
gullet Forestry 84 28
gull wing, inverted ~ 229 14
gully 12 44
gum 19 15
gun 218 50
gun, pneumatic ~ 94 3
gun, self-cocking ~ 87 23
gun, self-propelled ~ 255 57
gun barrel, rifled ~ 87 34
gun carriage 255 43
gun carriage, self-propelled ~ 255 49-74
gun dog 86 7
gunnel 283 30
gunport 218 59
gunport shutter 218 60
gun slit 86 52
gun turret 258 29
gunwale 283 30
gutta-percha tree 383 37
gutter Dwellings 37 6, 11
gutter Roof & Boilerr. 38 9
gutter Roof 122 28, 92
gutter Bookbind. 185 55
gutter Street Sect. 198 10
gutter, parallel ~ 122 83
gutter bracket 122 32
guy Wine Grow. 78 8
guy Camping 278 23
guy line 278 23
guy pole 152 31
guy wire Wine Grow. 78 8
guy wire Energy Sources 155 44

gybe **285** 28
gybing **285** 26
gymkhana **290** 32
gymnastic ball **297** 34
gymnastic club **297** 38
gymnastic hoop **297** 46
gymnastic ribbon **297** 49
gymnastics **297** 33-50
gymnastics, men's ~ **296** 1-11
gymnastics, Olympic ~ **296**
   1-11; **297** 1-6
gymnastics, women's ~ **297**
gymnastics apparatus **296**
   1-11; **297** 1-6
gymnastics kit **296** 61-63; **297**
   51-52
gym shoe **296** 63; **297** 52
gym trousers **296** 62
gypsum *Sculpt. Studio* **339** 29
gypsum *Crystals* **351** 24, 25
gypsum crusher **160** 14
gypsum powder **339** 29
gypsum store **160** 13
gyro compass **224** 31, 51-53
gyro compass unit **224** 51-53
gyrodyne **232** 29
gyro horizon **230** 3
gyro repeater **224** 52

H

habergeon **329** 51
habit **382** 53
habit, monk's ~ **331** 55
hack **186** 26
hacking knife **128** 37
hackney carriage **186** 26
hackney coach **186** 26
hacksaw **134** 3, 17; **136** 40;
   138 23; **140** 9; **150** 14
hacksaw frame **126** 71
haematite **108** 48
haft **137** 30
hail **9** 36
hail, soft ~ **9** 35
hair **16** 3
hair, bobbed ~ **34** 34
hair, closely-cropped ~ **34** 11
hair, curled ~ **34** 33
hair, curly ~ **34** 18
hair, long ~ **34** 1
hair, pinned-up ~ **34** 28
hair, shingled ~ **34** 34
hair, swept-back ~ **34** 28
hair, swept-up ~ **34** 28
hairbell **375** 14
hairbrush **28** 7; **105** 10
haircap moss **377** 17
hair clip **105** 11
hair curler **106** 31
haircut **106** 3
haircuts **34** 1-25
haircutting scissors **105** 7; **106**
   34
hair decoration **355** 82
hairdress **354** 9
hairdresser **105** 35; **106** 1
'hairdresser' *Airport* **233** 53
hairdresser, ladies' ~ **105**
hairdresser, men's ~ **106**
hairdresser's tools **105** 1-16
hairdressing salon, ladies' ~
   105 1-39
hairdressing salon, men's ~
   106 1-42
hair drier, hand-held ~ **105**
   33; **106** 22
hair element **10** 9
hair-fixing spray **105** 24
hair moss **377** 17
hairpin *Needlewk.* **102** 29

hairpin *Winter Sp.* **301** 69
hairpin work **102** 28
hair sieve **260** 66
hair spray **105** 24
hairstyle **106** 3
hairstyles **34** 1-25
hairstyles, girls' ~ **34** 27-38
hairstyles, ladies' ~ **34** 27-38
hairstylist **310** 36; **315** 48
hair tonic **106** 10
hair trigger **87** 12
hairworm **80** 51
hake **65** 19
hake chain **65** 17
half-barrier crossing **202** 45
half chicken **266** 56
half mask **306** 13
half-moon **4** 4, 6
half nonpareil **175** 20
half note **320** 14
half nut **149** 19
half rest **320** 22
half-step **320** 50, 52
half-title **185** 43, 44
halftone dot **178** 39
half-way line **291** 3
hall **41** 1-29
hall, main ~ **236** 1-30; **250**
   1-11
halliard **253** 2
hall manager **275** 7
hall mirror **41** 6
hall of mirrors **308** 55
Hallstatt period **328** 21-40
hallux **19** 52
halma **276** 26-28
halma board **276** 26
halma man **276** 28
halma piece **276** 28
halogen lamp **177** 31
halothane container **26** 26
halt **15** 27
halter **71** 7-11
halter top **31** 64
halved joint **121** 86
halving joint **121** 86
halyard **253** 2
ham **95** 51
hame **71** 14
hammer **85** 5; **126** 78; **134** 7;
   137 26; **139** 26
hammer *Army* **255** 4
hammer *Athletics* **298** 42
hammer *Music. Instr.* **322** 35;
   325 3
hammer *Graphic Art* **340** 14
hammer, anvil and stirrup **17**
   61
hammer, bricklayer's ~ **118**
   53
hammer, brickmason's ~ **118**
   53
hammer, carpenter's ~ **120** 74
hammer, flat-face ~ **137** 35
hammer, glazier's ~ **124** 18
hammer, iron-headed ~ **339**
   16
hammer, machinist's ~ *D.I.Y.*
   134 40
hammer, machinist's ~
   Metalwkr. **140** 23
hammer, shoemaker's ~ **100**
   37
hammer, stonemason's ~ **158**
   35
Hammer and Sickle **253** 21
hammer axe **300** 37
hammer blow **293** 78
hammer crusher *Quarry* **158**
   20
hammer crusher *Cement
   Wks.* **160** 2
hammer cylinder **139** 30

hammer drill **158** 11
hammer drill, electric ~ **134**
   43
hammer forging **139**
hammer guide **139** 29
hammer head *Airsports* **288** 4
hammer head *Athletics* **298**
   43
hammer head, felt-covered ~
   325 24
hammer jack **325** 30
hammer lever **325** 30
hammer mill **160** 2
hammer rail **325** 15, 26
hammer shank **325** 25
hammer throw **298** 42-47
hammock **278** 4
ham on the bone **96** 1; **99** 52
hamper **306** 11
hamster **366** 16
hand **16** 47, 48; **17** 15-17; **19**
   64-83
hand apparatus **297** 33-50
hand axe **328** 1
handball **292** 1
handball player **292** 2
hand bindery **183** 1-38
handbook **262** 17
hand bookbindery **183** 1-38
hand brace **140** 13
hand brake **187** 5; **191** 72; **212**
   33
hand brake lever **188** 33; **191**
   93
hand brake wheel **212** 64, 80
hand camera, large-format ~
   114 36
handcart **120** 6
handcart, wooden ~ **309** 86
hand circle **297** 47
hand circling **297** 37
handclap **117** 69
hand-composing room **174** 1
hand compositor **174** 5
hand control **195** 8
hand cream **99** 27
hand cultivator **55** 21
hand die **126** 85
hand die, electric ~ **125** 12
hand drill **140** 13
hand flat knitting machine
   167 35
hand gallop **72** 42
hand glass *Hairdresser* **105**
   23; **106** 7
hand glass *Opticn.* **111** 16
handgrip *Photog.* **114** 37
handgrip *Cine Film* **117** 5, 61
handgrip *Bicycle* **187** 3
handgrip *Navig.* **224** 9
handgrip *Films* **313** 21, 24, 38
hand guard **94** 10
hand hair drier **105** 33; **106** 22
hand hammer, blacksmith's ~
   137 23
hand harpoon **280** 40
handicraft **48** 3
hand-ironing pad **104** 30
hand-iron press **103** 18
handkerchief **33** 10
hand ladle **148** 23
hand lamp **270** 42
hand lance **83** 46
handle *Atom* **2** 39
handle *Hosp.* **26** 12
handle *Infant Care etc.* **28** 50
handle *Tablew. etc.* **45** 51, 59,
   62
handle *Household* **50** 9, 63
handle *Market Gdn.* **55** 27
handle *Agr. Mach.* **65** 2
handle *Agr. Impl.* **66** 17
handle *Pest Contr.* **83** 19

handle *Forestry* **85** 3
handle *Hairdresser* **106** 37
handle *Joiner* **132** 10, 18
handle *D.I.Y.* **134** 47
handle *Metalwkr.* **140** 5
handle *Carriages* **186** 12
handle *School* **260** 8
handle *Motorboats etc.* **286** 48
handle *Fencing* **294** 41
handle *Athletics* **298** 44
handle *Sports* **305** 57, 80
handle, bound ~ **89** 55
handle, cork ~ **89** 50
handle, double ~ **148** 15
handle, fixed ~ **129** 7
handle, insulated ~ **127** 54
handle, tubular ~ **50** 64
hand lead **224** 58
handlebar **187** 2; **188** 45
handlebar, adjustable ~ **188** 3
handlebar, semi-rise ~ **188** 11
handlebar fittings **188** 30-35
handlebar grip **187** 3
handlebar moustache **34** 8
handlebars **34** 8
handlebar stem **187** 10
hand lever *Joiner* **132** 55
hand lever *Bookbind.* **183** 31
hand-lever press **183** 26
hand luggage **194** 19
hand mirror *Hairdresser* **105**
   23; **106** 7
hand mirror *Opticn.* **111** 16
hand net **89** 2
handpiece **24** 6
hand press **340** 29
hand pump **83** 26; **269** 66
hand puppet **260** 74
handrail *Roof & Boilerr.* **38**
   28
handrail *Hall* **41** 23
handrail *Floor etc. Constr.*
   123 53, 79
handrail *Ship* **221** 122
handrailing **215** 70
hand rammer **148** 32
hand-removing tool **109** 10
handrest **112** 58
hand sail **302** 28
hand saw **120** 60; **126** 72; **134**
   27
handscrew **132** 14
handset **237** 7; **245** 15
handset cord **237** 14
handset cradle **237** 13
hand-setting room **174** 1
hand shank **148** 14
hand shears *Tailor* **104** 11
hand shears *Bldg. Site* **119** 87
hand signal **268** 33
handsledge **304** 29
hand spray *Pest Contr.* **83** 24
hand spray *Hairdresser* **105**
   30; **106** 13
hand spray *Painter* **129** 35
hand spray *Offset Platem.*
   179 7
handspring **297** 22
handstamp **236** 45
handstand **295** 27; **296** 52
handstand dive **282** 45
hand steel shears **119** 22
handstrap, leather ~ **296** 47
hand-to-hand throw **297** 33
hand towel **28** 9; **49** 23; **106**
   24
hand vice **140** 24
hand weapons **255** 1-39
handwheel *Shoem.* **100** 24
handwheel *Cooper* **130** 19
handwheel *Cotton Spin.* **163**
   18
handwheel *Knitting* **167** 7, 30

handwheel *Paperm.* 172 74
handwheel *Bookbind.* 183 23
handwheel *Road Constr.* 201 9
handwriting, English ~ 342 10
handwriting, German ~ 342 11
hang 296 33, 35; 298 41
hangar 287 14
hanger 215 41
hang glider 287 44
hang glider pilot 287 45
hang gliding 287 43
Hansa cog 218 18-26
Hansa ship 218 18-26
hansom 186 29
hansom cab 186 29
harbour 216 14; 225; 226
harbour ferry 225 11
harbour tunnel 225 55
hardboard 338 22
hardcore 123 12
hardener 130 33
hardie 137 32
hard-rock drill 158 11
hard-top 193 26
hardwood cutting 54 25
hardy 137 32
hare 86 35; 88 59
hare-and-hounds 289 41-49
harebell 375 14
hare call 87 44
hare hunting 86 34-39
harlequin 306 35
harmonica 324 35
harmonium 325 43
harmonium case 325 47
harmonium keyboard 325 48
harness *Horse* 71 7-25
harness *Airsports* 288 43
harness horse racing 289 23-40
harness of diving apparatus 279 12
harness racing 289 23-40
harness racing track 289 23
harp 323 60
harpoon 353 10
harpoon, bone ~ 328 3
harpoon thrower 328 5
harpsichord 322 45
harpsichord mechanism 322 48
harpy 254 35; 327 55
harrow, disc ~ 65 82
harrow, rotary ~ 65 89
harrow, spike-tooth ~ 65 88
harrow, three-section ~ 65 88, 89
hasp 71 14
hat 35 9
hat, Alpine ~ 35 23
hat, carpenter's ~ 120 13
hat, felt ~ 35 15, 24; 355 55
hat, fox ~ 35 19
hat, hard ~ 289 18
hat, huntsman's ~ 86 5
hat, iron ~ 329 59
hat, knitted ~ 35 10
hat, ladies' ~ 41 11
hat, lightweight ~ 35 37
hat, loden ~ 35 23
hat, men's ~ 35 13
hat, mink ~ 35 18
hat, mohair ~ 35 6, 11
hat, paper ~ 306 45
hat, picador's ~ 319 20
hat, sailor's ~ 309 63
hat, Thessalonian ~ 355 4
hat, three-cornered ~ 355 62
hat, trilby-style ~ 35 14
hat, Tyrolean ~ 35 24

hat, wide-brimmed ~ 35 38; 355 55
hat, woollen ~ 29 57; 35 10, 26
hat and light luggage rack 208 28
hat box 205 11
hatch *Roof & Boilerr.* 38 14
hatch *Roof* 122 24
hatch *Post* 236 30
hatchback 193 18
hatchboard 222 65
hatch coaming 222 64
hatch cover 222 65
hatcher 74 30
hatchery 89 11-19
hatchet 270 43
hatchet iron 125 5
hatching compartment 74 30
hatching jar 89 17
hatching tray 74 31, 32
hatchment 254 1-6
hatch platform 6 34
hatchway 222 64-65
hatchway, main ~ 259 86
H atom 1 26
hat peg 266 13
hats, ladies' ~ 35 1-21
hats, men's ~ 35 22-40
hat shop 268 38
hatter's shop 268 38
haubergeon 329 51
haulage *Forestry* 85 42
haulage *Rivers* 216 27
haulage cable *Railw.* 214 14, 26, 37, 42, 45
haulage cable *Winter Sp.* 301 63
haulage cable driving pulley 214 62
haulage cable guide wheel 214 61
haulage cable roller 214 32, 49, 60
haulage cable sleeve 214 73
hauling 216 27
hauling capstan 217 22
haulm conveyor 64 76
haulm conveyor agitator 64 77
haulm conveyor drive 64 78
haulm elevator 64 90
haulm stripper 64 73
haulm stripper, flexible ~ 64 76
haulyard 253 2
haunch *Horse* 72 35
haunch *Game* 88 21, 37
haunch jump 282 14
Hauptwerk 326 1
hautboy 323 38
haute école 71 1-6
Havana cigar 107 2
Hawaii girl 306 16
hawk, male ~ 86 46
hawkbells 276 45
hawker 308 12, 51
hawking 86 42-46
hawkmoth 82 27; 358 55; 365 9
hawksbill turtle 364 28
hawse 222 75
hawse hole 227 11
hawse pipe 222 76; 258 54
hawthorn 374 30
hay 75 13
hay, tedded ~ 63 25
hay fork, three-pronged ~ 66 3
hay harvest 63 19-30
haymaking 63 19-30
hay rack, double ~ 75 12
hayrake 66 23
hay tripod 63 30

hazard flasher 191 76
hazard flasher switch 191 68
hazel 59 49
hazel branch, flowering ~ 59 44
hazel bush 59 44-51
hazel grouse 88 69
hazel hen 88 69
hazel leaf 59 51
hazelnut 59 49
hazel tree 59 44-51
H-beam 143 6
head *Man* 16 1-18; 17 42-55
head *Arable Crops* 68 2
head *Horse* 72 1-11
head *House Insects etc.* 81 33, 36
head *Forest Pests* 82 2
head *Game* 88 12
head *Brew.* 93 31
head *Tobacc. etc.* 107 23
head *Carp.* 120 58
head *Roof* 122 87
head *Mach. Parts etc.* 143 14, 52
head *Weaves* 171 31
head *Composing Rm.* 175 39
head *Hydr. Eng.* 217 25
head *Restaurant* 266 4
head *Music. Instr.* 323 52; 324 10
head *Prehist.* 328 4
head *Articulates* 358 28
head, bald ~ 34 22
head, binocular ~ 112 12
head, cock's ~ 327 35
head, combined ~ 241 59
head, composite ~ 370 74
head, countersunk ~ 143 46
head, eagle's ~ 327 12
head, goat's ~ 327 18
head, human ~ 327 21
head, lion's ~ 327 17
head, partly bald ~ 34 20
head, pig's ~ 95 43
head, rotating ~ 64 52
head, shrunken ~ 352 30
head, woman's ~ 327 56
head and neck 19 1-13
head badge 187 15
headband 183 35
headband, padded ~ 241 67; 261 41
head bandage 21 3
head beam 183 21
headboard *Bedrm.* 43 6
headboard *Sailing* 284 47
headbox 173 11
head cellarman 79 17
headcheese 96 9
headdress 354 9; 355 65
headdress, feather ~ 352 12
headdress, ornamental ~ 352 12
head drum 243 19, 27
header *Carp.* 120 41
header *Roof* 121 71
header *Ball Games* 291 46
header joist 120 41
header tank 212 78
head frame 144 3
headgear 35; 144 1; 302 34
headguard 299 30
heading 130 10
heading bond 118 60
heading course 118 64
head interlocking point 171 34
headlamp 187 7; 189 10; 191 20
headlight 189 10; 191 20
head line *Man* 19 73
headline *Sea Fish.* 90 7

headline *Script* 342 44
head margin 185 56
head of department 271 60
head of railcar 197 3
headphone cable 241 71
headphone cable plug 241 70
headphone cord 241 71
headphones 241 66; 249 63; 261 38; 309 24
headphone socket 117 10; 249 68
headpiece 71 7-11
head piece 183 21
headpiece, padded ~ 241 67; 261 41
head post 123 54
headrace 91 41
head rail 120 58
headrest *First Aid* 21 13
headrest *Railw.* 207 67
headrest, adjustable ~ 191 33; 207 47
headrest, integral ~ 193 31
headrest cushion, down-filled ~ 207 68
head restraint, adjustable ~ 191 33
head restraint, integral ~ 193 31
head rule 342 40
headset 241 66; 249 63; 261 38; 309 24
headset socket 249 68
headspring 297 27
headstall 71 7-11
headstand 295 28
headstock 150 2
headstock, geared ~ 149 2
headstock, movable ~ 150 26
headstone 331 26
head support assembly 311 25
heald, wire ~ 166 27
heald eyelet 166 28
heald frame 166 4
heald frame guide 166 3
heald shaft 166 4
heald shaft guide 166 3
heald shaft guiding wheel 166 36
health insurance certificate 22 9
heap cloud 8 1, 2, 17; 287 22
heart 18 14; 20 8, 24-25, 45-57
heart cherry 59 5
hearth *Blacksm.* 137 1-8, 1; 138 34
hearth *Iron & Steel* 147 24
heart line 19 74
heart plank 120 93
heart rhythm 25 1
hearts 276 40, 44
heartsease pansy 60 2
heart-shield 254 17
heartwood *Carp.* 120 84
heartwood *Bot.* 370 13
heartwood plank 120 93
heat 1 55
heat colour 343 16
heater 172 32
heater, electric ~ 174 45; 179 3
heater, gas ~ 126 25
heater, water-controlled ~ 192 60-64
heater box 192 61
heater plug 190 55
heat exchanger *Nucl. Energy* 154 6, 44
heat exchanger *Coking* 156 27
heat exchanger *Cement Wks.* 160 4, 6
heat exchanger *Paperm.* 172 19

heat exchanger *Car* 192 61
heat exchanger *Railw.* 207 6;
  209 15; 212 36, 55
heat exchanger *Warships* 259
  66
heat exchanger, auxiliary ~
  212 43
heat exchanger exhaust 160 7
heat extractor 182 5
heath 15 5
heath and moor 15 5
heather 377 19
heating, underfloor ~ 356 18
heating box 183 27
heating coupling hose 208 20
heating element 172 32
heating engineer 126
heating oil 38 50
heating oil tank 212 75
heating pipe 55 8
heating regulator 207 54
heating system 207 6
heating system, hot-water ~
  38 38-81
heating unit, electric ~ 174 45
heat pump 155 22
heat pump system 155 1
heat reservoir 155 20
heat-sealing machine 76 27;
  226 12
heat shield *Motorcycles etc.*
  188 16
heat shield *Space* 234 5, 20;
  235 8, 40
heat space 259 93
heat transfer fluid 155 31
heaume 254 7
Heaviside-Kennelly Layer 7
  27
heavy-duty boot 101 39
heavy liquor pump 172 34
heavy vehicle elevator 221 56
heavy vehicle lift 221 56
heckelphone 323 38
heckler 263 15
heddle, wire ~ 166 27
heddle eyelet 166 28
hedge *Map* 15 98
hedge *Dwellings* 37 59
hedge *Fruit & Veg. Gdn.* 52 32
hedge, trimmed ~ 272 37
hedgehog 366 5
hedgehog fungus 381 31
hedge mustard 61 16
hedge shears 56 49
hedge trimmer 134 55
hedge trimmer, battery-
  operated ~ 56 17
hedge-trimming attachment
  134 55
heel *Man* 19 63
heel *Agr. Impl.* 66 15
heel *Bakery* 97 5
heel *Shoem.* 100 67
heel, high ~ 101 28
heel, raised ~ 101 33
heelbone 17 27
heel flap 286 58
heel trimmer 100 4
heel unit, automatic ~ 301 54
height adjuster 106 17
height-adjuster bar 106 17
height adjustment *Hosp.* 27 3
height adjustment *Photog.*
  116 34
height adjustment *Sawmill*
  157 49
height adjustment crank 64
  57
height adjustment wheel 132
  60
height and angle adjustment
  177 21

height gauge 22 69
height of shank 175 45
height of shoulder 175 45
height scale *Sawmill* 157 60
height scale *Athletics* 298 20
height to paper 175 44
helicon 323 44
helicopter deck 146 7
helicopter hangar 221 52; 259
  38
helicopter landing deck 228
  15
helicopter landing platform
  259 39, 53
helicopter platform 221 19
helicopters 232 11-25
heliostat 5 29
heliozoan 357 7
heliport 146 7
heliport deck 146 7
helium atom (model) 1 5
helium-neon laser 243 57
helium nucleus 1 30-31
helium pressure bottle 234
  14
helium pressure vessel 234
  43, 50
heller 252 27
hellhound 327 29
helm 218 13
helmet *Police* 264 35
helmet *Equest.* 289 18
helmet *Ball Games* 292 24
helmet *Chivalry* 329 39-42
helmet, barred ~ 254 8
helmet, fireman's ~ 270 38
helmet, grilled ~ 254 8
helmet, protective ~ *Police*
  264 21
helmet, protective ~
  Mountain. 300 53
helmet, protective ~ *Winter
  Sp.* 302 34
helmet affronty 254 9
helmet flower 379 1
helmet lamp 300 54
helmets 254 4,7-9
helms 254 4,7-9
helmsman 224 16
helper 21 19
helve 85 3
hemidemisemiquaver 320 19
hemidemisemiquaver rest
  320 27
hemihedron 351 24
hemipyramid 351 24
hemisphere, northern ~ 3
  1-35
hemline marker 271 40
hemlock 379 4
hemp 383 9
hem stitch work 102 14
hen 62 36; 73 19
hen, fattened ~ 98 7
henbane 379 6
hen pheasant 88 77
herald 329 75
heraldic beasts 254 15-16
heraldic tent 254 14
heraldry 254 1-36
herb, primulaceous ~ 53 5
herb, solanaceous ~ 53 6; 379
  7
Hercules 3 21
herd 86 15
Herdsman 3 30
Herero woman 354 25
herm 334 35
herma 334 35
hermes 334 35
heron 86 46; 359 18
herring 364 14
herringbone 301 26

herringbone stitch 102 9
herring drift net 90 2-10
herring lugger 90 1
Hessian fly 80 40
Heterocera 365 7-11
hexagon 351 15
hexagonal crystal system 351
  20-22
hexahedron 351 2
hexakis-octahedron 351 13
hexoctahedron 351 13
H-girder 143 6
hibernation cocoon 80 31
hide 88 56
hide, raised ~ 86 14-17, 14
hide beetle 81 22
hieroglyphics, ancient
  Egyptian ~ 341 1
Hi-Fi component 241 13-48
high 9 6
high-altitude anorak 300 6
highball 317 33
highball glass 267 56
high bar *Playground* 273 32
high bar *Gymn.* 296 7
highboard diver 282 5
highboard diving 282 40-45
high chair, baby's ~ 28 33
high-draft draw frame 164 14
high-draft speed frame 164
  19
high-draft system 164 14
high frequency 7 26
high-hat cymbals 324 50
high house 305 75
high jump 298 9-27
high jump apparatus 298 32
high jump equipment 298 32
high jumper 298 10
highland Indian 352 23
high-moor bog 13 19
high-mountain region 12
  39-47
high performance sailplane
  287 9
high-pile lining 101 3
high-pressure area 9 6
high-pressure belt 9 47
high-pressure manometer
  141 4
high-pressure xenon arc
  lamp 312 39
high-rise handlebar 188 57
high-riser 188 56
high school 261
high school riding 71 1-6
high seat 86 14
high-speed plate, automatic ~
  39 15
high-tension voltage
  indicator 211 29
high tide 280 7
high toss 297 35
high-water line 13 35
high-water mark 13 35
highway construction 201
  1-24
hiking boot 101 18
hiking stick 284 31
hiking strap 284 30
hill *Phys. Geog.* 13 66
hill *Films* 310 13
hillside spring 12 38
hill upcurrent 287 28
himation 355 6
hind 86 13
hind, young ~ 88 1
hinge 188 2
hip *Man* 16 33
hip *Horse* 72 32
hip *Roof* 121 12
hip bone 17 18
hip circle backwards 296 55

hip dormer window 121 13
hip end 121 11
hip grip 21 38
hipped-gable roof 121 16
hippocampus *Fabul. Creat.*
  327 44
Hippocampus *Fish etc.* 364 18
hippocentaur 327 52
hippodrome 308 59
hippogryph 327 26
hippopotamus 366 31
hip rafter 121 62
hip roof 37 64; 121 10, 60
hip tile 122 9
historical ship, types of ~ 218
hitch 65 61
hitch, adjustable ~ 64 60
hitch, front ~ 65 50
hitch-kick 298 40
hitch pin 325 14
hive 77 45-50, 52
hive-bee 77 1-25
hock 72 37
hockey 292 6
hockey ball 292 14
hockey player 292 15
hockey stick 292 13
hod 122 22
hod hook 122 23
hoe 66 24
hoe and fork, combined ~ 56
  7
hoe handle 66 2
hog 94 11
hogpen 62 8; 75 35
hoist *Oil, Petr.* 145 11
hoist *Flags* 253 22-34
hoist, builder's ~ 118 31
hoist, inclined ~ 158 16; 159 5
hoisting gear 206 56; 217 74
hoisting gear bridge 217 73
hoisting gear cabin 217 71
hoisting rope 120 37
hold 223 55, 75
hold, insulated ~ 223 56
hold, underfloor ~ 231 21
hold-down, automatic ~ 157
  65
holdfast *Carp.* 120 66
holdfast *Alp. Plants etc.* 378
  50
holding device 157 47
holding forceps 23 12
holding press 183 4
holding squad 270 17
hold pillar 222 61
hole *Phys. Geog.* 13 34
hole *Ball Games* 293 87
hole, elongated ~ 240 17
hole, square ~ 140 43
holes 293 79-82
holing out 293 86
hollowing tool 135 17
hollow of the throat 16 20
hollow-shaft boring bit 133 7
holly 374 9
holohedron 351 2
holster 264 24
Holy Bible 330 11
Holy Communion 332 26
Holy Scripture 330 11
holy table 330 4
holy water basin 332 47
home and overseas news
  section 342 62
home base 292 53
home plate 292 53
home port 286 8
homogenizer 76 12
homopteran 358 3
honey 77 33
honey, strained ~ 77 62-63
honey bag 77 18

honey-bee **77** 1-25
honey cell **77** 33
honeycomb **77** 31-43, 45
honeycomb, artificial ~ **77** 42
honeycomb, natural ~ **77** 60
honeycomb weave **171** 29
honeydew melon **266** 50
honey extractor **77** 61
honey fungus **381** 28
honey gland **59** 18
honey in the comb **77** 64
honey jar **77** 63
honey pail **77** 62
honey sac **77** 18
honey separator **77** 61
honeysuckle **374** 13
honey super **77** 45
honey wrack **378** 48
hood *Infant Care etc.* **28** 26
hood *Child. Clothes* **29** 2
hood *Ladies' Wear* **30** 69
hood *Headgear* **35** 2
hood *Blacksm.* **137** 7
hood *Carriages* **186** 42
hood *Car* **191** 8
hood *Garage* **195** 36
hood *Aircraft* **230** 39
hood *Mountain.* **300** 19
hood *Church* **331** 56
hood, collapsible ~ **186** 52;
  193 10
hood, convertible ~ **193** 10
hood, detachable ~ **31** 21
hood, falcon's ~ **86** 44
hood, folding ~ **28** 35
hood, protective ~ **157** 65
hood drawstring **29** 64
hood support **195** 37
hoof *Horse* **72** 26
hoof *Game* **88** 24
hoof, horse's ~ **327** 42
hoofprints **86** 8
hook *Roof & Boilerr.* **38** 22
hook *Horse* **71** 14
hook *Shoem.* **100** 62
hook *Sports* **299** 33
hook *Winter Sp.* **301** 61
hook *Sports* **305** 18, 46
hook *Music. Not.* **320** 5
hook, blunt ~ **26** 50
hook, butcher's ~ **96** 55
hook, closed ~ **89** 85
hook, concealed ~ **89** 75
hook, double ~ **89** 83
hook, open ~ **89** 83
hook, treble ~ **89** 85
hookah **107** 42
hook-and-ride band **140** 50
hook ball **305** 18
hook belt **270** 44
hook disgorger **89** 40
hook ladder **270** 16
hooks **89** 79-87
hoop *Airsports* **288** 67
hoop *Ball Games* **292** 78
hoop *Circus* **307** 58
hoopoe **359** 25
hoop of barrel **130** 8
hooter *Motorcycles etc.* **188** 53
hooter *Fire Brig.* **270** 7
hop boiler **92** 52
hop garden **15** 114
hop growing **83** 27
hopper *Agr. Mach.* **64** 59
hopper *Wine Grow.* **78** 18
hopper *Mills* **91** 13
hopper *Cotton Spin.* **163** 31
hopper *Music. Instr.* **325** 30
hopper, endless-floor ~ **64** 84
hopper barge **226** 46
hopper delivery roller,
  wooden ~ **163** 32

hopper feeder **163** 33
hopsack weave **171** 11
horizon **13** 21
horizon, artificial ~ **230** 3
horizon glass **224** 7
horizon light **316** 15
horizon mirror **224** 7
horizontal bar **296** 7
horizontal boring and milling
  machine **150** 25
horizontal deflection module
  240 10
horizontal eight **288** 2
horizontal linearity control
  module **240** 9
horizontally-opposed twin
  engine **189** 47
horizontal milling spindle
  150 39
horizontal slow roll **288** 8
horizontal synchronizing
  module **240** 7
horn *Horse* **71** 38
horn *Motorcycles etc.* **188** 53
horn *Car* **191** 60
horn *Railw.* **212** 70
horn *Fire Brig.* **270** 7
horn *Flea Market* **309** 34
horn *Music. Instr.* **323** 41
horn *Invertebr.* **357** 31
horn *Birds* **362** 16
horn, spirally twisted ~ **327** 8
hornbeam **371** 63
horned owl **362** 14
horns **88** 29-31
horse *Horse* **71**; **72**
horse *Dom. Anim.* **73** 2
horse *Carp.* **120** 18
horse *Gymn.* **296** 1; **297** 1
horse, armoured ~ **319** 18
horse, piebald ~ **289** 29
horse, toy ~ **47** 15
horse, wild ~ **328** 7
horse, winged ~ **327** 26
horse armour **329** 83-88
horse bean **69** 15
horse box **75** 2
horse brush **71** 55
horse chestnut **371** 60
horse chestnut tree **371** 58
horsefish **364** 18
horsehair **323** 15
horsehair brush **100** 12
horse latitudes **9** 47
horsemanship **289**
horse racing **289** 50
horse-radish **57** 20
horse's head **72** 1-11
horseshoe *Game* **88** 71
horseshoe *School* **260** 1
horseshoe arch **336** 30
horseshoe grip **298** 53
horseshoe marking **88** 71
horseshoe mount **113** 25
horseshoe mounting *Astron.*
  5 9
horseshoe mounting *Optic.*
  Instr. **113** 25
horse sleigh **304** 25
horse stall **75** 2
horsetail **376** 18
horst **12** 10
hose *Household* **50** 75
hose *Bldg. Site* **118** 38
hose *Serv. Stat.* **196** 2; **196** 23
hose *Fire Brig.* **270** 54
hose *Hist. Cost.* **355** 47
hose, rotary ~ **145** 13
hose carriage **270** 28
hose cart **270** 28
hose connection **83** 30
hose connector **56** 45
hose coupling **270** 29

hose layer **270** 53
hosepipe **118** 38; **196** 23
hose reel **56** 26; **270** 28
hose truck **270** 28
hose wagon **270** 28
hosiery **271** 56
hosiery department **271** 17
hosiery mill **167** 1-66
hosiery shelf **99** 25
hospital **25**; **26**; **27**
hospital bed **25** 10
hospital unit **228** 21
Host **331** 48; **332** 28, 35
hostess **318** 33
hot-air duct **139** 52
hot-air gun **130** 25
hot-air sterilizer **22** 71
hotbed **55** 16
hotbed vent **55** 17
hot-blast pipe **147** 19
hot-blast stove **147** 15
hotel **267**
hotel bar **267** 51
hotel bill **267** 11
hotel guest **267** 14
hotel lobby **267** 18-26
hotel manager **267** 19
hotel porter **204** 17
hotel register **267** 8
hotel restaurant **267** 20
hotel room **267** 27-38
hotel sticker **205** 9
hothouse **55** 4; **272** 65
hot-pipe space **259** 93
hotplate **39** 15; **207** 30
hotplate, electric ~ **45** 45
hot reservoir **155** 20
hot-shoe contact **114** 72
hot-shoe flash contact **115** 21
hot tap **126** 28
hot water supply **155** 26
hot water tank **38** 68
hot water tank *Brew.* **92** 10
hot water tank *Paperm.* **172**
  18
hound *Hunt.* **86** 33
hound *Sailing* **284** 14
hour and minute button **110** 3
hour axis **5** 8
hour axis drive **5** 7
hourglass **110** 31
hour hand **110** 13
house *Dwellings* **37** 54
house *Farm Bldgs.* **62** 1
house *Bldg. Site* **118** 1-49
house, detached ~ **37** 1-53
house, dikereeve's ~ **216** 45
house, duplex ~ **37** 64-68
house, ferryman's ~ **216** 45
house, semi-detached ~ **37**
  69-71
house, solar ~ **155** 17
house, solar-heated ~ **155** 17
house, terraced ~ **37** 58-63
house, timber ~ **37** 84-86
houseboat **353** 1
house cat **62** 3
housecoat *Underwear etc.* **32**
  20
housecoat *Hist. Cost.* **355** 66
house cricket **81** 7
house detective **275** 16
house dress **31** 36
housefly **81** 1, 2
house frock **31** 36
household appliances **50**
household utensils **50**
house insects **81** 1-14
houseleek **51** 7
house light dimmer **312** 17
houseplant **42** 36; **248** 14
houseplants **53**
house sparrow **361** 5

house spider **81** 9
house telephone **127** 3
house wall **120** 29
housewife **39** 1
housing *Meteorol. Instr.* **10** 18
housing *Iron Foundry etc.* **148**
  57
housing *Films* **312** 48
housing, protective ~ **10** 39
housing, soundproof ~ **310**
  48; **313** 16-18, 27
housing development **37**
  54-57
housing estate **37** 54-57
housing lock **313** 33
hover **74** 3
hovercraft **286** 63
hub **187** 26
hub, centre ~ **187** 59
hub, front ~ **187** 52
hub assembly, front ~ **187** 52
hub barrel **187** 69
hub body **187** 69
hub shell **187** 69
huckleberry **377** 23
hula-hula girl **306** 16
hula skirt **306** 18
hull *Aircraft* **232** 2, 9
hull *Warships* **258** 2; **259** 22,
  42
hull bottom **286** 32, 35, 39
hull frame **222** 29
human flea **81** 42
Humanist **342** 4
human louse **81** 40, 41
humblebee **358** 23
humerus **17** 12
humidifier **79** 22
hummock **13** 42
hump **206** 46
hundreds **344** 3
hunt **289** 41-49
Hunter *Astron.* **3** 13
hunter **86** 1
hunting **86** 1-52, 9-12, 14-17
hunting cap **289** 14
hunting cap, hard ~ **289** 18
hunting clothes **86** 2
hunting dog **86** 33
hunting equipment **87** 41-48
hunting horn **87** 60; **289** 44
hunting knife **87** 42
hunting knife, double-edged
  ~ **87** 41
hunting leopard **368** 7
hunting pink **289** 13, 42
hunting rifle **86** 4
hunting rifles **87** 1-40
hunting screen **86** 9
hunting weapons **87**
huntsman **86** 1
hurdle *Free Exerc.* **295** 12
hurdle *Athletics* **298** 8
hurdle position **295** 12
hurdle racing **298** 7-8
hurdles **298** 7-8
hurdy-gurdy **322** 25
hurst **91** 20
husk **59** 50; **68** 33
husk corn **68** 31
husky **70** 22; **353** 2
hut **300** 1
hut, beehive-shaped ~ **354** 28
hut, Indian ~ **273** 59
Hydra **3** 16
Hydra, Lernaean ~ **327** 32
Hydrallmania **369** 9
hydrangea **51** 11
hydrant key **270** 27
hydraulic engineering **217**
hydraulic lift pad **195** 27
hydraulic plant **92** 13
hydraulic plant room **316** 50

hydraulic system *Agr. Mach.* 64 65
hydraulic system *Paperm.* 173 37
hydraulic system *Army* 255 53
hydraulic system *Air Force* 257 16
hydrocyanic acid 83 15
hydro-extraction 169 23
hydro-extractor, pendulum-type ~ 168 14
hydro-extractor lid 168 18
hydroformer 145 47
hydrogenation 170 16
hydrogen atom 1 15; 242 62
hydrogen atom (model) 1 1
hydrogen balloon 10 56
hydrogen bomb explosion 7 12
hydrogen cooler 153 27
hydrogen inlet *Synth. Fibres* 170 15
hydrogen inlet *Chem.* 350 12
hydrogen sulphide scrubber 156 22
hydrogen sulphide wet collector 156 22
hydrogen tank 6 6
hydropathic 274 8
hydrophone 224 64
hydroplane 286 22
hydroplane, stepped ~ 286 38-41
hydroplane, three-point ~ 286 42
hydrosphere 11 2
hydroxylamine inlet 170 21
hyena 368 1
hygrograph 10 8, 50
hygrometer *Drawing Off.* 151 39
hygrometer *Offset Platem.* 179 28
hygrometer *Swim.* 281 23
hygrometer element 10 9
hymenium 381 17
Hymenoptera 358 21-23
hymn board 330 24
hymn book 330 30
hymn number 330 24
hyoid 20 2
hyperbola 347 26
hyperbolic position line 224 43, 44
hyphae 381 2
hyphen 342 28
hypocentre 11 32
hypocotyl 370 89
hypophysis cerebri 17 43
hypotenuse 346 32
hypotrachelium 334 22
hyrax 366 24
hyssop 374 5

I

ibex 367 7
ibis 359 5
ice 266 44
ice, glacial ~ 12 48-56
ice accident 21 28-33
ice axe 300 16, 31
ice axe, short-shafted ~ 300 36
iceboat 302 44
iceboating 302 44-46
icebox 39 2; 46 33; 317 10
ice breaker 221 50
ice bucket 267 67
ice cream 308 31
ice-cream cornet 308 31
ice-cream man 308 30

ice-cream sundae 266 76
ice-cream vendor 308 30
ice-crystal cloud 8 6
ice-crystal cloud veil 8 7
ice cube 266 44
ice hockey 302 29-37
ice hockey player 302 29
ice hockey set 302 23
ice hockey skate 302 23
ice hockey stick 302 30
ice ledge 300 4
ice pellets 9 35
ice piton 300 40, 41
ice racing 290 24-28
ice ridge 300 21
ice sailing 302 44-46
ice skater 302 1
ice skates 302 20-25
ice skating 302 1-26
ice skating boot 302 24
ice slope 300 14
ice speedway 290 24-28
ice step 300 17
ice stick 302 39
ice-stick shooter 302 38
ice-stick shooting 302 38-40
ice yacht 302 44
ice yachting 302 44-46
icicle 304 21
icing, chocolate ~ 97 34
icing sugar 98 54
icosahedron 351 11
icositetrahedron 351 12
identification mark 163 6
identification number 85 33
identification tally 74 55
idle air bleed 192 2
idle mixture adjustment screw 192 11
idling adjustment 190 51
idling air jet 192 2
idling jet 192 1
idol 328 20
igloo 353 4
igloo tent, inflatable ~ 278 58
ignition distributor 190 9, 27
iguana 364 32
ileum 20 16
ilium 17 18
illegal punch 299 34
illumination, incident ~ 112 59, 63
illumination, vertical ~ 112 59, 63
illumination beam path 112 6
illumination optics 112 7
illumination path 112 6
image beam 115 35
image converter 26 15, 18; 27 19
imago 358 10
imbrication 335 15
imitation motorcycle fork 188 58
immersion heater 40 17
immersion roller 165 45
immersion vibrator 119 88
impact crusher 158 20
impact wrench 195 44
impair 275 23
impeller wheel 217 52
Imperial Crown 254 38
impost 336 21
impounding reservoir 217 57
impregnating spray 50 40
impression-adjusting wheel 180 81
impression control 249 10
impression cylinder 180 35, 64; 181 2, 44, 59
impression-setting wheel 180 81
impression tray 24 56

imprint 342 40
imprint, publisher's ~ 185 48
impulse generator, programmed ~ 25 33
impulse meter, automatic ~ 25 42
incense boat 332 42
incense spoon 332 43
inchworm 80 17
incident light measurement 114 60
incident neutron 1 42
incisor 19 16, 34
inclined cable anchorage 215 48
inclined cable system 215 51
incubation tank, long ~ 89 18
incubator 261 30
incubator, Californian ~ 89 15
incus and stapes 17 61
indention 175 16
index 345 1, 2
index arm 224 3
index bar 224 3
index cards 22 7
index finger 19 65
indexing mark 249 74
indexing table, rotary ~ 150 42
index mirror 224 6
index plate 151 51
Indian 352 25
Indian chief 352 11
Indian corn 68 31
Indian cress 53 4
Indian meal moth 81 28
Indian Ocean 14 23
indicator *Hosp.* 26 28
indicator *Motorcycle* 189 37, 45
indicator *Tram* 197 22
indicator, rear ~ 189 42
indicator and dimming switch 191 59
indicator board *Station* 204 32
indicator board *Hotel* 267 5
indicator for rough and fine adjustment 148 65
indicator lamp *Sawmill* 157 62
indicator lamp *Cotton Spin.* 164 8
indicator lamp *Office* 249 71
indicator light *Hosp.* 25 6
indicator light *Motorcycle* 189 37, 45
indicator light *Serv. Stat.* 196 7
indicator light *Tram* 197 22
indicator light *Railw.* 203 14
indicator light *Audio* 241 55
indicator light *Office* 249 71
indicator light *Hotel* 267 6
indicator light *Fencing* 294 30
indicator light, front ~ 191 19
indicator light, rear ~ 189 42
indicator needle *Photog.* 114 58
indicator needle *Inf. Tech.* 242 76
indicator plate 203 12
indicator scale 114 58; 313 28
indigo dying and sizing machine 165 40
Indio 352 23
individual-section machine 162 21
indoor target rifle 305 35
indorsee 250 26
indorsement 250 25
indorser 250 27

induced-draught fan 152 14
induction coil 11 44
industrial plant 225 71
inert-gas atmosphere 162 16
inert-gas supply 142 34
inert-gas torch 142 33
inert-gas welding 142 33
inert-gas welding equipment 138 29
inertial measurement unit 6 43
inescutcheon 254 17
infant care 28
infants' wear 29 13-30
in-feed scale 157 61
infighting 299 31
infiltration drain 216 37
infinity 345 15
inflating bulb 25 17
inflator 22 37
inflections 320 50-54
inflight antenna 6 46
inflight refuelling probe 256 7
inflorescence 371 43, 48; 378 7, 53, 55; 382 38; 383 49; 384 31
inflorescence, female ~ 59 46; 68 32; 383 11; 384 50
inflorescence, male ~ 59 39; 68 35; 371 8; 372 17, 24; 383 13
inflorescences 370 67-77
'information' 233 31
information bureau 204 29
information clerk 204 49
information counter 250 9
information office 204 29
information plate 356 20
information position 237 34
information technology 242
infrared drier 173 32
infrared laser rangefinder 255 82
infrared sound headphones 242 30
infrared sound transmitter 242 29
infrared transmission 242 27
infraspinatus 18 53
infringement 291 50
infructescence 61 15; 371 22, 44, 69, 72; 373 8; 374 18; 383 56; 384 32
infusion apparatus 25 11
infusion bottle 25 12
infusion device 25 14
ingot 148 48
ingot mould 147 32
ingot tipper 148 49
ingress/egress hatch 6 38
ingress/egress platform 6 34
inhalation 274 7
inhalational therapy 274 6-7
inhalator 23 24
inhalatorium 274 6
inhaler 26 2, 29
inhaling apparatus 23 24
inhaling tube 26 2, 29
initial 175 1
initial position *Fish Farm.* 89 33
initial position *Fencing* 294 18
injection condenser 172 16
injection nozzle 190 32, 54
injection pump *Intern. Combust. Eng.* 190 65
injection pump *Railw.* 211 48
injection pump drive 190 57
injection timer unit 190 58
ink 260 83
ink ball 340 22
ink duct 180 22; 181 65

inker 180 21, 50, 60, 77
inker unit 180 6-13, 40, 51, 60, 71, 76; 181 7, 8, 19, 28, 50, 57; 249 51-52
ink fountain 180 22; 181 65
ink fountain roller 181 64
inking ball 340 22
inking roller 180 21, 50, 60, 77; 249 52
inking unit 180 6-13, 40, 51, 60, 71, 76; 181 7, 8, 19, 28, 50, 57; 249 51-52
ink pad 22 30
ink plate 181 8
ink roller 180 21, 50, 60, 77; 249 52
ink slab 181 8
ink unit, tubular ~ 151 68
inkwell 309 78
inlay 323 26
inlet Paperm. 172 77
inlet Chem. 349 21
inlet filter 146 26
inlet manifold 190 18; 192 13
inlet valve 242 52
inlet vent 191 47
inner tube 187 30
input 117 27
input keyboard 238 13
input/output device 237 59
input selector 241 44
input selector switch 238 49
input unit 176 30
inscription 252 11
insect, homopterous ~ 358 3
insect, orthopterous ~ 358 8
insectivores 366 4-7
insects 358 3-23
insects, dipterous ~ 358 16-20
insert, wood ~ 85 4
insertion ring 349 17
inshore fishing 90 24-29
inside defender 291 12
inside forward 291 15
insolation 155 18
insole 291 27
inspection apparatus 79 20
inspection window 38 62
inspector 205 44
instep 19 61
instruction, programmed ~ 242 16
instruction key 247 21
instruction laser 242 81
instrument, keyed ~ 325 1
instrument, plucked ~ 322 21
instrument basin 27 5
instrument cabinet 24 16
instrument housing Atom 2 5, 22
instrument housing Meteorol. Instr. 10 59
instrument panel Offset Print. 180 74
instrument panel Railw. 212 31
instrument panel Aircraft 230 1
instrument panel Airsports 288 11
instruments, dental ~ 24 4
instruments, orchestral ~ 323 1-62
instruments, retractable ~ 258 68; 259 74, 88-91
instruments for gynecological and proctological examinations 23 3-21
instruments for minor surgery 22 48-50
instrument table 22 45
instrument table, mobile ~ 26 37

instrument tray 24 5; 26 39
instrument unit 234 53
insufflator 23 18
insulating board 122 44
insulating casing 10 26
insulating tape 127 34
insulation Slaughterho. 94 10
insulation Energy Sources 155 36
insurance company office 268 40
intaglio printing 182
intaglio process 340 14-24
intake muffler 191 54
intake pipe 189 5
intake silencer 190 16; 191 54
integer 344 10
integral 345 14
integral sign 345 14
integration 345 14
intensive care unit 25 1-30
interceptor 256 1
Intercity train 205 34; 209 1-22
intercom Doc. 22 34
intercom Garage 195 55
intercom Computer 244 5
intercom Office 245 20; 246 10
intercommunication telephone 239 13
intercom system Railw. 202 48; 203 69
intercom system Computer 244 5
interest 345 7
interference technician 237 28
interior equipment 239 6
interlacing point 171 28
interleaving device 181 11
intermediate frequency amplifier module 240 4
intermediate image screen 113 37
internal combustion engine, single-cylinder ~ 190 6
internal combustion engine, two-stroke ~ 190 6
internal combustion engines 190
internal facing tool 149 51
International Signals Code 253 29
interrogation mark 342 20
interrogation point 342 20
interrupter 153 55
intersection 347 12
intersection of sets 348 4
interspacing 175 13
inter-stage connector 234 31, 36
inter-stage section 234 31, 36
inter-tank connector 234 16
inter-tank section 234 16
intervals 321 6-13
intestine 77 15
intestine, large ~ 20 17-22
intestine, small ~ 20 14-16
intestines 20 14-22
intestinum crassum 20 17-22
intestinum tenue 20 14-16
intrusion 11 30
inundation area 216 41
inverness 186 32
invertebrates 357
inverted comma 342 26
inverted flight 288 9
involucre 59 50
ion chamber 2 2, 17
ionization chamber 2 2, 17
ionizing particle 1 58
ionosphere Atmos. 7 23

ionosphere Post 237 55
iris Man 19 42
iris Flower Gdn. 51 27
iris Gdn. Flowers 60 8
iron Shoem. 100 9
iron Tailor 104 29
iron Ball Games 293 92
iron, electric ~ 50 6
iron, light-weight ~ 50 6
iron, molten ~ 148 11
iron, slater's ~ 122 84
iron, square ~ 143 9
Iron Age 328 21-40
iron and steel works 147
ironer 103 19
iron foundry 148 1-45
ironing board 50 16
ironing-board cover 50 17
ironing head 50 4
ironing machine, electric ~ 50 1
ironing surface Household 50 16
ironing surface Dressm. 103 23
ironing table 50 15
iron ladle 147 12, 21, 42
iron pyrites 351 8
iron runout 147 11
irons 50 1-20
iron well 50 18
irradiation table 2 36
irrigation, overhead ~ 67
irrigation system, portable ~ 67 3
irrigation unit, long-range ~ 67 18
ischium 17 19
island Phys. Geog. 13 6
island Warships 259 3
island Park 272 55
isobar 9 1
isocheim 9 42
isohel 9 44
isohyet 9 45
isometric crystal system 351 1-17
isosceles triangle 346 27
isoseismal 11 37
isothere 9 43
isotherm 9 42
issue desk 262 20
Italian ryegrass 69 26
italics 175 7
ITOS satellite 10 64
ivory carver 135

J

jack Ship 223 54
jack Army 255 68
jack Fire Brig. 270 12
jack Sports 305 23
jack Music. Instr. 322 50
jack, hydraulic ~ 85 45
jackal 367 11
jack boot 355 58
jack chain, endless ~ 157 17
jacket 29 51; 31 2; 33 2
jacket, baby's ~ 28 25; 29 9
jacket, casual ~ 33 39
jacket, cork ~ 282 19
jacket, denim ~ 33 21
jacket, leather ~ 33 43
jacket, metallic ~ 294 15
jacket, mink ~ 30 1
jacket, oilskin ~ 228 6
jacket, padded ~ 300 6
jacket, pile ~ 29 44
jacket, poplin ~ 31 37
jacket, short-sleeved ~ 33 26

jacket, suede ~ 30 58
jacket button 33 55
jacket crown 24 28
jacket flap 185 38
jack-in-the-box 306 56
jack panel 311 16
jack plane 132 16
jack rafter 121 61, 63
jack spur, screwed ~ 71 50
jack spur, strapped ~ 71 51
jackstaff 223 53; 258 4
jackstay 221 118
jacob's ladder 221 91
jai alai 305 67
jam 98 52
jam, whole-fruit ~ 98 51
jamb 118 11; 120 32, 51
jambeau 329 54
jam cleat 284 22
Jamestown weed 379 8
Japan Current 14 31
Japanese quince 373 17
japonica 373 17
jardin anglais 272 41-72
javelin 319 17
javelin throw 298 51-53
jaw Man 16 17
jaw Hosp. 26 46
jaw Joiner 132 33
jaw Metalwkr. 140 3
jaw, lower ~ Man 17 35
jaw, lower ~ Horse 72 11
jaw, upper ~ 17 36; 19 27
jawbone, lower ~ 17 35
jawbone, upper ~ 17 36
jaws, inside ~ 149 71
jaws, outside ~ 149 70
jaw trap 87 48
jay 361 1
jazz band instruments 324 47-78
jazz guitar 324 73
jazz trumpet 324 65
jeans 31 60; 33 22
jejunum 20 15
jellyfish 357 14
jelly roll 97 19
J-2 engine 234 19, 34
jenny 222 14, 28
jerboa 366 15
jerkin 355 45
jerkin head roof 121 16
jerk with split 299 4
jersey 291 56
jersey, padded ~ 292 26
jess 86 45
jester 306 38
jet 83 19
jet, main ~ 192 12
jet aeroplanes 231 7-33
jet airplanes 231 7-33
jet blower 281 34
jet condenser 172 16
jet engine 231 26
jet engines 232 33-50
jet fuel tank 146 18
jet nozzle 153 29
jet of water 272 22
jet planes 231 7-33
jet pump 216 62
jets 231 7-33
jet stream level 7 5
jet trainer 257 1-41
jet turbine 231 26
jet turbine engine 231 26
jet turbine engines 232 33-50
jet turbines 232 33-50
jetty Map 15 59
jetty Docks 225 30, 66
jetty Park 272 46
jetty Camping 278 13
jetty Rowing 283 19
jewel 110 33; 355 17

jewel box 36 31
jewel case 36 31
jewellery 36; 36 1
jewellery department 271 62
jewelry 36 1
jib *Bldg. Site* 119 36
jib *Ship* 220 2
jib *Docks* 226 24, 49
jib *Army* 255 95
jib *Sailing* 284 16; 285 3
jib, flying ~ 219 23
jib, inner ~ 219 21
jib, outer ~ 219 22
jib boom 218 51; 219 1
jib crane 222 34
jib downhaul 284 17
jibe 285 28
jibing 285 26
jib sheet 284 23
jib stay 219 14
jig 134 42
jiggering 161 14
jig saw 108 12
jigsaw puzzle 48 9
jigsaw puzzle piece 48 10
jimpson weed 379 8
jimson weed 379 8
job advertisement 342 70
jockey 22 68
jockey cap 35 8
jockey roller 181 45
jockey wheel 278 54
jogger 249 56
join 122 94
joiner 132 38; 133
joiner's tools 132 1-28
joining of modules 242 70
joint *Phys. Geog.* 13 50
joint *Plumb. etc.* 126 38
joint *Railw.* 202 11
joint *Industr. Plants* 383 63
joint, pre-packed ~ 96 22
joint, universal ~ 284 6
joint and side pasting
    attachment 185 28
joint cutter 201 16
joint-cutting blade 201 17
jointed charlock 61 21
jointer 133 37
joint vice 108 34
joist 121 54
joist shuttering 119 12
joke 306 56
jollying 161 14
Jordan 172 27, 60, 73, 83
Jordan refiner 172 27, 60, 73,
    83
journal 143 63
joust 329 71
jousting helmet *Heraldry* 254
    4
jousting helmet *Chivalry* 329
    77
judge *Cyc. Racing* 290 5
judge *Sports* 299 43
judo 299 13-17
judoist 299 14
judoka 299 14
judo throw 299 17
jug 39 30
jug, clay ~ 260 78
juice extractor 40 19
ju-jitsu 299 13-17
jumbo derrick boom 221 25,
    62
jumbo jet 231 14
jump 289 21
jumper *Child. Clothes* 29 43
jumper *Equest.* 289 9
jumper, child's ~ 29 47
jumper, cowl neck ~ 30 2
jumper, polo neck ~ 30 7
jumper, short-sleeved ~ 31 67

jumping 298 9-41
jumping hoop 307 58
jumping jack 306 52
jumping rope 273 15, 16
jumping saddle 289 10
jumping sheet 270 18
jump rope 273 16
jump-sit-spin 302 8
jump ski 286 62
jumpsuit 31 53
jump throw 292 3
junior hacksaw 127 52
juniper berry 372 52
juniper tree 372 47
junk 353 32
junk stall 308 60
Jupiter 4 48
just 329 71
justifying scale 174 35
jute 383 25

K

kail 57 34
kale 57 34
kangaroo 366 3
kapok tree 383 20
karabiner 300 46
karabiner hole 300 35
karate 299 18-19
karateka 299 18
karst formation 13 71-83
karst spring 13 74
kart 305 83
karting 305 82
kayak 283 4; 353 12
kayak, folding ~ 283 61, 62, 67
kayak, one-man ~ 283 54
kayak, two-seater ~ 283 61
kayaks 283 68-70
Keel *Astron.* 3 46
keel *Shipbuild.* 222 22
keel *Space* 235 7
keel *Rowing* 283 32
keel *Sailing* 285 32
keel, lead ~ 285 36
keel, vertical ~ 222 53
keel arch 336 36
keel block 222 39
keel-centreboard yawl 285
    37-41
keel plate 222 49
keelson 222 53; 283 50
keep 329 4
keep net 89 28
kegellade chest 326 12-14
kelly 145 14
kelson 222 53; 283 50
kerb 198 6; 272 25
kerbstone 198 7
kerbstone broker 251 5
kerbstoner 251 5
kerf 84 28
kernel 68 13; 383 44
kerosene 145 60
kerosene tank 234 9
kerria 373 28
ketchup 45 43
kettle, brass ~ 42 14
kettle, whistling ~ 39 16; 40
    10
kettledrum 323 57
Keuper 154 57
key *Map* 14 27-29
key *Town* 268 4
key *Metalwkr.* 140 33-35
key *Music. Instr.* 322 28, 38,
    49; 323 32, 35; 324 40; 326
    8
key, black ~ 325 5
key, ebony ~ 325 5
key, flat ~ 140 48

key, gib-headed ~ 143 74
key, iron ~ 328 32
key, ivory ~ 325 4
key, sunk ~ 143 73
key, white ~ 325 4
key action 325 22-39
keyboard *Composing Rm.* 174
    32, 37; 176 2
keyboard *Post* 236 44; 237 70
keyboard *Office* 245 27; 249
    2-6
keyboard *Music. Instr.* 322
    28; 324 40; 325 4-5
keyboard, lower ~ 322 47
keyboard, upper ~ 322 46
keyboard console 176 1
keyboard instrument 325 1
keyboard operator 176 4
keyboard send-receive
    teleprinter 176 31
keyboard side 324 39
keyboard unit 176 1
keyhole 140 40
keyhole saw 120 63; 126 70;
    132 3
key lever 322 38, 49; 326 8
key mechanism 325 22-39
key rack 267 3
keys *Mach. Parts etc.* 143
    73-74
keys *Music. Not.* 320 55-68
key seat 143 85
key signatures 320 50-54
key slot 143 85
keystone 336 23
keyway 143 66, 85
kick-back guard 132 47; 157
    59
kicker 292 10
kicking strap 284 21
kick stand 187 34
kickstarter 188 39, 43; 189 38
kidney, left ~ 20 30-31
kidney, right ~ 20 28
kidney dish 23 45
kidney vetch 69 6
kieselguhr 93 3
kieselguhr filter 93 4
kill *Hunt.* 86 38
kill *Bullfight. etc.* 319 30
killer 94 1
kiln 92 19
kiln, circular ~ 159 19
kiln, rotary ~ 160 8
kilning floors 92 16-18
kilns 161
kilometer *see* kilometre
kilometre sign 216 44
kimono 353 40
kindergarten 48
king 276 8
King Carnival 306 58
king cup 375 8
kingfisher 360 8
king penguin 359 4
king pin roof structure 121 42
king post 223 35
king post, ventilator-type ~
    221 58
king's fern 377 16
Kipp generator 350 59
Kipp's apparatus 350 59
Kirghiz 353 22
Kirschner beater 163 25
kit 322 20
kitchen 39
kitchen *Butch.* 96 31-59
kitchen *Railw.* 207 29, 80
kitchen, ship's ~ 223 42
kitchen appliances 40
kitchen cabinet 207 35
kitchen chair 39 43
kitchen clock 39 20; 109 34

kitchen cupboard 39 8
kitchen lamp 39 39
kitchen roll 40 1
kitchen scales 309 84
kitchen table 39 44
kitchen unit 46 29
kitchen utensils 40
kite *Playground* 273 41, 42
kite *Maths.* 346 38
kite *Birds* 362 11
kite, paper ~ 260 71
kite string 273 44
knapsack 86 3
knapsack sprayer, plunger-
    type ~ 83 43
knapweed 376 12
kneading machine 97 55
knee *Man* 16 50
knee *Horse* 72 22
knee-breeches 33 40
kneecap *Man* 17 23
knee cap *Chivalry* 329 53
kneeler 332 25
knee lever 325 45
kneeling front support 295 20
kneeling position *Free Exerc.*
    295 8
kneeling position *Sports* 305
    28
knee mounting 113 21
knee pad *Ball Games* 292 9
knee pad *Winter Sp.* 303 17
knee piece 329 53
knee roll 71 48
knee strap 33 41
knee swell 325 45
knife *Tablew. etc.* 45 7, 50
knife *Forestry* 85 11
knife *Paperhanger* 128 38
knife *Paperm.* 172 74
knife *Swim.* 279 8
knife, bookbinder's ~ 183 13
knife, bronze ~ 328 31
knife, butcher's ~
    Slaughterho. 94 15
knife, butcher's ~ *Butch.* 96
    37
knife, cobbler's ~ 100 50
knife, electrician's ~ 127 63
knife, gardener's ~ 56 9
knife, gilder's ~ 129 51
knife, hafted ~ 328 31
knife, shoemaker's ~ 100 50
knife, surgical ~ 26 43
knife blade 96 32
knife case 94 12
knife coulter 65 10
knife handle 96 34
knife rest 45 11
knife thrower 307 37
knight *Games* 276 11
knight *Chivalry* 329 67
knighting 329 66
Knight Templar 329 73
knit 101 43
knits 171
knits, basic ~ 171 30-48
knit stitch 101 43
knitting 167
knitting head 167 21
knitting machine, circular ~
    167 1
knitting machine, flat ~ 167
    18
knives, butcher's ~ 96 31-37
knob 359 17
knob, adjustable ~ 151 3
knobkerrie 354 33
knobkerry 354 33
knob-leaf capital 333 14
knockout 299 40
knock-over bit 167 52
knot *Meteorol. etc.* 9 12

knot *Ladies' Wear* 31 47
knot *Underwear etc.* 32 42
knot *Roof* 122 68
knot, French ~ 102 13
knot hole cutter 132 53
knot hole moulding machine 132 52
knot stitch, twisted ~ 102 13
knotted work 102 21
knotter 172 54; 173 13
knotting machine 85 18
knuckle *Man* 19 82
knuckle *Meat* 95 38, 42, 49
knuckle, fore ~ 95 5, 8
knuckle, hind ~ 95 1, 10
knuckle of pork 96 17
Kocher's forceps 22 49
kohlrabi 57 26
Kort vent 227 21
koruna 252 27
kraft pulp mill 172 1-52
KR-class 284 63
kris 353 44
krona 252 25
krone 252 24, 26
Krüger flap 229 55
krummhorn 322 6
Kuroshio 14 31
Kuro Siwo 14 31
kursaal 274 8
kymation 334 19

L

label 54 4
laboratory 23 41-59
laboratory, multi-purpose ~ 235 66
laboratory and research microscope 112 1
laboratory apparatus *Doc.* 23 57
laboratory apparatus *Paperm.* 173 2-10
laboratory apparatus *Chem.* 349 1-38; 350 1-63
laboratory equipment *Doc.* 23 57
laboratory equipment *Paperm.* 173 2-10
laboratory equipment *Chem.* 349 1-38; 350 1-63
laboratory microscope 112 1
laboratory technician 23 41
laboratory timer 116 18
laborer *see* labourer
labourer, bricklayer's ~ 118 19
labourer, builder's ~ 118 19
Labrador Current 14 40
labret 354 23
laburnum 374 32
labyrinth 17 62
lace 100 64; 291 32
lace, cotton ~ 31 32
lace, Venetian ~ 102 30
lace fastening 101 21
lackey 186 20
lackey moth 80 13
lacolith 11 30
lacquered work, incised ~ 337 6
lacquey 186 20
lactam oil 170 37
ladder *Moon L.* 6 35
ladder *Roof & Boilerr.* 38 15
ladder *Child. Rm.* 47 5
ladder *Fruit & Veg. Gdn.* 52 8
ladder *Bldg. Site* 118 42
ladder *Railw.* 211 43
ladder *Hydr. Eng.* 217 8
ladder *Space* 235 28

ladder, aluminium ~ 50 35
ladder, arched ~ 5 20
ladder, extending ~ 270 10
ladder, standard ~ 118 86
ladder, steel ~ 270 10
ladder dredge, multi-bucket ~ 216 56
ladder hook 122 15, 69
ladder mechanism 270 11
ladder operator 270 13
ladder scaffold 118 86-89
'ladies' 233 48
'ladies' toilet' 233 48
ladies' wear 30; 31
ladies' wear department 271 28
ladle 130 32
ladle, crane-operated ~ 147 60
ladle, drum-type ~ 148 6
ladle, mobile ~ 148 6
lady *Café* 265 23
lady *Hist. Cost.* 355 59, 64, 68, 70, 79
ladybird 358 37
ladybug 358 37
lady-finger 69 6
lady's finger 69 6
ladysmock 375 11
lady's slipper 376 27
lady's smock 375 11
lager 93 26
lager cellar 93 12
lagging 38 72
lagoon 13 33
lake 13 3
lake, coastal ~ 13 44
lake, ox-bow ~ 15 75
lake dwelling 328 15
lamantin 366 23
lamb 73 13; 75 11
lamb's lettuce 57 38
lamellicorn 82 1
lamellicorn beetle 358 24, 39
lamina 68 20; 370 28, 85
laminate 301 48
lamp *Dent.* 24 19
lamp *Dining Rm.* 44 12
lamp *Watchm.* 109 12
lamp *Carriages* 186 9
lamp *Street Sect.* 198 18
lamp *Nightclub* 318 26
lamp, directional ~ 22 44
lamp, fluorescent ~ 49 32; 271 23
lamp, front ~ 188 29
lamp, individual ~ 26 11
lamp, pendant ~ 44 12
lamp, rear ~ 187 46
lamp, side ~ 191 20
lamp bracket *Photomech. Reprod.* 177 16
lamp bracket *Bicycle* 187 6
lamp compartment 177 41
lampholder 127 60
lamphouse 112 28, 59; 116 29; 309 44; 312 39-44
lamphouse connector 112 60
lamp housing 116 29
lamp post 198 18
lam rod 166 54
lance *Gdn. Tools* 56 25
lance *Bullfight. etc.* 319 17
lance *Chivalry* 329 81
lance *Ethnol.* 353 9
lanceolate 370 32
lancer 319 16
lance rest 329 80
lancet arch 336 31
lancet window 335 39-41
land 87 39
landau 186 36
landaulette 186 36

land drill 282 20
landfill, sanitary ~ 199 10
landing *Floor etc. Constr.* 123 34-41
landing *Athletics* 298 19
landing, intermediate ~ 123 52-62
landing area 298 36, 39
landing beam 123 34, 55
landing beam, main ~ 123 66
landing craft 258 89; 259 46
landing flap 229 42; 230 53; 257 38; 288 29
landing gear, hydraulically operated ~ 235 31
landing gear, main ~ 235 31
landing gear, retractable ~ 232 10
landing gear housing 256 15
landing gear hydraulic cylinder 257 41
landing gear unit, forward-retracting ~ 257 40
landing gear unit, main ~ 230 41; 231 28; 257 40; 288 33
landing gear unit, retractable ~ 231 28
landing light 230 49; 257 37; 288 32
landing mat 296 13; 297 7
landing net 89 2
landing pad *Moon L.* 6 33
landing pad *Athletics* 298 36
landing pontoon 225 63
landing skid 232 15; 256 21
landing stage 225 63; 278 13; 283 19
landing unit, main ~ 256 26
landlord 305 7, 13
landside 65 5, 67
landslide 11 46
landslip 11 46
land surveying 14 46-62
land wheel 65 15
lane *Map* 15 112
lane *Forestry* 84 1
lane arrow 268 73, 74
lane timekeeper 282 24
language laboratory 261 35
languid 326 28
lansquenet 355 32
lantern *Carriages* 186 9
lantern *Ship* 218 44; 221 48
lantern *Navig.* 224 105
lantern *Art* 335 45
lantern, Chinese ~ 353 36
lantern, combined ~ 286 13
lantern, paper ~ 52 15; 306 4
lantern mast 224 82
lantern tower 224 82
lanyard 284 19
lap *Dom. Anim.* 73 23
lap *Roof* 122 100
lap *Cotton Spin.* 163 58, 64
lap, carded ~ 163 47
lapboard 136 7
lap cradle 163 15
lapel 31 23; 33 5
lapel, silk ~ 33 8
lapping plate 125 4
lap riveting 143 56
lap scorer 290 6
lap-turner, movable ~ 163 19
lapwing 359 21
larch 372 32
larch cone 372 36
lard 96 5
large cabbage white butterfly 80 47
larks 361 18-19
larkspur 60 13
larmier 88 14
larry 144 8; 156 6

larry car 144 8; 156 6
larva 58 64; 77 29; 80 6, 19, 36, 38, 41, 46; 81 20; 358 9, 19; 82 12, 25, 36
larva, first-generation ~ 80 23
larva, mature ~ 80 53
larva, second-generation ~ 80 24
larva, young ~ 77 28; 80 54
larynx 20 2-3
laser 242 81
laser beam 243 53
lashing *Bldg. Site* 118 30
lashing *Ship* 218 32; 221 119
lasso 319 40; 352 5
last 100 34
last, iron ~ 100 54
last, wooden ~ 100 32
latch bolt 140 37
latch needle 167 12, 56, 61
lateen sail 218 29; 220 3
lateen spanker 218 29
lateen yard 218 30
La Tène period 328 21-40
lateral 144 30
lath 123 70
lath, double ~ 122 43
lath, tilting ~ 122 43
lath, toothed ~ 122 26
lath axe 122 21
lathe 135 1
lathe, watchmaker's ~ 109 20
lathe bed 135 2; 149 31
lathe carrier 149 54
lathe foot 149 12
lathe spindle 149 20
lathe tool 149 48, 52
lathe tools 149 45-53
lathing 123 71
latissimus dorsi 18 59
latitude 14 6
latrine 118 49
lattice casing 221 84
lattice girder 235 12
lattice mast 258 18
lattice structures 1 9-14
lattice swing bridge 215 63
launch 225 25
launcher 258 49
launching container 258 32
launching housing 259 26
launching ramp 255 66
launch phase escape tower 234 66
lauter battery 92 51
lauter tun 92 50
lava plateau 11 14
lava stream 11 18
lavatories 317 31
lavatory 49 12; 146 29; 207 16, 42, 72; 211 59; 231 31; 278 5
lavatory, public ~ 268 62
lavender 380 7
lawn 37 46; 51 33; 272 36; 274 12
lawn aerator 56 15
lawn mower, electric ~ 56 31
lawn mower, motor ~ 56 28
lawn rake 51 3; 56 3
lawn sprinkler 37 43; 56 43
lay-by 217 27
layer 54 11, 12
layer, bast ~ 54 35
layer, bituminous ~ 200 58
layer, level ~ 123 39
layer, raffia ~ 54 35
layer, top ~ 123 41
layer cloud 8 3, 4, 8, 9, 10
layering 54 10
layette 28
layette box 28 18
lay figure 338 31

laying battery 74 19
laying hen 74 57
laying-on trowel 118 56
laying up 216 14
lay shaft 192 37
L-D converter 147 45-50
lead *Kitch.* 39 25
lead *Dog* 70 30
lead *Slaughterho.* 94 9
lead *Arc Weld.* 142 25
lead *Navig.* 224 59
lead, electric ~ *Household* 50 77
lead, electric ~ *Gdn. Tools* 56 32
lead, oval ~ 89 88
lead, pear-shaped ~ 89 90
lead, spare ~ 151 46
lead came 124 13
leader *Dwellings* 37 13
leader *Roof & Boilerr.* 38 10
leader *Fish Farm.* 89 78
leader *Photog.* 114 9
leader *Carriages* 186 46
leader *Mountain.* 300 25
leader *Script* 342 48
lead hammer 124 11
leading article 342 48
leading edge *Sailing* 284 42
leading edge *Gliding* 287 34
leading edge, carbon fibre reinforced ~ 235 32
leading-edge flap, profiled ~ 229 54
leading lady 310 27
leading light, higher ~ 224 102
leading light, lower ~ 224 101
leading lights 224 101-102
leading man 310 28
leading soloist 314 28
lead-in tube 153 40
lead knife 124 12
leadline 224 60
leads 89 88-92; 224 58-67
leadscrew 149 19, 32
leadscrew handwheel 149 13
leadscrew reverse-gear lever 149 6
lead shot 89 89
lead sinker 224 59
leaf 58 3, 53; 59 17; 68 8; 333 24; 370 19, 26; 371 21, 23, 27, 29, 68; 372 23; 373 3, 16, 25; 374 28; 375 2; 378 15, 18, 19, 41, 45; 384 55, 62
leaf, alternate pinnate ~ 59 40
leaf, basal ~ 375 9, 12, 15, 30; 383 2
leaf, pinnate ~ 57 3
leaf, sprouting ~ 59 29
leaf, ternate ~ 58 19
leaf, trifoliate ~ 58 19
leaf, young ~ 59 29
leaf axil 370 25; 375 38
leaf blade 68 20; 370 28, 85
leaf bud 59 47; 370 90
leaf cluster, rooted ~ 54 17
leaf drop 80 20
leaf fat 95 45
leaflet 263 9
leaf margin shapes 370 43-50
leaf ornament 334 40
leaf roller 82 43
leaf shapes 370 31-38
leaf sheath 68 9, 21; 370 83; 384 30
leaf stalk 370 27; 371 73
leaf tendril 57 4
leaf vegetables 57 28-34
leakage steam path 153 28
lean forward 301 36
lean-to roof 37 78; 121 7

leaping hind leg 358 11
learner-swimmer 282 17
learning programme, audio-visual ~ 242 7
lease rod 166 38
leash 70 30
leather beetle 81 22
leathers 290 26
leather side 131 13, 18
leaves 276 43
leaves, compound ~ 370 39-42
lebkuchen 97 51
lectern 262 4; 330 2, 37
lecture 262 1
lecture notes 262 5
lecturer 262 3
lecture room 262 2
lecture theatre 262 2
lederhosen 29 32
ledge *Photograv.* 182 23
ledge *Mountain.* 300 4
ledge, cushioned ~ 277 16
ledger 118 26
ledger tube 119 48
leeboard 220 7; 283 63
leech *Sailing* 284 45
leech *Invertebr.* 357 20
leech pocket 284 43
leek 57 21
lee waves 287 17
left 254 19, 21, 23
left corner pin 305 6
left front second pin 305 2
left hook 299 33
left luggage locker 204 21
left luggage office 204 27
left tank fuel gauge 230 16
leg *Man* 16 49-54; 17 22-25
leg *Game* 88 21, 37, 81
leg *Meat* 95 1, 38
leg *Mach. Parts etc.* 143 2
leg *Maths.* 346 27
leg, back ~ 82 8
leg, broken ~ 21 11
leg, downwind ~ 285 23
leg, first ~ 285 19
leg, fractured ~ 21 11
leg, front ~ 82 6
leg, hind ~ *Dog* 70 7
leg, hind ~ *Horse* 72 33-37
leg, hind ~ *Bees* 77 3, 6-9
leg, hind ~ *Game* 88 22, 63
leg, middle ~ 82 7
leg, second ~ 285 20
leg, third ~ 285 21
leg, tubular ~ 114 44
leg, vertical ~ 143 4
leg, windward ~ 285 22
leg armour 319 19
legato 321 33
leg boot, high ~ 101 7, 13
leg boot, men's ~ 101 7, 13
legend 252 11
leg feather 362 3
leggings 28 24; 29 45; 352 17
leg holder 23 11
leg of mutton piece 95 22, 29
leg ring 74 54
legs 82 6-8
leg space ventilation 191 81
leg support 23 10, 11
legume 57 6; 370 92
legume, immature ~ 374 22
legume, unripe ~ 374 22
Leguminosae 57 1-11
leg vice 140 10
Leine rock salt 154 64
leisure centre 281
lemon 384 23
lemonade 265 15
lemonade glass 265 16
lemon peel, candied ~ 98 10

lemon squeezer 40 9
lending library 262 18
length adjustment 100 20
lengthening arm 151 57
lengths of material 104 2
length stop 157 68
lens *Man* 19 48
lens *Photog.* 115 32, 84; 116 32
lens *Composing Rm.* 176 23
lens *Audiovis.* 243 2, 52
lens *Films* 313 2
lens *Crystals* 351 33
lens, bifocal ~ 111 15
lens, concave and convex ~ 111 41
lens, convex and concave ~ 111 42
lens, fisheye ~ 115 44
lens, flat ~ 111 38
lens, flush ~ 114 5
lens, interchangeable ~ 112 62; 115 43
lens, long focal length ~ 115 48
lens, long-focus ~ 115 49
lens, medium focal length ~ 115 47
lens, negative ~ 111 37
lens, normal ~ 115 3-8, 46; 117 49
lens, plano-concave ~ 111 39, 40
lens, positive ~ 111 37
lens, short focal length ~ 115 45
lens, special ~ 111 38
lens, standard ~ 115 3-8, 46; 117 49
lens, telephoto ~ 115 48
lens, variable focus ~ 117 2
lens, varifocal ~ 117 2
lens, wide-angle ~ 115 45; 117 48
lens barrel 115 3
lens carrier 177 27
lens case 115 104
lens head 117 46-49
lens hood 313 3, 10
lens hood barrel 313 5
lens hood bellows 313 39
lens panel 112 18
lens pouch, soft-leather ~ 115 105
lens standard 114 52
lens surface 111 37
lens system 242 83
lens turret 117 46; 313 32
lenticular 287 19
Lent lily 60 3, 12
Leo 3 17; 4 57
Leonberger 73 16
leopard 368 6
leotard 297 51
Lepidoptera 358 48-56; 365
lepton 252 39
lesene 335 11
Lesser Bear 3 34
lesser celandine 375 36
Lesser Dog 3 15
lesser housefly 81 1
less-than-carload freight 206 4
let-off motion 166 59
let-off weight lever 166 62
let-out section 131 7
let-out strip 131 7
letter 174 44
letter, capital ~ 175 11
letter, double ~ 175 6
letter, initial ~ 175 1
letter, lower case ~ 175 12
letter, small ~ 175 12

letter, upper case ~ 175 11
letter carrier 236 53
letter container 236 32
letter feed 236 31
letter flags 253 22-28
letter-folding machine 249 44
lettering 129 40
lettering brush 129 41
lettering stencil 151 69
letter matrix 174 47; 176 16
letterpress machine, rotary ~ 181 41
letterpress machine, web-fed ~ 181 41
letterpress press, rotary ~ 181 41
letterpress printing 181
letterpress printing machines 181 1-65
letterpress printing method 340 1-13
letter rack 267 2
letter-rate item 236 55
letters, illuminated ~ 268 45
letter scales 236 24
letter-sorting installation 236 31-44
letter spacing 175 13
letter tray 245 30; 248 41
lettuce 57 36
lettuce leaf 57 37
leucite 351 12
levade *Horse* 71 4
levade *Circus* 307 30
levee 13 9; 216 49
level 14 48
level, lower ~ 217 17
level, motor-driven ~ 112 69
level, upper ~ 217 25
level crossing 15 26
level crossing, protected ~ 202 39
level crossing, unprotected ~ 202 49
level crossings 202 39-50
level indicator 316 57
leveling *see* levelling
levelling 14 46
levelling and support shovel 255 94
levelling beam 201 3, 4
levelling blade 200 18
levelling staff 14 47
lever *Plumb. etc.* 126 19
lever *Sawmill* 157 46
lever *Cotton Spin.* 164 42
lever *Office* 249 50
lever *Graphic Art* 340 61
lever for normal and coarse threads 149 4
lever hang 296 56
lever mechanism 203 54
liberty horses 307 30-31
Libra 3 19; 4 59
librarian 262 14, 19
library, municipal ~ 262 11-25
library, national ~ 262 11-25
library, regional ~ 262 11-25
library, scientific ~ 262 11-25
library, ship's ~ 223 25
library ticket 262 25
library user 262 24
license plate 189 8
lichgate 331 19
licker-in 163 53
licker-in roller 163 53
licker-in undercasing 163 54
lid *Kitch. Utensils* 40 13
lid *Electrotyp. etc.* 178 37
lid *Chem.* 350 52
lid, glass ~ 269 56
lid, hinged ~ 127 24

lid, sliding ~ 179 2
lid clip 50 83
lido deck 223 22
Lieberkühn reflector 115 97
liege lord 329 67
lifebelt 221 124; 222 24; 280
3; 281 6
lifebelt light 221 125
lifeboat *Offshore Drill.* 146 19
lifeboat 221 78, 107; 223 19
lifeboat launching gear 221
101-106
lifebuoy *Ship* 221 124
lifebuoy *Shipbuild.* 222 24
lifebuoy *Bathing* 280 3
lifebuoy light 221 125
lifeguard 280 1
lifeguard station 280 46
life jacket 286 20
life jacket, cork ~ 228 9
life jacket, inflatable ~ 228 8
life line 19 72
lifeline 221 103; 228 12; 280 2
life preserver, cork ~ 228 9
life raft 228 19; 258 11; 286
19
life rocket 228 2
lifesaver 21 36; 280 1
life saving 228
life support pack 6 20
life support system 6 20
lift *Ship* 219 47
lift *Store* 271 45
lift *Theatre* 316 33
lift, hydraulic ~ 195 25, 26
lift, vertical ~ 170 36
liftback 193 29
lift bridge 225 70
lift cage 271 46
lift car 271 46
lift chair 214 16
lift chair, double ~ 214 17
lift controls 271 48
lift device 103 24
lift dump 229 42
lifter *Agr. Mach.* 64 59
lifter *Sawmill* 157 46
lifter rail 164 30
lifter roller 181 63
lifting arm 255 76
lifting bolt 164 37
lifting crane 270 48
lifting device 255 76
lifting gear 206 56
lifting hook 85 6
lifting motor 150 22
lifting platform 232 19
lifting rod 65 29
lifting rod adjustment 65 25
lifting spindle 217 36
lifting undercarriage 232 18
lift-off hinge 140 49
lift operator 271 47
lift platform 173 40
lift shaft 271 51
ligament, falciform ~ 20 34
ligature *First Aid* 21 14-17
ligature *Composing Rm.* 175
6
ligature-holding forceps 26
44
light 106 8; 210 46; 224 69
light, flashing ~ 270 6
light, fluorescent ~ 271 23
light, leaded ~ 124 14
light, polar ~ 7 30
light, rear ~ 187 46; 189 9
light, supplementary ~ 203 17
light ale 93 26
light and bell buoy 224 74
light and whistle buoy 224 68
light beer 93 26
light box 179 25

light bulb 127 69; 318 26
light-emitting diode readout
110 2
lighter 216 25; 225 8, 25
lighter, disposable ~ 107 30
lighter, tug-pushed ~ 221 94
lighterman 216 26
light face 175 8
lighthouse *Map* 15 8
lighthouse *Navig.* 224 103
lighting, external ~ 197 32
lighting, indirect ~ 317 12
lighting, internal ~ 197 32
lighting aperture 334 75
lighting bridge, travelling ~
316 19
lighting console 316 2
lighting control console 316 2
lighting effects 316 2
lighting electrician 310 37
lighting gallery, travelling ~
316 19
lighting man 310 37; 316 20
lighting operator 316 20
lighting plot 316 3
lighting station 226 27
lighting technician 307 4
lightning 9 39
lightning arrester 152 35
lightning conductor 38 30
lightning rod 38 30
light plot 316 3
light railway diesel
locomotive 200 24
light rays 1 62
light readout 195 9
lights, set of ~ 268 54
light section tube 112 38
light-sensitive section 77 22
lightship *Map* 15 13
lightship *Ship* 221 47
lightship *Navig.* 224 81
light source *Atom* 1 59
light source *Optic. Instr.* 112
52
light source, photometric ~
112 50
light stop 5 22
light vessel 221 47; 224 81
ligula 68 22; 370 84
ligule 68 22; 370 84
lily 60 12
lily of the valley 377 2
limb 370 5
limb, fractured ~ 21 10
limb, moon's ~ 4 41
limbing machine 85 18
limbs 16 43-54
lime 147 56
lime, reconverted ~ 172 52
lime bunker 147 62
lime kiln 15 86
limerick 89 84
lime slaker 172 51
limestone 160 1
lime tree 371 46
limiter display 238 44
limit switch 241 60
limousine 193 1
linden plant 53 9
linden tree 371 46
line *Horse* 71 33
line *Composing Rm.* 175 4
line *Carriages* 186 31
line *Railw.* 202 1-38
line *Theatre* 316 8
line *Maths.* 346 1-23
line, curved ~ 346 21
line, equinoctial ~ 3 3
line, horizontal ~ 344 15
line, local ~ 15 25
line, straight ~ 346 2-3, 5, 16
linear 370 31

line block 178 42
line-casting machine 174 19
line cut 178 42
line engraving 178 42
line etching 178 42
line glass 124 6
line guide 89 60
linen 206 11
linen, dirty ~ 50 22
linen bin 50 21
linen compartment 267 31
linen drawer 44 22; 47 22
linen goods 271 57
linen shelf 43 2
linen tester 177 23
line-of-battle ship 218 51-60
line of fencing 294 9
line of latitude 14 2
line of life 19 72
line of longitude 14 4
line of the head 19 73
line of the heart 19 74
line of the staff 320 43
line plate 178 42
liner 221 82; 225 32
lines *Horse* 71 25
lines *Rowing* 283 52
line shooting 89 20
linesman *Railw.* 202 44
linesman *Ball Games* 291 59;
293 69
lines of the hand 19 72-74
line space adjuster 249 23
line space and carrier return
key 249 4
line steam injector 210 41
line-throwing gun 228 1
lingerie 32 1-15
lining *Bldg. Site* 119 54
lining *Hist. Cost.* 355 57
lining, fireproof ~ 147 48
lining, knitwear ~ 101 17
lining, leather ~ 291 22
lining, refractory ~ 147 48
lining, tricot ~ 101 17
lining board *Bldg. Site* 118
41; 119 18
lining board *Floor etc. Constr.*
123 56
lining paper 128 5
lining paper, shredded ~ 128
8
link 36 39
link, lower ~ 65 28
link, top ~ 65 27
linkage, three-point ~ 64 45;
65 72
linking of modules 242 70
link-up of modules 242 70
Linotype line-composing
machine 174 19
Linotype matrix 174 29
lint 383 19
lintel 37 25; 118 9
lintel, reinforced concrete ~
118 13
Linz-Donawitz converter 147
45-50
Lion *Astron.* 3 17; 4 57
lion 307 56; 356 5; 368 2
lip, lower ~ *Man* 19 26
lip, lower ~ *Horse* 72 10
lip, lower ~ *Music. Instr.* 326
26
lip, upper ~ *Man* 19 14
lip, upper ~ *Horse* 72 8
lip, upper ~ *Music. Instr.* 326
27
lip of the pudendum 20 87
lip of the vulva 20 87
lip plug 354 23
liquefied-gas tanker 221 35
liqueur 98 58

liqueur decanter 45 48
liqueur glass 45 89; 317 7
liquid-column barometer 10
1
liquid crystal readout 110 2
liquid feed pipe 74 26
liquid hydrogen and liquid
oxygen tank, jettisonable ~
235 46
liquid hydrogen line 234 51;
235 50
liquid hydrogen pump, high-
pressure ~ 235 41
liquid hydrogen suction line
234 23
liquid hydrogen supply, main
~ 235 35
liquid hydrogen tank 234 26,
41
liquid level indicator 316 57
liquid manure channel 75 44
liquid manure silo 62 13
liquid oxygen line 234 52; 235
51, 56
liquid oxygen pump, high-
pressure ~ 235 42
liquid oxygen supply line 234
10
liquid oxygen tank 234 12, 24,
39
liquid stage 148 27
liquor 168 14
liquor, weak ~ 172 45
liquor preheater 172 8
liquor pump 172 33
liquor supply pipe 92 48
lira 252 20, 21
literature 330 57
literature stand 330 56
litho artist 340 45
Lithodes 369 16
lithographer 340 45
lithographic crayon 340 26
lithographic press 340 60
lithographic stone 340 25, 57
lithography 340 25-26
lithosphere 11 1
litter *Poultry Farm* 74 8
litter *Livestock* 75 6
litter *Town* 268 22
litter basket 37 63; 205 55;
272 43; 273 25
litter bin 37 63; 205 55; 268 5;
272 43; 273 25
litter receptacle 196 12; 207
55
Little Bear 3 34
little brain 17 45; 18 23
little cluster fungus 381 33
Little Dipper 3 34
Little Dog 3 15
little owl 362 19
livelong 377 9
live power take-off 65 31
live power take-off shaft 65
31
liver 20 10, 34-35
livery 186 21
live sound 117 100
livestock, small 213 28
livestock ramp 206 1
living quarters 224 108; 227
19; 259 84
living room 42
lizards 364 27,30-37
llama 366 28
load 73 5
load, driven ~ 226 19
load, foil-wrapped ~ 226 9
load, unitized ~ 226 9, 21
load hook 270 49
loading bridge 221 90; 226 2
loading chamber 116 6

loading crane 85 28, 44
loading deck 221 34
loading dock 206 9
loading door 207 23
loading foreman 205 30; 206 29
loading gauge 206 22
loading platform *Lorries etc.* 194 3
loading platform *Ship* 221 90
loading siding 206 17
loading strip 206 8
loading supervisor 206 36
loaf, French ~ 97 12
loaf, long ~ 97 8
loaf, round ~ 97 6, 7; 99 14
loaf, small ~ 97 7
loaf, white ~ 97 9
loaf of bread 97 2
loam 120 44; 159 2
loan, personal ~ 250 4
lobby 267 18-26; 315 12-13
lobe 229 30
lobe, pulmonary ~ 20 7
lobe, upper ~ 20 7
lobe of the liver 20 35
lobster fork 45 79
local-battery telephone 224 27; 238 9, 40
lock *Map* 15 58
lock *Hunt.* 87 9
lock *Hydr. Eng.* 217 20
lock approach 217 26
lock chamber 217 20
lock gate 217 18, 32
lock indicator panel 203 63
locking bolt 117 62
locking lever *Atom* 2 40
locking lever *Motorcycles etc.* 188 2
locking lever *Office* 247 42
locking mechanism 246 23
locking nut 143 30; 187 54
lock lever 203 55
locknut 143 30; 187 54
locksmith 140 1
lock washer 202 8
locomotive, articulated ~ 210 64
locomotive, electric ~ 205 35; 211 1
locomotive, elevation of ~ 212 51-67
locomotive, fireless ~ 210 68
locomotive, mainline ~ 212 1
locomotive boiler 210 2-37
locust tree 371 70
loft 37 4; 38 18
log *Forestry* 84 20, 31
log *Maths.* 345 6
log, mechanical ~ 224 54
log, sawn ~ 157 33
log, ship's ~ 224 22
logarithm 345 6
logarithm sign 345 6
log capacity scale 157 10
log chain, endless ~ 157 17
log clock 224 57
log dump 85 32; 157 31
log grips 85 29; 157 13, 39
log grips, pivoted ~ 157 29
logic element 242 68
logic module 242 68
log-kicker arm 157 19
log ladder 273 22
loin *Game* 88 18, 35
loin *Meat* 95 3
loin *Butch.* 96 4
loin, pork ~ 95 46
loincloth 352 38; 354 31
loins *Man* 16 24
loins *Horse* 72 30
loin strap 71 32

long-conductor antenna 230 66
long-distance racing 290 11-15
long-distance runner 298 5
long drink 317 32
long-eared bat 366 9
long-eared owl 362 14
long-fly 296 48; 297 20
long haul airliner 231 13, 14
long horse 296 1
longicorn 358 38
longicorn beetle 358 38
longitude 14 7
long johns 32 29
long jump 298 37-41
long line 90 28
long-line fishing 90 28-29
long-lining 90 28-29
long measure 294 10
long primer 175 27
long rifle cartridge 305 38
longship 218 13-17
long sitting 295 10
longwall face, cut ~ 144 34
longwall face, ploughed ~ 144 33
longwall faces 144 33-37
long-wire antenna 230 66
lookout platform 273 23
loom, automatic ~ 166 1, 35
loom framing 166 24
loop *Knitting* 167 62, 66
loop *Weaves* 171 39
loop *Airsports* 288 1
loop *Winter Sp.* 301 7; 302 15
loop, closed ~ 171 36
loop, open ~ 171 30
loop, platinum ~ 23 15
loop, primary ~ 154 2, 42
loop, secondary ~ 154 7, 45
loop antenna 223 5
loo paper 49 11
looper 80 17
loop fastening 30 41
loop formation 167 65
loop former 312 30
loose-leaf file 260 15
Lophocalyx philippensis 369 7
lopping 85 11
lords-and-ladies 379 9
Lord's table 330 4
lorries 194
lorry 226 19
lorry, heavy ~ 194 20; 200 7
lorry, light ~ 194 1, 5
lorry, toy ~ 47 38; 273 62
lorry tyre 273 19
lorry wheel 138 21
lorry with trailer 213 34
loser 292 5
lot 310 1
lottery booth 308 44
lottery ticket seller 266 20
lotus column 333 13
loud hailer 264 12
loud pedal 325 8
loudspeaker 42 10; 241 14; 264 12; 311 46; 317 15; 318 12
loudspeaker, built-in ~ 249 70
loudspeaker aperture 309 19
louis-d'or 252 5
Louis Seize table 336 14
lounge *Living Rm.* 42
lounge *Ship* 223 26
lounge *Airport* 233 18
'lounge' *Airport* 233 28
lourer 321 71
louvre shutter 304 12
love-lies-bleeding 60 21

low 9 5
low box 172 26
lower cable sleeve 214 74
lower fore topgallant sail 219 58
lower fore topgallant yard 219 35
lower fore topsail 219 56
lower fore topsail yard 219 33
Lower Keuper 154 57
lower main topgallant sail 219 64
lower main topgallant yard 219 41
lower main topsail 219 62
lower main topsail yard 219 39
Lower Muschelkalk 154 60
lower station platform 214 51
low house 305 76
low-moor bog 13 14
low-pressure area 9 5
low-pressure manometer 141 4
low-pressure regulator 190 59
low relief 339 33
low-speed aileron 229 41
low-temperature surface insulation 235 15
low tide 280 7
low-voltage bushing 152 44
low-voltage terminal 152 44
lozenge 346 35
L-seat 295 10
L-support 295 16
lubber's line 224 48
lubber's mark 224 48
lubber's point 224 48
lubricant pump, automatic ~ 210 42
lubricating nipple 143 81
lubricating oil 145 62
lubricating oil refinery 145 67
lubricating system, pressure-feed ~ 192 16-27
lubrication hole 187 62
lubrication system 65 45
lubricator 187 62, 65
lubricator, automatic ~ 210 42
lucerne 69 9
ludo 47 19
luff 284 42
luffing 285 9
luffing jib crane 222 23
luge 303 13
luge, junior ~ 303 3
luge toboggan 303 13
luge toboggan, junior ~ 303 3
luge tobogganer 303 12
luggage 205 7-12
luggage carrier 187 44
luggage clerk 204 9
luggage compartment *Car* 193 17, 23
luggage compartment *Lorries etc.* 194 13
luggage compartment *Railw.* 207 71; 208 15
luggage counter 204 4
luggage label 205 8
luggage locker 194 18
'luggage lockers' 233 39
luggage rack 207 51; 208 27
luggage receipt 204 8
luggage rest 204 43
luggage sticker 204 7
lugger 90 1
lugsail 220 4
lug strap 166 22
lumbar region 72 30
lumber 120 2
lumber, rough ~ 120 83
lumberer 84 18

lumbering 84 15-37
lumberjack 84 18
lumber-jacket 30 38
lumberman 84 18
lumber room door 38 20
luminescent 369 14
luminescent material 240 18
lump coal 156 14
lunar module 234 55
lunar module hangar 234 54
lunation 4 2-7
lung 18 13; 20 6-7
lung, right ~ 20 6
lunge 295 42
lunging 294 5
lunging position 294 5
lungwort 377 7
lunula *Man* 19 81
lunula *Prehist.* 328 25
lunula *Church* 332 36
lunule 19 81
lupin 51 23
lur 322 1
lute 324 1
lute pin 324 11
lycaenid butterfly 365 6
lychgate 331 19
Lyman series 1 20
lymph gland, submandibular ~ 19 10
lynx 368 8
lynx fur 131 20
lynx skin 131 15
lynx skin, let-out ~ 131 16
Lyoner sausage 96 10
Lyra 3 22
Lyre *Astron.* 3 22
lyre *Music. Instr.* 322 15
lyre flower 60 5

M

maar 11 25
macadam spreader 200 31
macaroni 98 33
macaroon, coconut ~ 97 37
mace 382 34
machicolation 329 23
machicoulis 329 23
machine, four-cylinder ~ 189 49
machine, heavy ~ 189 43
machine, heavy-weight ~ 189 43
machine, high-performance ~ 189 43
machine, multi-magazine ~ 174 19
machine base 168 15
machine bed 177 57
machine chest 172 86; 173 1, 13
machine control lever 167 44
machine drum 323 57
machine gun 255 8, 32
machine hood 173 27
machine housing 200 2
machine part 111 30
machine parts 143
machine processor 116 60
machinery and observation deck 224 107
machinery and observation platform 224 107
machinery shed 62 15
machine tap 150 44
machine tools 149; 150
machine wire 173 14
machining centre 150 41
mackerel sky 8 14
MacPherson strut unit 192 72-84

macramé 102 21
macro equipment 115 81-98
macro frame 117 56
macro lens attachment 117 55
macronucleus 357 11
Macropharynx longicaudatus 369 2
macrophoto stand 115 94
macro zoom lens 117 53
madeira glass 45 84
Madonna 330 51
Madonna lily 60 12
magazine Doc. 22 4
magazine Flat 46 20
magazine Hunt. 87 17
magazine Cine Film 117 45
magazine Office 249 33
magazine Army 255 15, 21
magazine Police 264 25
magazine Chivalry 329 13
magazine, rotary ~ 114 77
magazine, spring-loaded ~ 247 6
magazine back 115 80
magazine holder 255 7
magazine housing 313 9
magazine repeater 87 2
magazine rifle 87 2
magazine spring 87 18
magenta filter adjustment 116 43
maggot Gdn. Pests 80 19
maggot Articulates 358 19
'magic eye' 309 18
magmatism, plutonic ~ 11 29-31
magnesium plate 179 9
magnet 1 63; 2 51; 108 32; 212 38
magnetic disc store 244 1
magnetic film 311 21
magnetic film spool 311 2
magnetic head, four-track ~ 312 51
magnetic head cluster 312 28
magnetic head support assembly 311 3
magnetic sound amplifier 311 28
magnetic sound deck 311 20
magnetic sound head 312 50
magnetic sound recorder 310 58; 311 1
magnetic sound recording and playback deck 238 4
magnetic sound recording and playback amplifier 311 5
magnetic sound recording equipment 310 58; 311 1
magnetic sound unit, attachable ~ 312 50
magnetic sound unit, four-track ~ 312 50
magnetic tape 237 63; 238 4, 5; 244 2
magnetic tape dictating machine 249 62
magnetic tape loop 245 28
magnetic tape recording and playback equipment 238 55
magnetic tape reel 244 10
magnetic tape station 242 32
magnetic tape unit 244 9
magnifier 175 34
magnifying glass 175 34; 177 23
magnitude 3 14
magpie 361 3
magpie moth larva 58 5
maharaja 306 28
mahlstick 129 47

mail 329 62, 63
mail and cargo terminal 233 9
mailbag 236 54
mailbox 236 50
mail carrier 236 53
mailcoach 186 39, 53
mailcoach driver 186 40
mailman 236 53
mail van 236 52
main air pressure gauge 212 6
main air reservoir pressure gauge 212 8
main beam warning light 191 69
main course 218 33; 219 61
main drive unit 113 15
main engine revolution indicator 224 21
main engine room 223 72
main exchange line 237 18, 24
main line 203 45
mainmast 218 40; 219 5-7; 220 22
mainmast, lower ~ 219 5
main royal sail 219 66
main royal stay 219 13
main royal staysail 219 26
main royal yard 219 43
mainsail 218 33; 219 61; 220 11; 284 46; 285 2
mains button 195 11
mainsheet 284 28
mains power unit 311 11
mainstay 219 10
maintained lift 299 5
maintenance technician 237 28
main title 185 46
maintop 219 52
main topgallant mast 219 7
main topgallant rigging 219 18
main topgallant sail 218 53
main topgallant stay 219 12
main topgallant staysail 219 25
main topmast 219 6
main topmast crosstrees 219 53
main topmast rigging 219 17
main topmast stay 219 11
main topmast staysail 219 24
main topsail 218 38
main topsail yard 218 39
main yard 218 37; 219 38
maize 68 1, 31
maize billbug 81 26
maize cob 68 36
maize kernel 68 37
majorette 306 67
major keys 320 55-68
major second 321 7
major seventh 321 12
major sixth 321 11
major third 321 8
major triad 321 1
majuscule 175 11
maker-up 174 5
make-up artist 310 36; 315 1
make-up artist, chief ~ 315 47
make-up gown 315 44
make-up man, chief ~ 315 47
make-up table Offset Platem. 179 23
make-up table Theatre 315 45
Malacosteus indicus 369 10
malaria mosquito 81 44
malleolus, external ~ 19 59
malleolus, inner ~ 19 60
malleolus, internal ~ 19 60
malleolus, lateral ~ 19 59
malleolus, medial ~ 19 60

malleolus, outer ~ 19 59
malleolus fibulae 19 59
malleolus medialis 19 60
malleolus tibulae 19 60
mallet 118 54; 120 67; 125 18; 132 5; 158 36; 278 25; 339 21
malleus 17 61
malt 92 1-41
malt, green ~ 92 23
malt beer 93 26
malt elevator 92 35
maltese cross mechanism 312 38
maltese cross movement 312 38
malting 92 1-41
maltings 92 1
malting tower 92 1
malt silo 92 37
mamma 16 28-29
mammal, flying ~ 366 9
mammal, oviparous ~ 366 1
mammal, scaly ~ 366 10
mammals 366; 367; 368
mammals, insect-eating ~ 366 4-7
mammals, marsupial ~ 366 2-3
mammoth tree 372 69
Man 16; 17; 18; 19; 20
manager 299 45
manatee 366 23
manati 366 23
mandarin Carnival 306 29
mandarin South. Fruits 384 23
mandible Man 17 35
mandible Articulates 358 25
mandible, lower ~ 359 8
mandolin 324 16
mandrel 125 19
mane 72 13
mane, lion's ~ 368 3
man-eater 364 1
maneuver see manoeuvre
maneuvering see manoeuvring
mangelwurzel 69 21
manger board 258 7, 76
mangle 165 46
mangold 69 21
mangoldwurzel 69 21
manhole Roof & Boilerr. 38 45
manhole Brew. 93 13
manhole Cooper 130 18
manhole Space 234 30; 235 52
manhole Water 269 26, 51
manhole cover Roof & Boilerr. 38 46
manhole cover Cooper 130 19
manhole cover Street Sect. 198 17
manikin 338 31
manipulator 2 38
manipulator, mechanical ~ 139 32
manipulators 2 47
man-made fibres 169; 170
mannequin 338 31
manoeuvres, principal, of aircraft 230 67-72
manoeuvring keel 227 30
manoeuvring rocket assembly 234 63
manoeuvring rockets 6 5, 39
manometer 25 22; 67 10; 83 42; 178 8; 196 20; 349 19
manostat 269 47
manque 275 22
mansard dormer window 121 19

mansard roof 121 18
mantelpiece 267 24
mantelshelf 267 24
mantissa 345 6
mantle Phys. Geog. 11 3
mantle Iron & Steel 147 46
mantle Heraldry 254 3
mantle clock 42 16
mantling 254 3, 14
manual 325 48; 326 42, 43, 44, 45
manual, lower ~ 322 47
manual, upper ~ 322 46
manual feed station 184 2
manure 63 15
manure distributor 62 21
manure fork, four-pronged ~ 66 7
manure gutter 75 20
manure hoe 66 8
manure removal 74 23-27; 75 21
manure spreader 62 21; 63 39
manuscript 174 6; 176 3
manway 154 32
map Map 14; 15
map 204 15; 260 44; 268 2
maple seed 371 57
maple tree 371 53
map light 230 23
map of the world 14 10-45
mapping 348 9, 10
mapping, one-to-one ~ 348 11
mappings 348 9-11
map projections 14 8-9
map signs 15 1-114
map symbols 14 27-29; 15 1-114
maraca 324 59
marcando 321 27
marcato 321 27
mare 73 2
margarine 98 21; 99 48
margin 185 55-58
margin, back ~ 185 55
margin, inside ~ 185 55
margin, outside ~ 185 57
margin, upper ~ 185 56
margin control 180 5, 20
margin release key 249 6
margin scale 249 12
margin stop, left ~ 249 13
margin stop, right ~ 249 14
marguerite 51 24; 376 4
marimba, steel ~ 324 61
marimbaphone 324 61
marine sequence 310 11
mark 285 17
mark, port hand ~ 224 95
mark, starboard hand ~ 224 96
marker 85 12
marker, port ~ 224 100
marker, starboard ~ 224 99
market for securities 251 2
market garden 55 1-51, 3
market place 15 52
market square 15 52
market woman 308 65
markiert 321 27
marking, axillary ~ 88 74
marking hammer 85 12
marking iron 85 12
marking out 104 21
markings, graduated ~ 115 65
mark of omission 342 29
marks, diacritical ~ 342 30-35
marl 160 1
marmot 366 18
maroon 306 53
marquise 36 55
marriage ceremony 332 14

Mars 4 46
marsh *Phys. Geog.* 13 14-24
marsh *Map* 15 20
marshal 329 75
marshaling *see* marshalling
marshalling yard 206 42
marshalling yard signal box 206 44
marsh harrier 362 13
marshmallow *Bakery* 97 36
marshmallow *Med. Plants* 380 12
marsh plants 378 14-57
marsh tea 377 21
marsupials 366 2-3
marten 86 22
martens 367 14-17
martinet 218 36
marzipan 98 82
Masai warrior 354 8
mash 93 10
mash copper 92 44
masher 92 49
mashhouse 92 42-53
mashing process 92 42-53
mash kettle 92 44
mash thermometer 93 9
mash tub 92 43
mash tun 92 43, 44
mask *Hosp.* 27 48
mask *Swim.* 279 10
mask *Carnival* 306 7
mask *Films* 310 51; 313 4
mask *Sculpt. Studio* 339 37
mask, clay ~ 260 75
mask, pressure-equalizing ~ 279 10
mask, wooden ~ 354 16
mask drum 177 48
masked ball 306 1-48
masking frame 116 35
masking tape 128 16
mask-scanning head 177 47
masonry bonds 118 58-68
masonry dam 217 58
masquerade 306 1-48, 6-48
mass 11 43
mass, continental ~ 11 7
massage bath 281 33
mass book 330 38
masseter 19 7
massif 12 39
mast 219 1-9; 221 77; 284 4, 11
mast, full-rigged ~ 220 16
mast, half-rigged ~ 220 15
Master 289 45
master arm 2 42
master brewer 92 49
master butcher 96 38
master clock 245 18
master compass 224 51
master control panel 242 3
master furrow 91 18
master gyro compass 224 51
Master of foxhounds 289 45
master selector 195 8
master/slave manipulator 2 47
master station 224 40
master switch 153 2
master turner 135 20
master volume control 261 44
masterwort 376 7
mat 299 12
matador 319 2, 25, 31
match 107 22
matchbox 107 21
matchbox holder 266 24
match head 107 23
mate 276 15
maté 382 11
material *School* 260 81

material *Store* 271 59
material, basic ~ 169 1
material, radioactive ~ 1 28
materials store 146 6
maté shrub 382 11
mathematics 344; 345; 346; 347; 348
mathematics, higher ~ 345 11-14
matinée coat 29 3
matrix *Man* 20 79
matrix *Composing Rm.* 174 21, 31
matrix, punched ~ 175 37
matrix, stamped ~ 175 37
matrix-boring machine 175 49
matrix case 174 42, 46; 176 17
matrix clamp 175 59
matrix disc 176 20
matrix drum 176 27
matrix-engraving machine 175 49
matrix for hand-setting 174 28
matrix holder 24 55
matrix mimic board 153 8
mat sail 353 33
matte 313 4
matte box 313 3
matter 174 15; 181 37
matter, front ~ 185 43-47
matter, machine-set ~ 174 27
matter, preliminary ~ 185 43-47
matting, reed ~ 55 6
matting, straw ~ 55 6
mattress 47 3; 296 18
mattress, foam ~ 43 10
matt weave 171 11
maturing 169 7
mauerkrone 254 46
mausoleum 337 16
mavis 361 16
maw worm 81 31
maxilla 17 36; 19 27
maximum 347 19
maximum thermometer 10 53
may 374 30
Maya temple 352 20
May bug 82 1
mayfly 358 6
maypole swing 273 8
maze 272 5
M-cardan 67 29
meadow 13 13; 62 44; 63 22
meadow buttercup 375 8
meadow fescue grass 69 24
meadow flowers 375; 376
meadow foxtail 69 27
meadow grass 375 39
meadow grasshopper 358 8
meadow mushroom 381 1
meadow saffron 379 3
meal, complete ~ 266 17
meal, deepfreeze ~ 96 23
meal, deep-frozen ~ 96 23
meal, hot ~ 266 67
meal, ready-to-eat ~ 96 23
meal beetle 81 18
meal of the day 266 27
meal worm beetle 81 18
meander *Phys. Geog.* 13 11
meander *Art* 334 43
meander core 13 12
mean low water 15 9
mean sea level 146 39
measure *Hotel* 267 60
measure *Music. Not.* 320 28-42
measure line 320 42
measurement chamber 112 43

measurement dial 242 75
measurement range selector *Atom* 2 4, 23
measurement range selector *Optic. Instr.* 112 46
measurement range selector *Inf. Tech.* 242 74
measurement scale 242 75
measuring and control unit 178 3
measuring arm 142 38
measuring beaker 267 60
measuring cylinder *Doc.* 23 43
measuring cylinder *Photog.* 116 11
measuring cylinder *Paperm.* 173 4
measuring cylinder *School* 261 26
measuring cylinder *Chem.* 350 26
measuring device 112 51
measuring flask 350 27
measuring glass 10 47; 350 26
measuring instrument 153 30
measuring instrument platform 235 69
measuring instruments 149 56-72
measuring machine, universal-type ~ 112 67
measuring probe 234 42
measuring rod *Map* 14 47
measuring rod *Cine Film* 117 59
measuring rod *Quarry* 158 26
measuring scale 149 63
measuring tank 130 22
measuring tape 103 2; 271 38
measuring vessel 93 3; 130 33
measuring worm 80 17
meat 96 1-4, 59; 99 53
meat, canned ~ 98 20
meat, cold ~ 96 14
meat, minced ~ 96 16
meat, roast ~ 45 27
meat, smoked ~ 96 3
meat axe 94 18
meat chopper 40 39
meat counter 99 51
meat dish 266 55
meat grinder 96 53
meathook 96 55
meat inspector 94 24
meat joints 95
meat mincer 96 53
meat-mixing trough 96 40
meat plate 45 26
meat platter 45 26
meat product 99 53
meat salad 96 13
meat saw 94 20
mechanic 140 1
mechanical finger car 159 18
mechanical pulp mill 172 53-65
mechanism casing 255 10
medallion 339 36
Mediaeval 342 4
medical card 22 8
medical laboratory technician 23 41
medical record 22 8
medicament, water-soluble ~ 25 14
medicine 22 23
medicine cabinet 49 49
medicine case 24 7
medicine cupboard 22 35
medicine sample 22 41
Mediterranean 14 25

medium 308 9
medium haul airliner 231 12
medium measure 294 10
medulla oblongata 17 47; 18 24
medusa 357 14
meeting 263 8
meeting, public ~ 263 1-15
meeting point 233 29
meganucleus 357 11
megaphone 283 21
megaphone exhaust pipe 189 51
meiobar 9 3
Melanocetes 369 6
melodium 325 43
melody key 324 39
melody pipe 322 10
melody side 324 39
melody string 322 30; 324 24
melon 57 23
melter 148 7
melting bath 162 3, 14
melting furnace *Iron Foundry etc.* 148 1
melting furnace *Electrotyp. etc.* 178 19
melting plant 148 1-12
melting pot *Goldsm. etc.* 108 8
melting pot *Synth. Fibres* 170 30
member, diagonal ~ 215 35
member, upright ~ 119 59
member, vertical ~ 215 36
member of set 348 2
membership card 275 14
membrane 241 68
membrane, parchment ~ 324 31
membrane, periodontal ~ 19 28
membrane, tympanic ~ 17 59
membrane, vitelline ~ 74 64
membranophones 323 51-59
memorial chapel 331 12
memorial plate 331 14
memorial tablet 331 14
memory, main ~ 244 6; 245 28
memory key 247 22
memory typewriter 245 26
memory unit 176 11; 242 9
memo sheet 247 34
menagerie 307 63
menhir 328 18
menhir group 328 11
men's wear 33
men's wear department 271 12
menu 266 21
menu card 266 21
Mercator projection 14 9
Mercury 4 43
mercury barometer 10 1
mercury battery 25 32
mercury column 10 2
mercury manometer 25 18
meridian 14 4
meridian circle 113 26
meridian of Greenwich 14 5
meridian of longitude 14 4
meridians 14 1-7
meridian telescope 113 29
meringue 97 26; 265 5
merlin 362 1
merlon 329 7
mermaid 327 23
merman 327 23, 40
merry-go-round 308 2
mesa 13 59
mesh 171 37
mesh connection 153 21

mesh gauge 102 25
mesh pin 102 25
mesh ventilator 278 40
Mesolithic period 328 1-9
messroom 228 25
metacarpal 17 16
metal, noble ~ 237 42
metal-blocking device 111 34
metal feeder 174 26
metal feeder, automatic ~ 174 40
metal runner 147 35
metals 254 24-25
metal shears 108 23; 125 1
metalworker 140 1
metalwork shop 140 1-22
metatarsus 17 28
metazoans 357 13-39
meteor 7 18
meteorite crater 6 16
meteorological instruments 10
meteorological office 225 33
meteorological watch office 9 7
meteorology 8; 9
meter Atom 2 6
meter Photog. 114 62
meter Blacksm. 138 19
meter Serv. Stat. 196 14
meter Music. Not. 320 28-42
meter, customer's ~ 237 16
meter, multiple ~ 242 73
meter, private ~ 237 16
meter, rotary ~ 269 53
meter, subscriber's ~ 237 16
meter cell 114 3, 24; 115 37
metering pump 169 13
metope 334 16
metre tape measure 103 2
metronome 325 19
mezzanine 315 18
mezzo staccato 321 29
mezzotint 340 14-24
micro attachment 115 89
micro cassette recorder 246 32
microfilm card 237 38
microfilm file 237 37
microfilming system 242 31
microfilm reader 237 36
micrometer 142 37; 149 62; 173 10; 224 4
micrometer eyepiece 14 53
micrometer head 14 52
micronucleus 357 12
microphone 22 15; 117 8, 24, 74; 197 26; 209 31; 224 30; 230 29; 237 9; 241 49; 261 39; 263 7; 310 30; 317 20
microphone, built-in ~ 241 5; 243 3
microphone, umpire's ~ 293 21
microphone base 241 51
microphone boom 310 25
microphone boom, telescopic ~ 117 23
microphone cable 239 14; 310 32; 311 41
microphone connecting cord 117 25
microphone connecting lead 117 25
microphone cradle 249 65
microphone screen 241 50
microphone socket 249 69
microphone socket panel 238 36
microphone stand 241 51
microprism collar 115 54
microprism spot 115 58, 59, 62, 63

micropyle 383 57
microscope 111 19; 112 1
microscope, metallurgical ~ 112 23
microscope, surgical ~ 112 31
microscope, universal ~ 112 54
microscope, wide-field ~ 112 23, 54
microscope body 113 31-39
microscope camera, fully automatic ~ 112 64
microscope for reflected light 112 23
microscope stage 112 9
microscope tube 113 31-39
microwave treatment unit 23 36; 24 23
mid-channel 224 98
middle-distance runner 298 5
middle ground 224 91
middle ground to port 224 88
middle mast 220 33
Middle Muschelkalk 154 59
middle of the fairway 224 98
middle section 259 55-74
middling 91 2
midfield player 291 14
midge 358 16
midget 308 22
midi bus 194 34
midinette 306 21
mid-range speaker 241 16
midrib 370 30
mihrab 337 14
milch-cow 62 34; 75 17
mild 93 26
mildew 80 20
milestone 15 109
milk 266 60
milk, canned ~ 98 15
milk, homogenized ~ 99 44
milk, long-life ~ 99 44
milk, pasteurized ~ 99 44
milk, sterilized ~ 76 16
milk bag 99 45
milk carton 76 22
milk churn 309 89
milker 62 34; 75 17, 25
milk glass 124 5
milk heater 76 13
milking parlour 75 23
milk jug 44 31
milkman 75 25
milk pipe 75 27
milk pot 40 15
milk processing area 76 12-48
milk reception 76 1
milk tanker 76 2
milk tub filler 76 21
milkwort 377 3
Milky Way 3 35
mill 276 24
miller 91 15
millet 68 28
millibar scale 10 3
millimeter graduation 247 36
millimetre scale 10 3
milliner 35 1
milliner's shop 268 38
milling machine, rotary ~ 168 1
milling machine, universal ~ 150 32
milling machine table 150 33
milling roller, bottom ~ 168 4, 6
milling roller, top ~ 168 3
millrace 91 44
mills 91
mill spindle 91 12
millstone 91 16, 19, 21

millstone, upper ~ 91 22
millstone casing 91 20
millstone ruff 355 52
millstream 91 44
mill weir 91 42
mill wheel, breast ~ 91 37
mill wheel, middleshot ~ 91 37
mill wheel, overshot ~ 91 35
mill wheel, undershot ~ 91 39
milometer 187 33
mimbar 337 15
minaret 337 13
minbar 337 15
mince 96 16
mincemeat 96 16
mincer 40 39; 96 53
mincing machine 96 52, 53
mine 15 34
mine, disused ~ 15 35
mine car 144 45
mine fan 144 16
minehead buildings 154 70
mine hunter 258 80
minelayer 258 94
mineral bath, outdoor ~ 281 9
mineral spring 274 11
mineral water 266 61
minesweeper 258 84
mine-sweeping gear 258 87
mini 193 19
miniature film cassette 112 35
minibus 194 9; 195 47
minigolf course 272 68
minigolf hole 272 70
minigolf player 272 69
minim 320 14
minim rest 320 22
minimum 347 20
minimum thermometer 10 54
mining, underground ~ 144 21-51
minion 175 24
minionette 175 23
mink 30 60
mink skin 131 11
mink skin, let-out ~ 131 19
minnesinger 329 70
minor keys 320 55-68
minor planets 4 47
minor triad 321 2
minstrel 329 70
mintage 252 10, 40-44
minting dies 252 40-41
minting press 252 44
mint mark 252 10
minuend 344 24
minus blue filter adjustment 116 44
minuscule 175 12
minuscule, Carolingian ~ 341 18
minus green filter adjustment 116 43
minus red filter adjustment 116 45
minus sign 344 8, 24
minute hand 110 12
Mira 3 11
mirabelle 59 25
mire crow 359 14
mirror 43 29; 49 33; 105 20; 106 6; 111 4; 177 38; 188 35; 189 30; 207 49
mirror, angled ~ 177 28
mirror, auxiliary ~ 115 38
mirror, concave ~ 5 32; 308 56; 312 39
mirror, convex ~ 308 57
mirror, flat ~ 5 3
mirror, illuminating ~ 14 59
mirror, main ~ 5 1; 113 10
mirror, primary ~ 5 1; 113 10

mirror, right-angle ~ 261 10
mirror, rotating ~ 243 54
mirror, secondary ~ 5 2; 113 11
mirror, semi-reflecting ~ 243 55
mirror, triple ~ 104 1
mirror arc lamp 312 39
mirror assembly 176 21
mirror carp 364 4
mirror lens 115 50
mirror manometer 349 20
mirror reflex system 115 31
mirror spot 316 48
mirror spotlight 316 48
mirror system 176 24
missal 330 38
missile 258 49
missile, short-range ~ 259 26
missile, wooden ~ 352 39; 353 8
missile cruiser 259 21, 41
missile launcher, underwater ~ 259 37, 51
missile-launching housing 258 71
miter see mitre
miter angle 120 82
mitre 124 4
mitre block 124 30
mitre board 124 31
mitre box Glaz. 124 30
mitre box Joiner 132 43
mitre gate 217 19
mitre joint 124 4
mitre shoot 124 31
mitre square 120 82
mitring machine 124 7
mitt, catcher's ~ 292 60
mitt, fielder's ~ 292 59
mitten crab 358 1
mixed asphalt outlet 200 54
mixer Dent. 24 51
mixer Kitch. Utensils 40 45
mixer Cine Film 117 26
mixer Synth. Fibres 170 53
mixer Aircraft 232 48
mixer Broadcast. 238 25
mixer Films 311 21
mixer Disco 317 26
mixer, double shaft ~ 159 10
mixer, hand ~ 39 22
mixer, high-speed ~ 79 5
mixer, propeller-type ~ 79 5
mixer drum 200 15
mixer operator 118 32
mixer tap 39 36; 49 2; 106 14; 126 27
mixing 169 2
mixing chamber 83 62
mixing chest 173 1
mixing console Cine Film 117 26
mixing console Broadcast. 238 25
mixing console Films 310 56; 311 35
mixing console Disco 317 26
mixing desk Cine Film 117 26
mixing desk Broadcast. 238 25
mixing desk Films 310 56; 311 35
mixing desk Disco 317 26
mixing drum 118 34; 200 15
mixing faucet 39 36; 49 2; 106 14; 126 27
mixing machine 200 15
mixing plant, central ~ 201 19
mixing plant, stationary ~ 201 19
mixing room 311 34
mixing screw 83 59

mixing spoon 40 3
mixing tank 172 35
mixture, additive ~ 343 10
mixture, subtractive ~ 343 12
mixture control 230 31; 288
16
Mizar 3 29
mizen see mizzen
mizzen 218 29; 219 30
mizzen, lower ~ 219 8
mizzen mast 218 31; 219 8-9;
220 23, 24, 30, 34
mizzen stay 219 10
mizzen staysail 219 27
mizzen top 219 54
mizzen topgallant sail 218 54
mizzen topgallant stay 219 12
mizzen topgallant staysail 219
29
mizzen topmast 219 9
mizzen topmast rigging 219
17
mizzen topmast stay 219 11
mizzen topmast staysail 219
28
moat 329 33, 37; 356 3
mobile 260 70
moccasin 101 30; 352 18
moccasin flower 376 27
mock orange 373 9
model, clay ~ 260 67
model, dressmaker's ~ 103 6
model, nude ~ 338 32
model, plaster ~ 339 4
model, wax ~ 339 26
model aeroplane 273 37, 38
model aeroplanes 288 85-91
model coat 103 7
model dress 103 5
model flight, radio-
controlled ~ 288 85
model hat 35 7
modeling see modelling
modeller 339 6
modelling board 48 14; 339
34
modelling clay 48 12; 339 31
modelling stand 339 9
modelling substance 339 8
modelling tool 161 20
modelling tool, wire ~ 339 11
modelling tool, wooden ~ 339
10
model of set 315 42
model of skull 261 15
models of molecules 242
61-67
model stage 315 41
moderator 1 54
modular elements 242 68-72
module, electronic ~ 242 69
module, lunar ~ 6 12
module, magnetic ~ 242 72
moistener 247 31
moisturising cream 99 27
molar 19 18, 35
mold see mould
molder 97 57
mole Map 15 48
mole Hydr. Eng. 217 15
mole Docks 225 65
mole Mammals 366 4
molecular rearrangement 170
23
molluscs 357 27-36
monastery Map 15 63
monastery Church 331 52-58
monastery garden 331 53
money 252; 265 3
money, hard ~ 252 1-28
money, metal ~ 252 1-28
money, paper ~ 252 29-39
money compartment 271 6

money order 236 27
moneywort 375 26
monitor 23 27; 26 15, 16, 33;
27 23
monitor Cine Film 117 97
monitor Broadcast. 238 33
monitor Audiovis. 243 6
monitor Fire Brig. 270 66
monitor Theatre 316 18
monitor Fish etc. 364 31
monitor, six-channel ~ 27 31
monitoring and control panel
238 1, 7
monitoring controls 153 5
monitoring instrument 311
15
monitoring loudspeaker 239
9; 311 13
monitoring speaker 238 15
monitoring unit, mobile ~ 25
24
monitor lizard 364 31
monitor support, swivel-
mounted ~ 27 24
monitor unit 25 44
monk 89 9
monk, Benedictine ~ 331 54
monkey bridge 223 4-11; 227
24
monkey house 356 10
monkey nut 383 41
monkeys 368 12-13
monkshood 379 1
monochlorobenzene 170 9
monoclinic crystal system 351
24-25
monogram 36 41
mono-line control system
288 90
monolith 328 18
monoplane, high-wing ~ 229
1; 231 2
monoplane, low-wing ~ 229
5, 14; 231 1
monoplane, midwing ~ 229 4
monoplane, shoulder-wing ~
229 3
mono posto 290 34
monorail car 144 43, 44
monoski 286 56
mono sound 311 35
monotreme 366 1
monotype caster 174 39
monotype casting machine
174 39
monotype composing and
casting machine 174 32-45
monotype composing
machine 174 32
monsoon 9 52
monster 327 16
monster, winged ~ 327 55
monstrance 331 48; 332 34
montera 319 29
monument Map 15 92
monument Park 272 10
moon 4 1-9, 31, 45
moon, full ~ 4 5
moon, new ~ 4 2
moon, waning ~ 4 7
moon, waxing ~ 4 3
moon landing 6
moor buzzard 362 13
moor harrier 362 13
moor hawk 362 13
mooring 283 19
mooring bitt, cross-shaped ~
217 13, 14
mooring bitt, double ~ 217 14
mooring chain 224 72
mooring line 288 66
mooring sinker 224 73
moose 367 1

mop, gilder's ~ 129 54
mopboard 123 21, 63
moped 188 24
moped, battery-powered ~
188 20
moped headlamp 188 29
mopeds 188
Mopsea 369 8
moraine, lateral ~ 12 53
moraine, medial ~ 12 54
morainic filter layer 199 24
Morchella conica 381 27
Morchella esculenta 381 26
mordant 178 24; 182 16
mordent, inverted ~ 321 19
mordent, lower ~ 321 20
mordent, upper ~ 321 19
morel 381 26, 27
morello 59 5
morello cherry 59 5
morion 329 60
morse 367 20
morse lamp 223 7
mortadella 96 7
mortar Army 255 40
mortar Chem. 349 9
mortar bed 123 27
mortar pan 118 39
mortar trough 118 20, 39, 84
mortar tub 118 39
mortice see mortise
mortise, forked ~ 121 85
mortise and tenon joint 121
84, 85
mortise axe 120 72
mortise chisel 132 8
mortise lock 140 36-43
mortiser 120 17
mortising chain, endless ~
132 50
mortuary 331 21
mosaic 338 37
mosaic figure 338 38
mosque 337 12
mosquito 358 16
moss 377 17
moss phlox 60 14
moss pink 60 14
moth 58 64; 81 13; 82 15, 18,
45, 48
moth, female ~ 82 30
moth, male ~ 82 29
moth, night-flying ~ 82 14
moth, nocturnal ~ 82 14
mother 28 6; 272 71
mother-of-pearl 357 34
mother sheep 75 10
moths 358 48-56; 365 7-11
motif Child. Clothes 29 20
motif Art. Studio 338 27
motion, longitudinal ~ 149 17
motion picture camera,
lightweight ~ 313 20
motion picture camera,
narrow-gauge ~ 313 31
motion picture camera,
professional ~ 313 20, 31
motion picture camera,
soundproof ~ 310 47; 313
15
motion picture camera,
standard-gauge ~ 313 1
motion picture cameras 313
1-39
motion picture laboratory 310
2; 311 30
motion picture library 310 5
motion picture projection 312
1-23
motion pictures 310; 311;
312; 313
motion picture storage vault
310 5

motions, rotary ~ 4 22-28
moto cross 290 24-28
motor Forestry 84 34
motor Watchm. 109 13
motor Iron Foundry etc. 148
64
motor Weaving 165 12, 34
motor Electrotyp. etc. 178 14
motor Tram 197 5, 7
motor Water 269 45
motor, auxiliary ~ 211 17
motor, built-in ~ 164 2
motor, built-on ~ 164 33
motor, electric ~ Roof &
Boilerr. 38 59
motor, electric ~ Pest Contr.
83 53
motor, electric ~ Blacksm.
138 2
motor, electric ~ Weaving 166
18
motor, electric ~ Railw. 212
34
motor, electric ~ Ship 223 69
motor, synchronous ~ 176 19
motor, three-phase ~ 164 35
motor, two-stroke ~ 56 30
motor base plate 164 36
motor bedplate 164 36
motorboat 283 2
motorboat landing stage 216 7
motorboats 286 1-5
motor car 191 1-56; 192;
193; 195 34
motor car mechanic 195 53
motor coach 194 17
motor cruiser 286 4
motor cultivator 56 18
motorcycle 189; 268 35
motorcycle, heavyweight ~
189 31
motorcycle, light ~ 188 39;
189 1, 16
motorcycle, lightweight ~ 189
1
motorcycle, pacer's ~ 290 12
motorcycle chain 189 22
motorcycle racing 290 24-28
motorcycles 188
motorcycles, heavy ~ 189
31-58
motorcycles, heavyweight ~
189 31-58
motorcycles, large-capacity ~
189 31-58
motorcycle stand 189 21
motorcycle tyre 189 26
motorcyclist 268 34; 290 11
motor drive 115 76
motor drive, attachable ~ 115
78
motor drive gear 167 31
motor ferry 216 6
motor grader 200 19
motor pump 270 8
motor safety switch 269 46
motor saw 84 22, 27; 85 13
motor scooter 188 47
motor ship 223
motorsports 290 24-38
motor truck, heavy ~ 194 20
motor turntable ladder 270 9
motor uniselector 237 42
motor unit 50 82
motor vehicle mechanic 195
53
motorway Map 15 16
motorway Docks 225 54
motor winch 287 6
moufflon 367 6
mouflon 367 6
mould Bldg. Site 119 84
mould Iron & Steel 147 37

mould *Glass Prod.* 162 47
mould *Paperm.* 173 48
mould, fixed ~ 178 22
mouldboard 65 4, 64
moulder *Bakery* 97 57
moulder *Iron Foundry etc.*
  148 30
moulding, concave ~ 334 29
moulding, hollow ~ 336 10
moulding, ornamental ~ 336
  12
moulding box, closed ~ 148
  18
moulding box, open ~ 148 33
moulding department 148
  30-37
moulding press, hydraulic ~
  178 7
moulding sand 148 35
moulding shop 148 30-37
mould loft 222 3
mould wall 148 29
mound *Equest.* 289 8
mound *Prehist.* 328 16
mound *Art* 337 21
mountain ash 371 42
mountain climber 300 5
mountain climbing 300 1-57
mountaineer 300 5
mountaineering 300 1-57
mountaineering boot 300 42
mountaineering equipment
  300 31-57
mountain hut 300 1
mountain racing 290 24-28
mountain railroads 214 1-14
mountain railways 214 1-14
mountain range 12 39
mountain ridge 12 36
mountains, folded ~ 12 12-20
mountain slope 12 37
mountain top 12 35
mounting, German type ~
  113 16
mounting, mobile ~ 27 22
mounting, underfloor ~ 127
  22
mount of the frame 111 10
mourner 331 33
mourning cloak butterfly 365
  5
mourning veil 331 39
mousetrap 83 36
moustache, English-style ~
  34 19
moustache, military ~ 34 19
moustache, waxed ~ 34 13
mouth *Man* 16 13; 19 14-37
mouth *Horse* 72 9
mouth *Forestry* 84 28
mouth *Game* 88 13, 45
mouth *Joiner* 132 21
mouth *Airsports* 288 70, 81
mouth *Music. Instr.* 326 25
mouth, fork-tongued ~ 327 5
mouth band 322 5
mouth gag 22 48
mouth lamp 24 42
mouth mirror 24 41
mouth organ 324 35
mouthpiece *Hosp.* 27 38
mouthpiece *Tobacc. etc.* 107
  40
mouth piece *Electrotyp. etc.*
  178 17
mouthpiece *Post* 237 9
mouthpiece *Music. Instr.* 323
  36; 324 33, 72
mouthwash 49 36
movable-comb hive 77 45-50
movable-frame hive 77
  45-50
movable half 215 66

move 276 14
movie audience 312 5
moviegoer 312 5
movie house 312 1
movie projector 312 24
movie script 310 45
movie set 310 7
movie studios 310 1-13
movie theater 312 1
movie theater box office 312
  2
movie theater ticket 312 3
moving iron 137 39
mower, electric ~ 56 31
mower, hand ~ 56 34
mower, motor ~ 56 28
mower, riding ~ 56 37
mower, rotary ~ 63 19
mud drum 210 28
mudguard, front ~ 187 13
mudguard, rear ~ 187 43
mud pump 145 16
muffle furnace 140 11
muffler *Car* 191 29
muffler *Railw.* 209 12, 22, 24;
  211 49
muffler *Sports* 305 93
mulberry-feeding moth 358
  48
mule *Dom. Anim.* 73 8
mule *Shoes* 101 25
mule, open-toe ~ 101 22
mule cop 165 15
muleta 319 33
mull 183 33; 185 20
mullion *Dwellings* 37 35
mullion *Art* 335 41
mull roll holder 185 19
multiple cable system 215 51
multiple drying machine 169
  31
multiple-frame viewfinder
  114 41
multiple meter 127 41
multiple-unit train 211 60
multiplicand 344 25
multiplication 344 25
multiplication sign 344 25
multiplier 344 25
multiplier phototube 112 51
multiplier reel 89 59
multiplying 344 25
multirole combat aircraft 256
  8
multirole helicopter, light ~
  232 11
multi-tier transport 74 35
mummy 352 21
Munich beer 93 26
mural 338 40
Muschelkalk 154 58, 59, 60
muscle, contractile ~ 77 17
muscle, deltoid ~ 18 35
muscle, pectoralis ~ 18 36
muscle, sternocleidomastoid
  ~ 18 34; 19 1
muscle, sternomastoid ~ 18
  34; 19 1
muscle, temporal ~ 19 3
muscle, thenar ~ 18 41
muscles, ocular ~ 19 44
muscles of facial expression
  19 6
muscles of the neck 19 12
muscular system 18 34-64
musculature 18 34-64
musette 322 8
mushroom 381 2, 3
mushrooms, poisonous ~ 379
  10-13
musical instrument,
  automatic ~ 308 38
musical instruments 322;

323; 324; 325; 326
musical instruments, popular
  ~ 324 1-46
musical notation 320; 321
music recording studio 310 14
music recording theatre 310
  14
music rest 326 36
music stand 326 36
music systems 241
musk ox 367 10
mussel shell 357 36
mustang 352 4
mustard *Weeds* 61 16
mustard *Grocer* 98 28
mute 323 10; 324 68
mute swan 359 16
mutton spanker 218 29
mutule 334 13
muzzle *Dog* 70 3, 31
muzzle *Game* 88 45
muzzle *Army* 255 58
muzzle *Sports* 305 71
mycelium 68 4; 381 2
myrtle 53 11
Myrtus 53 11

N

Na atom 1 8
nacre 357 34
nadir 4 13
naiad 327 23
nail 19 80
nail, clenched ~ 285 52
nail, galvanized ~ 122 74
nail, riveted ~ 285 52
nail, wire ~ 121 95; 122 74;
  143 51
nail, wooden ~ 121 92
nail bag 122 72
nail claw 120 75
nail grip 100 56
nail polish 99 32
nail puller 100 47
nail punch 134 32
nail varnish 99 32
naked boys 379 3
naked lady 379 3
name plate 118 47; 285 46
Nansen sledge 303 18
nape of the neck 16 21
napkin 45 9; 266 47; 267 48
napkin ring 45 10
nappy, disposable ~ 28 22
narcissus 53 8; 60 3
narghile 107 42
narghileh 107 42
narrow-gauge diesel
  locomotive 200 24
narrow-gauge track system
  159 4
nasicorn 366 25
nasturtium 53 4
natural 320 45, 46, 54
natural-gas engine 155 5
naturist 281 16
naum keag 100 7
nave 334 62; 335 1
navel 16 34
navette 36 55
navigating bridge 223 14; 228
  22, 23, 24
navigating officer 224 37
navigation 224
navigational marks, floating
  ~ 224 68-108
navigational television
  receiver mast 221 37
navigation equipment 288 13
navigation light *Air Force* 257
  36

navigation light *Warships* 258
  56
navigation light *Airsports* 288
  31
navigation light, left ~ 230 50
navigation light, right ~ 230
  44
navigation light, side ~ 258 15
navigation light indicator
  panel 224 29
navigation lights 286 10-14
navvy 118 76
navy 258
navy plug 107 25
navy yard 222 1-43
Neanderthal man 261 19
neck *Man* 16 19-21
neck *Horse* 72 12, 15
neck *Game* 88 3
neck *Meat* 95 6, 20
neck *Mach. Parts etc.* 143 64
neck *Weaves* 171 33
neck *Rowing* 283 37
neck *Airsports* 288 70
neck *Music. Instr.* 324 7, 18
neck, cylindrical ~ 328 40
neck, ground glass ~ 350 37
neckband 36 16
neck brush 106 27
neckerchief 31 57
neck flap *Fire Brig.* 270 38
neck flap *Fencing* 294 14
neck guard *Fire Brig.* 270 38
neck guard *Fencing* 294 14
neck guard *Chivalry* 329 83
neck interlocking point 171
  35
necklace 36 2; 328 25; 352 14
necklace, coral ~ 36 34
necklace, cultured pearl ~ 36
  12
necklace, ivory ~ 36 28
necklace, pearl ~ 36 32
neckline *Ladies' Wear* 30 34
neck line *Airsports* 288 71
neck of violin 323 2
neck piece 329 83
neck ring, gold ~ 328 26
neck ring 71 30
necktie 319 38
nectary 59 18
needle *Mach. Parts etc.* 143 76
needle *Drawing Off.* 151 56
needle *Conifers* 372 11
needle, hypodermic ~ 22 65;
  24 54
needle, right-angle ~ 151 67
needle, surgical ~ 22 57
needle, tapered ~ 190 51
needle bar 167 28
needle bed 167 51, 55
needle butt 167 60
needle cage 143 75
needle cam 167 14
needle cylinder *Knitting* 167
  8, 11
needle cylinder *Bookbind.*
  185 21
needled part of the cylinder
  163 70
needle file 108 22
needle head 309 33
needle holder 22 59
needle holder, cylindrical ~
  167 8, 11
needle hook 167 64
needle-matching system 114
  29
needlepoint 102 30
needle point attachment 151
  54
needlepoint lace 102 30
needle-raising cam 167 59

needle roller bearing **143** 75-76
needles in parallel rows **167** 53
needle trick **167** 15
needlework **102**
negative carrier **116** 30
negative flight **288** 9
negligée **355** 66
negress **354** 22
negro **354** 13
negro hut **354** 21
nematode **80** 51
Neolithic period **328** 10-20
neon sign **268** 16
Neptune **4** 51
Nereid **327** 23
nerve **370** 30
nerve, auditory ~ **17** 64
nerve, femoral ~ **18** 31
nerve, optic ~ *Man* **19** 51
nerve, optic ~ *Bees* **77** 23, 24
nerve, peroneal ~ **18** 33
nerve, radial ~ **18** 28
nerve, sciatic ~ **18** 30
nerve, thoracic ~ **18** 26
nerve, tibial ~ **18** 32
nerve, ulnar ~ **18** 29
nerves **19** 33
nervous system **18** 22-33
nervure *Articulates* **358** 34
nervure *Bot.* **370** 29
nest **359** 28
nesting cavity **359** 29
Net *Astron.* **3** 48
net *Hunt.* **86** 27
net *Sea Fish.* **90** 8
net *Airsports* **288** 74
net *Ball Games* **293** 13
net-cord judge **293** 23
net curtain **42** 35; **44** 14
net fabric **167** 29
net post **293** 15
net sonar cable **90** 14
net sonar device **90** 17
net stocking **306** 10
net strap **293** 14
netting **102** 22
netting, wire ~ **339** 35
netting loop **102** 23
netting needle **102** 26
netting thread **102** 24
nettle **61** 33
net vault **336** 45
network **288** 74
neume **320** 1
neuropteran **358** 12
neutral conductor **127** 13
neutral corner **299** 38
neutral point **153** 22
neutron **1** 30, 39, 45, 52, 53
neutron bombardment **1** 36, 50
nevé **12** 48
new-born baby **28** 5
newel **123** 43
newel, open ~ **123** 76
newel, solid ~ **123** 77, 78
newel post **123** 43
Newfoundland dog **70** 34
news, miscellaneous ~ **342** 63
newscaster **238** 21
news dealer **205** 17; **268** 75
news in brief **342** 63
news item **342** 50
newspaper **182** 31; **205** 51; **265** 25; **342** 37-70
newspaper, folded ~ **181** 56
newspaper delivery unit **182** 29
newspaper heading **342** 39
newspaper holder **265** 26

newspaper page **342** 37
newspaper rack **265** 8
newspaper shelf **262** 16; **265** 8
newspaper typesetting **176** 29
newsreader **238** 21
newsreel camera **313** 26
New Stone Age **328** 10-20
news trolley **205** 16
news vendor **205** 17; **268** 75
New World opossum **366** 2
nib **122** 51
nib size **151** 40
niche **331** 60
nick **175** 47
nigger **310** 51
night-care cream **99** 27
nightclub **318** 1-33
nightdress **32** 16
nightgown **32** 16
nightie **32** 16
nightingale **361** 14
nightshirt **32** 37
night spot **318** 1-33
nightwear **32**
nightwear, ladies' ~ **32** 16-21
nightwear, men's ~ **32** 35-37
Nile crocodile **356** 13
nimbostratus **8** 10
nine-eight time **320** 39
nine-four time **320** 40
nine men's morris **276** 18, 23-37
nine men's morris board **276** 23
nipper, bottom ~ **163** 65
nipper, top ~ **163** 66
nippers **100** 40, 41
nipping press **183** 20
nipple **16** 28
nipple key **126** 63
nitrogen tetroxide tank **234** 59
nitrous oxide **26** 3
nix **327** 23
nixie **327** 23
nobleman **355** 44
nock **305** 63
node **68** 7
node, lymph ~ **19** 10
nodosity **80** 27
nogging piece **120** 55
noir **275** 21
nominal par **251** 12
non-belayer **300** 27
nonpareil **175** 23
noodle **98** 34; **99** 65
Norfolk Island pine **53** 16
North America **14** 12
North Atlantic Drift **14** 30
North Equatorial Current **14** 32
Northern Cross **3** 23
Northern Crown **3** 31
northern gannet **359** 9
northern pike **364** 16
north light **121** 21
north point **4** 16
North Pole **14** 3
North Sea **14** 26
North Star **3** 1, 34
Norton tumbler gear **149** 8
nose *Man* **16** 10
nose *Dog* **70** 4
nose *Horse* **72** 6
nose *Fish etc.* **364** 2
nose, false ~ **306** 46
nose cone, carbon fibre reinforced ~ **235** 20
nose gear flap **231** 24
nose landing gear unit, retractable ~ **231** 23

nosepiece, revolving ~ **112** 11, 30
nose rib **287** 36
nose-section fairing **235** 20
nose undercarriage flap **231** 24
nose undercarriage unit, retractable ~ **231** 23
nose wheel **288** 34
nose wheel, forward-retracting ~ **257** 3
nose wheel, hydraulically steerable ~ **235** 30
nose wheel, steerable ~ **230** 40
nosing **123** 20
nostril **72** 7
notation, mensural ~ **320** 2
notation, square ~ **320** 1
notch *Phys. Geog.* **13** 30
notch *Forestry* **84** 28
notch *Hunt.* **87** 66, 70
notch *Army* **255** 22
notch, wedge-shaped ~ **54** 38
note **185** 62
note, marginal ~ **185** 68
note, musical ~ **320** 3-7
notebook **47** 24; **260** 18
note head **320** 3
notepaper **245** 12
notes **252** 29-39
notes, medieval ~ **320** 1-2
note stem **320** 4
note tail **320** 4
note values **320** 12-19
'NOT GO' gauging member **149** 58
'NOT GO' side **149** 61
notice **356** 7
notice board **204** 12
nougat **98** 81
novice **319** 2
novillero **319** 2
nozzle *Moon L.* **6** 3
nozzle *Household* **50** 67
nozzle *Overh. Irrign.* **67** 33
nozzle *Pest Contr.* **83** 46
nozzle *Serv. Stat.* **196** 3
nozzle *Aircraft* **232** 39, 45, 49, 55
nozzle *Space* **234** 35; **235** 37
nozzle, pistol-type ~ **83** 28
nozzle, revolving ~ **56** 44
nozzle, swivelling ~ **235** 64
nozzle fuel tank **235** 45
nuclear energy **154**
nuclear power plant **154** 19
nuclear reactor casing **259** 67
nuclear research ship **221** 9
nucleus **1** 43
nucleus, atomic ~ **1** 2, 16, 29, 35, 49, 51
nude **338** 32
nudist **281** 16
nudist sunbathing area **281** 15
null hyperbola **224** 42
number *Equest.* **289** 33, 36
number *Cyc. Racing* **290** 28
number *Winter Sp.* **301** 37
number *Sports* **305** 84
number, abstract ~ **344** 3
number, cardinal ~ **344** 5
number, complex ~ **344** 14
number, concrete ~ **344** 4
number, even ~ **344** 11
number, four-figure ~ **344** 3
number, mixed ~ **344** 10
number, negative ~ **344** 8
number, odd ~ **344** 12
number, ordinal ~ **344** 6
number, positive ~ **344** 7
number, prime ~ **344** 13
number, whole ~ **344** 10, 18
number disc **189** 18

number-key *Office* **247** 18
number key *Store* **271** 3
number key *Flea Market* **309** 76
'number one' **283** 13
number plate **189** 8; **290** 28; **305** 84
numbers **344** 1-22
number sign **197** 21
number tab **267** 10
number tag **267** 10
numeral, Arabic ~ **344** 2
numeral, Roman ~ **344** 1
numeral pendants **253** 33-34
numeral pennants **253** 33-34
numerator **344** 15
nun **331** 50
nun moth **82** 17
nursery **47**
nursery child **48** 2
nursery education **48** 1-20
nursery gardener **55** 20
nursery hand **55** 45, 46
nursery sapling **83** 15
nursery teacher **48** 1
nut *Bldg. Site* **119** 75
nut *Music. Instr.* **323** 13, 20
nut *Bot.* **370** 98
nut *Industr. Plants* **383** 44
nut *South. Fruits* **384** 52, 58, 60
nut, castellated ~ **143** 24, 77
nut, castle ~ **143** 24
nut, hexagonal ~ **143** 18
nut, round ~ **143** 35
nutation **4** 24
nutcracker **361** 1
nutcrackers **45** 49
nuthatch **361** 11
nutmeg **382** 34, 35
nutmeg tree **382** 30
nuts **59** 59, 37-51
Nydam boat **218** 1-6
nylon **101** 4
nylon 6 fibres **170** 1-62
nylons pack **99** 26
nylon-thread cop **133** 4
nymph, artificial ~ **89** 66

O

oak **51** 12
oak apple **82** 34
oak gall **82** 34
oak-gall wasp **82** 33
oak tree **51** 12; **371** 1
oar **218** 5; **278** 19; **283** 14, 26, 35-38
oarlock **278** 18; **283** 29, 41
oarsman **218** 3; **283** 12
oasis **354** 4
oat-grass **69** 22
oat panicle **68** 27
oats **68** 1
oats, rolled ~ **98** 37
obelisk **333** 10
Oberwerk **326** 2
obi **353** 41
object ball, red ~ **277** 12
objective, interchangeable ~ **112** 62
objective aperture **113** 35
objective lens **113** 36
objective turret **112** 11, 30
object lens **114** 26; **313** 2
object stage **112** 9
oblique, external ~ **18** 43
obliquus externus abdominis **18** 43
oboe **323** 38
O'Brien technique **298** 50
observation opening **5** 13

observation port *Agr. Mach.* 64 27
observation port *Films* 312 15
observation room 5 33
observation shaft 5 30
observation telescope 351 31
observation window 25 8
observation window, forward ~ 235 25
observation window, upward ~ 235 24
observatory 5 1-16; 9 7
observatory, solar ~ 5 29-33
observatory dome 5 12
obstacle, almost-fixed ~ 289 8
obstacle, fixed ~ 289 20
obstruction 291 51
obverse 252 8
ocarina 324 32
occipitalis 18 50; 19 2
occipitofrontalis 19 4
occiput 16 2
occlusion 9 5
ocean *Phys. Geog.* 13 26
ocean *Map* 14 19-26
ocean current, cold ~ 14 27
ocean current, warm ~ 14 28
ocean currents 14 30-45
ocean drifts 14 30-45
Oceanid 327 23
ocean liner 221 82; 225 32
ocean nymph 327 23
ocean station vessel 9 7
ocellus *Dom. Anim.* 73 32
ocellus *Bees* 77 2
octagon 351 17
octahedron 351 6, 14, 16
Octans 3 43
Octant 3 43
octave, five-line ~ 321 50
octave, four-line ~ 321 49
octave, great ~ 321 44
octave, one-line ~ 321 46
octave, small ~ 321 45
octave, three-line ~ 321 48
octave, two-line ~ 321 47
octave engagement 294 50
odalisque 306 41
odd-pinnate 370 42
odds 289 37
odds-and-ends box 195 31
Oertz rudder 222 69-70
oesophagus *Man* 17 49; 20 23, 40
oesophagus *Bees* 77 19
offcut 120 96
off-end framing 165 14
offering 330 60
offertory bag 330 59
offertory box 330 55
office *Coal* 144 18
office *Station* 205 13
office *Railw.* 207 41
office *Office* 245; 246; 247; 248; 249
office *Camping* 278 1
office *Chivalry* 329 27
office, executive's ~ 246 1-36
office, manager's ~ 271 24
office, open plan ~ 248 1-48
office, physician's ~ 22 1-74
office, purser's ~ 223 45
office, receptionist's ~ 245 1-33
office, secretary's ~ 245 1-33
office building *Coal* 144 18
office building *Offshore Drill.* 146 14
office building *Docks* 225 53
office building *Films* 310 4
office calculator 245 31
office chair 248 25
office cupboard 248 12

office equipment 247 1-44
office furniture 248 39
office intercom 245 20; 246 10
office machinery 249
office materials 247 1-44
officer in charge 270 36
officer of the watch 221 126
offices 217 24; 310 4
offices, administrative ~ 222 1
office supplies 247 1-44
offset machine, four-colour ~ 180 30
offset machine, rotary ~ 180 1, 18
offset machine, sheet-fed ~ 180 30
offset machine, single-colour ~ 180 46, 59
offset plate 179 1
offset plate, coated ~ 179 16
offset platemaking 179
offset press *Paperm.* 173 21
offset press *Office* 249 48
offset press, four-colour ~ 180 1, 18, 30
offset press, rotary ~ 180 1, 18
offset press, sheet-fed ~ 180 30, 70
offset press, single-colour ~ 180 46, 59
offset printing 180
offshoot 370 21
offshore drilling 146
offshore drilling rig supply vessel 221 32
offside 291 42
off switch 10 15
ogee arch 336 36
ogee wing 229 22
oil 98 24
oil, crude ~ *Phys. Geog.* 12 31
oil, crude ~ *Oil, Petr.* 145 28-35, 36-64
oil, mineral ~ 145
oil, viscous ~ 84 35
oil and vinegar bottle 45 42
oil bag 228 11
oil bath air cleaner *Agr. Mach.* 65 54
oil bath air cleaner *Railw.* 212 79
oil bath air filter *Agr. Mach.* 65 54
oil bath air filter *Railw.* 212 79
oil bleeder screw 190 24
oil burner 38 58-60
oil can 196 16
oil-circulating pump *Power Plant* 152 45
oil-circulating pump *Railw.* 211 12
oil conservator 152 42; 153 9
oil cooler *Power Plant* 152 46
oil cooler *Car* 192 19
oil cooler *Railw.* 211 11
oil drain plug 190 24
oil drilling 145 1-21
oiler 109 4
oil filler neck 190 28
oil filter 190 43; 192 20
oil-firing system 199 30, 35
oil furnace 145 36
oil gallery, main ~ 192 21
oil gauge *Roof & Boilerr.* 38 54
oil gauge *Power Plant* 153 11
oil heating furnace 38 57
oil level pipe 38 53
oil paint 338 11
oil palm 383 54
oil pipe 190 13

oil pipeline 145 65
oil pressure gauge *Sawmill* 157 7
oil pressure gauge *Aircraft* 230 20
oil pressure limiting valve 190 67
oil pressure warning light 191 73
oil production 145 22-27
oil products 145 52-64
oil pump 190 42; 192 16
oil pump drive 190 25
oil refinery 145 65-74
oil reservoir 64 29, 93
oil rig 146 1-39
oil scraper ring 190 37
oilskins 228 4
oil stand 109 5
oilstone 340 21
oil sump *Agr. Mach.* 65 45
oil sump *Intern. Combust. Eng.* 190 41
oil sump *Car* 192 17
oil tank *Roof & Boilerr.* 38 44
oil tank *Agr. Mach.* 64 93
oil tank *Oil, Petr.* 145 34
oil tank *Motorcycle* 189 36
oil temperature gauge *Car* 191 38
oil temperature gauge *Aircraft* 230 21
oil temperature sensor 195 16, 40
oil-to-air cooling unit 209 18
ointment, tube of ~ 22 47
O-Joller 284 50
Old Stone Age 328 1-9
old woman's tooth 132 26
oleander 373 13
olive oil 98 24
olive tree 383 29
omnibus, horse-drawn ~ 186 37
on-board equipment 239 6
on-board telephone 239 13
one-design keelboat 284 62
one-half twist isander 282 41
Oneirophanta 369 18
one-second theodolite 112 73
one-two 291 49
one-way tap 350 42
on full point 314 19
on guard line 294 3
on guard position 294 18, 33
onion 57 24
onion skin 57 25
on-line disc storage unit 176 32
on-load tap changer 153 13
on/off switch *Railw.* 211 30
on/off switch *Audio* 241 63
on/off switch *Audiovis.* 243 16
on/off switch *Office* 247 16; 249 9, 37, 64
on/off valve 279 22
on-ramp 15 16
on-the-ground wrestling 299 8
open gate 301 65
open-hearth furnace 147 21-30
opening 122 24
opening, pharyngeal ~ 19 24
opening control 313 8
open-newel staircase 123 76
open-reel tape 241 58
open vertical gate 301 67
open work 102 27
opera glass 315 9
opera hat 35 36
operating cabin 228 21

operating handle 309 81
operating indicator 244 11
operating instructions 244 15
operating key 243 13, 41, 48; 246 19; 261 45
operating lamp 27 25
operating lamp, shadow-free ~ 26 10
operating lamp, swivel-mounted ~ 26 10
operating lever *Pest Contr.* 83 21
operating lever *Cine Film* 117 63
operating lever *Road Constr.* 201 12
operating mechanism housing 153 60
operating table 26 8, 36
operating table, pedestal ~ 26 5
operating theatre 26 1-33
operating valve 153 52
operation indicator 244 7
operations, arithmetical ~ 344 23-26; 345 1-10
operator *Post* 237 35
operator *Computer* 244 14
operator *Theatre* 316 59
operator, chief ~ 244 3
operator's position 237 34
operator's set 237 23
operculum 364 5
ophthalmic test stand 111 43
ophthalmometer 111 44
ophthalmoscope 22 62
opium poppy 380 15
opponent 293 18
optical bench 114 50; 242 79
optical instruments 112; 113
optical sound recorder 310 60; 311 6
optical sound recording 311 9
optical sound recording equipment 311 6
optical sound unit 312 45
optical system 242 41; 243 50
optician 111 1
optic plate, right-hand ~ 195 18
optometer 111 44
or 254 24
orange *Colour* 343 7
orange *South. Fruits* 384 23, 27
orange flower 384 25
orange peel, candied ~ 98 11
orangery 272 3
orange tip butterfly 365 3
orange tree 55 49
orang-outan 368 15
orang-utan 368 15
orbicular 370 33
orbicularis oculi 19 5
orbicularis oris 19 8
orbiculate 370 33
orbit, moon's ~ 4 1
orbital manoeuvring main engine 235 44
orb spinner 358 45
orchard 15 108
orchard sprayer, mobile ~ 83 38
orchestra *Theatre* 315 25
orchestra *Art* 334 47
orchestra pit 315 24
orchestrion 308 38; 309 14
orchid 376 28
orchis 376 28
order 250 19
ordinal 344 6
ordinate 347 10
ore 147 2

öre 252 24, 25, 26
ore deposit 11 31
organ 326 1-5, 1-52
organ, automatic ~ 308 38
organ, portable ~ 322 56
organ, portative ~ 322 56
organ, positive ~ 322 56
organ, suctorial ~ 81 36
organ case 326 1-5
organ console 326 36-52
organelle 357 5
organistrum 322 25
organ of equilibrium and
    hearing 17 56-65
organ pipes 326 17-35
organs, internal ~ 20 1-57
orifice, cardiac ~ 20 41
original 177 18
origin of ordinates 347 4
Orion 3 13
ornament, Rococo ~ 336 13
ornamental 53 16
ornamentation, Greek ~ 334
    38-43
ornamentation, Romanesque
    ~ 335 14-16
ornaments 321 14-22
orogenis 12 4-20
orogeny 12 4-20
orographic lift 287 28
orpine 377 9
orthopinacoid 351 25
orthopteron 358 8
ortolan 361 7
ortolan bunting 361 7
Orton cone 161 6
oscillation counter 110 17
osier branch 371 29
osier rod 136 15
osier stake 136 14
ossicles, auditory ~ 17 61
Ostiak 353 17
ostrich 359 2
ostrich egg 359 3
ostrich feather 254 30
Ostyak 353 17
os uteri externum 20 85
otter 367 17
otter boards 90 13
Otto-cycle engine 190 1
Otto-cycle internal
    combustion engine 190 2
outboard 278 15; 283 6, 7
outboard inflatable 286 1
outboard motor 278 15; 283
    7; 286 1, 21
outboard motorboat 283 6
outboard speedboat 283 6
outdrive motorboat 286 2
outer case 187 30
outfall 216 36
outfielder 292 41
outflow condenser 92 4
outhouse 62 14
outlet Electr. 127 5
outlet Paperm. 172 78
outlet Water 269 21
outlet, double ~ 127 6
outlet cock 178 34
outlet control valve 269
    30
outlet duct 92 19
outlet structure 217 44
outlet to brake line 192 53
outlet tunnel 217 62
outlet valve 269 31
outline drawing 129 46
output 117 28
output gear box 212 53
outrigger Rowing 283 42
outrigger Ethnol. 352 36
outrigger canoe 352 35
outriggers 283 9-16

outside broadcast vehicle 239
    1-15
outside defender 291 13
outside forward 291 16
outside grip 296 45
outsider 289 53
ovary Man 20 83
ovary Soft Fruit 58 40
ovary Bot. 370 54, 60
ovary Shrubs etc. 373 2, 5
ovary Flowers etc. 375 34
ovary, epigynous ~ 58 7
ovary, perigynous ~ 59 14
ovary cavity 370 62
ovary wall 370 61
ovate 370 36
oven 39 13; 97 66, 71
oven, electric ~ 207 30
oven window 39 14
overall 33 56
overalls, hairdresser's ~ 106 2
overalls, leather ~ 290 26
over-and-under shotgun 305 70
overblouse 31 61
overblouse, girl's ~ 29 48
overburden 158 2
overburden excavator 159 3
overdress 31 17
overfall 91 43
overfeed, initial ~ 168 26
overflow Roof & Boiler. 38
    69
overflow Bathrm. etc. 49 25,
    45
overflow Fish Farm. 89 5
overflow Water 269 33
overflow basin 272 23
overflow container 350 60
overflow pipe 38 69; 269 20,
    33
overflow spillway 217 60
overfold 12 14
overgown 355 36, 50
overgrasp 296 40
overhead bicycle kick 291 45
overhead camshaft 189 3;
    190 14
overhead contact wire 197
    41; 205 58
overhead line support 152 36
overhead projector 261 8
overhead spray washing plant
    169 29
overhead wire maintenance
    vehicle 211 41
overhead wire voltage
    indicator 211 28
overlap angle 128 51
overlay flooring 123 62
overload indicator 224 33
oversite concrete 123 13
overskirt, panniered ~ 355 83
over tile 122 58
overtop 29 48
overtop, knitted ~ 30 4; 31 65
oviduct 20 81
ovule 58 39; 59 14; 370 63
ovum 20 84
owl 252 2
owl-glass 306 38
owls 362 14-19
ox Dom. Anim. 73 1
ox Slaughterho. 94 2
ox Meat 95 14-37
oxer 289 8
ox eye 361 9
oxeye daisy 376 4
oxeye daisy, white ~ 51 24
Oxford 101 31
Oxford shoe 101 31
ox hide, painted ~ 354 11
oxidation 170 19
oxidation, controlled ~ 169 7

oxide ceramic 149 46
oxteam 63 16
oxygen apparatus Moon L. 6
    18
oxygen apparatus Fire Brig.
    270 20
oxygen atom 1 13
oxygen-blowing converter
    147 45-50
oxygen connection 141 30
oxygen control 141 29
oxygen cylinder Hosp. 27 45
oxygen cylinder Gas Weld.
    141 3, 21
oxygen cylinder Road Constr.
    200 40
oxygen flow meter 26 4
oxygen hose 141 10
oxygen inlet 350 11
oxygen jet 350 13
oxygen lance 147 49
oxygen molecule 242 65
oxygen supply 25 22
oxygen tank Moon L. 6 6
oxygen tank Space 234 61
oxygen tank Air Force 257 2
oxygen treatment 25 23
oxymeter 27 13
oxysphere 11 1
oyster 357 32
oyster fork 45 80
oyster round 95 11
ozone layer 7 13, 19

P

pace 72 40
pacemaker 25 36
pacemaker, cardiac ~ 25 31,
    37
pacemaker, internal ~ 25 37
pacemaker, short-term ~ 25
    25
pacemaker battery 25 51
pacemaker control unit 25 40
paeemaker impulse 25 44
pacemaker unit 25 30
pacer 290 11
Pacific Ocean 14 19
pack Dom. Anim. 73 5
pack Hunt. 86 33
pack Airsports 288 44
pack, disposable ~ 93 28
package, unitized ~ 226 21
package cargo transit shed
    225 9
package freight 206 4, 27
pack animal 354 3
packing, sterile ~ 26 31
packing box 210 33
packing box dispenser 74 53
packing machine 76 36
pack of hounds 86 33; 289 46
pack saddle 73 4
pad Horse 71 49
pad Game 88 46
pad Shoem. 100 16
pad Ball Games 292 9
pad Graphic Art 340 13
pad, bakelite ~ 166 64
pad, leather ~ Goldsm. etc.
    108 29
pad, leather ~ Weaving 166 64
pad, suctorial ~ 77 9
pad, unsterile ~ 26 23
pad bridge 111 12
padding, foam rubber ~ 291
    20
paddle Brew. 92 46
paddle Electrotyp. etc. 178 25,
    33
paddle Ship 218 8

paddle Ethnol. 353 14
paddle, double-bladed ~ 283
    39
paddle, double-ended ~ 283
    39
paddle, single-bladed ~ 283
    34
paddle boat 280 12
paddling pool 37 44; 273 28
paddock 319 15
padlock 38 21
page Bookbind. 185 53
page Hotel 267 18
page, double-column ~ 185
    64
page, front ~ 342 38
pageboy 267 18
pageboy style 34 35
page cord 174 16
page heading 342 52
page number 185 63; 251 14
page printer 237 66
pagoda, Indian ~ 337 21
pagoda, multi-storey ~ 337 1
pail 50 54
pailoo 337 3
pailou 337 3
paint 129 6, 7-8, 9; 338 10
paintbox 48 6; 338 10
paintbrush 48 7; 129 3; 260
    84
paint bucket 129 10
paint container 315 34
Painter Astron. 3 47
painter Painter 129 2
painter Art. Studio 338 2
painting 129 1; 260 27
painting, watercolour ~ 48 5
painting materials 338 6-19
painting surface 338 22
painting table 338 25
paint kettle 129 8
paint roller 129 11
paint room 315 28-42
paint scraper 129 22
paint trolley 315 36
pair 275 20
pairing season 86 9-12
pair skater 302 4
pajamas 32 17, 36
palace, Baroque ~ 272 7
palace, Renaissance ~ 335 47
palace buildings 333 29
palace gardens 272 1-40
Palaeolithic period 328 1-9
Palaeopneustes niasicus 369
    19
palate, hard ~ 19 20
palate, soft ~ 19 21
pale ale 93 26
palette 338 28
palette dipper 338 29
palette knife 338 14
paling 52 10
palisade Equest. 289 8
palisade Chivalry 329 36
palisading 329 36
palla 355 10
pallbearer 331 40
pallet Porcelain Manuf. 161
    20
pallet Station 206 32
pallet Docks 225 43; 226 7
pallet Music. Instr. 326 10
pallet, flat ~ 226 10
pallet, standard ~ 226 10
pallette 329 45
palm 88 41
Palma Christi 380 14
palma manus 19 71
palmate 370 39
palmation 73 36; 359 7
palm capital 333 25

palm column 333 17
palmette 334 41
palm frond 384 3
palm of the hand 19 71
palm rest 255 13, 19; 305 45
palm tree 354 5
palpebra, lower ~ 19 40
palpebra, upper ~ 19 39
pampas grass 51 8
pamphlet 330 57
pan Household 50 52
pan Carp. 120 59
pan School 260 60
panache 329 78
Panama hat 35 16
pan and tilt head 114 48; 313
   12
pancreas 20 44
Pandean pipes 322 2
pandora 322 21
pane 66 10; 137 27
panel 120 59
panel, front ~ 32 24
panel, mirrored ~ 267 66
panelboard 157 67
panelling, metal ~ 208 6
panelling, wood ~ 281 19
panelling, wooden ~ 266 37
panel pin 124 29
pane of glass 124 16
pangolin 366 10
pan grinding mill 159 8
Panhard rod 192 70
panicle 68 27; 370 69; 378 46;
   382 54
pan loaf 97 10
pannier 78 15
panpipes 322 2
pan set 40 12-16
pansy 60 2
pantaleon 325 1
pantaloons 306 42
pantie briefs 32 8
pantie-corselette 32 3
pantie-girdle 32 2
pantie-hose 29 42; 32 12
panties, long-legged ~ 32 10
pantile 122 54
pantograph Map 14 65
pantograph Composing Rm.
   175 58
pantograph Tram 197 23
pantograph carriage 175 53
pantry, ship's ~ 223 43
pants, long ~ 32 11
paper Photog. 116 50
paper Drawing Off. 151 14
paper Paperm. 173 2-10
paper Offset Print. 180 47
paper Letterpress 181 46
paper Office 249 57
paper, asphalted ~ 153 48
paper, blank ~ 180 2, 69; 181
   23, 30
paper, coated ~ 173 35
paper, cork ~ 128 18
paper, metallic ~ Paperhanger
   128 18
paper, metallic ~ Power Plant
   153 44
paper, metallized ~ 153 44
paper, natural ~ 128 18
paper, printed ~ 180 57; 181
   9, 25
paper, raw ~ 173 29
paper, unprinted ~ 180 2, 69;
   181 23, 30
paper, wood ~ 128 18
paper bag, cone-shaped ~ 98
   49
paper bail 249 17
paper chase 289 41-49
paper clip 247 1, 2

paper edge, butted ~ 128 20
paper feed 245 11; 249 45, 49
paper feed and delivery 181
   14
paper feeding and delivery
   unit 181 14
paperhanger 128
paper hanging 128 18-53
paperhanging brush 128 40
paperhanging kit 128 33
paper hunt 289 41-49
paper machine 173 11, 13-28
papermaking 172; 173
papermaking by hand 173
   46-51
paper punch 22 28
paper recorder 25 56, 57
paper recorder unit 27 33
paper reed 383 64
paper release lever 249 20
paper ribbon 174 34
paper roll 249 33; 309 75
paper roller 148 47
paper rush 383 64
paper size selection 249 34
paper speed scale 116 54
paper stand 151 13
paper tape 237 32
paper towel 196 11
paper-towel dispenser 196 10
paper tower 174 33, 43
pappus 375 34
pappus bristle 375 33
pappus tuft 378 11
paprika 57 42
papyrus column 333 15
papyrus plant 383 64
par 251 12
para 252 28
parabola 347 14
parachute Meteorol. Instr. 10
   57
parachute Airsports 288 37
parachuting 288 37-62
paraffin 145 60
paraffin lamp 278 29
paraffin oil 145 60
paragon 175 31
Paraguay tea 382 11
parallel 346 4
parallel bars 296 2
parallelepiped 347 36
parallel of latitude 14 2
parallelograms 346 33-36
parallels 14 1-7
Paramecium 357 9
parapet Dwellings 37 19
parapet Bridges 215 70
parapet Chivalry 329 21
parapet, battlemented ~ 329
   20
parasites 81
parasites of man 81 31-42
parasol mushroom 381 30
paravane 258 87
parcel Station 204 2
parcel Post 236 3, 6
parcel registration card 236 7
parcel registration slip 236 4
parcels counter 236 1
parcels office 204 1
parcels scales 236 2
parent 54 15
parentheses 342 24
parent plant 54 15
paring knife 100 51
parison 162 47
parison mould 162 26
park Map 15 97
park Park 272
park Ball Games 291 1; 292
   40-58
park, landscaped ~ 272 41-72

parka 29 66
parka coat 29 66
park bench 272 16, 42
park by-law 272 29
park chair 272 48
park entrance 272 32
park gardener 272 66
parking meter 268 1
park keeper 272 30
park path 272 38
park railing 272 33
park tree 272 59
parlour, herringbone ~ 75 23
parquet floor 123 74
parquet strip 123 62
parrot 363 1
parrying 294 6
parry of the fifth 294 24
parry of the quinte 294 24
parry of the tierce 294 8
parsley 57 19
parsonage 331 20
part, imaginary ~ 344 14
part, real ~ 344 14
parterre 272 39
Parthenon 334 1
partial-hip end 121 17
parting, centre ~ 34 9
parting, side ~ 34 14
parting kiss 205 52
parting-off tool 149 53
parting tool Turner 135 24
parting tool Mach. Tools 149
   53
partition 75 38
partition, framed ~ 120 48
partition, glass ~ 25 8
partition, sound-absorbing ~
   248 20
partition, wooden ~ 38 19
partition screen 248 1
partition wall Bldg. Site 119
   25
partition wall Office 248 1
part load 206 4
part-load goods 206 27
partridge 88 70
partridge call 87 47
party 263 20
party, private ~ 267 40-43
party blouse 30 55
party games 276
party skirt 30 56
par value 251 12
Paschen series 1 22
pas de trois 314 27-28
Pasiphaea 369 12
pass Phys. Geog. 12 47
pass Ball Games 291 47
pass, short ~ 291 49
passage 71 3
passage, barred ~ 307 51
passage grave 328 16
passe 275 19
passenger 204 24; 205 6; 208
   30; 221 97, 109
passenger aircraft 231 2
passenger cabin 231 22
passenger car 208 3
passenger coach 207 1-21;
   208 3
passenger compartment 207
   13
passenger door, centre ~ 231 25
passenger door, rear ~ 231 30
passenger ferry 216 1
passenger liner 221 82; 225
   32
passenger seat Car 191 36
passenger seat Lorries etc. 194
   14
passenger seat Aircraft 230
   38; 231 22

passenger sledge 353 18
passenger terminal 225 31
passenger vehicle 191 1-56;
   195 34
passerines 361
Passiflora 53 2
passion flower 53 2
passport 267 13
'passport check' 233 42
pastas 98 32-34
paste 128 26
paste, heavy-duty ~ 128 24
pasteboard 128 31
paste brush 128 27
pastel crayon 338 19
pastern 72 25
pasting machine 128 25
pastor Church 330 22
pastor Birds 361 4
pasture, rough ~ 15 5
patch pocket 29 68; 30 22; 31
   56; 33 38; 35 37
pâté 96 15
patella 17 23
paten 330 9; 332 51
patent 246 26
patent anchor 222 78; 258 5;
   286 17
patent key 187 50
patent log 224 54
patent valve 187 31
paternoster 332 31
path, central ~ 55 42
path, gravel ~ 272 18
path, unfenced ~ 15 102
patient 22 2, 3; 24 2;
   274 7, 18
patients file 22 6
patin 330 9; 332 51
patine 330 9; 332 51
patrician lady 355 48
patrol car 264 10
patrolman 264 13
patrol submarine 259 75
patten 355 43
pattern Iron Foundry etc. 148
   34
pattern Composing Rm. 175
   55
pattern, chequered ~ 335 14
pattern control chain 167 19
pattern repeat 171 12
pattern stencil 168 62
pattern table 175 56
pauldron 329 45
Pauli exclusion principle 1 7
Pauli principle 1 7
pause 321 25
pause sign 321 25
pavais 329 56
pavement 37 60; 198 8, 9
paving 198 8
paving, brick ~ 123 7
paving, flagstone ~ 123 26
paving brick 159 27
pavis 329 56
Pavo 3 41
paw 88 46, 50; 368 4
paw, hind ~ 70 8
pawn 276 13
payee 250 19
payer 250 20
paying agent 250 22
paying-in counter 236 25
paying-in slip 236 27
payload bay 235 26
payload bay door 235 14
payload bay insulation 235 13
payload manipulator arm 235
   29
pay phone 236 9; 237 3
pea 57 1, 7
peach 59 31

peach blossom 59 27
peach flan 97 22
peach flower 59 27
peach leaf 59 32
peach tree 59 26-32
Peacock Astron. 3 41
peacock Dom. Anim. 73 30
peacock butterfly 365 2
pea flower 57 2
pea jacket 221 127
peak 11 6; 12 40
peanut 45 41; 383 41
pear 58 33
pear blossom 58 38
pearl Jewell. 36 8
pearl Game 88 30
pearl Composing Rm. 175 22
pearl Invertebr. 357 35
pearl barley 98 35
pear pip 58 37
pears 99 87
pear-shape, faceted ~ 36 84
pear-shape, plain ~ 36 83
pear-shape, standard ~ 36 54
pear-shapes 36 82-86
pear stalk 58 34
pear tree 58 31, 32
peasecod 355 30
peat 55 31; 206 10
pea tendril 57 4
peavy 85 9
peba 366 8
pebble, painted ~ 328 6
pectoralis, greater ~ 18 36
pectoralis major 18 36
pedal Joiner 132 72
pedal Bicycle 187 40, 78
pedal Sports 305 85
pedal Music. Instr. 323 62;
  325 41, 46
pedal, adjustable ~ 298 2
pedal, left ~ 325 9
pedal, right ~ 325 8
pedal bracket 325 42
pedal car 273 55
pedal crank 188 25
pedal cylinder 163 27
pedal drive 188 25
pedal frame 187 83
pedal harp 323 60
pedal key 326 51, 52
pedal lever 163 28
pedal mechanism 324 54
pedal pipe 326 3
pedal roller 163 27, 28
pedal tower 326 4
peddle boat 280 12
pedestal Optic. Instr. 113 2
pedestal Office 248 37
pedestal Park 272 11
pedestal Circus 307 55
pedestal crane 146 3
pedestal grinding machine
  138 7
pedestal mat 49 18
pedestrian 268 18
pedestrian crossing 198 11;
  268 24, 51
'pedestrian crossing' sign 268
  29
pedestrian lights 268 55
pedestrian precinct 268 58
pedicel 59 4; 383 7
pediculate 369 6
pediment Phys. Geog. 13 65
pediment Art 334 3; 335 36
peduncle 59 4; 383 7
peeler 133 1
peeling machine 133 1
peen 66 10; 137 27
peewit 359 21
peg Floor etc. Constr. 123 11
peg Camping 278 24

peg Music. Instr. 323 18; 324
  11
Pegasus Astron. 3 10
Pegasus Fabul. Creat. 327 26
pegbox 323 19
pegbox, bent-back ~ 324 10
pegbox, swan-head ~ 324 10
pegdisc 324 19
pein 137 27
Pekinese dog 70 19
Peking man 261 18
pelargonium 53 1
pelican 359 5
pelican eel 369 2
pellitone 323 44
pelorus 224 53
pelota 305 67
pelota player 305 68
pelvis 17 18-21
pelvis, renal ~ 20 31
pen Livestock 75 36
pen Office 245 21
pen School 260 14
pen, ballpoint ~ 47 26
pen, felt tip ~ 47 26; 48 18
pen, metal ~ 341 25
penalty 291 40
penalty area 291 4
penalty kick 291 40
penalty line 292 5
penalty spot 291 6
pen and pencil case 260 12
pen and pencil tray 245 22;
  260 24
pencil 47 26; 129 41; 260 5
pencil, carpenter's ~ 120 77
pencil, clutch-type ~ 151 45
pencil, coloured ~ 48 11
pencil, lead ~ 118 51
pencil attachment 151 62
pencil box 309 73
pencil holder 22 31
pencil lead 151 46
pencil of rays 346 19
pencil point attachment 151
  55
pencil sharpener 247 25
pencil silhouette 31 14
pen clip 2 18
pendant 335 32
pendant, gemstone ~ 36 14
pendant, oblong ~ 253 28
pendants 253 30-32
pendeloque 36 54
pendentive 334 74
pendulum Atom 2 35
pendulum 110 27; 309 58
pendulum device 2 35
pendulum spray 83 27
penguin 359 4
peninsula 13 5
penis 20 66
penlight pocket 6 24
pen meter 2 15
pennant, oblong ~ 253 28
pennants 253 30-32
pennon 278 9; 280 11
pennon staff 280 10
penny, new ~ 252 37
pensions counter 236 25
Pentacrinus 369 3
pentagon 351 9
pentaprism 115 41, 70
pentaprism viewfinder,
  interchangeable ~ 115 69
penthouse 37 83
penthouse head 312 50
penthouse roof 37 55
pent roof 37 55, 78; 121 7
penumbra 4 34
peplos 355 2
pepper 382 39
peppercorn 382 39

peppermint 380 3
pepper plant 382 36
pepper pot 266 77
percentage focusing chart 177
  7
percentage key 247 23
percentage sign 345 7
percent key 247 23
perch 86 49
percolation of a river 13 73
percussion cap Hunt. 87 59
percussion cap Carnival 306
  49
percussion drill, electric ~ 134
  43
percussion instruments 323
  49-59; 324 47-58
percussion screwdriver 138 6
percussor 22 73
peregrine falcon 362 2
perennial 52 22
perennial, flowering ~ 52 9
perfect binder 184 1; 249 61
perfect fifth 321 10
perfect fourth 321 9
perfecting unit 181 49
perfecting unit for black 180
  12-13
perfecting unit for cyan 180
  8-9
perfecting unit for magenta
  180 10-11
perfecting unit for yellow 180
  6-7
perfect octave 321 13
perforated brick 159 21
perforation 236 62
perforator Paperhanger 128
  12
perforator Composing Rm.
  176 5
perfume bottle 43 27; 105 36
perfume spray 43 26; 106 21
pergola 37 80; 51 1; 272 17
pericarp 57 6
pericementum 19 28
perineum 20 64
period 342 16
periodical 262 15
periodicals rack 262 15
periodontium 19 28
periphery 346 44
peristomion 322 5
peristyle 334 2
peritoneum 20 58
perlon fibres 170 1-62
Permian 154 62
peroneus longus 18 64
perpendicular 346 6, 27, 28
perpetual frost climate 9 58
Persian cat 73 17
Persian lamb 30 60
personnel carrier, armoured
  ~ 255 91
Peru Current 14 42
pesade 71 4; 307 30
peseta 252 22
pest control 83
pestle 349 10
petal 58 43; 59 11; 370 59
petasus 355 4
pet foods 99 36-37
petiole 370 27
petri dish 173 7; 261 25
petrol can 196 25
petrol canister 84 36
petroleum Phys. Geog. 12 31
petroleum Oil, Petr. 145 41
petroleum gas, liquefied ~
  145 53
petroleum reservoir 12 27
petrol lighter 107 27
petrol motor 83 41

petrol pump 196 1
petrol pump, self-service ~
  196 8
petrol pump hose 196 2
petrol station 196 1-29
petrol tank 188 10, 28; 189 2;
  305 87
petticoat 355 37
petty cash 246 27
petty morel 379 5
petunia 53 6
pew 330 28
pewit 359 21
Pfund series 1 24
phaeton 86 18; 186 38
phalange 17 17, 29; 19 77
phalanx 17 17; 19 77
pharmacopoeia 22 23
pharynx 19 24
phases, lunar ~ 4 2-7
pheasant 88 77
pheasant cock 88 77
pheasant hen 88 77
pheasant's eye 60 4
phenol 170 3, 14, 16
phenol extraction 156 39
philomel 361 14
philomela 361 14
philtrum 16 12
phloem 370 9
phlox 60 14
Phoenix 327 9
phonetics 342 14
phonetic transcription 342 14
phorbeia 322 5
phoropter 111 44
phosphorescent material 240
  18
photocell 312 49
photocomposition 176
photocomposition system 176
  29
photodiode 114 70; 243 56
photoengraving, halftone ~
  178 38
photogrammetry 14 63-66;
  112 67
photographic plate 309 49, 50
photographic unit 176 14
photography 114; 115; 116
photography, underwater ~
  279 23
photogravure 182
photomechanical
  reproduction 177
photometer 23 54
photometer, microscopic ~
  112 49
photometry 23 52, 53
photomicrographic camera
  attachment 112 36
photomicro mount adapter
  112 64
photomicroscope 112 34
photomicroscope adapter 115
  89
photomultiplier 112 51
photosetting 176
photosetting system 176 29
phototheodolite 112 67
phototopography 14 63-66
phototypesetting 176 1
photo-unit 176 14
piaffe 71 1
pianino 325 1
pianissimo 321 36
pianissimo piano 321 37
piano Music. Not. 321 35
piano Music. Instr. 325 1, 40
piano accordion 324 36
piano action 325 2-18
piano case 325 6
pianoforte 325 1

piano keys 325 4-5
piano mechanism 325 2-18
piano pedal 325 9
piano pedals 325 8-9
piano string 325 7
pica 175 28
picador 319 16
piccolo 323 30
Piciformes 363 6
pick 158 31; 300 33
pick counter 166 2
picker 166 64
picker head 184 11
picking bowl 166 67
picking cam 166 66
picking knife 136 38
picking stick 166 17, 22
picking stick buffer 166 65
picking stick return spring
  166 68
pickpocket 308 16
pick stick 166 17
pickup attachment 62 41; 63
  27
pickup reel 64 4
pickup sucker 184 8
pickup truck 194 1, 5
pickup unit 240 36
pictographs 233 24-53
Pictor 3 47
picture 43 20; 246 28
picture, panoramic ~ 24 21
picture frame 43 21
picture gate 312 34
picture house 312 1
picture monitor 238 65; 239
  12
picture rail 128 29
picture tube 240 3
picture tube geometry 242 39
pier Bridges 215 21, 54
pier Docks 225 66
pier Airport 233 12
pier Art 336 25
pier, clustered ~ 335 34
pier, compound ~ 335 34
pier, reinforced concrete ~
  215 61
piercing saw 108 12
piercing saw blade 108 13
pierette 306 12
pierhead 233 13
pierrot 306 19
pies 97 22-24
pig Farm Bldgs. 62 10
pig Dom. Anim. 73 9
pig Livestock 75 39
pig Slaughterho. 94 11
pig Meat 95 38-54
pig Iron & Steel 147 40
pig, solidifying ~ 148 25
pig-casting machine 147
  34-44
pigeon 73 33; 359 23
pigeon hole 267 2
pig iron, molten ~ 147 55
pig iron ladle 147 12, 21, 42
pig iron runout 147 11
piglet 73 9; 75 42
pigment paper 182 1, 8, 10
pigmy 354 41
pigpen 62 8; 75 35
pigskin 292 27
pigsty 62 8; 75 35
pigtail Hairst. etc. 34 6
pigtail Tobacc. etc. 107 18
pigtail wig 34 5; 355 77
pig trap 146 31
pike Fish Farm. 89 17
pike Free Exerc. 295 38
pike Fish etc. 364 16
pike, spawning ~ 89 11
piked reverse hang 296 36

pike pole 319 17
pi-key 247 24
pilaster 335 46
pilaster strip 335 11
pile 226 40
pile, steel ~ 217 4
pile delivery unit 180 55
pile driver, floating ~ 226 36
pile driver frame 226 37
pile dwelling 328 15; 352 33
pile feeder 180 73
pile feeder, automatic ~ 180
  48
pile foundation 216 8
pile hammer 226 38
pile of arrow 305 61
pile shoe 269 61
pileus 381 4
piling 157 25
pillar Mach. Tools 150 21
pillar Shipbuild. 222 61
pillar Art 335 20
pillar, engaged ~ 335 35, 46
pillar guide 139 42
pillar stand Atom 2 29
pillar stand Optic. Instr. 112
  32
pillar tap 126 31
pillion footrest 188 44
pillion passenger 268 36
pillion rider 268 36
pillow 27 27; 43 12-13; 47 4
pillowcase 43 12
pillow lace 102 18
pillowslip 43 12
pilot Railw. 210 34
pilot Music. Instr. 325 33
pilot, automatic ~ 224 18
pilot boat 221 95
pilot chute 288 39
pilot flag 253 23
pilot light 50 10
pilot light, covered ~ 38 60
'pilot on board' 253 24
pilot tone cable 313 29
pilot tone generator 313 30
pilot tone socket 117 7
pilot wire 325 34
Pilsener beer 93 26
pimehinketone 170 20
pin Roof 121 93
pin Turner 135 9
pin Metalwkr. 140 47
pin Mach. Parts etc. 143 31
pin Sports 305 12
pin, bronze ~ 328 29
pin, cylindrical ~ 143 40
pin, diamond ~ 36 18
pin, front ~ 305 1
pin, grooved ~ 143 40
pin, split ~ 143 19, 25, 78
pin, tapered ~ 143 37
pinacoid, triclinic ~ 351 26
pinafore, bib top ~ 29 41
pinafore dress 29 13; 30 8; 31
  8
pin block 324 22; 325 18
pincers Shoem. 100 40, 41
pincers Plumb. etc. 126 65
pincers D.I.Y. 134 13
pincers Basketm. 136 37
pincers Metalwkr. 140 69
pincers, caudal ~ 81 12
pinch bar 158 32
pinchcock 350 30
pinch roller 243 25
pinch roller, rubber ~ 117 35
pincushion 104 20
pine 372 20
pineapple 99 85
pineapple flower 384 64
pineapple gall 82 40
pineapple plant 384 61

pine beauty 82 46
pine cone 372 26
pine hawkmoth 82 27
pine moth 82 28
pine weevil 82 41
pin groove 143 49
pin holder 109 16
pinion Game 88 76
pinion Mach. Parts etc. 143 92
pink Equest. 289 13
pink Colour 343 4
pinnacle 335 29
pinnate 370 41
pinnatifid 370 40
pinnipeds 367 18-22
pin slit 143 49
pin slot 143 49
pin vice 109 16
pin wire 124 28
pip 276 32
pipe Living Rm. 42 12
pipe Ship 221 3
pipe Music. Instr. 322 57; 326
  16, 29
pipe, briar ~ 107 39
pipe, cast-iron ~ 37 14
pipe, cement ~ 200 62
pipe, clay ~ 107 34
pipe, Dutch ~ 107 34
pipe, earthenware ~ 269 35
pipe, long ~ 107 35
pipe, magic ~ 354 42
pipe, perforated ~ 200 62
pipe, polyester ~ 67 26
pipe, short ~ 107 33
pipe, vertical ~ Dwellings 37
  14
pipe, vertical ~ Fire Brig. 270
  26
pipe bender 125 28
pipe-bending machine
  Plumb. 125 28
pipe-bending machine
  Plumb. etc. 126 82
pipe bowl 107 36
pipe cleaner 107 46, 48
pipe clip Roof 122 31
pipe clip Plumb. etc. 126 56
pipe connection, quick-
  fitting ~ 67 28
pipe cutter 126 84
pipe-cutting machine 126 10
pipeline 145 65
pipe of peace 352 6
pipe rack Living Rm. 42 11
piperack Offshore Drill. 146 4
pipe repair stand 126 11
pipes 326 17-35
pipe scraper 107 45
pipe stem 107 38
pipe still 145 36
pipe support 67 7, 25
pipe supports 126 53-57
pipette 22 72; 350 25
pipette, automatic ~ 23 44
pipette, graduated ~ 350 24
pipette stand 23 52
pipetting device, automatic ~
  23 47
pipe union 350 5
pipe vice 126 81
pipe wrench 126 61; 127 47;
  134 11
piping 30 13; 31 7
pirate Sailing 284 52
pirate Carnival 306 43
pirn 166 30
pirn, empty ~ 166 21
pirn holder, spring-clip ~ 166
  33
pirouette 314 24
Pisces 4 64
pisciculture 89 1-19

pistachio 382 51
pistachio nut 382 51
pistachio tree 382 49
piste 294 2
pistil 59 13
pistol 255 1
pistol, captive-bolt ~ 94 3
pistol grip Hunt. 87 6
pistol grip D.I.Y. 134 44
pistol grip Army 255 6, 38
pistol grip Police 264 23
piston Drawing Off. 151 60
piston Intern. Combust. Eng.
  190 37
piston Inf. Tech. 242 46
piston, hydraulic ~ 139 41
piston pin 192 26
piston pump lever 83 45
piston ring 190 37
piston rod Intern. Combust.
  Eng. 190 21
piston rod Car 192 75
piston rod Railw. 210 33
pit Blacksm. 138 17
pit Coal 144 1-51
pitcher Ball Games 292 50, 68
pitcher Prehist. 328 35
pitcher's mound 292 49, 69
pitching 230 67
pitching, stone ~ 216 55
pitch number 278 42
pitch of rivets 143 60
pith 370 14
pithead building 144 4
pithead frame 144 3
pithead gear 144 1
Pithecanthropus erectus 261
  16
pith ray 370 11
pit hydrant 270 25
piton 300 38
piton, ringed ~ 300 39
pitot-static tube 256 11; 257 1
pitot tube 256 11; 257 1
pivot Hairdresser 106 36
pivot Bridges 215 69
pivot Winter Sp. 302 6
pivot bearing 91 10
pivoting half 215 66
pivoting section 215 66
pivoting span 215 66
pivot pier 215 65
pix 330 8; 332 53
placard 263 13; 271 65; 308
  50
place 44 5; 45 3-12
place card 45 13
place mat 44 4
place of issue 250 13
place of payment 250 15
place setting 44 5; 45 3-12
placing judge 282 25
plaid strap 303 2
plain, alluvial ~ 13 10
plainclothes policeman 264
  33
plain part of the cylinder 163
  69
plains Indian 352 3
plainsong notation 320 1
plain-tile roofing 122 2
plait 97 41
plait, coiled ~ 34 38
plaiter 168 30, 35
plaiting-down platform 168
  37
plaits 34 30
plaits, coiled ~ 34 32
plan Drawing Off. 151 19
plan Railw. 207 10-21, 26-32,
  38-42, 61-72, 76
planchet 252 43
plane Carp. 120 64

plane *Aircraft* 230 67-72
plane *Maths.* 347 31
plane, abyssal ~ 11 10
plane, circular ~ 347 39
plane, high-wing ~ 229 1; 231 2
plane, horizontal ~ 4 12
plane, low-wing ~ 229 5, 14; 231 1
plane, midwing ~ 229 4
plane, propeller-driven ~ 231 1-6
plane, shoulder-wing ~ 229 3
plane, two-seater ~ 288 18
plane, types of ~ 231 1-33
plane geometry 346 1-58
plane iron 132 20
plane of symmetry 351 5
planer, two-column ~ 150 8
planer table 150 11
planes 132 15-28
planetarium 5 17-28
plane tree 371 67
plane triangles 346 26-32
planets 4 42-52
planing boats 286 38-44
planing machine, two-column ~ 150 8
plank 55 22; 118 87; 120 1, 91; 157 34, 35
plank, unsquared ~ 120 94
plank, wooden ~ 340 2
plank cut 340 4
planking 119 52
planking, inner ~ 285 57
plank platform 118 28
plank roadway 118 79
plan of locomotive 211 10-18
planographic printing method 340 25-26
plant 370 15; 382 53
plant, anagraceous ~ 53 3
plant, asclepiadaceous ~ 53 15
plant, climbing ~ 51 5; 52 5; 57 8
plant, cyperaceous ~ 53 17
plant, ericaceous ~ 53 12
plant, female ~ 383 10
plant, flowering ~ 58 17
plant, fruit-bearing ~ 58 17
plant, gesneriaceous ~ 53 7
plant, indoor ~ 42 36; 248 14
plant, insectivorous ~ 377 13
plant, liliaceous ~ 53 13
plant, pistillate ~ 383 10
plant, pneumatic ~ 92 12
plant, potted ~ 55 25
plant, ranunculaceous ~ 60 13
plant, tiliaceous ~ 53 9
plant, tuberous ~ 68 38
plantation, young ~ 84 11, 12
plant body 378 49
planter 248 13
plant in flower 378 36
plant louse 358 13
plants, alpine ~ 378 1-13
plants, aquatic ~ 378 14-57
plants, drupaceous ~ 59 1-36
plants, farinaceous ~ 68 1-37
plants, indoor ~ 53
plants, leguminous ~ 57 1-11
plants, medicinal ~ 380
plants, poisonous ~ 379
plants, pomiferous ~ 58 31-61
plants, propagation of ~ 54
plants, tropical ~ 382
plants of forest, marsh and heathland 377
plant stand 248 13
plants used in industry 383
plaque *Roulette* 275 12
plaque *Sculpt. Studio* 339 38
plaster *Hosp.* 26 54

plaster *Paperhanger* 128 2
plaster *Art. Studio* 338 42
plaster, adhesive ~ 21 7; 22 55
plaster cast 339 4
plaster cup 134 18
plasterer 118 83
plastering 118 83-91
plaster mould 161 15
plaster of Paris 128 2; 260 85
plasticine 48 12
plate 266 11
plate, baby's ~ 28 28
plate, bottom ~ 45 3
plate, curved ~ 178 21
plate, deep ~ 44 6; 45 5
plate, front ~ 85 35
plate, halftone ~ 178 38
plate, presensitized ~ 179 31
plate, rear ~ 85 40
plate, sliding ~ 183 28
plate, steel ~ 96 54
plate armour 329 65
plateau 13 46
plate clamp *Electrotyp. etc.* 178 27
plate clamp *Offset Platem.* 179 8
plate-coating machine 179 1
plate cylinder *Offset Print.* 180 25, 38, 53, 62
plate cylinder *Letterpress* 181 51, 60
plate cylinder *Office* 249 50
plate-drying cabinet, vertical ~ 179 27
plate girder bridge 215 52
plate magazine 113 40
plate mount 178 41
plate mounting 178 41
platen *Letterpress* 181 13, 15, 29
platen *Bookbind.* 183 24
platen *Office* 249 18
platen *Graphic Art* 340 31
platen knob 249 22
platen machine 181 13, 29
platen press 181 13, 29; 340 29
platen variable 249 25
plate rack 178 35
plate rod 178 6
plate whirler 179 1
platform *Wine Grow.* 78 20
platform *Shoes* 101 8
platform *Bldg. Site* 118 87; 119 52
platform *Station* 205 1, 14
platform *Swim.* 282 7, 8
platform *Circus* 307 5
platform *Art. Studio* 338 30
platform, continental ~ 11 8
platform, covered ~ 218 49
platform, intermediate ~ 145 5
platform, operator's ~ 168 23
platform, wave-cut ~ 13 31
platform clock 205 46
platformer 145 47
platform lighting 205 48
platform loudspeaker 205 27
platform mailbox 205 56
platform number 205 4
platform post box 205 56
platform railing 118 24
platform roofing 205 5
platform scale 204 5
platform seat 205 54
platform sole 101 8
platform telephone 205 57
platform truck 194 6
platypus 366 1
play area 272 44
playback deck 238 4
playback deck, single ~ 238 56

playback head 311 25
player 48 20
player's name 293 36
playgoer 315 8
playground, children's ~ 273
playing card 276 36
playing card, French ~ 276 37
play pen 28 39
playsuit 29 11, 19, 22
plaza de toros 319 5
pleasure boat 283 1
pleasure steamer 221 101-128; 225 29
pleasure vehicle 186 33
pleat, front ~ 31 25
plectrum 322 19; 324 20
Pleiades 3 26
Pleiads 3 26
pleiobar 9 2
plexus, brachial ~ 18 27
pliers, flat-nose ~ 126 62; 140 66
pliers, multiple ~ 134 12
pliers, round-nose ~ 126 64; 127 50
pliers, shoemaker's ~ 100 38
plinth *Dwellings* 37 17
plinth *Carp.* 120 28
plinth *Art* 334 31
plinth, natural stone ~ 37 85
Plough *Astron.* 3 29
plough *Agr.* 63 6
plough *Brew.* 92 24
plough, four-furrow ~ 63 40
plough, mounted ~ 65 62
plough, reversible ~ 65 62
plough, single-bottom ~ 65 1
plough anchor 286 16
plough beam 65 9, 71
plough bottom 65 4-8, 64-67
plough frame 65 70
plough handle 65 3
ploughshare 65 7, 65; 328 33
plough stilt 65 3
plovers 359 19-21
plow 63 6
plow *see* plough
plowshare 328 33
plucking device 322 19
Pluderhose 355 34
plug *Tobacc. etc.* 107 19
plug *Plumb. etc.* 126 55
plug *Metalwkr.* 140 45
plug, double-jointed ~ 89 70
plug, earthed ~ 127 9
plug, multi-pin ~ 241 70
plug, single-jointed ~ 89 69
plug, three-pin ~ 127 67
plugboard 242 69
plug gauge 149 56
plugging 123 69
plugging sand bucket 158 29
plug point 127 5
plug point, double ~ 127 6
plug socket 50 78
plum 59 25
plum, black-skinned ~ 59 20
plum, oval ~ 59 20
plumb bob 118 50, 71
plumber 125; 125 17; 126; 126 1
plumber's tools 126 58-86
plumbing fixtures 126 26-37
plume *Heraldry* 254 36
plume *Chivalry* 329 78
plumicorn 88 78; 362 16
plum leaf 59 21
plummet *Fish Farm.* 89 91
plummet *Bldg. Site* 118 50, 71
plum slice 97 43
plum stone 59 23
plum tree 59 19-23
plumule 370 90

plunger *Oil, Petr.* 145 23
plunger *Glass Prod.* 162 32
plunger *Car* 192 7
plus sign 344 7, 23
Pluto 4 52
pneumatic pick longwall face 144 35
pneumatophore 370 82
pneume 320 1
poacher 86 29
pochette 322 20
pocket, front ~ 30 23; 33 46; 260 10
pocket, inset ~ 29 63; 31 4
pocket billiards 277 7
pocket book 264 36
pocket calculator 246 12
pocket calculator, electronic ~ 247 14
pocket camera 114 16
pocket chamber 2 15
pocket flap 33 18
pocket meter 2 15
pocket timetable 204 42; 205 45
pocket torch 127 26
pocket train schedule 204 42; 205 45
pod 57 6; 61 20, 23; 69 8, 16; 370 92, 93; 378 33; 384 46
pod, immature ~ 374 22
pod, mature ~ 383 4
pod, pouch-shaped ~ 61 11
pod, ripe ~ 383 4
pod, unripe ~ 374 22
pod corn 68 31
poet's daffodil 60 4
poet's narcissus 60 4
point *Game* 88 10, 31
point *Mach. Parts etc.* 143 23, 54
point *Sculpt. Studio* 339 15
point *Maths.* 346 1-23
point, angular ~ 346 1
point, diamond ~ 24 40
point, equinoctial ~ 3 6, 7
point, front ~ 300 49
point, typographic ~ 175 18
pointer *Hosp.* 26 28
pointer *Dog* 70 40, 43
pointer *Photog.* 114 58
pointer *Inf. Tech.* 242 76
pointer *Chem.* 349 34
point guard 300 50
pointing 122 55
pointing sill 121 47
point lace 102 30
point light exposure lamp 179 21
point lock 202 28
point-of-aim mark 305 56
point of Aries 3 6
point of arrow 305 61
point of contact 346 49
point of hook 89 80
point of inflexion 347 21
point of intersection 346 1
point of release 89 34
point paper design 171 4, 27
points, equinoctial ~ 3 6-7
points, manually-operated ~ 202 16
points, remote-controlled ~ 202 27
points, single ~ 203 45-48
points change indicator 197 39
point shoe 314 30
point size 175 46
points knob 203 62
points lever 203 55
points mechanism, electric ~ 197 43

points mechanism, electrohydraulic ~ **197** 43
points mechanism, electromechanical ~ **197** 43
points motor **202** 35
points of sailing **285** 1-13
points of the horse **72** 1-38
point source lamp **182** 4
points signal **197** 38; **202** 19
points signal, electrically illuminated ~ **202** 33
points signal lamp **202** 19
points signals **203** 45-52
point wire **202** 30
poison gland **77** 14
poison sac **77** 13
poitrel **329** 85
poke bonnet **306** 23; **355** 71
poker **38** 41; **137** 5
polar bear **368** 11
Polaris **3** 1, 34
polarizer **112** 14
polarizing filter **112** 19
polar sledge **303** 18
polar wind zone **9** 51
pole *Fruit & Veg. Gdn.* **52** 28
pole *Horse* **71** 21
pole *Fish Farm.* **89** 30
pole *Mills* **91** 32
pole *Carriages* **186** 19, 30
pole *Rivers* **216** 16
pole *Athletics* **298** 28
pole, bamboo ~ **307** 46
pole, celestial ~ **3** 1; **4** 24, 26
pole, geographical ~ **14** 3
pole, hooked ~ **77** 55
pole, terrestrial ~ **14** 3
pole chain **71** 20
pole horse **186** 47
pole mast **358** 42; **259** 6
Pole Star **3** 1, 34
pole vault **298** 28-36
pole vaulter **298** 29
poleyn **329** 53
polhode **4** 28
police **264**
police badge **264** 27
police dog **70** 25; **264** 5, 6
police duties **264** 1-33
police helicopter **264** 1
police identification disc **264** 26
police launch **221** 100
policeman **264** 18, 34
police officer **264** 18
police patrolman **264** 13
police signalling disc **264** 14
police van **264** 38
policewoman **264** 37
polishing **109** 17
polishing and burnishing machine **108** 42
polishing bonnet, lamb's wool ~ **134** 21
polishing brush **100** 11
polishing iron **108** 51
polishing machine attachment **109** 15
polishing wheel **108** 44
polish rod **145** 27
political section **342** 51
Politzer bag **22** 37
polje **13** 72
pollen **77** 3, 35; **370** 65
pollen basket **77** 6
pollen comb **77** 7
pollen sac **372** 45, 50
pollen tube **370** 66
pollex **19** 64
polling booth **263** 23
polling card **263** 19
polling number **263** 19

polling place **263** 16
polling station **263** 16
polo jumper, striped ~ **30** 20
polo neck jumper **30** 7
polo outsole **101** 24
polo saddle, high-back ~ **188** 13
polyamide **170** 34, 35, 37, 41
polyamide chip, dry ~ **170** 39
polyamide cone **170** 51, 52
polyamide fibres **170** 1-62
polyamide filament **170** 43
polyamide staple **170** 61, 62
polyamide thread **170** 46
polyanthus narcissus **60** 4
Polycheles **369** 15
polyester resin **130** 17
polygon **346** 40
polygon, eight-sided ~ **351** 17
polygon, five-sided ~ **351** 9
polygon, regular ~ **346** 41
polygon, six-sided ~ **351** 15
polyhedron **260** 73
polyhedron, eight-faced ~ **351** 6
polyhedron, forty-eight-faced ~ **351** 13
polyhedron, four-faced ~ **351** 1
polyhedron, regular ~ **351** 11
polyhedron, six-faced ~ **351** 2
polyhedron, twenty-faced ~ **351** 11
polyhedron, twenty-four-faced ~ **351** 12
polymerization **170** 33, 54
polyp, hydroid ~ **369** 9
polypod **377** 16
polypody **377** 16
pome **370** 102
pomegranate **384** 16
Pomeranian **70** 20
pomes **58**
pommel **296** 6
pommel horn **71** 38
pommel horse **296** 5
pommer **322** 14
pompier **270** 43
pompier ladder **270** 16
pompon **29** 4
pompon dahlia **60** 23
poncho **352** 24
pond *Map* **15** 79
pond *Park* **272** 50
pons **17** 46
pons cerebelli **17** 46
pons cerebri **17** 46
pontic, porcelain ~ **24** 29
pontoon **226** 57
pontoon, bottom ~ **222** 38
pontoon bridge **15** 46
pontoon dock **222** 34-43; **225** 16
pony **75** 4
ponytail **34** 27
poodle **70** 36
pool, indoor ~ **281** 1-9
pool, non-swimmers' ~ **282** 21
pool, swimmers' ~ **282** 23
pool attendant **281** 4; **282** 15
pool billiards **277** 7
poolroom **277** 7-19
poop **223** 33; **258** 22
poor man's weatherglass **61** 27
popcorn **68** 31
pop group **306** 2
poplar **371** 15
pop musician **306** 3
poppy **51** 30; **61** 2
poppy flower **61** 4
poppy seed **61** 5

porcelain manufacture **161**
porcelain painter **161** 17
porcupine **366** 13
porifer **357** 13
pork **95** 38-54
pork, collared ~ **96** 9
porridge oats **98** 37
port *Ship* **220** 27
port *Docks* **225**; **226**
port administration offices **225** 36
portal **331** 16
portal, main ~ **333** 34
portal, recessed ~ **335** 24
portal figure **333** 36
portal frame **215** 38
portal relief **333** 35
portal spotlight **316** 21
portato **321** 29
portcullis **329** 24
port custom house **225** 6
port de bras à coté **314** 7
port de bras en avant **314** 9
port de bras en bas **314** 8
port de bras en haut **314** 10
porter *Brew.* **93** 26
porter *Station* **205** 31; **206** 33
porter *Hotel* **267** 17
porthole **117** 64
porthole, ornamental ~ **218** 57
port hospital **225** 26
portico **334** 50, 56
port liner **190** 73
port of registry **286** 8
ports de bras **314** 7-10
posaune stop **326** 17-22
position **224** 45
position indicator **246** 18
position light **257** 36; **288** 31
position light, left ~ **230** 50
position light, right ~ **230** 44
positions **314** 1-6
positions, arm ~ **314** 7-10
positive **322** 56
post *Dent.* **24** 34
post *Wine Grow.* **78** 7
post *Forestry* **84** 17; **85** 30, 47
post *Mills* **91** 34
post *Carp.* **120** 25
post *Roof* **121** 40, 81
post *Paperm.* **173** 50
post *Ball Games* **291** 37
post, broker's ~ **251** 3
post, principal ~ **120** 53
postage meter **22** 24; **236** 7
postage stamp **236** 61
postal code **236** 43
postal collection **236** 50-55
postal delivery **236** 50-55
postbox **236** 50
post code **236** 43
post crown **24** 31
poster **98** 2; **204** 10; **268** 71; **271** 25
posthorn **186** 41
post horse **186** 43
postman **236** 53
postmark, special ~ **236** 59
postmark advertisement **236** 56
postmarks **236** 56-60
post office **236**; **237**; **268** 68
post office box **236** 13, 14
post office savings counter **236** 25
post office van **236** 52
post-synchronization **311** 37-41
post-syncing **311** 37-41
post-sync sound **117** 101
post windmill **91** 31
pot *Kitch.* **39** 29

pot *Kitch. Utensils* **40** 12
pot *Plant Propag.* **54** 8
pot, baby's ~ **28** 47
pot, centrifugal ~ **169** 17
potash salt bed **154** 65
potash salt seam **154** 65
potato **68** 38, 40
potato, flat-oval ~ **68** 38
potato, Irish ~ **68** 38
potato, kidney-shaped ~ **68** 38
potato, long ~ **68** 38
potato, pear-shaped ~ **68** 38
potato, purple ~ **68** 38
potato, red ~ **68** 38
potato, round ~ **68** 38
potato, round-oval ~ **68** 38
potato, white ~ **68** 38
potato, yellow ~ **68** 38
potato apple **68** 43
potato basket **66** 25
potato beetle **80** 52
potato berry **68** 43
potato chipper **40** 43
potato crisp **45** 41
potato dish **45** 31
potato fork **66** 5
potato harvester **64** 59-84
potato haulm **68** 41
potato hoe **66** 24
potato hook **66** 6
potato plant **68** 38
potato planter **66** 21
potato rake **66** 20
potato server **45** 75
potato top **68** 41
potato tuber **68** 40
potential transformer **153** 59
pot-helm **254** 7
pot-helmet **254** 7
pot holder **39** 18
pot holder rack **39** 19
pot plant **39** 37; **44** 25; **55** 25
potsherd **161** 21
potter's wheel **161** 11
pottery **308** 66
pottery, chip-carved ~ **328** 35
pottery stand **308** 64-66
potting bench **55** 12
potting table **55** 12
potty **28** 47
pouch, gular ~ **359** 8
poulaine **355** 42
poulard **98** 7; **99** 58
poultry **73** 19-36
poultry farming **74** 1-27
poultry keeping **74**
poultry management, intensive ~ **74** 1-27
pounce bag **129** 49
pouncing **129** 48
pound, lower ~ **217** 29
pound, upper ~ **217** 37
pound lock gate **217** 31
pound sterling **252** 37
pouring end **147** 34
pouring floor, sinking ~ **148** 24
pouring ladle lip **147** 43
powder, black ~ **87** 53
powder, smokeless ~ **87** 53
powder box **43** 28; **49** 35
powder charge **87** 57
powder flag **253** 38
powder tin **99** 29
power **345** 1
powerboat racing **286** 21-44
powerboats **286** 1-5
power control **100** 22
power hacksaw **138** 23
power hammer **137** 9
power house *Hydr. Eng.* **217** 21

power house *Shipbuild.* 222 33
power house *Films* 310 8
power lift 65 24-29
power line 127 23
powerpack unit 114 66
power plant *Coal* 144 13
power plant *Power Plant* 152; 153
power plant *Glass Prod.* 162
power regulator 100 22
power saw *Forestry* 84 22, 27; 85 13
power saw *Blacksm.* 138 23
power screwdriver 195 23
power shovel 200 1
power source 110 7
power station *Coal* 144 13
power station *Offshore Drill.* 146 1
power station *Power Plant* 152; 153
power station *Glass Prod.* 162
power station *Hydr. Eng.* 217 64
power supply *Arc Weld.* 142 25
power supply *Energy Sources* 155 21
power supply, external 115 79
power take-off 63 21; 64 49
power take-off clutch 65 40
power take-off gear 65 38
power take-off gear-change 65 23, 40
power take-off shaft 63 21; 64 49
power transformer 152 30, 39
power unit 84 34
power zooming arrangement 117 19
prairie horse 352 4
pralltriller 321 19
pram *Infant Care etc.* 28 34
pram *Docks* 226 57
pram *Park* 272 71
pram *Playground* 273 31
pram, wicker ~ 28 30; 48 24
pram jacket 29 3
pram suit 29 1
prayer book 330 62
prayer tower 337 13
prayer wheel 353 29
preacher 330 22
precession 4 24
precipitation 8 18
precipitation, scattered ~ 8 19
precipitation, types of ~ 8 18-19
precipitation area 9 30
precipitation gauge 10 44
precipitator, electrostatic ~ *Power Plant* 152 13
precipitator, electrostatic ~ *Coking* 156 20
precipitator, electrostatic ~ *Cement Wks.* 160 7
precipitator, electrostatic ~ *Paperm.* 172 39
precision balance 108 35
precision bench lathe 109 20
precision file 140 8
precision lathe 138 20
predator, small ~ 86 19, 20, 22
pre-distributor channel 236 36
pre-drying 165 50
preheater 212 41
preheater, high-pressure ~ 152 26
preheater, low-pressure ~ 152 25
preheater pressure gauge 210 43

preheater unit 185 30
prehistory 328
prelims 185 43-47
pre-listening button 238 46
pre-listening speaker 238 50
premasher 92 42
premixer 97 58
pre-mixing room 238 54-59
premolar 19 18
préparation 314 23
preparation and sterilization room 26 34-54
preparation level 64 16
preparation of surfaces 128 1-17
preparation room 26 34-54
prepuce 20 70
presbytery 330 32
prescription 22 3, 20
present-day man 261 21
preserve 98 51
preserving jar 40 25
preset control 316 2
presorter 172 21
presorting 64 82
press *Joiner* 133 51
press *Ball Games* 293 32
press, first ~ 173 19
press, rotary ~ *Text. Finish.* 168 33
press, rotary ~ *Letterpress* 181 57
press, second ~ 173 20
press, web-fed ~ 181 57
press-and-blow process 162 30
press attachment 100 15
press bar 100 17
press bed 180 78; 181 17
press bowl, heated ~ 168 41
press camera 114 36
presser 103 19
'press facilities' 233 43
press finishing 168 38
pressing *Glass Prod.* 162 33
pressing *Paperm.* 173 50
pressing cloth 104 32
pressing cushion 104 28
pressing mechanism 184 13
pressing pad 104 28
pressman 340 35
press mould 162 34
press photo 342 58
press photographer 299 49
press roll 173 37
press roller 64 64
pressure, atmospheric ~ 9 4
pressure, barometric ~ 9 4
pressure adjustment 249 53
pressure adjustment, calibrated ~ 185 5
pressure bulkhead 231 32
pressure bulkhead, forward ~ 235 19
pressure chamber 83 44
pressure cloth 116 59
pressure cooker *Kitch. Utensils* 40 21
pressure cooker *Camping* 278 35
pressure cylinder 133 46
pressure foot 133 47
pressure fuelling point 257 33
pressure gas 156 28
pressure gauge *Hosp.* 25 53; 26 29
pressure gauge *Overh. Irrign.* 67 10
pressure gauge *Pest Contr.* 83 42
pressure gauge *Blacksm.* 138 15

pressure gauge *Electrotyp. etc.* 178 8
pressure gauge *Offset Print.* 180 74
pressure gauge *Garage* 195 29
pressure gauge *Serv. Stat.* 196 20
pressure gauge *Railw.* 211 24
pressure gauge *Theatre* 316 56
pressure graph 27 31
pressure hull 258 66; 259 55, 76
pressure indicator 25 55
pressure line 235 54, 57
pressure pipe *Market Gdn.* 55 8
pressure pipe *Hydr. Eng.* 217 50
pressure pipe *Theatre* 316 54
pressure pipeline 217 41
pressure piston 133 52
pressure plate 115 24
pressure point 21 14
pressure pot 129 31
pressure pump, hydraulic ~ 178 11
pressure-reducing valve 141 5
pressure regulator *Gas Weld.* 141 5
pressure regulator *Graphic Art* 340 38
pressure release valve 155 7
pressure tank 316 55
pressure trace 25 57
pressure transducer 27 32
pressure valve 40 22
pressure weight 168 2
pressurized gas delivery system 234 60
pressurized-water reactor 154 19
pressurized-water system 154 40
presto 321 28
pretzel *Bakery* 97 44
pretzel *Supermkt.* 99 16
preventer 270 15
preview monitor 238 60
price 289 37
price card 271 19
price display 196 6
price label 96 6
price list *Butch.* 96 19
price list *Grocer* 98 73
price list *Bank* 250 8
price offered 289 37
pricket 330 52
pricking off 54 5
pricking out 54 5
priest 330 39; 331 47
prima ballerina 314 27
primary 153 15
primary school 260 1-85
primary voltage bushing 152 43
primary voltage terminal 152 43
primates 368 12-16
prime focus cage 5 2
Prime meridian 14 5
primer 128 6
prime steam line 154 31
priming brush 338 9
primitive man 261 19
princess, German ~ 355 20
principal 345 7
principal diapason 326 31-33
print delivery 249 43
print drier, heated ~ 116 57
print drier, rapid ~ 116 57
printer *Garage* 195 6
printer *Office* 245 32

printer, rotating ~ 111 27
printery 340 27-64
printing, rotary ~ 178 21
printing cylinder 177 67
printing-down frame 179 13
printing element 178 39
printing image carrier 340 59
printing office 340 27-64
printing paper 180 47
printing paper, photographic ~ 116 51
printing plate 178 38
printing speed adjustment 249 55
printing surface 340 59
printing unit 180 41, 80
printing unit, first ~ 181 48
printing unit, lower ~ 180 7,9,11,13
printing unit, reversible ~ 182 26
printing unit, second ~ 181 52
printing unit, upper ~ 180 6,8,10,12
print-out machine 195 6
print quantity selection 249 35
print tongs 116 47
'Prinz Heinrich' cap 35 28
prism, hexagonal ~ 351 21
prism, monoclinic ~ 351 24
prism, quadratic ~ 347 34
prism, triangular ~ 347 37
private detective 275 16
privet 373 6
privet hawkmoth 358 55
prize 306 11; 308 48
probe *Dent.* 24 46
probe *Photog.* 114 63; 116 55
probe, bulb-headed ~ 22 53; 26 40
probe, hollow ~ 26 41
probe, olive-pointed ~ 22 53; 26 40
probe exposure meter 114 61
probe lead 116 38
proboscidean 366 20
proboscidian 366 20
proboscis *Articulates* 358 17, 56
proboscis *Mammals* 366 21
procaviid 366 24
process and reproduction camera, universal ~ 177 24
process camera, overhead ~ 177 1
process camera, vertical ~ 177 32
process control computer 236 37
processing drum 116 48
processing laboratory 310 2; 311 30
processing machine 179 31
processing plant 144 5
processing unit, central ~ 176 29
procession, religious ~ 331 42-50
processionary moth 82 14
processor, automatic ~ 116 60
processor, central ~ 244 6
proclamation 263 14
proctoscope 23 17, 19, 21
proctoscopy 23 18
Procyon 3 15
produce, agricultural ~ 68 1-47
producer 316 40
product 344 25
production control room 238 17
production line 173 13-28

production manager 310 26
production oil and gas
   separator 146 9
product register 309 82
profile 118 69
profile, basic ~ 229 45
profiling tool 161 14
profit 345 7
program see programme
program card 195 5, 10
program input 177 71
programme 315 13
programme, computer-
   controlled ~ 238 2
programme, educational ~
   261 7
programme dial 243 40
programmed individual
   presentation system 242 15
programme monitor 238 61
programmer 248 15
programme recorder 261 42
programme scale 243 40
programme selector 243 39
program selector control 50
   26
program selector switch 25 50
progress counter 242 5
projectile 255 26
projection Films 311 45
projection Art 335 43
projection, conical ~ 14 8
projection, cylindrical ~ 14 9
projection booth 5 27; 312 12
projection dome 5 21
projectionist 312 20
projection lamp 312 18
projection lens 261 10; 312 35
projection room 312 12
projection room window 312
   15
projection screen Optic. Instr.
   112 24
projection screen Broadcast.
   238 32
projection screen School 260
   36
projection screen Films 310
   16; 312 11
projection table 261 13
projection window 312 15
projector 5 23; 316 17
projector, lefthand ~ 312 13
projector, overhead ~ 242 6
projector, righthand ~ 312 14
projector attachment 112 55
projector gate 312 34
projector lens 312 35
projector mechanism 312
   25-38
projector switch 195 20
projector top 261 9
promenade 223 27
promenade deck 223 22-27
prominence, laryngeal ~ 19
   13
prominence, solar ~ 4 40
prompt book 316 41
prompt box 316 27
prompter 316 28
prompt script 316 41
prone position Free Exerc.
   295 45
prone position Sports 305 29
prong Tablew. etc. 45 60
prong Agr. Impl. 66 4
proof 340 43
proofing press 180 75
proof press 180 75
prop Household 50 37
prop Circus 307 13
prop Theatre 315 50
prop, front ~ 303 8

prop, rear ~ 303 9
propagation 54 10, 14, 27
propagation of plants 54
propane gas 278 33
propane gas bottle 278 34
propeller Brew. 92 46
propeller Energy Sources 155
   45
propeller Life-Sav. 228 26
propeller Aircraft 230 32
propeller Motorboats etc. 286
   64
propeller Airsports 288 36
propeller, feathering ~ 224 19
propeller, reversible ~ 224 19
propeller, ship's ~ 221 44; 222
   72; 223 62
propeller, three-blade ~ 223
   62
propeller, variable-pitch ~
   224 19
propeller bracket 223 61
propeller guard 258 40
propeller guard boss 258 63
propeller guard moulding 258
   74
propeller mixer 79 6
propeller pitch indicator 224
   20
propeller post 222 71
propeller pump 217 47-52
propeller shaft Car 192 30, 65
propeller shaft Ship 223 65
propeller shaft Aircraft 232
   60
propeller shaft Warships 259
   59
propeller strut 223 61
propeller-turbine engine 256
   16
propeller-turbine plane 231 4
propelling nozzle 232 39, 45,
   49, 55
property 315 50
proportion, simple ~ 345 8-10
proportional dividers 339 2
proprietor 248 29; 266 71
prop stand 187 34; 188 51
propulsion nozzle 232 39, 45,
   49, 55
propylaea 334 7
propylaeum 334 7
propylon 334 7
proscenium 315 15; 334 46
proscenium, adjustable ~ 316
   22
prostate 20 76
protection device 255 81, 90
prothorax 82 4; 358 29
proton 1 2, 16, 31
protoplasm 357 3
protoprism 351 19, 20
protopyramid 351 19, 20
prototype 290 38
protozoans 357 1-12
protractor 260 38
protrusion, massive ~ 11 29
protuberance, frontal ~ 16 4
prow, rounded ~ 218 25
pruner 56 11
pruning knife 56 9
pruning saw 56 16
pruning shears 56 50
prussic acid 83 15
pseudocarp 58 21; 384 12, 62
pseudopod 357 4
psychrometer 10 52
pubis 17 20
public conveniences 268 62
publicity calendar 22 10
puck 302 35
pudding fender 227 17
pudenda 16 39

puffball 381 19
puff paste 97 18
puff pastry 97 18
pug 70 9; 123 69
pug dog 70 9
pull 340 43
pull-down table 207 53
pullet 74 9
pullet fold unit 74 5
pulley Cotton Spin. 164 48
pulley Bicycle 187 9
pulley, glass ~ 169 16
pulley cradle 214 36, 53
pulley cradle, main ~ 214 67
pullover, heavy ~ 33 52
pullover, men's ~ 33 51
pullover, short-sleeved ~ 33
   32
pull rod Mach. Parts etc. 143
   101
pull rod Railw. 202 20
pull-switch 127 16
pull-through 87 64
pull-up phase 298 29
pulmonary function test 27 36
pulp 58 24, 35, 58; 59 6
pulp, chemical ~ 172 77, 78
pulp, dental ~ 19 32
pulp, mechanical ~ 172 77, 78
pulp-drying machine 172 61
pulper 172 80
pulpit 330 19; 337 15
pulpit balustrade 330 23
pulpit steps 330 18
pulp machine 172 61
pulpstone 172 71
pulp water pump 172 55, 63
pulsator 75 32
pulse cable 117 72
pulse-generating camera 117
   71
pulse generator 313 30
pulse generator socket 117 7
pulse rate 23 27
pulse shape 23 37
pump Agr. Mach. 65 45
pump Shoes 101 29
pump Oil, Petr. 145 22
pump Synth. Fibres 170 31
pump, centrifugal ~ Wine
   Cell. 79 7
pump, centrifugal ~ Rivers
   216 60
pump, centrifugal ~ Water
   269 44
pump, centrifugal ~ Fire Brig.
   270 8
pump, direct-connected ~ 83
   41
pump, hydraulic ~ Agr.
   Mach. 64 29, 91
pump, hydraulic ~ Theatre
   316 53
pump, main ~ 269 15
pump, motor-driven ~ 83 41
pump, portable ~ 270 52
pump, power take-off-driven
   ~ 67 14, 15
pump compass 151 59
pump compression spring 174
   41
pump connection 67 8
pumpernickel 97 49
pumping plant 217 39-46
pumping rod 145 25
pumping station Offshore
   Drill. 146 22
pumping station Hydr. Eng.
   217 43
pumping station Shipbuild.
   222 33
pumping station Spa 274 4
pumping unit 145 22

pumpkin 57 23
pump pressure spring 174 41
pump room Brew. 92 11
pump room Spa 274 8, 15
pumps 2 52
pump shaft 199 19
pump strainer 269 6, 14, 43
punch Shoem. 100 45, 46
punch Goldsm. etc. 108 19,
   30, 31
punch Office 247 3
punch Sculpt. Studio 339 15
punch, foul ~ 299 34
punch, hollow ~ 125 13
punch, illegal ~ 299 34
punch, revolving ~ 100 44
punch, rotary ~ 100 44
punch, round ~ 137 36; 140
   65
punch, steel ~ 175 36
punch, straight ~ 299 28
punch bag 299 21
punch ball 299 24
punch ball, spring-supported
   ~ 299 20
punch ball, suspended ~ 299
   23
punch blank 175 35
punch card 237 64
punch card reader 244 12
punch cutter 175 32
punched card 237 64
punched card reader 244 12
punched tape 176 6, 8, 12;
   237 62, 68
punched tape input 176 30
punched tape reader 176 13,
   15
punching bag 299 21
punch tape 176 6, 8, 12; 237
   62, 68
punch tape input 176 30
punch tape reader 176 13, 15
punctuation marks 342 16-29
punt 216 15; 283 1
punt pole 89 30; 216 16
pup 73 16
pupa 77 30, 32; 80 4, 25, 43;
   81 21, 24; 82 13, 21, 32; 358
   20; 365 11
pupa, coarctate ~ 81 3
pupil Man 19 43
pupil School 260 3
puppy 73 16
pure culture plant 93 6
purfling 323 26
purge valve 6 25
purified water tank 269 13
purlin 119 55; 121 39, 51, 76
purlin, concrete ~ 119 4
purlin, inferior ~ 119 3; 121
   44; 122 40
purlin roof 121 46
purlin roof structure 121 52,
   60
purple clover 69 1
purple medick 69 9
purse wig 34 4
push button 203 67; 237 18,
   19; 241 3
push-button keyboard 237
   10; 245 14; 246 14
push-button telephone 237
   20
pushchair 28 37
pushchair, doll's ~ 48 31
pusher ram 156 7
pushing frame 200 30
push sledge 304 29
push tow 225 60
push tug 221 93
putlock 118 27
putlog 118 27

putter 293 93
putting 293 86
putting green 293 82
putty 124 17
putty knife 124 27; 129 24
puzzle 48 9
pyelogram 27 6
pyelogram cassettes 27 14
pyelography 27 4
pygmy poodle 70 36
pyjamas 32 17, 36
pyjama top 32 18
pyjama trousers 32 19
pylon Railw. 214 31, 77
pylon Art 333 9
pylon, tubular steel ~ 214 78
pylorus 20 42
pyramid Fruit & Veg. Gdn. 52 16
pyramid Circus 307 28
pyramid Art 333 1
pyramid, glass ~ 5 19
pyramid, orthorhombic ~ 351 23
pyramid, quadrilateral ~ 347 46
pyramid, stepped ~ 333 22; 352 20
pyramid site 333 6
pyramid tree 52 16; 272 19
pyrheliometer 10 23
pyrite 351 8
pyrometer 178 16
pyx 330 8; 332 53
pyxidium 370 95

Q

quack grass 61 30
quadrant 347 5
quadraphonic system 241 13-48
quadra/stereo converter 241 46
quadrilateral, irregular ~ 346 39
quadrilaterals 346 33-39
quadruplet 321 23
quail 359 22
quail call 87 45
quake, tectonic ~ 11 32-38
quake, volcanic ~ 11 32-38
quantity, unknown ~ 345 4, 8
quant pole 89 30; 216 16
quantum jump 1 15
quantum jumps 1 20-25
quantum transitions 1 20-25
quarantine wing 225 27
quarrier 158 5
quarry Map 15 87
quarry Quarry 158 1
quarryman 158 5
quarry worker 158 5
quarte engagement 294 47
quarter Shoem. 100 61
quarter Carp. 120 25
quarter, first ~ 4 4
quarter, last ~ 4 6
quarter, third ~ 4 6
quarter baulk 120 90
quarter gallery 218 57
quarterings 254 18-23
quartering wind 285 13
quarter light 191 23
quarter note 320 15
quarter of beef 94 22
quarter piece 329 88
quarter rest 320 23
quarters, firemen's ~ 270 2
quarter vent 191 23
quarter wind 285 13
quartz 110 15

quartz-halogen lamp 179 21; 182 3
quartz watch, electronic ~ 110 14
quatrefoil 335 39
quaver 320 16
quaver rest 320 24
quay 222 5; 225 64
quayside crane 225 24
quayside railway 225 21
quayside road 225 38
quayside roadway 225 38
quayside steps 283 22
quay wall 217 1-14
queen Bees 77 4, 38
queen Games 276 9
queen bee 77 4
Queen Carnival 306 61
queen cell 77 37
queen-excluder 77 47
queen post 121 46, 52, 68
queen truss 121 65
Queen Victoria water lily 378 17
quenching car 156 10
quenching tower 156 11
quenching trough 137 8
question mark 342 20
queue 34 6; 319 26
quickbeam 371 42
quick grass 61 30
quick hitch 65 86
quicksand 227 3
quid 107 19
quill 341 26
quillons 294 42
quill pen 341 26
quill plectrum 322 53
quilting 29 39; 30 17
quilt stitching 29 39; 30 17
quince, apple-shaped ~ 58 49
quince, pear-shaped ~ 58 50
quince leaf 58 47
quince tree 58 46
quinquefoliolate 370 39
quintuplet 321 23
quipa 352 22
quitch grass 61 30
quiver 352 27
quoin 181 39
quoit 280 32; 308 47
quoits 280 31
quotation 250 8
quotation board 251 8
quotation mark, double ~ 342 26
quotation mark, French ~ 342 27
quotient 344 26

R

rabbet plane 132 25
rabbit 73 18; 86 23; 88 65
rabbit burrow 86 26
rabbit fence 84 7
rabbit hole 86 26
rabbit net 86 27
raccoon 368 9
race, inner ~ 143 72
race, outer ~ 143 71
race board 166 42
racehorse 289 51
raceme 58 15; 374 33
raceme, simple ~ 370 68
raceway 91 44
racical sign 345 2
racing 289 50
racing, motor-paced ~ 290 11-15
racing and passenger aircraft 230 1-31, 32-66; 231 1

racing bicycle 290 16
racing boats 283 9-16
racing car 290 36, 38
racing cars 290 34-38
racing cycle 290 15, 16
racing cyclist 290 8
racing dive 282 29
racing flag 284 48
racing handlebar 290 18
racing jersey 290 9
racing keelboat 285 35
racing motorcycle 290 27
racing motorcycle, streamlined ~ 290 31
racing motorcyclist 290 25
racing outboard motor 286 23
racing saddle 290 17
racing sculler 283 16
racing shell, eight-oared ~ 283 10
racing suit 301 31
racing toe clip 290 21
racing tyre 290 19
rack Kitch. Utensils 40 31
rack Composing Rm. 174 8
rack Garage 195 10
rack Railw. 214 9, 11
rack, removable ~ 40 24
rack and pinion 112 39
rack-and-pinion railway 214 4-5
rack-and-pinion railways 214 7-11
racket 293 29
racket handle 293 30, 46
racket press 293 32
rack for glasses 274 16
rack head 163 16, 18
racking back 118 61
rack mountain railway 214 4-5
rack railroad 214 4-5
rack railroad car 214 5
rack railroad locomotive, electric ~ 214 4
rack railway coach 214 5
rack railway locomotive, electric ~ 214 4
rack railways 214 7-11
rack railway trailer 214 5
rack track 217 69
racoon 368 9
racquet see racket
radar antenna 223 8; 224 104; 258 36; 259 8, 29, 48, 91
radar apparatus 224 10-13
radar display unit 224 12
radar dome Aircraft 231 18
radar dome Air Force 256 10
radar dome Warships 258 52, 77; 259 49
radar equipment 224 10-13
radar image 224 13
radar nose 231 18; 256 10
radar pedestal 224 10
radar picture 224 13
radar reflector 10 58
radar reflector, revolving ~ 224 11
radar scanner 223 8; 224 104; 258 36; 259 8, 29, 48, 91
radar screen 224 12
radial side of the hand 19 69
radiant energy 10 23
radiation, solar ~ 155 18
radiation detectors 2 1-23
radiation meters 2 1-23
radiation monitor 2 1
radiation shield 2 31, 46
radiation shielding 2 31
radiation unit 24 23
radiator Doc. 23 23
radiator Roof & Boilerr. 38 76

radiator Agr. Mach. 65 51
radiator Plumb. etc. 126 20
radiator Energy Sources 155 15
radiator Car 191 9
radiator Railw. 212 54
radiator bonnet 304 11
radiator brush 129 21
radiator grill 191 11
radiator heating 155 27
radiator hood 304 11
radiator rib 38 77; 126 21
radiators 6 8
radiator shutter 304 12
radical 345 2
radicle 370 88
radio 238; 239
radioactive waste storage 154 56
radio antenna 197 34
radio cassette recorder 241 1
radio communication set 197 28
radio compass 230 5
radio direction finder antenna 223 5; 224 106
radio direction finder frame 258 17
radio equipment 197 28; 230 22; 288 13, 17
radiographer 27 11
radio interference service 237 27
radiolarian 357 8
radio link, intercontinental ~ 237 54-55
radiometer 10 71
radio navigation equipment 230 22
radio OB van 239 1-15
radiophone 22 14
radio room 223 12
radioscope box 74 47
radioscope table 74 48
radiosonde 10 59
radiosonde assembly 10 55
radio station 238 1-6
radio switching centre control room 238 7-15
radio system 6 26
radio telephone 212 23
radish 57 15
radish, white ~ 57 16
radius Man 17 13
radius Mills 91 2
radius Maths. 346 47
radius of curvature 346 22
radome Aircraft 231 18
radome Air Force 256 10
radome Warships 258 52, 77; 259 49
raffia 136 29
raffle 306 11
raft 283 60
rafter 121 28, 36; 122 19
rafter, common ~ 121 56
rafter, principal ~ 121 55
rafter end 121 45; 122 41
rafter head 121 45; 122 41
rafter roof 121 27
rag bolt 143 43
rag felt 122 62
ragged robin 376 21
rail Atom 2 37
rail Livestock 75 16
rail Joiner 133 41
rail Mach. Tools 150 12
rail Station 205 59; 206 38
rail Railw. 214 10
rail Restaurant 266 72
rail Equest. 289 2
rail Birds 359 20

rail, triangular ~ 242 80
rail bottom 202 4
rail brake 206 48
railcar 205 25
railcar, articulated ~ 197 1, 13
railcar, front ~ 211 61
railcar, light ~ 208 13
railcar, short-distance ~ 208 13
railcar, six-axle ~ 197 13
railcar, twelve-axle ~ 197 1
rail clip 202 9
rail foot 202 4
rail guard 210 34
rail head 202 2
railing Bldg. Site 118 89
railing Park 272 34
rail joint 202 11
railroad see railway
railroad map 204 33
railroad policeman 205 20
railroad station 15 41
railroad ticket 204 36
railroad track 202; 203
rail service, interurban ~ 197 1
rail service, urban ~ 197 13
railway, funicular ~ 214 12
railway, light ~ 200 23
railway, main line ~ 15 21
railway, narrow-gauge ~ Map 15 90
railway, narrow-gauge ~ Road Constr. 200 23
railway guide, official ~ 204 50
railway information clerk 204 49
railway line 202; 203
railway map 204 33
railway policeman 205 20
railway siding 225 62
railway station 15 41
railway ticket 204 36
railway vehicles 207; 208; 209; 210; 211; 212; 213
rail web 202 3
rain 8 18; 9 32
rainbow 7 4
rainbow, colours of the ~ 343 14
rainbow dressing 221 85
rain cape 41 4; 196 26
rain cloud 8 10
raincoat 29 31
rain cover 10 41
rain gauge 10 38, 44
rainwater pipe 37 13; 38 10; 122 29
rain zone, temperate ~ 9 55
rain zone, tropical ~ 9 53
raisin 98 8
raising of livestock 75
raising to a power 345 1
rake Roof & Boilerr. 38 42
rake Gdn. Tools 56 4
rake Blacksm. 137 4
rake Roulette 275 5
rake Winter Sp. 303 24
rake, wire-tooth ~ 51 3; 56 3
rake, wooden ~ 66 23
raking back 118 61
Ram Astron. 4 53
ram Dom. Anim. 73 13
ram Blacksm. 137 10
ram Forging 139 12
ram Ship 218 9
ram Theatre 316 60
ram, lower ~ 139 7
ram, upper ~ 139 6
rambler 52 5
ram guide 139 8
ram longwall face 144 36

rammer 200 26
rammer, pneumatic ~ 148 31
ramp Bldg. Site 119 41
ramp Floor etc. Constr. 123 30
ramp Station 206 1
ramp Ship 221 55
ram piston 65 24
ramson 377 6
randing 136 1, 4
randing, oblique ~ 136 3
rangefinder 255 82
rangefinder, optical ~ 258 37
rangefinder window 114 40
range light, higher ~ 224 102
range light, lower ~ 224 101
range lights 224 101-102
range selector 114 59
range switch 114 59
rape 383 1
rapelling 300 28-30
rapid adjustment compass 151 64
rapid feeding system 74 23
rapid-filter plant 269 9
rapid heat-up cathode 240 25
rapid-loading system 115 25
rapid scale 98 12
rapid-veneer press 133 49
rapping iron 136 36
raptorial leg 358 5
Raschel fabric 167 29
rasp 260 55
rasp, shoemaker's ~ 100 49
raspberry 58 28; 370 101
raspberry bush 58 25
raspberry flower 58 26
ratan chair cane 136 32
rate-of-climb indicator 230 14
rate of interest 345 7
rattan chair cane 136 32
rattle Infant Care etc. 28 44
rattle Carnival 306 40, 47
rattle, baby's ~ 28 44
rat trap binding 301 15
Rautek grip 21 18
ravine 13 52
raw coal bunker 144 41
raw material Cement Wks. 160 1, 4
raw material Synth. Fibres 169 1-12
raw material store 160 3
raw meal silo 160 5
raw milk pump 76 3
raw milk storage tank 76 5
raw mill 160 4, 7
ray Church 332 37
ray Maths. 346 20
ray, medullary ~ 370 11
ray, vascular ~ 370 11
ray floret 375 31
rays, sun's ~ 4 9
razor, open ~ 106 38
razor, straight ~ 106 38
razor handle 106 39
R-class 284 59
reach, lower ~ 217 29
reach, upper ~ 217 37
reaching leg 285 24
reactor 154 3, 41, 50
reactor, nuclear ~ 1 48; 154 19
reactor building 154 20
reactor core 259 68
reactor pressure vessel 154 22
reader 260 16
reading adjustment 10 10
reading lamp 43 15
reading microscope 113 28
reading room 262 13
reading room staff 262 14
readout, digital ~ 110 2; 112 47

readout, fast ~ 195 12
ready position 305 72
reamer 109 8; 140 31
reamer, angled ~ 125 9
rear brace 329 47
rearing of livestock 75
rear of the railcar 197 4
rear seat headrest 193 8
rear seat head restraint 193 8
rearsight 255 22, 36
rear vault 297 32
rear-view mirror 188 35; 189 30
rear-view mirror, inside ~ 191 39
rearward horizontal stand 295 31
rearward swing 296 57
rear window heating switch 191 82
rebate plane 132 25
receipt 98 44; 271 7
receipt stamp 236 29
receiver Meteorol. Instr. 10 63
receiver Hunt. 87 16
receiver Docks 226 33
receiver Audio 241 40
receiver Office 246 16
receiver Ball Games 293 50
receiver Nightclub 318 18
receiver, tilting-type ~ 148 5
receiver cord 237 14
receiver surface, blackened ~ 155 29
receiving hopper 147 5
receiving table 249 54
receiving tray 249 47
receiving truck 226 15
receptacle 370 53
reception Doc. 22 5
reception Camping 278 1
reception hall 267 1-26
receptionist, chief ~ 267 7
recess 217 70
reciprocal 344 16
recirculation pump 154 43, 54
record 46 15; 309 32; 317 24
record chamber, automatic ~ 241 18
record changer, automatic ~ 241 52
recorder Meteorol. Instr. 10 61
recorder Hosp. 25 3
recorder Music. Instr. 322 7
recorder, eight-channel ~ 27 28
recorder, open-reel-type ~ 241 56
recorder, potentiometric ~ 23 55
recording, photographic ~ 27 33
recording amplifier 311 11
recording and playback deck, single ~ 238 58
recording and playback equipment 311 23
recording arm 10 7, 12, 15, 21
recording channel, central ~ 238 1-6
recording drum 10 5, 16, 20
recording engineer 310 23, 55; 311 36
recording head Cine Film 117 33
recording head Audio 241 59
recording head Films 311 25
recording instrument 10 61
recording level control 117 16
recording level display 243 15
recording level indicator 243 12; 311 14

recording level meter 241 35, 36, 61; 242 14
recording level meters 241 35-36
recording loudspeaker 238 37
recording mechanism 10 42
recording meter 138 19
recording paper 25 4; 27 29, 34, 40
recording pen 10 13
recording rain gauge 10 38
recording room 238 16; 310 54
recording room mixing console 238 25
recording sensitivity selector 117 16
recording space 177 49
recording speaker 238 37
recording tape 241 58
record keeper 299 48
record of posting book 236 18
record player 241 18; 317 19
record player base 241 19
record player housing 241 19
record rack 309 36
record storage compartment 241 48
record storage slot 241 48
record turntable 238 24
recovery parachute 235 60
recovery vehicle, armoured ~ 255 93
rectangle 346 34
rectifier Blacksm. 138 30
rectifier Electrotyp. etc. 178 2
rectifier Films 312 18
rector 330 22
rectory 331 20
rectoscope 23 16, 17
rectoscopy 23 18
rectum 20 22, 61
rectus abdominis 18 44
red 343 1
red admiral 365 1
red-billed toucan 363 6
redbreast 361 15
redcap 205 31
red card 291 63
red deer 88 1, 1-27
red flyer 366 3
red fox 88 42; 367 12
red kangaroo 366 3
red magnolia 373 15
redstart 360 3
red swing filter 116 46
reducing coupler 126 39, 41
reducing elbow 126 49
reducing socket 126 39, 41
reducing valve 141 5
reduction drive lever 149 3
reduction gear Paperm. 172 69
reduction gear Aircraft 232 59
reduction gear Warships 259 61
reduction gearing, multi-step ~ 64 71
red underwing 365 8
red whortleberry 377 23
red wine glass 45 83
reed Basketm. 136 28
reed Weaving 166 10
reed Music. Instr. 326 41
reed, double ~ 323 29
reed mace 136 27
reed mace bulrush 378 21
reed organ 325 43
reed pen 341 22
reed pipe, metal ~ 326 17-22
reed stop 326 17-22

reed-threading draft 171 6
reef 219 72
reefer 221 127
reel, fixed-spool ~ 89 32, 61
reel, multiplying ~ 89 59
reel, spring-tine ~ 64 4
reel, stationary-drum ~ 89 61
reel arm, foldaway ~ 117 92
reel drum 312 16
reel drum, fireproof ~ 312 25
reel gearing 64 5
reeling machine 173 41
reel of film 312 33
reel oven 97 71
reels 89 59-64
reel stand 180 3, 19
referee 291 62; 293 67; 299 16, 41
referee's position 299 8
reference book 262 17
reference library 262 17
refill 151 46
refill lead 151 46
refiner 172 84
refiner, conical ~ 172 27, 60, 73, 83
refining bath 162 4
reflected-light microscope 112 23
reflecting goniometer 351 28
reflector Atom 1 65
reflector Optic. Instr. 113 1
reflector Bicycle 187 45
reflector, glass ~ 187 86
reflector, swivel-mounted ~ 114 69
reflector pedal 187 78
reflex angle 346 10,11-12
reflex camera, twin-lens ~ 114 22
reflex finder 117 44
reflex mirror 115 33
reflex system 115 31
reformer 145 47
reformer, catalytic ~ 145 71
refractometer 111 44
refractometer, dipping ~ 112 48
refractor 113 16
refreshment kiosk 205 49
refreshment stall 308 3
refrigeration system 93 11
refrigerator 39 2; 46 33; 317 10
refrigerator car 213 39
refrigerator shelf 39 3
refrigerator van 213 39
refrigerator wagon 213 39
refuse 199 17
refuse, compacted and decomposed ~ 199 22
refuse collection vehicle 199 1
refuse container 199 4
refuse disposal 199
refuse incineration unit 199 28
regatta 283 1-18
regatta course 285 14-24, 16
register School 260 23
register Hotel 267 8
register Music. Instr. 322 51
register device 177 12
register mark 340 58
registration form 267 12
registration number Election 263 19
registration number Motorboats etc. 286 7
registration number Script 342 43
reglet 334 57
regula 334 17
regular crystal system 351 1-17

regular customer 266 39, 40
regular grade gasoline 145 54
regular grade petrol 145 54
regulating handle 133 14
regulating valve 38 75
regulator 109 32
regulator main valve 210 13
regulator valve 210 13
Regulidae 361 10
rehearsal 315 21-27
reheating 162 27, 35
reichstaler 252 6
rein 71 33; 186 31; 289 27; 303 4
reindeer 353 16
reindeer harness 353 15
reinforced concrete construction 119 1-89
reinforcement 119 54-76, 68
reinforcement, projecting ~ 119 10, 71
reinforcement, steel-bar ~ 123 37
reinforcement beading 125 8
reinforcement binding 119 66
reinforcement rod 119 23
reinforcing member, longitudinal ~ 230 47, 57
reinforcing rib Road Constr. 200 9
reinforcing rib Hydr. Eng. 217 78
reinforcing steel 119 23
reinforcing strut 315 31
reins 71 25, 33
rejects chest 172 59
relay 186 43
relay horse 186 43
release First Aid 21 34
release Weaving 165 35
release, delayed-action ~ 309 51
release binding 301 2
release grip 21 34
release lever Slaughterho. 94 6
release lever Office 247 42
release/lock lever 247 42
release phase 75 33
release valve 210 58
relief image carrier 340 2
relief printing method 340 1-13
relief tile, glazed ~ 333 20
remainder 344 24
remains 15 72
Remington cartridge 305 39
remitter 250 19
remnant 103 16
remote control jack 117 9
remote control panel 157 14
remote control radio 288 87
remote control socket 117 9
rendering, exterior ~ 122 38
rendering coat 123 6
rendezvous point 233 29
rendezvous radar antenna 6 42
reniform 370 38
rennet vat 76 48
repair bay 196 22
repair quay 222 10
repair shop 196 22
repeater 87 2
repeaters 253 30-32
repeating rifle 87 2
repeat mark 321 26
replenishing ship 258 97
report 342 54
reproducing head 241 59
reptile enclosure 356 12

reptiles 364 27-41
requin 364 1
re-recording 311 1-46
re-reeler 173 41
re-reeling machine 173 41
rescue 21 18-23, 28-33, 34-38
rescue cruiser 221 18; 228 14
rescue helicopter 221 20; 228 16
rescuer 21 29, 34
research laboratory 310 9
research microscope 112 1, 66
research microscope, binocular ~ 23 51
research rocket 7 24
reserve fuel tank 212 60
reserve tank 232 20
reservoir Hydr. Eng. 217 39-46
reservoir Air Force 257 16
reservoir, impounded ~ 217 57
reservoir rock 12 29
reset button Cine Film 117 86
reset button Car 191 77
resetting button 127 20
resetting spring 237 49
residential area 15 28
residue 145 43
resin 323 11
resin, synthetic ~ 130 26
resistor 153 56
resonating body 322 29; 323 3; 324 2, 15, 26
resonating chamber 322 18; 324 15, 63
resonating sound box 324 26
resonator 322 18, 29; 324 2, 15
resonator, tubular metal ~ 324 78
resonator wall 322 33
respiration, artificial ~ 21 24-27
respirator 21 27; 26 25
respiratory apparatus 21 27; 26 24
respiratory functions 23 31
respiratory machine 26 1
respiratory rate 23 27
respond 335 35
'restaurant' 233 50
restaurant 266 1-29
restaurant car 207 22-32
restaurant car, self-service ~ 207 73
rest cure 274 12-14
resting rail 322 42
restoring spring 237 49
restricted area 292 37
rests 320 20-27
result register 309 82
results of sets 293 35
resuscitation 21 24-27
resuscitation, mouth-to-mouth ~ 21 26
resuscitation, mouth-to-nose ~ 21 26
resuscitation apparatus 21 27
resuscitation equipment 270 20
resuscitator 21 27; 270 20
retailer 98 41
retail shop 98 1-87
retail store 98 1-87
retaining plate 167 56
retarder 206 42
reticella lace 102 30
reticule 115 61
Reticulum 3 48
retina 19 49
retort 349 13
retort ring 350 15
retoucher 182 14

retouching and stripping desk 177 19
retrieving 86 36
retrofocus position 115 84
return 38 79
return pipe 38 56, 79, 80; 126 24
return spring Knitting 167 37
return spring Car 192 55
return tap 350 49
Reuther board 296 12; 297 8
rev counter 189 41; 191 38; 212 22; 230 8
rev counter, electric ~ 191 70
rev counter, electronic ~ 188 40
reveal 37 26; 118 10; 120 31
revenue stamp 107 26
revers collar 30 9
reverse 252 9
reverse dive 282 41
reverse gear 192 44
reverse hang 296 34
reverse shaft 149 34
reversing catch 87 24
reversing clutch 115 27
reversing gear 210 18; 211 53; 212 74
reversing gears 65 41
reversing ring 115 83
reversing wheel 210 56
revertive signal panel 153 7
revetment 216 51-55
revolution counter 189 41; 191 38; 212 22; 230 8
revolution counter, electric ~ 191 70
revolution counter, electronic ~ 188 40
revolving die hammer 85 12
reward 86 43
rewind 114 6; 115 12
rewind bench 238 59; 312 21
rewind button 249 73
rewind cam 115 29
rewind crank 114 6; 115 12
rewinder Cine Film 117 93
rewinder Paperm. 173 41
rewind handle Photog. 114 6; 115 12
rewind handle Cine Film 117 93
rewinding 170 50
rewind release button 115 27
rewind station 173 41
rhesus macaque 368 12
rhesus monkey 368 12
rhinoceros 366 25
Rhiptoglossa 364 33
rhizome 58 18
rhizopod 357 1
rhomb 346 35
rhombic crystal system 351 23
rhombohedron 351 22
rhomboid 346 36
rhombus 346 35
rhubarb plan 97 22
rhynchophore 358 4
rib Meat 95 3
rib Floor etc. Constr. 123 36
rib Basketm. 136 24
rib Shipbuild. 222 58
rib Aircraft 230 46
rib Rowing 283 49
rib Sailing 285 51
rib Music. Instr. 322 33; 323 4, 25
rib Art 335 31
rib Bot. 370 29
rib, annular ~ 235 47
rib, false ~ 287 36
rib, flat ~ 95 21
rib, fore ~ 95 18

rib, main ~ *Space* 235 10
rib, main ~ *Gliding* 287 35
rib, middle ~ 95 19
rib, prime ~ 95 18
rib, top ~ 95 31
ribbon 34 7; 355 78
ribbon, corded ~ 35 13
ribbon, fancy ~ 35 14
ribbon cassette 249 16
ribbon of glass 162 10
ribbon selector 249 11
ribbon window 37 86
Ribes 58 1-15
ribgrass 380 11
rib randing 136 2
ribs, false ~ 17 10
ribs, true ~ 17 9
rib vault 336 43
rib weave, combined ~ 171 19
ribwort 380 11
ribwort plantain 380 11
rice *Arable Crops* 68 1; 68 29
rice *Grocer* 98 38
rice grain 68 30
rickshaw 353 34
rickshaw coolie 353 35
rickstand 63 28, 29
riddle 55 13
ride *Map* 15 112
ride *Forestry* 84 1
rider *Cyc. Racing* 290 25
rider *Chem.* 349 33
rider bar 349 31
rider holder 349 32
ridge *Phys. Geog.* 12 36; 13 60
ridge *Dwellings* 37 7
ridge *Roof* 121 2; 122 93
ridge *Mountain.* 300 21
ridge, concave ~ 302 22
ridge, hollow ~ 302 22
ridge beam 121 48
ridge board 121 48
ridge capping piece 122 99
ridge course 122 47, 79
ridge course tile 122 4
ridge cross 331 10
ridge hook 122 65
ridge joint 122 79
ridge purlin 121 43
ridge rope 221 118
ridge tent 278 21; 280 45
ridge tile 122 3, 8, 52
ridge turret 121 14
ridge vent 55 11
ridging hoe 56 5
riding animal 354 2
riding cap 289 14
riding seat 296 32
riding switch 289 22
riffler 172 2; 173 13
rifle, self-loading ~ 255 16
rifle, short ~ 86 30
rifle, single-loading ~ 87 1
rifle, triple-barrelled ~ 87 23
rifle barrel 87 26
rifle butt 255 24
rifle cleaning kit 87 61-64
rifle grip *Photog.* 115 100
rifle grip *Films* 313 37
riflescope 87 29; 305 49
rifle shooting 305 26
rifling 87 36
rifling calibre 87 37
rig 219 1-72
Rigel 3 13
rigging 219 1-72
rigging, running ~ 219 67-71
rigging, standing ~ 219 10-19
right 254 18,20,22
right angle 346 9, 32
right corner pin 305 8
right front second pin 305 4
right hook 299 33

right tank fuel gauge 230 17
rim *Bicycle* 187 28
rim *Motorcycle* 189 25
rim *Car* 191 16; 192 77
rim brake 187 5
rimfire cartridge 305 35
rind 120 86; 370 8
ring *Jewell.* 36 4
ring *Forestry* 85 4
ring *Fish Farm.* 89 56
ring *Cotton Spin.* 164 51, 54
ring *Sports* 299 35
ring *Circus* 307 21
ring *Bullfight. etc.* 319 9
ring *Church* 332 17
ring *Maths.* 346 57
ring *Chem.* 350 15
ring, all-round ~ 89 58
ring, annual ~ 84 24
ring, asymmetrical ~ 36 27
ring, diamond ~ 36 23, 24
ring, front ~ 113 7
ring, gemstone ~ 36 15
ring, man's ~ 36 20
ring, rubber ~ *Kitch. Utensils* 40 26
ring, rubber ~ *Bathing* 280 32
ring, spring-steel ~ 89 51
ring and bead sight, optical ~ 305 51
ring attendant 307 27
ring cake 97 33; 99 22
ringed snake 364 38
ring entrance 307 11
ring fence 307 22
ring file 260 15
ring finger 19 67
ring for the carrying strap 115 9
ring frame 164 34
ring gauge 108 25, 27
ring gemstones 36 72-77
ringmaster 307 31
ring net 90 25
ring plectrum 324 27
ring rail 164 42, 54
ring-rounding tool 108 26
rings 296 4
ring sight, optical ~ 305 50
ring snake 364 38
ring spindle, standard ~ 164 45
ring spinning frame 164 34
ring tube *Cotton Spin.* 164 52
ring tube *Weaving* 165 15
riot duty 264 15
riot gear 264 18
riot shield 264 20
rip panel 288 75, 83
rip panel, emergency ~ 288 72
ripper 200 20
ripping line 288 76
ripping line, emergency ~ 288 73
ripple marks 13 41
riprap 216 51
rise adjustment 133 21
rise adjustment wheel 133 22
rise and fall adjustment wheel 132 60
riser *Floor etc. Constr.* 123 33, 48
riser *Iron Foundry etc.* 148 22
riser *Water* 269 19
riser *Fire Brig.* 270 26
riser *Airsports* 288 42
riser *Sports* 305 55
riser gate 148 22
riser pipe 269 19
rise to straddle 296 49
rising 283 31
Rising Sun 253 20
ritual cart, miniature ~ 328 36

ritual chariot, miniature ~ 328 36
river *Phys. Geog.* 13 61
river *Map* 15 76
river *Rivers* 216 31
river, navigable ~ 15 45
river, subterranean ~ 13 83
river arm 13 2; 216 3
river arm, blind ~ 216 18
riverbank 216 5
riverbed 13 68
river bend 13 11
river branch 13 2; 216 3
river branch, blind ~ 216 18
river engineering 216
river ferry 216 10
river island 216 4
river islet 216 4
river mouth 13 1
river nymph 272 2; 327 23
river police 217 24
rivers 216
river terrace 13 49, 63
river tug 216 23
river valley 13 57-70
rivet 143 57-60
rivet head 143 57
riveting 143 56
riveting machine 138 27
rivet shank 143 58
riving hammer 85 5
rivulet *Phys. Geog.* 13 8
rivulet *Map* 15 80
road 37 61
road, bituminous ~ 200 55
road, good ~ 15 30
road, main ~ 15 83
road, metalled ~ 15 30
road, poor ~ 15 99
road, secondary ~ 15 36
road, unmetalled ~ 15 99
road bridge 15 55
road building 200; 201
road-building machinery 200 1-54
road coach 186 39
road construction 200; 201
road form 201 15
road layers 198 1-5
road making 200; 201
road-metal spreading machine 200 31
road over railway 15 22
road race 290 8-10
road race bicycle 290 16
road racer 290 8
road racing 290 16, 24-28
road ripper 200 20
road roller 200 36
roadster *Bicycle* 187 1
roadster *Car* 193 26
road surface 215 8; 217 1
road sweeper 199 5; 268 20
road-sweeping lorry 199 41
roadway, orthotropic ~ 215 2
road wheel 255 86
roast 45 27
roasting chicken 98 6
roasting drum 98 71
roasting round 95 11
robe de chambre 355 66
robes 330 22; 332 4
robin 361 15
robin redbreast 361 15
robot 273 36
rocaille 336 13
rock 13 25; 327 38; 356 2
rock, blasted ~ 158 4
rock, coal-bearing ~ 144 49
rock, impermeable ~ 12 23; 13 78
rock, impervious ~ 12 23; 13 78

rock, loose ~ 158 4
rock, piece of ~ 6 15
rock, sedimentary ~ 12 1; 13 48
rock, stratified ~ 13 48
rock bit 145 21
rock climbing 300 2-13
rocker *Child. Rm.* 47 16
rocker *Winter Sp.* 302 19
rocker *Music. Instr.* 326 39
rocker *Graphic Art* 340 19
rocker arm 190 33
rocker arm mounting 190 34
rocker switch 127 4
rockery 37 40; 51 6
rocket *Life-Sav.* 228 2
rocket *Army* 255 26, 65
rocket *Carnival* 306 54
rocket, short-range ~ 259 26
rocket apparatus 228 1
rocket cruiser 259 21, 41
rocket engine 6 3
rocket engine, liquid-fuelled ~ 235 36
rocket engine, main ~ 235 36
rocket gun 228 1
rocket launcher 255 64, 70
rocket launcher, underwater ~ 259 37, 51
rocket line 228 3
rocket stage, first ~ 234 3
rocket stage, second ~ 234 18
rocket stage, third ~ 234 33
rocket tube 255 71
rock face *Phys. Geog.* 12 43; 13 28
rock face *Quarry* 158 15
rock face *Mountain.* 300 2
rock garden 37 40; 51 6
rock goat 367 7
rocking chair 309 61
rocking tool 340 19
rock island 13 12
rock ledge 300 4
rock painting 328 9
rock plant 51 7
rock rose 377 20
rock salt 351 2
rockslide 11 46
rock slip 11 46
rock spike 300 9
rock terrace 13 47
rock tomb 333 38
rock wall 300 2
rod, carbon-fibre ~ 89 57
rod, glass ~ 89 49, 57
rod, iron ~ 130 3
rod, metal ~ 339 24
rod, polished ~ 145 27
rod, telescopic ~ 89 53
rodents 366 12-19
rodeo 319 34
rodeo rider 319 39
rod rest 89 23
rods 89 49-58
rod section 89 54
rod tip 89 35
roe *Game* 88 28-39
roe *Fish Farm.* 89 12
roe, female ~ 88 34
roebuck 86 17; 88 28
roe call 87 43
roe deer 88 28-39
roll *Kitch. Utensils* 40 31
roll *Tablew. etc.* 45 21
roll *Horse* 71 48
roll *Bakery* 97 13
roll *Supermkt.* 99 12
roll *Restaurant* 266 54
roll *Athletics* 298 17
roll, double ~ 97 15
roll, lower ~ 148 55
roll, upper ~ 148 54

roll, white ~ **97** 14
roll bar *Agr. Mach.* **65** 21
roll bar *Motorcycles etc.* **188** 18
roll bar *Car* **193** 13
roll bearing **148** 60
roll cutter **173** 42
roller *Hairdresser* **105** 12
roller *Cooper* **130** 26
roller *Glass Prod.* **162** 11
roller *Weaving* **165** 57
roller *Road Constr.* **200** 37
roller *Station* **206** 39
roller *Hydr. Eng.* **217** 65
roller *Office* **249** 17
roller *Cyc. Racing* **290** 13
roller *Graphic Art* **340** 12
roller *Birds* **359** 25; **360** 6
roller, bottom ~ **164** 10
roller, fluted ~ **164** 10
roller, grooved ~ **130** 30
roller, lambskin ~ **130** 31
roller, leather ~ **340** 23
roller, lower ~ *Iron Foundry etc.* **148** 55
roller, lower ~ *Cotton Spin.* **164** 10
roller, rubber ~ **182** 8
roller, rubber-disc ~ **64** 82
roller, steel ~ **164** 10
roller, submersible ~ **217** 68
roller, three-wheeled ~ **200** 36
roller, top ~ **164** 11
roller, upper ~ *Iron Foundry etc.* **148** 54
roller, upper ~ *Cotton Spin.* **164** 11
roller, wire-covered ~ **168** 34
roller bearing **164** 47
roller bit **145** 21
roller chain *Bicycle* **187** 36
roller chain *Intern. Combust. Eng.* **190** 25
roller chain, double ~ **190** 10
roller covering **50** 3
roller guide **201** 4
roller path **148** 50
roller postmark **236** 60
roller printing machine, ten-colour ~ **168** 53
rollers **148** 54-55
roller stamp **236** 46
roller table **157** 23
roller top **217** 66
roller trestle **157** 26
rollfilm **114** 19
rollfilm spool **114** 20
roll holder **40** 1
rolling **230** 71
rolling circle **288** 3
rolling dam **217** 65-72
rolling mill **148** 46-75
rolling plant **159** 9
rolling road **138** 16
rolling shutter frame **37** 29
rolling stock **207; 208; 209; 210; 211; 212; 213**
roll-on roll-off operation **225** 39
roll-on roll-off ship **226** 17
roll-on roll-off system **225** 39
roll-on roll-off trailer ferry **221** 54
rollover device **139** 43
rolls *Bakery* **97** 13-16
rolls *Iron Foundry etc.* **148** 54-55
roll stand **148** 56-60
roll unit **97** 61
roll-up door **245** 5
Roman **355** 11
Roman woman **355** 7

romper **29** 21
romper suit **29** 22
roof **37** 5; **38; 121; 122; 337** 2
roof, cement ~ **122** 97
roof, flat ~ **37** 77
roof, glass ~ **55** 5
roof, hipped ~ **37** 64; **121** 10, 60
roof, imperial ~ **121** 25
roof, mission-tiled ~ **122** 56
roof, pantiled ~ **122** 53
roof, paper ~ **122** 90
roof, pitched ~ **38** 12
roof, plain-tiled ~ **122** 50
roof, sliding ~ **193** 24; **194** 10; **213** 22
roof, Spanish-tiled ~ **122** 56
roof, split-tiled ~ **122** 45
roof, swivelling ~ **213** 26, 27
roof, tiled ~ **122** 1
roof beam **121** 29
roof board **122** 61
roof boarding **122** 61
roof cable **211** 5
roof cladding **38** 1
roof course **122** 78
roof covering **38** 1
roofer **122**
roof guard **38** 8
roof hook **38** 6
roofing, cement ~ **122** 90-103
roofing, paper ~ **122** 90-103
roofing felt **122** 62
roofing nail **143** 55
roofing paper **122** 62
roof ladder **38** 4; **122** 63
roof lashing **278** 51
roof opening **213** 23
roof rack **278** 50
roofs, styles and parts of ~ **121** 1-26
roof sheathing **122** 61
roof trestle **122** 66
roof truss **120** 7; **121** 78
roof valley **121** 15; **122** 11, 82
roof ventilator **278** 56
rook *Games* **276** 12
rook *Birds* **361** 2
room, double ~ **267** 27-38
room, heated ~ **169** 24
room divider **42** 19
room key **267** 9
room number **267** 10
room telephone **267** 34
room thermostat **38** 78
room trader **251** 6
room waiter **267** 33
rooster **62** 37; **73** 21
root *Man* **19** 36
root *Plant Propagn.* **54** 21
root *Arable Crops* **68** 17, 45
root *Horse* **72** 34
root *Maths.* **347** 12
root *Bot.* **370** 16-18
root *Industr. Plants* **383** 43
root, adventitious ~ **370** 78, 80
root, aerial ~ **370** 80
root, primary ~ **370** 16
root, secondary ~ **370** 17
root, tuberous ~ **370** 79
root crops **68** 38-45
rooter **200** 20
root gall **80** 27
root hair **68** 18; **370** 18
root louse **80** 26
roots **54** 12; **370** 78-82
rootstock **54** 33
root thorn **370** 81
rope *First Aid* **21** 30
rope *Weaving* **166** 61
rope *Swim.* **282** 32

rope *Gymn.* **296** 19; **297** 43
rope *Mountain.* **300** 12, 22-27
roped party **300** 22-27
rope ladder **221** 91; **273** 49; **307** 8
rope-pulley hoist **118** 91
ropes **299** 36
rope sling **300** 11
ropeway, aerial ~ **15** 67
ropeway, double-cable ~ **214** 25, 30
ropeway gondola **214** 52
ropeways **214** 15-38
ropeways, endless ~ **214** 15-24
ropeways, single-cable ~ **214** 15-24
ropeway support **214** 76
roping down **300** 28-30
ro-ro depot **226** 20
ro-ro-ship **226** 17
ro-ro system **225** 39
ro-ro trailer ferry **221** 54
rosary **332** 30
rose *Market Gdn.* **55** 28
rose *Game* **88** 5, 29
rose *Music. Instr.* **324** 5
rose, bush ~ **52** 13
rose, climbing ~ **52** 12
rose, double ~ **60** 17
rose, ivory ~ **36** 29
rose, rambling ~ **52** 12
rose, standard ~ **51** 25; **52** 21
rosebay **373** 13
rosebud **60** 16
rose cut **36** 45
rose-ear **70** 2
rose hip **370** 100
rose laurel **373** 13
rose thorn **60** 18
rose tree, standard ~ **52** 13, 21
rosette **306** 34
rose window **335** 23
rosin **323** 11
rostrum **263** 6; **316** 34
rotary engine, two-rotor ~ **190** 5
rotary-table machine **150** 41
rotary-table shot-blasting machine **148** 39
rotary turbine pump **259** 57
rotated grasp **296** 44, 46
rotation **298** 18
rotation axis **351** 4
rotator **224** 55
rotisserie **40** 32
rotogravure press, multicolour ~ *Photograv.* **182** 24
rotor *Clocks* **110** 32
rotor *Intern. Combust. Eng.* **190** 68
rotor *Aircraft* **232** 22
rotor *Gliding* **287** 18
rotor, main ~ **232** 12-13; **256** 19; **264** 3
rotor, tail ~ **256** 20
rotor, tilting ~ **232** 32
rotor blade *Energy Sources* **155** 45
rotor blade *Aircraft* **232** 12
rotor head **232** 13
rotor pylon **232** 23
rouge **275** 24
rough **293** 80
rough focusing indicator **224** 35
roughing file **134** 9
roughing-out hammer **195** 46
roughing wheel **111** 36
roulette *Roulette* **275** 1-33, 28
roulette *Graphic Art* **340** 18
roulette ball **275** 33

roulette bowl **275** 29
roulette layout **275** 9, 17
roulette player **275** 15
roulette table **275** 8
roulette wheel **275** 10, 28
round **95** 14
round, caseless ~ **305** 37
roundabout **308** 2
round bar reinforcement **119** 80
round-bilge boat **286** 32-34
round end **95** 52
rounding machine *Bakery* **97** 63
rounding machine *Plumb.* **125** 30
roundwood **120** 35; **157** 30
round worm **81** 31
route **203** 68
route indicator **203** 20, 21
route lever **203** 58
route of the paper **180** 26
route of the sheets **180** 33
route of the web **180** 26
router plane **132** 26
route sign **197** 21
route straight ahead **203** 45, 49, 50
roving **164** 29
roving bobbin **164** 23
row **312** 9
rowan **371** 42
rowboats **283** 9-15
rowing **283**
rowing boat **89** 27
rowing boat, Germanic ~ **218** 1-6
rowing boats **283** 9-15
rowing coach **283** 20
rowlock **278** 18; **283** 29, 41
row of needles **167** 27
row of needles, back ~ **167** 46
row of needles, front ~ **167** 47
row of seats, tiered ~ **261** 1
royal **88** 8
Royal Crown, English ~ **254** 42
royal fern **377** 16
royal osmund **377** 16
royal water lily **378** 17
rubber, synthetic ~ **164** 11
rubber belt, studded ~ **64** 79
rubber plant **383** 33
rubber solution **340** 49
rubber tree **383** 33
rubber tyre cable car **273** 53
rubber tyre swing **273** 18
rubbing strake, reinforced ~ **258** 81
rubbish **268** 22
rubble **11** 47
rubble, rough ~ **269** 37
ruby **175** 22
ruby, synthetic ~ **110** 33
Rückpositiv **326** 5
rucksack **283** 65
rudder *Ship* **218** 6, 24; **221** 43
rudder *Shipbuild.* **222** 69
rudder *Ship* **223** 63
rudder *Life-Sav.* **228** 26
rudder *Aircraft* **229** 25; **230** 60
rudder *Air Force* **257** 23
rudder *Rowing* **283** 51-53, 53
rudder *Sailing* **284** 9, 34; **285** 34
rudder *Motorboats etc.* **286** 65
rudder *Airsports* **288** 22
rudder, retractable ~ **285** 37
rudder, vertical ~ **259** 95, 96
rudder angle indicator **224** 17
rudder blade **221** 43; **222** 69; **223** 63; **283** 53; **284** 34
rudderhead **284** 33

rudder pedal **230** 27; **257** 10
rudder pedal, co-pilot's ~ **230** 28
rudder post **222** 70
rudder stock **222** 68; **284** 33
ruff *Carnival* **306** 20
ruff *Hist. Cost.* **355** 52
rugby **292** 19
rugby ball **292** 21
rugby football **292** 19
rule **151** 33
rule, folding ~ **120** 76; **134** 33
rule, glazier's ~ **124** 21
rule of three sum **345** 8-10
rule pocket **33** 49
ruler **151** 33; **247** 35
ruling pen **151** 49
ruling pen attachment **151** 58, 61
rum **98** 57
ruminant **73** 1
ruminants **366** 28-30; **367** 1-10
rummer **45** 87
rump *Horse* **72** 31
rump *Game* **88** 20, 36
rump *Meat* **95** 14, 35
rump piece **329** 88
runch **61** 18
rune **341** 19
rung **38** 17; **50** 38
runner *Plant Propagn.* **54** 14, 16
runner *Soft Fruit* **58** 20
runner *Mills* **91** 22
runner *Iron Foundry etc.* **148** 21
runner *Rowing* **283** 45
runner *Ball Games* **292** 45, 66
runner *Athletics* **298** 5
runner, movable ~ **303** 10
runner, outrigged ~ **302** 46
runner bean **52** 28; **57** 8
runner gate **148** 21
running **298** 1-8
running axle **210** 35
running-boar target **305** 33
running dog **334** 39
running gear, front ~ **191** 52
running head **185** 66
running light **258** 56
running light, side ~ **258** 15
running light indicator panel **224** 29
running posture **295** 2
running side **277** 5
running step **295** 41
running step indicator **211** 36
running take-off twist dive **282** 43
running three **305** 3, 5
running title **185** 66
running track **298** 6
running wheel **64** 41, 56; **214** 7, 70
runout **147** 54
runway *Hunt.* **86** 16
runway *Airport* **233** 1
runway *Gliding* **287** 15
rush *Phys. Geog.* **13** 17
rush *Basketm.* **136** 27
rusk **97** 54
Russula vesca **381** 23
rustication **335** 51
rustic work **335** 51
rutting mane **88** 27
rutting season **86** 9-12
rye **68** 1, 2
rye bread **97** 10, 49; **99** 14
rye-bread roll **97** 16
rye flour **97** 52
ryegrass, perennial ~ **69** 26

S

sabaton **329** 55
saber *see* sabre
sable *Ladies' Wear* **30** 60
sable *Heraldry* **254** 26
sable *Mammals* **367** 15
sabot **101** 47
sabre, light ~ **294** 20, 34
sabre fencer **294** 19
sabre fencing **294** 19-24
sabre gauntlet **294** 21
sabre glove **294** 21
sabre mask **294** 22
sabreur **294** 19
sack **38** 34
sacker **92** 39
Sacrament **331** 48
sacrarium **330** 32
sacristan **330** 26, 58
sacristy **331** 13
sacristy door **330** 17
sacrum **17** 21; **20** 59
saddle *Phys. Geog.* **12** 16, 42
saddle *Mach. Tools* **149** 13
saddle, adjustable ~ **188** 4
saddle, English ~ **71** 45-49
saddle, reciprocating ~ **185** 24
saddle, unsprung ~ **290** 17
saddle, western ~ **71** 37-44
saddle apron **149** 16
saddleback roof **37** 5; **121** 1
saddle bag **187** 25
saddle clip **126** 53
saddle-pad **71** 17, 31
saddle roof **37** 5; **121** 1
saddles **71** 37-49
saddle seat **71** 37
saddle spring **187** 23
saddle stitching **31** 45
saddle tree **374** 1
safe **246** 22
safelight **116** 21
safety bar **301** 58
safety binding **301** 2
safety bonnet **85** 36
safety brake **85** 15
safety catch *Atom* **2** 40
safety catch *Household* **50** 25
safety catch *Hunt.* **87** 8, 24
safety catch *Army* **255** 14
safety catch, sliding ~ **87** 25
safety chain **126** 3
safety current **127** 2
safety curtain **316** 24
safety device **290** 13
safety equipment **316** 18
safety glass **124** 5
safety glasses **140** 21
safety helmet **84** 23; **140** 22; **158** 10; **300** 53
safety helmet, shock-resisting ~ **127** 48
safety hood **85** 36
safety jet **301** 53
safety key **140** 48
safety latch **50** 25
safety lighting **312** 6
safety lock **140** 44
safety net *Warships* **259** 18
safety net *Circus* **307** 14
safety nut **187** 64
safety pin **328** 27
safety rail **119** 43
safety valve *Roof & Boiler.* **38** 70
safety valve *Railw.* **210** 3
safety wall **122** 35
saffron milk cap **381** 29
saggar **161** 2
sagger **161** 2
Sagittarius **3** 37; **4** 61
sagittate **370** 37

sago **98** 39
sago palm **383** 58
sail **219** 1-72; **283** 62; **284** 2; **285** 8
sail, ballooning ~ **285** 4
sail, brailed-up ~ **218** 21
sail, fore-and-aft ~ **220** 15
sail, furled ~ **218** 21
sail, square ~ **218** 21, 33; **219** 55-66; **220** 16
sail axle **91** 5
sailboat *Playground* **273** 29
sailboat *Camping* **278** 12
sailboat *Sailing* **284** 10-48
sailboat, single-masted ~ **220** 6-8
sailboats, mizzen-masted ~ **220** 9-10
sailboats, two-masted ~ **220** 11-17
sailing **284**; **285**
sailing barge, ketch-rigged ~ **220** 9
sailing boat *Playground* **273** 29
sailing boat *Camping* **278** 12
sailing boat *Sailing* **284** 10-48
sailing boat, single-masted ~ **220** 6-8
sailing boats, mizzen-masted ~ **220** 9-10
sailing boats, two-masted ~ **220** 11-17
sailing close-hauled **285** 10
sailing downwind **285** 1
sailing ship **219**; **220**
sailing ships, development of ~ **220** 35-37
sailing ships, four-masted ~ **220** 28-31
sailing vessels, three-masted ~ **220** 18-27
sailing with free wind **285** 12
sailing with wind abeam **285** 11
sailor suit **309** 62
sailplane **287** 3
sailplane, high-performance ~ **287** 9
sails, fore-and-aft ~ **219** 20-31
sail shapes **220** 1-5
sail top **91** 6
sainfoin **69** 10
saint, Buddhist ~ **337** 10
Saint Andrew's cross bond **118** 65
salad **266** 51
salad bowl **45** 23
salad chicory **57** 40
salad cream **96** 29
salad drawer **39** 4
salad fork **45** 68
salad oil **98** 24; **99** 66
salad plants **57** 36-40
salad servers **45** 24
salad spoon **45** 67
salamander **364** 22
salamanders **364** 20-22
sal-ammoniac block **125** 6
sales area **99** 4
sales check **98** 44; **271** 7
salesclerk **98** 13
sales counter **271** 42, 61
salesgirl **97** 1; **98** 31; **99** 17; **271** 18, 63
saleslady **97** 1; **98** 31; **99** 17; **271** 18, 63
salesman **309** 29
sales premises **111** 1-19
sales shelf **99** 23
sales statistics **248** 46
salicional **326** 23-30

salientians **364** 23-26
salina *Map* **15** 32
salina *Spa* **274** 1-7
sallow **371** 24
salon, men's ~ **106** 1-42
salon mirror **105** 20; **106** 6
saloon, lower ~ **194** 37
saloon, upper ~ **194** 38
saloon car **193** 4, 25
salt **98** 40
salt, common ~ **1** 9
salta **276** 20
salta piece **276** 21
salt cake storage tank **172** 36
salt cellar **266** 77
salt mine **154** 57-68, 72
saltstick **97** 31
salt water outlet **145** 33
salt water pipe **145** 33
salt water tank **146** 17
salt works *Map* **15** 32
salt works *Spa* **274** 1-7
salt works attendant **274** 5
saltzstange **97** 31
salvage **227**
salvage tug **227** 5, 16
salvaging **227** 1
Salvator beer **93** 26
salving **227** 1
sampan **353** 31
sample beam **115** 36
sample sagger **161** 2
sample scoop **98** 72
samson post **223** 35
samson post, ventilator-type ~ **221** 58
samurai **353** 37
sanctuary **330** 32
sanctuary lamp **330** 49
sanctus bell **330** 46
sand *Map* **15** 6
sand *Bldg. Site* **118** 36; **119** 26
sandal **101** 51
sandal, ladies' ~ **101** 49
sandal court shoe **101** 27
sandbag **216** 50; **288** 65
sandbank **227** 3
sand bed **123** 8
sand belt, endless ~ **133** 15
sand box *Railw.* **212** 59, 76
sandbox *Playground* **273** 64
sand delivery pipe **148** 38
sand deposit **216** 52
sand dome **210** 14
sander **129** 30
sander, orbital ~ **134** 53
sander, single-belt ~ **133** 30
sander control **211** 32
sander switch **211** 32
sandhill **273** 66
sand hills **15** 6
sanding **129** 28
sanding attachment, orbital ~ **134** 53
sanding belt, endless ~ **133** 15
sanding belt regulator **133** 14
sanding disc **134** 25
sanding dust extractor **133** 28
sanding machine, single-belt ~ **133** 30
sanding table **133** 35
sanding valve **210** 55
sanding wheel **133** 27
sand lizard **364** 27
sandpaper **128** 14; **129** 25; **135** 25
sandpaper block **128** 13; **129**
sand pipe **210** 15, 19
sandpit **273** 64
sand star **369** 11
sand table **173** 13
sand track racing **290** 24-28

sand trap *Paperm.* 173 13
sand trap *Ball Games* 293 81
sand tube 210 15
sandwich 45 39
sandwich, open ~ 45 37
sandwich board 308 50
sandwich man 308 49
sanitary articles 99 35
San-José scale 80 35
Sanserif 342 7
Sanserif type 342 7
Sanskrit 341 9
sap 120 85; 370 12
sappho 363 4
sapwood 120 85; 370 12
sarcophagus 335 53
sardine server 45 78
sardines in oil 98 19
Sargon's Palace 333 29
sartorius 18 45
Satan's mushroom 379 12
satchel 260 9
sate 137 34
satellite 4 45
satellite radio link 237 51-52
satellite sounding 7 33
satin stitch 102 10
Saturn 4 49
Saturn V 234 1, 2
sauceboat 45 17
sauce ladle 45 18
saucepan 40 16
saucer 44 30
sauna, mixed ~ 281 18
sauna stove 281 21
sausage 98 4; 99 54
sausage, broiled ~ 308 34
sausage, grilled ~ 308 34
sausage, pork ~ 99 55
sausage, scalded ~ 96 8
sausage fork 96 49
sausage fork 96 44
sausage meat 96 41, 52
sausages 96 6-11
sausage stand 308 32
sausage stuffer 96 49
sausage tongs 308 35
savings account 250 4
savoy 57 33
savoy cabbage 57 33
saw, butcher's ~ 94 19
saw, circular ~ 119 19; 125
    24; 134 50
saw, free-cutting ~ 84 32
saw, two-handed ~ 120 68
saw, vertical frame ~ 157 2
sawbill 359 15
saw blade 120 62; 150 16; 157
    3, 47; 260 54
saw carriage 132 71; 133 38
saw chain 84 35; 85 14; 85 15;
    120 16
saw frame 138 25; 150 17;
    157 8
saw guide 85 16
saw handle 132 4
sawing shed 120 3
sawmill 144 6; 157 1
saw rasp 134 6
saw set 132 42
saw-sharpening machine 157
    42
saw tooth 96 33
sawtooth roof 121 20
saxboard 283 43
saxifrage, rotundifoliate ~
    375 1
saxophone 324 69
scaffold 118 25; 122 34; 222
    18
scaffold, steel ~ 5 18
scaffold, supporting ~ 14 50
scaffold, tubular steel ~ 119 46

scaffold board 122 70
scaffolding 215 62
scaffolding, tubular steel ~
    119 46
scaffolding joint 118 30
scaffold pole 118 23
scaffold standard 118 23
scalding colander 96 45
scale *Map* 14 29
scale *Chem.* 349 35
scale *Fish etc.* 364 11
scale *Decid. Trees* 371 12
scale *Conifers* 372 34, 42, 45,
    50
scale, triangular ~ 151 34
scale, wax ~ 77 25
scale adjustment 116 34
scale armour 329 64
scaled prickle fungus 381 24
scale insect 80 35
scale louse 80 35
scale pan *Kitch. Utensils* 40
    37
scale pan *Chem.* 349 36
Scales *Astron.* 3 19; 4 59
scales *Doc.* 22 66
scales *Kitch. Utensils* 40 35
scales *Child. Rm.* 47 33
scales *Supermkt.* 99 88
scales *Photog.* 114 58
scales *Music. Not.* 320 45-49
scaling hammer 137 38
scallop shell 309 46
scalp 352 15
scalpel 26 43
scalper 340 7
scaly ant-eater 366 10
scanner 177 39
scanner film 177 72
scanning drum 177 45
scanning head 177 46, 63
scanning zone 243 47
scantling 120 10
scape 370 52
scapula 16 23; 17 7
scar 11 49
scarecrow 52 27
scarf *Ladies' Wear* 31 57
scarf *Men's Wear* 33 65
scarf *Headgear* 35 16
scarf *Bullfight. etc.* 319 38
scarf joint, oblique ~ 121 88
scarf joint, simple ~ 121 87
scarifier 200 20
scarlet pimpernel 61 27
scarlet runner 52 28; 57 8
scarlet runner bean 57 8
scarp 13 57
scatter cushion 42 27; 46 17
scauper 340 7
scaur 11 48
scaw 11 48
scene *Theatre* 316 36
scene *Art* 334 45
scene number 310 35
scene painter 315 35
scene-repeat key 243 42
scenery 316 35
scenery projector 316 17
scene shifter 315 28; 316 46
scenic artist 315 35
scenic railway 308 39
scent, artificial ~ 289 49
sceptre, fool's ~ 306 59
schalmeys 322 14
schedule 204 16
schedule, engineer's ~ 210 52
Scheidt globe 349 1
schilling 252 13
schizocarp 370 94
schnapps 98 56
schnauzer 70 35
schnecke 97 38

schnorkel *Warships* 259 72,
    90
schnorkel *Swim.* 279 11
schnorkel *Bathing* 280 39
school 260; 261
school bag 260 7
school book 47 25
school children's wear 29
    31-47
school figure 289 7
school horse 289 3
school satchel 260 9
schooner, four-masted ~ 220
    28
schooner, three-masted ~ 220
    18
schooner, topsail ~ 220 11-13
Schottel propeller 227 20
Schwellwerk 326 45
scion 54 37
scion bud 54 23, 34
scissor-blade 106 35
scissor jump 295 39; 298 22
scissors *Shoem.* 100 43
scissors *School* 260 49
scissors *Gymn.* 296 51
scissors *Athletics* 298 22
scissors, angled ~ 22 51
scissors, bull-nosed ~ 128 34
scissors, curved ~ 26 42
scissors movement 296 51
scoop *Doc.* 22 50
scoop *Hosp.* 26 52
scoop *Graphic Art* 340 8
scoop thermometer 92 53
scooter 188 47
scooters 188
scoreboard 293 34, 70
scorer 293 71
scoring equipment, electrical
    ~ 294 25-33
scoring equipment, electronic
    ~ 294 32
scoring light 294 28
scorper 340 7
Scorpio 3 38; 4 60
Scorpion *Astron.* 3 38; 4 60
scorpion *Articulates* 358 40
scorzonera 57 35
Scots pine 372 20
Scottish terrier 70 17
scouring machine, open-
    width ~ 168 8
scouring nozzle 216 62
scouring tunnel 217 62
scouring wheel 100 6
scout 278 11
scout camp 278 8-11
scrag 95 6
scrag end 95 6
scramble racing 290 24-28
scrambling motorcycle 189 16
scrap box 141 15
scraper *Butch.* 96 42
scraper *Paperhanger* 128 10
scraper *Painter* 129 23
scraper *Graphic Art* 340 63
scraper, pointed ~ 140 63
scraper, triangle ~ 140 63
scraper adjustment 340 62
scraper and burnisher 340 17
scraper blade 200 17
scraper floor, movable ~ 62
    24
scrap iron charging box 147
    26
scrap iron feed 147 65
scray entry, curved ~ 168 47
scree 11 47; 12 45; 13 29
screech owl 362 17
screed 123 41
screeding beam 201 14
screeding board 201 14

scree ledge 300 4
screen *Hunt.* 86 9
screen *Fish Farm.* 89 10
screen *Bldg. Site* 118 85
screen *Paperm.* 172 57
screen *Refuse Coll.* 199 11
screen *Post* 236 40
screen *Inf. Tech.* 242 84
screen *Swim.* 281 17
screen *Films* 310 16, 51; 312
    11
screen, all-matt ~ 115 58, 59,
    60, 65
screen, centrifugal ~ 172 22,
    56
screen, crystal glass ~ 179 24
screen, fluorescent ~ 74 40
screen, ground glass ~ 112 24;
    115 58, 59, 60, 61, 65, 66;
    177 2, 34
screen, illuminated ~ 177 20;
    264 30
screen, inner ~ 240 20
screen, lead ~ 259 70
screen, magnetic ~ 240 20
screen, matt ~ *Optic. Instr.*
    112 24
screen, matt ~ *Photog.* 115 61,
    66
screen, protective ~ 154 74
screen, rotary ~ 172 2
screen, secondary ~ 172 58
screen, vibrating ~ 158 21
screen curtain 312 10
screen frame, mobile ~ 168 60
screen holder, hinged ~ 177 3
screening 156 14
screening, inner ~ 240 20
screening, magnetic ~ 240 20
screenings 158 22
screen magazine 177 9
screen printing 168 59
screen printing operator 168
    65
screen table 168 63
screen work 136 4
screw *First Aid* 21 16
screw *Metalwkr.* 140 4
screw *Weaving* 165 36
screw *Life-Sav.* 228 26
screw, cheese-head ~ 143 36
screw, cross-head ~ 143 26
screw, feathering ~ 224 19
screw, hexagonal socket head
    ~ 143 27
screw, main ~ 148 62
screw, self-tapping ~ 143 26
screw, ship's ~ 221 44; 222 72;
    223 62
screw, slotted ~ 143 36
screw, three-blade ~ 223 62
screw-back 277 4
screw base 127 59
screw block 136 8
screw clamp 120 66
screw conveyor 92 26
screw-cutting machine 125
    27; 126 86
screw die 140 61
screw dive 282 44
screwdriver 109 6; 126 69;
    127 46; 134 4; 140 62
screwdriver, cross-point ~
    134 5
screwgate 300 47
screw groove 140 38
screw joint 126 42
screw log 224 54
screw post 222 71
screws 143 13-50
screw slit 143 38
screw slot 143 38
screw tap 140 60

screw thread **50** 50
screw wrench **126** 67
scrim **183** 33; **185** 20
scrim roll holder **185** 19
script *Films* **310** 45
script *Script* **341**; **342**
script, cuneiform ~ **341** 8
script, director's ~ **316** 44
script, Latin ~ **342** 12
script, producer's ~ **316** 44
script, Sinaitic ~ **341** 13
script, uncial ~ **341** 17
script girl **310** 39
scripts **341** 1-20
Scriptures **330** 11
scroll *Music. Instr.* **323** 17
scroll *Art* **333** 26; **334** 23
scroll, Vitruvian ~ **334** 39
scroll-opening roller **168** 13
scrollwork **336** 8
scrotum **20** 71
scrubber **156** 22, 23, 24
scrubbing agent **156** 37
scrubbing brush **50** 56
scrubbing oil tank **156** 43
scrub board **123** 21, 63
scrum **292** 20
scrummage **292** 20
scuba **279** 19
scull **283** 17, 35-38
sculptor **339** 1
sculpture **339** 32
sculpture, modern ~ **272** 64
scut **88** 19, 62
scutcher, double ~ **163** 14
scutcher lap **163** 47
scutcher lap holder **163** 48
scutch grass **61** 30
scutellum **82** 5; **358** 30
scythe **66** 12
scythe blade **66** 13
scythe sheath **66** 14
scythestone **66** 19
sea **13** 26; **14** 19-26
sea, epeiric ~ **14** 26
sea, epicontinental ~ **14** 26
sea, marginal ~ **14** 26
sea, open ~ **227** 4
sea anemone **369** 20
sea bear **367** 18
seabirds **359** 11-14
sea calf **367** 19
sea couch grass **61** 30
sea cucumber **369** 18
sea deity **327** 23
sea divinity **327** 23
sea dog **367** 19
sea fan **369** 8
sea feather **369** 14
sea fishing **90**
Sea Goat **3** 36; **4** 62
sea goddess **327** 23
sea grass **378** 54
sea hedgehog **357** 39; **369** 19
sea horse **364** 18
seakale beet **57** 28
seal **190** 69
seal, clay ~ **269** 39
seal, loam ~ **269** 39
sea ladder **221** 91
sea lead **89** 92
sea level **11** 11
sea lily **369** 3
sealing tape **126** 75
seals **367** 18-22
seam **144** 97
sea maid **327** 23
sea maiden **327** 23
seaman **327** 23
sea marks **224** 68-108
seam binding **103** 14; **104** 19
seamless engraving
    adjustment **177** 53

sea monster **327** 47
seam roller **128** 36
sea nymph **327** 23
sea otter **367** 17
sea ox **327** 47
sea pen **369** 14
seaplane **232** 1, 5
seaquake **11** 53
search **264** 31
searchlight **258** 28
Sea Serpent **3** 16
seaside pleasure boat **221** 15
sea star **357** 38; **369** 17
sea strait **14** 24
seat *Man* **16** 40
seat **24** 24; **41** 10; **44** 11; **65**
    22; **71** 45; **212** 63; **271** 35;
    273 58; **283** 28; **303** 6; **307**
    15; **312** 9; **315** 20
seat *Mach. Parts etc.* **143** 65
seat, back ~ **193** 22
seat, captain's ~ **235** 17
seat, child's ~ **187** 21
seat, circular ~ **281** 38
seat, coachman's ~ **186** 8
seat, commander's ~ **235** 17
seat, conical ~ **143** 67
seat, co-pilot's ~ **230** 37; **235**
    18
seat, cox's ~ **283** 27
seat, double ~ **197** 19; **207** 63
seat, driver's ~ **186** 8; **191** 34;
    210 59
seat, engineer's ~ **210** 59
seat, fireman's ~ **210** 39
seat, folding ~ **193** 22; **207** 12
seat, instructor's ~ **257** 7
seat, observer's ~ **257** 7
seat, pilot's ~ **230** 36; **235** 18;
    257 6
seat, rear ~ **191** 31
seat, reclining ~ **191** 34; **207**
    44, 64
seat, single ~ **197** 17; **207** 62
seat, sliding ~ **283** 41-50, 44
seat, student pilot's ~ **257** 6
seat, upholstered ~ **207** 44;
    208 25; **265** 10
seat cushion **42** 23
seated position **296** 31
seating **330** 28
seating group **42** 21-26
seat pillar **187** 24
seat stay **187** 19
seat stick **86** 10
seat tube **187** 18
seat upholstery **207** 65
sea urchin **357** 39; **369** 19
seawater desalination plant
    146 25
sea wave, seismic ~ **11** 53
sea wing **232** 3
secant **346** 50
secateurs **56** 50; **78** 12
second **299** 44
secondary **153** 16
secondary school **261**
second base **292** 43
second-class seating
    arrangement **211** 58
second-class section **207** 10;
    208 22
seconde engagement **294** 50
second-hand stall **308** 60
second indicator **110** 21
second man **300** 26
second-stage separation
    retro-rocket **234** 37
seconds timer **129** 39
secretary **209** 27
secretary, proprietor's ~ **248**
    31
section *Forestry* **84** 2

section *Drawing Off.* **151** 28
section *Bookbind.* **183** 12
section *Railw.* **203** 29
section, hollow ~ **215** 5
section, middle ~ **215** 68
section, tubular ~ **215** 5
section line *Map* **15** 112
section line *Forestry* **84** 1
section line *Drawing Off.* **151**
    27
section mark **342** 36
section of warp rib fabric **171**
    14
sections **143**
sections, conic ~ **347** 11-29
sector **346** 54
securities **251** 11-19
security **251** 1-10
security, fixed-income ~ **251**
    11-19
security, unlisted ~ **251** 5
security drawer **236** 22
sedan **193** 4, 25
sedge *Phys. Geog.* **13** 17
sedge *Indoor Plants* **53** 17
sedilia **330** 41
sediment *Phys. Geog.* **13** 69
sediment *Doc.* **23** 50
sediment filter, stainless steel
    ~ **79** 8
seed *Plant Propagn.* **54** 3
seed *Soft Fruit* **58** 23
seed *Drupes & Nuts* **59** 8
seed *Agr.* **63** 12
seed *Arable Crops* **68** 13, 15,
    25
seed *Bot.* **370** 86
seed *Decid. Trees* **371** 20, 65
seed *Conifers* **372** 9, 10, 15, 28,
    37, 54, 57, 60, 71
seed *Flowers etc.* **375** 25, 28
seed *Alp. Plants etc.* **378** 33, 34
seed *Trop. Plants* **382** 20, 34,
    35, 39, 45
seed *Industr. Plants* **383** 15,
    23, 24, 57
seed *South. Fruits* **384** 10, 20,
    21, 47, 52, 58
seed, foraminate ~ **383** 57
seed, oleiferous ~ **383** 3, 5
seedbed preparation **63** 31-41
seed capsule **61** 5
seed corn **63** 12
seed-dressing machine **83** 52
seed dusting **83** 52
seed fish **89** 13
seed-harrow, combination ~
    Agr. **63** 41
seed-harrow, combination ~
    Agr. Mach. **65** 87
seed hopper **65** 75
seed leaf **370** 87
seedling *Plant Propagn.* **54** 6
seedling *Market Gdn.* **55** 23
seedling *Forestry* **84** 7, 9
seedling box **55** 51
seedling nursery **84** 6
seedling plant **54** 6
seedlip **63** 11
seed lobe **370** 87
seed pan **54** 2
seed pike **89** 11
seed potato **68** 39
seed sowing **54** 1
seed tuber **68** 39
seed vessel **57** 6; **378** 5; **383** 8
seed vessel, circumscissile ~
    370 95
seesaw **273** 35; **307** 59
Seger cone **161** 6
seggar **161** 2
segment *Maths.* **346** 52
segment *Invertebr.* **357** 25

segment disc shutter **313** 8
seismograph, horizontal ~ **11**
    39
seismology **11** 32-38
seismometer **11** 39
seizing **90** 5
selector **237** 42
selector, electronic ~ **237** 42
selector fork **192** 42, 45
selector head **192** 44
selector motor **237** 48
self-discharge freight car **213**
    24
self-discharge wagon **213** 24
self-feeder **74** 13
self-heal **376** 16
self-rescue **21** 33
self-service restaurant **266**
    45-78
self-service station **196** 1-29
self-threading guide **165** 18
self-time lever **115** 15
self-timer **115** 15
selvedge **166** 11; **171** 20, 24
selvedge shaft **171** 22
selvedge thread draft **171** 20
semaphore arm **203** 2
semaphore arm,
    supplementary ~ **203** 8
semaphore signal **203** 1, 7, 12
semibold **175** 3
semibrew **320** 13
semibreve rest **320** 21
semicircle **346** 46
semicolon **342** 19
semidome **334** 73
semiquaver **320** 17
semiquaver rest **320** 25
semitone **320** 50, 52
semi-trailer *Lorries etc.* **194**
    30-33
semi-trailer *Station* **206** 59
semolina **98** 36
sending-off **291** 61
senna **380** 16
senna leaf **380** 16
sensing element **10** 22
sepal **58** 8, 44; **59** 12; **370** 58
separating funnel **349** 3
separating layer **7** 10
separating rail **164** 30
separation plant **199** 31
separation rocket motor, aft ~
    235 62
separation rocket motor,
    forward ~ **235** 60
separator *Bldg. Site* **119** 81
separator *Offshore Drill.* **146**
    28
separator *Cotton Spin.* **164** 43
separator *Paperm.* **172** 31
separator *Roulette* **275** 30
separator, centralized ~ **172**
    15
septimole **321** 23
septolet **321** 23
septum **77** 43
septum, interventricular ~ **20**
    52
septum, ventricular ~ **20** 52
septuplet **321** 23
sequestrum forceps **26** 45
sequoia **372** 69
seraglio, Sultan's ~ **306** 41
serial number *Stock Exch.*
    251 13
serial number *Money* **252** 36
series, arithmetical ~ **345** 11
series, geometrical ~ **345** 12
series, inner ~ **375** 32
series, outer ~ **375** 31
series of moulds **147** 36
Serpens **3** 20

Serpent *Astron.* 3 20
serpent *Gymn.* 297 48
serpent *Music. Instr.* 322 13
serpent, nine-headed ~ 327 33
serpent, paper ~ 308 14
serrate 370 44
serratus anterior 18 42
serrulate 370 44
server *Ball Games* 293 51, 62
server *Church* 330 40
service 293 42
service area 293 61
service bell panel 267 28
service bridge 217 72
service building 154 36
service bunker 156 3
service counter 250 4
service court 293 12
service girder, adjustable ~ 119 78
service line 293 6-7
service line judge 293 27
service module 6 2
service module main engine 234 57
service pistol 264 22
service riser 126 7
service room 329 27
service station 196 1-29
service tray 105 31
service vehicle 233 22
servicing craft 258 93
serviette 45 9; 266 47
serviette ring 45 10
serving, jute ~ 153 49
serving area 207 79
serving cutlery 45 69-70
serving fork 45 70
serving hatch 266 66
serving spoon 45 74, 75
serving trolley 45 32
servo-actuating mechanism 257 22, 23
servo cylinder 192 50
servo unit 192 50
sesame plant 383 45
sesquiplane 229 13
set *Plant Propagn.* 54 20
set *Blacksm.* 137 34
set *Composing Rm.* 175 48
set *Ball Games* 293 37
set *Maths.* 348 1, 3
set collar 143 33
set designer 310 43; 315 37
set hammer 137 33
set head 143 57
set of rolls 148 54-55
set piece 315 30; 316 47
sets 348
set screw 127 21
set square 151 7
set square, adjustable ~ 151 4
set square, steel ~ 108 28
sett 137 34
settee 42 24
setting 54 18
setting and hatching machine 74 28
setting lever 115 15
setting lotion 106 23
setting rule 174 14
setting stick 174 13
set trigger 87 12
set trigger, second ~ 87 11
Seven Sisters 3 26
seventh chord 321 5
sewer, combined ~ 198 27
sewing 183 8, 34
sewing cord 183 10
sewing frame 183 9
sewing machine *Dressm.* 103 8

sewing machine *Tailor* 104 12
sewing machine *Bookbind.* 185 16
sewing machine cotton 103 12
sewing machine drawer 104 18
sewing machine table 104 17
sewing machine thread 103 12
sewing mechanism 133 5
sewing needle 185 21
sewing silk 104 10
sewing thread 183 11
sex organs, female ~ 20 79-88
sex organs, male ~ 20 66-77
sextant 224 1
sextolet 321 23
sexton 330 26, 58
sextuplet 321 23
sgraffito 338 41
shading 55 6
shading panel 55 9
shadow 34 17
shadow mask 240 17
shadow mask mount, temperature-compensated ~ 240 22
shadow roll 289 30
shaft *Farm Bldgs.* 62 20
shaft *Agr. Mach.* 64 59
shaft *Mach. Parts etc.* 143 61
shaft *Nucl. Energy* 154 69
shaft *Cotton Spin.* 164 42
shaft *Weaving* 166 4
shaft *Carriages* 186 19, 30
shaft *Aircraft* 232 56
shaft *Rowing* 283 37
shaft *Ball Games* 291 26
shaft *Sports* 305 64
shaft *Art* 333 27
shaft, intermediate ~ 232 57
shaft, main ~ *Coal* 144 24
shaft, main ~ *Car* 192 40
shaft alley 223 66
shaft bossing 223 59
shaft chain 71 20
shaft furnace 147 1
shaft guide 166 3
shaft strut 223 61
shaft tunnel 223 66
shag *Tobacc. etc.* 107 25
shag *Birds* 359 10
shake 321 17, 18
shaker 324 59
shallot 326 18
shallows 224 87, 97
shaman 353 24
shampoo 106 20
shampoo basin 105 29; 106 12
shampoo bottle 105 32
shampooing head 50 79
shampoo spray 105 30; 106 13
shampoo unit 105 28; 106 11
shank *Man* 16 52
shank *Meat* 95 14, 33
shank *Shoem.* 100 68
shank *Metalwkr.* 140 33
shank *Mach. Parts etc.* 143 15, 53
shaper 150 45
shapes game 48 19
shaping, final ~ 162 28, 36
shaping hammer 108 40
shaping machine *Dairy.* 76 35
shaping machine *Mach. Tools* 150 45
shaping pad 104 23
shard 161 21
share *Agr. Mach.* 65 7, 58, 65
share *Stock Exch.* 251 11-19
share, chisel-shaped ~ 65 58
share, diamond-shaped ~ 65 58
share, pointed ~ 65 65
share, three-bladed ~ 64 67
share certificate 251 11

share register 251 14
share warrant 251 11
shark 364 1
sharp 320 50
sharpie 284 53
shave 136 39
shave, clean ~ 34 25
shaver, electric ~ 49 37
shaving 120 80
shavings 132 40; 135 26
shawl 31 71
shawm 322 14
shawm, double ~ 322 3
shearing train 148 74, 75
shears 128 34
shears, tinner's ~ 125 1
sheatfish 364 12
sheath *Arable Crops* 68 9
sheath *Forestry* 84 30
sheath, lead ~ 153 39, 47
sheath, leather ~ 283 41
sheathfish 364 12
sheathing paper 122 62
shed 166 40
shedding tappet 166 57
shed roof 37 78; 121 7
sheep 73 13
sheepdog 70 25
sheep pen 75 9
sheer 259 23
sheer strake 222 44
sheet *Household* 50 5
sheet *Offset Print.* 180 17, 47
sheet *Ship* 219 68
sheet *Office* 249 57
sheet *Fire Brig.* 270 18
sheet *Gymn.* 297 11
sheet, blank ~ 180 69; 181 23, 30
sheet, corrugated ~ 122 98
sheet, linen ~ 43 9
sheet, plastic ~ 76 28
sheet, printed ~ 180 55, 57; 181 25
sheet, single ~ 340 27
sheet, unprinted ~ 180 69; 181 23, 30
sheet cloud 8 3, 4, 8, 9, 10
sheet counter 181 54
sheet delivery 249 54
sheet feeder 180 31, 48, 68, 74; 181 24; 184 16; 185 25
sheet feeder, automatic ~ 181 5
sheet-feeding station 184 16
sheet glass 124 5
sheet glass production 162 1-20
sheeting support 119 86
sheet metal 128 17
sheet-metal screw 143 26
sheet of glass 162 10
sheet of stamps 236 21
sheet pile 119 17
sheet pile bulkhead 217 5
sheet pile wall 119 17; 217 5
sheet piling 119 17; 217 5
sheet shears 125 26
sheet zinc 122 14
shelf 44 19; 98 14; 100 36; 195 14; 271 27
shelf, continental ~ 11 8
shelf, revolving ~ 39 28
shelf, steel ~ 262 12
shelf, wall-mounted ~ 248 40
shelf for bottles 266 10; 267 64; 317 4
shelf for glasses 266 9; 267 65; 317 5
shelf unit 46 1
shell *Cooper* 130 23
shell *Shipbuild.* 222 44-49
shell *Rowing* 283 33, 48

shell *Ball Games* 293 33
shell *Invertebr.* 357 29
shell *Fish etc.* 364 29
shell, soft ~ 59 42
shell, steel ~ 154 21
shell bit 135 16
shell bossing 223 59
shell membrane 74 60
shell plating 222 44-49
shells 283 9-15
shelter 223 17
shelving 248 28
shepherd bird 361 4
shepherd's club 376 9
shepherd's purse 61 9
shepherd's weatherglass 61 27
sherd 161 21
sherry glass 45 84
shield *Game* 88 55
shield *Plumb. etc.* 126 33
shield *Ship* 218 17
shield *Heraldry* 254 5
shield *Ethnol.* 354 10
shield, concrete ~ 154 20
shield, concrete and lead ~ 1 57
shield, protective ~ 2 46
shield, round ~ 329 57
shield, sliding ~ 2 32
shield budding 54 30
shielding, protective ~ 2 46
shielding-gas supply 142 34
shielding wall, lead ~ 2 46
shield volcano 11 13
shifting spanner 126 68
shift key 249 3
shift lock 249 5
shift pattern 192 47
shikara 337 26
shin 95 22, 28
shinbone 17 25
shingle 34 34
shin guard 142 12; 291 34
shin pad 292 9; 302 33
ship, five-masted ~ 220 35
ship, four-masted ~ 220 31
ship, full-rigged ~ 220 24-27, 31, 35
ship, stranded ~ 228 10
shipbuilding 222
shipbuilding sheds 222 3-4
shipbuilding yard 222 1-43
'ship cleared through customs' 253 36
ship-drawing office 222 2
ship fix 224 45
ship of the line 218 51-60
shipper 206 28
shipping traffic radio telephone 224 28
ship run aground 227 2
ship under construction 222 30
shipyard 222 1-43
shirt 30 26; 291 56
shirt, boy's ~ 29 61
shirt, casual ~ 32 38; 33 37
shirt, check ~ 33 50
shirt, knitted ~ 33 36
shirt, short-sleeved ~ 33 33
shirt-blouse 30 40
shirt button 33 34
shirts, men's ~ 32 38-47
shirt top 30 45
shirtwaist 319 23
shirt-waister dress 30 10
Shiva 337 19
shoals 224 87, 97
shoat 75 42
shock absorber *Moon L.* 6 32
shock absorber *Car* 191 26; 192 69
shock absorber *Railw.* 207 4
shock absorber, telescopic ~

188 41; 189 23
shock treatment 25 26
shock wave 11 35
shoe *Mills* 91 14
shoe *Bldg. Site* 119 50
shoe, bast ~ 122 75
shoe, copped ~ 355 42
shoe, finished ~ 100 1
shoe, hemp ~ 122 75
shoe, high-heeled ~ 101 33
shoe, laced ~ 101 31
shoe, peaked ~ 355 42
shoe, piked ~ 355 42
shoe, repaired ~ 100 1
shoe, slater's ~ 122 75
shoe brake 143 97
shoe brush 50 41
shoe buckle 101 52
shoe care utensils 50 39-43
shoelace 100 64
shoemaker 100
shoe polish 50 39, 43
shoes 41 16; 101
shoe sieve 64 19
shoe spray 50 40
shoot 54 37; 370 19-25
shoot, female ~ 372 46, 48
shoot, long ~ 78 3
shoot, male ~ 372 44, 49, 56
shoot, short ~ 372 23, 31
shooting *Hunt.* 86 47-52
shooting *Films* 310 14-60,
  26-60
shooting, exterior ~ 310 18
shooting, outdoor ~ 310 18
shooting box 305 78
shooting brake 193 15
shooting gallery 308 58
shooting positions 305 27-29
shooting range 305 74
shooting script 310 45
shooting seat 86 10
shooting star 7 25
shooting station 305 78
shooting stick 86 10
shop 195
shop, goldsmith's ~ 215 33
shop assistant 97 1; 98 13, 31;
  99 17; 271 18
shop front 268 42
shopkeeper 98 41
shopper 50 87
shopping bag 98 45; 99 3; 268
  19
shopping trolley 50 87;
  99 1
shop shelf 47 36
shop sign 268 39
shop walker 271 33
shop window 268 10
shop window decoration 268
  12
shop window display 268
  11
shorthand 342 13
shorthand pad 245 29; 248
  32
shorthand writing 342 13
short measure 294 10
short/medium haul airliner
  231 4; 231 11
short run 184 1; 249 59
shorts 33 25; 291 57
shorts, children's ~ 29 25
shorts, ladies' ~ 31 39
shorts, leather ~ 29 32
short standing 75 22
short stop 292 42
short wave 7 26
short-wave station 237 54
short-wave therapy
  apparatus 23 22, 39
shot *Athletics* 298 49

shot *Sports* 305 52
shote 75 42
shot firer 158 25
shotgun, over-and-under ~
  87 33
shot number 310 35
shot put 298 48
shoulder *Phys. Geog.* 12 41
shoulder *Man* 16 22
shoulder *Horse* 72 18
shoulder *Game* 88 17, 38
shoulder *Meat* 95 5, 9
shoulder *Composing Rm.* 175
  40
shoulder balance 295 29
shoulderblade 16 23; 17 7
shoulder button 31 15
shoulder cape 355 39
shoulder girdle 17 6-7
shoulder guard 142 5
shoulder iron 38 33
shoulder landing 298 12
shoulder rest 255 9, 31, 39
shoulder stand 295 29
shoulder strap 260 11
shoulder strap, frilled ~ 29 14
shovel 55 14; 137 2; 200 1;
  255 77
shovel, mechanical ~ 118 81
shovel, wooden ~ 91 24
shovel bucket 118 82
show booth 308 6
showcase 271 13
shower *Meteorol.* 8 19
shower *Meteorol. etc.* 9 37
shower *Life-Sav.* 228 30
shower *Swim.* 282 2
shower, lukewarm ~ 281 29
shower adjustment rail 49 43
shower attachment,
  extendible ~ 126 30
shower base 49 44
shower bath 282 2
shower cubicle 49 39
shower curtain 49 40
shower head, adjustable ~ 49
  41
shower nozzle 49 42
'showers' 233 46
show jumping 289 8-14
showman 308 10
show people, travelling ~ 308
  25-28
shredding 169 6
shrew 366 7
shrew mouse 366 7
shrimp 369 12
shrine 337 21
shrine, Buddhist ~ 337 21
shrink foil 76 25
shrink ring 130 24
shrink-sealing machine 76 24
shroud 219 16; 284 18
shrub, anemophilous ~ 59
  44-51
shrub, ornamental ~ 272 14
shrub, wind-pollinating ~ 59
  44-51
shrub bed 55 37
shrubs, ornamental ~ 373;
  374
shuck 68 33
shunter 206 43
shunting engine 206 43
shunting locomotive 206 43
shutter *Market Gdn.* 55 9
shutter *Mills* 91 4
shutter, folding ~ 37 30
shutter, louvred ~ 212 84
shutter, rolling ~ 37 28
shutter, side ~ 119 55
shutter board 118 41; 119 18,
  76

shutter catch 37 31
shuttering 119 54-76; 123 10
shuttering, bottom ~ 119 54
shuttering board 119 76
shuttering strut 119 13
shutter opening 304 12
shutter release 114 12, 31;
  115 18; 117 6; 313 24, 38
shutter release button 114 12;
  115 18
shutter speed control 114 35;
  115 19
shutter speed setting knob
  115 19
shutter weir 217 65-72
shuttle *Needlewk.* 102 20
shuttle *Weaving* 166 9, 26
shuttle *Ball Games* 293 44
shuttle box 166 9
shuttlecock 273 7; 293 44
shuttlecock game 273 6
shuttle eye 166 29
shuttle tip, metal ~ 166 25
sickle 56 8
side *Man* 16 32
side *Opticn.* 111 13
side *Joiner* 132 23
side *Weaves* 171 32
side *Art* 336 40
side *Maths.* 346 26, 27
side, subordinate ~ 252 9
side, woven ~ 136 18
side batten 222 62
side blackboard 260 35
sideboard *Dining Rm.* 44 20
sideboard *Tablew. etc.* 45 44
side board *Farm Bldgs.* 62 25
sideboards 34 24
sideburns 34 24
sidecar 290 30
sidecar body 189 54
sidecar combination 290 29
sidecar crash bar 189 55
sidecar machine 189 53
sidecar wheel 189 57
sidecar windscreen 189 58
sidecar windshield 189 58
side cast, two-handed ~ 89 32
side ceiling 222 62
side comb 105 6
side control 180 5, 20
side drum 323 51
side elevation 207 1, 22-25,
  37, 60, 74
side flat 310 33
side frame 165 12; 167 20
side girder, longitudinal ~ 222
  52
side grafting 54 36
side grip 134 45
side horse 296 5
side joint 111 14
side lay control 180 5, 20
sidelight 189 56; 191 20; 223
  15
sidelight, green ~ 286 11
sidelight, headlight, and
  parking light switch 191 62
sidelight, port ~ 286 12
sidelight, red ~ 286 12
sidelight, starboard ~ 286 11
sideline 292 17; 293 2 - 3, 4 -
  5; 293 55
side margin control 180 5, 20
sidemarker lamp 189 56; 191
  20
side note 185 68
side of pork 94 23
side panel, removable ~ 188
  48
side parting 315 1
side planking 62 25

side pocket 33 12
siderostat 5 16
side rudder 218 6
side shoot 370 21
sideshow 308 24
side slit 30 49
side split 295 14
side stake 206 24
side stay 284 18
sidestep 301 27
sidestepping 299 29
side stop 200 34, 44
side straddle 295 3
side strake 222 45
side stringer 222 50
side stroke 282 36
side support *Shipbuild.* 222 40
side support *Free Exerc.* 295
  25
side thrust kick 299 19
side trappings 71 16
side view 207 1, 22-25, 37, 60,
  74
sidewalk 37 60; 198 9
sidewall *Electrotyp. etc.* 178
  45
sidewall *Railw.* 213 29
side wall *Music. Instr.* 323 4,
  25
side-whiskers 34 24
side window blower 191 61
siding 206 50
Siemens-Martin open-
  hearth furnace 147 21-30
sieve *Market Gdn.* 55 13
sieve *Graphic Art* 340 24
sieve, louvred-type ~ 64 17
sieve, reciprocating ~ 64 19
sieve, upright ~ 55 13
sieve extension 64 18
sifter 91 26
sight 87 65; 255 45
sight, front ~ 87 71; 255 3, 23,
  37; 305 42
sight, optical ~ 305 41
sight, telescopic ~ 87 29; 255
  28; 305 49
sight graticule 87 31-32
sighting mechanism 255 45
sighting notch *Hunt.* 87 66
sighting notch *Army* 255 22
sight scale division 87 68
sign, chequered ~ 203 30
sign, illuminated ~ 203 38
signal 205 42
signal, distant ~ 203 7-24
signal, main ~ 203 1, 1-6
signal, visual ~ 238 30
signal and radar mast 221 7
signal arm 203 2
signal box 15 24
signal box, electrically-
  operated ~ 203 61
signal box, manually-
  operated ~ 203 53
signal element 243 60
signal flags 253 22-34
signal generator 313 30
signaling *see* signalling
signal knob 203 62
signal lever 203 56
signal light *Power Plant* 153 3
signal light *Cotton Spin.* 164 8
signal light *Railw.* 212 15
signal light *Ship* 221 125
signalling equipment 203
signalling lamp 223 7
signalling mast 225 34
signal mast *Map* 14 51
signal mast *Docks* 225 34
signal position 203 4, 5, 10, 11
signals, supplementary ~ 203
  25-44

signal stay 223 11
signal tower 14 51
signal tower, electrically-
operated ~ 203 61
signal tower, manually-
operated ~ 203 53
signal track 243 59
signature *Bookbind.* 183 12;
185 69
signature *Stock Exch.* 251 15,
16
signature, cross-folded ~ 185
15
signature, parallel-folded ~
185 13
signature code 185 69
signboard 118 45
signet ring 36 40
sign for day running 203 36
sign for night running 203 38
sign of parallelism 345 21
sign of similarity 345 22
signs, conventional ~ 15
1-114
signs, zodiacal ~ 4 53-64
signs of the zodiac 4 53-64
signwriting brush 129 41
sikar 337 26
sikhara 337 26
silencer 191 29; 209 12, 22, 24;
211 49; 305 93
silhouette 25 39
silicon atom 1 14
siliqua *Weeds* 61 20, 23
siliqua *Bot.* 370 93
siliqua *Alp. Plants etc.* 378 33
siliqua *South. Fruits* 384 46
siliqua, mature ~ 383 4
siliqua, ripe ~ 383 4
silk-cotton tree 383 20
silk moth 358 48
silk taffeta 35 36
silkworm 358 50
sill *Phys. Geog.* 11 31
sill *Car* 193 21
sill rail 120 56
silo 225 68
silo, above-ground ~ 62 11
silo, polythene ~ 62 43
silo cylinder 225 69
silo pipe 62 12
silver 254 25
silver-disc pyrheliometer 10
23
silver fir 372 1
silverfish 81 14
silverleaf 371 23
silver owl 362 17
silver poplar 371 23
silverside 95 34
silversmith 108
sima 11 4
simple interest formula 345 7
simsim 383 45
Sinanthropus 261 18
sine 346 32
singer 315 22, 23
single, clinker-built ~ 283 18
single-hand control 185 7
single-loader 87 1
singles 293 4-5
single sculler 283 16
single-shot rifle 305 35
singles match 293 4-5
singles sideline 293 4-5
single-system recording 117 8
singlet 296 61
single-trip bottle 93 29
sinister 254 19,21,23
sink *Phys. Geog.* 11 49; 13 71
sink *Kitch.* 39 35
sink *Forestry* 84 28
sink *Bakery* 97 68

sink *Coal* 144 47
sink *Energy Sources* 155 16
sink *School* 261 6, 34
sink *Camping* 278 6
sinker *Sea Fish.* 90 10
sinker *Knitting* 167 58
sinker *Navig.* 224 73
sinker, oval ~ 89 88
sinkhole 11 49; 13 71
sink unit 39 33-36
Sinningia 53 7
sinter terraces 11 23
sinuate 370 48
sinus, frontal ~ 17 55
sinus, sphenoidal ~ 17 54
siphon barometer 10 1
siphon tube 10 43
siren *Ship* 223 3
siren *Fabul. Creat.* 327 58
siren, ship's ~ 224 32
sirenian 366 23
Sirius 3 14
sirloin 95 17; 96 4
sisal 35 13
siskin 361 8
site fence 118 44
site hut 118 48; 119 44
site of battle 15 93
site office 118 48
sit harness 300 57
situla, sheet-bronze ~ 328 34
Siva 337 19
six-day race 290 2-7
six-day racer 290 2
six-eight time 320 34
six-four time 320 35
sixte engagement 294 48
sixteenth note 320 17
sixteenth rest 320 25
six-to-pica 175 19
sixty-fourth note 320 19
sixty-fourth rest 320 27
size 128 4
size press 173 24
sizing 162 53
sizing and edging machine
132 57
sizing machine 165 52
skateboard 273 51
skate guard 302 25
skate sailing 302 27-28
skate sailor 302 27
skeet 305 70-78
skeet choke 305 71
skeet shooting 305 70-78
skeg 279 3; 286 61
skeletal 194 30-33
skeleton *Man* 17 1-29
skeleton *School* 261 14
skeleton *Winter Sp.* 303 22
skeleton, siliceous ~ 357 8
skeleton construction 119 1
skeleton rider 303 23
skeleton toboggan 303 22
skeleton tobogganing 303
22-24
skep 77 52
sketch for costume 315 40
sketch pad 338 35
skew notch 120 54
skew notch, double ~ 121 91
skew notch, single ~ 121 90
ski, compact ~ 301 1
ski, modern ~ 301 46
ski bag 301 28
ski bob 304 16
ski cap 35 39; 301 10
skid chain 304 10
skidder 85 34
skidder, short-haul ~ 85 27
skife knife 100 51
skiff 283 16
skiing 301 1-72

skiing boot, cemented sole ~
301 12
skiing cap 35 39; 301 10
skiing goggles 301 11
ski jumping 301 35
ski jumping boot 301 41
ski jumping ski 301 38
ski lift 301 57-63, 59
skim coulter 65 11
skimmer 96 43
skimmer, stepped ~ 286 38-41
skimmer rod 148 17
skimmers 286 38-44
skim milk tank 76 17
skin *Shipbuild.* 222 44-49
skin *School* 261 9
skin *Gliding* 287 40
skin, light alloy ~ 235 11
skin, outer ~ *Rowing* 283 33,
48
skin, outer ~ *Ball Games* 293
33
skin diver 279 7
skin diving 279 7-27
skip *Road Constr.* 200 25
skip *Railw.* 213 38; 214 34
skip *Gymn.* 297 42, 45
skip hoist *Iron & Steel* 147 3
skip hoist *Road Constr.* 200
14
ski pole 301 5
skipping 273 15
skipping rope 273 16; 297 43
skip rope 273 16
skip-winding system 144 25
skirt *Child. Clothes* 29 52
skirt *Ladies' Wear* 30 9; 31 3,
24
skirt *Army* 255 85
skirt *Motorboats etc.* 286 66
skirt *Airsports* 288 48
skirt, aft ~ 235 63
skirt, girl's ~ 29 46
skirt, grass ~ 306 18
skirt, inverted pleat ~ 30 51
skirt, loden ~ 30 67
skirt, long ~ 30 45
skirt, pleated ~ 30 32
skirt, wrap-around ~ 31 13
skirt, wrapover ~ 31 13
skirting 123 21
skirting board 123 21, 63
skirt suit 31 1
skirt suit, girl's ~ 29 50
ski stick 301 5
ski stop 301 56
ski suit, ladies' ~ 301 9
ski suit, one-piece ~ 301 9
skittle frame 305 1-11
skittles 305 1-13
skiving knife 100 51
ski wax 301 21
ski-waxing equipment 301
21-24
skull *Man* 17 1, 30-41
skull *School* 261 15, 17, 19, 21
skull *Rowing* 283 35-38
skull *Chivalry* 329 39
skull, australopithecine ~ 261
20
sky 3 1-8
sky, northern ~ 3 1-35
sky, southern ~ 3 36-48
sky blue 343 6
skydiving 288 37-62
skylight 38 2; 121 8; 122 12
skysail 220 32
slab 120 96
slab, reinforced concrete ~
123 28
slab, stone ~ 51 17; 331 61
slab, wooden ~ 324 62
slab cake 97 34; 99 21

slacks 29 49
slacks, lightweight ~ 31 52
slack suit 30 57
slade 65 6, 56
slag escape 147 9
slag ladle 147 10
slag spout 148 12
slalom 301 29, 64
slalom canoe 283 4
slalom ski 286 60
slant track 243 31
slapstick 306 48
slat 229 53
slat, extensible ~ 229 38
slate *Roof* 122 85
slate 309 72
slate hammer 122 73
slater *House Insects etc.* 81 6
slater *Roof* 122 71
slate roof 122 61-89
slath 136 21
slating batten 122 17
slaughterer 94 1
slaughterhouse *Slaughterho.*
94
slaughterhouse *Bullfight. etc.*
319 13
slaughterman 94 1
slave, female ~ 306 41
slave driver 218 47
slave galley 218 44-50
slave station 224 41
sled 303 1, 2
sled dog 353 2
sledge 303 1, 2
sledge dog 353 2
sledge hammer 137 22; 158 6
sleeper *Bldg. Site* 119 39
sleeper *Station* 205 60
sleeper *Railw.* 207 36
sleeper, concrete ~ 202 37
sleeper, coupled ~ 202 14, 38
sleeper, steel ~ *Railw.* 202 36
sleeper, steel ~ *Hydr. Eng.*
217 3
sleeper and strampler 29 23
sleeping bag *Infant Care etc.*
28 17
sleeping bag *Camping* 278 30
sleeping car 207 36
sleeping doll 47 11
sleeve 30 15
sleeve, batwing ~ 31 16
sleeve, braided ~ 186 24
sleeve, dagged ~ 355 46
sleeve, full ~ 355 60
sleeve, gallooned ~ 186 24
sleeve, kimono ~ 30 36
sleeve, petal-scalloped ~ 355
46
sleeve, protective ~ 142 6
sleeve, puffed ~ 31 27; 355
49, 60
sleeve, sliding ~ 192 32, 35
sleeve, turned-up ~ 31 62
sleeve, turnover ~ 30 6
sleeve, turn-up ~ 30 6
sleeve board 50 20
sleeve protector 324 17
sleigh, horse-drawn ~ 304 25
sleigh bell 304 26
slender funnel fungus 381 25
slewing crab 222 21
slew turntable 200 22
sley 166 41, 53
sley cap 166 6
slice *Bakery* 97 43
slice *Blacksm.* 137 2
slice, sugared ~ 97 43
slicer 96 31
slicker 81 14
slide *Inf. Tech.* 242 42
slide *Playground* 273 24

slide *Winter Countr.* **304** 17
slide *Music. Not.* **321** 16
slide *Music. Instr.* **322** 51; **323** 47; **326** 7, 33
slide, bed ~ **177** 59
slide bar **313** 10
slide calliper **85** 10
slide chair **202** 22
slide control **238** 47; **241** 8
slide-copying adapter **115** 88
slide-copying attachment **115** 87
slide holder **309** 43
slide projector **114** 76; **309** 42; **312** 23
slider **326** 7
slide rail **206** 38
sliding door **271** 50
sliding scale **349** 23
sliding weight **22** 68; **40** 36
sliding-weight scales *Doc.* **22** 66
sliding-weight scales **40** 35
sling *First Aid* **21** 2
sling *Mountain.* **300** 11
sling pump **101** 53
sling ring **87** 5
sling seat **300** 29
slip *Underwear etc.* **32** 13
slip *Plant Propagn.* **54** 20
slip *Roof* **122** 48
slip casting **161** 15
slip fault **12** 7
slip-off slope **13** 58
slipper *Shoes* **101** 41
slipper *Station* **206** 49
slipper animalcule **357** 9
slipper brake **206** 49
slip road **15** 16
slips **222** 11-26
slip sock, woollen ~ **101** 42
slipway **222** 11-18
slipway crane **222** 23
slipway floor **222** 17
slipway frame **222** 19
slipway portal **222** 11
slipways **222** 11-26
slit, side ~ **30** 49
slit gong **354** 18
slitter **181** 42
sliver **164** 15, 21
sliver, carded ~ **163** 38
sliver, carded and combed ~ **163** 72
sliver, coiled ~ **163** 35
sliver, doubled ~s **164** 12
sliver, thin ~ **164** 13
sliver can **164** 3, 20
sloe **374** 27
slope **347** 12
slope, continental ~ **11** 9
slope soaring **287** 27
slops **355** 34
slosh baffle system **235** 53
slot *Glass Prod.* **162** 9
slot *Weaving* **166** 32
slot *Garage* **195** 5
slot *Election* **263** 30
slot *Airsports* **288** 45
slotted board **2** 45
slouch hat **35** 21
slow motion control **243** 49
slow-running jet **192** 1
slowworm **364** 37
slubbing frame **164** 19
slug **174** 27
slug-casting machine **174** 19
slug-composing machine **174** 19
slug of clay **161** 10
sluice dam **217** 73-80
sluice gate **217** 53-56, 77
sluice valve **217** 53-56

slump fault **12** 7
slush **304** 30
slush pump **145** 16
smack **221** 49
small-arm **87** 2
small beer **93** 26
smallbore free rifle **305** 44
smallbore rifle **305** 48
smallbore standard rifle **305** 43
small cabbage white butterfly **80** 48
small ermine moth **80** 5
small of the back **16** 25
small of the butt **87** 7
small scabious **375** 29
small-shot cartridge **87** 49
small-shot charge **87** 51
smash **293** 17
smear **23** 15, 50
smelting section **147** 8
smith **137**; **138**
smith forging **139**
smock overall **31** 35
smock windmill **91** 29
smokebox door **210** 26
smoke canister **255** 83
smoke dispenser **255** 83
smoke extract **38** 81
smoke flap **352** 9
smoke house **96** 48
smoke outlet **38** 81; **210** 22; **353** 21
smoker's companion **107** 44
smokestack *Power Plant* **152** 15
smokestack *Railw.* **210** 22
smoke tube **210** 8
smoking requisites **107**
smoother **128** 11
smoothing blade **200** 18
smoothing plane **132** 15; **134** 1
snaffle **289** 12
snail **357** 27
snail, edible ~ **357** 27
snail shell **357** 29
snake, poisonous ~ **364** 40
snake, venomous ~ **364** 40
snake charmer **353** 45
snakes **364** 38-41
snakeweed **376** 10
snapdragon **51** 32
snap gauge **149** 59
snap lid **127** 24
snapping beetle **80** 37
snapping bug **80** 37
snare drum **323** 51
snath **66** 16
snathe **66** 16
snead **66** 16
sneath **66** 16
snedding machine **85** 18
snipe **88** 83
snorkel *Warships* **259** 72, 90
snorkel *Swim.* **279** 11
snorkel *Bathing* **280** 39
snout **73** 10; **88** 53; **364** 2
snow **8** 18; **9** 34; **304** 24; **353** 5
snow and ice climber **300** 15
snow and ice climbing **300** 14-21
snow and ice climbing equipment **300** 31-57
snow avalanche **304** 1
snowball *Winter Countr.* **304** 15
snowball *Shrubs etc.* **373** 10
snowball bush **373** 10
snowball fight **304** 14
snow blower **213** 17
snow bridge **300** 24
snow chain **304** 10

snow cornice **300** 20
snowdrift **304** 5
snowdrop **60** 1
snowfall **10** 48; **304** 4
snow fence **304** 6
snow forest climate **9** 56
snow gaiter **300** 55
snow goggles **300** 18
snow guard **38** 8
snow guard bracket **122** 16
snow hut **353** 4
snow ledge **300** 4
snowman **304** 13
snow plough, rotary ~ **213** 17
snow plough attachment **304** 9
snow plough signs **203** 34-35
snow push **304** 23
snow shovel **304** 23
snowshirt **300** 6
snowslide **304** 1
snow suit **29** 38
snuff **107** 20
snuff box **107** 20
soaking pit **148** 46
soaking pit crane **148** 47
soaking tub **136** 13
soap **49** 22
soap box **273** 33
soap dish **49** 21
soap dispenser **50** 27
soaring **287**
soccer **291**
soccer game **273** 10
sock **291** 58
sock, knee-length ~ **29** 53; **32** 32; **33** 42
sock, long ~ **32** 34
sock, surgical ~ **101** 50
socket *Hairdresser* **106** 15
socket *Plumb.* **125** 20
socket *Plumb. etc.* **126** 43
socket *Electr.* **127** 7
socket, double ~ **127** 6
socket, earthed ~ **127** 5, 6, 13
socket, four-way ~ **127** 8
socket, surface-mounted ~ **127** 13
socket, switched ~ **127** 7
socket, three-pin ~ **127** 66
socket, three-pole ~ **127** 13
socket, tinner's ~ **125** 20
socket, underfloor ~ **127** 22
socket outlet box **127** 25
socks, men's ~ **32** 32-34
soda bottle **42** 32
soda-lime absorber **27** 39
soda water **98** 87
soda water bottle **42** 32
sodium atom **1** 8
sodium chloride **1** 9; **170** 13
sodium ion **1** 11
sodium pump, primary ~ **154** 5
sodium pump, secondary ~ **154** 8
sodium sulphate storage tank **172** 36
sodium system, primary ~ **154** 2
sodium system, secondary ~ **154** 7
sofa **336** 17
sofa, two-seater ~ **246** 36
soffit **122** 27
soft corn **68** 31
soft pedal **325** 9
soil covering **200** 64
soil injector **83** 33
solan goose **359** 9
solar cell **155** 34
solar collector **155** 28, 32
solarium **281** 10

solar panel **10** 66
solar radiation shielding **10** 36
solar sensor **10** 69
solar spectrum **343** 14
solar system **4** 42-52
soldanella **378** 3
solder **108** 38
solder, tin-lead ~ **126** 76
soldering apparatus **125** 5-7
soldering borax **108** 39
soldering fluid **125** 7
soldering flux **108** 36
soldering gun *Goldsm. etc.* **108** 14
soldering gun *D.I.Y.* **134** 56
soldering iron *Plumb.* **125** 5
soldering iron *Plumb. etc.* **126** 73
soldering iron *D.I.Y.* **134** 19, 57
soldering iron, electric ~ **127** 45
soldering iron, high-speed ~ **134** 58
soldering stone **125** 6
solder wire, tin-lead ~ **134** 20
soldier, lead ~ **309** 52
soldier, tin ~ **309** 52
sole *Agr. Mach.* **65** 6, 66
sole *Shoem.* **100** 66
sole *Joiner* **132** 22
sole, cemented ~ **101** 11
sole, corrugated ~ **300** 43
sole, inner ~ **291** 31
sole, natural-colour ~ **101** 15, 38
sole, nylon ~ **291** 30
sole, plastic ~ **101** 2
sole, PVC ~ **101** 2
sole, rubber ~ **101** 38
sole, wooden ~ **101** 45
sole bar reinforcement **213** 12
sole leather **100** 31
sole-leather shears **100** 39
solenoid valve **139** 23
sole of the foot **19** 62
sole-plate *Household* **50** 7
sole-plate *Road Constr.* **200** 33
sole-plate *Railw.* **202** 5
sole press, automatic ~ **100** 14
sole stitcher **100** 26
sole-stitching machine **100** 26
sole trimmer **100** 5
solid-fuel rocket, recoverable ~ **235** 58
solidification **170** 35, 43
solid-newel staircase **123** 77
solid rocket booster **235** 58
solids **347** 30-46
solid stage **148** 26
solid-web girder **121** 72
solid-web girder bridge **215** 7
solifluction lobe **11** 51
solifluction tongue **11** 51
soling **284** 56
solleret **329** 55
solo machine **290** 27
solo organ **326** 45
solo seat **189** 19
solo skater **302** 1
solstice **3** 8
solution **345** 10
solution, viscous ~ **169** 15
solvent fumes **182** 25
Somali Current **14** 36
sombrero **35** 5
songbirds **360** 1,3,4,5,7,9,10; **361** 1-20
song thrush **361** 16
soot **38** 34
sordino **323** 10; **324** 68

Soricidae 366 7
sort 174 7, 28
sorter 172 57
sorter, rotary ~ 172 23
sorter, secondary ~ 172 58
sorting machine 74 38
sorting siding 206 47
sorting table 64 81
sound assistant 117 68; 310 57
soundboard *Music. Instr.* 323 24; 324 3
soundboard *Church* 330 21
sound box 322 18, 29; 323 3; 324 15, 63
sound camera 117 22; 313 26
sound camera, Super-8 ~ 117 1
sound coding equipment 242 11-14
sound connecting cord 117 8
sound control console 238 20, 41, 54; 239 8
sound control desk 238 20, 41, 54; 239 8
sound control engineer 238 19
sound control room 238 27; 239 7
sound dubbing 311 34-36
sound echo 224 63
sound editor 117 96
sound effect 310 30
sound effects box 238 35
sound engineer 238 19
sound film 117 82
sound film cartridge, Super-8 ~ 117 29
sound head *Cine Film* 117 33
sound head *Audiovis.* 243 35
sound head *Films* 312 47
sound head housing 241 59
sound hole 322 22; 323 6; 324 5
sound impulse 224 62
sounding balloon 7 17
sounding board 330 21
sound mixer 238 26
sound mixing 311 34-36
sound module 240 14
sound OB van 239 1-15
sound optics 312 46
sound production control room 238 27; 239 7
sound projector 117 81; 312 24
sound recorder, portable ~ 310 24
sound recording 311 1-46
sound recording camera 310 60; 311 6
sound recording equipment 117 7
sound recording level control 243 11
sound recording selector switch 117 13
sound recordist *Broadcast.* 238 26
sound recordist *Films* 310 23, 55; 311 36
sound source 117 27
sound source, external ~ 117 8
sound technician 238 26
sound track *Cine Film* 117 82
sound track *Audiovis.* 243 32
sound track system 117 21
sound transmitter 224 61
sound turntable, first ~ 117 100
sound turntable, second ~ 117 101

sound wave 224 62
sound wave propagation 7 14
soup ladle 45 14
soup plate 44 6; 45 5
soup seasoning 98 30
soup spoon 45 61
soup tureen 44 8; 45 15
soup vegetable 68 25
sources of energy, modern ~ 155
source water inlet 155 2
sour cherry 59 5
souring chamber 159 6
sour milk vat 76 42
South America 14 13
South Equatorial Current 14 34
Southern Cross 3 44
Southern Ocean 14 22
Southern Triangle 3 40
south point 4 17
South Pole 14 3
southwester 35 30; 228 5
souvenir plate 309 48
sou'wester 35 30; 228 5
sow *Dom. Anim.* 73 9
sow *Livestock* 75 41
sow *Hunt.* 86 32
sow *Game* 88 48, 51
sow bug 81 6
sower 63 10
sowing 54 1; 63 10-12
sow pig 75 42
spa 274
space *Composing Rm.* 175 5, 17
space *Music. Not.* 320 44
space, popliteal ~ 16 51
spaceband 174 24
space bar 249 2
space capsule 6 9, 10; 234 65
spacecraft 6 1
space flight 234; 235
spaceflight module 235 70
Spacelab 235 65
space laboratory 235 65
spacer 119 81
Space Shuttle-Orbiter 235 1-45
space station 235 65
space suit 6 18-27
space suit helmet 6 22
spacing bracket 126 54
spacing clip 126 57
spacing lines 10 58
spacing material 174 8
spade 56 2; 331 36
spade *Fish Farm.* 89 82
spade *Army* 255 55
spade, semi-automatic ~ 56 12
spade piston 255 56
spades 276 39
spadix 370 71; 378 22
spadix, female ~ 384 6
spadix, male ~ 383 55; 384 4
spa gardens 274 1-21
spaghetti 98 32
spale 136 12
spale basket 136 11
span *Bridges* 215 14
span *Aircraft* 229 2
span, clear ~ 215 13
span, wire rope ~ 221 102
Spandau 255 32
Spanish chestnut 384 48
Spanish paprika 57 42
spanker 219 30
spanker boom 218 28; 219 44
spanker boom topping lift 219 48
spanker gaff 219 45
spanker peak halyard 219 49

spanker sheet 219 69
spanker vang 219 70
span of oxen 63 16
spa orchestra 274 20
spa promenade 274 10
spar 230 45
spar, diagonal ~ 287 33
spar, integral ~ 257 28
spar, main ~ 287 30
spar buoy 224 79
spar ceiling 222 62
spare man 291 11
spare part *Watchm.* 109 22
spare part *Garage* 195 32
spare rib 95 47
spare tyre *Lorries etc.* 194 4
spare tyre *Cyc. Racing* 290 23
spare wheel 191 25; 194 33
spar arrester 210 24
spark gap 153 62
spark-ignition engine 190 1, 2
sparking plug 190 35; 242 48
spark plug 190 35; 242 48
spark-plug cap 188 27
Sparmannia 53 9
sparring partner 299 27
sparrow hawk 362 12
sparrow owl 362 19
spars 219 32-45
spatula *Dent.* 24 50
spatula *Hosp.* 25 7
spatula *Art. Studio* 338 15
spatula, plastic ~ 128 44
spawn 89 12
spawner 89 13
speaker *Living Rm.* 42 10
speaker *Election* 263 5
speaker *Hotel* 267 40
speaker *Disco* 317 15
speaker *Nightclub* 318 12
speaker, three-way ~ 241 14
speaking key 242 24
spear, long-bladed ~ 354 12
spear head, bronze ~ 328 21
spear thrower 352 40
special effects equipment 310 59
special offer 96 20; 271 65
specialty shop 195 1-55
specie 252 1-28
speciestaler 252 6
specimen insertion air lock 113 33
specimen stage adjustment 113 34
spectacle fitting 111 1-4
spectacle frame *Optician.* 111 5, 10-14
spectacle frame *Ship* 223 61
spectacle lens 111 15
spectacles 111 5, 9
spectator 308 29
spectator barrier 292 40
spectators' terrace 233 20
'spectators' terrace' 233 30
spectrograph 5 33
speculum, aural ~ 22 74
speculum, rectal ~ 23 19
speculum, vaginal ~ 23 13
speed ball 299 22
speed change lever 149 5
speed changer 241 29
speed code number 203 37
speed control 179 29
speed indicator 203 18
speed indicator, distant ~ 203 19
speedo 188 19, 34; 191 38, 74
speedometer *Motorcycles etc.* 188 19, 34, 40
speedometer *Motorcycle* 189 40

speedometer *Car* 191 38, 74
speedometer *Tram* 197 31
speedometer *Railw.* 211 35; 212 9
speedometer *Navig.* 224 54
speedometer, ship's ~ 224 22
speedometer drive 192 38, 39
speed recorder 210 54
speed restriction, permanent ~ 203 41, 42
speed restriction, temporary ~ 203 39, 40
speed restriction sign 203 36-38, 41, 44
speed restriction signs 203 36-44
speed restriction warning sign 203 43
speed selector 241 29
speed skate 302 20
speed skater 302 26
speed skating set 302 20
speedway 290 24-28
speedwell 375 22
speleothems 13 80-81
spelling book 260 17
spelt 68 24
spelt, green ~ 68 25
spencer 220 1
sperm whale 367 25
sphagnum mosses 13 20, 22
sphenoid 17 38
sphere 347 41
sphere, celestial ~ 4 23
sphere, plain ~ 36 82
sphere, solar ~ 4 36
spheres 36 82-86
sphere unit 2 38
spherical typing element 249 15
sphincter, anal ~ 20 63
sphinx *Fabul. Creat.* 327 20
sphinx *Articulates* 358 55
sphinx *Lepidopt.* 365 9
sphinx, Egyptian ~ 333 11
sphygmograph 26 32
sphygmomanometer 25 15
Spica 3 18
spice jar 39 32
spice packet 99 67
spice rack 39 31; 47 29
spices 382
spider legs 115 91
spiders 358 44-46
spider's web *Playground* 273 46
spider's web *Articulates* 358 47
spike *Arable Crops* 68 2
spike *Mountain.* 300 9
spike *Music. Instr.* 323 22
spike *Industr. Plants* 383 62, 66
spike, fleshy ~ 370 71
spike, racemose ~ 370 67
spikelet 68 3, 10; 69 23; 375 41, 42
spill light 310 51
spillway 217 60
spin *Roulette* 275 32
spin *Airsports* 288 7
spinach 57 29
spinal cord 17 48; 18 25
spindle *Watchm.* 109 17
spindle *Mach. Tools* 149 66; 150 27
spindle *Cotton Spin.* 164 43
spindle *Bookbind.* 183 22
spindle *Bicycle* 187 60, 80
spindle, horizontal ~ 150 40
spindle, main ~ 149 11
spindle, screwed ~ 149 66

spindle catch 164 49
spindle drive 164 31
spindle oil 145 61
spindle rail 164 50
spindle rotation speed 150 35
spindle shaft 164 46
spindle speed 164 38, 40
spindle top 126 32
spine *Man* 17 2-5
spine *Bookbind.* 183 14; 185
41
spine *Mammals* 366 6
spine label 247 38
spine of the book 183 1
spinet 322 45
spine tag 247 38
spinet piano 325 1
spinner *Fish Farm.* 89 74, 75
spinner *Aircraft* 230 33
spinner, long ~ 89 76
spinneret *Synth. Fibres* 169
14; 170 41
spinneret *Articulates* 358 46
spinneret hole 170 41, 42
spinning 170 57
spinning bath 169 15
spinning jet 169 14; 170 41, 42
spiraea 374 23
spiral *Photog.* 116 2
spiral *Airsports* 288 51
spiral *Gymn.* 297 50
spiral design pottery 328 13
spire 331 6
spire ball 331 5
spirit glass 45 90
spirit lamp 24 57
spirit level *Map* 14 61
spirit level *Bldg. Site* 118 55
spirit level *Plumb. etc.* 126 79
spirit level *D.I.Y.* 134 29
spirits 98 56-59; 318 19
spirograph 27 36
Spirographis 357 22
spirometer 23 31
spirometry 27 36-50
spit *Phys. Geog.* 13 5
spit *Kitch. Utensils* 40 33
spitz 70 20
splashboard 186 6
spleen 20 12, 27
splenius of the neck 18 51
splice, wet ~ 117 89
splice graft 54 39
splice grafting 54 39
splicer 117 89
splicing cement 312 22
splicing head 133 29
splint *First Aid* 21 12
splint *Sawmill* 157 16
splint, emergency ~ 21 10
splint bone 17 24
splinter 157 16
split-image rangefinder 115
55, 59, 64
splits 314 20
splitter 94 17
splitting hammer 85 5
spoil 226 47
spoiler 229 39; 287 38
spoiler, front ~ 193 36
spoiler, inner ~ 229 42
spoiler, rear ~ 193 34; 290 35
spoiler rim 193 30
spoil heap 144 19
spoke *Mach. Parts etc.* 143 88
spoke *Bicycle* 187 27
spoke *Motorcycle* 189 24
spoke end 187 29
spoke flange 187 29
spoke nipple 187 29
spokeshave 132 12
spoke wheel 289 25
sponge *Bathrm. etc.* 49 6

sponge *School* 260 42
sponge *Graphic Art* 340 25
sponge *Invertebr.* 357 13
sponge holder 23 12
sponge tray 260 41
spool 162 55
spool box 312 16
spool box, fireproof ~ 312 25
spool holder 185 17
spool knob 114 27
spoon *Tablew. etc.* 45 61
spoon *Fish Farm.* 89 73
spoon, wooden ~ 40 2
spoon bait 89 73
spoonbill 359 5
spoon bit 135 16
spoon bow 285 30
spoon chisel 339 18
spore 381 8, 13
sporting coupé 193 28
sporting gun 86 4
sporting guns 87 1-40
sporting rifle 86 4
sporting rifles 87 1-40; 305
40-49
sport parachute 288 45
sport parachuting 288 37-62
sports, various ~ 305
sportsboat, inflatable ~ 286 1
sportsboats *Rowing* 283 9-16
sportsboats *Motorboats etc.*
286 1-5, 10-14
sports news item 342 61
sports report 342 60
sports reporter 299 50
sports section 342 57
spot 276 32
spot, central ~ 115 65
spot, clear ~ 115 66
spot ball, white ~ 277 13
spotlight 307 3; 318 24
spotlight catwalk 310 53
spotted bruchus 81 19
spotted woodpecker 359 27
spotting position 297 16
spot welder, foot-operated ~
142 29
spot welding 142 22
spot welding electrode holder
142 23
spout 91 14
spout, swivel-mounted ~ 64
37
spout hole 367 26
spray *Doc.* 22 60
spray *Pest Contr.* 83 8
spray boom 83 3
spray can 106 23
spray canister 83 44
spraydeck 283 56
sprayer *Gdn. Tools* 56 24
sprayer *Letterpress* 181 10, 34
sprayer, semi-mounted ~ 83
47
sprayer, tractor-mounted ~
83 2
spray fluid tank 83 5, 50
spray gun *Pest Contr.* 83 18
spray gun *Painter* 129 32
spray gun *Letterpress* 181 34
spray gun, airless ~ 129 37
spraying 129 28
spraying tube 83 29
spray line, oscillating ~ 67 1
spray nozzle *Household* 50 13
spray nozzle *Intern. Combust.*
Eng. 190 54
spray pipe 172 72
spray tank 83 39
spray tube 83 22
spray unit *Pest Contr.* 83 58
spray unit *Offset Platem.* 179
5, 6

spray unit, airless ~ 129 36
spreader *Paperhanger* 128 46
spreader *Ship* 223 37
spreader *Sailing* 284 13
spreader cylinder 62 23
spreader unit 62 22
spreading flap 200 42
spring *Map* 15 82
spring *Metalwkr.* 140 46
spring *Knitting* 167 38
spring *Carriages* 186 15
spring, artesian ~ 12 26
spring, rubber ~ 297 13
spring attachment 11 42
spring barrel 110 38
springboard *Swim.* 282 9, 10
springboard *Gymn.* 296 12;
297 8
springboard *Circus* 307 36
springboard acrobat 307 35
springboard artist 307 35
springboard trampoline 297
14
spring bolt 140 37
spring bow compass 151 64
spring buffer 214 50
spring bumper 214 50
spring chest 326 12-14
springer 336 22
spring extension 309 28
spring fly 358 12
spring form 40 27
spring pin tool 109 9
spring ring hinge 151 65
spring snowflake 60 1
spring suspension 83 7
spring tine 65 57
spring tine, double ~ 64 42, 54
spring vice 140 10
spring washer 143 34; 202 8
sprinkler 55 19
sprinkler, oscillating ~ 56 46
sprinkler, revolving ~ 56 43;
62 29; 67 4, 32
sprinkler cart 62 27
sprinkler hose 62 30
sprinkler nozzle 67 27
sprinkler stand 62 28
sprinkler system 316 6
sprinkling can 51 21; 55 26
sprinkling device 55 19
sprinter 298 5
spritsail 218 43; 220 5
sprocket 143 90; 187 38, 74
sprocket piece 121 30
sprocket wheel 187 38
sprout *Veg.* 57 30
sprout *Bot.* 370 19-25
spruce 372 12
spruce cellulose 169 1
spruce cone 372 13
spruce fir 372 12
spruce-gall aphid 82 38
spruce needle 372 19
spur *Dom. Anim.* 73 26
spur *Game* 88 82
spur *Mountain.* 300 13
spurrey 69 12
spurs 71 50-51
spur vein 72 28
spur wheel, helical ~ 143 89
sputum 23 25
spyhole *Hall* 41 29
spyhole *Iron Foundry etc.* 148
4
squadron marking 256 2
square *Metalwkr.* 140 57
square *Maths.* 346 33; 347 31
square, black ~ 276 3
square, glazier's ~ 124 20
square, iron ~ 120 78
square, white ~ 276 2
squared timber store 157 32

square root 345 3
squash 57 23
squat 295 9
squat-style snatch 299 1
squat vault 296 53
squaw 352 10
squaw corn 68 31
squeegee *Photog.* 116 49
squeegee *Text. Finish.* 168 61
squeeze phase 75 34
squeeze roller 165 46
squirrel 366 19
squirrel's bread 381 16
stabilizer *Photog.* 116 10
stabilizer *Motorcycles etc.* 188
5
stabilizer *Railw.* 214 55
stabilizer *Navig.* 224 26
stabilizer *Air Force* 256 22
stabilizer *Winter Sp.* 301 49
stabilizer *Sports* 305 58
stabilizer, horizontal ~ 229
26; 230 62; 256 31; 288 23
stabilizer, vertical ~ 229 24;
230 59; 231 6; 232 7; 256
32; 288 21
stabilizer and rudder, vertical
~ 229 24-25; 230 58
stabilizer bar 192 71
stabilizing fin *Air Force* 256
22
stabilizing fin *Swim.* 279 3
stabilizing fin, aerodynamic ~
234 7
stabilizing layer 301 49
stabilizing panel 288 49
stabilizing surface 256 22
stabilizing wing 117 60
stable 62 2; 75 1
stable fly 81 4
stableman 186 27
staccato 321 34
stack *Forestry* 84 15
stack *Univ.* 262 11
stack bearer 157 37
stacker, intermediate ~ 236 34
stacker truck 159 18
stacking machine 162 20
stack of logs 84 16
staff 320 43-44
staff compartment 207 81
staff lavatory 207 82
staff toilet 207 82
staff washroom 207 26
staff WC 207 82
stag, rutting ~ 86 12; 88 4
stag beetle 358 24
stag call 87 46
stage *Films* 312 8
stage *Theatre* 315 14-27, 14
stage *Nightclub* 318 22
stage, mechanical ~ 112 10,
29; 115 98
stage, microscopic ~ 112 9
stage, revolving ~ 316 31
stage, universal ~ 112 17
stage base 112 15
stage carpenter 316 45
stagecoach 186 39
stagecoach, English ~ 186 53
stage curtain 312 10
stage designer 315 37
stage director 316 30
stagehand 315 28; 316 46
stagehouse 316 1-60
stage light 316 14
stage lighting 318 23
stage lighting unit 316 14
stage manager 316 30
stage plate 115 95
stage rehearsal 315 21-27
stage separation retro-rocket
234 8

staghorn 377 12
stag horn moss 377 12
staghound 289 47
staging *Photograv.* 182 12
staging *Shipbuild.* 222 18
stag jump 295 40; 302 7
stag leap 295 40; 302 7
stag's horn 377 12
stag's horn moss 377 12
staining dish 23 50
staining vat 130 15
staircase 37 72; 118 22
staircase, dog-legged ~ 123 42-44
staircase, outside ~ 333 33
staircase, quarter-newelled ~ 123 75
staircase, spiral ~ 123 76, 77
staircase, winding ~ 123 76, 77
staircase bolt 123 46
staircase construction 123
staircase of locks 217 17-25
staircase window 37 81; 123 65
stair light 41 22
stairs, concrete ~ 123 16
stair well 120 46
stake *Wine Grow.* 78 7
stake *Forestry* 84 17
stake *Plumb.* 125 23
stake *Basketm.* 136 6
stake *Roulette* 275 13
stake net 89 94
stalactite 13 80, 82
stalactite vault 337 17
stalagmite 13 81, 82
stalk 58 13, 34, 61; 68 6; 370 20; 378 31
stalk, herbaceous ~ 384 30
stalking 86 1-8
stall 75 2
stallion 73 2
stalls, front ~ 315 19
stall turn 288 4
stamen 58 45; 59 10, 39; 370 57, 60; 372 7, 18; 373 2, 5; 374 3
stamp *Doc.* 22 29
stamp *Slaughterho.* 94 24
stamp *Post* 236 21, 61
stamp *Bank* 250 24
stamp, impressed ~ 252 35
stamp book 236 20
stamp counter 236 15
stanchion 221 117
stanchion, hinged ~ 213 6
stanchion, steel ~ 213 6
stand *Hosp.* 25 11; 26 9, 29
stand *Overh. Irrign.* 67 2
stand *Shoem.* 100 54
stand *Opticn.* 111 5
stand *Optic. Instr.* 112 2
stand *Basketm.* 136 10
stand *Composing Rm.* 175 50
stand *Photomech. Reprod.* 177 29 ·
stand *Motorcycles etc.* 188 51
stand *Circus* 307 57
stand *Bullfight. etc.* 319 8
stand, hydraulic ~ 310 50
stand, raised ~ 86 14, 14-17
standard *Bldg. Site* 119 47, 59
standard *Forging* 139 19
standard *Photomech. Reprod.* 177 11
standard adjustment 114 51
standard lamp 46 37
Standard meridian 14 5
standard of the German Federal President 253 14
standby drive 214 64
standing-in position 297 16

standing matter 174 11
standing matter rack 174 9
standing position 305 27
standing press 183 20
standing room portion 197 18
standing stone 328 18
standing take-off pike dive 282 40
standing type 174 11
standing type rack 174 9
standing wrestling 299 6
standpipe *Farm Bldgs.* 62 12
standpipe *Oil, Petr.* 145 13
standpipe *Paperm.* 173 12
standpipe *Space* 234 25
standpipe *Fire Brig.* 270 26
standpipe coupler 67 5
stapelia 53 15
staple fiber lap 169 31
staple fibre 169 1-34
staple fibre, viscose rayon ~ 169 28-34
staple fibre layer 169 31
staple length 170 60
stapler 22 25; 247 4
staple shaft 144 27
stapling machine 247 4
star *Sailing* 284 55
star *Films* 310 27, 28
star, binary ~ 3 29
star, circumpolar ~ 3 5
star, double ~ 3 29
star, principal ~ 3 9
star, variable ~ 3 11
star connection 153 20
star finch 360 3
starfish 357 38; 369 17
starling 361 4
star map 3 1-35
star network 153 20
stars, fixed ~ 3 9-48
Stars and Stripes 253 18
Star-Spangled Banner 253 18
start *Motorboats etc.* 286 28, 29
start *Athletics* 298 1-6, 3
starter 282 30
starter, electric ~ 56 39
starter and steering lock 191 75
starter battery 212 46
starter button, electric ~ 189 52
starter motor *Intern. Combust. Eng.* 190 44
starter motor *Railw.* 212 30
starter pedal 188 25
starter's flag 273 34
starter switch 241 30
starting and braking device, automatic ~ 168 20
starting and finishing buoy 285 14
starting and stopping handle 166 8
starting and stopping lever 165 17; 180 80; 181 32
starting block *Swim.* 282 27
starting block *Athletics* 298 1
starting dive 282 29
starting gear ring 192 31
starting handle 163 17
starting lever 178 20
starting line 286 30
starting motor 190 44
starting place 282 27
starting position 295 1
starting price 289 37
starting resistance 135 3
starting resistor 135 3
starting rod 167 22
starting signal 205 47
start print button 249 38

start-stop lever 163 40
star wheel *Mach. Tools* 149 43
star wheel *Graphic Art* 340 39
Stassfurt salt 154 66
Stassfurt seam 154 65
stately home 15 96
statement of account 247 44
state of play 293 38
static air tank 196 19
station, coastal ~ 237 53
station, lower ~ 214 39
station, top ~ 214 57
station, upper ~ 214 57
stationary rings 296 4
station bookstall 204 26
station bookstand 204 26
station clock 204 30
station foreman 205 41
station hall 204
station mailbox 204 11
station of the Cross 330 54
station platform 205
station post box 204 11
station preset button 241 49; 243 17; 309 20
station restaurant 204 13
station selector button 241 4; 243 17; 309 20
station sign 205 30
station wagon 193 15
statistics chart 248 36
statue 272 10; 334 5; 339 32
statue, stone ~ 272 2
statuette, ivory ~ 328 8
stave *Cooper* 130 2
stave *Music. Not.* 320 43-44
stay, triatic ~ 223 11
stayer 290 14
stay pole 152 31
stay rope 299 37
stay-warm plate 28 28
stay wire 296 10; 297 5; 299 37
St. Bernard dog 70 37
steady, fixed ~ 150 30
steam 50 11
steam and recirculation water flow path 154 51
steam boiler 152 5
steam chest 210 31
steam collector 210 21
steam coupling hose 208 20
steam dome 210 12
steam extraction 103 26
steam extractor 103 25
steam-generating station 152 1-28
steam generator 154 9, 26, 44
steam heater 172 38
steam hole 50 14
steaming light 223 40; 258 55
steaming light mast 221 51
steam iron 103 20; 131 3
steam line 154 11
steam locomotives 210 1-69
steam pipe 172 64
steam pipe, high-pressure ~ 259 63
steam press 104 26
steam pressing unit 104 26
'steam radio' 309 16
steam reversing gear 210 18
steam slit 50 14
steam spray gun 131 2
steam sterilizer 22 39
steam storage locomotive 210 68
steam trawler 221 46
steam tube 210 17
steam turbine 152 23; 153 23-30; 154 14, 46, 52
steam turbine generator 259 58

steel 94 16
steel, finished ~ 148 68
steel bender 119 21
steel-casting ladle 147 31
steel grit delivery pipe 148 38
steel ingot 147 33
steel lattice bridge 215 34
steel-leg vice 126 80
steel-wheel glass cutter 124 26
steelworks 147 21-69
steep face 12 43
steeping 169 4
steeping floor 92 8, 28
steeping tank 92 8
steeple 331 2
steeplechase *Equest.* 289 20-22
steeplechase *Athletics* 298 7-8
steep liquor 92 6
steering, hydraulic power ~ 65 41
steering alignment 195 17, 22
steering alignment, visual ~ 195 41
steering and control position 224 14
steering arm 192 79
steering axle 64 32
steering column 192 56
steering column, controlled-collapse ~ 191 57
steering drop arm 192 58
steering gear 192 56-59
steering head 187 11
steering line *Rowing* 283 52
steering line *Airsports* 288 41
steering oar 218 6
steering rudder 283 51-53
steering runner 302 45
steering system, rear-wheel ~ 64 39
steering tube 187 14
steering wheel 191 37; 305 89
steering wheel spoke 191 58
steersman *Ship* 218 2
steersman *Winter Sp.* 303 20
stein 309 53
steinbock 367 7
Steinheim man 261 17
stela 330 43; 334 33
stele 330 43; 334 33
stem *Forestry* 84 19
stem *Tobacc. etc.* 107 38
stem *Metalwkr.* 140 33
stem *Ship* 218 4; 221 14, 83, 108; 258 3
stem *Chem.* 350 7
stem *Bot.* 370 2
stem *Edib. Fungi* 381 18
stem, bulbous ~ 222 74
stem, prostrate ~ 58 20
stem, straight ~ 285 40
stem, wire ~ 325 29
stem cutting 54 25
stemless alpine gentian 378 13
stemming sand bucket 158 29
stem post 218 4
stem rudder 218 24
stem stitch 102 4
stencil ejection 245 9
stencil knife 129 43
stencil lettering guide 151 69
stencil magazine, vertical ~ 245 8
stencil storage drawer 245 10
stenography 342 13
steno pad 245 29; 248 32
stenter 165 54; 168 21
stenter clip 168 24
stenter pin 168 24
step *Roof & Boilerr.* 38 27
step *Hall* 41 24

step *Carriages* 186 13
step *Tram* 197 15
step *Aircraft* 230 42
step *Swim.* 281 32, 37
step *Mountain.* 300 17
step, bottom ~ 123 18, 42
step, top ~ 123 19
step, wedge-shaped ~ 123 31
step bearing 91 10
step-cut, hexagonal ~ 36 62
step-cut, octagonal ~ 36 52
step-cut, rectangular ~ 36 50
step-cut, rhombus ~ 36 59
step-cut, round hexagonal ~ 36 64
step-cut, square ~ 36 51
step-cut, trapezium ~ 36 57
step-cut, triangular ~ 36 60-61
step fault 12 8
step irons 269 28
stepladder 50 35; 126 2; 129 5
steppe zone 9 54
stepping stones 37 45
steps *Dwellings* 37 39
steps *Household* 50 35
steps *Station* 204 25; 205 2
steps *Circus* 307 20
steps, front ~ 37 66
steps, wooden ~ 38 25
stereobate 334 4
stereo cassette deck 241 33
stereo component system, three-in-one ~ 241 52
stereo effect 310 30
stereo equipment 42 9; 317 22-23
stereo microphone jack 241 65
stereo microphone socket 241 65
stereomicroscope, wide-field ~ 112 61
stereoplanigraph 14 66
stereo receiver 241 52
stereoscope 14 64
stereo sound 311 35
stereo speakers 241 13-14
stereo system 42 9; 241 13-48; 317 22-23
sterilization room 26 34-54
sterilizer 76 12
sterilizer, small ~ 26 35
stern 222 66-72; 258 26; 285 29
stern, gilded ~ 218 55-57
stern, lower ~ 218 58
stern, square ~ 285 43
stern, upper ~ 218 55
sterncastle 218 23
stern fender 227 29
stern frame 222 70-71
stern gallery 218 56
stern light 258 62
stern light, white ~ 286 14
stern loading door 221 31
stern opening 221 55; 226 18
stern port 221 55; 226 18
stern post 218 1
stern ramp 221 88; 258 91
stern towing point 221 53
sternum 17 8
stethoscope 23 35
stetson hat 319 37
steward *Ship* 221 110
steward *Election* 263 10
steward *Cyc. Racing* 290 4
stick 322 35; 323 14, 56
stick, forked ~ 54 13
stick, French ~ 97 12
stick blade 302 32
sticker *Slaughterho.* 94 14

sticker *Music. Instr.* 325 30; 326 9
stick handle 302 31
sticking knife 94 14
sticking paper 260 50-52
sticking plaster 21 7; 22 55
stiffener 215 53
stiffening 101 37
stifle 72 33
stifle joint 72 33
stigma *Soft Fruit* 58 41
stigma *Drupes & Nuts* 59 16
stigma *Articulates* 358 32
stigma *Bot.* 370 56
stile *Roof & Boilerr.* 38 16
stile *Household* 50 36
stile *Carp.* 120 25
stile *Roof* 121 40
stiletto 102 12
stiletto beard 34 13
stiletto heel 101 28
stillhunting 86 1-8
stilling basin 217 61
stilling box 217 61
stilling pool 217 61
still life group 338 27
stilt 359 19
stilt bird 359 19
stilt plover 359 19
stilts 308 49
stimulants 382
sting 77 11
stinging nettle 61 33
stinging organs 77 10-14
sting sheath 77 12
stinkweed 379 8
stipe 381 18
stipple paint 129 53
stippler 129 18
stippling roller 129 13
stipule 57 5; 58 48; 371 73
stirrer *Dairy.* 76 43
stirrer *Paperm.* 172 47
stirrer *Chem.* 349 18
stirrup *Horse* 71 43
stirrup *Bldg. Site* 119 70
stirrup iron 71 43
stirrup leather 71 42
stitch, flat ~ 102 10
stitch, knotted ~ 102 13
stitch, ornamental ~ 102 3
stitch, overcast ~ 102 8
stitch, Russian ~ 102 9
stitching 183 8, 34
stitching, decorative ~ 31 5
stitching machine 100 21
stitching wire feed mechanism 184 18
stock *Plant Propagn.* 54 33
stock *Hunt.* 87 3,4,6,13
stock *Mills* 91 2
stock *Joiner* 132 24
stock *Paperm.* 173 1, 2-10
stock *Stock Exch.* 251 1-10
stock *Stock Exch.* 251 11-19
stock, round ~ 139 1
stock, square ~ 143 9
stockbroker, sworn ~ 251 4
stock certificate 251 11
stock chest 172 85; 173 1
stock cube 98 26
stock exchange 251 1-10
stock exchange agent 251 7
stock exchange attendant 251 9
stocking 318 32
stocking, knee-high ~ 32 9
stockings pack 99 26
stockjobber 251 6
stock ledger 251 14
stock list 250 8
stock preparation plant 172 79-86
stocks 222 11-26

stock saddle 71 37-44
stogy 101 39
stoker, travelling-grate ~ 152 3
stola 355 9
stole, fur ~ 318 30
stollen 97 11
stomach *Man* 16 35-37; 20 13, 41-42
stomach *Bees* 77 16
stomiatid 369 10, 13
stone *Agr.* 63 9
stone *Mills* 91 21
stone *Clocks* 110 33
stone *Quarry* 158 8
stone *Swim.* 281 22
stone *Sculpt. Studio* 339 5
stone *Shrubs etc.* 374 12
stone, crushed ~ 158 24
stone, dressed ~ 158 30
stone, lower ~ 91 23
Stone Age idol 328 8
stone block 339 5
stone catcher 64 9
stone chippings 158 23
stonecrop 51 7; 61 17; 375 21
stone-crushing plant 158 18
stone-dressing device 172 70
stone fruit 59 41, 43, 49; 370 99
stone lithography 340 25-26
stone marten 367 14
stonemason 158 34
stonemason's tools 158 35-38
stone pine 372 55
stones, faceted ~ 36 42-71
stone spreader 200 31
stone trap 64 9
stool 24 14; 27 50; 260 58
stop *Bookbind.* 185 11
stop *Railw.* 214 35
stop *Music. Instr.* 325 44; 326 6
stop *Chem.* 349 37
stop and start lever 163 31
stop and tail light 189 9
stop and tail light unit 188 38
stop bar 133 11
stop bath 116 10
stop board 203 25, 33
stop boards 203 31-32
stop button *Clocks* 110 22
stop button *Office* 249 73
stopclock 238 62
stopclock, electronic ~ 238 31
stopcock, flange-type ~ 130 21
stop-cylinder machine 181 20
stop-cylinder press 181 20
stop fillet 119 62
stop key 243 43
stop knob *Music. Instr.* 325 44; 326 6
stop knob *Chem.* 349 38
stop lever 324 42
stop line 268 50
stop motion 166 43
stop-motion device 168 19
stopper *Overh. Irrign.* 67 36
stopper *Iron & Steel* 147 31
stopper *Music. Instr.* 326 35
stopper *Chem.* 350 44
stopper, ground glass ~ 349 4
stopper, octagonal ~ 349 4
stopping device 168 19
stopping handle 164 6, 32
stopping point 203 25, 31-32
stop plate 157 18
stop rod blade 166 43
stops 342 16-29
stop signal 203 1
stop signal, electric ~ 203 3
stop signals 203 1-6

stop tab 326 39
stop valve *Plumb. etc.* 126 4
stop valve *Gas Weld.* 141 7
stop valve *Water* 269 48
storage area 246 5
storage bin 200 35
storage box *Child. Rm.* 47 2
storage box *D.I.Y.* 134 34, 39
storage cell 77 35
storage chamber 154 71, 76
storage container 130 17
storage cupboard 207 27
storage door 39 6
storage reservoir 217 57
storage shelf 174 10
storage siding 206 50
storage tank *Brew.* 93 13
storage tank *Oil, Petr.* 145 72
storage tank *Paperm.* 172 17, 41, 45, 46
storage tank *Docks* 225 72
storage tank gauge 76 10
storage unit *Dent.* 24 8
storage unit *Composing Rm.* 176 11
storage unit *Inf. Tech.* 242 9
storage vessel 10 46
store area 5 17
storehouse 329 13
storekeeper 98 41
store room 223 57
storey roof 337 2
storm front 287 24
storm-front soaring 287 23
storm lantern 278 29
storm signal 225 35; 280 4
stout 93 26
stove, cylindrical ~ 309 4
stove, tiled ~ 266 34
stove bench 266 36
stove door 309 7
stovepipe 309 5
stovepipe elbow 309 6
stove screen 309 8
stove tile 266 35
stowage 227 26; 228 27
straddle 298 23
straddle jump 298 23
straddle position 296 30
straddle seat 295 18
straight ball 305 17
straightedge *Paperhanger* 128 39
straightedge *Metalwkr.* 140 56
straightedge rule 179 26
straight hang 296 38
straight header 282 12
straight inverted hang 296 37
straight thrust 294 7
strainer *Paperm.* 172 54
strainer *Water* 269 32
strainer, basket ~ 67 12
strainer, rotary ~ 172 23
strain insulator 152 38
strait 14 24
Strait of Gibraltar 14 24
straits bridge 215 57
strake, outside ~ 285 50
stramonium 379 8
stramony 379 8
strampler 29 23
strand 162 54
strand of fruit 384 8
strand of moulds 147 36
strap *Clocks* 110 5
strap *Bldg. Site* 119 60, 65
strap *School* 260 11
strap *Cyc. Racing* 290 22
strap *Winter Sp.* 301 3
strap hinge 140 51
strap support 286 59
stratification 12 1
stratocumulus 8 3

stratosphere 7 8
stratosphere aircraft 7 15
stratovolcano 11 15
stratum, impermeable ~ *Phys. Geog.* 12 28
stratum, impermeable ~ *Water* 269 36
stratum, impervious ~ *Phys. Geog.* 12 28
stratum, impervious ~ *Water* 269 36
stratum, porous ~ 12 29
stratum, water-bearing ~ *Phys. Geog.* 12 22
stratum, water-bearing ~ *Water* 269 2, 38
stratus 8 4
straw *Agr.* 63 34, 36
straw *Livestock* 75 7
straw *Basketm.* 136 30
straw *Station* 206 23
straw *Restaurant* 266 46
straw baler 63 35
strawberry 58 21
strawberry flan 97 22
strawberry plant 58 16
straw fiddle 324 61
straw hive 77 52
straw press 63 35
straw shaker 64 14
strawwalker 64 14
straw yard system 74 1-17
stream *Phys. Geog.* 13 8
stream *Map* 15 80
stream *Park* 272 45
stream, subglacial ~ 12 52
stream, underground ~ 269 3
streamer 253 9
streamer, paper ~ 306 66
streamlining, integrated ~ 189 44
street 37 61; 198 13
street, cross-section of a ~ 198
street café 268 59
streetcar 197; 268 46
streetcar schedule 268 27
streetcar service 197 13
streetcar stop 268 25
streetcar stop sign 197 36; 268 26
streetcar track 268 23
street cleaner 199 41; 304 8
street cleaning 199
street-cleaning lorry 199 41; 304 8
street corner 198 12
street lamp 37 62; 268 6
street lamp, suspended ~ 268 49
street light 37 62; 268 6
street map 204 15; 268 2
street sign 268 7
street sweeper 199 5; 268 20
stretcher *Fire Brig.* 270 23
stretcher *Rowing* 283 47
stretcher, emergency ~ 21 23
stretcher, wedged ~ 338 20
stretcher bar 202 29
stretch girdle 32 5
stretching 170 46, 55
stretching, final ~ 170 47
stretching, preliminary ~ 170 45
stretching bond 118 59
stretching course 118 63
stretching machine 100 18
streusel cake 97 35
streusel slice 97 43
stridulating apparatus 81 8
stridulating mechanism 81 8
strike *Phys. Geog.* 12 2
strike *Composing Rm.* 175 37
striker *Hunt.* 87 21

striker *Ball Games* 291 15
striker pad 255 47
striking circle 292 16
striking force control 249 10
striking mechanism 325 3
striking of coins 252 40-44
striking surface *Tobacc. etc.* 107 24
striking surface *Ball Games* 293 31
striking weight 110 28; 309 60
string *Roof & Boilerr.* 38 26
string *Basketm.* 136 28
string *Sports* 305 59
string *Music. Instr.* 322 44, 55; 323 9, 61; 325 7
string, catgut ~ 324 6, 14
string, chalked ~ 128 45
string, fretted ~ 324 24
string, gut ~ 324 6, 14
string, nylon ~ 324 14
string, open ~ 324 25
string, outer ~ 123 44
string, stopped ~ 324 24
string, unfretted ~ 324 25
string, wreathed ~ 123 49
string briefs 32 23
string course 335 52
stringed instruments 323 1-27; 324 1-31
stringer *Roof & Boilerr.* 38 26
stringer *Shipbuild.* 222 50
stringer *Aircraft* 230 47, 57
stringer *Sailing* 285 55
stringer, outer ~ 123 44
string fastener 324 4
string holder 324 4, 13
strings 293 31
string vest 32 22
strip 148 66-75
stripe, magnetic ~ 117 82
striped hyena 368 1
strip flooring 123 62
stripper *Paperhanger* 128 1, 9
stripper *Nightclub* 318 27
stripping 89 11
stripping knife 128 15; 134 37
stripping table 179 23
strip steel 143 11
striptease act 318 27-32
striptease artist 318 27
striptease number 318 27-32
strip window 37 86
strobile 376 19
stroke *Rowing* 283 12
stroke *Music. Not.* 320 6
stroke, plain ~ 277 2
strokes 136 1-4
stroller 28 37
strong beer 93 26
strong man 308 27
strong room 250 11
structural parts of ship 222 44-61
structural system, Gothic ~ 335 27-35
structure, geological ~ 154 57-68
structure, longitudinal ~ 222 44-56
structures, molecular ~ 1 9-14
strut *Bldg. Site* 119 63, 67
strut *Carp.* 120 27, 54
strut *Roof* 121 58, 69, 82
strut *Ship* 223 61
strut *Aircraft* 229 11
strut *Rowing* 283 46
strut *Winter Sp.* 303 5
strut, diagonal ~ *Bldg. Site* 118 88
strut, diagonal ~ *Bridges* 215 4
stub 84 14

stub axle 192 78
stubble beard 34 23
stubble field 63 33
stub wing 232 3
stud *Carp.* 120 25
stud *Roof* 121 40
stud *Mach. Parts etc.* 143 22
stud, ornamental ~ 253 8
stud, rubber ~ 187 84
stud, screw-in ~ 291 28
student 262 9, 10
student input device 242 4
student response device 242 4
studio *Broadcast.* 238 18
studio *Art. Studio* 338 1-43
studio, artist's ~ 338
studio, sculptor's ~ 339
studio apartment 37 74
studio complex 310 1-13
studio easel 338 3
studio electrician 310 37
studio flat 37 74
studio lot 310 1
studio microphone *Broadcast.* 238 34
studio microphone *Films* 310 31
studio skylight 338 1
studio table 238 29
studio window 238 38
study in oils 338 36
study step counter 242 5
stuff 173 1, 2-10
stuff box 173 11
stuff chest 172 85, 86; 173 1, 13
stuffing box *Oil, Petr.* 145 26
stuffing box *Railw.* 210 33
stuffing box *Ship* 223 64
stuff preparation plant 172 79-86
stump 84 14
stump of tooth 24 27
stunner, electric ~ 94 7
stunning device 94 3
stupa 337 21, 28
Stuttgart Planetarium 5 17-28
sty 62 8
style 58 42; 59 15; 68 34; 370 55; 373 5; 378 5
style jump 288 50-51
styling scissors 106 34
stylobate 334 32
stylus 341 25
stylus, conical ~ 241 26
stylus, elliptical ~ 241 26
stylus, steel ~ 341 21
stylus force control 241 24
stylus pressure control 241 24
sub-base course, bituminous ~ 198 2
sub-base course, gravel ~ 200 60
sub-base course, hardcore ~ 200 60
subcontra octave 321 42
sub-drainage 200 61
subfloor 123 38, 73
subgrade grader 201 1
subheading 342 41
submarine 258 64
substation, outdoor ~ 152 29-35
substitute 291 54; 292 39
substitute flags 253 30-32
substitute signal 203 6
substructure *Oil, Petr.* 145 2
substructure *Offshore Drill.* 146 38
subtitle 185 47
subtracting 344 24
subtraction 344 24
subtrahend 344 24

succory 57 40; 376 25
sucker *House Insects etc.* 81 37
sucker *Optcn.* 111 23
sucker *Invertebr.* 357 21
sucker rod 145 25
sucking organ 358 17
suction 162 25, 28, 36
suction apparatus *Dent.* 24 11
suction apparatus *Poultry Farm* 74 41
suction box *Poultry Farm* 74 41
suction box *Cotton Spin.* 164 44
suction box *Paperm.* 173 15
suction control 50 72
suction control, fingertip ~ 50 74
suction control, sliding ~ 50 74
suction dredger 216 59
suction electrode 23 29
suction feeder 180 72
suction head 217 51
suction hose *Household* 50 75
suction hose *Fire Brig.* 270 67
suction hose, soft ~ 270 30
suction pipe *Roof & Boilerr.* 38 55
suction pipe *Docks* 226 32
suction pipe *Water* 269 5, 14, 41
suction pipe *Theatre* 316 52
suction pipe, trailing ~ 216 59
suction port 199 43
suction pump 216 62
suction roll 173 16
suction slot 168 43
suction tube 10 37
sugar 98 53-55
sugar, confectioner's ~ 98 54
sugar, refined ~ 98 55
sugar beet 68 44
sugar beet eelworm 80 51
sugar bowl 44 32; 265 20
sugar cane 382 52
sugar loaf 99 64
suit 33 1
suit, asbestos ~ 270 46
suit, casual ~ 33 17
suit, denim ~ 31 58; 33 20
suit, extra-vehicular ~ 6 18-27
suit, jersey ~ 29 17
suit, men's ~ 33 1
suit, one-piece ~ 29 17
suit, quilted ~ 29 38
suit, single-breasted ~ 33 1
suit, two-piece ~ 29 12
suitcase 194 19; 204 6; 205 7
suitcase, light ~ 267 15
suitcase, lightweight ~ 267 15
suite, upholstered ~ 42 21-26
suiting 104 3
suits 276 38-45
suits, German ~ 276 42-45
suit trousers 33 3
sulfate *see* sulphate
sulfide *see* sulphide
sulfur *see* sulphur
sulfuric *see* sulphuric
sulky 289 24
sulphate pulp mill 172 1-52
sulphur 351 23
sulphur-crested cockatoo 363 1
sulphuric acid 170 23, 24
sulphuric acid, production of ~ 156 34
sulphuric acid supply 156 33
sultana 98 8
sum 344 23
Sumatra cigar 107 2

summer 121 67
summer beam 121 67
summer blouse 31 22
summer coat 31 20
summer dike 216 48
summer dress 31 9
summerhouse 52 14
summer quarters 356 11
summer slacks 31 52
summer solstice 3 8
summer wear 31
summit 12 40
sump *Coal* 144 47
sump *Intern. Combust. Eng.*
190 41
sump filter 192 18
sun 4 10-21, 29, 36-41, 42
sun bather 281 12
sunbathing area *Dwellings* 37
46
sunbathing area *Spa* 274 12
sunbathing area *Swim.* 281
11; 282 4
sun bed 281 5
sun blind 37 71
sun canopy 274 14
sun deck 223 22
sundew 377 14
sundial 110 30
sun disc, winged ~ 333 12
sundress, child's ~ 29 13
sun filter 6 22
sunflower 51 35; 52 7; 69 20
sunflower oil 98 24
sunglasses 6 19; 111 6; 301 19
sunglass pocket 6 19
sun hat 29 16; 35 37
sunlight 155 18
sun lounge 37 70
sun parlor 37 70
sun ray lamp 281 13
sun roof 37 75
sunroof, steel ~ 193 24
sun rose 377 20
sun sensor 10 69
sunshade *Dwellings* 37 48, 71
sunshade *Town* 268 61
sunshade *Park* 272 58
sunshade *Films* 313 3
sun spectacles 111 6
sunspot 4 37, 38
sun terrace 37 75
supatap 126 35
super *Bees* 77 45
super *Theatre* 316 39
Super-calender 173 36
supercilium 19 38
super grade gasoline 145 55
super grade petrol 145 55
superheater 152 9
supermarket 99 1-96
supernumerary 316 39
superstructure *Weaving* 165 6
superstructure *Ship* 221 10, 69
superstructure, aft ~ 258 22
superstructure, compact ~
221 33
superstructure, forward ~ 259
45
superstructure deck 258 10
superstructures 258 10-28
Super-Vee racing car 290 37
supplementary angle 346 14
supply pipe *Butch.* 96 50
supply pipe *Plumb. etc.* 126 9
supply sprocket 312 26
supply table 74 51
supply vessel 221 32
support *Plant Propagn.* 54 33
support *Roof* 121 83
support *Knitting* 167 38
support *Offset Platem.* 179 20
support *Shipbuild.* 222 27

support *Circus* 307 29, 45
support, adjustable ~ 67 22
support, intermediate ~ 214
29, 76
support, single-pylon ~ 214
23
support, three-point ~ 349 28
support, tubular steel ~ 214 78
support cable 2 30
supporters 254 15-16
support guide rail 214 79
supporting cable 214 27, 38,
41, 44
supporting cable anchorage
214 59
supporting cable brake 214 71
supporting cable guide 214 58
supporting cable guide rail
214 79
supporting insulator 153 54
supporting pulley 163 46
supporting structure 337 9
supporting wall 121 77
support insulator 153 54
support roll 270 50
support truss 214 80
suppressor 190 35
surcoat 355 25
surf 13 27
surface, asphalt ~ 200 58
surface, bituminous ~ 198 5
surface, curved ~ 347 40
surface, flat ~ 111 39
surface, hatched ~ 151 29
surface, icy ~ 304 19
surface, lunar ~ 6 13
surface, nap ~ 168 31
surface, plane ~ 347 31
surface, raised ~ 168 31
surface, special ~ 111 40, 41,
42
surface boundary layer 7 7
surface chart 9 1-39
surface condenser 152 24
surface finisher 200 43
surface-finish microscope
112 37
surface hydrant 270 35
surface not to be machined
151 20
surfaces, plane ~ 346 24-58
surface skimmers 286 38-44
surface synoptic chart 9 1-39
surface-to-air missile
launcher 259 50
surface-to-air rocket
launcher 259 50
surface to be machined 151 21
surface to be superfinished
151 22
surface wave 11 36
surfacing 111 36
surfboard 279 1, 2; 280 15;
284 5
surfboarder 279 5; 280 14
surfer 279 5; 280 14
surfing 279 1-6; 280 13
surf riding 279 1-6; 280 13
surge baffle system 235 53
surge diverter 152 35
surgery 22 32-74
surge tank 217 40
surgical instruments 26 40-53
surgical unit 26 1-54
sur le cou-de-pied 314 14
surroyal 88 9
survey illumination 112 52
surveying 14 46-62
surveying, geodetic ~ 14
46-62
surveying level 14 48
surveyor's level 14 48
suspect 264 32

suspender *Underwear etc.* 32
6
suspender *Bridges* 215 41
suspender *Nightclub* 318 28
suspenders 29 26, 34; 32 30;
33 45
suspension 168 16
suspension, steel and rubber
~ 207 4
suspension and haulage cable
214 21
suspension arm, lower ~ 192
84
suspension bridge 215 39
suspension bridge, primitive
~ 215 15
suspension cable *Railw.* 214
27, 38, 41, 44
suspension cable *Bridges* 215
40
suspension cable anchorage
Railw. 214 59
suspension cable anchorage
Bridges 215 43
suspension cable bearing 214
33
suspension cable brake 214 71
suspension cable guide 214 58
suspension cable guide rail
214 79
suspension damper 192 76
suspension file 248 3
suspension file system 248 2
suspension gear 214 54
suspension gear bolt 214 72
suspension line 288 40
suspension line, double-cable
~ 214 25, 30
suspension line gondola 214
52
suspension lines, single-cable
~ 214 15-24
suspension line support 214
76
suspension rope 215 17
suspension spring 192 74
sustaining pedal 325 8
suture material 22 56; 26 21
swab 137 3
swab dispenser 22 36
swage block *Goldsm. etc.* 108
18
swage block *Blacksm.* 137 17
swage block *Metalwkr.* 140 14
swage head 143 57
swallow 361 20
swallowhole 11 49; 13 71
swallowtail 358 52
swallow-tail twin crystal 351
25
swamp 13 24
Swan *Astron.* 3 23
swan 272 54; 359 16
swan-neck 37 12; 122 30
swan's neck 37 12; 122 30
swarf 149 44
swarm cluster of bees 77 53
swarming net 77 54
swarm of bees 77 53
swath 63 23, 36
swathe 63 23, 36
swather 63 19
swather, rotary ~ 63 26; 64
40-45
swath rake 64 44
swath reaper 63 19
sweater 29 43; 31 51
sweater, short-sleeved ~ 33 32
sweepback, positive ~ 229 21
sweepback, semi-positive ~
229 20
sweeper, mechanical ~ 199 39
sweet 98 75, 80

sweet bread 97 40
sweet calamus 377 22
sweet cherry 59 5
sweet chestnut 384 48
sweet corn 68 31
sweet flag 377 22
sweet gale 373 33
sweet pepper 57 42
sweets 47 31, 32
sweet sedge 377 22
sweet syringa 373 9
sweet william 60 6
swell 325 45
swell organ 326 2, 44
swell pedal, balanced ~ 326 50
swift 359 24
swimming 282
swimming bath 281
swimming bath attendant 281
4; 282 15
swimming belt 282 19
swimming cap 280 29, 44
swimming instruction 282
16-20
swimming instructor 282 16
swimming lane 282 31
swimming pool 223 23; 281
1-9
swimming pool, open-air ~
282 1-32
swimming pool attendant 281
4; 282 15
swimming strokes 282 33-39
swimming teacher 282 16
swimming trunks 280 43
swimsuit 280 42
swing *Gymn.* 297 39
swing *Athletics* 298 30
swing, double ~ 273 39
swing boat 308 41, 42
swing bridge, flat ~ 215 67
swing door 207 18
swing-grippers 180 33
swing pipe 172 10
swing seat 273 40
swing wing 256 9
Swiss chard 57 28
Swiss cheese 99 41
Swiss roll 97 19
Swiss stone pine 372 29
switch *Electr.* 127 7
switch *Garage* 195 4, 12
switch *Aircraft* 230 26
switch, main ~ *Joiner* 132 58
switch, main ~ *Railw.* 211 3,
31
switch, main ~ *Office* 249 37
switch, manually-operated ~
202 16
switch, remote-controlled ~
202 27
switch, rotary ~ *Electr.* 127 18
switch, rotary ~ *Office* 245 28
switchback 308 39
switch blade 202 21
switchboard *Post* 237 17,
22-26
switchboard *Office* 245 13
switch engine 206 43
switcher 206 43
switches, single ~ 203 45-48
switching box 237 25
switching centre 237 25, 41
switching device 269 47
switching system 153 5
switching system, automatic
~ 237 25
switch knob 203 62
switch lever *Mach. Tools* 149
11; 150 35
switch lever *Railw.* 203 55
switch lock 202 28
switch signal 197 38; 202 19

switch signal, electrically
  illuminated ~ 202 33
switch signal lamp 202 19
switch signals 203 45-52
switch stand 202 17
switch tongue 202 21
switch tower 15 24
switch tower, electrically-
  operated ~ 203 61
switch tower, manually-
  operated ~ 203 53
switch yard 206 42
swivel Fish Farm. 89 77
swivel Oil, Petr. 145 10
swivel arm 26 13; 104 27; 105
  26
swivel chair 246 1; 248 25
swivel coupling 50 69 ∤
swivel head 50 60
swivel mechanism 65 73
swivel motor 132 69
swivel nozzle 235 64
swivel saddle 188 21
swivel tap 126 36
swop platform 194 23
sword 319 32
sword antenna 256 28
sword lily 60 11
swordsman 319 25
sword swallower 308 26
S-wrench, adjustable ~ 126
  66
symbol, algebraic ~ 344 9; 345
  5
symbols, geometrical ~ 345
  21-24
symbols, mathematical ~ 345
  15-24
symphisis, pubic ~ 20 65
symphonia 322 25
syncarp 384 63
sync head 243 34
synchro 153 32
synchromesh gearbox, four-
  speed ~ 192 28-47
synchronization 311 37-41
synchronization start 117 65
synchronization unit 117 77
synchronizing cone 192 33
synchronizing filter 311 27
syncing 311 37-41
syncline 12 18
sync pulse cable 313 29
sync start 117 65, 69
sync track 243 33
synthetic fibres 169; 170
syringe 22 54, 65
syringe, hypodermic ~ 24 53
syringe, multi-purpose ~ 24
  10
syrinx 322 2
system, ancillary ~ 211 34
system, planetary ~ 4 42-52
system camera 115 1-105
system-monitoring device
  234 17
system of accessories 115
  43-105
system of coordinates 347 8,
  11
system of flaps 229 37

T

tabard 30 50
tabby weave 171 1
tabernacle 330 42
table Forging 139 20
table Restaurant 266 74
table Playground 273 2
table Music. Instr. 324 3
table Art 336 14, 16

table, auxiliary ~ Blacksm.
  137 14
table, auxiliary ~ Mach. Tools
  150 28
table, director's ~ 316 42
table, flat ~ 36 46, 72, 73, 74
table, producer's ~ 316 42
table, revolving ~ 148 41
table, rotary ~ 145 15
tableau curtain 315 2
table bed 277 15
tablecloth 45 2
table decoration 45 19; 266
  78
table en cabochon 36 47
table en cabochon, antique ~
  36 76
table en cabochon,
  rectangular ~ 36 77
table feed drive 150 34
table lamp 46 24; 246 35
tableland 13 46
table leg 44 2
table linen 271 57
table napkin 45 9
table pedestal 26 6
table piano 325 40
table rise adjustment 133 23
table runner 46 35
table telephone, standard ~
  237 6
table tennis 293 45-55
table tennis ball 273 5; 293 48
table tennis bat 273 4; 293 45
table tennis game 273 1
table tennis net 273 3; 293 53
table tennis player 293 49
table tennis racket 273 4; 293
  45
table tennis table 293 52
table top Dining Rm. 44 3
table top Arc Weld. 142 14
table-top tripod 115 99
table tripod 115 99
tableware 45
tabulator clear key 249 8
tabulator key 249 7
tachograph 210 54
tachometer Weaving 166 2
tachometer Knitting 167 43
tachometer Letterpress 181 54
tachometer Car 191 38
tachometer Railw. 212 22
tachometer Aircraft 230 8
tack 285 25
tacking 285 25-28
tackle 219 1-72; 221 27, 104
taffrail log 224 54
tagetes 60 20
tail Horse 72 38
tail Game 88 19, 47, 49, 58, 62,
  67, 75, 80
tail Roof 122 89
tail Bookbind. 185 58
tail Birds 362 8
tail Mammals 367 29
tail, cruciform ~ 229 28
tail, curly ~ 73 12
tail, docked ~ 70 12
tail, dolphin's ~ 327 25
tail, falcate ~ 73 25
tail, fish's ~ 327 25, 43, 46, 49
tail, horizontal ~ 229 26-27,
  35; 230 61; 257 21
tail, normal ~ 229 23
tail, prehensile ~ 364 35
tail, raised ~ 229 35
tail, serpent's ~ 327 31
tail, tufted ~ 73 6
tail, vertical ~ 229 24-25; 230
  58
tailband 185 42
tail bracing wire 232 4

tailcoat 33 13
tail end shaft 223 60
tail fin Aircraft 229 24; 230
  59; 231 6; 232 7
tail fin Air Force 256 32
tail fin Airsports 288 21
tail fin Fish etc. 364 10
tail fluke 367 29
tailgate 193 16, 20; 195 50
tailings auger 64 21
tailings outlet 64 22
tail line 122 81
tail loading gate 232 25
tail margin 185 58
tail of kite 273 43
tailor 104 22; 271 37
tailor's chalk 271 39
tailor seat 295 11
tailpiece 323 7
tailpin 323 22
tailplane 229 26; 230 62; 256
  31; 288 23
tailpole 91 32
tail propeller 232 28
tail rotor 232 14; 264 4
tails 33 13
tail shaft 223 60
tail shapes 229 23-36
tail skid 256 23
tail slide 288 5
tail sting 358 43
tailstock Turner 135 7
tailstock Mach. Tools 149 29;
  150 5
tailstock Photomech. Reprod.
  177 62
tailstock barrel 149 27
tailstock barrel adjusting
  handwheel 149 30
tailstock barrel clamp lever
  149 28
tailstock centre 149 26
tail unit, cruciform ~ 229 28
tail unit, double ~ 229 32, 34
tail unit, normal ~ 229 23
tail unit, triple ~ 229 36
tail unit shapes 229 23-36
tail vice 132 37
tail wheel 256 27
take-down weight 167 32
take number 310 35
take-off 298 26, 37
take-off, balloon ~ 288 84
take-off board 298 38
take-off stand 165 41
taker-in 163 53
take-up reel 117 80
take-up spindle 312 37
take-up spool Photog. 115 25
take-up spool Cine Film 117
  32, 80
take-up sprocket 312 27
taking lens 313 2
talkback equipment 238 64
talkback microphone 238 10,
  53
talkback microphone,
  producer's ~ 238 39
talkback speaker 238 8, 52
talkback system 238 64
talk button 242 24
talk key 242 24
talon Stock Exch. 251 19
talon Birds 362 7
talus 11 47; 12 45
tambour door 245 5
tambourine Disco 317 27
tambourine Music. Instr. 324
  45
tamer 307 52
tamper 200 26; 201 13
tamping beam 200 32; 201 2
tandem 186 50

tandem kayak 283 5
tang 45 52, 60
tangent Music. Instr. 322 43
tangent Maths. 346 32, 48
tangent screw 14 56
tangerine 384 23
tank Cooper 130 1
tank Lorries etc. 194 30
tank Army 255 80
tank, bottom ~ 222 38
tank, concrete ~ 310 11
tank, side ~ 222 37
tank, spherical ~ 145 73; 221
  36
tank bottom valve 38 49
tank car 213 31
tank construction engineer
  130
tanker Docks 225 73
tanker Airport 233 22
tanker terminal 145 74
tank farm 225 61
tank for sterilized milk 76 16
tank furnace 162 1
tank inlet 38 47
tank locomotive 210 65
tank margin plate 222 51
tank reel 116 2
tank spiral, multi-unit ~ 116
  4
tank top 222 54
tank top plating 222 54
tank vent 234 44
tank wagon 213 31
tansy 380 9
tap Doc. 23 49
tap Metalwkr. 140 60
tap Power Plant 153 18
tap Spa 274 17
tap Disco 317 8
tap Chem. 349 5, 22; 350 44,
  53
tap, outside ~ 37 41
tap bar 148 9
tap changer 211 10
tap changer driving
  mechanism 211 13
tape Ball Games 293 73
tape Music. Instr. 325 36
tape, adhesive ~ 98 47; 134
  38; 247 29
tape, magnetic ~ 25 46
tape, varnished-cambric ~
  153 46
tape cassette 117 76
tape counter 241 64; 243 9
tape deflector roller 241 60
tape feed 243 29
tape guide 243 22
tape measure 103 2; 271 38
tape punch 176 5
taper, wax ~ 77 65
tape recorder 117 70; 317 21;
  318 17
tape recorder, four-track ~
  242 13
tape recorder, portable ~ 309
  37
tape recorder, two-track ~
  242 12
tape reel, open ~ 241 57
taper thread, female ~ 126 47
tape speed selector 241 62
tapestry wallpaper 128 18
tape threading indicator light
  243 14
tape wire 325 35
tapeworm 81 35
tap hole 147 50
tapir 366 26
tappet 166 57
tappet shaft 166 56
tapping 153 18

tapping a spring 269 24-39
tapping bar 148 9
tapping hole 147 50
tapping spout 148 3
taproot, swollen ~ 370 79
tap wrench 140 30
tar 170 4
tar and bitumen heater 200 46
target *Inf. Tech.* 242 84
target *Sports* 305 30, 32, 66, 77
target, bobbing ~ 305 33, 48
target, turning ~ 305 33, 48
target archery 305 52-66
target areas 294 51-53
target cross 288 56
target jack 305 22
target rectangle 292 34
targets 305 30-33
tar-spraying machine 200 46
tar storage tank 200 47
tarsus *Man* 17 26
tarsus *Birds* 362 4
tartlet 97 20
tasse 329 49
tassel *Headgear* 35 24
tassel *Arable Crops* 68 35
tassel *Hist. Cost.* 355 23
tasset 329 49
tatting 102 19
tatting shuttle 102 20
tattoo 306 44
tau cross 332 59
Taurus 3 25; 4 54
taxi 268 64
taxicab 268 64
taxi rank 268 63, 66
'taxis' 233 32
taxi sign 268 65
taxi stand 268 63, 66
taxi telephone 268 67
taxiway 233 2
T-cut 54 32
tea *Grocer* 98 65-68
tea *Supermkt.* 99 68-70
tea *Trop. Plants* 382 9
tea bag 98 68
teacher 260 21
teaching equipment 242; 242 45-84
teaching laser 242 81
teaching machine 242 1
teaching material 261 27
tea dance 267 44-46
tea leaf 382 9
team of oxen 63 16
tea packet 99 69
tea plant 382 7
tea plate 39 34
tear bag 88 14
tear-off edge 247 30
tea room 265 1-26
teat *Infant Care etc.* 28 20
teat *Livestock* 75 19
teat cup 75 30
teat cup cluster 75 26
tea tree 382 7
technical drawing 151 16
technical laboratory 310 9
Teclu burner 350 4
tectogenis 12 4-20
tedder, rotary ~ 63 24; 64 46-58
teddy bear 28 46; 273 26; 309 12
teddy bear, rocking ~ 48 30
tee 126 44, 47
tee *Ball Games* 293 90
teeing ground 293 79
tee-iron 143 3
teepee 352 7
tee-square 151 9
teeth 19 16-18
teeth, false ~ 24 25

teeth grinder 157 43, 45
teething ring 28 12
teeth of knock-over bit 167 52
telecobalt unit 2 28
telegraphy 237 30
telemetry antenna 10 70
telephone 22 18; 41 7; 202 48; 238 23; 246 13; 248 9
telephone, public ~ 236 9; 237 1, 3
telephone, toy ~ 47 35
telephone adapter socket 249 67
telephone answering and recording set 22 13
telephone answering device 22 13
telephone book 236 12; 237 5
telephone booth 204 46; 236 8; 237 1; 251 10; 268 56
telephone box 204 46; 236 8; 237 1; 251 10; 268 56
telephone cable 198 15
telephone cable pipeline 198 16
telephone casing 237 15
telephone connection 242 20
telephone cover 237 15
telephone customer 237 2
telephone directory 236 12; 237 5
telephone directory rack 236 10
'telephone - emergency calls only' 233 40
telephone exchange 237 27-41
telephone exchange, internal ~ 245 13
telephone index 22 21
telephone instruments 237 6-26
telephone kiosk 204 46; 236 8; 237 1; 251 10; 268 56
telephone line, customers' ~ 198 20
telephone line, subscribers' ~ 198 20
telephone list, internal ~ 245 17
telephone number 237 38
telephone receiver 237 7; 246 16
telephones 237 6-26
telephone service 237 41
telephone subscriber 237 2
telephone switchboard panel 238 14
telephone user 237 2
telephoto lens 117 47
teleprinter 176 31; 237 31, 61, 66; 238 12
telescope 14 60; 42 15; 224 8
telescope, gimbal-mounted ~ 235 68
telescope, monocular ~ 111 18
telescope, reflecting ~ 113 1
telescope, refracting ~ 113 16
telescope, surveyor's ~ 14 48
telescope magnifier 113 38
telescope mountings 113 16-25
telescope mounts 113 16-25
telescope sight 87 29; 255 28; 305 49
Teletype 176 31
teletypewriter 237 31
television 238; 239
television cabinet 240 2
television camera 10 67; 112 36; 154 78; 240 26
television disc system 243 37-45

television engineering 240
television mast 15 33
television OB van 239 1-15
television post-sync studio 238 27-53
television programmes 342 64
television receiver 242 28
television receiver, domestic ~ 243 6
television receiving aerial 239 4, 5
television reception aerial 239 4, 5
television set 42 8; 46 14; 242 28
television sound 242 27
television tube 240 3
telex link 237 65
telex message 237 69
telex service 237 41
telex tape 237 68
Telford base 200 60
teller 250 2
tempera 338 17
temperature 9 8
temperature gauge 179 4
temperature gauge, distant-reading ~ 210 48
temperature graph 7 37
temperature regulation flap 10 65
temperature regulator 191 84
temperature scale 7 36
temperature selector 50 8
tempest 284 54
template 126 83
template, circular ~ 141 35
temple *Man* 16 6
temple *Weaving* 166 13
temple *Art* 337 7
temple, Doric ~ 334 1
temple, Etruscan ~ 334 49
temple, funerary ~ 333 7
temple buildings 337 25
temple tower 333 32; 337 1, 26
temple wall 334 6
temporalis 19 3
tender *Railw.* 210 38
tender *Warships* 258 92
tender platform 210 2
tendo calcanaeus 18 48
tendril 57 4
tendril, thorny ~ 58 30
tennis 293 1-42
tennis ball 293 28
tennis court 293 1
tennis net 293 13
tennis player 293 16
tennis racket 41 13; 293 29
tennis shoe 101 36
tenon saw 132 44
tenor clef 320 11
tenor horn 323 39
tenor trombone 323 46
tenor viol 322 23
tenpin bowling 305 14-20
tens 344 3
tension and slub-catching device 165 13
tension bar 167 49
tension cable, inclined ~ 215 47
tension cable pulley 214 43
tension compensator 165 51
tension equalizer 165 51
tension hoop 324 56
tensioning device *Agr. Mach.* 64 94
tensioning device *Railw.* 208 18
tensioning lever 208 18
tensioning screw 323 53

tension roller *Joiner* 133 13
tension roller *Letterpress* 181 45
tension weight *Knitting* 167 50
tension weight *Railw.* 214 41, 42
tension weight shaft 214 40
tent 80 7
tent, four-pole ~ 307 1
tentacle 357 16, 31
tenter 165 54; 168 21
tenter clip 168 24
tenter pin 168 24
tent peg 278 24
tent pole 278 38; 307 2; 352 8
tent prop 307 13
tenuto 321 30
tepee 352 7
teres major 18 55
teres minor 18 54
tergites 358 31
term 344 23
terminal *Docks* 226 16
terminal *Airport* 233 15
terminal box 211 16
termination of speed restriction 203 40
tern 359 11
terrace 37 36
terracette 13 64
terrarium 356 14
terrestrial meridian 14 4
terrier 70 15, 16, 17, 18, 27, 39
terry towel 49 9
tessellation 338 37
tessera 338 39
tesseral crystal system 351 1-17
test equipment 195 17
testicle, right ~ 20 72
testing and control station 237 40
testing board 237 29
testing desk 237 29
testing device for waterproof watches 109 26
testing kit 138 14
testis 20 72
test meter, universal ~ 127 41
test oil and gas separator 146 10
test separator 146 10
test tube 350 34
test tube rack 173 8; 261 31; 350 35
tether 75 15-16
tetradrachm 252 1
tetragonal crystal system 351 18-19
tetrahedrite 351 1
tetrahedron 351 1
text 237 68
textbook 261 28
thalamus 370 53
thallus 378 49
Thaumatolampas diadema 369 4
T-head bolt 202 10
theater *see* theatre
theatergoer 315 8
theatre *Astron.* 5 26
theatre *Theatre* 315; 316
theatre, Greek ~ 334 44
theatre, open-air ~ 272 6
theatregoer 315 8
theatre projector 312 24
theatre seat 315 20
theatre ticket 315 11
thé dansant 267 44-46
theodolite 14 52-62
theorbo 324 1

thermal **287** 21
thermal protection shield **234** 5, 20
thermal soaring **287** 20
thermograph **10** 19, 51
thermometer *Meteorol. Instr.* **10** 25
thermometer *Infant Care etc.* **28** 29
thermometer *Text. Finish.* **168** 27
thermometer *Swim.* **281** 24
thermometer, ladle-type ~ **92** 53
thermometers **10** 53-54
thermometer screen **10** 49
thermometer shelter **10** 49
thermometric scale **7** 36
thermoplastic **130** 15
Thermos jug **40** 5
thermo time switch **190** 63
thickener **172** 24, 42, 44, 48, 62
thicknesser **132** 45
thicknessing machine **132** 45
thicknessing table **132** 46
thief **308** 16
thigh **16** 49; **17** 22
thigh bone **17** 22
thill **186** 19, 30
thiller **186** 28
thill horse **186** 28
thimble, graduated ~ **149** 64
thinner *Painter* **129** 16
thinner *Art. Studio* **338** 13
thinning **84** 37
thinning razor **105** 9; **106** 41
thinnings, small-sized ~ **84** 37
thinning scissors **105** 8; **106** 33
thinning shears **105** 8; **106** 33
third base **292** 47
third man **300** 27
thirty-second note **320** 18
thirty-second rest **320** 26
thistle **61** 32
Thomas converter **147** 55-69
thoracic shield **82** 4; **358** 29
thorax *Man* **16** 28-30; **17** 8-11
thorax *Articulates* **358** 29-30
thorn *Gdn. Flowers* **60** 18
thorn *Spa* **274** 2
thorn *Shrubs etc.* **374** 30
thorn apple **379** 8
thorn house *Map* **15** 32
thorn house *Spa* **274** 1
thousands **344** 3
thread *Overh. Irrign.* **67** 38
thread *Mach. Parts etc.* **143** 16, 68
thread *Glass Prod.* **162** 54
thread *Cotton Spin.* **164** 53
thread *Weaving* **165** 21
thread *Knitting* **167** 17, 36
thread *Bookbind.* **183** 11
thread, coarse ~ **149** 4
thread, female ~ **126** 41, 45
thread, glass ~ **162** 56, 57
thread, male ~ **126** 38, 51
thread, metal ~ **102** 30
thread, mycelial ~ **381** 2
thread, normal ~ **149** 4
thread, sleeved ~ **162** 57
thread chaser **135** 14
thread clearer **165** 20
thread container **22** 61
thread cop **185** 18
thread-cutting machine **125** 27; **126** 86
thread guide *Shoem.* **100** 30
thread guide *Knitting* **167** 3, 54, 64

thread head **187** 75
threading draft **171** 5
threading key **127** 30
thread interlacing **171** 26
thread pitch **149** 9
thread spool **185** 18
thread tapper **108** 15
threadworm **80** 51
three **302** 13
three-day event **289** 16-19
three-decker **218** 51-60
three-eight time **320** 36
three-four time **320** 37
three-masters **220** 18-27
three-phase generator **153** 26
three-phase plug **127** 14
three-two time **320** 38
threshing drum **64** 12
throat *Man* **16** 19; **19** 14-37, 24
throat *Horse* **72** 16
throat *Forestry* **84** 28
throatlash **71** 11; **72** 16
throatlatch **71** 11; **72** 16
throat piece **329** 42
throstle **361** 16
throttle control **230** 30; **288** 15
throttle lever **230** 30; **288** 15
throttle twist grip **188** 30; **189** 29
throttle valve *Hosp.* **27** 43
throttle valve *Car* **192** 9
through-the-lens reflex finder **117** 44
thrower **161** 9
throw-in **291** 53
throwing act **307** 43
throwing knife **354** 15
throwing ring **308** 47
throwing spear **328** 2
throwing stick **352** 40
thrush **360** 3
thrushes **361** 13-17
thrush nightingale **361** 17
thrust bearing **221** 29
thrust block **223** 67; **259** 60
thrust lever **257** 9
thrust mount, lower ~ **235** 6
thrust mount, upper ~ **235** 5
thrust nozzle **234** 35; **235** 37
thrust nozzle fuel tank **235** 45
thrust structure **234** 21
thrust vector control system **235** 43
thrust washer **190** 56
thrust weapon **294** 11, 36, 37
thuja **372** 39
thumb **19** 64
thumb hold **323** 45
thumb hole **305** 47
thumb nut **119** 75
thumb piston **326** 46
thundercloud **7** 2
thunderstorm **9** 38
thurible **332** 38
thurible bowl **332** 41
thurible chain **332** 39
thurible cover **332** 40
thwart **278** 17; **283** 28
thymele **334** 48
tiara, papal ~ **254** 37
Tibetan **353** 27
tibia **17** 25
tibialis anterior **18** 47
tick *Bedrm.* **43** 13
tick *Articulates* **358** 44
tick, drill ~ **43** 10
tick bean **69** 15
ticket **204** 36
ticket agent **204** 39
ticket-cancelling machine **197** 16

ticket clerk **204** 39
ticket counter **197** 33; **204** 35
ticket machine **268** 28
ticket office **204** 34
ticket printer, hand-operated ~ **204** 41
ticket-printing machine **204** 40
ticket-stamping machine **204** 40
tidal power plant **155** 37
tide level indicator **225** 37
tidemark **13** 35
tide table **280** 7
tie *Ladies' Wear* **30** 46
tie *Underwear etc.* **32** 41
tie *Bldg. Site* **119** 39
tie *Roof* **121** 59
tie *Station* **205** 60
tie *Music. Not.* **321** 24
tie, concrete ~ **202** 37
tie, coupled ~ **202** 14, 38
tie, diagonal ~ **121** 30
tie, double ~ **121** 50
tie, simple ~ **121** 49
tie, steel ~ **202** 36
tie beam **121** 53
tie belt **29** 55; **31** 19
tie fastening **101** 21
tiepin **36** 22
tier, lower ~ **228** 24
tier, upper ~ **228** 23
tierce engagement **294** 48
tiercel **86** 46
tie rod **65** 47
tier of oars **218** 12
tie shoe **101** 31
tie tube **119** 49
tie-up **171** 22, 23
tie-up of shafts **171** 9
tiger **307** 56; **368** 5
tightening screw **293** 33
tightrope **307** 41
tightrope dancer **307** 40
tights **29** 42; **32** 12
tilbury **186** 44
tilde **342** 35
tile *Bathrm. etc.* **49** 19
tile *Games* **276** 34
tile, flat interlocking ~ **122** 60
tile, interlocking ~ **122** 59
tile, plain ~ **122** 6, 46
tile beard **34** 16
tile cutter **122** 33
tile hammer **122** 20
tile roofings **122** 45-60
tiles **122** 45-60
tiling batten **122** 17
till **207** 86; **271** 5
till, electric ~ **271** 2
tillage **69** 1-28
tiller **218** 13; **284** 32; **286** 24
tiller extension **284** 31
tillering **68** 5
tilt **329** 71
tilt block **12** 9
tilting armour **329** 76
tilting device **147** 44, 59
tilting helmet **254** 4; **329** 77
tilting lance **329** 81
tilting shield **329** 79
tilting table **133** 17
tilting target **329** 79
tilt wing **232** 27
timbale **324** 57
timber **85** 42
timber, end-grained ~ **120** 92
timber, halved ~ **120** 88
timber, long ~ **120** 2
timber, round ~ **120** 35; **157** 30
timber, sawn ~ **157** 22
timber, small ~ **84** 37

timber, squared ~ **120** 10; **157** 36
timber, stacked ~ **84** 15
timber, standing ~ **84** 4
timber, undressed ~ **120** 83
timber, yarded ~ **84** 15
timber cutting **84** 15-37
timber dog **121** 97
timberjack **84** 18
timber joints **121** 84-98
timber planking **285** 50-57
time *Music. Not.* **320** 28-42
time *Maths.* **345** 7
time ball **280** 5
time indicator **289** 40
timekeeper **282** 24; **299** 47
timer *Doc.* **23** 40
timer *Hosp.* **27** 35
timer *Kitch.* **39** 21
timer *Watchm.* **109** 35
timer *Photog.* **116** 18
timer *Photograv.* **182** 20
timer *Billiards* **277** 17
timer, synchronous ~ **24** 52
timer switch, built-in ~ **243** 18
time scale *Meteorol. Instr.* **10** 17
time scale *Office* **249** 74
time scale stop **249** 75
time schedule **151** 12
time signatures **320** 28-42
timetable **204** 16, 18
timetable, driver's ~ **210** 52
timetable, official ~ **204** 50
time weight **110** 29; **309** 59
timing machine, electronic ~ **109** 27
timpano **323** 57
tin **129** 7
tin, molten ~ **162** 17
tinctures **254** 24-29
tine *Tablew. etc.* **45** 60
tine *Agr. Impl.* **66** 4
tine *Game* **88** 10, 31
tine bar **64** 53
tinner's snips **125** 1
tip, adjustable ~ **149** 47
tip, controlled ~ **199** 10
tip, cork ~ **107** 13
tip, gold ~ **107** 13
tip, oxide ceramic ~ **149** 47
tip, pointed ~ **253** 10
tip-cart, three-way ~ **62** 18
tip heap **144** 19
tipper **200** 7
tipper, three-way ~ **194** 24
tipper wagon **213** 37
tipping body *Lorries etc.* **194** 25
tipping body *Road Constr.* **200** 8
tipping bucket **214** 34
tipping car **147** 64
tipping cylinder **62** 19
tipping device **147** 44, 59
tipping truck **119** 28
tipping wagon **119** 28
tippler, three-way ~ **92** 34
tip tank **231** 9; **256** 30
tip-up seat **207** 12
tire *see* tyre
tired swimmer grip **21** 38
T-iron **143** 3
tissue, erectile ~ **20** 67
tit **360** 4; **361** 9
titan **327** 37
title block **151** 31
title bout **299** 35-50
title fight **299** 35-50
title page **185** 45
title panel **151** 31
titmouse **360** 4; **361** 9

tjalk 220 6
T-joint 126 44, 47
T-junction joint 126 44, 47
toad 364 23
toadstools 379 10-13
toast 45 34
toaster 40 30
toat 132 18
tobacco *Tobacc. etc.* 107 25
tobacco *Trop. Plants* 382 43
tobacco, raw ~ 83 13
tobacco beetle 81 25
tobacco factory 83 11
tobacco leaf 382 43
tobacco plant 382 40
tobacco pouch 107 43
tobacco presser 107 47
toboggan 303 1, 2, 13
toboggan, junior ~ 303 3
toboggan cap 35 39
toboggan slide 308 40
toe, big ~ 19 52
toe, first ~ 19 52
toe, fourth ~ 19 55
toe, great ~ 19 52
toe, little ~ 19 56
toe, second ~ 19 53
toe, third ~ 19 54
toecap 100 58; 101 16, 40
toecap remover 100 52
toe clip 290 21
toenail 19 57
toe piston 326 48
toe post sandal 101 48
toe stand 295 5
toestrap 284 30
toe unit 301 55
toffee 98 77
toga 355 13
toggle 340 30
toggle action *Letterpress* 181 16
toggle action *Bookbind.* 183 30
toggle fastening 30 66
toggle-joint action 181 16; 183 30
toggle-joint press 183 26
toggle-lever press 183 26
toilet 49 12; 146 29; 207 16, 42, 72; 211 59; 231 31; 278 5
toilet bowl 49 13
toilet cistern 126 14
toilet-cleaning vehicle 233 22
toilet lid 49 14
toilet pan 49 13
toilet paper 49 11
toiletries 99 27-35
toilet roll holder 49 10
toilets 317 31
toilet seat 49 15
toilet water 105 37; 106 9
tomahawk 352 16
tomato 57 12; 99 82
tomato plant 55 44
tomb 331 23; 337 16
tomb, giant's ~ 328 16
tomb, megalithic ~ 328 16
tomb, royal ~ 333 1
tombola 306 11
tombola booth 308 44
tomb recess 331 60
tombstone 331 26
tom cat 73 17
tom-tom 324 48, 49
tondo 339 36
tone 320 51, 53
tone arm 241 21
tone arm balance 241 53
tone arm lift 241 28
tone arm lock 241 27
tone generator 238 51

toner roll 249 41
tongs *Atom 2* 44
tongs *Glass Prod.* 162 44
tongs *Graphic Art* 340 50
tongs, concreter's ~ 119 85
tongs, flat ~ 137 24
tongs, round ~ 137 25
tongue *Man* 17 52; 19 25
tongue *Tablew. etc.* 45 52
tongue *Game* 88 2
tongue *Shoem.* 100 65
tongue *Shoes* 101 32
tongue *Music. Instr.* 322 52; 326 19
tongue, foam rubber ~ 291 24
tongue, forked ~ 327 6
tonsil 19 23
tonsil, palatine ~ 19 23
tonsure 331 57
tool 195 43
tool, stone ~ 328 1
tool bag 187 25
tool bit holder 149 45
tool box *D.I.Y.* 134 35
tool box *Mach. Tools* 150 13
tool box *Railw.* 212 45
tool cabinet 134 1-34
tool case 127 49
tool cupboard 134 1-34
tool grinder 137 18
tool-grinding machine 137 18
tool post 149 21
tool rest 135 5; 149 22
tools 119 77-89
tool shank 149 49
tool shed 37 32; 52 3; 55 1
tool slide 149 22
tool trolley 195 42
tooth *Man* 19 28-37
tooth *Mach. Parts etc.* 143 83
tooth *Composing Rm.* 174 30
tooth *Office* 249 31
tooth, bicuspid ~ 19 18
tooth, canine ~ 19 17
tooth, molar ~ 19 18, 35
tooth, porcelain ~ 24 29
tooth, premolar~ 19 18
toothbrush, electric ~ 49 29
tooth chisel 339 13
toothed 370 45
tooth glass 49 28
toothing, external ~ 143 96
toothing, internal ~ 143 95
toothing, spiral ~ 143 92-93
toothing plane 132 17
tooth mug 49 28
toothpaste box 99 31
toothpick holder 266 23
tooth pulp 19 32
tooth-root elevator 24 48
tooth scaler 24 45
top 12 40; 193 10; 323 24
top, collapsible ~ *Carriages* 186 52
top, collapsible ~ *Car* 193 10
top, convertible ~ 193 10
top, elasticated ~ 32 33
top, fireclay ~ 108 9
top, fixed ~ 186 14
top, folding ~ 194 10
top, hard ~ 193 27
top, humming ~ 309 71
top, leather ~ 35 19
top, marble ~ 265 12
top, shirred ~ 29 15
top clearer 164 22
top gases 145 38
top hat 35 36; 186 25; 289 6
top light, white ~ 286 10
top lighting, incident ~ 112 63
topmark 224 78, 90
topmark buoy 224 80
topmast 223 39

topography, fluvial ~ 13 1-13
topper 64 85
topping 266 54
topping knife 64 87
top rail 221 122
top ring 89 52
top roller, light ~ 164 18
tops 145 38
topsail schooner, three-masted ~ 220 19
top side *Meat* 95 37
top side *Paperm.* 173 31
top slide 149 22, 42
top stroke 277 3
top tube 187 16
torch 127 26
torch lighter 141 27
torcular 26 48
torero 319 21, 25
torii 337 11
torpedo boat 258 69, 75
torpedo housing, underwater ~ 259 36
torpedo tube 258 78; 259 79
torque converter 190 70
torque converter bearing 211 54
torque converter lever 65 34
torque wrench 195 45
torril door 319 11
torsional clamp 287 39
torso 339 7
Torsteel 119 82
torten 97 22-24
tortrix moth 80 9
torus *Art* 334 28, 30
torus *Bot.* 370 53
totalizator 289 35
totalizator window 289 34
tote 289 35
totem 352 2
totem pole 352 1
tote window 289 34
toucan 363 6
touch line 291 9
touch-me-not 377 11
touch-tone button 242 25
touch-tone pad 242 25
toupee wig 355 8
toupet 34 2
touring bicycle 187 1
touring boat 283 26-33
touring cycle 187 1
touring cycle handlebar 187 2
touring kayak 283 61, 70
touring moped 188 24
tourist 272 28
tourist guide 272 27
tournament 329 71
tournament pennon 254 33
tournament saddle 329 87
tourneur 275 3
tourney 329 71
tourniquet, emergency ~ 21 15
tourniquet, surgeon's ~ 26 48
tow 170 57, 58, 59, 60
towage 227
towel 106 25; 281 25
towel, paper ~ 40 1; 106 5
towel rail 49 8
tower *Map* 15 53
tower *Bldg. Site* 119 34
tower *Bridges* 215 42
tower *Airport* 233 17
tower *Gliding* 287 12
tower, central ~ 335 6
tower, lattice steel ~ 152 36
tower, stepped ~ 333 32
tower, terraced ~ 333 32
tower clock 331 7
tower crane 47 39; 119 31
tower platform 329 8

tower roof, pyramidal ~ 335 7
tower slewing crane 119 31
tower spotlight 316 21
tower tomb 333 21
tow hook 227 27
towing 216 27
towing engine *Rivers* 216 29
towing engine *Salvage* 227 7
towing engine *Warships* 258 86
towing gear 227 6, 6-15, 13
towing hawser 216 24; 227 8, 15
towing line 286 47
towing log 224 54
towing machine 227 7; 258 86
towing mast 216 28
towing path 216 30
towing plane 287 2
towing track 216 30
towing vehicle 194 21, 29
towing winch 227 7; 258 86
tow line 216 24; 227 8, 15; 286 47
town 15 51; 268
town banner 218 22
town centre 268
tow path 216 30
tow rope *Rivers* 216 24
tow rope *Salvage* 227 8, 15
tow rope *Gliding* 287 4
tow rope guide 227 9
toy, soft ~ 46 13; 47 6, 7, 41
toy, wooden ~ 260 80
toy duck 28 10
toys 48 21-32
toy shop 47 27
T position 288 62
trace 71 22, 24, 35
trace monitor 25 54
tracer 153 45
tracer element 153 45
tracery 335 39-40
tracery window 335 39-41
trachea 17 50; 20 4
tracing head 141 37
tracing leg 302 2
tracing wheel 129 42
track *Atom 2* 37
track *Hunt.* 86 8
track *Cine Film* 117 82
track *Railw.* 202 1-38
track *Station* 205 59-61
track *Army* 255 87
track *Equest.* 289 23
track *Cyc. Racing* 290 2
track *Winter Sp.* 301 60
track, cinder ~ 298 6
track, indoor ~ 290 1
track, sand ~ 290 24
track, synthetic ~ 298 6
track, unfenced ~ 15 102
track and field events 298
track and signal indicator 203 64
track-clearing vehicle 213 17
track diagram control layout 203 65
track diagram control panel 203 66
tracker action 326 6-16
track format 243 28
trackhound 70 42, 43
track indicator 65 81
track inspection railcar 213 32
track racer 290 2
track rider 290 2
track rider, motor-paced ~ 290 14
track rod 65 47
track-rod ball-joint 192 80
tracksuit 33 27

tracksuit bottoms 33 29
tracksuit top 33 28
trackwalker 202 44
tract 330 57
traction motor 211 6
traction motor blower 211 15
tractive effort indicator 211 26
tractive unit 194 21, 29
tractor 62 38; 64 46; 65 20; 67 17; 85 43; 194 21, 29; 273 55
tractor, narrow-track ~ 78 21
tractor driver 62 39
tractor unit 85 43
trader, itinerant ~ 308 51
trades 9 48, 49
tradesman 98 41
trade winds 9 48, 49
traffic control 264 9
traffic control cuff 268 31
traffic helicopter 264 1
traffic light post 268 53
traffic lights 268 52
traffic patrol 264 9
traffic policeman 268 30
traffic sign 268 66
trail 86 8
trail, scented ~ 289 49
trailer Farm Bldgs. 62 40
trailer Agr. 63 27, 38
trailer Blacksm. 138 10
trailer Lorries etc. 194 22
trailer Station 206 3, 35
trailer Camping 278 52
trailer, collapsible ~ 278 3
trailer, folding ~ 278 3
trailer, tip-up ~ 56 42
trailer frame 138 28
trailering 278
trailer wagon 200 25
trailing arm 191 27; 192 66
trailing cable hanger 133 39
trailing cable support 133 39
trailing edge Sailing 284 45
trailing edge Gliding 287 37
trailing link arm 192 81
trail rope 288 69
train 355 80
train, electric ~ 197
train, interurban ~ 197
train, local ~ 208 1-12
train, short-distance ~ 208 1-12
train, suburban ~ 205 25
train control system, inductive ~ 211 7, 38; 212 14, 38
train deck 221 80
trainee pastry cook 265 6
trainer Shoes 101 35
trainer Circus 307 31
train ferry Map 15 12
train ferry Ship 221 74
train heating generator 212 39
train heating system 212 17, 18
train heating system transformer 212 40
train heating voltage indicator 211 27
training apparatus 299 20-24
training equipment 299 20-24
training ship 258 95
training shoe 101 35
train plate, bottom ~ 110 37
'trains' 233 34
train schedule 204 50
train service, local ~ 208 1-30
trainset 209 1
trainset, experimental ~ 209 23

train set, wooden ~ 47 37; 48 29; 273 27
trajectory 89 36
tram 197; 268 46
tramline 268 23
trammel 125 11
trampoline 282 10; 297 10
tram service 197 13
tram stop 197 35; 268 25
tram stop sign 197 36; 268 26
tram timetable 268 27
transept 335 3
Trans-Europe Express 209 1-22
Trans-Europe Express, electric ~ 205 34
transfer blanket 249 40
transfer cylinder 180 36
transfer drum 180 36
transfer entry 250 25
transfer port 242 57
transformer Clocks 110 8
transformer Power Plant 153 9-18
transformer Railw. 211 10
transformer, high-tension ~ 211 4
transformer, mobile ~ 152 30, 39
transformer, transportable ~ 152 30, 39
transformer connection 153 19
transformer station Brew. 92 21
transformer station Hydr. Eng. 217 46
transformer tank 152 40
transforming section 23 56
transillumination 112 60
transistor, actuating ~ 195 19
Transitional 342 5
'transit passengers' 233 27
transit shed 225 9
transmission 209 18
transmission, multi-speed ~ 65 36
transmission cable 326 53
transmission line 154 16
transmission line, high-voltage ~ 152 32
transmission oil 209 15; 212 36, 43
transmission oil temperature gauge 212 20
transmissometer 10 60
transmitted-light microscope 112 14
transmitter 10 59, 62
transmitting antenna 288 88
transom Dwellings 37 35
transom Ship 221 42
transom Sailing 284 35; 285 49
transom Motorboats etc. 286 26
transom stern 221 42; 258 26; 259 11; 285 48
transparency 242 42
transparency arm 177 44
transparent gage 59 25
transplanting Plant Propagn. 54 5
transplanting Forestry 84 10
transport aircraft, medium-range ~ 256 14
transport and communications aircraft 256 24
transport and rescue helicopter 256 18
transporter, suction ~ 74 49
transporter container-

loading bridge 225 46; 226 2
transporter loading bridge 225 20
transport helicopter 232 21
transport lug 152 48
transport roller Cine Film 117 34
transport roller Joiner 132 72
transport sprocket 115 26
transport vehicle 62 18
transtainer 226 2
transtainer crane 226 2
transversal chicane 301 68
transverse motion 149 17
trap Bathrm. etc. 49 27
trap Hunt. 86 20
trap Plumb. etc. 126 26
trapdoor 38 13
trapercius 18 52
trapeze Sailing 284 12
trapeze Circus 307 6
trapeze artist 307 7
trapezium 346 37
trap opening 316 32
trapper 306 8
trapping 86 19-27, 19
trappings Horse 71 16
trappings Chivalry 329 74
trash bin Doc. 22 70
trash bin Butch. 96 46
trash can 199 3
trash conveyor 64 80
travel agency 271 24
travel centre 204 28
traveler see traveller
traveling see travelling
traveller Cotton Spin. 164 51, 55
traveller Sailing 284 27
Travellers' Aid 204 45
travelling bag 205 10
travelling box 77 44
traverse 152 37
traversing handle 255 48
trawler 90 11; 221 86
trawl fishing 90 11-23
trawling 90 11-23
trawl warp 90 12
tray Living Rm. 42 30
tray Pest Contr. 83 17
tray Game 88 8
tray Café 265 3, 14
tray Restaurant 266 19, 45, 63
tray Fair 308 52
tray, revolving ~ 204 37
tray, round ~ 44 24
tray counter 266 64
tray for purchases 271 15
tray thermometer 116 13
tread 50 38; 123 32, 47
tread, rubber ~ 187 85
treading water 282 39
treadle Poultry Farm 74 63
treadle Dressm. 103 11
treadle Tailor 104 13
treadle control 168 48
treadle lever 166 58
treadle sewing machine 309 1
treadling diagram 171 10
tread sledge 304 29
treasury notes 252 29-39
treble belly bridge 325 11
treble bridge 325 11
treble clef 320 8
treble control 241 31
treble coupler 324 41
treble plume 254 30
treble register 324 41
treble stop 324 41
treble string 325 10
treble tuning 241 43
treble viol 322 23

tree 272 59, 61; 370 1
tree, conical ~ 272 13
tree, globe-shaped ~ 272 12
tree, pyramidal ~ 52 16; 272 19
tree brush 56 23
tree cake 97 46
tree calliper, steel ~ 84 21
tree felling 84 15-37
tree frog 364 24
tree guard 118 80
tree nursery Map 15 111
tree nursery Market Gdn. 55 3
tree nursery Forestry 84 6, 10
tree of life 372 39
tree pruner 56 11
trees, coniferous ~ Map 15 1
trees, coniferous ~ Conifers 372 1-71
trees, deciduous ~ 371 1-73
trees, mixed ~ 15 14
trees, non-coniferous ~ 15 4
trees, ornamental ~ 373; 374
trees, young ~ 84 10-11
tree scraper 56 14
tree stake 52 31
tree stump 84 14
tree toad 364 24
treetop 272 60; 370 4
tree trunk 84 19; 370 2, 7
tree trunk, hollowed-out ~ 218 7
trefoil arch 336 32
trek, roped ~ 300 22-27
trellis 89 5
trellis, wire ~ 78 9
trembling poplar 371 21
trenchcoat 33 57
trestle Overh. Irrign. 67 7
trestle Carp. 120 18, 19
trestle Shipbuild. 222 27
trestle, paperhanger's ~ 128 52
trestle rope 122 67
triad 321 1-4
triakis-octahedron 351 10
trial 290 24-28
trial frame 111 3
trial lens case 111 45
triangle Fish Farm. 89 85
triangle Drawing Off. 151 7, 8
triangle Railw. 203 13
triangle School 260 37
triangle Music. Instr. 323 49
triangle, acute-angled ~ 346 28
triangle, equilateral ~ 346 26
triangle, obtuse-angled ~ 346 30
triangle, pipe clay ~ 350 17
triangle, right-angled ~ 346 32
triangle cut 36 67
triangles, plane ~ 346 26-32
triangle sign 203 13
triangle symbol 345 24
triangulation point 14 49; 15 71
triangulation station 14 49; 15 71
Triangulum Australe 3 40
triceps brachii 18 38
trick button 117 84
trick ski 286 56
triclinic crystal system 351 26
Tricolour 253 16
triforium 335 33
trigger Slaughterho. 94 6
trigger Army 255 5
trigger guard 87 10
trigger mechanism 255 20
trigger valve 270 62
triglyph 334 15

trilby hat **35** 22
trill **321** 17, 18
trim **46** 5
trimaran **278** 16
trimmer *Carp.* **120** 41
trimmer *Roof* **121** 71
trimmer *Paperhanger* **128** 43
trimmer joist **120** 41
trimming, fur ~ **30** 59
trimming, lace ~ **31** 32
trimming, leather ~ **30** 18
trimming blade **85** 22
trimming knife **128** 38
trimming machine **85** 18
trimmings **266** 55
trimming tab **288** 25, 30
trimming table **132** 64
trimming tool **162** 43
trim tab **288** 25, 30
triplane **229** 6
triple-spar tail construction **257** 20
triplet **321** 23
trip mileage recorder **191** 74, 77
tripod *Photog.* **114** 42; **115** 99
tripod *Paperm.* **173** 6
tripod *Chem.* **349** 15; **350** 14
tripod, wooden ~ **313** 13
tripod bush **115** 30
tripod crane **222** 6
tripod lattice mast **258** 41
tripod leg **114** 43
tripod socket **115** 30
tripod spotlight **310** 52
trireme **218** 9-12
triton **327** 40
trochilus **334** 29
troika **186** 45
trolley *Blacksm.* **138** 35
trolley *Lorries etc.* **194** 42
trolley *Tram* **197**
trolley *Station* **206** 14
trolley *Town* **268** 46
trolley, electric ~ **205** 29
trolley, metal ~ **74** 31
trolley bus **194** 40
trolley bus trailer **194** 44
trolley shoe **194** 42
trolley shoe, aluminium alloy ~ **197** 24
trolley shoe, carbon ~ **197** 24
trolley stop **197** 35; **268** 25
trolley stop sign **197** 36; **268** 26
trolley wire **197** 41; **205** 58
trolley wire contact point **197** 40
trombone **323** 46
trombone slide **323** 47
tropaeolum **53** 4
trophus **358** 26
trophy **352** 15, 30
tropic of Cancer **3** 4
tropics **14** 10
tropopause **7** 9
troposphere **7** 1
trot **72** 41
trotter *Meat* **95** 38, 42, 48
trotter *Equest.* **289** 28
trotting silks **289** 26
troubadour **329** 70
trough *Phys. Geog.* **12** 18
trough *Mills* **91** 14
trough *Railw.* **202** 34
trough *Art* **336** 48
trough, equatorial ~ **9** 46
trough, outdoor ~ **62** 9
trough gutter **122** 83
trough mixer, double shaft ~ **159** 17
trough plane **12** 19
trough surface **12** 19

trough valley **13** 55
trough vault **336** 47
trouser leg **33** 6
trouser pocket **33** 47
trousers, boy's ~ **29** 60
trouser suit **30** 57
trouser turn-up **31** 40
trout **364** 15
trout breeding **89** 14
trout fry **89** 16
trout pond **89** 6
trout rearing **89** 14
trowel *Gdn. Tools* **56** 6
trowel *Bldg. Site* **118** 52
trub **93** 2
trub removal **93** 1-5
truck *Bldg. Site* **119** 32
truck *Power Plant* **152** 41
truck *Sawmill* **157** 16
truck *Refuse Coll.* **199** 38
truck *Railw.* **207** 4; **208** 4; **212** 2; **213** 13
truck *Docks* **226** 4, 19
truck *Flags* **253** 1
truck, electric ~ **205** 29; **206** 2, 34
truck, heavy ~ **194** 20; **200** 7
truck, large-capacity ~ **158** 14
truck, light ~ **194** 1, 5
truck, toy ~ **47** 38; **273** 62
truck farm **55** 1-51, 3
truck garden **55**; **55** 1-51, 3
trucks **194**
truck tire **273** 19
truck-to-truck handling **226** 7
truck-to-truck operation **225** 41
truck-to-truck system **225** 41
truck with trailer **213** 34
trudgen **282** 37
trudgen stroke **282** 37
truffle *Grocer* **98** 86
truffle *Edib. Fungi* **381** 9, 10, 11
trumpet **318** 6; **323** 43
trumpet, bronze ~ **322** 1
trumpet daffodil **60** 3
trumpeter **318** 7
trumpet narcissus **60** 3
truncheon *Heraldry* **254** 31
truncheon *Police* **264** 19
trunk *Man* **16** 22-41
trunk *Forestry* **84** 19
trunk *Car* **191** 24; **193** 23
trunk *Mammals* **366** 21
trunk *Bot.* **370** 2
trunk, horse's ~ **327** 45
trunk, main ~ **88** 11
trunk, round ~ **120** 83
trunk, woman's ~ **327** 24
trunk-bending forwards **295** 33
trunk-bending sideways **295** 32
trunk call **237** 3
trunk-hose, paned ~ **355** 34
trunk-hose, stuffed ~ **355** 31
trunk lid **191** 7
trunk line **15** 21
trunk pipeline **145** 35
trunk road **15** 17
trunks **32** 27
truss **215** 3
trussed arch bridge **215** 23
trussed-rafter roof **121** 34
truss element **215** 24
trusser **130** 12
truss joint **215** 37
truss post **121** 68
truss tower **155** 43
trying plane **132** 39
trysail **220** 1

try square **120** 69; **132** 6; **134** 26
try-your-strength machine **308** 11
tsetse fly **81** 43
T-shirt **31** 38
T-shirt, children's ~ **29** 27
T-square **151** 9
tsunami **11** 53
T-tail **229** 29; **256** 31-32; **287** 10
T-tail unit **229** 29; **256** 31-32; **287** 10
tub *Market Gdn.* **55** 48
tub *Wine Grow.* **78** 10
tub, wooden ~ **91** 27
tuba **323** 44
tubaphone **324** 61
tube *Hosp.* **25** 13; **26** 17
tube *Pest Contr.* **83** 31
tube *Opt:cn.* **111** 18
tube *Optic. Instr.* **113** 8
tube *Bicycle* **187** 30
tube *Music. Instr.* **323** 29; **326** 22
tube *Invertebr.* **357** 23
tube *Edib. Fungi* **381** 17
tube, diaphragmed ~ **10** 27
tube, eustachian ~ **17** 65
tube, fallopian ~ **20** 81
tube, steel ~ **155** 30
tube, telescopic ~ **65** 77
tube, uterine ~ **20** 81
tube bin **255** 72
tube cap **260** 52
tube centre section **113** 9
tube clamp **40** 20; **350** 30
tube clip **40** 20; **350** 30
tube connection **6** 26
tube holder **22** 46
tuber *Arable Crops* **68** 40
tuber *Bot.* **370** 79
tuberose **60** 9
tuberosity **80** 27
tube support **27** 47
tube valve **187** 31
tube well **269** 60
tubing **145** 20, 24
tub plant **55** 47
tuck and miss stitch **171** 44, 47
tuck jump **282** 14; **295** 36; **297** 40
tuck stitch, pulled-up ~ **171** 45, 48
tuck stitch, staggered ~ **171** 46
tue iron **137** 6
tuff **11** 19
tuff deposit **11** 26
tuft **73** 7
tufted lark **361** 19
tuft of grass **375** 44
tug *Shipbuild.* **222** 42
tug *Docks* **225** 15
tug *Salvage* **227** 5, 16
tug *Gliding* **287** 2
tulip poplar **374** 1
tulip tree **374** 1
tulle background **102** 16
tulle lace **102** 15
tulle work **102** 15
tumble drier **50** 28
tumbler *Metalwkr.* **140** 38
tumbler *Restaurant* **266** 3
tumbler, seaward ~ **226** 23
tumbler, shore-side ~ **226** 28
tumbler lever **149** 10
tumbler reverse lever **149** 14
tumbler spring **140** 42
tumbling separator, mechanical ~ **64** 75
tumulus **328** 16
tun **92** 45

tun, wooden ~ **91** 27
tundra climate **9** 57
tuner **241** 9, 37; **317** 22
tuner, automatic ~ **23** 38
tunic *Ladies' Wear* **30** 29
tunic *Ship* **221** 115
tunic *Hist. Cost.* **355** 12, 25
tunic, long ~ **355** 19
tunica **355** 12
tunic dress **30** 29
tunic top **30** 29
tuning control **241** 9
tuning crook **326** 21
tuning device **326** 30
tuning dial **241** 7
tuning flap **326** 30
tuning fork element **110** 9
tuning fork principle **110** 6
tuning fork watch **110** 6
tuning hammer **325** 20
tuning hole **326** 33
tuning key **325** 20
tuning knob **241** 9; **309** 21
tuning meter **241** 39, 54
tuning peg **323** 18; **324** 11; **325** 17
tuning pin **324** 23; **325** 17
tuning screw **323** 59
tuning slot **326** 33
tuning tongue **326** 30
tuning wedge **325** 21
tuning wire **326** 21
tunnel *Map* **15** 70
tunnel *Soft Fruit* **58** 63
tunnel *Station* **204** 23
tunnel *Railw.* **214** 6
tunnel, plastic ~ **55** 40
tunnel, underground ~ **198** 29
tunnel entrance **233** 6
tunnel kiln **161** 5
tunnelling machine **144** 32
tunnel vault **335** 19; **336** 38
tup *Blacksm.* **137** 10
tup *Forging* **139** 12, 26
turban **353** 46
turbine **67** 20; **209** 18; **232** 40, 47
turbine, high and low pressure ~ **259** 62
turbine, high-pressure ~ **232** 53
turbine, low-pressure ~ **232** 54
turbine, reversible ~ **155** 39
turbine, supercharged ~ **212** 51
turbine engine **232** 17, 24; **257** 15
turbine exhaust **146** 5
turbine house **152** 22; **217** 43
turbine inlet **155** 40, 41
turbine monitoring panel **153** 30
turbine transmission **209** 10
turbine unit **209** 24
turbogenerator **154** 34
turbogenerator set **154** 33
turbogenerator unit **153** 23-30
turbojet engine **231** 26
turbojet engines **232** 33-50
turbopropeller engine **231** 5; **232** 30, 51
turbopropeller plane **231** 4
turboprop engine **231** 5; **232** 30, 51; **256** 16
turboprop plane **231** 4
tureen **45** 15
turkey **73** 28
turkey cock **73** 28
turkey hen **73** 28
turkey leg **99** 59
Turkish delight **308** 18

turk's cap 377 4
turk's cap lily 377 4
turn *Athletics* 298 24
turn *Music. Not.* 321 21
turnbuckle 130 4; 202 31
turner *Brew.* 92 24
turner *Turner* 135 20
turnery 135 1-26
turn indicator *Car* 191 76
turn indicator *Aircraft* 230 12
turn indicator light 189 37, 45
turn indicator light, front ~
191 19
turning head, multiple ~ 149
41
turning judge 282 26
turning tools 135 14,15,24
turnip moth 80 42
turnout 203 51, 52
turn slot 288 46
turntable *Porcelain Manuf.*
161 11
turntable *Electrotyp. etc.* 178
26
turntable *Lorries etc.* 194 31
turntable *Bridges* 215 64
turntable *Docks* 226 56
turntable *Audio* 241 20
turntable *Army* 255 73
turntable glazing machine
161 16
turn-up 30 35; 31 54; 33 35
turpentine separator 172 14
turret *Mach. Tools* 149 40
turret *Warships* 258 47, 67.
70; 259 31, 52, 71
turret *Chivalry* 329 28, 35
turret, aft ~ 259 44
turret, armoured ~ 255 84
turret, forward ~ 259 43
turret head 117 46; 313 32
turret lathe 149 38
turtle dove 359 23
tusk 88 54; 366 22; 367 22
tutu 314 29
tuyère 147 20
TV set 42 8; 46 14
tween deck 223 76
tweeter 241 15
tweezers 109 14; 174 18
twig 370 6
twilight area 4 21
twin anti-aircraft gun 258 31
31
twin anti-aircraft gun turret
259 30
twin anti-aircraft missile
launcher 259 25, 33
twin anti-aircraft rocket
launcher 259 25, 33
twin columns 336 6
twin edger 157 57
twin engine, horizontally-
opposed ~ 189 47
twin etching machine 178 30
twin hull 284 65
twin launching catapult 259
14
Twins 3 28; 4 55
twin seat 188 42
twin seat, racing-style ~ 189
14
twin set 31 49
twin-spar wing construction
257 27
twin tail unit 229 32, 34
twist bit 134 49; 140 59
twist drill 134 49; 140 59
twist grip *Pest Contr.* 83 19
twist grip *Motorcycles etc.* 188
31
twist grip throttle control 188
30; 189 29

twist of tobacco 107 18
twitch grass 61 30
two-eight time 320 28
two-four time 320 29
two-high mill 148 53
two-line brevier 175 30
two-line primer 175 31
two-pipe system 126 22
two-seater 193 28
two-stroke blending pump
196 13
two-toed sloth 366 11
two-two time 320 30
two-way tap 350 49
tympan 340 37
tympanum 335 26
type *Composing Rm.* 174 7,
15, 44; 175 1-17, 38
type *Letterpress* 181 37
type *Office* 249 15, 29
type *Money* 252 12
type, black-letter ~ 342 1, 2, 3
type, bold ~ 175 2
type, bold condensed ~ 175 10
type, boldfaced ~ 175 2
type, extra bold ~ 175 9
type, Gothic ~ 342 1
type, heavy ~ 175 2
type, italic ~ 175 7
type, light face ~ 175 8
type, Schwabacher ~ 342 2
type, semibold ~ 175 3
type area 185 59
type bed 180 78; 181 17
typecase 174 3
type casting 175 32-37
type character 174 7; 175 38
type cleaner 247 8
type-cleaning brush 247 7
type-cleaning kit 247 8
type disc 176 20
type face 174 31; 175 42
type faces 342 1-15
type forme 340 32
typefounding 175 32-37
type height 175 44
type line 175 43
type magazine 174 21
type matrix 174 47; 176 16
type matter 174 15; 175 1-17;
181 37
types 342 1-15
typescript *Composing Rm.*
174 6
typescript *Script* 342 9
typesetter 174 5
typesetting, computer-
controlled ~ 176 14
typesetting computer 176 10
type size 175 18, 46
types of ship 221
typewriter 209 28; 248 22;
309 79
typewriter, electric ~ 249 1
typewriter rubber 247 26
typewriting 342 9
typhoon wheel 308 46
typing compartment 209 26
typing desk 245 25; 248 26
typing opening 249 19
typing window 249 19
typist 248 21
typographer beetle 82 22
tyre 191 15
tyre, high-pressure ~ 187 30
tyre, pneumatic ~ 187 30; 305
86
tyre, rubber ~ 273 54
tyre, tubular ~ 290 19, 23
tyre chain 304 10
tyre pressure gauge 196 17
tyre tread 189 27

U

udder 75 18
ulna 17 14
ulnar side of the hand 19 70
ultra large crude carrier 221 1
umbel 383 65
umbel, simple ~ 370 72
Umbellula encrinus 369 14
umbo 329 58
umbra 4 35
umbrella *Hall* 41 15
umbrella *Station* 205 12
umbrella *Art* 337 22
umbrella *Invertebr.* 357 15
umbrella, telescopic ~ 41 12
umbrella stand 41 14
umpire 292 55, 65; 293 19, 68
unau 366 11
uncial 341 17
underbrush 84 5
undercarriage 194 32
undercarriage, retractable ~
232 10
undercarriage housing 256 15
undercarriage hydraulic
cylinder 257 41
undercarriage unit, forward-
retracting ~ 257 40
undercarriage unit, main ~
230 41; 231 28; 256 26; 257
40; 288 33
undercarriage unit,
retractable ~ 231 28
underclothes, ladies' ~ 32
1-15
underclothes, men's ~ 32
22-29
undercut *Forestry* 84 28
undercut *Meat* 95 13
undercut swing saw 157 24, 64
underframe 207 3; 208 5
undergown 355 37
undergrasp 296 41
undergrowth 84 5
underlip 72 10
under-ridge tile 122 5
undershirt 296 61
underside 173 34
underskirt 309 85
understructure 191 2
under tile 122 57
underwater case 117 57
underwater housing 117 57
underwater massage bath 281
31
underwater salvo missile
launcher 259 24
underwater salvo rocket
launcher 259 24
underwater swimmer 279 7;
280 37
underwater swimming 279
7-27; 282 38
underwater swimming set 279
8-22
underwear 32
underwear, ladies' ~ 32 1-15
underwear, men's ~ 32 22-29
underwing tank 256 4
underwood 84 5, 32
uneven bars 297 3
ungulates 366 25-31; 367
1-10
ungulates, even-toed ~ 366
28-31
ungulates, odd-toed ~ 366
25-27
unicorn 254 16; 327 7
uniform 264 7
uniform cap 264 8
Union Jack 253 15
union of sets 348 5-6

unison 321 6
unison interval 321 6
unit, assistant's ~ 24 9
unit, slide-in ~ 27 32
unit indicator 174 36
unit load 225 49; 226 9
unit load, foil-wrapped ~ 225
42
units 344 3
university 262 1-25
university lecturer 262 3
university library 262
11-25
university professor 262 3
unloading unit 62 42
unwind station 173 39
up-and-down roundabout
308 5
up-and-down slide 273 52
upcurrent, frontal ~ 287 vp
upholstery 134 59
upper, corduroy ~ 101 26
upper, rubber ~ 300 45
upper, soft-leather ~ 101 46
upper, terry ~ 101 23
upper arm hang 296 58
upper board 326 15
upper board groove 326 14
uppercut 299 32
upper fore topgallant sail 219
59
upper fore topgallant yard
219 36
upper fore topsail 219 57
upper fore topsail yard 219 34
upper hatch 6 45
upper-leather shears 100 42
upper main topgallant sail
219 65
upper main topgallant yard
219 42
upper main topsail 219 63
upper main topsail yard 219
40
Upper Muschelkalk 154 58
Upper Permian 154 62
upright *Gymn.* 296 9
upright *Athletics* 298 13, 33
upright *Music. Instr.* 325 1
upright kneeling position 295
7
upright spin 302 9
upsett 136 25
upsetting block 137 16
upstart 297 28
upward ventilator 154 81
U-rail 214 22
Uranus 4 50
ureter 20 32
urethra 20 68
urethroscope 23 20
urine sediment chart 23 58
urn 328 40; 331 31
urn, cinerary ~ 328 38
urn, domestic ~ 328 38
urn, embossed ~ 328 38
urn grave 328 39; 331 30
Ursa Major 3 29
Ursa Minor 3 34
ursine seal 367 18
usher 315 12
usherette 312 4
uterus 20 79
utility room door 118 6
utility room window 118 5
U-tube 349 2
U-valley 13 55
uvula 19 22

V

vacancy 342 70
vacuum 240 21
vacuum back 177 35
vacuum box 173 15
vacuum chamber 2 52; 83 12; 159 12
vacuum cleaner *Household* 50 80
vacuum cleaner *Goldsm. etc.* 108 43
vacuum cleaner, cylinder ~ 50 68
vacuum cleaner, upright ~ 50 58
vacuum equipment 145 51
vacuum film holder 177 8
vacuum frame 179 13; 182 2
vacuum line 74 50; 75 29
vacuum printing frame 179 13
vacuum pump *Intern. Combust. Eng.* 190 59, 60
vacuum pump *Water* 269 8
vacuum pump switch 179 19
vacuum ripening tank 169 11
vacuum timing control 190 9
vagina 20 86
Valasian dulcimer 322 34
Valenciennes 102 18
valerian 380 5
valley *Phys. Geog.* 13 52-56
valley *Roof* 121 15; 122 11, 82
valley, dry ~ 13 75
valley, synclinal ~ 13 56
valley, U-shaped ~ 13 55
valley, V-shaped ~ 13 53, 54
valley bottom 13 67; 215 60
valley floor 13 67
valley glacier 12 49
valley rafter 121 64
valleyside 13 57-70
valley station 214 39
valley station platform 214 51
valley temple 333 8
value 250 18
value, note's ~ 320 7
valve *Roof & Boilerr.* 38 73
valve *Bicycle* 187 31
valve *Airsports* 288 77
valve *Ball Games* 291 18
valve *Music. Instr.* 323 40; 324 66
valve, aortic ~ 20 49
valve, atrioventricular ~ 20 46, 47
valve, bicuspid ~ 20 47
valve, mitral ~ 20 47
valve, pulmonary ~ 20 50
valve, sliding ~ 217 55
valve, tricuspid ~ 20 46
valve control house 217 42, 63
valve horn 323 41
valve house 217 42, 63
valve housing 217 54
valve line 288 78
valve sealing cap 187 32
valves of the heart 20 46-47
valve tube 187 31
vambrace 329 47
vamp *Shoem.* 100 60
vamp *Carnival* 306 32
vamplate 329 82
van, medium ~ 194 7
Vandyke beard 34 13
vane, curved ~ 91 38
vane, flat ~ 91 40
vang 284 21
vanilla 382 48
vanilla plant 382 46
vanilla pod 382 48
vans 194

vaquero 306 31
variable 345 14
variable depth sonar 259 40
variable focus lens 313 23
variable platen action lever 249 24
varifocal lens 313 23
variometer 230 14
varnish 338 12
varnishing 129 14
vas deferens 20 74
vase, Greek ~ 334 37
vase, hand-painted ~ 161 18
vase, porcelain ~ 337 5
vase, stone ~ 272 35
vastus lateralis 18 46
vastus medialis 18 46
vat *Fish Farm.* 89 4
vat *Paperm.* 172 25; 173 47
vat, concrete ~ 79 3
vat, stainless steel ~ 79 4
vatman 173 46
vault 79 1
vault, cloistered ~ 336 41
vault, groined ~ 336 42
vault, ribbed ~ 336 43
vault, stalactitic ~ 337 17
vault, stellar ~ 336 44
vault, types of ~ 336 38-50
vaulter *Athletics* 298 29
vaulter *Circus* 307 32
vaulting 298 9-41
vaulting, Romanesque ~ 335 17
vaulting horse 296 1; 297 1
vaulting pole 298 28
V-belt 64 78
V-belt drive 180 58
V-cardan 67 31
VCR cassette 243 5
veal 95 1-13
vee-belt drive 180 58
vee-neck 31 68
vee-tail 229 31
Vega 3 22
vegetable, frozen ~ 99 61
vegetable basket 99 81
vegetable crate 55 43
vegetable dish 45 25
vegetable garden 52
vegetable oil 98 23
vegetable patch 52 26
vegetable plants 57
vegetable plate 45 33
vegetable platter 45 33
vegetable plot 52 26; 55 39
vegetables 57
vegetables, canned ~ 96 27
vegetable spoon 45 74
vegetarian meal 266 62
vehicle 195 47
vehicle, articulated ~ 194 28
vehicle, electrically-powered ~ 188 20
vehicle ferry 15 47
vehicle ramp 206 1
vehicles 186 1-54
vehicles, horse-drawn ~ 186 1-54
vehicle tanker 194 28
veil 381 5
veil, bridal ~ 332 20
veil, widow's ~ 331 39
vein 370 29
vein, frontal ~ 18 6
vein, iliac ~ 18 18
vein, jugular ~ 18 2
vein, portal ~ 20 39
vein, pulmonary ~ 18 12; 20 56
vein, subclavian ~ 18 8
vein, temporal ~ 18 4
velum 381 5

velum palati 19 21
vena cava, inferior ~ 18 15; 20 57
vena cava, superior ~ 18 9; 20 53
venation 370 29
vendor 308 17
veneer 133 2
veneer-peeling machine 133 1
veneer-splicing machine 133 3
V-engine 190 1
vent *Phys. Geog.* 11 28
vent *Airsports* 288 82
vent, volcanic ~ 11 17
ventilating tile 122 7
ventilation control knob 26 27
ventilation drum 74 29
ventilation drum motor 74 33
ventilation flap *Market Gdn.* 55 41
ventilation flap *Railw.* 213 16, 29, 30
ventilation shaft *Brew.* 92 14
ventilation shaft *Coal* 144 21
ventilation slit 50 30
ventilation switch 191 83
ventilation system 6 26
ventilation system, automatic ~ 191 30
ventilation window 55 10
ventilator *Bathrm. etc.* 49 20
ventilator *Poultry Farm* 74 10, 17
ventilator *Railw.* 207 9
ventilator *Ship* 221 41
ventilator *Water* 269 27
ventilator *Disco* 317 30
ventilator *Zoo* 356 17
ventilator, hinged ~ 55 10
ventilator grill 258 43
ventilator lead 223 41
ventilator opening 258 43
ventilators 55 10-11
vent mast 221 38
vent pipe 155 11
vent prop 55 18
ventral part 95 39
ventricle 20 51
vents 55 10-11
venturi 192 8
venturi throat 190 15
Venus *Astron.* 4 44
Venus *Prehist.* 328 8
Venus's flytrap 377 14
Venus's slipper 376 27
verge 37 8; 121 3
verger 330 26, 58
Vermes 357 20-26
vermouth 98 62
vernier *Metalwkr.* 140 55
vernier *Navig.* 224 5
vernier calliper gauge 140 52; 149 67
vernier depth gauge 140 54; 149 72
vernier scale 149 69
vert 254 29
vertebra, cervical ~ 17 2
vertebra, coccygeal ~ 17 5; 20 60
vertebra, dorsal ~ 17 3
vertebra, lumbar ~ 17 4
vertebra, thoracic ~ 17 3
vertex *Man* 16 1
vertex *Maths.* 346 26; 347 16, 28
vertex refractionometer 111 33
vertical backward somersault 297 17

vertical deflection module 240 8
vertical drive head 150 38
vertical flick spin 288 6
vertical milling spindle 150 37
vertical/short take-off and landing aircraft 232 26-32
vertical speed indicator 230 14
vertical tangent screw 14 54
vesicle, germinal ~ 74 66
vesicle, seminal ~ 20 77
vessel, completed ~ 162 29, 37
vessel, damaged ~ 227 2; 228 10
vessel, funerary ~ 328 34
vessels, ecclesiastical ~ 332 34-54
vessels, liturgical ~ 332 34-54
vessel with spiral pattern 328 13
vest *Infant Care etc.* 28 23
vest *Underwear etc.* 32 7
vest *Men's Wear* 33 4, 15
vest *Gymn.* 296 61
vest *Hist. Cost.* 355 75
vest, envelope-neck ~ 29 7
vest, knitted ~ 33 53
vest, short-sleeved ~ 32 28
vest, sleeveless ~ 29 6; 32 25
vest, wrapover ~ 29 8
vest and shorts set 32 21
vestibule *Railw.* 207 21
vestibule *Hotel* 267 1-26
vestments 330 22; 332 4
vestry 331 13
vestry door 330 17
VHF and UHF tuner 240 6
VHF antenna 257 25
VHF station selector button 241 38
viaduct 215 59
vibrating beam 201 13
vibrating cylinder 119 89
vibrating head 119 89
vibrating poker 119 89
vibration, macroseismic ~ 11 38
vibration damper 190 26
vibrator 201 13
vicar 330 22
vicarage 331 20
vice 109 28; 134 10; 138 24; 260 47, 56
vice, front ~ 132 30
vice, parallel-jaw ~ 140 2
vice bar 260 48
vice handle 132 31
vice screw 132 32
Victoria regia water lily 378 17
video cassette 242 18
video cassette recorder 243 7
video cassette recorder system 243 5-36
video coding station 236 39
video controller 239 11
video control room 239 10
video data terminal 238 2, 11
video disc 243 38, 44, 58
video disc jacket 243 45
video disc player 243 37, 46
video head 243 26, 36
video head movement, direction of ~ 243 30
video long play video disc system 243 46-60
video monitor 238 2
video recorder, portable ~ 243 4
video signal 243 58
videotape recorder, portable

~ 243 4
video telephone 242 21
video telephone screen 242 26
video track 243 31
vielle à roue 322 25
Vienna sausage 96 8
view, front ~ 151 17
view, lateral ~ 27 3
view, side ~ 151 18
viewer editor 117 91
viewfinder, rectangular ~ 114 14
viewfinder, right-angle ~ 115 71
viewfinder, universal ~ 114 41
viewfinder eyepiece *Photog.* 114 2; 115 22
viewfinder eyepiece *Films* 313 6
viewfinder hood 114 23; 115 68
viewfinder image 115 51
viewing lens 114 25
viewing screen 117 94
view point 15 68
Viking ship 218 13-17
village 15 105
vine *Wine Grow.* 78 2-9
vine *Pest Contr.* 83 51
vinegar 98 25
vine layer 83 15
vine leaf 78 4
vine pests 80 20-27
vine root louse 83 33
vine shoot 78 2
vine stem 78 6
vine tendril 54 22
vineyard *Map* 15 65
vineyard *Wine Grow.* 78 1, 21
vineyard area 78 1-21
vineyard tractor 83 48
viniculture 78
viniculturist 78 13
viol 322 23
viola 323 27
viola da gamba 322 23
viol bow 322 24
violet 343 9
violin 323 1
violin, miniature ~ 322 20
violin body 323 3
violin bow 323 12
violin-bow fibula 328 27
violin bridge 323 5
violin clef 320 8
violinist 267 45
violin string 323 9
violoncello 323 16
violone 322 23; 323 23
vipers 364 40-41
Virgin 3 18; 4 58
virginal 322 45
Virginia creeper 51 5; 374 16
Virgin Mary 330 51
Virgo 3 18; 4 58
vis-à-vis 186 51
viscose 169 13-27, 15
viscose process 169 1-34
viscose rayon 169 1-12, 34
viscose rayon cake 169 18
viscose rayon thread 169 13-27
viscose spinning solution 169 10, 28-34
viscous drive 190 8
vise *see* vice
vision controller 239 11
vision control room 239 10
vision mixer 238 63
vision-mixing console 238 63
vision-mixing desk 238 63
visitor 356 6

visor *Forestry* 84 23
visor *Heraldry* 254 9
visor *Chivalry* 329 40
visual display 23 27
visual display unit 248 16, 44
viticulture 78
viticulturist 78 13
vitreous body 19 46
vixen 88 42
VLP video disc 243 51
V-neck 31 68
vocal pouch 364 25
vocal sac 364 25
Voith transmission 209 14; 212 74
vol-au-vent 97 18
volcanism 11 13-28
volcano, active ~ 11 15
volcano, composite ~ 11 15
volcano, extinct ~ 11 25, 28
volcano, subterranean ~ 11 20
vole and mole trap 83 37
volley 293 41
volley, forehand ~ 293 41
volleyball 293 56-71, 58, 59
voltage meter 212 17
voltage regulator, automatic ~ 153 31
voltage transformer 153 59
voltmeter 326 38
volume, respiratory ~ 26 28
volume control 117 85; 241 41
volume control, pupil's ~ 261 43
volume control, student's ~ 261 43
volume readout 196 5
volumetric flask 350 28
volume unit meters 241 35-36
volute 333 26; 334 23
volute cushion 334 24
VOR antenna 257 26
VOR radio direction finder 230 51
voter 263 22
voter, qualified ~ 263 24
votive candle 330 53
voussoir 336 22
V-seat 295 13
V-support 295 17
V-tail 229 31
vulcanicity 11 13-28
vulva 16 39
V-valley 13 53
V-way *Joiner* 132 61
V-way *Composing Rm.* 175 54

W

wad, felt ~ 87 52
wafer *Bakery* 97 45
wafer *Church* 332 28
wafer, sacred ~ 332 48
waffle 97 45
waffle iron, electric ~ 40 34
waggonette 186 2
wagon 213 18
wagon, flat ~ 206 21, 24; 213 5, 11, 40
wagon, large-capacity ~ 213 28
wagon, open ~ 213 33
wagon, special ~ 213 33
Wagoner 3 27
wagon load 206 52
wagon truck 200 25
wagtail 360 9
waist *Man* 16 31
waist *Shoem.* 100 68
waist, corseted ~ 355 53

waistband *Ladies' Wear* 31 41
waistband *Men's Wear* 33 23
waistcoat 33 4, 15
waistcoat, denim ~ 31 59
waistcoat, embroidered ~ 355 75
waistcoat, knitted ~ 33 53
waistcoat, quilted ~ 30 16
waist longeron 235 9
waist slip 32 14; 309 85
waiter 267 47
waiter, head ~ 266 30
waiting room *Doc.* 22 1
waiting room *Station* 204 14
waiting room *Airport* 233 18
'waiting room' *Airport* 233 28
waitress 265 13; 266 18
wake 223 58
wake-robin 379 9
waldhorn 323 41
walk 71 2; 72 39
walk, gravel ~ 272 18
walkie-talkie set 270 41
walking stick 41 5
walking-stick umbrella 205 12
walkway *Dwellings* 37 60
walkway *Street Sect.* 198 9
walkway *Hydr. Eng.* 217 72
wall *Map* 15 95
wall *Carp.* 120 29
wall *Equest.* 289 8
wall *Ball Games* 291 44
wall, brick ~ 118 8; 123 29; 260 45
wall, concrete ~ 123 1
wall, framed ~ 120 48
wall, glass ~ 37 16
wall, hollow-block ~ 118 15
wall, inner ~ 329 19
wall, mirrored ~ 317 28
wall, outer ~ 121 32, 77; 122 37
wall, Rococo ~ 336 9
wall, rubble concrete ~ 119 7
wall, side ~ 42 2; 46 4; 222 37
wall, slatted ~ 213 29
wall, stone ~ 337 23
wall, timber ~ 119 25; 120 9
wall barley 61 28
wall bars 296 20
wall brush, flat ~ 129 17
wall calendar 22 17; 245 3; 248 42
wall candelabrum 330 16
wall chart 195 32
wall clock 109 32; 309 87
wall connection 25 23
wall cupboard 39 8; 46 30
wall desk 267 16
wall espalier 52 1
wall fountain 272 15
wall gecko 364 36
wall joist 120 39
wall lamp 265 9
wall lining, 'acoustic' ~ 310 15
wall map 260 44
wall memorial 331 14
wall mirror 309 3
wall-of-death rider 308 54
wall outlet 127 5
wall outlet, double ~ 127 6
wallower 91 11
wallpaper 128 18, 19
wallpaper, synthetic ~ 128 18
wallpaper-cutting board 128 41
wallpapering 128 18-53
wallpaper paste 128 23
wallpaper-stripping liquid 128 1
wallpaper-stripping machine 128 9

wall pepper 51 7
wall plaster 123 60
wall plate 120 40, 49
wall shelf 104 8
wall shelf unit 104 8
wall socket 39 26; 127 5
wall socket, double ~ 127 6
wall stone 331 14
wall string 123 45
wall stringer 123 45
wall switch 127 16
wall unit 42 1; 44 17; 46 1
wall ventilator 266 15
walnut 59 41, 43
walnut tree 59 37-43, 37
walrus 367 20
wane 120 89
waney edge 120 89
Wankel engine, two-rotor ~ 190 5
wapiti 367 2
ward, inner ~ 329 2
ward, outer ~ 329 31
wardrobe 43 1
wardrobe door 46 2
wardrobe trunk 267 29
warehouse *Station* 206 53
warehouse *Docks* 225 23
warhead 255 65
war horn, ivory ~ 354 39
warm-air brush 106 30
warm-air comb 105 22; 106 29
warm-air curtain 271 43
warm-air regulator 191 87
warm house 55 4, 32
warm-up regulator 190 50
warning cross 202 41
warning light 191 67, 72, 76, 80; 202 46, 50; 224 69; 230 64; 270 6
warning sign 280 6
warp *Sea Fish.* 90 12
warp *Weaving* 165 43; 166 39
warp *Knitting* 167 24
warp *Weaves* 171 14
warp *Hydr. Eng.* 217 23
warp, wire ~ 90 15
war paint 352 13
warp beam 165 29, 42; 166 48; 167 24
warp beam, sized ~ 165 56
warping capstan 217 22
warping machine 165 22
warping machine frame 165 27
warp-knitting machine 167 23
warp let-off motion 166 61
warp rib fabric 171 14
warp rib weave 171 13
warp thread 166 39; 171 1-29, 2, 17, 18
warp thread, lowered ~ 171 8
warp thread, raised ~ 171 7
warren 86 23
warship, Roman ~ 218 9-12
warships 258; 259
washbasin 24 15; 49 24; 126 27, 31; 278 6
washbasin, double ~ 267 32
washbasin pedestal 49 27
washboard *Floor etc. Constr.* 123 21, 63
washboard *Flea Market* 309 70
wash-bottle 349 8
washer *Photog.* 116 15
washer *Mach. Parts etc.* 143 17, 34
washer *Sawmill* 157 21
washer *Bicycle* 187 55
washer, lead ~ 122 103

washing 169 19; 170 48, 56
washing and toilet facilities
278 5-6
washing basin 309 65
washing bottle 261 32
washing drum 50 24
washing floor 92 3, 27
washing line 38 23; 50 33
washing machine 157 21
washing machine, automatic
~ 50 23
washing machines 50 23-34
washing set 309 64
washing trough 165 49
washing unit, compressed-air
~ 92 3
washing-up area 207 28
washing-up brush 50 51
wash liquor, weak ~ 172 44
washroom 207 15; 278 5
washstand Railw. 207 40
washstand Flea Market 309
67
wash tank Photog. 116 15
wash tank Oil, Petr. 145 30
washtub 309 69
wash water, weak ~ 172 44
wasp 82 35
wasp waist 355 53
waste 144 37
waste, medium-activity ~ 154
72
waste, nuclear ~ 154 57-68
waste, radioactive ~ 154
57-68, 77
waste bin 22 70; 96 46
waste-gas heat exchanger 155
9
wastepaper basket 46 25; 248
45
waste pipe Bathrm. etc. 49 45
waste pipe Street Sect. 198 26
waste steam exhaust 210 22
waste tray, mobile ~ 26 22
waste water discharge 156 38
waste water outlet 217 62
waste water pump Paperm.
172 63
waste water pump Refuse
Coll. 199 20
watch, automatic ~ 110 32-43
watch, waterproof ~ 109 26;
279 16
watchdog 62 32; 70 25
watches 110
watchglass-fitting tool 109
11, 29
watchkeeper 221 126
watchmaker 109 1
watchman 329 9
watch strap 110 5
watch strap, metal ~ 109 19
watch-testing machine 109
24
watch-timing machine 109
25
watchtower 329 35
water 48 8
water, artesian ~ 12 21
water, baptismal ~ 332 12
water, entrapped ~ 13 16
water, raw ~ 269 4
water, rising ~ 12 26
water, running ~ 89 1
water, shallow ~ 224 87, 97
water, underlying ~ 12 32
water and brine separator 145
32
water appliances 126 12-25
water ballast 223 78
water barrel 52 4
water bath 132 12; 349 14
water bath, constant

temperature ~ 23 48
Water Bearer 4 63
water bottle 290 10
water buffalo 367 8
water bug 358 4
water butt 52 4
water canister 83 57
water cannon 270 66; 316 18
Water Carrier Astron. 4 63
water carrier Camping 278 32
water channel 334 54
water circuit, auxiliary ~ 259
63
water circuit, primary ~ 259
65
water circuit, secondary ~ 259
63
water-collecting tank 92 5
watercolour 260 27; 338 18
water connection 179 5
water container 103 22
water cooler 189 35
water-cooling system Moon
L. 6 26
water-cooling system Iron
Foundry etc. 148 28
watercress 378 30
water cruet 332 45
water elf 327 23
water extractor 281 39
waterfall 11 45
waterfall, artificial ~ 272 9
water feed pipe 103 21
waterfowl 272 51-54
waterfowling 86 40
water gauge Map 15 29
water gauge Roof & Boilerr.
38 63
water gauge Railw. 210 45
water gauge Chem. 349 16
water glass 24 13
water heater 145 31
water heater, electric ~ 126 13
water heater, gas ~ 126 12
water heater, instantaneous ~
126 12-13
watering can 51 21; 55 26
water inlet Fish Farm. 89 7
water inlet Plumb. etc. 126 18
water inlet Water 269 54
water inlet pipe 168 11
water jet pipe 281 40
water jet pump 23 49
water jug 309 66
water jump 289 20
water level 13 77
water lily 51 18; 272 56
waterline 258 27; 285 31
water main 198 22
watermark 252 31
water meter 269 53
water-meter dial 269 58
watermill Map 15 77
watermill Mills 91 35-44
water molecule 242 67
water moth 358 12
water newt 364 20
water nixie 327 23
water nymph Fabul. Creat.
327 23
water nymph Articulates 358
3
water outlet Fish Farm. 89 8
water outlet Energy Sources
155 23
water outlet Water 269 57
water outlet pipe 116 17
water overfall 91 43
water ox 367 8
water pipe Market Gdn. 55 30
water pipe Poultry Farm 74 7,
26
water pipe Tobacc. etc. 107 42

water pipe Power Plant 152 7
water pipe Paperm. 172 65
water pipe School 261 4
water plantain 378 44
water plants 378 14-57
water polo 282 46-50
water polo ball 282 48
water preheater 152 10
waterproofing 123 5
water pump 190 61
waters, coastal ~ 286 10-14
waters, inshore ~ 286 10-14
water scorpion 358 4
water ski 280 16
water ski, types of ~ 286
56-62
water skier 286 45
water skiing 286 45-62
water slater 358 2
Water Snake Astron. 3 16
water snake Fish etc. 364 38
water supply 27 46; 269
water supply, individual ~
269 40-52
water supply pipe Brew. 92 48
water supply pipe Photog. 116
16
water table 13 77; 269 1, 42,
63
water tank Market Gdn. 55 2,
29
water tank Gas Weld. 141 17
water tank Refuse Coll. 199
27
water tank Railw. 210 66
water tank School 261 33
water tank Theatre 316 51
water tanker 233 22
water tap 39 36; 49 26; 126 31
water temperature 280 8
water temperature gauge 191
38, 66
water tender 270 51
water tower Map 15 81
water tower Market Gdn. 55 2
water tower Coal 144 14
water tower Water 269 18
water trough 137 8
water tub 281 26
water-tube boiler 152 5
water vole 366 17
waterway engineering 217
water wings 281 7; 282 18
Watling Street thistle 61 32
wattle 73 24
wave 13 36; 287 17
wave, seismic ~ 11 36
waves, artificial ~ 281 1-9
wave soaring 287 16
wave system 287 17
waxing cork 301 23
waxing iron 301 22
wax scraper 301 24
wax separation 145 50
waxworks 308 68
waybill 206 30
wayside flowers 375; 376
WC 49 12; 207 16, 42, 72; 211
59; 231 31; 317 31
weaponry 255 1-98
weapons, heavy ~ 255 40-95
weapon system radar 258 35
weasel 367 16
weather 8 1-19
weather chart ~ 9 1-39; 342 66
weather cloth 223 17
weathercock 331 3
weather map 9 1-39; 342 66
weather radar antenna 231 18
weather report 342 65
weather satellite 10 64
weather ship 9 7
weather station 9 7; 225 33

weather vane 121 26; 331 4
weave, plain ~ 171 1, 4, 24
weaver 136 5
weaves Basketm. 136 1-4
weaves Weaves 171 1-29
weaving 165; 166
weaving draft 171 29
weaving machine 166 1, 35
web Dom. Anim. 73 36
web House Insects etc. 81 10
web Paperm. 173 30, 45
web Letterpress 181 43, 58
web Railw. 202 3
web Gymn. 297 11
web Articulates 358 47
web Birds 359 7
webfoot 359 6
web-offset press 180 1, 18
wedding ceremony 332 14
wedding ring 36 5; 332 17
wedding ring box 36 6
wedding ring sizing machine
108 24
wedge 119 15; 132 19; 158 7
wedge, hardwood ~ 121 96
wedge, optical ~ 176 22
wedge heel 101 55
wedge stone 336 22
weed 379 8
weeding hoe 51 22
weeds 61
weekend house 37 84-86
weeping willow 272 63
weevil 80 10, 49; 82 42
weft feeler 166 31
weft feeler, electric ~ 166 14
weft pirn 166 7
weft replenishment 166 5
weft thread 171 1-29, 3
weft thread, lowered ~ 171 15
weft thread, raised ~ 171 16
weft yarn 163 2
weigela 373 23
weigelia 373 23
weighbridge 206 41
weighbridge office 206 40
weighing apparatus 92 32;
170 29
weighing bottle 349 24
weighing bunker 225 22
weighing machine 206 31
weighing platform 22 67
weigh office 199 12
weight Roof & Boilerr. 38 32
weight Sea Fish. 90 10
weight Clocks 110 32
weight Railw. 202 18
weight Athletics 298 49
weight, iron ~ 90 21
weight belt 279 14
weighting disc 165 21
weightlifter 299 2
weightlifting 299 1-5
weights, lead ~ 89 88-92
weir Rowing 283 60
weir Hydr. Eng. 217 65-72
weir sill 217 79
welder electrode arm 142 30
weld gauge 142 36
welding bench 141 13;
142 21
welding glove, five-fingered
~ 142 32
welding glove, three-fingered
~ 142 8
welding goggles 141 24
welding lead 142 19
welding nozzle 141 33
welding paste 141 18
welding pressure
adjustment 142 31
welding rod 141 12

welding table **142** 13
welding torch **141** 11, 19, 28
welding transformer **125** 29; **142** 1, 27
well *Astron.* **5** 24
well *Map* **15** 100
well *Carp.* **120** 46
well *Joiner* **132** 35
well *Oil, Petr.* **145** 17
well *Water* **269** 40
well, artesian ~ **12** 25
well, driven ~ **269** 60
well, glass-roofed ~ **271** 11
well casing **269** 64
well head **269** 65
wellington boot **101** 14
Wellingtonia **372** 69
wels **364** 12
welt, knitted ~ **29** 65; **31** 70
welt, stretch ~ **31** 43
welt cutter **100** 48
welt pincers **100** 38
West Australian Current **14** 45
westerlies **9** 50
Western roll **298** 16
west point **4** 15
West Wind Drift **14** 44
westwork **335** 22
wet and dry bulb thermometer **10** 52
wet bulb thermometer **10** 35
wet felt, first ~ **173** 17
wet felt, second ~ **173** 18
wet oil tank **145** 30
wetsuit, neoprene ~ **279** 9
wetting trough **165** 44
Weymouth pine **372** 30
Whale **3** 11
whales **367** 23-29
wharve **164** 48
wheat **68** 1, 23
wheat and rye bread **97** 6, 8
wheat beer **93** 26
wheat flour **97** 52; **99** 63
wheatgerm bread **97** 48
wheatgerm oil **98** 24
wheel *Overh. Irrign.* **67** 24
wheel *Clocks* **110** 11
wheel *Bicycle* **187** 1
wheel *Aircraft* **230** 24
wheel, back ~ **186** 17
wheel, co-pilot's ~ **230** 25
wheel, front ~ **186** 4; **187** 26-32
wheel, light alloy ~ **189** 48
wheel, rear ~ **186** 17
wheel, rubber-tyred ~ **64** 32
wheel, ship's ~ **224** 15
wheel, spoked ~ **289** 25
wheel adjustment **64** 58
wheel alignment **195** 17, 21
wheel alignment, visual ~ **195** 41
wheel and axle drive **212** 28
wheel and axle set **212** 3; **213** 3
wheelarch doorway **278** 39
wheelbarrow **56** 47; **118** 37; **119** 42
wheelbarrow sprayer **83** 38
wheel brush, wire ~ **134** 24
wheel cover **322** 27
wheel cylinder **192** 54
wheel disc, plastic ~ **289** 12
wheeler **186** 47
wheel flange lubricator **211** 52
wheel guard *Tram* **197** 11
wheel guard *Music. Instr.* **322** 27
wheelhead slide **150** 3

wheelhorse **186** 47
wheelhouse **223** 18; **224** 14-38
wheel lock **187** 49
wheel mirror **195** 41
wheel nut **187** 53
wheel of fortune **308** 45
wheel plough **65** 1
wheel ratchet **110** 10
wheel rim **187** 28; **189** 25; **191** 16; **192** 77
wheelsman **224** 16
wheel tapper **205** 39
wheel-tapping hammer **205** 40
whelp **73** 16
whetstone **66** 19
whetting anvil **66** 11
whetting hammer **66** 9
whip *Bldg. Site* **118** 30
whip *Equest.* **289** 43
whip *Circus* **307** 53
whip antenna **258** 60
whip line **228** 3
whipper-in **289** 43
whipping unit **97** 70
whip stall **288** 5
whirler **179** 1
whirligig **308** 2
whirlpool, hot ~ **281** 31, 35
whirlpool separator **93** 2
whisk **39** 23
whiskers *Hairst. etc.* **34** 12
whiskers *Mammals* **367** 21
whisky **42** 31
whisky glass **267** 57
whistle *Kitch. Utensils* **40** 11
whistle *Railw.* **211** 9; **212** 49
whistle *Navig.* **224** 70
whistle lever **211** 40
whistle valve handle **210** 51
white *Poultry Farm* **74** 62, 67
white *Heraldry* **254** 25
white *Colour* **343** 11
white bear **368** 11
white clover **69** 2
white light, supplementary ~ **203** 15
white line **268** 72
white owl **362** 17
white oxeye daisy **376** 4
white pelican **359** 5
white pine **372** 30
white poplar **371** 23
white-tailed eagle **362** 5
white-tailed sea eagle **362** 5
white wagtail **360** 9
white water lily **378** 14
white water pump **172** 63
white wine glass **45** 82
whitewood **374** 1
wholemeal bread **97** 48
whole note **320** 13
whole rest **320** 21
whortleberry **377** 23
wick **107** 29
wickerwork **136** 4, 16
wicket **292** 70
wicket keeper **292** 73
wide screen camera **310** 47
width *Roof* **122** 91, 95
width *Composing Rm.* **175** 48
width adjustment **100** 19
width scale **157** 58
width-setting tree **100** 55
Wiener **96** 8
wig **105** 38; **315** 49
wig, full-bottomed ~ **34** 2
wig, partial ~ **355** 8
wig block **105** 39
wiggler **89** 72
wigwam **352** 7
wild animal cage **307** 49

wild animal tamer **307** 52
wild arum **379** 9
wild barley **61** 28
wild boar **86** 32; **88** 51
wild briar **373** 26
wild camomile **380** 1
wild cherry **59** 5
wild chicory **376** 25
wild endive **376** 25
wildfowling **86** 40
wild morning glory **61** 26
wild mustard **61** 18
wild oat **61** 29
wild orchid **376** 28
wild pear tree **58** 31
wild radish **61** 21
wild sow **86** 32; **88** 51
wild strawberry **58** 16
wild-water racing kayak **283** 69
willow rod **136** 15
willow stake **136** 14
Wilson chamber **2** 24
Wilson cloud chamber **2** 24
winch **270** 56
winched launch **287** 5
winch house **226** 54
wind arrow **9** 9
wind avalanche **304** 1
wind box **147** 69
wind chest **326** 12, 12-14
wind chest box **326** 12
wind cone **287** 11
wind cripple **13** 43
wind direction **9** 9-19; **285** 6
wind-direction indicator **10** 31
wind directions **285** 1-13
wind-direction shaft **9** 9
wind-direction symbols **9** 9-19
windflower **375** 5; **377** 1
wind gauge **10** 28
wind generator **55** 34; **155** 42
winding, low-voltage ~ **153** 16
winding, primary ~ **153** 15
winding, secondary ~ **153** 16
winding crown **110** 42
winding engine house **144** 2
winding gear **217** 74
winding handle **117** 50
winding inset **144** 26
wind knob **110** 23
windlass **223** 49; **258** 6
windmill *Map* **15** 31
windmill *Mills* **91** 1-34
windmill *Fair* **308** 15
windmill, Dutch ~ **91** 29
windmill, German ~ **91** 31
windmill arm **91** 1
windmill cap, rotating ~ **91** 30
windmill sail **91** 1
windmill vane **91** 1
window **2** 16; **6** 40; **25** 8; **28** 36, 49; **75** 31; **77** 50; **186** 10; **268** 14; **284** 38
window, circular ~ **335** 12
window, double casement ~ **37** 22
window, heated ~ **191** 80
window, lead glass ~ **154** 75
window, pedimental ~ **355** 49, 50
window, rear ~ **191** 32, 80
window, side ~ **231** 29
window, single casement ~ **37** 23
window, sliding ~ **207** 7
window, transparent ~ **278** 41; **284** 3
window box **268** 15

window breast **37** 24
window decoration **260** 68; **268** 12
window display **98** 1; **268** 11
window frame **133** 44
window glass **124** 5
window head **37** 25; **118** 9; **120** 57
window jamb **120** 51
window ladder **296** 21
window ledge **118** 12; **120** 33
window lintel **120** 57
window opening **120** 30
window painting **260** 26
window shutter **37** 30
window sill **37** 24; **118** 12; **120** 33
window vent **55** 10
windpipe **17** 50; **20** 4
wind power plant **155** 42
wind pump **15** 73
windrow **63** 36
wind screen **5** 15
windscreen, panoramic ~ **191** 21
windscreen wiper **191** 41; **197** 32
wind shaft **91** 5
windshield **5** 31
windshield, panoramic ~ **191** 21
windshield wiper **191** 41
wind sock **287** 11
wind speed **9** 10
wind-speed barb **9** 10
wind-speed feather **9** 10
wind-speed indicator **10** 29
wind-speed meter **10** 29
windsurfer **284** 1
windsurfing **284** 1-9
wind systems **9** 46-52
wind trunk **326** 11
wind vane **10** 32; **55** 36; **331** 4
wind wheel **55** 35
wine **99** 76; **266** 43
wine, bottled ~ **98** 60-64
wine, red ~ **98** 64
wine, sparkling ~ **98** 63
wine, white ~ **98** 60
wine bar **266** 30-44
wine bottle **79** 14
wine carafe **266** 32
wine cask **79** 2
wine cellar **79** 1-22
wine cooler **266** 42
wine cruet **332** 46
wineglass **44** 9; **45** 12, 82, 83; **79** 19; **266** 33; **317** 7
wine grower **78** 13
wine growing **78**
wine in bottles **98** 60-64
wine jug **79** 15
wine list **266** 31
wine press, horizontal ~ **79** 21
wine restaurant **266** 30-44
wine tasting **79** 16
wine vat **79** 3
wine vault **79** 1-22
wine waiter **266** 30
wing *House Insects etc.* **81** 8
wing *Game* **88** 76, 79
wing *Sea Fish.* **90** 16
wing *Aircraft* **230** 43
wing *Airsports* **288** 27
wing *Fabul. Creat.* **327** 15, 28, 51, 60
wing *Decid. Trees* **371** 57
wing *Conifers* **372** 9
wing, bat's ~ **327** 4
wing, central ~ **229** 8
wing, cranked ~ **229** 14
wing, elliptical ~ **229** 15
wing, front ~ **191** 3

wing, hind ~ **358** 33
wing, lower ~ **229** 9
wing, membranous ~ **82** 11
wing, middle ~ **229** 8
wing, multispar ~ **287** 29
wing, ogival ~ **229** 22
wing, rectangular ~ **229** 16
wing, rotary ~ **232** 12
wing, swept-back ~ **229** 20, 21
wing, tapered ~ **229** 17
wing, upper ~ **229** 7
wing case **82** 10
wing configurations **229** 1-14
Winged Horse **3** 10
winger **291** 16
wing mirror, left-hand ~ **191** 40
wing mirror, right-hand ~ **191** 56
wing nut **143** 42; **187** 39
wing of bridge **223** 16
wing rail **202** 25
wings **307** 12
wing shapes **229** 15-22
wing span **229** 2
wing suspension, inner ~ **257** 34
wing suspension, outer ~ **257** 35
wing tally **74** 55
wing tank **256** 4
wing tank, integral ~ **257** 29
wing tip **287** 42
wing-tip tank **231** 9; **256** 30
wing wall *Rivers* **216** 35
wing wall *Hydr. Eng.* **217** 80
winker **71** 26
winner **299** 39
winner's price **289** 39
winners' table **289** 38
winning peg **292** 77
winnowing **64** 15
winter boot **101** 1
winter coat **30** 61
winter dike **216** 32
winter dress **30** 12
winter green **57** 34
winter moth **80** 16
winter slacks **30** 19
winter sports **301**; **302**; **303**
winter wear **30**
wiper *Post* **237** 44
wiper *Graphic Art* **340** 13
wiper/washer switch and horn **191** 60
wire *Paperm.* **173** 14
wire *Fencing* **294** 31
wire, gold ~ **108** 3
wire, iron ~ **143** 12
wire, overhead ~ **194** 43
wire, silver~ **108** 3
wire and sheet roller **108** 1
wireless mast **15** 33
wireman **127** 1
wire side **173** 34
wire spool, spring-loaded ~ **294** 29
wire stripper and cutter **134** 15
wire strippers **127** 64
wireworm **80** 38
witch **306** 6
witchgrass **61** 30
withers *Dog* **70** 11
withers *Horse* **72** 17
witloof **376** 25
witness **332** 23
wobbler, double-jointed ~ **89** 70
wobbler, round ~ **89** 71
wobbler, single-jointed ~ **89** 69
wolf **367** 13

wolfsbane **379** 1
womb **20** 79
wood *Forestry* **84** 1-34
wood *School* **260** 82
wood *Ball Games* **293** 91
wood *Sculpt. Studio* **339** 27
wood, coniferous ~ **15** 1
wood, deciduous ~ **15** 4
wood, mixed ~ **15** 14
wood, open ~ **326** 31-33
wood, rough ~ **135** 21
wood anemone **377** 1
woodbind **374** 13
woodbine **51** 5; **374** 13, 16
wood carver **339** 28
wood carving **260** 77
wood chip paper **128** 18
wood chisel **339** 19
wood cut **260** 83
wood cutting *Forestry* **84** 15-37
woodcutting *Graphic Art* **340** 2
wood engraving **340** 1, 1-13
wood file **132** 2
wood grouse **88** 72
wood haulage way **84** 3
wood ibis **359** 5
woodland strawberry **58** 16
woodlark **361** 18
wood louse **81** 6
woodpecker **359** 27
wood pulp, chemical ~ **172** 77, 78
wood pulp paper **128** 18
wood rasp **132** 1; **134** 8; **260** 55
wood screw **122** 101; **132** 41; **143** 45
wood screw thread **143** 47
wood sculptor **339** 28
woodsman **84** 18
wood stork **359** 5
wood tick **358** 44
wood-turning lathe **134** 51; **135** 1
woodwind instruments **323** 28-38
woodwinds **323** 28-38
woodworking adhesive **134** 36
woofer **241** 17
woolly apple aphid **80** 32, 33
woolly apple aphid colony **80** 34
woolly milk cap **379** 13
woolpack cloud **8** 1; **287** 22
work **118** 17
workbench **97** 60, 62; **100** 33; **104** 7; **108** 20; **109** 2; **111** 20; **124** 15; **125** 10; **137** 21; **140** 7; **260** 46
workbench, collapsible ~ **134** 41
workbench lamp **109** 12
workboard **136** 7
work clamp *Joiner* **132** 51
work clamp *Arc Weld.* **142** 35
worker *Bees* **77** 1, 6-9, 10-19
worker *Articulates* **358** 22
worker bee **77** 1
worker cell **77** 34
work folder **261** 27
working, open-cast ~ **158** 1
working area **162** 5
working bath **162** 5
working deck **221** 19, 34
working face **158** 3
working passage **75** 24
working platform **118** 17; **145** 5; **211** 42; **234** 28, 46
workings, underground ~ **144** 21-51

working surface, tiled ~ **261** 5
working top **39** 11
workman's cap **35** 40
workpiece **104** 25; **133** 44; **139** 46; **140** 6; **141** 20; **142** 28; **148** 51; **150** 20
workpiece, blocked ~ **139** 28
workpiece, preshaped ~ **139** 28
work platform **118** 17; **211** 42; **234** 28, 46
workroom, dressmaker's ~ **103** 1-27
workroom, furrier's ~ **131** 1-25
workroom, tailor's ~ **104** 1-32; **268** 17
works **15** 37
workshop **62** 17; **146** 30; **310**. 6; **315** 28-42
workshop, bootmaker's ~ **100** 1-68
workshop, carpenter's ~ **120** 4
workshop, cooper's ~ **130** 1-33
workshop, fitter's ~ **140** 1-22
workshop, glazier's ~ **124** 1
workshop, joiner's ~ **132** 1-73
workshop, locksmith's ~ **140** 1-22
workshop, mechanic's ~ **140** 1-22
workshop, optician's ~ **111** 20-47
workshop, orbital ~ **235** 66
workshop, shoemaker's ~ **100** 1-68
workshop, tank construction engineer's ~ **130** 1-33
workshop, turner's ~ **135** 1-26
workshop area **5** 17
workshop door **120** 5
workshop trolley **109** 22
work top **50** 31
worm **192** 59
worm-and-nut steering gear **192** 56-59
worm gear sector **192** 57
wormhole **58** 65
worms **357** 20-26
wormwood **380** 4
worshipper **330** 29
wort **92** 50, 51, 52
wort boiler **92** 52
wort cooler **93** 5
wort cooling **93** 1-5
wound **21** 8
wrap, coloured ~ **355** 10
wrapper *Tobacc. etc.* **107** 5
wrapper *Bookbind.* **185** 37
wrapping, jute ~ **163** 4
wrapping counter **271** 14
wrapping material **98** 46-49
wrapping paper **98** 46
wreath **123** 52
wreath, bridal ~ **332** 19
wreath of the colours **254** 2
wreath piece **123** 49
wreck **224** 84
wrecking crane **270** 47
wreck to port **224** 86
wreck to starboard **224** 85
wren **361** 12
wrench **134** 14
wrench, open-end ~ **134** 2
wrest **325** 20
wrestler **299** 7
wrestling **299** 6-12
wrestling, Greco-Roman ~ **299** 6-9
wrestling mat **299** 12
wrest pin **324** 23; **325** 17
wrest pin block **324** 22; **325** 18

wrest plank **324** 22; **325** 18
wrist *Man* **19** 76
wrist *Horse* **72** 22
wristband **296** 64
wrist joint **2** 41
wrist sling **300** 32
wristwatch, automatic ~ **110** 32-43
wristwatch, electronic ~ **110** 1
writing, English ~ **342** 10
writing, German ~ **342** 11
writing cane **341** 23
writing surface **47** 23; **246** 3
writing system, pictorial ~ **341** 1
writing unit **46** 21
wrought-iron craftsman **140** 1
wryneck **359** 27

X

xanthate **169** 10
X-contact **115** 14
xenon lamp **177** 17
xenon lamp housing **177** 42
X-radiation **1** 33, 56
X-ray **25** 39
X-ray apparatus **24** 21; **27** 6
X-ray cassette **27** 2
X-ray control unit, central ~ **27** 9
X-ray examination table **27** 1
X-ray generator **24** 22
X-ray head **27** 18
X-ray image intensifier **27** 16
X-ray support, telescopic ~ **27** 8
X-ray technician **27** 11
X-ray tube **27** 17, 18
X-ray unit **27** 1-35
xylography **340** 1-13
xylophone **324** 61

Y

yacht **273** 29; **278** 12; **284** 10-48
yacht classes **284** 49-65
yacht hull, types of ~ **285** 29-41
yachting **284**; **285**
yachting cap **35** 29
yacht stern **285** 42
yacht stern, types of ~ **285** 42-49
yacht tacking **285** 7
yankee corn **68** 31
yard **276** 27
yardmaster **206** 45
yard radio **212** 50; **213** 4
yarn **164** 53, 56; **167** 17, 36; **169** 17, 25
yarn, doubled ~ **164** 60
yarn, glass ~ **162** 56, 57
yarn, inlaid ~ **171** 43
yarn, sleeved ~ **162** 57
yarn, viscose rayon ~ **169** 1-34, 27
yarn count **164** 40
yarn-distributing beam **167** 25
yarn-dividing beam **167** 25
yarn feeder **167** 6
yarn-forming frame, intermediate ~ **164** 27
yarn guide *Shoem.* **100** 30
yarn guide *Knitting* **167** 3, 54, 64
yarn guide support post **167** 2
yarn length recorder **165** 28

yarn package **165** 15; **170** 48
yarn package container **165** 16
yarn-tensioning device **167** 5
yarrow **376** 15
yawing **230** 69
yawl **220** 10
y-axis **347** 3
Y-connection **153** 20
Y-cross **332** 61
yeast **93** 6
yeast, baker's ~ **97** 53
yeast bread **97** 11
yeast propagation **93** 6
yellow *Heraldry* **254** 24
yellow *Colour* **343** 2
yellow bunting **361** 6
yellow card **291** 63
yellow coral fungus **381** 32
yellow filter adjustment **116** 44
yellow flag **60** 8
yellow-flowered jasmine **373** 4
yellowhammer **361** 6
yellow iris **60** 8
yellow light **203** 16
yellow lupin **69** 17
yellow meal beetle **81** 23
yellow owl **362** 17
yellow prickle fungus **381** 31
yellow water flag **60** 8
yerba maté **382** 11
yew tree **372** 61
yoghurt maker **40** 44
yoke *Bldg. Site* **119** 64
yoke *Power Plant* **153** 14
yoke *Rowing* **283** 51
yoke, adjustable ~ **65** 14
yoke, bolted ~ **119** 74
yoke, front ~ **33** 19
yoke, kimono ~ **31** 18
yoke elm **371** 63
yoke mount, English-type ~ **113** 23
yoke mounting, English-type ~ **113** 23
yolk **74** 68
yolk sac **74** 64
Y-tube **350** 56
yucca **373** 24
yurt **353** 19
yurta **353** 19

Z

zap flap **229** 50
Z-drive motorboat **286** 2
zebra **366** 27
zebra crossing **198** 11; **268** 24
Zechstein, leached ~ **154** 62
Zechstein, lixiviated ~ **154** 62
Zechstein shale **154** 68
zenith *Astron.* **4** 11
zenith *Hunt.* **87** 77
zero **275** 18
zero adjustment **2** 7
zero isotherm **9** 41
zero level **7** 6, 20
ziggurat **333** 32
zimmerstutzen **305** 35
zinc plate **179** 9; **180** 53; **340** 52
zinc plate, etched ~ **178** 40
zinc plate, photoprinted ~ **178** 32
zink **322** 12
zinnia **60** 22
zip **31** 55; **33** 28; **260** 13
zip, front ~ **29** 18
zip, inside ~ **101** 6
zip code **236** 43

zircon **351** 19
zither **324** 21
zone, arid ~ **9** 54
zone, paved ~ **268** 58
zone, tropical ~ **9** 53
zoo **356**
zoological gardens **356**
zooming lever **117** 54; **313** 22, 36
zoom lens **112** 41; **240** 34; **313** 23
zoom lens, interchangeable ~ **117** 2
zoom stereomicroscope **112** 40
Zulu **354** 36